MW01049433

DIAGNOSIS AND TREATMENT OF MENTAL DISORDERS ACROSS THE LIFESPAN

Stephanie M. Woo, PhD
Carolyn Keatinge, PhD

WILEY

John Wiley & Sons, Inc.

This book is printed on acid-free paper. ⊗

Copyright © 2008 by John Wiley & Sons, Inc. All rights reserved

Published by John Wiley & Sons, Inc., Hoboken, New Jersey
Published simultaneously in Canada

No part of this publication may be reproduced, stored in a retrieval system, or transmitted in any form or by any means, electronic, mechanical, photocopying, recording, scanning, or otherwise, except as permitted under Section 107 or 108 of the 1976 United States Copyright Act, without either the prior written permission of the Publisher, or authorization through payment of the appropriate per-copy fee to the Copyright Clearance Center, Inc., 222 Rosewood Drive, Danvers, MA 01923, (978) 750-8400, fax (978) 646-8600, or on the web at www.copyright.com. Requests to the Publisher for permission should be addressed to the Permissions Department, John Wiley & Sons, Inc., 111 River Street, Hoboken, NJ 07030, (201) 748-6011, fax (201) 748-6008, or online at http://www.wiley.com/go/permissions.

Limit of Liability/Disclaimer of Warranty: While the publisher and author have used their best efforts in preparing this book, they make no representations or warranties with respect to the accuracy or completeness of the contents of this book and specifically disclaim any implied warranties of merchantability or fitness for a particular purpose. No warranty may be created or extended by sales representatives or written sales materials. The advice and strategies contained herein may not be suitable for your situation. You should consult with a professional where appropriate. Neither the publisher nor author shall be liable for any loss of profit or any other commercial damages, including but not limited to special, incidental, consequential, or other damages.

For general information on our other products and services or for technical support, please contact our Customer Care Department within the United States at (800) 762-2974, outside the United States at (317) 572-3993 or fax (317) 572-4002.

Wiley also publishes its books in a variety of electronic formats. Some content that appears in print may not be available in electronic books. For more information about Wiley products, visit our web site at www.wiley.com.

Library of Congress Cataloging-in-Publication Data:

Woo, Stephanie M.
   Diagnosis and treatment of mental disorders across the lifespan /
Stephanie M. Woo, Carolyn Keatinge.
       p. ; cm.
    ISBN 978-0-471-68928-7 (cloth : alk. paper)
   1. Psychology, Pathological.   2. Mental illness–Diagnosis.   3. Mental illness–Treatment.   I. Keatinge, Carolyn.   II. Title.
    [DNLM: 1. Mental Disorders–diagnosis.   2. Mental Disorders–therapy. WM 141 W873d 2008]
    RC454.W64 2008
    616.89–dc22   2007022151

Printed in the United States of America

10 9 8 7 6 5

To my parents, Larry and Delia Woo, for always believing in me; my husband Kenneth, for your constant support and love; and my children Daniel and Tatiyana, for the joy you bring me each and every day.
—SMW

To John, as promised, thank you for being you. Love and thoughts always, Mum. To Dr. Lois Mendelson and the staff of the JCC therapeutic nursery, who everyday bring hope to children with autism and their families.
Thank you for the hope.
—CK

Contents

Preface

Understanding the origins of psychological distress and how to ameliorate its symptoms has been both a source of fascination and a challenge since time immemorial. Today, mental health professionals are able to benefit from a rapidly growing understanding of the features, etiology, course, and treatment of mental disorders that has been informed by modern research methodologies utilizing cutting-edge, state-of-the art science and improved assessment measures and diagnostic systems. Our knowledge of how to best work with people struggling with the often devastating effects of mental illness has also been aided by the wealth of information gleaned from the decades of experience of astute clinicians treating clients on the front lines. For the mental health clinician, whether a student just starting out on his or her professional journey or an experienced therapist, the task of grasping and integrating these diverse sources of information can be daunting. Our purpose in writing this text was influenced by our experiences teaching graduate courses in introductory psychopathology and the need for a clinical diagnostic training text for beginning mental health clinicians that could also serve as an essential reference for experienced therapists. By integrating the key information necessary for clinical practice for a wide range of disorders across the continuum of development we also hoped to focus on clinical populations that are sometimes overlooked and often underserved. Our intent is to present the information in a practical, applied, and accessible manner that also incorporates current advances in the field.

OUTLINE OF THIS VOLUME

This book is divided into two parts, which are intended to facilitate the learning experience. The first four chapters of the book focus on essential clinical skills that lay the foundation for the evaluation and treatment of mental disorders. Included are chapters on "Intake and Interviewing," "Crisis Issues," "Essentials of Diagnosis," and "Fundamentals of Treatment Planning." These chapters draw from clinical and research literature and contain practical strategies and tips for dealing with a wide range of clients. The format of these chapters is designed to orient and guide the novice clinician through the skills needed for clinical practice and to serve as useful reminders to experienced clinicians. Basic and advanced information is organized in an easily accessible format to enhance clinical utility and recall. Information regarding the role that cultural factors play in the evaluation, diagnosis, and treatment process is woven throughout the text.

The second part of the book addresses clinical disorders and illustrates the application of the clinical principles reviewed in Part I to specific forms of psychopathology. Importantly, the chapters in Part II provide a comprehensive overview of the disorders most commonly encountered in clinical practice (e.g., disruptive behavior, mood and anxiety disorders). Information is provided on the clinical presentation, associated features, course, epidemiology, etiology, diversity considerations, assessment, treatment of a wide range of disorders, and the therapeutic challenges encountered by clinicians. Important aspects of the developmental presentation of psychopathology (i.e., in children and adolescents as well as older adults) are also summarized throughout the chapters. Clinical diagnosis and the clinical disorders are discussed in terms of the *Diagnostic and Statistical Manual of Mental Disorders,* fourth edition, text revision (*DSM-IV-TR*) system, the classification system that is the current standard in the field, and the limitations and strengths of this system are reviewed. Discussion of treatment issues in the clinical disorders chapters are informed by evidence-based approaches (e.g., cognitive-behavioral treatment for mood disorders, exposure-based treatments for anxiety disorders, multidisciplinary treatment for Schizophrenia, autism, and dementia due to Alzheimer's disease), but also integrates the real-world approaches taken by today's clinicians. Both psychosocial and pharmacologic interventions are discussed, and each disorder is considered from a multidisciplinary framework that teaches the novice clinician ways to interface and benefit from contact with a variety of health professionals and services, including psychologists, physicians, social workers, and local agencies. Each clinical disorders chapter ends with an advanced topic, which presents information on a specialized issue related to assessment, diagnosis, or treatment. Collectively, these topics cover a wide range of subjects, from early intervention and multisystemic treatment for disruptive behavior disorders, to the epidemic of meth-amphetamine abuse and dependence, to postpartum mood disorders, which we hope will be of interest to today's mental health professional. Finally, an appendix provides an overview of psychopharmacology. Our hope is to provide a book that will introduce new clinicians to the field and serve as their resource book as they challenge themselves to work with different populations and add their contribution to our clinical knowledge.

Acknowledgments

This book could not have been completed without the support and encouragement of many important people in our personal and professional lives. Special thanks is given to Dean Margaret Weber and Associate Dean of Psychology Robert de Mayo of Pepperdine University's Graduate School of Education and Psychology (GSEP), whose support allowed us to complete this book while continuing to teach the classes we love. We are grateful to our GSEP colleagues who provided the intellectual and collegial support that encouraged us to continue to write. To our mentors, Dr. Michael Goldtstein, Dr. Keith Nuechterlein, Dr. Joan Asarnow, Dr. Cheri Adrian, Dr. Linda Weinberger, Dr. Cary Mitchell, and Dr. Michael Jenike, who showed the way, we will always be grateful for your guidance. We also are deeply indebted to the clients we have treated over the years, whose courage in seeking help and willingness to let us to accompany them on their journey toward mental health has taught us much. Thank you to our families and friends for their love, laughter, patience, and support that made it all possible. To the editorial staff at John Wiley & Sons, and in particular to Tracey Belmont, for supporting our idea for this text, our editor, Lisa Gebo, whose patience allowed it to come to fruition, and editorial staff members Sweta Gupta and Kate Lindsay for their editorial and production assistance, thank you. Special thanks to Cheryl LaSasso for her contribution of the chapter on "Eating, Sleep, Sexual, and Gender Identity Disorders." Thanks also to Dr. Kenneth Subotnik for his valuable feedback on the chapters covering diagnosis and psychotic disorders. We also thank our tireless research assistants, Jen Carusone, Sarah Metz, Valerie Sims, Kim Stanley, Julie Cooney, and Stephanie Kremer for their great work, endless energy, and good ideas. Finally, to our students who inspired and challenged us to write a textbook that they could use as clinicians, we thank you.

PART I

FUNDAMENTAL CLINICAL SKILLS

Chapter 1 ———————————————————

INTAKE AND INTERVIEWING

A good clinician is like a detective trying to solve a mystery. Clues must be gathered, facts ascertained, leads followed up, a time line of events created, and pieces of a puzzle eventually put together to tell a story that hopefully answers some important questions. But whereas a detective strives to answer the question "*Who* dunnit?" the clinician must answer questions such as "*What* is this person's diagnosis?" "*When* did these problems begin?" "*Why* is this person seeking help now?" and "*How* can I best help?" Like the detective, the clinician needs a specific set of skills and tools to answer these questions. The four chapters in Part I review the essentials necessary to diagnose and treat a wide array of clients. This chapter reviews one of the most fundamental of these skills: the ability to conduct a comprehensive intake interview. A well-done intake interview provides clients an opportunity to tell their own stories, including information about self-concept, values, self-expectations, and the meaning of the symptoms and experiences (S. B. Miller, 1987). The information collected creates nothing less than the road map that ultimately guides the clinician and client toward an appropriate diagnosis and treatment plan. When an interview is poorly conducted and treatment decisions subsequently made are based on incomplete or inaccurate information, a client's well-being is directly threatened (S. M. Turner, Hersen, & Heiser, 2003).

This chapter addresses the fundamentals of a good intake interview. The chapter begins with factors to consider prior to the interview itself. A separate section is devoted to legal and ethical considerations in interviewing and addresses such important issues as client confidentiality, communication between treatment providers, and records release. This is followed by a discussion of process issues involved in interviewing, including the establishment of rapport and listening and questioning skills. Next, content areas that should be addressed in a standard intake interview are reviewed, as well as details of conducting a mental status exam. Consideration of the benefits and drawbacks of conducting structured versus unstructured interviews follows, and the chapter ends with a discussion of how the interviewing skills and content areas discussed should be adapted when working with individuals at either end of the life span spectrum: children and older adults.

Before delving into this information, a general piece of advice is offered. If you want to become a skilled interviewer, the key is repeated practice. As will become evident in reading this chapter, interviewers must possess a variety of skills and be able to accomplish multiple tasks at once. Skill in dealing with one client does not necessarily generalize across clients. Differences in presenting problems, verbal skills, insight, and cultural factors can all influence a client's manner of relating as well as the specific skill set required to conduct an effective interview. Thus, during one's training it is wise to take advantage of as many opportunities as possible to conduct supervised interviews in order to develop and maintain skills in this most important of clinical areas.

PREPARING FOR THE FIRST INTERVIEW

Determine What You Know and Don't Know About Your Client

Depending on the setting in which you work, you may have very little or quite a bit of information about a new client prior to the first meeting. Clients seen through outpatient clinics have often been through a telephone screening with a staff person, and information on the presenting problem, past treatment, current medication, and much more may be available. In contrast, a private practice clinician may opt to do relatively little screening over the telephone and will have only the most basic idea of the client's presenting complaint prior to the first meeting. In either case, it is helpful before the first session to begin building a profile of what is known about your client and what you need to find out (Lukas, 1993). For example, if phone intake notes indicate that the client has recently been hospitalized, during the intake interview you will want to be certain to find out the reason(s) for the hospitalization (including any thoughts and behavior indicating an intent to harm self or others), the length of stay, whether the hospitalization was voluntary, diagnoses rendered, medications the client was treated with, and if this was the client's first inpatient stay.

Although the client's diagnosis and full range of presenting problems may not be known before the first meeting, you will likely have some idea of the general type of problems or symptoms the client is experiencing. It is therefore useful to refamiliarize yourself with diagnostic criteria for disorders that are likely to be under consideration. For example, if you know that the client has a history of depression and multiple sclerosis, familiarity with the symptoms, prognoses, and typical treatments for both, as well as ways the conditions can affect each other is helpful. Reviewing past treatment records (obtained with the client's permission) is a good way to do this advance preparatory work. However, one should not overly rely on such records in forming an impression of the client since the utility of the information contained in them is highly dependent on the competence and insight of those who reported it (Lukas, 1993). Also, some clients may be reluctant to release records to a clinician they have not met in person and are not certain they will continue seeing.

With this said, it is important to be flexible and remain open to attending to and following up on information that may contradict any preconceived ideas about the client's problems or diagnosis. Effective interviewers take care to avoid the *confirmatory bias effect*, or asking only questions that will confirm diagnostic preconceptions, as well as the *halo effect*, in which an initial impression of the client guides subsequent questioning and diagnostic decision making (e.g., deciding that a client who presents as irritable and difficult to interview must have personality pathology). The power that mistaken initial impressions can have on subsequent conceptualizations of clients is aptly illustrated by a study that found a group of psychoanalytically oriented therapists were more likely to rate a male interviewee seen in a videotape as disturbed when he was labeled as a "patient" compared to when he was labeled as a "job applicant" (Langer & Abelson, 1974). This finding does not mean that members of one theoretical orientation are more likely than others to draw biased conclusions about individuals they see, but merely illustrates the need to be vigilant to the tendency to jump to conclusions based on limited information.

Consider How the Setting Will Guide the Interview

Later in this chapter key areas typically addressed during a first interview will be reviewed. The areas that are emphasized and the time spent on them may vary considerably depending on the interview setting. Therefore, you should spend time deciding on the type of interview structure and style that will most likely achieve the goals dictated by your work setting. Table 1.1 compares presenting client issues in three different treatment settings and suggests interview formats for each.

Consider Issues That Could Impact Interview Effectiveness

Our past experiences (e.g., events, relationships), current needs, motivations, physical state, cultural assumptions, biases, and blind spots can all affect the quality of the relationship that is established with the client, which in turn can affect the quality of information obtained in the initial interview (J. Sommers-Flanagan & Sommers-Flanagan, 1993). These problems may come to the clinician's awareness only during or after the initial interview. However, it is sometimes possible to anticipate such issues ahead of time, make a concerted effort to remain aware of them during the interview, and therefore reduce the likelihood that they will adversely impact the initial working relationship with the client. For example, suppose a 28-year-old male clinician is scheduled to meet a 56-year-old male client for an intake interview. Prior to the session the therapist reflects on how he typically interacts with older male clients or older men in general, and recognizes that he often feels insecure, is often overly deferential, and tends to be hyperattuned to any verbal or nonverbal signs that they are disappointed or irritated with him. Awareness of these reactions may lead the clinician to take such steps as role-playing before the interview how he might ask questions, making a list of specific questions he thinks he might (un-)consciously be reluctant to ask, exerting a special effort to catch himself and question his motives when he decides not to ask the client a particular question, and practicing cognitive reframing of possible client reactions ("If the client frowns during the interview that doesn't necessarily mean I've asked the wrong question; he may just be remembering something upsetting").

The astute clinician is mindful throughout treatment (not just in preparation for or during the first interview) of the ways personal reactions to clients can affect clinical impressions, diagnostic decisions, and treatment interventions. *Countertransference* is a psychoanalytic concept that refers to the development of feelings in a therapist about a client that are similar to those the therapist has had toward someone from his or her past. One does not have to be working from a psychodynamic framework to experience such feelings, and countertransference will be experienced with all clients to some degree (Leon, 1982). However, when left unchecked, countertransference reactions can obscure clinical judgment and lead to inappropriate diagnosis and/or treatment (Wiger & Huntly, 2002). An extreme example would be a therapist who mistakenly diagnoses a client as

Table 1.1   A comparison of three interview settings

Emergency Diagnostic Centers/Crisis Settings	Outpatient (Clinics/ Private Practice)	Medical Settings
Goal:	*Goal:*	*Goal:*
Address crisis issues (e.g., suicidality). Gain enough information for diagnosis and immediate disposition.	Learn as much as possible about client's emotional functioning to determine reasons for seeking consultation.	Gain enough information for diagnosis and immediate disposition.
Additional considerations:	*Additional considerations:*	*Additional considerations:*
Clients may be frightened by their symptoms and agitated; intimidated by the interview setting.	Client problems are likely to be less acute/ severe than seen in crisis settings.	Clients often not self-referred (referred by treating physician).
Adopt a calm, structured, reassuring manner to put client at ease.	Devote ample time to establishment of rapport and a strong therapeutic relationship.	Clients may have questions or doubts about the need for psychological treatment and consequently may be reluctant to be interviewed.
Client ability to clearly provide history may be diminished.	More time is available for detailed questioning.	Format and length of questioning may be affected by client pain, fatigue, physical discomfort.
Decrease emphasis on obtaining a detailed psychosocial history.	Client is likely to request information on clinician's diagnostic impressions, treatment recommendations, prognosis.	Interviewing process may be protracted. Clinician may need to slowly approach idea of psychological (versus solely medical) factors contributing to client functioning.
A mental status examination is important.		
Clinician will likely need to supplement information from client with other sources (e.g., family, police).		Client may try to get clinician to side with him or her against treating physician.

From "The Interviewing Process" (pp. 3–20), by S.M. Turner and M. Hersen in *Diagnostic Interviewing,* third edition, M. Hersen and S. M. Turner (Eds.), 2003, New York: Kluwer Academic Publishers. Adapted with kind permission of Springer Science and Business Media.

having Borderline Personality Disorder primarily based on countertransference feelings of anger or hatred (Reiser & Levenson, 1984). Research suggests that therapists rated as having good self-awareness and reduced countertransference potential are more likely to be viewed as excellent therapists (Van Wagoner, Gelso, Hayes, & Diemer, 1991). Thus, when strong reactions are aroused by a client, consultation with a colleague or supervisor may lend insight into why these feelings are being aroused and how they might be affecting the treatment process. Among therapist factors identified as being helpful in the management of countertransference feelings are self-insight, empathy, self-integration (i.e., healthy character structure), anxiety management (i.e., ability to experience, control, and understand one's anxiety), and conceptualizing ability (i.e., ability to theoretically understand what is happening in the therapeutic relationship; Gelso & Hayes, 2001). In cases when a clinician has continued difficulty working through countertransference issues, personal psychotherapy may be the best avenue through which to address and hopefully resolve these feelings. In some cases, the clinician may ultimately need to refer the client to another treatment provider if countertransference issues continue to adversely affect the client's treatment (R. Sommers-Flanagan & Sommers-Flanagan, 1999). Although it may seem that countertransference is always an obstacle to therapy (this was actually Freud's view), many contemporary psychoanalytic theorists point to the valuable information that can be gleaned from scrutiny of these feelings. For example, countertransference reactions can clue the clinician into understanding the client's impact and effect on others, which can be particularly helpful in assessing problematic aspects of the client's personality (McWilliams, 1994).

Good interviewers recognize that not only can their behavior be affected by characteristics of the client, but interviewer variables such as gender, ethnicity, age, and other demographics can differentially influence the behavior, comfort level, and openness of clients. Although findings from the literature are mixed, there is evidence that treatment length is improved for African American, Mexican American, and Asian American adult and adolescent clients when there is a match with their therapist in terms of ethnicity or language (Flaskerud & Liu, 1991; Fujino, Okazaki, & Young, 1994; Gamst, Dana, Der-Karabetian, & Kramer, 2000; Rosenheck, Fontana, & Cottrol, 1995; Sue, Fujino, Hsu, Takeuchi, & Zane, 1991; Yeh, Eastman, & Cheung, 1994). This does not imply that therapists should treat only individuals from the same ethnic or linguistic background as themselves, nor does research suggest that ethnicity and language factors are the top criteria ethnic minority clients cite when asked about therapist characteristics that are important to them (attitudes, educational level, personality, and maturity have been found to rank higher; H. Coleman, Wampold, & Casali, 1995). However, these research findings call attention to the need to be sensitive to *potential* impediments to the therapy process when treating a client whose ethnic or linguistic background is different from one's own and the necessity to educate oneself (through reading, workshops, supervision, etc.) about a client's cultural background.

Consider Physical Presentation and Surroundings

When interacting with clients it is important to be well groomed and professionally dressed. The therapy room is not the place to make a fashion statement, and care must be taken to consider how a variety of clients might interpret your dress. For example, novice therapists who look very young and are planning to work with adult clients may wish to avoid dressing in clothes or wearing a hair style that accentuates their youth. As a safety consideration, avoid wearing anything that could be used to inflict harm (i.e., long necklaces, pins).

Equally important as one's physical presentation is the impression that the physical environment of the therapy room makes. Ideally the therapy room should be a comfortable refuge that helps put the client at ease and encourages open dialogue. An uncomfortable, dirty, or inappropriately furnished room reflects poorly on one's professionalism, is likely to distract the client and discourage disclosure, and decreases the likelihood that the client will return for treatment. While personal taste and desires in terms of decor need not be sacrificed, the clinician should reflect on whether any furnishings, pictures, or photographs would be likely to offend, disturb, or overly distract clients. For example, although a clinician may cherish a photograph of herself hugging her 5-year-old daughter, placing this picture in clear view of a client may invite trouble, including unwanted personal questions about her family life or client reluctance to divulge troubling feelings about parenting issues for fear of therapist disapproval or disappointment.

Furniture in the therapy office should be clean, comfortable, and arranged in such a way that the client and clinician do not have to sit too close together (e.g., feet almost touching) nor too far apart. Allowing clients a personal space of about 3 feet around their body should be sufficient (Twemlow, 2001). Tissue should be available in the event a client cries during the session. Keep paperwork and client files you are working on so that they cannot be seen when the client enters the office or is seated. If child clients are seen, age-appropriate toys, books, and furniture (e.g., low table and small chairs) should be available. Lighting should be moderate; strong overhead fluorescent lights that can impart an institutional feeling should be avoided whenever possible. Conversely, a darkened therapy room with minimal light or use of lit candles as accessories can evoke an inappropriately intimate atmosphere. The therapy office should afford privacy and protection from interruptions, and to these ends care should be taken to ensure that there is adequate soundproofing, that the telephone ringer is turned off, and that others are instructed not enter the office (Phares, 1992).

Attend to Safety Issues

All clinicians, regardless of the setting in which they work, should take steps to keep themselves safe from potentially aggressive or violent clients. Unfortunately, assaults (verbal and physical) by clients are not entirely rare and are probably underreported (Owen, Tarantello, Jones, & Tennant, 1998). Surveys of psychiatric residents suggest that between one third and one half have been assaulted during their training (K. J. Black, Compton, Wetzel, Minchin, & Farber, 1994; Chaimowitz & Moscovitch, 1991; Coverdale, Gale, Weeks, & Turbott, 2001; D. Fink, Shoyer, & Dubin, 1991; T. L. Schwartz & Park, 1999). A study of patient assaults experienced by marriage and family therapists found that 44% reported being assaulted at least once (this included property damage, pushing, grabbing, holding, and being knocked down, kicked, slapped, scratched); 35% of these assaults occurred in the therapists' offices, and another 14% occurred in the reception areas and/or hallways. Despite these sobering statistics, many mental health professionals receive no or inadequate training on dealing with verbally or physically aggressive clients (Coverdale et al., 2001). Chapter 2, "Crisis Issues," provides a detailed review of steps for dealing with potentially homicidal clients, but some general principles for dealing with aggressive clients during the intake and interview phase of treatment will now be reviewed.

If a clinician suspects that a client may pose a danger, intake or waiting room staff should be questioned prior to the interview about behavioral manifestations of agitation (e.g., pacing, verbally threatening behavior) and whether the client appears intoxicated, psychotic, or in possession of a weapon or other potentially dangerous object. The clinician and intake staff should also continually stay alert for changes in the client's demeanor and signs of escalation and increased agitation. When working with impulsive clients, an awareness of physical surroundings, including knowledge of emergency alert procedures and access to the door, panic buttons, and distress codes, is essential. If the clinician has concerns about the client's level of agitation, arrangements should be made for the interview to be conducted in the vicinity of other staff members. A quiet corner of the waiting room, where the client's confidentiality may be maintained and visibility with other staff members ensured, may be appropriate. New clients should always be scheduled at times when staff are present and support is available.

In the therapy room, the clinician should avoid sitting so that access to the door is blocked and should consider removing any items that could be used to inflict injury (e.g., letter openers, paperweights, decorative items such as vases; Twemlow, 2001). The clinician's hands should be visible, and he or she should make no abrupt gestures. A physically safe distance from the client is often considered "two quick steps" from the client, since this allows one to easily avoid or intervene should the client's behavior escalate. A sideways stance also avoids the potential for a direct body assault (Eichleman, 1996). Finally, rather than sitting directly opposite the client, which may be perceived as confrontational, the clinician may favor sitting at a lesser angle, suggesting a supportive nonverbal tone.

When interacting with an agitated client, the tendency to match the client's level of heightened emotionality and to rush through the interview should be avoided. Instead, a relaxed, natural, nondefensive manner should be displayed that imparts a sense that the clinician is knowledgeable and in control, and the client should be firmly told that violence is not acceptable. Maintaining a verbal and emotional tone that is below the client's in intensity also serves to model appropriate affect, and most clients who are feeling out of control will find a clinician who is calm and in control reassuring (Hipple, 1983). Genuine interest and concern in the client's story can further help reassure the client that the interview is a safe environment and discourage the use of inappropriate ways of communicating distress. Twemlow (2001) suggests that "rational maneuvering" or pointing out the consequences of a client's violent actions in a nonthreatening manner can also help with de-escalation. Emotionally charged material should be approached cautiously and only after rapport has been established and the client calmed down in order to minimize the likelihood of escalation. One guideline for working with agitated clients is that the therapist be active for 10 seconds of every minute (Eichleman, 1996). Agitated clients with cognitive limitations may require frequent restating, paraphrasing, and reaffirming of what has been said. If the client appears psychotic, the interviewer can provide reassurance about the purpose of the interview in a straightforward manner, thus assisting the client's reality testing. The clinician should assess the client's ability to respond to verbal limitations and interventions (e.g., Is the client calmed or further agitated when the clinician attempts to change topics or asks the client to breathe deeply and collect his or her thoughts?). If escalation occurs, the clinician may need to change topics or end the interview altogether. The interview may also need to be stopped if the client is intoxicated or extremely psychotic (e.g., highly disorganized or paranoid; McNeil, 1998).

Table 1.2   Basic safety strategies

Know the agency's emergency and security procedures.
Review prior records and intake information.
Be sensitive to scheduling and availability of others.
Be aware of physical surroundings, door access, and furnishings.
Conduct interview in a safe environment.
Use appropriate interviewing techniques.
Observe a safe distance when approaching client.
Do not make abrupt moves; approach in a calm, nonthreatening manner.
Attend to verbal and nonverbal cues.
Do not make provocative or threatening comments.
Calm and reassure the client, and assist the client's reality testing.
Address threats directly; explore veiled or indirect threats.
Be alert for escalating emotions or loss of control.
Leave physical restraint to those trained in the procedures.

In summary, clinicians should trust their gut instinct regarding danger, and if at all concerned have another person present or move the interview to a more secure setting. Obtaining training in basic self-defense strategies is a good idea for clinicians, particularly those who work in settings where agitated or potentially violent clients are frequently seen. Several safety guidelines to minimize the risk to therapist safety are summarized in Table 1.2.

Gather Relevant Paperwork

Basic paperwork, such as the consent to treatment form, Health Insurance Portability and Accountability Act (HIPAA) forms, release of information forms, clinician's business card and emergency contact information, and information regarding clinic policies and procedures, should be readied for the client prior to the initial interview. Because a great deal of information is typically gathered in the first session, an interview form on which notes can be written and organized is highly recommended. While it is helpful to jot down key phrases or descriptions that the client uses or any instances of unusual language use (see section on the mental status exam, later in this chapter), avoid trying to write down verbatim everything that the client says, as this will make it difficult for you to adequately listen to the client, observe his or her behavior, and make appropriate eye contact (Phares, 1992). Clients usually will not mind if notes are taken during the interview. In fact, some clients may resent the clinician who writes nothing down during the interview and may interpret this to mean that the clinician does not take their comments seriously (H. I. Kaplan & Saddock, 1998). Packets of necessary paperwork can be made in advance so that one can be assured of always having all necessary forms before going into the first interview. It is also helpful to have an up-to-date referral notebook available that contains the business cards or names and phone numbers of fellow treatment providers who may be able to provide adjunctive services (e.g., psychiatrists who can conduct medication evaluations) or to whom referral of the client might ultimately need to be made.

LEGAL AND ETHICAL ISSUES IN INTERVIEWING

Informed Consent

Just as the decision to enter psychotherapy is not made lightly by most individuals, clinicians too must take seriously their obligation to provide prospective clients with sufficient information that will allow them to make an informed decision about pursuing treatment. According to Welfel (2002), disclosure and free consent are two key aspects of informed consent; that is, clients should be provided with full information about issues that could affect their decision to engage in treatment, and their decision to enter treatment should not be the result of coercion or undue pressure (e.g., warning clients that they will not get better unless they enter treatment with you). Major mental health professional organizations, including the American Psychological Association (APA), American Counseling Association (ACA), American Association of Marriage and Family Therapists (AAMFT), and the National Association of Social Workers (NASW), contain within their ethics codes guidelines regarding informed consent. The language used in these codes varies somewhat, but important principles emphasized in them include (a) obtaining informed consent during treatment, (b) providing adequate information to the client in developmentally and culturally appropriate language, (c) ensuring that the client has the capacity to consent, (d) avoiding coercion of the client and communicating the right of the client to refuse or withdraw from services, and (e) documenting client consent (AAMFT, 2001; ACA, 2005; APA, 2002; NASW, 2000).

What constitutes adequate information in the context of informed consent? Clients should be informed, for example, of your credentials and training, information relating to the process of treatment (e.g., goals, therapy techniques), confidentiality, and practical issues such as your fee, cancellation policy (e.g., how far in advance appointments must be canceled to avoid being charged), and how to contact you in an emergency or after hours. Table 1.3 lists elements that are recommended for inclusion in an informed consent process. The use of the term *process* here stresses that informed consent is not solely

Table 1.3   Elements to include in an informed consent process

Clinician's education and training (including licensure, status as a trainee)

Purposes, goals, procedures, and techniques of therapy

Treatment length (e.g., length of sessions, estimated length of overall treatment)

Risks and benefits of treatment

Treatment alternatives

Confidentiality and its limits (e.g., mandated reporting)

Involvement of third parties (e.g., insurance claims, coordination among treatment providers, supervision, consultation)

Fees and billing arrangements (including actions to be taken in the event of nonpayment)

Cancellation policies

Emergency and after-hours contact procedures and information

Access to treatment records

Right to ask questions and receive answers regarding treatment

How disputes and complaints will be handled

What happens in the event clinician becomes disabled or dies addressed at the start of treatment or through the signing of an informed consent form, but should be considered an ongoing dialogue as issues, goals, risks, and benefits of treatment change over time (Handelsman, 2001). However, it is important to initially address the issue of informed consent as early as possible in the treatment relationship so that the client is made aware of information that could affect his or her willingness to pursue treatment with you. Although state laws vary regarding the requirement to document informed consent in writing, it is good practice to provide clients with a written informed consent form that they sign and receive a copy of, rather than solely relying on an oral consent procedure. Sole reliance on an oral consent procedure is problematic for several reasons, including the difficulty most clients would have in remembering everything that should be covered in an informed consent procedure and the possibility that a client who chooses to sue a clinician may deny having ever given oral consent (Sales, Miller, & Hall, 2005).

In addition to documenting informed consent through the use of a signed form, any discussions that pertain to issues of informed consent that occur throughout treatment should be clearly documented in the client's case notes. Indeed, clinicians are likely to find that certain issues that are relevant to informed consent (e.g., psychotherapy duration, goals, and activities) are not easily addressed at the start of treatment and are likely to be meaningfully discussed only as the treatment progresses and the client's background and presenting problems are more fully understood (Pomerantz, 2005).

It is important to ensure that an individual has the capacity to consent. If an individual is deemed unable to meaningfully provide consent because of psychiatric, developmental, or cognitive limitations, consent must be obtained by a legally authorized individual. Children, for example, are not recognized as being legally capable of providing informed consent because of limitations in judgment and experience. As such, consent must be provided by the child's legal parent or guardian. If parents share custody of a child, obtaining the consent of both parents is advisable (Welfel, 2002). Sales et al. (2005) note the importance of determining the custodial status of any parent seeking to place a child in treatment as some states will allow only a parent with legal custody to consent to treatment and/or will allow a noncustodial parent to consent to treatment only in certain emergency situations. Under certain circumstances a child (i.e., person under the age of 18) may be able to consent to mental health services. For example, certain states recognize the rights of emancipated minors to consent to mental health treatment services. Some states also allow unemancipated minors to consent to certain forms of treatment such as contraceptive services, testing and treatment for HIV and other sexually transmitted diseases, prenatal care and delivery services, and treatment for alcohol and drug abuse. Clinicians who treat minors should become familiar with state laws concerning these issues.

Even when an individual cannot legally provide informed consent, it is advisable to obtain his or her *assent* to treatment. This means that the client agrees to services even though the agreement is not legally recognized (Handelsman, 2001). The information imparted to an individual in such a situation must obviously be tailored to his or her psychological capacities (APA, 2002). For example, although very young children may not be able to meaningfully understand what agreeing to treatment means, Morrison and Anders (1999) suggest that beginning around age 7 children are able to reasonably participate in discussions of issues such as confidentiality. As Welfel (2002) notes, in the case of older adolescents the information imparted in an assent procedure will increasingly approximate what is included in a typical informed consent process with an adult client.

Confidentiality

Most clients enter psychotherapy with an expectation that what they disclose will be kept strictly confidential (D. J. Miller & Thelen, 1986). Although this expectation is reasonable for the most part, clinicians have legal and ethical responsibilities both to maintain confidentiality and also to breach it under certain circumstances. For example, all 50 states require mental health professionals to report cases of suspected child abuse or neglect, and most states have similar mandated reporting laws for cases of suspected elder or dependent abuse (although the precise wording of such laws varies by state). Similarly, when a client discloses a threat to harm a specific individual, laws specify the steps clinicians must take to protect these potential victims, which may include breaching confidentiality. Confidentiality may also be breached if an individual is at risk of self-harm (e.g., a clinician can discuss the client's case with other treatment professionals in arranging for an involuntary hospitalization). If a client initiates legal action against a therapist, client confidentiality is waived to allow the clinician to defend himself or herself by discussing details of the treatment in court. Also, if a client is involved in litigation in which he or she is claiming psychological harm (and citing treatment with you in building his or her case), confidentiality is not protected (Welfel, 2002). Clinicians can also be compelled by a court order to produce treatment records or give testimony about a client. In certain states, if a client discloses the intent to commit a crime in the future and the client is being investigated by law enforcement officials, the clinician may be compelled to report this to the officials (Glosoff, Herlihy, & Spence, 2000). In certain states, confidentiality of an individual's positive HIV status cannot be guaranteed. For example, some states require new HIV-positive test results (including the names of affected individuals) to be reported to governmental agencies, and some states require disclosure of HIV-positive status to an individual's sexual partner (Sales et al., 2005).

The preceding discussion is not an exhaustive list of situations in which confidentiality may be breached, and it is beyond the scope of this text to provide such a review (for further information, see Sales et al., 2005; Welfel, 2002). It is probably safe to say that most clients will not be aware of the many circumstances in which confidentiality cannot be assured, and as such these exceptions should be discussed with the client and clearly documented in a written informed consent to treatment form that the client reads and signs at the start of treatment. The preceding discussion also emphasizes the importance of clinicians taking responsibility for becoming familiar with the laws governing confidentiality in the state in which they practice and keeping abreast of statutes and case law relating to this issue. The latter is probably most efficiently and easily achieved by participating in continuing education workshops and through updates provided by one's professional organization (Glosoff, Herlihy, Herlihy, & Spence, 1997). Clinicians should also be familiar with their professional organization's ethics code as it relates to issues of confidentiality (AAMFT, 2001; ACA, 2005; APA, 2002; NASW, 2000).

As previously noted, a child is rarely able to consent to treatment. This raises interesting questions about the confidentiality of the child's disclosures in treatment. From a legal perspective, if a parent consented to treatment on behalf of the child, the parent will have the right to access the child's treatment records. However, parents and guardians consenting to treatment may also have an expectation that beyond this, you will discuss with them everything the child says in sessions with you. Parents and guardians need to understand that if such an agreement is made, it is very likely the child will not be forthcoming with you and that this could adversely affect the course of treatment. Of course, parents and guardians have a right to know if a child discloses anything in a session that indicates the child's health or well-being is in jeopardy (e.g., if the child expresses suicidal ideation, if the child reports abuse, if the child is taking drugs; Morrison & Anders, 1999). This should be explained to the parents and guardian and the child client, along with the fact that certain disclosures required by law (e.g., child abuse) necessitate that third parties be informed.

In cases where confidentiality must be breached, it is important to fully document the rationale and the steps taken in reaching this decision in the client's case notes. Such documentation can show that a clinician thoughtfully considered issues pertaining to the client's confidentiality and are valuable should questions later arise as to the appropriateness of a clinician's actions (Reamer, 2005).

Health Insurance Portability and Accountability Act

In 1996, the U.S. Congress enacted the Health Insurance Portability and Accountability Act, Public Law 104–191, in an effort to improve the efficiency and effectiveness of the health care system. More specifically, HIPAA was designed to facilitate the transfer of health care benefits from one employer to another (hence the name "portability"), to give individuals greater access to their own medical records and increased control over how personally identifiable health information is used, and to reduce administrative paperwork and decrease fraud within the health care system (Brendal & Bryan, 2004). Although HIPAA is intended to improve aspects of the health care system related to the storage and transmission of patient health information, it has been criticized for being convoluted, difficult to comply with, and misleading with regard to how well the privacy of health information is actually protected (Kuczynski & Gibbs-Wahlberg, 2005). Nevertheless, HIPAA is now the law of the land, and individuals or organizations considered to be "covered entities" must comply with its provisions. A covered entity is any health plan, health care clearinghouse, or health care provider who conducts certain transactions (e.g., claims, inquiries regarding eligibility and benefits, enrollment information, referral and authorization requests, payments) electronically (e.g., through the use of computers and computer networks).

An important part of HIPAA is the Privacy Rule, which took effect in April 2003. This rule outlines for covered entities who can and cannot receive an individual's protected health information, requires that reasonable administrative, technical, and physical safeguards be put in place to protect the privacy of such information, and mandates that clients be notified of their health care provider's privacy policies. With regard to the last item, HIPAA requires that a good faith effort be made to obtain clients' written acknowledgment of receipt of such notice. The notice of privacy policies informs clients of how their personally identifiable health information may be used and disclosed and specifies those situations in which written authorization from the client is required for disclosure and when disclosures of information can be made without the client's authorization (Sales et al., 2005). Thus, if you determine that you or the organization for which you work is a covered entity, you will need to provide your client with notice of your privacy policies and document the client's receipt of it.

Clinicians who are considered covered entities or who work in a setting that is considered a covered entity by HIPAA should familiarize themselves with all applicable HIPAA provisions. Detailed information about HIPAA is available through the U.S. Department of Health and Human Services' website (www.hhs.gov/ocr/hipaa/). In addition, one's professional organization can be consulted for HIPAA-relevant information.

Release of Information

It is not uncommon during the course of an intake interview to determine that it is useful or necessary to gather additional information about the client from a knowledgeable third party. This might be a prior therapist, a past or current psychopharmacologist, a general physician, or a family member or significant other. In some cases, the purpose of these contacts is to obtain additional information that will aid in diagnosis and/or treatment planning; in other cases, contact with collateral sources is needed to coordinate treatment. In any case, it is necessary to obtain the client's (or parent's or guardian's) signed consent to contact these individuals. A release of information form accomplishes this purpose. Even when a client has provided verbal permission to contact a third party, this should be memorialized in the form of a signed release form.

The HIPAA regulations discussed previously outline the elements that should be included in a valid written authorization to release information. These include the name of the client, the name and address of the facility or person from whom information will be obtained and to whom information will be released, the purpose of the disclosure, limitations of the disclosure (e.g., regarding the type of information to be released), a statement that the client can revoke the authorization, and the length of time for which the authorization will be valid (e.g., 1 year). If a clinician is not subject to the HIPAA provisions (i.e., is not a covered entity), the elements of a release of information specified under the HIPAA provisions provide a reasonable standard to follow, and we recommend including these in any written release of information form. The release form should be signed and dated by the client or his or her legal guardian (e.g., in the case of a child client or a client under conservatorship). When requesting information from a third party, always send a copy of the release of information to the individual or agency from whom information is being requested and keep the original in the client's file.

Sometimes clients are hesitant to have others contacted as part of the intake process. There may be reluctance to reveal being in treatment to others, or, if there were conflicts with previous treatment providers, there may be concern about how these individuals will portray the client. Such concerns should not be summarily dismissed by simply insisting that additional information from collateral sources is necessary. While such information may be very important for understanding the client's current situation, the client's concerns must first be addressed. For example, you can explain exactly what kinds of information you are hoping to obtain from collateral sources and the limits of information that will be provided to these sources (e.g., obtaining only historical information from the client's sister but disclosing nothing to her about the reasons the client is seeking treatment).

INTERVIEWING THE CLIENT

Establishing Rapport

The new client, however motivated for treatment, faces a daunting task in the first session: He or she must be prepared to reveal to a virtual stranger highly personal thoughts, feelings, and experiences, many of which may be distressing or embarrassing. For clients to lower their defenses enough to provide meaningful information to assist in diagnosis and treatment planning, they must feel sufficiently safe with the clinician (Wiehe, 1996). The establishment of rapport and a good working relationship with the client is a necessary component of this process. Rapport can be defined as the feeling of harmony and confidence that exists between client and clinician (Morrison, 1995b). Rapport helps put a client at ease, contributes to feeling that one's worldview and suffering are understood, and instills hope that the clinician has the insight and expertise to help (Ivey & Matthews, 1984; Othmer & Othmer, 1989). As Phares (1992, p. 166) aptly notes, "Rapport . . . is not a state wherein the clinician is always liked or always regarded as a great person. It is, rather, a relationship founded upon respect, mutual confidence, trust, and a certain degree of permissiveness. It is neither a prize bestowed by an awed client nor a popularity contest to be won by the clinician." Rapport and a strong therapeutic alliance are not only critical for eliciting information during the initial interview, but also consistently predict more positive overall outcomes in psychotherapy (Constantino, Castonguay, & Schut, 2002; Horvath, 1994; D. N. Klein et al., 2003; P. Solomon, Drain, & Delany, 1995; Sue, 1988). Thus, the establishment of rapport is not just a goal to be sought during the initial interview, but an ongoing process that operates throughout treatment (C. Rogers, 1992; Utay & Utay, 1999).

Skills such as listening, reflecting and summarizing, asking pertinent and correctly timed questions, and displaying appropriate nonverbal behavior contribute to the process of establishing rapport. Not surprisingly, such interpersonal process skills have been found to highly correlate with client satisfaction (Bögels, van der Vleuten, Kreutzkamp, Melles, & Schmidt, 1995). However, clinicians often do not closely monitor and evaluate these skills, because many (e.g., nonverbal behavior) occur with little conscious awareness and greater attention is usually allocated to *what* areas will be addressed in the interview rather than *how* they will be approached (i.e., content versus process skills). Thus, it is helpful to review fundamental skills of good interviewing before addressing specific content areas that should be covered in the initial interview.

Setting the Tone

The verbal style adopted in the interview does much to facilitate or hamper the establishment of rapport. For example, an overly casual style ("Hi, Mary" versus "Hello, Mrs. Martinez") may be viewed as nonprofessional by some clients. When in doubt about how to address a client, the least offensive alternative should be adopted, which usually means using the most formal and/or conservative option (R. Sommers-Flanagan & Sommers-Flanagan, 1999). However, recognize that some clients (e.g., adolescents) may feel the clinician is out of touch with their experiences if more casual terminology or vernacular with which a client is comfortable is not used. The wording a clinician uses throughout the interview (in asking questions, making comments, providing information) should be appropriate to the client's cognitive and developmental level, and care should be taken to avoid the use of technical words that the client may misunderstand or not know (Morrison, 1995b).

Introducing the Interview

Information on the purpose and format of the interview should be presented before delving into questions about why a client is seeking treatment or about his or her background.

As mentioned under "Legal and Ethical Considerations," information about confidentiality and its limits should be offered up front. The client should be told how long the interview will last, what you hope to accomplish, and how you will go about trying to achieve these goals (e.g., taking notes, use of a fairly structured interview style). Because so much is covered in the initial interview it is helpful for clients to know that at certain points you may interrupt them to ask about something else, and that this is not meant to convey disinterest in what is being discussed, but rather to ensure that you have a thorough understanding of their situation and the background context against which current concerns are occurring. If you work in a clinic setting, where the clinician conducting the intake interview may not be the person who ends up treating the client, you should indicate this at the start of the interview. Although some clients may be anxious to begin telling you why they are there, most will appreciate waiting a few minutes to hear you discuss how the session will be structured. We favor establishing a collaborative tone with the client and in this spirit recommend asking the client what he or she hopes to get out of the interview. This simple question can reveal the client's expectations, pressing concerns, and misperceptions of the interview process. If the client expresses goals that are clearly not possible to achieve (e.g., "I want you to tell me whether I should leave my wife"), the clinician can correct such expectations up front and avoid a situation where the client feels frustrated or duped at the end of the session. By finding out what the client expects and desires to occur during the first interview, the clinician can structure the time so that both client and clinician goals can be met to the fullest degree possible.

Listening

Listening is arguably the most important skill the clinician brings to the interview situation. Although effective and accurate listening may, on the surface, appear to be a relatively easy and somewhat passive activity, in reality it is an active process that challenges the clinician to simultaneously attend to a number of different tasks. In addition to noting the content and emotional tone of a client's responses, the clinician must formulate questions, integrate information as the interview progresses, and make note of any inconsistencies or issues needing clarification. As McWilliams (2004, p. 133) notes, "Listening in a professional capacity is a disciplined, meditative, and emotionally receptive activity in which the therapist's needs for self-expression and self-acknowledgment are subordinated to the psychological needs of the client."

A good way to begin an interview is to allow some unstructured, uninterrupted time that allows clients to present their story. Not only does this facilitate the development of rapport, but it allows the clinician an opportunity to observe the client's manner of relating, the organization of thought processes, mood, and other important behaviors that are key elements of the mental status exam, discussed later in this chapter. Effective listeners flexibly adapt questions based on the story they hear from the client. To be a receptive listener, the clinician should not be distracted by extraneous thoughts or an uncomfortable physical state such as extreme fatigue or hunger. For this reason, allow sufficient time prior to client sessions to collect your thoughts, rest, and get something to eat or drink if necessary. Scheduling sessions too closely together without a break or when rushing from another appointment greatly increases the likelihood that you will not be in a frame of mind to be focused on your client and able to accurately listen to him or her.

Another aspect of effective listening is becoming comfortable with periods of silence. Silence allows clients space to consider their thoughts and feelings, to reflect on something they or the clinician has just stated, to free-associate, or to recover from difficult material that has been discussed (R. Sommers-Flannagan & Sommers-Flannagan, 1999). In their examination of 59 therapy interviews, Sharpley, Munro, Elly, and Martin (2005) determined that periods rated high in rapport were associated with greater lengths of silence compared to those rated low in rapport, and that therapist-initiated but client-terminated silences were more likely to contribute to rapport than silences that were both initiated and terminated by the therapist. Although silences are important, overuse in the very early phases of treatment can be counterproductive because the client may experience considerable anxiety in response to them (McWilliams, 2004).

Clinicians convey that they are listening through verbal and nonverbal channels. Leaning toward a client, maintaining a relaxed and attentive posture, placing legs and feet unobtrusively, minimizing extraneous movements, sitting an arm's length from the client, using smooth, unobtrusive hand gestures, and maintaining facial expressions that are congruent with feelings expressed by oneself or the client are positive interviewer behaviors that convey that the therapist is attuned to the client (J. Sommers-Flanagan & Sommers-Flanagan, 1993). Other nonverbal behaviors that have been empirically demonstrated to further the therapeutic process include frequent but not staring eye contact, a warm, relaxed vocal tone, and a moderate degree of head nodding and smiling (J. A. Hall, Harrigan, & Rosenthal, 1995). Because more than 60% of communication is estimated to take place via nonverbal means (Burgoon et al., 1993), one should not underestimate the power that nonverbal communication plays in establishing rapport with the client. In fact, nonverbal behavior has been found to play a dominant role in the expression of empathy (Tepper & Haase, 1978). A clinician who is listening but fails to indicate this through his or her nonverbal behavior (i.e., fails to make appropriate eye content, does not nod) can mistakenly convey inattention to the client. Because we are often unaware of our own nonverbal actions, it is exceedingly helpful (with a client's permission) to videotape at least one interview to review this important class of interpersonal behavior.

Facilitative comments (e.g., "Mm-hmm"; "Tell me more") also communicate that you are listening. Sharpley and McNally's (1997) finding that experienced clinicians use such minimal verbal encouragers more frequently and are rated more highly in terms of client-perceived rapport than their less experienced counterparts suggests that the use of minor verbalizations by a skilled interviewer can effectively maximize rapport. Listening can also be conveyed to the client verbally through appropriately timed questions that (a) incorporate information that has been given, (b) seek to clarify ("Do you mean . . . ?"), and (c) provide additional information ("Tell me more about that"). Listening is also conveyed through reflections and interpretations.

Reflections and Interpretations

When clinicians use a reflection, they are restating or rephrasing something the client has expressed. There are different levels of reflective responses: verbatim repetition of or paraphrasing something the client has said, restatement of an emotion the client has clearly stated or that is obvious he or she is experiencing in the moment, restating meaning that is implied by the client's statements, and summarizing major themes or pieces of information the client has disclosed over the course of the interview (R. Sommers-Flannagan & Sommers-Flannagan, 1999). Some examples of reflections are:

> *Client:* I don't know if I should change jobs. I like the financial security of my work, but I'm constantly behind on deadlines and everything I do just keeps piling up. I used to think what I did was interesting but not anymore.
>
> *Verbatim Reflection:* You're not certain if this job is for you. There are some things, like the money, that are good, and other things, like the deadlines you have to meet and what you do at work that you don't like.
>
> *Reflection of Feeling:* It sounds like you feel quite ambivalent about your job and often overwhelmed.
>
> *Reflection of Meaning:* It sounds like you no longer find your work meaningful and that you're not sure that financial security is enough reason to stay at something you don't really like.

These kinds of statements let clients know that you have been listening to what they have said, enhance rapport, encourage discussion of an issue, and allow the clinician to check that the client has been correctly heard.

Interpretations differ from reflections by going beyond a mere restatement of what the client has expressed in an attempt to uncover the underlying deeper meaning and/or feelings. R. Sommers-Flanagan and Sommers-Flanagan (1999) classify interpretations as directive listening responses or responses designed to direct a client toward certain material. Interpretations attempt to provide explanations of behavior that a client may not have considered and involve renaming the client's thoughts and feelings from the viewpoint of the clinician (Compas & Gotlib, 2002). Caution should be exercised in using interpretations during the initial interview because they can adversely affect rapport if the client is not ready to hear them (Morrison, 1995b). Remember too that the process of extracting key underlying themes or issues from the surface content requires not only skill, but a certain degree of knowledge about the client; because of this you may not have enough information to make meaningful interpretations in the initial interview.

Questioning

Effective questioning enhances the clinician's ability to collect specific information, control the quantity or quality of information, reveal the client's feelings and motives, and encourage the client to disclose general information. Questions allow the clinician to develop a structure or agenda for the interview, redirect the interview, and obtain a deeper understanding of information revealed by the client. However, when questions are overused, the client may feel offended, bombarded, or confused (Pederson & Ivey, 1993). Successful questioning is predicted on good listening skills. As a client is interviewed, cues that follow-up questioning is needed include client responses that are (a) vague ("I was *sort of* anxious"), (b) use extreme terminology ("That relationship was the *worst*"; "I can *never* concentrate"), (c) seem overly minimizing ("My depression *wasn't that bad*"), (d) contain psychological or diagnostic jargon or terminology ("I had a *nervous breakdown*"; "When the *panic attacks* happened . . . "), or (e) use words (e.g., *hopeless*) or are accompanied by affect (e.g., crying) indicating strong emotional content.

A very basic distinction in questioning is between open-ended and closed-ended questions. Closed-ended questions can be answered using only one or two words (e.g., "When did you meet your husband?"), whereas open-ended questions require longer responses (e.g., "Please describe your relationship with your husband"). There are a number of advantages in using open-ended questions during the initial interview. They can broaden the scope of information obtained from the client, convey interest in hearing the client's story, allow more opportunities to observe the client's behavior, encourage the free expression of feelings, and be better received by clients who have complex or ambivalent feelings about a topic (Morrison, 1995b). However, a good interviewer does not necessarily solely or even primarily use open-ended questions, and care must be taken to avoid asking too many broad, nondirective questions so that control of the interview is lost. Instead, an effective interviewer flexibly utilizes both open- and closed-ended questions to match the verbal skills, emotional state, attentional abilities, and cognitive capacities of the client. For example, reliance on primarily structured, closed-ended questions may be needed for guarded or reticent clients, persons of limited cognitive capacity, or individuals who are extremely tangential or disorganized and who cannot be easily redirected to answer the original question. As Pederson and Ivey (1993) note, a really good question will not have a simple answer, but will encourage a great deal of constructive exploration.

There are certain types of questions that should be used judiciously. Some believe that "why" questions should be avoided during the initial interview because answering these (a) requires a level of insight that the client may not yet possess, (b) may lead the client to feel inadequate if he or she does not know the answer, and (c) may result in the client's feeling prematurely intruded upon to share highly personal feelings (Lukas, 1993). However, appropriately timed "why" questions may help to uncover a client's motives (Pederson & Ivey, 1993). Hipple and Hipple (1983) suggest that asking "How can you account for that?" is a more acceptable alternative to "Why?" that may yield more information. Questions of a confrontational nature should generally be avoided during the first interview or should be restricted to one or two key issues about which there are contradictions. In broaching such questions, avoid an adversarial tone in favor of one that expresses genuine puzzlement and a desire to understand exactly what the client meant; this may help to avoid putting the client on the defensive and breaching rapport (Morrison, 1995b). With agitated clients, confrontation must be used very cautiously as this could increase the likelihood of aggressive escalation.

Clinicians should also avoid leading questions and instead strive to be neutral in the way questions are posed so that a preferred answer is not suggested to the client (Leon, 1982). Failure to do so may result in questionably valid information that reflects what the client thinks the clinician wishes to hear rather than the reality of the situation. However, there are times when it may be appropriate to suggest possible responses to a client who is having a particularly difficult time answering a question ("Did your sister's disapproval about your engagement anger or sadden you, or cause some other feeling?"). This could occur when interviewing clients with impoverished thinking (e.g., an individual with Schizophrenia who has prominent negative symptoms) or limited cognitive abilities, those who experience difficulty describing emotional states (a condition sometimes referred to as alexythymia), and clients who are difficult to engage. In an attempt to gather as much information as possible in the limited time of an initial interview, novice clinicians often err on the side of asking multiple questions at once ("Can you tell me about the problems you have been having at work? Are these something new or have you had them before? And what has your boss said to you?"). This can be very problematic for clients who are nervous or who have attention or concentration difficulties. Leon recommends rehearsing questions mentally before asking them to reduce the possibility of such compound questions.

Answering Client Questions

During the initial interview one should expect to be asked some questions by the client. Although some schools of therapy discourage answering clients' questions to avoid fostering dependence and circumventing self-examination and self-inquiry (Pederson & Ivey, 1993), you are ethically bound to respond to certain questions such as your training and experience, the type of therapy you practice, and how you propose to treat the client (i.e., treatment plan). Similarly, information should be provided about fees, cancellation policy, and procedures for contacting the clinician in an emergency; as previously reviewed, this sort of information should also be included in the consent to treatment form. How questions regarding your diagnostic impressions and treatment recommendations are handled is important in helping the client develop a realistic perspective on his or her treatment (what can and cannot be done) and prognosis (S. M. Turner et al., 2003).

Some client questions may involve requests for the clinician to self-disclose personal information (e.g., details of one's life, one's feelings about a particular issue). Inquiries about a clinician's personal life usually reflect a broader underlying concern or issue; for example, questions about marital status or children may indicate concern about the clinician's ability to understand, empathize, or help with family-related concerns. Redirecting clients toward discussing these underlying issues is generally more helpful than answering their initial question. However, in some cases, therapists may choose to disclose their own feelings or personal information as a means of strengthening the working relationship with a client. For example, the disclosure of a therapist's feelings in the present moment can be a powerful intervention that can enhance rapport and can model how to talk about one's emotions (Compas & Gotlib, 2002). In fact, some theorists contend that self-disclosure enhances rapport by decreasing the power differential and hierarchical nature of the client-therapist relationship and by demystifying the therapy process (Mahalik, van Ormer, & Simi, 2000). However, the disclosure of personal feelings or information should be done with a clear therapeutic purpose in mind and not to fulfill the needs of the therapist. Among the dangers of therapist self-disclosure are (a) creating in clients a need to take care of the therapist's feelings and censoring what is mentioned in treatment, (b) making clients feel as if a boundary has been violated, (c) overtaking or infringing on a client's story, (d) making it difficult to determine whose agenda is being addressed because the client's and therapist's stories have become too intertwined, and (e) making a client believe the therapist is redirecting interest away from the client and toward the therapist (J. Roberts, 2005). Clients frequently come to the first session in distress and looking for answers that will help alleviate their suffering as soon as possible. As a result, you may be asked for direct advice on how to handle a particular problem the client is experiencing. Although directive guidance and active intervention are appropriate in some circumstances, such as dealing with clients in crisis (see Chapter 2, "Crisis Issues"), in most cases the first session should be devoted to information gathering. Furthermore, most schools of therapy caution against direct advice giving, preferring for solutions to emanate from clients themselves. Premature intervention can lead to inappropriate treatment and may cause the client to feel misunderstood or rushed (J. Sommers-Flanagan & Sommers-Flanagan, 1993).

INTERVIEWING THE CLIENT: WHAT TO ASK

Goals of a standard outpatient intake interview include identifying, evaluating, and exploring the client's primary complaint and treatment goals, getting a sense of the client's interpersonal skills and style, obtaining information about the client's personal history, and evaluating the client's current life situation (R. Sommers-Flanagan & Sommers-Flanagan, 1999). Another goal of the intake interview is to determine whether you (or someone in your agency) have the appropriate knowledge and skills to treat the client (Phares, 1992). The more information you can obtain during the initial interview, the more likely that timely decisions regarding diagnosis and treatment disposition can be made. Another reason to maximize the information gathered during the first interview is because clients are often most receptive to discussing their presenting problems and history during the first session because of the distress they feel; between the first and second sessions some clients may develop significant resistance toward the therapeutic process and may be less forthcoming (Siassi, 1984). This portion of the chapter reviews the essential topics that should be covered in the initial intake interview. Table 1.4 summarizes the main content areas that you will typically want to cover in the initial interview. The initial interview can be expected to take 50 to 90 minutes. Although you should aim to gather as much information as possible during this time, more than one meeting may be required depending on a number of factors, including but not limited to the complexity of the client's history and presenting problems, cognitive and verbal abilities, level of insight, comfort level with you, and whether the client is in a crisis state (S. M. Turner et al., 2003). Also, be flexible and recognize that depending on the situation, it may not be possible or even initially necessary to gather information in all of the areas listed in Table 1.4.

Before reviewing these areas in depth, a word of caution is in order. It is natural to focus on just getting the facts for all these areas. However, failure to attend to feelings in

Table 1.4   Areas to cover in the initial interview

Demographics
Presenting problem(s)
Past psychiatric history (including family history)
Medical history (including family history)
Educational and work history (including military service)
Social history (family relationships, friendships)
Dating and marital history (including sexual functioning)
Ethnic, cultural, and spiritual identity
Legal history (including any current litigation)
Recent significant life events
Traumatic events
Coping
Resilience, competencies, and accomplishments

the pursuit of information about events can lead clients to feel misunderstood, reduce the likelihood of disclosure of important information, and result in missed opportunities for understanding the emotional experiences connected with certain topics. As Leon (1982) notes, questions about feelings often yield specific information about events, but solely asking about events will not always lead to the disclosure of feelings.

How Theoretical Orientation Affects Interview Content

The areas of inquiry we suggest for inclusion in an initial interview are ones that would be part of most standard diagnostic interviews. Such an interview is presumed to be fairly directive and structured and will contain many questions for the client. While nondirective interviews have been found to produce similar numbers of reported problems compared to directive interviews, the latter tend to also elicit more extensive, detailed, and better quality information about reported problems (A. Cox, Holbrook, & Rutter, 1981).

The interview framework we review here is not intended to reflect a particular school of therapy, and theoretical orientation will influence which of the areas receive the greatest emphasis, as well as the specific type and amount of information gathered for each. For example, in listening to a client's description of problems, a behaviorally oriented clinician will be attuned to and will direct questions toward obtaining descriptions of current, observable problematic behaviors and information on the antecedent conditions that facilitate these behaviors and understanding sources of positive or negative reinforcement that help maintain the behaviors—a process collectively known as a *functional analysis* (Acierno, Hersen, & Van Hasselt, 1998). The behavioral therapist may also use role-plays to assess specific skills and imaginal exposure techniques to evaluate beliefs and emotional reactions to specific stimuli (D. A. Beach, 1989). The cognitive therapist will try to determine the thoughts and/or images that accompany a client's negative emotional states (e.g., all-or-nothing thinking as related to depression) and through Socratic questioning will attempt to get the client to recognize the long-standing dysfunctional beliefs and schemas that underlie these thoughts and images (J. S. Beck, 1995). The psychodynamically oriented therapist may utilize less directive questioning and give the client greater latitude in taking the initiative and determining the content of the session (Strupp & Binder, 1984). Compared to other theoretical orientations, there may also be more questions aimed at understanding the nature and quality of relationships with early caregivers.

Demographics

Be sure to gather some basic demographic information about your client at the first interview if you do not already have this from some other source (e.g., phone intake form, past records). Demographic information that should be noted in each client's file includes age, gender, marital or partner status, number and ages of any children, occupation, religious affiliation, and self-identified ethnic/cultural group. With regard to the last, it is important not to assume that you know what a client's ethnic or cultural background is based on appearance or name. For example, a biracial individual may have a bicultural self-identity or may identify more strongly with one biological heritage or neither (C. I. Hall & Turner, 2001; Stephan, 1992).

Presenting Problem

One of the first areas to inquire about is the reason prompting the client's decision to seek treatment. The answer to a question such as "What problems brought you here today?" can reveal a host of information, including the concerns that are uppermost in the client's mind, level of insight or denial about problems, and aspects of the client's personality and mental status (e.g., mood, behavior, thought processes). To obtain this wealth of information, experienced interviewers often allow clients as much as 10 minutes of uninterrupted free speech to answer an initial question about the presenting problem and will make note of the client's exact words in describing the reason for seeking treatment (Morrison, 1995b). Jumping in too quickly when clients are describing why they came to therapy can result in a loss of valuable information and redirect the clients away from the problems they view as most pressing (D. A. Beach, 1989).

The mnemonic CLIENTS can be used to remember several dimensions about which to then inquire when exploring the presenting problem (see Table 1.5). The client's perception of the Cause of a problem can reveal the level of insight and knowledge he or she may have about her difficulties. For example, a client who is convinced that he will contract HIV from touching a door knob in a public building unless he washes his hands for 10 minutes afterward demonstrates less insight into his Obsessive-Compulsive Disorder symptoms than the client who recognizes that this belief is unfounded yet feels compelled to engage in repeated hand-washing. Asking questions about the source or cause of a client's difficulties, if the problem has a name, the symptoms associated with the problem, and what kind of treatment the client thinks the problem requires can also reveal culture-specific formulations or interpretations of symptoms and experiences (Twemlow, 1995). Failure to consider the client's conceptualization of his or her problems may result in nonadherence to recommended treatments or premature termination from therapy.

Questions regarding the Length of time a problem has been present provide information on chronicity, which may in turn give a rough indication of how lengthy the treatment is likely to be. Generally speaking, the longer the client has experienced the problems, the more difficult they will be to change. The scope of Impairment is a particularly crucial dimension to find out about, and almost all disorder criteria in the *Diagnostic and Statistical Manual of Mental Disorders* (*DSM-IV*; American Psychiatric Association, 2000b) require evidence of significant impairment in functioning (e.g., social, occupational)

Table 1.5 Client problems: ask about these dimensions

Cause: What does the client think has caused the problem?

Length: How long has this been a problem (chronic versus recent onset)?

Impairment: What areas of the client's life have been negatively affected by the problem (e.g., work or school, relationships, finances)?

Emotional impact: In what ways has the client's problem impacted him or her emotionally?

Noticed: Have other people noticed changes in the client's mood or behavior?

Tried: Has the client tried anything to alleviate the problem? How successful have these attempts been?

Stopped: In what ways would the client's life be different if his or her problem stopped or were no longer present?

before a diagnosis can be made. Remember to ask about impairment in a variety of domains, including school or work, family and romantic relationships, friendships, household maintenance, personal health and hygiene, and finances. Questions about the Emotional impact that a client's problems have caused can provide clues to possible diagnoses (e.g., anxiety, depression). Inquiries about changes others have Noticed in the client not only can provide convergent evidence supporting the client's observations of his or her own functioning, but can expose denial or lack of insight, as suggested in the following exchange:

Clinician: Has your depression affected your work?
Client: No, I manage to hold it together pretty good at work and still get things done. Outside of work I'm not doing as well.
Clinician: What do others think about your work?
Client: Well, I got passed up for a promotion last month because I missed some deadlines and left out some items on reports. But that's got nothing to do with my depression; my boss is just a picky jerk.

Knowing about what the client has Tried to alleviate or fix the problem is useful since this tells you about his or her coping strategies and resourcefulness and can steer you away from interventions with a history of limited effectiveness. Be sure to inquire about formal (e.g., previous psychotherapy, talking to a family physician, taking medication) as well as informal (e.g., talking to family or friends, reading self-help books, searching for information on the Internet, praying, journaling) attempts to deal with the problem. If the client is taking psychotropic medications, be sure to write down their names, the length of time the medication has been taken, side effects experienced, and to what extent the client has adhered to the prescribed medication regimen. In such cases, the clinician should plan to coordinate treatment efforts with the prescribing physician and obtain the necessary releases of information from the client to contact other treatment providers.

Finally, it is interesting to ask clients to imagine what life would be like if the problems for which they are seeking treatment Stopped and were no longer present. Although clients may primarily mention positive changes that would result, it is helpful to ask about new difficulties or challenges that might be created (e.g., having to return to work or socialize more with others). Answers to such questions can uncover possible reinforcers for the problem and may help expose any function the problem might be serving in the client's life.

A sound understanding of the client's presenting problem not only is important for the initial stages of treatment planning, but can guide the clinician through difficulties during later stages of treatment. This is illustrated by Yalom's (2002) example of a female therapist who sought consultation about a therapeutic impasse with a male client. The client was demanding hand-holding and comforting hugs as part of his treatment. Yalom encouraged the therapist to recall the initial reasons the client came to treatment, which included complaints that relationships with women failed because he insisted on getting exactly what he wanted at all times. By recalling this initial, presenting complaint, the therapist subsequently gained insight into the client's current insistent behavior with her and was able to use this information as leverage in helping him gain a better understanding of how his behavior impacted others.

History

To determine the most appropriate diagnosis and plan for treatment, it is necessary to understand how the client's current difficulties fit into the larger framework of psychiatric, medical and developmental, social, cultural, and religious history.

Psychiatric History

While the problems and symptoms a client initially presents may directly relate to his or her ultimate diagnosis, this is not inevitably the case. A common error made by novice interviewers is to rely excessively or exclusively on information presented early in the interview to form diagnostic opinions (*primacy effect*). When a diagnostic impression is formed very early in the interview, subsequent questions may be geared primarily toward confirming this impression while neglecting to ask questions that may disconfirm it (*confirmatory bias*; Groth-Marnat, 2003). A study examining the concordance between information provided by clients in the first 5 minutes of a psychiatric interview and their final clinical diagnoses found correspondence in only 58% of cases (Herrán et al., 2001). This highlights the importance of devoting sufficient time and questions to understanding the range of psychiatric symptoms the client has experienced, both currently and in the past. It is a good idea to ask a screening question about each of the following major domains of psychiatric symptomatology: (a) *mood symptoms* (including depression and mania); (b) *anxiety symptoms* (including excessive worrying, phobias and fears, obsessive thoughts and compulsive behavior, panic attacks); (c) *symptoms and dissociative experiences related to Posttraumatic Stress Disorder (PTSD)*; (d) *psychotic experiences* (hallucinations, delusions); (e) *substance use*; (f) *eating problems*; (g) *impulse-control problems* (including suicidal or other self-injurious behavior, anger control problems or aggressive acting-out, and other impulsive behaviors such as excessive gambling or spending); (h) *cognitive problems* (e.g., memory problems, learning difficulties); (i) *sexual difficulties or conflicts*; and (j) *sleep disturbances*. Detailed follow-up questions regarding specific disorders can then be asked if the client endorses any symptoms in the screening questions. Clients should be asked if any symptoms they endorsed are currently a problem, how these symptoms have interfered with functioning (in the past or currently), and what treatment, if any, has been sought to alleviate these symptoms (including medication). Finally, it is important to find out about any history of psychiatric hospitalizations, including the approximate dates and lengths of stay, the circumstances leading to the hospitalization, treatments received in the hospital, and whether the hospitalization was voluntary.

Do not forget to ask about family history of psychiatric problems. Many psychiatric disorders have a strong heritable component, and a notable family history of a particular type of disorder can be an important piece of information when making diagnostic decisions. A general question, such as "Did anyone in your family ever have emotional problems or problems with drugs or alcohol that they sought treatment for or that you or someone else thought they could or should have sought treatment for?" can often reveal familial history of psychopathology. Gather information on diagnoses and/or symptoms, any treatments received, and the level of the family member's impairment (e.g., recurrently hospitalized, unable to work, impaired relationships).

Medical History

Gathering information about the client's current health status (including approximate date and results of the last physical exam, chronic conditions, current medical treatments, including medications), past significant illnesses, accidents, injuries, and hospitalizations, and family medical history is important for a number of reasons. Knowledge of a client's current health status provides information on potential stressors he or she is facing. In addition, some medical conditions can cause symptoms that mimic psychiatric conditions (e.g., hypothyroidism can mimic symptoms of depression, including anhedonia, forgetfulness, diminished concentration, low energy, and sleep disturbance). If a client presents with emotional or behavioral symptoms that may be attributable to a medical condition, the clinician should refer the client for a medical evaluation if one has not recently been conducted. Also, certain psychological syndromes (somatoform disorders) are associated with physical symptoms that are determined to have no organic basis. Such disorders might become diagnostic possibilities if a client describes a history of seeking medical attention for physical symptoms (e.g., pain) that have repeatedly been found to have no medically known cause. Of course, psychological symptoms can develop secondary to a medical condition and complicate its course, as in the case of a client who develops depression following a diagnosis of Type II diabetes and becomes unmotivated to monitor his or her daily blood sugar and make dietary changes.

Information about past health concerns or problems can lead to questions about how this affected the client's emotional, physical, and social development. A question such as "How was your physical health growing up?" or "Did you have any health problems as an infant, child, or teenager?" will usually suffice to gather this information. When asking these questions, it is appropriate to also inquire about the client's birth history. Many adult clients will not have detailed information on their own developmental history but will generally be able to report whether their mother had any significant problems during the pregnancy, if there were complications with the labor and/or delivery, and if there were any notable problems during the neonatal period. Clients may not be able to recall the precise ages at which various developmental milestones were reached, and this degree of detail for an adult client is typically not needed; instead, clients are more likely to recall parental comments such as "She walked early" or "She talked late," and this degree of detail is usually sufficient to get a general sense of the client's developmental history. Similarly, clients are likely to be able to report on what their parents or caregivers mentioned about their temperament and personality growing up. A more detailed developmental history is usually desired when interviewing a child, and information on this topic is presented later in this chapter.

Family medical history can reveal stressors (either past or current) that may have affected the client's development or current functioning (e.g., Did the client grow up with a chronically ill mother? Is the client the primary caretaker for his father with Alzheimer's disease?). In addition, family medical history may reveal conditions the client is at risk for and about which he or she is worried (e.g., a 50-year-old woman whose mother, sister, and grandmother all developed breast cancer in middle age). Finally, inquiries about medical conditions and their treatment may reveal general attitudes about treatment providers, treatment adherence, and so on. Although there is not necessarily a one-to-one correspondence between a client's attitudes toward physicians or compliance with medical treatment and analogous issues in psychotherapy, understanding a client's experiences, thoughts, and feelings about these issues can help a clinician understand how positive or negative the client's past treatment-related relationships have been.

If your client is currently taking medications for a medical condition, note the medication name, amount, length of time taken, and any side effects that have been experienced. Consultation with a text such as the *Physician's Desk Reference* (2007) following the session can assist you in learning more about the purposes, possible side effects (including psychological symptoms), and potential complications (e.g., overdose potential) of any medications your client is taking.

Social History (Family Relationships, Friendships)

As alluded to earlier, the amount and quality of information sought regarding a client's social history may vary depending on the theoretical orientation of the clinician. Yet, no matter what a clinician's theoretical framework, it is helpful to gather at least some basic information on the client's important social relationships and experiences, including basic facts about the client's family composition (e.g., family size, marital status of parents, whether significant family members are deceased), where the client was born and raised, and parental educational levels and occupations. When gathering information about the client's personal history, an initially nondirective stance should be adopted as this allows one to learn which relationships and experiences the client sees as most salient and significant (R. Sommers-Flanagan & Sommers-Flanagan, 1999). Eventually, more directive questions can be asked to address information not mentioned by the client. Siassi (1984) recommends obtaining *objective* information about significant individuals in the client's life, as well as the client's *subjective* impression of them. With regard to the latter, a simple question such as "Tell me three adjectives that would best describe your mother" can be used to quickly gather preliminary information on a client's view of important figures in his or her life. Similarly, Maxmen and Ward (1995) suggest asking clients to name the three to four most crucial turning points in their lives and to describe the most significant or memorable event during each major developmental period (e.g., childhood, adolescence, early adulthood, middle adulthood) as a time-efficient way to gather relevant information about a client's social history. Ideally, inquiries should be made about the quality relationships with parents and caregivers, siblings, important extended family members, and anyone else who played a significant role in the client's upbringing, including how these relationships have changed over time. If time permits, asking a few questions concerning the values emphasized in the family, how family members spent time together, important family traditions, similarities and differences among family members, and what each person's role in the family was perceived to be are exceedingly helpful in painting a fuller picture of the environment in which the client grew up. Construction of a genogram (i.e., a graphic representation of family relationships that resembles a family tree and uses symbols such as circles, squares, and different line styles) can aid the clinician in keeping track of complex family relationships and may uncover repetitive patterns, events, and themes in family relationships. It is beyond the scope of this chapter to review the construction and use of genograms, but the interested reader is referred to McGoldrick, Gerson, and Shellenberger (1999) for a thorough discussion of this topic.

Questions should also be directed toward gathering information about the client's friendships, both past and current. Because clients may be reluctant or embarrassed to admit to having few or no friends, a face-saving way to elicit such information is to neutrally structure questions so that either end of the relationship spectrum appears acceptable (e.g., "Some people like having a lot of friends and being around others, and other people may have fewer friends or do things more on their own. How was it for you growing up?"). It is important to follow up responses indicating that a client had few or no friends with a question as to whether this was the client's preference or if he or she wished things had been different; this distinction can have important diagnostic implications (e.g., suggesting schizoid versus avoidant characteristics).

Dating and Relationship History (Including Sexual Functioning)

Questions regarding a client's dating and relationship history should address the length and level of satisfaction of any current romantic relationship, as well as the history of significant past relationships. Remember that some clients experiencing relationship distress may focus primarily on negative aspects of their current relationship at the expense of reporting any positives that exist, so it may be necessary to probe for this information. Conversely, individuals whose primary complaint does not involve relationship issues may underreport problems in this area in order to appear more socially desirable or to save face. Victims of domestic violence may not spontaneously mention maltreatment for a number of reasons, including fear of the consequences of disclosing abuse and decreased awareness that such behavior is problematic. Asking about strengths of the relationship as well as areas in need of improvement can help to provide a balanced view. General screening questions about how conflicts are resolved and whether either member of the couple has been verbally or physically aggressive with the other may help to uncover any potentially abusive behavior that should be followed up. (Chapter 2, "Crisis Issues," addresses the topic of partner abuse in greater detail.)

When inquiring about relationships, do not neglect questions about sexual functioning. This can include questions about the frequency of sexual activity, level of satisfaction with sexual activity, whether client and partner agree on the frequency and nature of their sexual contact, changes in sexual behavior, and history of any sexual symptoms (e.g., premature ejaculation, lack of sexual desire). Additional information on questions pertinent to uncovering sexual difficulties or disorders is discussed in Chapter 13, "Eating, Sleep, Sexual, and Gender Identity Disorders." It is important to become comfortable asking clients about their sex lives without appearing embarrassed or judgmental. Recognize that because of the sensitivity of this topic, questions about sex are best saved until later in the interview, when you have better knowledge of the client and the client has developed a degree of comfort with you (Morrison, 1995b). An exception to this general rule is if a client's presenting problem concerns sexual issues. Finally, be sure not to assume what a client's sexual orientation is. For example, even a seemingly straightforward question about what type of birth control a sexually active female client uses upon closer analysis reveals a presumption that the client is having sex with a male partner (H. I. Kaplan & Saddock, 1998). When assumptions about heterosexuality are made, homosexual or bisexual clients may understandably feel that the clinician is uncomfortable with other orientations and may avoid discussion of this important aspect of their life. If a client is homosexual or bisexual, it is helpful to understand the degree to which the client feels comfortable with his or her sexual orientation and whether the client has come out to others and, if so, the degree of acceptance and support the client has received in response.

This may also lead into a discussion of how societal attitudes toward homosexuality may have affected the client either while growing up or currently.

Educational and Work History

Questions about a client's educational history should include the highest educational level completed and general performance in school (e.g., history of grade retention or grade skipping). In cases where cognitive functioning is of concern, or when a client is a child or adolescent, more detailed information on academic history will be needed. This could include best and worst subjects, performance on standardized tests, and special educational services received. When asking any client about educational history, it is useful to include questions pertaining to relationships with teachers and peers, as well as any history of behavioral difficulties (e.g., detention, suspensions, truancy).

Some time should be spent in the initial interview finding out about the client's current and past employment. For any significant employments, the clinician should obtain brief descriptions of job responsibilities and work schedules, length of employment, promotions, presence of any work-related difficulties (e.g., being fired, coworker conflicts), level of job satisfaction and stress, and reasons for leaving. The clinician can also evaluate such factors as whether the client seems under- or overqualified for his or her current position, which may provide interesting avenues for exploration in future sessions (e.g., Is the client's consistent history of employment in jobs that are below his or her level of training and education related to low self-esteem or fears of failure?). Inquiries about employment can also yield fruitful information about ability to handle responsibility, interpersonal skills, stress tolerance, persistence, and motivation.

Inquiries should also be made regarding any military service completed by the client. Relevant questions would include the branch of the military in which the client served, length and location(s) of service, highest rank attained, job responsibilities, disciplinary actions, commendations received, combat experience, and discharge status (e.g., honorable). Combat experiences should prompt later follow-up questions regarding PTSD symptomatology since rates of this disorder are elevated among combat veterans and associated with particularly high rates of disability (Kulka et al., 1990; Prigerson, Maciejewski, & Rosenheck, 2001).

Legal History

Some questions should relate to past or current legal troubles or actions, such as excessive traffic tickets, arrests, incarcerations, and litigation (either initiated by the client or which the client was subject to). Inquiries in this area can lead to diagnostic possibilities that should be explored; for example, an individual who reports being charged with driving under the influence should be thoroughly assessed for past and current alcohol abuse or dependence. Reports of illegal activity or repeated physical altercations should prompt exploration of diagnostic possibilities such as Conduct Disorder or Antisocial Personality Disorder. Current litigation is important to know about since a client may have some expectation that records from treatment either will or will not be used in the legal proceedings.

Racial, Ethnic, and Cultural Identity

Despite the importance of understanding how one's racial, ethnic, and cultural background influences self-identity and worldview, many therapists neglect to ask about these important aspects of a client's background. Clinicians may be uncomfortable asking clients questions about race, ethnicity, or culture for any of a number of reasons, including lack of training on how to do this, mistaken assumptions that such questions are somehow racist (i.e., that the therapist should somehow be color-blind), or conflicts clinicians may experience regarding their own ethnic identity. If a client senses this discomfort or seeming unwillingness to openly address issues of race, ethnicity, and culture, the therapeutic alliance may be undermined. A broad (and admittedly oversimplified) dichotomy for thinking about questions related to culture, ethnicity, and spirituality is (a) how these factors may influence the client's conceptualization of therapy and the client-therapist alliance, and (b) how these factors influence one's understanding of the client's presenting problems.

With regard to the first point, the clinician should consider the meaning to the client of seeking help from a psychotherapist, and how this experience fits into the client's larger worldview. For example, among Asian communities, seeking mental health treatment is frequently associated with stigma and shame, and Asian individuals often enter treatment with more severe symptoms because they delay getting help (Okazaki, 2000; Yamashiro & Matsuoka, 1997). Similarly, delays into treatment entry, poorer treatment outcomes, and decreased satisfaction with treatment outcome have been noted in Hispanic communities and speculated to relate, in part, to factors such as incongruities between typical treatment approaches and client cultural values (e.g., individualistic versus collectivistic orientation, self-reliance) as well as linguistic issues (Alegria et al., 2002; Antshel, 2002; Paris, Añez, Begregal, Andrés-Hyman, & Davidson, 2005). Also, as mentioned earlier, research evidence suggests that at least for some clients, a cultural/ethnic match with their therapist may be a significant factor associated with therapeutic outcome. Thus, when there is not a match, clients should be asked about their feelings in working with a therapist who is of a different cultural/ethnic background. The clinician should not shy away from asking directly about acceptable beliefs, behavior, and values among the client's ethnic or cultural group and the extent to which the client accepts these and identifies with his cultural/ethnic group. However, do not mistake this encouragement as license to avoid doing your own homework on learning about a client's cultural/ethnic background. Consultation with clinicians who are of the same cultural/ethnic background as your client and obtaining relevant readings in the clinical literature as well as more general sources are some ways of obtaining information on the beliefs, value systems, and traditions of particular groups (the same can be said of religious groups, which is discussed next). Do not neglect the sociopolitical environment in which your client was raised and how world events may have shaped the client's belief systems and identity (Hays, 2007).

The culturally competent interviewer will consider the role that a client's ethnic/cultural and/or religious background plays in understanding the client's presenting problems and symptoms. Discussions of race and ethnicity with clients can reduce the likelihood of stereotyping and can help the clinician understand important contextual elements in which presenting problems are embedded (Cardemil & Battle, 2003). To this point, P. A. Hays (2007) provides an example of a 40-year-old biracial (Cuban Irish), Catholic woman with two children who sought help for chronic back pain. The client's therapist initially conceptualized the woman's problems as depression characterized by somatization. However, an investigation of the client's cultural and spiritual beliefs and family relationships ultimately led to a reconceptualization of the woman's problems as stemming from emotional pain related to the conflict she felt between being divorced and the religious and cultural values that had been instilled in her related to marriage, family relationships, and motherhood.

A thorough cultural conceptualization of a client's presenting problems will also take into consideration the level of acculturation among clients who were not born or raised in the United States. Acculturation can be defined as "the process of cultural exchange by which immigrants modify their attributes, beliefs, cultural norms, values, or behaviors as a result of interaction with a different culture" (Heilemann, Lee, Stinson, Koshar, & Goss, 2000, p. 118). The acculturation process may result in assimilation to the dominant society and a relinquishing of one's original culture, integration resulting in the adoption of dominant culture behaviors and the retention of aspects of the original culture, separation from the dominant culture and a retention of one's original culture, or rejection of the dominant culture but failure to retain one's original culture as well (referred to as marginalization; Dana, 1993). The last outcome is presumed to place an individual at particular risk for mental health problems (J. W. Berry & Sam, 1997). In addition, stressors can occur at any point in the acculturation process and may be accompanied by expressions of distress and the development of psychological difficulties for some individuals (Organista, Organista, & Kurasaki, 2003). Interestingly, recent research findings suggest that higher levels of acculturation may be associated with increasing rates of psychopathology and that adherence to traditional culture may provide some protection against the development of mental health problems (Escobar, Nervi, & Gara, 2000). Understanding whether the acculturation process has been voluntary or involuntary and undertaken within a framework of support networks and traditional resources (e.g., existing cultural institutions) are important considerations in this regard (Dana, 1993). Assessment or acculturation can include questions about adherence to cultural traditions, social affiliations, preferred foods and dress, language usage, group identity (including cultural identification and pride), generation and geographic history, and attitudes toward acculturation. Use of formal acculturation measures may be helpful in this process, and the interested reader is referred to Dana (1993) for a review.

Finally, it is helpful to be familiar with the research literature on diagnostic challenges and common errors that occur with different ethnic groups. As examples, Schizophrenia has been found to be overdiagnosed among African Americans, whereas anxiety and mood disorders are often underdiagnosed (D. Coleman & Baker, 1994; Strakowski, Flaum, et al., 1996). As previously noted, Asians often delay entry into mental health treatment due to stigma and shame associated with admitting to psychological problems, and thus may come to treatment displaying greater symptom severity and impairment (K. Lin, Inui, Kleinman, & Womack, 1982; Okazaki, 2000). In addition, the tendency to view the mind and body as intimately connected can result in more frequent reporting of somatic symptoms versus emotions, which can further contribute to misdiagnosis by clinicians not sensitive to this perspective (K. Lin & Cheung, 1999). Such findings underscore the importance of carefully and systematically evaluating symptoms and understanding the difference between abnormal behaviors and culturally normative experiences before coming to diagnostic conclusions. S. M. Turner et al. (2003) suggest that the use of structured interviews with ethnic minority populations may help to guard against the overpathologizing bias by forcing clinicians to ask certain questions and ensure that specific criteria are met. The importance of including a cultural formulation in the diagnostic process is further addressed in Chapter 3, "Essentials of Diagnosis."

Religious and Spiritual Identity

Religion is an important part of the lives of many individuals and can be a major factor that shapes values, behavior, coping strategies, and thinking patterns. Religious belief can profoundly influence how psychological difficulties are viewed and handled. There are over 2,000 identifiable religious groups in the United States (Keller, 2000), and between 80% and 90% of Americans identify themselves as associated with a religion (Kosmin, Mayer, & Keysar, 2001; Roof, 1999). An even higher percentage (94%) report a belief in God (Roof, 1999). Despite the important role that religious belief and spirituality play in the lives of many clients, questions about these areas are often neglected during the intake interview. This seems to reflect a more general inattention to the psychology of religious experience in clinical textbooks and training programs. Indeed, many mental health professionals feel inadequately prepared to discuss issues related to spiritual or religious development, despite recognizing that this area is clinically relevant (Shafrankse & Maloney, 1990).

Although a complete understanding of the role that religious belief plays in a client's life may not occur until treatment has been under way for some time, examples of appropriate inquiries in the initial interview include (a) past and present religious experience and affiliation, (b) the evolution of one's religious practice, (c) how religion influences identity and day-to-day life and religious training, (d) familial attitudes toward religion, (e) use of religious resources during challenging and crisis periods, (f) perceived relationship to God or deities, (g) participation in a faith community, (h) observance of religious rituals and holidays, (i) relationship with spiritual advisors and teachers, (j) conflict versus congruence between values prescribed by religion and how one's life is lived, and (k) how religion may affect the client's conceptualization of his or her difficulties and their solution (Hedayat-Diba, 2000; H. I. Kaplan & Saddock, 1998; Richards & Bergin, 1997; Shafrankse, 2000). Also remember that clients may identify themselves as spiritually oriented but not fully or even partially ascribe to any organized religion. In such cases, a careful and sensitive approach is needed to evaluate the meaning and tenets of such private spirituality (Lovinger, 1996).

One should not automatically assume that religion plays either a constructive or an unhelpful role with regard to the client's presenting complaints, and it is especially important to be mindful of how one's own feelings and beliefs about religion and spirituality could influence such assumptions. Instead, it is useful to consider, for example, whether clients' religious beliefs appear to have helped them confront or evade issues with which they are grappling, enhanced interpersonal intimacy or fostered social isolation, and increased self-care or contributed to self-neglect (Finn & Rubin, 2000). Just as psychopathology must be viewed through the lens of culture, so too should it be viewed within the context of religious belief. The clinician should strive to determine if experiences that might be otherwise labeled as psychopathology are acceptable and normative within the client's religious community. An example is the phenomenon of speaking in tongues, or glossolalia, that is practiced by some Pentecostals; this involves the utterance of ecstatic speech that is unintelligible to others. While this behavior could be mistaken for symptoms of thought disorder in the context of psychosis, Dobbins (2000, p. 176) notes that its function is actually to provide "relief from times of extreme tension and anxiety [and it] . . . also provides Pentecostal believers a way to pray . . . and commit to God's care those overwhelming concerns that are difficult or impossible to articulate in a known language." However, separating out psychopathology from religious experience can be challenging as some individuals vulnerable to certain psychiatric symptoms (e.g., psychosis, schizotypal symptoms) may gravitate toward religion to provide meaning for unusual experiences and thoughts (Farias, Claridge, & Lalljee, 2005; Feldman & Rust, 1989; Maltby & Day, 2002). In addition, philosophical questions can be raised as to whether it is appropriate to consider as nonpathological (e.g., nondelusional) any belief that is culturally sanctioned by a religious subgroup (Meissner, 1996). Lovinger (1996) offers 10 markers of what he terms "probable religious pathology" as well as "mature religious adjustment" that are summarized in Table 1.6.

Recent, Significant Life Events

Research has demonstrated that for a variety of psychiatric conditions, including mood, anxiety, substance use, and eating disorders, the occurrence of significant life events can place an individual at risk for symptom exacerbations (El-Shikh, Fahmy, Michael, & Moshelhy, 2004; Faravelli, Paterniti, & Servi, 1997; Hammen, 2005; Paykel, 2003; Raffi, Rondini, Grandi, & Fava, 2000). Even disorders that we typically think of as being strongly biologically driven, such as Schizophrenia, are adversely affected by significant life stressors (Norman & Malla, 1993). In addition, enduring stressful life events are associated with increased risk of physical illness as well as early death (S. Cohen, 2002; Creed, 1985). All of this points to the importance of understanding what recent stressful life events your client has experienced and how these may relate to his or her presenting problems.

Although your client may cite a specific recent stressor as a reason for coming into treatment, do not assume that this is the only stressful life event that the client has experienced within the past 6 to 12 months. Instead, be sure to ask clients about *any* significant events or changes that have happened over the past year. Remember that events that we normally think of as positive (e.g., marriage, birth of a child, going to college, getting a new job or promotion) can be as stressful as events we typically think of as negative. In addition to considering the role that acute stressors may have in client functioning, consider chronic stressors your client may be facing, such as economic hardship or poor physical health. Because it can sometimes be difficult for clients to remember all of the significant life events that have occurred over a period as long as a year, it can be helpful to present a list of such events to clients and have them indicate which ones they have experienced. Measures such as the Social Readjustment Rating Scale (T. H. Holmes & Rahe, 1967) and the Family Inventory of Life Events (FILE; McCubbin, Patterson, & Wilson, 1983) are useful for this purpose. The Social Readjustment Rating Scale asks respondents to indicate which of 43 life events occurred over the previous 6- or 12-month period. The FILE consists of a list of 71 stressful family-oriented life events (e.g., marital strains, illness, financial stressors) that are differentially weighted based on the relative magnitude and intensity of the stressor (e.g., death of a family member has greater weight than a family member losing a job). The respondent indicates which stressors occurred, and a total score can be generated.

Finally, recognize that in some cases the stressor that may have precipitated the client's problems may not be a recent acute stressful event or a chronic stressor, but something

Table 1.6 Religiosity: potential markers of pathology and adjustment

	Potential Indicator of Pathology		Indicators of Mature Adjustment
Self-oriented display	Religion used to satisfy narcissistic needs	**Awareness of complexity or ambiguity**	Ability to appreciate ambiguities inherent in most religions based on the complexity of the human condition
Religion as reward	Religion used as a substitute for the satisfaction of human relationships	**Choice in religious affiliation**	Evidence that a meaningful decision has been made to commit to a particular religion (versus affiliation with no investment)
Scrupulosity	Intense focus on avoiding sin or error that may have obsessive-compulsive features and/or be accompanied by significant underlying hostility	**Value-behavior congruence**	Reasonable congruence between the values prescribed by one's religion and one's personal behavior
Relinquishing responsibility	Client feels responsible for what he or she could not have been responsible for or does not accept responsibility for actions	**Recognition of shortcomings**	Ability to recognize one's failings without being excessively punitive or readjusting standards
Ecstatic frenzy	Needs careful evaluation; could reflect unregulated emotional expression that is a precursor to decompensation	**Respect for boundaries**	Ability to respect others' wishes to not share one's religious experiences
Persistent house-of-worship shopping	Inability to find a religious community or house of worship that is satisfactory for more than a few months at a time; could reflect difficulties maintaining stable relationships		

(Continued)

Table 1.6 (Continued)

	Potential Indicator of Pathology	Indicators of Mature Adjustment
Indiscriminate enthusiasm	Insistence on sharing religious experiences with others who have consistently indicated such disclosures are unwelcome; may reflect self-doubt, questions, uncertainties	
Hurtful love in religious practice	Using religion to justify hurtful, damaging, or painful experiences with others	
Religious texts as moment-to-moment guides to life	Tendency to surrender self-direction, self-responsibility by viewing religious texts as providing direction on every decision one makes in daily life	
Possession	Requires careful evaluation; may reflect psychosis, hysteria, dissociative reactions (including DID), borderline disorders	

Source: From "Considering the Religious Dimension in Assessment and Treatment" (pp. 327–364), by R. J. Lovinger, in *Religion and the Clinical Practice of Psychology*, E. P. Shafranske (Ed.), 1996, Washington, DC: American Psychological Association Press. Adapted with permission.

more subtle, such as the anniversary of a significant event (e.g., death of a loved one). Such anniversary reactions may occur out of the client's conscious awareness and thus may not always be readily apparent from information gathered in the initial interview (Siassi, 1984).

Traumatic Experiences

An area of inquiry often neglected by beginning clinicians is a client's history of traumatic experiences. Included here are a history of physical, emotional, or sexual abuse in child-hood, adolescence, or adulthood and exposure to natural or man-made life-threatening experiences (e.g., earthquake, car accident, mugging). Remember too that an individual does not have to be the direct victim of a threatening experience in order to be traumatized by it; the woman who saw her younger brother beaten on a regular basis by her father and the store clerk who witnessed a customer getting shot during a store robbery may be highly traumatized by these events. Also, do not solely think of the term "trauma" as it is defined under the diagnostic criteria for PTSD in the *DSM-IV* (American Psychiatric Association, 2000b), namely, an event involving actual or threatened death or serious injury or a threat to the integrity of self or others. Experiences outside of the boundaries of this definition may also be perceived as highly traumatic or life-altering to a client. In fact, some research indicates that stressful life events (e.g., divorce, unemployment) can be associated with at least as many, and in some cases more, posttraumatic symptoms than traumatic events as defined in the *DSM-IV* (Mol et al., 2005).

Considerable care must be taken in how questions about these sensitive topics are broached. Unless an individual specifically presents with complaints that stem from a traumatic experience, questions about traumatic events should be saved until sufficient rapport has been established. Thus, such questions may need to await later treatment sessions. A history of traumatic experiences warrants follow-up questions regarding how these experiences have affected the client, including PTSD symptomatology.

Coping

It is exceedingly useful for treatment planning to find out something about how a client copes with stress, and information about coping strategies may be obtained at various points throughout the interview. As previously mentioned, clients should be asked how they have coped with the problems cited as the reason for seeking treatment. Similar questions can be asked about any stressful or problematic experience, current or past, that a client mentions during the interview (e.g., job loss, divorce). Questions can also be directed toward finding out how a client deals with lower-level, everyday stresses (e.g., "What do you do to relax or unwind at the end of a busy day?"). There are many ways to conceptualize coping. For example, in problem-focused coping an individual tries to solve the problem perceived to be at the source of the stress, whereas in emotion-focused coping, the individual tries to deal with the negative emotional consequences that a stressor produces (Folkman, 1984; Moos & Billings, 1982). An individual may try to cognitively reframe difficult situations so that they are less stressful (sometimes subsumed under the rubric appraisal-focused coping; Moos & Billings, 1982). Coping can also involve turning to social supports (e.g., family, friends, community supports) or spirituality or religion (e.g., prayer). One can also deal with stress through potentially harmful means such as rumination, distraction, or engaging in risky behaviors (e.g., drug or alcohol use; Nolen-Hoeksema, 1987). If a client relies primarily on maladaptive ways of dealing with stress, this can become an area to focus on in treatment.

Resilience, Competencies, and Accomplishments

As mental health professionals, we are trained to focus on problems so that we can understand their scope, possible causes, and consequences in order to ultimately try to help resolve them. This focus can, however, blind us from seeking information on client strengths. In fact, therapists may subtly encourage clients to primarily discuss negative behaviors by providing greater verbal attention to negative self-statements than to positive self-statements (D. A. Beach, 1989). Therefore, it is important to not only take note of positive behaviors and attributes that are revealed during the course of the interview, but to specifically direct questions to elicit this information if it is not spontaneously mentioned by the client. Gathering this information serves two purposes. First, it informs the clinician about client strengths that can be marshaled in treatment. For example, the client who displays a good sense of humor during the interview may be able to use that humor to cognitively reframe difficult situations in a manner that makes them easier to handle. Second, gathering information on strengths and competencies reminds clients that they are not defined solely by their problems and may aid in the recognition of a more balanced view of the self. Questions relating to important achievements or accomplishments and what the client likes to do for fun or relaxation may reveal client competencies. Table 1.7 presents examples of positive qualities to look for in the initial interview.

Table 1.7   Positive qualities to look for in the initial interview

Intelligent
Displays sense of humor
Insightful
Candid
Empathic
Persistent
Optimistic
Responsible
Able to be spontaneous
Can form close relationships with others (e.g., friends, romantic partners)
Courteous
Flexible
Creative
Cooperative
Confident
Thoughtful
Assertive
Displays self-control
Resourceful

The Mental Status Exam

Up to this point, we have primarily focused on the collection of information from clients about various aspects of their current and past functioning. Such information constitutes the *subjective* portion of the interview because we must rely on clients' accounts of their experiences without having directly observed the events and situations they describe (A. J. Levenson, 1981). However, a comprehensive initial interview also contains an *objective* portion composed of the clinician's observations of the client's behavior, appearance, and manner of relating during the interview. When such observations are categorized with the aim of identifying the clinical entities and diagnoses that best describe the client, a *mental status examination* (MSE) is being conducted (E. Schwartz, 1989). The MSE is rooted in psychiatry, where it remains an essential part of the psychiatrist's armamentarium of clinical procedures. Nowadays, MSEs are routinely conducted by other mental health professionals as well and can be done at various points during treatment, not just at the initial interview. Mental status exams provide snapshots of the client's presentation at a particular point in time; when serial MSEs are available, they can help the clinician see how a client's behavior has changed over time (Lukas, 1993). The information obtained during an MSE can also be particularly helpful in determining the validity of the information reported by the client in the interview. For example, if a client is noted on an MSE as having disorganized thought processes, being extremely guarded, or exhibiting extreme emotional lability, additional information from collateral sources should be gathered since the quality of historical information provided by the client may be compromised. In cases where a client is confused or extremely uncooperative, the MSE may constitute the total initial evaluation (Siassi, 1984).

Areas covered in an MSE can be roughly divided into noncognitive and cognitive. Table 1.8 summarizes noncognitive areas typically covered in an MSE conducted by a mental health professional and provides information on specific elements to assess in each. Table 1.9 reviews areas of cognitive functioning that may be evaluated as part of an MSE if a client is suspected of cognitive impairment (e.g., appears confused or disoriented or displays impaired memory).

Table 1.8   Noncognitive areas typically covered in a mental status examination

Area	What to Evaluate
Physical appearance	☐ Ethnicity ☐ Height and weight ☐ Notable physical characteristics ☐ Clothing ☐ Grooming ☐ Health status ☐ Age
Psychomotor behavior	☐ Agitation ☐ Retardation ☐ Gait ☐ Posture ☐ Unusual movements or mannerisms
Emotional state	☐ Mood ☐ Affect
Speech	☐ Rate ☐ Volume ☐ Prosody ☐ Fluency ☐ Speech impediments or paraphasias ☐ Regional or cultural factors
Thoughts	☐ Process ☐ Content
Sensory disturbances	☐ Hallucinations ☐ Illusions
Manner of relating to clinician	☐ Eye contact ☐ Openness ☐ Cooperation ☐ Anger or hostility ☐ Passivity ☐ Boundary issues ☐ Ability to express warmth ☐ Response to empathy

Table 1.9   Cognitive areas typically covered in a mental status examination

Cognitive Function	Definition	Examples/How to Evaluate
Consciousness	Assessed on continuum from alert to comatose	***Fully alert:*** Able to respond quickly to environment; aware of surroundings. ***Drowsy:*** Awake but less than fully alert. ***Stuporous:*** Partially aroused; may need vigorous physical stimulation to respond. ***Coma:*** Unable to be aroused by any stimuli (pain, odor).
Orientation	Awareness of oneself in relation to person, time, and place ("oriented × 3")	***Person:*** Does client know his or her name? ***Time:*** Does client know date (month, day, year, day of week, time of day)? ***Place:*** Does client know location of interview? ***Situation:*** Does client know what the purpose of the interview is?
Attention and concentration	Ability to focus on topic at hand and sustain focus over time	***Serial 7s:*** Ask client to count aloud backward by 7s beginning at 100. ***Digit repetition:*** Ask client to repeat aloud strings of digits of increasing length (5-8, 3-9-12, etc.). ***Registration:*** Ask client to repeat a list of three common objects.
Language	The ability to use and understand spoken and written language	***Comprehension*** (receptive language): Does client understand questions, simple commands? ***Expression:*** Does client's speech flow easily without evidence of unusual word usage, long pauses or response latencies, poverty of content, etc.? Can test by asking client to name various objects. ***Repetition:*** Can client repeat single words, simple phrases, complex sentences stated by examiner?
Memory	Ability to remember information presented during exam, in recent past, or long ago	***Immediate memory:*** Ability to remember things presented within the past few seconds. Can test through digit repetition or ability to recall a series of three common subjects. ***Recent memory:*** Ability to recall information after minutes, hours, or days. Can test through ability to recall a series of three common objects after a few minutes, asking questions about recent meals or activities (must be able to verify responses).

(Continued)

Table 1.9 (Continued)

Cognitive Function	Definition	Examples/How to Evaluate
		Remote memory: Ability to recall information or events that occurred in previous years. Can test through questions about important personal facts (date of marriage, high school graduation) or historical events (names of past presidents).
Constructional ability	The ability to draw or construct 2- or 3-dimensional shapes or figures	Ability to copy simple shapes such as vertical diamond (◇), 2-D cross (✝), or 3-D cube (❑), clock face, or intersecting pentagons.
Intelligence	Gross estimate of client's overall intellectual abilities (e.g., above average, average, below average)	May be inferred from: *Client's vocabulary:* Complexity and range. *Educational and occupational achievement* *Abstract reasoning:* Interpret proverbs; identify common concept linking objects (e.g., "How are car and airplane alike?"). *General fund of knowledge:* For example, "Name four presidents since 1940"; "What is the capital of Spain?"; "Who wrote *Macbeth*?
Judgment	Ability to make sound, reasonable decisions that are adaptive	*Infer from client history:* Is there evidence of repeated poor judgment (e.g., drinking and driving, staying in problematic relationships, getting fired for poor work performance)? *Pose hypothetical questions:* "What would you do if you saw smoke and fire in a theater?"
Insight	Client's awareness and understanding of his or her problems	Does client have a reasonable understanding of cause(s) of his or her problems? Does client feel he or she needs treatment? Does client have realistic expectations regarding treatment?

Note that the MSE includes statements about various aspects of the client's physical presentation, such as general descriptions of health status (e.g., robust, gaunt, sallow-complexioned), age (including whether the client looks much younger or older than his or her stated age), height, weight, grooming (e.g., appropriateness and cleanliness of clothing, body odor), and unusual or notable physical characteristics (e.g., tattoos, body piercings). A statement is usually included in the MSE that addresses aspects of the client's psychomotor behavior. For example, was the client agitated (e.g., pacing, fidgeting) or moving and talking very slowly (i.e., psychomotor retardation)? Were there any abnormalities in the client's gait, posture, or mannerisms?

A statement about the client's emotional presentation is always included in an MSE and identifies the client's mood (i.e., self-reported emotional state) as well as affect (i.e., the emotional tone observed by the interviewer and manifest in behaviors such as facial expression, voice tone, gestures, and posture; M. Zimmerman, 1994). Aspects of speech that are typically evaluated in an MSE include the rate and speed, clarity (e.g., Are there speech impediments?), volume (overly soft or loud), fluency (amount of speech and ease of production), and prosody. Prosody refers to the rise and fall or musicality that is inherent in normal speech. Individuals who speak in a monotone or robotic voice or who evidence other peculiarities in the lilt of their speech (that are not due to cultural factors such as a foreign-language accent) may be broadly described as *dysprosodic*. Descriptions of a client's speech may also make note of regional or cultural factors such as accented speech and use of slang or colloquialisms. In evaluating a client's speech, clinicians should also note the use of any abnormal words (paraphasias).

The client's thinking is remarked on in an MSE by noting two aspects: process and content. Comments about *thought process* address the client's ability to answer questions and relate information in a relatively straightforward and organized manner (sometimes referred to as "linear and goal-directed"), as opposed to thought processes marked by frequent digressions that either eventually return to the original point (i.e., circumstantiality) or do not (tangentiality). Additional descriptions of client thought processes include *flight of ideas* (continuous, overproductive speech that reflects fragmented ideas), *loose associations* (a lack of logical relationship between thoughts), *clang associations* (combining unrelated words because of similar sounds or rhyming), and *mutism* (complete verbal nonexpression; R. Sommers-Flanagan & Sommers-Flanagan, 1999). Statements about *thought content* concern notable themes that occurred in the course of the interview. Usually this includes notation of any psychotic thought processes (e.g., delusions), expressions of fears or phobias, depressive thoughts, obsessions, and suicidal or homicidal thoughts. It is imperative to *always* inquire about suicidal and homicidal thoughts in any intake interview and to carefully document the client's responses in the case notes and intake report. If the client indicates that suicidal or homicidal thoughts are present, the clinician must immediately shift gears and focus on determining whether the client is in immediate danger of harming self or others. Chapter 2 ("Crisis Issues") addresses how to handle clients in such crisis situations. The MSE may also include a statement regarding whether the client exhibited any evidence of perceptual disturbances such as hallucinations (i.e., perceptual experiences occurring in the absence of sensory stimulation, such as hearing or seeing things that are not really there) or illusions (i.e., misperceptions of actual sensory stimuli, such as mistaking a cane for a snake).

The MSE should document the client's manner of relating to the examiner, which can encompass level of cooperation, openness in answering questions, respect for boundaries, ability to respond to empathy, and ability to convey warmth. As R. Sommers-Flanagan and Sommers-Flanagan (1999) note, it is important to not readily assume that the client's behaviors toward the clinician reflect general patterns of responding to others or personality traits, unless there is sufficient evidence from the history to do so. How a clinician perceives a client is also influenced by the clinician's own personality, background, motivations, and issues. Thus, a soft-spoken, low-key clinician may be more put off by a loquacious, highly gregarious client than would a clinician with a similar personality and interpersonal style.

The level of detail included in an MSE can vary considerably depending on the setting in which a clinician works and the type(s) of clients typically seen. One aspect of the MSE where this is particularly true concerns evaluation of the client's cognitive abilities. A formal MSE includes statements about the client's attention and concentration, memory (immediate, recent, remote), estimated intelligence, insight, and judgment. These mental functions will usually be evaluated by a series of brief tasks, such as those outlined in Table 1.7. Several structured MSEs exist that primarily assess these cognitive aspects. These instruments contain specific questions and scoring directions for client responses. A popular example of such an MSE is the Folstein Mini-Mental Status Exam (M. F. Folstein, Folstein, & McHugh, 1975), which briefly and grossly evaluates orientation, attention and concentration, memory, receptive and expressive language, and visuomotor skills through the use of items that ask the interviewee to identify the date and location of the interview, name common objects, repeat and remember the names of three objects, follow a written command, copy a picture or intersecting pentagons, and so forth. Structured cognitive MSEs typically utilize cut scores intended to detect individuals who are likely to have an organic brain disorder (e.g., dementia) so that the clinician can refer such persons for further in-depth evaluation. Studies on the psychometric properties of structured cognitive MSEs have generally found that they possess high reliability (e.g., produce consistent results across repeated testing [test-retest reliability] and across different raters [interrater reliability]) and are useful for documenting cognitive changes in moderately to severely demented individuals. However, the ability of cut scores to accurately identify demented individuals has been more variable, with some instruments producing high percentages of false-negative cases (i.e., individuals identified as nonimpaired who have true cognitive impairment; R. Rogers, 2001). Thus, a negative finding on a cognitive MSE does not always rule out the need for further cognitive evaluation, particularly if there are other indicators of cognitive impairment from either the interview or history. In general, it is important to remember that even when formal tasks, such as those found on structured cognitive MSEs, are used to assess client functioning, the results are only gross estimates of ability in the tested areas. Furthermore, some tasks used to evaluate cognitive functioning on MSEs can be strongly influenced by educational and cultural factors. For example, if one chooses to estimate general intelligence by asking the client a series of general fund of knowledge questions (e.g., "Name four individuals who have been president of the United States since 1940"), it is important to ensure that the client has had a reasonable opportunity to learn this information (i.e., intelligence should be assessed relative to an individual's premorbid life experiences; E. Schwartz, 1989). Thus, asking such a question of a recent immigrant from Honduras with 4 years of formal education would likely not be appropriate.

Whether you conduct a full, formal MSE that includes an evaluation of the client's cognitive functioning will largely depend on the setting in which you work and the types of clients seen. For example, in most general outpatient settings, clinicians are less likely to evaluate aspects of the client's cognitive functioning through the administration of formal tasks, and any written statements about the client's attention, verbal ability, suspected level of intellectual functioning, and so on are likely to be based on how he or she responded to questions in the interview (e.g., Did the client need questions repeated? Were his or her responses clear and well-organized?). Morrison (1995b) identifies several situations in which all portions of a formal mental status exam should be administered: (a) when used as a forensic or other legal exam (e.g., competency evaluations, commitment proceedings), (b) when a baseline of client functioning is needed to evaluate treatment effects, (c) when a client is suicidal or has threatened violence, (d) for evaluations of inpatients, (e) when major Axis I diagnoses must be investigated, and (f) when brain injury is suspected. In contrast, individuals seen for general outpatient psychotherapy who are not suspected of having major mood, perceptual, thinking, or cognitive disturbances are not likely to require administration of a formal MSE. Results of an MSE are usually summarized in an intake report under a separate heading that may be identified as MSE or by a label such as "Behavioral Observations."

This last observation raises the more general point that although information gathered from the MSE can assist in making a diagnosis, it should never be the only information used for this purpose. For example, brightly colored clothes could suggest mania, and inappropriate clothing could reflect psychosis (Morrison, 1995b), but these are not pathognomonic signs. As Lukas (1993) notes, a client who comes to a summer appointment dressed in a heavy winter coat may not be exhibiting bizarre behavior reflecting psychosis, but instead could be poor and own only one coat or may be a victim of abuse attempting to cover bruises. Particularly important in this regard is the consideration of cultural and ethnic variations in interpersonal behavior. In some cases, infrequent eye contact might be interpreted as signs of shyness, poor social skills, or evidence of psychopathology, but such behavior may be considered respectful and therefore perfectly appropriate in certain cultures (e.g., among Asian individuals).

ENDING THE INTERVIEW

Intake interviews should never be ended abruptly. It can be extremely disconcerting for a client who has spent a good hour or more disclosing information to you to be unexpectedly told that time is up. At least 10 minutes prior to the end of the session, the client should be informed that your time together will soon be ending. This allows an opportunity for you to summarize what has been discussed in the interview and for the client to ask any questions. It is reasonable for a client to expect that you will be able to provide some information on what the next steps in the treatment process will be (e.g., further interview, proceeding to therapy sessions, referral to another treatment provider). A client may also have questions about how the treatment might proceed, what the clinician thinks about the problems the client is having, how long the treatment might last and what the prognosis might be, and possible diagnoses. You may not be able to provide firm answers for all these questions, but you should be prepared to give clients answers that you are reasonably certain of and explain when you might be able to address their other inquiries. In some cases, a client may ask you questions that you cannot possibly answer as they have been posed, and you should tell the client this, as in the example below:

Client: Am I going to get worse?
Clinician: I understand how upsetting this is, and often when individuals are in the midst of a crisis it feels like things are not going to get better. However, coming to talk

to someone is the first step. You have given me a lot of very helpful information and I am committed to working with you [this will vary if you may not see the person in therapy] to find ways that you can cope and not feel so upset or overwhelmed.
Client: That sounds great. So when do we start?

At the end of the interview provide the client the opportunity to tell you about anything you did not ask about that the client feels is important for you to know. Always thank the client for participating in the interview and being willing to disclose information to you. Even when a client has been challenging to interview (e.g., reticent, argumentative), it is usually possible to come up with an appreciative comment to make (e.g., "I know that answering all of these questions was not easy and I appreciate your willingness to discuss some of the things I asked about. I also appreciate your honesty in letting me know that you're not yet comfortable talking about certain issues, like your relationship with your husband.").

STRUCTURED INTERVIEWS

Beginning in the late 1960s researchers began to recognize that information obtained from unstructured interviews often resulted in poor diagnostic reliability and validity (C. H. Ward, Beck, Mendelson, Mock, & Erbaugh, 1962). This is because unstructured interviews vary widely from clinician to clinician in terms of the methods used, content areas covered, specific questions asked, and the manner in which formal diagnostic criteria are applied. Spurred on largely by a desire to improve the research value of psychiatric interviews, significant efforts were undertaken in the 1970s and 1980s to develop structured psychiatric interviews that would ensure consistency in both the procedures used to evaluate clinical symptoms and specific areas covered. R. Rogers (2001) defines a structured interview as a method of systematic evaluation that standardizes the language used to question clients, the sequence in which questions are presented, and the quantification of the client's responses. Some structured interviews (e.g., Structured Clinical Interview for *DSM* Axis I Disorders [SCID]) utilize a branching format in which the interviewer is led to certain questions based on the client's responses to previous questions; such a format allows, for example, interviewers to skip a particular diagnostic section if the essential criteria for a disorder are not met (D. L. Segal, 1997). Dozens of structured clinical interviews are now available to evaluate psychiatric symptoms in adults and children, and some of these are summarized in Table 1.10. Some (e.g., SCID, Kiddie Schedule for Affective Disorders and Schizophrenia) are broad-based and evaluate a range of different conditions, whereas others (e.g., Anxiety Disorders Interview Schedule) focus on specific disorder categories or diagnoses. Among the advantages of structured clinical interviews over their unstructured counterparts are (a) comprehensive coverage of disorders, (b) reduced likelihood of clinician bias or lack of knowledge influencing results, (c) consistency in interview content and diagnostic decision making across interviewers, and (d) improved ability to assess change across settings and time. There is also evidence that structured interviews may yield more accurate diagnoses than unstructured interviews with ethnic minority clients (Neighbors, Jackson, Campbell, & Williams, 1989).

Table 1.10 A sample of structured clinical interviews

Interview	Authors	Target Population	Time to Complete	Areas Covered
Diagnostic Interview for Children (DICA)	Herjanic & Reich, 1983a, b	Children (6–17)	45 min	Various clinical syndromes (e.g., affective disorders, anxiety disorders, mania, substance abuse). Originally designed for administration by lay interviewers.
Diagnostic Interview Schedule for Children (DISC-IV)	Shaffer, Fisher, Lucas, Dulcan, & Schwab-Stone, 2000	Children (6–17)	90–120 min	Six diagnostic sections (anxiety, mood, disruptive, substance use, Schizophrenia, and miscellaneous disorders). Disorders are evaluated for presence within the past year and currently (past 4 weeks). Can also evaluate lifetime presence of disorders. Parent, youth, and teacher versions available.
Structured Interview for *DSM-IV* Personality Disorder (SIDP)	Pfohl, Blkum, & Zimmerman, 1997	Adults	60–90 min for client interview 20 min for interview of significant informants 20 min to complete summary sheet	Covers all *DSM-IV* Axis II disorders as well as three personality disorders proposed for further study in *DSM-IV* (i.e., self-defeating, depressive, negativistic).

Hamilton Rating Scale for Depression (HAM-D)	Hamilton, 1960	Adults	20–30 min	17- or 21-item instruments designed to assess depression. Higher scores equal greater depression severity. Questions relate to symptoms of depressed mood, guilt, sleep problems, weight loss, anxiety, and suicidality. Longer version briefly evaluates additional symptoms such as paranoia, depersonalization, and Obsessive-Compulsive Disorder.
Anxiety Disorders Interview Schedule (ADIS)	DiNardo, Brown, & Barlow, 1994	Adults		Assesses *DSM-IV* anxiety disorders and other select disorders (e.g., mood, somatoform); allows for determination of severity ratings for each disorder.
Present State Examination (PSE)	Wing, Cooper, & Sartorious, 1974; World Health Organization, 1994	Adults	60–90 min	Extensive coverage of psychotic and neurotic symptomatology associated with Axis I disorders; greater emphasis on symptom evaluation versus diagnosis. Linked to *International Classification of Diseases (ICD)* system; has been translated into several languages and used with diverse cultures in epidemiological research.

(Continued)

Table 1.10 (Continued)

Interview	Authors	Target Population	Time to Complete	Areas Covered
Structured Clinical Interview for the *DSM-IV* (SCID)	First, Spitzer, Williams, & Gibbon, 1997	Adults	60–180 min	Axis I disorders not first evident in childhood; also excludes cognitive and dissociative disorders. Interviews are also available for Axis I dissociative disorders (Steinberg, 1993) and Axis II disorders (First, Spitzer, Gibbon, Williams, & Lorna, 1994).
Schedule for Affective Disorders and Schizophrenia (SADS)	Endicott & Spitzer, 1978	Adults	60–120 min	Axis I psychotic and affective disorders plus other select disorders (e.g., anxiety); current, lifetime, and change versions available
Diagnostic Interview Schedule (DIS)	Robins, Cottler, Bucholz, & Compton, 1995	Adults	90–120 min	Axis I and Axis II disorders. Focuses on current and past (1 year) symptoms. Originally designed to be administered by nonprofessional interviewers for epidemiological studies. A child version (DISC) is also available (Shaffer, et al. 2000).
Kiddie Schedule for Affective Disorders and Schizophrenia (K-SADS)	Puig-Antich & Chambers, 1978; Ambrosini, 1992	Children (6–18)	60–75 min	Mood, psychotic, anxiety, and disruptive behavior disorders. Administered to child and parent. Versions available to assess present and/or lifetime symptoms and for epidemiological research.

However, there are also some disadvantages in using structured interviews. Many require significant training to ensure accurate administration. It may be more difficult to establish rapport using a highly structured interview that requires the clinician to read questions verbatim and follow a strict sequence of questioning. A clinician who uses only a structured interview may miss opportunities to learn about unique experiences or beliefs of a client that will not be tapped by a standard set of symptom-based questions, and research suggests that such clinically significant, idiosyncratic information is commonly reported by clients when they are provided the opportunity (A. Cox, Rutter, et al., 1981). In addition, such interviews lessen opportunities to examine how well clients can organize and structure their behavior without the aid of the clinician (Hughes & Baker, 1990). Finally, highly structured interviews may be inappropriate to use with highly emotional clients or those in crisis.

In truth, the decision to use structured and unstructured interview formats is not an either/or choice. An interviewer may decide to utilize a fairly unstructured format to gather certain pieces of information, to put the client at ease, and to establish rapport, but then move into a more structured modality to inquire about the presence, duration, and severity of specific symptoms. If using a highly structured interview format, it is useful to inform the client beforehand of the manner in which the interview will be proceeding.

LIFE SPAN CONSIDERATIONS IN INTERVIEWING

The information discussed thus far has been presented with interviewing a young to middle-aged adult client in mind. While many areas of inquiry previously reviewed would also be included in an interview of a child, adolescent, or older adult, other areas would not, or would require significant modification. Interviewing individuals at either end of the life span spectrum requires sensitivity to and an appreciation for how developmental changes and aging can affect a client's reactions to and understanding of a therapy interview and how building rapport and establishing trust may be uniquely different for our youngest and oldest clients.

Interviewing Children and Their Families

Interviews with children can be challenging on several fronts, including the nature of child referrals, how the child client understands the initial visit, and issues related to the multiple systems with which the clinician must interact.

How Child Referrals Differ from Adult Referrals

Children rarely refer themselves for treatment, and so, unlike most adults, the child client may have little understanding of why he or she is seeing you or may actively disagree with parents or caregivers that he or she needs to see you at all. The reasons children are referred for treatment are quite varied, and in some cases, as when evaluating very young children (e.g., toddlers), the purpose of the interview may not even be to assess psychopathology in the child per se, but to identify problems in parents, to develop an early intervention plan to prevent permanent damage in the child, or to assess risk in siblings or other children in the home (Morrison & Anders, 1999). If a child disagrees with the idea that he or she is experiencing some sort of difficulty that requires your help or has been told by parents that the visit is intended to set him or her straight or to give him or her a good talking to, it will be more difficult to establish rapport and obtain information.

Children's Understanding of Treatment and the Initial Interview

Whereas most adults may have some idea of how psychotherapy works (even if it is as basic as conceptualizing therapy as a place where you talk to someone about things that bother you), many children have no idea what psychotherapy is. If you are a doctoral-level practitioner, a child client may think that going to see "the doctor" means having to remove his or her clothes and get a shot. Based on negative portrayals in popular culture, older children and adolescents may associate seeing a mental health professional with being crazy or insane (P. Barker, 1990).

This underscores the importance of giving parents and caregivers adequate instructions on how to prepare their child in advance for an interview and suggestions about what to say. For example, parents can tell their child that the visit to the clinician is to meet some-one who will talk with the child about his or her feelings and how things have been going at school and home (distinguish visit from a routine doctor's appointment), that the child is not being taken to the appointment as any kind of punishment, that part of the time the clinician will be talking with the parents and child together and then with the child alone, and that the child will be returning home after the appointment (unless an evaluation is being done for residential or inpatient placement; Morrison & Anders, 1999).

Working with Multiple Systems and Reconciling Informant Discrepancies

Clinical evaluations of children should be conceptualized as working with multiple sys-tems and obtaining information from multiple informants. In addition to providing con-sent for the child to receive treatment, parents and guardians provide much-needed history about the child's current difficulties and past history and are likely to be crucial partners in the treatment (e.g., helping to carry out treatment recommendations at home, monitoring the child's behavior outside of sessions). Because most children spend a sig-nificant portion of their day in school, it is also necessary to obtain information from the child's teachers (with the consent of the child's parents or guardians). And of course, direct interviews with children themselves are important not only to observe behavior, but as a source of information about the child's experiences and history. It was once assumed that children were not accurate reporters of their feelings and behaviors, but we now know that, in some cases, children provide more clinically meaningful and accurate information about themselves than do the adults in their lives (e.g., parents, teachers; Hughes & Baker, 1990). For example, children may be more accurate reporters than parents of child inter-nalizing problems such as depression and anxiety (Edelbrock, Costello, Dulcan, Conn-over, & Kalas, 1986; Kazdin, 1987) and qualities such as shyness (Spooner, Evans, & Santos, 2005).

Establishing a strong working relationship with multiple individuals and evaluating information obtained from them can be challenging when parents do not see eye to eye on the nature, severity, possible causes, or consequences of a child's problems, when pa-rental and teacher reports of problems conflict, or when the parents and child see things very differently from one another. Clinicians should not be surprised by a lack of concordance between child and parent reports of child problems, as the low correlation between these sources of information has been repeatedly noted in the research literature (Achenbach, McConaughy, & Howell, 1987; De Los Reyes & Kazdin, 2005). Studies suggest that parents and children fail to agree on a single problem to target in treatment between 63% and 77% of the time, and may not even agree on the general area to focus on in treatment up to 44% of the time (Hawley & Weisz, 2003; Yeh & Weisz, 2001). A large-scale study by Roberts, Alegria, Roberts, and Chen (2005) that examined parental and adolescent reports of youth emotional and behavioral problems suggests that such parent-child discrepancies may be even more common for Latino and African American youth.

According to De Los Reyes and Kazdin's (2005) ABC model, discrepancies between child and parent reports are theorized to result from differences in the attributions that each party makes as to the cause of the child's problems. Specifically, it is assumed that parents and teachers are more likely to attribute child problems to dispositional causes that in turn require the child to be treated. In contrast, children are posited to view their problems as stemming more from situational or contextual variables and may therefore see individual treatment as less likely to solve their problems. It is believed that these differing perspectives result in memory biases for both parents and children whereby information about child problems is recalled in a manner that supports the informant's belief about where the genesis of the problems lies. The model further assumes that factors such as parental psychopathology and stress affect reports of problems in a manner that will make them more discrepant from other informants (e.g., the child himself or herself, the child's teacher). A clinical implication of this model is that clinicians should understand informant attributions for child problems; this can be achieved by asking informants why they believe the child is exhibiting problematic behaviors and what the solution might be (i.e., Do problems warrant treatment?). The model also suggests that it is important for clinicians to balance asking general questions about the child's behavior (e.g., being oppositional around people the child does not know) with questions about the contexts or situations in which these behaviors do or do not occur (e.g., being oppositional around people the child does not know on the playground or at family gatherings). De Los Reyes and Kazdin note that failure to account for both the dispositional and contextual aspects of the child's behavior can lead to over- or underidentification of problems, which in turn can adversely affect treatment decisions.

The ABC model for understanding discrepancies in informant reports highlights the notion that in child evaluations there should be no presumption that one informant's perspective is the gold standard against which the veracity of other information should be judged (Kazdin & De Los Reyes, 2005). Although discrepancies may be reduced by gathering information relevant to both dispositional and contextual elements from all informants, some disagreement will inevitably remain. However, differing perspectives can, in and of themselves, be useful in the treatment planning process. For example, even if a piece of historical information provided by a child is determined to ultimately be factually inaccurate, it is still important to understand the child's construal and interpretation of events in his or her environment.

Interviewing Parents

Usually child clients should initially be seen with their parents, and a brief interview should be conducted with the parents alone. A separate interview with the child alone can follow. Interviewing parents first allows them to feel that their views, observations, concerns, and opinions are valued and will be taken seriously and provides an opportunity for the clinician to establish rapport with them. It also provides an opportunity to observe how the parents interact with each other and the degree of agreement between parents on child management behaviors and beliefs (Hughes & Baker, 1990). This strategy also gives the child time to become acclimated to the office surroundings. Even though the parents will be interviewed first, the clinician should explain to the child why he or she is being seen and what the session will involve (e.g., talking together with Mom and Dad a bit first, and then talking with the child alone). The importance of telling parents how to prepare their child for the interview was previously noted, but one cannot assume that parents always follow this instruction. Highly sensitive topics or those that would be inappropriate to discuss directly in front of the child (e.g., the quality of the parents' relationship) should not be addressed in the portion of the session where the child is present, but can be discussed at another time when only the parents are present.

Once exception to the general rule of interviewing the parents first is when the client is an adolescent. Among the developmental challenges facing adolescents are identity formation and the dependency/independence conflict. Adolescents desire recognition of their own unique identity, views, and interests, and they may actively reject the conceptualizations that parents or other adults have of them. Thus, interviewing adolescent clients before interviewing their parents sends a message that learning about the adolescent's thoughts and feelings is valued (P. Barker, 1990).

When interviewing the parents in the child's presence, observations should be made of how they interact with the child (such observations can also begin when the child and parents are initially greeted in the waiting room). If children are old enough (e.g., 7 years or older), they and their parents can be asked questions that focus on the family in general, rather than just those pertaining to the child's identified problems. Discussions of this kind can help reveal the family's power structure, alliances and coalitions, and cultural mores, as well as bring to light specific conflicts that may exist between family members (Krill, 1968). Another way to obtain data on parent-child interactions is to observe the parents and child engaged in an activity, such as a simple game, playing with toys, or planning a meal. Examples of qualities to note in parent-child interactions are summarized in Table 1.11.

We have already reviewed the general content areas that are covered in an initial interview, and most of these should also be covered when interviewing parents about their child. Obviously, some areas of inquiry will be modified; for example, the clinician will not ask about work history for a young child, but will ask fairly extensive questions about school history. This would include the age at which the child began school, academic performance (strengths and weaknesses, grades, standardized test scores if applicable), history of grade retention or grade skipping, history of learning problems and any evaluations or interventions conducted in response to them, history of behavioral difficulties in school, and peer and teacher relationships. Additional modifications regarding interview content areas will now be addressed.

The mnemonic CLIENTS presented earlier can easily be adapted when asking parents about the reasons they are seeking treatment for their child. As with adult clients, be sure to ask about significant changes and life events (either positive or negative) that may have coincided with the onset or worsening of the child's symptoms or difficulties. When

Table 1.11 Observations to make during parent-child interactions

Are the child's attempts to gain attention or solicit help noticed? How are they responded to?

What is the general emotional tone of the parents' behavior toward the child (e.g., happy, interested, anxious, distracted, irritated), and vice versa?

What are the parents' reactions to the child's positive emotional expressions (e.g., interest, excitement, happiness)?

What are the parents' reactions to the child's negative emotional expressions (e.g., sadness, anger, irritation, fear)?

How do the parents set limits or discipline the child, and is this done in a consistent manner?

What are the child's reactions to praise, limit setting and discipline, frustration, novelty?

Are there recurring themes or topics in the child's interactions or play?

How easily does the child separate from parents?

inquiring about the child's medical history, time should be devoted to obtaining a thorough developmental history. This information is best gathered when parents are interviewed separately from the child. A developmental history consists of historical data about the child's earliest environment and includes information pertaining to all major periods of the child's development, including the circumstances of conception and details about the gestational period, infancy, toddlerhood, early childhood, and adolescence. Questions about the parents' recollection of their child's behavior, temperament, attachment to caregivers, achievement of developmental milestones, and reactions to significant personal and family events (e.g., birth of a sibling) and potentially traumatic experiences (e.g., medical problems, accidents and injuries, losses) are part of this history. As Lukas (1993) notes, the developmental history also represents an opportunity for the clinician to learn about the parents' feeling toward and expectations about their children.

When asking when developmental milestones were achieved, try to get parents to recall specific ages rather than using general terms like "late" or "early" as some parents may have an inaccurate idea of what constitutes delayed or accelerated development. Because freely recalling detailed information on early development can be difficult for many parents, it can be helpful to ask them to bring in a baby book in which various milestones and other observations were recorded so that possible distortions due to retrospective recall of information from the distant past are minimized. The clinician should know at what ages different developmental milestones are expected to be achieved; a summary of some of these is presented in Table 1.12. This knowledge is useful both when the clinician interviews parents about the child's behavior and when directly observing the child. Note that the ages listed in this table represent when each milestone is *typically* achieved and that for many milestones there is a fairly wide range of ages in which it is normal for the behavior to appear. For older children and adolescents it is important to keep in mind the developmental tasks faced during these periods so that you will be in a good position to know if behaviors a child is exhibiting are normal for a particular stage of development. Severe separation anxiety in a child in middle school, for example, is a red flag requiring further investigation since such behavior is unusual at this age (P. Barker, 1990).

A useful question that can yield much information and provide segues into specific areas of inquiry is to ask the child's parents to describe a typical day in the life of their child. For very young children (e.g., toddlers) questions may center around activities such

Table 1.12   Developmental milestones

Milestone	Age (in months)
Social smiling	3
Reaches for dangling objects	3
Holds a rattle	4
Sits with support	4
Babbles	5
Pays attention to small objects	5
Rolls over and back	6
Makes two-syllable sounds	6
Responds to name	6
Plays peek-a-boo	7
Can self-feed some foods	7
Begins to show stranger anxiety	7
Sits unsupported	8
Begins to show separation anxiety	8
Picks up tiny objects	9
Goes from stomach to sitting by self	9
Crawls on hands and knees	9
Pulls self to standing	10
Points	10
Waves bye-bye	10
Cruises (i.e., walks while holding onto furniture, etc.)	11
Says "Mama" and "Dada"	12
Takes first steps alone	12
Fearful of strangers	12
Can say several simple words	15
Scribbles well	18
Can say 10 to 50 words	18
Can point to own body parts	18
Runs	19
Can throw a ball overhand, kick a ball	20
Can follow a 2-step request	22
Can draw a straight line	22
Can make short sentences (e.g., 2 words)	23–24
Walks downstairs	24
Builds a tower of 5 to 6 blocks	25–26
Speaks clearly most of the time	25–26
Can name several body parts	25–26
Uses 4 to 5 words in a sentence	30
Separates fairly easily from parents	35–36
Begins toilet training	24–36
Can feed self without spilling	36
Can imitate vertical and horizontal lines	36
Has working vocabulary of 1,000+ words	36
Able to use objects to represent people in play	36

as eating and sleeping schedules and play activities the child enjoys, whereas for older children, information can be gathered about school and recreational or extracurricular activities and friends. Descriptions of a typical day may also offer some insight into the organization of the household and patterns of family interaction that establish the context in which a child's difficulties will need to be considered.

Interviewing the Child

P. Barker (1990) suggests conceptualizing the child interview as having three stages: (1) introduction, (2) information gathering and giving, and (3) termination. During the introductory stage, the clinician should orient the child to what will occur during the session. Even if an explanation of the reasons the child is seeing you was offered when the initial meeting with the parents occurred, it is a good idea to reiterate that information when you are meeting alone with the child. Before offering this information, it is useful to ask children why they think they are meeting you; this allows you to correct any misconceptions they may have. Older children and adolescents can be asked if there is anything they hope to achieve during the interview. If the interview is conducted in a playroom (as with a younger child), the clinician can review any rules, such as that the children are allowed to play with anything they like but cannot break anything or hurt themselves or you (Greenspan, 1981).

During the introductory phase, basic information about the child that is not already known can be gathered, and questions about the school the child attends, extracurricular activities, pets, hobbies, interests, and so forth can be asked. If you plan to devote a significant part of your clinical work to treating children, you should become familiar with games, television shows, music, and celebrities popular with the age groups you treat. Speaking the same language as your child client can greatly aid in the establishment of rapport. Providing games and toys to play with can help ease younger children into the interview process. Such play also provides the clinician an opportunity to observe gross and fine motor development, ability to play by rules, cooperativeness, and frustration tolerance. If a child enjoys drawing, the clinician can employ projective drawing techniques (e.g., kinetic family drawing, house-tree-person). Analysis of the details of a drawing, as well as responses the child may give to questions asked about it, can potentially yield a wealth of clinical information about the child's preoccupations, drives, and mood state. It is beyond the scope of this chapter to review projective drawing techniques; the interested reader is referred to Malchiodi (1998) and Oster and Gould (1987).

During the information-gathering and -giving stage of the interview, the clinician is likely to give a child client greater latitude than with adult clients in initiating discussion of various topics and the format in which this communication takes place (e.g., talking, play; Hughes & Baker, 1990). Greenspan (1981) cautions again too highly structuring the initial moments of the interview as this may preclude opportunities to examine how children organize themselves in an ambiguous situation. The manner in which the child interview is structured will also depend on the emotional and cognitive level of the child. The younger the child client, the more inferential and nondirective the interview will be and the more frequently primarily closed-ended questions will be used (P. Barker, 1990; Morrison & Anders, 1999). When interviewing children, care should be exercised to avoid asking multiple questions at once, asking leading questions, and asking multiple-choice questions (unless the interviewer can be fairly certain that all possible relevant responses are included). Questions should be geared so that the child is able to easily understand them, and the clinician should have some idea of the quality and complexity of responses that can be expected from children of different ages.

In interviewing a toddler or preschool-age child, one should use short, simple questions and expect that responses will be brief and concrete. Toddlers require more verbal probes than older children, and it may be difficult to obtain reliable information from them (Morrison & Anders, 1999). Furthermore, children of this age will not be able to deal with abstractions, and examination of play content may be more likely to yield information than the child's responses to interview questions (P. Barker, 1990). The play interview is an ideal format for interviewing young children because children's familiarity with play can help allay their anxiety and facilitate the transition into the interview setting; also, by expressing things indirectly through the play materials (e.g., dolls, puppets), the child is able to maintain a safe distance from troubling emotions and concerns. It is beyond the scope of this chapter to review how to conduct a play interview with a young child, but the interested reader is referred to Morrison and Anders (1999) and O'Conner and Braverman (1996).

For a client who is in middle childhood (i.e., the period between the beginning of formal schooling and puberty), it may be possible to conduct the interview entirely through talking (or through a combination of play and talking), and the child will likely be able to provide clinically rich responses to projective-like questions, such as "If you had three wishes, what would they be?" or "If you were shipwrecked on a desert island and could have any three people in the world with you, who would you pick?" (P. Barker, 1990). Children at this age are able to report facts fairly accurately, especially if asked open-ended questions, but may still have difficulty accurately making judgments of events or situations (e.g., Did something happen often or infrequently?; Morrison & Anders, 1999).

As children enter into adolescence their ability to report on events in their lives becomes increasingly similar to adults' ability, which allows the clinician to gather more history directly from them compared to younger children. The ability to think abstractly also widens the scope of questions a clinician can ask. Morrison and Anders (1999) suggest addressing several content areas with adolescents, including (a) identity formation; (b) self-esteem; (c) independence/dependence issues; (d) friendships and activities with peers (especially important given the influence friends exert during this time period); (e) use of drugs, alcohol, and tobacco; (f) sexual knowledge and experiences; (g) empathy and conscience; (h) delinquent behavior; and (i) family life.

Table 1.13 summarizes what developmental variations clinicians can expect from children's interview responses.

If, prior to the interview, the clinician knows that particular subjects are likely to be very sensitive ones for the child, it is probably best to wait until later in the interview to address these topics, after sufficient rapport has been established. An exception to this would be in cases where it is clear that the child is anxious to discuss a problematic issue (e.g., an adolescent child who strongly desired referral for treatment of a specific concern; P. Barker, 1990). For an adequate assessment of child problems to be made, clinicians must be willing to tolerate their own discomfort in allowing the extent of the client's psychopathology to become manifest (Greenspan, 1981). Thus, while it is important to recognize when intervention is needed to calm, comfort, and keep a child safe, it is also critical to avoid prematurely jumping in to try to avert the first sign of a child's distress because of one's own countertransference reactions.

Table 1.13   Interviewing children: developmental variations in relevant cognitive processes

Age	Description
Preschool	Descriptions of people are undifferentiated, concrete (e.g., focused on physical characteristics, behavior), limited in number. Perceptions of people exist on global dimensions (i.e., good-bad; strong-weak). Impressions are strongly biased by observable, immediate events. May not be able to express feelings with words.
Kindergarten	Believe feelings are provoked by events rather than through internal states (e.g., thoughts, memories). Feelings provoked by a current event override competing feelings from the past. Inability to integrate contradictory feelings leads to all-or-nothing expressions of feelings that are temporary (e.g., "I hate Mommy").
Middle childhood	Understands that two contradictory feelings can exist about the same object or person at the same time and that contradictory feelings modulate each other. Able to provide longer descriptions of others, acquire more complete conceptions of social roles, make more inferences about others, and use more constructs. Able to report facts fairly accurately, but may still have difficulty accurately making judgments of events or situations (e.g., judging often versus infrequently).
Adolescence	Can inductively reason about people (e.g., determine someone is shy after multiple observations). Increasingly able to think abstractly. May still not be fully capable of reflecting on experiences and articulating feelings.

As with adult clients, it is important to avoid ending an interview with a child abruptly. Appreciation should be expressed for the child's willingness to participate in the interview, time should be allowed for the child to ask questions or add any information that he or she wants the clinician to know, and information should be provided on what the next step in the treatment process will be.

Interviewing Older Adults

Although interviews with older adult clients may appear similar in many ways to those conducted with younger or middle-aged adults, there are important differences in terms of content areas covered and therapist techniques used. First, older adults may come to therapy knowing less about what to expect and experiencing a greater sense of stigma or embarrassment than younger adults. Seeking help for emotional problems is not likely to be a behavior many older adults grew up viewing as acceptable. Thus, more time may need to be spent explaining the therapy process and addressing concerns the client may have about seeking treatment. When a treatment provider is significantly younger than the client, questions may be raised about the clinician's ability to understand or help due to a generational gap. In such situations, it is best to nondefensively acknowledge lacking the same life experiences as someone who is the client's age, but at the same time provide information about skills and experiences that will allow you to help the client (e.g., specialized training or education, work with similar clients). This is not meant to imply that treatment with older adults is less likely to succeed; in fact, some have argued that older adults who enter therapy may be less prone to dropping out and more compliant with treatment than younger individuals (Kennedy, 2000).

Other differences in the manner in which the initial interview with an older adult will be approached may include using more formal means of address (e.g., "Mrs. Jones" rather than "Lucy"), allowing greater time to gather information, conducting the interview at a slower pace, shortening session times because of client fatigue, repeating information more frequently, using a louder speaking voice if there is suspicion or knowledge of a hearing impairment, and allowing time for clients to reminisce while recounting their history (Hipple, 1983). Use of a cognitive MSE may be more of a necessity when interviewing older adults because memory problems or confusion are more likely to occur in this client population than in younger adults. (Chapter 7, "Cognitive Disorders," reviews cognitive disorders common among older adults, including dementia and delirium, and discusses specific intake strategies to employ in suspected cases.) Issues of capacity to consent to treatment may arise more frequently for the clinician who treats older adults. Evaluating capacity to consent to treatment can be complex and establishing specific criteria difficult. In considering this issue, it is helpful to think about the characteristics of decisionally capable individuals, which include the ability to understand that a choice is being made and to express a decision consistently, appreciation for the nature of one's condition (e.g., diagnosis, prognosis, potential treatments), capability to weigh risks and benefits of different choices, ability to apply a reasonably stable set of values in making decisions, and capacity to communicate the rationale behind choices made (Kennedy, 2000). Use of formal assessment instruments such as the MacArthur Competency Assessment Tool (Grisso & Appelbaum, 1998), a 20-minute semi-structured interview that quantitatively evaluates capacity to consent to treatment, may be helpful in evaluating decisional capacities of older adults.

With a client of any age it is important to recognize the unique physical and social changes and challenges that each life cycle stage brings and to understand presenting problems within this biopsychosocial matrix. One way of organizing thoughts about an interview with an older adult is to consider theoretical frameworks that address the psychological and physical challenges faced by older adults. Erikson's (1993) stages of psychosocial development identify the challenge of integrity versus despair and isolation as the major task to be resolved for persons over 65. At this stage in life, people become aware of their own mortality and will naturally begin to review their lives. A healthy resolution of this stage occurs when a person is able to reflect on his or her life with a sense of contentment and meaning. The individual is able to take responsibility for his or her life and accept the inevitability of death. When this ego integrity is achieved, wisdom results. In contrast, a failure to resolve this stage of development results in feelings of despair and a fear of death. Hopelessness, depression, bitterness, and anxiety may occur if an individual feels life has been meaningless or full of regret, failures, and unfulfilled aspirations (H. I. Kaplan & Saddock, 1998). Building on Erikson's work, Peck (1968) identified three additional developmental tasks facing older adults. Ego differentiation versus work role preoccupation concerns whether one is able to develop new interests and aspects of one's identity when work roles end (as a result of retirement, grown children leaving the home, etc.), or whether self-esteem and identity are too strongly tied to these old roles and one is unable to fill the void left by their loss. Body transcendence versus body preoccupation has to do with the ability to overcome preoccupation with the physical ailments and deterioration of the body that naturally accompany aging and accept and make use of those capabilities that remain in order to enjoy life. Finally, ego transcendence versus ego preoccupation refers to whether the older adult is able to look past the inevitability of death and appreciate the contributions and legacy of his or her life to world.

These theoretical models help us to understand the meaning and challenges posed by the many changes that aging brings. These changes include role changes (e.g., worker to retiree, parent to grandparent, spouse to caregiver), financial changes (e.g., reduced income, greater medical expenses), decline of physical health (e.g., onset of age-related illnesses, worsening of preexisting conditions), and loss and isolation (e.g., deaths of spouse, siblings, or friends; children moving away). In addition, issues arising in any one of these areas can create a ripple effect that results in changes in other areas. For example, an older adult who is slowly losing his or her hearing may experience greater isolation when around others because of an inability to hear conversations (Hipple, 1983).

Health problems, a common concern among the elderly, may be at the root of why the client is seeking treatment (e.g., depression resulting from chronic pain) or maybe an issue that impacts the presenting concerns (e.g., a retiree struggling to find meaning in life after leaving a job and is unable to pursue certain new activities due to rheumatoid arthritis). Because of the importance of health issues in the older adult's life, it is important to devote sufficient time during the initial interview to explore the client's physical health and the impact of any ailments on the client's physical and emotional functioning. Obtaining a list of current medications is important, as many older adults are on multiple medications. It has been estimated that each year noninstitutionalized older adults use an average of 10.7 prescription medications (Yee, Williams, & O'Hara, 1990). Physiological changes associated with aging can affect the absorption, distribution, and metabolism of medications and make it more likely that older adults will experience side effects, drug toxicity, and unexpected reactions (Saxon & Etten, 2002). This is one reason that collaboration with the client's primary physician is important; releases should be secured to allow open communication among care providers to take place. Older adults typically expect that the therapist will communicate with the primary care provider (Kennedy, 2000).

One cannot underestimate the impact that larger sociocultural attitudes toward aging may have on a client's self-perception and emotional well-being. The emphasis in Western culture on youth and the concomitant attitude that aging is to be dreaded and staved off as long as possible can send messages to older adults that the later years of one's life are not to be primarily valued but feared. It is helpful to explore these issues with the older adult client, and for clinicians to consider the impact that ageism has on their own views of older adults. Examination of stereotypic assumptions (e.g., older adults aren't sexually active; older adults aren't productive or capable of change) and countertransference reactions (e.g., unresolved dependency conflicts, parental rejection, parental idealization) is important to prevent such feelings from undermining the therapeutic process (Kennedy, 2000; Schwiebert & Myers, 2001).

Finally, when interviewing older adults the clinician should be attentive to any information (e.g., client appearance or disclosures, aspects of the history) suggesting that elder abuse may be occurring. Such abuse may take many forms, including physical or emotional abuse or neglect, as well as financial abuse (e.g., withholding funds that should be rightfully accessed by the elder). Chapter 2 ("Crisis Issues") reviews signs of elder abuse and neglect in detail and outlines appropriate steps to take in response.

SUMMARY: STRATEGIES AND TIPS FOR SUCCESS

Information obtained during the initial intake interview with a client helps create a road map for diagnosis and future treatment, and therefore represents a critically important point of contact with the client. Adequate preparation for the interview encompasses a review of information that is available about the client; willingness to engage in self-reflection to identify potential biases, assumptions, and blind-spots that may adversely affect rapport established with the client and the quality of the information obtained; attention to the appropriateness of one's physical presentation and office surroundings; awareness of potential safety issues; gathering relevant paperwork; and knowledge of appropriate legal and ethical issues in the interview process. The last item encompasses the importance of obtaining the client's informed consent to treatment, reviewing limits to confidentiality with clients, compliance where applicable with laws (e.g., HIPAA) regarding the storage and transmission of client information, and obtaining client consent in contacting third parties (e.g., former treatment providers, family members). Adequate information will not be obtained in an intake interview if there is a failure to establish sufficient rapport with the client. Rapport is established through both nonverbal and verbal means and should be considered a process that operates continually throughout the therapy process.

Although interview content may be affected by theoretical orientation, it is useful to obtain information from the client in a number of standard areas, although more than one meeting may be necessary to gather this information based on the client's developmental and cognitive capacity, emotional state, and physical condition. The interview represents an opportunity not only to inquire about problems and potential pathology, but to understand client resiliencies, strengths, and accomplishments. Presenting problems must be considered within the larger matrix of the client's culture and religious background, areas often neglected in the interview process. The mental status examination provides a means for systematically evaluating dimensions of a client's cognition, emotions, and general behavior at the time of the interview, and is an important component of the interview process. Structured interviews can assist clinicians in obtaining information relevant to diagnosis and can help avoid biases that result in incomplete information being gathered on a client; however, they may have limited application for clients in crisis and may reduce opportunities to learn about unique aspects of a client's life.

Interviewing techniques must be modified when dealing with clients at either end of the age spectrum. Interviews with children, for example, include consultation with parents and observation of parent-child interactions, in addition to a direct interview with the child. Issues of confidentiality, developmental variations in children's cognitive processes, and the unique circumstances under which child clients come in for treatment (e.g., typically referred by others, lacking in knowledge of the therapy process) are among the unique challenges clinicians face when conducting pediatric interviews. For older adult clients, the interview process may need to be adjusted for physical and sensory limitations, and the stigma of seeking professional help may be salient. Greater emphasis on understanding the impact of role changes, loss, and physical illness and decline is needed in interviewing older adult clients. Use of life cycle stage models (e.g., Erikson, 1993; Peck, 1968) can be useful in providing a framework for areas of inquiry when working with this population.

During the course of an initial interview (and certainly at other points during treatment), clinicians may learn of life-threatening crises faced by clients, including disclosures of suicidal or homicidal ideation and reports of abuse or neglect. Such issues require an immediate response that is thoughtful, thorough, and designed to maximize client safety. These issues are addressed in Chapter 2, "Crisis Issues."

Chapter 2

CRISIS ISSUES

Dealing with issues of suicidality, violence or homicidality, and abuse can create a sense of urgency that is intimidating and overwhelming for the novice clinician. The need to respond rapidly can inadvertently contribute to the neglect of salient information and result in the provision of inadequate care. This chapter focuses on the management of these crisis issues and how they impact the initial interview and clinical decision-making process. The clinical skills required involve the ability to prioritize and discern the relevant issues and to formulate and implement a plan of action while trying to contain the client's feelings of emotional turmoil.

CLINICIAN AND THERAPEUTIC ISSUES

When a client is suicidal, poses a danger to others, or has been abused, be prepared to conduct an appropriate assessment of risk and lethality and to rapidly develop a plan to protect and treat. If the client is impulsive or agitated, you must also be ready to deal with the possibility of aggressive behavior. Thus, even before meeting with a client for the first time, review available records for possible indicators of impulsivity and aggression potential (see Table 2.1) and be familiar with the basic safety guidelines outlined in Chapter 1.

When conducting the initial interview, clinicians frequently omit or fail to ask about suicidal and violent or homicidal ideation and behavior, and physical, sexual, or emotional abuse or neglect. Consequently, the seriousness of potential risk and safety issues may be underestimated and treatment decisions made based on incomplete information (S. C. Shea, 1999). Because crisis-related information can present itself unexpectedly, always be attuned to information that warrants a direct response and be prepared to respond quickly.

Although many clients in crisis are motivated to be open and honest to obtain help, this is not always the case. Court-mandated clients, paranoid individuals, those with poor insight, persons experiencing intense feelings of hopelessness and futility, and those fearing involvement of the legal system may not readily disclose information regarding harm to self or others (R. G. Meyer & Deitsch, 1996; R. I. Simon & Gutheil, 2002). In these cases, you should openly acknowledge the difficulties the client may have in disclosing information, but also explain that openness and honesty will ultimately enable you to most effectively help the client. However, in spite of such encouragement, some clients will continue to be evasive regarding risk issues. Concerns about the veracity of a client's report should be carefully and fully documented.

Table 2.1   What to look for in a review of client records

Historical/Behavioral Data	Diagnoses
Juvenile history	Antisocial Personality Disorder
Previous violence, altercations	Narcissistic Personality Disorder
History of impulsive acts, behavior	Borderline Personality Disorder
Driving under the influence	Alcohol or substance abuse
Work problems, suspensions	Intermittent Explosive Disorder
Restraining orders	Schizophrenia
Hot tempered or history of anger	Delusional Disorder
Poor or impaired judgment	Bipolar Disorder, manic
Suicidal ideation, attempts	Dementia
Homicidal ideation, plans	CNS damage and headaches
Gambling or bankruptcies	Head injury
If inpatient: A record of holds and restraints	

Dealing with clients who engage in dangerous behaviors can lead to feeling ill at ease or uncomfortable about one's abilities and to fear for one's own safety. Clinicians working in stressful settings with clients who have severe problems often express anger, anxiety, and despair, and it is not unusual to experience intensely negative emotions when treating suicidal clients (Maltsberger & Buie, 1974). These emotions can find expression in such therapy-interfering behaviors as taking excessive calls and pages from a client, being chronically late, eating or drinking in session, or falling asleep during sessions (Linehan, 1997; Maltsberger & Buie, 1989). If you need to continually consider your own safety, as in the case of treating an impulsive, explosive client, there is apt to be a significant negative impact on the therapeutic relationship. You may, for example, avoid discussion of important issues for fear of upsetting or provoking the client, experience problems setting limits, and collude with the client's tendency to minimize or deny problems. However, if you are lulled into a false sense of security by the client, you may fail to take adequate action to ensure safety (Leenaars, 1994).

Given the clinical issues presented by clients who pose a danger to themselves and others, it is wise to limit the number of these individuals in one's caseload to prevent burnout. Negative feelings that arise in working with clients in crisis must be acknowledged and addressed so that they do not adversely impact your ability to provide effective treatment (Kleespies, Deleppo, Mori, & Niles, 1998). This can be achieved by seeking support via supervision, professional peers, and personal psychotherapy.

SUICIDE

It is highly likely that you will, at some point in your career, deal with an actively suicidal client (Baerger, 2001). Suicide is the ninth leading cause for death in the United States and the third leading cause in 15- to 24-year-olds, and it is estimated that an average of 83 Americans kill themselves daily (J. L. McIntosh, 1991; A. L. Miller & Glinski, 2000; Moscicki, 1997). The suicide rate for Caucasian males over 85 is 6 times the average rate

(Hoyert, Smith, Murphy, & Kochanek, 2001). The highest rate for completed suicides is for Caucasian males; Hispanic youth have the highest rate of suicide attempts, and for African American males the rate for suicide has consistently risen over the past 2 decades (Johr, Harstein, & Miller, 2002). Despite these sobering statistics, suicide is a relatively rare event with considerable individual variation, which makes its prediction akin to hitting a moving target (Kral & Sakinofsky, 1994). Individuals differ in how they become suicidal. For some, there is a gradual progression toward suicide that culminates in the act itself, while others experience frequent suicidal storms of volatility and impulsivity (S. C. Shea, 1999). Within the same individual there are temporal fluctuations in suicidal state, and during stressful times and changing life circumstances the client's level of risk must be reassessed and monitored.

Suicide Myths

Suicide myths are fallacies that exist in the general public and even among clinicians that can result in failures to provide appropriate assistance and intervention to clients. The first myth is that individuals who are contemplating suicide will not tell anyone, and that people who kill themselves do so without warning. In fact, most suicidal people communicate their intent either directly, by talking about it, or indirectly through their behavior. A review of psychological autopsies of suicide victims found that more than 60% had directly or indirectly communicated suicidal intent to others within 6 months of their death; 40% to 60% of victims had contacted a physician (although in most cases it was not a mental health physician); and most individuals had communicated their intent to family and friends (Fawcett, Clark, & Busch, 1993).

Another myth is that females only threaten suicide, whereas males actually carry it out. Women do *attempt* suicide more often than males (usually by a ratio of 4:1) and tend to use less reliably lethal means (e.g., pills) compared to those typically chosen by men (e.g., guns, hanging; Krueger & Wollersheim, 1993). It is also true that most completed suicides occur in men over 45 years of age, with the greatest rate being for White males over 65. Yet, in spite of these statistics, do not automatically conclude that a suicide attempt by a woman is less dangerous or serious than that by a man (J. Sommers-Flanagan & Sommers-Flanagan, 1993).

Related myths are that a dramatic, nonlethal attempt is attention-getting, manipulative, and not to be taken seriously, and that people who attempt suicide are crying for help and don't really want to kill themselves (Krueger & Wollersheim, 1993). Any suicide attempt, regardless of the demographics of the client or the nature of the attempt, should be treated as a serious clinical emergency.

Some believe that all suicides are well planned and that only high-risk individuals kill themselves. In fact, some suicides are impulsive acts in which the individual did not clearly think through the decision to die, and some involve nonlethal means that accidentally go wrong (S. C. Shea, 1999). It was also once believed that children did not commit suicide. It is true that children under 7 may not understand the concept of death and, until age 13, are likely to see death as a temporary state. However, between 1980 and 1992, the suicide rate among children ages 10 to 14 in the United States increased by 120%, and children as young as 4 have successfully killed themselves (Jaimson, 1999; Lukas, 1993).

A myth especially prevalent among novice clinicians is that talking about suicide (e.g., asking about details of a suicide plan) will give clients ideas about how to kill themselves and will increase suicide risk. There is no evidence to support this idea (Pipes & Davenport, 1990). In fact, clients may feel judged and remain secretive about suicidal thoughts and behaviors if they believe a clinician is reluctant to talk about these issues. Thus, by *avoiding* the topic of suicide the opportunity to intervene and prevent self-harming actions may be lost.

Other fallacies are that competent therapists never have clients who commit suicide, and a good clinician can stop a client who wishes to die. In reality, if individuals truly wish to end their life they will find a way to do so. During their careers, 20% of psychologists (PhD) and 50% of psychiatrists will lose a client to suicide (Baerger, 2001; Bongar, Greaney, & Peruzzi, 1998).

Interviewing Skills

Whether it arises during the course of an interview or as a side comment at the end of a session, whenever a client mentions self-harm, a thorough risk assessment must be conducted (Bongar, 1992). Therefore, it is necessary to become comfortable discussing the painful issues that invariably accompany suicidal ideation. It is important to listen for and follow up on expressions of hopelessness, pessimism regarding the future, feelings of worthlessness, and refusal to discuss these issues as these may belie suicidal ideation. Open discussion of suicidal thoughts and feelings will help you understand the depth of the client's suicidal state and will convey a sense of empathy and concern (S. C. Shea, 1999). Care must be taken to avoid colluding with a client's denial, minimization, or avoidance of these topics, and encouragement to disclose may be facilitated by normalizing the client's feelings (R. I. Simon & Gutheil, 2002; Sommers-Flanagan & Sommers-Flanagan, 1995). Indeed, a common problem in dealing with psychiatric emergencies such as suicidal thoughts and behavior is the failure to sufficiently engage the client and significant others (D. C. Clark, 1998). Given the common tendency to withhold information about suicidal thoughts and behaviors, a helpful rule of thumb is to always ask about suicide attempts at least twice in an interview (S. C. Shea, 1999).

Common errors in suicide assessment and intervention include being defensive, offering superficial reassurance and trivialized prepackaged solutions, giving premature advice, distancing oneself from strong feelings by using intellectualization, and adopting a passive, interpretative stance instead of providing directive, structured guidance (Neimeyer & Pfeiffer, 1994). Similarly, S. C. Shea (1999) describes how clinicians can fall prey to a "deadly trio" of errors when eliciting suicidal ideation: omissions or failing to ask, distortion (mishearing), and assumptions. Clinician errors (see Table 2.2) in the assessment of suicide often relate to the misapplication of clinical skills or a failure to obtain information or to implement an appropriate intervention (Bongar, Greaney, et al., 1998).

To minimize clinician's errors, S. C. Shea (1999) recommends using a highly structured interview format known as the Chronological Assessment of Suicidal Events (CASE) when assessing a suicidal client. This interview focuses on four specific areas: (1) presenting suicidal ideation and behavior, (2) recent (prior 2 months) suicidal ideation and behavior, (3) past suicidal ideation and behavior, and (4) immediate suicide plans and their implementation. While conducting this assessment the clinician needs to be alert for

Table 2.2   Clinician's common errors in suicide assessment

Assessment Failures (Failure to)[*]	Clinical Errors[**]
Evaluate need for appropriate medication.	Superficial reassurance and minimization
Specify or implement hospitalization criteria.	Avoidance of strong feelings
Maintain appropriate therapeutic relationship.	Distancing using professionalism
Seek consultation and supervision.	Inadequate assessment of suicidal intent
Evaluate suicide risk on intake.	Failure to identify precipitating events
Evaluate suicide risk at transitions.	Adopting passive or interpretive stance
Obtain prior records and adequate history.	Insufficient directiveness
Conduct a mental status examination.	Advice giving
Diagnose appropriately.	Stereotypic responses
Establish a treatment plan.	Defensiveness
Ensure a safe environment.	Poor preparation and errors of omission
Document rationale and clinical judgment.	Distortions and assumptions

[*]From "Risk Management with the Suicidal Patient" (pp. 199–216), by B. Bongar, S. Greaney, and N. Peruzzi, in *Emergencies in Mental Health Practice: Evaluation and Management*, P. M. Kleespies (Ed.), 1998, New York: Guilford Press. Adapted with permission.

[**]From "The Ten Most Common Errors of Suicide Interventionists" (pp. 207–224), by R. A. Neimeyer and A. M. Pfeiffer, in *Treatment of Suicidal People*, A. A. Leenaars, J. T. Maltsberger, and R. A. Neimeyer (Eds.), 1994, Philadelphia: Taylor & Francis. Adapted with permission.

any underlying patterns in the client's behavior, any efforts to conceal suicidal intention, any rehearsal behavior, and any changes in suicide method (e.g., progressively more lethal means being considered). Using the CASE format, the interviewer should be able to determine the most serious attempt, the approximate number of past attempts or gestures, how serious the most recent attempt was, and the ways the client has tried to cope with suicidal feelings. A poorer prognosis and higher level of lethality is associated with individuals who have a history of multiple attempts, poor coping skills, substance abuse, and a family history of suicide (Kral & Sakinofsky, 1994).

Clinician Responsibilities

In addition to the emotional ramifications of losing a client to suicide, clinicians may worry whether they will be found legally responsible for the client's death should litigation be pursued by the client's family or loved ones. While the courts recognize the difficulty of predicting suicide, the definition of standard of care includes the concepts of foresight (Was an adequate assessment conducted?) and causation (Was an appropriate plan to protect implemented?) (Baerger, 2001; Bongar et al., 1998). To conduct an adequate assessment, one must recognize that suicide is a multifaceted, multidimensional, and multicausal concept. It includes predisposing vulnerabilities, suicidal intent and behavior, psychiatric diagnosis, precipitants, hopelessness, agitation, perturbation, cognitive constriction, self-control, and the presence of supportive or protective factors (Bongar et al., 1998; Maltsberger, 2001). When a client is suicidal or engaging in self-injurious behavior the clinician's responsibilities are fourfold: (1) Assess risk factors and precipitants, (2) evaluate the individual's level of risk and lethality, (3) implement a plan to protect and treat, and (4) document all of these actions (see Table 2.3).

Table 2.3   Responsibilities when a client is suicidal

Assessment	Evaluate Risk	Plan to Protect
Gather history	Assess mental state and intent	Decide disposition
Obtain records	Determine access to means	Remove means
Contact others	Assess lethality	Contract for safety
Evaluate risk factors	Evaluate prior behavior	Consider medication referral
Screen for precipitants	Assess level of self-control	Create crisis contact card
Administer suicide scales	Consider level of support	Increase supports
Consult	Determine risk	Implement interventions

Document, Monitor and Follow Up

Assessing Risk Factors and Precipitants

A number of client characteristics (historical, personal, psychosocial-environmental, and clinical) have been correlated with completed suicide. Some risk factors represent acute conditions, whereas others reflect chronic stressors or characteristics. Risk factors have also been conceptualized as background (demographic) or subjective (the personal meaning and experience of distress) factors that can be mitigated by protective factors such as social support, employment, and religious beliefs (Kral & Sakinofsky, 1994; Sanchez, 2001). Unfortunately, no one risk factor is pathognomonic of suicide, and suicide remains difficult to foresee even with the best of predictors (Motto, 1989; Roy, 1989, 1992). The client's level of self-disclosure and the amorphous nature of suicidality also impact the assessment of risk (Kral & Sakinofsky, 1994; Rudd, Joiner, & Rajab, 2001). Nevertheless, it is important to be familiar with the most common suicide risk factors. A helpful mnemonic for remembering is **HIDE** the Bullet **CLIPS** (Table 2.4).

Table 2.4   Suicide risk factors and suicide plan assessment

Suicide Risk Factors	
History: familial and individual	**C**ommunicates desire to die
Ideation and intention	**L**ack of support and loss
Diagnosis	**I**nflexibility of cognitions
Emotional state	**P**recipitants and losses
Behavior	**S**tatistics and suicide scales

Mnemonic: **HIDE** the Bullet **CLIPS**

Suicide Plan Assessment[*]

Specificity: What are the details of the client's plan?
Lethality: How quick and likely is death?
Availability: Does the client have access to the means and their immediate implementation?
Proximity: How close by or available are family, friends, social, or helping resources?

Mnemonic: **SLAP**

[*]Adapted.

Table 2.5   Assessment of suicide attempt and ideation

Assessment of Suicide Attempt[*]	Assessment of Suicidal or Violent Ideation
What was the method used?	What is the nature or content of the ideation?
How serious was the action?	What is the frequency and intensity of the
To what extent did the client intend to die?	ideation?
What are his or her feelings about the unsuccessful attempt?	Are the thoughts fleeting or pervasive?
Was the attempt impulsive or well planned?	When did client last think about suicide or violence?
Did the attempt involve alcohol or drugs?	Is the ideation related to a particular trigger or stressor?
Were interpersonal factors involved in the attempt?	How comfortable is the client with the ideation: Is it ego syntonic?
Was there an identifiable stressor or group of stressors?	Do delusions and hallucinations accompany the ideation?
How hopeless did the client feel at the time of the attempt?	Is the ideation bizarre, paranoid, or psychotic?
What happened to cause the attempt to fail?	Does the client feel he or she has to act on the ideation?
Has the client made other attempts?	
Does the client currently have a plan and access to the means to carry it out?	

[*]From *The Practical Art of Suicide Assessment: A Guide for Mental Health Professionals and Substance Abuse Counselors*, by S. C. Shea, 1999, New York: Wiley. Adapted with permission.

History

A family history of suicide or suicide attempts is significant, and the clinician should inquire about anniversaries and how old family members were when these events occurred (J. J. Mann, Waternaux, Haas, & Malone, 1999; Roy, 1992). It is also significant if the client's family has a history of using suicidal actions as a coping mechanism, problem-solving strategy, or source of relief from suffering. Additional familial factors that increase suicide risk are family instability, parental rejection, and early parental loss (H. I. Kaplan & Saddock, 1998). With regard to parental loss, if a parent commits suicide when a child is less than 5 years old, the surviving child is 9 times more likely to commit suicide (Krueger & Wollersheim, 1993).

The client is also at higher risk for self-harm if he or she has a personal history of suicide attempts or self-mutilation (Fawcett et al., 1993; Joiner & Rudd, 2000; R. Maris, 1992). Inquiries about previous suicide attempts should probe factors contributing to the attempt, level of planning, means employed and lethality, consequences of the attempt, and reaction of both the client and significant others. If the method or attempt was bizarre, psychosis should be assessed. A detailed account of prior attempts can be obtained by asking the client to walk the clinician through what happened step-by-step, describing feelings at each point along the way. S. C. Shea (1999) also recommends asking the client a specific series of questions, which are summarized in Table 2.5.

Ideation and Intention

A cornerstone of a suicide assessment is a thorough review of the client's thoughts about suicide, how the client has coped with them, and the level of acceptance, preoccupation, or obsession with the suicidal ideation (see Table 2.5). The importance of inquiring about suicidal ideation is reflected in a study finding that more than 50% of mentally ill individuals and 92% of alcoholics who committed suicide expressed suicidal ideation prior to their deaths (Fawcett et al., 1993). Attempts should be made to quantify suicidal ideation by asking about the frequency, duration, and intensity of the thoughts. The client should be asked who else has been told about the suicidal thoughts, and what the client thinks the impact of the suicide will be on others, such as family members, friends, and pets. Exploration of these consequences can sometimes lead to the discovery of underlying motivations or wishes (e.g., "My family will finally realize how important I was to them") that can then be explored and processed more constructively in therapy. It is also critical to inquire about deterrents to suicide such as future life goals, cultural and religious beliefs, and fears of pain or suffering that might prevent the client from acting on the thoughts (Gibbs, 1997; Lester, 2001).

Suicidal intent implies that the client is acting or talking in a way that suggests he or she intends to commit suicide. Intent can be determined from client report, peer or family report, or behavioral observations. In an interview, intention can be assessed by evaluating if the client's thoughts are passive or active ("I wish I would get into an accident" versus "I want to kill myself") and how detailed and complex the suicide plan is. Be very specific and ask the client to outline the particulars of the plan, the proposed time frame, whether steps have been taken to prevent discovery, and if there are backup plans or alternative methods should the attempt be unsuccessful. Having a backup plan suggests a particularly high level of risk. Although the level of planning is often a good indicator of the seriousness of the intention, many successful suicides are achieved with minimal planning using highly lethal means. In this regard, it is important to determine the client's tendency toward impulsive behavior, antisocial tendencies, history of impaired judgment, access to the means of suicide, and the involvement of alcohol or substance use. Alcohol and substances can act as disinhibitors that physiologically and psychologically facilitate impulsive behavior and impact the individual's ability to think logically (Fawcett et al., 1993; Lukas, 1993). In summary, the more intense the ideation, the more thorough and elaborate the plan; the greater the loss of cognitive control, the more suicide risk increases. Be certain to document the specific content of the client's ideation and intent.

Diagnoses

The presence of depression or melancholia in individuals who attempt suicide is almost universal, and the suicide risk for depressed persons is 30 times greater than in the general population (Bongar, 1992; J. Sommers-Flanagan & Sommers-Flanagan, 1995). Comorbid anxiety may lead to severe psychic pain that, in turn, becomes a precipitant to suicide (Fawcett et al., 1993). In general, a psychiatric diagnosis constitutes a suicide risk factor, and multiple diagnoses increase the risk (Sanchez, 2001). Reviews of completed suicides among young adults indicate that the presence of a recent psychiatric illness was a primary factor in 93% of suicides, with Major Depression accounting for 40% to 60% of cases, chronic alcohol abuse for 20% of cases, and a diagnosis of Schizophrenia for 10% of cases (Fawcett et al., 1993). The combination of alcohol or substance abuse, a history of suicide attempts, and the presence of psychotic features has been referred to as a triad of lethality (S. C. Shea, 1999). With regard to substances, the abuse of *both* drugs and alcohol results in a ten-fold increase in risk for suicide (A. L. Miller & Glinski, 2000;

Sanchez, 2001). Schizophrenics are more likely to commit suicide during periods of improvement rather than psychotic exacerbations because when active symptoms abate and lucidity returns, psychotic individuals often become depressed (Fawcett et al., 1993; J. F. Westermeyer, Harrow, & Marengo, 1991). Among individuals with Bipolar Disorder, 25% to 60% attempt suicide at least once, and 19% of deaths among this population are due to suicide (Fawcett et al., 1993; F. K. Goodwin & Jamison, 1990). Combat-related Posttraumatic Stress Disorder (PTSD), head injury, and anxiety disorder (specifically panic attacks) are also related to higher suicide risk (Sanchez, 2001).

The rate of personality disorders among completed suicides is as high as 30% to 40%, with Borderline and Antisocial Personality Disorders associated with the most lethal attempts. A history of child abuse has also been linked to increased suicide risk, and child sexual abuse has been found to be an even stronger predictor of current suicidality than depression (Read, Agar, Barker-Collo, Davies, & Moskowitz, 2001).

Among adolescents, the majority who commit suicide (90% to 97%) have a psychiatric illness at the time of death, and as diagnostic comorbidity increases, so does the frequency and lethality of suicide attempts (A. L. Miller & Glinski, 2000). There may also be a pattern of lifelong coping difficulties in this population (Kral & Sakinofsky, 1994). Common diagnoses among adolescents who have attempted or committed suicide include Major Depression and other mood disorders, antisocial behavior, anxiety, Borderline Personality Disorder, Conduct Disorder, and alcohol or substance abuse. It has been estimated that in 38% of adolescent suicide attempts alcohol was consumed within 6 hours of the attempt (A. L. Miller & Glinski, 2000).

The clinician should also be aware that suicide risk varies with the duration and stage of illness. Among depressed clients, for example, individuals who are considered at short-term risk (i.e., of committing suicide within 1 year) frequently have panic attacks or other severe anxiety, problems with concentration, psychomotor agitation, sleep difficulties, alcohol abuse, and severe anhedonia (loss of pleasure). In contrast, depressed individuals at risk for committing suicide at a later date (between 2 and 10 years) often present with severe hopelessness, suicidal ideation, and a history of suicide attempts (Fawcett et al., 1993). It is well known that severely depressed clients are at higher risk for suicide when their mood improves and energy returns, particularly if they had been suffering from vegetative symptoms. Be particularly alert to abrupt improvement from depression, as this may precede suicide. Individuals who have been recently discharged from a psychiatric inpatient facility are often at high risk in the period subsequent to release (Fawcett et al., 1993; Maxmen & Ward, 1995).

Emotional State

Imminent suicide is an episodic phenomenon linked to a client's emotional state, which can fluctuate significantly. It is therefore important to assess the volatility and depth of the client's emotional experience when conducting a suicide assessment. This information can be obtained from observations of the client's verbal and nonverbal behavior. States such as deep depression, agitation, self-hatred, anguish, anxiety, shame, and exhaustion are associated with a heightened risk for suicide. Research consistently demonstrates that loss of pleasure, a sense of hopelessness or helplessness, extreme guilt, and despair are among the best predictors of suicide (Beck, Steer, Beck, & Newman, 1993; Bonner, 1990; Kral & Sakinofsky, 1994). Therefore, listen for indications that the client feels life is too painful and unbearable (perturbation), that he or she can't go on, and that treatment is a waste of time (Shneidman, 1985, 1993). For some individuals, self-hatred or contempt, combined with a sense of aloneness and emotional abandonment, can create a lethal pain ("psychache") for which suicide is seen as a welcome escape (Maltsberger, 2001; Shneidman, 1993). Perceiving oneself as a disappointment, burden, or source of shame to others also places the individual at risk for suicide, as can the desire to seek revenge on those who have disappointed one. For individuals in treatment, a lack of change in their level of hopelessness is highly predictive of completed suicide on discharge (Dahlsgaard, Beck, & Brown, 1998).

To assess the client's ability to regulate strong emotions at critical times, queries should be made about the client's past responses to stress and life challenges. A history of dealing with stress by escape or avoidance is associated with increased suicide risk (Maltsberger, 2001). Difficulties with emotional self-control may also be indicated by a history of frequent altercations, violent verbal or physical outbursts, alcohol or substance abuse, and participation in high-risk behaviors (Plutchik & van Praag, 1995). The individual's perception of their level of self-control can provide information on insight and judgment.

Behavior

It is necessary to fully explore the presence of behaviors that suggest the client has made a decision to die. If the individual has recently and unexpectedly made a will, started to give away possessions (especially pets), or begun to sever relationships, one should be alerted to an increased risk for suicide. Fantasizing how others might react to one's death, writing a suicide note, or appearing preoccupied by morbid thoughts also suggests the possibility of suicidal thoughts and intention. According to Leenaars and Lester (1995), sudden behavior changes in the client should be suspect. An unexplained, inappropriate, sudden calm or cheerfulness after a long period of depression or despair can indicate that the client has made a decision about death and has the energy to act on it. If the client has access to the means to kill himself or herself and has started to rehearse the plan (experimental actions), there is a strong possibility of imminent suicide (D. C. Clark, 1998). In such cases, you should query what factors are stopping the client when he or she thinks of the plan. It is also helpful to determine what proactive, appropriate coping methods the client has used to stay in control during previous challenging moments (e.g., move to college, death of a loved one) and to encourage their use again. If the client's history or significant others indicate a pattern of leaving rather than resolving issues, it is necessary to assess the tendency to see suicide as an escape (Maltsberger, 2001).

Communication

The majority (80%) of individuals who kill themselves have told others of their intent (R. G. Meyer & Deitsch, 1996). This may be in the form of a suicide note, a farewell or goodbye phone call, or statements made to friends or significant others in passing. Clients may state a desire to end it all or a feeling that they have had enough (Krueger & Wollersheim, 1993). Inquiries (with permission) of friends or family can be made to determine whether clients have said they wish to die or see death as an escape and solution to distress. If the individual has actually written a suicide note you may ask to see it and inquire about the response that is expected. Although many suicidal individuals communicate their intent, not all do. Individuals suffering from a vegetative depression, for example, may present as noncommunicative and withdrawn. In such cases, be alert for mental status exam indicators such as psychomotor retardation, slowed speech, long response latency, agitation, and restlessness. In a 10-year follow-up of psychiatric inpatients who attempted suicide, more than half had denied suicidal ideation or stated that suicidal thoughts were rare to experienced interviewers (Fawcett et al., 1993). Similarly, a number of individuals who committed suicide shortly after hospital discharge had prior to discharge denied suicidal ideation, a plan, or intent (R. I. Simon & Gutheil, 2002).

Lack of Support

Lack of a therapeutic alliance, estrangement from friends or family, a recent geographic move, being imprisoned, the breakup of a relationship, or the death of a loved one (even a pet) all increase suicide risk (H. I. Kaplan & Saddock, 1995). These factors share the common threads of isolation and a lack of social support. It has been estimated that a quarter of individuals who die from suicide experienced an interpersonal loss in the 6 weeks prior to their death (G. E. Murphy & Wetzel, 1990). Among individuals with affective disorders, the absence of the responsibility of a child is associated with higher suicidal risk (Fawcett et al., 1993). As noted by Bonner (1990), suicidal intention does not exist in a vacuum. It exists in a psychosocial context and occurs when the individual feels isolated and hopeless and that the problems of life have become overwhelming (Maltsberger, 2001).

Given this, a suicide assessment should include an evaluation of the number and quality of an individual's social relationships. In particular, any recent conflicts with friends or family (and whether any have committed suicide) should be ascertained since withdrawal from loved ones has been found to be an important predictor of suicide risk (Fawcett et al., 1993). Even if there appears to be a caring extended family available, the client may still feel isolated and without support. Rejection or betrayal by others may not be a reality, but it is the individual's *perception* that is important. Profoundly depressed individuals, for example, may have an unrealistic appraisal about who loves or cares for them (Maltsberger, 2001). For psychiatric inpatients, detachment characterized by withdrawal, isolation, and a failure to form a therapeutic relationship has been correlated with high suicide risk (R. I. Simon & Gutheil, 2002). In the course of the interview, questions can be asked about whom the client talks to and shares information with to determine if there is a comfort person who might act as a deterrent to the client's suicide. The presence of significant relationships, a satisfying social life, and familial and nonfamilial support systems can act as protective factors for suicide risk (Sanchez, 2001).

Inability to See Alternatives

A suicidal client often presents with cognitive rigidity and an unwillingness to view alternatives (Leenaars & Lester, 1995; Shneidman, 1985). Such cognitive constriction is positively correlated with the lethality of suicide attempts (Paludszny, Davenport, & Kim, 1991). In cognitive-behavioral terms, thinking becomes black and white, and the world is viewed in all-or-nothing terms. The client may state that everything has been tried, nothing has worked, and suicide is the only rational, viable solution. Such thinking is aptly illustrated in a suicide note (Bell, 1992, p. 226) left by the author Virginia Woolf for her husband prior to her death by drowning:

> I feel certain I am going mad again. I feel we can't go through another of those terrible times. And I shan't recover this time . . . So I am doing what seems the best thing to do . . . I know that I am spoiling your life, that without me you could work . . . I can't go on spoiling your life any longer.

The inability to see alternatives can lead to feelings of hopelessness, which have been found to be a more accurate predictor of suicide risk than overall level of depression (A. T. Beck et al., 1993). Because hopelessness may also cause the client to drop out of treatment or reject interventions (Maltsberger, 2001), such expressions should be a signal to both inquire about suicidality and redouble efforts to keep the client engaged in the therapy (e.g., more frequent sessions).

If the individual is experiencing a debilitating or chronic physical illness, death may be viewed as the only solution to end the suffering or pain. In some cases, the client's cognitive rigidity is tinged with magical thinking and leads to the belief that death is a welcome relief that will fix insolvable problems or allow a peaceful escape from an impossible situation. In this way, the suicide option becomes akin to Ulysses' sirens' song for the client: clever, comforting, beautiful, and convincing (D. C. Clark, 1998). Gently challenge such beliefs by pointing out the realistic consequences of both the physical act of taking one's life (e.g., pain) and the ramifications for friends and loved ones. According to Kral and Sakinofsky (1994), the two most important questions the clinician needs to ask in determining suicide risk are "Is suicide an option?" and "Is it the only option?"

Other Precipitants

Recent interpersonal losses can be precipitating events to suicide, as can anniversaries of such losses; this is particularly true for individuals with alcohol-related disorders (Fawcett et al., 1993). Other precipitants to suicide are changes in financial status or employment (especially for clients who define themselves in terms of work or who are very invested in the status their jobs provide). The diagnosis of a medical or physical illness can be a major precipitant, particularly if the condition is chronic and deteriorating or will involve considerable suffering and/or a loss of function. For example, a diagnosis of AIDS is associated with a 7- to 36-fold increase in risk for suicide (Cote, Biggar, & Dannenberg, 1992). Admission to or discharge from an inpatient psychiatric facility can often be a precipitant to suicide. In particular, unmarried, unemployed, recently discharged patients who have previously attempted suicide, are chronically mentally ill, have a history of depression, and live alone are at high risk (Fawcett et al., 1993). For individuals with a history of affective disorder the periods of greatest suicide risk are during the early stages of recovery, including the week following hospital admission, and the first month and first year after hospital discharge (Fawcett et al., 1993).

Statistics and Scales

It is helpful to know basic demographic variables that have been linked to suicide risk. High-risk populations include men 45 years or older and women older than 55. If an individual is separated, widowed, or divorced, the risk for suicide increases, particularly if there has been a recent change in marital status (Krueger & Wollersheim, 1993; Sommers-Flanagan & Sommers-Flanagan, 1995). In general, men commit suicide more frequently than women (3:1), and more women attempt suicide. Never married, White males ages 15 to 24 are at particularly high risk, with suicide being the third leading cause of death for this age group (National Center for Health Statistics, 1996). The difference in rates of suicide between males and females increases markedly with age, rising to a ratio of 12:1 for individuals 85 years and older. Older White males have the highest suicide rate, in part because they tend to communicate their intent less and to use highly lethal means such as guns or hanging. Among women, the highest rate of suicide attempts occurs in those younger than 30. However, the risk of successful suicide for women is increasing, particularly among the elderly. Gender differences observed in attempted versus completed suicides may be due to the higher rates of depression among women, the greater likelihood that men will feel stigmatized by a failed suicide attempt, and the lower likelihood that men will seek help for psychiatric problems (Jamison, 1999).

In terms of ethnicity, the vast majority (90%) of suicides are committed by Whites (R. G. Meyer & Deitsch, 1996). In all age groups Whites exceed non-Whites for suicide, except between the ages of 15 and 29, when Native Americans and African Americans have higher rates (Garrison, 1992). However, there is also variability in suicide rates *within* ethnic groups; for example, the Navajo have relatively low rates of suicide, whereas Inuit tribes in Alaska have a much higher suicide risk (I. N. Berlin, 1987; Kral & Sakinofsky, 1994). Immigrants have a higher rate of suicide than native-born individuals, and Europeans, Scandinavians, and Japanese are at particularly high risk (H. I. Kaplan & Saddock, 1995). Cultural prohibitions or taboos against suicide, including religious beliefs, can act as deterrents to suicide and are important to inquire about (Kral & Sakinofsky, 1994). The extremes of social class are also risk factors for suicide. In addition, being recently unemployed (particularly if the client is a professional) and living in an urban area also result in a higher risk.

For older adults in general there has been a threefold increase in suicide rate over the past 25 to 30 years. Significant risk factors for this age group include depression, alcohol use, medical or physical illness or concerns, social and occupational losses, isolation, and a lack of social support (Fawcett et al., 1993; Kral & Sakinofsky, 1994). Although suicide is rare under 10 years of age, the clinician should assess for it in 6- to 12-year-olds who present with a mood disorder, Conduct Disorder, and antisocial traits. The risk for adolescent suicide over the past 30 years has risen 300% for males and 200% for females (Krueger & Wollersheim, 1993). Developmentally, adolescents may represent a high-risk group because they are more likely to engage in dichotomous thinking, have difficulty considering alternatives, see time as relative and now as forever, and are often overly critical, lonely, and isolated (J. Callahan, 1993; Eyman, Mikawa, & Eyman, 1990). Similar to the pattern seen in adults, adolescent males outnumber females (4:1) for completed suicides, but females are more likely to attempt suicide. White male adolescents have the highest rate, followed by African American males; African American females have the lowest rate (Eyman et al., 1990; Grosz, Zimmerman, & Asnis, 1995). There are few studies on rates of suicide among Hispanic youth. When Hispanics are separated based on cultural subgroup, national origin, and immigration status, there are few differences from

White or African American suicide rates (Vega, Gil, Warheit, Apospori, & Zimmerman, 1993).

In surveys of suicidal thinking among adolescents, 40% to 60% admitted to considering suicide, and 8% to 10% attempted suicide (J. Callahan, 1993; Eyman et al., 1990). Psychological autopsies of completed suicides indicate that in the 12 months preceding death, 16% of adolescents had a well-formulated plan, thus dispelling the popular belief that adolescent suicide is almost always an impulsive, poorly planned act (Centers for Disease Control, 1998; Shafii, 1989). Most suicidal adolescents communicate their intent to others, and most suicide attempts occur in the family home (Kral & Sakinofsky, 1994). It can be difficult to evaluate suicidal ideation in adolescents because they are often reluctant to disclose and may provide conflicting information to a perceived authority figure. In addition, depression may be masked and present as an eating disorder, substance abuse, aggression, school problems, and sexual acting-out or promiscuity (Leenaars & Lester, 1995). The precipitants to adolescent suicide are often conflicts with parents, loss of a boyfriend or girlfriend, and school or relationship problems (J. Callahan, 1993). Suicidal adolescents' families are often characterized by a lack of communication, a blurring of generational boundaries, and enmeshed parent-child relationships (J. K. Zimmerman & Asnis, 1995). Fortunately, social support can act as a protective factor and as a moderator variable for life stress and suicide (Grosz et al., 1995).

The use of standardized scales to assess suicidality can be helpful for assessing risk of engaging in self-harming behaviors and for documenting the range and severity of a client's hopelessness, suicidal behaviors, and suicidal ideation. The Scale for Suicide Ideation (A. T. Beck, Kovacs, & Weisman, 1979) is a 21-item interviewer-administered (10 minutes) rating scale that assesses suicidal ideation and previous attempts. It is widely used, has excellent reliability and validity, and has predictive validity for completed suicides (A. T. Beck, Brown, Steer, Dahlsgaard, & Grisham, 1999; G. K. Brown, Beck, Steer, & Grisham, 2000). A self-report version, the Beck Scale for Suicide Ideation (A. T. Beck & Steer, 1991), also has good reliability and validity and assesses the individual's specific attitudes and plans to commit suicide during the past week. Two other scales that have good reliability and are valid for the assessment of suicidal ideation and behaviors are the Reynolds' (1991) Adult Suicidal Ideation Questionnaire (ASIQ) and the Suicidal Behavior Questionnaire (Linehan, 1996). The Beck Hopelessness Scale (A. T. Beck & Steer, 1988) is a 20-item self-report with excellent psychometric properties that is widely used and had been found to be predictive of suicide (A. T. Beck, Brown, Berchick, Stewart, & Steer, 1990; A. T. Beck & Steer, 1989; Dahlsgaard et al., 1998). G. K. Brown (2000) provides a very practical review of available suicide assessment measures for use with adults and older adults. For children and adolescents, Goldston (2000) reviews and critiques most of the current available measures for the assessment of suicide. These scales can be incorporated into an intake assessment or introduced during the course of treatment. In the latter case, anticipate resistance by some clients if completion of questionnaires to track treatment progress has not been a standard part of therapy. In such cases, frame the use of scales as a way for both you and the client to more fully understand the depth of the client's feelings around the issue of suicide. From a risk management perspective, the use of such scales can demonstrate that active, concrete steps were taken to explore and document the client's suicidal ideation and behavior.

While it is important to be familiar with such measures, they should not be overly relied on. Although suicide scales can assist in determining risk and lethality, it is still the clinician's responsibility to develop and implement an individualized plan to protect the client.

Evaluating Level of Risk and Lethality

To form an overall suicide risk profile, evaluation of the aforementioned risk factors is combined with specific information about a client's suicidal plans and behavior (Sanchez, 2001). One method for evaluating aspects of a client's suicide plan (see Table 2.4) is to use the SLAP criteria (M. Miller, 1985).

Specificity refers to how detailed and well thought out the individual's plan is: The more detailed and clearer the plan, the greater the risk. Because the details of the client's plan are an indication of the level of premeditation and immediate danger, no detail is too small for the clinician to inquire about. Evaluate the client's level of preparedness to act on this plan by asking how, what, and when (S. C. Shea, 1999). Exploring details of the client's suicide plan can be one of the most difficult aspects of conducting a risk assessment due to the uncomfortable nature of the questions that must be asked. However, it is critical to make it easy for the client to talk about these issues. To facilitate the client's disclosure, J. Sommers-Flanagan and Sommers-Flanagan (1995) suggest the use of open-ended questions, normalizing, and reassuring the client that it is okay to talk about the details.

Lethality refers to the likelihood and speed with which the suicide plan will result in death. Joiner and colleagues (Joiner, Walker, Rudd, & Jobes, 1999) recommend considering the client's "resolved plans and preparation factor" to assess lethality. Specifically, the client should be queried about all suicide methods under consideration, including whether there is a backup plan and if steps have been taken to avoid discovery. Methods such as shooting, hanging, and jumping are highly lethal, whereas medication or drug overdose is less reliable. However, in comparison to pathologists, laypersons have been found to have a less accurate understanding of the lethality associated with various methods of suicide. They often overestimate the deadliness of medication overdose and wrist cutting, and may underestimate the lethality of guns (Jamison, 1999). To encourage discussion of these issues, ask about specific, concrete behaviors and thoughts (behavioral incidents and symptom amplification), use unconditional positive regard when querying about guilt- or shame-inducing topics (shame attenuation), normalize thoughts and feelings, and utilize gentle assumption (S. C. Shea, 1999). The latter refers to nonforcefully assuming certain thoughts or actions on the client's part in order to assist disclosure of difficult topics (although when using this technique, always check with the client to ensure the accuracy of any assumptions made). These techniques can also be used to obtain a more accurate assessment of impulsivity.

Availability relates to how readily accessible the means to carry out a suicide plan are. Clients should be asked if they have practiced the suicide plan since one of the strongest clues of suicidal intent is when the client moves from tentative thoughts and plans to actual rehearsal (J. Callahan, 1993; D. C. Clark, 1998). Also consider the client's level of control and the presence of others who might prevent the client from accessing the means and implementing the plan (Kral & Sakinofsky, 1994).

Table 2.6 Continuum of suicide risk

Suicide Risk	Presentation
Nonexistent	No identifiable suicidal ideation or plans exist.
Mild	Suicidal ideation is of limited frequency, intensity, and duration. There are no specific or concrete plans or intent. Mild symptomatology is present, as is good self-control. There are few risk factors, and there are identifiable protective factors.
Moderate	Suicidal ideation is frequent, but with limited intensity and duration. There are some specific plans or a general plan. Self-control is intact. Limited symptomatology is present, as well as some risk factors. However, the client has some reasons for living, does not intend to commit suicide, and there are some identifiable protective factors.
Severe	Suicidal ideation is frequent, intense, and enduring. The suicide plan is specific and lethal, and the means are available. Intent may be questionable (i.e., no subjective intent, but objective indicators such as means to complete attempt are present). Self-control is impaired and there is severe symptomatology. Few, if any, helping resources are nearby. Protective factors are limited and multiple risk factors are present.
Extreme	Suicidal ideation is frequent, intense, and enduring. The suicide plan is specific, lethal, and the means to carry it out are available. There is clear subjective and objective intent. Self-control is impaired and severe symptomatology is present. There are many risk factors and no protective factors. The client intends to kill him/herself when the first opportunity arises (i.e., as soon as possible).

Source: From *Treating Suicidal Behavior: An Effective, Time-Limited Approach,* by M. D. Rudd, T. Joiner, and M. H. Rajab, 2001, New York: Guilford Press. Adapted with permission.

Proximity focuses on whether there are supports such as family, friends, or neighbors available and close by. The further away these supports are, the greater the suicide risk. It is important not to confuse geographic proximity with availability. The latter can be ascertained by questioning the client about the actual frequency of contact and availability of assistance from others with even mundane tasks. Proximity also refers to access to social or helping resources such as support groups or therapy (M. Miller, 1985).

Having assessed the client's risk factors, precipitants, and level of lethality, a decision regarding intervention must be made. The appropriate level of intervention will be based on the client's overall suicide risk, which should take into account both intent and protective factors (Rudd et al., 2001). A model is presented in Table 2.6 that allows the client to be placed on a continuum ranging from nonexistent to extreme suicide risk and serves as a decision-making guide for treatment interventions. If a client is at risk for suicide, there is a legal responsibility to develop a plan to protect before allowing the client to leave (Bongar, 1991; Bongar, Maris, Berman, & Litman, 1998).

Implementing a Plan to Protect and Treat

If a client is suicidal, an initial decision that must be made is whether he or she can be managed on an inpatient or outpatient basis. This decision is, in part, determined by the client's level of risk, ability to cooperate with treatment (e.g., agree to a no-suicide

Table 2.7   Interventions for suicidal clients

Practical	Support	Therapeutic
Consultation	Contact others	Rapport and relationship
Disposition decision	Identify supports	Increase contact
Ensure safety	Involve monitor	Explore client's perceptions
Remove means and contract	Strengthen support	Self-monitoring
Medication evaluation	Contact card	Identify alternatives
Reassess need for hospital	24-hour crisis support	Build coping strategies
Ongoing monitoring of risk	Related services	Target disruptive behaviors
Documentation	Follow through	Reassess goals

contract), and the degree to which the client is honest and can be trusted. There is no single method of treatment for suicidal clients, and the nature and level of intervention is determined by the immediacy of the situation, the availability of support and resources, and the client's clinical state (Joiner et al., 1999). However, all interventions (see Table 2.7) share the common goal of keeping the client alive (Bongar, 1992; Lester, 2001; Shneidman, 1981).

When treated on an outpatient basis, the suicidal client may need to be seen daily, and those experiencing intense depression, anxiety, sleep disturbance, or other debilitating symptoms should also be referred for a medication evaluation. Therapeutic interventions to treat the most disruptive symptoms, specifically those that impair daily functioning, should be immediately implemented. Adoption of a crisis intervention model (discussed in Chapter 4), in which immediate coping is reestablished, is helpful (Leenaars, 1994). Such a model incorporates a series of steps, including the establishment of rapport, exploration of the nature of the client's problems and previous coping, and identification of cognitive constriction and underlying feelings of helplessness and hopelessness. You will also want to help generate alternatives to suicide and provide support, including developing a suicide prevention contract, a concrete, step-by-step plan to address the immediate crisis; mobilizing social support resources; and determining the need for hospitalization (see Chapter 4). A follow-up plan to check on progress and verify that the interventions have been implemented should also be developed (Leenaars, 1994; Rudd et al., 2001; J. Sommers-Flanagan & Sommers-Flanagan, 1995).

In a critical review of interventions with suicidal patients, a strong therapeutic relationship characterized by trust and caring was found to be crucial (Baerger, 2001; Rudd et al., 2001). This allows the client to experience support, hope, acceptance, relief from despair, and a lifesaving connection. Actions that can facilitate therapist attachment and alliance are emergency availability, flexibility regarding session length and frequency, and the prompt return of phone calls. By adopting a very active approach in establishing rapport and exploring and redefining the client's problems, one can focus on reducing anguish and fostering life-sustaining actions. A plan of action can be developed that mobilizes and identifies people available to help, thus increasing the client's sense of choice and being supported (Leenaars, 1994; J. Sommers-Flanagan & Sommers-Flanagan, 1995). Encourage the client to talk to others (e.g., commit to calling a significant other each evening) and to identify a monitor who will never leave the client unattended, as serious suicide attempts rarely occur in the company of loved ones (Fawcett et al., 1993). Supportive persons should be informed of warning signs of suicide and should be instructed to help clients structure their day. Assigning even mundane household chores can help the client feel part of the family and break the cycle of inertia that often accompanies suicidal ideation (Jacobs, 1995).

The client can be provided with a wallet-size emergency card that outlines several mutually agreed upon, concrete steps to be taken to ensure safety and that includes several contact numbers and 24-hour emergency contacts (Joiner et al., 1999). In the presence of the clinician, the client should rehearse and practice the steps outlined on the card, and a copy should be provided to the client's supports. Access to 24-hour emergency services in the year following a first suicide attempt has been found to significantly decrease the number of subsequent attempts. Failure to provide a suicidal client with after-hours access to help may be seen as patient abandonment (Rudd et al., 2001).

Suicide prevention contracts serve as a lifeline between the therapist and the client. The most effective contract occurs in the context of a solid therapeutic relationship. Although a contract provides no guarantees for a client's safety, it can function as a deterrent, provide valuable information about the bond between therapist and client, and give a sense of the client's true suicidal intent (S. C. Shea, 1999). Contracts should be avoided with individuals with characterological disorders (e.g., borderline, passive aggressive clients), particularly if there is a manipulative component to their presentation. In these situations the negotiation of the contract may be counterproductive and result in power struggles in the therapeutic relationship (Stanford, Goetz, & Bloom, 1994).

An individual's lethality can be reduced by decreasing perturbation and cognitive constriction through a variety of therapeutic techniques, including ventilation, transfusion of hope, interpretation, and identifying alternatives (Joiner et al., 1999; Leenaars, 1994). Cognitive-behavioral interventions can be useful in addressing the constriction and all-or-nothing thinking that characterizes suicidal ideation. Short-term (less than 6 months) cognitive-behavioral therapy with a focus on problem solving has been shown to decrease suicidal ideation, depression, and hopelessness but not necessarily attempts. Reducing attempts requires longer term treatment focused on skill building around emotion regulation, anger management, and distress tolerance (Rudd et al., 2001). Approaches such as Linehan's (1993a,b, 1997) dialectical behavioral therapy (DBT), which is specifically tailored for chronically suicidal borderline clients, may be particularly helpful. This treatment views suicidal behaviors as maladaptive means to regulate affect and to escape or avoid intensely negative emotions. It involves a year of weekly individual and didactic group therapy and employs four behavioral-skills-oriented modules focusing on (1) mindfulness, (2) emotion regulation, (3) distress tolerance, and (4) interpersonal effectiveness. The therapist uses acceptance strategies (e.g., validation) and change strategies (e.g., behavioral analysis and cognitive modification) to reinforce the acquisition and generalization of these adaptive skills (Linehan, 1993a,b, 1997).

When a client cannot contract for safety, is experiencing an acute episode of a psychiatric illness, or is chronically suicidal and experiencing an exacerbating stressor, hospitalization needs to be considered. Juhnke (1994) developed a brief semi-structured interview to assess suicide risk and need for hospitalization based on W. M. Patterson, Dohn, Bird, and Patterson's (1983) SAD PERSONS scale. The latter considers the following 10 literature-identified suicide risk factors: **S**ex, **A**ge, **D**epression, **P**revious attempt, **E**thanol abuse, **R**ational thinking loss, **S**ocial supports lacking, **O**rganized plan, **N**o spouse, and

Sickness. Although voluntary hospitalization is preferable, suicidal clients may lack insight, be in denial, or be determined to kill themselves, and may consequently refuse to consider hospitalization. In such instances, involuntary commitment can be initiated. Because the laws concerning involuntary hospitalization vary with different jurisdictions, become familiar with local laws and your agency's policies. The clinician or family members should not personally transport the client to the hospital, as he or she may attempt suicide in transit or resist being transported; instead, emergency services should be contacted.

Once the client is hospitalized, his or her level of suicidality will need to be continually monitored, and the client may be placed on a one-to-one suicide watch. The postdischarge period can be a particularly high-risk period, and plans should be made to see the client frequently. Research on high-functioning inpatients who committed suicide shortly after discharge reveals that they were withdrawn, detached, and isolative while hospitalized, failed to build a therapeutic alliance or presented with a sham alliance, were affect-intolerant, and were noncompliant with and avoidant of treatment. Prior to discharge these patients passively agreed to a no-suicide contract, denied suicidal intent or plan, and frequently petitioned for discharge (R. I. Simon & Gutheil, 2002).

Whenever a child or adolescent is treated for suicidal ideation or behavior, interventions should be conceptualized as multimodal and involving parents and school resources (teachers, counselors). In addition, when disclosures about suicide are made, the child or adolescent should be reassured that something is being done, that the suicidal urges are real, and that although the urges may not disappear immediately, help is available (Gilliland & James, 1988). Unfortunately, suicidal adolescents tend to have poor treatment compliance, and there is a lack of treatment programs targeting this population (A. L. Miller & Glinski, 2000). A modified, 12-week DBT intervention for suicidal adolescents and parents has demonstrated some promising initial results (A. L. Miller, Rathus, Linehan, Wetzler, & Leigh, 1997). This shorter duration program includes parents and family members in the skill-training groups and individual therapy sessions. The number of skills taught is reduced and the language is simplified to facilitate skill acquisition and to match the adolescent's developmental level. In addition, a follow-up group is offered to enhance the generalization of these skills to the adolescent's life. Another innovative youth intervention under investigation is C. A. King's (1999) Connect Five program, the goal of which is to empower at-risk youth by creating a supportive network of two to four individuals, including friends, adults, and health professionals. By increasing adolescents' sense of connectedness to others, the hope is to decrease their social isolation and suicide risk (A. L. Miller & Glinski, 2000).

Documentation

When documenting a suicide assessment (see Table 2.8) the following information should be included: relevant history, pertinent information from previous treatment records, a description of the direct evaluation of the client's suicidal thoughts and impulses, the implementation of an appropriate suicide intervention, resources provided to the client, and any contact made with the authorities and family members (J. Sommers-Flanagan & Sommers-Flanagan, 1995).

Table 2.8   12-Step documentation for suicidal or dangerous clients

1. Obtain adequate and relevant historical information.
2. Obtain previous treatment records.
3. Contact collateral sources and significant others.
4. Conduct a thorough suicide and dangerousness assessment.
5. Directly evaluate suicidal and violent thoughts and impulses.
6. Discuss limits of confidentiality with the client.
7. Consider duty to warn and protect.
8. Consult one or more professionals.
9. Implement an appropriate suicide or dangerousness intervention plan.
10. Provide appropriate resources, including telephone numbers.
11. Consider contacting authorities, hospital personnel, and family members for high-risk clients.
12. Conduct ongoing monitoring of risk and appropriate follow-up.

In addition, when dealing with suicidal or violent clients, it is crucial to consult with colleagues. Ideally this consultation should be formal and documented, as there must be a written record for it to be legally recognized. The content of the consultation should cover a range of issues, including overall management of the case, the clinician's feelings about the client's treatment progress, the role of medication, confidentiality, informed consents, and hospitalization (Bonger, 1991). The consultation serves the twin functions of providing professional support and feedback on best clinical practices and standards of care.

DANGEROUSNESS

In addition to considering the client's risk for self-harm, evaluate all impulsive clients for their risk of harm or danger to others. Although most mentally ill individuals are neither criminal nor violent (Marzuk, 1996), and most clients seen as outpatients are not at risk of harming others (S. Eddy & Harris, 1998), it is still necessary to know how to assess and respond to dangerousness. The prediction of violence is one of the most complex and controversial issues in the field of mental health (Borum, 1996). Until recently, it was believed that the prediction of dangerousness to others was an inexact, subjectively driven science in which the clinician's prediction rate was worse than chance. Many early studies of predictive risk provided limited insight because they were restricted to chronically institutionalized males (Pagani & Pinard, 2001; Sheldrick, 1999; Tardiff, 1989). In attempting to predict a low base rate behavior, problems with false positives (i.e., mistakenly identifying a nonviolent person as violent) and false negatives (i.e., mistakenly identifying a violent person as nonviolent) emerged. Reviews of the literature indicate that predictive ability is improving, and clinicians are now able to differentiate between nonviolent and violent individuals at a better than chance rate, particularly if the focus is on the prediction of short-term risk (i.e., a few hours to a week; McNeil, 1998). There has also been a shift in the field away from more dichotomous predictions of whether or not the client is dangerous to the broader issue of assessing degree of risk. Violence potential is now conceptualized on a continuum, and dangerousness is seen as an attribute that can fluctuate over time and vary depending on changes in the client's symptoms and life's circumstances (Pagani & Pinard, 2001; Sheldrick, 1999).

Clinician Responsibilities

The assessment of lethality and risk of harm to others, like suicide, involves consideration of both legal and clinical responsibilities. These primarily involve issues of confidentiality and the duty to warn. Confidentiality is the foundation of the therapeutic relationship and needs to be maintained in most cases. However, danger to others is one of the circumstances under which confidentiality may need to be broken. Mandated reporting laws and the duty to warn may supersede the clinician's obligation to confidentiality. Prior to the landmark *Tarasoff* rulings (*Tarasoff v. Regents of University of California*, 1974, 1976), clinicians could, according to their code of ethics, breach confidentiality at their professional discretion. Only hospital-based clinicians were held liable for the damages caused by dangerous clients (S. Eddy & Harris, 1998). The *Tarasoff* decision was a California ruling in which clinicians were found to have a legal duty to the potential victim of their dangerous clients; professional discretion was replaced by a mandated responsibility of "duty to warn." Specifically, when a client makes a threat of harm against an identifiable victim, clinicians are mandated to take preventive measures to protect an intended victim (e.g., warning the police, warning the potential victim). Although most states recognize a *Tarasoff*-type duty on the part of therapists, states differ in the actions required of the clinician, in the actual details for notifying the victim, and situations in which the duty-to-warn responsibility is triggered (e.g., some states include threats made against property). Consequently, it is necessary to be familiar with the laws in the state in which you practice.

At the first meeting with the client, issues of confidentiality should be discussed and circumstances in which confidentiality must be breached (e.g., mandated reporting) should be thoroughly reviewed (see Chapter 1). When dealing with a client who poses a danger or threat to others, the clinician's responsibilities are fourfold: (1) Assess risk factors and precipitants, (2) evaluate the client's plan and lethality, (3) develop and implement a plan to protect, and (4) document all actions taken (see Table 2.9).

Assessing Risk Factors and Precipitants

Paralleling the approach for dealing with a suicidal client, the first step in evaluating dangerousness is to evaluate the client's risk factors. As with suicide, there is no one risk factor that definitively predicts danger to others; rather, the presence of many cumulative

Table 2.9   Responsibilities when a client is a danger to others

Evaluate the Threat	Assess the Lethality	Plan to Protect
Refer for medical evaluation	Evaluate specific plan	Ensure safety
Obtain history and records	Consider access to means	Decide disposition
Contact collaterals	Consider past behavior	Refer for medication evaluation
Consider risk factors	Determine level of control	Develop nonviolence contract
Identify trigger events	Identify the victim	Set limits and monitor
Document critical data	Consider duty to warn	Implement interventions
Obtain consultation	Determine risk	Strengthen supports

Document and Follow Up

Table 2.10 Assessment of dangerousness and model of violence risk

Assessment of Dangerousness

Risk factors

History, Intent, Diagnosis, Emotional ability, Behavior, Grew up in violent family and gangs, Statistics and scales, and Precipitants or triggers,

Mnemonic: HIDE Bullets, GunS and Poison

Trigger situations

Loss or breakup of a relationship. Client is obsessed with someone. Client has made verbal threats and/or a third party reports a threat. Client has a gun collection. Client lost an important job. Client is hot-tempered. Client has been recently released or discharged from a facility.

Categorical Model of Violence Risk[*]

Category 1—Low violence risk

Few risk factors are present. No further inquiry into violence risk or special preventative actions are indicated.

Category 2—Moderate violence risk

Several risk factors are present. Gather additional information and monitor the individual more closely than usual.

Category 3—High violence risk

A number of key risk factors are present. Give priority to gathering additional information and closely monitor client. Make preparations for preventive action should situation deteriorate.

Category 4—Very high violence risk

Many key risk factors are present. Enough information is available to make a decision to take preventive action immediately. Intensive case management needed. Involuntary or voluntary hospitalization should be considered. Warning potential victim may be necessary.

[*]From "Violent Storms and Violent People: How Meteorology Can Inform Risk Communication in Mental Health Law," by J. Monahan and H. J. Steadman, 1996, *American Psychologist, 51,* pp. 931–938. Adapted with permission.

factors results in greater risk. Evaluation of these risk factors involves several steps, including a review of existing records and interviews with the client, significant others, and third parties. Such a comprehensive assessment is most likely to occur at intake or at the first point in treatment when the clinician becomes concerned about a client's potential for violence (see Table 2.10). Thereafter, risk assessments for violence are likely to be briefer and will build on and utilize information gathered from the initial, comprehensive risk assessment.

Combining self-reports of violence with information from other sources such as arrest records, previous treatment records, and collateral informants (e.g., family members) can result in a more accurate assessment of risk than by relying on the client's report alone (W. Gardner, Lidz, Mulvey, & Shaw, 1996; Monahan, 1994). Highlighting the value of seeking additional sources of information is the observation that although rates of violence reported by the client and family or friends may be similar, the *specifics* of the incidents are often different (W. Gardner et al., 1996). If the client is reluctant to allow the clinician to contact others, concerns about the client's veracity are raised.

Several risk factors for violent behavior in clinical populations have been identified, including dispositional (demographic, personality, and cognitive); historical (social, work, educational, treatment, and criminal); contextual (perceived stress, social support); and psychiatric (diagnosis, alcohol or substance abuse; Monahan, 1994). Yet, to date, no single best indicator has emerged, and the emphasis has shifted to identifying *a set* of indicator variables that are associated with an increased risk of violence (Bjorkly, 1997; Pagani & Pinard, 2001; Sheldrick, 1999). Some of the most common risk factors identified in the literature are summarized in Table 2.10. A useful mnemonic for remembering these risk factors for danger to others is **HIDE B**ullets, **G**un**S** and **P**oison.

History

A past history of violence has consistently been found to be an important factor associated with future violent behavior and may be a more accurate predictor than clinical judgment (Sheldrick, 1999; Steadman et al., 1998; Truscott, Evans, & Mansell, 1995). Therefore, gather a detailed account of the frequency and severity of any prior acts of violence or aggression. Prior to intake it is helpful to review previous records for this information (Faulk, 1994) and to focus on admission and discharge reports if time constraints are a factor. Reliance on collateral sources of information is important since it can be easy for individuals to minimize or deny prior aggressive behavior at intake. For example, studies of psychotic patients experiencing aggression-inducing auditory hallucinations have revealed that many minimize or deny such symptoms, and a significant percentage (50%) did not inform their treating therapist of these experiences (Bjorkly, 1997; Meloy, 1995; R. Rogers, Gillis, Turner, & Friese-Smith, 1990). A technique that can facilitate disclosure if there is reluctance to discuss past behavior is to initially ask if the client has ever been the *victim* of violence (Monahan, 1994).

As information is gathered about previous episodes of violence, look for a consensus or pattern of findings. In conducting this review, it may be helpful to conceptualize violence on two levels. Level 1 encompasses the more serious forms of violence, including use of a weapon, sexual assault, and any form of physical violence that resulted in injury. Level 2 is a less serious form of violence characterized by throwing, grabbing, or hitting that caused no injury to the victim (Sheldrick, 1999). Particular attention should be paid to when the events occurred and whether any occurred in the past 6 months. What was the context in which the events happened, the client's level of premeditation, the degree of injury inflicted on any individuals, use of weapons, property damage, and consequences, e.g., arrest, restraining orders (Limandri & Sheridan, 1995; Sheldrick, 1999)? It is also important to determine whether the client acted alone or with others (e.g., gang affiliations), and if drugs or alcohol were involved. Any bizarre aspects of previous offenses can alert the clinician to assess for the presence of psychosis or a severe personality disorder.

The client should also be asked about any past juvenile or childhood history of violence or other behavioral problems, property destruction, fire-setting, and cruelty to others or animals (see Table 2.11). Higher risk of future violent behavior is associated with early age at which offenses occurred, higher number of previous arrests, and greater frequency of offending (Pinard & Pagani, 2001; Sheldrick, 1999; Steadman et al., 1998). According

Table 2.11   Assessment of prior violent behavior

Nature of Offense*	Seriousness*	Prior History
Verbal or physical violence	Premeditated or impulsive	Juvenile record
Personal or property	Weapon used	Cautions or warnings
Predatory or random	Intention or motivation	Restraining orders
Role in offense	Recency, frequency, or episodic	Conditional release
Solitary or group	arrests or incarcerations	Self-reported offending
Stressors or triggers	Extent of victim's injury	Pattern of offending
Alcohol or substances involved	Empathy or concern	Compliance with treatment
Victim class and characteristics	for victim	
	Behavior after offense	
	Perception of consequences	

*Index offense and other offenses.

to McNeil and Binder (1994), the presence of three or more of the following five items from the client's records or interview is associated with a high risk for inpatient violence: (1) a history of physical attack or fear-inducing behavior 2 weeks prior to admission, (2) an absence of suicidal behavior 2 weeks prior to admission, (3) a diagnosis of Schizophrenia, (4) being male, and (5) currently married to or living with the victim of previous violence.

The client should be asked to reflect on past violent events and their consequences to determine his or her level of insight and judgment. Does the client express empathy for the victim(s)? Have any efforts at restitution been made? It is important to realize that lack of remorse may not be a good indicator for future risk because amnesia or the defense mechanism of denial may be mistaken by the clinician for callous indifference or fake remorse. The lack of capacity for compassion is a better indicator of the potential for violence (Bjorkly, 1997; Sheldrick, 1999). Adopting an entitled attitude, blaming others, minimizing one's role and/or the consequences of one's actions, and describing the victim as deserving the abuse or as an object (rather than a human) are key indicators of risk for future dangerous behavior (Hare, 1991).

Intent

When conducting an assessment of dangerousness, the client needs to be directly asked about any intent and plan to harm others and the frequency of these thoughts. The means to carry out the plan (and access), the identity of and access to the targets, and the time frame in which the client is planning to act should all be assessed. Attention should be paid to the client's affect, emotional lability, level of control, insight, and judgment when describing these thoughts, and whether the client's intent relates to reality-based issues or is influenced by an underlying paranoid, delusional, or psychotic process (Bjorkly, 1997). Questions should be asked regarding any preparatory actions the client has taken to implement a plan to harm, and whether the client has been following or stalking the intended victim(s). Once the individual has moved from talking and thinking about violence to acting on it, the risk of doing so in the future greatly increases (Sheldrick, 1999).

Diagnoses

Initially it was believed that there was no significant relationship between mental illness and violence when other variables were controlled. The base rates of violence were believed to be so low that it would be impossible to predict which mental disorders posed a significant risk (Borum, 1996; Monahan, 1993). In addition, early studies yielded conflicting findings on the relationship between clinical diagnosis and violence because acute and nonacute patients were combined in analyses, making intergroup comparisons difficult (McNeil, 1998). Clinicians in the past also have tended to overestimate the risk among non-Whites and underestimate the risk among female patients (McNeil, 1998; Pagani & Pinard, 2001).

Although most mentally ill individuals are not violent, recent epidemiological studies indicate that mentally ill individuals are statistically at a higher risk than others for violence, and the risk for violence increases with the number of diagnoses (Link & Stueve, 1994; Steadman et al., 1998; Swanson, 1994). For example, over a 1-year follow-up period, 18% of individuals with a major mental disorder, 31% of individuals with a substance abuse disorder and mental disorder, and 43% of individuals with substance abuse, a mental disorder, and a personality disorder perpetrated violence (Pagani & Pinard, 2001). Substantial percentages of psychiatric emergency room patients (45%) have been found to commit violence over a 6-month follow-up period (Lidz, Mulvey, & Gardner, 1993). It has been estimated that among psychiatric inpatients, 15% to 28% have engaged in physically assaultive behavior, and 40% to 50% have engaged in dangerous behavior (Otto, 1992). Swanson and colleagues (Swanson, Holzer, Ganju, & Jono, 1990) found that more than half of psychiatric patients released into the community who reported violent behavior met *DSM* criteria for more than one diagnosis (Swanson et al., 1990). The association between mental illness and violence is stronger among less well-educated young adults (Stueve & Link, 1997).

In terms of specific disorders, the diagnoses most frequently associated with dangerous or violent behaviors are Antisocial Personality Disorder and substance-related disorders (Klassen & O'Connor, 1994; Sheldrick, 1999; Steadman et al., 1998). There is a strong relationship between predatory crime and polysubstance abuse (especially heroin), and an increased risk of violence is associated with cocaine and stimulant abuse (Chaiken & Chaiken, 1990; McNeil, 1998; D. J. Smith, 1995). The potential for violence increases with the use of alcohol or other substances, even among individuals without a psychiatric diagnosis (Marzuk, 1996; Swanson, 1994). For example, it has been estimated that in approximately 50% of homicides the perpetrators and victims were intoxicated at the time of the killing (Eichleman, 1996).

With regard to psychosis, the greatest risk for violence is among individuals who are experiencing active symptoms, have a comorbid substance abuse problem, and have a history of antisocial behavior (Limandri & Sheridan, 1995; Litwack & Schlesinger, 1999; Swanson, Borum, Swartz, & Monahan, 1996). It is important to evaluate the presence of delusions involving themes of threat or persecution or feeling controlled by others, as well as any obsessions with weapons (Link & Stueve, 1994; Meloy, 1995; P. J. Taylor, 1995). A diagnosis of paranoid Schizophrenia is regarded as a serious risk factor since the preserved ability to plan and organize one's behavior increases the likelihood that delusional material can effectively be acted on (Wessely, Castle, & Douglas, 1994). If delusional material that may provoke violent behavior is discovered, a careful assessment should be undertaken to evaluate the rigidity of the client's belief (i.e., the ability to entertain alternative hypotheses) and any sadness, fear, or anxiety induced by the belief (Link, Andrews, & Cullen, 1992). There is clinical lore that command hallucinations are an important factor in provoking violence among psychotic patients, although research has not unequivocally established the truth of this common clinical belief (McNeill & Binder, 1994; Link et al., 1992; P. J. Taylor, 1995). Also be alert to the potential for violence with diagnoses of Bipolar Disorder, Major Depression, postpartum depression, and Delusional Disorder (Pinard & Pagani, 2001).

In children and adolescents, the presence of Oppositional Defiant Disorder and Conduct Disorder is associated with a risk of acting-out, particularly when the disorders have an early onset. Initial findings on the triad of childhood bedwetting, fire-setting, and cruelty to animals as predictors of violence have not been consistently supported (Bjorkly, 1997). There are few studies of adolescents at risk for violence who are psychotic or experiencing prodromal symptoms. However, hyperactivity, impulsivity, and attentional problems have been found to be important predictors of delinquency for this age group (Farrington, 1995).

Among older adults there is a higher likelihood of violence associated with organic disorders such as dementia, particularly when the client is agitated, hallucinating or delusional, or is disoriented (McNeil, 1998). Older adults who are paranoid and delusional and have access to weapons may also present with a heightened risk for violence.

Emotional Lability

Emotional dysregulation is associated with a higher risk for violence, and the presence of emotional detachment may indicate that the client is becoming more focused on his or her intent to harm (Meloy, 1995; Tardiff, 1991). Therefore, during the interview, be particularly aware of the client's mood and the lability of emotions (Bjorkly, 1997). In particular, note if the client becomes defensive or hostile, rapidly switches moods, or becomes easily agitated or aggressive. Also consider any personal feelings of discomfort or intimidation that are aroused by the client. The client should be questioned about past and current incidents involving an emotional loss of control (e.g., in the workplace, in personal relationships) and whether these involved alcohol or substance use. Because clients may be reluctant to discuss these topics, it is sometimes helpful to ask them how they would describe themselves from an emotional perspective or how others might describe them. This can lead to asking the client to describe what a loss of control is like and the frequency and consequence of such incidents in the past. Asking a benign question such as "How do you handle your anger?" or "Have you ever broken things when you are angry?" may facilitate the disclosure of violent tendencies (Maxmen & Ward, 1995). The emphasis the client places on being in emotional control and the techniques used to remain in control will give insight into the client's perceptions and coping strategies.

Behavioral Impulsivity

A past unstable school or occupational history should alert the clinician to inquire about behavioral impulsivity (Le Blanc, 1994). In addition to violently impulsive behavior such as fights and assaults, the clinician should look for evidence of overspending, bankruptcies, stealing, reckless driving, automobile accidents, and drug or alcohol use. Two classic patterns of violent outbursts are characterized by (1) ongoing suppression of anger punctuated by episodic sudden eruptions, and (2) routine, regular outbursts of anger (Maxmen & Ward, 1995). Concerns about betrayal or narcissistic injury from an interpersonal or occupational source that could be precipitants to violent behavior should be evaluated. Behaviors suggesting stalking or obsessional following should be fully explored (Meloy, 1995; Pinard & Pagani, 2001). Indicators of imminent potential for violence include signs of emotional arousal such as agitation, pacing, clenching fists, explosive language, and explicit threats and gestures.

Growing Up with Violence or Gang Involvement

Frequently, individuals involved in violent crimes were exposed to violence in their childhood (McNeil, 1998). Therefore, inquire about a family history of violence, including the means of discipline used by the client's parents or caregivers, family tolerance or acceptance of violent behavior, assaultive behavior by family members, and any arrests or incarcerations of relatives. Such questioning may uncover intergenerational cycles of violence. Poor parental child rearing, harsh and authoritarian discipline, poor supervision, parental conflict, cruel or sadistic behavior directed toward a child, physical or sexual abuse, family instability, and separation from parents for reasons other than death or hospitalization are correlated with the age at which violent offenses were committed (Farrington, 1995; Faulk; 1994).

In addition, if the client is a member of or affiliated with a gang, the level of involvement and commitment need to be fully evaluated. The client's age when initiated into the gang, means of initiation, specific gang activity engaged in, and the number of friends or family members with gang affiliations need to be queried. Friends may be the instigators of violence rather than a source of positive social support. Aggression, if it appears early and is maladaptive, is likely to persist (Farrington, 1995). Risk for violence is increased when there has been exposure to a violent, male-dominated subculture in which there are limited educational and employment opportunities. Having weapons available and a family that accepts violence as a means of problem resolution also contributes to a higher risk (McNeil, 1998).

Statistics and Scales

The most critical demographics that predict who may be a potential perpetrator of violence are young age (under 35 years), male sex, lower socioeconomic status (SES), disadvantaged minority status, less well-educated, lower intellectual level, unstable work or school history, alcohol or substance abuse, and prior history of violence (including juvenile violence). Also critical are a prior history of suicide attempts, a history of family violence, soft neurological signs, and a hospital discharge diagnosis that includes paranoia or command hallucinations (McNeil, 1998; Monahan, 1994; Pinard & Pagani, 2001). The peak risk period for violence is young adulthood; aggression has been found to decrease dramatically after age 40 (Bjorkly, 1997). Men commit the majority of violent crimes in every culture (Marzuk, 1996). The highest male risk group consists of young, lower SES individuals who have few social supports and a past history of violence and impulsive behaviors such as gambling and substance abuse (Klassen & O'Conner, 1994;

McNeil, 1998). Interestingly, in outpatient samples males and females have been found to have comparable rates of violence, with younger clients being at greater risk of committing violence (Pagani & Pinard, 2001). Among hospitalized individuals, males have been found to be more threatening but females more physically violent (Binder & McNeil, 1990).

When psychiatric diagnosis is controlled for, culture does not appear to be a significant factor in predicting violence (Pagani & Pinnard, 2001). Lower intelligence in acutely mentally ill individuals is associated with a heightened risk for violence (McNeil, 1998; Swanson, 1994). Having a mental health professional in an individual's social network lowers the client's risk for violence, which underscores the importance of treatment for potentially violent individuals (McNeil, 1998).

Considerable research has focused on the prediction of violence and the development of actuarial models to improve prediction, but the results are still inconsistent (Dolan & Doyle, 2000; K. S. Douglas, Yeomans, & Boer, 2005; Szmulker, 2001). Whereas these models are frequently used in research and do appear to improve the prediction of violence, their application to clinical settings has been limited by their cumbersome nature (Borum, 1996). For example, the Violence Prediction Schema (Webster, Harris, Rice, Cormier, & Quinsey, 1994) has been found to result in a 75% accurate classification of potential for violence over an average follow-up of 81.5 months (Borum, 1996). However, this complex model combines 12 separate factors from the client's history (e.g., evidence of psychopathy, separation from parents at 16 years or younger, Schizophrenia diagnosis, never married status), making it somewhat impractical for clinicians to use on a regular basis. A more detailed review and discussion of these issues is beyond the scope of this chapter but is provided by Monahan (2003).

Other Precipitants and Triggers

In addition to risk factors, it is necessary to assess the presence of recent or chronic precipitants or common trigger situations for violent behavior (see Table 2.10). The recent loss of employment, particularly if the client's self-image was strongly determined by the job, can be a major precipitant. If the individual has made sacrifices to focus on work, experienced a termination that was sudden and unforeseen, and has few transferable skills, the risk for becoming angry and experiencing narcissistic injury is increased (Pagani & Pinard, 2001). Recent rejection and perceived betrayal in interpersonal relationships are considered significant precipitants and are often precursors to spousal abuse and domestic violence (Riggs, Caufield, & Street, 2000). If the client is hot-tempered, makes verbal threats, or is obsessed with a particular person, the risk for violence is also increased. Gun ownership increases lethality potential (McNeil, 1998; Truscott et al., 1995). Ongoing family and relationship difficulties are examples of chronic precipitants that may provoke violent behavior. Indeed, more than half of the violence perpetrated by mentally ill individuals is directed at family members, with the greatest risk to the primary caregiver. Therefore, the level of family conflict and family history of violence should be assessed to determine if the client's aggression is targeted toward family members (Binder & McNeil, 1986; Estroff & Zimmer, 1994).

Heightened risk periods for violent behavior are just prior to a psychiatric hospitalization, during emergency room (ER) visits, and during a psychiatric hospitalization itself (Steadman et al., 1998). Approximately 10% to 20% of patients are physically assaultive prior to hospitalization. Further, it has been estimated that 4% to 8% of patients bring weapons with them into psychiatric ERs and that these patients are often male substance abusers (American Psychiatric Association, 1992). During short-term hospitalization, 30% to 35% of individuals on civil commitments engage in fear-inducing behavior, and 15% are physically assaultive (McNeil, 1998). Having been recently discharged from a very structured living situation such as jail or prison or an inpatient unit also places the client at higher risk for acting in an impulsive manner.

Evaluating Plan and Lethality

Many of the same principles outlined earlier for assessing a suicide plan can be applied to the evaluation of plans to harm others. Specifically, information needs to be gathered on the means being considered to commit violence and the client's access to them. Details such as intended victim(s), the time frame in which the client plans to act, and whether the client has thought through the specific steps to be followed in carrying out the plan should also be evaluated. As with suicide, the more detailed and specific the plan, the greater the risk for acting on it, especially if there has been any rehearsal behavior. While lethality should also be evaluated when a client expresses plans to harm others, the key issue is whether the client's planned actions are likely to result in injury (not necessarily death) to others. A client who says she is planning to go into work and yell at her boss (and nothing more) would not trigger a *Tarasoff*-type duty to warn, whereas statements that she was planning to attack him with a baseball bat would.

Information about the client's plans for violence can be combined with information from a risk factor assessment to make an overall determination of the client's potential for violence. As with a suicide assessment, consideration should be given to protective factors that might attenuate the risk for violence. These could include the presence of supportive others to whom the client can turn to express frustrations, fears of the legal consequences of acting on violent thoughts, presence of constructive coping methods, and empathic capacity. In making a dangerousness assessment, it is critical to obtain consultation from colleagues or supervisors. Monahan and Steadman (1996) have formulated a helpful model for communicating risk for violence in which individuals are assigned to one of four categories based on the presence of risk factors (refer back to Table 2.10). Limandri and Sheridan (1995) suggest following a seven-step pathway when assessing a client's potential for violence: (1) Clarify the threat, (2) assess the lethality, (3) identify a specific or intended victim, (4) obtain specific information about the victim, (5) determine the client's relationship to the victim, (6) assess the need for family intervention, and (7) evaluate the need for hospitalization.

Implementing a Plan to Protect and Treat

Once a risk of dangerousness has been identified, a plan to protect must be developed, implemented, and documented (Applebaum & Gutheil, 1991; McNeill, 1998). A very concrete, action-oriented intervention approach to de-escalate the situation should be adopted (see Table 2.12). If the client's behavior is inappropriate, clear limits should be set and a concrete contract to maintain self-control developed. In treating court-mandated clients, therapeutic rapport may be particularly difficult to establish, and consultation from a colleague or supervisor is essential in these difficult cases.

Table 2.12   Interventions for dangerous clients

Practical	Support	Therapeutic
Consult	Contact others	Maintain rapport
Decide disposition	Identify supports	Target disruptive behaviors
Ensure safety	Involve monitor	Work on anger control
Nonviolence contract	Provide contact card	Address substance abuse
Reassess need for hospital	24-hour crisis support	Teach self-monitoring
Refer for medication evaluation	Establish support group	Identify alternatives
Avoid high-risk people and places	Need for adjunct services	Explore client's perceptions
Ongoing monitor violence risk	Follow through	Address compliance

Documentation

Incorporated into a plan to protect are any legal obligations to warn the victim and notify the appropriate law enforcement agency under the duty-to-warn laws. While it may be necessary to alert the potential victim and provide sufficient information to ensure safety, efforts should be made to maintain the client's privacy by disclosing only essential information (Eddy & Harris, 1998). Having to break confidentiality to warn may significantly impact rapport with the client, and once the confidence is broken, the client's trust in the therapist and in psychotherapy may be lost (Truscott et al., 1995). If confidentiality is to be broken, it is necessary to explain why the breech was necessary, but not to be overly focused on the legal reasons supporting the breach. While it is important to cite this obligation, it is equally important to explain how warning others will help to keep the client out of even greater trouble (e.g., going to jail) and how the client might actually feel worse about himself or herself if the violence to others was actually committed.

Concerns about dangerousness should also prompt consideration of whether the client is in need of a medical evaluation to rule out an organic etiology for violent behavior (Eichelman, 1996). This is especially important in cases where the client presents with a sudden change in mental status and/or with uncharacteristic aggression that appears unrelated to the provoking incidents (Kausch & Resnick, 1999). Medical conditions such as head injuries, organic brain disease, brain lesions, viral encephalitis, tumors, renal disease, toxic poisoning, heavy metal exposure, and a range of dementias are associated with increased risk for violence (McNeil, 1998; Pagani & Pinard, 2001; Tardiff, 1991). A medication evaluation may also be required if the client displays significant mood or anxiety symptoms, agitation, sleep disturbance, disorganized behavior, or evidence of psychosis. The use of or withdrawal from alcohol or substances such as PCP (phencyclidine), amphetamines, or cocaine can cause disinhibition, agitation, or confusion that can result in greater risk for violence (McNeil, 1998; Swanson, 1994). Behavioral indicators of acute intoxication vary depending on the substance, but common signs include dilated or bloodshot pupils, tremors, slurred speech, unsteady gait, disorientation, disheveled personal appearance, fluctuating course of symptoms, and uncoordination. Some indicators of withdrawal are sweating, hypervigilance, and a racing heart (see Chapter 8 for additional information).

One of the crucial treatment decisions to be made is whether the client can be managed in the community or other open setting. In determining the level of security that the client requires, take into consideration the client's current clinical condition (e.g., impulsivity, emotional dysregulation, symptoms), ability to contract for safety, availability of support and supervision, and the seriousness of previous violent behavior (Sheldrick, 1999). Hospitalization must be considered if the client cannot be maintained on an outpatient basis. Hospitalization can provide containment of risk, the opportunity for a thorough diagnostic evaluation, and rapid intensive treatment (McNeil, 1998). Ideally, the client will concur with the clinician and agree to be admitted on a voluntary basis. However, if the client is reluctant to be hospitalized and presents a threat to others, an involuntary hold should be initiated. For those who pose a high risk of harm to others, Monahan (1993) recommends three interventions: (1) incapacitation or hospitalization on a secure ward, (2) warning the target, and (3) intensification of subsequent treatment by increasing the frequency of sessions, providing a medication evaluation, and strengthening the client's supports. Once the client has been hospitalized, he or she may need to be placed on a one-to-one monitoring status to prevent violence, assault, property damage (e.g., arson), or elopement. When safety has been ensured, a treatment plan can be formulated and a determination made as to which risk factors can be treated or attenuated. Unfortunately, simple effective treatments do not exist for dangerousness (Eichleman, 1996). Medication, seclusion, restraint, a rapid differential to eliminate medical organic causes, and verbal interventions focusing on limit setting and identifying the consequences of behavior are all interventions that can be administered if required in an inpatient setting.

When treatment occurs on an outpatient basis, the client should agree to sign a nonviolence contract. Lethality is reduced if the means to complete a violent act are removed, the individual makes a commitment to postpone the lethal act, and the individual is under constant observation (Slaikeu, 1990). The nonviolence contract can include impulse delay procedures (e.g., calling the therapist when overcome by violent thoughts) and other commitments such as not to drink or abuse substances. It is essential that the client contract to avoid high-risk, provocative places and people. Risk reduction can include family or significant others and possibly police in implementing preventive measures (Estroff, Zimmer, Lachicotte, & Benoit, 1994; Truscott et al., 1995). A significant other, for example, can be recruited to serve as a one-to-one monitor (S. Eddy & Harris, 1998).

Establishing and maintaining the therapeutic alliance is a critical foundation for all interventions and may be particularly challenging with clients who are angry and/or impulsive (Truscott et al., 1995). If anger control issues, underlying psychiatric disorders, alcohol and substance abuse problems, and family difficulties are contributing to the client's dangerousness, treatment should address these problems (Sheldrick, 1999). Helpful therapeutic interventions include assisting the client in identifying underlying emotions, cultivating alternative emotional outlets, and developing concrete coping strategies for anger control (e.g., using self-observation and contingency management strategies; Eichleman, 1996). With regard to the latter, many violent patients have poor self-regulation and experience internal warning signs before aggressive episodes occur (Eichleman & Hartwig, 1995). Providing the client with insight into these sensations can aid in the development of self-control strategies and can assist in the identification of triggers and situational variables that play a role in patterns of violence (Eichleman, 1996; McNeil, 1998). Referral to anger control workshops or groups may also be beneficial. Cognitive-behavioral interventions focused on cognitive restructuring, coping and communication skills training, and enhancement of social supports and self-esteem are also useful. Family interventions can focus on educating family members on patterns of violence, communication strategies, and parenting skills (McNeil, 1998).

Throughout the treatment the clinician needs to monitor ongoing risk. During periods of increased stress or exposure to anger triggers, the frequency of therapeutic contact should be increased: Be continually on the alert for signs of decompensation (Factor & Diamond, 1996). The client can be provided with an emergency contact card similar to that described for suicidal clients. This helps clients remember how to reach out, and to whom, when they are having trouble coping with difficult emotions or stressful situations. When there are changes in the client's clinical presentation that result in an increased risk or danger to others, the responsibility to alert identifiable victims must be considered (Grisso & Tomkins, 1996).

When treating potentially violent clients, do not overlook threats and compliance problems and be particularly attentive to boundary issues. With regard to the latter, many violent or aggressive clients are manipulative, and clear expectations must be set at the start of treatment regarding attendance, participation, and the consequences for noncompliance (e.g., discharge from treatment). All direct threats should be addressed as they occur, with clear limits and consequences. Threats are boundary issues, which many therapists deal with by denial. However, effective treatment cannot occur in an environment where the therapist feels threatened or afraid (Eichleman, 1996). It is helpful to have a solid relationship with law enforcement and to have practiced an emergency plan should the client escalate. The treatment plan should also include a rigorous reevaluation component and follow-up procedures to check progress and monitor ongoing risk. Given the risks of working with violent clients, those who are not court-ordered to treatment should be discharged from treatment if noncompliant. However, treatment should not be abruptly stopped, as this could be perceived as client abandonment. If the patient is discharged from treatment prematurely, an invitation can be provided to return when the client is willing to comply with recommendations (Eichleman, 1996). Throughout the process, be certain to document risk, interventions, compliance, and the rationale for actions taken (Pinard & Pagani, 2001).

ABUSE

The term *abuse* involves a range of victims, including children, elders, spouses or partners, and dependents. Types of abuse include physical, sexual, emotional, and fiduciary abuse and neglect. Abuse or neglect occurs when a child, elder, partner, or dependent adult's physical or mental health or welfare is harmed or threatened by a parent, caregiver, or other responsible person (Veltkamp & Miller, 1994). Estimates that approximately 10 out of 1,000 children are abused and neglected each year and that there are at least 1 million abused or neglected children in the United States are sadly regarded as the tip of the iceberg (Veltkamp & Miller, 1994). In addition, each year over 10 million Americans experience domestic violence (J. Schaefer, Caetano, & Clark, 1998). Finally, it has been estimated that there are up to 1.1 million victims of elder abuse nationwide (Breckman & Adelman, 1992). Individuals who are abused or neglected frequently experience a wide range of psychological, academic or occupational, and social problems (Lundy & Grossman, 2001; Wurtele & Miller-Perrin, 1992).

From a diagnostic perspective, the *DSM-IV-TR* (American Psychiatric Association, 2000b) defines abuse to include physical abuse of a child or adult, sexual abuse of a child or adult, and neglect of a child. All of these are included as V codes (coded on Axis I) under the section entitled "Other conditions that may be a focus of clinical attention." While specific reporting laws vary, in most states a child is defined as a person under 18 years of age and an elder is an individual 65 years or older. Dependent adults have mental or physical limitations that restrict their ability to carry out normal activities and make decisions concerning their welfare. General descriptions of neglect and abuse are reviewed next; however, clinicians should become familiar with the specific definitions used by the state and jurisdiction in which they practice.

Child Abuse and Neglect

Physical and Sexual Abuse

Child physical abuse refers to the intentional infliction of overt physical violence and/or injury upon a child (Wiehe, 1996; Wolfe & McEachran, 1997). Physical abuse can include beating, squeezing, lacerating, burning, suffocating, binding, poisoning, exposure to excessive temperatures, sensory overload, and sleep deprivation (D. J. Hansen & Warner, 1992). Injuries may be apparent or hidden. A less frequent and very extreme form of physical (and psychological) abuse is Munchausen Syndrome by Proxy (see Chapter 12, "Somatoform and Related Disorders"), in which a parent or caregiver seeks to get attention from medical personnel by intentionally making a child sick. In these cases, the parent may resort to harming the child through poisoning, administration of inappropriate medications or substances, physical force, or partial suffocation (D. Jones, 1994).

Physically abused children frequently do not tell others of their abuse, may offer benign explanations for their injuries, or may attribute the abuse to their own "bad" behavior. Children who have been physically abused or neglected present with a wide range of behavioral and emotional problems (see Table 2.13). These include low self-worth, internalizing disorders (e.g., depression), externalizing disorders (e.g., disruptive behavior disorders), feelings of hopelessness, lower scores on tests of academic achievement, higher rates of perceptual-motor deficits, and regressive behaviors such as bedwetting, head banging, thumb sucking, and rocking (D. J. Hansen & Warner, 1992; D. Jones & McGraw, 1987; Vondra, Kolar, & Radigan, 1992).

Typically, as abused children become older they experience shame and fear of humiliation, of further harm, or of destroying the family should outsiders learn of the abuse (Lukas, 1993). Female children tend to experience physical abuse more than males and are at highest risk at younger ages (birth to age 2 years being the greatest risk period). In a significant portion of child physical abuse cases (67%), the parent is a substance abuser and young mother at the time of the child's birth. Immaturity, lack of education, low income, social isolation, and lack of sufficient support services or networks are additional characteristics observed among perpetrators of child physical abuse (Wiehe, 1996).

Sexual abuse refers to the use of a child for sexual purposes or gratification, and includes a broad range of behaviors, from exposure to pornography, inappropriate touching to rape. When committed by a family member, it is referred to as incest or familial abuse (Wurtele & Miller-Perrin, 1992). Victims of child sexual abuse range in age from

Table 2.13   Physical abuse, sexual abuse, and neglect indicators

Physical Abuse

There is evidence of burns, specific pattern burns, bites, bruises, dislocations, or fractures.

Injuries are consistent with being beaten with an object and somatic symptoms.

Child is *accident-prone* or presents with multiple atypical accidents.

Child is fearful, shrinks from adult or physical contact, is guarded or overly aggressive.

Child is overly compliant, clingy, overly dependent, and seeks constant affection.

Child is isolated and anxious when other children get hurt.

Child engages in self-harming behavior or attempts suicide.

Child dresses inappropriately or wears excessive clothes to cover body.

Child lags in development or there is regression of age-appropriate behavior and activities.

Child displays marked aggressiveness toward people and objects.

Child withdraws from age-appropriate activities, avoids being at home, or runs away.

Child is agitated or hyperactive and has temper tantrums or poor attention span.

Caretaker has unrealistic expectations of child and *parentifies* the child.

Parent or caretaker uses physical discipline and child is seen as *bad*.

Caretaker may be a substance abuser, unable to control child, possibly isolated, and abused as a child.

Sexual Abuse

Child appears to regress; has bedwetting, sleep, or eating problems, frequent vomiting.

Child suddenly becomes isolated, withdrawn, or engages in extreme secrecy.

Child is overly concerned about cleanliness; engages in excessive bathing.

Child appears fearful, hypervigilant, excessively withdrawn, or overly conscious about body.

Child appears sexually precocious, sexually preoccupied, or acts in overly sexualized manner.

Child reports or evidence is found of infections, sexually transmitted diseases, or pregnancy.

Child runs away; is involved in drugs, promiscuous behavior, or self-mutilation; attempts suicide.

Child shows role reversal.

Child appears more worldly than friends; engages in provocative or promiscuous sexual patterns (especially if under 7).

Child suddenly possesses money or merchandise that may have been used as a bribe.

Neglect Indicators

Child wears inappropriate clothing or has poor personal hygiene and grooming.

Child appears malnourished, tired, listless, or sleepy.

Child seems to need dental, medical, or vision treatment.

Child might steal food, appear ravenous, or be worried about food.

Child is frequently missing school or schoolwork and materials.

Child appears isolated or overly self-reliant.

Child is abandoned, left alone, lacks adequate supervision, has a chaotic home, or has an absent father.

Caretaker is critical or hostile to child; lacks parenting skills.

Caretakers appear disorganized, uninterested, and unconcerned about child's welfare.

Caretaker frequently abuses substances or is depressed or stressed.

There is a dysfunctional parent-child relationship and disengaged family.

The family experiences poverty and social isolation.

From *Where to Start and What to Ask: An Assessment Handbook,* by S. Lukas, 1993, New York: Norton. Adapted with permission.

newborn to young adulthood and are from all ethnicities and socioeconomic groups. Most perpetrators (75% to 80%), whether female or male, are known to the victim and are often in a trusted role, such as stepparent, family friend, coach, or babysitter (Wiehe, 1996). Incestuous relationships are frequently characterized by a series of escalating contacts, starting with sexualized fondling or caressing and progressing to actual intercourse. Perpetrators often use intimidation, from threats to withdrawing attention or affection to threats on the child's life, to coerce their young victims (McLeer & Rose, 1992).

Child sexual abuse is grossly underreported, and victims often encounter disbelief and blame (Veltkamp & Miller, 1994; Wurtele & Miller-Perrin, 1992). Very young children may not understand what has happened to them, and only later in adolescence or adulthood experience confusion and betrayal when the inappropriateness of what has occurred is realized (Damon, Card, & Todd, 1992). Longer periods of abuse result in greater trauma. The presence of threat or aggression, the nature of the child's relationship with the adult, and the degree and frequency of sexual activity with the perpetrator also affect the extent of subsequent harm and traumatization (see Table 2.15). The trauma can also be deepened and feelings of vulnerability intensified if the child tells an adult of the abuse and is not believed or is blamed. Victims of sexual abuse often present with ambivalence, trust issues, and emotional detachment (N. King, 2000). If sexual abuse occurs in the context of enticement and subsequent entrapment, the victim often experiences self-blame (Summit, 1983). Potential indicators of sexual abuse are summarized in Table 2.13.

Adult survivors of sexual abuse can present with a wide range of psychological problems, including posttraumatic reactions, self-harming behaviors (e.g., substance abuse, suicidal behavior, self-mutilation), mood disturbance, interpersonal problems (e.g., insecurity, feelings of inadequacy), and sexual difficulties (e.g., sexual dysfunction, distress or confusion about sexual orientation). These individuals may enter therapy following an event that was in some way reminiscent of the earlier abuse, including aversive reactions during sexual activity, anniversary dates of abusive events, or media coverage of abuse cases (Jehu, 1992).

Emotional Abuse

Psychological or emotional abuse includes attacks on the child's self-esteem and social competence. These incidents may occur in isolation or concurrently with other forms of abuse. Blaming, belittling, degrading, exploiting, labeling, humiliating, terrorizing, threatening, denigrating, or rejecting a child are examples of emotional abuse. Similarly, refusing to help a child, forcing a child to be withdrawn, or treating the child differently from siblings and in a manner suggesting dislike are also forms of emotional abuse (Brasssard & Gelardo, 1987). Emotional abuse can also encompass behaviors such as denial of the child's emotional needs and emotional unresponsiveness such as ignoring the child's attempts to interact (Veltkamp & Miller, 1994; Wiehe, 1996). Psychological maltreatment deeply and adversely affects a child's sense of self and relationship security, which, in turn, can lead to the development of further maladjustment (Vondra et al., 1992). Adverse outcomes associated with emotional abuse include extreme passivity, low self-esteem, depression, suicidal ideation or behavior, anxiety, somatic complaints, aggressiveness, hyperactivity, and conduct problems such as lying, stealing, and demandingness (Broadhurst, 1984).

Neglect

Whereas abuse refers to acts of commission (i.e., harm inflicted by doing something), neglect involves acts of omission (i.e., harm incurred by *not* doing something, such as failing to provide adequate care for a child). Child neglect is the most common form of maltreatment reported to child protective agencies and accounts for approximately 63% of all substantiated cases of child abuse (www.preventchildabuse.com). Neglect is frequently characterized by an ongoing pattern of inadequate care and may initially be noticed by relatives, neighbors, teachers, day care personnel, or physicians. It is important to recognize the role that poverty may play in adversely affecting parenting abilities, and not to confuse this with willful neglect (Veltkamp & Miller, 1994). There are five types of neglect: physical, medical, emotional, and educational neglect, and inadequate supervision, including child abandonment (Wiehe, 1996).

Physical neglect includes failing to provide basic necessities such as food and shelter, leaving a child alone or with an inappropriate caregiver (e.g., a young sibling), or placing a child in a physically dangerous environment (e.g., exposure to drug paraphernalia). Physical neglect often subsumes inadequate supervision and child abandonment. The latter includes behaviors such as not allowing a runaway child to return home or expelling a child from the home. Physical neglect may be apparent from a child's appearance (e.g., inappropriate, insufficient clothing; emaciation; Lukas, 1993). There may also be growth problems or delays that result from caregiver failure to meet the nutritional needs of the child. In infants and very young children this is sometimes referred to as failure to thrive (FTT) and can be associated with developmental delays. It is important to remember that FTT is not always due to neglect and may be secondary to real medical problems or due to poverty. In cases of nonorganic FTT, it has been estimated that up to 70% of cases are related to accidental feeding problems (i.e., parents are uninformed about adequate dietary guidelines) or are associated with parental depression and substance abuse problems (Jaudes, Ekwo, & Voorhis, 1995; Schmitt & Mauro, 1989). Suspected FTT should always prompt a referral for a thorough medical evaluation.

Medical neglect should be considered when a child presents as malnourished or sickly. Medical neglect includes not obtaining appropriate medication or treatment for an ill child even though the caregiver or parent is financially able and treatment is available. The decision to withhold medical care due to religious or cultural beliefs is generally not considered neglect, although in some cases court intervention may be sought to compel parents or caregivers to provide treatment that is deemed lifesaving.

Emotional neglect occurs when the parent ignores, threatens, humiliates, or isolates the child. Failure to provide needed psychological treatment when such services are available and affordable, exposure to spousal abuse, and allowing a child to engage in dangerous or self-destructive behavior (e.g., drug use) are other forms of emotional neglect. Failure to see that a child attends school and allowance of repeated truancy are examples of educational neglect (Wiehe, 1996).

Contributing Factors

The causes of child abuse and neglect are multifactorial and include but are not limited to severe emotional or social pressure or burdens of caregivers, poverty, negative parental attitudes, family stress, and multigenerational patterns of abuse (Wurtele & Miller-Perrin,

1992). Although the majority of parents with a personal abuse history do not abuse their own children, the presence of such a history increases the risk for abuse proneness (S. Jackson et al., 1999). Families at high risk for child abuse and neglect are often characterized by intrafamilial abuse, parents with unmet needs and high stress levels, maternal depression and substance abuse, and isolation of both the child and family from others (Ethier, Lacharite, & Couture, 1995; Wiehe, 1996). Some cases of abuse are precipitated by life crises such as the loss of a job or parental injury resulting in home confinement. Mothers' neglect of children has been associated with depression, substance abuse problems, absence of a father, parental disengagement, negative family interactions, poverty, unemployment, and social isolation and alienation (Ethier et al., 1995; Jaudes et al., 1995; Wiehe, 1996).

Abusive parents may have unrealistic ideas about how their children ought to behave and frequently have deficits in areas such as child management, parent-child interaction, anger and stress control, and problem solving (S. Jackson et al., 1999; Wiehe, 1996). They may rely on harsh, unreasonable discipline, and as children felt unable to obtain love from their own parents. They may be especially prone to displaying abusive behavior toward children who exhibit physical, psychological, or developmental problems (e.g., prematurity, hyperactivity; Lukas, 1993). Abusive families often have one parent who is overly involved in activities outside of the home, while the other parent is overly involved with the children. There is frequently marital discord and/or a lack of intimacy between the parents, who may individually have low self-esteem, inadequate coping abilities, and an alcohol or substance use problem (Wiehe, 1996). The general family environment may lack order and responsibility, there may be difficulty with task accomplishment, and parent-child role reversal may be present (Sirles & Franke, 1989). Violence may be viewed as a familiar and acceptable way of resolving disagreements (Veltkamp & Miller, 1994). A telephone survey of factors that place parents at risk for abusing children indicated that parental attitudes and the child's age are important variables to consider (S. Jackson et al., 1999). The younger the child, the more likely the parent was to have a positive attitude toward the use of physical discipline. In contrast, older children who were verbal and not as socially isolated were at lower risk for abuse.

Elder and Dependent Adult Abuse

This category includes physical, sexual, emotional, and fiduciary abuse and neglect. The following information focuses primarily on elder abuse; however, similar issues arise in dealing with the abuse of dependent adults. As with child abuse, the clinician has the responsibility to conduct an appropriate assessment, make clinical decisions that may include mandated reporting, and develop a disposition plan to ensure the safety of the individuals involved. Clients may be reluctant to admit to abuse, and, as with child abuse, they may be fearful of retaliation by the abuser. The elder, unlike the child, has the right to refuse to allow an abuse investigation to continue; however, the clinician may still be mandated to report the abuse. Elder abuse may be perpetrated by a spouse, an adult child or other relative, or by an unrelated individual, such as a nursing home staff member or caregiver. Abuse is most likely to be committed by the person with whom the elder lives and to be characterized by a pattern of violence that increases in severity and frequency over time (Breckman & Adelman, 1992). Signs of abuse and neglect may be observed,

Table 2.14   Potential indicators of elder abuse

Bruises, buckle or belt marks, lacerations, bed sores, and other open wounds
Injuries to breasts, genitals could reflect sexual abuse
Sprains, broken or fractured bones
Bloodied clothing, bandages or concealing clothing
Inadequate medical care, untreated medical conditions, problems with medication use
Signs of malnourishment including extreme weight loss
Poor hygiene (e.g., soiled clothing, body odor)
Unexplained sexually transmitted disease, anal or vaginal bleeding
Emotional or behavioral changes (e.g., agitation, distress, withdrawal)
Overly controlling behavior by caregivers
Caregiver appears reluctant to have older adult interviewed alone
Older adult appears fearful and hesitant to talk or describes being exploited
Elder reports physical, sexual, emotional abuse or neglect
Missing valuables or reported loss of items
Evidence of financial irregularities (e.g., unauthorized withdrawals of funds, unpaid bills despite
 adequate funds)
Unexpected changes in wills or other financial or legal documents

such as unexplained bruises or sores and malnutrition, or the abuse may be observed directly (see Table 2.14).

If there are physical signs or injuries, it is important to obtain appropriate medical attention for the client. Indicators of neglect in an elderly client not only point to the possibility of maltreatment by others, but may also indicate a deteriorating ability of the client to care for himself or herself. In such cases, you may want to assess the client's cognitive abilities and be alert for early signs of dementia (see Chapter 7). Several factors correlated with risk for elder mistreatment have been identified. Abusers often have serious psychiatric disorders, including drug and/or alcohol abuse, and frequently have a personal history of abuse. Additionally, these individuals are often experiencing significant external stress such as caregiver burden or financial difficulties, and they are frequently dependent on their abuse victim in some way (e.g., for financial support). Finally, abusers and their victims are often socially isolated, which increases opportunities for abuse that will go undetected (Pillemer, 1986).

Domestic Violence

Until the 1970s the extent of violence against women in the United States was not fully acknowledged. We now know that domestic violence is the leading cause of injuries to women ages 15 to 44 years, with many women being repeatedly victimized at least 3 to 4 times per year (Lundy & Grossman, 2001). In 1996, 840,000 women were assaulted by husbands, ex-boyfriends, or boyfriends, and 26% of female murder victims were killed by a partner (U.S. Department of Justice, 1998). Some studies have reported high rates of female-to-male violence (Straus & Gelles, 1990), which is a reminder that perpetrators of domestic violence are not solely male. However, the consequences of such violence may be quite different from the consequences of male-to-female violence given the greater size and strength of men (Bachman & Pillemer, 1992); women are injured more often than men in domestic disputes (American Medical Association [AMA], 1992; Sorenson, Upchurch, & Shen, 1996). Also, a great deal of the violence against male partners is committed in retaliation or self-defense (Aldarondo & Sugarman, 1996). Domestic violence occurs in both heterosexual and homosexual relationships. However, more research is needed on the extent of abuse in same-sex relationships. Because domestic violence often accompanies child abuse and neglect, whenever partner violence is discovered the range of abuse that may be occurring in the home should be explored. An effective brief screening to assess for domestic violence is to ask "Have you ever been hit, slapped, kicked or otherwise been physically hurt by someone in the past year?" (Barthauer, 1999, p. 35).

Psychological abuse almost invariably accompanies partner physical abuse (Tolman, 1992). Examples of psychological abuse include threats (e.g., to harm one's partner, his or her family, children); isolation (e.g., restricting contact with friends, limiting outside activities); economic abuse (e.g., denial of access to checking accounts, credit cards); degradation (e.g., making partner perform humiliating acts); monopolization (e.g., being exclusively possessive); emotional withholding (e.g., giving partner "the silent treatment"); and psychological destabilization (e.g., acts designed to make partner doubt his or her perceptions; Tolman, 1992).

Studies of domestic violence between intimate adults indicate that women ages 17 to 28 are at increased risk, as are pregnant women and those who are separated from violent partners (D. G. Dutton, Saunders, Starzomski, & Bartholomew, 1994; Lystad, Rice, & Kaplan, 1996; M. Wilson & Daly, 1993). Several studies have consistently found rates of domestic violence decrease with age (Bachman & Pillemer, 1992). A review of the literature indicates that the predictors of domestic violence and victimization are inconsistent (Riggs et al., 2000). Nevertheless, a number of risk factors have been identified. Not surprisingly, relationships in which partner abuse occurs have been characterized by distress, conflict, and negative interactions (Lystad et al., 1996). Although domestic violence occurs in all social classes, socioeconomic disadvantage increases the risk of partner assault, and a nationally representative household survey indicated an inverse relationship between domestic violence and social class (R. C. Kessler, Molnar, Feurer, & Applebaum, 2001). Findings of higher rates of domestic violence among Hispanics and African Americans disappear when income and education are controlled (R. C. Kessler, Molnar, et al., 2001).

As with child abuse, victims of domestic violence are often reluctant to report abuse out of shame, fear of punishment, loyalty to the abuser, feelings of guilt and responsibility, and a desire to avoid painful memories (D. G. Saunders, 1992). Depression, suicidal ideation, self-esteem problems, anxiety, learned helplessness, and PTSD are among some of the psychological sequelae that may be experienced by victims of domestic violence. Battered woman syndrome, observed in some women who have been repeatedly abused by their partner, is characterized by fear of unavoidable physical aggression and unpredictable physical aggression (L. E. Walker, 1989). This syndrome has been cited as a mitigating factor in many legal cases of women who have killed their allegedly abusive husband (O'Leary & Murphy, 1992), and it highlights the importance of assessing the victim's potential for killing his or her partner. Inquires can be made as to whether the victim's life has been threatened by the abuser, if the victim has fantasies about killing his or her partner, if there is a specific plan and access to the means to carry it out, and if the victim feels all other means of protection have been exhausted (D. G. Saunders, 1992).

Factors that have been found relevant in cases of women who kill their partner include threats to kill the woman, suicide attempts or threats by the woman, severity of the woman's injuries, the frequency of physical and sexual assaults, and the frequency of the man's intoxication or drug use (Browne, 1987).

With regard to specific characteristics of perpetrators, no single profile of an abusive partner has been identified. Abusers run the gamut from seemingly model citizens to obviously aggressive, domineering individuals to those who are unassertive and meek outside of the home (D. G. Saunders, 1992). Nevertheless, some characteristics have been identified that increase the risk of abuse, such as extreme jealousy, use of abusive or threatening language, threats or fear of abandonment, and a previous history of relationship aggression (D. G. Dutton et al., 1994). One study found that of men who were violent prior to marriage, 51% were aggressive within 18 months of the marriage (O'Leary et al., 1989). Men who abuse are frequently angry loners who lack an adequate social support system (D. G. Saunders, 1992). Among the most dangerous offenders are those who were severely abused in childhood, abuse drugs and alcohol, and are violent outside the home (D. G. Saunders, 1992). Many perpetrators of domestic violence were exposed to or were victims of violence growing up, and such exposure can be a risk factor for the early onset of mental illness (National Co-Morbidity Survey on Domestic Violence; Riggs et al., 2000). Yet, interestingly, the majority of male offenders do not suffer from severe mental disorders, although many have personality disorders (e.g., narcissistic, borderline, negativistic traits) or personality traits such as unpredictability and distrust of others (Aldarondo & Sugarman, 1996; D. G. Dutton et al., 1994; D. G. Saunders, 1992). In general, past violent behavior and environmental factors are better predictors of domestic violence than the presence of psychopathology (D. G. Saunders, 1992). Some studies have found an increased risk of male violence associated with a history of nonaffective psychosis, head injury, mood disorder, or anxiety disorder (Pan, Neidig, & O'Leary, 1994; Riggs et al., 2000). With regard to anxiety disorders, a veteran with PTSD is twice as likely to be violent with a partner as non-PTSD veterans (Riggs et al., 2000). Alcohol and substance use also increase the risk of domestic violence (AMA, 1992; Lystad et al., 1996). For example, it has been estimated that alcohol is involved in 85% of cases of domestic abuse (M. Slade, Daniel, & Hoisler, 1991), and one study found that 66% of married male alcoholics seeking treatment engaged in domestic violence (C. M. Murphy & O'Farrell, 1994).

Responsibilities

The major responsibilities in relation to abuse and neglect cases relate to legal and clinical issues and involve conducting an appropriate assessment, developing a plan to ensure safety, and implementing appropriate interventions (see Table 2.15).

Most of the time the clinician's role is not to prove abuse, but to assess and contact the relevant agencies. In most states, the standard that triggers mandated reporting is "reasonable suspicion" that abuse has occurred or that there may be other children or vulnerable individuals at risk. In most communities reports are made to child protective services, the Department of Children's Services, adult protective services, or the police department. Some of these agencies have teams of professionals who interview the victim and coordinate all the necessary services. It is important to try to prevent the victim being interviewed

Table 2.15   Responsibilities when a client is being abused and traumatic effects of abuse

Assessment	Immediate Issues	Long-Term Issues
Interview issues	Ensure safety	Therapeutic factors
Mandated reporting	Refer for medical attention	Interventions
Confidentiality	Determine if others are at risk	Individual needs
Consultation	Monitor suicide risk	Support and recovery issues
Collateral contacts	Plan to protect	Family considerations

Document and Follow Up

Factors Associated with Traumatic Effects of Abuse

Abuse over a substantial time period
Many episodes of abuse
Abuse by several perpetrators
Victim physically hurt
Victim threatened or traumatized
Abuse by natural father, mother, or loved one (especially if still loved and separated from them)
Continuing abuse when victim is old enough to experience guilt
Victim does not have access to loving, secure family structure
Treatment was delayed or of poor quality
Victim made to feel responsible for subsequent family disruptions
Victim had aversive experience with the legal system or perpetrators found not guilty

multiple times and undergoing repetitious assessments that may be retraumatizing. Clear documentation is essential, as is maintaining an intake or interviewer role (i.e., avoid engaging in therapy or advocacy) and collecting unbiased, uncontaminated information, which may later be used in legal proceedings (R. G. Meyer & Deitsch, 1996; Wurtele & Miller-Perrin, 1992). It is necessary to be aware of one's own biases and issues and how they may impact the ability to be an objective evaluator in cases of abuse; consultation or supervision should be sought if this become a problematic concern. If in a training role, it is imperative to seek consultation from a supervisor or agency contact person.

Assessment Strategy

According to R. G. Meyer and Deitsch (1996), an initial assessment strategy for evaluating child abuse should include two steps: (1) documenting the chronology, context, and consistency of the abuse, and (2) gathering uncontaminated data and recording all the relevant information. This strategy may be used in the assessment of all abuse or neglect cases. While it is beyond the scope of this chapter to comprehensively address these assessment strategies, some additional general guidelines follow. Emphasis is placed on assessment of child abuse and neglect.

Behavioral and Physical Indicators of Abuse and Neglect

Review of prior records is essential to determine if there are any reports of documented or suspected maltreatment or previous behavioral indicators that could suggest possible abuse (Lukas, 1993; Wurtele & Miller-Perrin, 1992). An example of information that may raise suspicion of possible child abuse is a history of the family repeatedly seeking treatment at a variety of locations for a child's injuries. In addition to such "hospital shopping," the child may be withdrawn from or frequently miss school, or the family may relocate entirely. Because victims of abuse and neglect will frequently not volunteer this information and may be too frightened to talk, be familiar with potential signs of abuse (see Tables 2.13 and 2.14). Signs of physical abuse or injury should always be questioned, such as the four Bs: unexplained **b**urns, **b**leeding, **b**ald spots, and **b**ruises (particularly bruises to the head or face or multiple bruises). If injuries resemble the shape of an object, such as a belt buckle, or the patterning of bruises is not consistent with an accidental injury or with the victim's, caregiver's, or spouse's explanation, concern should be high (Lukas, 1993; Veltkamp & Miller, 1994). The presence of indicators of physical abuse should prompt inquiries about other forms of abuse and neglect.

Neglect can be formally assessed by several methods: interviews of parents and children, home visits, and behavioral monitoring by parents, children, or teachers (D. J. Hansen & Warner, 1992). To assess neglect, the children or parents can be asked to describe their current living situation, including when they last ate and bathed; to provide a general description of the home environment, including eating and sleeping arrangements; and to identify who cares for the child. Regarding care, if the child is left with an older sibling, the age of the sibling and whether appropriate safety arrangements are in place need to be considered.

Among children, regression to an earlier developmental stage, loss of a previously acquired skill such as toilet training, significant behavioral or temperament changes, poor school performance (e.g., failing grades, truancy), and displays of aggressive behavior, fearfulness, depression, and withdrawal are some behavioral indicators that should prompt an exploration of possible abuse (Lukas, 1993; Wurtele & Miller-Perrin, 1992). However, it is important to remember that none of these is a pathognomonic sign of child abuse. The most commonly reported indicator used to substantiate allegations of child sexual abuse is age-inappropriate sexual knowledge (Damon et al., 1992), so it is important to be particularly alert for this, as well as reports and observations of sexualized behavior in children. The impact of abuse on battered women is similar to the trauma experienced by rape victims; they present with constant terror, severe agitation, anxiety, fear of imminent doom, nightmares, helplessness, somatic complaints, depression, and suicidal behavior (Lystad et al., 1996; Riggs et al., 2000). Potential signs of elder abuse are summarized in Table 2.14. Possible indicators of elder neglect include dehydration, malnutrition, untreated bed sores, and poor personal hygiene; unattended or untreated health problems; hazardous or unsafe living conditions (e.g., no heat or running water); and unsanitary living conditions (e.g., dirt, fleas, lice, soiled bedding, fecal or urine smell).

Victims of physical or sexual abuse may require referral for a medical examination. With regard to child sexual abuse, McLeer and Rose (1992) recommend that the child be taken to a center that specializes in the examination of victims of sexual assault, rather than to the child's pediatrician or family physician since the latter may lack specific training in the medical evaluation of sexual abuse and may unwittingly conduct an inadequate medical evaluation.

Interview Strategies

Effectively interviewing abuse victims requires considerable skill and knowledge (R. G. Meyer & Deitsch, 1996; Wurtele & Miller-Perrin, 1992). For example, individuals who conduct child abuse interviews need to be familiar with normal child development and the abuse literature (e.g., know common signs and sequelae of abuse). The amount of information abuse victims divulge and the manner in which information is shared vary widely. Some victims may respond directly when questioned, but many will deny or minimize their abuse histories (Lukas, 1993). Battered women, for example, rarely consult mental health professionals and often only after enduring long periods of violence (Barthauer, 1999). Abuse victims may be particularly reluctant to disclose if they have been directly threatened with harm by the perpetrator (Wiehe, 1996). With regard to child abuse, as children get older and become more aware of societal norms, they may be ashamed, embarrassed, and fearful of the consequences of disclosure and be unwilling to share information. Many child victims present with child sexual abuse accommodation syndrome, which is characterized by secrecy, helplessness, and delayed, conflicted testimony, often accompanied by retractions (Summit, 1983).

When interviewing a possible abuse victim, questioning needs to be conducted in a sensitive, supportive, tactful manner that is cognizant of cultural differences in disclosing personal information (see Chapter 1). Also be aware of cultural practices that might be mistaken for abuse. For example, the traditional Asian medical practice of coining, in which warm oil or ointment is rubbed on the skin and the skin firmly abraded with a coin or special instrument, can result in lesions or even scars that could be mistaken for signs of physical abuse.

The victim and family members should be interviewed separately. Information related to three areas should be obtained: abuse-related information, victim factors, and family factors. The assessment may involve direct questioning of the victim, history taking, and observation of the victim's behavior (Wiehe, 1996). Assess the victim's psychological status and evaluate symptoms of the comorbid disorders previously reviewed that often accompany abuse (Lystad et al., 1996). It should be remembered, however, that not all symptoms an abuse victim displays are necessarily sequelae of the abuse; some may represent preexisting or independent conditions. Nevertheless, it is important to know about these in order to develop an effective treatment plan.

Interviews with the victim should first focus on general questions (e.g., inquiring about living situation, family members, friends, pets) and establishing rapport, before inquiries about possible abuse are made (Lystad et al., 1996). The victim should be made to feel comfortable and relaxed; for younger children, an initial period of free play may be helpful (Lukas, 1993). Do not assume the child or older adult understands all the terms used, and take care to gear questions toward the victim's cognitive level. For example, older adults may need more time to retell events, and one should be alert for signs of fatigue or memory impairment. Among young children, the use of multiple-choice questions can be problematic; a child may select a response option because it was the most easily remembered or the most recently presented choice and not because it was accurate (Damon et al., 1992). In addition, young children often have difficulty with temporal sequencing but can be helped by asking them to place events in relation to common experiences and events (e.g., "Was it before or after you watched your favorite cartoon?"). If a child's account appears to be developmentally inappropriate or rehearsed, consider the possibility that the child has been coached. In general, young children's accounts tend to be disjointed and may include odd comments that relate to tactile or olfactory experiences (G. S. Goodman, Rudy, Bottoms, & Aman, 1990; D. Jones & McGraw, 1987).

Recognize that the disclosure of abuse may be a protracted process, so allot ample time for the interview. In evaluating incest in young children, Damon and colleagues (1992) suggest that a minimum of two interviews be conducted, and a referral for extended evaluation and therapy be provided if the child does not disclose within a maximum of six sessions.

Throughout the evaluation take care to avoid contamination of the victim's report. In particular, avoid leading questions (e.g., "Your mother hit you hard enough to bruise you, didn't she?"), disconfirmation ("Did that really happen?"), repeating questions, or other coercive techniques. Despite concerns that children are particularly susceptible to the effects of leading questions (and therefore at risk for making false abuse allegations), studies have shown that even very young children (e.g., 4 years old) are both quite accurate in their ability to recall emotionally upsetting events and resistant to suggestions (G. S. Goodman et al., 1990). Furthermore, children are more likely to make errors of omission than commission (R. G. Meyer & Deitsch, 1996). This has led some to question the practice of solely or primarily utilizing open-ended questions (as opposed to more specific, contextual questions) when interviewing child abuse victims (McLeer & Rose, 1992). Focused questions (e.g., "Tell me about some things you don't like that Mom or Dad do") may be particularly helpful (Damon et al., 1992). For young children, specialized interview techniques, such as drawings and the use of anatomically correct dolls, should be used only by clinicians familiar with the normative data for these techniques. Although the use of anatomically correct dolls in the evaluation of sexual abuse has been controversial, research indicates that nonabused and abused children do differ with regard to how they play with such dolls and that such dolls do not increase the likelihood that nonabused children will make false abuse allegations (McLeer & Rose, 1992).

In general, a strategy of starting with general questions and then honing in on more specific abuse-related issues can be helpful when interviewing both abuse victims and alleged perpetrators. For example, with victims of domestic violence, initial questions can include "What are arguments like?" and "What happens when you fight?" (Barthauer, 1999). Then follow up with in-depth questions that address the frequency of the violence, the directionality of violence, the severity of violence (i.e., injury-producing potential), specific details concerning past abuses, whether there are children at risk, and what was done in the past for self-protection (Lystad et al., 1996). Positive feelings about the abuser and negative feelings toward authorities suggest the presence of a symbiotic dependent relationship or traumatic bonding (D. Dutton & Painter, 1981). When such ambivalent feelings or strong positive attachment is present, the victim is less likely to report abuse (Veltkamp & Miller, 1994). In these cases, a supportive, empathic approach is more effective than direct questioning.

When assessing alleged perpetrators where there is a high likelihood of a negative outcome, in the form of incarceration or criminal charges, concern for the veracity of information provided should be raised (R. G. Meyer & Deitsch, 1996). Care should be taken to obtain specific, concrete details and examples in response to questions. Be aware that the alleged perpetrator may utilize euphemisms or other distortions when describing behaviors (e.g., "Sometimes I have to hold her during an argument or she gets out of control"; Lystad et al., 1996). Finally, be alert for any duty to warn responsibilities that may arise as a result of the perpetrator's disclosures. Interview significant others and talk to the primary care physician (with releases) and, where appropriate, to other family members.

Mandated Reporting

All states have mandated abuse reporting laws that require mental health and other professionals (e.g., physicians, teachers) to report cases of suspected abuse discovered in the course of one's professional duties to a designated agency (e.g., child protective services, adult protective services). However, state laws vary (e.g., not all states require mental health professionals to report spousal abuse); therefore, clinicians should be aware of the required reporting for the state in which they practice. Mandated reporting laws are structured such that the clinician need only have a reasonable suspicion that abuse is occurring rather than definitive proof, and reporters are afforded protection from criminal or civil liability unless it is determined that the reporter knowingly made a false report. Typically, a telephone report will be made that is then followed up with a written report (using forms designated by the protective services agency), filed within a specific time frame (e.g., 36 hours). Specific information needs to be gathered for reporting purposes, such as the victim's name and whereabouts, age, address, living situation, parents (in the case of child abuse), and other family members' names and ages (Lukas, 1993; R. G. Meyer & Deitsch, 1996). Information must be provided on why you believe abuse is occurring (e.g., child's report, evidence of bruises), and you should be prepared to provide descriptions of the alleged abuse, including the most recent incident. Details such as the frequency, timing, and duration of abuse may also be requested. The identity of the alleged perpetrators and his or her whereabouts should also be provided. It is especially important to determine if other individuals are at risk. Even if all of the aforementioned information is not available, it is still necessary to make a report to the designated agency within the required time frame. You can also call protective service agencies when you are uncertain as to whether a child or elder abuse report needs to be filed. Be familiar with and follow specific guidelines provided by your agency or workplace regarding filing abuse reports. If your agency does not provide guidelines, Table 2.16 provides an outline of how to report. This framework should be modified to reflect the standards of care in your community.

Although not required by reporting agencies, it is clinically recommended that the client always be informed that a report is being filed. Even though clients should be informed at the start of treatment that suspected abuse can lead to a mandated breach of confidentiality, they may be very upset or even surprised when an abuse report is actually filed. Considerable time may need to be spent processing the client's negative feelings, which may include anger, fear, shame, and even a sense of being betrayed by the clinician. In the case of abuse victims, reassurance should be provided that the disclosure of abuse to an outside agency is an important first step in stopping future abuse. In counseling abuse perpetrators, reporting can be framed in terms of the need for the perpetrator to obtain help in stopping the abusive behavior. In addition to filing abuse reports with the relevant agencies, it is necessary to develop a plan to protect the victim, and the victim should not leave unless you are certain that safety can be ensured.

Table 2.16   10 Steps in reporting

1. Conduct an appropriate assessment.
2. Document information, underlining key information.
3. Review with supervisor or consult colleague.
4. Follow agency guidelines and forms.
5. Call appropriate local agency.
6. Identify self, agency, contact number, and reporter (if mandated).
7. Provide the following information:
   Victim's name, age, address, DOB, parents' names
   Names and ages of other at-risk individuals living in home, any others in residence
   Address and telephone number of alleged victim
   Parents' or significant others' telephone numbers
   Name of alleged perpetrator
   Date, time, location, and description of alleged incident(s)
   Any corroborating information and any description of precipitants or other witnesses
8. Obtain the name of person taking the report and the case number assigned.
9. Clarify actions to be taken and time frame, and discuss information with victim.
10. Develop a plan to protect, follow up, and document.

Source: From *Where to Start and What to Ask: An Assessment Handbook,* by S. Lukas, 1993, New York: Norton. Adapted with permission.

Treatment

Once the determination has been made that abuse has occurred, it is imperative to ensure that the victim obtains appropriate medical attention and is safe from further abuse and that there are no other victims at risk. This protective action may involve referral to community services such as shelters or family services. You can also help the client develop a safety plan. Victims of domestic violence can be assisted in developing strategies for staying safe during arguments (e.g., avoiding rooms with weapons or without easy access to an outside door); when preparing to leave (e.g., having extra money, copies of important documents ready); and when living away from the abusive partner (e.g., changing locks, installing alarm system). For most victims of abuse, appropriate treatment involves a combination of modalities (see Table 2.15). These include crisis intervention and individual, couple, family, and group therapy. In addition, if the abuse occurs in the context of the family, referral to parenting programs, a parent support group, and substance abuse treatment may also be warranted (Lystad et al., 1996).

A nested model with multiple layers of intervention that provides treatment in the context of the individual's life and utilizes community resources such as shelters, police, and psychological services has been found to be effective for abuse victims (Heise, 1998). During the acute period many victims of abuse are at high risk for suicide and need to be closely monitored. For some, hospitalization may be needed as a temporary safe refuge that will allow the victim to establish therapeutic and supportive alliances, provide time to decide on a plan of action, and enable treatment plan coordination with local agencies prior to discharge (Lystad et al., 1996).

The type of abuse will impact the type of intervention seen as helpful. For example, among emotionally abused women, self-esteem issues are crucial, whereas for physically abused women, danger and safety considerations are primary. The victim may need to be placed in a shelter or given an emergency phone number for community resources to ensure her safety (Riggs et al., 2000). Sexual abuse victims need the severity of the problem to be acknowledged and help with breaking the isolation barrier (B. Hamilton & Coates, 1993; Wurtele & Miller-Perrin, 1992). Children who have been abused should be encouraged to identify and express feelings (e.g., guilt, sadness) and fears and be told clearly that they were not responsible for the abuse and had a right to disclose the abuse (Geffken, 1998).

Be aware of the far-reaching effects that abuse can have on victims and be prepared to address these issues in treatment; these can include guilt, fear, depression, low self-esteem, poor social skills, trust issues, role confusion, and feelings of being damaged goods (Geffken, 1998). Regardless of the form of abuse, the most important stance to adopt is to be respectful and empathic and to listen to the individual's story. It is important to be aware of the factors that contribute to a traumatic response in abuse cases (see Table 2.15). Support groups can provide victims with the opportunity to talk, receive validation, draw emotional support, and identify coping strategies, all of which can counteract social isolation and immobilization (Bowker & Maurer, 1986; N. King, 2000). Groups can also help with issues of self-esteem, anger, and depression. Cognitive-behavioral groups have been found to reduce PTSD symptoms (Lubin, Loris, Burt, & Johnson, 1998; Lundy & Grossman, 2001), and in victims' self-reports, self-help groups are rated as particularly helpful (B. Hamilton & Coates, 1993).

For abusing parents, family therapy, parent training, and participation in support systems (such as Parents Anonymous, Parents United, or community-based support groups) are helpful. Focusing on social skills and cognitive-behavioral interventions, including parent education, is also effective. Couples therapy in spousal abuse cases is highly controversial, in part because of a high dropout rate and also because of safety considerations. A temporary separation or time-out is encouraged in domestic violence. Social services advocacy services can assist in safety planning and linking the victim to community resources. For the perpetrator of domestic violence, behavior and insight-oriented psychotherapy focusing on expressing feelings, mastery over anger, and behavioral alternatives to violence are useful. When treating the batterer, a goal-setting, action-oriented approach with adjunctive services (e.g., vocational counseling) is effective. Role-playing how to stop arguments and resolve conflicts can be helpful. However, batterers generally refuse to come voluntarily to treatment unless court-ordered.

Once the issues of danger to self and others have been addressed, the focus needs to shift to determining the appropriate diagnosis and treatment planning.

Chapter 3 ————————————————————————————————

ESSENTIALS OF DIAGNOSIS

Once information has been gathered from the initial interview, the clinician can begin the process of formulating a diagnosis that will aid in the development of a treatment plan. According to Barlow (1991, p. 243), "Classification is at the heart of any science," and this process plays a crucial role linking psychiatric research to mental health service delivery (H. E. Adams, Luscher, & Bernat, 2001; Jablensky, 1998). Diagnostic classification enhances unambiguous communication, which in turn facilitates the understanding of treatment options and prognosis and encourages systematic research (Rutter, 2002; Thangavelu & Martin, 1995). The use of a classification system also allows for the calculation of the economic impact of mental illness, the reimbursement of providers, and access to benefits (e.g., children needing special services), and can be used for forensic purposes (S. E. Hyman, 2002).

Despite these potential benefits, our view of any diagnostic classification system must be tempered with an understanding that a diagnosis represents an *interpretation* of an individual's experience that is influenced by many factors, including the clinician's training, specialization, institutional setting, and cultural background (Hersen & Turner, 2003; Kleinman, 1988). The level of rapport, the strength of the therapeutic alliance, and the individual's comfort with you also significantly influence his or her willingness to share critical diagnostic information (Othmer & Othmer, 2002). This chapter covers the fundamentals of diagnosis and describes the essential skills necessary to develop as a diagnostician. The history of classification and the development of the current diagnostic system, the *DSM-IV-TR*, are reviewed with a focus on conceptual understanding and clinical application. Particular emphasis is placed on rendering a diagnosis and dealing with the complex issues of diagnostic uncertainty and comorbidity.

THE HISTORY OF CLASSIFICATION

Classification can be defined as a method for constructing categories or groups and assigning either persons or disorders to these categories on the basis of shared attributes, with the resulting nonarbitrary sets of categories forming a classification system (Millon, 1991). It provides a context for the individual's unique signs and symptoms and allows clinicians and researchers to communicate in a common nomenclature (Langbucher & Nathan, 2006; Volkmar, Paul, Klin, & Cohen, 2005). Early classification systems of mental disorders were often linked to theories of etiology that reflected the climate and values of their times. These theories included beliefs that mental illness could be caused by possession by evil spirits, wandering wombs, and zodiac signs (LaBruzza &

Mendez-Villarrubia, 1997). Among the Greeks, Hippocrates (460–355 BC) was the first to propose that mental illness was a disease of the brain. He hypothesized that an imbalance of four essential bodily fluids caused disorders or diseases, such as mania, melancholia, depression, and paranoia (Zuckerman, 1999). Although these specific theories were incorrect, they served as the forerunners of current theories regarding the role of biological influences on human behavior.

The birth of psychiatric classification is attributed to Emil Kraepelin (1855–1926), who proposed that mental disorders are rooted in the brain; he recommended a fundamentally behavioral and descriptive approach based on systematic observation and documentation (Blashfield & Livesley, 1999). Using Sydenham's (1666) concept of discrete disease entities, he statistically recorded the signs, course, and outcome of clinical syndromes. His goal was to identify similarities in onset and presentation that suggested common etiologies and prognoses (Zuckerman, 1999). His early classification efforts focused on a small number of psychiatric inpatients with severe psychopathology and relied on posthoc theories to explain variations in clinical presentations (Millon, 1991). Kraepelin's findings were reported in a 13-chapter clinical psychiatry textbook that pioneered principles of psychiatric nosology still applicable today (Kraepelin, 1913). He emphasized the importance of obtaining a thorough history of medical and psychiatric problems, including a mental status examination, the observation of signs and symptoms to establish a diagnosis, and a consideration of longitudinal course as well as cross-sectional observations (First, 2002; Langenbucher & Nathan, 2006). Kraepelin's student Bleuler (1857–1937) continued his work, focusing on the identification of central, defining, or characteristic features of symptom constellation for various mental disorders (Bleuler, 1911/1950; First, Frances, & Pincus, 2004). This laid the foundation for the later development of research and diagnostic criteria for specific psychiatric disorders.

By the early twentieth century, hospitals and clinics were using idiosyncratic diagnostic categories based on the patients seen and the hospital's theoretical training model. In an attempt to encourage the use of a standardized diagnostic terminology, the New York Academy of Medicine sponsored a National Conference on Nomenclature in 1928. Subsequently, in 1932, the *Standard Classified Nomenclature of Diseases* was published; it focused on diagnosing patients with severe psychiatric disorders in public mental hospitals (American Psychiatric Association, 2000b; LaBruzza & Mendez-Villarrubia, 1997). In 1948, the World Health Organization (WHO) published the *International Classification of Diseases,* sixth edition (*ICD-6*), with a section on mental disorders (American Psychiatric Association, 2000b; First, Frances, & Pincus, 2002). This text contained a comprehensive listing of conditions that were the cause of significant death and disability. Several mental disorders, including psychotic disorders (e.g., schizophrenia, manic-depressive reaction), "psychoneurotic reactions" (e.g., obsessive compulsive reaction, neurotic-depressive reaction), and "disorders of character, behavior, and intelligence" (e.g., antisocial personality, passive dependency, borderline intelligence, specific learning defects) were listed (WHO, 1948).

The Diagnostic and Statistical Manual of Mental Disorders

In 1952, the American Psychiatric Association formed a Committee on Nomenclature and Statistics that reviewed the existing diagnostic systems, including the *ICD-6,* and created the *Diagnostic and Statistical Manual of Mental Disorders* (*DSM-I;* American Psychiatric Association, 1952). This was a 130-page book of 106 diagnoses, which was strongly influenced by Freudian theories and those of the Swiss-born American psychiatrist Adolf Meyer (Alarcon, 1995; Skodol Wilson & Skodol, 1994; Zuckerman, 1999). Meyer theorized that mental disorders were a reaction to biological and psychological factors that resulted in a failure to adapt to the environment (First et al., 2004). This emphasis on theory as part of the definitional diagnostic conceptualization served to impede research and contributed to the manual's lack of acceptance, particularly among clinicians (Volkmar & Klin, 2005). The *DSM-I* itself was criticized because the signs and symptoms of the disorders were not empirically based; the vague descriptions negatively impacted on the reliability, validity, and clinical utility of the diagnostic categories; and its idiosyncratic nature made it incompatible with *ICD-7* (Alarcon, 1995; Langenbucher & Nathan, 2006).

In an effort to make the *DSM* system more consistent with international standards and to increase its acceptance the *DSM-II* was published in 1968 (American Psychiatric Association, 1968). This 134-page book reviewed 182 disorders (Garfield, 2001). The Meyerian term "reaction" and other psychoanalytic concepts were removed, thus starting a return to a more descriptive, pragmatic Kraepelinian disease model approach and away from an etiologically focused nosology (Zuckerman, 1999). However, because of its continued poor interrater reliability and limited clinical validity, the *DSM-II* was also not widely accepted (LaBruzza & Mendez-Villarrubia, 1997; Skodol Wilson & Skodol, 1994). The *DSM-I* and *DSM-II* were small books whose diagnostic criteria were not empirically derived and lacked interrater and clinician reliability, consistency, and validity (A. T. Beck, Ward, Mendelson, Mock, & Erbaugh, 1962; Nathan, Andberg, Behan, & Patch, 1969; Zubin, 1967). This lack of empirical support raised ethical concerns about the impact of psychiatric labeling and the potentially dehumanizing and stigmatizing role of diagnostic classification. These concerns were described in Thomas Szasz's (1961) *The Myth of Mental Illness*, Karl Menninger's (1963) *The Vital Balance*, and Ken Kesey's (1962) novel *One Flew Over the Cuckoo's Nest*. These issues were further highlighted in 1973 when a psychologist had eight normal subjects seek admission to psychiatric hospitals with the presenting complaint of hearing a voice saying "Thud." All were admitted and received a discharge diagnosis of Schizophrenia in remission. The results were published in *Science* in an article entitled "On Being Sane in an Insane Place" and became one of the most widely cited studies in the field (Rosenhan, 1973).

MODERN PSYCHIATRIC CLASSIFICATION SYSTEMS

In the late 1950s the WHO recognized that the *ICD* classification system was not being widely used in the field of mental health and commissioned the British psychiatrist Erwin Stengel to identify the factors contributing to its lack of adoption. He recommended that if a system was to be internationally accepted it would have to be a descriptive classification that eschewed etiological theory and contained operational definitions or descriptions in a glossary (Stengel, 1959). These recommendations were not implemented until 1974, when the *ICD-8* was published (First, 2002). In the 1960s and 1970s, in an attempt to develop an internationally agreed upon diagnostic nosology, the WHO sponsored a series of studies on cultural differences in diagnosis (First, 2002). The U.S.–U.K. study conducted by J. E. Cooper and colleagues (1972) found significant diagnostic disparities in that American clinicians had an overly inclusive concept of Schizophrenia compared to their British counterparts. They also found that psychiatrists using the same symptoms came up with different diagnoses, which appeared to be influenced in part by the client's ethnicity (Blashfield & Livesley, 1999). These findings questioned the utility of clinical diagnoses and highlighted the need for the development of reliable diagnostic criteria that were clinically valid (Fabrega, 2001).

In 1972, a group of researchers at Washington University led by Feighner and known as the Neo-Kraepelinians developed explicit, standardized, descriptive, rule-driven criteria for psychiatric diagnoses. The development of specific statistics, for example, Kappa, to measure interdiagnostician agreement paved the way for research on the reliability and empirical validity of psychiatric disorders (Zuckerman, 1999). This was a turning point or paradigm shift in the field; now there was a move away from theories of etiology and a return to Kraepelinian descriptive psychopathology (First, 2002). The Washington University group collaborated with a group from New York State Psychiatric Institute under the leadership of Spitzer, Endicott, and Robins and expanded and modified Feighner's operational diagnostic criteria to form the basis of the research and diagnostic criteria (RDC) in 1975 (Spitzer, Endicott, & Robbins, 1975, 1978). The development of specific diagnostic criteria to describe psychopathology, in terms of objective symptoms and signs, resulted in the construction of standardized structured interviews and a range of epidemiological studies (Langenbucher & Nathan, 2006). This emphasis on standardized assessment, clearly defined diagnostic criteria, and interrater reliability strongly influenced the empirical basis of the *DSM-III* and the birth of modern classification (Maxmen & Ward, 1995).

DSM-III

In 1980, the *DSM-III* was published (American Psychiatric Association, 1980). Spearheaded by Spitzer and colleagues, it was a radical departure from previous classification systems and represented a fundamental shift in the field of psychiatric classification (Bertelsen, 1999). This edition drew heavily from Feighner's criteria and the RDC (First, 2002; Zuckerman, 1999). Using Stengel's earlier recommendations, this third edition of the *DSM* emphasized descriptive diagnoses determined by explicit operationalized diagnostic criteria. These criteria were derived from observable behaviors and discrete clinical findings and could be applied across most theoretical orientations (Skodol Wilson & Skodol, 1994; Volkmar & Klin, 2005). The diagnostic categories were defined in terms of core features for each disorder, allowing for the variability of clinical presentations. The atheoretical emphasis meant that clinicians could agree on the identification of the disorders based on their clinical manifestations while disagreeing on causality. This feature resulted in its acceptance and use by a wide range of clinicians from a variety of backgrounds (Regier, Narrow, First, & Marshall, 2002). The primary goals of the *DSM-III* were to enhance communication, facilitate research, and educate students by providing a standard medical nomenclature for clinicians and researchers (L. A. Clark, Watson, & Reynolds, 1995; First, 2002; Spitzer, 1991).

According to Millon (1991), the *DSM-III* focused on observable phenomena from an atheoretical stance. Subjective and vague glossary definitions were replaced by diagnostic criteria, which were operationalized based on the empirical findings of research and field trials. Technical terms were defined. A multiaxial approach to diagnosis was presented, which encouraged a more comprehensive assessment and ensured that personality and other factors were considered and not overlooked (Kastrup, 2002). An innovative, albeit controversial, feature in the *DSM-III* was the inclusion of decision trees for differential diagnosis, with flowcharts that presumed that each branch point would lead down a sequential path to a more specific and differentiated disorder.

The *DSM-III* was revised in 1987 to form the *DSM-III-R* (American Psychiatric Association, 1987). In this revision the conceptual basis of the five axes of the multiaxial system was described. There was also a shift away from seeing the diagnostic categories as classic categories of homogeneous disorders with well-defined boundaries to conceptualizing them as being organized around best examples or prototypes (First et al., 2004). This prototypic approach recognized the existence of boundary cases, where the individual's clinical presentation included features that were shared or overlapped with different disorders, and spectrum and subthreshold cases, where some core but not all the diagnostic characteristics were met. These changes allowed for considerable variability and heterogeneity of the disorders within each category and were thought to be more representative of clinical reality (Fauman, 2002). There was a de-emphasis on the hierarchical nature of the system, and it was stated that it was not assumed that each disorder was a discrete entity with sharp boundaries. Additionally, for many disorders exclusionary criteria were modified or omitted, and there was a move toward assigning multiple diagnoses when applicable to individuals (LaBruzza & Mendez-Villarrubia, 1997). To enhance clinical utility and reliability the format of several diagnostic categories, including the personality disorders, changed to a *polythetic format,* which listed a range of diagnostic criteria of which the individual had to meet only a subset (L. A. Clark et al., 1995; First et al., 2004). Some of the diagnostic criteria were also revised to improve clarity and validity, and the text descriptions of the disorders were updated (Skodol Wilson & Skodol, 1994).

The *DSM-IV* and *DSM-IV-TR*

Work on the *DSM-IV* started in 1988, with the main goal being to facilitate compatibility with the international system (*ICD*) and thus provide a common framework and diagnostic language that could be used by "adherents of different theoretical points of view" (Volkmar & Klin, 2005, p. 12). To provide a stronger scientific rationale to justify changes in the classification system, a three-stage methodology was developed (Langenbaucher & Nathan, 2006). First, a comprehensive systematic literature search aimed at determining the empirical support for existing categories and changes was undertaken. Then alternative proposals were tested by reanalyzing the existing data and incorporating new findings from unpublished studies. Finally, 12 field trials were conducted in 81 settings involving over 7,000 individuals to validate certain diagnoses and focus on specific issues (First & Pincus, 1999). In addition, a higher threshold for change was utilized, and the systematic review of the relevant empirical information and the rationale for changes were published in a four-volume series of sourcebooks edited by Widiger and colleagues (1994, 1996, 1997, 1998). A new diagnosis was considered for inclusion only if it was sufficiently supported by existing research studies and consideration was given to diagnoses already in the *ICD-10*. The major differences between the *DSM-IV* (published in 1994) and its predecessors were the level of research conducted, the systematic manner in which evidence was gathered, and the adherence to a methodology for making changes (LaBruzza & Mendez-Villarrubia, 1997). The *DSM-IV* was updated in 2000 to form the *DSM-IV-TR* (fourth edition, text revision), in which factual errors in the text were corrected and text and diagnosis code information consistent with the *ICD* system was included (First & Pincus, 2002).

Looking Ahead: *DSM-V*

The research and planning group for the development of the *DSM-V* was formed in 1999, and the next revision focuses on six specific areas (Regier, Narrow, First, & Marshall, 2002):

1. Nomenclature, specifically to make the *DSM* diagnostic definitions comparable to the *ICD*
2. The nature of the interaction between symptoms and disability and impairment
3. Current gaps in classification, limitations of existing diagnostic criteria, specifically for personality disorders, the placement of spectrum disorders and relational disorders
4. The nature of the development of psychopathology across the life span
5. The role of genetics, including vulnerability to mental disorders and neurobiological markers for diagnosis and treatment
6. The impact of cross-cultural and contextual factors in the expression of mental illness

Whereas many applaud the work being undertaken with the *DSM-V* and emphasize the need to address *ICD* or *DSM* discrepancies, cross-cultural applications, and its utility in nonpsychiatric settings, Rounsaville and colleagues (2002) recommend a highly conservative approach to revision, that only compelling changes be made. Several excellent texts provide more detailed information on the challenges and dilemmas confronting the next edition of the *DSM,* including those by S. R. Beach and colleagues (2006), K. A. Phillips and colleagues (Phillips, First, & Pincus, 2003), Helzer and Hudziak (2002), and Widiger and colleagues (Widiger, Simonsen, Sirovatka, & Regier, 2007). Additionally, Kupfer, First, and Regier's (2002) *Research Agenda for the DSM-V* is available online at www.appi.org.

STRENGTHS AND LIMITATIONS OF THE *DSM-IV-TR*

The *DSM-IV-TR* is an evolving system of diagnostic classification, and although each revision improves upon the previous edition, it has limitations. The *DSM-IV-TR* itself acknowledges four major weaknesses: the use of a categorical approach to diagnosis, the reliance on the use of clinical judgment, the use of the *DSM* in forensic settings, and ethnic and cultural considerations (American Psychiatric Association, 2000b). As a clinician it is important to be familiar with the advantages and disadvantages of using the *DSM*

Table 3.1 *DSM-IV-TR* advantages and disadvantages

Advantages	Disadvantages
Communication system	Cumbersome and inconsistent format
Atheoretical	Atheoretical and medical model
Categorical model	Heterogeneity and comorbidity
Descriptive and objective criteria	Relies on consensus and clinical judgment
Nonetiological diagnostic criteria	Exclusion criteria
Scientific basis and terms defined	An appearance of clarity and scientific basis
Increased diagnostic reliability	Reliability at the expense of validity
Multiaxial assessment	Focus on impairment and distress
Cultural and diversity considerations	Limited applications to diverse groups
Correlates with treatment	Self-fulfilling and a focus on labeling
Relationship to *ICD-10* and revisions	Reification of classification and instability

system for diagnosis; these are summarized in Table 3.1 and will now be discussed in more detail.

Atheoretical Communication System

The main strength of the *DSM-IV-TR* is as a communication tool. Over 90% of its text describes aspects of psychiatric disorders, including the clinical course, presentation, and associated features (First, 2002). As its title suggests, it aspires to be a diagnostic and statistical manual, providing a common language based on consistently agreed-upon diagnostic criteria for the surface manifestations of psychiatric disorders (Skodol Wilson & Skodol, 1994). It is a rule-based system. It contains operational definitions that eschew etiologic theory and facilitate the compilation of statistics on psychiatric illnesses (Zuckerman, 1999). It has reduced the scope of idiosyncratic teaching and increased interclinician agreement by providing an international reference system and is widely accepted by a range of mental health professionals, due in part to its atheoretical stance regarding etiology (Regier et al., 2002). In addition, it has also improved communication with consumers and the public, thus demystifying psychiatry (Bertelsen, 1999; Jablensky, 1998). The *DSM-IV-TR* has become the standard language in the United States for psychiatric diagnosis and has been translated into 13 other languages (First, 2002). International reviews indicate that 95% of clinicians use the *DSM* system for teaching, 97% for research, and 81% for clinical practice (Nelson-Gray, 1991). The extensive documentation and rigorous development of the *DSM-IV* has enhanced its credibility and acceptance in the research and scientific community. Its impact on education is evidenced in the overwhelming sales numbers of related texts (First, 2002).

Despite its widespread acceptance and numerous modifications it is still cumbersome (980 pages), and the organization of the diagnostic categories is inconsistent even in format. The frequent revisions have resulted in a pragmatic heterogeneous system lacking clearly elucidated etiologies for the major *DSM* disorders (Regier et al., 2002). Nelson-Gray (1991) contends that it represents an inherent medical model based on medical assumptions and content about abnormal behavior and suggests medical or psychophar-macological interventions.

Categorical Model: Implications for Heterogeneity and Comorbidity

The use of categories is essential for epidemiology and research as it facilitates the separation of conditions into discrete entities. A major limitation of the *DSM-IV* is its reliance on the underlying assumptions associated with a categorical model (Carson, 1991; Faul & Gross, 2006; Garfield, 2001; M. B. Johnson, 1998). A categorical model runs the risk of minimizing the differences between individuals who have the same condition (Volkmar & Klin, 2005). The designers of the *DSM* have been criticized for overemphasizing the discreteness of the diagnostic categories. The presence of comorbidity and heterogeneity of clinical presentation in individuals with the same disorder represent inherent challenges to this model (Maser & Patterson, 2002). Whereas comorbidity was barely recognized prior to the 1980s, it has become one of the strongest challenges to the validity of the *DSM* categorical classification system (Maser & Patterson, 2002). The National Comorbidity Study (1990–1992) conducted by R. C. Kessler and colleagues (1994, 1995, 1996, 1997, 1998, 2001) highlighted the extent of this issue and yielded a wealth of clinical, descriptive, and epidemiological data (Langenbucher & Nathan, 2006). Even in the disorders of childhood and adolescence high rates of comorbidity have been noted (J. Costello, Mustillo, Erkanli, Keeler, & Angold, 2003; Lillienfeld, 2003). The modification and removal of many of the exclusion criteria, the de-emphasizing of the diagnostic decision trees and hierarchical decision making, and the emphasis on the assignment of multiple diagnoses may have further compounded this problem (Zuckerman, 1999). In addition, the *DSM* categories have been criticized as not reflecting a unifying integrated scientific classification of psychiatric disorders, but an eclectically pragmatic system for filing diagnoses, where the primary concern is differential diagnosis (L. A. Clark et al., 1995, p. 125). Assigning a diagnosis based on a subset of diagnostic criteria (polythetic criteria sets) has also been criticized given the heterogeneity of the diagnostic categories' defining features and the mixed symptom presentations of boundary cases (Carson, 1991; First et al., 2002). The presence of this type of heterogeneity in the *DSM* appears to defeat the purpose of diagnosis to inform treatment or predict course and suggests that there are inherent incompatibilities between the nature of psychopathology and categorical taxonomies (L. A. Clark et al., 1995). Thus the *DSM* appears to violate the fundamental categorical classification requirement that categories are mutually exclusive and jointly exhaustive (Jablensky, 1998).

The use of a categorical model creates the additional problem for personality disorders of imposing an artificial boundary where no natural boundary exists, which may also contribute to the proliferation of comorbidity (Jablensky, 2002). Kendell and Jablensky (2003) note that most currently recognized mental disorders are not separated by natural boundaries. Over the years there has been a call for a dimensional approach to psychiatric classification, replacing the large number of diagnostic categories with fewer dimensions and including measures of severity and distress (P. A. Bank & Silk, 2001; Widiger et al., 2007). Whereas a dimensional model may increase reliability, it would be at the expense of clinical utility, and there is lack of consensus and insufficient empirical support to determine which dimensional approach is most appropriate for diagnosis (American

Psychiatric Association, 2000b). Some argue that a spectrum-type dimensional model is a more valid model of psychopathology and better accounts for subthreshold symptoms (Maser & Patterson, 2002). Earlier, Frances and colleagues (Frances, First, & Pincus, 1995) noted that dimensional models are more cumbersome than useful, would be unfamiliar to most clinicians, and likely would be rejected as irrelevant to their clinical needs. Currently, the *DSM-IV-TR* uses a categorical model for personality disorders; however, the text presents a discussion of a dimensional model that is under active consideration with the *DSM-V* Task Force (American Psychiatric Association, 2000b; Kupfer, First, et al., 2002; Widiger et al., 2007).

Diagnostic Criteria and Clinical Judgment

One of the goals with the continued revisions of the *DSM* was to develop specific and observable empirically based sets of diagnostic criteria, which, like earlier criteria (Feigher et al., 1972), were a distillation of clinical research and field experience (First, 2002; Widiger & Trull, 1993). The present diagnostic criteria have been criticized because they do not adequately sample all the relevant clinical diagnostic information, are not readily operationalized, and are not sufficiently specific to be useful (Nelson-Gray, 1991). Morrison (1995a) notes that few of the 300 diagnoses have been studied enough to have scientific legitimacy, and many were formulated and written by committees where the objective criteria often represented a compromise of widely disparate views. In fact, the *DSM* has been criticized as creating new illnesses by committee consensus agreement of operational criteria that lack clinical validity (P. J. Caplan, 1991; Carson, 1991; Kirk & Kutchins, 1992). Also, the early task groups were composed predominantly of psychiatrists, thus neglecting the role of other clinicians. The lack of a more broad-based approach and the omission of studies from epidemiology, genetics, and the social and behavioral sciences diminish the reliability and validity of some diagnoses and may result in their inappropriate use by more inexperienced clinicians (Regier et al., 2002).

One of the *DSM-IV*'s advantages was the open disclosure of the rationale for nosologic changes in the sourcebooks (Widiger et al., 1994, 1996, 1997, 1998). However, despite this emphasis on empirical research, the *DSM* still relies on clinical judgment in determining a diagnosis, and the use of this in psychiatric classification runs counter to scientific nosology (H. E. Adams et al., 2001; Garfield, 2001). The cutoff points that characterized most of the *DSM* categories have been criticized as somewhat arbitrary (S. E. Hyman, 2002). The lack of severity thresholds, resulting in a tendency to expand the boundaries into normal functioning, has been seen as contributing to an overestimation of psychiatric illness (Preskorn, 1995). The consistent use of exclusion criteria by both the *ICD* and the *DSM-IV* may also result in systematic exclusion errors and a serious bias in the selection of populations for clinical research (Jablensky, 1998).

Furthermore, despite advances in the *DSM* system, psychiatric clinical diagnosis is still dependent on the clinician's ability to elicit the relevant information via the individual's readiness to disclose and discuss their subjective experience. Thus the key components of most of the *ICD* and *DSM-IV* diagnoses rely on phenomenological, behavioral communication and trained introspection rather than objective signs or tests (Jablensky, 1998). According to Skodol Wilson and Skodol (1994), defining a mental disorder is a matter of subjective clinical consensus, not science; the diagnostic criteria can be viewed as guidelines that should be implemented using clinical judgment. They caution against their misuse or misapplication in a cookbook fashion with either extreme flexibility and or in an idiosyncratic manner. The *DSM*'s ongoing reliance on clinical judgment implies it is most appropriately used in clinical, educational, and research settings, and only by individuals who have appropriate clinical training and experience.

Reliability at the Expense of Validity?

The use of descriptive nonetiologically based diagnostic criteria and the definition of diagnostic terms have facilitated research on interclinician agreement. This research has generally shown that satisfactory to good interrater reliability can be obtained for most *DSM* diagnoses and good predictive validity for a range of disorders; these are significant strengths of the system (T. A. Brown, Di Nardo, Lehman, & Campbell, 2001; Kim-Cohen et al., 2003; Simpson et al., 2002; Yen et al., 2003). Nevertheless, L. A. Clark and colleagues (1995) caution that there is a danger of reductionism with the *DSM-IV*, and the attempt to reduce phenomena to a few fundamental categories may result in the reification of nosological categories that lack validity (Twemlow, 1995). Both the *ICD-10* and *DSM-IV* have good reliability, but this does not imply validity (S. E. Hyman, 2002). In fact, both systems of necessity were developed based on expert consensus, not empirical validation. Thus the DSM's title, organization, and content suggest a scientific basis that is currently lacking. Another major criticism is that the *DSM* has begun to drive science, and the official taxonomy has become an "unintended straightjacket" for researchers that limits them to studying only *DSM* disorders and criteria (L. A. Clark et al., 1995, p. 123). Interestingly, even the developers of the current *DSM* in their "last words" state, "Do not be a *DSM-IV* idolater who allows clinical observation and common sense to be distorted by a need to shoehorn patients into the *DSM-IV* pidgeonholes, independent of whether they fit or not. At the same time, avoid being a *DSM* heretic who derides the whole system" because it does not always provide the appropriate diagnosis for every individual (A. Frances et al., 1995, p. 24).

On a more specific level, Nelson-Gray (1991) reviewed the methodology associated with the development of the *DSM-IV* and describes as problematic the measurement of interdiagnostician reliability using videotapes of patients undergoing the Structured Clinical Interview for *DSM* Axis I Disorders. Reliance on prerecorded interviews does not assess the diagnostician's skill in eliciting symptom information and is not the typical format for a clinical interview. Spitzer (1991) concurs with this criticism and adds that the lack of attempts to use the free-form interview preferred by many clinicians is a concern.

Multiaxial and Diversity Considerations

The adoption of a multiaxial format (*DSM-III*) represented a major paradigm shift to include such factors as medical conditions and psychosocial stressors into diagnostic consideration (American Psychiatric Association, 1980). Thus problems and disorders could be conceptualized in the context of the individual's physical health and life situation. However, the *DSM-IV-TR* has been criticized for generically introducing the diagnostic criteria requiring evidence of clinically significant distress or impairment to all disorders without fully assessing the implications of this diagnostic requirement (Spitzer & Wakefield, 1999).

One of the major innovations of the *DSM-IV* was the inclusion of cultural and diversity considerations in the assignment of psychiatric diagnosis (Mezzich, Berganza, & Ruiperez, 2001). The *DSM-IV-TR* addresses these considerations as a subsection for each disorder and in an appendix of culture-bound syndromes, which includes a cultural formulation (American Psychiatric Association, 2000b). The cultural formulation supplements the multiaxial system and allows the clinician to systematically assess and consider the role of cultural factors in the individual's clinical presentation (American Psychiatric Association, 2000b). These modifications have been criticized as being an afterthought and inadequate, and the *DSM-IV* specifically has been criticized as a North American culture-bound document (LaBruzza & Mendez-Villarrubia, 1997). Its application to young children is also limited as it lacks information on developmental and life span issues, and there is a paucity of diagnostic criteria for very young children (Dunitz, Scheer, Kvas, & Macari, 1996; Faul & Gross, 2006). It has also been criticized as too jargonish and not suited to nonpsychiatric settings such as medical primary care settings, where a full psychiatric evaluation may not be feasible (S. Lee, 2002). Additionally, the *DSM-IV* does not provide criteria to identify high-risk individuals, although this omission may be due in part to the paucity of high-quality high-risk identification and early intervention studies (Regier et al., 2002).

Correlates with Treatment and Self-Fulfilling Prophecy

One of the purposes of the *DSM* classification system was to facilitate open communication, which would foster systematic research into effective interventions and thus enhance treatment (Langenbucher & Nathan, 2006; Rutter, 2002; Thangavelu & Martin, 1995). To this end, the *DSM-IV* has become an invaluable tool in guiding treatment, for communicating with colleagues, predicting illness course, and educating family members (Morrison, 1995a,b). However, there is a lack of clear evidence that treatment response is specific to diagnosis. Also, the relationship of specific *DSM* disorders to the new psychotropic medications that are effective across a wide range of conditions remains unclear (Regier et al., 2002).

Over the years there have been major controversies over the definition of psychopathology, the classification of what is abnormal, and the impact of labeling (H. E. Adams et al., 2001; Barlow, 1991; Zuckerman, 1999). Specifically, classification systems have been criticized for not considering the unique nature of the individual. Labeling individuals with psychiatric diagnoses has been described as unnatural, arbitrary, unnecessary, and often dehumanizing (Fabrega, 2001; Szasz, 1961). These issues have significant implications for children and adolescents and their families when a diagnostic label elicits responses from others that encourage or excuse the child's maladaptive behavior, thus creating a self-fulfilling prophecy (Faul & Gross, 2006; Rutter & Gould, 1985). There is also concern that diagnoses may be used as labels to exclude individuals from services and programs and curtail their ability to purchase insurance and health coverage (Volkmar & Klin, 2005).

Compatibility with the *ICD* and Revisions

Despite the high levels of concordance of many of the *DSM-IV* and *ICD-10* diagnostic categories, minor differences in the systems' diagnostic criteria remain (Andrews, Slade, & Peters, 1999; Ottosson, Ekselius, Grann, & Kullgren, 2002). Both systems have been described as separate dialects rather than separate languages; however, having two diagnostic systems in and of itself undermines the goal of fostering communication among professionals and researchers (First & Pincus, 1999; Thangavelu & Martin, 1995). First (2002) states that the challenge for the future is to eliminate the differences that are insignificant, highlight the meaningful differences, and develop a unified international system.

The frequent revisions and updates of the *DSM* have had a disruptive impact on research and have hindered comparative diagnostic studies (First, 2002). The tendency to constantly change diagnostic criteria without a compelling reason and the absence of "a modicum of stability" has resulted in a database whose boundaries are subject to frequent and capricious changes (Carson, 1991, p. 305; Garfield, 2001). The major goals in revising the *DSM* over the years have included making it less cumbersome, enhancing its clinical utility, simplifying the diagnostic criteria, incorporating feedback from clinicians in the field, providing an empirical foundation, and maintaining compatibility with the *ICD* (Regier et al., 2002). S. E. Hyman (2002) recommends that the existing system should not be modified without a high threshold for changes, and Garfield (2001) concurs. It should be noted that this approach was implemented in the development of the *DSM-IV-TR* (American Psychiatric Association, 2000b).

In summary, the major criticisms of the *DSM-IV* are the inappropriate assumption of a categorical model, the persistence of traditional diagnostic categories, excessive changes and concern with clinician acceptance, and interdiagnostician reliability at the expense of construct validity (Carson, 1991). Despite these limitations, there is reason for optimism: A more logical, valid, coherent system will emerge with time and research. Currently, it is helpful to envision the *DSM* as its framers intended, as a way station or a work in progress to be replaced with more inclusive models of classification as research develops (L. A. Clark et al., 1995). However, it is also important not to reify the *DSM-IV-TR* as a diagnostic tool and to be mindful of the still unaddressed concerns for validity. The *DSM-IV-TR* is the standard of care and the system for communication in the field; therefore, it is important for us as clinicians to understand and become proficient in its use while being mindful of its limitations.

CLINICAL SKILLS: DIAGNOSIS

One of the main functions of psychiatric diagnosis is to provide a succinct means to communicate a large amount of information about an individual. It can be viewed as a shorthand notation for a syndrome or a cluster of clinical signs and symptoms that commonly occur together (Fauman, 2002). Deciding on a diagnosis can appear to the novice clinician to be an overwhelming task. It involves the distilling, culling, and condensing of a multitude of data into a meaningful conceptualization of the presenting symptomatology (First et al., 2002). A correct diagnosis is a prerequisite for proper treatment (Bertelsen, 1999). Thus diagnosis serves as a communication tool allowing for the identification of appropriate interventions and the prediction of treatment response and outcome (A. Frances & Ross, 2001; Othmer & Othmer, 2002).

The diagnoses in the *DSM-IV-TR* have been described as ready-made suits that come in a variety of styles and sizes (Fauman, 2002). The clinician's role is to identify the individual's clinical presentation, characteristic signs, and symptoms and then match them to a specific predefined psychiatric diagnostic category. The process of this diagnostic fitting is guided in part by the organization and structure of the *DSM-IV-TR*. The skills necessary to become a competent diagnostician include a familiarity with diagnostic terminology, an understanding of the overall conceptualization of the disorders, and an applied knowledge of multiaxial assessment. Also required is the ability to identify diagnostic clues or signs and symptoms that suggest specific diagnoses, common core syndromes, and the features that allow you to differentiate between disorders.

Key Diagnostic Terminology

The *DSM-IV-TR* defines a *mental disorder as:*

> a clinically significant behavioral or psychological syndrome or pattern that occurs in an individual and that is associated with present distress (e.g., a painful symptom) or disability (i.e., impairment in one or more important areas of functioning) or with a significantly increased risk of suffering death, pain, disability or an important loss of freedom. These disorders must be present at a clinical significant level of distress or impairment or risk of personal suffering. "In addition, this syndrome or pattern must not be merely an expectable or culturally sanctioned response to an event." Neither deviant behavior nor the result of conflicts between the individual and society is included in this definition unless it is a symptom of the individual's dysfunction (American Psychiatric Association, 2000b, p. xxxi.) Whereas the term mental disorder implies a difference between physical and mental disorders, the *DSM-IV-TR* recognizes that this distinction is reductionistic and no longer meaningful. It also notes that there is no consistent operational definition of mental disorder that defines precise boundaries and can be applied across all situations (American Psychiatric Association, 2000b; First et al., 2004). Thus the term mental disorder, which has been criticized extensively, persists because there is no good alternative or substitute currently available (Blashfield & Livesley, 1999; Spitzer & Wakefield, 1999). The focus of the *DSM-IV-TR* is on the classification of disorders that occur in individuals (rather than in families or groups).

Diagnostic Categories

In the *DSM,* disorders are organized into *diagnostic categories* based on defining or *essential features,* for example, the presence of psychotic symptoms for Schizophrenia and other psychotic disorders (American Psychiatric Association, 2000b). These features represent core symptoms or prominent aspects of the clinical presentation, which capture the diagnostic essence around which the disorders are clustered. Thus, within the categories there may be several disorders that share common or cardinal features, for example, the presence of a disturbance of mood in Dysthymic Disorder and Bipolar Disorder I in the mood disorders category (First, 2002). The essential features of the diagnostic categories are often stated in the opening description of the disorder in the *DSM-IV-TR* text. There are 16 major diagnostic categories and one additional section. The first category, "Disorders Usually First Diagnosed in Infancy, Childhood or Adolescence," consists of a wide range of disorders, grouped solely on the basis of age of onset or first presentation

(Fauman, 2002). The use of age for categorization is merely a matter of convenience, as individuals may also present with these disorders in adulthood. The next three categories—Delirium, Dementia, and Amnestic and Other Cognitive Disorders; Mental Disorders Due to a General Medical Condition (GMC) Not Elsewhere Classified; and Substance-Related (SR) Disorders—are placed before the other categories because the clinician needs to consider these at the onset of diagnostic decision making (First & Tasman, 2004). The disorders within each of these categories have similar etiologies in that they are caused by or due to specific identifiable factors (American Psychiatric Association, 2000b; First et al., 2004). The following 12 categories consist of disorders grouped according to shared phenomenology (L. A. Clark et al., 1995; First et al., 2002). The exception is the Adjustment Disorders category, which includes disorders that may look (phenomenologically) very different, though they share a common etiology and are a maladaptive reaction to a stressor (LaBruzza & Mendez-Villarrubia, 1997). Each *DSM-IV-TR* diagnostic category includes diagnoses for disorders due to a GMC, a substance-induced disorder, and a Not Otherwise Specified (NOS) diagnosis. The section "Other Conditions That May Be a Focus of Clinical Attention" includes problems that are a focus of attention but are not diagnosable according to *DSM-IV-TR* specifications. The Additional Codes category includes codes often used to indicate diagnostic uncertainty or the absence of psychopathology (i.e., unspecified, deferred, or no diagnosis).

Syndromes

The *DSM-IV-TR* describes disorders as clusters of *signs* and *symptoms* that are organized around commonalities (essential features) that form a specific symptom constellation. The choice of signs and symptoms is necessary to account for the variability inherent in most psychiatric disorders (Fauman, 2002). Signs are defined as observable disturbances of behavior or changes in state or function, for example, crying or agitation. They can be assessed on intake, during the clinical interview or the mental status examination, or by laboratory tests (Maxmen & Ward, 1995). In contrast, symptoms are experienced subjectively and consist of the individual's self-report, conscious recollections, and recorded experiences (Millon, 1991). Often described as intangible and subtle, symptoms can be physiological and/or psychological; in and of themselves they are not considered mental illness (Alarcon, 1995; Maxmen & Ward, 1995). It is only when they form part of a *syndrome,* a cluster of signs and symptoms that commonly occur together and are characteristic of a specific disorder, that they become associated with mental illness (Fauman, 2002). Many of the *DSM-IV-TR* disorders are organized as syndromes, which include a core cluster of symptoms as a model or *prototype.* Individuals who present with signs and symptoms similar to the prototype receive the same diagnosis. Overall, the *DSM*'s approach is a descriptive one that emphasizes observed or reported clinical features and adheres to a categorical approach in which an individual either meets or does not meet the diagnostic criteria.

Diagnostic Criteria

The *diagnostic criteria* can be conceptualized as the rules that define or describe a clinical disorder. They specify the type, intensity, and duration of various behaviors and symptoms required for diagnosis (Fauman, 2002). Currently most of the duration and threshold diagnostic criteria lack empirical validation and are somewhat arbitrary. Signs and symptoms form the basis for diagnostic criteria that describe both the prototypic cases and the clinical variants, thereby allowing for variability in clinical presentation (Fauman, 2002; First et al., 2004). Thus individuals with similar diagnoses may not have identical features but may be similar in terms of cardinal or core symptoms. It is important to note that the diagnostic criteria are not mutually exclusive, and several occur in multiple diagnostic categories, for example, hypersomnia, weight fluctuations, and depressed mood (Fauman, 2002). The goal for the future is to refine the diagnostic criteria over time with research and the accumulation of clinical information (First, 2002).

For most categories the *DSM-IV-TR* is organized using *monothetic* or *polythetic* decision rules for classification (LaBruzza & Mendez-Villarrubia, 1997). Monothetic classification requires that each one of several diagnostic criteria have to be present in order to make a diagnosis; hence the criteria are jointly necessary and sufficient (Blashfield & Livesley, 1999). Thus, before a diagnosis of Depersonalization Disorder can be assigned, all four diagnostic criteria must be met. This approach works best when disorders are homogeneous: In relation to their defining features, each category is mutually exclusive and the boundaries distinguishing different disorders are clear (L. A. Clark et al., 1995). Although the categorical monothetic approach tends to increase the reliability of diagnosis, this may be at the expense of validity and clinical utility. It also runs the risk of reifying diagnostic categories and reduces the need for clinical judgment or inferences (LaBruzza & Mendez-Villarrubia, 1997).

As the *DSM* has evolved to increase its clinical utility, some diagnostic categories have adopted a more polythetic approach involving many possible signs or symptoms as diagnostic criteria (First et al., 2004; Skodol Wilson & Skodol, 1994). This format lists a range of symptoms and signs, not all of which are required for a diagnosis; an individual may be assigned a diagnosis based on a subset of possible diagnostic features that were sufficient to meet the diagnostic threshold (LaBruzza & Mendez-Villarrubia, 1997). Consequently, two people may have the same diagnosis and yet may have only a single diagnostic criterion in common and may differ in terms of defining features, symptoms, and the course of the disorder (Millon, 1991). This organization allows for a more open diagnostic system that can account for the natural heterogeneity of psychiatric disorders. Within the *DSM-IV-TR*, polythetic diagnostic sets are used extensively with the disruptive behavior disorders, the substance-related disorders, and the personality disorders. Whereas this approach improves the clinical utility of diagnosis, the use of polythetic rules and diagnostic criteria that are not mutually exclusive increases the complexity and heterogeneity of the diagnostic categories (LaBruzza & Mendez-Villarrubia, 1997). This approach has also resulted in considerable diagnostic overlap and may have contributed to spurious high rates of comorbidity (Blashfield & Livesley, 1999).

Exclusion Criteria

Many *DSM-IV-TR* diagnostic categories also include *exclusion criteria,* which identify diagnostic hierarchies, establish the boundaries between diagnoses, clarify differential diagnosis, and list alternative diagnoses that must be excluded (American Psychiatric Association, 2000b; First et al., 2004). These exclusion criteria often involve specific wording, such as "Criteria have never been met for," to clarify the lifetime hierarchy between disorders. Phrases such as "Criteria are not met for" or "Does not occur exclusively during the course of" are used to differentiate between difficult boundary diagnostic cases or establish the precedence of the more pervasive disorder over the less pervasive disorder with similar defining features (American Psychiatric Association, 2000b, p. 6). The phrase "Not due to the direct physiological effects of a substance or a general medical condition" serves to discriminate between disorders with similar symptoms but different etiologies. The phrase "Not better accounted for" emphasizes the need for clinical judgment and the consideration of alternative diagnoses (American Psychiatric Association, 2000b, p. 6; First, 2002). Thus the diagnostic criteria for each disorder in the *DSM-IV-TR* represents a set of to-be-included and to-be-excluded defining features that follow certain specific rules (Millon, 1991). The lack of a standard format (currently there are 10 different phrases) for the exclusionary criteria used in the *DSM-IV* is problematic (T. Slade & Andrews, 2002). However, these criteria are useful in differential diagnosis and in resolving diagnostic uncertainty, determining comorbidity, and preventing the assignment of multiple incompatible diagnoses.

Subtypes and Specifiers

The *DSM-IV-TR* diagnostic categories may also include diagnostic criteria known as *subtypes, specifiers,* or *modifiers,* which serve to subgroup individuals within the categories into more homogeneous combinations or to identify additional features of the disorder. Not all *DSM-IV-TR* disorders have subtypes or specifiers. Subtypes are mutually exclusive phenomenological subgroupings within a specific disorder in that the individual is assigned to only one subtype. Thus individuals with a diagnosis of Schizophrenia may be further differentiated into Paranoid or Catatonic Type. Specifiers are used to define or describe specific features of the clinical presentation, such as with Depressive Features with Poor Insight, and to predict commonalities in the severity (*mild, moderate, or severe*) or course of the disorder (First et al., 2004). To assign a severity modifier, the individual must currently meet the full diagnostic criteria for the disorder. To determine the severity level, the clinician considers the number and intensity of signs and symptoms and the resultant level of impairment in occupational or social functioning. The *DSM-IV-TR* offers the following guidelines: Mild is used when there are few diagnostic criteria beyond those minimally required for a diagnosis and/or minor impairment. Moderate is in between mild and severe. Severe represents the presence of many signs or symptoms in excess of those required to make a diagnosis or several very severe or apparent symptoms and marked impairment in occupational or social functioning (American Psychiatric Association, 2000b). The clinician is encouraged to consider the severity specifiers for all of the *DSM-IV-TR* diagnostic categories (First et al., 2004).

Course specifiers focus on the history of the disorder rather than on the intensity of the clinical presentation and include *in partial remission, in full remission,* and *prior history.* In partial remission implies that the client met some of the criteria for the disorder but no longer meets the full criteria that were present when the diagnosis was originally made. In full remission indicates that the signs and symptoms of the disorder have cleared or are no longer present, but the diagnosis is still clinically relevant. According to the *DSM-IV-TR,* after a period of time in full remission, the individual may be considered to be recovered

(American Psychiatric Association, 2000b). To make a determination of recovery, as opposed to remission, the clinician needs to consider several factors, including the course of the disorder, the individual's response to treatment, ongoing need for treatment, the severity of symptoms, and the duration of time without symptoms (American Psychiatric Association, 2000b). *DSM-IV-TR* diagnoses typically refer to the individual's current clinical presentation. The past or prior history modifier is used if the individual is determined to have recovered from a disorder, but a history of the disorder is still clinically salient or significant. After a period of remission or recovery some individuals may experience a recurrence of the original disorder but do not meet the necessary diagnostic criteria for a diagnosis. In these cases the clinician can assign a provisional diagnosis based on prior history or consider the NOS category. Several of the *DSM-IV-TR* diagnostic categories, such as the mood disorders, include specific details about particular course specifiers in the introductory descriptive text.

Diagnostic Principles

In an effort to facilitate differential diagnosis, early versions of the *DSM* organized the diagnostic categories using a *hierarchical system* (First & Tasman, 2004; Millon, 1991). The use of decision trees as flowcharts or algorithms of branching logic was intended to help in the identification of the best disorder or the one that accounts for all symptoms and to facilitate the differentiation of diagnoses (First et al., 2002). The decision trees in the *DSM-IV-TR*'s Appendix A do not follow a fixed methodological approach but function as a guide to assist clinicians in discriminating between diagnoses and understanding the hierarchical nature of classification (R. D. Morgan, Olson, Krueger, Shellenberg, & Jackson, 2000). The organization of the hierarchical system involves two guiding principles: *parsimony* and *precedence*. The principle of parsimony implies that the clinician should seek the most efficient, economical, and elegant diagnosis that accounts for all the clinical information (Maxmen & Ward, 1995). If more than one diagnosis is being considered, the clinician should identify the fewest number of diagnoses using the decision tree flowcharts. The precedence principle suggests that when two diagnoses share common defining diagnostic criteria, the most severe or pervasive is assigned (American Psychiatric Association, 2000b; Fauman, 2002). Pervasive refers to how extensively the symptoms permeate the individual's life in terms of duration and intensity. Specifically, when an individual has more than one diagnosis, the clinician can use the exclusion criteria to establish the rules of diagnostic precedence. The organization of the diagnostic categories in the *DSM-IV-TR* and the recommended diagnostic decision trees encourage the clinician to consider disorders in order of declining severity (American Psychiatric Association, 2000b; Fauman, 2002). After the category Disorders of Infancy, Childhood, and Adolescence, the next three categories (Delirium, Dementia, Amnesia and Other Cognitive Disorders; Mental Disorders Due to a GMC; and SR Disorders) are the first considerations or rule-out conditions in determining a diagnosis. These are followed by the categories Psychotic, Mood, Anxiety, Somatoform, Factitious, Dissociative, Sexual, Eating, Sleep, Impulse-Control, Adjustment, and Personality Disorders, Other Conditions, and finally no mental disorder (American Psychiatric Association, 2000b; First, 2002).

While the *DSM-IV-TR* still endorses the use of decision trees in differential diagnosis, there has also been a shift toward making multiple diagnoses when the patient meets the criteria of more than one disorder (Jablensky, 1998). There are three exceptions to this practice. If the disorder is due to a GMC or SR, it precludes the diagnosis of an additional mental disorder. When a pervasive disorder has among its defining or associated symptoms the defining symptoms of a less pervasive disorder, then only the pervasive disorder is diagnosed. Thus Asperger's Disorder is not assigned to a child who already meets the criteria for Autistic Disorder. Finally, when there is not a clear differentiation between competing diagnoses (boundary cases), clinical judgment should be used to determine the most appropriate diagnosis. Specifically, the "Not better accounted for" exclusionary criteria needs to be considered (Fauman, 2002).

When an individual presents with multiple diagnoses, the clinician needs to identify the diagnosis that brought the client to therapy or that is the focus of attention. The *DSM-IV-TR* recommends that in inpatient settings the diagnosis responsible for the psychiatric admission be listed as the *principal diagnosis.* If the client is seen on an outpatient basis, the diagnosis that is the focus of attention is coded as the *reason for visit.* The *provisional* diagnosis specifier may be noted if the clinician is uncertain about whether to assign a diagnosis or not because the individual may not meet the full diagnostic criteria or the duration of the symptoms may not have been met (Morrison, 1995a, b). This is particularly applicable if the clinician strongly suspects that with more information or a longer time frame the client would meet the full diagnostic criteria (American Psychiatric Association, 2000b).

ORGANIZATION OF THE *DSM-IV-TR*

While the *DSM-IV-TR* diagnostic criteria attempt to codify the diversity of human emotional and behavioral problems, their primary purpose is to help clinicians establish a diagnosis, choose appropriate treatment, and communicate with one another (First et al., 2004). In terms of the organization or structure of the classification system, there are two major components you need to be familiar with: the organization of the manual and the organization of the specific chapters that deal with the diagnostic categories. Whereas the current diagnostic categories have good reliability and useful clinical descriptions, there are major differences in the organization of some categories and a lack of unifying decision-making rules.

The introduction of the manual includes a brief historical review, descriptions of the revision process (including the criteria for change), and the relationship of the *DSM-IV-TR* to the international system (*ICD-10*). This is followed by a definition of mental disorder, a description of the limitations of the forensic application of the *DSM-IV-TR,* ethnic and cultural considerations, and treatment planning issues. An overview of the organization of the manual is then presented with a cautionary statement that the diagnostic criteria are guidelines that enhance interclinician agreement and their use requires training and clinical skills. Thus, whereas the system represents "a consensus of the current formulation of evolving knowledge in our field," it does not purport to be all-inclusive (American Psychiatric Association, 2000b, p. xxxvii).

The section "Use of the Manual" is crucial for the clinician, as it outlines the format for coding and reporting disorders, the use of the NOS categories in cases of diagnostic uncertainty, exclusion criteria, and the criteria for substance-induced disorders and a mental disorder due to a GMC. A description of the types of information in the *DSM-IV-TR* and its organizational plan are also provided. The chapter entitled "*DSM-IV-TR* Classification" lists all of the diagnostic categories and diagnoses with their appropriate codes and page references. This provides a visual overview of the clustering of the disorders according to diagnostic category and the appropriate code numbers that are often required for reimbursement. The chapter "Multiaxial Assessment" provides a detailed explanation of how to use the different axes to assess an individual's clinical presentation, which emphasizes the underlying biopsychosocial approach of the *DSM*. In most treatment settings, a multiaxial assessment is required. The concluding statements address how to diagnose individuals using a nonaxial format.

Organization of the Diagnostic Category Chapters

The core and most essential parts of the *DSM-IV-TR* for the clinician are the diagnostic category chapters; these contain the information for specific disorders. Each chapter is organized into nine subsections. As the organization of the *DSM-IV-TR* is not uniform, the diagnostic categories may omit certain of these sections if there is no information available. The introduction to the chapter describes the general class of the disorders and reviews common shared features. For some disorders, such as mood and anxiety disorders, there is a features section on the clinical presentation of clusters of signs and symptoms.

The section entitled "Diagnostic Features" includes a more detailed description of the symptoms and signs that are listed in the diagnostic criteria. Here tips for diagnosis, the definition of terms, and illustrative examples are provided. The "Subtypes and/or Specifiers" section describes relevant specifiers and instructs the clinician to "specify if" they are present and code this information on the fifth digit of the diagnostic code. The coding of the disorder is reviewed in the "Recording Procedures" section, which includes the numerical code, the *DSM-IV-TR* name, and the *International Classification of Diseases* 9th edition Clinical Modification (*ICD-9* CM) codes. Most *DSM-IV-TR* disorders get a four-digit code. A fifth digit is added for greater specificity to indicate subtypes or the severity or course of the disorder (American Psychiatric Association, 2000b).

In terms of your developing skills as a diagnostician, crucial information is presented in the section called "Associated Features and Disorders." Here the clinical features that are commonly associated with the disorders but that are not essential or necessary for a diagnosis are reviewed. The information is organized into three clusters: associated descriptive features and mental disorders, associated laboratory findings, and associated physical examination findings and GMCs. The first cluster may include signs, symptoms, and frequent comorbidity considerations, other disorders that have precedence or that can co-occur or follow the disorder, and predisposing factors. When applicable, the complications or untoward effects of the disorder, for example, hopelessness or suicide, are also noted. The associated laboratory findings section discusses diagnostic or research findings associated with complications of the disorder, for example, abnormal elevations. For the categories of mental retardation and learning disorders, specific required diagnostic testing is identified here. The associated physical examination findings and GMCs section provides information on medical conditions that are implicated in the cause of the disorder, that may contribute to the disorder's symptoms, or that are complications of the disorder (American Psychiatric Association, 2000b). These conditions are regarded as significant associated features of the disorder but are not essential for a diagnosis, for example, sleep EEG abnormalities or transient tachycardia.

The section "Specific Culture, Age and Gender Features" provides information about the impact of these factors on the individual's clinical presentation, including age of onset and variations associated with different developmental stages. When available, the "Prevalence" section has information on how frequently the disorder is seen in the community or a variety of clinical settings. It includes the incidence (number of new cases), point prevalence (proportion of individuals in the population who have the disorder at a specific time), and lifetime prevalence (all individuals who have ever had the disorder in their lifetime; American Psychiatric Association, 2000b). This information is very helpful when considering the frequencies of disorders at a given point for different clinical settings. Most of this information has been accumulated from the large-scale epidemiological studies of the 1980s, the Epidemiological Catchment Area Study, the National Comorbidity Study, and the National Household Drug Survey (First et al., 2004)

The "Clinical Course" section provides information on the typical lifetime presentation of the disorder and how it evolves. The typical age, mode of onset, if it was insidious or abrupt, the nature of the disorder if it is episodic or continuous, and whether it is characterized by single or recurrent episodes are all discussed. The typical length or duration of the illness and its progression or trend over time is described (whether it stabilizes, improves, or worsens). For some diagnostic categories this information is presented graphically, as in mood and substance-related disorders. The "Familial Pattern" section includes data on the frequency of disorders in first-degree relatives as compared to the general population. Data from genetic research (twin and adoption studies) on the heritability of the disorder and information on disorders that tend to occur in family members are also presented when available. The final section, "Differential Diagnosis," provides very useful tips on diagnostic differentiation and identifies ways to distinguish among disorders with similar presentation. This section, in combination with the earlier mentioned diagnostic exclusion criteria and decision tree information, are essential aids for the clinician to use in differential diagnosis.

Appendixes

Finally, the manual includes 11 appendixes that address a range of issues. "Appendix A: Decision Trees for Differential Diagnosis" reflects the *DSM*'s earlier approach to diagnostic hierarchies and provides diagnostic decision trees for six disorders based on presenting symptomatology (American Psychiatric Association, 2000b). "Appendix B: Criteria Sets and Axes Provided for Further Study" includes diagnostic criteria that were suggested for inclusion, alternative descriptors for Schizophrenia and Dysthymic Disorder, and three additional scales to assess level of functioning. "Appendix C: Glossary of Technical Terms" is an invaluable aid to understanding the terminology of the *DSM* system. Also worth noting is "Appendix I: Outline for Cultural Formulations and Glossary of Culture-Bound Syndromes," which provides a framework for considering the role of cultural factors in diagnostic formulation and a synopsis of descriptors of syndromes that occur in particular cultures. The remaining Appendixes (D–H, J, and K) focus on highlights of the revisions and the diagnostic codes of the *DSM-IV-TR* and *ICD-10.*

MULTIAXIAL DIAGNOSIS

Multiaxial diagnosis attempts to describe an individual in several areas or domains that are assumed to be of high clinical relevance, thus dealing more effectively with the complexity of clinical conditions. By considering factors in addition to psychiatric disorders, more specific and appropriate treatment recommendations may be made that will fully address the individual's needs (Mezzich & Schmolke, 1995). The first multiaxial system (Essen-Moller & Wohlfahrt, 1947) included separate axes for symptoms and etiology (Blashfield & Livesley, 1999; Kastrup, 2002). Over time this model was adapted to include severity, course, and time frame as separate axes. The adoption of a multiaxial system by *DSM* enables clinicians to evaluate not just current acute problems, but also underlying personality characteristics, relevant medical or physical conditions, psychosocial stressors, and the client's highest level of functioning (Blashfield & Livesley, 1999). The choice of axes was based on the consensus of the experts and the premise that the individual's clinical psychiatric status could be more accurately and completely reported along several dimensions thought to be important in treatment planning and predicting outcome (First et al., 2004). The final choice of the number of axes was somewhat arbitrary but reflected a desire to make the system utilitarian, but not too cumbersome (LaBruzza & Mendez-Villarrubia, 1997). The first three axes relate to diagnostic issues, and the last two relate to psychosocial stressors and level of functioning (see Table 3.2). The use of the multiaxial format is optional; however, most agencies and practitioners who use the *DSM* use it.

Axis I

All psychiatric disorders, with the exclusion of Mental Retardation and personality disorders, are coded on Axis I. The 16 clinical disorders on Axis I are broad categories of clinical syndromes organized around essential clinical features or defining characteristics using a prototype model. Exceptions are the disorders of childhood, where the unifying concept is the age of onset, and adjustment disorders, where the commonality is the presence of trauma. The term *clinical disorders* is a misnomer as the disorders on Axis II and III are also considered clinical disorders (First et al., 2004).

Other conditions that may be a focus of clinical attention (see Table 3.3) do not necessarily involve a mental disorder but are conditions that warrant diagnosis or treatment, as their presence may interfere with treatment, constitute additional risks, or exacerbate symptoms (American Psychiatric Association, 2000b) These conditions are a range of problems, including psychological factors affecting medical condition, medication-induced disorders (such as neuroleptic-induced tardive dyskinesia), and a group of problems often referred to as V codes. The diagnostic code number for these conditions is preceded by the letter *V* and includes such issues as relational problems and problems related to abuse or neglect. Perpetrators and victims of abuse are identified using different code numbers, as in the relational unit within which the abuse occurred. Additional V codes include maladaptive behaviors or coping problems such as noncompliance with treatment, malingering, adult antisocial behavior, bereavement, and occupational and acculturation problems. If the conditions represent psychosocial and environmental problems, they are also coded on Axis IV. Additional conditions coded on Axis I include

Table 3.2   *DSM-IV-TR* multiaxial assessment

Axis I Clinical Disorders (15 Disorders)
Disorders Usually First Diagnosed in Infancy, Childhood, or Adolescence
Delirium, Dementia, and Amnestic and Other Cognitive Disorders
Mental Disorders Due to a GMC Not Elsewhere Classified
Substance-Related Disorders
Schizophrenia and Other Psychotic Disorders
Mood Disorders
Anxiety Disorders
Somatoform Disorders
Factitious Disorders
Dissociative Disorders
Sexual and Gender Identity Disorders
Eating Disorders
Sleep Disorders
Impulse-Control Disorders Not Elsewhere Classified
Adjustment Disorders

Other Conditions That May Be a Focus of Clinical Attention (13 Conditions)

Axis II Personality Disorders (10 Disorders)
Paranoid, Schizoid, Schizotypal, Antisocial, Borderline, Histrionic, Narcissistic, Avoidant, Dependent,
    Obsessive-Compulsive
Mental Retardation
Borderline Intellectual Functioning
Maladaptive Personality Traits
Defense Mechanisms

Axis III General Medical Conditions

Axis IV Psychosocial and Environmental Problems
Problems with primary support group
Problems related to social environment
Educational problems
Occupational problems
Housing problems
Economic problems
Problems with access to health care service
Problems related to interaction with the legal system/crime
Other psychosocial and environmental problems

Axis V Global Assessment of Functioning (GAF) (0–100)
Optional scales: Defensive Functioning Scale (DFS)
                 Global Assessment of Relational Functioning Scale (GARF)
                 Social and Occupational Functioning Assessment Scale (SOFAS)

Adapted with permission from the *Diagnostic and Statistical Manual of Mental Disorders,* fourth Edition, Text Revision (Copyright 2000). American Psychiatric Association.

Table 3.3   Other conditions that may be a focus of clinical attention

Psychological Factors Affecting GMC	Medication-Induced Movement Disorders
Mental disorder	Neuroleptic-induced parkinsonism
Psychological symptoms	Neuroleptic malignant syndrome
Personality traits or coping style	Neuroleptic-induced acute dystonia
Maladaptive health behaviors	Neuroleptic-induced acute akathisia
Stress-related physiological response	Neuroleptic-induced tardive dyskinesia
Other or unspecified factors	Medication-induced postural tremor
Other Medication-Induced Disorder	Medication-induced movement disorder NOS
Adverse effects of medication NOS	

V Codes

Relational Problems	Problems Related to Abuse or Neglect
Related to a mental disorder or GMC	Physical abuse of a child
Parent-child	Sexual abuse of a child
Partner	Neglect of a child
Sibling	Physical abuse of adult
Relational problem NOS	Sexual abuse of adult

Additional Conditions That May Be a Focus of Clinical Attention

Noncompliance with treatment	Academic problem
Malingering	Occupational problem
Adult antisocial behavior	Identity problem
Child or adolescent antisocial behavior	Religious or spiritual problem
Borderline intellectual functioning	Acculturation problem
Age-related cognitive decline	Phase of life problem
Bereavement	

Adapted with permission from *Diagnostic and Statistical Manual of Mental Disorders,* fourth edition, revised, by American Psychiatric Association, 2000b, Washington, DC: Author.

unspecified mental disorder (nonpsychotic), no diagnosis or condition on Axis I, and diagnosis or condition deferred on Axis I. Typically these codes are used to indicate diagnostic uncertainty or incomplete information.

Axis II

Personality disorders (10 in all), Mental Retardation, maladaptive personality features, defense mechanisms, and borderline intellectual functioning are all placed on Axis II. According to First and colleagues (2004), the rationale for placing these disorders on Axis II is not based on any compelling logic. Rather, the purpose is pragmatic or functional in ensuring that consideration is given to disorders that otherwise may be overlooked or ignored given the florid presentation of Axis I psychopathology (Morrison, 1995a,b; M. T. Shea & Yen, 2003). These disorders often do not have clear onsets and tend to be lifelong problems. Borderline intellectual functioning is the only disorder in the category of other conditions that may be a focus of clinical attention that is coded on Axis II. Problematic personality features such as maladaptive personality traits and habitual defense mechanisms can also be listed here but are not assigned a diagnostic code (American Psychiatric Association, 2000b).

Traditionally, Axis I disorders have been described as more acute, episodic, florid, variable in duration, and responsive to treatment and are more often associated with the transient features of illness. In contrast, personality disorders are often conceptualized as being consistent, chronic, and resistant to treatment (Maxmen & Ward, 1995; M. T. Shea & Yen, 2003). Current longitudinal studies on the temporal stability of Axis I versus Axis II disorders question these assumptions and conclude that stability is not meaningful as an interaxis discriminator and that the distinction between the two axes may be functional rather than reflecting inherent differences or natural groupings (M. T. Shea & Yen, 2003). L. A. Clark and colleagues (1995) reviewed the separation of Axis I and Axis II disorders and concluded that the division exists for pragmatic rather than scientific reasons and that the primary function for placement of the disorders is to facilitate recall. Additional codes on Axis II include no diagnosis or condition on Axis II and diagnosis or condition deferred on Axis II. More than one diagnosis can be coded on Axis II; the clinician identifies the principal diagnosis or reason for the visit in parentheses.

Axis III

Medical conditions that relate to psychiatric disorders in terms of etiology, prognosis, relevance to treatment, and understanding the individual's functioning are coded on Axis III, using *ICD-9* CM codes (Mezzich & Schmolke, 1995). Individuals with severe psychiatric disorders have been found to have a higher incidence of medical illness than the general population (LaBruzza & Mendez-Villarrubia, 1997). According to the *DSM-IV-TR,* these conditions can impact Axis I disorders in several ways. They may be directly related to the cause of an Axis I condition, for example, Delirium Due to Hypoglycemia (the Delirium is coded on Axis I as Delirium Due to a General Medical Condition, and the Hypoglycemia on Axis III). An Axis I condition may develop as a psychological response to the medical illness, for example, depression following the diagnosis of AIDS. The illness may have implications for prognosis and treatment in that it may need ongoing monitoring or influence the choice of psychiatric medication (American Psychiatric Association, 2000b). Thus Axis III includes concurrent medical conditions, current medical problems, and any physical illnesses that have a direct bearing on Axis I and Axis II disorders. Clinicians may also use this axis to note significant physical symptoms or symptoms that need further evaluation. The source of the information, for example, client report, referring physician, and medical records, is noted in parentheses following the condition.

Axis IV

Psychosocial and environmental problems that impact the diagnosis, treatment, and prognosis of Axis I and Axis II disorders are coded on Axis IV (Fauman, 2002; First et al., 2004). This includes all clinically significant, relevant, positive (eustress), and negative (distress) stressors that have been present during the preceding year. If the problem occurred prior to this time and still impacts the clinical disorder or has become a focus of attention, it will also be noted here. Problems or stressors that have become a focus of clinical attention are coded on Axis I and Axis IV. Psychosocial stressors and environmental problems can act as a magnifier, a consequence, a trigger, or a cause of clinical disorders (Othmer & Othmer, 2002). The determination of the role of the stressor involves skill as a diagnostician. The *DSM-IV-TR* lists nine categories of psychosocial and environmental problems, including educational problems and problems accessing health care services (see Table 3.2). The categories are self-explanatory, and detailed description and specific examples are provided. With multiple problems, the clinician determines and lists all those that are relevant to the current clinical presentation.

Axis V

Axis V allows the clinician to assess the individual's overall level of functioning, excluding any impairment due to physical limitations or environmental problems, using a single rating scale (the Global Assessment of Functioning Scale [GAF]). The GAF evaluates the individual's psychological, social, and occupational functioning on a continuum from 1 to 100 (Fauman, 2002; First et al., 2004). Administration of the scale requires clinical judgment and experience; the manual provides a 4-step method to ensure that no element is omitted from consideration (American Psychiatric Association, 2000b). The GAF is divided into ten 10-point segments describing different levels of symptom severity and functioning. Individuals' rating is determined if either their level of functioning or their symptom severity falls within the range. If different criteria are met, the lowest level is assigned. A score of 0 is given if the clinician has inadequate information. A score of 1 to 10 is indicative of serious suicidal acts or the inability to maintain even minimal hygiene. In contrast, a score of 91 to 100 represents superior functioning or the absence of any significant impairment (American Psychiatric Association, 2000b). The time frame used (current, past week, past year, etc.) depends on the clinical setting and on the reason for the assessment. The GAF can be administered reliably after minimal training and significantly relates to ratings of symptoms and social behavior on follow-up (Startup, Jackson, & Bendix, 2002). The GAF is also useful for treatment planning and measuring changes in current overall functioning in global terms. In contrast to its predecessors, which simply rated overall stressor severity on Axis V, the *DSM-IV-TR* has three additional optional scales (*DSM-IV-TR* Appendix B) that assess level of functioning.

   The use of multiaxial assessment has been criticized for being cumbersome and creating a distinction between Axis I and Axis II that may be made more pronounced than exists in reality (L. A. Clark et al., 1995). Yet the recognition of the impact of medical factors, psychosocial stressors, and level of impairment of functioning allows for a more comprehensive evaluation of the individual. There are concerns that the differentiation of Axis I from Axis II and from Axis III conditions may contribute to differential reimbursement from insurance companies. The placement of some disorders, particularly neurological conditions (Rett's Disorder) and personality disorders (Schizotypal), continues to be a focus of debate (First et al., 2004).

DETERMINING A DIAGNOSIS

Determining a diagnosis is a clinical process that is strongly influenced by the personal contact between the clinician and the individual (Alarcon, 1995; Othmer & Othmer,

2002). The establishment and maintenance of adequate rapport is crucial. Ideally, information should be obtained from several sources: the individual, collateral contacts, and records (Hersen & Turner, 2003). Not all information and informants are equally reliable, and it is important to assess the quality of the gathered information. Current information is considered more accurate than retrospectively recalled details (Morrison, 1995b). As clients may lack insight or experience difficulty expressing their feelings, observable signs are regarded as more reliable than symptoms or subjective reports. Objective data may be more valid than intuitive or interpretative information, and data gathered during crises may be susceptible to distortions. For some individuals, collateral contacts may be more informative than recalled memories, and prior records can help reconstruct a diagnosis and indicate responsiveness to treatment and effectiveness of medications (Maxmen & Ward, 1995; Othmer & Othmer, 2002).

Having evaluated the accuracy and reliability of the individual's data in light of additional information from others and prior records, you then need to identify the diagnostic clues, distinctive features, and prominent symptom clusters in the individual's clinical presentation. Mezzich and Schmolke (1995) describe diagnostic conceptualization as an evolving informational statement about the patient's condition, which progressively increases the clinician's level of understanding and, though it is never perfect, is continually susceptible to improvement. An ideal diagnosis should be broad, precise, clear, reliable, valid, and based on well-defined criteria (Alarcon, 1995). The importance of an accurate diagnosis cannot be overstated: Diagnostic errors are often difficult to reverse and can result in delays in treatment and inappropriate interventions (Morrison, 1995b).

During the intake interview, diagnostic clues can be identified from the individual's report of discomfort or impairment, the chief complaint, and observed clinical signs or reported symptoms (Othmer & Othmer, 2002). The chief complaint can include patterns of maladjusted behavior, stressors, and interpersonal conflicts. According to Ahrens and Stieglitz (1998), when making a diagnosis it is important for clinicians to base their assessment on the number of symptoms and on information about the course of the disorder and etiology. Thus, it is crucial to determine how long the key features have been present, their severity, the abruptness of onset, the presence of factors that impact prognosis, the level of distress or clinical impairment, and any psychiatric or family history. The diagnostic interview can be used to identify the anatomy of clinical disorders, namely, the presence and severity of essential (core) symptoms and associated features (Othmer & Othmer, 2002). Essential or key symptoms are necessary but not sufficient for a diagnosis of a disorder, and associated features are specific signs and symptoms that occur only if specific essential symptoms are present (American Psychiatric Association, 2000b). In most cases, classification is based on a cross-sectional assessment of the diagnostic clues, which the clinician then matches to the key or essential features of a specific *DSM-IV-TR* diagnostic category.

In terms of diagnostic conceptualization, several different models have been proposed. Othmer and Othmer (2002) describe a model for gathering relevant information and making a diagnostic decision, which includes collecting the data, checking the diagnostic criteria, assigning a diagnosis using a multiaxial format, and assessing prognosis. The *DSM-IV-TR* also provides general guidelines for diagnostic decision making (American Psychiatric Association, 2000b). A. Frances and Ross (2001) describe a more detailed approach, arguing that no one clinical presentation is cut-and-dried, and diagnostic boundary cases and multiple diagnoses are common. They outline six practical, logical, and well-organized steps for differential diagnosis:

Step 1: Rule out the possibility of a substance-related etiology.

Step 2: Evaluate the presence of a GMC etiology.

Step 3: Determine the specific primary disorder.

Step 4: Consider if an adjustment or NOS disorder is warranted.

Step 5: Assess the level of impairment or distress.

Step 6: Consider and exclude the presence of a factitious disorder or malingering.

Variations of these steps have been widely used by others in the field (First et al., 2002; A. Frances & Ross, 2001; Maxmen & Ward, 1995). These models have been combined into a more specific integrated approach to differential diagnosis and multiaxial assessment (see Table 3.4).

In this model the determination of a diagnosis involves seven fundamental steps, which can be conceptualized as a series of basic questions that guide decision making: Is the disorder caused by a general medical condition? Is it due to a substance? Are there any cultural, diversity or developmental considerations? What are the defining key or essential features of the client's clinical presentation, and which *DSM-IV-TR* diagnostic categories do they match? Which diagnostic criteria best fit the diagnostic clues? Are there any coexisting conditions? And finally, what is the level of impairment or distress?

Step 1: Consider General Medical or Physical Causes

The first step is a difficult discrimination to make and involves determining whether the symptoms are due to a GMC (First & Tasman, 2004). Many individuals with a GMC develop psychiatric symptoms as a complication of their illness, and individuals with psychiatric disorders often have an underlying GMC. Almost any psychiatric presentation can be caused by a GMC, and physical disorders may complicate or mimic psychiatric disorders (First et al., 2004; Othmer & Othmer, 2002). Medical conditions that present with psychiatric symptoms are summarized in Table 3.5. In addition, the GMC can cause psychiatric symptoms through direct physiological effects on the central nervous system (CNS) or result in psychological reactions such as anxiety. Neurological disorders may present with psychiatric symptoms, for example, temporal lobe epilepsy or lupus. Determining the cause of the psychiatric disorder can be complicated by the fact that the symptoms might be identical, for example, fatigue or weight loss (A. Frances & Ross, 2001).

The general diagnostic rule is to consider a GMC if there is an atypical presentation of the psychiatric features, for example, age of onset or the associated features are unusual, symptoms appear suddenly or are disproportionately severe, or if a GMC has been listed at the outset (A. Frances & Ross, 2001). The *DSM-IV-TR* recommends looking for evidence of the role of a GMC in the individual's history, physical examination, and any laboratory tests that may have been conducted (American Psychiatric Association, 2000b). First, the clinician needs to establish that an individual has a GMC that could account for the observed psychiatric symptoms and determine whether the relationship is reasonably well established in the medical literature (First et al., 2002). Mood disturbance caused by hypothyroidism (GMC) is well documented. In contrast, peptic ulcer is not

Table 3.4   Seven steps to diagnosis

Step 1—Consider General Medical or Physical Condition

Determine whether there is a general medical or physical condition that could account for observed psychiatric symptoms.

Review if the relationship is reasonably well established in the medical literature.

Consider if there is a close temporal relationship between the course of the psychiatric symptoms and the GMC.

Step 2—Consider Substance-Induced or -Related Disorder

Determine whether the psychiatric symptoms occur only with substance use.

Determine whether there is a close temporal relationship between the substance use and psychiatric symptoms.

Evaluate the likelihood that the pattern of abuse causes the psychiatric symptoms.

Consider whether the symptoms may be better accounted for by a disorder that is not substance-related.

Step 3—Consider Cultural and Developmental Factors

Review relevant *DSM* text, including Appendix I.

Consider using a cultural formulation.

Review information on developmental stages.

Use age-specific measures and diagnostic criteria.

Step 4—Determine Axis I and/or Axis II Disorders

Identify diagnostic clues.

Compare diagnostic clues to key or essential features.

Determine which diagnostic categories are relevant.

Review diagnostic criteria.

Consider exclusion criteria.

Outline a decision tree.

Engage in diagnostic decision making.

Step 5—Resolve Diagnostic Uncertainty

Gather additional specific information.

Consider NOS categories.

Examine unspecified mental disorder (nonpsychotic).

Review V codes and disorders under further study (see Appendix B).

Assess diagnosis deferred on Axis I and/or Axis II.

Consider provisional diagnosis (specific disorder).

Evaluate no diagnosis on Axis I or Axis II.

Consider malingering.

Step 6—Consider Comorbidity and Associated Features[*]

Determine whether comorbid conditions cause or predispose the individual to either diagnosis.

Determine whether an independent underlying condition may cause or predispose the individual to either or both conditions.

Determine whether the comorbid conditions are a complex unified syndrome that is artificially split by the diagnostic system.

Determine whether the relationship between the comorbid conditions is artificially enhanced by definitional overlap.

Consider if the presence of the comorbid conditions is a chance co-occurrence of a high base rate disorder.

Step 7—Assess Level of Distress and/or Impairment

[*]From *DSM-IV-TR: Handbook of Differential Diagnosis,* by M. B. First, A. Frances, and H. A. Pincus, 2002, Washington, DC: American Psychiatric Press. Adapted with permission.

Table 3.5   Medical conditions resembling psychiatric disorders

Psychosis

Adrenal insufficiency, AIDS, brain tumor, cerebrovascular accident, congestive heart failure, Cushing's syndrome, deafness, epilepsy, head trauma, herpes encephalitis, Huntington's disease, hyperthyroidism, hypothyroidism, kidney failure, premenstrual syndrome (PMS), rheumatoid arthritis, sleep apnea, syphilis

Mood Disorders: Major Depressive Disorder, Bipolar Disorder I, and Bipolar Disorder II

Adrenal insufficiency, AIDS, brain tumor, cancer, cerebrovascular accident, congestive heart failure, Cushing's syndrome, diabetes mellitus, epilepsy, fibromyalgia, head trauma, Huntington's disease, hydrocephalus, hyperthyroidism, hypothyroidism, Klinefelter's syndrome, liver failure, Lyme disease, Meniere's syndrome, menopause, migraines, multiple sclerosis, Parkinson's disease, PMS, postoperative states, rheumatoid arthritis, sickle cell disease, sleep apnea, syphilis, systemic lupus erythematosus, Wilson's disease

Anxiety Disorders

Generalized Anxiety Disorder: Adrenal insufficiency, AIDS, cancer, cardiac arrhythmia, cerebrovascular accident, congestive heart failure, Cushing's syndrome, deafness, diabetes mellitus, fibromyalgia, head trauma, herpes encephalitis, hyperthyroidism, Lyme disease, menopause, mitral valve prolapse, Parkinson's disease, PMS, pneumonia, postoperative states, sleep apnea, thiamine deficiency

Panic Attacks/Disorder: Cancer, congestive heart failure, diabetes mellitus, fibromyalgia, hyperthyroidism, Lyme disease, pneumonia

Obsessive-Compulsive Disorder: Hypoparathyroidism, Lyme disease
Post-traumatic Stress Disorder: Cancer

considered to be a well-established cause of depression. Second, it needs to be determined whether there is a close temporal relationship between the course of the psychiatric symptoms and the course of the GMC. Or does the onset of the symptoms follow the onset of the medical condition and wax and wane with the severity of the medical condition? A temporal relationship is not always a good indicator of etiology as psychiatric symptoms may be the first observable signs of a GMC, as in some cases of Parkinson's disorder depression is often the first indicator. Psychiatric symptoms can also be a sign of undetected medical disorders (First et al., 2004). Third, it is important to evaluate if there is a reasonable alternative explanation; for example, did the individual have a history of depression prior to the medical condition? Family psychiatric history can also be used to confirm a psychiatric diagnosis and to predict the course of the disorder in a young patient as well as an individual's response to treatment (Hersen & Turner, 2003; Othmer & Othmer, 2002).

For older adults presenting with psychiatric symptoms, you need to consider the role of a GMC when there is no personal or family history of psychiatric disorders. If the symptoms occur in unusual combinations, with an unexpected course, or the onset is late for that particular disorder, also consider a GMC. It is helpful to assess whether the individual's symptoms are temporally related to beginning a new medication and cease with the discontinuation of medication. For older adults medication side effects may be mistaken and misdiagnosed for symptoms of a psychiatric disorder (Hersen & Turner, 2003; Othmer & Othmer, 2002).

Step 2: Consider Substance-Induced or -Related Disorder

According to First and colleagues (2002), the single most common diagnostic error made in clinical practice is to miss a substance etiology (see Table 3.6). Almost any presentation of psychiatric symptoms can be caused by substance use, which can also exacerbate symptoms of a preexisting mental disorder and complicate treatment and is a common comorbid condition (First et al., 2002). The first task is to determine if the individual has been or is currently using a substance (for specific assessment techniques, see Chapter 8, "Substance-Related Disorders"). The clinician should be alert for physical signs of intoxication (slurred or constricted speech or dilated pupils). The individual's chart may

Table 3.6   Diagnostic tips for general medical conditions or substance-related disorders

Consider general medical condition or substance-related disorder if:
   Atypical presentation
   GMC listed at intake
   Sudden atypical onset
   Trauma or toxins exposure noted
   Unusual associated features
   History of substance abuse
   Disproportionately severe symptoms
   Physical examination or laboratory results

Possible relationship:
   Determine if GMC/SR causes the psychiatric symptoms by a direct physiological effect on the brain.
   Assess if GMC/SR causes psychiatric symptoms through a psychological mechanism.
   Consider if medication taken for GMC causes psychiatric symptoms.
   Evaluate if psychiatric symptoms cause or adversely affect GMC.
   Examine if psychiatric symptoms and GMC/SR are coincidental or independent.
   Determine the nature of the temporal relationship.

If substance-induced or -related:
   Identify the nature, amount, and pattern of abuse.
   Are the symptoms consistent with self-medicating by substance use?
   Evaluate if the substance use is the consequence of the symptoms or an associated feature.
   Review if the symptoms are due to medications, exposure to toxins, or from an exogenous psychoactive substance that is exerting direct effect on CNS.

Indicators that symptoms may not be GMC, substance-induced, or substance-related:
   Negative laboratory or medical test results.
   Family history positive for psychiatric symptoms.
   Psychiatric symptoms preceded the onset of substance or medication use.
   Psychiatric symptoms occur in the absence of any identifiable substances.
   Symptoms persist after cessation of acute withdrawal or severe intoxication.
   Psychiatric symptoms excessive for the type, duration, or amount of substance used.
   Other evidence suggests independent nonsubstance-related disorder.
   Psychological assessment results suggest the role of other factors or disorders.

Source: From *DSM-IV-TR: Handbook of Differential Diagnosis,* by M. B. First, A. Frances, and H. A. Pincus, 2002, Washington, DC: American Psychiatric Press. Adapted with permission.

indicate that a urine or toxicology screen has been administered. You also need to consider whether the psychiatric disorder might be medication- or toxin-induced, which, although less common forms of SR disorders, are often overlooked and misdiagnosed (First et al., 2002). Critical diagnostic information to gather includes the nature, amount, and duration of the substance use and the type of response to the substance (First et al., 2004). Also consider whether the substance is causing the symptoms or the drug use is a consequence of a primary psychiatric disorder, as with a self-medicating psychotic individual, or whether both conditions are unrelated or caused by a third disorder (First et al., 2002; A. Frances & Ross, 2001). Some of these issues may be addressed by taking a careful history and conducting laboratory tests and a physical examination.

Establishing whether there is a close temporal relationship between the substance use and the psychiatric symptoms is critical (First et al., 2004). However, this may be difficult to determine, as the drug use and clinical symptoms may overlap. Also, the initial onset of psychiatric problems and substance abuse is often around the same time in adolescence. If the substance abuse and psychiatric conditions are unrelated, a detailed history should indicate nonoverlapping episodes of psychiatric symptoms and episodes of substance abuse. Individuals' retrospective recall of this information may be unreliable, especially if they are still using. Interviewing significant others who know the client well may clarify these issues and what the person is like when he or she is not using. Consulting past medical records can help determine if there were episodes of psychiatric symptoms without concomitant substance abuse. If the pattern of substance use could have resulted in the symptoms seen and if the symptoms persist beyond periods of intoxication and withdrawal, it may suggest that the psychopathology is not primarily due to substance use (First et al., 2004; First & Tasmen, 2005). The *DSM-IV-TR* suggests that psychiatric symptoms due to substances are likely to remit within 4 weeks of acute intoxication, withdrawal, or medication use (American Psychiatric Association, 2000b). This guideline is controversial, and many clinicians instead consider a 6- to 8-week window to make this determination. Two exceptions are Substance-Induced Dementia and Substance-Induced Amnestic Disorder, which often persist long after the acute effects because of permanent CNS damage (First et al., 2002).

Finally, if there is no evidence in the literature of a relationship between the substance use and the psychiatric symptoms, the clinician needs to consider alternative explanations. These may include the presence of an independent nonsubstance-related disorder, for example, a history of recurrent depressive episodes with no associated drug use (First et al., 2002, 2004).

Step 3: Consider Cultural and Developmental Factors

The clinician needs to be mindful of cultural, developmental, and diversity considerations that influence the expression or diagnosis of clinical symptoms. Culture impacts diagnostic decision making through variations in clinical presentation and the manner in which the client relates to the mental health practitioner. When the clinician and the client are from different cultures, misdiagnosis and over- and underestimation or neglect of psychopathology are potential problems. When both the clinician and the client are from the same culture, the clinician may be susceptible to a cultural blind spot and overlook culture as a consideration (Alarcon, 1995). Throughout the world, clinical presentations that conform to *DSM-IV-TR* categories have been identified (Zuckerman, 1999). Within the *DSM-IV-TR* text there is information on specific culture, age, and gender features for each diagnostic category describing differences in clinical presentation (Twemlow, 1995). In addition, Appendix I is a glossary of culture-bound syndromes, terms, and idioms of distress that do not conform to *DSM* diagnoses. These terms can be clustered into two broad groupings: brief acute psychotic-like reactions (e.g., bilis, amok) and somatoform-like syndromes (e.g., brain fog). In all, there are 25 conditions described that can be assigned the NOS diagnostic category (American Psychiatric Association, 2000b).

One of the major innovations of *DSM-IV* was the introduction of a cultural formulation or ideographic statement to reflect individuals' personal perspective on their experience and their cultural reference group (Mezzich et al., 2001). This formulation involves five steps (see Table 3.7) and complements the multiaxial assessment (Mezzich & Schmolke, 1995).

Table 3.7   Cultural formulation

1. Cultural Identity of the Individual
Includes information on the individual's ethnic or cultural reference group. For immigrants, ethnic minorities, and refugees, the level of acculturation, specifically the degree of involvement with culture of origin and host culture, is recorded. The individual's language usage, abilities, and preferences are also noted.

2. Cultural Explanations of the Individual's Illness
Predominant idioms of distress used by the individual to express symptoms or obtain social support (e.g., "nerves") are identified. The meaning and perceived severity of the individual's symptoms are noted in comparison to the cultural reference group. Familial and community explanations and perceived causes of the illness are described. It is helpful to be familiar with culture-bound syndromes that might be applicable (see the Glossary of Culture-Bound Syndromes, Appendix I). The individual's current and past experiences with professional and popular sources of care are reviewed.

3. Cultural Factors Related to Psychosocial Environment and Levels of Functioning
Culturally relevant interpretations of social stresses, including stresses in the family, kin, or local community are considered. Culturally relevant health providers or social supports (e.g., shaman) are also described. The role of religion or spirituality and the supportive role of kin and religious networks are also noted. The individual's level of functioning and disability is reviewed in the cultural context.

4. Cultural Elements of the Relationship between the Individual and the Clinician
Differences in the culture and social status of the individual and the clinician are recorded, specifically, how cultural factors affect the individual-clinician relationship in terms of diagnosis and treatment. This includes but is not limited to language or idiomatic differences that make communication difficult, rapport issues, differences affecting the individual's level of and willingness to disclose, and the identification of normal versus pathological symptomatology.

5. Overall Cultural Assessment for Diagnosis and Care
This is the conclusion of the cultural formulation and should include a discussion of how the cultural considerations impact the individual's diagnosis and care.

Adapted with permission from *Diagnostic and Statistical Manual of Mental Disorders,* fourth edition, revised, by American Psychiatric Association, 2000b, Washington, DC: Author.

In diagnosing children, developmental issues need to be considered as well as the categories within the disorders of childhood and adolescence. Many of the disorders of childhood involve observations and evidence of impairment in multiple settings, as well as multi-informant assessment. Children can be diagnosed using all of the diagnostic categories in the *DSM-IV-TR,* although their clinical presentation may be different from that of adults and the duration of the illness may be shorter; for example, Dysthymic Disorder requires a 2-year duration for adults and 1 year for children. In the *DSM,* the age considerations section discusses important differences in the clinical presentation at different developmental stages. The assignment of a personality disorder diagnosis to a child or adolescent is strongly discouraged unless there is evidence of a pervasive pattern that is long-standing and unless the symptoms are present in a range of situations. Antisocial Personality Disorder *cannot* be given to anyone under the age of 18 years (American Psychiatric Association, 2000b).

In very young children (0 to 3 years), there is a lack of diagnostic information, and until recently, there has been a hesitancy to label or pathologize a child's behavior (Dunitz et al., 1996; J. Thomas & Clark, 1998). However, with the surge in early intervention programs, particularly for children with developmental delays, there has been a need to assess children at an earlier age. The Zero-to-Three Diagnostic Classification System was introduced in 1994; according to Guedeney and colleagues (2003), it is compatible with *DSM-IV-TR* but places more emphasis on the parent-child relationship.

There are no specific diagnostic criteria for older adults, although significant relevant information is described in the sections for each diagnostic category. Diagnosing older adults tends to be more challenging, as coexisting medical conditions, the side effects of medication, and comorbid conditions often complicate the presentation (Hersen & Turner, 2003). The presence of cognitive problems may also hamper the gathering of diagnostic information from older adults. (See Chapter 7 for specific strategies that are helpful with this group.) A summary of developmental considerations that influence diagnosis across the life span is presented in Table 3.8.

Step 4: Determine Axis I and/or Axis II Diagnoses

To identify the most appropriate diagnosis, it is useful to organize the diagnostic information with the goal of pinpointing the relevant categories for consideration. Knowledge of the key, essential, core, or discriminating features of the major *DSM-IV-TR* categories is critical for this task. According to Maxmen and Ward (1995), the following questions are helpful to consider: Is the clinical presentation indicative of cognitive impairment or psychotic symptoms? Is there grossly impaired reality testing, such as delusions or hallucinations? Is the predominant feature a disturbance of mood? Is the disorder a nonpsychotic neurotic disorder or an ego-dystonic syndrome that can be disabling? Is there irrational anxiety, avoidance behavior, increased arousal, or physical complaints? Several strategies for diagnostic decision making are summarized in Table 3.9.

By comparing the diagnostic information to the prominent symptom clusters, the most relevant *DSM-IV-TR* diagnostic categories can be identified. This information can then be used with the differential diagnosis decision trees (*DSM-IV-TR,* Appendix A) to differentiate between diagnostic categories (A. Frances & Ross, 2001). When determining the diagnosis, it is helpful to be mindful of the guiding principles of parsimony and the

Table 3.8   Developmental or life span considerations

Diagnosis: Children

Conduct parent and child interviews and child and parent-child observations.
Modify interview format to match child's developmental and linguistic levels.
Consider the role of developmental factors and stages.
Obtain a development history; include baby book, home video, etc.
Use multi-informant assessment; include parent and teacher checklists.
Be alert for confidentiality issues and obtain releases.
Conduct multisetting evaluation; use varied levels of structure.
Be alert for diagnostic overlap; use time lines to clarify sequence.
Review disorders of childhood and adolescence.
Consider other disorders; check childhood presentation.
Consider other factors that are the focus of clinical attention.
Be hesitant to assign a personality disorder.

Diagnosis: Adolescents

Interview parents and adolescent separately.
Obtain knowledge of adolescence and developmental issues.
Conduct multi-informant and -setting evaluations.
Consider checklist and self-report measures.
Consider role of developmental factors.
Be alert for underlying learning disorder or cognitive challenges.
Assess for alcohol and substance abuse disorders.
Be alert for diagnostic overlap; use time lines to clarify sequence.
Consider disorders of childhood and adolescence.
Also consider other disorders and other factors that are the focus of clinical attention.
Check other disorders of childhood presentation.
Be hesitant to assign a personality disorder.

Diagnosis: Older Adults

Modify the intake and interview using extended time and several sessions.
Be alert for the impact of cognitive deficits and physical impairments on competence.
Consider the role of medical factors.
Be alert for the impact of medication or side effects.
Be alert for depression masking other issues.
Obtain collateral information.
Consider developmental factors, stressors, life changes, and losses.
Consider cohort effects and comfort with assessment and self-report measures.

hierarchical format and organization of the *DSM-IV-TR*. Thus GMC or SR disorders are considered first, followed by most of the Axis I disorders, then personality disorders, adjustment disorders, other conditions, and finally, the absence of major pathology or no mental disorder (Maxmen & Ward, 1995). A common mistake that novice clinicians make is failing to consider the category of disorders of childhood or adolescence when considering adult clients and vice versa, as adults can present with autism and Attention-Deficit/Hyperactivity Disorder and children can be depressed and psychotic.

Table 3.9   Diagnostic decision making

Between Diagnostic Category Determination
    Identify core symptoms and signs.
    Determine that the symptoms are not due to GMC or SR.
    Review the diagnostic categories' essential features.

Within Diagnostic Category Determination
    Review discriminating features.
    Identify differentiating criteria.
    Consider exclusion criteria.

Diagnostic Differentiation
    List included, excluded, and unexplored diagnoses.
    Review diagnostic and exclusion criteria.
    Consider temporal and severity criteria.
    Outline a decision tree.
    Consider precedence and parsimony.
    Modify lists of diagnoses.
    Consider comorbidity.
    Determine working diagnoses.

Diagnostic Details
    Assign subtype.
    Consider specifiers.
    Note diagnostic code.

Within-Category Diagnostic Differentiation

Once the diagnostic categories have been identified, it is important to review the relevant *DSM-IV-TR* chapters. The introductory text and the sections on diagnostic features, associated features, and differential diagnosis provide invaluable information on clarifying diagnostic decisions. The diagnostic criteria for each disorder represent the core symptoms and signs. Diagnostic definitions of disorders recognize that most patients with the same disorder do not have identical clinical features; they may share certain core features but have different associated symptoms. When reviewing the relevant diagnostic criteria remember to clarify their duration and assess the temporal relation of the symptoms to each other (Othmer & Othmer, 2002). Many disorders have limitations specifying the duration of the symptoms; these, with the exclusion criteria and specifiers, can assist in differentiating and narrowing your diagnostic considerations (Fauman, 2002). If the individual reports sufficient symptoms to meet the diagnostic criteria, then the diagnosis is assigned. Finally, consider whether the reported symptoms and observed signs meet the criteria for more than one disorder (Othmer & Othmer, 2002). Differential diagnosis is the process of choosing the correct diagnosis from conditions with similar features. Once all of the relevant Axis I disorders have been reviewed, consider the presence of Axis II disorders, including personality disorders, Mental Retardation, and borderline intellectual functioning. The diagnoses of Mental Retardation and borderline intellectual functioning are based solely on the measurement of adaptive and cognitive functioning as determined by psychological assessment.

To diagnose a personality disorder, it is necessary to obtain a detailed history and identify diagnostic clues, such as repeated interpersonal conflicts and patterns of maladjustment with a long-standing history (Hersen & Turner, 2003; Morrison, 1995b). Othmer and Othmer (2002) describe lifelong patterns of maladjusted behaviors that are often ego syntonic and impact several areas of functioning, including work, love, and leisure. Observing the way the individual relates and responds in the interview situation is also diagnostic. Specific interview strategies are provided in Chapter 14, "Personality Disorders." The *DSM-IV-TR* cautions the clinician not to diagnosis an Axis II disorder in the midst of a florid Axis I disorder unless there is knowledge of the individual's prior history (American Psychiatric Association, 2000b). If the symptoms occur only during Axis I disorder episodes, then an Axis II disorder should not be considered (American Psychiatric Association, 2000b). The age of onset and course of the disorder may help with this differentiation. Most Axis I disorders appear episodic, with periods of remission or recovery; in contrast, personality disorders are described as having an early onset and being stable and pervasive (American Psychiatric Association, 2000b; Morrison, 1995b). The high rates of comorbidity between personality and Axis I disorders makes this diagnostic differentiation all the more complicated (P. A. Bank & Silk, 2001; Oldham et al., 1995). The use of structured interviews as described in the intake chapter can be particularly helpful with these cases.

Once all the relevant diagnoses have been identified, they can be compiled into a list of included diagnoses (diagnoses for consideration), excluded diagnoses, and unexplored diagnoses (Morrison, 1995 a,b; Othmer & Othmer, 2002). At the onset it is better to be over-inclusive than overexclusive; Morrison (1995b) recommends considering every diagnosis possible, even remote ones. As the included psychiatric diagnoses increase, the number of unexplored diagnoses will decrease. According to Othmer and Othmer, the average patient fulfills criteria for two to three diagnoses during his or her lifetime. The most appropriate diagnosis is the one that best explains all the historical data, all the signs and symptoms, and all the elements of the mental status exam and supports the differential diagnosis (Othmer & Othmer, 2002). If there is uncertainty or a chance that the initial diagnosis may be incorrect, list it as a rule-out consideration. In terms of deciding which diagnoses to include, Morrison (1995b) recommends considering the frequency of the occurrence of disorders in clinical settings. All things being equal, the most common diagnoses for the population served should be at the top of your diagnostic hierarchy (see Table 3.10).

The diagnostic rules of precedence and parsimony should be applied in this decision making (Fauman, 2002). If there is more than one diagnosis, do not assign mutually exclusive diagnoses (check the diagnostic exclusion criteria). Priority is given to the

Table 3.10 Common psychiatric disorders in different settings

Psychiatric Inpatient	Community Outpatient	General/Medical Hospital
Schizophrenia	Major Depressive Disorder	GMC conditions
Major Depressive Disorder	Substance use disorders	Substance use disorders
Bipolar Disorder	Bipolar Disorder	Somatoform disorders
Alcohol Dependence	Schizophrenia	Anxiety disorders
Personality disorders	Somatization	Dementias
Anxiety disorders	Borderline Personality Disorder	Eating disorders

disorder that is present for the longest time (chronology rule). In 80% of cases the individual meets the major diagnostic criteria and the diagnosis is clear-cut and is one on which the majority of clinicians would agree. For the remaining 20% there may be insufficient information or the individual may appear to meet several diagnostic criteria (Morrison, 1995b). Diagnosing these more complex cases involves considerable skill and practice.

Step 5: Resolve Diagnostic Uncertainty

Clinical presentations of psychiatric symptoms vary, and clinicians differ in the amount of information they collect, their use of observation and interpretation, and their application of the diagnostic criteria. They may also selectively seek information to merely confirm an original or initial diagnosis or end the interview before obtaining adequate information (Maxmen & Ward, 1995). There may be a lack of data from other sources or conflicting information, and the clinician's diagnostic decisions may be influenced by halo, primacy, or recency biases. All of these sources of variance combine with difficulties of diagnostic fit to create diagnostic uncertainty (Fauman, 2002). Missing records and the individual's inability to provide sufficient or accurate information can further compound these problems (see Table 3.11). The actual clinical presentation may be atypical or may fluctuate in severity and nature, and it is not unusual for early features of the disorder to be different from the more established forms (Hersen & Turner, 2003). For many individuals, precipitating or aggravating factors are common, further complicating diagnostic differentiation (Maxmen & Ward, 1995). Thus, while some individuals fit the prototype, many vary; some appear to be on the boundary of diagnostic categories while others appear to belong to multiple categories (Morrison, 1995b). Clinical presentations are not as cut-and-dried as the *DSM-IV-TR* criteria would suggest (A. Frances & Ross, 2001). According to Fauman, the three most common types of "diagnostic fit difficulties" are individuals who do not quite fit the criteria, individuals who fulfill the criteria for more than one disorder in the same category, and individuals who have more than one psychiatric disorder.

If the individual's presentation appears to meet most of the criteria (but not the full criteria) or there is a history of a disorder, the clinician can still assign a diagnosis if the signs and symptoms are of sufficient severity (American Psychiatric Association, 2000b). Many of the *DSM-IV-TR* diagnostic criteria are soft and subjective and rely on clinical judgment, with some symptoms being weighed more heavily when the individual does not quite fit or fulfill all the criteria (Fauman, 2002).

For individuals whose clinical presentation fulfills the criteria for more than one disorder in the same category, it is critical to determine if these disorders are mutually exclusive. When the individual has symptoms of more than one psychiatric disorder but does not meet the criteria for any specific disorder, it is important to assess whether the symptoms occur in the context of a disorder from another diagnostic category.

Overall, the best course when dealing with uncertainty is to gather more or very specific information, interview others, or obtain additional history. Information on the length of the illness, the number of symptoms, and the presence of typical and absence of atypical features can be compared directly to the diagnostic criteria and may help to differentiate between disorders (Morrison, 1995b). The use of structured interviews and self-report measures can help in gathering diagnosis-specific information, as can psychological assessment, particularly when clients present with emotional or cognitive challenges that

Table 3.11   Diagnostic uncertainty

Causes
Clinician biases and premature closure of intake interview.
Variations in interviewer skills, style, and application of diagnostic criteria.
Atypical clinical presentation.
Symptoms of multiple diagnoses that fluctuate in severity and nature.
Early and established forms of the disorder differ in presentation.
Clinical presentation does not meet or fit diagnostic criteria.
Precipitating and aggravating factors are common.
Inadequate data, unavailability of records, conflicting and misleading information.

Common Clinical Omissions
Failing to consider alcohol or substance abuse.
Neglecting medical and medication issues.
Omitting the impact of trauma and cognitive disorders.
Ignoring diversity and developmental factors.
Not considering disorders of childhood and adolescence for adults and vice versa.

Strategies
Gather more information and contact collaterals.
Administer assessment measures or request psychological assessment.
Consider the number of symptoms and the length of the illness.
Identify the presence of typical features, and absence of atypical features.
Review the relevant diagnostic exclusion criteria.
Determine the individual's response to treatment.

Diagnosis to Consider
Provisional.
Unspecified mental disorder (nonpsychotic).
V codes.
Diagnosis or condition deferred.

Consider NOS If:
The disorder is phenomenologically similar but subthreshold.
It is a culture-bound syndrome or other condition.
The cause or etiology is uncertain.
It is not clear if disorder is primary SR or secondary to a GMC.
There is insufficient information to make a specific diagnosis.
The available information is incomplete or there is no access to information.

For Comorbid Diagnoses:
Review the exclusion criteria and associated features.
Map a decision tree of diagnoses using the rules of precedence and parsimony.
Do not assign mutually exclusive disorders.
Identify principal diagnoses.

impact their ability to provide information or when they lack insight into the nature of their problems. Remember: The chief complaint reflects only what the individual is willing to disclose. The individual's response to psychiatric medication may also help to clarify the diagnostic picture. However, a given medication may not be specific to an illness but affect several disorders. Some individuals improve with or without medication, and other factors not considered, for example, compliance or family factors, can impact outcome (Morrison, 1995b).

If there is uncertainty, it is important to note this and use the undiagnosed category (or a variant) that allows for identifying the individual as ill without forcing a potentially inaccurate diagnosis. This approach leaves the question of diagnosis open and allows time for additional consideration (Morrison, 1995b). The *DSM-IV-TR* has several ways to indicate uncertainty, with the categories not otherwise specified (NOS), provisional, diagnosis deferred, and no diagnosis (American Psychiatric Association, 2000b).

Not Otherwise Specified

In the *DSM-IV-TR,* each diagnostic category contains at least one NOS diagnosis (57 in all). This is a catchall diagnosis, which ensures at least a common denominator for an individual who exhibits the predominant symptoms of a diagnostic group even if the clinical presentation is subthreshold, atypical, or mixed (American Psychiatric Association, 2000b; Fauman, 2002). The NOS disorders have no diagnostic criteria sets; consequently, individuals who receive this diagnosis are a far more heterogeneous group in regard to symptoms. The NOS category is also used to identify disorders that are specific to a particular culture or subculture, that is, culture-bound syndromes (Appendix I), and for disorders that were not included in the diagnostic categories but are still under consideration (American Psychiatric Association, 2000b). To maintain compatibility with the *ICD-10,* the threshold for the inclusion of new disorders in the *DSM-IV-TR* was high. Many of the excluded disorders are described in the *DSM-IV-TR*'s Appendix B.

The NOS code can also be used to indicate uncertainty about causal factors, for example, if the disorder is substance-induced or due to a GMC. For some individuals, past records may be unavailable, the individual may be unable to provide sufficient information, significant others may be unavailable to interview, or the individual may refuse to consent for the clinician to contact others. In other cases, the available information is incomplete, inconsistent, or contradictory, or the clinician does not have access to relevant information. In all of these situations, the use of the NOS category is warranted (First et al., 2004). When assigning an NOS diagnosis, it is important to explore any associated symptoms and the severity of these symptoms. Atypical or isolated signs and symptoms are often indicators of the presence of a GMC, indicating the need for referral for a medical evaluation.

There is controversy in the field concerning the use of the NOS category. The framers of the *DSM-IV* encourage the use of these categories (American Psychiatric Association, 2000b; First et al., 2004), whereas others feel that the category should be used sparingly, if at all, as it has become an overused "waste basket" with little predictive value for response to treatment or prognosis (Blashfield & Livesley, 1999; Fauman, 2002). However, the use of the NOS category is one way of dealing with diagnostic uncertainty and filling the gaps in the diagnostic system (LaBruzza & Mendez-Villarrubia, 1997).

Provisional Diagnosis

A provisional diagnosis is assigned when there is a strong presumption that the individual will eventually meet the full criteria or the required duration of the illness (American Psychiatric Association, 2000b). Thus, the term provisional can be used when the duration of the disorder is too short or there are not a sufficient number of criteria to make the diagnosis. This may happen when the interviewer is able to assess some symptoms but a lack of cooperation prevents the determination of the full syndrome, or when there is a lack of documentation or adequate information. The term provisional is listed in parentheses following the diagnosis and indicates that the diagnosis needs to be ruled out.

V Codes and Unspecified, Deferred, and No Diagnosis

Specific V codes (refer back to Table 3.3) are used when there is insufficient or inadequate information to know whether or not a presenting problem is attributable to a mental disorder, (e.g., academic problem). When the clinician is certain the individual has a mental disorder that is not characterized by psychosis but the specific type is unclear, the category *unspecified mental disorder* is used. Similarly, *psychotic disorder unspecified* is used if the clinician is certain that the individual has a mental disorder that includes psychotic symptoms. The V codes of *diagnosis deferred* on Axis I or Axis II can be used if there is inadequate information for making or ruling out any of the diagnoses listed.

Establishing the boundary with symptoms that are not sufficiently impairing to warrant a psychiatric diagnosis is an essential step in diagnostic differentials (A. Frances & Ross, 2001; Morrison, 1995b). A *no diagnosis* code can be assigned when an individual presents with clinical symptoms or signs but demonstrates no distress or impairment in functioning. This latter situation may be difficult to assess as many mental disorders are characterized by a lack of insight, for example, substance-related disorders and bipolar manic episode. In such circumstances, it behooves the clinician to do a thorough evaluation of current and past levels of functioning and evaluate how disabling the symptoms are to the individual. Assigning no disorder on Axis I or Axis II is different from deferred diagnosis on Axis I or Axis II. Listed in the Additional Codes section, a no diagnosis code should be considered if the individual presents with signs and symptoms that are not of the severity, frequency, intensity, or nature to warrant a diagnosis or even a deferred diagnosis. In making this decision it is important to consider the differential with an adjustment disorder or the NOS diagnostic category. For a mental disorder to be identified as an adjustment disorder the symptoms must be determined to be a maladaptive response to a psychosocial stressor.

The veracity of the clinical information provided by the individual is also a consideration. If the individual presents with atypical symptomatology, a unique course or onset, and fluctuating symptoms that appear resistant to treatment, and secondary gain is present, then the clinician needs to assess for malingering (A. Frances & Ross, 2001). In these situations it is imperative to obtain additional information from sources other than the client, particularly other treating professionals. It may be that the individual is consciously feigning the symptoms in order to assume the sick role, as in the case of factitious disorders. If the motivation appears to be unconscious, consider the assignment of a conversion disorder or another somatoform disorder (First et al., 2002). These difficult differentials are discussed further in Chapter 12 on the somatoform disorders.

Step 6: Consider Comorbidity and Associated Features

When confronted by a mixed or an atypical clinical presentation, the clinician should consider the presence of comorbidity. Epidemiological studies have consistently found high rates of individuals with a *DSM* disorder having at least one other diagnosis (Faul & Gross, 2006; Langenbucher & Nathan, 2006; Zuckerman, 1999). Community samples of individuals with psychiatric disorders found the majority also had chronic medical conditions, and comorbidity appeared to be the norm (Bassett, Chase, Folestien, & Regier, 1998). Thus an uncomplicated, pure presentation appears to be the exception, with most disorders presenting with high risks of comorbidity and the highest rates occurring for the most severe diagnoses (L. A. Clark et al., 1995; Oldham et al., 1995). In general, individuals with comorbid disorders have a poorer response to treatment, a more complicated and chronic course, higher rates of suicide and suicidal ideation, and a more negative prognosis (Milos, Spindler, Buddeberg, & Crameri, 2003; Reich, 2003).

Although comorbidity appears prevalent, its occurrence is not random. L. A. Clark et al. (1995) propose that there are consistent associations of disorders with one another, and certain diagnoses present with diagnostic affinities. Individuals with an Axis II disorder are at a higher risk for comorbidity than those with an Axis I disorder. Also, there is a significant association between most Axis I disorders and Axis II disorders (Othmer & Othmer, 2002; M. T. Shea & Yen, 2003; Zuckerman, 1999). Within the Axis II personality disorders, comorbidity appears pervasive, with 85% of individuals who are diagnosed with Borderline Personality Disorder meeting the criteria for another personality disorder (Grilo, McGlashan, & Skodol, 2000). It may be that the nature of psychiatric disorders is that they occur in clusters (Jablensky, 1998) and that psychiatric symptoms may mimic multiple syndromes (Preskorn, 1995). Comorbidity may also reflect the natural co-occurrence of one or more disorders that represent the presence of a shared vulnerability in the individual (L. A. Clark et al., 1995; Maxmen & Ward, 1995). Comorbid disorders can also develop secondarily to a complication of the first disorder, for example, depression and substance abuse after Social Phobia (Maxmen & Ward, 1995). Common comorbid conditions are discussed in each of the following clinical chapters.

According to Jablensky (1998), given that *DSM-IV-TR* diagnostic categories are not mutually exclusive, comorbidity may be a product of a diagnostic classification system that fails to discriminate between spurious and true comorbidity. Thus the various presentations of the same disorder are mistaken for independent disorders (spurious comorbidity). Or comorbidity may be an artifact of a diagnostic system that does not preclude multiple category membership and allows two separate diagnoses to be coded for what may be the presentation of the same disorder. Since the abandonment of the diagnostic hierarchical rules, there has been a proliferation of comorbid diagnoses, reflecting an unsatisfactory diagnostic fit for 18% to 22% of cases (L. A. Clark et al., 1995). It has also become common practice to list disorders as comorbid without attempting to use diagnostic hierarchical rules (Jablensky, 1998).

Methodological variables such as the time frame studied (concurrent or lifetime), level of severity of the criteria chosen (the inclusion of subthreshold cases), and the range of disorders considered (Axis I and/or Axis II) all influence the reported rates of comorbidity (L. A. Clark et al., 1995). The diagnostic methods used may also confound the findings, as self-report measures yields higher rates than structured interviews. Comorbidity has been found to vary with the population being studied and the setting of the investigation, and help-seeking behavior may contribute to the higher comorbidity rates in clinical samples (Oldham et al., 1995). Lahey and colleagues (Lahey, Miller, Gordon, & Riley, 1999) note that the higher comorbidity rates in clinical samples may reflect a sampling bias that is not representative of the general population (Berkson's bias) and may contribute to an over-estimation of comorbidity for children with Oppositional Defiant Disorder.

From a diagnostician's perspective, when confronted with comorbidity the first step is to determine the nature of the relationship between the comorbid conditions. This is often difficult to assess. First and colleagues (2002) identified six different ways the comorbid disorders may be related: (1 & 2) Either disorder may cause or predispose the individual to the other disorder; (3) there may be an underlying third condition that predisposes the individual to both disorders; (4) both disorders may be part of a more complex unified syndrome that was artificially split by the diagnostic system; (5) the relationship between the two disorders may be enhanced by definitional overlap; or (6) the comorbidity may be caused by the chance co-occurrence of high base rate disorders (First et al., 2002).

An examination of the diagnostic criteria for each disorder under consideration may clarify the diagnostic picture. Many disorders have exclusion criteria that list alternative diagnoses that must be excluded. The exclusion criteria often involve specific wording that helps to define the lifetime diagnostic hierarchies between disorders, establish inter-diagnosis boundaries, and clarify differential diagnosis. These criteria can also help to differentiate between difficult boundary cases or establish the precedence of the more pervasive disorder over the less pervasive disorder with similar defining features. Finally, they can facilitate the discrimination between disorders with similar symptoms but different etiologies. Several diagnostic categories have diagnostic criteria that specify the duration of symptoms and clinical course that can also be used to differentiate among disorders. Having considered all of this information, it is helpful to also review the diagnostic decision trees (*DSM-IV-TR,* Appendix A). If the client still meets the criteria for more than one disorder, several disorders can be assigned, being mindful of the rules of precedence and parsimony. Do not assign mutually exclusive disorders, always assign the more pervasive condition, and indicate which disorder is the principal diagnosis or the reason for the visit.

Step 7: Assess Level of Distress and/or Impairment

For a *DSM-IV-TR* diagnosis to be assigned, there must be clinically significant distress or impairment (A. Frances & Ross, 2001). The assessment of the individual's degree of suffering or impairment requires clinical judgment and inference; considering the areas described earlier by the mnemonic CLIENT can be very helpful. The individual's psychiatric, social, and occupational history may indicate premorbid functioning, and a comparison of the individual's highest level of premorbid functioning to functioning during the illness will indicate the impact of the disorder on the person's life. The course of the disorder can also provide information on the level of impairment, as the prodromal state of the illness may vary from several weeks to a lifetime and be characterized by a chronic, progressive course with exacerbations. If there is a discrepancy between the reported age of onset and the age at which the individual felt healthy, this may suggest a condition with an insidious onset (Othmer & Othmer, 2002). The course specifiers outlined in the *DSM-IV-TR* also provide information on the level of impairment (American Psychiatric Association, 2000b). However, it is important to realize that the level of impairment during a single episode is not a good indicator of long-term prognosis as disorders may be episodic. Objective measures of impairment include the individual's report

Table 3.12   Assessment of impairment

1. Has your (diagnosis) ever interfered with your school or employment?
2. Has your (diagnosis) ever caused you any problems with your family or caused your family to worry about you?
3. Has your (diagnosis) ever interfered with your social activities or friendships?
4. Have you ever gotten into trouble with authorities because of your (diagnosis)?
5. Has your health suffered from your (diagnosis)?
6. Have you received medication or treatment for your (diagnosis)?
7. Have you been hospitalized for your (diagnosis)?
8. When you had your (diagnosis), were you able to live alone?

Source: From *The Clinical Interview Using the DSM-IV: Vol. 1. Fundamentals,* second edition, by E. Othmer and S. C. Othmer, 2002, Washington, DC: American Psychiatric Press. Adapted with permission.

and his or her current mental status. Othmer and Othmer suggest asking the individual a series of eight questions to determine the level of impairment (see Table 3.12). It is also helpful to consider associated features, as many of these conditions impact the individual's level of functioning.

The *DSM-IV-TR* also assesses the individual's level of functioning using the GAF (American Psychiatric Association, 2000b). There have been few studies that have examined the clinical utility of the GAF. A small study by Frazee and colleagues (Frazee, Chicota, Templer, & Arikawa, 2003) found the majority of psychologists surveyed did not find the scale useful in making clinical decisions.

The *DSM-IV-TR* includes, in Appendix B, three additional scales of functioning (see Table 3.2) a global assessment of relationship functioning (GARF), a measure of social and occupational functioning (SOFAS), and a defensive functioning scale (DFS; American Psychiatric Association, 2000b). The GARF evaluates the overall functioning (0 to 100) of the family, couple, or other relational unit and includes the quality of problem solving, organization, and emotional climate in the family. The SOFAS (0 to 100) measures the social and occupational functioning and considers the role of the individual's general medical condition but does not include the severity of psychiatric symptoms. The GARF and SOFAS were added in *DSM-IV* in an effort to separate out the role of psychiatric symptoms from relational, social, and occupational functioning. These two domains were developed so the clinician could assess areas of functioning independent of impairment and symptoms. The DFS addresses the concerns of psychodynamic clinicians by measuring the level of defense mechanisms utilized by individuals. It includes seven defensive levels, ranging from higher adaptive level to defensive dysregulation. It also provides a glossary of specific defense mechanisms and coping styles that have been found to be useful in treatment planning (American Psychiatric Association, 2000b).

Hilsenroth and colleagues (2000) found that the GAF, SOFAS, and GARF can be scored reliably, represent different constructs, and are valid measures of global psychopathology, problems of social, occupational, and interpersonal functioning, and personality pathology, respectively. In a 2-year follow-up, the SOFAS had the strongest concurrent and predictive validity for general psychiatric inpatients both for initial hospital stay and 2-year outcome (Hay, Katsikitis, Begg, Da Costa, & Blumenfeld, 2003).

Distress and level of impairment are also impacted by the presence of psychosocial or environmental stressors (see Table 3.2), which are to be listed on Axis IV (American

Psychiatric Association, 2000b). As problems can impact the onset, course, or treatment of a disorder the clinician should evaluate the role of the problem or the nature of the stressor. The individual's history, family history, and mental status examination may assist in distinguishing the role of psychosocial stressors. The *DSM-IV-TR* provides a list of problems and stressors in the description of Axis IV. Typically only stressors occurring in the past year are considered relevant. However, if these stressors were experienced prior to the past year but still influence the individual's psychological functioning, or if the stressors are chronic, they can be considered relevant (American Psychiatric Association, 2000b).

TIPS AND STRATEGIES FOR MASTERY

As this chapter has illustrated, becoming a competent diagnostician is a skill-building process that involves knowledge, clinical experience, and practice. Although the *DSM-IV-TR* has its limitations (e.g., it is atheoretical, reliability comes at the expense of validity, and it still relies on clinical judgment), it is the standard in the field. Initially the *DSM-IV-TR* can be both overwhelming and confusing, but with practice and use your level of familiarity and comfort will increase. As an initial step, we recommend that you review and focus on understanding the terminology and organizational structure of the system (e.g., the use of a multiaxial diagnostic system, polythetic criteria sets, the hierarchical nature of the diagnostic process). Next, learn the essential or key features of the diagnostic categories and practice using the diagnostic decision trees to gain an understanding of the relationship of the diagnostic categories to one another. R. D. Morgan and colleagues (2000) found the use of the diagnostic decision trees not only increased clinicians' confidence but when combined with practice also increased diagnostic accuracy and decreased diagnostic time. Familiarity with the *DSM-IV-TR* diagnostic criteria provides you with an overall picture of each disorder, enabling you to recognize the disorder's common symptoms and defining features (Maxmen & Ward, 1995). According to Fauman (2002), clinicians initially learn best when they learn to recognize the typical or prototypical patient who fits the diagnostic criteria for a given disorder. Once this skill level is attained, mastery should focus on becoming familiar with variations in clinical presentation and boundary or atypical cases. At this more advanced stage of differential diagnosis, first focus on between-category differentiation (e.g., mood versus anxiety disorder), followed by within-category differentiation (Major Depressive Disorder versus Dysthymic Disorder). The seven steps outlined in Table 3.4 will facilitate learning these skills. Also consider complex and mixed cases and become familiar with the issues of comorbidity.

It is very important to remember the factors that contribute to diagnostic uncertainty (see Table 3.11) and your own limitations. Clinician omissions such as failing to consider diversity and developmental factors often result in misdiagnosis. Conducting brief or rushed intake interviews results in inadequate data, contributing to diagnostic uncertainty. Finally, be mindful of First and colleagues' (2002) advice to temper the temptation to use the *DSM-IV* in a rote or cookbook fashion and to instead learn to use it without becoming enslaved to it.

Once you have determined the individual's diagnosis, the next step is to assess the need for treatment and to formulate a treatment plan.

Chapter 4

FUNDAMENTALS OF TREATMENT PLANNING

The provision of direct clinical services is the primary career focus of many mental health professionals, and mastering the complex set of skills required to effectively treat others is one of the most challenging, yet rewarding learning experiences that a clinician will face. Adding to this challenge is the fact that the clinical treatment arena has undergone significant changes over the past several decades. Empirically based disorder-specific treatments have been developed that are rapidly becoming the standard of care in the field (Fongay, Target, Cottrell, Phillips, & Kurtz, 2002; Norcross, 2002a; A. Roth & Fongay, 2006; Stout & Hayes, 2005). There is increased recognition for the need to provide services to populations that have historically been neglected, including those lacking basic resources who have been marginalized and disenfranchised from society (Fakhoury & Priebe, 2002; Terry, 2005; A. S. Young & Magnabosco, 2004). Today's clinician is likely to encounter an increasingly diverse range of clients and may be particularly challenged when clients present with issues beyond their area of expertise or theoretical orientation (Ingram, 2006). The rich array of treatment interventions now available for specific clinical problems is discussed in detail in each of the clinical disorder chapters, along with current advances in the field. The current chapter focuses on a review of practical, general strategies that should be considered in treating all clients. Treatment challenges such as premature termination, countertransference, and practical issues such as dealing with noncompliance, documentation, and interfacing with health management organizations (HMOs) are also reviewed.

INITIAL CONSIDERATIONS IN EVALUATING TREATMENT NEEDS

Clients in Crisis

When an individual presents for treatment in the midst of a crisis or because of a traumatic experience, this needs to be addressed prior to making any other treatment decisions. A crisis state can be defined as a brief, personal psychological upheaval or reaction of severe distress caused by a stressor or "hazard" that results in intense emotional turmoil and impairment in daily coping (G. Caplan, 1964; Feinstein & Carey, 1995; Westefeld & Heckman-Stone, 2003). Individuals in crisis can present with a range of symptoms that can include feelings of pain, confusion, anxiety, crying, depression, being mute, and suicidal (Lindemann, 1944; A. R. Roberts, 2000). For some, these symptoms may ultimately be relatively short-lived (e.g., 6 weeks). For others, a range of outcomes may be experienced, including improved functioning, incomplete recovery and a vulnerability to future crises, a stable but lower level of functioning, and severe impairment (G. Caplan, 1964). Early research in this area suggested that clinical outcome is determined by the severity of the stressor experienced, the individual's personal reaction to it, and the impact the trauma had on one's supports (Lindemann, 1944).

Over the years, several different models of crisis intervention have developed which can guide clinicians in providing effective treatment. Baldwin (1979) described a 4-step model consisting of (1) catharsis and assessment, (2) focusing or contracting, (3) intervention or resolution, and (4) termination or integration. Westefeld and Heckman-Stone (2003) proposed an integrated problem-solving model (IPSM), a 10-step approach to crisis intervention that places strong emphasis on explicitly and immediately establishing rapport; focuses on empowerment and cultural context; draws on cognitive-behavioral, narrative, solution-focused theories; and moves a client through processing trauma in a series of graduated steps (e.g., establishing safety and stabilization, processing trauma, generating and implementing options). By combining these models with Feinstein and Carey's (1995) research on the key clinical issues in crisis intervention, several very practical strategies for crisis resolution can be identified (see Table 4.1).

When dealing with an individual in crisis, the clinician must adopt a very active approach to ensure safety, de-escalate the crisis, and identify the most appropriate interventions (James & Gilliland, 2005; Kanel, 2006). As clients in crisis are often distressed and vulnerable and may be distrustful of the clinician's ability to help, rapport building is a crucial early step in the treatment process. The use of attending and listening skills, expressions of empathy and encouragement, reflection of affect, and provision of support and hope all facilitate the development of a trusting relationship (Cloitre, Stovall-McClough, & Chemtob, 2004; C. E. Hill & O'Brien, 1999; Westefeld & Heckman-Stone, 2003).

The client's level of impulse control, tendency to engage in high-risk behaviors, and the presence of maladaptive coping patterns (e.g., relying on alcohol and substances) must be continually assessed and monitored (Othmer & Othmer, 2002). As many individuals in a crisis rely on a single coping style that may be maladaptive and lack the capacity or flexibility to change, the clinician initially needs to focus on enhancing coping and providing a framework for goal setting (Westefeld & Heckman-Stone, 2003). Toward these ends, the therapist can teach new coping strategies for crisis resolution by noting examples of adaptive coping such as asking others for support and establishing priorities (Feinstein & Carey, 1995). Attention should also be paid to practical issues such as the need for shelter, and the client should be encouraged to identify, contact, and talk to available, capable supports (Feinstein & Carey, 1995). The trauma that led to the client's crisis state should be addressed after the clinician has attended to these and other safety issues, such as suicidality, dangerousness, abuse, and the need for medical evaluation (Lukas, 1993; S. M. Turner et al., 2003; see also Chapter 2, "Crisis Issues").

In the beginning of treatment, clients in crisis should be afforded the opportunity to express feelings of guilt, rage, and anxiety (Maxmen & Ward, 1995). Toward these ends, cognitive-behavioral approaches have been found to be effective, as they are active, directive, structured, and usually time-limited and psychoeducational in nature (Westefeld & Heckman-Stone, 2003). An assessment of the personal meaning of the events is crucial to

Table 4.1 Key crisis intervention strategies

Establish and maintain rapport.
Ensure safety.
Assess and monitor suicide and impulse control.
Recognize early warning signs of crisis.
Encourage the client to talk to supports (physician, family, friend, clergy).
⇓
Assess client and gather information.
Begin processing the trauma.
Discuss painful feelings and emotions.
Identify stressors and the impact on life.
⇓
Draw support network map.
Formulate crisis and prioritize issues.
Gather information for crisis resolution.
Identify coping style.
Set goals.
Generate options.
Evaluate options.
⇓
Select specific plan and coping style.
Determine sequence of actions.
Implement plan.
⇓
Evaluate the outcome.
Assess results.
Address future coping strategies.
Follow up.

Source: From J. Westefeld & C. Heckman-Stone The integrated problem-solving model of crisis intervention: Overview and application. (*The Counseling Psychologist*, Volume *3*, Issue 2) pp. 221–239, © 2003 by SAGE Publications, Inc. Adapted with permission of SAGE Publications, Inc.

understanding the role of precipitants and events contributing to the client's current distress. However, care must be taken not to retraumatize the individual by initially over-focusing on details (Rheingold & Acierno, 2003). A time line of events, a selective relevant psychiatric history, and a focus on the present can help the individual to recognize the impact of the crisis and identify the early warning signs of feeling overwhelmed (Feinstein & Carey, 1995). Gathering information, including material from significant others (with the client's permission), can assist in determining the unique way the individual deals with stress and his or her repertoire of coping skills (Freuh, Elhai, & Hamner, 2003).

The identification and setting of solution-focused goals, such as processing emotions and improving coping and self-care, begins the process of helping the individual work through the crisis. Although clients in crisis may readily turn to the clinician to make decisions, it is imperative to *collaboratively* generate goals and decide on the plan of execution that will ultimately be followed (Westefeld & Heckman-Stone, 2003). It is crucial for the resolution of the crisis that the outcome and options are continually evaluated and the plan is modified when necessary. Finally, termination and follow-up can be implemented, with particular attention to providing the individual with preventive strategies for the future (Feinstein & Carey, 1995). A more detailed discussion of crisis intervention is provided in James and Gilliland (2005) *Crisis Intervention Strategies*, Kanel's (2006) *A Guide to Crisis Intervention*, and A. R. Roberts's (2000) *Crisis Intervention Handbook: Assessment, Treatment and Research*.

Medical Referrals

An important part of the initial treatment process is to determine whether involvement of a medical professional is necessary in the client's assessment or ongoing treatment. As reviewed in Chapter 3, the possibility that a general medical condition (GMC) may be the cause of or an exacerbating factor contributing to a client's psychological symptoms must always be considered in the diagnostic process. In such cases, appropriate intervention will involve treatment of the underlying GMC (H. I. Kaplan & Saddock, 1996). In addition, it is not unusual for clients with emotional problems to neglect their physical health or to develop secondary physical problems for which medical treatment is warranted. Clients can also present to therapy on medication, as noncompliant with medication, or in need of a medication evaluation, all of which require a referral to a physician (Horne, 1998; O'Neal, Talga, & Preston, 2002; Perkins, 2002). Older adults may be on a regimen of medications to treat physical ailments, and the side effects of these agents may mirror or contribute to psychiatric conditions (Edelstein, Koven, Spira, & Shreve-Neiger, 2003). If referral to a physician is deemed appropriate, the clinician should be certain to obtain the client's consent and authorization to release information to the physician (see section on "Release of Information" in Chapter 1).

Addressing Cultural Competence

Given that ethnic minorities currently compose 25% of the U.S. population and that by 2050 more that 50% of all U.S. residents will be minorities, there is a high probability that a clinician practicing today will treat a diverse group of clients (La Roche, 2005). The impact of culture is consistently present in the therapeutic relationship and is a complex, dynamic factor that needs to be acknowledged and incorporated coherently (see Table 4.2) for treatment to be effective (Hanna, Bemak, & Chung, 1999; La Roche, 2005). As discussed in Chapter 1, from the outset, it is necessary to be sensitive and attuned to clients' cultural or ethnic identity and their comfort level with you as a clinical provider (McKitrick & Jenkins, 2000). The client's language of choice may be different from yours, and the client may have gender, age, or religious preferences for a therapist that need to be inquired about and considered (Hays, 2007). Even when a clinician is able to communicate with a client in his or her preferred language, it is important not to assume that basic linguistic competence implies familiarity with the subtle nuances that often characterize emotionally laden speech.

When working with any client it is important to appreciate his or her individuality, personal perspective and understanding of presenting issues, and the unique context in which these problems emerge (W. M. Liu & Clay, 2002; McKitrick & Jenkins, 2000).

Table 4.2   Steps to incorporate diversity into treatment planning

Determine which diversity factors are relevant.

Assess the level of skill and information necessary for competent treatment.

Determine the need for possible referral or consultation.

Evaluate the impact of diversity factors on the establishment and maintenance of rapport.

Consider the role of these factors on information gathering.

Determine when and how to incorporate diversity issues.

Examine the potential treatments and the cultural assumptions for each factor.

Consider the cultural role of supports.

Implement treatment using the individual's cultural strengths.

ADDRESSING (acronym for within-group) Diversity Factors[*]

Age and generational influences

Developmental and acquired

Disabilities

Religious and spiritual orientation

Ethnic and racial identity

Socioeconomic status

Sexual orientation

Indigenous heritage

National origin

Gender

Cultural Questions to Consider[**]

Do the individual's beliefs and values reflect his or her culture?

Do these beliefs and values influence his or her openness to treatment?

Does the individual see culture as important?

Are the individual's beliefs and behaviors influenced by culture?

Do cultural issues impact on treatment acceptability and treatment goals?

[*]From *Addressing Cultural Complexities in Practice: Assessment, Diagnosis, & Therapy*, by P. A. Hays, 2007, Washington, DC: American Psychological Association. Adapted with permission.

[**]From "Multicultural Counseling Competencies: Guidelines in Working with Children and Adolescents," by W. M. Liu and D. L. Clay, 2002, *Journal of Mental Health Counseling, 24*(2), pp. 177–187. Adapted with permission.

Considering the client as the expert on his or her culture and asking about his or her cultural beliefs may facilitate rapport and client involvement in the therapeutic process. This is even more crucial when the individual is in any way different from you and those differences have resulted in previous experiences of discrimination, labeling, stigmatization, and other adverse life consequences. These issues not only significantly impact your ability to establish and maintain rapport but also have major implications for the choice and effectiveness of therapeutic interventions and the client's participation. Hays (2007) describes the importance of respect as a central value in many cultures and recommends avoiding psychological jargon, being aware of the different meanings of nonverbal communication, and considering within-group diversity (see Table 4.2). Similarly, Lo and Fung (2003) recommend that the clinician develop generic and specific cultural competence skills that can be applied across psychotherapy from engagement to termination. These skills include cultural sensitivity, curiosity, perceptiveness, respect, an understanding of different cultural explanatory models, and an awareness of the importance of cultural identity and connection to the community at large. Multicultural competence, according to W. M. Liu and Clay (2002, p. 178), involves "having the knowledge, awareness and skills to know when and how culture can be best used" rather than indiscriminately incorporating it. Prior to starting therapy it is important to educate yourself on different cultural norms and expectations and conduct a self-audit of your own biases and worldviews. This may appear to be a daunting task, but a very practical starting point is to use census profile data to identify the populations you will be providing services to and educate yourself about these cultures (W. M. Liu & Clay, 2002).

Addressing Life Span Issues

When working with any client it is important to consider if there are any developmental or life span considerations that need to be included in treatment planning (see Table 4.3). For adolescents, issues of trust and privacy are often paramount. Many states have specific confidentiality considerations relating to adolescents who seek treatment for substance use and pregnancy (see Chapter 1). Providing services to children involves being competent in multi-informant and multisetting assessments and being familiar with the impact of developmental issues on diagnostic presentation and therapeutic effectiveness (Douglas & Davies, 2004; Kazdin & Weisz, 2003). Young children often warrant the use of specific interventions that require specialty training such as play therapy, sand trays, and storytelling (Kaduson & Schaefer, 2000; O'Conner & Schaefer, 1994; Schaefer & Cangelosi, 2002). If there are multiple clients, for example, a family or couple, your decision concerning how to structure treatment needs to be guided by what is in the individual's best interest, an awareness of boundary issues, and the conflict inherent in functioning in multiple roles (Lukas, 1993).

At the opposite end of the age spectrum, negative stereotyping, ageism, the reluctance to seek treatment, and the disinclination of care providers to refer for treatment are often barriers that limit older adults' access to psychotherapy (Edelstein et al., 2003). Research shows that older adults who are able to access psychotherapeutic help often have higher attendance and lower dropout rates, and their outcome is comparable to if not better than younger adults (J. Garner, 2003; Klausner & Alexopoulous, 1999).

Table 4.3   Life span and developmental considerations in treatment planning

Consider the individual's chronological, developmental, and cognitive age.
Modify intake and therapeutic interventions to reflect the individual's abilities.
Familiarize yourself with developmental and generational issues.
Clarify client's understanding of problems and knowledge of treatment.
Explore attitude and motivation toward therapy.
Consider stage of development and relevant life span issues in treatment planning.
Integrate knowledge of the disorder's course into treatment plan.
Select and stagger goals based on a developmental life span perspective.
Ensure that goals of autonomy and independence reflect developmental and life span issues.
Vary involvement of support system to reflect developmental issues.
Consider cohort effect.

Clinician Factors That May Impact Treatment

Providing treatment beyond your skill or competence level is unethical, according to the ethics code guidelines of the American Psychological Association (APA, 2002), American Counseling Association (ACA, 2005), American Association of Marriage and Family Therapists (AAMFT, 2001), and the National Association of Social Workers (NASW, 1999). Thus, when choosing to work with a particular client, it is essential to be familiar with the relevant diagnostic considerations (e.g., *DSM-IV-TR*), the standards of care, and the current research on effective and most appropriate interventions (American Psychiatric Association, 2000b; Kazdin & Weisz, 2003; Luborsky et al., 2003; A. Roth & Fongay, 2006). While your case conceptualization and treatment approach may be guided by your theoretical orientation, it should also include consideration of diversity, developmental, and medical issues and recognition of the complexity of the case in its presenting context (Hays, 2007). In addition, Beutler, Moleiro, and Talebi (2002) note that among the elements necessary for productive therapeutic change are such basic clinician competencies as an attitude conducive to the establishment of warmth, genuine interest, and empathy and a knowledge of the principles of change.

Having feelings toward the client that impair your ability to function in an objective, professional manner or responding to the individual's presenting problems in a nontherapeutic way can negatively impact the therapeutic process. For example, research shows that the clients of therapists who experience negative feelings or who lack feelings of competence are more likely to terminate prematurely (Truant, 1998a,b). Psychodynamic theorists identify this as *countertransference* (J. A. Hayes, Riker, & Ingram, 1997; Rosenberger & Hayes, 2002; I. Weiner, 1998). Being aware of and managing these issues (e.g., through consultation, supervision, personal therapy) is crucial to your development as an effective clinician (J. Hayes, Gelso, Van Magoner, & Diemer, 1991; I. Weiner, 1998).

In some cases, there may be existing relationships that result in a dual relationship, a conflict of interest, or a blurring of professional boundaries. This may happen when you know the client from another setting (e.g., school, local business), as can often happen in smaller, closely knit communities. Pope and Vasquez (2001) define a *dual relationship* in psychotherapy as one in which the clinician is in another, significantly different relationship with a client. In such dual relationships, the client's emotional reaction to the therapist may become confused, and the power differential already inherent in a treatment setting may become amplified (e.g., a client is reluctant to be open in treatment for fear of jeopardizing the other relationship he or she has with the therapist outside of the treatment setting; Welfel, 2005). Other problems include distortion and erosion of the professional nature of the therapeutic relationship and the clinician's professional judgment and objectivity. This may result in the possibility that the clinician may begin to seek out clients with whom additional relationships outside of the therapy setting can occur (e.g., looking for potential business partners or friends; Pope & Vasquez, 2001). For these reasons, it is important to avoid such conflicts whenever possible and to be aware of the therapeutic ramifications of functioning in multiple roles (AAMFT, 2001; ACA, 2005; APA, 2002; NASW, 1999). One form of dual relationship that is strictly prohibited is developing a sexual relationship with a client who is in treatment with you. All the ethical codes of all major mental health practitioner organizations explicitly prohibit sexual relationships with current clients. Although some codes discuss circumstances in which sexual contact with a client following the termination of treatment may occur (e.g., after no less than a minimum of 2 years following the termination of therapy), their wording essentially conveys the message that sexual contact with former clients is very likely to be harmful and unethical, and that only under the most extraordinary of circumstances would such a situation not be considered unacceptable (ACA, 2005; APA, 2002; Welfel, 2005).

Client Factors That May Impact Treatment

As clinicians it is important to realize the realties of client attrition. Research indicates that between 30% and 60% of clients drop out of treatment (Corning & Malofeeva, 2004). Truant (1998a,b) recommends assessing individuals at the onset for their suitability for psychotherapy by gathering information from three areas: (1) the traditional interview and diagnosis, (2) a conceptualization of how the individual functions psychologically, and (3) a determination of the individual's ability to engage in the psychotherapeutic process. The client's clinical history can provide information that has prognostic implications, such as prior response to treatment, idealization or devaluation of a previous therapist, the course of the disorder, or underlying long-standing patterns of inconsistent follow-through (Lukas, 1993; R. Sommers-Flanagan & Sommers-Flanagan, 1999). A history of premature termination or discharge against medical advice or of relapse for substance abuse may indicate the need for more structured intervention.

At the onset of treatment it is helpful to consider whether there are any contraindicators for therapy (see Table 4.4). This information can guide your discussion with the client concerning the need for and commitment to treatment and your selection of the most appropriate interventions. Other factors to consider in assessing appropriateness for therapy include the individual's relational history, motivation, and supportive life circumstances. During the initial interview the clinician should note the ease with which rapport was developed; the individual's responses to open-ended questions, clarifications, and interpretations; the client's psychological-mindedness (including capacity for introspection and insight); the client's ability to acknowledge maladaptive behavior patterns; and the degree of honest communication (Othmer & Othmer, 2002; Truant, 1998a). Individuals at risk for dropping out of treatment prematurely include those who are spontaneously hostile or resistant or have difficulty engaging with the clinician. Self-involved individuals with a history of chaotic relationships, withdrawn clients who dread self-disclosure, and those who promiscuously disclose and have unrealistic intimacy expectations also have difficulty committing to therapy (Truant, 1998a,b). When considering the individual's interpersonal history, the clinician should look for the presence of at least one meaningful sustained relationship that was characterized by the presence of intimacy, trust, and the ability to confide in another and resolve conflicts (Truant, 1998a). Individuals who do not have sufficient financial, familial, and occupational support or who complain of having limited time may also have difficulty completing therapy (Truant, 1998a).

When potentially negative prognostic indicators to treatment are identified, this does not mean the clinician should conclude that therapy is not worth pursuing or that it will inevitably fail. Instead, such information should be used to tailor the treatment plan in a way that can help maximize its success. For example, for clients with a history of repeated premature "flights into health," the clinician can gently but directly address this early in treatment by saying something like the following:

Table 4.4   Therapy considerations

Contraindicators for Therapy

Client Factors	Therapist Factors	Other Factors
Severe pathology	Inexperience	Level of care
Cognitive challenges	Countertransference	Setting limitations
Denial, lack of insight	Dual relationship	Financial constraints
Noncompliant	Limited availability	Time and location
Unmotivated	Overextended	Hostile supports
Unrealistic expectations		
Mandated to treatment and hostile		

Brief Therapy Exclusion Criteria*

Entangled family problems
Drug addiction and chronic alcoholism
Suicide high risk, serious attempts
Severe Psychopathology: psychotic disorders, long-term hospitalization, more than one course of electroconvulsive therapy, incapacitating depression without precipitant stressors, chronic obsessional or phobic symptoms, gross self-destructive acting-out, extensive early trauma or inadequate memory and concentration

When to Consider Hospitalization

Specific plan to harm self or others and access to means
Inability to contract for safety
Gross inability to care for self (e.g., inability to feed oneself, seek shelter)
Grossly disorganized, psychotic behavior
Rapidly deteriorating psychological condition
Inability to utilize basic coping skills
Inability to maintain sobriety
Unable to continue to participate in needed treatment
Unavailable, chaotic, or dysfunctional support system

Psychological Clues That Facilitate Therapy

Individual's locus of responsibility	Affective triggers and critical issues
Habitual view of helping figures	Recurrent associations and themes
Defense mechanisms and coping patterns	Clinician's reaction to client
Individual's expectations of treatment	

*Adapted with permission of the Association for the Advancement of Psychotherapy, from "Assessment of Suitability for Psychotherapy: Pt. I. Introduction and the Assessment Process," by G. S. Truant, 1998a, *American Journal of Psychotherapy, 52*(4), pp. 397–411.

I understand that in the past when you have started to feel better you have often decided to leave treatment. However, the fact that you have returned suggests that the issues you were seeking help for are not resolved as completely as you might have hoped. I am glad that we will have the opportunity to try to address some of these concerns together. However, my guess is that, as in the past, when you begin to feel better, you will want to leave treatment again, and I want to encourage you to discuss these feelings with me before deciding to stop coming to therapy.

Practical considerations can also impact the decision to treat: Your clinical practice may not be equipped to provide the range or level of required services, or the client may have financial, time, work, or social constraints or transportation and scheduling issues that may adversely impact treatment follow-through. Clients may have physical and cognitive challenges (dementia), emotional or motivational issues, or a clinical presentation (e.g., active psychosis, intoxication, immature defense systems) that impact their ability to meaningfully participate in both intake and treatment and complicate the formation of a therapeutic alliance (Maxmen & Ward, 1995; Othmer & Othmer, 2002; J. C. Perry, 2001; Piper, McCallum, Joyce, Azim, & Ogrodnickzuk, 1999).

Some clients are not self-referred, and though in need of treatment are resistant or unwilling to engage in a therapeutic relationship. Many of these clients may have been mandated to treatment by another agency, such as judicial or family services, and compliance may be based on a secondary gain (e.g., possible sentence reduction for a DUI). Individuals may have sought help under emotional or interpersonal duress, such as a spouse threatening to leave, or may have been actively brought against their will, such as with an oppositional-defiant adolescent. In such cases, high levels of hostility and resistance are often apparent on intake and characterized by a failure to establish rapport (Othmer & Othmer, 2002). The clinician's challenge is in such cases to be highly active in establishing and continually assessing the level of rapport and evaluating if the interventions can be effective. The client's level of impulse control, judgment, insight, and commitment to treatment should also be assessed (Lukas, 1993). Acknowledging the less than favorable circumstances that may have led to treatment and the client's feelings about them are important; however, this should be balanced with attempts to help the client identify personally meaningful goals for the therapy in spite of a reluctance to be in treatment in the first place.

Disposition Decisions

Outpatient Treatment versus Hospitalization

In most cases, the client will be seen as an outpatient; however, for some individuals, inpatient hospitalization needs to be considered. When treating clients who actively pose a danger to themselves or others despite a plan to protect, who demonstrate a gross inability for self-care, or whose condition is deteriorating and resulting in an inability to comply with treatment, hospitalization may be necessary (see Table 4.4). This option should also be explored if the home environment is chaotic and presents a danger to the individual, such as a recovering alcoholic or substance user returning to an environment where there is continued use. Ways and Banks (2001), in a study of admissions to urban psychiatric emergency services, found that danger to self, psychosis, depression, lack of impulse control, and low ability to care for self were among the most likely factors leading to admission to an inpatient setting. Another review of admissions to a psychiatric emergency room found that referral by police or health professionals (in contrast to self-referral or referral by relatives), current psychotic diagnosis, and previous hospitalizations are the most powerful predictors of hospitalization (Schnyder, Klaghfor, Leuthold, & Buddeberg, 1999). In the majority of cases, the reported stressors that precipitated the admission crisis involved problems and conflicts with close relationships. Interestingly, in contrast, the presence of a precipitating stressor related to a social support network was found to decrease the likelihood of hospitalization in a study by Schydner et al. (1999).

It is important to be knowledgeable about your local mental health facilities, including emergency room procedures. Some hospitals allow outpatient therapists to admit clients and encourage a continuity of care. If you are not experienced or do not wish to provide inpatient treatment, you may want to collaborate with colleagues who provide these services. If the client is in need of hospitalization but is unwilling to be admitted, you may need to contact your local psychiatric emergency team to initiate hospital admission and an involuntary hold. In all cases where psychiatric hospitalization is pursued, the clinician's decision-making process and any actions taken should be clearly documented in the case notes.

Referral to Other Providers

Some clients require a referral to another professional. For example, if you cannot provide services that the client is deemed in need of, if there are practical barriers to the client's being in treatment with you (e.g., client determines your office is too far away), or if an insufficiently strong therapeutic alliance is determined to be present that is hampering treatment progress, a referral to another treatment provider will be needed. The standards of care suggest that you should provide a client with at least two referrals and that ethically you cannot have a personal relationship with these individuals or receive any form of compensation for the referral (AAMFT, 2001; ACA, 2005; APA, 2002; NASW, 1999). Ideally, you should have some knowledge of the individual's professional training, expertise, and availability. In making referrals, one should consider the format or modality that is most appropriate for the client given his or her presenting problem. Remember that the frequency and type of therapy provided is likely to be influenced by the clinician's orientation, and parameters of the client's insurance (if this is to be used to pay for treatment) may place limitations on the type and scope of services sought (Lubrosky, 2001; Sandell, Blomberg, & Lazar, 2002). Factors you may want to consider at the beginning of treatment are outlined in Table 4.5.

Building the Relationship

The crucial first step or therapeutic task in treatment is the establishment and maintenance of rapport and a therapeutic alliance (R. Elliott, Watson, Goldman, & Greenberg, 2004). I. Weiner (1998, p. 3) aptly writes of psychotherapy as "an interpersonal process in which therapists communicate to their patients that they understand them, respect them, and want to be of help to them." Goldfried and Davila (2005) describe the therapeutic alliance as the presence of a personal bond between the individual and therapist in which the therapist is viewed as caring, knowledgeable, and understanding. The client and therapist together agree on treatment goals and the means to achieve these goals, and the alliance provides the context in which interventions are implemented (Goldfried & Davila, 2005).

Basic rapport-building tools include using attending and listening skills, reflecting affect, offering encouragement and support, and instilling hope (Ivey & Ivey, 1999). When clients seek treatment they often report feeling vulnerable, distressed, distrustful, and fragile; your expression of empathy is crucial in relationship building (Ackerman &

Table 4.5   Commencement checklist and factors for change

Commencement Checklist

Assess for crisis issues.
Establish and maintain rapport.
Rule out medical or medication concerns.
Assess presence of substance-related disorders.
Address diversity and life span issues.
Obtain releases to contact others (e.g., family).
Gather additional history and coordinate treatment.
Address contraindications and client and clinician factors.
Address legal, ethical, competence, and informed consent considerations.
Evaluate symptoms and impact on treatment.
Determine disposition decision and modality.
Create a problem list.
Identify goals, strengths, and resources (including family support).
Formulate a case conceptualization.
Write a treatment plan.
Develop and sign a treatment contract.

Factors That Facilitate Change[*]

Facilitate the expectation that therapy will help: Build hope, positive expectation, optimism, and motivation to engage in therapy.
Establish the optimal therapeutic alliance: Develop a personal bond and agreement on goals and interventions.
Offer feedback to increase awareness of problems and contributing or causal factors.
Continually emphasize reality testing to increase awareness leading to corrective experiences.
Encourage corrective experiences.

[*]From "The Role of the Relationship and Technique in Therapeutic Change," by M. R. Goldfried and J. Davila, 2005, *Psychotherapy: Theory, Research, Practice Training, 42*, pp. 421–430. Adapted with permission.

Hilsenroth, 2003; C. E. Hill & O'Brien, 1999). Personal attributes that facilitate the establishment of a positive relationship are flexibility, experience, trustworthiness, confidence, clear communication, enthusiasm, warmth, and interest (Ackerman & Hilsenroth, 2003). Additional therapeutic techniques that enhance the therapeutic alliance are accurate interpretation, affirmation, exploration, facilitation of affect expression, and understanding of and attention to the individual's experience (Ackerman & Hilsenroth, 2003). Also crucial are conveying concern for the client's safety and welfare and consideration of the cultural, developmental, societal, and diversity factors that impact the individual's experience and expression of distress (Hays, 2007; Lukas, 1993). Other factors that contribute to a productive therapeutic relationship include close matches for race, sex, and culture between the individual and the therapist and agreement on the goals and expectations of therapy (Cartwright, 2004). Some general strategies and techniques that the clinician can use to foster change and that can be applied across all theoretical orientations are presented in Table 4.5. The importance of the therapeutic alliance cannot be emphasized enough; it is one of the most widely documented factors that impact treatment outcome across all theoretical orientations (Norcross, 2002a,b).

DEVELOPING THE TREATMENT PLAN

The individualized treatment plan is based on an assessment of the individual's strengths, weaknesses, abilities, and preferences and serves to formulate strategies or interventions to target problems and therapeutic goals (Wiger, 2005). This is most effective if it is an interactive process between the clinician and the client, thus ensuring that both are on the same page at the outset. Typically, the clinician reviews the intake and diagnostic information and then collaboratively develops the treatment plan with the client. Maxmen and Ward (1995) note that every client's treatment plan should include the type and amount of therapy, the focus of treatment or the specific problems to be addressed, the goals or objectives for each therapy, and the timing and sequence of treatment. New clinicians often find treatment planning a daunting task and struggle with knowing where to begin and what to do next (Ingram, 2006). This task can be conceptualized as involving several different steps that begin with problem selection and definition, followed by goal development and the identification of the appropriate interventions to achieve each goal (Jongsma & Peterson, 2003).

Identifying and Prioritizing Problems

Problem List Identification

Identifying a comprehensive and detailed list of the individual's problems or concerns is the first step in case conceptualization. This helps focus therapy and serves as the basis for evaluating therapeutic effectiveness and the individual's progress (Persons, 1989; Woody, Detweiler-Bedell, Teachman, & O'Hearn, 2003). Writing an explicit problem list can minimize the potential for missing important problems and is a useful communication tool for other involved professionals. It suggests a clear agenda for therapy, provides structure across sessions, and enhances the therapeutic relationship by engendering a sense of concern, confidence, and hope (Woody et al., 2003).

Relevant information for a problem list can be obtained from the intake interview, collateral reports, previous records, results of any psychological assessments, and your clinical observations (Wiger, 2005). By constructing the problem list collaboratively, the vague concerns of an overwhelmed client can be organized and operationalized, thus making them more accessible and fostering the client's hope and motivation (Woody et al., 2003). Clients differ in their ability to construct a problem list; for example, some tend to become overly focused on one or two problems and avoid important issues that feel insoluble. For clients presenting with an abundance of problems, it may take considerable clinical skill to help them organize and prioritize (this is discussed further under "Prioritizing Problems"). Some individuals may want to start therapy straight away and skip the step of generating a problem list; however, failure to take this step jeopardizes treatment by leading to a hit-or-miss approach to interventions that is likely to be ineffective (Persons, 1989). It is also important from the onset to be aware of any limitations on treatment such as limited health coverage or time constraints (e.g., a student client who is graduating and will no longer be eligible for services at a university-based clinic), as these factors will also impact your selection of problems to address.

Remember that the issues that eventually are added to the problem list may not all be generated from clients themselves. For example, there may be problems that the individual has limited insight into or is not ready to report (e.g., substance abuse, inability to read, past suicidal attempts) that you learn of through observations of the client's behavior, review of past records, or contacts with significant others. Clients' interaction with you and the pattern of interpersonal difficulties in their background information may highlight underlying personality problems (Othmer & Othmer, 2002). When the clinician observes a problem that the individual does not report, it is a good idea to point these out and discuss them so they can be added to the list (Persons, 1989). Individuals' willingness to discuss these issues may indicate their level of insight and readiness to engage collaboratively in therapy.

The identification of a problem list is a good focus for the first session if it has not already been developed in the intake interview. Although the goal is to compile as comprehensive a list as possible, this does not mean that all the problems can or will be actively addressed in treatment (Persons, 1989; Woody et al., 2003). It is helpful at the beginning to identify 8 to 10 problems that can provide the focus for therapeutic interventions (Persons, 1989). Some of the domains for consideration when constructing a problem list are presented in Table 4.6; this is by no means an exhaustive list but provides general areas of concern (Woody et al., 2003). The problem list is not a one-time list but will change as therapy progresses. As the individual develops a greater sense of trust, it is not unusual for additional problems to emerge, and new problems can develop as a result of life circumstances or changes the individual makes.

In the beginning of therapy it can be very helpful to obtain quantitative information about the behavioral, cognitive, and mood aspects of the individual's problems by having the client complete specific self-report measures. This information can help you understand the nature of the problem, assist with case conceptualization, and provide a baseline to evaluate progress and the effectiveness of treatment (Persons, 1989). Measures frequently used include the Beck Depression Inventory, second edition (A. T. Beck, Steer, & Brown, 1996), a 21-item self-report measure that assesses the severity and symptoms of depression; the Burns Anxiety Inventory (Burnes, 1984), a 33-item self-report measure that assesses the cognitive, physical, and mood aspects of anxiety; and the Fears Survey Schedule (Wolpe & Lang, 1997) that lists 108 commonly feared events or objects. Maruish's (2004) three-volume *The Use of Psychological Testing for Treatment Planning* is an excellent source for additional measures.

Prioritizing Problems

Having constructed a comprehensive problem list, the next task, in collaboration with the client, is to narrow the list, prioritize the problems, and determine those that can be addressed in treatment and those that warrant a referral or consultation (Wiger, 2005; Woody et al., 2003). Problems that need immediate attention are placed at the top of the list, and then the others are rank-ordered based on several factors (see Table 4.7). The reason for referral or chief complaint identifies the client's primary concern or the impetus for seeking treatment. Those problems that create the greatest distress or impairment or have the greatest impact on functioning are often given a higher priority than other problems (Woody et al., 2003). Among those problems that significantly impact functioning, those that have a good prognosis or are likely to show quick progress should be addressed earlier, as this can boost the client's motivation for treatment, create a sense of

Table 4.6   Problem list domains or target areas

Injurious and Impulsive Behaviors	Medical, Medication, and Physical Health
Suicidal ideation or behavior	Recent physical examination to rule out GMC
Homicidal ideation or behavior	Medical conditions and management
Self-mutilation or injurious behavior	Medications and compliance
Impulsivity, flight, or elopement risk	Physical fitness and exercise
Alcohol or substance use or abuse	Nutrition and eating habits
Unsafe or inappropriate sexual behavior	Appropriateness of help-seeking behavior
Aggressive or explosive behavior	Use of legal drugs: caffeine, nicotine, diet pills
Gambling or financial impulsivity	Sleep problems
Thrill seeking or illegal activities	
Clinical Considerations	**Family and Interpersonal Functioning**
Presenting problem	Relationship with family members
Chief complaint	Family crisis, trauma, abuse, or neglect
Diagnostic considerations	Parenting skills and issues
Comorbid conditions	Adjustment to interpersonal stressor (e.g., loss)
Associated features	Quality of supports and frequency of contact
Distress or clinical acuity	Excessive interpersonal isolation
Diagnoses onset and time line	Excesses and deficiencies in social skills
Self-concept and Identity	Overly dependent inability to function autonomously
Low self-esteem or self-confidence	Unstable marriage or relational difficulties
Unclear or unstable sense of self or identity	Oppositional and hostile in relationships
Dissociation disrupting self-concept or identity	Extreme distrust, hypersensitivity, or self-centeredness
Uncertain sexual identity	Poor family alliance with treatment team
School/Occupational Functioning	**Cultural, Spiritual, and Other**
Attendance	Cultural influences and difficulties
Performance	Involvement with faith or institutions
Disciplinary action, behavioral problems	Existential questions and challenges
Overall school or job stability	Moral dilemmas and issues
Financial status in relation to occupation	Developmental or phase of life issues
Satisfaction with role or performance	Transition or migration issues
Thinking and Cognition	**Adaptive or Life Skills**
Impaired contact with reality and testing	Impairment in daily living activities
Disorganized thinking or loose associations	Poor treatment or medication compliance
Failure to adapt to cognitive deficits	Difficulty providing for basic needs, food, and housing

Source: From "A Psychodynamic Approach to the Master Treatment Plan," by J. G. Allen, J. R. Buskirk, and L. M. Sebastian, 1992, *Bulletin of the Menninger Clinic, 56,* pp. 487–510. Adapted with permission.

efficacy and mastery in the client, and weaken resistance to address more difficult problems (Woody et al., 2003).

A diagnostic formulation (e.g., using the *DSM-IV-TR* system) can further aid in prioritizing problems (Wiger, 2005). The *DSM* terminology can be useful in defining problems in a manner that enhances communication between professionals and provides a means of assessing the impact of mental disorders on an individual's relational, social, occupational, and defensive functioning (American Psychiatric Association, 2000b). The use of the mnemonic CLIENT (reviewed in Chapter 1) and information on recent stressors, the

Table 4.7   Factors to consider in prioritizing problems and tips for goal setting

Factors to Consider in Prioritizing Problems

Immediacy or severity of problem
Individual's acknowledgment of problem
Case formulation or linchpin concept
Impact of problem on individual's functioning
Probability of success in addressing problem, especially given time constraints
Client readiness or motivation to address problem
Likelihood of improvement from one problem generalizing to other problems—ripple effect
Whether the problem currently maintains the client's dysfunctional state
Clinical symptoms that are amenable to therapeutic intervention
Assets and supports
Degree to which caregivers or supports are involved

Tips for Goal Setting

Be realistic, flexible, and judicious.
Review previous records for goal attainment.
Involve the client and assess insight and commitment to goals.
Operationalize goals in clear, attainable objectives.
Determine simultaneous or staggered goals.
Monitor symptom reduction.
Involve supports.
Focus on relapse prevention.
Develop backup or fallback plan.
Clarify follow-up.
Document.

onset, course, associated features, and of a client's disorder can be invaluable in determining the severity and immediacy of presenting symptoms and can further help prioritize problems. It is crucial to also consider the presence of comorbid disorders, as overlooking these can lead to ineffective treatment. If you are working as a member of a multidisciplinary team or with other professionals, it is important to collaborate on the prioritizing of problems and goals, thus ensuring that goals are not mutually exclusive or counterproductive.

Assets and Resources

In the beginning of therapy it is critical to have an understanding of the individual's strengths, resources, and patterns of prior effective coping, as this will influence the need to involve additional services. Often when individuals are experiencing emotional problems they forget or minimize their strengths and previous adaptive coping strategies. The nature of some emotional disorders (e.g., mood or substance abuse disorders) may be characterized by a lack of insight, a negative outlook on the future, and lack of hope, which makes it more likely that clients will not spontaneously consider or mention their positive attributes (First & Tasman 2004; Maxmen & Ward, 1995; Othmer & Othmer, 2002). Asking clients to describe their strengths and how they have coped with difficult situations in the past provides information on their insight, resources, and skills.

Individuals' capacity for cognitive flexibility or rigidity is an indicator of their degree of willingness to change. Significant others can also provide critical information on the availability of family, community, and cultural supports to facilitate recovery (Lukas, 1993).

The Role of Psychological Assessment

Psychological assessment is an invaluable tool in evaluating the severity of the overall symptomatology and the individual's strengths and coping and cognitive styles (Olin & Keatinge, 1997). Assessment results can also clarify diagnostic concerns and determine the individual's level of impulsivity and potential for high-risk behaviors (e.g., suicidality). Cognitive and neuropsychological assessment can provide a comprehensive review of the client's areas of cognitive challenges or deficits and provide a critical measure of baseline functioning, which can be used to monitor cognitive deterioration or improvement (Horton, Wedding, & Webster, 1997). Although a comprehensive or full psychological assessment may be time-consuming (often requiring several sessions), the results can yield a wealth of information to aid in case formulation, target areas of intervention, and identify therapeutic challenges (Maruish, 1999, 2004). Psychological assessment can be incorporated into the treatment plan at any time. It can be useful when therapy reaches an impasse, when clients appear as treatment-resistant, and when undiagnosed comorbid conditions are suspected (e.g., cognitive deficits, personality pathology). If there is a need for rapid intervention (e.g., hospitalization, restricted number of therapy sessions due to insurance constraints) and the individual presents as diagnostically and therapeutically challenging, the results of psychological assessment can be crucial in quickly focusing interventions and providing information relevant to treatment planning (Maruish, 1999, 2004). If a comprehensive psychological assessment is desired, you may need to refer the client to a psychologist who specializes in this type of evaluation (e.g., a neuropsychologist for an in-depth cognitive evaluation or a psychologist who specializes in the administration of projective measures like the Rorschach Inkblot Test). A more comprehensive description of the types of psychological assessment and the types of measures that are used is available from Groth-Marnat's (2003) *Handbook of Psychological Assessment*. The use of assessment measures to evaluate treatment progress and outcome is discussed later in this chapter.

Case Conceptualization and Orientation

According to Eells (1997, p. 1), the case formulation is a "hypothesis about the causes, precipitants, and maintaining influences of a person's psychological, interpersonal and behavioral problems." It ties together the individual's problems, reconciles diagnostic information, and helps you to choose a treatment modality, intervention point, and strategy. In short, the case conceptualization serves as the clinician's compass (Persons, 1989). Additionally, it can help to predict behavior, understand and manage treatment adherence and relationship difficulties, address extratherapeutic issues (e.g., modifying payment plans), redirect unsuccessful treatment, and identify key or underlying problems (Woody et al., 2003).

The first step in developing an optimal case formulation involves fully ascertaining the facts of the case, differentiating between what is relevant and irrelevant, identifying what is cause and what is effect, and understanding the common pathway that links prior influences to current consequences (Bergner, 1998). Typically, a written case formulation begins with a descriptive phenomenological statement about the client's presenting problem. This includes the nature and severity of the problems and the presence of any precipitants. The facts are then organized into an explanatory model that briefly outlines the development and maintenance of the individual's difficulties. This is often the most difficult part of the case formulation. One way to do this is to identify the central underlying mechanism or "linchpin factor" that is at the heart of the client's problems. Bergner (1998) describes the linchpin conceptualization as being similar to Schacht and colleagues' (Schacht, Binder, & Strupp, 1984) "dynamic focus" or the repeating pattern that is central to the individual's problems in family therapy. An examination of the problem list may identify themes, patterns of behavior, and nuances or clues about a unifying construct. Consider asking "What do these problems have in common?" to aid in this process. Also, the chief complaint, the words the client uses to describe it, and the individual's associated automatic thoughts may reflect a central underlying belief.

Another way to conceptualize the facts into an explanatory model is to use prominent theories or a clinical orientation. If a theoretical orientation is used to understand the individual's problems it is important to continually check to see that it is consistent with your observations, whether it accounts well for all the facts, and whether the results of your intervention are what you would expect based on your theoretical conceptualization (Bergner, 1998). When using a theoretical model it is also important not to allow theoretically preferred variables to limit your conceptualization or choice of interventions, but to also consider alternative explanations.

Once you determine how to conceptualize the case, you need to evaluate whether it provides a good explanation of or fit to the client's data. Bergner (1998) suggests that you first ask yourself a series of questions (see Table 4.8), review all of the client's problems, and try to tell a story to see if the proposed formulation fits the individual's description of the events precipitating the current problem in an understandable way.

The case formulation may also include a treatment and prognosis section that identifies the proposed interventions, anticipated outcome, and predicted obstacles to treatment (Persons, 1989; Woody et al., 2003). Sharing the case formulation with clients can help them organize their understanding of their problems and identify the focal point on which they can focus their energies for change. Thus, it places the individual in a position of power and decreases feelings of fear, helplessness, and hopelessness (Bergner, 1998). The next step is to identify goals.

Selecting Goals

Using the problem list, the clinician and client mutually identify realistic short- and long-term goals. This involves focusing on all aspects of the presenting problems, including the behavioral, emotional, and cognitive symptoms associated with each disorder and the therapeutic, social, and interpersonal impact of the individual's problems. Setting mutually agreed-upon realistic goals enhances the client's investment in treatment.

Table 4.8   A case formulation outline

Case Conceptualization*

1. Ascertain facts of the case; differentiate relevant from irrelevant.
2. Identify common pathway, repeated patterns, and cause-and-effect relations.
3. Develop an explanatory mode or conceptualization.
4. Identify underlying mechanism, linchpin factor, dynamic or central focus.
5. Test conceptualization by considering:
   a. How well does it account for all the problems on the problem list?
   b. Is it consistent with the client's report of the presenting problem?
   c. Can it make predictions that can be tested?
   d. What was the client's reaction to the formulation?
   e. Is the outcome of therapy consistent with the formulation?

Outline for a Case Formulation Report

Identifying information
Chief complaint
Problem list
Hypothesized mechanism
Relation of mechanism to problems
Precipitants of current problems
Origins of the central problem
Treatment plan
Predicted obstacles to treatment

---

*Produced with permission from the Association for the Advancement of Psychotherapy. From "Characteristics of Optimal Clinical Case Formulations. The Linchpin Concept," by R. M. Bergner, 1998, *American Journal of Psychotherapy, 52*(3), pp. 287–300.

Wiger (2005) defines goals as the desired outcomes of therapy, and objectives as the means to achieve these outcomes, which can be operationalized as a series of incremental steps. He suggests developing two written objectives per goal and including a target date for attainment and reevaluation, at which time progress is assessed and the treatment plan is revised. Moran (2000) notes that three goals at a time are manageable and recommends making sure that they are observable and measurable. For individuals with problems in multiple areas (e.g., hospitalized clients), the focus should be on pivotal areas of impairment, and the clinician should develop a series of behaviorally stated short-term goals or a series of graded steps that link together to attain the overall outcome (J. G. Allen, Buskirk, & Sebastian, 1992). Bergner (1998) suggests selecting goals that target issues that create the "biggest ripple factor," are helping to maintain a dysfunctional state, are amenable to intervention, and are the most likely to resolve the client's problems. Goals can focus on symptom management, reduction, and relief; relapse prevention; adherence; improved coping; and alleviating impairment and/or distress. In selecting goals, remember to be realistic; recognize that goals can be staggered, adopted simultaneously, or approached sequentially. The timing of treatment and the number of objectives identified to reach therapeutic goals will be influenced by the client's level of impairment, motivation, insight, and rapport with the clinician, the treatment setting, and the number of sessions allowed (Wiger, 2005). The standards in the field include guidelines developed by the Joint Commission on Accreditation of Healthcare Organizations (JCAHO, 2004) for treatment planning that include short- and long-term goals. According to the JCAHO, goals should target the removal of unwanted symptoms and be linked to learning, living, and work activities.

Selecting Intervention Strategies

Preliminary Considerations

Before selecting specific interventions it is helpful to have an overall plan to identify all the areas of treatment that need to be addressed. Ingram (2006) describes matching the treatment plan to the needs of each client using core clinical hypotheses to generate integrated case formulations and an individualized plan. A comprehensive treatment plan should address symptom management, family, and adjunct referrals (see Table 4.9). For many clients, symptom management involves the identification of characteristic symptoms and prodromes and a referral for a medication evaluation to treat presenting problems. If the client is currently on medication, a review of medication adherence issues should be incorporated into the plan (M. J. Gitlin, 1996; Horne, 1998; O'Neal, Talga, & Preston, 2002). Educating clients about their illness, its nature, course, associated features, and appropriate treatments, and what to expect about the therapeutic process more generally is also essential (Cartwright, 2004). When individuals have significant social supports or family members who are available and willing to be involved in treatment,

Table 4.9   Treatment interventions

Area	Interventions
Symptom management	Medication evaluation and review (including medication adherence)
	Psychoeducation about illness and treatments
	Identification of characteristic symptoms and prodromes
	Assessment and treatment of comorbid conditions
	Determination of the need for Abstinence model
	Evaluate the need for behavioral interventions
	Coordination of treatment plan with other team members
Therapeutic interventions	Rapport issues
	Client acceptance of illness and ongoing education
	Emotional aspects of illness
	Enhancement of self-esteem
	Teaching adaptive coping strategies
	Assess effectiveness
	Modify treatment goals
Family/support interventions	Education
	Communication training
	Problem-solving training
	Adjunctive family support groups, organizations
Quality of life	Social services (living and support services)
	Adjunct referrals
	Occupational and vocational counseling
	Enrichment activities: volunteering, interests, social clubs

the provision of similar education about the client's illness (and possibly referrals to family support groups) can be helpful. It can also be very helpful to liaise with social services or community agencies for living and support services and to include adjunct referrals for occupational and vocational counseling.

Strategies for Intervention Selection

Having selected and prioritized the goals and agreed with the client on the issues that will be the focus of attention, you must now consider which interventions are most appropriate. This is often described as the nuts and bolts of treatment planning. G. L. Paul's (1967, p. 111) early, insightful question about the process of treatment selection still resonates today: "What treatment, by whom, is most effective for this individual with that specific problem, and under which set of circumstances?"

Beutler et al. (2002) recommend that the clinician adopt a systematic approach to treatment selection and consider which combination of interventions best addresses particular aspects of the client's problem (e.g., chronicity, coping style, level of social support). Your therapeutic orientation, case conceptualization (including clinical presentation and diagnosis), and knowledge of research on treatment effectiveness will guide the selection of interventions (Ingram, 2006; A. Roth & Fonagy, 2006). Practical factors such as available time and resources will also impact your choice. In addition, clients may have a very clear sense of what interventions they are interested in based on prior treatment experiences or from Internet research they have done on the nature of their problems and available treatments. However, for many clients, part of your role as a clinician is educating them about the nature of their disorder, the range of treatments available, and the most effective interventions (Castonguay & Beutler, 2006; Norcross, 2002a,b; A. Roth & Fonagy, 2006). Being able to provide clients with literature and access to a support group such as AA, NA, or Alliance for the Mentally Ill can be invaluable in destigmatizing their problems and increasing their involvement in their recovery.

An individual's level of functional impairment and coping style should also be considered in selecting interventions (Beutler, Brookman, Harwood, Alimohamed, & Malik, 2001). Functional impairment is measured by the severity of problems and the range of areas of reduced functioning, including disruptions in intimate attachments, work, leisure, and home life. It can be assessed using the GAF (American Psychiatric Association, 2000b) or the Social Adjustment Scale Self-Report (Weissman & Bothwell, 1976). The negative effects of functional impairment can be addressed by increasing the length or duration of psychotherapeutic interventions (Beutler & Harwood, 2000). Coping style is the individual's way of relating to others (e.g., internalizing versus externalizing style). Overall, individuals with good interpersonal supports, a single diagnosis, and acute problems are the most likely to benefit from psychotherapy, while more functionally impaired individuals demonstrate lower rates of improvement and poorer outcome regardless of type of disorder or treatment (Beutler et al., 2001). In looking at the impact of matching individual variables (including coping style) with treatment type, Beutler and colleagues found that medication was most effective for individuals with high levels of functional impairment and social support. Interpersonal and insight-oriented treatments were recommended for internalizing individuals, and symptom-focused and behavioral treatments were better for externalizing individuals. Makover (2004) describes effective treatment as being based on clinical judgment about the desired overall outcome, which may include resolving the distress that precipitated the need to seek help, restoring the individual to previous level of functioning, and allowing the individual to make further progress and growth.

When choosing interventions it is crucial to consider research findings on efficacious and appropriate interventions for specific disorders and to avoid the use of treatments that are contraindicated for specific clinical populations (Wiger, 2005). There is a wealth of treatment manuals and information on empirically validated treatments that can be overwhelming for the novice clinician to wade through. When selecting treatment options it is important to consider the details of research cited in support of the interventions, which is typically provided in the manual itself or in the manual's reference list. In particular, note the size of sample that was used, including demographics (including issues of diversity), diagnoses, the presence of comorbid conditions, exclusionary criteria, and use of control or comparison groups. Attend to the setting in which the intervention took place, the skill level and training of the clinicians utilized in the study, how outcome was measured, how effectiveness was determined (including consideration of statistically versus clinically significant change), and the degree to which details of the intervention (e.g., session content) are provided. Strengths and limitations of intervention research will be revealed by careful consideration of these variables. More detailed consideration of these issues is provided by Norcross (1999, 2002b), Castonguay and Beutler (2006), and Beutler, Consoli, and Lane (2005). When selecting treatments you also need to evaluate your personal training, skill level, and experience with specific interventions. A wide range of organizations offer continuing education courses that teach empirically validated therapeutic techniques, and many of the treatment manuals provide information on training opportunities. Using techniques or interventions that you are unfamiliar with is not only likely to be ineffectual but is also unethical (AAMFT, 2001; ACA, 2005; APA, 2002; NASW, 1999).

Duration of Treatment

The duration of therapy is influenced by the clinician's theoretical orientation, the client's presenting problem, financial considerations, the development and maintenance of a therapeutic relationship, the existence of appropriate and effective interventions, session frequency, treatment adherence history, client preferences, and the therapy setting (Mathews, 1989). Research suggests that long-term therapy can have lasting effects especially for individuals with chronic problems such as a personality disorder (Luborsky, 2001; Sandell et al., 2002; D. A. Shapiro et al., 2003). However, there is no set effective number of sessions for all clients, and both short- and long-term therapies can be effective for different individuals and disorders (Luborsky, 2001; Sandell et al., 2002). If the treatment plan includes the involvement of other professionals, it is helpful to determine how information will be shared and progress will be evaluated and to consider the confidentiality and HIPPA issues discussed in Chapter 1.

Selecting Therapeutic Interventions for Older Adults

J. Garner (2003) found that a wide range of analytic and cognitive-behavioral therapies are effective for older adults. He recommends that work with older adults initially focus on the rationale for treatment, a discussion of ageism and other biases (e.g., being too old to change) that could impede treatment, and the setting of realistic, concrete goals that involve activity and behavior change rather than cognitive restructuring. Presenting problems for older adults are usually multifaceted, and often more complex than for younger adults, so it is especially important to prioritize problems (Secker, Kazantzis, & Pachana, 2004).

When working with older adults it is imperative that the clinician respect the client without appearing patronizing and focus on learning new skills or rediscovering discarded ones. Any meaningful psychotherapeutic approach must take into consideration the psychological tasks of the older adult's developmental stage, including redefining one's sense of self in the context of multiple losses and changes in the psychological, physical, and social spheres (Nordhus, Nielsen, & Kvale, 2003). Indeed, it is helpful to explicitly address developmental issues, such as the loss of friends or the impact of retirement, and to incorporate reflection on past events (e.g., reminiscence therapy), life review, and the use of repetition, written materials, and photographs or objects as recall cues in working with elderly clients (Klausner & Alexopoulous, 1999; Nordhus et al., 2003). The pacing of session content is also crucial, and the clinician may want to consider reducing the amount of material addressed, decreasing session length and increasing session frequency, and gradually tapering sessions when treatment is nearing a close (J. Garner, 2003; Secker et al., 2004). When the client has difficulty staying focused, setting and adhering to an agenda can be very helpful, as well as using techniques such as a therapy diary to bridge sessions. Older adults are often vulnerable to feelings of hopelessness, depression, and isolation, which increase their risk for suicide. Grief is often a focus of therapy, and suicide risk should be continually monitored (Klausner & Alexopoulous, 1999; Nordhus et al., 2003). The use of systematic family therapy, especially focusing on improved communication, transitions, and dealing with age-related disorders such as Alzheimer's disease, has been found to be effective (J. Garner, 2003). In fact, psychotherapy for older adults not only decreases psychopathology, somatic complaints, pain, and disability, but also improves compliance with medical regimens and is an effective intervention for bereavement-related depression and caregiver burden (Nordhus et al., 2003). Klausner and Alexopoulous (1999) report that psychosocial interventions also play a crucial role in the treatment of psychiatric symptoms in older adults. Therapy can be beneficial in developing coping mechanisms to deal with life's adversities, stress from increased disability, and psychosocial impoverishment.

Writing the Treatment Plan

Treatment plans are the most consulted part of a client's chart and provide "examples of behaviors for which changes will be documented to validate therapeutic progress" (Wiger, 2005, p. 125). A major point in documentation is to demonstrate the effectiveness of treatment; thus, treatment plans are not set in stone but are revised as the client meets therapy objectives (Wiger, 2005). To facilitate communication and obtain third-party reimbursement the written treatment plan should include a *DSM-IV-TR* diagnosis (American Psychiatric Association, 2000b). The plan's time frame may span several months or be condensed into several sessions. Most agencies require treatment plans to be updated after a certain number of sessions. For long-term cases the treatment plan can be revised incrementally, at least every 3 months. The format of treatment plans can vary depending on the clinical site in which you work. In describing how the Menninger Clinic developed a psychodynamic treatment plan format, J. G. Allen et al. (1992) note that many clinics' and hospitals' treatment plans are determined by third-party accreditation or reimbursement organizations such as JCAHO, Medicare, or a managed care organization. A good treatment plan should at a minimum include sections addressing symptoms, areas of functional impairment, goals or objectives, treatment strategies, and methods of assessing effectiveness (Maxmen & Ward, 1995; Wiger, 2005). Wiger recommends that the clinician specify the type of therapy (individual, family, or group), the theoretical orientation or school of thought that will guide the interventions (e.g., cognitive-behavioral, psychodynamic), and the specific therapeutic techniques or interventions to be used (e.g., interpretation, systematic desensitization, role-playing). Homework assignments and any other interventions outside of the sessions that are going to be implemented should also be noted. Some clinicians include the time frame for each objective in a column form; others use a time period or number of sessions for the overall plan rather than individual objectives. The treatment plan should also incorporate information on the individual's assets and strengths. Some clinicians write the treatment plan in the form of a treatment contract that both the clinician and the client sign at the onset of treatment and refer to frequently during treatment.

In writing the treatment plan, keep in mind basic report writing skills such as remembering the audience for whom the treatment plan is intended, avoiding jargon and redundancy, and being logical, clear, and concise. Writing a good treatment plan is an invaluable skill that, like others, takes time and practice to develop. If you are still in training, one of the ways to familiarize yourself with this skill is to obtain clinic forms and to ask your supervisor for examples of completed treatment plans to review. Over the past several years a range of treatment planners have been developed (e.g., Jongsma & Peterson, 2003) to help clinicians conceptualize interventions in a ready-made format.

Some common problems clinicians encounter in writing treatment plans relate in part to an attitude that such plans are unnecessary and should be completed only when mandated by a third party. Typically, clinicians are not trained specifically in writing treatment plans, and this skill requires a knowledge of psychopathology, client-change factors, creativity, ability to integrate diagnosis and treatment interventions, and writing ability (Wiger, 2005). The lack of a treatment plan can result in unfocused, poorly defined interventions and objectives. Elements to include and common pitfalls to avoid in the formulation and writing of a treatment plan are presented in Table 4.10.

ASSESSING TREATMENT EFFECTIVENESS AND OUTCOME

Regardless of your orientation or choice of interventions, you need to determine the means and methods for assessing therapeutic effectiveness and outcome for each individual client (Tillet, 1996). Initially, it is helpful to review the presenting problems, progress toward goals, the appropriateness and effectiveness of interventions, and factors that relate to treatment outcome (Table 4.11). The use of formal assessment measures can aid in establishing a baseline of symptomatic status and functioning and tracking treatment progress over time.

Table 4.10   Treatment plan essentials

Writing a Treatment Plan

State reason for referral.

Document relevant history succinctly.

Address crisis issues.

Identify target behaviors.

Determine and describe goals and objectives.

Describe resources and supports.

Specify interventions.

Document challenges and contraindications.

Outline evaluation measures or criteria for achievement.

Include referrals to adjunct services.

Monitor compliance and follow-through.

Outline of a Typical Treatment Plan

Identifying information: Basic demographic, referring and treating clinician, case number or identification

Reason for referral: Very succinct synopsis (often omitted)

Problems or concerns: Prioritized, clear

Goals and objectives: Operationalized, clear, and concise

Interventions: Nature, frequency, and format

Measures: Assessment of outcome/progress reliable, valid, and appropriate

Time frame

Clinician's signature

Pitfalls to Avoid[*]

Vague, incomplete, or unclear assessment

Diagnosis and interventions not integrated

Nonmeasurable objectives

Undefined treatment strategies

Nonstandard interventions

Plan- and *DSM*-discordant

Effectiveness of interventions unclear

Strengths and weakness not incorporated

Functional impairments not addressed

Not accessible

Unrealistic: Under- or overambitious in scope

[*]From *The Psychotherapy Documentation Primer*, second edition, by D. E. Wiger, 2005, Hoboken, NJ: Wiley. Adapted with permission.

The majority of psychotherapy outcome studies use symptom reduction as a measure of treatment effectiveness, which may be influenced by several factors, including the duration of treatment and the nature of the disorder being treated (Kazdin, 1997b). In evaluating treatment outcome in children, Kazdin (1997b) notes that it is important to consider family functioning and the impact of the symptoms on other systems, such as school and special services utilization. Beyond symptomatic status, the clinician can consider assessing relationship functioning, work or educational performance, and ability to carry out activities of daily living.

Table 4.11   Factors in evaluating treatment progress

Factors in Evaluating Treatment Progress

Reduction of problems

Management of symptoms

Client reports of improvement

Third-party or significant other's reports of improvement

Decrease in subjective distress or impairment

Objective assessment of improvement and outcome

Increase in functioning

Increase in insight and awareness

Improved coping strategies

Decrease in associated features

Decrease in comorbid conditions

Attainment of goals

Factors to Consider for Children and Adolescents[*]

1. Child's or adolescent's functioning

   a. Clinical and behavioral symptoms

   b. Level and pervasiveness of impairment

   c. Mental and physical health

   d. Prosocial competence and social relationships

   e. Academic functioning

2. Parent and family functioning

   a. Dysfunction symptoms, behaviors, and patterns

   b. Contextual influences: Stress, quality of life, poverty of community

   c. Factors for adaptation: Family support, quantity, and quality time

3. Social impact measures

   a. Consequences on systems: School attendance, activities, truancy

   b. Changes in services utilization: Special education or other services

[*]From "A Model for Developing Effective Treatment: Progression and Interplay of Theory, Research, and Practice," by A. E. Kazdin, 1997b, *Journal of Clinical Child Psychology, 26,* pp. 114–129. Reproduced with permission.

In reviewing treatment outcomes for more than 11,000 individuals over a range of settings, Finch, Lambert, and Schaaljie (2001) found that the largest gains occur in the early stages of treatment; however, for individuals with serious disorders, the treatment benefits accumulated over time. Similarly, Leibert (2006) reported that 50% of individuals with anxiety and depression improve by sessions 8 to 13, and those with borderline psychosis reached similar improvement in sessions 13 to 52, suggesting that more severe psychopathology and characterological problems require longer treatment. Findings from this study also demonstrated that higher levels of initial distress required more sessions for clinical improvement, and that those individuals who presented initially with more severe disturbances changed more over the course of treatment, but that individuals with fewer symptoms initially remained better after therapy. In addition, whereas clinical symptoms (e.g., depression) tended to improve quickly once therapy was initiated, occupational improvement was most apparent after 4 to 6 months, and interpersonal and social improvement often was not apparent until after 6 to 8 months of treatment.

Subjective Units of Distress

A common means of assessment used in inpatient settings is subjective units of distress (SUDs). Using this method, the clinician asks clients to rate their level of distress on a scale from 0 to 100 for a range of symptoms, including their presenting problem (e.g., anxiety), at different times or in different situations. Clients are reassessed several times, and the results can be presented graphically (Wiger, 2005). These SUDs ratings are frequently used in cognitive-behaviorally oriented treatments for conditions such as anxiety disorders. When relying on the individual's self-report you need to consider factors that influence the veracity of the data, including reluctance to be critical, desire to please the therapist, and the tendency to be hypercritical if the therapist is confrontational (Leibert, 2006). Some clinicians opt to assess outcome using client satisfaction surveys; however, these often do not assess symptom change and have a very low return rate (5% to 10%; Leibert, 2006).

Multidimensional and Symptom-Specific Measures

Leibert (2006) recommends considering global measures of outcome such as the Symptom Checklist 9—Revised (Derogatis, 1983) that can be used across diagnoses. He notes that using a range of brief measures that can be repeated facilitates assessing the breadth of the individual's clinical improvement. Toward these ends, Woody and colleagues (2003) describe and provide a range of measures that can be used to assess the client's progress that are brief, easy to administer, and have good psychometric properties. Examples include the NIMH's Center for Epidemiological Studies Depression scale (Radloff, 1977), a 20-item measure of depression; the Rosenberg Self-Esteem Scale (Rosenberg, 1965), a 10-item scale that assesses global self-esteem; the Brief Psychiatric Rating Scale (Overall & Gorham, 1962), an 18-item measure of global functioning most suitable for clients with severe forms of psychopathology such as Schizophrenia or Bipolar Disorder; the Psychotic Symptoms Rating Scales (Haddock, McCarron, Tarrier & Faragher, 1999), a 17-item scale assessing hallucinations and delusions; and the Yale-Brown Obsessive-Compulsive Scale (Goodman, Price, Rasmussen, Mazure, Fleischmann, Hill, et al., 1989), a 10-item scale to assess for Obsessive-Compulsive Disorder. The clinical disorders chapters in this text review additional assessment measures for specific disorders.

Considerations in Selecting an Assessment Measure

Over the past few years there has been a proliferation in the number of measures to assess treatment effectiveness and outcome, and it may be difficult for the clinician to decide which ones to select. There are a number of factors the clinician should consider in making this decision. First, the measure should assess variables relevant to the problematic symptoms or behaviors for which the client is seeking treatment. Second, practical considerations, such the length of a measure, its required reading level, and the ease with which it can be administered (e.g., whether standardized instructions are provided), scored, and interpreted will also influence measure selection (Groth-Marnat, 2003). Third, whether or not the clinician has sufficient training and expertise to use a measure must be taken into account. Some assessment instruments (e.g., the Minnesota Multiphasic Personality Inventory 2) require considerable training to use competently and should not be administered by individuals unfamiliar with them unless they are closely supervised by a knowledgeable clinician and educate themselves (e.g., through courses, readings, workshops) about the measure.

Clinicians should also be familiar with the psychometric properties of the measures they are considering, including whether there is documented evidence of reliability and validity. *Reliability* refers to the degree to which a test's scores are free from measurement error (Groth-Marnat, 2003). There are many forms of reliability, including *test-retest* (which assesses the consistency of scores across time), *split-half* (which assesses the internal consistency of items within a measure), and *interrater* (which assesses the degree of score agreement between different raters). Reliability estimates are expressed as correlation coefficients and when .80 or higher are generally considered strong (Groth-Marnat, 2003). The *validity* of a test concerns the degree to which a test actually assesses what it intends to measure. As with reliability, there are many forms of validity. For example, *content validity* relates to whether a measure contains items that sufficiently represent the behavior domain being assessed, for example, does a measure of panic attacks sufficiently cover relevant symptoms and features associated with this clinical phenomenon? *Criterion validity* examines whether the results of a measure are consistent with scores on another outside measure (Groth-Marnat, 2003); for example, does a measure of dementia severity predict nursing home placement? *Construct validity* may be determined in multiple ways, including examination of whether a measure correlates highly with theoretically related variables but demonstrates a low correlation with theoretically dissimilar variables (*convergent* and *discriminate validity*, respectively), or whether a measure is able to detect change following a treatment intervention (Leibert, 2006); for example, do scores on a marital satisfaction inventory improve among individuals who undergo couples therapy? The *sensitivity* and *specificity* of a measure concern its ability to accurately identify cases and noncases of a disorder, respectively. The reader is referred to Groth-Marnat (2003) for a more in-depth discussion of reliability and validity.

Many measures used to assess clients involve a comparison of the client's scores to a larger group of individuals who also took the test (known as the standardization sample or normative sample). Thus, another psychometric consideration in evaluating a measure is whether the standardization sample is sufficiently representative of the clients with whom you are intending to use the measure. For example, if you are planning to use a measure with ethnic minority clients, it is important to determine whether published normative data include an adequate representation of those ethnic groups. To the extent that a client is very different from the profile of the individuals composing the normative sample, the normative data may not provide a fair basis of comparison for your client's scores. For additional information on selecting measures to assess treatment progress, see Maruish's (2004) *The Use of Psychological Testing for Treatment Planning*.

DOCUMENTATION

Most agencies require that all contact with clients be documented; even if one is working as a private practitioner this is a good practice to adopt. Good documentation is the clinician's primary responsibility to his or her patients, peers, and the institution for which he or she works (Horner, 2000). Treatment plans should be revised and updated during the course of treatment, often every 60 to 90 days (Wiger, 2005). Horner describes a 20-day review period for individuals in partial hospitalization programs and a 120-day review for outpatient treatment. Revisions to the treatment plan may include changes that occurred since the original plan was written, updated information on the client's current functioning, and the delineation of new goals if originally outlined objectives have been met. If interventions were unsuccessful and objectives were not met, new interventions may be incorporated and the goals modified. Depending on clinic policy, updates may be incorporated into the chart progress notes or included on a treatment plan update form.

While the treatment plan serves to document the course of treatment, progress notes record that the plan is being implemented and followed. Progress notes help to document baseline behavior, change, insight, and treatment compliance and attendance. Think of the progress note as the clinician's behavioral evidence of therapeutic progress (Wiger, 2005). Many clinical settings have set formats for progress notes, and it is important to familiarize yourself with these. Progress notes may follow a SOAP (subjective, objective assessment plan) or DAP (data assessment plan) format that has been adopted across many mental health disciplines and used in medical settings as well (Wiger, 2005). For example, using the SOAP format, information included under *subjective* would include clients' subjective report of their functioning (e.g., presenting complaints, self-reported mood). Under *objective*, the clinician documents observations on the client's clinical presentation (e.g., affect, mental status, symptoms). Clinical observations should be related to the individual's presenting problems and diagnosis. The *assessment* section will include information on therapeutic progress, the client's cooperation, effectiveness of therapeutic interventions, and any necessary modifications or revisions to the treatment plan. Finally, the *plan* section of the note addresses homework assignments, referrals, and the focus of future sessions (Wiger, 2005).

Progress notes should provide documentation on the occurrence, length, and content of the therapy sessions, including problems or objectives that were the focus of clinical attention, interventions used, and information on the client's progress (Wiger, 2005). They should also document the client's level of functioning and current symptomatology, any setbacks encountered, and client strengths and limitations (Wiger, 2005). Issues that warrant concern and continued monitoring, such as problems with impulse control (e.g., suicide risk, substance use), medication compliance, and crisis issues, should always be documented. Such issues often warrant modification of the treatment plan or additional interventions. Any referrals and homework assigned outside the session should also be noted. Although this sounds like a lot of information, it should not take an excessively long time to write a good progress note, and may take as little as 5 to 10 minutes. A good habit to get into is to write the progress note immediately after the treatment session has ended, while the details of what transpired are still fresh in your mind. Common clinician errors in writing progress notes include vagueness and noting information that is unrelated to treatment goals (Wiger, 2005). Information should be summarized and presented in an objective, factual, clear, and concise manner. Many third parties require the continued documentation of the medical or functional necessity for treatment in order to obtain reimbursement for services (Wiger, 2005). Remember that progress notes as part of the individual's file are confidential, need to follow HIPAA regulations, and can be used to evaluate the treatment you provided. They establish a level of clinical accountability and are invaluable in facilitating recall of clinical information when reviewed prior to the therapy session, when transferring a case, or when conveying information to other professionals involved in an individual's clinical care. When completed, notes should be signed and your credentials or title and the date included.

CHALLENGES TO TREATMENT IMPLEMENTATION

Premature Termination

A strong therapeutic alliance appears to be the best predictor of a positive outcome in psychotherapy (Cartwright, 2004; Truant, 1998a,b). The failure to establish and maintain adequate rapport often results in the client dropping out of treatment, missing appointments, or failing to follow through on recommendations (Gabbard, 2000). In these instances, it is not unusual for the clinician to feel at a loss for what to do and unsure how to proceed. Premature termination is defined as the client's leaving therapy before reaching a requisite level of improvement or completing therapy goals (Hatchett & Park, 2003). It not only renders therapy ineffective but can also be very demoralizing to the therapist. Despite decades of research, no consistent indicators of premature termination have emerged (Cartwright, 2004; Corning & Malofeeva, 2004). Premature termination has been described as one of the greatest single obstacles to the effective delivery of mental health services, with 20% to 60% of adults with a range of problems dropping out of therapy (Cartwright, 2004; Venable & Thompson, 1998). Brogan and Prochaska (1999) found that 20% to 57% of outpatients terminate against a therapist's advice after the first session, and 30% to 60% drop out of treatment prior to completing therapeutic goals (Corning & Malofeeva, 2004). Survival analysis indicates that the rate of premature termination is higher at the beginning of therapy and highest when few sessions have been attended. In contrast, the rate for mutually agreed-upon termination is low at the beginning of treatment, increases slightly until the 8th session, and then decreases and plateaus until the 28th session, after which it increases sharply (Corning & Malofeeva, 2004).

The dropout rates for children, adolescents, and their families have been estimated at between 40–60%, with the parent usually making the decision for their child to enter and terminate treatment (Kazdin, 1997b; Venable & Thompson, 1998). Uncooperative parents, those with psychological problems themselves (e.g., depression), and those reluctant to accept change are more likely to cause the child to drop out of treatment prematurely (Kazdin, 1997b). The mother's attitude toward treatment may also be a factor in premature termination. Caretakers with high levels of self-criticism and delusional guilt were found to have higher levels of premature termination (Venable & Thompson, 1998). Additionally, depressed caretakers may be likely to withdraw their child from treatment if the child does not appear to respond within a brief time. These findings suggest that providing counseling at the outset to parents who present as depressed and self-depreciating may decrease the likelihood that the child's counseling is prematurely terminated. These findings also emphasize how important it is to have achievable goals that the caretaker can view as related to specific successes (Venable & Thompson, 1998).

Rigorous selection screening for treatment and the early detection of repetitive behaviors and motives that serve to sabotage therapy is crucial (Cartwright, 2004). From the beginning, you need to recognize and address anxieties and other factors that may have a negative impact on the therapeutic process and on the individual's ability to work collaboratively, and to continually remain alert to these issues as therapy progresses. In the early stages, it is natural for clients to express skepticism; however, it is important that this does not develop into problems of misalliance and a negative transference (Cartwright, 2004).

Cartwright (2004) described several techniques to prevent premature termination, including the use of anticipatory interpretations and cautionary tales early in therapy. *Anticipatory interpretations* convey concern about the future of the therapeutic relationship and address areas of resistance that impact premature termination in a manner that is understandable and usable for the client (Cartwright, 2004). They involve three essential elements. First, there should be a clear reference to themes that pinpoint anxieties leading to resistances; specifically, the therapist comments on imminent anxieties that may be difficult for the client to articulate and that may cause avoidance or abandonment of the therapeutic process. Second, a future-oriented focus that raises awareness about issues that interfere with the therapeutic process is adopted; the therapist encourages open communication and acknowledges the importance of factors that influence termination. Third, the therapist affirms the difficulty the client may be experiencing, but also provides statements encouraging the client's willingness to engage in therapy and asks the client to reflect on feelings or motives and affirms that these may be obstacles to the therapeutic process. Thus, the clinician recognizes and validates the individual's difficulty in seeking treatment in a supportive manner that communicates respect and understanding (Cartwright, 2004).

In utilizing *cautionary tales*, the therapist addresses the client's initial anxieties about treatment and therapy and his or her tendency to isolate, retreat from difficult situations, or display signs of impulsiveness. Cartwright (2004) recommends addressing these concerns before they consume the therapeutic process in an unproductive manner. He also encourages the clinician to reflect when the client acts out in this manner outside the therapeutic session because this is when the client is the most vulnerable to terminating. The early recognition of repetitive behaviors may also enhance the client's feeling of being understood.

Countertransference

I. Weiner (1998) defines countertransference as inappropriate or irrational reactions by the therapist to a patient's behavior. Such reactions are based on the therapist's unresolved conflicts or issues or are triggered by client content or skill deficits (Rosenberger & Hayes, 2002). J. Hayes et al. (1991) note that countertransference occurs when empathy or the ability to identify with the client goes awry and the therapist is unable to disengage from the identification. Countertransference has also been conceptualized as avoidance behavior, as the tendency to over- or underemphasize the client's emotionally threatening material, and as a withdrawal of the clinician's involvement (Rosenberger & Hayes, 2002). Countertransference reactions can be acute or chronic and vary in how directly they are expressed and how obvious their meaning is (Kernberg, 1999). When countertransference occurs, it always involves a prevailing tone that casts the client in either a

186 Fundamental Clinical Skills

favorable or unfavorable light. It is essentially negative in that it distorts reality and suspends a therapist's attention to helping the client toward self-understanding (I. Weiner, 1998).

Therapists' awareness of their feelings, especially in conjunction with their ability to use a theoretical framework in which to understand these feelings, plays a critical role in managing countertransference (Rosenberger & Hayes, 2002). Additionally, therapists' empathy and capacity for self-integration inversely relates to countertransference behavior. In general, the better the therapists' understanding of themselves and the more experience they have with different types of clients, the more adept they will be at recognizing, anticipating, and controlling countertransference reactions. I. Weiner (1998) also recommends being circumspect in terms of what personal information the therapist reveals to the client regarding such reactions. J. Hayes and colleagues (1991) identified five factors that experts identify as central in managing countertransference: (1) self-awareness or self-integration (i.e., the therapist's sense of self and of boundaries); (2) anxiety management; (3) conceptualizing skills; (4) empathy; and (5) self-insight. The last variable includes the clinician's awareness of blind spots or limits of therapeutic effectiveness, an awareness of one's feelings elicited by the client, the capability to reflect on one's own feelings, and an awareness of personal areas of unresolved conflict. Empathy can also be a moderator of countertransference, resulting in sensitivity to others' emotions and an awareness of one's own feelings. In cases of chronic stalemate, Kernberg (1999) recommends that therapists imagine what a normal interaction would be like, and then use cognitive clarity, contained emotional concern, and courage to interpret the situation.

Medication Nonadherence

Bebbington (1995, p. 41) described compliance as "adherence to a prescribed and appropriate treatment." Noncompliance or nonadherence with medication increases the risk not only for relapse but also for hospitalization, a longer length of stay, and the potential for revolving-door treatment (Perkins, 2002). In short, no medication is effective unless it is taken (Perkins, 2002). Medication adherence is influenced by many factors (see Table 4.12), including individuals' cognitive beliefs about medication, their perception of the benefits of treatment and the risks of illness versus the costs of treatment, and the views of significant others (Horne, 1998; Perkins, 1999, 2002). Medication nonadherence is common among individuals with severe psychopathology such as Schizophrenia, Bipolar Disorder, and comorbid alcohol and substance abuse (Bebbington, 1995; W. Fenton, Blyler, & Heinssen, 1997; Raimirez Basco & Rush, 1995). In a comprehensive review of medication nonadherence in Schizophrenia, Lacro, Dunn, Dolder, Leckband, and Jeste (2002) found the most consistent factors predicting this behavior included poor insight, negative attitude or subjective response to the medication, prior nonadherence, substance use, shorter duration of illness, poor therapeutic alliance, and inadequate discharge planning or aftercare environment. Lack of insight and denial, particularly in the early stages of mental illness, contribute to nonadherence, and adherence tends to also decline with increasing length of a medication regimen. For the homeless, practical barriers (including access to medication) and financial burden are particularly salient factors in nonadherence.

Table 4.12   Factors in treatment of nonadherence

| | Factors in Medication Noncompliance | |
Patient-Related	Medication-Related	Clinician or Environment-Related
Lack of insight and information	Dysphoric side effects	Poor therapeutic alliance
Substance abuse comorbidity	Subtherapeutic dosage	Inadequate supervision
Negative attitude to medication	Excessively high dosage	Social isolation
Greater symptom severity	Adverse side effects (e.g., weight gain)	Practical barriers
Paranoia, grandiosity	Parkinson effects	Medication access
Disorganization, cognitive deficits	Sleep difficulties	Poor aftercare
Prior noncompliance	Complicated regimen	Family beliefs
Decreased functioning		Discharge plan inadequate
Decreased quality of life		
Shorter duration of illness		

| | Strategies for Improving Compliance | |
Patient-Related	Medication-Related	Clinician or Environment-Related
Screen and treat comorbidity	Identify and treat side effects	Strong therapeutic alliance
Cognitive therapy	Minimiz impact of side effects on individuals life	Patient-centered approach
Active participant in planning	Minimize regimen complexity	Active discussion of compliance
Education about illness	Titrate to optimum dose	Education and support of family/others
Education benefits treatment	Clear instructions on use	Assertive case management
Anticipatory planning	Use minimal side effects medications	Improve access to mental health services (including times and locations)
Identify cues and memory aids	Consider medication restrictions (e.g., diet)	Improve services coordination
		Stronger discharge and aftercare planning, including home visits

Whereas a poor therapeutic alliance is frequently linked to nonadherence, a warm, empathic relationship enhances trust and open communication about medication concerns and may enhance adherence (Fleischhacker, Meise, Gunther, & Kurz, 1994; Paykel, 1995; Zygmunt, Olfson, Boyer, & Mechanic, 2002). Indeed, empirical studies indicate that therapists who are successful in achieving medication adherence have been found to give their clients more reassurance and hope and discuss adherence in an open, nonpunitive fashion (Fawcett, 1995; Horne, 1998; Ramirez Basco & Rush, 1995). Defining the treatment goals and actively involving the patient in treatment and regular discussions of adherence issues should be inherent in any treatment plan (Raimirez Basco & Rush, 1995).

Family and social support can help with medication administration and enhance outpatient compliance (W. Fenton et al., 1997). Describing over 15 years of outpatient treatment at Western Psychiatric Institute, E. Frank, Kupfer, and Siegel (1995) found that for mood disorder clients, reframing adherence as an alliance resulted in a low patient dropout rate (10%) and high medication adherence (>85%). The essential elements of their approach are educating clients about the illness and treatment and engaging them as active participants or coinvestigators in their recovery. A strong effort was also made to engage the family in treatment, using family psychoeducational workshops; as the authors noted, informed family members rarely undermine treatment.

ENDING TREATMENT: TERMINATION

The manner in which the therapeutic relationship is brought to a close has a significant impact on the outcome of therapy, the individual's posttherapy adaptation, and whether the therapeutic changes become life-enriching, meaningful experiences (Garcia-Lawson & Lance, 1997; I. Weiner, 1998). Termination may be a mutually collaborative decision, something that either the therapist or the client initiates, something that has been predetermined by insurance factors, or an event that is abrupt and unplanned. The factors in private practice that impact how long you work with a client include theoretical orientation, the client's presenting problems, financial considerations, and development and maintenance of the therapeutic alliance (Mathews, 1989). Abrupt, premature, and unplanned (e.g., due to therapist death) terminations can result in profoundly negative feelings on the part of the client (Garcia-Lawson & Lance, 1997). Completion of therapy may represent the cessation of a learning experience; incomplete termination or good-byes may adversely impact individuals so that they are reluctant to seek help at a later date when they need it (Mathews, 1989). There is a paucity of literature on termination guidelines and procedures, which may in part be due to the lack of a systematic conceptualization of the reasons for termination, which should include both client and clinician perspectives (Corning & Malofeeva, 2004; Mathews, 1989; Todd, Deane, & Bragdon, 2003). In a comparison of therapist and client reasons for termination, Todd et al. found that whereas therapists were more likely than clients to endorse improvement, clients were more likely to endorse environmental factors such as a move, transportation problems, or financial, insurance, or time limitations as reasons for termination.

The decision to terminate therapy involves a series of questions that at the most basic level include "When should therapy stop?" and "How do you decide when therapy should end?" (Auld, Hyman, & Rudzinski, 2005). Several factors to consider when terminating with a client are outlined in Table 4.13. In reviewing earlier literature on termination, Garcia-Lawson and Lane (1997) cite Freud, who described treatment concluding when the unconscious became conscious and the ego replaced the id. However, from the therapist's perspective, no single criterion applies to all circumstances; the criteria for termination include considering the individual's ability to love and work, symptom disappearance, resolution of issues, progress toward goals, structural personality changes, and countertransference issues (Auld et al., 2005; Garcia-Lawson & Lane, 1997). I. Weiner (1998) describes three minimum criteria that should be considered if termination is being considered: (1) some substantial progress has been made toward therapeutic goals; (2) the individual is capable of working independently on his or her problems; and (3) the patient's transference relationship is sufficiently resolved. Clients' responses to ending

Table 4.13   Termination checklist

Review treatment plan.

Reevaluate symptoms and impact.

Reassess any suicide, dangerousness, substance-related, or high-risk behaviors.

Assess progress to goals.

Determine need for follow-up.

Assess need for adjunct services or referral.

Address termination with client.

Monitor countertransference.

Remain alert for regression, maladaptive behaviors, or acting-out.

Review progress.

Discuss new and alternative coping strategies.

Identify red flags for relapse.

Discuss prevention strategies.

Review and identify supports.

Clarify tune-up sessions or contact policy.

Discuss follow-up.

Say good-byes.

therapy is impacted by the success of the treatment, their history of earlier losses, whether the decision was mutual, and whether it occurs at a difficult or favorable time in their life (Garcia-Lawson & Lane, 1997).

Setting a termination date initiates a chain reaction, and it is important to stick to the time frame and to work through the issues. The appearance of new or reemergence of old problems does not necessarily contraindicate the decision to end therapy (I. Weiner, 1998). The length of the termination phase is determined by several factors, including the therapist's orientation and length of treatment. It can be as short as several sessions or several months with decreasing frequency of sessions. I. Weiner cautions against terminating therapy during the session when this issue is first raised, as this precludes time for consolidation and review. In general, the more intensely involved the individual has been in the treatment, the stronger the reaction to termination is likely to be. The individual's reaction to the termination of long-term therapy may resemble the stages one experiences when dealing with a death (i.e., denial, anger, depression, and bargaining; Garcia-Lawson & Lane, 1997). In short-term counseling there may be less frequent discussion of the ending of therapy and a review of the course of therapy and of the client's emotions or reactions to termination, although it is important that some time be devoted to a review of these topics (Quintana & Holahan, 1992). Rather than setting a date for the end of therapy, some clinicians use a spaced termination process in which the time between sessions is gradually increased, allowing for the client's response to be monitored (I. Weiner, 1998). Whereas setting a termination date works well in uncovering therapy, spaced termination is helpful for individuals in more supportive forms of psychotherapy (I. Weiner, 1998).

Depending on the nature and duration of treatment, you may spend one or several sessions reviewing the course of treatment with the client, emphasizing the progress made and highlighting in a constructive manner the issues that still need to be addressed (I. Weiner, 1998). This is also a good time to review relapse prevention strategies, identify with the client red flags or indicators of the reoccurrence of problems, and alternative adaptive coping strategies (Wachtel, 2002). Both clinicians and clients may experience mixed feelings, and it is not unusual for the client to regress or present with previously resolved clinical issues as termination draws near. Patience, empathetic understanding, encouraging the client to verbalize these feelings and fears, and monitoring of your own countertransference issues are essential for successful closure. For most cases, termination is a time for both pride in one's work and for humility (Wachtel, 2002).

Therapist-Initiated Termination

Therapist-initiated terminations can be the consequence of a variety of factors, including client resistance (e.g., acting-out or intolerable anxiety), client nonadherence or lack of commitment, a breach of the therapeutic contract, therapy reaching a dead end, or non-payment of fees. A clinician may also consider terminating treatment for personal reasons, including unmanageable countertransference reactions that are adversely impacting treatment, pregnancy, a move, or completion of training (Auld et al., 2005; Mathews, 1989). In such cases, it is important to remember it is unethical to abandon your client (AAMFT, 2001; ACA, 2005; APA, 2002; NASW, 1999). If a client continues to be in need of clinical services, you should help him or her find an appropriate referral and be available to help make the transition to the new treatment provider as smooth as possible, e.g., be willing to discuss the client's case with the new provider, encourage the client to make an initial appointment with the new therapist while still seeing you so that there is not a gap in treatment (Welfel, 2005). If the client is being transferred, you need to document the follow-up plan. Typically, individuals who are reassigned or transferred experience feelings of anxiety, insecurity, and rejection, and the new therapist needs to be aware that transferred clients are often initially challenging to treat (Garcia-Lawson & Lane, 1997). Successful therapist-induced termination involves skills in effecting the closure of unfinished business. You need to be alert for countertransference feelings of rushing to terminate with frustrating or irritating clients or unnecessarily prolonging the therapy of clients you like (I. Weiner, 1998). Gaining satisfaction from your work, being aware of your own issues and history with attachments and separation, regular education or supervision, and an optimally filled appointment schedule are safeguards against the unhealthy retention of clients (Auld et al., 2005). Mathews (1989) recommends continually examining client termination issues from the framework of considering what you would do if you had a waiting list of clients. This technique may guard against keeping clients in treatment longer than is warranted.

Client-Initiated Termination

In terminations initiated by the client, a thorough review of the therapeutic changes should be conducted (I. Weiner, 1998). In these situations, the therapist may interpret the client's decision to leave treatment as a personal affront, and it is important to monitor your countertransference reactions in this regard (Mathews, 1989). Overly solicitous behavior or improper attempts to encourage the client to continue (e.g., offering additional services at a reduced fee or prematurely severing relationship out of sadness or anger) are unethical. Solo practitioners who are overly dependent on clients may be particularly vulnerable to these ethical breaches, and it may be helpful to seek consultation with colleagues to examine your response to your client's departure (Mathews, 1989). In cases where the client cancels, stops showing up, or prematurely terminates the treatment, you have a responsibility to reinstate contact with a follow-up phone call or letter to suggest that the client return for a final session. Your feelings must not undermine sound clinical practice, and you have an ethical responsibility not to abandon a client. If the client fails to show up for treatment or decompensates after termination and there was not an adequate follow-up plan in place, you could be held responsible.

Forced Termination

Forced termination occurs when therapy is ended in a nonnegotiable manner for reasons beyond the control of the therapist or the client, such as therapist illness or death. These situations can result in the client's experiencing profound grief, disappointment, and bitterness (Garcia-Lawson & Lane, 1997). As a clinician you have a responsibility to have a professional will that includes naming colleagues responsible for contacting clients and a system for handling process notes, files, billing, and the disposition of your books (Garcia-Lawson & Lane, 1997).

Discharge Summary

When terminating or ending therapy, a discharge summary should be written. This is a synopsis of treatment; it may include a brief summary description of the presenting problems and intake diagnosis. The course of treatment should be described, including interventions that were successful and goals that were met and those that were not achieved. Complications or challenges to treatment should also be described. The discharge summary should clearly outline any follow-up plan, including referrals that were made to the client and any additional treatment that is recommended. Some clinicians provide the client with a copy of the discharge plan.

WORKING WITH HEALTH MAINTENANCE ORGANIZATIONS

Hoyt and Austad (1995) note that more than 30 million Americans are covered by HMOs, and according to Sauber (1997), the focus on cost containment is here to stay, with reimbursement being based on medical or functional necessity. As such, clinical practice has been reshaped with a focus on efficacy and efficiency. The essence of good HMO therapy is short-term modes of treatment (Hoyt & Austad, 1995; Sauber, 1997). When working in a managed care environment, one must recognize that arrangements that regulate the nature, length, cost, site, and utilization of services are often determined by individuals other than the clinician and client (Hoyt, 1995). Therefore, to be successful, the therapist needs to be aware of informed consent issues; understand how to obtain authorization, which include articulating the medical necessity of treatment; be time-sensitive, pragmatic, targeted, and cost-effective in providing treatment; focus on the client's strengths and resources rather than looking at underlying pathology; and embrace a higher level of record keeping (Hoyt, 1995; Moran, 2000; Sauber, 1997). Sauber further recommends that therapists think prospectively, maximize health benefits by adopting a proactive approach to utilization review, establish a billing and case review system, become involved with the managed care organization, and ensure that one's credentialing is sufficient. He also suggests thinking of your long-term relationship with the HMO and developing a strong continuum of care for your clients.

Moran (2000) notes that most managed care organizations allow at least eight therapy sessions before case review. Although treatment termination today is based not only on the clinical needs of the individual, but also on the financial needs of the insurance company, caution is required in reducing the number of therapy sessions to avoid clinical mismanagement of a case (Wachtel, 2002). Remember that clinicians are ethically and legally obligated to appeal a managed care decision to deny medically necessary treatment. However, it is also unethical to "up-code" or to describe the client's condition as more serious than it is to obtain more sessions (Hoyt, 1995). Hoyt and Austad (1995) recommend appearing judicious and flexible to the managed care company by not using or needing to go beyond the maximum number of sessions available (usually 20) when feasible and allowing some time for follow-up. It is important to be aware of appropriate documentation that many HMOs require; a typical format is presented in Table 4.14.

Hoyt and Austad (1995) identify eight common trends in managed care that are useful to consider when working with these organizations: (1) rapid setting of specific goals with an orientation toward brief therapy and problem solving and involving other therapies or different modalities; (2) use of an early or crisis intervention approach to prevent problem entrenchment and the development of secondary problems; (3) clearly defining the responsibilities of the therapist and client, including an explicit understanding of the purpose of, schedule, and duration of therapy, as well as structured treatments and interventions in which the client actively participates (such as completing homework assignments); (4) the flexible and creative use of length, frequency, and timing of sessions to fit with the client's needs and a focus on the most parsimonious, least intensive, intrusive, and expensive interventions; (5) interdisciplinary cooperation, including allied professionals and psychopharmacologists; (6) sequential or concurrent involvement of multiple treatment formats and modalities, including individual, family, group, or community

Table 4.14   Third-party or managed care issues

Competence: Provider has appropriate credentials and expertise in treatment.

Medical necessity: Document dysfunction or functional impairment caused by a mental disorder (*ICD* or *DSM* diagnostic code). Provide evidence of impact on individual's daily living.

Goals/objectives: Document specific, attainable, observable, and measurable goals and objectives.

Treatment: Level and amount are consistent with intensity of impairment. Type is consistent with acceptable procedures and reliably predict outcome. Treatment is directed to active signs and symptoms of the disorder.

Ongoing documentation: Progress notes follow specific treatment plan objectives targeting functional impairments that have been clearly documented in assessment and treatment plan.

General concerns: Confidentiality, ethical and clinical issues.

Source: From *The Psychotherapy Documentation Primer,* second edition, by D. E. Wiger, 2005, Hoboken, NJ: Wiley. Adapted with permission.

groups (e.g., AA); (7) a family practitioner model of intermittent serial or distributed treatment; and (8) orientation toward accountability and documentation of treatment results (e.g., outcome measures and utilization review).

Brief therapy is the backbone of managed care. Hoyt and Austad (1995) provide several suggestions for effective short-term treatment. They emphasize engendering hope and monitoring progress throughout treatment, using the middle phase of treatment to work through the major tasks and increase awareness (e.g., confirming the problem or focus of attention; prioritizing and redefining treatment goals), and utilizing termination to review work completed on issues addressed and providing a plan for follow-through to address longer-term issues.

TIPS AND STRATEGIES FOR MASTERY

Establishing a strong therapeutic relationship and rapport with your client is the first step in providing good treatment. Considering the context of the individual's problems and his or her unique perspective is crucial for effective treatment planning. Having an accurate diagnosis, considering associated features, and being alert for common comorbid conditions that may undermine therapeutic interventions are also essential. Treatment planning involves the ability to identify and prioritize problems and select the interventions that are not only the most effective but that match your client's needs and situation. When developing a case conceptualization it is important to consider the client's strengths and assets as well as problems and challenges. Encouraging the client's involvement in setting goals and having realistic expectations for goals and compliance also enhance follow-through. Being successful with small, well-defined goals can provide a foundation for future growth, whereas failure with overly ambitious goals can be disheartening and devastating for clients. Awareness of different treatment modalities, the research on evidence-based interventions, and your own competence and limitations is crucial. Good treatment also involves continually reassessing the effectiveness of your interventions and being flexible to modify treatment plans as needed. Successful treatment planning also includes monitoring the factors that may adversely impact rapport and contribute to premature termination of therapy. One of the most essential skills for a clinician to develop is being able to write a good treatment plan and to effectively implement it. This takes practice, and in the beginning consultation from experienced colleagues can be invaluable. The ability to coordinate and collaborate with other professionals in providing integrated treatment is also crucial. The next chapters will address the major *DSM-IV-TR* diagnostic categories and integrate the clinical skills reviewed in the previous chapters.

PART II

CLINICAL DISORDERS

Chapter 5 ———————————————————

DISORDERS OF CHILDHOOD I: PERVASIVE DEVELOPMENTAL DISORDERS

Volkmar, Lord, Bailey, Schultz, & Klin (2004) describe pervasive developmental disorders (PDDs) as a group of childhood-onset neurodevelopmental disorders that are characterized by both delays and deviance in the unfolding of basic social, communicative, and cognitive skills and are often associated with other conditions such as mental retardation and epilepsy. Although children with these disorders present with impairments in social interactions, communication, and language, and with stereotyped behaviors and interests, there is considerable heterogeneity in the severity of symptoms, cognitive abilities, and adaptive functioning (American Psychiatric Association, 2000b; First & Tasman, 2004). The *DSM-IV-TR* category includes five disorders: Autistic Disorder, Asperger's Disorder, Rett's Disorder, Childhood Disintegrative Disorder (CDD), and a PDD Not Otherwise Specified (NOS; American Psychiatric Association, 2000b). Since the 1980s there has been a dramatic increase in the prevalence rate of autism, from 2 to 5/10,000 to 40/10,000 and from 4 to 5/10,000 to 60/10,000 for the broader autistic spectrum disorders (Fombonne, 2003a,b, 2005; Willemsen-Swinkles & Buitelaar, 2002; Yeargin-Allsopp et al., 2003). In the United States in 2002 approximately 284,000 to 486,000 individuals under 20 have a PDD (Fombonne, 2005).

Reviews of family studies show an underlying vulnerability that is transmitted from one generation to the next (Rutter, 2005; Volkmar, Klin, & Paul, 2005). Having a child with autism is a profoundly painful experience for family members, and the emotional toll on all involved brings "a fair share of disappointment, sadness and emotional scarring" (Volkmar, Klin, & Paul, 2005, p. xviii). Over the past decade, secondary to the family advocacy groups such as Cure Autism Now (CAN), the Autism Society of America, and the National Alliance for Autism Research, public knowledge of these disorders has increased. The placement of CAN posters in the popular television series *E.R.*, the movie *Rain Man* (1988), best-selling books like Mark Haddon's (2003) *The Curious Incident of the Dog in the Night* and Temple Grandin's (1995) autobiography *Thinking in Pictures and Other Reports from My Life with Autism* have also increased public awareness (Rapin, 2005). In 2006, both *Time* and *Newsweek* magazines featured cover stories on autism. Lobbying by family groups has resulted in the establishment of and government funding for centers and programs like the Collaborative Program for Excellence in Autism and the Studies to Advance Autism Research and Treatment.

Current treatment for these disorders is multidisciplinary and systemic, focusing on early identification and intense intervention (D. A. Allen & Mendelson, 2000; Arick, Krug, Fullerton, Loos, & Falco, 2005; Olley, 2005; Volkmar, Paul, et al., 2005). Early intervention for every child who achieves normal functioning can result in a net savings of $1.5 million (J. W. Jacobson & Mulick, 2000). Unfortunately, even though early intensive intervention produces significant and sustainable benefit to these children, the lack of available funding and insurance reimbursements means it is inaccessible to many children with PDDs (CDC, 2006; Gunter, 2004; Mandalawitz, 2005; McEachin, Smith, & Lovaas, 1993; Scheinkopf & Siegel, 1998). There is no cure for autism, which is a lifelong disabling condition (Howlin, 2005; V. Shea & Mesibov, 2005). Long-term follow-up studies show that a small minority of higher functioning individuals (10%) live independently but continue to experience social challenges throughout their life (Howlin, 2003; Howlin, Goode, Hutton, & Rutter, 2004). While tremendous advances have been made in early intervention, resulting in a decreasing number of individuals remaining mute and being identified with severe mental retardation, there is currently a dearth of programs servicing adolescents and young and older adults (R. Paul & Sutherland, 2005; Rapin, 2005; V. Shea & Mesibov, 2005). Consequently, the majority of individuals with PDDs remain unemployed and reliant on others and experience ongoing loneliness and isolation (Howlin, 2005).

Genetic research has identified the underlying mechanism for Rett's Disorder (Van Acker, Loncola, & Van Acker, 2005). With scientific advances, the hope is that other disorders may be detected at birth and that early intervention followed by programs that target specific developmental challenges will minimize the lifelong negative sequelae (Rapin, 2005). According to Volkmar and colleagues (Volkmar, Klin, et al., 2005, p. xvii) the effectiveness of early intervention programs and cultural changes in attitudes to individuals with disabilities have resulted in a shift, and a "philosophy of despair has given way to one of hope." Whether or not this statement is premature remains to be seen.

HISTORICAL OVERVIEW

Throughout literature there are recurrent stories and folk tales from places as diverse as Malta and India of individuals who appear innocent-like, "blessed fools" who lack social awareness, are overly concrete in thought, have bizarre behaviors, and are insensitive to pain (Frith, 1989). According to Happe (1998), many of these individuals appear to fit the current description of autism, as do many of the wild or feral children (Volkmar & Klin, 2005). The actual term autism comes from the Greek word *autos* meaning "self" and was first used by E. Bleuler (1911/1950) to describe the unusual self-centered quality and social withdrawal seen in Schizophrenia (Rapin, 2005; Szatmari, 2000a,b). In 1943, Leo Kanner, a Baltimore child psychiatrist, in his landmark study of 11 preschool children entitled "Autistic Disturbances of Affective Contact," used the term *autism* to convey the children's apparent unusual lack of social interest. He believed that autism was a congenital condition. His descriptions highlighted many characteristics that are still relevant today: a profound lack of affective contact, repetitive routines, need for the preservation of sameness, mutism, language not intended for communication with others, and an early onset (usually before 30 months). Basing his observations on the developmental theories of Gesell (Gesell & Ilg, 1940), Kanner described autism as a failure of development, in contrast to Schizophrenia, which was seen as a developmental regression (Volkmar & Klin, 2005).

A year later, Hans Asperger (1991/1944), a Viennese child psychiatrist, unaware of Kanner's work, wrote a medical school dissertation research report on four older school-age children. He described these children as eccentric, having normal IQ, fluent language, poor conversation skills with odd pedantic speech, little facial expression, motor clumsiness, resistance to change, with circumscribed interests, pronounced social impairment, and a marked lack of common sense (Myhr, 1998; Wing, 2005). He referred to their condition as an autistic personality disorder in childhood or autistic psychopathy (Klin, McPartland, & Volkmar, 2005; Szatmari, 2000a,b). The report was written in German and not widely known until after 1981, when Wing (1981, 1991) published an influential review citing Asperger's case studies and describing several adults previously diagnosed with autism as having "Asperger's syndrome" (Szatmari, 2000a,b).

For many decades psychogenic theories were proposed that linked the development of autism to parental ineptitude, or the "refrigerator mother" and maternal depravation (Rapin, 2005; B. Siegel, 1996). The treatment of choice was psychoanalysis of the mother or removal of the child to long-term psychodynamic programs (Bettelheim, 1967). These approaches have been subsequently described "as misdirected and ultimately harmful" and remain a black mark on the field (Gerhardt & Holmes, 2005, p. 1089; Volkmar, 2005). The finding in the 1960s of elevated whole-blood serotonin levels in individuals with autism and a landmark book by a parent advocate emphasized the biological basis for autism and the need for empirical research and treatment (Rimland, 1964; Schain & Freedman, 1961; Volkmar, 2005). Research in the 1970s demonstrated that mothers of autistic children were not inept; rather, these children often had significant intellectual and social deficits and were at higher risk for epilepsy and abnormal brain functioning (DeMyer et al., 1972; Deykin & MacMahon, 1979; Rapin, 2005). Current research clearly indicates that autism and PDDs are characterized by alterations and delays in early brain development caused by complex polygenic influences, the expression of which is influenced throughout childhood and later by chance environmental events (Rapin, 2005).

Prior to 1980, childhood Schizophrenia was the only officially recognized diagnostic category for severely disturbed children, and children with autism were often diagnosed with this disorder (Rapin, 2005). Wing and Gould (1979) noted that children in special education classes with repetitive stereotyped behaviors often had deficits in social understanding, communication, and symbolic play or imagination; these three core deficits were identified as characteristic of autism and later became known as "Wing's triad." These early observations and subsequent research led Wing (1991) to described autism as a spectrum disorder that was more closely linked to mental retardation than to Schizophrenia (Szatmari, 2000a). Autism has become increasingly recognized in clinical practice, with a higher number of children with higher functioning autism (HFA) being identified who are often difficult to differentiate from children with Asperger's Disorder (Klin et al., 2000; Szatmari, 2000a). The shared common features and phenomenological similarities have resulted in conceptualizing these disorders as on a spectrum; though not an official diagnosis, the term *autism spectrum disorder* (ASD) has become synonymous with the term PDD and has widespread use (First & Tasman, 2004; Volkmar, Paul, et al., 2005).

AUTISTIC DISORDER

Historically, autism is one of the most reliably empirically based and validated childhood disorders, yet it has a heterogeneous clinical presentation (First & Tasman, 2004; Sponheim, 1996; Volkmar & Klin, 2005; Willemsen-Swinkles & Buitelaar, 2002). Since they were first identified by Kanner in 1943 there has been agreement on the core autistic symptoms (Sponheim, 1996). The broad range of clinical signs and symptoms that are characterized by linguistic and cognitive deficits change with age and developmental level, making this diagnosis very challenging, especially for novice clinicians (Klin, Lang, Cicchetti, & Volkmar, 2000). Autism was first officially included in the *DSM-III* in 1980 under the newly coined pervasive developmental disorders, which described the characteristic features as an impairment in the development and unfolding of several areas of functioning or developmental delays in a range of different domains (American Psychiatric Association, 1980; Volkmar and Klin, 2005; Willemsen-Swinkels & Buitelaar, 2002). It was called *infantile autism,* reflecting the emphasis on prototypical cases with early onset, usually before 3 years (Sponheim, 1996). Dustin Hoffman's portrayal of Raymond Babbit in the film *Rain Man* vividly captured many of the clinical features. Children with autism appear normal and often physically attractive; however, they present with significant pervasive delays that impact several areas of functioning (Chudley, Guitierrez, Jocelyn, & Chodirker, 1998). Described by Kanner as an inborn dysfunction impacting affective management, autism included such features as failing to "mold" against their mother's body when held or to reach out to a caregiver, resulting in extreme aloneness and social withdrawal (Volkmar & Klin, 2005). Impairments in social interaction are considered by many to be the primary or core characteristic of autism (C. T. Jackson et al., 2003; Volkmar & Klin, 2005). For the majority of children with autism, these deficits are apparent in their first year and include failures to make eye-to-eye contact or to orient to social stimuli or to their name and little interest in parents, siblings, or the human face (Chawarska & Volkmar, 2005; Volkmar, Lord, Bailey, Schultz & Klin, 2004).

Early research (Lord & Rutter, 1994) found that about half of children with autism were mute. More recently, this number is significantly decreasing secondary to the impact of early identification and intense intervention. The current consensus is that language in autism is extremely variable, with subgroups within the disorder having distinctive linguistic profiles (H. Goldstein, 2002; Tager-Flusberg, Paul, & Lord, 2005). These children may also express an anxiously obsessive desire for the preservation of sameness; small changes in routine or environment are extremely upsetting, resulting in tantrums that may be accompanied by self-injurious behaviors such as head banging and hand biting (Frick & Silverthorn, 2001; Howlin, 1998b). Some children experience unusual sensitivities to sensory stimuli and present with a restricted range of interests and activities and a limited variety of spontaneous activity; these, however, are not regarded as robust defining features of autism (Loveland & Tunali-Kotoski, 2005; Volkmar & Klin, 2005).

Boys typically present with autism more frequently than girls; a male-to-female ratio of 4.4:1 has been noted, which decreases to 1.3:1 as the severity of cognitive impairment increases (Yeargin-Allsopp et al., 2003). Kanner (1943) believed that the outstanding memory and the fine motor dexterity he observed in some children reflected superior intellectual abilities (the notion that these children "could if they would"). However, we now know that the majority (68% to 75%) of children with autism exhibit cognitive impairment, and though these numbers are significantly decreasing and are thought to be considerably lower, there is within the disorder considerable cognitive heterogeneity, ranging from childhood savants to children with profound mental retardation (Chudley et al., 1998; V. Shea & Mesibov, 2005; Yeargin-Allsopp et al., 2003). The clinical variability in intellectual and communicative functioning and developmental changes in symptom presentation makes the early identification and assessment of this disorder challenging (Klin, Lang, Cicchetti, Volkmar, 2000; Sponheim, 1996). The use of the *DSM-IV* diagnostic criteria for autism, especially by inexperienced clinicians, significantly improves diagnostic reliability over reliance on clinical judgment alone (Klin et al., 2000). Given the importance of early diagnosis, the clinical presentation will be discussed in detail.

Clinical Presentation

Social Deficits

The clinical presentation of Autistic Disorder involves three clusters of impairment: social, including reciprocal social interactions; language or communication; and play and behavioral or interest (American Psychiatric Association, 2000b). Social deficits are regarded as the defining feature of the disorder (Klin, Jones, Schultz, & Volkmar, 2003; Vig & Jedrysek, 1999). The manifestation of these deficits may vary across children and even within the same child over time (First & Tasman, 2004; Willemsen-Swinkles & Buitelaar, 2002). During their first months, children with autism, in contrast to typically developing children, demonstrate a lower sensitivity to the salience of social stimuli (Chawarska & Volkmar, 2005). In first birthday and earlier home videos, these children show delays in eye-to-eye gaze and a failure to orient to social stimuli or to look at others; they appear to seek help and smile at others less and have fewer vocalizations (Mastero et al., 2002; Osterling & Dawson, 1994). In comparison to matched Down syndrome and typical peers, children with autism more often failed to orient to social stimuli, and those who did look took a longer time to do so (G. Dawson, Meltzoff, Osterling, Rinaldi, & Brown, 1998). Gaze and eye-tracking research suggests that by age 2, children with autism demonstrate abnormal eye gaze, including frequently avoiding eye contact, failing to shift gaze in response to a social cue, and failing to establish mutual gaze with their caregivers (A. S. Carter, Ornstein Davis, Klin, & Volkmar, 2005). In visual scanning studies, children with autism demonstrate difficulty in the basic processing of social stimuli such as faces, often focusing on the mouth more than the eyes and showing deficits in facial recognition (Klin, Jones, Schultz, & Volkmar, 2005; Schultz & Robbins, 2005). G. Dawson and colleagues (2005) interpreted this impaired face and emotion memory and atypical strategies for processing faces as an inefficient processing strategy that may reflect aberrant neural circuitry. Of note, both high- and low-functioning children with autism were found to be equally impaired in social referencing, or looking to adults for social cues (Bacon, Fein, Morris, Waterhouse, & Allen, 1998; Carver & Dawson, 2002).

In terms of social gestures, parents of infants with autism more frequently report that their child never shows anticipation of being held, affection to or reaches for familiar others, interest in children other than siblings, or interest in playing simple interactional games. In contrast, parents of matched developmentally delayed peers did not report these deficits (Klin, Volkmar, & Sparrow, 1992). Deficits in gestures to regulate social interactions and social engagement are regarded as early clinical signs of difficulties in social reciprocity and have been identified as early indicators of autism (A. S. Carter et al., 2005; Chawarska & Volkmar, 2005; Hobson, 2005). Many children with autism fail to develop peer relationships and may demonstrate a lack of interest in or awareness of other children or peers (American Psychiatric Association, 2000b; Howlin, 2005; Orsmond, Krauss, & Seltzer, 2004). These children may want friends, but often they do not understand the concepts of reciprocity and sharing interests and ideas, and they frequently isolate, watching television or playing video games for hours (Filipek et al., 1999; Loveland & Tunali-Kotoski, 2005). Some see these social challenges as reflecting difficulties with intersubjectivity, emotional perception, and the understanding of others' feelings as characteristic core deficits (Baron-Cohen, 1995; A. S. Carter et al., 2005).

Joint attention is the ability to coordinate attention between interactive social partners with respect to objects or events in order to share an awareness of the objects or events (Mundy Sigman & Kasari, 1994). These behaviors are strongly predictive of the development of receptive and expressive language. Individuals with autism experience difficulty using these skills adaptively and spontaneously throughout their life (Chawarska & Volkmar, 2005; Mundy & Burnette, 2005). Baron Cohen and colleagues' (Baron-Cohen, Allen, & Gillberg, 1992) early research suggested that impairments in joint attention, proto-declarative pointing, and pretend play underlie the child's difficulties in understanding others' thoughts. Others theorize that the problems in joint attention occur at an earlier age and relate to difficulties of social engagement and a failure to self-generate social experiences, which results in suboptimal neurodevelopment (Mundy & Burnette, 2005). All agree that these deficits and the lack of spontaneous sharing with others are central defining symptoms of autism (Vig & Jedrysek, 1999).

Social interaction literature describes children with autism as less likely to respond to positive, neutral, or distressing stimuli or conversational bids from others, having impaired ability to carry on conversations and to sustain pretend play, and overall less socially engaged. These deficits are apparent even when the children are compared to peers with mental retardation (C. T. Jackson et al., 2003). Thus, although children with autism may learn rote social skills such as simple conversation, the subtle nuances of play interactions are more difficult and harder to sustain (C. T. Jackson et al., 2003). It is important to note that, despite their marked impairments in social functioning, children with autism are not globally socially impaired and can and do form secure attachments. The risk for insecure attachment in children with autism was found to be related to the presence of cognitive deficits (A. S. Carter et al., 2005).

These children have marked difficulty imitating others, which persists across their life; oral-facial imitation deficits are particularly severe (Chawarska & Volkmar, 2005; S. J. Rogers, Cook, & Meryl, 2005). The ability to imitate is an important skill that may help infants understand the relationship between themselves and others; early infant motor imitation skills have been found to relate to later social responsivity to a caregiver (S. J. Rogers et al., 2005). Difficulties in body imitation have been found to influence the child's expressive language skills, and failures in object imitation may also impact the later acquisition of play skills and symbolic play. When children with autism are asked to spontaneously produce a particular emotional expression, the resulting expressions are more bizarre and mechanical and more difficult to identify and classify than those of normal peers (Hobson, 2005). This failure to imitate may contribute to joint attention deficits, difficulty understanding others' emotional states, and lack of emotional reciprocity (Osterling, Dawson, & McPartland, 2001; S. J. Rogers et al., 2005).

Language

Abnormalities, delays, or the total lack of spoken language (not accompanied by compensatory strategies such as gestures) are common. Initially, Lord and Rutter (1994) found that about half of the children with autism were mute; now, however, this number is significantly decreasing secondary to the success of early intervention (H. Goldstein, 2002). Typically, children with autism have difficulty using language to communicate; they present with delayed echolalia (repeating earlier heard language) and bizarre, idiosyncratic speech with intonation peculiarities including monotony (Kanner, 1943; Loveland & Tunali-Kotoski, 2005; Tager-Flusberg et al., 2005). When language does develop, the grammatical structures are often immature, stereotyped, and characterized by extreme literalness and difficulties with pronoun use (First & Tasman, 2004; Myhr, 1998; Tager-Flushberg et al., 2005). The child may repetitively use language in a nonsensical, ritualized manner, such as repeating memorized TV commercials, phrases of others, or video scripts. Those who develop speech show immediate or delayed echolalia, which some see as a communicative strategy used by children who do not understand what is said or lack the ability to consistently produce spontaneous speech (Loveland & Tunali-Kotoski, 2005; Prizant & Wetherby, 2005). It is important to note that echolalia is also seen in normal children, and its use by older, previously mute autistic children may indicate progress in language development (Volkmar & Klin, 2005). Abnormal pronoun use, including confusion and reversals, are common and decrease with age and increasing linguistic skill; they have been related to the child's deficits in understanding and taking another's perspective (Tager-Flusberg et al., 2005).

Almost universally there are impairments in comprehension, resulting in difficulty understanding simple questions or directions (Howlin, Mawhood & Rutter, 2000). These children tend to be overly literal in their understanding of language and have difficulty understanding nonliteral aspects of speech, including irony and implied meaning. A 5-year-old boy with autism who saw the "bump ahead" sign on the sidewalk proceeded to bump his head against the sign. Myhr (1998) found that even highly verbal children with autism had difficulty using language to engage others and to meet their needs; Myhr reports on an earlier study in which children with autism learned sign language but tried to sign with their back to others.

These children will often interject irrelevant details, such as someone's age or the date of an event, into conversations. They may persist in talking about a topic regardless of the listener's interest, ignoring the other person's conversational initiations, and have difficulty gracefully ending topics (Chuba, Paul, Miles, Klin, & Volkmar, 2003). Even verbally fluent children with autism show a fundamental lack of understanding of speaker-listener social discourse rules and a basic difficulty in establishing and maintaining conversational reciprocity or mutually cooperative social dialogue (Tager-Flusberg et al., 2005). These children tend not to use their language to provide new information during a conversation or to elicit new information from others; they use fewer "wh-" (who, what, when, where) questions, and their pragmatic or social practical use of language is often markedly impaired. Understanding conversational language represents a significant challenge for individuals with autism, as the semantic and pragmatic aspects are so closely linked to nonverbal communication and social adaptation (Tager-Flusberg et al., 2005).

Play

The lack or absence of varied, spontaneous make-believe, social-imitative, or symbolic play is apparent in the nonuse of small toys or dolls in pretend play. This is one of the unique features of autism that has been universally supported (American Psychiatric Association, 2000b; S. J. Rogers et al., 2005; Wing, Gould, Yeates, & Brierley, 1977). Children with autism may persist longer with and derive pleasure from sensory play, the earliest form of play in infants and toddlers that involves repetitive motor behaviors. These children may use toy figures in a repetitive, reflexive manner but appear unable to make up new scenarios (Filipek et al., 1999; B. Siegel, 1996). Highly verbal children may invent a fantasy world, which becomes the sole focus of repetitive play, or precisely re-enact or recite play scenarios from favorite videos, such as the storm scene in "Howl's Moving Castle." Typically in social interactions they do not actively participate in simple social games or play; they may use others as "tools," mechanical aids, or as "assistants," without attending to the other child's suggestions. They tend to rely on the physical properties of the object for simple manipulative play, in contrast to portraying symbolic play, and may spend many hours alone, building and rebuilding Legos, playing video games, engaged in purposeless or no activity (Lord & Magill-Evans, 1995; Vig & Jedrysek, 1999). Both the symbolic and nonsymbolic play of children with autism show similar deficits, including more repetition, less novelty, and diversity of play themes that are more immature when compared to typical peers (S. J. Rogers et al., 2005).

Stereotypies and Preoccupations

The presence of restrictive, repetitive, and stereotyped patterns of behavior, interests, activities, and preoccupations that are abnormal in focus or intensity are common (American Psychiatric Association, 2000b). The child may repeatedly ask the same questions on a particular subject, such as U.S. presidents, or develop highly circumscribed interests, such as the solar system. Some preschoolers become zealous fans of *Wheel of Fortune* or *Jeopardy* (Filipek et al., 1999). They may engage in repetitive, stereotyped motor mannerisms, referred to as *stereotypies*, such as rocking, spinning, toe walking, arm flapping, and hand clapping, or performing peculiar finger movements in front of their face or in their peripheral vision (First & Tasman, 2004, 2005; Frick & Silverthorn, 2001). Filipek (2005) reports that 37% to 95% have hand or finger mannerisms, body rocking, or unusual posturing, which is usually evident during the preschool years. These movements may serve a self-regulating function when a child is overly stimulated (B. Siegel, 1996). The frequencies of such behaviors as hand flapping, rubbing surfaces, ignoring the examiner, eye contact, repeating sounds, and the lack of social smile have been used to differentiate preschool children with autism from peers with cognitive deficits (Vig & Jedrysek, 1999). Some restricted, repetitive, stereotyped activities are not seen in autistic children who are of very low cognitive ability or are under 3 years of age (Charman & Baird, 2002; Moore & Goodson, 2003; Volmar & Klin, 2005). M. Turner (1999b) notes that low-level repetitive behaviors (e.g., repetitive motor movements) can be differentiated from those that are more cognitively complex (e.g., insistence on sameness or routine). Children with lower verbal abilities exhibit more motor stereotypies, and the clinical presentation may change with development, going from repetitive sensory motor activities to more elaborate ritualistic behaviors as the child ages (Militerni, Bravaccio, Falco, Fico, & Palermo, 2002; Waterhouse et al., 1996). There may be an adherence to nonfunctional routines or an insistence on sameness (American Psychiatric Association, 2000b). The child may wear only one particular blue T-shirt, may insist on taking only a certain route to school, and transitions, changes, or new experiences may be accompanied by temper tantrums (First & Tasman, 2004; Wing, 1996).

There may be persistent preoccupations with parts of objects, and the child may collect unusual things (pieces of string or lint), become fascinated with water, or love spinning wheels (American Psychiatric Association, 2000b; Volkmar, Cohen, & Paul, 1986). It is not clear how much repetitive or restricted interests are core deficits of autism; however, these are among the earliest symptoms observed. Also, whereas a child's preoccupation or unusual interest in physical objects is highly suggestive of autism, it is not invariably present, and when presents it tends to occur in younger children (Volkmar & Klin, 2005).

Onset

The onset of the clinical symptoms is prior to 3 years of age (American Psychiatric Association, 2000b). As onset may be difficult to identify, particularly for individuals first seen as adolescents or adults, some have suggested that age of recognition may be a more appropriate criterion than age of onset (Wing, 2005). It is now common for children to be seen in specialized diagnostic centers at 2 years or younger. Of children with autistic symptoms identified at age 2, 88% to 100% remain autistic on follow-up (Baron-Cohen et al., 1996; A. Cox et al., 1999; Moore & Goodson, 2003; W. L. Stone et al., 1999). The *DSM-IV-TR* criteria require the direct observation of the child and assume that the examiner has some clinical expertise with diagnosing children under 3, which is often difficult and complex (W. L. Stone et al., 1999; Vig & Jedrysek, 1999; Volkmar & Klin, 2005). Additionally, some of the diagnostic criteria (e.g., failure to develop peer relationships, impaired conversational skills, insistence on routine) are not applicable to very young children and the behaviors may change with developmental level (Volkmar & Klin, 2005). Also, although some of the social deficits may improve after 2 years of age, repetitive behaviors typically do not develop before 3 years of age (Lord, 1995; R. Rogers, 2001; Volkmar & Klin, 2005). Thus, for many children the full scope of symptoms and impairment may not be evident until about 3 to 4 years. W. L. Stone et al. (1999) found that agreement between clinicians when evaluating children under 3 was in the moderate range between experienced clinicians, but below chance when one of the clinicians had less experience dealing with very young children. In an effort to address these issues, the Center for Clinical Infant Programs in 1994 developed diagnostic guidelines for children 0 to 3 years (Zero to Three, 1994). This classification system is compatible with the *DSM*. Maldonado-Duran and colleagues (2003) have described its use in a community infant mental health clinic. Overall, the sensitivity and discriminatory power of the *DSM-IV* criteria for autism are very high (greater than .80), and there is high overall agreement with other measures, including the Childhood Autism Rating Scale (CARS: Schopler, Reichler, & Renner, 1988) and Autism Behavior Checklist (ABC; Buitelaar & van der Gaag, 1998; Sponheim, 1996).

Additional Characteristics

Cognitive Variability

Impaired intellectual functioning is not required for a diagnosis of autism. Children with autism are a cognitively heterogeneous group, ranging from those with profound mental retardation to those with superior intellect (Schultz & Robins, 2005; Willemsen-Swinkles & Buitelaar, 2002). In a metropolitan prevalence study of children with autism, and an IQ or developmental test 68% were found to have cognitive impairment. Of those with psychometric test results: 20% had mild mental retardation, 11% moderate, 7% severe, and 3% had profound mental retardation, and 28% were unspecified (Yeargin-Allsopp et al., 2003). These figures should be viewed with caution in light of the validity of using traditional verbally mediated measures of intelligence with children with autism (Howlin, 2005). Secondary to the availability of early intervention and special education, the prevalence of mental retardation in children with autism has been significantly declining (V. Shea & Mesibov, 2005). In comparing children born between 1974 and 1984 to those born before 1960 and those born between 1960 and 1972, L. C. Eaves and Ho (1996) found that of the later born children only 62% had a Verbal IQ and 52% had a Performance IQ less than 70. Similarly, in California 50% of individuals diagnosed with autism born between 1983 and 1985 were diagnosed with mental retardation, whereas only 22% of those born between 1993 and 1995 received both diagnoses (Byrd, 2002). The term *high functioning* (IQ > 70; HFA) is often used to describe children whose deficits resemble those of older children with Asperger's Disorder; *low functioning* (IQ < 70) is used to describe younger children with autism who have clinical features similar to those in Kanner's group (Tsatsanis, 2005).

Children with autism often demonstrate uneven cognitive abilities, with relative strengths in visual and visuospatial skills in comparison to deficits in verbal skills, regardless of the child's overall intelligence level (Ghaziudin & Moutain-Kimchi, 2004; Mayes & Calhoun, 2003; Volkmar & Klin, 2005). On measures of cognitive functioning children with autism often have difficulty on subtests assessing social judgment and social norms and do well on visual analysis and spatial integration tasks (Tsatsanis, 2005). Even preschool children with autism show this uneven cognitive pattern, with verbal skills being weaker than nonverbal skills. The lower the child's IQ, the more severe the autistic symptoms (Vig & Jedrysek, 1999).

Functional neuroimaging studies indicate many areas of spared functioning, suggesting that autism is not incompatible with superior cognitive functioning (Schultz & Robins, 2005). There also may be areas of exceptional talent or special cognitive skills, referred to as splinter or savant skills, such as drawing, calculation, music, calendar calculation, outstanding rote memory, decoding ability, and hyperlexia (American Psychiatric Association, 2000b; Tager-Flusberg et al., 2005). Savant skills occur in 1 in 10 individuals with autism and are 10 times more common in these individuals than in others with cognitive disabilities (Happe, 2005). In the past, these skills were frequently ignored, as they often failed to relate to general intellectual and functional abilities; more recently, they have been used as starting points for teaching more adaptive functioning (Tager-Flusberg et al., 2005). The current knowledge concerning cognitive abilities in individuals with autism suggests a scattered profile, where cognitive abilities are not well integrated but suggest isolated strengths and a broad range of deficits (Tsatsanis, 2005).

Self-Injurious Behavior

Individuals with autism may engage in behaviors such as head banging, tantrums, finger or hand biting, and hair pulling when they are frustrated or have no other means to communicate their feelings or needs. Although self-injury may be one of the most troubling behaviors, there is no simple formula for symptom management (Towbin, 2005). Howlin (1998b) notes that, given the severity of the communication and social deficits and the child's need for routine and rituals, many children with autism express fewer challenging behaviors than might be expected. It is important to assess for the presence of an underlying physical illness, as 10 out of 13 children referred for self-injurious behavior were found to have a physical basis for their behaviors, including ear infections and medication complications (Howlin, 1998b). Many of these challenging behaviors serve a communicative function, such as seeking help to wanting to escape from a certain situation, and may be the only way a child with severe linguistic challenges can control his or her world (Howlin, 1998b).

Sleep and Eating Disturbances

Research shows that the majority of children with autism have sleep problems, which are frequently severe and characterized by abnormalities in the sleep-wake cycle (Didde & Sigafoos, 2001; Filipek, 2005; Polimeni, Richdale, & Francis, 2005; Stores & Wiggs, 1998). It is not uncommon for parents to report their autistic children as having significant difficulties falling and staying asleep, as well as early-morning awakening. Total hours of sleep are often greatly reduced, in some cases to 4 hours per night (Schreck & Mulick, 2000; Wiggs & Stores, 2004). Rates of sleep problems in autistic children have been estimated to range from 44% to 83% and often contribute to significant parental stress (Richdale, 1999; Richdale, Francis, Gavidia-Payne, & Cotton, 2000). Sleep problems frequently appear prior to age 8 and may improve as the child grows older and reaches adolescence. Additionally, many children with autism have unusual obligatory bedtime routines, including time of going to bed, positioning of bedding, and involvement of family members (Filipek, 2005; Richdale, 2001).

Parents also report significant feeding problems, often centered around food preferences that are determined by type, texture (e.g., only smooth foods), or color, which are accompanied by food refusal and very restricted diets (Field, Garland, & Williams, 2003; Filipek, 2005). At an earlier age these children may have eaten a range of foods and become more selective and restrictive in range and type only as their autism became more pronounced. There may also be an insistence on certain rituals (e.g., food must be cut into triangles) or on certain brands and a reluctance to try new foods. In studying autistic children with sensory hypo- and hypersensitivities, Talay-Ongan and Wood (2000) found that all parents reported their children had a limited diet (with food texture being the main reason for food rejection) and an unwillingness to try other foods, which may reflect sensory integration and processing problems.

Sensory Integration Deficits and Sensory Sensitivities

Sensory integration is the ability to take in information through the senses (touch, movement, smell, taste, vision, and hearing), to put it together with prior information, memories, and knowledge stored in the brain, and make a meaningful response. It occurs in the central nervous system and is generally thought to take place in the midbrain and brain stem levels in complex interactions of the portions of the brain responsible for such things as coordination, attention, arousal levels, autonomic functioning, emotions, memory, and higher level cognitive functions. Between 42% and 88% of individuals with autism exhibit sensory processing abnormalities. These include under- or overreactivity to noise or sounds, such as appearing deaf, complaining that sounds are painful, sensitivities to clothing (e.g., tags), or a preoccupation with the sensory features of objects (Baranek, 2002; Filipek, 2005; Kientz & Dunn, 1997). These behaviors occur across all sensory modalities, the most common being auditory sensitivities of which hyperacuity is the most prominent (Baranek, Parham, & Bodfish, 2005; Talay-Ongan & Wood, 2000). Parents comment that their child is visually fixated, is tactile defensive in responding, experiences distress with innocuous experiences (e.g., getting wet), falls frequently, appears oblivious to personal space, and is insensitive to pain (Schreibman & Charlop-Christy, 1998; Talay-Ongan & Wood, 2000). Controlled studies of children with autism identified as being underresponsive to pain actually demonstrated heightened pain responses in comparison to normal peers (Nader, Oberlander, Chambers, & Craig, 2004). Some children may develop unusual fear of everyday objects, such as clothing, elevators, and vacuum cleaners (Frick & Silverthorn, 2001; Klinger & Dawson, 1996). Talay-Ongan and Wood (2000) hypothesized that children with autism experience an overwhelming barrage of sensory information that their neurological subsystems inadequately regulate and that this may contribute to deficits in promoting social interactional behaviors. Unusual sensory deficits are not unique to autism; hypersensory responsiveness may occur in many developmentally delayed individuals. However, hyporesponsiveness may be more characteristic of autism (Baranek et al., 2005). Observational studies using retrospective video analysis show that during infancy, even before parents notice developmental delays, there are subtle sensory symptoms associated with autism, including over- and underreactivity to sound and touch aversion (Baranek et al., 2005). Sensory deficits are well documented in clinical and anecdotal literature, yet there is a dearth of systematic research (Bristol-Powers & Spinella, 1999).

Onset, Course, and Life Span Considerations

Onset

There appear to be two different courses for autism; one is apparent at birth and the other is characterized by normal development followed by a developmental regression at 18 to 20 months (Bristol-Powers & Spinella, 1999). In the latter scenario, the child appears to acquire language and then lose it, shows a decreased social interest, and starts to withdraw from others. This regression, also referred to as "the setback phenomenon," occurs in 20% to 40% of children with autism and is controversial and poorly understood (Chawarska & Volkmar, 2005; Volkmar & Klin, 2005). These occurrences are usually based on parents' retrospective reports and include descriptions of developmental stagnation or a dramatic regression; in the latter cases the diagnostic differential with CDD must be considered (Siperstein & Volkmar, 2004). A retrospective analysis of early childhood videos has supported parental reports of a late-onset autism (Davidovitch, Glick, Holtzman, Tirosh, & Safir, 2000; Werner, Dawson, Osterling, & Dinno, 2000).

Table 5.1   Early indicators of autism

Lack of Reciprocal or Social Interaction

Deficits in joint or shared attention	Lack of or abnormal eye contact
Lack of anticipation of being picked up	Rarely looks at others
Difficulty relating to social stimuli	Does not point
Abnormal nonverbal communication	Interpersonal aloofness
Lack of affection toward familiar others	Content to be alone
Restricted emotional expression	Little interest in reciprocal games
Social smile absent	No fear of strangers
Poor motor imitation	Repetitive limited formal play
Lack of shared enjoyment	No pretend play

Language Delays or Disturbances

Delayed or lack of speech	Does not use language to communicate
No babbling by 12 months	No compensating gesture
No gesturing (pointing, waving) by 12 months	Nonresponsive to name
No single words by 16 months	Speech not used to direct adult attention
No 2-word spontaneous phrases by 24 months	Failure to respond to others' speech
Stereotyped or repetitive use of language	Unresponsive to others' gestures
Idiosyncratic use of words	Uses others' bodies as tools
Pronoun reversal (saying *you* for *I*)	Failure to share interest with others
Abnormalities of prosody (pitch stress intonation)	Conversation not initiated or sustained

Sensory and Conceptual Difficulties

Oversensitivity to light, texture	Cognitive rigidity
Stereotypic movements (twirling)	Need for sameness or order
Fascination with objects	Intolerant of change
Hand or finger mannerism	Restricted diet
Toe walking, twirling	Repetitive and restrictive interests

Source: Portions from "Practice Parameters: Screening and Diagnosis of Autistic Spectrum Disorders" (A Multi-Society Consensus Statement), by P. A. Filipek, P. J. Accardo, G. T. Baranek, E. H. Cook, Jr., G. Dawson, B. Gordon, et al., 1999, *Neurology, 55,* pp. 468–479. Adapted with permission.

For most individuals, autism has an onset in infancy and early childhood. Many parents (30% to 54%) express serious concerns during their child's first year of life, and the majority (80% to 90%) recognize abnormalities by 24 months (Chawarska & Volkmar, 2005; De Giacomo & Frombonne, 1998; Howlin & Asgharian, 1999). Early concerns focus on the lack of communication, emerging social interaction, play, or social responsiveness and the presence of abnormalities or repetitive behaviors (A. S. Carter et al., 2005). From birth, children with autism appear to lack a preference for speech sounds and interest in listening to speech sounds (A. S. Carter et al., 2005). When called, they may not respond to their own name, a phenomenon known as *verbal auditory agnosia*. This lack of response to name persists, and combined with the behaviors of looking at people and looking at objects held by others differentiates children with autism from typical peers and those with developmental delays (Chawarska & Volkmar, 2005). A summary of early indicators of autism is presented in Table 5.1.

Baron-Cohen and colleagues (1992) found that 18-month-old children at risk for autism demonstrate reflecting deficits in proto-declarative pointing, gaze monitoring, and pretend play and concluded that pretend play deficits were a key indicator of subsequent diagnosis of autism. An early diagnosis of autism based on clinical observation is stable, with 75% to 90% of children retaining this diagnosis on follow-up (Chawarska & Volkmar, 2005). However, for many children early diagnosis may be hampered by primary health clinicians opting to wait to refer until after the first year, hoping that the problems will resolve themselves (Maldonado-Duran et al., 2003).

Course

The course of autism and the child's pattern of development is impacted by the child's level of cognitive functioning and the degree of language delay (Loveland & Tunali-Kotoski, 2005). An IQ below 50 at school age predicts severe restriction of social and adaptive functioning later in life and dependence in adulthood. The more severe the cognitive deficits, the less likely the development of speech (V. Shea & Mesibov, 2005). The absence of communicative speech at 5 to 6 years is significantly indicative of a poorer long-term overall outcome (Howlin, 2005; Lord & Bailey, 2002; Rutter, 1997a; Rutter, Greenfield, & Lockyer, 1967). With the increased knowledge of the brain plasticity of very young children and the advent of specialized intensive early interventions, significant improvements in language functioning and cognitive and social adaptive skills acquisition have occurred, suggesting that the prognosis for autism may be improving (National Research Council, 2001; W. L. Stone, Coonrod, & Ousely, 2000). Myhr (1998) noted that participation in early intensive intervention results in gains in the acquisition of developmental skills and improved peer relationships; children who are younger make the most progress. Thus an important factor in predicting future outcome is the age at which intervention is started (S. L. Harris & Handleman, 2000). W. L. Stone and colleagues (1999) suggest that early intervention may not only facilitate optimal neurological development but also decrease the occurrence of the long-term secondary negative sequelae associated with autism.

As children with autism become older, problems in communicating and stereotyped language use and mannerisms may become more common (Volkmar & Klin, 2005). In school, difficulties in social functioning may be mediated by the child's level of cognitive functioning and the presence of severe language difficulties (Howlin, Mawhood, & Rutter, 2000; Volkmar & Klin, 2005). Socially, the child may appear as aloof, actively avoiding social contact; passively accepting others with little interest or pleasure in social contact; or as an actively odd child who is socially engaging, especially with adults, in a peculiar, inappropriate idiosyncratic style (Wing & Gould, 1979). Waterhouse and colleagues (1996) described two overlapping clusters for children with autism. The first group were active but odd, had significantly higher cognitive and adaptive functioning with fewer autistic features, and had speech with bizarre features, impaired prosody, and preservative behaviors. The second cluster had lower cognitive and adaptive functioning, more autistic behaviors, motor and sensory abnormalities, motor stereotypies, impaired language comprehension and social imitation, and were more aloof (Waterhouse et al., 1996). Parent history and clinical interviews of children with autism show problems with empathy, difficulties appreciating and understanding the subtleties and reciprocal nature of social interaction, and the wish for relationships but a lack of know-how (Fitzgerald, 1999).

Given the wide variability in children's cognitive abilities, children with autism encounter a range of academic and school-related challenges that change as the child moves from elementary to middle school. In the past children with autism often did not complete school and were educated separately from normally developing peers. The emphasis on inclusion and education in the least restrictive setting has resulted in many more children with autism staying longer (10 versus 5 years) and completing school (Howlin, 2005). However, as Howlin (2005, p. 206) notes, despite these trends, "full inclusion in schools still appears to be the exception rather than the rule" and acceptance by teachers and mainstream peers decreases as the child ages.

For children without mental retardation the outcome is variable. There may be a period of substantial improvement, with adolescence characterized by improved language use and ability to communicate, reduced idiosyncratic speech, and an abatement or significant symptom reduction as assessed by the Autism Diagnostic Interview (Kanner, Rodriguez, & Ashenden, 1972; Seltzer et al., 2003; V. Shea & Mesibov, 2005). Parental surveys report improvements in communication (82% to 88%), socialization (82% to 83%), and behaviors (55% to 75%) from school age to late adolescence (Byrd, 2002; Piven, Harper, Palmer, & Arndt, 1996). However, many adolescents, even those considered high functioning, continue to struggle with peer relationships, and the majority report having few friends (V. Shea & Mesibov, 2005). While there have been reports of the success of research intervention programs targeting peer and social skills, to date many of these programs are unavailable to most adolescents with autism (A. S. Carter et al., 2005; S. Rogers, 2000).

Of adolescents with autism, 12% to 22% experience a cognitive or behavioral deterioration; one study found that 32% showed behavioral deterioration, characterized by increased hyperactivity, aggression, ritualistic behavior, and loss of previously acquired language peaking at ages 12 to 13 years (L. C. Eaves & Ho, 1996; Kobayashi, Murata, & Yoshinaga, 1992; Nordin & Gillberg, 1998). In some cases, this deterioration coincides with the onset of neurological problems such as seizures, although in other cases the cause is unclear (Byrd, 2002; Kobayashi et al., 1992; V. Shea & Mesibov, 2005). Research suggests that 20% to 35% of children with autism will develop seizure disorders during adolescence, which contributes to a poorer prognosis (Frick & Silverthorn, 2001; Lord & Bailey, 2002; Werry, 1996). Even in cases where the adolescents' problem behaviors decrease, it may be more difficult for family members to cope given the adolescent's increased stature, and there may be more parent and sibling burnout (V. Shea & Mesibov, 2005).

Life Span Considerations

There is currently a dearth of programs for young adults and adults with autism that facilitate their move to independence, employment, and self-reliance. Consequently, independent living or living with peers is rare (Howlin, 2005; V. Shea & Mesibov, 2005). In the past many adults with autism were placed in long-term state hospitals, where they were classified as having Schizophrenia, Simple Schizophrenia, or Schizoid Personality Disorder and were believed to be treatment-resistant (Fitzgerald, 1999). Since the 1980s there has been a decline from 40% to 50% to 6% of these placements, with many adults with autism (23% to 54%) now residing with their family (Howlin et al., 2004; Seltzer, Krauss, Orsmond, & Vestal, 2001). For adults, particularly those who also have mental retardation, the nature of their behavioral problems and lack of social skills make placement in community-based programs difficult, and they frequently reside in residential placements that are often difficult to obtain (Howlin, 2005; Nordin & Gillberg, 1998). Looking at clinical deterioration during adulthood, Hutton (1998) found that over a third of adults with autism developed new behavioral and psychiatric symptoms, including tics and social withdrawal, at 26 or before 30 years of age.

Only a small percentage (5% to 15%) of individuals with autism show positive outcomes, as demonstrated by the ability to maintain some social relationships and perform adequately in a job setting (Osterling et al., 2001). Even for adults without mental retardation, the severity of ritualistic and stereotyped behaviors may swamp the benefits of a higher IQ, and only a small percentage (<5%) marry or have long-term relationships (Howlin et al., 2004). Many of these relationships tend to be less empathic and supportive, and many adults with autism report being less likely to enjoy social interaction for its own sake (Baron-Cohen & Wheelwright, 2003). The majority have limited social contacts and experience ongoing social and communication difficulties (Howlin, 2005; V. Shea & Mesibov, 2005). Of note, there are also very few follow-up studies of adults with autism older than their early 30s (Howlin, 2005).

Some high-functioning adults become employed, and the availability of specialized vocational training programs and support services significantly improves their success. A few also attend college and complete graduate degrees, typically in the sciences and engineering and technology fields (Howlin, 2005; V. Shea & Mesibov, 2005). Temple Grandin's (1995) autobiography is an inspirational account outlining the remarkable achievement and significant challenges she had to overcome to become a leading researcher in agricultural studies and a national spokesperson for adults with autism. Reviewing follow-up studies, Howlin notes that the trend over the past 2 decades has been toward an overall improvement in outcome. She found that the number of poor outcomes is decreasing, with some high-functioning adults achieving social independence by going to college (0% to 50%, with a mean of 12%) or by being employed (4% to 47%, mean of 24%). For many seeking employment the job interview is often very challenging, and many adults with autism end up with menial, underpaid jobs, often relying on family or friends for employment (Howlin, 2005; Howlin & Goode, 1998). Only recently have supported employment model programs focusing on job placement and ongoing support been used with individuals with autism (Howlin, 2005). These programs have been successful in finding not only employment for adults with autism but higher wages; they report high levels of satisfaction from both employers and employees with autism. In fact, in one study, more than 50% of the initial placements were made permanent and additional employment was offered to other adults with autism (Mawhood & Howlin, 1999). The future prognosis for many individuals with autism may be determined in part by the availability of such programs and the individual's ability to access and participate in them.

In terms of mortality, although autism is not a degenerative disease and is not fatal, there is evidence of an increased mortality rate. In a 24-year follow-up study of 207 cases, Isager and colleagues (Isager, Mouridsen, & Rich, 1999) found a crude mortality rate of 3.4%, which was double the expected rate; the highest rate was for individuals with higher and severe-profound cognitive functioning. Shavelle and colleagues (Shavelle, Strauss, & Pickett, 2001) also found a mortality rate double the rate of the general population, highest for those who were either very high functioning or profoundly impaired. The associated conditions of epilepsy and mental retardation have also been linked to a significantly decreased life expectancy (V. Shea & Mesibov, 2005). Given that individuals first diagnosed with autism in the 1940s are only now reaching their age of mortality, the research in this area is still very limited.

In summary, while the core deficits of social relatedness in autism may remain present throughout the course of the disorder, the nature of the outcome is not only heterogeneous but is also significantly changing (Howlin, 2005; V. Shea & Mesibov, 2005). Consistently, the level of mental retardation and presence of other comorbid conditions such as epilepsy are important factors in predicting outcome. One of the best and most consistent predictors of favorable outcome is the development of communicative speech prior to age 5 and higher intellectual abilities, specifically an IQ of 70 or above (Howlin, 2005; Lord & Bailey, 2002). Szatmari (2000a) notes that a key determinant of the child's developmental pathway is the timing of the acquisition of fluent language. These findings emphasize the importance of early identification and intervention to maximize the potential for a long-term positive prognosis. Educational placement and number of years of and involvement in mainstream schooling are also associated with more positive outcomes (Howlin, 2005). There is a subgroup of children who do not acquire language and have a childhood IQ of less than 70 whose prognosis is poorer and who need a higher level of care throughout their lives. The crucial issue is to identify the factors that influence the trajectory of this disorder in individuals and the presence of any additional skills or interests that facilitate their integration and participation in society (Howlin, 2005).

ASPERGER'S DISORDER

In 1944, Hans Asperger first described four children ages 6 to 11 who appeared to have adequate verbal and cognitive abilities yet significant difficulty with social relationships (Klin, McPartland, et al., 2005). Asperger's Disorder was not widely recognized until after Wing's (1981) influential review and its inclusion in the *DSM-IV* in 1994, which resulted in a burgeoning of research (American Psychiatric Association, 1994). Prior to the *DSM-IV* five different sets of diagnostic criteria were in use, and there remains considerable controversy over the disorder's existence as a discrete entity or as part of spectrum of disorders that includes autism and PDD-NOS (First & Tasman, 2004; Frith, 2004; Klin, McPartland, et al., 2005). There has also been increased interest in the overlap of Asperger's with HFA and the identification of specific unique features or differences in neuropsychological profiles, psychiatric comorbidity, family genetics, and outcome (Klin, McPartland, et al., 2005; Volkmar & Klin, 2005). This differentiation is discussed further in the diagnostic differential section.

Many of Asperger's (1944/1991) original observations concerning the clinical presentation of the disorder are still relevant today. These include the presence of impaired nonverbal communication; a limited diversity of facial expression; verbal idiosyncrasies, including circumstantial utterances and pedantic speech; poor empathy; intellectualization of affect; clumsiness; and behavioral problems (Frith, 1989, 2004; Hippler & Klicpera, 2003; Klin, McPartland, et al., 2005). He also noted that the disorder was predominantly present in males (95% of his original and later cases were boys) and had a familial pattern, and while the onset was in childhood, curiosity and interest in the world and people were present at an early age (Frith, 1989, 2004; Hippler & Klicpera, 2003). Differences in the diagnostic definition of the disorder have made the calculation of the prevalence difficult; however, a rate of 2.6/10,000 has been reported, and as with other PDDs, this rate is reported to be rising (Fombonne, 2005; Fombonne & Tidmarsh, 2003; Klin, McPartland, et al., 2005). Asperger's is a lifelong disorder with a stable course, and the prognosis is believed to be better than in autism, with some studies showing some individuals being capable of gainful employment and personal self-sufficiency (Gillberg, 1998). However, other studies suggest that despite high cognitive potential, many individuals remain at home and few marry and have regular employment (Klin, McPartland, et al., 2005).

Clinical Presentation

Social Deficits

The deficits in social impairment for Asperger's Disorder are the same as those for Autistic Disorder; however, a fewer number of symptoms (two as opposed to six) are required for a diagnosis (American Psychiatric Association, 2000b). Hence the earlier detailed clinical descriptions are relevant for children with Asperger's Disorder. Social deficits were identified by Asperger as the defining feature of this disorder; these deficits are severe, have an early onset, and significantly impact the individual's daily functioning throughout life (Klin, McPartland, et al., 2005). There may be subtle qualitative differences in the expression of these social deficits by children with autism that are different from those in children with Asperger's; however, these are not addressed in the current diagnostic criteria (Klin, McPartland, et al., 2005). Early studies suggest that individuals with Asperger's may wish to be friendly, approach others in an odd or eccentric manner, making unusual overtures, and fail to establish relationships. They are often interested in social interaction, whereas individuals with autism have been described as appearing to disregard others (Tantam, 1988; Van Krevelan, 1971). In conversations and interpersonal interactions children with Asperger's may be pedantic, longwinded, and overly reliant on rigid social conventions and formal rules of behavior; they may also have poor intuition and appear somewhat socially naive (Klin, McPartland, et al., 2005; Klin & Volkmar, Sparrow, 2000).

Stereotypies and Preoccupations

The restrictive, repetitive, stereotyped behaviors, patterns, interests, and activities that are often present in children with Asperger's are identical to those for Autistic Disorder (American Psychiatric Association, 2000b). However, in Asperger's these behaviors are often accompanied by encompassing preoccupations, unusual and circumscribed interests or topic-based obsessions that dominate the child's life and social exchanges and consume their attention and motivation, thus interfering with the acquisition of other skills (Klin, McPartland, et al., 2005; Romanowski Bashe & Kirby, 2001). These children often have cognitive strengths in verbal abilities such as vocabulary and auditory rote memory that may be apparent in their ability to acquire large amounts of factual knowledge, often without a broader understanding (Klin, McPartland, et al., 2005). The intensity with which the preoccupations are pursued helps differentiate them from normal age-appropriate hobbies and interests. According to Baron-Cohen and colleagues (Baron-Cohen, Wheelwright, Stone, & Rutherford, 1999), many individuals with Asperger's have a learning style suited to technical knowledge and skills.

The child's lack of common or intuitive sense and ability to adapt spontaneously results in poor insight, and their overreliance on rigid rules may appear to others as insensi-
tivity, thus contributing to significant difficulties in establishing and maintaining
friendships (Romanowski Bashe & Kirby, 2001). This social ineptitude and naiveté may
result in victimization and bullying (Klin, McPartland, et al., 2005). Given their adherence
to rules, individuals with Asperger's tend to be rigidly law-abiding; however, their preoccupations and perseverative interests may result in difficulties with the legal system
(Howlin, 2005; V. Shea & Mesibov, 2005).

Language

Typically in Asperger's there are no clinically significant delays in early language; single
words are used by age 2, and communicative phrases are used by age 3 (American Psychiatric Association, 2000b). The apparently normal development of early language is in
contrast to autism, and the presence of communication deficits early in life precludes a
diagnosis of Asperger's Disorder (Frick & Silverthorn, 2001; Gilchrist et al., 2001; Szatmari, 2000a,b). The child's language is still noticeably odd, however. Klin and colleagues
(2005) identify three ways in which the speech of individuals with Asperger's is clinically
significant. First, prosody may be poor, and there may be a restricted range of intonation.
Thus, though the intonation and inflection may not be as monotonic or rigid as in autism,
there is a constricted range of intonation that often appears unrelated to the speaker's remarks. This is particularly apparent when humor is used (Ghaziuddin & Gerstein, 1996).
There may be a lack of fluency, speech rate may be unusual and appear jerky, and often
there are difficulties with volume modulation, with the child appearing to shout at a listener standing nearby. Second, speech may appear circumstantial or tangential. These children often fail to demonstrate changes in topics, provide background information, or
suppress verbalizations associated with thoughts, all of which contribute to an egocentric
one-sided monologue style of conversation. Third, although children with Asperger's are
usually very verbose, their speech often appears incessant, with a marked disregard for the
listener. The child appears to talk at listeners and ignores attempts by listeners to comment or change topics. The monologues rarely come to a point or conclusion, and it is
difficult to change topic (Klin, McPartland, et al., 2005). The *DSM-IV* has been criticized
for including no significant delay in language in the diagnostic criteria for the
disorder and not addressing the peculiarities of language that have been consistently observed in clinical studies (Eisenmajer et al., 1998; Fitzgerald, 1999; Klin, McPartland,
et al., 2005).

Cognitive Abilities

Compared to Autistic Disorder, in Asperger's there is a greater preservation of cognitive
abilities and no significant delay in cognitive functioning or in age-appropriate self-help
skills or adaptive behavior (American Psychiatric Association, 2000b). Asperger's earlier
and subsequent work found almost all children had normal to above normal full-scale IQ;
54% showed excellent verbal abilities, with deficits in nonverbal skills such as visual-
spatial abilities (Hippler & Klicpera, 2003). Individuals with Asperger's Disorder consistently demonstrate higher verbal IQ and greater strength in fund of general knowledge and
vocabulary in comparison to individuals with HFA (Ghaziuddin & Mountain-Kimchi,

2004; Reitzel & Szatmari, 2003). For a diagnosis of Asperger's there must also be no significant delay in self-help or adaptive behavior skills, excluding social skills (Willemsen-Swinkles & Buitelaar, 2002).

These clinical symptoms are not the result of another PDD or schizophrenia, and Autistic Disorder takes diagnostic precedence over Asperger's Disorder (American Psychiatric Association, 2000b). Unlike autism, a diagnosis of Asperger's does not require significant delays present before the age of 3. Thus, if in clinical practice concerns are noted about social interaction, communication, symbolic play, or cognitive or adaptive functioning prior to age 3, a diagnosis of Asperger's should not be assigned (American Psychiatric Association, 2000b). This and the other *DSM-IV* criteria have been criticized as being too restrictive and making the diagnosis of Asperger's unlikely to be assigned (Klin, McPartland, et al., 2005; Mayes, Calhoun, & Crites, 2001; J. Miller & Ozonoff, 2000). Whereas a number of early case reports suggested that individuals with Asperger's may be at increased risk for psychosis or Schizophrenia and their excessive verbalization and poor social skills may be mistaken for schizophrenic thought disorder, the preponderance of empirical research does not support this association (Klin, McPartland, et al., 2005).

Additional Characteristics

Clumsiness and Behavioral Deficits

Motor clumsiness has been consistently identified as a clinical feature of Asperger's; motor coordination problems are apparent in the majority (50% to 90%) of children (Fitzgerald, 1999; Klin, McPartland, et al., 2005). The child's history may reveal difficulties acquiring skills such as throwing a ball, riding a tricycle, climbing play equipment, opening jars, and problems with self-help skills and writing (Romanowski Bashe & Kirby, 2001; Volkmar & Klin, 2005). Rigid gait, odd posture, poor fine motor skills, including handwriting, and deficits in visuomotor coordination and visuospatial skills may also be reported (Gillberg, 1990). Children with Asperger's Disorder may have difficulties in proprioception and often have difficulties on tests of apraxia, balance, tandem gait, and finger-thumb coordination (Weimer, Schatz, Lincoln, Ballantyne, & Trauner, 2002). These features are not included in the current diagnostic criteria, and no consistent motor and neuropsychological skills have been identified that can differentiate between individuals with Asperger's and HFA (Klin, McPartland, et al., 2005; I. M. Smith, 2000; Willemsen-Swinkles & Buitelaar, 2002).

Variability of Cognitive Functioning and Preoccupations

Reviewing neuropsychological studies, Klin and colleagues (Klin, McPartland, et al., 2005) report that individuals with Asperger's demonstrate significant strengths in verbal abilities on measures of cognitive functioning. Typically they have difficulty on tasks assessing fine and gross motor skills, nonverbal concept formation, visual-motor integration, visual-spatial perception, and visual memory and tend to do well on tests that assess general factual knowledge and knowledge of verbal concepts (Ghaziuddin & Mountain-Kimchi, 2004). The child's circumscribed interest may spuriously inflate these scores, and these cognitive strengths often do not necessarily reflect a genuine understanding. Such strengths can be an impediment to the child's learning and can significantly negatively impact the ability to engage peers in a reciprocal manner (Klin, McPartland, et al., 2005).

Onset, Course, and Life Span Considerations

Onset

Initially Asperger's disorder was thought to be unrecognizable before 3 years, and the lack of early problems made it relatively rare for children to be recognized prior to this age (Klin, McPartland, et al., 2005). Generally parents do not report concerns about their child's development early in life, because language and other cognitive functions appear normal, as do self-help skills and adaptive behavior (American Psychiatric Association, 2000b). In fact, these children may be reported as precocious in talking, often acquiring complex adultlike words quickly and speaking in a very formal manner. Some children have an early fascination with letters and are able to decode words but have little or no understanding of their meaning (a condition known as *hyperlexia*). Attachment to family members is often unremarkable, and there may be few signs of social deficits in the home setting (Romanowski Bashe & Kirby, 2001).

Course

As the child begins socializing with others in nursery or preschool, social deficits become apparent. These children may appear socially awkward, use others in play instrumentally rather than reciprocally, speak loudly, and become upset when others are not interested in their interests (Klin, McPartland, et al., 2005). During this time the child may develop intense preoccupations, such as for U.S. presidents or Thomas the Tank Engine, about which they accumulate vast amounts of knowledge, often to the exclusion of more appropriate learning (Romanowski Bashe & Kirby, 2001). The child may adhere to and appear to need rigid rules and to be fascinated with unchangeable stimuli, such as letters and numbers. These latter behaviors have been related to the children's lack of intuitive skills and difficulty understanding their experiences; such behaviors may serve to ground these children in an otherwise overwhelming, changing social world (Klin, McPartland, et al., 2005). These children's rigidity and good language skills may result in teachers and others mistakenly assuming that their problem behavior is due to stubbornness or willfulness (American Psychiatric Association, 2000b).

Interest in forming social relationships may increase in adolescence, although social problems may result in the adolescent gravitating toward younger or significantly older, more sensitive peers (Romanowski Bashe & Kirby, 2001). Asperger noted that these children were often bullied and teased mercilessly by peers, resulting in interpersonal aggression and poor social adjustment (Klin, McPartland, et al., 2005). Many children with HFA, Asperger's, and PDD-NOS may also fall through the cracks in the education system (Myhr, 1998). As Howlin (2005) notes, their good cognitive skills and apparent linguistic competence mean they often fail to receive much-needed support. Others' expectations are often unrealistically high, and their significant limitations with the subtleties of social interaction can result in profound sadness, isolation, and very low self-esteem. Given these issues, their risk for suicide should not be underestimated (Howlin, 2005).

Life Span Considerations

In his early and subsequent research, Asperger proposed a positive outcome for individuals with this disorder; however, whether this is a consequence of the early preservation of cognitive and language skills is unclear (Klin, McPartland, et al., 2005). Despite good cognitive skills most individuals remain at home, and only a minority obtain regular employment and marry (Klin, McPartland, et al., 2005). As the individual ages, the differentiation of Asperger's from HFA becomes impossible (Howlin, 2003). Trying to determine where individuals with Asperger's Disorder go after age 40, Fitzgerald (1999) hypothesized that in the past they, like adults with autism, may have resided in state psychiatric hospitals and been misdiagnosed as simple schizophrenics. He also notes that many individuals diagnosed with Schizoid Personality Disorder might be more appropriately given the diagnosis of Asperger's, and there is still controversy about the differentiation between Asperger's Disorder and Schizoid Personality Disorder (Fitzgerald, 1999).

OTHER PERVASIVE DEVELOPMENTAL DISORDERS

Childhood Disintegrative Disorder

According to Volkmar, Koenig, and State (2005), the Viennese educator Theodore Heller in 1908 first described six children who initially developed within normal limits but then underwent profound and enduring developmental regression; describing their condition as "dementia infantilis." Also known as "Heller's disorder" or "disintegrative psychosis," it was officially classified as Childhood Disintegrative Disorder in the *DSM-IV* (Volkmar & Klin, 2005). One tenth as common as autism, CDD is a rare disorder; as of mid-1999 only 126 cases have been identified worldwide, primarily in developed countries (Volkmar & Cohen, 1989). It is characterized by a rapid regression or disintegration of mental functions and derailment of future functioning (Volkmar, Koeing, et al., 2005). The hallmark signs are pervasive losses in acquired skills in all areas, including verbal and nonverbal communication, social relationships, play, motor, and adaptive or self-care behavior (American Psychiatric Association, 2000b). The regression also includes a loss of previously normal language and the occurrence of repetitive, restrictive behaviors, stereotyped behaviors, or resistance to change, as is seen in autism (American Psychiatric Association, 2000b). According to the *DSM-IV-TR* (American Psychiatric Association, 2000b) the striking and profound loss of previously acquired abilities takes place after 2 years but before age 10, after a period of normal development of at least 2 years. Heller (1930) originally described the onset as between 3 to 5 years, and this is still considered the case. There are several different patterns of onset; the disorder can occur slowly over a period of weeks to months, or it can be abrupt and rapid over a period of days to weeks. The onset may come after a period of marked deterioration, when the child is anxious and irritable, or after a medical event or a common stressor, such as the death of a family member or birth of a sibling (Volkmar, Koeing, et al., 2005).

The child's parents often note the dramatic loss of social interaction skills and general loss of interest in the environment; in this way the clinical presentation once the disorder is established resembles autism (Volkmar, Koeing, et al., 2005). However, unlike autism, self-help skills, motor skills, and bladder and bowel control are also often lost (First & Tasman, 2004; Volkmar, Koeing, et al., 2005). Following the initial severe regression, the course for the majority of cases (75%) tends to plateau or involve minimal to mild improvement (American Psychiatric Association, 2000b; Volkmar, Koeing, et al., 2005). In a few cases, the deterioration may continue and early death may result, especially if comorbid neurological or medical conditions are present (Volkmar, Koeing, et al., 2005). For most children, life expectancy is normal, although the disorder can be accompanied by seizures and has been linked to a range of medical conditions, including tuberous sclerosis, infections, and encephalitis. In most cases, CDD appears to arise from nowhere (First & Tasman, 2004; Malhotra & Gupta, 2002; Volkmar, Koeing, et al., 2005). The majority of children with CDD (75%) are mentally retarded, often in the severe (IQ 35–40) to profound (IQ below 20 or 25) range (American Psychiatric Association, 2000b). In these cases, the CDD would be coded on Axis I and the mental retardation on Axis II. Overall, children with CDD have a more severe prognosis than children with autism in that they are more likely to be mute and reside in residential facilities and a higher number (77% versus 33%) develop seizures (Willemsen-Swinkles & Buitelaar, 2002).

Rett's Disorder

In 1966, Andreas Rett first observed two girls in his waiting room with similar hand-wringing mannerisms and then identified 22 cases with a similar clinical presentation, including stereotypic hand movements, autistic behavior, dementia, and cortical atrophy. As Rett's original report was in German, widespread recognition of the syndrome did not occur until Hagberg, Aicardi, Dias, and Ramos (1983) reported on an additional 35 cases (Van Acker et al., 2005). Rett's is a rare, primarily female disorder characterized by arrested neurodevelopment with a highly distinctive pattern of cognitive and developmental stagnation, followed by regression and deterioration (American Psychiatric Association, 2000b). The majority of cases (37% to 87%) are caused by mutations of the X chromosome's MECP2 gene (First & Tasman, 2004; Van Acker et al., 2005). There was some controversy about including Rett's in a manual of psychiatric disorders, as it seems to be a primarily neurological disorder and can appear with and without autism (Sponheim, 1996; Volkmar & Klin, 2005). Given that it can be confused with autism in the first years of life, a decision was made to include it in the *DSM-IV*. According to Rutter (1994) the placement of disorders such as Rett's often has to do with the practical issue of usage. Its placement in the PDD category facilitated research by Amir and colleagues (1999) and Hoffbuhr and colleagues (2001) into the genetic mechanisms of the disorder and the ultimate discovery of a gene linked to the cause of the disorder (Volkmar & Klin, 2005). Rett's is second only to Down syndrome as the most common cause of mental retardation in females (Ellaway & Christodoulou, 1999).

The hallmark features of Rett's Disorder are multiple specific deficits after a period of normal development (American Psychiatric Association, 2006b). The *DSM-IV-TR* specifies that the child has apparently unremarkable prenatal and perinatal development, and normal psychomotor development for at least 5 months (American Psychiatric Association, 2000b). On closer scrutiny of home videos, some minor problems, including tremulous neck movements and unusual hand use and language development, have been noted during the pre- and perinatal periods (Burford, Kerr, & Macleod, 2003). At birth the child has a normal head circumference; then, beginning between 5 and 48 months, head growth begins to decelerate. Between 5 and 30 months there is slowing, cessation, or stagnation in the acquisition of developmental milestones (American Psychiatric Association, 2000b). This is followed by a rapid deterioration and loss of previously acquired purposeful hand skills and speech and the development of stereotyped hand movements such as hand-wringing, hand washing, or clapping (American Psychiatric Association, 2000b). Although the girls maintain eye contact, they begin to lack interest in others, and there is also a loss of social engagement. The onset is usually prior to 4 years, usually in the second or third year of life (American Psychiatric Association, 2000b). The disorder may present as early as 6 to 8 months of age. Early warning signs include excessive hand patting, wrist twisting, and nonspecific circulating hand-mouth movements (Van Acker et al., 2005). The deterioration is rapid, usually within a year, and results in severe to profound impairments, including severely impaired expressive or receptive language; distinctive motor problems, such as poorly coordinated gait or trunk movements; and aberrant breathing patterns. Increased irritability, spontaneous tantrums, screaming, and sleep abnormalities may also be present, and seizures occur in 80% of children (Van Acker et al., 2005).

The course of the condition is one of progressive deterioration interspersed with periods of plateau (during the early school years) and very occasional stabilization or modest improvement. The *DSM-IV-TR* notes that in the preschool years, children with Rett's may exhibit social deficits similar to that seen in autism, but that these deficits are often of a transient nature (American Psychiatric Association, 2000b). Early research by Hagberg and Witt-Engerstrom (1986) describes a four-stage model of clinical course for the disorder from onset to adolescence that has wide acceptance in clinical practice. Whereas impairments are lifelong, some modest developmental gains may be observed and social interest may improve; however, increased motor deterioration after age 10 often results in decreased mobility. Given the nature of the clinical presentation and severity of cognitive and motor impairments, adults with Rett's Disorder require a high level of support and supervision. Additional associated features include bruxism, breathing problems (periods of apnea alternating with hyperventilation), scoliosis, spasticity, seizures, and abnormal EEG for almost all individuals (American Psychiatric Association, 2000b). There is also a risk of sudden death associated with cardiac disturbances and breathing abnormalities (Van Acker et al., 2005).

Pervasive Developmental Disorder Not Otherwise Specified

First coined in the *DSM-III-R,* PDD-NOS is a catch-all category for severe and pervasive impairments in reciprocal social interaction, with impairments in either verbal or nonverbal communication skills or the presence of stereotyped behaviors, interests, and activities (American Psychiatric Association, 1987). In these cases, the clinical presentation does not meet criteria for Autistic Disorder, Asperger's, or another PDD (American Psychiatric Association, 2000b). This residual category includes what used to be called "atypical" autism (Buitelaar & Van der Gaag, 1998). The diagnosis can be given when the child fails to have an onset prior to age 3, or when the clinical presentation consists of atypical symptoms. The presentation is considered atypical if it does not fit the criteria for another disorder or is subthreshold (i.e., having less than the required number of symptoms; American Psychiatric Association, 2000b).

The use of this category has been described as problematic and underresearched (Volkmar & Klin, 2005; Willemsen-Swinkles & Buitelaar, 2002). It has no explicit criteria, and no threshold is given to differentiate between PDD-NOS and non-PDD-NOS, resulting in a very heterogeneous grouping (L. S. Walker, Claar, & Garber, 2002). For many, what is particularly problematic is the high number of unspecified or spectrum disorder cases, resulting in the number of children with nonautistic PDD outnumbering the number of children with autism (Buitelaar & Van der Gaag, 1998; Fombonne, 2003a; Myhr, 1998). Initially the category was considered to be inherently vague and too heterogeneous to be meaningful; however, genetic and family history research suggest the presence of biological features and genetic risks similar to autism, but to a milder degree (Fitzgerald, 1999; Towbin, 2005). The few studies on natural history and outcome demonstrated that individuals with PDD-NOS fared better than individuals with autism but worse than individuals with Asperger's. These differences in outcome were found to be directly correlated with cognitive and language abilities and were more related to functional abilities than diagnosis per se (Towbin, 2005).

W. J. Mahoney and colleagues (1998) found that although there is 91% interrater agreement among experienced clinicians distinguishing PDD from non-PDD cases, this drops to 73% when the differentiation was between PDD-NOS and other PDDs. According to Fitzgerald (1999), the wording of the disorder's description greatly dilutes the meaning of the category and grossly widens it. He states that many clinicians use two of the diagnostic criteria from autism as a cutoff. A scoring rule based on a short set of the seven *DSM-IV* criteria with a mandatory cutoff of three items and one social interaction item has been suggested as the best balance between high sensitivity and specificity to prevent overdiagnosis (Buitelaar & Van der Gaag, 1998). D. R. Walker and colleagues (2004) suggest that, after ruling out all other PDDs, the clinician should use three *DSM-IV* Autistic Disorder criteria, one of which must be social impairment, to determine a diagnosis. Using this approach, the age of onset criterion in some cases may be omitted. Given the absence of diagnostic criteria and the ambiguity, Towbin (2005) suggests that it is helpful to consider the PDD-NOS category as a work in progress, with more work being required to reach a consensus on its operational definition. He recommends using PDD-NOS under four conditions: (1) as a temporary designation or delaying strategy as a default diagnosis when information is inadequate or as a last resort when developmental history is unreliable; (2) when the impairments are too mild to be considered by another disorder (subthreshold) but too severe to be considered normal; (3) for individuals with late onset of autistic symptoms after the 3-year age requirement; and (4) for early-onset symptoms that are characterized by impairments in social reciprocity or relatedness, which may include other disorders such as childhood schizoid disorders or Multiple Complex Developmental Disorder.

EPIDEMIOLOGY

Autism

Epidemiological studies of autism started in England in the mid-1960s (Fombonne, 2005). Most of the studies have focused on the prevalence rate as measured by the number of individuals receiving services, and the rate has varied depending on the population studied and the diagnostic criteria used. Early studies reported prevalence ranges from about 2 to 20 cases per 10,000, with the *DSM-IV-TR* noting the median to be about 5 cases per 10,000 (American Psychiatric Association, 2000b; Wing, 1993; Yeargin-Allsopp et al., 2003). In reviewing epidemiological studies (1966 to 2004) of autism from 14 countries, including the United States, France, Finland, Japan, and Hong Kong, Fombonne found consistency across all studies in the clinical presentation of autism and gender differences. With changes in case definition and improved recognition, he noted, the median prevalence rates increased from 4.7/10,000 in studies from 1966 to 1993 to 12.7/10,000 for studies published in 1994 to 2004. He estimated a minimum conservative prevalence for autism to be between 10 and 16/10,000 or 13/10,000. Using a multimethod case ascertainment approach, Yeargin-Allsopp and colleagues (2003) found a prevalence rate of 34/10,000, which was significantly higher than earlier rates (prior to 1980). It was, however, consistent with Bertrand and colleagues' (2001) study in New Jersey, which found prevalence rates of 40/10,000 for autism or 67/10,000 for spectrum disorders.

In 1999, the California Department of Disabilities (CDER) in a report to the legislature reported a 273% increase in the number of individuals with autism seeking services between 1987 and 1998 (CDD, 2003). Such a dramatic increase in prevalence rates caused considerable controversy in the field, giving rise to the public perception of an "autism epidemic" and resulted in a congressional hearing in April 2002 on the topic (Croen, Grether, Hoogstrate, & Selvin, 2002a,b). The studies using the CDER report were criticized as having methodological limitations. These included the lack of equivalency between the CDER and *DSM-IV* criteria, not considering California's population increase in calculating the change in prevalence rates, the lack of diagnostic uniformity across California's regional centers, and the *DSM* changes during the study period (Fombonne, 2005). The increases in prevalence were attributed to the broadening of the diagnostic criteria to include spectrum disorders, greater public awareness, the success of early intervention services, and the expansion of special education services to include autism (Croen et al., 2002a,b; Gurney et al., 2003; Yeargin-Allsopp et al., 2003). It was also theorized that the increases reflected a reclassification of cases. When earlier (1987 to 1994) prevalence data were reanalyzed there was evidence of diagnostic substitution, wherein the prevalence of autism increased from 5.8 to 14.9/10,000 and the prevalence from mental retardation decreased from 28.8 to 19.5/10,000 (Fombonne, 2003a,b). However a reexamination of the data determined that the increase was not attributable to a broadening of the diagnostic criteria, reclassification of children with mental retardation, or migration but rather reflected a true increase in the prevalence of this disorder in California (Byrd, 2002; MIND Institute, 2002). There is evidence to suggest that improved research design involving multiple ascertainment, differences in case identification, greater public and professional awareness of autism, and the availability of and improved access to effective early intervention services may contribute to higher prevalence rates (Fombonne, 2005; Yeargin-Allsopp et al., 2003). These factors may not be a sufficient explanation for the perceived autism "epidemic," and confusing the prevalence rates with the incidence rate or the number of new cases may also have contributed to some of the lack of clarity in the field (Fombonne, 2005, p. 38). To date there are few current incidence studies on autism or other PDDs. Fombonne (2005) reviewed three current studies (J. Kaye, Melero-Montes, & Jick, 2001; J. Powell et al., 2000; Smeeth et al., 2004) and noted that incidence rates for PDDs increased as much as ten-fold. He concluded that the effect of the changes in the diagnostic criteria over time, the increased awareness, and the availability of services on the rate of autism still needs to be determined.

Asperger's and Other Pervasive Developmental Disorders

Earlier epidemiological studies (prior to 1985) found that if the wider definition of spectrum disorders based on the presence of the Wing triad is used, the prevalence is approximately 4 to 5/10,000 (Fombonne, 1997; Wing, 1996; Yeargin-Allsopp, 2003). More recent studies have found the prevalence rate for spectrum disorders to be 1.5 to 2.5 times higher than the rate for autism, or a rate as high as 67 to 91/10,000 (Bertrand, Mars, Boyle, Bove, Yaergin-Allsopp, et al., 2001; Yeargin-Allsopp et al., 2003).

For Asperger's the lack of consistent definitions and disagreements about the basic diagnosis have contributed to confusion and a lack of consistent data on prevalence (American Psychiatric Association, 2000b; Klin et al., 2005). Earlier studies reported rates varying from 0.3 to 48.4/10,000, reflecting significant diagnostic and methodological differences (Fombonne & Tidmarsh, 2003; Willemsen-Swinkles & Buitelaar, 2002). Only two studies specifically focused on the prevalence of Asperger's, and the numbers were too small to yield a precise estimate (Fombonne, 2005). Using the data from autism surveys, which identified a subgroup of children with Asperger's, Fombonne (2005) calculated the prevalence rate for Asperger's to be 2.6/10,000. As with other PDDs, the rates of Asperger's are reported to be increasing (Klin et al., 2005).

Both CDD and Rett's Disorder are very rare (Szatmari, Jones, Zwaigenbaum, & McLean, 1998). Only 1 CDD case occurs for every 65 cases of autism, and the *DSM-IV-TR* notes that the condition is underdiagnosed (American Psychiatric Association, 2000b; Fombonne, 2005). Burd, Fisher, and Kerbeshian (1989) found a prevalence rate for CDD of 0.1/10,000, while Fombonne's (2005) review of five available studies reported a prevalence estimate of 1.1 to 9.2/10,000, or a pooled estimate of 1.9/10,000. These rates must be interpreted with caution given the lack of familiarity of many clinicians with this disorder (Volkmar et al., 2005). The prevalence rate for Rett's is not listed in the *DSM-IV-TR*, which notes that data are limited mostly to case studies (American Psychiatric Association, 2000b). According to Van Acker and colleagues (2005), Rett's Disorder is universal and has been reported in most countries; they report on three prevalence study rates of 1 per 15,000, 1 per 12,000 to 13,000, and 1 per 22,800 of live female births.

ETIOLOGY

Autism

Biological Theories

Kanner (1943) observed mild autistic features such as social difficulties and detachment in the families of autistic children, suggesting a possible genetic basis for the disorder. Since then, genetic and family studies show a significant familial loading for autism, with high concordance rates (60% to 90%) for autism and autistic spectrum disorders among monozygotic twins (E. H. Cook, 2001). These rates may be an underestimation, as many twins who were discordant for autism matched for another PDD disorder. If one considers concordance for impaired sociability, cognition, or language, the rate increases to over 90% (First & Tasman, 2004; Rutter, 2005).

Autistic Disorder is 15 to 30 times more frequent in siblings of children with autism than in the general population, and 3% to 5% of siblings have the disorder (American Psychiatric Association, 2000b; First & Tasman, 2004; Rutter, 2005). Waterhouse and colleagues (1996) found a sibling concordance rate of 6.6% for autism or other PDD. Siblings also show higher than expected rates of other developmental difficulties, even if they do not have autism per se (American Psychiatric Association, 2000b). In reviewing the literature, Howlin (1998b) concluded that genetic factors are implicated in the majority of cases of autism. Szatmari and colleagues (1998) concluded that there was widespread agreement that the PDDs are caused in part by genetic factors. Combining all the studies of risk for autism, they found a sibling risk of 2.2% and an increased risk for siblings for nonautistic forms of PDD. They note that this may be an underestimation of sibling risk, given that many parents of autistic children choose not to have more children or have one and then stop, often referred to as stoppage rules. They also noted that autism, Asperger's Disorder, and atypical autism demonstrated significant familial aggregation and risk and that the pattern of risk falloff from first- to second- to third-degree relatives is inconsistent with a single major gene but suggests multiple interacting genes or complex genetic transmission. Pickles and colleagues (2000) suggest that 2 to 10 genes may be involved, but more likely 3 to 4 genes; others suggest there may be as many as 10 to 20 autism susceptibility genes (Minshew, Sweeny, Bauman, & Webb, 2005; Rutter, 2005). Reichenberg and colleagues (2006) have found that advancing paternal age is associated with increased rates of autistic spectrum disorders and postulated that this may be secondary to genetic mutations. The heterogeneity of the clinical presentation and wide phenotypic variations seen in autism may be related to variations in the expression of these susceptibility genes, which in turn may produce a variety or spectrum of handicaps. Current research suggests that autism involves multiple susceptibility genes. Genome-wide scans of siblings have found potential loci on chromosomes 7, 2, 16, 1, 3, 13, 5, 17, 19, and X (First & Tasman, 2004; Rutter, 2005).

Brain Growth and Abnormalities   Increased head size is a well-established correlate of autism. Kanner (1943) noted it in five of the original 11 children, and 20% of children with autism have a head size more than 2 standard deviations above the mean (> 97%; Lainhart, 2003; Rutter, 2005). Early research by Chudley and colleagues (1998) found that all children with a PDD had a head circumference above the mean and hypothesized that a macrocephaly defect in regional neuronal development may represent a vulnerability to PDDs. In a similar vein, Courchesne and colleagues (Courchesne, Carper, & Akshoomoff, 2003) found that a small head circumference at birth followed by a sudden and excessive increase during the first year (onset 6 to 14 months) is linked to the development of autism. They noted that the head size of children with autism at birth was, on average, in the 25th percentile, then sudden, rapid, and excessive brain growth placed them in the 85th percentile by 12 to 14 months of age. Minshew and colleagues (2005) estimate the onset of these changes in neuronal and brain development to be no later than 30 weeks gestation and that this premature accelerated brain growth coincides with the onset of autistic symptoms. The rate of excessive brain growth predicted the severity of autism, and children with a more severe form demonstrated a faster and greater rate of brain overgrowth during their first year of life, compared to that of children with a milder form of the disorder (Courchesne et al., 2003). This early acceleration in brain growth leads to increased brain volume, which several studies have found may normalize as the child ages. Brain growth decelerates and is normal by late childhood (Aylward, Mishew, Field, Sparks, & Singh, 2002; Courchesne et al., 2001, 2003; Minshew et al., 2005). Courchesne and colleagues (2003) found that 90% of children with autism ages 2 to 4 years had larger than normal brain volume, with a 12% increase in gray matter and an 18% increase in white matter. Using factor analysis to study the size of brain structures, Herbert and colleagues (2002) found that cerebral white matter tended to be dispropor- tionately larger in children with autism. In contrast, the cerebral cortex-hippocampus- amygdala tended to be disproportionately smaller and the central white-gray matter (excluding the caudate) had significantly larger volume.

In normal brain development, neurons proliferate and then become interconnected, and as certain connections are strengthened, some neurons die off (a process called pruning). It appears that this growth and pruning process is abnormal in autism; some areas are left with too many neurons and others are left with too few or abnormal connections. Minshew and colleagues (2005) note that functional MRIs show altered activation in the cortical gray matter and its white matter projections. They also describe an increase or enlargement of the outer zone of radiate white matter, which consists of connections between adjacent cortical regions and longer intrahemispheric connections (which mature postnatally), which may relate to the development of autism. These abnormalities are per- vasive and impact brain functions that involve a high degree of integration. They con- cluded that although the pathogenesis of the brain enlargement is unknown, it may reflect the presence of a greater number of neurons and/or glia, early and rapid proliferation of synapses, axonal and dendritic arbors, and/or greater myelination. They note that the lim- bic system of brains of individuals with autism is characterized by truncated dendritic tree development, small neuronal cell size, and increased cell packing, which may contribute to a curtailment in the development of cerebral and cerebellar circuitry. They also noted intact connectivity for early information processing and simple cognitive abilities, and that areas of superior or intact abilities have enhanced local connectivity. In contrast, there were pervasive deficits or reductions in functional connectivity in complex or higher- order tasks, including deficits in abstraction, conceptual reasoning, higher-order interpre- tative language, and memory for complex material (Minshew et al., 2005). This under- development of functional connectivity is consistent with findings of neuropsychological functioning in children with autism, which demonstrates a profile of deficits in complex or higher-order cognitive and neurological abilities (Minshew et al., 2005).

Postmortem studies failed to find any consistent abnormalities of gross brain structure, and numerous methodological limitations resulted in inconclusive and contradictory evi- dence and a lack of replication for findings on the role of several structures, including the hippocampus, amygdala, basal ganglia, and cerebellum (Minshew et al., 2005). The cor- pus callosum was found to have a reduced size, which may contribute to decreased intra- hemispheric connectivity (Minshew et al., 2005). In the language-related cortices M. R. Herbert and colleagues (2002) found reversed language-related asymmetry, which was consistent with earlier findings of left temporal language region deficits as underlying autistic language difficulties (Schultz & Robins, 2005). Social deficits have been linked to impairments in facial recognition and deficits in perspective taking, social cognition, and social motivation. Research is now focusing on areas of the brain such as the fusiform (FFA) and the STS that interpret dynamic social signals such as facial expression and eye gaze. It remains to be determined what is the role of the orbital and medial prefrontal cortex, the amygdala, and the frontal cortex mirror neuron networks in the significant impairments in empathy, social relatedness, and reciprocity (Schultz & Robins, 2005).

Other Biological Factors   In terms of neurotransmitters, elevated levels of blood serotonin (5-HT) or hyperserotonemia have been observed in 50% of individuals with PDDs. A familial aggregation of elevated 5-HT has been found consistently and replicated for autistic disorder (G. M. Anderson & Hoshino, 2005; First & Tasman, 2004). Elevated platelet serotonin has been identified as a well-established correlate of autism, and research suggests there is an alteration in how the platelet handles the 5-HT (G. M. Anderson & Hoshino, 2005; Rutter, 2005). Serotonin is involved in a wide range of experiences: sleep, pain and sensory perception, motor functioning, learning, and memory. It may also play a critical role in embryogenesis and the development of the nervous system (G. M. Anderson & Hoshino, 2005). Currently one of the highest priorities for research on autism is the identification of a biological marker that can differentiate between the developmental disorders (Bristol-Powers & Spinella, 1999).

Early research suggested that birth and obstetric complications were related to autism; however, a systematic examination of these factors by P. F. Bolton and colleagues (1997) concluded that it was unlikely that such an association existed. Similarly, Szatmari and colleagues (1998) concluded that no single complication arises as a consistent risk factor for children with autism.

Looking at sensory sensitivities in children with autism, Talay-Ongan and Wood (2000) hypothesize that these children experience an overwhelming barrage of sensory information, and their neurological subsystems are not adequately regulating and promoting social interactional behaviors. Thus the child's sensory sensitivities make responsiveness to auditory and visual joint attention bids nonviable. This in turn impacts and reduces the child's early interactions and opportunities for linguistic scaffolding, which is essential for the acquisition of language.

Psychological Theories

Kanner believed that autism was congenital; he also observed that the parents of his initial cases were frequently intellectual and remarkably successful educationally and professionally. The role of potential parental psychological factors in autism was espoused by several professionals in the past and became a contentious issue and also extremely painful for parents who were blamed for their child's autism (Volkmar & Klin, 2005). In the 1960s Bettelheim (1967) speculated that autism was a maladaptive response to a threatening and unloving environment. Parents were assumed to be overly intellectual and cold, with limited interest in people, including their spouse and children. There was no research or empirical evidence to support this type of severe personality pathology among parents of children with autism (DeMyer et al., 1972; Deykin & MacMahon, 1979; Rapin, 2005). In fact, research on children with autism demonstrated that the interactional problems arise on the child's side, not the parents' (Volkmar & Klin, 2005). Currently, there is strong evidence for a genetic basis for a biological vulnerability for autism and the role of dysfunction in the basic brain systems as the causes of the disorder (Volkmar et al., 2004).

Over the years several cognitive theories have developed to explain the underlying core deficits in autism. In 1985, Baron-Cohen and colleagues proposed a theory of mind (ToM) to explain how children with autism interpret the world and their inability to attribute independent mental states to others in order to predict and understand behavior. In normal children the ability to think about things that are not really there (metarepresentational thought) gradually develops from infancy on and is firmly established by 3 to 4 years of age. It is a prerequisite for pretend play (around 18 months), enabling a banana to be a telephone and teddy bears to cry and for the ability to "mind-read" or understand others' feelings. Children with autism have been described as "mind blind," lacking in metare-presentations and unable to think about others' mental states (Baron-Cohen, 1995).

Early evidence of ToM deficits came from the Sally Ann studies. A simple version involves showing a child two dolls: Sally, who has a basket, and Ann, who has a box. As the child observes, Sally places a marble in the basket and then leaves; then Ann moves Sally's marble from the basket to her box. When Sally returns, the child is asked, "Where will Sally look for her marble?" Baron-Cohen (1995) found that 80% of children with autism (mental age over 4 years) failed to appreciate Sally's false belief that the marble is still in the basket and said that she would look in the box, where the marble really was. In contrast, almost all of the children with Down syndrome and lower mental ages and typical 4-year-olds succeeded on the task. This finding has been replicated with several variations, including using real people and a control group of language-impaired children to rule out a language deficit explanation. This fundamental deficit is evident as early as 18 months and can be used to explain Wing's triad of impairments in social and communication functioning and in symbolic play (Baron-Cohen et al., 1996; Charman et al., 2002). Some children (15% to 60%), often with HFA, have been found to pass the Sally Ann test by hacking out a solution that may not reflect a true understanding of others' mental states. ToM performance has been linked to verbal IQ, suggesting that this skill is delayed rather than absent in children with autism (Happe, 1995; Sparrevohn & Howie, 1995).

This earlier work was expanded into an empathizing-systematizing theory, which looked at the occurrence of deficits in emotional or affective reaction to others and strengths in systematizing skills in individuals with spectrum disorders (Baron-Cohen, 2002). This was further expanded to explain gender differences in empathy and eye contact and describe autism in terms of an extreme male brain theory (Baron-Cohen, 2002; Baron-Cohen et al., 2005). These researchers noted that among children with autism or a spectrum disorder, 28.4% had at least one relative who was an engineer. Science students at Cambridge University were found to have a sixfold increase in the rate of autism in family members (Baron-Cohen et al., 1998, Baron-Cohen, Wheelwright, Stott, Bolton, & Goodyear, 1997).

Other cognitive theories that have been used to explain the core deficits in autism include the executive function theory, the weak central coherence theory, joint attention, and the enactive mind. The executive function theory describes how individuals with autism present with deficits in mental flexibility, which may relate to the repetitive behaviors seen in autism (Pennington & Ozonoff, 1996; M. Turner, 1997, 1999b). This theory has been criticized, as executive dysfunction is not specific to autism but occurs in children with a range of other disorders (Ozonoff, South, & Provencal, 2005). The weak central coherence model proposes that the strengths and deficits in autism all relate to a core cognitive style of processing information, where the details are focused on to the exclusion of the bigger picture (Frith, 1989; Happe, 1996, 2000). Though intriguing, this theory remains to be empirically supported. Joint attention models address deficits in the interactive process between children and their environment, focusing on the fundamental deficits in joint attention or the children's ability to coordinate their visual attention with another. For the child with autism these deficits in early social behavior repertoire may contribute to long-term disturbances in their social experience. The relationship of these deficits to the impairments characteristic of autism and children's development is under active investigation (Mundy & Burnette, 2005). Klin and colleagues (Klin, Jones, et al., 2005) have used the enactive mind theory to explain how individuals with autism and normal IQ present with significant deficits in social reasoning and have difficulty responding spontaneously or in social situations. This research is in its infancy and needs to be conducted in naturalistic settings.

Asperger's and Other Pervasive Developmental Disorders

Asperger's (1944/1991) earlier observation that the children's fathers often had similar characteristics has been supported by research indicating a strong genetic predisposition for this disorder (Rutter, 2005). Klin, McPartland, et al. (2005) note that nearly half of families surveyed reported the presence of Asperger's, spectrum disorders, and autism in first-degree relatives. In looking at the family clustering of PDDs, Volkmar and Klin (2000) concluded that there is a stronger genetic contribution in families of individuals with Asperger's than for individuals with autism. Research, including that by Tentler and colleagues (2003) on chromosome 17, is focusing on the identification of genetic abnormalities and gene susceptibility candidates.

Studies on identifying brain structural differences that are characteristic of Asperger's have been complicated by the difficulties in differentiating individuals with this disorder from those with HFA (Klin, McPartland, et al., 2005). D. G. Murphy and colleagues (2002) found that individuals with Asperger's in comparison to typical controls had higher levels of neurotransmitters (NAA), which has been associated with obsessional behavior and abnormalities in the prefrontal cortex, which have been linked to social functioning. In an interesting study, Lotspeich and colleagues (2004) found differences in typical controls and individuals with autism and Asperger's in terms of cerebral gray matter. They hypothesized that symptom severity may be related to cerebral gray matter and suggested that Asperger's might represent the mild end of a range of cognitive symptom severity. In reviewing all children referred for a PDD evaluation, Chudley and colleagues (1998) found that 8.2% of families had an affected sibling. They concluded that the excessive clustering of PDDs in siblings suggests a genetic predisposition, and a multifactorial inheritance seems likely.

Classically, Rett's Disorder is observed in females; a mutation of the regulating X-linked MECP2 gene plays a critical role in the development of the disorder (Van Acker et al., 2005). Bieber Nielsen and colleagues (2001) found that the MECP2 gene mutation accounts for 87% of classic Rett's cases and 50% of variant cases. Rett's Disorder is characterized by abnormalities in the substantia nigra, a structure located in the midbrain, part of the basal ganglia, associated with voluntary movement, which produces dopamine, and may be associated with the movements associated with this disorder (Van Acker et al., 2005). Results from autopsy studies suggest that the brain of individuals with Rett's weighs less than normal brains, suggesting arrested brain development (D. Armstrong, 2001). Examination of cortical neurons in individuals with Rett's indicates that they are less mature, with significantly less dendrite branching, which is associated with reduced synaptic input. There is also evidence of continued neuronal and mitochondrial deterioration even after the disorder has stabilized (Van Acker et al., 2005).

For CDD there is a lack of family clusters or multigeneration families, and the disorder appears sporadically in families. Volkmar, Koenig, et al. (2005) describe it as a complex disorder, caused either by the chance accumulation of rare genetic events; by an unknown environmental precipitant, which alone or with a genetic liability results in the sporadic expression of the disorder; or from a new, unique genetic mechanism. No specific neuropathological condition has been associated with CDD, and the extensive medical evaluations, typically undertaken at the onset of the pervasive regression and deterioration of ability, typically fail to reveal the presence of a medical condition (Volkmar, Koenig, et al., 2005). In cases where a medical condition that may play an etiological role is found (e.g., metachromatic leukodystrophy, subacute panencephalopathy), this is noted on Axis III. There is some evidence that the older a child is at the time of illness onset, the more likely the disorder is associated with a neurological condition. When associated with a neurological condition, the disorder is more likely to have a deteriorating course. Other than studies showing EEG abnormalities associated with this disorder, little else is known about the neurobiology of CDD, including information on possible neuroanatomical, neurochemical, and other neurophysiological abnormalities (Volkmar, Koenig, et al., 2005). The *DSM-IV-TR* theorizes that CDD may be the result of an insult to the brain, but to date the etiology is unclear (American Psychiatric Association, 2000b). Early case and parental reports suggested that the onset of CDD coincided with a psychosocial stressor such as the birth of a sibling; Shinnar and colleagues (2001) suggest there may be some significance to this, but there are limited supporting data (Volkmar, Koenig, et al., 2005).

Environmental Factors: Vaccines

When Wakefield and colleagues (1998) reported that 9 of 12 children within 24 hours to a few weeks of MMR vaccination experienced intestinal abnormalities, resulting in impaired intestinal function and developmental regression, concern was raised that the vaccine may be causally linked to autism. The validity of this finding was later called into question when the findings could not be replicated and 10 of the 13 authors retracted their interpretation, stating that the data were insufficient to establish a causal link between MMR vaccine and autism (Murch et al., 2004). In 1999, the British Committee on Safety of Medicines convened a Working Party on MMR Vaccine; they concluded that available information did not support associations between MMR and autism and other disorders. Several other studies (Fombonne & Chakrabarti, 2001; B. Taylor et al., 2002) found no association between developmental regression and gastrointestinal symptoms or the existence of a new syndrome of MMR-induced Inflammatory Bowel Disease and autism. In a subgroup of boys ages 2 to 5 years, J. Kaye and colleagues (2001) in the United Kingdom found that the risk of autism increased almost fourfold from 1988 to 1993, but MMR vaccination coverage remained constant at approximately 95% over these same years. In the United States, among children born between 1980 and 1994 and enrolled in California kindergartens, there was a 373% relative increase in autism cases, though the relative increase in MMR vaccine coverage by the age of 24 months was only 14% (Dales, Hammer, & Smith, 2001). Madsen et al. (2002) conducted a study of all children born in Denmark from January 1991 through December 1998. There were a total of 537,303 children in the study; 440,655 of the children were vaccinated with MMR and 96,648 were not. The researchers did not find a higher risk of autism in the vaccinated than in the unvaccinated group. The rate of autism in Japan has continued to rise even after the MMR vaccine was discontinued (Honda, Shimizu, & Rutter, 2005).

Some believe that thimerosal, a preservative used in vaccines (but no longer routinely used), may have been the causative factor. Several studies have looked at this relationship and failed to find any strong evidence supporting a link, including studies that looked at differences in trends in incidence rates of autism in Denmark, where thimerosal-free vaccine was used from April 1992 to January 1997 (Rutter, 2005). The National Childhood Encephalopathy Study also found no indication that measles vaccine contributes to the development of long-term neurological damage, including educational and behavioral deficits (B. Taylor, Miller, Farrington, Petropoulos, Favot-Mayaud, Li, et al., 1999). It is important to realize, however, that many parents remain concerned about this issue and clinicians need to address it with sensitivity. More information about this topic can be found on the CDC's web page on research on vaccines and autism (www.cdc.gov/nip/vacsafe/concerns/autism/autism-research.htm/).

DIVERSITY CONSIDERATIONS

Boys are more frequently diagnosed with autism than girls. The male-to-female ratio decreases from 4.4:1 to 1.3:1 as the severity of cognitive impairment increases (Fombonne, 1997, 2005; Yeargin-Allsopp et al., 2003). Females are overrepresented in the lower ranges of mental ability, which often have higher rates of structural abnormalities, epilepsy, and identified neurological conditions (B. Siegel, 1996; Szatmari et al., 1998). Szatmari and colleagues theorize that this sex difference in rates of autism with mental ability level suggests the role of genetic factors or mechanisms. It may be that females are more strongly affected by genes implicated in the disorder, or milder forms relate to incomplete genetic penetration being seen in boys.

Kanner's original observations that all of his cases were professionals from upper-income households likely reflected a referral bias, as there is no strong evidence of a social class differential distribution for autism (Waterhouse et al., 1996). Yeargin-Allsopp and colleagues (2003) found comparable prevalence rates for autism among African American and White children in Atlanta and that schools were the most important referral source for younger, less educated African American single mothers and their children. Overall, there is a lack of research on low-income and ethnic minority families who have children with autism and PDDs (Bernheimer, Weisner, & Lowe, 2003; Fombonne, 2005). These families may face additional challenges when raising a child with autism, as many work full time yet do not have adequate benefits or security or flexible hours and frequently lack adequate transportation and child care (Bernheimer et al., 2003; Sherman, Amery, Duffield, Ebb, & Weinstein, 1998). Language differences and lack of knowledge about available resources may also impede the child's family from gaining access to early appropriate intervention.

INTAKE AND INTERVIEWING CONSIDERATIONS

Rapport

The intake process for children with PDDs involves two major tasks: the assessment and evaluation of the child and the support and education of the family. You need to establish and maintain rapport with the child and the parents, as the cooperation of both parties is essential for effective treatment. Given the wide variability in clinical presentations, obtaining a comprehensive assessment of the child's strengths and challenges and the needs of the family at the onset is crucial to individualize the intervention strategies and access the most appropriate services. For the novice clinician this can be a daunting task; it is helpful to adopt a very systematic approach (see Table 5.2).

Table 5.2   Pervasive developmental disorders intake issues

Conduct a comprehensive multidisciplinary assessment.

Include cognitive, behavioral, linguistic, and sensory assessments.

Rule out medical disorders and physical causes.

Gather a detailed developmental history, including family videos of first years.

Consider a screening measure and parent questionnaire, preferably
multi-informant.

Conduct child interview and observation, preferably multisetting.

Modify intake interview given child's lack of language, play, and behavioral
issues.

Identify strengths and resources (including family support).

Determine challenges and delays.

Assess risk for aggressive, self-injurious, repetitive, stereotyped behaviors.

If present, assess function and role of behaviors:

    To indicate the need for attention or help.

    To escape from stressful activities or situation.

    To obtain a desired object.

    To protect against unwanted events or activities.

    To obtain stimulation.

Evaluate ability for self-care.

Provide family support and education.

Identify appropriate interventions and early intensive intervention programs.

Outline short-term and long-term intervention plans.

Assess eligibility for funding and support programs.

Consider the involvement of a regional center, school, or other agencies.

Document and determine follow-up.

Interview and Assessment Strategies

Young children with autism present as an assessment and diagnostic challenge, as they may be largely or totally mute and have significant social interactional and motivational issues (Coonrod & Stone, 2005; Volkmar & Klin, 2005). They may have poor eye contact, present with behavioral rigidities, and appear anxious, fearful, or difficult to engage. The disorders within this category are characterized by severe deficits in social reciprocal interaction skills, which by definition makes the establishment of rapport challenging (Chawarska & Volkmar, 2005). The child's cognitive and linguistic challenges will determine the nature of the assessment techniques and measures used and provide a framework within which the child's unique profile may be understood (Klin, Salnier, Tsatsanis, & Volkmar, 2005; R. Paul, 2005). Being knowledgeable about the best practice assessment guidelines and evidence-based measures for children with PDDs is crucial. Toward these ends, the studies by the National Research Council (2001), Ozonoff and colleagues (Ozonoff, Goodlin-Jones, & Solomon, 2005), and Volkmar and colleagues (Volkmar, Paul, et al., 2005) are invaluable. A developmental perspective is essential as the child's clinical presentation will vary based on his or her cognitive, linguistic, and developmental abilities, across settings, and even across a day (Burack, Iarocci, Bowler, & Mottron, 2002; Klin, Salnier, et al., 2005). Thus multisetting, multi-informant evaluations are necessary, as is the involvement of the child's parents to describe variations in the child's behavior and whether the intake behavior is representative of the child's daily functioning (Lord & Corsello, 2005; Ozonoff, Goodlin-Jones, et al., 2005). The speech of children with Asperger's may be tangential, circumstantial, and incoherent, and their egocentric conversational style and intense preoccupations and circumscribed interests may make it difficult to establish and maintain rapport (Klin, McPartland, et al., 2005).

Ideally, children with PDDs should be evaluated by a multidisciplinary team with expertise and experience with spectrum disorders, who collaborate using a transdisciplinary framework to administer and compile an integrated assessment report and series of recommendations (Klin, Salnier, et al., 2005; Ozonoff, Goodlin-Jones, et al., 2005). This minimizes the duplication and fragmentation of effort and the likelihood of presenting conflicting information to the child's parents. The range of professionals involved may include developmental pediatricians, child psychologists, speech therapists or speech pathologists, child psychiatrists, pediatric neurologists, occupational and physical therapists, and other specialists. Having one team member coordinate the evaluations facilitates this process and is essential for compiling an integrated report and helping the parents through this often overwhelming task (First & Tasman, 2004; Ozonoff, Goodlin-Jones, et al., 2005). If you are not part of an early intervention program or university- or hospital-based program where these professionals are readily available, you will need to coordinate several adjunct referrals. At a minimum, you need to follow the guidelines for the assessment of children with spectrum disorders, as described by Volkmar and colleagues (Volkmar, Cook, Pomeroy, Realmuto, & Tanguay, 1999) for the American Academy of Child and Adolescent Psychiatry, or the multidisciplinary panel guidelines described by Filipek et al. (1999). In recent years, many state agencies, such as the California Department of Developmental Services, have developed best practice guidelines for the assessment of children with autistic spectrum disorders that are available on their websites (CDD, 2002). Obtaining a comprehensive assessment can be daunting for many parents, and you need to be familiar with the different components so you can discuss these and offer guidance. Typical elements of a multidisciplinary assessment are described briefly; a more detailed account is provided in the *Handbook of Autism and Pervasive Developmental Disorders* (Volkmar, Paul, et al., 2005).

Medical Evaluation

As with all disorders, it is important to refer the child for a full medical evaluation to rule out the presence of an underlying medical condition. A research review found that 5% to 33% of individuals with autism had a medical condition, and the rate of underlying medical conditions increased to 50% for individuals with severe and profound mental retardation (Filipek, 2005; Scott, 1994). Earlier research by Rutter and colleagues (Rutter, Bailey, Bolton, & Le Couteur, 1994) found that about 10% of children with autism had a known medical condition, including genetic disorders, Fragile X, and central nervous system diseases; 25% who had no previous evidence of neurological problems developed epileptic attacks by adulthood. They concluded that a thorough medical assessment is warranted in cases where individuals are presenting as severely or profoundly retarded, epileptic, and with atypical autism. An audiological evaluation may be useful to determine if hearing issues account for the infant's apparent lack of responsiveness, and a lead screening is important for very young children who have pica or frequently put things in their mouth (Filipek, 2005; Filipek et al., 1999; Shannon & Graef, 1997). At present, the case for more extensive invasive medical procedures, such as lumbar puncture, structural brain imaging, and metabolic studies, being routinely included in the assessment of autism has not been made, unless there are specific concerns (Rutter, 2005). As discussed earlier, a large head size is an established finding for children with autism but does not in itself warrant additional neuroimaging workup (Filipek, 2005; Miles, Hadden, Tahashashi, & Hillman, 2000). Extensive neurological and medical investigations involving brain scans (MRI, CT) and/or EEG may be needed in cases with an unusual or very late onset or an unusual pattern of findings or if there is any question of developmental regression or a comorbid seizure disorder (Filipek, 2005). Genetic testing may be useful to assess for the presence of chromosomal abnormalities such as Fragile X if there is a family history of genetic disorders (Filipek, 2005; Rutter, 2005).

Developmental Assessment

As a clinician, your primary role will be conducting a developmental assessment of the child. Typically, this will involve several interviews with the parent, observations of the child, and administration of screening and assessment measures (Klin, Salnier, et al., 2005). Parent interviews should include a review of the pregnancy and neonatal period, early development, and a medical and family history, including history of genetic disorders or developmental delays (Filipek et al., 1999). You will also want to gather information on the child's social skills, such as interest in social interaction, eye contact, differential attachments, communication (including verbal, nonverbal, and preverbal skills), responses to the environment, and any unusual behaviors such as hand-washing stereotypies and unusual breathing patterns (Volkmar et al., 1999; Volkmar, Paul, et al.,

2005). It is important to prepare the parents for the intake interview ahead of time, have them talk to significant others who know the child, and prepare a list of contacts who may provide valuable information. Retrospective recall and parental information may be unreliable and inaccurate, so it is important to facilitate the process by using parental memory aids (Volkmar & Klin, 2005). Having the parents bring in baby diaries, memory books, and home movies can provide important historical information regarding developmental milestones (E. Brown, Dawson, Osterling, & Dinno, 1998). On first birthday home videos, children with autism compared to children without a PDD show significantly fewer social and joint attention behaviors, such as pointing, showing objects, looking at others, and orienting to name (Osterling & Dawson, 1994). In one study, none of the children later diagnosed with autism pointed. In fact, how often a child looked at others was the best predictor of later diagnosis; when this was combined with behaviors of showing, pointing, and failing to orient to name, 91% of children were correctly classified as autistic (Osterling & Dawson, 1994).

Being aware of, listening for, and specifically asking about parental concerns that are associated with autism is crucial (Filipek et al., 1999). Parents of children with autism with an onset prior to 12 months often report concerns about temperamental issues, describing extreme irritability or passivity, and the absence of fear of strangers, which is present in normal children at age 8 months (Chawarska & Volkmar, 2005). Infants with autism may show deficits in synchronizing intentional gestures and eye gaze, may smile less at others, may not reciprocate in lap play, and may not spontaneously seek others or share enjoyment and interests with others (Chawarska & Volkmar, 2005; Mastero et al., 2002; Mundy et al., 1994). These early developing abilities and joint attention skills are considered to be important precursors to language and communication abilities. Significant impairments in joint attention have been documented at 12 to 18 months and may be particularly pronounced among autistic children with an IQ score below 70 (Mundy, Sigman, & Kasari, 1994). Children with Asperger's or PDD-NOS may not be identified until after 4 years, and parental concerns may focus on difficulties with change, social skills, and overactivity or preoccupations (Gilchrist et al., 2001; Ozonoff, Dawson, & McPartland, 2002).

Being familiar with normal childhood development is critical, as you will have to determine whether the child's behavior represents a delay or a deficit or is atypical. If you are unfamiliar with normal child development, D. Davies's (1999) *Child Development* text is excellent, and Volkmar and colleagues' (Volkmar, Paul, et al., 2005) text provides detailed descriptions of specific developmental delays and challenges for children with autism and PDDs. Although children with autism typically sit, crawl, and walk at the expected ages and many will also produce a few words at developmentally appropriate times, the words will seldom develop into useful early language. They may not show anticipatory social responses before 6 months, and the emergence of a social smile between 6 and 12 months may be delayed or absent. Several specific behaviors, such as pretend play, joint attention, social interest, and proto-declarative pointing, have been used to differentiate children with autism from developmentally matched controls (Baron-Cohen et al., 1992; B. Siegel, 2004; W. L. Stone et al., 2000). Impaired use of nonverbal behavior and lack of social or emotional reciprocity are among the *DSM-IV* criteria most frequently endorsed by clinicians evaluating very young children (i.e., under 3) who were ultimately diagnosed with autism (W. L. Stone et al., 1999). Delayed spoken language was the language symptom most often endorsed by clinicians assigning young children a diagnosis of autism (W. L. Stone et al., 1999). Filipek and colleagues (1999) identified several developmental milestones as nearly universally present by certain ages; they suggest that failure to meet these milestones warrants further assessment and is an indication that a child is in need of an evaluation. Most of the early signs of autism (refer back to Table 5.1) appear to be in the realm of social and communicative competence; red flags include lack of following gaze, proto-declarative pointing, and interest in toys and symbolic play (B. Siegel, 2004; B. Siegel & Ficcaglia, 2006).

The assessment of the child with a PDD should include an intake interview and observations in a range of settings, including home and school. The nature and format of the sessions need to accommodate the child's developmental level and cognitive, linguistic, adaptive, and motivational challenges and may include the use of play materials, puppets, and toys. If your intake interview is taped, it can be reviewed later for social interaction responses such as responding to clinician requests, initiation, and turn-taking (Mundy et al., 1994; Vig & Jedrysek, 1999). When interviewing the child, pay particular attention to the child's eye contact, joint attention behaviors, ability to show you things and point, response to his or her name, and orienting to speech. Using a three-item screen comprising pointing at an object to direct another's attention (proto-declarative pointing), gaze monitoring, and pretend play with a teacup, Baron-Cohen and colleagues (1992) identified children with autism; and the diagnosis was maintained for the majority of children 2 and 6 years later (Baird et al., 2000).

Essential elements of any assessment and a prerequisite for treatment planning are a functional analysis of the child's behavior and an assessment of adaptive functioning (Klin, Salnier, et al., 2005; Ozonoff, Goodlin-Jones, et al., 2005). These assessments evaluate the child's everyday real-life adjustment and social skills and relate to their ability to function independently or need for support. The information can be gathered from the parent interview, information from others, and the administration of measures of adaptive functioning. These are frequently part of a more extensive psychological assessment to evaluate for the presence of mental retardation and will be discussed later in the chapter. It is crucial to also assess for any underlying causes of challenging behaviors and rituals and the impact of these behaviors on the child's life. Howlin (1998b) recommends ruling out the presence of an underlying physical illness and using a questionnaire developed by Schuler, Peck, Willard, and Theimer (1989) to assess the communicative function of inappropriate disruptive behaviors such as tantrums and screaming.

Assessment Measures

Accurate historical information on the onset and nature of the clinical presentation is critical for differential diagnosis. The use of specific autistic screening measures with parents or caregivers can identify areas to be further investigated during the interview (Coonrod & Stone, 2005; Klin, Salnier, et al., 2005; Lord & Corsello, 2005). Additionally, both screening measures and behavioral checklists can identify the areas that the clinician can focus on and target for further assessment in conducting behavioral observations of the child. Given the importance of early diagnosis for children with PDDs, an overview of several widely used measures is presented in Table 5.3. Some screening measures (often referred to as Level 1) are brief and can be completed by the clinician or parent on or prior to intake; others are more detailed structured interviews and assessments (Level 2) that

Table 5.3 Screening and assessment measures for autism

Assessment Measure Age Range (Administration Time)	Format	Level of Clinician Experience Required
Checklist for Autism in Toddlers (CHAT) 18 months	Parent report and interactive items	Minimal
Modified CHAT (M-CHAT) 24 months	Parent questionnaire	None
Pervasive Developmental Disorders Screening Test Stage 1 (PDDST-Stage1) Under 6 years (5 minutes)	Parent questionnaire preliminary stages	None or minimal
Level 2 Screening		
Autism Diagnostic Interview— Revised (ADI-R) 18 months to adult (1–2.5 hours)	Parent report and interview	Experience needed, training video available
Autism Screening Questionnaire and Social Communication Questionnaire (ASQ, SCQ) 4 years and older (10 minutes)	Parent questionnaire	None or minimal
Childhood Autism Rating Scale (CARS) 2 years to adult (5–10 minutes)	Behavioral checklist and observation	Minimal or moderate, video available.
Autism Diagnostic Observation Screening (ADOS) (30–50 minutes)	Direct testing	Experience needed, training video available
Screening Tool for Autism in Two-year-olds (STAT) 24–36 months (20 minutes)	Direct observation, interactive	Training required
Gilliam Autism Rating Scale (GARS) 3–22 years	Parent behavioral checklist	Minimal

Source: From "Screening for Autism in Young Children" (pp. 707–729), by E. C. Coonrod and W. L. Stone, in *Handbook of Autism and Pervasive Developmental Disorders,* third edition, F. R. Volkmar, R. Paul, A. Klin. and D. Cohen (Eds.), 2005, Hoboken, NJ: Wiley. Adapted with permission.

can be administered as secondary measures after the initial interview. This is by no means an all-inclusive list but rather the most widely used measures that have been established as evidence-based or have strong research support and good clinical utility. More detailed reviews are provided by Coonrod and Stone (2005), Lord and Corsello (2005), and Ozonoff and colleagues (Ozonoff, Goodlin-Jones, et al., 2005).

The Checklist for Autism in Toddlers (CHAT), developed by Baron-Cohen and colleagues (Baird et al., 2000; Baron-Cohen, et al., 1992, 1996), is recommended as a first-stage screening for children with autism and can be used at 18 months on medical or well-child visits (Vig & Jedrysek, 1999). The parents are asked nine questions about play, pointing, social interest, and joint attention. The clinician observes the child's eye contact, ability to follow adult's pointing, pretend play, and pointing to specific object. The screening identified 83% children who later received a diagnosis of autism (Baird et al., 2000; Baron-Cohen, et al., 1992, 1996). The M-CHAT (Robbins et al., 2001) is an extended parent report version of the CHAT for which initial empirical reports are promising.

The Pervasive Developmental Disorders Screening Test (PDDST) is an unpublished parent report measure focusing on areas of parental concern for children under 6 years. It has three separate versions for use in primary care pediatric settings, developmental clinics, and specialty clinics (B. Siegel, 1996). It has good sensitivity and specificity but limited psychometric data (B. Siegel & Hayer, 1999; W. L. Stone et al., 1999, 2000).

A more specific detailed evaluation can be obtained by administering Level 2 measures. The Autism Diagnostic Interview—Revised (ADI-R) is a more extensive and widely used semi-structured interview that elicits information from the parent or caregiver on the child's developmental history and current behavior (LeCouteur, Lord, & Rutter, 2003). The revised clinical version can be used for individuals 18 months to adulthood. It has 93 items, administration time is 90 to 120 minutes, and the clinician's participation in training workshops is required (Ozonoff, Goodlin, et al., 2005). It is linked to the *DSM-IV* and *ICD-10*, has been translated into 11 languages, and is regarded in many countries as the gold standard for the diagnosis of autism (Lord & Corsello, 2005). It has very strong empirical support, with good to excellent interrater reliability and internal consistency; however, it has limitations for children with lower functioning (IQ less than or equal to 20).

The Social Communication Questionnaire (SCQ), previously known as the Autism Screening Questionnaire (ASQ), is a parent report questionnaire which uses items from the ADI-R but in a briefer, yes/no format (Berument, Rutter, Lord, Pickles, & Bailey, 1999; Rutter et al., 2003). There are two versions, one for current behavior and one for lifetime. It has two different cutoffs: a score of 15 identifies children with an autism spectrum disorder and a cutoff of 22 identifies children with autism distinct from the other PDDs (Ozonoff, Goodlin-Jones, et al., 2005).

The Childhood Autism Rating Scale (CARS), developed by Schopler, Reichler, and Renner (1988), is based on direct observation, parent report, and case history. It assesses 15 behavioral areas and rates the child in a range from normal (1) to severely impaired (4). It is a well-established measure for the diagnosis for autism, with documented reliability and validity, but it may overidentify 2-year-olds and lower functioning nonverbal children (Sponheim, 1996).

The Autism Diagnostic Observation Schedule (ADOS), developed by Lord and colleagues (2000), is a semi-structured interactive assessment of autism spectrum symptoms which yields a *DSM-IV/ICD-10* diagnosis (Ozonoff, Goodlin-Jones, et al., 2005). It takes an hour to administer. The examiner presents the child with multiple opportunities for social interaction, communication, imitation, and play and evaluates the child's spontaneous behavior. There are four different modules for different developmental and linguistic levels, including the prelinguistic (PL-ADOS), which can be used for children under 6 with significant language impairments (DiLavore, Lord, & Rutter, 1995).

The Screening Tool for Autism in Two-Year-Olds (STAT) differentiates children with autism from those with other developmental disorders (W. L. Stone et al., 2000; W. L. Stone, Coonrod, Turner, & Pozdol, 2004; W. L. Stone & Ousley, 1997). This 12-item measure focuses on interactional items such as play, motor imitation, directing attention, and requesting items for children 24 to 36 months. The test items do not require language comprehension. In a small population-based clinic sample (40 children) it was found to correctly identify autistic children in 100% of cases and nonautistic children in 91% of cases. The STAT also provides information for early intervention in three areas: imitation, play, and communication (both requesting and directing attention).

The Gilliam Autism Rating Scale (GAR; Gilliam, 1995) is a 56-item questionnaire completed by parents of 3- to 22-year-olds. It is becoming very widely used and consists of four scales: Social Interaction, Communication, Stereotyped Behaviors, and Developmental Disturbances (Ozonoff, Goodlin-Jones, et al., 2005). It relates directly to *DSM-IV-TR* symptoms; the results are presented as an autism quotient or the likelihood of autism. Current norms are available; however, there is limited empirical information, the validity data are disappointing, and its high rates of false positives and negatives lead Lord and Corsello (2005) to recommend that it not be used alone to determine diagnosis. An earlier, widely used scale, the Autism Behavior Checklist (ABC; Krug, Arick, & Almond, 1980), was found to have high false-positive and -negative rates and is not recommended as a diagnostic measure (Ozonoff, Goodlin-Jones, et al., 2005).

The differentiation between individuals with HFA and Asperger's is controversial, and research suggests that the two disorders are more similar than different (Howlin, 2003). Several screening measures have been developed to assess autism spectrum disorders and Asperger's Disorder: the Autism Spectrum Screening Questionnaire (S. Ehlers, Gillberg, & Wing, 1999), the Gilliam Asperger's Disorder Scale (Gilliam, 2001), and the Asperger Syndrome Diagnostic Scale (Myles, Bock, & Simpson, 2001). However, as Ozonoff and colleagues (Ozonoff, Goodlin-Jones, et al., 2005) note, none of the scales provides adequate differentiation between HFA and PDD-NOS and Asperger's. The latter two scales also lack basic information on psychometric properties such as reliability and validity (Ozonoff, Goodlin-Jones, et al., 2005).

Other Evaluations

A comprehensive psychological assessment can provide invaluable information on the child's cognitive strengths and adaptive functioning, which is essential to determine the presence of mental retardation. The nature of this assessment is described further under "Advanced Topics." As one of the primary deficits for most children with PDDs is the absence, delay, loss, or abnormality of speech, it is critical that the child be given a comprehensive speech and language evaluation at the onset (Filipek et al., 1999; Klin, Salnier, et al., 2005; Ozonoff, Goodlin-Jones, et al., 2005; R. Paul, 2005). Ideally, this evaluation should be conducted by a speech therapist familiar with autism and spectrum disorders who is available to function as a member of a multidisciplinary intervention team in compiling a report and intervention plan. Emphasis should be placed not only on the child's level of language, speech peculiarities, and oddities but also on the child's expressive and receptive linguistic skills and the more difficult issue of pragmatic speech (Filipek et al., 1999; Ozonoff et al., 2005; R. Paul, 2005). This area is often the core of the evaluation, and it is vital that a comprehensive assessment is conducted as this is often the central target of early intervention (Klin, Salnier, et al., 2005; Prizant & Wetherby,

2005; Prizant, Wetherby, & Rydell, 2000). Many Asperger's children present with advanced language skills, such as a large vocabulary, but still have significant pragmatic and prosodic deficits that should be fully assessed (R. Paul, 2005). Given the crucial role the acquisition of language plays in the child's future, it is imperative to identify and work closely with a language specialist who is experienced in assessing and working with children with PDDs. If the child is nonverbal, a form of augmentative or alternative communication will have to be established (R. Paul, 2005).

As described earlier, it is not unusual for children with PDDs to have sensitivities to the environment and motor coordination issues characterized by clumsiness and gait abnormalities. These issues and the presence of sensory integration deficits often warrant an evaluation by a developmental occupational or physical therapist. Talay-Ongan and Wood (2000) suggest the use of the Sensory Sensitivity Questionnaire—Revised, which assesses auditory, gustatory, olfactory, tactile, vestibular, and visual sensitivities in children with autism and sensory hypo- and hypersensitivities.

Family Support and Education

On intake the child's parents may present as overwhelmed, angry, self-blaming, or sad, and may have difficulty accepting a diagnosis that challenges their hopes and dreams for their child (Marcus, Kunce, & Schopler, 2005; Sanders & Morgan, 1997). Part of your role as a clinician is to help them express their feelings, including grief over the loss of their child's normal childhood, their fears for the future, concerns about stigmatization, and misconceptions about their child's disorder (S. Cohen 1998; Ozonoff et al., 2002). Your goal is to educate the parents and help them mobilize and access all the support and resources they can to ensure the best future possible for their child (B. Siegel, 2003). It is important from the beginning not to minimize the challenges they will face and the emotional, physical, and financial toil and toll it will involve for them, their other children, and everyone involved with their child's life (Romanowski Bashe & Kirby, 2001; Schall, 2000; Volkmar, Klin, et al., 2005). Providing accurate information about their child's disorder can decrease parental stress and facilitate realistic expectations based on their child's capabilities. Obtaining an assessment and diagnosis is often extremely stressful for parents and can often be delayed by professionals minimizing their concerns, leading to further frustration and delays in access to intervention (Marcus et al., 2005). For parents of children with Asperger's who are often diagnosed later, the process can be even more frustrating (Howlin & Asgharian, 1999).

It is equally important to use education and support to instill hope and encourage the parents to recognize their child's unique strengths as well as challenges (Powell-Smith & Stollar, 1997). Recognizing the parents as experts and active collaborators and encouraging their participation in the assessment and treatment planning for their child counteracts feelings of powerlessness and frustration and is vital in facilitating their development as active advocates (Marcus et al., 2005; Powell-Smith & Stollar, 1997). A strong collaboration with the child's parents is also essential given the amount of parental resources that will be needed during the assessment phase, to research and access appropriate interventions, and to monitor the daily implementation requirements of many of these programs (S. Cohen, 1998; Gunter, 2004; S. L. Harris, Handleman, & Jennett, 2005; J. W. Jacobson & Mulick, 2000).

Crisis, Legal, and Ethical Issues

For children with PDDs an immediate concern is safety. In a preschool setting, young children with these disorders may wander, may not respond to their name when called, and may be unaware of safety rules. Among older children, language challenges and lack of awareness of social judgment require additional attention to safety, such as stranger rules. Many children with PDDs also present with co-occurring conditions and associated features such as self-injurious behaviors and mental retardation; these complicate the prognosis and may warrant continual supervision (Bregman, Zager, & Gerdtz, 2005; Towbin, 2005).

Given the involvement of multiple professionals and agencies determining the child's eligibility for funding and early intervention programs, issues of confidentiality will need to be continually considered. Parents also require information about their legal rights and provisions for their child under federal and state laws to take on a more proactive role in their child's education (Mandalawitz, 2005; Marcus et al., 2005; Powell-Smith & Stollar, 1997). The major concern of most families is accessing appropriate services in terms of both funds and appropriate placement, and many engage an advocate to assist with educational placement in the least restrictive settings and funding for intense early intervention.

DIAGNOSTIC CONSIDERATIONS

Common Comorbidities

Although autism has been noted to co-occur with developmental, psychiatric, and medical conditions, its presence in the past may have been masked by other difficulties, and few studies have considered greater than chance associations (Dykens, 2000; Gillberg & Coleman, 2000). As these comorbid conditions often complicate treatment and contribute to ineffective interventions, their early identification is critical.

Mood and Anxiety Disorders

The most prevalent comorbid psychiatric disorders for the PDDs are anxiety and depression (Howlin, 2005). The rate for depression ranges from 4% to 58%, and it may manifest in a worsening of behaviors, agitation, social withdrawal, changes in sleep and appetite, and compulsions (Lainhart, 1999). Whereas anxiety may be characterized by feelings of being overwhelmed, depression often develops in higher-functioning individuals in adolescence as they become more aware of their differences from others and experience interpersonal and friendship difficulties (Klin, Jones, et al., 2005). There is also some evidence of increased risk for depressive disorders in adolescents with Asperger's Disorder (Klin, Volkmar, et al., 2000).

Medical Conditions

Various medical conditions have been associated with autism, with 10% of individuals having an underlying medical condition and 25% to 35% developing a seizure disorder and epilepsy in adolescence or adulthood (Bristol-Powers & Spinella, 1999; Volkmar & Klin, 2005). On average, 6% of medical conditions have causal significance, including tuberous sclerosis, epilepsy, and cerebral palsy. Certain genetic conditions such as Fragile X syndrome are associated with autistic-like symptoms of poor eye contact, repetitive speech, difficulty adjusting to change, and frequent mental retardation. Higher rates (approaching 50%) of associated medical conditions are found in individuals with severe or profound mental retardation (Filipek, 2005).

DIFFERENTIAL DIAGNOSIS

Pervasive Developmental Disorders versus Other Psychiatric Disorders

In addition to considering the presence of comorbid disorders, the discrimination of the PDDs from other psychiatric disorders, most notably mental retardation, is essential and for the clinician is particularly challenging. The similarities and differences between the PDDs and other major disorders are presented in Table 5.4.

A significant proportion of individuals with autism have some form of mental retardation (American Psychiatric Association, 2000b). In reviewing the earlier research Fombonne (2005) noted, studies used a wide range of assessment measures and often pooled

Table 5.4   Between-category diagnostic differentials

Disorder	Similarities with Pervasive Developmental Disorders	Differences from Pervasive Developmental Disorders
Mental Retardation	Cognitive impairment Adaptive functioning impairment Onset before 18	Impairment consistent with IQ No splinter skills Social functioning consistent with IQ Language consistent with IQ No additional social deficits or impairment in gaze, eye contact, or play,
Communication Disorder	Language deficits Delayed speech Processing deficits Nonresponsive to verbal cues	Deficits specific to communication No social deficits Symbolic play present Intent to communicate present
Childhood Schizophrenia	Interpersonal detachment Social difficulties	Normal development Characteristic psychotic features Language intact Impaired reality Later onset
Schizoid Personality	Interpersonal detachment Poor reciprocal skills	No impairment in language Symbolic play present Later onset
Learning Disorder	Significant academic challenges	Deficits limited to academic functioning Normal development No language or social deficits

broad ranges of intellectual functioning, and consequently recommended caution in interpreting the findings. He reports median results of 29.6% (range: 0–60%) without intellectual impairment, 29.3% (range: 6.6–100%) with mild to moderate, and 38.5% (range: 0–81.3%) for severe to profound mental retardation. Recent studies indicate that the rate is significantly declining (Byrd, 2002; L. C. Eaves & Ho, 1996; Yeargin-Allsopp et al., 2003). This decrease in rate has been attributed to several factors, including increased diagnosis of higher functioning autistic individuals, effective early interventions, and an awareness of the inappropriate use of verbal-based assessment of intellectual functioning for children with significant verbal delays or lacking in verbal skills (Howlin, 2005; V. Shea & Mesibov, 2005). Mental retardation is the most common comorbid condition, most difficult, diagnostic differential, and is discussed further in the Advanced Topics section.

Communication Disorders

Expressive Language Disorder and Mixed Expressive-Receptive Language Disorder are not accompanied by impairments in social interaction and restricted patterns of behavior and interests, as exhibited in autism (American Psychiatric Association, 2000b). By definition all of the PDDs are characterized by significant impairment in language or the use of idiosyncratic language, however, the clinical presentation additionally includes deficits in nonverbal social reciprocal skills. Children with autism also fail to develop compensatory communication skills, and their difficulties with joint attention suggest preverbal deficits that are absent in children with communication disorders.

Childhood Schizophrenia

Childhood Schizophrenia usually has an onset in early childhood, though later than autism, which is typically prior to 3 years of age. There is usually a history of relatively normal development, followed by an onset of hallucinations and delusions (First & Tasman, 2004). In Schizophrenia, although oddities of behavior may be present, there is also often a loosening of associations, or incoherence. In autism, none of the psychotic symptoms associated with Schizophrenia are evident and there is no increased incidence of Schizophrenia in the familial histories of autistic children (American Psychiatric Association, 2000b; Klin, Jones, et al., 2005).

Schizoid Personality Disorder

The relationship between Asperger's and Schizoid Personality Disorder is unclear, as there are too few studies on the developmental histories of Schizoid Personality Disorder (Towbin, 2005). Both disorders are associated with social difficulties, but the deficits in Asperger's are usually more severe and of earlier onset.

Among the Pervasive Developmental Disorders

Autism versus Asperger's

The continuity between autism and Asperger's Disorder remains a topic of much debate, and the differentiation between individuals with HFA and Asperger's is controversial.

Table 5.5   Pervasive developmental disorders: key and discriminating features

Disorder	Key Features	Discriminating Features
Autism	Pervasive delays Impaired reciprocal skills Delays or no language Lack of symbolic play	Pervasive delays Age identified: 0–36 months Lack of or severe delays in language Seizure disorder common Enlarged head
Asperger's	Impaired social functioning Limited imaginative play Preoccupations, interests No impairment in cognition No delay in self-help adaptive skills Curiosity intact	Language may be intact Age identified: usually >36 months Marked circumscribed interests Seizure disorder uncommon Inflexible adherence to rules Clumsiness
Childhood Disintegrative Disorder (CDD)	Normal functioning Marked regression Loss of language, social, motor, and adaptive skills Loss of bladder and bowel control	Period of normal functioning Regression in functioning Specific onset and course Age identified >24 months Seizure disorder common
Rett's Disorder	Normal functioning Decelerated head growth Loss of skills Stereotyped hand movement Poor gait or trunk control Impaired language	Period of normal functioning Age identified 5–30 months Specific course Predominantly female Seizure disorder frequent Decelerated head growth

Source: Adapted with permisson from *Diagnostic and Statistical Manual of Mental Disorders,* fourth edition, text revision, by American Psychiatric Association, 2000b, Washington, DC: Author. Adapted with permission.

Some researchers view Asperger's as a milder form of autism, while others emphasize the disorders' different developmental pathways and trajectories (S. E. Folstein & Mankoski, 2000; Myhr, 1998; Szatmari, 2000a; Szatmari, Archer, Fisman, Streiner, & Wilson, 1995; Volkmar & Klin, 2005). The *DSM* diagnostic criteria for both disorders are identical, except there is no significant cognitive or language delay for Asperger's and the hierarchical rule specifies that the diagnosis of Asperger's or PDD-NOS cannot be assigned if the diagnostic criteria for autism are met (American Psychiatric Association, 2000b [see Table 5.5]; Myhr, 1998). The lack of Asperger's-specific items makes the differentiation of these two disorders challenging and has added to the considerable ongoing controversy in the field (Klin, McPartland, et al., 2005; Mayes et al., 2001). Myhr concluded that the *DSM-IV* identifies a lower functioning group with Autistic Disorder and a higher functioning group with Asperger's, which is not clearly distinguishable from Autistic Disorder or PDD-NOS. Both disorders are characterized by social handicaps that persist throughout life, poor eye contact, stereotypies of language and movement, and marked resistance to change. The most difficult differential is between autism associated with milder impairments of socialization and communication or HFA and Asperger's. According to Howlin

(1998a) there are few substantive differences between these groups other than that individuals with Asperger's lack early language delays and have relatively normal cognitive development. Current research suggests that the two disorders are more similar than different (Howlin, 2003). When differences are present they are more apparent in the early years, with both disorders converging phenomenologically with age (Howlin, 2003; Ozonoff, South, & Miller, 2000; Starr, Szatmari, Bryson, & Zwaigenbaum, 2003).

Autism versus Rett's and Childhood Disintegrative Disorder

The within-category diagnostic differential with Rhett's and CDD can be very difficult to discern in the early stages of these disorders (American Psychiatric Association, 2000b). The lack of a period of normal development followed by a characteristic regression and the presence of a poorly understood developmental regression in 20% to 25% of children with autism make this differential more complex (Volkmar & Klin, 2005). Research on the genetic basis for Rett's Disorder has resulted in the development of revised diagnostic criteria, which may clarify the diagnostic picture in the future (Van Acker et al., 2005). Whereas autism and Asperger's affect a preponderance of males, Rett's occurs almost exclusively in females. Rett's Disorder also has highly characteristic symptoms, such as head size deceleration and development of unusual stereotyped hand movements (e.g., hand washing), loss of purposeful hand movements, abnormal trunk and gait movements, and gross impairments in language and communication (American Psychiatric Association, 2000b; Van Acker et al., 2005).

In autism the developmental abnormalities are usually observed much sooner than 2 years, and the *DSM-IV-TR* notes that when information on early development is unavailable or when it is not possible to document the required period of normal development for CDD, a diagnosis of Autistic Disorder should be made (American Psychiatric Association, 2000b). This is presumably because CDD is so much rarer than autism. Whereas autism is conceptualized as a developmental disorder: There is something wrong with development from the beginning. CDD is characterized by apparently normal development for at least 2 years and then deterioration characterized by a loss of language (both expressive and receptive), of motor, social, and adaptive skills, and of bladder and bowel control (Volkmar, Koeing, et al., 2005). For Rett's the rule-outs are CDD, a much shorter period of normal development (usually 5 months), and a very specific clinical presentation.

TREATMENT

General Principles in Treating Pervasive Developmental Disorders

Appropriate early and vigorous intervention that addresses behavioral, language, and social reciprocal skills at an age when brain development is rapid and plasticity substantial stands the greatest chance of effecting a more positive prognosis for children with PDDs (Volkmar, Paul, et al., 2005). Children with PDDs are unable to learn from their environment in the manner most of us do; therefore, intensive intervention is necessary to expose them to the environmental richness and intensity of learning opportunities that are available to typical peers (B. Siegel & Ficcaglia, 2006). The clear consensus in the field is that the treatment and lifetime planning for individuals with PDDs needs to facilitate normal development, promote problem-solving skills, decrease behaviors that impede learning, provide family support, and focus on the ideals of autonomy and community-based living and working (Howlin, 2005; Gerhardt & Holmes, 2005; Marcus, Kunce & Schopler, 2005; Volkmar, Paul, et al., 2005). Partnership with parents and their involvement are crucial, as treatment is lifelong and will vary depending on the developmental challenges the individual encounters. An overview of treatment interventions is presented in Table 5.6.

Given the heterogeneity of clinical presentations, the first task and the key to effective treatment is a comprehensive evaluation that will inform treatment and provide a baseline

Table 5.6   Treatment interventions for pervasive developmental disorders

Area	Interventions
Assessment	Multidisciplinary assessment
	Specific language, occupational therapy, behavioral, education evaluations
	Detailed history and family education and involvement
	Eligibility for early intervention
	Development of intervention plan
Symptom management	**Language acquisition**
	Assessment of language and need for communication system
	Target individual speech delays and deficits
	Emphasis on social pragmatic speech, including questions
	Interpersonal reciprocity
	Establish eye contact, shared focus, gaze, and reciprocal skills
	Face emotion training
	Play-based intervention (e.g., floor time)
	Social skills training, including learning social rules
	Behavioral interventions
	Stop self-injurious behavior
	Limit self-stimulating and isolating behaviors
	Increase frustration tolerance and decrease rigidity
	Increase attending; use visual skills to build auditory skills
	Reinforce observational learning
	Develop behaviors to ensure safety (e.g., stranger rules)
Family interventions	Education
	Referral to adjunctive family support groups, organizations
	Focus on independence
Adjunct referrals	Regional center
	Speech and language therapist
	Educational psychologist
	Advocacy or legal support
	Adaptive physical education or occupational therapist for sensory integration
	Music, art, and dance classes to build social skills and self-esteem
	Social services (living and support services)
	Occupational and vocational counseling

for evaluating treatment effectiveness. The assessment report describes the child's unique profile of cognitive, linguistic, and adaptive functioning skills, identifying areas of strengths, challenges, and targets for intervention. This forms a framework around which realistic goals can be constructed. The initial assessment occurs when the child is first identified (0 to 2 years); as the child ages, assessments are repeated on a yearly or less frequent basis, targeting different areas of intervention and crucial skills depending on the child's development and progress. The information garnered in this manner can be used to monitor the child's progress, include successes, and adapt the treatment plan to address new challenges as they emerge.

Providing emotional support for the child's family, linking them to support groups and helping them determine a realistic appraisal of the intensity of intervention is crucial, as to date there is no good evidence of miracle cures for autism or other PDDs (Howlin, 2005; Marcus et al., 2005). Given the pervasive nature of the child's challenges, the most efficacious approach for treating a child with PDD is participation in a good appropriate early intervention program. Coordinating treatment without a program involves at a minimum several speech and language sessions per week, behavioral interventions, school placement, physical and play therapists, and daily structured activities, which is beyond the emotional and financial resources of most families (S. Cohen, 1998; Gunter, 2004; Mandalawitz, 2005; Romanowski Bashe & Kirby, 2001).

Parent organizations like the Autism Society of America, Cure Autism Now, and groups such as the Foothill Alliance for Autism in Los Angeles or Center for Outreach and Services for the Autism Community (COASC) in New Jersey provide support, referral lists, and resource guides that are invaluable for families. The wide range of interventions may be overwhelming and confusing for families; some are well researched, others are not yet as successful. Resource websites such as the Online Asperger Syndrome Information and Support (OASIS) can provide crucial information. B. J. Freeman's (1997) early article on evaluating intervention programs and Handleman and Harris's (2001) book on preschool programs may also be helpful. Intervention programs can be accessed and evaluated using the Internet; many have parent visiting days. Many early intervention services are offered through early educational (0 to 3) programs or regional centers, and some are affiliated with universities; the range and quality of services differ dramatically (Arick et al., 2005; G. Dawson & Osterling, 1997; S. L. Harris et al., 2005). As children reach 3 they may be eligible for services through their local school district. Some states (e.g., New Jersey, North Carolina, Colorado, and California) have a range of programs targeting children with PDDs. However, funding for public education is decreasing, and it is becoming more difficult for parents to access the intensity and quality of services needed for their children (Mandalawitz, 2005).

Clinicians should familiarize the parents with the essential elements of good intervention programs and how to determine if a program will meet their child's needs and their expectations. This knowledge also provides hope to the parents and empowers them as active participants in their child's treatment. In reviewing psychological and educational treatments for autism, Howlin (1998b) concluded that no single mode of treatment is effective for all children and their families. She recommends approaching intervention from a functional analysis of the child's behaviors. The child's comprehensive assessment report enables the parents to consider their child's unique needs and to compare these to the program's curriculum. When evaluating a program the parents need to consider several

Table 5.7 Early intervention programs

Questions to Consider When Evaluating Intervention Programs[*]

For whom is the intervention effective?

What are the characteristics of those for whom the intervention did not work?

Does it work better with younger or older children?

Is it more effective for verbal or nonverbal children?

Is it better for more cognitively able children?

What sort of pretreatment assessments were used, and what were the outcome measures?

What happens to children with autism as they grow older?

What is the overall financial cost of the intervention?

How much time will be involved, and what are the restrictions on family life?

How does program participation impact the child?

Can the child cope with the change or separation?

Are there local facilities?

Elements of Effective Early Intervention Programs[**]

Element 1: Curriculum content emphasizes five basic skills:

   a. The ability to attend to the environment

   b. The ability to imitate others, which includes verbal and motor imitation

   c. The imitation of motor skills

   d. The ability to comprehend and use language

   e. The ability to socially interact with others

Element 2: A highly supportive teaching environment that includes generalization strategies

Element 3: Predictability and routine

Element 4: A functional approach to problem behaviors

Element 5: A transition from the preschool classroom program

Element 6: Family involvement.

Additional factors to consider: available techniques to facilitate acquisition of

play and language

[*]From "Practitioner Review: Psychological and Educational Treatments for Autism," by P. Howlin, 1998b, *Journal of Child Psychology and Psychiatry and Allied Disciplines, 39*(3), pp. 307–322. Adapted with permission.

[**]From "Early Intervention in Autism: Effectiveness and Common Elements of Current Approaches" (pp. 307–326), by G. Dawson and J. Osterling, in *The Effectiveness of Early Intervention: Second Generation Research,* M. J. Guralnick (Ed.), 1997, Baltimore: Paul H. Brookes. Adapted with permission.

factors, including the characteristics of the children for whom the treatment program was or was not successful, the impact of the program on the family, and whether it will help with the transition to regular school. Some helpful questions to consider are presented in Table 5.7.

Elements of Effective Psychosocial Interventions

In their landmark review of effective early intervention programs, G. Dawson and Osterling (1997) identified six common elements that characterized effective early intervention programs (see Table 5.7). The programs reviewed provided services to children with autism and PDDs across the United States and included university-, center-, and school-based programs. According to Dawson and Osterling, these elements represent guidelines, the minimum requirements that parents should consider when evaluating a program for their child, and what "parents should reasonably expect a school system to provide for their child." These elements will be reviewed in detail, as they are the essential foundation for effective early intervention.

First, the curriculum content needs to emphasize five basic or core skills that children with autism have difficulty with and that are critical for the acquisition of knowledge. These are attention, imitation, communication, appropriate toy play, and social skills. Children need to be taught how to attend to their environment, including social stimuli, facial expressions, gestures, and speech. The program needs to teach and encourage children to imitate others' verbal and motor behaviors, including using echolalic tendencies as a critical first phase of early language acquisition. Deficits in motor skill imitation can be targeted through either operant conditioning methods or structured social play that sets the stage for spontaneous imitation.

Many children with autism have a lack or poverty of language and limited linguistic comprehension, and typically they are not motivated to communicate or share information and experiences. Many effective programs provide immediate reward for the child's smallest attempt to communicate (whether by glance, voice, or gesture) and include exposure to a range of communicative modalities, including visual symbols. Effective programs also use and integrate visual and verbal cues in play sequences and classroom routines to facilitate the acquisition of language. The program's curriculum needs to address the core challenge for children with PDDs: the ability to socially interact with others. This may begin by teaching children specific skills such as turn-taking and sharing in the context of adult-child interactions and then systematically generalizing these skills to child-child interactions. The use of video, role-playing, and the opportunity to interact with typically developing peers in a variety of settings, including structured and unstructured activities, all aid the development of social behavior.

The second element the parents need to consider is the presence of a highly supportive teaching environment that includes systematic strategies for the child to generalize the five basic skills to more complex natural environments. Thus initially, the child may interact directly with a trained therapist or teacher in an environment that minimizes distraction and maximizes attention to specific stimuli. Effective classrooms have small numbers of students (4 to 8) and intensive teaching with a low staff-to-child ratio (1:2 or 1:1), especially during skill acquisition and use techniques, such as repetition, predictability, and salience, including placing the stimulus directly in the child's visual field to enhance skill building. Fading prompts and gradually increasing the complexity or only changing one feature of the child's environment at a time during the process of generalization also enhances the transfer of skills to different settings. Having the classroom aide work with the child in a small, highly structured setting and then in the larger classroom also assists in the child's use and transfer of acquired skills.

The third program element parents need to evaluate is the presence of predictability and routine. Children with autism and PDDs become more socially responsive and attentive and are less likely to tantrum or behave in a disruptive manner when information is provided in a highly predictable manner. Transitions are especially challenging, even from one activity to another, and many programs provide highly structured routines with clear visual cues to label and define specific activities and activity centers. Programs may have daily photo or written calendars that are posted and reviewed, with ample time being provided for transitioning between activities. The child may be allowed to carry a transitional object as he or she moves to another activity or engage in a familiar ritual such as singing a song during the transition.

Fourth, the program should have a functional approach to problem behaviors. If problem behaviors persist, a functional assessment of the child's behavior should be conducted to determine the situations in which the behavior occurs, the antecedent conditions, and the consequences of the behavior. It is important that the program try to understand what function the behavior is serving (e.g., "I need help," or "I don't like this") and teaches the child adaptive, alternative behaviors. The program may also change classroom conditions as necessary to facilitate adaptive behavior. Thus, if children throw toys because they are unable to deal with the lack of structure in free play and are frustrated at their inability to choose an activity, a board showing two activities from which children may choose may be set up.

The fifth element the parents need to consider is whether the program has a clearly identified strategy for addressing the transition to preschool or school, which often needs to be accomplished gradually and systematically. This transition is a critical point in a child's education and it is important that it is as smooth and successful as possible. Some programs systematically decrease the time in preschool while time in kindergarten is increased; others have a split- or alternate-day approach. The program should also take an active role in assisting parents and school districts in finding an appropriate placement for the child. Once an appropriate placement is found, the intervention team staff—through class observation—determine the skills needed for the child to function independently and incorporate these skills into the child's program. Systematically teaching, prompting, and reinforcing skills such as saying the teacher's name and requesting a bathroom pass in the smaller, more structured setting enhances the child's acquisition of these necessary daily adaptive skills. Teaching the child to function as independently as possible and to use classroom survival skills such as turn-taking, listening to directions, sitting quietly, raising a hand to get attention, picking up toys after use, and walking in a line are all essential.

Many programs advocate the use of typically developing peers as promoters of social behavior and encourage or facilitate experiences in small integrated activities groups (Strain, McGee, & Kohler, 2001). This can also provide invaluable information on the child's functioning and the skills still needed to be successful. Effective programs encourage parents to enroll their children in small group inclusion activities such as gymnastics, dance, art, and music classes to facilitate the child's involvement with normal peers and to foster interests that bring ongoing joy and acceptance to the child's life. Given that some children with PDDs have areas of talent or skill, these can also be used to foster peer acceptance and enhance the child's self-esteem.

Finally, effective programs also need to include a format for family involvement. Because parents spend so much time with their child, they can provide unique insights into their child's needs and help continue work that is done in the program at home, thus maintaining gains. Parents' inclusion in programs increases their feelings of relatedness with their child and can increase their sense of competence as parents and their ability to advocate for their child. Effective programs may include parent training in behavioral techniques and other intervention strategies, which may be conducted at home, at school, or both (Smith, Groen, & Wynn, 2002). Many programs also include a parent support group or some other type of support for family members, a major component of which is education. G. Dawson and Osterling (1997) note that another important element that the parents need to consider is the intensity of the program. Their review, consistent with earlier research, including Lovaas's (1987) work, suggests that effective programs provide 20 or more hours per week of intervention. They also recommend considering whether the program utilizes adjunctive resources such as occupational therapists.

Approaches to Intervention

In addition to knowing the elements of effective intervention, parents need to know the approaches to intervention and the nature of the available programs for children with PDDs. According to Siegel, Hayer, and Tanguay (2001), in the past decade three trends are apparent in the treatment of autism. First, the early diagnosis of developmental disorders has resulted in public funding through the Individuals with Disabilities Education Act (IDEA) for the diagnosis and treatment of younger children (0 to 3 programs). Second, research on early neuromaturation, neurodevelopmental factors, neuroplasticity, and the transfer of function has emphasized the importance of early intervention. Third, there has been a move toward the development and implementation of more autism-specific interventions and treatment matched to symptom profiles that have produced significant gains and improved the prognosis and quality of life of children with these disorders. The past two decades have seen a proliferation of these programs; for a comprehensive list, see G. Dawson and Osterling (1997), Handleman and Harris (2001), and S. L. Harris et al. (2005). There has been a lack of research on programs specific to the other PDDs; however, many of the programs for autism target core deficit areas and accept children who have Asperger's, PDD-NOS, and other PDD diagnoses. One of the major decisions a family will have to make is whether to opt for home-based, center-based, school-based, or a combination intervention program.

Home-Based Interventions   Home-based interventions tend to be behavioral or relationship-play-based. Behavioral approaches use a detailed assessment (functional analysis) of the child's behaviors and, using operant techniques, strengthen adaptive behaviors and decrease or eliminate maladaptive ones (Bregman et al., 2005; M. Campbell, Schopler, Cueva, & Hallin, 1996). Operant methods include positive and negative reinforcement, extinction, and time-out, which target and reduce or eliminate self-injury and stereotyped behaviors or establish and maintain imitation, eye contact, communication, and self-help skills (Bregman et al., 2005).

Applied behavior analysis (ABA) is the most widely researched operant behavior treatment modality for young children (2 to 5 years old) with autism and was the basis for the pioneering work of Ivar Lovaas and colleagues in the Young Autism Program at the University of California–Los Angeles (Lovaas, 1981, 1987). This home-based program uses a structured teaching sequence known as discrete-trial training (DTT) that targets a single specific skill area, such as eye contact or imitation of speech or movements (Erba, 2000). Each discrete trial consists of a stimulus–response–consequence sequence; the child is given an instruction (stimulus) such as "Look at me," and their response is followed by an immediate consequence, either positive, neutral, or corrective. Using a highly structured protocol that describes and organizes activities in a hierarchical fashion, parents and caregivers are trained to use DTT. A trained behavioral aide works with the families at home to provide a minimum of 40 hours per week over a 1- to 2-year period. Typically, there is an emphasis on reducing self-stimulatory and aggressive behaviors and increasing compliance, imitation, and appropriate play during the first year. In the second year the emphasis shifts to expressive language and peer interaction. The program also includes a component for transitioning to preschool in which the behavioral aide accompanies the child and is then gradually phased out.

Forty-seven percent of children who received intensive behavioral therapy (40 hours per week) for 2 years achieved "normal functioning," or were placed in a regular class-room (Lovaas, 1987). The majority (53%) of control children who received 10 hours per week of behavioral treatment or community support were placed in classes for children with autism or mental retardation, and 45% were placed in language and learning disabled classrooms. On reevaluation at age 13 years, the treatment effects persisted: The initial IQ gains (30 points higher) were maintained, eight of the nine children still attended regular classrooms, and all the control children were in special education classes (McEachin et al., 1993). Howlin's (1998b) review of earlier research found that 42% of children (ages 2 to 4 years) who received 40 hours per week for at least 2 years of intensive home-based behavioral intervention maintained normal functioning on follow-up. Lovaas's (1981, 1987) study involved a treatment manual, trained behavior therapists, and an adequate group size. However, children were matched rather than randomly assigned to groups, and there was a lack of information on the amount of treatment provided and the use of adjunctive services (S. J. Rogers, 1998). The issue of selection bias resulting in a nonrepresentative, relatively high-functioning group has been raised as a criticism, as has the possibility that regular classroom placement of the children reflected parent advocacy rather than actual clinical improvement. Findings of replication studies have been limited by small sample size and methodological difficulties. Although DTT results in significant improvements, some children continue to have autistic behaviors and do not, as claimed earlier, "recover" (Gresham, Beebe-Frankenberger, & MacMillan, 1999; S. J. Rogers, 1998). Behavioral interventions aimed at encouraging the reacquisition of some lost skills and in managing behavior problems may benefit children with CD. However, given the rarity of the disorder there are no data currently available.

Another behavioral-based home intervention is pivotal response training (PRT), based on Koegel and Koegel's (1995) earlier research at the University of California–Santa Barbara identifying pivotal behaviors or core areas of autism that impact a wide range of functioning, such as motivation, responsivity to multiple cues, and self-management. By targeting and changing these pivotal responses, a wide range of symptoms, including nontargeted behaviors, may be altered. To increase responsiveness to general environmental stimuli and to enhance the ongoing development of skills, the intervention strategies are implemented throughout the child's day (Koegel, Koegel, & McNerney, 2001). Parent training is a central component, allowing PRT to be used in the child's home. This approach proposes that because of their developmental delays, children with autism experience failure and become unmotivated, which is often expressed in socially and academically disruptive behavior. Using PRT children are prompted until tasks are correctly completed, thus increasing exposure to response-reinforcement contingencies, and they are allowed to choose preferred and novel tasks interspersed with mastered tasks to increase motivation (Koegel et al., 2001). To help the children self-manage their behavior, PRT also uses behavior analysis techniques, such as response counting, and targets social communicative behaviors such as eye contact and gestures. In general, targeted behaviors tend to improve rapidly and generalize to other areas, including pragmatic language and voice volume.

Floor time is an in-home developmental relationship therapeutic intervention based on Greenspan and Wieder's (1998) work that emphasizes building emotional reciprocity and the connection between socialization and communication. As the name suggests, the clinician or parent sits on the floor with the child and follows the child's lead, initially nonverbally, using joint attention and shared interest to establish two-way communication. The goal is the development of a secure relationship that provides the basis for the opening and closing of naturalistic communication circles and addresses the child's emotional needs, as well as challenging his or her problem-solving skills (Greenspan & Wieder, 1998). This approach uses child-directed play periods with the parents as primary play partners. It targets attention and intimacy, two-way communication, the expression of feelings and ideas, and logical thinking (Erba, 2000). In a chart review 58% of the children given floor time were found to have significant improvements; however, there is a lack of empirical studies on this approach (Erba, 2000; Greenspan & Wieder, 1998).

Center-Based Programs   Lovaas's (1981) program spurred the establishment of several center-based programs, including those at the Princeton Child Development Institute, the Douglass Developmental Center at Rutgers University (Harris, Handleman, Arnold, & Gordon, 2001), the May Institute, and the Alpine Learning Center (G. Dawson & Osterling, 1997; S. L. Harris et al., 2005). These are state-of-the-art programs that meet many of the earlier described elements of effective programs. Each program is different in its own right, but all are centered on an ABA model and include small classes with separate and inclusive or integrated programs, very high staff-to-student ratios (often 1:1 or 2:1), a strong school transition program, and parental support or home programs. To date, limited available data on the outcome of these programs suggest evidence of substantial gains in intellectual and language functioning and a significantly higher likelihood of attending normal school on program completion (S. Harris, Handleman, Gordon, Kristoff, & Fuentes, 1991; S. L. Harris et al., 2005).

Major limitations of these programs are that they accept very few children (2 to 4) per year, they have long waiting lists (often 2 years long), they prefer to accept very young children (children identified at 4 are often too old), and they are very expensive. More information is also needed on pretreatment characteristics that are associated with program success or failure to better delineate which subgroup(s) of autistic children will benefit from them. C. T. Jackson and colleagues (2003) in looking at sustained interactions and play in children with autism suggested that although behavioral programs may successfully teach the skills to sustain a short conversation, these skills may not generalize to play exchanges.

Other center-based programs focus on the acquisition of language and social development skills using interpersonal relationships, incidental learning, and play as a means to engage the child, and structure and routine in the classroom to teach skills. These programs often integrate speech therapists into the classroom, and teaching occurs individually or in small groups, with an emphasis on pragmatic language and building social skills. The program may be half-day and the child may attend a school-based program in the afternoon. Parents are often actively involved and may attend the program with the child. The Walden Early Childhood Programs at Emory University (G. G. McGee & Morrier, 2001) and the JCC Therapeutic Nursery (D. A. Allen & Mendelson, 2000) are two examples of language play-based intervention programs that also meet G. Dawson and Osterling's (1997) criteria for effective intervention programs. There is limited empirical outcome research on language play-based intervention programs; however, parents report high levels of satisfaction and success in the placement of children in regular school.

School-Based Programs   The University of Pittsburgh's Western Psychiatric Institute's Learning Experiences: An Alternative Program for Preschoolers and Parents was the first program in America to integrate typical peers with children with autism as part of the curriculum (S. L. Harris et al., 2005). This is an integrated school-based program that uses naturalistic ABA techniques and peer modeling to teach children with autism and includes a parent behavior skills training component. The program has been adopted by the Denver Public School System. Although the program elements have empirical support, there is a lack of controlled outcome research (Gresham et al., 1999; S. L. Harris et al., 2005).

The Denver Health Sciences Center Program, started in 1981 by S. J. Rogers and colleagues (S. J. Rogers, Hall, Osaki, Reavan, & Herbison, 2001; S. J. Rogers & Lewis, 1989), is a developmentally based program. It uses play, relationships, and structure and routine in the classroom to teach pragmatic language, communication skills, and abstract thinking to children with autism. Children who attended the program were found to have significant increases in language, cognitive, social, emotional, and self-care skills, and the results have been replicated (S. L. Harris et al., 2005).

Treatment and Education for Autistic and Communication Handicapped Children (TEACCH) was developed by Schopler (Marcus, Schopler, & Lord, 2001) at the University of North Carolina and has been implemented statewide. It is not a specific technique but a way of thinking about children with autism that emphasizes early identification, parent training, education, the development of social and leisure skills, and vocational training (Siegel et al., 2001). Education is a core element, and learning environments are modified based on the strengths of autistic children, emphasizing visual aids and very structured, usually self-contained classrooms. S. L. Harris and colleagues (2005) note that the use of structured teaching at home has been found to be effective, but they could not find studies on classroom effectiveness.

Medications

The history of medication usage in PDDs has often been characterized by initially promising drugs being shown to be ineffective when further study is conducted and rushes to use new psychotropic medications prior to adequate clinical trials (Siegel et al., 2001). Although psychopharmacology is a common treatment for children with PDDs, there are insufficient numbers of controlled studies and limited empirical support. Medications can be used to target specific symptoms; however, they appear to have little to offer in ameliorating social relationship difficulties in autism (Scahill & Martin, 2005). A study of medication usage among individuals with high-functioning PDDs by A. Martin and colleagues (A. Martin, Scahill, Klin, & Volkmar, 1999) found that psychotropic medication use was common; the most common drugs used were selective serotonin reuptake inhibitors (SSRIs), consistent with findings of serotonin dysregulation in autism. There have not been enough double-blind, placebo-controlled studies in this area, but there are some promising indications that SSRIs such as fluvoxamine are more effective than placebos in improving repetitive thoughts and behavior, maladaptive behavior and aggression, and, to a lesser degree, social relatedness. However, earlier trials were associated with increased hyperactivity, insomnia, worsening symptoms, and side effects (Awad, 1996; Scahill & Martin, 2005).

The next most common medications used were stimulants, not because of any controlled study findings supporting this drug class but often these are given for attentional problems. Clonidine has been shown in some studies to improve hyperactivity, irritability, inattention, and impulsivity and is most commonly used in pediatric psychiatry to treat Tourette's Disorder and other tic disorders. Neuroleptics were the third most common medication and were generally used for disruptive, aggressive, and self-injurious behaviors. The Research Units on Pediatric Psychopharmacology (2002) Autism Network completed a multisite trial of risperidone in children with autism with aggressive behaviors and found significant decreases in the target behaviors of aggression and tantrums. There was no change in adaptive functioning, and the medication was associated with weight gain, increased fatigue, tremor, and drooling (Scahill & Martin, 2005). For individuals with CDD, there are some reports of antipsychotics (e.g., haloperidol, olanzapine) being helpful in managing overactivity, aggression, and other behaviors. Anticonvulsants are often used to treat comorbid seizure disorders.

Education

The most effective educational interventions are those that involve an individualized education plan that addresses not only the academic but also the social and emotional challenges that the child encounters and provide social skills training in the school (M. Dunn, 2004). Children with PDDs are entitled to a free and appropriate public education under the IDEA. Typically, schools spend $8,000 to $12,000 per child per year on special education, whereas early intensive intervention programs start at $30,000 per year. Consequently, most school districts' early and special education programs often do not offer evidence-based, state-of-the-art interventions, and there is frequent dispute over the provision and quality of services and reimbursement (Jacobson & Mulick, 2000; Mandalawitz, 2005). In many cases, the costs of implementing an intensive early intervention program for children with PDDs falls to the parents. Families of young children with autism often are desperate to do all they can in what is perceived to be a narrow window of time and may move across the country if their child is offered a place at an early intervention program. In these cases, they often have to bear the brunt of the financial burden as local school districts are frequently unwilling to pay for children who move for early intervention.

For children with Asperger's the goal is to be mainstreamed with normal children as much as possible, but careful planning and extra resources may be needed to enable such integration to occur smoothly (Handleman, Harris, & Martins, 2005). The child's parents may need to educate teachers and administrators about the disorder so that the child's placements are appropriate. Interventions that facilitate the inclusion of the child with typical peers include peer modeling, social skills groups, peer buddies for all students, and behavioral self-management skills (Handleman et al., 2005). For children with PDDs, attention also needs to be paid to the development of social communication skills and pragmatic language (Marans, Rubin, & Laurent, 2005). Your role as a clinician may include helping the family obtain supportive services and educating them about their alternatives (S. Cohen, 1998; Ozonoff et al., 2002; Romanowski Bashe & Kirby, 2001; B. Siegel, 2003).

Family Support

As Marcus and colleagues (2005) emphasize, parent-clinician collaboration in autism intervention is paramount, and parental involvement is a key factor in the child's success in early intervention and access to future services (Romanowski Bashe & Kirby, 2001; B. Siegel & Ficcaglia, 2006). Parents of children with PDDs report higher levels of stress, and mothers report less parenting competence, less marital satisfaction, more family cohesion, and less family adaptability than parents of unaffected children or those with Down syndrome (Sanders & Morgan, 1997). Given the pervasive nature of the child's problems and the intensive nature of the intervention required, there may be additional financial burdens, fatigue, loss of leisure time, and increased marital and family conflicts (Marcus et al., 2005; Powell-Smith & Stollar, 1997). Parents of children with CDD may feel extremely burdened by the care of their child, and supportive and educational interventions are essential. Providing the family with referrals to support groups and information on the nature and course of the disorder and practical strategies for home management are invaluable and empower the parents to become active participants in their child's and the family's recovery. Several strategies for supporting families are provided by Randall and Parker (1999) and Marcus and colleagues (2005), including addressing the lack of perceived support from relatives and dealing with the child's behavior in public. Holidays and family reunions may be particularly stressful, and grief may be reexperienced when other family members note the accomplishments of their nondisabled children or make insensitive comments. Parent guides on autism (S. Cohen, 1998; B. Siegel, 2003) and Asperger's (Ozonoff et al., 2002; Romanowski Bashe & Kirby, 2001) can provide the parents with tools to cope with these emotions and situations (Powell-Smith & Stollar, 1997).

It is also important not to overlook the impact of having a sibling with a PDD on other members of the family. Marital stress negatively impacts the sibling relationship, and due to the increased caregiving demands siblings may spend less time in social activities with their peers or less time outside the family (Powell-Smith & Stollar, 1997; Rivers & Stoneman, 2003). Siblings of children with autism were more likely to report feeling lonely, and their mothers were more likely to report more peer problems in comparison to peers with a sibling with mental retardation or an unaffected sibling (Hastings, 2003). They may feel embarrassed by their sibling's problems; educating them about the nature of the disorder in a developmentally appropriate manner and providing social support can mediate these factors (Rivers & Stoneman, 2003; B. Siegel & Ficcaglia, 2006).

Over the course of the child's development the family's socioemotional needs will change as they face additional different challenges (Powell-Smith & Stollar, 1997). Treatment for children with PDDs and their families involve a life span developmental approach. Several areas to target for intervention are outlined in Tables 5.8 and 5.9.

Life Span Developmental Approach

In 2002, according to the California Department of Developmental Service (2003), approximately 18% of children (0 to 14 years) and 57% of young adults (15 to 29)

Table 5.8   Treatment interventions for pervasive developmental disorders: early years

Intake (Ages 0–4)

Comprehensive developmental assessment: including medical, speech, developmental, psychological, adaptive, and behavioral functioning, and occupational therapy evaluations.

Multisetting and multi-informant: play and social assessment observed at home, with siblings, and in peer groups.

Child's individualized profile: include strengths, challenges, and intervention plan.

Family support: parent education, advocacy, support group.

Identification of available, appropriate interventions and resources.

Implement intervention plan and identify evaluation measure.

Early Years (Ages 2–6)

Intensive, integrated, individualized early intervention.

Focus on the acquisition of language, social reciprocal, and play skills.

Identification and training with appropriate assisted communication device.

Decrease maladaptive behaviors.

Occupational therapy sensory integration addressing: balance, coordination, and motor skills.

School inclusion, partial program, individualized small group.

Sports skills to facilitate participation with peers.

Music, dance, or art classes related to splinter skills, interests, and to provide small group normal peer experiences.

Yearly comprehensive assessment to target areas of intervention and monitor progress.

Grade School Years (Ages 6–10)

Individualized education plan prior to school entry.

Transition to school plan focused on mainstreaming and inclusion with support.

Classroom support with experienced aide 1:1.

Phase out classroom support over 2–3 years.

Classroom accommodations (e.g., seating, visual cues, calendars, and schedules).

Separate individualized skill building in pull-outs.

Balance staggered goals focusing on the whole child and a range of skills.

Ongoing speech therapy in individual and group settings focusing on acquisition and pragmatics.

Educational assessment and monitoring of areas of academic difficulty.

Remain alert for challenges—reading comprehension, abstract math, especially fourth grade.

Organizational skills, occupational therapy, and adaptive physical education focus on flexibility and playground skills.

Social and play skills to enhance interactions with peers.

Ongoing assessment, minimum yearly individualized education plan.

Comprehensive evaluation every 2 to 3 years.

with autism were in residential care, costing from $80,000 to $100,000 per year (CDC, 2003). Living an independent life requires the ability to manage money and a home and having some basic cooking and self-protection skills, which are often absent even in capable adults with autism. Few programs provide this type of training or support (Howlin, 2005; V. Shea & Mesibov, 2005). Additionally, many individuals need support with self-help skills such as personal hygiene and issues related to sexual behavior (V. Shea & Mesibov, 2005). Encouraging parents to have children learn to cook, do laundry, shop for groceries, and plan family outings as early as possible are

Table 5.9   Treatment interventions for pervasive developmental disorders: adolescence to adulthood

Adolescence

Education and transition plans for middle and high school.

Yearly individualized education plans and educational reevaluation, assessment, and updating of goals.

Ongoing academic accommodations, including organizational aids.

Continued academic counseling and provision of supports.

Social skills training addressing sexuality and friendship building.

Individual education concerning self-esteem, difference, and the nature of the PDD.

Involvement in peer support group.

Encouraging the development of interests and participation in peer groups (e.g., music).

At-home focus on self-help, daily living, and social planning skills.

Staggered participation in independent activities (e.g., sleepovers, camps).

Medical monitoring, ongoing alert for seizures.

Evaluate need for out-of-home placement or alternative residential setting.

Long-term plan updated.

Young Adulthood

Continued focus on the development of independent living skills.

Access community programs such as regional center.

Job coach, vocational counseling, and training.

Development and implementation of employment or educational plan.

Life coach: develop living and transportation plan.

Encourage ongoing interests that give life meaning and enjoyment; consider a pet.

Monitor presence of mood or other disorders.

Support involvement in social and support groups.

Parents and individual financial planning, including long-term decisions.

Long-term plan updated.

Middle Adulthood

Ongoing vocational support and counseling.

Ensure consistent living arrangement.

Ongoing support by a social worker or case manager.

Encourage continued interests and social activities.

Address death of parents and caretaker decisions.

Long-term plan updated.

crucial skills that can impact their child's future. For individuals with PDDs there needs to be a lifelong focus on the acquisition of basic skills in social interactions and other areas of functioning (see Tables 5.8 and 5.9). "Social stories" involving scripts to teach these skills can be helpful, as can role-play and verbal rehearsal. The application of rules may be helpful and can capitalize on Asperger's Disorder individuals' verbal skills and tendency to rely (rigidly) on rules (Olley, 2005).

It is important to teach others who are involved with individuals with PDDs that the intact cognitive abilities of children and adolescents with HFA and Asperger's do not necessarily relate to ability to apply their knowledge. These individuals often need help with social skills and building a network of supports (Howlin, 2003). For individuals with PDDs a concrete, problem-solving approach is typically more helpful than intensive, insight-oriented treatment. Of individuals followed into adolescence and early adulthood, 60% to 75% showed poor or very poor outcome, and only 5% to 15% of those with classical childhood autism were found to lead independent adult lives (Nordin & Gillberg, 1998). Whether these rates decrease subsequent to the availability of early intervention remains to be seen. Regardless, vocational training and counseling is critical (see Table 5.9). Many adults with autism when employed appear able to deal with a range of tasks as long as there is a schedule and a predictable routine to follow and the expectations are clear (Keel, Mesibov, & Woods, 1997).

Social difficulties and eccentricities can lead employment counselors to assume that individuals with HFA or Asperger's are less capable cognitively than they really are and result in referrals to manual labor jobs, which may be far below their cognitive abilities and are likely to aggravate their difficulties. One of the few job support programs for high-functioning adults with spectrum disorders found that providing specialist support resulted in significantly higher wages for these individuals and higher job satisfaction among both employees and employers. Additionally, 80% of the placements were in accounting, administration, or computing, and 50% of the jobs resulted in permanent work (Howlin, 2005). These programs are rare and even with such impressive results, parents should be also encouraged to financially plan for their child's future on their death.

According to Howlin (1998a,b), most children with autism who do not develop speech by 6 or 7 years remain impaired in verbal communication, and alternative communication systems using either signing, pictures, or writing may need to be considered. For these individuals and those with significant mental retardation programs like TEACCH, which incorporate visual strategies and structured teaching, have been very successful; however, the jobs are often at a low level (V. Shea & Mesibov, 2005). The early acquisition of language, high cognitive abilities, and the absence of epilepsy, mental retardation, and comorbid medical conditions have all been linked to a more positive outcome for children with PDDs (Howlin, 2005; B. Siegel & Ficcaglia, 2006). While the current lack of programs other than residential placement for adolescents and young adults with PDDs continues to compromise their future, parent involvement and advocacy may change this in the next decade. As a clinician it is important to instill realistic hope and provide these families with the knowledge and access to support that can result in an optimal outcome for their child.

ADVANCED TOPIC: THE ASSESSMENT OF DEVELOPMENTAL CHALLENGES

The PDDs are characterized by pervasive delays in development, which for some include significant cognitive delays. Mental retardation is characterized by global impairments in cognitive and adaptive functioning. In contrast, learning disorders are characterized by narrow cognitive deficits that result in specific challenges in learning. These disorders can occur as comorbid conditions, and the heterogeneity of cognitive ability in children with PDDs makes diagnostic differentiation difficult. As the interventions warranted for each of these disorders are very different, it is important to be familiar with their clinical presentation.

Mental Retardation

Mental retardation (MR) has a prevalence of approximately 1%. It is not a disease or an illness but is caused by a heterogeneous group of conditions ranging from genetic and metabolic disorders to functional changes that follow trauma to the nervous system at birth or later, during the developmental period (American Psychiatric Association, 2000b). There is no single cause, mechanism, clinical course, or prognosis for mental retardation (First & Tasman, 2004). Prenatal, perinatal, postnatal, and other external causes, including infection, trauma, toxins, birth complications, and prematurity, account for a third of all cases (Dykens & Hodapp, 2001; Ratey et al., 2000). Genetic causes are implicated in 35%, fewer than 10% have a malformation syndrome of unknown origin, and of clinical cases 30% to 40% have no clear etiology (American Psychiatric Association, 2000b).

The child's level of cognitive functioning can affect the clinical presentation and types of behavioral features seen in this disorder; the lower the IQ, the more severe the symptom expression (Bebko & Weiss, 2006). According to A. S. Carter and colleagues (1998), the most widely accepted definition of mental retardation is the *DSM-IV-TR*'s, which includes an onset before 18, the presence of subaverage cognitive functioning (about 2 SDs below the mean, IQ 70 or lower), and deficits in adaptive behavior (American Psychiatric Association, 2000b). It is important to note that this diagnosis is not made solely on the basis of low IQ, which is a required but not sufficient criterion for a diagnosis. Given the measurement error inherent in assessing intelligence, individuals who fall in the IQ range of 70 to 75 can be diagnosed with MR if they exhibit significant deficits in adaptive functioning. The *DSM-IV-TR* requires deficits in two areas of adaptive functioning: communication, self-care, home living, social and interpersonal skills, use of community resources, health, and safety. Typically, adaptive functioning is assessed using a structured interview and observational measures such as the Vineland Adaptive Behavior Scales (Sparrow, Balla, & Cicchetti, 1984). This involves interviewing a caregiver or significant other who can comment on the individual's abilities. An alternative, widely used definition is that of the American Association on Mental Retardation (2002) which states "Mental retardation is a disability characterized by significant limitations both in intellectual functioning and in adaptive functioning as expressed in conceptual, social and practical adaptive skills." This diability originates before age 18 (AAIDD, 2007). States differ in their definition of impairment of adaptive functioning; some require adaptive functioning to be below the fourth percentile (Standard Score 70 to 75) in two areas, for example, communication and daily living skills or self-help skills (A. S. Carter et al., 1998), so it is important to be familiar with your state's laws.

Mental retardation is coded on Axis II, and any comorbid conditions can be coded on Axis I or, if it is a personality disorder, on Axis II. Individuals with MR have a prevalence of comorbid psychiatric disorders that is 3 to 4 times that of the general population (American Psychiatric Association, 2000b). The full range of mental disorders can be diagnosed for individuals with MR; however, evaluating comorbid psychiatric disorders requires additional special considerations and often more reliance on outside informants. When considering the presence of an additional disorder, you must first account for all the symptomatology that can be primarily attributed to MR; in cases where IQ is below 30 (i.e., in the severe range), such multiple diagnoses may be meaningless (J. W. Jacobson &

Mulick, 1996). Individuals with MR are at greater risk for physical and sexual abuse and are at increasing risk for mental disorders that develop as sequelae of these experiences. Common comorbid mental conditions are tic disorders, Stereotypic Movement Disorder, mood disorders, and pervasive developmental disorders (American Psychiatric Association, 2000b). These individuals are often at risk for depression, loneliness, and negative psychosocial experiences, such as repeated failure and disapproval (J. W. Jacobson & Mulick, 1996; Tonge & Enfield, 2003). These may relate to the presence of problematic characteristics, including affective instability, explosive and disruptive behaviors, overdependency, low ideal self-image, and limited levels of aspiration.

When providing treatment to individuals with MR it is important to adapt and match psychotherapeutic techniques to the individual's cognitive and developmental level. The goals are to reduce or eliminate the impact of the disability (First & Tasman, 2004). Using syntactically simple language, providing concrete examples in an understandable context, taking a directive approach, and verifying that the individual has understood what has been discussed are all helpful strategies. As a clinician it is important to recognize one's own personal distortions and biases regarding providing help, being mindful of desires to "rescue" and thereby infantilize the individual or increase dependency. Individuals with mild MR may be very aware of negative interpersonal responses and may be sensitive to being labeled mentally retarded. At the onset the clinician should carefully explain the rules and structure of therapy and establish firm but appropriate limits for aggressive, destructive, or overly affectionate behavior. The length and frequency of sessions should be tailored to the individual; more frequent and briefer sessions may be needed, and maintaining flexibility in choice of treatment methods is crucial. Behavioral interventions and the use of operant techniques have been found to increase adaptive behaviors and decrease maladaptive behaviors, such as stereotypic behaviors and noncompliance.

Along with disability counseling, the therapist may provide ability counseling by helping these individuals place their overall disability into perspective and helping them recognize their value as individuals (Zigler, 2001). Family and individual therapy are often combined to provide consistency and the consolidation of new skills. Families also require support in identifying resources, and parenting skills can be a focus of treatment (Hauser-Cram et al., 2001).

Learning Disorders

Children with language and learning disorders (LLD) are the greatest users of special education services in schools, accounting for 75% of all children or adolescents in special education and 4% to 6% of all students (Beitchman & Young, 1997; A. A. Silver & Hagin, 2002). Many of these children are referred secondary to behavioral problems in preschool, conflicts concerning school attendance or home or school work, or an undetected learning disorder. Half have a comorbid Axis I disorder, the most common being ADHD, disruptive disorders, anxiety, and, to a lesser extent, mood disorders; mood disorders are often overlooked or masked by other issues (Beitchman & Young, 1997; Frick & Silverthorn, 2001; Heath & Ross, 2000; Howard & Tryon, 2002). The presence of an LLD complicates treatment and contributes to the persistence of the problems (First & Tasman, 2004). The *DSM* defines a learning disorder as a significant discrepancy (of the magnitude of greater than 2 SDs) between intellectual ability and academic achievement as determined by standardized tests (American Psychiatric Association, 2000b). The National Joint Committee for Learning Disorders defines a learning disorder as a heterogeneous grouping of disorders in listening, speaking, reading, writing, or math, with a presumed central nervous system dysfunction (T. G. Bowers & Derr Bailey, 1998). Legal definitions and federal guidelines presume a neurological basis for the disorders, and most states require 1 to 2 SDs between achievement and IQ (Loomis, 2006).

Treatment for children with learning disorders needs to be individualized and aimed at minimizing the disability and maximizing the child's potential (Loomis, 2006). It is important for the clinician to work in collaboration with the family and school personnel in identifying the most efficacious interventions, which often target problem-solving skills, social support, and study habits. Providing encouragement and recommending involvement in extracurricular activities such as drama, art, and sports that can enhance the child's self-esteem are also important (Gans, Kenny, & Ghany, 2003; A. A. Silver & Hagin, 2002). Counseling and help with education and career decisions, family support, and academic support are crucial in that the most successful individuals with learning disorders were found to be those who recognized, understood, and accepted their learning challenges (Gerber & Brown, 1997). Developing adaptive coping strategies, creativity, problem solving, and the proactive development of compensatory strategies, including finding mentors and developing support networks, all facilitate success (T. G. Bowers & Derr Bailey, 1998). Success is also associated with early intervention in elementary and middle school, supportive tutoring, and counseling. College success is facilitated by a reduced academic load and a later college completion date (T. G. Bowers & Derr Bailey, 1998).

Psychological or Psychoeducational Assessment

The diagnostic determination of mental retardation and learning disorders is based on the administration of a battery of standardized psychological tests. This assessment can also facilitate the differentiation of autism from these disorders and can identify the child's strengths, which may not be apparent with a florid clinical presentation. An overview of some of the more common evidence-based assessment measures used in diagnostic differentiation and the assessment of a PDD is presented in Table 5.10. The determination of cognitive ability is in many cases based on the administration of traditional tests of intelligence such as the Wechsler scales (Wechsler, 2003), the Stanford-Binet (G. H. Roid, 2003), and the Differential Abilities Scales (C. Elliott, 1990). It is important that the test administered is appropriate for the child; many common measures of intellectual functioning are verbally based and not valid for children with significant language delays. For children with more profound attentional, behavioral, and communication deficits Tsatsanis (2005) recommends using a nonverbal measure of intellectual functioning such as the Leiter International Performance Scale—Revised (G. Roid & Miller, 1997). Younger children may need to be assessed with scales such as the Bayley Scales of Infant Development (Bayley, 1993) or the Mullen Scales of Early Learning (Mullen, 1995).

Adaptive functioning is most frequently assessed using the Vineland, which has specific norms developed by A. S. Carter and colleagues (1998) for children with autism. Academic achievement can be assessed by the Woodcock-Johnson scales (Woodcock,

Table 5.10 Psychological assessment measures for Autism, MR & LD

Assessment Measure	Format	Information Provided
Overall cognitive measures		
Bayley Scales for Infant Development 1–42 months	Mainly nonverbal tests	IQ and mental ages
Mullen Scales of Early Learning Birth–68 months	Non verbal language and motor skills	Early learning composite domain scores
Wechsler Intelligence Scale for Children (WISC-IV) 6–16 years 11 months	Verbal and non verbal subtests	Full-Scale IQ, index scores, subtests
Wechsler Preschool and Primary Intelligence Scale (WIPPSI-III) 2 years 6 months–7 years 3 months	Verbal and non verbal subtests	Full-Scale IQ, index scores, subtests
Stanford-Binet-V (SB-V) 2–85 years	Verbal and non verbal tests	IQ, subtests
Leiter International Performance Scale Battery-R (Leiter-R) 2–20 years 11 months	Non verbal tests	Non verbal full IQ, brief IQ: reasoning scores
Differential Abilities Scales (DAS) 2 years 6 months–17 years 11 months	Intellectual and academic skills	General conceptual ability, verbal, nonverbal, and spatial cluster scores
Adaptive functioning		
Vineland Adaptive Behavior Scales Birth–18 years 11 months	Motor, social, communication, daily living skills	Standard scores and age equivalents

Assessment Measure	Format	Information Provided
Academic achievement tests		
Woodcock Johnson Tests of Achievement	Range of academic skills	Standard scores, percentiles, age and grade equivalents
Wechsler Individual Achievement Test (WIAT-II) 4–85 years	Range of academic skills	Age and grade standard scores, composite scores, percentile ranks, stanines
Tests of Language and Play		
Peabody Picture Vocabulary Tests (PPVT-4) 2 years 6 months–90 years	Measures receptive language	Age and grade equivalents, percentiles and stanines.
Preschool Language Scales (PLS-4) Birth–6 years 11 months	Measures expressive and receptive language	Total language, standard scores, percentiles, language age equivalents
Clinical Evaluation Language Fundamentals CELF-P 3–6 years 11 months (CELF-4) 3–21 years	Measures range of language deficits	Core and index scores, percentiles, age equivalents, and stanines
Expressive One Word Vocabulary Test (EOWPVT) 13 months–12 years extended 18–35 years	Expressive language	Standard scores, percentiles, and age equivalents
Test of Language Competence (TLC) Level 1 5–9 years; Level 2 10–18 years	Pragmatic speech	Composite and subtests scores, percentiles, standard and age equivalent scores
Symbolic Play Test-2 1–3 years	Measures spontaneous pretend play	Play test age

McGrew, & Mather, 2001a,b), which provide a wide range of information on academic skills and abilities. Additional measures that can identify some of the language and play deficits characteristic of children with PDDs include the Peabody Picture Vocabulary Test (for expressive language; L. M. Dunn & Dunn, 1997), the Preschool Language Scales (for expressive and receptive language; I. L. Zimmerman, Steiner, & Pond, 2002), the Children's Communication Checklist (for pragmatic speech; Bishop & Baird, 2001), and the Symbolic Play Test—Revised (for play; M. Lowe & Costello, 1995). Ozonoff and colleagues (2005) provide an in-depth discussion of these and other evidence-based measures that are appropriate for children with PDDs.

Chapter 6 ——————————————————————

DISORDERS OF CHILDHOOD II: ATTENTION-DEFICIT/HYPERACTIVITY DISORDER AND OTHER DISRUPTIVE BEHAVIOR DISORDERS

These disorders first identified during childhood are characterized by persistent patterns of difficulties with attention, hyperactivity, impulsivity, behavioral control, and defiant behavior (American Psychiatric Association, 2000b). They are the most frequent reason children and adolescents are referred for services. It is estimated that between 5% and 35% of children under age 17 have Attention-Deficit/Hyperactivity Disorder (ADHD), or one to two students per classroom (Barkley, 2005). The majority (75% to 80%) of those diagnosed as children continue to experience symptoms, resulting in prevalence rates of 1% for adults and 2% to 7% for the total population (M. D. Garber & Garber, 1998). They are also at high risk for developing comorbid conditions, including learning, mood, anxiety, and substance abuse disorders, and experiencing myriad associated problems, including school dropout, accidents, unplanned pregnancy, and incarceration (Willoughby, 2003).

Disruptive behavior disorders include Conduct Disorder (CD) and Oppositional Defiant Disorder (ODD). Conduct Disorder describes a chronic pattern of behaviors that violate the norms and rules of society or the rights of others and antisocial behavior, such as vandalism, truancy, fighting, fire-setting, lying, stealing, assault, and rape (Bassarath, 2001; Frick, 2001). In 2000 alone there were 2.4 million arrests of minors who committed 16% of all violent crimes and 32% of all property crimes. Juvenile offenders' most frequent murder victims were 14 years old (Loeber & Farrington, 2000; H. Snyder, 2002; H. N. Snyder & Sickmund, 2006). Between 1988 and 1997 arrests of young offenders ages 7 to 12 increased by 45%, and drug abuse violations for these children rose 165% (H. Snyder, 2001). Oppositional Defiant Disorder is characterized by a recurrent pattern of negativistic, defiant, disobedient, and hostile behavior toward authority figures and is most commonly diagnosed in preschoolers (American Psychiatric Association, 2000b; Lavigne, Gibbons, Christoffel, Arend, Rosenbaum, et al., 1996). The *DSM-IV-TR* category for attention-deficit and disruptive behavior disorders includes ADHD, CD, ODD, ADHD-NOS, and Disruptive Behavior Disorder Not Otherwise Specified (DBD-NOS; American Psychiatric Association, 2000b).

HISTORICAL OVERVIEW REVIEW

According to Barton (2001), problems with attention and staying focused were popularized in Shakespeare's *Henry IV*, and hyperactivity and inattentiveness were described in German doctors' notes from 1848. Children who survived the brain infection encephalitis epidemic of 1917 to 1918 in North America were noted to have high levels of distractibility, impulsivity, and hyperactivity (Barkley, 2005). These behaviors were identified as similar to the restlessness and difficulty sustaining interest that were observed in primates with frontal lobe lesions (Levin, 1938). The concept of the "brain-injured child" became popular in the 1940s, as did the notion of "minimal brain dysfunction," which was vague and often applied without a clear history or evidence of cognitive damage (Barkley, 2005). In the 1950s the terms hyperkinetic impulse disorder and hyperkinetic syndrome were used to describe central nervous system deficits that caused an overstimulation of the brain that were postulated to relate to hyperactivity in children (Barkley, 2005). A clearer clinical picture developed with Chess's (1960) behavioral description of the hyperactive child. The disorder was differentiated from those syndromes caused by brain damage, and several interventions, including therapy, special education, and parent counseling, were recommended. In 1968, "hyperkinetic reaction of childhood" was included in the *DSM-II* (American Psychiatric Association, 1968); this description was subsequently broadened to include attention deficits (V. I. Douglas, 1980, 1983).

E. J. Costello and Angold (2000) report that CD is the oldest diagnostic category used in contemporary child psychiatry. They describe memorable early examples of antisocial behavior, including Agamemnon's abduction of Achilles' slave girl Briseis (*Iliad*, 800 BC); Buddha encountering a group of greedy, rough, quick-tempered, spoiled boys who went about plundering, devouring food, and being physically assaultive to girls (600 BC); the advice in Deuteronomy (21:18–21) to the parents of an oppositional, stubborn son is to seek support from the city elders and to consider stoning him. Antisocial behavior has classically been viewed as a failure of moral development or "moral insanity" (Prichard, 1837). Early attempts to deal with this behavior generally consisted of incarceration, "moral conversion," and/or deportation to the colonies (E. J. Costello & Angold, 2000). Literature of the day abounded with examples of these individuals and society's response, including Jane Austen's (1817/1997) description of the Musgraves' very troublesome, hopeless, and unmanageable son, Victor Hugo's novel *Les Miserables* (1982), and Charles Dickens's *Oliver Twist* (2003) and *Great Expectations* (2002).

According to Barkley (2005) in 1902, Still described 43 children, mainly boys, who were defiant, aggressive, and resistant to discipline, who showed little "inhibitory volition" and appeared to have a major defect in the ability to conform their behaviors for the common good. Still noted that the families of these children were characterized by high rates of alcoholism, criminality, and affective disorders (e.g., depression and suicide) and proposed a biological predisposition that was probably either hereditary or the result of pre- or postnatal injury. He assumed that the deficits in moral control, sustained attention, and inhibitory volition were related to one another and to the same underlying neurological deficiency (Barkley, 2005). In a similar vein, in the early twentieth century Chicago's Juvenile Court Psychopathic Institute's director noted that juvenile delinquents came from defective homes, often with alcoholism and defective heredity (Healy, 1915).

The discussion of the origins of delinquent behavior gained momentum with the publication in 1935 of a series of case histories by Aichorn titled *The Wayward Youth*. Subsequently, Bowlby (1944) related early trauma in the form of disrupted attachments or maternal deprivation to delinquent character development. These studies questioned the view that the asocial behaviors were simply moral deficiencies, suggesting instead a developmental framework and a range of risk factors. Early epidemiological studies found that children of constantly absent or neglectful parents were most likely to have antisocial behaviors (J. D. Cummings, 1944; McFie, 1934). Research on the Y chromosome and subsequent family and twin studies, including the Virginia Twin Studies, supported the inheritance of aggressive behaviors (Simonoff, 2001b; J. M. Meyer et al., 2000). Using social learning theory, G. R. Patterson and colleagues (G. R. Patterson, 1982, 1986; G. R. Patterson, Capaldi, & Bank, 1991; G. R. Patterson, Reid, & Dishion, 1992) described a coercion hypothesis in which the child's behavior contributed to negative aversive parental interactions, increased parental anger, and negative discipline. In an effort to identify those children with an early onset and more severe outcome, research on psychopathy in adult offenders was linked to temperamental style in toddlers (Cleckley, 1976; Frick & Morris, 2004; Hare, 1998, 1999). Current research, while supporting a genetic and familial component of antisocial behavior, has emphasized the role of the environment and developmental pathways in the expression of these behaviors (Frick & Morris, 2004; Simonoff, 2001a). Specifically, longitudinal follow-up studies such as the Pittsburgh Youth Study describe the heterogeneity of the clinical presentation, outcome, and different developmental pathways (Loeber, Keenan, Lahey, Green, & Thomas, 1993; Moffitt, 2003). In 1968, the *DSM-II* first mentioned CD (American Psychiatric Association, 1968); subsequently, specific diagnostic criteria were developed based on Robbins's behavioral descriptions from his study of "deviant children grown up" (Atkins & McKay, 1996).

Of more recent origin is ODD, which for many years was clustered with CD in a general category of disruptive disorders. In the mid-1960s the Group for the Advancement of Psychiatry used the term oppositional personality disorder to describe children who expressed aggressiveness through oppositional behavior. The introduction of ODD in the *DSM-III* (1980) was intended to capture aggressive behavior manifestations that are exhibited in early to mid-childhood. Though children with ODD are described as displaying persistently disobedient, negativistic, and provocative behavior to authority figures, many of the clinical features are ubiquitous in young children in general. Subsequent clinical and research studies have established it as a disorder distinct from CD and ADHD (Angold & Costello, 1996; Loeber, 1991; Loeber, Lahey, & Thomas, 1991; Waldman & Lilienfeld, 1991). This differentiation has facilitated research and the development of creative interventions, including that of Webster-Stratton and colleagues (Webster-Stratton, Reid, & Hammond, 2001a, 2001b) targeting preschool children.

ATTENTION-DEFICIT/HYPERACTIVITY DISORDER

Attention-Deficit/Hyperactivity Disorder is one of the most common disorders of childhood and is the most prevalent childhood disorder among school-age children (Doggett, 2004; Unnever & Cornell, 2003; Willoughby, 2003). A comparison of physician practices from 1986 and 1999 found that the diagnosis of ADHD increased threefold, and available treatment services increased tenfold (Hoagwood, Kelleher, Feil, & Comer, 2000). In 1995, the cost to public education in the United States for students identified with ADHD exceeded $3 billion (NIH Consensus Developmental Panel, 2000). Attention-Deficit/ Hyperactivity Disorder is a developmental disability with a childhood onset that has a chronic and pervasive pattern of multiple impairments in a wide range of areas of daily and adaptive functioning (J. Murphy, 2005). Despite the name of the disorder, hyperactivity does not always have to be present; typically there are chronic difficulties with inattention and/or hyperactivity-impulsivity (Barkley, 2005). Initially conceptualized as a male disorder limited to middle childhood, for the majority of children it is a chronic disorder that persists into adulthood with negative developmental outcomes, including both school and family problems (Wilens, Biederman, & Spenser, 2002; Willoughby, 2003; Wolf & Wasserstein, 2001). It is associated with executive functioning and cognitive deficits and a higher risk for comorbid psychiatric conditions such as depression and substance abuse (Barkley, Fischer, Smallish, & Fletcher, 2002; Gallagher & Blader, 2001; Kinsbourne, De Quiros, & Tocci Rufo, 2001; Leibson, Katusic, Barbaresi, Ransom, & O'Brien, 2001). For girls ADHD dramatically increases the risk of unplanned pregnancies (38% versus 4%), sexually transmitted diseases (17% versus 4%) and the number of sexual partners (19 versus 7) as compared to non-ADHD age-matched controls (Barkley, 2005). It has been referred to as an invisible disability, with the individual experiencing an ongoing sense of demoralization, discouragement, and intense frustration engendered by persistent shortcomings. The symptoms and particularly the behaviors are often blamed on bad character, low motivation, and willful misconduct rather than the recognition that it is the consequence of subtle neurological deficits in the prefrontal cortex (Barkley, 1997a). Family and patient support organizations such as Children and Adults with ADD have contributed to a greater public recognition of this disorder and political activity that has resulted in increased eligibility of individuals with ADHD for entitlements and legal protections under the Americans with Disabilities Act of 1990. The importance of understanding how comorbidity influences family functioning, academic success, and outcome has made the early diagnosis and intervention of this disorder crucial (C. Johnston & Marsh, 2001).

Clinical Presentation

Attentional Difficulties

The nature of the individual's clinical presentation consists of two clusters: either inattention or hyperactivity-impulsivity, with six or more symptoms being present for at least 6 months (American Psychiatric Association, 2000b). Parents and teachers describe a child with these attentional problems as *never finishes assignments and chores, doesn't follow instructions, daydreams, often loses things, can't concentrate, can't work without supervision*, or *doesn't seem to listen* (Eiraldi, Power, & Maguth Nezu, 1997; Owens & Hoza, 2003). The child's greatest difficulties are encountered on tasks requiring sustained attention, or vigilance, and the behavioral manifestations are particularly pronounced in situations involving repetitive, dull tasks (e.g., chores and schoolwork; Barkley, 2005). In free play, these children may rapidly shift from toy to toy or between activities; their work can appear dirty, sloppy, or careless; assignments and books are frequently lost; and due dates are often missed. The reasons for not following through and for avoiding tasks are not due to oppositionality, defiance, or a failure to understand directions (American Psychiatric Association, 2000b). The diagnostic criteria, which were derived primarily from studies with boys, have been criticized for not being sufficiently validated for girls (Delligatti, Akin-Little, & Little, 2003) and for including insufficient criteria to reflect what McBurnett, Pfiffner, & Frick (2001) describe as the sluggish cognitive tempo (SCT) characteristics of inattentive girls.

Hyperactivity and Impulsivity

The clinical expression of hyperactivity and impulsivity may vary with the child's developmental level. The core symptoms need to be persistent, maladaptive, and beyond what is considered normal for the child's developmental stage (Barkley, 2005). Parents of a preschooler may report that the child is unable to sit still, that he or she never stops or runs or climbs excessively. As the child ages, the hyperactivity may present as restlessness (Owens & Hoza, 2003). The lack of an operational definition of what constitutes developmentally inappropriate behavior led Barkley (2005) to recommend the use of behavior rating scales and standardized cutoffs on dimensions of relevant symptoms. Others have called for developmentally and gender-sensitive norm-referenced diagnostic criteria (Faraone, 2000; Wasserstein, 2005; Widiger & Clark, 2000). Barkley (2005) notes that problematic behaviors of preschoolers have a high likelihood of remitting within 12 months and suggests increasing the required symptom duration to 12 months to decrease the likelihood of overdiagnosis.

Age of Onset

At least some impairing symptoms must be present before age 7 (American Psychiatric Association, 2000b). In children younger than 3, separating hyperactive-impulsive behavior from aggression or defiant behavior or behavioral immaturity may be difficult, and Barkley (2005) suggests limiting the lower age for diagnosis. Due to the variability of symptoms, the small number of attentional demands placed on younger children, and the lack of parental exposure to peer comparisons formal diagnosis prior to age 4 or 5 is challenging (American Psychiatric Association, 2000b). Most young children are not in situations requiring sustained attention until they attend school, and parents and teachers have a differential sensitivity to ADHD symptoms as a function of the child's age (Milich, Balentine, & Lynam, 2001; Nolan, Volpe, Gadow, & Sprafkin, 1999). Twins study research suggest that the clinical presentation may change with age and that a number of older children show higher levels of inattention or impulsivity or hyperactivity with an onset after age 7 (Biederman, Mick, & Faraone, 2000; Larsson, Larsson, & Lichtenstein, 2004). Thus requiring an onset before age 7 may exclude individuals with the predominantly inattentive type, which often presents at a later age (Barton, 2001; Cuffe et al., 2001). There have also been calls for diagnostic criteria that are more developmentally sensitive, allowing for the identification of adults with ADHD (Faraone, 2000; Widiger & Clark, 2000; Willoughby, 2003).

Impairment

The clinical symptoms must cause impairment in at least two settings (e.g., home, school, work). This may be difficult to assess as there is often low parent and teacher agreement

(.30 to .50) on ratings of the child's behavior (Barkley, 2005). Barkley (2005) recommends that pervasiveness of problems should be interpreted to mean a history of symptoms in multiple settings. In free play or situations with low demand for inhibition, such as lunch, children with ADHD will often not appear significantly different from non-ADHD peers in terms of activity level (Breen & Altepeter, 1990). Increases in the levels of task complexity (e.g., reading and math periods) and group settings requiring the regulation of behavior (e.g., the classroom) result in greater performance differences (Barkley, 2005). It is also not unusual for a child to demonstrate few symptoms when being assessed in a novel, one-on-one situation with interesting tasks (e.g., a therapist's office) or when frequently rewarded, as when playing video games (Barkley, 2005; Emes, 1997).

The clinical symptoms must also cause significant impairment in two or more areas of functioning, for example, academic, occupational, and social life (American Psychiatric Association, 2000b). This does not necessarily mean that the level of impairment will be the same or even apparent in all settings. Children with ADHD who have normal intelligence often have deficits in adaptive functioning, and clinic-referred boys with ADHD are likely to experience impairment in many areas of functioning that cause significant adjustment problems later in life (Marshal, Molina, & Pelham, 2003). For both boys and girls the clinical symptoms may contribute to academic difficulties that are further compounded by additional emotional problems that develop secondary to the disorder (Barriga et al., 2002; Hinshaw, 2002). These children also experience difficulty making and maintaining friendships, resulting in their often feeling lonely and isolated (Blachman & Hinshaw, 2002; Hoza, Owens, et al., 2000). Court records indicate that ADHD is associated with criminal activity, serious offenses, and institutionalization (S. Young, 2000).

Very bright children in an understimulating environment or those from chaotic home environments may also present with attentional problems, and it can be difficult to differentiate between children who cannot as opposed to those who refuse to do the work (Doggett, 2004). Typically children with ADHD have difficulties secondary to disorganization and distractibility, and the omission of details is due to inattentiveness or forgetfulness. In contrast, gifted children appear more bored and impatient (Doggett, 2004).

Subtypes

One of three subtypes (Combined, Predominantly Inattentive, or Predominantly Hyperactive-Impulsive) is assigned based on the predominant pattern of symptom presentation during the 6 months that precede diagnosis (American Psychiatric Association, 2000b). This subtype may change over time (e.g., Predominantly Hyperactive-Impulsive may later become Combined Type).

Combined Type

This is assigned if six or more inattention and six or more hyperactive-impulsive symptoms persist for at least 6 months (American Psychiatric Association, 2000b). This subtype accounts for 50% to 70% of individuals with ADHD and is associated with the most overall impairment (Eiraldi et al., 1997; Nolan et al., 1999; Wolraich, Hanah, Pinnock, Baumgaertel, & Brown, 1996). It has a higher likelihood of comorbid and externalizing disorders as well as conduct and delinquency problems and has an earlier age of onset and referral (Lahey & Willcutt, 2002; Milich et al., 2001; A. E. Morgan, Hynd, Riccio, & Hall, 1996). These children are also more frequently male, younger, more academically impaired, more often rejected by peers, and twice as likely to meet the criteria for concomitant ODD (Eiraldi et al., 1997). From teacher and parent ratings, the symptom expressed by "runs and climbs excessively" strongly predicts a diagnosis of Combined Type (Owens & Hoza, 2003). Barkley (2005) proposes that the underlying deficits in children with this type are with the persistence of effort or sustained attention and the presence of distractibility. Nigg and colleagues (Nigg, Blaskey, Huang-Pollock, & Rappley, 2002) found that even after controlling for comorbid ODD/CD, the Combined group had deficits in behavioral inhibition, whereas no such deficit was apparent in the Inattentive group, suggesting that this may be a discriminating feature between the two types.

Predominantly Inattentive Type

This is used if, for at least 6 months, six or more inattention symptoms and fewer than six hyperactive-impulsive symptoms are present (American Psychiatric Association, 2000b). This is the second most common subtype, accounting for 25% to 31.5% of clinical cases and 4.5% to 9% of a community sample (Faraone, Biederman, Weber, & Russell, 1998; Lahey et al., 1994; M. Weiss, Worling, & Wasdell, 2003). The primary deficit for these children is in focused, or selective, attention and involves sluggish information-processing speed. The onset is often several years later than for the other types (Barkley, 2005; Nolan et al., 1999). Some individuals will present with purely attentional/arousal problems; for others, hyperactivity may still be a significant clinical factor but at a subthreshold level (Wasserstein, 2005). Nonhyperactive children have been described as daydreamy, more cognitively slowed, and more likely to have anxiety, depression, and social withdrawal (Eiraldi et al., 1997; McBurnett et al., 2001). In comparison to the Combined Type, Inattentive children were older, more frequently female, and less impaired overall with fewer early impulsive symptoms. They were also more likely to have learning disorders and math disability, were shy and withdrawn, and were referred to speech and language services more frequently (Barton, 2001; Milich et al., 2001; M. Weiss et al., 2003). Inattentive boys were found to have lower levels of delinquency, aggression, and Conduct Disorder problems but did not differ significantly from the other two subtypes in symptoms of anxiety, depression, psychosomatic problems, or social problems (Paternite, Loney, & Roberts, 1996). The greater academic impairment of Inattentive children underscores the relationship between inattention and academic problems. In comparison to controls, Inattentive children had more externalizing behaviors, which were expressed more at home than in school, resulting in higher parent than teacher ratings (Eiraldi et al., 1997). Parents described these children as excessively inattentive, distractible, forgetful, and disorganized, which may contribute to increased parental conflict. Of the children with this type, 19% met the criteria for ODD, whereas none of the controls did (Eiraldi et al., 1997).

The separation of the Combined and Inattentive subtypes has been controversial. In an effort to have similar inattentive symptoms for all subtypes, the *DSM-IV* field trials excluded the symptoms drowsy and daydreamy. This may have artificially attenuated the inter-subtype differences and contributed to a less clear clinical description of the Predominantly Inattentive subtype (Milich et al., 2001). Additionally, the *DSM* field trials found that only 57% of ADHD Inattentive Type met the age criteria, whereas 82% of ADHD Combined met it. The earlier ages of onset (age 2.9 ADHD/C versus age 4.0 ADHD/I) and referral (6.4 ADHD/C versus 9.2 ADHD/I) of the Combined Type may reflect a referral bias, as disruptive problems are often noticed at an earlier age (Faraone et al., 1998; Milich et al., 2001). Also, if inattention is not developmentally apparent until the school-age years, this means the Combined subtype cannot be diagnosed until a child is older. Thus the distinction between the Hyperactive and Combined subtypes may be an artifact of developmental changes in symptom presentation.

Predominantly Hyperactive-Impulsive Type

This subtype describes individuals who have six or more hyperactive-impulsive symptoms and fewer than six inattention symptoms for at least 6 months. This is the least common type, accounting for fewer than 15% of cases (C. L. Carlson, Shin, & Booth, 1999). It is characterized by motor- and impulse-control difficulties, behavioral problems accompanied by few academic difficulties, and low levels of anxiety and depression, which may be an artifact of the young referral age (Barton, 2001; Wasserstein, 2005). Although hyperactivity and impulsivity are the predominant feature, it is rare that inattention is absent (Owens & Hoza, 2003). In general, hyperactive-impulsive symptoms are more common among preschoolers (3- to 5-year-olds) and appear to decline with age (Nolan et al., 1999). Barkley (2005) sees this type as a developmental precursor to the Combined Type at school age. These children are more likely to be neurologically impaired, impulsive, distractible, and aggressive. They are likely to have more conduct symptoms, experience more peer rejection, and are at significantly greater risk for disruptive behavior disorders (DBDs). They are also at higher risk for placement in programs for behaviorally disturbed children, for school suspensions, and for receiving psychotherapeutic interventions, in comparison to children without the hyperactivity component (Wolraich et al., 1996). Differences in the clinical correlates and the treatment responses of individuals with and without hyperactivity-impulsivity has led some to believe that these two subtypes should be considered separate and unique disorders and not subtypes of an identical attention disturbance (Barkley, 2005). The *DSM-IV* field trials found that the Predominantly Hyperactive subtype was primarily found in preschool children and the Combined subtype in school-age children, suggesting that there may be developmental differences when symptoms come online such that motor hyperactivity might come first (American Psychiatric Association, 2000b).

Attention-Deficit/Hyperactivity Disorder Not Otherwise Specified

If the individual does not meet the full diagnostic criteria for ADHD but the clinical presentation includes prominent symptoms of inattention or hyperactivity-impulsivity, or if the onset of symptoms is after age 7, the NOS category is assigned (American Psychiatric Association, 2000b). The diagnosis Attention-Deficit/Hyperactivity Disorder in Partial Remission is assigned if an individual previously diagnosed with the disorder still experiences significant clinical symptoms but no longer meets the full diagnostic criteria (American Psychiatric Association, 2000b). How remission is defined impacts the number of individuals identified as adults with this disorder (Barkley et al., 2002).

Additional Characteristics

Cognitive Challenges

S. Young (2000) contends that hyperactive children's cognitive impairments begin earlier and are often apparent prior to school entry. While children with ADHD represent the entire spectrum of intellectual development, they are more likely to be behind in intellectual development than normal children, averaging 7 to 15 points below control groups on standard intelligence tests (Barkley, 2005). These differences appear to be related to problems with verbal working memory, or the capacity to hold information, and difficulties with freedom from distractibility. The working memory deficits may reflect problems with executive or frontal lobe functioning, which result in the child's not using feedback on previous mistakes to alter subsequent performance (Barkley, 2005). Children with ADHD are not more distractible than non-ADHD peers to extra-task stimulation; rather, they have diminished persistence on tasks with little intrinsic appeal or immediate consequences and frequently shift tasks. According to Barkley (2005), this off-task shift relates to the greater appeal or reward associated with the newly attended to activity and deficits in behavioral inhibition (Wilens, Biederman, & Spencer, 2002). Paternite et al. (1996) found no differences among the subtypes with regard to IQ scores or in academic skills as assessed by a very broad measure of academic functioning (i.e., Wide Range Achievement Test 3). Similarly, A. E. Morgan et al. (1996) found no differences in the Inattentive or Combined subtypes on measures of general intellectual functioning but did find more math learning disabilities among the Inattentive individuals. These cognitive deficits that include executive functioning difficulties persist throughout the child's life (Gallaher & Blader, 2001).

Self-Regulation and Rule-Governed Behavior

Many of the interpersonal difficulties ADHD children experience relate to the self-regulation of emotion (e.g., low frustration tolerance, temper outbursts, bossiness, stubbornness, and excessive and frequent requests; Barkley, 2005; Braaten & Rosen, 2000). Anecdotal and objective studies have shown that these children often express greater emotional reactivity and are more likely to express irritability and excitability (Hoza, Owens, et al., 2000). They are often described as not listening to or following rules and lacking in conscientiousness (De Wolfe, Byrne, & Bawden, 2000; Sonuga-Barke, Dalen, Daley, & Remington, 2002). They have greater difficulty following rules when the reinforcement for rule following is delayed and when there are more immediate, tangible consequences for not following rules (Barkley, 2005). Even when taught rules they have difficulty applying them and organizing their behavior to coming up with problem-solving strategies to deal with different situations. Thus, while children with ADHD appear to be no less knowledgeable about safety or accident prevention, they are more likely to get into accidents than non-ADHD peers, which may relate to a more general difficulty with behavioral inhibition (Barkley, 2005). As many as 57% are described as accident prone, and 15% having had at least four serious accidental injuries such as broken bones, accidental poisonings, lost teeth, or head injuries (Barkley, 2005; Leibson et al., 2001). Adolescents with ADHD who underwent treatment in substance-abuse programs were found to have a higher rate of early termination and to be twice as likely to relapse in the first 6 months after treatment as compared to their non-ADHD peers. Adolescents and young adults with ADHD have a higher risk for traffic accidents; those with comorbid ODD and CD are at the highest risk for driving-related problems and have a significantly higher rate of crashes and license revocations or suspensions (Barkley, 2005; P. S. Jensen, Martin, & Cantwell, 1997; B. H. Smith et al., 2000).

In reviewing ADHD as a risk factor for criminal activity, S. Young (2000) found that ADHD children were 4 to 5 times more likely to be arrested for a serious offense and 25 times more likely to be institutionalized than non-ADHD peers. In terms of occupational difficulties, more individuals with ADHD had lower-status jobs, and there were fewer professionals; of note, a higher number were self-employed. Nigg and colleagues (2002) found that when the effects of comorbid conditions are controlled, some of the problems and impairment associated with ADHD disappear.

Academic and School Difficulties

Academic underachievement appears to be the hallmark of ADHD. Nearly all clinic-referred ADHD children do poorly in school and have great difficulty with academic performance in reading and math and suffer significant language delays (Doggett, 2004). Such performance is typically believed to be a result of inattentive, impulsive, and restless behavior in the classroom. As a result, 56% of ADHD children may require academic tutoring, 30% may repeat a grade in school, and 30% to 40% may be placed in a special education program (Barkley, 2005). Children with ADHD also demonstrate higher rates of learning disabilities, including reading and math disabilities and spelling disorders (P. S. Jensen et al., 1997; Milish et al., 2001; Nigg et al., 2002). Compounding these problems, school authorities may attribute performance variability and difficulties in sustaining attention as willful behavior on the part of the child. While inattention appears to be a strong correlate of academic problems, school impairment was found to vary with the subtype (K. R. Murphy, Barkley, & Bush, 2002). Grade failure related to the presence of hyperactivity, and 15% of children with ADHD/H were suspended at least once and were more likely to receive behavior school placement (Barkley, 2005; P. S. Jensen et al., 1997; Milich et al., 2001). Barkley (2005) reports that ADHD/H and ADHD/I children performed worst on tests of reading achievement and spelling. Those with ADHD/I did worst on measures of math achievement, and the subtype ADHD/C was more likely to have the codiagnosis of language and stuttering disorders. In reviewing the research, Milich and colleagues (2001) concluded that the processing deficits of the Combined versus the subtype may differ from the Inattentive Type's right-hemispheric deficits, which are characterized by problems with memory, reading, spelling, and written language.

Family and Social Difficulties

Parents of children with ADHD often have their own emotional problems, including un-diagnosed ADHD, which may contribute to child-rearing difficulties (Morrell & Murray, 2003; Sonuga-Barke et al., 2002). In terms of family history, children with ADHD/H are more likely to have maternal relatives with substance-abuse problems and paternal relatives with attention deficits and hyperactivity and depression (Nadder, Rutter, Silberg, Maes, & Eaves, 2002; Nigg & Hinshaw, 1998; Rutter, Silberg, O'Conner, & Simonoff, 1999). For children with ADHD without hyperactivity, their maternal relatives were more likely to have anxiety and learning disorders and they were more likely to have a sibling with a learning disorder (Milich et al., 2001). Parents of preschool children with ADHD report more stressful parenting, with a need to give more commands, criticism, and punishment and to provide more supervision (Morrell & Murray, 2003). The child's behavior is often unpredictable or out of control emotionally and physically, exhausting the family's coping abilities and creating a volatile situation of arguments and destructive comments made out of frustration and anger (McCleary, 2002; Podolski & Nigg, 2001). There are frequent conflicts over responsibilities and chores, resulting in parent arguments over discipline and a sense that nothing works, resulting in increased parental stress that may be accompanied by alcohol use (Pelham & Lang, 1999). Parents spend hours helping with homework, often to the exclusion of other family members. The ongoing stress caused by the child's academic and social problems makes family gatherings unpleasant and contributes to the child's feeling sad and depressed. The clinical symptoms of inattention and hyperactive-impulsive behaviors lead to stress and the impairment of child-parent interaction and ultimately result in counterproductive, maladaptive parenting (Chronis, Chacko, Fabiano, Wymbs, & Pelham, 2004; C. Harrison & Sofronoff, 2002). For many parents, the variability in symptom expression creates conflict and tension, as it is hard to understand how a child who plays video games uninterrupted for 3 to 4 hours can have attention problems. Parents often respond negatively to their ADHD children's impulsive, intrusive, disorganized, inattentive behavior with greater negativity, less responsiveness to their questions, resentment, and antagonism (American Psychiatric Association, 2000b; Morrell & Murray, 2003). These negative interactions are even more likely when the child has comorbid ODD, which is related to greater maternal depression and marital discord. The presence of depression also contributes to mothers reporting the presence of more severe ADHD symptoms in their child (Chi & Hinshaw, 2002).

One of the major challenges confronting children with ADHD is establishing and maintaining healthy peer relationships (Barkley, 2005; Blachman & Hinshaw, 2002; Hodgens, Cole, & Boldizar, 2000). Social information-processing deficits, impulsive, sensation-seeking behaviors, and difficulties regulating emotions during social interactions result in problems with taking turns, listening to instructions, and awareness of social reciprocal rules in conversation (Hoza, Waschbush, Pelham, Molina, & Milich, 2000; S. Young, 2000). In addition, the child's impulsivity often results in engaging in high-risk activities without considering the consequences (dangerous bike or skateboard tricks, reckless climbing, and dare games). This creates myriad issues with establishing friendships and participating in social activities. Consequently, problems with peer relationships plague children with ADHD, and even those without significant aggressive behavior are at risk for peer disapproval. Children with ADHD struggle with social interactions and appear less friendly and responsive, often resulting in increased isolation and loneliness (Blachman & Hinshaw, 2002; Hinshaw, 2002; Hoza, Waschbush, et al., 2000). When the clinical symptoms of ADHD are in remission there is ongoing evidence of poor personal, interpersonal, and occupational adjustment. In a study of bullying among middle school students, Unnever and Cornell (2003) found that students who were on ADHD medication were at increased risk for bullying and victimization by bullies secondary to their low self-control.

While all the types of ADHD are characterized by impaired interpersonal functioning, there are some subtle differences in the nature of the social problems. Children with

Predominantly Inattentive symptoms are somewhat unpopular, often anxious and shy, and have difficulties with sports and school performance due to their slower, lethargic cognitive tempo (Doggett, 2004). Boys with ADHD/I were found to be more solitary, socially withdrawn, and engaged in high levels of onlooking behavior with low levels of sustained interaction. Their passive, withdrawn behavior was associated with low popularity, and they tended to be neglected by peers. In contrast, ADHD/H children were described as the least liked, most unpopular, most frequently engaged in fighting, and with the most inappropriate social skills (Milich et al., 2001). Teachers rated ADHD/C children as least liked and higher in social problems. Milich and colleagues (2001) found that this group used more aggressive solutions, such as fighting, to deal with social problems, showed more negative behavior following disappointment, and were actively disliked and rejected by their peers.

Overall, children with ADHD were more likely to become immersed in a deviant peer group, to use controlled substances, and to be more vulnerable to the negative influences of the group than non-ADHD peers (Marshal et al., 2003). The connection between deviant peer affiliation and self-reported substance abuse was stronger for children with ADHD, suggesting a heightened susceptibility to peer influence and tighter peer modeling of this behavior.

Onset, Course, and Life Span Considerations

Onset

As Maxmen and Ward (1995) note some mothers report that their ADHD children were very active before birth ("womb kickers") and overresponsive during infancy to noise, light, and frequently crying and becoming agitated. However, other children appear to sleep a lot and develop more slowly for the first few months of life (Maxmen & Ward, 1995). Severe infant sleep problems and difficulties being soothed have been associated with subsequent development of ADHD at 5 years of age (Thunstrom, 2002). Wilens and colleagues (2002) noted that preschool children identified with ADHD had rates of comorbidity similar to that for school-age children and had significant impairment in school, social situations, and overall functioning. In fact, few preschool (26%) and school-age (21%) children with ADHD had no psychiatric comorbidity. The Combined and Inattentive Types were the most likely to have comorbidity. The early-onset forms of ADHD were the most virulent, with the majority of children also having ODD (Nolan et al., 1999). J. M. Thomas and Guskin (2001) noted the presence of comorbid depression as early as 5 years and suggested that it is not just a complication of untreated ADHD. For preschool children presenting at psychiatric clinics, ADHD was found to be highly comorbid, typically chronic, underrecognized, characterized by social impairment, and having an onset of 3 years prior to evaluation (M. F. Green et al., 1997). The delay in the identification and treatment of these children contributes to increased risk for the development of deviant behavior, substance abuse, and family problems. Social dysfunction and ADHD were found to be strong predictors of later behavioral problems and substance abuse (Greene, Biederman, Faraone, Sienna, & Garcia-Jetton, 1997). Additionally, when treated with stimulants these preschool children with ADHD were found to have higher side effects and were less responsive to treatment (Wilens & Spencer, 2000).

Course

During middle childhood, children with ADHD are likely to experience considerable difficulties and challenges, especially when they enter elementary school. The requirements to sit still, obey, share, be attentive, and play well with other children make school particularly difficult (Barkley, 2005). This is not to mention the difficulties in achievement and the problems with cognitive skills needed to master the school curriculum and frequent standardized testing. By the time they reach adolescence just over a third will be receiving some formal special educational assistance for their academic difficulties (Barkley, 2005). Problems with academics and poor peer and family relationships may lead to increasing depression, lower self-esteem, and a higher risk for psychiatric comorbidity and non-psychiatric medical conditions (Leibson et al., 2001; Willoughby, 2003). By later childhood, the patterns of academic failure and family and social conflicts will have become well established, and at least 40% to 85% will develop ODD, and 25% to 50% are likely to develop CD and antisocial behaviors (Barkley, 2005). S. Young (2000) found that a high percentage of children with ADHD experience long-term difficulties and that hyperactivity is associated with continued symptomatology, antisocial and criminal behavior, educational and occupational failure, and social problems. Whereas motor symptoms often attenuate with age, symptoms such as lying, petty theft, and resistance to the authority of others may increase, and it is the minority of ADHD children who do not develop some comorbid psychiatric or academic disorder (Barkley, 2005). Additionally, the core symptoms of inattention—impulsiveness and restlessness—persist and contribute to ongoing psychosocial difficulties (S. Young, 2000).

Willoughby (2003) found across research studies that only a minority of ADHD children recover from or outgrow ADHD in the transition to adolescence, while the remainder experience a moderate decline in symptoms accompanied by continued problems or substantial problems with a minimal decline in symptoms. In fact, the consensus of longitudinal studies is that at least half of those children diagnosed with ADHD continue to meet the criteria as adolescents. This is a chronic disorder persisting past childhood into adolescence and adulthood, with only the minority receiving treatment (Barkley, 2005; Willoughby, 2003). In a longitudinal twin study of changes in ADHD symptoms between ages 8 and 13 years, Larsson and colleagues (2004) found a relatively high stability of symptoms, with 70% to 80% of ADHD children likely to continue displaying symptoms of ADHD into adolescence. Barkley (2005) reports that more than 59% of children with ADHD hyperactive type had comorbid ODD (compared to 11% in a control group), and 43% had comorbid CD. This latter group of hyperactive children with CD had substance use rates two to five times that of hyperactive children without CD and normal children (Barkley, 2005). Teenagers with ADHD were more likely than their non-ADHD peers to get into auto accidents, receive speeding tickets, have lower academic outcome, and have more frequently failed a grade, been suspended from school, or been expelled (Barkley, 2005). The presence of comorbid CD was found to account for the higher rate of expulsions from school, and hyperactivity entirely accounted for the increased risk for having to repeat a grade (Barkley, 2005). Thus children with ADHD continue to struggle with symptoms that persist through adolescence to adulthood and place them at increased risk for impairment in several areas of life, including educational, occupational, and psychosocial (Barkley et al., 2002; Gadow & Weiss, 2001).

Life Span Considerations

The diagnosis of adult ADHD has been validated as a chronic disorder that impacts both sexes (Biederman & Spenser, 2000; Willoughby, 2003). Approximately 2% of adults may suffer from ADHD, yet it remains hidden for many, making it a common, though under-identified, adult psychiatric disorder (Biederman & Spencer, 2000; Wasserstein, 2005). Of childhood-onset cases, 10% to 60% persist into adulthood, and 4- to 12-year follow-up studies show diagnostic retention rates of 80% (Willoughby, 2003). Reviewing symptom trajectory studies, Willoughby found that the hyperactive-impulsive symptoms decline with age, while the attentional problems remain constant. Although the core childhood symptoms shift, the impulsivity may present as overt executive function difficulties (planning, forethought, self-control, and delayed gratification), which may result in problems with adaptive functioning (e.g., difficulties holding a job or staying in a marriage; Wasserstein, 2005; Wolf & Wasserstein, 2001). Adults with ADHD may present with affective lability (hot tempers and explosive, short-lived outbursts), disorganization, poor stress tolerance, or emotional overactivity. Many adults report problems with impulse control, including a tendency to blurt out answers, difficulty waiting turns, trouble with driving, and poor inhibition of emotional reactions to others (Barkley, 2005; Faraone, Biderman, & Monuteaux, 2002; K. R. Murphy & Barkley, 1996). Other, more subtle symptoms such as low levels of alertness and increased restlessness may emerge with time (Whalen, Jamner, Henker, Delfino, & Lozano, 2002). The pattern of subtypes for adults was similar to that seen in childhood, and the Combined Type remains the most impairing and the most vulnerable to having comorbid conditions (Barton, 2001). In a review of adult outcomes, Hechtmen (1999) found that 1% to 30% have no major impairment; 50% to 60% have substantial difficulties, including emotional problems and multiple jobs; and 10% to 15% have severe depression or Antisocial Personality Disorder. The greater the severity of initial ADHD symptomatology, the more likely the disorder will persist into adulthood (Steinhausen, Drechsler, Foldenyi, Imhof, & Brandeis, 2003).

Academic attainment is likely to continue to be poor in adulthood. Many individuals attend special schools, fail grades, drop out with no qualifications, and do not go on to college (S. Young, 2000). Of that small number of individuals with ADHD that attempt college, very few actually obtain a degree. In a cross-national (Italy, New Zealand, United States) study of university students with ADHD, DuPaul and colleagues (2001) found that students with ADHD are at higher risk for academic impairment. The Hyperactive-Impulsive Type was the most common, followed by the Inattentive Type. The authors concluded that the lower number of students with the Combined Type may be a function of the more significant impairment associated with this subtype.

While adults with ADHD on follow-up have been found to be gainfully employed, many report more work-related problems or are working at a lower level and are less likely to be in a professional position (S. Young, 2000). They are also likely to be negatively rated by employers in areas such as working independently, level of work performance, task completion, relationship with supervisor, and fulfilling job demands (Barkley, 2005). Adults with ADHD are also more likely to switch jobs, have difficulty organizing time and money, fail to file taxes, and even become bankrupt (Wasserstein, 2005; Wolf & Wasserstein, 2001). For those who continue to experience ADHD symptoms, there are ongoing interpersonal difficulties. Young adults with the Combined Type often begin dating early, whereas those with the Inattentive Type were more withdrawn and passive. The research is limited in this area but does suggest higher rates of divorce and separation among those with ADHD (S. Young, 2000).

CONDUCT DISORDER

Though young males (12 to 24) make up only 8% of the population, they are responsible for committing almost half the violent crimes in the United States, and a single youth engaging in 14 years of delinquent offenses can cost society up to $2.4 million (M. A. Cohen, 1998). Bassarath (2001) found that 5% to 8% of offenders committed the majority of criminal offenses, and almost all of these youths would meet *DSM-IV-TR* criteria for Conduct Disorder. Community samples estimate the prevalence of CD for youth to be between 2% and 4% (Loeber, Burke, Lahey, Winters, & Zera, 2000). The persistent aggressive and disruptive behaviors that characterize conduct problems are the most frequent reasons for referral for children and adolescents to mental health and community clinics and residential and inpatient programs (Frick & Silverthorn, 2001; Lyman & Campbell, 1996). Conduct Disorder is the second most common psychiatric disorder among young girls. Their poor outcome is characterized by failure to complete high school, sexual promiscuity, unwed pregnancy, contracting sexually transmitted diseases, substance abuse and dependence, arrest, adult Antisocial Personality Disorder (ASPD), and an early violent death (Delligatti et al., 2003). The cost to society includes incarceration to prevent further offenses; damage to property, schools, and homes; the emotional cost to victims; and the resulting unsafe school and recreational environments for others (Kimonis & Frick, 2006; Loeber & Farrington, 2000).

Clinical Presentation

Problematic Behaviors

Diagnosis of CD requires the presence of at least three of 15 problematic behaviors that are organized into four clusters: aggression toward people and animals, destruction of property, deceit or theft, and serious violations of rules (American Psychiatric Association, 2000b). At least one of the problematic behaviors has to have been present for the past 6 months. Behaviors associated with CD are typically apparent at the following ages: for lying, age 8; for bullying, age 9; and for stealing, age 12. The *DSM-IV-TR* diagnostic criteria may have limited utility, as they measure behaviors that peak at an early age and they fail to differentiate between covert CD behaviors, property crimes, and status offenses. Loeber and colleagues (Loeber, Burke, et al., 2000) found that cruelty to people and weapon use by boys younger than 13 were the best predictors of a later CD diagnosis; physical fighting and an ODD diagnosis were the best predictors of the onset of the disorder. For girls, running away and breaking into a building were the best predictive factors. Physical fighting is common in many preschool boys, but those at highest risk for later maladjustment were the persistent or stable fighters who engaged in proactive, rather than reactive, aggression. These children often expressed a high degree of anger associated with rumination, maintenance of grudges, and the desire for revenge (Loeber, Green,

Lahey, & Kalb, 2000). Conduct problems are expressed differently over time, with more severe behaviors being preceded by minor behaviors, starting with anger in infancy, bullying in childhood, and then the use of weapons (Frick & Morris, 2004; Moffitt, 2003). The clinical symptoms may also have distinct developmental pathways, with childhood forms of aggression or fighting decreasing, and status violations, or authority conflicts, and serious physical aggression, such as rape, significantly increasing in adolescence (Lahey et al., 2000; Loeber et al., 2000; Maughan, Rowe, Messer, Goodman, & Meltzer, 2004). The *DSM* criteria have been criticized because they appear to be based on a collection of behaviors that do not speak to the dynamics (impulsive-affective versus controlled-predatory aggression), the underlying causes, or the developmental changes in clinical presentation (Frick, 1998; Kimonis & Frick, 2006; Lynam, 1997).

Gender Differences

There appear to be gender differences in the expression of aggression that the diagnostic criteria do not address (Zoccolillo, Tremblay, & Vitaro, 1996). For some boys aggression emerges early and is accompanied by ODD symptoms. In contrast, girls tend to use indirect aggression and behaviors that are not included in the *DSM* (e.g., alienation, ostracism, and character defamation), directed at relationships with friends rather than physical aggression (J. Hill, 2002). The most common reasons for referral tend to be sexual misconduct for girls and aggression and theft for boys. Once the disruptive behaviors are apparent they tend to be stable in presentation. Diagnostic criteria that emphasize behavior more typical of boys, such as confrontational, violent acts, may also contribute to a gender bias in diagnosis (Kazdin, 1997a). Kazdin (1997a) notes CD in girls may also be underestimated because of a later age of onset (14 to 16 versus 10), and the rates of non-aggressive status violations, like truancy or running away, increase at a later age (from 4% among ages 4 to 11 to 7% in 12- to 16-year-olds). Delligatti et al. (2003) noted that girls have more highly honed social skills and heightened interpersonal awareness. Thus it is easier for them to deviate from social expectations and escape detection, and they are also more likely to practice covert relational aggression (e.g., malicious gossip, covert deceitfulness, and theft). The authors suggest that there are different gender developmental pathways for the expression of aggression that are influenced by gender differences in socialization. They identified two types of CD presentation for girls. One is similar to boys and is characterized by severe and persistent aggressive behavior. The other presents as subtle social aggression, ostracism of others, and defiance (Delligatti et al., 2003). They recommend expanding the *DSM* criteria to include relational aggression and note that for girls, the nonaggressive diagnostic criterion of running away has a later onset age of 12 to 13.

Impairment and Severity

To warrant diagnosis, the behaviors of CD have to cause significant impairment in social, academic, or occupational functioning. Children are not considered to have CD unless the behaviors are quite severe and/or the overall functioning of the child is compromised (American Psychiatric Association, 2000b). In reviewing 70 years of research, including international studies, Robins (1999) concluded that all studies show the powerful impact of CD on a wide range of adverse outcomes.

A CD diagnosis is not to be given if an individual is 18 years or older and meets the criteria for ASPD (American Psychiatric Association, 2000b). Risk-taking is part of growing up, and a clinician who evaluates this behavior must elicit a careful history and take into consideration the context in which the behavior occurs within an individual's personal development (Boggs, Griffin, & Gross, 2003). The importance of the recognition of the role that environmental circumstances may play in affecting the emergence of antisocial behavior is reflected in the following statement in the *DSM-IV*: "Concerns have been raised that the CD diagnosis may at times be misapplied" (American Psychiatric Association, 2000b, p. 96). However, as Hinshaw (1992) notes, it can be extremely difficult to tease apart cultural, environmental, and intra-individual causal factors for any one individual.

The severity of the clinical presentation is assessed, based on the number of conduct problems present and the degree of harm inflicted on others, and one of three *severity specifiers* is used: mild, moderate, or severe. If an individual does not have many conduct problems in excess of those required for diagnosis but the degree of harm is significant, one should assign Severe. Mild should only be assigned when the number of conduct problems is relatively low and the degree of harm to others is mild (American Psychiatric Association, 2000b). A high degree of frequency, pervasiveness, intensity, and severity of acts is a consistent predictor of poor outcome (Kimonis & Frick, 2006).

Subtypes

One of three subtypes is then assigned based on the age of onset, which has been found to be an indicator of the severity of symptoms and chronicity (Atkins & McKay, 1996). In Childhood-Onset Type, at least one characteristic behavior is present before the age of 10. These are more often boys with high levels of aggression, opposition to authority, frequent displays of physical aggression toward others, impaired peer relationships, and lower levels of affective morality and guilt, and they are more likely to later receive an adult ASPD diagnosis (Cimbora & McIntosh, 2003). Early onset is associated with lower IQ, more attentional and impulsivity problems (more ADHD), higher rates of neurological deficits, more adverse family conditions, and poorer peer relationships (Loeber et al., 2002; Loeber & Farrington, 2000; Moffitt & Caspi, 2001; Moffitt, Caspi, Dickson, Silva, & Stanton, 1996).

If there are no characteristic CD behaviors before age 10, then the presentation is described as Adolescent-Onset Type (American Psychiatric Association, 2000b). This later onset group is characterized by lower aggression, less antisocial behavior as adults, and a minimal relationship to childhood ODD (Cimbora & McIntosh, 2003; Moffitt, 2003). Angold and Costello (2001) found that those who present in adolescence or adulthood without a prior history of antisocial behavior may have a better outcome, better social relationships, and a lack of neurocognitive deficits; this group may also have a more balanced sex ratio. Adolescents with these later onset antisocial behaviors have been described as being unable to achieve to their expectations; and secondary to the social influences or their association with other delinquent youth, they seek social status through crime (Kimonis & Frick, 2006; Moffitt, 2003; Moffitt, Caspi, Harrington, & Milne, 2002). In comparison to peers without behavioral problems, the late-onset group was more antisocial; had more recorded offenses, depression, anxiety, and problems with alcohol and controlled substances; and were more likely to use physical aggression in partner relationships (Moffitt et al., 2002). According to Moffitt, the distinction between the two groups is broadly supported and allows for comparisons of the two types in terms of risk factors and trajectory pathway (Kimonis & Frick, 2006). Nonetheless, this simple partition into early- and late-onset has been criticized as an oversimplification (Frick & Ellis, 1999).

If the information concerning age of onset is unknown or unavailable, then Unspecified-Onset Type is assigned (American Psychiatric Association, 2000b). The use of age of onset has also been criticized because of its reliance on recall and on a single indicator of the presence or absence of symptoms before a certain age and because it lacks empirical prognostic use for girls. The average earlier age of onset for boys has also not been supported uniformly (Loeber et al., 2000).

Child or Adolescent Antisocial Behavior

When antisocial behavior does not represent the pervasive pattern seen in CD and is not in response to an identifiable stressor, the V-Code child or adolescent antisocial behavior may be appropriate (American Psychiatric Association, 2000). According to the American Psychiatric Association (2000b, p. 740), "This category can be used when the focus of clinical attention is antisocial behavior in a child or an adolescent that is not due to a mental disorder." This can include isolated antisocial acts of children and adolescents that are not a pattern of antisocial behavior.

Additional Characteristics

Lack of Empathy and Poor Peer Relationships

Individuals with CD often misperceive others' intentions and may respond with unwarranted hostility or threats to the actions of others (American Psychiatric Association, 2000b). They can appear psychopathic or egocentric, manipulative, callous, lacking feelings of guilt or remorse, having little trust and loyalty, and willingly informing on and blaming others. According to Loeber and colleagues (2000) this is the most serious outcome of the DBDs and has been described as a failure to inhibit aggression and a reduced autonomic reactivity to others' distress cues (Frick & Ellis, 1999; Frick & Morris, 2004). Looking at emotional responsiveness, Cimbora and McIntosh (2003) found that youth with childhood-onset CD reported the lowest levels of guilt and the presence of psychopathic traits in boys as young as 7 to 12 with CD predicts serious stable antisocial traits and interpersonal exploitiveness. Frick and colleagues (2003; Barry et al., 2000) report that children with callous, unemotional traits, such as a lack of empathy, are similar to children with comorbid hyperactivity or attention and conduct problems. However, they tend to have more varied severe problems, earlier contact with police, fewer verbal deficits, and conduct problems, and are less associated with dysfunctional parenting. Of clinic-referred individuals, those with ADHD/C and CD had the highest levels of callousness and lack of emotion. They were noted to have poorer peer relationships, experienced greater peer rejection than non-CD peers and poorer interpersonal relations characterized by socially ineffective interactions with adults (J. Hill, 2002; Kazdin, 1997a, 1998).

From around 5 years, antisocial, aggressive children appear attracted to each other and reinforce one another's deviant behavior. These children make many social overtures that are more likely to be unsuccessful, and other nondeviant children are more likely to be unresponsive or rejecting of them (Dodge & Pettit, 2003; Vitaro, Tremblay, & Bukowski, 2001). By the fourth to the seventh grade, the presence of deviant peers is significantly associated with the onset of overt and covert antisocial problems (Hill, 2002). Antisocial friendships were noted to reinforce rule-breaking talk and delinquent behavior for both boys and girls, and peer approval for law violations was particularly salient (Capaldi & Shortt, 2003). Bullying in middle school was found to be associated with a more general antisocial rule-breaking pattern, which impulsive aggressive children were more likely to engage in. The level of deviancy of the 10-year-old child's best friend was predictive of the child's later delinquency, though this association did not hold for children with strong parental attachment (J. Hill, 2002). This suggests that an affective bond with parents may buffer deviant peers' influence on teenagers. Hill (2002) noted that rejected boys expressed excessive anger when unsuccessful in competitive games and pleasure when things went their way. He hypothesized that the combination of the lack of interpersonal sensitivity and emotional regulation results in both peer and conduct problems. The combination of aggression and rejection resulted in increased externalizing behaviors among adolescent boys. Hostile talk about females with a peer in late adolescence was found to predict partner violence 3 years later. Youth with CD are more likely to engage in antisocial acts in a peer context (Capaldi, Dishion, Stoolmiller, & Yoerger, 2001; Fergusson, Swain, & Horwood, 2002). These findings convey a more pervasive problem whereby children with CD experience ongoing interpersonal problems, which may be compounded by assortive mating in adulthood (Farrington, Jolliffe, Loeber, Stouthamer-Loeber, & Kalb, 2001; Simonoff, 2001a). Inner-city adolescents with CD frequently drop out of high school, engage early in sexual relationships, and become parents in adolescence. This accelerated movement into adult roles, while associated with difficulties for adolescent mothers, often served to extricate them from their antisocial peer group and decrease their delinquent acts. In contrast, many adolescent fathers were found to fail in this role; within 2 years 40% of them had no contact with their child (Capaldi & Shortt, 2003).

Substance Use

Children with CD tend to have parents who abuse substances and engage in antisocial acts (Lahey, Loeber, Burke, & Rathouz, 2002). Concurrent and longitudinal research indicates that CD has a distinct tendency to cluster with substance use and abuse disorders and early sexual activity. For girls, this combination contributes to a more rapid transition into adulthood, early onset of sexual activity, and alcohol and cannabis use. For boys with CD early onset and continued use of substances may increase their risk for adult ASPD (Modestin, Matutat, & Wurmle, 2001). Angold and Costello (2001) found that children who later have problems with alcohol and substance abuse also have antisocial, rebellious, aggressive behavior, high rates of school dropout, poor achievement, delinquency, and family problems. Among offenders, twice as many initiate drug use after delinquent behavior as opposed to those who initiate delinquent behavior after drug use. The number of conduct problems predicted future substance abuse for those first using before age 20. Of adolescents with seven or more conduct problems, more than half developed substance abuse problems before the age of 15, whereas only 5% of those with one conduct problem developed substance abuse before age 15 (Robins & McEvoy, 1990).

Onset, Course, and Life Span Considerations

Onset

Within the group of early-onset conduct disorders two distinct temperamental styles have been identified early in life (Kimonis & Frick, 2006). One group is characterized by angry reactivity and problems with emotional regulation, which can contribute to difficulties internalizing parental norms and coercive parenting relationships (Dodge & Pettit, 2003; Kruh et al., 2005; G. R. Patterson, 1986). These individuals often demonstrate aggression and conduct problems when emotionally aroused without thinking of the consequences (Hubbard et al., 2002). Their aggression tends to be reactive, and they are highly responsive to distress in others and are remorseful afterward (Frick et al., 2003; Looney, Frick, Clements, Ellis, & Kerlin, 2003; Pardini, Lochman, & Frick, 2003). In contrast, the second group present with more covert antisocial acts; these children have low behavioral inhibition and fearfulness, may have difficulties developing empathy and guilt, and often have severe forms of antisocial and aggressive behavior (Frick & Morris, 2004; Kimonis & Frick, 2006). They appear less responsive to parental socialization, less distressed by the impact of their behaviors, less able to identify distress in others, and less reactive to threatening and emotional stimuli and have more impaired moral reasoning (Blair, Colledge, Murray, & Mitchell, 2001; Pardini et al., 2003). Thus one temperamental style is associated with emotion regulation problems and anger reactivity, the other with low fearfulness, inhibition, and responsiveness (Kimonis & Frick, 2006). These children may also experience parental anger, harsh discipline, and coercive, erratic, and ineffective parenting, resulting in escalating power struggles (Dodge & Petit, 2003). In describing young fledgling psychopaths, Lynam (1997, 1998) notes that they often came from families with parent psychopathology, including alcoholism; antisocial behavior; harsh, lax, or inconsistent parenting; insufficient acceptance of children in the household; less affection and unsatisfactory emotional support; minimal warmth; and defensive communication. Dodge and colleagues (2003) attribute the tendency to favor aggressive responses to social challenges to repeated exposure to physical maltreatment. They found that conduct problems in third and fourth grade related to documented physical abuse in kindergarten.

Webster-Stratton (2005) describes how children with early-onset CD show an emergence of ODD in early preschool years. She notes that 4- to 7-year-olds expelled from two or more preschools experience significant early peer and teacher rejection. These experiences set the stage for future school behavior and the parents' future attitude toward their school experience. The child's oppositional behavior progresses in middle childhood to aggressive and nonaggressive symptoms. A follow-up study of boys through high school found that 4% continued aggressive behavior from kindergarten through adolescence (Bassarath, 2001). J. Hill (2002) notes that aggressive children tend to overestimate their academic, behavioral, and social capabilities, their cognitive competence, and the quality of their peer relationships and have aggressive outbursts when their inflated, but fragile, self-appraisal is threatened. Very young girls with CD were found to have higher intelligence than the controls, and only 25% of this group continued the CD behaviors into adulthood (Fagot & Leve, 1998).

Course

The Pittsburgh Youth Study (Loeber, Farrington, Stouthamer-Loeber, & Van Kammen, 1998; Loeber & Stouthamer-Loeber, 1998) found that CD among boys can take three pathways. The first is an overt course beginning with minor aggression, then physical fighting, followed by violence. The second is a covert pathway before age 15, with minor covert behaviors followed by property damage and moderate to serious forms of delinquency. The third path is characterized by conflicts with authority before age 12, stubborn defiance prior to authority avoidance, running away, and staying out late. The authors concluded that the most disturbed adolescents present with problems characteristic of multiple pathways. Bassarath (2001) describes two developmental pathways to CD that are characterized by different behaviors. The first is a persistent life course beginning around age 4 with biting and hitting, transitions by age 10 to include shoplifting and truancy, and developing by age 16 into acts of selling drugs, stealing cars, robbery, and rape. In adulthood (at studied ages of 22, 30, and 40), the behaviors encompass child abuse, fraud, violent assault, and drunk driving. Those with adolescent-limited or adolescent-onset CD have a less remarkable early history of conduct difficulties; offenses are mainly with peers, and these children may be well behaved in school or at home (Bassarath, 2001). This type of CD has been described as more ecologically sensitive or more likely to be caused or influenced by environmental factors, such as deviant peer groups. It is associated with higher IQ, less comorbidity, lower levels of aggression, and a lower likelihood of a family history of disruptive disorders. The middle teenage years are a high-risk time for conduct problems in girls who have high levels of familial conflict with their parents, in particular with mothers (Capaldi & Shortt, 2003; Moffitt et al., 2001). For girls adolescence-limited antisocial behavior and low educational achievement predict teenage pregnancy (Nagin & Tremblay, 2001). In the past, low intelligence was thought to be a precursor to disruptive behavior, yet when ADHD was controlled for, the results were found to be nonsignificant (Hogan, 1999). Of children identified with CD, 40% to 70% also meet the criteria for ADHD; these children had the worst outcome and were more likely to show academic deficits, be left behind in grades, display lower academic achievement, and end schooling sooner than matched peers for boys (J. Hill, 2002). In clinic-referred boys, an improvement over 4 years was related to above-average IQ and a lack of parental ASPD (J. Hill, 2002).

The frequency of many forms of physical aggression was found to decline between childhood and adolescence, while nonaggressive status violations, levels of truancy, the acts of staying out late and running away all increase significantly with age (Maughan et al., 2004). Loeber, Burke, et al. (2000) found that aggression such as fighting decreased, but more serious forms, such as rape, increased in adolescence. Children with CD are also more likely to engage in vandalism, shoplifting, and truancy, to be convicted of at least one crime before age 24, and to have three or more convictions than nondeviant peers (Unnever & Cornell, 2003).

Conduct Disorder is the most stable of all childhood psychiatric diagnoses. Lahey and colleagues (2002) reviewed longitudinal studies on population-based samples that showed that 35% to 45% of the children with CD met the criteria on follow-up. They then conducted a 7-year follow-up of clinic-referred CD boys and found that most showed persistent, but fluctuating, levels of CD, with fewer than 25% sufficiently improved to be considered recovered. Improvement was predicted by a lower initial severity of CD and fewer ADHD symptoms. This was related to higher verbal intelligence, higher family socioeconomic advantage, older maternal age at first birth, and the child's mother being highly educated. Antisocial personality in biological mothers and biological fathers combined additively to predict poor outcome, and boys who were older at the start exhibited fewer symptoms, which were also less persistent (Lahey et al., 2002).

Life Span Considerations

Robin's (1966) classic study of antisocial youths found that fewer than 50% continue as antisocial adults, and one of the best predictors of how aggressive a boy will be is how aggressive his father was at the same age. In general, adults with early-onset CD continue to present with more persistent symptoms, higher self-reported rates of violent crime, and higher conviction rates for violent offenses. They are more likely to have used controlling violence in their partner relationships, and they have significantly higher rates of hitting children as well as more disagreements with coworkers and supervisors (Moffitt, 2003; Moffitt et al., 2002). As adults girls with CD are at high risk for anxiety, mood and somatoform disorders, and suicide attempts (Kimonis & Frick, 2006). Adolescent-onset CD is also associated with a range of negative outcomes, including early pregnancy, marriage to antisocial partners, high rates of marital violence, school dropout, involvement in family court, unstable work history, higher use of welfare services, and higher mortality (Connor, 2004). Bassarath (2001), in reviewing the risk factors for CD, found that of boys convicted of a violent crime between the ages of 10 and 16, 50% were convicted again of violence before age 24, in contrast to 8% of nonconvicted youth. As adults, if not incarcerated these individuals will continue to experience occupational and social dysfunction and unemployment, collect welfare, not own their own home, and die an early death from unnatural causes (Connor, 2004; Laub & Valliant, 2000).

OPPOSITIONAL DEFIANT DISORDER

The key feature of ODD is a recurrent pattern of negativistic, defiant, disobedient, and hostile behavior toward authority figures (American Psychiatric Association, 2000b). It is the most common diagnosis for preschoolers. Children with this disorder are described as persistently stubborn, resistant to following directions, unwilling to compromise, and constantly testing limits (Lavigne et al., 2001). It is estimated that 2% to 35% of clinic-referred children receive a diagnosis of ODD (Gadow & Nolan, 2002). J. Hill (2002) reports that 0.5% to 10% of children ages 8 to 16 have significant persistent oppositional, disruptive, or aggressive behavior problems. The symptoms, which are apparent at an early age, also appear to persist and become more severe as the child matures (Maughan et al., 2004; Speltz, McClellan, De Klyen, & Jones, 1999). Oppositional Defiant Disorder is a precursor to childhood-onset CD, and although most children (two thirds) do not go on to develop CD, they continue to exhibit ongoing oppositional behavior (Greene et al., 2002; Loeber, Burke, et al., 2000). For years the impact of ODD has been difficult to assess, as it was not differentiated from conduct problems or CD and was classified as a disruptive disorder or an externalizing disorder (Angold & Costello, 2001; Greene, 2006). Oppositional Defiant Disorder rarely occurs on its own and is often comorbid with ADHD and anxiety and mood disorders (Greene, 2006; Lavigne et al., 2001). Behaviors can be highly context-sensitive and are more prevalent in families where harsh, inconsistent, or neglectful child-rearing practices are common and where there is serious marital discord (J. M. Eddy, Leve, & Fagot, 2001; Stormshak, Bierman, McMahon, & Lengua, 2000). Parents of oppositional children are more likely to criticize, belittle, and blame their children and are more likely to use mental heath services than parents of children with other disruptive disorders (Greene et al., 2002). These children have been described as "chronically inflexible" and explosive and are often very difficult to parent, particularly when the parent lacks skills (M. F. Green, 2001). Clinicians need to be alert for possible child abuse and familiar with mandated reporting requirements (see Chapter 2).

Clinical Presentation

Defiance

These children are described by parents as being "argumentative," having "an attitude," and "never listen[ing]," resulting in frequent school referral for disciplinary action and the child's being unpopular and ostracized by peers (American Psychiatric Association, 2000b). Stubbornness in children later diagnosed with ODD is likely to be apparent by age 3; defiance and temper tantrums appear by age 5, and argumentativeness by age 6 (Conner, 2004). The persistence (6 months or longer) of the problematic behaviors and atypical frequency are often indicators that can help differentiate normal acting-out or nondysfunctional reactions to environmental conditions (a high-crime community) from more problematic forms (American Psychiatric Association, 2000b). The use of a duration criterion has been questioned, as the symptoms tend to be long-standing (Loeber, et al., 2000).

To diagnose ODD, the determination is made at the therapist's discretion that the behavior is more frequent than is typical given the child's age and developmental stage. One must be very careful in diagnosing ODD, as many of the behaviors listed are developmentally normal at certain ages, for example, defiance and conflict in toddlers and adolescents (First et al., 2004). For typical children oppositional and defiant behaviors under the progressive influence of parent and school socialization diminish starting at age 6 and continue to decrease through grade school (Conner, 2004; NaNagin & Tremblay, 1999). Angold and Costello (1996) note that there are also developmental changes in clinical presentation: Arguing becomes more common with increasing age, whereas annoying behavior decreases with age. A certain degree of noncompliance and defiance is normal in toddlerhood, particularly for boys, and reflects the child's assertiveness and search for autonomy or ignorance of what parents are prepared to accept. Indeed, prosocial behaviors (e.g., sharing and cooperation) appear to increase up to the age of 3 and then decline as children begin to learn that they do not always need to be "good" (Rey & Walter, 1999). Hinshaw (1992) notes that it would take an extremely high level and severity of such oppositional behavior (compared to age and sex norms) at this stage to warrant a diagnosis. In adolescence there is an emphasis on individuation, which often results in adolescent rebellion and conflict with parents, in turn reflecting a healthy process of identity formation.

Impairment

The disruptive problems must cause clinically significant impairment in areas of academic, occupational, or social functioning to warrant a diagnosis (American Psychiatric Association, 2000b). In contrast to ADHD, there is no pervasiveness requirement that behaviors must occur across multiple settings. In fact, situational variability is common; some children show oppositional behavior only at home (American Psychiatric Association, 2000b). In general, children with ODD are more likely to display these behaviors with people they know, people unlikely to characterize them as oppositional, and those who see the behaviors as justified (e.g., in response to unreasonable demands). Therefore, the reliability of assessment is likely to increase when the clinician uses information from multiple sources: parents, teachers, rating scales, and questionnaires. Rey & Walter (1999) note that it is unlikely that oppositional behaviors will be apparent only in school with teachers; when this is the presentation, the presence of a learning disorder or other academic problem should be considered. Oppositional Defiant Disorder occurs with significant social dysfunction and impairments in adaptive and family functioning (Greene et al., 2002). As the *DSM-IV-TR* precludes an ODD diagnosis with CD, which takes diagnostic precedence, thus the rates for ODD, appear to decrease with age. However, age trend data show that clinically significant oppositionality persists beyond childhood and increases in severity (Maughan et al., 2004).

Disruptive Behavior Disorder Not Otherwise Specified

When individuals present with conduct and oppositional-defiant behavior that results in significant clinical impairment and fail to meet the full diagnostic criteria for CD or ODD, they are assigned Disruptive Behavior Disorder Not Otherwise Specified (DBD-NOS; American Psychiatric Association, 2000b).

Parent-Child Problems

It can be difficult to determine if a child should be given a diagnosis of ODD or a relational problem (V-Code), or whether both should be considered. First et al. (2004, p. 386) note that this decision is difficult because "informants may have their own axe to grind," and the lack of clearly effective and specific treatments for ODD adds to the ambiguity of this disorder.

Additional Characteristics

Self-Esteem Issues

The *DSM-IV-TR* notes that low self-esteem, or in some cases an inflated sense of self-esteem, may be associated with ODD (American Psychiatric Association, 2000b). August and colleagues (August, Realmuto, MacDonald, Nugent, & Crosby, 1996) screened more than 7,000 first through fourth graders and found that preschool disruptive behaviors, such as tantrums and noncompliance, were linked to poor peer relationships, peer rejection, and academic underachievement in elementary school. Mood lability and low frustration tolerance are also often seen in these cases, and ODD children appear at increased risk for using illicit drugs, tobacco, and alcohol. They are also at high risk for depression and school dropout (Greene et al., 2002). The aggression and oppositional behavior that are apparent in school interactions often result in referral for mental health services. Teachers rate them as more stressful to teach (Greene, 2006).

Onset, Course, and Life Span Considerations

Few studies have reported on ODD alone. Most tend to cluster it with CD and report on results for disruptive or externalizing behaviors. Longitudinal studies show that ODD symptoms tend to be quite stable (Maughah et al., 2004). Preschool children with ODD are likely to continue to have symptoms, increasing comorbidity with ADHD, and significant impairment on follow-up (Angold & Costello, 1996; Lavigne et al., 2001). In preschool, the combination of hyperactivity and disruptive behaviors was strongly predictive of later antisocial behavior (Speltz et al., 1999). J. D. Burke, Loeber, and Birmaher (2002) report that the manifestations of the disruptive behavior change with age, suggesting continuity rather than stability. As a child ages, there is an orderly unfolding of disruptive behaviors, with less serious symptoms followed by moderate and then serious symptoms. First and Tasman (2004) describe nonaggressive oppositional behavior in one group of children peaking at 8 years and subsequently declining. However, children with ODD and physical aggression are more likely to engage in delinquent behavior and progress into more severe conduct problems, and the presence of comorbid ADHD tends to increase this escalation. Conner (2004) describes how in a "normative pathway" infant oppositional behavior decreases with socialization, and in adolescence drinking, curfew violations, and minor transient delinquency associated with peers may occur. In contrast, in the more "deviant pathway," childhood oppositional behavior develops into defiant, disobedient behavior, followed by aggressive acts that escalate into more violent antisocial behavior in adolescence.

In one of the few studies to look at ODD independent of its relationship to CD, Greene and colleagues (2002) found that children with ODD alone had significantly higher rates of ADHD, mood disorders (major depression and bipolarity), and multiple anxiety disorders. Individuals with both ODD and CD had significantly higher rates of mood disorder than those with ODD alone. The combination of ODD, ADHD, and major depression was found to be a significant predictor of social problems at school. The combination of ODD, CD, and language impairment was a significant predictor of problems with peers. And while ODD and CD combined was the only predictor of problems with siblings and with parents, ODD was the only predictor of family conflict. The authors concluded that with ODD alone, there were significant high rates of comorbidity, greater social impairment, and family dysfunction, as characterized by poorer family cohesion and higher conflict. Thus, ODD was found to have detrimental effects on children in multiple domains of functioning, independent of the impact of CD or the impairment accounted for by other psychiatric disorders (Greene et al., 2002).

EPIDEMIOLOGY

ADHD

The *DSM-IV-TR* lists the prevalence of ADHD as 3% to 7% in school-age children, depending on the diagnostic criteria and the diagnostic instruments used (American Psychiatric Association, 2000b). Overall in the community-based samples 5% to 10% of school-age youth meet the diagnostic criteria for ADHD (Scahill & Schwab Stone, 2000). Of note, Cuffe and colleagues (2001) found that the prevalence of ADHD in community samples of older adolescents doubled if late-onset symptoms were included in the assessment. Burt and colleagues (Burt, Krueger, & McGue, 2001) found that the lifetime prevalence for ADHD was 6.9% for boys and 3.5% for girls. Studies indicate fairly consistent rates of ADHD throughout the world: Germany, 4.2%; Canada, 6%; New Zealand, 7%; and Puerto Rico, 10% (Wilens, Biederman, & Spencer, 2002). In developing countries, such as Brazil, there is a 6% prevalence of ADHD in outpatient programs and schools, with a high comorbidity (47.8%) with the disruptive disorders (Rohde, 2002). It is important to consider the roles in these countries of malnourishment, inadequate educational systems, scarce mental health services, and mental health professionals' reluctance to diagnose ADHD when the clinical symptoms occur in close temporal proximity to psychosocial stressors (Rohde, 2002). Prevalence rates for ADHD are affected by age, with younger groups demonstrating higher prevalence than older groups. (American Psychiatric Association, 2000b; Barkley, 2005). The community prevalence of ADHD shows a 3:1 ratio of males to females and between 6:1 and 9:1 for clinic samples (Gaub & Carlson, 1997). The lower referral rate for girls may reflect an underestimation, neglect of the problem in this group, or a referral bias secondary to differences in clinical presentation. That is, girls present with learning problems, whereas boys express more disruptive behaviors in structured settings. The gender differences in rates of ADHD appear to be more consistent in younger children (4 to 11). The 3:1 male-to-female ratio decreases to a ratio of 2.1:1 for older children (12 to 16), and the male-to-female ratio for college students was found to be equivalent (Lahey et al., 1999). K. R. Murphy and Barkley (1996) estimate the prevalence of adult ADHD in the community to be about 4.7%. They asked ADHD individuals who were renewing a driver's license about childhood-onset symptoms and current symptoms of ADHD. Of course, it is difficult to know whether the individuals' retrospective recall of experiences was accurate. The *DSM-IV* notes that sufficient information on the prevalence of adulthood ADHD is lacking. Of the ADHD subtypes, Milich and colleagues (2001) found that ADHD/I was the most prevalent in community samples and was twice as common as ADHD/C. In clinical samples, ADHD/C was found to be 1.5% more prevalent than ADHD/I, suggesting that the more disruptive the behavior, the higher the likelihood to be referred for treatment (C. L. Carlson & Mann, 2000). Males are more prevalent in all ADHD subtypes, but both in the community and in clinical samples there is a greater proportion of males in the Combined Type as opposed to the Inattentive Type.

Conduct Disorder

The *DSM-IV-TR* lists the prevalence rate for CD as between 1% and 10% (American Psychiatric Association, 2000b). In the general population, CD has rates of 1% to 9% (Essau,

2003). The lifetime prevalence for CD was found to be 7.4% for boys and 1.1% for girls (Burt et al., 2001). More males than females tend to be diagnosed with CD; the ratio varies from 3:1 to 5:1, and there is some evidence that the ratio decreases during adolescence. Delligatti et al. (2003) found CD rates for males under age 18 to be 6% to 16% in the general population. For females, the rates were 2% to 9%, which is believed to be an underestimation because of the tendency for research to focus on males. In a longitudinal study, the difference between CD rates for boys and girls was found to narrow in the mid-teens, suggesting that girls are at particular risk for CD in the peripubertal period (Moffitt & Caspi, 2001). Kazdin (1997a) cites earlier studies of community samples of school-age children where CD rates were 2% to 6% for boys, which were 3 to 4 times higher than the rates for girls. In a national sample in the United Kingdom, Maughan and colleagues (2004) also found that CD was more common in boys and increased in prevalence with age. Whereas aggressive symptoms decreased, nonaggressive conduct status violations increased. The *DSM* diagnostic criteria may be gender-biased, in that girls are more likely to engage in covert crimes, relationship aggression, or prostitution, which are not included. In their review of epidemiological studies of disruptive disorders, Lahey and colleagues (1999) note that most studies did not include youth residents in correctional facilities, which they cite as being 0.5% of all Black youth and 0.1% of all White youth in the United States according to the 1997 census. This omission significantly underestimates CD rates in communities and does not present a true picture of the pervasiveness or the severity of these problems.

Oppositional Defiant Disorder

According to the *DSM-IV-TR*, estimates of the prevalence of ODD range from 2% to 16% depending on the sample and the method of assessment used to collect the data (American Psychiatric Association, 2000b). In the general population, prevalence rates for ODD are between 1.5% and 15.6%, with the rates varying depending on the diagnostic criteria, assessment instrument, and number of informants used and if impairment was included as a diagnostic criterion (Loeber, et al., 2000). Looking at large-scale epidemiological studies using community surveys, Essau (2003) reports a prevalence rate for ODD of 2%. Burt and colleagues (2001) found rates for ODD of 9.2% for boys and 4.8% for girls. In clinically referred children, 2% to 30% received a diagnosis of ODD (Gadow & Nolan, 2002)

ETIOLOGY

Biological Factors

Genetic Factors

Twin, family, and adoption studies strongly indicate that genetic factors play a strong role in the etiology of ADHD (Kuntsi & Stevenson, 2000; Larsson et al., 2004; Tannock, 1998). The high concordance rate for monozygotic twins compared to dizygotic twins (81% versus 29%) has led to the suggestion that the majority of variance in the hyperactivity-impulsivity trait is due to genetic factors (80%) and that this increases with the severity of the trait. If both parents have ADHD, the risk to offspring is 57%; 31% of children with ADHD had one ADHD parent, and male siblings were 3 times more likely than female siblings to have ADHD (Barton, 2001; Erk, 1997; Maxmen & Ward, 1995; Rohde, 2002). In reviewing the earlier research on the relationship between family genetic and environmental risk factors, P. S. Jensen and colleagues (1997) concluded that the influence of family genetics on ADHD was important over and above the effects of psychological adversity. Genetic research suggests that the strongest link is between ADHD and the dopamine receptor 7-repeat allele of the DRD4 and the dopamine transporter 10-repeat allele of DAT1 as potential candidate genes (First & Tasman, 2004; Levy, Barr, & Sunohara, 1998; Simonoff, 2001a).

Burt et al. (2001) used the Minnesota Twin Study to look at the covariance in ADHD, ODD, and CD, and found that 29% to 72% of individuals with one of these disorders had another one. They concluded that, although each of the disorders was influenced by genetic and environmental factors, the largest contribution to the covariance in the different disorders could be explained by a shared environmental factor. G. R. Patterson, DeGarmo, and Knutson (2000) suggest that a common vulnerability is the shared mechanism between antisocial and hyperactive behavior. In looking at a nonclinical sample of twins in Finland, Dick and colleagues (2005) concluded that the comorbidity between ADHD, CD, and ODD is primarily explained by shared genetic influences and that each disorder possessed some unique genetic influence that supports the distinct nature of each.

Early Swedish and Danish twin and adoption studies consistently showed that antisocial behaviors tend to run in families and that parental criminal behavior and alcoholism place children at risk for CD (Bohman, 1995; Brennan, Mendick, & Jacobsen, 1995; R. Cadoret, 1986). Farrington and colleagues (2001) found that antisocial and disruptive behavior aggregated in families and that adolescent-onset CD was associated with a parental history of antisocial behavior. Studies of twins and their families (Marmorstein & Iacono, 2004) indicate that the presence of CD or ODD in adolescents was related to paternal antisocial behavior and maternal depression. The Virginia Twin Study (Silberg et al., 1996a,b). showed that the genetic influences are strongest for youth with multiple symptoms and/or the combination of hyperactivity and CD. Viding and colleagues (Viding, Blair, Moffitt, & Plomin, 2003) conducted one of the few twin studies to look at the subgroup of antisocial children with callous unemotional traits. They found that genetic factors accounted for 81% of the variance for this group, in comparison to 30% for children with conduct problems but without the callous traits. In a large (2,682) community sample of twins in Australia, Slutske and colleagues (1997) found a significant genetic influence (accounting for 71% of the variance) of the risk for CD, which was similar for boys and girls, and a small modest effect for a shared environment. In reviewing earlier work, they noted that childhood antisocial behaviors appeared to aggregate in families and that the association between parent characteristics and parenting behaviors in CD children may be due to genetics rather than shared environmental factors. Similarly, Simonoff (2001a) quoted genetic studies that found the hereditability for CD to be 60% to 90% through gene-environment interaction and that the child's behavior influenced the experience of parenting and the mother's behavior toward the adopted child. J. Hill (2002) cited earlier Swedish adoption studies that found that an adoptee of nonantisocial biological parents in a low-risk environment had a 3% risk for adult criminality, which increased to 6% in a high-risk family. Adoptees of antisocial biological parents had a rate of 12% in low-risk environments and 40% when there were high-risk environmental factors. Reiss and Neiderhiser (2000) noted that there is now substantial evidence that social experience can alter gene expression at the molecular level and impact the developmental fate of inherited behavioral and cognitive characteristics. D. L. Foley and colleagues (2004), using twins from the Virginia longitudinal study, looked at the heritability of CD and the impact of adverse environmental factors. They found that the risk associated with a specific genotype differs qualitatively in relation to different environments and that specific genotypes that represent a risk for psychiatric disorder may vary depending on environmental exposure. The authors hypothesized that genotypic effects are reordered in response to variations in environmental risks. Thus, individuals with a low-activity genotype for CD are at risk for CD only when exposed to severe environmental adversity (D. L. Foley et al., 2004).

In terms of genetic influences on ODD and CD, J. Hill (2002) concluded from twin and adoption studies that there is now substantial evidence that these disorders are heritable, with estimates of heritability varying from .2 to .8 and with the majority clustering around .4 to .7. Similarly, J. D. Burke and colleagues (2002) reviewed research on the risk factors for ODD and CD, citing earlier twin studies research (L. Eaves et al., 2000) that found a high genetic correlation across sexes for ODD and CD. They concluded that genetic factors also explained the association between familial negativity and adolescent antisocial behavior. The *DSM-IV-TR* notes that ODD is more common in individuals with a parental history of any one of a number of disorders, including ADHD, ODD, ASPD, CD, and mood or substance-related disorders (American Psychiatric Association, 2000b).

Neurotransmitters, Brain Structure, and Functioning

Biological theories of ADHD focus on the role of neurotransmitters, such as serotonin, which may exert an inhibitor influence on behavior, and dopamine dysfunction, which may contribute to ADHD clinical symptoms (Quist & Kennedy, 2001; Simonoff, 2001a). Genetically engineered mice with high levels of dopamine exhibit ADHD characteristics, suggesting that this is a heterogeneous disorder with several biochemical or genetic defects resulting in a similar clinical presentation (Gainetdinov & Caron, 2001). Genetic research also suggests that ADHD is a complex trait involving many genes, including the dopamine receptor genes (DRD4) that contribute to susceptibility for ADHD (Barr, 2001). Neuroimaging (MRI and PET) studies suggest that ADHD is associated with a decreased size of certain frontal regions of the brain. These findings include a smaller right prefrontal cortex, abnormal asymmetry of frontal lobes, immature incomplete functions of the cerebellum, and significant differences in the corpus callosum (Barton, 2001; Erk, 1997; Y. Frank & Pavlakis, 2001). There is also evidence of decreased blood flow to the prefrontal regions and of lower glucose metabolism in frontal and striatal regions of the brain (Barton, 2001; Erk, 1997; Hale, Hariri, & McCracken, 2000). According to Erk, these findings suggest that ADHD is not necessarily associated with gross brain damage but rather some sort of brain dysfunction. The current prevailing view is that ADHD is caused by a deficit in neurobiological brain functioning in the prefrontal cortex (Doggett, 2004).

There appears to be a complex relationship between neurotransmitters and executive brain function that results in behavior dysregulation (Davidson, Putnam, & Larson 2000; Pliszka, 1999). According to J. Hill (2002), CD is likely to be multidetermined. It is unclear to what extent neurotransmitter systems are affected in CD. However, J. D. Burke and colleagues (2002) report that low levels of serotonin have been associated with con-current and future aggressive behaviors, such as fire-setting, impulsivity, sensation seeking, and alcohol abuse. Mpofu and Conners (2003) found comorbidity in 90% of children referred for CD treatment and 20% to 60% of children with ODD. They hypothesized that the abnormalities in serotonin conductance and norepinephrine may explain the high rates of comorbidity. Neuroanatomy damage to, deficits in, and atypical functioning of the frontal lobes have been associated with aggression and negative-affective-style violence (Baving, Laucht, & Schmidt, 2000; Brower & Price, 2001; Pliszka, 1999). The limbic system (the amygdala, the septal area, and the hypothalamus) has also been identified as important in the activation and inhibition of aggression; higher cortical centers help to interpret stimuli and mediate aggressive responses. More specifically, impairments in the amygdala have been related to difficulty with the interpretation of social cues (Davidson et al., 2000). Adolescents with CD have weaker autonomic sympathetic response to fear-arousing stimuli and show more rapid habituation in skin conductance to intense or aversive stimuli (Frick & Silverthorn, 2001). Pliszka (1999) found that children with disruptive behaviors evidenced underarousal of the autonomic nervous system (ANS). Individuals with childhood-onset CD show this pattern of decreased ANS arousal. However, it does not appear that adolescent-onset CD shows this same pattern of ANS underarousal. J. D. Burke and colleagues (2002) hypothesized that these low levels of anxiety tend to inhibit children from criminal or disruptive behaviors. In reviewing the earlier studies of cognitive deficits associated with CD, Toupin and colleagues (Toupin, Dery, Pauze, Mercier, & Fortlin, 2000) found that most did not adequately control for the presence of ADHD. They found at 1-year follow-up that children with CD were significantly impaired on four of five measures of executive functioning, even when ADHD and socioeconomic status (SES) were controlled for. They also found that these executive functioning cognitive deficits could distinguish between children with CD and non-CD controls as early as 10 years of age. They concluded that most children with CD end up in disadvantaged schools that may further stunt their development of verbal skills (Toupin et al., 2000).

Other Biological Factors

Younger maternal age, unusually short or long labors, fetal distress, toxemia, eclampsia, and low birth weight have been associated with ADHD (Barkley, 2005). Low birth weight may reflect intellectual and neuromotor delays linked to prematurity (Breslau, Johnson, & Lucia, 2001; Nadeau, Boivin, Tessier, Lefebrve, & Robaey, 2001). The presence of un-diagnosed sleep disorders, which, when appropriately treated, resulted in decreased ADHD symptoms, has been noted in a significant number of children, as has the improved attention of children following tonsils and adenoid removal (Chervin, Dillon, Bassetti, Ganoczy, & Pituch, 1997; N. A. Goldstein, Post, Rosenfeld, & Campbell, 2000).

Heavy alcohol or substance use during pregnancy and toxin exposure (e.g., high levels of lead in poor housing conditions) have been related to higher levels of aggression and delinquency (Mick, Biederman, Faraone, Sayer, & Kleinman, 2002). J. M. Williams and Dunlop (1999) found that being early or late (off-time) in pubertal development contributes to deviant social status and antisocial behavior, which suggests the role of hormonal factors.

Earlier research in Denmark found a significant interaction between birth complications, early childhood rejection, and violent criminal offenses at ages 17 to 19 years (R. McGee & Williams, 1999). In reviewing the studies on birth complications and disruptive disorders, J. Hill (2002) noted that even when a range of factors, such as maternal smoking and prematurity, were controlled, birth complications were associated with an increased risk for these disorders. Convictions for violent offenses were predicted by the combination of maternal rejection and birth complications combined, but not as individual factors. Smoking in pregnancy increased the risk for conduct problems, and in the group with birth complications it was associated with violent crime. In fact, the combination of smoking during pregnancy and birth complications predicted the most serious forms of violent offense, including rape, robbery, and murder, and was related to rates of violence before age 18. Smoking in pregnancy was found to be an independent predictor of problems in boys with parental criminal behavior, boys who were exposed to physical punishment, and boys who had a history of child sexual abuse (Hill, 2002). Other factors associated with birth complications, including young maternal age, poor antenatal care, and alcohol and substance abuse during pregnancy, were also found to contribute to the risk for future antisocial behavior. Hill (2002) concluded that these factors in combination with hostile and inconsistent parenting might increase the child's vulnerability for disruptive behaviors.

Psychological Theories

Current theories of ADHD include Barkley's (2005) theory of behavioral disinhibition, which suggests that hyperactivity and impulsivity may reflect a common deficit in the inability to inhibit behavior and that this is the core and distinguishing feature of this disorder. M. D. Levine's (2002) attentional model emphasizes that attention is multidimensional, including such factors as mental energy controls, alertness, and mental effort. He describes ADHD children as similar to computers in that they have trouble "booting up" and maintaining a steady, reliable, predictable flow of the mental energy needed for cognitive work output and for getting good sleep. He found that ADHD children also have difficulty distinguishing between important and unimportant information, linking incoming information with prior knowledge and experience, and sustaining and monitoring concentration for a long enough period of time. M. D. Levine notes that impulsivity associated with inattention may not necessarily manifest in all activities. In other words, there may be more of a problem in less structured environments, such as home, than in more structured environments, such as school. Earlier research on temperament and ADHD failed to produce consistent findings (J. Hill, 2002).

In contrast, research on temperament and childhood externalizing behavior found that negative emotionality, intense reactive responding, and inflexibility were predictive of later disruptive behaviors (Sanson & Prior, 1999). Moffitt (2003) describes how a temperamentally difficult and vulnerable child experiences inadequate parental rearing. The child has problems with behavioral and emotional regulation, resulting in impulsive, aggressive, and antisocial unplanned acts. The child also has difficulty controlling anger and is often remorseful and susceptible to perceived provocation from peers. As the child is missing the precursors to the development of empathetic concern and is insensitive to the prohibitions or sanctions of the parents and other socializing agents, the child then develops an interpersonal style focused on the rewards of using aggression with a disregard to the consequences to others. Moffitt also reports that within the group with childhood onset, there is a subgroup of callous, unemotional children whose behavior is strongly related to a temperament characterized by low inhibition, psychological underactivity, low fearfulness in novel or threatening situations, poor response to punishment cues, and a preference for thrill seeking. This conceptualization has been supported by Frick and colleague's work (Barry et al., 2000; Frick et al., 2003; Frick & Morris, 2004).

Children with conduct problems have been found to have higher rates of deficits in language-based verbal skills and executive functioning, which remain significant even when other variables such as social class and race are controlled for. These deficits may decrease the child's capacity for self-control and impact problem-solving abilities, as in learning contingency rules (Lynam & Henry, 2001). In fact, aggressive children were found to generate fewer verbal solutions and more action-oriented solutions in response to social dilemmas and to misconstrue others' behaviors as hostile and negative meaning. Whereas children with ODD and CD do not differ in the number of solutions or the number of aggressive solutions with peers, CD boys used more aggression with teachers and parents (Pardini & Lochman, 2003).

The role of empathy and the presence of a hostile intention attribution bias have been linked to the development of CD, the expression of interpersonal aggression, and deficits in prosocial behavior and the ability to identify interpersonal cues (Pardini et al., 2003). Incarcerated delinquent boys were found to consistently attribute hostile intention to others (Eisenberg, 2000). In reviewing the information-processing model theory of disruptive disorders, J. Hill (2002) noted that these children made more encoding errors, suggesting that they are less accurate in their interpretation of the facts of a situation rather than deficient in interpreting social cues. Pardini and Lochman (2003) proposed that these children present with difficulties in social information processing at six stages: (1) encoding social cues, (2) making attributions and interpretations concerning social infomation, (3) identifying goals in the social situation, (4) generating solutions to interpersonal problems, (5) using the perceived consequences to determine which plan to act on, and (6) implementing that plan. They describe these children as consistently more likely than normal peers to interpret and attribute hostile intention to others, expect and value positive consequences for aggression, and endorse social goals destructive to interpersonal relationships. They tend to encode fewer social cues and generate fewer positive problem-solving strategies and are more confident in aggressive responses to a variety of social situations. They perceive themselves to be as socially acceptable as normal children and appear to overestimate their social competence, which the authors felt was a defense against loneliness (Pardini & Lochman, 2003). This internalization of the world as hostile results in the children's developing coercive, aggressive behavior to obtain their needs, which leads to deleterious interpersonal consequences such as peer rejection and isolation (Keiley, 2002).

To date there is no evidence that poor parenting plays a causal role in ADHD. However, social factors are likely to affect the severity of ADHD symptoms expressed, the types of secondary symptoms that may occur, and the outcome of the disorder (Frick & Silverthorn, 2001). The range of family factors associated with conduct problems includes parental criminality and psychopathology, large family size and parental discord, and hostile and coercive parenting (J. Hill, 2002). J. D. Burke and colleagues (2002) reviewed the role of psychosocial factors in ODD and CD and concluded that parental psychopathology was a stronger determinant of the offspring's disruptive behavior than parenting style. They note that punitive discipline was a common risk factor for children with a range of disruptive and internalizing behaviors and that the use of punishment reflected a general pattern of inept child-rearing practices that tended to escalate into coercive and aggressive behaviors by encouraging maladaptive cycles. Bassarath (2001) found that early aggression was related to maternal reports of persistent attention seeking at 12 months and noncompliance at 18 months, and aggression at 24 months related to externalizing behavior at 36 months. Stormshak and colleagues (2000) hypothesized that the relationship between the child's conduct and the family parenting style was dynamic and reciprocal and links the child's aggression with physical aggressive punishment, and oppositional behavior with low physical warmth. Adoption studies also found that genetically at-risk antisocial adoptees were more likely to receive negative parenting in their adoptive home. Children with CD elicited more negative interactions from all groups of parents, with the most negative interactions coming from their own parents (J. Hill, 2002; Simonoff, 2001a). Family conflict research indicates that harsh, inconsistent discipline and poor supervision increase the risk for both ODD and CD, and parental criticism and harsh punishment of 5-year-old children predicts the emergence of defiant, disruptive behaviors (Atkins & McKay, 1996; Simonoff, 2001a,b). Ineffective, punitive parenting practices and negative maternal control also relate to a higher number of later conduct problems (F. E. M. Gardner, Sonuga-Barke, & Sayal, 1999; Kimonis & Frick, 2006; Oxford, Cavell, & Hughes, 2003). Mothers of children with CD did not differ in the number of positive strategies they used in parenting but showed fewer preemptive strategies in disciplining the child at the age of 3 (J. Hill, 2002). According to R. McGee and Williams (1999), inconsistent parenting may lead to a failure to inhibit reward seeking and increase the risk of stealing. Coercive parenting has been shown consistently to result in aggressive behaviors, and abusive, harsh parenting, child abuse, and childhood victimization increase the risk of CD in children and of ASPD in adults (J. D. Burke et al., 2002; J. M. Eddy et al., 2001). J. Hill (2002) described Patterson's seminal description of the coercive family, in which the antisocial child's parents are inconsistent disciplinarians who use unclear commands and respond to their child on the basis of their mood rather than the child's behavior. They are unresponsive to prosocial behavior, which reinforces negative behavior, and are less likely to monitor their child's whereabouts, resulting in an increase in aggressive and oppositional behavior. As the oppositional behaviors are pervasive, these children are at risk for being overly punished across multiple settings, which the child finds incomprehensible and unfair and contributes to negative cognitions such as "It is always my fault" and a negative reaction to authority that persists into adulthood (Greene, 2006).

Bowlby's (1944) early study on the role of attachment was the foundation for research on the role of the parent-child relationship in the later development of delinquency. Pardini and Lochman (2003) note that the insecure attachment to their mother of preschool children with ODD may relate to maternal depression or stress. J. Hill (2002) also surmised that the negative communication associated with critical parenting and the mother's low responsivity to children with behavioral problems was associated with the presence of maternal depression. The presence of parental depression has been linked to development of CD in girls (Delligatti et al., 2003). In reviewing the literature, Keiley (2002) suggests that disruption in the attachment bond and affect regulation may underlie the development of CD. Attachment difficulties are attenuated when the child reaches adolescence and there is a failure to maintain relatedness, which further deteriorates with involvement in the juvenile justice system. Few families can extract themselves and break the cycle of repeated probation and incarceration, and the negative impact on familial attachments serves to escalate the cycles of negative affect and conflict (Keiley, 2002).

In examining the role of parental psychopathology and parent-child conflict in the development of CD, Marmorstein and Iacono (2004) found that the family environments of delinquents were less accepting, affectionate, emotionally supportive, and warm and involved less supervision. Studies of the child's role in the parents' monitoring behavior suggest that at-risk children tell their parents less about what they are doing, indicating that parents have less knowledge of the child's whereabouts at an early age (Stattin & Kerr, 2000). Some parents give up or cease to monitor their children, and many disruptive children have antisocial or substance-abusing biological parents (J. M. Meyer et al., 2000). Their mother gives birth at a young age, and the children tend not to live with their biological father. Family instability and parental disagreement on discipline by the time the child is 5 relates to antisocial behavior at 11 (Toupin et al., 2000). In males, the likelihood of a conviction for a violent offense by age 18 is related to parental lack of control and the number of changes in the parental figure before age 13, which also correlate with the prevalence of a DBD. Kazdin (1997a) noted that stable one- and two-parent families were less likely to have children with behavioral problems than families where the custodial parent had more than one partner. He also noted a referral bias in that clinic-referred DBD children had parents who have higher rates of antisocial behavior, substance abuse, and depression. Single-parenting was related to a threefold later risk for CD, and the context in which parental separation occurs has been identified as a risk factor for disruptive behaviors (R. McGee & Williams, 1999). A meta-analysis of the relationship between parental divorce and disruptive or antisocial behaviors found the association to be modest and that not controlling for maternal preexisting conditions may have created a spurious relationship (Amato, 2001; Emery, Waldron, Kitzman, & Aaron, 1999). Moffitt (2003) described early-onset, life-course-persistent delinquent boys from adverse, conflict-laden, low-SES backgrounds and CD girls with significantly higher levels of conflict with parents who may be less accepting of their behavior. He saw these children as caught in a cycle of conflict and disobedience. J. M. Meyer and colleagues (2000) reviewed data from the Virginia Twin Study on the role of genetic and family factors in CD development and found that family discord and maladaptation resulted in a twofold-increased risk for symptomatology. The authors also found that individuals with CD had a tendency to marry and have children with antisocial partners. As adolescents they are often part of an antisocial peer group, tend to marry impulsively and early, and lack planning in relation to key life decisions (J. M. Meyer et al., 2000).

Several aspects of peer relationships impact the development and maintenance of CD behaviors. Peer rejection is consistently identified as occurring in young children with conduct problems, and when a child associates with deviant peers this contributes to the initiation of deviant behavior (J. D. Burke et al., 2002; Dodge & Petit, 2003). Early onset of puberty in girls has been linked to the onset of deviant behavior. The effects of social disadvantage may also reemerge as a factor in high school, where the influence of a peer group, social mixing, and the youth culture creates a snowball effect. Moffitt (2003) describes adolescent-onset CD as an exaggeration of normal identity-formation issues, whereby the antisocial behaviors represent a misguided attempt to gain a sense of maturity and status from an antisocial peer group. In contrast, children with early-onset CD who show aggressive and antisocial behavior prior to joining a peer group may seek deviant peers secondary to rejection by normal peers and a lack of parental supervision (Kimonis & Frick, 2006).

Over the years numerous psychosocial or risk factors that contribute to the development of these disorders, particularly ODD and CD, have been identified (see Table 6.1). Kazdin (1997a) notes that risk factors tend to be less important in isolation, but when they cluster in packages they become interrelated over time and may interact with one another and that ultimately their effects are cumulative. Children involved in delinquency are characterized by the presence of multiple risk factors, including social and material disadvantage, familial instability and change, parental marital conflicts, parental criminality and substance abuse, impaired parenting, inadequate child-rearing practices, and poor parental supervision (Farrington & Loeber, 1998; Moffitt, 2003). Both CD and ODD have similar risk factors, and the accumulation of risk factors was found to be significant, although ODD without CD is associated with different and fewer risk factors, which are related to low intrafamily social support (J. D. Burke et al., 2002).

R. McGee and Williams (1999) reviewed longitudinal studies on environmental factors that relate to ODD and CD and quoted Farrington's (1995) seminal work by stating that there is a clear correlation between the sociocultural environments in which children are raised and antisocial behavior as expressed in CD and delinquency. The effects of living in public housing were found to counteract the presence of any individual protective factors that were present (Wikstrom & Loeber, 2000).

Loeber, Burke, and colleagues (2000) found that ODD and CD were more prevalent in the lower classes and were especially concentrated in neighborhoods characterized by high crime, social disorganization, and high numbers of juveniles arrested and involved in violent crime. Living in poor and disadvantaged neighborhoods characterized by higher density, older rental units, poorer schools with available drugs, community adults involved in crime, and racial prejudice is also associated with higher rates of later violence (Hawkins et al., 1998; Herrenkohl et al., 2000). While rates of ADHD, ODD, and CD are higher among children of lower SES, they do not relate to whether the parent is a recipient of public financial assistance but do relate to broader factors, such as parental education, employment, and occupational status. J. D. Burke et al. (2002) reviewed earlier research and identified a range of community factors, including living in public housing, level of disorganization, availability of drugs, and duration of poverty, that were linked to disruptive behavior (Hawkins et al., 1998; Herrenkohl et al., 2000; McLeod & Shanahan, 1998). McLeod and Shanahan (1996), looking at developmental trajectories of antisocial behavior and children's experience of poverty, found that unremitting poverty was associated with the highest rates of antisocial behavior. The authors hypothesized that persistent poverty increases parental stress, which impacts parenting skills and exposes the child to unsafe settings. In addition, limited access to health care may reflect parental psychopathology and poorer educational skills. Schools that are in poor physical condition, where little emphasis is placed on academic work, and where teachers are unavailable, have low expectations, and rarely use praise have been associated with CD (Little, Akin-Little, & Mocniak, in press). Thus the environmental factors of poverty, familial disharmony, and violence-prone neighborhoods all play a role in the development of CD (Mpofu,

Table 6.1   Risk and protective factors for disruptive disorders

Strongly Predictive Risk Factors
Prior antisocial behavior
Antisocial peers
Low popularity with few social ties or peer rejection
Higher levels of aggressive externalizing behavior
Early alcohol and substance use, particularly before age 12
Male sex
Maternal depression
Paternal antisocial behavior
Parental rejection and punishment
Poor supervision
Cognitive deficits in executive functioning

Moderate Risk Factors
Early aggression
Low familial SES
Poor parent-child relationship
High activity level
Risk-taking or impulsiveness
Short attention span
Minimal parental involvement or lack of supervision
Low familial emotional warmth
Parental negative attitude to child
Low school achievement
School dropout
Lower verbal IQ and higher nonverbal IQ
Early medical insult or neuropsychological factors

Environmental Predictors
Socioeconomic disadvantage or lower SES
Parent less than 21 years old when child is born
Low maternal education
Single-parent family status, including parental separation
Low intrafamily support and maternal depression
Parent-child interaction high on authoritarianism

Protective Factors
Female sex
High intelligence
Parental warmth and control
Warm, supportive relationships with adults
Positive social orientation
Resilient temperament
Competence at a skill
Presence of anxiety
Individual and familial commitment to prosocial norms and academic achievement
Recognition for involvement in extracurricular activities or larger social programs

Source: From "Conduct Disorder: A Biopsychosocial Review," by L. Bassarath, 2001, *Canadian Journal Psychiatry, 46,* pp. 609–616. Adapted with permission.

2002). J. Hill (2002) concluded that the greatest number of risk factors clustered in the group with the lowest social competence resulted in the highest number of behavioral problems on follow-up.

Several factors appear to be protective against the development of disruptive behaviors, and it is the accumulation of factors that is important (Connor, 2004). Positive personal relationships with at least one parent, family member, or important adult, prosocial peer relationships, and a positive school environment that emphasizes responsibility and self-discipline act as buffers against delinquency. Children who do not become delinquent are more likely to be firstborn, to be perceived by their mother as affectionate, and to have higher self-esteem and above-average intelligence. They also had a caretaker in the family, often a same-sex role model, who was not a parent and who was supportive of them and played an important part in their lives. These children presented with competence in several areas, including schoolwork and friendships, and were described as having an easygoing temperament (Connor, 2004).

DIVERSITY CONSIDERATIONS

The predictors and outcomes for CD are similar across all cultures in which it has been studied, and ethnicity did not relate to the prevalence of CD in the Epidemiological Catchment Area (ECA) study (Robins, 1999). Atkins and McKay (1996) found that the stressors of urban living, such as neighborhood violence and poverty, confounded the findings on diversity and economic hardship. All youth—White, African American, and Hispanic—showed a significant association between neighborhood violence and aggression. African American adolescents were found to experience the greatest economic hardship, which was linked to the highest rates of aggression. The authors cited earlier findings: 67% of urban (Chicago and Washington, DC) children witnessed serious assault; 33%, a homicide; 33% to 50% were victims of violence; and the rate for childhood externalizing behaviors was 4 times higher in urban areas than the national average (Atkins & McKay, 1996). Gorman-Smith and Tolan (1998) found that 65% of inner-city African American and Hispanic boys had been exposed to violence during the past year and had at least one family member who had been attacked or robbed. Among girls, the more severe the initial exposure to violence, the greater the future exposure to violence, and the early exposure to violence predicted subsequent violent behavior. In a survey of 8,000 residents in 300 Chicago neighborhoods, Sampson, Raudenbush, and Earls (1997) found that socioeconomic disadvantage and residential stability, as reflected in neighborhood social cohesion and informal social control, related to violent crime. They also found that ethnicity differences were confounded by social disadvantage. Of note is the finding that cultural identity and cultural values are protective factors against antisocial behavior.

There are also significant gender differences in the expression of these disorders. In girls ADHD is often a hidden disorder and underestimated, as the symptoms are less overt and often masked by comorbid conditions such as anxiety, moodiness, learning disorders, and substance abuse (Quinn, 2005). An earlier meta-analysis of the literature on gender differences (Gaub & Carlson, 1997) found a lack of difference in a range of factors, including impulsivity, academic functioning, and parental depression. However, differences did emerge among girls with ADHD, demonstrated by greater intellectual impairment, lower levels of hyperactivity and externalizing behaviors, and fewer CD problems. The authors reported that the higher inattention found in clinic-referred girls may reflect the role of referral bias (Gaub & Carlson, 1997). Quinn contends that the symptoms of anxiety, low self-esteem, disorganization, and forgetfulness are less overt than classically male disruptive behaviors. Also, girls are more likely to internalize symptoms, resulting in anxiety, depression, and social withdrawal as they enter adolescence or in substance abuse and early sexual activity. The girls may exert considerable energy to cope and to maintain a semblance of normalcy. In looking at the developmental progression of clinical symptoms, Quinn notes possible differences in the course of the disorder based on the presence of inattention symptoms that are often not apparent until the demands of middle school and the onset of puberty. The presence of good grades may not be indicative of the absence of ADHD, as these children may spend excessive time compensating. However, as academic demands increase, particularly in college, they may have more difficulty coping. Willoughby (2003) suggests that ADHD symptomatology in females may be more persistent and more impairing and notes that females outnumber males in seeking treatment for ADHD. Previous research (Nolan et al., 1999) shows that only the more severely impaired girls were referred to clinics. Cantwell (1997) found that gender is considered a moderating factor for ADHD, and clinic-referred girls with ADHD had more comorbidity and more severe symptoms than epidemiologically identified girls. Women with ADHD who were not diagnosed until adulthood had a higher risk of divorce and single parenthood, were less consistent parents, and experienced difficulties in home and occupational functioning (K. Nadeau, 2002).

Atkins and McKay (1996) found in their review of CD and ODD that girls are not well understood and often are overlooked in studies. Also, aggression and defiance in girls do not show the same continuity as for boys. Although aggression and disruptive behaviors are stable by fourth to fifth grades, the transition from childhood to adolescence suggests gender differences in comorbid conditions. As with boys, a core group remain aggressive; however, the larger group presents with more of the subtle socialized interrelationship aggression based on ostracism. In addition, a significant number drop out secondary to teenage pregnancy. Girls with a diagnosis of ADHD had a higher likelihood of a diagnosis of CD. The presence of depression appears to aggravate the relationship between CD and substance abuse for adolescent girls, resulting in more experimentation with nonprescription diet pills and nicotine dependence. They were also at higher risk for anxiety and depression, somatization disorders or somatic complaints, and headaches and stomach aches (Loeber, Burke et al., 2000; Loeber, Green et al., 2002).

INTAKE AND INTERVIEWING CONSIDERATIONS

Rapport

Establishing rapport may be difficult, as many children with these disorders are referred secondary to behavioral or disciplinary problems and the threat of expulsion from school. As a result, they may be reluctant to participate fully in an intake interview. For some families a sense of shame, feelings of parental failure, desperation, and anger at the

Table 6.2   Intake issues for ADHD and disruptive disorders

Be alert for rapport, compliance, and follow-through issues.

Rule out the role of medical conditions and substance-related disorders.

Determine risk for suicide, dangerousness, or impulsive high-risk behaviors.

Screen and assess for comorbid symptoms and disorders, especially learning, substance-related, mood, and anxiety disorders.

Consider confidentiality issues, third-party involvement, school and legal system.

Gather detailed history, including prior educational, court, and child protective services records.

Develop diagnostic time line identifying symptom onset, course, social stressors, and transitions.

Consider the role of developmental, cultural, familial, and peer factors.

Conduct a multi-informant and multisetting assessment.

Assess risk for school failure, dropout, and disciplinary problems.

Identify strengths and resources (including family support).

Assess family factors, parenting, and disciplinary practices.

Administer assessment measures, including self-report and rating scales.

ongoing family conflicts may accompany their child's referral. For others, there may be a high tolerance for the child's behavior, a tendency to minimize and disengage, which may be accompanied by resistance, expressed in scheduling difficulties and missed and late appointments. It is important not to overlook the genetic evidence on the familial clustering of these disorders and the role of parental pathology (Barkley, 2005; Meyer et al., 2000; Simonoff, 2001a,b). Thus, it is not unusual for an ADHD teenage son to present with clinical symptoms that his own father experienced but never had identified. Also, as described earlier, many of these problems are associated with maternal depression, parental substance-related disorders, and ASPD (Burke et al., 2002; J. Hill, 2002; Lahey et al., 2000). Given the heterogeneity of clinical presentations and the range of behavioral issues that need to be addressed during the intake, it is helpful to have an overview of the issues involved (see Table 6.2).

For those children presenting with attentional difficulties or who are very young, it is advisable to shorten the interview and schedule it early in the day. Many clinicians who work with these families arrange for a separate interview with the parents or have the parents complete a developmental questionnaire prior to the interview. As these disorders are often underrecognized and some clinical symptoms, such as inattention, can be misinterpreted as willfulness, the time of referral may be the culmination of several years of frustration and conflictual parent-child interactions. In many cases, the clinician will be working with both the child and the parent and will need to establish and maintain rapport with both (Boggs et al., 2003). The clinician needs to be very careful not to appear to take sides and not to play the role of the adolescent's friend or another parent. From the beginning the clinician must clarify the procedures for sharing information and review a policy of no secrets, as described in Chapter 1.

The very hallmark of ODD is defiance, and by definition the child may present as resistant, angry, hostile, and unwilling to communicate with the therapist as an authority figure (Greene, 2006). The establishment of a therapeutic alliance is difficult. In extreme cases, the child may refuse to attend, may leave abruptly, or may be extremely pleasant and compliant with the therapist, which serves to further antagonize the parent.

Trust is a pivotal issue in working with children with CD. Anything the child perceives as misrepresentation by the clinician, even if unintentional and seemingly harmless, is likely to validate the youth's impression that, as with everyone else, the clinician is bound to fail him or her. Rey and Walter (1999) note that the clinician is likely to be faced with multiple inconsistencies and contradictions during the evaluation. However, premature confrontation may lead to early and possibly irreparable alienation. These children also test limits, disregard boundaries, and ignore rules. Hence the therapist needs to be direct and consistent in responding to such behaviors and clearly document all interventions. Working with children and adolescents with disruptive disorders is difficult, for these clients often engender strong feelings and reactions in the therapist that can cause countertransference. Children and adolescents with CD often present with bravado or threatening behavior, and those who feel the most helpless in their situations are the ones most likely to threaten, manipulate, or stonewall the clinician. This may cause the clinician to experience a range of negative feelings, including anxiety and frustration, in response to the adolescent's story. If the clinician appears afraid, angry, or judgmental, this may elicit a negative, menacing, and possibly assaultive response from the patient. It is important to be careful to avoid over- or underresponding to the adolescent's or child's antisocial behavior and to remember that it is the youth who must learn to gain control.

In addition to addressing issues of behavioral impulsivity and danger to others, the clinician needs to be alert for the youth's self-directed danger, either through suicidal behavior or by engagement in high-risk behavior. These children are also at high risk for involvement in substance abuse, which should be assessed at the onset and throughout therapy. As many of these families are at high risk for dropping out before the evaluation is completed, the clinician needs to address this in a proactive manner at the start of treatment using the techniques discussed in Chapter 4.

Interview and Assessment Strategies

Parent and Child Clinical Interviews

The clinician needs to determine the age of onset and be aware of what constitutes appropriate behavior for different developmental stages. Both ADHD and CD assign a specific age of onset, and, as previously discussed, it is important to identify that the core clinical symptoms have been present since childhood. A diagnosis of ADHD also requires evidence that the symptoms cause impairment in several settings and that the evaluation includes information from several informants (American Psychiatric Association, 2000b). Barkley's (2005) text provides an excellent description of the core features of this disorder and strategies for assessment and treatment. Given the strong genetic contribution for all three disorders, a comprehensive family history and a history of learning disabilities are essential. Accurate diagnosis of adult ADHD can be a clinical challenge as it is often a hidden disorder; a good marker for risk is low self-esteem against a background of solid abilities (Wasserstein, 2005). A careful clinical history is the backbone of an assessment for ADHD, which needs to be multimodal (Barton, 2001). M. D. Garber and Garber (1998) identify several diagnostic steps that are helpful for clinicians, starting with ruling out the presence of medical, hearing, and vision problems. It is important to also be alert for medical mimics and the most common causes of acquired inattention, such as head injury, lead toxicity, and seizure and sleep disorders. As Wasserstein (2005) indicates, there are currently no objective biological tests for ADHD. These disorders have a high base rate for allergies, and a detailed family psychiatric and neuropsychiatric history may be helpful.

The next step is to determine the nature of the primary emotional problem, including identifying the presence of learning disabilities, gaps in knowledge, academic weakness, and processing deficits. Many students may attempt to hide their deficits by acting out. It is essential to take a complete history identifying the onset and the nature of symptoms and the duration and course of the presenting problems, while being alert for comorbid conditions and associated features. Cantwell (1997) suggests considering ADHD from eight aspects that can be helpful in systematically gathering clinical information: the clinical picture, demographic factors, psychosocial factors, biological factors, family genetic factors, family environment factors, natural history of the disorder, and management of the symptoms. When assessing problem behaviors such as inattention, defiance, and aggression it is important to query about their frequency, intensity, and duration and to attend to the impact of these behaviors on the parents and other family members. The child's ability to follow rules, the parenting strategies used, and the consequences for noncompliance and parental supervision or monitoring should also be assessed. Given that these children are often exhausting to parent, levels of marital and family stress and discord need to be evaluated. It is also helpful to the parents to have them identify their child's positive qualities or strengths and end the interview on this note.

Wasserstein (2005) recommends that the evaluation include, in addition to clinical symptoms, an assessment of the current level of functioning and that the clinician be alert for underreporting. Clinical interviews with the individual and significant others can help evaluate the degree of functional impairment. The clinician needs not only to assess the amount of distress and dysfunction caused by symptoms but also be alert for any significant health risks or involvement in high-risk behaviors (e.g., risky driving, substance abuse). It is helpful to consider whether the individual is working excessively, at great personal and social cost, to compensate for the underlying cognitive challenges.

Clinicians treating adults also need to establish a childhood history of the disorder (American Psychiatric Association, 2000b). When reviewing the personal history, be alert for particular developmental markers that are suggestive of the presence of ADHD. In preschool, was there poor cooperation with peers or noncompliance and difficulties with transitions and focused group activities, as in circle time? At school age, were there problems with distractibility, hyperactivity, impulsivity, and the development of daily living routines, such as sleeping and toilet training? During grade school, was there trouble acquiring basic skills, poor handwriting, specific learning difficulties, disorganization, or signs of underachievement (Barkley, 2005; Weiss & Weiss, 2004)?

It is also important to screen for inattentive behaviors even at a very young age and especially in girls. Previous research (Nolan et al., 1999) shows that only the more severely impaired girls are referred to clinics, while many are overlooked. During adolescence, the markers for these disorders include appearing immature, engaging in more conflict with parents, maintaining poor social skills, partaking in high-risk activities, and having difficulty completing homework and long projects (Barkley, 2005). Adolescent boys with ADHD Combined Type tend to be more isolated, while girls with ADHD and CD tend to be more hypersocial. A highly organized home life can often mitigate the expression of many ADHD symptoms. In general, ADHD problems become more apparent as environmental demands become more complex and as external supports are removed (Barkley, 2005). Whereas the core symptoms of restlessness, distractibility, and impulsivity persist, many adults develop coping strategies, and a thorough evaluation, including work history and samples and interviews with significant others, is essential (L. A. Adler, 2004; Wasserstein, 2005; M. D. Weiss & Weiss, 2004).

Atkins and McKay (1996) suggest several specific considerations when diagnosing children with CD and ODD. They encourage clinicians to consider information from school-based assessments, including behavioral observations and peer and teacher ratings and reports. They note that, although the relationship between ODD and CD may be overstated, attention to ODD symptoms as early indicators of CD can result in interventions and an improved outcome for early-onset CD. It is also important not to ignore the nonaggressive pathway to CD that has few ODD symptoms. By using multi-informant and repeated assessments to evaluate the stability of symptoms, the influence of rater bias may be minimized. Community factors that impact on CD may also suggest the need for group intervention, in addition to targeting the most aggressive children (Atkins & McKay, 1996). The variability over time of the clinical presentation with girls emphasizes the need for repeated assessments from multiple sources (Delligatti et al., 2003). The co-occurrence of academic difficulties with CD and ODD warrants an educational assessment, a review of academic records, and a curriculum-based assessment. Rey et al. (1999, 2000) recommend that an evaluation of a child with CD also include a thorough physical examination and an evaluation of attendant health risks (e.g., sexually transmitted disease).

Diagnostic Interviews and Assessment Measures

Given the diagnostic complexity of these disorders, using a structured interview as described in Chapter 1 and obtaining a developmental history from parents is crucial. There are several standardized diagnostic interviews, including the NIMH Diagnostic Interview Schedule for Children Version IV, the Child and Adolescent Psychiatric Assessment, the Schedule for Affective Disorders and Schizophrenia for School-Age Children, and the ADHD Clinic Parent Interview, all of which may be helpful. The *DSM-IV-TR* requires a multi-informant assessment, and the correlation between different informants is often low. Children's and adolescents' lack of insight into their problems and tendency to overestimate their abilities make their self-report unreliable (Hoza, Waschbush, Pelham, Molina & Milich, 2000, 2002). As many children are referred secondary to a teacher's complaint it is important to obtain a teacher rating (Pelham, Fabiano, & Massetti, 2005a). Loeber and colleagues (2000) point out that different sources provide different types of useful child information that serve a variety of purposes in determining the level of impairment (Nolan et al., 1999). P. S. Jensen and colleagues (1999) examined data from the Methods for the Epidemiology of Child and Adolescent Mental Disorders Study on 9- to 17-year-olds and their parents. They found that for most disorders, when structured diagnostic interviews were used, the parent and child rarely agreed on the presence of diagnostic symptoms. The authors concluded, however, that the discrepancies reflect meaningful clinical concerns.

Because multi-informant evaluations are necessary for a diagnosis, teacher interviews are critical. Rating scales from multiple sources—parents and teachers—can facilitate the appropriate diagnosis and a comprehensive assessment. A number of questionnaires and checklists can supplement information gathered from interviews, such as the Child Behavior Checklist (CBCL), the Conners Rating Scales, and various depression scales (e.g., Center for Epidemiologic Studies Depression Scale). The CBCL does not include many items relevant to the *DSM* diagnosis of ODD, but the Conners Scales have items very similar to the *DSM* diagnostic criteria. Children with ODD often have high scores on the Aggressive and Social Problems scales of the CBCL. For adults, the Brown Attention-Deficit Disorder Scales are a 40-item self-report measure that addresses executive functioning, affect regulation, and inattention. The use of a standardized, retrospective self-report questionnaire, such as the Wender-Utah Rating Scale, is strongly predictive of an accurate diagnosis of ADHD and a good response to stimulant medication in adults. However, it is limited in its assessment of impulsivity and hyperactivity symptoms (Wasserstein, 2005). Evidence-based measures for the assessment of ADHD include scales that relate to the *DSM-IV* such as the SNAP (Swanson, Nolan and Pelham rating scale), the Disruptive Behavior Disorders, the ADHD Rating Scale, and the Vanderbilt Rating Scale. Other broad measures of ADHD that are evidence-based are the Child Behavior Checklist, the Child Attention Problems test, the Behavior Assessment for Children, and the Conners Parent and Teacher Rating Scales. More detailed descriptions of these measures for ADHD is provided by Pelham and colleagues (Pelham, Fabiano, Gnagy, Greiner, & Hoza, 2005). For conduct problems evidence-based measures include the Behavioral Assessment System for Children, the Achenbach System of Empirically Based Assessment, the Early Childhood Inventory 4, the Conners Rating Scales, and the Revised Behavior Problem Checklist. McMahon and Frick (2005) provide a comprehensive review of these measures.

The high level of comorbidity and associated learning problems for all three disorders indicate that a full psychological, educational, or neuropsychological evaluation may be necessary. In such cases, a comprehensive evaluation is important because it provides a description of the child's strengths and weaknesses, which can act as a baseline from which to monitor medication and therapeutic change. This assessment can also provide evidence for mandated accommodations and academic supports that may enhance academic success. Computerized tests of sustained attention can be used to discriminate normals from individuals with ADHD (Baker, Taylor, & Leyva, 2006). Although neuropsychological testing is not relied on in making a diagnosis of ADHD and there is no consensus on a neuropsychological profile for ADHD, such testing can identify the presence of any cognitive weaknesses and comorbid learning disabilities.

According to August and colleagues (1996), the assessment of risk and protective factors for these disorders is crucial as they provide targets for intervention. Thus, the mothers of children with ADHD alone or with ADHD and internalizing disorders may need a different type of intervention than mothers of children with ADHD and externalizing behaviors.

Crisis, Legal, and Ethical Issues

As many of these children are referred for treatment by a third party (i.e., the school or juvenile justice systems), the clinician needs to be very familiar with rules of confidentiality. The limits of confidentiality and the current HIPAA laws governing client information should be reviewed carefully with the client (see Chapter 1). Interviewing typically in-volves multi-informant and multisetting evaluations, so it is important at the outset to obtain all the necessary releases of information to gather any required reports. Given that the clinician will be coordinating interventions and working with different parties (pa-rents, schools, and juvenile justice), the role of the clinician and the nature of the shared information should be clarified and documented at the outset. Secondary to ongoing con-flicts with the child, the parents are at risk for relying on coercive discipline and harsh punishment; thus the clinician needs to stay alert for any indicators of child abuse. Because impulsive or oppositional children often engage in acting-out or high-risk self-destructive behaviors, the signs of such behaviors need to be continually monitored. Substance use, sexual acting-out, and any antisocial acts that pose a danger to others may warrant reporting to a third party (see Chapter 2). Although adolescents with CD may appear tough, they often have low self-esteem and are at increased risk for suicidal ideation, suicide attempts, and completed suicide.

DIAGNOSTIC CONSIDERATIONS

Common Comorbidities

As multiple diagnoses are far more common than single disorders for this category, on intake the clinician should probe for the presence of other disorders (Barkley, 2005; Greene et al., 2002; Maughan et al., 2004). Gadow and Nolan (2002), in studying comor-bidity in preschoolers ages 3 to 6, concluded that the clinical impact of comorbidity is additive, with the highest rating of symptom severity given to ODD combined with ADHD. In general, comorbid psychiatric symptoms are more frequently associated with ODD rather than ADHD. In contrast to children with ADHD alone, children with ODD and ADHD are more likely to present with depression and learning and communication disorders (Gadow & Nolan, 2002). The nature of the child's difficulty with peers and dif-ferences in developmental deficits (defiance versus inattention) reported by parents versus teachers can help differentiate ODD from ADHD. The reason for referral may also be different, as parents of children with ODD may seek help if their child is defiant primarily at home, whereas parents of a child with ADHD may seek help if school performance is suffering. Wasserstein (2005) recommends performing a general psychological evalua-tion, including a standardized checklist (e.g., SCL-90-R [Symptom-Checklist-90-Revised], Beck Anxiety or Depression Scales), which may be helpful in the assessment of comorbid anxiety and depression. It is important for the clinician to check if the symp-toms are constant comorbid symptoms or secondary to lifelong ADHD. Also, the presen-tation of comorbid disorders may change with age. That is, preschoolers with ADHD present with high rates of PDD-NOS, while school-age children with ADHD/I present with nonverbal learning disabilities.

The three disorders in this category are characterized by high rates of comorbidity with each other, with estimates ranging from 54% to 67% of clinic-referred children with ADHD who also have ODD (American Psychiatric Association, 2000b; P. S. Jensen et al., 2001; Newcorn, Spencer, Biederman, Milton, & Michelson, 2005). Looking at the longitudinal stability of ODD in preschoolers, Lavigne and colleagues (2001) found that not only was the disorder stable, but with time there was increasing comorbidity with ADHD and anxiety and mood disorders. The overlap of ADHD with disruptive behaviors is particularly true for the Hyperactive subtype (Barkley, 2005; Eiraldi et al., 1997; M. Weiss et al., 2003). Early literature consistently found that ADHD comorbid with CD or ODD was more common in boys than in girls and related to negative outcomes beyond the home, namely, school suspension, expulsion, and dropout (August et al., 1996; P. S. Jensen et al., 1997). Maughan et al. (2004) found a strong overlap between ODD or CD and ADHD for significant comorbidities and gender differences in 11 out of 14 studies. Studies of the overlap between ODD and CD suggest that in boys ODD may be a developmental precursor to CD, and the relationship of ODD and ADHD appears to be stronger for girls. They also found that 62% of children with a *DSM-IV* CD diagnosis also met the criteria for ODD, and 39% of girls and 46% of boys with CD met the criteria for another nonantisocial *DSM* disorder (Maughan et al., 2004). P. S. Jensen et al. (2001) concluded that the presence of ODD or CD in children with ADHD had been well established for several decades. The role of childhood ADHD in the development of CD remains controversial; what is clear that when both disorders are present there is a much earlier age of onset of disruptive behaviors and a poorer outcome (Loeber et al., 2000). However, the clinician needs to be cautious in interpreting these high rates of comorbidity, given that the 1990s is widely regarded as the decade of comorbidity and there is significantly higher comorbidity in clinical samples than in the general population (Berkson's bias; P. S. Jensen et al., 1997). Earlier research by August and colleagues (1996) found comorbidity rates of only 12% for ADHD and CD in the general population. Having said this, the identification of CD as a comorbid condition is important, given its association with poor prognosis and heightened risk for dropping out or being expelled from school and developing addictions. In a 10-year review of comorbidity and CD, N. D. Stahl and Clarizio (1999) concluded that comorbidity varies with age, sex, informant and diagnostic criteria, and sample type. The most malignant combination is CD or ODD and ADHD (Angold & Costello, 2001; August et al., 1996). Rutter (1997b) theorized that ADHD and antisocial behavior might represent different phases or manifestations of the same underlying liability.

Substance-Related Disorders

A review of community studies indicated that 60% of youth with substance use, abuse, or dependence disorders had a comorbid diagnosis, and CD and ODD were the most common (T. D. Armstrong & Costello, 2002). Early-onset substance abuse has been found to predict later criminality, and it is likely that the relationship is reciprocal, with each disorder exacerbating the expression of the other (Loeber, Green, et al., 2002). For children with ADHD the research is mixed, and few studies have examined the relationship independent of the presence of CD. In a small study (142 children with ADHD and 100 controls), Marshal and colleagues (2003) found that children with ADHD were more likely to become involved with deviant peers and consequently more likely to use substances.

Anxiety and Mood Disorders

Mood and anxiety disorders were found to occur particularly with the Inattentive Type of ADHD. These individuals may present with low energy and low arousal level and are often misdiagnosed as dysthymic (M. Weiss et al., 2003). Those with a hyperactive-impulsive clinical presentation are sometimes misdiagnosed as bipolar. Angold and Costello (2001) found that 14% of ODD and 14% of ADHD children had anxiety and 9% had a comorbid depressive disorder. It remains to be seen if depression develops as a result of ADHD or independent of it. Nonetheless, the presence of internalizing comorbid disorders increases the likelihood of nonresponsiveness to traditional stimulant medication. Sachs and colleagues (Sachs, Baldassano, Truman, & Guille, 2000) found that 62% of bipolar individuals also had ADHD. They cited an earlier study indicating that 94% of children treated at a pediatric psychopharmacology clinic met the criteria for mania and ADHD. Barton (2001), in reviewing the earlier research, found that 90% of children with early-onset Bipolar Disorder (BD) had ADHD as a comorbid diagnosis; the common symptomatology makes diagnostic differentiation difficult.

Angold and Costello (1996) found that although depression has little effect on the course of CD, the combination of CD and depression is strongly associated with suicide, especially when combined with alcohol abuse. An anxiety disorder combined with CD is associated with less impairment and lower rates of aggression and violent crime. In fact, childhood anxiety disorders appear to protect against the development of antisocial behavior through inhibition as a protective factor rather than withdrawal (Angold & Costello, 1996).

Other Diagnostic Considerations

Children with ADHD often present with a range of comorbid learning and language disorders (Barkley, 2005). On intake, 21% of children with ODD were found to also have a language disorder, suggesting that this may be underdiagnosed and the child's difficulties may be misinterpreted as noncompliance or inattentiveness (Speltz et al., 1999). M. D. Garber and Garber (1998) found that complicated speech and language disorders were more pervasive among children with ADHD; 20% to 30% had learning difficulties, and an even greater percentage had more specific academic skill deficits. They also found that 50% of children with Tourette's Disorder also have ADHD (M. D. Garber & Garber, 1998). Given the parenting challenges with these disorders, a history of child physical or sexual abuse and neglect should also be considered.

DIFFERENTIAL DIAGNOSIS

Attention-Deficit/Hyperactivity Disorder and Disruptive Behavior
Disorders versus Other Psychiatric Disorders

Typically, the differentiation of the disorders from other diagnostic categories involves the determination of whether the presenting symptoms are limited to illness episodes (for mood and anxiety disorders, see Table 6.3). If the problems of inattention or disruptive behavior occur independent of mood or level of anxiety, then a disruptive disorder is the most appropriate diagnosis (American Psychiatric Association, 2000b). The symptoms of irritability and inattention may be common to many clinical disorders; however, the pervasiveness of the presentation and characteristic clinical course can be used to differentiate between disorders. In addition, both ADHD and CD have age requirements before

Table 6.3   Between-category diagnostic differential

Disorder	Similarities with ADHD and DBD	Differences from ADHD and DBD
Substance-related	Agitation, hyperactivity, distractibility, antisocial behaviors	Symptoms are related to the direct effects of or use or acquisition of a substance.
Parent-child	Parent-child conflict	Lower persistence and intensity of defiant behaviors.
Learning disorders	Academic difficulties School problems	Discrepancy between ability and achievement. Circumscribed deficits not necessarily behavioral problems.
Anxiety disorders	Distractibility Inattention	Clinical symptoms are episodic and limited to periods of anxiety.
Mood disorders (e.g., Dysthymic Disorder, Bipolar Disorder)	Inattention, motoric slowing, irritability, agitation, grandiosity	Symptoms occur during and related to mood episodes. Later sudden onset, episodic, family history of mood disorder.
Mental retardation	Cognitive deficits Difficulty with executive functions	Significant cognitive impairment. Impairment in adaptive functioning.
Pervasive developmental disorders (PDD)	Inattentive, rigidity may appear as oppositionality Poor social skills	Characteristic impairment in several areas, including social reciprocal interactions, symbolic play, cognitive, language, and stereotypic movements. Earlier onset.

which clinical symptoms must be apparent. Unlike ADHD and many of the others disorders of childhood, ODD does not have a minimum age of onset.

Bipolar Disorder

The overlap between ADHD and Adolescent Bipolar Disorder (ABD) is of recent scientific and clinical interest. The rates of comorbid ADHD range from 70% to 90% for bipolar children and 30% to 60% for bipolar adolescents (Kowatch & Fristad, 2006). While cases of hyperactive children who develop Bipolar Disorder have been reported, research suggests that when ABD has an onset in adolescence there is a lower likelihood of comorbid ADHD (Biederman et al., 1996). There is overlap in the clinical characteristics of these disorders such as increased motor activity, irritability, hostility, and impulsivity or distractibility. Wilens, Biederman, and Spencer (2002) contend that symptom overlap alone does not account for the assignment of a comorbid diagnosis of ADHD and ABD:

ADHD is primarily characterized by the presence of cognitive and hyperactive or impulsive features; in contrast, BD is characterized by mood instability, pervasive irritability, cyclicity, possible psychosis, and a lack of response to structure. E. Y. Kim and Miklowitz (2002), in reviewing the difficulties with the diagnostic differentiation of these disorders, noted that ADHD and CD are regarded as developmental disorders, whereas BD is an episodic illness with a more abrupt onset and a mixed and rapid-cycling clinical presentation. They suggest that the bipolar episodes can be used to differentiate BD from ADHD and CD. According to these authors, the low base rate of childhood BD may contribute to clinicians' lack of exposure to it. In addition, the lack of appropriate diagnostic criteria and the salience of the acting-out disruptive behavior over mood symptoms may lead to an underdiagnosis of mania for these children (E. Y. Kim & Miklowitz, 2002). Differences between the disorders include nonoverlapping diagnostic criteria—euphoria and grandiosity—and an abrupt onset, which are characteristic of mania. In contrast, for CD there is a progression of rule-breaking behaviors and a lengthy prodromal period. The clinician also needs to consider the family context for both disorders: ADHD with comorbid BD presents as a distinct family subtype, with relatives having both a higher risk for ADHD and BD and an earlier age of onset; for BD individuals, there is a higher risk among relatives for Major Depressive Disorder (Barton, 2001).

Among the Disruptive Behavior Disorders

The differential of the disorders within this category is very complex (see Table 6.4) and is confounded by the high level of comorbidity and the controversy over the relationship of the disorders to one another. The *ICD-10* contends that ODD and CD are part of the same dimension of behavior, and that ODD is a milder version of CD, typically seen in children younger than 10. Early work by Angold and Costello (1996) proposed that there is a developmental pathway from oppositional problems in childhood through adolescent CD to adult antisocial behavior. J. D. Burke et al. (2002) reviewed a decade of research on ODD and CD and concluded that there is a lack of convincing evidence of a causal link between the two disorders. Loeber and colleagues (2000) also reviewed the research; they concluded that the results supported differentiating the two disorders but added that there is controversy as to whether aggressive behaviors should be considered part of CD or ODD. J. Hill (2002) reports that children who have both ODD or CD and ADHD have more ODD or CD symptoms and worse outcomes than either condition alone. According to Maughan and colleagues (2004), few studies present data on ODD and CD separately. One that did, the Virginia Twin Study, found that oppositionality may be a predisposing factor or a marker of broader behavioral and emotional dysregulation, including CD and a wide range of childhood disorders. They also noted distinct age profiles, with ODD rates remaining stable, while CD rates increase in the teens, and the majority of CD children had high levels of oppositional behavior that did not vary with age (Maughan et al., 2004).

Although ADHD is often comorbid with CD, the behavioral problems seen in ADHD rarely involve the violation of societal norms and the basic rights of others. Individuals with ODD may have significant difficulty getting along with others but are not apt to show the physical aggression toward people and animals or the more serious violations of others' rights associated with CD (American Psychiatric Association, 2000b), nor are they likely to engage in theft or deceit. As defined, ODD includes primarily verbal aggression and discordant interpersonal relationships. In contrast, CD includes a range of physical

Table 6.4   ADHD and disruptive disorders: key and discriminating features

Disorder	Key Features	Discriminating Features
ADHD Inattentive Type	Primarily inattentive Drowsy daydreaming Slowed cognitive tempo	Later onset Predominantly female Deficits in focused, select attention Greater academic difficulties Comorbid anxiety and mood disorders
ADHD Hyperactive-Impulsive Type	Excessive energy Difficulty sitting still Interrupts and intrusive	Earlier onset Predominantly male More motor, impulse control difficulties Behavioral problems
ADHD Combined Type	Features of both inattention and hyperactivity or impulsivity	Younger and male Deficits in behavioral inhibition Higher comorbidity with externalizing behaviors Higher peer rejection and problem behaviors Poorer prognosis
Oppositional Defiant Disorder	Recurrent pattern of negativistic, defiant, hostile, disobedient behavior to authority figures	Early onset, behaviors interpersonally focused Includes temper tantrums Defiant oppositional attitude may target specific individual Greater psychiatric comorbidity
Conduct Disorders	Persistent repetitive pattern of the violation of the rights of others and social rules	Greater number and intensity of aggressive and antisocial acts May be callous or lack empathy Adolescent onset: later onset and often peer influenced

Adapted with permission from *Diagnostic and Statistical Manual of Mental Disorders,* fourth edition, revised, by American Psychiatric Association, 2000b, Washington, DC: Author. Adapted with permission.

aggression, from bullying to rape to antisocial acts such as theft, fire-setting, and violation of age-normative rules (e.g., truancy; Simonoff, 2001a). Parents are more likely to tolerate ODD symptoms than CD symptoms, though this is not to say that parents do not become exasperated by their ODD child's behavior. Pardini and Lochman (2003), in examining the relationship of CD to ODD, state that while the two disorders share several correlates—low SES, parental ASPD, and poor parenting—CD is more related to adverse environmental factors than ODD. There is also a distinct group of ODD children who do not go on to have CD. The clinical symptoms of anger and spite are the most useful for predicting ODD diagnosis, and ODD symptoms are more prevalent than CD in preadolescent children. Pillow, Pelham, Hoza, Molina, and Schultz (1998) note that ODD children tend to purposefully interrupt and intrude on others, whereas ADHD children violate social norms unintentionally and engage in behaviors out of restlessness. Both ODD and CD exhibit forms of aggressive behavior; however, ODD has a more positive prognosis than CD, and it appears earlier and is less entrenched than CD.

TREATMENT

General Principles in Treating Attention-Deficit/Hyperactivity Disorder and Disruptive Disorders

The disorders within this category are often the most challenging for clinicians to address. The children and their parents may come to treatment with a history of family stress and conflict, school problems, and untreated comorbid mood and anxiety disorders. They may not be coming voluntarily but be mandated secondary to legal proceedings or under the duress of school suspension. These children are at risk for acting-out and engaging in impulsive, dangerous behaviors and are at high risk for school dropout and becoming involved with substances. In addition to continually assessing and treating the child's level of impulse control and comorbid conditions, the clinician needs to engage family members who may have challenges of their own, as effective treatment involves intervention in the home and school. Additionally, the time commitment in the early stages of treatment, low motivation, and parental lack of knowledge may present as barriers to treatment (B. H. Smith et al., 2000). An overview of the general elements of a treatment plan (see Table 6.5) and more disorder-specific intervention will now be discussed, followed by early and multisystemic interventions under "Advanced Topics."

Disorder-Specific Treatments

Attention-Deficit/Hyperactivity Disorder

Despite the multitude of problems experienced by children with ADHD and the chronicity of this disorder, few receive appropriate treatment (Barkley, 2005). In summarizing the literature on treatments for ADHD, Hinshaw and colleagues (2000) noted that treatment can be difficult as noncompliance and dropout are ongoing risks.

Medication   The standard in the field, as well as the most common intervention, for the past 50 years has been to treat ADHD with medication (Dodson, 2005; First & Tasman, 2004). The so-called first-line medications are methylphenidate (MPH), which is prescribed as Ritalin, Ritalin-SR, Metadate, and Concerta; amphetamine (AMPH), which is prescribed as Dexedrine, Adderrall, and Dextrostat; and pemoline, prescribed as Cylert. B. H. Smith, Waschbusch, Willoughby, and Evans (2000), in reviewing the effectiveness of medication for ADHD, concluded that it was a safe, well-established treatment that results in significant improvement. They found that the majority of children were prescribed one of two psychostimulants, MPH or AMPH, a decision that was influenced by the individual's preference for one over the other.

   McGoey and colleagues (McGoey, Eckert, & Dupal, 2002) found that low-dose pharmacological interventions reduced ADHD symptoms and increased on-task activity and compliance; the likelihood of medication side effects increased with the dosage. These medications have been found to increase blood flow to the prefrontal areas of the brain,

Table 6.5   General treatment interventions for ADHD and disruptive disorders

Area	Interventions
Individual therapeutic issues	Rapport issues. Monitor compliance and follow-through. Assess and monitor impulsive high-risk behaviors. Be alert for high risk for dropout and noncompliance. Assess comorbid learning, mood, and substance-related disorders.
Symptom management	Identify appropriate interventions. Consider multimodal approach. Refer for a medication evaluation. Manage comorbid conditions. Identify behavioral, cognitive, and psychosocial interventions. Facilitate school support, tutoring, and modifications. Establish collaborative relationships with allied professionals. Coordinate interventions.
Family interventions	Educate child and family. Treat coexisting family conditions. Family interventions, including communication and parenting issues. Refer to adjunctive family support groups.
Adjunct referrals	Encourage self-esteem-enhancing activities. Coordinate academic skill building. Include involvement in sports or social skill-building programs. Consider socialization experiences.
ADHD	Early assessment and diagnosis. Refer for medication evaluation. Facilitate individualized support and strategies. Refer to education and family support groups. Organize academic accommodations and organization tools. Teach social skills. Be alert for depression and anxiety.
Oppositional Defiant Disorder	Consider psychosocial interventions. Teach social skills and anger management. Refer to parent programs (e.g., parent management training, parent-child interaction therapy, and problem-solving skills training). Be alert for school dropout and depression.
Conduct Disorder	Early intervention for early onset. Assess role of peer group, parenting group. Consider intensive intervention (e.g., multisystemic therapy).

and for 3 in 4 children with ADHD they significantly reduce the core clinical symptoms (Greenhill et al., 2001; B. N. Kim, Lee, Cho, & Lee, 2001). They have been found to decrease hyperactive symptoms, such as fidgeting and off-task behavior, classroom disruptive behaviors, and problematic behavior, during parent-child interactions (Barkley, 2005; First & Tasman, 2004). N. Purdie, Hattie, and Carroll (2002), in a meta-analysis of interventions for ADHD, found that pharmacological interventions were more effective than other approaches and that they impacted behavioral symptoms (e.g., hyperactive-impulsive behavior). The medication does not typically decrease long periods of inattention or result in an increase in the initiation of interpersonal interactions, but it does result in improved relationships, with less aggressive and more appropriate interactions (Connor, Glatt, Lopez, Jackson, & Melloni, 2002). Medication has also been found to be effective in reducing the impulsivity and the poorly regulated behavior associated with ADHD, which results in decreased conflicts with parents and teachers and improved peer relationships. The effects of medication are often quick. Within a few days, significant changes in behavior can be observed, but there is no evidence to suggest that these improvements persist after the medication is discontinued.

The *Physician's Desk Reference* (*PDR*; 2006) reports that these medications produce few side effects, including mild transient loss of appetite, mild dysphoria, jittery feelings, headaches, and irritability. Other side effects can include gastrointestinal upset, sleep difficulty, blood glucose changes, increased glaucoma, hypertension, high blood pressure, and ticking for those with comorbid Tourette's Disorder (Biederman & Spencer, 2000). Cylert, which has been associated with potential liver toxicity and liver function disease, needs to be monitored biweekly and may not be practical for children who are afraid of needles. In rare cases, Cylert has also been associated with mortality and carries an FDA warning that has significantly decreased its use (First & Tasman, 2004; D. J. Safer, Zito, & Gardner, 2001). With these medications some individuals may experience moodiness, paranoia, and anxiety symptoms and in rare cases psychotic features (Cherland & Fitzpatrick, 1999). Screening for a history of these disorders and treating coexisting depression, anxiety, or psychosis can minimize these effects. Contrary to popular myth, the use of stimulant medication does not predispose the adolescent to substance abuse but rather acts as a protective factor, and there is little evidence that children develop tolerance to the medication (Barkley, Fischer, Smallish, & Fletcher, 2003; Faraone & Wilens, 2003). For many parents, however, lingering concerns about stimulants as controlled substances, their misuse, and the risk for substance abuse create a barrier to effective treatment (Bussing et al., 2003). It used to be thought that stimulants might adversely affect the release of growth hormones, because some children showed a growth rebound after discontinuing medication; these findings are not consistently supported (First & Tasman, 2004). Many parents prefer to have children stop taking medication during holiday periods because of concerns of potential medication side effects such as decreased appetite, sleep problems, stunted growth, and weight loss.

B. H. Smith and colleagues (2000) noted that problems with noncompliance and inconvenience reduce the efficacy of psychopharmacological interventions. Biederman and Spencer (2000) found that the multiple doses required by short-acting stimulants create problems of compliance for children who, by definition, are disorganized and inattentive, whereas long-acting stimulants adversely impact sleep. If the medication is administered late in the day, there is an increased risk of insomnia and loss of appetite. Some families have also expressed concerns about stigmatization of children at school. Extended-release medications are felt to enhance privacy. Biederman and Spencer found that although stimulants are effective and often the treatment of choice, at least 30% of individuals with ADHD do not adequately respond or are intolerant of the medication. Children with comorbid depression and anxiety, which in some studies is as high as 75% of ADHD children, typically have a lower response to stimulants.

Milich and colleagues (2001) found that there were few studies on the differential treatment response of ADHD subtypes, and it appears that the groups are equally sensitive to medication across doses. They note that hyperactive or impulsive symptoms were a greater predictor of negative outcome than inattention, and differences in medication responsiveness may reflect the greater severity of symptoms of the Combined subtype. Barkley (2005) notes that more information is needed on which types of treatment may be most effective for the different subtypes of ADHD. He reports that those who are Predominantly Inattentive benefit from stimulant medication but often need lower doses, which may minimize the impact of side effects and increase compliance. Most studies on medication effectiveness are on elementary school children, and medication effects may change after puberty. Also, there are few studies on the differences in treatment responsiveness for girls or the efficacy of stimulants in much younger children (younger than 6) and in adults. J. Stevens and Ward-Estes (2006) quote earlier research that found African American parents had low expectations for the medication (DosReis et al., 2003), and they note that the lack of information on the long-term functional outcome for children taking these medications is a serious limitation. In their meta-analysis, Faraone and colleagues (Faraone, Spenser, Aleardi, Pagano, & Biederman, 2004) concluded that stimulants were the most studied treatment and were effective for adults with ADHD; even though some individuals are nonresponsive or experience adverse side effects, few alternatives have been tried (Spencer, 2004).

Tricyclic antidepressants (TCAs)—imipramine, nortriptyline, desipramine, and others—are a consideration for those individuals who do not respond to stimulants. These medications have a longer half-life (12 hours) to decrease rebound effects, have better effects on mood and hyperactivity than on inattention, and are less likely to exacerbate comorbid tics. However, they also have severe side effects, including cardiac arrhythmias that can result in sudden death, and are associated with risks for lethal overdosing (Biederman & Spencer, 2000; Popper, 1997; B. H. Smith et al., 2000). In their review of effective treatments for ADHD, B. H. Smith and colleagues (2000) concluded that TCAs had minimal empirical support and debatable safety in their use for ADHD.

Strattera (atomoxetine) is a nonstimulant medication that blocks the noradrenergic transporter and has been found to decrease inattentive and hyperactive-impulsive symptoms (First & Tasman, 2004; Michelson et al., 2001). Its side effects are mild and similar to those of the stimulants, and it may be more acceptable to parents who do not want their children on stimulants (Caballero & Nahata, 2003). Spencer (2004) in reviewing the research notes that the child's ADHD symptoms decrease and functional outcome improves with atomoxetine, and the parents also report decreased stress and worry.

Multimodal Treatment   Dodson (2005) notes that psychopharmacotherapy may be the first step, but pills don't give skills, and longitudinal studies show how devastating untreated ADHD can be to children and their families (M. D. Garber & Garber, 1998). Concerns that medications have been overprescribed and inappropriately administered and that there is a subgroup of children unresponsive to medication led M. D. Garber and Garber (1998) to recommend a multimodal approach as the most effective long-term treatment for ADHD. This approach includes medication, psychological therapy, educational interventions, strategic tutoring, and social skills training. J. Murphy (2005) concurs that the most comprehensive approach to ADHD is a multimodal intervention that combines psychoeducation, medication, psychotherapy, compensatory behavioral self-management skills, tutoring, technological tools, and educational or occupational accommodations. The combination of interventions may also enable the child to take a lower dose of medication while improving the overall level of functioning (M. D. Garber & Garber, 1998). Barton (2001) describes an effective multimodal approach as involving different professional disciplines working together over longer time intervals, with periodic interventions. According to Quinn (2005), the use of a multimodal approach makes ADHD a very treatable condition in adolescence, and yet it is rarely considered (Gaub & Carlson, 1997).

The largest clinical trial of a multimodal treatment to date was the MTA Study (1999a), which was conducted for 5 years across six sites involving 579 elementary school children (ages 7 to 9.9 years old) with ADHD/C, of whom 70% had another Axis I condition. The children were randomly assigned into one of four conditions (each lasted 14 months): medication, behavioral management, combined (medication and behavioral management) therapy, and community treatment. The results, which were gathered at 14, 24, and 36 months, showed that medication had the most improvement across all groups and produced significant improvement in comparison to behavioral and community treatments. Medication combined with behavioral treatment was the most effective treatment. Specifically, 56% of children on medication alone showed a loss of symptoms; after 24 months this decreased to 38%. For those children assigned to the combination group of medication and therapy, 68% showed a loss of symptoms, which after 24 months dropped to 48%. The children in this group were on 20% less medication than the medication-only group, some of whom experienced adverse growth side effects. Of those given only behavioral treatment, 34% showed a loss of symptoms, which decreased to 32% after 24 months. When therapy and medication stopped, the benefits also stopped. The dropoff rate for those who continued to show a loss of symptoms was more dramatic for the medication conditions (alone or combined) than the behavioral-alone group. The children that fared worst were those in the community-referred group, who received no treatment despite having evaluations that documented a diagnosis of ADHD/C. Compared to a medication-only treatment, the behavioral program was twice as favorable among parents. Rowland and colleagues (2002) noted that, while medication was found to reduce ADHD symptoms, the combined treatment also improved social skills and parent-child relationships. The study has been criticized because the behavioral treatment was faded out but the medication treatment was not tapered off, and the psychosocial treatment package did not include cognitive-behavioral skills therapy (CBST) interventions.

P. S. Jensen and colleagues (2001) looked at the role of comorbid conditions in treatment responses for the different groups in the MTA Study. The authors concluded with a simple rule of thumb: If the child presents with ADHD and anxiety, all interventions are likely to be effective. If the clinical presentation consists of ADHD only or ADHD and ODD or CD, then medication is the most effective treatment and behavior therapy alone is contraindicated. For individuals with ADHD, anxiety, and ODD or CD, a combination of treatments that includes therapy offers substantial advantage over other treatments, particularly in terms of overall impairment and functioning outcomes. More recently there has been a move to develop treatment algorithms that integrate research and clinical findings into medication decision trees, including one for ADHD and its comorbid conditions (First & Tasman, 2004; Pliszka, Greenhill, Crismon, Sedillo, Carson, et al., 2000a, 2000b).

Psychosocial Interventions   There are a range of psychosocial treatments available for ADHD, yet only a handful have empirical support (Pelham, Wheeler, & Chronis, 1998; B. H. Smith et al., 2000). Behavior and contingency management (CM) interventions focus on increasing on-task behavior with the use of positive reinforcement, the appropriate use of reprimands, and the immediate effective utilization of response cost. Parents and teachers can be trained in CM principles to implement the interventions at home and in school. These programs can increase on-task behavior and decrease ADHD symptoms (Dogggett, 2004; DuPaul & Eckert, 1997). However, the results have been criticized as transient in nature as opposed to long term (Barkley, 2005; First & Tasman, 2004). M. D. Levine (2002) emphasizes that children learn in many different ways, and rather than allowing ADHD to become a catchall, it is important to identify the individual learning profile of the child.

Approaches involving cognitive-behavioral skills (CBST) include teaching children to give themselves instruction and helping them self-monitor their behavior. These skills can be taught in individual and group formats; however, they have not consistently produced significant change in ADHD-related behavioral problems. Barkley (2005) argues that training a child in more knowledge skills is not as helpful as trying to alter the motivation parameters associated with the performance of adaptive behaviors through operant procedures. However, others argue that ADHD is a heterogeneous disorder, and there may be those children who, because of developmental lags, have a skills deficit and not a performance deficit and could benefit from a therapeutic approach that attempts to teach such skills (Biederman et al., 2000). J. Murphy (2005, p. 611) characterizes CBST as particularly well suited to individuals with ADHD, since they respond best to an active pragmatic behavioral approach, which he describes as a "roll up your sleeves and get busy approach." He contends that cognitive strategies can be particularly helpful in erasing longstanding negative messages, faulty cognitions, and catastrophic thinking and emphasizes the importance of the instillation of hope for the individual and family (J. Murphy, 2005).

Family Interventions   J. Hill (2002) suggests that positive parenting techniques, reasoning, and negotiation all help the child understand social rules, gain responsibility, and witness positive maternal control strategies. Compromise and the use of preemptive strategies increase compliance. Behavioral parent training (BPT) and parent management training (PMT) programs (see Table 6.6) have a long history of success as empirically supported interventions for parents of children with ADHD, ODD, and CD (Chronis et al., 2004). These programs provide parents with explicit behavioral modification techniques based on the social learning of Patterson's group at the Oregon Social Learning Center and Kazdin and colleagues' work at Yale.

These programs have been described as step-by-step methods of teaching parent skills. Parents are taught to identify problem behaviors, to introduce stimuli (e.g., prompts, instructions, and modeling), to facilitate desirable behavior, and to use positive reinforcement. They also learn different methods of monitoring behavior, such as narrative record

Table 6.6   Typical parent training intervention

Overview of the disorder, social learning theory, and behavior management principles.

Develop daily home and school report card, checklist, and rewards.

Focus on attending to appropriate behavior and compliance, ignoring inappropriate behavior (e.g., whining).

Learn to give effective commands and reprimands.

Determine and implement rules and contingencies (e.g., when . . . then).

Develop and implement time-out procedures.

Establish home reward and response-cost system.

Focus on generalized contingencies outside the home, anticipating misbehavior outside home.

Learn problem-solving techniques.

Maintenance of program after weekly therapist contact ends.

Source: From "Enhancements to the Behavioral Parent Training Paradigm for Families of Children with ADHD: Review and Future Directions," by A. M. Chronis, A. Chacko, G. A. Fabiano, B. T. Wymbs, and W. E. Pelham, 2004, *Clinical Child and Family Psychology Review, 7,* pp. 1–27. Adapted with permission.

keeping, which can help establish the antecedents and consequences of problem behavior. The parents are educated on the link between their perception and response and the child's disruptive behavior. The typical program involves 6 to 12 sessions with the goal of providing the child with consistent parenting, clear boundaries, and consequences for noncompliance. Parents of children with ADHD learn how to observe the effects of medication at home and at school, provide daily positive reinforcement for appropriate on-task behavior, and create opportunities to enhance social functioning.

The strongest empirical support for BPT is with elementary school children with ADHD. The child's father's involvement was found to be a predictor of continued family engagement. Chronis et al. (2004) found that when BPT is coupled with school interventions and brief behavioral consultations it can be a part of a sustained multimodal intervention that is effective for children with ADHD. When behavioral social skills training is combined with BPT, there are greater gains and generalization. Pelham and colleagues (Pelham, Greiner, & Gnagy, 1997; Pelham et al., 2005) report on the effectiveness of an intensive 8-week summer treatment program that focused on social skill building in children with ADHD. The program had high parent participation and satisfaction, indicating it was an effective adjunct to BPT. In their review of BPT programs Chronis and colleagues (2004) also addressed the issue of the chronic nature of ADHD and the need for a maintenance program that helps parents deal with developmental transitions after the initial parenting intervention. Eyberg and Boggs (1998) suggest that the clinician incorporate periodic contact, parent self-monitoring, and booster sessions to enhance maintenance. The factors contributing to nonoptimal results and higher dropout rate include environmental stressors such as low SES, marital discord or a single-parent household, and parental problems such as psychopathology and maternal depression, which are often barriers to treatment (Chronis et al., 2004). The mother's low self-esteem, father's low parental efficacy, and his attribution concerning the child's noncompliance resulted in poorer response to treatment across interventions for children with ADHD (Hoza et al., 2000). Parental ADHD may also contribute to difficulty with adherence to the treatment plan; the parents of these children with ADHD were found to drink more alcohol than parents of non-ADHD children. The clinician needs to be alert for the presence of these disorders and marital dissatisfaction or conflict, which can undermine treatment. The MTA Study found that parents' expectations of themselves and their ADHD children and their parenting style impacted the treatment outcome (Hinshaw et al., 2000).

Oppositional Defiant Disorder

Medication   There is a lack of information about the response of children with ODD to medication. Rey and colleagues (1999) recommend reserving medication for situations where there is a comorbid condition, requiring medications such as are used for ADHD or depression. Newcorn and colleagues (2005) found that atomoxetine caused significant improvement in quality of life issues for individuals with ADHD and comorbid ODD. Similarly, Greene and colleagues (2002) found that treating children with ODD and ADHD with stimulant medication resulted in significant improvement in oppositional and ADHD-related behavior. The diagnosis of ODD confers significant clinical risk for psychiatric comorbidity, particularly for Major Depressive Disorder and Bipolar Disorder, and the treatment of these comorbid conditions with appropriate medication is essential for the treatment of the primary condition to be effective.

Psychosocial Interventions   For ODD children and their families the most successful treatments have coupled behavior management training for parents and child-based interventions aimed at correcting maladaptive social cognitive processes and problem solving in the children (Pardini & Lochman, 2003). These include using behavioral, structural, and strategic techniques to improve communication and reciprocity among family members, as well as how to be consistent and to resist coercion. Referred to as PMT, these are regarded as the most effective and well-established interventions for disruptive behaviors; however, many families still demonstrate only marginal improvements (Brestan & Eyberg, 1998; Greene & Doyle, 1999). In an excellent review of treatments for children with ODD, Pardini and Lochman (2003) identified Kazdin's problem-solving skills training (PSST) and PMT programs as two parent-training programs that are well established and empirically supported. The primary focus of these programs is the development of prosocial behavior and treating youth ages 7 to 13 diagnosed with ODD and CD. The child attends 25 individual sessions once a week focusing on problem-solving skills. The parents are taught to help the child use these skills at home and in the community. The PMT program consists of 16 individual sessions of a home behavioral component support; these are 2 hours long and run for 6 to 8 months (Kazdin, 1997b). Parents are taught how to develop and implement contingency management in the home, improve child-parent interactions, change behavioral antecedents, enhance the likelihood of prosocial behaviors, and improve the parents' monitoring, supervision, and discipline strategies. Both programs have been demonstrated to produce significant improvement in global functioning on follow-up. The PSST program was found to also improve the child's social competence and decrease self-reports of aggressive and delinquent behavior (Kazdin, Seigel, & Bass, 1992). Similar factors that impact BPT interventions were found to be related to a negative outcome: high rates of parents dropout; lack of effectiveness for dysfunctional families; and the more severe the CD, the less effective the treatment (Schoenwald & Henggeler, 1999). The results suggest the need to consider the interventions in a broader family context, including consideration of factors such as parental depression, substance abuse, and marital conflict (Schoenwald & Henggeler, 1999). Three other PMT programs for younger children with ODD or CD that have been demonstrated to be effective are McMahon & Forehand's (2005) Helping the Noncompliant Child (3- to 8-year-olds), Patterson's Oregon Social Learning Center Program (OSLC, 2007) for 3- to 12-year-olds based on Patterson's earlier work (1981, 1986), and Barkley's (1997c) Defiant Children (2- to 12-year-olds). Conner (2004) provides a detailed review of these programs.

Parent-child interaction therapy (PCIT) is an established program for preschool children diagnosed with ODD (Schulmann, Foote, Eyberg, Boggs, & Algina, 1998). It consists of 1-hour-per-week sessions until the parents master skills in naturalistic play settings. It begins by having a parent engage the child in direct free play; the parent is then guided in play to focus on positive interactions, which strengthen the parent-child relationship. Families demonstrated significant improvement; even with clinic-referred cases, child conduct problems were lowered and compliance was increased, in comparison to wait-list families (Eyberg & Boggs, 1998; Pardini & Lochman, 2003; Schulmann et al., 1998). Reviews of the research indicate that PCIT is an effective intervention for young children and their families with CD and ODD (Brinkmeyer & Eyberg, 2003; Rayfield, Monaco, & Eyberg, 1999).

The Anger Coping Program (P. C. Kendall, Reber, Mcleer, Epps, & Ronan, 1990; Lochman, Coie, Underwood, & Terry, 1993) is a school-based intervention modified for outpatient use for fourth through sixth graders with ODD and CD (Pardini & Lochman, 2003). Group sessions last for 45 to 60 minutes in school and 60 to 90 minutes in clinic settings, with a focus on anger control, coping strategies, problem solving, and use of self-thought and distraction to deal with anger. This program was further extended to enhance outcome, and individual and parent group sessions were added. In its new configuration, it is called the Coping Power Program (Lochman, Barry, & Pardini, 2003). Initial results showed improvements in the child's social competence and aggressive behavior and in parent parenting practices (Pardini & Lochman, 2003).

The Montreal Delinquency Prevention Program is a 2-year intervention for second and third graders (Pardini & Lochman, 2003). It includes a parent-training component based on Patterson's earlier model and a social skills and self-monitoring component for the child. The child component consists of a 45-minute once-a-week group of four to six children that includes prosocial peers. Several longitudinal studies have found that this program can reduce antisocial behaviors in childhood and adolescence, and the benefits were found to be long term rather than acute. Additionally, boys who received the intervention before age 12 had lower levels of delinquency and substance abuse and were less likely to have serious adjustment problems in school or to be involved in gangs and have antisocial friends (Pardini & Lochman, 2003).

For adolescents with severe ODD problems, hospitalization should be reserved for when outpatient treatment has failed or problem behaviors are escalating out of control (Rey et al., 1999).

Many of the programs just described initially used clinic-based families, and there were high dropout rates, limiting the ability to generalize results. Over the years the format was changed to incorporate group training and to utilize more cost-effective variations, such as videos and online feedback, which were found to be effective for families needing more intensive intervention (Eyberg & Boggs, 1998). Cunningham, Bremner, and Secord (1997) found that a community-based, group-training format (with about 27 participants) was associated with greater parent participation and child improvement, as compared to a clinic-based individual parent-training program. Chronis and colleagues (2004) describe a 9-week program called Strategies to Enhance Positive Parenting (STEPP) that involves a combination of didactic teaching, modeling, coping, and smaller single-mother subgroups to enhance retention and group-based PCIT. A variation of this program, called Coaching Our Acting-Out Children and Heightening Essential Skills (COACHES), is an 8-week behavioral parent-training program that uses in vivo sports experiences targeting fathers of children with ADHD.

Conduct Disorder

Medication   Stimulants have been found to be effective in reducing antisocial behavior and aggression in youth with or without ADHD. Steiner and colleagues (Steiner, Petersen, Saxena, Ford, & Matthews, 2003) found, in a fully controlled, double-blind, randomized study of youth with a diagnosis of CD and at least one crime conviction, that the seizure disorder medication divalproex sodium had a high success rate and few side effects. The results showed significant improvement in clinician-rated and self-reported impulse control and self-restraint. Of the clinic-referred children with CD, 60% to 90% also had ADHD; the medication was found to have little effect on CD without ADHD. While medication can be helpful in the control of affective aggression and pathological levels of anger, it is important for children with CD to develop internal controls, and thus medication should be used wisely and not viewed as a panacea. Mpofu (2002) reviewed medication studies for CD and found that, while low-dose neuroleptics have been found effective in reducing aggressive behaviors, the limited number of studies and the adverse side effects outweigh the effectiveness of the use of medication. He reports that antidepressants may be effective for 19% of children with CD and comorbid depression, but lithium was not found to be any more effective than a placebo. He notes that, given the side effects, psychostimulants should be considered only for children with comorbid ADHD. Though 25% to 35% of children with chronic behavioral problems respond to psychopharmacological intervention, the studies are limited and the side effects with this age group are as yet unknown (Mpofu, 2002). J. D. Burke and colleagues (2002) note that there are few randomized controlled studies assessing the effectiveness of medication for CDs.

Based on the theories that CD children have deficits in interpreting, processing, and encoding social cues and tend to attribute hostile intent to ambiguous situations, cognitive-behavioral interventions, which focus on social skill deficits, have been developed. These interventions concentrate on teaching the child in a small group format to inhibit aggressive or impulsive responses and develop anger-coping techniques, alternative strategies, and skills. The major limitation of this approach is the difficulty in generalizing and maintaining skills over a long period. Reviewing behavioral treatments for CD, Mpofu and Crystal (2001) report that failures are notoriously high. They reviewed specific cognitive-behavioral programs, including anger-coping interventions, problem-solving skills training, and attribution retraining. They found that treatment effects erode over time and that cognitive-behavioral methods achieve short-term gains and are unsuccessful with severe forms of CD or comorbid conditions. They concluded that problems with treatment compliance and motivation caused by external factors contributed to the poor outcomes. In addressing the barriers to treatment for referred CD children, Kazdin and

Wassell (1999) found that the child's dysfunction, the parent's psychopathology and stress, and the family's socioeconomic disadvantage were barriers to participation and adversely impacted therapeutic change.

Schoenwald and Henggeler (1999), in reviewing effective interventions for children with CD and substance abuse, describe functional family therapy (FFT), which combines social learning and family system interventions and focuses on reorganizing family relationships. For an average of 16 sessions in five and a half months, a therapist provides in-home family sessions lasting 90 minutes for families of children with CD. Participants rated the FFT intervention favorably, and on follow-up children were found to have misdemeanor but not felony recidivism. Keiley (2002) discussed a modification of these techniques, multidimensional family therapy (MDFT), which focuses on reattaching parents and adolescents and shifting from anger to fear and from hurt to healing. Schoenwald and Henggeler (1999) found that MDFT resulted in significant improvement in parenting but not always a change in the substance-abusing adolescent's behavior. They concluded that some adolescent maladaptive patterns are too firmly entrenched and that for chronic delinquency and serious substance abuse, the intervention was too little, too late (Schoenwald & Henggeler, 1999).

Keiley (2002) noted that the exclusive emphasis on parent training is only marginally effective in modifying delinquent behavior because of high dropout rates, additional confounding factors, lack of community support, high neighborhood violence, and poor schools (Cunningham & Henggeler, 2001). Moreover, he notes many of these programs neglected to address the underlying process that serves to continue the aversive behavior cycle and the maintenance of CD. He maintains that a multidimensional approach is necessary for treatment to be effective (Keiley, 2002).

Educational and Practical Interventions   Erk (1997) reports that ADHD children often do not understand their disorder; they spend hours of frustration at home and in school, and it affects all members of the family and causes myriad problems, including dysfunctional interactions and high degrees of conflict. A crucial first step in the long-term effective treatment of ADHD is educating the child and family about the nature of the disorder (Barkley, 2005). The clinician has to address preconceived notions, since misunderstandings play a significant role in compromising compliance and success. The family needs to understand that ADHD is a biological disorder and, to some extent, the ability to control attention, concentration, impulsivity, and restlessness is beyond the individual's grasp. Given that effective ADHD treatment is time-consuming in the early stages, parental encouragement and guidance are necessary for the child or adolescent to participate and complete treatment (B. H. Smith et al., 2000). As there is no cure for ADHD, it is important for parents to see treatment in relation to symptomatic relief and learn how to manage symptoms across the life span (J. Murphy, 2005). In the MTA study, parent satisfaction was found to be higher when parents received psychosocial treatment instead of medication alone (MTA, 1999a,b). Most parents report experiencing relief when their child is diagnosed by a professional; psychoeducation is important for families to understand the pervasiveness of the disorder. Presenting information on the disorder as a neurological condition helps the child or adolescent as well as the family to understand and fosters open communication and partnership with the clinician to work as a team to gain control over ADHD; this is invaluable in the building of hope. The clinician can provide a referral to and encourage involvement in family support groups such as Children and Adults with Attention Deficit Disorder (CHADD: www.chadd.org) or the Attention Deficit Disorder Association (ADDA: www.adda.org). For spouses or significant others, education is crucial. It is also critical that the non-ADHD partner believe in the ADHD partner's serious and committed effort at behavior change (J. Murphy, 2005). Marital or family counseling may also help, as ADHD is a considerable stress factor for significant others (Barkely, 2005; J. Murphy, 2005).

Young children with ADHD are at risk for expulsion from preschool secondary to disruptive noncompliance behaviors, thus limiting the child's exposure to preacademic instruction, socialization, and a structured classroom experience (McGoey, Eckert, & DuPaul, 2002). Barkley (2005) reports a screening prevalence of 18.2% for all types of ADHD for preschool children and notes that the most common problem encountered in these children is the inability to modulate behavior in response to different situational demands. In boys, difficulty remaining seated is often described as noncompliant or defiant behavior. These findings and the ongoing academic difficulties ADHD children experience, including the higher risk for school dropout, highlight the need for school-based interventions, such as effective contingency management for older children (DuPaul & Eckert, 1997).

To be effective for children with attentional and disruptive disorders the clinician needs to work with school personnel to build a successful intervention plan for the child. Under the Americans with Disabilities Act any individual with a legitimate disability, including ADHD, has the right to accommodations. To be eligible persons must disclose and document their disability and the extent of the functional impairment (J. Murphy, 2005). Assessment for eligibility can be done by school personnel or private psychologists and involves the administration of a battery of standardized psychoeducational and psychological measures. A typical battery includes measures of cognitive functioning or ability and achievement or academic skills. The results of the evaluation are shared at a meeting with the parents, school personnel, and involved clinicians, and an individualized education plan (IEP) is developed for the child. Academic accommodations may include extra time on standardized tests, testing in quiet distraction-free setting, course substitutions, books on tape, pairing with a model peer, priority registration, and special orientation support. It is important at the onset of this process that the clinician is very clear with the parents regarding what information is shared with the school and their role in this process. As working with school districts may be challenging for the novice clinician, some general guidelines are presented in Table 6.7.

The clinician will want to work closely with school counselors and teachers to ensure that the child is as successful as possible and to develop interventions to decrease disruptive classroom behavior. Awareness of the task and situational factors that enhance performance can help the clinician work with parents and teachers in modifying the child's school requirements and schedule to compensate for difficulties with sustaining attention and regulating activity level. Barkley (2005) recommends that difficult, complex, or tedious tasks be organized into smaller units, provided with greater clarity, and enhanced with more immediate and salient reinforcers for task completion. Given the findings on the variability in performance associated with time of day, activities that require greater attention and behavioral control should be scheduled early in the day. Parents need to help with homework planning and consider the child's need for breaks and difficulty completing

Table 6.7   Considerations when working with schools

Clarify your role and be aware of confidentiality issues.
Be cognizant of the nature of the evaluation and the information being shared.
Conduct a comprehensive evaluation with multi-informant and multisetting information.
Identify strengths and challenges in the child, content, curriculum, application, process, and skills.
Consider school and staff scheduling requirements, academic time lines, and transitions.
Know the child's rights and special education law.
Consider available, alternative, and community resources and adjunct referrals.
Identify preplanning strategies and backup plans.
Focus on concrete operationalized objectives; stagger goals and interventions.
Consider long-term objectives and goals (e.g., 1 year from now).
Obtain baseline measures; determine a system of follow-through and accountability.
Include review, monitoring, and feedback components.
Address need for individual, classroom, and testing accommodations.
Provide academic supports, skill-building services, and technology.
Evaluate recess needs, physical education, social, and summer support.
Identify subsequent meeting and reassessment time frame.
Consider the role of advocacy.
Clearly document and maintain comprehensive, current records.

work later in the evening. Scheduling homework in the late afternoons or early evenings, permitting some motion or talking during task completion, and interspersing periods of sitting with periods of exercise or movement can help (Barkley, 2005). These children may also benefit from peer-focused strategies that address social skill deficits, the school curriculum and life management skill acquisition. Effective environmental modifications for the classroom might include seating at the front of the class, away from windows or doors, and beside a good peer model. Restructuring assignments and implementing organizational strategies and routines, such as the use of day planners, at home and in school can be helpful. For students with CD, who are frequently low academic achievers and have poor relationships with peers and teachers, academic tutoring in math and reading can be effective, as can social skills training to improve academic success and peer ratings.

Adults with Attention-Deficit/Hyperactivity Disorder

When working with adults with ADHD it is important to be aware of differences in clinical presentation and to assess and treat comorbid mood and anxiety disorders (M. D. Weiss & Weiss, 2004). Stimulants have been found to be effective for adults with ADHD (Faraone et al., 2004). J. Murphy (2005) suggests very practical self-management skill building for adults with ADHD to deal with the disorganization and time management problems characteristic of the disorder. He suggests the following specific techniques: taking time in the evenings to practice proactive planning for the next day, making multiple copies of daily prioritized to do lists, using a planner to record appointments, learning and practicing time management skills, and using a watch and an alarm clock. The clinician may provide a brief 10-minute daily phone call and individual weekly sessions. Personal digital assistants (PDAs), such as Palm Pilots, can help clients stay organized, as can the use of Post-its for low-tech visual reminders. School and workplace accommodations may involve the use of assistive devices or technology.

For many, college offers myriad distractions, and it is not unusual for students with ADHD to become overwhelmed and to fail. Exploring nontraditional or smaller colleges may enhance success. J. Murphy (2005) notes that adults with ADHD who are successful in college accept their disorder and seek support to develop adaptive coping strategies.

As many individuals with ADHD experience significant impairment in occupational functioning secondary to disorganization and tardiness, career counseling may be beneficial. The lack of follow-through can create problems with peers and supervisors, which is compounded by the difficulty of tolerating a daily repetitive routine. Adults with ADHD may also receive workplace accommodations; a quiet nondistracting work environment, more frequent feedback reviews, flex time, restructuring job requirements, and access to more effective technology can all be helpful.

It is important to remember that ADHD is a lifelong neurobiological disorder that creates significant challenges for adolescents and adults, and as a clinician you need to adopt a developmental life span approach to intervention (J. Murphy, 2005).

ADVANCED TOPIC: EARLY INTERVENTION AND MULTISYSTEMIC TREATMENT

The early identification of ODD symptoms in preschoolers has provided a unique opportunity for intense intervention to alter future trajectories for delinquent behavior (Greene, 2006). The Incredible Years Project, started by Webster-Stratton (2005), is a 20-year ongoing study targeting preschool children at risk for ODD and CD. It developed into additional programs to meet the needs of children and their families with innovative ways of providing treatment, including the use of videos. Webster-Stratton noted that aggressive children at a very early age are at increased risk for being rejected by peers, for being abused by parents, and for dropping out of school. Additionally, very few of these children who needed services were receiving them. Building on Patterson's work, she developed the parenting clinic program, which includes videotaped modeling for families of at-risk children. The original program (BASIC) consisted of 26 hours of parent training over the course of 13 to 14 weeks. A therapist led discussions in small parent support groups of 8 to 10 parents and used videotapes for training, with the goal of supporting and empowering parents. On follow-up 1 year later, 93% demonstrated significant improvement in parental attitudes, child-parent interactions had a decreased reliance on violent disciplinary measures, the child's conduct problems were reduced, and the intervention proved more cost-effective than individual therapy. Three years later, however, 25% to 46% of parents and 26% of teachers still reported difficulties with the child's behavior. Webster-Stratton and colleagues (Webster-Stratton, 1996; Webster-Stratton, Reid & Hammond, 2001a) then looked at the factors that characterized the 30% to 50% of families who relapsed or failed to show long-term benefits. They found that these families were often divorced or single-parent households and that there was evidence of marital distress, increased maternal depression, lower SES, and high levels of stressors and alcohol, substance, and spousal abuse. Using these findings they developed the ADVANCE program, which was a 14-session addition to the BASIC program that focused on personal self-control, communication skills, problem-solving skills, and strengthening social support and self-care. Of note, only one family dropped out of this intervention.

When conducting follow-up interviews on these programs, Webster-Stratton and colleagues (Webster-Stratton, 1996) found that 58% of parents requested help with their child's homework, so they developed the SCHOOL program, which was an additional four to six sessions focusing on collaboration with teachers and the school to build good learning and homework skills (Webster-Stratton, Reid & Hammond, 2001a). In summarizing the results of the interventions, they found that 65% of families achieved sustained improvement in the child's behaviors, but they felt that their model for conduct problems was incomplete, as many of the children relapsed and failed to generalize their skills. Consequently, they developed a 4- to 6-day teacher-training program to teach effective classroom strategies for preventing peer rejection and behavior management. The addition of this component resulted in a decrease in aggressive behavior, an increase in positive social and academic behaviors, and a significantly higher parent-teacher bond (Webster-Stratton, 1996; Webster-Stratton & Reid, 2003).

In reviewing the earlier research of Moffitt and Lynam (1994), Webster-Stratton and colleagues (Webster-Stratton, Reid & Hammond, 2001a,b) noted that children with CD had significant social deficits. In response, they developed a 22-week social skills and problem-solving intervention, called the Dinosaur School, which was further modified to the Dinosaur Classroom-based Curriculum. The Dinosaur School is a program for 4- to 7-year-old children diagnosed with ODD or CD and their parents. The child attends Dinosaur School for 22 2-hour sessions, where videos and life-size puppets are used to model social skills, which the child then practices. The parent-training components consist of groups of 10 to 12 parents also for 22 2-hour sessions, which utilize videotapes and therapist-led discussion. Three years later there were overall improvements in parent ratings of their child's behavior, a significant reduction in conduct problems at home, and increased problem solving compared to wait-list controls (Webster-Stratton, 1996, 2005). The program was found to be effective in reducing conduct problems and increasing problem-solving skills even when the PMT was not part of the program (Pardini & Lochman, 2003). On follow-up the children were found to have increased problem-solving and conflict-management skills, and these improvements were maintained 1 year later. These interventions are now being applied in school settings and in collaboration with Head Start programs, and additional long-term follow-up studies are being conducted (Webster-Stratton, Reid & Hammond, 2001a). Webster-Stratton (2005, p. 548) emphasizes the interrelatedness of child, parent, teacher, and peer risk factors in the development of CDs and the need for a continuum of services provided to young children to "break the link in the cycle of disadvantage."

Multisystemic Treatment

Multisystemic therapy (MST) is an intensive, time-limited treatment approach of 3 to 5 months. It targets interventions within the family and between the family and other systems (Schoenwald & Henggeler, 1999). The goal is to empower the parents with skills and support to cope with raising an adolescent and to empower youths to handle the range of problems they encounter at home, from peers, and in the neighborhood. It is offered in the home, school, community, and neighborhood and involves intensive services of 2 to

15 hours a week per family. It provides around-the-clock availability of clinicians who, by design, have small caseloads for 4- to 6-month periods (Schoenwald & Henggeler, 1999). The program aims at targeting variables associated with delinquency and delivering services in the family's environment for the greatest outcome. It was initially developed in a university setting, and subsequent studies were conducted in the community using a master's-level case manager to coordinate treatment that included social workers, probation officers, specialized classroom interventions, and afterschool programs. Results for serious juvenile offenders and their families show reduced criminal behavior 4 years after treatment (Schoenwald & Henggeler, 1999). In a 4-year follow-up, 26% of those adolescents who underwent MST were rearrested compared to 71% of the control group. Adolescents who had multiple arrests and were treated with MST at the community mental health clinic were incarcerated 73 fewer days and had half as many arrests as non-MST peers. For children and families from divergent backgrounds, the intervention was found to be equally effective in reducing drug use, incarceration, and out-of-home placement 1 year later. Unlike other studies that were undermined by family dropout, this program resulted in a 98% completion rate by focusing on engagement and alliance (Schoenwald & Henggeler, 1999). The chief barriers to implementation of this form of treatment are the cost and the paucity of suitably trained therapists. Yet, as Schoenwald and Henggeler report, the cost of MST ($3,500) is significantly lower than the cost of incarceration or institutional care ($17,769 per offender per year in South Carolina).

Another long-term, multicomponent, multisite intervention is the Families and Schools Together (FAST) Track program, which targets children with severe conduct problems at school entry. It was developed by the Conduct Problems Prevention Group (1992) and involves intensive intervention during kindergarten to promote competence in the child, family, and school. It consists of 22 PMT group sessions, individual CBST child interventions focusing on anger management and problem-solving skills, guided small group peer play, academic tutoring in beginning reading, a case management component, and biweekly home visits. The goal is to intervene early through community-based intervention and to target the processes that play a role in the development of CD. In the early stages, the child is seen individually. After the initial intensive phase, there is ongoing follow-up contact by the case manager. There is also a strong treatment evaluation component. Follow-up results show that after the first year the children showed better coping skills, had better grades, and had positive peer relations, and parents demonstrated more warmth and involvement with their children. Aggressive disruptive behavior improved on 4 of 10 measures (Conduct Problems Prevention Group, 1999a,b).

Schoenwald and Henggeler (1999) review a range of alternative treatments for CD youth, including family preservation services (FPS) and therapeutic foster care. In the FPS model, the family is seen as a source of strength. Counseling and concrete interventions are implemented at home, involving crisis-based and family treatment interventions that typically last 4 to 6 weeks. The failure rates among FPS programs are high (Schoenwald & Henggeler, 1999). Therapeutic foster care either in a group home or in an individual foster family has been proposed as an alternative to institutionalization (Schoenwald & Henggeler, 1999). In extreme cases, residential placement made privately or with assistance from family or juvenile services may be necessary. These programs typically employ a strongly behavioral orientation and utilize treatment modalities such as group therapy and vocational training. A major problem with this form of treatment is the high staff turnover rate due to low wages, which makes it difficult for the youth to develop a meaningful therapeutic relationship with stable, caring adults.

Frick (2001) concluded that there are several significant limitations to the existing treatment programs for CD. Notably, a significant number of children do not respond to these interventions, and even among responders the behaviors are not reduced to a normative level. The greatest improvement is in children younger than 8 years old with less severe problems. For most interventions, the ability to generalize is poor, and the improvements are difficult to maintain over time, especially with older children from dysfunctional families. Frick (2001) contends that most treatments fail to address the causal factors in the development of CD, such as the psychosocial context and the transactional nature of the processes. He concluded that CD is a heterogeneous, multidetermined interaction of individual vulnerabilities including child-rearing problems, social-environment stressors, poverty, and poor schools. These factors do not operate independently but in a mutually dependent way. Thus, no single intervention will be effective for all children with CD. According to Frick (2001), the implications and the clinical challenge are in tailoring the treatment to the individual needs of the child; the clinician must be flexible and have a very clear conceptualization of the child that involves a multidisciplinary approach to treatment. There is also a need for information on effective treatment to be disseminated (Frick, 2001). Toward this end, the Center for the Study and Prevention of Violence at the University of Colorado at Boulder has developed a website for the dissemination of information on well-evaluated intervention programs called Blueprints for Violence Prevention Program (www.colorado.edu/cspv/blueprints/).

A great deal of money is still spent emphasizing the imprisonment of law-offending youth rather than rehabilitation or prevention intervention. Until this approach changes, the number of incarcerated adolescents will continue to rise.

Chapter 7

COGNITIVE DISORDERS

The Office of the U.S. Surgeon General (U.S. Department of Health and Human Services, 1999) estimates that severe cognitive disorders affect nearly 8% of the adult population. The risk of many cognitive disorders (e.g., dementia, delirium) increases with age, and ongoing medical advances continue to result in an unprecedented ability to extend life. Thus the prevalence of cognitive disorders will only continue to rise. For example, whereas only about 5% of men and women between the ages of 65 and 74 have Dementia of the Alzheimer's Type, nearly half of those age 85 and older may have the disease (National Institute on Aging, 2006). Thus, for the foreseeable future, cognitive disorders will represent a major health crisis. Treatment of cognitive disorders should be conceptualized as multidisciplinary; a clinician involved in the treatment of cognitively disordered clients can expect to interact with primary care physicians, neurologists, psychiatrists, and occupational therapists. For clients in the early stages of dementia or whose cognitive disorder involves relatively circumscribed cognitive impairment, psychotherapy can address coping with the realization of lost or dwindling abilities and fears about the future, psychoeducation regarding the illness, preparations for the future, determining ways in which deficits may be compensated for, and encouraging as much functional independence as is safely and practically possible. However, in some cases (e.g., delirium, severe dementia), treatment will be carried out primarily by medical professionals, and the clinician's work will center on helping family members cope with the tremendous emotional and practical aftermath of witnessing a loved one change, both in terms of abilities and personality. It is imperative for clinicians to be aware of the symptoms and signs associated with various cognitive disorders, which can share similar features but have very different treatment approaches and prognoses. For example, recognition of delirium is important since this condition is largely reversible and reflects an underlying medical condition that requires prompt treatment. This chapter addresses the clinical presentation, diagnosis, and treatment of delirium, dementia (i.e., Vascular Dementia, Dementia of the Alzheimer's Type, which together account for the most cases of dementia), and amnestic disorder.

HISTORICAL OVERVIEW

Cognitive disorders such as dementia and delirium have likely afflicted human beings since time immemorial. Some of the earliest written accounts of dementia and delirium date to the first century AD (Boller & Forbes, 1998; Lipowski; 1990). Although called by different names, descriptions of these conditions were often remarkably similar to what is observed today. For example, Greek and Roman medical writers described an acute condition called *phrenitis* that could be brought on by factors such as fever and that was associated with disruptions in cognition, behavior, and sleep; this appears quite similar to our current concept of delirium (Lipowski, 1990).

The seventeenth and eighteenth centuries, which were marked by medical advances such as increased knowledge of the structure and function of the brain, saw increasingly detailed descriptions of cognitive disorders such as delirium and dementia. Delirium, for example, was hypothesized to result from a variety of conditions beyond fever, and additional symptoms (e.g., perceptual disturbances) besides confusion were documented. However, in contrast to current conceptualizations, the term delirium was also broadly used to describe agitation and disorganized behavior associated with severe mental illness (Rockwood & Lindesay, 2003). Although the use of the term dementia (*démence*) is found in fourteenth-century French writings, it became more popular in the eighteenth century, when physicians such as Phillipe Pinel and Jean Etienne Esquirol provided detailed written accounts of dementia and its purported causes (Torack, 1983). At that time it was believed that not only factors such as head injuries, old age, and certain diseases (e.g., syphilis) could cause dementia, but also unhappy love, unfulfilled ambitions, menstrual disorders, and political upheavals (Boller & Forbes, 1998). Despite the inaccuracy of some of these beliefs, early descriptions of dementia were often highly insightful and consistent with modern-day observations; Esquirol, for example, described dementia as "a cerebral disease characterized by an impairment of sensibility, intelligence, and will" (Boller & Forbes, 1998, p. 127).

In the nineteenth century, further refinements were made to the concepts of delirium and dementia. The preeminent German psychiatrist Emil Kraepelin distinguished dementia associated with old age from other conditions such as Schizophrenia (what Kraepelin termed *dementia praecox*) that were characterized by deterioration in mental functioning among relatively young individuals. The American psychiatrist Benjamin Rush introduced the term dementia in the United States and also wrote about the phenomenology of delirium in the first American psychiatry textbook. Writings on delirium tremens, a form of delirium associated with excessive alcohol use, also appeared during this time, as well as treatises on the pathophysiology and treatment of delirium more generally (Lipowski, 1990).

In more recent times, cognitive disorders such as dementia and delirium were frequently referred to as *organic* disorders, such as in early versions of the *Diagnostic and Statistical Manual of Mental Disorders* (e.g., *DSM-III;* American Psychiatric Association, 1980; *DSM-III-R,* American Psychiatric Association, 1987). This was in contrast to so-called *functional* disorders such as Major Depressive Disorder or Schizophrenia. However, the distinction between organic and functional conditions is no longer used (e.g., these terms were eliminated from the *DSM* system beginning with *DSM-IV;* American Psychiatric Association, 2000b) because as research on mental disorders progressed, it became increasingly clear that this dichotomy was neither useful nor meaningful. Many nonorganic disorders (e.g., Schizophrenia, Bipolar Disorder), for example, clearly had biological underpinnings and involved dysfunction in different brain areas, and for organic disorders environmental factors could interact with biological factors to affect outcome (A. Frances et al., 1995). For additional information on the historical evolution of cognitive disorders, the interested reader is referred to a number of excellent reviews (Boller & Forbes, 1998; Lipowski, 1990; Rockwood & Lindesay, 2003).

DELIRIUM

The term delirium refers to an acute confusional state characterized by changes in cognitive functioning, mood, thinking, perception, and sleep that occur over a short period of time (Trzepacz, 1996). Terms that have been used interchangeably with delirium include *acute brain syndrome, acute confusional states, metabolic encephalopathy,* and *acute brain failure* (H. I. Kaplan & Saddock, 1998). The use of such diverse terminology has been criticized as a factor contributing to the lack of clarity about the defining features of the delirium syndrome. Lipowski (1992), the prominent delirium researcher, asserts that the only acceptable synonym for delirium is *acute confusional states.* Delirious individuals display alterations in their level of consciousness and appear highly distractible, inattentive, and cognitively impaired. Behavioral and emotional changes may also be apparent, and the symptoms tend to fluctuate throughout the course of the day. Delirium can arise from many different causes, including underlying medical conditions or diseases, drugs, and toxins. Prompt medical evaluation and treatment generally result in a rapid amelioration of symptoms, but when left untreated, a delirium can result in coma, seizures, or death (American Psychiatric Association, 1999). Thus, unlike a dementia, which is irreversible, a delirium is largely considered a reversible condition, which underscores the importance of recognizing this disorder and referring the affected client for prompt medical evaluation.

Clinical Presentation

Problems with Consciousness and Attention

According to the *DSM-IV-TR,* a cardinal feature of a delirium is a disturbance of consciousness accompanied by a reduced ability to maintain attention (American Psychiatric Association, 2000b). The importance of *both* disturbances in attention and consciousness in the current *DSM* represents a change from earlier versions (e.g., *DSM-III* and *DSM-III-R*) that placed greater weight on attentional difficulties compared to problems with consciousness. In a clinical interview, problems with consciousness and attention may be manifest by a client's inability to tune out extraneous noise or other stimuli, answer questions, or follow instructions, or by the tendency to give perseverative responses (A. Frances et al., 1995). If asked to carry out a nonsensical command such as "Put your right hand on your right elbow," a delirious individual may attempt to carry it out without realizing it is impossible (M. G. Wise, Hilty, & Cerda, 2001). Inattention is common among children and adolescents with delirium and may be apparent in very young children (e.g., toddlers) as difficulty engaging them, and in older children and adolescents as distractibility and an inability to focus on a particular activity (Turkel & Tavaré, 2003). Although delirious individuals may also look sluggish, the impairment of consciousness is less likely to progress to stupor or coma (Trzepacz, 1996).

Other Cognitive Changes

Symptoms such as disorientation, memory impairment, language disturbance, and perceptual abnormalities (e.g., hallucinations, illusions) are commonly encountered in delirious individuals. With regard to the first of these, *disorientation* to time or place and an inability to recognize familiar people may be seen, but it is rare for delirious individuals to be so disoriented that they cannot correctly identify their own name (American Psychiatric Association, 1999; M. G. Wise et al., 2001). Disorientation in young children suspected of delirium can be difficult to assess, but when it can be evaluated (e.g., by asking questions pertaining to orientation to person and place), it is often abnormal (Turkel & Tavaré, 2003).

Delirious individuals often have problems with recent *memory,* experience difficulty registering, retaining, and recalling new information, and may make up information (i.e., confabulate); however, remote memory is usually intact (Lipowski, 1992). Memory problems can obviously be compounded by inattention and disorientation. Memory impairment appears to be more readily identifiable in older compared to younger children (Turkel & Tavaré, 2003). After the delirium resolves, an individual may be amnestic for (i.e., have no memory of) the delirium or may have only a spotty memory for certain events during that time.

Despite the fact that *language disturbances* have been estimated to occur in 41% to 93% of delirium cases, this symptom has not received major attention in the research literature (Meagher & Trzepacz, 1998). Language in delirious individuals may be incoherent, disorganized, and rambling, and impairments in understanding language (receptive language) may also be seen (H. I. Kaplan & Saddock, 1998). J. L. Cummings and Benson (1992) also note that whereas delirious patients may exhibit relatively mild naming problems but impaired articulation (e.g., slurred speech), the opposite pattern is more likely to be seen in dementia. However, individuals with subcortical dementias may exhibit features similar to those seen in delirious individuals (e.g., speech disturbances, less impaired language functioning), making a differential diagnosis between these two conditions more difficult (J. L. Cummings & Benson, 1992). Language abnormalities in delirium may also be evident through impaired writing ability (dysgraphia; American Psychiatric Association, 2000b). An example of language impairment is provided by Prugh, Wagonfeld, Metcalf, and Jordan's (1980) description of a 7-year-old child with severe delirium, who, in response to a question about his hospital experience, responded, "Whose funeral—all the cars around mean a funeral—I was in the hospital 2 or 3 days."

Delirious individuals (particularly those with more hyperactive versus hypoactive features) may develop *psychotic symptoms* such as delusions and hallucinations (American Psychiatric Association, 2000b; Meagher, O'Hanlon, O'Mahony, Casey, & Trzepacz, 2000; C. A. Ross, Peyser, Shapiro, & Folstein, 1991). Sandberg, Gustafson, Brännström, and Buch (1999) reported psychotic symptoms in 43% of their sample of elderly delirious patients, and Turkel and Tavaré (2003) reported an identical rate in their sample of children and adolescents diagnosed with delirium. Hallucinations and illusions result from abnormalities in perception that lead to difficulties meaningfully discriminating and integrating incoming stimuli; for example, the delirious individual may be unable to clearly separate dreams from actual perceptions (Lipowski, 1992). Hallucinations in the context of a delirium are usually visual and/or auditory and can range from simple shapes or spots to objects, people, and even complex scenes; delusions often develop in relation to hallucinations and are typically persecutory but unsystematized and fleeting. The development of organized delusions in delirious children appears rare (Turkel & Tavaré, 2003).

Symptoms of delirium develop over a short period of time (usually hours to days) and tend to fluctuate during the course of the day. The rapid onset and usually short course of a delirium are reasons why it is frequently referred to as an acute syndrome (Lipowski, 1992). Because the symptoms of delirium fluctuate during the day, the affected individual may sometimes appear lucid and relatively intact cognitively, which can complicate the diagnostic process. The greatest periods of lucidity are usually in the morning or midday, whereas symptoms are likely to worsen at night, which is known as "sundowning" (S. A. Jacobson, 1997).

Additional Characteristics

Sleep-Wake Cycle Changes

Disturbances in the sleep-wake cycle are common in both adults and children with delirium and may result in an individual's being very sleepy during the day but active and agitated at night (Turkel & Tavaré, 2003; M. G. Wise et al., 2001). Sleep, if it can be achieved, is likely to be fragmented. Delirious individuals can awaken from dreams that subsequently merge with hallucinations, leading some patients to describe delirium as being like a "bad dream" (Lipowski, 1992). Hypoactive delirious individuals are less likely than their hyperactive counterparts to exhibit pronounced sleep-wake cycle disturbances (Meagher et al., 2000). Although considered an associated feature rather than a core sign of delirium, according to the *DSM-IV-TR* (American Psychiatric Association, 2000b), sleep-wake cycle disturbances have been observed to be part of the delirium syndrome for centuries and should be considered an essential feature (Lipowski, 1992).

Emotional Changes

Delirious clients may exhibit a wide range of abnormal emotional responses that range from affective flattening to irritability, agitation, and rage, with apathy and fear being among the most common (Lipowski, 1992; Marin, 1990). A study of over 300 delirious seniors found that pronounced emotional symptoms were present in over 75% of cases, which underscores how common affective changes are in this syndrome (Sandberg et al., 1999). Similarly, Turkel and Tavaré (2003) reported affective lability in 79% of a sample of delirious children and adolescents, with apathy and anxiety present in 68% and 61% of their sample, respectively. Because these prominent emotional changes are often highly salient to care providers, misdiagnosis of a primary psychiatric disorder (e.g., depression) often occurs (Valan & Hilty, 1996).

Additional Neurological Symptoms

In addition to displaying the problems with consciousness, attention, and cognition previously mentioned, delirious individuals may also exhibit a number of other neurological signs, such as coarse tremor (common in sedative-hypnotic and alcohol withdrawal delirium), incoordination, incontinence, nystagmus (involuntary, rhythmical, repeated oscillations of one or both eyes, often seen in delirium associated with medication intoxication), asterixis (inability to maintain a fixed posture against gravity, common in delirium due to metabolic encephalopathy), and cranial nerve palsies (often seen in Wernicke's encephalopathy; American Psychiatric Association, 1999; H. I. Kaplan & Saddock, 1998; Lipowksi, 1992).

Psychomotor Disturbances

Delirious individuals often display abnormal psychomotor activity. In some cases, the individual may appear lethargic and sluggish, whereas in other cases, agitation and excitement can occur (American Psychiatric Association, 2000b). While hypoactive delirious clients may display greater persistence of their delirium and, according to some studies, greater cognitive impairment than hyperactive delirious clients, they are also more likely to be overlooked by treatment providers because of the less florid nature of their symptoms (Kelly et al., 2001; Koponen & Riekkinen, 1993). An open-label trial of olanzapine for the treatment of delirium found that hypoactive patients were significantly less likely to show a resolution of their delirium than those with hyperactive features, suggesting that this clinical feature may predict differential treatment response (Breitbart, Tremblay, & Gibson, 2002). Interestingly, it appears that the experience of a hypoactive delirium is just as distressing as that of a hyperactive delirium for the affected individual (Breitbart et al., 2002). It is notable that upwards of 50% of delirious individuals show a mixed pattern characterized by hyperactive and hypoactive states, whereas purely hypoactive or hyperactive subtypes represent smaller minorities of patients (Meagher et al., 2000; Meagher & Trzepacz, 1998).

Onset, Course, and Life Span Considerations

Onset

As noted earlier, a delirium typically develops rapidly (i.e., over the course of hours or days), but in some cases it may evolve more slowly (although it is rare for a delirium to develop over a period of more than a few weeks; Koponen, Rockwood, & Powell, 2002). A prodromal phase, marked by alterations in behavior, mood, and sleeping, may occur prior to the full onset of symptoms (Meagher & Trzepacz, 1998). This phase may last several days and may be marked by anxiety, drowsiness, insomnia, restlessness or lethargy, irritability, withdrawal, disturbing dreams, transient hallucinations, and increasing difficulty concentrating and judging the passage of time (Koponen et al., 2002; Lipowski, 1992). Symptoms of delirium typically resolve in reverse order of their appearance, and the time course varies depending on factors such as the underlying causes of the delirium (S. A. Jacobson, 1997; Rolfson, 2002). Some studies have shown that hyperactive delirious patients have shorter hospitalizations and lower mortality rates compared to mixed or hypoactive presentations (Liptzin & Levkoff, 1992). In general, a delirium will typically resolve within 1 to 2 weeks and usually will not last longer than 1 month (American Psychiatric Association, 1999; Lipowksi, 1992). It has been estimated that approximately 15% of delirious individuals have symptoms lasting up to 30 days or more (Sirois, 1988). Although a full-blown delirium may be relatively short-lived, some symptoms of delirium may persist for weeks to months after an acute illness has been treated (Marcantonio, 2002).

Course

Individuals who are delirious are severely impaired. Their level of confusion and cognitive disturbance make it impossible for them to carry out even routine tasks effectively or safely. Most studies have found that hypoactive and hyperactive delirious patients tend to display similar levels of cognitive impairment (Meagher & Trzepacz, 1998). Symptoms such as hallucinations, delusions, and emotional agitation increase risks to the affected individual's safety because they may lead to impulsive, ill-judged behavior (e.g., running out of the hospital and into the street). Delirious individuals may become transiently incontinent (especially common among the elderly) due to a decreased ability to recognize the need to use the bathroom and/or an inability to effectively communicate such needs to others (Marcantonio, 2002). They are also at risk for malnutrition and dehydration due to an inability to adequately attend to feeding and drinking because of severe attentional deficits, and may be likely to fall or injure themselves due to poor attention, psychomotor agitation, and lack of judgment (Marcantonio, 2002; Saravay et al., 2004).

The presence of a delirium is a poor prognostic indicator for medically ill individuals and has been repeatedly associated with longer hospitalizations, increased postoperative complications, and increased risk of mortality both during and following hospital admission (Ely et al., 2004; Inouye, Rushing, Foreman, Palmer, & Pompei, 1998; M. P. Rogers et al., 1989; van Hemert, van der Mast, Hengeveld, & Vorstenbosch, 1994). Delirium is also a poor prognostic indicator among the elderly and is associated with longer hospital stays (even when controlling for severity of comorbid medical conditions), greater likelihood of nursing home placement following hospital discharge, and greater mortality (J. Frances & Kapoor, 1990; Koponen et al., 1989; Levkoff et al., 1992; O'Keefe & Lavan, 1997; Saravay et al., 2004).

Although most cases of delirium are reversible, some individuals will not completely recover. Studies of nondemented delirious individuals have revealed that they are much more likely to evidence cognitive impairment at follow-up intervals ranging from 6 months to 2 years compared to nondelirious controls (J. C. Jackson, Gordon, Hart, Hopkins, & Ely, 2004). Although the causes of this phenomenon are undoubtedly varied and complex, this could occur if the delirium arose from a serious medical condition that involved irreversible damage to an organ system. In situations where the underlying cause seemed to be effectively treated, it is possible that the delirium process itself could have a toxic effect on brain functioning that is not yet fully understood (Marcantonio, 2002). In some cases, persistent cognitive decline following a delirium may reflect the long-term neuropsychological effects of anesthetics, sedatives, narcotics, and other drugs commonly used in medical settings on vulnerable individuals, such as the very old (Ancelin et al., 2001). Finally, the persistence of cognitive impairment following resolution of an acute delirious state may reflect an underlying, evolving dementia (Eikelenboom & Hoogendijk, 1999; Meagher & Trzepacz, 1998). It has been suggested that a delirium that lasts several weeks to a month should more properly be classified as a dementia, but this is still open to debate (Lipowski, 1992).

Life Span Considerations

It should be clear from the discussion to this point that old age is a risk factor for delirium. In older patients, delirium is often associated with a prolonged course that may exceed 1 month (American Psychiatric Association, 1999). Delirium in elderly individuals may present differently than in younger persons and appear less florid. Whereas poor attention, slow or vague thinking, incoherent speech, and increased psychomotor activity (e.g., plucking at bedclothes) are often seen, delusions, hallucinations, excitement, and aggression are less common in the elderly (Rockwood & Lindesay, 2003). At the opposite end of the age spectrum, delirium in children is generally considered rare, but its diagnosis and treatment are likely underrecognized (Turkel, Braslow, Tavaré, & Trzepacz, 2003). The *DSM-IV-TR* notes that children may actually be more susceptible than adults to delirium (e.g., in the context of febrile illnesses or from taking certain medications) due to physiological differences, including children's immature brain development (American Psychiatric Association, 2000b). Symptoms of delirium in children may be wrongly attributed to uncooperativeness, but the inability of familiar persons to console a child who is at risk for delirium should raise the index of suspicion for this disorder (American Psychiatric Association, 2000b). As with adults, delirium in children is associated with increased risk of mortality. Turkel and Tavaré (2003) reported a mortality rate of 20% in their sample of 84 cases of child and adolescent delirium, with the highest rates found among those with autoimmune disorders, organ failure, and organ transplants.

DEMENTIA

The term dementia refers to a syndrome affecting multiple areas of cognitive functioning that can arise from many causes. In the *DSM* system, the term dementia first appeared in the *DSM-II* (American Psychiatric Association, 1968). The two forms of dementia reviewed in this chapter, dementia due to Alzheimer's disease (AD) and Vascular Dementia, were first differentiated from one another in *DSM-III* (American Psychiatric Association, 1980). Regardless of the cause, the hallmark of all dementias is memory loss that is accompanied by significant impairments in other areas of cognition such as language, visuospatial functioning, and executive functioning (e.g., abstract reasoning, judgment, problem solving; Nixon, 1996). After the age of 60, dementia doubles in frequency every 5 years (J. L. Cummings, 2003); thus, as noted in the introduction to this chapter, dementia will continue to be a major public health issue because increasingly greater numbers of the population are surviving into old age. Annual costs associated with the diagnosis, treatment, and care of individuals with Alzheimer's disease exceed $100 billion (Ernst & Hay, 1994), and annual costs per patient (including direct and indirect costs) are estimated to range between $15,000 and $91,000 (Bloom, de Pouvourville, & Straus, 2003).

Beyond the financial burden associated with dementia is the significant emotional toll this disorder takes on affected individuals and their families. Those diagnosed with dementia must come to terms with the gradual waning of their ability to take care of daily activities, which results from progressive cognitive decline. In addition, there are likely to be marked changes in behavior and personality and an increasing vulnerability to the effects of any coexisting medical conditions or medications (Rabins, Lyketsos, & Steele, 1999). The strain is also great on family members, and most caregivers can expect to face between 3 and 15 years of exposure to the physical, psychosocial, and emotional demands of caring for a person with dementia (Vitaliano, Zhang, & Scanlan, 2003).

Many different factors can give rise to a dementia, including degenerative brain diseases (e.g., Alzheimer's disease), cerebrovascular disease (e.g., stroke), infectious diseases (e.g., HIV), traumatic brain injury (e.g., closed head injury), exposure to toxins (e.g., heavy metals, alcohol), and cerebral tumors. It is beyond the scope of this chapter to extensively review dementias caused by all of these factors; thus emphasis will be placed on a review of the two of most common forms of dementia: Dementia of the Alzheimer's Type (DAT) and Vascular Dementia (VD). The special topics section at the end of this chapter will review a common diagnostic challenge encountered in evaluating an individual suspected of dementia: differentiating dementia from depression.

Clinical Presentation

Memory Impairment

Problems with memory are a characteristic feature of dementia. The *DSM-IV-TR,* for example, requires the presence of memory impairment for a diagnosis of dementia, in addition to at least one other cognitive impairment (e.g., aphasia, apraxia; American Psychiatric Association, 2000b). Memory impairment in dementia is typically characterized by initial problems recalling recent information and utilizing working memory skills (i.e., the ability to temporarily store information in memory so that it can be manipulated; Andreasen, 2001). Long-term memories (i.e., information that has been stored for long periods of time) are initially preserved but eventually are affected in the later stages of dementia, to the point where severely demented individuals may not remember family members, friends, or basic information such as where they were born. For forms of dementia such as DAT, the progression of memory impairment is slow and insidious, which can make it difficult for the affected person, family members, and friends to recognize there are problems. If memory problems are recognized, they may be erroneously attributed to normal age-related declines in memory (i.e., benign senescent forgetfulness; H. I. Kaplan & Saddock, 1998). Affected individuals may also try to hide evidence of memory problems by choosing to discuss things that they can still remember well. However, as a dementia progresses, the individual's memory impairment will begin to interfere with activities of daily living and increasingly impair functioning. For example, demented individuals may show dwindling knowledge of current and recent events, impaired concentration, and decreased ability to travel, handle finances, or perform complex tasks (K. G. White & Ruske, 2002). Memory impairment can become physically hazardous; for example, a demented individual may leave the stove or iron on, forget to remove house keys from the front door lock, or forget to eat.

Individuals with VD characterized by cerebrovascular insults that are primarily in subcortical regions of the brain (the most common areas affected in this type of dementia) tend to display memory impairment that is not as severe as that seen in DAT; for example, such individuals may have difficulty freely recalling new information but are more likely to have intact recognition and to benefit from cues (e.g., will be able to select information that was recently presented to them from a list of choices; Erkinjuntti & Pantoni, 2000). However, to the extent that ischemic brain injury involves cortical areas of the brain, memory impairment may be more extensive and similar to what is seen in cortical dementias.

Aphasia

Demented individuals may also display language impairment or *aphasia.* Individuals in the early phases of DAT exhibit word-finding difficulties and circumlocutory speech characterized by the frequent use of nonspecific words, such as "thing" and "it" (American

Psychiatric Association, 2000b). Early in the course of DAT, affected individuals do better on a task asking them to name as many animals as they can in 1 minute compared to naming as many words as they can that begin with a particular letter (J. L. Cummings & Benson, 1992). However, eventually the ability to carry out both of these tasks becomes impaired, and as DAT progresses, the individual will also display increasing inability to name objects appropriately, even when given choices of words. In contrast, repetition ability and the ability to read aloud may remain relatively intact (J. L. Cummings, 2003). In later stages of the disease, DAT patients may simply repeat what is said to them or what they themselves say (known as echolalia and palilalia, respectively). Eventually the patient may become mute or able to make only unintelligible sounds. In contrast to DAT, those with VD are more likely to display impairments in speech *mechanics* such as articulation, prosody, and rate (A. L. Powell, Cummings, Hill, & Benson, 1988). However, when areas such as the middle cerebral artery are affected, aphasic syndromes such as Broca's aphasia and Wernicke's aphasia may be seen (J. L. Cummings, 2003).

Agnosia

Another cognitive deficit that may be seen in dementia is the inability to recognize objects in spite of intact sensory perception, termed *agnosia*. For example, a demented individual may not recognize faces of familiar people (*propagnosia*). A person with DAT may eventually exhibit a "mirror sign," which involves reacting to one's own mirror image as if it were another person (J. L. Cummings & Benson, 1992). Agnosia syndromes are particularly likely in VD when occlusion of the middle cerebral or posterior cerebral arteries leads to right hemispheric damage (J. L. Cummings, 2003).

Apraxia

Dementia can also be associated with an inability to execute motor activities in spite of intact sensory function, motor abilities, and comprehension, which is known as *apraxia*. An individual may be able to spontaneously perform a particular action but will be unable to do so on command. Thus, when asked to show an examiner how liquid would be poured from a teapot, apraxic individuals might indicate that they understand what is being asked but are unable to execute this request. Apraxia can be seen in both DAT and VD. Although not one of the early signs of DAT, this loss of knowledge about how to do things is likely to attract the attention of loved ones and family members that something may be seriously wrong with their relative (Andreasen, 2001).

Executive Functioning Deficits

Another area commonly affected in dementia is executive functioning, a broad term that encompasses cognitive functions related to goal-directed behavior, such as planning, reasoning, logical analysis, and mental flexibility. Executive functioning problems may be apparent early in the course of DAT and may be evident on neuropsychological tests that require the individual to use working memory abilities, shift cognitive set, divide attention, or reason abstractly (Logie, Cocchini, Delia Sala, & Baddeley, 2004; R. J. Perry & Hodges, 1999). In everyday life, problems in executive functioning may become apparent through increasingly poor decision making and judgment. In fact, impaired performance on cognitive tests that assess executive functioning has been correlated with reduced capacity to make competent legal decisions, such as consenting to treatment (Marson, Cody, & Ingram, 1995). Impairments in executive functioning may also manifest themselves through emotional changes (discussed further later in the chapter), such as disinhibition or apathy. Executive functioning deficits are also seen in VD, with the nature of the deficit being dependent on the brain areas affected by the cerebrovascular disease. For example, VD associated with subcortical involvement has been linked to deficits in working memory, response preparation, and context-nonspecific interference (Lamar, Swenson, Kaplan, & Libon, 2004). In a review of studies comparing individuals with DAT and VD matched for age, education, and severity of dementia, Looi and Sachdev (1999) found that VD patients exhibited more impairment in frontal executive functioning compared with DAT patients.

THE NINCDS-ADRDA CRITERIA FOR ALZHEIMER'S DISEASE

In addition to the *DSM-IV-TR* criteria for DAT, another commonly used criteria set is that developed by the National Institute of Neurological and Communicative Disorders and Stroke/Alzheimer's Disease and Related Disorders Association, known as the NINCDS-ADRDA criteria (McKhann et al., 1984), which is summarized in Table 7.1. The NINCDS-ADRDA criteria differ from the *DSM-IV* criteria in two important ways: (1) They differentiate between definite, probable, possible, and unlikely cases of DAT; and (2) they include laboratory and test findings among the criteria (e.g., definite DAT requires histopathologic evidence from biopsy or autopsy, probable DAT requires confirmation of dementia via neuropsychological testing). Widely used in clinical and research settings, the accuracy rates of these criteria in identifying cases of probable DAT varies between 65% and 92% (Klatka, Schiffer, Powers, & Kazee, 1996); however, they may not be able to adequately differentiate between cases of DAT and other cortical dementias, such as frontotemporal dementia (A. R. Varma et al., 1999).

Additional Characteristics

Emotional Changes

A range of emotional changes are common among demented individuals, including irritability, agitation, disinhibition, apathy, withdrawal, depression, and anxiety. Often, these symptoms (as well as psychotic symptoms, discussed later) are among the most distressing to family members. While emotional changes can reflect independent comorbid conditions, they can also be a manifestation of underlying cognitive impairments. For example, Binswanger's disease, a type of VD associated with white matter ischemic injury, is associated with neuropsychiatric changes that include diminished motivation and apathy (J. L. Cummings, 2003).

Apathy is one of the most common neuropsychiatric symptoms observed in demented individuals and may occur in over one third of demented individuals (Lyketsos et al., 2002). Clinicians may assume that a lack of interest in usual activities, social withdrawal, and decreased emotional engagement are manifestations of depression; although depression is commonly comorbid with dementia, these signs may actually be manifestations of apathy (J. L. Cummings, 2003).

Table 7.1   NINCDS-ADRDA diagnostic criteria for Alzheimer's disease

1. Criteria for the clinical diagnosis of *probable* AD:
Dementia established by clinical examination and documented by Mini-Mental Test, Blessed
  Dementia Scale, or similar examination and confirmed by neuropsychological tests.
Deficits in two or more areas of cognition.
Progressive worsening of memory and other cognitive functions.
No disturbance of consciousness.
Onset between ages 40 and 90, most often after age 65.
Absence of systemic disorders or other brain diseases that in and of themselves could account for
  the progressive deficits in memory and cognition.

2. The diagnosis of *probable* AD is supported by:
Progressive deterioration of specific cognitive functions such as language (aphasia), motor skills
  (apraxia), and perception (agnosia).
Impaired activities of daily living and altered patterns of behavior.
Family history of similar disorders, particularly if confirmed neuropathologically.
Laboratory results of:
  Normal lumbar puncture as evaluated by standard techniques;
  Normal pattern or nonspecific changes in EEG (e.g., increased slow wave activity);
  Evidence of cerebral atrophy on computed tomography with progression documented by serial
    observation.

**3. Other clinical features consistent with the diagnosis of *probable* AD, after exclusion of causes
of dementia other than AD:**
Plateaus in the progression of illness.
Associated symptoms of depression; insomnia; incontinence; delusions; illusions; hallucinations;
  catastrophic verbal, emotional, or physical outbursts; sexual disorders; and weight loss.
Other neurological abnormalities, especially with more advanced disease, including motor signs
  such as increased muscle tone, myoclonus, or gait disturbance.
Seizures in advanced disease.
Computed tomography that is normal for age.

4. Features that make the diagnosis of *probable* AD uncertain or unlikely:
Sudden, apoplectic onset.
Focal neurological findings such as hemiparesis, sensory loss, visual field deficits, and in
  coordination early in the course of the illness.
Seizures or gait disturbances at the onset or very early in the course of the illness.

5. Clinical diagnosis of *possible* AD:
May be made on the basis of the dementia syndrome; in the absence of other neurologic,
  psychiatric, or systemic disorders sufficient to cause dementia; and in the presence of variations
  in the onset, in the presentation, or in the clinical course.
May be made in the presence of a second systemic or brain disorder sufficient to produce dementia,
  which is not considered to be the cause of the dementia.
Should be used in research studies when a single, gradually progressive severe cognitive deficit is
  identified in the absence of other identifiable causes.

6. Criteria for diagnosis of *definite* AD:
Clinical criteria for probable AD met.
Histopathologic evidence of AD obtained from a biopsy or autopsy.

7. Classification of AD for research purposes should specify features that may differentiate subtypes of the disorder, such as:

Familial occurrence.

Onset before age 65.

Presence of trisomy 21.

Coexistence of other relevant conditions such as Parkinson's disease.

Source: "Clinical Diagnosis of Alzheimer's Disease: Report of the NINCDS-ADRDA Work Group Under the Auspices of Department of Health and Human Services Task Force on Alzheimer's Disease," by G. McKhann, D. Drachman, M. Folstein, R. Katzman, D. Price, and E. M. Stadlan, 1984, *Neurology, 34,* pp. 939–944. Reprinted with permission.

Demented individuals often display *agitation* that can range from pacing and repeatedly asking questions to more aggressive forms that include hitting, pushing, and cursing. Lyketsos et al. (2002) reported a prevalence rate of agitation or aggression in 30% of demented individuals and noted that this was the third most commonly occurring neuropsychiatric symptom in their study. The more severe an individual's cognitive impairment, the greater the likelihood that physically aggressive behavior will be displayed (Nasman, Bucht, Eriksson, & Sandman, 1993). Individuals may also become agitated as a result of experiencing psychotic symptoms such as delusions and hallucinations. G. R. Ford, Goode, Barrett, Harrell, and Haley (1997) found that agitated behavior was one of the top six most distressing patient behaviors according to dementia caregivers (other behaviors included dangerous behaviors, embarrassing behaviors, suspicious or accusatory behaviors, getting lost, and waking others at night).

Disinhibition may also be seen in demented individuals and be manifest in inappropriate behaviors such as acting in an overtly sexual manner with family members, friends, or even strangers, or making socially inappropriate comments. Common in forms of dementia such as frontotemporal dementia, disinhibition can also be seen in DAT and VD (J. L. Cummings, 2003). *Anxiety* is also fairly common in people with dementia and is often seen in the early stages of the disorder (Folks, 1999). In many cases, symptoms such as cognitive decline or the appearance of psychotic symptoms can trigger anxiety responses. Estimates of the rates of anxiety among individuals with dementia vary widely and have been reported in as few as 12% to as many as 69% of cases (Bolger, Carpenter, & Strauss, 1994; Jost & Grossberg, 1996). In DAT, anxiety is more common among those whose disorder begins prior to age 65 (J. L. Cummings, 2003). The relationship between *depression* and dementia is the focus of the "Advanced Topics" section at the end of this chapter.

Psychotic Symptoms

Individuals with dementia can experience psychotic symptoms, including hallucinations and delusions. It has been estimated that up to two thirds of those with DAT develop psychotic symptoms (Andreasen, 2001). Lyketsos et al. (2002) found that the prevalence of hallucinations and delusions was not significantly different among DAT patients and those with other forms of dementia (including VD). Furthermore, the phenomenology of psychosis in DAT and VD does not appear markedly different (Leroi, Voulgari, Breitner, & Lyketsos, 2003). More has been written about psychotic symptoms in the context of DAT than VD, so the information presented here primarily reflects this literature.

Common delusions in dementia include beliefs that things are being stolen from the individual, that the spouse or partner is unfaithful, and that family members or loved ones are not who they claim to be (J. L. Cummings, 2003). *Capgras syndrome* refers to a delusion in which the affected individual believes that someone he or she knows (e.g., spouse) has been replaced by an imposter who is an exact double. Harwood, Barker, Ownby, and Duara (1999) found a 10% rate of Capgras syndrome among individuals with DAT, which was correlated with the presence of other delusions, lower Mini Mental State Exam (MMSE) scores, higher Blessed Dementia Scale scores, and later illness stage.

Delusions among demented individuals may be precipitated by memory or sensory impairment. For example, demented individuals may believe that the reason they cannot find something in their home is because someone has stolen it, rather than realizing that their memory impairment is to blame. Similarly, a demented individual with sensory impairment, such as poor hearing, may misinterpret sounds and conversations in the environment, which then become incorporated into a delusion. Visual hallucinations are most common in dementia, followed by auditory hallucinations (Bassiony & Lyketsos, 2003). Although delusions become more common among individuals in the more advanced stages of dementia (J. L. Cummings, 2003), psychotic symptoms can be present at the time of diagnosis and may represent the reason the individual was referred for evaluation (Jost & Grossberg, 1996). In some cases, psychotic symptoms are time-limited, but they can also recur for years (Hope, Keene, Fairburn, Jacoby, & McShane, 1999). Because psychotic symptoms in older adults can be caused by medications (e.g., anticholinergics, antiparkinsonian drugs, anticonvulsants, stimulants, steroids), it is important for the client's treating physician to rule these out as causes (E. K. Mahoney, Volicer, & Hurley, 2000).

Visuospatial Difficulties

Individuals with DAT show impairments in visuospatial functioning early in the disorder that result in getting lost in familiar environments or getting lost when driving (J. L. Cummings & Benson, 1992). On neuropsychological testing, individuals with DAT show increasing impairments on tasks such as putting blocks together to replicate 2- and 3-dimensional designs and drawing geometric shapes (Guérin, Belleville, & Ska, 2002; Larrabee, Largen, & Levin, 1985; Malloy, Belanger, Hall, Aloia, & Salloway, 2003). Significant visuospatial impairment can also characterize individuals with VD, depending on the brain areas that have been affected by cerebrovascular insult. In cases where VD has affected subcortical white matter areas, these deficits may be even more pronounced than those seen in DAT (R. Q. Freeman et al., 2000; Libon, Malamut, Swenson, & Cloud, 1996).

Motor Problems

Severe motor difficulties are typically not seen in the early stages of DAT; however, motor slowing that is more pronounced than in normal controls may be seen during this time (Goldman, Baty, & Buckles, 1999). Extrapyramidal symptoms such as bradykinesia (slowed ability to start and stop movements), postural instability, abnormal gait, and rigidity are also not uncommon in DAT (Tsolaki et al., 2001). In later phases of DAT, motor abnormalities such as myoclonic jerks (i.e., unsustained, sudden muscular contractions) may be seen (J. L. Cummings & Benson, 1992). Motor symptoms such as limb rigidity, hyperreflexia (i.e., overactive or overresponsive reflexes), gait abnormalities, extensor plantar responses (also known as Babinski's reflex), and spasticity are common among individuals with VD (J. L. Cummings & Benson, 1992). *DSM-IV-TR* diagnostic criteria for vascular dementia require the presence of focal neurological signs and symptoms, such as abnormal motor functioning, for a diagnosis to be made (American Psychiatric Association, 2000). J. L. Cummings (2003) notes that gait disturbance, marked by hesitation and diminished stride length and step height, is a common sign of subcortical white matter ischemic injury.

Onset, Course, and Life Span Considerations

Dementia of the Alzheimer's Type is a progressive dementia in which the affected individual will exhibit a slow but steady decline in cognitive abilities over the course of the illness; thus, a sudden onset of significant symptoms would make a diagnosis of DAT unlikely (Knopman & Selnes, 2003). Because the onset of DAT is gradual, affected individuals initially exhibit mild cognitive impairment (MCI) that can be distinguished from normal aging but that is not severe enough to meet formal diagnostic criteria for dementia. This period may last for quite some time (e.g., up to 6 years) and is typically characterized by mild memory impairment (including impairments in delayed free recall and recognition; Bäckman, Small, & Fratiglioni, 2001). It has been estimated that of patients with MCI, approximately 10% to 15% per year will progress to a diagnosis of DAT; however, not everyone who has MCI will develop dementia (J. L. Cummings, 2003; Petersen et al., 1999). Poor performance on neuropsychological tests assessing executive functions (e.g., initiation and perseveration) and visual memory, as well as emotional symptoms such as depression and apathy, have been found to discriminate individuals with MCI who convert to DAT (H. R. Griffith et al., 2006; Mondrego & Fernandez, 2004; Robert et al., 2006).

Although DAT does not progress through discrete stages that are readily discernable from one another, staging paradigms have been developed to illustrate patterns of cognitive decline in this disorder and help illuminate the relationship between cognitive and functional impairment (Zarit & Zarit, 2006). Table 7.2 provides an example of such a guide. Early or more severe language impairment (e.g., naming ability, word fluency) has been found in some studies to predict more rapid decline among DAT patients (Boller et al., 1991; Huff, Belle, Shim, Ganguli, & Boller, 1990). In addition, MRI indicators such as degree of high signal intensities and ventricular volume have been found to predict rate of decline in DAT (Adak et al., 2004). Recent evidence indicates that levels of tau protein, a substance that is a component of the characteristic neurofibrillary tangles seen in the brains of individuals with DAT (see "Etiology," in this chapter) may serve as a biochemical correlate of severity and number of DAT symptoms, and that low levels of the ß-42 amyloid peptide may indicate a higher risk of early death (Wallin, Blennow, Andreasen, & Minthon, 2006).

The onset of VD is more likely to be abrupt and characterized by a stepwise deterioration in functioning (i.e., functioning that plateaus for a period of time and then abruptly declines) rather than the slow, gradual deterioration seen in DAT (Hachinski, Lassen, & Marshall, 1974). Because steps can be taken to treat underlying factors contributing to

Table 7.2   Stages of dementia due to Alzheimer's disease

Stage 1: Individual may appear clinically normal and does not complain of memory deficits. Clinical interview does not reveal evidence of a memory deficit.

Stage 2: Subjective complaints of memory problems are present. Most often, complaints are of forgetting names formerly known well or where familiar objects have been placed. No objective evidence of memory deficit in clinical interview. No objective deficits in social or employment situations. Individual displays appropriate concern about symptoms.

Stage 3: Objective evidence of memory deficit revealed in clinical interview conducted by a trained interviewer. Mild cognitive deficits may include (1) concentration problems, (2) difficulty remembering names of individuals just met, (3) word-finding problems, (4) difficulty retaining information from a recently read passage, (5) losing or misplacing valued objects, and (6) becoming lost in an unfamiliar location. Individual may deny cognitive problems and may experience mild to moderate anxiety in response to symptoms. Decreased performance evident in demanding work or social situations.

Stage 4: Moderate cognitive deficits manifest in many areas and are apparent in a carefully conducted clinical interview. Deficits likely to be seen include (1) concentration problems (e.g., evident on serial 7 subtraction task), (2) decreased knowledge of current events or recent events in own life, (3) deficits in memory of personal history, (4) problems traveling alone or managing finances, and (5) general difficulty performing complex tasks accurately and efficiently. Individuals remain well oriented to person and time, are able to readily distinguish familiar persons from strangers, and are able to travel to familiar locations without notable problems. Denial common at this stage. Flattened affect and withdrawal from previously challenging situations may also be evident.

Stage 5: Early dementia characterized by moderately severe cognitive decline. Individual can no longer function without some assistance. Deficits likely to be seen include (1) inability to recall a major relevant aspect of one's current life (e.g., individual may be unable to recall or may misreport address or phone number, names of family members, name of high school or college attended), (2) some disorientation to time (i.e., date, day of week, season) or place, (3) difficulty with serial subtraction tasks (e.g., counting backward from 40 by 4s or from 20 by 2s), and (4) some difficulty choosing proper clothing and/or clothing self properly (e.g., may put shoes on wrong feet).

Stage 6: Middle phase of dementia characterized by severe cognitive deficits. Deficits may include (1) occasionally forgetting the names of very familiar individuals (e.g., spouse), (2) unawareness of recent personal events and experiences, (3) very sketchy memory of previous personal history, (4) unawareness of surroundings (including year, season), and (5) difficulty counting backwards from 10 (and sometimes forward). Individual requires substantial assistance with activities of daily living (e.g., may be incontinent), requires assistance in traveling, and may exhibit disruptions in diurnal rhythms. Ability to recall own name still typically intact, as well as the ability to frequently distinguish familiar from unfamiliar people. Personality and emotional changes are often evident and may include (1) delusional behavior (e.g., accusations that spouse is an imposter), (2) anxiety, agitation, and/or previously nonexistent violent behavior, (3) obsessive symptoms (e.g., repetition of simple cleaning activities), (4) loss of willpower that results from an inability to carry a thought long enough to determine a purposeful course of action (i.e., cognitive abulia).

Stage 7: Late dementia characterized by very severe cognitive decline. All verbal abilities are lost and only grunting may be evident. Individual is incontinent of urine and requires assistance with toileting and eating. Ability to walk may be lost. Generalized cortical and focal neurologic signs and symptoms are frequently present. Individual's brain appears no longer able to tell body what to do.

Source: From "The Global Deterioration Scale for the Assessment of Primary Degenerative Dementia," by B. Reisberg, S. H. Ferris, J. J. Leon, and T. Crook, 1982, *American Journal of Psychiatry, 139,* pp. 1136–1139. Adapted with permission from the American Psychiatric Association.

cerebrovascular disease (e.g., hypertension, diabetes), early diagnosis can be key in decreasing risk of further brain damage, which can in turn lessen impairment and morbidity associated with this form of dementia (Burruss, Travella, & Robinson, 2001). The average duration of subcortical forms of VD has been estimated to be approximately 5 years, with patient survival being less than that seen for DAT (Hebert & Brayne, 1995). However, others report that survival rates and rates of cognitive decline are similar for DAT and VD (Agüero-Torres, Winblad, & Fratiglioni, 1999). Poor prognosis in VD has been linked to low education, poor neuropsychological test performance, and male sex (Hier, Warach, Gorelilck, & Thomas, 1989). The presence of symptoms such as delusions and hallucinations has been correlated with early institutionalization and more rapid dementia progression (Bassiony & Lyketsos, 2003).

AMNESTIC DISORDERS

Amnestic disorders are characterized by significant impairment in memory that is not due to either a delirium or dementia, and they differ from each another in terms of the etiology of the memory deficit (American Psychiatric Association, 2000b). For example, memory problems may be due to the persisting effects of a substance or may result from a medical condition such as head trauma or a seizure disorder (for additional information, see "Etiology" in this chapter). These disorders are seen less frequently in clinical practice compared to delirium and dementia but have provided important information on the anatomical substrates of memory (de Renzi, 2000). While the degree of impairment seen among patients with amnestic disorders varies depending on the location and extent of brain injury, these disorders are often extremely debilitating because the affected individual cannot effectively learn new information and may have difficulty recalling previously learned information.

Clinical Presentation

All amnestic disorders are characterized by impaired ability to learn and recall new information (referred to as anterograde amnesia), but an inability to recall previously learned information (retrograde amnesia) may also be present depending on the areas of the brain affected and the associated degree of damage (American Psychiatric Association, 2000b). For example, individuals with Korsakoff's syndrome (an amnestic disorder caused by thiamine deficiency that usually stems from chronic alcoholism) have damage in the hippocampus, thalamus, and frontal cortex and display both anterograde and retrograde amnesia. Even when memory for previously learned information is affected, memories from the very distant past (e.g., childhood) often remain intact (First & Tasman, 2005). Interestingly, amnestic individuals are typically able to perform normally on tasks that require the *immediate* repetition of information that can be held in short-term memory (e.g., a sequence of digits). However, if the information to be retained exceeds the short-term memory store or must be transferred to long-term memory (e.g., asking a client to remember a list of items after a short delay), the client will likely be unable to perform the task (de Renzi, 2000). Implicit memory, or memory for procedures (e.g., remembering how to drive or ski), is usually unaffected in amnesia.

Additional Characteristics

Other Cognitive Impairment

According to the *DSM-IV-TR* criteria (American Psychiatric Association, 2000b), the memory impairment seen in an amnestic disorder cannot be better accounted for by another cognitive disorder such as dementia and delirium. However, amnestic disorders may be accompanied by additional signs of cognitive difficulties (e.g., confusion, attentional difficulties, disorientation), which can be mistaken for symptoms of other cognitive disorders and thus complicate the diagnostic process (American Psychiatric Association, 2000b). For example, relative to normal controls as well as nonamnestic individuals and abstinent alcoholics, individuals with Korsakoff's syndrome not only display impairments in memory, but also deficits in frontal lobe functions such as fluency, cognitive flexibility, perseveration, ability to make affective judgments, and cognitive estimation (e.g., ability to judge attributes such as size, weight, quantity, and time; Brand et al., 2003; Oscar-Berman, Kirkley, Gansler, & Couture, 2004). Individuals with Korsakoff's syndrome may also display impairments in fine motor performance (e.g., finger tapping) that are possibly related to frontal lobe-mediated task initiation and persistence (Welch, Cunningham, Eckardt, & Martin, 1997). However, the primary and most significant impairment of amnestic disorders involves memory.

Confabulation

Individuals with amnestic disorder will often attempt to hide their poor memory by confabulating or creating detailed, seemingly credible accounts of their experiences to cover gaps in their memory. When an individual confabulates, he or she may tell a different story each time. These plausible types of confabulations that occur in response to questions the patient cannot answer are referred to as *provoked confabulations* (de Renzi, 2000). In contrast, *spontaneous confabulations* are often grandiose, bizarre, and fantastical fabrications that appear mediated by damage to the frontal lobes (de Renzi, 2000; Schnider, 2001). Interestingly, there is evidence that amnestic individuals can confabulate both verbal and visual material. For example, an amnestic individual may insist that drawing errors made on a visual memory task accurately depict previously presented visual stimuli (Welch, Nimmerrichter, Gilliland, King, & Martin, 1997). Confabulation may appear in the earlier stages of an amnestic disorder, but disappear over time (American Psychiatric Association, 2000b). Remember that confabulations are not unique to amnestic disorder and have been observed in other cognitive disorders such as DAT (J. M. Cooper, Shanks, & Venneri, 2006).

Emotional Changes and Lack of Insight

Individuals with amnestic disorders may display changes in emotional functioning that include diminished affective range, lack of motivation, and agitation (American Psychiatric Association, 2000b; Lindqvist & Malmgren, 1993). In some patients, depression and anxiety may occur secondary to memory loss or disorientation (Blansjaar, Takens, & Zwinderman, 1992). However, other individuals with amnestic disorders may appear unconcerned about their memory impairment and/or fail to recognize the severity of their deficits. For example, when being evaluated with a mental status examination, an amnestic individual may insist that incorrect responses are right (First & Tasman, 2005).

Onset, Course, and Life Span Considerations

The course of amnestic disorders is variable, with onset being abrupt in some cases and insidious in others, depending on the presumed cause of the amnesia. In some cases, amnesia may be chronic (defined in the *DSM-IV-TR* [American Psychiatric Association, 2000b] as lasting 1 month or more); in others, the condition is transient. Although the scope of the affected individual's cognitive impairment is, by definition, limited to memory (as opposed to a demented individual, who will display significant deficits across a number of different cognitive functions), amnestic persons are typically disabled by their disorder and frequently spend much of their life in a dependent role if their condition is chronic (W. J. Burke & Bohac, 2001).

For example, a prospective study of 44 individuals with alcohol-induced amnestic disorder characterized by severe anterograde and retrograde amnesia but no major loss of other intellectual functions, found that cognitive functioning remained relatively stable over a 3-year period and that 90% of patients continued to have impaired social (especially occupational) role functioning. This study also found that individuals who were in a nursing home or similar setting were particularly apt to evidence deterioration in social functioning, whereas patients in a sheltered accommodation that provided encouragement to actively take part in household-type activities were more likely to improve (Blansjaar et al., 1992).

Perhaps the most famous case of an amnestic disorder that illustrates the degree of impairment that can be caused by memory loss was described by Scoville and Milner (1957) in the 1950s. Their patient, H.M., underwent a temporal lobe resection in an attempt to eliminate recurrent, worsening seizures. The surgery removed his hippocampi, brain structures now known to be crucial in the transfer of short-term memories into long-term memory storage, and as a result H.M. developed global anterograde amnesia. Following the surgery, H.M. was unable to remember information recently presented to him (e.g., lists of words, pictures of faces, names of new people), although his memory for events prior to the surgery (particularly those older than 2 to 3 years before the operation) was generally intact. Although he was estimated to be of above-average intelligence, the only work H.M. was capable of doing after his surgery consisted of repetitive tasks at a state rehabilitation center, such as mounting cigarette lighters on cardboard display frames (Kolb & Winshaw, 1990). He was unable to live independently following the surgery and currently resides in a nursing home.

With regard to life span considerations, Sumner (1998) notes that older adults may be at particular risk for developing benzodiazepine-induced persisting amnestic disorder compared to individuals in younger age groups. Older adults are often prescribed benzodiazepines for complaints such as sleep difficulties but are likely to have greater difficulties than younger people in processing and eliminating such medications due to changes in gastrointestinal, liver, and renal functioning. It may be difficult to detect amnestic disorders in such cases because the older adult may not even realize that benzodiazepine medications are adversely affecting his or her memory. Because of this, it is important to conduct a baseline mental status exam and regular assessment of cognitive impairment with any older adult who is taking medication that carries a risk of memory impairment (Sumner, 1998).

EPIDEMIOLOGY

Delirium

At any one point in time, delirium is estimated to affect 0.4% of adults (18 years or older), and 1.1% of those 55 years or older (American Psychiatric Association, 2000b). As previously noted, old age is a risk factor for delirium, and the prevalence of delirium among the hospitalized elderly and nursing home residents has been estimated to be between 10% to 40% and 60%, respectively (American Psychiatric Association, 2000b; M. G. Wise et al., 2001). Delirium is also common among hospitalized medically ill patients (10% to 30%), those with AIDS (30% to 40%), cancer patients (25%), the terminally ill (up to 80%), and cardiac surgery patients (13% to 67%; M. G. Wise et al., 2001). Individuals who have a preexisting dementia are also at great risk for developing a superimposed delirium, with estimates that as many as half of those admitted to the hospital for treatment of delirium will have an underlying dementia (F. R. Purdie, Honigman, & Rosen, 1981). The prevalence of delirium is affected to some degree by the specific diagnostic criteria utilized to identify cases. According to a study of hospitalized and nursing home elders, utilization of *DSM-IV* criteria for delirium resulted in the highest number of identified cases (24.9%) compared to *DSM-III-R* criteria (18.8%) or *DSM-III* criteria (10.1%; Laurila et al., 2004b). Epidemiological statistics regarding delirium must be tempered by the fact that it is likely underreported in many settings. For example, Laurila, Pitkala, Strandberg, and Tilvis (2004a) independently identified delirium in approximately 35% of a sample of hospitalized elderly, but this diagnosis was recorded in fewer than half of these patients' medical charts.

Although rarely reported, delirium can also occur in children. A study of over 1,000 consecutive psychiatric consultations over a 4-year period at a large urban children's hospital found that 8% of children and adolescents (ages 6 months to 18 years) qualified for a *DSM-III-R* diagnosis of delirium (Turkel & Tavaré, 2003). Obtaining accurate estimates of the prevalence of delirium is made difficult by the fact that this condition is frequently not recognized and is consequently underdiagnosed in as many as one third to two thirds of cases (Meagher & Trzepacz, 1998).

Dementia

Dementias of all etiologies are estimated to collectively affect 5% to 10% of the elderly population in industrialized countries (Kukull & Ganguli, 2000). It has been estimated that by the year 2040, 7 to 10 million people in the United States will suffer from severe dementia (U.S. Congress, Office of Technology Assessment, 1987). The risk of dementia increases dramatically with age up to 90 to 95 years, and the prevalence of dementia doubles with every 5-year increase in age (Jorm, Korten, & Henderson, 1987). Thus, whereas 5% to 8% of individuals 65 or older have dementia, 18% to 30% of those over 75 have dementia, and 35% to 40% of those over 85 are demented (Rabins et al., 1999).

Although estimates vary somewhat across studies, DAT and VD have been estimated to account for up to 60% to 70% and 15% to 30% of cases of dementia, respectively (J. L. Cummings, 2003). Estimates of the relative proportion of VD and DAT among dementia cases are complicated by the fact that dementia can be due to multiple etiologies. The term *mixed dementia* is often used to refer to individuals whose dementia is thought to be the result of cerebrovascular and primary degenerative features (e.g., both VD and DAT). Estimates of the number of VD cases may be significantly affected in a given study depending on whether investigators count such mixed cases as VD cases or as due to another etiology (Rocca & Kokmen, 1999).

As with delirium, dementia is often underreported, so the aforementioned prevalence statistics may be underestimates. In a sample of hospitalized elderly diagnosed by Laurila and colleagues (2004a) as demented, only slightly more than 50% had this diagnosis in their medical chart and cognitive testing had been performed by hospital staff in fewer than half of these cases. Epidemiologic efforts in regard to dementia have frequently been hampered by lack of clear diagnostic criteria and difficulties developing effective means of identifying affected individuals (including problems using techniques such as neuroimaging in large-scale studies; Rocca & Kokmen, 1999).

Amnestic Disorder

The *DSM-IV-TR* does not report prevalence rates for amnestic disorders, which reflects the fact that these conditions have not been as well studied as dementia or delirium (American Psychiatric Association, 2000b). The prevalence of Wernicke's encephalopathy, a common cause of Korsakoff's syndrome, has been estimated to be 0.05% in general hospital settings (Nakada & Knight, 1984). In general, little is known about the prevalence of amnestic disorders that are due to general medical conditions (W. J. Burke & Bohac, 2001).

ETIOLOGY

Delirium

Many different medical conditions and situations can bring about a delirium. Infections, medication toxicity or withdrawal, fluid or electrolyte imbalances, metabolic derangements, conditions that result in insufficient oxygen delivery to the central nervous system, and severe pain are among some of the general factors that can give rise to a delirium. The most severe manifestation of alcohol withdrawal is *delirium tremens*, which carries a mortality rate of more than 10%. This syndrome is characterized by delirium, agitation, changes in blood pressure, tremor, rapid heart rate, sweating, fever, nausea, and irritability that may begin within several hours or days after consumption of alcohol in physiologically dependent individuals ceases (Marcantonio, 2002). Individuals with impaired cerebral functioning (including those with dementia) are at high risk for becoming delirious in the face of stressors such as acute illness (Laurila et al., 2004b). Delirium is also common among terminally ill patients at the end of life and may reflect the body's protective mechanism against the anguish and pain of death (Marcantonio, 2002). Causes of delirium in children include fever, systemic infections, organ failure, chemotherapy, closed-head injury, AIDS, postoperative recovery from anesthesia, near drowning, asphyxiation, hypoxia due to status asthmaticus (a type of life-threatening asthma attack), CNS viral infections, substance use (e.g., alcohol use, inhalants), and seizures (M. G. Wise et al.,

2001). In a study of delirium in children and adolescents, the most common cause of delirium was infection (e.g., bacterial, viral, fungal, parasitic), followed by drug-induced cases (Turkel & Tavaré, 2003). Table 7.3 lists common causes of delirium. It should be noted that in most cases, multiple causal factors are implicated in a delirium, with single causes accounting for fewer than half of all cases (F. R. Purdie et al., 1981).

Delirium caused by metabolic problems, infections, or alcohol withdrawal is likely to be hypoactive, whereas delirium secondary to closed head injury or anticholinergic drug intoxication is more likely to result in a hyperactive presentation (Meagher & Trzepacz, 1998; O'Keefe & Lavan, 1999; C. A. Ross et al., 1991). In addition, the scope and severity of symptoms may be greater for a delirium arising from a drug-related etiology compared to other causes (e.g., metabolic or electrolyte imbalances, brain injury, hypoperfusion; Meagher & Trzepacz, 1998).

Although we know of many conditions that can give rise to delirium, knowledge of the pathophysiology of delirium is limited compared to other psychiatric disorders (Meagher & Trzepacz, 1998). Neural pathways (particularly right hemispheric structures) that include the prefrontal cortices, anterior and right thalamus, right basal ganglia, right posterior parietal cortex, and right basilar mesial temporoparietal cortex appear to play a significant role in the pathogenesis of delirium caused by diverse etiologies and are consistent with findings that imbalances in cholinergic and dopaminergic neurotransmitter systems have been linked to delirium (Fleminger, 2002; Trzepacz, 1999b, 2000). Acetylcholine plays an important role in attention, normal cognitive functioning, and sleep-wake cycles (all of which are adversely affected in delirious individuals; Lipowski, 1992), and it is also well known that drugs that exert anticholinergic effects (i.e., reduce availability of acetylcholine) can precipitate a delirium (Blazer, Federspiel, Ray, & Schaffner, 1983; Tune, 2001). Because the CNS cholinergic system is adversely affected by degenerative brain disease and aging, older individuals and those with compromised cerebral functioning are often very sensitive to the effects of anticholinergic drugs and are at increased risk for this type of drug-induced delirium (Lipowski, 1992). Excessive amounts of dopamine have also been implicated in delirium, and dopamine-activating medications are considered to constitute a medium-risk group for the development of delirium (Karlsson, 1999; Meagher & Trzepacz, 1998). Other neurotransmitter changes that have been documented in association with delirium involve gamma amino-butyric acid (GABA), serotonin, glutamine, and histamine (Trzepacz, 1999b). Electroencephalogram (EEG) recordings of delirious individuals typically show generalized slowing of background rhythm; however, superimposed fast wave activity is found in individuals with delirium secondary to alcohol withdrawal (Meagher & Trzepacz, 1998).

Dementia

Dementia of the Alzheimer's Type

Dementia of the Alzheimer's Type is referred to as a cortical dementia because the brain areas initially involved are located in the cortical mantle or the upper layers of the brain (i.e., gray matter). This is in contrast to subcortical dementias (e.g., dementia associated with Parkinson's disease or Huntington's disease) that primarily affect structures and neuronal circuits beneath the cortex. Alzheimer's disease is named after the German

Table 7.3   Some causes of delirium

Disease	Substance
Anemia	Alcohol, amphetamine, cannabis, cocaine,
Cancer	hallucinogens, inhalant, opioid, PCP, sedative/
Disease	hypnotic, anxiolytic intoxication
Electrolyte imbalances and dehydration	Alcohol, sedative, hypnotics, anxiolytic
Encephalitis	withdrawal
Epilepsy	Anesthetics
Head trauma	Anticholinergics
Hypertensive encephalopathy	Antihistamines
Metabolic conditions (e.g., thyroid, renal,	Antihypertensives
or hepatic dysfunction; hypoglycemia)	Antiparkinsonian drugs
Huntington's disease	Gastrointestinal drugs
Creutzfeld-Jakob disease	Immunosuppressants
Cardiac problems (e.g., congestive heart	Insulin
failure, myocardial infarction)	Lithium
Meningitis	Muscle relaxants
Multiple sclerosis	Neuroleptics
Normal pressure hydrocephalus	Nonsteroidal anti-inflammatory drugs
Postoperative states	Pain medications
Pulmonary conditions (e.g., chronic obstructive	Steroids
pulmonary disease)	Toxins (e.g., carbon monoxide, insecticides)
Stroke	
Subdural hematoma	
Systemic infection	
Thiamine deficiency	

neuropathologist and psychiatrist Alois Alzheimer, who, in 1907, described the case of a 51-year-old woman who presented with disorientation, memory impairment, delusions, hallucinations, and language disturbance characterized by inappropriate word substitutions (i.e., paraphasic errors) and impaired comprehension; however, the woman's motor functioning (i.e., gait, coordination, and reflexes) was normal. Following the woman's deterioration and death 4.5 years later, an autopsy of her brain revealed several important changes, including general atrophy, neurofibrillary tangles, and neuritic plaques (J. L. Cummings & Benson, 1992). Interestingly, it was not until the late 1970s that research on Alzheimer's disease began in earnest; prior to 1976 there were only 42 published papers on this topic (Boller & Forbes, 1998).

The pathological brain changes Alzheimer originally observed remain important characteristics of DAT. Due to the significant neuronal loss that occurs as the disease progresses, the brains of individuals with DAT may weigh less than 1,000 grams at death, with atrophy most pronounced in the temporoparietal and anterior frontal regions of the brain (Andreasen, 2001). A particularly high rate of atrophy is observed in the entorhinal cortex (located in the ventromedial portion of the temporal lobe), which has reciprocal connections with the hippocampus and other cortical and subcortical areas involved in memory. The significant neuronal loss observed in the entorhinal cortex suggests that pathological changes associated with DAT may begin here (de Toledo-Morrell,

Goncharova, Dickerson, Wilson, & Bennett, 2000; Du et al., 2004). The plaques and tangles Alzheimer described are now recognized as hallmarks of DAT. Neurofibrillary tangles are insoluble, twisted fibers found inside the brain's cells. They are primarily composed of an abnormal variant of tau protein and appear to interfere with the transportation of nutrients and other important substances in the cell (J. L. Cummings, 2003). Tangles in DAT are found in several areas of the brain, including the neocortex, hippocampus, and amygdala. Although DAT is characterized by neurofibrillary tangles, they are not unique to this disease and have been observed in other neurological conditions, suggesting that their development may be a nonspecific neuronal response to injury (J. L. Cummings & Benson, 1992). Neuritic plaques are accumulations of the protein substance beta amyloid (a breakdown product of amyloid precursor protein) and other cellular material such as degenerative nerve endings (Zarit & Zarit, 2006). These plaques, which look like puddles of sludge under the microscope, form near the spaces between nerve cells (i.e., synapses) and interfere with normal neuronal communication (Andreasen, 2001, p. 264). Beta amyloid production occurs in all brains, but unlike cells that are able to clear out excess accumulations, cells in the brain affected by DAT cannot effectively perform this function. As the disease progresses, plaques are seen in many areas of the brain. The highest concentrations are found in the temporal and occipital lobes, with an intermediate amount in the parietal lobes, and the lowest densities in the frontal cortex and limbic cortex (J. L. Cummings, 2003). As with neurofibrillary tangles, plaques are seen in other dementing illnesses such as Creutzfeld-Jakob disease and dementia pugilistica (C. M. Clark & Karlawish, 2003).

Because plaques and tangles can be revealed only through a microscopic study of brain tissue, a definitive diagnosis of DAT is possible only following death, when the brain can be autopsied. Technically, it would be possible to examine brain tissue in a patient suspected of Alzheimer's while still alive, but this would require a brain biopsy; such an invasive procedure is generally thought to have risks that substantially outweigh its benefits. Thus, a diagnosis of DAT while the patient is alive is made by ruling out other possible causes of the dementia and observing whether the pattern and constellation of signs and symptoms typically associated with DAT is observed in the patient. Such probable cases can be identified with as high as 90% accuracy (Small et al., 1997).

The location of the abnormal brain changes associated with Alzheimer's disease helps to explain the symptoms observed in DAT. Pathology in the hippocampus and entorhinal cortex is associated with memory impairment, abnormal changes in the temporal lobe lead to language disturbance, and cell loss in the parietal lobes results in visuoperceptual disturbances (Rabins et al., 1999). The pathological cellular changes that occur in the brains of DAT-affected individuals are also associated with abnormalities in neurotransmitter systems, most notably deficits in acetylcholine. Autopsy studies indicate that DAT is associated with decreased acetylcholine activity in the cerebral cortex and hippocampus (E. K. Perry, 1980). Acetylcholine has been linked to the encoding component of working memory, which is the main characteristic of the memory deficit among individuals with DAT (K. G. White & Ruske, 2002).

There is no single cause of DAT; rather, this form of dementia can arise from different genetic and nongenetic causes (St. George-Hyslop, 2000). Some individuals may develop DAT and have no known history of dementia in their family, whereas other individuals (particularly those with early-onset DAT) may have a strong family history of the disorder. An early clue that Alzheimer's could involve a genetic component came from observations that individuals with Down syndrome, who have an extra copy of chromosome 21, are at risk for developing Alzheimer's disease in early to mid-adulthood (Holland & Oliver, 1995). Eventually, mutations on chromosome 21 that code for amyloid precursor protein, the substance from which the characteristic plaques of DAT are derived, were found to account for some familial cases of Alzheimer's disease (Goate, Hardy, & Owen, 1991). In addition, genetic mutations associated with the production of the proteins presenilin 1 and presenilin 2 on chromosomes 14 and 1, respectively, have now been implicated in other cases of early-onset familial DAT (i.e., onset prior to age 60; Levy-Lahad, Tsuang, & Bird, 1998). The mutations on chromosomes 21, 14, and 1 follow an autosomal dominant pattern of inheritance; this means that individuals who inherit copies of any of the mutations on these three chromosomes will almost invariably develop DAT. Familial forms of DAT account for a relatively small percentage of cases (i.e., 5% to 10%), and mutations in presenilin 1 are the most frequent (Tedde et al., 2003).

The apoliopoprotein E (APOE) gene, which provides a blueprint for a protein that carries cholesterol in the bloodstream, has three major alleles; ε2, ε3, and ε4. The ε-4 allele of the apoliopoprotein E gene (APOE 4) located on chromosome 19 is associated with an increased risk for late-onset DAT, but the presence of this allele does not ensure that DAT will develop, as is the case with the mutations noted for chromosomes 1, 14, and 21. Upwards of 50% of DAT cases in the United States are associated with the presence of the ε-4 allele (Raber, Huang, & Ashford, 2004). Epidemiologic studies indicate that individuals are 3 times more likely to have DAT when carrying one copy of the ε-4 allele and 9 times more likely when carrying two copies of this allele (Lindsay et al., 2002; Roses, 1997). In addition, the presence of the ε-4 allele has been found to predict more rapid cognitive decline and conversion to dementia in individuals with mild cognitive impairment (Aggarwal et al., 2005). This allele may facilitate the accumulation of beta-amyloid as well as the formation of neurofibrillary tangles (J. L. Cummings, 2003; Warzok et al., 1998). Whereas the ε-4 allele is considered a risk factor for DAT, the ε-2 may actually decrease risk for this disorder.

Vascular Dementia

Vascular Dementia can be caused by a number of vascular mechanisms and changes in the brain. The two most common causes of VD are multiple large or small strokes and ischemic white matter lesions (I. Skoog, 1998). Although cerebrovascular disease is considered to underlie VD, different diagnostic criteria sets for VD vary in their requirement of how this is to be documented. For example, diagnostic criteria for VD developed by the National Institute of Neurological Disorders and Stroke and the Association Internationale pour la Recherche et l'Enseignement en Neurosciences, the most widely used criteria in clinical trials on VD, require evidence of vascular disease on CT or MRI of the brain (Román et al., 1993). In contrast, the broader and less detailed *DSM-IV-TR* (American Psychiatric Association, 2000b) criteria for VD do not have such a neuroimaging requirement, but instead indicate that evidence of cerebrovascular disease may be revealed either by laboratory evidence (e.g., neuroimaging) or via focal neurological signs or symptoms as might be revealed during a neurological exam. Because cerebrovascular changes can affect varying areas of the brain, the manifestations of VD are quite broad, and the specific clinical picture seen will depend on the areas of the brain where vascular changes have occurred. For example, in cases where vascular changes primarily involve subcortical areas of the brain (e.g., Binswanger's disease), the clinical profile is apt to include motor hemiparesis (i.e., weakness of one side of the body), dysarthria (difficulty with articulation), gait disturbance, bulbar signs (e.g., difficulty swallowing), extrapyramidal signs (e.g., rigidity), memory impairment that is less severe than that seen in DAT (e.g., relatively intact recognition memory, ability to benefit from cues), and deficits in executive functioning (Erkinjuntti & Pantoni, 2000). As Knopman and Selnes (2003) note, an individual with cerebrovascular disease can also develop VD from single strategically placed lesions in areas such as the thalamus, hippocampus, or parietal lobes. In general, compared to DAT, VD is associated with greater white matter pathology, including myelin loss and vacuolization (i.e., formation of holes in cells; J. L. Cummings, 2003).

As previously noted, there is increasing recognition that many individuals with a primary degenerative dementia such as DAT also have cerebrovascular factors that contribute to their dementia (so-called mixed dementia cases; Agüero-Torres et al., 1999). Postmortem examinations of individuals with DAT have found that the comorbid presence of infarcts is associated with more severe symptoms, including poorer cognitive functioning (Snowdon et al., 1997). In addition, cases of dementia due solely to vascular pathology are estimated to be half as common as cases in which such pathology is also accompanied by signs of DAT pathology (C. Holmes, Cairns, & Lantos, 1999). The APOE-ε4-allele, a well-known risk factor for DAT, is also more common in cases of VD compared to in control subjects (Hsiung, Sadovnick, & Feldman, 2004; Treves et al., 1996); however, this finding is somewhat controversial since a number of researchers have not found a link between APOE-ε-4 and VD (Molero, Pino-Ramirez, & Maestre, 2001; Slooter et al., 1997; Traykov et al., 1999). Because the APOE-ε-4 allele is also considered a risk factor for the development of atherosclerosis, this allele may serve as a primary risk factor for VD as well as for DAT. The association observed between the APOE-ε-4 allele and VD cases could also reflect individuals at risk for the eventual development of DAT who first develop VD because of strokes or other cerebrovascular pathology. The ways cerebrovascular factors interact with risk factors for primary degenerative dementias such as DAT are not yet well understood, and further study of these mixed cases is needed. Finally, the coexistence of vascular and Alzheimer's pathology in many individuals highlights potential problems with current diagnostic systems, such as the *DSM-IV-TR* (American Psychiatric Association, 2000b), that specify that cognitive deficits associated with DAT cannot be attributable to cerebrovascular factors (R. Stewart, 1998).

Amnestic Disorders

Amnestic disorders can be caused by both medical factors or conditions and the persisting effects of drugs, including substances of abuse and medications. One of the more common causes of persisting amnesia is *Korsakoff's syndrome*, which typically results from thiamine deficiency associated with chronic alcohol use. This vitamin deficiency results from poor nutrition, decreased absorption of thiamine from the gastrointestinal tract, and impaired thiamine utilization in the cells resulting directly from the alcohol consumption (P. R. Martin, Singleton, & Hiller-Sturmhofel, 2003; McKinley, 2005). Malnourishment from other conditions such as HIV-related disease can also lead to Korsakoff's syndrome (First & Tasman, 2005). The development of Korsakoff's syndrome is often preceded by an episode of the neurological condition *Wernicke's encephalopathy*, which is characterized by mental confusion, eye movement abnormalities (e.g., nystagmus, paralysis of the eye muscles), and ataxia (i.e., lack of coordination, gait abnormalities). Prompt thiamine administration may prevent the progression from Wernicke's encephalopathy to Wernicke-Korsakoff syndrome or lessen the severity of the latter condition but is unlikely to reverse existing deficits in patients who already have Korsakoff syndrome (B. K. Phillips, Ingram, & Grammer, 2004).

Other substances of abuse, including cocaine, solvents, methamphetamine, and ecstasy, can cause substance-induced persisting amnestic conditions (Meredith, Jaffe, Ang-Lee, & Saxon, 2005; O'Malley, Adamse, Heaton, & Gawin, 1992; Ron, 1986; Vik, Cellucci, Jarchow, & Hedt, 2004). Other causal factors are toxin exposure (e.g., carbon monoxide poisoning), cerebrovascular disease (e.g., left or bilateral posterior cerebral artery infarct), infective and inflammatory conditions such as herpes simplex encephalitis, head trauma, hypoxia, seizures, multiple sclerosis, and use of medications such as benzodiazepines (de Renzi, 2000). Amnestic disorders are associated with brain damage in areas that mediate memory functioning, including the hippocampus, fornix, mammillary bodies, and thalamus; some forms of amnestic disorder are also associated with frontal lobe damage (Benson et al., 1996; de Renzi, 2000; Kopelman et al., 2001; Matsuda et al., 1997; Sahin, Gurvit, Bilgic, Hanagasi, & Emre, 2002). Left hemispheric structures appear to be particularly important in the etiology of memory disorders (First & Tasman, 2005).

Risk Factors for Cognitive Disorders

Delirium

M. G. Wise et al. (2001) identified the following groups as being at increased risk for delirium: older adults, individuals with decreased cerebral reserve (e.g., due to aging, disease, injury), drug-dependent individuals undergoing withdrawal, and burn or postcardiac surgery patients. Changes in brain function, increased likelihood of brain disorders such as dementia, reduced ability to metabolize medication, frequent use of multiple medications, and multisensory declines are among the reasons older adults are at particular risk for delirium (American Psychiatric Association, 1999). Among the elderly, the frail elderly are especially vulnerable to developing delirium in the face of even minor physical insults due to their diminished physical and nutritional status (J. C. Jackson et al., 2004).

Dementia

Age constitutes a primary risk factor for both DAT and VD, as the incidence of both forms of dementia increases with increasing age (Jorm & Jolley, 1998; Rocca & Kokmen, 1999). Low education level, female sex (see "Diversity Considerations" later in this chapter), family history of DAT, head trauma associated with loss of consciousness, and possibly depression, small head size, and exposure to certain environmental factors such as organic solvents and aluminum are among the risk factors that have been identified for DAT (Kukull & Ganguli, 2000; Launer et al., 1999). Many factors that used to be thought of as primarily increasing risk for VD now also appear to increase risk for late-onset DAT, including hypertension, peripheral arterial disease, certain cardiovascular disorders, smoking, and diabetes mellitus (I. K. Skoog, Raj, & Breteler, 1999). Diabetes has been associated with impairments in cognitive processes such as decreased verbal memory, working memory, processing speed, and visuospatial functions (Arvanitakis, Wilson, Bienias, Evans, & Bennet, 2004; Messier, 2005). Insulin dysregulation may contribute to DAT pathology by decreasing utilization of glucose in areas such as the hippocampus and entorhinal cortex, contributing to the formation of neurofibrillary tangles, increasing the accumulation of beta-amyloid (the substance from which plaques are composed), and through increased oxidative stress (Geroldi et al., 2005; H. Grossman, 2003). The link between diabetes and dementia is complicated by the fact that depression, a common comorbid condition in diabetes that can also impact cognition, has not always been sufficiently assessed and controlled for in these studies (Franco & Branson, 2005). Dietary habits such as a moderate to high intake of saturated fats may increase the risk of dementia and DAT (Laitinen et al., 2006). Recent research has linked high dietary intake of copper in conjunction with a diet high in trans- and saturated fats to accelerated cognitive decline that may be related to DAT (Morris et al., 2006).

Risk factors for VD include coronary artery disease, cerebrovascular disease, hypertension, obesity, arrhythmia, diabetes mellitus, hyperlipidemia (i.e., high cholesterol and triglycerides), alcohol-related disorders, low education, and smoking (Burruss et al., 2001; J. L. Cummings, 2003; Gorelick et al., 1999; Duthie & Glatt, 1988). Among individuals who have had a stroke, a number of factors have been identified that increase the risk of subsequent development of VD, including advanced age, lower educational level, non-White ethnicity, diabetes, more severe neurological impairment at the time of medical admission, larger size of stroke-related lesions, hemispheric (versus brain stem or cerebellar) lesions, left (versus right) hemispheric lesions, and presence of silent (i.e., asymptomatic) infarcts on neuroimaging (J. L. Cummings, 2003). Table 7.4 summarizes risk factors for delirium and dementia.

In addition to risk factors for dementia, a number of protective factors have been identified as well. These include greater educational attainment, higher socioeconomic status, presence of the APOE-ε-2 allele, use of antioxidants (e.g., vitamins E, C), use of estrogen supplements in women, use of nonsteroidal, anti-inflammatory drugs, emotional support, and moderate alcohol use (Hendrie et al., 2006; Kukull & Ganguli, 2000). Regular physical exercise also appears associated with a lower risk of cognitive impairment and dementia (Laurin, Verreault, Lindsay, MacPherson, & Rockwood, 2001). Risk for dementia appears to be reduced with participation in cognitively stimulating activities such as reading newspapers, magazines, or books; solving crossword puzzles; visiting museums; and following a diet characterized by moderate intake of unsaturated fats. Because many of the risk factors for VD (e.g., hypertension, obesity, diabetes) are controllable, theoretically it should be possible to avoid, delay, or slow the onset of many cases of VD, which underscores the importance of educating physicians and the public about VD (Erkinjuntti & Pantoni, 2000).

DIVERSITY CONSIDERATIONS

The prevalence of dementia in different countries around the world has been reported to vary widely, particularly for VD (Rocca & Kokmen, 1999; Suh & Shah, 2001). In some cases, this may be due to variability in study methodology (e.g., diagnostic criteria) across

Table 7.4   Risk factors for delirium and dementia

Delirium	Dementia	
	DAT	VD
Old age (especially frail elderly)	Age	Age
Decreased cerebral reserve (e.g., due to dementia, head injury, CNS lesions)	Family history, genetic factors (e.g., APOE-ε-4 allele)	Coronary artery disease
Medical illness (e.g., systemic infections, AIDS, cancer)	Low education	Hypertension
Drug withdrawal	Female sex	Stroke
Surgical patients (especially hip surgery, cardiotomy, organ transplant)	Head trauma with loss of consciousness	Obesity
Burn victims	Hypertension	Hypertension
Dialysis patients	Peripheral arterial disease	Hyperlipidemia (high cholesterol/triglycerides)
Terminal illness	Diabetes mellitus	Diabetes mellitus
	Cardiovascular disease	Smoking
	Depression	Arrhythmia
	Small head size	Coronary artery disease
	Environmental exposures (e.g., aluminum)	Alcohol-related disorders
	Diet	Low education

studies. However, real differences in etiologic and risk factors (e.g., hypertension, atherosclerosis) across different countries as well as survival rates may also play a role. For example, during the 1980s a pattern of higher rates of VD versus DAT was observed in some Far Eastern countries (e.g., China), whereas the opposite pattern was observed in Western European countries and in the United States. This finding may in part be due to differences in diet, cigarette and alcohol use, and the prevalence and treatment of hypertension in different parts of the world (Li, Shen, Chen, & Zhao, 1989; Shibayama, Kasahara, & Kobayashi, 1986). With regard to survival rates, DAT has been reported to have a fairly low prevalence in countries such as Nigeria (Ogunniyi, Osuntokun, Lekwauwa, & Falope, 1992); this may be partly explained by the fact that fewer individuals would be expected to enter into the age of risk for DAT given that the average life expectancy in this nation in the 1990s was less than 60 years (Suh & Shah, 2001).

Differences in the prevalence of different types of dementia have been reported for different ethnic groups within the same country. Cumulative risk for and incidence rates of DAT appear to be higher among African Americans relative to Caucasians (R. C. Green et al., 2002; Gurland et al., 1999; Tang et al., 2001). In addition, African Americans also tend to have higher rates of VD compared to Caucasians (Auchus, 1997; A. Heyman, Fillenbaum, Prosnitz, & Raiford, 1991). This may be due to the higher rates of diabetes, hypertension, and stroke in the African American community, since these conditions are all risk factors for the development of VD.

Rates of DAT are often reported to be higher for women than men; however, this finding may be attributable to women's greater longevity and consequent higher representation in age groups at greater risk for dementia, as well as higher likelihood of seeking out or being referred for medical care (Kukull & Ganguli, 2000). This finding may also be linked to loss of a possible protective role played by estrogen following menopause (Fratiglioni et al., 1997). Further, certain other risk factors for DAT may be different among men and women; for example, it appears that a history of head injury may be a risk factor for the later development of DAT for males, but not females (Fleminger, Oliver, Lovestone, Rabe-Hesketh, & Giora, 2003). Gender has also been found to be a significant predictor of survival for DAT. In a large-scale study that enrolled patients with DAT across 21 U.S. medical centers (the Consortium to Establish a Registry for Alzheimer's [CERAD] study), the median period of survival from time of entry was significantly shorter for men compared to women (5.7 years and 7.2 years, respectively; A. Heyman, Peterson, Fillenbaum, & Pieper, 1996). With regard to VD, there appear to be no appreciable differences in rates for women and men (Andersen et al., 1999) but possibly higher rates in men at younger ages (Jorm & Jolley, 1998).

INTAKE AND INTERVIEWING CONSIDERATIONS

Rapport

When the level of a client's cognitive impairment is extreme (e.g., severely demented or delirious) it will be difficult to meaningfully establish rapport. Challenges are also faced prior to this point, since individuals experiencing even mild cognitive decline may be reluctant to admit to difficulties they are experiencing. Some may refuse to be tested via a mental status exam even if they are anxious and distressed by their symptoms (Koponen et al., 2002). Individuals with DAT may admit to memory problems if directly asked, but may not spontaneously offer this information (M. F. Folstein, 1997). Of course, an inability to clearly and comprehensively report information may also be directly due to memory and other cognitive problems, and the clinician may need to rely more heavily on additional informants to obtain relevant information about previous and current symptoms and functioning. However, the prospect of contacting significant others to inquire about the client's difficulties may further raise the client's anxiety and increase reluctance to engage with the clinician. Such behaviors can be exasperating for clinicians and can stimulate notable negative countertransference reactions.

In spite of these challenges, devoting time and attention to the establishment of a good working relationship with the client is critically important when working with cognitively impaired clients. To the extent that the client is evasive and guarded and/or the clinician has unchecked negative reactions to the client, the quality of any data gathered from a mental status exam could be seriously compromised, and the clinician may be unable to accurately determine the extent of cognitive difficulties (J. L. Cummings & Benson, 1992). Gently easing into discussions of problems, asking about areas of strength and competence, and normalizing emotional reactions to difficulties may aid in the process of building rapport. It is also important to spend time inquiring about the client's previous experiences in psychotherapy to determine the degree to which the client may need to be socialized to the process of therapy. As Zarit and Zarit (2006) note, the nature of psycho-therapy and our understanding of mental disorders have greatly changed over time, and some older adults may have highly negative views of treatment based on outdated theories of psychological difficulties or a very restricted concept of what psychotherapy entails (e.g., psychoanalysis only). Providing clients with information about what to expect in therapy may make the experience less daunting and may increase the client's sense of connection with the clinician. For additional general strategies for establishing rapport with older adults, see Chapter 1.

Interview and Assessment Strategies

Medical Concerns

When an individual is suspected of a delirium, this is a medical emergency and imme-diate referral to a physician or hospital is necessary so that this can be properly eval-uated. Individuals suspected of dementia or an amnestic disorder should similarly be referred to a physician to rule out medical factors that may be causing or exacerbating their symptoms.

Gathering Information about Cognitive Problems

When evaluating individuals suspected of a cognitive disorder, the clinician can begin to gather informal information about the client's cognitive ability (e.g., alertness, memory, organization of thought) by observing how the client recalls, sequences, and makes sense of events when giving a history (Koponen et al., 2002). If the client is accompanied by a spouse or other family member, it is important to avoid allowing this other person to con-stantly fill in the client's sentences, interrupt the client to correct a fact, or engage in sim-ilar compensatory behaviors because this will interfere with the ability to obtain a clear picture of the client's cognitive abilities. Gathering supplemental information from family members (with the client's consent) after the interview can help to fill in missing information.

In obtaining a history of cognitive problems, it is important to ask very specific ques-tions about the type of problems the client may be experiencing and their timing (e.g., "When did the problems with language start?"; M. F. Folstein, 1997). Inquiries about the client's ability to complete basic and more advanced self-care skills (often referred to as activities of *daily living* [ADLs] and *instrumental activities of daily living* [IADLs]) should be made. The former include activities such as bathing, dressing, and feeding skills; IADLs include behaviors such as financial management, marketing, and food preparation. A num-ber of scales are available to evaluate ADLs and IADLs and are typically completed with or by a caregiver or family member who knows the client well. Another method of assess-ment is to watch the client actually perform a particular task, but this can be time-consum-ing, highly influenced by the client's motivation, and affected by the artificiality of the setting in which the performance test takes place (Lehfeld & Erzigkeit, 2000).

Mental Status Examination

Administration of a formal mental status exam that includes standardized questions that assess different aspects of cognition is very helpful. The most commonly used general mental status exam is the Folstein Mini-Mental Status Exam (M. F. Folstein et al., 1975), which contains 30 items that grossly assess the client's orientation, attention, learning and recall, language (e.g., naming, repetition, writing, verbal and written comprehension), and copying skills. Individuals with a variety of cognitive disorders, including delirium, dementia, and amnestic syndromes, are likely to score in the abnormal range on this measure (typically considered a score of 23 or less), so it is best viewed as a gross screening instrument that can point to the need for further testing. The Folstein MMSE can also be used as a general means of tracking cognitive decline over time; individuals with DAT can be expected to decline on the Folstein MMSE at a rate of about 3 to 4 points per year, with early-stage patients scoring between 20 and 23 points, middle-stage patients scoring 10 to 19 points, and late-stage patients scoring 0 to 9 points (M. F. Folstein, 1997). Even when an individual is unable to participate in an interview or mental status exam, observation of behavior may be sufficient to reveal severe impairment, disorganization, and confusion (S. A. Jacobson, 1997).

Other Assessment Measures

Delirious individuals will frequently have difficulty with simple tasks such as drawing a clock face with hands at a particular time on a page with an empty circle (M. G. Wise et al., 2001). In addition, a number of specific instruments are available for evaluating the presence and severity of delirium. Many were developed for use by medical personnel such as physicians and nurses, but others can be utilized by nonmedical professionals if sufficient training is provided. It is recommended that the results of two or more assessment methods be used to evaluate suspected cases of delirium (e.g., administration of a standardized mental status examination and a delirium-specific rating scale; Robertsson, 2003). A general criticism of delirium assessment measures is that they often place greater emphasis on florid symptoms such as behavioral agitation, which can make evaluation and detection of hypoactive delirious states more difficult (Meagher & Trzepacz, 1998). In addition to standard mental status exams such as the Folstein MMSE, other brief instruments that can provide a preliminary evaluation of dementia are available. A summary of some of these measures is included in Table 7.5.

Neuropsychological testing should also be pursued when the suspicion of dementia is strong. This type of testing is far more extensive than the administration of a mental status exam or dementia rating scale and involves giving standardized tests (typically with age- and education-based normative data) to evaluate various domains of cognitive functioning (e.g., global intellectual level, attention and concentration, memory, language, visuospatial functioning, executive functioning, motor skills; J. L. Cummings, 2003). This testing should be conducted by a psychologist who has specialized training in the evaluation of brain-behavior relationships. In addition to determining whether a client has deficits that would meet criteria for a cognitive disorder such as dementia, neuropsychological testing provides a profile of the client's cognitive strengths and weaknesses and level of impairment, which can be used both for treatment planning and as a baseline against which future testing can be compared to determine improvement, stability, or decline. When an individual is severely demented and difficult to evaluate using traditional cognitive tests, it may still be possible to evaluate cognitive functioning. For example, the Severe Impairment Battery, a 57-question, 20-minute cognitive battery that evaluates orientation, attention, language, praxis, and visuospatial,

Table 7.5   Some delirium and dementia assessment measures

Delirium Rating Scale (Trzepacz, 1999a)	10 items total. 2 items assess temporal onset of symptoms and their relationship to a physical condition. 8 items evaluate major symptoms of delirium, including perceptual disturbances, delusions, hallucinations, cognitive dysfunction, sleep-wake cycle disturbance, mood lability, and symptom variability. Score range is 0–32, 13+ indicating a likely diagnosis of delirium.	Translated into several languages. Found to have excellent reliability and very good validity. Although originally designed to be administered to adults, it has also been reported useful with children.
Confusion Assessment Method (CAM) (Inouye, vanDyck, Alessi, Balkin, Siegal, & Horowitz, 1990)	Brief screening measure with 2 forms (4 and 9 items, respectively). Assesses features such as acute onset and fluctuating course, inattention, disorganized thinking, and alterations in level of consciousness. Positive findings should trigger a more complete evaluation of the client to confirm the delirium diagnosis.	Training is needed before competent administration of this measure can be achieved.
Delirium Index (DI) (McCusker, Cole, Bellavance, & Primeau, 1998)	7 items. Items assess inattention, disorganized thinking, disorientation, altered consciousness, memory impairment, motor disturbances, perceptual disturbances. Used in conjunction with the Folstein MMSE (M. F. Folstein et al., 1975), which serves as basis for observing patient's behavior.	Adapted from CAM for use by nonprofessionals (e.g., research assistants). Can be completed by observing the patient, without obtaining additional information from the medical chart, nursing staff, or patient's family. Evidence of strong interrater reliability (for trained, experienced research assistants), good internal consistency reliability; evidence of construct validity.
Mattis Dementia Rating Scale (DRS) (Mattis, 1976) (Mattis, Jurica, & Leitten, 2002)	36 tasks assessing attention, initiation/perseveration, construction, conceptualization, and memory presented in a fixed order.	One of most widely used dementia rating instruments. Strong evidence of reliability and validity.

(Continued)

Table 7.5   (Continued)

	Testing time shortened by beginning with the most difficult items within each domain so that easier items can be skipped.	Revised DRS-2 (2002) provides more comprehensive information about select areas of cognitive functioning (e.g., executive functioning) than standard mental status exams such as the Folstein MMSE. Has also been found useful in tracking symptom course in mild to moderately impaired individuals.

constructional, memory, and social orientation abilities, has been found to differentiate among demented individuals scoring between 0 to 5 points on the Folstein MMSE and those scoring between 6 to 11 points (Panisset, Roudier, Saxton, & Boller, 1994). It is beyond the scope of this chapter to comprehensively review the multitude of neuro-psychological tests that are typically used in a battery to evaluate dementia and the various patterns of test results that would be expected for different types of dementia (interested readers can consult DeBettignies, Swihart, Green, & Pirozzolo, 1997; Knopman & Selnes, 2003; Nixon, 1996).

A number of psychometrically sound measures exist for evaluating psychotic symptoms and behavioral disturbances associated with dementia (Bassiony & Lyketsos, 2003). Many of these measures (e.g., Neuropsychiatric Inventory, Dementia Behavior Disturbance Scale, Columbia University Scale of Psychopathology in Alzheimer's Disease) take only 10 to 15 minutes to administer and some can be completed by caregivers. Other measures, such as the 187-item Present Behavioral Examination (Hope & Fairburn, 1992), are more comprehensive and require a trained rater to complete.

Laboratory Tests

In the case of delirium, laboratory tests likely to be carried out to determine the underlying causes include serum electrolyte levels, serum glucose, urinalysis, blood urea nitrogen, hemogram, chest radiograph, and an electrocardiogram (Lipowksi, 1992). Although not always routinely used, an EEG recording can be helpful in diagnosing a delirium since this will typically show slowing of background activity (although alcohol withdrawal delirium is usually characterized by low-voltage fast wave activity; Lipowski, 1992). When an individual is suspected of dementia, it is likely that the treating physician will also order a battery of laboratory tests that include blood tests (e.g., complete blood count, serum electrolytes, serum chemistries, thyroid testing, serum medication levels) and urinalysis to determine if a medical condition could account for the patient's symptoms or be exacerbating them (Rabins et al., 1999). A thorough medical evaluation for an individual suspected of dementia is important given the many medical conditions that can cause symptoms mimicking this degenerative condition, including medication problems, vitamin B12 deficiency or other poor nutrition issues, urinary tract infections, pneumonia, normal pressure hydrocephalus, uncontrolled diabetes, electrolyte imbalances, hyper- or hypothyroidism, hyper- or hypoglycemia, alcoholism, neurosyphilis, and subdural hematoma. Additional tests, such as HIV testing, may be ordered to determine medical conditions that may account for the client's cognitive decline.

There is no additional definitive laboratory test for DAT, except for genetic testing to determine the presence of specific genes that have been determined to account for autosomal dominant cases of the disorder (J. L. Cummings, 2003); however, as was discussed under "Etiology," this represents a very small percentage of all DAT cases. Neuroimaging may be ordered in cases of suspected DAT. Computerized tomography (CT) or magnetic resonance imaging (MRI) studies of an individual with DAT are likely to reveal mild to severe cortical atrophy, and evidence of coexisting cerebrovascular disease may also be found through such scans (J. L. Cummings, 2003). Functional neuroimaging studies of individuals with DAT, such as positron emission tomography (PET), typically show bilateral temporoparietal hypometabolism (Gill, Rochon, Guttman, & Laupacis, 2003). However, the cost of functional studies is likely to preclude their being routinely ordered in cases of suspected DAT.

Neuroimaging is considered a critical component in diagnosing cases of VD (J. L. Cummings, 2003). As previously noted (see "Etiology"), although current *DSM-IV-TR* criteria for VD do not require data from neuroimaging to make this diagnosis (American Psychiatric Association, 2000b), MRI or CT scans can reveal evidence of strokes or other cerebrovascular pathology in cases where VD is suspected. Functional imaging methods such as PET and single photon emission computerized tomography (SPECT) that allow physicians to examine glucose metabolism and regional blood flow, respectively, can also help to identify cerebrovascular abnormalities (J. L. Cummings, 2003).

Crisis, Legal, and Ethical Issues

Elder Abuse

Family members caring for cognitively impaired individuals at home are likely to experience high levels of stress that, in some cases, may result in abusive or neglectful behavior toward the impaired relative (Hallberg, 2002). Thus a clinician working with individuals who are cognitively impaired should be alert to the signs of potential elder abuse and neglect that were reviewed in Chapter 2. The "Treatment" section of this chapter highlights family-based interventions that may help to ease caregiver burden and decrease the likelihood of abusive and neglectful behavior occurring.

Harmful Behavior to Self and Others

As previously noted, emotional changes are often pronounced in delirium, and affected individuals may become so distressed that they attempt to kill themselves. Fortunately, as Koponen et al. (2002) note, the delirious state itself (with the attendant disorganization in thinking and behavior) will generally interfere with successful suicide completion; nevertheless, any suicidal behavior in a delirious individual should be taken very seriously. It is also possible that an agitated, delirious individual might become aggressive toward hospital staff, although such violent behavior is less common among delirious elders (Koponen et al., 2000). Delirious individuals can also engage in ill-judged behavior that risks serious *self-injury* due to heightened levels of disorganization and agitation (Marcantonio, 2002; Saravay et al., 2004).

Because receiving a diagnosis of a dementing disorder can be devastating, clinicians should inquire about suicidal ideation among individuals in the mild to moderate stages of the illness (i.e., when cognitive functioning is still sufficiently intact so that such questions can be understood). Among the medically ill, delirious individuals and those with dementia have been identified as posing an elevated suicide risk when increased agitation and impulsivity are present (J. L. Levenson & Bostwick, 2005). Although it has been reported that suicide risk for demented individuals is lower than that for other psychiatric illnesses (E. Harris & Barrowclough, 1997), clinicians should not be lulled into thinking that demented individuals do not kill themselves. A study of 200 individuals 65 years or older who completed a questionnaire assessing opinions about being told the diagnosis of DAT versus cancer found that most indicated they wanted to be told if they had either diagnosis; for a small minority of respondents, a reason for wanting to be informed included consideration of suicide (Turnbull, Wolf, & Holroyd, 2003). Furthermore, a 10-year retrospective analysis of all elderly dementia patients admitted to a large urban mental health center found that among those diagnosed with DAT, 7.4% were admitted immediately following a suicide attempt and that higher level of daily functioning and previous suicide attempts were associated with increased suicidal risk (Barak & Aizenberg, 2002). Individuals with dementia who have greater insight and awareness of their cognitive deficits are more likely to experience feelings of hopelessness, which is a risk factor for suicide (Harwood & Sultzer, 2002). Additional risk factors are access to firearms, frank paranoid delusions, and the resurgence of painful past memories (Hierholzer, 2001). Strategies for assessing and treating suicidal ideation among demented individuals are similar to those used for nondemented persons and may include psychotherapy, pharmacotherapy, increased supervision, removal of potentially lethal items, and hospitalization (American Psychiatric Association, 1997).

Capacity to Consent

An important ethical consideration in evaluating individuals suspected of significant cognitive impairment is whether the individual is capable of providing informed consent or whether a guardian or conservator may be needed. For a conservator or guardian to be appointed to an individual, a petition must be filed with the court requesting this action, and a hearing conducted in which the proposed ward and other interested parties are in attendance (Sales et al., 2005). State law determines who is able to petition the court for conservatorship and guardianship of an individual. Because the decision to take away freedom from an individual through a process such as the appointment of a guardian is momentous, Welfel (2006) asserts that in cases where there is a question about ability to consent to treatment, it is prudent to attempt to go forward with the consent process to the greatest extent possible and to concurrently obtain consultation from someone who is skilled and knowledgeable enough to objectively evaluate the client's capacity.

In the case of an acutely delirious individual (who is more likely to first be seen in a medical setting such as a doctor's office or hospital rather than a mental health clinic or private practice setting), it is unlikely that informed consent can be meaningfully obtained. In such cases, it is ideal if the individual has previously signed an advanced directive that identifies who can make medical decisions for him or her in the event of incapacitation, but medical personnel may need to rely on next of kin in the absence of such legal documentation (Marcantonio, 2002). The common law doctrine of implied consent allows for medical care to be given in an emergency situation when next of kin are unavailable to provide consent on the patient's behalf; this doctrine asserts that appropriate care that a reasonable person would want can be given in this type of situation (American Psychiatric Association, 1999).

In a troubling study by Auerswald, Charpentier, and Inouye (1997) that examined the medical records of elderly hospitalized patients who developed delirium, there were no documented assessments of competency or decisional capacity, and 19% of the delirious patients had no documentation of any consent. In addition, cognitive assessments had been documented in only 4% of cases and legal consultations in only 1%. This underscores that adequately attending to issues of informed consent and patient decision-making capacity remain a challenge for those who assess and treat delirious individuals. In a series of case studies, Bostwick and Masterson (1998) discuss the use of flumazenil (a benzodiazepine antagonist) to temporarily restore mental functioning in four delirious individuals (ranging in age from 41 to 85 years) to obtain their informed consent to undergo lifesaving but high-risk surgical interventions.

Even when a client suspected of cognitive impairment appears sufficiently intact to understand the nature of psychological treatment and the limits of confidentiality, clinicians are very likely to need contact with others in the client's life (e.g., family members, medical treatment providers) to obtain information to fill in gaps in the client's recollection and to coordinate treatment efforts (e.g., to keep abreast of any medical issues or conditions experienced by the client). Identifying these individuals early in the treatment process and obtaining appropriate consent is therefore imperative. Also, it is important to periodically reevaluate capacity to consent among individuals suspected or known to have cognitive impairment, as illustrated in a study by Moye, Karel, Gurrera, and Azar (2006), which found that a significant percentage of mild to moderately demented individuals developed clinically significant impairments in reasoning ability over a 9-month follow-up period.

Ideally, early on in the course of dementia, discussions should take place with patients and their families about financial and legal issues to ensure that appropriate plans can be made for updating wills, establishing resources for paying for care (e.g., respite care, in-home care, nursing home) and making arrangements for a durable power of attorney to make medical and legal decisions when the patient becomes incapacitated.

Safety at Home and in the Community

Individuals who are cognitively impaired are at greater risk for engaging in behaviors that are potentially dangerous. As previously noted, for example, delirious individuals have great difficulty carrying out even basic tasks of daily living due to inattention, disorientation, and memory difficulty. Treatment professionals working with cognitively impaired individuals must therefore be vigilant for signs that an individual's cognitive symptoms have led to an inability to safely carry out tasks of daily living without supervision. Family members can be instructed about the degree of supervision that is required for the patient and the steps that need to be taken to make the home environment safe (e.g., removal of dangerous items such as power tools, curtailing use of the stove, accompanying the demented individual on walks). The use of identification bracelets or necklaces or sewing labels inside of clothing that include the individual's name and contact information can be useful for demented individuals prone to wandering (E. K. Mahoney et al., 2000). Because individuals with dementia are at increased risk of falls (which could result in serious medical problems such as head trauma or hip fractures), loose rugs, low tables, and other obstacles should be removed from the individual's dwelling and consideration given to the use of canes, nightlights, lowered beds, bedrails, and bedside commodes (American Psychiatric Association, 1997). Agitation or combativeness (likely in the later stages of a dementing illness) can pose hazards to the affected individual as well as those around him or her and may require transfer to a supervised setting (e.g., hospital, nursing home) if these behaviors cannot be controlled through environmental or psychopharmacologic interventions.

Demented individuals are at increased risk for traffic accidents should they continue driving. Moderately to severely demented individuals should not drive, and even mildly demented individuals should be encouraged to stop driving or to severely limit driving to safe situations (American Psychiatric Association, 1997). Some states require health professionals to report individuals to the Department of Motor Vehicles when a diagnosis of dementia has been made, and it is important to be aware of the existence of such laws in your state and whether you would be considered a mandated reporter. The patient may require help understanding the reasons for suspension of driving privileges, and the clinician should validate the client's understandable feelings of sadness, anger, and disappointment that come with this loss of independence. It is important to also discuss with family members the need to curtail driving privileges since, in some cases, they may actively need to take steps to prevent the demented individual from attempting to drive (e.g., hide keys, lock car doors).

Other Issues

Unique ethical issues can arise in the context of treating delirium at the end of life. As previously noted, delirium is common among terminally ill individuals. Patients (and often their family members) may have to wrestle with choices such as whether to receive continuous sedation to attain a "good death" or forgo these measures to remain aware but risk becoming delirious (Caraceni & Luigi, 2003). Further, it can at times be difficult to achieve adequate pain control without sending a patient into a delirium, raising other difficult decisions for the patient and his or her family members (Caraceni & Grassi, 2003). Table 7.6 summarizes key intake issues to consider in evaluating a client suspected of having a cognitive disorder.

DIAGNOSTIC CONSIDERATIONS

Cognitive Disorders versus Other Psychiatric Disorders

Mood Disorders

Cognitive disorders such as delirium and dementia can be difficult to distinguish from depression, particularly in older adults, because a severe affective disturbance can be

Table 7.6   Intake issues: cognitive disorders

Gently ease into discussions of cognitive difficulties.
Ask about areas of strength or competence, not just problems.
Normalize emotional reactions to cognitive difficulties.
Refer for medical evaluation (critical for delirium).
Consider referral for medication evaluation (dementia).
Inquire about difficulties in specific domains of cognitive functioning.
Inquire about ability to complete basic and advanced self-care tasks; assess ability of client to be alone at home safely.
Evaluate emotional-behavioral symptoms (e.g., depression, anxiety).
Evaluate suicidal ideation.
Consider referral for neuropsychological testing (dementia, amnestic disorder).
Carefully evaluate capacity to consent to treatment.
Obtain corroborating historical information from collateral sources (with client permission).
Coordinate care with medical providers.

associated with significant cognitive impairments. To complicate matters further, mood disorders are frequently comorbid with cognitive disorders. For example, late-life depression may make an individual vulnerable to developing a comorbid delirium since the former is frequently associated with self-neglect and physical illness, which can create risk factors for the development of a delirium.

A hypoactive delirium is associated with a lack of florid behavioral disturbance, which can easily be misdiagnosed as depression or undiagnosed altogether (Meagher & Trzepacz, 1998; Nicholas & Lindsey, 1995). In addition, certain features of severe late-life depression can be mistaken for delirium; these include agitation or retardation, slow thinking, impairments in concentration, disrupted sleep, persecutory auditory hallucinations and delusions, behavioral disturbances (e.g., screaming), and diurnal variations in symptoms (Koponen et al., 2002). When there is (a) a history of depression; (b) a slower, insidious onset of symptoms; and (c) evidence from testing that cognitive impairments are mild compared to the disturbances in mood, psychomotor behavior, and psychotic symptoms, it is more likely that the individual is depressed rather than delirious (Koponen et al., 2002).

Making a differential diagnosis between depression and dementia is a commonly encountered clinical challenge that can be quite complicated and is the subject of the "Advanced Topics" section at the end of this chapter.

Psychotic Disorders

Delirious individuals who are agitated and experiencing psychotic symptoms may be misdiagnosed as having Schizophrenia or another primary psychotic disorder. Although some psychotic individuals display grossly disorganized, inappropriate behavior, they are not apt to show the fluctuating impairments in attention, concentration, and level of consciousness that are seen in delirium. In addition, whereas delusions in primary psychotic disorders are typically persistent and often quite elaborate or systematized, delusions in the context of delirium are typically fleeting, unsystematized, and bound by stimuli in the patient's immediate environment (Lipowski, 1992). In the differential between delirium and a primary psychotic disorder, an EEG may be useful since it is likely to be normal in a psychotic disorder but characterized by slowed background activity in a delirious individual (Lipowski, 1992).

As noted earlier, it is fairly common for demented individuals to develop psychotic symptoms such as delusions and hallucinations that could be mistaken as evidence of a primary psychotic disorder. However, primary psychotic disorders typically have an onset in late adolescence or early adulthood, in contrast to the typical age of onset for dementing illnesses, which occur later in life. The profile of delusions and hallucinations seen in dementia is also different from that seen in Schizophrenia; in the latter disorder, delusions are more likely to be complex and bizarre, whereas in dementia delusions are typically paranoid, simple, and nonbizarre. In addition, whereas hallucinations are more likely to be auditory in Schizophrenia, they are more likely to be visual in dementia (Montzer & Targum, 2003). Although individuals with disorders such as Schizophrenia may experience cognitive impairments in areas such as working memory and executive functioning, these are not as profound as those seen in dementia, and psychotic individuals typically do not show progressive deterioration in cognitive functioning, which is one of the characteristics of dementias such as DAT. Knopman and Selnes (2003) note that when psychotic symptoms occur in late middle-aged or elderly persons who have no history of psychiatric illness, it is very likely that these behaviors reflect an underlying dementia.

Substance Use Disorders

When individuals are experiencing the acute effects of intoxication or withdrawal from substances, aspects of their cognitive functioning, including memory, may appear impaired. However, if an individual's cognitive impairment occurs only during a period of intoxication or withdrawal, a diagnosis of a dementia or amnestic disorder would be inappropriate. Although not reviewed in this chapter, dementia syndromes can be caused by excessive exposure to alcohol and other substances. Thus, when an individual meets criteria for dementia, it is clear the cognitive impairments are not transient in nature and the assumed cause is a substance (e.g., alcohol, substance of abuse, medication, toxin), a diagnosis of Substance-Induced Persisting Dementia can be given. Substance intoxication and withdrawal can lead to delirium, so the clinician evaluating a client in these circumstances would need to determine if the criteria for a delirium (i.e., disturbance of consciousness, change in cognition, development over a short period of time) are present and in excess of what would typically be seen in a withdrawal or intoxication syndrome for a particular substance (American Psychiatric Association, 2000b).

Mental Retardation

Individuals with mental retardation exhibit impairments in cognitive functioning. However, in contrast to an individual with dementia, these impairments are present at an early age and are nonprogressive (Kennedy, 2000). In addition, subaverage intellectual functioning in the context of mental retardation does not necessarily include memory impairment, which is a core symptom of dementia. Individuals with mental retardation also would not be expected to show impairments in arousal and orientation that are seen in delirious individuals.

Malingering and Factitious Disorder

Some individuals may feign cognitive impairment for secondary gain (e.g., to receive disability payments, to avoid legal responsibility for criminal action), known as *malingering,* or for attention from physicians and other treatment providers, known as *Factitious Disorder.* In contrast to those with bona fide cognitive impairment (such as dementia, delirium, or an amnestic disorder), individuals feigning cognitive impairment may (a) exhibit a marked inconsistency between their level of impairment according to self-report or performance on cognitive testing (i.e., very impaired) and their clinical presentation or recent history; (b) report or exhibit patterns of cognitive impairment that are inconsistent over time; or (c) exhibit unexpected patterns on neuropsychological testing, such as obtaining correct answers on more difficult items yet failing much easier items, or failing very basic cognitive tasks that even those with true cognitive impairment are able to complete (American Psychiatric Association, 2000b; R. Rogers, 1997). In the case of a feigned amnestic disorder, there will be a lack of evidence of an identifiable cause of the memory loss (H. I. Kaplan & Saddock, 1998).

Dissociative Disorders

Because dissociative disorders involve a disturbance in consciousness, memory, perception, or identity, these clinical conditions can be mistaken for a primary cognitive disorder (American Psychiatric Association, 2000). Dissociative Amnesia involves an inability to recall important personal information that cannot be explained by ordinary forgetfulness; Dissociative Fugue involves sudden and unexpected travel away from home and a concomitant inability to remember portions or the entirety of one's past. It is easy to see how such disorders could be mistaken for an amnestic disorder due to either a general medical condition or the lingering effects of a substance. In both dissociative disorders and cognitive disorders such as amnestic disorders, affected individuals may be unaware of their memory deficits, which further complicates the differential diagnosis. However, a key difference between amnestic and dissociative disorders is that the latter often occur following a traumatic experience and the forgotten material usually has a high emotional valence. Thus, in the case of dissociative disorders there is a presumption that the etiology of the amnesia is psychogenic, and in contrast to an amnestic disorder, there will be no evidence of an organic cause such as a brain injury, general medical condition that can affect cognition, or exposure to substances or toxins that can cause memory impairment. In addition, individuals with dissociative disorders such as Dissociative Amnesia typically will not have difficulty learning new material and instead are amnestic for information that has occurred in the past (i.e., retrograde amnesia; First & Tasman, 2005). Table 7.7 summarizes this differential diagnostic information.

Cognitive Disorders

Delirium versus Dementia

A common differential diagnosis among the cognitive disorders is whether an individual has delirium or dementia or whether a delirium is superimposed on a preexisting dementia (American Psychiatric Association, 1999). The ability to accurately differentiate between

Table 7.7   Between-category diagnostic differential

Disorder	Similarities with Cognitive Disorders	Differences from Cognitive Disorders
Substance intoxication/ withdrawal	Memory disturbance and other cognitive deficits	Occurs only during periods of intoxication or withdrawal
		Deficits are not excessive (e.g., compared to delirium)
Mood disorder (e.g., Major Depressive Disorder)	Attention or concentration difficulties	Likely to overestimate cognitive difficulties
	Slow thinking	Acutely sensitive to failures on cognitive testing
	Possible memory complaints	Mood symptoms may be more prominent than cognitive impairments
	Lack of motivation, apathy	History of depression (though not always a distinguishing feature)
	Agitation or retardation	Better comorbid functioning and abrupt onset of cognitive symptoms
	Disruptions in sleep	More likely than individuals with DAT to benefit from cues in memory testing
Psychotic disorder (e.g., Schizophrenia)	Multiple cognitive impairments	Age of onset typically in late adolescence or early adulthood
	Decline in functioning	Cognitive impairment typically less severe compared to dementia
	Presence of psychotic symptoms (seen in delirium, later stages of dementia)	Psychotic symptoms a prominent part of clinical presentation
		Delusions highly systematized EEG normal
Mental retardation	Impairments in wide range of cognitive functions	Cognitive impairment has onset prior to age 18
		Memory impairment may not be present
		Nondeteriorating course. Impairments in consciousness or arousal not expected
Malingering or Factitious Disorder	Cognitive impairments that are reported to interfere with functioning	Cognitive deficits often not consistent over time or with symptom patterns seen in bona fide cognitive disorders

		Reported impairments typically worse than observed functioning
		Issues of secondary gain are notable (malingering)
Dissociative disorders	Impairment in consciousness, memory, perception	Impairments likely to begin after traumatic experience
	May be unaware of memory deficit	Psychogenic versus medical cause
		Forgotten material often has emotionally symbolic meaning
		Typically no difficulty learning new material (i.e., amnestic for past information)

delirium and dementia is an important but challenging task. Because a delirium is potentially reversible if appropriate treatment for the underlying cause is provided, timely identification of this condition is especially important. Part of what makes differentiating between delirium and dementia difficult is that both conditions involve global cognitive impairment and both become increasingly common in older populations (Lipowski, 1992). Furthermore, delirium is a common comorbid condition in dementia (sometimes referred to as *beclouded dementia*), particularly in VD and late-onset DAT, and acute delirium may actually be an early sign of an underlying dementia (H. I. Kaplan & Saddock, 1998; Laurila et al., 2004b; Robertsson, 2003).

The onset and resolution of symptoms can usually help to differentiate a delirium from a dementia, because symptoms of delirium have a rapid onset (i.e., usually within hours to days), whereas the symptoms of dementia frequently have a gradual onset. However, it should be recognized that the time course for symptom onset among different types of dementias varies, and while the progression of DAT is often gradual, the symptoms of VD can be much more rapid, depending on the location and extent of brain injury due to infarctions (Rockwood & Lindesay, 2003). Abrupt onset can also characterize other dementias, such as Lewy body dementia (Meagher & Trzepacz, 1998). As has been noted, delirium is largely considered a reversible syndrome, whereas dementia is not.

Demented individuals (e.g., those with Alzheimer's disease) can experience increased agitation at night that may appear similar to the sleep-wake cycle problems seen in delirium. Estimates of sundowning in demented individuals range from 12% to 28% (Little, Satlin, Sunderland, & Volicer, 1995). However, demented individuals are usually alert and aware during the daytime and will not show the disturbances in arousal or consciousness that characterize delirious individuals (American Psychiatric Association, 1999). Finally, whereas delirious individuals will show fluctuations in such symptoms throughout the day, this is not typical of dementia (Bliwise, 1994; Lipowksi, 1992).

It can be particularly challenging to identify delirium among individuals with known dementia because delirium superimposed on dementia does not necessarily look qualitatively different from a delirium that occurs in the absence of dementia. In their study of

over 300 elderly patients, Cole, McCusker, Dendukuri, and Han (2002) found that delirium appeared phenomenologically similar among patients with and without dementia,
although patients with dementia exhibited more psychomotor agitation at the time of diagnosis and more disorganized thinking and disorientation at a second assessment
24 hours later. Trzepacz et al. (1998) found that while delirious demented individuals had
lower MMSE scores than purely delirious individuals, no differences were found in total
scores on the Delirium Rating Scale or the Brief Psychiatric Rating Scale, or in EEG
findings. Signs such as perceptual and motor disturbances, disorientation, and impairments in memory or abstract thinking may raise the index of suspicion for delirium in
nondemented individuals, but they are of less diagnostic value in identifying a *comorbid*
delirium in a demented individual since many of these signs are quite common in dementia alone (Laurila et al., 2004b). S. A. Jacobson (1997) suggests that deterioration in function or changes in behavior (e.g., incontinence, refusal to walk) may point to comorbid
delirium in elderly patients with known dementia. The difficulty of differentiating delirium from dementia and in determining if the two conditions are comorbid underscores the
importance of obtaining information from collateral sources (e.g., family members, previous treatment providers) to establish if there was evidence of dementia prior to the onset
of symptoms of delirium.

Amnestic Disorder versus Dementia or Delirium

The memory impairment associated with amnestic disorder can be mistaken for dementia.
However, unlike dementia, the cognitive impairment in amnestic disorder does not involve multiple areas (e.g., language, executive functioning) and is instead restricted to
significant memory impairment. Similarly, while delirium can be characterized by memory impairment, this syndrome differs from an amnestic disorder in that it is also characterized by impairments in attention and consciousness (American Psychiatric Association,
2000b). Typically, amnestic individuals have an unclouded sensorium, are cooperative,
and are able to concentrate (de Renzi, 2000). Key features that characterize delirium, dementia, and amnestic disorders and characteristics that help differentiate between these
disorders are presented in Table 7.8.

TREATMENT

General Principles in Treating Cognitive Disorders

The treatment of cognitive disorders is multidisciplinary and involves close coordination
of care among several disciplines. Mental health counselors will need to develop strong
alliances with various physicians (including internists, psychiatrists, and neurologists)
and nursing staff and should also view the active involvement of family members and
caregivers as critical for good client care. For clients not severely impaired by their cognitive deficits, psychotherapy may be appropriate. However, the more cognitively impaired
the client is, the less intense the clinician's role will be in the client's direct care; instead,
primarily physicians and nursing staff will be involved. However, mental health clinicians
may still play an important role in the client's care by helping family members deal with
the stress and negative emotional consequences that occur when a loved one is cognitively

Table 7.8   Cognitive disorders: key and discriminating features

Disorder	Key Features	Discriminating Features
Delirium	Disturbance of consciousness. Change in cognition.	Disturbance develops over short time. Symptoms tend to fluctuate during course of day. Reversible.
Dementia	Multiple cognitive deficits that include memory impairment. Deficits represent a decline from previous level of functioning.	Temporal onset typically more gradual than delirium. Sleep-wake cycle less likely to be impaired than in delirium. Irreversible.
Amnestic disorder	Memory impairment (inability to learn new information or recall previously learned information). Memory impairment represents a decline from previous level of functioning.	Cognitive impairment restricted to memory. Sensorium typically unclouded. Irreversible.

Source: From *Diagnostic and Statistical Manual of Mental Disorders,* fourth edition, text revision, by American Psychiatric Association, 2000b, Washington, DC: Author. Adapted with permission.

impaired. Specific treatments for delirium, dementia, and amnestic disorder will be presented, followed by general information about family and caregiver interventions and support groups.

Delirium

Delirium is a medical emergency and, as such, its treatment is carried out primarily by physicians and other medical professionals. Nevertheless, mental health professionals should be knowledgeable about the signs and symptoms of delirium so that they can recognize suspected cases and quickly refer them for appropriate medical care. In addition, mental health professionals can provide family members with support and can help affected individuals process their experiences following resolution of the delirium.

When delirium has been diagnosed, the medical team's first charge is to determine the underlying cause (e.g., infection, electrolyte imbalance, medication toxicity) so that it can be effectively treated. Common causes of delirium are presented in Table 7.3. Because medications are among the most common causes of delirium, a careful review of all medications (including nonprescription medications) is undertaken, with particular attention paid to dosages and recent changes or discontinuation, newly prescribed medications, and potential drug interactions. If medications are implicated in a delirium, they may be discontinued or administered at a much lower dosage, or a lower risk drug may be substituted. If the delirium is due to drug *withdrawal* (e.g., sedatives), the offending class of drug may actually be reinstituted to stop the delirium (Marcantonio, 2002). Even when an individual has had no recent changes in medications and has tolerated the current medication regimen well in the past, changes in physical condition (e.g., due to illness, disease, or age) can result in changes in the body's ability to metabolize medications and result in an increased risk of developing a delirium. Because delirium can be life-threatening, nursing staff must frequently monitor the patient's medical condition, including fluid intake and output, vital signs, and oxygenation (American Psychiatric Association, 1999).

Medication

Antipsychotic medications are the preferred pharmacologic agents for treating delirium (see Lipowski, 1992; Trzepacz, 1996). Although much of the evidence supporting this comes from case studies, a randomized, double-blind comparison study examining delirium among AIDS patients found that treatment with the neuroleptics haloperidol or chlorpromazine resulted in significant improvement in delirium symptoms and a very low rate of *extrapyramidal side effects* (Breitbart et al., 1996). Indeed, haloperidol is the most frequently used medication to treat delirium since it has few cholinergic side effects, a short half-life, and carries a lower likelihood of sedation than other antipsychotics (American Psychiatric Association, 1999). However, in some cases neuroleptic medications may actually prolong delirium and increase a patient's stupor (Marcantonio, 2002; Meagher, 2001), and older, so-called first-generation antipsychotic medications also carry higher risks of extrapyramidal side effects, tardive dyskinesia, and neuroleptic malignant syndrome than newer-generation, atypical antipsychotics (Trzepacz & Breitbart, 1999). With regard to the latter, recent studies indicate that risperidone and olanzapine may effectively treat delirium (Han & Kim, 2004; C. Y. Liu, Juang, Liang, Lin, & Yeh, 2004; Sipahimalani & Massand, 1998). Many of these studies have utilized relatively small sample sizes, but a larger uncontrolled, open-label study of olanzapine in the treatment of delirium in hospitalized cancer patients found that more than 75% experienced a resolution of their delirium within 7 days of study entry, and that patients younger than 70 showed a particularly good response (i.e., >90% experienced delirium resolution). Patients in this study were treated with relatively low doses of medication and experienced an exceptionally low rate of side effects (including no extrapyramidal side effects; Breitbart et al., 2003).

Benzodiazepines may also be used to treat delirium, but may overly sedate the patient or produce a paradoxical excitatory effect (Flacker & Marcantonio, 1998). In addition, Brietbart and colleagues (1996), in a randomized, double-blind, comparison trial, found benzodiazepines less effective than antipsychotic medications (haloperidol and chlorpromazine) in treating delirium. However, there are certain situations in which benzodiazepines may be preferred to an antipsychotic, including in the treatment of alcohol or benzodiazepine withdrawal and in cases where it is necessary to raise the seizure threshold (since antipsychotics lower seizure threshold; American Psychiatric Association, 1999). In some situations, both classes of drugs may be used in combination to treat a delirium. A potential drawback of utilizing psychotropic medications to treat delirious individuals (whether children or adults) is that their use can make accurate evaluation of changing cognitive function more difficult due to the medication's effects on mental status (Meagher, O'Hanlon, O'Mahony, & Casey, 1996; Prugh et al., 1980). Furthermore, in some cases such medications may be primarily used for reasons other than direct benefit to the patient, such as easing family members' discomfort about the patient's agitation (Fainsinger, Tapper, & Bruera, 1993). Interestingly, although the pathogenesis of delirium (especially medication-induced delirium) has been associated with anticholinergic mechanisms, relatively few studies have been conducted examining the effectiveness of cholinergic drugs; however, the results of these studies have been promising and indicate a need for future research in this area (American Psychiatric Association, 1999).

Environmental Interventions

Because sensory deprivation can worsen a delirium (and in rare cases be the sole or primary cause), it is important for delirious patients to be frequently reoriented to their surroundings and to have familiar objects or persons around them. An otherwise unfamiliar or sterile-looking hospital room can be altered by having pictures of family members and loved ones and other familiar objects from home by the bedside; large clocks and wall calendars can help orient the patient; and incandescent lighting and soft music can create a more home-like atmosphere that can relax the patient (Marcantonio, 2002). If the affected individual normally uses glasses or a hearing aid, these should be provided to avoid further sensory impairment (S. A. Jacobson, 1997). Staff members should frequently orient the patient to his or her surroundings (e.g., remind the patient of where he or she is, the date). Similarly, family members can reorient the patient when they visit and should be instructed to keep communication simple, concise, and clear. Ideally, efforts should be made to avoid excessive staff changes, and noise levels (e.g., from radios, televisions) should be minimized on wards where delirium patients are being treated (Meagher et al., 1996). Because the sleep-wake cycle is so often disrupted during a delirium, lowering lights and minimizing extraneous sounds at night can help promote sleep in the evening. Unfamiliar individuals (e.g., doctors, nursing staff) should always introduce themselves and explain what they are doing with the patient (e.g., checking vital signs) in a quiet, gentle, and reassuring manner that avoids the use of medical jargon the patient is unlikely to understand (Marcantonio, 2002). Although many of the aforementioned strategies are aimed at reducing overstimulation, it is important to recognize that understimulation can also be problematic, and a regular degree of modest visual, tactile, and vocal stimulation should be utilized with delirious individuals (American Psychiatric Association, 1999). Behavioral agitation is important to control among delirious persons to avoid injuries that could be caused by falls or pulling out IV lines or catheters.

Some of the aforementioned environmental interventions (e.g., making surroundings more familiar, speaking to the patient in a calm, reassuring tone) may help prevent or de-escalate agitation; however, in some cases physical restraints or use of medications (sometimes referred to as chemical or pharmacological restraints) may be necessary. In the case of the former, because restraints carry a risk of injury and can increase the patient's agitation, they are considered only when other means of controlling the patient's behavior have been ineffective (American Psychiatric Association, 1999).

Medical staff should routinely evaluate the delirious patient's ability to carry out basic activities of daily living. Although the patient may be unlikely to carry out any self-care activities initially, as the delirium begins to resolve it becomes important to encourage the patient to adopt an increasingly greater role in his or her self-care to prevent a cycle of dependence from occurring and to maximize functional independence and recovery (Marcantonio, 2002). It is important to provide delirious individuals with reassurance regarding their symptoms. This can take the form of information that such symptoms are common among individuals with similar medical issues and should abate with treatment of the underlying conditions that caused them. Patients may be especially distressed by cognitive symptoms and, if appropriate (e.g., if there is no evidence that the delirium is due to a stroke or injury to the brain; if there is not suspicion of an underlying dementia), reassurance can be given that these deficits are typical of what occurs in a delirium and are temporary (American Psychiatric Association, 1999).

Postdelirium Care

Although memory is often impaired in a delirium, some clients may recall significant portions of their delirium experience and be quite distressed by it. In fact, a minority of patients may be so distressed by their recollections of the delirium experience that their reaction may resemble Posttraumatic Stress Disorder (S. A. Jacobson, 1997). The clinician may therefore need to spend time processing the experience with the client, exploring concerns about the consequences of the delirium (e.g., "Will this happen again?"), and addressing fears that this experience may have stimulated about issues such as becoming ill or infirm, losing control, or being dependent on others. It is also necessary to ensure that patients have received appropriate education regarding the causes of their delirium so that they are aware of risk factors that could result in another delirium in the future (American Psychiatric Association, 1999).

Dementia

Unfortunately, there is no cure for dementia. Thus treatment is aimed at trying to slow the rate of cognitive decline and help the affected individual remain as functional as is safely possible for as long as possible. It is also critical that the individual's physician closely monitor and treat any comorbid medical conditions that may be exacerbating dementia symptoms or contributing to associated behavioral disturbances. To effectively monitor cognitive functioning and the development of noncognitive psychiatric symptoms, demented individuals will generally be seen by their treating physicians at least every 4 to 6 months, or more frequently should there be changes in treatment regimens, complex symptom presentations, or evidence of dangerous symptoms or behaviors (American Psychiatric Association, 1997).

J. L. Cummings (2003) identified the following four components of treatment for DAT: (1) cholinesterase inhibitor therapy to improve, temporarily stabilize, or temporarily reduce the rate of cognitive decline; (2) disease-modifying therapies (e.g., vitamin E) intended to reduce the progression of DAT; (3) psychotropic medication to treat neuropsychiatric symptoms and behavior disturbance; and (4) working with caregivers to address their emotional needs and to develop an alliance to optimize patient care. Goals for the treatment of VD are similar, but different medications and approaches may be used in an attempt to slow the rate of cognitive decline.

Acetylcholinesterase Inhibitors

As noted previously, dementia is associated with decreases in acetylcholine. When acetylcholine is released by neurons, it is eventually broken down by the enzyme acetylcholinesterase; acetylcholinesterase inhibitors enhance cholinergic functioning by preventing this breakdown from occurring and allowing greater amounts of acetylcholine to remain in the synapse (i.e., space between neurons) to interact with postsynaptic receptors. Four acetylcholinesterase inhibitors are currently available for the treatment of dementia: tacrine, donepezil, galantamine, and rivastigmine. The oldest of these agents, tacrine, is associated with increased risk of liver toxicity and has a short half-life, and therefore is now rarely used (J. L. Cummings, 2003).

Acetylcholinesterase inhibitors cannot halt cognitive decline nor dramatically improve cognitive functioning. However, use of these medications in mild to moderately demented individuals improves or maintains cognitive functioning (as measured by neuropsychological testing, MMSE scores, etc.) by an amount that would be expected to be lost over 6 months in an untreated case, and is also associated with improvements in measures of global functioning and psychiatric and behavior disturbances, delays in nursing home placement, and decreased nursing home mortality rates (Gasper, Ott, & Lapane, 2005; Geldmacher, Provenzano, McRae, & Ieni, 2003; Kurz, Farlow, Quarg, & Spiegel, 2004; Lopez-Pousa et al., 2005; Paleacu, Mazeh, Mirecki, Even, & Barak, 2002; Trinh, Hoblyn, Mohanty, & Yaffe, 2003; Whitehead et al., 2004; Wilkinson & Murray, 2001). Results from longer-term studies further suggest that acetylcholinesterase inhibitors can be safely used and tolerated by patients for periods of a year or more and that modest improvements in cognitive functioning continue to be seen relative to untreated individuals (Almkvist, Darreh-Shori, Stefanova, Speigel, & Nordberg, 2004; Dengiz & Kerhsaw, 2004; Lyketsos, Reichman, Kershaw, & Zhu, 2004). For some patients, the medication may maintain some level of effectiveness for several years. Therefore, it is recommended that treatment with an acetylcholinesterase inhibitor be initiated as soon as a diagnosis of DAT is made and should be continued until the patient reaches the advanced stages of the disease (J. L. Cummings, 2003). These medications may take up to 6 weeks before improvement in baseline memory or behavior is evident and months before symptom stabilization is evident (S. M. Stahl, 2006).

A meta-analysis of randomized, placebo-control treatment studies utilizing donepezil, rivastigmine, or galantamine found that all were similarly efficacious and superior to placebo in improving cognitive functioning, and that larger effects were seen with higher doses of donepezil and rivastigmine (Ritchie, Ames, Clayton, & Lai, 2004). Another meta-analytic study comparing donepezil and galantamine similarly concluded that neither drug was superior to the other in affecting cognitive functioning and that both produced modest improvements in cognitive functioning in individuals diagnosed with DAT (Harry & Zakzanis, 2005). Thus, the decision of which specific acetylcholinesterase inhibitor to use is likely to be guided by factors such as side effect profile, individual patient tolerance, and dosing considerations (e.g., donepezil requires only once per day dosing). Nausea, vomiting, loose stools, decreased heart rate, headache, sweating, and dizziness are among some of the side effects reported by users of acetylcholinesterase inhibitors, although these are often transient and tend to occur when treatment is initiated (Kennedy, 2000). Because rivastigmine appears to cause weight loss to a greater degree than other acetylcholinesterase inhibitors, this needs to be monitored closely in patients (especially females) on this medication (J. L. Cummings, 2003). Finally, although acetylcholinesterase inhibitors have been studied primarily in relation to DAT, evidence is emerging that these medications may also improve cognitive functioning (e.g., working memory, delayed recognition memory, general cognitive functioning) among those with VD

(Kurz, Erkinjuntti, Small, Lilienfeld, & Damaraju, 2003; Malouf & Birks, 2004; Moretti, Torre, Antonello, Cazzato, & Bava, 2003; Thomas, Libon, & Ledakis, 2005).

Other Agents

In 2003, the U.S. Food and Drug Administration (FDA) approved memantine for the treatment of moderate to severe DAT. This medication is an N-methyl-D-aspartate (NMDA) antagonist believed to attenuate toxic effects of increased calcium flow into neurons through the blockade of NMDA receptors (Schatzberg, Cole, & DeBattista, 2005). Like acetylcholinesterase inhibitors, memantine cannot reverse the degenerative process associated with dementia, but may slow disease progression (although this may take months to notice). Randomized, double-blind controlled clinical trials have found that memantine resulted in significantly better global, behavioral, and cognitive outcomes than placebo and has low rates of discontinuance due to adverse effects (Peskind et al., 2005). Memantine has been reported to be effective among a range of community-dwelling and institutionalized patients, including newly diagnosed individuals and those previously or concurrently taking acetylcholinesterase inhibitors (Bullock, 2006). Memantine also appears effective for VD (Wilcock, Möbius, & Stöffler, 2002; Winblad & Jelic, 2003).

Disease-Modifying Treatments

For individuals considered at risk for or who are in the early stages of dementia, treatments designed to delay the onset or to slow the rate of cognitive decline may be considered. Among such treatments for DAT are antioxidants, anti-inflammatory agents, hormones, and antihypertensives. Some of these same treatments have also been used for VD.

Dementia of the Alzheimer's type appears to involve oxidative injury to brain cells (Markesbery, 1999). Recent evidence suggests that VD may also be associated with oxidative stress and the depletion of antioxidant micronutrients and oxidative modification (Polidori et al., 2005). Interest has therefore centered on the role that *antioxidants* may play in slowing the onset or progression of dementia; this has primarily been studied in relation to DAT. The first study demonstrating the potential positive benefits of antioxidants found that 1,000 IU of vitamin E (α-tocopherol) or a 5mg twice daily dosage of selegiline were equally efficacious in delaying severe dementia by approximately 8 months in patients with moderate DAT, and that the combination of these agents was not more efficacious than either used alone (Sano et al., 1997). In a large-scale study of elderly individuals in Utah, Zandi et al. (2004) found that a combination of vitamins E and C (ascorbic acid) supplements was associated with reduced DAT prevalence and incidence assessed 3 years later. A retrospective chart review study comparing 130 DAT patients treated with the cholinesterase inhibitor donepezil and vitamin E to patient data collected prior to the availability of these treatments found that those on the combination therapy declined at a significantly lower rate (Klatte, Scharre, Nagaraja, Davis, & Beversdorf, 2003). It should be noted, however, that other studies have failed to find a link between antioxidants and DAT or cognitive decline. Engelhart and colleagues (2005), for example, found that higher plasma levels of vitamins A and E were not significantly associated with lower prevalence of DAT (or cognitive decline in nondemented subjects) when adjusting for factors such as age, sex, and total cholesterol. Although the evidence is equivocal, the generally favorable cost and safety profile of vitamin E makes this a likely recommendation for most individuals with mild to moderate DAT (Knopman, 2002). However, it should be noted that high doses of vitamin E are associated with reduced blood coagulation and potential problems with blood clotting, so this treatment must be used with caution in those who have bleeding disorders, are receiving anticoagulation therapy, or who have liver disease (Masterman & Cummings, 2001).

Epidemiological studies suggest that use of *anti-inflammatory drugs,* such as nonsteroidal anti-inflammatory drugs (NSAIDs), may be associated with reduced risk of developing DAT (see McGeer, Schulzer, & McGeer, 1996, for a review). However, randomized controlled trials of such agents have largely yielded negative findings (Aisen et al., 2003; Reines et al., 2004). Yet, findings from the Rotterdam study that NSAID use was associated with significantly reduced risk of developing DAT in those who used the drug for 2 or more years suggest that to be effective NSAID therapy for DAT may require prolonged use (In t' veld, Ruitenberg, Hofman, Stricker, & Breteler, 2001). It should be noted that this same study found that risk reduction associated with NSAID use was most pronounced for VD. Based on the collective findings of research in this area, use of anti-inflammatory agents is not currently considered a preventive or therapeutic treatment for DAT (Masterman & Cummings, 2001).

Interest in the use of *hormone replacement therapy* as a means to delay onset of cognitive decline associated with dementia was spurred by observations that women have a higher prevalence of DAT and are also estrogen-deficient following menopause. Unfortunately, the role of hormone replacement therapy as either a preventive measure to forestall the onset of DAT or as a disease-slowing agent in the treatment of known cases of DAT now appears uncertain. While some studies of women receiving hormone replacement therapy indicate a decreased risk of developing DAT (Yaffe et al., 2005), a recent study of long-term use of estrogen replacement in older postmenopausal women found no protective effects on cognition and a heightened risk of dementia (Rapp et al., 2003). However, the latter finding may suggest that hormone replacement therapy initiated in old age with the hope of preventing DAT is not likely to be successful, whereas the protective benefits of such treatment may be seen with earlier use (Breitner & Zandi, 2003). Studies of estrogen replacement therapy in women with known mild to moderate DAT have also failed to show significant delays in progression of cognitive deterioration compared to placebo (Henderson et al., 2000; A. J. Levine & Battista, 2004; Mulnard et al., 2000). Thus, although hormone replacement therapy may play a role in delaying the onset of dementia, strong evidence is lacking regarding the ability of this treatment to significantly modify the course of the disease in already diagnosed patients.

Given that hypertension is a risk factor for dementias, including DAT and VD, use of antihypertensive agents as a means to delay onset of dementia is logical to consider. Research evidence suggests that a variety of blood pressure-lowering medications, including ACE (angiotensin-converting enzyme) inhibitors, calcium channel blockers, beta blockers, and diuretics, may slow progression of cognitive decline among elderly individuals and protect against the development of dementia (Forette et al., 2002; Rozzini et al., 2006). Khachaturian and colleagues (2006) demonstrated that while use of any antihypertensive medication was associated with a decreased incidence of dementia, potassium-sparing diuretics were associated with the greatest reduction in risk of DAT.

Additional aggressive management of cardiovascular risk factors and steps to prevent stroke have been recommended for the treatment of VD (Burruss et al., 2001; Haan & Wallace, 2004). This can include lifestyle changes and/or medications for risk factors such as high cholesterol or triglycerides and diabetes, identification and treatment of conditions such as atrial fibrillation and carotid vascular occlusive disease, and use of anticoagulation therapy, among others (Burruss et al., 2001; Langa, Foster, & Larson, 2004). The evidence that cholesterol-lowering drugs known as *statins* are associated with decreased risk of dementia and slower disease progression in those already diagnosed with dementia is mixed (Miida, Takahasi, Tanabe, & Ikeuchi, 2005; Patatanian & Gales, 2005). Thus at the current time, it appears premature to routinely recommend this class of drug to either prevent or aid in the treatment of DAT until research further clarifies the relationship between cholesterol and cognitive decline.

Psychotropic Medications

Antipsychotic medications may be prescribed for demented individuals experiencing behavioral symptoms such as agitation, aggression, sleep disturbance, and wandering and/or psychotic symptoms. With regard to psychosis, prior to prescribing neuroleptics it is important for the treating physician to first rule out treatable medical causes that could be at the root of such symptoms (e.g., medications, drugs) as well as factors such as poor vision or hearing that can contribute to the development of psychotic symptoms. Psychotic symptoms that do not have an adverse impact on the client (e.g., hallucinations that are comforting) may not warrant pharmacologic intervention; in such cases, intervention with family members and caregivers around their discomfort with such behavior may be more appropriate (Cohen-Mansfield, 2003). Although demented individuals exhibiting agitation or psychosis may be treated with first-generation antipsychotic medications (e.g., haloperidol), side effects such as akathisia, tardive dyskinesia, and parkinsonism are common (L. S. Schneider, Pollack, & Lyness, 1990). In the treatment of primary psychotic disorders (e.g., Schizophrenia) second-generation (atypical) antipsychotic medications are generally favored because they carry a lower risk of extrapyramidal symptoms (e.g., parkinsonism) and tardive dyskinesia. However, a review by Ballard and Waite (2006) of randomized, double-blind studies utilizing atypical antipsychotic medications in the treatment of dementia indicated that while risperidone and olanzapine result in improvement in aggression and risperidone decreases psychotic symptoms, a significantly higher incidence of serious adverse cerebrovascular events was associated with risperidone. Similar conclusions were reached in a meta-analysis undertaken by the U.S. Food and Drug Administration (FDA & Public Health Advisory, 2005), which found an elevated death rate among individuals treated with atypical antipsychotic drugs compared to those given placebos. Subsequently, manufacturers of atypical antipsychotics have been required by the FDA to place a black box warning on packages indicating this risk and stating that these medications are not approved for the treatment of dementia. Because of this risk, use of atypical antipsychotics in patients with dementia is likely to be considered only when patients display a serious, life-threatening risk to themselves or others and after nonpharmacologic options (e.g., adhering to predictable routines, utilizing environmental interventions to reduce confusion and restlessness, simplifying tasks) have been exhausted (S. S. Jones, 2006).

Psychosocial Interventions

General Cognitive Stimulation and Reality Orientation Interventions   These interventions attempt to improve overall cognitive and social functioning among individuals with dementia. Rather than narrowly focus on memory functioning, these interventions utilize tasks that tap a range of cognitive functions (e.g., attention, memory, language, problem solving) because it is assumed that memory does not operate in isolation, but is instead integrated in a complex way with other mental abilities (Clare & Woods, 2004). Reality orientation paradigms involve the presentation and repetition of information designed to help orient individuals to their environment (this may take place throughout the day or in specific group or classroom meetings; Spector et al., 2003). Unfortunately, there have been relatively few well-conducted, randomized, controlled trials of such interventions. An exception was a large, randomized, controlled, multisite, single-blind study by Spector et al. that compared an empirically grounded cognitive stimulation and reality orientation intervention to a usual activities control group in a sample of approximately 200 demented individuals (mean MMSE score = 14), none of whom were taking an acetylcholinesterase inhibitor. The selection of specific activities included in the 7-week, 14-session intervention was influenced by previous findings in the literature, and examples included reminiscing about the past, using objects (e.g., CD player), discussing pictures of individuals, guessing the cost of various items, and creating maps. The program also included a reality orientation board that displayed both personal and orientation information (e.g., the group's name). The nature of the usual activities control condition varied across sites and ranged from essentially no activities to arts and crafts, bingo, and music. At the end of treatment, the cognitive stimulation group had significantly higher scores on two measures of cognitive functioning (MMSE and Alzheimer's Disease Assessment Scale—Cognition) and on a quality of life measure. However, no differences in anxiety, depression, functional behaviors (e.g., eating, dressing), or ratings of overall dementia severity were observed between the groups. It is not yet clear whether benefits derived from such interventions are attributable to the direct focus on cognitive functioning per se, the social interaction that is fostered in the intervention, or some combination of both (Clare & Woods, 2004).

Cognitive Training Methods   These techniques involve guided practice on tasks thought to utilize specific domains of cognitive functioning such as memory, attention, or executive functioning. A variety of formats may be used (e.g., computerized tasks, paper-and-pencil activities, tasks that simulate activities of daily living), and presentation may be in either an individual or a group format. Underlying assumptions of these programs are that regular practice can help to improve or maintain specific cognitive functions and effects will generalize beyond the training sessions (Clare & Woods, 2004). Unfortunately, a meta-analytic review of six randomized, controlled clinical trials failed to find significant differences between cognitive training and control conditions on variables such as global dementia severity, memory test scores, verbal fluency scores, depression self-ratings, and general behavior ratings (Clare, Woods, Moniz-Cook, Orrell, & Spector, 2003). However, as Clare and Woods (2004) point out, methodological limitations across studies may obscure possible beneficial effects of cognitive training programs; these limitations include reliance primarily on neuropsychological measures to assess outcome (which in essence is a measure of training generalization and not necessarily the impact on practical day-to-day functioning), comparison to other active treatments rather than placebo conditions (which makes detection of cognitive training effects harder), difficulty designing placebo conditions that do not activate or stimulate participants' cognitive resources (e.g., viewing videos, engaging in unstructured conversations), limited statistical power due to small sample sizes, and possible choice of an insufficient dose (frequency, intensity, and duration) of intervention. Although concerns have been raised about potential negative side effects of cognitive training methods (e.g., patient frustration, depression), Clare and colleagues (2003) did not find such side effects to be common in the randomized, controlled trials they reviewed.

Cognitive Rehabilitation Programs   This type of program, if of sufficient duration and supported by the involvement of caregivers, may be useful for individuals in the early stages of dementia (De Vreese, Neri, Fioravanti, Belloi, & Zanetti, 2001). Cognitive rehabilitation programs offer an individualized approach to help build on areas of strength (e.g., preserved cognitive abilities) and develop compensatory strategies to deal with areas of impairment to enhance or maintain everyday functioning and well-being, reduce excess disability, and reduce strain for family caregivers (Clare & Woods, 2004). Cognitive rehabilitation interventions try to directly address difficulties considered most relevant by the person with dementia and his or her family members and caregivers and target everyday situations in real-life contexts. Goals are selected collaboratively, interventions are typically conducted individually, and tasks in such programs may involve associative memory strategies (e.g., memorizing names of individuals in one's environment using photographs; Clare, Wilson, Carter, Hodges, & Adams, 2001). Techniques such as errorless learning and spaced retrieval may be used to facilitate client performance on memory tasks. Rather than teaching by trial and error, errorless learning paradigms present the correct response in a way that minimizes the possibility of client mistakes (Page, Wilson, Shiel, Carter, & Norris, 2006). This technique is based on the observation that individuals with memory problems have difficulty remembering and correcting errors during the learning process; thus, it is best to avoid errors whenever possible (Evans, Levine, & Bateman, 2004). Spaced retrieval is a method of learning and retaining information that requires an individual to recall information over increasingly longer periods of time (Camp, Foss, O'Hanlon, & Stevens, 1996). These teaching strategies may be effective for individuals with dementing illnesses such as DAT because they appear to rely on implicit memory, a form of unconscious retention that appears to be initially preserved in DAT. Compensatory strategies that might be used in a cognitive rehabilitation paradigm include placing frequently used objects in the same place, using notes and calendars as reminders, utilizing printed labels for objects, maintaining a bulletin board with a list of daily activities and schedules, using photographs as prompts for long-term memory, breaking down tasks into simple steps, and placing a card with important information in one's pocket or wallet (Camp et al., 1996). Randomized, controlled trials are needed, but existing evidence suggests that individuals in the early stages of dementia can learn or relearn personally relevant information, maintain it over time, and apply it in everyday contexts (Clare & Woods, 2004). Such interventions may also increase the quality of interactions between patients and caregivers (Bourgeois, Dijkstra, Burgio, & Allen-Burge, 2001). Interestingly, it appears that demented individuals with higher levels of awareness of their deficits may be particularly likely to benefit from cognitive rehabilitation strategies (Clare, Wilson, Carter, Roth, & Hodges, 2004).

Other Stimulation-Oriented Approaches   Interventions such as *music therapy* and *art therapy* have been used to provide stimulation and enrichment of the demented individual's environment and hopefully stimulate cognitive resources (American Psychiatric Association, 1997). There is limited evidence that such interventions help improve mood and decrease behavioral disturbances. Yet, despite a lack of compelling findings, these interventions seem to carry low risk to clients and have been suggested for inclusion in treatment plans out of humane and commonsense considerations (American Psychiatric Association, 1997).

Exercise may play a role in improving mood and daily functioning of demented individuals. A randomized, controlled trial comparing an intervention consisting of behavioral management training for caregivers and a 3-month home-based patient exercise program to a usual treatment control group demonstrated improved physical functioning, decreased depression, and a trend toward lower rates of institutionalization (at a 2-year follow-up) for individuals with DAT (Teri et al., 2003). Lack of exercise is also correlated with the development of depression among individuals with DAT (Regan, Katona, Walker, & Livingston, 2005). Hypotheses about the positive impact physical activity may have on DAT include (a) cortical stimulation (including increased profusion of oxygen to the brain), (b) promotion of immune system functioning, (c) a possible moderating role on the arteriosclerotic disease process of the brain, and (d) increased plasma levels of sex hormones (Akishita et al., 2005; Bonner & Cousins, 1996; Eggermont, Swaab, & Luiten, 2006).

Amnestic Disorder

Selective serotonin reuptake inhibitors have been used to treat amnestic disorder with mixed success. Unfortunately, relatively few studies have been done in this area, and those have employed small samples of patients. P. R. Martin et al. (1995) and Stapleton et al. (1988) both reported significant improvements in memory function for amnestic patients treated with fluvoxamine (ranging from 200 to 400 mg per day) in small, double-blind, crossover studies, whereas O'Carroll et al. (1994) found no improvement in memory or verbal performance with this same medication. Preuss and Soyka (1999) reported a case study in which paroxetine treatment resulted in memory improvement in a patient with Korsakoff's syndrome. Case reports suggest that galantamine may be beneficial in treating certain forms of amnestic disorder, such as Korsakoff's syndrome (B. K. Phillips et al., 2004).

Family-Based Interventions for Cognitive Disorders

Family members frequently play an important role in the treatment of cognitively impaired individuals. If the affected individual is not in a hospital or nursing home, family members (most often a wife or daughter) frequently become the primary caretakers (Rabins et al., 1999). It has been estimated that 7 of every 10 individuals with DAT in the United States live at home and that 75% of those with DAT are cared for by family members or friends (Alzheimer's Association, 2005). Because of their central role in the cognitively impaired individual's daily care, family members can provide valuable information to a treatment team regarding the client's history and current functioning, which in turn can aid diagnosis and monitoring of progress or decline. Thus family members should be viewed as key collaborators in the treatment process and their views taken into consideration whenever treatment and discharge decisions are made (Hallberg, 2002). C. M. Callahan et al. (2006) found that a collaborative care model for patients with Alzheimer's disease that included an interdisciplinary team led by an advanced practice nurse working with family caregivers resulted in decreased caregiver distress and improvement in caregiver depression.

Because of the tremendous physical and emotional strain that caring for a cognitively impaired relative can create, family members also need support, education, and assistance accessing interventions that may lessen their stress. The information that follows primarily comes from literature on caregiver interventions in dementia since relatively little has been written about these issues with regard to delirium or amnestic disorders (Hallberg, 2002). However, many of the general principles outlined are applicable to families caring for any seriously cognitively impaired individual.

As has been noted, having a relative with a serious cognitive disorder such as delirium or dementia can be highly stressful. In the case of delirium, the rapidly evolving nature of symptoms can be extremely upsetting to family members and loved ones, who may wonder if the patient's current state represents a permanent change in functioning. Additionally, family members may be very distressed about whatever serious underlying trauma, disease, or other condition gave rise to the delirium, and may be physically taxed if involved in keeping watch over the delirious individual to prevent self-harm (Hallberg, 2002). Neuropsychiatric and behavioral symptoms that often occur in syndromes such as delirium and dementia (e.g., agitation, psychotic symptoms) are also particularly difficult to deal with and may substantially increase caregivers' sense of burden (Haput, Romero, & Kurtz, 1996; Zarit, Todd, & Zarit, 1986). When such behavioral disturbances (e.g., aggressive, disruptive, unpredictable behavior) occur early in the course of a relative entering the caregiver role, earlier institutionalization of the demented individual is likely to occur (Gaugler, Kane, Kane, & Newcomer, 2005; Gaugler, Zarit, & Pearlin, 2003).

Studies of caregivers reveal that they have elevated rates of emotional problems (e.g., depression), are often socially isolated, and experience significant personal, financial, and social stressors associated with caring for their impaired family member (Covinsky et al., 2003; Rosenthal, Sulman, & Marshall, 1993; Wayte, Bebbington, Skelton-Robinson, & Orrell, 2004). Relative to noncaregiver controls, caregivers also report more physical symptoms and exhibit a poorer immune response (Glaser & Kiecolt-Glaser, 1994; Schulz & Matire, 2004). Other variables, such as lack of participation in regular exercise, lack of support, and feelings of captivity in the caregiver role, have been found to correlate with caregiver burden and depression (Alspaugh, Stephens, Townsend, Zarit, & Greene, 1999; Gaugler, Anderson, et al., 2004; Karlin, 2004).

The impact of caregiving stress can express itself differently for female and male caregivers of demented individuals. Fitting and colleagues (Fitting, Rabins, Lucas, & Eastham, 1986) found that female caregivers were more likely to report depressive symptoms and marital deterioration, even though the subjective degree of burden expressed by wives and husbands was similar, and that younger wives and older husbands experienced a high degree of burden.

Some longitudinal studies indicate that caregiver burden, stress, and depression may eventually decrease over time as acclimation to the ill relative's situation occurs (Gaugler,

Davey, Pearlin, & Zarit, 2000; D. Roth, Haley, Owen, Clay, & Goode, 2001). However, other research suggests that these findings apply to only a subset of caregivers and that many may leave the caregiver role early in their relative's illness due to feeling overwhelmed (and thus be lost to follow-up in long-term studies of caregiver stress and burden; Gaugler et al., 2005). Thus, how family members initially cope with the stress of taking care of a cognitively impaired relative may strongly influence the trajectory of their long-term caregiving role vis-à-vis their ill relative.

The experience of caring for a demented family member appears to vary among different ethnic groups. A multisite study comparing dementia caregivers (Project REACH: Resources for Enhancing Alzheimer's Caregiver Health) found that Latina caregivers reported lower appraisals of stress, greater use of religious coping, and greater perceived benefits of caregiving compared to Caucasian caregivers (Coon et al., 2004). Latina caregivers also delayed institutionalization of their demented relative longer than Caucasian female caregivers, and those Latinas who identified greater benefits or more positive aspects of the caregiving process were especially less likely to institutionalize their relative. The inverse relationship found in this study between positive views of the caretaker role and acculturation suggests that traditional Latino values such as *familismo* (placing the family above individual, personal interests), *respeto* (respect for older persons), and *dignidad* (maintaining dignity) play important roles in shaping appraisals of the caregiver role (Mausbach et al., 2004). Other data from the Project REACH initiative revealed that African American caregivers reported better well-being, more benign stress appraisals, lower anxiety, less use of psychotropic medications, greater perceived benefits of caregiving, and more frequent use of religious coping and participation than Caucasian caregivers (Haley et al., 2004). However, Gaugler, Leach, Clay, and Newcomer (2004) found that among African American caregivers, those who experienced high levels of burden and difficulty adapting to their role as caregivers were most likely to expedite the placement of the ill relative in a nursing home.

A stress/health model has been used to guide thinking about the nature and consequences of caregiving stress among dementia caregivers. This model assumes that caregiver stressors can be broadly divided into primary stressors that are directly related to providing care to a demented individual (e.g., dealing with symptoms, behavioral problems) and secondary stressors such as decreased relationship quality, conflict with other family members, and job-related difficulties (e.g., missing work, being overly tired at work). Negative outcomes, such as the problems with physical and emotional health previously noted, are assumed to result when perceived stress overwhelms available coping strategies, leading to unhealthy emotional, behavioral, and physiologic responses (Schulz & Martire, 2004). It is assumed that interventions such as family counseling, provision of social support, education, skills training, preventive health practices, and communication can help to mitigate these negative caregiver outcomes.

Although caregiving experiences may be somewhat different across families based on factors such as caregiver demographics (e.g., gender, cultural background), coping strategies, and the severity of the ill relatives' symptoms (particularly behavioral disturbances), some key elements of family interventions have been identified. These include provision of support, the opportunity to verbalize feelings, education to family members about their ill relative's condition, emphasis on the need for family members to seek respite care, and referral to support groups (L. R. Phillips, 1987). We would add to this list strategies to improve caregiver health and well-being. These elements will now be reviewed in greater detail.

Provision of Support and Opportunities to Verbalize Feelings

Family members of seriously cognitively impaired individuals are likely to experience myriad negative emotions that may feel overwhelming and frightening and about which they may be embarrassed to talk. Family therapy and counseling can provide an avenue for caregivers to express such feelings of distress. Family members may experience *chronic grief* throughout their impaired relative's illness and cycle through periods of numbness, anger, and demoralization (Rabins et al., 1999). As noted earlier, rates of *depression* are elevated among caregivers compared to controls; Wisniewski et al. (2003), in a sample of over 1,200 dementia caregivers studied in 6 sites throughout the United States, found that 41% had scores indicating a risk of clinically significant depression on a standardized depression screening instrument. Similarly, Covinsky et al. (2003), in a study of over 5,000 caregivers of persons with dementia, found that nearly 33% endorsed items on a self-report measure indicative of clinically significant depression. Among the caregiver characteristics that predicted depression in this study were relationship to the ill individual (i.e., wife or daughter), low levels of financial resources (income), more hours spent caregiving, and poor caregiver functional status (i.e., ability to carry out ADLs). These findings underscore the importance of being alert to signs that a caregiver may be experiencing a clinical depression that requires specific psychotherapeutic or pharmacologic intervention and recognizing that certain caregivers may be particularly vulnerable to depression.

Anger is another common feeling caregivers should be encouraged to discuss. As Rabins et al. (1999) note, anger and frustration may be experienced toward the patient, other family members or friends, the disorder itself, treatment professionals, and society at large. Discussion of these feelings can help normalize them and provide opportunities for the clinician and family member to evaluate whether anger is reaching a level where adverse emotional or psychological consequences for the family member or ill relative (i.e., abuse) are of concern.

Finally, many family members of seriously cognitively impaired individuals will experience significant *guilt* during the course of their relative's illness. This guilt may be associated with having to make painful decisions that their ill relative cannot understand are necessary, such as restriction of driving privileges, enrollment in an adult day care center, or nursing home placement (Zarit & Zarit, 2006).

Psychoeducation

Providing education to the family is important so they will know the name of their loved one's disorder, its symptoms, available treatments, and prognosis, how to best interact with their ill relative, and to remain vigilant for any worsening of the patient's mental status or ability to engage in basic daily activities (e.g., feeding, self-care). Accurate information can help dispel family members' misconceptions of the client's condition. For example, some family members of demented individuals may need help understanding that when their relative repeatedly asks questions it is not to annoy them but because of memory problems about which the affected individual may have limited awareness (Zarit & Zarit, 2006). In some cases, education about the illness can provide family members a sense of relief, such as information regarding the reversibility of most deliriums with appropriate treatment. Clinicians providing education to family members should recognize that information may need to be repeated several times before it is fully absorbed, that utilization of written materials (e.g., pamphlets, handouts) can help aid discussion of the ill member's condition and facilitate understanding, and that anticipation of family members' questions (i.e., "A lot of people have questions about . . . ") may be needed to overcome feelings of being intimidated by professionals (Rabins et al., 1999). Formal studies of psychoeducational interventions have found that they tend to produce small to moderate effect sizes on variables such as caregiver burden, depression, and perceived ability and knowledge (Sörensen, Pinquart, & Duberstein, 2002). Burns, Nichols, Martindale-Adams, Graney, and Lummus (2003) found that a primary care-based intervention that provided targeted educational materials on dementia resulted in better outcome in general well-being and a trend toward increased risk of depression when a stress management component was added. This highlights the need for psychoeducational interventions to focus both on care recipient behavior *and* caregiving issues to maximize the positive impact on caregiver distress.

Problem Solving

Family members may be uncertain how to respond to changes in behavior, such as agitation, that accompany cognitive disorders. In addition to providing psychoeducation about common symptoms of disorders such as dementia and appropriate responses, it may be helpful to teach family members a general problem-solving strategy that can be utilized to manage problem behaviors in their affected relative. Zarit and Zarit (2006) describe a 6-step problem-solving process that family members of demented individuals can apply to a variety of difficulties they may encounter that emphasizes understanding the conditions that give rise to the behavior and the consequences that may be inadvertently reinforcing it. The steps are (1) pinpointing the behavior and conducting an assessment of how often and when it occurs, (2) identifying antecedent conditions that precede the behavior and consequences of the behavior, (3) brainstorming possible intervention strategies, (4) selecting a strategy to implement based on an evaluation of the pros and cons of each solution generated during brainstorming, (5) planning and rehearsing the implementation of the strategy, and (6) implementing the strategy and assessing its effectiveness. A series of studies examining a Project REACH caregiver program that provided education on modifying the home environment to maximally support the day-to-day functioning of a demented family member found this intervention resulted in improvements in caregiver-reported skills, decreased need for help providing assistance, fewer problematic behavioral occurrences, fewer declines in patients' IADLs, less decline in self-care, and fewer behavior problems relative to a control condition (L. N. Gitlin, Corcoran, Winter, Boyce, & Hauck, 2001; L. N. Gitlin, Hauck, Dennis, & Winter, 2005). Spouses in this intervention also reported being less upset with disruptive behaviors, and female caregivers also demonstrated improvements in affect, overall well-being, and mastery (L. N. Gitlin et al., 2003).

Respite Care

Family members caring for a cognitively impaired relative should be made aware of and encouraged to utilize *respite care*. Respite care, defined as temporary, planned relief for a primary caregiver through the provision of substitute care (D. M. Petty, 1990), encompasses a variety of services that include in-home personal and nursing care, adult day care, and institutional-based care. Such care can be for a certain number of hours during the day, and overnight, weekend, or longer stays can be arranged in cases of emergency or to provide caregivers with a vacation. Taking breaks from the caregiving role is important not only to help protect the physical and emotional health of the caregiver, but also to protect the patient. Exhausted caregivers may forget to administer medications or other treatments properly and are at greater risk for neglecting or abusing their ill family member (Saveman as cited in Hallberg, 2001).

Interestingly, studies examining utilization of respite care have frequently reported low rates among family members, even when concerted outreach efforts are made and financial barriers to accessing these services diminished (C. Cox, 1997). This may reflect reluctance on the part of family members to give up even a small portion of time spent caring for their impaired relative because of feelings of responsibility, guilt, or concerns about the quality or nature of the care that would be provided by nonfamily members. In fact, family members often wait a considerable amount of time (e.g., more than 4 years) before utilizing respite care services (Kosloski & Montgomery, 1993). When caregivers do use respite care it is often for relatively short periods of time, and the most common reason for stopping is to place the impaired family member in long-term residential care, suggesting that family members may view respite care primarily as a means to determine their own and the patient's ability to adjust to a permanent, out-of-home placement (Gottlieb & Johnson, 2000). Although respite care as a transitional step to long-term placement may be appropriate for some families, this relatively narrow focus points to the need for interventions that encourage earlier, more intensive use of respite services as a means of reducing caregiver burden, increasing caregiver well-being, and increasing ability to endure in the caregiving role, particularly for family members who do not have imminent plans for permanent out-of-home placement. Gottlieb and Johnson note a number of important points in this regard: (a) the need to allay fears that program enrollment will result in the caregiver losing control over decision making for their relative, (b) that enrollment is the first step toward long-term placement, and (c) that respite use signifies a failure in coping on the caregiver's part. They further suggest that detailed program information, including use of videos depicting a typical day, would be helpful in achieving these aims.

Eventually an individual may become so impaired that home care becomes impossible. Adult children of demented individuals, for example, may be increasingly torn between responsibilities to their own spouse and children and caring for aging parents. Similarly, older adults caring for a partner who has become demented may have their own physical, mental, and medical limitations that will severely limit the degree of care they can provide and are likely to have fewer resources to rely on in times of emergency (Buckwalker, Smith, Maas, & Kelley, 1998). This may lead to the decision to place the cognitively impaired individual in a long-term care facility (e.g., nursing home). Clinicians should recognize that although family members may experience some relief when their relative is placed in such a setting, the decision to do so is highly stressful and a significant level of anxiety and perceived burden in family members is likely to remain (Albinsson & Strang, 2003; Elmstahl, Ingvad, & Annerstedt, 1998).

Support Groups

Encouragement should be given to family members to utilize support groups for family members, loved ones, and caregivers of persons with cognitive impairment. The Alzheimer's Association, for example, provides information and resources for individuals with DAT and their family members, raises money for research, and is involved in public policy advocacy for affected individuals and their families. This organization has local chapters throughout the United States that sponsor support groups for families and caregivers. Participation in such groups can help to ease feelings of isolation, provide validation of thoughts and feelings, be a source of information exchange on treatment and community resources and strategies for dealing with the illness, and suggest ways to improve caregiver well-being and functioning (Zarit & Zarit, 2006). With the advent of the Internet, support chat rooms have expanded opportunities for family members to seek support and information from others in a similar situation. A study of a telephone-based support group used by an ethnically diverse sample of dementia caregivers found that 80% of participants found the group valuable and that the majority reported increased knowledge and skills as caregivers (A. L. Bank, Arguelles, Rubert, Eisdorfer, & Czaja, 2006). Reductions in caregiver anxiety, depression, and sense of mastery were also noted in this intervention, with wives further exhibiting a significant reduction in ratings on the bothersome nature of caregiving (D. F. Mahoney, Tarlow, & Jones, 2003). Although participation in support groups has been found by some to be less effective than individual and family counseling, they can serve as a useful adjunct to these services (Toseland, Rossiter, Peak, & Smith, 1990). In a study of 406 spouses of individuals with DAT, participants who received a combination of individual and family counseling plus participation in a weekly support group exhibited significantly fewer depressive symptoms after the intervention than did the control subjects receiving usual care, and these effects were sustained for approximately 3 years after baseline (Mittelman, Roth, Coon, & Hayley, 2004).

Strategies to Increase Caregiver Health and Well-Being

Because caregivers of demented individuals are at risk for adverse physical and psychological outcomes, programs designed to directly improve these variables are a potentially valuable component of caregiver interventions. A 12-month, randomized, controlled trial of female caregivers of dementia patients demonstrated that a nutrition education program and a moderate-intensity, home-based, telephone-supervised exercise program significantly reduced reported psychological distress, and participation in the exercise condition was also associated with improvements in energy level, stress-induced blood pressure reactivity, and sleep quality (A. C. King, Baumann, O'Sullivan, Wilcox, & Castro, 2002). Similarly, a small-scale study found that a 6-week yoga intervention significantly reduced anxiety and depression and increased self-efficacy among a sample of Latina and Caucasian caregivers of DAT patients. The intervention included instruction on meditation, hatha yoga, breathing techniques, guided imagery, mantra repetition, discussion of the application of techniques to the caregiving role, and encouragement of regular at-home audiotape-guided practice (Waelde, Thompson, & Gallagher-Thompson, 2004). Finally, the addition of a coping and stress management component to a psychoeducational intervention for caregivers of patients with DAT resulted in significantly better overall outcome and reduced depression risk for caregivers treated in a primary care setting (Burns et al., 2003). Table 7.9 summarizes key elements in the treatment of individuals with cognitive disorders.

Table 7.9   Treatment interventions for cognitive disorders

Area	Interventions
Therapeutic issues	Maintenance of functional independence for as long as possible
	Safety monitoring
	Psychoeducation
	Establishment and maintenance of an alliance with patient's family
	Ongoing monitoring of cognitive, behavioral, and emotional symptoms
	Mourning loss of functioning and independence
	Preparing for future legal and financial issues (e.g., power of attorney, guardianship)
Adjunctive interventions	Medical evaluation and medication referral
	Exercise (dementia)
	Stimulation-oriented approaches (e.g., music, art therapies; dementia)
	Consultation with physician about nutritional supplements, other nonpharmacologic interventions (dementia)
	Legal and financial planning
Family interventions	Psychoeducation on aspects of dementia and delirium and strategies for dealing with behavioral disturbances, loss of function, and cognitive impairment in loved one
	Caregiver interventions (e.g., coping, stress management, exercise) to reduce burden, distress, depression, and other adverse psychological and physical outcomes
	Referral to support groups and organizations
	Discussion of legal and financial planning issues
Disorder-Specific Interventions	
Delirium	Immediate referral to physician or hospital
	Prompt, thorough medical workup to determine cause of delirium
	Low stimulation, frequent reorienting
	Immediate, close monitoring for safety issues
Dementia	Acetylcholinesterase inhibitors or memantine to slow rate of cognitive decline; other medications as needed to treat neuropsychiatric symptoms
	Compensatory strategies and environmental manipulation to maintain functional independence
	Neuropsychological testing to establish baseline cognitive functioning and subsequent stabilization or decline

ADVANCED TOPIC: DEPRESSION AND DEMENTIA

> The patient becomes slow to grasp essentials, thinking is laboured, and behavior becomes generally slipshod and inefficient. Events fail to register either through lack of ability to attend and concentrate or on account of the patient's inner preoccupations. In consequence he may show faulty orientation, impairment of recent memory, and a markedly defective knowledge of current events. The impression of dementia is sometimes strengthened by the patient's decrepit appearance due to self-neglect or loss of weight. (Lishman, 1987, p. 410)

Although this quotation seems to be an accurate portrayal of a demented individual, it is in fact describing the cognitive changes that can be seen in the context of depression. Determining whether a patient is demented or depressed is a challenging but common differential diagnostic question that arises when working with older adults. Elderly demented individuals can display emotional changes (e.g., apathy), changes in appetite, sleep difficulties, and diminished interest that may mistakenly be attributed to a primary psychiatric disorder such as depression, and any accompanying cognitive impairment may also wrongly be ascribed to a presumptive mood disorder (E. K. Mahoney et al., 2000). Conversely, older individuals who are depressed may be misdiagnosed as demented because cognitive changes associated with depression such as mental slowing, forgetfulness, and impairments in executive functioning can be readily mistaken for signs of dementia. Indeed, depression often presents atypically in older adults, with cognitive, somatic, and behavioral symptoms more notable than affective symptoms, which further contributes to potential misdiagnosis of a primary dementing disorder (Murray, 2002). The term *pseudodementia* has been used to describe cases in which prominent cognitive symptoms similar to those seen in dementia are present, but are instead attributable to a primary psychiatric disorder such as depression (Lishman, 1987). Further complicating this differential is the fact that depression is a common symptom in the early to middle stages of dementias such as DAT (M. F. Folstein, 1997); thus in some cases, an individual may qualify for diagnoses of both a dementing disorder and a mood disorder.

Differentiating Depression from Dementia

Because depression can be associated with real and significant cognitive changes in areas such as *attention, psychomotor activity,* and *memory* (Gallassi, Monrreale, & Pagni, 2001), many take exception with the term pseudodementia to refer to these problems because it suggests there is something false about the nature of changes observed in a patient's mental status (J. L. Cummings & Benson, 1992). Instead, the term *depression-associated cognitive decline* has been proposed to refer to cases in which depression involves cognitive changes that result in clinically significant impairment; this term has advantages over other alternatives, such as *dementia syndrome secondary to depression,* because cognitive decline associated with depression rarely meets criteria for a diagnosis of dementia despite the significant impact on functioning that can result (van Gorp, Root, & Sackheim, 2004).

Accurate diagnosis of depression is critical given that improvement in both mood and cognition can often be achieved with appropriate treatment. Misdiagnosis of depression as an irreversible dementia is costly for a number of reasons: (a) providing inappropriate medical treatment; (b) giving the patient and family an inappropriate prognosis in which problems are expected to get worse instead of better; (c) making an inaccurate determination of legal competency; (d) incorrectly placing the patient in a nursing home; and (e) putting the patient at increased risk of suicide because of untreated depression (Murray, 2002). Although appropriate acute and continuation-phase treatment for depression can result in significant improvement in both mood and cognitive symptoms for older depressed adults, some individuals will continue to experience ongoing cognitive impairment despite depression treatment. Bhalla and colleagues (2006) found that after 1 year 45% of their sample of depressed older adults remained cognitively impaired despite remission of depression, with deficits in visuospatial ability, information-processing speed, and delayed memory being most frequent. The persistence of cognitive impairment among depressed elderly is a risk factor for poor depression outcomes; such individuals require aggressive clinical monitoring and management of both their cognitive and affective symptoms (Steffens et al., 2006). Depression severity has also been identified as a risk factor for the development of cognitive decline and dementia, further highlighting the need to carefully monitor depressed elderly over time (Gatz, Tyas, St. John, & Montgomery, 2005).

Nixon (1996) summarized a number of factors that may be helpful in differentiating between depressed and demented individuals. Individuals with cognitive impairments due to depression are likely to have an onset that is more acute than that seen in dementing disorders such as DAT. In cases of depression, a family history of affective disorders (e.g., Major Depressive Disorder, Bipolar Disorder) is also likely. The last observation is complicated by the fact that some research suggests that demented individuals with depression are more likely to have a family history of mood disorders than nondepressed demented individuals (M. E. Strauss & Ogrocki, 1996). The depressed client may be more likely to complain of memory or other cognitive impairment and may overestimate the severity of these deficits. Mental status exam results may be variable across administrations, in contrast to the consistently impaired performance seen among demented individuals. On neuropsychological testing, the depressed individual may exhibit a lack of motivation, be acutely sensitive to failures, and frequently respond to questions with "I don't know." Demented individuals, on the other hand, are more likely to display good cooperation and to appear genuinely frustrated by their poor performance. On memory tests, depressed individuals are likely to exhibit deficits in free recall but may display intact or better recognition memory and are more likely than individuals with DAT to benefit from cues to help recall previously learned information (D. A. King, Caine, Conwell, & Cox, 1990). In contrast, individuals with DAT will show impairments in both recall and recognition memory (Traykov et al., 2002). Murray (2002) found that individuals in the early stages of DAT performed significantly worse on tests of *complex attention functions* (e.g., attention-switching accuracy, focused and divided attention), working and episodic memory, and high-level language comprehension and formulation abilities compared to depressed elderly, whose performance was not distinguishable from normal controls; however, depressed subjects exhibited impaired performance on tests of performance speed and accuracy compared to normal controls.

It should be noted that depression can be particularly difficult to distinguish from subcortical dementias (e.g., dementia due to Parkinson's disease, some forms of VD) since these conditions share features such as generally intact language functions and motor praxis, difficulties with inattention and slow mental processing, and deficits in free recall, but better or intact recognition memory (Caine, 1981; Pillon, Deweer, Agid, & DuBois, 1993; Traykov et al., 2002).

Comorbid Depression and Dementia

Although the preceding focused on the differential diagnosis between depression and dementia, it is important to keep in mind that these conditions are commonly comorbid. In a multisite, longitudinal study of neuropsychiatric symptoms among cognitively impaired individuals, Lyketsos et al. (2002) found that 32% of demented individuals had symptoms of depression, and in most cases these symptoms were clinically significant. Comorbid depression in demented individuals is associated with a worsening of cognitive symptoms. For example, those with DAT and depression have been found to perform significantly worse than nondepressed individuals with DAT on tasks of visuoconstructive ability and speed of information professing (Wefel, Hoyt, & Massman, 1999). Comorbid depression in demented individuals is also associated with greater functional impairment, more rapid functional decline, and earlier institutionalization, thus underscoring the need to identify and treat this condition in demented individuals (Dorenlot, Harboun, Bige, Henrard, & Ankri, 2005; Kales, Chen, Blow, Welsh, & Mellow, 2005; Pearson, Teri, Reifler, & Raskind, 1989; Ritchie, Touchon, & Ledéset, 1998).

The cognitive impairment associated with dementia makes accurate evaluation of depression difficult because affected individuals may be unable to adequately recall and articulate depressive symptoms they have experienced, including the time frame in which symptoms occurred and their severity (Teri, McKenzie, & LaFazia, 2005). Research suggests that an important factor predicting inaccurate self-reported depression is not dementia per se, but deficit awareness, such that individuals who have poor awareness of the impairments associated with their dementia are more likely to be poor reporters of depressive symptoms (Snow et al., 2005).

Level of insight and severity of illness were found by W. J. Burke and colleagues (1998) to be associated with larger discrepancies between self-reported depressive symptoms among demented individuals and symptoms reported by family members, with family members consistently perceiving more depressive symptoms than did patients. Because of potential difficulties with self-reported depression among demented individuals, clinicians should routinely seek additional information from collateral sources, such as family members.

Chapter 8 ———————————————————————

SUBSTANCE-RELATED DISORDERS

Perhaps no other mental health topic provokes as much debate among laypersons and professionals alike as drug abuse and how society ought to best deal with this problem. At various times, addiction has been conceptualized as a manifestation of immoral conduct, a disease, and a maladaptive behavior problem (Thombs, 2006). The spectrum of views on this subject range from the belief that drug use is a war in which prosecution and confinement are the best deterrents, to the assertion that it is a problem whose ill effects may be largely ameliorated through drug legalization. One certainty amid this gamut of opinions is the tremendous cost associated with drug abuse. Statistics reported by the National Institute on Drug Abuse (NIDA, 2004) indicate that total economic costs associated with alcohol and drug abuse in 1992 exceeded $245 billion; this figure included costs associated with drug-related crime, substance abuse treatment and prevention costs, other health care costs, and factors such as reduced job productivity and lost earnings. Undoubtedly this figure would be much higher today. Another staggering statistic concerns the amount of money Americans spend on the abuse of drugs; between 1988 and 1995 it was estimated that $57.3 billion was spent on the use of illicit substances and the misuse of legal drugs (NIDA, 2004). A 2005 survey of adolescents and adults estimated that 22.2 million (or 9.1% of the population) of Americans age 12 or older qualified for a substance dependence or abuse diagnosis; this includes 3.3 million who have both drug and alcohol use disorders, 3.6 million with drug use disorders only, and 15.4 million with alcohol use disorders only (Substance Abuse and Mental Health Services Administration [SAMHSA], 2006). From a mental health perspective, substance use disorders are not only themselves associated with significant morbidity and mortality, but also greatly complicate and impede the course and treatment of co-occurring disorders such as depression, anxiety, and psychotic conditions. The primary focus of this chapter is on the diagnosis and treatment of what are termed *substance use disorders* as defined in the *DSM-IV-TR* (American Psychiatric Association, 2000b), namely, abuse and dependence. Information is also provided on intoxication and withdrawal syndromes, which are classified as *substance-induced disorders* in the *DSM-IV-TR* system (American Psychiatric Association, 2000b), but less emphasis is placed on these conditions relative to the discussion of substance use disorders. The *DSM-IV-TR* (American Psychiatric Association, 2000b) discusses all substance-related disorders in relation to 11 separate classes of substances: (1) alcohol, (2) amphetamines (or similarly acting sympathomimetics), (3) caffeine, (4) cannabis, (5) cocaine, (6) hallucinogens, (7) inhalants, (8) nicotine, (9) opioids, (10) phencyclidine (PCP) or similarly acting arylcyclohexylamines, and (11) sedatives, hypnotics, and anxiolytics. Because it is beyond the scope of this chapter to provide comprehensive information on each substance group separately, the organization of this chapter will be somewhat different from that of other clinical disorder chapters. For example, information regarding onset, course, and life span considerations is presented as a single section, within which important distinctions among various classes of substances are discussed (however, nicotine- and caffeine-related disorders are not discussed). Information on intake and treatment considerations is presented with a focus on *general principles* that are important to address in treating a client with a substance use problem and is supplemented where appropriate with information that is unique to the treatment of specific populations of substance users (e.g., alcohol, opiates). The "Advanced Topic" section focuses on the current epidemic of methamphetamine abuse and concludes the chapter.

HISTORICAL OVERVIEW

Since ancient times alcohol and other psychoactive substances have been viewed as possessing the ability to heal and enlighten, as well as wreak havoc in the lives of those who use them to excess. Writings of the ancient Chinese, Sumerians, Egyptians, Greeks, and Romans discussed the medicinal use of cannabis and opium, and the ancient Mayans, Aztecs, and Incas utilized mushrooms, peyote, and coca leaves (from which cocaine is derived) for sacred as well as healing purposes and to make hard labor or long hunts tolerable (Dobkin de Rios, 1990; Madden, 1999; Westermeyer, 2005). Yet the historical record reveals that writers such as Hippocrates, Aristotle, and Celsus warned of the adverse physical and emotional effects that substances such as alcohol could cause (Madden, 1999). Abstinence from alcohol was also advocated in the early writings of diverse religious traditions, including Hinduism, Buddhism, and Islam (Westermeyer, 2005).

Fast-forwarding to the eighteenth century, the addictive properties of alcohol were described by many writers, and the immoderate use of spirits such as gin, whisky, and rum was thought to lead to adverse behavioral outcomes such as lying, fighting, swindling, burglary, murder, and suicide, as well as physical maladies such as jaundice, epilepsy, melancholy, madness, and even death (Lettsom, 1789). Excessive alcohol consumption was often viewed as a moral failing and a public nuisance, but not necessarily as a disease requiring treatment. One of the first individuals to articulate the latter position was the American physician-surgeon Benjamin Rush (often considered the father of the temperance movement in the United States). Rush advocated for an asylum system to treat alcoholics in which social support, consideration, and respect were deemed important; he also suggested a forerunner of modern-day aversion therapy that involved pairing rum with a tartar emetic (Madden, 1999; Westermeyer, 2005). Rush's (1793) influential publication, *An Inquiry into the Effects of Ardent Spirits on the Human Body and Mind*, warned of social ills that could result from unrestrained drinking (e.g., insanity, poverty, crime, disease) and even provided estimates of deaths in the United States attributable to alcoholism.

In the nineteenth century the notion that alcoholism was a disease gained greater acceptance; the writer Thomas Trotter, in his 1804 *Essay on Drunkenness,* described symptoms such as tolerance, withdrawal tremors, distress, anxiety, depression, and fetal damage that could arise from excessive alcohol consumption (Madden, 1999). The concept of delirium tremens was also formally introduced by Thomas Sutton in 1813. The invention of the hypodermic needle and the use of morphine to treat battle wounds among soldiers in the Civil War led to rising rates of opiate addiction in the second half of the nineteenth century. During this time, the temperance movement gained momentum in the United States. Although they initially were advocates of moderation in alcohol consumption, temperance movement members eventually emphasized complete abstinence from alcohol and other drugs that were considered addictive (e.g., opium and morphine), and they began to lobby for government control over the sale of alcohol. During this time, a "disease-moral model" of substance use was adopted in which conditions such as alcoholism were confusingly viewed both as a disease and a moral failing or sin (Thombs, 2006). Other important developments included the coining of the term "alcoholism" by the Swedish physician Magnus Huss in 1851, and the description of Wernicke's encephalopathy and Korsakoff's syndrome in the late 1880s (i.e., the acute syndrome associated with severe alcohol withdrawal, and the persisting amnestic condition that can follow; Madden, 1999).

The early twentieth century was marked by continuing attempts in the United States to curb the consumption of alcohol, which culminated in passage of the 18th Amendment to the U.S. Constitution, which prohibited the import, export, transport, sale, and manufacture of alcohol (although private possession and consumption were still legal), and enforcement of the National Prohibition Act (also known as the Volstead Act) in 1920. Although lawmakers hoped that the national prohibition of alcohol would decrease crime rates and solve a host of social and financial problems, consumption actually ended up increasing during this period, organized crime took over the production and distribution of alcohol, serious crime rates rose, court and prison systems became overloaded, and rampant corruption of public officials occurred (M. Thornton, 1991). Eventually in 1933 the 18th Amendment was repealed by the 21st Amendment.

In the psychiatric and medical communities, the disease conceptualization of substance dependence continued to gain favor and was embodied in the work of individuals such as Jellinek, whose 1960 text, *The Disease Concept of Alcoholism,* identified five subtypes of alcoholics designated by one of five Greek letters (alpha, beta, gamma, delta, and epsilon). Jellinek contended that gamma, delta, and epsilon alcoholics, who all displayed tolerance and physical dependence, suffered from a disease. This was in contrast to alpha and beta alcoholics, who could experience adverse medical events (e.g., cirrhosis) and social problems as a result of drinking, but were not assumed to have a physical addiction to alcohol or a loss of control around their drinking habits. Self-help groups to aid individuals who excessively used drugs and alcohol began forming in earnest in the United States during the Depression and following World War II. These groups focused on abstinence, social support or fellowship, and reliance on a superior spiritual force in the recovery process (Westermeyer, 2005). The best known of these is Alcoholics Anonymous (AA), which was founded in the 1930s by Bill Wilson, a New York Wall Street stock speculator, and Dr. Bob Smith, an Ohio physician and surgeon. Alcoholics Anonymous and related 12-step programs continue to play an important role in the contemporary treatment of substance use disorders and are discussed in the "Treatment" section of this chapter.

Before moving on to a discussion of substance use disorders, a word should be said about the varying terminology that one encounters in the field of substance use treatment. In the 1970s terms such as *drug abuse, substance abuse,* and *addiction* were typically used with reference to illicit substances, while *chemical dependency* was used to refer primarily to the harmful use of alcohol and sedative-hypnotic drugs; however, beginning in the 1980s such distinctions between classes of substances faded (Ashenberg-Straussner, 2004). Currently, in addition to terms such as *substance use disorder, substance dependence,* and *substance abuse* (encountered in the *DSM* system; American Psychiatric Association, 2000b), harmful use of mood-altering substances is also commonly referred to by terms such as *psychoactive substance use disorders* and *alcohol and other drug use* (AOD) *disorders* (Ashenberg-Straussner, 2004).

SUBSTANCE ABUSE AND DEPENDENCE

Substance Abuse

If one conceptualizes drug or alcohol use as falling along a continuum, substance abuse is considered less severe than dependence but more serious and problematic than experimental use or recreational use (Lessa & Scanlon, 2006). In the *DSM* system, the diagnostic distinction between substance abuse and dependence was first introduced in the *DSM-III.* According to the *DSM* system, for a given substance, an individual cannot be diagnosed with both abuse of and dependence on the substance (e.g., cocaine dependence and cocaine abuse); if present, a diagnosis of dependence overrides the diagnosis of abuse for a given substance (American Psychiatric Association, 2000b).

According to the *DSM-IV-TR,* substance abuse is characterized by at least one of four recurrent, significant adverse consequences stemming from drug or alcohol use that has occurred within the past year; examples include using a substance in a situation that is physically hazardous and continuing to use in spite of interpersonal or social problems resulting from the substance use (American Psychiatric Association, 2000b). The recurring nature of the problematic consequences helps to differentiate substance abuse from nonproblematic types of use (e.g., experimental, recreational; A. Frances et al., 1995). However, in contrast to the more pervasive problems associated with substance dependence, substance abusing individuals still exercise a degree of choice and control over their substance use (Lessa & Scanlon, 2006). However, the *DSM-IV-TR* (American Psychiatric Association, 2000b) also states that the pattern of use must be *maladaptive* and the resulting problems must be *recurrent,* which helps to differentiate abuse from nonproblematic types of use (e.g., experimental, recreational; A. Frances et al., 1995). The *DSM-IV-TR* indicates that recurrent substance-related legal problems are a symptom of substance abuse; however, this symptom has been found to be among the poorest discriminators of problematic alcohol use (Saha, Chou, & Grant, 2006), which suggests that this criterion be reevaluated in future editions of the *DSM* for its ability to provide information about severity of substance use.

Saha et al. (2006) investigated the question of whether *DSM-IV-TR* substance abuse criteria represent milder symptoms than substance dependence criteria in a study of 22,526 adults identified as current drinkers (i.e., defined as having had 12 or more drinks in the preceding year and having drunk more than 5 drinks on at least one occasion). When structured interview responses pertaining to the 7 substance dependence and 4 substance abuse criteria outlined in the *DSM-IV-TR* were subjected to an item response theory model, the majority of abuse and dependence criteria fell along such a continuum of severity. However, it was not consistently the case that substance abuse criteria fell at the lower end of the use continuum and that dependence criteria always reflected more severe use. For example, the criteria of failure to fulfill major role obligations was one of the best discriminators of severity of use, suggesting that this item taps a fairly advanced stage of drinking; it is therefore ironic that this item was actually moved from the dependence criteria in *DSM-III-R* to the abuse criteria in *DSM-IV-TR* (American Psychiatric Association, 1987, 2000b). The study also concluded that there is a high degree of redundancy among the *DSM-IV-TR* dependency and abuse criteria (i.e., items tapping the same underlying construct) and that, at least for alcohol use disorders, more criteria tapping the mild to moderate end of the use spectrum are needed (e.g., drinking in excess of nationally recommended guidelines). Although this research focused solely on alcohol use disorders, the findings call into question the use of a categorical system to represent what may very well be a dimensional phenomenon across substances, and suggests that *DSM-IV-TR* substance use criteria need to be closely examined to determine how well they reflect points along a spectrum of problematic use.

Substance Dependence

Clinical Presentation

Substance dependence refers to a group of cognitive, behavioral, and physiological symptoms indicative of continued substance use despite significant substance-related problems (American Psychiatric Association, 2000b). Terms such as *alcoholism* and *drug addiction,* common in everyday clinical parlance, can be considered synonymous with substance dependence (Ashenberg-Straussner, 2004). Clinicians often equate substance dependence with phenomena such as the development of tolerance (i.e., the need for increasingly greater amounts of a substance to achieve the same effect) and withdrawal (i.e., characteristic physical and/or psychological symptoms that occur when a substance is no longer present in the system). While these symptoms often characterize substance dependence, they *are not* necessary for such a diagnosis to be made, according to the current *DSM* system. In the *DSM-III,* a diagnosis of substance dependence required the presence of either tolerance or withdrawal (American Psychiatric Association, 1980); however, this requirement was changed in the *DSM-III-R* such that tolerance and withdrawal remained symptoms of substance dependence but were not required for a diagnosis (American Psychiatric Association, 1987). Substance dependence, according to the *DSM-IV-TR,* requires that at least 3 of 7 symptoms be present over the same year-long period (American Psychiatric Association, 2000b). These symptoms can be conceptualized in two clusters: those related to physiological dependence and those pertaining to compulsive use (A. Frances et al., 1995).

Tolerance and Withdrawal

Physiologic dependence on alcohol or drugs is indicated by *tolerance* or *withdrawal.* Physiologic dependence on a substance often implies a severe form of substance dependence characterized by greater medical, psychiatric, and psychosocial problems (Sofuoglu, Dudish-Poulsen, Brown, & Hatsukami, 2003).

Tolerance can be manifest in either the need for markedly increased amounts of a substance to achieve intoxication or a desired effect or markedly diminished effect with continued use of the same amount of the substance (American Psychiatric Association, 2000b). In addition to a client reporting this phenomenon, tolerance may also be indicated by an absence of expected signs of intoxication despite high blood levels of a drug, although this can be complicated by preexisting variability in inborn tolerance (A. Frances et al., 1995). *Cross-tolerance* is said to occur when the use of one substance produces tolerance to a pharmacologically similar substance; for example, an individual who has developed tolerance to alcohol will also show cross-tolerance to substances such as barbiturates and benzodiazepines (i.e., will require higher than usual dosages to demonstrate a desired effect). Tolerance can also be influenced by environmental cues. This has been demonstrated in animal studies with rats who were given heroin and placebo in separate, distinct settings; when some of these animals were administered a high heroin dose in the placebo setting, significantly more fatalities occurred compared to rats given the high heroin dose in the usual heroin setting (i.e., 64% versus 32%, respectively; S. Siegal, Hinson, Krank, & McCully, 1982). This "situational specificity" of tolerance has been demonstrated for diverse classes of substances, including alcohol, opiates, benzodiazepines, and phencyclidine (S. Siegal, 2001), and may help explain why some substance abusers overdose in new environments on drug amounts they had previously been able to tolerate (Gutierrez-Cebollada, de la Torre, Ortufio, Garces, & Cami, 1994).

Symptoms of withdrawal vary by class of substance. In some cases, physical symptoms (e.g., nausea, insomnia, autonomic changes) predominate, whereas for other drugs withdrawal is associated primarily with psychological symptoms. An example of the latter is stimulant (e.g., cocaine) withdrawal, which is characterized by anxiety, irritability, and depression (Haney, 2004). Generally speaking, withdrawal syndromes are associated with an onset of symptoms within 24 to 48 hours following cessation of use, peaking of symptoms within 2 to 4 days, and a return to baseline within 1 to 3 weeks (Budney, 2006). However, drugs with a longer duration of action (i.e., longer half-lives) are associated with longer periods of time between the cessation of use and the onset of withdrawal symptoms, as well as a longer withdrawal course (American Psychiatric Association, 2000b). Additional information on withdrawal symptoms by different drug classes is presented in "Intoxication and Withdrawal" later in this chapter.

Withdrawal syndromes are controversial for some substances. For example, the *DSM-IV-TR* (American Psychiatric Association, 2000b) does not include cannabis withdrawal as a diagnostic category because compelling evidence supporting this phenomenon was deemed insufficient. However, Budney, Moore, Vandrey, and Hughes (2003) found that 78% of a sample of former heavy marijuana users reported experiencing at least 4 symptoms of a withdrawal syndrome characterized by anger or irritability, aggression, restlessness, decreased appetite, sleep disturbance, and strange dreams. Budney (2006) has further argued that the current "with/without physiologic dependence" specifiers that are given with a *DSM-IV-TR* substance dependence diagnosis should be replaced by "with/without significant withdrawal" because the latter terminology encompasses the emotional and behavioral symptoms frequently associated with withdrawal that may be even more potent factors than traditional physiologic symptoms in precipitating dependence and relapse.

Dupont and Dupont (2005) note that physical dependence (as indicated by phenomena such as tolerance and withdrawal), though often a sign of a substance use disorder, is not equivalent to addiction, which implies out-of-control drug use despite clear-cut evidence of drug-related problems; for example, an individual being treated for severe pain may develop physical dependence on opiate medication yet not be considered to have a substance use disorder. Similarly, methadone maintenance treatment for heroin addiction involves continuing physical dependence on a substance, but in the service of reducing the impact of a preexisting addiction. Thus, it has been argued that the diagnostic terms of drug and alcohol dependence be replaced with the more accurate descriptor *addiction* (Potenza, 2006).

Compulsive Use

Individuals who are dependent on drugs or alcohol exhibit a pattern of compulsive use that is marked by an intense preoccupation with using, to the exclusion of other important personal, social, and occupational activities. Several symptoms of substance dependence in the *DSM-IV-TR* relate to compulsive use; for example, substance-dependent individuals may have a history of unsuccessful attempts to quit, may end up drinking or taking much more of a drug than they initially intended, and may use despite knowledge of the adverse effects the alcohol or drug has on their physical or emotional problems (American Psychiatric Association, 2000b). However, if the client lacks insight into the extent of his or her substance use problem, it may be difficult for the clinician to evaluate this out-of-control pattern of behavior since the client may not view as problematic activities such as taking more of a substance than intended. Although substance-dependent individuals frequently spend a great deal of time trying to obtain substances (American Psychiatric Association, 2000b), clinicians should recognize that this symptom will vary depending on how difficult it is to procure the substance. For example, it would be rare for an inhalant user to spend a great deal of time trying to obtain this type of substance because inhalants are readily available in the form of any number of low-cost, common household items (e.g., glue, cleaning agents, paint, gasoline; American Psychiatric Association, 2000b).

Additional Characteristics

Health Problems and Increased Mortality   Substance use disorders are frequently associated with medical problems that are the direct result of drug and/or alcohol use. Drugs that can be injected, such as heroin, cocaine, and methamphetamine, are associated with increased risk of contracting illnesses such as hepatitis and HIV (Copenhaver et al., 2006; Maher, Jalaludin, & Chant, 2006). Substance use can also lead to risky sexual behavior, such as having unprotected sex or trading sex for drugs, that can in turn increase the risk of contracting HIV and other sexually transmitted diseases (Staton et al., 1999; Tortu, McCoy, Beardsley, Deren, & McCoy, 1998). Use of substances that are smoked (e.g., marijuana, certain forms of cocaine) can lead to respiratory disease and increased risk of certain forms of cancer.

Substance use disorders are, in general, associated with increased risk of mortality. For example, it has been estimated that alcohol-related deaths account for 5% of all deaths in the United States (Stinson & DeBakey, 1992). Mortality rates have been estimated to be 13 times greater than the norm among opioid users (Hulse, English, Milne, & Holman, 1999) and 8 times higher among crack cocaine users (Ribeiro, Dunn, Laranjeira, & Sesso, 2004). Use of multiple drugs (particularly combinations involving alcohol, opiates, and cocaine) has been linked to increased risk of fatal overdose (Coffin et al., 2003). Factors such as poverty and economic disadvantage further heighten mortality rates among substance users (Hannon & Cuddy, 2006). With regard to life span issues, Moos, Brennan, and Mertens (1994) found that the mortality rate among middle-aged and older substance abusers (55+ years) was almost 3 times greater than the expected rate for this age group; among the predictors of earlier mortality in the substance-abusing group were nonmarried status, older age, comorbid organic brain disorder diagnoses, and medical diagnoses such as cancer, liver cirrhosis, and respiratory disorders. Vaillant (2003) found that by age 70 to 80 the mortality rates in two samples of alcoholic men were $1\frac{1}{2}$ to 2 times greater than in nonalcoholic comparison cohorts. Table 8.1 summarizes some of the adverse physical outcomes that can result from use of different substances.

Increased Lethality   High rates of suicidal behavior have been reported in drug- and alcohol-dependent individuals (Modesto-Lowe, Brooks, & Ghani, 2006). When a

Table 8.1   Medical complications that can arise from substance use

Alcohol	Blackouts, liver cirrhosis, gastroesophageal reflux disease, gastritis, aspiration pneumonia, cerebellar degeneration, pancreatitis, cardiomyopathy, persistent amnestic disorder, dementia
Amphetamines and Cocaine	Myocardial infarction, chest pain, strokes, transient ischemic attacks, deterioration of nasal septum (due to snorting), pulmonary disorders (e.g., collapsed lung, pulmonary infarction) secondary to smoking, hepatitis, HIV, and other blood-borne diseases (secondary to intravenous use)
Cannabis	Lung infection, bronchitis, obstructed airway, possible increased risk of certain cancers (e.g., respiratory, cervical, prostate, head, neck), increased risk of heart attack
Inhalants	Skin damage (e.g., burns, eczema, dermatitis), cardiovascular damage (e.g., myocardial ischemia, arrhythmias), pulmonary problems (e.g., emphysema, pneumonia).
	Long-term use: hearing loss, peripheral neuropathy, liver damage, acute renal failure, complications secondary to bone marrow suppression (e.g., anemia, leukemia), central nervous system and brain damage (including dementia)
Opioids	Constipation, respiratory depression, reduced thyroid activity, kidney damage, scarred and/or collapsed veins, bacterial infections of blood vessels/heart valves, hepatitis, HIV, and other blood-borne diseases (secondary to intravenous use), pulmonary problems (e.g., tuberculosis, pneumonia), coma and death (in overdose)
PCP	Seizures, ischemic or hemorrhagic stroke, hyperthermia, coma and death
Sedatives, Hypnotics, and Anxiolytics	Gastrointestinal difficulties, respiratory and cardiac depression, liver damage, dementia

Note: This table does not include a listing of withdrawal symptoms, which can be found in Table 8.3.

substance use disorder begins prior to adulthood or has been of long duration, risk for suicide increases (Landheim, Bakken, & Vaglum, 2006). In addition, when compared to nonattempters, suicide attempters with substance use disorders are more likely to be young, single or separated, have a history of prior attempts, and exhibit higher rates of psychiatric comorbidity (particularly depressive disorders, personality disorders, and personality traits such as impulsivity, sociopathy, and deviance; D. W. Black, Yates, Petty, Noyes, & Brown, 1986; Burch, 1994; Modesto-Lowe et al., 2006). In a study of 500 alcoholics followed over a 33- to 42-year period, R. M. Costello (2006) found that deaths attributable to suicide, homicide, accidents, and AIDS frequently occurred in the earlier years of the follow-up and were disproportionately prevalent among younger and ethnic minority (i.e., African American and Hispanic) individuals. In a comprehensive review of studies on suicide and drug/alcohol use disorders published between 1994 and 2002, Wilcox, Conner, and Caine (2004) found that suicide mortality rates associated with alcohol use disorders and opioid use disorders represented 10- and 13-fold increases, respectively, over expected rates, and that intravenous drug use and mixed drug use were associated with 13- and 17-fold increases over expected rates. These authors noted that the literature is sparse in regard to the association between suicide risk and cannabis or cocaine use.

Neuropsychological Impairment

Alcohol Chronic use of alcohol and drugs can be associated with impairment in cognitive functioning. Excessive alcohol use has been linked to impairments in problem solving, abstract thinking, perceptual motor ability, and short- and long-term verbal and (particularly) nonverbal memory (D.N. Allen & Landis, 1998). Eckhardt, Stapleton, Rawlings, Davis, and Grodin (1995) examined cognitive performance in a sample of abstinent younger alcoholics (ages 18 to 35) who had alcohol-related problems for an average of 6 years. Although the majority performed within normal limits on a neuropsychological battery assessing language skills, attention, motor skills, intelligence, memory, and frontal systems and executive functioning, greater lifetime consumption predicted lower test scores. In some cases, enduring neuropsychological deficits, most notably frontal lobe dysfunction, may be seen even in alcohol-dependent individuals who have achieved sobriety (Ihara, Berrios, & London, 2000; Noel et al., 2001). Such deficits may persist even among apparently physically and mentally healthy abstinent alcohol-dependent individuals (S. J. Davies et al., 2005). In addition, alcohol withdrawal is associated with increased cortisol production, which can have a deleterious effect on hippocampal neurons, suggesting that repeated untreated alcohol withdrawals may lead to damage in this area of the brain (National Institute on Alcohol Abuse and Alcoholism [NIAAA], 1989; Sapolsky, Krey, & McEwen, 1986). A persistent amnestic condition known as Korsakoff's syndrome can develop after a prolonged period of heavy alcohol use. Symptoms include severe retrograde and anterograde amnesia, confabulation, attentional deficits, and impairment in executive and frontal systems functions. *Korsakoff's syndrome* is preceded by an acute disorder known as *Wernicke's encephalopathy,* which is caused by a lack of thiamine (often the result of dietary deficiency associated with chronic alcohol use). Wernicke's encephalopathy is characterized by mental confusion, ataxic gait, nystagmus, and ophthalmoplegia (i.e., paralysis or weakness of the eye muscles; D. N. Allen & Landis, 1998). Chronic alcohol use can also lead to alcohol-induced dementia.

Cocaine and Stimulants In a unique study of 50 twins in which only one member was a heavy stimulant abuser (i.e., cocaine and/or amphetamines), Toomey et al. (2003) found that those with a history of substance abuse performed significantly worse than their twin sibling on tests of attention and motor skills. Because those with a history of abuse had been abstinent for 1 year prior to the study, these results suggest that cognitive deficits associated with stimulant abuse may be persistent. Recent research among HIV-positive individuals further suggests that in addition to exerting direct neurotoxic effects on the brain, cocaine may contribute to the development of HIV-related dementia by modifying the toxicity of the virus and increasing its expression in the brain (Gekker et al., 2004).

Opiates Studies of opiate abusers have documented impairments in psychomotor speed, working memory, and executive functions such as decision making (Mintzer & Stitzer, 2002). P. E. Davis, Liddiard, and MacMillan (2002) found that approximately two-thirds of their sample of opiate-dependent individuals demonstrated impaired performance (defined as at least 2 standard deviations below published normative data) on two or more neuropsychological tests. In their study of both amphetamine and opiate abusers, Ersche, Clark, London, Robbins, and Sahakian (2006) found that both current and former users of these two substance classes demonstrated significant impairments on tests of frontal systems functioning and visual memory, suggestive of neuropathology in the frontal and temporal cortices. The lack of significant differences between currently dependent individuals and former users in this study again suggests that impairment in cognitive functioning associated with stimulants and opiates may persist even after a period of abstinence.

Benzodiazepines In a meta-analysis of 13 studies examining neuropsychological performance of long-term (i.e., average of 10 years) benzodiazepine users, M. J. Barker, Greenwood, Jackson, and Crowe (2004) found that the substance users were consistently more impaired than control subjects across a variety of cognitive domains, including sensory processing, memory (working, verbal, nonverbal), processing speed, attention and concentration, problem solving, and motor performance. Impairments in verbal memory, motor control and performance, and nonverbal memory have been documented to persist in some individuals after more than 6 months of abstinence (M. J. Barker, Greenwood, Jackson, & Crowe, 2005).

Other Substances Long-term cannabis use is associated with impairments in verbal memory and psychomotor speed, and shorter-term heavy users as well as long-term users display deficits on tasks of verbal fluency, verbal memory, attention, and psychomotor speed (Messinis, Kyprianidou, Malefaki, & Papathanasopoulos, 2006). Chronic inhalant use has been linked to problems with memory, visuomotor skills, visual processing, and attention (Brouette & Anton, 2001; Zur & Yule, 1990). In extreme cases, use of toluene may lead to a subcortical dementia syndrome that includes psychomotor and attentional deficits, depression, insomnia, and irritability (Brouette & Anton, 2001). Chronic PCP use is also associated with neuropsychological deficits, the most prominent of which are impairments in immediate and short-term verbal memory; however, abstinence or greatly reduced use has been correlated with improved functioning in these areas and on tasks of visuomotor tracking, set shifting, and psychomotor speed (Cosgrove & Newell, 1991).

SUBSTANCE INTOXICATION AND WITHDRAWAL

Intoxication refers to a reversible syndrome resulting from the *ingestion of or exposure to* a substance; withdrawal describes a syndrome that results from the *cessation* of a substance following prolonged and heavy use (American Psychiatric Association, 2000b). The *DSM-IV-TR* classification system allows clinicians to give intoxication and withdrawal diagnoses for a number of different substances. Five specific substance classes (i.e., alcohol, amphetamines, cocaine, opioids, and sedatives/hypnotics/anxiolytics) have criteria for both intoxication and withdrawal. For five others (i.e., caffeine, cannabis, hallucinogens, inhalants, PCP) there are criteria sets for intoxication only because evidence of clinically relevant withdrawal syndromes is not considered compelling (American Psychiatric Association, 2000b); future versions of the *DSM* may end up including withdrawal syndromes for some of these substances (e.g., cannabis) if sufficient research evidence accumulates. Finally, for nicotine, specific criteria for withdrawal are identified but not for intoxication (American Psychiatric Association, 2000b). As previously noted, withdrawal can be an indicator of substance dependence, but for an individual who is displaying withdrawal symptoms to receive an additional *DSM-IV-TR* diagnosis of substance dependence, at least two other symptoms reflecting a maladaptive pattern of substance use must be present (e.g., tolerance, unsuccessful attempts to control use, continued use despite recurrent adverse psychological or physical effects; American Psychiatric Association, 2000b). Tables 8.2 and 8.3 summarize intoxication and withdrawal symptoms for different classes of psychoactive substances. The information in these tables is broader than that included in the substance-specific intoxication and withdrawal criteria sets in the *DSM-IV-TR* and is intended to illustrate the wide range of symptoms that may be seen among individuals who are intoxicated or withdrawing from various substances.

Alcohol

The alcohol contained in beer, wine, and spirits is ethanol and is produced through fermentation. *Fermentation* is the process by which yeast breaks down sugar (e.g., from grapes, barley) into carbon dioxide and alcohol. Vodka and other spirits are produced by an additional process known as *distillation* in which fermented liquid is heated so that the evaporated ethanol can be caught, cooled, and condensed. The term *proof* refers to how much ethanol (ethyl alcohol) is contained in a distilled alcoholic beverage and is roughly twice the percentage of alcohol by volume. Thus, 100-proof distilled liquor contains 50% ethanol. The percentage of ethanol in white and red wines is roughly 12% and 14%, respectively, whereas the alcohol content of beer varies between 3% and 8%. The term *standard drink* refers to a fixed measure of pure *beverage alcohol* and is used to calculate alcohol intake; this amount varies across different countries and in the United States usually refers to 14g of ethanol. Table 8.4 presents information on standard drink equivalents for different types of alcoholic beverages.

When alcohol is consumed, intoxicating effects can be observed after as little as one standard drink (which usually produces a blood alcohol concentration [BAC] of 0.015 to 0.020 g/dL), although much of the United States legally defines intoxication as a BAC of 0.08 g/dL (Schuckit & Tapert, 2004). Blood alcohol levels will typically peak within 30 to

Table 8.2   Intoxication symptoms by drug class

Substance	Symptoms
Alcohol	Slurred speech, disinhibition, motor incoordination (e.g., unsteady gait), impaired judgment, cognitive impairment (e.g., attention, memory), nystagmus, mood lability, stupor, coma
Amphetamines and Cocaine	Euphoria, increased energy, elevated or lowered blood pressure, elevated body temperature, perspiration and chills, increased or slowed or irregular heart rate, dilated pupils, depressed respiration, chest pain, increased sex drive, psychomotor agitation or retardation, insomnia, irritability, panic, paranoia, hallucinations, nausea and vomiting, weight loss, muscular weakness, confusion, seizures
Cannabis	Mild euphoria, feelings of relaxation, giggling, time perception distortion, alteration of sensory acuity (e.g., colors seem brighter), dry mouth, tachycardia, increased appetite, hypervigilance and panic (higher doses)
Hallucinogens	Perceptual changes (e.g., hallucinations, illusions, derealization, depersonalization, synesthesia, prolonged afterimages), tremors, dilated pupils, increased heart rate and palpitations, sweating, incoordination, restlessness, blurred vision, euphoria and elation, tension, anxiety, panic
Inhalants	Euphoria, impaired motor control, gait disturbance, slurred speech, disinhibition, belligerency, nystagmus, hallucinations and delusions, lethargy, dizziness, incoordination, tremor, slowed reflexes, psychomotor retardation, muscle weakness, blurred vision, stupor, coma
Opioids	Analgesia, drowsiness, slurred speech, pupillary constriction (dilation associated with overdose), euphoria, impaired concentration, attention, and memory, depressed respiration
PCP	Derealization and depersonalization; disorganized thinking; euphoria or affective dulling; increased sense of strength, power, invulnerability; psychotic symptoms; elevated blood pressure; increased heart rate; muscle rigidity; numbness; decreased pain responsivity; dysarthria; nystagmus; ataxia; nausea; sweating
Sedatives, Hypnotics, and Anxiolytics	Relief of tension and anxiety, euphoria, drowsiness and sleepiness, incoordination, unsteady gait, slurred speech, impaired attention and memory, nystagmus, stupor and coma

45 minutes after ingesting an alcoholic beverage. Intoxicating effects occur when an individual's ability to metabolize alcohol (which occurs at the rate of about one third to one fourth ounce per hour) is exceeded by the amount consumed, thus resulting in increased BAC levels. However, the same amount of alcohol will not necessarily produce the same BAC level in all individuals; factors such as height, weight, sex, and stomach contents affect this variable. For example, smaller individuals usually achieve higher BAC levels than larger individuals after drinking the same amount of alcohol because of the lower blood volume with which the alcohol can mix. Women will typically achieve a higher BAC than men after drinking similar amounts because of their lower levels of alcohol dehydrogenase (an enzyme that removes alcohol from the blood) and higher body fat content (which decreases the degree to which alcohol becomes diluted in the body). When an

Table 8.3   Withdrawal symptoms by drug class

Substance	Symptoms	Typical Onset Time Following Cessation of Use
Alcohol	Tremor, anxiety and agitation, sweating, increased pulse and respiration, elevated blood pressure, nausea, vomiting, light and sound sensitivity, insomnia, hallucinations and illusions, seizures (severe withdrawal), delirium tremens (severe withdrawal)	6–24 hours
Amphetamines and Cocaine	Sleep disturbance (e.g., insomnia, hypersomnia), hyperphagia, agitation or psychomotor retardation, depression, irritability, anergia and fatigue, cravings, vivid unpleasant dreams, concentration problems	8 hours to 4 days
Opioids	Dysphoria, muscle aches, headaches, nausea and vomiting, anorexia, anxiety, irritability, diarrhea, tear secretion, runny nose, fever, sweating, insomnia, pupillary dilation, yawning, increased respiration, restlessness, abdominal cramps, sleep disturbance, increased pulse, elevated blood pressure, hot or cold flashes, muscle spasms, muscle and bone pain, goosebumps	8–10 hours (heroin and other short-acting opioids) 24–72 hours (methadone and other longer-acting opioids)
Sedatives, Hypnotics, and Anxiolytics	Anxiety, insomnia, tremors, postural hypotension, anorexia, elevated pulse, sweating, agitation, nausea and vomiting, sensitivity to light and sound, transient hallucinations and illusions, delirium, seizures	Sedatives/Hypnotics: 12–16 hours (short-acting agents) 2–5 days (long-acting agents)

individual has a full stomach, alcohol absorption into the bloodstream is slowed down, which results in a lower BAC than drinking on an empty stomach. The symptoms of alcohol intoxication are similar to those seen for benzodiazepines, barbiturates, and other sedatives, and urine toxicology screens can be useful in differentiating among these conditions (First & Tasman, 2005).

Alcohol intoxication lowers inhibitions, increases irritability and dysphoria, and is associated with greatly increased risk of suicide and violence toward others (including homicide) and involvement in accidents (American Psychiatric Association, 2000b). It has been estimated that alcohol-related deaths exceed 200,000 per year (Stoudemire, Wallack, & Hedenark, 1987). In their meta-analytic review of 30 experimental studies, Bushman and Cooper (1990) concluded that alcohol does indeed cause aggression, and in a review by MacDonald (1961), over 50% of individuals who committed homicide had been drinking at the time of their crime. The prevalence of suicidal ideation and suicide attempts has also been correlated with degree of alcohol use (Windle, Miller-Tutzauer, & Domenico, 1992). The relationship between alcohol use and accidents is illustrated by the finding that the majority of individuals with traumatic brain injuries have detectable levels of alcohol

Table 8.4   Standard drink equivalents

Type of Drink	Alcohol Percentage	Ounces	Number of Standard Drinks
Beer or wine cooler	5	12	1
		16	1.3
		22	2
		40	3.3
Malt liquor	7	8–9	1
		12	1.5
		16	2
		22	2.5
		40	4.5
Table wine	12	5	1
		25 (750 ml bottle)	5
Hard liquor (80 proof spirits)	40	1 mixed drink	1 or more[*]
		16 (1 pint)	11
		25 (a fifth)	17
		59 (1.75L)	39

Note: Estimates are approximate. Different types of beverages and brands vary in actual alcohol content.
[*]A mixed drink may be equivalent to 1–3 standard drinks depending on the type of spirits used and the drink recipe.
From *A Pocket Guide for Alcohol Screening and Intervention,* by the National Institute on Alcohol Abuse and Alcoholism, 2005, Rockville, MD: NIAAA Publications. Adapted with permission.

in their system at the time of hospital admission (Bombardier, Temkin, Machamer, & Dikmen, 2003). At high BAC levels, intoxication becomes life-threatening. For example, at BAC levels of .30 reflexes may be diminished and an individual may be semiconscious; loss of consciousness and limited reflex responses occur at BAC levels of .40, and death is likely at BAC of .50 or higher (although for some individuals, lower BAC levels can lead to death).

In heavy users of alcohol, withdrawal symptoms may occur within 6 to 48 hours after alcohol consumption is drastically reduced or stopped and BAC levels drop. The symptoms of alcohol withdrawal (e.g., autonomic hyperreactivity, agitation, anxiety, tremor) reflect an overactivation of the central nervous system that occurs when the inhibitory effect of alcohol on nerve cells is disrupted by cessation of use (Morrow, Suzdak, Karanian, & Paul, 1988). *Delirium tremens* refers to a form of severe alcohol withdrawal that affects approximately 5% of alcohol-dependent persons and is characterized by tremor, severe autonomic hyperactivity, agitation, and hallucinations (Schuckit & Tapert, 2004). Severe alcohol withdrawal may also include seizures. Usually there is one seizure characterized by a shaking of the legs and arms and a loss of consciousness; in some cases, a second seizure follows within approximately 6 hours of the first. Multiple seizures, though rarer, can lead to a potentially fatal condition known as *status epilepitcus* in which there are continuous seizures (Saitz, 1998).

Amphetamines and Cocaine

Amphetamines and cocaine are considered psychostimulants that increase central nervous system activity and produce a powerfully addictive high characterized by euphoria, increased energy, extreme self-confidence, and feelings of greatly increased strength (Coombs & Howatt, 2005; Kosten & Sofuoglu, 2004). Methamphetamine is another stimulant whose use has become epidemic; this drug is the focus of the "Advanced Topics" section at the end of this chapter.

First synthesized in Germany in 1887, amphetamine is structurally related to adrenaline (the body's fight-or-flight hormone) and ephedrine (a natural, plant-based stimulant). Amphetamine was originally used for medicinal purposes to treat a host of conditions, such as asthma, hay fever, depression, epilepsy, travel sickness, and impotence. Currently, amphetamine and other psychostimulants (e.g., methylphenidate, dextroamphetamine) are legitimately used to treat ADHD and narcolepsy.

Coca leaves, from which cocaine alkaloids are derived, were routinely used in pre-Hispanic America by cultures such as the Incas for religious and medicinal purposes. In the nineteenth century, cocaine was chemically isolated and produced in a powdered form that could be snorted, injected, or mixed in a tonic (Dackis & O'Brien, 2003). The addictive properties of cocaine were not well recognized until the early twentieth century; during the second half of the nineteenth century cocaine was viewed as having valuable therapeutic properties (e.g., treating morphine addiction), praised by prominent figures such as Sigmund Freud, and even added to the original formulation of Coca-Cola. Known by street names such as *coke, blow, snow,* and *flake,* cocaine can be snorted, smoked (known as freebasing), or injected. *Crack* refers to a form of cocaine that has been processed using baking soda or ammonia to remove hydrochloride. The resulting form has a rocklike appearance and is typically smoked; the term "crack" derives from the crackling sound that the drug makes when it is heated. Because crack cocaine is easily produced, it can be bought cheaply, resulting in widespread use in inner-city areas beginning in the 1980s.

Although stimulant intoxication is associated with euphoria and other pleasurable symptoms, restlessness, irritability, anxiety, and psychotic symptoms such as paranoia and hallucinations can also occur with repeated use (NIDA, 2006b). Stimulant use is also associated with increased risk of heart attack and other cardiac complications, headaches, and gastrointestinal complications such as nausea and abdominal pain. Stimulant delirium may be seen among chronic users of cocaine or amphetamine; this is characterized by disorientation, confusion, excitement, and fear and is associated with a heightened risk of serious medical complications such as seizures, cardiac arrhythmias, pulmonary complications, and stroke (Kosten & Sofuoglu, 2004). The rapidity with which intoxicating effects of stimulants are experienced depends on the route of substance administration. Intravenous use and smoking result in the fastest and most intense effects. One study of cocaine users found that the average time for peak effects to be reached was 1.4 minutes, 3.1 minutes, and 14.6 minutes when the drug was smoked, injected, or snorted, respectively (Volkow et al., 2000). However, the faster the absorption, the shorter the duration of effects; thus, a high from smoking cocaine may last only 5 to 10 minutes, whereas that from snorting will last 15 to 30 minutes (Coombs & Howatt, 2005). Although cocaine and amphetamine produce similar symptoms of intoxication, these substances are structurally dissimilar to one another and have different half-lives. As a result, the high that is produced by cocaine is significantly shorter than that produced by amphetamine (i.e., minutes versus hours), and therefore cocaine users are more likely than stimulant users to go on drug binges (Ockert, Baier, & Coons, 2004). Cocaine binges typically average 12 hours but can last as long as a week (M. C. Acosta, Haller, & Schnoll, 2005).

Following stimulant use, a "crash" is typically experienced that is characterized by depression, anxiety, cravings, and agitation; this may last 5 to 10 days if stimulant use ceases. Fatigue, lack of mental and physical energy, decreased interest in the environment, and increasingly intense cravings characterize the intermediate and later phases of stimulant withdrawal, which can linger as long as 1 to 10 weeks (M. C. Acosta et al., 2005; Kosten & Sofuoglu, 2004). During the period of dysphoric mood following cessation of stimulant use, suicidal ideation can occur. Cocaine withdrawal is not associated with the autonomic hyperreactivity that characterizes withdrawal from substances such as alcohol or opiates, and therefore typically does not have to be treated on an inpatient basis. However, severity of stimulant withdrawal symptoms has been correlated with premature treatment dropout and failure to maintain abstinence (Kampman et al., 2002).

Cannabis

As with many substances discussed in this chapter, the history of cannabis use dates back thousands of years, to ancient civilizations in China and India (Gold, Frost-Pineda, & Jacobs, 2004). Cannabis is derived from the hemp plant *cannabis sativa;* cannabinoids are found in the leaves, stalks, and flowers of this plant, as well as in the resin and seeds of the female plant.

Marijuana (also known as *pot, grass, weed, ganga, MJ,* and *mary jane*) is the most commonly used form of cannabis and refers to the shredded and dried stems, leaves, seeds, and flowers of the hemp plant, which are smoked via a cigarette (*joint*), cigar (*blunt*), pipe, or water pipe (*bong*). Hashish (*hash*) is derived from the dried resin of the flowers of the female hemp plant. Although many compounds are contained in marijuana and other forms of cannabis, and controversy exists as to the scope of active ingredients in marijuana smoke, the major active ingredient in marijuana and hashish is delta-9-tetrahydrocannabinol or THC (Gold et al., 2004). The potency of marijuana has changed dramatically over the past 30 years and has increased from 1% TCH to 7% to 20% TCH.

Use of marijuana or hashish causes THC to bind to cannabinoid receptors in the brain and facilitates the release of dopamine, which in turn causes sensations such as euphoria, relaxation, sedation, and time distortion. Individuals may also experience increases in self-confidence, talkativeness, appetite, and libido. In some cases, anxiety, paranoia, and panic can occur (Lessa & Scanlon, 2006). Effects of smoked cannabis occur quickly (within minutes) and peak approximately one half hour after use begins. Cannabinoid receptors are located throughout the brain but are heavily concentrated in areas such as the hippocampus, which is involved in learning and memory. Thus, use of cannabis is associated with short-term problems with memory, learning, thinking, and problem solving (NIDA, 2006d). The *DSM-IV-TR* does not specify a withdrawal syndrome for cannabis (American Psychiatric Association, 2000b); however, according to several studies, withdrawal symptoms are commonly reported among adolescent and adult users (Budney, Novy, & Hughes, 1999; Nocon, Pfister, Wittchen, Zimmermann, & Lieb, 2006; Vandrey, Budney, Kamon, & Stanger, 2005). Specifically, heavy marijuana users report that symptoms such as aggression, anger, decreased appetite, irritability, nervousness and anxiety, restlessness, shakiness, sleep difficulty, stomach pains, and sweating occur 1 to 3 days after marijuana use ceases, peak between 2 to 6 days following last use, and can persist up to 2 weeks (Budney et al., 2003).

Hallucinogens

As the name implies, hallucinogens are drugs that produce profound alterations in perceptions of reality; these substances can also produce rapid and intense emotional swings (NIDA, 2001). Pechnick and Ungerleider (2004) note that the term hallucinogen may be a misnomer because the most common effects experienced with such substances are *illusions* or a perceptual distortion of something that is actually in the environment rather than bona fide hallucinations (i.e., perceptual experiences in the absence of external stimuli). Hallucinogens (which are also known as psychedelics) include lysergic acid diethylamide (LSD), mescaline, and psilocybin.

The hallucinogen LSD (*acid*) is a highly potent synthetic compound that was created in the late 1930s by the Swiss chemist Albert Hoffman. Although it was originally hoped that LSD could treat conditions such as circulatory and respiratory problems, alcoholism, and even Schizophrenia, this substance currently has no medically recognized use. It is typically ingested orally in pills, capsules, gelatin squares (*window panes*), drug-laced sugar cubes, or, most commonly, by placing under the tongue specially treated blotter paper containing the drug. Powerful hallucinations, illusions, and delusions occur within 30 to 90 minutes of taking LSD that may be perceived as pleasurable or interesting (e.g., experiencing the feeling that one can hear colors or see sounds [synesthesia]; experiencing prolonged afterimages; heightened sense of touch, smell, taste, and hearing; seeing stationary objects undulate). However, these experiences can also be disturbing, frightening, and disorienting (a *bad trip;* Pechnick & Ungerleider, 2004). Effects typically peak 2 to 4 hours after use, but may persist in some form for as long as 12 hours (Coombs & Howatt, 2005). In some cases, frank panic may result during use, and an individual may engage in unpredictable behavior that carries risk of harm to self or others.

Some hallucinogens are derived from natural sources such as plants and mushrooms. Mescaline, a dark brown powder, is derived from the peyote plant and is typically taken orally and often mixed with juice or tea to mask its bitter taste. Psilocybin is a mushroom (*magic mushrooms*), typically chewed or brewed in tea. The use of hallucinogens in religious ceremonies has been documented over centuries, and Native Americans can legally use peyote for religious purposes (Furst, 1990). The ability to experience feelings such as the dissolution of boundaries between oneself and others, awe, and elation that are associated with the use of hallucinogens can contribute to intense mystical or spiritual experiences (Coombs & Howatt, 2005). A unique study of religious or spiritually active hallucinogen-naive adults who were given psilocybin under controlled conditions found that the participants rated their experiences with the drug as having substantial personal meaning and spiritual significance (Griffiths, Richards, McCann, & Jesse, 2006). However, as with LSD, paranoia and disturbing hallucinations can occur with the use of these natural forms of hallucinogens, particularly if high doses are taken.

Other physical effects of hallucinogens include increased body temperature, pupillary dilation, nausea, perspiration, dizziness, and increased heart rate and blood pressure. However, lethal overdose on hallucinogens is rare (Pechnick & Ungerleider, 2004). Hallucinogens affect serotonin in the brain, which is a neurotransmitter involved in the control of perceptual, behavioral, and regulatory systems. Tolerance to hallucinogens develops quickly, requiring the use of increasingly greater amounts of the drug to produce the desired effects. In addition, tolerance to one hallucinogen (e.g., LSD) will produce tolerance to other hallucinogens (e.g., mescaline). However, tolerance is rapidly lost if an individual stops using for several days (NIDA, 2001). No consistent withdrawal syndrome has been identified for the hallucinogens.

Perhaps one of the most troubling effects of hallucinogen use is the occurrence of long-term persistent psychotic symptoms and flashbacks. Flashbacks refer to recurring sensory distortions like those experienced during periods of active drug use, and they may last for years after use of hallucinogens has stopped. During flashbacks, an individual might experience visual disturbances such as colored or bright flashes, halos or trails attached to moving objects, intensified colors, and afterimages (American Psychiatric Association, 2000b; NIDA, 2001). This phenomenon does not appear to be directly correlated with the extent of hallucinogen use (e.g., a person who has used LSD one time could experience flashbacks). While fatigue and other stressors may precipitate flashbacks in some cases, many times they occur suddenly and unpredictably, which can be highly distressing for the affected individual (Pechnick & Ungerleider, 2004). The *DSM-IV* contains a diagnostic category, Hallucinogen-Persisting Perception Disorder, that can be given to individuals who experience flashbacks (American Psychiatric Association, 2000b). Following the use of hallucinogens, some individuals experience persisting psychotic symptoms that are accompanied by dramatic mood swings; such symptoms can occur for many years after active use of hallucinogens has stopped and can occur in persons with no prior history of psychotic symptoms or other symptoms of a psychological disorder (NIDA, 2001). Although a Hallucinogen-Persisting Psychotic Disorder was considered for inclusion in the *DSM-IV,* a decision was ultimately made against its inclusion due to insufficient empirical evidence. If a clinician suspects that persisting psychotic symptoms are directly the result of hallucinogen use, an appropriate *DSM-IV-TR* diagnosis would be Hallucinogen-Related Disorder Not Otherwise Specified (A. Frances, First, & Pincus, 1999).

Inhalants

Inhalants refer to chemicals that are volatile at room temperature, misused for their psychoactive effects, and taken via inhalation through the nose or mouth (Brouette & Anton, 2001; Kilmer, Cronce, & Palmer, 2005). *Huffing* refers to breathing an inhalant from a cloth soaked with the substance, and *bagging* involves inhaling concentrated vapors from a bag (Crowley & Sakai, 2004). Subcategories of inhalants include volatile solvents, nitrites, gases, and aerosols (NIDA, 2000b). Inhalants include chemicals such as acetone, hexane, butane, xylene, benzene, amyl nitrate, nitrous oxide, propane, and toluene, and can frequently be found among common household items such as lighter fluid, gasoline, nail polish remover, paint thinner, glue, felt-tip markers, correction fluid, cleaning products, and whipped cream dispensers (Kilmer et al., 2005). Street names for inhalants include *whippets, poppers,* and *snappers.*

Substances such as solvents produce effects quickly; for most abused solvents, only 15 to 20 inhalations are needed to evoke euphoria and drowsiness, which may come on in seconds to minutes. Slurred speech, gait disturbances, psychomotor retardation, disorientation, and even visual hallucinations (at higher levels of exposure) can occur. Nitrites produce short-lived but potent effects within seconds of inhalation that include floating sensations, heightened sexual arousal, reduced sexual and social inhibitions, and increased skin perception (Brouette & Anton, 2001). In many ways, intoxication from inhalants appears similar to alcohol intoxication (Crowley & Sakai, 2004). Loss of sensation or anesthetic effects and loss of consciousness can also occur (NIDA, 2006c). Withdrawal criteria are not included in the *DSM-IV-TR* for inhalants because research has not established a well-defined withdrawal syndrome for this class of drugs, even though tolerance has been reported among individuals with a history of heavy use (American Psychiatric Association, 2000b). Among symptoms that have been proposed as part of a withdrawal syndrome associated with inhalants are nausea, inattention, diarrhea, tremor, sleep disturbance, anxiety, and irritability (Brouette & Anton, 2001; Crowley & Sakai, 2004). As noted in Table 8.2, severe medical complications can result from inhalant use. "Sudden sniffing death" caused by heart failure can occur within minutes of repeated inhalations of highly concentrated amounts of chemicals (particularly those found in aerosols, butane, and propane); death can also occur from inhalant use via suffocation, when oxygen in the lungs is displaced by the inhaled chemicals (NIDA, 2006c).

Opioids

This class of highly addictive drugs (also referred to as narcotics) includes both illegal substances such as heroin (known by the street names *smack, ska, junk,* and *H*) and prescription pain medications such as codeine, morphine, fentanyl, oxycodone (OxyContin), and meperidine (Demerol). Opioids are so named because they are derived from opium or its natural or synthetic derivatives. In the United States medical use of opioids (morphine and codeine) became common in the 1800s, particularly after the introduction of the hypodermic needle in 1843, which allowed for quick administration and more rapid drug effects to occur. During the Civil War, use of opioids to treat injured soldiers was common; many became physiologically addicted and were referred to as having "soldier's illness" (Friedman & Wilson, 2004).

Prescription opioids are mostly administered in pill form or injected, and heroin may be snorted, smoked, or taken intravenously. Use of opioids produces intense feelings of euphoria and pleasure that are often accompanied by warm flushing of the skin, limb heaviness, and a dry mouth (Coombs & Howatt, 2005). Nausea and vomiting may also occur. These drugs produce drowsiness, slowed respiration, and decreased mental alertness that may last for several hours; in some cases, breathing can be slowed to the point of death (NIDA, 2005).

Opioid withdrawal symptoms include restlessness, anxiety, depression, headache, yawning, insomnia, diarrhea, vomiting, abdominal cramping, bone and muscle pain, goose bumps, and leg movements and muscle spasms (i.e., "kicking the habit"; Collins & Kleber, 2004; NIDA, 2005). The nature and severity of opioid withdrawal is linked to factors such as the specific drug used (drugs that are rapidly metabolized lead to shorter but more severe withdrawal symptoms), amount of daily use (higher daily use tends to lead to more severe withdrawal), duration and regularity of use (daily use for at least 2 to 3 weeks is typically required before withdrawal symptoms will be experienced), and psychological factors (e.g., anticipatory anxiety about withdrawal seems to heighten its severity; Collins & Kleber, 2004). For example, heroin withdrawal symptoms may be apparent as early as 8 hours after the last dose was taken, will peak at approximately 48 to 72 hours, and gradually subside after 5 to 7 days (Jaffe & Jaffe, 2004). Cravings for opioids and subtle mood and sleep disturbances can occur many weeks or months after withdrawal symptoms have subsided (Collins & Kleber, 2004).

Phencyclidine and Similarly Acting Arylcyclohexylamines

Developed in the 1950s as a surgical anesthetic, phencyclidine (PCP) is often referred to as a *dissociative anesthetic* because of its sedating and trance-like effects that can cause users to experience an out-of-body phenomenon and detachment from the environment (NIDA, 2001). Ketamine, developed in the mid-1960s, is a shorter acting and less potent PCP derivative. Phencyclidine is known by the street names *angel dust, ozone, rocket fuel, embalming fluid, wack,* and *Shermans.* It was eventually abandoned for legitimate medical uses due to dangerous side effects such as delirium and agitation, but began to be widely abused in the 1960s. Available in powdered and tablet form, PCP can be orally ingested, smoked (e.g., in marijuana cigarettes laced with the drug, called *supergrass*), snorted, or injected intravenously. The most rapid onset of effects (i.e., occurring within seconds to a few minutes) is associated with injection, smoking, and snorting, and symptoms may last for up to 1 hour (Schnoll & Weaver, 2004). In addition to dissociative symptoms, users experience feelings of numbness and a sense of heightened invulnerability, strength, and power (NIDA, 2001). Individuals under the influence of PCP may exhibit poor judgment and become hostile, agitated, violent, or suicidal. Even though negative experiences with the drug frequently occur, some users cite the unpredictability of the drug experience as one of the attractions for use (Schnoll & Weaver, 2004). Changes in blood pressure, respiration, and heart rate, nausea, dizziness, lack of coordination, nystagmus (i.e., a rapid, involuntary oscillation of the eyes), and sweating are among some of the physiological changes associated with PCP use. High doses can result in psychotic symptoms such as hallucinations, paranoia and other delusions, and disorganized speech. Although tolerance to PCP can develop, a clearly defined withdrawal syndrome in humans has not been established. Long-term use is associated with memory loss, problems with speech and thinking, weight loss, and depression that may persist up to a year after PCP use has ceased (NIDA, 2001).

Sedatives, Anxiolytics, and Hypnotics

This class of substances includes many different drugs, some legal and some illicit, that share the ability to ameliorate anxiety and induce sleep (Smith & Wesson, 2004). Among the drugs that fall under the umbrella of sedatives, anxiolytics, and hypnotics are benzodiazepines (e.g., diazepam, alprazolam, flunitrazepam), benzodiazepine-like drugs (e.g., zolpidem), barbiturates (e.g., secobarbital, pentobarbital), carbamates (e.g., meprobamate), and barbiturate-like hypnotics (e.g., methaqualone; American Psychiatric Association, 2000b). Street names for barbiturates include *barbs, block busters, Christmas trees, goof balls, pinks, red devils, reds and blues,* and *yellow jackets;* benzodiazepines may be referred to as *nerve pills, downers, tranks, xanies* (alprazolam), *vals* (diazepam), and *ruffies* (flunitrazepam). Although pharmaceutical companies in the United States have discontinued the manufacture of some sedative and hypnotic drugs such as methaqualone (*Quaaludes*), imports from other countries and illegal manufacture have resulted in continued availability (Shader, Ciraulo, & Greenblatt, 2003). These substances can be ingested orally or injected intravenously. Most drugs in this class produce calming and soporific effects by increasing the activity of *gamma-aminobutyric acid* (GABA), a primary inhibitory neurotransmitter. Because of their depressive effects on central nervous system functioning, high doses of sedatives, anxiolytics, or hypnotics can be fatal, particularly when used in combination with other substances that are depressants (e.g., alcohol, pain medications) or with antihistamines (often found in cold, sinus, and allergy medications; Coombs & Howat, 2005). Individuals intoxicated from sedatives, anxiolytics, or hypnotics will often appear drowsy and display slurred speech, nystagmus, and ataxia (i.e., shakiness, unsteadiness); mood may be labile, and some individuals can be aggressive and uncooperative (Shader et al., 2003).

As seen in Table 8.3, the withdrawal symptoms associated with sedative, hypnotic, and anxiolytic drugs are similar to those seen in alcohol withdrawal. A danger of withdrawal from a central nervous system depressant is that rebound brain activity can trigger seizures. These may take the form of grand mal convulsions and, if present, are often seen within a week after the withdrawal symptoms begin. For some substances in this class (barbiturates), the progression of withdrawal symptoms can lead to delirium, cardiovascular collapse, and death (Shader et al., 2003).

ONSET, COURSE, AND LIFE SPAN CONSIDERATIONS

Onset

Drug and alcohol use is often conceptualized in terms of a developmental pathway that typically begins in adolescence. However, beliefs about and attitudes toward different substances may be formed at even earlier ages, and this priming can have a significant impact on subsequent initiation and experimentation during the teenage years (Pandina & Johnson, 1999). In a study examining elementary school-age children's knowledge, future intentions to use, and actual use of a variety of substances, *intention* to use alcohol and cigarettes as a teenager or adult significantly predicted use of these substances 3 years later, indicating that early intent to use substances may represent a significant risk factor for later drug and alcohol use (Andrews, Tildesley, Hops, Duncan, & Severson, 2003).

A period of heightened risk for the initiation of substance use is the middle school years; during this time cigarette, alcohol, and marijuana use among youth increases significantly (D'Amico, Ellickson, Wagner, et al., 2005; L. D. Johnston, O'Malley, Bachman, & Schulenberg, 2005; Simons-Morton et al., 1999). Use of inhalants often also begins in adolescence because this class of substances provides an inexpensive, convenient alternative to alcohol (NIDA, 2006c). In a study of over 3,000 individuals ages 12 to 18, substance use progressed in a linear fashion across adolescence. For example, whereas only 1.6% and 28% of 12-year-olds reported having ever tried marijuana and alcohol, respectively, these rates were 12% and 52% for 14-year-olds, and 49% and 90% for 18-year-olds. Furthermore, experimentation, rather than specialized use, was typical among the adolescents, and diagnoses of abuse and dependence became increasingly more common among the older age groups (S. E. Young et al., 2002).

Early experiences with alcohol (e.g., intoxication prior to age 16) and cigarette smoking have been linked to increased risk of abuse and dependence diagnoses for substances such as alcohol and cannabis (Clapper, Buka, & Goldfield, 1995; Lewinsohn, Rohde, & Brown, 1999; SAMHSA, 2006). Similarly, early use of cannabis (e.g., by age 17) is associated with significantly increased risk of progression to other drug use, alcohol dependence, and drug abuse and dependence (Lynskey et al., 2003). Data from the National Survey on Drug Use and Health (NSDUH) indicate that the average age of initiation for use of inhalants, marijuana, PCP, and LSD is late adolescence (16 to 18); for cocaine, stimulants, ecstasy, and pain relievers it is the early 20s; and for heroin, tranquilizers, and sedatives it is between 22 and 26 (SAMHSA, 2006).

As will be discussed under "Etiology," accumulating research evidence indicates that genetic factors, particularly those related to the expression of certain personality traits, appear to exert a stronger influence on the *initiation* of substance use than on the transition to abuse or dependence (Cloninger, 2004). An example of how personality factors may influence preferences to begin using specific drugs is illustrated by J. B. Adams et al.'s (2003) finding that marijuana, alcohol, and sedatives were preferred by individuals who scored low on a measure of novelty seeking and who endorsed a desire to avoid negative emotions and life experiences as a motivation for use, whereas those who scored high on novelty seeking and who cited obtaining positive rewards as a primary motivation for use gravitated toward the use of stimulants and endorsed a wider range of preferred substances.

Course

The course of substance abuse is typically milder and less persistent than that of substance dependence, and for many individuals abuse will not progress to dependence. Among studies of individuals with a diagnosis of alcohol abuse, the rate of progression to alcohol dependence over 1 to 5 years is approximately 4% to 11% (Hasin, Van Rossem, McCloud, & Endicott, 1997; Schuckit, Smith, et al., 2001; Schuckit, Smith, & Landi, 2000). Furthermore, while roughly 33% of those with alcohol abuse diagnoses can be expected to still meet criteria for this disorder at a 1- to 5-year follow-up, about 50% to 60% no longer will (Hasin et al., 1997; Schuckit, Smith, et al., 2001). Vaillant (2003), in a 60-year follow-up of alcoholic men, found that among those with *DSM-III* alcohol abuse diagnoses who survived to age 80, over half (i.e., 53%) were still abusing alcohol but showed no evidence of worsening drinking behavior. In contrast, substance dependence is a more chronic and severe disorder. Drawing from the alcohol literature, roughly 66% of those with alcohol dependence diagnoses will continue to meet at least one abuse or dependence criteria at follow-up periods of 1 to 5 years, indicating failure to achieve remission (Hasin et al., 1997; Schuckit et al., 2000; Schuckit, Smith, et al., 2001).

Studies of the general population indicate that many individuals with problematic alcohol use will eventually become abstinent or greatly reduce their level of drinking (i.e., engage in nonhazardous levels of use), even though they may never seek treatment (Sobel, Cunningham, & Sobell, 1996). Among alcoholics with a history of treatment, remission rates ranging from 21% to 83% have been reported for follow-up periods of 8 years or more (Finney, Moos, Timko, 1999; Vaillant, 1996). In a long-term follow-up of alcoholic men, roughly half with initial *DSM-III* diagnoses of alcohol dependence had been able to achieve stable abstinence of 3 years or more when monitored until age 70 or death. However, only a very small percentage of alcohol-dependent men were able to maintain significant periods of controlled drinking, and periods of intermittent abuse typically led to a return of serious symptoms such as morning drinking (Vaillant, 2003).

In a follow-up of Vietnam veterans who were also illicit drug users, Price, Risk, and Spitznagel (2001) found that patterns of use for sedatives, stimulants, marijuana, cocaine, and opiates were relatively stable and typically extended into middle age, and that substances were used during approximately 25% of participants' adult lives. Of all substances tracked, marijuana use was associated with the fewest symptoms of abuse and dependence during active periods of use, but also the longest duration of use, lowest mean number of remissions, and one of the shortest mean remission times. Opioid use was associated with the lowest rates of spontaneous remissions, which is consistent with the highly addictive nature of this class of substance.

A number of personal and environmental factors may converge to influence the course of drug and alcohol use problems. Stice, Myers, and Brown (1998) found that among adolescents, increased use of alcohol was predicted by perceived peer use, parental control, and externalizing symptoms, and that escalating use of illicit substances was predicted by perceived peer use, negative affectivity, internalizing symptoms, and alcohol use. In a longitudinal study of 18-year-olds followed over an 11-year period, D'Amico, Ellickson, Collins, Martino, and Klein (2005) found that an early pattern of heavy drinking, the presence of pro-drug social influences among peers, and history of poor mental health during adolescence were significant predictors of substance dependence at age 29. Data from over 4,000 individuals with past-year diagnoses of alcohol dependence, obtained as part of the National Epidemiological Survey on Alcohol and Related Conditions (NESARC), revealed that a history of a personality disorder, greater dependence symptom severity (i.e., 10 or more lifetime dependence symptoms), and illicit drug use (particularly dependence) were among the factors that predicted continued or recurring alcohol dependence, and that risk of dependence decreased with age, marriage, and graduation from high school (D. D. Dawson et al., 2005). Personality characteristics such as high emotional instability, behavioral disinhibition, and low persistence have also been associated with relapse to alcohol and other drugs (L. A. Fisher, Elias, & Ritz, 1998; Janowsky, Boone, Morter, & Howe, 1999).

Life Span Considerations

Children and Adolescents

As previously noted, initiation and experimentation with alcohol and drugs typically begins in adolescence, and social learning variables are particularly important sources of influence in this regard. Preston and Goodfellow (2006) found that frequency of alcohol use among adolescents ages 12 to 17 increased with peer approval for alcohol use and the number of peers who got drunk at least once a week. In a longitudinal analysis of data from three studies of Caucasian, African American, Puerto Rican American, and Colombian youth, peer deviance, including peer smoking and marijuana use, increased the odds of the adolescents' own marijuana use, whereas having high-achieving peers significantly reduced this risk (Brook, Brook, Arencibia-Mireles, Richter, & Whiteman, 2001). D'Amico & McCarthy (2006) found that among youth ages 10 to 15, initiation of alcohol use was predicted by perceived peer use of alcohol, and initiation of marijuana use was predicted by perceived peer use of alcohol and marijuana. Perceived use of alcohol by peers also predicted an escalating pattern of marijuana and alcohol use, and perceived peer marijuana use predicted increased personal alcohol use. Peer use may influence adolescents' alcohol and drug use through direct modeling of substance use behaviors, conveying an acceptance of substance use and increasing the availability of alcohol or drugs; conversely, lower peer use may decrease sources of social reinforcement for use, provide positive role models (regarding lifestyle, coping strategies, etc.), and limit the availability of substances (Stice et al., 1998).

It is important to understand how parental variables may influence initiation of substance use among youth. Permissive attitudes toward substance use, parental substance use and abuse behaviors, and impairments in the quality of parent-child interaction (including abuse, neglect, and lack of parental supervision) predict the initiation of substance use among adolescents (Kaminer & Bukstein, 2005). When parents use substances, modeling opportunities are provided for vulnerable youth, and negative sequelae associated with parental substance use (e.g., emotional and physical unavailability, poor coping) can create an environment that may push youth toward their own use of substances. Blanton, Gibbons, Gerrard, Jewsbury-Conger, and Smith (1997) found that parental substance use and negative parent-child interactions indirectly exerted influence on adolescent substance use by precipitating adolescents' affiliation with peers who drank or smoked. Older siblings' substance use and behavioral willingness to use substances have also been found to predict substance use among adolescents, and the presence of a nonusing sibling or a sibling who indicates a low willingness to use may provide a buffer against peer influences (Brook, Whiteman, Gordon, & Brook, 1990; Griffin, Botvin, Scheier, & Nichols, 2002; Pomery et al., 2005).

Older Adults

The prevalence of alcohol and substance use disorders is lower in older age groups compared to younger adults (Harford, Grant, Yi, & Chen, 2005). Similarly, fewer older adults present to mental health facilities with substance use problems, as revealed by a 2001 survey of federally funded substance abuse treatment programs which found the admission rate for 30- to 54-year-olds was 17 times higher than that of adults ages 55 and older (Arndt, Gunter, & Acion, 2005). Thus, it can be easy for clinicians to overlook or fail to ask about symptoms of substance use disorders in older adults. In addition to stereotyped notions of what a person with drug or alcohol problems will look like, additional factors contributing to inadequate evaluation of substance use disorders in the elderly are assumptions that substance use disorders invariably "burn out" in old age, and prematurely concluding that symptoms such as slurred speech, depression, falling, memory problems and decline in hygiene are due to dementia and related disorders rather than substance use (Zarit & Zarit, 1998). A study of emergency center visits to a large, urban hospital over an 8-year period found that although older adults ($\geq$ 65 years) with substance use problems were less likely to be hospitalized for these conditions compared to older adults with cognitive, psychotic, and bipolar disorders, the prevalence of substance use problems was approximately 18% (Cully et al., 2005). This indicates that substance abuse in older adults is a growing problem that health professionals must be prepared to detect and treat. Among risk factors for substance abuse in older adults are role changes and loss (e.g., loss of spouse, friends, job), feelings of loneliness and grief, and medical or other health problems (e.g., insomnia; Farkas, 2004).

Alcohol and prescription opiates and benzodiazepines are among the more commonly misused substances in older adults (Christensen, Low, & Anstey, 2006; Shader et al., 2003). Older adults may be particularly sensitive to the acute effects of even small amounts of drugs and alcohol due to their slower metabolism and the potential interactions with prescription medications, which in turn can lead to serious health consequences (Zarit & Zarit, 1998). In a study of over 83,000 older adults, Pringle, Ahern, Heller, Gold, and Brown (2005) found that among individuals who were prescribed alcohol-interactive medications (i.e., those that could lead to adverse effects when taken with alcohol), almost 20% reported concomitant alcohol use and 6% reported problematic alcohol use.

The course of substance use disorders among older adults is variable. For example, in some cases, alcohol use may decline with age because of decreased income, fewer social opportunities, or increasing health problems (Farkas, 2004). Problematic alcohol use among older adults is also related to the extent to which drinking is accepted within the individual's social network, as well as personal attitudes regarding the acceptability of drinking (Preston & Goodfellow, 2006). Age of onset of substance use is correlated with prognosis. Individuals with an early onset of substance use problems (e.g., ≤ 40 years old) are more like to have a family history of alcoholism and more psychological instability compared to those with later onset (Atkinson, Turner, Kofoed, & Tolson, 1985). Individuals with late-onset alcohol or drug use problems are more likely to have begun this behavior in reaction to life stressors. Because these individuals typically do not have a long history of using substances as a coping mechanism, impaired relationships due to substance use, or mental or physical problems caused by drugs or alcohol, their prognosis is more promising (Farkas, 2004). Generally speaking, older age is associated with increased rates of remission from drug and alcohol problems and improved treatment outcomes such as greater treatment length, adherence, and attendance (Lemke & Moos, 2003; Oslin, Pettinati, & Volpicelli, 2002; Weisner, Ray, Mertens, Satre, & Moore, 2003). Factors that have been identified as predictors of good outcome among younger adults have also been found relevant for the elderly, including longer duration in treatment, greater involvement in self-help groups such as Alcoholics Anonymous, increased self-efficacy, and nonavoidant coping strategies (Lemke & Moos, 2003).

EPIDEMIOLOGY OF SUBSTANCE USE DISORDERS

Much of the data that follow on prevalence rates of use of specific substances comes primarily from three sources: (1) the Monitoring the Future survey, (2) the NIAAA's NESARC, and (3) the 2005 NSDUH, sponsored by the SAMHSA. The Monitoring the Future study is an ongoing study funded by the NIDA of behaviors, attitudes, and values of American youth; each year approximately 50,000 8th-, 10th-, and 12th-grade students are surveyed regarding their lifetime, past year, and past month substance use behavior (L. D. Johnston, O'Malley, Bachman, & Schulenberg, 2006). The NESARC is a general population survey of over 43,000 individuals 18 years or older selected randomly from the U.S. population who were administered a structured interview (the NIAAA Alcohol Use Disorder and Associated Disabilities Interview Schedule IV) assessing *DSM-IV*-defined alcohol and substance use disorders for 10 classes of drugs (Stinson et al., 2005). The NSDUH survey annually questions approximately 67,500 individuals from the civilian, noninstitutionalized population of the United States ages 12 and older about their use of drugs and alcohol (SAMHSA, 2006). It should be noted that this section of the chapter provides information about the rates of abuse and dependence diagnoses for various substances as well as statistics on general use (the latter are not necessarily indicative of *DSM-IV*-defined substance use disorders).

Alcohol

Approximately 7% of the population ages 12 or older in the United States are current drinkers of alcohol (SAMHSA, 2006). Data from the 2005 NSDUH found that in the month prior to the survey 6.6% of individuals ages 12 or older engaged in heavy drinking (i.e., 5 or more drinks on one occasion on each of 5 or more days), and approximately 23% had engaged in binge drinking (i.e., 5 or more drinks on one occasion; SAMHSA, 2006). Data from the most recent Monitoring the Future surveys indicate that although alcohol use among teenagers has declined from rates noted in the 1980s and early 1990s, it remains relatively widespread, with approximately 75% of respondents indicating that they have consumed alcohol by the end of high school. Reported prevalence rates of being drunk at least once in the prior month were 6%, 19%, and 30% for 8th, 10th, and 12th graders, respectively (L. D. Johnston et al., 2006; NIDA, 2006a).

With regard to alcohol use disorders, according to data from the National Institute of Mental Health (NIMH) Epidemiologic Catchment Area (ECA) survey, the lifetime prevalence rate for alcohol dependence or abuse is 13.5% (Regier et al., 1990). Data from the 2001–2002 NESARC survey estimated the 12-month prevalence rate of alcohol dependence to be 3.81% and alcohol abuse to be 4.65%. For both dependence and abuse, prevalence rates were significantly higher for men than women (dependence: men = 5.42%, women = 2.32%; abuse: men = 6.93%, women = 2.55%). The overall 12-month prevalence rate for alcohol dependence in 2001 to 2002 represented a decline from the rate of 4.38% that had been noted in the NESARC survey from a decade earlier. Consistent with information presented earlier regarding life span considerations, rates of alcohol dependence and abuse steadily declined across age groups in the 2001–2002 NESARC data. For example, 12-month prevalence rates of alcohol dependence for 18- to 29-year-olds, 30- to 44-year-olds, 45- to 64-year-olds, and those 65 and older were 9.24%, 3.77%, 1.89%, and 0.24%, respectively. Rates of alcohol abuse across these same age groups were 6.95%, 5.95%, 3.45%, and 1.21%, respectively (B. F. Grant et al., 2004).

Amphetamines and Cocaine

In 2005, 2.4 million persons were current cocaine users, including 682,000 current crack users; 872,000 individuals were new users of cocaine (SAMHSA, 2006). Among youth, data from the 2005 Monitoring the Future survey showed that between 3.7% and 8.0% of 8th to 12th graders had used cocaine during their lifetime, and between 2.5% and 5.1% had used cocaine within the past year (L. D. Johnston et al., 2006). Lifetime prevalence rates of cocaine use for youth ages 12 to 17 and adults ages 18 to 25, 26 to 34, and 35 or more were 2.3%, 15.1%, 15.9%, and 15.1%, respectively, according to data from the 2005

NSDUH. Rates of lifetime use of crack for these same four age groups were 0.4%, 3.5%, 4.5%, and 3.4%, respectively (SAMHSA, 2006).

Data from the 2001–2002 NESARC survey found that lifetime prevalence rates for cocaine dependence and abuse were 0.98% and 1.83%, respectively, while lifetime prevalence rates for amphetamine dependence and abuse were 0.60% and 1.40%, respectively (Conway, Compton, Stinson, & Grant, 2006). Using data from the same survey, 12-month prevalence rates of cocaine dependence and abuse were both 0.13%, and were 0.09% and 0.07% for amphetamine dependence and abuse, respectively (Stinson et al., 2005). According to NSDUH statistics, approximately 1.5 million Americans (age 12 or older) qualified for a diagnosis of cocaine abuse or dependence in 2005, making this illicit drug second only to cannabis in terms of the number of diagnosed individuals.

Cannabis

According to data from the Monitoring the Future study, cannabis use among youth markedly increased during the 1990s but began to decline after 1996 and now appears to be holding steady. Despite this stabilized trend, lifetime and 12-month use prevalence rates are much higher than for other drugs, highlighting the fact that marijuana is one of the most commonly used substances among youth. Specifically, data from the 2005 Monitoring the Future study indicate lifetime use rates for 8th, 10th, and 12th graders were 16%, 34.1%, and 44.8%, respectively; 12-month use prevalence rates for these same groups were 12.2%, 26.6%, and 33.6%, respectively (L. D. Johnston et al., 2006). Data from the 2005 NSDUH showed rates of lifetime marijuana use among individuals 12 to 17, 18 to 25, 26 to 34, and 35 or older were 17.4%, 52.4%, 49.8%, and 39.0%, respectively (SAMHSA, 2006).

Lifetime rates of *DSM-IV*-defined cannabis dependence and abuse have been estimated to be 7.16% and 1.38%, respectively, and 12-month rates for dependence and abuse are 0.32% and 1.13%, respectively (Conway et al., 2006; Stinson et al., 2005). According to data from the 2005 NSDUH, marijuana is the illicit drug that accounts for the highest number of abuse and dependence cases in the United States (i.e., over 4 million individuals ages 12 or older; SAMHSA, 2006).

Hallucinogens

Rates of hallucinogen use among adolescents have been on the decline since the 1990s, particularly for LSD (L. D. Johnston et al., 2006). Data from the 2005 Monitoring the Future study found that rates of 12-month use of hallucinogens for 8th, 10th, and 12th graders were 2.4%, 4.0%, and 5.5%, respectively, and that rates of lifetime use for these three age groups were 3.4%, 6.1%, and 8.3%, respectively. According to data from the NSDUH, lifetime rates of any LSD use for individuals 12 to 17, 18 to 25, 26 to 34, and 35 or older were 1.1%, 10.5%, 14.8%, and 9.0%, respectively (SAMHSA, 2006).

Lifetime prevalence rates for *DSM-IV* hallucinogen dependence and abuse are likewise low and have been reported to be 0.24% and 1.45%, respectively (Conway et al., 2006). Twelve-month prevalence rates for hallucinogen dependence and abuse, according to the NESARC survey, are 0.02% and 0.12%, respectively (Stinson et al., 2005).

Inhalants

Relative to other substances, the prevalence of inhalant use is relatively low. Data from the Monitoring the Future survey found that 12-month prevalence rates of inhalant use among 10th and 12th graders in 2004 (5.9% and 4.2%, respectively) declined in comparison to rates in these age groups observed a decade earlier (9.6% and 8%, respectively; L. D. Johnston et al., 2006). However, inhalant use among 8th graders in 2004 increased from the previous year from 15.8% to 17.3% (NIDA, 2006c). Data from the 2005 NSDUH found that lifetime, past year, and past month rates of inhalant use among 12- to 17-year-olds were 10.5%, 4.5%, and 1.2%, respectively, and for 18- to 25-year-olds were 13.3%, 2.1%, and 0.5%, respectively.

The NESARC study found the lifetime and 12-month prevalence rates of *DSM-IV*-defined inhalant abuse among adults were 0.30% and 0.02% among the 43,093 respondents surveyed (Conway et al., 2006; Stinson et al., 2005). The National Comorbidity Survey (Anthony, Warner, & Kessler, 1994) estimated the lifetime prevalence rate of inhalant dependence at 0.3%.

Opioids

After holding steady for many years (throughout the late 1970s and 1980s), use of heroin among youth in the United States began to rise starting in 1993, stabilized around 2000, declined in 2001, and has been fairly stable since that time, according to data from the Monitoring the Future study (L. D. Johnston et al., 2005). Lifetime use prevalence rates for heroin among 8th, 10th, and 12th graders in 2005 were 1.5% for all groups, and 12-month use prevalence rates were 0.8% for all groups. According to data from the NSDUH, lifetime rates of any heroin use among 12- to 17-year-olds, 18- to 25-year-olds, 26- to 34-year-olds, and those 35 or older were reported to be 0.2%, 1.5%, 1.6%, and 1.6%, respectively (SAMHSA, 2006).

Lifetime rates of *DSM-IV*-defined opioid dependence and abuse have been estimated to be 0.34% and 1.08%, respectively, whereas 12-month rates for dependence and abuse are 0.11% and 0.24%, respectively (Conway et al., 2006; Stinson et al., 2005).

Phencyclidine and Similarly Acting Arylcyclohexylamines

Use of PCP among youth and young adults is low compared to other illicit drugs. For example, data from the 2005 Monitoring the Future study found that lifetime and annual use rates of PCP among high school seniors were 2.4% and 1.3%, respectively (L. D. Johnston et al., 2006). Data from the NSDUH found low rates of lifetime use among 12- to 17-year-olds (i.e., 0.7%), 26- to 34-year-olds (2.0%), and those 35 and older (3.3%). A higher rate of lifetime use was found for adults ages 18 to 25 (i.e., 10.5%; SAMHSA, 2006). Unfortunately, systematic study of the prevalence of PCP abuse and dependence disorders has not been undertaken (American Psychiatric Association, 2000b).

Sedatives, Hypnotics, and Anxiolytics

According to data from the NSDUH, lifetime rates of tranquilizer use among 12- to 17-year-olds, 18- to 25-year-olds, 26- to 34-year-olds, and those 35 and older were 3.0%,

13.4%, 10.5%, and 8.1%, respectively. Lifetime rates of sedative use among these four age groups were 0.9%, 2.0%, 1.6%, and 5%, respectively (SAMHSA, 2006).

Lifetime rates of *DSM-IV*-defined sedative dependence and abuse have been estimated to be 0.25% and 0.82%, respectively, whereas 12-month rates for dependence and abuse are 0.07% and 0.09%, respectively. With regard to tranquilizers, rates for lifetime dependence and abuse (0.22% and 0.76%, respectively) and 12-month dependence and abuse (0.05% and 0.08%, respectively) are similar to that seen for sedatives (Conway et al., 2006; Stinson et al., 2005).

ETIOLOGY

Biological Factors

Biological factors associated with substance use disorders are discussed next primarily in terms of two topics: the neurobiology of addiction (i.e., the effects of alcohol and drugs on the brain) and genetic influences in the development of substance use disorders. With regard to the former, the powerfully reinforcing effects of drugs and alcohol are due to their ability to stimulate reward centers in the brain associated with feelings of pleasure. These areas include the medial forebrain bundle, nucleus accumbens, and ventral tegmentum. The medial forebrain bundle contains nerves that connect areas of the brain's limbic system, including the amygdala, septum, nucleus accumbens, hypothalamus, and the ventral tegmentum. Dopaminergic projections that connect these areas are stimulated by most drugs of abuse (Koob et al., 1999). Cocaine, for example, blocks the reuptake of dopamine from the synaptic cleft. When opiates are ingested they bind to μ opioid receptors in the brain, which in turn facilitates the release of dopamine and decreases release of the neurotransmitter GABA, which normally inhibits dopamine release (Kosten, George, & Kleber, 2005). With repeated substance use a homeostatic process known as *neuroadaption* occurs in the brain, which can result in a decrease in the number and sensitivity of dopamine receptors in key areas and decreased dopamine release to compensate for chronically high levels of dopamine (Lessa & Scanlon, 2006; Thombs, 2006). The altered neurobiology of dopamine neurons has been referred to as the "changed set point model," and there are a number of hypotheses about the precise manner in which such adaptations take place. For example, in one scenario, use of substances such as opiates bypasses neuronal autoreceptors that ordinarily shut down further release of dopamine when concentrations become excessive; over time this may cause the brain to increase the number and strength of such autoreceptors to the point that resting levels of dopamine release are inhibited and cause the addicted individual to take more of the drug to achieve desired effects (tolerance; Kosten et al., 2005). When ingestion of an abused substance suddenly stops, the body is not able to rapidly revert back to the preuse production levels of neurotransmitters and other neurochemicals affected by the drug use; these decreased levels then trigger symptoms associated with withdrawal (Lessa & Scanlon, 2006). It has also been hypothesized that individuals susceptible to drug or alcohol addiction may have abnormalities in the prefrontal cortex, particularly with regard to the ability of this brain area to send inhibitory signals to the brain's reward center (e.g., to stop or delay impulsive, pleasure-seeking behavior; Kosten et al., 2005).

With regard to genetic factors implicated in the development of substance use disorders, evidence is strong that such influences are more important in understanding the *initiation* of substance use than the progression from use to abuse or dependence and generally do not appear to be substance-specific (Cloninger, 2004). Promising chromosome regions have been identified that appear linked to either protecting against or increasing the risk of substance use disorders (e.g., chromosomes 3, 4, 9, 10, 11, 12, 13, 16, and X); in some cases, these regions are linked to personality traits associated with increased risk of substance use disorders such as novelty seeking (see Cloninger, 2004, for a review). It is likely that genetic influences for substance use involve multiple genes that may operate in a number of ways, including additive effects, locus heterogeneity (i.e., more than one gene could trigger a syndrome), threshold effects (i.e., a certain number of genes needed), interaction effects (i.e., a particular set of genes is needed), or some combination of these (Schork & Schork, 1998). Although the genetic heritability for alcoholism has been estimated to be as high as 40% to 60% according to individual studies (McGue, 1999), a meta-analysis of alcohol-related genetic studies (including family, twin, and adoption studies) published between 1970 and 2000 placed heritability estimates in the more moderate range of 20% to 26% (and at 30% to 36% for males with severe alcohol dependence; G. D. Walters, 2002).

These findings highlight the important role that *nongenetic* factors play in influencing substance use disorders. The fact that alcohol and drug use disorders frequently run in families can be understood both in terms of genetic and psychosocial influences. An example of the interaction between genetic and environmental factors is exemplified in Cloninger's typology of alcoholism that was based on studies of Swedish male adoptees (Bohman, Cloninger, Sigvardsson, & von Knorring, 1987; Cloninger, Bohman, & Sigvardsson, 1981). Specifically, Cloninger identified what he termed *milieu-limited* or *Type 1 alcoholics* and *male limited* or *Type 2 alcoholics*. The Type 1 alcoholics displayed a milder form of alcohol abuse that had an onset in adulthood, typically did not require hospital treatment, and lacked criminality or legal problems. This form of alcoholism was viewed as requiring sufficient environmental stressors or "provocation" to trigger the underlying diathesis or vulnerability, with the severity of the resulting alcohol problems strongly related to environmental factors. Type 1 alcoholics were presumed to have personality characteristics such as low novelty seeking (i.e., low in impulsive aggressive traits), high harm avoidance (i.e., low risk taking), and high reward dependence. In contrast, Type 2 alcoholics were characterized by personality traits such as high novelty seeking, low harm avoidance, and low reward dependence. These individuals also typically had a biological father who frequently had an onset of alcoholism in adolescence and a history of serious criminality and extensive alcohol treatment. The heritability of Type 2 alcoholism was thought to be transmitted from fathers to sons.

One of the most important studies to examine the role of genetic and environmental influences on drug use was the Harvard Twin Study of Substance Abuse, which studied members of the Vietnam Era Twin (VET) registry (comprising over 8,000 male twins who served in the U.S. military from 1965 to 1975) (Tsuang, Bar, Harley, & Lyons, 2001). Individuals from the VET registry were interviewed regarding their use of illicit and licit substances and history of psychopathology. Monozygotic (identical) twin pairs were significantly more likely to be concordant for *DSM-III-R* substance abuse or dependence diagnoses than dizygotic twin pairs (26.2% versus 16.5%, respectively). However, findings from this study support *both* genetic and environmental influences on the abuse of substances such as heroin and other opiates, stimulants, sedatives, marijuana, and PCP and other psychedelics. When substances were considered as a whole, the percentage of variance in lifetime risk of drug abuse or dependence accounted for by genetic factors, shared environmental factors, and unique environmental influences were 34%, 28%, and 38%, respectively. Examination of specific substance classes revealed that each was associated with unique vulnerability factors, but shared vulnerability factors (i.e., factors that cut across substances and predispose a person to substance abuse more generally) accounted for the majority of the variance in risk for abuse for all drugs studied except heroin. The last finding suggests that genetic linkage studies of heroin abuse and dependence are particularly important to pursue given the greater proportion of unique genetic vulnerabilities apparently associated with this drug.

Psychological Factors

Psychodynamic and Psychoanalytic Theories

These theories of substance use have variously conceptualized addiction as a manifestation of an unconscious death wish driven by the id, an indication of severe personality disturbance and impaired ego functioning, an attempt to replace missing or defective self-objects, a consequence of arrested psychological development that leads to inadequate self-care functions, and a defense mechanism designed to protect against unacceptable sexual or aggressive drives and negative emotional states such as anxiety, depression, shame, guilt, boredom, helplessness, and powerlessness (i.e., the self-medication hypothesis; Dodes, 1996; Kohut & Wolf, 1978; H. Krystal, 1995; Thombs, 2006; Wurmser, 1984). H. Krystal (1978) contends that individuals with drug and alcohol problems suffer from alexithymia, or an inability to verbalize feelings, and thus turn to substances to ameliorate the arousal of undifferentiated emotional states. A common thread throughout many psychoanalytic theories is that substance use disorders are preceded and facilitated by underlying severe psychopathology (e.g., narcissism). Some have further suggested that specific substances are chosen for use because of their ability to alleviate symptoms stemming from certain forms of psychopathology. For example, Khantzian (1980) describes the appeal of the sedating and relaxing effects of opiates and heroin for individuals who experience overwhelming anger, rage, and depression caused by disorganized, regressed, and dysphoric ego states. Anecdotal reports of clients using substances to cope with intolerable emotions, as well as findings from epidemiologic studies that substance use typically follows rather than precedes the onset of forms of psychopathology such as anxiety disorders would seem to lend support to self-medication hypotheses. However, research findings that use of substances such as cannabis and nicotine predict depression (but not vice versa) run counter to a self-medication hypothesis (E. Goodman & Capitman, 2000; Patton et al., 2002). It is also clear that many factors can affect the substances that individuals choose to use, including social pressures, availability, and cost. Furthermore many individuals do not report that specific substances alleviate specific symptoms, but instead note more generally that use of alcohol and drugs help a variety of problems (Mueser, Drake, & Wallach, 1998). Findings that schizophrenic individuals frequently abuse drugs that carry the potential to worsen psychotic symptoms (e.g., cocaine) further run counter to the self-medication hypothesis (Dixon, Haas, Weiden, & Frances,

1991). Psychoanalytic perspectives on substance use disorders have additionally been criticized for relying too heavily on clinical reports and case studies for supporting evidence rather than larger scale investigation with adequate control groups, and also for failing to adequately articulate models of treatment (Leeds & Morgenstern, 2003).

Cognitive and Behavioral Theories

These theories of substance use rest on several assumptions, as outlined by Rotgers (2003): (a) Human behavior is largely learned; (b) learning processes that create problem behaviors can be used to change them; (c) behavior is primarily determined by environmental and contextual factors; (d) covert behaviors (e.g., feelings, thoughts) can be changed through the application of learning principles; (e) engaging in new behaviors in the settings in which they are supposed to occur is an important part of the behavior change process; (f) clients are unique and must be evaluated in their individual contexts; and (g) treatment rests on a thorough cognitive-behavioral assessment. From a behavioral perspective, principles of both classical and operant conditioning can be applied to understand how substance use disorders developed and are maintained.

Classical (Pavlovian) conditioning paradigms provide a way of understanding phenomena such as cravings (i.e., strong desire to use) and relapse in the presence of stimuli that have been associated with prior use. For example, if an individual always used heroin while sitting on a particular park bench, it is likely that she will experience cravings or a strong desire to use when confronted with this stimuli. The heroin serves as an unconditioned stimulus that provokes the unconditioned response of euphoria and other sensations associated with getting high. The bench becomes a conditioned stimulus through repeated pairings with the drug's effects and is able to elicit a conditioned response that triggers feelings similar to the unconditioned response and that increase the motivation to use. Cue exposure treatments attempt to break the association between formerly neutral stimuli and drug use and essentially follow a Pavlovian model of extinction (Bradizza, Stasiewicz, & Maisto, 1994). Classical conditioning can also help explain the phenomenon noted earlier in this chapter regarding environmental influences on tolerance (see section on "Substance Dependence").

With regard to *operant conditioning,* it is assumed that the pleasurable sensations associated with drinking and drug use serve as powerful reinforcers that increase the likelihood of continued substance use behavior. Although there may be negative effects of substance use (e.g., relationship problems, health consequences), these are not as immediate as the reinforcing aspects of substance use and may not serve as sufficiently strong deterrents for use, at least initially. Furthermore, there may be a lack of positive reinforcement for alternative behaviors that do not involve using drugs or alcohol, and the rewards for maintaining sobriety may be quite delayed (Thombs, 2006). Another aspect of operant conditioning, negative reinforcement, can be applied to understanding an individual's behavioral response to withdrawal symptoms. If a person who is physically dependent on alcohol or another drug begins to experience uncomfortable withdrawal symptoms, he or she is likely to use again to ameliorate these symptoms. In behavioral terms, we would say that continued substance use behavior was negatively reinforced by the removal or alleviation of the painful withdrawal symptoms.

Social learning theory, as articulated by Albert Bandura (1977), emphasizes that modeling and imitation play important roles in learning new behaviors. Individuals are particularly likely to imitate models who are similar to them or whom they see as attractive, trustworthy, competent, or of higher social status (Bandura, 1977; McCullagh, 1987; B. J. Zimmerman & Koussa, 1979). This theory can be applied to understanding the critical role that peer influences have on the development of substance use disorders among adolescents (Newcomb & Bentler, 1986). The likelihood of drug and alcohol use is increased among adolescents when their peer networks exhibit positive attitudes toward substance use and engage in substance use (Brook et al., 2001; Preston & Goodfellow, 2006). Parental drug and alcohol use have also been identified as risk factors for adolescent substance use, and while genetic factors may play some role in this association, the impact that modeling may have on such behavior cannot be overlooked (Brook et al., 2001). Modeling is also utilized in many behaviorally oriented interventions for substance abuse, such as in teaching social skills, anger management skills, assertiveness training, and use of relaxation strategies (Rotgers, 2003).

Cognitive theories of substance abuse emphasize the role that beliefs about the use of drugs or alcohol can play in perpetuating problematic patterns of use. In A.T. Beck's (Beck, Wright, Newman, & Liese, 1993) model of substance abuse, it is assumed that some individuals have developed a cognitive vulnerability to drug abuse that results in the activation of beliefs (e.g., "I can't socialize without getting high") that increase the likelihood of substance use. The circumstances that trigger these beliefs may be internal states such as depression or boredom, or external events such as being around others who are using. The beliefs that are activated in response to such triggers may fall into one of three categories: (1) anticipatory beliefs that involve an expectation about drug use (e.g., "I feel like superman when I use"); (2) relief-oriented beliefs that substances will alleviate an uncomfortable physical state (e.g., "My urges and cravings won't go away unless I use"); and (3) facilitative or permissive beliefs that contend drug or alcohol use is acceptable even if there could be negative consequences (e.g., "I deserve this because I have worked hard, and there is nothing wrong with taking a risk"; F. D. Wright, Beck, Newman, & Liese, 1993). The potency of expectancy effects has been demonstrated in the laboratory by showing, for example, that men led to believe they had consumed alcohol subsequently report experiencing less social anxiety regardless of whether alcohol or a placebo was actually administered (G.T. Wilson & Abrams, 1977).

Figure 8.1 illustrates the cognitive model and shows that once thoughts stemming from drug-related beliefs are activated, cravings and urges to use increase. This leads to the activation of additional thoughts that further facilitate drug use. In turn, behaviors are generated that lead to the search for and ultimately use of drugs. Importantly, the actual use of drugs or alcohol is posited to serve as yet another circumstance that triggers additional beliefs (e.g., "I've ruined my abstinence so I might as well binge") that lead to a vicious cycle of further drug use (F. D. Wright et al., 1993).

Beliefs related to self-efficacy have been hypothesized to be powerful mediators of alcohol and drug use behavior. Bandura (1999) has noted that addicted individuals who have low self-efficacy are likely to avoid or drop out of treatment prematurely and are more likely to relapse if they stay in treatment. It has also been suggested that individuals with low self-efficacy may be prone to blaming socially problematic behavior on the alcohol or drug use as a way to avoid further negative self-evaluation, or they may develop positive beliefs or expectancies about the ability of alcohol or drugs to soothe distress or alleviate tension (G. T. Wilson, 1987).

Figure 8.1   The cognitive model of substance abuse.

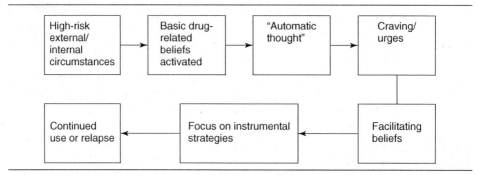

Source: "Cognitive Therapy of Substance Abuse: Theoretical Rationale," by F. D. Wright, A. T. Beck, C. F. Newman, and B. S. Liese, *NIDA Research Monograph, 137,* pp. 123–146. Reprinted with permission.

Family Environment Models

Understanding substance use from a family systems perspective requires consideration of the interpersonal and social matrix in which individual drug and alcohol use is embedded. Systemic models of substance abuse examine both the influence that environmental factors can have on the initiation of drug or alcohol use, as well as the subsequent impact that substance use disorders can have on significant others. There is a considerable body of research demonstrating a connection between the quality of the family environment and subsequent risk of substance use in adolescents. Variables such as decreased parental involvement and monitoring, parental displays of hostility and lack of warmth, low family cohesion, and higher rates of family conflict are associated with greater adolescent use of alcohol and marijuana, as well as poorer recovery among adolescents who have received treatment for substance use problems (Bray, Adams, Getz, & Baer, 2001; Godley, Kahn, Dennis, Godley, & Funk, 2005; Nation & Heflinger, 2006). Information presented under "Onset, Course, and Life Span Considerations" further illustrated that parental substance use is a risk factor for the development of substance use in children; this relationship may be mediated by decreased closeness and parental support, increased risk of seeking out deviant peer groups, modeling of substance use behavior, and facilitation of beliefs regarding the acceptability of drug or alcohol use (Barnes, Reifman, Farrell, & Dintcheff, 2000; Gerrard, Gibbons, Stock, & Vande Lune, 2005).

Much has been written in the clinical literature on the impact that growing up with an alcoholic parent may have on self-esteem, emotional functioning, and the development of cognitive relationship rules. Theories on adult children of alcoholics (ACOA) hypothesize that the inconsistency and chaos associated with parental substance abuse results in the development of insecurity, fear, self-blame, and unexpressed anger among children, which can then persist into adulthood (Deutsch, 1982). It has further been suggested that such children may come to adopt characteristic roles as a result of living with an alcoholic parent, such as the "hero" or "placater," who garners positive attention through achievement behaviors; the "responsible child," who adopts a parentified role within the family; the "lost child" or "adjuster," who fades into the background; and the "mascot" or "problem child," who diverts attention away from problems created by parental alcoholism through his or her own acting-out behavior or clowning around (C. Black, 1982; Wegsheider, 1981). It is hypothesized that while such roles are intended to minimize conflict within the family and serve a protective function for the child, individual growth is inhibited and the formation of future healthy relationships is impeded (Beesley & Stoltenberg, 2002). Research literature does not firmly support the notion that ACOAs have a consistently identifiable personality type (George, LaMarr, Barrett, & McKinnon, 1999; Lewis-Harter, 2000). Criticisms have been raised that attributes that supposedly characterize ACOAs (e.g., taking care of others in a crisis, taking on more than one's fair share of work, sensitivity to the difficulties of others, hiding true feelings) are so broad that almost anyone could identify with at least some of them (the so-called Barnum effect; George et al., 1999; Logue, Sher, & Frensch, 1992). However, ACOAs do appear to be at greater risk for the development of substance use problems than those who did not grow up in households where alcohol was abused (Jacob, Windle, Seilhamer, & Bost, 1999; M. Russell, 1990). Other research finds that ACOAs report greater need for control in relationships, less relationship satisfaction, difficulties trusting others, higher rates of psychopathology (e.g., depression, anxiety), decreased behavioral control, and lower educational attainment (Beesley & Stoltenberg, 2002; Jacob et al., 1999). Yet several studies have failed to find significant differences in personality traits, psychopathology, or adjustment differences between ACOAs and others (Berkowitz & Perkins, 1988; Churchill, Broida, & Nicholson, 1990; George et al., 1999; Jarmas & Kazak, 1992). Differences in subject samples (e.g., ACOAs in treatment or who have a parent in active treatment versus ACOA college students) may account for some of the variability of findings across studies. Kashubeck and Christensen (1992) found that ACOAs who were participants in 12-step support groups reported higher levels of psychological distress, lower satisfaction with perceived social support, lower hardiness, and more negative attitudes, feelings, and behaviors regarding parental alcoholism than a comparison group composed of ACOA college students.

DIVERSITY CONSIDERATIONS

Ethnicity and Culture

Variability in the patterns of drug and alcohol use among different ethnic groups has been well documented in the empirical literature. These relationships are complex and are undoubtedly impacted and complicated by factors beyond cultural differences in the meaning of and acceptability of substance use, such as family-of-origin issues, political and economic climates, acculturative stress, religion and spirituality, educational and occupational issues, and community environment (Franklin & Markarian, 2005). It is beyond the scope of this chapter to thoroughly review so multifaceted a topic, and hence the focus here is on general findings from the research literature. An important caveat to keep in mind is that within any broadly designated ethnic or cultural group, considerable heterogeneity exists. To illustrate, while rates of illicit drug use among Asian American communities are typically lower than national averages, rates among some subgroups (e.g., Koreans) more closely approximate general U.S. population figures (NIDA, 2003).

T. J. Young (1988) also notes that among Native American tribal groups, views on the use of alcohol vary widely, with some (e.g., Navajo) viewing alcohol use as acceptable and others (e.g., Hopi) condemning it.

African Americans

Many studies suggest that among African American youth, rates of drinking are significantly lower compared to Caucasian youth, and that drinking increases at a slower rate across adolescence relative to Caucasian and Hispanic youth (Bray et al., 2001). In a survey of over 4,000 adolescents ages 12 to 17 (National Survey of Adolescents), Kilpatrick and colleagues (2000) found that after controlling for demographic factors and history of victimization (e.g., physical or sexual assault), African Americans were 3 to 9 times less likely to meet criteria for substance abuse or dependence diagnoses relative to Caucasians. Although risk of substance use disorders may be lower for African American youth in some studies, use of alcohol and street drugs predicts risk-taking behavior (including sexually risky behavior) in this population, which increases the risk of adverse outcomes (e.g., contraction of sexually transmitted diseases; Busen, Marcus, & von Sternberg, 2006). Furthermore, African American youth who use alcohol and marijuana and lack regular family interactions are at increased risk for progressing to harder drug use (e.g., crack cocaine; Bowser & Word, 1993).

Rates of substance use problems increase in adulthood for African Americans. It has been suggested that discrimination, feelings of powerlessness, poverty, and limited employment and educational opportunities may become more salient in adulthood and help to explain this trajectory (Franklin & Markarian, 2005; Terrell, 1993). Data from the 2001–2002 NESARC study found that the 12-month prevalence rate of any alcohol use disorder was significantly lower among African Americans adults compared to Caucasians (6.9% versus 8.9%, respectively), but 12-month prevalence rates of any drug use disorder were comparable between these two groups (2.4% and 1.9%, respectively; B. Huang et al., 2006). Furthermore, the use of crack cocaine has become widespread in many African American communities, particularly in impoverished inner-city areas (Dunlap, Golub, & Johnson, 2006). Crack users are more likely than nonusers to have multiple sex partners, have unprotected sex, and to trade sex for drugs, all of which increase the risk of sexually transmitted diseases such as HIV, which has become a major health crisis in the African American community (Bowser & Word, 1993). Finally, African Americans experience a disproportionately high rate of adverse health consequences from substance use such as cancer, cirrhosis of the liver, and pulmonary disease, are more likely to be victims of drug-related crimes, and are more likely to be incarcerated for drug-related offenses than to receive treatment (D'Avanzo, Dunn, Murdock, & Naegle, 2000).

Asian Americans

As previously noted, lower rates of drug and alcohol use have typically been reported for Asians compared to other ethnic groups. Data from the 2001–2002 NESARC study found that the 12-month prevalence rates for any alcohol or drug use disorder were 4.5% and 1.4%, respectively, for Asians; the alcohol use disorder rate was significantly lower than that for African Americans, Caucasians, Hispanics, and Native Americans, and the rate of drug use disorders was significantly lower than that for Native Americans (B. Huang et al., 2006). Despite the relatively low rates of substance use disorders frequently observed among Asian Americans, they appear to be at increased risk for substance-related (particularly alcohol) medical problems, including certain forms of cancer (Munaka et al., 2003; Salaspuro, 2003; Yokoyama & Omori, 2003). The presence of fewer risk factors associated with drug use (e.g., parental or peer models who use, impaired family relationships, sensation seeking) has been posited to explain the lower rates of substance use among Asian Americans (Wall, Shea, Chan, & Carr, 2001). The importance of considering acculturation in understanding substance use among Asian Americans was demonstrated in a study by Hahm, Lahiff, and Guterman (2003), which found that alcohol use was highest among highly acculturated Asian American youth (i.e., those who spoke English at home and were born in the United States). Interestingly, parental attachment moderated this effect such that highly acculturated youth with poor parental attachment were 11 times more likely to use alcohol than the least acculturated group (i.e., no use of English at home and born outside the United States), but the odds of use among highly acculturated youth with medium or high parental attachment were not significantly greater than those found for the least acculturated group.

Biological factors are also important to consider in examining patterns of alcohol use among individuals of Asian heritage. Specifically, much attention has focused on the mutant ALDH2*2 allele for the acetaldehyde dehydrogenase gene, which is possessed by approximately 50% of individuals of Chinese, Korean, and Japanese heritage. Acetaldehyde dehydrogenase is an enzyme that oxidizes ethanol (alcohol) into acetaldehyde, which in turn is converted to acetic acid. Unlike acetic acid, which is harmless, acetaldehyde can cause a number of aversive physical reactions if it accumulates in the body. Among those who possess the ALDH2*2 allele, the conversion of alcohol to acetic acid is less effective, and therefore consumption of alcohol is associated with symptoms such as flushing of the skin, increased respiration and heart rates, nausea, and vomiting. Not surprisingly, these individuals are less likely to regularly consume alcohol, to engage in binge drinking, or to develop alcohol use disorders than persons who do not possess the mutant allele (Takeshita & Morimoto, 1999; Wall et al., 2001). In addition, Wall et al. (2001), in a study of young Asian American adults with and without the ALDH2*2 allele, found that possession of the ALDH2*2 allele was associated not only with lower alcohol use, but also with lower likelihood of regular tobacco use. This raises interesting questions about the protective role this biological factor may play regarding escalation to harder drug use given that alcohol and cigarette use frequently precede the use of illicit substances.

Although substance use disorders appear less prevalent in many Asian American communities, those who do have these conditions are less likely than their Caucasian counterparts to seek treatment (particularly if they are highly educated and born outside of the United States; Sakai, Ho, Shore, Risk, & Price, 2005). Because of shame and embarrassment, family members may collude with the affected individual in ignoring or denying substance use problems, and seeking help from those outside of the extended family or local community may be viewed as a last resort (Franklin & Markarian, 2005). Thus clinicians need to be aware that an Asian client with a substance use disorder may present with more severe symptomatology related to this problem and to any comorbid conditions because entry into treatment has been delayed.

Hispanics

Data from the 2005 Monitoring the Future survey found that rates of substance use among Hispanic eighth graders were higher than that for African American or Caucasian youth for nearly all classes of drugs studied except amphetamines, and that by 12th grade Hispanics demonstrated higher rates of use of crack, heroin, methamphetamine, and Rohypnol (L. D. Johnston et al., 2006). Among adults, data from the 2001–2002 NESARC survey indicated the rate of any drug use disorder among Hispanic respondents was 1.7%, which was significantly lower than for African American and Native American respondents. The rate of any alcohol use disorder was 7.9%, which was significantly higher than that for Asian Americans, lower than that for Native Americans, and comparable to rates for Caucasians and African Americans (B. Huang et al., 2006). Although statistics regarding patterns of drug and alcohol use and the prevalence of substance use disorders are typically presented for Hispanics as a broad group, notable differences among subgroups of Hispanics exist that become obscured by such aggregate reporting. For example, Mexican Americans and Puerto Ricans appear to have higher rates of alcohol-related problems than Cubans and those from Central or South America (Amaro, Whitaker, Coffman, & Hereen, 1990; NIDA, 2003). In addition, a marked difference has been observed in drug and alcohol problems between women and men in the Hispanic community, with men reporting higher rates of problematic drug and alcohol use than their female counterparts (S. A. Black & Markides, 1993; Hines & Caetano, 1997). However, differences across subgroups of Hispanic individuals as well as between men and women may be less apparent when treatment populations are studied. In a study of Mexican, Cuban, and Puerto Rican Americans in substance abuse treatment, Alvarez, Olson, Jason, Davis, and Ferrari (2004) found no significant differences between ethnic groups for years of alcohol use or number of days of alcohol use in the 30 days prior to treatment, and no significant differences in the number of days alcohol, heroin, or cannabis was used in the month prior to treatment.

In working with lower-income Hispanic clients, factors such as economic stressors, educational limitations, and gang influences must be considered in understanding risks for substance use disorders. Childhood maltreatment is another risk factor for the development of substance use disorders, including polysubstance use, among Hispanic individuals (Hodson, Newcomb, Locke, & Goodyear, 2006). Early drug use also predicts participation in risky sexual behaviors that place Hispanic youth at risk for contracting HIV and other sexually transmitted diseases (Locke, Newcomb, & Goodyear, 2005).

Native Americans

Rates of drug and alcohol use among the American Indian and Native Alaskan communities have been repeatedly documented to be higher than rates observed among other ethnic minority groups, as well as Caucasians.

For example, rates of alcohol, nicotine, marijuana, and cocaine use among Native American youth are significantly higher than among their Hispanic, African American, and Caucasian counterparts, and substance use frequently begins at an earlier age among Native Americans. Rates of heavy drinking have been reported to be particularly high among some Native American groups, including the Sioux (9% to 24%), Navajo (14%), and Ojibwa (42%; T.J. Young, 1988).

According to statistics from the 2005 NSDUH, the rate of substance dependence or abuse was highest among American Indians and Alaska Natives (21%) compared to Hispanics, African Americans, and Asian Americans, and this rate is more than twice the national average (SAMHSA, 2006). Data from the 2001–2002 NESARC study found that among five ethnic groups studied (i.e., African Americans, Asian Americans, Caucasians, Hispanics, and Native Americans) the highest rates of past-year alcohol use and drug use disorders were observed among Native Americans (i.e., 12.1% and 4.0%, respectively). Furthermore, the rate of drug use disorders among Native Americans was significantly higher than that for the other four ethnic groups, and for alcohol use disorders was significantly higher than that observed for African Americans, Asian Americans, and Hispanics. It is notable that rates of mood, anxiety, and personality disorders (15.3%, 15.3%, and 24.1%, respectively) were also highest among Native Americans and were significantly higher than corresponding rates for African Americans, Asian Americans, and Hispanics (B. Huang et al., 2006).

Many hypotheses have been put forth to explain these higher rates of substance use disorders, and in particular problem drinking, among Native American communities. These include (a) the introduction of alcoholic beverages by Europeans and the associated lack of cultural mechanisms within tribal communities to restrict or moderate excessive alcohol use; (b) acculturative stressors and the mourning of the loss of cultural traditions that has occurred through historical events such as forced tribal relocation, population loss through wars and disease, harassment by the government and military, separation of families, and removal of traditional means of livelihood; (c) positive views that may be associated with alcohol and substance use; and (d) genetic vulnerability to alcoholism (see T. J. Young, 1988, for a review). Family studies of Native Americans suggest that alcohol dependence, marijuana and stimulant dependence, and regular tobacco use show evidence of moderate genetic influences (Wilhelmsen & Ehlers, 2005). Other risk factors for substance abuse that are not unique to the Native American population but that may be overrepresented in this community include personal history of trauma, poverty, inadequate resources, and discrimination (B. Huang et al., 2006; Russo, Purohit, Foudin, & Salin, 2004).

Although the need to address the sizable problem of substance use disorders among Native Americans remains a challenge for the mental health community, rates of help-seeking behavior among Native Americans for substance use problems appear commensurate with national averages when diverse sources of assistance, including biomedically oriented treatment facilities, 12-step groups, and traditional healers, are included (Beals et al., 2006). In a large-scale study examining the correlates of help-seeking behavior for substance use problems among over 2,800 members of two tribal groups, Beal and colleagues found (a) those with co-occurring mental or physical health problems were especially likely to seek help, (b) general spirituality was associated with greater likelihood of utilizing 12-step programs or help from a variety of treatment sources beyond solely biomedical services, and (c) individuals who placed importance in their lives on culture-specific spiritual traditions tended to utilize traditional healing sources. These findings point to the need for integrated treatments that incorporate dimensions such as spirituality and traditional cultural beliefs as options for Native Americans seeking help for drug and alcohol use disorders. The importance of developing biculturally oriented treatment approaches that combine empirically supported treatments with traditional practices has been noted by others (M. Brady, 1995; Schinke, Tepavac, & Cole, 2000).

Gender

Generally speaking, rates of substance use disorders are higher among men than women. Data from the 2005 NSDUH, for example, showed that males ages 12 years and older were approximately twice as likely to be diagnosed with substance abuse or dependence than females (12% versus 6.4%, respectively), although rates among youth ages 12 to 17 were more comparable for males and females (7.8% and 8.3%, respectively; SAMHSA, 2006). Similar results were obtained from the 2001–2002 NESARC data, which found the lifetime rate of any *DSM-IV* drug use disorder was 13.8% for men and 7.1% for women (Conway et al., 2006). Among older adults, males who abuse or are dependent on alcohol outnumber females by as much as 3:1 (Preston & Goodfellow, 2006). However, women are more likely than men to become dependent on sedatives or other substances intended to treat sleep problems and anxiety (NIDA, 2000a). The higher rates of substance use disorders among men may have more to do with increased opportunities for use rather than a difference in susceptibility to substance use disorders (Van Etten & Anthony, 1999; Van Etten, Neumark, & Anthony, 1999).

However, research has emerged demonstrating that there are physiologic differences in the way that alcohol and other drugs affect men and women. Correcting for body weight, when men and women are given equivalent amounts of alcohol, women attain higher blood alcohol levels than men. This is related to factors such as the higher proportion of body fat and lower body water level in women, and faster metabolism of alcoholism in men due to higher levels of alcohol dehydrogenase in the gastric system (Blume & Zilberman, 2005). With regard to other substances, women have been found to rate their subjective experiences of using cocaine more positively (in terms of mental and physical well-being) than men, which could increase the risk of toxicity for women if they are not as aware of physiologic signals indicating a need to stop using (McCance-Katz, Hart, Boyarsky, Kosten, & Jatlow, 2005). In addition, PET scans of the brains of men and women experiencing cocaine cravings show that while both groups exhibit similar activation in areas such as the nucleus accumbens, women demonstrate significantly less activation of the amygdala, which may be related to greater activation of the frontal cortex (Kilts, Gross, Ely, & Drexler, 2004).

When they enter treatment for substance use, women are more likely to report a wider range of psychosocial problems compared to men, including children being removed from their custody, termination of parental rights, other family members abusing substances, being the recent victim of physical or sexual abuse, and being on public assistance (men are more likely to report greater involvement in criminal activity and contacts with the criminal justice system; Hser, Evans, & Huang, 2005). Women addicted to drugs or alcohol are also more likely to have comorbid disorders such as mood and anxiety disorders, Posttraumatic Stress Disorder (PTSD), and eating disorders, and more health problems (Blume & Zilberman, 2005; NIDA, 2000a). In spite of the fact that women often enter treatment with a greater number of poor prognosis factors, they do not appear to relapse faster than men with regard to alcohol use, and actually appear to relapse less than men with regard to other substance use (Walitzer & Dearing, 2006). Furthermore, gender-related differences in risk factors for relapse have been identified. For example, whereas marriage appears to be a protective factor for men against alcohol-related relapse, it has been found to be a risk factor for women (e.g., marital stress precipitates relapse).

Similarly, negative mood states such as depression are associated with increased risk of (nonalcohol) substance use relapse for women, but positive mood states may pose a greater risk for men (Walitzer & Dearing, 2006).

INTAKE AND INTERVIEWING CONSIDERATIONS

General Considerations

The approach that is taken during the intake period and subsequent treatment planning will very much depend on the client's level of insight into the substance use problem, motivation to change, the point in the illness course at which help is being sought (e.g., early versus advanced stage), the current drug use phase (e.g., withdrawal, remission, relapse), demographics (e.g., age, gender), and cultural or ethnic background (e.g., acceptability of different levels of substance use, willingness to disclose problematic aspects of use to a mental health professional; Greenfield & Hennessy, 2004). It is common for individuals with substance use problems to deny or underreport their level of use and/or the resulting negative consequences. In some cases, problems with substance use will not be among the client's self-reported presenting problems; instead, the client may enter treatment for a co-occurring condition such as depression or anxiety or a problem in daily functioning (e.g., relationships, work) that is later determined to be related to drug or alcohol use. Even when individuals are willing to share details of their substance use experiences, memory difficulties surrounding periods of use may adversely impact the accuracy of their self-report. Thus, when evaluating individuals suspected of a substance use disorder, the clinician will likely gather information from a wider range of sources than might occur for clients with other psychiatric problems (First & Tasman, 2005).

Rapport

Clients who come into treatment for a substance use problem will vary in their motivation to change their drinking and/or drug use patterns. Some may have hit rock bottom and experienced a number of dramatic health, interpersonal, occupational or educational, financial, legal, or other consequences that now compel them to address their substance use disorder. In many ways, it is easier to establish rapport with these individuals compared to clients whose motivation to change and insight into the destructive effects of drug or alcohol use are substantially lower. The latter clients may feel coerced into treatment (e.g., by family, the courts), see therapy as unnecessary, and view the therapist with skepticism and perhaps hostility. The challenge in treating clients with substance use disorders is to meet them where they are in the recovery process. Rapport with clients who are resistant to examining their drug or alcohol use will be more quickly established if the clinician acknowledges the client's ambivalence and expresses empathy for this position, rather than trying to sell the therapy or convince the client of the need for change. This type of approach to working with substance-abusing clients is exemplified in motivational interviewing (W. R. Miller & Rollnick, 2002), which will be discussed shortly.

Many substance-abusing clients present with a grandiose or self-assured style that can be off-putting and make the establishment of rapport difficult. However, this bravado often masks feelings of worthlessness, self-hatred, and expectations of rejection by others

(Ashenberg-Straussner, 2004). For other clients, particularly older adults, shame or embarrassment about the extent of drug or alcohol use leads to a reluctance to engage in treatment (Dearing, Stuewig, & Tangney, 2005; Farkas, 2004). Some clients may wonder whether therapists who have not themselves struggled with addiction can really understand or help them. While it is common to find substance abuse counselors who have personally gone through the recovery process, one need not have experienced either the highs or lows of drug or alcohol use to work effectively with clients who have drug or alcohol use disorders. What is important is the adoption of a nonjudgmental and open attitude toward hearing about an individual's use experiences. Of course, this carries with it the potential for strong negative countertransference feelings to develop, such as if one hears of children who were abused or neglected as a direct result of the client's substance use, or if the client discloses a history of criminal behavior to support a drug habit. It is also possible to develop positive countertransference reactions to the substance-abusing client, such as feeling the need to rescue the client or to be the client's role model (Vannicelli, 2001). All such reactions must be continually monitored and dealt with (e.g., through professional consultation, personal psychotherapy) to avoid making the treatment counterproductive.

Many different therapeutic approaches have been utilized to effectively treat substance use disorders; however, one that we do not recommend is a highly confrontational style. This approach is based on a philosophy that stern challenges, inducing shame and guilt, making clients uncomfortable, anxious, or scared, and using other similarly punitive measures will create sufficient motivation for behavior change. It is our opinion that such tactics run counter to such basic therapeutic principles as establishing rapport and a strong working alliance with a client, demonstrating respect, and expressing interest in the client's view of his or her difficulties. The so-called boot camp approaches to the evaluation and treatment of substance use disorders have rarely been subjected to rigorous scientific study, and extant research indicates they are generally ineffective in producing lasting, positive behavior change among clients (Cowles, Castellano, & Gransky, 1995).

Interview and Assessment Strategies

A client's substance use can be evaluated in a number of different ways including interviews, self-report measures (questionnaires), biometric measures (e.g., urine toxicology screen), behavioral observations, and interviews with collateral sources. Each source has strengths and limitations.

Client Interview

Any standard intake interview should include at least a screening question about drug and alcohol use. Ashenberg-Straussner (2004) recommends that questions about potential substance abuse be asked of anyone who has a history of unpredictable, highly volatile behavior and/or occupational, financial, legal, or interpersonal problems. Indicators among older adults that a substance use disorder may be present include chronic insomnia or fatigue due to poor sleep, failure of normally treatable medical conditions to respond to treatment, cognitive deterioration (e.g., confusion, memory loss), diarrhea, urinary incontinence, malnutrition or weight loss, anxiety complaints and frequent use of anxiolytics, sedative, or hypnotics, and (among surgical patients) unexplained postoperative anxiety, confusion, agitation, or recent-onset seizures in the absence of known cerebrovascular disease (Egbert, 1993).

Clients may be more willing to first discuss their use of alcohol rather than drugs because most people drink (Ashenberg-Straussner, 2004). Even slight differences in how questions are phrased (e.g., "*How often* do you drink alcohol?" versus "*Do you* drink alcohol?") can result in different client perceptions of the acceptability of disclosing substance use. Zimberg (2005) suggests a number of questions that may be helpful in establishing a diagnosis of an alcohol or substance use disorder in an older adult, which are presented in Table 8.5.

When an individual reports using alcohol or other drugs, it is necessary to determine the quantity and frequency with which the substances are used. A useful approach to gathering this information is the time line follow-back (TLFB) method developed by Sobell and Sobell (1992). This technique involves asking clients to recall their pattern of substance use over the preceding 6 months using a calendar; clients indicate on the calendar the number of days a substance was used and approximately how much was used on those days. It may be easiest for clients to recall in detail the pattern of their substance use over the preceding month. For more distant months it may be necessary to ask clients to compare their use at those times to more current patterns of use or to utilize memory prompts such as anchoring substance use to events like holidays or birthdays (Greenfield & Hennessy, 2004). The TLFB method has demonstrated good test-retest reliability and validity among a range of clinical populations, including primary substance users, homeless individuals, and psychiatric outpatients (Carey, 1997; Ehrman & Robbins, 1994; Maisto, Sobell, Cooper, & Sobell, 1982; Sacks, Drake, Williams, Banks, & Herrell, 2003). Strengths of the TLFB include the ability to document drinking patterns that can be linked to nondrinking events in the client's life, flexibility to summarize drinking data over different time intervals, sensitivity to the range of quantities a client has consumed, and the yield of a large amount of data that can be used in treatment planning (Carey, 1997).

Table 8.5   Questions that may assist in evaluating substance use disorders in older adults

Has there been any recent marked change in behavior or personality?
Are there recurring episodes of memory loss and confusion?
Has the person become more socially isolated and begun to stay at home most of the time?
Has the person become more argumentative and resistant to offers of help?
Has the person tended to neglect personal hygiene, not been eating regularly, and not kept appointments, especially doctor's appointments?
Has the individual been neglecting his or her medical treatment regimen?
Has the individual been neglecting to manage his or her income effectively?
Has the individual been in trouble with the law?
Has the individual caused problems with neighbors?
Has the individual been subject to excessive falls or accidents?
Does the individual frequently use a benzodiazepine (Valium, Librium, Xanax)?
Has drinking been associated with any of the above situations?

Source: "Alcoholism and Substance Abuse in Older Adults" (pp. 396–410), by S. Zimberg, in *Clinical Textbook of Addictive Disorders,* third edition, R. J. Frances, S. I. Miller, and A. H. Mack (Eds.), 2005, New York: Guilford Press. Reprinted with permission.

Interview questions about substance use should also tap the client's perception of adverse consequences that have resulted from use. To address this, Lessa and Scanlon (2006) suggest that *DSM-IV* symptoms of abuse and dependence simply be formulated as questions (e.g., asking if a client has ever tried to cut down or control use of marijuana, or if alcohol has caused any recurrent legal problems). In addition to the standard questions included in any intake interview (see Chapter 1), additional areas of inquiry for clients suspected of having drug or alcohol use problems should include the age when substance use began, changes in the types or amounts of substances used across the client's life, history of treatment (e.g., inpatient detoxification, residential or sober living settings, outpatient), participation in self-help groups such as AA, length of abstinence (most recent and longest periods), factors (e.g., life events, emotional states) that were associated with periods of relapse, and family history of substance use. Greenfield and Hennessy (2004) note that the age when nicotine was first used is important because of the observed association between nicotine use and subsequent experimentation with illicit drugs. Because of the high rates of comorbidity (see "Diagnostic Considerations" in this chapter), it is important to obtain a thorough history of psychiatric problems beyond substance use disorders. Similarly, medical problems that may be either causally related to substance use or exacerbated by it should be investigated. Asking about the route through which a substance is taken (e.g., intravenously, smoked, inhaled) can clue the clinician into potential medical complications or risks that the client might face (e.g., HIV, hepatitis for IV drug use). Questions about the quality of friendships and romantic relationships, as well as the degree of drug and alcohol use within the client's social network are important because a lack of social support and substance use problems among significant others are risk factors for client use (Tucker et al., 2005). Finally, it is helpful to assess coping skills that can be marshaled in treatment, such as the ability to cognitively reframe difficult situations, use of religion or spirituality, and seeking social support.

A frequently used semi-structured interview that covers some of the aforementioned areas is the Addition Severity Index (ASI; McLellan, Luborsky, O'Brien, & Woody, 1980). The ASI takes approximately 60 minutes to complete and contains questions about drug and alcohol use, as well as general medical status (e.g., chronic medical conditions, current medications), employment and financial support (e.g., education, occupation, sources of monetary support), legal history (both substance and nonsubstance related), family and social history (e.g., close relationships, history of serious conflicts, history of abuse), and psychiatric status (e.g., gross screening for mood, anxiety, psychotic, cognitive problems; history of psychiatric treatment). Quantitative scores can then be generated indicating problem severity for the preceding 30 days and for lifetime problems. This measure has demonstrated good reliability and validity (Kosten, Rounsaville, & Kleber, 1983; Stöffelmayr, Mavis, & Kasim, 1994).

Screening Tests and Other Self-Report Measures

A number of widely used, psychometrically sound self-report measures are available to assist the clinician in evaluating the extent and severity of a client's substance use problems. These measures can be useful supplements to the clinical interview. While it is beyond the scope of this chapter to comprehensively review these instruments, a few are summarized in Table 8.6.

Table 8.6 Some substance-use screening measures

CAGE (Ewing, 1984)	• Commonly used screening measure for problematic alcohol use
	• Consists of the four questions assessing:
	  1. attempts to **C**ut down drinking
	  2. others being **A**nnoyed by client's drinking
	  3. feeling **G**uilty about drinking
	  4. drinking in the morning (**E**ye Opener)
	• Affirmative answers to one or more questions indicate high probability that an alcohol use disorder is present.
	• Among older adult alcoholics, questions 1 and 3 are frequently answered yes
		Easy to administer
		Good psychometric properties in clinical settings
		• Limitations: Lack of focus on current drinking, inability to assess levels of alcohol consumption and binge drinking, concerns about usefulness in general population surveys
		• Variant for use with pregnant women (TWEAK) has been developed (Russell, Martier, & Sokol, 1984)

Michigan Alcohol Screening Test (MAST) (Selzer, 1971)	• Widely used screener for alcohol-related problems
	• Consists of 25 questions covering:
	  1. self and others' perceptions of degree of use
	  2. guilt
	  3. withdrawal symptoms
	  4. informal and formal treatment
	  5. inability to control drinking
	  6. interpersonal, occupational, health, and legal problems associated with alcohol use
		• MAST A/D available for those with alcohol and/or substance use disorders. (Westermeyer, Yargic, & Thuras, 2004)
		• Version suitable for use with geriatric clients is available (MAST-G) (Blow et al., 1992)

Alcohol Use Disorders Identification Test (AUDIT) (J. B. Saunders, Aasland, Babor, de la Fuente, & Grant, 1993)	• Screening instrument for problem drinking • Initially validated on primary care patients in six countries (i.e., crossculturally appropriate) • 10 items ask about: alcohol use (3 questions), alcohol-related problems (3 questions), and dependence symptoms (4 questions) • Score of 8 or more indicates harmful levels of alcohol use or possible dependence. • Shorter version (AUDIT-C) performs similarly to the AUDIT in detecting heavy drinking and/or active abuse or dependence. • On AUDIT-C, a score of 3 or more, or a report of drinking 6+ drinks on one occasion in past year, triggers concern about problematic alcohol use	• Psychometrically sound • Can be administered in interview format or as self-report questionnaire • Advantages of questionnaire format: shorter and easier administration, potentially more accurate answers • Interview format appropriate for individuals suspected of limited reading ability; also allows for clarification of ambiguous answers and chance to give feedback and treatment suggestions to positive screeners

Biometric Measures

These measures attempt to detect the presence of substances of abuse through the analysis of a biological sample, such as urine, blood, saliva, hair, or sweat. The most common biometric tests for drugs and alcohol involve analysis of urine samples—typically, an initial enzyme immunoassay that, if positive, is followed by a confirmatory gas chromatography-mass spectroscopy test (Baron, Baron, & Baron, 2005). A strength of biometric measures is their ability to detect recent ingestion of certain substances among individuals who may have denied use.

Just because biometric measures are not vulnerable to some of the biases associated with self-report measures (e.g., conscious minimization or denial of use), one should not generalize that they are problem-free. Substances can typically be detected by biometric markers only for short periods of time following ingestion (e.g., 1 hour for blood tests, 1 to 2 days for saliva tests, 1 to 7 days for urine tests). They are of limited utility in quantifying the extent of use over a long period of time (Lennox, Dennis, Scott, & Funk, 2006). Furthermore, differences in the metabolism rates of drugs across individuals can muddy comparisons with self-reported measures of use. Less expensive and/or faster screening tests that do not use gas chromatography-mass spectrometry may produce invalid results. Also, the quality of samples may be compromised because of processing delays, handling errors, or tampering (Lennox et al., 2006). With regard to the last, a variety of adulterants can be used to alter the results of a drug test, ranging from common household items (e.g., lemon juice, salt, bleach, vinegar) to expensive chemicals marketed specifically for this purpose. Some individuals may attempt to circumvent a drug test by utilizing biological samples that are not their own (Baron et al., 2005). On the other end of the spectrum are persons who did not use illicit substances but who test positive on a drug test because of prescription or over-the-counter medications or medical conditions that produce false-positive results on a test (e.g., allergy medications or liver disease that may produce false-positive results on a test screening for amphetamine use). Finally, a biometric measure may screen for only a limited number of substances and thereby fail to detect recent use of an illicit substance; for example, thin-layer chromatography, a relatively inexpensive, comprehensive drug screen, does not detect substances such as marijuana, mescaline, 3,4-methylenedioxy-N-methylamphetamine (MDMA), LSD, or PCP; drug testing done in workplace environments typically screens only for marijuana, cocaine, amphetamines, opiates, and PCP (Baron et al., 2005).

Behavioral Observations

Familiarization with symptoms commonly seen in intoxication and withdrawal syndromes for different substances enables a clinician to more easily spot potential signs of drug abuse. General observations of a client's physical presentation may also reveal signs that strongly suggest drug use is present and prompt follow-up questions (see Table 8.7). However, care must be taken to avoid assuming that these signs invariably indicate substance abuse; for example, jaundice may be due to hepatitis not caused by injection drug use.

Motivational Interviewing

A counseling style that has proven effective in encouraging clients to change problem drinking and/or drug use is motivational interviewing (MI; S. B. Miller & Rollnick,

Table 8.7   Physical indicators suggesting possible drug use

Indicator	Comment
Needle puncture marks	Typically found over veins; usually on backs of hands, forearms, crook of the arm, but could be any place where a vein can be accessed.
Track marks	Hyperpigmented, linear scars along veins; associated with injection drug use; caused by deposits of carbon when needles are sterilized with matches, etc. and from nonsterile injections; may fade over time but not totally disappear. Tattoos may be used in an attempt to cover tracks.
Thrombophlebitis	An inflammation or blockage of veins often found on the limbs of injection drug users; caused by unsterile injections and drug adulterants.
Hand edema	Swelling of the hands that can occur from use of veins on the back of the hands to inject drugs.
Abscesses and ulcers	Open sores often caused by the injection of chemical irritants in drugs such as barbiturates or heroin.
Cigarette burns or scars from old burns	May be the result of drug-induced drowsiness when smoking (there is a high rate of comorbidity between drug/alcohol abuse and dependence and smoking).
Ulcerations or perforation of nasal septum	Frequent cocaine use can lead to perforation of the septum; frequent heroin use to septum ulcerations.
Cheilosis	Cracking of the skin at the corners of the mouth often seen among opioid-addicted individuals prior to or during detoxification and among chronic amphetamine users.
Contact dermatitis	Often seen around the nose, mouth, hands of inhalant users (e.g., "glue sniffer's rash") or in injection users secondary to chemicals used to cleanse skin.
Piloerection	Goosebumps seen on the arms and trunk in individuals undergoing opioid withdrawal.
Jaundice	Often secondary to hepatitis that results from sharing unsterilized needles and syringes.
Monilial infection	A fungal infection, usually oral thrush, common among individuals with AIDS.

Source: "Opioids: Detoxification" (pp. 265–289), by E. D. Collins and H. D. Kleber, in *Textbook of Substance Abuse Treatment,* M. Galanter and H. D. Kleber (Eds.), 2004, Washington, DC: American Psychiatric Press. Adapted with permission.

2002), a procedure influenced by existential and humanistic schools of therapy and by Prochaska and DiClementi's (1992) *stages of change (transtheoretical) model.* The transtheoretical model assumes that when individuals exhibit a problematic behavior requiring change, they can be in any one of several stages. In the *precontemplation* stage, individuals are not thinking about changing their behavior within the next 6 months. The *contemplation* stage is characterized by intentions to begin behavior change sometime within the next 6 months and is associated with an active consideration of the pros and cons associated with change. In the *preparation* stage, individuals intend to change their behavior within the next 30 days and begin to demonstrate some behavioral steps in this direction. During the *action* stage, individuals are actively changing their behavior but have done so for less than 6 months, whereas in the *maintenance* stage they have been engaged in behavioral change for 6 months or more. The stages of change model does not assume that individuals progress through these stages in a linear fashion (i.e., moving steadily from one stage to the next); rather, the pattern of progression is more like a spiral (i.e., individuals move to a higher stage, but may then experience setbacks that lead them back to a lower stage, after which they return to the higher stage, and so on).

Motivational interviewing recognizes that individuals with problems such as excessive drinking or drug use may be at any of these points in the change process when they come into contact with a mental health professional and attempts to move individuals toward more active stages of change. It has been defined by its founders as "a client-centered, directive method for enhancing intrinsic motivation to change by exploring and resolving ambivalence" (S. B. Miller & Rollnick, 2002, p. 25). Although discussed under "Intake and Interviewing," MI can be conceptualized not only as a prologue to another treatment intervention (e.g., cognitive-behavioral therapy), but as a counseling style that will permeate the entire treatment (and is thus applicable beyond the initial intake period). It is beyond the scope of this text to fully describe MI, but key elements of this approach will be summarized. Interested readers are referred to S. B. Miller and Rollnick for further information.

Motivational interviewing rests upon the assumption that individuals have an inherent ability to change that can be marshaled in treatment, and that this intrinsic motivation to change can be *elicited* by a skilled therapist in a directive, empathic manner. Motivation to change, therefore, does not have to be imposed externally through social pressure, punishment, or rearranging the individual's social environment (S. B. Miller & Rollnick, 2002). Four general principles of MI are (1) expressing empathy, (2) developing discrepancy, (3) rolling with resistance, and (4) supporting self-efficacy. The *expression of empathy* is a reflection of the client-centered therapeutic approach from which MI heavily draws. Techniques such as active listening, use of reflections, and acknowledgment that having ambivalent feelings about behavior change is normal, all fall under the rubric of expressing empathy. *Developing discrepancy* involves creating and amplifying the discrepancy between the client's current behavior or situation and what he or she would like these to be like to overcome the tendency to remain stuck in the status quo. Rather than having the therapist enumerate arguments in favor of changing behavior, it is considered imperative to have this emanate from clients themselves. *Rolling with resistance* refers to developing an attitude in which client resistance is not met with attempts to argue or cajole the client into seeing things differently or to adopt the stance of an all-knowing expert. Rather than pathologizing resistance, the clinician views it as an indicator that different responses to the client are required. The client is viewed as an autonomous individual who should be actively involved in the problem-solving process and the one who must ultimately determine how situations should be handled. *Self-efficacy* refers to the belief that one can achieve a desired goal or outcome. In MI, the counselor imparts that the client is responsible for and capable of change. This view can create a sense of hope that helps sustain participation in treatment.

Crisis, Legal, and Ethical Issues

Suicide Risk

Earlier in this chapter, the issue of heightened suicide risk among individuals with substance use disorders was discussed (see "Additional Characteristics"). For both youth and adults, when substance use is comorbid with other psychiatric disorders, suicide risk is further increased (L. L. Davis et al., 2006; Foley, Goldston, Costello, & Angold, 2006). Thus the presence of a substance use disorder, whether alone or in combination with other psychiatric disorders, raises a red flag for the clinician to regularly monitor suicidal ideation. Chapter 2 reviewed general strategies for evaluating and managing suicidal clients.

Child Abuse and Neglect

If a client is actively using drugs or alcohol and is taking care of minor children or elderly or dependent adults, it is important to evaluate the impact of the client's use on these other individuals and to determine whether abuse or neglect is occurring. State laws require mental health professionals to report cases of suspected child abuse or neglect, and many states have similar mandated reporting laws for suspected abuse or neglect of elderly or dependent adults. Children exposed to parents who are actively using drugs or alcohol face a number or risks: lack of adequate supervision, neglect of physical needs (regular meals, grooming, appropriate clothing), exposure to physical violence or emotional abuse associated with a caregiver's altered mental and emotional state, possible exposure to criminal activity such as selling drugs, and modeling of permissive attitudes toward substance use (Haight, Ostler, Black, Sheridan, & Kingery, 2007). Helping clients to recognize the adverse emotional and physical consequences of their substance use on loved ones, particularly children, and the possibility that children may be removed from the home by the authorities when abuse or neglect is evident can be powerful motivating factors for treatment.

It is also crucial to recognize that many individuals who have substance use disorders have themselves been victims of child abuse. Substance abusers who were abused as children are more likely than those who were not abused to have low self-esteem, to have difficulty establishing trust and intimacy in relationships, to engage in high-risk behavior that increases the likelihood of HIV infection, to engage in suicidal behavior, and to suffer from comorbid PTSD (Swan, 1998). Thus, when a clinician learns of a client history of child abuse, this raises a host of issues that become important to explore in treatment and should also prompt exploration to ensure that the perpetrator of the abuse is no longer in contact with other children who could be at risk.

Mandated Treatment

Some clients with drug or alcohol use disorders will end up being channeled into treatment through the legal system. Society continues to debate the issue of how to best deal with individuals who use illicit drugs or who engage in illegal activity in which alcohol or drugs (licit or illicit) are implicated. From a mental health perspective, any proposed solution that does not include addressing an individual's substance use problems through treatment is unlikely to result in favorable outcomes. Increasingly, many states recognize the important role that drug and alcohol treatment plays in a comprehensive law enforcement approach to substance-related offenses. So-called drug treatment courts (DTCs) involve a system of local law enforcement, courts, and community substance abuse treatment centers working collaboratively to initiate and supervise the treatment of certain substance-using offenders (Sales et al., 2005). The form of treatment mandated through DTCs varies, but is most often designed to last at least 1 year and to involve outpatient or inpatient counseling, random drug testing, and participation in 12-step recovery groups (Sales et al., 2005). These courts are associated with lowered recidivism rates and have demonstrated cost-effectiveness (Mack, Frances, & Miller, 2005).

DIAGNOSTIC CONSIDERATIONS

Common Comorbidities

Substance use disorders (abuse and dependence) are commonly comorbid with one another. The prevalence of comorbid alcohol disorders among those with another substance use disorder is nearly 50%, with risk being particularly high for those with cocaine abuse or dependence diagnoses (Regier et al., 1990). Data from the NESARC similarly found that rates of alcohol use disorders among those with specific drug use disorders were high, particularly for hallucinogen dependence and abuse (100% and 77%, respectively), cocaine dependence and abuse (89% and 69%, respectively), amphetamine dependence (78%), opioid dependence (74%), and cannabis dependence (68%). Among those with alcohol use disorders, the rate of any comorbid drug use disorder was 13% (Stinson et al., 2005). Terms such as *polydrug use, polysubstance use, polysubstance abuse,* and *polyaddiction* are often used in reference to clients who are dependent on multiple substances (Rosenthal & Levounis, 2005). It should be noted that the *DSM-IV-TR* diagnosis of Polysubstance Dependence does not refer to individuals who meet substance dependence diagnostic criteria for multiple substances, but instead refers to those who repeatedly use three or more substances over a 12-month period, do not predominantly use any one substance, and meet the substance dependence criteria only when all substances used are collectively considered (American Psychiatric Association, 2000b). The utility of this diagnosis has been called into question because of its low prevalence rate (Schuckit, Danko, et al., 2001).

Two thirds of individuals with substance use disorders are likely to meet criteria for another, nonsubstance-related psychiatric diagnosis at some point during their life (R. C. Kessler, Nelson, McGonagle, Liu, et al., 1996). Data from the ECA survey estimated that among individuals with a mental disorder, the lifetime prevalence of a drug or alcohol use disorder was approximately 29%. This same study found that the comorbidity rate of nonsubstance use disorders among those with alcohol dependence was 37%, and among those with (nonalcohol) substance dependence was 53% (Regier et al., 1990). When an individual has three or more psychiatric disorders, the risk of substance dependence is 14 times greater than among individuals without this number of disorders (C. P. O'Brien et al., 2004). Finally, it has been estimated that approximately 50% of individuals with severe mental disorders will develop an alcohol or substance use disorder during their lifetime (Cuffel, 1996). In a long-term follow-up of abstinent individuals formerly in treatment for detoxification, approximately one fourth were dead at a 15-year follow-up, and psychiatric status at a previous 5-year follow-up was predictive of 15-year mortality (Fridell & Hesse, 2006). Similarly, Moos et al. (1994) found that among middle-aged and older substance abusers (age 55+), lower mortality rates were associated with higher rates of prior outpatient mental health care. Co-occurring substance use disorders typically complicate treatment of other mental disorders and predict poorer prognosis for the other disorders (Schaar & Öjehagen, 2001), which highlights the importance of integrated treatment models that aggressively address both types of disorder. Unfortunately, only one fourth of individuals with co-occurring disorders receive treatment for *both* their substance use disorder and other psychiatric disorders (R. C. Kessler, Walters, & Wittchen, 2004).

Mood Disorders

The NIAAA's NESARC study found that the risk of comorbid mood disorders was significantly increased for individuals with substance use disorders (27.5%) or comorbid substance and alcohol use disorders (35.3%) compared to those with alcohol-only use disorders (16.4%; Stinson et al., 2005). Data from the National Comorbidity Survey (R. C. Kessler, Crum, et al., 1997) found that among those with an alcohol dependence disorder, 28% of men and 53% of women met criteria for an affective disorder diagnosis, with the majority of these diagnoses being Major Depressive Disorder. Among populations of individuals with mood disorders, rates of substance use disorders are high; specifically, it has been estimated that almost one third of those with an affective disorder have a comorbid substance use disorder (Regier et al., 1990). Data from the ECA study found that 56% of those with Bipolar Disorder and 27% of individuals with Major Depressive Disorder met criteria for an alcohol or drug use disorder. C. P. O'Brien et al. (2004) note that the relationship between mood disorders and substance use is bidirectional, such that mood disorders predict increased risk for later substance abuse and vice versa. A diagnosis of depression or the presence of significant depressive symptomatology has been found to predict increased risk of relapse and shorter time to relapse among individuals with alcohol use disorders (Bobo, McIlvain, & Leed-Kelly, 1998; Curran, Flynn, Kirchner, & Booth, 2000; Hasin et al., 1996).

Anxiety Disorders

It has been well documented that substance use disorders are commonly seen among individuals with anxiety disorders (R. C. Kessler, Nelson, McGonagle, Edmund, et al., 1996; 2001; Regier et al., 1990). The onset of anxiety disorders typically precedes the onset of substance use disorders (Merikangas et al., 1998). According to the NIAAA's NESARC, the lifetime prevalence rates of any anxiety disorder among individuals with substance abuse and dependence disorders were 24.1% and 47.2%, respectively. With regard to specific anxiety disorders, lifetime rates for those with substance abuse versus dependence disorders were as follows: Specific Phobia, 13.9% versus 26.7%; Social Phobia, 8.0% versus 18.8%; Generalized Anxiety Disorder (GAD), 6.4% versus 17.7%; Panic Disorder without Agoraphobia, 6.8 versus 15.4%; and Panic Disorder with Agoraphobia, 2.0% versus 8.1%. Data from the National Comorbidity Study indicate that the odds of a PTSD diagnosis among those with alcohol abuse and dependence were .45 and 3.30, respectively. Research evidence suggests that early trauma may predispose adolescents to both depression and later substance use disorders (D. B. Clark, DeBellis, Lynch, Cornelius, & Martin, 2003; Libby, Orton, Stover, & Riggs, 2005). Collectively, these statistics demonstrate that risk of comorbid anxiety disorders is significantly higher for substance dependence compared to abuse. Panic Disorder with Agoraphobia appears strongly related to tranquilizer, opioid, and marijuana dependence, while GAD is strongly related to tranquilizer dependence (Conway et al., 2006). Such associations raise hypotheses about the self-medicating function that such substances may play in relation to anxiety symptoms, which longitudinal research could help answer. Data from the NESARC also demonstrated that comorbid anxiety disorder diagnoses were more common in individuals with substance use disorders (24%) or comorbid substance and alcohol use disorders (26.5%) compared to individuals with alcohol-only disorders (15.6%; Stinson et al., 2005).

Psychotic Disorders

The prevalence of substance abuse among individuals diagnosed with Schizophrenia is estimated to be 47% (Regier et al., 1990). Psychosis proneness in early adulthood has also been identified as a predictor of subsequent drug and alcohol problems over a 10-year period (Kwapil, 1996). Commonly abused drugs among psychotic individuals are alcohol, cannabis, and cocaine. Although it has been hypothesized that some psychotic individuals may use substances in an attempt to self-medicate symptoms (e.g., using cocaine to alleviate depressive symptoms; Sevy, Kay, Opler, & Van Praag, 1990), substance use by psychotic persons often exacerbates their psychiatric symptoms. Substance use among psychotic individuals has additionally been linked to increased rates of hospitalization, poor medication and other treatment compliance, and increased likelihood of homelessness and violent crime victimization (Dixon, 1999; Drake, Osher, & Wallach, 1989; Lyons & McGovern, 1989).

Personality Disorders

Personality disorders are commonly encountered among those with substance use disorders. Morgenstern, Langenbucher, Labouvie, and Miller (1997) found that over half of their sample of substance abusers in treatment met criteria for at least one personality disorder. Significantly higher rates of comorbid personality disorders have been reported for individuals with substance use (44%) and comorbid substance and alcohol use disorders (50.8%) compared to those with alcohol-only disorders (25.3%; Stinson et al., 2005).

Among those with personality disorders, the presence of comorbid substance use disorders is associated with poorer prognosis (including stability of diagnosis), increased suicidality, poorer treatment compliance, and higher rates of hospitalization (Links, Heslegrave, Mitton, van Reekum, & Patrick, 1995; S. Ross, Dermatis, Levounis, & Galanter, 2003; Skodol et al., 2002; Yen et al., 2003). Among youth, the presence of personality disorders in early adolescence, including Schizotypal, Borderline, Narcissistic, Histrionic, and Passive-Aggressive Personality Disorder, increase risk for subsequent substance use disorders, as well as predict persistence of substance use problems into adulthood (P. Cohen, Chen, Crawford, Brook, & Gordon, 2007).

Antisocial Personality Disorder (ASPD) and Borderline Personality Disorder are among the most common Axis II diagnoses among those with substance use disorders.

For example, the rate of comorbid substance use among those with ASPD has been estimated at 84% (Regier et al., 1990). Individuals with ASPD who have comorbid affective disorder diagnoses have a lower risk of relapse, suggesting that ASPD individuals who are able to articulate their emotional symptoms may be able to form a more effective working alliance in treatment and experience better outcomes (Bradizza, Stasiewicz, & Paas, 2006).

Differential Diagnosis

Substance Use Disorders versus Other Psychiatric Disorders

Substance intoxication and withdrawal states often include psychiatric symptoms (e.g., anxiety, depression, irritability, euphoria) that can easily be mistaken for a primary non-substance-related psychiatric disorder (see Tables 8.2 and 8.3). Thus a clinician should always rule out the possibility that alcohol or drugs are responsible for a client's presenting symptoms. To determine if a substance-induced disorder diagnosis such as intoxication or withdrawal is warranted, the clinician must establish that there is an etiological relationship between the substance use and the client's symptoms (A. Frances et al., 1999). First, the clinician must determine whether the client has used a substance prior to the onset of the observed or reported psychiatric symptoms (i.e., Is there a close temporal relationship between the substance use and the onset of symptoms?). Next, the clinician must determine that the substance in question (both type and amount) could have reasonably caused the client's symptoms (e.g., Are the client's symptoms consistent with the documented effects of the substance under question?). Complicating factors can arise at several points along this process, including the inability to clearly ascertain from the client the sequence of substance use and symptom onset (e.g., client is a poor historian, is defensive), or the possibility of substance use exacerbating symptoms of a preexisting psychiatric condition. If the client has had similar symptoms in the past and clearly was not under the influence of or withdrawing from any substance, this would raise suspicion that the current symptoms are due to a primary psychiatric disorder rather than to a substance. When a clinician is still not certain as to whether drugs or alcohol are the cause of the client's symptoms, it may be necessary to wait until the effects of the substance have worn off or withdrawal symptoms abate to determine if the psychiatric symptoms in question persist. The *DSM-IV-TR* suggests that substance-related symptoms should remit within 4 weeks following the onset of intoxication or withdrawal symptoms; however, some contend that this suggested window may be too brief and recommend that 6 to 8 weeks may be more appropriate (A. Frances et al., 1999).

Among the Substance-Related Disorders

When deciding between a diagnosis of substance abuse or dependence, the clinician must consider the pattern and consequences of an individual's substance use and must therefore gather detailed information about these issues from the client or collateral sources. Impairment is common to both substance abuse and dependence diagnoses, but a dependence diagnosis involves a more pervasive, compulsive, and out-of-control pattern of substance use compared to abuse and may also be accompanied by symptoms of physiologic dependence.

The key difference between the two substance-induced disorders reviewed in this chapter—intoxication and withdrawal—concerns the timing of symptoms in relation to ingestion of the substance. Intoxication is associated with the effects of recent use of the substance, whereas withdrawal symptoms occur when a substance that has been regularly used is abruptly stopped. Not all classes of substances outlined in the *DSM-IV-TR* have a characteristic withdrawal syndrome.

It is important to recall that substance use disorders and substance-induced disorders are not automatically linked to each other. Thus, if a clinician assigns a substance use diagnosis, a substance-induced disorder may or may not also be given. For example, a client might meet criteria for alcohol dependence, yet if he or she never presents to the clinician in either an intoxicated state or as suffering from withdrawal symptoms, diagnoses of alcohol intoxication or withdrawal would not be given. Conversely, if a client presented to a clinic under the influence of drugs, an intoxication diagnosis would be appropriate to consider, but the client may or may not meet criteria for an abuse or dependence diagnosis (although one of these additional diagnoses may be quite likely and should certainly be pursued as treatment proceeds). In the case of a client who presents with symptoms consistent with withdrawal from either alcohol or a drug, consideration of a diagnosis of substance dependence is warranted, but again cannot automatically be assumed. According to *DSM-IV-TR* criteria, withdrawal is only one of seven possible symptoms of substance dependence, and three are required for diagnosis (American Psychiatric Association, 2000b). To illustrate, suppose a client who experiences chronic pain and has been taking an opiate-based medication for several months presents with reports that she has been trying to cut back on her medication but has begun to experience symptoms consistent with opioid withdrawal. Although it is clear that this client is physiologically dependent on the medication, it does not automatically follow that she displays the compulsive drug-seeking and -using behavior that is associated with substance dependence. Careful questioning would be needed to determine whether the client had been taking more of the drug than prescribed, engaging in behaviors such as trying to get multiple concurrent prescriptions from different doctors, and experiencing problems in social or occupational activities as a direct result of drug-seeking or -using behavior (this is different from impairment due to her chronic pain).

TREATMENT

General Principles in Treating Substance Use Disorders

Two concepts encountered in the literature on substance use disorders treatment are *abstinence* and *harm reduction approaches*. Abstinence-based approaches strive to help clients stop using drugs or alcohol completely. In contrast, harm reduction approaches operate from the belief that complete abstinence from drugs or alcohol may not be a reasonable or practical goal for many individuals. If a person does not believe that his drinking is causing significant impairment, he is likely to have low motivation to completely abstain from alcohol. Proponents of harm reduction might argue that for this person, decreasing risks to health, psychological well-being, and daily functioning will more likely be achieved by encouraging a reduction in alcohol consumption rather than complete abstinence. Additional examples of harm reduction approaches include needle exchange programs for injection drug users and drug substitution treatments such as methadone or levo-alpha acetyl methadol (LAAM; Coombs & Howatt, 2005). Harm reduction approaches may be most suitable for clients who are not seeking to completely discontinue their use of drugs or alcohol and who meet *DSM-IV* abuse criteria or minimal dependence criteria (Kellogg, 2003). Clients may feel that harm reduction-oriented treatment is more accepting of who they are, their needs, and their goals than approaches that emphasize complete abstinence (Tatarsky, 2003). Interestingly, however, it is not uncommon for individuals to elect abstinence when offered a chance to moderate their substance use (Marlatt, Somers, & Tapert, 1993). Kellogg notes that the neutral stance harm reduction approaches take with regard to eventual abstinence may lead to treatment stagnation, and proposes a "gradualism" (or an "abstinence eventually") approach to bridge harm reduction and abstinence models of treatment. Such a paradigm would combine the central tenet of abstinence-based models, that addictive or abusive use of substances cannot contribute to growth and well-being, with key elements of harm reduction approach such as outreach, and an emphasis on gradual healing and incremental change.

Pharmacologic Treatments

Medical Detoxification

As has already been discussed, physiological dependence on alcohol and drugs can result in withdrawal symptoms that are uncomfortable and potentially life-threatening. Detoxification is the process by which the addicted person's body is freed from physiological dependence on drugs and involves the administration of medications to safely manage the withdrawal process and its associated discomfort (Friedman & Wilson, 2004). Detoxification is an important initial step in the recovery process, but is rarely an effective treatment alone because it does not address behavioral, psychological, and social problems associated with addiction (NIDA, n.d.). Detoxification should therefore be accompanied by interventions (e.g., group and individual therapy, psychoeducation) designed to facilitate the client's entry into ongoing addiction treatment (American Society for Addiction Medicine, 1996).

Detoxification is most commonly discussed in relation to depressants (i.e., alcohol, sedative-hypnotics) and opiates, can take place on either an outpatient or inpatient basis, and should always be medically supervised. Although outpatient detoxification allows an individual to carry out his or her daily activities, it is a slower process than inpatient detoxification and is associated with lower completion rates, exposure to greater temptations to use, and more difficulty managing any concomitant medical conditions (Kleber, 2001). However, this level of care may be appropriate for those at minimal risk for severe relapse and who demonstrate sufficient motivation to undergo the detoxification process and willingness to follow treatment recommendations, and have the presence of a supportive other who can encourage compliance and help monitor the client (Lessa & Scanlon, 2006). Residential and inpatient detoxification programs represent increasingly more intensive levels of clinical service that have a higher degree of involvement of medical professionals; in the most intensive of inpatient detoxification settings, 24-hour-a-day nursing and physician care are available. Clients at risk for severe withdrawal, pregnant women, persons with compromised neurological functioning (e.g., recent head trauma or loss of consciousness) or cardiac status, older adults, and those with underlying serious medical conditions that may be exacerbated by the withdrawal process are among those best served by intensive inpatient detoxification (Lessa & Scanlon, 2006).

The specific drugs used for treating withdrawal are those that have demonstrated cross-tolerance with the substance in question. For example, individuals withdrawing from alcohol may be administered benzodiazepine (chlordiazepoxide, diazepam, clonazepam) in doses that are gradually tapered over a 3- to 5-day period. Additional medications (e.g., antipsychotics, antiepileptics) may be administered to treat severe symptoms of alcohol withdrawal such as agitation, psychosis, and seizures. Opiate withdrawal is often treated with a long-acting opiate such as methadone, which is typically given twice daily in gradually decreasing amounts. Other approaches include the use of the antihypertensive clonidine or the mixed opiate agonist-antagonist buprenorphine. Withdrawal from benzodiazepines may involve decreasing the agent of dependence and then substituting and gradually tapering a long-acting barbiturate (e.g., phenobarbital). In the case of concomitant alcohol and benzodiazepine dependence, gradually decreasing doses of the long-acting benzodiazepine chlordiazepoxide may be administered (Gallant, Smith, & Wesson, 2001).

Maintenance Treatment

Disulfiram (Antabuse) is sometimes used as a maintenance treatment to discourage further alcohol use; this drug produces symptoms such as flushing, headache, nausea, and vomiting within 15 to 20 minutes after ingesting alcohol. The major drawback of this treatment is that the medication must be taken consistently to work; an individual simply needs to stop taking it to no longer experience the adverse symptoms associated with alcohol consumption (disulfiram remains in the system for up to 2 weeks following the last ingested dose). Thus this medication is best reserved for individuals who are highly motivated to maintain sobriety and who have a significant other, family member, or friend who can help monitor compliance (the medication can be taken daily or in larger doses three times per week; Chick, 1999).

Naltrexone is an opiate antagonist (i.e., binds to opiate receptors in the brain) and reduces the reinforcing effects of drugs such as heroin by blocking dopamine release (Modesto-Lowe & VanKirk, 2002). Naltrexone has also been used in the maintenance treatment of alcoholism and decreases cravings for alcohol. It is given orally either daily or three times per week. If opiates or alcohol are used when naltrexone has been taken, the client will not experience nausea or other uncomfortable physical effects, but the euphoric effects of these substances will be blocked. Similar to disulfiram, a primary drawback of naltrexone is that it is easy for an individual to stop taking it and within 2 to 3 days experience the full euphoric sensations of an opiate or alcohol. Unfortunately, adherence is a major problem with naltrexone and other treatments that block the reinforcing effects of opioids; it has been estimated that only 10% to 15% of opioid-dependent clients are willing to take such medications (Rounsaville, 1995). However, a meta-analysis of randomized controlled trials of naltrexone revealed that it was superior to placebo in reducing opioid use (as measured by urine toxicology screens) in groups with high retention rates. Notably, this analysis also found that contingency management techniques (discussed later under "Psychotherapeutic Interventions") were associated with increased retention and greater naltrexone use (Johansson, Berglund, & Lindgren, 2006). Studies of naltrexone treatment for alcohol dependence suggest it is a moderately effective intervention, but compliance problems and, in some cases, poor tolerability (e.g., gastrointestinal and neuropsychiatric side effects) have been significant problems (Kranzler & VanKirk, 2001; Modesto-Lowe & VanKirk, 2002). Interestingly, two groups for which good retention rates have been observed are opioid-dependent individuals who are professionals or those who are inmates or parolees. For both of these seemingly disparate groups, compliance with naltrexone treatment can avert immediate negative consequences (e.g., loss of professional licensure, revocation of parole), which may explain their higher compliance rates (Modesto-Lowe & VanKirk, 2002).

Acamprosate, a taurine analog, is another medication increasingly used in the treatment of alcohol dependence; it was approved by the FDA in 2004. Like naltrexone, acamprosate reduces craving for alcohol and therefore can be a useful agent in the maintenance treatment of alcoholism. A disadvantage of this medication over naltrexone is that it must be given in three daily divided doses, which may pose a compliance problem for some individuals (Schatzberg et al., 2005). Meta-analytic studies of acamprosate for maintenance treatment of alcohol-dependent individuals find superior abstinence rates compared to placebo for time periods ranging from 3 to 12 months, and percentages of completely abstinent individuals during the duration of different studies have varied between 18% to 61% for acamprosate versus 4% to 45% for placebo (Boothby & Doering, 2005; K. Mann, Lehert, & Morgan, 2004). The combination of acamprosate and naltrexone appears to produce superior outcomes compared to placebo and acamprosate monotherapy (Kiefer & Wiedemann, 2004).

Since the 1960s, *methadone* (a μ-receptor opioid agonist) has been used in the treatment of heroin and other opiate addictions (Dole, Nyswander, & Keek, 1966). Methadone relieves opioid withdrawal, reduces craving, attenuates the subjective and reinforcing effects of continued opioid use, and normalizes physiological functions deranged by opioid use (Donny, Brasser, Bigelow, Stitzer, & Walsh, 2005). Methadone treatment is normally administered in a clinic setting, where the client must go to take a daily dose; in some cases, clients who are stabilized and doing well may be given a "take-home" dose on alternating days so that clinic visits can occur less frequently (Schatzberg et al., 2005). Methadone is administered orally, and because it is used in the treatment of substances (e.g., heroin) that are often taken intravenously, has been associated with decreased rates of blood-borne diseases such as HIV and hepatitis (Ball, Lange, Myers, & Friedman, 1988; J. Ward, Mattick, & Hall, 1998). However, cocaine use is common among methadone-treated individuals, and if cocaine is used intravenously or leads to risky sexual behavior such as not using condoms, the risk for HIV and other diseases is increased (Bux, Lamb, & Iguchi, 1995). It is estimated that approximately 20% of heroin addicts in the United States receive methadone maintenance treatment (American Methadone Treatment Association, 1999). Advocates of methadone maintenance programs point to its cost-effectiveness, ability to improve health and daily functioning, lack of serious side effects, and treatment format (i.e., required clinic visits) that puts clients in contact with health care professionals (Friedman & Wilson, 2004). Critics note that methadone maintenance does not necessarily facilitate change but simply makes the addicted person more comfortable and suggest that because physiological dependence to methadone occurs, the treatment simply substitutes one addiction for another (Friedman & Wilson, 2004). Continuing use of methadone will result in a withdrawal syndrome if the medication is abruptly stopped or drastically decreased, and because methadone is longer acting than opiates such as heroin, the withdrawal process is more protracted. Withdrawal symptoms typically occur 24 to 72 hours after the last dose, peak within 5 to 6 days, and last as long as 14 to 21 days (Jaffe & Jaffe, 2004). Individuals wishing to stop methadone maintenance treatment should be medically supervised during this process and may need to enter a detoxification center. There is some evidence that long-term methadone maintenance therapy is associated with cognitive impairments in areas such as psychomotor speed, working memory, and decision making and other executive functions; however, the degree to which such impairments reflect the acute versus chronic effects of methadone and/or the effects of prior substance abuse has yet to be clarified (Mintzer & Stitzer, 2002).

Levo-alpha acetyl methadol is another opiate agonist used in the maintenance treatment of opiate dependence that was FDA-approved in 1993. An advantage of LAAM over methadone is that it is longer acting and needs to be administered only three times per week (Schatzberg et al., 2005). Although this lower dosing rate can provide advantages to both client (daily life is disrupted less due to fewer required clinic visits) and provider (additional treatment slots are freed up for more individuals), individuals who are in crisis or unstable may benefit more from the increased structure that daily methadone maintenance entails (Friedman & Wilson, 2004). In a meta-analysis of 15 studies of LAAM (including randomized controlled trials and controlled prospective studies), N. Clark et al. (2002) concluded that LAAM may be more effective than methadone at reducing heroin use.

In 2002, the FDA approved *buprenorphine,* a mixed opiate agonist-antagonist, for the maintenance treatment of opiate dependence. This medication is taken sublingually on a daily basis and is a viable alternative to methadone maintenance therapy (Schatzberg et al., 2005). Unlike methadone and LAAM, which in the United States can be administered to clients only through designated opiate treatment programs, buprenorphine can be prescribed by qualified physicians in an office-based setting (Marsch et al., 2005). Another potential advantage of buprenorphine is that its pharmacologic properties decrease risk of abuse and overdose (Marsch et al., 2005). In a meta-analysis of 13 randomized clinical trials, buprenorphine was deemed superior to placebo medication in client retention rates, and at high doses suppressed heroin use significantly more than placebo (Mattick, Kimber, Breen, & Davoli, 2004).

Psychotherapeutic Interventions

Contingency Management

Contingency management (CM) applies principles derived from operant conditioning theory to help clients reduce or abstain from using drugs or alcohol. Intervention techniques involve providing reinforcement to clients for achieving goals related to the reduction or cessation of substance use; some programs also use positive reinforcement when the client complies with other aspects of treatment (e.g., treatment attendance; Parks, Anderson, & Marlatt, 2004). Techniques of CM also assist clients in restructuring their environment so that rewards associated with drug or alcohol use are diminished and costs of this activity are increased (Hunt & Azrin, 1973; Parks et al., 2004). Operant conditioning theory indicates that behaviors followed by positive reinforcers are more likely to recur in the future (G. Martin & Pear, 1999). Thus, if behaviors such as obtaining a negative urine toxicology test (i.e., indicating substances were not recently used) and attending treatment sessions are rewarded, there is an increased likelihood that the client will exhibit these behaviors in the future.

Reinforcement used in CM may take many forms, including points or vouchers that can be traded in for retail goods and services, awards of privileges, and provision of verbal praise (from treatment providers, program staff, family, friends, etc.). Examples from three studies help to illustrate this point. In their treatment study of individuals with marijuana dependence, Budney, Moore, Rocha, and Higgins (2006) used vouchers with a predetermined monetary value (e.g., $1.50) that clients could earn for a negative urine toxicology screen (testing was done twice weekly). The value of the vouchers increased for each consecutive negative urine specimen, and a $10 bonus could be earned for two consecutive negative specimens. Vouchers could be traded in for retail goods (e.g., movie passes, sporting goods, vocational class). In contrast, Petry, Martin, Cooney, and Kranzler (2000) utilized prizes as reinforcers in their treatment study of individuals with alcohol dependence. Clients were tested daily with a breathalyzer to determine breath alcohol content (BAC). A negative BAC test (indicating no recent use of alcohol) earned an opportunity for a drawing from a prize bowl that contained 250 paper slips (some of which were winning slips). Winning slips listed either a small (e.g., $1 gift certificate, bus tokens) or medium (e.g., radio, $40 gift certificate, arts and crafts supplies) prize, and 1 slip had a large prize (e.g., handheld television). Drawing opportunities could also be earned for meeting other agreed-upon treatment goals (attendance at AA meetings, taking steps to return to work or school). K. Silverman, Svikis, Robles, Stitzer, and Bigelow (2001) provided clients in methadone maintenance therapy access to a data entry vocational training program contingent upon providing drug-free urine specimens. Additionally, vouchers could be earned by clients in the training program for such behaviors as displaying a professional demeanor, attending work shifts, accomplishing learning objectives, and for work productivity. Some programs have utilized direct money payments as positive reinforcers, but there is concern about whether this could facilitate subsequent drug use. Drebing et al. (2005) reported the successful use of cash payments in maintaining abstinence from drug and alcohol use and taking steps toward obtaining competitive employment among dually diagnosed veterans; however, to avert misuse of funds, this CM program included a provision that cash payments could not be earned following recent drug use.

If punishments are used in CM interventions, they typically take the form of *punishment by removal* (e.g., taking away points or vouchers, withdrawing attention, restricting privileges) rather than punishment by application (i.e., the application of aversive stimuli). Another important part of CM is to work with the client to develop alternative sources of reinforcement in the environment that can compete with reinforcement associated with drug use (Petry et al., 2000). Such procedures should not be confused with aversion therapies, which use aversive stimuli and are based on classical conditioning theory. Such treatments pair an aversive unconditioned stimulus (disulfiram, mild electric shock) with the use of alcohol or drugs so that the pleasurable sensation usually associated with ingestion of the alcohol or drug now becomes associated with an aversive reaction (Parks et al., 2004).

Approaches employed in CM have been used to treat a variety of substance use problems, such as alcohol, stimulant (including cocaine), opioid, marijuana, and tobacco use disorders, and have been applied in both inpatient and outpatient settings (K. M. Carroll et al., 2006; J. D. Griffith, Rowan-Szal, Roark, & Simpson, 2000; Higgins, Roll, Wong, Tidey, & Dantona, 1999; Petry et al., 2000; Shoptaw, Jarvik, Ling, & Rawson, 1996). Contingency management has also been successfully used in the treatment of special populations, such as dually diagnosed individuals and homeless persons with substance abuse problems (Schumacher et al., 2003; Shaner, Tucker, Roberts, & Eckman, 1999). A meta-analysis of CM programs for the treatment of drug and alcohol use disorders published between 1970 and 2002 found that they generally produced positive results compared to control group conditions and were more effective in treating opiate or cocaine use than tobacco use or polydrug use. By helping clients maintain abstinence, CM approaches can help them take greater advantage of other clinical treatment interventions, and adding CM to existing treatments frequently enhances the effects of the other approaches (e.g., cognitive-behavioral therapy, coping skills, motivational approaches, pharmacologic treatments such as naltrexone; Budney, Higgins, Radonvich, & Novy, 2000; K. M. Carroll et al., 2006; K. M. Carroll, Sinha, Nich, Babuscio, & Rounsaville, 2002; Prendergast, Podus, Finney, Greenwell, & Roll, 2006). The addition of CM approaches to existing treatment programs also increases program completion rates (Higgins et al., 1994; Petry et al., 2000).

When used as a stand-alone treatment, CM approaches compare favorably to other treatment modalities. For example, in a randomized clinical trial of CM and cognitive-behavioral therapy (CBT) approaches for the treatment of stimulant abusers, Rawson and colleagues (2006) found that during the 16-week study period, CM produced better retention and lower rates of stimulant use, and that at subsequent follow-ups the CM and CBT groups had comparable outcomes on variables such as self-reported stimulant use and urinalysis data. Similarly, Budney et al. (2006) found that an abstinence-based voucher intervention for cannabis dependence produced significantly greater abstinence rates during treatment compared to CBT, and that the proportions of abstinent individuals in both treatment groups were similar at 3-, 6-, 9-, and 12-month follow-ups. This study also found that a combined CBT + voucher condition was associated with significantly greater posttreatment abstinence than CBT alone and was associated with a trend toward greater abstinence than the voucher condition alone. Such findings suggest that while CM strategies help to increase initial abstinence during the period of active treatment, adjunctive therapies (such as CBT) may help to maintain gains posttreatment.

Despite the empirically demonstrated efficacy of CM programs, they have not been widely adopted in community substance abuse treatment programs. A survey of substance abuse treatment providers found that despite agreement with an average of 67% of survey statements reflecting a positive view of CM programs, only a little more than half of respondents were in favor of adding a CM intervention to their treatment program (Kirby, Benishek, Dugosh, & Kerwin, 2006). Among commonly cited objections were concerns about cost, failure to address the underlying problems of addiction, and not addressing multiple behaviors (e.g., programs providing reinforcers for abstinence-related behaviors but not other treatment-related behaviors). The survey results also revealed that treatment providers often had misconceptions about CM, such as believing that providing incentives for attendance would not result in improved attendance (empirical evidence suggests the opposite) or did not understand how CM interventions could be flexibly applied. This indicates a need for more practical, straightforward dissemination of empirical findings on CM to those on the front lines treating substance abuse clients.

Cognitive-Behavioral Therapy and Relapse Prevention

Cognitive-behavioral therapy has proven to be an efficacious intervention for persons dealing with alcohol and drug use problems. Relapse prevention (RP), a treatment incorporating cognitive and behavioral principles, is a particularly effective approach that will be addressed here. Relapse prevention has two primary goals: (1) preventing a lapse in sobriety and maintaining goals related to abstinence or harm reduction, and (2) teaching tools to manage a lapse (should it occur) and to prevent further relapse (Marlatt & Witkiewitz, 2005). Relapse prevention attempts to reduce exposure to drugs and alcohol; increases motivation for abstinence (helping clients weigh the pros and cons of use); teaches strategies for monitoring behavior, thoughts, and feelings; helps clients identify thinking patterns associated with increased risk for relapse; provides methods for coping with negative mood states and cravings; and establishes a crisis plan should relapse occur (McGovern, Wrisley, & Drake, 2005).

During RP treatment the client and therapist work together to determine situations that pose a high risk of relapse (i.e., the resumption of drug and/or alcohol use) and identify client factors that may contribute to or protect against putting the client in such situations. Thus the client is educated about the relapse process and learns that a return to drug or alcohol use does not simply occur out of the blue, but instead is triggered by identifiable and predictable events. These can include situations (e.g., locations where one used to drink or use, hanging out with friends who use), emotional states (e.g., depression, anger, boredom, loneliness), interpersonal conflict, and cognitive factors, to name a few (Donovan, 2005). Specific examples of cognitive factors include self-efficacy, outcome expectancies, and motivation. With regard to the first two of these, drug- or alcohol-addicted individuals who do not believe in their ability to effect change and accomplish goals are more likely to relapse, as are individuals who have positive expectations regarding outcomes associated with drinking or drug use (Marlatt & Witkiewitz, 2005). To the extent that a client is ambivalent about giving up drugs or alcohol, the motivation to remain abstinent will be limited and relapse more likely to occur. How clients cope with situations that may lead to use is important in predicting relapse (Marlatt & Witkiewitz, 2005).

With CBT, the client is taught strategies for dealing with high-risk situations that may produce cravings and urges to use. This can include cognitive reframing of maladaptive or inaccurate thoughts and challenging positive outcome expectancies for use (e.g., "That drink will relax me," "One hit of marijuana won't hurt"; Donovan, 2005). Coping strategies for dealing with urges and cravings to use could include avoiding situations that trigger these thoughts and feelings (i.e., stimulus control techniques), recalling unpleasant consequences associated with use, behavioral rehearsal and role-playing (e.g., saying no to an offer of drugs), employing cognitive strategies and imagery to get through urges and cravings (e.g., conceptualizing cravings as waves that will rise but eventually crest and fall), and utilizing coping cards on which coping strategies are recorded (Haug, Sorenson, Gruber, & Song, 2005; Kadden & Cooney, 2005). Cue exposure techniques may also be employed that involve developing a hierarchy of cues that have been associated with past substance use and that trigger cravings, and repeatedly exposing the client to these cues (in vivo or imaginally) while preventing access to substances in order to break the conditioned associations between the cues and drug or alcohol use (K. M. Carroll & Rawson, 2005). Clients are also taught to maintain lifestyle balance through relaxation training, stress management, exercise, and time management (Donovan, 2005). In addition, clients are prepared for handling a lapse if it happens. Understanding the abstinence violation effect (AVE) is a critical piece of this process. The AVE refers to a constellation of cognitive and affective experiences that typically follow a lapse. An individual may have a thought such as "I've completely ruined my sobriety because I'm a failure who can't be fixed." This is likely to lead to guilt, self-blame, and additional thoughts that the lapse is due to internal, global, and uncontrollable factors, all of which increase the likelihood that the lapse will lead to a full-blown relapse (Marlatt & Witkiewitz, 2005).

Some have criticized the RP model as paying insufficient attention to the role of interpersonal factors such as social support (e.g., the quality and nature of social relationships) in the relapse process (Stanton, 2005). Nevertheless, there is strong empirical support for RP-based treatments, indicating the superiority of this approach over no-treatment control conditions and demonstrating that it is as effective as other active interventions for drug and alcohol use disorders (K. M. Carroll, 1996; Marlatt & Witkiewitz, 2005). In particular, clients in RP treatment appear to sustain gains at posttreatment follow-ups and may actually exhibit improvements in functioning over time (K. M. Carroll, 1996). A meta-analytic review of 26 published and unpublished studies (collectively involving over 9,000 participants) concluded that RP interventions were efficacious in reducing substance use and improving psychosocial adjustment. This review found that relapse prevention was most effective in the treatment of alcohol or polysubstance use disorders with adjunctive medication use (Irvin, Bowers, Dunn, & Wang, 1999).

Family and Couples Interventions

When an individual is addicted to or abusing drugs or alcohol, it creates a ripple effect that negatively impacts spouses, parents, children, and other close relationships. As has been previously discussed, parental substance use may provide children with models of maladaptive coping, send messages about the acceptability of substance use, increase the potential for child abuse and neglect, and create emotional instability and chaos in the home. Family-based interventions can therefore be a valuable component to the treatment plan for drug- and alcohol-addicted individuals. These approaches do not view drug and alcohol addictions as solely or even primarily residing within the substance-using individual, but rather as problems embedded within a system of ongoing interactions and interpersonal relationships (Rohrbaugh & Shoham, 2002). A nonblaming attitude is adopted toward the substance-using client and family, and confrontational tactics are avoided (Stanton & Heath, 2005). Emphasis is placed on getting control of the substance use problem before addressing other issues that may be of concern in the family. In couples and family work the therapist must be able to diffuse the hostile or depressive reactions among family members that may occur if drinking or drug use resumes during treatment and be able to convey a hopeful message to the using client and the spouse or family that such behavior does not mean that treatment has failed and all is lost (O'Farrell & Fals-Stewart, 2003b).

There are many variations of family-based treatment for drug and alcohol abuse. For example, Rohrbaugh and Shoham (2002) discuss a 20-session couples treatment for alcoholism based on an integration of systemic and strategic models of family therapy. The treatment involves three phases: consultation, treatment, and restabilization and relapse prevention. In the consultation phase, the therapist gathers detailed information about the addicted individual's substance use (amounts used, situations in which use occurs, impairment caused by use), the meaning of the substance use to the couple, typical interaction patterns with and without substances, and what the couple imagines life would be like without the use of alcohol. The therapist also strives to understand the alcohol problem within the larger framework of the couple's social network and individual family histories. Afterward, a treatment plan is presented to the couple based on the information obtained in the consultation phase. Treatment involves a multistep process of *family detoxification* in which substance use ceases and the family environment becomes alcohol-free. The therapist works with the couple or family to strategize about specific steps that will be taken to ensure that substances are not available for the addicted member to use and, in the process, encourages the formulation of new solutions rather than a repetition of old, unsuccessful interaction sequences. Attention is paid to how the couple or family will deal with high-risk situations for use outside of the family home (e.g., with friends, coworkers), and the family is encouraged to *externalize* the drug or alcohol problem as something that is both alien to their relationships with one another and that must be actively fought against.

Techniques from problem-focused and solution-focused therapies are used to help the couple recognize and change problematic interpersonal interactions with one another that lead to substance use. Should the couple express reservations about the treatment or insist that drinking or drug use is not really a problem in the relationship, the therapist returns to a position of *continued consultation* to move the couple back into active treatment. For example, the therapist might paradoxically reframe reluctance to engage in treatment in terms of loyalty to unhealthy family tradition (i.e., substance use). The final phase of treatment entails helping the couple deal with selected problems that may have emerged when drinking stopped and how to deal with future high-risk situations.

In *behavioral family or couples therapy,* treatment also begins with gathering a comprehensive history of the substance use problem and the couple's relationship. O'Farrell and Fals-Stewart (2003b) outline a number of unique treatment techniques that are used in behaviorally oriented couples work, including the use of behavioral contracts to establish explicit shared goals. An example is a daily sobriety contract that outlines goals for the using partner (e.g., abstaining from alcohol and drugs, attending 12-step meetings, and acknowledging the partner's support) and the nonusing partner (e.g., not mentioning past drinking, attending an Al-Anon meeting). The therapist also helps the couple determine sequences of behaviors and events that lead to substance use and how each member of the couple can change his or her behavior to avert this outcome. Couples are also taught problem-solving skills and general strategies for increasing the amount of positive reinforcement they receive from each other and plan pleasant activities to do together. Communication skills training, including teaching active listening skills, how to express positive and negative feelings, and how to make specific requests, is also typically part of treatment. Such interventions help to decrease stress within the couple's relationship and therefore presumably guard against relapse. Many of these techniques can be easily adapted for use with families. Research evidence indicates that family and couples intervention is effective in treating substance use disorders, with particularly strong support for behaviorally oriented relationship therapies (Kaufman & Brook, 2004; W. R. Miller, Wilbourne, & Hettema, 2003; O'Farrell & Fals-Stewart, 2003a).

Another family-based procedure that may be utilized in the treatment process for drug- and alcohol-dependent individuals is an *intervention,* originally developed by the Johnson Institute (Faber & Keating-O'Connor, 1991). Involvement in an intervention is not restricted to family members, but can include friends, coworkers, employers, and anyone else who has directly witnessed and been affected by the adverse consequences of an individual's substance use. An intervention is essentially a method for motivating substance-dependent individuals to enter treatment. A therapist works with the group of individuals who will be involved in the intervention to plan a meeting at which the substance-abusing individual will be confronted with the consequences of his or her drug use. Intervention participants are asked to make a list of specific incidents that illustrate the negative impact of the substance user's behavior on them and to practice how they will tell the user about this (Fals-Stewart, O'Farrell, & Birchler, 2003). In addition, an intervention involves the presentation of consequences that the concerned others will institute should the addicted individual refuse to enter treatment (e.g., refusal to see the client). Concerned others can also communicate during the intervention what they hope life will be like if the addicted individual is able to get control over his or her substance use in order to provide hope to the client and increase his or her motivation (McIntyre, 2004).

In conducting an intervention, the therapist and others involved make it clear that the client *does* have a choice as to whether or not to pursue treatment, but that a decision not to pursue treatment will be associated with extreme and adverse consequences (McIntyre, 2004). As Fals-Stewart et al. (2003) note, ethical concerns can emerge in the execution of an intervention, including confidentiality issues (i.e., the client's lack of control over who is included in the planning and carrying out of the intervention) and the aftermath for the client should a decision to pursue treatment be refused and the negative consequences discussed in the intervention occur.

12-Step Groups

As mentioned at the beginning of this chapter, the formation of Alcoholics Anonymous in the United States in the 1930s marked an important development in the history of substance abuse treatment. Alcoholics Anonymous defines itself as

> a fellowship of men and women who share their experience, strength and hope with each other that they may solve their common problem and help others to recover from alcoholism. The only requirement for membership is desire to stop drinking. (AA General Service Office, 2005, p. 6)

As of 2005, it was estimated that there are approximately 52,651 AA groups in the United States that collectively compose a membership of 1,190,637 individuals (AA General Service Office, 2005). Alcoholics Anonymous is referred to as a 12-step group because it espouses a path to recovery that involves working through a series of 12 steps that were outlined by the founders of the program. In addition, AA is based on 12 traditions that were considered by the founders and early members of the organization to be crucial for the group's survival (e.g., an emphasis on anonymity, the importance of remaining a nonprofessional group, the need for AA groups to be financially self-sustaining). The 12 steps and 12 traditions of AA, along with information about the history and founders of AA, alcoholism, and stories of recovery are contained in the text, *The Twelve Steps and Twelve Traditions* (AA, 2002) that was originally published in 1952 and is commonly referred to as "the Big Book" by AA members. Table 8.8 lists the 12 steps of AA. The religious nature of many of the steps reflects the influence of the Oxford Group, a Christian movement, of which AA founding member Bill Wilson was a part (Spiegel & Fewell, 2004). However, AA membership does not require its members to be affiliated with any religion; while many in AA believe that recovery from alcoholism is dependent upon a power greater than the individual, there is an acknowledgment that members may define such a power in their own unique way, which may or may not include references to religion or spirituality. Important tenets underlying the philosophy of AA include an understanding that life with a substance use problem is unmanageable, acceptance that willpower is not effective in fighting a drug or alcohol addiction, and recognition that the support of others is key in the recovery process (Nowinski, 2003).

Alcoholics Anonymous meetings are not moderated or led by mental health or other professionals, but are conducted by members themselves. Officers (e.g., chairperson, secretary, treasurer) are elected every 6 months. Meetings may either be open or closed. Anyone can attend an open meeting (e.g., a person with a drug or alcohol problem, a family member or friend of such a person), whereas closed meetings are reserved for those with an alcohol problem. During closed meetings, individuals share their stories about their problems and struggles with alcohol and how they are trying to maintain sobriety. An important part of the AA tradition is sponsorship. New members are encouraged to find a sponsor, or an experienced AA member who has been able to maintain sobriety for at least 1 year and who is generally of the same sex. The sponsor provides support and encouragement to the new member in his or her quest to maintain sobriety, encourages

Table 8.8   The 12 steps of Alcoholics Anonymous

1. We admitted we were powerless over alcohol—that our lives had become unmanageable.
2. Came to believe that a Power greater than ourselves could restore us to sanity.
3. Made a decision to turn our will and our lives over to the care of God *as we understood Him*.
4. Made a searching and fearless moral inventory of ourselves.
5. Admitted to God, to ourselves, and to another human being the exact nature of our wrongs.
6. Were entirely ready to have God remove all these defects of character.
7. Humbly asked Him to remove our shortcomings.
8. Made a list of all persons we had harmed, and became willing to make amends to them all.
9. Made direct amends to such people wherever possible, except when to do so would injure them or others.
10. Continued to take personal inventory and when we were wrong promptly admitted it.
11. Sought through prayer and meditation to improve our conscious contact with God as we understood Him, praying only for knowledge of His will for us and the power to carry that out.
12. Having had a spiritual awakening as the result of these steps, we tried to carry this message to alcoholics and to practice these principles in all our affairs.

The Twelve Steps are reprinted with permission of Alcoholics Anonymous World Services, Inc. (AAWS) Permission to reprint the Twelve Steps does not mean that AAWS has reviewed or approved the contents of this publication, or that AAWS necessarily agrees with the views expressed herein. A.A. is a program of recovery from alcoholism only—use of the Twelve Steps in connection with programs and activities that are patterned after A.A., but which address other problems, or in any other non-A.A. context, does not imply otherwise.

attendance at AA meetings and working through the 12 steps, shares his or her experiences in recovery, and helps introduce the new member to other AA members (AA, 1983).

Many other 12-step groups designed to provide support for individuals in recovery from other substances have developed from the AA model, including Narcotics Anonymous, Cocaine Anonymous, and Heroin Anonymous. Groups to help family members and friends of substance users include Al-Anon, Alateen, and Adult Children of Alcoholics. Because AA is the prototype, the remaining discussion of 12-step programs will refer to this group.

There are many potential benefits to participation in a 12-step group such as AA. Spiegel and Fewell (2004) contend that the unconditional acceptance of individuals into the structured and consistent environment of AA meetings provides a secure holding environment for the newly recovering substance user that facilitates the transition from an attachment to drugs and alcohol to an attachment to supportive others. Research findings indicate that participation in AA generally enhances positive outcomes for those who are receiving professional treatment. Moos and Moos (2005) found that alcoholic individuals who participated in AA concurrently with professional treatment within the first year of seeking help were more likely to achieve remission compared to individuals who sought professional treatment only. Attendance has also been linked to increased social support resources, greater use of approach versus avoidant coping, and less use of drinking as a coping mechanism (Timko, Finney, & Moos, 2005). Participation in AA following cessation of active professional treatment has also been found to correlate with abstinence (Morgenstern, Labouvie, McCrady, Kahler, & Frey, 1997; Thurstin, Alfano, & Nerviano, 1987). Longer participation in AA is associated with improved treatment outcomes for both younger and older adults with alcohol use disorders (Lemke & Moos, 2003). Witbrodt and Kaskutas (2005) found the number of 12-step meetings attended and number of prescribed 12-step activities engaged in predicted abstinence not only for alcoholics, but for those with drug dependence diagnoses and comorbid drug and alcohol dependence. These researchers found that sponsorship and participating in service-related activities through the 12-step programs were especially important components in predicting abstinence among all client groups.

Project MATCH was a unique, multisite study that investigated whether it was possible to develop guidelines for matching clients with alcohol use disorders to appropriate treatment modalities based on client characteristics. Three manual-guided, 12-week treatments were investigated: (1) CBT, (2) motivational enhancement, and (3) 12-step facilitation therapy. The CBT intervention focused on skill acquisition for dealing with high-risk situations that could lead to drinking. The motivational enhancement therapy, based on techniques of motivational interviewing, emphasized client responsibility for change and enhancing client self-efficacy and resource mobilization for facilitating abstinence. The 12-step facilitation treatment helped clients work on the first five steps espoused in the AA tradition and encouraged active participation in AA groups (Project MATCH Research Group, 1993). Overall, the study did not find that any one of these treatments was superior to the others in terms of producing clinically meaningful outcomes across clients with a range of alcohol dependence severity. However, some interesting findings emerged relevant to recommendations for and against client referrals to 12-step groups. Specifically, individuals whose social support networks encourage or support continued drinking are likely to have better outcomes when they participate in AA compared to a motivational enhancement or CBT-based intervention. Similarly, inpatients with a high dependence on alcohol are likely to do better in a 12-step treatment program following discharge compared to a CBT intervention. In contrast, individuals who are angry at the start of treatment are apt to fare better in a treatment that is less confrontational, such as motivational enhancement, as compared to either CBT or a 12-step program (Project MATCH Research Group, 1997, 1998; Zywiak, Longabaugh, & Wirtz, 2002). Given the strong emphasis on spirituality that is part of the AA tradition, another interesting finding to emerge from the Project MATCH study was that AA attendance was significantly associated with increased abstinence and reductions in drinking intensity regardless of whether clients believed in God or not, and no differences in percentage of days abstinent or in drinking intensity were found between atheist or agnostic versus spiritual or religious clients (Tonigan, Miller, & Schermer, 2002). These findings indicate that clinicians should not automatically assume that nonreligious clients cannot benefit from participation in 12-step groups.

The correlation between participation in 12-step programs and improved substance use outcomes does not necessarily imply a causal relationship between the two. However, in an analysis of data from over 2,000 veterans participating in 12-step groups across 15 Veterans Administration settings followed for a 2-year period, McKellar, Stewart, and Humphreys (2003) utilized structural equations modeling and found that higher first-year levels of AA involvement predicted better second-year alcohol-related outcomes, but that first-year outcomes did not predict AA involvement. These findings support a causal link between AA involvement and substance use outcomes by demonstrating that improved outcomes seen among individuals affiliated with AA were not simply related to more successfully abstinent individuals choosing to participate in AA in the first place. The impact of AA and other 12-step programs on substance use outcomes may be mediated by effects on change processes such as motivation and commitment to achieving goals, self-efficacy, and use of active coping (Morgenstern, Labouvie, et al., 1997). Interestingly, cognitive and behaviorally oriented treatments for substance use problems often target similar processes, suggesting there may be some overlap between 12-step programs and certain psychotherapeutic interventions. The need for further head-to-head comparisons between 12-step programs and psychotherapy interventions are needed to determine unique versus common benefits to each approach (McKellar et al., 2003). Table 8.9 summarizes essential elements in the treatment of substance use disorders that have been reviewed in this chapter.

ADVANCED TOPIC: METHAMPHETAMINE ABUSE AND DEPENDENCE

Methamphetamine is a powerful stimulant that is chemically similar to amphetamine but produces more pronounced effects and carries an especially high risk for abuse and dependence. This drug, which is known by the street names *crank, crystal, ice,* and *speed,* can be snorted, smoked, ingested orally, or injected. Data from the 2005 NSDUH indicate that 10.4 million Americans age 12 and older have tried methamphetamine at least once in their lifetime. Methamphetamine is considered one of the fastest growing illicit drugs in the United States (Drug Enforcement Administration, n.d.).

Table 8.9   Treatment interventions for substance use disorders

Area	Interventions
Therapeutic interventions	Motivational interviewing (enhancing motivation to change, increasing self-efficacy) Behavioral contracting (e.g., agreement to remain sober) Cognitive-behavioral interventions (e.g., recognizing and labeling distortions, cognitive reframing, evaluating positive expectancy outcomes) Relapse prevention (lapse versus relapse; education regarding AVE; recognizing triggers for use) Coping skills training for dealing with high-risk situations and triggers and resulting cravings and urges (e.g., behavioral rehearsal, stimulus control, visualization, coping cards) Relaxation training Contingency management
Adjunctive interventions	Detoxification (e.g., for alcohol, sedatives or hypnotics, opiate dependence) Consideration of medication referral (for maintenance therapy [naltrexone, acamprosate, methadone] or comorbid conditions) Collaborative relationship with psychiatrist (if medications are prescribed) Urine toxicology screening 12-step groups (e.g., AA, Narcotics Anonymous)
Family interventions	Family therapy Couples therapy (e.g., behavioral marital therapy) Psychoeducation Communication skills training Problem-solving training Relapse prevention planning Participation in support groups (e.g., Al-Anon, Alateen)
Disorder-Specific Interventions	
Alcohol dependence	Maintenance pharmacologic treatments such as disulfiram, acamprosate, naltrexone
Opiate dependence	Maintenance pharmacologic treatments such as methadone, LAAM, buprenorphine, naltrexone

The history of methamphetamine dates to the late nineteenth century, when it was first synthesized from ephedrine in Japan (Suwaki, 1997). During the 1940s, methamphetamine was used by the military in the United States, Japan, and Germany to treat combat fatigue and enhance performance (Meredith et al., 2005). Today, methamphetamine is occasionally prescribed to treat conditions such as narcolepsy and ADHD, but the vast majority of users take illegally produced forms of the drug. Illegal methamphetamine production is widespread and ranges from super labs in areas such as California and Mexico, to small mom-and-pop laboratories throughout the United States, particularly in rural areas (NIDA, 2004).

The abuse of methamphetamine has become a public health crisis that has been facilitated by the ease with which the drug can be produced. Chemicals found in over-the-counter diet pills and cold medicines and in household products such as tincture of iodine, hydrogen peroxide, gasoline, paint thinner, acetone, lye-based cleaners, and fertilizers can be used to create methamphetamine with equipment that can be stored in places as small as a shed or car. Many of the chemicals used to create methamphetamine are caustic and volatile and pose significant health risks not only to those who directly handle them, but to individuals in the surrounding environment (e.g., via explosions and fires, inhalation of toxic chemicals). Data collected between 2001 and 2004 by the U.S. Centers for Disease Control (2005) found a significantly higher percentage of injuries associated with methamphetamine-related incidents reported to the Agency for Toxic Substances and Disease Registry compared to nonmethamphetamine drug-related events (31% versus 7%, respectively) and demonstrated that those most frequently injured were police officers and members of the general public.

The ability to cheaply and easily produce methamphetamine resulted in the signing into law in 2006 of an anti-methamphetamine bill (the Combat Methamphetamine Epidemic Act of 2005) as part of the U.S. PATRIOT Improvement and Reauthorization Act of 2005. This legislation, modeled after existing laws in several states, places restrictions on the purchase of over-the-counter cold medications containing pseudoephedrine, which can be used in the production of methamphetamine; for example, retailers are required to keep these products behind the counter, and consumers may have to sign log books when purchasing them.

A short but extremely intense high is produced when methamphetamine is smoked or injected intravenously (known as a *rush* or *flash*). When methamphetamine is taken orally or snorted, a longer lasting, less intensely euphoric state occurs that begins within 3 to 20 minutes of ingestion and which can persist for up to half a day or longer (NIDA, 2006f; Wray, 2000). In addition to these effects, use of methamphetamine is associated with appetite suppression and increases in wakefulness and energy levels. However, prolonged use can result in irritability, aggression, agitation, anxiety, depression, and psychotic symptoms that include intense paranoia and delusions (Maxwell, 2005). The drug's negative effects can be amplified by the 1- to 3-week binge-crash cycle that typifies methamphetamine use (Cretzmeyer, Sarrazin, Huber, Block, & Hall, 2003). Withdrawal effects from methamphetamine, including lack of mental energy and dysphoria, are more severe than that observed in cocaine withdrawal and can wax and wane for many months (C. Davidson, Gow, Lee, & Ellinwood, 2001).

The typical portrait of a methamphetamine user is a young Caucasian female. However, during the late 1980s and early 1990s, intensified use of methamphetamine in smoked form (i.e., *ice*) was observed among areas with predominantly Asian populations, including Guam, Saipan in the Mariana Island chain of western Micronesia, and Hawaii (NIDA, 2003). Furthermore, as Brecht, O'Brien, von Mayrhauser, and Anglin (2004) note, the population of methamphetamine users is expanding to include other minority groups, such as Hispanics, as well as adolescents, gay and bisexual men, and older arrestees. Women are most likely to be introduced to using the drug by a spouse or boyfriend, whereas initiation of use among men is typically facilitated by friends and later maintained by coworkers (Brecht et al., 2004).

As many as two thirds of methamphetamine users are introduced to this drug prior to the age of 16, and there is frequently a history of alcohol, tobacco, and marijuana use predating its start (Cretzmeyer et al., 2003). Although the percentage of methamphetamine users who also make the drug is low, over half of all users may end up selling the drug (for male users this often occurs early in the history of use; Brecht et al., 2004). Methamphetamine users frequently report experiencing work, financial, and legal difficulties and problems with violence (Brecht et al., 2004). Children of methamphetamine users are at risk for abuse and neglect, and if a user is also involved in the manufacture of the drugs, children are exposed to toxic and highly volatile chemicals that pose a direct threat to their safety. Information is limited regarding the developmental problems that may occur in children born to methamphetamine-addicted mothers, but there is evidence of deficits in visual recognition memory, executive dysfunction, and behavioral dyscontrol (e.g., hyperactivity and aggressive behavior; Billing, Eriksson, Jonsson, Steneroth, & Zatterstrom, 1994; R. Hansen, Struthers, & Gospe, 1993).

Ongoing use of methamphetamine is associated with a number of adverse health outcomes, including increased risk of HIV infection (through the sharing of infected needles, unprotected sex) and other sexually transmitted and blood-borne diseases, stroke, impaired lung functioning, cardiac valve stenosis, and pulmonary hypertension (N. V. Harris, Thiede, McGough, & Gordon, 1993; Maxwell, 2005). Among the most troubling consequences of methamphetamine use are the neurotoxic effects the drug has on the brain and subsequent adverse effects on cognitive functioning. Methamphetamine can cause degeneration of portions of dopaminergic neurons in the corpus striatum, nucleus accumbens, and neocortex and in serotonergic neurons throughout the brain, and may affect glutamatergic neurons as well; although some of the damaged neuronal areas may regenerate, the connections that are reestablished between neurons are not the same, and hence permanent changes in neural circuitry occur (D. O. Frost & Cadet, 2000). Individuals who abuse methamphetamine exhibit a number of deficits on neurocognitive testing, including problems with working memory, information manipulation, processing speed, perceptual motor speed, response inhibition, delayed recall, mental flexibility, verbal and nonverbal fluency, and abstract thinking (Chang et al., 2002; Kalechstein, Newton, & Green, 2003; Monterosso, Aron, Cordoova, Xu, & London, 2005; R. D. Rogers et al., 1999; S. L. Simon et al., 2000). Problems with learning and memory, spatial processing, decision making, and inhibiting irrelevant information may persist even after abstinence is achieved (S. L. Simon et al., 2000). This has led some to suggest that cognitive compensatory strategies be included in the treatment of methamphetamine users (S. L. Simon, Davey, Glynn, Rawson, & Ling, 2004).

Despite the many negative consequences associated with methamphetamine, many users continue to believe that the drug helps them to function, and an average of 9 years may pass from the time the drug is first used to when treatment is finally sought (Brecht et al., 2004). Many methamphetamine users also use other drugs or alcohol, which should be considered in developing a treatment plan with these clients. Treatment for methamphetamine-addicted clients has been based primarily on existing treatments for cocaine abuse and dependence (since both drugs are stimulants). Although still in the nascent stages, outcome research suggests that standard treatments employing relapse prevention methods, motivational interviewing, 12-step groups, family education, psychoeducational skills training, and contracting appear effective with this population (see Cretzmeyer et al., 2003, for a review). Although aversion therapy has also been reported effective in an uncontrolled trial (Frawley & Smith, 1992), there are questions about the acceptability of this form of treatment to potential clients. In a randomized multi-site trial, Roll, et al. (2006) compared the addition of 12 weeks of contingency management (CM+) to existing comprehensive psychosocial treatments (e.g. CBT and relapse prevention approaches) for individuals with methamphetamine abuse or dependence. Those who received CM+ were abstinent more frequently and continuously compared to those in usual care at most sites that already consisted of elements empirically documented as effective in promoting abstinence. Also, Shoptaw and colleagues (2006) conducted a randomized, placebo-controlled, double-blind trial of sertraline and contingency management for methamphetamine users. Clients at an outpatient clinic were randomly assigned to one of four conditions for a 12-week treatment period: (1) sertraline + contingency management (S + CM), (2) sertraline alone (S), (3) placebo + contingency alone (P + CM), and (4) placebo only (P). All clients participated in thrice-weekly 90-minute relapse prevention groups. The CM intervention consisted of providing vouchers (redeemable for goods and services) for clean urine samples that increased in monetary value for each consecutive methamphetamine metabolite-free sample given, plus the opportunity to earn a bonus voucher. Although no significant main effect for CM was observed in the study, a greater proportion of those who received this intervention produced three consecutive weeks of methamphetamine-free urine samples compared to those in non-CM conditions. In addition, the use of sertraline appeared to dampen the effects of the relapse prevention groups and was associated with greater amphetamine use. These results indicate that antidepressant medication, though seemingly a logical intervention for the depression that typically accompanies cessation of methamphetamine use, does not appear to be effective in the acute treatment of methamphetamine addiction, and that empirically supported psychosocial interventions (e.g., relapse prevention) are more likely to lead to positive outcomes. Other research supported the use of CM in the treatment of methamphetamine abuse (Shoptaw et al., 2005). Thus, CM appears to be an important treatment modality in the armamentarium of interventions that can be used with the ever-increasing treatment population of methamphetamine-addicted individuals.

Chapter 9

SCHIZOPHRENIA AND OTHER PSYCHOTIC DISORDERS

Lay conceptions of psychosis frequently conjure up images of strange, unkempt individuals who inhabit an alternate reality—conversing with others who are neither seen nor heard, acting on bizarre and fantastic beliefs, and behaving in ways that are oblivious to societal conventions regarding manners, speech, and dress. Psychotic individuals are often portrayed in the popular media as childlike, intellectually naive individuals or, more frequently, as sociopathic, potentially homicidal fiends whose disturbing behavior is attributable to a lack of willpower, poor parenting, moral decrepitude, or the absence of a loving and understanding partner, family member, or therapist. Such stereotypes and misconceptions about individuals with psychotic disorders have profound implications for mental health treatment providers because they contribute to the significant obstacles often encountered in the assessment, diagnosis, and treatment of affected individuals.

What is it really like to have a disorder such as Schizophrenia? Some have likened the experience to dreaming but being wide awake (Mueser & Gingrich, 1994), although perhaps being in a nightmare is a better analogy. Just as the appearance of fantastic, bizarre, or impossible occurrences seem real to a dreamer, so too do the psychotic phenomena experienced by the schizophrenic individual. One individual (Anonymous, 1990, p. 165) described the beginning of her first psychotic episode, which occurred at age 19 while on her way to a military college, as follows:

> During my drive, I notice I am "seeing" things that are not there. Rabbits, cats, bugs appear and disappear. I see people from my past, whom I know to be dead or hundreds of miles away, driving the vehicles on the highway next to me. I believe the FBI is following me, because I notice that black cars with no license plates are taking turns driving behind me. I am not alarmed. I attribute the sights to fatigue and it makes sense to me that the FBI is tailing me since I am going to a high-security school.

This description illustrates some of the classic symptoms associated with Schizophrenia—delusions and hallucinations—that will be discussed further in this chapter, and provides a glimpse into the disturbing nature of the clinical phenomena that must be endured by clients with this fascinating and challenging disorder. This chapter reviews the clinical presentation, diagnosis, and recommended treatments for psychotic disorders described in the *DSM-IV-TR* and the challenges faced by clinicians at each of these stages. The chapter is organized around and focuses primarily on Schizophrenia, which serves as a prototype and is used to differentiate among the remaining psychotic disorders (i.e., Schizophreniform Disorder, Brief Psychotic Disorder, Schizoaffective Disorder, Delusional Disorder, and Shared Psychotic Disorder). Schizophrenia is also the most researched psychotic disorder and the one most likely to be encountered in clinical practice.

HISTORICAL OVERVIEW

Written accounts from diverse, ancient cultures (e.g., Egypt, India, Greece, and China) that describe syndromes characterized by bizarre, apparently delusional behavior suggest that psychotic conditions have existed for thousands of years. Yet the roots of our modern taxonomy of psychotic disorders are of relatively recent origin and date to the nineteenth and early twentieth centuries. Prior to this time, conditions that would today be characterized as psychotic were often subsumed under the general and unhelpful term "madness" (Leff, 2001), and purported causes included imbalances of bodily humors, poisons, fecal matter, demonic possession, punishment for sinful behavior or wrongdoing, and the effects of the moon ("lunacy"). In medieval Europe, individuals whose mental illness was thought to reflect demonic possession were often tortured or killed, and so-called treatments from the Renaissance through the nineteenth century frequently involved little more than restraining the ill in chains and subjecting them to squalid conditions, bleeding with leeches, and beatings (Gottesman, 1991; D. S. Holmes, 2001).

The late nineteenth- and early-twentieth-century pioneers Pinel, Esquirol, and Morel advocated a more rational, biological, and humane approach that focused on differentiating psychotic conditions from other mental disorders (e.g., melancholia, mania, and mental retardation) in terms of phenomenology and course, and distinguishing among the ways psychosis could present (e.g., delusional versus catatonic states). Esquirol's (1838) text was the first to promote an objective and rational view of mental disorders. Morel's (1860) description of *démence précoce* or early dementia (i.e., modern-day Schizophrenia), a degenerative condition characterized by insanity that struck seemingly healthy individuals early in life (e.g., adolescence), was innovative because it emphasized a deteriorating course that stood in contrast to the apparent stability of other conditions such as "idiocy" (mental retardation) and postulated a hereditary basis for this disorder.

Morel's work strongly influenced the German psychiatrist Emil Kraepelin, who classified the different manifestations of dementia praecox into subtypes (e.g., hebephrenic, paranoid, catatonic, and simple) in the early twentieth century, and who described the common threads of frequent relapse and poor prognosis that seemed to link the different subtypes to a single disease entity that was distinguishable from manic-depressive illness. Kraepelin (1919) also advanced the concept that neurological abnormalities or impairment (i.e., damage or destruction of cells in the cerebral cortex) were implicated in the genesis of dementia praecox.

In 1911, the Swiss psychiatrist Eugene Bleuler (1950) introduced the term schizophrenia (from the Greek, *schizo* = to split, *phrene* = mind) to replace dementia praecox. This term captured the fragmentation of psychic functions and thought processes that were hallmarks of the disorder and moved away from the Kraepelinian notion that deterioration was an inevitable feature of this condition. Rather than emphasizing a single disease entity, Bleuler wrote about the "schizophrenias," which he believed were associated with potentially different etiologies and prognoses. This emphasis on the heterogeneity in Schizophrenia presentation is still reflected in the *DSM* system (*DSM-IV-TR*; American Psychiatric Association, 2000b).

Bleuler also described a set of core features or disturbances (the "4 A's") he believed were essential to the various manifestations of Schizophrenia:(1) **a**ffect (e.g., blunted, inappropriate thoughts), (2) **a**ssociations (e.g., loose, unconnected thoughts), (3) **a**mbivalence (i.e., inability to make up one's mind), and (4) **a**utism (i.e., social aloofness, inadequate contact or connectedness with the outside world). These fundamental symptoms could be contrasted with "accessory" or "secondary" symptoms (e.g., hallucinations, delusions), which were often the cause for hospitalization or institutionalization. Bleuler insightfully observed that symptoms at the heart of the disease process (i.e., the 4 A's) were often not obvious targets for treatment (E. Bleuler, 1950; M. F. Green, 2001).

In 1959, the German psychiatrist Kurt Schneider described a set of "first-rank" symptoms of Schizophrenia that were thought to be pathognomonic for the disorder and were subsequently accorded particular importance in American diagnostic procedures beginning with *DSM-II* (American Psychiatric Association, 1980). Table 9.1 presents examples

Table 9.1   Examples of Schneiderian first-rank symptoms

Symptom	Definition
Thought broadcasting	Delusional belief that one's thoughts are being broadcast aloud so that others can hear them. Not to be confused with the belief that others can read one's mind.
Thought insertion	Delusional belief that thoughts that are not one's own are being inserted into one's mind. Not to be confused with the delusional belief that one's mind is being *influenced* by an outside force (e.g., the devil) but that one's thoughts are still self-generated.
Thought withdrawal	Delusional belief that thoughts have been removed from one's head. The individual may suddenly stop talking and when questioned report that thoughts were removed from his or her head.
Delusions of external control	Delusional belief that one is not acting volitionally, but is instead being controlled by an external force, person, etc. The individual may report that his or her movements, voice, etc. are being controlled by an outside force.
Auditory hallucinations of voice(s) conversing about the individual or keeping up a running commentary on the individual's actions	Conversing voices are often reported as talking about the individual in the third person. When a running commentary is heard, it may be a single voice that comments on what the individual is doing (e.g., "She's getting up and walking to the window").

of Schneiderian first-rank symptoms. Although it is now clear that first-rank symptoms are neither necessary nor sufficient for a diagnosis of Schizophrenia (e.g., they can occur in psychotic mood disorders; they have relatively low base rates among schizophrenic individuals), their presence still indicates that Schizophrenia is a strong diagnostic possibility (Andreasen & Flaum, 1991). First-rank symptoms are discussed further under "Clinical Presentation" for Schizophrenia.

The definition and boundaries of psychosis have been rigorously debated over time, and the pendulum of thought has alternately swung between broad and narrow conceptualizations, with no one definition receiving universal acceptance (American Psychiatric Association, 2000b). Changes in the conceptualization of psychotic disorders can be seen in the evolution of these conditions within the *DSM* classification system, where the emphasis has been to increasingly subdivide disorders into distinct and somewhat narrowly defined conditions. In early versions of the *DSM* (*DSM-I* and *DSM-II*), any condition that caused serious functional impairment could be considered to reflect psychosis (American Psychiatric Association, 1952, 1968). A distinction was made, however, between psychotic conditions stemming from organic causes (e.g., dementia, epilepsy) and so-called functional psychoses such as Schizophrenia. Beginning with the *DSM-III*, detailed and explicit criteria sets replaced the brief and vague descriptions that had characterized psychotic disorders in earlier editions (American Psychiatric Association, 1980). This sea change followed the realization that the broad definition of Schizophrenia used in the United States was different from that used internationally and was adversely affecting the reliability of the diagnostic process (e.g., large numbers of individuals were receiving Schizophrenia diagnoses when they were not necessarily warranted; Kuriansky, Deming, & Gurland, 1974).

Overall, beginning with *DSM-III*, a shift was made to more restrictive conceptualizations of psychosis that focused on severe disturbances in cognitive and perceptual processes and resulted in symptoms such as hallucinations, delusions, and an inability to distinguish reality from fantasy. The current American definition of Schizophrenia is narrower than that used by much of the rest of the world (*International Classification of Diseases* [*ICD-10*]); the latter places greater emphasis on Schneiderian symptoms, requires a shorter duration of symptoms for a diagnosis to be made, and includes a greater range of disorder subtypes (e.g., simple Schizophrenia) than the *DSM-IV* (Andreasen & Flaum, 1991). This chapter focuses on psychosis as described by the *DSM-IV-TR*, with particular emphasis on the most characteristic and well researched of the psychotic disorders: Schizophrenia.

SCHIZOPHRENIA

Schizophrenia is arguably the most severe and devastating of all mental disorders, with yearly direct costs associated with treatment totaling $19 billion and indirect costs (e.g., lost productivity, lost time from work for caregivers, social services and criminal justice resources) estimated at $46 billion (American Psychiatric Association, 1996). Schizophrenia is a particularly devastating disorder because it typically strikes during late adolescence and early adulthood, often tragically derailing education, work, romantic and other relationships, and the myriad exciting changes and pursuits that typify these life stages.

Clinical Presentation

Schizophrenia is characterized by a number of symptoms, including hallucinations, delusions, disorganized speech, disorganized behavior or catatonia, and negative symptoms. According to the *DSM* system, at least two such active symptoms, lasting for most of a 1-month period, are required for a diagnosis, but only one symptom is required if delusions are bizarre or hallucinations consist of (a) a voice keeping a running commentary on the client's behavior or (b) voices conversing with one another (i.e., Schneiderian first-rank symptoms). Continuous signs of the illness (including prodromal or residual symptoms) must be present for a total of 6 months (American Psychiatric Association, 2000b). The symptom list for Schizophrenia includes a combination of what are referred to as *positive* and *negative symptoms*. Derived from terminology first used by the neurologist Hughlings Jackson, positive symptoms represent an exaggeration of mental functions, whereas negative symptoms are characterized by the absence or loss of normal mental functions. Table 9.2 presents a division of the signs and symptoms that are observed in Schizophrenia according to this positive/negative dichotomy.

Positive Symptoms

This class of symptoms can be divided into two clusters: (1) hallucinations and delusions and (2) disorganized thinking or speech (also known as positive thought disorder) and behavior (e.g., displays of inappropriate affect, unusual mannerisms). Positive symptoms are associated with active episodes of Schizophrenia, are dramatic and bizarre, and are what most people associate with severe mental illness. While they can cause significant impairment, positive symptoms have traditionally been more responsive to pharmacologic intervention than negative symptoms. The presence of positive symptoms does not imply disorientation, delirium, or confusion, and individuals who are actively hallucinating or who are delusional are generally oriented to person, place, and time and typically display reasonably organized behavior (e.g., catching a bus, driving a car, buying food at the store, carrying on a conversation; Gottesman, 1991).

Delusions refer to patently false beliefs that can develop around any issue or theme, are not accepted within an individual's social or cultural environment, and are held with conviction even in the face of contradictory evidence. Common examples are presented in Table 9.3. Delusions are often difficult to distinguish from *overvalued ideas*. The latter have been defined as solitary beliefs that are not considered senseless by an individual, often develop from a specific emotional experience, eventually determine a person's actions, and are often associated with preexisting personality pathology (R. W. Butler &

Table 9.2   Positive and negative symptoms of Schizophrenia

Positive Symptoms	Negative Symptoms
Hallucinations	Alogia
Delusions	Avolition
Disorganized thinking	Flattened or blunted affect
Grossly disorganized behavior	Anergia
	Anhedonia
	Social withdrawal

Table 9.3   Common delusional themes

Delusion Type	Definition	Examples
Erotomanic	Belief that another person (usually of higher status) is in love with you from afar.	"I know that Robert De Niro is in love with me because when I got his autograph he took extra long to sign it."
Grandiose	Belief that you have powers, knowledge, or abilities that are in excess of what reality indicates. Belief that you know or are associated with a famous or influential person or figure with no supporting evidence.	"I have been selected to be God's special emissary on earth and to bring peace to all war-torn countries."
Jealous	Belief that your partner (e.g., wife, boyfriend) is unfaithful in the absence of any supporting evidence.	"I'm sure my husband doesn't have a business meeting on Monday nights— he's meeting his mistress and his boss is just covering for him."
Persecutory	Belief that a person, group of persons, or entity is intentionally trying to harm you.	"I drink only bottled water because the government is carrying out experiments on people in my town by putting harmful viruses in the water system."
Somatic	The belief that you have a physical abnormality (e.g., parts of your body are not working properly) or medical condition with no supportive medical evidence.	"My intestines are slowly rotting away from gangrene."
Reference	The belief that persons, objects, occurrences, etc. in your environment have special meanings.	"When I saw that the sixth slot machine in my row at the casino had a jackpot of $66,000 I knew it was the Devil trying to tempt me."
Control	The belief that some force outside of you is controlling your actions, movements, etc.	"A satellite is making me move and talk to you."[*]

[*]This is a type of Schneiderian first-rank symptom.

Braff, 1991). Examples of disorders that involve overvalued ideas are Hypochondriasis, Anorexia Nervosa, and Obsessive-Compulsive Disorder.

Delusions can be classified as nonbizarre or bizarre, with the latter considered more pathological because they concern ideas that are not at all plausible, such as the belief that a computer chip controlled by a satellite has been implanted in one's brain. The Schneiderian delusions of thought insertion, thought broadcasting, and thought removal are examples of bizarre delusions. Nonbizarre delusions concern something that could conceivably happen (e.g., being followed by the police; being a government spy or a professional baseball player). The distinction between bizarre and nonbizarre delusions has diagnostic significance in the *DSM-IV-TR* because the presence of a bizarre delusion is sufficient to satisfy the symptom criterion for Schizophrenia, whereas another sign or symptom (e.g., hallucinations, grossly disorganized behavior) is required if a nonbizarre delusion is present (American Psychiatric Association, 2000b). However, it is not always easy to determine if a delusion is bizarre or nonbizarre. For example, a religious clinician might characterize a delusion of demonic possession as nonbizarre based on the belief that such a phenomenon is theoretically possible, whereas another clinician might label it bizarre. In evaluating a delusion, consideration must also be given to whether the belief is acceptable or normative within the client's cultural, social, or religious group. Clinicians should not automatically label as delusional any belief that they personally consider implausible (e.g., a common belief in many non-Western societies is that the dead can interact with and possess the living; K. M. Lin & Lin, 2001).

Hallucinations are sensory experiences that occur in the absence of appropriate stimuli (e.g., hearing a voice when no one is around) and can occur in any sensory modality (e.g., visual, auditory, tactile, gustatory, olfactory). Auditory hallucinations are most common in Schizophrenia. True hallucinations occur when the client is in a clear state of consciousness, and can thus be distinguished from hallucinatory experiences, such as hearing one's name being called, that can occur when drifting off to sleep (hypnagogic hallucinations) or awakening (hypnopompic hallucinations). Hallucinations are also different from sensory misperceptions such as *illusions* (e.g., mistaking a tree branch lying on the ground for a snake). To be considered evidence of psychosis, hallucinations must not represent culturally or religiously accepted phenomena, and in the case of substance-induced hallucinations the individual must not have insight that the hallucinations are the result of ingesting a drug (American Psychiatric Association, 2000b).

Auditory hallucinations in Schizophrenia generally consist of one or more voices that have a distinct auditory quality, often described as being akin to hearing actual voices, as opposed to indistinct sounds or noises (M. F. Green, 2001). A voice that keeps a running commentary of the individual's actions ("He's getting up to turn on the TV, now he's going to the kitchen") and voices that converse with each other are examples of Schneiderian first-rank symptoms, and the presence of either type of hallucination is enough to fulfill the *DSM-IV-TR* symptom criterion for Schizophrenia (American Psychiatric Association, 2000b). Command hallucinations can be especially troubling to a client because these instruct a person to act in a particular manner. These can range from the relatively harmless (e.g., "Turn the TV channel") to the extremely dangerous ("Kill yourself"). Although many clients ignore command hallucinations (e.g., if they have good insight, if the symptoms have been present for a long period of time), one study found that nearly 40% of clients with command hallucinations obeyed them (Junginger, 1990). Individuals who have only recently begun to experience command hallucinations, have poor insight into their symptoms, and/or use ineffective methods for coping with such hallucinations are at greater risk for acting on them. Violent command hallucinations typically instruct the individual to harm himself or herself rather than others (Resnick, 1997).

The rabbits and dead people mentioned by the author of the first-person account cited earlier are examples of visual hallucinations. Visual hallucinations are typically characterized by normal-size people and objects seen in color (D. W. Goodwin, Alderson, & Rosenthal, 1971). Flashing lights, shadows, and other indistinct perceptions may reflect substance use or neurological or ophthalmologic pathology, and are sometimes reported by acutely decompensated individuals with severe personality or dissociative disorders (e.g., Borderline Personality Disorder, Dissociative Identity Disorder). Olfactory, tactile, and gustatory hallucinations can occur in Schizophrenia but are much less common than auditory or visual ones, and their presence raises concern about possible neurological disease or substance use (e.g., parasitosis, or the sensation of bugs crawling on the skin associated with cocaine use). Dramatic, atypical hallucinations should raise suspicions of malingering. Resnick (1997, p. 54) cites the case of a criminal defendant, later found to have been malingering psychotic symptoms, who reported the following visual hallucinations: "a green laughing devil, a god with a flowing white beard, a black Doberman pinscher dog, and President Ronald Reagan."

Clients can have a wide range of reactions to hallucinations. Although many react with distress, hallucinations consisting of benign or positive voices or images may be perceived as providing comfort and even companionship. One factor related to how distressing a hallucination is perceived to be is the degree to which the client believes the hallucination (Gaudiano & James, 2006). Also, as illness chronicity increases, clients may become more habituated to hallucinatory experiences. Clients often utilize a variety of coping strategies to deal with hallucinations, such as listening to music or watching TV, changing position (e.g., lying down or walking), seeking out interpersonal contact, and taking medication (Falloon & Talbot, 1981). Jenner, Niehuid, van de Willige, and Wiersma (2006) reported increased control over auditory hallucinations and reductions in positive symptoms, perceived distress, and subjective burden among medicated Schizophrenia patients who received an intervention known as HIT (hallucination-focused integrative treatment) that utilized cognitive-behavioral interventions, coping skills training, family-based interventions, and crisis intervention techniques to help individuals cope with psychotic symptoms.

Disorganized speech is a manifestation of *thought disorder*, which refers to severely disorganized thought processes. Thought disorder is considered by some to be the single most important feature of Schizophrenia and is typically inferred through the quality and coherence of a client's speech (American Psychiatric Association, 2000b). Thought-disordered individuals are difficult to understand because they may jump from topic to topic in an unrelated manner (i.e., exhibit loose associations or derailment), begin to answer a question but quickly get off topic (i.e., tangentiality), eventually answer a question after repeatedly going off on peripheral details (i.e., circumstantiality), select words or phrases based on rhyming or punning rather than on meaning (i.e., clanging), or use made-up words (i.e., neologisms). In very extreme cases, a client's speech may be completely incomprehensible ("word salad") and resemble a fluent aphasic disorder. Marengo and Harrow (1997, p. 276) provide the following example of severe thought disorder exhibited by a schizophrenic individual attempting to answer the question "Why are people who are born deaf usually unable to talk?": "When you swallow in your throat like a key it comes out, but not a scissors. A robin, too. It means spring."

Although thought disorder can occur in mania and nonschizophrenic psychoses, it is estimated that 80% or more of schizophrenic individuals display signs of thought disorder during acute illness episodes (Marengo, Harrow, & Edell, 1993). For many schizophrenic individuals, residual signs of thought disorder may persist between active illness episodes despite treatment with neuroleptic medication (Marengo & Harrow, 1987). Docherty and colleagues (Docherty, Cohen, Nienow, Dinzeo, & Dangelmaier, 2003) found that while ratings of formal thought disorder varied with clinical state (i.e., were positively correlated with ratings of other positive symptoms), they also showed moderate stability over a 9-month period. This research team also found that certain referential disturbances (i.e., specific language disturbances related to a failure to transmit meaning) were fairly stable across time and may reflect an enduring traitlike cognitive vulnerability marker among persons with Schizophrenia. Additional research suggests that the etiology of thought disorder may be closely linked to executive functioning and semantic processing deficits rather than directly to impairments in general cognitive functioning or specific language functions (Stirling, Hellewell, Blakely, & Deakin, 2006).

Another symptom of Schizophrenia is *grossly disorganized behavior*. As noted in the *DSM-IV-TR*, this may take many forms, ranging from childlike silliness to extreme and unpredictable agitation (American Psychiatric Association, 2000b). Such behavior can seriously interfere with the individual's ability to effectively carry out even basic tasks of daily living such as maintaining appropriate hygiene, eating, and dressing properly. Wandering in a disheveled state, randomly accosting strangers, or standing on a street corner staring at the sun are examples of grossly disorganized behavior (A. Frances et al., 1995).

Interestingly, *catatonic behavior* and grossly disorganized behavior are listed together in the *DSM-IV-TR* as a class of characteristic symptoms of Schizophrenia even though catatonia is quite different from the examples of grossly disorganized behavior previously noted (American Psychiatric Association, 2000b). Catatonia refers to motor behaviors characterized by marked rigidity and resistance to being moved, waxy flexibility, purposeless excessive activity, and unusual or bizarre postures (American Psychiatric Association, 2000b). Catatonia is not specific to Schizophrenia and can occur in neurological disorders and other mental disorders such as mood disorders. It can also be characterized by staring, social withdrawal, mutism, echolalia, meaningless and stereotyped repetition of words (known as verbigeration), scrambled speech (known as schizophasia), and refusal to eat (G. Bush, Fink, Petrides, & Francis, 1996). There is some evidence that "negative" catatonic signs are more likely to be correlated with negative symptoms of Schizophrenia (to be discussed shortly) and cognitive impairment, and for "positive" catatonic signs to be more highly correlated with formal thought disorder among acute as well as chronically ill patients (Mortimer, Lund, & McKenna, 1990). Schizophrenic individuals with catatonic features have been observed to have an earlier age of onset, worse illness course, more hospitalizations, and poorer functional status compared to those without catatonia (Mimica, Folnegovic-Smale, & Folnegovic, 2001; Ungvari, Leung, Ng, Cheung, & Leung, 2005). D. Cohen et al. (2005) found that among hospitalized adolescents, catatonia in Schizophrenia (versus other disorders) was associated with male sex, insidious onset, longer duration, and greater symptom severity at hospital discharge.

Negative Symptoms

These symptoms are characterized by a diminution or loss of normal mental functions and include *blunted or flattened affect, social and emotional withdrawal, anhedonia* (lack of interest or pleasure in activities), *avolition* (lack of motivation), and *alogia* (decreased fluency of thought and speech). Schizophrenic individuals with prominent negative symptoms often appear interpersonally disconnected, bland, and zombie-like. Their cognitive style is usually simple, concrete, and repetitive, and these difficulties appear related to dysfunction of the dorsolateral prefrontal cortex (Weinberger, Berman, & Zec, 1986). Taciturn responses to questions and lack of spontaneous verbalizations give the impression that individuals with prominent negative symptoms are disinterested and uncommunicative. Feelings are likely to be unarticulated or poorly described (e.g., vague dysphoria rather than anxiety, depression, or guilt). In sum, interacting with such individuals may leave one feeling bored, sleepy, and stimulus-deprived (McGlashan, Heinssen, & Fenton, 1990). If family members and others in the schizophrenic individual's environment are not educated about negative symptoms, they may incorrectly attribute these symptoms to being under the client's control and have hostile or critical reactions to them.

The severity of negative symptoms will not necessarily be correlated with the degree of reported distress associated with these symptoms, and clinicians are apt to encounter a range of client reactions to them. Selten, Wiersma, and van den Bosch (2000) found that high self-reported distress about negative symptoms was best predicted by a combination of high depression scores and high scores for insight into positive symptoms.

Although less conspicuous than positive symptoms, negative symptoms are considered central to the disease process of Schizophrenia. These negative symptoms are sometimes referred to as "primary" in the research literature, and are distinguished from "secondary" negative symptoms that stem from causes such as long-term hospitalization, depression, and medication side effects. Whereas positive symptoms may wax and wane across the course of the disorder, the negative symptoms of Schizophrenia tend to be fairly stable (Pogue-Geile & Harrow, 1985) and are less commonly encountered in cases of late-onset Schizophrenia (American Psychiatric Association, 2000b). The presence of prominent and enduring primary negative symptoms constitutes the "deficit syndrome" of Schizophrenia (Carpenter, Heinrichs, & Wagman, 1988), which is discussed further under "Subtypes" and "Onset, Course, and Life Span Considerations." It is estimated that this syndrome accounts for 17% of schizophrenic individuals in general epidemiologic samples, and 25% to 30% in samples of chronically ill patients (B. Kirkpatrick, Buchanan, Ross, & Carpenter, 2001; B. Kirkpatrick, Ross, Walsh, Karkowski, & Kendler, 2000). An important change to the diagnostic criteria for Schizophrenia in the *DSM-IV-TR* was the addition of negative symptoms as one of the characteristic type of symptoms of the disorder (American Psychiatric Association, 2000b).

Finally, a rare schizophrenic syndrome known as *Simple Schizophrenia*, characterized by progressive deterioration in functioning, prominent negative symptoms, and an absence of positive symptoms, has also been observed. Simple Schizophrenia is currently listed in the *DSM-IV* under criteria sets requiring further study (American Psychiatric Association, 2000b).

Subtypes

The *DSM-IV* specifies five Schizophrenia subtypes that are based on the predominant symptom picture presented at the time the client is evaluated (thus, the subtype may change over time). They are *catatonic, disorganized, paranoid, undifferentiated*, and *residual*. The subtypes follow a hierarchically arranged algorithm that is summarized in Table 9.4.

It was hoped that the use of subtypes would help subdivide the heterogeneous population of schizophrenic individuals into meaningful subgroups that shared common clinical features and possibly similarities in course and prognosis. Empirical evidence indicates that the paranoid and catatonic subtypes are associated with the best prognosis, the undifferentiated subtype with an intermediate prognosis, and the disorganized subtype (also known as hebephrenic Schizophrenia) with the poorest prognosis (A. Frances et al., 1995). However, criticism has been raised regarding the reliability, stability, and predictive value (e.g., regarding illness correlates and treatment response) of the *DSM-IV*

Table 9.4   Hierarchical algorithm for *DSM-IV* Schizophrenia subtypes

Catatonic type: (*Two of the following*)
Motoric immobility (e.g., catalepsy or stupor)
Excessive motor activity (purposeless)
Extreme negativism (e.g., resistance to instructions), mutism
Peculiar voluntary movements (e.g., mannerisms, posturing, grimacing, stereotyped, movements)
Echolalia or echopraxia[*]
⇓
Disorganized type: (*All of the following*)
Disorganized speech
Disorganized behavior
Flat or inappropriate affect
⇓
Paranoid type: (*All of the following*)
Preoccupation with one or more delusions or frequent auditory hallucinations
No prominent disorganized speech, disorganized or catatonic behavior, or flat or inappropriate affect
⇓
Undifferentiated type:
Criteria for paranoid, disorganized, catatonic types not met
⇓
Residual type:
Absence of prominent delusions, hallucinations, disorganized speech, and grossly disorganized or catatonic behavior
Continuing evidence of disturbance indicated by negative symptoms or two or more Criterion A symptoms for Schizophrenia in attenuated form

[*]Echolalia refers to repetition of words/phrases said by others. Echopraxia refers to repetition (via imitation) of another's movements.
Adapted with permission. American Psychiatric Association (2000b). *The Diagnostic and Statistical Manual for Mental Disorders*, fourth edition (Revised). Washington, DC: American Psychiatric Association.

subtypes, as well as other subtype groupings based on clinical presentation that have been discussed in the literature (e.g., positive/negative; Andreasen, Flaum, & Schultz, 1997; Heinrichs & Awad, 1993). The distinction between deficit and nondeficit syndrome cases of Schizophrenia has received support from studies showing that the deficit syndrome is associated with more prominent anhedonia, greater treatment resistance, poorer social functioning, and less depression, paranoia, and substance abuse than other subtypes. Neurocognitive studies indicate that the deficit syndrome is characterized by eye-tracking deficits and impairments on tasks of executive functioning, sustained attention, and general ability suggestive of frontotemporoparietal dysfunction superimposed on a background of more global impairment (Jablensky, 2006).

Empirical techniques (e.g., factor analysis of symptom measures) have also been used, alone and in combination with rational approaches, to identify subgroups of individuals with Schizophrenia (M. D. Bell, Lysaker, Beam-Goulet, Milstein, & Lindenmayer, 1994; S. K. Hill, Ragland, Gur, & Gur, 2001; Kay & Sevy, 1990; Mueser, Curran, & McHugo, 1997). In some cases, subtypes derived from these methods have been correlated with different illness characteristics such as performance on neuropsychological assessment measures. To illustrate, S. K. Hill et al. (2001) divided schizophrenic individuals into negative, disorganized, mild, paranoid, and Schneiderian subtypes. They found that all subgroups displayed impairments in executive functioning, but that paranoid individuals displayed fewer impairments in verbal memory and spatial abilities compared to the disorganized subtype, better attention compared to the negative subtype, and better motor skills compared to both of these other subtypes. In fact, differences in patterns of neurocognitive deficits have been proposed as a promising basis on which to determine more useful Schizophrenia subtypes. Relevant to this point, Jablensky (2006) discusses the notion of the *endophenotype*, borrowed from genetics, as a useful organizing principle by which to determine subtypes for Schizophrenia. An endophenotype is characterized by (a) association with a clinical disorder but not necessarily a diagnostic criterion for it, (b) heritability, (c) state independence (i.e., is present during active illness phases and remission), (d) cosegregation with illness in families, and (e) appearance among unaffected family members of probands at a higher rate than in the general population (Gottesman & Gould, 2003). It would appear that the various neurocognitive deficits that have been identified among subgroups of schizophrenic individuals meet many of these criteria (Jablensky, 2006). Neurocognitive sequelae of Schizophrenia are discussed further under "Etiology."

Additional Characteristics

Poor Insight

Although not a diagnostic criterion, lack of insight into the fact that one has a mental disorder (also referred to as unawareness) is present in the vast majority (e.g., 85%) of schizophrenic individuals (Carpenter, Strauss, & Bartko, 1973). Poor insight is also one of the features that best discriminates between Schizophrenia and affective disorders (World Health Organization [WHO], 1975). Insight is considered by some to be a multidimensional construct that encompasses not only illness awareness, but factors such as the ability to recognize and define cardinal illness features (e.g., delusions, hallucinations) and to acknowledge the value of treatment (Amador et al., 1993; David, 1990). Not surprisingly, poor insight has been linked to a number of negative outcomes in Schizophrenia, including reduced treatment compliance, worse course, higher incidence of violent life events, and poorer social functioning (C. Goodman, Knoll, Isakov, & Silver, 2005; Lysaker, Bell, Bryson, & Kaplan, 1998; McEvoy et al., 1996).

The etiology of poor insight among persons with Schizophrenia is unclear; it appears that both neurocognitive and psychological variables may be at play. With regard to the former, some studies have found that deficits in executive functioning, memory, and attention are correlated with poor insight in schizophrenic individuals (Drake & Lewis, 2003; Lysaker & Bell, 1995; Lysaker, Bryson, & Bell, 2002; McEvoy, 1996; T. E. Smith, Hull, Israel, & Wilson, 2000; Subotnik et al., 2005; Voruganti, Heslegrave, & Awad, 1997), although negative findings have also been reported (Aleman, de Haan, & Khan, 2002; Dickerson, Boronow, Ringel, & Parente, 1997; R. W. Goldberg, Green-Paden, Lehman, & Gold, 2001; C. Goodman et al., 2005; C. H. Kim, Jayathilake, & Meltzer, 2003; Rossell, Coakes, Shapleske, Woodruff, & David, 2003). Methodological factors such as small sample sizes, variability in the way insight is defined and measured, differences in the assessment of neurocognitive variables, and heterogeneity of patients across investigations may account for some of the inconsistency observed across studies (C. Goodman et al., 2005).

Psychological factors have also been hypothesized to play a role in some cases of impaired insight in Schizophrenia. Startup (1996) contends that schizophrenic persons with generally intact neurocognitive abilities may display a severe form of psychologically-based denial that serves the purpose of keeping out of awareness painful information regarding the reality of having a debilitating mental illness. In contrast, other schizophrenic individuals evidence a moderate degree of impaired insight that is directly attributable to neurocognitive deficits (i.e., these individuals will be able to comprehend some, but not all, of their illness because of their cognitive impairments). In support of this model, research by Lysaker, Bryson, Lancaster, Evans, and Bell (2003) found that Schizophrenia patients with good neurocognitive functioning and poor insight endorsed items on a coping inventory indicating that they emotionally distanced themselves from the psychological impact of life events. Similarly, Subotnik et al. (2005) found that during periods of symptom remission, poor insight was related to neurocognitive deficits (e.g., sustained attention, working memory), but that during periods of active psychosis, poor insight was more strongly related to psychological defensiveness, as manifest in such characteristics as attempts to present oneself in a socially desirable manner, guardedness, tendencies to acquiesce to avoid social conflict, and denial of common personal failings (as measured by the Minnesota Multiphasic Personality Inventory-2 [MMPI-2]).

Suicide

Clinicians working with schizophrenic individuals need to be aware of the high risk for suicide in this population: 10% of individuals with this disorder commit suicide, and 20% to 40% make at least one attempt during the course of the illness (American Psychiatric Association, 2000b). Although it is not possible to predict with a high degree of accuracy whether an individual client will attempt suicide, a number of empirically derived risk factors for suicide among individuals with Schizophrenia have been established (see Table 9.5).

Individuals who are early in the course of the illness are at greatest risk. Westermeyer et al. (1991) found that 60% of clients who committed suicide did so within 6 years of their first hospitalization. However, the danger of suicide does not completely dissipate as a schizophrenic individual grows older, which suggests that emotional responsiveness (including the capacity to suffer) does not burn out as a schizophrenic ages, as had been suspected (M. Bleuler, 1978). Along these lines, Nyman and Jonsson (1986) identified two different types of schizophrenic individuals at risk for suicide: those in the early stages of the illness who experience anxiety, hopelessness, and a sense of being different from others, and those in the later stages of illness whose course has been chronic and resistant to treatment and who have poor social adjustment. It appears that the greater the disparity between premorbid and postillness functioning, the greater the risk for suicide. Compared to chronically low-functioning individuals, previously high-functioning individuals are likely to experience a more significant decline in several areas of functioning. The personal expectations such individuals may have had prior to their illness onset, combined with the realization that they must now contend with a chronic and often debilitating illness, can lead to hopelessness, despondency, and depression. Similarly, the finding that schizophrenic individuals with higher IQs are at increased risk for suicide has been

Table 9.5   Risk factors for suicide among individuals with Schizophrenia

Demographic

Male	Caucasian
Unmarried	Unemployed
20–39 years old	Higher level of education, intelligence

Illness and Treatment Characteristics

High level of premorbid functioning	Chronic illness with multiple relapses
Within first 10 years of illness	Recent hospital discharge
Comorbid depressive symptoms	History of previous suicide attempts
Active psychosis	Longer duration of untreated psychosis
Frequent, short hospitalizations	
Major loss experienced early in illness	

Emotional and Cognitive State

Suicidal ideation (even low levels may predict suicidal behavior better than depression)	Impulsivity
Awareness of deterioration or debilitation associated with Schizophrenia	Negative attitudes about or loss of faith in treatment
Feelings of hopelessness and despair (often linked to chronicity of disorder, decreased quality of life associated with illness)	Noncompliant with medication

interpreted as reflecting a greater ability to realize what has been or may be lost because of the illness (DeHert, McKenzie, & Peuskens, 2001).

In a transcultural study of suicide in Schizophrenia that examined individuals from North and South America, Western and Eastern Europe, and South Africa, common risk factors (e.g., history of substance or alcohol abuse and current smoking) were found across most groups, but differences were discovered as well. These included more frequent attempts by male patients in the North American and European samples only, and an earlier age at first attempt and higher number of previous attempts in the North American sample only (Altamura et al., 2007).

Clinicians should always evaluate suicidal ideation when their schizophrenic clients appear depressed (see Chapter 2 for additional information on conducting a suicide assessment). However, it is important to remember that suicidal ideation is not inevitably linked to depressed mood, and the absence of obvious depression does not negate the risk for suicidal ideation or behavior. F. J. Acosta et al. (2006), in a sample of schizophrenic inpatients who had attempted suicide, identified a "psychotic motivation" subgroup that, compared to a "depressive motivation" subgroup, exhibited lower levels of depression, shorter duration of illness, lower educational attainment, and fewer previous suicide attempts. In their study of recent-onset schizophrenics, A. S. Young et al. (1998) found that mild suicidal ideation was a better predictor than depression of future significant suicidal ideation and behavior. These researchers found that suicidal ideation changed rapidly from week to week in some individuals, suggesting that clinicians be attuned to potential suicidal ideation on a regular basis throughout treatment and encourage their clients to openly discuss suicidal thoughts and feelings whenever they arise. As with other clinical populations, hopelessness is strongly associated with suicidality among persons with Schizophrenia, and this factor appears to be independent of any particular symptom dimensions or illness profile (F. J. Acosta et al., 2006; Kaneda, 2006).

Cognitive Difficulties

Schizophrenia is best conceptualized as a brain disorder that is neurodevelopmental in origin (see "Etiology"). A number of studies have demonstrated that individuals with Schizophrenia display impairments in a variety of cognitive domains, although there is no single profile of such deficits that is peculiar to the illness. Individuals with Schizophrenia have been found to perform poorly on tests assessing abstract thinking and problem solving (i.e., executive functions), visual processing, sustained attention, processing speed, and verbal and visual memory (Braff, Saccuzzo, & Geyer, 1991; Hoff, Riordan, O'Donnell, & DiLisi, 1991; T. Sharma & Antonova, 2003).

Individuals with a history of poor premorbid functioning in areas such as the quality and number of peer relationships and psychosocial adaptation to school have been found to display greater neurocognitive deficits in areas such as attention and executive functioning than those with a better premorbid history, even when clinically and pharmacologically stable (Silverstein, Mavrolefteros, & Close, 2002).

One cognitive deficit that many clinicians are likely to observe in schizophrenic individuals is difficulty recognizing and understanding emotional expression. A person with Schizophrenia may exhibit poor social skills, including the inability to pick up on subtle emotional cues emitted by others (Mueser, et al., 1996). These cognitive deficits do not appear to be the result of active psychotic symptoms or medication use, but instead appear to reflect a neurocognitive vulnerability or predisposition to Schizophrenia (M. F. Green, 2001). With regard to Schizophrenia subtypes, although it has often been assumed that individuals with the paranoid subtype display higher general intelligence than individuals diagnosed with nonparanoid forms of the disorder, a comprehensive review of the literature found little supportive evidence (Zalewski, Johnson-Selfridge, Ohriner, Zarrella, & Seltzer, 1998).

Although the cognitive deficits associated with Schizophrenia appear to unfold across development, it does not appear that there is a continual and progressive decline that extends into old age, as would be seen in a progressive dementing condition (Abi-Dargham, Jaskiw, Suddath, & Weinberger, 1991; Burton et al., 1990; T. E. Goldberg, Hyde, Kleinman, & Weinberger, 1993; Weinberger, Jeste, & Wyatt, 1987). Significant, progressive declines in cognitive functioning in elderly schizophrenic individuals may be more closely related to other neurological insults resulting from comorbid medical conditions, systemic illnesses, history of head trauma, or substance abuse than to the Schizophrenia process itself (T. E. Goldberg et al., 1993).

Onset, Course, and Life Span Considerations

Onset

Although men and women appear equally affected by Schizophrenia, the age of onset is often later for women (i.e., median onset age = late 20s) than men (i.e., median onset age = early to mid-20s; American Psychiatric Association, 2000b). In late-onset cases, a higher female-to-male ratio is seen. Cases of childhood and late onset (i.e., prior to age 15 and after age 45, respectively) are rare and will be addressed shortly.

Course

Schizophrenia is a chronic illness, and the most productive years of an individual's life are affected. It has been estimated that 50% of individuals diagnosed with Schizophrenia become significantly and permanently disabled by the disorder (Rupp & Keith, 1993). Individuals with prominent negative symptoms are particularly likely to experience severe functional impairment that may lead to irreversible disability (Fenton & McGlashan, 1991). Impairment in vocational ability appears strongly tied to neurocognitive deficits. For example, impairments in attention, cognitive flexibility, and verbal memory predict poorer work performance (Bryson & Bell, 2003).

Longitudinal studies of psychosis illuminate the course and outcomes associated with disorders such as Schizophrenia, but they are difficult to conduct and compare because of the heterogeneity of cohorts studied, differences in diagnostic methods utilized, and variability in how outcome is defined and evaluated (McGlashan, 1988; Ram, Bromet, Eaton, Pato, & Schwarz, 1992; Westermeyer & Harrow, 1988). Because effective medications to treat Schizophrenia have been available for several decades, it is difficult to know what the "natural" course of this disorder is in large numbers of untreated individuals. The Iowa 500 study (1934–1944), which provides a close approximation to the natural course of Schizophrenia, found that the illness was associated with significantly poorer outcome compared to individuals with other mental disorders or medical illnesses (Tsuang, Woolson, & Fleming, 1979). Other researchers have found that in comparisons with Schizoaffective Disorder, Schizotypal Personality Disorder, Borderline Personality Disorder, and unipolar and bipolar affective disorders (Tsuang et al., 1979), those with Schizophrenia have poorer outcome (see McGlasahan, 1988, for a review).

Although outcome tends to be worst for Schizophrenia when all psychotic disorders are considered, the progressive deterioration in functioning that Kraepelin initially asserted as a key feature of the illness has not been borne out by long-term follow-up studies. Instead, it appears that the deterioration in functioning that occurs early in the illness process plateaus at about 5 to 10 years after the illness has been clearly established (Carpenter & Strauss, 1991; McGlashan, 1988); however, some studies have documented continued deterioration 14 to 17 years postonset (Jonsson & Nyman, 1990). The majority of individuals diagnosed with Schizophrenia will experience persistent or episodic symptoms that will significantly interfere with psychosocial functioning (e.g., work, relationships). However, the percentage of schizophrenic individuals who are so disabled by their symptoms as to require continuous, institutional care appears to be low (Westermeyer & Harrow, 1988).

Outcome in Schizophrenia is characterized by considerable heterogeneity, with as many as one fourth of patients experiencing a complete symptomatic remission (Merry & Werry, 2001). Predictors of Schizophrenia outcome can be classified under several categories: illness characteristics, psychosocial factors, and family history (Table 9.6).

Prominent negative symptoms have been repeatedly linked to poor outcome. For example, Fenton and McGlashan (1991) found that Schizophrenia characterized by many negative symptoms was associated with poor premorbid functioning, insidious onset, partial or no remissions during the first several years of illness, and in the majority of cases a

Table 9.6   Predictors of outcome in Schizophrenia

Good	Poor
Female	Male
Good premorbid functioning (e.g., work, social relationships)	Poor premorbid adjustment
Higher IQ	Poor academic functioning
Acute onset	Early or insidious onset
Short illness	History of institutionalization
Prominent positive symptoms	Prominent negative symptoms
Family history of affective disorder	Family history of Schizophrenia
Highly systematized delusions	Disorganized thinking
Cohesive family available	Family disruption
Supportive, low-key family environment	Critical or overinvolved family
Early and available treatment	Delayed entry into treatment
Resides in developing country	Disorganized or undifferentiated subtype
	Emotional blunting
	Assaultiveness
	Schizoid personality or being a loner

progressive course leading to permanent disability. The deficit syndrome mentioned previously has been associated with cognitive deficits (especially on tasks that assess frontal and parietal lobe functions; Bilder, Mukherjee, Rieder, & Pandurangi, 1985; R. W. Buchanan et al., 1994), poor premorbid adjustment and outcome (Pogue-Geile & Harrow, 1984, 1985), neuropathological and neurological abnormalities (Johnstone et al., 1978; Katsanis & Iacono, 1991; Marks & Luchins, 1990; Stevens, 1982), and poor response to neuroleptic medication (Angrist, Rotrosen, & Gershon, 1980). Although Schizophrenia is considered to be a disorder with strong biological underpinnings (discussed under "Etiology"), it is worth noting the influence that the social environment can have on the course of this disorder. This is demonstrated most robustly in a series of studies on expressed emotion (EE), which have demonstrated a significantly higher relapse rate among clients residing in high EE home environments (i.e., characterized by elevated levels of criticism, hostility, and emotional overinvolvement) compared to clients residing in low EE homes (Butzlaff & Hooley, 1998). It is important to remember that prognosis is a dimensional phenomenon that is influenced by a multitude of factors, such that there is no categorical set of criteria that define good or poor prognoses (McGlashan, 1988). Predictors also appear to vary with regard to which particular outcomes they best predict (e.g., premorbid social functioning may do a better job at predicting postillness social functioning but not symptomatic relapse) and over what time period their prognostic power is greatest (e.g., premorbid functioning strongly predicts outcome within the first decade or so of illness, whereas genetic predisposition may have greater predictive power 3 decades or more after an index episode; McGlashan, 1986a, 1986b). Factors that have linked to poor and good outcome in Schizophrenia are summarized in Table 9.6.

Because Schizophrenia is a disorder typically characterized by a relapse-remission course, it is important to intervene at the earliest possible sign of an impending relapse to prevent its occurrence or shorten its duration. A number of investigations have examined whether exacerbation of psychotic symptoms is preceded by characteristic symptoms and behaviors, collectively known as a *prodrome* (from the Greek word *prodromos* or "running before").

Some studies have shown that a high percentage of clients (e.g., upwards of 80%) are able to identify such characteristic symptoms, and there is often a high degree of agreement between clients and family members about the symptoms noted (Herz & Lamberti, 1995; Herz & Melville, 1980; Kumar, Thara, & Rajkumar, 1989). Prodromal symptoms can be idiosyncratic, may include milder versions of psychotic phenomena, and commonly involve nonpsychotic changes in mood and behavior such as moderate to severe dysphoria, anxiety, social withdrawal, irritability, sleep disturbance, loss of appetite, restlessness, concentration difficulties, agitation, and loss of interest (Herz & Lamberti, 1995; Subotnik & Nuechterlein, 1988). Identification of prodromal signs can help the schizophrenic client develop greater insight into and understanding of his or her illness and can lead to the development of specific coping strategies and preventative measures.

Life Span Considerations

Childhood-onset Schizophrenia, typically defined as onset prior to age 15, is an extremely rare but especially devastating disorder. The prevalence rate is estimated at .14 cases in 1,000, which is almost 50 times lower than the prevalence rate for adult-onset cases (McKenna, Gordon, & Rapoport, 1994). Males tend to predominate in cases of childhood Schizophrenia where onset is prior to age 14 (Remschmidt, Schulz, Martin, Warnke, & Trott, 1994). Childhood-onset Schizophrenia appears to exist on the same illness spectrum as adolescent- and adult-onset Schizophrenia, but likely reflects a stronger biological predisposition than the latter and is associated with an insidious onset, poor course, and bleak prognosis (J. R. Asarnow, Tompson, & Goldstein, 1994; A. T. Russell, 1994). Some studies have found that acute onset of symptoms and predominance of positive symptoms are associated with more favorable prognosis compared to those with slow onset, continuous cognitive impairment, and/or depressive states (Remschmidt et al., 1994). Systematic investigation of childhood Schizophrenia has been complicated by changes in how this disorder has been conceptualized. Prior to the *DSM-III* (American Psychiatric Association, 1980), the term "childhood schizophrenia" was used to refer to children with Schizophrenia, autism, and other severe mental disorders. Although subsequent editions of the *DSM* have differentiated childhood Schizophrenia from the pervasive developmental disorders, attempts to reliably and adequately define this disorder have been hampered by the illness's rarity, children's developmental limitations in describing complex symptoms, and the challenges faced in differentiating psychotic phenomena (e.g., hallucinations, delusions) from normal childhood experiences (A. T. Russell, 1994). With regard to the last, it is important not to confuse psychotic symptoms with imaginary companions, which young children often report.

These limitations notwithstanding, studies of children with Schizophrenia have shown that they can exhibit a wide range of psychotic symptoms that are qualitatively similar to symptoms seen in adults, although developmental variations will be present. As with adults, children with Schizophrenia experience auditory hallucinations more often than visual or other types of hallucinations. Children are likely to be frightened by such hallucinations, which are often negative or threatening in nature and may be of the command type (E. K. Spencer & Campbell, 1994). Schneiderian symptoms of voices maintaining a running commentary or conversing with each other occur less frequently (A. T. Russell, 1994). Delusions (e.g., persecutory, somatic) are common in children with Schizophrenia and tend to be less complex and less fixed at younger ages. As with adults, delusions often occur in the context of hallucinations; for example, E. K. Spencer and Campbell describe a 5-year-old boy who believed that there was a baby inside his throat who told him to kill himself. Rates of formal thought disorder in children with Schizophrenia vary widely across studies (e.g., 40% to 100%), but difficulties in defining and measuring thinking disturbances in children may account for these discrepant estimates (A. T. Russell, 1994). Flattened or inappropriate affect is frequently observed, whereas grossly disorganized behavior appears less common. Studies of neurocognitive functioning in children with Schizophrenia reveal similar impairments as individuals with adult-onset Schizophrenia (e.g., attention, learning, abstraction), particularly difficulty with tasks that make heavy demands on information-processing resources (R. F. Asarnow et al., 1994; Kumra et al., 2000). Neuroimaging studies suggest that childhood-onset Schizophrenia is associated with abnormalities that are similar to those associated with adult-onset forms of the illness, such as decreased gray matter and caudate volumes and increased ventricles (Mehler & Warnke, 2002).

The average age of onset of psychotic symptoms for childhood Schizophrenia has been reported to be between 7 and 9 years of age, although nonpsychotic symptoms may be apparent 2 or more years earlier (reflecting an insidious onset; A. T. Russell, 1994). Because the disorder is so rare, it may be mistaken for other clinical conditions such as a pervasive developmental disorder or a disruptive behavior disorder, and accurate diagnosis may not take place for more than a year after the onset of psychotic symptoms. A significant percentage of children with childhood Schizophrenia are likely to meet criteria for other disorders as well, including conduct and mood disorders (J. R. Asarnow et al., 1994; A. T. Russell, 1994).

Treatment of childhood Schizophrenia involves neuroleptic medication to control symptoms; in cases of chronic psychosis, depot neuroleptic medication (i.e., medication administered via injection that is subsequently slowly released in the body over several weeks) may need to be considered. In terms of psychotherapeutic treatment, Remschmidt et al. (1994) identify provision of information about the disorder and related problems to parents and clients (the latter in a developmentally appropriate manner) as the primary goal, and supportive interventions designed to assist the child and family in learning to cope with stress in a way that prevents relapses and symptom exacerbations as additional important treatment components. Family counseling can target the emotional sequelae of the child's diagnosis and can teach parents practical skills for dealing with their child's behavior.

In late life, elderly schizophrenics appear to have fewer active positive symptoms and more residual or negative symptoms compared to when they were younger, and the appearance of new symptoms is rare (Belitsky & McGlashan, 1993; Ciompi, 1980). Although many individuals with Schizophrenia experience an attenuation of their illness as they age, elderly schizophrenics who have not fully recovered or stabilized into a mild residual state remain at elevated risk for institutionalization (Mulsant et al., 1993). It has been estimated that 23% of schizophrenics have a late onset of the disorder (i.e., after 40 to 45 years of age), although estimates vary across studies due to differences in case-finding methodologies and diagnostic methods (M. J. Harris & Jeste, 1988). The proportion of females to males is greater in late-onset Schizophrenia than earlier onset cases, and while individuals with late-onset Schizophrenia are more likely to have been married than their earlier onset counterparts, they are still more socially isolated and impaired compared to the general population (American Psychiatric Association, 2000b). Compared to their earlier onset counterparts, those with late-onset Schizophrenia are more likely to experience persecutory delusions, visual and olfactory hallucinations, partition delusions (i.e., belief that living organisms, radiation, other materials, can pass through objects normally considered barriers to them), and auditory hallucinations that involve a running commentary or accusatory or abusive communications (Moran & Lawlor, 2005). Some studies have suggested that late-onset psychosis is associated with sensory impairments (e.g., hearing loss) that may facilitate the development of psychotic symptoms through such mechanisms as sensory deprivation, social isolation, and misinterpretation of environmental stimuli; however, several studies in this area are marred by methodological limitations (e.g., lack of case-control design or standardized procedures for assessing psychiatric diagnosis and sensory impairment; Prager & Jeste, 1993).

Evidence is mixed regarding the relationship of dementia to late-onset Schizophrenia. Some studies have found the cognitive deficit profile of late-onset Schizophrenia cases more similar to earlier onset cases than to degenerative dementia and no significantly increased risk for developing a degenerative dementia compared to late-onset cases of other psychiatric disorders. However, other investigations have found increased risk of developing dementia of the Alzheimer's type in late-onset schizophrenics relative to healthy controls (see Moran & Lawlor, 2005, for a review).

SCHIZOAFFECTIVE DISORDER

Prior to the *DSM-III*, the presence of mood-incongruent psychotic symptoms in individuals with affective disorders typically led to a diagnosis of Schizoaffective Disorder. However, beginning with the *DSM-III* (American Psychiatric Association, 1980), Schizoaffective Disorder was conceptualized in terms of the timing and duration of mood and psychotic symptoms relative to one another, rather than the content of psychotic symptoms, and a specific criteria set for Schizoaffective Disorder was established in the *DSM-III-R* (American Psychiatric Association, 1987). The confusion about the diagnostic criteria for Schizoaffective Disorder reflects the lack of clarity regarding the degree to which Schizophrenia and psychotic mood disorders are truly separate conditions (A. Frances et al., 1995).

Clinical Presentation

Concurrent Psychotic and Mood Symptoms

Schizoaffective Disorder is characterized by the co-occurrence of psychotic and affective symptoms. According to the *DSM-IV-TR*, the individual must meet symptom criteria for Schizophrenia, while at the same time meeting criteria for a manic, mixed, or depressive episode (the last must include depressed mood rather than a loss for interest in activities, since the latter symptom is a common negative symptom of Schizophrenia). In addition, across the entire course of the individual's illness, mood symptoms must be present for a substantial proportion of the time (American Psychiatric Association, 2000b). This requirement is a reminder that the mere presence of affective symptoms (e.g., either depression or mania) in someone who is schizophrenic does not automatically indicate a Schizoaffective Disorder. For example (as discussed under "Common Comorbidities"), depression is fairly common in Schizophrenia, and not all schizophrenic individuals who experience depression during the course of their illness would qualify for a diagnosis of Schizoaffective Disorder according to *DSM-IV-TR* criteria. Unfortunately, the *DSM-IV* does not operationalize what is meant by mood symptoms being present for a substantial portion of the entire illness, but A. Frances et al. (1995) suggest using the rule of thumb that mood symptoms should constitute at least 10% of the total illness duration.

Psychosis in the Absence of Mood Symptoms

Another important aspect of Schizoaffective Disorder is the occurrence of psychotic symptoms in the absence of prominent mood symptoms during an illness episode. The *DSM-IV-TR* specifies that during the same illness episode in which psychotic symptoms and mood symptoms have co-occurred, there must be at least 2 weeks when psychotic symptoms (e.g., delusions, hallucinations) were present in the absence of significant mood symptoms (American Psychiatric Association, 2000b). These psychotic symptoms might precede or follow the period during which there is overlap between the mood and psychotic symptoms.

Onset, Course, and Life Span Considerations

Onset

The onset of Schizoaffective Disorder is typically in early adulthood and may be preceded by Schizoid, Schizotypal, Paranoid, or Borderline Personality Disorder (American Psychiatric Association, 2000b). In addition, it is not uncommon for individuals initially diagnosed with Schizoaffective Disorder to change diagnoses over time. Samson, Simpson, and Tsuang (1988) estimated that approximately 10% of individuals diagnosed with Schizoaffective Disorder shift their diagnosis over time, with their symptoms either becoming predominantly affective or psychotic. J. E. Schwartz et al. (2000) found the instability of Schizoaffective Disorder diagnoses quite high, with only 36% maintaining this diagnosis over a 2-year period.

Course

Outcome is variable due to the heterogeneous group of clients who end up with a diagnosis of Schizoaffective Disorder. Recovery rates have been estimated to be as high as 85% in short-term studies to 50% in long-term studies, with 25% estimated to exhibit a deteriorating course (Samson et al., 1988). Comparisons with Schizophrenia have usually found that schizoaffective clients exhibit less or sometimes equal impairment in terms of occupational and symptomatic functioning, and rarely as a group do worse (Harrow & Grossman, 1984). The outcome of Schizoaffective Disorder, bipolar type (i.e., where mood symptoms include manic or mixed episodes) may be better than for the depressive type (American Psychiatric Association, 2000b). Although the results are not entirely consistent, in general it appears that compared to affectively disordered individuals, persons with Schizoaffective Disorder tend to show greater global impairment, are similar in terms of symptomatic measures of outcome, and tend to have similar or worse social and occupational functioning (Samson et al., 1988). The presence of mood-incongruent psychotic features has been shown to predict poorer outcome in this group (L. S. Grossman, Harrow, Fudala, & Meltzer, 1984).

Life Span Considerations

Relatively little has been written specifically about Schizoaffective Disorder among either children or older adults. For both children with Schizoaffective Disorder and those with Schizophrenia, there is often a long delay between when either parents first notice something is wrong with their child or psychotic symptoms appear and when an eventual diagnosis of a psychotic disorder is made (e.g., 2 and 4.5 years, respectively; J. C. Schaeffer & Ross, 2002). Data from the Child and Adolescent First-Episode Psychosis Study, a multicenter, longitudinal project of youth with psychotic disorders, revealed that a diagnosis of Schizoaffective Disorder was relatively rare in a sample of 110 children ages 9 to 17 who presented following a first episode of psychosis. Only 4.5% of the sample were diagnosed with Schizoaffective Disorder, and the most common diagnoses were Psychotic Disorder NOS (35.5%) and Schizophreniform Disorder (24.5%); individuals with Schizophrenia accounted for 10% of the sample. Interestingly, affective disorder diagnoses accounted for nearly one fourth of the sample, which the study authors note is consistent with other research finding that children with psychotic symptoms are often initially diagnosed with mood disorders (Castro-Fornieles et al., 2007).

Studies examining long-term outcome in Schizophrenia often group together individuals with Schizophrenia and those with Schizoaffective Disorder based on the close relationship the two disorders are hypothesized to have given treatment response and family studies (Bartels, Mueser, & Miles, 1997). In a long-term follow-up of individuals with Schizophrenia or Schizoaffective Disorder treated at Chestnut Lodge (a residential facility that pioneered work in the intensive treatment of serious mental illness), few differences were observed between the groups, with the exception of a finding that a measure of global functioning was significantly correlated with age in the schizoaffective but not the schizophrenic group. This suggests that advancing age may be more likely to be associated with improvements in general functioning for individuals with Schizoaffective Disorder (McGlashan, 1988). However, in a study examining subsyndromal affective symptoms in a sample of chronically ill individuals with *DSM-IV* diagnoses of Schizophrenia or Schizoaffective Disorder (mean age 53 years), Zisook et al. (2006) found that those with Schizoaffective Disorder appeared more depressed, obtained higher scores on a brief depression assessment instrument, and endorsed more intense "guilty" ideas than those with Schizophrenia; however, the two groups obtained similar scores on other depression symptoms. The study authors concluded that increased depressive symptoms may be a core feature of Schizoaffective Disorder and that further study is needed to determine the value of symptoms such as guilty ideas of reference in predicting individuals prone to future major depressive episodes.

SCHIZOPHRENIFORM DISORDER AND BRIEF PSYCHOTIC DISORDER

Schizophreniform Disorder

Clinical Presentation

According to the *DSM-IV-TR*, diagnostic criteria for Schizophreniform Disorder are identical to those for Schizophrenia, except the total duration of illness is at least 1 month but no longer than 6 months (this includes prodromal, active, and residual phases of the illness), and there is no requirement that social or occupational functioning be impaired during the duration of the illness (although this can occur; American Psychiatric Association, 2000b). In essence, then, Schizophreniform Disorder is like Schizophrenia, but of brief duration. This diagnosis may be given to individuals who have fully recovered from their symptoms by the 6-month mark, or those who have not yet reached this time requirement and therefore have not been ill long enough to meet diagnostic criteria for Schizophrenia (American Psychiatric Association, 2000b). When the *DSM-IV-TR* diagnostic system is used, the clinician can also indicate whether the diagnosis of Schizophreniform Disorder is associated with good prognostic features (e.g., good premorbid functioning) or without.

Onset, Course, and Life Span Considerations

As noted in the *DSM-IV-TR* (American Psychiatric Association, 2000b), there is a paucity of information available on the course of Schizophreniform Disorder. It is estimated that one third of individuals with this diagnosis recover during the 6-month period demarcated in the diagnostic criteria, and two thirds go on to receive a diagnosis of Schizophrenia or Schizoaffective Disorder.

In a study by Naz, Bromet, & Mojtabai (2003), compared to first-admission patients diagnosed with Schizophrenia, those with Schizophreniform Disorder were somewhat younger, were more likely to be working full time or in school, and had better GAF test scores prior to an index admission. Those with Schizophreniform Disorder were also hospitalized earlier in their psychosis, had less prominent negative symptoms at a baseline assessment, and were more likely to experience full remission of symptoms over a 2-year period compared to those with Schizophrenia.

Questions have been raised as to whether Schizophreniform Disorder might actually represent an atypical variant of affective disorders (Hirschowitz, Casper, Garver, & Chang, 1980). In one study, 70% of individuals who had been diagnosed with Schizophreniform Disorder with good prognostic features went on to receive affective disorder diagnoses at a 6-year follow-up (Benazzi, 1998). It is likely that the schizophreniform diagnostic category captures a heterogeneous group of individuals, some of whom have a developing Schizophrenia, some of whom will go on to develop a primary affective disorder, and still others who will display a time-limited psychotic disorder (Strakowski, 1994).

The literature on Schizophreniform Disorder at either end of the age spectrum is limited. There is evidence that as children, adults later diagnosed with Schizophreniform Disorder display notable impairments in cognitive development, neuromotor abilities, and receptive language that are not directly related to factors such as socioeconomic variables or obstetric complications (Cannon et al., 2002). Similarly, a study by Poulton et al. (2000) found that self-reported hallucinatory experiences and delusional beliefs in

11-year-old children were associated with increased risk of a Schizophreniform Disorder diagnosis at age 26 and that children with prominent psychotic symptoms were 16 times more likely to have a Schizophreniform Disorder diagnosis in adulthood.

Brief Psychotic Disorder

Clinical Presentation

Brief Psychotic Disorder, according to the *DSM-IV-TR*, is characterized by at least one of four symptoms (e.g., delusions, hallucinations, grossly disorganized behavior or speech) that lasts at least 1 day but less than 1 month, and is followed by a return to the premorbid level of functioning (American Psychiatric Association, 2000b).

Onset, Course, and Life Span Considerations

Brief Psychotic Disorder is an illness of very short duration that typically occurs among young adults (American Psychiatric Association, 2000b). Much less has been written about Brief Psychotic Disorder relative to other psychotic conditions such as Schizophrenia and Schizoaffective Disorder. Some of what is known about this disorder comes from the literature on acute transient psychosis, a diagnostic category included in the *ICD-10* (WHO, 1993), which is a broader diagnostic category that also includes cases of *DSM-IV*-defined Schizophreniform Disorder.

In general, acute and transient psychotic disorders, including Brief Psychotic Disorder, are often associated with good premorbid functioning, female gender, and a high prevalence (i.e., 63%) of personality disorders, with no one personality disorder category predominating (Jorgensen, Bennedsen, Christensen, & Hyllested, 1996). The disorder may follow the occurrence of an acute stressor, such as the death of a loved one, combat experiences, and even typically positive events such as the birth of a child (American Psychiatric Association, 2000b). Postpartum psychosis is a rare but dangerous condition that is estimated to affect 0.01% of the population (Halbreich, 2005). Women with postpartum psychosis may develop delusional beliefs about their infant that place the child at risk (e.g., believing the baby is evil), and therefore aggressive and immediate treatment is imperative to assure the safety of both mother and child.

The *DSM-IV-TR* allows the clinician to use specifiers when assigning a diagnosis of Brief Psychotic Disorder to indicate the occurrence of a stressor in association with the disorder's symptoms (American Psychiatric Association, 2000b). Interestingly, although psychotic symptoms may develop following an acute stressor, Jorgensen et al. (1996) found that acute transient psychotic disorders were associated with no or minor or moderate stressors in samples they studied.

Transient psychotic disorders are associated with more favorable outcomes compared to disorders such as Schizophrenia, and, as previously noted, an eventual return to premorbid levels of functioning is a required symptom for Brief Psychotic Disorder. Pillmann and Marneros (2005) found that at three follow-up periods (covering either a 7- or 12-year period after the index episode), individuals with *ICD-10*-defined acute, transient psychotic disorders did not exhibit deterioration in functioning, in contrast to a comparison group of persons with Schizophrenia. In addition, at the end of the follow-up period, 31% of those with acute, transient psychotic disorders were functioning well without medication compared to 0% of the Schizophrenia comparison group. Despite long-term outcome being generally favorable for transient psychotic states, risk of suicide is of concern. The prevalence of suicidal behavior among those with transient psychotic disorders is estimated to be approximately 36%, with the greatest risk being during the period of acute psychotic symptomatology (Pillmann, Balzuweit, Haring, Bloink, & Marneros, 2003).

DELUSIONAL DISORDER

Clinical Presentation

Presence of Nonbizarre Delusions

As the name implies, the central feature of a Delusional Disorder is an encapsulated, false, nonbizarre belief or set of beliefs held with delusional intensity. *DSM-IV-TR* diagnostic criteria require that the delusion be present for at least 1 month (American Psychiatric Association, 2000b). Although more than one type of delusion (e.g., erotomanic, grandiose, jealous, persecutory, somatic) may occur in Delusional Disorder, delusions tend to cluster around a single, overarching theme. Examples of delusions from many of these categories were presented earlier in Table 9.3. Using the *DSM-IV-TR* system, a clinician must specify the type of delusion that the client endorses when assigning a Delusional Disorder diagnosis.

It can be especially difficult to differentiate a delusion from an overvalued idea in a person suspected of Delusional Disorder because, by definition, the delusion must concern something that is plausible (i.e., nonbizarre). For example, imagine during an intake interview that an appropriately groomed, well-mannered, articulate male client who is a successful small business owner tells you that he is certain his wife of 10 years is being unfaithful to him (although he reports that she adamantly denies this). He cites as his only evidence a few hang-up calls he has received at home and several occasions when his wife has arrived home slightly later than expected from her job across town. Is this man delusional, or does his jealously represent a strongly held belief that has not quite reached the threshold of a delusion? It can also be challenging to differentiate Delusional Disorder from nonpsychotic disorders such as Body Dysmorphic Disorder, Somatization Disorder, Hypochondriasis, and Obsessive-Compulsive Disorder, all of which are characterized by strongly held beliefs for which there is no clearly supportive evidence.

Absence of Other Psychotic Symptoms

Individuals with Delusional Disorder do not experience prominent hallucinations or other signs that are characteristic of Schizophrenia (e.g., grossly disorganized speech or behavior). The *DSM-IV-TR* Delusional Disorder criteria indicate that if tactile or olfactory hallucinations are present, they are related to the delusional theme (American Psychiatric Association, 2000b). Munro (1999) asserts that other types of hallucinations can occur in Delusional Disorder besides olfactory and tactile, even though this is not explicitly mentioned in the *DSM-IV-TR*; however, in all cases, the hallucinations are generally not intrusive.

Psychosocial Functioning

Unlike individuals with Schizophrenia, who are typically markedly impaired by their symptoms, those with Delusional Disorder typically do not display notably unusual behavior or significant functional impairment. In fact, the *DSM-IV-TR* requires that functioning be relatively unimpaired for a diagnosis to be made (American Psychiatric Association, 2000b). Because of the encapsulated nature of the psychotic symptoms, the delusion is not likely to interfere with the client's general logical reasoning abilities, and the delusion itself is apt to be logical in construction and internally consistent (even though the content may sound unbelievable or strange; Munro, 1999). A delusional person may also be able to blend in by joining a group with a belief structure that is broadly supportive of his or her views (e.g., an individual with conspiratorial delusions about the government may join a political action group), further making detection of any problem difficult.

Onset, Course, and Life Span Considerations

The onset of a Delusional Disorder can vary from adolescence to late life and may be gradual or acute. The course of the disorder is chronic and frequently lifelong. Men and women appear equally affected; many individuals with the disorder are unmarried, separated, divorced, or widowed; and the premorbid personality is likely to be isolative and asocial (Munro, 1999). Treatment of Delusional Disorder is difficult because these clients rarely seek out treatment and are likely to express considerable distrust of the clinician if they do agree to treatment. Considerable time will need to be spent earning the client's trust, and it may take several sessions to convince the client to consider a medication (neuroleptic) trial. Even if the client agrees to such a trial, there is a high likelihood of eventual noncompliance. However, if a client is willing to comply with treatment, the prognosis for Delusional Disorder is reasonably good across subtypes (Munro & Mok, 2006). In a summary of published cases of nonorganic Delusional Disorder, Manschreck and Khan (2006) found that 50% exhibited a positive response to pharmacologic interventions, which consisted of treatment with a first- or second-generation antipsychotic medication. There have also been case reports of the successful use of electroconvulsive (shock) therapy to treat Delusional Disorder (Ota et al., 2003). Cognitive-behavioral approaches may be helpful in the treatment of delusions, but exploratory, "uncovering" psychotherapy is contraindicated (Munro, 1999).

EPIDEMIOLOGY

Schizophrenia

The lifetime prevalence rate for Schizophrenia is approximately 1% (range = 0.5% to 1.6%; Jablensky, 1995), and rates of the disorder are fairly consistent around the world. For example, data from the World Health Organization's large-scale epidemiologic study of Schizophrenia in 13 catchment areas spread across North and South America, Europe, West Africa, Japan, and the Indian subcontinent demonstrated that when a narrow definition of Schizophrenia is utilized (e.g., characterized by Schneiderian first-rank symptoms), reported rates range from .7 to .14 per 1,000, with no statistically significant differences observed between sites. This study found that although lifetime risk for the illness was approximately equal for men and women, men were overrepresented in the 15- to 24-year-old age group and women in the 35- to 54-year-old group (Jablensky et al., 1992). The fairly consistent rates of Schizophrenia that have been reported across epidemiologic studies can be interpreted as indirectly supporting a common, fundamental genetic basis of the illness or might indicate a syndromal admixture effect, whereby Schizophrenia is the final common pathway for varying combinations of low-incidence syndromes of heterogeneous etiology but similar phenotypic expression (Jablensky, 1997).

Schizoaffective Disorder

The *DSM-IV-TR* does not specify the prevalence of Schizoaffective Disorder, noting only that it is less common than Schizophrenia (American Psychiatric Association, 2000b). Part of the difficulty in determining rates of Schizoaffective Disorder concerns changes in the conceptualization and definition of this condition over time (First & Tasman, 2005). Examining data across studies, it appears that the lifetime prevalence of Schizoaffective Disorder is approximately 0.5% (Kempf, Hussain, & Potash, 2005).

Schizophreniform Disorder and Brief Psychotic Disorder

The prevalence of Schizophreniform Disorder may be as much as 5 times less than that of Schizophrenia, and Brief Psychotic Disorder is rarely encountered in the United States (American Psychiatric Association, 2000b). Pillmann and Marneros (2005) estimate that *ICD-10*-defined acute and transient psychotic disorders (which would subsume Schizophreniform Disorder and brief reactive psychosis) may account for between 8% and 9% of all psychotic disorders. Interestingly, psychotic conditions lasting between 1 and 6 months appear more common in developing countries, which may be due to the more benign course (and hence greater remission rate of symptoms) often seen in these regions (American Psychiatric Association, 2000b).

Delusional Disorder

The prevalence for Delusional Disorder is estimated to be 0.03% and to account for 1% to 4% of hospital admissions (American Psychiatric Association, 2000b). The disorder is more commonly diagnosed in women than men, by some accounts at a 3:1 ratio (Kelly, 2005). Clinicians' lack of familiarity with the illness and a tendency to misdiagnose Delusional Disorder as one of the more well-known psychotic disorders such as Schizophrenia may contribute to an underestimation of the this disorder's prevalence (Munro, 1999).

ETIOLOGY

Schizophrenia

The speculation by Kraepelin and Bleuler that Schizophrenia is a brain disease must have been a radical assertion in the early twentieth century, but it is now commonly accepted among members of the mental health community. Although we do not yet know the precise causes of Schizophrenia, research evidence indicates that the disorder is developmental in origin and involves the interaction of a number of factors (genetic, biological, environmental) that alter the path of normal brain development. Although research on psychosocial stressors suggests that aspects of the social environment may heighten an existing risk for the disorder or affect illness course, purely psychogenic theories of Schizophrenia (prominent in the 1940s and 1950s) that implicated inadequate parenting (e.g., the "schizophrenogenic mother") and disturbed family relationships and communication patterns as the primary causes of the disorder are no longer considered credible.

Although Kraepelin and Bleuer suspected that Schizophrenia runs in families, they did not have the benefit of a modern science of genetics to verify their intuition. Several decades later, Meehl (1962) postulated that Schizophrenia arose from a genetic predisposition (*schizotaxia*) that he believed could interact with other genetic and environmental factors to produce a latent (unobservable) personality organization (known as *schizotypy*) that placed an individual at risk for developing Schizophrenia. Depending on a number of factors, a *schizotype* could go on to develop Schizophrenia or Schizotypal Personality Disorder or might manifest symptoms (e.g., cognitive slippage, anxiety, depression, interpersonal aversion, behavioral eccentricities) that did not rise to the level of a diagnosable mental disturbance (Lenzenweger, 1998; Meehl, 1990). Evidence from twin, family, adoption, and longitudinal studies has substantiated many of Meehl's hypotheses (Gottesman, 1991; Lenzenweger, 1998). Biological relatives of schizophrenic individuals have a much greater risk for developing schizophrenia spectrum disorders (e.g., Schizophrenia, Schizotypal Personality Disorder, Paranoid Personality Disorder) than the general population, and the risk of developing Schizophrenia increases with the degree of genetic relatedness with an affected individual (Gottesman & Moldin, 1998; Kendler & Diehl, 1993). The chance of developing Schizophrenia with no family history of the illness is approximately 1%; the chance increases to about 3% if one has a schizophrenic uncle or aunt (i.e., second-degree relative); 5% to 10% if one has a schizophrenic parent, sibling, or nonidentical (dizygotic) twin; 15% to 20% if both parents are schizophrenic; and 48% if one has an identical (monozygotic) twin with the disorder (Gottesman & Moldin, 1999; Mueser & Gingrich, 1994). Studies of identical twins reared apart and adoption studies demonstrate that the elevated rates of Schizophrenia among biologically related individuals cannot primarily be attributed to shared environmental factors (Heston, 1966; Kety, 1988; Lowing, Mirsky, & Pereira, 1983). In addition, a significant percentage of unaffected biological relatives of schizophrenics exhibit cognitive deficits similar to those displayed by people with Schizophrenia, including impairments in eye-tracking ability (e.g., difficulty smoothly following a moving target with the eyes), motor ability (e.g., gait and balance disturbances, poor coordination), perceptual motor speed, short-term memory, sustained attention, verbal ability (e.g., loose associations, word-finding difficulty, conceptual disorganization), and executive functions (i.e., problems in cognitive abilities related to planning and abstract thought; Faraone, Green, Sidman, & Tsuang, 2001; Nuechterlein, 1985).

Unlike disorders such as Huntington's disease, Schizophrenia appears to involve multiple genes based on the complicated patterns in which the disorder and conditions related to it aggregate in families (Gottesman, 1991). Several potentially promising chromosomal regions that may be linked to Schizophrenia have been identified, but no specific genes have yet been definitively implicated in the disorder (Andreasen, 2001). The fact that the concordance rate (i.e., the percentage of twin pairs in which both individuals are affected by the same disorder) for Schizophrenia among monozygotic twins is not 100% indicates that genes are not the only relevant factor in this illness. The *diathesis-stress model* of Schizophrenia (Zubin & Spring, 1977) suggests that a biological vulnerability is necessary but not sufficient for the development of the disorder, and additional factors (stressors) are needed for the illness to manifest itself. Gottesman likens the risk for Schizophrenia to a balance sheet composed of genetic and environmental assets and liabilities (each with different weights, because all factors are not equal in influence); when an individual's "bottom-line value" exceeds a particular threshold value, Schizophrenia will result.

Mednick's "two-hit" model (Mednick et al., 1998) proposes that Schizophrenia results from a combination of two sets of factors, or "hits": the first is a liability for Schizophrenia that is genetically inherited or that is caused by a teratogenic factor such as maternal influenza exposure in the second trimester of pregnancy. Such teratogens are thought to mimic or exacerbate genetic effects. The first hit disrupts normal development of fetal brain areas relevant in Schizophrenia (e.g., prefrontal cortex), which increases the risk for developing the disorder by making the affected individual more vulnerable to "second hit" environmental stressors such as maternal starvation (especially in the first trimester), obstetrical complications at birth (e.g., anoxic or hypoxic episodes), or severe early childhood stress (e.g., institutional care). An individual who has the first hit but is lucky enough to escape the second hit is hypothesized to be at risk for developing a less severe Schizophrenia spectrum disorder such as Schizotypal Personality Disorder. This model underscores the idea that Schizophrenia is characterized by aberrant brain development that begins at the earliest stages of life.

Several lines of evidence support the idea that Schizophrenia is a neurodevelopmental disorder, including neuroimaging studies of individuals recently diagnosed with Schizophrenia that reveal brain abnormalities such as enlarged ventricles and sulci, decreased overall brain volume, and decreased volume of the prefrontal cortex and hippocampus. As these were first-episode individuals examined shortly after their illness onset, the observed brain abnormalities are likely to be developmental in origin and not due to the effects of chronic illness or long-term medication use (Andreasen, 2001). Several other brain abnormalities that have been found in individuals with Schizophrenia are in hemispheric asymmetry, increased size of basal ganglia structures (although this may be due to neuroleptic medication response), and reduced size of the thalamus, posterior temporal gyrus, and superior temporal gyrus (Cornblatt, Green, & Walker, 1999). The superior temporal gyrus is linked to auditory processing; abnormalities in this brain area are believed to relate to formal thought disorder and hallucinations (M. F. Green, 2001).

Longitudinal studies of children at risk for developing Schizophrenia (i.e., born to a schizophrenic mother; Fish, 1987) and studies of the childhood home movies of adult schizophrenics (E. F. Walker, Grimes, Davis, & Smith, 1993) have found evidence of emotional, motor, and reflex abnormalities (e.g., unusual foot postures or gait, abnormal muscular tone, nystagmus) that far predated the onset of overt symptoms of Schizophrenia. Such children frequently have attentional problems, poorer school performance, impaired social adjustment, and lower IQ scores relative to controls (Niemi, Suvisaari, Tuulio-Henriksson, & Lönnqvist, 2003).

In addition, schizophrenics show elevated rates of minor physical anomalies (MPAs) and fingerprint abnormalities (e.g., greater inconsistency in the number of ridges between left- and right-hand fingerprints). The MPAs are subtle, physical aberrations that typically are not readily noticeable to others (e.g., eyes that are too close or too widely set apart, head circumference that is too large or small). Such findings suggest second trimester problems in fetal neurological development because MPAs and fingerprint abnormalities develop in utero at the same time that critical development of the nervous system takes place (M. F. Green, 2001; Mellor, 1992). These findings underscore that the roots of Schizophrenia extend back into the earliest periods of development, but it is likely that the disorder affects many stages of central nervous system development, up until the time such growth stops (i.e., the late teens to early 20s; Andreasen, 2001).

Schizophrenia is also associated with a number of neurotransmitter abnormalities. Early antipsychotic medications (also known as neuroleptics) were found to have an antagonistic effect on dopamine (i.e., blocked dopamine receptors on neurons), and it was assumed that Schizophrenia involved an excess of dopamine, which became known as the *dopamine hypothesis of schizophrenia* (Carlsson, 2001). This hypothesis was supported by findings that compounds (e.g., amphetamine) that were dopamine agonists (i.e., that bind to and stimulate dopamine receptors) could produce psychotic symptoms in some individuals. Theories about the role of dopamine in Schizophrenia have shifted from assumptions that there is a simple excess of dopamine (not always supported in the research literature; see Lieberman & Koreen, 1993) to exploration of abnormalities in dopamine receptors (e.g., receptor hyperactivity). Studies suggest that Schizophrenia is associated with an excess or increased ratio of a particular subtype of dopamine receptors (the D2 receptors; Joyce, Lexow, Bird, & Winkour, 1988; Tune et al., 1993). Increases in dopamine receptor density may be linked to prenatal exposure to stress hormones such as cortisol (Cornblatt et al., 1999). Recent research also indicates that, in addition to dopamine, other neurotransmitters are implicated in Schizophrenia, including GABA (an inhibitory neurotransmitter), glutamate, and serotonin (Cornblatt et al., 1999).

Schizoaffective Disorder

Schizoaffective Disorder has sometimes been dubbed a "wastebasket" diagnostic category into which individuals are placed who have significant psychotic and affective symptoms but who do not clearly meet criteria for a primary psychotic disorder (e.g., Schizophrenia) or a primary mood disorder (e.g., Bipolar Disorder with psychotic features). Theories of Schizoaffective Disorder range from viewing the illness as a variant of either Schizophrenia or a mood disorder, to being intermediate to both of these conditions and on the same continuum (First & Tasman, 2005). As M. F. Green (2001) notes, such varying conceptualizations have resulted in Schizoaffective Disorder being "the Alsace Lorraine of psychiatry." Family studies indicate an increased risk of Schizoaffective Disorder in first-degree relatives of schizophrenic probands that ranges from 1.4% to 3.0% (Kempf et al., 2005), which suggests a potential shared etiological basis for these two disorders. However, Schizoaffective Disorder also appears to share genetic risk with affective disorders, as demonstrated by findings of increased rates of affective illnesses (e.g., Bipolar Disorder) among the first-degree relatives of schizoaffective probands (Gershon et al., 1988). Indeed, genetic studies of Schizophrenia and Bipolar Disorder indicate that there is some overlap between genomic regions believed to be involved with both disorders (e.g., chromosomes 22q, 18q, 13q, 10p, 10q, 6q, and 5q; Berrettini, 2000; Kelsoe, 1999). These findings suggest the possibility that the same genes in these regions predispose to Schizophrenia *and* Bipolar Disorder, although it is also possible that separate genes controlling each disorder are coincidentally near one another (Kelsoe, 2003). Similarities in neuroanatomical abnormalities in Schizophrenia and psychotic affective disorders (Major Depressive Disorder and Bipolar Disorder) also suggest the possibility that these disorders may share some etiologic bases. Enlarged ventricles have been observed in Schizophrenia and psychotic depression, and reduced left frontal and temporoparietal white matter volume and high dopamine D2 receptor densities have been observed in Schizophrenia and Bipolar Disorder with psychotic features (see Kempf et al., 2005, for review).

Schizophreniform Disorder

As noted earlier, it appears that the population of individuals meeting criteria for this disorder is heterogeneous and that a certain percentage go on to develop affective disorders, suggesting that in some cases Schizophreniform Disorder may represent an atypical variant of an affective illness (Hirschowitz et al., 1980). However, the fact that a sizable proportion of those with Schizophreniform Disorder go on to meet diagnostic criteria for Schizophrenia obviously suggests the potential for shared etiologic factors between these disorders. In support of this is evidence that Schizophreniform Disorder has been associated with childhood developmental deficits in several areas, including neuromotor, language, cognitive, and interpersonal functioning, that are similar to those associated with Schizophrenia (Cannon et al., 2002). This also provides additional support for a neurodevelopmental model for Schizophrenia spectrum disorders.

Delusional Disorder

Because Delusional Disorder is not common and affected individuals do not routinely present for treatment, there is a dearth of empirical studies on the etiology of the disorder. It is not clear if Delusional Disorder is genetically related to Schizophrenia, as some studies have found a higher than expected incidence of Schizophrenia in the families of individuals with Delusional Disorder (Schanda, Berner, Gabriel, Kronberger, & Kufferle, 1983), whereas others have not (Kendler & Hays, 1981; Munro, 1982). A small-scale genetic study (Debnath, Das, Bera, Nayak, & Tapas, 2006) found an association between the HLA*A*03 allele and both Delusional Disorder and paranoid Schizophrenia, suggesting the possibility of a common genetic liability for both illnesses, although larger studies are needed to replicate this finding. There is also some evidence that Paranoid Personality Disorder and Avoidant Personality Disorder occur with an increased frequency in the families of individuals diagnosed with Delusional Disorder (American Psychiatric Association, 2000b). A number of difficulties are faced in trying to determine genetic underpinnings of Delusional Disorder, including the difficulty of ascertaining cases (which makes obtaining sufficiently large samples challenging) and the rarity of multiply affected families (which prohibits linkage studies; Cardno & McGuffin, 2006).

A neuropsychological study of 21 individuals with Delusional Disorder demonstrated deficits in metaphorical speech comprehension and executive functioning relative to normal controls, which suggests that this disorder may be characterized by subtle cognitive deficits; interestingly, this study found that performance on an emotional recognition task, an indicator of social cognition, was unimpaired (Bömmer & Brüne, 2006). Some cases of late-onset Delusional Disorder have been linked to subcortical cerebral lesions and insults (Botteron, Figiel, & Zorumski, 1991; Munro, 1999). If a neurological condition such as a head injury or stroke was causally related to the onset of delusional symptoms, the appropriate diagnosis, according to the *DSM-IV*, would be a Psychotic Disorder Due to a General Medical Condition.

DIVERSITY CONSIDERATIONS

Ethnicity and Culture

Although the clinical presentation of Schizophrenia is remarkably similar across diverse cultures (K. M. Lin & Kleinman, 1988), qualitative differences in symptoms across ethnic/cultural groups have been documented. For example, delusional content may be influenced by an individual's cultural background. Mexican American individuals diagnosed with Schizophrenia have reported a greater frequency of somatic symptoms, such as hypochondriacal concerns, and to less frequently report delusions involving persecution (e.g., by family members) or science fiction themes compared to their Anglo-American counterparts (Escobar, Randolph, & Hill, 1986; Weisman et al., 2000). K. Kim et al. (1993) found that the content of delusions across three groups of Asian schizophrenic persons varied and appeared influenced by sociocultural and political situations that differed across the three groups studied: Koreans living in South Korea and Chinese and Korean Chinese living in China. Common delusions among those in South Korea involved religious matters and economic and business matters, whereas delusions of political themes were most frequent in Korean Chinese (including persecutory delusions involving the army, police, and secret agents); somatic delusions of bloodsucking, brain or viscera extraction, and poison were most prominent in the Chinese patients. Few studies have conducted cross-cultural comparisons of negative symptoms, despite the increased interest in this symptom domain as a core feature of Schizophrenia. Dassori et al. (1998) found that Hispanic individuals with Schizophrenia obtained scores similar to Caucasian patients' on scales of a negative symptoms measure assessing alogia, avolition, and flat affect, but obtained higher scores on a cognition subscale that evaluated symptoms such as abstraction difficulties, temporal disorientation, and memory problems (although differences in level of education may have contributed to the latter finding).

Ihara, Berrios, and McKenna (2003) found that negative symptoms in individuals diagnosed with Schizophrenia were associated with everyday impairments in executive functioning in a similar manner for Japanese and British patients, suggesting that culture may not significantly influence negative symptoms.

It appears that schizophrenic individuals residing in developing countries (e.g., India, Nigeria, Colombia) exhibit a more favorable illness course than their counterparts in industrialized countries (Sartorius, Gulbinat, Harrison, Laska, & Siegel, 1996). The demands of living in a fast-paced industrialized society that emphasizes individuality and competition, combined with the erosion of extended family and social support networks in such environments, may create stressors that adversely affect the prognosis for schizophrenic individuals living in industrialized countries. The importance of an extended social support network in affecting the course of Schizophrenia is suggested by a study by Prince (2006), which found that 3 months following an index hospitalization, African American Schizophrenia patients reported a higher subjective quality of life compared to Caucasian Schizophrenia patients, even after controlling for potentially confounding variables such as symptom scores, global functioning, and the presence of comorbid substance use disorders. These findings were interpreted as potentially being related to the extended family networks that are more likely to be found in the African American community. However, Prince suggested that lowered expectations resulting from oppression and institutionalized racism could have also contributed to these findings.

As noted earlier (see "Onset, Course, and Life Span Considerations"), a family atmosphere characterized by high levels of criticism or emotional overinvolvement (high EE) is predictive of relapse among individuals with Schizophrenia (Butzlaff & Hooley, 1998). However, additional research suggests that among certain ethnic groups, such familial criticism may be less predictive of relapse. Kopelowicz and colleagues (2002) found that high EE predicted relapse for Caucasian Schizophrenia patients but not for Mexican American patients, and that Mexican American patients and their relatives reported lower rates of high EE than did their Caucasian counterparts. Similarly, López et al. (2004) found that high levels of familial criticism predicted exacerbations of psychotic symptoms following an index hospitalization for Caucasian Schizophrenia patients but not Mexican American patients, and that family warmth was a protective factor against relapse among the Mexican American but not the Caucasian patients. These researchers speculated that differing cultural values might explain these findings and hypothesized that among Mexican American families the emphasis placed on family ties might subsequently make a lack of familial warmth a significant stressor that carries a risk of inducing relapse, whereas for Caucasian families a greater emphasis on independence and autonomy might make personal criticisms by family members particularly stressful.

Gender

Women with Schizophrenia generally have a later age of onset and more favorable illness course than their male counterparts. Female schizophrenics are less likely to show evidence of early brain insults, to display antisocial behavior, and to abuse substances compared to male schizophrenics (Bardenstein & McGlashan, 1990). Negative symptoms also appear to be less common among women (Castle, Wessely, & Murray, 1993). Women with Schizophrenia also have lower rates of hospitalization and relapse, and they are more likely than men with Schizophrenia to be married, to have a better premorbid history, and to exhibit better social and overall functioning (e.g., achieving personal independence, being employed) during the course of their illness (Angermeyer & Kühn, 1988; Bardenstein & McGlashan, 1990; Häffner, 2003; Harrison, Croudace, Mason, Glazebrook, & Medley, 1996; Moldin, 2000). Some research suggests that women may cope better with the disabilities caused by Schizophrenia (e.g., adopting somewhat reduced expectations in a number of life areas; Häffner, 2003). There is also some evidence that medication and psychosocial interventions are more effective in women than men. Finally, the mortality rate (from suicide and other causes) is lower for females than for males with Schizophrenia (Bardenstein & McGlashan, 1990). It appears that over long follow-up periods, differences in outcome by gender become more attenuated (J. M. Goldstein, 1988; Opjordsmoen, 1991).

Many hypotheses have been put forth to explain the gender differences observed in Schizophrenia, including theories regarding variations in stress levels associated with different societal expectations for men versus women and the role that gender-based socialization differences may play in symptom expression. Biological theories have focused on neurologic and neuroendocrine bases for gender differences in illness expression and course, including the possible role that estrogen may play in reducing vulnerability to psychosis (by affecting dopamine in a manner similar to neuroleptic medication; Bardenstein & McGlashan, 1990; Häfneret al., 1998; Seeman & Lang, 1990). It has been suggested that the protective role of estrogen may help explain the later age of onset of Schizophrenia in women and may indirectly contribute to the higher psychosocial functioning seen in female Schizophrenia patients by allowing a higher level of social, cognitive, and personality development to occur before the illness strikes (Häffner, 2003).

INTAKE AND INTERVIEWING CONSIDERATIONS

Rapport

In the case of evaluating a potentially psychotic individual, the clinician's job is made particularly difficult because such persons may have limited insight into their symptoms, may be guarded due to paranoia, and may exhibit extremely disorganized thought processes that make it difficult to obtain clear, coherent answers to questions. The intrusion of psychotic symptoms may not only make information gathering quite difficult, but also may complicate the establishment of rapport. Therefore, patience is required to allow the client to become comfortable and develop a sense of trust in the clinician. Adopting an attitude of interested curiosity in the client's experiences is helpful in encouraging discussion of delusional material and unusual perceptual experiences. With paranoid individuals, it is important to be open and forthcoming about the process of the initial interview and how information will be handled and to encourage the client to ask questions about the treatment process. For clients with prominent negative symptoms, closed-ended questions may be more efficient and effective in gathering information. Clinicians unaccustomed to working with schizophrenic individuals with negative symptoms are prone to mistakenly assume that the clinical relationship is not important to them based on their apparent lack of overtly observable emotional responsiveness (Herz & Marder, 2001). It is likely that collateral informants such as family members, close friends or roommates, and prior treatment providers will need to be contacted to obtain additional information about the client. However, a client who is paranoid with poor insight may not consent to this and/or may not have regular contact with these individuals.

Perhaps more than any other clinical population, it can be easy for clinicians to define psychotic individuals solely in terms of their illness. Instead, one must strive to understand the person with a psychotic disorder as a complete person who, in addition to vulnerabilities and struggles, possesses strengths, aspirations, and goals (Herz & Marder, 2001).

Interview and Assessment Strategies

Although a variety of neuropsychological impairments and brain abnormalities have been documented in Schizophrenia, there is no cognitive test or brain imaging procedure that can be used to definitively diagnose this disorder. Thus diagnosis rests on clinical observation of the client and obtaining a thorough history of symptoms and the degree of associated impairment. When a psychotic disorder is high on the list of suspected diagnoses, the clinician must not only inquire about psychotic symptoms, but must also explore other diagnostic domains since psychosis can be induced by substances or a medical condition or may accompany mood disorders (e.g., Bipolar Disorder with psychotic features). In addition, the symptoms of some disorders (e.g., Obsessive-Compulsive Disorder [OCD], Body Dysmorphic Disorder) are characterized by unusual beliefs that may be mistaken for delusions.

Table 9.7 lists key points to cover in an intake interview when a psychotic disorder is suspected. These are intended to supplement more general information on what should be covered in any intake interview (see Chapter 1).

Rule Out Substances and Medical Conditions as Primary Cause of Symptoms

When evaluating a client who presents with psychotic symptoms, consideration should first be given to whether substance use or a general medical condition is the cause of the symptoms. Several substances and medical conditions (Table 9.8) can cause psychotic symptoms that appear indistinguishable from those caused by a primary psychotic disorder. For example, amphetamine use can produce symptoms that are nearly identical to those seen in paranoid Schizophrenia.

The clinician should be alert for atypical presentations such as the sudden onset of psychotic symptoms in individuals who have no history of mental problems or significant social impairment, or who are past the age of risk (i.e., adolescence, early adulthood) for the onset of a psychotic disorder. Unusual symptoms such as olfactory or gustatory hallucinations could implicate a medical condition as the cause of the psychotic symptoms

Table 9.7   Intake issues: Schizophrenia

Rule out medical or substance-related disorders.

Assess positive symptoms and impact on intake.

Evaluate negative symptoms.

Determine risk for suicide or dangerousness.

Screen for comorbid symptoms and disorders.

Inquire about level of functioning.

Identify strengths and resources (including family support).

Review medication issues: need for and compliance.

Make appropriate referrals for adjunctive treatment (e.g., medication, vocational rehabilitation).

Obtain releases to contact other treatment team members and knowledgeable others (e.g., family) to coordinate treatment and gather additional history.

Table 9.8   Substances, medications, and medical conditions that can cause psychotic symptoms

Drugs	Medical Conditions
Alcohol (withdrawal hallucinosis)	Embolism
Amantadine	Aqueduct stenosis
Amphetamine	Ischemia
Atropine	Trauma (especially temporal lobe)
Bromide	Tumor (especially limbic and basal ganglia)
Bromocriptine	Epilepsy (especially of the temporal lobe)
Cannabis (marijuana)	Narcolepsy
Carbon monoxide	Encephalitis (e.g., post-influenza)
Cimetidine	Vitamin B12 deficiency
Clonidine	AIDS
Cocaine or crack	Syphilis
Corticosteroids (ACTH, cortisone, etc.)	Tuberculous meningitis
Dexatrim	Pellagra (vitamin B6 deficiency)
Diazepam (Valium)	Hypoglycemia
Digitalis	Hyperthyroidism
Disulfiram (Antabuse)	Hepatic (liver) encephalopathy
Ephedrine	Lead poisoning
Ibuprofen	Lupus erythematosus
Indomethacin	Multiple sclerosis
Isoniazid	Uremia
Levodopa	Vasculitis
Lidocaine	Huntington's disease
LSD	Acute intermittent porphyria
MAO inhibitors	Phenylketonuria
Methamphetamine	Wilson's disease
Pentazocine (Talwin)	Metachromatic leukodystrophy
Phencyclidine (PCP, angel dust)	XXY Klinefelter karotype
Phenelzine (Nardil)	XYY karotype
Propoxyphene (Darvon)	XXX karotype
Propranolol (Inderal)	XO Turner or Noonan syndrome
Tricyclic antidepressants	Ischemia

Adapted from *Schizophrenia Genesis: The Origin of Madness*, by Irving I. Gottesman, © 1991 by Irving I. Gottesman. Used with permission of Worth Publishers.

(e.g., neurological disease or injury). Thus, if a client has not had a recent medical evaluation, the clinician should refer him or her to a physician.

Given the high incidence of comorbid substance abuse in Schizophrenia, the presence of a positive urine toxicology screen or admission by the client that he or she has recently used drugs that could produce psychotic symptoms does not rule out the possibility of a primary psychotic disorder diagnosis. In such cases, the clinician must try to determine whether the client has a history of psychotic symptoms that occurred during periods when substances were not being used or withdrawn from, and if the current psychotic symptoms are in excess of what would be expected given the type, amount, and time period over which the substance was used. This is addressed further under "Differential Diagnosis."

Evaluate Positive Symptoms

During the interview, the clinician should determine the scope, quality, and duration of hallucinations and delusions and note the quality of the client's speech and behavior. Care should be taken to obtain *specific* examples of any symptoms endorsed. As previously noted, the quality of hallucinations (vague versus clear, unusual or dramatic) can suggest diagnoses other than a primary psychotic disorder (e.g., neurological condition, substance use, malingering) and can help differentiate among the *DSM-IV* psychotic disorders. Recall that only one type of symptom is sufficient to fulfill the *DSM-IV-TR* symptom criteria for Schizophrenia: if it is a bizarre delusion or an auditory hallucination that involves conversing voices or a voice keeping a running commentary on the client's activities (American Psychiatric Association, 2000b). Remember too that for Delusional Disorder, the client's delusional belief must be nonbizarre and hallucinations should not be prominent. Finally, the content of psychotic symptomatology (e.g., what the voices are saying, what the delusion is about) can suggest possible areas of psychological conflict, preoccupation, or concern (van de Loo & Eurelings-Bontekoe, 1990).

Clinicians need to approach discussion of delusions and hallucinations with care and sensitivity. Although some clients may freely discuss their delusions and clearly describe hallucinatory experiences when asked, many clients (particularly if they are paranoid) will be reluctant to discuss these beliefs and experiences with a new clinician. Therefore, the clinician needs to be alert to statements or behaviors that could suggest psychotic symptoms, and allusions to experiences that were unusual, weird, or out of the ordinary should be carefully followed up. Clues may be more subtle than this, as in the case of a client who mentioned spending a longer than usual time driving home from work and who later discloses upon careful questioning that she is taking different routes home to throw off the government officials who are following her. Similarly, the clinician may note changes in the client's behavior during the interview that may be indicators of psychotic symptoms. If the client suddenly seems unable to concentrate on questions and appears preoccupied, he could be responding to a hallucination (sometimes referred to as responding to internal stimulation).

Direct, argumentative challenges to delusional material ("Mr. Jones, it is physically impossible for radio waves to be controlling your movements") will do little to contribute to a therapeutic alliance and instead will likely result in the client's shutting down and refusing to answer additional questions. However, it is important for the clinician to determine the strength of a client's beliefs (Table 9.9) because delusions are considered erroneous beliefs that are held with *conviction*. One way to evaluate the strength of a delusional belief without directly challenging its veracity is to ask the client if anything else could explain or account for the experiences that the client cites in support of his or her delusion (e.g., "Mrs. Lee, is it possible that the person in the car that slowly passed by your house was looking for another address, and was not a plainclothes policeman checking up on you at home?").

Finally, remember that beliefs that are commonly held or accepted by the individual's cultural or religious subgroup are not considered delusions. Therefore, it is important to ask whether others in the client's family or community have questioned his or her beliefs or expressed an inability to understand them. Such questioning can also help to reveal a possible Shared Psychotic Disorder (e.g., a client mentions something that sounds

Table 9.9   Suggested indicators for identifying delusions

The client expresses an idea or belief with unusual persistence or force.

The idea exerts an undue influence on the client's life; the client's life is altered to an inexplicable extent.

Although there is profound conviction, the client may be secretive or suspicious when questioned about it.

The client may lack a sense of humor or be overly sensitive, especially around the belief.

The client accepts relatively unquestioningly things that sound strange or unlikely.

The client reacts strongly (e.g., with hostility, irritability) to attempts to contradict the belief.

The belief seems unlikely.

The client is overly emotionally invested in the belief (it overwhelms other elements of his or her psyche).

Actions carried out as the result of the delusion may appear abnormal or out of character (even though they may be consistent with the delusion's content).

Individuals who know the client well describe the belief (and associated behaviors if it is acted on) as uncharacteristic and alien (except in the case of Shared Psychotic Disorder).

Associated features such as suspicion, evasiveness, hauteur, grandiosity, mood change, or threatening or eccentric behaviors may be present, as well as hallucinations, thought disorder, or mood change.

From *Delusional Disorder: Paranoia and Related Illnesses*, by A. Munro, 1999, New York: Cambridge University Press. Adapted with permission.

delusional, admits that others have a hard time believing this, but notes that his sister is the only person who adamantly believes him). If the clinician is uncertain about whether a belief cited by a client is commonly held by a particular ethnic, cultural, or religious group, he or she should seek consultation with a knowledgeable individual.

In evaluating possible thought disorder, clinicians should remember that it is common for people to be somewhat tangential and circumstantial when they speak. Therefore, clinicians should have a fairly high threshold for concluding that the *DSM-IV* Schizophrenia symptom of disorganized speech has been met (i.e., speech must be sufficiently disorganized to impair effective communication). Clinicians must also be careful not to misattribute common linguistic errors committed by nonnative English speakers to thought disorder. Although thought disorder is considered by many to be a central symptom of Schizophrenia, remember that it is commonly encountered in other clinical conditions, such as mania. However, it appears that remission of thought disorder is more likely between active illness episodes in conditions such as Schizoaffective Disorder and mania compared to Schizophrenia (Harrow & Marengo, 1986; Marengo & Harrow, 1997).

As with disorganized speech, the clinician should have a fairly high threshold for concluding that the symptom of grossly disorganized behavior has been met and should remember that all bizarre behavior is not grossly disorganized. A delusional individual may act in extremely odd ways (e.g., dressing up in an elaborate disguise to evade detection by the CIA), but such behavior is organized in the sense that it directly relates to and is consistent with a delusional belief.

Evaluate Presence and Extent of Negative Symptoms

Negative symptoms can be challenging to evaluate because they are more subtle than positive symptoms, occur on a continuum with normality, are nonspecific, and can be caused by a variety of factors (American Psychiatric Association, 2000b). Although some negative symptoms can be evaluated through specific questions (e.g., assessing anhedonia by inquiring about typical activities and interests), most negative symptoms are evaluated by observing the client's interpersonal behavior with the interviewer or others. It can be helpful to tell or ask the client to relate a funny story or joke to evaluate the range and appropriateness of affect. After determining that a negative symptom is present, the clinician must try to establish whether it is being caused by some factor other than a psychotic disorder. If a negative symptom is determined to result from depression, environmental understimulation or isolation, or medication side effects, it is not to be counted toward a diagnosis of Schizophrenia. It may be necessary for the nonphysician mental health professional to consult with the client's psychiatrist to discuss whether the type or pattern of negative symptoms observed would be consistent with the dose and combination of medications the client is taking.

Because clients with prominent negative symptoms may say little and be emotionally nonresponsive, it can be difficult for the therapist to get a sense of such clients and the world they inhabit. In such cases, it may be helpful to ask a series of highly detailed questions that can be answered by clients with relatively few words to obtain details about their daily activities (McGlashan et al., 1990).

Screen for Comorbid Mood Symptoms

It can be easy for a novice clinician evaluating an individual suspected of having Schizophrenia to focus primarily on those symptoms that relate directly to the psychotic disorder. After all, these symptoms are apt to be the most debilitating and troublesome to the client, and their compelling nature makes it likely that these aspects of the clinical presentation will occupy the majority of the clinician's attention. However, mood symptoms should also be carefully evaluated, particularly with regard to their intensity, timing, and duration relative to psychotic symptoms. As will be discussed under "Differential Diagnosis," such assessment is key in making a differential diagnosis between Schizophrenia, Schizoaffective Disorder, and mood disorders with psychotic symptoms. Significant mood symptoms also have implications for psychotherapeutic and pharmacologic interventions.

Inquire about Social, Academic or Work, and Occupational Functioning

It is important to inquire about the amount and quality of social relationships and activities, interests and hobbies, school and/or work performance, and self-care skills (e.g., grooming, hygiene) prior to the onset of frank psychotic symptoms to gain a sense of the length of a possible illness prodrome. Valuable information about the client's social skills can be gleaned from the intake interview itself, and deficits may suggest the need for social skills training interventions.

A potentially important resource is the client's family. As discussed in the section on treatment, the client's family can play a pivotal role in many aspects of treatment. In the intake phase, family members (contacted with the client's permission) can help to fill in gaps or verify information provided by the client about his or her psychiatric, medical, and social history. It is important to find out about the quality of clients' family relationships, particularly if they have significant contact with the family. As previously noted, a large body of research on the concept of *expressed emotion* has demonstrated a robust association between symptomatic relapse and family environments characterized by elevated levels of criticism, hostility, and emotional overinvolvement (for a review, see Butzlaff & Hooley, 1998).

Assess Resources, Coping, and Other Strengths

In a diagnostic or intake interview it can be easy to focus solely on problems and pathology because the client has presumably come to treatment due to experiencing difficulties and is in distress (or someone else who knows the client well believes this to be the case). This bias can be especially pronounced when interviewing a psychotic individual, and novice clinicians often make the mistake of equating the presence of florid psychotic symptoms with poor prognosis. In addition to evaluating and documenting symptoms and impairment, it is imperative for the clinician to evaluate the strengths and abilities that the client brings to treatment. For example, different coping methods used by individuals to deal with their psychotic symptoms have been documented and include cognitive (e.g., shifting attention, self-instruction, positive reframing), behavioral (e.g., seeking or withdrawing from social contact, changing postural position), sensory (e.g., listening to loud music, limiting sensory input by closing eyes), and physiological (e.g., exercising, practicing relaxation exercises) strategies (van de Loo & Eurelings-Bontekoe, 1990). In addition, the presence of skills and interests has been found to be a positive prognostic indicator for Schizophrenia (McGlashan, 1988), so the clinician should inquire about hobbies, interests, and skills related to academic, work, or recreational pursuits.

Review Medication Issues

It is beyond the scope of practice for the nonphysician clinician to make recommendations as to the specific medications that might be appropriate for a psychotic client, but it is crucial for the clinician to inform clients about the availability of pharmacologic treatment and to encourage a medication evaluation if this has not already been sought. If a client has a history of taking medication, the clinician should find out the names of the medications, when they were taken, their effects (i.e., both in terms of ameliorating symptoms as well as side effects), and the extent to which the client took the medication as prescribed. Addressing medication adherence is extremely important because a substantial percentage of clients become nonadherent at some point in their illness; among individuals with Schizophrenia, estimates range as high as 75% over 2 years (Weiden, Mott, & Curcio, 1995). A variety of factors, including intolerable side effects, lack of insight into the need for medication, misinformation about the effects of medication, encouragement by others in the client's environment to stop medication, and difficulty in the physician-client relationship, can be involved. Contacting the client's psychiatrist (after obtaining the client's consent) is helpful in verifying the client's medication regimen and issues of adherence, treatment response, and side effects. A strong working relationship with the client's psychiatrist should be developed; it is important to contact this individual sooner rather than later so that the client's treatment is coordinated.

Psychological Testing

Psychological testing may help to document the presence of certain response patterns that are suggestive of a psychotic disorder (e.g., an elevated Scale 8 and/or Scale 6 score on the MMPI-2; a high percentage of poor form quality responses and an elevated number of Special Scores on the Rorschach Inkblot Test), and may be helpful in providing information about comorbid symptoms (e.g., anxiety, mood) that may aid in the differential diagnostic process. However, because there is no psychological test profile that is pathognomonic for a specific psychotic disorder, the results of psychological testing cannot be used alone to diagnose a specific psychotic disorder. For example, although it is well known that individuals with Schizophrenia often display certain cognitive deficits in areas such as attention, memory, information processing, abstract reasoning, and planning, attempts to identify a pathognomonic neuropsychological profile for Schizophrenia have been unsuccessful (Cornblatt et al., 1999). Thus test results may provide corroborative evidence in support of a particular disorder suggested by the history and clinical presentation of the client, rather than being sufficient to render a diagnosis in and of themselves. Psychological testing may also be used to evaluate coping resources and other strengths or impairments (e.g., cognitive impairments revealed through neuropsychological testing) that can aid in making treatment recommendations.

Symptom Rating Scales

Symptom rating scales, such as the Brief Psychiatric Rating Scale (Lukoff, Nuechterlein, & Ventura, 1986; Overall & Gorham, 1962) and the Scales for the Assessment of Positive and Negative Symptoms (Andreasen, 1981, 1984) can be helpful in documenting the severity of specific symptoms. When completed at regular intervals during the client's treatment, such measures can help to objectively document the course of a psychotic disorder and may assist in the early identification of impending symptomatic relapses so that aggressive intervention can be initiated. Scales evaluating some of the previously discussed prognostic indicators in Schizophrenia have been developed (Fenton & McGlashan, 1987; J. S. Strauss & Carpenter, 1974) but have been utilized primarily in research settings.

Crisis, Legal, and Ethical Considerations

Danger to Self

Earlier in this chapter, the elevated rate of suicide among individuals with Schizophrenia was discussed. Clinicians should become familiar with the risk factors shown in Table 9.5. With regard to clinical presentation, remember that although significant depressive symptoms place a client with a psychotic disorder at risk for suicidal ideation and attempts, these risks can occur in other states as well, such as when a client is actively psychotic or is feeling hopeless. It is therefore of paramount importance to assess suicidality when you interview an individual with Schizophrenia or another psychotic disorder, and to regularly evaluate this throughout the course of treatment. If a client is experiencing violent command hallucinations (to harm self or others), the clinician should determine the client's degree of insight into and distress caused by these symptoms, as well as any history of acting on such hallucinations. The same should be done for delusions that involve depressive, violent, or threatening content or themes. The presence of significant depressive symptoms places the client at risk for suicidal ideation and attempts, which underscores the importance of evaluating depression when treating a schizophrenic individual. Chapter 2 reviews in detail the steps for conducting a suicide assessment and dealing with a suicidal client.

Danger to Others

Depictions of severely mentally ill individuals in film and television, combined with highly publicized crimes involving mentally ill suspects, might readily lead to the conclusion that violent behavior is a fundamental attribute of persons with Schizophrenia and other psychotic disorders. Indeed, although the general public today is more likely to espouse a scientifically based view of mental illness compared to attitudes in the 1950s, they are also more likely to consider mentally ill persons suffering from psychosis to be violent (Phelan, Link, Stueve, & Pescosolido, 2000). In contrast, studies conducted prior to the widespread de-institutionalization movement of the 1960s that found lower arrest rates among the mentally ill compared to the general population have often been cited in support of the claim that seriously mentally ill individuals are not more violent or dangerous than most other people (P. Brown, 1985). The truth regarding violence proneness among individuals with severe mental illness appears to lie between these two extremes, and clinicians should become familiar with some of the variables that have been linked to violence proneness among individuals with psychotic disorders. Studies of rates of violence among seriously mentally ill individuals in the United States since 1990 collectively indicate that each year 5% to 10% commit acts of serious violence, and that treatment with antipsychotic medication is associated with significantly reduced violence risk (Torrey, 2006).

In a review of research examining this issue from multiple perspectives (e.g., studies of the psychiatric status of arrested or incarcerated individuals, investigations of violent behavior among psychiatric inpatients and outpatients, rates of violence reported by the family members of mentally ill individuals), Torrey (1998) concluded that the vast majority of individuals with serious mental illnesses such as Schizophrenia are not more dangerous than the general population. Torrey also concluded that, in the United States, alcohol and drug abusers are, on the whole, more violent than persons suffering from serious mental illness. However, other studies suggest that individuals with Schizophrenia are more likely to engage in assaultive and destructive behavior than individuals with other psychiatric disorders (H. K. Lee, Villar, Juthani, & Bluestone, 1989; Noble & Rodger, 1989; Odejide, 1981), and Torrey acknowledges that there is a subgroup of seriously mentally ill individuals who are more violent than the general population. In addition to a psychotic disorder diagnosis, these individuals are likely to be male, to have a history of violence and concurrent drug and/or alcohol abuse, and to be medication noncompliant. Schizophrenic persons with psychopathic traits are also more likely to be violent (Abushua'leh & Abu-Akel, 2006). Interestingly, while a positive correlation between neurological impairment and violence has been reported among schizophrenic inpatients (Krakowski, Convit, Jaeger, Shang, & Volka, 1989), a negative relationship has been reported between these variables in schizophrenic outpatients (LaPierre et al., 1995). Relevant to the latter point, Munro (1999) asserts that the potential for dangerousness may be particularly increased for an individual with a paranoid Delusional Disorder for a number of reasons, including the relative preservation of reasoning and intellectual ability that allow the individual to weave events together in a complex manner to support the delusion.

Such seemingly contradictory findings regarding the role of cognitive factors and violence prediction point to the apparent heterogeneity among psychotic individuals who commit violent acts. Some clients with psychotic disorders may be at risk for violent behavior due to cognitive impairments that lead to poor frustration tolerance, severe symptoms, and impulse control (and a greater likelihood of hospitalization), whereas higher functioning psychotic clients may be susceptible to violent behavior because of greater exposure to aggression-provoking situations that may be aggravated by substance-induced disinhibition (LaPierre, et al., 1995; Räsänen et al., 1998). Teplin, Abram, and McClelland (1994) found that although a diagnosis of Schizophrenia did not predict the probability of arrest or number of violent crimes over a 6-year follow-up period, the presence of psychotic symptoms was associated with a marginally increased rate of violent crime, suggesting that specific symptoms rather than a particular diagnosis may have more predictive value with regard to violent behavior.

Lack of insight may also play a significant role in predicting violence among severely mentally ill individuals since poor insight has been empirically linked to poor treatment compliance and can potentially lead to decreased ability to monitor and modulate affect and impulses (Torrey, 1998). Neurological impairment and delusions that one's mind is being controlled have been identified by other researchers as additional predictors of violence among seriously mentally ill persons (P. J. Taylor, Mullen, & Wessely, 1993). These findings underscore the importance of assertive case management that includes active interventions for increasing medication compliance and addressing comorbid substance abuse.

Informed Consent

When clients make a decision to enter psychotherapy they have the right to know about the services they are purchasing, including the techniques and procedures to be used, goals, risks and benefits, confidentiality limits, the therapist's training, fees and billing, and access to records so that informed consent for treatment can be given (Welfel, 2002). Questions have been raised about the ability of persons with chronic and severe mental illnesses such as Schizophrenia to adequately provide consent; much of what has been written on this topic deals with the capacity of such persons to consent to participate in research, but many of the issues also apply to consent to treatment in clinical settings. First, it is important to avoid assuming that all individuals with psychotic disorders such as Schizophrenia are decisionally impaired and to recognize that the evaluation of capacity to consent must be undertaken on an individual, case-by-case basis. Second, it appears that *cognitive* variables rather than symptom variables are more highly correlated with decisional capacity; a client who is delusional, for example, may still be quite capable of adequately processing information related to treatment because his or her delusional system does not necessarily influence all spheres of cognition (Carpenter & Conley, 1999; Palmer, Dunn, Applebaum, & Jeste, 2004).

With this said, significant numbers of clients with psychotic disorders evidence difficulties comprehending what is involved in giving informed consent. Prentice, Bellack, Gold, and Carpenter (2003) found that 75% of patients with Schizophrenia scored below the average control subject on a measure assessing decisional capacity to consent to participation in research. Assuming parallels to consent to treatment in clinical settings, such findings highlight the need to take steps to maximize the likelihood that the client will have an adequate understanding of the parameters of treatment and can make an informed decision about whether he or she wishes to participate. Positively, research indicates that decisional capacity can be improved among individuals with Schizophrenia. Prentice et al. (2003) found that a two-session intervention in which patients were taught key elements in the decision-making process for research participation demonstrated a 20% increase in decisional capacity compared to an 8% increase in a comparison group provided with a social skills training intervention of equivalent duration. Other research has found that schizophrenic patients' comprehension of informed consent forms for a research study was enhanced by using a procedure in which information in the consent form was repeatedly presented and explained until 100% of the items on a questionnaire about the consent form were answered correctly. While 90% of the sample in this study required two or more presentations of the material to reach this criterion, comprehension improved from the first presentation of the material to a test conducted 1 week later, and 96% of patients reported feeling adequately informed (Wirshing, Wirshing, Marder, Liberman, & Mintz, 1998). In another study, Wirshing, Sergi, and Mintz (2005) found that schizophrenic patients who watched a videotape providing detailed information about the consent process in treatment and research demonstrated a greater understanding of informed consent than a comparison group that watched a videotape presenting general information about bioethical issues in research. Finally, Jeste and colleagues (2003) found that an enhanced informed consent process in which an audiovisual presentation containing bulleted summary points of key information enhanced Schizophrenia patients' comprehension of the material compared to standard informed consent procedures. The implication of such research for the practicing clinician is that comprehension and retention of information presented in a consent document is likely to be enhanced through repetition of information, questioning to assess understanding, and use of visually presented bulleted points or other methods of summarizing key pieces of information.

DIAGNOSTIC CONSIDERATIONS

Common Comorbidities

Substance Use Disorders

Substance abuse is a common problem in individuals diagnosed with Schizophrenia. According to community-based epidemiologic studies, the prevalence of comorbid substance abuse or dependence among those with Schizophrenia is approximately 47%, and young male clients are particularly at risk (Mueser et al., 1990; Regier et al., 1990). Among the substances commonly abused by those with Schizophrenia are stimulants, hallucinogens, alcohol, and nicotine, and polysubstance abuse is frequently encountered (Mueser et al., 1990). Nicotine dependence is the most common substance use disorder in Schizophrenia; rates of smoking in this population are estimated to be 70% to 90% (Ziedonis & George, 1997).

Many substances (e.g., alcohol, amphetamines, hallucinogens, cannabis) can worsen psychotic symptoms, and comorbid substance use is generally associated with a poorer illness outcome (e.g., increased risk of relapse and hospitalization, poor self-care, homelessness; Drake et al., 1989; Mueser et al., 1990). Studies reporting an earlier age of onset and better premorbid functioning among dually diagnosed individuals suggest that substance use may play a role in the onset of illness in some cases (Tsuang, Simpson, & Kronfol, 1982). Dually diagnosed individuals receiving disability payments intended to provide for basic necessities may instead spend these funds on illicit substances, thereby beginning a revolving-door cycle in which symptom exacerbations lead to repeated hospitalizations (Shaner et al., 1995). Substance abuse can also aggravate and precipitate the appearance of tardive dyskinesia and has been reported to lead to alterations in the mesolimbic dopaminergic system, which can lead to nonresponse to neuroleptic medication (M. B. Bowers, Mazure, Nelson, & Jatlow, 1990; Dixon, Haas, Weiden, Sweeney, & Frances, 1992; Wilkins, 1997). Depressive states have been associated with chronic use of alcohol and withdrawal from cocaine and nicotine, while an anergic state that in many ways appears similar to depression has been associated with chronic cannabis use (Siris, 1995).

Some schizophrenic individuals report using illicit substances to self-medicate anxiety, dysphoria, negative symptoms, and medication side effects (Dixon et al., 1992; Hansell & Willis, 1977). Ironically, substances that may provide relief from certain types of symptoms or side effects can end up exacerbating other symptoms. Substances such as nicotine and amphetamine facilitate dopamine release, which may affect the dopamine deficiency in prefrontal cortical regions thought to underlie negative symptoms, yet may also exacerbate positive symptoms thought to be related to hyperfunctional mesolimbic dopamine systems (Ziedonis & George, 1997). Cigarette smoking can also lower blood levels of antipsychotic medications (Ziedonis & George, 1997). In addition to self-medication, there are many other factors that contribute to substance abuse and the particular class of substances used, including enjoyment of the intoxicated state, a way to escape problems, social pressure to use, and substance availability (Dixon et al., 1991; Fowler, Carr, Carter, & Lewin, 1998).

The evaluation of substance abuse among schizophrenic individuals is complicated because many clients underestimate or deny substance use and its consequences. Such underreporting may be due to psychological defensiveness, social desirability factors, or neuropsychological impairments that affect the ability to identify relationships between substance use and adjustment difficulties (Drake et al., 1990). Thus the clinician should not rely solely on self-reported use; intensive case management approaches, in which there is frequent contact with the client, may aid in making more reliable and valid assessments of the extent of substance use and associated impairments. Laboratory tests, such as urine toxicology screens, can also provide objective indicators of substance use.

Depression

Because depression is a commonly associated feature of Schizophrenia, and because Schizoaffective Disorder or a psychotic mood disorder is a competing diagnostic consideration in any differential diagnosis involving Schizophrenia, the clinician must evaluate the presence, extent, and pattern of mood symptoms. A mistake that novice clinicians frequently make is jumping to the conclusion that the mere presence of any significant mood symptoms automatically means the client has a psychotic mood disorder or Schizoaffective Disorder. The clinician should also consider whether drugs or alcohol are playing a role in producing the depressive symptoms. In addition, because depressive symptoms often accompany psychotic decompensation and are among the earliest prodromal symptoms noticed by clients and their relatives, the possibility of a psychotic relapse should be considered when depressive symptoms emerge in schizophrenic patients (Herz & Lamberti, 1995; Herz & Melville, 1980; Siris, 1995).

Estimates of the incidence of so-called secondary depression in Schizophrenia, or depression that typically develops following the remission of active-phase symptoms, range from as little as 7% to as high as 70% of clients, with a modal estimate of 25% (Siris, 1991). Although early studies suggested that the presence of depressive symptoms in Schizophrenia was a positive prognostic indicator (McGlashan & Carpenter, 1976; Vaillant, 1964), more recent studies indicate that depression that follows the resolution of active psychotic symptoms is associated with poorer prognosis (e.g., increased risk of relapse, higher suicide rates; R. E. Becker, Singh, Meisler, & Shillcutt, 1985; Heilä, et al., 1997; Mandel, Severe, Schooler, Gelenberg, & Mieske, 1982).

It can be challenging to determine whether a client is experiencing symptoms of depression or is instead exhibiting negative symptoms (e.g., anhedonia) or neuroleptic side effects such as *akinesia* and *akathesia* that can mimic depressive symptomatology. Akinesia and akathesia are two types of extrapyramidal side effects that are associated with neuroleptic use. Akinesia is characterized by anergia and anhedonia and a failure to initiate or sustain activities. Akathesia is characterized by extreme subjective feelings of restlessness that may be accompanied by motoric restlessness (pacing, tapping legs or feet). Akathesia is often associated with extreme dysphoria and can be mistaken for agitated depression. The clinician may need to consult with the client's psychiatrist if there is any question about whether symptoms that appear to be depression are neuroleptic-induced side effects, and an intensive trial of antiparkinsonian medication may be needed to resolve this issue. Another difficult differential concerns a syndrome of demoralization that often occurs in Schizophrenia and that is characterized by chronic feelings of discouragement, but that is not necessarily accompanied by clinical depression or the vegetative symptoms of depression (Siris, 1991).

The presence of any significant depressive symptoms should immediately alert the clinician to the need to assess suicidal ideation since suicide is a significant cause of death among individuals with Schizophrenia. Persisting depression may warrant the addition of antidepressant medication to the client's pharmacologic regimen and should be discussed with the client's psychiatrist.

Clinicians should be particularly attentive to evaluating depression among ethnic minority individuals. Depression is diagnosed less frequently among African American individuals compared to Caucasians, and this pattern appears to also be true among African Americans diagnosed with Schizophrenia (Delahanty et al., 2001). While it is possible that comorbid depression may be less prevalent among minorities diagnosed with Schizophrenia, factors such as cultural distance between clinician and client, biases or stereotypes regarding psychopathology expression, and other nonillness factors may be contributing to underdiagnosis of an important clinical syndrome among some schizophrenic individuals.

According to the *DSM-IV-TR*, in cases where mood symptoms that meet full criteria for a mood episode are superimposed on Schizophrenia and are of clinical significance (but do not fulfill criteria for Schizoaffective Disorder), it is appropriate to give a comorbid diagnosis of Depressive Disorder NOS or Bipolar Disorder NOS in addition to Schizophrenia (American Psychiatric Association, 2000b). Postpsychotic depressive disorder of Schizophrenia is currently among the criteria sets in the *DSM-IV-TR* that have been identified as warranting further study for possible inclusion among the Axis I syndromes (American Psychiatric Association, 2000b).

Anxiety Disorders

Anxiety disorders are comorbid in up to 60% of individuals with Schizophrenia (Braga, Mendlowicz, Marrocos, & Figueira, 2005). The rates of comorbidity for specific disorders are estimated at up to 35% for OCD, 3% to 34% for Panic Disorder, 12% to 31% for GAD, 28% for Agoraphobia, 3% to 31% for Simple Phobia, 13% to 40% for Social Phobia, and 5% to 17% for Agoraphobia without panic (for reviews, see Braga et al., 2005; Braga, Petrides, & Figueira, 2004). The wide ranges for many of these disorders likely reflect methodological issues such as small sample sizes and heterogeneous patient groups (e.g., using differing diagnostic criteria, including Schizophrenia spectrum cases). It does not appear that anxiety symptoms in schizophrenic persons can be attributed solely to the presence of symptoms such as hallucinations or delusions (Tibbo, Swainson, Chue, & LeMelledo, 2003). It can be easy to overlook comorbid anxiety symptoms in an individual with a disorder such as Schizophrenia due to the more florid nature of psychotic symptoms.

An anxiety disorder commonly comorbid with psychotic disorders, but often missed is Post Traumatic Stress Disorder (PTSD). Mueser and colleagues (1998) examined the prevalence of PTSD in a mixed sample of inpatients and outpatients with severe mental illness, a third of whom had Schizophrenia or Schizoaffective Disorder. They found a current PTSD rate of 28% and 37% for the Schizophrenia and Schizoaffective subgroups, respectively. Although the rate of trauma exposure for the sample overall was extremely high (i.e., 98%), only 2% of chart diagnoses reflected a diagnosis of comorbid PTSD, which indicates that PTSD is seriously underdetected among the severely mentally ill.

Some studies have found that comorbid anxiety disorders are not associated with worse outcome in Schizophrenia, and may even be associated with better outcome (Strakowksi et al., 1993; Tibbo et al., 2003). Yet other research has found that schizophrenic individuals with these conditions appear to be at increased risk for suicide (Pallanti, Quercioli, & Hollander, 2004; Sevincok, Akoglu, & Kokcu, 2007; Siris, Mason, & Shuwall, 1993). In addition, comorbid anxiety is a significant predictor of poorer quality of life among schizophrenic individuals (Braga et al., 2005; Huppert & Smith, 2001). Braga and colleagues found that schizophrenic patients with comorbid anxiety disorders were more impaired in global functioning and exhibited significantly more limitations in their work and social lives compared to patients without these conditions. Despite the mixed nature of the research findings in this area, it is important to be aware that anxiety disorders can and do exist among individuals with Schizophrenia, have the potential to adversely impact functioning, and should therefore be detected and treated.

DIFFERENTIAL DIAGNOSIS

Schizophrenia versus Other Psychiatric Disorders

Mood Disorders

Mood disorders such as Major Depressive Disorder and Bipolar Disorder may be characterized by psychotic features that appear qualitatively similar to those seen in Schizophrenia, including mood-incongruent hallucinations, Schneiderian first-rank symptoms, grossly disorganized behavior and speech, and catatonia. In addition, severe depression can be characterized by symptoms such as anhedonia and flattened affect that appear similar to the negative symptoms of Schizophrenia (Lake & Hurwitz, 2006). As such, it is likely to be difficult to make a differential diagnosis between Schizophrenia and mood disorders with psychotic features based on clinical presentation alone. Instead, it is necessary to gather information from the client or reliable collateral sources about the timing of psychotic symptoms such as hallucinations or delusions and mood symptoms. In mood disorders with psychotic features, such symptoms will be present only during periods of mood disturbance and should remit when the mood episode resolves. In cases where psychotic symptoms persist in the absence of mood symptoms, the clinician should consider diagnoses of Schizophrenia and Schizoaffective Disorder. As discussed in the next section, a primary factor differentiating Schizophrenia from Schizoaffective Disorder is the amount of time prominent mood symptoms have occurred over the course of the entire illness. When a reliable history of symptoms cannot be obtained, the clinician may need to wait until the mood episode is adequately treated to determine if psychotic symptoms are still present.

Cognitive Disorders

Disorders such as dementia and delirium can be associated with psychotic symptoms such as hallucinations or delusions. However, a key feature distinguishing these conditions from psychotic disorders such as Schizophrenia is the degree of cognitive impairment. Delirium is associated with a disturbance of consciousness, inability to sustain, focus, or shift attention, and other changes in cognition such as memory or language disturbance. Although cognitive impairments are frequently associated with Schizophrenia, they are not typically as severe as those seen in a delirium; for example, a delirious individual may be disoriented to time and place, whereas this would be much rarer in Schizophrenia. Also, symptoms in delirium fluctuate over the course of a day, whereas those in Schizophrenia are more stable. Finally, delusions in the context of delirium are typically fragmented and unsystematized (American Psychiatric Association, 2000b). With regard to dementia, the level of cognitive impairment is typically much greater than that seen in Schizophrenia. Also, the age of onset for these disorders is usually quite different, with Schizophrenia typically having an onset in late adolescence to early adulthood and dementia most often having an onset in old age.

Substance-Induced Disorders

Intoxication from substances such as cocaine and other amphetamines, LSD, and PCP can cause delusions and hallucinations. Among the prescription medications that can cause psychotic symptoms are steroids, ACE inhibitors, beta blockers, and antihistamines (refer to Table 9.8 for additional information). The key to differentiating between substance-induced psychotic symptoms and a disorder such as Schizophrenia is establishing whether the psychotic symptoms have been present only during periods of substance use. This can be accomplished by taking a careful history, but if the client is an unreliable historian and other sources of information (e.g., past treatment records, knowledgeable others such as family members, friends, or prior treatment providers) are unavailable, the clinician may need to wait until the effects of a substance have completely dissipated. Although the amount of time that a substance can continue to exert effects on the brain after active use has stopped varies across drugs, the *DSM-IV-TR* suggests that symptoms persisting beyond 1 month of the end of active use or the cessation of withdrawal symptoms indicate that a primary psychotic disorder may better account for the symptoms (American Psychiatric Association, 2000b). It should be noted that use of hallucinogens (e.g., LSD) can result in persistent and recurrent flashbacks or perceptual disturbances; this disorder is referred to as Hallucinogen Persisting Perception Disorder in the *DSM-IV-TR* (American Psychiatric Association, 2000b). This disorder may appear more difficult to differentiate from a primary psychotic disorder due to the persistence of hallucinatory phenomena long after use of a hallucinogenic substance has ceased. However, in Hallucinogen Persisting Perception Disorder, the affected individual realizes that the perceptual experiences are drug effects, whereas in a primary psychotic disorder the affected individual often believes that the hallucinatory experiences represent external reality (American Psychiatric Association, 2000b). Table 9.10 summarizes information pertinent to making a differential diagnosis between psychotic disorders and other psychiatric conditions.

Table 9.10   Between-category diagnostic differential

Disorder	Similarities with Psychotic Disorders	Differences from Psychotic Disorders
Mood disorders	Flattened affect, anhedonia, lack of motivation Hallucinations, delusions may be present in Major Depressive Disorder or Bipolar Disorder with psychotic features Thought disorder (Bipolar Disorder with psychotic features)	Symptoms such as flattened affect, anhedonia restricted to periods of mood disturbance Positive symptoms (e.g., hallucinations, delusions) restricted to periods of mood disturbance
Cognitive disorders	Hallucinations, delusions may be present during course of dementia Apathy	More severe cognitive impairment Consciousness disturbed (delirium) Underlying medical condition is cause (e.g., Alzheimer's disease) More likely to be initially diagnosed in old age (dementia)
Substance intoxication or withdrawal	Psychotic symptoms (e.g., hallucinations, delusions) Negative symptoms	Symptoms are related to the direct effects of a substance Symptoms follow ingestion or (in dependent individuals) withdrawal of substance Symptoms are known to be associated with substance effects Symptoms remit when intoxication or withdrawal syndromes remit

Among the Psychotic Disorders

As should be apparent from the preceding discussion of the symptoms of Schizophrenia and the other psychotic disorders, these conditions differ from one another primarily in terms of the scope of psychotic symptoms, the duration of symptoms, and their relationship to other clinical states (e.g., depression, mania). Table 9.11 presents a summary of the key and discriminating features of the psychotic disorders.

Schizophrenia versus Schizoaffective Disorder

Schizophrenia is differentiated from Schizoaffective Disorder by the absence of prominent mood symptoms during the course of the disorder. Recall that both conditions are characterized by symptoms that include hallucinations, delusions, grossly disorganized speech or behavior, catatonia, and negative symptoms. However, Schizoaffective Disorder is further characterized by the presence of a concurrent mood episode (i.e., major depressive episode, manic episode, mixed episode) a period of delusions and hallucinations in

Table 9.11 Psychotic disorders: key and discriminating features

Disorder	Key Features	Discriminating Features
Schizophrenia	*Two or more of:* Delusions Hallucinations Disorganized speech Grossly disorganized behavior Negative symptoms (one if bizarre delusion or hallucinated voices keep a running commentary or converse with each other)	Active symptoms present at least 1 month Continuous signs of illness (prodromal, active, residual symptoms) present at least 6 months Mood symptoms, if present, are not present for significant part of illness
Schizophreniform Disorder	Same as for Schizophrenia	Disorder episode (including prodromal, active, residual symptoms) lasts at least 1 month but less than 6 months
Brief Psychotic Disorder	*One or more of:* Delusions Hallucinations Disorganized speech Grossly disorganized behavior	Symptoms present for at least 1 day but less than 1 month Eventual return to premorbid level of functioning
Delusional Disorder	Presence of nonbizarre delusion of at least 1 month duration Total duration of mood symptoms, if present, has been brief relative to duration of delusional period	No prominent hallucinations, disorganized speech, disorganized behavior, catatonia, negative symptoms Functioning not markedly impaired; behavior not obviously bizarre or odd

From *Diagnostic and Statistical Manual for Mental Disorders*, fourth edition, text revision, by American Psychiatric Association, 2000b, Washington, DC: Author. Adapted with permission.

the absence of prominent mood symptoms for at least 2 weeks during the same illness episode, and the presence of mood symptoms for a substantial portion of the illness. In Schizophrenia, one may see comorbid mood symptoms (as was discussed for depression under "Common Comorbidities"), but the total duration of these should be brief when looked at in the context of the entire period of illness.

Schizophrenia versus Brief Psychotic Disorder and Schizophreniform Disorder

The primary difference between Schizophrenia and either Brief Psychotic Disorder or Schizophreniform Disorder is the duration of symptoms. Both Schizophreniform Disorder and Brief Psychotic Disorder are of relatively short duration. Specifically, if psychotic symptoms have been present for less than 6 months and there is no prior history of a psychotic disorder such as Schizophrenia, the clinician should consider the possibility of a Brief Psychotic Disorder or Schizophreniform Disorder. For Brief Psychotic Disorder, symptoms such as delusions, hallucinations, grossly disorganized behavior, or catatonic behavior must be present for at least 1 day but less than 1 month, whereas in Schizophreniform Disorder, psychotic symptoms have been present for at least 1 month but less than 6 months. In addition, for a diagnosis of Schizophreniform Disorder to be made, the client's symptoms must meet the symptom criteria for Schizophrenia (American Psychiatric Association, 2000b).

Schizophrenia versus Delusional Disorder

The primary differences between Schizophrenia and Delusional Disorder concern the scope of psychotic symptoms and the impairment caused by them. In Delusional Disorder, the affected individual endorses one or more nonbizarre delusions but does not have other psychotic symptoms such as prominent hallucinations, grossly disorganized speech or behavior, catatonia, or negative symptoms. Recall that Delusional Disorder is often associated with generally unimpaired functioning (i.e., only those aspects of the client's functioning that are directly related to the delusion may be impaired). As noted in the *DSM-IV-TR* (American Psychiatric Association, 2000b), it may be difficult to differentiate the paranoid subtype of Schizophrenia from Delusional Disorder because this subtype is not associated with symptoms such as disorganized speech or behavior or flat or inappropriate affect and is often associated with better functioning compared to other subtypes of Schizophrenia.

TREATMENT

General Principles in Treating Schizophrenia and Other Psychotic Disorders

This section focuses on treatment of Schizophrenia, but the principles discussed are relevant to other psychotic disorders as well. Treatment for Schizophrenia and other psychotic disorders is best conceptualized as long term, multimodal, and involving several areas of intervention and focus. Table 9.12 summarizes some of the key elements in the treatment of Schizophrenia. Medication is a necessary component of treatment, and psychosocial interventions appear to produce an additive or positive synergistic effect on

Table 9.12   Treatment interventions for Schizophrenia

Area	Interventions
Therapeutic interventions	Psychoeducation about illness (helpful to present in a stress-vulnerability framework) and pharmacologic treatments
	Identification of characteristic symptoms and prodromes
	Assessment and treatment of comorbid conditions
	Monitor suicide risk
	Client acceptance of illness and ongoing education
	Monitor medication adherence
	Cognitive behavioral approaches
	Social skills and social awareness training
	Enhancement of self-esteem through teaching adaptive coping strategies
Adjunctive interventions	Medication referral
	Coordination of treatment plan with other team members
	Social services (living and support services)
	Assertive community treatment (ACT), clubhouse model
	Occupational and vocational counseling or rehabilitation
Family interventions	Education
	Communication training
	Problem-solving training
	Referral to adjunctive family support groups, organizations

outcomes (Falloon & Liberman, 1983; Mojtabi, Nicholson, & Carpenter, 1998; Schooler & Keith, 1993). Treatment of the other psychotic disorders—Schizophreniform Disorder, Brief Psychotic Disorder, Delusional Disorder, and Schizoaffective Disorder—will follow many of the principles to be outlined for Schizophrenia, including medication to control symptoms and a structured, supportive psychotherapeutic approach that emphasizes illness education and development of coping strategies. For Schizoaffective Disorder, particular emphasis on cognitive techniques to deal with affective symptoms may be helpful in psychotherapy with these individuals. Mood stabilizers and/or antidepressants are often used in conjunction with neuroleptics to treat Schizoaffective Disorder (Gitlin, 1996). The treatment emphasis for Schizophreniform Disorder and Brief Psychotic Disorder is on rapid intervention to minimize the impact of the illness and to reduce the possibility of chronicity.

Individuals with Schizophrenia require a variety of services, and treatment models, which comprehensively integrate multiple services for clients are more consistently effective than less intensive, individual case management strategies. An example of such an integrated approach is the assertive community treatment (ACT) model developed by L. I. Stein and Test (1980), which is similar to the clubhouse model (Heydebrand, 2002). The ACT model involves provision of a comprehensive range of treatment, rehabilitation, and support services utilizing multidisciplinary teams based in the community. Assertive outreach, continuous responsibility and staff continuity over time, high staff-to-client ratios, brief but frequent contacts, use of a wide range of community services, and close liaison with the client's support system (including provision of psychoeducation) are among the defining features of the ACT model (Herz & Marder, 2002; Scott & Dixon, 1995). Interventions are individually tailored to the client and attempt to capitalize on strengths rather than employing a sole emphasis on remediating deficits (Herz & Marder, 2001). The ACT programs have been found to reduce psychiatric symptoms, improve social functioning and treatment compliance, enhance residential stability, and promote independent living (Bond, McGrew, & Fekete, 1995; Lehman, Dixon, Kernan, DeForge, & Postrado, 1997; Test, 1992).

Because treatment of psychotic disorders is collaborative, signed releases should be obtained from the outset of treatment to begin the process of open, ongoing communication among treatment team members (e.g., psychiatrist, social worker). Regular communication with other treatment team members will help coordinate care and avoid unnecessary duplication of effort or contradictory treatment recommendations.

Medication

It is important for all members of the client's treatment team to be aware of the types of medications used to treat psychosis, their general effectiveness, and common side effects. Although nonphysician mental health professionals are not responsible for prescribing such medications, their frequent therapeutic contact with the schizophrenic client allows therapists to (a) help monitor client adherence with medication, (b) assist in evaluating medication effectiveness (e.g., impact on symptoms), (c) encourage discussion of medication issues in the therapy session, and (d) work with the client to discuss with his or her psychiatrist side effects and other medication concerns. Nonphysician clinicians have an ethical responsibility to recognize the limits of their expertise and training and should not make recommendations to the client about changes in medication or offer medical opinions (e.g., treatment suggestions) about possible side effects the client may be experiencing.

Medications to effectively treat psychotic symptoms (typically referred to as *neuroleptics* because of their dopamine agonist properties) have been in existence for over half a century. In the early 1950s, the drug chlorpromazine (Thorazine) was found to significantly reduce psychotic symptoms such as delusions and hallucinations. Although this medication had ameliorative effects on the positive symptoms of Schizophrenia, it often caused uncomfortable side effects that led to medication nonadherence (e.g., dizziness, dry mouth, constipation, and excessive sedation—hence the name "major tranquilizers").

Since that time, a number of other antipsychotic medications have been developed that carry more favorable side effect profiles, although most are similar to one another and to older medications in how effectively they treat psychotic symptoms. The availability of a number of effective antipsychotic medications means that if a client is unable to tolerate a particular medication because of problematic side effects, there is a good chance he or she may respond to another drug. In selecting an appropriate medication, the client's psychiatrist will typically take into account past response and side effects (M. J. Gitlin, 1996). In addition, there is evidence that the newer, so-called *second-generation* or *atypical antipsychotic medications* improve some of the neurocognitive deficits associated with Schizophrenia (e.g., verbal learning and memory, executive functioning, working memory), which may be an additional consideration in medication selection (M. F. Green et al., 1997; Kern et al., 1999; Meltzer & McGurk, 1999).

The Appendix summarizes several neuroleptic medications in terms of typical dose, common side effects, and trade and generic names. Although these medications have proven effective in treating symptoms of Schizophrenia and other psychotic disorders, they neither represent a "cure" for these conditions, nor are they 100% effective for all clients (i.e., breakthrough symptoms can and do occur even when a client faithfully adheres to his or her medication regimen, and some clients are treatment refractory and do not adequately respond to any medication for a sustained period of time). For clients who experience intolerable side effects, a number of medications can be prescribed to address them (e.g., anticholinergics, benzodiazepines, beta blockers, and dopamine agonists), which can help increase the likelihood of adherence.

First- versus Second-Generation Neuroleptics

Neuroleptic medications can be divided into two broad classes: *first-generation* or *conventional* and *second-generation* or *atypical agents.* The former includes medications released before 1990; among these are haloperidol, fluphenazine, loxapine, thiothixene, thioridazine, and trifluoperazine. Among the second-generation or atypical antipsychotic medications are clozapine, risperidone, olanzapine, quetiapine, ziprasidone, and aripiprazole. Although second-generation agents are considered first-line treatments for Schizophrenia, many individuals continue to be treated with first-generation neuroleptics. Among the advantages of first-generation antipsychotic medications are their lower cost and availability of intramuscular and depot formulations (DeOliveira & Juruena, 2006; Schatzberg et al., 2005). Conventional neuroleptics are referred to as either *low-potency* or *high-potency* depending on the number of milligrams required to achieve an effective therapeutic dose. High-potency conventional neuroleptics may be favored over their low-potency counterparts because they cause less sedation and anticholinergic side effects (e.g., blurred vision, dry mouth, constipation, sweating), but they can also cause more extrapyramidal side effects (EPS; discussed further below; Schatzberg et al., 2005).

Atypical and conventional neuroleptics differ in their effects on neurotransmitter systems. Conventional neuroleptics primarily block D2 dopamine receptors, whereas atypical neuroleptics have weaker effects on D2 dopamine receptors, stronger effects on D1 dopamine receptors, and also block serotonin receptors (M. J. Gitlin, 1996). Major advantages of atypical antipsychotic medications are that they can effectively treat psychosis without the EPS experienced with conventional antipsychotics and they may have beneficial effects on cognitive functioning in Schizophrenia (P. D. Harvey, 2006; P. D. Harvey, Bowie, & Lobel, 2006; Meltzer & McGurk, 1999). A study of patient perceptions of atypical and conventional antipsychotic medications also demonstrated strong preference for atypical agents (Karow, Schnedler, & Naber, 2006). All of the atypical antipsychotics are effective in treating positive symptoms of Schizophrenia and take full effect within 4 to 6 weeks, so the decision as to which of these agents to use is likely to be guided by side effect profiles. For example, clozapine, which is helpful for treatment-resistant clients and appears to have beneficial effects on the negative symptoms of Schizophrenia (Kane, Honigfeld, Singer, Meltzer, & the Clozaril Collaborative Study Group, 1988), carries the risk of a potentially life-threatening side effect known as agranulocytosis, a condition characterized by a marked decrease in white blood cells that can place a client at risk for life-threatening infections. Although agranulocytosis is observed in only a small percentage (i.e., under 1%) of individuals treated with clozapine, the potentially fatal nature of this side effect requires that the client undergo weekly blood counts when this medication is prescribed. Older clients and women appear to be at a heightened risk for this side effect (M. J. Gitlin, 1996). Thus the use of this agent is usually reserved for clients who have not adequately responded to other antipsychotic medications. Weight gain and sedation are among the problematic side effects associated with olanzapine and quetiapine (Schatzberg, et al., 2005). Another significant concern associated with the use of olanzapine is an increased risk of developing Type II diabetes. In their review of studies examining this issue, Ramaswamy, Masand, and Nasrallah (2006) concluded that olanzapine, but not risperidone, is associated with a significantly increased risk of new-onset diabetes and that this risk may be higher for women; conclusions could not be reached for clozapine and quetiapine because of limited data.

Aripiprazole is sometimes referred to as a third generation antipsychotic agent and has a somewhat different pharmacologic profile from other neuroleptics. This drug has a high affinity for dopamine D2 and D3 receptors and serotonin 5-HT1A, 5-HT2A, and 5-HT2B receptors, and it can both enhance and inhibit the release of dopamine in specific brain areas (Schatzberg et al., 2005). Aripiprazole appears to be similarly efficacious to first- and second-generation antipsychotics and has a generally favorable side effect profile (El-Sayeh & Morganti, 2004). For example, it is less sedating than many other antipsychotic medications, is not associated with significant weight gain, and may carry a lower risk for the development of diabetes (S. M. Stahl, 2006). It also appears to have beneficial effects on cognition that are on par with olanzapine (Kern et al., 2006).

Extrapyramidal Side Effects

Antipsychotic medications carry the risk of inducing EPS, which are neurological side effects caused by the blockade of dopamine type 2 (D2) receptors in areas of the extrapyramidal motor system, which disrupts neural pathways involved in the control of voluntary and involuntary movement (H. I. Kaplan & Saddock, 1998). Among the acute side effects that can result are tremor, muscular rigidity, akinesia (i.e., decreased spontaneous facial expressions, gestures, speech, or body movement), dystonic reactions (i.e., brief or prolonged muscle contractions resulting in abnormal postures, tongue protrusion, eye movements), and akathesia (i.e., subjective feelings of restlessness that may be accompanied by objective signs such as pacing, inability to sit still, rocking). Although low-potency first-generation neuroleptics carry a lower risk of EPS than their high-potency counterparts, the assumption that second-generation medications are uniformly superior to these older, low-potency agents with regard to EPS does not appear warranted. In their meta-analysis of randomized controlled trials comparing low-potency first-generation agents with second-generation medications, Leucht, Wahlbeck, Hamann, and Kissling (2003) concluded that only clozapine was associated with significantly fewer EPS and higher efficacy than low-potency conventional drugs.

A very serious, nonacute neurological side effect that can occur after months of neuroleptic use is tardive dyskinesia (TD), a potentially irreversible condition involving abnormal, involuntary movements of the jaw (e.g., chewing, lip smacking), tongue (e.g., tongue thrusting), trunk, or extremities. Tardive dyskinesia is estimated to affect 20% to 30% of individuals on long-term neuroleptic treatment (American Psychiatric Association,

2000b). Risk factors for TD include older age, female sex, longer time on neuroleptic medication, higher doses of neuroleptic medication, and carrying a nonschizophrenic diagnosis (e.g., mood disorder; M. J. Gitlin, 1996). The symptoms of TD may wax and wane over time, are worsened by stress and anxiety, and may respond to a limited extent to client attempts to voluntarily suppress them. Consistently effective treatment for TD has yet to be discovered, but adjunctive use of beta blockers, stimulants, benzodiazepines, and cholinergic drugs, among others, are sometimes helpful. Reduction in the dose or complete discontinuation of antipsychotic medication may cause TD symptoms to improve or disappear (Gardos et al., 1994), but complete cessation of neuroleptic treatment is typically not advisable for clients diagnosed with chronic psychotic disorders because other effective pharmacologic treatments for psychosis are not available. Clozaril appears to carry a much lower risk of TD compared to conventional and other atypical neuroleptics, but the need for weekly blood draws may make this an infeasible first-choice medication.

Despite the availability of effective medications, significant nonadherence is estimated to be as high as 50% among schizophrenic individuals over 1 year and 75% over 2 years (Weiden et al., 1995). Common reasons underlying and general principles for addressing problems with medication adherence were reviewed in Chapter 4. These strategies and concepts apply to individuals with Schizophrenia and other psychotic disorders. In addition, medication nonadherence factors such as lack of insight into the illness and inability to remember to take medication may be especially pronounced in clients with psychotic disorders due to the nature of the symptoms and the cognitive deficits associated with these conditions (e.g., actively psychotic individuals may develop a delusional belief that their doctor is trying to poison them with the medication).

Psychotherapy

Psychotherapy is a potentially useful adjunct that may augment the effects of medication and provide the client with illness education, support, and skills and strategies for dealing with symptoms, stress, social and vocational issues, and illness-related cognitive deficits. Psychosocial interventions can also be used to target symptoms that have traditionally been less amenable to pharmacologic intervention (e.g., negative symptoms). A meta-analysis found that the average schizophrenic client who received psychosocial treatment in addition to medication was more improved than 65% of clients who received medication only, and that these gains were maintained across a median 12-month follow-up period (Mojtabai et al., 1998).

When surveyed, the overwhelming majority of respondents with Schizophrenia (i.e., 85%) indicated a preference for brief, less frequent sessions of reality-oriented therapy (i.e., focused on pragmatic issues, involving advice giving) over more frequent sessions of insight-oriented treatment (Coursey, Keller, & Farrell, 1995). Despite the preference for briefer, less frequent sessions, clients reported multiple issues as being important to address in treatment, including illness-intensified life issues (e.g., independence, self-esteem, depression), adverse secondary consequences (e.g., lack of work, stigma), management of the disorder (e.g., symptoms, hospitalization, medication), and coming to terms with one's disability (Coursey et al., 1995).

Individual Cognitive-Behavioral Therapy

Over the past decade, increasing interest has developed in applying principles of cognitive-behavioral therapy (CBT) to the treatment of psychotic disorders. Several clinical trials indicate that CBT combined with usual care (i.e., medication and case management) is superior to usual care alone in reducing positive symptoms in schizophrenic individuals (see Tarrier & Haddock, 2002). Garety, Fowler, and Kuipers (2000) conceptualize CBT for Schizophrenia as involving the following 6-stage process that can be flexibly applied over the course of 6 to 12 months of treatment: (1) engagement and assessment, (2) coping strategy work, (3) developing an understanding of the psychotic experience, (4) working on delusions and hallucinations, (5) addressing mood and negative self-evaluations, and (6) managing risk of relapse and social disability.

Treatment engagement of individuals diagnosed with psychotic disorders can be particularly challenging since high levels of illness-related suspiciousness and hostility may be present. Goals of the engagement phase include establishment of rapport and a strong working alliance, evaluation of the scope and severity of the client's psychotic symptoms (including details such as the internal and external antecedent conditions that precipitate symptoms, and the client's cognitive, emotional, behavioral, and physiological response to symptoms), and strategies the client typically employs to cope with symptoms. These goals may take several sessions to achieve, and the therapist is discouraged from adopting an overly confrontational approach with the client (e.g., trying to convince the resistant client that a particular diagnosis is warranted; Garety et al., 2000; Tarrier & Haddock, 2002).

Adaptations to CBT for psychotic disorders recognize that all individuals, including those experiencing symptoms such as hallucinations and delusions, try to cope with and make sense of troubling experiences. Coping interventions attempt to teach and enhance strategies that clients can use to deal with symptoms. Examples of coping strategies are teaching clients to refocus attention on pleasant images or thoughts in response to positive symptoms, instructing clients to narrow the focus of attention in response to symptoms (to decrease stimulus overload), engaging in activities (including social contacts) to divert attentional resources from positive symptoms, practicing breathing and other simple relaxation exercises to decrease arousal, and utilizing internal self-statements to cope with symptoms (Tarrier & Haddock, 2002).

Educational interventions can assist clients in developing a new, more accurate understanding of the symptoms they are experiencing and can lay the groundwork for interventions focused on belief and attribution modification of delusions and hallucinations. As in traditional CBT approaches, clients are encouraged to critically examine the evidence that supports faulty beliefs related to positive symptoms and to set up behavioral experiments to test the veracity of these beliefs. If no or limited evidence is found to support the beliefs, clients are encouraged to develop alternative explanations for their symptomatic experiences. However, in contrast to traditional CBT approaches in which the therapist strives to have clients formulate the rational responses themselves, the therapist may need to engage in more prompting and direct suggestion of alternative beliefs when working with psychotic clients (Tarrier & Haddock, 2002). The tools developed for challenging beliefs related to psychotic symptoms can also be extended to address negative self-evaluations and depressive cognitions that frequently accompany psychotic disorders (e.g., helping clients to reframe their illness-related experiences as demonstrating strength in dealing with adversity rather than as evidence of being a failure or a worthless person; Garety et al., 2000). Social skills training can also be employed to address negative symptoms later in the treatment (Gaudiano, 2005). In the final stages of CBT for psychotic disorders, strategies learned throughout treatment are reviewed and relapse prevention strategies are discussed (i.e., identifying signs of potential relapse, developing a plan to initiate skills learned in treatment to deal with symptom exacerbations).

Controlled trials indicate that upwards of 60% of clients may significantly benefit from CBT interventions (Herz & Marder, 2001). Meta-analyses of randomized controlled trials indicate this treatment produces significant reductions in positive and negative symptoms, has favorable effects on mental state ratings, and is effective for chronic patients (Rector & Beck, 2001; Cormac, Jones, Campbell, & Silveira da Mota Neto, 2003). Although CBT approaches hold promise for treating individuals with Schizophrenia and other psychotic disorders, these interventions are likely to be difficult to carry out with clients who lack insight into their illness, who are unwilling to entertain alternative explanations for their delusional beliefs, or who do not appear overtly distressed by their psychotic symptoms (e.g., grandiose delusions; Chadwick & Lowe, 1990; Garety et al., 2000). Ford (2005) also points out that CBT approaches for schizophrenia should develop intervention methods that are noted in the research literature on information processing and other neurocognitive deficits in this disorder.

Psychoeducation

An important aspect of treatment with schizophrenic individuals is providing education about the nature of their illness. This should include discussion of the characteristic symptoms that the client displays, why their pattern and course suggests a diagnosis of Schizophrenia (or another psychotic disorder), recommended treatments (including medication), and what is known about the causes and general course of the illness. Such education will take place throughout the course of treatment and serves as the foundation for helping clients identify when they are experiencing exacerbations of symptoms or prodromal signs that require more vigorous intervention. Individuals with Schizophrenia are a heterogeneous group and will display a range of cognitive abilities and levels of insight regarding their illness; thus the clinician must tailor the educational information presented to suit these client characteristics. It is important to not mislead clients into believing that there is a cure for Schizophrenia. Currently, medications and psychotherapeutic interventions are designed to *manage* symptoms and hopefully limit future relapses, but treatments have not been perfected to the point where clients can be guaranteed that they will be symptom-free if compliant with treatment.

Although most individuals with Schizophrenia do not marry and only 20% of males and 40% of females with Schizophrenia have one or more children (Gottesman & Moldin, 1999), the question of having children may arise when discussing issues such as the role that genetic factors play in the etiology of the illness. Individuals who have Schizophrenia in their family but who are not themselves schizophrenic may also raise this question. Such a decision is obviously very personal and important, and it is not the therapist's job to provide a direct answer. A clinician will be able to best help a client who raises such a question by explaining what is known about the risk of developing the illness when a family member has Schizophrenia (see section on etiology) and how the genetics of Schizophrenia, while not yet completely understood, are not similar to the genetics of disorders such as Huntington's disease (50% chance of developing the disorder if a parent is affected) or Tay-Sachs. It is also important to engage clients in a discussion of whether they feel emotionally ready to have a child (including the ability to tolerate the stress parenting responsibilities bring) and have the resources and abilities to adequately care for a child. Ultimately such decisions must be made by the client and his or her partner.

Social Skills Training

Many individuals with Schizophrenia exhibit impairments in social skills. As previously noted, these deficits may be related to neurocognitively based problems with recognizing and understanding emotional expression. For more than 3 decades social skills training (SST) programs have been developed and refined that are designed to teach social and independent living skills to schizophrenic individuals utilizing behavioral principles such as rehearsal, modeling, prompting, positive reinforcement, and homework assignments. Social skills training attempts to improve the clients' overall functioning in major life domains by teaching more effective and appropriate social and interpersonal behaviors, and has been found to provide benefits beyond medication alone and to have positive effects on client self-perception (Dilk & Bond, 1996; Heinssen, Liberman, & Kopelowicz, 2000; Mueser, Drake, & Bond, 1997; S. Pratt & Mueser, 2002).

Typically, SST begins with an assessment of a variety of domains of interpersonal functioning, such as comfort in social situations, range and appropriateness of interpersonal behaviors (e.g., eye contact, ability to initiate and sustain conversations), grooming and hygiene, and scope of prosocial activities and hobbies. Interviews with the client and significant others, completion of standardized instruments (e.g., Social Behavior Schedule: Wykes & Sturt, 1986), observation in naturalistic settings (e.g., clinic, board and care residence), and structured role-plays with the therapist are among the ways such an assessment can be carried out. From this initial evaluation, social skills requiring remediation can be identified for intervention.

Although SST can be done individually, it is most often conducted in groups (ideally with four to eight people) lasting 45 to 90 minutes per session, which is cost-efficient and provides opportunities for peer modeling and socialization experiences (S. Pratt & Mueser, 2002). For each social skill reviewed, the therapist helps clients identify the reason the skill is important, reviews the steps involved in the skill (these are often written on a large board or poster), and facilitates role-plays in which the clients practice and receive feedback on the skill. Skills taught can range from the simple (e.g., maintaining appropriate eye contact during a conversation) to the complex (e.g., assertiveness skills), with the latter being broken down into constituent parts and taught in a graded manner using repetition, rehearsal, and practice outside of sessions to reinforce learning (Heinssen et al., 2000).

Problems with generalization of skills over time and across settings have been reported in SST programs (Benton & Schroeder, 1990). This underscores the importance of ensuring that there are opportunities outside of the SST group sessions for clients to practice skills and receive positive reinforcement. Individuals who exhibit cognitive impairments in areas such as verbal memory, sustained and selective attention, and abstract reasoning are likely to have greater difficulty learning and retaining skills taught in such programs (Bowen et al., 1994; Kern, Green, & Satz, 1992; Mueser, Bellack, Douglas, & Wade, 1991). In a review of the literature on social skills training interventions for Schizophrenia, Bellack (2004) concluded that this treatment has a significant positive impact upon behavioral skills, social role functioning (particularly regarding defined skill areas), client self-efficacy, and client satisfaction, but is not substantially effective in preventing relapse or reducing symptoms.

Family-Based Interventions

Because as many as 60% of schizophrenic individuals live with their relatives, the client's family represents a potentially vital treatment resource (Goldman, 1982). Family members, more than anyone else, may have the most frequent contact with the client. The family's ongoing observations of the client's symptoms and functioning can help the treatment team closely evaluate the effectiveness of pharmacological and psychotherapeutic interventions so that swift intervention can take place if signs of impending relapse occur. Family members can encourage participation in treatment and are often an essential source of emotional and practical support for the client. Over the past few decades, family-based interventions that are primarily cognitive-behavioral and psychoeducational in nature have been developed for individuals with Schizophrenia and have largely proven effective in reducing rates of relapse compared to standard care. For example, relapse rates within the first year of treatment delivery have been reported to be 41% to 60% for clients receiving standard care, but only 8% to 19% for those receiving family treatment as an adjunctive treatment (Falloon, Hahlweg, & Tarrier, 1990). One impetus for developing family-based psychoeducational treatments grew out of findings from studies of the concept of expressed emotion. This index of critical, hostile, and emotionally overinvolved attitudes expressed by family members about a psychiatrically ill relative has been shown to predict client relapse over 9 to 12 months (Butzlaff & Hooley, 1998). Unfortunately, the EE literature has often been mistakenly interpreted as blaming the family for client relapses, even though current thinking in this area readily acknowledges that EE is likely tapping into a transactional process whereby client behaviors may both be affected by and influence family members' affective attitudes (Rosenfarb, Goldstein, & Nuechterlein, 1995; Woo, Goldstein, & Nuechterlein, 1997). In some cases, the hostile, critical reaction by family members may be a response to dealing with a chronically mentally ill family member, underscoring the need for education and support (McCreadie, Williamson, Athawes, & Connolly, 1994).

When a schizophrenic client's relatives are actively involved in his or her treatment, it can be helpful for the clinician to individually evaluate family members' thoughts about the client (e.g., the extent to which they feel burdened by the client's illness), the impact the client's symptoms have had on the family, family members' understanding of the nature and course of the client's illness, and how family members typically communicate with their ill relative. With regard to communication, the therapist may ask the client and his or her family to spend a brief time (e.g., 10 minutes) discussing an issue that has been identified as a problem in the family in order to observe how the family communicates. The therapist should be particularly attuned to globally critical, hostile, or overly intrusive (e.g., mind-reading) statements made by relatives, as well as problematic behaviors exhibited by the client (e.g., hostile, odd, or unusual behaviors) to understand how negative interactional cycles might begin or be maintained within the family.

If the clinician determines that family-based interventions may be helpful, a cognitive-behavioral, psychoeducational intervention model is recommended because this approach has been found effective in decreasing relapse, reducing family burden, improving client work functioning, and enhancing treatment compliance (Dixon, Adams, & Lucksted, 2000). This model typically emphasizes three elements: (1) psychoeducation about the illness (e.g., utilizing a stress-diathesis conceptualization), (2) communication training (to decrease the likelihood of arguments and misunderstandings that can result from faulty communication), and (3) structured problem solving (to provide the client and his or her family with a strategy for resolving both illness- and nonillness-related problems in the family; Falloon, 2002). This treatment can be conducted with individual families or with groups of families and usually takes place over 9 months, with session frequency titrated from weekly to bimonthly to monthly over the course of treatment. The CBT or psychoeducational approach is an active family treatment that requires the client and the family to participate in in-session role-plays (e.g., practicing communication skills such as active listening, making positive requests, and expressing negative feelings) and complete homework assignments in which skills are practiced to increase generalization of learning. The intervention also includes formulation of a relapse drill or a structured plan outlining client warning signs that could be indicative of an impending relapse and steps that the client and family will take in response to these signs (Mueser & Glynn, 1995). The Schizophrenia Patient Outcomes Research Team has recommended that any schizophrenic client who has ongoing contact with his or her family should be offered a family psychosocial intervention that is at least 9 months in duration and provides illness education, crisis intervention, problem-solving training, and family support (Lehman, Steinwachs, & PORT Co-investigators, 1998).

However, clinicians must recognize that engagement of the client's family in the treatment process can be complicated by several factors. Family members may fear being blamed by mental health professionals for their relative's illness, may harbor concerns about shame and stigma associated with having a seriously mentally ill relative, or may deny the illness or its severity. The clinician may also encounter complicated time and scheduling constraints in planning family sessions. Finally, relatives may wish to distance themselves from the affected individual because of the emotional, physical, and/or financial toll the illness has taken on them. A 1987 survey of members (primary family members of individuals with Schizophrenia) of the National Alliance for the Mentally Ill (a support organization for family members of mentally ill individuals) found that, on average, annual family costs associated with caring for a mentally ill family member totaled $3,539 and that close to 800 hours per year were spent in caregiving-related activities (which totals approximately $8,000 additional if time is conservatively valued at $10/hour; Franks, 1987, as cited in McGuire, 1991). These cost estimates would undoubtedly be far higher today. As discussed in the treatment chapter, involvement of the family in support groups is crucial. The struggle and frustrations that family members so often face are reflected in the following comments by a woman whose mother was schizophrenic and who is now herself the mother of a schizophrenic daughter (Aldridge, 2000; pg. 937):

Despite the effectiveness of today's anti-psychotic medications, [my husband] and I have gradually realized that [our daughter's] care remains our day-to-day responsibility—one unlikely to end while we live. Yes, there is community mental health care . . . but it's fragmented and under-funded. Professionals in one corner have no idea how to link clients' to other corners, and agencies are trying so hard to keep afloat that money, not client care, is often the prime concern.

Vocational Rehabilitation

Individuals with Schizophrenia are often chronically disabled by their symptoms and have difficulty finding and maintaining employment. However, several types of vocational rehabilitation programs have been developed to aid these individuals in acquiring job skills and finding work in settings that range from sheltered workshops to volunteer experiences to competitive employment in the community. Herz and Marder (2001) note that among the developments that have encouraged interest in improving vocational functioning among persons with Schizophrenia are the beneficial effects associated with second-generation neuroleptic medication (e.g., in terms of improvements in neurocognitive functioning and negative symptoms and milder side effect profiles) that may increase clients' interest in work, and federal legislation (e.g., the Americans with Disabilities Act) that encourages the employment of those with disabilities.

The best practice principles that have been identified by experts in the field of vocational rehabilitation as holding the greatest promise for assisting clients include (a) situational assessment, (b) competitive or supported employment, (c) rapid placement, (d) ongoing vocational support, and (e) tailoring job development and support to individual client preferences (J. A. Cook & Razzano, 2000).

Situational assessment refers to the evaluation of vocational skills and potential in actual or simulated work environments. Targets of evaluation can include specific work tasks (e.g., filing), work attitude, interpersonal skills exhibited with coworkers and supervisors, and work quality. It appears that more favorable outcomes are achieved when clients are placed in competitive or supported employment settings where they are able to earn at least minimum wage, rather than receiving training and placement in sheltered workshops (Wehman & Moon, 1988). Competitive employment placements increase opportunities for positive role-modeling (through working with nondisabled coworkers), provide economic incentives for clients, and allow clients to practice vocational skills they have learned in the very settings in which they are required (J. A. Cook & Razzano, 2000). The rationale behind rapid placement in employment settings is that long preemployment training periods may lead clients to feel demoralized and to have more difficulty applying the skills they have learned to actual work settings (J. A. Cook & Razzano, 1995). Ongoing vocational support is recommended once a client has gotten a job because the enduring nature of the social and cognitive deficits associated with Schizophrenia are likely to pose ongoing challenges for clients in work settings (Wehman & Moon, 1988). Although it makes intuitive sense, vocational rehabilitation programs have not always stressed placing clients in employment situations that are consistent with their preferences. However, when clients are able to obtain work that is inherently desirable to them, greater job satisfaction and lengthier employment have been reported (D. Becker, Drake, Farabaugh, & Bond, 1996).

Financial Issues and Disability

Due to the debilitating nature of many psychotic disorders, particularly Schizophrenia, many individuals with these illnesses are eligible for state and/or federally funded monetary benefits, including food and housing assistance. Clinicians who plan to work regularly with individuals with psychotic disorders should familiarize themselves with the rules, regulations, and procedures for applying for such benefits, as they may be called on to provide documentation of a client's disabilities to justify an award of benefits and may need to help the client and his or her family navigate the various agencies and organizations that provide aid. With regard to federal benefits, many persons who are disabled by and prevented from maintaining employment because of a chronic mental illness are eligible for Social Security Disability Insurance (SSDI) and Supplemental Security Income (SSI). Individuals are eligible for SSDI if they have worked in the past and contributed money to Social Security, whereas past work history is not required for eligibility for SSI. Another difference between these benefit sources is that SSDI is awarded independently of whether an individual has other (nonemployment-related) sources of income, whereas an individual is ineligible for SSI if his or her income exceeds a certain amount (Mueser & Gingrich, 1994). Financial assistance provided at the state or county level varies depending on location. It may be particularly difficult to secure such assistance to homeless individuals, underscoring the importance of community-based comprehensive mental health care programs based on the ACT or clubhouse model. In some cases, an individual with a severe mental illness, such as a psychotic disorder, may be unable to effectively make decisions regarding his or her personal affairs, including financial matters and medical and mental health treatment. In such cases, it may be necessary to seek a conservator to manage the client's monetary affairs and make treatment decisions (see Chapter 5).

ADVANCED TOPIC: SHARED PSYCHOTIC DISORDER

First described in the late nineteenth century, Shared Psychotic Disorder (also known as *folie à deux*, French for "madness of two") is an infrequently encountered syndrome in which an individual (often referred to as the secondary or inductee) comes to believe in a delusion held by another person (often referred to as the primary or inducer) with whom he or she has a close relationship (Lasègue & Falret, 1877/1964). In the majority of cases, the shared delusion is persecutory and nonbizarre.

Precise estimates regarding prevalence are lacking, in part because individuals with Shared Psychotic Disorder rarely seek out treatment, although the disorder appears somewhat more common in women than men (American Psychiatric Association, 2000b). While cases involving two people are most common, those involving larger numbers (e.g., entire families) have also been reported. Cults such as the Heaven's Gate group, in which 39 individuals committed mass suicide in 1997 believing they would join a spacecraft traveling behind the Hale Bopp comet, may reflect a form of this disorder, although the boundary between such large-scale phenomena and Shared Psychotic Disorder remains unclear (H. I. Kaplan & Saddock, 1998). Consideration of the cultural context in which seemingly psychotic experiences occur is important, and commonly accepted beliefs held by large numbers of individuals within a particular ethnic, cultural, or religious group are not examples of Shared Psychotic Disorder (e.g., speaking in tongues among certain Pentecostal Christian groups).

Persons who develop Shared Psychotic Disorder typically have a long-standing history of social isolation and share an intensely close relationship with one another. Early psychodynamic theories, which have not been supported by recent research (Silveira & Seeman, 1995), emphasized the role that dominance and submissiveness played in the development of the disorder, with women and young individuals viewed as particularly susceptible to becoming secondaries because of their assumed submissiveness vis-à-vis the primary. Typically, the primary suffers from a psychotic disorder such as Schizophrenia or Delusional Disorder, although some experts believe that nonpsychotic disorders (e.g., OCD, Somatoform Disorder) may be found in association with Shared Psychotic Disorder (Munro, 1999). Shared Psychotic Disorder most commonly develops among pairs of individuals from the same family, with such cases being fairly evenly divided among married or common-law, sibling, and parent-child dyads (Silveira & Seeman, 1995). Cases involving larger groups of individuals, such as an entire family, are rarer, but have been reported (Oshodi, Bangaru, & Benbow, 2005; Wehmeier, Barth, & Remschmidt, 2003).

It has been reported that most secondaries are not truly psychotic and that their delusional beliefs may remit upon being separated from the primary (Munro, 1999). However, approximately two thirds of reported familial cases of Shared Psychotic Disorder involve biologically related individuals, raising questions about possible genetic underpinnings of this illness. Schizophrenia, considered to have a strong heritable component, is the most commonly reported diagnosis in primaries, and almost one third of published case studies have reported hallucinations in the secondary (Silveira & Seeman, 1995). These observations suggest that some secondaries may possess a preexisting biological vulnerability to developing psychosis, which is then triggered by a close, isolative relationship with a psychotic individual.

Psychiatric comorbidity in the secondary appears common, with relatively high frequencies of depression, dementia, and mental retardation reported (Ghaziuddin, 1991; Mazzoli, 1992; Silveira & Seeman, 1995). Thus some secondaries may be vulnerable to impaired reality testing and the imposition of another's delusion by virtue of compromised cognitive functioning. The assertion that personality traits such as excessive dependency may make an individual susceptible to becoming a secondary makes intuitive clinical sense, although supporting empirical evidence is needed.

A ubiquitous feature of Shared Psychotic Disorder is the social isolation experienced by the affected individuals, which likely facilitates the development of the shared delusion by restricting access to other sources of reality testing. Such isolation also makes it less likely that individuals suffering from Shared Psychotic Disorder will present for treatment. Treatment of the primary is guided by the principal psychiatric diagnosis that is determined to be contributing to the delusion, and use of antipsychotic medication is common. While the delusional beliefs of the secondary may remit upon separation from the primary, effective treatment often requires use of neuroleptics as well (Silveira & Seeman, 1995). Reintroduction to reality via decreasing social isolation is an important goal of treatment for both the primary and the secondary, but resistance and attempts to sabotage treatment are likely if the affected individuals show limited insight into the irrationality of their beliefs (Munro, 1999).

Chapter 10 ————————————————————————

MOOD DISORDERS

Mood disorders are often the primary complaint of many clients seeking treatment and commonly coexist with other disorders for which the client may initially seek help. The *Report of the Surgeon General—Executive Summary,* a comprehensive summary of information relating to the epidemiology, etiology, and treatment of a variety of mental disorders, estimated that within any 1-year period in the United States, mood disorders collectively affect 7.1% of adults ages 18 to 54, 6.2% of children ages 9 to 17, and 4.4% of adults age 55 or older (U.S. Department of Health and Human Services, 1999). In birth cohorts since the 1940s the prevalence of mood disorders has been increasing and the age of illness onset decreasing, leading some to dub this period the "age of melancholy" (Gershon, Hamovit, Guroff, & Nurnberger, 1987; Klerman, 1978; Lewinsohn, Rohde, Seely, & Fischer, 1993). While the causes of this phenomenon remain unclear (hypotheses range from changes in genetic loading for disorders across generations to the breakdown of societal supports and stressors associated with changes in social roles), what is certain is that the treatment of mood disorders will remain one of the most important public health issues for years to come (First & Tasman, 2005). The primary focus in this chapter is on Major Depressive Disorder, Dysthymic Disorder, and Bipolar Disorder.

HISTORICAL OVERVIEW

Numerous descriptions can be found in ancient literature of conditions that would be labeled mood disorders today. Many date to the ancient Greeks, when illnesses such as *melancholia* (akin to our notion of depression) and *mania* were first described. The Greeks conceptualized mental disturbances as biological phenomena that arose from derangements in essential bodily humors (blood, black bile, yellow bile, and phlegm); melancholia was believed to result from an excess of black bile, and mania occurred because of an excess of yellow bile (F. K. Goodwin & Jaimison, 1990). Although such etiological theories bear little resemblance to current thinking about mood disorders, these ancient writers' descriptions of the presentation of melancholia and mania were often remarkably close to what we see today. For example, melancholia was described by writers such as Hippocrates (c. 460–337 BC), Aretaeus (c. AD 50–130), and Galen (c. AD 129–199) as a frequently chronic, recurrent condition involving despondency, dissatisfaction with life, sleep problems, restlessness, irritability, difficulties with decision making, desire to die, and, in extreme cases, the development of psychotic features (e.g., delusions; Jackson,

1986; Porter, 1999). Aretaeus also wrote extensively about mania and noted its myriad manifestations, such as excitement, cheerfulness, euphoria, grandiosity, and angry furor (Porter, 1999). Aretaeus drew linkages between melancholia and mania and suggested that in some cases mania could follow a period of melancholia or vice versa (Porter, 1999). He also differentiated between biological causes of melancholia and reactive depression, and hypothesized that the latter was caused by psychological or environmental factors (Angst & Marneros, 2001).

At other points throughout history, conditions such as depression and mania were attributed to other worldly causes such as demonic possession, the influence of evil spirits, or punishment from God (F. K. Goodwin & Jaimison, 1990). However, during the late Renaissance, extensive writings on depression and mania appeared, and a movement toward more scientific conceptualizations of these conditions emerged. Descriptions of the phenomenology of depression and mania often closely paralleled modern-day conceptualizations, as in Plater's (1536–1613) observation that manic individuals were prone to uncharacteristic behavior such as hypersexuality (Porter, 1999). During this period, Robert Burton (1577–1640) published his voluminous *Anatomy of Melancholy*, in which he outlined causal factors for melancholia, including temperament, biological rhythms, diet, alcohol, and emotional factors (e.g., passions of intense love; Kiessling, Faulkner, & Blair, 1990).

The term *depression* replaced melancholia in the mid-nineteenth century and was viewed as a potentially reversible condition characterized by sadness, lack of initiative, and gloomy thoughts (Berrios, 1999). During this time, Flaret, Baillarger, and Griesinger also recognized that depression and mania could co-occur in a single disease state that was thought to be chronic and have a poor prognosis (J. Angst & Marneros, 2001; F. K. Goodwin & Jaimison, 1990). Important work in the historical evolution of mood disorders was done by the German psychiatrist Emil Kraepelin in the late nineteenth and early twentieth centuries. Kraepelin, often referred to as the father of modern-day psychiatry, drew a distinction between *manic-depressive insanity* and *dementia praecox* (i.e., Schizophrenia); he believed that the former was more likely to have an episodic course that carried a better prognosis (Berrios, 1999a). While Kraepelin conceptualized manic-depressive illness as having biological origins, he also believed that psychological factors could play a role in precipitating illness episodes (F. K. Goodwin & Jaimison, 1990), which foreshadowed the modern stress-diathesis (or stress-vulnerability) model of mental illness. Although Kraepelin acknowledged the existence of forms of depression not linked to mania, he conceptualized most forms of melancholia as part of manic-depressive illness.

In early versions of the *DSM* (e.g., *DSM-I*; American Psychiatric Association, 1952), the terms *manic-depressive reaction* and *depressive-reaction* appeared. The word *reaction* reflected the influence of Adolf Meyer, a Swiss-born neurologist and psychiatrist who immigrated to the United States in the late nineteenth century and became a highly influential figure in American psychiatry. Meyer believed that psychopathology could best be understood as a reaction resulting from the interaction among biological, psychological, and psychosocial factors (F. K. Goodwin & Jaimison, 1990). This term was dropped in subsequent versions of the *DSM* and replaced by terms such as *depressive neurosis* (*DSM-II*; American Psychiatric Association, 1968). The more familiar term *affective disorders* appeared in the *DSM-III* (American Psychiatric Association, 1980), along with specific, atheoretical diagnostic criteria sets for disorders that improved the reliability of diagnoses. The *DSM-III* also introduced the *unipolar-bipolar* distinction among the mood disorders, which reflected the work of Leonhard, Angst, Perris, and others who observed differences in the histories of individuals with depression versus Bipolar Disorder that appeared to warrant such a division (e.g., the higher incidence of mania in the families of individuals with Bipolar Disorder; F. K. Goodwin & Jamison, 1990).

Many questions remain unanswered regarding various subgroups of mood disorders that are not well represented in the current *DSM-IV-TR* nomenclature. For example, argu ments have been made for expanding the continuum of bipolar spectrum disorders to include recognition of conditions such as recurrent major depressive episodes superimposed on a hyperthymic temperament, recurrent depression that switches to hypomania with antidepressant use, and recurrent depressions in the absence of spontaneous hypomanic episodes but in the context of a family history of Bipolar Disorder (Akiskal & Pinto, 1999). Other mood disorders requiring further study (e.g., minor depressive disorder) are summarized under *DSM-IV* Appendix B: Criteria Sets and Axes Provided for Further Study, and further research will ultimately determine whether any of these are incorporated into future revisions of the *DSM*.

DEPRESSIVE DISORDERS

Major Depressive Disorder

A major depressive episode is the building block of the Major Depressive Disorder diagnosis. According to the *DSM-IV-TR* system, a diagnosis of Major Depressive Disorder requires a history of one or more major depressive episodes, no history of mood episodes that would indicate Bipolar Disorder (e.g., a hypomanic, manic, or mixed episode), and no symptoms that would indicate another disorder of which significant depressive symptoms could be a part (e.g., Schizoaffective Disorder; American Psychiatric Association, 2000b).

Clinical Presentation

Mood Changes   Major depressive episodes are characterized most prominently by mood changes that are manifest as sad or depressed mood and/or significantly decreased interest in usual or pleasurable activities. The centrality of these features is highlighted by the requirement in the *DSM-IV-TR* that at least one of these two symptoms be present for major depressive episode criteria to be met (the symptom criteria list for a major depressive episode consists of nine symptoms and a total of five are required for diagnosis; American Psychiatric Association, 2000b). In children and adolescents, depression may be manifest primarily in irritable mood.

The term *anhedonia*, which is used to denote a complete loss of pleasure in activities, is notably excluded from the *DSM-IV-TR* criteria for a major depressive episode; this is because depressed individuals often retain *some* capacity for experiencing pleasure, even though it may be greatly diminished (Frances et al., 1995). Often, depressive changes in mood are noticed by others, so it is helpful to ask the client about the perceptions of family members, friends, or coworkers.

Vegetative Symptoms   Major depressive episodes are also characterized by additional symptoms such as motoric changes (e.g., retardation or agitation), impaired sleep, appetite disturbance, and fatigue or decreased energy that are collectively referred to as vegetative symptoms. When severe, such symptoms can be highly disabling, and pharmacologic intervention may be required to ameliorate them. Although depressed individuals often complain of *decreases* in appetite and/or sleep (e.g., difficulty falling asleep, staying asleep, awakening too early), some individuals have the opposite experience and will eat and sleep more than usual. Such increases can suggest the presence of atypical features, which are discussed further under "Subtypes." Recent research indicates that depressed individuals report poorer perceptions of sleep quality compared to normal controls, even when sleep timing perceptions are similar between groups, which suggests that faulty cognitions may play a role in how certain vegetative symptoms are perceived (Mayers & Baldwin, 2006).

Cognitive Changes   Depressed individuals frequently report cognitive changes that include impaired attention, concentration, and decision making. These problems may be suggested by the client's report of being unable to pay attention or remember something that has just been read or seen on television, difficulty completing even simple tasks at work, and inability to decide what to wear in the morning or what to eat. Studies of depressed people's performance on formal tests of attention reveal significant impairment relative to normal controls (Landrø, Stiles, & Sletvold, 2001). Against a background of generalized attentional deficits, both medicated and unmedicated unipolar depressed persons also exhibit a mood-congruent attentional bias (Erickson et al., 2005; Murphy et al., 1999). Erikson et al. found that unmedicated depressed individuals administered an attention task requiring responses to words of a certain valence and response suppression to words of the opposite valence made more omission errors when responding to happy than to sad words and responded more quickly to sad targets than to happy targets (control subjects showed the opposite pattern). It appears that some degree of attentional deficits (e.g., in sustained and divided attention) may persist even when a major depressive episode has remitted (Paelecke-Habermann, Pohl, & Leplow, 2005).

Negative Self-Evaluation and Suicidal Ideation   Negative thoughts about oneself are very common in depression and may take the form of an extreme and exaggerated sense of guilt or worthlessness (American Psychiatric Association, 2000b).

Whenever a client presents with depression, it is imperative to inquire about suicidal ideation and attempts. Chapter 2 reviewed in detail the steps for evaluating suicidality. As will be addressed later (under "Associated Features"), depression is associated with a significantly elevated risk of suicide. Individuals with mood disorders are approximately 15 to 20 times more likely than others in the general population to commit suicide (Jaimison, 1999).

Depression Subtypes

Melancholic Depression   Individuals with melancholic depression experience a loss of pleasure in all or almost all activities or are nonreactive to usually pleasurable activities (i.e., the individual's mood does not brighten at all or brightens only minimally in response to them; American Psychiatric Association, 2000b). In addition, according to the

DSM-IV-TR (American Psychiatric Association, 2000b), the individual must display three or more symptoms from a list of six, such as worsening depression in the morning, early morning awakening, significant weight loss or anorexia, and the perception that one's mood is qualitatively different from that experienced in other contexts (e.g., after the death of a loved one). The vague definition of the last symptom makes it difficult to evaluate. For example, the *DSM-IV-TR* notes that descriptions of mood as simply being more severe, longer lasting, or occurring without reason are not sufficient to qualify as being distinct in quality (American Psychiatric Association, 2000b). Thus, calls have been made to remove this item from the *DSM* symptom list for melancholic depression (Parker et al., 1997). In the *DSM-IV-TR* system, *melancholic features* is a specifier that can be attached to depressive episodes that occur in the context of a diagnosis of Major Depressive Disorder or Bipolar I or II Disorder and is used to refer to the client's current or most recent depressive episode.

Melancholic depression (also known as endogenous depression) is considered a severe form of affective illness. Suicide risk may be elevated when specific symptoms of severe anhedonia, hopelessness, and inappropriate guilt are present, and there is evidence that the *lethality* of suicide attempts among those with melancholic depression is greater than that seen in nonmelancholic depression, despite overall suicide rates being lower in the former group (Grunebaum et al., 2004; Leventhal & Rehm, 2005; M. Zimmerman, Coryell, Pfohl, & Stangl, 1986). Although comorbid personality disorders have been reported to be less common among persons with melancholic depression (Charney, Nelson, & Quinlan, 1981), this finding has been disputed (Tedlow et al., 2002). Other features typically associated with melancholic depression are older age, stronger family history of depression, lower family history of alcoholism and antisocial personality, lower prevalence of divorce and marital separations, better social support, higher frequency of neuroendocrine or other biologic abnormalities, poorer response to psychotherapy, and better response to pharmacotherapy (M. Zimmerman et al., 1986). Individuals with melancholic features respond less well to selective serotonin reuptake inhibitors (SSRIs) compared to nonmelancholic individuals and better to tricyclic antidepressants (TCAs) and electroconvulsive therapy (ECT; Pagnin, de Queiroz, Pini, & Cassano, 2004; Parker, Roy, Wilhelm, & Mitchell, 2001; P. Perry, 1996). Although melancholic depression may appear strongly biologically driven, recent research suggests that nonsevere, stressful life events may play a role in precipitating mood episodes in these individuals (Harkness & Monroe, 2006). Finally, questions have been raised about the descriptive validity of the melancholic features specifier based on research findings that the rates of persistence of these features across time is relatively low, and that consistent differences between *melancholic* and *nonmelancholic* depressed patients in rates of current comorbid Axis I or II disorders or the course of depression have not been firmly established (Melartin, Leskelä, et al., 2004).

Atypical Depression   Atypical major depression is characterized by mood reactivity (i.e., mood brightens in response to positive events) and additional features such as excessive sleep, weight gain, a heavy, leaden feeling in the extremities (known as leaden paralysis), and a history of rejection sensitivity (even during periods of normal mood; American Psychiatric Association, 2000b). In the *DSM-IV-TR* system, *atypical features* is a specifier that can be attached to depressive episodes that occur in the context of a diagnosis of Major Depressive Disorder or Bipolar I or Bipolar II Disorder and is used to refer to the client's current or most recent depressive episode. "The atypical features specifier can also be applied to a DSM-IV-TR diagnosis of Dysthymic Disorder." (American Psychiatric Association, 2000b). The term atypical is not meant to imply that these features are unusual or rare, but instead was originally meant to distinguish such presentations from more classical endogenous or melancholic depression (American Psychiatric Association, 2000b). Thus, atypical depression is noted to have "reverse" vegetative symptoms such as hypersomnia and increased appetite; atypical depression is also characterized by the presence of somatic anxiety, fatigue, evening worsening of mood, initial insomnia, and poor response to ECT and certain antidepressant drugs (R. W. Lam & Stewart, 1996). Atypical depression responds better to monoamine oxidase inhibitors (MAOIs) and less well to TCAs (Henkel et al., 2006). Outpatient studies suggest that nearly 30% of depressed clients meet criteria for atypical depression (Asnis, McGinn, & Sanderson, 1995). Atypical depression is diagnosed more frequently in women and has been linked to greater likelihood of Panic Disorder, somatization, substance use comorbidities, and an earlier age of onset (H. I. Kaplan & Saddock, 1998). A study examining atypical depression in individuals with either Major Depressive Disorder or Bipolar II Disorder found the overall frequency of atypical depression was 43% in their combined sample, the frequency was especially high among those with Bipolar II Disorder, and the number of atypical features displayed was strongly related to a family history of Bipolar Disorder (Akiskal & Benazzi, 2005). Collectively, these findings suggest that atypical depression could be an indicator of an undiagnosed Bipolar II Disorder in some individuals (Akiskal & Benazzi, 2005).

Seasonal Affective Disorder   Some individuals experience recurrence and remission of depressive symptoms at predictable seasons of the year. The most typical pattern for seasonally linked depression is onset during the winter months and remission during the spring. The prevalence of seasonal affective disorder (SAD) in the United States is estimated to be less than 1% (Blazer, Kessler, & Swartz, 1988). In the *DSM-IV-TR* system, a seasonal pattern specifier can be assigned to a diagnosis of recurrent Major Depressive Disorder (as well as to Bipolar I and II Disorder; American Psychiatric Association, 2000b). Faedda and colleagues (1993) found that SAD accounted for 10% of all mood disorders (and of this group, half had Major Depressive Disorder), and affected individuals were most likely to be women. Among those presenting for treatment of SAD, over one third will eventually develop a nonseasonal pattern to their affective episodes (Partonen & Lönnqvist, 1998). Features of SAD are very similar to atypical depression and include hypersomnia, hyperphagia (i.e., increased eating), carbohydrate craving, and fatigue. Among the factors that have been implicated in the development of SAD are abnormal phase-delays in circadian rhythms, increased melatonin secretion during winter months, seasonally linked neurotransmitter fluctuations, and genetic factors (R. W. Lam & Levitan, 2000).

Dysthymic Disorder

Dysthymic Disorder is a chronic illness characterized by depressed mood. Although the symptoms of Dysthymic Disorder may be less severe than those encountered in illness episodes of Major Depressive Disorder, the morbidity associated with this illness is high (B. Bell et al., 2004). As will be discussed under "Common Comorbidities" later in this chapter, Dysthymic Disorder frequently co-occurs with other Axis I and II disorders and can therefore easily be overlooked and undertreated by clinicians who may be focused on more florid symptoms associated with a comorbid condition (D. N. Klein & Santiago, 2003).

Clinical Presentation

Mood Changes   According to the *DSM-IV-TR*, Dysthymic Disorder is characterized by a 2-year period during which an individual is depressed most of the time (for children and adolescents, mood can be irritable and the duration requirement is a minimum of 1 year instead of 2; American Psychiatric Association, 2000b). Additionally, an individual cannot be without mood or other symptoms of dysthymia for more than 2 months at a time in order for a diagnosis to be made. During the first 2 years of the disorder (1 year for children), a major depressive episode cannot have occurred, although after this time, superimposed major depressive episodes are allowed for a Dysthymic Disorder diagnosis. Dysthymic Disorder cannot be diagnosed if there is a history of hypomanic, manic, or mixed episodes.

Additional Symptoms   In addition to chronically depressed mood, *DSM-IV-TR* criteria require that two of a list of six additional symptoms must also be present. These symptoms reflect vegetative symptoms (disturbances in eating, sleeping) as well as cognitive-emotional changes (e.g., low self-esteem, decision-making difficulty). Although only two symptoms are required, dysthymic individuals frequently experience many more than this (D. N. Klein & Santiago, 2003).

Individuals with Dysthymic Disorder tend to report cognitive and emotional changes more frequently than vegetative symptoms (Barzega, Maina, Venturello, & Bogetto, 2001; Keller et al., 1995; Serretti et al., 1999). Results of the *DSM-IV* field trials indicated that a different set of the additional symptoms of dysthymia, one that emphasizes cognitive and emotional symptoms, may more accurately capture the types of symptoms commonly experienced by dysthymic individuals; however, further research supporting this alternative criterion set is needed before it can be officially incorporated into the *DSM-IV* proper. Among dysthymic children, commonly reported symptoms include irritability, fatigue, low energy, depressed mood, guilt, concentration difficulties, hopelessness, and anhedonia (Masi et al., 2003).

Association with Major Depression   Dysthymic Disorder is frequently comorbid with Major Depressive Disorder, a condition referred to as *double depression*. For example, 75% to 90% of those with Dysthymic Disorder report a history of major depression at some time during their illness (Keller et al., 1995; Klein, Schwartz, Rose, & Leader, 2000). Approximately 25% of those presenting with a history of a major depressive episode have a history of an antecedent Dysthymic Disorder (D. N. Klein & Santiago, 2003). Among children and adolescents with Dysthymic Disorder, 42% to 75% have a superimposed Major Depressive Disorder (Kovacs, Akiskal, Gastonis, & Parrone, 1994).

Additional Characteristics

Increased Mortality   The mortality rate among individuals diagnosed with depressive disorders is significantly higher than for the general population (estimates range from

36% to 100%), and suicide accounts for much of this increase (F. Angst, Stassen, Clayton, & Angst, 2002; Guze & Robins, 1970). F. Angst et al., in a longitudinal follow-up study of formerly hospitalized individuals with mood disorders, found the rate of suicide was 27 times higher than in the general population. Rates of suicide attempts and of completed suicide among individuals with unipolar depression have been reported to be 56% and 7% to 22%, respectively (Berglund & Nilsson, 1987; F. K. Goodwin & Jamison, 1990; Kiloh, Andrews, & Neilson, 1988). More conservative estimates of suicide risk among those with depressive disorders indicate a risk of 3.4% overall, 1% for women, and 7% for men (Blair-West, Cantor, Mellsop, & Eyeson-Annan, 1999). Men under age 25 with depression are over 10 times more likely to die by suicide compared to women in the same age group (Blair-West et al., 1999). Among psychiatric inpatients who commit suicide, the percentage of individuals with depression ranges from 11% to 77% (Krupinski et al., 1998). A depressive disorder diagnosis is also a risk factor for suicide among adolescents (Fergusson & Lynskey, 1995; Lewis, Johnson, Cohen, Garcia, & Velez, 1988; Reinherz et al., 1995). To illustrate, Lewinsohn, Seeley, Buckley, and Klein (2002) reported a suicide attempt rate of 21.8% in a community-derived sample of adolescents with Major Depressive Disorder who were followed into early adulthood. At the opposite end of the age spectrum, Barrow and Linden (2000) found that a diagnosis of major depression in community-dwelling elders was associated with a 40-fold increased risk of showing signs of suicidality, but only was 3 times higher when a nonmajor depressive disorder psychiatric diagnosis was present.

The 6 to 12 months following hospital discharge represents a period of particularly high risk for suicide attempts by those with depressive disorders (Fawcett, Scheftner, Hedeker, Gibbons, & Coryell, 1987). However, a subset of depressed individuals has a nearly constant risk of suicide across their lifetime (possibly due to a genetic or biological predisposition), and lifelong therapeutic precautions are needed for these individuals (F. Angst et al., 2002). Additional predictors of suicide among those with depressive disorders include prior suicide attempts, hopelessness, loss of pleasure or interest, anger or impulsivity, agitation, panic, hypochondriacal concerns or delusions, acute onset, mood cycling during the index episode, discontinuation of medication, and comorbid conditions such as substance use disorders, personality disorders, or anxiety (Berglund & Nilsson, 1987; Fawcett et al., 1987; Krupinski et al., 1998; A. Rihmer, 2007; B. Schneider, Philipp, & Müller, 2001; Sher, Oquendo, & Mann, 2001; Yerevanian, Koek, Feusner, Hwang, & Mintz, 2004). Long-term treatment with antidepressant medication has been shown to significantly lower suicide risk among adults with unipolar affective disorders (F. Angst et al., 2002).

Psychosis   It is estimated that as many as 20% of depressed individuals experience psychotic symptoms such as hallucinations or delusions during the course of their mood disturbance (Ohayon & Schatzberg, 2002). Delusions are frequently nihilistic and center on themes of worthlessness, guilt, and hypochondriacal or somatic concerns (Maher, 2001). Individuals with psychotic depression appear to differ in important ways from those with nonpsychotic depression. Longitudinal studies of psychotic depression show that affected individuals remain well for shorter periods of time than depressed persons with no history of psychosis, exhibit greater psychosocial impairment, and have a suicide risk that is as much as 5 times higher than in nonpsychotic depression (Coryell et al., 1996; Roose,

Glassman, Walsh, Woodring, & Vital-Herne, 1983). Neuropsychological studies demonstrate that depression with psychotic features is associated with greater impairments in psychomotor speed and verbal memory compared to nonpsychotic depression (Fleming, Blasey, & Schatzberg, 2004). In addition, psychotic depression appears associated with hyperreactivity of the hypothalamic-pituitary-adrenocortical axis (Duval et al., 2006; this axis is discussed further under "Etiology"). Psychotic symptoms are most likely to recur in subsequent severe episodes of depression. In the *DSM-IV-TR* system, the presence of psychotic symptoms associated with a mood disorder diagnosis is indicated by use of a severity specifier (American Psychiatric Association, 2000b).

Catatonia Major depression may be accompanied by catatonia, which is defined by the *DSM-IV-TR* (American Psychiatric Association, 2000b) as encompassing features such as motoric immobility, purposeless motor activity, and unusual voluntary movements (e.g., unusual mannerisms, grimacing). Catatonic individuals often appear extremely still or immobile and may hold positions they are posed in (known as waxy flexibility or catalepsy), but may also appear agitated. Among inpatients with catatonic features, the majority are diagnosed with mood disorders (American Psychiatric Association, 2000b). Catatonic features may respond to ECT or the administration of benzodiazepines (e.g., lorazepam, diazepam; Hung & Huang, 2006). In the *DSM-IV-TR* system, catatonic features are considered a specifier that can be attached to a client's current or most recent major depressive episode in the context of Major Depressive Disorder, or Bipolar I or II Disorder. The catatonic features specifier can also be attached to the current or most recent mixed, or manic episode occuring in the context of Bipolar I or Bipolar II Disorder (American Psychiatric Association, 2000b).

Onset, Course, and Life Span Considerations

Onset According to the Epidemiologic Catchment Area (ECA) study, the median age of onset for depression in adults is 23 years for women and 25 years for men, with notable increases in onset observed for both sexes during the 15- to 19-year-old period (K. C. Burke, Burke, Regier, & Rae, 1990). Earlier age of onset is correlated with a history of depression in a first-degree relative (e.g., a parent; Weissman, Merikangas, & Wickramaratne, 1986).

When a *DSM-IV-TR* diagnosis of Dysthymic Disorder is given, the clinician must specify whether the illness onset is early (i.e., prior to age 21) or late (i.e., at 21 years of age or later; American Psychiatric Association, 2000b). The age demarcating early and late onset dysthymia in the *DSM-IV* is somewhat arbitrary and not universally accepted, as is evident when one examines *ICD-10* criteria, which defines late-onset dysthymia as occurring between 30 and 50 years of age (World Health Organization, 1992). Some studies report a greater percentage of cases of earlier-onset dysthymia (e.g., 73%; D. N. Klein, Schatzberg, McCullough, Keller, et al., 1999), whereas other studies report the opposite (e.g., 24%; Barzega et al., 2001). In a longitudinal study of individuals with dysthymia, D. N. Klein, Shankman, and Rose (2006) found that the mean age of onset of those with early-onset dysthymia was approximately 11 years.

Course Major depression is the cause of significant mortality and morbidity. In industrialized countries, disability associated with this disorder is second only to that caused by ischemic heart disease (Murray & Lopez, 1996). In a longitudinal study assessing the impact of depression among employed primary care patients, depressed individuals (including those with dysthymia and double depression) experienced multiple persistent job-related problems compared to both healthy controls and medically ill individuals (i.e., persons with rheumatoid arthritis) in areas such as interpersonal functioning, time management, work output, ability to complete mental and physical tasks, and job turnover rates. In addition, even depressed patients who met criteria for clinical improvement performed worse relative to healthy controls (Adler et al., 2006; Lerner et al., 2004).

When untreated, a major depressive episode may last anywhere between 6 and 12 months (H. I. Kaplan & Saddock, 1998). Although depression is considered a highly treatable disorder, it is a recurrent illness. Half of those seeking treatment for depression can be expected to experience recurrent episodes (Keller, Lavori, Lewis, & Klerman, 1983). The risk of recurrence following recovery from an index episode is approximately 30% after 6 months and almost 40% after 1 year, with multiple (e.g., three or more) major depressive episodes predicting faster recurrence (American Psychiatric Association, 1993). A 10-year follow-up study of 318 individuals with Major Depressive Disorder found an average of two episodes occurred during the follow-up period, recurrence risk decreased as length of recovery increased, and the probability of recurrence increased by 16% for each successive recurrence (e.g., an individual with five lifetime depressive episodes would be more than 2 times as likely to have a recurrence compared to someone with only one lifetime episode; Solomon et al., 2000).

The course and prognosis of major depression are related to a number of factors. In general, *earlier age of onset* is associated with a poorer prognostic picture characterized by longer episode and total illness duration, greater symptom severity (including suicidality), and more psychiatric comorbidity and irritability, agitation, and atypical features (D. N. Klein, Schatzberg, McCullough, Dowling, et al., 1999; Zisook et al., 2004). As alluded to previously, the *number of previous episodes* is also related to the course of depression. Approximately 50% of individuals who experience one major depressive episode are likely to experience another, whereas 70% to 80% of those experiencing two or more depressive episodes are likely to experience another (Keller et al., 1983). These statistics point to the importance of prompt and effective treatment of the first episode of depression since this represents a crucial turning point in establishing the course of a depressive disorder (Z. V. Segal, Pearson, & Thase, 2003). *Axis I and Axis II comorbidity* are also associated with longer episode duration and more frequent recurrences (Melartin, Rystälä, et al., 2004). The presence of co-occurring dysthymia is associated with particularly poor prognosis and low remission rates among individuals with major depression (Wells, Burnam, Rogers, & Hays, 1992).

It can be easy to think of dysthymia as less impairing than Major Depressive Disorder; however, impairment in interpersonal, marital and family, and occupational functioning is at least as great as that seen in unipolar depression (D. N. Klein & Santiago, 2003). In addition to utilizing a higher proportion of health and social services and having higher annual health care costs and more indirect costs (e.g., lost wages) compared to those without psychiatric disorders, persons with dysthymia have been found to worry more about their health, report worse health status, exhibit lower social role functioning and adjustment, and possess poorer coping ability (B. Bell et al., 2004).

In the first long-term follow-up study of adults with either dysthymia or double depression, D. N. Klein et al. (2006) reported that the estimated rate of recovery over a 10-year period was approximately 74%, with the average time to recovery from the point of study entry being slightly under 5½ years (recovery was defined as at least 2 consecutive months with no more than one to two mild depressive symptoms). However, among those who attained recovery, the estimated risk of subsequent relapse was about 71%, highlighting the recurrent nature of Dysthymic Disorder. Recovery was most likely to occur within the first 3 years of follow-up, and recovery after 6 years was quite low. Among those who experienced a relapse, approximately one fourth met full *DSM-IV* criteria for Dysthymic Disorder, one fourth met diagnostic criteria for a major depressive episode, and one half experienced significant depressive symptoms that did not meet the diagnostic threshold for either Dysthymic Disorder or Major Depressive Disorder. In addition, many individuals experienced subthreshold depressive symptoms in between periods of recovery and relapse. Finally, this study found that in comparison to individuals with nonchronic Major Depressive Disorder, those with Dysthymic Disorder demonstrated a slower rate of symptomatic improvement over time, exhibited a higher level of symptoms at the final 10-year follow-up assessment, and spent a greater proportion of the follow-up period meeting diagnostic criteria for a depressive disorder (60% versus 21%, respectively). Rates of hospitalization and suicide have also been reported being higher among those with Dysthymic Disorder compared to those with major depression (Klein et al., 2000).

Life Span Considerations   Depression in children and adolescents is frequently a recurrent and persistent condition. The development of depressive disorders in youth is undoubtedly influenced by many factors, both biological and environmental. Risk factors for the development of depression in children and adolescents include a family history of depression, maladaptive parenting style, child abuse, and negative life events (Waslick, Kandel, & Kakouros, 2002). Depression in children and adolescents is often associated with school problems (e.g., academic underachievement, poor attendance, lack of motivation), family conflict, somatic symptoms (e.g., headaches, stomachaches), and increased risk of drug and alcohol use (Waslick et al., 2002). It is estimated that one half of youth with elevated levels of depressive symptoms will continue to endorse high levels of depression 6 to 24 months later (J. Garber, Keiley, & Martin, 2002). Although many depressed children and adolescents experience improvement in their depressive symptoms with appropriate follow-up care, initial diagnoses of chronic depressive conditions, such as Dysthymic Disorder, are associated with persistence of symptoms. For example, over a 5-year period, children and adolescents with a Dysthymic Disorder diagnosis can be expected to show some degree of symptoms 70% of the time (Nobile, Cataldo, Marino, & Molteni, 2003).

Risk of relapse among depressed children and adolescents has not been studied as extensively as in adults, but community- and clinic-based studies have reported fairly high rates, ranging from 46% to 63% (B. A. Brent, Birmhauer, Kolko, Baugher, & Bridge, 2000; Lewinsohn, Rohde, Seeley, Klein, & Gotlib, 2000; Weissman et al., 1999). Lewinsohn, Rohde, et al., in a longitudinal study of 274 depressed adolescents, found that multiple depressive episodes in adolescence, Borderline Personality Disorder symptoms, a family history of recurrent Major Depressive Disorder, and (for females only) increased conflict with parents predicted reoccurrence of major depression into early adulthood (i.e., through age 24). Stressful life events and maternal history of depression also predict higher levels of depression among adolescents, and the presence of a negative attributional style in depressed adolescents is associated with increasing levels of depressive symptoms across adolescence compared to depressed youth who exhibit a more positive attributional style (J. Garber et al., 2002).

Among the elderly, risk factors for depression include cognitive impairment, previous depressive episodes, female sex, stressful life events (e.g., death of a spouse or loved one), reduced social support or contact, physical or medical illness or injury, functional decline or disability, and lower socioeconomic status (Blazer, 2004; Bruce, 2002). In general, one third of elderly individuals with depression can be expected to recover within 1 year and remain well, one third will experience a partial recovery, and one third will have a chronic course (Blazer, 2004). As with younger populations, depression among the elderly is associated with increased mortality from a variety of medical causes (Schulz, Drayer, & Rollman, 2002; Vinkers, Stek, Gussekbi, van der Mast, & Westendorp, 2004; Yaffe, Edwards, Covinksy, Lui, & Eng, 2003) and from suicide. Among older adults with depression, risk of poor outcome is significantly increased when a comorbid Dysthymic Disorder is present (Hybels, Blazer, & Steffens, 2005). Poor outcome is also associated with increased limitations in mobility and capacity to carry out activities of daily living, poor self-perceived health, life dissatisfaction, and cardiac problems (Hybels et al., 2005).

BIPOLAR DISORDERS

Bipolar I Disorder and Bipolar II Disorder are based on the occurrence of manic or hypomanic episodes, respectively. More specifically, according to the *DSM-IV-TR* (American Psychiatric Association, 2000b), a diagnosis of Bipolar I Disorder can be made when there is a history of at least one manic or mixed episode, whereas a diagnosis of Bipolar II Disorder requires a history of at least 1 hypomanic episode, 1 major depressive episode, and no manic or mixed episodes (American Psychiatric Association, 2000b). Remember that although Bipolar I Disorder is characterized by manic or mixed episodes, an individual with this diagnosis may also exhibit hypomanic episodes during the course of the illness.

Clinical Presentation

Manic versus Hypomanic Episodes

According to the *DSM-IV-TR*, a manic episode can be distinguished from a hypomanic episode based on (a) the minimum number of days symptoms must be present and (b) the degree of impairment caused by symptoms (American Psychiatric Association, 2000b). Indeed, the symptom lists (i.e., Criteria A and B) for mania and hypomania are essentially identical. Both, for example, require the presence of a persistently elevated, expansive, or irritable mood and the presence of three additional symptoms from a list of seven (four if mood is predominantly irritable); however, for mania, symptoms must be present for at least 1 week (or less, if the individual is hospitalized), and for hypomania for *at least* 4 days (American Psychiatric Association, 2000b). With regard to hypomania, novice clinicians often mistakenly interpret this criterion to mean that a hypomanic episode can last no longer than 4 days; however, mood symptoms may persist longer than this time. In addition, mania must result in markedly impaired functioning (e.g., the individual may become psychotic or need to be hospitalized), whereas hypomania is associated with un-equivocal change in functioning (e.g., noticed by others) that is not associated with sig-nificant impairments in occupational or social functioning (American Psychiatric Association, 2000b). It should be noted that the decision to set the minimum temporal duration of a hypomanic episode to 4 days was somewhat arbitrary, and arguments have been made to lower it to 2 days to capture more individuals who lie along the spectrum of Bipolar Disorders (Akiskal et al., 2000). In a prospective longitudinal study of individuals diagnosed with Bipolar II Disorder, long-term symptom status, chronicity, and other course characteristics were not significantly different when hypomanic episodes were de-fined as brief (2 to 6 days) versus longer (7+ days; Judd, Akiskal, et al., 2003).

Mood Changes

In the early stages of mania, feelings of euphoria and extreme well-being are not likely to be viewed as problematic by the affected individual or even others. However, if left un-treated, such pleasant feelings are likely to give way to increasingly negative emotions. Based on longitudinal observations of untreated manic episodes, G. A. Carlson and Goodwin (1973) identified three stages through which mania progresses. Stage 1 is char-acterized by feelings of euphoria, overconfidence, and expansiveness. Stage 2 is marked by increasing hostility and anger that may be accompanied by aggressive outbursts. In stage 3, the individual is likely to experience feelings of panic and may be floridly psychotic.

Cognitive Changes

Mania and hypomania are also characterized by cognitive changes that are reflected in symptoms such as grandiosity, racing thoughts (or flight of ideas), increased talkativeness, and distractibility. Manic and hypomanic individuals may present as being extremely self-confident and may harbor beliefs that they are the best and the brightest. They have an excessively positive view of themselves, the future, and the world at large that is charac-terized by irrepressible optimism and an underestimation of the negative consequences of their behavior (Basco & Rush, 2007). In mania, self-confidence can give way to grandiose ideation that becomes delusional (e.g., beliefs that one has special powers or is famous). The speech of a manic individual is likely to be pressured and difficult to follow or inter-rupt. In some cases, speech may be so disorganized that it resembles the type of thought disorder seen in Schizophrenia. However, in comparison to Schizophrenia, thought disor-der in mania is more likely to be characterized by pressured pace, flight of ideas, combi-natory and overly inclusive thinking, grandiosity, and an affective element that includes playfulness, flippancy, and humor (F. K. Goodwin & Jamison, 1990). Hypomanic individ-uals typically do not experience the degree of disorganization in thought or speech that is seen in mania. As many as 71% of manic persons report distractibility and impairments in concentration, which may be revealed through behaviors such as difficulty answering questions or finishing their thoughts (F. K. Goodwin & Jamison, 1990).

Changes in Activity Levels

Behavioral changes seen in mania include markedly decreased need for sleep, increases in goal-directed activities, and excessive involvement in activities that carry a high potential for negative consequences. Sleep disturbance is one of the most common symptoms of mania; approximately 4 out of 5 individuals with Bipolar Disorder report insomnia or decreased need for sleep (F. K. Goodwin & Jamison, 1990). Despite sleeping little or not at all, a manic individual typically reports feeling rested and energized. Sleep cycles and patterns appear to be abnormal in bipolar individuals (even when euthymic) and are characterized by longer periods of sleep, longer onset latencies, greater variability in sleep across nights, and impaired sleep efficiency (A. G. Harvey, Schmidt, Scarná, Semler, & Goodwin, 2005; Millar, Espie, & Scott, 2004). Sleep disturbances have also been observed in relatives of individuals with Bipolar Disorder, suggesting that disturbed sleep patterns may be a vulnerability marker for this illness (Lauer, Schreiber, Holsboer, & Krieg, 1995). Individuals with Bipolar Disorder are particularly susceptible to changes that cause disruptions to circadian rhythms (i.e., the internal clock that regulates behaviors, including sleep, over a 24-hour period). For example, sleep deprivation is known to increase the risk of inducing a manic episode (Barbini, Bertelli, Colombo, & Smeraldi, 1996; Wehr, Sack, & Rosenthal, 1987).

Manic individuals frequently channel their increased energy into taking on an uncharacteristically large number of projects or activities. In the early stage of mania, an individual may indeed be more productive than usual, but as the mania progresses, behavior will become increasingly disorganized and chaotic. Manic individuals also frequently engage in highly pleasurable activities that nevertheless are likely to result in negative consequences; this includes hypersexual behavior, excessive spending, and speeding while driving. Such behaviors can be especially detrimental to relationships with family, significant others, and friends, who must often pick up the pieces and try to repair damage done as a result of these behavioral excesses.

During hypomanic episodes it is not uncommon for a person to feel productive, creative, self-confident, and socially skilled. The absence of notable disability during hypomanic episodes may lead the affected individual to regard treatment as unnecessary and undesirable.

Mixed Episodes

Some individuals with Bipolar I Disorder may experience one or more mixed episodes during the course of their illness. In the *DSM-IV-TR*, a mixed episode is defined as period of at least 1 week during which the criteria are simultaneously met for both a manic and a major depressive episode nearly every day (American Psychiatric Association, 2000b). Note that the 2-week duration requirement for a major depressive episode is waived under the criteria for a mixed episode (i.e., the depressive symptoms need be present for only 1 week). Mixed states are associated with rapidly fluctuating moods that include euphoria, irritability, and sadness. These mood episodes are commonly encountered in women, those who have had depressive symptoms during previous manic episodes, and those with comorbid substance abuse (Benazzi, 2001; McElroy et al., 1995). Mixed states typically take longer to resolve than pure manias and have been linked to greater chronicity and suicide risk (Bolland & Keller, 1999; Strakowski, McElroy, Keck, & West, 1996). With regard to the latter, mixed episodes are particularly dangerous because an individual with suicidal ideation will have the energy and impulsiveness to act on these thoughts. Interestingly, Cassidy, McEvoy, Yang, and Wilson (2001) found that bipolar individuals in a mixed episode demonstrated greater insight into their illness and more accurate self-evaluation compared to individuals in pure manic episodes.

Depressive Episodes in Bipolar Disorder

Differences have been noted in major depressive episodes occurring in the context of Major Depressive Disorder and Bipolar Disorder. Specifically, compared to unipolar depression, *bipolar* depression is more likely to be associated with hypersomnia, motor retardation, mood lability, morning worsening of symptoms, periods of derealization, and atypical features (Berk & Dodd, 2005; Bowden, 2005; P. B. Mitchell et al., 2001). Rubinsztein, Underwood, Tempest, and Sahkanian (2006) found that whereas depressed bipolar patients demonstrated cognitive impairments in attention and decision making, they did not exhibit the mood-congruent affective attentional bias observed in unipolar depressed individuals (i.e., responding more quickly and accurately to stimuli that have a negative emotional valence compared to a positive one).

Although it may sound surprising, compared to individuals with unipolar depression, those with Bipolar I or II Disorder have been observed to have a greater number of depressive episodes across similar time periods (Coryell et al., 1989). Depressive episodes in Bipolar Disorder are typically longer than manic episodes and develop more slowly (e.g., over a period of weeks; F. K. Goodwin & Jamison, 1990); however, the length of depressive episodes in bipolar depression is likely to be shorter than in unipolar depression (P. B. Mitchell et al., 1992).

The first episode in Bipolar Disorder is most likely to be a depressive episode; this is especially true for women (H. I. Kaplan & Saddock, 1998). In a sample of 61 medicated bipolar individuals, the average length of depressive episodes in the 28 months following a hospitalization was 1.75 months (range = 1 to 11 months) and 1.15 months for manic episodes (range = 1 to 3 months; I. W. Miller, Uebelacker, Keitner, Ryan, & Solomon, 2004). *Untreated* manic episodes are estimated to last, on average, approximately 3 months (H. I. Kaplan & Saddock, 1998). It is estimated that over a 5-year period, 5% to 15% of individuals with Bipolar II Disorder will experience a manic episode and thus convert to a diagnosis of Bipolar I Disorder (American Psychiatric Association, 2000b).

Rapid Cycling

According to the *DSM-IV-TR*, the specifier *rapid cycling* may be given with a diagnosis of either Bipolar I or II Disorder, which indicates the occurrence of at least four distinct mood episodes (depressive, manic, hypomanic, or mixed episodes) within a 1-year period (American Psychiatric Association, 2000b). The definition of rapid cycling in the *DSM-IV-TR* stems from early work by Dunner and Fieve (1974), who found that a significant percentage of individuals for whom lithium maintenance treatment was ineffective had four or more illness episodes per year, and subsequent studies have linked rapid cycling to poorer outcome (Maj, Magliano, Pirozzi, Marasco, & Guarneri, 1994). Reported prevalence rates for rapid cycling among individuals with Bipolar Disorder vary widely (e.g., 13% to 56%; Schneck et al., 2004). Rapid cycling may be more common among individuals with Bipolar II Disorder (Baldessarini, Tondo, Floris, & Hennen, 2000), although this is not a consistent finding (Coryell et al., 2003; Schneck, 2004). Research has consistently found that women account for 70% to 90% of rapid cyclers, and there is evidence that a history of thyroid dysfunction is also a risk factor for rapid cycling (Dunner, 1999). It appears that highly recurrent refractory depression may be a hallmark of rapid-cycling Bipolar Disorder (Calebrese et al., 2005). The term *ultra-rapid cycling* is used to describe individuals who experience very frequent mood shifts (e.g., multiple shifts across a week-long period). Ultra-rapid cycling is not currently a designation found in the *DSM-IV*, and it is likely that some individuals who have been described as such in research studies might be given a *DSM-IV-TR* diagnosis of Cyclothymic Disorder (Dunner, 1999). It should be noted that once an individual becomes a rapid cycler, he or she may not always meet this criterion in future illness episodes.

Additional Characteristics

Increased Lethality

As with Major Depressive Disorder, a diagnosis of either Bipolar I or II Disorder is associated with increased suicide risk. It is estimated that during their lifetime, 80% of individuals with Bipolar Disorder will exhibit suicidal behavior, 50% will attempt suicide, and between 10% and 15% will kill themselves (Goodwin & Jamison, 1990; Valtonen, et al., 2005). Compared to Major Depressive Disorder, those with Bipolar Disorder have been found to collectively make more lethal suicide attempts (Raja & Azzoni, 2004). Overall, suicide attempts among individuals with Bipolar Disorder are 20 times more likely than those in the general population, and suicidal acts frequently occur early in the illness course, in association with severe depressive and mixed episodes, and particularly following repeated severe depressions (Tondo, Isacsson, & Baldessarini, 2003). Comorbid substance abuse also increases the risk of suicide in individuals with Bipolar Disorder (Swann, Dougherty, Pazzaglia, Pham, & Moeller, 2004), as do comorbid anxiety disorders (Simon, Hunkeler, Fireman, Lee, & Savarino, 2007). The lifetime risk of suicide has been reported higher in individuals with Bipolar II Disorder compared to Bipolar I Disorder (Z. Rihmer & Pestality, 1999), which may be related to the longer time the former individuals spend in depressive episodes (Frye et al., 2004). Lewinsohn et al. (2002) reported a suicide attempt rate of 44% among adolescents with Bipolar Disorder and noted that the rate among those with subthreshold Bipolar Disorder was approximately 18%. A re-analysis of the ECA study data similarly found that adults with subsyndromal bipolar symptoms had a significantly higher lifetime prevalence rate of suicide attempts compared to a no-mental-disorder control group (8% versus 2%, respectively; Judd & Akiskal, 2003). The risk of suicide among older adults with Bipolar Disorder appears lower than that for younger age groups (i.e., under 35; Tsai, Kuo, Chen, & Lee, 2002).

Psychosis

By definition, an individual with Bipolar II Disorder cannot experience psychotic symptoms during a hypomanic episode, but such individuals may experience psychotic symptoms during a major depressive episode. Those with Bipolar I Disorder can experience psychotic symptoms during either a manic or a major depressive episode. It is estimated that 47% to 75% of individuals with Bipolar I Disorder have experienced psychotic symptoms sometime during the course of their illness, with delusions being more commonly experienced than hallucinations (F. K. Goodwin & Jamison, 1990). Grandiose delusions are most common, but persecutory and paranoid delusions also occur with some frequency. The presence of first-rank Schneiderian symptoms (e.g., delusions of being controlled by an external force, thought insertion or withdrawal, thought broadcasting, hearing hallucinated voices commenting on one's thoughts or actions or having a conversation with one another), once thought to be pathognomonic for Schizophrenia, can occur in Bipolar Disorder as well. Approximately 20% of individuals with Bipolar I Disorder report a history of first-rank symptoms occurring at some point in their illness (F. K. Goodwin & Jamison, 1990). The presence of first-rank symptoms has been found to correlate with poorer psychosocial functioning after 12 months (Conus, Abdel-Baki, Harrigan, Lambert, & McGorry, 2004). Mood-incongruent psychotic symptoms have also been linked to poorer functioning at short- (e.g., 8 months) and long-term (e.g., 4 years) follow-ups (Strakowski et al., 2000; Tohen, Tsuang, & Goodwin, 1992).

Onset, Course, and Life Span Considerations

Onset   The average age of onset for Bipolar Disorder is approximately 18 to 20 years of age (American Psychiatric Association, 2000b; Berk & Dodd, 2005). However, misdiagnosis is common, and can result in long delays between the emergence of the disorder and the initiation of appropriate treatment. A survey of National Depressive and Manic Depressive Association members found that over two thirds of respondents reported being misdiagnosed (most with unipolar depression or an anxiety disorder), and one third of respondents reported delays of up to 10 years between the time of symptom onset and correct diagnosis (Hirschfeld, Lewis, & Vornik, 2003). These findings are consistent with other research demonstrating that an average of 8 years passes between the time an individual first experiences symptoms and when a final diagnosis of Bipolar Disorder is made and that a high percentage of individuals are initially misdiagnosed with unipolar depression (Baldessarini, Tondo, & Hennen, 1999; Ghaemi, Sachs, Chiou, Pandurangi, & Goodwin, 1999; Lish, Dime-Meenan, Whybrow, Price, & Hirshfeld, 1994). Individuals with Bipolar II Disorder are also likely to be misdiagnosed as having a personality disorder (e.g., Borderline Personality Disorder; Berk & Dodd, 2005).

Course   Depressive and manic episodes are typically preceded by a prodrome, which is a 1- to 2-week period in which abnormal changes in emotion, cognition, and mood occur (Swann, 2005). Although the specific prodromal symptoms can vary widely across individuals, for any one individual the features of the depressive and manic prodromes tend to remain stable across episodes. For this reason, an important part of treatment involves helping clients identify the symptoms that are characteristic of their particular prodrome. For most individuals with Bipolar I or II Disorder, depressive episodes outnumber manic episodes (J. Judd, Schettler, et al., 2002; Judd, Akiskal, et al., 2003). Studies have found that approximately 20% of individuals with a history of unipolar depression will eventually experience a manic episode and thus convert to a Bipolar I Disorder, and between 9% and 27% will convert to Bipolar II Disorder (Akiskal et al., 1983, 1995; J. F. Goldberg, Harrow, & Whiteside, 2001). Among children with depression, as many as one third may eventually be diagnosed with Bipolar I Disorder within a 10-year period and an additional 15% with Bipolar II Disorder (B. Geller, Zimermann, Williams, Bolhofner, & Craney, 2001).

Despite the availability of psychopharmacologic and psychotherapeutic interventions, 70% to 80% of individuals with Bipolar Disorder will experience at least one mood episode within 5 years of an index episode (Gitlin & Hammen, 1999; Keller, Lavori, Coryell, Endicott, & Muller, 1992; Tohen, Waternaux, & Tsuang, 1990). The percentage of time that individuals with Bipolar Disorder are fully symptomatic has been reported to be around 7% to 8%, and subsyndromal levels of symptoms are present as much as 22% to 33% of the time (Judd et al., 2002; I. W. Miller et al., 2004). The recurrence risk for Bipolar I and II Disorders has been estimated to be twice that of depression (J. Angst, Gamma, Sellaro, Lavori, & Zhang, 2003). Even among aggressively treated individuals who have adhered to their medication regimen, relapse and the persistence of subsyndromal symptoms is common. In a study of 82 outpatients with Bipolar Disorder treated through a specialty mood disorders clinic for at least 2 years, the rate of relapse within 5 years among continuously treated clients was 73% (with 37% of relapses occurring within the first year). Furthermore, 70% of those who relapsed had multiple mood episodes during the study period, and almost half of those who did not relapse continued to show subsyndromal symptoms of depression or mania (Gitlin & Hammen, 1999). Interestingly, Bipolar II Disorder may be associated with greater risk of recurrence than Bipolar I Disorder as measured by the number of depressive, hypomanic, and total episodes and episode length (i.e., shorter in bipolar II; Ayuso-Gutierrez & Ramos-Brieva, 1982). One long-term study that followed individuals with Bipolar II Disorder for almost 14 years found these individuals were symptomatic for more than half of all follow-up weeks (Judd, Akiskal, et al., 2003).

In 1991, the cost of Bipolar Disorder in the United States was estimated at $45 billion ($7 billion in direct patient care costs and $38 billion in indirect costs such as lost productivity of affected individuals and their caregivers; Wyatt & Henter, 1991). A more recent analysis of data provided by 3,000 persons self-identified as having Bipolar Disorder revealed that, despite the fact over 60% have completed some college and 30% completed college, 64% were unemployed (Kupfer, Frank, et al., 2002). The World Health Organization has ranked Bipolar Disorder 6th among the top 10 causes of disability worldwide among 15- to 44-year-olds; this illness is associated with greater disability than chronic medical conditions such as diabetes, asthma, and osteoarthritis (Murray & Lopez, 1996). Gitlin & Hammen (1999) found that occupational outcome was deemed poor in 35% of their sample of continuously treated individuals with Bipolar Disorder and that the number of previous depressive episodes was significantly related to family dysfunction and social maladjustment.

Caregivers of those with Bipolar Disorder report less reward, more subjective burden, and worse *family functioning* than depression caregivers at an index of hospitalization (Heru & Ryan, 2004). Targum, Dibble, Davenport, and Gershon (1981) found that spouses reported a significant level of burden associated with their partner's Bipolar Disorder, and were particularly troubled by manic symptoms such as poor judgment, impulsive spending, decreased need for sleep, potentially violent outbursts, and talkativeness and depressive symptoms such as suicide attempts, low self-esteem, hopelessness, and social withdrawal. Perhaps most striking was the finding that 53% of these spouses indicated that they would not have married their partner had they known more about Bipolar Disorder beforehand, and 47% indicated they would not have had children.

Prognosis for Bipolar Disorder appears related to a number of factors. Earlier age of onset is associated with more severe illness course, poorer treatment response, and poorer psychosocial functioning and quality of life (Engstrom, Brandstrom, Sigvardsson, Cloninger, & Nylander, 2003; R. H. Perlis, Miyahara, et al., 2004; Schulze et al., 2002). Poorer prognosis and decreased treatment response have also been correlated with the greater number of untreated episodes an individual has experienced and longer delays in treatment (Franchini, Zanardi, Smeraldi, & Gasperini, 1998), although these findings have not been uniformly supported (Baethge et al., 2003; Baldessarini, Tondo, & Hennen, 2003b). A large study examining correlates of outcome over 1 year in Bipolar Disorder found that mania severity was associated with poor occupational functioning at study entry, comorbid substance use, and a history of more than 10 prior manic episodes; depression severity was similarly associated with a history of more than 10 prior depressive episodes and poor occupational functioning. The total number of overall illness episodes was associated with a positive family history of drug abuse, a history of prior rapid cycling, poor occupational functioning, and a history of childhood abuse (Nolen et al., 2004). Some studies indicate that the presence of mood-incongruent psychotic features may be associated with poorer outcome compared to mood-congruent psychosis (Miklowitz, 1992; Tohen et al., 1992). However, others report that psychotic features may have limited prognostic significance with regard to the course of Bipolar Disorder (Keck et al., 2003; MacQueen, Young, Robb, Cooke, & Joffe, 1997). Nevertheless, the presence of first-rank Schneiderian symptoms has been found to correlate with poorer psychosocial functioning after 1 year and may identify a subgroup of patients with more severe presentation and poorer outcome (Conus et al., 2004).

Life Span Considerations

Although it was once believed that Bipolar Disorder could not have an onset in childhood, we now know that children as young as 4 or 5 can be diagnosed with this illness (Wozniak, 2005). Because childhood Bipolar Disorder presents quite differently from classic Bipolar Disorder in adults it is frequently misdiagnosed, most often as ADHD (Craney & Geller, 2003). Whereas adults with Bipolar Disorder may present with discrete mood episodes that have acute onsets, children with Bipolar Disorder are more likely to display continuous periods of mood instability that appear similar to rapid cycling or mixed states, and switches from elevated mood to depression can occur over relatively short periods of time (e.g., numerous times a day; Geller & Luby, 1997). Marked irritability, aggression, and rage are also common and are more likely to be seen than euphoric states (G. A. Carlson, 2002; Wozniak, 2005). In a 4-year prospective study of children with Bipolar Disorder, B. Geller, Tillman, Craney, and Bolhofner (2004) found that the average episode duration of baseline manic episodes was 79 weeks, which underscores the chronic and unremitting nature of childhood-onset Bipolar Disorder.

Part of the difficulty of diagnosing Bipolar Disorder in children using the *DSM-IV-TR* system is that examples of how manic symptoms may present in children are not provided (American Psychiatric Association, 2000b). Work by B. Geller et al. (2002) has yielded useful examples of how various bipolar symptoms may manifest differently in children and adults (see Table 10.1).

Table 10.1   Examples of manic symptoms in childhood-onset bipolar disorder

Symptom Domain	Normal Child Example	Child with Bipolar Disorder Example
Elated mood	Extreme happiness expressed in relation to special events, situations (e.g., trip to Disneyland, Christmas, visits from favorite people).	Elation for no apparent reason (e.g., giggling hysterically in class or church when no one else is; dancing around after being suspended from school).
Grandiosity	Age-appropriate pretend play (e.g., a 7-year-old boy pretending to be a fireman). Child realizes that he is not really a fireman.	Child steals from a store, knowing that stealing is considered wrong, but believes it is not wrong for him to steal. Child failing school spends evenings discussing how she will become president of the United States in the future; believes this is possible in spite of poor school performance.
Sleep	Needs 8–10 hours of sleep to feel rested; if deprived of sleep will feel tired.	Child stays up until 2 a.m. playing games, wakes up a few hours later ready to go to school; throughout day does not appear tired or fatigued from lack of sleep the previous night.
Hypersexuality	A young child plays doctor with an opposite sex playmate; a young adolescent finds and looks at a parent's adult magazine.	Child makes sexual gestures (e.g., provocatively gyrating, grabs crotch or breasts) and/or uses sexually explicit language or propositions in front of other children or adults, calls sex phone lines, draws explicit pictures of naked people saying they are the child's future husband or wife.
Racing thoughts	Generally not reported.	Child describes needing a stoplight to stop thoughts that are coming fast; says there is an "Energizer Bunny" in his or her head, or that thoughts have broken the "speed limit" or "sound barrier."

Source: From "Phenomenology of Pre-pubertal and Early Adolescent Bipolar Disorder: Examples of Elated Mood, Decreased Need for Sleep, Racing Thoughts, and Hypersexuality," by B. Geller, B. Zimerman, M. Williams, M. P. Delbello, J. Frazier, and L. Beringer, 2002, *Journal of Child and Adolescent Psychopharmacology, 12*, pp. 3–9. Adapted with permission.

Temperamental characteristics such as inflexibility and oppositionality, oversensitivity to stimuli, and histories of fussiness, marked separation anxiety, and sleep problems in infancy have also been noted among children with Bipolar Disorder (Papolos & Papolos, 1999). Childhood Bipolar Disorder is frequently comorbid with ADHD and Oppositional Defiant Disorder. Although mood-stabilizing medications such as lithium and anticonvulsants are first-line treatments for Bipolar Disorder, they appear less effective in treating children with Bipolar Disorder (Kowatch et al., 2000). Instead, atypical antipsychotics such as risperidone and olanzapine have been found to be produce better results, but large-scale, randomized, controlled trials are needed (Wozniak, 2005).

In general, age of onset for Bipolar Disorder is an important variable that is associated with differences in clinical presentation and course. Onset in youth has been linked to increased suicidality, greater likelihood of psychotic symptoms during mood episodes, and higher rates of comorbid conditions such as substance use disorders and Panic Disorder (Leboyer, Paillere-Martinot, & Bellivier, 2005). In a study of 983 individuals with Bipolar Disorder, Perlis and colleagues (R. H. Perlis, Miyahara, et al., 2004) found rates of Axis I comorbidity were highest in a very early onset group (defined as first episode occurring prior to age 13), followed by an early-onset group (defined as first episode occurring between 13 to 18 years of age). In addition, compared to an adult-onset group, both of the early-onset groups had a greater number of lifetime episodes (both manic and depressed), greater likelihood of suicide attempts, and poorer quality of life and functioning at the time of study entry (after controlling for age at study entry and illness duration). In their study of Bipolar Disorder among high school students, Lewinsohn et al. (2002) reported that significant impairment in school functioning and social functioning was observed in 83% and 67% of adolescents, respectively. The presence of psychotic symptoms in childhood Bipolar Disorder is correlated with poorer recovery (B. Geller et al., 2004). These findings collectively point to the importance of prompt treatment for the disorder when it first appears.

Far less is known about Bipolar Disorder in older adults compared to younger populations, and research studies in this area are often difficult to interpret because of small sample sizes, overreliance on inpatient samples, use of different illness definitions, lack of standardized measures to assess symptoms and functioning, failure to report distinctions between Bipolar I and II Disorder, use of retrospective chart review, and a dearth of longitudinal studies (Depp & Jeste, 2004). In a review of a large database that included over 65,500 veterans diagnosed with Bipolar Disorder, older adults composed nearly one fourth of this population (Sajatovic, Blow, Ignacio, & Kales, 2005). Although not common, Bipolar Disorder can have an onset in middle to old age. The term *late-onset Bipolar Disorder* is often used to refer to cases where a diagnosis is made at age 50 or later (Van Gerpen, Johnson, & Winstead, 1999). Late-onset cases have been reported to constitute between 6% and 11% of samples of older adults with Bipolar Disorder (Almeida & Fenner, 2002; Cassidy & Carroll, 2002; Sajatovic et al., 2005).

Although Bipolar Disorder is reported to equally affect men and women in younger age groups, samples of older adults have a 2:1 ratio of women to men (Depp & Jeste, 2004). In a comparison of young (18 to 39 years), middle-aged (40 to 59 years), and older (60+ years) adults with Bipolar Disorder drawn from a large public mental health system database, Depp et al. (2004) found that the older individuals were less likely than their younger counterparts to have a comorbid substance use disorder and were less likely to use emergency psychiatric services. However, the older age group was more likely to have a comorbid cognitive disorder and lower GAF scores. In general, outcome among older adults with Bipolar Disorder appears better than for older adults with Schizophrenia but worse than for older adults with unipolar depression. It does not appear that Bipolar Disorder burns out in old age, and the majority of affected individuals continue to have residual or recurrent symptoms (Depp & Jeste, 2004).

EPIDEMIOLOGY OF MOOD DISORDERS

Major Depression

According to the *DSM-IV-TR*, the lifetime risk of major depression is 10% to 25% for women and 5% to 12% for men, and point prevalence rates are 5% to 9% for women and 2% to 3% for men (American Psychiatric Association, 2000b). However, in their recent review of epidemiological studies of mood disorders in adults, Waraich, Goldner, Somers, and Hsu (2004) observed a wide range of prevalence estimates for major depression across studies published between 1980 and 2000. They note, for example, that the lifetime prevalence rates for Major Depressive Disorder ranged from .88 per 100 in Taipei, Taiwan, to 29.6 per 100 in Montreal, Canada, which represents a more than 33-fold difference. Pooling data across studies resulted in 1-year and lifetime best estimate prevalence rates for Major Depressive Disorder of 4.1 per 100 and 6.7 per 100, respectively. Consistent with the *DSM-IV-TR* (American Psychiatric Association, 2000b), Waraich and colleagues found prevalence rates for Major Depressive Disorder were 1.5 to 2.5 times higher for women compared to men.

Among youth, point prevalences for depression range from 1% to 3% for children and 3% to 9% for adolescents, with more females than males diagnosed following puberty (Waslick et al., 2002). Lifetime prevalence of depression in older adolescents has been reported to be as high as 20% to 25% (Lewinsohn, Hops, Roberts, Seeley, & Andrews, 1993). Depression in older adults is fairly common, with most prevalence estimates of clinically significant depressive symptoms among community-dwelling elders ranging from 8% to 16% and in institutional settings between 25% and 35% (Blazer, 2004).

Dysthymic Disorder

A review of epidemiologic studies conducted between 1980 and 2000 confirmed that dysthymia is approximately half as common as Major Depressive Disorder (Waraich et al., 2004). Community-based estimates of Dysthymic Disorder range from 3% to 6% (R. C. Kessler, McGonagle, Zhao, Nelson, et al., 1994; Weissman, Leaf, Bruce, & Florio, 1988). As with major depression, one encounters a rather wide range of lifetime prevalence estimates (e.g., 1% to 14%) for this disorder across epidemiological studies (Waraich et al., 2004). Clinical studies place the prevalence of dysthymia among outpatients at between 22% and 36% (D. N. Klein, Dickstein, Taylor, & Harding, 1989; Markowitz, Moran, Kocsis, & Francis, 1992). A fairly consistent finding across studies is that prevalence rates are 1.5 to 2.5 times higher for women than men (Waraich et al., 2004). For example, data from the National Comorbidity Study (NCS) revealed an 8.1% lifetime rate of dysthymia among women compared to 4.8% for men (Parker & Hadzi-Pavlovic, 2001). Among children, point prevalence estimates for Dysthymic Disorder range from 0.6% to 4.6% in children and 1.6% to 8% in adolescents (Nobile et al., 2003).

Bipolar Disorder

According to the *DSM-IV* (American Psychiatric Association, 2000b), the collective lifetime prevalence of the Bipolar Disorders (types I and II) is approximately 1% to 2%

(i.e., 0.4% to 1.6% for Bipolar I Disorder and 0.5% for Bipolar II Disorder). The ECA and NCS studies estimated the prevalence for Bipolar Disorders at .08 and 1.6%, respectively (R. C. Kessler, McGonagle, & Zhao, 1994; Robins & Regier, 1991). In a sample of young American adults (ages 17 to 39), B. S. Jones, Brody, Roper, and Narrow (2003) found a 1.6% lifetime prevalence for any Bipolar Disorder (i.e., Types I and II). Based on pooled data from epidemiologic studies conducted between 1980 and 2000, Waraich et al. (2004) estimated the lifetime prevalence of Bipolar Disorder at .82 per 100. Bipolar Disorder prevalence estimates among those over age 65 are between 0.1% and 0.4% (Van Gerpen et al., 1999). Community-based studies indicate that the prevalence in older adults is significantly lower than that seen in younger age groups and is about one third less prevalent (Depp & Jeste, 2004; Hirschfeld, Lewis, et al., 2003; Weissman, Leaf, Bruce, et al., 1988), although in clinical settings, differences in the proportions of younger versus older individuals with this disorder are more comparable (Schulman, 1996). Rates of Bipolar Disorder among children and adolescents are low. Lewinsohn et al. (2002), in a community sample of approximately 1,700 high school students, reported a point prevalence of Bipolar Disorder of 0.6%, which increased to 0.7% when the cohort was reevaluated at age 24.

In summary, narrowly defined Bipolar Disorders appear fairly rare, affect less than 2% of the adult population, and do not appear to be significantly different between men and women (B. S. Jones et al., 2003; Waraich et al., 2004). However, if one takes into account cases across the continuum of what has been termed the *bipolar spectrum*, which includes conditions such as recurrent brief hypomania and antidepressant-induced mania, prevalence estimates for Bipolar Disorders increase substantially to approximately 5% to 8% (J. Angst, 1998; Lewinsohn, Seeley, & Klein, 2003). In a reanalysis of the ECA data that included individuals with a history of subsyndromal manic symptoms (defined as two or more lifetime manic symptoms, without meeting a full diagnosis of a manic or hypomanic episode), Judd and Akiskal (2003) found the lifetime prevalence of bipolar spectrum disorders to be 6.4% and estimated subsyndromal cases to be 5 times more prevalent than cases carrying traditional Bipolar I or II Disorder diagnoses.

ETIOLOGY

Biological Theories

Depressive Disorders

Theories regarding a *genetic basis* for some cases of depressive illness stem from findings of family and twin studies. A meta-analysis of family studies of depressed individuals found that the likelihood of affective illness was nearly 3 times greater for the first-degree relatives of depressed individuals compared to individuals from the general population, medical patients, and surgical patients, and that recurrent major depression in particular is associated with increased familial risk (P. F. Sullivan, Neale, & Kendler, 2000). Because related individuals share environment as well as genes, such studies do not solely implicate genetic factors in the etiology of depression. Several environmental risk factors have been associated with depression, including early trauma and loss, child-rearing patterns, and low socioeconomic status (First & Tasman, 2005). Therefore, twin studies can provide further clarification on this point. These have demonstrated a significantly higher degree of concordance for affective illness among identical (monozygotic) twins than dizygotic (fraternal) twins, although not as pronounced as that seen in Bipolar Disorder (P. F. Sullivan et al., 2000). It should be noted that these studies have primarily examined twins reared together, which again means environmental influences cannot be completely ruled out (e.g., identical twins may be treated more similarly than nonidentical twins). Adoption studies can disentangle the confluence of environmental and genetic factors, but the few existing studies examining concordance rates for major depression have yielded mixed results. Cadoret (1978) found significantly higher rates of depression in adoptees who had a biological parent with depression, and Wender et al. (1986) determined that biological relatives of depressed adoptees had an eightfold higher rate of depression than the biological relatives of nondepressed adoptees. However, von Knorring, Cloninger, Bohman, and Sigvardsson (1983) did not find a significant correlation between depression in adoptees and their biological parents. Nevertheless, family and twin studies collectively indicate that the heritability of major depression is likely to fall in the range of 31% to 42% (P. F. Sullivan et al., 2000).

It is well established that depressive disorders are associated with abnormalities in several *neurotransmitter systems*, most notably serotonin. Supportive evidence of abnormalities in serotonin (also known as 5-hydroxytryptamine, or 5-HT) in depression includes the following: (a) reduced availability of tryptophan, the precursor of serotonin; (b) abnormalities in the metabolism of serotonin; (c) postmortem observations of increased number serotonin receptors (possibly a response to lowered levels of circulating serotonin); (d) postmortem findings of decreased cerebrospinal fluid levels of 5-HIAA, the principal metabolite of serotonin; (e) blunted prolactin response to the fenfluramine challenge test; and (f) effectiveness of medications that block the reuptake of serotonin (i.e., SSRIs; Cleare, 2004; First & Tasman, 2005). In addition to serotonin, deficits in other monoamines have been implicated in depression. For example, MAOIs, which block the metabolism of neurotransmitters such as dopamine, serotonin, and norepinephrine, have been successfully used in the treatment of depression (Schatzberg et al., 2005). Noradrenergic dysfunction also appears relevant in depression, as evidenced by the effectiveness of medications that block the reuptake of noradrenaline (e.g., TCAs such as desipramine and newer medications such as venlafaxine and reboxetine; Schaztberg et al., 2005). Finally, low plasma levels of the inhibitory neurotransmitter GABA may serve as a marker for vulnerability to affective disorders, including Major Depressive Disorder and Bipolar Disorder (F. Petty, Kramer, Fulton, Moeller, & Rush, 1993; F. Petty & Sherman, 1984).

Neuroendocrine abnormalities have also been linked to depressive disorders, including dysfunction in the hypothalamo-pituitary-adrenal (HPA) axis, part of the neuroendocrine system that controls reactions to stress. The HPA axis is a complex series of interconnections between the brain and the adrenal glands. A key component of this system is the stress hormone cortisol, which is secreted by the adrenal glands. The release of cortisol is ultimately controlled by the hypothalamus and neurons in the prefrontal and limbic cortices. These structures initially secrete corticotrophin-releasing hormone (CRH), which triggers the release of adrenocorticotropin hormone from the pituitary gland, which in turn stimulates the adrenal glands to secrete cortisol. In the dexamethasone suppression test, the administration of the synthetic glucocorticoid dexamethasone typically results in a decrease in measured levels of cortisol. However, among a high percentage of melancholic depressives and depressive persons with psychotic features, this suppression does not take place (Duval et al., 2006). These abnormalities implicate impaired HPA axis functioning in a subset of depressed persons. Increased levels of CRH and cortisol can lead to sleep abnormalities seen in depression, as well as decrements in the transmission of serotonin (Howland & Thase, 1999). It is not clear what causes abnormalities in the HPA axis to begin with, but intriguing research suggests that one potential causative factor may be severe early life stress (e.g., child abuse), which has been correlated with long-term changes in the corticotropin-releasing factor neuronal systems (Heim et al., 2000).

Abnormalities have also been noted in the hypothalamic-pituitary-thyroid axis among mood disordered individuals. This system involves the release of thyrotropin-releasing hormone (TRH) by the hypothalamus, which stimulates the pituitary gland to release thyroid-stimulating hormone (TSH), which then causes the release of hormones T3 and T4. Irregularities in thyroid functioning (e.g., hypothyroidism) can cause depressive symptoms, and there is evidence that a subset of depressed individuals exhibit subtle thyroid abnormalities, such as subclinical hypothyroidism (First & Tasman, 2005). Indeed, between 25% and 40% of depressed people exhibit a blunted TSH response when given a TRH stimulation test (Howland & Thase, 1999). Thyroid hormones have been successfully used to augment TCAs and SSRIs in the treatment of refractory depression (G. Abraham, Milev, & Lawson, 2006; Aronson, Offman, Joffe, & Naylor, 1996).

Imaging studies of depressed individuals reveal *structural brain abnormalities* such as ventricular enlargement, cortical atrophy, sulcal widening, reduced volume of the frontal lobes and caudate nucleus, and increased frequency of white matter hyperintensities (the last particularly in geriatric depression). In addition, decreased frontal metabolism in areas such as the dorsolateral prefrontal cortex, orbitofrontal cortex, and thalamus have been found (Howland & Thase, 1999).

Bipolar Disorders

As with the depressive disorders, research has consistently shown that Bipolar Disorder runs in families. The risks of developing Bipolar I or II Disorder among first-degree relatives of affected individuals are 3% to 15% and 2% to 10%, respectively, and early age of onset in the proband (e.g., <25 years) is associated with greater morbidity risk among relatives (Howland & Thase, 1999; Shih, Belmonte, & Zandi, 2004). Elevated rates of *depressive* disorders are also observed among the first-degree relatives of bipolar probands, with morbidity risk estimates ranging from 12% to 19% (Shih et al., 2004). This is in marked contrast to unipolar depression, where the rates of Bipolar Disorder among first-degree relatives are only 2% to 4%. Significantly higher rates of Major Depressive Disorder and subthreshold Bipolar Disorder have also been found among the first-degree relatives of adolescents diagnosed with Bipolar Disorder (Lewinsohn et al., 2002). These findings indicate that Bipolar Disorder does not breed true; there is a higher probability that someone with bipolar disorder will have a child with a unipolar mood disorder than a Bipolar Disorder (First & Tasman, 2005).

Additional evidence supporting a *genetic underpinning* to Bipolar Disorder comes from twin studies that have found concordance rates among monozygotic twins ranging from 20% to 75% and rates among dizygotic twins between 0% to 8% (Shih et al., 2004).

The difference in concordance rates between identical and nonidentical twins is markedly greater for Bipolar Disorder compared to major depression, which suggests that bipolar illness may be more strongly influenced by genetic factors than unipolar illness (Howland & Thase, 1999). Two adoption studies (Mendlewicz & Rainer, 1977; Wender et al., 1986) reported significantly higher rates of Bipolar Disorder in the biological parents of bipolar probands (i.e., 5% to 7%) compared to the adoptive parents (2% to 3%), which also implicates genetic factors in this illness. It has been suggested that the etiology of late-onset Bipolar Disorder may be more strongly linked to underlying neurological factors than genetic mechanisms, and findings of elevated rates of comorbid neurological conditions, vascular risk factors and disorders, and lower likelihood of family history of mood disorders support this contention (Cassidy & Carroll, 2002; Moorhead & Young, 2003; Van Gerpen et al., 1999). However, others have failed to find significant differences between elderly individuals with Bipolar Disorder who have early versus late onset in terms of factors such as family history, cognitive functioning, and depressive symptoms (Depp et al., 2004).

Neurotransmitter abnormalities in monoamine systems (e.g., serotonin, norepinephrine) are believed to be associated with Bipolar Disorder. For example, SSRIs are routinely used in the treatment of depressive states in Bipolar Disorder and therefore implicate dysfunction in this neurotransmitter system (Blackwood & Muir, 2004). Although dopamine has been studied less extensively in Bipolar Disorder compared to Schizophrenia, it is well known that agents that are dopamine agonists (e.g., stimulants such as cocaine and TCAs) can precipitate manic states in individuals with Bipolar Disorder (Ackenheil, 2001). This suggests that dysregulation of dopaminergic systems may be at play in Bipolar Disorder, but further investigation is needed (Blackwood & Muir, 2004). Based on postmortem studies, defective transmission of the neurotransmitter GABA has also been implicated in Bipolar Disorder (Benes & Berretta, 2001).

Much attention has also focused on dysfunction in so-called *second-messenger systems* in Bipolar Disorder. When neurotransmitters (sometimes referred to as first systems) are released by a nerve cell and bind to postreceptors on other nerve cells, a series of complex cellular changes occurs that allows the signal from the first nerve cell to be communicated to the second nerve cell (second messengers diffuse within the second cell and alter its behavior). Important components of second-messenger systems are substances known as g-proteins. Abnormalities in g-protein levels have been observed among individuals with Bipolar Disorder, and it is thought that the therapeutic effects of drugs such as lithium may involve effects on these systems (Brunello & Tascedda, 2003; Manji & Potter, 1997).

Another biologically based theory of Bipolar Disorder is the *kindling model* proposed by R. Post, Rubinow, and Ballenger (1986). This is a behavioral sensitization model that contends that repeated mood episodes occurring in response to stressors will eventually result in the triggering of spontaneous, increasingly frequent mood episodes similar to the kindling effect for seizures that has been observed in laboratory animals repeatedly exposed to electrical brain stimulation (R. Post, Rubinow, & Ballenger, 1985). Support for this hypothesis comes from the therapeutic effects of anticonvulsant medications for Bipolar Disorder and from observations that illness episodes in the disorder often increase in number and frequency across time (First & Tasman, 2005).

Psychological Theories

More has been written about psychological theories of depressive disorders compared to Bipolar Disorder, and the following discussion reflects this emphasis.

Cognitive Theories

Cognitive theories of mood disorders have primarily focused on the role that negative cognitions can play in creating a vulnerability to depression and maintaining a depressive state. Aaron Beck is the most famous and influential figure in this area; his conceptualization of depression is the basis for one of the most efficacious nonpharmacologic treatments for depression: cognitive-behavioral therapy (see "Treatment"). *Beck's cognitive theory of depression* holds that how an individual perceives and interprets events in his or her environment powerfully shapes his or her mood and behavior. He believed that depressed individuals are prone to a cognitive set (referred to as a cognitive triad) in which the individual, world, and future are viewed negatively. Thus, depressed persons may consider themselves inadequate, unworthy, and defective; their interactions with the world are likely to be construed in terms of defeat, deprivation, and obstacles; and they are likely to anticipate a future filled with hardship, frustration, and suffering (A. T. Beck, 1967). According to Beck's theory, depressed individuals' view of their situation is likely to be based on a distortion or misinterpretation of reality rather than objective facts. Thus, depressed individuals are prone to making a number of characteristic cognitive errors in processing information, such as selective abstraction (i.e., focusing on only select aspects of a situation that confirm a negative conclusion), overgeneralization (i.e., assuming that one negative event or outcome is indicative of all future outcomes), mind reading (i.e., in the absence of direct, objective evidence, assuming others are making negative judgments about oneself), and arbitrary inference (i.e., drawing unwarranted connections between ideas that are not logically related). Beck believed that a vulnerability to depression could be created early in life if individuals developed negative thoughts about themselves and the world that continued to be reinforced. These beliefs could initially result from early negative experiences with parents and other significant figures in the child's life (e.g., being criticized or rejected; Power, 2004). Eventually such beliefs would become "structuralized" into enduring, fixed cognitive structures that Beck called schemas. These depressogenic schemas could remain dormant for long periods but could be reactivated by stressful life events, particularly those reminiscent of the original experiences that led to the development of the negative beliefs comprising the schema (A. T. Beck, 1967). Beck hypothesized that when these negative schemas were reactivated, related negative automatic thoughts would occur that might remain out of the individual's conscious awareness but could negatively affect mood (e.g., increase depression; A. T. Beck, Rush, Shaw, & Emery, 1979).

Another cognitive model of depression is *Seligman's learned helplessness model*. The foundations of Seligman's theory are based in animal research demonstrating that dogs exposed to inescapable electric shock did not try to escape subsequent shocks when provided with the opportunity to do so, but instead simply lay down. From these observations, Seligman extrapolated that individuals who believe they are helpless to control negative situations in their lives are vulnerable to becoming depressed (M. E. Seligman, 1975). In 1978, Abramson, Seligman, and Teasdale expanded the learned helplessness model to include a cognitive component—namely, the type of causal attributions that may contribute to negative emotional states such as depression. Specifically, it was hypothesized that depressed individuals tend to attribute negative outcomes to internal, stable, and global factors. According to this model, a student who received a poor grade on a college algebra exam and concluded that she does not have the ability to succeed in the class (internal), will never be able to learn algebra (stable), and is not capable of succeeding in *any* college-level math or science course (global) is vulnerable to experiencing depressed mood (Abramson et al., 1978). Early empirical support for this *reformulated learned helplessness theory* comes from a study finding that depressed college students were more likely than their nondepressed counterparts to attribute negative outcomes to internal, stable, and global causes and were also more likely to attribute positive outcomes to external and unstable factors when presented with a series of hypothetical events (e.g., "You go out on a date and it goes badly"; M. E. Seligman, Abramson, Semmel, & vonBaeyer, 1979). Since that time several studies have demonstrated the tendency for both depressed adults and youth to adopt the internal, stable, global attributional style in explaining negative events and external, unstable, specific attributions for positive outcomes (for meta-analytic reviews, see Gladstone & Kaslow, 1995; Sweeney, Anderson, & Bailey, 1986). In 1989, Abramson, Alloy, and Metalsky put forth another reformulation of the learned helplessness model that is referred to as the *hopelessness model of depression*. This model hypothesizes that a depressogenic attributional style, in combination with negative life events, can lead to any of a number of cognitive conclusions (e.g., stable, global attributions for negative events, inferred negative characteristics of oneself regarding the event, inferred negative consequences of the negative event), which then lead to feelings of hopelessness. Such feelings are assumed to lead to the development of a particular form of depression, referred to a "hopeless depression," that is characterized by symptoms of sad affect, lack of energy, psychomotor retardation, slowed initiation of voluntary responses, suicidal ideation, apathy, sleep disturbance, concentration difficulties, mood-exacerbated negative cognitions, and possibly lowered self-esteem and dependency (Abramson et al., 1989).

Lewinsohn's behavioral model of depression contends that a lack of response-contingent reinforcement in an individual's environment can lead to depression (Lewinsohn, 1974). Put more simply, a depressed individual does not engage in enough sufficiently rewarding activities and because of this lack of pleasure is vulnerable to depression. This model assumes several ways this lack of reinforcement might occur. An individual could live in an environment in which there is a dearth of positive reinforcers; examples include someone who lives in an impoverished environment or who experiences many stressful life events. Alternatively, an individual might lack the skills to acquire positive reinforcement from the environment; for example, a person with poor social skills could have difficulty establishing and maintaining interpersonal relationships that are a source of pleasure. Finally, reinforcers may be available in the environment, but the individual is unable to access them; for example, a person could be too socially anxious to engage in activities that could be pleasurable but that require being around others (Lewinsohn, 1974). There is also an assumption that depressive behaviors may themselves actually get reinforced (at least in the short run) through attention and sympathy from caring others. In 1985, Lewinsohn expanded his model to include cognitive and environmental elements (Lewinsohn, Hoberman, Teri, & Hautzinger, 1985). This reformulation contends that stressful life events may precede the onset of a depressive episode in a vulnerable individual (e.g., one who does not have adequate coping mechanisms) and that depressed mood and disruptions in daily life contribute to a loss of response-contingent reinforcement. Resulting behavioral (e.g., social withdrawal) and cognitive changes (e.g., adoption of negative, self-critical, pessimistic thinking patterns) then further contribute to a deepening, downward spiral of depression (Ingram, Scott, & Siegle, 1999).

With regard to Bipolar Disorder, A. T. Beck (1967) discussed the tendency for depression to be associated with tendencies toward extreme dependence and mania to be associated with autonomous tendencies. Expanding on this, K. Wright and Lam (2004) propose that individuals with Bipolar Disorder often display excessively high achievement-oriented attitudes and ambivalence regarding the need to depend on others for validation and desires for independence. They postulate that such cognitive tendencies can lead an individual to engage in behaviors (e.g., excessive work, erratic daily routines, and disruption of the sleep-wake cycle) that can lead to increased risk of manic or hypomanic episodes.

Psychodynamic Theories

Psychodynamic theories of mood disorders hypothesize that persons become vulnerable to depression when they have experienced a real or imagined loss (e.g., through separation, death, rejection) of an important person or "object" (e.g., the mother) early in life. Karl Abraham, for example, contended that the depressed individual is fixated at the oral stage of psychosexual development and as a result of frustrating experiences with important figures early in life, alternatively experiences a desire to orally repossess the loved object or reject it. Depressive symptoms such as guilt could be viewed as a consequence of having hostile feelings toward the loved object; self-denigration could be conceptualized as a projection inward of hostile feelings toward the loved object; and lack of appetite or food refusal might be seen as a defense against wishes to symbolically orally incorporate the loved object (Gotlib & Hammen, 1992). Sigmund Freud (1917), in his classic paper "Mourning and Melancholia," also emphasized the theme of loss in the development of depression. Although Freud observed certain similarities between depressed and grieving individuals, he also noted that the depressed individual is more likely to be highly self-critical. This self-critical tendency can be understood as a result of hostile feelings turned toward an internalized representation of the lost love object. Another distinction between depression and mourning noted by Freud is that in grief, the external world is perceived as diminished (i.e., because of the loss of a valued person), whereas in depression one primarily feels that what has been damaged or lost is part of the self (McWilliams, 1994).

Later psychoanalytic theorists emphasized disruptions in the quality of the early mother-child relationship as a basis for the development of depression. Melanie Klein posited that affective symptomatology could result from an inability to establish a representation of a good inner object in infancy and a failure to work through the "depressive position," a developmental phase occurring during the second 6 months of life in which the infant gains increased realization that the concepts of a "good" and "bad" mother do not represent different entities, but instead are parts of the same whole object (Glovinsky, 2002). This realization is accompanied by the recognition that the child is dependent on this separate person, who has her own feelings, experiences, and relationships with others, and results in the infant feeling ambivalence toward the mother. The infant is postulated to experience feelings of loss, sadness, and guilt over having aggressive impulses toward the mother and because of the realization of dependency on her. Impairments in the quality of the child's relationship with the mother (e.g., failure to feel loved or good about oneself) could lead to an inability to overcome this infantile depression and a consequent vulnerability to affective disorders, such as depression or manic-depression (H. Segal, 1979). For example, such an individual could resort to so-called manic defenses such as identification with the superego, extreme idealization, and omnipotence to deal with unresolved feelings.

John Bowlby, a British psychiatrist who was psychoanalytically trained (and was clinically supervised by Melanie Klein), also wrote of the role that impaired early mother-child relations play in the genesis of depression. Unlike Klein, who placed greater emphasis on the role that fantasies generated from internal conflict between aggressive and libidinal drives played in creating psychological disturbance, Bowlby focused more on the actual family experiences of an individual to understand the development of psychopathology. Specifically, Bowlby was concerned with the quality of the infant's attachment to his or her mother. Bowlby believed that human infants, like other mammals, developed through evolution and natural selection certain behaviors that ensure caretakers will stay in close proximity to attend to and care for their basic needs. Bolwby contended that a person's good mental health was dependent on experiencing a "warm, intimate, and continuous relationship with his mother (or permanent mother substitute) in which both find satisfaction and enjoyment" (Bowlby, 1951, p.13). If there are disruptions in the quality of this attachment, an individual could become vulnerable to psychological disorders such as depression and anxiety.

Psychoanalytic conceptualizations of Bipolar Disorder typically view hypomanic and manic states as defenses against fears of object loss (M. Klein, 1940). In addition, individuals with Bipolar Disorder are regarded as having intense fixations on love objects and insatiable narcissistic needs that, when unfulfilled, can lead to rageful responses (K. Abraham, 1911/1927; Freud, 1917). Impaired family dynamics are also viewed as contributing to the origins of Bipolar Disorder (M. B. Cohen, Baker, Cohen, Fromm-Reichmann, & Weigert, 1954; Freud, 1917; Gibson, 1958). For example, the families of bipolar individuals have been viewed as socially isolated, emotionally rigid systems in which parental identities are sharply split between the presence of a domineering, orderly, decisive parent and a weak, passive parent. Manic and depressive episodes can then be understood as individualized expressions of the polarized emotional positions and bipolar tendencies (i.e., reserved, depressed, emotionally distant versus unreliable, flighty, and impulsive) adopted by the individual's parents (Stierlin, Weber, Schmidt, & Simon, 1986).

Interpersonal Theories

Interpersonal theories of depression emphasize the role that impairments in social relationships can have on the onset and perpetuation of depressive episodes. Coyne's interpersonal theory of depression contends that individuals may become depressed in response to interpersonal losses. The depressed person then seeks excessive reassurance and support from those in his or her environment. Although such support is likely to be forthcoming initially (and to potentially reinforce the expression of depressive symptoms), such reassurance seeking eventually becomes difficult for others to tolerate and leads to rejection. The theory also assumes that interactions with the depressed person over time will lead to the induction of negative mood in the other person (Coyne, 1979). Research suggests that excessive reassurance seeking is associated with rejection of adults and youth (Joiner, 1999; Joiner, Alfano, & Metalsky, 1992) and has also found that living with a depressed person is often associated with feelings of distress, low enjoyment, greater displays of aggressive behavior, higher rates of conflict, and more feelings of burden (Coyne, Thompson, & Palmer, 2002; Hokanson, Rubert, Welker, Hollander, & Hedeen, 1989). Depressive symptoms that appear to be particularly burdensome for family members are feelings of worthlessness, constant worrying, and lack of energy (Benazon & Coyne, 2000). However, evidence supporting the mood contagion aspect of Coyne's theory (i.e., that interacting with a depressed person results in one experiencing depressed mood as well) has received mixed support (Benazon & Coyne, 2000; Whisman, Weinstock, & Uebelacker, 2002). In addition, it has been suggested that a primary mechanism by which depressed individuals elicit rejection by others may be something other than excessive reassurance seeking, and instead may relate to social skills deficits that make it difficult for the depressed individual to meet the social needs of others (Segrin & Abramson, 1994).

DIVERSITY CONSIDERATIONS

Ethnicity and Culture

An unfortunately common theme observed in the literature on bipolar and depressive disorders is the high rate of misdiagnosis among members of ethnic minority groups. In their review of records of individuals diagnosed with Bipolar Disorder, Mukherjee and colleagues (Mukherjee, Shukla, Woodle, Rosen, & Olarte, 1983) found that Hispanic and African American clients were at higher risk for misdiagnosis than Caucasians, particularly if they were young and experienced psychotic symptoms. Kupfer and colleagues (Kupfer, Grochocinski, Houck, & Brown, 2005) found that a high proportion of a sample of 208 African Americans with Bipolar Disorder had a personal history of antipsychotic medication treatment and a family history of Schizophrenia, suggesting many of these individuals may have been misdiagnosed with a primary psychotic disorder.

Patterns of misdiagnosis have been observed at both ends of the life span spectrum. Similar to findings reported for adults, DelBello, Lopez-Larson, Soutullo, and Strakowski (2001) found that young African American males were more commonly diagnosed with schizophrenic spectrum disorders compared to African American women, Caucasian men, and Caucasian women. In contrast, Caucasians were more commonly diagnosed with depression and alcohol use disorders. Misdiagnosis of Major Depressive Disorder in low-income Hispanic youth with Bipolar Disorder has been reported by Dilsaver and Akiskal (2005), who found that 51.5% of the girls and 62.5% of the boys in their sample met the *DSM-IV* criteria for Bipolar Disorder. Most of these youth had a history of unruly, aggressive behavior (including encounters with the juvenile justice system), and there was a relative absence of euphoric mania in their clinical presentations, underscoring the need to carefully evaluate bipolarity (e.g., via a structured interview) among youth who present with concurrent depression and aggressiveness. A study of older African Americans with

Bipolar Disorder found that they were more likely to received a diagnosis of mutually exclusive disorders such as Schizophrenia compared to Caucasians (Kilbourne, Haas, Mulsant, Bauer, & Pincus, 2004).

Diagnostic errors are concerning because they may reflect clinician bias, inadequate assessment, or lack of client access to quality evaluations, and because of the elevated rates of suicide attempts and substance use disorders among some ethnic minority communities (e.g., African Americans with mood disorders; Kilbourne et al., 2005; Kupfer et al., 2005).

Differences in clinical presentation of affective symptoms may also contribute to misdiagnosis. With regard to depression, ethnic minority clients (e.g., African Americans, American Indians, Hispanics) may be particularly likely to present with somatic and neurovegetative symptoms (Fabrega, Mezzich, & Ulrich, 1988). A study of Southeast Asian refugees found that depression is likely to be expressed in a syndrome accompanied by significant anxiety and somatic symptoms (similar to the concept of neurasthenia; Chung & Singer, 1995). Wohl, Lesser, and Smith (1997) found that compared to Caucasian outpatients, depressed African Americans were less likely to present with observed or articulated depressive mood, agitation, suicidal thoughts, and anxiety, which underscores the need to evaluate these symptoms carefully in this population since they may be underreported. Severe sleep disturbance may be more commonly reported among depressed African American outpatients and should therefore trigger inquiries about mood disturbance if mentioned in an intake interview (C. Brown, Schulberg, & Madonia, 1996). Kennedy, Boydell, van Os, and Murray (2004) found that, compared to Caucasians, African Americans with Bipolar Disorder were more likely to experience a manic episode as their first presentation of the illness and to have psychotic features. This is consistent with reports by others that African Americans with Bipolar Disorder may experience a predominance of manic symptoms during the course of their illness (Kirov & Murray, 1999).

In a cross-cultural study of depressive symptoms among undergraduates in the United States, Argentina, and Japan, Iwata and Buka (2002) found a number of interesting differences across groups. For example, Argentinians and Anglo-Americans were generally similar in the types of depressive symptoms endorsed, although Argentinians also exhibited the lowest levels of depression of all the student groups studied. Total depression scores on a self-report inventory were similar between Native American and Japanese individuals and significantly higher than the groups from Argentina and the United States; however, notable qualitative differences were also apparent between Japanese and Native American students. For example, the Native American students endorsed more somatic rather than affective symptoms, whereas the Japanese students obtained significantly higher scores on a composite measure of low positive affect. The study authors hypothesized that sociocultural factors might explain some of these results. For example, Japanese individuals may be less inclined to engage in frequent overt expressions of positive feelings, and the inhibition of positive affect may be more likely viewed as a desirable behavior that facilitates social harmony.

Gender

Gender differences have been observed for both depressive and bipolar disorders. Starting around puberty, women are much more likely to report depression and are twice as likely to be diagnosed with Major Depressive Disorder compared to men (American Psychiatric Association, 2000b). Women are also more likely to be diagnosed with dysthymia than men. Depressed females are more likely to report symptoms such as guilt, body image dissatisfaction, self-blame, self-disappointment, feelings of failure, concentration problems, difficulty working, sadness or depressed mood, sleep problems, fatigue, and health worries than depressed males, who may be more likely to report symptoms such as anhedonia, depressed morning mood, and morning fatigue (Bennett, Ambrosini, Kudes, Metz, & Rabinovich, 2005).

Although rates of Bipolar I Disorder are similar among women and men, women are more likely than men to be diagnosed with Bipolar II Disorder. Among the other gender differences noted for Bipolar Disorder are that women are more likely to have their first illness episode be depressive rather than manic, have more refractory episodes during their illness, and be rapid cyclers (Roy-Byrne, Post, Uhde, Porcu, & Davis, 1985; Tondo & Baldessarini, 1998; Viguera, Baldessarini, & Tondo, 2001). Women are also more likely than men to experience mixed episodes as well as dysphoric mania (i.e., mania with depressive symptoms that do not reach criteria for a major depressive episode; Leibenluft, 2000). The initial presentation of Bipolar Disorder in women is likely to be mistaken for unipolar depression, a comorbid Axis I disorder, an Axis II personality disorder, or a general medical disorder (McElroy, 2004). Higher rates of alcohol use disorders have been reported among women with Bipolar Disorder compared to men (Frye et al., 2003). Men are more likely to have an earlier age of onset of the illness (and of mania) than women, as well as a history of childhood antisocial behavior (Kennedy et al., 2005).

Mood Disorders and Pregnancy

Women who have a history of mood disorder are at increased risk for exacerbations of their affective illness during pregnancy (Petrillo, Nonacs, Viguera, & Cohen, 2005). Women who discontinue psychotropic medication for depression or Bipolar Disorder during pregnancy appear to have particularly high rates of relapse, especially in the first trimester (L. S. Cohen et al., 2004; Viguera, Nonacs, & Cohen, 2000). The importance of trying to prevent symptomatic relapse during pregnancy is highlighted by findings that women with Major Depressive Disorder or Bipolar Disorder are more likely to experience postpartum depression if they experience a relapse during their pregnancy (Viguera, Cohen, Nonacs, & Baldessarini, 2005). The clinical management of mood disorders is challenging because of risks to both maternal and fetal morbidity that can result from poorly controlled mood disorder symptoms, which must be balanced against potential adverse consequences of psychopharmacologic agents on the developing fetus. For example, inadequately treated depression may result in poor maternal nutrition, inadequate compliance with prenatal care, and a greater likelihood of engaging in health-harming behaviors (Zuckerman, Amaro, Bauchner, & Cabral et al., 1989). In addition, clinical states such as depression may exert negative effects on the developing fetus, as suggested by studies linking maternal depression with adverse neonatal outcomes (e.g., preterm birth, low birth weight; S. Orr & Miller, 1995). However, many expectant mothers with a history of mood disorders express understandable concerns about the consequences of taking psychotropic agents during pregnancy. Factors to consider in planning medication treatment during pregnancy include the estimated safety of pharmacologic interventions and details of the client's illness history, including frequency and severity of past illness episodes, duration of clinical stability with and without medication, history of medication discontinuation attempts, prodromal signs of relapse, time to relapse, and time to recovery following relapse (Viguera et al., 2005).

For some women, it may be possible to discontinue psychotropic medication entirely during pregnancy (e.g., in the case of mild depression). For these women, psychotherapy and other forms of psychosocial intervention may reduce the risk of symptomatic recurrence, although this has not been rigorously studied (Nonacs, Cohen, Viguera, & Mogielnicki, 2005). On the other hand, for women who have treatment-refractory mood disorders or a history of readily relapsing when medication has been discontinued, use of medication during pregnancy may be viewed as the best available option (Nonacs et al., 2005). No psychotropic medication has been categorized by the U.S. Food and Drug Administration (FDA) as safe for use during pregnancy (category A of the FDA's five-risk category system [A, B, C, D, and X]), and most have been classified as category C (i.e., agents for which human studies are lacking and for which risks cannot be ruled out). Although this may sound ominous, studies of some mood disorder medications (e.g., TCAs) indicate that they appear to be relatively safe to use during pregnancy (Nonacs et al., 2005). Although SSRIs had been considered relatively safe during pregnancy, recent research suggests a correlation between increased risk of fetal abnormalities (e.g., cardiac, digestive, bone or tissue malformations) and SSRI use early in pregnancy (e.g., second or third month), although it is not clear if the medications played a causal role in these findings or if they are attributable to the underlying condition for which women were being treated (A. R. Dobson, 2006). Bérard and colleagues (2006) also reported an association between SSRI use and congenital abnormalities; they found that women who took more than 25 mg per day of paroxetine during the first trimester had a threefold increased risk of having a child with a major cardiac anomaly. With regard to mood stabilizers used to treat Bipolar Disorder, the teratogenic effects associated with lithium also appear to be less common than once thought, although anticonvulsants such as carbamazepine and divalproex appear less safe and have been associated with a number of congenital abnormalities (e.g., neural tube defects) when used during pregnancy (Viguera et al., 2005). Information on the safety during pregnancy of newer anticonvulsant medications used to treat Bipolar Disorder, such as topiramate, gabapentin, lamotrigine, and oxcarbazepine, is limited. Thus, women with affective disorders receiving pharmacotherapy who are planning to conceive or who are already pregnant must work closely and collaboratively with their psychiatrist to determine the best course of treatment that will minimize the risks to both mother and child.

INTAKE AND INTERVIEWING CONSIDERATIONS

Rapport

One of the factors influencing the ease with which rapport can be established with a client is the level of motivation to seek treatment. Depressed individuals are often, though not always, very motivated to seek help because of the great emotional, physical, cognitive, and social toll their mood symptoms have taken on their life. However, this observation must be tempered with a recognition that pessimistic thoughts are part and parcel of the depressive experience, and clients may therefore come to treatment desperately wanting help, yet very uncertain as to whether anything the therapist has to offer will do much good. Although clients may express extreme thoughts that appear inaccurate or unbalanced (e.g., "I can't do anything right"), they may be highly sensitive to and feel misunderstood as a result of any direct challenges of the veracity of these views at the start of treatment. Thus, in establishing rapport with depressed clients, you must strive to empathically express understanding of their negative thoughts without conveying that you believe these thoughts are necessarily accurate, and try to convey a sense of hope that, despite how difficult or painful it may be for them to discuss their experiences with depression, this condition is treatable. The psychological meaning of events that may have preceded the depressive episode and/or occurred as a consequence of it may also affect how the client approaches the treatment situation. For example, it may be difficult to engage individuals in the therapeutic process whose depression is triggered by some real or perceived achievement failure (what A. T. Beck, 1967, would refer to as "autonomous" individuals), as they might view the need for treatment as humiliating or embarrassing (Power, 2004).

Similar considerations should be taken into account when treating a client with Bipolar Disorder who is presenting with depression. Additional, unique issues faced in establishing rapport with a client with Bipolar Disorder relate to the impact of manic or hypomanic episodes and the client's insight regarding this. Clients who have had severe manic episodes in which they were psychotic or engaged in behavior that resulted in extreme interpersonal, financial, or occupational consequences (e.g., spending thousands of dollars, engaging in promiscuous sexual encounters, getting fired from a job) may experience a phenomenon seen in Posttraumatic Stress Disorder, in which there is emotional numbness, fears of symptom recurrence, and a desire to avoid situations that are reminders of the episode (Miklowitz & Goldstein, 1997). Conversely, some clients with Bipolar Disorder may associate few adverse outcomes with episodes of mania or hypomania, and instead may view aspects of such episodes positively (e.g., noting the benefits of increased energy on work productivity, feeling more socially confident). It is a challenge to help these clients come to grips with the need for treatment and to balance out the picture of the illness with acknowledgments of its detrimental aspects. Many individuals with Bipolar Disorder will be mourning the loss of the healthy self, as realization of the impact the disorder can have on daily functioning and the necessity of ongoing monitoring and treatment becomes clearer (Frank, Swartz, & Kupfer, 2000). Helping the client through this grief process and providing a sense of hope for the future are important therapeutic tasks.

Interview and Assessment Strategies

In interviewing a client suspected of a mood disorder, it is important to get details about the scope, severity, and timing of mood symptoms as these are important dimensions along which diagnostic criteria for mood disorders in diagnostic systems such as the *DSM-IV-TR* differ from one another. For example, recall that hypomanic episodes differ from manic episodes in terms of the minimum amount of time that symptoms need to be present and the degree of impairment caused by symptoms. It is often most helpful to begin this discussion by asking open-ended questions, such as, "What is it like when you are feeling depressed?" or "When you've had periods when you felt emotionally high, what were those like?" This provides an opportunity for you to observe what symptoms the client spontaneously mentions, which can then be followed up with more specific inquiries about symptoms the client did not mention. It is also important to understand how mood symptoms impact daily functioning. This may be achieved through questions such as, "How does being depressed (or high or elated) affect how you interact with others (get things done at work, get things done around the house, take care of yourself)?" or "What have other people told you they have noticed about you during these times?" If clients have difficulty responding to such questions, it may be helpful to ask them to walk you through the details of what happened on a recent day when their mood was low or high (e.g., What time did they get up, and how much sleep did they get the night before? What activities were done in the morning, afternoon, and so on? Did the client eat regular meals?). Getting details about the impact of symptoms on day-to-day functioning also allows you to determine how pervasive mood symptoms are throughout the day (e.g., Is depressed mood present most of the day, most days each week?).

Another way to assess the impact of mood symptoms on daily functioning is to ask clients to imagine what their life would be like without these symptoms. For example, "What would your life look like if you were no longer depressed? What would be different? What would you be doing?" This type of questioning can also help identify treatment goals (e.g., work issues for the client who says, "I would probably decide to look into changing my job to something I'd like better"). It is possible that clients who have experienced mania or hypomania will say they like these periods because they are associated with increased energy, creativity, and confidence. This will help the clinician understand if the client is ambivalent about treatment. In response to client statements about enjoying or desiring manic or hypomanic experiences, the clinician may wish to ask whether others in the client's life have responded favorably to the client during these times (in many cases, others are likely to be distressed, annoyed, or concerned about the client's behavior).

Life Charting

Life charting is a technique that is often used in the evaluation of individuals with Bipolar Disorder, but it can also be usefully applied to the evaluation of an individual with Major Depressive Disorder. A life chart is a visual depiction of a client's mood episodes over time that allows both client and clinician to observe the pattern, severity, and timing of symptomatic periods. In constructing a life chart, a horizontal line is drawn to represent time, and manic and depressive episodes are noted as curves that extend above and below the line, respectively. The farther above the horizontal time line a curve is drawn, the more severe the mood episode being depicted; similarly, the greater the distance over which a curve extends, the longer the mood episode represented (Basco & Rush, 2007). Typically, the most recent mood episodes are charted first, and the client then works backward in time to fill in previous episodes. Information on life events and any treatment received or stopped at the time of episodes is also usually recorded on the life chart, which enables client and clinician to observe potential triggers associated with the onset of symptoms (Basco & Rush, 2007).

There are a number of assessment measures that can aid the clinician in diagnosing mood disorders in clients as well as tracking symptom change over time. Some of these measures are summarized in Table 10.2; the interested reader is referred to Nezu, Ronan, and Meadows (2006) for a more in-depth discussion of a number of different mood measures.

Table 10.2   Some depression and mania assessment measures

Beck Depression Inventory (BDI) (BDI: A. T. Beck, Ward, Mendelson, Mock, & Erbaugh, 1961) (BDI-II: A. T. Beck, Steer, & Brown, 1996)	BDI-II is a 21 item scale. Inquires about depressive symptoms over the preceding 2 weeks. Takes approximately 5 to 10 minutes to complete. Individual items cover symptoms such as mood, sense of failure, pessimism, self-dislike, suicidal ideation, appetite disturbance. Total score ranges from 0 to 63, with higher scores indicating more severe depression.	Revision designed to make item content consistent with *DSM-IV* symptoms. Easy to use and score. Useful for tracking treatment progress. Strong psychometrics (e.g., good test-retest and internal consistency reliability; validity demonstrated by strong correlations with other measures of depression). Because it has high face validity it is easy for individuals to exaggerate or minimize their level of depression (i.e., "fake bad" or "fake good").
The Hamilton Rating Scale for Depression (HRSD or HAM-D) (M. Hamilton, 1960)	Administered by a clinician or other trained observer. Based on interview and observation of a client, responses are made to 21 items. First 17 items concern common depression symptoms. Remaining items assess the presence of rarer symptoms such as paranoia, depersonalization, and obsessionality. Heavy emphasis on somatic symptoms (so good for severe depression). Takes approximately 20 to 30 minutes to complete.	Used in research and sometimes considered a gold standard against which other depression measures are compared. Internal reliability, convergent and discriminant validity are adequate. Psychometric problems include inadequate test-retest reliability, poor interrater reliability, questionable content validity, and many scale items are poor contributors to depression severity measurement. Other drawbacks: length of time required for administration, need for a clinician or trained rater.
Patient Health Questionnaire (PHQ-9) (Spitzer, Kroenke, & Williams, 1999)	Brief self-report measure with 9 items directly paralleling *DSM-IV* diagnostic criteria for a major depressive episode. Originally developed and tested for use with medical patients. Frequently used in primary care settings.	Substantially shorter than most depression screening measures and consistent with *DSM-IV* depression criteria. Excellent test-retest reliability and internal consistency estimates. Evidence of validity includes strong correlations with well-established measures of depression.

(Continued)

Table 10.2   (Continued)

	Scores range from 0 to 27, with higher scores indicating greater symptom severity. Categorical algorithm for diagnosing Major Depressive Disorder also available.	The utility in evaluating depression among different ethnic groups (e.g., African Americans, Hispanics, Chinese, and Nigerians) has been documented.
Mood Disorder Question-naire (MDQ) (Hirschfeld et al., 2000)	Yes/no, 13-item self-report measure. Screens for lifetime history of manic or hypomanic syndromes derived from both *DSM-IV* criteria and clinical experience. Also queries functional impairment due to symptoms. 11-item, clinician-rated measure.	Widely used. Appropriate for primary care settings. Easy to complete and score. Excellent internal consistency and reliability. Good sensitivity and specificity ratings.
Young Mania Rating Scale (YMRS) (R. C. Young, Biggs, Ziegler, & Meyer, 1978)	Evaluates the presence and severity of mania-related symptoms over the preceding 48-hour period. Items cover elevated mood, motor activity/energy, sexual interest, sleep, irritability, speech, language or thought disorder, thought content, disruptive or aggressive behavior, appearance, and insight. Higher scores indicate a greater severity of manic symptoms.	Strong internal reliability and consistency coefficients and good interrater reliability estimates. Correlates with other clinician-rated measures of mania. Easy to administer, brief, and widely accepted use. Limited usefulness with diagnostic populations other than mania.

Crisis, Legal, and Ethical Issues

Suicide

As previously noted, a common feature associated with both unipolar and bipolar mood disorders is suicidality. It has been estimated that 60% of all individuals who commit suicide have a mood disorder diagnosis at the time of death (Maris, Berman, & Silverman, 2000). For children, adolescents, and adults, the risk of suicidal ideation, suicide attempts, and completed suicide is significantly increased when a lifetime diagnosis of Major Depressive Disorder is present (D. A. Brent et al., 1993; M. S. Gould et al., 1998). In their study of individuals with Bipolar I and II Disorders, Valtonen et al. (2005) found that during an index episode, 20% had attempted suicide and 61% had suicidal ideation, and that during their lifetime, 80% had suicidal behavior and 51% had attempted suicide.

Thus, whenever a client suspected of a mood disorder is evaluated, questions about suicidal ideation and suicide attempts must be asked.

Chapter 2 reviews strategies for assessing and responding to suicidal clients and reviews risk factors for suicide. However, it is helpful here to highlight those factors that have been correlated with increased risk of suicide specifically among those with mood disorders. A prospective study of 280 patients with major depression found that at a 5-year follow-up, approximately 6% had killed themselves and that the most potent predictors of suicide were feelings of hopelessness, thoughts of suicide or suicide attempts, and hypochondriacal preoccupations during an index episode of depression (B. Schneider et al., 2001). The presence of alcohol abuse, substance use, and Cluster B personality disorders is also associated with increased suicide risk among affectively disordered individuals (Cornelius et al., 1995; Oquendo, Malone, & Mann, 1997). Some studies have found psychotic symptoms to be a risk factor for suicide; Roose, Glassman, Walsh, Woodring, and Vital-Hern (1983) found that delusional depressed patients were 5 times more likely to commit suicide than nondelusional individuals. Other factors that have been identified in the literature as suicide risk factors for those with affective disorders include family history of suicide, low CSF 5-HIAA levels, alcohol and/or substance abuse, Cluster B personality disorder, chronic physical illness, marital isolation, parental loss before age 11, childhood history of physical and sexual abuse, and not living with a child under age 18 (Sher et al., 2001). The most common precipitants of suicidal acts in mood disorders are financial problems, interpersonal losses or conflicts, and job difficulties (Sher et al., 2001).

Individuals who begin to experience improvement in some but not all of their depressive symptoms (e.g., increased energy but continued low mood) are often considered at heightened suicide risk. Various theories have been put forth to explain this phenomenon: (a) The resolution to commit suicide results in increased energy due to resolving ambivalence and a sense that relief from suffering is at hand; (b) the improvement in some depressive symptoms results in demoralization as support systems pull back and the affected individual realizes that obstacles and problems contributing to the depression are still present or recurring; and (c) psychomotor agitation, masquerading as increased energy, adds an intensely distressing element to the depression that becomes intolerable (Joiner, Pettit, & Rudd, 2004). Interestingly, Joiner and colleagues found that the pattern of improved energy in the context of continuing depression was a relatively rare symptom constellation and occurred in only 7% of a sample of over 100 depressed suicidal young adults. Furthermore, these researchers failed to find evidence, based on a temporal analysis of serial BDIs, of heightened suicide risk among individuals who demonstrated the increased energy with continuing depression pattern versus those who did not. The conclusion reached in this study was that there may not be a special relationship between suicide risk and increased energy in the context of persistent depressive symptoms and suicide. Instead, patients who fit the latter clinical profile may represent one of many subgroups of depressed persons who experience incomplete remissions and that careful, ongoing evaluation of suicide risk is recommended when depressive symptoms persist despite sufficient treatment trials.

Depressed elderly who express suicidal ideation or thoughts of death appear to respond more slowly to treatment (both pharmacotherapy and psychotherapy) and exhibit a less robust response compared to depressed older adults who are not suicidal (Szanto, Mulsant, Houck, Dew, & Reynolds, 2003). Older suicidal adults are also more likely to need augmentation of their medication regimen during treatment and are at greater risk of relapse than their nonsuicidal counterparts (Szanto et al., 2001). Thus, the presence of suicidal ideation among depressed older adults is likely to indicate the need for aggressive and sustained treatment.

Among those with Bipolar Disorder, monitoring suicidal ideation is important particularly during depressive episodes and especially if a mixed episode is present, as it has been estimated that approximately 20% of deaths in this clinical population are the result of suicide during these types of episodes (Tondo & Baldessarini, 2000). The presence of a mixed episode is also a risk factor for suicide attempts among children with Bipolar Disorder, as are psychosis, hospitalization, self-injurious behavior, Panic Disorder, and substance use disorder (T. R. Goldstein et al., 2005).

When a client endorses suicidal ideation, the clinician must carefully and systematically evaluate the intensity of the ideation, the presence of a suicide plan, the availability of means to carry out the plan, potential deterrents, and additional factors that might facilitate the carrying out of a suicide plan (e.g., emotional lability or agitation, substance use, social isolation). Clinicians must work with their clients to develop a safety plan, which might include a no-suicide contract, increased frequency of sessions, telephone contact outside of sessions, and, in extreme cases, hospitalization. It is best for clients to agree to hospitalization voluntarily, but if they are not willing to do so, involuntary commitment may be necessary. Clinicians should be familiar with the laws in their respective states regarding the individuals who are authorized to initiate such an action (e.g., police, members of a psychiatric emergency team).

Severe Vegetative Symptoms

Clinicians working with depressed individuals should also carefully evaluate the severity of vegetative symptoms, such as alterations in sleep and eating patterns. When such symptoms are severe, referral for a medication evaluation is indicated. Biological treatments may be needed to enable such a client to meaningfully participate in and benefit from psychotherapy.

A summary of key intake and interviewing issues to keep in mind when seeing clients suspected of a mood disorder can be found in Table 10.3.

Table 10.3   Intake issues for mood disorders

Assess severity of affective symptoms (e.g., presence of severe vegetative symptoms).

Gather information on timing, duration, and severity of past mood symptoms and precipitating factors (e.g., complete life chart).

Consider cultural and familial factors in symptom presentation.

Refer for medical evaluation to rule out medical or substance-related etiology.

Evaluate suicidality.

Assess for comorbid conditions (e.g., substance use, anxiety).

Evaluate interpersonal precipitants and sequelae of mood episodes.

Consider medication referral.

Coordinate care with other treatment providers (e.g., psychiatrist).

DIAGNOSTIC CONSIDERATIONS

Common Comorbidities

Anxiety Disorders

Anxiety disorders are among the most common comorbid conditions found among those with mood disorders, particularly among those with depressive disorders. Among persons with a lifetime history of Major Depressive Disorder, nearly 60% have a lifetime history of a comorbid anxiety disorder (R. C. Kessler et al., 2003). Epidemiological studies indicate that among the most common anxiety disorders in those with Major Depressive Disorder are Panic Disorder (56%), Social Phobia (26.5%), and GAD (17.2%; R. C. Kessler, Stang, Wittchen, Stein, & Walters, 1999).

Among dysthymic persons, as many as three fourths will meet diagnostic criteria for an anxiety disorder, and those with double depression appear to be at particularly high risk (Yerevanian, Koek, & Ramdev, 2001). With respect to specific disorders, it is estimated that 13% to 33% have comorbid Panic Disorder, 53% to 65% have comorbid GAD, 4% to 13% have comorbid OCD, and 9% to 26% have comorbid simple phobia (Pini, Cassano, Savino, Russo, & Montgomery, 1997; Yerevanian et al., 2001). In a sample of 100 clinic-referred children and adolescents diagnosed with Dysthymic Disorder without comorbid Major Depressive Disorder, 59% had GAD, 28% had Simple Phobia, 18% had Separation Anxiety Disorder, 14% had OCD, 13% had Social Phobia, and 10% had Panic Disorder (Masi et al., 2003).

Studies of Bipolar Disorder reveal rates of comorbid anxiety disorders that range from 37% to 93%. The comorbidity rates for specific disorders have been reported to range from 21% to 37% for Panic Disorder, 32% to 43% for GAD, 47% for Social Phobia, 9% to 39% for PTSD, and 5% to 67% for Simple Phobia (Chen & Dilsaver, 1995; R. C. Kessler, Rubinow, et al., 1997; Pini et al., 1997; Yerevanian et al., 2001; L. T. Young, Cooke, Robb, Levitt, & Joffe, 1993). Rates of OCD among individuals with Bipolar Disorder I are low (Yerevanian et al., 2001). Rates of comorbid anxiety disorders in adolescents with Bipolar Disorder have been reported to be as high as 32% to 45% (Lewinsohn et al., 2002).

Comorbid anxiety symptoms are frequently correlated with poorer outcome among those with mood disorders, including premature termination from treatment, greater symptom severity, higher suicide risk, poorer medication and psychotherapy treatment response, longer time to recovery, and greater role impairment (C. Brown, Schulberg, Madonia, Shear, & Houck, 1996; Roy-Byrne et al., 2000). Similar findings have been reported for affectively disordered older adults with regard to suicidal ideation, somatic symptoms, social functioning, and, in some cases, antidepressant treatment response (Allgulander & Lavori, 1993; Dew et al., 1997; Flint & Rifat, 1997; Lenze et al., 2000). Anxiety symptoms among older adults being treated for depression (with either medication alone or in combination with psychotherapy) have also been found to remit more slowly than core mood symptoms of depression and sleep disturbance (Dombroski et al., 2006).

Substance Use Disorders

Substance use disorders are common comorbid conditions for both unipolar and bipolar mood disorders. It has been estimated that 1 in 4 individuals with Major Depressive Disorder has a current substance use disorder (R. C. Kessler et al., 2003). This statistic is similar to that reported by L. L. Davis et al. (2005) in a study of 1,500 outpatients with nonpsychotic Major Depressive Disorder, which found that 28% endorsed symptoms indicative of a current substance use disorder. That study further found that compared to those without a concurrent substance use disorder, those with such a disorder were more likely to be male, divorced or never married, have a younger age of onset of depression, higher rates of suicidal ideation and previous suicide attempts, higher levels of anxious mood and insomnia, and greater illness-related functional impairment.

Estimates of comorbid substance use disorders among adults with Bipolar Disorder are as high as 50% to 61% (Berk & Dodd, 2005; R. C. Kessler et al., 1997). Alcoholism is estimated to occur in approximately 30% of individuals with Bipolar Disorder (Winokur et al., 1998). Lewinsohn et al. (2002) reported a 22.2% rate of comorbid substance abuse or dependence in their sample of bipolar adolescents drawn from a community-based sample. Older adults with Bipolar Disorder are less likely to abuse substances than their younger counterparts (Depp & Jeste, 2004). Use of alcohol, sedatives, tranquilizers, and opioids appears to be particularly high among individuals with Bipolar Disorder (Conway et al., 2006; Regier et al., 1990), raising interesting questions about attempts at self-medication. Comorbid substance use disorders are associated with poor outcome in Bipolar Disorder, particularly when more than one substance is abused (Salloum & Thase, 2000).

Personality Disorders

As many as one half to three fourths of those with major depression may have a comorbid personality disorder (Brieger, Ehrt, Bloeink, & Marneros, 2002; M. T. Shea et al., 1990). So-called Cluster B (i.e., Borderline, Histrionic, Narcissistic, Antisocial) and Cluster C (i.e., Avoidant, Dependent, Obsessive-Compulsive) Personality Disorders are the most common among individuals with major depression. For example, in a sample of depressed inpatients, approximately 32% were diagnosed with Borderline Personality Disorder, 25% with Dependent Personality Disorder, and 14% with Obsessive-Compulsive Personality Disorder (Schiavone, Dorz, Conforti, Scarso, & Borgherini, 2004). Grilo et al. (2005) reported comorbidity rates for four selected personality disorders among adults diagnosed with Major Depressive Disorder: Borderline Personality Disorder (22.5%), Avoidant Personality Disorder (22.5%), Obsessive-Compulsive Personality Disorder (16%), and Schizotypal Personality Disorder (11%).

Personality disorders may be even more common among those with Dysthymic Disorder than those with Major Depressive Disorder (Sansone, Gaither, & Rytwinski, 2004). Data from the NESARC found that 55% of those with diagnosable dysthymia met criteria for a concurrent personality disorder; rates reported for 7 personality disorders were Paranoid (29.5%), Obsessive-Compulsive (28.4%), Avoidant (20.6%), Schizoid (19.2%), Antisocial (13.5%), Histrionic (8.8%), and Dependent (6.6%).

Rates of personality disorders among those with Bipolar Disorder are somewhat variable but generally high. Among inpatient samples, between 50% and 89% of those with Bipolar Disorder can be expected to meet diagnostic criteria for at least one personality disorder (Brieger et al., 2002; Schiavone et al., 2004; Turley, Bates, Edwards, & Jackson, 1999). Among euthymic outpatients, a little less than one third may be diagnosed with a comorbid personality disorder (George, Miklowitz, Richards, Simoneau, & Taylor, 2003).

As with unipolar depressive disorders, Cluster B and C personality disorders are the most commonly encountered comorbid conditions. In their sample of inpatients, Schiavone and colleagues found the most frequently diagnosed comorbid personality disorders were Borderline (41%), Narcissistic (21%), Dependent (13%), and Histrionic (10%). Similar findings were reported by Turley et al. in their inpatient sample: Narcissistic (47%), Antisocial (47%), Histrionic (37%), and Passive-Aggressive (37%). In a sample of bipolar outpatients participating in a family-based treatment, George et al. found the two most commonly occurring comorbid personality disorders were Histrionic and Obsessive-Compulsive (each observed in 18% of their sample). Rates of bipolarity in samples of individuals with Borderline Personality Disorder have been reported as high as 69% (Deltito et al., 2001).

Axis II personality disorders have often been associated with a poorer prognosis for both unipolar and bipolar mood disorders. For example, comorbid personality disorders among depressed individuals are linked to earlier age of onset, more previous depressive episodes, shorter time to relapse, worse response to treatment, longer use of psychotropic medication, and increased risk of suicide (Brieger et al., 2002; Casey et al., 2004; Cyranowski et al., 2004; P. E. B. Hansen, Wang, Stage, & Kragh-Sorensen, 2003). In particular, Grilo and colleagues (2005) found that the presence of Schizotypal Personality Disorder, Borderline Personality Disorder, and Avoidant Personality Disorder predicted longer time to remission than depressed individuals without a comorbid personality disorder. This is consistent with the work of Brieger et al., who found that depressed individuals with a comorbid Cluster A (i.e., Schizotypal, Schizoid, or Paranoid) or Cluster B personality had a history of more suicide attempts compared to individuals with a comorbid Cluster C personality disorder. Among those with Bipolar Disorder, the presence of comorbid personality pathology has been linked to poorer recovery (including higher levels of residual symptomatology), increased suicide risk, greater likelihood of comorbid substance abuse, and poorer psychosocial outcomes (e.g., work functioning; Dunayevich et al., 2000; Garno, Goldberg, Ramirez, & Ritzler, 2005; George et al., 2003; J. H. Kay, Altshuler, Ventura, & Mintz, 2002).

Differential Diagnosis

Mood Disorders versus Other Psychiatric Disorders

Psychotic Disorders   Depressed individuals can present with emotional flattening and anhedonia that appear similar to negative symptoms of Schizophrenia (e.g., blunted affect, avolition). Similarly, positive symptoms such as delusions and hallucinations characterize both primary psychotic disorders and psychotic mood disorder, and first-rank Schneiderian symptoms, once thought to be pathognomonic for Schizophrenia, can also occur in mood disorders with psychotic features. Furthermore, the flight of ideas seen in mania can be mistaken for thought disorder in Schizophrenia (F. K. Goodwin & Jamison, 1990). These facts can make the differential diagnosis between mood disorders and psychotic disorders quite difficult. A key to distinguishing between primary psychotic disorders, such as Schizophrenia, and mood disorders is the sequencing and overlap of affective and psychotic symptoms. In mood disorders, the appearance of any psychotic symptoms will be restricted to periods of mood disturbance (i.e., depression, mania, or mixed states). If psychotic symptoms occur during periods of relatively euthymic mood, the clinician will lean toward a diagnosis of a primary psychotic disorder, assuming that a general medical condition or substance has been ruled out as a causative factor. By definition, Schizoaffective Disorder is characterized by the prominence of both mood and psychotic symptoms, thus making the differential with either Major Depressive Disorder or Bipolar Disorder especially challenging. However, a *DSM-IV-TR* diagnosis of Schizoaffective Disorder requires that, in addition to an overlapping period during which psychotic and mood (i.e., manic, mixed, or depressive episode) symptoms are concurrently present, there must also be a period of at least 2 weeks during the same illness episode in which prominent mood symptoms are absent (American Psychiatric Association, 2000b). Thus the presence of psychotic symptoms not restricted to periods of disturbed mood helps distinguish Schizoaffective Disorder from either Major Depressive Disorder or Bipolar Disorder.

In addition to examining the timing of psychotic symptoms relative to mood symptoms, examination of family history may also be helpful in differentiating between mood and psychotic disorders; for example, F. K. Goodwin and Jamison (1990) suggest that clinicians be cautious in diagnosing Schizophrenia in an individual who has a history of Bipolar Disorder in a first-degree relative.

Cognitive Disorders   Depression can be associated with cognitive changes such as impaired attention and concentration, difficulties in decision making, and memory problems that can be mistaken for a cognitive disorder such as dementia, particularly in older adults. The term *pseudo-dementia* has been used to refer to the cognitive changes that can be seen in the context of depression (Lishman, 1987). Conversely, demented individuals may display emotional changes, such as apathy, that can easily be mistaken for depression. The *DSM-IV-TR* (American Psychiatric Association, 2000b) notes that the onset of cognitive changes associated with depression is generally more abrupt than those seen in dementia; this would be particularly true for cortical dementias, such as Dementia Due to Alzheimer's Disease, which have a slow and insidious onset. The extent of cognitive impairment in dementia is also typically greater than that seen in depression. The "Special Topics" section of Chapter 7 reviews the differential diagnosis of depression and dementia, and the reader is referred there for a fuller discussion of this issue.

Mood Disorders due to General Medical Conditions or Substances   As noted in the *DSM-IV-TR*, mood symptoms are often associated with intoxication and withdrawal states from various substances (American Psychiatric Association, 2000b). For example, amphetamine intoxication is associated with symptoms such as euphoria, grandiosity, talkativeness, and increased energy and activity that could be mistaken for a manic episode. Similarly, withdrawal from cocaine is associated with dysphoria that might appear similar to a depressive episode. Certain medical conditions can also cause affective symptoms that can be mistaken for a primary mood disorder; for example, hypothyroidism may be accompanied by symptoms such as depressed mood, fatigue, difficulties concentrating, and feelings of worthlessness. When deciding between a diagnosis of a primary mood disorder and a substance-induced mood disorder or a mood disorder due to a general medical condition, the clinician must determine if an etiological relationship between the mood symptoms and the substance or medical condition exists. A. Frances et al. (1995) note that an etiological relationship between a substance or medical condition and psychiatric symptoms may be suggested by a close temporal relationship in which the symptoms follow rather than precede the ingestion or withdrawal of a substance or the onset of a medical condition and cease when the effects of the substance (or its withdrawal) are no longer present or the medical condition has been successfully treated. In addition, there must be evidence from the clinical literature that the substance or medical condition in question could reasonably cause the psychiatric symptoms seen. It is also important to determine whether the psychiatric symptoms in question have ever occurred in the absence of the substance or medical condition; for example, the presence of major depressive episodes that occurred in the absence of drug use makes it more difficult to rule out a primary mood disorder in an individual presenting with depressive symptomatology and recent cessation of cocaine use.

Borderline Personality Disorder Both Bipolar Disorder and Borderline Personality Disorder are associated with affective instability that may make these conditions difficult to distinguish from one another. In addition, as noted under "Common Comorbidities," these diagnoses often co-occur in the same individual, although there is debate in such cases as to whether these represent truly separate conditions or are part of the same affective spectrum. In differentiating between these conditions, F. K. Goodwin and Jamison (1990) note that the lability associated with Borderline Personality Disorder makes it more likely that shifts in mood will be more rapid (e.g., occurring on a day-to-day or even hour-to-hour basis) than what is typically seen in Bipolar Disorder and that such shifts are more apt to be tied to environmental factors. They also note that the hyperphagia and hypersomnia associated with depressive states in Bipolar Disorder, as well as symptoms such as flight of ideas or decreased need for sleep associated with (hypo)manic episodes, are less likely to be seen in Borderline Personality Disorder.

Bereavement Following the death of a loved one, it is common to feel depressed. The presentation of bereavement may appear clinically quite similar to major depression. The *DSM-IV-TR* includes bereavement under the so-called V-Codes, located in the section entitled "Other Conditions That May Be a Focus of Clinical Attention (American Psychiatric Association, 2000b)." When an individual meets criteria for a major depressive episode but the onset of the symptoms occurs within 2 months following the death of a loved one, the clinician may choose to diagnose bereavement rather than a mood disorder. However, the *DSM-IV-TR* notes that the presence of any of a number of symptoms and features may lead to the decision to diagnose Major Depressive Disorder even when symptoms occur shortly after a death, such as hallucinations other than thinking one hears the voice or transiently sees the image of the deceased person, marked psychomotor retardation, and significant functional impairment (American Psychiatric Association, 2000b). Also, if symptoms that meet criteria for a major depressive episode extend *beyond* 2 months of the date of the loved one's death, a diagnosis of Major Depressive Disorder is typically given if the other criteria for this disorder are also met. Studies of bereaved individuals indicate that as many as one fourth to one third experience chronically elevated levels of depressive symptoms prior to the death of their loved one; in these cases, bereavement may be better conceptualized as an extension of a prebereavement depressive condition (Bonnano, 2005). It is important to keep in mind cultural variations in the grieving process in evaluating the individual's grief reaction and deciding on a diagnosis of bereavement versus a primary mood disorder. Table 10.4 summarizes differential diagnostic information for mood disorders.

Table 10.4   Between-category diagnostic differential

Disorder	Similarities with Mood Disorders	Differences from Mood Disorders
Psychotic disorders	Flattened affect, anhedonia, lack of motivation. Hallucinations, delusions (Major Depressive Disorder or Bipolar Disorder with psychotic features). Thought disorder (Bipolar Disorder with psychotic features).	Negative symptoms (e.g., flattened affect, anhedonia) not restricted to periods of mood disturbance. Positive symptoms (e.g., hallucinations, delusions) not restricted to periods of mood disturbance.
Cognitive disorders	Memory complaints. Attention or concentration difficulties. Decision-making problems. Apathy.	Onset of cognitive changes may have a slower, insidious onset (e.g., Dementia Due to Alzheimer's Disease). Extent of cognitive impairment in dementia is also typically greater than that seen in depression. Client more likely to underestimate cognitive difficulties. Mood symptoms may be absent or much less prominent than cognitive impairments. Less likely to benefit from cues in memory testing (e.g., Dementia Due to Alzheimer's Disease).
Substance intoxication or withdrawal	Affective symptoms. Possibly other cognitive (e.g., attention problems) and somatic symptoms (e.g., sleep disturbances).	Symptoms follow ingestion or (in dependent individuals) withdrawal of substance. Symptoms are known to be associated with substance effects. Symptoms remit when intoxication or withdrawal syndromes remit.
Medical conditions	Affective symptoms. Possibly other cognitive and somatic symptoms.	Symptoms follow onset of medical condition. Symptoms are known to be associated with medical condition. Symptoms remit when medical condition is successfully treated.
Borderline Personality Disorder	Affective instability (Bipolar Disorder).	Mood shifts typically more rapid than in Bipolar Disorder and tied to environmental factors. Vegetative symptoms (e.g., changes in sleep and appetite) less likely than in Bipolar Disorder.

Table 10.4 (Continued)

| Bereavement | Affective symptoms. Possibly other cognitive and somatic symptoms. | Always followed by death of significant individual in client's life. Severe symptoms (e.g., psychotic symptoms) typically absent. Symptoms typically resolve within 2 months. |

Among the Mood Disorders

Table 10.5 presents key and discriminating features among the mood disorders. Although major depression and dysthymia frequently co-occur, they can be differentiated from one another based on the severity, chronicity, and persistence of mood symptoms (American Psychiatric Association, 2000b). Although there is overlap among the symptoms of both disorders, Major Depressive Disorder is characterized by the presence of symptoms that occur nearly every day, for most of the day, over a minimum of a 2-week period. In contrast, Dysthymic Disorder is characterized by symptoms that are typically less severe (e.g., occur more days than not but not necessarily every day) but that occur over an extended period of time (i.e., at least 2 years). The *DSM-IV-TR* criteria for dysthymia prohibit the presence of a major depressive episode during the first 2 years of the disorder (1 year for children and adolescents) and also require that if a major depressive episode occurred *prior* to the onset of the dysthymia, a period of full remission (i.e., no signs or symptoms of

Table 10.5 Mood disorders: key and discriminating features

Disorder	Key Features	Discriminating Features
Major Depressive Disorder	Presence of at least one major depressive episode (MDE)	No history of a manic, hypomanic, or mixed episode
Bipolar Disorder I	History of at least one manic or mixed episode	Manic symptoms cause impairment
Bipolar Disorder II	History of at least one MDE History of at least one hypomanic episode	Hypomanic symptoms cause noticeable change but do not cause significant impairment
Dysthymic Disorder	Depressed mood more days than not for at least 2 years (in children and adolescents, mood can be irritable and duration must be at least 1 year) Depressed mood does not meet criteria for an MDE (MDE can be superimposed on dysthymia after the first 2 years of the illness)	During 2 years, not without symptoms for >2 months at a time (1 year for children and adolescents) No MDE during the first 2 years of illness (1 year for children and adolescents) If MDE present prior to onset of illness, there was a full remission from the MDE

Source: From *Diagnostic and Statistical Manual for Mental Disorders*, fourth edition, text revision, by American Psychiatric Association, 2000b, Washington, DC: Author. Adapted with permission.

Table 10.6   Factors that may indicate Bipolar Disorder in a client presenting with Depression

Mood lability
Atypical depressive features (e.g., hypersomnia, overeating)
Presence of psychomotor retardation
Presence of psychosis
Medication-induced hypomania
Sudden episode onset
Earlier age of onset
Early onset of depressive symptoms (<25 years)
Shorter well intervals; more tempestuous course of illness
History of temperamental instability
Family history of Bipolar Disorder

Source: From "Unmet Needs in Bipolar Depression," by M. A. Frye, M. J. Gitlin, and L. L. Altshuler, 2004, *Depression and Anxiety, 19*, pp. 199–208, and "Bipolar II Disorder: A Review," by M. Berk and S. Dodd, 2005, *Bipolar Disorders, 7*, pp. 11–21. Adapted with permission.

depression for at least 2 continuous months) must have preceded the onset of the dysthymia. These stipulations attempt to differentiate Dysthymic Disorder from an evolving Major Depressive Disorder. For example, if an individual experiences a major depressive episode just prior to the onset of symptoms that appear to meet criteria for Dysthymic Disorder, one could argue that the subsequent dysthymic symptoms simply represent a partially remitted major depressive episode. Conversely, if a major depressive episode occurs within the first 2 years of an apparent Dysthymic Disorder, it is possible that the dysthymic symptoms were merely the prodromal phase of the major depressive episode.

As previously noted, many individuals with Bipolar Disorder are frequently misdiagnosed, most commonly with unipolar depression (Hirschfeld, Lewis, et al., 2003). Because most individuals with Bipolar I or II Disorder have depressive episodes that outnumber manic or hypomanic episodes, it is quite likely that an individual with Bipolar Disorder will initially present for treatment with depression. Frye et al. (2004) identified a number of factors that should raise the index of suspicion that an individual presenting with depressive symptoms may actually have Bipolar Disorder. These are presented in Table 10.6. In addition, the occurrence of four or more episodes per year that meet full criteria for a major depressive episode is relatively rare among individuals with Major Depressive Disorder and should trigger suspicion of an undiagnosed rapid cycling Bipolar Disorder (Dunner, 1999).

TREATMENT

General Principles in Treating Mood Disorders

In treating affectively disordered clients, an initial goal should be the stabilization of acute symptoms. Referral for a medication evaluation should be given to any client suspected of Bipolar Disorder and may also be warranted for individuals with unipolar depression if severe vegetative symptoms or suicidal ideation is present. Because affective disorders are recurrent and carry a high risk of relapse, attention should be paid to monitoring symptoms and helping the client develop strategies to identify and cope with early warning signs that depression or (hypo)mania are returning. As stressed throughout this chapter, affective disorders carry a high risk of suicide, so regular monitoring of suicidal ideation is imperative. Given the adverse impact that mood disturbance can have on interpersonal relationships (as well as the role that interpersonal stressors and conflict may play in exacerbating these symptoms), attention to the relational issues and the interpersonal sequelae of the mood disorder should receive attention in treatment. Because the use of medication can play an important role in the treatment of mood disorders, it is critical to have a good working relationship with the client's psychiatrist, including regular communication about the client's clinical status and any changes made to the medication regimen. Because psychotherapists typically see a client more frequently and for a longer period of time at each contact than the psychiatrist does, the therapist is likely to have valuable insights and observations as to the client's symptomatology and functioning that will aid the psychiatrist in developing the client's medication treatment plan.

Although it is not the nonphysician mental health practitioner's role to provide clients with detailed information or recommendations about medication, monitoring adherence and exploring the client's thoughts and feelings related to the need for medication are certainly topics that can be discussed in psychotherapy. Indeed, medication nonadherence is a common factor complicating treatment of many affectively disordered clients, particularly those with Bipolar Disorder. For example, in a study of over 400 individuals with Bipolar Disorder who attended a lithium clinic for up to 30 years, the suicide rate among those who left the clinic and stopped taking medication increased by 80% compared to those who remained adherent to their lithium regimen (Kallner, Lindelius, Petterson, Stockman, & Tham, 2000). A clinician can assist in the identification of factors that may be contributing to nonadherence, such as intrapersonal variables (e.g., no longer seeing the need for medication), treatment variables (e.g., intolerable side effects), social system variables (e.g., discouragement from family or friends to take medication), interpersonal variables (e.g., poor rapport with prescribing physician), and cognitive factors (e.g., belief that taking medication is a sign of weakness; Basco & Rush, 2007). The clinician can then help the client develop plans for resolving these obstacles (e.g., make plans to discuss unwanted side effects with one's psychiatrist, assertively respond to others who discourage medication use, utilize cognitive techniques to address faulty beliefs about taking medication).

Depressive Disorders

Depression is frequently associated with dramatic impairment in psychosocial functioning that can create a ripple effect, adversely affecting not only the client, but his or her family, community, and the larger society as a whole. However, many effective treatments, including medication and psychotherapy, exist for depression that can substantially reduce the severity of symptoms and the likelihood of recurrence. From a public health perspective, treatment of depression is associated with reduced costs to employers and health care providers and is a wise societal investment whose cost is exceeded by money saved in the form of work productivity and decreased absenteeism (Beuzen,

Ravily, Souetre, & Thomander, 1993; Katzelnick, Kobak, Greist, & Jefferson, 1997; Pyne et al., 2003).

Medication

Antidepressant medications represent one of the most commonly prescribed drug classes in the United States, accounting for some $12 billion in annual sales (Schatzberg et al., 2005). Many different types of antidepressants are available to treat depression, including TCAs, SSRIs, MAOIs, and miscellaneous drugs such as venlafaxine (a mixed serotonin-norepinephrine reuptake inhibitor, or SSNRI), reboxetine (a selective norepinephrine reuptake inhibitor, or SNRI), and buproprion (a norepinephrine and dopamine reuptake inhibitor, or NDRI). The focus of this section is on the TCAs, SSRIs, and MAOIs. Pharmacotherapy of depression is based on the premise that this condition is associated with a deficit in various neurotransmitters known as monoamines, such as noradrenalin, serotonin, and dopamine (i.e., the "monoamine hypothesis of depression"), and the aforementioned medications affect these neurotransmitter systems in different combinations and to varying degrees (Ebmeier, Berge, Semple, Shah, & Steele, 2004). Overall, 50% to 65% of individuals can be expected to respond to any given trial of an antidepressant medication (Schatzberg et al., 2005).

In prescribing an antidepressant medication, a physician must take into consideration a number of factors, such as the drug's side effect profile and potential for toxicity or overdose, as well as characteristics of the client such as medical status, age, and depression presentation (Schatzberg et al., 2005). The atypical subtype has been demonstrated to respond better to MAOIs (and possibly the SSRIs) compared to TCAs, and the melancholic subtype to TCAs versus SSRIs (Henkel et al., 2006). In terms of age, response time may be substantially longer for older adults. Typically, antidepressant medications can take 6 to 8 weeks before notable symptom relief is achieved, but conventional clinical wisdom has been that up to 12 weeks of treatment may be necessary before a full response is seen in an older adult (Young & Meyers, 2004). However, some studies suggest that therapeutic effects in older adults may occur at rates that are not highly dissimilar to those seen in younger individuals (Flint & Rifat, 1996; Halpern & Glassman, 1990), thus raising questions about the value of routinely extending an antidepressant trial beyond 8 weeks in an older adult who is clearly nonresponsive (Roose & Sackheim, 2004).

The *TCAs* represent one of the oldest classes of medications used to treat depression and are currently considered second- or third-line agents (i.e., typically used if an individual has not responded to or cannot tolerate one of the newer generation drugs such as an SSRI). Examples of TCAs are amitriptyline, desipramine, imipramine, nortriptyline, and clomipramine. The therapeutic effects of TCAs may be evident within 2 to 4 weeks of taking the drug, but 6 to 8 weeks may be needed to determine if a trial has been adequate (Stahl, 2006). Randomized controlled trials have demonstrated that TCAs are superior to placebo and equally efficacious as SSRIs (Arroll et al., 2005; Bech et al., 2000; Boyce & Judd, 1999). TCAs also appear more effective than SSRIs for severe depression. However, primary drawbacks of the TCAs are their side effect profiles and safety considerations, which include anticholinergic effects such as constipation, dry mouth, blurred vision, sedation, and weight gain that can lead to reduced compliance. For example, in studies demonstrating similar efficacy between TCAs and SSRIs in the treatment of depression, dropout rates due to side effects are typically significantly higher in the TCA-treated groups (Mulsant et al., 2001; Nelson et al., 1999). The TCAs also carry a risk of serious cardiovascular complications, including cardiac slowing and arrhythmias, which makes prescription of these medications to individuals with cardiac conditions risky. It is also relatively easy to overdose on a TCA, with as little as three times the prescribed daily dose resulting in fatality (Roose & Sackheim, 2004). Among older adults, TCAs have been established as effective for depression, but the side effects associated with this drug class may make them a less desirable alternative compared to SSRIs. Among the TCAs, nortriptyline is the preferred agent for older adults due to its lower likelihood of inducing orthostatic hypotension and clear therapeutic window that aids in dosing (Roose & Sackheim, 2004).

The *SSRIs* are now the most widely used class of antidepressant medications. These medications primarily target serotonin and increase the availability of this neurotransmitter by inhibiting its reabsorption from the synaptic cleft; however, these medications also affect other neurotransmitter systems to some degree (e.g., high doses of paroxetine block norepinephrine reuptake; Schatzberg et al., 2005). Among the SSRIs are fluoxetine, sertraline, paroxetine, fluvoxamine, citalopram, and escitalopram. The popularity of SSRIs is due both to their demonstrated effectiveness in treating mild to moderate depression and their more favorable side effect profile relative to TCAs and MAOIs. A meta-analysis of 20 short-term comparative studies of five SSRIs (i.e., citalopram, fluoxetine, fluvoxamine, paroxetine, and sertraline) demonstrated no difference in efficacy between agents, but a slower onset of action and more frequent occurrence of certain side effects (e.g., agitation, weight loss, dermatological reactions) for fluoxetine (Edwards & Anderson, 1999). Up to 50% of individuals who do not respond to one SSRI will show a response when switched to another SSRI; thus, this class of medications provides several options for a treating physician should one agent fail to be effective (Schatzberg et al., 2005). Although atypical depression has been extensively noted to respond to MAOIs, there is some evidence from randomized controlled trials that this subtype also appears to respond favorably to SSRIs; however, larger studies are needed (Henkel et al., 2006). The SSRIs may not be as effective as the TCAs in treating very severe depression (Boyce & Judd, 1999).

The SSRIs are associated with fewer problematic side effects and do not have the overdose potential associated with the TCAs. Common side effects of the SSRIs include gastrointestinal distress (e.g., gas, cramping, diarrhea, nausea, heartburn), jitteriness, agitation, and insomnia. One of the most troubling side effects for many individuals taking SSRIs is sexual dysfunction (e.g., decreased libido, delayed ejaculation, failure to achieve orgasm), which may affect upwards of 30% to 40% of patients (Schatzberg et al., 2005). Sexual side effects may be ameliorated for some individuals with the use of buspirone, sildenafil, yohimbine, ginko biloba, amantadine, bromocriptine, or amphetamine, but well-controlled clinical trials in this area are lacking (Schatzberg et al., 2005). Although fatal overdoses of SSRIs have been reported, they are exceptionally rare. Schatzberg et al. note that overdoses up to 30 times the prescribed dose are typically associated with only minor symptoms such as vomiting, nausea, tremor, and sedation, but that at very high dosages (greater than 75 times the prescribed dose) cardiovascular events, seizures, and altered consciousness have been noted.

A recent controversy surrounding SSRIs is whether their use increases suicidal ideation in children, adolescents, and adults. Beginning in 2004, the FDA began to review reports of suicidality in pediatric patients diagnosed with Major Depressive Disorder who were participating in clinical trials for different antidepressant drugs (including SSRIs and atypical antidepressants such as buproprion, venlafaxine, nefazodone, and mirtazapine; no actual suicides occurred in these studies). Although a causal link between SSRI use and suicidal thinking or behavior could not be definitively established, a decision was eventually made to require a black-box warning on all antidepressant medications about the potential for an increased risk of suicidality among children and adolescents (the decision to include this warning for *all* antidepressants was based on the FDA's assertion that available data were insufficient to exclude any single medication from the increased risk of suicidality; FDA, 2004). Questions remain as to whether antidepressant medications might increase suicide risk by, for example, decreasing indecision and psychomotor retardation before suicidal and depressive symptoms improve, or as a result of triggering intolerable side effects such as akathesia (a subjective feeling of extreme restlessness or inability to sit still that is often accompanied by anxiety and dysphoria). A meta-analytic review of published and unpublished data from randomized controlled trials on the efficacy of SSRIs in the treatment of depressed children and adolescents found evidence that only fluoxetine was associated with a favorable risk-benefit ratio (i.e., evidence of clinically meaningful treatment response and lack of significant adverse events) and that risks outweighed benefits in trials of paroxetine, sertraline, citalopram, and venlafaxine. The authors of this review noted that in light of the ongoing questions about the relationship between suicidal ideation and SSRI use, the lack of strong findings supporting the use of SSRIs other than fluoxetine in the treatment of child and adolescent depression should caution against the use of SSRIs other than fluoxetine in the treatment of depression in this population (Whittington et al., 2004).

The *MAOIs* work by blocking monoamine oxidase from breaking down a number of neurotransmitters, including serotonin, norepinephrine, and dopamine, thereby boosting the transmission of these substances (Stahl, 2006). Isocarboxazid, phenelzine, and tranylcypromine are MAOIs. As previously noted, MAOIs have been found particularly effective in the treatment of atypical depression (Henkel et al., 2006). Because of problematic side effects, they are typically prescribed only when trials of other medications (e.g., SSRIs or TCAs) have failed. The most dangerous side effect associated with MAOIs is the risk of hypertensive crisis (which in extreme cases can lead to stroke, delirium, coma, and death) when foods or medications containing significant amounts of tyramine are eaten. Because MAO helps to degrade tyramine in the intestinal tract, the use of MAOIs increases the risk that excessive amounts of tyramine will be absorbed into the system, which in turn can elevate blood pressure (Schatzberg et al., 2005). Thus, individuals taking MAOIs must alter their diets to avoid certain tyramine-containing foods (e.g., beer, red wine, aged cheese, fava beans, smoked fish, dry sausage) and medications, which in turn can create adherence problems.

Electroconvulsive Therapy

Available since the 1930s, ECT involves passing an electric current through the brain to produce a convulsion or seizure in a patient who has first been given an anesthetic and muscle relaxants (Greenhalgh, Knight, Hind, Beverley, & Walters, 2005). Seizures of 25 to 30 seconds in duration are typically considered sufficient. A usual course of ECT consists of 6 to 12 treatments given twice a week; this is generally carried out on an inpatient basis. Currently, ECT is rarely used as a first-line treatment in depression. Guidelines published by the American Psychiatric Association (2001) indicate that ECT should be considered primarily when there is a need for rapid response because of the severity of an individual's psychiatric condition (e.g., a depressed patient with catatonic features or who is refusing to eat or drink), when the risks of other treatments outweigh the risks of ECT, when there is a history of poor medication response, or when the patient requests this treatment (American Psychiatric Association, 2001). A risk of ECT is impaired cognitive functioning, particularly memory loss for the period immediately preceding the treatment (retrograde memory loss) and impaired ability to learn new information during the period immediately following each treatment and at the end of the treatment course (anterograde memory impairment; Bidder, Strain, & Brunschwig, 1970; Sackeim et al., 2000; R. D. Weiner, Rogers, Davidson, & Squire, 1986). Impairments in long-term personal memories have been reported 6 months following ECT treatment (R. D. Weiner et al., 1986). Use of bilateral electrodes (i.e., electrodes placed on both sides of the head) has been consistently shown to produce greater impairment in retrograde and anterograde memory and orientation and to be associated with greater subjective cognitive complaints by patients (Greenhalgh et al., 2005). As such, placement of electrodes is now typically unilateral, even though there is evidence that this method may produce a less robust antidepressant effect. However, bilateral ECT may be indicated in cases where quick and thorough response is paramount, when unilateral ECT has failed, or when previous use of bilateral ECT has produced a good response with no memory impairment (Greenhalgh et al., 2005).

A recent review examining the efficacy and cost-effectiveness of ECT found that this treatment was more effective than pharmacotherapy (including use of TCAs and SSRIs) for severely depressed and treatment-resistant patients. For example, analyses of pooled data from studies conducted in the United Kingdom estimated that approximately 77% of patients treated with ECT were less depressed at the end of treatment than the average patient treated with drug therapy (Greenhalgh et al., 2005). However, the authors of this review note that studies in this area were frequently marred by methodological problems, including a failure to clearly specify diagnostic criteria used to evaluate participants, inadequate information on the dosage of ECT used (making comparisons to usual clinical practice difficult), and not consistently comparing ECT to a sufficiently high dosage of medication (e.g., amounts expected to be prescribed in cases of treatment-resistant depression). Furthermore, examination of long-term outcome data indicates that the antidepressant benefits of ECT are limited primarily to the duration of treatment and must be followed by pharmacologic treatment or maintenance ECT in order for improvement to be maintained (Greenhalgh et al., 2005). It should also be noted that while ECT has been acutely associated with a lowered risk of subsequent suicide attempts (Sharma, 2001), the *severity* of a suicide attempt following this form of treatment may be greater than that associated with antidepressant medication treatment (Brådvik & Berglund, 2006).

Psychotherapy

Cognitive-Behavioral Therapy   One of the most effective forms of psychotherapy for treating depression is cognitive-behavioral therapy (CBT). Based on ideas articulated in A. T. Beck's (1967) cognitive model of depression previously discussed, CBT is conceptualized as a short-term (e.g., 12 to 16 sessions) treatment that focuses on teaching a client how behaviors and thinking patterns contribute to and maintain depression (Leahy & Holland, 2000).

Power (2004) identified the following as key elements of CBT for depression: (a) psychoeducation, (b) monitoring daily activities, (c) monitoring thoughts and feelings, (d) exploring schemas of the self and others, and (e) addressing termination issues, including relapse prevention. With regard to psychoeducation, it is important to not only explain the cognitive-behavioral model, but also provide information about the symptoms and course of depression. Monitoring activities is important because depressed individuals frequently stop doing things that are pleasurable or that provide a sense of competence or mastery, which in turn can exacerbate depression (Lewinsohn, Muñoz, Youngren, & Zeiss, 1986). Thus, finding out about the quantity and quality of a depressed client's daily activities can enable the therapist and client to design interventions to increase participation in healthy activities (e.g., activity scheduling, challenging negative thoughts about the value of engaging in activities, conducting graded task assignments that break down activities into small, manageable steps).

The monitoring of thoughts and feelings is an important ongoing activity that illustrates to clients the relationship between thinking patterns and mood. Typically, clients are asked to keep a thought record or diary outside of sessions in which they record details of situations in which a negative mood such as depression occurred. In separate columns, the date, situation, and emotions experienced are recorded, as well as the specific thoughts that the client had at the time. Clients are also often asked to record how firmly they believe the thoughts that are recorded. As the therapy progresses, clients are taught strategies for identifying and labeling dysfunctional, depression-inducing thoughts and ways to challenge and replace them with more adaptive, realistic thoughts. These strategies can include examining the evidence as to whether or not a thought is true and setting up behavioral experiments to test the veracity of a thought (e.g., going to a party to test the thought "No one will talk to me because I am boring"). As clients learn these strategies, additional columns are added to the thought record that provide space for recording replacement thoughts (including how much they are believed) and noting the effect these new thoughts have on their mood (J. S. Beck, 1995). In the therapy sessions themselves, negative automatic thoughts can be uncovered by looking for shifts in a client's mood and asking about accompanying thoughts or by listening carefully to the client's verbalizations for examples (e.g., "I'll never be able to find a job I like").

Eventually, it is important for the therapist to help clients discover the underlying core beliefs or schemas that give rise to their negative automatic thoughts so that these can be addressed and modified in treatment. Sometimes the "downward arrow technique" is used to uncover these beliefs; this involves asking the client about the personal meaning of a negative automatic belief (e.g., "What would it mean if your friend thought you were inconsiderate?") and continuing to ask these questions after the client's successive responses in order to arrive at the underlying core belief. As treatment nears an end, a review of the strategies the client has learned for changing thoughts and behaviors that typically lead to depression is undertaken in combination with the improvements that the therapist and client have noted during the course of treatment. The recurrent nature of depression is used as a basis for discussing the very real possibility of a return of mood symptoms and the subsequent steps that a client can take, utilizing the tools learned in therapy, to avert progression to a full-blown major depressive episode. In some cases, periodic booster sessions (e.g., 3 to 6 months after therapy) may be offered to shore up client skills and address any difficulties that were encountered when the active treatment was no longer in place (Power, 2004).

In delivering a CBT intervention, it is important for the therapist to provide (a) a convincing rationale for the intervention (e.g., explaining how thoughts influence mood so it is clear why changing thinking patterns is a target of treatment); (b) training in practical skills to change mood-related thoughts and behaviors; (c) encouragement of skills practice outside of therapy sessions (in the form of homework or practice assignments); (d) an attribution of improvement to the use of the skills and not to contact with the therapist (Zeiss, Lewinsohn, & Muñoz, 1979).

One of the earliest studies to examine the effectiveness of CBT in the treatment of depression was the National Institutes of Health Treatment of Depression Collaborative Research Program. This multisite, randomized, controlled trial examined the effectiveness of two 16-week psychotherapeutic interventions for depression, CBT and interpersonal psychotherapy, as well as standard pharmacologic treatment with imipramine, and a placebo plus clinical management condition among 250 patients who met Research Diagnostic Criteria for major depression. Results of the study showed that while medication treatment resulted in the best outcome in terms of reduction of depressive symptoms at the end of treatment, both of the psychotherapeutic treatments resulted in significant patient improvement as well; for example, the percentage of patients with Hamilton Depression Rating scores of 6 or less was 42% for the imipramine condition, 43% for interpersonal therapy, and 36% for CBT. When data were analyzed by depression severity, CBT was not found to be as effective as medication or interpersonal psychotherapy for severe depression (Elkin et al., 1989). However, the latter finding has been the subject of debate because of methodological problems (including significant site-by-treatment-by severity effects) that complicate the interpretation of the data (e.g., in one site CBT performed as well as imipramine in the treatment of severely depressed individuals; Craighead, Hart, Craighead, & Ilardi, 2002). Other studies have found CBT to be effective in the treatment of severe depression (Hollon, DeRubeis, & Evans, 1992).

Since the NIMH collaborative study, many other randomized, controlled clinical trials of CBT have convincingly demonstrated the effectiveness of this treatment for depression in adults. Meta-analytic studies of CBT for depression have found it to be superior to untreated controls, wait-list control conditions, attentional control conditions, and in some cases pharmacotherapy (Butler, Chapman, Forman, & Beck, 2006; K. S. Dobson, 1989; Gloaguen, Cottraux, Cucherat, & Blackburn, 1998). However, there is not strong evidence supporting the superiority of CBT over behaviorally oriented treatments for depression (Gloaguen et al., 1998).

When individuals receiving medication for depression also take part in CBT during the acute phase of their depression, subsequent relapse rates have been found to be significantly lower and to range from 15% to 28% over a 1- to 2-year period compared to a 32% to 66% relapse rate for individuals treated with medication alone (Evans et al., 1992; Simons Simons, Murphy, Levine, & Wetzel, 1986), which suggests that CBT may have a protective effect against future depressive episodes. When depressed individuals have been successfully treated with medication, the addition of CBT appears to confer protection against future relapse, as demonstrated in studies by Fava and colleagues (Fava, Grandi, Zielezny, Rafanelli, & Canastrari, 1996; Fava, Rafanelli, Grandi, Canastrari, &

Morphy, 1998) which found a 35% relapse rate for CBT-treated individuals versus 70% for those treated with medication (where pharmacotherapy was tapered prior to follow-up) over a 4-year period.

A recent meta-analysis of randomized controlled trials of psychotherapy for depressed children and adolescents found an effect size of .35 for treatments employing a cognitive emphasis (i.e., changing unrealistic, negative cognitions), which falls in the small to medium range (Weisz, McCarty, & Valeri, 2006). This indicates that while cognitively oriented treatments produced improvements in depression that were significantly greater than a control condition (e.g., wait-list, nondirective supportive therapy, treatment as usual), the effects were not highly dramatic and are somewhat less than what has been reported in previous meta-analytic studies that used a smaller database and relied only on published studies (Lewinsohn & Clarke, 1999; Reinecke, Ryan, & DuBois, 1998). Nevertheless, according to the Treatment for Adolescents with Depression Study (TADS) CBT has demonstrated evidence of being effective in the treatment of depression in youth, particularly when combined with medication therapy (Treatment for Adolescents with Depression Study Team, 2004). This multisite study enrolled a sample of 439 adolescents (ages 12 to 17) diagnosed with Major Depressive Disorder and compared 12 weeks of fluoxetine alone, CBT alone, fluoxetine + CBT, and a medication placebo. Although fluoxetine (60.6% response rate) was found to be superior to CBT alone (43.2% response rate), the combination of fluoxetine and CBT (71% response rate) was superior to fluoxetine alone; in addition, CBT produced significantly better outcomes than placebo (34% response rate).

Interpersonal Psychotherapy   As previously noted, IPT was one of the psychotherapeutic treatments studied in the NIH Treatment of Depression Collaborative Research Program that was found to be particularly efficacious (compared to a placebo control condition) in the treatment of severe depression (Sotsky et al., 1991). Like CBT, IPT is a time-limited, focused, and practical psychotherapy that focuses primarily on the here and now. Based on the interpersonal school of psychotherapy founded by Adolf Meyer and Harry Stack Sullivan, IPT emphasizes the reciprocal interaction between mood and current life events and encourages clients to make changes in problematic roles and relationships thought to contribute to depressive symptomatology (Swartz, Markowitz, & Frank, 2002). The foundations of IPT were also influenced by empirical research (e.g., the work of Coyne), which highlighted the profoundly negative impact that depression can have on psychosocial relationships, as well as the protective role that social support can play in depression (Weissman, Markowitz, & Klerman, 2000).

As in many other forms of treatment, IPT begins with a thorough clinical interview that evaluates the client's current symptoms and functioning and gathers historical information. However, unique to IPT is the completion of an interpersonal inventory, in which detailed information is gathered about all significant past and present relationships, including variables such as the quality, unmet expectations, and satisfying and unsatisfying aspects of the relationships. The information from this initial evaluation is used to develop an interpersonal case formulation that involves identification of one of four interpersonal problem areas as the primary focus of treatment (grief, role disputes, interpersonal role transitions, or interpersonal deficits; Swartz et al., 2002). Table 10.7 summarizes these areas and specific issues that may be addressed in each. It should be noted that although

Table 10.7   Elements of interpersonal psychotherapy for depression

IPT Problem Area	Examples of Treatment Strategies and Goals
Grief: Onset of depression related to death of an important person	Facilitation of the mourning process by reviewing the relationship with the deceased Encouraging expression of previously suppressed affect to bring about catharsis Assistance in recognizing distorted (positive and negative) memories of the deceased Encouragement to undertake role changes to reengage in activities and relationships
Role dispute: Relationship characterized by nonreciprocal, conflicting expectation	Identification of dispute and development of a plan for change Modification of communication patterns Modification of role expectations Utilization of strategies such as role-play, communication analysis, exploration of realistic options
Role transition: Major life changes such as moving to a new city, getting a new job, being diagnosed with an illness, retiring	Focus on realistic appraisal of new and old roles Establishment of a more balanced view of each role Mourning the loss of the old role Development of skills necessary to manage the new role more successfully
Interpersonal deficits: Long history of impoverished or unsuccessful interpersonal relationships is present and no acute precipitant (e.g., grief, role dispute, role transition) is evident	Expansion of social skills Understanding the link between social impairment and mood symptoms Use of role play, hypothetical social situations, and examination of the relationship with the therapist to enhance client's repertoire of social skills

Source: From "Interpersonal Psychotherapy for Unipolar and Bipolar Disorders" (pp. 131–158), by H. A. Swartz, J. C. Markowitz, and E. Frank, in *Treating Chronic and Severe Mental Disorders*, S. G. Hofmann and M. C. Tompson (Eds.), 2002, New York: Guilford Press. Adapted with permission.

IPT emphasizes the interpersonal context of depression, it also rests on the medical model of depression; clients are provided with education that characterizes depression as a treatable medical illness with a specific constellation of symptoms that are related to biological processes.

Techniques such as the following are used in IPT: (a) obtaining considerable detail about a client's interpersonal interactions (including contextual information, thoughts and feelings the client had, and the relationship between mood and events); (b) helping clients generate options when they feel trapped in a particular situation; and (c) maintaining an optimistic stance (e.g., encouraging clients to take interpersonal risks to achieve interpersonal goals, providing unflagging support and encouragement for remaining in treatment, and amply reinforcing signs of change and improvement). These are used in combination with techniques commonly employed in other forms of therapy such as empathic listening, open-ended questions, affect expression and exploration, role-playing, behavioral activation, and decision analysis (Swartz et al., 2002).

Behavioral Marital Therapy   Depression is associated with perceptions of increased burden among spouses (e.g., restricted social activities, financial problems), may precipitate marital distress, and appears to increase risk of divorce (Coyne et al., 2002; Dew & Bromet, 1991; Fadden, Bebbington, & Kuipers, 1987). The marriages of depressed persons are also frequently characterized by greater use of maladaptive coping strategies during times of conflict and higher rates of conflict in areas such as child care, division of responsibilities, sexual satisfaction, and issues directly relating to the depressive illness itself. Data from the New Haven Epidemiologic Catchment Area program showed that marital dissatisfaction was associated with an almost 3 times higher risk of developing a major depressive episode over the course of a 1-year period, and approximately 30% of the new occurrences of major depressive episodes identified during this time were associated with marital dissatisfaction (Whisman & Bruce, 1999). For these reasons, psychotherapeutic interventions targeting relationship issues are important to consider in the overall treatment plan for a depressed person.

Behavioral marital therapy (BMT) is a psychotherapeutic approach that has empirically demonstrated effectiveness in treating couples in which there is a depressed partner. This therapy is short term and time limited (e.g., 15 sessions), designed to increase marital cohesion, increase self-esteem support, and reduce or eliminate severe and recurrent marital stressors (O'Leary, 2002). Approaches involve teaching behavior exchange, problem-solving, and communication strategies. Behavior exchange strategies attempt to increase the amount of positively reinforcing exchanges between a couple and concomitantly decrease negative, punishing interactions. Couples are encouraged to begin engaging in simple, positively oriented behaviors on a regular basis (e.g., every day) that are likely to be pleasing to each partner. A structured problem-solving method is also taught that encourages couples to identify specific problems that need resolution, brainstorm solutions, collectively weigh the pros and cons of each solution to select the most promising one, and develop a plan to implement the mutually agreed upon solution. Communication skills such as active listening, using reflections and paraphrasing, using "I" statements, and checking out the accuracy of what one's partner has said are also taught (Baucom & Epstein, 1990).

Jacobson, Dobson, Fruzzetti, Schmaling, and Salusky (1991) examined the impact of BMT on both depression and marital distress in a sample of women diagnosed with Major Depressive Disorder. Three treatments were compared: BMT, traditional cognitive therapy (CT), and a combined treatment (BMT + CT). Results demonstrated that for depressed women who reported significant levels of marital distress, BMT was as effective as CT in reducing depressive symptoms and the combined treatment did not confer any advantage in ameliorating depression; CT was more effective than BMT in reducing depression among depressed women who did not identify themselves as maritally distressed. Among maritally distressed couples, BMT also produced significant reductions in marital distress. In a similar investigation, O'Leary and Beach (1990) found that depressed women randomly assigned to BMT demonstrated significant and clinically meaningful decreases in depressive symptomatology (as measured by the BDI) that were on par with those found among women randomly assigned to CT (both treatment groups demonstrated greater improvement than a wait-list control group). In addition, women participating in BMT exhibited greater improvement in marital satisfaction than women in either the CT or wait-list control group, which was maintained at a 1-year follow-up.

Despite the effectiveness of BMT approaches in reducing marital distress and improving depression, there are situations in which individual therapy for depression is more appropriate as the primary treatment. Specifically, BMT would be contraindicated as the initial or primary treatment if the depressed individual (a) acknowledges marital difficulties but does not see them as one of the most salient issues contributing to the depression, (b) does not view the marital problems as preceding or potentially playing a causative role in the depression, (c) is intensely suicidal, or (d) has a partner with a low commitment to the relationship (Beach, 2001). It should also be noted that thus far, BMT interventions for depressed persons have utilized traditionally administered BMT that has not been specifically modified to address depression per se, and the need for BMT treatments tailored to this specific clinical population may increase the effectiveness of couples' oriented treatment for depression even further (Gilliam & Cottone, 2005).

Bipolar Disorder

Medication

Pharmacotherapy is a key element in the treatment of individuals with Bipolar Disorder. Medication is taken prophylactically, meaning that it is taken not only when symptoms of depression or mania emerge, but during euthymic periods as well. As such, pharmacologic treatment for this illness should be conceptualized as potentially lifelong, which may be particularly difficult for clients to accept and therefore is a topic appropriate for exploration in psychotherapy. Bowden and Singh (2005) note that the pharmacologic treatment of Bipolar Disorder has undergone the following major paradigm shifts over the past decade: a greater focus on maintenance versus acute treatment, emphasis on functional recovery versus simply syndromal recovery, and a focus on the illness as a whole rather than on discrete episodes. What follows is a discussion of the most commonly used medications to treat Bipolar Disorder. Because as many as one third of individuals with this disorder will not respond to the use of a single medication (i.e., monotherapy), a combination of medications is often used (Schaztberg et al., 2005).

Lithium was the first pharmacologic treatment discovered to be effective in treating Bipolar Disorder and continues to be used today. John Cade, an Australian physician, originally observed that lithium, a naturally occurring salt, had a calming effect on guinea pigs. Cade (1949) went on to test the use of this compound in a small sample of manic individuals, found that it had similar effects, and in the late 1940s published the first paper on the use of lithium for this purpose. In the 1960s the Danish psychiatrist Morgans Shou conducted further research on lithium's effects on mania and found that it was not only effective in treating acute mania but also decreased recurrences of manic episodes when used long term (Andreasen, 2001). In 1970, lithium was given FDA approval for treatment of mania. The mechanism whereby lithium controls manic episodes and influences affective disorders is not yet known, but recent interest has focused on the role it may play in affecting second-messenger systems (Brunello & Tascedda, 2003).

Studies of lithium treatment for acute mania have consistently found high response rates that range from approximately 50% to 80% (Ketter, Nowakowska, Marsh, Bonner, & Wang, 2005). Dosages to treat a manic episode are typically titrated up until therapeutic efficacy is achieved, and it may take up to a few weeks before effects are seen (Ketter et al., 2005). In cases of severe acute mania, the American Psychiatric Association's (2002) practice guidelines for Bipolar Disorder suggest utilizing a combination of lithium and an antipsychotic (e.g., risperidone, olanzapine, and quetiapine).

Despite the documented effectiveness of lithium in treating manic episodes, this medication appears less effective in treating depressive episodes associated with Bipolar Disorder. Although the American Psychiatric Association's (2002) practice guidelines recommend lithium as an initial treatment for mild to moderate depression in Bipolar Disorder, it is estimated that half of bipolar individuals who are depressed experience only a partial response to this medication (Frye et al., 2004). Antidepressant effects of lithium may be greatest when relatively high serum levels are achieved, as demonstrated in a double-blind, placebo-controlled study that found combination treatment for bipolar depression using either paroxetine or imipramine plus lithium was not more efficacious than lithium alone when serum lithium levels were high (Nemeroff et al., 2001). A review of pharmacologic treatment studies indicate that acute mixed states do not respond well to lithium (Krüger, Young, & Braünig, 2005). Nevertheless, lithium has been found effective in reducing suicide rates during long-term treatment of patients with Bipolar Disorder (F. Angst et al., 2002; F. K. Goodwin, 2002; Kallner et al., 2000; Tondo & Baldessarini, 2000). Interestingly, this reduced suicidality may not be directly attributable to a general reduction in symptoms, and the precise mechanism by which the suicide-lowering effect of lithium works remains unknown, but may be related to an anti-aggressive potential that is mediated through serotonergic mechanisms (McIntyre, Mancini, Parikh, & Kennedy, 2001).

With regard to long-term maintenance, a meta-analysis of five randomized, controlled trials that collectively had 770 participants demonstrated that lithium was more effective than placebo in preventing all relapses, particularly manic relapses (Geddes, Burgess, Hawton, Jamison, & Goodwin, 2004). Randomized, controlled trials of lithium compared to the anticonvulsants valproate and carbamazepine in the maintenance phase of Bipolar Disorder have generally documented similar efficacy, although lithium has been noted to have a worse side effect profile (J. M. Davis, Janicak, & Hogan, 1999; Macritchie, Geddes, Scott, Haslam, & Goodwin, 2001). In general, lithium tends to work best for individuals whose illness is characterized by the following: (a) euphoric manias (versus mixed states or dysphoric manias); (b) absence of rapid cycling; (c) a longitudinal course in which manias are followed by depressions, which are in turn followed by normal mood; (d) previously good response to lithium; (e) clear-cut episodes interspersed with relatively symptom-free periods; (f) fewer previous illness episodes; (g) absence of comorbid substance abuse; (h) absence of psychotic symptoms during illness episodes; and (i) a strong family history of Bipolar Disorder (F. K. Goodwin, 2002; Miklowitz, 2002). Because abrupt discontinuation of lithium is associated with a high risk of relapse (particularly in the period immediately following discontinuation), and because individuals often stop taking lithium because of intolerable side effects, careful monitoring of and prompt attention to side effects is necessary. Poor adherence suggests a contraindication for the use of this agent (Carney & Goodwin, 2005; Cavanagh, Smyth, & Goodwin, 2004).

Indeed, an important factor psychiatrists consider in selecting a medication for long-term maintenance pharmacotherapy in Bipolar Disorder is not only how effective the medication is, but how well it will be tolerated by the client (Bowden & Singh, 2005).

When individuals begin lithium treatment it is necessary to check serum concentrations frequently to ensure that they are within a therapeutic window. More specifically, blood draws are typically done twice weekly for the first 2 weeks, once per week for the next 3 to 4 weeks, and every 2 weeks for the next 2 months. Once an individual is in the maintenance phase of treatment, blood draws may be done on a monthly basis or even less frequently (e.g., every few months; no less than every 6 months). Common side effects associated with lithium include tremor, polydypsia (i.e., drinking water more frequently than usual), polyuria (urinating more frequently than usual), nausea, hypothyroidism (which more commonly affects women than men), cognitive slowing, and weight gain. At higher serum concentration levels more severe side effects may occur, such as severe diarrhea, drowsiness, vomiting, blurry vision, impaired coordination, and muscular weakness. Individuals taking lithium are advised to contact their psychiatrist immediately if they experience any of these more severe side effects, as they could be early indications of lithium toxicity—a potentially life-threatening condition that can progress to seizures, cardiovascular abnormalities, and coma. The serum levels at which toxicity can occur are actually quite close to the therapeutic window, making monitoring and prompt reporting of such side effects especially important. Package information for lithium includes warnings about toxicity and indicates that individuals with significant cardiovascular or renal disease, severe dehydration or sodium depletion, or severe debilitation are at increased risk for toxicity and should therefore avoid the use of this medication. Drug interactions, certain medical conditions, and advanced age can also increase serum lithium levels (Ketter, 2005).

A number of *anticonvulsants* or antiseizure medications are used to treat Bipolar Disorder, including valproate, carbamazepine, lamotrigine, gabapentin, topiramate, oxcarbazepine, and tiagabine. Interest in the use of anticonvulsants to treat Bipolar Disorder stemmed from observations that psychiatric symptoms associated with temporal lobe epilepsy were similar to those seen in primary mood disorders and theories that symptoms of Bipolar Disorder might arise from limbic seizures or kindling phenomena (Schatzberg et al., 2005). In addition to their use as treatments for acute mood episodes and prophylactic maintenance, there is some evidence that anticonvulsant medications may be as effective as lithium in reducing suicide risk among individuals with Bipolar Disorder (Baldessarini, Tondo, & Hennen, 2003a; Ginsberg, 2003; Yerevanian, Koek, & Mintz, 2003).

Among the anticonvulsants, valproate is the most commonly used to treat Bipolar Disorder. It is FDA approved for the treatment of acute mania, and randomized controlled trials have repeatedly shown this medication to be superior to placebo and as effective as lithium in such cases, with antimanic effects generally seen within as little as a few days of treatment (Bowden & McElroy, 1995; Pope, McElroy, Keck, & Hudson, 1991). Mixed states and rapid cycling also typically respond well to valproate (Calabrese, Markovitz, Kimmel, & Wagner, 1992). In contrast, evidence is mixed regarding the effectiveness of valproate in treating depressive episodes in Bipolar Disorder, with some studies demonstrating effectiveness compared to placebo (Bowden et al., 2000). Valproate can be used as a maintenance treatment for Bipolar Disorder (M. J. Gitlin, 2006) and has been found effective when combined with agents such as lithium (D. Lin, Mok, & Yatham, 2006).

Carbamazepine has also been demonstrated in controlled clinical trials to be effective in the treatment of acute mania as well as for rapid cycling and mixed states (Coryell, 2005). As with valproate, carbamazepine appears more effective in the treatment of mania than depression among individuals with Bipolar Disorder. Although carbamazepine is used in the long-term treatment of this disorder, it appears less efficacious than lithium but may be effective in individuals with atypical presentations, such as rapid cycling (D. Lin et al., 2006).

Lamotrigine, a newer anticonvulsant medication, compares favorably to lithium in the treatment of Bipolar Disorder and appears to be particularly effective in treating rapid cycling Bipolar Disorder, treatment-resistant Bipolar Disorder, mixed states, and depression in Bipolar Disorder (Calabrese et al., 2000). With regard to maintenance therapy, randomized, double-blind, placebo-controlled studies among stabilized individuals with Bipolar I Disorder have found lamotrigine equally efficacious as lithium in prolonging time to intervention for any mood episode, and particularly effective at delaying time to a depressive episode (Bowden et al., 2003).

Gabapentin, a newer anticonvulsant medication with relatively benign side effect and drug interaction profiles, has demonstrated promise in treating Bipolar Disorder, but large-scale randomized, controlled trials are needed (Schatzberg et al., 2005). Existing studies indicate that gabapentin is helpful in the treatment of acute mania, mixed states, and bipolar depression, particularly when used in combination with other medications. Gabapentin monotherapy for Bipolar Disorder is not recommended (Schatzberg et al., 2005).

Like gabapentin, topiramate is a more recently utilized mood stabilizer that is best considered an adjunctive treatment to other mood-stabilizing medications. Topiramate is often used to counteract weight gain associated with other mood-stabilizing agents since weight loss is a common side effect of this medication. However, a recent review of studies examining the efficacy of topiramate in the treatment of acute mood episodes in Bipolar Disorder concluded that there is insufficient evidence to recommend its use in any phase of bipolar illness, either in monotherapy or as an adjunctive treatment (Vasudev, Macritchie, Geddes, Watson, & Young, 2006).

Side effects for the anticonvulsants include gastric distress, weight gain, sedation or fatigue, dizziness, headache, and vision problems. Rare but potentially life-threatening side effects associated with some anticonvulsants include hepatotoxicity (valproate), pancreatitis (valproate), agranulocytosis (carbamazepine), aplastic anemia (carbamazepine), and potentially fatal rashes such as those associated with Stevens-Johnson syndrome (lamotrigine). It is not uncommon for individuals with Bipolar Disorder to be placed on a combination therapy that includes use of, for example, lithium and a mood stabilizer. Advantages of such an approach include synergistic interaction between medications, potentially greater efficacy than monotherapy, and lower risk of cycle acceleration or mania induction, whereas disadvantages include higher treatment dropout rates (Frye et al., 2004).

Antipsychotics

Atypical antipsychotics such as olanzapine, risperidone, and quetiapine can be used effectively in the treatment of acute mania, and studies of this class of agents suggest that they are as efficacious as lithium and anticonvulsant medications and twice as effective as placebo (D. Lin et al., 2006). Results of recent double-blind, placebo-controlled studies

suggest that olanzapine and quetiapine may be effective agents in treating depressive episodes in Bipolar Disorder, but further study is needed (Gao, Gajwani, Elhai, &
Calabrese, 2005). In terms of maintenance treatment, olanzapine has demonstrated superiority over placebo in delaying symptomatic relapse (D. Lin et al., 2006).

Antidepressants

Individuals with Bipolar Disorder who are experiencing depression that is not well controlled by a mood stabilizer such as lithium may be given an adjunctive antidepressant.
This strategy requires close monitoring by the individual's psychiatrist since all antidepressant medications are associated with the risk of triggering a manic episode in an individual with Bipolar Disorder (Frye et al., 2004); as such, monotherapy with
antidepressants is not recommended for Bipolar Disorder. Among the antidepressants, the
SSRIs appear less likely to induce mania compared to the TCAs in individuals who are
also receiving adjunctive mood-stabilizing therapy (Peet, 1994). Use of TCAs can also
precipitate mixed states and, if used to treat mixed episodes, may actually worsen intra-
episodic mood lability (Altshuler et al., 1995; Krüger et al., 2005). In contrast, a recent
study examining the use of a combination of the SSRI fluoxetine and the neuroleptic olanzapine found this combined treatment did not present a greater risk of treatment-emergent
mania compared to olanzapine or placebo over 8 weeks of acute treatment for Bipolar I
Depression (Keck et al., 2005). The olanzapine + fluoxetine combination was also reported to be superior to olanzapine alone in the treatment of bipolar depression in an 8-
week placebo-controlled, randomized, double-blind trial (Tohen et al., 2003).

Psychotherapy

Cognitive-Behavioral Therapy   Individual CBT interventions, modeled after those developed for depression, have demonstrated promise in the treatment of Bipolar Disorder.
Basco and Rush (2007) identified the following five goals of CBT for Bipolar Disorder:
(1) education of clients and significant others about the disorder, including available treatments and common problems encountered in the illness; (2) instruction on a method for
monitoring manic and depressive symptoms (e.g., occurrence, severity, and course);
(3) facilitation of adherence to prescribed medication regimens; (4) provision of nonpharmacologic strategies for coping with mood, behavioral, and cognitive problems associated
with bipolar symptomatology; and (5) instruction in strategies to help clients cope with
stressors that may precipitate mood episodes and/or interfere with treatment. As with
treatment of depression, CBT for Bipolar Disorder is a time-limited intervention that typically consists of 12 to 20 sessions (Basco & Rush, 2007; D. H. Lam et al., 2003). Manuals for CBT treatment that have been developed for Bipolar Disorder present a fairly
structured treatment in which specific tasks and goals are outlined for each session (Basco
& Rush, 2007; D. H. Lam, Jones, Hayward, & Bright, 1999). However, the collaborative
approach that is fundamental to CBT more generally is utilized, and clients should be
encouraged to participate in agenda setting for sessions as well. The learning that takes
place in CBT treatment is apt to be most effective when the client is not experiencing
significant manic or hypomanic symptoms, since these states are likely to be associated
with poorer insight into the need for treatment and difficulties with attention and concentration. It is beyond the scope of this chapter to review CBT treatment for Bipolar

Disorder in detail, but some representative examples of interventions typically used in this approach will give the reader a sense of how the treatment is carried out.

In addition to providing clients with psychoeducational material about Bipolar Disorder, the importance of helping clients understand their own unique experience with the illness is conveyed through activities in which clients review the course of their illness (e.g., using the life charting method discussed earlier), recording symptoms typically associated with normal, depressed, and (hypo)manic states, and prospectively tracking mood in relation to daily activities to better understand the relationship with environmental factors that may precipitate illness episodes (Basco & Rush, 2007; D. H. Lam et al., 1999). The identification of mood, behavioral, and cognitive changes associated with depressed and (hypo)manic states is an important step in determining prodromes for mood episodes. Future recognition and timely intervention in response to the appearance of these prodromes is considered key in averting full-blown symptomatic relapses (Lam & Wong, 1997). The identification of a *constellation* of symptoms, extending beyond mood changes, that may herald an oncoming illness episode is also helpful in counteracting the hypervigilance to mood changes that frequently develops among individuals with Bipolar Disorder (i.e., assuming that any upward or downward change in mood automatically signals an impending illness episode; Schwannauer, 2004). As with CBT for depression, clients are encouraged to record thoughts in between sessions that are associated with notable mood shifts and to examine their accuracy and utility. Many of the same kinds of cognitive errors observed among unipolar depressed individuals have relevance for depressed individuals with Bipolar Disorder. In addition, thoughts related to perfectionism and social approval may also have particular salience for this population (Scott, Stanton, Garland, & Ferrier, 2000). A. T. Beck (1979) postulated that during (hypo)manic phases, persons with Bipolar Disorder are likely to display a cognitive style that reflects overly optimistic views of oneself, the world, and the future (the opposite of the negative cognitive triad articulated with respect to depression). In addition to cognitive interventions, behavioral strategies are employed to help activate clients who are depressed and to slow down those who are becoming or are already (hypo)manic. Examples of the latter would be prioritizing interests, activities, and responsibilities so that all are not undertaken at once, minimizing sleep disruptions, and engaging in relaxation exercises (Basco & Rush, 2007). Interventions may also address interpersonal problems that may have precipitated or resulted from the illness (Schwannauer, 2004). Clients with Bipolar Disorder may experience significant blows to their self-esteem and sense of self-efficacy as a result of their illness episodes and need help in processing the emotional aftermath of such experiences and challenging any maladaptive cognitions about themselves, others, or their future that may have developed. Treatment typically ends with a review of gains made and skills learned and how the client will handle the return of any symptoms in the future (i.e., relapse prevention work).

Although randomized, controlled trials are far fewer for this form of treatment compared to analogous treatments for depression, results have thus far been encouraging. For example, in a study of 103 individuals with Bipolar I Disorder randomized into a CBT group (averaging 14 sessions) or control group, D. H. Lam et al. (2003) found that the CBT group experienced significantly fewer bipolar episodes, fewer days in bipolar episodes, and fewer hospitalization admissions and displayed significantly higher social functioning over a 12-month period. A subsequent 30-month follow-up study found that although the CBT group demonstrated significantly better outcome in terms of time to relapse, this effect was most pronounced during the first 12 months, and the treatment did not significantly impact relapse reduction in the last 18 months of the study period (D. H. Lam, Hayward, Watkins, Wright, & Sham, 2005). The authors interpreted this finding to suggest that maintenance therapy or booster sessions may be necessary to solidify the gains made during the initial treatment phase. Pavuluri, et al. (2004) found that a developmentally sensitive CBT approach incorporating family focused interventions was associated with significant decreases in symptom severity and overall functioning in a small sample of bipolar children concurrently treated with medication.

Interpersonal and Social Rhythm Therapy An intriguing intervention that integrates interpersonal psychotherapy (previously reviewed in relation to depression treatment) with theories regarding the role that environmental events such as life stressors, medication noncompliance, and social rhythm disruption can play in the generation of mood episodes in Bipolar Disorder is interpersonal and social rhythm therapy, or ISRT (E. Frank, 2005). This therapy employs components already reviewed with regard to CBT for Bipolar Disorder, including illness psychoeducation and the identification of prodromal symptoms. Providing clients with information about the nature of and treatment for their disorder is assumed to assist in enhancing medication adherence (Swartz et al., 2002). Two additional, unique aspects of ISRT are the focus on regulating social rhythms and the incorporation of techniques related to interpersonal psychotherapy. The first of these interventions is predicated on theories that abnormalities in the body's biological clock (i.e., sleep-wake cycles and circadian rhythms) underlie Bipolar Disorder (F. K. Goodwin & Jamison, 1990). For example, if an individual with Bipolar Disorder is sufficiently deprived of sleep, vulnerability to a (hypo)manic episode is likely to ensue. Thus, ISRT assumes that the maintenance of regular routines and schedules lowers the risk of mood episodes (especially [hypo]manic episodes). The concepts of *zeitgebers* and *zeitstörers* are also important in understanding the regulation of the biological clock. Zeitgebers are the psychosocial, physical, or chemical events that help to maintain biological functions on a regular schedule, whereas zeitstörers disrupt biological rhythms (Swartz, Frank, Spielvogle, & Kupfer, 2004). An example of a zeitstörer might be a conflict with a significant other that causes an individual to stay up late in angry rumination and thus experience disruption in sleep routines. Clients in ISRT are taught to monitor their daily mood and activities using a social rhythm metric, a structured self-report measure that asks clients to record the time they got out of bed, their first contact with another person, whether various activities occurred alone or with others, mood symptoms, and so on (Swartz et al., 2004). Review of the social rhythm metric allows both client and therapist to see the relationship between mood symptoms and activities and serves as the basis for implementing interventions to stabilize daily rhythms (e.g., setting regular sleep times, avoiding overstimulation, monitoring the intensity and frequency of social interactions; Swartz et al., 2002). Treatment also incorporates the elements of IPT reviewed earlier regarding depression treatment, including completion of an interpersonal inventory and selection of a key area (grief, role transitions, interpersonal role disputes, or interpersonal deficits) as a target for treatment. Key differences between ISRT for Bipolar Disorder and IPT for depression identified by Swartz et al. (2004) include (a) the view that life events can be both sources of mood dysregulation and triggers of disruptions in social rhythms, (b) the use of both IPT and behavioral strategies to address interpersonal problems, and (c) an emphasis on gradual change that seeks to balance spontaneity and stability rather than encouraging the client to take interpersonal risks in the service of change (as the latter might create destabilizing effects). In addition, ISRT is designed to be a longer treatment (approximately 2 years) compared to 12 to 16 weeks of IPT for depression.

Empirical studies of ISRT are under way, most notably in a large-scale trial comparing ISRT with intensive clinical management in a sample of individuals with Bipolar I Disorder receiving adjunctive pharmacotherapy (E. Frank et al., 1997). Preliminary findings indicate that individuals assigned to ISRT showed significantly greater stability of daily routines with increasing time in treatment compared to no significant change in the social routines of individuals in the intensive clinical management condition (E. Frank et al., 1997).

Family-Focused Treatment   Family-focused treatment (FFT; also known as Behavioral Family Management or Behavioral Family Therapy) is a behaviorally oriented, structured, 9-month treatment for Bipolar Disorder clients and their families that is theoretically rooted in family-based interventions originally designed for persons with Schizophrenia (Miklowitz, 2002). Miklowitz and Goldstein (1997) outline six objectives of FFT for Bipolar Disorder: (1) integrating experiences associated with episodes of Bipolar Disorder, (2) accepting the notion of a vulnerability to future episodes, (3) accepting a dependency on psychotropic medication for symptom control, (4) distinguishing between the affected person's personality and his or her Bipolar Disorder, (5) recognizing and learning to cope with stressful life events that trigger recurrences of Bipolar Disorder, and (6) reestablishing functional relationships after the episode. This treatment attempts to achieve these goals through three primary therapeutic phases: (1) psychoeducation, (2) communication skills training, and (3) problem-solving training. A stress-diathesis model of Bipolar Disorder acknowledges the biological underpinnings of the disorder as well as the psychosocial factors that can influence its expression and course. By providing persons with Bipolar Disorder and their families with information about the illness and practical tools to help reduce stress within the family environment, it is hoped that future relapses can be averted or attenuated. The important role that the quality of family relationships can play in affecting the course of Bipolar Disorder has been demonstrated by studies examining the concept of Expressed Emotion (EE) in Bipolar Disorder. Expressed Emotion is an index of hostile, critical, and emotionally overinvolved attitudes that family members hold toward a psychiatrically ill relative. Studies have shown that high levels of such attitudes (i.e., high EE attitudes) in a bipolar person's family are associated with greater risk of patient relapse over a 9-month period following an index hospitalization. The EE construct is further reviewed in Chapter 9.

Empirical investigations of FFT have involved the delivery of the treatment by a team of two co-therapists over a titrated schedule (i.e., 3 months of weekly sessions, 3 months of biweekly sessions, and 3 months of monthly sessions; Rea et al., 2003; Miklowitz et al., 1988; Miklowitz, Simoneau, George, Suddath, & Wendel, 2000). These components are reviewed in detail in Chapter 9. Miklowitz and Golstein (1997) note that in comparison to treating individuals with Schizophrenia and their families using a similar form of treatment, the clinician can expect that persons with Bipolar Disorder and their families may prefer being more spontaneous and engaging in active, lively interchanges (thus requiring

Table 10.8   Treatment interventions for mood disorders

Area	Interventions
Therapeutic interventions	A sense of hope that mood disorders are treatable. Stabilization of acute mood state. Regular assessment of mood state. Prodrome identification (especially important for Bipolar Disorder). Cognitive strategies (e.g., techniques to combat distorted patterns of thinking, challenging maladaptive cognitive schemas). Behavioral interventions (activation strategies for depression; decreasing activity for mania). Examination of interpersonal precipitants and consequences of mood episodes. Processing emotional and interpersonal aftermath of manic episodes. Regular suicide assessment. Medication adherence (for clients receiving adjunctive pharmacotherapy). Relapse prevention.
Adjunctive interventions	Consideration of medication referral. Collaborative relationship with psychiatrist (if medications are prescribed).
Family interventions	Family therapy (e.g., FFT). Couples therapy (e.g., BMT). Psychoeducation. Communication skills training. Problem-solving training. Relapse prevention planning. Disorder-Specific Interventions
Depression	Consideration of antidepressant medication.
Bipolar Disorder	Stabilization of social rhythms (regularizing routines, decreasing overstimulation, establishing regular sleep pattern). Help client grieve loss of healthy self. Mood stabilizers.

the clinician to be somewhat flexible in how this structured treatment is delivered). In addition, they note that the typically higher functioning associated with Bipolar Disorder compared to Schizophrenia is likely to be reflected in a greater desire for the affected individual to play a more active role in the management of his or her illness. Couples, not only parents and an adult child, are participants in the treatment.

Empirical studies of FFT, including two randomized trials, have demonstrated that compared to case management plus medication, this treatment is effective in reducing the risk of relapse (especially depressive relapses), time to relapse, and hospitalizations among individuals also receiving adjunctive medication (Miklowitz & Golstein, 1990; Miklowitz et al., 2000; Rea et al., 2003). A small open trial of FFT for pediatric patients, in combination with mood stabilizing medications, resulted in reduction in mania, depression, and parent-rated behavior problems over a 2-year period (Miklowitz, Biuckians, & Richards, 2004).

Table 10.8 summarizes general elements of the treatment of mood disorders.

ADVANCED TOPIC: MOOD DISORDERS AND THE POSTPARTUM PERIOD

The birth of a child is a life-changing experience that triggers a host of emotions, including happiness, excitement, anxiety, and sometimes sadness. Upwards of 70% women experience "the baby blues," or transient depressive symptoms following the birth of a child that may include tearfulness, sadness, problems with concentration, lack of motivation, diminished interest in food or self-care, and loss of interest in the new baby (Baker et al., 2005). For approximately 10% to 15% of women, depressive symptoms following the birth of a child will be severe enough to indicate a postpartum depression is present (O'Hara, Neunaber, & Zekoski, 1984).

The *DSM-IV-TR* does not contain separate criteria sets for mood disturbances that develop during the postpartum period. Instead, the clinician can utilize the specifier "with postpartum onset" for Major Depressive Disorder and Bipolar I or II Disorder (American Psychiatric Association, 2000b). Although the *DSM-IV-TR* defines the postpartum period as 4 weeks, symptoms of postpartum depression typically have an onset anywhere from 1 to 3 months after delivery, and the year following the birth may be a period of heightened risk for some women (Nonacs, 2005). Although postpartum depression often spontaneously remits within 4 to 6 months, the emotional toll on the new mother and her family can be considerable. For example, depressed mothers are less likely to exhibit positive affective expressions (e.g., smiling), vocalizations, touching, and contingent responses toward their infants (Cohn, Campbell, Matias, & Hopkins, 1990). In turn, infants of mothers with postpartum depression have been found to display lower rates of positive behavior, higher rates of crying, and more feeding and sleeping disturbances (Righetti-Veltema, Conne-Perreard, Bousquet, & Manzano, 2002). Husbands of women with postpartum depression have been reported to have higher rates of depressive disorder, nonspecific psychological problems, and problematic fatigue compared to men whose partner did not have postpartum depression (S. L. Roberts, Bushnell, Collins, & Purdie, 2006).

Cultural Considerations

Some studies have found differences in the rates of postpartum depressive symptomatology or postpartum depression among various ethnic groups. Rich-Edwards et al. (2006) found a higher prevalence of postpartum depressive symptoms among African Americans and Hispanics compared to Caucasian mothers, but Segre, Losch, and O'Hara (2006) found that African American women were more likely and Hispanic women less likely to report postpartum depressed mood compared to Caucasian women. However, these associations appear to be related to other variables such as lower income, financial hardship, and increased rates of negative pregnancy outcomes among minority women, as well as differing levels of social support (Rich-Edwards et al., 2006; Segre et al., 2006). Rates of postpartum depression among American Indian women have been reported to be as high as 23% (Baker et al., 2005).

It is important to consider cultural issues when working with a woman who may be experiencing postpartum depression for several reasons: first, because cultural differences in the expression of depression or distress (e.g., via somatic symptoms) and acculturation issues can make the detection of depressive symptoms challenging (Bashiri & Spielvogel, 1999); second, because different cultural rituals, values, and beliefs regarding childbirth and the postpartum period may serve as protective factors (e.g., elaborate postnatal rituals that provide attention and support to new mothers) or vulnerability factors (e.g., higher value attached to the birth of a son versus a daughter) for depression (Saravanan, 2002).

Illness Recurrence in Women with Affective Disorders

For women with a known history of Bipolar Disorder, the risk of relapse is particularly high during the postpartum period. Recent studies indicate illness recurrence rates in the first 3 to 6 months postpartum range from 67% to 82% (Viguera, Cohen, Baldessarini, & Nonacs, 2002). Up to one quarter of women with a history of unipolar depression can be expected to develop postpartum depression (O'Hara et al., 1984). Postpartum depression is phenomenologically similar to non-postpartum depressive episodes, but may also be accompanied by ruminative thoughts regarding ambivalent feelings about the baby, questions about one's ability to take care of the baby, and significant anxiety symptoms that may meet criteria for a comorbid anxiety disorder (e.g., GAD; Nonacs, 2005). An especially dangerous postpartum psychiatric disturbance is postpartum psychosis; although rare in the general population (affecting 0.1% to 0.2% of women), this condition is much more common among women with affective disorders, particularly Bipolar Disorder (i.e., occurring in 10% to 20% of women; Viguera et al., 2000). Postpartum psychosis is associated with rapid onset (within 2 weeks of delivery) and has a clinical presentation similar to a delirium, or a manic or mixed episode with psychotic features (i.e., agitation, confusion, rapidly shifting mood, insomnia, delusions). Women with postpartum psychosis may develop delusional beliefs about their newborn that place the infant at risk of harm (e.g., believing the baby is the devil), and thus are in need of prompt and aggressive treatment. The risk of recurrence of postpartum psychoses in affected women is as high as 90% (D. E. Stewart, 1988).

Treatment

Treatment of postpartum depression can include pharmacologic as well as psychotherapeutic interventions. Depression in the postpartum woman should be treated as aggressively as any other depressive episode because the earlier treatment is initiated, the better the outcome is likely to be (Nonacs, 2005). Women with more severe symptoms or preexisting illness that has been exacerbated by childbirth may be more likely to need pharmacologic intervention. Although SSRIs are often first-line treatments for postpartum depression, the selection of medication is apt to be guided by factors such as any previous positive response to medication, the nature of the client's symptoms (e.g., TCAs may be helpful for women with prominent sleep disturbance), and concerns regarding breastfeeding (Nonacs, 2005).

Psychotherapy may be the primary treatment for women experiencing mild to moderate symptoms of postpartum depression and/or who have concerns about taking psychotropic medications while breastfeeding. Brief CBT approaches (e.g., 6 sessions) have been reported to be as effective as fluoxetine in the treatment of postpartum depression

(Appleby, 1998). In addition, IPT has been adapted for use with women suffering from postpartum depression and was found to positively affect maternal mood and social functioning (Stuart & O'Hara, 1995). In a randomized, controlled trial involving 193 women with postpartum depression, P. J. Cooper, Murray, Wilson, and Romaniuk (2003) compared the effectiveness of three different 10-week interventions (CBT, psychodynamic therapy, nondirective counseling) and a usual care control condition in women diagnosed with postpartum depression. Follow-ups were conducted at 4.5, 9, 18, and 30 months. Results revealed that all three active treatments had a significant positive impact on maternal mood (self-reported postpartum depression symptoms) relative to the control condition, but only psychodynamic treatment produced a reduction in depression diagnoses that was greater than that seen in the control group. However, treatment benefits were no longer apparent at 9 months due to the rates of spontaneous remission in the control group, and none of the treatments was associated with reduced likelihood of subsequent depressive episodes relative to the control condition. Similarly, the three active treatment interventions were found to have positive effects on the maternal-child relationship, as indexed by mothers' reports at 4.5 months of fewer difficulties in the relationship with their children and experiencing as less problematic play, separation issues, and management of the child's needs for the mothers' attention. However, at later follow-up these beneficial effects of the treatment on the mother-child relationship and on child development were not found (Murray, Cooper, Wilson, & Romaniuk, 2003). Collectively, these findings suggest that brief postpartum psychotherapeutic treatments are very likely to be effective in the short run but may have limited long-term effects, and that follow-up intervention may be necessary to reduce the risk of future depressive episodes in mothers and to sustain positive child development.

Chapter 11 ————————————————————————

ANXIETY DISORDERS

Anxiety is the hand maiden of creativity.
T. S. Eliot

The bow too tensely strung is easily broken.
Publius Syrus

Part of the everyday landscape of life, anxiety is one of the most common human emotions that can be, as the quotes above suggest, both friend and foe. Anxiety and arousal are elements of our ancient reflexive ability to recognize and respond to dangerous situations, which has facilitated our survival as a species. A certain degree of anxiety can help us to complete tasks and come up with solutions to problems. At the same time, the worries and concerns that seem to plague so many people in our current Age of Anxiety can be overwhelming and debilitating, and disorders involving anxiety are among the more frequently encountered conditions in clinical practice. The *Report of the Surgeon General— Executive Summary* (U.S. Department of Health and Human Services, 1999) summarizing epidemiologic data on a range of mental disorders, reported that the best estimate 1-year prevalence rate of anxiety disorders among adults is 16.4%. Among older adults (age 55 and above) the rate is 11.4%, and among children the rate is 13%. Anxiety disorders typically follow a chronic course and are associated with significant impairment and decreased quality of life. They are costly to society as well. A comprehensive study of this issue published in the late 1990s (Greenberg et al., 1999) estimated the annual cost of anxiety disorders was over $42 billion in the United States; undoubtedly, this figure would be even higher today. In a large-scale study of the impact of physical and mental disorders on disability and quality of life in six European countries, Panic Disorder, Social Phobia, Agoraphobia, and PTSD were among the top 10 disorders with the highest impact on lost work days. Furthermore, three of the five mental disorders associated with the greatest adverse impact on a composite index assessing mental and physical quality of life and missed work days were anxiety disorders (i.e., Social Phobia, Panic Disorder, and PTSD) (Alonso et al., 2004). Among youth the presence of anxiety disorders poses a significant risk factor for poor educational attainment. One study found that approximately half of youth with anxiety disorders reported leaving school prematurely, and nearly one fourth of these individuals cited anxiety as the primary reason prompting this decision (Van-Amerigen, Mancini, & Farvolden, 2003). This chapter discusses the clinical presentation, etiology, course, and treatment of several anxiety disorders, including Panic Disorder with Agoraphobia, Specific Phobia, Social Phobia, Obsessive-Compulsive Disorder, Posttraumatic Stress Disorder, and Generalized Anxiety Disorder.

HISTORICAL OVERVIEW

For many centuries, expressions and discussions of the experience of anxiety were more commonly encountered in the arts and in literature than in medical writings (M. J. Clark, 1999). In the 1800s, documentation of anxiety-related conditions became more prominent in the medical literature. For example, Esquirol described a case of *monomania* that was likely Obsessive-Compulsive Disorder, and Morel described similar patients and others experiencing general anxiety and phobic symptoms, all of whom he believed suffered from *délire emotif*, a condition thought to be linked to abnormalities in the autonomic nervous system (see Berrios & Link, 1999, for a review). As time went on, chronic anxiety became associated with a number of different maladies, such as hysteria, hypochondriasis, neurasthenia, and melancholia. In the late 1800s Freud published an influential paper arguing for consideration of a new class of anxiety disorder, *anxiety neurosis*, that was distinguishable from neurasthenia, the popular and ubiquitous diagnosis of the day. Freud observed that anxiety neurosis was characterized by not only emotional features, but physical symptoms such as cardiac and respiratory problems, tremors, dizziness, sweating, and diarrhea (symptoms similar to those seen in panic attacks; see M. J. Clark, 1999, for a review). Freud initially contended that anxiety neurosis stemmed from sexual causes, but later acknowledged that this was not likely the sole etiologic factor in this condition. Descriptions of posttraumatic reactions to accidents and other stressors also emerged in the late nineteenth century. In particular, the diagnosis of *railway spine* was popular; this condition was so named because of its frequent occurrence in victims of railway accidents and was characterized by both physical and emotional symptoms (e.g., agitation, mood lability, inability to work) believed caused by a chronic inflammation of the spinal membrane and cord (E. Brown, 1999). In 1915, Charles Myers used the term *shell shock* to describe combat soldiers who displayed symptoms such as amnesia, sleep problems, and visual problems. This condition was the forerunner of modern conceptualizations of PTSD.

In early versions of modern diagnostic systems, such as the *DSM* (see *DSM-I* and *DSM-II*), most conditions characterized by prominent anxiety were classified as neurotic disorders and were included alongside conditions marked by mood, somatic, and dissociative features (American Psychiatric Association, 1952, 1968). Beginning with the *DSM-III* (American Psychiatric Association, 1980), we see the organization and enumeration of anxiety disorders that more closely resemble current diagnostic categories (e.g., Social Phobia, Simple Phobia, Panic Disorder, Obsessive-Compulsive Disorder). Childhood disorders characterized by anxiety were noted separately (e.g., Separation Anxiety Disorder). Refinements to diagnostic conceptualizations continued to be made in subsequent editions of the *DSM*, and where relevant these changes will be discussed in the remainder of this chapter.

PANIC DISORDER

Clinical Presentation

Panic Attacks

According to the *DSM-IV-TR*, an essential feature of Panic Disorder is recurrent *unexpected* or *uncued* panic attacks, that is, attacks that do not appear to be triggered by any situation, event, or object but seem to come out of the blue. A panic attack is characterized by a variety of physical symptoms as well as cognitive symptoms, which collectively develop abruptly and reach a peak within a short period of time. For example, the *DSM-IV-TR* criteria for Panic Disorder require at least 4 of a list of 13 symptoms to reach a peak within a 10-minute period (American Psychiatric Association, 2000b). Thus, a panic attack can be differentiated from chronic high levels of anxiety by this sudden onset and rapid crescendo of symptoms. This is crucial to note because clients may colloquially use the term "panic attack" to refer to high general anxiety experienced throughout the day. Among the most commonly experienced symptoms reported during panic attacks are heart palpitations, dizziness, trembling, shortness of breath, sweating, hot or cold flashes, feeling faint, and fear of losing control (Barlow, 2002d).

It is important to remember that panic attacks can occur in the context of many psychiatric disorders (e.g., other anxiety disorders, mood disorders, Schizophrenia), and so their presence does not invariably indicate a Panic Disorder diagnosis; however, such attacks are typically *cued* by specific objects or situations. Additionally, there appear to be qualitative differences in panic attacks experienced in the context of Panic Disorder versus other anxiety disorders, as illustrated in a series of two studies by Rapee, Sanderson, McCauley, and DiNardo (1992). The first examined differences in the frequency and intensity of specific panic symptoms endorsed by the different clinical groups (i.e., Panic Disorder, Specific Phobia, Social Phobia, Obsessive-Compulsive Disorder). Those with Panic Disorder were more likely to report cognitive symptoms (i.e., fear of dying, going crazy, losing control), parathesias, dizziness, faintness, feelings of unreality, and shortness of breath; however, when symptom *severity* ratings were compared among the diagnostic groups, no differences emerged for any Panic Disorder symptom. The second study examined differences in cued panic attacks versus situationally triggered fears experienced by individuals with Panic Disorder and another comorbid anxiety disorder (i.e., Specific Phobia, Social Phobia, or Obsessive-Compulsive Disorder). Fears of dying, losing control, and parathesias were more commonly reported in association with uncued panic attacks, and trembling and dizziness were reported to be more intense during this type of attack.

Although Panic Disorder is characterized by uncued panic attacks, affected individuals may also have *situationally predisposed attacks* in which a panic attack is *likely* to occur on exposure to a particular trigger situation but does not invariably happen (American Psychiatric Association, 2000b). Some individuals may also experience *limited symptom attacks*, which differ from full-blown panic attacks primarily in their intensity and severity (Uhlenhuth, Leon, & Matuzas, 2006). Barlow (2002d) classified limited symptom attacks into two types: (1) those occurring among clients with a history of full panic attacks (e.g., interspersed among full panic attacks), and (2) those involving isolated but severe symptoms (e.g., diarrhea and sweating) that result in an avoidance of going out (i.e., agoraphobic avoidance) for fear of having an attack.

Anxious Apprehension

Panic Disorder is also associated with anxious apprehension about the likelihood of future panic attacks or the consequences of having had a panic attack. The *DSM-IV-TR* criteria for Panic Disorder require evidence of such apprehension for a diagnosis to be made (American Psychiatric Association, 2000b). Such apprehension usually takes the form of becoming hypervigilant to any fluctuations in physical state, and then misinterpreting normal physiological variations as threatening (Barlow, 2002c,d). For example, the individual may worry about whether the attack is an indicator of a serious physical (e.g., heart attack) or mental (e.g., an indicator of becoming insane) condition. Although there is increased attention to bodily sensations, individuals with panic disorder are also likely to then try to divert their attention from such sensations, thereby resulting in decreased accuracy in evaluating the severity or frequency of such symptoms (Barlow, 2000c). Somewhat less common are individuals who experience panic attacks not accompanied by subjective reports of fears of dying, losing control, or going crazy; instead, these individuals experience distress primarily centered on the discomfort caused by certain somatic symptoms (e.g., chest pain). These individuals have been referred to as having *nonfearful Panic Disorder* and are likely to exhibit behavioral change following panic attacks (e.g., escape or avoidance behavior) rather than worry about having another attack or about the implications or consequences of an attack (Barlow, 2002d). As will be discussed next, an extreme form of behavioral change that may be triggered by having unexpected panic attacks is Agoraphobia.

Agoraphobia and Other Forms of Avoidance

A common condition that co-occurs with Panic Disorder is Agoraphobia. According to the *DSM-IV-TR*, the key features of Agoraphobia are anxiety about being in a situation or places from which escape might be embarrassing or difficult or in which help may be unavailable in the event of a panic attack or panic-like symptoms, and subsequent avoidance of these situations or marked anxiety and distress if one is in such a situation (American Psychiatric Association, 2000b). Individuals with Agoraphobia may avoid crowds, standing in lines (e.g., at stores, post offices, banks), bridges, elevators, and traveling on buses, trains, planes, or ships (American Psychiatric Association, 2000b; Jansson & Öst, 1982). Agoraphobia exists on a continuum of severity, with some individuals able to tolerate (albeit with difficulty) being in such situations and others being completely housebound. Some agoraphobic individuals engage in "safety behaviors," such as carrying a bottle of water or medication, when in feared situations because they believe these will prevent a panic attack from occurring or will help them when an attack happens (K. S. White & Barlow, 2002). Others may delineate a safety zone in which they will freely roam, but beyond whose boundaries they will not venture.

Agoraphobia is now generally conceptualized as a form of avoidance behavior that develops out of concern over having panic attacks, and most individuals with Panic Disorder display at least mild agoraphobic avoidance (K. S. White & Barlow, 2002). Although it is quite rare to encounter an individual in a clinical setting who has Agoraphobia without a history of Panic Disorder, community epidemiological studies have found this to be more common (R. C. Kessler, McGonagle, Zhao, Nelcon, et al., 1994). This discrepancy has been at the center of an ongoing debate regarding the nature of

Agoraphobia and its relationship to Panic Disorder. Nevertheless, our focus here is on Agoraphobia as it relates to Panic Disorder.

Given the many places feared by panic disordered individuals with Agoraphobia, their mobility can be severely limited. Studies comparing panic disordered individuals with Agoraphobia to those without Agoraphobia have found that the former are more often in the presence of family members; are less likely to be alone; spend less time at work, in public places, or in transportation situations; and spend more time at home. However, there appear to be few differences between these two groups of clients in terms of the frequency, duration, or intensity of panic attacks (Dijkman-Caes, Kraan, & DeVries, 1993). Individuals with Panic Disorder with Agoraphobia are more likely to seek treatment, have an earlier age of symptom onset and first treatment, longer episodes, and more severe disability, impairment, panic symptomatology, and Axis I and II comorbidity than those with Panic Disorder without Agoraphobia (B. F. Grant et al., 2006).

In addition to agoraphobic avoidance, individuals with Panic Disorder frequently avoid situations that may cause symptoms reminiscent of a panic attack. This is referred to as *interoceptive avoidance*; examples include avoidance of (a) physical activity (e.g., walking or running upstairs, aerobic exercise, participation in sporting activities); (b) situations that lead to being hot or overheated (e.g., being in a hot, stuffy car or room, being in a sauna, wearing heavy clothing); (c) emotionally arousing events (e.g., watching a horror movie, having sex); and (d) eating hot, spicy, or caffeine-containing foods. Interoceptive avoidance is a major target of cognitive-behaviorally oriented exposure treatments for Panic Disorder that will be discussed later in this chapter.

Onset, Course, and Life Span Considerations

Onset

Panic Disorder typically has an onset in the mid-20s, although the Epidemiologic Catchment Area study found age of onset presented as a bimodal distribution, with one peak occurring between 15 and 24 years of age and another between 45 and 54 (Eaton, Kessler, Wittchen, & Magee, 1994). As with other anxiety disorders, the onset of Panic Disorder is often preceded by negative life events and interpersonal and situational stressors (White & Barlow, 2002). Manfro and colleagues (1996) found that 80% of individuals with Panic Disorder reported a negative life event in the year preceding the onset of their illness, and the highest rates of such events were found among those with comorbid depression in adulthood and those with a history of two or more childhood anxiety disorders. The last finding could reflect an increased sensitivity to the effects of life stress and a vulnerability factor for development of additional anxiety disorders in adulthood; however, the possibility that such individuals overreported or were overly focused on negative life events in retrospectively recalling their relationship to the onset of Panic Disorder cannot be discounted. Additional risk factors for Panic Disorder include a family history of Panic Disorder (and possibly other anxiety and mood disorders), behaviorally inhibited temperament, maladaptive parenting styles (e.g., overprotection, rejection), anxiety sensitivity, and somatic conditions (e.g., respiratory illness; R. D. Goodwin et al., 2005).

Course

Studies on the course of Panic Disorder indicate remission rates of 17% to 37% at 1 year and 39% at 5 years, although the probability of symptom recurrence or relapse is high (e.g., .65 to .75 for women and .39 to .47 for men; K. S. White & Barlow, 2002). In a long-term follow-up of individuals with Panic Disorder (mean follow-up time = 47 years), Rubio and López-Ibor (2007) found that individuals with "uncomplicated panic disorder" experienced exacerbations of panic attacks every 1 to 2 years (over periods of 3 to 6 months) and that periods of total remission of panic attacks were infrequent. Panic Disorder with Agoraphobia was characterized by symptom exacerbations that lasted 6 to 9 months, and although the intensity of panic attacks and agoraphobic avoidance decreased over time, Agoraphobia remained chronically present. Eighty percent of the sample had comorbid psychiatric disorders, with other anxiety disorders, mood disorders, and (among women) somatoform disorders being most common. With the exception of Simple Phobia and Social Phobia, most of these comorbid conditions emerged after the appearance of the Panic Disorder. Poor prognostic factors included lack of regular treatment compliance, developing Agoraphobia during the course of Panic Disorder, greater number of episodes of Panic Disorder (where episodes were demarcated by the onset of symptoms and clinical remission of symptoms compatible with normal performance of occupational and social activities), and a family history of anxiety disorders.

Collectively, these findings highlight the chronic and often debilitating nature of Panic Disorder. In fact, Panic Disorder ranks among the five mental disorders with the strongest impact in terms of lost work days and reduced quality of life (R. D. Goodwin et al., 2005). Unfortunately, clients with Panic Disorder often do not seek treatment until several years have passed from the time the symptoms first appeared. A troubling finding from the long-term follow-up study by Rubio and López-Ibor (2007) was that 60% of participants reported leaving treatment prior to completion, 25% of those receiving pharmacotherapy reported a tendency to take less than their prescribed dosages of medication, and only 15% complied with treatment recommendations.

Life Span Considerations

Although Panic Disorder can occur in children, it is not common. When Panic Disorder does occur in pediatric populations, it is most likely to be seen among adolescents (Birmaher & Ollendick, 2004). Panic attacks among children and adolescents appear to be qualitatively similar to those seen in adults, but cognitive symptoms such as fears of going crazy or losing control are less common (Ollendick, Mattis, & King, 1994). Indeed, young children may not possess the cognitive ability to readily make the catastrophic misinterpretations of physical symptoms that are a hallmark of Panic Disorder (Nelles & Barlow, 1988). Risk factors for the development of Panic Disorder in youth include female sex, comorbid Major Depressive Disorder, family history of Panic Disorder and Major Depressive Disorder, and high anxiety sensitivity (i.e., increased tendency to respond fearfully to symptoms of anxiety; Birmaher & Ollendick, 2004). Biederman and colleagues (2005) found that Separation Anxiety Disorder, Obsessive-Compulsive Disorder, Social Phobia, and Bipolar Disorder in parents with Panic Disorder were associated with increased risk for childhood-onset Panic Disorder in their offspring, and that this risk was especially high if both parents had Social Phobia. As with adults, high rates of comorbidity (e.g., 90%) are found among youth with Panic Disorder; common comorbid conditions include other anxiety disorders (especially Generalized Anxiety Disorder and Separation Anxiety Disorder), Major Depressive Disorder, and externalizing disorders (e.g., ADHD, Oppositional Defiant Disorder; Birmaher & Ollendick, 2004).

With regard to older adults, as individuals with Panic Disorder age, their symptoms typically attenuate. In their long-term follow-up study, Rubio and López-Ibor (2007) found that spontaneous panic attacks disappeared in 78% of their sample by approximately 53 years of age. Sheikh, Swales, Carlson, and Lindley (2004) found that older adults (age 60 and above) with Panic Disorder reported fewer panic symptoms, less severe Panic Disorder, lower levels of depression, less anxiety and arousal, and higher levels of functioning compared to younger individuals. In addition, when the older adult group was subdivided into early versus late onset, the latter group reported less distress related to body sensations, emotions, and cognitions during panic attacks. It can be challenging to differentiate Panic Disorder from other anxiety disorders such as Generalized Anxiety Disorder in older adults due to the increase in nonspecific symptoms (e.g., fatigue) and concomitant decreases in symptoms of physiological arousal that frequently occur in the elderly (Mohlman, et al., 2004). In their comparison of older adults with Panic Disorder versus Generalized Anxiety Disorder, Mohlman and colleagues found these groups could not be differentiated from one another on the basis of levels of uncontrollable worry or trait anxiety, but that individuals with Panic Disorder exhibited higher scores on measures of sympathetic nervous system arousal and agoraphobic avoidance and had higher rates of comorbid Somatization Disorder and Alcohol Dependence than those with Generalized Anxiety Disorder.

SPECIFIC PHOBIA

Specific Phobia (formerly known as Simple Phobia) is a persistent and marked fear of a circumscribed object or situation. As many as 60% of the general population have at least one "unreasonable fear" (Davey, 2004), but a far smaller percentage would qualify for a formal diagnosis of Specific Phobia according to a system such as the *DSM-IV-TR* (American Psychiatric Association, 2000b). This is because many individuals with specific fears are able to avoid contact with the object or situation that makes them anxious and thus never or rarely experience impairment from the fear. In contrast, the diabetic patient who refuses to take daily blood sugar readings because they require a needle prick, or the individual who has repeatedly been denied a desired promotion at work because of a staunch refusal to fly for business trips would likely qualify for a diagnosis of Specific Phobia.

Clinical Presentation

Situation-Specific Fear

According to the *DSM-IV-TR*, Specific Phobia is characterized by a marked, persistent, yet unreasonable fear triggered by exposure to a specific object or situation (or anticipation of such exposure; American Psychiatric Association, 2000b). Adults with Specific Phobia understand that their fears are excessive. Further, Essau, Conradt, and Petermann (2000) found that over 80% of their sample of adolescents (ages 12 to 17) with Specific

Phobia acknowledged their fears as being excessive and unreasonable. However, younger children may lack this insight. The array of situations or objects that could become the focus of Specific Phobia is endless; however, common fears include animal phobias (e.g., spiders, snakes, rodents, bugs), heights, enclosed spaces (claustrophobia), water, blood, injury, and inoculation (Davey, 2004). Among children, common phobias include the dark, small animals, insects, heights, needles and injections, flying, vomiting, swimming or being near or in deep water, and enclosed spaces (Last, 2006). The fear experienced by a person with Specific Phobia has an immediate and automatic quality and may be so intense as to result in a cued panic attack. More than three fourths of those with blood and injury, animal, and height phobias and nearly half of those with driving phobias report experiencing an intense, paniclike rush upon exposure to the feared stimulus, which suggests that situationally cued panic attacks are common in Specific Phobia (Antony & Barlow, 2002). Many phobic individuals will try to completely avoid the feared object or situation; some can endure exposure but experience intense anxiety or distress in the process. Thus clinicians should be careful to avoid dismissing from consideration a Specific Phobia diagnosis simply because the client is able to tolerate some contact with the feared stimulus. The key is to find out what the client's emotional reaction is in that situation.

Subtypes

Phobias can be grouped according to the type of situation feared. For example, the *DSM-IV-TR* utilizes a system of specifiers that include animal type, situational type (e.g., airplanes, elevators, enclosed places), natural environment type (e.g., heights, storms, water), and blood-injection-injury type (herein referred to as BII; American Psychiatric Association, 2000b). Research evidence suggests that some subtypes of Specific Phobia (e.g., animal, natural environment, BII types) are associated with different patterns of age of onset, gender distribution, comorbidities with other anxiety disorders, physiological response, and the focus of the client's apprehension (e.g., external situational characteristics versus internal physical sensations; Antony & Barlow, 2002). For example, animal and BII phobics typically have an onset of symptoms in childhood, are less likely to experience panic symptoms during carbon dioxide (CO_2) inhalation challenge tests, and are less likely to experience unexpected panic attacks under natural conditions; in contrast, situational phobics usually begin experiencing symptoms in young adulthood, are more likely to experience panic during CO_2 inhalation, and are more likely to experience unexpected panic attacks (Fyer, 1998; Lipsitz, Barlow, Mannuzza, Hofmann, & Fyer, 2002).

Those with BII phobia also may experience a unique physiological response upon exposure to feared stimuli, which involves an initial increase in blood pressure and/or heart rate followed by sudden decreases in these physiological indices and a high likelihood of fainting (Öst, Sterner, & Lindahl, 1984). However, Lipsitz and colleagues (2002) did not find significant differences between the animal, natural environment, BII, or situational phobias in terms of mode of onset (despite other reports indicating that situational phobias are less likely to be associated with a specific precipitating event than other types of phobias). These authors suggest that conflicting results across studies may be partially attributable to differences in the particular types of phobics included in different subtype groups (e.g., many studies have mostly included claustrophobia in the situational phobia group, fears of heights in the natural environment group, and fears of small animals [insects or rodents] in animal phobia groups), and they note that relatively little is known about how well phobias cluster within each subtype.

It should be noted that most individuals who qualify for a Specific Phobia diagnosis will have more than one diagnosable phobia. Approximately 50% of clients with this disorder have two to four specific phobias, and approximately 17% have more than four specific phobias (Curtis, Magee, Eaton, Wittchen, & Kessler, 1998).

Disgust Sensitivity

Although not a diagnostic criteria or associated feature in the DSM system (2000b), animal and BII phobias appear to be associated with disgust sensitivity as well as fear. Disgust sensitivity has typically been measured using questionnaires that assess disgust toward stimuli such as contaminated food rather than to stimuli directly related to the respondent's phobia. For animal fears, disgust appears more highly correlated with small, relatively harmless animals (e.g., spiders, cockroaches, maggots, rats) than with predatory animals (e.g., bears, sharks, lions; Matchett & Davey, 1991). From an evolutionary standpoint, disgust may have developed to these kinds of small animals because of their association with spreading disease or with sources of contamination or dirt (the so-called disease-avoidance model), or because they have features (e.g., mucus, resemblance to feces) that naturally elicit feelings of disgust (Davey, 1992). Davey, Forster, and Mayhew (1993) found that disgust sensitivity in parents was a significant predictor of animal phobia in offspring, suggesting that this characteristic may mediate the transmission of certain phobia types in families; however, whether this occurs by genetic or environmental means remains unclear. Mulkens, de Jong, and Merckelbach (1996) found that compared to controls, spider phobic women had higher self-reported disgust and contamination sensitivity ratings and displayed greater aversion to eating a cookie after it had been touched by a spider. The phobic women did not, however, show greater aversion to drinking tea from a dirty cup than control women. This study demonstrates that disgust sensitivity in phobic individuals may directly or closely relate to perceptions of finding the phobic stimuli disgusting, and that such sensitivity may not be so broad as to make other unpleasant, nonphobic-related stimuli seem disgusting. Mulkens et al. (1996) suggest that high disgust sensitivity may contribute to the development of spider phobia because it leads to an avoidance of settings in which spiders are likely to live (due to an aversion to features of these settings), which results in a lack of familiarity with spiders and subsequently renders the individual more vulnerable to conditioning processes involving spiders. Conditioning models of phobias are discussed further under "Etiology" later in this chapter. Disgust sensitivity may also help to *maintain* an animal phobia by intensifying avoidance of the feared animal (e.g., spider), thereby reducing functional exposure to it.

Onset, Course, and Life Span Considerations

Onset

Specific Phobia frequently has an early age of onset, particularly the animal (e.g., 4 to 7 years), natural environment (e.g., 12 years old), and BII (e.g., 7 to 9 years) subtypes (Lidell & Lyons, 1978; Marks & Gelder, 1966; Öst, 1987, 1991). In a study of adolescents with Specific Phobia, all subjects with animal and natural environment phobias and 80%

of those with BII phobias reported an onset prior to age 10 (Essau et al., 2000). However, situational phobias tend to begin at later ages. For example, Himle, McPhee, Cameron, and Curtis (1989) reported that situational phobias had a mean age of onset of 27 years, and the average age of onset for heights and driving phobias has been reported to be 24 and 32 years of age, respectively (Antony, Brown, & Barlow, 1997). In a sample of German women, E. S. Becker and colleagues (2007) reported somewhat earlier ages for the onset for elevator (9 years), flying (15 years), and driving phobias (16 years).

Course

A relatively long time (e.g., 9 years) may pass between the time symptoms of a phobia first appear and the point at which significant impairment and distress are caused (Antony & Barlow, 2002). Relatively few individuals seek treatment primarily for Specific Phobia, and the disorder is apt to be chronic if untreated. When onset is in childhood, Specific Phobia has one of the poorest recovery rates of all the anxiety disorders (Last, Perrin, Hersen, & Kazdin, 1996). On average, Specific Phobia is associated with reduced quality of life and at least moderate impairment across a number of domains, including social, leisure, and work or school (E. S. Becker et al., 2007; Essau et al., 2000; Magee, Eaton, Wittchen, McGonagle, & Kessler, 1996). Despite the potential for chronicity and impairment, Chioqueta and Stiles (2003) found that Specific Phobia was the only anxiety disorder associated with a significantly lower risk of suicide.

When Specific Phobia is the *primary* diagnosis, it is less likely that a client will be diagnosed with any other anxiety disorder; however, if Specific Phobia is not the primary diagnosis, it is much more likely that it will be a comorbid condition with other anxiety disorders (Antony & Barlow, 2002).

Life Span Considerations

Transient fears are commonly encountered in children that often resolve spontaneously within several months, so care should be taken to avoid pathologizing such short-lived fears. The *DSM-IV-TR* (American Psychiatric Association, 2000b), for example, requires that a fear be present for at least 6 months before it can be considered indicative of Specific Phobia in children and adolescents.

When phobic children come into contact with the feared stimulus or situation, their response may be different from that seen in older adolescents or adults and may include tantrums, screaming, crying, adopting a rigid posture or freezing, clinging to caregivers, or thumb sucking (N. J. King et al., 2004). Panic symptoms are also common; in a sample of adolescents with Specific Phobia, commonly reported panic symptoms experienced upon exposure to the feared situation or object included palpitations, trembling or shaking, nausea, and fear of losing control or going crazy (Essau et al., 2000). Although specific phobias commonly co-occur with one another (i.e., an individual will meet criteria for more than one subtype), according to studies with adults, Essau and colleagues found that only 17% of adolescents with Specific Phobia met criteria for two or more subtypes.

For children whose fears are excessive and warrant a diagnosis of Specific Phobia, the resulting impairment can be severe and may result in behaviors such as refusal to attend school, inability to concentrate at school, declining academic performance, and refusal to play outside or visit friends' homes, depending on the nature of the feared object or situation (Last, 2006). In their study of adolescents with Specific Phobia, Essau et al. (2000) found that 100% of the sample reported impairment in functioning during the worst episode of their phobia, and during the month preceding the study, the percentages reporting impairment in school, leisure, and social functioning were 11% to 27%, 13% to 64%, and 0% to 27%, respectively. These researchers also found that comorbid anxiety disorders were common, including PTSD (14%), Obsessive-Compulsive Disorder (11%), and Anxiety Disorder NOS (11%).

G. A. Carlson and Weisbrot (2004) observe that our understanding of phobias in the context of complex psychiatric comorbidities in children is limited. For example, they note that unusual, intense fears (e.g., of ceiling fans, imaginary characters) are common among children with autistic spectrum features, severe anxiety and mood symptoms, and atypical psychotic features, but that research on the nature of these fears, their comorbidities, and treatment is sparse. They further note that fears in children with serious illness (e.g., fears of needles, death) are often assumed to merely be inherent aspects of having a medical condition and, as such, are underrecognized as potential phobias and undertreated.

Research suggests that the types of phobia commonly encountered are somewhat different in older versus younger adults. In a sample of over 700 randomly selected adults ages 18 to 70, Fredrikson, Annas, Fischer, and Wik (1996) found that younger adults (average age 29 years) rated fear of spiders significantly higher than older adults (average age 53 years), and that older adults rated fear of lightning, heights, and flying higher than younger adults. With regard to diagnosable phobias, the situational type was significantly more common among the older age group (i.e., 16.8%) compared to the younger group (9.4%), which was primarily accounted for by differences in the frequency of height and lightning phobias. It should be noted that these researchers included in the situational phobia category some situations that would normally be considered natural environment phenomena according to the *DSM-IV-TR*, such as lightning, darkness, and heights. In a sample of 345 women and 200 men administered a fear survey, Kirkpatrick (1984) found variable patterns for fears rated as producing terror across different age groups (i.e., 15 to 17, 18 to 24, 25 to 34, 35 to 44, 45 to 54, and over 54). This study did not focus solely on fears that would typically qualify as phobias according to the *DSM-IV-TR* (American Psychiatric Association, 2000b) and did not use formal diagnostic criteria for phobias; instead, it focused on fears rated by respondents as producing the highest levels of fear. Among women, a pattern of decreasing terror ratings was noted for fears of an untimely or early death, being punished by God, and dead people, whereas increasing terror ratings across age groups were seen for fears of deep water, looking down from high buildings, fire, and strange dogs. A decreasing pattern that then increased in the oldest age group was observed for fears of the death of a loved one, illness or injury to loved ones, and ideas of possible homosexuality. Among men, different patterns were seen: Decreasing terror scores were noted for fears of untimely or early death, masturbation, ideas of possible homosexuality, being punished by God, prospect of a surgical operation, and taking written tests, whereas a pattern of decreasing terror scores that then increased for the oldest two age groups was noted for being punished by God and death of a loved one. These results demonstrate that the common clinical assumption that anxiety invariably decreases with age is not true. Clinicians may develop the mistaken impression that Specific Phobia is rare among older adults because affected individuals rarely seek treatment for this disorder.

SOCIAL PHOBIA

Many individuals experience anxiety in certain social situations, such as speaking in public. A study of adolescents and young adults, for example, found that 27% (32% of females and 22% of males) reported having at least one socially related fear (e.g., eating or drinking in public, public speaking, talking with others) during their lifetime (Wittchen & Fehm, 2001). However, the diagnosis of Social Phobia (also known as social anxiety disorder) should be considered only when an individual's social anxiety is severe enough to result in notable functional impairment or distress.

Clinical Presentation

Socially Based Fear

The key feature of Social Phobia is a fear of social or performance situations that involve exposure to unfamiliar people or possible scrutiny by others; the affected individual fears that he or she will act in a manner or display anxiety symptoms that will result in humiliation or embarrassment (American Psychiatric Association, 2000b). The range of social situations that may be feared by those with Social Phobia is broad, but some of the more common include public speaking, informal meetings or speaking, eating or drinking in public, writing in public, initiating or maintaining conversations, and attending parties (S. M. Turner, Beidel, & Townsley, 1992). Social phobics not only fear situations in which performance will be scrutinized, but in some cases may also experience dread in relation to any situation in which social interaction may occur (Beidel & Turner, 1998). Thus, a socially phobic individual may experience significant anxiety simply walking down the street because others may see him or her (Rapee & Heimberg, 1997). Like the individual with Specific Phobia, the socially phobic person will experience anxiety almost immediately upon every exposure to the feared situation. Thus, someone who occasionally experiences anxiety in a social situation such as speaking in front of or with others would not qualify for a diagnosis of Social Phobia. Adults with Social Phobia generally recognize that their fears are excessive, although children may not. Complete avoidance of social situations may be seen, but an ability to tolerate being in a social situation despite high levels of distress is not a contraindication of a Social Phobia diagnosis. Most individuals with a diagnosis of Social Phobia (e.g., 70% of adults, 46% of adolescents, and 89% of children) fear many social situations and therefore qualify as having what the *DSM-IV-TR* terms the *generalized subtype* of the disorder (American Psychiatric Association, 2000b; Beidel et al., 2004).

Additional Characteristics

Cognitive Features

Individuals with Social Phobia engage in a style of information processing characterized by negative self-appraisals, such as distorted evaluations of their social performance and beliefs that the social expectations of others cannot be met. Rapee and Heimberg's (1997) model of Social Phobia contends that the socially phobic individual's internal mental representation him/herself, which is likely inaccurate, is based on how the person believes *others* view him or her (not necessarily how he or she views himself or herself), exaggerates or is overly focused on negative characteristics, and is uniquely focused on social aspects of behavior. This model hypothesizes that considerable attentional resources are allocated to monitoring this internal mental representation to determine if elements are present that would elicit negative reactions from others, as well as scanning the social environment for evidence of negative evaluation from others. Anxious symptoms occur when socially phobic persons compare the internal self-representation to what they believe the "audience" expects, and perceive a discrepancy (e.g., see themselves as falling short of this standard).

The ideas that Social Phobia involves fears of being acceptable to others and that the consequences of negative social interactions will be disastrous are shared by other cognitive theories of the disorder (D. M. Clark & Wells, 1995). Empirical studies support the hypothesis that Social Phobia is characterized by a biased information-processing style. Those with generalized Social Phobia rate their behavior in social interactions more negatively than outside observers, discount their own displays of social competence, exhibit a positive bias when rating other people's behavior in social interactions, and experience excessively negative and distorted images of themselves during social interactions (Alden & Wallace, 1995; Hirsch & Clark, 2004; Rapee & Lim, 1992; Stopa & Clark, 1993). Even when socially phobic people experience positive social interactions, they are likely to have negative emotional reactions due to thoughts that others will set higher expectations in the future that they will be unable to meet (Wallace & Alden, 1997). Social phobics have also been found to rate the probability of negative social interactions happening higher than nonanxious controls and other clinical groups (e.g., those with Obsessive-Compulsive Disorder or Agoraphobia), and to rate the costs associated with negative social interactions higher (see Hirsch & Clark, 2004, for a review). Some studies have also found that social phobics rate the likelihood of *positive* social interactions happening to them lower than nonanxious controls (Gilboa-Schechtman, Franklin, & Foa, 2000; Lucock & Salkovskis, 1998). Persons with Social Phobia further tend to interpret ambiguous social situations in a negative manner, although they may not display such a bias when evaluating the behavior of others in ambiguous social situations or of themselves in ambiguous nonsocial situations (N. Amir, Foa, & Coles, 1998).

Evidence is mixed as to whether people with Social Phobia exhibit a memory bias that involves negative information being recalled more readily than positive information. Lundh and Öst (1996) found that social phobics are more likely to remember critical versus accepting faces in laboratory memory tasks. However, Rapee, McCallum, Melville, Ravenscroft, and Rodney (1992) failed to find evidence of a memory bias among individuals with Social Phobia across four different tasks assessing memory for threatening words, recall of feedback from a hypothetical public performance, and autobiographical memory for social and neutral situations.

Social Skills Deficits

Some studies have found that relative to nonanxious controls, those with Social Phobia display less adequate social abilities when interacting with a confederate (Alden & Wallace, 1995; Stopa & Clark, 1993). However, other studies have not found socially phobic individuals to be more globally deficient in social skills relative to nonanxious controls

(Rapee & Lim, 1992; Strahan & Conger, 1998). Although social skills training interventions have proven effective with socially phobic individuals, such results cannot be taken as conclusive evidence that Social Phobia is invariably associated with social skills deficits. This is because, for some individuals, the problem may be an inability to apply existing social skills knowledge due to overwhelming anxiety rather than a lack of social skills knowledge per se (J. D. Herbert et al., 2005). Social skills deficits are also most likely to be apparent in situations with low structure or that are highly feared by the individual, and among persons whose social skill development has been hampered by chronically socially avoidant behavior (Rapee & Heimberg, 1997). With regard to the latter, social skills deficits are more likely to be associated with the generalized subtype of Social Phobia (Beidel & Turner, 1998). Strahan and Conger (1999), applying Fazey and Hardy's (1988) performance catastrophe model, suggest that performance deficits among socially anxious individuals are also particularly likely to occur when there is a combination of both negative cognitions and high physiological arousal; they speculate that the ability to manage arousal, even in the presence of negative cognitions regarding performance, should make impaired social performance less likely. Social skills in Social Phobia are discussed further under "Treatment."

Onset, Course, and Life Span Considerations

Onset

Data from clinical studies suggest that the initial onset of symptoms of Social Phobia is between 13 and 24 years (Hazen & Stein, 1995), whereas epidemiologic studies indicate a slightly lower age range (i.e., 10 to 16 years; Wittchen & Fehm, 2003). However, much younger individuals (e.g., elementary-school-age children) may qualify for a Social Phobia diagnosis, and many people with Social Phobia report having been socially anxious for much of their life (Beidel & Turner, 1998). Data from the ECA study indicate that in addition to a peak in onset age during adolescence, another earlier peak at less than 5 years of age exists (Juster & Heimberg, 1995). It is rare for Social Phobia to have an onset after age 25; when such cases occur, the social anxiety is usually secondary or part of another mental disorder (e.g., depression, psychotic disorders, eating disorders; Wittchen & Fehm, 2003). The generalized subtype of Social Phobia often has an earlier age of onset than the nongeneralized subtype (e.g., by >2 years) and is generally considered to be a more severe disorder with greater comorbidity (Beidel & Turner, 1998).

Course

A typical course for Social Phobia is the emergence of the disorder in the early teenage years, a progressive worsening or persistent course by age 19, a waxing and waning of symptoms during the late adolescent and early adult years, and a more stable and persistent course emerging by the mid-20s, with few cases of spontaneous remission (Wittchen & Fehm, 2003). Thus, when untreated, Social Phobia is a chronic condition marked by significant risk of impairment in multiple spheres of functioning (Juster & Heimberg, 1995). Individuals with Social Phobia miss more days of work, have poorer work quality, are more likely to be unemployed, often have more limited educational or vocational attainment, and are more likely to be single than their nonphobic counterparts (Alonso et al., 2004; Wittchen & Fehm, 2003). They have also been found to rate their quality of life (in domains such as friends, partner, and childhood memories) worse than did patients with other anxiety or mood disorders (Bech & Angst, 1996). Those with the generalized subtype of Social Phobia tend to have greater symptom persistence, higher rates of co-morbidity, more severe functional impairment, higher treatment rates, and a more frequent parental history of mental disorders than those with nongeneralized Social Phobia (M. B. Stein, McQuaid, Laffaye, & McCahill, 1999; Wittchen, Stein, & Kessler, 1999). However, in a longitudinal study of the course of Social Phobia, Reich, Goldenberg, Vasile, Goisman, and Keller (1994) found no significant difference in remission rates between the generalized and nongeneralized (specific) subtypes over a 65-week follow-up period. Although three fourths of individuals followed in the study were receiving treatment of some kind, complete remission was achieved in only 12% of the generalized subgroup and 11% in the specific subgroups.

Unfortunately, many individuals with Social Phobia do not seek treatment. In a longitudinal study of a Swiss community sample that included individuals with Social Phobia, only slightly more than one third had received treatment, despite the significant impairment associated with the disorder (Merikangas, Avenevoli, Acharyya, Zhang, & Angst, 2002). Another study found that clients with Social Phobia being treated at a specialty anxiety clinic had experienced symptoms for an average of 13 years prior to being seen at the clinic, had symptoms for an average of 4 years prior to seeking help from a family physician, and in 73% of cases had received no psychological diagnosis from the family physician (Wagner, Silove, Marnane, & Rouen, 2006). There are probably many reasons why such long delays occur. In addition to primary care providers potentially being unfamiliar with the symptoms of Social Phobia, individuals with this condition may be reluctant to disclose their social discomfort, and because of their general social avoidance may be less likely to receive encouragement from others to seek help (Wagner et al., 2006).

It is estimated that 80% of social phobics meet criteria for a lifetime comorbidity, and depression, substance use, and other anxiety disorders are common (Merikangas & Angst, 1995). In a prospective, naturalistic, longitudinal study of anxiety disorders, fewer than one fourth of those diagnosed with Social Phobia had no current or lifetime comorbid anxiety disorder. Among those with a lifetime diagnosis of Social Phobia, 42% had comorbid Panic Disorder with Agoraphobia, 35% had GAD, and 21% had Simple Phobia (Goisman, Goldenberg, Vasile, & Keller, 1995). Social Phobia typically precedes the onset of mood and substance use disorders, as well as most comorbid anxiety disorders, with the exception of Simple Phobia (Merikangas et al., 2002). Axis II comorbidity is also common among those with Social Phobia. S. M. Turner, Beidel, Borden, Stanley, and Jacob (1991) found that 37% of their sample of social phobics met *DSM-III-R* criteria for an Axis II personality disorder, and that when subthreshold cases were included, this figure jumped to 88%; the most commonly encountered personality disorders were Avoidant Personality Disorder and Obsessive Compulsive Personality Disorder. In a sample of individuals with Social Phobia who also had a comorbid psychiatric disorder, quality of life was markedly impaired in 31.4% and severely impaired in 51.0% (Wittchen, Fuetsch, Sonntag, Müller, & Liebowitz, 2000). Social phobics with an additional Axis I disorder diagnosis are also more distressed than those with Social Phobia alone, as indexed by clinician ratings of depression and anxiety and by self-report indices of interpersonal sensitivity, neuroticism, and Agoraphobia (S. M. Turner et al., 1991).

Table 11.1   Situations commonly feared by children with social phobia

Reading aloud in front of the class
Performing at musical or athletic events
Joining in a conversation
Speaking to adults
Starting a conversation
Writing on the blackboard
Ordering food in a restaurant
Attending dances or activity nights

From "Social Phobia" (pp. 141–163), by D. C. Beidel, T. L. Morris, and M. W. Turner, in *Anxiety Disorders in Children and Adolescents*, T. L. Morris and J. S, March (Eds.), 2004, New York: Guilford Press. Adapted with permission.

Life Span Considerations

Youth with Social Phobia experience distress in a number of different interpersonal situations (some of which are summarized in Table 11.1), with the majority of these occurring in school (Beidel et al., 2004). Children with Social Phobia may express their anxiety by crying, tantrumming, freezing, or shrinking from social situations involving unfamiliar people (American Psychiatric Association, 2000b). In addition, they may experience a variety of physiological symptoms, most notably heart palpitations, shakiness, chills and flushing, nausea, and sweating (Beidel et al., 2004).

As with adults, children and adolescents with Social Phobia frequently have comorbid psychopathology, including depression, somatoform disorders, substance use disorders, and other anxiety disorders such as Specific Phobias and overanxious disorder or Generalized Anxiety Disorder (Beidel et al., 2004; Essau, Conradt, & Petermann, 1999). Impairment due to Social Phobia in youth may take the form of poor academic performance, missed days of school and school refusal, and problems with peers (Beidel & Turner, 1998). VanAmerigen et al. (2003) examined educational attainment in a sample of youth with anxiety disorders and found that of the participants who left school prematurely, 62% had a lifetime diagnosis of Social Phobia. Although impairments in social skills have not been consistently found among adults with Social Phobia, such problems appear common among youth with the disorder. Compared to control children, those with Social Phobia have been found to rate themselves as less socially skilled and to be so rated by parents and outside raters observing them during actual social interactions (Spence, Donovan, & Brechman-Toussaint, 1999).

Relatively little has been written about Social Phobia among the elderly. Gretarsdottir, Woodruff-Borden, Meeks, and Depp (2004) examined the phenomenology and prevalence of social anxiety in a sample of 283 older adults (mean age 74 years) and a comparison group of 318 young and middle-aged adults. Scores on a self-report measure of social anxiety were significantly lower for the older adult group, and for more than half of the social situations inventoried younger individuals endorsed more anxiety than did the older adults. The study authors suggest that these findings may be attributable to factors in the older age group of lower social involvement, decreased emotional responsiveness, increased emotional control, better coping skills, underreporting of anxiety symptoms, confounding medical or cognitive impairment, and use of a self-report measure not well validated among the elderly. However, this study also found that elderly adults scoring in the range indicative of significant social anxiety also obtained higher scores on additional measures assessing anxiety, depression, subjective health, and medical conditions compared to older adults who scored below this cutoff point, and that scores on these additional measures were similar to those for younger adults who also scored above the cutoff for high social anxiety. This suggests continuity in the clinical presentation of high social anxiety from young adulthood and middle age through old age.

OBSESSIVE-COMPULSIVE DISORDER

Obsessive-Compulsive Disorder (OCD) is a fascinating yet often highly debilitating condition characterized by recurrent, intrusive thoughts and impulses and associated mental or physical behaviors that are performed in reaction to them. Once considered rare, OCD is increasingly being diagnosed in both children and adults and is now one of the most common mental disorders in the United States, with an estimated 3 million Americans suffering from the disorder at any given time (Steketee & Pigott, 2006).

Clinical Presentation

Obsessions

Obsessive-Compulsive Disorder is characterized by recurrent thoughts, impulses, or images perceived as undesirable, unacceptable, and inconsistent with one's view of oneself. These obsessions are not simply worries about everyday, real-life concerns. Although obsessions are experienced as ego-dystonic, the affected individual recognizes that they are products of his or her own mind, as opposed to, for example, having a psychotic delusion that the thoughts, images, or impulses have been inserted into one's mind from some outside source. Table 11.2 summarizes some key characteristics of obsessions in OCD.

Many individuals with OCD are embarrassed by the content of their obsessions, which can relate to themes that the person finds repugnant (e.g., obsessions regarding contamination by fecal matter), violent (e.g., stabbing a loved one), or morally reprehensible (e.g., committing a blasphemous act, having sex with an animal). However, it is useful to inform clients with OCD that it is common for "normal" individuals to periodically experience obsessions similar to those seen in OCD. This is illustrated by Rachman and de Silva's (1978) study that surveyed a sample composed primarily of university students about the nature and frequency with which a number of obsessions were experienced. Over 80% of respondents indicated having experienced intrusive, unacceptable thoughts or impulses (with thoughts being somewhat more frequently experienced than impulses). Examples of the types of thoughts and impulses endorsed by these normal subjects were thoughts of harm befalling a loved one, thoughts of "unnatural" sex acts, thoughts of being poisoned by chemicals, impulses to violently attack and kill another person or an animal, and impulses to say rude or unacceptable things. Interestingly, clinicians with experience in treating clients with obsessions could not consistently discriminate between

Table 11.2   Ways in which obsessions in obsessive-compulsive disorder can present

Type of Obsession	Description
Ideas	Thoughts (words, phrases, rhymes) intruding into conscious awareness that interfere with the normal flow of thoughts. Content is frequently obscene, nonsensical, or blasphemous.
Images	Repetitive vivid images that often depict disturbing scenes that may be violent, aggressive, or disgusting.
Convictions	Beliefs that are founded on irrational assumptions (e.g., "if I read or touch an obituary in the newspaper, someone in my family will die").
Ruminations	Ponderous worrying intended to prevent a feared outcome or imagined harm (e.g., "Did I turn off the oven?").
Impulses	Unwanted impulses about harming oneself or another person (e.g., jumping off the roof of a building, pushing a child down the stairs) or engaging in potentially embarrassing behaviors (e.g., shouting obscenities in a house of worship).
Fears	Intense anxiety about specific items or objects (e.g., dirt, feces, germs, animals), situations (e.g., public bathrooms), or performing particular acts (e.g., handling objects others have touched).

From *Obsessive-Compulsive Disorder: The Latest Assessment and Treatment Strategies*, by G. Steketee and T. Pigott, 2006, Kansas City, MO: Compact Clinicals. Adapted with permission.

obsessions or impulses endorsed by normal subjects and those endorsed by obsessional patients. These findings illustrate that the experience of obsessive thoughts is fairly common in the general population and that the content of such thoughts among individuals without OCD is not vastly different from those with the disorder. Key differences, however, are the degree to which such thoughts can be readily dismissed and the frequency with which they are experienced. Rachman and de Silva (1978), found that between 80% and 88% of those who had experienced obsessive thoughts and impulses found them easy to dismiss, and that 78% to 95% had obsessive thoughts or impulses 10 times per month or less. In contrast, those with OCD find it exceedingly difficult to ignore obsessions and hence experience a great deal of distress from them. They may also spend hours a day engaged in compulsive behaviors.

Compulsions

When persons with OCD experience obsessions, they will typically attempt to decrease the resulting intense anxiety by engaging in some form of compulsion. Compulsions are defined as either repetitive behaviors or mental acts that must be carried out in a specific manner to reduce anxiety, distress, or some feared outcome (American Psychiatric Association, 2000b). In some cases, the form of the compulsion will be directly linked to the obsession; examples are a hand-washing compulsion in response to an obsession of contamination by dirt or germs and a checking compulsion related to an obsession that one has left electrical appliances (e.g., iron, stove) turned on. In other cases, the compulsion is not clearly thematically related to the obsession to which it is linked; an example is tapping one's fingers four times in response to obsessions that harm might come to a loved one. It is important to remember that compulsions can take the form of *mental rituals* not readily observable to others: counting, reading or rereading things, or repeatedly thinking a certain "lucky" or "safe" word or phrase. Mental compulsions can sometimes be challenging to treat because the clinician may not be aware when the client is doing them.

A compulsive behavior easily missed by both novice clinicians and family members is repeatedly *asking for reassurance*. For example, a client who believes that she may have run over someone while driving may compulsively retrace the route to check for the person believed to have been hit. Eventually she may return home and begin repeatedly asking her family members, "It's not really possible that I could have hit someone, is it?" Family members may feel that answering this question (presumably with "No") is helping the client with reality testing. In actuality, the asking for reassurance is likely a compulsion that will get reinforced by the provision of reassurance.

As with other anxiety disorders, adults with OCD at some point typically recognize that their obsessions and compulsions are excessive and unreasonable, although children with the disorder may not. However, it is not unusual to encounter clients with OCD who firmly contend that their compulsions are not unreasonable responses to an obsessive thought (e.g., the individual who insists that it is necessary to wash his hands 30 times in a row to kill contaminating germs). Such clients are often referred to as having *overvalued ideas* or beliefs that are not completely rejected as unreasonable or excessive, but that are held with less than delusional intensity (A. Frances et al., 1999). Admittedly, drawing the line between an overvalued idea and a delusion is quite difficult. The *DSM-IV-TR* (American Psychiatric Association, 2000b), allows the specifier "with poor insight" to be given with a diagnosis of OCD if the clinician determines that a client does not recognize the obsessions and compulsions are excessive or unreasonable. As noted by A. Frances et al. (1999), although consideration had been given to including a psychotic subtype of OCD in the *DSM-IV*, this was ultimately decided against because more evidence is needed regarding similarities and differences between psychotic and nonpsychotic forms of OCD. For now, if a client's OCD symptoms are determined to be of delusional intensity, in addition to utilizing the specifier "with poor insight" the clinician can also give a comorbid diagnosis of Delusional Disorder. Such a diagnosis is somewhat awkward and should not be taken to mean that two different pathological processes are the cause of the client's symptoms (A. Frances et al., 1999).

Cognitive Features

Many individuals with OCD, particularly those with checking compulsions, exhibit *pathological doubt* regarding whether an action or event has actually occurred. Individuals may, for example, doubt whether or not they really locked the door and will repeatedly test the handle. Different mechanisms that may underlie such doubt have been proposed, including actual memory deficits and decreased belief in one's memory in spite of adequate memory functioning. With regard to the first of these, findings across studies examining memory impairment among those with OCD have yielded mixed results. This may, in part, be due to methodological issues such as small sample sizes (and associated lack of statistical power) and a focus on *general* memory tasks versus those with stimuli *specifically related* to the content of an individual's OCD symptoms. However, in their meta-analysis of OCD memory studies, Woods, Vevea, Chambless, and Bayen (2002) noted the following: (a) OCD checkers display worse performance than noncheckers on a range of memory tasks, including those assessing short-term or working memory, free recall, cued recall, and visual recognition; (b) these memory deficits are not severe enough to constitute a clinically significant amnestic syndrome; (c) effect sizes for these findings are small to medium, which indicates that memory impairment may be moderately associated with checking but is not the only factor contributing to the development or maintenance of this behavior; (d) the relationship between memory impairment and checking may be moderated by a third variable (e.g., high anxiety, depression, other neurologic deficits); and (e) in some cases, memory deficits may be secondary to OCD symptoms (e.g., distraction by symptoms leads to impaired performance on memory tests). This meta-analysis also included studies examining OCD clients' *confidence* in their memory and found that checkers were not as confident in their verbal and visual recognition abilities as were noncheckers.

Individuals who engage in compulsive behavior may also have difficulty tolerating the uncertainty that is stimulated by their OCD symptoms. *Intolerance of uncertainty* is a construct that has been explored in relation to other anxiety disorders, such as Generalized Anxiety Disorder (see later in this chapter). Tolin, Abramowitz, Brigidi, and Foa (2003), in a study of individuals with OCD and normal controls, found that scores on a self-report measure of intolerance of uncertainty were significantly higher for checkers than noncheckers and normal controls, and that this result remained after controlling for depression (which was higher in the checker group). In addition, repeating rituals (e.g., feeling the need to repeat an action until it feels right) were significantly associated with intolerance of uncertainty. These findings suggest that pathological doubt in OCD may be influenced by both memory factors and an emotional component (i.e., intolerance of uncertainty).

Excessive responsibility is another cognitive feature commonly encountered among those with OCD. This may occur because persons with OCD frequently believe that simply having a thought means the action or event embodied in the thought will actually occur (referred to as *thought-action fusion*); thus, to the individual with OCD, personal thoughts take on a great deal of importance. Cognitive models of OCD contend that excessive responsibility schemas are at the core of the disorder, such that affected individuals evaluate intrusive thoughts in terms of possible harm that may befall themselves or others, which then triggers the occurrence of other uncomfortable, obsessive thoughts that the individual attempts to neutralize through compulsive behaviors (Salkovskis, 1985, 1989). Experimental manipulations that reduce OCD clients' sense of responsibility have been found to reduce compulsive behavior (Lopatka & Rachman, 1995). It appears that *perfectionism* and excessive responsibility may be related to obsessive symptoms, with excessive responsibility mediating the relationships between perfectionism and behaviors such as checking and cleaning (Bouchard, Rhéaume, & LaDouceur, 1999; Yorulmaz, Karanci, & Tekok-Kiliç, 2006).

Onset, Course, and Life Span Considerations

Onset

The onset of OCD symptoms usually begins in late adolescence or early adulthood, although between one-third and one-half of affected individuals report symptoms occurring in childhood (Steketee & Pigott, 2006). Although men and women are equally affected, symptoms may have an earlier onset in men (Rasmussen & Eisen, 1989). This is a chronic disorder often characterized by a fluctuating course (e.g., symptoms wax and wane; Rasmussen & Tsuang, 1986). However, in a 40-year follow-up study of individuals with OCD, G. Skoog and Skoog (1999) found that although 48% had OCD for more than 30 years, 83% of the sample exhibited improvement, which included recovery in 48% (recovery with subclinical symptoms = 28%, complete recovery = 20%). Among the factors that predicted worse outcome were low social functioning at baseline, a history of a chronic course early on, and magical obsessions and compulsive rituals. Among children with OCD, symptoms often remit prior to adulthood in as many as two thirds of cases (Berg et al., 1989).

Symptoms of OCD can be highly debilitating, and the disorder has been identified as the 10th leading cause of disability attributable to a medical condition in the industrialized world (Murray & Lopez, 1996). In addition to the amount of time obsessions and compulsions can take up each day, further impairment can occur if the individual begins to avoid situations that could potentially trigger obsessions (Steketee & Pigott, 2006). In some cases, this could involve making drastic life changes; for example, a person could refuse to ever use a public restroom and would therefore be severely limited in how long he or she could be away from home. In a study of close to 200 adults with OCD, Eisen et al. (2006) found impairment and lower quality of life were evident in multiple domains, including role performance, work and school functioning, general physical and emotional health, household responsibilities, recreational activities, relationships with family and friends, global social adjustment, and overall satisfaction. Substantial impairment was also apparent from the mean *DSM-IV* Global Assessment of Functioning and Social and Occupational Functioning Assessment Scale scores (i.e., approximately 51 and 54 points out of 100, respectively). The study further found that a little over 33% of participants were unable to work and 14% were receiving disability income.

Life Span Considerations

Obsessive-Compulsive Disorder is increasingly being recognized in children. Onset in childhood typically occurs between 10 and 12 years of age, but in some cases may be even earlier (Albano, Chorpita, & Barlow, 2003). Although the disorder in adults appears to affect men and women equally, cases of OCD in children are characterized by a preponderance of boys over girls (Heyman et al., 2001). Children may be particularly embarrassed or ashamed to admit obsessive thoughts (e.g., those involving harming a loved one) and may think that other children could not possibly also have such experiences. Thus, it is particularly important for the clinician interviewing a child suspected of OCD to indicate that such symptoms are not rare and to be flexible in the way that inquiries about symptoms are made (e.g., asking the child about the occurrence of specific obsessions and compulsions rather than posing open-ended questions, allowing the child to write down his or her fears rather than having to say them aloud; March & Franklin, 2006). The clinical presentation of OCD in children is similar to that seen in adults; common compulsions include hand washing (typically associated with contamination obsessions), checking (typically designed to avert a feared catastrophe of some kind), hoarding, counting, and ordering (Franklin, Rynn, Foa, & March, 2004). However, developmental factors can influence *qualitative* aspects of children's symptoms. For example, a child with a checking compulsion is more likely to worry about something getting lost from a book bag than from a car, or a young child may have difficulty identifying an obsession that precedes the performance of a compulsive behavior (Franklin et al., 2004). A child may be able to articulate only feeling that things will "not be right" unless the compulsion is performed (I. Heyman, 2005). In some cases, obsessions and compulsions may seem to have a bizarre, magical, or superstitious quality in children. It can at times be difficult to differentiate OCD symptoms from developmentally normal rituals, desires for routine, and behavioral preferences commonly seen in older toddlers and young children. However, such normal behaviors are not typically associated with extreme distress if a behavioral sequence is interrupted; they are not excessive and tend to disappear by age 9 (Albano et al., 2003). As with OCD in adults, the disorder can be extremely debilitating in children, interfering with school, family life, and social relationships. The course of the disorder in children is typically characterized by waxing and waning symptoms, although Berg et al. (1989) found that at a 2-year follow-up only one third of their sample continued to meet diagnostic criteria for the disorder.

In children, OCD is frequently comorbid with other psychiatric disorders, including externalizing disorders and tic disorders. With regard to the latter, rates of current comorbid tics and lifetime history of tic disorders range from 20% to 38% and 26% to 59% of cases of OCD, respectively, leading to speculation that some cases of childhood-onset OCD may have an etiology that is different from adult cases and which is related to tic disorders (Eichstedt & Arnold, 2001). This hypothesis is compatible with observations that childhood-onset OCD is associated with increased familial risk for *both* tic disorders and OCD (Leonard et al., 1992; Riddle et al., 1990). Children with OCD and comorbid tics typically have a less robust response to pharmacologic treatment with SSRIs compared to those without tics and may benefit from the augmentation of an SSRI regimen with a dopamine antagonist (I. Heyman, 2005).

Research on OCD among older adults is limited. However, given the frequently chronic nature of OCD, one would anticipate some degree of symptoms as affected individuals age, although improvement may be noted over time (Skoog & Skoog, 1999). Steketee, Frost, and Kim (2001) point out that behaviors such as compulsive hoarding can create particular problems for the elderly, including increased risk of falls, sanitation problems, and fire. It has been suggested that concerns about declining cognitive capacities (even in the absence of objective evidence of such deficits) may partially mediate obsessive thoughts and OCD symptoms. For example, if an older adult believes that thoughts are extremely important and is obsessively concerned with being able to track and control them, subjective concerns about declines in cognitive ability might lead such a person to repeatedly check his or her actions, order his or her life, and respond with extreme distress to the occurrence of normal unwanted, intrusive thoughts (Teachman, 2007).

POSTTRAUMATIC STRESS DISORDER

Estimates of the percentage of the general population who have been affected by at least one traumatic stressor range from 39% to 75% (Briere, 2004). For most of these individuals, the consequences of such experiences will not lead to enduring symptoms that are distressing or impairing. But for a smaller percentage, the occurrence of a traumatic event will lead to a constellation of signs and symptoms of sufficient severity and duration to warrant a diagnosis of PTSD.

Clinical Presentation

Trauma Exposure

As Briere (2004) notes, PTSD is one of the few disorders in the *DSM* where a specific causal factor for symptoms must be identified in order for a diagnosis to be made. According to this diagnostic system, individuals must have been exposed to a traumatic event involving a threat to their own or another's life or physical integrity or to an actual death, and must have experienced feelings of intense fear, helplessness, or horror (American Psychiatric Association, 2000b).

Defining a traumatic stressor has been a complicated issue for the framers of the *DSM*. The current definition of a traumatic stressor represents a change from that articulated in the *DSM-III-R*, where the precipitating event was somewhat more vaguely defined as involving an event outside the range of human experience that would be distressing to almost anyone (American Psychiatric Association, 1987). Although the current definition of a traumatic stressor may appear narrower by virtue of the specification that it involve death, injury, or threats to physical integrity, a careful reading of the *DSM-IV-TR* text clarifies that one *does not* have to directly witness the traumatic event but could *learn* of an experience that happened to someone else (American Psychiatric Association, 2000b). McNally (2003) argues that this definition of a traumatic event is unnecessarily broad and leads to a grouping of qualitatively different experiences under the same rubric, which in turn complicates the identification of common psychobiologic mechanisms of symptom expression. On the other hand, what is notably absent from the current definition of trauma in the *DSM* system are threats to *psychological* integrity (e.g., emotional abuse, major losses, humiliating events; Briere, 2004), and arguments have been made that experiences such as repeated exposure to sexually inappropriate joking in the workplace should qualify as a stressor capable of producing PTSD (Avina & O'Donohue, 2002).

Relevant to this issue is a study conducted by Gold, Marx, Soler-Baillo, and Sloan (2005) that examined PTSD symptoms in college students who had either experienced *DSM-IV*-defined traumatic stressors (trauma-congruent group) or other stressors (e.g., parental divorce, bereavement; trauma-incongruent group). Contrary to expectation, those in the trauma-incongruent group endorsed more severe symptoms on a well-validated self-report measure of PTSD than the trauma-congruent group. In addition, a greater number of individuals in the trauma-incongruent group met *DSM-IV* criteria for PTSD than those in the trauma-congruent group. Although this study was based on a fairly limited, homogeneous sample and relied on data derived from a self-report measure to assess PTSD, it raises intriguing questions about the definitional boundaries of traumatic stressors.

Notwithstanding the controversy regarding how a traumatic stressor should be defined, a wide range of stressors capable of producing PTSD have been repeatedly documented in the literature, and some of these are summarized in Table 11.3. Men are more likely than women to experience trauma related to combat exposure, whereas women are more likely than men to experience trauma involving childhood sexual abuse, intimate partner abuse, and rape. Such differences in exposure to traumatic stressors may be one factor contributing to the higher incidence of PTSD seen in women compared to men (Nemeroff et al.,

Table 11.3 Examples of stressors that can produce Posttraumatic Stress Disorder

Natural disasters (e.g., earthquakes, hurricanes)
War
Torture
Transportation accidents (e.g., plane crashes, car accidents)
Terrorist attacks
Emergency worker trauma exposure
Crime victimization
Child abuse
Domestic violence
Rape and sexual assault
Life-threatening illness
Sex trafficking

2006). Although not everyone exposed to a traumatic stressor will develop PTSD, when an event is prolonged, particularly horrific, gruesome, or brutal (e.g., torture), the chances of developing PTSD greatly increase no matter how psychologically healthy or stable the individual was prior to the trauma (Keane & Barlow, 2002; Sutker & Allain, 1996).

Reexperiencing the Trauma

Posttraumatic Stress Disorder may manifest in a number of different symptoms, which have been grouped in the *DSM-IV-TR* criteria into three clusters, the first of which includes symptoms related to reexperiencing the traumatic event. This can take the form of intrusive thoughts or distressing dreams and flashbacks that can be associated with extreme psychological distress or physiologic arousal. Herman (1997) notes that traumatic memories, unlike ordinary verbal memories, tend to be encoded in the form of intense visual images and sensations, lack a verbal narrative, and have a stereotyped quality (e.g., an intrusive nightmare may play itself out in exactly the same way each time it is experienced; in recollecting a traumatic memory, an individual may use the same words and gestures every time). Traumatic memories are also usually experienced with the same emotions that were present at the time of the original event (A. Ehlers & Clark, 2006). The visual nature of traumatic memories is exemplified in flashbacks, which have been found to compete for not only verbal processing resources, but visuospatial ones as well (e.g., poorer performance has been observed on tasks of visuomotor skill following a flashback; Hellawell & Brewin, 2002). ·

Flashbacks are perhaps the symptom most likely to be a source of confusion to clinicians who are not highly familiar with the clinical presentation of PTSD. The text accompanying the diagnostic criteria for PTSD in the *DSM-IV-TR* defines flashbacks as "dissociative states that last from a few seconds, to several hours, or even days, during which components of the event are relived and the person behaves as though re-experiencing the event at that moment" (American Psychiatric Association, 2000b, p. 464). Flashbacks typically come on suddenly, often without warning, and are experienced like a movie playing before the person's eyes; the realism of the experience may be heightened by sensory phenomena, such as sights, sounds, smells, tastes, and even tactile sensations that are like those experienced at the time of the trauma (Bremner, 2002; Keane & Barlow, 2002). Although these experiences can be terrifying because they seem real, elements of flashbacks are often distorted (e.g., sensations of time slowing down, colors seeming either brighter or diminished, distortion of shapes; Bremner, 2002; Scaer, 2001).

Although not listed among *DSM-IV-TR* criteria for PTSD, there are other ways in which trauma reenactment can take place; for example, an individual with a history of sexual abuse might engage in dangerous, risk-taking behavior, or a person who was physically abused might assume the role of a violent aggressor in an adult relationship (Herman, 1997; Scaer, 2001). The reliving of traumatic experiences has been conceptualized as an attempt to integrate and master the overwhelming feelings associated with the trauma. However, as Herman notes, reexperiencing is typically extremely distressing, and consequently the affected individual will often try to actively avoid triggering such traumatic memories.

Avoidance of Trauma Reminders

Individuals with PTSD often attempt to avoid thoughts, feelings, places, and people associated with their traumatic experiences and may have problems remembering details of the trauma. They may also become emotionally detached from the world around them and affectively numb (American Psychiatric Association, 2000b). Although not listed in the *DSM-IV-TR* as an avoidance symptom of PTSD, drugs and alcohol may be used to achieve an altered state of consciousness that facilitates escape from traumatic memories. Avoidance symptoms can be viewed as a form of behavioral, emotional, and cognitive shut-down whose purpose is to compensate for chronic states of hyperarousal (van der Kolk, 1997). Herman (1997) notes that these "constrictive symptoms" or detached states of consciousness share features that are akin to hypnotic trance states and represent the body's attempt to protect itself against unbearable emotional pain. Ironically, persistent avoidance strategies are believed to perpetuate PTSD symptoms because they prohibit the emotional processing and modification of the network of traumatic memories (Foa, Steketee, & Rothbaum, 1989).

The emotional numbing and detachment seen in PTSD can take an especially heavy toll on the client's interpersonal relationships, as it may be difficult for the person with PTSD to experience positive emotions such as love, contentment, satisfaction, and happiness (Keane & Barlow, 2002). Research confirms that PTSD appears associated with abnormal responses to positively valenced stimuli (e.g., rating pleasant pictures as nonarousing and showing decreased physiological responsiveness to such stimuli; Litz, Orsillo, Kaloupek, & Weathers, 2000; Spahic-Mihajlovic, Crayton, & Neafsey, 2005).

Increased Arousal

The third cluster of symptoms delineated in the *DSM-IV-TR* definition of PTSD involves increased arousal (e.g., problems falling asleep, hypervigilance, exaggerated startle response). Arousal symptoms have been found to predict substance abuse, suggesting the possibility that some individuals may turn to drugs or alcohol to ameliorate this specific symptom class (McFall, Mackay, & Donovan, 1992; Shiperd, Stafford, & Tanner, 2005).

Substance Use

It is common for clients with PTSD to have comorbid substance use disorders. For example, rates of comorbid drug abuse or dependence among veterans with PTSD range from
40% to 44%, and rates of comorbid alcohol abuse or dependence range from 64% to 84%
(Steward, Pihl, Conrod, & Dongier, 1998). Alternatively, when examining substance-
abusing populations, a history of PTSD is frequently encountered. For example, data from
the National Comorbidity Survey found that among individuals with a lifetime diagnosis
of Alcohol Dependence, 26% of women and 10% of men also had a history of PTSD
(R. C. Kessler, Crum, et al., 1997). Comorbidity rates among clinical populations of substance-abusing individuals are even higher and range from 25% to 55% (P. J. Brown &
Ouimette, 1999).

Steward et al. (1998) propose several ways in which substance use disorders and PTSD
may be related and note that these various pathways should not be considered mutually
exclusive: (a) Substance intoxication heightens the likelihood of trauma exposure (indirectly increasing the risk for PTSD); (b) substance abuse may directly increase susceptibility to PTSD (e.g., by inducing a chronically hyperaroused state that increases
vulnerability to PTSD following exposure to a traumatic event); (c) substance use may
develop secondary to PTSD in an attempt to self-medicate symptoms of intrusions,
arousal, or numbing, or to facilitate avoidance; (d) once PTSD has developed, substance
abuse might exacerbate or prolong PTSD symptoms by preventing habituation to traumatic memories or by interfering with the emotional processing of the traumatic experience; and (e) because of similarities between PTSD symptoms and certain substance
withdrawal symptoms (e.g., sleep disturbance, autonomic overarousal), the latter may be
mistaken for signs of anxiety or may serve as reminders of the trauma, thereby increasing
arousal and motivating further substance use.

Comorbidity of PTSD and substance use disorders is associated with poorer treatment
response, including less successful acquisition of adaptive coping skills and development
of helpful cognitions during treatment, greater psychological distress, less social support,
higher unemployment, greater psychiatric comorbidity, and increased risk of relapse at
1- and 2-year posttreatment follow-ups compared to substance-abusing clients without
PTSD (Ouimette, Ahrens, Moos, & Finney, 1997; Ouimette, Finney, & Moos, 1999).
Those with comorbid PTSD and substance use disorders are prone to also use less helpful
ways of coping with stressful situations, including avoidance coping and emotion discharge coping (Ouimette et al., 1999). With regard to relapse, situations involving the
experience of unpleasant emotions, conflict with others, and physical discomfort pose especially high risk for a return to substance use among those with PTSD (Sharkansky,
Brief, Peirce, Meehan, & Mannix, 1999).

Onset, Course, and Life Span Considerations

Onset

It is very common for individuals exposed to extreme stressors to develop PTSD-like
symptoms in the immediate aftermath of the event. What leads some individuals to experience persistent symptoms and develop PTSD and others to avoid the development of this
disorder has been the topic of much research. A number of risk factors have been

identified that increase the likelihood of PTSD developing following exposure to a stressor; these factors can be divided into those related to (a) the nature of the stressor, (b) variables related to the victim, (c) subjective responses to the stressor, and (d) the reaction of others to the victim (Briere, 2004).

The greater the magnitude or intensity of the stressor, the greater the likelihood that PTSD will develop. The following are empirically documented factors that increase the magnitude or intensity of stressors: (a) presence of threats to life, (b) intentional acts of violence, (c) physical injury, (d) sexual victimization, (e) loss of a friend or loved one, (f) unpredictability and uncontrollability, (g) witnessing death, (h) witnessing a grotesque death, and (i) extensive combat exposure (Briere, 2004). Characteristics of the victim that have been identified as risk factors for the development of PTSD include female sex, pre-trauma history of psychiatric illness, ethnic minority status, lower SES, and family history of psychopathology (Keane & Barlow, 2002; Nemeroff et al., 2006). Certain psychiatric disorders such as substance use disorders, Bipolar Disorder, and ADHD have also been associated with increased likelihood of being exposed to traumatic events (Breslau, Davis, Andreski, & Peterson, 1991; Cuffe, McCullough, & Pumariega, 1994; Wozniak et al., 1999), which in turn could lead to the development of PTSD.

Among the responses to the stressor that are relevant to the subsequent development of PTSD are physiological reactions at the time of trauma exposure. Specifically, lower cortisol levels shortly after trauma exposure, higher resting heart rate in the period immediately following the stressor, and panic attacks during trauma exposure increase the likelihood of developing PTSD and Acute Stress Disorder (Bryant, 2003). Dissociative reactions at the time of the trauma also predict greater likelihood of PTSD and are theorized to interfere with the individual's ability to process traumatic memories (Briere, 2004). Disengagement from attempts to cope with traumatic events has also been linked to PTSD (R. C. Silver, Holman, McIntosh, Poulin, & Gil-Rivas, 2002), as has lower social support (Briere, 2004; Nemeroff et al., 2006).

Cognitive interpretations of a traumatic event in the days and weeks following the event (e.g., the extent to which the trauma results in negative beliefs about oneself or the world, about one's symptoms in the aftermath of the trauma, and about other people's reactions to the trauma) have been found to predict the development of PTSD severity at 6 months and 1 year follow-up (A. Ehlers & Clark, 2006). This is consistent with the emotional processing theory of PTSD (discussed later under "Etiology"), which contends that the fear structure associated with this disorder is characterized by beliefs that the self is totally incompetent and that the world is completely dangerous (Foa, Huppert, & Cahill, 2006).

In some cases, symptoms meeting diagnostic criteria for PTSD may not develop until 6 months or more after the traumatic event (this would be designated as PTSD with delayed onset in the DSM-IV-TR system) (American Psychiatric Association, 2000b). Rates of delayed onset PTSD have generally been reported to be low and in the range of 2% to 6% (Bryant & Harvey, 2002; Buckley, Blanchard, & Hickling, 1996; Ehlers, Mayou, & Bryant, 1998). However, in many cases delayed onset PTSD is associated with notable subsyndromal symptoms (e.g., symptoms in 2 of the 3 DSM-defined symptom domains) in the months prior to meeting a formal diagnosis for the disorder and physiological findings such as higher resting heart rate in the month following trauma exposure (Bryant & Harvey, 2002; Carty, O'Donnell, & Creamer, 2006).

Course

Posttraumatic Stress Disorder is characterized by high rates of comorbidity, including increased rates of Major Depressive Disorder, substance use disorders, Bipolar Disorder, and a number of other anxiety disorders (e.g., GAD, Panic Disorder with Agoraphobia, Social Phobia, Specific Phobia, and OCD; American Psychiatric Association, 2000b). The pattern of comorbidity is somewhat different for women and men with PTSD; for example, women have been found to have lower (though still significant) rates of alcohol use disorders than men (27.9% versus 51.9%, respectively), but higher rates of other anxiety disorders, such as Panic Disorder and Agoraphobia (12.6% versus 7.3% and 22.4% versus 16.1%, respectively; R. C. Kessler et al., 1995). Not surprisingly, chronic PTSD is frequently associated with impaired work functioning and unemployment, marital problems and divorce, the development of substance use problems, and increased suicide risk (Galovski & Lyons, 2004; Vieweg, et al., 2006). Literature on male veterans with PTSD indicates that they may become aggressive or abusive toward family members and/or emotionally detached from them (including loss of sexual intimacy with partners; Frederikson, Chemberlain, & Long, 1996; Rosenheck & Thompson, 1986; Z. Solomon, 1988). The partners of veterans with PTSD are themselves at risk for developing a host of psychological problems, including depression, anxiety, hostility, and somatization (see Galovski & Lyons, 2004, for a review).

When PTSD symptoms have been present for less than 1 month, a diagnosis of Acute Stress Disorder may be appropriate. The *DSM-IV-TR* criteria for Acute Stress Disorder are in many ways similar to those for PTSD (e.g., required symptoms include those relating to the reexperiencing of the trauma, avoidance of trauma-related stimuli, and increased arousal), but particular emphasis is placed on dissociative symptoms (e.g., emotional numbing, derealization, depersonalization; American Psychiatric Association, 2000b). The latter symptoms are thought to reflect a form of cognitive avoidance that prevents the emotional processing of the trauma and may impede recovery (Spiegel, Koopman, Cardeña, & Classen, 1996). The Acute Stress Disorder diagnosis is controversial and has been the subject of criticism because even though it tends to be a good predictor of the subsequent development of PTSD, many persons with PTSD do not initially meet the criteria for Acute Stress Disorder (Bryant, 2003). This is likely due to the Acute Stress Disorder requirement that prominent dissociative symptoms are present even though such symptoms are not invariably part of the evolving picture of PTSD.

Life Span Considerations

While the symptomatic presentation of PTSD in children is in many ways similar to that seen in adults, some important developmental differences should be noted. In addition to intrusive memories and thoughts of the trauma, children with PTSD may also experience recurrent nightmares that, in younger children, may have generically frightening themes (e.g., monsters) rather than being solely focused on the trauma (J. A. Cohen & Mannarino, 2004). Developmental limitations may make it difficult for some youth with PTSD to articulate symptoms such as a sense of a foreshortened future or emotional numbing (Cohen & Mannarino, 2004). With regard to the latter, children may describe not wanting to know how they feel or engaging in behaviors designed to keep feelings from emerging (e.g., sitting alone in a corner; McKnight, Compton, & March, 2004). Themes noted in children's play may help identify trauma-related material. Like adults, youth with PTSD may turn to drugs or alcohol to deaden feelings or avoid traumatic memories. Avoidance may become so generalized that the child drastically reduces participation in most activities or avoids pleasurable or unfamiliar activities that evoke feelings of excitement and fear because of their ability to trigger recollections of the trauma (McKnight et al., 2004). In children PTSD is associated with significant comorbidity, including other anxiety disorders, depressive disorders, externalizing disorders, and substance use disorders.

Although there is a relative paucity of research on PTSD in older adults, the study of this disorder in the elderly is expected to assume increasing importance as Vietnam-era veterans age (U.S. Department of Health and Human Services, 1999). Prevalence rates of PTSD among World War II and Korean War veterans have been estimated to range from as little as 3% to as high as 56%, and in a study of 72 Holocaust survivors the rate of PTSD was 57% (Averill & Beck, 2000; Yehuda et al., 1995). Comorbidity among older adults with PTSD is common, with depression, alcohol use, and other anxiety disorders (e.g., Panic Disorder, GAD) frequently seen (Averill & Beck, 2000).

It appears that in old age, individuals who were traumatized early in life experience an episodic course of their PTSD symptoms, characterized by periods of exacerbation and remission. Common recurrent symptoms include intrusive thoughts, avoidance, hyperarousal, estrangement from others, social isolation, sleep disturbance (including nightmares), dissociation, emotional numbing, and survivor guilt (Averill & Beck, 2000). When trauma exposure occurs late in life, the clinical presentation of PTSD may be somewhat different compared to that of younger individuals exposed to the same stressor and may include notable preoccupation with the trauma and greater avoidance, sleep disturbance, intrusive thoughts, hyperarousal, and crying spells (Averill & Beck, 2000). In their study of older adult crime victims, Gray and Acierno (2002) found that commonly endorsed symptoms were somatic in nature, including shortness of breath, trembling, fatigue, accelerated heart rate, and sleep problems.

It is likely that PTSD is underrecognized among the elderly, and it can be easy for the clinician to overlook evaluation of this potentially debilitating disorder. Older adults may be unlikely to spontaneously report traumatic experiences for a number of reasons: (a) general reluctance to report emotional and psychological problems, (b) age-related forgetfulness for traumatic events that may have occurred in the distant past, (c) increased tendency to avoid trauma-related cues and discussions, (d) self-blame or credibility concerns regarding traumas such as sexual assault, and (e) failure to report an event as a crime due to rigid, preexisting beliefs (e.g., that rape is perpetrated only by strangers; Gray & Acierno, 2002).

GENERALIZED ANXIETY DISORDER

In early versions of the *DSM*, GAD was vaguely conceptualized and had corresponding poor reliability (Di Nardo, O'Brien, Barlow, Waddell, & Blanchard, 1983). This resulted in questions about the utility of this diagnosis (Breier, Charney, & Heninger, 1985). However, starting with *DSM-III-R* and continuing with *DSM-IV*, modifications were made to the diagnostic criteria that were based on empirical research and that resulted in improved reliability (Mennin, Heimberg, & Turk, 2004). It is also now possible to diagnose GAD in children, who formerly would have been diagnosed with Overanxious Disorder of Childhood using earlier versions of the *DSM* (e.g., *DSM-III* and *DSM-III-R*; American Psychiatric Association, 1980, 1987).

Clinical Presentation

Uncontrollable Worry

Generalized Anxiety Disorder is characterized by excessive, uncontrollable worry about everyday concerns such as work or school, interpersonal issues, family-related concerns, finances, and illness and health matters (American Psychiatric Association, 2000b; Craske, Rapee, Jackel, & Barlow, 1989; Sanderson & Barlow, 1990). Craske and colleagues found that those with GAD endorsed worrying about health, illness, and safety matters a greater proportion of the time than normal controls, suggesting that this may be an area of particular concern for many with this disorder. The *DSM-III-R* (American Psychiatric Association, 1987) required that the worry associated with GAD be "unrealistic" and concern two or more areas. However, these criteria were dropped in *DSM-IV* based on research findings that whether a worry was unrealistic or not had little ability to discriminate among those with GAD and those without the disorder, and a recognition that pervasive worry could occur no matter how many life areas were the subject of concern (Mennin et al., 2004).

Those with GAD tend to worry about their worrying. For example, M. M. Ruscio and Borkovec (2004) found that compared to nonanxious individuals and even high worriers not diagnosed with GAD, those with GAD were more likely to perceive worrying as negative, harmful, associated with disastrous consequences, and uncontrollable. Similarly, Craske et al. (1989) found that although individuals with GAD and nonanxious controls were similar in their reports of how anxious they became when worrying and how much they tried to resist worrying, those with GAD reported having less control over their worrying, being less successful in resistive attempts, and having more worries without precipitants (which may increase perceived lack of control over worries).

Additional Emotional, Physical, and Cognitive Symptoms

A *DSM-IV-TR* diagnosis of GAD requires that at least three of six additional symptoms be present in conjunction with excessive anxiety or worry. Several of these symptoms are related to motor tension (e.g., muscle tension, restlessness, fatigue) or vigilance and scanning (e.g., difficulty concentrating, disturbed sleep); irritability is also included. This list of symptoms represents a marked reduction from what appeared in the *DSM-III-R*, which had included symptoms of autonomic hyperreactivity (e.g., sweating, heart palpitations, shortness of breath) and had a total of 18 symptoms (American Psychiatric Association, 1987). That list was problematic for a number of reasons: It was cumbersome for clinicians to use, had substantial overlap with symptoms of panic attacks, and was not empirically supported (A. Frances et al., 1999). Research evidence indicates that individuals with GAD are more likely to experience increased muscle tension relative to controls but not increased autonomic activity (Hoehn-Saric, McLeod, & Zimmerli, 1989).

Additional Characteristics

Cognitive Features

There is a large body of research demonstrating that individuals with GAD display a bias toward selectively processing threat-related information and also tend to interpret ambiguous information as threatening. A number of experimental paradigms have been utilized to show that individuals with GAD perform less well than nonanxious controls on tasks that require the ability to ignore stimuli with a negative or threatening emotional valence. An example of such a task is the emotional Stroop paradigm, in which an individual must name aloud the color of ink that threatening words are printed in while ignoring the word (MacLeod & Rutherford, 2004). In addition, individuals with GAD have been repeatedly found to display enhanced performance on tasks that require attention to threatening stimuli (e.g., negatively valenced words; MacLeod & Rutherford, 2004). Mogg, Millar, and Bradley (2000) found that when presented with four types of faces (threatening, sad, happy, and neutral), individuals with GAD were more likely to look first toward the threatening faces instead of the neutral faces and to shift their gaze more quickly toward the threatening faces rather than away from them compared with normal controls and individuals with Major Depressive Disorder. Collectively, these findings suggest that GAD is associated with a tendency to allocate attentional resources to information that is threatening. As will be discussed shortly, GAD also appears to be associated with difficulty tolerating ambiguity. In the face of uncertainty, those with GAD are likely to assume that negative outcomes will be the most likely to occur and that such outcomes will be personally very costly (Dugas, Buhr, & Ladouceur, 2004). The tendency to interpret ambiguous situations in a negative or threatening way has been demonstrated in the laboratory. As an example, on a spelling task requiring subjects to write down auditorily presented words, if the words can be spelled two ways—one of which has a threatening interpretation and the other a neutral interpretation (e.g., die and dye)—individuals with GAD will tend to write down the word with the threatening meaning to a greater extent than nonanxious controls (see MacLeod & Rutherford, 2004, for a review).

Intolerance of Uncertainty

Because those with GAD often have great difficulty tolerating events or situations that are uncertain, some have speculated that this may be a central feature of the disorder. Dugas et al. (2004) note the following characteristics of clients with GAD that point to intolerance of uncertainty: (a) difficulty making decisions because of uncertainty that a chosen solution may not lead to the best outcome; (b) a preference for a sure outcome to occur, even if it is negative, rather than having to tolerate an uncertain outcome; and (c) inability of standard cognitive correction procedures (e.g., generating realistic estimates of the likelihood of catastrophic events) to decrease worry because such strategies do not lead to *absolute* guarantees against the occurrence of negative events. In their review of research in this area, Dugas and colleagues (2004) note that a relationship between worry and intolerance of ambiguity has been clearly documented in nonclinical samples and among those with GAD. They further suggest that this characteristic may serve as a cognitive filter through which those with GAD process information; it may therefore help explain the persistence of worry in this disorder. For example, intolerance of ambiguity may contribute to an avoidance of threatening mental images associated with feared outcomes and thereby preclude emotional processing of such fears by preventing somatic arousal, leading to maintenance of worry (Dugas et al., 2004). Similarly, an intolerance of uncertainty may lead to worry and hypervigilant behaviors as a means to try to exert some control over or prepare for the possibility of aversive future events or situations (Holoway, Heimberg, & Coles, 2006). Indeed, high intolerance of uncertainty appears more strongly related to making threatening *interpretations* of *ambiguous* situations than do worry, anxiety, or depression (Dugas et al., 2004). It does not appear that intolerance of uncertainty is a feature unique to GAD; research suggests that it characterizes other disorders, such as OCD (Holoway et al., 2006; Steketee, Frost, & Cohen, 1998). Nevertheless, interventions aimed at increasing tolerance for uncertainty have been associated with improvements in GAD symptoms, including worry, and highlight the value of considering this dimension in the treatment of GAD (Dugas & Ladouceur, 2000; Dugas et al., 2003).

Onset, Course, and Life Span Considerations

Onset

Typically, onset of GAD is in the late teenage years to early 20s, with relatively few cases having an initial onset after the mid-30s (R. C. Kessler et al., 2004). Many individuals with GAD report having been anxious for much of their lives; this suggests that many cases of the disorder have a gradual, insidious onset (Noyes et al., 1992). Age of onset appears to be related to whether GAD is a primary or a secondary disorder; in cases where the GAD is secondary to another disorder, the onset tends to be later (e.g., 30 years of age; M. P. Rogers, et al. 1999).

Course

This is a chronic disorder that lasts, on average, 20 years. Only one third of cases spontaneously remit (Wittchen, Zhao, Kessler, & Eaton, 1994; Yonkers, Warshaw, Massion, & Keller, 1996). The disorder tends to follow a waxing and waning course, and exacerbation of symptoms is likely during times of increased life stress (S. C. Newman & Bland, 1994). Even during periods of remission (i.e., when full criteria for the disorder are not met), many individuals continue to experience subsyndromal symptoms that adversely impact functioning (Judd et al., 1998). Given the extent and scope of worry that characterizes GAD, it is perhaps not surprising that the disorder is associated with reduced quality of life. Stein and Heimberg (2004) found that individuals with GAD were significantly more likely to report dissatisfaction with their main activity, family life, and overall well-being compared to those without the disorder, and these findings were apparent even when independent effects of comorbid depressive disorders were controlled. In a study examining work-related impairment, 34% of subjects with *DSM-IV*-defined GAD and 48% with GAD plus comorbid Major Depressive Disorder reported experiencing impaired functioning for at least 6 days in the previous month, and almost one third of the GAD group and one half of the GAD plus depression group also reported some reduction in work activity during the preceding month (Wittchen, Carter, Pfister, Montgomery, & Kessler, 2000).

Comorbidity is exceedingly common in GAD. Data from the National Comorbidity Survey showed that 90% of those with a lifetime history of GAD had a lifetime history of at least one other psychiatric disorder, and two thirds of those with current GAD had a comorbid disorder (Wittchen et al., 1994). Common comorbid conditions include Major Depressive Disorder and other anxiety disorders such as Social Phobia, Simple Phobia, Panic Disorder, and Agoraphobia. Studies of clinical samples reveal similarly high rates of comorbidity (with Major Depressive Disorder being most commonly encountered) and rates of lifetime comorbid Social Phobia, Panic Disorder, and Specific Phobia each ranging from approximately 50% to 60% (Nutt, Argyropoulos, Hood, & Potokar, 2006). The presence of GAD appears to be a risk factor for the development of other disorders, with severity of active GAD predicting the onset of later secondary anxiety and mood disorders (A. M. Ruscio et al., 2006). As with many other disorders, the presence of comorbid psychiatric illness in GAD is associated with poorer prognosis, including greater occupational and social impairment (Judd et al., 1998).

Life Span Considerations

Prior to the *DSM-IV*, excessive worry in children and adolescents would have been diagnosed as Overanxious Reaction (*DSM-II*) or Overanxious Disorder (*DSM-III-R*; American Psychiatric Association, 1980, 1987). The latter category was removed with the publication of the *DSM-IV* because of problems of vague criteria, poor interrater reliability, overlap with other disorder symptoms, and high numbers of children without significant pathology who evidenced symptoms of the disorder (Flannery-Schroeder, 2004). Despite the change in diagnostic classification and criteria, there is a high degree of similarity between cases of overanxious disorder and childhood GAD (Kendall & Warman, 1996).

Children with GAD frequently worry about personal health, family, and school-related issues (Pina, Silverman, Alfano, & Saavedra, 2002). Masi et al. (2004) found that tension, apprehensive expectations, need for reassurance, irritability, negative self-image, and physical complaints were reported in more than three fourths of their sample of children and adolescents with *DSM-IV*-defined GAD. In a study by Alfano, Beidel, Turner, and Lewin (2006), parents reported that their children with GAD had more nightmares, had more trouble sleeping, and were more often overly tired without good reason compared to children with other anxiety disorders. Estimates of sleep disturbance in GAD youth range from 42% to 56% for children and 49% to 57% for adolescents (Masi et al., 2004; Pina et al., 2002). In general, younger children with GAD are likely to report fewer symptoms than older children and adolescents with the disorder (Kendall & Pimentel, 2003; C. Strauss, Lease, Last, & Francis, 1988). In addition, child and parent reports regarding somatic symptoms are likely to be significantly different, with children reporting far fewer of these types of symptoms than their parents. Kendall and Pimentel (2003) found that whereas 72% of their sample of children and adolescents with GAD reported two or fewer somatic symptoms (e.g., muscle aches, inability to sit still), 76% of parents reported three or more such symptoms in their children. With regard to specific symptoms, parents and children differed significantly in their report of inability to concentrate or pay attention, inability to sit still or relax, irritability, muscle aches, and sleep disturbance, with parents consistently reporting these symptoms as being more frequent.

Detection of GAD in children and adolescents may be hampered when adults perceive features commonly seen in association with the disorder as desirable, such as perfectionism, rule conformity, concerns about meeting deadlines and appointments, and inquiries about the safety of various situations (Flannery-Schroeder, 2004). However, GAD can significantly impair functioning in children and is often comorbid with other psychiatric disorders, including depression, other anxiety disorders, and externalizing disorders (Masi et al., 2004).

Despite the fact that GAD has not been extensively studied among older adults, it appears to be one of the most frequent anxiety disorders among the elderly (Beekman et al., 1998). Six-month and lifetime prevalence rates for this disorder among the elderly have been estimated to be 1.9% and 4.6%, respectively (Blazer, George, & Hughes, 1991). Compared to younger individuals, older adults with GAD may actually worry more and for longer periods of time (Wittchen & Hoyer, 2001). One of the challenges in diagnosing GAD in older adults is that many of the disorder's symptoms (e.g., concentration difficulties, fatigue, restlessness) may be mistaken for normal age-related changes or attributed to the effects of associated medical conditions and/or medications (Wetherell, Le Roux, & Gatz, 2003). In addition, the elderly face a number of stressors (e.g., health decline; death of friends, spouse, family; financial concerns) that are apt to engender worry that may be difficult to establish as excessive.

However, research has demonstrated important ways in which older adults with GAD differ from normal, nonanxious elderly. Wetherell and colleagues (Wetherell, Le Roux, et al., 2003) compared three groups of older adults: (1) those with GAD, (2) nonanxious controls, and (3) individuals responding to a treatment advertisement for anxiety but who did not meet criteria for any *DSM-IV* anxiety disorder. Although these groups did not differ from one another on the basis of marital status (e.g., widowhood), retirement status, number of medical conditions, contact with primary care providers in the preceding 6 months, or cognitive impairment, the GAD group reported more frequent and uncontrollable worry about more topics than those without GAD. Worry topics related to minor matters, finances, social and interpersonal matters, and personal health distinguished the GAD group from the other groups. In addition to the frequency and uncontrollability of worry, degree of distress or impairment, muscle tension, and sleep disturbance distinguished older adults with GAD from the normal older adults and the subsyndromal treatment-seeking group.

As with younger persons with GAD, older adults with this disorder experience a reduced quality of life compared to nonanxious controls. Bourland and colleagues (2000) found that older adults with GAD scored significantly lower on two standardized measures of quality of life compared to both a normal elderly control group and to published normative data on elderly and younger nonpsychiatric controls.

EPIDEMIOLOGY OF ANXIETY DISORDERS

Panic Disorder

The lifetime prevalence of Panic Disorder with Agoraphobia is estimated to be between 1.5% and 4% (B. F. Grant et al., 2006; K. S. White & Barlow, 2002). In their review of European epidemiologic studies, R. D. Goodwin and colleagues (2005) found the 12-month prevalence rate for Panic Disorder was approximately 2%. The prevalence of Panic Disorder among women has consistently been reported to be double that seen in men, regardless of whether samples are drawn from the general community or from treatment-seeking populations (K. S. White & Barlow, 2002). The prevalence of Panic Disorder among children and adolescents has been reported to range from 0.5% to 5% (Birmaher & Ollendick, 2004).

Specific Phobia

Specific Phobia is quite common in the general population. Epidemiological surveys place the 12-month prevalence rate at 6% to 9% (Bilj, Ravelli, & van Zessen, 1998; Offord et al., 1996). The lifetime prevalence of Specific Phobia has been estimated to be 9% to 11% (Conway et al., 2006; Kessler et al., 1994). As noted in the *DSM-IV-TR* (American Psychiatric Association, 2000b), women are more commonly diagnosed with Specific Phobia compared to men by a ratio of 2:1. However, the pattern of gender differences varies somewhat according to phobia subtype. Women are more likely than men to have situational and animal phobias, whereas rates for BII phobias are more comparable between the sexes (Fredrikson et al., 1996). The prevalence of Specific Phobia among children and adolescents is estimated to be between 2% and 12% and is more common in girls than boys (Emmelkamp & Scholing, 1997; Essau et al., 2000).

Social Phobia

Early studies on the prevalence of Social Phobia suggested that it was a relatively rare disorder. The ECA survey, for example, placed the prevalence rate of Social Phobia at 2% to 3% using *DSM-III* diagnostic criteria (Schneier, Johnson, Hornig, Liebowitz, & Weissman, 1992). However, subsequent editions of the *DSM* highlighted generalized forms of Social Phobia (i.e., social fears that are not restricted narrowly to specific performance situations) that likely contributed to increasing prevalence estimates for this disorder, such that it is now considered one of the most common of all the anxiety disorders. For example, 1-year and lifetime prevalence rates were reported to be 7.9% and 13.3%, respectively, according to the National Comorbidity Study (NCS; Kessler, McGonagle, & Zhao, 1994). The NCS study utilized *DSM-III-R* criteria, which are quite similar to the *DSM-IV* criteria. Epidemiological studies of Social Phobia using *DSM-IV* criteria indicate lifetime prevalence rates ranging from 5% to 12% (Conway et al., 2006; Wittchen & Fehm, 2001). M. B. Stein, McQuaid, et al. (1999) reported a 7% point prevalence of Social Phobia in a primary care setting. Prevalence rates for women outnumber those for men by a ratio of 1.5:1 in epidemiologic studies (Moutier & Stein, 1999), but in clinical samples, rates are comparable for males and females or are higher for males (American Psychiatric Association, 2000b).

Accurate rates of Social Phobia in children are more difficult to determine, in part because prior to *DSM-IV*, socially anxious children could be given diagnoses of Social Phobia, Avoidant Disorder of Childhood, or Overanxious Disorder (Beidel & Turner, 1998). Studies of clinical samples have reported drastically increased rates of Social Phobia (e.g., more than doubling) when *DSM-IV* versus *DSM-III-R* criteria were used (Kendall & Warman, 1996). Wittchen et al. (1999) reported lifetime prevalence of Social Phobia of 9.5% in females and 4.9% in males in a sample of adolescents and young adults ages 14 to 24.

Obsessive-Compulsive Disorder

The lifetime prevalence rate for OCD has been estimated at 2.5% according to data from the ECA survey (Karno, Golding, Sorenson, & Burnam, 1988). Weissman and colleagues (1994) found that the lifetime prevalence rate of OCD across seven international sites (i.e., United States, Canada, Puerto Rico, Germany, Taiwan, Korea, and New Zealand) ranged from 1.9% to 2.5%, and annual prevalence rates ranged from 1.1% to 1.8%; rates were fairly consistent across sites in this study, except for Taiwan, where the lifetime and annual prevalence rates were significantly lower (i.e., 0.7% and 0.4%, respectively). Both of these studies utilized the Diagnostic Interview Schedule (Robins, Helzer, Croughan, & Ratcliff, 1981). Several other epidemiologic surveys of OCD (mostly in Europe) have been conducted using the Composite International Diagnostic Instrument (Robins et al., 1988); these place the lifetime prevalence of OCD at between 0.7% and 2% (see Fontenelle, Mendlowicz, & Versiani, 2006, for a review). A study utilizing the Schedule for Affective Disorders and Schizophrenia (Endicott & Spitzer, 1978) found a lifetime prevalence rate for OCD of 1.8% (Mohammadi et al., 2004). The 6-month prevalence of OCD among individuals older than 65 has been estimated to be 1.5% (Bland, Newman, & Orn, 1988). Among children, point prevalence rates for OCD range from 0.5% to 1% (Flament et al., 1988). Although rates of OCD are comparable in women and men, in pediatric cases, boys outnumber girls (Steketee & Pigott, 2006).

Posttraumatic Stress Disorder

The lifetime prevalence rate for PTSD is quite high, estimated at nearly 8% (Kessler, Sonnega, Bromet, Hughes, & Nelson, 1995). Twelve-month prevalence rates have been reported to range from 1.3% to 3.6% (S. Klein & Alexander, 2006). Rates of PTSD are higher in women than men; for example, data from the NCS reported PTSD lifetime prevalence rates of 10.4% versus 5.0% for women and men, respectively (R. C. Kessler et al., 1995). Estimates of the rate of PTSD in pediatric populations are lacking, but a British study found that 0.4% of children between the ages of 11 and 15 years displayed symptoms of PTSD (Meltzer, Gatward, Goodman, & Ford, 2003). The rates of PTSD are high among populations exposed to extreme stressors, such as combat veterans (31% to 37%), rape victims (50%), traffic accident victims (12%), and nonsexual assault victims (12% to 31%; S. Klein & Alexander, 2006).

Generalized Anxiety Disorder

After GAD was introduced in the *DSM-III* (American Psychiatric Association, 1980), the diagnostic criteria changed with each subsequent edition; this affects prevalence estimates that have been published for the disorder. R. C. Kessler et al. (2004) note that lifetime prevalence estimates of GAD based on *DSM-III* and *DSM-III-R* criteria are between 4% and 7%, and 12-month prevalence estimates range from 3% to 5%. Using *DSM-IV* criteria, lifetime prevalence is between 4% and 6%, and 12-month prevalence is 3% (Conway et al., 2006; A. M. Ruscio et al., 2006). The disorder is two thirds more common in women than men, according to epidemiologic studies, although in clinical samples this disparity is somewhat less pronounced (e.g., women compose 55% to 60% of samples; American Psychiatric Association, 2000b).

The *DSM-IV-TR* (American Psychiatric Association, 2000b) requires that worry be excessive for a diagnosis of GAD to be made and that symptoms be present for at least 6 months; however, these are not necessary for a diagnosis using the *ICD-10* criteria. A. M. Ruscio et al. (2006), utilizing data from the U.S. National Comorbidity Survey replication study, calculated lifetime prevalence estimates of GAD when the excessive worry and duration requirements were altered and compared this to rates obtained using full *DSM-IV* criteria. If the 6-month duration requirement is decreased to 1 month, the lifetime prevalence rate of GAD increases from approximately 6% to 9%. When the excessiveness criterion is excluded, the lifetime prevalence rate increases to 8%. If both of these criteria are excluded, the lifetime prevalence rate more than doubles to 13%. Cases of GAD in which the excessiveness criterion is met have been found to have a more chronic course that begins earlier in life, greater symptom severity, and more psychiatric comorbidity than nonexcessive GAD; however, nonexcessive cases are also characterized by considerable impairment and symptom persistence, high rates of treatment seeking, greater comorbidity than those without GAD, and similarities with excessive cases in terms of sociodemographic characteristics and familial aggregation of GAD (A. M. Ruscio et al., 2005). This suggests that the current *DSM-IV* GAD requirements that worry be excessive and symptoms be present for at least 6 months exclude a considerable number of individuals who resemble excessive worriers in a number of ways and experience notable impairment (A. M. Ruscio et al., 2006).

ETIOLOGY OF ANXIETY DISORDERS

Neurobiological Factors

Our understanding of the neurobiological mechanisms underlying anxiety has greatly increased during the past 15 years. Although it is beyond the scope of this chapter to provide a thorough review of this area, important basic information will be summarized.

From an evolutionary standpoint, it is important for humans to be biologically wired for the activation of survival-oriented emotional, behavioral, and physical reactions in response to threat. When confronted with danger, humans instinctively experience a fear response that often is translated into a behavioral action tendency that has been referred to as the "fight or flight" mechanism, "alarm reaction," or "emergency reaction"; although this response may manifest itself as confrontation and engagement with the source of threat (i.e., fighting), more commonly it is translated into an overwhelming urge to escape (i.e., flight; Barlow, 2002d). Anxiety disorders have been linked to a *misfiring* of the brain's fear circuit, and similarities between the subjective experience of fear and that of panic have been noted (Barlow, 2002d).

There are several brain areas that play key roles in the activation of the fear response, including the locus coeruleus, a nucleus located in the brain stem that is involved in triggering symptoms associated with the body's fight-or-flight response through its release of norepinephrine and subsequent activation of the autonomic nervous system via stimulation of epinephrine released from the adrenal glands. Abnormalities in the prefrontal cortex have also been observed in the anxiety disorders. This area of the brain plays a critical role in the modulation and interpretation of anxiety-provoking experiences and appears to show different patterns of dysfunctional activation in different anxiety disorders (e.g., hyperactivation in GAD, hypoactivity in Panic Disorder and PTSD; J. Kim & Gorman, 2005). The anterior cingulate gyrus, which serves as a bridge between the prefrontal cortex and amygdala, also plays an important role in the fear response and has been linked to emotional discomfort and problems in behavioral extinction observed in OCD (J. Kim & Gorman, 2005). Surgical disabling of the cingulate gyrus is occasionally used to treat highly treatment-refractory OCD, although such treatment is not considered standard.

Recently, much interest has focused upon the amygdala, bed nucleus of the stria terminalis (BNST), and hypothalamic-pituitary-adrenal (HPA) axis/corticotrophin-releasing factor (CRF) system. The amygdala, located deep within the medial temporal lobe, is part of the limbic system, the emotional center of the brain. The amygdala appears to serve a mediating or switchboard role, through which other brain areas involved in the fear response are activated (J. Kim & Gorman, 2005). One function performed by the amygdala is storage of memories associated with fear; this is adaptive because it enables an individual to readily recall such memories to deal with similar threats in the future (Gold, 2005). Amygdala hyperresponsivity has been hypothesized to play an etiological role in anxiety disorders; supportive evidence for this comes from neuroimaging studies demonstrating increased activity in the amygdala among PTSD sufferers exposed to trauma reminders (Rauch, Shin, & Phelps, 2006). However, studies have not been consistent in this area; thus, whereas some investigators have reported increased amygdala activity in OCD patients, others have observed a pattern of hyporesponsivity (Cannistraro et al., 2004). Therefore, the amygdala's potentially differential role across the anxiety disorders remains to be clarified.

The BNST is an area adjacent to the amygdala with similar projections to limbic and cortical regions involved in the so-called fear circuit (e.g., hypothalamus, locus coeruleus, ventral tegmental area, and periaqueductal gray matter). The BNST is involved in modulating the startle response and appears to play a role in activating worry over long periods of time (Cozolino, 2006). It has been hypothesized that repeated stimulation of the BNST by CRF as a result of stress may lead to persistent activation of this area and ongoing anxiety (Barlow, 2002e).

Neuroendocrine factors are also implicated in anxiety, and most attention has focused on the HPA axis, which is involved in controlling reactions to stress. When a threat is detected by the amygdala, a message is sent to the hypothalamus, which in turn releases CRF and arginine vasopressin; these peptides work together to stimulate the secretion of adrenocorticotropin hormone (ACTH) from the pituitary gland, which, upon arriving at the cortex of the adrenal gland, stimulates the synthesis of stress hormones, including cortisol. Cortisol abnormalities have been observed in individuals with anxiety disorders; specifically, some studies have found a weak or nonexistent increase in cortisol production in response to exposure to stressors among individuals with PTSD, Social Phobia, and Panic Disorder. This seemingly paradoxical observation has been interpreted as an indicator of a strong negative feedback system in these anxiety disorders, which inhibits cortisol production as an adaptation to initially elevated levels of CRF production (Barlow, 2002e).

In addition to its role in regulating the release of stress hormones, attention has also increasingly focused on the unique role CRF may play in the anxiety disorders. Corticotrophin-releasing factor is found not only in the hypothalamus, but also in other brain areas that are part of the fear circuit, including the amygdala and BNST, and there is now evidence that neurotransmitters implicated in anxiety disorders (e.g., serotonin, GABA, and norepinephrine) affect CRF secretion from the hypothalamus (Barlow, 2002e). Individuals with PTSD have been shown to display an attenuated ACTH response to CRF, and a similar relationship may be present for panic disordered individuals as well.

A number of neurotransmitter abnormalities are associated with the anxiety disorders that involve serotonin, norepinephrine, and GABA. As will be discussed under "Treatment," medications that increase the availability of serotonin have been found effective for anxiety disorders, thus highlighting the importance of this neurotransmitter in anxiety disorder pathology. Recent evidence suggests that some anxiety disorders (e.g., Panic Disorder) may be associated with fewer overall serotonergic receptors in the brain (J. Kim & Gorman, 2005). As previously noted, norepinephrine plays an important role in helping to trigger symptoms of the fight-or-flight response through its association with the locus coeruleus. The inhibitory neurotransmitter GABA is involved in the induction of relaxation and prevention of overexcitation; GABA receptors are located in a variety of brain regions implicated in anxiety disorders, and activity of this neurotransmitter appears reduced in anxiety disorders (J. Kim & Gorman, 2005). Drugs that are GABA antagonists increase anxiety, whereas medications such as benzodiazepines, which enhance GABA functioning, decrease anxiety (Barlow, 2002e).

Genetic Influences

Extant research indicates that genetic influences in anxiety disorders are of moderate magnitude and less than that for Schizophrenia (Leonardo & Hen, 2006). Much of the information provided here comes from a meta-analysis of family and twin studies of Panic Disorder, GAD, phobias, and OCD conducted by Hattema, Neale, and Kendler (2001), which sought to address two issues: (1) the magnitude of the familial aggregation of anxiety disorders and (2) the relative contribution of genetics and environment to the etiology of these disorders. The authors found strong evidence for a familial component in the liability for Panic Disorder, with an aggregated risk of 10% for first-degree relatives of panic disordered individuals compared to only 2.1% among first-degree relatives of comparison subjects. When data from twin studies were jointly considered, the overall heritability estimate for Panic Disorder was placed at .48. For GAD, approximately 32% of the variance in liability to developing this disorder was determined attributable to genetic factors. Although individual family studies of OCD have yielded mixed results regarding the familial aggregation of this disorder, when considered collectively the data point to an increased risk of developing the disorder for first-degree relatives of affected probands (8.2% versus 2.0% among comparison relatives). With regard to phobias, limited data available on individual phobic disorders necessitated the aggregation of data from studies examining Simple Phobia, Social Phobia, and Agoraphobia. Results again indicated a significant association between a phobia diagnosis among probands and their first-degree relatives, with 20% to 40% of variance in liability to developing a phobic disorder attributed to genetic factors.

Considered as a whole, the heritability estimates for all anxiety disorders studied were determined to fall in the range of 30% to 40%; however, the authors noted that this may be an underestimate due to factors in the statistical models used. They suggest that, correcting for this factor, phobia heritability estimates are, for example, likely to be 50% to 60%. The Hettema et al. (2001) meta-analysis did not include studies related to PTSD. However, a study by True and colleagues (1993), utilizing data from the Vietnam Veteran Twin Registry, reported heritability estimates for several PTSD symptoms, ranging from .21 to .37. It has also been well documented that the risk of developing PTSD is elevated in those with a family history of anxiety disorder and depression, and possibly also psychotic disorders (see Radant, Tsuang, Peskind, McFall, & Raskind, 2001, for a review).

Certain temperamental styles posited to have a strong genetic component may represent a vulnerability factor to the later development of anxiety disorders. An example is *behavioral inhibition*, which refers to quiet withdrawal in response to strangers and novel inanimate stimuli (Kagan, 1994). This temperamental style has been observed in approximately 15% to 20% of 2-year-old Caucasian children in the United States and is associated with a number of biological correlates that include high stable heart rate, increased salivary cortisol levels, increased muscle tension, greater pupil dilation, and increased levels of urinary catecholamines (Barlow, 2002b). Studies of behaviorally inhibited children demonstrate that these characteristics are stable over time and that approximately one third will go on to develop an anxiety disorder later in life (Biederman et al., 1990).

Other Biological Factors

Recently, attention has focused on the role that streptococcal (strep) infections may play in triggering OCD symptoms in some children. Specifically, in some children with OCD, a sudden onset or exacerbation of symptoms follows strep infections (a similar pattern has also been seen for other disorders, such as Tourette's Disorder). Although still in the relatively early stages of investigation, it is thought that in these children the body's immune response goes awry, causing the antibodies to mistakenly attack the basal ganglia; the name Pediatric Autoimmune Neuropsychiatric Disorders Associated with Strep (PANDAS) is used to refer to such cases (Swedo & Grant, 2004).

Learning Theory Paradigms

Principles derived from learning theory have repeatedly been applied to understanding the development and maintenance of fears associated with anxiety disorders. Specific Phobia will be used as a prototypical disorder to demonstrate important concepts related to conditioning models of anxiety.

There are many theories regarding how phobias are acquired, but those relevant to a discussion of learning models include (a) direct conditioning experiences (e.g., a fear of dogs develops after being bitten by one and getting hurt), which may be facilitated by biological predispositions; (b) modeling or seeing others exhibit fearful responses (i.e., a parent models fear of elevators to a child by refusing to ever enter one); and (c) informational transmission (e.g., a fear of flying develops after hearing news stories about plane crashes; Rachman, 1977).

With regard to the first of these, an illustrative example is provided by Watson and Raynor's (1920) classic study of Little Albert. In this investigation, Albert, an 11-month-old infant, was exposed to a white rat, to which he had formerly displayed no aversive reaction. The rat was presented to the child at the same time as a loud sound (a hammer hitting a metal bar). The sound served as an unconditioned stimulus that caused Albert to exhibit an unconditioned (unlearned) fear response (e.g., crying, attempts to flee). When the sound was repeatedly paired with the rat (i.e., over seven trials), Albert developed a conditioned fear response to the rat, such that when the rat was presented alone, the child cried, trembled, and looked fearful. Although this type of classical conditioning paradigm provides a plausible explanation for phobia development, it has two problems: (1) Many people with phobias cannot recall a specific conditioning experience associated with the development of their phobia, and (2) although it is theoretically possible for a phobia to develop to practically any stimulus, most do not commonly develop to all sources of potential danger (e.g., electrical outlets) and instead cluster around a small number of themes (the subtypes discussed earlier; Fyer, 1998). This suggests that conditioning phenomena must be considered in the context of other factors.

The concept of *biological preparedness* can help explain why certain types of phobias are more common than others. M. E. Seligman (1971) proposed that from an evolutionary standpoint, it is adaptive for humans to quickly learn to associate certain stimuli with potentially dangerous consequences and for these associations to be resistant to extinction; an example is learning to be fearful of snakes, which can be poisonous. The preparedness hypothesis is supported by studies demonstrating that lab-reared monkeys without prior snake experience develop fear of them after watching videos of other monkeys responding fearfully to snakes; however, such monkeys do not develop fears to flowers after watching videos of other monkeys responding fearfully to those objects (Mineka & Cook, 1993). The relationship between disgust sensitivity and the development of small animal phobias (e.g., spiders, rats) noted earlier could also have evolutionary value by encouraging avoidance of potential disease carriers.

Modeling influences may also facilitate the development of a phobia. Returning to primate studies, monkeys who have never been exposed to snakes but view a video of monkeys interacting with snakes in a *nonfearful* manner are less likely to develop a fearful response to snakes after viewing a second video showing other monkeys responding *fearfully* to snakes, compared to monkeys who viewed the second video only (Mineka & Cook, 1993). Such findings highlight the role observational learning can play in the development of fears. However, such vicarious experiences (including acquiring a phobia through informational transmission) appear to occur relatively infrequently among most phobic individuals (Antony & Barlow, 2002).

Mowrer's (1939) *two-factor theory* combines classical conditioning and operant conditioning principles to explain how phobias are acquired and maintained. This model assumes that phobias are acquired through classical conditioning (as previously discussed) and contends they are maintained through operant conditioning. Operant conditioning theory holds that the likelihood of a behavior occurring in the future increases if the behavior has been followed by reinforcement in the past. Reinforcers can be of two general types, positive or negative, and it is negative reinforcement that applies to the second part of Mowrer's two-factor theory. Thus, a dog phobic, upon seeing a dog, will exhibit a conditioned fear response (e.g., accelerated heart rate, desire to flee) and will quickly leave the site where the dog is located. The individual will then experience a reduction in the uncomfortable feelings, thoughts, and physical reactions that had been stimulated upon seeing the dog. The removal or termination of this aversive state of affairs is a negative reinforcer that increases the likelihood that the same avoidance behavior vis-à-vis dogs will be exhibited in the future. Unfortunately, by avoiding contact with the feared stimulus, the individual does not have the opportunity to learn new, nonfearful associations to it. Exposure-based treatments for anxiety disorders provide just such opportunities to break old associations and replace them with new, adaptive ones.

Cognitive Theories

Cognitive theories of anxiety disorders emphasize the role that inaccurate and maladaptive thoughts play in the genesis and maintenance of anxiety. The work of Aaron T. Beck will serve to illustrate important principles embodied in cognitive approaches to anxiety disorders. While Beck recognized the evolutionarily adaptive value of innate fear responses, he believed that under circumstances in which emotional responses were exaggerated, inappropriate, or otherwise dysfunctional, cognitive factors (i.e., thoughts, beliefs) play a central role. A. T. Beck and Emery (1985, p. 31) noted that anxious individuals, in particular, are overly attuned to perceived sources of danger or threat and that anxiety disorders can be conceptualized as a "hypersensitive alarm system" in which

> the anxious patient is so sensitive to any stimuli that might be taken as indicating imminent disaster or harm that he is constantly warning himself, as it were, about the potential dangers. Because almost any stimulus can be perceived by him as dangerous and can "trip off" the alarm, the anxious patient experiences innumerable "false alarms," which keep him in a constant state of emotional stress and turmoil.

They further noted that individuals with anxiety disorders (a) experience decreased ability to logically evaluate the danger posed by different situations; (b) tend to catastrophize or dwell on the worst possible outcome in a situation and to overestimate the probability of such an event occurring; (c) selectively abstract from a situation those elements that confirm a belief that danger is present and ignore disconfirming elements; (d) appraise events in dichotomous terms (i.e., safe versus not safe), with no room for tolerating ambiguity; and (e) interpret information through a set of rules characterized by a heightened sense of danger and personal vulnerability. For example, a person with GAD might abide by personal rules such as "Any strange situation should be regarded as dangerous," "It is always best to assume the worst," and "My security and safety depend on anticipating and preparing myself at all times for possible danger" (Beck & Emery, 1985). Cognitive-behavioral forms of therapy, which have proven highly effective in the treatment of anxiety disorders, emphasize learning to recognize, label, and replace such inaccurate thoughts with ones that reflect a more realistic appraisal of oneself, others, and the environment.

Emotional Processing Theory

Over the past 20 years, Foa and Kozak's (1986) emotional processing theory has become increasingly influential in advancing our understanding of anxiety disorders. This theory is based on Lang's (1977) earlier conceptualization of fear structures (i.e., cognitive representations of objects or situations that have been associated with danger). Such structures are thought to be composed of a network of elements that include representations of the feared stimulus itself, response elements (e.g., physiological and behavioral reactions to the stimulus), and meaning propositions (e.g., interpretations regarding the degree of threat posed by the stimulus). When faced with a situation with features that match elements in an existing fear structure, these elements become activated; this activation then spreads to associated representations so that the entire fear structure is accessed. The fear structure can be likened to a computer program or data file that provides direction on how to respond (behaviorally, emotionally, and cognitively) to a given stimulus (Barlow, 2002a). Lang postulated that treatment of anxiety disorders involves a reorganization of the propositions contained in fear structures so that the emotional valence of their elements is changed.

Emotional processing theory extended Lang's work by focusing on the distinction between normal or adaptive fear structures and pathological ones, and noted that the latter are characterized by distortions of reality and excessive response elements such as avoiding situations most people would consider safe (Foa et al., 2006). Furthermore, it is assumed that pathological fear structures are resistant to modification because the affected individual typically engages in behavioral and cognitive forms of avoidance and displays information-processing biases that prevent the acquisition of corrective information that contradicts propositions of the fear structure (Foa et al., 2006).

Thus, emotional processing theory holds that to modify maladaptive fear structures two things must occur: (1) The fear structure must be activated, and (2) new information that is incompatible with maladaptive elements of the fear structure must be acquired (Foa et al., 2006). This theory provides a foundation for understanding the effects of exposure-based therapies; such treatments presumably activate fear structures by placing the individual in a situation with features that resemble those associated with the fear structure. However, Foa and colleagues note that if the fear structure is activated but no information-disconfirming propositions of the fear structure are presented (e.g., because the person avoids attending to such information through distraction or tries to escape the situation), the fear structure will not change and may even become stronger.

Emotional processing theory was initially applied to understanding Specific Phobia, Panic Disorder with Agoraphobia, and OCD, but has now been extended to the other major anxiety disorders.

INTAKE AND INTERVIEWING CONSIDERATIONS

Rapport

As has been reviewed, several years may pass between the time anxiety disorder symptoms first appear and when formal help is finally sought. Yet once individuals with anxiety disorders enter treatment, their motivation is often high and fueled by a desire to experience relief from the extreme distress they are experiencing. However, even these clients may be reluctant to openly talk about their anxiety symptoms because of embarrassment (e.g., about obsessions and compulsions, social fears) or concerns that discussing the symptoms and situations that provoke them will create more distress (e.g., in PTSD). Thus, it is important to adopt a patient attitude and to normalize the client's experiences (e.g., acknowledge the development of avoidance symptoms after a traumatic event). Because they may be experiencing extreme distress, anxious clients may express a desire to obtain some kind of relief as soon as possible. While it is important to provide these clients with realistic expectations regarding the pace of treatment and the likely time frame in which goals can be met, it is also helpful for the clinician to actively begin helping clients develop ways of coping with their symptoms. Providing education about the nature of the client's disorder and its symptoms can often provide a sense of relief, as can teaching simple relaxation strategies (e.g., diaphragmatic breathing). Because many of the recommended treatments for anxiety disorders involve exposure techniques that will require the client to purposefully confront feared situations, it is important to spend sufficient time explaining the rationale for this type of intervention and to convey a sense of confidence in the client's ability to complete exposure assignments.

Some clients with anxiety disorders engage in intellectualized rumination during treatment sessions, in which endless minute details of situations are rehashed with little connection to the associated emotional experiences. This avoidance of affect is important to eventually address. Emotional processing theory (reviewed earlier under "Etiology") reminds us that the ability to fully access all elements of fear structures is necessary to modify their pathological elements (Foa et al., 2006).

Interview and Assessment Strategies

An intake interview with a client suspected of an anxiety disorder should follow the basic outline presented in Chapter 1; however, the following points are particularly important to note. First, when a client expresses experiencing significant anxiety or fear, it is crucial to find out what *specific* objects, situations, or events trigger the fear and what the ultimate focus of the fear is (i.e., What is the client most afraid will happen if he or she comes in contact with the feared situation or object?). These pieces of information are necessary for the differential diagnostic process. Sometimes the response to these questions seems to provide a diagnostic answer, but closer scrutiny reveals that further inquiries are needed. This is discussed further under "Differential Diagnosis."

Because a history of childhood anxiety disorders and a family history of anxiety (and sometimes mood) disorders have been identified as poor prognostic factors for some anxiety disorders, it is important to inquire about these during the intake interview. It is also important to determine family members' reactions to the client's symptoms and to determine if they are a supportive resource for the client. In some cases, family members inadvertently reinforce the client's symptoms, as was reviewed earlier regarding the provision of reassurance to clients with OCD. It may be most useful to contact family members directly to obtain this information (with the client's permission). In such discussions, it is important not to convey a blaming attitude toward family members; in most cases, any reinforcement of the client's anxiety symptoms by relatives is not done purposefully, but is more likely to stem from a genuine desire to lessen the client's distress. Family members may be helpful allies in the treatment and can, for example, encourage and support the client in completing exposure-based homework assignments.

Structured Interviews and Self-Report Measures

Several good measures exist for evaluating anxiety disorders, including structured interviews such as the Structured Interview for the *DSM-IV* (SCID-IV; First, Spitzer, Williams, & M. Gibbon, 1995), Kiddie Schedule for Affective Disorders and Schizophrenia (K-SADS; Kaufman et al., 1997), and the child and adult versions of the Anxiety

Disorders Interview Schedule (ADIS; T. A. Brown, DiNardo, & Barlow, 1994; ADIS-IV-C, W. K. Silverman & Albano, 1996). As discussed in Chapter 1, structured measures have the advantage of providing a comprehensive evaluation of symptoms and decrease the likelihood that clinician bias or lack of knowledge will influence the interview results. Because anxiety disorders are frequently comorbid with other psychiatric conditions, it is important to inquire about symptoms in clinical domains other than anxiety. Omnibus structured interviews such as the SCID, K-SADS, and Diagnostic Interview Schedule for Children are useful in this regard because they do not solely focus on anxiety disorders. The ADIS primarily focuses on anxiety disorders, but also includes questions about conditions commonly comorbid with anxiety or that may have a clinical presentation similar to anxiety disorders (e.g., mood, somatoform, and substance use disorders). Table 11.4 summarizes a number of measures designed to assess specific anxiety disorders or features relevant to them. For additional information on these and other measures, the interested reader is referred to Antony, Orsillo, and Roemer (2001); Briere (2004); Keane and Barlow (2002); W. K. Silverman and Ollendick (2005); and C. L. Turk, Heimberg, and Mennin (2004).

Behavioral Avoidance Tests

A common characteristic of anxiety disorders is avoidance of situations, people, objects, or events that provoke high levels of anxiety. Although determining the extent of a client's avoidance behaviors can be accomplished simply by asking clients about situations they avoid, the use of a behavioral avoidance test (BAT) is also helpful. These tests are commonly used in the treatment of Panic Disorder with Agoraphobia, Specific Phobia, Social Phobia, and OCD. An example of a BAT in the evaluation of Panic Disorder with Agoraphobia provides an illustration of this technique (K. S. White & Barlow, 2002). From a hierarchy of situations in which the client fears having a panic attack, a representative sampling of about five items are selected that include those anticipated to provoke high levels of anxiety (e.g., standing in line at the supermarket, driving on the freeway). Over the course of about 1 to 2 hours, clients are asked to complete each item on the hierarchy and try to stay in the situation for a sufficient length of time and rate their anxiety at regular intervals throughout. Clients are allowed to terminate the test (or any portion of it) if the anxiety becomes unbearable. Ideally, clients complete the BAT without the therapist present to avoid the therapist serving as a safety signal that might enable clients to approach situations that they could not on their own. In addition to providing pretreatment baseline information about the degree of behavioral avoidance, a BAT can also be useful in tracking treatment progress.

Crisis, Legal, and Ethical Issues

Suicide Risk

For some clients with anxiety disorders, the distress caused by their symptoms and the associated impairment may lead to feelings of hopelessness and increase the risk for suicide. It is therefore important to evaluate current and past suicidal ideation and suicide attempts in clients suspected of or known to have an anxiety disorder. The empirical research on whether anxiety disorders are associated with increased risk of suicide has been

Table 11.4 Examples of anxiety assessment measures

Disorder	Measure (Authors and Publication Date)	Areas Assessed	Comments
Panic Disorder	Panic Disorder Severity Scale (PDSS) Shear et al. (1992)	Assesses 7 areas of Panic Disorder with Agoraphobia as experienced in the previous month (e.g., frequency of panic attacks, distress during attacks, interoceptive and situational avoidance).	Administered by a clinician with a completion time of 10–15 minutes; a self-report version has been developed and is undergoing evaluation.
Panic Disorder	Panic Attack Questionnaire—Revised (PAQ-R) B. J. Cox, Norton, and Swinson (1992)	Provides information related to the phenomenology of panic attacks, such as symptoms, situational triggers, and coping styles. Also evaluates past history and future expectancies regarding having panic attacks, course of panic attacks, functional impairment, and suicidal ideation.	Can be administered in 20–30 minutes; often used in research.
Specific Phobia	Fear Survey Schedule (FSS) Geer (1965; FSS-II); Wolpe and Lang (1997; FSS-III)	Two versions available (II and III), containing 51 and 72 items, respectively. Assesses fears associated with a number of situations relevant to Specific Phobia (e.g., airplanes, injections), Social Phobia, and Agoraphobia.	Examination of scores on specific items may be more useful than total score; often used in research; both versions have been translated into a number of different languages.
Specific Phobia	Fear Survey Schedule for Children Ollendick (1983)	Eighty-item inventory that assesses fears in a number of domains, including fear of danger or death, fear of the unknown, medical fears, fear of small animals, and fear of failure and criticism.	Based on the FSS; appropriate for ages 7–18.
Social Phobia	Social Phobia and Anxiety Inventory (SPAI) S. M. Turner, Beidel, and Dancu (1996)	Assesses cognitive, behavioral, and somatic aspects of Social Phobia across a range of settings; measure contains two subscales: Social Phobia and Agoraphobia.	Measure has been translated into several languages, including Spanish, French, Dutch, Swedish, Portuguese, and Icelandic.

Disorder	Measure	Description	Notes
Social Phobia	Social Phobia and Anxiety Inventory for Children (SPAI-C) Beidel, Turner, and Morris (1995)	Assesses situations that are often distressing for children with Social Phobia. Contains three subscales: Assertiveness/General Conversation, Traditional Social Encounters, and Public Performance.	Child version of the SPAI; appropriate for ages 8–17.
Obsessive-Compulsive Disorder (OCD)	Yale Brown Obsessive-Compulsive Scale (Y-BOCS) W. K. Goodman et al. (1989); Baer (2000); Scahill et al. (1997)	Contains sections assessing obsessions and compulsions; separate severity scores derived for each of these broad domains based on factors such as frequency, duration, interference, control over, distress, and resistance; additional questions asses associated features (e.g., insight, pervasive doubt, slowness).	Available in interview and self-report formats; child version available; administration time approximately 30 minutes; scores of 16 or higher on adult version and 15 or more on child version typically used to identify clinically elevated symptom levels.
OCD	Vancouver Obsessional Compulsive Inventory (VOCI) Thordarson et al. (2004)	Provides an assessment of a range of obsessions, compulsions, avoidance behavior, and personality characteristics of known or theoretical importance in OCD. Contains scales assessing contamination, checking, obsessions, hoarding, feeling things must be just right, and indecisiveness.	An updated version of the Maudsley Obsessional Compulsive Inventory, a measure widely employed in research studies to assess OCD symptoms.
Posttraumatic Stress Disorder (PTSD)	Trauma Symptom Inventory (TSI) Briere (1995)	One-hundred-item questionnaire that assesses symptoms related to PTSD and other problems that can occur in traumatized individuals. Contains 3 validity scales and 10 clinical scales. Examples of the clinical scales include Anxious Arousal, Intrusive Experiences, Defensive Avoidance, Dissociation, Depression, Anger/Irritability, Sexual Concerns.	Takes approximately 20–30 minutes to complete; child version also available.

(Continued)

Table 11.4 Examples of anxiety assessment measures

Disorder	Measure (Authors and Publication Date)	Areas Assessed	Comments
PTSD	Post-traumatic Diagnostic Scale (PDS) Foa, Cashman, Jaycox, and Perry (1997)	Contains checklist of traumatic events and client's reaction to them, as well as 17 symptoms of PTSD (rated on a scale assessing intensity and frequency); also assesses impairment in nine areas of life functioning.	Items derived directly from *DSM* criteria; can be administered in 10–15 minutes; also available in interview form.
Generalized Anxiety Disorder (GAD)	Generalized Anxiety Disorder Questionnaire-IV M. G. Newman et al. (2002)	Nine-item questionnaire assessing the uncontrollability and excessive worry and severity of related physical symptoms (including one open-ended question asking for a list of most frequent worry topics).	Assesses *DSM-IV* symptoms of GAD; client must meet cutoff scores on various item groups for a diagnosis of GAD to be indicated.
GAD	Penn State Worry Questionnaire (PSWQ) T. J. Meyer, Miller, Metzger, and Borkovec (1990); Stöber and Bittencourt (1998); Chorpita, Tracey, Brown, Collica, and Barlow (1997)	Sixteen-item scale assessing the extent to which worry is uncontrollable, excessive, and pervasive.	Used extensively in research studies on GAD; a weekly version, suitable for tracking progress in treatment, is available; a child and adolescent version is available; the measure has been translated into several languages (e.g., Chinese, German, French, Spanish).

somewhat inconsistent and, for some disorders, not well investigated. Coryell, Noyes, and House (1986) reported a 20% suicide rate among individuals with Panic Disorder when they were followed over a 35-year period, and Weissman, Klerman, Markowitz, and Ouellette (1989), in an analysis of data from the ECA survey, also reported the rate of lifetime suicide attempts among those diagnosed with Panic Disorder was 20%. However, following these studies debate ensued; some studies found that suicide attempts among anxiety disordered individuals occurred only among those with comorbid conditions, such as depression, whereas others found that elevated risk of suicide remained even in the absence of such comorbidity (see Barlow, 2002a). Suicide risk has not been well studied in anxiety disorders such as GAD and OCD. However, a recent study that analyzed the FDA database containing information on participants from clinical drug trials found that suicide risk among patients with anxiety disorders is higher than in the general population by a factor of 10 or more and that suicide risk was high regardless of the type of anxiety disorder (Khan, Leventhal, Khan, & Brown, 2002).

Ruling Out Medical Concerns

Symptoms of anxiety disorders can be mimicked by potentially serious medical conditions and the effects of certain substances. For example, among the medical disorders that can produce symptoms resembling those seen in Panic Disorder are cardiovascular diseases (e.g., mitral valve prolapse, myocardial infarction, congestive heart failure), neurological diseases (e.g., epilepsy, multiple sclerosis, brain tumors, cerebrovascular disease), pulmonary diseases (e.g., asthma, pulmonary embolus), endocrine diseases (e.g., diabetes, thyroid disorders, hypoglycemia), electrolyte imbalances, systemic infections, and systemic lupus erythematosus (H. I. Kaplan & Saddock, 1998). Panic Disorder symptoms can also be caused by intoxication from drugs, including amphetamines, cocaine, marijuana, hallucinogens, nicotine, and amyl nitrate, and from withdrawal from alcohol, opiates, and sedative hypnotics (H. I. Kaplan & Saddock, 1998). Because medical conditions may cause anxiety symptoms that can be reversed with appropriate treatment, and because some of these medical conditions can be extremely serious (e.g., heart condition, neurological disorders), it is imperative for a clinician to determine if the client has recently seen a physician to evaluate the possibility of a medical condition or substance playing an etiologic role in the client's symptoms and to refer the client for such an evaluation if one has not been recently completed.

Mandated Reporting That May Arise from Trauma Interviews

When evaluating a history of trauma and PTSD-related symptoms, a clinician may encounter reports of child physical or sexual abuse. Obviously, if the client is a child or adolescent (i.e., under age 18), the clinician will be required to report the abuse to the appropriate authorities under the child abuse reporting laws that exist in each state. However, if the client is an adult, the clinician should be familiar with appropriate state laws regarding the need to report the alleged perpetrator of the abuse if it is determined that this individual continues to have contact with minors. In addition, as previously noted, some individuals with PTSD (e.g., male veterans) may exhibit increased impulsivity and aggressiveness following the trauma and may become abusive toward family members. Thus, evaluation of potential child and partner abuse is warranted if there are any indicators of anger control problems or impulsivity.

DIAGNOSTIC CONSIDERATIONS

Common Comorbidities

Depression

Major Depressive Disorder is the most common comorbidity observed among the anxiety disorders. In a sample of 968 individuals diagnosed with *DSM-IV*-defined anxiety disorders the rates of current comorbid depression for individual anxiety disorders were as follows: Panic Disorder with Agoraphobia 24%, Panic Disorder without Agoraphobia 23%, Social Phobia 14%, GAD 26%, OCD 22%, Specific Phobia 3%, and PTSD 69%. Lifetime prevalence rates of comorbid Major Depressive Disorder in this same sample are even more striking: Panic Disorder with Agoraphobia 52%, Panic Disorder without Agoraphobia 50%, Social Phobia 44%, GAD 64%, OCD 61%, Specific Phobia 27%, and PTSD 77% (Brown & Barlow, 2002). The frequent co-occurrence of depression and anxiety has raised as yet unanswered questions about the relationship between these two classes of disorders. The *DSM-IV* Task Force (Frances et al., 1992) noted that the relationship between anxiety and depression could reflect (a) distinct but coexisting syndromes, (b) syndromes that predispose to one another, (c) overlap in the definition of symptoms of each class of disorder, or (d) symptoms that have different external manifestations but a shared underlying cause.

With regard to the second of the *DSM-IV* Task Force's points, epidemiologic studies have found that prior anxiety disorder history is a strong predictor of subsequent Major Depressive Disorder (R. C. Kessler, Nelson, McGonagle, Liu, et al., 1996). Related to this, there is some evidence that the preponderance of female versus male depression may be partially accounted for by the higher frequency of anxiety disorders in women (Parker & Hadzi-Pavlovic, 2001). Bittner and colleagues (2004) found that among individuals with anxiety disorders, the risk of developing Major Depressive Disorder was significantly increased when any of the following were present: more than one anxiety disorder, comorbid panic attacks, and (in particular) severe impairment due to the anxiety disorder. Comorbid anxiety and depression are associated with greater impairment in psychosocial functioning and higher utilization rates of mental health resources compared to those with either depression alone or anxiety alone (Wittchen & Essau, 1993). When a depressive disorder is a primary diagnosis, the presence of comorbid anxiety is associated with higher levels of hopelessness and suicidal ideation (Chioqueta & Stiles, 2003). In any client presenting with comorbid anxiety and depression it is important to assess suicidal ideation. In addition, if the comorbid depression is severe, the client may feel unmotivated to complete anxiety-provoking exposures that form the basis of many recommended anxiety treatments, and it may be necessary to first address and stabilize the client's depressive symptoms before proceeding with the anxiety disorder treatment.

Substance Use Disorders

Substance use disorders are commonly encountered in many anxiety disorders. As was noted in the earlier discussion of the PTSD, rates of substance use disorders among this clinical population are high. With regard to anxiety disorders more generally, data from the ECA survey found that among individuals with any anxiety disorder, there were 50% and 70% increases in the odds of receiving an alcohol disorder diagnosis or a substance use disorder diagnosis, respectively. Panic Disorder and OCD were among the specific anxiety disorders associated with increased odds of receiving a diagnosis of alcohol or drug dependence (Reiger et al., 1990). Findings from the National Comorbidity Survey found that Social Phobia, Simple Phobia, Agoraphobia, and GAD were associated with significantly increased odds of being diagnosed with Alcohol Dependence (R. C. Kessler, Crum, et al., 1997). Data from the 2001–2003 NESARC provides information on the co-morbidity rates of *DSM-IV*-defined substance use disorders for Panic Disorder, Social Phobia, Specific Phobia, and GAD. The NESARC is a large-scale survey of over 43,000 adults drawn from the U.S. civilian, noninstitutionalized population. Rates of any drug use disorder (i.e., dependence or abuse) were Panic Disorder with Agoraphobia 34.2%, Social Phobia 22.3%, Specific Phobia 18.8%, and GAD 23%. The most common specific class of substance use disorders in these groups was marijuana use disorders (Panic Disorder with Agoraphobia 25.6%, Social Phobia 17.8%, Specific Phobia 14.9%, and GAD 18.5%). Panic Disorder with Agoraphobia was also characterized by an elevated rate of sedative use disorders (19.5%; Conway et al., 2006).

The relationship between anxiety disorders and drug and alcohol disorders may reflect any of a number of causal hypotheses: (a) Self-medication relieves anxiety symptoms; (b) Pathological alcohol or drug use directly promotes the development of anxiety disorders; or (c) Shared biological (e.g., genetic) and/or psychosocial factors predispose an individual to develop both types of disorder (Kushner, Abrams, & Borchardt, 2000). Kushner et al. propose an integrative feed-forward model for comorbid anxiety and alcohol use disorders in which drinking is initially maintained by the immediate negative reinforcement of anxiety reduction. However, prolonged alcohol use is postulated to worsen anxiety symptoms, potentially through biological changes (e.g., lower plasma levels of GABA, increased norepinephrine activity during withdrawal states), psychosocial factors (e.g., increasing number of stressful life events that may precipitate exacerbations in anxiety), and psychological factors (e.g., decreasing or narrowing attention, which may facilitate focus on environmental threat cues). This worsening anxiety is then thought to promote further drinking and create a vicious cycle.

Personality Disorders

There is a high co-occurrence of Axis II personality disorders, particularly Avoidant Personality Disorder and Dependent Personality Disorder, among individuals with anxiety disorders. Data from the 2001–2003 NESARC provides information on the comorbidity rates of *DSM-IV*-defined personality disorders for Panic Disorder, Social Phobia, Specific Phobia, and GAD. Low rates of personality disorders were observed among those with Specific Phobia (ranging from 2.9% for Antisocial Personality Disorder to 5.4% for Histrionic Personality Disorder). For those with Panic Disorder with Agoraphobia, GAD, and Social Phobia, the highest rates of Axis II comorbidity were seen for Avoidant Personality Disorder and Dependent Personality Disorder. For Avoidant Personality Disorder, prevalence rates were Panic Disorder with Agoraphobia 21%, GAD 14.2%, and Social Phobia 27.3%. For Dependent Personality Disorder, prevalence rates were Panic Disorder with Agoraphobia 37.2%, GAD 18.6%, and Social Phobia, 17.2% (B. F. Grant et al., 2005). Other studies have found Avoidant and Dependent Personality Disorders to be most common among those with OCD, with rates being as high as 27% to 56% and 39% to 56%, respectively, according to some studies (see Steketee, 1993). Obsessive-Compulsive

Personality Disorder is not one of the more common Axis II comorbidities for OCD, despite their similar-sounding names. Among those with Cluster B personality disorders, PTSD is frequently comorbid. Among those with Borderline Personality Disorder, rates of concurrent PTSD are high, ranging from 25% to 56% (Golier et al., 2003; Mueser, Goodman, et al., 1998; Zanarini et al., 1998). Those with a history of pervasive and prolonged trauma that began at an early age (e.g., severe childhood physical and sexual abuse) are likely to present with what Herman (1992) calls "complex PTSD" or a complex constellation of symptoms (e.g., PTSD, other anxiety disorders, mood disorders, somatoform disorders) that may include borderline personality pathology. Individuals with PTSD and comorbid Borderline Personality Disorder report significantly higher levels of general distress, anxiety, depression, and physical illness than those with Borderline Personality Disorder alone (E. E. Bolton, Mueser, & Rosenberg, 2006).

It should be noted that the high co-occurrence of Social Phobia and Avoidant Personality Disorder has raised questions about the relationship of these two disorders, particularly with regard to the generalized subtype. Examination of the diagnostic criteria for Avoidant Personality Disorder (e.g., avoidance of interpersonal activities because of fears of criticism, rejection, or disapproval; preoccupation with being criticized in social situations; viewing oneself as socially inept, unappealing, or inferior to others) reveals obvious similarities to the diagnostic criteria for Social Phobia. Some contend that these two disorders cannot be meaningfully differentiated from one another on the basis of factors such as clinical presentation, response to medication or psychotherapeutic treatment, course, and patterns of comorbidity with other Axis II disorders (Reich, 2000). It has also been suggested that Social Phobia and Avoidant Personality Disorder represent different points on the same underlying continuum of social anxiety (Hofmann & Barlow, 2002). This diagnostic classification controversy notwithstanding, Beidel and Turner (1998) note that clients presenting with Social Phobia and a comorbid diagnosis of Avoidant Personality Disorder pose particular challenges to therapists because of these clients' extreme level of sensitivity, which may translate into a "paranoid-like" style of thinking, particularly under periods of stress. Such clients may need to be reassured that exposure activities in therapy are not intended to humiliate them, but instead are intended to help them overcome their fears of social situations.

Differential Diagnosis

Anxiety Disorders versus Other Psychiatric Disorders

Mood Disorders   Depressed individuals may present with ruminations, anxious affect, concentration difficulties, social withdrawal, and somatic symptoms (e.g., sleep disturbance, fatigue) that can appear similar to symptoms seen in several anxiety disorders. Making this distinction more challenging is the fact that anxiety and depressive disorders are frequently comorbid. With regard to specific disorders, the social withdrawal seen in depression could be mistaken for social avoidance associated with Social Phobia, or the reluctance to leave one's home mistaken for Panic Disorder with Agoraphobia or pure Agoraphobia. An important difference between avoidance associated with anxiety disorders and that seen in depression is that in the latter this behavior is observed in the context of sad mood and/or anhedonia and is likely to improve when the depression lifts.

Similarly, the concentration problems seen in depression, which might be difficult to distinguish from OCD- or GAD-related ruminations, are more likely to be associated with depressive, self-deprecating themes and to dissipate with improvement in mood.

Psychotic Disorders   Conditions such as Schizophrenia, Schizoaffective Disorder, and Delusional Disorder are characterized by unusual beliefs and perceptions that may sometimes be difficult to distinguish from those that can be seen in some anxiety disorders. Obsessions in OCD that are firmly held may appear similar to delusions. However, delusions in psychotic disorders are not typically linked to the performance of compulsions or rituals. Furthermore, whereas those with OCD recognize that their obsessive thoughts are a product of their own mind, some (but not all) psychotic individuals may believe that delusional thoughts have been placed in their mind by some other source. Individuals experiencing PTSD-related flashbacks may appear similar to persons with psychotic disorders who are having hallucinations, and during such episodes client behavior may seem chaotic and disorganized. A difference between these conditions is that in PTSD the symptoms are typically triggered by exposure to cues that are reminiscent of a prior trauma; in addition, one would not expect to see delusions, grossly disorganized speech, or prominent negative symptoms in an individual with PTSD (although symptoms of emotional numbing could appear similar to the restricted affect observed in some psychotic disorders). Psychotic individuals are sometimes socially avoidant, which could be mistaken for social avoidance seen in the context of anxiety disorders such as Social Phobia and Panic Disorder with Agoraphobia. Similarly, some persons with psychotic disorders may express fear of and avoid specific situations or objects, in a manner that might appear similar to what is seen in a Specific Phobia. However, among psychotic individuals, one will also see associated symptoms (e.g., delusions, hallucinations, grossly disorganized speech) that are not associated with anxiety disorders. For example, a psychotic individual may avoid snakes because he is convinced they are agents of the devil, whereas an individual with Specific Phobia avoids them because she is afraid the snake may bite or harm her.

Somatoform Disorders   The multiple physical complaints and associated worry seen in Somatization Disorder may be difficult to differentiate from anxiety disorders such as Panic Disorder and GAD, which also have physical symptoms as part of the clinical picture. However, the prominent somatic symptoms of Panic Disorder are typically present only during periods of panic attacks. In GAD, although physical complaints may be present along with worry, the worry is not confined to concerns about one's physical health, as it is in Somatization Disorder and Hypochondriasis. It can be quite challenging to differentiate the preoccupations with physical health or with a perceived physical defect that characterize Hypochondriasis and Body Dysmorphic Disorder, respectively, from obsessions associated with OCD. What can be helpful is to thoroughly assess the presence of other nonbody- or health-related obsessions, which could then point to a primary or possibly comorbid OCD diagnosis. Steketee and Pigott (2006) further note that in contrast to Hypochondriasis, most clients with OCD recognize that their obsessive thoughts are excessive. They also note that when checking behavior is present in Hypochondriasis (e.g., checking the body for potentially cancerous moles), an alternative or secondary diagnosis of OCD should be considered.

Adjustment Disorder　A *DSM-IV* diagnosis of Adjustment Disorder can be considered when an individual develops emotional or behavioral symptoms in response to and within 3 months of an identifiable stressor, and the *DSM-IV* indicates that such a disorder may be marked by prominent anxiety symptoms such as nervousness, worry, or jitteriness (American Psychiatric Association, 2000b). Symptoms of an Adjustment Disorder must not persist beyond 6 months after the stressor (or its consequences) has terminated (American Psychiatric Association, 2000b). An Adjustment Disorder diagnosis should not be given when the client's symptoms meet the criteria for another Axis I anxiety disorder or it is clear that the presenting symptoms represent an exacerbation of a known preexisting anxiety disorder. Novice clinicians often make the mistake of assuming that if a client's anxiety symptoms developed at the time that an identifiable stressor was present, this means an Adjustment Disorder is indicated. Axis I anxiety disorders can develop at a time when notable stressors are present in an individual's life and, of course, a diagnosis of PTSD or Acute Stress Disorder require that the individual was exposed to a stressor.

Anxiety Disorders Due to a General Medication Condition or Substances　As has been noted, a wide variety of medical conditions and substances can cause symptoms that appear similar to those seen in primary anxiety disorders, and these causes must always be considered and ruled out in a client presenting with anxiety symptoms. In making such a differential diagnosis, the clinician must consider the timing of the onset of the medical condition or substance use relative to the onset of the anxiety symptoms, whether the medical condition or substance in question could have reasonably caused the anxiety symptoms seen, and if there has ever been a period when the anxiety symptoms were present but the client was not under the influence of or withdrawing from any substance nor suffering from a medical condition that could produce anxiety symptoms. A detailed discussion of making a differential diagnosis between a primary psychiatric disorder and a substance-induced psychiatric disorder is provided in Chapter 8.

Table 11.5 summarizes differential diagnostic information for the anxiety disorders.

Among the Anxiety Disorders

Table 11.6 presents key and discriminating features among the anxiety disorders. The following discussion is prefaced with a reminder to the clinician that anxiety disorders frequently co-occur with one another. Apprehension and avoidance characterize all of the anxiety disorders, and it is our experience that beginning clinicians sometimes become overly focused on the avoidance factor when making a differential diagnosis among the anxiety disorders and do not obtain sufficient information about what is at the center of the client's fears and apprehension. For example, if a clinician learns that a client is afraid of traveling on airplanes, he or she may automatically assume that a Specific Phobia is present. The clinician might then conclude that additional symptoms, such as experiencing intense anxiety when in a plane, avoidance of flying, recognition that the fear is excessive, and impairment and distress, confirm the presence of a Specific Phobia, situational type. However, what is missing is an exploration of *why* the client is fearful of flying. What is the client afraid will happen if he or she flies? Suppose that the client discloses any one of the following: (a) The fear is related to a concern that the client will

Table 11.5   Between-category diagnostic differential

Disorder	Similarities with Anxiety Disorders	Differences from Anxiety Disorders
Mood disorders (Depression)	Social withdrawal Concentration problems Ruminations Somatic complaints (e.g., fatigue, sleep disturbance)	Symptoms are linked to dysphoric mood and/or anhedonia and are alleviated when mood improves. Ruminations are likely to have depressive, self-deprecating quality.
Psychotic disorders	Unusual or irrational beliefs Social avoidance Seemingly disorganized behavior (PTSD) Hallucinatory experiences (PTSD)	Unusual beliefs are held with delusional intensity. Presence of hallucinations, grossly disorganized speech and/or behavior, prominent negative symptoms (for differential with PTSD: hallucinatory experiences and disorganized behavior are not confined to trauma-cued flashbacks).
Somatoform disorders	Physical symptoms Excessive worry	Physical symptoms are not confined to panic attacks (differential with Panic Disorder). Worries are focused on health and not other areas or about having a panic attack or consequences of a panic attack (differential with GAD and Panic Disorder).
Substance intoxication or withdrawal	Affective symptoms Possibly other cognitive (e.g., attention problems) and somatic symptoms (e.g., sleep disturbance)	Symptoms follow ingestion or (in dependent individuals) withdrawal of substance. Symptoms are known to be associated with substance effects. Symptoms remit when intoxication or withdrawal syndromes remit.
Medical conditions	Affective symptoms Possibly other cognitive (e.g., attention problems) and somatic symptoms (e.g., sleep disturbance)	Symptoms follow onset of medical condition. Symptoms are known to be associated with medical condition. Symptoms remit when medical condition is successfully treated.
Adjustment disorder with anxiety	Anxiety symptoms (worry, nervousness, jitteriness) Symptoms develop in response to identifiable stressor (required for Adjustment Disorder, PTSD, and Acute Stress Disorder; identifiable stressor may be present at onset of other anxiety disorders as well)	Symptoms do not meet criteria for an Axis I anxiety disorder. Symptoms remit within 6 months of termination of stressor.

Table 11.6   Anxiety disorders: key and discriminating features

Disorder	Key Features	Discriminating Features
Panic Disorder (with or without Agoraphobia)	Recurrent, unexpected panic attacks	Fear of having additional attacks, worry about the implication of having additional attacks, or significant change in behavior related to having panic attacks.
Specific Phobia	Marked persistent fear that is excessive or unreasonable Stimulus-response type reaction to fear (i.e., fear provoked almost immediately on exposure to phobic stimulus Recognition that fear is unreasonable	Fear is cued by presence or anticipation of a specific object or situation.
Social Phobia	Marked persistent fear that is excessive or unreasonable Stimulus-response type reaction to fear (i.e., fear provoked almost immediately on exposure to phobic stimulus Recognition that fear is unreasonable	Fear is cued by social or performance situations involving unfamiliar others or possible scrutiny by others. Individuals fear they will do something humiliating or embarrassing in social situations.
Obsessive-Compulsive Disorder (OCD)	Obsessions and compulsions Recognition that fear is unreasonable	Obsessions and compulsions are time-consuming and cause impairment or distress.
Posttraumatic Stress Disorder (PTSD)	Exposure to traumatic event Persistent reexperiencing of traumatic event (e.g., intrusive thoughts, nightmares, flashbacks) Avoidance behavior Increased arousal symptoms following trauma (e.g., exaggerated startle response)	Avoidance behavior is related to stimuli associated with the trauma. Diminished emotional responsiveness to the world (e.g., emotional numbing, sense of foreshortened future).
Generalized Anxiety Disorder (GAD)	Excessive anxiety and worry Worry is difficult to control At least three associated physical or cognitive symptoms (e.g., restlessness, fatigue, concentration problems)	Worry concerns multiple life circumstances (e.g., work, family relationships, financial concerns, health).

Reprinted with permission from the *Diagnostic and Statistical Manual of Mental Disorders, fourth Edition, Text Revision* (Copyright 2000). American Psychiatric Association.

be exposed to contaminating germs from the recirculating air on the plane; (b) the fear is connected to a previous experience in which the client was on a plane that was hijacked; or (c) the fear is related to being in a place from which it would be difficult to escape if the client had a panic attack. These alternative scenarios would dramatically change the diagnostic possibilities: *a* suggests OCD, *b* suggests PTSD, and *c* suggests Panic Disorder with Agoraphobia. Thus, in evaluating anxiety disorders it is critical to determine not only the situations that an individual may be avoiding because of his or her apprehensions or fears but also what is the central focus of the apprehension or fear.

TREATMENT

General Principles in Treating Anxiety Disorders

J. R. T. Davidson (2006) identified seven broad goals of the treatment for Social Phobia, which are useful to apply to the anxiety disorders more generally: (1) Reduce fear, (2) correct maladaptive cognitive patterns, (3) reduce avoidance, (4) reduce physiological arousal, (5) reduce comorbid disorders, (6) restore daily functioning, and (7) improve quality of life. Because many recommended psychotherapy treatments to be discussed involve the purposeful and systematic exposure to situations or objects that are the focus of fear and that are likely being avoided, many clients may express reluctance to engage in this form of treatment. Providing education on the role that avoidance plays in maintaining anxiety symptoms is therefore crucial to increasing the likelihood of treatment adherence. Treatment will be more complex and challenging when another Axis I or II disorder is present since comorbidity has been linked to poorer treatment outcome.

Pharmacologic and psychotherapeutic treatments for anxiety disorders will now be reviewed in detail. Table 11.7 provides a general summary of treatment interventions for anxiety disorders.

Medication

Medications most often used to treat clients with anxiety disorders are benzodiazepines, antidepressants, and the novel compound buspirone (U.S. Department of Health and Human Services, 1999). Each of these drug classes will be briefly reviewed. However, a few preliminary points should be noted. First, pharmacologic treatment of Specific Phobia will not be discussed because this class of anxiety disorder is not routinely treated with medication. Occasionally, benzodiazepines or beta blockers are prescribed for a phobic individual to take in the feared situation, but these medications are generally not considered effective in the long run and may prevent the emotional processing of fear that is considered to be a critical mechanism underlying exposure-based treatments (Antony & Barlow, 2002). Second, nonpharmacologic somatic treatments for OCD will not be discussed because these are beyond the scope of this chapter and some of these treatments are rarely used (e.g., neurosurgical approaches such as cingulotomy and capsulotomy), have not proven to be effective for large numbers of individuals (e.g., ECT), or are still in the early stages of investigation (e.g., transcranial magnetic stimulation, deep brain stimulation). Finally, adjunctive medications such as mood stabilizers and antipsychotics will not be reviewed. Antipsychotics may be used to treat comorbid, psychotic-like features in PTSD or anxiety symptoms that have been refractory to other medications, and mood stabilizers may be used to treat mood instability

Table 11.7　Treatment interventions for anxiety disorders

Area	Interventions
Therapeutic interventions	Psychoeducation
	Exposure to stimuli that provoke anxiety and avoidance behavior
	Symptom monitoring (e.g., tracking frequency and severity of symptoms)
	Cognitive restructuring
	Relaxation exercises (e.g., progressive muscle relaxation, diaphragmatic breathing)
	Homework assignments to apply skills learned in session to real-world settings (e.g., exposure assignments)
	Use of behavioral avoidance tests to assess baseline levels of avoidance and track treatment progress
	Suicide assessment
Adjunctive interventions	Medical referral to rule out general medical conditions as cause of anxiety symptoms
	Possible medication referral
Family interventions	Involvement of family members to assist clients in carrying out treatment homework assignments
	Psychoeducation
	Family therapy and/or support groups if client's anxiety disorder has had significant negative impact on family functioning (e.g., PTSD)
	Disorder-Specific Interventions
Social Phobia	Possible social skills training
Obsessive-Compulsive Disorder (OCD)	Prevention of compulsive behaviors and rituals during exposure treatment (i.e., exposure and *response prevention*)
Posttraumatic Stress Disorder (PTSD)	Eye movement desensitization and reprocessing (EMDR)

(Vieweg et al., 2006). Antipsychotic agents may also be used as adjunctive therapy for OCD.

Benzodiazepines

Benzodiazepines are widely prescribed medications that can rapidly produce anti-anxiety and sedative-hypnotic effects, presumably by enhancing the inhibitory neurotransmitter systems involving GABA. Among the benzodiazepines most commonly prescribed for anxiety disorders are alprazolam, lorazepam, clonazepam, and diazepam. The first two of these agents have short half-lives (i.e., 6 to 12 hours and 10 to 20 hours, respectively), whereas the latter two have longer half-lives (30 to 40 hours and 20 to 100 hours, respectively). Diazepam has been found to be more slowly metabolized by Asians, such that lower doses may achieve the same blood concentrations as in Caucasians (Burroughs, Maxey, & Levy, 2002). The primary advantage of benzodiazepines is their rapid onset of action, which will provide clients with more immediate symptomatic relief than antidepressants (which may take several weeks to work). However, a drawback of benzo-diazepine use is the potential for drug dependence to develop (particularly for those agents that have more rapid onset of effects). Although tolerance to the sedative effects of benzodiazepines can occur, tolerance to the *anxiolytic effects* is of less concern (K. S. White & Barlow, 2002). Of greater concern are the withdrawal symptoms that can occur if the medication is abruptly discontinued (e.g., anxiety, restlessness, dizziness, tremor, sleep disturbance). Therefore, when a decision is made to stop benzodiazepine treatment, the medication must be tapered slowly, and education should be provided to the client about what to expect during the withdrawal process (e.g., possible withdrawal symptoms; Kasper & Resinger, 2001). Many individuals will have difficulty tolerating the withdrawal process and end up taking the medication again (Gosselin, Ladouceur, Morin, Dugas, & Baillargeon, 2004). Sometimes benzodiazepines are used in conjunction with antidepres-sants and are slowly tapered after the antidepressant begins to take effect. Benzodiaze-pines do not have strong anti-obsessional effects and are generally not used to alleviate symptoms in either OCD or PTSD (but may be prescribed as a palliative treatment to relieve but not eliminate symptoms; U.S. Department of Health and Human Services, 1999).

Panic Disorder   A number of benzodiazepine medications have been used in the treat-ment of Panic Disorder, including alprazolam (the first medication approved by the FDA for the treatment of Panic Disorder with Agoraphobia), clonazepam, lorazepam, and dia-zepam (for reviews, see White & White, 2002; C. J. Cox, Endler, Lee, & Swinson, 1992; Kasper & Resinger, 2001). Randomized controlled trials of these medications have found them superior to placebo in treating symptoms such as generalized anxiety, panic-related symptoms, and phobic avoidance; in lessening the frequency of panic attacks; and in re-ducing illness-related disability. Side effects commonly reported by participants in clini-cal trials include drowsiness and sedation, incoordination, slurred speech, fatigue, memory problems, and sexual problems (Kasper & Resinger, 2001). Up to one third of individuals with Panic Disorder who are treated with benzodiazepines develop physical dependence on the medication, with higher dosages and longer time taking the medication being more likely to lead to dependence (Pecknold, 1993).

Social Phobia   There have been few double-blind, controlled trials of benzodiazepine treatment for Social Phobia, and their results provide mixed support for this use of this medication class. J. R. T. Davidson et al. (1993) found that 78% of patients receiving clonazepam were much improved or very much improved compared to only 20% in the placebo condition. Those in the clonazepam group also exhibited greater improvement on measures of work and social functioning. In contrast, Gelernter and colleagues (1991), in a double-blind study of alprazolam, phenelzine, placebo, and CBT, found that only 38% of patients on alprazolam were considered treatment responders at 12 weeks (compared to 69% for phenelzine).

Generalized Anxiety Disorder   Studies of benzodiazepine treatment for GAD have found it to be an effective treatment (J. R. Davidson, 2004; Lydiard, Brawman-Mintzer, & Ballenger, 1996). However, antidepressants are typically favored over benzodiazepines, particularly if long-term treatment is anticipated, due to the former's ability to address comorbid depression that may emerge (Lydiard & Monnier, 2004). In addition, concerns about dependence may arise. A recent study examined the effectiveness of including a CBT intervention with a medication-tapering protocol among individuals with GAD who had been using the medication for more than 1 year. Participants were randomly assigned into the medication taper + CBT condition or a medication taper + nondirective supportive therapy condition. Results demonstrated that nearly 75% of participants in the CBT condition completely stopped using benzodiazepines, compared to 37% in the control condition. Data from 3-, 6-, and 12-month follow-ups confirmed the maintenance of complete benzodiazepine cessation, found that discontinuation rates remained twice as high in the CBT condition, and determined that the number of patients who no longer met GAD criteria was also greater in the CBT condition (Gosselin, Ladouceur, Morin, Dugas, & Baillargeon, 2004).

Posttraumatic Stress Disorder   Although benzodiazepines may reduce anxiety and improve sleep among those with PTSD, they may not eliminate or control the core triad of PTSD symptoms (i.e., reexperiencing, avoidance, and hyperarousal), and their use may interfere with the cognitive processing of the trauma (Vieweg et al., 2006). In addition, the potential for abuse of this medication class is of concern given the high rates of comorbid substance use disorders seen among individuals with PTSD.

Antidepressants

Because of their anti-anxiety, antipanic, and anti-obsessional effects, combined with the lack of addiction potential, antidepressant medications are commonly used in the treatment of a range of anxiety disorders and are generally favored over benzodiazepines. When an antidepressant is effective in treating anxiety, it is typically continued for a minimum of 4 to 6 months; if a decision is made to stop medication treatment, the drug is slowly tapered to avoid activation of anxiety symptoms. Although tricyclic antidepressants have been found to be effective in treating several anxiety disorders, they are typically considered second-line agents behind the SSRIs (American Psychiatric Association, 1998). Tricyclics have problematic side and safety effect profiles, including anticholinergic side effects (e.g., constipation, dry mouth), sedation, and weight gain. They are also associated with a risk of serious cardiovascular complications, including cardiac slowing and arrhythmias, and it is relatively easy to fatally overdose on a TCA.

Panic Disorder   The TCA clomipramine has demonstrated efficacy in reducing the frequency of panic attacks, anticipatory anxiety, and associated disability of Panic Disorder (Bakker, van Dyck, Spinhoven, & van Balkom, 1999; Fahy, O'Rourke, Brophy, Schazmann, & Sciascia, 1992), although the placebo-controlled study by Bakker and colleagues found no difference between the clomipramine and placebo groups in the percentage of individuals who were free of panic at 12 weeks. Fairly high dropout rates (e.g., 45%) due to adverse side effects have been reported in clomipramine treatment studies, and common side effects include dry mouth, constipation, tremor, nausea, vomiting, orthostatic hypotension, and metallic taste in the mouth (Kasper & Reisinger, 2001). The SSRIs paroxetine, sertraline, fluoxetine, and fluvoxamine are very effective in the treatment of Panic Disorder. Results from randomized, controlled trials have demonstrated the superiority of the SSRIs over placebo in treating panic-related anxiety, frequency of panic attacks, anticipatory anxiety, and associated depression and in reducing illness-related disability and global impairment (Kasper & Reisinger, 2001).

Social Phobia   Paroxetine was approved by the FDA for treatment of Social Phobia in 1999, and results of placebo-controlled, double-blind studies have found it superior to placebo, with as many as 70% of patients exhibiting a treatment response. Sertraline has also been found to produce significant changes on measures of Social Phobia symptoms compared to placebo (see Blanco, García, & Liebowitz, 2004, for a review). In addition, Blomhoff and colleagues (2001) found that combined sertraline and exposure treatment and sertraline alone were significantly superior to placebo. Studies of fluvoxamine have found that 43% to 46% of patients respond to treatment, compared to 7% to 23% of those on placebo (M. B. Stein, Fyer, Davidson, Pollack, & Wiita, 1999; van Vliet, den Boer, & Westenberg, 1994). The MAOI phenelzine has also demonstrated effectiveness in treating Social Phobia in two double-blind, placebo-controlled trials (Gelernter et al., 1991; Heimberg et al., 1998). However, phenelzine has been associated with greater relapse rates compared to CBT treatment following a treatment-free follow-up period (Hofmann & Barlow, 2002).

Obsessive-Compulsive Disorder   The SSRIs fluoxetine, sertraline, paroxetine, and fluvoxamine and the TCA clomipramine have all been proven effective in the treatment of OCD (Steketee & Barlow, 2002). In their review of medication treatments for OCD, Steketee and Pigott (2006) concluded that SSRIs reduce OCD symptoms by approximately 30% over baseline levels. In comparison to anxiety disorders such as Panic Disorder, SSRI treatment for OCD generally requires higher doses for effectiveness. Therapeutic effects may not be seen for up to 10 weeks. Although clomipramine has amply demonstrated effectiveness in the treatment of OCD, it has a less favorable side effect profile compared to the SSRIs and thus is now considered to be a second-line treatment for the disorder. Those who respond to clomipramine are likely to benefit from an SSRI such as fluoxetine (Steketee & Pigott, 2006). Problems with clomipramine include fatal overdose potential, risk of seizures, and risk of abnormal heart rhythms. There is emerging evidence that the SSRI citalopram may be effective in treating treatment-refractory OCD (Marazziti et al., 2001) and pediatric OCD (Mukaddes, Abali, & Kaynak, 2003).

Posttraumatic Stress Disorder   Controlled and uncontrolled trials have been conducted examining the efficacy of a number of TCAs (including imipramine, desipramine, and amitriptyline) in the treatment of PTSD. In general, TCAs have demonstrated some beneficial effects on intrusion symptoms and avoidance symptoms, as well as general anxiety and depression in samples that include chronic PTSD sufferers; however, due to the less than favorable side effect profiles associated with these TCAs, dropout rates from studies have been high (approaching 50% in some cases; Albucher & Liberzon, 2002). The MAOIs have also been used in the treatment of PTSD. Results from a small number of controlled trials and a larger number of uncontrolled studies examining the use of MAOIs have yielded mixed but generally favorable findings; however, the dietary restrictions associated with this medication as well as the potential for misuse among impulsive clients suggest a limited role in the treatment of PTSD (Albucher & Liberzon, 2002). The nature of these dietary restrictions is reviewed in greater detail in Chapter 10.

There is now a substantial research literature on the treatment of PTSD with SSRIs that includes several controlled trials. Collectively, these studies demonstrate that medications such as fluoxetine, sertraline, and paroxetine are superior to placebo in treating PTSD symptoms (e.g., numbing, hyperarousal, and avoidance), depression, and PTSD-associated disability, and compare favorably to or outperform TCAs and MAOIs (see Albucher & Liberzon, 2002, for a review). The SSRIs may also help with the comorbid substance abuse so frequently encountered among those with PTSD (Schatzberg et al., 2005). Sertraline was officially approved by the FDA for the treatment of PTSD in 1999.

Generalized Anxiety Disorder   Because of the high rate of comorbidity with depression, so-called broad spectrum antidepressant medications, including the SSRIs and the serotonin-norepinephrine reuptake inhibitor venlafaxine, have been recommended as first-line drug treatments for GAD; benzodiazepines such as alprazolam and clonazepam are now primarily used as adjunctive medications for those who are nonresponsive to or cannot tolerate antidepressants (Lydiard & Monnier, 2004). Among specific SSRIs that have been studied in randomized, controlled trials and shown to be effective in reducing symptoms and associated impairment are paroxetine (Rickels et al., 2003; Pollack et al., 2001), sertraline (Allgulander et al., 2002), and escitalopram (J. R. Davidson et al., 2004; J. R. Davidson, Bose, & Wang, 2005). Although the TCA imipramine has been reported to be an effective GAD treatment, its less favorable side effect and safety profiles relative to the SSRIs make it a less attractive pharmacologic treatment option.

Buspirone

Buspirone is a nonsedating anti-anxiety medication that is not chemically or pharmacologically related to benzodiazepines, barbiturates, or other sedative or anxiolytic drugs. Buspirone has a safety profile comparable to that of the SSRIs, greater tolerability than the TCAs, and (in contrast to the benzodiazepines) has no abuse potential (Albucher & Liberzon, 2002). Buspirone was approved by the FDA in the mid-1980s as an anxiolytic medication. Currently this medication is used to treat GAD, but it has received mixed support regarding its superiority over placebo (see Lydiard & Monnier, 2004). In addition, buspirone has less robust effects on depression compared to TCAs, and this fact may limit its usefulness as a primary treatment for GAD because of this disorder's high comorbidity with depression (Lydiard & Monnier, 2004); however, it can be used as an adjunctive treatment. Buspirone does not appear to be effective in treating Panic Disorder, Social Phobia, or OCD (Grady et al., 1993; Schweizer & Rickels, 1988; vanVliet, den Boer, Westenberg, & Pian, 1997). It has demonstrated some beneficial effects on PTSD symptomatology in small, uncontrolled trials, but more study of this population is necessary (Albucher & Liberzon, 2002).

Psychological Treatments

Panic Disorder

Cognitive-Behavioral Treatment   Cognitive-behavioral therapy for Panic Disorder with and without comorbid Agoraphobia that utilize exposure have been found to be highly effective. One such example is the panic control treatment (PCT) program by Craske,

Barlow, and Meadows (2000). This is a time-limited, structured, manualized treatment with four key elements: (1) psychoeducation, (2) relaxation training, (3) cognitive restructuring, and (4) interoceptive exposure.

The treatment begins with a *psychoeducational component* that conceptualizes panic attacks as a misfiring of the body's built-in fear system. Attempts are made to normalize the Panic Disorder symptoms to which clients typically have catastrophic associations. For example, the rapid heart rate that is frequently experienced in panic attacks is explained in terms of a normal, adaptive response made by the body when preparing for an emergency that is designed to pump oxygen-rich blood to needed areas in the body. Clients are asked to track their panic symptoms in-between sessions so that both therapist and client can begin to understand how frequently they occur, their severity, and the circumstances in which the attacks happen and to increase the client's sense of control. As the treatment progresses, clients continue to be educated about panic attacks and learn that following the initial panic attack a form of conditioning takes place in which a fear response becomes linked to physical symptoms, such that the future experience of even subtle symptoms can trigger a panic attack that seems to be uncued. *Relaxation techniques* are taught to reduce general levels of anxiety that might produce the kinds of physical symptoms that can trigger panic attacks. *Cognitive work* is incorporated into the treatment to help the client learn how maladaptive thinking patterns (e.g., overestimating catastrophic outcomes) exacerbate and maintain symptoms. Later in treatment, *interoceptive exposure* exercises are introduced that are designed to break the fearful associations that clients have to bodily sensations associated with panic attacks. These exposure sessions, which are first led by the therapist and later completed alone by the client, involve having clients do any of a number of activities that will purposefully bring about symptoms that are most characteristic of their panic attacks. For example, clients might be asked to spin around in a chair if a prominent symptom of their panic attacks is dizziness. Clients learn to tolerate the anxiety that is initially created by these experiences and learn that it eventually decreases with repeated exposure. Clients are later asked to carry out interoceptive exposures in the actual settings in which panic attacks typically occur. An important message that is given to the client throughout this treatment is that symptoms of a panic attack are not something to be fearful of, and they do not indicate a catastrophic consequence will occur. Additional CBT and exposure work can also be undertaken for clients who exhibit agoraphobic avoidance. Before treatment ends, gains that have been made are reviewed and steps for dealing with symptoms in the future are discussed.

Initial studies of the PCT program have found it a highly effect treatment, with upwards of 85% to 87% of treated clients being free of panic attacks at the end of treatment, compared to 36% from a wait-list control group (Barlow, Craske, Cerny, & Klosko, 1989). Treatment gains (e.g., fewer panic attacks) also appear to be maintained over time (e.g., 2-year follow-up), and the treatment compares favorably to medication (e.g., alprazolam; Craske, Brown, & Barlow, 1991; Klosko, Barlow, Tassinari, & Cerny, 1990). Results from a large-scale, multicenter clinical trial that compared PCT, imipramine, PCT + imipramine, placebo, and PCT + placebo found that both PCT and imipramine and their use in combination were superior to placebo following the acute 3-month treatment phase, but that PCT + imipramine was not more effective than either of these treatments alone or when compared to the PCT + placebo combination (Barlow, Gorman, Shear, & Woods,

2000). After a subsequent 6-month maintenance phase (during which responders were seen on a monthly basis), all treatments studied continued to outperform the placebo condition, and at a final 15-month follow-up that occurred 6 months after all treatments ended, PCT was significantly more effective than the other conditions, whereas gains made by those taking imipramine (with or without PCT) had lost the gains they had made.

Specific Phobia

The highly circumscribed nature of Specific Phobia can make it relatively easy for affected individuals to organize their lives so that contact with the feared object or situation is avoided or greatly minimized. This helps to explain why relatively few individuals with Specific Phobia (i.e., 20% or less) seek formal treatment (Fyer, 1998). However, very effective treatments for this disorder exist.

Systematic Desensitization   The most commonly used and best researched interventions for treating Specific Phobia involve exposure-based techniques. One of the oldest of these is systematic desensitization, which was pioneered by Joseph Wolpe. Systematic desensitization involves four basic steps: (1) creation of a series of images related to the phobic object or situation that gradually increase in the degree of anxiety or fear evoked (i.e., a phobia hierarchy created using the Subjective Units of Distress Scale [SUDS]); (2) learning a relaxation technique (e.g., progressive muscle relaxation); (3) inducing a state of relaxation prior to vividly imagining the first scene in the phobia hierarchy and maintaining relaxation while the mental exposure to the feared scenario is occurring; and (4) after a scene no longer provokes notable anxiety, continuing to the next image in the hierarchy and repeating step 3. Systematic desensitization is based on the concept of *reciprocal inhibition* or counterconditioning, which assumes that the strength of association between a phobic object or situation and the emotional reaction of anxiety can be weakened if a reaction that is incompatible with anxiety (i.e., relaxation) is made to occur in the presence of the feared stimulus (Wolpe, 1958).

Research studies on the effectiveness of systematic desensitization have primarily involved individuals with animal, natural environment (e.g., heights), or situational (e.g., flying, enclosed spaces) phobias. In their review of studies comparing systematic desensitization to a placebo, wait-list control, or another active treatment condition, Choy, Fyer, and Lipsitz (2007) concluded that in the majority of studies, participants consistently reported improvements in subjective anxiety following treatment, but that evidence was less compelling regarding the impact on subsequent behavioral avoidance. Furthermore, while some studies found that 60% to 70% of participants maintained gains at varying follow-up periods, most did not include a long-term follow-up component, which makes it difficult to adequately assess the extended impact of this treatment form. Barlow and Antony (2002) note that systematic desensitization has begun to be viewed less favorably as a phobia treatment for three reasons: (1) research evidence indicating in vivo exposure is more effective than imaginal exposure in reducing fear, (2) decreased treatment time associated with in vivo exposure because relaxation training is not required, and (3) limited evidence that the inclusion of relaxation in the treatment of Specific Phobia significantly improves outcomes over exposure-based treatments that do not employ this component.

In vivo Exposure In contrast to imaginal exposure techniques, in vivo exposure involves actually having the client come into contact with the feared object or situation. As with systematic desensitization, a hierarchy of feared situations involving the phobic stimulus is typically created, but the client will actually encounter instead of only imagining each of the items on the hierarchy. For the treatment to be effective, exposure sessions need to be of sufficient length; typical treatment protocols that have been subjected to empirical study are either a series (e.g., five) of 1-hour sessions or one long session (e.g., 3 hours; Choy et al., 2007). It is important that such exposures not be terminated when the client is still experiencing high levels of anxiety, as this is more likely to lead to poor outcomes. Results of controlled trials comparing exposure therapy for a variety of phobias (e.g., animal, water, heights, enclosed spaces, driving) have consistently found exposure therapy to be superior to control conditions in terms of producing decreases in subjective anxiety and avoidance of feared stimuli (e.g., ability to complete a behavioral avoidance task at the end of treatment). Furthermore, in head-to-head comparisons with systematic desensitization and vicarious exposure (e.g., watching someone else encounter the feared object or situation, either live or via videotape) treatments, exposure therapy has been found to be more effective (for a review, see Choy et al., 2007). In contrast to systematic desensitization, several long-term follow-up studies of exposure therapy for Specific Phobia have been conducted, with the majority utilizing BATs as the outcome measure. The collective results of these studies, which followed participants over periods ranging from 6 to 14 months, indicate that for phobias involving animals, heights, enclosed spaces, and darkness, treatment gains were maintained or improved over time, but that results for flying phobias are mixed, with most studies reporting improvements in self-reported anxiety or flying activity, but one study finding a decrease in the percentage of individuals able to complete a BAT (i.e., test flight) from posttreatment to a 1-year follow-up (see Choy et al., 2007, for a review).

Applied Tension One group of clients who benefit less from traditional exposure-based treatments only are BII phobics. Instead, the treatment of choice for these individuals is a *combination* of exposure and applied tension. The latter is based on the observation that persons with BII phobias display a physiologic response of decreases in heart rate and blood pressure and fainting when exposed to phobic stimuli. Applied tension involves teaching clients to tense muscles in their body to raise blood pressure and instructing them to use these techniques during exposure-based treatment (Antony & Barlow, 2002). Applied tension treatments have been primarily studied by Öst and colleagues (Öst, Fellenius, & Sterner, 1991; Öst, Sterner, & Fellenius, 1989) who have found this to be more effective than in vivo exposure alone and to take fewer treatment sessions to produce a response. This treatment can also produce effective results in as little as a single session lasting no more than 2 hours (Hellström, Fellenius, & Öst, 1996).

Virtual Reality Therapy One of the newer variants of exposure-based treatments utilizes virtual reality (VR) technology to put clients in simulated environments that expose them to feared objects/situations. Rothbaum (2006, p. 228) defines VR as consisting of

> human-computer interactions in which the user becomes an active participant in a three-dimensional computer-generated virtual world. The user experiences visual, auditory, and often

tactile stimuli that serve to immerse him or her in the computer-generated environment and create a sense of presence or immersion within the environment.

This form of treatment is particularly useful for phobias that pose practical or financial challenges in creating exposure scenarios (e.g., certain natural environment phobias; flying fears) and provides the therapist with the opportunity to control variables that may have particular relevance for a client and hence make the exposure more effective (Rothbaum, 2006). Studies of VR technology in the treatment of Specific Phobia have primarily centered on fears of heights and flying, but reports have also been published on the treatment of claustrophobia, driving fears, and animal phobias (see Weiderhold & Weiderhold, 2005). Choy and colleagues (2007) summarized the results of seven controlled studies of VR therapy that compared this treatment to in vivo exposure, systematic desensitization, and control conditions (e.g., wait-list, relaxation condition), and concluded: (a) VR was equally effective as in vivo exposure in terms of ability to complete a BAT at the end of treatment and reducing self-reported anxiety; (b) VR was as effective as systematic desensitization in decreasing subjective anxiety, but more effective in decreasing behavioral avoidance; (c) the majority of studies comparing VR to control conditions found VR to be superior in terms of decreasing subjective anxiety and behavior avoidance; and (d) VR appears to be an effective adjunctive treatment to CBT.

Social Phobia

Because Social Phobia so frequently has its onset during the teenage years or earlier, it is important to initiate treatment as soon possible after the disorder is detected to avert the likelihood that maladaptive patterns of thinking and behavior will become chronic and comorbid conditions will develop (J. R. T. Davidson, 2006). Among the most common and best studied psychotherapeutic treatments for social phobia are exposure-based treatments, cognitive restructuring, and social skills training (or some combination of these elements). The first two of these treatments are often subsumed under the broader umbrella term of cognitive-behavioral therapy. Meta-analytic studies of psychotherapy for Social Phobia (Fedoroff & Taylor, 2001; Feske & Chambless, 1995; R. A. Gould, Buckminster, Pollack, Otto, & Yap, 1997; S. Taylor, 1996) indicate that exposure-based techniques and combined exposure + CBT treatments are both effective and produce equivalent results, that social skills training and CBT without exposure are associated with somewhat smaller effect sizes than treatments that utilize exposure, and that individual and group format treatments appear equivalent. The Gould et al. (1997) meta-analysis examined CBT (including exposure-based interventions) and pharmacologic treatments and found no significant difference in effect size between these two intervention forms; however, Fedoroff and Taylor (2001) reported that pharmacologic interventions were the most consistently effective treatment for Social Phobia. In the meta-analysis by S. Taylor (1996), cognitive restructuring, exposure treatment, and social skills training were all found superior to wait-list control conditions, but only CBT plus exposure produced significantly superior results compared to placebo-control conditions. A recent study that added a social skills training component to an empirically validated group CBT intervention found that this combined intervention produced superior results across a number of measures (including those assessing social anxiety symptoms, depression symptoms, illness-related disability or impairment, and objective ratings of participants' performance in social situations) compared to CBT alone for individuals with the generalized subtype of Social Phobia (J. D. Herbert et al., 2005). The results of this study are particularly promising given findings that despite the general effectiveness of CBT interventions for Social Phobia, clients with the generalized subtype typically do not do as well as those with the nongeneralized subtype.

What follows is a brief description of the three major psychotherapeutic interventions for Social Phobia: exposure therapy, cognitive restructuring, and social skills training.

Exposure Therapy   This form of treatment involves gradually exposing a client to a series of feared social situations that are hierarchically arranged from the least to the most anxiety-provoking. The assumption is that with repeated opportunities to confront feared social situations, the client's anxiety response will habituate (Barlow, Raffa, & Cohen, 2002). An important part of any exposure therapy is to ensure that the client stays in the anxiety-producing situation long enough for habituation to occur; if the client prematurely leaves the situation still experiencing a high level of anxiety, this will only increase the likelihood that fear will return in the future (Craske & Rachman, 1987). Exposure treatment sessions are therefore often longer than the typical 50-minute psychotherapy session, and may last 90 minutes or more. Exposures can be imaginal or in vivo.

Beidel and Turner (1998) provide an excellent review of exposure techniques, some of which will now be reviewed. First, they note that for imaginal exposures, it is critically important to include in the imagined scene the client's core fear and other relevant variables (e.g., particular symptoms the client would be likely to experience in the social situation, such as physiologic responses). Elements of a social situation that make up the core fear will vary across individuals; for example, for some people what is most anxiety-provoking about public speaking is being in front of a large audience, whereas for others it may be the composition of the audience (e.g., presence of people who are highly knowledgeable about the topic on which the client will be speaking). In addition, in imagining the feared scene, the client is discouraged from using strategies to attenuate anxiety such as distraction or imagining the interaction going smoothly.

For many clients, a combination of imaginal and in vivo exposures will be used. In vivo exposures can be more difficult to create, and clients may be reluctant to engage in these on their own (i.e., away from the presence of the therapist). In such cases, role-plays with the therapist or another willing aide can be arranged to supplement imaginal exposures. When a client is not able to imagine scenes vividly and does not seem to benefit from imagery training to facilitate this skill, it may be necessary to use in vivo exposures only. Homework is typically assigned that involves conducting some exposures (whether imagined or in vivo) away from the therapy office; this provides the client with additional opportunities for social anxiety to habituate and aids in the generalization of results to the natural environment. Because exposure-based treatments require clients to fully experience anxiety associated with their most feared social situations, dropout rates can be high.

Cognitive Restructuring   As was previously discussed, persons with Social Phobia tend to make a number of information-processing errors that include holding overly negative self-views, assuming that social partners have expectations or standards that cannot be met, and judging as high the likelihood that something catastrophic will occur during a social encounter. Such thoughts increase anxiety, and these types of thinking patterns are targeted in cognitive restructuring. This type of intervention may be used alone or in conjunction with other techniques such as exposures and social skills training, and involves the following elements: (a) identification of negative thoughts that occur before, during, or after anxiety-provoking situations; (b) evaluation of the accuracy of thoughts given data derived from Socratic questioning or behavioral experiments; and (c) generation of rational alternative thoughts based on the acquired information (Heimberg, 2002). Behavioral experiments consist of activities that are designed to determine the veracity of clients' beliefs. For example, a client who believes that she could never initiate a conversation with a fellow student in a lecture hall would be asked to try this the next time she is in this situation. As Heimberg notes, behavioral experiments inherently include an exposure component, but what differentiates this type of exercise from exposure therapy is that the goal of a behavioral experiment is to collect information that will assist the client in revising inaccurate beliefs regarding social situations.

Social Skills Training   Although not invariably the case, some persons with Social Phobia demonstrate deficits in social skills (e.g., particularly those with the generalized subtype) and therefore stand to benefit from social skills training. Development of skills such as initiating and maintaining conversations, attending to and remembering information, acting assertively, maintaining friendships, and giving presentations or speeches may be targeted (Beidel & Turner, 1998). General information about the importance of attending to nonverbal behavior (e.g., eye contact, facial expression, proximity to social partners) and paralinguistic features of speech (e.g., volume, voice tone, timing) are also typically included. Social skills training is usually done in group settings, which provides natural opportunities for practicing skills with and in front of others. Clients are provided with education about and demonstrations of various social skills, practice them in role-plays, and receive coaching and feedback from the therapist and feedback from other group members. Homework assignments provide opportunities to practice skills in real-life settings.

Obsessive-Compulsive Disorder

Exposure and Response Prevention   The psychotherapeutic treatment of choice for OCD is exposure and response prevention (ERP). This intervention is often combined with cognitive-behavioral therapy strategies, which will be discussed shortly. As the name implies, ERP treatment has two primary components: in vivo and/or imaginal exposure to stimuli that provoke obsessions, and the prevention of rituals and compulsions that would normally follow the obsession. These elements achieve two important goals: (1) disconnecting obsessions from the distress with which they are associated, and (2) eliminating ritualistic behaviors that negatively reinforce the client's obsessive fears (Steketee, 1993). Providing the client with a clear explanation early on of the rationale for the treatment is important because many individuals become upset on hearing that the treatment will involve the purposeful exposure to situations they have probably been trying very hard to avoid. Much of the following description of specific methods used in ERP was drawn from Steketee's excellent text on the treatment of OCD, and the interested reader is referred to this source for further information.

Typically, ERP begins with a thorough assessment of the client's symptoms, using an assessment measure such as the Y-BOCS (see Table 11.4; Baer, 2000; W. K. Goodman et al., 1989). The client and therapist then begin constructing hierarchies of situations that will form the basis for exposures. Clients are asked to rate (using a SUDS) how anxious they would become if placed in a variety of situations and prevented from engaging in any compulsions or rituals, and these situations are rank-ordered to form a hierarchy. A different hierarchy for each obsessive theme can be constructed; the therapist and client may decide to work on more than one hierarchy at once, or just one at a time. An item is then selected for an exposure and clients are asked to rate their anxiety using the SUDS prior to the exposure and approximately every 10 minutes after the exposure begins. This enables the client to see that anxiety eventually decreases without a compulsive behavior being performed, and also provides an indicator of when it is appropriate to terminate the exposure (e.g., when subjective anxiety ratings go down to half of their initial level). The client is encouraged not to carry out the compulsion as soon as the exposure is done, as this could defeat the purpose of the exposure. In some cases, however, it may not be practical to prohibit a client from engaging in any form of the compulsive behavior, so instructions can be given to perform the behavior in an attenuated form. For example, clients who have hand-washing compulsions can be instructed that it is permissible to wash their hands after using the bathroom, prior to eating, and after handling visibly dirty or greasy objects, and explicit directions given on the length of time such washing should take (Steketee, 1993).

Exposures often need to be done outside the office to place the client in contact with situations that provoke obsessions and are carried out for prolonged periods of time (e.g., 90-minute sessions), which makes ERP treatment sessions somewhat different from standard 50-minute psychotherapy sessions. Initially, the therapist should be present when the exposures are implemented to ensure that the client is carrying them out correctly and not engaging in subtle forms of avoidance behavior (e.g., trying to keep distracted by engaging in unrelated small talk) or "compartmentalization" (e.g., during a contamination exposure, keeping a finger of one hand from touching an object to avoid feeling completely contaminated). During an exposure, the therapist also asks clients to articulate their thoughts and feelings and to focus on the obsession triggered by the exposure in order to fully activate their fear structure. Eventually clients should be able to carry out exposures on their own as homework. Once clients can enter the exposure situation without experiencing undue anxiety, they can move on to the next item in the hierarchy.

Sometimes it is not practical to carry out in vivo exposures because of the nature of the situations that provoke obsessions (e.g., contamination fears associated with being in a hotel room). In such cases, imaginal exposures can be useful. This typically takes the form of creating a detailed script describing the feared situation, including what the client is ultimately afraid will happen if a compulsion is not performed. While the writing of the script can be considered a form of exposure in and of itself, clients are also asked to record the script on an audiotape and listen to it repeatedly (e.g., for an hour) as an exposure. Imaginal exposures are also useful for clients who perform mental rituals because it is harder for them to engage in such a compulsion if they have to concentrate on listening to the recorded script. Because of the difficulty of controlling mental rituals, treatment of clients who primarily present with this form of compulsion is somewhat less successful than those who have other forms of compulsive behavior (Steketee & Pigott, 2006).

Several randomized, controlled trials of ERP have been conducted, and meta-analytic studies of exposure-based behavioral treatments for OCD indicate that they are highly effective, produce significant improvements in clinician and client reports of symptoms, and are of equivalent and possibly superior efficacy to pharmacologic treatments (e.g., SSRIs; Abramowitz, 1997; Van Balkom et al., 1994). Even clients with severe symptoms and psychiatric comorbidity can achieve substantial reductions in OCD and related (e.g., depressive) symptoms following ERP (Franklin, Abramowitz, Kozak, Levitt, & Foa, 2000). Steketee and Pigott (2006), in summarizing the results of these meta-analytic studies, concluded that among those who complete ERP treatment, 90% experience positive results ranging from moderate improvement to recovery by the end of treatment. Clients particularly likely to benefit from behavioral approaches to the treatment of OCD are those with aggressive checking, contamination or cleaning, and symmetry or ordering symptoms (Steketee & Pigott, 2006). Finally, it appears that ERP is effective regardless of whether or not adjunctive medication is prescribed (Franklin, Abramowitz, Brux, Zoellner, & Feeny, 2002).

Cognitive-Behavioral Treatment   Obsessive-Compulsive Disorder is characterized by a number of thinking errors: overestimation of harm, excessive responsibility, thought-action fusion (i.e., belief that having a thought about doing an action is the same as doing the action), the belief that having complete control over one's thoughts is possible and necessary, intolerance of uncertainty, hypervigilance to avert disaster, and perfectionism (Steketee & Pigott, 2006). As such, CBT has proven useful in the treatment of OCD. Interventions involve helping the client to identify unhelpful thoughts that are associated with obsessions and generate more accurate, adaptive alternatives. An example of a specific CBT technique is probability estimation. Here, the therapist works with the client to identify the chain of events necessary for a feared outcome to occur, assign realistic probabilities to each step, and multiply these out to arrive at the final probability associated with the feared outcome. In this way, the real risk of the feared outcome can be compared with client's initial overestimation (Steketee & Pigott, 2006).

Research suggests that CBT interventions are effective in the treatment of OCD and, according to some reports, produce effects that are of similar magnitude to those seen with exposure and response presentation (Abramowitz, 1997). Other reports have found that although CBT is more effective than placebo conditions, it is somewhat less effective than ERP (van Balkom et al., 1994). Nevertheless, given that upwards of 25% of clients with OCD refuse exposure-based behavioral treatments, CBT offers a viable therapeutic alternative; CBT techniques can also be readily incorporated into ERP treatment paradigms and may be an appropriate starting point for clients who are unwilling to initially undertake ERP treatment.

Posttraumatic Stress Disorder

Currently, exposure-based therapies have garnered the most empirical support for the treatment of PTSD. These treatments are typically subsumed under the CBT umbrella, although additional CBT treatments primarily focused on changing maladaptive thoughts related to trauma have also been studied. Collectively, these studies indicated that CBT techniques (e.g., exposure, cognitive therapy, stress inoculation, or anxiety management) produce significant reductions in PTSD and associated symptoms (e.g., depression), are superior to wait-list conditions, produce treatment gains that are maintained over time, and can be utilized with a range of trauma survivors (for reviews, see Keane & Barlow,

2002; Hembree & Feeny, 2006). Approaches utilizing psychoeducation, gradual exposure techniques, cognitive reprocessing of the traumatic experience, and stress reduction training (e.g., relaxation strategies, positive self-talk) have also been demonstrated to produce superior outcomes to nondirective supportive therapy and wait-list control conditions (see J. A. Cohen & Mannarino, 2004, for a review). Although many clinicians utilize psychodynamic approaches during the treatment of individuals with PTSD, empirical studies examining this modality of treatment are lacking (Nemeroff et al., 2006).

Exposure Therapy   Emotional processing theory contends that avoidance symptoms of PTSD interfere with recovery from the disorder by preventing emotional habituation to trauma-related stimuli and correction of erroneous cognitions stemming from the trauma (Foa & Kozak, 1986; Hembree & Feeny, 2006). In exposure therapy, clients are purposefully and systematically exposed to trauma-related memories and reminders in order to correct the pathological elements of their fear structure through the integration of corrective information (Rothbaum, Meadows, Reisck, & Foy, 2000). An example of the elements that can be incorporated in exposure treatment is provided by Foa and Rothbaum's (1998) prolonged exposure therapy (see also Hembree & Feeny, 2004, for a summary). This is a 9- to 12-session treatment that involves psychoeducation about PTSD and reactions to traumatic experiences, breathing retraining, and in vivo and imaginal exposure. Therapy sessions are typically 90 to 120 minutes long. In vivo exposures usually begin in the second session and are based on a hierarchy created with the client of low-risk situations the client avoids because of their ability to trigger memories and feelings associated with the trauma. Items are ordered on the hierarchy based on how much anxiety the client anticipates experiencing when actually in the situation. Clients are instructed to select an item on the hierarchy to work on outside of the session (usually one that does not provoke a high level of anxiety, which increases the likelihood of success in completing the exposure). Clients are told to stay in the exposure situation for a sufficient length of time to allow anxiety to notably decrease (e.g., 30 to 45 minutes). Imaginal exposure begins in the third session and requires clients to provide a 45- to 60-minute detailed narrative description of the traumatic event in the present tense. Clients keep their eyes closed and are asked to describe not only the facts of what occurred during the trauma, but the emotional reactions experienced and the sensory reactions that occurred at the time, so that the retelling is as vivid as possible (thereby allowing full emotional engagement of trauma-related memories). During this time, the therapist monitors the client's anxiety level, offers support and encouragement to continue, but does not verbally engage the client at length to avoid interfering with the emotional processing of the trauma memories. The therapist needs to carefully watch the client's reaction to the exposure to ensure that there is sufficient engagement in the task but that the client is not overwhelmingly distressed. The session is typically audiotaped so that the client can repeat the imaginal exposures on a daily basis at home. Following the imaginal exposure, therapist and client discuss the client's reactions, emotional habituation that may have begun, and changes in the client's interpretation of the trauma and its aftermath. Remaining treatment sessions involve continued imaginal exposure work (e.g., on trauma aspects that are the most distressing or difficult) and postimaginal processing, review of exposures done as homework, and ongoing discussion of changes occurring at a cognitive, emotional, and behavioral level as a result of processing the trauma. The treatment ends with a review of what has been learned in treatment and reinforcement of the message that avoidance will maintain fear, whereas confronting reminders and memories of the trauma enables recovery and mastery (Hembree & Feeny, 2004).

Randomized, controlled trials show that exposure-based treatments produce greater posttreatment improvements on symptom-relevant measures compared to wait-list conditions, produce superior results at follow-ups when compared to both wait-list conditions and supportive counseling, and compare favorably to CBT-only treatments (see Keane & Barlow, 2002, for a review). Because exposure treatments, by definition, involve having the client directly confront situations that will evoke traumatic memories, some have raised concern that this will make clients feel worse and increase the likelihood of treatment dropout (Kilpatrick & Best, 1984). Although it appears that reliable increases in symptoms of anxiety and depression may occur following initial exposures for a small minority of clients, this does not predict poorer treatment response and does not appear to be associated with higher treatment dropout rates (Foa, Zoellner, Feeny, Hembree, & Alvarez-Conrad, 2002).

Cognitive-Behavioral Therapy   Traditional CBT approaches to the treatment of PTSD aim to help clients (a) understand how beliefs and interpretations of events can affect emotional reactions to them, (b) identify trauma-related erroneous thoughts or beliefs that precipitate negative emotions (e.g., fear, rage) and/or avoidance behaviors, and (c) challenge these beliefs and assumptions using logical, evidence-based methods (Hembree & Feeny, 2004). As in other forms of CBT, the client is asked to complete homework assignments in-between sessions to reinforce information discussed in sessions and to demonstrate that problematic ways of thinking about the trauma can be changed. The cognitive restructuring techniques of CBT can be particularly useful given the ways traumatic events frequently alter clients' fundamental concepts of themselves, others, and the world around them. For example, traumatized clients may begin to believe they should have been able to foresee or somehow control the traumatic event, may hold themselves excessively responsible for the outcome of events, may view the world as an unsafe and completely unjust place, and may view themselves as excessively vulnerable (E. M. Carroll & Foy, 1992). Additional elements that are often included in CBT treatment packages for PTSD are anxiety management training (e.g., relaxation techniques, breathing retraining, anger management skills) and relapse prevention work (e.g., management of anniversary reactions and other trauma cues, review of coping strategies, mobilization of support systems, communication skills to access assistance from others when needed; Keane & Barlow, 2002). In addition, exposure techniques, such as those outlined previously, can also be utilized.

Eye Movement Desensitization and Reprocessing   This form of treatment was developed by F. Shapiro (1989) and involves asking the client to evoke a trauma-relevant memory or image along with associated physical sensations and hold these in mind while articulating beliefs about the traumatic incident, including adaptive alternative interpretations. As clients do this, they are asked to simultaneously track the therapist's finger as it is rapidly moved in a lateral direction in sets of 10 to 20 strokes. The mechanism behind eye movement desensitization and reprocessing (EMDR) is not fully understood. F. Shapiro (1995) has speculated that eye movements may shift information that is dysfunctionally blocked in the nervous system or serve some sort of rebalancing mechanism, but such hypotheses have been criticized as lacking a sound neurobiological basis (J. G. Allen & Lewis, 1996). That the treatment lacks a theoretical basis is another point of controversy and a reason EMDR has been criticized, and attention has been drawn to the need for more basic research investigating the effects of eye movements on anxiety and other emotional problems (Keane & Barlow, 2002). Indeed, it is not clear whether the provocation of saccadic eye movements, clearly the most unusual feature of the treatment, is actually necessary to produce significant effects (Cusack & Spates, 1999; Feske & Goldstein, 1997). If it is not, the remaining treatment elements would render EMDR similar to other CBT approaches that utilize imaginal exposure and cognitive restructuring. A recent meta-analysis of 35 EMDR treatment studies (most of which were focused on anxiety-disordered populations) concluded the following about EMDR: (a) It is more effective compared to no treatment and to nonspecific therapies, (b) it is not superior to exposure-based treatments, (c) there is no strong evidence that eye movements or other alternating stimuli are necessary for treatment effects to occur, (d) there is no evidence that superior outcomes are obtained by therapists trained through Shapiro's EMDR Institute, and (e) the treatment does not appear to be more effective with certain clinical populations compared to others (P. R. Davidson & Parker, 2001). There are some reports of EMDR being effective for children with PTSD (e.g., comparing favorably to CBT and being superior to a wait-list control condition), but further research is needed before recommendations about its use in pediatric populations can be made (J. A. Cohen & Mannarino, 2004).

Generalized Anxiety Disorder

Cognitive-Behavioral Therapy   Cognitive-behavioral therapy is the most common approach in the treatment of GAD and typically includes elements such as psychoeducation, cognitive restructuring, exposure techniques, relaxation training, anxiety management, and problem-solving skills. Among the conclusions reached in a recent meta-analysis of published studies comparing CBT to control conditions in the treatment of GAD were the following: (a) Treatments that combine cognitive and behavioral interventions appear more effective than treatments that utilize cognitive interventions alone, relaxation training alone, or behavioral interventions alone; (b) group CBT is associated with low dropout rates (i.e., mean dropout rate across studies = 11.4%); (c) there is no significant difference between treatments administered in a group versus an individual format; (d) gains made during treatment are maintained at follow-up periods of at least 6 months; and (e) although many individuals treated with CBT demonstrate improvement, percentages of those who exhibit high end-state functioning are often very modest, which indicates a need to refine treatments to further increase their effectiveness. It is beyond the scope of this chapter to review the many versions of CBT that have been studied in relation to GAD, but some of the common elements across treatments will be briefly reviewed.

Given the information-processing biases that characterize GAD, cognitive restructuring approaches are a logical treatment approach for this disorder. The provision of education about the disorder is an important first step in dispelling misconceptions clients may have about GAD. Clients are taught methods for identifying cues (e.g., situational, cognitive, emotional, somatic) that trigger perceptions of threat and subsequent worrying. The therapist can then begin working with the client to examine mistaken beliefs that trigger worry, including thoughts related to function and consequences of worrying itself (i.e., metacognitions). For example, clients may believe that their worrying, though emotionally distressing, serves a necessary or important purpose such as helping to prepare them for an inevitable, negative outcome or magically preventing a feared outcome. Conversely, clients may believe they cannot control their worry, that their worrying is somehow physically harmful or damaging, or that the only way to stop worrying is to have absolute certainty. The CBT therapist can begin to help clients to challenge faulty perceptions through the use of skillful questioning that asks clients to examine the evidence that supports their beliefs; teaching clients to apply logical analysis to their assumptions, label cognitive errors, and decatastrophize; and setting up behavioral experiments to test beliefs (e.g., using worry diaries to predict the likelihood of various feared negative outcomes occurring and then determining if they come true) (Borkovec, Newman, Pincus, & Lytle, 2002; Leahy, 2004). Dugas and colleagues (2004) emphasize helping clients distinguish between worries about *current* problems and worries about *potential* problems, and applying different cognitive strategies to each—specifically, problem-solving training for the former and worry exposure for the latter.

In contrast to other anxiety disorders in which avoidance of specific situations or cues that trigger anxiety or fear is common and obvious, behavioral avoidance in GAD appears to occur less frequently and is more subtle when it does happen (Behar & Borkovec, 2006). Thus designing in vivo exposures may be less useful than utilizing imaginal exposures with this client population. In *worry exposure*, the client is asked to vividly imagine a scene (derived from a hierarchical list developed with the therapist) that provokes anxiety and worry, to remain focused on the scene for up to 30 minutes, and to generate alternative outcomes for the imagined situation (Lang, 2004). The client can be instructed to utilize relaxation techniques during exposures to decrease anxiety (Borkovec & Matthews, 1988). Exposures are repeatedly done until the imagined scene no longer provokes significant levels of anxiety and worry.

Progressive muscle relaxation (PMR) is frequently used as a behavioral intervention in CBT to target the symptom of increased muscle tension seen in GAD. As clients learn to release tension through PMR exercises, they can be encouraged to similarly let go of negative thoughts, feelings, and images associated with their worry (Behar & Borkovec, 2006). Clients are instructed to practice PMR twice daily and may also be taught additional relaxation techniques such as diaphragmatic breathing and meditation. In an applied relaxation approach, clients are instructed to use PMR and other relaxation techniques whenever internal or external cues that typically trigger worry arise; before, during, and after stressful events; and throughout the day, even when not anxious, so that they become competent at noting when tension is present and become able to quickly and effectively induce a state of relaxation (Borkovec & Ruscio, 2001). The feelings of relaxation promoted through techniques such as PMR will induce uncomfortable feelings in some clients. Relaxation-induced anxiety has been found to predict poorer response in treatments that utilize a relaxation component (Borkovec et. al., 1987; Borkovec & Matthews, 1988).

Additional Comments   Cognitive-behavioral therapy has been found to be effective in the treatment of GAD among older adults, but appears to produce less robust effects relative to active comparison treatments. Stanley et al. (2003) compared a CBT treatment that included psychoeducation, progressive deep muscle relaxation, cognitive restructuring, and exposure to a minimal contact condition (MCC) consisting of weekly telephone calls to assess symptom severity and need for immediate care. These researchers found that CBT produced improvement on measures of worry, anxiety, and quality of life following treatment, whereas the MCC did not, and 45% of CBT participants were designated as treatment responders, in comparison to only 8% of participants in MCC. Significantly fewer participants in the CBT condition met criteria for GAD at the end of treatment compared to those in the MCC (55% versus 81%). Although treatment gains were maintained over 6- and 12-month follow-up periods, only 7% and 19% of CBT participants achieved high-endstate functioning at these time points, respectively.

In another randomized trial that compared a manualized CBT treatment (including relaxation training, cognitive restructuring, and worry exposure) adapted for older adults to a discussion group intervention (focusing on worry-provoking topics and provision of validation and supportive listening) and a wait-list control condition, Wetherell, Gatz, and Craske (2003) found that individuals in the CBT condition improved more than wait-list participants on measures of GAD severity, worry, depression, role functioning, and energy, and showed greater improvement than the discussion group on a measure evaluating the percentage of the day spent worrying. However, at a 6-month follow-up there were no differences on outcome measures between the CBT and discussion group participants, and nearly equal percentages of participants in each group were classified as treatment responders (i.e., 50% and 53%, respectively). Thus, when compared to a more active treatment, CBT for older adults with GAD appears to show less pronounced effects, which suggests that therapeutic approaches found effective for younger individuals with GAD may not be equally effective in older populations without significant modification. Wetherell et al. (2005) found that homework completion was significantly correlated with improvement among older GAD clients treated with CBT, underscoring the importance of emphasizing this component of treatment in work with this client population. These researchers also found that GAD severity and the presence of comorbid conditions were also associated with greater improvement in CBT, which suggests the possibility that older clients with more severe symptoms may be more motivated in treatment.

ADVANCED TOPIC: UNDERSTANDING ANXIETY IN A CULTURAL CONTEXT

As was noted earlier in this chapter, a significant percentage of the general population will, at some point in their lives, be exposed to a stressor capable of producing PTSD. Unfortunately, the experience of natural disasters, war, assaults, life-threatening accidents, physical and sexual abuse, and other extreme events knows no geographical boundaries. A survey of epidemiologic studies of PTSD from around the world underscores this fact. For example, high rates of PTSD have been noted among such culturally diverse groups as Cambodian refugees (86%), immigrants from Central America (49% to 52%) and Mexico (25%), Israelis evacuated during the Gulf War (80%), Croatian prisoners of war (34%), Australian firefighters (22% to 36%), and French rape victims (37%; see Girolamo & McFarlane, 1996, for a review).

In treating a client who is an immigrant, it is important to learn about the history of his or her country of origin and to become familiar with natural and man-made trauma-relevant events to which the client may have been exposed. Cultural attitudes may also reveal the potential for increased risk for certain forms of trauma. For example, D. Varma, Chandra, Thomas, and Carey (2007), in a study of pregnant women in India, found that 14% reported physical abuse, 15% psychological abuse, and 9% sexual coercion, with 50% of the women experiencing ongoing abuse during pregnancy. These authors noted the need to consider sociocultural factors that could influence these high rates of intimate partner violence, including traditional gender roles espoused by the society at large (which might predispose men to aggress against women in times of stress), as well as stressors linked to poverty (e.g., crowding, loss of hope).

As Friedman and Marsella (1996) note, the ways PTSD symptomatology manifests cross-culturally is dependent on many factors: (a) religious and cultural beliefs that influence the subjective experience and meaning of trauma (e.g., Is a physically excruciating event a rite of passage or traumatic?); (b) cultural practices that could affect the direct experience of symptoms (e.g., the karmic meaning of a traumatic event for a Buddhist); (c) the safety and stability of the family and community environment; (d) the degree to which the client's family and larger culture view traumatic experiences and victims of trauma (e.g., Is survivorship honored or stigmatized? Are posttraumatic problems normalized or pathologized?); and (e) the existence of cultural traditions designed to deal with the impact of traumatic events and experiences (e.g., the Navajo Enemy Way ceremony to assist warriors in readjusting to peace-time society).

Our understanding of the consequences of traumatic experience will be restricted if we do not consider the larger communal context in which the personal trauma is embedded. For example, Kirmayer (1996, p. 155) highlights the "collective loss of meaning and social structure" that are part of the experience of Cambodian refugees who escaped the killing fields of the Khmer Rouge. Indeed, more attention deserves to be paid to the macro level at which traumatic experiences may impact an entire nation or society (Jenkins, 1996). With regard to the African American experience, one must consider how factors such as underemployment and poverty, medical morbidity, crime, single-parent households, and racism combine to create a traumatogenic backdrop against which the risk of developing PTSD increases (I. M. Allen, 1996). Similar issues (e.g., relating to migration and immigration experiences, language barriers, prejudice, and limited financial resources) have been raised in understanding the experience of Latinos and the elevated rates of PTSD that have been observed in this population (Hough, Canino, Abueg, & Gusman, 1996).

High rates of comorbidity (e.g., depression, anxiety, somatization, and drug and alcohol use disorders) with PTSD have been observed in epidemiologic studies conducted in diverse regions of the world, but many questions remain regarding the relationship between these and other comorbid conditions and PTSD, including their onset and potential etiological role vis-à-vis one another (Girolamo & McFarlane, 1996). Unfortunately, scant attention has been paid to the development of culturally sensitive measures of PTSD symptomatology, so it is difficult to know whether results obtained with measures standardized on primarily Caucasian individuals living in industrialized Western countries fully capture important elements of the psychological sequelae of trauma exposure among ethnic and culturally diverse populations (Marsella, Friedman, & Spain, 1996).

Although PTSD has been observed all around the world, some of the aforementioned factors that may shape the experience of trauma and resulting symptoms among those who develop a traumatic stress disorder raise questions about the applicability of the *DSM* criteria for PTSD in a cross-cultural arena. Jenkins (1996) suggests that perhaps it is best to conceptualize PTSD as a group of stress-related disorders that may have somewhat different manifestations. She cites as a supportive example her study of Salvadoran female refugees living in North America. In this investigation, Jenkins found that although some *DSM-III-R* PTSD criteria were commonly reported in these women (including intrusive experiences and to a certain degree increased arousal), avoidance symptoms were not commonly endorsed. Part of the difficulty of evaluating this symptom cluster was determining which events symbolized or resembled the traumatic event (recall that such symbols or reminders are the stimuli that typically trigger PTSD-related memories) and required an understanding, from a cultural perspective, of how environmental stimuli are classified and interpreted by different groups.

Although variations may be evident in the manner in which PTSD symptoms are displayed, similar underlying processes that influence the generation and perpetuation of symptoms may be evident across cultures. An example is provided by Hinton, Hsia, Um, and Otto's (2003) study of Cambodian refugees diagnosed with PTSD. These researchers found a 58% rate of anger-induced panic attacks in this population. The high rate of panic attacks produced by the specific emotional trigger of anger was tied to the cognitive interpretation of this emotion from a Cambodian cultural perspective. Specifically, anger-related autonomic arousal in this population is commonly interpreted as carrying the potential to lead to any of a number of life-threatening conditions, such as cardiac arrest due to heart abnormalities (*geung beh doung*), bursting of the neck vessels (*dac sosai go*), and chest blood overload (*go chieum*). Recall that cognitive conceptualizations of panic used in CBT treatments emphasize the role that catastrophic interpretations of bodily symptoms play in increasing the likelihood that a benign physical symptom will escalate into a panic attack. The findings of the Hinton et al. study fit nicely with this model and suggest that for Cambodian PTSD sufferers, fear and catastrophic interpretation of symptoms related to anger-induced arousal play an important role in generating panic attacks. This investigation indicates that we need not abandon existing models of anxiety to understand the development of this pathology in other cultures, but that we must seek to understand how cultural experience molds perceptions of threat and vulnerability.

Chapter 12

SOMATOFORM AND RELATED DISORDERS

Over 400 million clinic visits in the United States each year can be accounted for by somatic concerns; for at least 20% to 30% of these, a physical etiology cannot be identified (Kroenke & Swindle, 2000; Rief & Sharpe, 2004). Somatic symptoms are the most common clinical form of the expression of emotional distress, and somatization accompanied by medical help seeking occurs across all cultures (Kirmayer & Young, 1998). Folks (1995, p. 267) describes somatization as "the process by which an individual consciously or unconsciously uses the body or bodily symptoms for psychological purposes or personal gain." Community surveys indicate that 85% to 95% of individuals report at least one physical symptom every 2 to 4 weeks, and 30.3% of individuals in primary care settings and 70% of psychiatric patients present with somatic concerns (Holder-Perkins & Wise, 2001; Issac, Janca, & Orley, 1996). Barsky, Orav, and Bates (2005) found somatizing individuals had more primary care physician and specialty visits, hospital admissions, and higher inpatient and outpatient costs even when comorbid anxiety, depression, and major medical conditions were controlled. They estimated that somatization alone results on a national level in $265 billion a year medical care costs.

The term *somatoform* was first included in the *DSM-III* (American Psychiatric Association, 1980; Mayou, Levenson, & Sharpe, 2003). The defining feature of the somatoform disorders category is a physical complaint or bodily concern not better accounted for by a general medical condition (GMC) or other mental disorder (American Psychiatric Association, 2000b). These are diagnoses of exclusion that are characterized by individuals with an illness-affirming clinical presentation (Bouman, Eifert, & Lejuez, 1999). They may be the most prevalent psychiatric disorders in general medical practice, with 1 in 6 patients presenting with a somatoform disorder, and a prevalence rate of 16.5%, which increases to 21.9% when a mild impairment criteria is used (De Waal, Arnold, Eekhof, & Van Hemert, 2004). When *DSM-IV* diagnostic criteria were applied to a group of medical inpatients, 20.2% could be diagnosed with somatoform disorders (P. Fink, Hansen, & Oxhoj, 2004).

Individuals with somatoform disorders are wed to physical explanations of their symptoms and relentlessly seek medical evaluations (Escobar, 1996). They are often referred by a primary care or other physician after presenting in nonpsychiatric settings with one or more unexplained physical symptoms, persistent worry about physical complaints, or bodily preoccupations (Hurwitz, 2004). They tend to be distrustful of clinicians, are high users of health services, have multiple caregivers, use myriad medications, have poor follow-through, and are resistant to any psychological interpretations or interventions

(Escobar, 1996; Rief & Hiller, 2003; J. Stone et al., 2002). These individuals' physical symptoms are seen as nonintentional and involuntary; they genuinely believe they are ill, and this belief causes distress, impairment, and the adoption of the sick role in the absence of a medically recognized disease (Bouman et al., 1999; Dhossche, van der Steen, & Ferdinand, 2002). The determination of intentionality may be difficult and must be inferred from the context in which the symptoms present (First & Tasman 2004; Sharpe & Mayou, 2004).

The grouping of the somatoform disorders in the *DSM-IV-TR* is based on clinical utility rather than the assumption of a common etiology or common family history, resulting in a diagnostically heterogeneous category (First & Tasman, 2004; Wijeratne, Brodaty, & Hickie, 2003). Within this category, there are six disorders and an NOS diagnosis: Somatization Disorder, Undifferentiated Somatoform Disorder, Conversion Disorder, Pain Disorder, Hypochondriasis, and Body Dysmorphic Disorder (American Psychiatric Association, 2000b). One of the major challenges for the clinician is the differentiation of these disorders from the related disorders of psychological factors affecting a medical condition, factitious disorders, and malingering.

HISTORICAL OVERVIEW

The prevalence of individuals presenting to primary physicians with somatic complaints as expressions of psychological distress has been identified as anywhere between 25% and 72%, yet controversy remains as to how best to conceptualize these disorders (Chaplin, 1997; De Gucht & Fischler, 2002). Somatoform disorders have been described as straddling the boundary between physical and psychological ill health and are viewed differently by biomedically oriented physicians and psychosocially oriented clinicians (Guerje, Simon, Ustun, & Goldberg, 1997). Conversion Disorder and Hypochondriasis were identified by the Greeks; are closely associated with the development of the field of psychiatry and, as Escobar (1996, p. 590) describes, are part of the "golden era of descriptive psychopathology." Somatization Disorder and Pain Disorder are of more recent origin. Over the years, while the descriptions of the clinical presentation have been consistent, the names of the disorders have undergone considerable change, reflecting differing theories of etiology; and the definitions have frequently overlapped or been misused, resulting in diagnostic confusion (Holder-Perkins & Wise, 2001; G. Taylor, 2003).

The first known written recording of the term *hysteria* was on an Egyptian papyrus in 1900 BC. It was then used by the Greeks to describe a variety of physical symptoms in women, which often presented dramatically and were believed to be caused by the wanderings of the uterus (P. Fink, 1996; First & Tasman 2004; Trillat, 1995). By the Middle Ages hysteria was believed to be caused by demonic possession, and there are descriptions of cases of mass psychogenic illness and dancing manias (Kent, Tomasson, & Coryell, 1995). Maldonado and Spiegel (2001, p. 103) describe how in the seventeenth century, Thomas Sydenham (1666) proposed that hysteria was a psychological disorder and a condition that could mimic all physical diseases from which man is heir. The French neurologist Charcot (1889) described a neurological basis for the disorder, theorizing that the clinical symptoms were caused by an inherited degenerative process of the nervous system. He also believed that traumatic events could result in functional or dynamic lesions in the brain and that hysteria was a special type of consciousness, whereby highly suggestible individuals actually experienced a lack of physical functioning. He suggested that hypnotizability be seen as pathognomonic for hysteria. His student Janet (1920) extended these theoretical formulations to include a description of how information kept out of an individual's awareness continues to exert sensory and motor effects via unconscious mechanisms as a dissociative phenomenon (P. Fink, 1996).

Freud (1955) brought the phenomenon of *conversion* to the forefront by theorizing that emotions or internal conflicts not expressed or discharged could be channeled or con verted into physical symptoms that had symbolic significance (First et al., 2004; Iezzi, Duckworth, & Adams, 2001). In his classic case of Dora, Freud described a young woman who lost her voice when her loved one was away on a business trip, as speech had no value when he was not there (LaBruzza & Mendez-Villarrubia, 1997). Thus affect that could not be expressed because of moral or ethical concerns was repressed and converted into somatic-hysterical symptoms. These symptoms were often accompanied by the individual appearing to be unperturbed by her symptoms, described later as "la belle indifference" (G. Taylor, 2003). Using hypnosis, Freud demonstrated that the recollection of past memories and experiences could alleviate the somatic symptoms (Maldonado & Spiegel, 2001). Early clinical indicators of hysteria included the presence of a "battlefield abdomen," reflecting the scars not of combat but of the multiple surgeries conducted by caring physicians responding to their clients' pain complaints (Covington, 2000). *Conversion reaction* first identified in the *DSM-I,* was replaced with Conversion Disorder in the *DSM-III* (American Psychiatric Association, 1968, 1980; Zuckerman, 1999). The disorder in the *DSM-IV-TR* includes only symptoms or deficits affecting the voluntary motor or sensory systems with associated psychological factors (American Psychiatric Association, 2000b; R. L. Martin, 1995).

Hippocrates in AD 200 first used the term *hypochondrium* to describe the area under the rib cage, as the source of disordered emotions (Berrios, 2001). Later, hypochondria was regarded as a severe form of melancholia caused by excessive black bile (Bouman et al., 1999); as a disease of the brain; as the male equivalent of hysteria, characterized by two symptom clusters, one related to digestive problems and the other describing melancholia caused by blocked spleen; and as a disorder of animal spirits (Cullen, 1827; Sydenham, 1850). The clinical presentation included symptoms such as vomiting and convulsions (Berrios & Mumford, 1995). It was referred to as the "English malady" and considered a disease that affected very intelligent individuals from the upper class or a form of insanity caused by excessive worry about health, rich food, and an abundance of alcohol (Fallon & Feinstein, 2001). The afflicted individuals were described as the despair of doctors (Berrios, 2001; Cheyne, 1733; Morel, 1860). In the seventeenth century, the term *hypochondriasis* was used to describe the fear or belief that one had a serious disease. By the nineteenth century it was defined as a nervous disorder or form of insanity, only to be reconceptualized by Freud in the twentieth century as a neurosis (Berrios & Mumford, 1995). Psychodynamic theorists saw Hypochondriasis as a defense against low self-esteem, in that a sick body was less stigmatizing than a sick mind; however, these theories lacked empirical support (Bouman et al., 1999).

Somatization Disorder was originally called Briquet's syndrome after the French physician who in 1859 described patients with a chronic course of numerous unexplained medical or somatic complaints, including muscle pain and weakness, vomiting, aphonia (inability to produce sounds), and paralyses (Bouman et al., 1999; Kent et al., 1995). Stekel (1943), a colleague of Freud, had used the term *somatization* to describe a deep-seated neurosis caused by the conversion or transposition of repressed emotions into physical symptoms (Berrios & Mumford, 1995; De Gucht & Fischler, 2002). In the early 1950s a series of published papers, including a study of textile workers with high rates of absenteeism and unexplained medical complaints, offered the first contemporary conceptualization of what is now called Somatization Disorder (Holder-Perkins & Wise, 2001; G. Taylor, 2003). A list of clinical symptoms was developed and refined over the next 3 decades by Guze, Feighner, and colleagues to form the basis of the *DSM-III* criteria for Somatization Disorder (Bouman et al., 1999; First & Tasman, 2004; R. L. Martin, 1995). The major difference between Briquet's syndrome and the current Somatization Disorder is the absence of anxiety and depressive symptoms in the diagnostic criteria (De Gucht & Fischler, 2002). The current diagnostic criteria are based on a very simple but effective algorithm developed by Cloninger and Yutz (1993) that has a high correspondence with the original criteria and was based on the presence of 4 pain, 2 gastrointestinal, 1 sexual, and 1 pseudo-neurological symptoms, (First & Tasman, 2004).

Pain was first described by Aristotle as an emotion, and then by Descartes as being caused by physical stimuli impacting the body (Bouman et al., 1999). Pain for psychological reasons has been described for centuries as a symptom of hysteria and not significantly different from conversion symptoms (Birket-Smith & Mortensen, 2002). G. E. Engel (1959) described individuals with chronic pain as having pain-prone personalities characterized by pessimism, depression, and the unconscious belief that they did not deserve happiness. In a study of individuals with medically unexplained pain, A. Walters (1969) differentiated conversion hysteria and psychogenic regional pain on the basis of the absence or presence of a symbolic content to the pain. Verhaak, Kerssens, Dekker, Sorbi, and Bensing (1998, p. 231) note in 1986, the International Association for the Study of Pain defined pain as "an unpleasant sensory and emotional experience that is associated with actual and potential tissue damage." Biopsychological models have been proposed by Flor, Birbaumer, and Turk (1990), who describe pain as a complex, multi-determined response that can be learned and is precipitated and facilitated by stress in a biologically predisposed individual. Similarly, Verhaak, Kerssens, Decker, Sorbi, and Bensing (1998) describe Loeser's earlier model of pain, which places the physical origin of the pain at its core, surrounded by layers of pain experience and suffering that cumulates in pain behavior. It was not until recently that pain was recognized as a separate and distinct psychiatric condition (Bouman et al., 1999). Pain Disorder was adopted in the *DSM-IV* and was expanded to include medical conditions that contribute to the pain, given that psychological factors are determined to play a role in symptom expression (American Psychiatric Association, 2000b). Acute and chronic specifiers were added to allow for a description of the duration of the illness (R. L. Martin, 1995). The current definition of pain has been criticized as being so broad that it lacks specificity and its assessment is difficult (Santos, Schwarz, & Aladjem, 2002).

The clinical symptoms of excessive concern with an imagined or greatly exaggerated physical defect, characteristic of Body Dysmorphic Disorder (BDD) have a long history in both European and Asian literature. Various terms have been used, including dermatologic hypochondriasis, imagined ugliness disease, and beauty hypochondria (K. A. Phillips, 2001). The term *dysmorphophobia* was coined by Enrico Morselli (1886) to describe an obsessional preoccupation with a physical defect or feeling of ugliness despite a normal appearance (Berrios & Mumford, 1995; Rivera & Borda, 2001). In Freud's case of the Wolfman, the individual had what could be considered a dysmorphic preoccupation with his nose (First & Tasman, 2004). The specific diagnostic criteria for BDD first occurred in the *DSM-III-R* (American Psychiatric Association, 1987). It was redefined as a separate disorder within the somatoform disorders category in the *DSM-IV,* and the preoccupation was allowed to be held at delusional intensity without precluding a BDD diagnosis (American Psychiatric Association, 2000b; R. L. Martin, 1995).

The goal of the *DSM-III*'s introduction of the somatoform disorders category was to facilitate differential diagnosis by clustering together disorders with physical symptoms, where the common diagnostic issue was the exclusion of a physical cause (R. L. Martin, 1995). In the *DSM-IV* the disorders were arranged based on a rationale relating to the pervasiveness of presentation, chronicity, and the nature of the complaints. Thus Somatization Disorder, characterized by a chronic course of multiple complaints, is followed by the similar but less severe Undifferentiated Somatoform Disorder. Conversion and Pain Disorders, which are characterized by very specific types of symptoms, are followed by Hypochondriasis and Body Dysmorphic Disorder, which emphasize a preoccupation with or misinterpretation of bodily symptoms (R. L. Martin, 1995). The last disorder is the residual or NOS syndrome (American Psychiatric Association, 2000b).

Despite their long history, somatoform disorders remain to date difficult to diagnosis and classify (Iezzi et al., 2001; T. N. Wise & Birket-Smith, 2002). Many of the category's diagnostic criteria refer to normative patterns of behavior such as medical help seeking and checking appearance that are never defined, and there is considerable overlap of the disorders within this category (Bouman et al., 1999). There is also an overreliance on physical symptoms as reliable and valid diagnostic criteria, which may be influenced by the clinician's disease preoccupation and the patient's suggestibility and may underestimate the role of behavioral and social factors (Bouman et al., 1999; P. Fink, 1996). Rief and Sharpe (2004) concluded that the term somatoform lacks acceptance in most areas of medicine and psychiatry and is rarely used by medical doctors because the current classification is inadequate. In contrast, Wijeratne and colleagues (2003) contend that there is a misperception that somatoform disorders are rare disorders that have not been validated as independent entities, and this has impeded the consideration of these disorders particularly in older adults. In recommending changes for the *DSM-V,* Mayou and colleagues (2003; Mayou, Kirmayer, Simon, Kroenke, & Sharpe, 2005) state that the current classification system results in the inconsistent diagnosis of physical symptoms, an overreliance on symptoms counting for Somatization Disorder, and a lack of reliability, validity, and clinical utility for Hypochondriasis and BDD.

SOMATIZATION DISORDER

The key feature of Somatization Disorder is a pattern beginning before age 30 of recurring, multiple, clinically significant somatic complaints that cannot be fully explained by any known medical condition, that result in significant impairment in functioning or distress (American Psychiatric Association, 2000b; Hurwitz, 2004). The polysymptomatic clinical presentation includes a combination of pain (which can arise from different sites), gastrointestinal, sexual, and pseudo-neurological symptoms, which result in excessive medical help-seeking behavior (First & Tasman, 2004). Individuals with this disorder are high users of medical services, seeking numerous medical examinations, laboratory tests, medications, and potentially dangerous surgical procedures (Asaad, 2000; De Waal et al., 2004). They account for 20% of distressed, frequent primary care services users, and the quality of their life is often poor and with extensive periods of disability (Ladwig, Marten-Mittag, Erazo, & Gundel, 2001; Looper & Kirmayer, 2002). Frequently found in general medical settings, these individuals rarely seek psychiatric treatment unless urged to do so by their primary physician (Holder-Perkins & Wise, 2001). Cross-culturally, individuals with somatic concerns are at increased risk for a negative perception of their health, co-morbid anxiety, depression, significant disability, and self-reported disease burden (Gureje, Simon, Ustun, & Goldberg, 1997).

Clinical Presentation

Physical Symptoms

Somatization Disorder is characterized by an early onset (before 30), chronicity (several years), and marked impairment. Full remission occurs rarely, if ever (First & Tasman, 2004). This diagnosis is not meant to describe mild, brief, or late-onset presentations of unexplained physical symptoms (First et al., 2004). It is assigned only when the physical complaints result in the individual's seeking treatment or cause clinically significant impairment or distress (American Psychiatric Association, 2000b). Grabe and colleagues (2003) found that the criteria of significant impairment and distress differentiated individuals with unexplained somatic symptoms from those that have a more severe form in the general population. Children and adolescents can present with a range of somatic complaints; however, the requirement of several years' duration makes this disorder very rare in this age group (Bursch, 2006).

The clinical symptoms and signs are clustered into four thematic areas (pain, gastro-intestinal, sexual, and pseudo-neurological), based on the approximate order of their reported frequency (Morrison, 1995a). There must be a history of pain involving at least four different sites or functions, such as head, back, and extremities. At least two gastro-intestinal symptoms, such as bloating and diarrhea, at least one sexual symptom, such as sexual indifference or excessive menstrual bleeding, and at least one pseudo-neurological symptom, such as paralysis, blindness, or seizures, must also be present (American Psychiatric Association, 2000b). The clustering of symptoms aims to facilitate the clinician's recall and improve the reliability and clinical utility of the diagnosis (Holder-Perkins & Wise, 2001). However, the diagnostic criteria have been criticized as overly restrictive, still focusing on symptom counting (4P2G1S1P) and not including aspects of the disorder that relate to behavior, cognitive attributions, and personality (LaBruzza & Mendez-Villarrubia, 1997; T. N. Wise & Birket-Smith, 2002). There has been a call for the *DSM-V* to consider classifying the physical symptoms on a severity continuum rather than relying on symptom counting (Mayou et al., 2003, 2005; M. D. Sullivan, 2000). Also although the current criteria require fewer symptoms than in the past, they have also been criticized as relying on symptoms that are "uncommon in routine clinical practice" (Wijeratne et al., 2003, p. 814). Epidemiological research (Rief, Hessel, & Braehler, 2001) indicates that the most frequent presenting symptoms in the general population are pain symptoms, specifically back pain (30%), followed by joint pain (25%) and pain in the extremities (20%). These are followed by dysphagia, nausea, bloating, constipation, palpitation, dizziness, and shortness of breath (Looper & Kirmayer, 2002). Of note, while presenting with multiple somatic complaints, these individuals do not have more physical illnesses than individuals in the general population (Noyes, 2001).

Somatization Disorder can be diagnosed only when a GMC has been ruled out (American Psychiatric Association, 2000b; Bouman et al., 1999). If the client has an existing medical condition, the presentation must be in excess of what would be expected (American Psychiatric Association, 2000b; Morrison, 1995a). Additionally, the presence of a substance-related disorder, Factitious Disorder, or malingering must also be ruled out (American Psychiatric Association, 2000b).

Undifferentiated Somatoform Disorder

If the full diagnostic criteria for Somatization Disorder are not met in terms of number, duration, and severity of symptoms or age of onset, a diagnosis of Undifferentiated Somatoform Disorder can be assigned (American Psychiatric Association, 2000b; Marmer, 1999). This may include one or more physical complaints that persist for 6 months or longer that cannot be explained by a GMC or are in excess of what is expected. The symptoms cause clinical distress or impairment and are not intentionally produced or accounted for by another mental disorder (American Psychiatric Association, 2000b). The four most common presenting symptoms are decreased appetite, stomach upset, genito-urinary complaints (irritable bowel syndrome), and unexplained or chronic fatigue (First & Tasman, 2004; LaBruzza & Mendez-Villarrubia, 1997). The placement of fatigue symptoms in this residual category has been criticized as contributing to an underestimation of these symptoms in primary care settings, particularly of the elderly, where rates of 24% to 37% of persistent fatigue have been reported (Wijeratne et al., 2003). Included here are a wide range of somatization symptoms that account for the majority of somatoform disorders seen in medical practice and the general population (Grabe et al., 2003; G. E. Simon, 2002.).

Additional Characteristics

Vague, Exaggerated Communication Style

Although individuals with Somatization Disorder have numerous somatic complaints, when asked to describe details they are inconsistent historians. Their reports may be characterized by colorful terms, an overall dramatic style lacking in specific factual information, and symptoms that change upon repeated interviews (American Psychiatric Association, 2000b). Several studies (Garralda, 1996; Issac et al., 1996) suggest that the tendency to somatize may be associated with alexithymia (the inability to verbalize one's emotions). This is characterized by having difficulty differentiating between bodily sensations of emotional arousal and feelings, limited emotional functioning, a restrictive imaginative process, and a reality-based concrete presentation (L. Seligman, 1998). However, the role of alexithymia in the etiology of somatoform disorders is controversial (First & Tasman, 2004).

Multiple Doctor Visits

In reviewing the pattern of clinical presentation, Looper and Kirmayer (2002) describe how initially the primary care physician's concern is one of ruling out treatable medical conditions. When none are found, the focus becomes containing the perceived excessive help-seeking behavior, and the doctor-patient relationship deteriorates. The referral to mental health services may be perceived as a questioning of the individual's veracity or abandonment, as these individuals have little insight into the role that psychological factors play and their motivation for such treatment is limited (Asaad, 2000; De Waal et al., 2004).

Individuals with Somatization Disorder also often present with complex medical histories characterized by inconsistencies between their subjective complaints and the objective findings (A. Frances & Ross, 2001). In their quest to identify a medical basis for their symptoms, they frequently visit many doctors who may not be aware of one another's treatment, resulting in a potentially hazardous combination of treatments (American Psychiatric Association, 2000b). The physician's inability to form a diagnosis and inadequate medical advice may also prolong the symptoms (Haugaard, 2004). These individuals have a threefold higher use of ambulatory medical services and a ninefold higher overall cost for health care than nonsomatically preoccupied patients (Holder-Perkins & Wise, 2001). Their medical visits are often associated with unnecessary medical procedures, such as X-rays and laboratory exams, and may result in surgeries (Fink et al., 2004). When compared to patients with chronic medical conditions (e.g., hypertension, rheumatoid arthritis), Somatization Disorder clients typically rate their health as worse. Their distrust and the negative nature of their relationships with their providers often contribute to "lousy" care, poor follow-through, and the prescription of medication that contributes to a substance-related disorder and reinforces the individual's illness beliefs (Bouman et al., 1999; Maxmen & Ward, 1995).

Chaotic Lives

The lives of individuals with Somatization Disorder are often disorganized, chaotic, and marked by impulsivity and failure to cope with life's stresses (Bouman et al., 1999; L. Seligman, 1998). Relationship discord in the form of multiple divorces and remarriages and work problems involving frequent absences for medical appointments and high rates of disability are common. Often bedridden for 2 to 7 days per month, they are notoriously difficult to treat and often refractory to treatment, incurring 6 to 14 times the per capita annual health care expense (L. A. Allen et al., 2001). They may also attempt or threaten suicide (First & Tasman, 2004). Thomassen, van Hemert, Huyse, van der Mast, and Hengeveld (2003) found that those with Somatization Disorder referred to a consultation and liaison service were more frequently disabled and unemployed than individuals with any other psychiatric disorder.

Onset, Course, and Life Span Considerations

Onset

The symptoms of Somatization Disorder are present before age 30, with the initial symptoms often presenting by adolescence (First & Tasman, 2004; H. I. Kaplan & Saddock,

1996). The presence of somatization in young children may be influenced by their immature cognitive and verbal skills and limited emotional vocabulary, which may contribute to an impaired ability to verbalize distress (Garralda, 1996). In a prospective-longitudinal community follow-up study in Germany, Lieb and colleagues (2002) found an incidence rate of 25.7% for somatoform disorders in adolescents. Menstrual difficulties can frequently be an early sign, and sexual symptoms accompanied by marital discord are often the initial presenting problem.

Course

The course of the disorder is chronic, with new symptoms developing during times of emotional distress. Clinical symptoms may fluctuate, but the disorder itself rarely remits (American Psychiatric Association, 2000b; Groholt, Stigum, Nordhagen, & Kohler, 2003). There are no consistent findings on how long an illness episode lasts, but clinical reports suggest 6 to 9 months. Few individuals go for a year without seeking some type of health care or developing new symptoms, and they are at significant risk for impaired health perception on follow-up a year later (Fink et al., 2004). The development of new symptoms and additional conditions has been linked to lower class female status, the presence of mood, anxiety, and substance abuse symptoms, and the experience of physical threat or traumatic sexual experience (Groholt et al., 2003). Somatization Disorder is relatively stable for a substantial proportion of individuals, with 76.3% meeting the diagnostic criteria after a 4-year follow-up (Lieb et al., 2002). In comparison to individuals presenting with Pain and Conversion Disorders, individuals with Somatization Disorder present with higher levels of anxiety, depression, and personality disorder traits (Birket-Smith & Mortensen, 2002).

Life Span Considerations

Contrary to expectation, the reporting of physical complaints does not increase with age. Sheehan and Banerjee (1999) suggest that in fact, elderly individuals may downplay symptoms and use medical as opposed to psychiatric services. The lower elderly rates for this disorder may reflect a referral bias and the lack of research on this age group (Wijeratne et al., 2003). The diagnostic criteria may also be unsuitable for use with this population, in that some of the diagnostic pseudo-neurological symptoms (blindness and deafness) and nonspecific symptoms of weakness are more likely to be endorsed by older adults in general (Wijeratne et al., 2003).

CONVERSION DISORDER

Conversion Disorder remains an elusive and controversial entity even though conversion phenomena have been described throughout the medical literature since antiquity (Maldonado & Spiegel, 2001). Typically an individual presents with voluntary motor and sensory deficits that appear to be related to psychological factors and do not follow known anatomical pathways unless the individual is privy to medical training (A. Frances & Ross, 2001). The clinical presentation is predominantly sign-based, involving psychogenic motor-sensory or neurological deficits that have a clear symbolic meaning and are fewer than required for Somatization Disorder (Brasic, 2002; Holder-Perkins & Wise, 2001; Hurwitz, 2004).

Clinical Presentation

Motor and Sensory Symptoms

The key feature of a Conversion Disorder is the presence of one or more symptoms or deficits affecting voluntary motor or sensory function that suggest a neurological condition or other GMC (American Psychiatric Association, 2000b). These symptoms are often referred to as pseudo-neurological. The most common motoric symptoms are weakness, paralysis, muscular spasm, dysphagia, and involuntary movements (Looper & Kirmayer, 2002). These motor symptoms or deficits, which are often coarse, tend to worsen when attention is directed at them and may include tics, jerks. and catatonic-like postures (Maldonado & Spiegel, 2001). Sensory deficits can occur in any sensory modality and are often inconsistent with anatomical sensory pathways; over time they can present with an idiosyncratic pattern, such as glove or stocking paralysis (Maldonado & Spiegel, 2001; Morrison, 1995a). Common sensory deficits involve the loss of touch or pain sensation, double vision, seizures, and convulsions (American Psychiatric Association, 2000b). Conversion seizures (also called pseudo-seizures or nonepileptic seizures) are typically longer and more frequent than epileptic seizures; they tend to occur in the presence of others and can be characterized by bizarre and unusual behavior (O'Shea, 2003). Typically they have a variable gradual onset, with bodily movements that appear coordinated and synchronous; they are rarely associated with injury, postictal confusion, or abnormal EEG or accompanied by incontinence and can be linked with an acute environmental stressor (Maldonado & Spiegel, 2001).

Psychological Factors

Psychological factors are thought to be involved with the symptom or deficit, based on the observation that the initiation or exacerbation of the symptoms is preceded by conflicts or other stressors (American Psychiatric Association, 2000b). In most cases, the individual is unaware of the psychological basis of the symptoms, and the causal link between the stressor and symptom can be very difficult to determine (Bouman et al., 1999; Morrison, 1995a). First and Tasman (2004) conclude that the determination of the role of psychological factors is highly subjective and of questionable reliability and validity. Kirmayer and Tillefer (1997) note that although in some cases the symptoms may have a symbolic meaning, in most they are more readily attributable to available models of illness (e.g., patients with true seizure disorder may develop pseudo-seizures) and often follow an extreme stressor (e.g., death of a loved one). An exploration of the family history may reveal a family member with an illness after which the patient's symptoms are modeled. For motor Conversion Disorder, the use of psychological factors, conflicts, and other stressors has been criticized as having psychoanalytic overtones and is not specific enough to discriminate these disorders from Somatization Disorder or malingering (Krem, 2004).

Misdiagnosis

The exclusion of an underlying or contributing GMC is often difficult (Iezzi et al., 2001; LaBruzza & Mendez-Villarrubia,). In a review of available studies, Moene and colleagues

(2000) found anywhere from 4% to 67% of individuals diagnosed with Conversion Disorder were later found to have had an organic condition, and 11.8% of individuals initially diagnosed with a Conversion Disorder were found to have a neurological disorder on follow-up reassessment. The high percentage (70%) of individuals with a Conversion Disorder and coexisting neurological disorders (Maldonado & Spiegel, 2001) may contribute to the high rates (30%) of individuals misdiagnosed with a Conversion Disorder who were later found to have an organic illness (Hurwitz, 2004). These diagnostic challenges led Kent and colleagues (1995) to conclude that the diagnosis of Conversion Disorder in comparison to Somatization Disorder carried greater diagnostic uncertainty, was more unstable, and was more likely to have a medical illness underlying the chief complaint. More recently, the rate of misdiagnosis may be decreasing secondary to advances in diagnostic technology and greater awareness of rare neurological disorders (Looper & Kirmayer, 2002). The exclusion of culturally sanctioned behavior or experiences highlights the need for the clinician to review the *DSM-IV-TR*'s descriptions of culture-bound syndromes and to consider the cultural context of the individual's clinical presentation (Chaplin, 1997). The diagnostic differential with factitious disorders and malingering is complicated and is addressed later in this chapter.

Because conversion symptoms are part of Somatization Disorder, if the other criteria for Somatization Disorder are met, Conversion Disorder is not diagnosed (American Psychiatric Association, 2000b). In comparison to Somatization Disorder, Conversion Disorder requires less long-term morbidity, impairment, and disability, and the clinical symptoms tend to be self-limiting and do not lead to disability or physical changes (First & Tasman, 2004; Kent et al., 1995).

Additional Characteristics

These individuals' presentation may vary from what appears to be a lack of concern about their symptoms ("la belle indifference") to a dramatic or histrionic reaction (American Psychiatric Association, 2000b). The so-called hysterical personality is rarely seen, and its prevalence is as low as 8% in both adult and pediatric Conversion Disorder cases (Bursch, 2006; Maldonado & Spiegel, 2001). There is no one pathognomonic presentation for Conversion Disorder, and many medical patients may appear stoic, making the use of "la belle indifference" less useful as a discriminating feature (Bloom, 2001; Hurwitz, 2004).

Onset, Course, and Life Span Considerations

Onset

The age of onset may be in late childhood through early adulthood and rarely occurs prior to age 10 or after age 35 (Maldonado & Spiegel, 2001). There are few studies on childhood Conversion Disorder, and many cases go undiagnosed or may be misdiagnosed (Brasic, 2002). For children, this diagnosis is often shrouded in uncertainty, lacking in satisfactory explanations, doctor-patient hostility, shame, and family silence (Kozlowska, 2003). Early recognition and prompt intervention can result in recovery in the majority (85% to 97%) of childhood cases, with the illness being as short as a few days (Leary, 2003). Conversion symptoms in children are usually limited to gait problems or seizures

(American Psychiatric Association, 2000b). The age of onset may be somewhat later for men (e.g., 25) than women (e.g., 17), and there is often a 6- to 8-year delay before Conversion Disorder is actually diagnosed (Maldonado & Spiegel, 2001). There are also reports that clinical symptoms can have an onset in middle or late adulthood (H. I. Kaplan & Saddock, 1996).

Course

In most cases, the symptoms come on abruptly and then resolve within a short time, with patients hospitalized for conversion symptoms usually experiencing a remission within 2 weeks (American Psychiatric Association, 2000b). The recurrence of symptoms is common; 20% to 25% will have another episode within a year of the first episode (Maldonado & Spiegel, 2001). For motor Conversion Disorder, recovery may occur within days or months and may be complete or incomplete (Krem, 2004). Certain symptoms, such as paralysis, blindness, and aphonia, seem to be associated with a better outcome, whereas tremor and seizures and polysymptomatic presentation are not (H. I. Kaplan & Saddock, 1996). Acute onset, the presence of a clearly identified precipitant, a short duration between onset and treatment, and the absence of comorbid conditions all relate to a more favorable prognosis (Krem, 2004; Leary, 2003). In a 4-year follow-up of children and adolescents with Conversion Disorder, Pehlivanturk and Unal (2002) found that the majority (85%) who were diagnosed within a month of onset recovered within 3 months. The rate and the time of recovery and a favorable outcome were related to a short interval between symptom onset and diagnosis and good premorbid functioning. However, even after recovery, there was an increased rate of mood and anxiety disorders, with the rate being highest (100% versus 23.5%) for those who did not recover. In looking at recovery from pseudo-seizures in children using a 6-year symptom survival analysis, Gudmundsson, Prendgast, Foreman, and Cowley (2001) found that the majority recovered and resumed regular school. Hurwitz (2004) describes a subgroup (20%) of treatment-resistant individuals with Conversion Disorder who failed to recover as "invalids of choice." Those who develop a chronic course tend to have a greater comorbidity of psychiatric and medical conditions, experience and report multiple somatic symptoms, poor insight, and severe family dysfunction and conflict, and may eventually go on to meet the diagnostic criteria for Somatization Disorder (First & Tasman, 2004; Kent et al., 1995).

PAIN DISORDER

The presence of pain is one of the most common reasons individuals seek medical treatment (Birket-Smith & Mortensen, 2002). The key feature is the presence of pain at a level of severity that necessitates clinical attention; it can be from multiple sites and take different forms and is triggered or exacerbated by psychological factors (Asaad, 2000). The pain can serve both as a defense against stress and anxiety and as a symptom of stress; it is both a sensation and an emotion (Covington, 2000; H. I. Kaplan & Saddock, 1996). Perquin and colleagues (2000, 2003) report that children and adolescents frequently report stomachaches, headaches, and limb and other body pain, which can become chronic and persistent. In fact, abdominal pain accounts for a significant number of all pediatrician visits, and the majority of cases (75%) have no identifiable disease (Bursch, 2006).

According to L. Seligman (1998), for some individuals with a medically diagnosed physical condition, a Pain Disorder may develop from the physician's minimization or inadequate treatment of the underlying pain. In industrialized countries, chronic pain is a major health concern, with 25% to 30% of the population reporting experiencing chronic pain (Verhaak et al., 1998). Contemporary theories conceptualize chronic pain as multidimensional, including the underlying disorder or structural problem, the experience of the pain, and the associated features of impairment, disability, and emotional distress (Masheb & Kerns, 2000).

Clinical Presentation

Presence and Nature of Pain

The main focus of Pain Disorder is severe pain from one or more anatomical sites that warrants clinical attention (American Psychiatric Association, 2000b). The presence of pain as a presenting clinical symptom in other somatoform disorders contributes to considerable diagnostic overlap and a questioning of the validity of a separate Pain Disorder (T. N. Wise & Birket-Smith, 2002). The most prevalent form of pain is back or joint (musculoskeletal) pain, with headaches and stomach pain also frequently reported (Verhaak et al., 1998). The pain must cause significant distress or impairment. In their community study, Grabe and colleagues (2003) found that one third of individuals with chronic pain had significant impairment and distress.

Psychological Factors

For a diagnosis of Pain Disorder, psychological factors must be judged to have an important role in the pain symptoms (American Psychiatric Association, 2000b; Sharpe & Williams, 2002). These factors may or may not be of sufficient severity or nature to warrant a separate Axis I or Axis II diagnosis. Grabe and colleagues (2003) have criticized this criterion as being difficult to assess and confirm in the general population. In their community survey of individuals with chronic pain, they found only 25% could assign psychological factors to their pain. The role of psychological factors in the attenuation of pain often relies on clinical judgment and is complicated by the subjective nature of pain and the lack of specific organ pathology in many chronic pain patients (Wijeratne et al., 2003). M. D. Sullivan (2000) criticizes the DSM's lack of guidance on how to evaluate the role of psychological factors and states that the diagnosis is fundamentally flawed because it places medical and psychological causes for pain in opposition to one another.

Other Types of Pain

The clinician must determine that the pain is not intentional or feigned or not better accounted for by another disorder such as anxiety, mood, or psychotic disorders, which take diagnostic precedence (American Psychiatric Association, 2000b). If the pain is restricted to sexual intercourse, then the sexual disorder Dyspareunia is assigned. These diagnostic differentials are often based on highly subjective decisions (First & Tasman, 2004). The clinician then codes the disorder to differentiate whether the clinical presentation occurs with psychological factors, with a GMC, or a combination. An acute course specifier is assigned when the duration is less than 6 months; if longer than 6 months a chronic course specifier is assigned. The medical condition or site of the pain is also coded on Axis III (American Psychiatric Association, 2000b). The *DSM-IV-TR* includes a section on Pain Disorder associated with a GMC, where psychological factors are determined not to be involved (American Psychiatric Association, 2000b). This condition is not a mental disorder per se; however, individuals with this clinical presentation are often treated by mental health professionals (A. Frances & Ross, 2001). The *DSM-IV-TR* also describes a five-axis system for the classification of chronic pain that was proposed by the International Association for the Study of Pain (American Psychiatric Association, 2000b).

Additional Characteristics

Chronic, uncontrolled, and prolonged pain can alter both the central and peripheral nervous systems and become a disease in its own right and associated with other psychiatric disorders, as in unexplained facial pain, which frequently results in high rates of depression (First & Tasman, 2004; Hersen & Turner, 2003). Pain can also be associated with fatigue, inactivity, social isolation, and reduced physical endurance; pain associated with severe depression and terminal illness is related to a higher risk for suicide (Bouman et al., 1999; C. Ford, 1995). Individuals with both acute and chronic pain often experience sleep problems, including frequent awakenings, nonrestorative sleep, and difficulty falling asleep (American Psychiatric Association, 2000b). In an effort to obtain relief from their chronic pain, these individuals frequently doctor-shop, have multiple providers, are at risk for abusing pain medication, and often engender hostility in caregivers who feel thwarted and refer to their clients as "crocks" (Covington, 2000).

Onset, Course, and Life Span Considerations

Onset

While Pain Disorder can occur at any age, it is more common in women than in men, with a typical onset in early adulthood (H. I. Kaplan & Saddock, 1996). Pain Disorder associated with both psychological factors and a GMC is the most common form of illness that results in work and domestic responsibilities being neglected (A. Frances & Ross, 2001). For many individuals, the fear of what is causing the pain and fear of developing a serious disability result in their decreasing normal activity or avoiding specific activities or movements, which further worsens the situation (Bouman et al., 1999; Sharpe & Williams, 2002). The onset of disabling pain is strongly associated with adverse work conditions such as stress, dissatisfaction, and perceived income inadequacies (L. Seligman, 1998). Occupational factors such as the overuse of a body part from repetitive lifting have been related to the development of specific pain syndromes (Bouman et al., 1999).

Course

These factors and the individual's tendency to catastrophize and somatize contribute to the progression of the pain to a chronic course (Covington, 2000). The prevalence of chronic pain increases with age, with the peak prevalence occurring between age 45 and 65 (Verhaak et al., 1998). As the symptoms persist there may be increasing levels of incapacitation and impairment and more frequent use of pain medication and health services

(C. Ford, 1995). In some cases, this may result in complete invalidism, with the individual becoming homebound (Morrison, 1995a).

Life Span Considerations

Kashikar-Zuck, Vaught, Goldschneider, Graham, and Miller (2002) found that chronic pain significantly impacted children's daily lives, and the presence of depression was related to greater disability. In a community sample of children with unexplained chronic physical pain, Hunfeld and colleagues (2002) found that family life was adversely impacted by the child's pain, with the mother reporting a restriction of social life and increased personal strain.

HYPOCHONDRIASIS

The essential feature of Hypochondriasis is a preoccupation with fears of having a serious disease, or that one has a disease based on a misinterpretation of one of more bodily symptoms; thus a cold becomes a sign of lung cancer (American Psychiatric Association, 2000b; Asaad, 2000). Individuals with this disorder have been described as having a bodily preoccupation, disease phobia, disease conviction or a morbid fear of having a disease, health anxiety, or illness worry (Berrios, 2001; Shearer & Gordon, 2006). Between 4% and 10% of general medical patients experience some degree of hypochondriacal symptoms (Bouman, 2002). The clinical presentation is predominantly symptom based, in that an otherwise healthy person reports persistent unfounded fears, unreasonable conviction, and preoccupations, which results in impairment (Hurwitz, 2004; Morrison, 1995a). Factor analyses suggest three dimensions are typically involved: a bodily preoccupation, a disease phobia and conviction of the presence of a disease, and nonresponsiveness to reassurance (Starcevic, 2001). These features may exist in differing degrees, such that an individual with significant bodily preoccupation may check his or her body repeatedly or emphasize physical ailments when talking to others. In contrast, an individual with a high level of disease phobia might avoid seeing a physician. Individuals with a high level of disease conviction are often the most difficult for physicians to tolerate because they tend to respond with hostility to reassurances that no disease is present (Fallon & Feinstein, 2001). The urgency of the clinical presentation, the strongly expressed concern and anxiety about what is wrong, the history of numerous negative medical tests, and covert and overt seeking of reassurance are all indicators of this disorder (Sharpe & Williams, 2002). For many it is a disabling, chronic condition that is generally refractory to pharmacological and psychological interventions (Barsky & Ahern, 2004).

Clinical Presentation

Preoccupations

The hallmark of Hypochondriasis is the presence of a preoccupation with fears of having, or the idea that one has, a serious disease based on a misinterpretation of bodily symptoms (American Psychiatric Association, 2000b). According to Fink and colleagues (2004), rumination about illness is one of the central clinical features and may involve several body systems or may be restricted to a single organ or to a specific disease. The focus of attention may be on bodily functions such as heartbeat, minor physical abnormalities such as a small sore, or vague and ambiguous sensations like aching veins (American Psychiatric Association, 2000b). The inclusion of the presence of bodily symptoms has been controversial as it excludes individuals who are convinced of having a serious disease in the absence of physical symptoms, such as individuals who fear they have HIV because of presumed exposure (First & Tasman, 2004). Currently, these individuals would be diagnosed with Somatoform Disorder NOS (American Psychiatric Association, 2000b). The use of preoccupation and fears interchangeable with ideas or beliefs to describe the same disorder, rather than discrete subtypes, has been criticized; diagnostic criteria also fail to differentiate having a *fear of a disease* from *the conviction* that one has a disease (Bouman et al., 1999; Starcevic, 2001). The preoccupation should not be restricted to a circumscribed concern about appearance, as in Body Dysmorphic Disorder (American Psychiatric Association, 2000b). Also, the preoccupation must not occur solely in the presence of an anxiety or mood episode (American Psychiatric Association, 2000b). Determining the chronology of the clinical symptoms and using a symptom time line can assist in discriminating between different conditions (First & Tasman, 2004). Unlike Somatization Disorder, the focus of Hypochondriasis is on the fear of an illness rather than concern about the physical complaints.

Reassurance

It is not unusual for these individuals to seek numerous medical consultations and unnecessary laboratory tests and to remain fixed in their belief despite contradictory medical findings (American Psychiatric Association, 2000b). The *DSM-IV-TR*'s requirement that the individual does not respond to appropriate medical reassurance has been criticized as being overly restrictive and necessitates disagreement between the individual and the physician before the disorder can be assigned (American Psychiatric Association, 2000b; Fink et al., 2004). What constitutes appropriate medical reassurance is also not defined (Starcevic, 2001).

Delusions

Although the intensity of the individual's belief may appear similar to somatic delusions, this differentiation is essential (American Psychiatric Association, 2000b). Unfortunately, there is no clear boundary between a compelling but nondelusional idea (an overvalued idea) that one has a medical condition and the unshakable conviction (somatic delusion) that one has a disease (First et al., 2004). The intensity of these preoccupations and the individual's openness to contrary information can wax and wane over the course of the illness (American Psychiatric Association, 2000b). This distinction is likely to come down to a judgment call that is dependent on consideration of factors such as the severity, duration, degree of conviction, and presence of other characteristic symptoms. If the concerns are of delusional intensity, Hypochondriasis should not be diagnosed (First & Tasman, 2004). If for most of the current episode the person does not recognize that the concern about having a serious illness is excessive or unreasonable, the specifier *with poor insight* is assigned (American Psychiatric Association, 2000b). The use of this specifier has been criticized as confusing as it implies that there are individuals who recognize that their concerns are excessive and unreasonable, which does not seem to be the case for the majority of individuals (Starcevic, 2001).

Impairment

The clinical symptoms must cause significant distress and impairment (American Psychiatric Association, 2000b). Individuals with Hypochondriasis spend inordinate amounts of time engaging in repetitive checking patterns and seeking reassurance and medical evaluations, which result in significant interpersonal and occupational impairments (Fallon & Feinstein, 2001). The requirement that symptoms persist for at least 6 months has been criticized as being arbitrary, having limited validity in nonpsychiatric settings, and by definition excluding acute cases that may benefit from early intervention (Fink et al., 2004).

Additional Characteristics

Cognitive Style

Individuals with Hypochondriasis frequently present with an anxious cognitive style characterized by catastrophizing, doubts, preoccupations, and, at times, obsessional thoughts (Bouman, 2002). They tend to feel uncertain in appraising situations most people would find nonthreatening and have a persistent tendency to misinterpret innocuous physical symptoms as evidence of serious disease or illness (Magarinos, Zafar, Nissenson, & Blanco, 2002). Becoming overly focused on their bodily sensations, they selectively attend to illness-related information, make incorrect assumptions about health and illness, and tend to have more negative perceptions of their own health (Bouman et al., 1999; Magarinos et al., 2002).

Reassurance and Checking Behaviors

In an effort to allay their fears of having an illness, these individuals may try to impose excessive structure on their life, often developing a variety of inflexible rules. They may perform repetitive checking behaviors, including continually asking family and clinicians for reassurance, scheduling multiple doctor appointments, consulting medical books, and checking their body for disease (Fallon & Feinstein, 2001). They may become alarmed on reading or hearing about a disease or knowing someone who is sick, and fears of aging and death are common (American Psychiatric Association, 2000b). They may spend hours on the Internet and in chat rooms checking for illness signs and symptoms (Carrns, 1999; Shearer & Gordon, 2006).

Interpersonal Problems

Not surprisingly, interpersonal relationships are often strained as individuals with Hypochondriasis are often angry and hostile (L. Seligman, 1998). Health concerns may be their primary topic of conversation, and they may expect to be treated differently because of their presumed health maladies (American Psychiatric Association, 2000b). They are more frequent users of health services, take more medication, perceive themselves as more ill and more disabled, and receive excessive medical evaluations (First et al., 2004). The diagnosis of Hypochondriasis is by definition based on disagreement with the physician (Pilowsky, 2001). Doctor shopping and poor doctor-patient relationships are common; they more often disagree with their doctor over health status, feel they were not properly evaluated, and are more likely not to keep appointments (Lipsitt, 2001; Noyes, 2001). Many engender hostility in their treating physicians, who perceive them as uncooperative, using medical services inappropriately, and refusing to accept reassurance and referral to a psychiatrist, which can result in treating professionals acting blatantly disrespectfully toward the client (Pilowsky, 2001).

Onset, Course, and Life Span Considerations

Hypochondriasis can start at any time, but early adulthood is most common (Fallon & Feinstein, 2001). It is a chronic disorder (lasting at least 6 months) whose course waxes and wanes with remissions; the majority of individuals experience a chronic fluctuating course and a smaller percentage (36.5%) present with a transient form (Magarinos et al., 2002; Starcevic, 2001). Looper and Kirmayer (2002) note that many individuals present with acute hypochondriacal concerns in primary care settings, which resolve spontaneously or with physician reassurance; these individuals have overall less psychiatric comorbidity. In general, the disorder tends to be very stable, with 64% of medical outpatients initially diagnosed still fulfilling the diagnostic criteria 5 years later (Lieb et al., 2002). In a large international study of primary care patients, 45% on follow-up had persistent Hypochondriasis with a high overlap with anxiety and depressive disorders (G. E. Simon, Guerje, & Fullerton, 2001). Because of its chronicity, some view the disorder as having prominent trait-like characteristics and have questioned its validity as a separate disorder rather than a variant of Somatization Disorder (Starcevic, 2001). Life stressors are usually associated with exacerbation. Illness and medical appointments often interfere with work, and job performance is often impaired (Noyes, 2001). A subgroup of individuals (36.5%) characterized by less psychiatric comorbidity and more medical morbidity may experience a briefer transient form of Hypochondriasis (Magarinos et al., 2002).

Good prognosis is associated with the presence of anxiety or depression, sudden onset, young age of onset, high social class, and the absence of cognitive deficits or a personality disorder. In inpatients with Hypochondriasis Hiller, Leibbrand, Rief, and Fitcher (2002) found that the severity of the disorder, prior hospital utilization, and the level of pretreatment of Hypochondriasis were negative predictors for treatment outcome. They also found that the strongest predictors of poor outcome in short-term treatment were dysfunctional cognitions and disability at work.

BODY DYSMORPHIC DISORDER

Body Dysmorphic Disorder tends to be underrecognized, underreported, frequently misdiagnosed, and to present primarily in medical settings (A. Frances & Ross, 2001). These physically normal individuals present with a belief that some part of their body is ugly, deformed, hideous, and or misshapen (Morrison, 1995a). This faulty or disturbed belief involves a body dysperception that becomes a chronically disabling preoccupation that intensifies in social situations and results in social withdrawal and isolation (Rivera & Borda, 2001). Cororve and Gleaves (2001) suggest it is helpful to conceptualized BDD as a body image disorder with psychological, social, and even biological influences involving a perceptual, attitudinal, and affective component. The development of numerous associated compulsive behaviors results in notably impaired functioning, often accompanied by intense feelings of shame and humiliation. Many individuals become housebound (31%) and may be misdiagnosed as agoraphobic or admitted to psychiatric hospitals. There is a 48% lifetime prevalence rate (K. A. Phillips, Menard, Fay, & Pagano, 2005; M. Zimmerman & Mattia, 1998). These individuals are often embarrassed and reluctant to seek help and are chronically plagued by emotional desperation, recurrent preoccupations, and compulsive behaviors that frequently involve self-mutilation and at times death (Sarwer, Creand, & Didie, 2003). Nearly all children diagnosed with BDD (94%) experienced significant social and academic impairment, 18% had dropped out of school, and 21% had attempted suicide (Albertini & Phillips, 2001; K. A. Phillips, 2000). The providers of choice are dermatologists or cosmetic surgeons; many of those with BDD undergo multiple procedures or surgeries, the vast majority (83%) of which lead to no change, increased BDD symptoms, and high levels of dissatisfaction (76%; Sarwer et al., 2003).

Clinical Presentation

Excessive Concern

The key feature of BDD is a preoccupation with an imagined defect in appearance; if a slight physical anomaly is present, the person's concern is markedly excessive (American Psychiatric Association, 2000b). The issue is not unhappiness with one's appearance or a focus on an actual abnormality but rather the intensity of the individual's perception of and belief in the level of severity of the abnormality (Bouman et al., 1999). The complaint can be specific or vague, and any part of the body may become a focus of attention. The most common concerns are the skin (61%), hair (55%), some aspect of the face or head, that is, facial asymmetry, or the shape and size of features such as the nose or eyes (Albertini & Phillips, 2001). Most individuals with BDD are concerned with three to four features, and concern can shift from one feature to another, with some concerns disappearing altogether (Sarwer et al., 2003; Veale et al., 1996). The preoccupation is not the dissatisfaction with body shape and size that occurs in Anorexia Nervosa (American Psychiatric Association, 2000a); however, when overall body size is of concern, this differential may be difficult to make.

Impairment

The preoccupation causes clinically significant distress or impairment in social, occupational, or other important areas of functioning (American Psychiatric Association, 2000a,b). While the boundary between "normal" concerns and more pathological dissatisfactions about appearance can be hard to draw, this diagnosis should be reserved for individuals who become significantly preoccupied and tormented by their supposed deformity, which is experienced as repulsive or unacceptable (First et al., 2004). A clue to the diagnosis of BDD is when these individuals' worries about appearance become a dominant focus of their life, to the point that they are unable to stop thinking about it and nothing else has significance (Sarwer et al., 2003). Albertini and Phillips (2001) found that 68% of their BDD sample spent more than 3 hours a day thinking about the defect,

59% engaged in excessive grooming, and 25% compulsively picked at their skin for more than 8 hours a day. Individuals may also develop elaborate masking and camouflaging strategies or engage in time-consuming compulsive behaviors, including looking in the mirror or other reflective surfaces to examine the perceived defect. The preoccupation contributes to intense feelings of shame, defectiveness, and unworthiness and can result in an avoidance of social situations. K. A. Phillips (2000) describes one adolescent aptly stating, "My life is like hell on earth." Even when receiving treatment, individuals with BDD are characterized by significantly poor functioning and quality of life (K. A. Phillips et al., 2005).

Delusions

A chart review by K. A. Phillips, Albertini, Siniscalchi, Khan, and Robinson (2001) indicated that 38% of BDD inpatients were delusional at the time of the study. Thus the preoccupation can occur on a continuum of insight, ranging from obsessional uncertainty to overvalued ideas to delusional certainty (Rivera & Borda, 2001). Rather than a dichotomous variable, the delusionality in BDD may be more accurately conceptualized as ranging from obsessional thoughts accompanied by good insight to overvalued ideas to delusional thoughts (K. A. Phillips, 2000). The individual's insight may also shift over the course of the disorder and is influenced by stress and social exposure. There may be a psychotic subtype of BDD (K. A. Phillips, 2000). Earlier research found that delusional individuals with BDD presented with more severe levels of psychopathology, and the presence of psychotic features was associated with a poorer outcome and greater impairment (K. A. Phillips, McElroy, Keck, Hudson, & Pope, 1994). Unlike Hypochondriasis, both BDD and Delusional Disorder are coded when the beliefs or preoccupations are of sufficient severity to warrant both diagnoses (Cororve & Gleaves, 2001; First & Tasman, 2004; Morrison, 1995a).

Additional Characteristics

Compulsive Behaviors

Although not included in the diagnostic criteria for BDD, compulsive behaviors such as camouflaging and hiding the perceived defect are found in the majority (more than 90%) of adults with BDD (Cororve & Gleaves, 2001). All of the children (ages 12 to 17) studied by Albertini and Phillips (2001) presented with compulsive behaviors such as camouflaging with clothes (94%), comparing themselves with others (87%), mirror checking (85%), and repeatedly questioning others about their appearance, sometimes as frequently as 30 times per day (73%). They may wear wigs, hats, or sunglasses, frequently change clothes, buy excessive beauty products, and perform self-surgeries or use harsh household chemicals to remove the perceived defect (Sarwer et al., 2003). They frequently pick at their skin in the hope of improving its appearance, which unfortunately leads to skin lesions and often permanent scarring (Rivera & Borda, 2001). Veale and colleagues (1996) found that 26% had undergone one or more surgeries. When these individuals seek surgical correction for the presumed defect they are often dissatisfied and may become litigious.

Suicide Risk

In a 4-year prospective study, K. A. Phillips and Menard (2006) found high rates of suicidal ideation and attempts and a preliminary high rate of completed suicide in individuals with BDD. K. A. Phillips and colleagues' (K. A. Phillips, 2000; K. A. Phillips, Menard, Fay, & Pagano, 2005; K. A. Phillips & Menard, 2006) research has consistently found high rates of attempted suicide and Veale and colleagues (1996) found that 24% had a history of past suicide attempts. Of children and adolescents diagnosed with BDD, 21% were found to have made a serious suicide attempt; there were also high rates of suicidal ideation and physical violence (with destruction of property) secondary to BDD symptoms (Albertini & Phillips, 2001).

Onset, Course, and Life Span Considerations

Onset

Usually, BDD begins in adolescence, with a mean age of onset of 16 and a modal age of onset of 13; 70% of cases begin before the age of 18 (Albertini & Phillips, 2001; K. A. Phillips, 2000). In contrast, the average age of patients in published clinical studies is early to mid-30s, suggesting that a considerable amount of time elapses between onset and treatment. This may also reflect the years the individual spends seeking nonpsychiatric treatment as a first resource. Early childhood experiences, such as being teased about one's appearance, feeling unloved, neglected, and rejected by family members, and parents' excessive preoccupation with appearance ("BDD by proxy") have all been linked to the development of BDD (Cororve & Gleaves, 2001; Rivera & Borda, 2001).

Course

Unfortunately, the course of the disorder appears to be unremitting and chronic and tends to persist for years, if not decades, with a mean duration of 16 years (Rivera & Borda, 2001). Symptoms and severity wax and wane; 60% of individuals report a worsening of symptoms over time, and remission without treatment appears infrequent (Sarwer et al., 2003). In their study of children with BDD, Albertini and Phillips (2001) found that 18% had dropped out of school and 94% experienced social impairment. Berrios and Mumford (1995) describe an earlier review of 150 papers, including 300 cases of dysmorphophobia, an average 8-year delay in seeking treatment. The course could be divided into three groups: continuous (41%), relapsing (31%), and full remission (18%). Individuals with an earlier age of onset had a more chronic illness course and were more likely to have been treated with medication. Marriage was identified as a protective factor and anxiety was found to be a good prognostic indicator. However, social impairment is almost universal with BDD; thus individuals may avoid dating and other social interactions, have few or no friends, or experience marital problems or divorce. Most individuals with BDD (74% to 90%) are single or divorced, suggesting significant difficulties in establishing and maintaining intimate relationships (K. A. Phillips, 2000; Veale et al., 1996). Work and educational endeavors may also suffer because of avoidance, time-consuming rituals, and poor concentration secondary to BDD obsessions, all resulting in high rates of unemployment (K. A. Phillips, 2000). Individuals with BDD were found to be significantly impaired across several areas of psychosocial functioning, with a pervasive poorer quality of life than individuals with mood disorders or acute and chronic medical illness (K. A. Phillips et al., 2005).

Somatoform Disorder Not Otherwise Specified

When an individual does not meet the criteria for a specific somatoform disorder, Somato-form Disorder NOS is assigned. No minimal duration for symptoms is required (First & Tasman, 2004). This category includes the rare disorder pseudocyesis (the false belief of being pregnant), transient (less than 6 months) hypochondriacal states, total environmental allergy syndrome, and chronic fatigue syndrome (American Psychiatric Association, 2000b; Morrison, 1995a).

EPIDEMIOLOGY

The occurrence of somatoform disorders varies significantly depending on the setting, with the highest clustering of cases occurring in medical or specialty clinics and university or research hospitals (Escobar, 1996). In primary care settings, 20% to 25% of consultations were for somatoform disorders; 26% of new referrals to a general medical outpatient clinic and 20% of internal medicine inpatients could also be diagnosed with one of these disorders (Fink et al., 2004; Ladwig et al., 2001). In a community sample in Germany, 12.5% reported experiencing at least one somatoform disorder or syndrome during their lifetime, with pain being the most prevalent (Lieb et al., 2002). Individuals ages 14 to 24 years report a 12% lifetime prevalence of at least one somatoform disorder (Dhossche et al., 2002).

Somatization Disorder

When all of the diagnostic criteria are met for Somatization Disorder, it is a relatively rare disorder. It has a prevalence of 0.13% in the general population and a lifetime prevalence between 0.2% and 2% for women and less than 0.2% for males in the United States; no study reported on younger children (American Psychiatric Association, 2000b; Bursch, 2006; Rief et al., 2001). When Cloninger, Reich, and Guze (1975) considered the method of assessment and the individual's age, they found that the lifetime risk for women in the United States for Somatization Disorder was 2% (First & Tasman, 2004). Rates of 0.7% have been found in an Italian community-based survey, and 1.84% in a German community sample (Ladwig et al., 2001). In an extensive general population study in Finland, Karvonen and colleagues (2004) found a prevalence of 1.1% for Somatization Disorder. Somatization Disorder may account for 7% to 8% of all females who visit mental health clinics and be as high as 14% of all psychiatric consultations for medical or surgical patients (Maxmen & Ward, 1995; Morrison, 1995a). In the specialty care sector, where patients seek treatment for conditions such as irritable bowel syndrome, chronic pain, and neurological disorders, the rates are even higher (P. Fink, Sorensen, Enberg, Holm, & Munk-Jorgensen, 1999; P. Fink, Hansen, & Soudergaard, 2005; Iezzi, Duckworth, & Adams et al., 2001).

Undifferentiated or subsyndromal somatoform disorder is far more prevalent, with rates of 4.4% to 20% reported for adults (Lieb et al., 2002). C. Ford (1995) reports that the prevalence of subsyndromal Somatization Disorder is as great as 30 to 100 times that of the full-blown disorder, suggesting that it may be the most common somatoform disorder (Escobar, 1996; Holder-Perkins & Wise, 2001). These individuals have family histories similar to those with Somatization Disorder but fewer comorbid disorders (C. Ford, 1995).

Conversion Disorder

The reported rates of Conversion Disorder vary widely depending on the site of the study. The *DSM-IV-TR* reports rates of 0.01% to 0.5% (American Psychiatric Association, 2000b). Krem (2004) describes incidence rates varying from 0.5% to 2.5%, with 0.05% to 0.1% being the most common estimate and a prevalence of 0.04% for the general population. He found that the incidence increased to .02% to 12% among hospital inpatients and 1% to 14% of neurology and psychiatry patients. Rates of up to 3% have been reported in outpatient mental health clinics (Santos et al., 2002). In specialized treatment settings, the rates of Conversion Disorder are much higher; for example, one study found that of patients admitted to general hospital neurology wards for evaluation of seizures, 44% received a diagnosis of psychogenic seizures (Maldonado & Spiegel, 2001). C. Ford (1995) quotes studies of lifetime prevalence of conversion symptoms in postpartum normal women of 33%, while neurologists report rates of 1% to 3% and a range of 1.2% to 11.5% for medical and surgical inpatients who receive psychiatric consultations.

Pain Disorder

Although the prevalence of Pain Disorder is unclear, according to the *DSM-IV-TR* the occurrence of pain that causes distress or impairment is widespread (American Psychiatric Association, 2000b). It is the most common complaint that individuals present to physicians, and 80% of medical doctor consultations are for pain-related complaints (C. Ford, 1995; Maxmen & Ward, 1995). Although pain is a common condition (33.7% lifetime prevalence), it creates significant distress or impairment in only a third of these individuals (Grabe et al., 2003). According to First and Tasman (2004), in any given week in the United States 10% to 15% of adults are on work disability because of work pain. A review of epidemiological studies indicated wide variations (2% to 40%) in the reported prevalence of pain and concluded that prevalence of chronic pain of 10% was a cautious estimate (Verhaak et al., 1998). Of adults in the United States 10% to 15% are estimated to experience Pain Disorder (Santos et al., 2002). Pain Disorder tends to be diagnosed more often in women than men and often follows an accident or medical illness (Morrison, 1995a). Of school-age children and adolescents, 15% to 20% report at least three episodes of significant stomach pain within a 3-month period (Bursch, 2006).

Hypochondriasis

Although Hypochondriasis was not included in the ECA study, the prevalence in the general population has been estimated to be between 0.8% and 4.5% and between 8% to 10.3% among general medical patients (Margarinos, Zafar, Nissenson, & Blanco, 2002; Noyes et al., 1994). Looper and Kirmayer (2002) report a prevalence of 0.2% in a community survey and 0.8% in an international primary care study. C. Ford (1995) reports prevalence rates between 3% and 14% in primary care settings and between 4% and 6% of internal medicine patients, and Santos and colleagues (2002) report rates between 4%

and 9% in general medical practices. Using a structured interview, Noyes (2001) reports higher rates in medical specialty clinics (13% otolaryngology) and prevalence rates of 13% in unselected psychiatric outpatients and 30% to 45% for psychiatric inpatients. In reviewing Hypochondriasis in primary care settings, Escobar (1996) found rates of 4.5% when *DSM-IV* criteria were used. Men and women appear equally affected by Hypochondriasis, although there is a higher prevalence for females among medical inpatients (Fink et al., 2004). There are also higher rates for younger, less educated females with a history of childhood illness or abuse (Magarinos et al., 2002). Interestingly, individuals with frequent exposure to medical settings (e.g., medical students) have been found to have increased health concerns (Bouman et al., 1999).

Body Dysmorphic Disorder

General population studies found prevalence rates for BDD between 1% and 2%, with higher rates being reported in medical clinical settings (4% to 5%), where it is frequently missed (K. A. Phillips, 2001). M. Zimmerman and Mattia (1998) found that 3% of psychiatric outpatients could be diagnosed as BDD; they concluded that this disorder is underrecognized in outpatients and even when present is rarely the principal reason for seeking treatment. Given that many individuals with this condition are reluctant to seek help because of embarrassment, and their comorbid anxiety and depressive symptoms are easier to identify than BDD, they are often misdiagnosed or not diagnosed. Therefore, these rates may significantly underrepresent the true extent of the problem (Sarwer et al., 2003). In a community sample, 2.3% of adolescents were identified with this disorder (Mayville, Katz, Gipson, & Cabral, 1999). In clinical settings, rates of BDD with mood or anxiety disorders range from 8% to 42% (K. A. Phillips, 2001). It is most common in cosmetic surgery (7% to 15%) and dermatology practices (12% to 15%; K. A. Phillips, 2001; Sarwer et al., 2003). Bohne, Keuthen, Wilhelm, Deckersbach, and Jenike (2002) found that 4.0% of college students met the criteria for BDD. Men and women are equally affected by BDD, but there are gender differences in the focus of the preoccupations; females tend to present with more concern about hips, legs, breasts, and weight, whereas men focus on height, genitals, and hair (Morrison, 1995a; Sarwer et al., 2003).

ETIOLOGY

Biological Models

The *DSM-IV-TR* somatoform disorders are not clustered based on a common theory of etiology. As early as Freud and Charcot, there have been theories of a "constitutional diathesis" for somatization, and though evidence exists for biological and psychosocial factors, to date the etiology of these disorders remains unknown (First & Tasman, 2004). Genetic research indicates familial patterns with Somatization Disorder occurring in 10% to 20% of the female first-degree biological relatives of women with Somatization Disorder (H. I. Kaplan & Saddock, 1996). Having a biological or adoptive parent with an Antisocial Personality Disorder, substance-related disorder, or Somatization Disorder increases the likelihood of developing a somatoform disorder (American Psychiatric Association, 2000b; Maxmen & Ward, 1995). Adopted female children of biological parents with antisocial behaviors revealed a higher-than-expected rate of multiple unexplained somatic complaints, suggesting that sociopathy and somatization may have a common etiology (Guze, 1993; Holder-Perkins & Wise, 2001). Delinquent girls have been found to be at higher risk for developing Somatization Disorder as adults, and female relatives of male felons also have higher rates of Somatization Disorder (LaBruzza & Mendez-Villarrubia, 1997; Maxmen & Ward, 1995). After reviewing the available genetic research, Guze (1993) concluded that a familial association between Somatization Disorder and alcoholism and Antisocial Personality Disorder has been established. Individuals with Somatization Disorder and Antisocial Personality Disorder also have similar patterns of hemispheric impairments, further supporting the link between these disorders (First & Tasman, 2004).

In an effort to identify the biological underpinnings of the somatoform disorders, Rief, Pilger, Ihle, Verkerk, Scharpe, et al. (2004) have hypothesized that a dysfunction in the serotonergic amino acids relates to the experience of multiple unexplained somatic symptoms. They also postulate that the processes involve not only brain mechanisms but also the peripheral muscles' level of energy metabolism. Individuals with somatization have higher levels of physiological arousal, which, when combined with a tendency to amplify somatic sensations, may result in a hypersensitivity to bodily experiences (Bouman et al., 1999). These individuals, described as "somatosensory amplifiers," may also have a congenital hypersensitivity to sensations and bodily functions, a biological predisposition, or a low pain threshold, and thus experience more intense symptoms or misinterpret common body sensations (C. Ford, 1995; Garralda, 1996; H. I. Kaplan & Saddock, 1996; Terre & Ghiselli, 1997). Haugaard (2004) describes individuals who may present with an "organic vulnerability" as having a greater susceptibility to disease, increased sensitivity to internal states, and a vulnerability to stress, exacerbating somatic symptoms. He suggests that the clustering of somatic complaints and depression and anxiety in children may reflect the role of neurotransmitters (e.g., serotonin) in the development of headaches and stomachaches.

The biological causes of Conversion Disorder are unknown. There is some limited evidence of familial aggregation and increased risk in monozygotic twin pairs compared to dyzygotic twin pairs (American Psychiatric Association, 2000b). Relatives of individuals with Conversion Disorder present with higher rates of conversion symptoms, and individuals with neurological deficits such as frontal lobe trauma were found to present with an increased susceptibility for Conversion Disorder (H. I. Kaplan and Saddock, 1996; Toone, 1990). In summarizing available research, Bouman and colleagues (1999) note that individuals with Conversion Disorder show more anxious arousal and generally fail to habituate to stressors; however, they are not rated as more anxious by clinicians. They also report that given that conversion symptoms occur more often on the left side of the body, they could be linked to emotional arousal, as the right hemisphere has the capacity to generate more unpleasant emotions. The role of conscious active inhibition in the psychogenic deficits characteristic of Conversion Disorder has been proposed as the biological mechanism for the development of these symptoms (Hurwitz, 2004).

Familial studies indicate that there are higher rates of Alcohol Dependence and depressive mood disorders in first-degree relatives of individuals with chronic pain (American Psychiatric Association, 2000b; Maxmen & Ward, 1995). It has been hypothesized that stress and pain can trigger elevated muscle tensions and contractions, which result in the release of pain-inducing substances that contribute to further muscular and sympathetic hyperactivity and a vicious pain cycle (Bouman et al., 1999). Children with recurrent abdominal pain have been described as having hyperactive sympathetic nervous system arousal to environmental stressors and to experience a disrupted recovery from these stressors (Compas & Boyer, 2001). Research suggests the role of a system involving a neurological pathway that descends from the cortex and medulla, which, when activated, inhibits the pain transmission neurons from firing and which is mediated by endorphins and serotonin in the etiology of pain (Cloninger, 1993; First & Tasman, 2004). A gate control model has also been proposed to describe how psychological processes and biological factors are linked in the perception of pain (First & Tasman, 2004).

Bienvenu and colleagues (2000) reported on the familial clustering and higher frequency of Hypochondriasis in individuals with OCD and their first-degree family members. However, overall, the research on familial studies of Hypochondriasis has been mixed, with the most consistent findings suggesting that Hypochondriasis and Somatization Disorder are closely related. The relatives of individuals with Hypochondriasis consistently score higher on measures of mistrust and antagonism in interpersonal relationships and toward doctors (Noyes, 2001). Evidence of the therapeutic effectiveness of SSRI medication for Hypochondriasis suggests the role of serotonin dysregulation in etiology (First & Tasman, 2004).

Body Dysmorphic Disorder is likely to be multiply determined, with biological and environmental factors playing a role (Rivera & Borda, 2001). Neuropsychological studies suggest that dysfunction in the executive system or frontal lobes may be implicated (Rivera & Borda, 2001). The success of pharmacological treatment implies that serotonin may also be involved (Cororve & Gleaves, 2001; H. I. Kaplan & Saddock, 1996). Studies of the biological relatives of individuals with BDD indicate a high prevalence of OCD (K. A. Phillips, 2000). The similarities in clinical presentation, including inflexible ideation, stereotypic behaviors, and repetitive time-consuming behavior, led Rivera and Borda (2001) to posit that the two disorders may be related and that BDD might be better conceptualized as an OCD spectrum disorder.

Psychological Models

There are numerous psychoanalytic and psychodynamic theories of the etiology of somatoform disorders, but to date they lack empirical support (First & Tasman, 2004). Early psychoanalytic theory suggested that unexplained somatic symptoms were caused by the operation of defense mechanisms such as repression designed to keep painful conflicts from awareness (G. Taylor, 2003; Trillat, 1995). Pain was seen as the symbolic representation of intrapsychic conflicts and the consequence of directing repressed or suppressed anger toward others at oneself, due to a punitive self (H. I. Kaplan & Saddock, 1996). Conversion Disorder was described as representing a compromise between the need to express ideas or feelings that are unconscious and the fear of expressing them. Freud believed these feelings and impulses were sexual in nature; later theorists contended that other emotions such as aggression or dependency needs were involved (G. Taylor, 2003). The symptom was seen as a direct result of the psychological trauma or as symbolically representing the unconscious conflict (Bouman et al., 1999). Freud speculated that Hypochondriasis stems from a turning inward of libidinal energy from external objects onto organs of the body, creating a bodily tension that demands the patient's full attention (Trillat, 1995). Subsequent analytic theory elaborated on this premise and described how, rather than openly complain, the individual displaces onto the body repressed hostility over having been disappointed, hurt, abandoned, or unloved (Fallon & Feinstein, 2001). Psychoanalytic theories of BDD center on the symbolic meaning of the chosen body part and the unconscious displacement of emotional or sexual conflict or guilt (Cororve & Gleaves, 2001).

Current psychological models of the etiology of the somatoform disorders emphasize cognitive-behavioral and family models. It has been suggested that somatization results from the learning or modeling of illness behavior (e.g., from parents who are ill) and the reinforcement of illness and medical help seeking (First & Tasman, 2004; Garralda, 1996; Holder-Perkins & Wise, 2001). Somatizing behavior has also been described as a behavior driven by a maladaptive attachment style (Stuart & Noyes, 1999). In reviewing studies on somatization in children, Haugaard (2004) suggests that the primary psychological process may be learning and that reinforcement comes from many sources, as symptoms can divert attention and bring the child and parent closer. He noted that 54% of children with Conversion Disorder had symptoms that mimicked their parent's illness, supporting the role of learning and modeling from sick family members. Earlier work by Brodsky (1984) described the impact of growing up in a family of somatizers, with parents who are uncaring and demanding when the child is well and caring and loving when the child is ill. Terre and Ghiselli (1997) cite Minuchin's classic theory that the child's somatic concerns serve as a homeostatic mechanism for conflict avoidance in enmeshed, rigid, and overprotective families.

Libow's (2002) study of illness falsification in children suggested four mechanisms in which children may learn illness behavior: (1) Parental attention and caring and escape from school can reinforce the sick role; (2) children learn symptom amplification by being overfocused and hypervigilant to unpleasant bodily sensations; (3) by observing a somatizing parent, children are vulnerable to learning to express emotional states in somatic complaints; and (4) the parent may actively coach the child to present with and develop symptoms. For many children, well-meaning parents and health professionals may perpetuate the downward spiral of disability and symptoms by fostering the child's dependency or by increasing the child's distress (Bursch, 2006). Somatization in parents is often accompanied by high levels of disability, an increased salience of somatic symptoms, parental reinforcement of or closeness around somatic complaints, and the discouragement of coping (Garralda, 1996). Terre and Ghiselli (1997) found the expression of somatic complaints has also been found to differ with distinctive aspects of family style and developmental stages. Junior high adolescents expressed somatic complaints when there was a high level of familial disorganization and a low level of family cohesion. For high school students, gender and familial orientation toward cultural and intellectual pursuits were the determining factors. Thus, for high school girls, somatic complaints were found to be associated with the perception that the family was less interested in intellectual and cultural activities. For college students, somatic complaints were linked to a family focus on achievement, competitiveness, and conflict.

It has also been hypothesized that individuals who somatize have negative and distorted cognitions about physical sensations, have schemas of vulnerability, and tend to misinterpret and catastrophize somatic symptoms based on past illness experiences, all of which contributes to further anxiety and feelings of dysphoria (L. A. Allen et al., 2001; Looper & Kirmayer, 2002). Somatization has been linked to a social communication model and deficits in information processing whereby individuals learn to express their needs and failure to cope in excessive, vague somatic complaints, which, combined with difficulties with impulsivity and monotony intolerance, result in interpersonal impairments (Bouman et al., 1999; First & Tasman, 2004). The individual's poor health becomes an excuse for poor performance and the development of a "sick role," which is further reinforced by poor treatment (Bouman et al., 1999).

After studying Conversion Disorder in "good children," Kozlowska (2003) concluded that conversion symptoms do not occur in a vacuum but are embedded in a life context. Key issues include fear of parental anger or rejection, entrapment in problematic relationships, isolation, and unresolvable predicaments. In many cases, individuals with Conversion Disorder are in chaotic family and work situations (First & Tasman, 2004). Conversion symptoms may become paired with reductions in anxiety (primary gain) or modeled from ill family members and may also be a way of communicating helplessness, thereby fostering an environment that reinforces dependency and inhibits aggressive impulses. Thus the individual may be relieved of certain responsibilities and duties (secondary gain) and others may be supportive if he or she is perceived to have a "legitimate" medical illness (Maxmen & Ward, 1995). Often there is also a close temporal relation between the symptom and the intense emotion, conflict, trauma, or stress (Bouman et al., 1999; H. I. Kaplan & Saddock, 1996). In their study of children and adolescents with Conversion Disorder, Pehlivanturk and Unal (2002) found that the onset of symptoms was related to a specific event or psychosocial stressor in the majority of cases (90%); for most (52.5%), this involved relationship problems with family and or peers. Wyllie, Glazer, Benbadis, Kotagal, and Wolgamuth (1999) examined pediatric cases of pseudoseizures who were also diagnosed with Conversion Disorder. They found histories of sexual abuse, physical abuse, and severe family stressors. Roelofs, Keijsers, Hoogduin, Naring, and Moene (2002) found a history of childhood abuse in individuals diagnosed with Conversion Disorder.

The presence of interpersonal concerns and marital conflict in individuals with Pain Disorder has led some to posit that pain can act to stabilize a fragile marriage (H. I. Kaplan & Saddock, 1996). Thus somatic symptoms may be seen as a means to divert attention from family conflict (Haugaard, 2004). Both classical and operant learning theories have been used to explain how pain-related behaviors are acquired and maintained in familial and occupational settings (First & Tasman, 2004). Bouman and colleagues (1999) note that pain behavior has been found to be particularly susceptible to social reinforcement and that perceived competence significantly influences the intensity of the pain experienced and the individual's coping. They also describe a psychobiological model of chronic pain as a complex, multidetermined response that includes motor-behavioral, subjective-psychological, and physiological-organic components (Bouman et al., 1999). In clinical samples, rumination, magnification, helplessness, and pain catastrophizing are significantly related to the individual's pain experience and pain-related disability (M. J. Sullivan et al., 2001). In a chart review of children and adolescents meeting the somatoform Pain Disorder disability criteria, P. E. Hyman and colleagues (2002) found that many of the children presented with perfectionism, unrealistically high goals, early childhood pain experiences, and dependent coping style. The parents of these children often had chronic illness and marital conflict. The majority of children were found to have experienced multiple triggering events, including viral illness and school change. Interestingly, L. S. Walker, Smith, Garber, Van Slyke, and Claar (2001) found that daily stressors, including parental illness, were more important than major stressors in triggering abdominal pain in children.

Some studies have found that individuals with Hypochondriasis have a history of childhood illness or serious illness in their family and that hypochondriacal fears may be related to these diseases (Morrison, 1995a,b; Stuart & Noyes, 1999). Noyes and colleagues (2003) have described and empirically tested an interpersonal model of Hypochondriasis whereby early exposure to illness increases the likelihood that distress will be experienced somatically and the individual's insecure attachment results in abnormal care seeking and interpersonal difficulties. Individuals in families with high levels of illness may also develop physical vulnerability schema, which predispose them to develop Hypochondriasis (Robbins & Kirmayer, 1996). Thus these individuals may pay selective attention to even minor bodily sensations, present as overly concerned about bodily functions, and appear to habituate less to somatosensory input (Hiller et al., 2002). According to Visser and Bouman (2001), bodily sensations are the main triggers for the individual developing catastrophic interpretations that result in emotional distress and anxiety. These feelings then lead to the characteristic hypochondriacal behaviors of avoidance of disease-associated stimuli, checking, and reassurance seeking. Additionally, this fear activates a "better safe than sorry" cognitive strategy, in which the individual becomes hypervigilant and behaviorally preoccupied with his or her health status (Fallon & Feinstein, 2001). Visser and Bouman also describe a vicious cycle whereby such illness behaviors as selective attention and the presence of a confirmatory bias in relation to the individual's catastrophic misinterpretations contribute to further distress and anxiety, which often result in additional somatic symptoms. To allay this distress and anxiety, individuals with Hypochondriasis seek reassurance, engage in doctor shopping, and use excessive health care services, which add to significant impairments in psychosocial functioning (Hiller et al., 2002).

Cognitive-behavioral models of the development of BDD emphasize the interaction of cultural factors, such as the importance of appearance and physical attractiveness, and childhood experiences, including adolescent fears of rejection and familial criticism (Bouman et al., 1999; Cororve & Gleaves, 2001; Sarwer et al., 2003). In addition to feeling rejected and unloved by their family, individuals with BDD present with a tendency for shyness, introversion, unusually high personal standards, perfectionistic features, and sensitivity to rejection (R. O. Frost, Williams, & Jenter, 1995; Rivera & Borda, 2001).

Risk Factors for Somatoform Disorders

Research over the years has identified a range of factors that may predispose individuals to be vulnerable to the expression of emotional distress in the form of physical complaints (see Table 12.1). These include having an individual or family history of physical illness, a lack of education, the presence of alexithymia, and lower socioeconomic status (C. Ford, 1995; Garralda, 1996; Holder-Perkins & Wise, 2001; Hurwitz 2004). In a community sample, Ladwig et al. (2001) found that the risk for somatization was 1.6-fold

Table 12.1   Risk factors for somatoform disorders

Adult Risk Factors and Behaviors Associated with Somatization
Previous history of injury or illness
Significant individual and family psychiatric disorders
Family culture or atmosphere of illness
Close contact with and high rates of physical and psychological illness
Predisposition or vulnerability and sensitivity to pain
Tendency to channel psychological conflicts into physical symptoms
Cultural sanctions against emotional expression
History of child abuse, trauma, or neglect
Family history of antisocial personality disorder or antisocial behaviors
Interpersonal relationship problems, anxious tendency to withdraw
Comorbid depression or anxiety
Lower social class and lack of education
Employment in the medical profession
Alexithymia, difficulty with expressing emotions

Child Risk Factors and Behaviors Associated with Somatization
Severe family and individual psychopathology
History of somatization in child, parent, or other significant adult
Complaint appears to result in personal, family, or social gain
Symptom has some symbolic meaning to the child or family
Idiosyncratic family relationships with emotional distance in communication
Complaint or symptom intensity varies with family, personal, or social factors
Parental concerns and responses to child's physical symptoms appear excessive
Frequent discussions about specific body area or physical symptoms
Reassurance by trusted adult about perceived physical complaint has little influence
Symptom violates known anatomical or physiological pattern
Time relationship between stressors and the onset and exacerbation of somatic
   symptoms
Difficulties in social relationships, personality, and temperament
Educational, social, and precipitating life stresses
Child engages in excessive checking of specific body area
Physical symptom responds to placebo or psychological intervention

higher for women than men. When being female was combined with high emotional distress and low social class, the risk factor increased fourfold. They concluded that the predisposing factors for Somatization Disorder were lower social class, less education, and culturally acquired attitudes, which may be heightened by emotional distress. In a prospective longitudinal community study of *DSM-IV* somatoform disorders, Lieb and colleagues (2002) found that being female, having a preexisting substance use, anxiety, or mood disorder, and experiencing physical threat resulted in a higher risk for these disorders in adolescence and young adulthood. The occurrence of sexual abuse or assault was positively related to the onset of new somatoform disorders, whereas high education level and social class were negatively related to the onset of new disorders (Bursch, 2006; Campo, Comer, Jansen-McWilliams, Gardner, & Kelleher, 2002). In a similar vein, Holder-Perkins and Wise (2001) report that 55% of women with Somatization Disorder reported a history of sexual abuse, compared to 16% of women with affective disorders.

The *DSM* diagnostic criteria for the somatoform disorders were developed for adults, and though they can be applied to children there is a lack of child-specific criteria, making the assessment and assignment of these disorders to children and adolescents somewhat limited (Bursch, 2006). Haugaard (2004) reports that while it is developmentally appropriate for young children to express emotional distress as physical symptoms, these disorders are in fact rare in this population. Somatization in children has been associated with the presence of mood disorders and the prominence of fatigue as the key presenting symptom in severe cases (Bursch, 2006; Garralda, 1996). Early life experiences such as serious childhood illnesses or trauma, inadequate parenting, a history of physical or sexual abuse, and severe maltreatment have also been identified as contributing to the development of Somatization Disorder and Hypochondriasis (Bouman et al., 1999; C. Ford, 1995; Haugaard, 2004; Wyllie et al., 1999). Surveying couples in the community, Waldinger, Schulz, Barsky, and Ahern (2006) found that a history of childhood trauma was associated with higher levels of adult somatization. Kozlowska (2003) notes two very different clusters of family risk factors for Conversion Disorder. One is characterized by high levels of psychopathology and chaotic family and social circumstances. The other is the "supernormal presentation of good children," where there is an apparent lack of difficulties. Family life appears harmonious and respectful, with a high emphasis on achievement; however, there is often a high level of illness anxiety and hostility in the doctor-parent relationship. For BDD, family history data suggest that risk factors include a familial preoccupation with appearance and appearance-related teasing in childhood and adolescence (Sarwer et al., 2003). In reviewing the research on somatization in the elderly, Sheehan and Banerjee (1999) note the scarcity of available studies and the oversimplification of conceptualizing these behaviors merely as masked depression. For this age group, risk factors included anxiety, depression, medical illness, and personality characteristics.

Living in a culture or having religious beliefs that do not condone emotional displays or that see psychological distress as a sign of weakness and condone the physical expression of distress and being socially isolated may also increase an individual's risk for somatization (Folks, 1995; Hurwitz, 2004). The stigmatization of psychiatric conditions and lack of available psychiatric services, as well as differential reimbursements by insurance companies and increased availability of medical services, may result in diagnosing the more acceptable medical condition. During the intake interview the clinician will want to explore in considerable detail the role of these factors in the development and maintenance of the presenting clinical symptoms.

DIVERSITY CONSIDERATIONS

Culture plays an important role in the expression and diagnosis of somatic symptoms, and clinical presentations can vary dramatically, with pseudo-neurological symptoms such as insects under the skin or worms in the brain being more common in Africa and reproductive concerns dominating in India (American Psychiatric Association, 2000b). While unexplained medical symptoms and worries about health may be "idioms of distress" or culturally sanctioned means of expressing problems, they do not necessarily represent psychopathology (American Psychiatric Association, 2000b, p. 897). In a review of culture and somatization, Kirmayer and Young (1998) suggest that the concept of somatization reflects the inherent dualism in Western psychiatry that is notably absent in other cultural medical traditions. They also identified several culture-specific somatic manifestations, including the Korean concept of *hwa-byung* (suppressed anger or rage), the East African *brain fag* (typically associated with studying), and the Puerto Rican *ataques de nervios* (loss of control) that represent different styles of expressing distress. Chaplin (1997) contends that Asian clients presenting with somatic complaints may be influenced by their exposure to traditional Chinese medicine and that physical complaints are more socially acceptable and endorsed by Chinese media as expressions of unacceptable feelings such as aggression. The cultural and social isolation experienced by many refugees may also contribute to the increased rates of somatization for these groups (Chaplin, 1997). In their review of culture-bound syndromes and the universal nature of somatization, Issac et al. (1996) note that the lack of specific words to describe emotions in certain languages (e.g., Farsi) may relate to higher rates of somatic complaints in these cultures.

The World Health Organization's collaborative study of somatization in primary care settings found differences in the occurrence of somatic illness across 14 countries. However, apart from elevated rates in South American countries, the differences did not fit a neat cultural explanation (Gureje, 2004; Gureje et al., 1997). They did find that patients who lacked a close relationship with their doctor were more likely to present with multiple somatic complaints, suggesting that the nature of the patient-doctor relationship may influence the expression of somatic complaints (Gureje, 2004). There is significant variability across different cultures, with higher frequencies of somatic complaints reported for Greek and Puerto Rican males (American Psychiatric Association, 2000b). Chaplin (1997) hypothesized that the higher reported rates of somatic complaints among Puerto Rican males may be related to the stigmatization of mental illness and their sanctioned entry into health care. Typically, more women than men are diagnosed with Somatization Disorder, with ratios of between 10:1 and 5:1 reported, and the lower ratios occurring in primary care settings (Fink et al., 2004; Karvonen et al., 2004). Higher hormonal or other physiological differences have been hypothesized to play a role, as have gender differences in illness and help-seeking behavior and gender bias in the diagnostic process (Fink et al., 2004). Individuals who meet the full diagnostic criteria for Somatization Disorder have been described as poorly educated, non-White, unmarried, from rural areas, and congregating in primary care settings and general hospitals (C. Ford, 1995).

It is important not to diagnose Conversion Disorder for visions, spells, or dissociative experiences that have a strong somatic component, for example, loss of consciousness or seizure-like behaviors that may be considered normative in certain religious traditions or healing rituals (American Psychiatric Association, 2000b). A diagnosis of Conversion Disorder is warranted only when the symptoms exceed what would be culturally expected or if there is significant distress or impairment. Women more than men tend to be affected by Conversion Disorder, with the reported ratios varying from 2:1 to 10:1. For men Conversion Disorder is often seen in the context of industrial accidents or the military (Maldonado & Spiegel, 2001). Conversion Disorder is less common in the United States than in other cultures. In fact, conversion reactions are observed more frequently in lower SES, medically unsophisticated, uneducated individuals who reside in rural areas or countries where medical practice is developing (A. Frances & Ross, 2001; Morrison, 1995 a,b). These are often more bizarre and dramatic clinical presentations; in contrast, more highly educated individuals tend to present with symptoms that more closely simulate a physical disease. First and Tasman (2004) note that as countries develop and access to education and medical and psychological sophistication increase, the incidence of these disorders may decrease.

K. A. Phillips (2001) notes that case reports from around the world suggest that the clinical features of BDD are similar across cultures, but that culture produces nuances on a basically invariant or universal theme. For example, *koro*, a culturally bound syndrome found in Southeast Asia, may be related to BDD; it is characterized by a belief that genitals in men or breasts in women are shrinking and retracting into the abdomen, resulting in death.

INTAKE AND INTERVIEWING CONSIDERATIONS

On intake, individuals with somatoform disorders are challenging, and it is important for the clinician to adopt a very organized approach, addressing the relevant intake issues (see Table 12.2) while ensuring the establishment and maintenance of rapport. Given the focus on physical complaints and the need to coordinate care, the clinician has to have some knowledge of medical conditions and feel comfortable working with physicians and a range of medical specialists.

L. Seligman (1998) describes skills necessary to clinicians as being adept at rapport building and having the ability to rapidly establish a therapeutic relationship with clients who will be resistant, lack insight, and may not be psychologically minded. Clinicians will be most effective if they adopt a concrete, structured, yet flexible approach and carefully monitor and limit the client's discussion of somatic complaints. For many individuals with somatoform disorders, referral to a mental health professional can be misinterpreted as a dismissal or rejection (L. Seligman, 1998; J. Stone et al., 2002). To establish rapport, the clinician needs to attend to these feelings and the circumstances of the referral at the beginning of the interview (G. E. Simon, 2002). Symptom magnification

Table 12.2 Intake issues for somatoform disorders

Rapport difficult; lack of insight; denial; hostile, vague, exaggerated style.
Need to be alert for countertransference.
Obtain medical evaluation to rule out medical or substance-related etiology.
Assess congruence with known condition, anatomy, and physiology.
Evaluate symptom consistency over time and the context of symptom occurrence.
Consider cultural and familial factors in symptom presentation.
Poor and inconsistent informants; collateral information and detailed history essential.
Assess impulse control and suicide risk, especially for BDD and Somatization Disorder.
Collaboration with physician is crucial; often numerous prior medical procedures.
Coordinate care from multiple caregivers with releases.
Assess doctor seeking, checking, and compulsive behaviors.
Consider other disorders that present with physical symptoms (mood, anxiety).
Rule out Factitious Disorder and malingering.
Assess for risk factors, including recent and past trauma or stressors.
Be alert for compliance issues and follow-through problems.

or excessive and exaggerated pain behavior or symptomatology can occur when the client feels discounted, distrusted, or poorly cared for (Covington, 2000). If the therapist is perceived as unsympathetic, the individual may terminate the interview. The need to view problems as somatic rather than psychological is part of the nature of these disorders and, according to Pilowsky (2001), can be conceptualized as the surface manifestation of the individual's attempt to alleviate internal pain.

Hersen and Turner (2003) describe individuals with somatoform disorders using the acronym SHAFT: sad, hostile, anxious, frustrated individuals who tenaciously hold on to the medical doctor and their belief in a medical etiology. The clinician's acceptance that these individuals are suffering may temper their hostility, help to avoid confrontation, and facilitate the establishment of a therapeutic relationship (Campo & Fritz, 2001). Many of these clients are used to a passive role; thus an effective strategy is to approach these individuals as collaborators and recognize that their insight and participation is crucial if treatment is to be successful (Hersen & Turner, 2003). While it is important even in the intake interview to start to identify possible links between symptoms and psychological factors, do not expect the client to necessarily accept or to share your assumptions.

Working with individuals with somatoform disorders can be frustrating. Difficulties in establishing and maintaining rapport may result in mutual rejection between client and clinician (Holder-Perkins & Wise, 2001). Therefore, it is essential that the clinician continually be aware of and monitor not only clients' resistance but also any countertransference reactions they may experience (Hersen & Turner, 2003).

Consideration of a General Medical Condition

The *DSM-IV-TR* recommends considering a somatoform disorder rather than a GMC in three conditions: (1) when many organ systems are involved, (2) when there is a chronic course with early onset without structural abnormalities or physical signs, and (3) when laboratory or test results that would indicate the presence of a GMC are absent (American Psychiatric Association, 2000b). Unlike in cases of medical conditions, when interviewing individuals with somatoform disorders the clinician may experience the "reverse funnel effect" as the number of diagnostic considerations increases with more extensive investigations (First & Tasman, 2004). The exclusion of a medical cause is a key step in the diagnosis of a somatoform disorder (Wijeratne et al., 2003). The clinician should refer these individuals for a thorough physical examination to rule out the possibility of an actual disorder and to establish a bond of trust and caring (Magarinos et al., 2002). The clinician must walk a fine line between communicating reassurance to the patient and not dismissing the patient's complaint as unfounded while performing only those laboratory tests and diagnostic and surgical procedures that are indicated (Magarinos et al., 2002). Early neurological symptoms can signify a developing neurological condition, and it is important not to misdiagnose hypochondriacal individuals.

According to A. Frances and Ross (2001), one of the crucial issues is "to do no harm" by either under- or overestimating the role of a GMC. Inadequately assessing for the presence of a genuine GMC or other mental disorder, or overlooking the onset of a new medical condition because "it is all in your head," only further complicates treatment. The clinician's evaluation must include a detailed history of the individual's medical condition and concerns and a mental status exam. Contact with the general medical provider and a review of the patient's medical records are essential for obtaining clarification and the coordination of interventions. Previous records can also indicate the adequacy of care and difficulties with follow-through, doctor-seeking behavior, and family or other factors that may contribute to ineffective interventions. The differentiation between unexplained and explained medical symptoms may be influenced by the timing of the medical consultation, availability, and access to diagnostic facilities (Wijeratne et al., 2003).

In many of the somatoform disorders a history of child abuse represents a significant risk factor. Identifying these disorders in children who have been severely abused may be very difficult as frequently these children often sustain significant physical damage (Haugaard, 2004).

Clinical Interview

Focusing on the individual's experience of, interpretation of, and response to the symptoms rather than symptom counting is critical in the assessment of somatoform disorders (Bouman et al., 1999; P. Fink, 1996). As Fauman (2002) indicates, many of the disorders within the somatoform category require evidence that psychological factors play a role in the exacerbation or initiation of the clinical symptoms. Whereas a close temporal relationship between the stressors, conflicts, needs, and symptoms may be identified, a causal relationship is often impossible to prove (First & Tasman, 2004). The presence of alexithymia, the tendency to focus and amplify somatic sensations and misconstrue them as signs of a disease, makes the assessment of symptoms and level of impairment even more difficult (Bursch, 2006; G. Taylor, 2003).

The experience of pain is influenced by several factors, including the individual's psychological makeup, family members' reactions to the pain behavior, and the effectiveness of distractors (Morrison, 1995b). For individuals with chronic pain the assessment of pain beliefs and coping strategies is essential (Hersen & Turner, 2003). Covington (2000) suggests several helpful strategies. He recommends determining how congruent the presentation is with known conditions, determining the consistency of symptoms over time and situations, evaluating symptom consistency with anatomy and physiology, obtaining confirmatory information from significant others, and assessing excessive illness behavior.

For individuals with Hypochondriasis, Sharpe and Williams (2002) recommend asking about beliefs, the reasons the individual associates with their concerns, ruling out the presence of delusional beliefs, and evaluating concerns about catastrophic and fatal developments. They suggest doing a detailed assessment of self-checking behaviors and being alert for the presence of anxiety and depressive symptoms. Many individuals with BDD may present as ashamed, embarrassed, and reluctant to discuss their concerns, and their clinical presentation is often masked by the occurrence of comorbid mood and anxiety disorders. Therefore, it is important to directly ask about the symptoms pertaining to diagnostic criteria (Albertini & Phillips, 2001). K. A. Phillips (2000) suggests asking five specific questions on intake: Are you very worried about your appearance? Does this concern preoccupy you? What effect has this preoccupation on your life? Have your appearance concerns caused you a lot of distress? Have these appearance concerns affected your family or friends?

Cultural Factors

Because cultural factors influence the expression of somatic complaints, Chaplin (1997) recommends adopting several specific interview strategies. The clinician needs to have an awareness of the common prevalence or ubiquitous nature of somatization. A detailed interview should include gathering collateral information and being familiar with the individual's use and knowledge of psychosocial constructs. Cultural stereotypes that often obscure the important aspects of the clinical presentation should be avoided. In addition, caution should be used when assigning a somatoform disorder diagnosis, particularly in cultures where the presentation of somatic complaints is the only means to obtain medical or psychiatric care or attention; where the prevalent cultural concerns or idioms of distress involve physical complaints; or where there are endemic recurrent medical conditions that impact multiple systems, such as parasitic or infectious conditions and poor nutrition. Finally, where religious and healing rituals involve disassociation or seizure-type behavior, the clinician needs to be attuned to these issues and not overpathologize or misdiagnosis as Conversion Disorder (First et al., 2004).

Assessment Measures

The use of self-report or semistructured interviews for individuals with somatoform disorders can help with diagnostic differentiation and assessing the nature of the individual's experience and level of impairment. Holder-Perkins and Wise (2001) reviewed a range of scales that can be used as a screening for Hypochondriasis, such as the Whiltley Index (Pilowsky, 1967; Speckens, Spinhoven, Sloekers, Bolk, & van Hemert, 1996; Speckens, van Hemert, Spinhoven, & Bolk, 1996) and the Health Attitude Survey (Noyes, Langbehn, Happel, Sieren, & Muller, 1999) that assesses somatization. A structured screening interview such as the West Haven–Yale Multidimensional Pain Inventory can be used to help with the selection of treatment interventions (Kerns, Turk, & Rudy, 1985; D. C. Turk & Okifuji, 2001). Hersen and Turner (2003) recommend assessing pain behavior using a pain diary (M. P. Jensen & Karoly, 2001). Including in the interview such measures as the McGill Pain Questionnaire (Melzack, 1975), the Survey of Pain Attitudes (Tait & Chibnall, 1997), the Pain Beliefs and Perceptions Inventory (D. A. Williams & Thorn, 1989), the Stages of Pain Questionnaire (Kerns, Rosenberg, Jamison, Caudill, & Haythornthwaite, 1997), and the Coping Strategies Questionnaire (Rosensteil & Keefe, 1983) provides a more comprehensive understanding of the clinical presentation. D. C. Turk and Melzack's (2001) *Handbook of Pain Assessment* has a more detailed description of these measures.

CRISIS, LEGAL, AND ETHICAL ISSUES

Given the complexity of these cases, the clinician may become overly focused on the presence of somatic concerns and treatment history and not adequately assess for danger to self. Individuals with BDD and Somatization Disorder are at high risk for suicide, and it is imperative that the clinician not overlook the presence of suicidal ideation and behavior or of impulse control issues (First & Tasman, 2005; K. A. Phillips & Menard, 2006). It is important to ask about suicide at least twice during the interview.

Although somatoform disorders can be diagnostically challenging it is important not to use up the intake interview focusing on differential diagnosis, but to also address compliance and follow-through issues. As many of these individuals are inconsistent informants and have difficulty providing specific factual information, obtaining collateral information is essential. Interviewing family members and available supports can provide significant information, and their involvement is often crucial to ensure the effectiveness of treatment. The role of secondary gain or the reinforcement of illness behavior by family members should also be explored. For older adults, the assessment of somatoform disorders has often been hampered by inappropriate medical diagnosis and incorrectly attributing the presence of somatic complaints to aging, resulting in the neglect of these disorders (Wijeratne et al., 2003). Many individuals with somatoform disorders have negative treatment experiences, engender hostility in their care providers, and are often litigious. Obtaining ongoing consultation when treating these clients and clearly documenting all interventions and implementation issues is crucial. Particular attention should be paid to obtaining informed consents for treatment and releases of information to contact other service providers prior to treatment.

DIAGNOSTIC CONSIDERATIONS

Common Comorbidities

Axis I Disorders

Comorbidity tends to be the rule rather than the exception for the somatoform disorders, with 83% to 100% of individuals with a Somatization Disorder in primary care facilities presenting with comorbid conditions (P. Fink et al., 1999). Somatoform disorders have concurrent high rates of mood, anxiety, and personality disorders (Bouman et al., 1999; P. Fink et al., 1999). Hence, during the interview the clinician needs to assess for all comorbid conditions and discern that the symptoms do not occur only in the presence of these disorders. There is also emerging evidence to suggest that undiagnosed Pervasive Development Disorder may be underrecognized in individuals with somatoform disorders (Bursch, Ingman, Vitti, Hyman, & Zeltzer, 2004). De Waal and colleagues (2004) report that anxiety and depressive disorders were 3.3 times more likely with somatoform disorders than by chance, and more than 50% of the individuals with an anxiety or depressive disorder also had a somatoform disorder. Among internal medical patients identified with Somatization Disorder, 36% actually had another psychiatric disorder (Fink et al., 2004). This high level of comorbidity led Dhossche and colleagues (2002) to recommend that the clinician confronted by a high number of unexplained medical symptoms should also consider assessing for the presence of anxiety and depressive symptoms.

For Conversion Disorder the most common comorbid disorders are anxiety and depression (Bloom, 2001). C. Ford (1995) found that 56.2% of these individuals presented with depressive symptoms, 62.5% had anxiety, and 14.9% had an alcohol or substance dependence disorder. Similarly, Krem (2004) found one third of individuals with motor Conversion Disorder had a comorbid Axis I disorder, with Major Depressive Disorder being the most common. Half had a comorbid Axis II disorder.

For chronic pain the most common Axis I disorders are Major Depressive Disorder (85%) and Dissociative, Panic, Posttraumatic Stress, and substance-related disorders

(Maldonado & Spiegel, 2001). Of general medical patients, 62% of those with Hypochondriasis also presented with another condition, the most frequent being Major Depressive Disorder. Interestingly, Noyes and colleagues (1994) found that Major Depressive Disorder tended to occur after the Hypochondriasis, whereas anxiety disorders tended to occur before it. Of note also is the finding that 15% to 30% of individuals with Hypochondriasis had actual physical problems (H. I. Kaplan & Saddock, 1996).

According to Cororve and Gleaves (2001), BDD is almost never found without comorbidity. Major depression is the most common disorder, with reported rates varying from 8% to 42% (K. A. Phillips, 2000) and a lifetime prevalence of 82% (Gunstad & Phillips, 2003). Social Phobia was found to be common (38%), as was social anxiety and isolation, which often occur because of the excessive concern over appearance. Substance disorders co-occurred with BDD in 36% of cases, and OCD was also present in 30% of cases (Gunstad & Phillips, 2003). For most individuals the Social Phobia developed prior to the onset of the BDD, typically in the early to middle teens, whereas Major Depressive Disorder had an onset in the mid-20s and substance use disorders occurred after the development of BDD. Case reports suggest that individuals with BDD may use alcohol and drugs as a means of coping with their disorder (Sarwer et al., 2003). For children and adolescents with BDD, there was a current prevalence rate of 70% for Major Depressive Disorder and a lifetime rate of more than 91% for mood disorders. Anxiety disorders had a current rate of 61%, with OCD being the most frequent (36%) type (Albertini & Phillips, 2001). In their review of comorbidity studies, Sarwer and colleagues (2003) also note gender differences, with females more frequently presenting with a history of eating disorders, Panic Disorder, and Generalized Anxiety Disorder. In contrast, males were more likely to have a history of substance abuse or dependence and Bipolar Disorder. Rivera and Borda (2001) report that females have a higher comorbidity rate with anxiety disorders and eating disorders, and males have higher comorbid rates of Bipolar Disorder.

Axis II Disorders

Given that many of the somatoform disorders present with long histories and persistent patterns of behaviors, it is important not to overemphasize the overlap with personality disorders (Bouman et al., 1999). Having said that, it is estimated that 61% of individuals with Somatization Disorder have a comorbid Axis II disorder, including Histrionic, Borderline, and Antisocial Personality Disorder. Of individuals with chronic pain, 58.4% met the criteria for a personality disorder, the most frequent being Dependent, Histrionic, and Passive-Aggressive Disorder (C. Ford, 1995). Although there are no consistent data that demonstrate a personality pattern characteristic of Hypochondriasis, individuals with this disorder have been reported to have obsessive-compulsive traits, narcissistic traits, passive dependent, and borderline features (Iezzi, Duckworth, Adams, et al., 2001). For Conversion Disorder, the most frequently co-occurring personality disorders are Histrionic, Antisocial, Borderline, and Dependent. According to Veale and colleagues (1996), the majority of individuals with BDD (72%) have a coexisting Axis II disorder, the most common being Avoidance (38%), followed by Paranoid (38%), and then Obsessive-Compulsive (28%). K. A. Phillips and McElroy (2000) suggest that the high comorbidity between BDD and Avoidant Personality Disorder (43%) characterizes high levels of self-consciousness, obsessive-compulsiveness, worry, avoidance, introversion, rejection sensitivity, and social anxiety. Also, the high level of rejection sensitivity and referential thinking in BDD, specifically thinking that others are noticing and mocking one because of one's appearance, is similar to that found in Avoidant Personality Disorder and other Cluster C personality disorders.

Differential Diagnosis

First and colleagues (2004) identified four essential steps to establish the presence of a somatoform disorder. Initially, the clinician should determine that the subjective symptoms are not due to the presence of a medical condition, then assess if another *DSM-IV* disorder may be causing the clinical symptoms (see Table 12.3). Next, the clinician needs to evaluate if the symptoms are intentional and if they are associated with a Factitious Disorder. Finally, the clinician should determine which somatoform disorder best accounts for the symptoms (see Table 12.4).

Somatoform Disorders versus General Medical Condition

As somatoform disorders can be diagnosed only when a GMC has been ruled out; this fosters an either/or mentality and may result in overlooking treatable medical conditions that coexist with somatoform disorders (Bouman et al., 1999; Looper & Kirmayer, 2002). Additionally, these individuals typically, tend to be shuttled between medical and psychiatric settings, further contributing to misdiagnosis and unnecessary medical procedures (First et al., 2004; Looper & Kirmayer, 2002). In many cases, somatization may mask an underlying physical condition. In 25% to 50% of Conversion Disorder cases a true organic condition or medical or physical illness was eventually diagnosed (C. Ford, 1995; H. I. Kaplan & Saddock, 1996). Krem (2004) reports that the presence of mild brain injury may predispose individuals to Conversion Disorder and that 1% to 9% of neurology patients can also be classified as conversion patients. Maldonado and Spiegel (2001) cited earlier research which found that approximately 70% of patients diagnosed with Conversion Disorder also had evidence of a preceding or coexisting neurological disorder. They found that 44% of individuals with conversion symptoms had neurological disorders; the incidence of true medical or neurological symptoms was 20%, with a history of head trauma being the most common.

It can be very difficult to determine whether a GMC fully accounts for the individual's condition. Even in cases in which the medical condition is judged to be primarily responsible for the symptoms observed, psychological factors may play a role in the initiation and course of the illness and response to treatment. In such cases, the diagnostic category *psychological factors affecting medical condition* needs to be considered (First et al., 2004). A prior history or suspicion of a neurological disorder, an older age of symptom onset, and longer duration of symptoms are more indicative of an underlying neurological disorder than a Conversion Disorder (Moene et al., 2000). First and colleagues note that certain medical conditions such as multiple sclerosis, porphyria, systemic lupus erythematosus, and hyperparathyroidism are particularly likely to have an atypical presentation and a course marked by numerous medical symptoms that may be mistakenly diagnosed as Somatization Disorder. Differentiating pain that has a medical basis from Pain Disorder is also often difficult. H. I. Kaplan and Saddock (1996) suggest that constant pain that does not fluctuate with the use of medication, time, or the individual's emotional state is

Table 12.3   Between-category diagnostic differential

Disorder	Similarities with Somatoform Disorders	Differences from Somatoform Disorders
General medical condition (GMC)	Multiple physical complaints	Identified medical condition fully accounts for physical complaints. Significant laboratory or physical findings of GMC. Psychological factors not salient.
Substance-related disorder	Physical and neurological symptoms	Symptoms are related to the direct effects of or use of a substance.
Major Depressive Disorder (MDD)	Somatic symptoms such as headaches, unexplained pain, gastrointestinal problems	MDD: Somatic symptoms are limited to periods of depressed mood. Not likely to have a lifelong history of unexplained somatic symptoms. SD: Somatic symptoms are recurrent throughout most of individual's life and are not restricted to periods of depressed mood.
Anxiety disorders (AD; e.g., Panic Disorder, GAD, OCD)	Multiple somatic symptoms such as muscle tension, fatigue, concentration difficulties	AD: Symptoms present during panic attacks or anxiety. A history of unexplained somatic complaints unlikely. Anxiety and intrusive thoughts are not limited to physical symptoms or to disease or defect. SD: Symptoms are present at other times and panic attacks may be absent.
Eating disorders (ED; e.g., Anorexia Nervosa)	Preoccupation with body, weight, and appearance	ED: Concerns limited to body weight and shape, restrictive eating, and refusal to maintain weight. SD: Concerns include other perceived defects.
Schizophrenia	Somatic delusions may be present	Delusions are likely to have bizarre quality. Characteristic other symptoms not associated with SD (e.g., hallucinations, disorganized speech or behavior, negative symptoms).
Factitious disorders	Multiple unexplained somatic complaints	Symptoms are consciously or intentionally produced to assume the sick role.
Malingering	Vague, inconsistent, and unexplainable physical and psychological symptoms	Symptoms are consciously or intentionally produced for secondary gain or external incentives.
Psychological conditions that impact a medical condition	Physical symptoms	Presence of an identified medical condition.

Table 12.4   Within-category diagnostic differential

Disorder	Key Features	Discriminating Features
Somatization Disorder	Multiple physical complaints No medical basis Early onset Chronic course	Focus on symptoms: 4 pain, 2 gastrointestinal, 1 sexual, 1 pseudo-neurological Onset before age 30, duration several years
Undifferentiated Somatoform Disorder[*]	Multiple physical complaints No medical basis	Focus on fewer symptoms, briefer duration—6 months or more
Conversion Disorder[*]	Physical complaints No medical basis Role of psychological factors	Focus on symptoms that are limited to voluntary motor or sensory functions
Pain Disorder[*]	Pain complaints No medical basis Role of psychological factors	Symptoms limited to and focused on pain Not multiple sites and symptoms
Hypochondriasis	Fear, preoccupation, or concern Misinterpretation of bodily symptoms	Focus on disease or having a serious physical illness Duration at least 6 months
Body Dysmorphic Disorder	Fear, preoccupation, or concern	Focus on physical defect Preoccupation with imagined defect If anomaly present, concern excessive
Somatoform Disorder NOS	Physical complaints No medical basis	Does not meet specific diagnostic criteria for another Somatorm Disorders Briefer duration

[*]Somatization Disorder takes precedence over these disorders.
Adapted with permission from the *Diagnostic and Statistical Manual of Mental Disorders, fourth edition, text revision,* by American Psychiatric Association, 2000b, Washington, DC: Author.

more likely psychogenic, especially if there is a dramatic flair to the clinical presentation. These findings underscore the importance of ruling out a GMC and making a somatoform diagnosis only with caution and after a careful physical examination and review of the individual's medical history (Bouman et al., 1999).

Somatoform versus Other Psychiatric Disorders

Mood and Anxiety Disorders   Comorbid mood and anxiety disorders are common, making diagnostic differentiation difficult and resulting in some cases of multiple diagnoses being assigned (First et al., 2002). For all of these disorders the clinical presentation can include multiple somatic complaints, early onset, and a persistent course. In mood or anxiety disorders the somatic complaints and concerns are likely to be restricted to periods of sad mood or anxiety and tend to abate when the underlying condition abates or is treated (Holder-Perkins & Wise, 2001; Magarinos et al., 2002). More specifically, individuals with Somatization Disorder complaining of depression may present with greater levels of depressive symptomatology than for those with Major Depressive Disorder (First & Tasman, 2004). Unlike Hypochondriasis, in GAD the individual tends to worry about a variety of things, while for those with Panic Disorder the primary fear is of having future panic attacks. Noyes (2001) notes that individuals who present with both Hypochondriasis and Panic Disorder tend to have these disorders separately rather than concurrently. Reliance on the objective observation of the individual rather than subjective report and the use of a longitudinal history or time line of onset and course of the disorders will help with these difficult discriminations. Crucial to this differentiation is whether the somatic complaints occur during episodes when the anxiety and mood symptoms are not present or if they persist after the other disorders have been successfully treated (First & Tasman, 2004).

Individuals with Hypochondriasis and OCD both experience recurrent intrusive thoughts; their excessive fears may be obsessional, and they may also use behavioral compulsion such as going to the doctor to deal with their anxiety (Maxmen & Ward, 1995). In Hypochondriasis, individuals are afraid they already have some disease, whereas in a specific phobia or OCD persons are fearful they may contract a disease. Thus, individuals with Hypochondriasis embark on a quest of doctor visits to elicit confirmation of their worst fears. In contrast, individuals with illness phobia or OCD exhibit excessive maladaptive avoidance behaviors to prevent exposure to the feared disease or engage in compulsive behaviors to try to deal with their anxiety about contracting the disease. The individual with the disease fear presents with fewer and less severe anxiety symptoms but more significant illness behaviors than those with panic-related disorders (Bouman et al., 1999). If the clinical presentation includes nonhealth-related obsessions and compulsions, then an additional diagnosis of OCD must be considered (First & Tasman, 2004).

The social withdrawal and avoidance of individuals with BDD is similar to that seen with Social Phobia and Avoidant Personality Disorder; however, the underlying motivation is different. In Social Phobia the individual is self-conscious rather than focused on an imagined defect. As both of these disorders frequently co-occur, if the individual meets the criteria for both disorders both may be assigned (First & Tasman, 2004). The high comorbidity between BDD and Social Phobia has led some to suggest that the two disorders are related (Cororve & Gleaves, 2001). In their study of children and adolescents with BDD, Albertini and Phillips (2001) concluded that the high rates of comorbidity suggest that BDD is related to depression, Social Phobia, and OCD. Despite BDD being more similar in phenomenology and treatment response to OCD and Social Phobia, it is included in the somatoform disorders (First et al., 2004). An additional diagnosis of OCD can be given only if there is evidence that there are obsessions or compulsions about concerns other than appearance (American Psychiatric Association, 2000b). The similarities in the clinical presentation and high level of comorbidity have led several researchers to hypothesize that BDD is better conceptualized as an OCD spectrum disorder (M. Zimmerman & Mattia, 1998). In reviewing the similarities, K. A. Phillips (2000) concluded that although the disorders were alike in terms of demographics, neuropsychological deficits, and treatment response, there were notable differences. Individuals with BDD were more likely than those with OCD to be unmarried (39% versus 13%), to have suicidal ideation (70% versus 47%), to have attempted suicide (22% versus 8%), and to have a higher lifetime prevalence of Major Depressive Disorder (85% versus 55%) with an earlier onset (18.8 years versus 25.3 years). They were also more likely to have first-degree relatives with substance-related disorders, have poorer insight, and have a higher prevalence of ideas of references than individuals with OCD (A. Frances & Ross,

2001; K. A. Phillips, 2000). Rivera and Borda (2001) suggest that individuals with OCD are bothered by pervasive and persistent obsessional intrusions; in contrast, it is the content of the intrusions that is disturbing for the individual with BDD.

Psychotic Disorders   The differentiation between Hypochondriasis and Delusional Disorder is based on the intensity of the individual's beliefs or convictions and can be particularly difficult when the individual also has poor insight. Individuals with Hypochondriasis may at times consider alternative explanations of their symptoms, whereas individuals who are psychotic or have Delusional Disorder may not (Maxmen & Ward, 1995). Individuals with Schizophrenia or a mood disorder with psychotic features present with characteristic symptoms (psychomotor agitation or retardation or disorganized speech or blunted affect) that are not associated with Hypochondriasis. The differentiation of delusional ideation from somatic preoccupations can also be difficult (First et al., 2004). The *DSM-IV-TR* glossary describes a delusion as a false belief based on incorrect inference about external reality, which is held despite other beliefs, incontrovertible evidence, or obvious proof to the contrary and is not accepted by the individual's culture (American Psychiatric Association, 2000b). The conviction occurs on a continuum and can be inferred from the individual's behavior (American Psychiatric Association, 2000b). For many individuals, the intensity of these cognitive processes often wax and wane over the course of the disorder. Delusional Disorder of the somatic type can be given as a comorbid diagnosis if the preoccupation with the imagined defect, as in BDD, is held with delusional intensity (Cororve & Gleaves, 2001).

Among the Somatoform Disorders

The six disorders within the somatoform category share the common feature of unexplained physical symptoms or concerns that lack a medical basis or physiological mechanism (H. I. Kaplan & Saddock, 1996). Additionally, Somatization and Conversion Disorder and Somatization Disorder and Hypochondriasis are frequently comorbid (Fink et al., 2004; Hersen & Turner, 2003; Magarinos, Zafar, Nissenson, & Blanco, 2002). The clinician can initially differentiate between these disorders by identifying the nature of the clinical presentation and the individual's focus of concern (see Table 12.4). Hypochondriasis and BDD have been described as the obsessional and cognitive cluster, whereas Somatization and Pain Disorders have been described as the somatic and sensory cluster that involves a loss or alteration of bodily functions and a focus on somatic sensations that are experienced as unpleasant (Cromer, 1995; Wijeratne et al., 2003). Concern about a serious physical illness and general health is the hallmark of Hypochondriasis, and concern about a physical defect and physical appearance is the defining feature of BDD (Magarinos et al., 2002). For both Hypochondriasis and BDD, the preoccupations may be experienced as intrusive, unpleasant thoughts that are accompanied by the compulsive behaviors of needing to check one's appearance for reassurance and a fear or avoidance consequent to a negative bodily appraisal (Fallon, 2004). In both Hypochondriasis and Somatization Disorder there is a course of symptoms waxing and waning in severity and duration. For Somatization Disorder, the individual is preoccupied with the discomfort from physical complaints and does not have a clearly defined conception of what is causing the problem (Fallon, 2004). Here the focus is on the symptoms themselves, and the presentation is characterized by a multiplicity of complaints involving multiple organ systems (H. I. Kaplan & Saddock, 1996). According to Holder-Perkins and Wise (2001), individuals with Somatization Disorder seek sanctions for the sick role, in contrast to individuals with Hypochondriasis, who tend to seek reassurance and explanations rather than treatment (Noyes, 2001). In the most typical case of Hypochondriasis, the persistent fear or idea that a serious illness is present overshadows the individual's concerns about physical complaints. Individuals with Hypochondriasis may present with high levels of anxiety; in contrast, this anxiety may be absent in individuals with Somatization Disorder (Bouman et al., 1999). When there is overlap in clinical presentations, Somatization Disorder takes priority over a diagnosis of Hypochondriasis, Conversion Disorder, and Pain Disorder (Fauman, 2002).

Concern about physical symptoms is characteristic of Somatization Disorder, Undifferentiated Somatization Disorder, Pain Disorder, and Conversion Disorder. In Somatization Disorder the clinical presentation is multiple physical complaints presented in a vaguely exaggerated fashion with a gradual onset. In Pain and Conversion Disorders, the focus is a specific symptom (Holder-Perkins & Wise, 2001). Individuals with Conversion Disorder tend to minimize clinical symptoms, which often have a sudden onset, are confined to the motor and sensory systems, and are often dramatic and discrete (Maxmen & Ward, 1995). In contrast, in both Pain Disorder and Somatization Disorder, the primary focus or the cause of the distress is the symptoms themselves. In comparing Conversion Disorder and Somatization Disorder, G. Taylor (2003, p. 494) notes that individuals with Somatization Disorder experience and express somatic distress with symptoms that appear in the body and follow somatic pathways, whereas conversion symptoms appear to "leap from the mind to the body," not corresponding to known neurological pathways. He also notes that in Conversion Disorders the symbolic nature of the symptoms is intact, whereas in Somatization Disorder psychological issues are not well represented symbolically.

A common thread among the somatoform disorders is that the symptoms appear related to psychological factors and are associated with the presence of stress in individuals who have difficulty articulating their distress. Thus, psychological pain is expressed in physical symptoms (Fauman, 2002). Individuals with Conversion Disorder often present with little or no anxiety, whereas individuals with Hypochondriasis have excessive concerns; and the latter has been described as an illness-affirming disorder (Bouman et al., 1999). For both Conversion and Pain Disorder psychological factors must be identified as playing a role in the development or maintenance of the symptoms; this criterion, however, has been criticized as empirically untestable (Birket-Smith & Mortensen, 2002).

TREATMENT

General Principles in Treating Somatoform Disorders

Well-designed, controlled treatment studies for the somatoform disorders are scarce, with the majority focusing on educative, cognitive, behavioral, or a combination of these approaches. According to Holder-Perkins and Wise (2001), the clinician's main tasks in

Table 12.5   Treatment interventions for somatoform disorders

Area	Interventions
Therapeutic interventions	Establish firm therapeutic alliance.
	Accept that client is truly suffering and offer reassurance.
	Set up regular appointments and coordinate care.
	Provide ongoing client education and recognition of illness.
	Prevent the adoption of sick role.
	Consider cognitive-behavioral approaches, including ERP.
	Consider somatic interventions, such as relaxation.
	Set realistic concrete goals with clear follow through.
	Remain alert for dropout and compliance issues.
	Treat comorbid and associated features, (i.e. depression, anxiety, and anger).
Adjunct interventions	Establish a collaborative relationship with physician.
	Coordinate care; minimize unnecessary procedures.
	Educate about illness and pharmacologic treatments.
	Medication evaluation and review, including adherence and compliance.
	Be alert for psychological dependence on medication.
	Assess anti-anxiety or sleep medication use.
Family interventions	Educate family members about disorder and adaptive response strategies.
	Use concrete behavioral interventions.
	Decrease illness talk and focus and redirect to primary care physician.
	Focus on independence and assertiveness.
	Make referrals to adjunctive family support groups.
	Consider family therapy.
Adjunct referrals	Physical therapist and rehabilitation services.
	Biofeedback and relaxation training.
	Alternative therapies: hypnosis, acupuncture, holistic healing, meditation, and yoga.
Disorders	**Specific Interventions**
Somatization Disorder	Reassurance, reeducation, support, and suggestion.
Pain Disorder	Referral to pain management program.
Conversion Disorder	Symptom removal: psychotherapy and rehabilitation services referrals.
Hypochondriasis	CBT, ERP, and SSRI evaluation.
Body Dysmorphic Disorder	High-dose SSRI, CBT, and ERP.

treating individuals with somatoform disorders are to decode the individual's disguised communication and to formulate a treatment plan that addresses the client's specific needs while attending to environmental stressors and comorbid disorders. To be most effective, several clinical management interventions need to be implemented at the beginning of treatment (see Table 12.5).

Development of a Strong Relationship with Patient

These disorders may be fascinating, yet they can also cause considerable friction between treatment providers and patients (L. Seligman, 1998). The therapist, like the physician, will need to provide reassurance and acceptance that the client is truly suffering; recognizing and validating the individual's experience is essential to establishing rapport (Asaad, 2000; G. E. Simon, 2002). It is helpful to acknowledge the patient's distress, but suggest that the symptoms will resolve. The clinician's goal is to gradually decrease the time spent focusing on somatic symptoms and to establish an effective therapeutic alliance by explaining that stress—both psychological and environmental—can cause physical symptoms. The challenge is to balance the provision of empathic support, an understanding of the client's health concerns, and an overall focus on improving functioning rather than reducing physical symptoms (L. Seligman, 1998). It is important to communicate a belief that the client can learn to cope with stress and negative feelings and that physical changes or symptoms are not necessarily indicative of a catastrophic illness. Hearing this reassurance, the individual may gradually shift focus from the somatic complaints to personal and interpersonal issues (First & Tasman, 2004). Covington (2000) emphasized that clinicians need to monitor their negative feelings, understand the contributing factors in the client's life, respect the individual's dignity, and help decrease clients' suffering and improve the quality of their lives. By working collaboratively on mutually agreed treatment goals and focusing on symptom management rather than diagnosis and cure, a strong relationship can be established (G. E. Simon, 2002).

Scheduling Regular Appointments and Coordination of Care

Many individuals with somatoform disorders present with the belief that they will be seen or attended to only if they are sick; that is, they have an "admission ticket mentality" and have developed a variety of doctor-seeking behaviors. Scheduling regular appointments that are not related to the severity of clinical symptoms, having little contact outside of sessions, and limiting subspecialty and diagnostic testing referrals can redirect the individual toward more adaptive, healthy coping strategies (Kroenke & Swindle, 2000; Magarinos et al., 2002). This can help break the cycle of clients feeling they must develop a new symptom in order to be seen by a clinician.

Engaging these clients in treatment and maintaining a therapeutic alliance is most likely to be effective if the therapist works collaboratively with the referring medical professionals or primary care physician, utilizing a shared-care or team approach (Looper & Kirmayer, 2002; L. Seligman, 1998). These individuals often resist psychological treatment and their referral to mental health services is often fraught with difficulty; however, in a strong long-term medical doctor-patient relationship, therapy may be introduced as a way to deal with stress (Escobar, 1996). It is important that the individual's potential feelings of rejection are discussed from the beginning. Clients with these disorders do best when seen by a single identified primary physician who recognizes the role of emotional issues in the expression of somatic complaints (First & Tasman, 2004; Holder-Perkins & Wise, 2001; H. I. Kaplan & Saddock, 1996). The most effective care is for the primary care physician to stay involved by having regular follow-up appointments with set agendas, with a focus limited to objective findings and relating stress to physical symptoms and using caution in prescribing multiple medications (Holder-Perkins & Wise, 2001).

Quill (1985), in describing the most helpful intervention for the physician, recommends a caring, respectful, long-term medical, relationship that, "is not linked to testing of surgery, or focused primarily on the the resolution of symptoms." Consulting with the primary care provider and presenting information on the nature of somatoform disorders was found to decrease the individual's health care utilization (a 53% decrease in gross health care expenditure) and doctor-seeking behaviors (L. A. Allen et al., 2001; Looper & Kirmayer, 2002). If there is an underlying medical condition that requires treatment by specialists, regular, ongoing collaborative communication to avoid mixed messages or potentially harmful combinations of procedures is essential (Magarinos, Zafar, Nissenson, & Blanco, 2002).

For children, having one physician as the primary person interacting with the child and family and a clinician as a consultant may be a particularly effective model (Haugaard, 2004). This honors the child's and parent's perceptions that the symptoms involve physical problems, while including a mental health professional underscores the role of psychological factors and thus facilitates the family expanding their understanding of the problems.

Education and Preventing the Adoption of the Sick Role

Educating the client about the mind-body connection, the role that stress can play in exacerbating or contributing to symptoms, presenting both the physiological and psychological components of treatment as an integrated plan, promotes compliance and a successful outcome (L. Seligman, 1998). Educational interventions are advantageous in that they are brief and actively involve individuals in their own recovery. In reviewing effective treatments, Maxmen and Ward (1995) suggest six steps: (1) providing individuals with facts about their symptoms; (2) differentiating pain from the experience of pain; (3) detailing how one's emotional state impacts the perception of pain; (4) describing how suggestion and selective attention can heighten the awareness and focus on a symptom; (5) emphasizing coping and the fact that life continues despite physical problems; and (6) relating with empathy for and acceptance of the individual's disorder. Clients can also be educated about how current attempts to reduce anxiety through checking, reassurance seeking, or doctor's visits often bring temporary relief but do not get at the root of the problematic beliefs and underlying fears that one has an illness. Overall, the primary goals for treatment with these disorders are the prevention of the adoption of the sick role and the development of chronic invalidism (First & Tasman, 2004).

Treating Comorbid Conditions

As a comprehensive strategy for the somatoform disorders, Holder-Perkins and Wise (2001) recommend a conservative medical approach and a vigorous treatment of comorbid disorders. Given the high rates of comorbid conditions, the identification and treatment of these conditions are essential to ensure therapeutic effectiveness (Asaad, 2000; Magarinos et al., 2002). Effective treatment of the most common comorbid disorders, that is, mood and anxiety, can also result in a decrease in somatic symptoms (Fallon, 2004; G. E. Simon, 2002).

Medication

To date there is a lack of a specific effective pharmacotherapy and few medications that are effective for all the disorders within this category (First & Tasman, 2004; Wijeratne et al., 2003). Recent research (Fallon, 2004) found that individuals presenting with the obsessional cluster, that is, Hypochondriasis and Body Dysmorphic Disorder, have been found to respond well to SSRIs. Combining antidepressant medication with cognitive-behavioral interventions has been found helpful in treating these disorders (Karvonen et al., 2004). However, some individuals may refuse medication because they are fearful or sensitive to the side effects. Clinicians who are knowledgeable about these reactions can encourage the discussion of these effects with the primary physician (Escobar, 1996). Medications with risk for dependence or overdose (e.g., benzodiazepines) should be prescribed with caution as these individuals often develop psychological dependency (H. I. Kaplan & Saddock, 1996).

Psychological Interventions

Although specific treatment approaches to somatoform disorders have not been well studied, there is some evidence that CBT approaches may be helpful (De Waal et al., 2004). Typically, CBT approaches involve cognitive restructuring aimed at modifying automatic, distorted thoughts and catastrophizing and addressing learned past illness schemas. Behavioral techniques may include desensitization, decreasing illness behaviors, graded activity, and response prevention (Looper & Kirmayer, 2002). The use of behavioral logs and symptom diaries can help the individual understand the role of stress, emotional reactions, and coping mechanisms (Holder-Perkins & Wise, 2001). A critical review of studies of CBT for clients with somatization found that 71% of individuals improved more than controls, and that the treatment benefits persisted into follow-up in all but one study (Kroenke & Swindle, 2000). L. A. Allen and colleagues (2001) describe how a manualized CBT intervention (10 weekly sessions), focusing on relaxation, activity regulation, and cognitive restructuring, resulted in significant improvement for severe somatizers. In reviewing randomized, controlled studies of the effectiveness of CBT interventions, Looper and Kirmayer (2002) found these interventions to be effective for Hypochondriasis, BDD, and Undifferentiated Somatoform Disorder. They also found group CBT to be effective for BDD and Somatization Disorder. Although CBT has been found to be effective it tends to be underutilized, often limited to highly skilled therapists in academic institutions rather than general practitioners, making its availability limited, in particular to the elderly (Rief & Sharpe, 2004; Wijeratne et al., 2003).

Exposure and response prevention (ERP) has been found to be effective for Hypochondriasis (Visser & Bouman, 2001). This approach involves using exposure exercises, for example, visiting hospitals, reading relevant medical literature, repeatedly writing about fears; response prevention is deterring patients from seeking reassurance. Using a modification of an earlier intervention for OCD, Visser and Bouman (2001) found that in vivo exposure and response prevention was effective in decreasing hypochondriacal behaviors, specifically checking, reassurance seeking, and the avoidance of internal and external stimuli.

Family and Group Interventions

Family interventions typically focus on educating the family about the disorder and the role of physical symptoms as a method of dealing with stressful or upsetting affects and providing cognitive-behavioral interventions (Bursch, 2006). Practical interventions may include decreasing illness talk and focus, while increasing and encouraging autonomy, assertiveness, and independence (Jongsma & Peterson, 2003). Family support groups may also be helpful.

With children and adolescents, a strong relationship between the primary care physician and the parents is crucial, particularly in terms of educating the parent about the links between stress, psychological functioning, and physical pain (Garralda, 1996). Multifaceted treatment that involves changing reinforcement patterns, for example, encouraging the child's involvement in social activities, reducing somatic complaints, and increasing physical relaxation, have also been found to be effective (Haugaard, 2004). The child can be taught coping strategies, including relaxation and refocusing techniques, and the family and others can be shown how to reinforce the child's joining activities (Haugaard, 2004). For children with BDD, education and family involvement in interventions to facilitate treatment compliance and decrease ritualistic behavior is crucial (K. A. Phillips, 2000).

The clinician needs to be cautious in recommending individuals with a somatoform disorder for group therapy as they may be susceptible to mimicking symptoms (A. Frances & Ross, 2001). Group treatment focusing on sharing methods for coping with physical symptoms, increasing ability to perceive and express emotion, teaching assertiveness training and problem solving, increasing positive activities, and providing an atmosphere of general peer support can be helpful. Group therapy members reported better physical and mental health, and there is an associated saving on health care costs (Kashner, Rost, Smith, & Lewis, 1992).

Adjunct Referrals

Interventions such as biofeedback, meditation, yoga, relaxation training, exercise, and massage can be incorporated into the treatment plan for somatoform disorders. These techniques may be helpful in reducing levels of arousal and anxiety that may persist throughout the day. Referral to rehabilitation services can be invaluable as a face-saving means for the individual to recover (First & Tasman, 2004). Hypnosis (a form of heightened concentration or an alert state of focused awareness with concomitant physical relaxation) has been used in the past as an adjunct to the treatment of Conversion Disorder (Maldonado & Spiegel, 2001). This often involves several phases: exploration of the meaning of the symptom and symptom alteration, or taking the individual's mind away from symptoms and allowing him or her to find a more appropriate way to cope with anxiety; increasing the level of functioning through strengthening defenses; and posthypnotic suggestions of recovery, including thoughts about improved well-being (Maxmen & Ward, 1995). Krem (2004) found that results for hypnosis are inconsistent and contradictory concerning recovery for motor Conversion Disorder.

Disorder-Specific Treatments

Somatization Disorder   There are no medications currently available specifically for the treatment of Somatization Disorder, and individuals often take a variety of medications for their various somatic complaints (First & Tasman, 2004; Holder-Perkins & Wise, 2001). While medications can be helpful for comorbid conditions, ideally one physician should manage the prescription of medication. When treating individuals with Somatization Disorder, First and Tasman (2004) suggest the focus of treatment needs to be on symptom management rather than finding a cure; they recommend adopting an approach that minimizes distress and functional impairment and emphasizes reeducation, reassurance, and suggestion. They describe how after the establishment of a strong therapeutic alliance, a full investigation may be conducted, and once a diagnosis has been determined all subsequent tests are limited. Clients are then educated about their "medically sanctioned illness" and provided with a realistic discussion of prognosis and treatment. Maxmen and Ward (1995) recommend focusing on improving the level of functioning and not the elimination of physical complaints. They also caution the clinician to avoid raising false hope or making unrealistic promises that the individual is going to feel better and recommend that clinicians check repeatedly their annoyance level. The overall emphasis needs to be on ignoring complaining behavior, reinforcing more adaptive, noncomplaining communications, and working with the family to do likewise. This conservative approach involving the minimal use of new medication and a consistent level of contact with a caring physician independent of symptom severity has been found to improve outcomes (G. E. Simon, 2002). Having a family meeting and encouraging both the individual and family to talk only to the expert (the primary care doctor) about the illness and identifying family patterns around the illness behavior is crucial (Jongsma & Peterson, 2003).

Escobar (1996) noted the effectiveness of a highly structured, short-term (8 group therapy sessions) psychoeducational intervention that resulted in improvements in individuals' physical and mental health ratings and a decrease (52%) in medical expenditure. There was, however, a very low session attendance (2.2), reflecting the difficulty with treatment compliance for this population. Similarly, Looper and Kirmayer (2002) found few studies on the effectiveness of individual CBT for Somatization Disorder, and the high dropout rate was a limitation of the available research. Holder-Perkins and Wise (2001) reported on the effectiveness of a brief (8 to 16 sessions) group therapy program that integrated stress management and social skills; they concluded that reassurance and encouraging normal activity can be an effective intervention for individuals with Somatization Disorder.

For individuals with Undifferentiated Somatization Disorder, group CBT was found to be effective in one study; however, these results need to be replicated (Looper & Kirmayer, 2002). Given the diagnostic heterogeneity of this disorder, there is a lack of empirical research on therapeutic effectiveness. Many individuals spontaneously recover without treatment; for others, brief supportive and educative therapy provided in the context of a strong therapeutic relationship has been found to be effective (First & Tasman, 2004).

Conversion Disorder   The high rates of spontaneous remission and the lack of randomized controlled studies on the effectiveness of psychotherapy for Conversion Disorders make it difficult to draw conclusions about treatment recommendations (Looper &

Kirmayer, 2002). Conversion symptoms often occur in suggestible individuals, and the best approach is for the clinician to adopt a positive expectation and provide the client with a face-saving means of recovery (e.g., physical rehabilitation; A. Frances & Ross, 2001). As First and Tasman (2004) suggest, a conservative approach of reassurance, relaxation, and suggestion may be useful in symptom removal. Thus a therapeutic alliance that allows the client to recover with dignity and without losing face is crucial (Hurwitz, 2004). Insight-oriented psychotherapy may be useful for gaining an understanding of the dynamics behind the conflicts. G. Taylor (2003) makes a strong case for the use of psychoanalytic therapy given the symbolic nature of the clinical symptoms. It is important not to imply that the individual has been faking symptoms as the goal is to build rapport, not invalidate the client's symptoms (L. M. Cohen & Chang, 2004). However, A. Frances and Ross (2001) note that these individuals may not respond to insight-oriented therapy and may feel blamed.

As the symptoms often occur in the context of psychosocial stresses, environmental manipulation, cognitive and behavioral techniques, the education of supports, family therapy, and teaching coping skills are essential (Hurwitz, 2004). In general, the faster the resolution of the symptoms, the better the client's prognosis (Maldonado & Spiegel, 2001). Treatment is best if carried out in collaboration with a primary care physician, internist, or neurologist, using a joint approach that includes adequate medical intervention directed at diagnosing the cause of the patient's symptoms and alternative ways of dealing with affect. Sometimes hypnosis (or, less commonly, a medication-assisted interview such as a sodium amytal interview) is used to facilitate this process. Physical therapy combined with strategies for behavioral reinforcement, problem solving, stress management, and hypnosis have all been found to be effective in the treatment of Conversion Disorder (Looper & Kirmayer, 2002). Bragier and Venning (1997) described a very effective graded physiotherapy program for adolescents with Conversion Disorder that involved a reward system administered by a caring physiotherapist.

In reviewing the literature on the treatment of motor Conversion Disorder characterized by gait abnormalities, Krem (2004) suggested that the health care provider withdraw both medical and social attention from abnormal movements and gait by accepting symptoms and refocusing on physical rehabilitation. Then, using physical and occupational therapy, retrain the individual for normal gait. Finally, provide psychotherapeutic treatment that focuses on developing coping skills and strategies to deal with the stress. A better prognosis is associated with a sudden onset, the presence of psychological stressors prior to onset, a short delay between onset and treatment, high intelligence, the absence of comorbid psychiatric conditions, and aphonia as the presenting problem (Krem, 2004). When treating hospitalized adolescents with disabling Conversion Disorder, the goal is to restore functioning as rapidly as possible and hypnosis may be used as part of a multidisciplinary treatment plan (Bloom, 2001).

Pain Disorder   It is important for the clinician to accept that the pain is genuine and focus on strategies that help the individual assume responsibility for coping with pain, encourage activity, and maintain functioning (Covington, 2000; First & Tasman, 2004). In a review of randomized, placebo-controlled antidepressant studies, antidepressants were found to significantly decrease pain intensity (Fishbain, Cutler, Rosomoff, & Rosomoff, 1998). For acute pain, a major goal is the relief of pain; however, this is often mismanaged by undermedication or not providing medication on an as needs basis (First & Tasman, 2004; Maxmen & Ward, 1995). The individual's level of suicidality should be continually assessed as chronic pain also increases suicide risk. Cognitive-behavioral techniques, including distraction, stress management, relaxation, sleep management, and visualization, have been found to be effective (Covington, 2000; A. Frances & Ross, 2001). Masheb and Kerns (2000), in reviewing treatment interventions for chronic pain, describe the effectiveness of a CBT model that involves three interrelated phases: reconceptualization, skills acquisition, and a skills practice phase. Using this model, individuals learn to understand the multidimensional nature of their pain and the relationship between thoughts, feelings, and behaviors and their impact on exacerbating pain, disability, and distress. The skills training phase attempts to break the cycle of helplessness and focuses on effective self-management of pain, including behavioral goals and cognitive restructuring (Masheb & Kerns, 2000). The use of a pain diary, in which the individual records activities, level of pain, and coping strategies to deal with pain, can also be helpful. Sharpe and Williams (2002) recommend setting appropriate and explicit goals that include gaining increased control over the pain, recovery as much as possible, and increasing independence and simultaneously using several treatment modalities that have the same goals. For some, referral to biofeedback or a support group may be helpful; others may benefit from referral to specialized pain management programs, which include education, pain coping strategies, and medication (First & Tasman, 2004; Jongsma & Peterson, 2003; Maxmen & Ward, 1995).

Family therapy, which targets changing the family's responses by focusing on reinforcing adaptive behavior and decreasing the pain talk, can be an effective adjunct intervention. By focusing on and praising involvement in nonpain activities, ignoring pain-focused behavior, and making rest contingent on not complaining of pain, more adaptive coping may be developed.

Hypochondriasis   No matter what intervention is utilized with the hypochondriacal patient, the patient-therapist relationship must be strong (Fallon & Feinstein, 2001). The referral for psychological services may be presented in terms of dealing with the stress secondary to medical problems and comorbid conditions (Magarinas et al., 2002). Fallon and Feinstein (2001) suggest using the term "heightened illness concern" rather than Hypochondriasis when talking with individuals about their concerns because of the pejorative associations with the latter term. In the process of building trust, a careful history of previous medical work-ups should be investigated. This will help to strengthen the therapeutic bond and give the individual the sense that the treatment provider is interested in what he or she has gone through. Helpful in this process is trying to place the health concerns in a wider context by finding out about the circumstances that lead to increased worrying about health issues and reactions by others in the patient's environment (Magarinos et al., 2002). It is important to consider that over the course of 1 year, one third of individuals with Hypochondriasis were found to spontaneously recover (Fallon, 2004).

Initially, medication was regarded as unsuccessful in the treatment of Hypochondriasis; however, more recent research has indicated that SSRIs have been effective (Fallon & Feinstein, 2001). There is some controversy about the role that providing reassurance plays in the treatment of Hypochondriasis, in part because reassurance has not been operationally well defined. Some individuals have advocated for its use in the form of explanatory therapy and have noted that it resulted in a 50% reduction in physician visits and therapeutic gains that were maintained at 6-month follow-up (Looper & Kirmayer, 2002). Others believe an important aspect of the treatment management of individuals with Hypochondriasis is limiting reassurance seeking; toward these ends Sharpe and Williams (2002) recommend that symptoms should not automatically be met with further investigation or tests.

For individuals with Hypochondriasis, CBT and in vivo ERP have been found to be equally effective (Visser & Bouman, 2001). Cognitive-behavioral techniques may help patients to reattribute their false beliefs about physical symptoms and health concerns and to learn to recognize and label their tendencies to engage in all-or-nothing thinking, catastrophizing, and overgeneralizing. The in vivo ERP model involved constructing an individual hierarchy focusing on checking, reassurance seeking, and avoidance of related stimuli and the use of response prevention homework assignments (Visser & Bouman, 2001). Looper and Kirmayer (2002) describe the effectiveness of a combination of cognitive strategies (16 sessions over 4 months) similar to explanatory therapy and response prevention, which resulted in a 76% improvement in global problem severity compared to a 5% improvement with controls. Brief, time-limited (12 sessions over 3 months) CBT can result in significant clinical improvement, which was maintained at 7-month follow-up (Visser & Bouman, 2001). This model focused on the cognitive aspects of the hypochondriacal pattern and involved the identification of the catastrophic misinterpretations or dysfunctional automatic thoughts. The therapist then verbally challenged the basic assumptions and tenability of the hypochondriacal automatic thoughts and assisted the individual in formulating more functional or realistic beliefs. Behavioral experiments were developed to test the credibility of the thoughts, and these were practiced using homework assignments. Though brief (6 session), CBT significantly lowered and altered hypochondriacal thinking and beliefs, health-related anxiety, and social impairment, the hypochondriacal somatic symptoms were not significantly impacted at a 12-month follow-up (Barsky & Ahern, 2004). In a review of the effectiveness of CBT in the treatment of Hypochondriasis, Fallon and Feinstein (2001) note the importance of cognitive components focusing on irrational beliefs, self-monitoring, education, and the exposure and prevention of ritualistic behavior. Given that insight waxes and wanes with Hypochondriasis, the clinician also needs to consider that cognitive interventions are less likely to be effective when the patient is in the throes of poor insight.

In examining the effectiveness of intensive inpatient psychotherapy for individuals with Hypochondriasis, Hiller et al. (2002) found that 60% demonstrated significant improvement. Nonresponders were found to have higher pretreatment rates of Hypochondriasis, more somatic complaints, greater general psychopathology, dysfunctional cognitions about bodily functioning, greater impairment, and higher health care utilization. In the Netherlands, Bouman (2002) used a short-term (6 two-hour sessions) cognitive-educational small group for self-referred individuals with Hypochondriasis; this study found a significant decrease in clinical symptoms and medical service utilization (about 40%). The author noted the importance of individuals feeling they were listened to, their complaints acknowledged and taken seriously (Bouman, 2002).

Although not well studied, there is evidence that group-based CBT treatment is effective for decreasing illness attitudes, fears, and dysfunctional beliefs (Looper & Kirmayer, 2002). Such group programs are usually short term (e.g., 6 to 9 sessions) and often involve cognitive restructuring, learning to tolerate uncertainty, relaxation exercises, education about somatic symptoms, and identification of reassurance-seeking behavior. Supportive therapy focusing on life stressor management and education is an effective intervention for individuals with Hypochondriasis (Fallon & Feinstein, 2001). In reviewing CBT studies for individuals with Hypochondriasis, Magarinos and colleagues (2002) concluded that it is an efficacious treatment, and though there is stronger evidence for individual therapy, group CBT also appears to be useful.

Body Dysmorphic Disorder   K. A. Phillips and colleagues (2001) reviewed the charts of patients treated for up to 8 years with BDD and concluded that the majority of individuals (63.2%) on SSRIs improved in terms of symptomatology and comorbidity. However, dosages higher than that needed for depression are required, and given the high relapse rate (83.8%) with medication discontinuation, long-term treatment is necessary. Significant and sustained improvement in comorbid depressive and anxiety symptoms has also been found with SSRI treatment of BDD (K. A. Phillips, 2001). Educating the individual about the potential for psychological treatment to decrease level of preoccupation and increase functioning is also recommended (K. A. Phillips et al., 2001). For mild BDD without comorbid conditions CBT can be used as a first-line approach (K. A. Phillips, 2000). For individuals with severe BDD, the maximum recommended tolerated dose of SSRIs should be used for 12 to 16 weeks before determining whether the medication is ineffective. A combination of CBT therapy with medication and EPR is also an effective form of treatment for this group. With BDD treatment-resistant or noncompliant individuals who are experiencing significant life stressors, have personality disorders or traits, and need couples or family therapy, K. A. Phillips (2000) suggests adding supportive or insight-oriented therapy and using booster or maintenance sessions to prevent relapse. For children and adolescents with BDD, use of SSRIs have resulted in a sustained response over several years (Albertini & Phillips, 2001). After reviewing randomized, controlled studies, Looper and Kirmayer (2002) conclude that CBT is effective in both individual and group format for individuals with BDD. Similarly, Cororve and Gleaves (2001) found the most common effective treatment strategies for individuals with BDD were cognitive restructuring and ERP with in vivo and imaginary exposure involving response hierarchies, self-monitoring and psychoeducation. These interventions included limiting grooming time, having individuals sit in crowded places, and covering mirrors, and improvement was found with both behavioral and cognitive treatments. Supportive psychotherapy or insight-oriented treatments do not appear to be particularly effective for the treatment of BDD, but studies of these approaches are extremely limited (Sarwer et al., 2003). In summarizing the available research, A. Frances and Ross (2001) conclude that there is little systematic study and limited data on reassurance, which is usually not effective; antidepressant medication is somewhat effective; and a combination of CBT techniques including self-esteem building and modification of distorted thinking is effective. Of concern is the fact that individuals with BDD often present with high rates of treatment dissatisfaction and tend to not attend treatment. In Veale et al.'s (1996) study 92% of individuals with BDD who had received psychological and psychiatric treatment reported being dissatisfied or very dissatisfied. In addition, 26% of the sample had seen a dermatologist or cosmetic surgeon at least once for their problem, and 81% were unhappy with the outcome of the visit or operation. In fact, these individuals consistently report high degrees of dissatisfaction with the results of surgical procedures even though procedures are technically correct; for the majority of the clients cosmetic medical procedures resulted in no change or an exacerbation of the BDD symptomatology (Sarwer et al., 2003). In an interesting retrospective review of treatment response of individuals with severe BDD in comparison to individuals with severe OCD in a university-based partial hospitalization program, Saxena and colleagues (2001) found that a comprehensive multimodal approach that had been used for refractory OCD was effective for both groups.

Treatment Challenges

The lack of insight, overfocus on medical etiology, and poor compliance with treatment all create difficulty with implementing effective interventions for individuals with somatoform disorders. In addition, a reluctance to participate in exposure-based treatments, nonadherence to treatment recommendations, and high dropout and relapse rates often complicate treatment (Masheb & Kerns, 2000). For many cases, treatment must also address ways to reduce reinforcement for illness behaviors and provide the individual with face-saving opportunities to relinquish the somatic symptoms. Many individuals with chronic Pain Disorder define themselves in terms of their disability and may receive compensation for their level of impairment, which may create an obstacle to treatment (Masheb & Kearns, 2000). It is important to realize that relying on the self-report of symptom amelioration as a measure of treatment effectiveness may not be useful. Kroenke and Swindle (2000) found in a review of the effectiveness of CBT for clients with somatic complaints that improvement in physical symptoms can occur independent of reported changes in psychological distress. Escobar (1996) suggests that more appropriate measures of treatment outcome may be to assess functional capacity, the duration of sick leave and hospital stay, frequency of medical visits, and health care expenditures rather than focusing on self-reported symptoms. The inclusion of relapse prevention strategies, such as identifying high-risk situations and rehearsing cognitive and behavioral skills, is also crucial for the effectiveness of treatment (Masheb & Kerns, 2000).

According to Asaad (2000), the most common complication of somatoform disorders is the development of severe marital, family, and financial problems. Family members often attempt to compensate for the individual's disability, which may reinforce pain and illness behaviors (Masheb & Kerns, 2000). The chronic and disabling nature of many of the disorders in this category also contribute to significant high rates of unemployment and significant medical expenses. The tendency for managed care providers to cover medical procedures and specialists while being hesitant to cover long-term psychiatric or psychological care may further complicate recovery for these individuals (Asaad, 2000).

ADVANCED TOPICS: DIFFERENTIAL DIAGNOSIS

Psychological Factors Affecting a Medical Condition

Previously referred to as psychosomatic disorders, the key feature of these disorders is the presence of one or more behavioral or psychological factors that adversely impact a GMC (American Psychiatric Association, 2000b). These factors can interfere with the course or treatment of the medical condition, pose an additional health risk, or cause stress-related responses that precipitate or exacerbate the GMC. The *DSM-IV-TR* identifies six types of psychological factors: mental disorder, psychological symptoms, personality traits or coping styles, maladaptive health behaviors, stress-related physiological response, and other or unspecified factors (American Psychiatric Association, 2000b). The disorder is coded on Axis I and the medical condition is coded on Axis III. While the clinical presentation of this disorder may be similar to somatoform disorders, there is an identifiable medical condition that can account for the physical symptoms (American Psychiatric Association, 2000b).

Somatoform Disorders versus Factitious Disorders versus Malingering

The presence of unconfirmed symptoms is similar for somatoform disorders, factitious disorders, and malingering; the key to this differential is the intentionality of behavior (First et al., 2004; Hurwitz, 2004). According to Eisendrath (2001), it is helpful to conceptualize these disorders on a continuum of unconscious, unintentional production of symptoms (somatoform disorders), to intentional production to assume the sick role for what may be unconscious motives (factitious disorders), to intentional faking for secondary gain (malingering). To differentiate effectively between these disorders the clinician needs to be familiar with feigned symptoms and the nature of the different clinical presentations (see Table 12.6).

Fabrication of Symptoms

A very unusual clinical presentation that may conform to popular misconceptions (media or televised talk shows) that increases in severity when being observed should alert the clinician to feigned symptoms (A. Frances & Ross, 2001). Individuals who feign symptoms may engage in self-injurious behavior or ingest substances surreptitiously to create symptoms that mimic psychiatric conditions, such as stimulants to produce agitation and restlessness or hallucinogens to impair their reality testing (Eisendrath, 2001). They often have extensive medical or psychiatric knowledge, seek numerous medical consultations, undergo multiple invasive surgeries, and seem indifferent to painful medical procedures, frequently adding symptoms to their presentation (A. Frances & Ross, 2001). Their clinical presentation is limited only by their medical knowledge, and all organ systems are susceptible. The clinical presentation may not match diagnostic criteria, but it will mimic the individual's understanding or impression of the disorder (American Psychiatric Association, 2000b).

As with somatoform disorders, these individuals often present in a dramatic, vague, and inconsistent manner. Their answers to questions assessing cognitive capacities may be approximate (e.g., 9 times 9 is 82). Knowledgeable individuals may discern from the examiner which questions to endorse, or they may be hostile or negativistic. They may present as pathological liars who have the capacity to intrigue and engage the listener and may claim a different identity (impostership). The *DSM-IV-TR* describes this as "pseudologia fantastica or exaggerated lies the individual believes or invented exaggerated life histories" (American Psychiatric Association, 2000b, p. 515).

Table 12.6 Differentiating between somatoform disorders, factitious disorders, and malingering

When to Be Concerned About Your Client's Veracity

The client is a court-mandated or legal referral.

Client has a diagnosis of malingering, alcohol or substance-related disorder, or Antisocial Personality Disorder.

Clinician has difficulty establishing rapport and feels threatened.

Past treatment review suggests compliance problems.

Client has marked concern about confidentiality.

Client refuses to or is hesitant to sign releases.

Client is overly concerned about clinician obtaining corroboration from others.

Client lacks insight, minimizes problems, uses denial and blame.

There is marked distancing by client both physically and emotionally.

Client's account is superficial, lacks details, and appears implausible.

Client's account varies and contains marked inconsistencies.

There are discrepancies between client's account and past records.

Indicators of Factitious Disorder

Lack of referral letter or collaborative support for medical history.

Pathological lying (pseudologia fantastica) and inconsistent information.

Nonresponsive to standard treatment; peregrination (wandering).

Recurrent feigned, simulated, or induced illness.

High degree of medical knowledge or employed in medical profession.

Clinical presentation changes with technological advances.

Considerable medical treatment during childhood.

Particular relationship with a doctor or career in health care.

Minor injuries result in amputation or invasive procedures.

Bodily scarring (e.g., battlefield or gridiron abdomen).

Family detached, cold, lonely, rejecting, withholding, explosive, or abusive.

Belief that one is cared for only in medical system or during critical incident.

Fears of abandonment and rejection when well.

Tendency to channel psychological conflicts into physical symptoms.

Need to be taken care of or attended to.

Indicators of Malingering

Previous history of injury or illness.

Legal context to referral.

Bizarre, absurd symptoms with atypical onset and presentation.

Symptoms nonresponsive to treatment.

Significant noncompliance and lying to health care providers.

Inconsistencies on objective measures and observed symptoms.

Identified secondary gain to avoid responsibility or obtain financial or other incentive.

Drug seeking or diagnosis of Antisocial Personality Disorder.

Employed in the medical profession.

The most frequently feigned symptoms are command hallucinations, PTSD, and Dissociative Identity Disorder symptoms. In reviewing malingered psychosis, Resnick (1997) describes the motivators as including feigning incompetence or insanity to avoid trial or punishment, to mitigate sentencing, or to obtain financial gain or disability compensation, drugs, or "three hots and a cot." Malingered delusions often have a sudden onset, and the individual tends to overact the part or is eager to call attention to his or her symptoms, reporting more frequently visual hallucinations with a florid and dramatic content. In contrast, genuine delusions develop over weeks and are relinquished gradually, with most individuals being reluctant to discuss their clinical symptoms. Fake auditory hallucinations tend to be continuous rather than intermittent and often include stilted language. The individual is usually unable to report strategies used to diminish the hallucinations and has difficulty faking schizophrenic thought processes and negative signs such as blunted affect (Resnick, 1997). Interviews with others often reveal the nature of the individual's illness; thus the verification of facts is essential.

During the interview, it is important to maintain a neutral attitude, avoid confrontation, and conduct a careful clinical evaluation, noting inconsistencies between behavior and complaints (H. I. Kaplan & Saddock, 1996). Fauman (2002) suggests using the following series of questions in assessing the presence of a feigned disorder: Is the individual very knowledgeable about the clinical presentation? Does he or she suggest appropriate procedures? Do the symptoms appear unresponsive to treatment? Is there evidence that the individual has misrepresented important details about his or her history or appears vague and inconsistent? When confronted or when the staff become suspicious, does the individual become angry, verbally abusive, and suddenly self-discharge? Do observations indicate that the symptoms disappear or diminish when the individual is under constant observation or does not have access to personal belongings?

When the disorder is recognized by the staff, these individuals often question the staff's competence, threaten to take legal action, discharge themselves against medical advice, and travel to another hospital (Bouman et al., 1999). It is not unusual for these clients to have multiple hospital admissions in different cities and states. If the clinician suspects the symptoms are feigned, the diagnosis of Factitious Disorder or malingering needs to be considered.

Factitious Disorder

Originally referred to as Munchausen syndrome after Baron Von Munchausen, a world-renowned teller of tall tales (Asher, 1951), Factitious Disorder's key feature is the intentional production, feigning, or faking of physical or psychological symptoms in order to assume the sick role, often with a chronic unremitting course (Bauer & Boegner, 1996; Kinsella, 2001). This may be the most underdiagnosed condition in psychiatry, as most clinicians' nature and training is to trust the veracity of the client's report (A. Frances & Ross, 2001). The presence of factitious symptoms does not preclude the presence of true physical or psychological symptoms (American Psychiatric Association, 2000b). Individuals may provide a fictitious history, simulate or exaggerate symptoms, aggravate conditions, or self-induce diseases (Eisendrath & McNeil, 2004; Krahn, Li, & O'Connor, 2003). Evidence of several inconclusive hospitalizations, multiple scars, inconsistencies in the individual's history, or employment as a health care worker should alert the clinician (see Table 12.6) to consider Factitious Disorder (A. B. Goldstein, 1998). According to Kinsella, 0.2% to 1.5% of psychiatric consultation and liaison referrals can be attributed to individuals with this disorder, many of whom are health care and mental health professionals. Krahn and colleagues suggest that clinical suspicion is highest for female health care workers in their 40s, often well educated, who are employed or are full-time students.

For many individuals, the factitious symptoms provide socially sanctioned approval; hospitalization becomes the primary goal and a way of life, with external incentives playing a secondary role or being absent (Eisendrath & McNeil, 2004; Marmer, 1999). The need here is to be taken care of, to be nurtured; these individuals are compelled to be patients and often seek out dangerous procedures for reasons beyond their control (First et al., 2004; O'Shea, 2003).

The onset of Factitious Disorder is usually in adolescence or early adulthood (Libow, 2002) and often follows a hospitalization for a medical or mental illness; there is usually a significant delay (6 to 10 years) before appropriate diagnosis and intervention (Eisendrath & McNeil, 2004; Kinsella, 2001). Libow's (2003) review of illness falsification in children suggests that 41% of these individuals developed Munchausen's by age 18, with many showing the early signs of the illness in adolescence but remaining undetected for years. A course of intermittent episodes is common; with chronicity a pattern of frequent hospitalizations may occur, as the individual moves from a fabricated history to feigning symptoms to self-inducing illness, indicating a poorer prognosis.

Factitious Disorder can be conceptualized in two forms: one group (10%) contains middle-aged males, similar to the classic Munchausen syndrome with a dramatic presentation characterized by wandering or peregrination (Eisendrath, 2001). The second group is made up of stable, nonwandering young females, often unmarried, who seek medical treatment in their own community and have had a previous career in the health care or medical field (First & Tasman, 2004; C. Ford, 1995). A. B. Goldstein (1998) describes an acute presentation as a means to cope with a current life stressor, and the chronic type "life response individuals" that can be differentiated in terms of demographics, the presence of a psychosocial stressor, and clinical presentation. The life pattern response is similar to classic Munchausen's with a chronic history, including comorbid conditions, pseudologia fantastica, no immediate psychosocial stressor, and seeking medical attention to reaffirm their sense of identity (A. B. Goldstein, 1998). A very rare form of Factitious Disorder (Ganser's syndrome) is characterized by individuals simulating mixed affective, organic, and psychotic illnesses, presenting with approximate answers or narrowly incorrect or ridiculous answers to simple questions (Folks, 1995). The identification of factitious psychological disorders may be more difficult than for physical disorders as the assessment and verification of symptoms often rest primarily on the client's self-report (Eisendrath, 2001).

Given the misrepresentation of symptoms, traveling, and significant delay (often 6 to 10 years) before diagnosis it is difficult to accurately assess the true prevalence of this disorder (Bauer & Boegner, 1996; Eisendrath, 2001; Eisendrath & McNeil, 2004). These clients may be reluctant to authorize the release of medical records, making the diagnosis more difficult (Krahn et al., 2003). The best estimation is about 1% of individuals who consult mental heath professionals and 5% to 10% of all hospital admissions, with a higher number in highly specialized medical settings, university teaching, or research hospitals (American Psychiatric Association, 2000b; H. I. Kaplan & Saddock, 1996; Maxmen & Ward, 1995). Common comorbid conditions include substance-related disorders (especially opioids) and personality disorders (especially Borderline Personality Disorder; 53%), issues of abandonment, unstable relationships, chronic anxiety, alcohol abuse, and antisocial behavior (First & Tasman, 2004; A. B. Goldstein, 1998). Verification that the individual's intention is to assume the sick role rather than access to drugs is critical

(Krahn et al., 2003). These individuals also have a high suicide risk, and risk of death if they undergo life-threatening surgeries (H. I. Kaplan & Saddock, 1996). Of those involved in litigation, 20% died as a result of their Factitious Disorder (Eisendrath & McNeil, 2004).

As these clients are motivated to remain ill, they are not the most reliable informants and may be invested in undermining treatment (First & Tasman, 2004). It is also not unusual for them to develop additional new "disorders du jour" during the course of their treatment and seek multiple medical opinions (Krahn et al., 2003; Morrison, 1995a). According to O'Shea (2003), the only pathognomonic sign is residual dye from earlier intravenous procedures. The clinician may develop strong feelings of anger, so countertransference should be monitored. The difficulty for the clinician is missing a genuine medical condition or ordering extensive evaluations and missing the Factitious Disorder. Confrontation does not necessarily lead to patient acknowledgment and frequently results in flight (Kinsella, 2001; Krahn, Li, & O'Connor, 2003).

Factitious Disorder or Munchausen's Disorder by Proxy

First recognized in 1964 and called Munchausen's Disorder by Proxy (MPD) by Meadow in 1977, this disorder is included in Appendix B of the *DSM-IV-TR* (O'Shea, 2003). This disorder describes individuals who intentionally feign or produce physical or psychological symptoms or both in another who is under their care, usually a child (see Table 12.7),

Table 12.7   Indicators of factitious disorder by proxy

Clinical Presentation

Bizarre, unusual, rare symptoms with atypical onset and presentation
Persistent and recurrent illness or injuries
Laboratory or physiological findings consistent with induced illness
Symptoms nonresponsive to treatment
Illness and symptoms abate in absence of parent or caretaker
Indicators of recurrent feigned, simulated, or induced illness
Another child in family with unexplained illness or death
Absence of external incentives

Perpetrator Mother or Caregiver

Provides false family medical history
Multiple prior hospital admission with against medical advice discharges
Inconsistent or failure to follow through on discharge recommendations
Unwilling to allow contact with prior medical care providers
Presents with a high degree of medical knowledge
Often suggests medical procedures
Overattentive or refuses to leave child
Appears unconcerned about prognosis
Intense close relationship with a doctor or nursing staff
Family detached, cold, lonely, rejecting, withholding, explosive, or abusive
History of Factitious Disorder or somatization
Multigenerational history of illness falsification
When confronted leaves hospital abruptly or drops out of treatment

and has been described as a subtype of the battered-child syndrome (Bouman et al., 1999). The characteristic features include a parent or caretaker simulating or producing an illness in a child, or persistent presentations for medical evaluation or treatment (Libow, 2003; Meadow 1982). The clinical presentation is influenced by the perpetrator's medical knowledge and opportunity to induce illness and general forms of parental fabrication, include poisoning, suffocation, tampering with medical lines and specimens, withholding or tampering with medication, and symptom exaggeration (Libow & Schreier, 1986; Schreier, 2002; Schreier & Libow, 1994). The perpetrator continually denies any knowledge of the etiology of the illnesses, and the symptoms abate when the victim is separated from the perpetrator (R. Rogers, 2004). The purpose here is to indirectly assume the patient role or become involved in the drama of medical care, thus vicariously assuming the sick role (Pankratz, 1999). Mothers are often young (early 20s), articulate, middle class, married, with pathological attachments to their children (Folks, 1995). Typically, the perpetrator (usually the mother or caregiver; 98%) will induce and stimulate the illness in the child; this can involve poisoning, suffocation, and tampering. In preverbal children symptoms may be caused by active illness induction and suggest feeding and growth problems; for older children and adolescents, parental exaggeration and some degree of cooperation or collusion on the child's part may be involved and should be assessed (Libow, 2002). According to Folks (1995), the clinical presentations cluster into two patterns. The first, more often seen in infants, includes apnea and seizures. The second pattern, common in older children, frequently involves diarrhea and vomiting. There are significant mortality rates (9%) associated with this diagnosis for both the presenting child and siblings (Eisendrath, 2001; Pankratz, 1999). Should the victim survive, he or she is at increased risk for developing Factitious Disorder or a range of emotional and behavioral problems and sustaining permanent disfigurement (Folks, 1995; Libow, 2002). Typically the child is a preschooler, and within a family, one victim is focused on at a time (Libow, 2002). Perpetrators may have a diagnosis of Factitious Disorder, which is quiescent as long as they can induce illness in the child. Von Hahn and colleagues (2001) found that there is often evidence of chronic family dysfunction, an intergenerational vulnerability to somatoform disorders and preoccupation with illness, and even a multigenerational pattern of illness falsification (Libow, 2003). The perpetrator may present with pathological lying and become angry, depressed, suicidal, drop out of the assessment, or seek care at considerable distance when confronted, resulting in considerable delay in the identification of this disorder (Von Hahn et al., 2001). The parent may appear as a devoted caregiver: very loving, overly concerned, frequently bonding with and offering assistance to hospital staff (O'Shea, 2003; Pankratz, 1999). These individuals may be charged with child abuse or face criminal charges related to the injury or murder of a child (American Psychiatric Association, 2000b).

Malingering

The *DSM-IV-TR* includes malingering under other conditions that are a focus of clinical attention, and although no specific diagnostic criteria are provided, several indicators are presented (American Psychiatric Association, 2000b). The key elements of the *DSM-IV-TR* description involve a clinical judgment about the person's intention, the presence of false or grossly exaggerated symptoms, and external incentives or secondary gain

(Bordini, Chaknis, Ekman-Turner, & Perna, 2002). Thus the clinical presentation of malingering, as with factitious disorders, involves intentional or feigned physical and/or psychological symptoms for which there is no medical basis, the difference being the motivator, which is external versus internal (LoPiccolo, Goodkin, & Baldewicz, 1999). These individuals may self-inflict injury and stage accidents, and once the external reward has been achieved the fabricated illness usually remits (Eisendrath & McNeil, 2004; Hanson, Kerkoff, & Bush, 2005). H. I. Kaplan and Saddock (1996) cluster the external motivators into three groups: the avoidance of danger, punishment, or responsibility, including the legal consequences of actions (i.e., competency to stand trial or be executed); a desire to receive compensation, drugs, or free room and board; or retaliation after a loss. Malingering has been described as related to antisocial behavior and even as an adaptive response to extreme settings such as military service during war time (M. Turner, 1999a). It is diagnosed based on the clinician's suspicion (Bogduk, 2004), and several factors serve to alert the clinician to malingering (Table 12.6). It can co-occur with genuine medical and psychiatric conditions; however, unless one has an atypical referral source or is working primarily in a medical-legal setting, it is a relatively low base rate disorder (Sweet, 1999). Higher base rates of probable malingering or symptom exaggeration have been reported in settings involving litigation or compensation, such as personal injury (29%), disability (30%), and criminal cases (19%; Mittenberg, Patton, Canyock, & Condit, 2002). It is also common in industrial, military, and prison settings.

Symptoms are often vague, poorly localized, described in great detail, exaggerated, and hard to assess or measure objectively. Rare, absurd, bizarre symptoms, the endorsement of improbable clinical symptoms, and rapidly fluctuating complaints all suggest that malingering needs to be considered (A. R. Gerson, 2002). It can appear to be a very complex symptom presentation and warrants not only a comprehensive evaluation but also data from multiple sources (Hanson et al., 2005). Early research attempts to identify nonphysical findings (Waddell signs) that were indicative of secondary gain and malingering have been unsuccessful (Fishbain, Cutler, Rosomoff, & Rosomoff, 2004). In reviewing advances in the assessment of malingering versus brain injury, Bordini and colleagues (2002) recommend the evaluation include neuropsychological testing, a comprehensive history including medication effects, pre- and postinjury records, and the role of external stressors in recovery. They also recommend skepticism when considering collateral records and that consideration be given to the use of standardized measures and structured interviews. In many cases, the key to the diagnosis of malingering is the confirmation of the suspicion of the feigning of symptoms that can be achieved by observation and inferences and the identification of the external incentive (LoPiccolo et al., 1999; R. Rogers, 1997).

Differential Diagnosis

Somatoform and factitious disorders and malingering all present with unexplained physical complaints and can be differentiated based on the consequences of the action or the function and purpose of the clinical presentation. On intake the clinician needs to evaluate the context in which the symptoms occur and the goal of the symptoms (A. Frances & Ross, 2001; Pankratz, 1999). The hallmark of malingering and Factitious Disorder is the feigning (simulation) or concealment of symptoms (i.e., dissimulation; O'Shea, 2003).

LoPiccolo, Goodkin, and Baldewicz (1999) describe malingering as being a conscious intent to deceive to obtain a known result or gain. In contrast, for somatoform disorders there is a lack of conscious intention to deceive, and they can be conceptualized as a narrowly defined symbolic reaction to stress (Marmer, 1999). This discrimination is often difficult, if not impossible, in individual cases as hospitalizations tend to be brief, and while pathological organic findings cannot be identified there is usually no clear evidence for the psychogenic nature of the symptoms (Bauer & Boegner, 1996). Individuals with somatoform disorders feel they are doomed to be sick, whereas individuals with factitious disorders seek out the sick role and those with malingering pretend to be sick especially when someone is watching (Pankratz, 1999). Factitious disorders and malingering may also have an onset at any time, whereas Somatization Disorder has to occur before age 30 (Marmer, 1999). Individuals with somatoform disorders complain; however, they lack duplicity and often appear overly revealing and naive and present with a lifestyle focused on illness and complaints about ineffective treatment (Pankratz, 1999). As L. M. Cohen and Chang (2004) note, the presence of deception and active dissimulation is also the key to differentiating between Factitious and Conversion Disorders. Kinsella (2001) notes that individuals who somatize are often more concerned about the adverse impact of the symptoms and less aware of the mechanisms underlying the symptom presentation.

For individuals with malingering the focus may be on cash rather than cure; their physical complaints may be time-limited and environmentally opportunistic, difficult to pin down, and wax and wane with the status of their legal case (A. R. Gerson, 2002). Often there is a cost benefit, in that the illness mimicked involves little personal cost, and they usually do not cooperate with invasive medical procedures unless they are crucial to secondary gain, as when qualifying for disability insurance or obtaining monetary compensation (Eisendrath, 2001; Hanson et al., 2005; Pankratz, 1999). Unlike patients with factious disorders, these individuals will avoid treatment for fear of exposure and will demonstrate poor follow-through. When questioned they often become irate and demand another clinician. In contrast, Factitious Disorder clients will actively seek out treatment, present with a complex presentation, and comply with recommendations, as they are invested in remaining ill and the hospital becomes a haven or refuge (Marmer, 1999; Pankratz, 1999).

Individuals with factitious disorders and malingering are often seen in outpatient settings at times when the staff may be overworked or less experienced (e.g., holiday shifts; Bauer & Boegner, 1996; Eisendrath, 2001). Typically the diagnosis of these disorders involves an index of suspicion, excluding other causes, and obtaining direct evidence of motivating factors (Folks, 1995). For factitious disorders, the primary unconscious gain relates to the need to be taken care of or paid attention to. In contrast, for malingering there is a secondary gain involving obtaining something wanted or avoiding something undesirable (Marmer, 1999). Whether the intention to deceive is conscious or unconscious becomes less clear when individuals with factitious disorders deliberately self-harm to maintain the sick role (LoPiccolo et al., 1999).

Factitious Disorder should be considered if the individual clinical presentation is dramatic, florid, atypical for a medical condition, and does not conform to known medical conditions, and if the symptoms and behaviors wax and wane depending on whether the individual is being observed or is the focus of attention (American Psychiatric Association, 2000b). An extensive history of traveling, few visitors, a reluctance to provide collateral contacts, and an extensive medical knowledge should all alert the clinician to consider these disorders. Sweet (1999) suggests that it is important for the clinician to focus on excessive inconsistencies, compare test data to real life, and differentiate between self-serving and real-life losses.

Finally, in all of these disorders, it is important to maintain clear documentation, as the clinician may be involved with legal action if the individual's claims are intentionally fraudulent.

Chapter 13

EATING, SLEEP, SEXUAL, AND GENDER IDENTITY DISORDERS

CHERYL LA SASSO

EATING DISORDERS

Weight preoccupation and weight gain have, in the past few decades, become a national obsession. It has been estimated that on any given day, a quarter of American men and nearly half of American women are dieting (Gordon, 2001). According to the Center for Disease Control's Youth Risk Behavior Survey, which monitors health risk behaviors of high school students, approximately 2 out of 3 females and 1 out of 4 males have consistently reported trying to lose weight (Commission on Adolescent Eating Disorders, 2005). The desire for weight loss becomes pathological when the preoccupation evolves into an obsession and atypical or excessive behaviors are engaged in to implement overvalued ideas about weight and body image. Eating disorders, which the *DSM-IV-TR* defines as Anorexia Nervosa, Bulimia Nervosa, and Eating Disorder Not Otherwise Specified, are not common in the general population, but they are prevalent in specific groups, affecting between 5 and 11 million young American women each year (American Psychiatric Association, 2000c). Three percent of women may be impacted by eating disorders during their lifetime (B. T. Walsh & Devlin, 1998), and the impact on individuals and their families can be distressing at best, and devastating at worst. In addition to the life-threatening medical issues and the social and psychological impact of eating disorders in general, Anorexia Nervosa has the highest mortality rate of any mental illness (P. F. Sullivan, 1995). Furthermore, this group of disorders exacts a toll on both the health care and managed care systems despite the fact that only one third of individuals with anorexia and 6% of those individuals with bulimia in the community receive mental health care (Hoek & van Hoeken, 2003). There has been an influx of research since eating disorders became a part of cultural awareness beginning in the 1970s, but much of the resulting data have been conflicting, confusing, and inadequate, and a great deal more investigation is needed.

Historical Overview

Eating disorders have been formally recognized as a clinical entity only since the second half of the twentieth century, although disordered eating behavior has been chronicled for several thousand years. Spiritual or religious fasting relating to asceticism and the warding off of demonic influences and "bad humors" dates back to Roman times, as does self-induced vomiting subsequent to gluttonous binges (Pearce, 2004). These behaviors appear to have been socially acceptable practices, and any similar behaviors occurring outside of this context were attributed to medical problems (Van Deth, Vandereycken, & Parry-Jones, 1995). A case of nervous consumption described by Richard Morton in 1689 is considered the first published report of Anorexia Nervosa in which a young woman wasted away due to eating problems (J. A. Silverman, 1997). Her symptomatology included amenorrhea, fainting, and hypothermia, and her death was ascribed to emotional disturbance as no physical organicity was identified. Well into the nineteenth century, food avoidance and voluntary starvation were observed in syndromes variously described as hysteria, love sickness, mania, melancholy, and dementia (Bemporad, 1996; Van Deth et al., 1995). Despite cases in both the American and French literature of young women who refused to eat in order to gain attention, this syndrome was mainly ignored by the medical community until 1873 and 1874, when separate publications from British physician William Gull and French internist Ernest-Charles Lasegue described *anorexia hysterica* and *anorexie hysterique*, respectively, and provided descriptions of "extreme emaciation" mainly seen in females in the 16 to 23 age range (Pearce, 2004). Lasegue, in particular, noted the frustration of medical and familial attempts to treat the individual, whether through support or intimidation. Furthermore, bingeing behavior was observed in some of these cases, but it was considered a variant of anorexia. Despite this historical legacy, Anorexia Nervosa did not warrant significant attention until the 1960s, when psychiatrist Hilde Bruch introduced core psychiatric features such as low self-esteem, an unrelenting desire to be thin, and body image disturbance, which, in essence, created our current formulation of the disorder (Fairburn, Shafran, & Cooper, 1999; McDermott, Harris, & Gibbon, 2002).

Bulimia Nervosa has historical roots that have been variously traced to a Plutarch reference in which *bulimos* was considered an "evil demon" related to famine, as well as to the Greek words for ox (*bous*) and hunger (*limos*), implying one was hungry enough to eat an ox (Vandereycken, 1985). Although preoccupation and dissatisfaction with body image and utilization of weight control measures like dieting and self-induced vomiting are considered more modern clinical manifestations that seem to predominate in Westernized countries, issues surrounding body shape, obesity fears, and techniques to limit food intake (including drinking vinegar) were observed in cases from the mid-seventeenth to the nineteenth century (Yates, 1989). During the eighteenth century, bulimia was associated with extreme hunger, "fainting from hunger," and "overeating with vomiting," and by the twentieth century, such behavior was considered a common attribute in hysterical females (Nasser, 1993; Van Deth & Vandereycken, 1995). However, it was still believed to be a symptom rather than a syndrome and, like anorexia, was primarily ascribed to medical issues, most often stemming from gastric difficulties. Unlike anorexia, however, many of the cases were male. Bulimia Nervosa as a term was introduced in 1979 by British psychiatrist Gerald Russell, who described it as a variant of Anorexia Nervosa. He combined the symptoms of the desire to overeat (binge) with the fear of becoming fat and its subsequent compensatory strategies (purging) in those who were of normal weight (G. Russell, 1979).

Our conceptualization and understanding of eating disorders has undergone significant modifications, an evolution reflected in the various incarnations of eating disorders in the *Diagnostic and Statistical Manual of Mental Disorders*. Revisions have occurred with each publication, most often centering on severity criteria (Striegel-Moore & Cachelin, 2001). The only acknowledgment of eating disorders in *DSM-I* (American Psychiatric Association, 1952) and *DSM-II* (American Psychiatric Association, 1968) were a *disturbance of metabolism, growth, or nutrition* subsumed under organic brain syndrome and *feeding disturbance*, a special symptoms category, respectively. These early texts did not provide descriptions or criteria for these diagnoses. Eating disorders first appeared as a category in *DSM-III* (American Psychiatric Association, 1980) under disorders of infancy, childhood, or adolescence and included diagnoses such as Anorexia Nervosa and bulimia, as well as childhood eating disorders such as pica. Disorder criteria became increasingly refined and narrowed with subsequent editions of the *DSM*, and disorder descriptions were increasingly influenced by developments resulting from eating disorders research. For example, for Anorexia Nervosa, the intense fear of becoming obese was changed to gaining weight or becoming fat, and the criterion for amenorrhea (three consecutive absences of a menstrual cycle) was introduced (Bulik, Sullivan, & Kendler, 2000). Perfectionism was added as an associated feature of Anorexia Nervosa, rectal prolapse was added to the associated physical findings, and it was noted that a personality disorder is commonly associated with this eating disorder. Another important change in the *DSM-IV* included a provision that Anorexia Nervosa and Bulimia Nervosa could no longer be comorbidly diagnosed with one another, but were now considered distinguishable by newly introduced subtypes and specifiers (American Psychiatric Association, 1994).

Anorexia Nervosa

The term anorexia means loss of appetite, and Anorexia Nervosa translates as a nervous lack of appetite (D. A. Klein & Walsh, 2004). The disorder involves an unhealthy preoccupation with body weight and shape that manifests as a disturbed eating pattern in which food is restricted and dysfunctional behaviors are engaged in. Although considered to be an uncommon disorder with an average prevalence rate of 0.3% (Hoek, 2006), the mortality rate for Anorexia Nervosa—12 times higher than that for adolescent and young adult women in the general population—makes it a very serious disorder (Pompili, Mancinelli, Girardi, Ruberto, & Tatarelli, 2004).

Clinical Presentation

Intentional Weight Loss   The primary feature of Anorexia Nervosa is that an individual exhibits intentional, severe weight loss. The standard provision for determining this criterion is an individual's refusal to maintain his or her weight at 85% of what would be expected for his or her age and height (American Psychiatric Association, 2000b). For individuals who are still in a period of growth, the same percentage applies in terms of *expected* weight gain. However, these numbers serve as guidelines only; clinical judgment is required to accommodate individual differences (such as body build and ethnicity). The *DSM-IV-TR* (American Psychiatric Association, 2000b) recommends utilizing the Metropolitan Life Insurance table or a pediatric growth chart for this purpose, but widespread variability exists in terms of weight determination practices (Commission on Adolescent Eating Disorders, 2005). Another approach involves the Body Mass Index (BMI), which is a common practice in the research literature. Calculated by dividing weight in kilo-grams by height in meters squared, BMI is expected to be equal to or greater than 18.5.

Psychological Features   Individuals with anorexia have a profound disturbance in the perception and experience of their body, an overreliance on body image in determining self-worth, and/or denial of the seriousness of the weight loss (American Psychiatric Association, 2000b). The perceptual disturbance encompasses the experience of feeling fat even when the mirror and scale show otherwise. This distortion may refer to an overall feeling or to specific body areas (e.g., thighs, buttocks, abdomen; M. N. Miller & Pumariega, 2001). The overinvestment in attaining a severely exaggerated thin ideal is inextricably tied to self-esteem and typically results in incessant self-evaluation that is expressed through checking rituals such as continually weighing oneself, measuring body parts, or compulsively pinching skin in certain areas to feel how fat it is (J. C. Rosen, 1997). When weight loss or decreased shape occurs, there is a satisfying feeling of accomplishment, self-discipline, and control. Conversely, when weight gain or an increase in shape occurs, it is experienced as a personal failure, a lack of discipline, and a loss of control (G. T. Wilson, Becker, & Heffernan, 2003). Even with the sense of accomplishment, there is typically a subsequent desire to exert even more control and lose more weight in a vicious cycle.

Another related psychological feature of Anorexia Nervosa is the intense fear of gaining weight or becoming fat (American Psychiatric Association, 2000b). The worry is incessant, and the fear persists even after weight loss occurs. Although there may be some acknowledgment of being thin, most individuals will deny the gravity and severity of their situation even in the face of concerned others objectively attempting to explain that the weight loss has become unhealthy and harmful (Michel, 2002). The concern may, in fact, be inversely reactive: The individual may grow more vigilant as weight loss occurs and become even more determined to avoid putting on weight (Fairburn, Shafran, et al., 1999). The fear of gaining weight or becoming fat may have less applicability to males and those with a non-Caucasian, non-Western background (S. Lee, Ho, & Hsu, 1993; Khandelwal, Sharan, & Saxena, 1995). The manner in which psychological elements vary for different demographic groups is discussed in greater detail later in the chapter.

Physiological Dysfunction   Amenorrhea—the absence of menstrual cycles—is a common result of weight loss and reduced body fat, which causes a reduction in the secretion of gonadotropin-releasing hormone (Golden & Shenker, 1994). This, in turn, influences additional hormonal levels (progesterone, testosterone, estrogen) that also serve to regress the body to a prepubertal state. The *DSM-IV-TR* (American Psychiatric Association, 2000b) includes amenorrhea as a diagnostic criterion for postmenarcheal females, but this is controversial as studies have shown few differences between individuals with and without amenorrhea (Cachelin & Maher, 1998; Garfinkel et al., 1996) and because it excludes both males and prepubertal females. It also centers on the assumption that amenorrhea is a consequence of weight loss when, for some, it may precede the weight loss. Devlin, Jahraus, and Dobrow (2005) suggest that this implicates stress factors (e.g., hormonal or neurotransmitter disturbances) in producing amenorrhea along with other contributory factors such as excessive exercise and/or caloric restriction. While the absence of at least three consecutive menstrual cycles is considered a diagnostic indicator of Anorexia

Nervosa, this may be misleading when attempting to determine a state of remission. The menstrual cycle typically returns with weight gain, but it may take up to 6 months to reappear.

Subtypes In the *DSM-IV-TR* (American Psychiatric Association, 2000b), there are two subtypes that may be assigned to Anorexia Nervosa based on the category of behaviors in which an individual engages. These subtypes have been shown to be clinically different and can impact treatment planning (Herzog, Field, et al., 1996). The *restricting type* applies to weight loss methods confined to food limitation or avoidance and an extreme level of exercise. Individuals with this subtype tend to be overly controlled, rigid, and obsessive (G. T. Wilson et al., 2003). For a significant number of individuals, the restricting type may develop into Eating Disorder NOS or Bulimia Nervosa once they engage in binge-eating and/or purging behaviors and experience a weight gain that would render a diagnosis of anorexia inappropriate (Tozzi et al., 2005). Those with the *binge-eating/purging type* consume copious amounts of food that may or may not be accompanied by elimination behaviors, although such behaviors are typically the case. Purging predominantly involves self-induced vomiting, but laxatives (including herbals), diuretics, and enemas are also utilized. Those who binge/purge tend to have stronger familial histories of obesity, greater mood lability, higher rates of suicide attempts, more severe psychopathology, and additional medical complications (Favaro & Santonastaso, 1997; D. M. Garner, 1993). They tend to vacillate between periods of control and impulsivity (the latter of which may include reckless behavior such as theft, substance abuse, and self-harm), are often misdiagnosed as bulimic, are more likely to be diagnosed with Borderline Personality Disorder, and tend to have a worse prognosis (Tozzi et al., 2005).

Onset and Course

The *DSM-IV-TR* establishes the age of onset for Anorexia Nervosa to be in the 14- to 18-year-old range (American Psychiatric Association, 2000b), although retrospective reports and adult community samples (Commission on Adolescent Eating Disorders, 2005; Fairburn, Cooper, & Doll, 1999) set a slightly older range of 16 to 21. Impairment in social, occupational, and interpersonal areas can be substantial as individuals withdraw from their normal activities and often become isolative. Much of the anorexic's energy and focus is directed at food and weight obsessions, and interacting with others implicitly carries the threat of the symptoms and behaviors being discovered and interfered with by others (M. N. Miller & Pumariega, 2001). Although many anorexic individuals report symptoms of depression and/or anxiety, they generally present as overcontrolled or with flat or restricted affect. The desire to obtain a lower and lower weight goal is unrelenting; anorexic individuals believe the possibility of being too thin will never apply to them despite their outward appearance. Instead, there is often a need for control and a belief that attaining an appropriately low weight will bring happiness and a resolution to problems (Fairburn, Shafran, et al., 1999).

Some individuals with anorexia limit their diet to specific foods such as broccoli or restrict certain types of foods such as carbohydrates, whereas others will severely reduce the amount of food and water they ingest (D. A. Klein & Walsh, 2004). Typically, individuals begin by restricting specific foods from their diet, particularly high-calorie items, which escalates into restricting more categories of foods and consuming smaller quantities

(D. A. Klein & Walsh, 2004). Early, subtle signs may include eating very slowly or in a ritualized manner, cutting food into minute pieces, and drinking either very large or very small quantities of liquid. Individuals may hide unwanted food in pockets or under plates, engage in extreme calorie counting, or use work or study priorities as an excuse for not eating (D. M. Garner & Magana, 2002). As noted previously, the weight loss may or may not be accompanied by purging and/or excessive exercise. When confronted about their behavior, individuals often engage in denial and become more secretive, eating meals alone or during off hours. Exercise often accompanies these food restrictions and might take the form of a structured workout (e.g., jogging, aerobics) or simply extend into daily activities (e.g., walking instead of driving, taking stairs rather than elevators). Exercise can also be utilized as a contingency to allow for eating something, as a punishment for having eaten something, or as an incompatible behavior to avoid eating entirely (Beumont, 2002).

The course of Anorexia Nervosa is variable. It may remit after one episode with full recovery, partially remit (i.e., improve but exhibit residual symptoms), or evolve into a fluctuating pattern with periods of relapse that could require hospitalization depending on the severity of the weight loss (G. T. Wilson et al., 2003). Studies have shown recovery rates of 50% to <70%, partial recovery rates of approximately 33%, and chronic illness in 10% to 20% (W. H. Kaye & Strober, 2004; Herpertz-Dahlmann, Wewetzer, Schulz, & Remschmidt, 2001; Steinhausen, 2002). The standardized mortality rate is approximately 5% per decade of illness, while for hospitalized individuals the long-term mortality is over 10% (Herzog et al., 2000; D. A. Klein & Walsh, 2003; P. F. Sullivan, 1995). Common causes of death include suicide and starvation sequelae or medical complications. The suicide rate is 57 times greater than that in the general population for women of comparable age (Keel et al., 2003). Long-term outcome studies indicate that factors contributing to a good prognosis include early onset, diagnosis, and treatment, as well as short duration of illness. Poor prognosis indicators include extreme low weight, comorbidity, and long duration of illness (Zipfel, Lowe, Reas, Deter, & Herzog, 2000). Little is known about the outcome for adolescents as most long-term outcome studies are based on adults, but prognosis appears to improve over time. Strober, Freeman, and Morrell (1997) found that in adolescents a 1% probability for recovery at 3 years increased to a 72% probability for recovery after 10 years.

Referral for treatment is often initiated by friends or family rather than the individual and, given that years may pass before the illness comes to the attention of others, the disorder is often firmly entrenched by the time intervention begins. As a result, physical and medical issues, some life-threatening, are a predominant element in this picture, necessitating coordinated care through a multidisciplinary treatment team (American Psychiatric Association, 2000b).

Bulimia Nervosa

Over the years, Bulimia Nervosa has mostly been regarded as a variant of Anorexia Nervosa. Under the current conceptualization, the core distinction between the disorders is weight; individuals with bulimia are typically within normal weight expectancies with slight variations or fluctuations, making them ineligible for a diagnosis of Anorexia Nervosa (American Psychiatric Association, 2000b). Bulimia Nervosa is also more common than Anorexia Nervosa, with a lifetime prevalence of 1.1% to 4.2%, and it carries a better prognosis (Cubic & Bluestein, 2004). Individuals with bulimia engage in an eating cycle that vacillates between restriction (i.e., dieting) and excess, commonly referred to as a "binge."

Clinical Presentation

Bingeing   Binge eating (or reactive hyperphagia) is a recurrent eating pattern character- ized by the consumption of a large amount of food in a discrete period of time (e.g., with in any 2-hour period). The time span serves to distinguish Bulimia Nervosa from behavior in which extended periods of snacking occur, resulting in a large consumption of food that would not, in fact, be considered bingeing. "Large" is relatively determined in compar- ison to what most individuals would consume given a similar time period and context. Binge duration has consistently been found to last between 30 minutes and 1 hour (Jansen, van den Hout, & Griez, 1990; B. T. Walsh, Kissileff, Cassidy, & Dantzic, 1989). The amount of caloric intake can vary tremendously, but binges tend to average more than 1,000 calories per episode (Guertin, 1999). However, it is also possible for the amount of food in a binge to be of normal quantity if the binge is accompanied by a sense of loss of control in which the individual feels he or she cannot exercise restraint in terms of the act, the amount, or the content of what he or she is consuming. Many experience a feeling of numbness or a dissociative quality either during or following the episodes (Vanderlinden, Vandereycken, & Probst, 1995). Currently, some controversy exists as to whether the amount of food or the sense of loss of control is the more appropriate diagnostic stipula- tion (Beglin & Fairburn, 1992; E. M. Pratt, Niego, & Agras, 1998).

Bingeing behavior commonly occurs during or after dieting and, as the disorder pro- gresses, may evolve into more of an impulse that is difficult to resist rather than an acute, unavoidable compulsion (Beumont, 2002). Bingeing may or may not be planned, although most individuals will arrange for the appropriate circumstances to avoid detec- tion. It was previously thought that individuals who binged were more likely to crave carbohydrates or high-calorie sweets than noneating-disordered individuals, but empirical support has been lacking (B. T. Walsh, 1993; Woell, Fichter, Pirke, & Wolfram, 1989). Individuals may, however, gravitate toward "forbidden" or "reward" foods such as those high in fat or sugar (E. F. Kales, 1990). Nevertheless, food amount rather than food type is the more salient consideration. Termination of a binge episode often occurs as a result of physical discomfort.

Psychological Factors   Bulimia Nervosa shares with Anorexia Nervosa a self- evaluation component in which the individual is disproportionately influenced by body shape and weight, particularly in terms of manifesting or exacerbating negative or low self-esteem (Williamson, Cubic, & Gleaves, 1993). There may be distorted body image or a preoccupation or dissatisfaction with certain body areas that are impacted by weight gain or loss. Adverse emotional states and emotional dysregulation often act as triggers for binges, including boredom, depressed mood, anxiety, frustration, and rejection, and the way one looks is often implicated as a causative factor (S. F. Abraham & Beumont, 1982). Furthermore, individuals typically feel guilty about bingeing without recognizing that there is an intense need to reduce tension. Consequently, they berate themselves over their lack of control and then initiate a purge to obviate the guilt and alleviate the physical discomfort of stomach distension. The belief that they will not gain weight as a result of the purge often leads to a sense of satisfaction, but it is quickly followed by disgust over the fact that they vomited, resulting in further self-depreciation and low self-esteem (D. A. Klein & Walsh, 2004).

Weight Gain Prevention Behaviors   The behavioral component of the desire to prevent weight gain is both recurrent and inappropriate. The underlying purpose of these behaviors is to reduce the physical discomfort as well as the guilt over engaging in an act that could produce weight gain. Typically, individuals will employ self-induced vomiting, fasting, and excessive exercise, as well as misuse of laxatives, diuretics (to reduce fluid weight), appetite suppressants, enemas, and purgatives (to induce diarrhea). These latter methods are often utilized under the mistaken belief that they will stop the absorption of calories when in fact they cause dehydration (Beumont, 2002). Medications such as thyroid hormones and insulin have also been misused in an attempt to avoid gaining weight (Devlin et al., 2005). Although a combination of behaviors is typical, self-induced vomiting is the most common method (80% to 90% of those who present for treatment engage in vomiting), which over time can become a practice that is produced at will. Although rare, regurgitation of food (chewing and then spitting out food rather than swallowing it) has been observed (D. M. Garner & Magana, 2002). Exercise is considered excessive if it significantly impedes individuals' ability to conduct their normal daily activities or is inappropriately engaged in given the exigencies of time, place, or personal health (i.e., a willingness to risk or ignore injury or medical complications). The *DSM-IV-TR* (American Psychiatric Association, 2000b) sets a frequency guideline for both the bingeing episodes and the purging and/or nonpurging behaviors. It is expected that these will occur, on average, at least twice a week for 3 months. This level is somewhat arbitrary as there is wide-ranging variability in the frequency of bingeing and purging behavior among individuals, and the meaningfulness of this criterion is still subject to debate (Garfinkel, 2002; Guertin, 1999; Mehler, 2003).

Subtypes   The *DSM-IV-TR* identifies two subtypes of Bulimia Nervosa. The *purging type* describes individuals who regularly engage in compensatory behaviors involving the expulsion of food from the body. Individuals with this subtype tend to have less body weight, a higher likelihood of electrolyte imbalances, and greater comorbidity (D. A. Klein & Walsh, 2004). The *nonpurging type* refers to the regular engagement of compensatory methods other than purging; most often this involves fasting or excessive exercise. Individuals with this subtype often experience more severe depressive symptoms and a greater degree of preoccupation with body image and weight (Favaro et al., 2005).

Onset and Course

The typical age of onset for Bulimia Nervosa is late adolescence to early adulthood. The vast majority of individuals engage in dieting behavior prior to diagnosis, and they can become preoccupied with the thought of food because of the self-imposed restrictions, which then stimulate or trigger a binge (Mizes & Bonifazi, 2000). A pattern emerges in which they are restricting and gorging with no sense of moderation or balance. As the disorder progresses, a vicious cycle is generated that can interfere with daily activities and relationships. The bingeing/purging behavior can consume a significant amount of time depending on the frequency of the episodes. Individuals may begin to avoid social situations involving food and eventually avoid social interaction altogether (Beumont, 2002).

Despite being considered the milder eating disorder, Bulimia Nervosa can be significantly impairing in social, emotional, occupational, and interpersonal realms (Lewinsohn, Striegel-Moore, & Seeley, 2000) and may cause serious physical and medical harm. For individuals who engage in bingeing, dysphoria that can trigger binge episodes may be only briefly assuaged, leading to feelings of depression and self-loathing for having binged, thus leading to even more dysphoria. The shame and secrecy encompassing the disorder can be extremely debilitating (G. T. Wilson et al., 2003); a sense of disgust and fear of stigmatization engender a reluctance to reveal the problem and seek help, which, much too often, causes a delay in treatment.

The course of Bulimia Nervosa may be chronic or intermittent, and periods of remission may alternate with recurrences. In general, recovery rates range from 35% to 75% at 5 or more years (Fairburn, Cooper, & Doll, 2000; Herzog et al., 1999), but relapse can be chronic, and one third of individuals typically relapse within the first or second year. However, longer term follow-up has shown a reduction of symptoms typically occurs. A meta-analysis of 88 outcome studies found that 50% of individuals experienced full recovery after 5 to 10 years, 30% experienced a relapse of symptoms, and 20% still met full criteria (Keel, Mitchell, Miller, Davis, & Crow, 1999). A better prognosis is indicated when there is a shorter duration of illness, milder symptoms, early detection and treatment, simultaneous intervention for comorbid conditions, and motivation for treatment (Polivy, Herman, & Boivin, 2005). Poor prognosis is often associated with low self-esteem, longer duration of illness, more frequent or severe binge eating, comorbidity, substance abuse, parental obesity, and a history of personal obesity (Bulik, Sullivan, Joyce, Carter, & McIntosh, 1998; Fairburn, Stice, et al., 2003). Suicide attempts have been found to occur in 24% to 35% of individuals (Franko & Keel, 2006).

Eating Disorder Not Otherwise Specified

The catch-all *DSM-IV-TR* (American Psychiatric Association, 2000b) diagnostic category Eating Disorder NOS (herein referred to as ED-NOS) is the most common diagnosis made under the category of eating disorders, yet it is the least researched (Fairburn & Harrison, 2003; G. T. Wilson et al., 2003). It is an extremely heterogeneous category whose purpose is to provide a method for labeling symptom presentations that do not fulfill or match the criteria for Anorexia Nervosa or Bulimia Nervosa. This may include individuals with combined subthreshold features, symptomatology that is not completely expressed, or binge eating that occurs without inappropriate compensatory behaviors. The latter is listed in the current *DSM* as Binge-Eating Disorder and is a proposed diagnosis in need of further study (American Psychiatric Association, 2000b). Determining the appropriate eating disorder diagnosis can be problematic, particularly in distinguishing subthreshold from full diagnostic criteria. Sloan, Mizes, and Epstein (2005) performed a cluster analysis of data obtained from eating disordered individuals that included items from the Eating Disorders Inventory, a self-report measure of psychological and behavioral characteristics of eating disorders, and measures of weight fluctuation, weight goal, weight dissatisfaction, BMI, lowest and highest adult BMI, and average number of self-reported binges and purges per week; these investigators found that the data did not aggregate in a manner that necessarily matched eating disorder diagnoses in the *DSM*. Crow, Agras, and Halmi (2002) found that anorexia, bulimia, and binge-eating disorder were distinguishable, but full and subthreshold anorexia and binge-eating were not. While the nosology merits further discussion and examination, it is important to recognize that ED-NOS diagnoses can be just as impairing as the other eating disorders and require interventions tailored to the individual's specific constellation of symptoms (M. N. Miller & Pumariega, 2001).

Additional Characteristics of Anorexia Nervosa and Bulimia Nervosa

Medical Complications   Eating disorders may present with a vast array of associated laboratory findings, physical examination findings, and general medical conditions (American Psychiatric Association, 2000b). Medical complications are most often attributable to a state of malnutrition and/or weight-control behaviors (Cubic & Bluestein, 2004). In general, the medical conditions associated with bulimia tend to be less severe than those seen in anorexia. The age of the individual is a significant area of concern given that the younger the individual, the more severe the impact in terms of affecting growth and development (i.e., bone mass, puberty, structural brain changes). Many of these complications, however, are reversible through improved nutrition and a resolution of symptoms (Mehler, 2003). Tables 13.1 and 13.2 present common examples of medical conditions that may be observed or occur concurrently with eating disorder diagnoses.

Epidemiology

The epidemiology of eating disorders is heavily impacted by age and sex, but research in this area is rather limited and rates should be considered estimates (or even underestimates) due to the variability in and limitations of the current research. Different assessment measures, diagnostic criteria, methodologies, and population and sample sizes have

Table 13.1   Conditions and symptoms associated with undernourishment, starvation, and malnutrition

Condition	Definition
Hypercarotenemia	Dry, yellowish skin
Lanugo	Fine, downy hair on the face, body, and extremities
Alopecia	Hair loss
Osteopenia	Reduced bone mass
Osteoporosis	Decreased bone density; can cause low back pain, fractures
Cardiovascular dysfunction	Cardiac arrest or arrhythmias; congestive heart failure
Bradycardia	Low heart rate due to poor circulation
Hypothermia	Sensitivity to cold
Hyperadrenocorticism	Metabolic disturbance caused by excess cortisol production
Hypercholesterolemia	High levels of cholesterol in the blood
Leukopenia and mild anemia	Low white blood cell count; lethargy or fatigue
Amenorrhea	Absence of menstruation
Abdominal pain	Bingeing may cause abdominal rupture
Constipation and bloating	Delayed gastric emptying and increased intestinal motility

Table 13.2   Conditions and symptoms associated with purging

Condition	Definition
Gastrointestinal dysfunction	Severe constipation, hemorrhoids, colon damage, or renal failure from laxative withdrawal
Enlarged (hypertrophy) salivary glands	Puffy cheeks
Dehydration	Excessive loss of water
Menstrual irregularity or amenorrhea	Absence of menstruation
Loss of dental enamel, tooth decay	A result of the acid in vomit
Calluses on hands, Russell's sign	Due to scraping against the teeth when inducing vomiting
Esophageal dysfunction	Gastric reflux, esophagitis, tears, and possible bleeding or esophageal rupture
Electrolyte imbalances:	
Hypokalemia	Potassium depletion in the blood; increases the risk of renal failure and cardiac arrhythmia
Metabolic encephalopathy	Acute cerebral dysfunction or confusion often due to severe hypoglycemia
Hyponatremia	Low sodium levels from excessive drinking of water; can cause seizures
Hypochloremia	Decreased levels of chloride in the blood
Metabolic alkalosis	Significant loss of acid in the body that can lead to coma and death

made it difficult to achieve consensus in this area. Some prevalence studies utilize retrospective data, which may be less reliable, and studies that find higher rates of eating disorders over time may reflect improved treatment services, greater awareness in medical environments and the community, greater willingness to report, and improved diagnostic ability rather than true increases in the number of affected individuals.

Anorexia Nervosa

The incidence rate for Anorexia Nervosa for females is 8 to 10 per 100,000 per year, and 0.5 to <1 per 100,000 per year for males (Devlin et al., 2005; Nielsen, 2001; van Hoeken, Seidell, & Hoek, 2003). Lucas, Crowson, O'Fallon, and Melton (1999) studied incidence rates for females across age ranges and found rates of 9.5 in women 30 to 39, 5.9 in women 40 to 49, 1.8 in women 50 to 59, and 0.0 in women over 60, with the highest incidence rates in the 15- to 19-year-old age group (135.7 for 1980 to 1989). There are more studies on prevalence than on incidence, but few are based on nationally representative samples. Currently, the prevalence rate of Anorexia Nervosa in females is believed to range from 0.2% to 1% (D. A. Klein & Walsh, 2003; M. N. Miller & Pumariega, 2001), with much higher rates in the 15- to 19-year age range, which make up 40% of all cases (van Hoeken et al., 2003).

Bulimia Nervosa

There have been even fewer incidence studies on Bulimia Nervosa given its relatively recent introduction as a diagnosis into nosological systems such as the *DSM*, but rates currently range from 12 to 15 per 100,000 in females and approximately 0.8 per 100,000 in males (Devlin et al., 2005; Soundy, Lucas, Suman, & Melton, 1995; van Hoeken et al., 2003). The highest risk group is considered to be females ages 20 to 24 (with average rates of 82 per 100,000). From 1988 to 1993 the incidence rate increased from 14.6 to 51.7 in 10- to 39-year-old females (Turnbull, Ward, Treasure, Jick, & Derby, 1996). Rates of 8.3 for women over 35, and 1.7 for men and women over 40 have been reported (Hoek, 1993; Turnbull et al., 1996). The prevalence rate for Bulimia Nervosa in adolescent and young adult females ranges from 0.7% to 5% (Garfinkel et al., 1995; M. N. Miller & Pumariega, 2001; van Hoeken et al., 2003) and between 0.1% and 0.4% in males (Evans et al., 2005).

Etiology

Despite a great deal of hypothesizing, clinical research, and case studies, we do not yet have a definitive understanding of the causal pathway to an eating disorder. Given the multitude of risk factors that have been posited and explored, there are many people in the population at large who could be considered to be at risk for but never develop an eating disorder. Clearly, then, eating disorders develop from an interaction of many risk factors (Yager & Andersen, 2005). Moreover, it has proven extremely difficult to differentiate the factors that may be *causative* or *predispose* an individual to an eating disorder, from those that might *maintain* the eating disorder, from those that are a *consequence* of the behaviors being engaged in (Commission on Adolescent Eating Disorders, 2005). Research has shown that a biopsychosocial model may be the most appropriate conceptualization because eating disorders comprise psychological, sociocultural, and biological factors, and several studies argue for a cumulative effect of these risk factors (Fairburn, Cooper, et al., 1999; C. B. Wilson et al., 1998).

Biological

While it is generally acknowledged that eating disorders have a heritability factor (Lilenfeld et al., 1998; Strober, Freeman, Lampert, Diamond, & Kaye, 2000) and relatives of eating disordered individuals are more likely to develop an eating disorder than people in the general population (Bulik, Sullivan, Wade, & Kendler, 2000), there has been tremendous variability and inconsistency in such estimates due to methodological, diagnostic, and sample limitations. In their examination of twin studies, Fairburn, Cowen, and Harrison (1999) found contrasting results, with heritability rates for Anorexia Nervosa ranging from 0% to 70% and rates for Bulimia Nervosa ranging from 0% to 83%. Klump, Kaye, and Strober (2001) found heritability to be approximately 76% in a population-based twin sample, and female relatives of those with either Anorexia Nervosa or Bulimia Nervosa had a 7 to 20 times greater lifetime risk for an eating disorder than the general population. In female relatives of probands diagnosed with Anorexia Nervosa, rates were 11.3 for Anorexia Nervosa and 4.2 for Bulimia Nervosa higher than the control probands. In female relatives of probands diagnosed with Bulimia Nervosa, rates were 12.3 for Anorexia Nervosa and 4.4 for Bulimia Nervosa higher than the control probands (Strober, Freeman, Lampert, Diamond, & Kaye, 2000). Other studies have shown that behaviors such as binge eating and self-induced vomiting have a heritable component (46% and 70%, respectively; P. F. Sullivan, Bulik, & Kendler, 1998). The proportional contribution of genes versus environment remains unknown as more large-scale twin studies are needed, but this research supports neurobiological contributions and implicates genes in creating a vulnerability for developing an eating disorder.

Given the potential genetic component of eating disorders, it is important to understand the biological abnormalities that may occur as a reflection of the expression of certain genes. The serotonergic and noradrenergic systems have been implicated in both Anorexia Nervosa and Bulimia Nervosa as they are involved in the regulation of food intake and are associated with mood states (Monteleone, Brambilla, Bortolotti, & Maj, 2000; Pirke, 1996). Bingeing and purging behaviors may be a means of modulating dysregulation in these areas (Ferguson & Pigott, 2000; W. H. Kaye, Gendall, & Strober, 1998). Low norepinephrine and serotonin levels have been found in association with eating disorders, but not consistently (Collier, 2002). Associations have also been reported for melanocortin, leptin, and estrogen, which influence mood and body weight regulation and feeding (B. T. Walsh & Devlin, 1998). For example, dieting affects 5-HT (5-hydroxytryptamine) neurotransmission in women (A. E. Walsh, Oldman, Franklin, Fairburn, & Cowen, 1995), and studies have suggested trait abnormalities that may create a genetic vulnerability (Fairburn, Cowen, et al., 1999). Physiological changes in Bulimia Nervosa as a result of dieting and bingeing/vomiting can cause biological changes such as an enlarged stomach capacity, delayed stomach emptying, and hormonal changes that create disturbances in feelings of satiety (W. H. Kaye & Weltzin, 1991). In consideration of this, appetite and weight-regulating peptides are also being studied for their possible etiological link to eating disorders, as opposed to being a consequence of physiological changes due to weight loss. Further research is necessary to tease out the possibility of the biological mechanisms causing the eating disorder or the dysregulated eating behavior creating the biological abnormalities.

Cognitive-Behavioral Theories

According to cognitive-behavioral conceptualizations of eating disorders, the thoughts, feelings, and behaviors of eating disordered individuals are believed to be a dysfunctional loop of cognitive distortions, negative affect, and maladaptive responses (Mizes & Bonifazi, 2000). An individual develops a self-schema of a disturbed body image (which may be elicited by any number or combination of risk factors), which is then activated by various stimuli that are processed and interpreted in a biased manner, leading to cognitive distortions (selective attention for body weight or shape information, body size overestimation, internalized thin body ideal, etc.). These faulty beliefs then lead to negative emotionality, although it has been hypothesized that affect may activate the distortions (Williamson, White, York-Crowe, & Stewart, 2004). The tendency for dichotomous thinking is central to a belief about having to be thin, and cognitive rigidity leads individuals to create stringent rules regarding eating and food. Particularly for those who binge, there is an uninterrupted cycle of dysphoric thoughts and feelings: Their disappointment with their body image and low self-esteem leads to dieting, which leads to intense hunger and disappointment that they do not look different, which leads to bingeing, which leads to distress and guilt when they lose control and binge, which leads to lowered self-esteem (and disturbance of mood), which leads to less ability to control the impulse to binge (Sherwood, Crowther, & Wills, 2000; Stice, 2001). Purging becomes a way to relieve the guilt and reduce anxiety and anger and is therefore negatively reinforcing (W. G. Johnson, Jarrell, Chupurdia, & Williamson, 1994; Polivy & Herman, 2002). The idealized body weight image leads to such restricted dieting that there is a psychological and/or physiological vulnerability to loss of control in eating. The purging, which is enlisted to compensate for the excess eating, is reinforcing because it reduces the anxiety and guilt surrounding the binge. Both behaviors cause distress and low self-esteem, which leads to more restrictive dieting and binge eating, setting in motion a vicious cycle. Self-schema therefore serves as a maintenance factor in the eating disorder.

Psychodynamic Theory

Given the typical early adolescent age of onset and the preponderance of females that make up the eating disorder population, age and sex are considered prominent risk factors (Wakeling, 1996). One of the commonly acknowledged psychosocial tasks of adolescence is identity formation. Insecurity may influence a desire for external validation and a reliance on how others view the self. Physical appearance provides a much more tangible and potentially malleable form around which to develop control, self-esteem, and an identity (Bulik & Kendler, 2000; Striegel-Moore, 1993). Psychodynamic theorists have implicated developmental transitions as increasing the risk for developing an eating disorder with disturbances in identity as a key etiological factor (Caparrotta & Ghaffari, 2006). In adolescent girls, physical maturation can significantly affect self-image, and conflicted feelings about sexuality can make this transition difficult. Previously, Anorexia Nervosa was viewed as an unconscious attempt to return to a prepubertal state in terms of a "phobic avoidance" of maturation and sexuality (Crisp, 1997). Disordered eating has also been conceptualized as a method for managing emotional dysregulation stemming from insecure attachment (A. Ward, Ramsay, Turnbull, Benedettini, & Treasure, 2000). Self-starvation becomes a way to control overwhelming experiences, avoid intense emotions and conflict, and gain some self-control. Some argue that parent-child conflict (which may involve a struggle for independence) disrupts the self-concept development (Goodsitt, 1997); others have argued that a genetically based personality style is problematic (Strober, 1991). Nevertheless, familial dysfunction may be correlational or secondary to the eating disorder rather than causative (A. Ward et al., 2000).

Personality Characteristics

Specific personality traits have been found to aggregate in the eating disorders, including negative self-evaluation, low self-esteem, perfectionism, obsessionality, harm avoidance, neuroticism, social isolation, impulsivity, and negative affect (Fairburn, Cooper, et al., 1999; Lilenfeld et al., 2000; Polivy & Herman, 2002). In addition, specific to Anorexia Nervosa, individuals tend to be overly disciplined, rigid, conscientious, perfectionistic, compliant, anxious, low in novelty seeking, compulsive, and less self-directed (Klump et al., 2000). Traits generally considered to be associated with Bulimia Nervosa include impulsivity, stress reactivity, novelty seeking, affective lability, and compulsivity (Diaz-Marsá, Carrasco, & Sáiz, 2000; Lilenfeld et al., 2000; Wonderlich & Mitchell, 2001). Further research is needed to determine if these traits precede the disorder or are an effect of having the disorder, but thus far studies are pointing toward the former. For example, Stice (2002) reported in a meta-analysis that traits such as perfectionism and impulsivity are risk factors for eating disorders, and Halmi et al. (2000) found perfectionism to be a genetic vulnerability marker for Anorexia Nervosa.

Familial Factors

One's family environment is considered to be a risk factor for eating disorders, as a relationship has been found between difficult meal times and food struggles or conflicts from early childhood and subsequent eating disordered behavior (Kotler, Cohen, Davies, Pine, & Walsh, 2001). An overly critical, hostile, coercive parental style and/or overly enmeshed families have been found to be common in eating disorders. Familial criticism of body shape, weight, or eating behaviors tends to be more prevalent in Bulimia Nervosa (Fairburn, Cooper, et al., 1999), which may be due to the fact that the behaviors and weight issues are more observable or because weight loss is typically praised and/or more easily hidden. There is also a greater likelihood of childhood and parental obesity in individuals with Bulimia Nervosa (Fairburn et al., 1998).

Cultural Influences

Although cultural influences are believed to contribute to the development and maintenance of eating disorders (Stice & Shaw, 1994), the argument for causation is currently unsupported. In Western culture, particularly modern American culture, a slim and perfect body ideal has been established that was, to a large extent, created and reinforced by the print and media images prominently displaying and promoting this ideal. Ironically, this is occurring in a nation with a tremendous variety and availability of food resources and a high prevalence of obesity. Internalizing such a cultural valuation of thinness can lead to body dissatisfaction and dieting behavior (A. E. Becker & Fay, 2006). It is estimated that 50 million Americans will attempt to diet in a given year, but clearly dieting alone is not causative, as only a small portion of the population develops eating disorders (Polivy & Herman, 2004). Nevertheless, women in particular are socialized from an early age to evaluate themselves from a physical appearance perspective, which can result in low self-esteem and negative body issues—factors that share a correlational relationship with and appear to play a role in the development of eating disorders. Several prospective studies have shown that body dissatisfaction is a consistent predictor of eating disordered behavior (Thompson, Heinberg, & Altabe, 1999), and studies of clinical samples have implicated dieting as a behavioral antecedent, particularly in Bulimia Nervosa (Fairburn, Cowen, et al., 1999). Some researchers have posited that negative self-concept makes individuals more vulnerable to sociocultural pressure, which then contributes to eating disordered behavior (K. F. Stein & Corte, 2003). What has yet to be established is where normal dieting becomes pathological, how it progresses to the level of an eating disorder, and what combination of factors might lead to an eating disorder, including sociocultural influences. In an often cited study conducted in Fiji (A. E. Becker, Burwell, Gilman, Herzog, & Hamburg, 2002), researchers argued that culture was an important risk factor given that eating disorders became more prevalent once Western culture was introduced into a nonindustrialized society. However, both Anorexia Nervosa and Bulimia Nervosa occur in nonindustrialized countries, and ethnic and cultural aspects are beginning to elicit much more attention and research.

Diversity Considerations

Ethnicity

In previous decades, the prevailing conceptualization of eating disorders was as a culture-bound syndrome primarily affecting young, upper-middle-class, Caucasian females from Western, industrialized countries. Numerous studies have demonstrated ethnic and socioeconomic diversity in the occurrence of eating disorders, as Anorexia Nervosa has been documented in the Middle East, Asia, Eastern Europe, Latin America, and Africa (Gard & Freeman, 1996; C. I. Hall, 1995; Keel & Klump, 2003; Khandelwal et al., 1995; M. N. Miller, Verhegge, Miller, & Pumariega, 1999; Mitrany, Lubin, Chetrit, & Modan, 1995; Nadaoka et al., 1996; Ngai, Lee, & Lee, 2000; Rosenvinge & Gresko, 1997). Additionally, the clinical manifestation of the disorder has proven to be somewhat variable in that in several studies, weight concerns were not cited as a motivating factor or trigger. Rather, disordered eating behavior was attributed to digestive discomfort or loss of appetite, which could indicate cultural differences in reporting symptoms or cultural differences specific to this particular diagnostic feature (Holden & Robinson, 1988; S. Lee et al., 1993).

Consequently, although Anorexia Nervosa may not be an entirely culture-bound syndrome, sociocultural context clearly plays a role, as non-Western individuals sent to Western regions show higher rates of Anorexia Nervosa than indigenous people (Fichter, Elton, Sourdi, Weyerer, & Koptagel-Ilal, 1988; Nasser, 1986). Bulimia Nervosa, conversely, has mainly been observed in countries with a Western influence and is therefore considered to have a stronger sociocultural component (Keel & Klump, 2003). Supporting this hypothesis are prevalence data, which have shown lower rates of Bulimia Nervosa than Anorexia Nervosa in non-Western countries, which is opposite that found in Western countries. Additionally, unlike the dissimilar clinical presentation found with Anorexia Nervosa, individuals in non-Western countries with Bulimia Nervosa are apt to cite weight concerns as a factor in their behavior. Nevertheless, more epidemiological research is needed in this area before any firm conclusions can be drawn.

Within ethnic groups in the United States, it is generally agreed that eating disorders are on the rise among minority groups, which may be due to increased reporting and detection. Others have postulated the increase to be a function of assimilation to Western culture and ideals (Abrams, Allen, & Gray, 1993; Pumariega, Gustavson, Gustavson, Motes, & Ayers, 1994). However, most studies have operationally defined acculturation or assimilation as the number of years living in the United States, which may not be an accurate reflection of those concepts, underscoring the complexity of this issue. Additionally, some researchers have hypothesized that the stress of being an ethnic minority (Smolak & Striegel-Moore, 2001) plays a role in the genesis of eating disorders, but the question remains as to the nature of this stress and any potential contributions from, for example, the stress of discrimination and (for immigrants) the stress of the move itself and exposure to a new culture with different ideals regarding achievement, beauty, and acceptance. Research on eating disorders among different minority groups is still in its infancy, and methodological issues abound. Most of the assessment instruments for detecting eating disorders are not culturally sensitive (and therefore may not tap into the different ethnic presentations of these disorders), translations may not be valid, and samples are often nonrepresentative (Striegel-Moore & Smolak, 2002). As a result, findings have been inconsistent and varied.

Nevertheless, Zhang and Snowden (1999) found that African Americans had lower rates of Anorexia Nervosa than Caucasians, and Caucasians had rates similar to those of Asian Americans. Crago, Shisslak, and Estes (1996) also found lower rates of Anorexia Nervosa and eating disorders in African Americans than Caucasians and reported rates for Caucasians to be similar to those of Native Americans and Hispanics.

Gender

Although eating disorders predominantly affect females, male cases were observed as early as the seventeenth century (Fichter & Krenn, 2003). Males are believed to compose 5% to 10% of Anorexia Nervosa cases and 10% to 15% of Bulimia Nervosa cases (A. E. Becker, Grinspoon, & Klibanski, 1999; Carlat, Camargo, & Herzog, 1997; Garfinkel et al., 1995). In male adolescents, Ricciardelli, Williams, and Kiernan (1999) found rates of 0.1% to 0.7% for Bulimia Nervosa. However, these rates are likely to be underestimates given the shame and secrecy that accompany these disorders and their general perception as a "female" disorder, making males far less likely to seek treatment in an effort to avoid embarrassment or stigma. The eating disorders tend to manifest similarly between the sexes physiologically and psychologically, including body dissatisfaction, comorbidity, sociocultural factors, course, and outcome, although data are limited (Olivardia, Pope, Mangweth, & Hudson, 1995; Sharp, Clark, Dunan, Blackwood, & Shapiro, 1994; Soundy et al., 1995). However, a few differences have been noted. Males tend to engage more in compensatory behaviors such as excessive exercise than in self-induced vomiting, laxative use, and dieting; their age of onset tends to be higher than for females (i.e., 18 to 26 years); and premorbid weight is often in the overweight or obese realm (Braun, Sunday, Huang, & Halmi, 1999; Carlat et al., 1997; Garfinkel et al., 1995; Sharp et al., 1994). Furthermore, rather than a desire to attain a thin body ideal, males tend to desire muscle and leanness (A. E. Andersen & Holman, 1997). Sexual orientation is considered by some to be a risk factor for eating disorders in males because several studies have demonstrated higher rates for homosexual men than heterosexual men (A. E. Andersen, 1999; Buroughs & Thompson, 2001; Fichter & Daser, 1987). Similar findings in population-based studies of adolescents focusing on abnormal or disordered eating and body dissatisfaction have been found (French, Story, Remafedi, Resnick, & Blum, 1996; Lock & Steiner, 1999). It has been postulated that this may be reflective of an emphasis on physical appearance and attractiveness within the gay culture (Carlat et al., 1997; Walcott, Pratt, & Patel, 2003).

Both male and female athletes appear to be at higher risk for eating disorders, but prevalence data are inconsistent and extremely limited due to methodological factors such as sampling and sample size, diagnostic criteria, assessment instruments, and cross-sport versus intrasport analysis (Byrne, 2002). Athletics are believed to be a risk factor because weight control is an important aspect in many sports, including, but not limited to, rowing, wrestling, horse racing (i.e., jockeys), boxing, swimming, gymnastics, running, dancing (particularly ballet), and ice skating. Several studies have shown the prevalence among athletes to be higher than in the general population (Patel, Greydanus, Pratt, & Phillips, 2003; Smolak, Murnen, & Ruble, 2000), and higher in females than males (although very little attention has been focused on male athletes; Brownell & Rodin, 1992). Sundgot-Borgen's (1994) study of 522 elite female athletes across 35 sports found 18% of the athletes to have eating disorders versus 5% of the nonathletic control group.

While athletes tend to share in the high-achieving, perfectionistic traits that are found in eating disordered individuals, they generally report higher self-esteem, less depression, and less body dissatisfaction than nonathletes with eating disorders, which suggests a somewhat different motivational profile for the weight loss (Smolak et al., 2000; Sundgot-Borgen, 1994). They may feel they need to adhere to strict weight limitations, or that they are being aesthetically judged (i.e., skating, dancing), or that their disordered eating helps them enhance their performance. In rarer cases, they may be looking for a way to undermine their participation in the sport (either for fear of failure or lack of desire; Sundgot-Borgen, Skarderud, & Rodgers, 2003). While abnormal eating behavior may seem transient or occur solely within the context of the sport or season, it would be imprudent to ignore potential signs of an eating disorder in an athlete given that subclinical symptoms may predispose the individual to the eventual development of a clinical eating disorder and because of the potential for medical complications (e.g., risk of fractures associated with Anorexia Nervosa) and health risks that could physically weaken the athlete and negatively affect his or her performance (D. M. Garner, Rosen, & Barry, 1998).

Intake and Interviewing Considerations

Individuals with eating disorders rarely self-refer for treatment with mental health professionals and, instead, commonly present to primary care physicians for associated symptoms (medical, psychological, somatic). When they do seek help, there is usually a significant delay from the onset of symptoms; for example, individuals with Anorexia Nervosa generally experience very little subjective distress concerning weight loss and may in fact feel a sense of accomplishment or pride in becoming thinner (Bryant-Waugh, Lask, Shafran, Shafran, & Fosson, 1992). Eating disordered individuals' behavior can be highly reinforcing as compliments on their looks are received or a sense of control or relief is gained. As a result, affected individuals may hide their symptoms out of fear that they will be prevented from continuing their behavior or feel tremendous ambivalence about giving it up and resist acknowledging the problem (Michel, 2002). Individuals with Bulimia Nervosa or Anorexia Nervosa, binge-eating/purging type, are often ashamed or disgusted by their behavior and will hide their symptoms out of embarrassment. They may be willing to change the binge/purge cycle, but they may not be so willing to confront their body image issues and dieting practices (Devlin et al., 2005; J. Geller, Williams, & Srikameswaran, 2001). Quite often, family members or friends are the ones responsible for an individual seeking help, which can certainly impact the affected person's motivation and desire to disclose information in an intake interview as well as consent to and participate in treatment. An overview of intake considerations for individuals with eating disorders is presented in Table 13.3.

Rapport

It is very important that the clinician acknowledge the individual's potential ambivalence about the treatment process and demonstrate understanding, support, and empathy to gain the individual's trust and form a cooperative alliance. Forming a therapeutic relationship with adolescents, in particular, may be difficult given their desire to be independent of authority figures and the likelihood that they may be engaged in the process of searching

Table 13.3   Intake considerations: eating disorders

Arrange for medical consultation to evaluate the presence of medical complications.

Arrange for medical assessment of current state of physical health.

Assess need for hospitalization and determine disposition decision.

Evaluate risk for suicide and consider high rates of mortality.

Assess impulsivity and impulsive behaviors, particularly for individuals with bulimia.

Attend to building and maintaining rapport.

Reduce the stigma of the disorder and the individual's sense of shame.

Assess substance abuse, including laxative and diet pill abuse.

Evaluate eating history and habits.

Quantify behaviors using food record or diary.

Remain alert for disorder-related behaviors (e.g., overexercising, hoarding).

Consider the individual's cultural expectations around food, rituals, and body image.

Explore the individual's sense of self and beauty or ideal.

Identify pathological eating patterns, including any ritualized patterns and cognitive distortions.

Assess family factors, familial food habits, and interactional patterns.

Consider referral for family therapy.

Involve nutritionist and multidisciplinary team.

Consider and assess for comorbid conditions and disorders.

Assess need for medication evaluation.

Develop relapse prevention program.

Agree on intervention if weight loss continues or individual is noncompliant.

for their own sense of independence. Control issues are often endemic in these cases, and the clinician should be mindful of the fact that the disorder may be an attempt to gain autonomy (Cubic & Bluestein, 2004). It is important to respect the individual's control over his or her body while also actively confronting any self-injurious behaviors. A nonjudgmental approach and an acknowledgment of the courage it took to seek treatment are highly recommended (Strober, 2004). Clinicians should be clear about what the therapy goals are, what treatment will entail, and what the therapy time frame will be to allow for realistic expectations and to dispel any preexisting misconceptions about treatment (American Psychiatric Association, 2000b). Individuals should be asked what they want or hope to achieve in treatment versus what others might want. In treating adolescents, the clinician will need to be particularly careful to navigate the potential minefield of being in an alliance with both the family and the adolescent, who may be at odds with one another. Third-party involvement (significant others, family, friends) is relevant to the treatment of both youth and adults and should be thoroughly discussed, especially as it may prove beneficial in terms of providing context for the clinician and support for the individual. Motivational interviewing, psychoeducation, and parental involvement are typically utilized to ameliorate an individual's ambivalence and the negative impact it can have on compliance (Treasure & Bauer, 2003). All options should be presented to the individual—including no treatment at all. By confronting the meaning of maintaining their current behavior with worsening consequences, individuals may be better able to face the possibility and come to appreciate the value of change.

Interview and Assessment Strategies

Gathering Information about Disordered Eating   While the clinician should work toward a trusting alliance to allow for appropriate disclosure in the intake, the presence of minimal or absent insight and denial or shame can make individuals with eating disorders poor historians. It may be necessary to have multiple informants or collateral sources (parents, siblings, significant others, friends, medical personnel) to obtain a complete evaluation (American Psychiatric Association, 2000b). A referral for a medical examination (including a dental exam and appropriate lab tests) is crucial to rule out an organic etiology for the weight loss or symptoms as well as to detect potential medical complications or comorbid medical illnesses (Pritts & Susman, 2003). The intake interview for individuals with an eating disorder requires assessment in several domains beyond the standard interview. These domains encompass the psychological, behavioral, and nutritional and medical features of disordered eating. Lifetime changes in weight (including physical and sexual growth, onset of menses, etc.) and current weight with actual measurements of height and weight (for BMI) are important in being able to establish a diagnosis. Past and current eating patterns should be discussed, including both dieting and bingeing behavior (daily caloric intake, foods being restricted or avoided, amount and type of food being consumed, food rituals, etc.; M. N. Miller & Pumariega, 2001). If bingeing is occurring, a detailed description of the context in which it is occurring is needed. This level of detail is important to obtain an objective view of the bingeing behavior, which may be different from the client's subjective view; for example, an individual's distorted perceptions could lead to a description of a normal (or less than normal) meal being labeled a binge (D. A. Anderson, Lundgren, Shapiro, & Paulosky, 2004). Similarly, eating large quantities of food may be normative in situations such as holidays or in certain cultural contexts. The clinician should also ask in detail about the use of techniques for weight control or weight loss other than dieting (e.g., vomiting, laxatives, diuretics, enemas, exercise, diet pills, syrup of ipecac).

Beliefs and attitudes about weight and body image are essential psychological features to assess, and the individual should be asked about his or her own conception of ideal weight in order to gain a sense of the individual's motivation and distortion. Assessment of comorbidities is key given their impact on diagnosis and treatment planning (Herzog, Keller, Sacks, Yeh, & Lavori, 1992). Current family functioning as well as social and psychological functioning should be evaluated, including self-esteem and potential social impairment (given that food consumption is very often a social activity, disordered eating could be causing social avoidance and isolation). Precipitating and/or maintenance factors or triggers for disordered eating should be inquired about as these can be very idiosyncratic (e.g., stress, interpersonal conflict, relationship loss, physical changes, guilt, control, numbing emotions, pleasure; Vanderlinden et al., 2004). It is also important to evaluate the family's history of eating patterns and weight as well as their thoughts and feelings about eating in general and their child's eating in particular as it is not uncommon to find distorted thinking or behavior within the family itself that will also need to be addressed (D. M. Garner & Magana, 2002). Assessment may include psychological testing, which can provide a context of potential characterological features that might be contributing to or maintaining the eating disorder as well as additional issues that may be a focus of individual family therapy (W. A. Bowers, Evans, le Grange, & Andersen, 2003; Michel, 2002).

Assessment Measures The clinical interview is the gold standard for diagnosing eating disorders, but there are several excellent assessment measures that can be clinically beneficial for both screening and treatment progress purposes. One of the most commonly utilized instruments is the Eating Disorders Examination, which is available in both adult and child versions and is a well-validated, semistructured interview that uses a categorical approach to diagnosis and covers the range of psychopathology and behaviors associated with eating disorders (D. A. Anderson et al., 2004; Fairburn & Cooper, 1993). Another diagnostic measure with good psychometric support is the Interview for the Diagnosis of Eating Disorders, which relates to *DSM-IV* criteria and is helpful in differential diagnosis. Numerous self-report measures are also available, including the Eating Attitudes Test, the Eating Disorders Inventory, and the Eating Disorder Diagnostic Scale, all of which have adequate psychometrics (Garfinkel & Newman, 2001; Stice, Telch, & Rizvi, 2000). T. M. Stewart and Williamson (2004a) provide further information on these and additional measures.

Crisis, Legal, and Ethical Issues

Capacity to Consent

In the intake session, the clinician should assess the individual's ability to consent to treatment (i.e., Does he or she have the psychological capacity for appropriate decision making? Is there confusion or an inability to process choices and consequences?; Nicholls & Bryant-Waugh, 2003). Consent is typically a more prominent issue in Anorexia Nervosa given that these individuals are often minors and may have cognitive problems secondary to starvation. The individual should be both fully informed and a willing participant in the treatment.

Hospitalization

Among psychiatric disorders, eating disorders have some of the highest rates of morbidity and mortality (E. C. Harris & Barraclough, 1998). Thus, the areas of immediate concern in an intake include medical risk and potential involuntary hospitalization, which also invoke legal and ethical issues. There are no U.S. guidelines for involuntary treatment, but the standard regarding least restrictive care still applies (Anonymous, 2006). Inpatient treatment should generally be considered in cases in which a client weighs less than 75% to 85% of his or her normal weight or, if treating children and adolescents, there is severe and rapid weight loss occurring (Devlin et al., 2005; Yager & Andersen, 2005). Given the arbitrary nature of weight levels, clinical judgment in these cases is crucial. Hospitalization may also be warranted in the event of medical emergencies, if the individual is critically ill (i.e., malnutrition, cardiac dysfunction, esophageal ruptures), or if there are significant comorbidities with potentially dangerous features such as suicidality, self-harm, substance abuse, or psychotic depression (Halmi, 2004).

Suicidality and Impulsivity

The clinician should always conduct a standard suicide assessment (particularly with Anorexia Nervosa), as well as evaluate high-risk behaviors (see Chapter 2) when evaluating a client suspected of an eating disorder. In Bulimia Nervosa, impulsivity can be a serious factor in several different realms, such as suicide attempts, drug abuse, stealing, shoplifting, self-harm, and casual sex (Wiederman & Pryor, 1996).

Diagnostic Considerations

Common Comorbidities

Comorbid conditions in the eating disorders can have a tremendous impact in terms of understanding the disorder's course, designing interventions, and assessing the effectiveness of treatment. However, although there is agreement that the most common comorbidities are mood, anxiety, substance use, and personality disorders, there is tremendous variability across studies in terms of the rates of these comorbidities (Herpertz-Dahlmann et al., 2001; Herzog, Nussbaum, & Marmor, 1996; Pearlstein, 2002; K. M. O'Brien & Vincent, 2003; Wonderlich & Mitchell, 1997). This is primarily due to changes in diagnostic criteria, utilization of different screening measures, varying sample sizes, study attrition rates, and methodological heterogeneity, with many of the studies based on clinical samples. The dearth of comparable and controlled studies highlights an important area for future research, and the ranges discussed here should be viewed, in this context, as estimates.

Overall, when presenting for treatment, 66% of individuals with Anorexia Nervosa and 50% of individuals with Bulimia Nervosa report a mood disorder; 5% of individuals with Anorexia Nervosa and 34% of individuals with Bulimia Nervosa report substance use disorders; 56% of both diagnoses report anxiety disorders, and 27% to 77% of individuals are found to have a co-occurring Axis II disorder (Braun, Sunday, & Halmi, 1994; Herpertz-Dahlmann et al., 2001; Herzog, Keller, Lavori, & Kenny, 1992; Wonderlich & Mitchell, 1997). Interestingly, many studies have revealed significant differences in the various comorbid conditions based on the eating disorder type and subtype (K. M. O'Brien & Vincent, 2003). Furthermore, it is important to note that the sequence of onset for each comorbidity may differ, which impacts conceptualization and treatment in terms of comorbidities as predisposing factors or coping strategies. Given that substance use disorders often appear after, anxiety disorders often appear before, and mood disorders can occur before, after, or concurrently with eating disorders, there is an ongoing need to assess for co-occurring symptomatology throughout treatment (Brewerton et al., 1995; Commission on Adolescent Eating Disorders, 2005).

Mood Disorders   Within the mood disorder spectrum, depression is the most common comorbid disorder. Lifetime prevalence rates range from 46% to 74% in Anorexia Nervosa, although rate differences by subtype have been reported: 46% to 80% for those who binge and purge versus 15% to 50% for those who are restrictive (Herzog, Keller, Sacks, et al., 1992; Herzog, Nussbaum, et al., 1996; Lewinsohn, Striegel-Moore, et al., 2000; Pearlstein, 2002). Controversy exists as to whether the eating disorders exacerbate an existing predisposition for depression and to what degree the neuroendocrine abnormalities of eating disorders contribute to the depressive symptomatology, but a causal relationship has yet to be found. Individuals may appear dysphoric or irritable, experience sleep and sex drive disturbances, have poor attention and concentration, and engage in social withdrawal (Fairburn, 1985). Current research is ongoing in terms of investigating potential shared genetic influences between eating and mood disorders, but twin studies have shown correlations between Anorexia Nervosa and depression in terms of genetic risk factors (Wade, Bulik, Neale, & Kendler, 2000). Among those with Bulimia Nervosa, the lifetime prevalence rate of major depression is estimated to be between 50% and 65% (Brewerton et al., 1995; Herzog, Keller, Sacks, et al., 1992; Herzog et al., 1996; Pearlstein, 2002). While the literature on comorbid Bipolar Disorder and eating disorders is sparse, a recent review of the literature found mainly subsyndromal associations, particularly for hypomania and Bulimia Nervosa, which suggests more rigorous studies involving full diagnostic criteria are warranted (McElroy, Kotwal, Keck, & Akiskal, 2005).

Anxiety Disorders   Lifetime prevalence rates of comorbid anxiety disorders range from 20% to 65% in Anorexia Nervosa and 13% to 75% in Bulimia Nervosa (Godart, Flament, Perdereau, & Jeammet, 2002; Herzog, Keller, Sacks, et al., 1992; Pearlstein, 2002; Wonderlich & Mitchell, 1997). Using a large sample of individuals from a genetics study, Kaye, Bulik, Thornton, Barbarich, and Masters (2004) found lifetime prevalence rates for anxiety disorders and eating disorders to be approximately 64%. The most common anxiety diagnoses are Obsessive-Compulsive Disorder (25% to 69%) and Social Phobia (17% to 59%; Lepine & Pelissolo, 1996; Wonderlich & Mitchell, 1997). It is important to note that to be considered comorbid with OCD, obsessions and compulsions should be unrelated to food. Although it was previously thought that sexual abuse (and concomitantly, in many cases, PTSD), were comorbid with eating disorders, research has shown that sexual abuse is no more likely to co-occur with eating disorders than with other psychiatric disorders, although the presence of a sexual abuse history is associated with more serious psychopathology and has been broadly acknowledged to be a general risk factor (J. C. Carter, Bewell, Blackmore, & Wodside, 2006; Dansky, Brewerton, Kilpatrick, & O'Neil, 1997; Mantero & Crippa, 2002).

Substance Use Disorders   Substance abuse is more commonly encountered in Anorexia Nervosa, binge/purge type, and Bulimia Nervosa than in Anorexia Nervosa, restricting type, most likely due to the impulsivity and compulsivity associated with the former disorders. Lifetime rates of substance abuse in Anorexia Nervosa range from 12% to 21% and 30% to 70% in Bulimia Nervosa (Braun et al., 1994; Herpertz-Dahlmann et al., 2001; Pearlstein, 2002; Stock, Goldberg, & Corbett, 2002). Comorbidity rates of alcohol use disorders in those presenting for treatment of Bulimia Nervosa range from 30% to 50% (Dansky, Brewerton, Kilpatrick, et al., 1997). In considering the impact of comorbid substance use and eating disorders, it is important to determine how debilitating the substance use is as it may be more appropriate to make it the primary treatment goal. If it is severe, it could be a predictor of death in Anorexia Nervosa. If it is not severe, both disorders may be treated simultaneously (Keel et al., 2003; G. T. Wilson & Fairburn, 2002).

Personality Disorders   Cross-sectional studies of comorbid personality disorders and eating disorders demonstrate a range from 27% to 77% (Matsunaga, Kiriike, Nagata, & Yamagami, 1998; Wonderlich, Fullerton, Swift, & Klein, 1994; Wonderlich & Mitchell, 2001). A meta-analysis by Rosenvinge, Martinussen, and Ostensen (2000) reported that

58% of eating disordered individuals had one or more personality disorders; prevalence rates were 49% for outpatients and 75% for inpatients. So-called Cluster B personality disorders (i.e., Antisocial, Borderline, Histrionic, Narcissistic) are more typically seen in Bulimia Nervosa and Anorexia Nervosa, binge/purge type, while Cluster C disorders (i.e., Avoidant, Dependent, Obsessive-Compulsive) are more typical of Anorexia Nervosa, restrictive type (J. M. Carroll, Touyz, & Beumont, 1996; Herzog, Keller, Lavori, et al., 1992; Schmidt & Telch, 1990). Individuals with Bulimia Nervosa often meet criteria for one or more personality disorders, with Borderline Personality Disorder being the most common (K. M. O'Brien & Vincent, 2003; C. Thornton & Russell, 1997). More generally, low self-esteem, low self-efficacy, impulsivity, self-mutilation, interpersonal conflicts, and suicidal ideation are traits often observed among those with Bulimia Nervosa. Common traits found in individuals with Anorexia Nervosa are rigidity, shyness, controlled affect and cognition, a lack of spontaneity, a sense of inefficacy despite high performance goals and expectations, and interpersonal restraint (K. M. O'Brien & Vincent, 2003; C. Thornton & Russell, 1997).

Other Disorders Although few studies exist on the comorbidity between eating disorders and Body Dysmorphic Disorder, some conflicting data suggest the need for further examination. Using *DSM-IV* criteria and a large sample, Ruffolo, Phillips, Menard, Fay, and Weisberg (2006) found 32.5% of BDD individuals had a comorbid eating disorder (9% Anorexia Nervosa, 6.5% Bulimia Nervosa, and 17.5% ED-NOS). In a previous study in which individuals with Anorexia Nervosa were screened, 39% were diagnosed with comorbid BDD, and weight issues were not the bodily preoccupation (J. E. Grant, Kim, & Eckert, 2002). The latter study's results may be reflective of the severity of the psychopathology and the clinical setting, or they may indicate higher comorbidity of BDD in those with Anorexia Nervosa than vice versa. Nevertheless, in both studies, the BDD preceded the onset of the eating disorder in the majority of the individuals. In the J. E. Grant et al. (2002) study, those with comorbid Anorexia Nervosa and BDD demonstrated a higher degree of BDD delusions, more severe symptomatology, a greater number of hospitalizations, and triple the number of suicide attempts than those with Anorexia Nervosa alone. Ruffolo et al. (2006) were able to replicate a high degree of mental health treatment, but they did not find greater delusionality or a greater likelihood for suicide attempts. While it may be easy to overlook this type of comorbidity given the shared preoccupation with one's physical condition, the research on the comorbidity of eating disorders and BDD raises important questions whose answers may significantly impact both etiologic and treatment considerations.

Differential Diagnosis

Eating Disorders versus General Medical Conditions Eating disorder diagnoses need to be differentiated from possible medical and neurological conditions resulting in weight loss, such as brain (e.g., hypothalamic or pituitary) tumors, certain malignancies, thyroid disease, gastrointestinal disease, Kleine-Levin syndrome, Crohn's disease, cystic fibrosis, inflammatory bowel disease, peptic ulcer disease, parasitic infections, and drug-induced weight loss, among others (Devlin et al., 2005). As previously mentioned, referral for a complete physical exam is highly recommended for both differential diagnosis and treatment purposes.

Eating Disorders versus Other Psychiatric Disorders
MOOD DISORDERS

Major Depressive Disorder and, to a lesser extent, Bipolar Disorder include criteria involving weight loss or gain and appetite disturbance, but not the requisite body image disturbance and compensatory behaviors of the eating disorders (American Psychiatric Association, 2000b). In addition, disruptions in eating and appetite that occur in the context of mood disorders will be accompanied by other symptoms (e.g., depressed mood, loss of interest in usual activities, concentration difficulties, sleep disturbance) that will not necessarily be seen in a primary eating disorder. Eating disturbance in the context of a mood disorder would also be expected to remit once the mood symptoms are alleviated.

ANXIETY DISORDERS

Persistent, obsessive thoughts about food and dieting accompanied by compulsive behavior may be present in eating disorders, but would be differentiated from Obsessive-Compulsive Disorder due to their circumscribed nature. For an additional diagnosis of OCD to be warranted, one would expect to see nonfood- or weight-gain-related obsessions and associated compulsions (e.g., contamination obsessions, checking compulsions). Avoidance of eating in public or in front of others might resemble a criterion for Social Phobia; however, in Social Phobia, an individual's reluctance to eat in front of others stems from concerns about doing something embarrassing or humiliating in front of another person and about being scrutinized by others. Such an individual would not likely restrict eating when alone. In contrast, an individual with an eating disorder such as Anorexia Nervosa is likely to restrict eating in front of others as well as when alone, and the desire to avoid eating is motivated by concerns about gaining weight or becoming fat.

OTHER DISORDERS

For some psychotic spectrum disorders, delusions can include food or eating issues such as the fear of being poisoned, magical beliefs about food that lead to avoidance, or somatic delusions that might resemble body image disturbance (American Psychiatric Association, 2000b). However, many psychotic individuals will also display symptoms that are not associated with eating disorders, such as hallucinations, grossly disorganized thinking or behavior, or negative symptoms such as anhedonia, avolition, and flattened affect.

Body image disturbance, preoccupation with appearance, and compulsive behaviors appear in both Body Dysmorphic Disorder and the eating disorders. Although not always the case, the primary difference is one of generality and specificity: In the eating disorders the concern is overall weight, as opposed to a preoccupation with a specific body part or dissatisfaction in body shape or size, as in BDD (J. E. Grant et al., 2002).

The best method for appropriately ruling out all of these competing diagnoses is to fully assess for Anorexia Nervosa and Bulimia Nervosa symptomatology. The clinician should be particularly sensitive to intentional weight loss behaviors, negative thoughts surrounding body image, and a fear of gaining weight.

Among the Eating Disorders

The distinction between Anorexia Nervosa and Bulimia Nervosa is an important one, particularly in regard to treatment considerations. Whereas Anorexia Nervosa tends to be ego-syntonic in nature, Bulimia Nervosa is ego-dystonic; that is, individuals might be fearful or ambivalent about giving up the disorder, but they are typically far less resistant and are therefore more compliant with and responsive to treatment (Fairburn & Harrison, 2003). The most distinguishing characteristic, however, is weight, particularly in differentiating Bulimia Nervosa and Anorexia Nervosa, binge/purge type. The *DSM-IV-TR* (American Psychiatric Association, 2000b) stipulates that Bulimia Nervosa does not occur exclusively during episodes of Anorexia Nervosa. In other words, binge eating may not take place in the context of severe weight loss. In previous versions of the *DSM*, bulimia and anorexia could be comorbid diagnoses, but this changed in the *DSM-IV* (American Psychiatric Association, 1994). Anorexia requires a body weight less than 85% of ideal weight and the presence of amenorrhea. The severe weight loss that occurs with Anorexia Nervosa may require hospitalization, and the immediate goal of treatment, whether inpatient or outpatient, is weight gain. Individuals with Bulimia Nervosa may have abnormal menstrual cycles, but they are typically not underweight for their age and height (Mehler, 2003). If there is bingeing and weight gain, the individual becomes eligible for a diagnosis of Bulimia Nervosa. Anorexia Nervosa, restrictive type, can transition into Anorexia Nervosa, binge/purge type, and it is not uncommon to see Anorexia Nervosa, binge/purge type, become Bulimia Nervosa (Devlin et al., 2005). K. T. Eddy et al. (2002) found that more than 50% of Anorexia Nervosa, restrictive type, individuals developed bulimic symptomatology and went on to develop Bulimia Nervosa, whereas approximately 33% of individuals with Bulimia Nervosa had a prior diagnosis of Anorexia Nervosa. In terms of differentiating those with ED-NOS from those dieting normally, the distinction is based on the level of severity and the inability to control or avoid the compulsiveness of the dieting behaviors.

Treatment

General Principles in Treating Eating Disorders

Coordination of Care   Treatment for eating disorders requires a multidisciplinary team approach, necessitating a coordinated effort among various professionals in the mental health, physical health, diet and nutrition, and social service realms. Consultation with or referral to an eating disorder specialist for his or her expertise and experience is highly recommended. The team may include any combination of a psychologist, psychiatrist, psychiatric nurse, pediatrician or physician, nutritionist or dietitian, social worker, family therapist, and occupational or recreational therapist. A close working relationship with the physician is important in determining the type, level, and intensity of care as eating disorders require a great deal of monitoring and management given the numerous precipitant and maintenance factors (Cubic & Bluestein, 2004). The physician's role is to monitor the individual's physical and medical sequelae or complications, including cardiac problems, electrolyte levels, dehydration, malnutrition, and bone scans. The nutritionist's role is to provide nutritional interventions and information on creating and implementing a healthy diet. The social worker's role is to support the family's needs and functioning, and the occupational or recreational therapist's role is to provide psychosocial rehabilitation, such as exercise, activities, and coping skills. In regard to the mental health practitioners, the overall goals in treating eating disorders involve normalization of the disturbed eating behavior and weight restoration, if necessary; treatment of psychological issues such as disturbed body image; and treatment of comorbidities (Cubic & Bluestein, 2004).

Psychotherapy can be delivered in individual, family, and/or group modalities. However, for both Anorexia Nervosa and Bulimia Nervosa, instilling regular eating patterns is paramount (American Psychiatric Association, 2000b). Meals are scheduled at specific times and spaced throughout the day. Foods that were previously avoided are incorporated into these meals. Interventions may include a food hierarchy regarding feared foods, behavioral contracts with reinforcers for weight gain or symptom reduction, and individual monitoring of food intake, behaviors, and emotional triggers to provide a sense of control and ownership of recovery (Halmi, 2004). Treatment may span a continuum ranging from self-help or support groups to weekly outpatient treatment to intensive outpatient status to day hospital treatment to inpatient hospitalization (A. S. Kaplan, Olmsted, Carter, & Woodside, 2001).

Disorder-Specific Treatments

Anorexia Nervosa

WEIGHT GAIN

The primary treatment goal in Anorexia Nervosa is to attain a healthy target weight in a safe and effective manner, particularly as a life-saving measure but also to enhance participation in other treatment modalities, which can be hindered by starvation sequelae such as impaired concentration and thought processes (Devlin et al., 2005). Target weight is usually determined by height-weight-age charts, and should proceed slowly for medical purposes. Strong consideration should be given to an individual's body build, pubertal status, and age in determining these weight goals, which might require recalculation over time. In an inpatient setting, the American Psychiatric Association (2000b) practice guidelines suggest 1,000 to 1,600 kcal/day to achieve a weight gain of 2 to 3 pounds per week, decreasing to 1 to 2 pounds per week for partial hospitalization and 0.5 to 1 pound per week for individual outpatient treatment. The minimum acceptable target for discharge from inpatient treatment is typically equal to or greater than 90% of the individual's height-weight-age average.

Maintaining an appropriate caloric intake and stabilizing the nutritional, fluid, and electrolyte status of the individual can be particularly difficult. Common obstacles hindering treatment compliance include the individual's denial of the problem, intense fear of gaining weight, and manipulative behavior (Michel, 2002). In most cases, it is necessary to reduce or completely stop exercise for a period of time while being aware of the potential for clandestine or compulsive attempts to engage in such behavior. Exercise management may allow for activity to be phased in gradually at a low level (stretching, low-impact aerobics), but it should be scheduled and specifically delineated as to type and duration (Rosenblum & Forman, 2002; Stewart & Williamson, 2004a). As individuals with Anorexia Nervosa often give the appearance of improvement and active participation in treatment, weight monitoring is essential in tracking progress.

THERAPEUTIC INTERVENTIONS

Family Therapy. Treatment research on Anorexia Nervosa is very limited due to low prevalence rates, the severity of the illness, length of treatment, and individual ambivalence, particularly for adolescents and children. Family therapy is the most researched treatment modality and therefore is viewed as the most effective. Outcome studies have shown a 60% to 90% recovery rate for family interventions in general (Eisler, le Grange, & Asen, 2003). In treating adolescents with Anorexia Nervosa, family therapy has been found to be effective (M. J. Kaplan, 2002) and is considered the treatment of choice, although its efficacy as compared to individual therapy is still unknown. Treatment with the family should include each individual living in the house and any additional relatives or others who spend a significant amount of time with the individual. Family therapy for Anorexia Nervosa typically follows the Maudsley method, which has been manualized and is currently the only family therapy with empirical support (Lock, le Grange, Agras, & Dare, 2001). It consists of three stages: refeeding, defining and developing new familial dynamics or relationships, and managing adolescent issues and treatment termination. Using psychoeducation and skills training, the parents are at first put in control of the affected individual's eating, and then the individual is taught how to manage his or her own weight. The focus then shifts to family issues and individual concerns in terms of boundaries, interactions, emotional expression, autonomy, and self-empowerment. Ultimately, the goal is to foster more effective communication within the family. The family's expectations or desire for change may differ from the individual's, and these elements are dealt with to avoid negative expressed emotion or counterproductive confrontation, including the family's potential to reinforce the eating disordered behavior.

Individual Therapy. Individual therapy is an adjunctive, long-term intervention with the goal of improving psychological functioning. The objective is to have the individual develop healthy eating attitudes and a better self-concept. Typically, this is addressed through exploration of identity issues, attachment and individuation, boundary setting, and interpersonal communication (Ortmeyer, 2001). The process promotes an understanding and discovery of the self within a healthy rather than distorted framework and emphasizes self-esteem building such that the individual no longer determines self-worth based on appearance alone. Similarly, body image disturbance is confronted by neutralizing and reducing the individual's fears and concerns, recognizing and altering maladaptive thoughts and biased information processing, and promoting body acceptance (Mehler, 2003). Individuals may focus on acknowledging rigid and obsessive behaviors, identifying and expressing emotions, and learning adaptive ways to cope with distress and negative affect.

Group Therapy. Group therapy generally involves several different contextual formats, including psychoeducation, mindfulness, skill-building and problem-solving groups, as well as recovery and relapse prevention (Stewart & Williamson, 2004a). There are also exposure and behavioral groups, interpersonal or process therapy groups, family groups, and creative therapy groups to provide creative outlets and teach individuals coping skills (Stewart & Williamson, 2004b). In group treatment, individuals find empathy and cohesion; learn about the disorder, themselves, and others; and improve their interpersonal skills: Seeing and pointing out others' behavior can make them more aware of their own (W. A. Bowers et al., 2003). Group work also helps eating disordered clients reduce their isolation by allowing them to share their issues and gain support from others with similar problems.

Cognitive-Behavioral Therapy.   In general there is a lack of large-scale randomized trials of CBT for Anorexia Nervosa. A CBT program was developed by D. M. Garner and Bemis (1982) that utilizes behavioral interventions (i.e., food journals to assess and target eating disordered behavior) and cognitive interventions (i.e., automatic thought records to target distorted assumptions and modify core beliefs), but controlled studies on this treatment are lacking.

Small studies have investigated CBT for anorexic adults and suggest that although the treatments show moderate effects (e.g., improved self-esteem), there is insufficient evidence to recommend them over other forms of therapy (Gowers, 2006). Behavior family system therapy and ego-oriented individual therapy were compared in a randomized clinical trial (Robin et al., 1999), and both were found to be generally effective for adolescents, including at 1-year follow-up, suggesting a worthwhile area for future studies.

MEDICATION

In terms of pharmacological treatments, there is a dearth of randomized, controlled medication trials for Anorexia Nervosa. Neuroleptics were previously found to have no significant effect (Roerig, Mitchell, Myers, & Glass, 2002). Antidepressant medications have shown only slight effects and are not empirically supported in adults or adolescents. Fluoxetine, however, has been found to be useful for preventing relapse after weight has been restored, and some case studies and open trials of atypical antipsychotic medications such as olanzapine (which is associated with weight gain) have shown improvement in children, adolescents, and adults (Boachie, Goldfield, & Spettigue, 2003; La Via, Gray, & Kaye, 2000; Powers, Santana, & Bannon, 2002). More research is needed for more conclusive results, particularly in determining the possible benefits of antidepressants in reducing relapse and mediating comorbid conditions.

Bulimia Nervosa
WEIGHT STABILIZATION

The major goal in treating Bulimia Nervosa is weight stabilization rather than weight gain, as individuals are often within the general parameters of age-height-weight standards. For Bulimia Nervosa and Anorexia Nervosa, binge/purge type, treatment involves nutritional counseling to moderate unhealthy habits and dieting behaviors. Meals are planned (by time and content) to create a regular eating pattern and regulate satiety. Avoiding hunger means avoiding subsequent bingeing behaviors. For Bulimia Nervosa, careful monitoring is required after eating the planned meals to ensure that the individual does not engage in vomiting and instead tolerates the feeling of fullness (Devlin et al., 2005). Strict limits need to be set on behaviors such as exercising. The clinician also needs to be mindful of heightened levels of resistance (panic or dysphoria) as the weight goal is nearly achieved.

MEDICATION

The majority of the empirical evidence on pharmacologic interventions for Bulimia Nervosa has focused on antidepressants. Many placebo-controlled, double-blind studies for adults with Bulimia Nervosa support the efficacy of antidepressant drugs, even in the absence of depression (Bacaltchuk, Hay, & Mari, 2000; D. J. Goldstein, Wilson, Ascroft, & Al-Banna, 1999; Zhu & Walsh, 2002). The SSRIs are the first pharmacological treatment of choice, but the U.S. FDA has approved only one, fluoxetine, for the treatment of Bulimia Nervosa, and the recommended dosage is significantly higher than that used for major depression. In controlled studies, the reduction in bingeing and purging was found to be between 50% and 75%. Antidepressants also serve to reduce obsessive thoughts about food as well as body image dissatisfaction. Overall, however, psychotherapy is generally considered to produce better long-term results, and there is evidence that the combination of cognitive-behavioral therapy and antidepressants is superior to either modality alone (Narash-Eisikovits, Dierberger, & Westen, 2002). Given that pharmacotherapy may only marginally improve an individual's status, consideration of the risks and benefits is important. Use of psychopharmacotherapy will depend on an individual's willingness, but it is commonly recommended for those who are nonresponsive or treatment-resistant with regard to psychotherapeutic approaches, or in cases in which comorbidity is interfering with treatment.

THERAPEUTIC INTERVENTIONS

Cognitive-Behavioral Therapy.   A great deal of empirical support has shown that psychotherapy, particularly CBT, is highly effective in treating Bulimia Nervosa and appears to also significantly reduce comorbid depression in this population (Gowers, 2006; J. E. Mitchell, Raymond, & Specker, 1993; Waller & Kennerley, 2003; B. T. Walsh et al., 1997). Cognitive-behavioral therapy for Bulimia Nervosa has now been identified as a gold standard treatment, and National Institute of Clinical Excellence (2004) guidelines recommend time-limited (e.g., 16 to 20 sessions spread over 4 to 5 months) CBT for adults with this disorder.

It is worth noting that most of the research applies to the purging rather than nonpurging subtype of Bulimia Nervosa. Cognitive-behavioral therapy for Bulimia Nervosa is conceptualized as time-limited and problem-focused and can be delivered in individual, group, or guided self-help formats. Well-supported by empirically validated research, CBT is the treatment of choice to reduce dietary restraint and the binge/purge cycle by creating a pattern of regular eating that includes previously avoided foods, targeting distorted beliefs regarding food and body image, raising awareness of emotional stimuli and other triggers that initiate and maintain disordered eating, providing coping skills for potential situations leading to bingeing and purging, and developing relapse prevention strategies (P. J. Cooper, Coker, & Fleming, 1994; Fairburn, 1985; Leung, Waller, & Thomas, 2000). Studies have shown a 75% reduction of symptoms and an abstinence level of 25% to 50% for those who participate in CBT, with maintenance over the long term (Peterson & Mitchell, 1999). In controlled outcome studies, bingeing and purging behavior was reduced by 80% or more in all individuals and completely eliminated in 30% to 50% of individuals. Cognitive-behavioral therapy also assists in ameliorating other types of symptomatology and improves self-esteem (Vitousek, 1996; G. T. Wilson, 1999). It has been shown to be as effective as or more effective than other treatments, including antidepressant medications, supportive psychodynamic psychotherapy, stress management, and behavior therapy (B. T. Walsh et al., 1997; Whittal, Agras, & Gould,

1999). Although randomized controlled trials of CBT for bulimic adolescents are lacking, the strong empirical support from the adult literature suggests that this treatment strategy holds promise for younger populations and should be vigorously investigated (Gowers, 2006).

Interpersonal Psychotherapy.   Interpersonal psychotherapy has also been used to treat Bulimia Nervosa. It conceptualizes both the development and maintenance of eating disorder symptoms as extensions of interpersonal problems. The focus when devising interventions, therefore, is on the individual's relational context (McIntosh, Bulik, McKenzie, Luty, & Jordan, 2000; Weissman, Markowitz, & Klerman, 2000). Self-esteem, negative affect, and interpersonal stressors are targeted. Formulation of target treatment areas generally derive from one of four possible domains: grief, interpersonal deficits, interpersonal role disputes, and role transitions (Weissman et al., 2000). Outcomes studies have shown interpersonal psychotherapy to be less effective than CBT in the short term, but similarly effective in the long term (Agras, Walsh, Fairburn, Wilson, & Kraemer, 2000; Peterson & Mitchell, 1999). Interpersonal psychotherapy is discussed in greater detail in Chapter 10.

Family Therapy.   While the Maudsley family therapy method is being adapted for the treatment of Bulimia Nervosa (le Grange, Lock, & Dymek, 2003), there is currently a paucity of research on its efficacy with this disorder.

Adjunctive Treatments   More refractory or complex cases of Bulimia Nervosa may require a slightly different approach to treatment. Fairburn, Cooper, and Shafran (2003) have developed a manual-based form of CBT that provides a transdiagnostic model of eating disorders in which interventions are matched to clinical features of the disorder rather than to a specific diagnostic category, allowing for the targeting of certain features, which may prove particularly applicable for ED-NOS cases. Adjunctive or integrative types of treatment often require clinical judgment because these cases are typically not included in the research studies. Comorbidities such as substance abuse or trauma, maladaptive personality characteristics, and impulsivity issues may require different strategies, such as dialectical behavior therapy (D. L. Safer, Telch, & Agras, 2001; Waller, 1997), to address interpersonal relations, affective experience, and self-regulation. Substance abuse may be more appropriately treated through a concurrent 12-step program or via concomitant CBT for substance abuse and CBT for Bulimia Nervosa (Mizes & Bonifazi, 2000). Choice of treatment, particularly the use of medication, will depend on a thorough assessment of the clinical presentation.

Relapse Prevention   Another important step in the process of recovery for both disorders is relapse prevention. What constitutes relapse, however, is highly variable, making the establishment of guidelines extremely difficult. The initial step involves identifying the potential obstacles that may deter progress, and then devising strategies for managing them, including the use of psychosocial support (Agras & Apple, 2002). Individuals need to understand that setbacks will occur and they must work toward the process of recovery with realistic expectations. Recognizing the difference between a minor setback and relapse can be crucial in responding appropriately (Mizes & Bonifazi, 2000). The Maudsley family therapy success rate is significant: 75% of adolescents (Lock et al., 2001).

However, data on effective prevention of relapse with this method are limited to a group that is younger than 18 at diagnosis and has a short duration of illness (3 years). Both CBT and interpersonal therapy are considered potentially effective for relapse prevention for adults as they both show similar rates of relapse at 1-year follow-up. There is a significant rate of relapse for individuals on antidepressant medication, but the rate increases if the pharmacotherapy is not maintained (Romano, Halmi, Sarkar, Koke, & Lee, 2002). The necessary duration for a maintenance regimen is still unclear, and more longitudinal studies are needed.

SLEEP DISORDERS

Sleep disturbance affects between 5% and 35% of the U.S. population (M. T. Smith & Perlis, 2002), resulting in approximately 70 million Americans experiencing clinically significant sleep problems (Czajkowski, Casey, & Jones, 2004). The sleep state involves five nonsequential stages, with one categorized as rapid eye movement (REM) and the other four as nonrapid eye movement (NREM). These stages form a pattern over the course of the night that is known as an individual's sleep architecture. Given that sleep duration is highly variable among individuals and may also vary across an individual's life span, quality, time of day, and effect of sleep are often more salient in determining if a person feels rested and refreshed after sleeping. Sleep disorders traverse gender, age, socioeconomic status, and ethnicity, and can impact physical, psychological, occupational, and social functioning (Haynes, 2005; Pilcher & Huffcutt, 1996). Across the disorders, the level of impairment may be severe: Individuals with sleep complaints have been documented as having twice as many hospitalizations and medical visits as those without them (Leger, Guilleminault, Bader, Levy, & Paillard, 2002; G. E. Simon & VonKorff, 1997). Furthermore, sleep disorders are a burden on the health care system, with direct economic costs in the $30 billion range and indirect costs estimated at over $100 billion (Chilcott & Shapiro, 1996; Sivertsen et al., 2006).

It is often difficult to identify sleep disorders, as many people assume that disturbed sleep is a consequence or symptom of another disorder and present to physicians with problems other than sleep issues (Ancoli-Israel & Roth, 1999). Treatment for sleep disorders typically involves specialized care and may require referral to a specialty clinic. Consequently, this section focuses on clinical presentation and evaluation and treatment.

Historical Overview

The scientific study of sleep is a twentieth-century phenomenon that fully established itself in the 1950s, when Nathaniel Kleitman and Eugene Aserinsky made the discovery of REM and NREM sleep stages (Aserinsky & Kleitman, 1953). In 1971, the first international congress of sleep research was convened in Scotland, and the American Sleep Disorders Association was established in 1975 (Sassin & Mitler, 1987). The Association of Sleep Disorders Centers, which was also founded in 1975, proposed the concept of an institutional model for researching and treating sleep disorders as a response to the need for interdisciplinary interaction involving psychologists, psychiatrists, neurologists, pediatricians, gastroenterologists, and cardiologists (Karacan, Williams, & Moore, 1989).

Over the next 30 years, sleep research and clinical interest in sleep disorders proliferated, resulting in the 1990 publication of the International Classification of Sleep Disorders (ICSD, 1990) *Diagnostic and Coding Manual* and the establishment of hundreds of sleep clinics throughout the United States (Kryger, Lavie, & Rosen, 1999; Morin, Savard, Ouellet, & Daley, 2003).

Sleep disorders first appeared in the *DSM-III-R* in 1987 (American Psychiatric Association, 1987) and were organized by presenting complaint into four categories: insomnia, hypersomnia, sleep wake schedule disorder, and parasomnias. In the *DSM-IV*, an attempt was made to become more synchronous with the ICSD by classifying diagnoses according to pathophysiology, and guidelines were created to distinguish primary sleep disorders from sleep disorders associated with mental disorders, medical conditions, and substance-induced disorders (Nofzinger, Buysse, Reynolds, & Kupfer, 1993). The *DSM-IV-TR* (American Psychiatric Association, 2000b) divides sleep disorders into three groupings based on presumed etiology: *primary sleep disorders*, which include internally derived disturbances due to abnormalities in physiologic processes; *sleep disorders related to another mental disorder*, which include disturbances caused by other psychological issues but that require their own individual focus and treatment; and *other sleep disorders*, which include disturbances arising from general medical conditions or substance use. Primary Sleep Disorders are further divided into *dyssomnias* and *parasomnias*, which include 10 individual diagnoses.

Dyssomnias

Clinical Presentation

Primary Insomnia is characterized by a disturbance in sleep or sleep that is nonrestorative (i.e., there is an inferior level of sleep quantity or quality that impacts functioning). Generally, it presents as a latency in the ability to fall asleep, accompanied by several brief or lengthy awakenings during the night, resulting in several hours less sleep than would satisfy requirements for normal functioning. This disturbance can manifest individually or in combination as initial or sleep-onset insomnia (the inability to fall asleep), middle or maintenance insomnia (the inability to stay asleep), and terminal insomnia (the tendency to wake early and not be able to get back to sleep; Van Brunt & Lichstein, 2000). Significant distress or impairment is required to distinguish this diagnosis from individual complaints of dissatisfaction with sleep, which may be mild or moderate insomnia (American Psychiatric Association, 2000b). According to the *DSM-IV-TR* (American Psychiatric Association, 2000b) criteria, the disturbance must be present for at least 1 month, although several months or years are not uncommon (M. T. Smith & Perlis, 2002). The effects of *Primary Insomnia* can include fatigue, anergy, cognitive inefficiency, and emotional and mood changes (J. K. Walsh & Üstün, 1999). The "primary" label is intended to differentiate this diagnosis from insomnia secondary to a medical condition, psychiatric condition, or substance use.

Approximately one third of individuals presenting with sleep problems suffer from occasional insomnia (Czajkowski et al., 2004). The onset of Primary Insomnia is often sudden but can be gradual; the course may be chronic or episodic and is commonly fluctuating (P. M. Becker, 2005). The age of onset may influence the course of the disorder as different challenges and stressors at different phases of life can influence sleep patterns

(Neubauer, 2003). Symptom presentation also tends to differ with age. For example, in adolescents, insomnia can manifest as behavioral problems such as academic difficulties, peer conflict, or truancy, with irritability and moodiness that are often misdiagnosed as depression, laziness, or rebelliousness (Stores, 2001). The disorder generally affects more women than men (D. E. Ford & Kamerow, 1989; Ohayon & Caluet, 1996; J. K. Walsh & Üstün, 1999), and prevalence increases with age (Foley et al., 1995).

Primary Insomnia typically manifests as having a history of poor sleep and acute, transient bouts of insomnia prior to developing the persistent, chronic type that becomes a disorder. Both depression and anxiety symptoms are common and may precede the disorder or be a consequence of it (Ohayon, Caulet, & Lemoine, 1998). Many individuals become anxious about not getting enough sleep, which can exacerbate the sleep problem. The prognosis for Primary Insomnia is considered to be good overall, but difficult to estimate given the idiosyncrasies of each individual's circumstances. Frequently, the original stressor resolves but the insomnia persists. In a longitudinal study, Hohagen et al. (1994) found that only 35% of individuals were reporting the same type of sleep complaint (initial, maintenance, or terminal) at 4-month follow-up as they had at presentation.

The etiology of Primary Insomnia is considered to be multifactorial and may include sleep-related breathing disorders (apneas), medical conditions (pregnancy, illness, migraines), neurological conditions (stroke, multiple sclerosis, head injury), poor sleep hygiene (e.g., excessive time in bed, noise), substances (including sleep medications), personality traits, external stressors (divorce, bankruptcy), and other mental health issues (P. M. Becker, 2005).

Primary Hypersomnia has an onset typically in the 15- to 30-year-old range and is characterized by excessive sleepiness that occurs either during the day or as an extension of nightly sleep. It must persist for at least 1 month, and other causes, such as another sleep or psychiatric disorder, a medical condition, or a consequence of substance use, must be ruled (American Psychiatric Association, 2000b). The quality of sleep is not at issue in Primary Hypersomnia, but waking up is often difficult. During the day, individuals may unintentionally nod off or schedule naps into their routine that are lengthy, not particularly refreshing, and fail to help with the level of alertness (First & Tasman, 2004). Similar to the effects of insomnia, hypersomnia can affect social and occupational functioning with fatigue that is more severe than that seen in insomnia (Billiard, 2003). The course is generally steady, but it may also present in a periodic manner; thus the *DSM* system allows for the diagnostic specifier "recurrent" (American Psychiatric Association, 2000b).

Narcolepsy is generally considered to be a neurological condition characterized by excessive daytime sleepiness that appears as fatigue or tiredness. Despite nocturnal sleep that is normal in quantity and quality, individuals may experience sleep attacks—frequent episodes of falling asleep inappropriately (i.e., while driving, talking, eating)—which can be acute and difficult to control (Czajkowski et al., 2004). They may also experience cataplexy, a sudden loss of muscle tone, which can be as overt as a fall to the floor or as subtle as knees buckling. Narcolepsy is often triggered by sudden or strong emotion, and the frequency of episodes ranges from occasional to 15 to 20 or more per day (Reite, 1998). Both sleep paralysis and hypnogogic hallucinations are common, but they are not exclusive to this diagnosis or to sleep disorders in general (Wills & Garcia, 2002). The former, which occurs in about one fourth of individuals, results in a transitory inability to move any muscle except the eyes and is usually experienced while in the process of falling asleep or upon awakening. The latter involves vivid dreams or hallucinatory imagery (lasting a few seconds to a few minutes) in which one sees, hears, or smells things that are not actually present, usually as one falls asleep (Ohayon, Priest, Caulet, & Guilleminault, 1996). The onset of Narcolepsy typically occurs in the early teenage years, but it has been observed in those over 50. This disorder demonstrates a generally stable course, and a genetic component has been implicated in its etiology; one third of narcoleptic individuals show a family history of symptoms (Ohayon & Okun, 2006). Polysomnography and multiple sleep latency tests are used for diagnosis. The treatment for Narcolepsy often involves stimulant medication to obtain a near-normal level of alertness (M. H. Silber, 2001). Tricyclic REM suppressants or MAOIs may be prescribed to manage cataplexy. Individuals also need to be educated about potential safety issues (such as driving) and proper sleep hygiene.

Breathing-Related Sleep Disorder, also known as obstructive sleep apnea (OSA), is characterized by a chronic disruption of airflow that can be a partial obstruction, a prolonged (1 minute or more) collapse of the airway, or a mix of the two during sleep. The restricted or obstructed airflow decreases blood oxygen saturation, and the individual awakens multiple times throughout the night to restore normal breathing, although there is generally no awareness of most of the awakenings (Guilleminault & Bliwise, 1994). Because of the physiologic processes involved, this disorder is also coded on Axis III when using the *DSM* system (American Psychiatric Association, 2000b). The presentation of Breathing-Related Sleep Disorder usually includes loud snoring, gasping for air, and/or grunting or snorting. Collateral sources (e.g., significant others) can be extremely helpful informants in evaluating symptomatology. The persistent sleep interruptions result in nonrestorative sleep, daytime sleepiness, irritability, depression, decreased cognitive and work performance, morning headaches, and even personality changes (Czajkowski et al., 2004; Guilleminault & Bliwise, 1994). This disorder is most often seen in middle-aged males who are overweight and hypertensive. Breathing-Related Sleep Disorder, although infrequent in women, is more likely to occur after menopause. It has also been documented in children, usually due to tonsil and adenoidal enlargement (El-Ad & Lavie, 2005). Potentially lethal medical conditions may result from Breathing-Related Sleep Disorder given that cardiovascular problems can lead to congestive heart failure, stroke, or myocardial infarction (W. C. Orr, 1997). The disorder typically has an insidious onset and chronic course, and a diagnosis requires polysomnographic testing to record the frequency, duration, and type of apneas (Chesson et al., 1997). Treatment typically involves weight loss and continuous positive airway pressure (CPAP), which is administered via a face mask affixed with a tube that forces the appropriate amount of air pressure through the airway. In some cases, surgery (particularly for tonsil hypertrophy) and dental devices (for overbite or other anatomical abnormalities) are utilized.

Circadian Rhythm Disorder occurs from a desynchronization between a person's desired sleep-wake cycle and the exigencies of everyday life. Individuals may experience excessive sleepiness and insomnia but do not have difficulty maintaining sleep. Etiology is believed to involve a dysregulation in the suprachiasmatic nuclei of the hypothalamus (M. T. Smith & Perils, 2002). There are several types of Circadian Rhythm Disorders articulated in the *DSM-IV-TR* (American Psychiatric Association, 2000b). *Delayed sleep phase syndrome* is difficulty falling asleep at the desired time. Onset occurs in adolescence or early adulthood (Regestein & Monk, 1995), and the disorder generally remits over time or resolves when the individual is able to set his or her own schedule. Sleep deprivation may occur due to chronicity or severity of symptoms. *Jet-lag type* occurs from traveling through different time zones. *Shift work type* results from evening or rotating employment schedules that obviate any opportunity to adjust to or create a sleep pattern. *Unspecified type* includes *advanced sleep phase* (going to bed early and arising early, which is more prominent after middle age), *non-24-hour-sleep-wake pattern* (an endogenous circadian rhythm schedule that is slightly over 24 hours), and *irregular sleep-wake pattern* (which results from no discernable sleep schedule). Sleep diaries are often helpful in diagnosis and treatment of these disorders. Furthermore, as light impacts the synthesis and distribution of melatonin in the body (causing sleepiness), light exposure can modulate these disorders (although melatonin itself is still an unproven intervention; Lee-Chiong & Sateia, 2006). Treatment involves pharmacotherapy and bright light chronotherapy, exposing an individual to a specific light source at a particular time of day, along with a schedule change and/or implementation of proper sleep hygiene techniques (Chesson et al., 2000). Generally prognosis is average, with a 50% response rate observed in clinic settings (Regestein & Monk, 1995).

Additional Dyssomnias   Restless legs syndrome (RLS) is a discomfort that may be experienced as a tightness or crawling sensation deep in the legs that is briefly relieved by frequent movements (i.e., twitching or jerking). It can lead to insomnia and daytime sleepiness and fatigue. The etiology may be idiopathic or related to a medical or neurological condition; it is often associated with pregnancy, iron deficiency, uremia, and peripheral neuropathy (Chahine & Chemali, 2006). Onset is typically prior to age 50, and it has been observed in children (Kotagal & Silber, 2004). Symptoms tend to worsen with age (Ohayon & Roth, 2002), and a familial history is common. The majority of individuals with RLS will experience periodic limb movements, but this phenomenon is not reciprocal (Van Brunt & Lichstein, 2000).

Periodic limb movement (PLM) is a brief, rhythmic jerking of the limbs (typically the legs) that significantly disturbs sleep by causing repeated brief awakenings. The number of events per night varies, and the individual is generally unaware of the movements (Grenier, 2003). Onset is unknown, but the disorder affects more men than women and may be seen in a normal population, in the elderly, and in those suffering from Narcolepsy, RLS, and apneas (Czajkowski et al., 2004).

Diagnosis for RLS is clinically determined, and a polysomnography or multiple sleep latency test is required for diagnosing PLM. Both disorders are treated with dopaminergic medications such as levodopa and dopamine agonists, although opioids and benzodiazepines are also used (Hening, Allen, Earley, Picchietti, & Silber, 2004).

A summary of the dyssomnias is presented in Table 13.4, including key and discriminating features and epidemiological data.

Parasomnias

Clinical Presentation

The parasomnias are defined as unusual or abnormal motoric behaviors or physiological events occurring in the context of sleep (American Psychiatric Association, 2000b). An overview of these disorders is provided in Table 13.5.

Table 13.4 Overview of sleep disorders: dyssomnias

Sleep Disorder	Epidemiology*	Key Features	Discriminating Features
Primary Insomnia	10%–20% 25% in the elderly	Excessive sleepiness; nonrestorative sleep	Difficulty falling or staying asleep for 1 month; not due to other sleep or mental disorder, substance use, or GMC
Primary Hypersomnia	0.3%–16.3%	Excessive daytime sleepiness; unintentional sleep episodes; nonrestorative naps; normal quality of nocturnal sleep; difficulty awakening	Excessive sleepiness for at least 1 month; not better accounted for by another sleep disorder or sleep deprivation; not due to a substance, GMC, or another mental disorder
Narcolepsy	0.02%–0.16%	Excessive sleepiness; discrete sleep attacks; cataplexy; dreamlike hallucinations; sleep paralysis; normal quality and quantity of nocturnal sleep	Irresistible attacks of refreshing sleep that occur daily over at least 3 months; presence of cataplexy and the recurrent intrusions of REM sleep into the sleep-wake transition (i.e. sleep paralysis or hallucinations); not due to substance use or GMC
Breathing-Related Sleep Disorder	1%–10% OSA: 9% women, 24% men ages 30–60	Obstructed breathing leading to sleep disruption; excessive sleepiness or insomnia; unrefreshing naps; loud snoring; dry mouth; headaches; physical characteristics: obesity, hypertension, cardiovascular issues, anatomical abnormalities	Sleep disruption due to sleep-related breathing condition leading to excessive sleepiness or insomnia; not better accounted for by substance use or GMC
Circadian Rhythm Sleep Disorder	Not established; delayed sleep phase: 0.1%–4% adults 7% adolescents	Unable to manage sleep-wake cycle with that of work or social circumstances: delayed sleep phase, advanced sleep phase, shift work, jet lag, non-24-hour-day syndrome, periodic limb movements in sleep; daytime sleepiness from abnormal sleep-wake cycle; impaired performance	Pattern of sleep disruption due to sleep-wake schedule mismatch between environment and circadian rhythms that leads to excessive sleepiness or insomnia; is not due to another sleep disorder, substance use, or GMC
Dyssomnia NOS	0.5%–15% RLS 2%–10% PLM 3.9%	Subthreshold criteria or unclear diagnosis Examples: restless legs syndrome (RLS) periodic limb movement (PLM)	

*The epidemiology of most sleep disorders is unknown; as such, these rates are based on estimates from the research literature and the *DSM-IV*.

Source: Diagnostic and Statistical Manual of Mental Disorders, fourth edition, text revision, by American Psychiatric Association, 2000b, Washington, DC: Author. Reprinted with permission.

Table 13.5   Overview of sleep disorders: parasomnias

Sleep Disorder	Epidemiology[*]	Key Features	Discriminating Features
Parasomnias	1%–15% in children	Abnormal behavior or physiological events occur with sleep	
Nightmare Disorder	more common in 3- to 6-year-olds 1/week in 5% adults	Recurrent frightening dreams; occur during REM sleep; vivid imagery; complete awakenings; dream recall; mild autonomic arousal	Repeated awakenings from sleep or nap with recall of frightening dreams and postawakening alertness; not due to a GMC, mental disorder, or substance use
Sleep Terror Disorder	1%–17.3% in children <1%–2.2% in adults	Sudden partial awakenings with disorientation; intense fear and panic; occur during NREM sleep; significant autonomic arousal with possible motoric activity; minimal recall or amnesia for the event	Repeated abrupt awakenings from sleep with a panicky scream, intense fear, and autonomic arousal, nonresponsive to others and amnestic for the event; not due to a GMC or substance use
Sleepwalking Disorder	1%–5% of children 1.9%–3.2% of adults	Recurrent motoric behavior; occur during NREM; organized motor behavior with mild autonomic arousal; minimal recall or amnesia for the event	Repeated risings from bed while asleep; generally unresponsive and difficult to awaken; amnesia for the event; no mental impairment within minutes of awakening from episode; not due to a GMC or substance use
Parasomnia NOS	.8% sleep paralysis, 5% REM sleep behavior disorder	Subthreshold criteria or unclear diagnosis Examples: sleep paralysis REM sleep behavior disorder	

[*]The epidemiology of most sleep disorders is unknown; as such, these rates are based on estimates from the research literature and the *DSM-IV.*

Source: Diagnostic and Statistical Manual of Mental Disorders, fourth edition, text revision, by American Psychiatric Association, 2000b, Washington, DC: Author. Reprinted with permission.

Nightmare Disorder may occur multiple times during REM sleep episodes and involves frightening dreams that wake an individual to alertness. This diagnosis does not include nightmares that may occur as the result of substances, medical illness or conditions, or another mental disorder. Individuals can usually recount the nightmare content in detail, which is often dangerous, threatening, or embarrassing and causes lingering anxiety (Vecchierini, 2003). It is also possible for the nightmares to occur during NREM sleep, which is more commonly seen following a traumatic event. This disorder is predominantly observed in children and is considered developmentally normative unless the nightmares persist or cause significant distress.

Sleep Terror Disorder, also known as "night terrors," involves repeated sudden awakenings from NREM sleep (generally occurring in the first few hours of sleep), accompanied by autonomic arousal (e.g., panicky screams, sweating, heavy breathing, rapid heartbeat, crying out, thrashing or sitting up, feelings of terror or panic). The individual may motorically respond or attempt to get out of bed, raising the possibility of injury to self or others (G. M. Rosen, Kohen, & Mahowald, 2003). Episodes may last up to 20 minutes and typically occur only once per night (Vecchierini, 2003). It may be difficult to wake the individual to a state of alertness. Immediate recall is usually an image or a fragment as opposed to a detailed dream, with subsequent amnesia for the event. This disorder is most common in children ages 4 to 12, and distress and impairment often manifest as avoidance of sleep situations involving others (e.g., sleepovers, camp; First & Tasman, 2004). The etiology of Sleep Terror Disorder is unknown, but risk factors can include sleep deprivation, excessive exercise, stress, fever, and substance use (Mahowald & Schenck, 2005). A clinical interview is sufficient for diagnosis. Most children outgrow sleep terrors; adults may have a more chronic course with waxing and waning episodes (Vecchierini, 2003). Sleep terror or sleepwalking is commonly reported in the family history. Behavioral therapy and scheduled awakenings are used to treat severe or chronic cases (N. C. Frank, Spirito, Stark, & Owens-Stively, 1997). Psychotherapy and/or hypnosis have been attempted with adults to target stressful triggers or events. In very severe cases, benzodiazepines or tricyclics may be used (Mahowald & Schenck, 2005).

Sleepwalking Disorder, or *somnambulism,* is similar to and often co-occurs with sleep terrors; it also involves arousal during NREM sleep, during which the affected individual is nonresponsive and lacking in awareness or memory of the event, although vague, fragmented recall may occur (Reite, 1998). However, in sleepwalking, the motoric behavior is more organized and intricate and can range from simple movement such as standing near the bed to complex activity such as eating, talking, responding to others, or ambulating up and down stairs or out of the house (First & Tasman, 2004). The disorder tends to occur in children and adolescents. Episodes may last from a few minutes to a half hour, and may be terminated by an awakening or a return to sleep either in bed or elsewhere. Sleepwalking is somewhat normative; 15% to 40% of children have had at least one episode, and 3% to 6% have had more than one episode (G. M. Rosen, Ferber, & Mahowald, 1996). Distress and impairment usually arise from avoidance of situations in which others will become aware of the behavior, but there is also a risk of physical harm depending on the individual's surroundings. Although the etiology of Sleepwalking Disorder is unclear, there appears to be a familial component (R. M. Berlin & Qayyum, 1986; Vecchierini, 2003). Typically, childhood sleepwalking spontaneously remits, although a recurrent course is possible, waxing and waning through adulthood. Polysomnography can track sleepwalking episodes and may be necessary for individuals who live alone, but information from collateral sources is usually sufficient for diagnosis. As with sleep terrors, treatment is generally not required for children (M. H. Silber, 2001), except in cases of potential danger or self-injury in which protective measures are considered.

Additional Parasomnias   The REM sleep behavior disorder is similar to sleepwalking, but the individual is more easily awakened and has detailed recall of the event. Additionally, the behavior occurs during REM sleep and tends to involve more violent behaviors (Wills & Garcia, 2002). Polysomnography can be helpful with diagnosis as well as neurologic evaluation to rule out neurodegenerative diseases (Olson, Boeve, & Silber, 2000). Another common syndrome is sleep paralysis, which can be a symptom of Narcolepsy or an individual diagnosis. Episodes may be hypnagogic (occur at sleep onset) or hypnopompic (occur with awakening; Wills & Garcia, 2002) and typically involve anxiety or a sense of foreboding (Vecchierini, 2003).

Etiology

In addition to some of the etiologic factors previously mentioned, a commonly accepted general etiologic model for sleep disorders proposed by Spielman, Caruso, and Glovinsky (1987) conceptualizes sleep disorders in terms of predisposing (trait), precipitating (state), and maintaining and perpetuating factors. Predisposing elements are similar to triggers and may include the personality types considered to be worriers or night owls, chronic coffee drinkers, or individuals with established sleep patterns from childhood that are dysfunctional in adulthood. Precipitating factors are triggers that set the disorder in motion. Perpetuating factors usually develop after the triggering event and may even represent a person's attempts to cope with the initial problem, such as an individual who drinks alcohol to aid in falling asleep. The latter often maintains the disorder beyond resolution of the original trigger. In such cases, the individual may be spending too much time in bed while awake, or taking naps, or drinking more coffee during the day. For many individuals, preoccupations with needing to fall asleep and thoughts of losing sleep cause anxiety and frustration that can become a vicious downward spiral that continues to adversely affect sleep. This, in turn, creates even more negative expectations regarding future sleep episodes, increasing anger, fatigue, and concern during the day and anxiety at night, leading to magnification of the consequences of lost or poor sleep. This ultimately causes a conditioned arousal tendency that is attached to the bedroom environment.

Intake and Interviewing Considerations

The assessment and evaluation of sleep disorders needs to be detailed and thorough to determine any possible etiology and maintenance factors as well as implement a treatment plan that comprehensively addresses the clinical picture (Czajkowkski et al., 2004). For most sleep disorders, diagnosis is derived from the clinical history. In addition to the standard information obtained in a typical clinical interview, the clinician should inquire about the circumstances surrounding onset, severity, and frequency of symptoms, effects on functioning (daytime fatigue and cognitive, mood, and performance issues), past treatments (professional or personal, including medication and other sleep aids), and potential maintenance factors (diet, exercise; Grenier, 2003; Spielman, Nunes, & Glovinsky, 1996). A sleep history questionnaire can be helpful in many cases, and evaluation should also include a physical exam, psychopathology screen, and collateral reports.

Assessment Measures

There are several self-report measures that may be useful tools in the evaluation of sleep disorders. Instruments with good psychometric properties include the Epworth Sleepiness Scale, a brief questionnaire that assesses an individual's level of daytime sleepiness in various situations, and the Pittsburgh Sleep Quality Index, which assesses insomnia complaints (Buysse, Reynolds, & Monk, 1989). The Stanford Sleepiness Scale is similar to the Epworth Sleepiness Scale, has shown good reliability, and is often used in conjunction with multiple sleep latency tests (Bae & Golish, 2006). These measures, however, do not replace a thorough history and the usefulness of a sleep diary.

A sleep diary is an invaluable tool in contextualizing an individual's sleep disturbance and is generally completed over a 2-week time period (Espie, 2000; Van Brunt & Lichstein, 2000). The information gathered in this manner provides a comprehensive picture of an individual's sleep-wake cycle, work or school schedule, sleep environment and habits, and the effect of lifestyle and coping strategies. Specifically, a diary can illustrate both sleep patterns and changes in daytime functioning and commonly includes detailed information as to time to bed, time to wake, sleep latency, frequency of nightly awakenings, wake time after sleep onset, total sleep time, early morning awakenings, medications or substances taken before bed, activities done before bed, activities done in bed, daytime napping (frequency and duration), sleep environment (snoring partner, pet or child needing attention, noisy neighborhood, etc.), and subjective assessments of sleep quality and daytime functioning (i.e., fatigue levels; Hooper, 2001). Sleep diaries can provide prospective information for treatment planning purposes, assist in creating treatment modifications, and serve as a useful tool for outcome measurement.

Life Span Considerations

Diagnostically, age is an important consideration in any sleep disturbance as sleep cycles vary considerably across the life span; different developmental stages require different amounts of sleep. During adolescence, a normal phase delay occurs in the circadian rhythm (i.e., biologically speaking, adolescents would rather stay up later at night and wake up later in the morning), whereas the elderly experience a phase advance (i.e., a preference for going to bed early and arising early; Neubauer, 2003). However, sleep maintenance is the most common complaint in the older adult age group (Carskadon, Wolfson, Acebo, Tzischinsky, & Seifer, 1998; Foley, Monjan, Simonsick, Wallace, & Blazer, 1999).

Sleep Clinics

Assessment that involves referral to a sleep clinic for a polysomnographic evaluation is not required for all sleep disorders, including chronic insomnia (Nowell, Buysse, Morin, Reynolds, & Kupfer, 2002; M. T. Smith & Perlis, 2002), but it is indicated for potential organic causes (such as in apnea and PLM). Polysomnographic study can also measure REM latency, which may assist in ruling out depression, and is helpful in cases of diagnostic uncertainty (Espie, 2000). Polysomnography requires an overnight stay at the sleep clinic, and measurements often include electroencephalogram, eye movements, heart rate, muscle activity, electrocardiogram, blood oxygen levels, and airway flow in the process of tracking sleep physiology and sleep stages (Van Brunt & Lichstein, 2000). Scoring and interpreting these tests can take several days, and results are reviewed in the context of the client's history and presentation (Sassin & Mitler, 1987). Once a diagnosis is made, a treatment plan is formulated that may include follow-up by various physicians at the sleep center.

Diagnostic Considerations

Differential Diagnosis

Sleep Disorders versus Other Psychiatric Disorders   For within-class differential diagnosis, please refer to Tables 13.4 and 13.5 for key and discriminating features of the sleep disorders. With regard to a differential diagnosis between sleep disorders and other psychiatric conditions, if insomnia or hypersomnia occurs exclusively during the course of another mental disorder (i.e., is causally or temporally linked to another psychiatric condition), the diagnosis of Insomnia/Hypersomnia Related to Another Mental Disorder is made (American Psychiatric Association, 2000b). A dual diagnosis may be designated, however, if the insomnia is not a manifestation of any other mental disorder and has an independent course. This can be an incredibly difficult distinction to make, but an individual with a predominant complaint of severe insomnia as well as depressed mood would generally fit this criteria (C. F. Reynolds, 1999).

Sleep disturbance can be found in a wide range of psychiatric conditions, including psychotic, somatoform, adjustment, and impulse disorders, but insomnia is most often seen in conjunction with mood and anxiety disorders (Moul & Buysse, 2006). Several researchers have reported that a psychiatric disorder is associated with insomnia complaints in 30% to 40% of individuals, with the most common being depression (D. E. Ford & Kamerow, 1989; Nowell et al., 2002; Reite, 1998). Currently, it is still unclear in which instances insomnia is a consequence of depression versus a precursor or risk factor for depression, as it is possible these conditions share a common vulnerability (Riemann & Voderholzer, 2003). A large study involving four European countries showed that insomnia tends to precede or co-occur with mood disorders but co-occurs or follows anxiety disorders (Ohayon & Roth, 2003). Insomnia is common in Generalized Anxiety Disorder, OCD, Panic Disorder, and PTSD. In particular, initial and maintenance insomnia and nonrestorative sleep are found. Typically, the anxiety should involve concerns about life circumstances and sleep to be considered a comorbid disorder.

Sleep Disorders versus Medical Conditions   Sleep disturbance is ubiquitous in medical conditions (Moul & Buysse, 2006). When it has been assessed as being the direct physiological consequence of an illness or condition, a diagnosis of Sleep Disorder Due to a General Medical Condition is made using the *DSM* system, and one of four subtypes within this diagnostic category can be specified: insomnia, hypersomnia, parasomnia, and mixed type (American Psychiatric Association, 2000b). Sleep maintenance insomnia is the most common symptom in those with medical or pain conditions such as hyperthyroidism, pregnancy, fibromyalgia, chronic fatigue syndrome, iron deficiency, cardiac failure, or gastroesophageal reflux disease (McCrae, & Lichstein, 2001; Moul & Buysse, 2006; Reite, Ruddy, & Nagel, 2002). A sleep complaint that is assessed as being a physiological effect of a substance should be diagnosed as Substance-Induced Sleep Disorder (which carries the same list of subtypes used with the GMC) using the *DSM* system

(American Psychiatric Association, 2000b). The substances may refer to recreational or prescription drugs, tobacco, caffeine, or even toxins, and the *DSM* includes specifiers for onset during intoxication as well as onset during withdrawal.

Treatment

General Principles in Treating Sleep Disorders

Treatment for sleep disorders generally involves a multidisciplinary team that might include a neurologist, psychiatrist, cardiologist, and pulmonary or other specialist depending on symptomatology (First & Tasman, 2004). When there is a physiological component (e.g., restless legs, apnea), referral to a sleep specialist is advised. Multimodal treatment for sleep disorders often includes behavioral strategies and/or medication implemented in a manner that both allows for appropriate changes and adjustments as well as provides a means for marking progress (Spielman & Glovinsky, 1997). The American Academy of Sleep Medicine and empirical data have shown sleep restriction, stimulus control, and CBT to be efficacious in treating insomnia (Chesson et al., 1999; Murtagh & Greenwood, 1995). In treating parasomnias, nonpharmacological methods such as relaxation and hypnosis at bedtime, as well as scheduled awakenings in 15- to 30-minute increments before the behaviors generally occur have been shown to be helpful (P. M. Becker, 2005).

Behavioral Interventions

Sleep Restriction The goal of sleep restriction therapy is to limit the time spent in bed to the actual behavior of sleeping (Van Brunt & Lichstein, 2000). For many individuals, this may sound counterintuitive because the process initially decreases the individual's sleep time in order to increase sleep efficiency (Spielman, Saskin, & Thorpy, 1987). Consequently, the arise time remains constant but the bedtime is moved to later in the night. Naps or resting during the day are not allowed. Over the course of several days, this will actually decrease the time it takes the individual to fall asleep and therefore decrease arousals (First & Tasman, 2004). Once this target have been achieved, the bedtime is moved earlier in 15- to 20-minute increments until the individual reaches the desired bedtime while still falling asleep quickly and staying asleep throughout the night. Typically, a consistent 85% to 90% (or higher) level of time in bed should be spent asleep to start increasing the sleep window increments. If the time spent asleep drops below the 85% level, the individual returns to the mean total sleep time (Morin, 2003).

Stimulus Control This is a method of disassociating the inappropriate conditioned cues an individual has developed over time to sleep-related stimuli, and involves removing any stimuli that are not associated with sleep to recondition sleep patterns and habits (Edinger & Means, 2006; Lacks, Bertelson, Sugerman, & Kunkel, 1983). Particular rules are then established surrounding sleep behavior. For example, a consistent bed time is set each night to help eventuate a consistent sleep-wake cycle. The only behaviors that are allowed to take place in the bedroom are sleep and sex, and the individual is not to sleep anywhere other than the bed (i.e., not on a couch or lounge chair). If there are nighttime awakenings, the individual is to get out of bed after 15 to 20 minutes and return only when he or she feels ready to fall asleep again. Through this method, the bedroom becomes the conditioned stimulus for sleep.

Cognitive-Behavioral Therapy   Many individuals with sleep disturbance carry dysfunctional thoughts or beliefs about their sleep problems. This type of thinking creates anxiety that can occur prior to sleep or prior to arousal upon intermittent awakening throughout the night (L. Harvey, Inglis, & Espie, 2002). The thoughts are often ruminative or perseverative, reflecting an individual's concerns about not getting work done, getting fired, or being unable to perform adequately as a result of lack of sleep. Cognitive-behavioral therapy attempts to identify any existing maladaptive thoughts and then challenge and restructure them to create more realistic expectations about the consequences of disturbed sleep (Means & Edinger, 2006). To uncover cognitive distortions, individuals should be asked what they think about their sleep and any attendant issues with losing sleep. Cognitive-behavioral therapy has been found to be as effective as medication and appears to be more effective over the long term (Espie, Inglis, Tessier, & Harvey, 2001).

Additional Interventions   Typically an adjunct intervention, sleep hygiene (see Table 13.6) examines and alters the individual's behaviors and habits that negatively impact sleep quantity and quality (Morin, Hauri, et al., 1999). This might include a wide range of practices such as the quantity and timing of drinking coffee or caffeinated beverages, the consumption of alcohol (particularly as a sleep aid), smoking or the use of stimulant drugs (prescription or recreational), and the timing of exercise, reading, and other activities that generally tend to cause arousal rather than sedation (Neubauer, 2003). Relaxation training is also often used to support other treatments and may involve progressive muscle relaxation, biofeedback, guided imagery, and diaphragmatic breathing (Morin, 2003). The purpose is not to make the individual sleepy, but to release tension and decrease arousal. The strategies discussed earlier under "Stimulus Control" are sometimes subsumed under the rubric of sleep hygiene techniques.

Although researchers (Morin, Colecchi, Stone, Sood, & Brink, 1999; M. T. Smith & Perlis, 2002) have reported greater efficacy with behavioral approaches over drug interventions, a large percentage of people with disturbed sleep rely on medications, such as over-the-counter sleep aids, which may prove helpful in cases of transient or mild sleep disturbance but are not efficacious for sleep disorders. Prescription medications are considered effective in the short term, but more studies are needed that focus on treatment gains longitudinally (Stepanski & Perlis, 2003). Benzodiazepine and benzodiazepine-receptor agonists such as zolpidem and zaleplon are empirically validated and widely used (M. L. Perlis, McCall, Krystal, & Walsh, 2004), although this class of drugs can cause tolerance, abuse, or dependence and side effects such as next-day sedation. They are less effective on sleep maintenance problems and may result in rebound insomnia after termination (Rosenberg, 2006). Recently, the FDA approved eszopiclone, a cyclopyrrolone nonbenzodiazepine agent, for long-term use (A. D. Krystal et al., 2003). Sedative hypnotics and antidepressants such as trazadone and nefazodone can provide fast relief, with a 50% decrease in symptom severity in the short term (2 to 4 weeks; Lee-Chiong & Sateia, 2006), but these medications do not impact the factors that may be sustaining the insomnia and therefore represent a short-term solution.

Table 13.6   Sleep hygiene basics (dos and don'ts)

BEFORE SLEEP

Do recognize that sleep cycles and needs are individualistic.

Do exercise at a consistent time in the morning or afternoon.

Do have a light snack prior to going to bed, thus avoiding a full digestion process.

Do avoid recreational drugs or medications that are stimulants, including tobacco.

Do realize that alcohol is not a sleep aid and, in fact, worsens rather than improves sleep.

Do make a to-do list or concerns (well before bedtime) and put it aside for the next day.

Do keep to a schedule to maintain a consistent sleep time—including weekends.

Do limit quantity and terminate consumption of caffeine at least 6 hours prior to bedtime.

Don't assume that you require 8 hours of sleep.

Don't engage in stimulating activities just prior to bed (i.e., exercise, talking on the phone, working, playing video games).

Don't eat in bed or just prior to bed.

Don't take contraindicated substances or medications.

Don't drink alcohol before bed.

Don't bring your worries to bed.

Don't go to bed at different times.

DURING SLEEP

Do go to another part of the house until you feel ready to fall asleep and return to bed.

Do see bed as appropriate for two activities only: sleep and intimate relations.

Do establish the bedroom as a quiet, dark place with appropriate temperature (consider ear plugs, sleep mask).

Do practice thought stopping, as obsessing on negative thoughts does not facilitate sleep.

Don't lie in bed awake.

Don't engage in stimulating activities (apart from sexual) while in bed.

Don't ignore a poor sleep environment (inside and outside the bedroom).

Don't become preoccupied with thoughts of needing to be asleep.

AFTER SLEEP

Do keep to a schedule to maintain a consistent wake time; avoid weekend catch-up sleep.

Do realize your functioning may be mildly affected; you can work with less sleep.

Do limit sleep to nighttime only; daytime naps often perpetuate the problem.

Don't allow different wake times.

Don't catastrophize social and occupational functioning due to a lack of sleep.

Don't take naps.

Don't drink too much coffee or caffeine.

Treatment Challenges

The general treatment challenges commonly seen in sleep disorders involve motivation and compliance, particularly as symptoms tend to initially worsen rather than improve. It is essential to educate clients about their disorder and explain the various interventions that may be attempted as well as acknowledge the difficulties that may be encountered (M. T. Smith, Smith, Nowakowski, & Perlis, 2003). The clinician should make clear that the therapy will be a process requiring adjustments and solicit from the individual any expectations and concerns. Similarly, the clinician should actively engage clients in taking responsibility and control of their treatment by tailoring interventions to their lifestyle and exploring different habit changes they express a willingness to implement (Moul & Buysse, 2006), as these will be much more difficult than simply taking a pill and falling asleep.

One of the salient concerns with a combination of behavioral and pharmacologic therapy is that individuals who commence treatment with medication will not comply with the behavioral therapy (M. T. Smith et al., 2003). Therefore, it may be best to wean individuals off the medications prior to starting the behavioral interventions to avoid a potential setback in the midst of trying to demonstrate the efficacy of such nonpharmacologic interventions. In this way, medication can provide more immediate results and thus improve motivation for the more difficult and longer time to effectiveness of the behavioral interventions, which then provide long-term effectiveness.

Compliance with CPAP for those with sleep apnea is also particularly difficult (Zozula & Rosen, 2001) as individuals generally find the mask too intrusive or uncomfortable. Design adjustments have been implemented in recent years, but being aware of the positive and negative characteristics of any particular intervention will help the individual's motivation and stamina (Stepanski & Perlis, 2003).

Knowledge about the choice of interventions and the attributes of various treatment options, as well as appropriate clinician-client rapport can all have a positive impact on compliance and keep the individual involved until at least modest gains have been attained.

SEXUAL AND GENDER IDENTITY DISORDERS

Sexual functioning involves a complex interplay of biological, interpersonal, and individual factors. For most individuals, the personal experience of sex remains personal; most sexual disorders are not known by the general populace, nor are they well understood or assessed by a large proportion of those in the medical or mental health fields. Despite a high number of sexual complaints, these disorders appear infrequently in clinical practice, are underrecognized due to poor or nonexistent assessment, and are best treated in specialty programs or by those with specialty training (Laumann, Paik, & Rosen, 1999; Mercer et al., 2003). Consequently, the purpose of this section is to provide a brief review of sexual and gender identity disorders with a focus on identification and assessment and treatment. For more comprehensive coverage, the reader is referred to Stayton (1996), Leiblum and Rosen (2000), Laumann et al. (1999), J. V. Becker and Johnson (2004), and Atwood (2003).

Historical Overview

Sexual disorders were brought to the forefront of psychiatry by Sigmund Freud, who associated them with developmental stages that individuals were presumed to pass through on their way to adulthood. The psychoanalytic formulation and treatment of these disorders dominated until the mid-twentieth century, when more behavioral-oriented interventions were explored (J. P. Brady, 1966; A. J. Cooper, 1969; Wolpe, 1958). Alfred Kinsey's groundbreaking work on sexuality in the 1930s set the stage for Masters and Johnson, in the 1960s and 1970s, to revolutionize our understanding of sexual problems by delineating the *sexual response cycle* (T. Segraves & Althof, 2002; West, Vinikoor, & Zolnoun, 2004). The subsequent emergence of a psychobiological conceptualization coalesced in 1998 with the FDA's approval of sildenafil citrate, commonly known as Viagra, for the treatment of erectile dysfunction.

Sexual disorders first appeared in the *DSM-III* (American Psychiatric Association, 1980), and two new diagnoses—Substance-Induced Sexual Disorder and Sexual Disorder Due to a General Medical Condition—were added in the subsequent edition (American Psychiatric Association, 1994). The *DSM-IV-TR* groups dysfunctions and disorders in the sexual response cycle according to the psychophysiologic phases of desire, arousal, and orgasm (American Psychiatric Association, 2000b). A disturbance in sexual functioning may be composed of one or more of these phases, or may arise from pain that is experienced in the context of sexual activity (Clayton, 2003). The *disorders of desire* are Hypoactive Sexual Desire Disorder and Sexual Aversion Disorder. *Disorders of arousal* are Female Sexual Arousal Disorder and Male Erectile Disorder. *Disorders of orgasm* are Female Orgasmic Disorder, Male Orgasmic Disorder, and Premature Ejaculation. All of these sexual disorders are highly interrelated and can co-occur (K. B. Segraves & Segraves, 1991). The *sexual pain disorders* are Dyspareunia (which can occur in both sexes) and Vaginismus (which is exclusive to females). Both of the sexual pain disorders can be a symptom as well as a diagnosis, and each may serve as a causal factor for the other (First & Tasman, 2004).

Sexual Dysfunction

Clinical Presentation and Diagnostic Considerations

Given the heterogeneity, diagnostic overlap, and co-occurrence factors, the prevalence of sexual disorders has been difficult to determine (Clayton, 2003). Hypoactive Sexual Desire and Premature Ejaculation are two of the most common sexual dysfunctions diagnosed in women and men, respectively (Broderick, 2006; West et al., 2004). The course of sexual disorders can be extremely varied, and the *DSM-IV-TR* provides diagnostic specifiers to distinguish between acquired and lifelong, generalized or situational, conjoint or solitary, and psychological or combined factors (American Psychiatric Association, 2000b). Etiology is often multifaceted, and neurological, infectious, endocrine, and vascular conditions, among many others, can affect sexual functioning (Clayton, 2003). Consideration should be given to psychological aspects (i.e., performance anxiety, guilt, poor body image, or self-esteem issues) and comorbid psychiatric problems. For example, Major Depressive Disorder and eating disorders reduce sexual desire, and Schizophrenia can affect orgasmic dysfunction (Aizenberg, Zemishlany, Dorfman-Etrog, & Weizman, 1995; M. J. Kaplan, 2002; W. K. Reynolds, 2006). Cultural context may play a role as individuals often obtain their knowledge of sex and develop their sexual values through sources such as the family, the community, and religious tenets. Interpersonal dynamics may be a primary or contributory cause stemming from power struggles, a lack of communication, and/or abandonment or trust issues.

One of the crucial considerations in diagnosing a sexual disorder is that it not be better accounted for by substance use or a medical condition, either or both of which are commonly implicated. Numerous illnesses and various classes of drugs (prescribed and recreational) can negatively impact sexual functioning. The *DSM-IV-TR* provides specific diagnostic codes for substance-induced sexual dysfunction due to the following substances: alcohol, amphetamines, cocaine, opioids, sedatives, hypnotics, and anxiolytics (American Psychiatric Association, 2000b). Commonly prescribed medications such as antihypertensives, diuretics, vasodilators, antidepressants, neuroleptics, anabolic steroids, and anticonvulsants have also been shown to induce or exacerbate sexual dysfunction (First & Tasman, 2004; Schiavi & Segraves, 1995). Disease or illness such as diabetes mellitus, multiple sclerosis, Crohn's disease, thyroid dysfunction, and hypogonadism are often associated with sexual disorders (Clayton, 2003; McConaghy & Lowy, 2000; Sun et al., 2006), and desire disorders in particular can be affected by chronic pain or fatigue.

Paraphilias

Clinical Presentation and Diagnostic Considerations

A second grouping of sexual disorders, known as *paraphilias*, represent the seeking of sexual pleasure in unusual or unconventional ways, and are overwhelmingly found to occur in men. Paraphilias may be impulsive behaviors (such as Exhibitionism) or planned behaviors (such as Pedophilia). The various disorders involve both criminal acts (Pedophilia, Sexual Sadism, Exhibitionism, Voyeurism, Frotteurism), and noncriminal behavior (Fetishism, Transvestic Fetishism, Sexual Masochism; Seto, 2004). Usually, two or more paraphilias are exhibited together. Individuals typically come to the attention of treatment providers after being referred by the legal system (Maletzky, 2002). However, an essential diagnostic consideration in this context is the use of clinical judgment in regard to the continuum of what is normal and what is abnormal regarding sexual activity. Assigning a diagnosis may generally be based on the potential to cause harm or the presence of significant personal or societal distress. Pertinent questions to consider are: Does the paraphilia supersede or displace normal sexual behavior? and Is there an aggressive or dehumanizing aspect to the behavior? Key features of the sexual disorders can be found in Table 13.7.

Gender Identity Disorders

Clinical Presentation

Much like the sexual disorders, *gender identity disorders* are not rare, but they are rarely discussed in the clinical literature or diagnosed (First & Tasman, 2004). Also, similar to the sexual disorders, gender identity occurs on a continuum. These individuals may not feel stereotypically male or female, but they may not experience marked distress over it or they may exhibit socially acceptable behaviors (i.e., girls who are labeled "tomboys"). Gender identity, which derives from one's self-perception as male or female, is influenced by both biological and environmental factors (Risen, 1995). In this diagnostic category, it is important to recognize that homosexuality is an orientation, not a gender identity. Thus, an individual with a gender identity disorder might be homosexual, heterosexual, bisexual, or asexual. A multitude of factors may be implicated in gender identity disturbance, ranging from temperament, attachment difficulties, parental or familial issues, trauma, illness, and social and environmental characteristics (R. A. Carroll, 2000).

Table 13.7   Sexual disorders: key features

Hypoactive Sexual Desire Disorder	Lack of sexual desire or fantasies
Sexual Aversion Disorder	Aversion or avoidance of genital sexual contact with a partner
Female Sexual Arousal Disorder	Failure to attain or maintain appropriate sexual excitement response
Male Erectile Disorder	Failure to attain or maintain sufficient level of erection
Female Orgasmic Disorder	Absent or delayed orgasm following normal level of excitement
Male Orgasmic Disorder	Absent or delayed orgasm following normal level of excitement
Premature Ejaculation	Ejaculation that occurs before, during, or just after penetration
Dyspareunia	Genital pain occurring/associated with sexual intercourse (male or female)
Vaginismus	Involuntary vaginal spasm that interferes with sexual intercourse
Exhibitionism	Exposing one's genitals to strangers
Fetishism	The use of objects or devices for sexual stimulation
Frotteurism	Touching or rubbing against a nonconsenting person
Pedophilia	Sexual activity with a prepubescent child by one who is minimally 16 years of age and 5 years older than the child
Sexual Masochism	Being humiliated, bound, beaten, or otherwise made to suffer as part of sexual activity
Sexual Sadism	The suffering of another is sexually stimulating
Transvestic Fetishism	Heterosexual males using crossdressing as sexual stimulation
Voyeurism	Watching others who are nude or engaged in sexual activity and are unaware of the observation

Intake and Interviewing Considerations

The crucial first step in a sexual disorders evaluation is to refer the individual for a complete physical examination to rule out medical illness and/or substance use as the source of the dysfunction. The most challenging aspect of the intake is that, for many individuals, sex can be a difficult topic to discuss. Several strategies and issues to consider are presented in Table 13.8. Clinicians themselves may find it problematic to broach the subject without appearing too intrusive (Clayton, 2003). They may think that they lack appropriate knowledge or feel uncomfortable or concerned that they will cause a sense of arousal or interest by inquiring about sex (Risen, 1995). Attaining a comfort level requires self-examination by the clinician as well as recognition of the clinical utility in performing a thorough assessment. Given these issues, rapport is exceedingly important in a sexual disorders evaluation, and the clinician should be sensitive to the potential for embarrassment, guilt, shame, fear, ignorance, and feelings of inadequacy (Clayton, 2001).

An unstructured interview typically works best and allows the clinician to determine the context of the individual's problems (McConaghy, 2002). Individuals should be asked to describe their symptoms and why they are seeking treatment at this time. Questions should be directed toward ascertaining the onset, frequency, duration, setting, and

Table 13.8   Intake considerations: sexual and gender identity disorders

Be respectful; broach topics according to patient's comfort level and willingness to divulge.
Refer for medical evaluation to rule out organic causes and current medical health.
Assess for possible contributions of medications or illness.
Assess for comorbid conditions, especially mood, anxiety, and substance-related disorders.
Use appropriate language (i.e., not overly clinical or slang terms).
Use sensitivity in regard to client's fears of inadequacy, embarrassment, etc.
Consider ethnic, sociocultural, religious factors.
Employ open-ended questions.
Evaluate sexual practices and functioning: desire, arousal, orgasm, satisfaction.
Obtain prior sexual history: frequency and type of experiences.
Obtain sexual medical history, including STDs, surgeries.
Ask about high-risk sexual or impulsive behaviors.
Assess past or current sexual abuse.
Assess sexual expectations (may be unrealistic; performance varies with age).
Evaluate gender identity and sexual orientation.
Explore beliefs about sexual intimacy.
Inquire about how the individual communicates sexual feelings and wishes to others.
Explore fantasies and sexual behavior to reveal paraphilic intent.
Assess potential emotional factors: anxiety, depression, anger, etc.
Assess environmental and lifestyle changes or stressors: job change, marital discord, new baby, etc.
Meet with couple conjointly and individually for potential privacy.
Be aware that adolescents may be reluctant to discuss these issues.
Do not assume that older adults are not sexually active.

circumstances of the sexual dysfunction (see Table 13.8). For example, Does it happen during every sexual experience? With a partner only? During masturbation and/or intercourse? During a particular time of day or night? In addition to the standard components of any assessment (current and past medical, psychiatric, educational, occupational, and psychosocial history, substance use, etc.), the presenting problem needs to be evaluated in terms of the actual behavior, possible stimulus triggers, similar problems or treatment, current stressors or lifestyle changes, and sexual history (Risen, 1995). First sexual memories, degree of parental displays of affection toward one another, familial attitudes toward sex, experiences with masturbation, age at first sexual experience with a partner, sexual orientation, dating and relationship history, history of sexually traumatic experiences, and history of sexual difficulties are among some of the areas that should be inquired about (L'Abate & Bagarozzim, 1993). The level of the client's impairment may be circumscribed to the personal realm and include embarrassment, pain, and/or self-esteem issues, or it may involve an interpersonal component in which frustration, anger, or disappointment is experienced by one or both partners (Broderick, 2006; Clayton, 2003). Furthermore, the impact of the disorder on other forms of functioning may help discern possible etiologies or coexisting problems that are related to affective, interpersonal, or characterological issues, all of which can influence the course, treatment, and outcome of a sexual disorder (McConagy & Lowy, 2000).

Another important aspect in taking a sexual history is an exploration of the individual's beliefs about what normal sexual functioning entails. The clinician should be aware that psychoeducation may be necessary if assumptions are made regarding not meeting a certain standard or if there are expectations that are inappropriate for that individual (e.g., sex a certain number of times per week or duration of sexual activity). Interviewing collateral sources, such as a partner, can be invaluable; however, be aware that a symptomatic individual may not want to share certain information in front of his or her partner. Emotional and relationship difficulties or issues may be the primary problem for some clients presenting with sexual dysfunction, and sexual difficulties can exist as a result of an extramarital affair, incompatibility of sexual identity, or childhood abuse (Laumann et al., 1999). The clinician should be sensitive to the individual's issues and needs and modify the evaluation accordingly (i.e., individual interview only, individual and then conjoint interview). As in all assessments, age, culture, ethnicity, religion, and sexual history will play a role in the decision to assign a sexual disorders diagnosis.

Treatment

General Principles in Treating Sexual Disorders

There are currently no widely used standardized treatments for sexual disorders and, consequently, there is a lack of information on prognosis (R. C. Rosen & Leiblum, 1995). Although treatment was formerly etiologically driven, with mental health professionals handling the psychological dysfunctions and medical professionals (such as urologists) managing the organic conditions, mental health providers are currently considered integral to the treatment of all these disorders due to the involvement of psychological factors in the treatment process (T. Segraves & Althof, 2002). If there is an organic basis, the clinician should work in tandem with the physician to treat the underlying problem with medication and/or surgery and concomitantly deal with interpersonal issues that may be associated with or exacerbating symptoms. In psychogenic cases, there may be a need to explore the possible functionality of the problem or the potential underlying meaning of the sexual symptom (Risen, 1995).

Disorder-Specific Treatments

Sexual Dysfunction   The essential goal of treatment is to restore the individual's sexual function and satisfaction, and treatment models span the pharmacologic, cognitive-behavioral, and psychodynamic realms. An important corollary of any sexual disorder therapy is the role of the partner in the treatment process (First & Tasman, 2004). The partner's active involvement in certain disorders is imperative, particularly in terms of relapse. Most forms of sexual disorder are likely to affect two people, and contributory or maintenance factors may be a result of interpersonal dynamics (Bancroft et al., 2003). Community surveys have shown that sexual satisfaction has more to do with the "emotional relationship" rather than the actual sexual dysfunction (McConaghy, 1993). In some cases, sexual dysfunction will spontaneously remit or remit slowly over time.

Psychotherapy is particularly pertinent if there is a history of sexual trauma (L. A. Berman, Berman, Bruck, Pawar, & Goldstein, 2001). For the desire disorders, treatment is usually long term and often includes couples therapy, given the likelihood of individual or interpersonal issues that exist in the context of the dysfunction. These require time to be uncovered and processed. Therapy may also be short term and symptom-focused and often utilizes psychoeducation to help mitigate cultural inhibitions and, in some cases, ignorance of bodily needs and sensations. The effectiveness of hormone replacement therapy, which was historically prescribed, is still inconclusive (O'Carroll, 1991; R. C. Rosen & Leiblum, 1995). In cases of premature ejaculation, behavioral techniques such as desensitization, the stop-start technique, and sensate focus may be used along with hypnosis (Zilbergeld & Hammond, 1988), guided fantasy exercises, and assertiveness training (McCabe, 1992). Many of these techniques also apply to the treatment of pain disorders. External vacuum devices, intracavernosal injection, and penile prostheses are the common treatments used for erectile dysfunction (T. Segraves & Althof, 2002). Medication may be prescribed for some disorders; both estrogen and bupropion have been shown to aid desire disorders (J. R. Berman et al., 2001; R. T. Segraves et al., 2001; Shifren et al., 2000), and serotonergic medications and sildenafil are widely used for the treatment of premature ejaculation and erectile dysfunction, respectively (Broderick, 2006; I. Goldstein et al., 1998).

Paraphilias   Generally, a multimodal approach is appropriate for treating paraphilias and may comprise psychotherapy, medication, and external controls. Cognitive-behavioral interventions (e.g., aversive therapy) and behavioral treatments (e.g., social skills training) are often combined with group therapy and/or marital therapy, with an emphasis on recognizing the victimization the paraphilia can cause rather than rationalizing it away (Maletzky, 2002). Aversion therapies are based on classical conditioning theory and involve pairing an aversive stimulus with a deviant sexual response to decrease the likelihood that the deviant sexual behavior will occur again. Aversive agents have included electric shock and imagined aversives (e.g., visualizing an embarrassing or physically painful scene in association with a deviant sexual fantasy); the latter process is known as *covert sensitization* and also typically includes visualization of a relief scene in association with nondeviant behavior (Maletsky, 2002). In *positive conditioning techniques* clients are reinforced for nondeviant sexual behavior (e.g., asked to masturbate using deviant fantasies to the point of climax and then switch to visualizing a nondeviant scene) or for removing themselves from a situation with the potential for deviant behavior (e.g., having clients imagining successfully leaving a situation in which they were about to expose themselves; Maletsky, 2002).

Pharmacologically, serotonergic agents and gonadotropin-releasing blockers are sometimes used (First & Tasman, 2004). For those individuals whose paraphilias have brought them into conflict with the legal system, mandated treatment can be a difficult and frustrating process. Treatment with offenders may take place in group settings, which has the advantage of being an efficient forum in which to disseminate psychoeducational information (e.g., the rationale for aversive conditioning) and for challenging the denial and minimization clients may engage in regarding the consequences of their behavior (Maletsky, 2002). However, individual treatment sessions often supplement group work and allow opportunities to focus on the unique set of historical, psychological, biological, and behavioral variables that have contributed to a client's deviant sexual behavior. There is a paucity of studies on treatment effectiveness and outcomes for paraphilias, rendering generalizations somewhat inappropriate.

Gender Identity Disorder   Treatment for Gender Identity Disorder can be a long and complicated process and often includes either family members or partners (R. A. Carroll, 2000). The approach is multidisciplinary and requires a mental health team and medical specialists. At the extreme end of the treatment spectrum, the individual undergoes a gender transformation process, which commences with a thorough evaluation and self-analysis and proceeds to cross-dressing (to experience life as the chosen gender), hormone therapy, a year spent living as the chosen gender, and surgery to become the chosen gender (known as sex reassignment surgery [SRS]). Because of the radical nature of SRS and the potential medical complications that go along with any major surgery, consideration of this procedure, as well as for the less drastic hormone replacement treatment, require written referrals by qualified psychotherapists who have treated the client (G. R. Brown, 2001). Psychotherapy focuses on providing psychoeducation to the client, an exploration of feelings of secrecy, shame, and guilt that frequently permeate the lives of these individuals from an early age, conveying that clients have rights to make lifestyle choices that respect their cross-gender feeling and may include living in the preferred gender role, and discussing treatment and lifestyle options (e.g., cross-dressing privately, living publicly as a cross-dressing individual, undergoing SRS; G. R. Brown, 2001). An excellent source for standards of care in this treatment can be found through the Harry Benjamin International Gender Dysphoria Association (S. B. Levine, et al., 1998).

Life Span Considerations

An important consideration in sexual and gender identity disorders is the impact of life span issues (Laumann et al., 1999). Many individuals fail to recognize that sexual changes over the life span are normal and that each age group tends to have a different, albeit potentially overlapping, emphasis. For adolescents, it is about forming a sexual identity; for young adults, it is about exploring boundaries and growing comfortable as a sexual being; for those in middle adulthood, it is handling the intimacy and complexities of maintaining a long-term relationship as well as learning to cope with psychological and external impingements; and for those in late adulthood, it is dealing with the inability to maintain previous functioning given biological factors (e.g., aging, menopause) and sequelae of illness (including medication and surgery; Leiblum & Segraves, 2000). Gender Identity Disorder typically manifests in the adolescent years but may not become problematic until young adulthood or beyond. Individuals generally present for treatment just after they first start engaging in sexual behavior, but many individuals will present later in life, delaying treatment for years until they are in a significant long-term relationship that draws attention to the need to resolve the issue.

ADVANCED TOPIC: EATING DISORDERS ACROSS THE LIFE SPAN

Infancy and Childhood

Although the majority of eating disordered individuals fall in the adolescent to young adult age range, the disorder can manifest, albeit rarely, in children. The *DSM-IV-TR* (American Psychiatric Association, 2000b) diagnostic criteria for Anorexia Nervosa specifically addresses pediatric and developmental growth issues for those younger than the typical age of onset due to the need to address unique medical complications such as reduced bone mass, growth retardation, and pubertal delay or arrest that may occur (Nicholls & Stanhope, 2000). Although research on this population is scarce, the clinical presentation of

Anorexia Nervosa and Bulimia Nervosa in young children appears to be very similar to that in adults in terms of disordered eating, compulsive behaviors, and a preoccupation with body weight and shape (Watkins & Lask, 2002). In younger children, excessive exercise and self-induced vomiting tend to be more common than laxative or diuretic use (Bryant-Waugh & Lask, 2002). No evidence-based treatments currently exist, but both assessment and intervention would necessitate consideration of the child's developmental issues and psychosocial context, with an emphasis on familial dynamics and the home environment given that the child's caregivers will be helping to manage the child's treatment.

Pica, Rumination Disorder, and Feeding Disorder of Infancy or Early Childhood were previously subsumed under the eating disorders category in the *DSM* until being reclassified as *feeding and eating disorders of infancy or early childhood* in 1994. Before diagnosing any of these disorders, a full medical evaluation is recommended to rule out potential physiological causes (Rudolph & Link, 2002). Pica is the repeated eating of nonnutritive substances, such as paint, plaster, hair, string, animal feces, sand, and rocks (American Psychiatric Association, 2000b). This disorder is more prevalent in lower socioeconomic communities and in developing countries (Wren & Tarbell, 1998) and is rarely observed in adolescents and adults. Although the etiology is currently unknown, risk factors include an impoverished environment, neglect and maltreatment, poverty, and family or parental issues (Hakim-Larson, Voelker, Thomas, & Reinstein, 1997). Pica can result in medical complications such as bowel obstruction or lead poisoning and is an associated feature of Pervasive Developmental Disorder and mental retardation. The disorder typically remits after several months. Treatment tends to focus on improving the environment and parental supervision as well as behavioral interventions (K. E. Bell & Stein, 1992; W. W. Fisher et al., 1994).

Rumination Disorder is characterized by the repeated regurgitation of food and weight loss (American Psychiatric Association, 2000b). Regurgitation is defined as partially digested food that is brought back up into the mouth and subsequently ejected or rechewed and swallowed. The regurgitation may cause malnutrition and can result in weight loss and even death (G. T. Wilson et al., 2003). Rumination is a rare disorder that is primarily seen in infants and occurs more commonly in males and in those with mental retardation (Wren & Tarbell, 1998). The onset is typically between 3 and 12 months, with a course that can be either continuous or intermittent and frequently has spontaneous remission. Risk factors for this condition include lack of stimulation, neglect, stress, and parent-child relational problems. Interventions may involve parent training and the employment of incompatible behaviors (Linscheid & Bennett-Murphy, 1999).

Feeding Disorder of Infancy or Early Childhood, or "failure to thrive," involves a persistent failure to eat adequately, resulting in insufficient weight gain or significant weight loss (American Psychiatric Association, 2000b). All of these infants suffer from malnutrition, which may be life-threatening, but problems may also span the psychological, developmental, and social realms. Prevalence rates vary depending on the setting (Drotar, 1995; Linscheid & Bennett-Murphy, 1999), but the disorder has been observed equally in males and females. The etiology is unclear, but common risk factors include problematic caregiver-child interaction, infant characteristics, family problems, and an impoverished and/or stressful environment (Benoit, 2000; Chatoor, Ganiban, Colin, Plummer, & Harmon, 1998; Valenzuela, 1990). Treatment is multidimensional, with a focus on responding to the family's needs, particularly in terms of addressing the provision of an appropriate environment for the child.

Although not a disorder in the *DSM*, *childhood obesity* has been the focus of recent concern as a growing epidemic, with a dramatic increase in prevalence over the past few decades (Wilfley & Saelens, 2002). The state of being overweight does not necessarily imply disordered eating, and an assessment of a child's genetics, metabolism, level of exercise, and diet (in terms of content and quantity) should be an initial consideration (Nicholls & Bryant-Waugh, 2003). It remains to be seen what impact the current level of childhood obesity will have on eating disorders.

Middle Adulthood and the Elderly

Eating disorders can manifest in older adults, and although an onset of Anorexia Nervosa after age 40 is very rare, case studies of anorexia in the elderly have been reported, including new onset in a 92-year-old (Mermelstein & Basu, 2001; Pobee & LaPalio, 1996). Many eating disorders in the geriatric population are more commonly observed as food refusal, which differs from the eating disturbance in younger age groups due to a lower degree of weight preoccupation and disturbed body image (E. M. Berry & Marcus, 2000).

Perhaps the most common diagnosis for this age range, however, is binge-eating disorder, a research category in the *DSM-IV-TR* (American Psychiatric Association, 2000b) that is similar to bulimia in its binge-eating presentation but differs due to the absence of compensatory strategies. Onset occurs in adulthood for approximately half of these individuals, and it is diagnosable as an ED-NOS (Abbott et al., 1998). Binge-eating disorder affects both men and women of different ethnicities, and most are obese. Prevalence varies from 2.0% to 4.6% in community samples (Spitzer et al., 1992) to 15% to 70% for those seeking weight control treatment (such as Overeaters Anonymous; M. B. Schwartz & Brownell, 1998; Spitzer et al., 1993). Similar to the theories underlying Bulimia Nervosa, dietary restraint and interpersonal vulnerability (i.e., insecure attachment and affective dysregulation) have been posited as etiologically salient (M. B. Schwartz & Brownell, 2001). Both CBT and interpersonal therapy have been shown to be effective (Wilfley, Stein, & Welch, 2003). Controlled medication trials have also shown antidepressants to be efficacious in the treatment of binge-eating disorder (Arnold, McElroy, Hudson, Welge, & Bennett, 2002; McElroy, Hudson, Malhotra, Welge, & Nelson, 2003).

Chapter 14

PERSONALITY DISORDERS

Webster's (1999) defines *personality* as "the state or quality of being a person and those special characteristics that distinguish a person." Our individual personality defines our identity and describes our unique way of interpreting and interacting with the world. It influences our expression of emotions, our response to adversity, our selection of friends, our decisions and life choices, how we define and see ourselves. It grows and changes as we do and it is not maladaptive by nature, except when it sets us apart and fails to adapt to the vagaries and vicissitudes of life. The *DSM-IV-TR* describes a personality disorder (PD) thus: "An enduring pattern of inner experience and behavior that deviates markedly from the expectations of the individual's culture"; "the enduring pattern is inflexible and pervasive," has an onset in adolescence or early adulthood, is stable over time, and leads to distress or impairment (American Psychiatric Association, 2000b, p. 689).

B. F. Grant and colleagues (Grant, Hasin, Stinson, Dawson., Chou, & Ruan, 2004) found that in the general population in 2000 to 2001, 14.79% of Americans, or 30.8 million, met the diagnostic criteria for at least one PD. In reviewing epidemiological research, Torgersen (2005) notes that PDs occur in more than 1 in 10 adults, are most prevalent in lower educated individuals who live alone in urban areas, and are associated with significant social and occupational impairment. Individuals usually do not seek treatment for their PD, and it is rarely a focus of treatment, which is often directed at comorbid Axis I disorders. Failure to identify the presence of a PD, particularly in the context of an Axis I disorder, can adversely impact the therapeutic alliance, resulting in ineffective treatment and compliance issues, with the individual being labeled as treatment-resistant or dropping out of therapy (McClanahan et al., 2003; J.C. Perry & Bond, 2000). The presence of PDs in clinical practice has also been underestimated because of the lack of comprehensive assessments and the limited financial resources available for appropriate treatment (First & Tasman, 2004; Levy & Scott, 2006).

In an effort to draw attention to these disorders, the *DSM* placed PDs on a separate axis (Axis II); however, this is controversial, with many clinicians still calling for a dimensional approach (Livesley, 2001; Widiger & Mullins-Sweatt, 2005). The *DSM-IV-TR* describes 10 disorders: Paranoid, Schizoid, Schizotypal, Antisocial, Borderline, Histrionic, Narcissistic, Avoidant, Dependent, and Obsessive-Compulsive (American Psychiatric Association, 2000b). Of individuals in clinical settings, more than 50% can be diagnosed with a PD, and 47% to 50% of correctional facility inmates may receive an Antisocial PD diagnosis (Coid, 2005; First & Tasman, 2004; Widiger & Corbitt, 1995). As many as 60% of psychiatric inpatients may meet criteria for Borderline PD (American Psychiatric Association,

2000b; Gunderson, 2001; Mattia & Zimmerman, 2001) and individuals with Dependent, Borderline, Obsessive-Compulsive, Avoidant, and Schizotypal PDs are overrepresented in clinical populations (Torgersen, 2005). For most individuals treatment is long term and may involve hospitalization and concurrent medication (Gabbard, 2000a; Gunderson, Gratz, Neuhaus, & Smith, 2005; A. Roth & Fonagy, 2006). Given the pervasive and inflexible nature of the clinical presentation, these are often the most challenging clients for clinicians (Gutheil, 2005). Suicidal behavior is found in the histories of 55% to 70% of individuals with a PD, and in 60% to 78% of individuals with a Borderline PD. Individuals with Borderline PD account for 12% of all psychiatric emergency room visits and represent 9% to 33% of all suicides (Links & Kolla, 2005). These are also the clients who often provoke the strongest reactions and boundary violations in clinicians, from the need to rescue to hatred, and even inappropriate sexual relationships (Gutheil, 2005).

HISTORICAL OVERVIEW

Personality functioning has been of interest to human beings as early as Hippocrates, who in the fifth century BC described four personality styles related to imbalances among the four humors of the body (McClanahan et al., 2003). The overly optimistic or extroverted, sanguine type was caused by blood imbalances, and the pessimistic or melancholic type related to excessive black bile. Yellow bile resulted in the irritable, hostile, or choleric type, and lymph imbalances contributed to the apathetic or phlegmatic type. Since then personality types have been linked by Gall to differences in skull contours (phrenology), by Sheldon to morphology or body type, by Freud (1952) to stages of psychosexual development, and by Erikson (1950) to stages of ego development (First et al., 2004). Building on earlier theories of attachment and object relations, Schore (1994) integrated empirical research from developmental psychology to describe the development of personality. With the development of psychological assessment measures, theories have emerged describing personality in terms of underlying factors and dimensions. The most prominent of these include Millon's (1996) evolutionary-based social learning theory, Cloninger's (2000) character model, Widiger and colleagues' (Widiger, Trull, Clarkin, Sanderson, & Costa, 2002) application of the five-factor model to PDs, and Morey's (1991) and Livesley and colleagues' (Livesley, Jackson, & Schroeder, 1992) research using assessment measures. Initially, this research focused on the nonpathological development of personality; more recently, these theories and measures have been incorporated into the study of PDs and clinical populations, as in the Collaborative Longitudinal Personality Disorders Study (First & Tasman 2004; Gunderson, Shea, Skodol, et al., 2000; Widiger, 2005). The disorders in this category do not share a common origin, and although some have been known for several decades and have been the subject of theoretical models, particularly psychoanalytic, many of these theories lack empirical support and have yet to be validated (Levy & Scott, 2006). A brief review of the history of each PD helps to frame the discussion of the current diagnostic conceptualization.

Paranoid

The term *paranoid* comes from the Greek term *paranous*, meaning "beside the mind" (LaBruzza & Mendez-Villarrubia, 1997; Regehr & Glancy, 1999). According to Lewis

(1970) and M. B. Miller, Useda, Trull, Burr, & Minks-Brown (2001), in 1818, Heinroth described paranoia as primarily affecting the individual's ability to understand, and as co-occurring with delusions, bizarre behavior, and mood disorders. Heinroth identified several types of paranoia including a gross distortion of reality due to a single misconception, delusions of the supernatural, and megalomania. Later Esquirol (1838) wrote about a group of disorders (monomania) that were characterized by delusions with no impairment in cognition or behavior (Regehr & Glancy, 1999). In 1921, Kraepelin coined the term *paranoid personality* and identified several types of paranoia, including the presence of a persistent or insidious fixed delusional system without hallucinations or personality deterioration (Akhtar, 1990; Manschrek, 1979, 1992). Continuing in this vein, his student E. Bleuler described individuals who presented with suspiciousness, grandiosity, and feelings of persecution as having "contentious psychopathy" or "paranoid constitution" (Akhtar, 1990). Freud (1952) theorized that the defense mechanism of projection facilitated paranoid tendencies. He later noted the role of an aggressive disposition and early experiences of threat in the development of paranoia (Regehr & Glancy, 1999). Further clinical descriptions were provided by Leonhard (1959), Shepherd (1961), and Polatin (1975), who described individuals who were suspicious, critical, constantly felt mistreated, blamed their failures on others' ill will, accumulate trivial incidents as proof of their accusations, and were emotionally undemonstrative. The first version of the *DSM* included a brief description of Paranoid Personality (American Psychiatric Association, 1952). Beginning with the *DSM-III*, diagnostic criteria were based on clinical literature, and the defining features included a pervasive, unwarranted mistrust of others, hypersensitivity to criticism, antagonism, aggressiveness, hypervigilance, rigidity, and excessive need for autonomy (M. B. Miller et al., 2001).

Schizoid

E. Bleuler (1922) coined the term *schizoid* to describe individuals who were turned inward, away from the world, and appeared indifferent to others and to pleasure. Their expression of emotions was muted, and they appeared aimless, dull, and had underdeveloped interests (Bernstein & Travaglini, 1999; Levy & Scott, 2006). Later, British object relation theorists (Fairbairn, 1952; Guntrip, 1969; Winnicott, 1991) broadened the description to include individuals who have difficulty with intimacy and a broad range of behavioral peculiarities, including depersonalization, derealization, and a fragmented sense of self (Levy & Scott, 2006). A brief description of Schizoid PD was first introduced in *DSM-I* emphasizing inherent traits, such as the avoidance of close relationships with others (American Psychiatric Association, 1952; M. B. Miller et al., 2001). Specific diagnostic criteria were developed with the *DSM-III*, which focused on emotional coldness, aloofness, lack of tender feelings for others, and an indifference to praise and criticism and to the feelings of others (American Psychiatric Association, 1980).

Schizotypal

The major early precedent for Schizotypal PD was Bleuler's concept of latent Schizophrenia, which he applied to individuals who exhibited mild or attenuated symptoms of Schizophrenia but did not deteriorate in the classic manner described by Kraepelin (M. B.

Miller et al., 2001). Rado (1953) first used the term *schizotype* as an abbreviation of schizophrenic phenotype (First et al., 2004). Early clinical studies (Meehl, 1962; Spitzer, Endicott, & Gibbon, 1979) used the terms schizotypy, borderline, ambulatory schizophrenic, and pseudo-neurotic schizophrenic to describe individuals who had a genetic predisposition to developing Schizophrenia but who displayed only mild symptoms (Bernstein & Travaglini, 1999; Levy & Scott, 2006). Kety, Rosenthal, Wender & Schulsinger (1968) and Kety, Wender, et al. (1994), in their remarkable series of Danish adoption studies, identified similar clinical presentations in the biological relatives of chronic schizophrenics. These individuals presented with features including peculiar ideas and inappropriate affect, but did not have the frank psychotic features associated with Schizophrenia (Kety et al., 1968; Kety et al., 1994). The term Schizotypal PD was first introduced in the *DSM-III* and was used as it suggested Schizophrenic-like, which was consistent with the clinical presentation of a phenotypic resemblance to Schizophrenia (Oldham, 2005). The diagnostic criteria were derived from descriptions of the relatives of chronic schizophrenics in the Danish adoption studies (Spitzer et al., 1979). The *DSM-IV* considered whether Schizotypal PD should be moved to Axis I and included it in the Schizophrenia and other psychotic disorders section, thus recognizing the spectrum relationship between it and Schizophrenia. In the *ICD-10*, Schizotypal is included as an early-onset disorder that is a variant of chronic Schizophrenia (First & Tasman, 2004). However, as First and colleagues (2004, p. 358) note, "For no compelling reason the Task Force decided to keep Schizotypal PD in the PD section of the *DSM-IV*."

Antisocial

According to Levy & Scott (2006) antisocial traits and behaviors have been described in literature from the earliest time and by most of the fathers of psychiatric classification, including Pinel (1809), Kraepelin (1921), K. Schneider (1923), and A. Meyer (1957). Starting from the concept of impulsion or impulsive insanity, which was later replaced by psychopathy, a range of terms have been used over the years, including sociopathy, moral insanity, and dyssocial personality disorder (*ICD*). Early influential research describing psychopathy was provided in Cleckley's (1941) book *The Mask of Sanity,* by Hare's (1970) theory and research on psychopathy, and by Robbins's (1966) study on the development of sociopathic personality. The designation Antisocial PD was introduced into the *DSM-II* and included inferences and traits closely tied to Cleckley's description of psychopathy (Sutker & Allain, 2001). In the *DSM-III* the diagnosis was assigned based on a frequency count using a long checklist of antisocial behaviors based on Robins's (1966) research, on deviant children and sociopathy including an onset before 15 years (American Psychiatric Association, 1980; First et al., 2004; Sutker & Allain, 2001). There was widespread criticism of the validity, length, and complexity of these criteria, their neglect of psychopathy, and their tendency to overdiagnose in criminal and forensics settings and to underdiagnose in noncriminal settings and white-collar crime (First et al., 2004; Levy & Scott, 2005). With the *DSM-IV* an effort was made to reflect the traits of psychopathy and to simplify the criteria without substantially changing the diagnosis. The field trials failed to provide conclusive support for including psychopathy items, and, given the high threshold for change, they were not included in the final diagnostic criteria (Sutker & Allain, 2001).

Borderline

The term *borderline* was first used by the psychoanalyst Stern (1938) to describe individuals on the border between neurosis and psychosis. These individuals presented with a range of characteristics, including psychic bleeding and rigidity, negative therapeutic reactions, inordinate hypersensitivity, affective lability, and chronic suicide attempts (H. E. Adams, Bernaty, & Luscher, 2001; Paris, 1999). Kernberg (1975a, 2004) subsequently used the term to describe a primitive level of personality organization. A major advance in the conceptualization of the disorder occurred when Gunderson and Singer (1975) operationalized the definition, and it was subsequently reliably distinguished from other disorders (Gunderson & Kolb, 1978; Paris, 1999; Perry & Klerman, 1978). In 1979, Spitzer and colleagues surveyed members of the American Psychiatric Association and asked them to rate their patients using items that then formed the basis of the *DSM-III* Borderline PD diagnostic criteria (M. B. Miller et al., 2001). The term Borderline PD was retained as the survey also indicated its common clinical usage; however, this remains controversial and in the *ICD-10* Borderline PD is classified as an "emotionally unstable personality" (Paris, 1999; Spitzer et al., 1979).

Histrionic

Histrionic PD was previously known as Hysterical PD. The early roots of this disorder are linked to Hippocrates' use of the Greek term *hystera* in describing a womb that wandered too close to the brain and caused excessive and wild emotionality or hysterical behavior (Bornstein, 1999; Levy & Scott, 2006). Over the centuries it has described a range of behaviors, including extreme fickleness, sexual provocativeness, immaturity, self-centeredness, and suggestibility (S. M. Johnson, 1994). Bornstein (1999) notes that the development of psychoanalytic theory was, in fact, based on Breuer and Freud's (1895) clinical work with individuals with hysteria. Later psychoanalytic theorists describe the clinical presentation as including compliance accompanied by swift deprecation, baseless disparagement, and rigid, maladaptive defenses that serve to keep oral and dependency fantasies out of awareness (Bornstein, 1999; Marmor, 1953; Reich, 1933). There was considerable diagnostic confusion with the term hysteria, and the *DSM-III* replaced Hysterical PD with Histrionic PD, in part because of the former term's historical and sexist connotations. The current diagnostic criteria for Histrionic PD may still represent exaggerated stereotypic feminine traits, and there is an absence of masculine parallels (First et al., 2004; LaBruzza & Mendez-Villarrubia, 1997). The term *histrionic* itself is derived from Latin-Etruscan roots and refers to "a stage player," thus emphasizing the theatrical, overemotional characteristics of the histrionic individual (LaBruzza & Mendez-Villarrubia, 1997; M. H. Stone, 1993). Millon and Davis (2000) describe a manipulative interpersonal style in which these individuals run the risk of alienating others and being left without the excitement they crave.

Narcissistic

The concept of narcissism or self-adoration comes from the Greek myth of Narcissus, who fell in love with his own reflection, pined away, and died (Levy & Scott, 2006; Maxmen & Ward, 1995). The term was initially introduced into psychological literature in case studies and descriptions of male sexual perversions (Ellis, 1898; Nacke, 1899). The first psychoanalytic paper describing different forms of self-love was written by Rank in 1911. Freud (1952) described narcissism initially as a phase in psychosexual development where the self becomes the libidinal object; he then described the development of primary and secondary narcissism, narcissistic object choice, and a narcissistic libidinal character type. Subsequent psychoanalytic writings by Horney (1939), Reich (1960), and Pulver (1970) described the role of narcissism as a defense against threats to the self-esteem and the development of pathological self-esteem. Bernstein and Travaglini (1999) note that throughout the literature a variety of other terms have been used to describe the presentation of this personality style, including God complex, Nobel Prize or Icarus complex, and the glass bubble fantasy (we still await the Oscar complex). The next decades saw two major schools of thought, with Kernberg (1975b, 1989, 1990) developing the concept of Narcissistic PD based on ego psychology and object relations theory. While Kohut (1968, 1971, 1972, 1977) saw narcissism as an arrest or divergent path in the development of the self and founded the self psychology movement. In the 1990s, patterns of early infant-caregiver interactions were identified as influencing the child's biopsychological development and character development (Schore, 1994), and maladaptive cognitive schema were identified as characteristic of narcissistic individuals (J. Young, 1998). Building on early conceptualizations, Millon (1998) described the Narcissistic PD as including such key concepts as inflated sense of self-worth and exploitive interpersonal style. According to A. Frances (1980), the inclusion of Narcissistic PD in the *DSM-III* was based on the increased clinical psychoanalytic literature and its presence in psychological personality studies. The clinical presentation includes grandiosity, preoccupation with fantasies of success and brilliance, feelings of entitlement, interpersonal exploitiveness and devaluation of others, and lack of empathy (American Psychiatric Association, 1980; Widiger & Bornstein, 2001). Of note, this is the only PD not recognized in the *ICD,* and some theorists have suggested it is a distinctly Western cultural manifestation, reflecting a focus on self-centered materialism with a decreasing emphasis on familial and interpersonal ties (Widiger & Bornstein, 2001).

Avoidant

The concept of Avoidant PD was proposed by Millon (1981) to describe those individuals who presented with active detachment, pervasive social inhibition, and low self-esteem (Levy & Scott, 2006). It was related to the earlier clinical and theoretical literature on individuals who were overly sensitive to rejection, highly self-critical, and aversive to interpersonal closeness while longing for it (Bernstein & Travaglini, 1999; Kretschmer, 1925). According to First and colleagues (2004), terms that have been used in the past to describe similar clinical symptoms are aesthetic psychopath (K. Schneider, 1923), phobic character (Fenichel, 1945), and active-detached personality syndrome (Millon, 1981). Research has focused on the role of an inhibited temperament, early adverse experiences, and the role of paternal overprotectiveness in the development of Avoidant PD (Bernstein & Travaglini, 1999). Avoidant PD was first used in the *DSM-III* to describe individuals who were socially withdrawn, hypersensitive to rejection, and isolated because of social anxiety (American Psychiatric Association, 1980). These individuals could be differentiated from Schizoid PD on the basis of the cause of the social isolation. Yet this differentiation remains controversial (M. B. Miller et al., 2001). With the addition of Avoidant and Schizotypal PD to the *DSM-III* there was a marked decrease in the number of cases classified as Schizoid (First et al., 2004), leading Bernstein and Travaglini (1999, p. 524) to wonder if Schizoid PD has not been "gerrymandered out of existence."

Dependent

Early psychoanalytic conceptualizations of pathological dependency focused on oral dependency and the individual's belief that there will always be someone there to play the role of his or her caretaker (K. Abraham, 1911/1927; Fenichel, 1945; Freud, 1952). In the past, individuals with excessive dependency have been described as "shiftless" (Kraepelin, 1913), "weak-willed" (K. Schneider, 1923), gullible, compliant, immature, and easily exploited. In looking at the development of personality styles, Millon and Davis (2000) proposed that a central component for the dependent individual is the need for affection from, security in, and leadership by others. Cognitive theorists have emphasized the core self-belief "I am helpless"; the world is cold, frightening, and lonely, and I need another in order to cope (Bernstein & Travaglini, 1999). Borenstein (1996) integrated early object relations with developmental and cognitive theories and hypothesized that overprotective authoritarian parenting and the socialization of sex roles related to the development of Dependent PD. The term dependent PD was first included in the *DSM-II* and the diagnostic criteria that were developed in the *DSM-III* have been criticized as overly narrow (Widiger & Bornstein, 2001; Zuckerman, 1999).

Obsessive-Compulsive

Obsessive-Compulsive PD is closely linked to Freud's (1909) early descriptions of individuals fixated at the anal stage of psychosexual development who are extremely orderly, rigidly controlling, and parsimonious (Levy & Scott, 2006). It has also been referred to in the *ICD* as the anakastic personality, which is related to K. Schneider's (1923) description of an overly correct and controlling personality (Bernstein & Travaglini, 1999). K. Abraham (1921) and Reich (1933) expanded on Freud's anal character, emphasizing the obsessional and compulsive characteristics as they relate to indecision, self-doubt, and the lack of initiative. Erikson (1950) further developed these concepts and theorized that excessive parental criticism resulted in an overemphasis on self-control and discipline. Salzman (1980) and Storr (1980) hypothesized that these individuals become overly cautious, perfectionistic, and focused on stability as a reaction to perceived external threats to their security. Millon and Davis (2000) describe an integrated model that includes a constricted cognitive style, compartmentalization of feelings and thoughts, and a solemn, tense mood (Bernstein & Travaglini, 1999). It was initially described as compulsive personality in the *DSM-I*, was renamed Obsessive-Compulsive in the *DSM-II*, and the diagnostic criteria were expanded in *DSM-III-R* to include fears of separation and feelings of submissiveness (American Psychiatric Association, 1968; Widiger & Bornstein, 2001; Zuckerman, 1999).

In the *DSM-IV-TR* two additional PDs, Passive-Aggressive (Negativistic) and Depressive, were included in Appendix B for proposed further study (Oldham, 2005). The limitations of a categorical approach to the classification of personality disorders were also

reviewed in the *DSM-IV-TR*, and a section on a dimensional approach to personality classification is included in the text (American Psychiatric Association, 2000b). One of the
major focuses for the *DSM-V* research group is the determination of the status of the PDs
and whether to include dimensional, prototype, or other models or to maintain the multiaxial system (Kupfer, First, et al., 2002).

GENERAL DESCRIPTION

In the *DSM-IV-TR*, the PD category is organized differently from the other disorders:
There is a set of five general diagnostic criteria that are similar to the five distinctive
features (early onset, stability and persistence, pervasiveness, interpersonal focus, and impairment) of personality disorders identified by Livesley, Schroeder, Jackson, and Jang
(1994). Each of the 10 PDs is then described on the basis of a grouping of specific diagnostic criteria listed in order of decreasing diagnostic importance, which reflect the
unique clinical presentation or consistent theme (Fauman, 2002; First et al., 2004). The
10 PDs (see Table 14.1) are described and clustered into three groups based on common
or shared clinical features or phenotypic similarities (M. B. Miller, 2001). The first cluster

Table 14.1   Personality disorders: key features

Personality Disorder	Cluster and Disorder Descriptions
Cluster A	
Odd and eccentric	*Socially detached, restricted affect, suspiciousness*
Paranoid	Pervasive distrust and suspiciousness; interprets others as malevolent
Schizoid	Interpersonal indifference, persistent detachment, emotional restriction
Schizotypal	Social discomfort, cognitive and perceptual distortions, odd and eccentric
Cluster B	
Dramatic and erratic	*Impulsive, superficial, manipulative, volatile, needing attention*
Antisocial	Pervasive pattern of disregard for the rights of others and antisocial acts
Borderline	Chronic instability of interpersonal relationships, self-identity, emotions; marked impulsivity
Histrionic	Excessive emotionality and attention seeking
Narcissistic	Grandiosity, lack of empathy, craves attention or admiration from others
Cluster C	
Anxious and fearful	*Anxious, socially avoidant or dependent, perfectionistic, and controlling*
Avoidant	Social inhibition, hypersensitive to others' negative evaluation, feels inadequate
Dependent	Excessive need to be taken care of, submissive, reliant on others, clingy
Obsessive Compulsive	Preoccupation with order and control, perfectionistic, inflexible, emotionally restricted

Adapted with permission from the *Diagnostic and Statistical Manual of Mental Disorders, fourth edition, text revision.* American Psychiatric Association, 2000b Washington, DC: Author.

(A), often referred to as the odd and eccentric, includes Paranoid, Schizoid, and Schizotypal PDs. The second cluster (B), known as the dramatic and erratic, includes Antisocial, Borderline, Histrionic, and Narcissistic PDs. The final cluster (C), referred to as the anxious and fearful, includes Avoidant, Dependent, and Obsessive-Compulsive PDs (American Psychiatric Association, 2000b). Determining the cluster the PD belongs to narrows your diagnostic choice and allows you to focus on within-cluster differentiation (Fauman, 2002). However, it is important to remember that although this clustering can be helpful in arriving at a diagnosis, the clusters are controversial and lack empirical support (American Psychiatric Association, 2000b).

The *DSM-IV-TR* describes a PD as an enduring pattern of inner experience and behavior that is markedly different from cultural expectations (American Psychiatric Association, 2000b). The PDs are the disorders most tied to cultural expectations (First et al., 2004). Hence it is critical to consider the individual's ethnic, cultural, and social background, with particular sensitivity to issues of acculturation, immigration, habits, customs, and values of the individual's culture of origin and to be cautious about not overpathologizing adaptive or culturally condoned behaviors (Alarcon, 2005; Paris, 2004b). The pattern must be apparent in two or more of the following areas: cognitions, affectivity, interpersonal functioning, or impulse control (American Psychiatric Association, 2000b). It is the intensity of the individual's behavior or cognition that sets the individual apart and often warrants a PD diagnosis (Fauman, 2002). The enduring pattern must be inflexible and pervasive across a broad range of personal and social situations (American Psychiatric Association, 2000b). By definition, individuals with PDs have difficulty responding flexibly and adaptively to changes and demands that are part of everyday life. This inflexibility is often the reason the behavior pattern is maladaptive and enduring and results in "vicious cycles in interpersonal relationships" (First et al., 2004, p. 350). The individual's behaviors cannot be restricted to one person or relationship and must be an ingrained part of the individual and not merely a reaction to the demands of a particular situation or role (Othmer & Othmer, 2002). A key to the diagnosis of a PD is the pervasive nature of the maladaptive behavior, which is commonly and frequently exhibited across many different settings (Fauman, 2002).

The enduring pattern must also lead to clinically significant distress or impairment in social, occupational, or other important areas of functioning (American Psychiatric Association, 2000b). For most individuals, personality features typically involve characteristics that are accepted as an integral part of the self (e.g., ego-syntonic) and do not create distress (American Psychiatric Association, 2000b). Impairment in personality functioning exists on a continuum, and the *DSM-IV-TR* does not provide clear-cut guidelines on the extent to which a behavior must be maladaptive, impairing, or distressing to warrant a PD diagnosis (Magnavita, 2005). The assessment of impairment can be confounded by the individual's limited self-awareness, lack of empathy, and disregard for others (Othmer & Othmer, 2002). Thus individuals with Antisocial or Narcissistic PD may minimize or rationalize their behaviors, attributing blame to others, and individuals with Obsessive-Compulsive PD may value their perfectionism and incessant devotion to work as an indication of scrupulousness and dedication rather than as an impairment (First et al., 2004). Because individuals with PDs rarely seek treatment on their own or see themselves as impaired, a detailed history and collateral contacts may be the only way to assess the level of impairment (Othmer & Othmer, 2002).

The personality pattern should be typical of the individual's long-term functioning and have an onset that can be traced back to at least adolescence or early adulthood (American Psychiatric Association, 2000b). Time is needed to determine if a pattern is enduring; PDs are not time-limited and do not refer to discrete episodic illnesses, but are insidious disorders with an early onset (First et al., 2004). In the past, their stability and duration were used to differentiate PDs from the Axis I disorders; however, as First and Tasman (2004) note, with every edition of the *DSM* this distinction has been harder to apply. According to Fauman (2002), the clinical symptoms in PDs form an enduring and pervasive part of the individual's repertoire of behaviors. However, the validity of lifelong patterns of maladjustment as an essential feature of personality disorders has not been well established (P. A. Bank & Silk, 2001; M. T. Shea & Yen, 2003).

Childhood psychopathology is often unstable and self-limited, and problematic behaviors may occur during a particular developmental stage and then resolve (First et al., 2004). As many childhood personality traits do not persist into adulthood, a PD should be *rarely* diagnosed in children and "only in those relatively unusual instances in which the individual's particular maladaptive personality traits appear to be pervasive, persistent, and unlikely to be limited to a particular developmental stage or an episode of an Axis I disorder" (American Psychiatric Association, 2000b). If a PD diagnosis is to be assigned to a child, the personality features must be present for at least 1 year, and Antisocial PD cannot be diagnosed in anyone under 18 (American Psychiatric Association, 2000b).

The personality traits must be differentiated from responses to stressors or transient mental states, such as Axis I disorders (American Psychiatric Association, 2000b). The *DSM* notes specifically that some PDs have a spectrum relationship with Axis I disorders based on "phenomenological or biological similarities or familial aggregation." Such is the relationship of Schizotypal PD and Schizophrenia and Avoidant PD and Social Phobia (American Psychiatric Association, 2000b, p. 688). First and colleagues (2004) caution that it is important not to reify the difference between Axis I and Axis II disorders, as in many cases the boundary between the disorders is inherently impossible to determine and the differentiation becomes meaningless. The differentiation can be very difficult, especially when the individual is presenting with or is in the midst of an Axis I episode. It is best to be very cautious in diagnosing a PD in an individual you have not observed over time, unless the history is very clear that there are recurrent, persistent problems related to personality traits, which are present even when the Axis I symptoms remit (First et al., 2004; Othmer & Othmer, 2002). In such cases, obtaining information from collateral sources or reviewing previous treatment is invaluable.

The enduring pattern must not be caused by the direct physiological effects of a substance, including a medication, or a GMC (American Psychiatric Association, 2000b; First & Tasman, 2004). The relationship between substance use and PDs is complicated. Both are common comorbid disorders. The substance use may also reflect the PD individual's lack of impulse control or attempts at self-medication. If the individual undergoes a change in personality, not just a worsening of features previously present, it is important to consider a medical evaluation to evaluate the presence of a GMC. Personality changes due to a GMC rarely conform to the specific clinical presentations that are characteristic of the 10 *DSM-IV-TR* PDs; rather they often have an atypical onset and course (First et al., 2004).

Personality disorders are always coded on Axis II. If the individual meets the criteria for more than one disorder, these should all be listed in order of importance (American Psychiatric Association, 2000b). The principal diagnosis or reason for the visit, which is usually the focus of treatment and attention, should be clearly identified in parentheses following the relevant disorder. If the individual has a chronic Axis I disorder (e.g., Schizophrenia) that was preceded by a preexisting PD (e.g., Schizoid), this should be indicated by writing "Premorbid" after the PD (American Psychiatric Association, 2000b).

CLUSTER A PERSONALITY DISORDERS

This cluster contains Paranoid, Schizoid, and Schizotypal PDs, which are characterized by the presence of odd and eccentric thoughts and/or behaviors and difficulty relating to others. When under stress, individuals with these PDs can experience brief transient psychotic episodes (American Psychiatric Association, 2000b; Fauman, 2002). The individual's peculiar thoughts, idiosyncratic fantasies, and odd and eccentric mannerisms may result in ostracism, which contributes to further suspiciousness (American Psychiatric Association, 2000b; First & Tasman, 2004). The significant deficits in social relatedness may be apparent since childhood and range from distrusting and seeing others as malevolent to a disinterested detachment (American Psychiatric Association, 2000b; Levy & Scott, 2006; M. B. Miller et al., 2001). The common features of distrust and avoidance of or indifference to others means that these individuals rarely seek treatment and are often most prevalent among society's most marginalized groups, such as the homeless, chronically mentally ill, treatment-refractory clients, and skid row residents (B. F. Grant et al., 2004; Maxmen & Ward, 1995).

Paranoid Personality Disorder

Paranoid PD is based on one of the oldest and most familiar psychiatric symptoms: paranoia. Its core clinical presentation is historically consistent, and it is considered among the most severe PDs, yet it remains the most understudied (Akhtar, 1990; M. B. Miller et al., 2001; Regehr & Glancy, 1999). The lack of empirical literature may reflect the disorder's key features of mistrust, antagonism, suspiciousness, hypersensitivity to criticism, hypervigilance, and the need to distance from others who are perceived to be exploitive or harmful (Kazdin, 2000; Levy & Scott, 2006). These individuals rarely seek treatment, and when they do, they present with a lack of insight, a tendency to blame others, and a belief that their ego-syntonic mistrust is an accurate perception of a dangerous world (First & Tasman, 2004; M. B. Miller et al., 2001). An angry, litigious nature and an incessant need to seek out confirmation of their beliefs often accompanies their suspiciousness. They continually feel attacked and threatened, reading malevolent intent even in the most innocent remarks. This makes the establishment of rapport extremely challenging (Bender, 2005). Their prolonged hostility, pathological jealousy, and feelings of being deeply harmed by others means they often live solitary, angry lives (M. B. Miller et al., 2001). In clinical practice, a "pure" Paranoid PD is rare, with two thirds of clinical cases meeting criteria for another PD, the most common being Schizotypal, Narcissistic, Borderline, and Avoidant (Bernstein, Useda, & Siever, 1995; M. B. Miller et al., 2001).

Clinical Presentation

Distrust   Paranoid PD is characterized by a pervasive distrust and suspiciousness of others, which begins by early adulthood and occurs in a variety of contexts (American Psychiatric Association, 2000b; First et al., 2004). This distrust significantly deviates from the individual's culture; it is enduring and inflexible and results in distress and impairment (American Psychiatric Association, 2000b; Fauman, 2002). In diagnostic conceptualizations, cultural differences in the expression of trust and mistrust and the fact that paranoid traits may be adaptive in certain threatening settings must be considered (American Psychiatric Association, 2000b; Blaney, 1999; Kazdin, 2000). These individuals perceive and interpret others' responses as malevolent, which contributes to fears and behaviors aimed at self-protection, minimizing self-disclosure, and the ongoing maintenance of suspicions, grudges, justified jealousy, and aggression (American Psychiatric Association, 2000b; Levy & Scott, 2006). Distrust makes it unlikely that these individuals will check their maladaptive, inflexible beliefs with others. The resultant antagonistic stance often provokes hostile reactions, thus confirming that the world is harsh and threatening (Kazdin, 2000; M. B. Miller et al., 2001). These individuals feel deeply and irreversibly injured by others and are preoccupied with unjustified doubts of the loyalty and trustworthiness of their associates (American Psychiatric Association, 2000b). They are quick to counterattack and vigilantly screen in minute detail the actions of others for hostile intent, interpreting compliments as criticism and perceiving demeaning and threatening hidden meanings in benign remarks and honest mistakes (American Psychiatric Association, 2000b; Blaney, 1999). They may also present as intolerant of ambiguity, with rigid value systems. Their lack of insight, antagonistic style, and lack of self-disclosure may make the determination of distress and impairment difficult (First & Tasman, 2004; Skodol, 2005).

Lack of Close Relationships   The personal histories of individuals with Paranoid PD often emphasize themes of betrayal, deceit, and pride in self-reliance, with few social relationships (McClanahan et al., 2003; Morrison, 1995b). They are emotionally cold and have an excessive need to be autonomous and superior, which may be expressed in their projecting malevolent motivations to others and embracing negative stereotypes of others (American Psychiatric Association, 2000b; M. B. Miller et al., 2001). They have enemies rather than friends, disdain weakness, think in hierarchical terms (always noting who is superior and in control), can be pathologically jealous, desire total interpersonal control, and often suspect their partners of infidelity (LaBruzza & Mendez-Villarrubia, 1997; Maxmen & Ward, 1995). They continually interpret others' actions as deliberately demeaning and threatening. Thus their interpersonal hostility, pathological suspiciousness, and jealousy make it difficult for them to relate to others and maintain relationships (American Psychiatric Association, 2000b; A. Roth & Fonagy, 2005).

Onset, Course, and Life Span Considerations

In childhood, individuals with Paranoid PD demonstrate significant difficulties with social relationships, characterized by isolation, hypersensitivity, social anxiety, and angry hostility. This often develops into a lack of social connectedness and interpersonal distance that pervade their personal and occupational functioning (American Psychiatric Association,

2000b). The clinical symptoms typically do not improve over time, but become more pronounced, as demonstrated in a 12-year follow-up study (Seivewright, Tyrer, & Johnson, 2002). However, there is a lack of long-term outcome follow-up studies for this disorder (Kazdin, 2000; M. B. Miller et al., 2001). Their lack of trust, pathological jealousy, reluctance to be close, and feeling of being deeply hurt by others often result in their living isolated, guarded lives (Levy & Scott, 2006; M. B. Miller et al., 2001). Their need to control those around them and their rigid cognitions limit their ability to consider others' perspectives and make it difficult to collaborate, resulting in ongoing occupational impairment (M. B. Miller et al., 2001). B. F. Grant and colleagues (2004) found that Paranoid PD was significantly associated with disability. If they do maintain steady employment, they are inflexible and critical, tend to blame coworkers, and are likely to become involved in acrimonious, protracted legal disputes (First & Tasman, 2004). Often acutely aware of power and status, they attribute malevolent intent to others and may be at risk for being perceived by others as "fanatics" or joining or forming cults (American Psychiatric Association, 2000b). As they rarely seek help, they often tend to live marginalized lives alone (Paris, 2003). By joining a paranoid group, however, they may find some solace in belonging and being with like-minded individuals (Robins & Post, 1997).

Schizoid Personality Disorder

The term schizoid was first used by E. Bleuler (1922) to describe individuals who appeared to turn inward, indifferent to interpersonal relationships and pleasure, and who were emotionally restricted (Levy & Scott, 2006). They have also been described as "shut-in" and "autistic" personality types (Hoch, 1910; Kraepelin, 1913). Schizoid PD has been included in the *DSM* since its inception, but diagnostic changes and the introduction of Avoidant and Schizotypal PDs have resulted in this now being the rarest of the PDs (Bernstein & Travaglini, 1999; First & Tasman, 2004).

Individuals with Schizoid PD are more frequently males, who appear introverted, low on gregariousness, and lacking warmth, positive emotions, and an openness to feelings. The characteristic symptoms are social detachment and emotional restriction (Skodol, 2005; Widiger et al., 2002). There is a high overlap with Avoidant PD (53%) and Schizotypal PD (38%), giving rises to concerns that these may not be separate diagnostic entities (Bernstein & Travaglini, 1999). As immigrants and individuals moving to metropolitan cities from small rural communities may present as detached, defensive, solitary, and "emotionally frozen," it is crucial to consider the individual's life situation before diagnosing this disorder (American Psychiatric Association, 2000b).

Clinical Presentation

Detachment   The key feature of Schizoid PD is a pervasive pattern beginning in early adulthood and occurring across settings of detachment from social relationships and a restricted emotional expression in interpersonal settings (American Psychiatric Association, 2000b; Fauman, 2002). This odd, isolated, and suspicious pattern includes a lack of desire for intimacy, an indifference to relationships with others, a preference for solitude and isolation, emotional coldness, and bland or flat affect (American Psychiatric Association, 2000b; Skodol, 2005). These individuals experience significant discomfort in social interactions and appear cold, distant, and aloof, with an anhedonic detachment that is ego-syntonic (American Psychiatric Association, 2000b; First & Tasman, 2004). They present as loners who have no friends, appear ignorant to the subtleties of social interaction, rarely reciprocate with social gestures or appropriate facial expressions, and thus seem cold, self-absorbed, aloof, and apathetically indifferent (American Psychiatric Association, 2000b; First et al., 2004; M. B. Miller et al., 2001). They may excel at occupations that involve minimal social contact and require abstract skills, such as mathematics, computer, or technological knowledge (American Psychiatric Association, 2000b; First & Tasman, 2004). They appear ambivalent, lacking affective involvement in social relations, and are unable to take pleasure in basic physical, social, and sexual activities. Bernstein and Travaglini (1999, p. 525) so aptly note that for these individuals, "The world is experienced in shades of gray rather than color."

Lack of Close Relationships   Individuals with Schizoid PD present with a level of comfort with long-standing isolation and an indifference to social needs that is present in all aspects of their lives, suggesting lifelong loners who date infrequently and appear cold and reclusive (American Psychiatric Association, 2000b; Morrison, 1995b). Their extreme social anxiety and the discomfort they feel because of their suspiciousness of others' motives result in their having few close relationships other than first-degree relatives. They appear to be bland individuals, drifting directionless, detached, and disconnected from the world around them (American Psychiatric Association, 2000b; Bernstein & Travaglini, 1999). They seem uninterested in developing intimate or sexual relationships and rarely marry (Levy & Scott, 2006; M. B. Miller et al., 2001). It is important not to discount their desire for a solitary life or to assume that they are distressed by this lack of contact (McClanahan et al., 2003).

Onset, Course, and Life Span Considerations

The majority of those diagnosed with Schizoid PD in late childhood retain this diagnosis 10 years later (Bernstein & Travaglini, 1999). As adolescents they are often teased and ostracized. Their difficulty expressing anger may contribute to their withdrawing, reacting passively to adverse life events, and appearing to drift aimlessly (American Psychiatric Association, 2000b). The lack of capacity for emotional warmth characteristic of this disorder makes sustaining meaningful, emotionally intimate relationships very difficult (First & Tasman, 2004). This, combined with their extreme difficulty with social relationships, results in their having few friendships, rarely marrying, and seeking occupations that do not involve interaction with others and allow them to work in isolation (First & Tasman, 2004; Levy & Scott, 2006). Over time, highly intelligent individuals with Schizoid PD may show some educational and occupational improvement; however, they will continue to experience ongoing emotional and interpersonal difficulties (Bernstein & Travaglini, 1999).

Schizotypal Personality Disorder

Individuals with Schizotypal PD present with a reduced capacity for close relationships and exhibit a number of oddities in behavior, speech, thought, and perception (First et al., 2004; M. B. Miller et al., 2001). Earlier studies by both Kraepelin and Bleuler described similar odd, eccentric, nonpsychotic individuals in the families of their chronic schizophrenic patients (LaBruzza & Mendez-Villarrubia, 1997). This disorder has been described as on a continuum with Schizophrenia, but is identified as a PD because of its early onset and pervasive, ego-syntonic, stable nature and course (First & Tasman, 2004; M. B. Miller et al., 2001; M. H. Stone, 2001). Individuals with Schizotypal PD may present with magical thinking, believing that their thoughts have the power to cause events to happen, and may also appear preoccupied with paranormal phenomena (American Psychiatric Association, 2000b; Levy & Scott, 2006). These beliefs are not held with delusional conviction and are inconsistent with subculture norms, such as speaking in tongues, shamanism, Santeria, clairvoyance, telepathy, a "sixth sense," and beliefs about health and illness (American Psychiatric Association, 2000b; M. B. Miller et al., 2001). When assessing for this disorder, knowledge and consideration of the individual's cultural, religious, and spiritual beliefs are essential, and it is important not to overpathologize beliefs concerning faith healing, the presence of spirits, and the powers of rituals as magical thinking (American Psychiatric Association, 2000b). Those with Schizotypal PD often seek treatment for comorbid Major Depressive Disorder (American Psychiatric Association, 2000b; Skodol, 2005).

Clinical Presentation

Eccentricities   Typically, there are significant social and interpersonal deficits, accompanied by cognitive and perceptual distortions, eccentricities of behavior, and acute excessive discomfort with others (American Psychiatric Association, 2000b; Fauman, 2002). There may be ideas of reference and suspiciousness, and they may dress and act in a bizarre, inappropriate manner with ill-fitting, mismatched, stained, unkempt clothes (American Psychiatric Association, 2000b; First et al., 2004; Skodol, 2005). They may express feelings that others are taking special notice and misinterpret casual incidents and external events as having a particular and unusual meaning or relevance; thus the news has special personal significance or importance (American Psychiatric Association, 2000b; Skodol, 2005). They may also report unusual perceptual experiences, such as sensing the presence of others not present or hearing their voice being whispered. They often express paranoid ideation (American Psychiatric Association, 2000b; Othmer & Othmer, 2002). Their speech may be coherent but hard to follow, vague, circumstantial, metaphorical, overly elaborate, stereotyped, and with unusual word usage (American Psychiatric Association, 2000b; Maxmen & Ward, 1995). Their affect may be inappropriate or constricted, and they may have difficulty reading social and emotional cues or determining others' emotional states; they appear inattentive to social conventions (Bender, 2005; M. B. Miller et al., 2001).

Lack of Close Relationships   The interpersonal histories of individuals with Schizotypal PDs reflect few long-standing relationships and high levels of social anxiety (American Psychiatric Association, 2000b; McClanahan et al., 2003). Although they may express a desire for more friends or greater closeness with others, they appear to have a decreased desire for intimate contacts and have few friends other than first-degree relatives (A. Roth & Fonagy, 2005). They avoid others, often reporting that they "don't fit in," and experience excessive social anxiety that does not diminish with familiarity or time and is associated with paranoid fears rather than negative self-judgments (M. B. Miller et al., 2001). Their idiosyncratic style and eccentricities in appearance and behavior make maintaining interpersonal relationships difficult, and they are likely to be rejected, socially humiliated, ostracized, and isolated (McClanahan et al., 2003; M. B. Miller et al., 2001).

Onset, Course, and Life Span Considerations

As children, individuals with Schizotypal PD may appear interested in esoteric fantasies and peculiar interests that further isolate them from peers (First & Tasman, 2004). Because of their magical thinking and their peculiar interests, they may appear odd to peers and may associate with fringe groups who endorse their aberrant beliefs (First & Tasman, 2004).

The course of Schizotypal PD is fairly stable; the individual's symptoms do not remit with time, and only a small proportion go on to develop a full-blown psychotic disorder such as Schizophrenia (American Psychiatric Association, 2000b; Raine, Lencz, & Mendick, 1995). They rarely achieve close relationships, they tend to isolate themselves, and most remain withdrawn, transient, and marginally employed, working in occupations below their potential throughout their lives (First & Tasman, 2004). Some may be attracted to and join esoteric groups, which may result in further deterioration and cognitive loosening and slippage (First & Tasman, 2004). Those few individuals who show marked improvement and treatment gains on follow-up often had empathy, emotional warmth, or the capacity for interpersonal relatedness. Most individuals, however, experience continued interpersonal and occupational difficulties (Levy & Scott, 2006; McGlashan, 1986a,b; M. H. Stone, 2001).

CLUSTER B PERSONALITY DISORDERS

The most prominent pervasive characteristics of Cluster B PDs, which include Antisocial, Borderline, Histrionic, and Narcissistic, are the presence of dramatic and erratic behaviors (American Psychiatric Association, 2000b). The presence of impulsivity, interpersonal exploitiveness, superficiality, and a reduced capacity for empathy place these individuals at high risk for harming themselves and others and engaging in high-risk behaviors (Fauman, 2002; Gutheil, 2005; Skodol, 2005). Their level of entitlement and lack of insight often provoke strong reactions in their therapists, who are at risk for making poor clinical decisions, engaging in unethical behavior, and boundary violations (Fauman, 2002; First et al., 2004).

Antisocial Personality Disorder

Individuals who violate and disregard the rights of others have been with us since the beginning of time, but despite being the oldest and most researched PD, Antisocial PD continues to spark controversy over how best to define it (LaBruzza & Mendez-Villarrubia, 1997; Sutker & Allain, 2000). The hallmarks of this disorder are impulsivity, exaggerated sensation-seeking needs, intolerance of boredom, and eagerness for gratification (Sutker & Allain, 2001). This is the adult development of Conduct Disorder, and only 2% of those diagnosed with it remit (Maxmen & Ward, 1995). These individuals tend to live violent lives, marry one another, engage in domestic violence, have children they do not care for, have high rates of sexually transmitted disease, die early and violently, and if not murdered spend large periods of their life incarnated (Coid, 2005; Levy & Scott, 2006). While charming and resourceful, their relationships are shallow. They lack the capacity for empathy, shame, guilt, and commitment. These factors make the establishment of a therapeutic relationship almost impossible, and the level of associated aggression makes this the most difficulty PD to treat (First & Tasman, 2004; Gunderson & Gabbard, 2000; M. H. Stone, 2005). Those with Antisocial PD rarely seek treatment as they have limited insight and often embrace their personality features. They are at high risk for comorbid substance abuse and depression, which, with pending legal cases, are often the precipitants for treatment (First & Tasman, 2004).

Clinical Presentation

Antisocial Behavior   Since at least the age of 15 these individuals present with a pervasive, enduring, inflexible, and long-standing disregard for and violation of the rights of others, which deviates from their culture (American Psychiatric Association, 2000b). This includes a failure to conform behavior to social norms, repeatedly performing illegal activities, and a reckless disregard for the rights of others (Fauman, 2002; Levy & Scott, 2006). They may have a lack of empathy, an inflated, arrogant self-image, and be cynical, callous, and contemptuous of others, often reveling in their exploits and crimes (First & Tasman, 2004; Skodol, 2005). M. H. Stone (2005) describes the current diagnostic criteria as including the personality features of deceitfulness, impulsivity, a reckless disregard for others' safety, a lack of remorse, and repeated acts that serve as grounds for arrest. These individuals frequently engage in physical altercations, blame others for their actions, and disavow any responsibility (M. H. Stone, 2005). They repeatedly fail to follow through on personal, familial, financial, and occupational responsibilities, demonstrating consistent extreme irresponsibility (Levy & Scott, 2006). Deceitfulness, interpersonal manipulation, and lack of insight are central features, and these individuals will lie or con to gain personal advantage; thus, gathering collateral information is imperative (American Psychiatric Association, 2000b; Othmer & Othmer, 2002). The current *DSM* criteria have been criticized as cumbersome, overly complex, and focusing on overt criminal acts and irresponsible behaviors (First et al., 2004; Levy & Scott, 2006).

Psychopathy   Cleckley (1941) and Hare (1998) used the term *psychopathy* to describe cold, charming, manipulative individuals who appear lacking a conscience, engage in antisocial acts, and use violence and intimidation to satisfy their own needs. Coid (2005) notes that 79% of individuals identified with psychopathy receive a diagnosis of Antisocial PD, and 30% of those with Antisocial PD also have psychopathy. The presence of these traits have been linked to a higher risk for violence, a greater range and frequency of violent acts, and recidivism for violent offending, particularly the predatory type (Coid, 2005; Monaghan et al., 2001). Cold emotional traits have also been identified in a subgroup of early-onset Conduct Disorder children, who present with more severe forms of antisocial and aggressive behavior, appear less responsive to parental socialization, and are less distressed by the impact of their behaviors on others (Kimonis & Frick, 2006). The *DSM-IV-TR* does not include psychopathic traits such as arrogant self-appraisal, lack of empathy, and superficial charm, but it does note that these traits can be particularly useful in predicting recidivism and in identifying Antisocial PD in forensic settings, where delinquent aggressive acts are common (American Psychiatric Association, 2000b; Sutker & Allain, 2001). The presence of psychopathy warrants a continual assessment and monitoring of the individual's risk of danger to others (M. H. Stone, 2005).

Superficiality of Relationships Individuals with Antisocial PD relate to others with superficial charm; however, they are interpersonally manipulative and may be physically violent, often engaging in multiple sexual relationships (Coid, 2005; M. H. Stone, 2005). Typically, they are focused on their own pleasure and rationalize their mistreatment of others by blaming the victim (American Psychiatric Association, 2000b; Scott & Levy, 2006). Those individuals with Antisocial PD and a callous lack of empathy may see others as objects and may violently victimize them to obtain their desires (Hare, Cooke, & Hart, 1999).

Onset, Course, and Life Span Considerations

By definition, individuals with Antisocial PD have received a previous diagnosis of Conduct Disorder (American Psychiatric Association, 2000b). As children, these individuals lie, steal, are truant, exploit parental affection, run away, defy authority, and associate with like-minded peers (Coid, 2005; Levy & Scott, 2005). By adolescence they are frequently involved with substance use, have disciplinary action or expulsions from school, delight in terrorizing others, and engage in a wide range of antisocial acts (Bassarath, 2001; Moffitt, 2003). The presence in childhood of callous unemotional traits and of multiple delinquent behaviors before 10 is linked to the continuation of these behaviors into adulthood (Frick & Ellis, 1999; Lynam, 1996). These individuals crave stimulation, live in the present, make decisions impulsively, consider work to be boring and dull, rarely persevere, abandon jobs, and may see unemployment as preferable to working (Levy & Scott, 2006). Consequently, their occupational history suggests irresponsibility (American Psychiatric Association, 2000b; Othmer & Othmer, 2002). Some individuals who are characterized by high levels of conscientiousness may be able to successfully express their psychopathic tendencies in a legitimate occupation (Widiger & Lynam, 1998). There may also be evidence of financial irresponsibility, such as defaulting on debts, failing to pay child or spousal support, and failing to pay compensation or make amends. As parents they may exploit their children, fail to provide adequate caretaking for them, and squander money for necessities (American Psychiatric Association, 2000b). Their relationships with others are exploitive, often with multiple concurrent sexual relationships (Othmer & Othmer, 2002). B. F. Grant and colleagues (2004) found that Antisocial PD was a significant predictor of long-term impairment in functioning and disability. There may be a gradual decrease in overt criminal acts as the individual ages (Sutker & Allain, 2001). Some individuals may burn out in middle age, losing the energy to sustain their antisocial life. If not incarcerated, they may exist on skid row, in low-paying jobs, with marked occupational and social impairment (Coid, 2005). They may continue to experience relationship and work problems, often having multiple marriages, divorces, and a history of family violence. Ultimately, 5% commit suicide (Maxmen & Ward, 1995; Paris, 2003).

Borderline Personality Disorder

This is the most common personality disorder seen in clinical settings; the rates increase from 2% in the general population, to 11% in outpatient settings, to 19% in inpatient settings (H. E. Adams et al., 2001). The core features of affective instability, impulsivity, intense and inappropriate anger, and suicidal and self-mutilating behavior make these the most challenging clients even for experienced clinicians (Paris, 1999). Characteristic impulsive behaviors include cutting oneself, binge eating, overdosing, gambling, substance abuse, reckless driving, and promiscuous sexual activity (First et al., 2004; Gunderson, 2001). Individuals with this PD are at high risk for suicide, particularly in their 20s: 10% will commit suicide, and 70% will engage in self-harming behaviors (J. Gerson & Stanley, 2002; Paris, 2002a; M. H. Stone, 2001). Interpersonal relationships are chaotic, often characterized by splitting (i.e., using idealization and devaluation), intense fears of abandonment, and dissociation or paranoid ideation during stressful periods (American Psychiatric Association, 2000b; Othmer & Othmer, 2002). Additionally, this disorder rarely occurs in isolation and is frequently comorbid with Narcissistic, Histrionic, and Antisocial PDs and Axis I mood disorders, particularly Major Depressive Disorder (Trull, Stepp, & Solhan, 2006). Longitudinal research suggests that the occurrence of Major Depressive Disorder may be related to the individual's interpersonal difficulties and emotional sensitivity and may be related to identifiable events or stressors (Gunderson, Morey, Stout, Skodol, Shea, et al., 2004).

Initially seen as predominantly (75%) a female disorder, this may reflect a gender bias in clinical samples, as community samples show no gender difference in prevalence rates (American Psychiatric Association, 2000b; D. M. Johnson, Shea, Yen, Battle, Zlotnick, et al., 2003; Skodol & Bender, 2003; Torgersen, Kringlen, & Cramer, 2001). Borderline PD does appear to cluster in families with high rates of impulsivity, including alcohol- and substance-related disorders, antisocial behavior, and depressive mood disorders (Paris, 1999). There is consistent evidence of the role of psychological factors, particularly childhood trauma (physical and sexual abuse, parental loss), disturbed family setting or invalidating environments, and abnormal bonding in the development of this disorder (H. E. Adams et al., 2001; Linehan, 2000; Paris, 1999). These individuals have a tendency to undermine themselves and often drop out of treatment or regress significantly prior to attaining a goal or treatment termination (American Psychiatric Association, 2001a; Gunderson, 2001). For individuals who chronically engage in self-injurious behavior and suicidal attempts, hospitalization may be contraindicated (J. Gerson & Stanley, 2002; Paris, 2002a). The majority of those who receive treatment appear to outgrow their disorder and develop less chaotic relationships and become less suicidal in middle age (Paris, 1999). There are few studies focusing on individuals with Borderline PD and limited resources. According to M. H. Stone (2001, p. 266), few of these individuals in adulthood "escape the misery of their earlier years." As individuals with Borderline PD often engender strong negative reactions in care providers, it is essential to pay ongoing attention to professional boundaries and monitor one's countertransference (Gunderson, 2001; Gutheil, 2005; Jordon, 2004).

Clinical Presentation

Instability   The key feature of Borderline PD is a pervasive pattern since early adulthood of instability of interpersonal relationships, self-image, affects, and impulsivity (American Psychiatric Association, 2000b; First et al., 2004). These individuals are prone to dramatic, sudden shifts in their appraisal of others, including the therapist, are exquisitely sensitive to interpersonal stresses, and often express extreme anger (Gunderson, 2001; Skodol, 2005). The clinician's subjective experience of an individual with Borderline PD is one of anger, emptiness, and loneliness (Trull et al., 2006). The combination or co-occurrence of the personality traits of impulsivity and emotional dysregulation is a characteristic feature

(Gurvits, Keoenigsberg, & Siever, 2000; Paris, 2000; Silk, 2000). They are not only chronically impulsive, but are also at high risk for suicide and may experience cognitive dysregulation in the form of transient quasi-psychotic symptoms, paranoid ideation, and dissociative experiences (American Psychiatric Association, 2000b; Paris, 1999; M. H. Stone, 2001). Compounding this, they often present with severe issues and confusion over self-identity and may report identity disturbance or an absence of a sense of self (Linehan, 2000; Skodol, 2005). They may experience this identity disturbance as "a black hole of emptiness" or as feelings of worthlessness and extreme self-loathing, which has been related to the individual's inability to integrate the disparate positive and negative parts of self-identity (Gunderson, 2001; Wilkinson-Ryan & Westen, 2000).

Abandonment   Interpersonal relationships of individuals with Borderline PD are, by nature, explosive, stormy, and unstable; intimate relationships are established rapidly and with intensity, often followed by a questioning of the other's commitment (First & Tasman, 2004; Trull et al., 2006). They may alternate between feeling consumed to feeling abandoned by others, and long-standing difficulties with interpersonal relationships are common (H. E. Adams et al., 2001). There may be frantic efforts to avoid real or imagined abandonment, identity disturbance, chronic feelings of emptiness, and behavioral impulsivity (American Psychiatric Association, 2000b). A friend's leaving on vacation or a partner's arriving home late or not returning a call is interpreted based on an intense fear of abandonment and rejection, which in turn may result in self-injurious behaviors (Gunderson, 2001; Linehan, 2000).

Affect Lability and Impulsivity   Affective lability, characterized by intense and chronically fluctuating emotions, is one of the defining features of Borderline PD (Gunderson, 2001). Widiger and colleagues (2002) describe these individuals as experiencing the most extreme and highly maladaptive variations of emotional instability. This lability is often expressed in relationships, including in therapy, resulting in the individual's elation and idealization turning dramatically to intense, inappropriate rage within moments (Gutheil, 2005; Trull et al., 2006). Individuals with Borderline PD experience their extreme emotions as reactions to events or interpersonal difficulties and feel helpless or unable to control the intensity of their feelings (Paris, 1999). Their anger may be expressed as bitterness, physical aggression, extreme sarcasm, accusations, and hostility. Although many individuals experience anger and anxiety, the more prominent emotions are depression, sadness, dysthymia, emptiness, and loneliness, which are experienced as intolerable (Paris, 1999). Unable to tolerate the intensity of the dysphoric affect, the individual acts out impulsively or in a self-destructive or harming manner (M. Z. Brown, Comtois, & Linehan, 2002). Self-cutting or burning and suicidal gestures can serve a distracting purpose, and become, for some, an addictive pattern of affect regulation (Linehan, 1997). Stanley and Brodsky (2005b) describe the self-injurious behavior as serving several functions, including affect regulation, distraction, self-punishment, concrete proof of emotional distress, exertion of control, alleviation of numbness and depersonalization, and ventilation of anger. It is important for clinicians to differentiate suicide attempts from those self-mutilation gestures that often do not involve suicidal intent, but rather serve an affect-regulating, emotional-numbing, or dissociating or distracting function (M. Z. Brown et al., 2002; Linehan, 1993a).

Dissociative States   The *DSM-IV-TR* describes dissociation as "a disruption in the usually integrated functions of consciousness, memory, identity, or perception of the environment," which may be gradual, transient, or chronic (American Psychiatric Association,
2000b, p. 822). According to Wildgoose, Waller, Clarke, and Reid (2000), the presence of
dissociation has been identified as the single factor that differentiates Borderline PD
from the other PDs. In comparison to controls, Zanarini Ruser, Frankenburg, Hennen, and
Gunderson (2000) found that individuals with Borderline PD had significantly higher
levels of dissociation (26% versus 3%). These researchers also identified inconsistent
caretaker treatment, caretaker sexual abuse, witnessing sexual violence as a child, and an
adult rape history as risk factors for dissociation in these individuals. Earlier research by
Brodsky, Cloitre, and Dulit (1995) found that 52% of individuals with Borderline PD and
high levels of dissociation reported a history of self-mutilation, and 60% reported a history of childhood sexual or physical abuse. Self-mutilation was found to be the most
powerful predictor of dissociation. Although the relationship between self-injurious behavior and affect regulation has been established in the literature, the role of dissociation
in this process remains to be determined (Linehan, 1997).

Onset, Course, and Life Span Considerations

Onset   A small percentage of children and adolescents may present with borderline
behaviors, such as chaotic impulsivity and intense affectivity for short periods of time,
but only a small percentage of these retain the diagnosis of Borderline PD years later
(Trull et al., 2006). In childhood, more boys than girls are given a Borderline PD diagnosis (Paris, 1999). It is important not to confuse normal adolescent rebellion, identity confusion, and relationship issues with borderline symptoms (Ad-Dab'bagh & Greenfield,
2001; Gunderson, 2001). An adolescent diagnosis of Borderline PD is less stable than an
adult diagnosis, and for all individuals the symptoms appear to remit over time (Paris,
2003; Paris & Zweig-Frank, 2001). For most individuals, the clinical symptoms appear in
early adulthood.

Course   There is limited research on the natural course of Borderline PD, with the majority of studies focusing on individuals in private psychiatric programs (H. E. Adams
et al., 2001). Young adults with Borderline PD often present with poor impulse control,
suicidal behavior, substance abuse, and concurrent eating and mood disorders that often
warrant multiple hospitalizations. The 20s are a high-risk time for suicide attempts, with
most suicides occurring within the first 5 years after diagnosis (H. E. Adams et al., 2001;
Paris, 1999; M. H. Stone, 2001). By the age of 30, 3% to 10% will have committed suicide, and those with comorbid substance abuse are at even higher risk for suicide
(Gunderson, 2001; Paris, 1999). These individuals have chaotic, explosive, and unstable
interpersonal relationships and demonstrate significant impairment in occupational functioning (Gunderson, 2001). Over the course of 6 years, 75% were found to experience a
remission; the most likely symptoms to remit are impulsive behaviors, self-mutilation,
help-seeking suicidal behaviors, quasi-psychotic thoughts, and substance abuse. In contrast, affective symptoms persisted and individuals with Borderline PD were more generally impaired and showed more impairment in social and occupational functioning than
individuals with other PDs or Major Depressive Disorder (Skodol, Gunderson, et al.,

2002a; Zanarini, Frankenburg, Hennen, & Silk, 2004). The remission of symptoms for the majority of individuals was found to be consistent across four major follow-up studies after 15 years and was found to be stable, with only 6% experiencing symptom resurgence (Paris, 1999; Zanarini, 2005). For individuals with comorbid Major Depressive Disorder, when Borderline PD symptoms improved, the mood symptoms were also found to improve (Gunderson et al., 2004).

Life Span Considerations   For most individuals, the borderline symptoms remit by middle age; however, functional and long-term recovery is rarely complete (H. E. Adams et al., 2001). If these individuals find a supportive partner and are able to maintain that relationship, there is evidence of improvement (Daley, Burge, & Hammen, 2000; M. H. Stone, 2001). Early severe Borderline PD symptoms, early severe childhood sexual abuse, global impairment, substance abuse, aggression in relationships, magical thinking, and paranoid features are all associated with a poorer prognosis (Skodol et al., 2002a,c; M. H. Stone, 2001). The prognosis is better for individuals who are bright, attractive, creative, and likeable. Individuals with Borderline PD are less likely to marry or have children. They may become less impulsive if they have children or by not involving themselves in intimate relationships. Yet severe stressors such as divorce or the death of a loved one can result in increased symptomatology (First & Tasman, 2004; Paris, 1999). In reviewing the literature on outcome, M. H. Stone (2001, p. 266) notes that there are many individuals with Borderline PD who are never diagnosed or who receive treatment in free or low-cost clinics; these persons can "never look forward to the mellowing" or decrease of symptoms enjoyed by their more well-off peers.

Histrionic Personality Disorder

Originally called Hysterical PD and linked to the Greek description of overly dramatic female behavior, this disorder was renamed Histrionic PD to avoid the earlier implied gender bias (LaBruzza & Mendez-Villarrubia, 1997; Levy & Scott, 2006). However, this is the only disorder in the *DSM* tied to the individual's physical characteristic of seductiveness, and it occurs more frequently in men and women of above average physical attractiveness (Bornstein, 1999). These individuals present with rapidly shifting, intense emotional reactions and a tendency to act impulsively (Skodol, 2005). Before assuming that traits such as emotionality, seductiveness, and dramatic interpersonal style are evidence of Histrionic PD, it is important to evaluate whether they cause clinically significant impairment or distress (American Psychiatric Association, 2000b; Othmer & Othmer, 2002). Treating individuals with Histrionic PD can be challenging, as they often are at high risk for suicide attempts and gestures and comorbid substance abuse and Borderline and Narcissistic PDs (Levy & Scott, 2006; Links & Kolla, 2005). Given the individual's flamboyant interpersonal style and need to control others, it is crucial for the clinician to be very consistent and clear with boundaries (Gutheil, 2005).

Clinical Presentation

Excessive Emotionality and Need for Attention   The clinical presentation consists of a pervasive, long-standing pattern of excessive emotionality and attention seeking that results in distress and impairment (American Psychiatric Association, 2000b; First et al., 2004).

The diagnostic criteria have been criticized as continuing to represent an exaggerated version of stereotypical feminine traits and placing too little emphasis on exaggerated masculine traits (First et al., 2004). They describe interpersonal interactions characterized by being uncomfortable in situations when not the center of attention; inappropriate, sexually seductive, or provocative behavior; and a style of speech that is excessively impressionistic, lacks detail, and displays a rapidly shifting and shallow expression of emotions (American Psychiatric Association, 2000b; Skodol, 2005). These individuals' cognitive style is diffuse, global, superficial, and impressionistic, making the gathering of information difficult (Fauman, 2002; Othmer & Othmer, 2002). While initially they may appear superficially charming, appealing, fun-loving, and exciting, they crave novelty and quickly become bored with the routine or normal, and their emotionality is often accompanied by irrational outbursts and temper tantrums (Levy & Scott, 2005). They tend to make impulsive decisions that have dramatic or melodramatic repercussions on their lives (First & Tasman, 2004). Their need for attention can result in impulsive acting-out gestures and a presentation that continually offers new symptoms, which undermines effective treatment (American Psychiatric Association, 2000b; Bender, 2005). As the *DSM-IV-TR* notes, individuals with Histrionic PD are very suggestible, easily influenced by others, including the clinician, and may be overly trusting of strong authority figures, whom they see as being able to magically solve their problems (American Psychiatric Association, 2000b).

Superficiality of Relationships   Individuals with Histrionic PD have relationships that are superficial and focused on their own needs (American Psychiatric Association, 2000b). With friends, their overly seductive manner may be off-putting. Difficulties with delaying gratification and problems with boredom cause them to continually replace existing relationships. They have a pathological need to be loved (Widiger & Bornstein, 2001), but they fall in and out of love quickly, tiring of old relationships, and their shallow superficiality contributes to difficulties establishing emotional intimacy. They also suffer impaired relationships with same-sex friends, as their competitive, sexually provocative interpersonal style is considered threatening (American Psychiatric Association, 2000b; First & Tasman, 2004).

Lability   Excessive emotionality and attention-seeking behavior, including public temper tantrums, are among the characteristic features of Histrionic PD (American Psychiatric Association, 2000b; Skodol, 2005). These individuals engage others in ongoing melodramas that provide a continual distraction against the cognitive recognition of underlying conflicts (M. H. Stone, 1993). Their strong emotions may seem to be turned on and off quickly, making significant others doubt that these feelings are deeply felt, or causing them to perceive the emotions as fake or phony (Levy & Scott, 2006). However, these individuals may be unaware that they are exaggerating their emotions, and if confronted about this will often seem genuinely confused, surprised, and flustered and may not be troubled by their diffuse cognitive style (D. Shapiro, 1965; Skodol, 2005). They appear vain and self-indulgent, crave excitement, and engage in suicidal gestures, which not only creates turmoil but may also serve a defensive function of keeping deeper, upsetting thoughts and feelings about the self and others out of awareness. Actual risk of suicide in Histrionic PD is not clear, yet this is the most common personality disorder (22%) among those who present with self-injurious behaviors but did not intend to die. Of those who committed suicide after age 60, 4% had a Histrionic PD (Links & Kolla, 2005).

Onset, Course, and Life Span Considerations

As children, these individuals may present as immature and demanding; as adolescents, they tend to be flamboyant and flirtatious (Bornstein, 1999; First & Tasman, 2004). They establish intimate relationships and friendships rapidly and become demanding and self-absorbed and constantly need reassurance and attention (Skodol, 2005). They have a naive, somewhat romantic view of the world, often sense intimacy where none exists, and may spend excessive time and finances on their appearance in an effort to impress others (American Psychiatric Association, 2000b; LaBruzza & Mendez-Villarrubia, 1997). Though they initiate activities, they may lose interest, lack follow-through, and are often intolerant of delayed gratification, unreliable, and irresponsible. They present with erratic work histories, sometimes becoming sexually involved with work colleagues (First et al., 2004; Othmer & Othmer, 2002). Given their high level of suggestibility, they are at risk for becoming involved in fads and making impulsive decisions (First & Tasman, 2004). Among older adults, the sexual seductiveness may decrease as it becomes less effective, and there may be a shift to a guilt-inducing parental style (Bornstein, 1999; Widiger & Bornstein, 2001).

Narcissistic Personality Disorder

This is among the least frequently diagnosed PD in clinical settings, as it is often ego-syntonic, and treatment is rarely sought unless there is a medical issue undermining the individual's grandiosity or a depression secondary to narcissistic injury (Ronningstam, 1999; Widiger & Bornstein, 2001). This disorder has come to be associated with an exaggerated sense of self-importance, self-absorption, and a lack of empathy for others (LaBruzza & Mendez-Villarrubia, 1997; Skodol, 2005; Westen & Shedler, 1999b). For individuals with Narcissistic PD, the outward inflated sense of self masks a very fragile self-esteem, which is propped up with a grandiose sense of entitlement; thus these individuals appear arrogant, haughty, and demeaning to others (Levy & Scott, 2006; A. Roth & Fonagy, 2005). Believing their needs are special and their grandiose self-concept is enhanced by their idealization of those they associate with, they may challenge and devalue the clinician's credentials and competence, making genuine rapport difficult and often engendering intense countertransference reactions (American Psychiatric Association, 2000b; Bender, 2005; Gutheil, 2005). Further complicating treatment, individuals with Narcissistic PD are prone to mood and eating disorders and abusing substances, especially cocaine (First & Tasman, 2004). Individuals with Narcissistic PD can present with suicidal behavior, which can take the form of ego-syntonic, self-directed aggression and may be a way of avoiding a disappointing reality. They are particularly prone to this in middle age, related to the need to feel in control of life, and may exhibit nondepressed, sudden, deadly suicidal behavior in response to interpersonal stress (Links & Kolla, 2005; Ronningstam & Maltzberger, 1998).

Clinical Presentation

Grandiosity   The individual presents with a pattern of grandiosity, an excessive need for admiration, and lack of empathy that begins in early adulthood and is pervasive across settings (American Psychiatric Association, 2000b). This is often characterized by a grandiose sense of self, preoccupations with fantasies of brilliance, feelings of special-ness, a sense of entitlement, and envy of others. The current diagnostic criteria have been criticized as reflecting predominantly male expressions of the disorder, relying too much on the overt superficial forms of narcissism rather than the more subtle manifestations, such as dependency conflicts and the inability to stay in love (First et al., 2004; Ronning-stam, 1999). The core criteria of grandiosity and lack of empathy are recognized by 97% of clinicians as Narcissistic PD (Linde & Clark, 1998). In early work looking at discrim-inating characteristics for pathological narcissism, Ronningstam and Gunderson (1990) identified boastful and pretentious, self-centered, self-referential behavior and the envious reaction to others as crucial. These behaviors, as well as the individual's need to be ca-tered to and the assumption that one's own needs surpass others', may create difficulty in even scheduling the intake interview (Othmer & Othmer, 2002). Their inflated image masks a very fragile sense of self and the presence of extreme emotional reactions to any-thing that threatens the vulnerable self-image and a significant need for interpersonal con-trol and interpersonal hostility are also characteristic features (Morey & Jones, 1998; Skodol, 2005). These individuals' inability to tolerate feedback and their hypersensitivity to perceived criticism from others may result in disdain, rage, and withdrawal from treat-ment (American Psychiatric Association, 2000b).

Interpersonal Exploitiveness   For individuals with Narcissistic PD, others serve as admirers; their narcissistic vulnerability makes them exquisitely sensitive to others' criticism and evaluation, which can provoke rage and intense envy (Fauman, 2002; LaBruzza & Mendez-Villarrubia, 1997). They are contemptuous and insensitive to others' needs. Oblivious to their hurtful behavior, they may exploit and take advantage of others. There also is an emotional coldness and a lack of reciprocal interest (American Psychiat-ric Association, 2000b). These individuals greatly overestimate their successes and fail-ures; fantasies of fame substitute for reality; they crave attention; and appearance is more important than substance. Thus they appear interpersonally selfish, frequently slipping from idealization to devaluation (Maxmen & Ward, 1995; Skodol, 2005).

Onset, Course, and Life Span Considerations

A certain level of narcissism is developmentally appropriate in young children (Maxmen & Ward, 1995). During adolescence, these individuals may appear assertive, self-centered, dominant, and even arrogant (First & Tasman, 2004). Unlike the other Cluster B PDs, individuals with Narcissistic PD tend to have more stable lives, tend to be less impulsive, and their interpersonal exploitiveness is more likely expressed as issues of power and control (Fauman, 2002). They are often preoccupied with achievement, fame, and wealth; they place excessive emphasis on the trappings of success and feel entitled to special privileges (American Psychiatric Association, 2000b). An exaggerated sense of self-importance is adaptive and may lead to success in certain professions (Widiger et al., 1995). However, while these individuals may demonstrate high levels of achievement, their success may be marred by their self-centered egotism and difficulty accepting and addressing criticisms and setbacks (Skodol, 2005). Their overestimation of their abilities and underestimation of the contributions of others may also result in occupational impairment.

They have difficulty developing relationships, and they are often unable to maintain the ones they do have, unless their partner is dependent and deferential. If they are parents, they tend to live through their children, seeing them as an extension or reflection of themselves (First & Tasman, 2004). There is some evidence that less severe forms of narcissism may decrease with age and become more treatable, and some may present with physical symptoms (Levy & Scott, 2006). However, there may also be increased difficulties as the individual ages and has trouble with the associated physical and occupational limitations (American Psychiatric Association, 2000b). Severe Narcissistic PD appears highly resistant to change and may worsen with time, with greater levels of contempt, envy, and disillusionment associated with higher rates of rehospitalization and lower levels of social and global functioning (Ronningstam, 1999).

CLUSTER C PERSONALITY DISORDERS

The disorders in this cluster—Avoidant, Dependent, and Obsessive-Compulsive—are characterized by ego-syntonic, anxious, and fearful behaviors (American Psychiatric Association, 2000b). They also have a high comorbidity with Axis I mood and anxiety disorders, which often precipitate treatment and increase with age (First et al., 2004; Levy & Scott, 2006).

Avoidant Personality Disorder

Avoidant PD has considerable overlap with both Axis I Social Phobia and Schizoid and Dependent PDs, and controversy still surrounds its status as a separate disorder or as a spectrum anxiety disorder (Coles & Horng, 2006; Rettew, 2000; C. T. Taylor, Laposa, & Alden, 2004). Prior to its introduction in the *DSM-III*, individuals who were timid, socially inept, excessively self-conscious, self-critical, and aversive to interpersonal relationships were clustered with the Schizoid or Inadequate PDs. They were described as aesthetic and phobic, with an active-detached personality syndrome (Bernstein & Travaglini, 1999; First et al., 2004; LaBruzza & Mendez-Villarrubia, 1997). They compose 5% to 25% of all PDs that seek treatment and 10% of individuals in outpatient mental health clinics, and they frequently seek treatment for comorbid anxiety disorders (American Psychiatric Association, 2000b; First & Tasman, 2004). They live shy, lonely lives; they are constantly vigilant and anticipating others' criticism, fearing painful rejection. Their extreme interpersonal sensitivity results in significant social and occupational impairment (American Psychiatric Association, 2000b; Kantor, 2003; Levy & Scott, 2006) and has been described as a form of hypervigilant narcissism. They appear to crave admiration to bolster their fragile self-concept (Dickenson & Pincus, 2003; Gabbard, 2000). Given different cultural values related to diffidence and avoidance, it is important to assess the client's background and be particularly hesitant in applying this diagnosis to immigrants who may be experiencing acculturation difficulties (American Psychiatric Association 2000b; Bernstein & Travaglini, 2000). Children and adolescents may experience developmentally appropriate shy and avoidance behaviors. Hence, particular attention needs to be directed to an awareness of normative development and assessing the behavior in the context of peer comparisons (American Psychiatric Association, 2000b). These individuals' social sensitivity and fear of others' criticism may make the establishment of rapport and obtaining information difficult (Bender, 2005; Othmer & Othmer, 2002).

Clinical Presentation

Interpersonal Sensitivity There is a pervasive pattern that is present since early adulthood of social inhibition, feelings of inadequacy, and hypersensitivity to negative evaluation that occurs across a range of settings (American Psychiatric Association, 2000b; Fauman, 2002). As the disorder's name suggests, the predominant behavior pattern is avoidance, which pervades all social relationships. These are the chronically shy, who, as Maxmen and Ward (1995) note, are the constant cast members of Garrison Keillor's Lake Wobegon. There is a pattern of interpersonal restraint, avoidance of interpersonal risks, and unwillingness to become involved based on fear of negative evaluation, rejection, criticism, or not being liked (American Psychiatric Association, 2000b; Fauman, 2002). They overvalue acceptance and are so preoccupied with others' negative evaluation that they appear hypersensitive to interpreting any signs of disapproval, reacting strongly to the subtlest of social cues; they often misconstrue others' comments as derogatory (American Psychiatric Association, 2000b; C. T. Taylor et al., 2004). They prefer to be invisible and are reluctant to share intimate details because they believe that attention will result in further degradation and rejection. Thus they avoid humiliation and rejection by being absent from society (Levy & Scott, 2006). Their shyness is pervasive and involves feelings of interpersonal insecurity, accompanied by feelings of inadequacy and low self-esteem (First & Tasman, 2004; Widiger, 2001). These maladaptive patterns become particularly pronounced when they are dealing with strangers or new situations, where they are reluctant to take risks or join group activities and place their fate in someone else's hands (American Psychiatric Association, 2000b; Levy & Scott, 2006). Even though they have a strong desire for and almost crave affection, they engage only when they are certain of uncritical acceptance; consequently, they rarely have close friends or confidants (Othmer & Othmer, 2002; C. T. Taylor et al., 2004). They may fantasize about relationships, yet they have difficulty initiating them, and when in relationships, they demonstrate strong dependency features, often appearing to cling to others (Fauman, 2002; First et al., 2004). They present as distressed by their social isolation, and their superficial indifference may mask a profound and intense wish for closeness (Bernstein & Travaglini, 1999).

Hypersensitivity to Criticism Fearing others' criticism, disapproval, or rejection, individuals with Avoidant PD experience pervasive social inhibition and social discomfort (American Psychiatric Association, 2000b). They are painfully self-conscious, and casual conversations become excruciating, as innocuous remarks are scrutinized for criticism and disapproval (Bernstein & Travaglini, 1999). There may also be underlying fears of being inept, embarrassed, shamed, and feeling socially incompetent, personally unappealing, ridiculed, or inferior (American Psychiatric Association, 2000b; Skodol, 2005). They spend their lives avoiding activities with interpersonal contact and restricting their lives to minimize the potential of being criticized, humiliated, or rejected by others (Levy & Scott, 2006). Thus they deal with the fears of negative evaluation and rejection by eliminating or reducing their exposure to social situations (McClanahan et al., 2003). Their avoidance in part is fueled by beliefs that whatever they say or do will be wrong. Consequently, they constantly dissect their own behavior for embarrassing mistakes, and they exaggerate the potential negative consequences (American Psychiatric Association, 2000b; Bernstein & Travaglini, 1999).

Onset, Course, and Life Span Considerations

Avoidant PD has an onset in childhood and tends to have a long stable pattern that does not remit with age (Paris, 2003; Levy & Scott, 2006). Follow-up at 12 years showed increased isolation, unhappiness, and comorbidity with anxiety and mood disorders (Seivewright et al., 2002). B. F. Grant and colleagues (2004) found that Avoidant PD was a significant predictor of disability. Personal histories of individuals with Avoidant PD include long periods of painful shyness and isolation, restricted interpersonal contact, difficulty initiating relationships, and significant distress in the early stages of relationships (McClanahan et al., 2003). Their fearful, tense, shy, timid demeanor may elicit ridicule from others, which confirms their fears of interpersonal rejection (American Psychiatric Association, 2000b). Adolescence is a significantly difficult time, and they are frequently isolated; with few friends on whom they are dependent, they may fantasize about relationships and be devastated when they end (First & Tasman, 2004). As they avoid relationships, their social skills fail to develop, and this further impairs their ability to form long-term attachments. For some, the symptoms may remit with age (American Psychiatric Association, 2000b). Their fear of others' criticism and avoidant behavior interferes with work performance, especially if it involves interviews, presentations, or social events. Conversely, their work may become a distraction from their loneliness, and they may be successful in their jobs (First & Tasman, 2004).

Dependent Personality Disorder

Pathological dependency has its roots in the descriptions of Kraepelin's (1913) shiftless and K. Schneider's (1923) weak-willed individuals and in the psychoanalytic concept of oral dependency proposed by Freud (1909/1952), K. Abraham (1911, 1927), and Fenichel (1945; Bornstein, 1999). These individuals present with an optimistic belief that there will always be someone who will provide for them, which condemns them to inactivity. This is the most frequently diagnosed PD. The current criteria have been criticized as being gender-biased in that they reflect stereotypically female traits and underidentify masculine dependency as characterized by domineering behaviors (First et al., 2004; Widiger & Bornstein, 2001). Further complicating the diagnosis, dependency symptoms show noticeable variations as a function of age, ethnicity, and gender (Widiger & Bornstein, 2001). Cultures show marked differences in their endorsement of dependency and autonomy, and an immigrant's level of acculturation may also affect the expression of these behaviors. Thus it is crucial to consider the context of the clinical presentation and to not misclassify culturally endorsed or developmentally appropriate dependent behavior as pathological (American Psychiatric Association, 2000b; Bornstein, 1999).

Clinical Presentation

Needs and Fears These individuals have a pervasive, excessive need to be taken care of, which results in submissive and clinging behavior and fears of separation beginning in early adulthood (American Psychiatric Association, 2000b; First et al., 2004). Clinical symptoms may include difficulties making decisions without advice and reassurance, trouble initiating and completing tasks independently, excessive reliance on and deference to others, and the need for nurturance (American Psychiatric Association, 2000b; Fauman, 2002; Skodol, 2005). Underlying these behaviors are pessimism, extreme self-doubt, excessive and unrealistic fears of being unable to cope without others, and an unwillingness to express disagreement for fear of abandonment (American Psychiatric Association, 2004b; A. Roth & Fonagy, 2005). It is important to differentiate this reluctance to get angry from the realistic fear of retribution in abusive relationships (American Psychiatric Association, 2000b). These fears must be determined to be excessive and unrealistic, not related to condition or disability (American Psychiatric Association, 2000b). Viewing themselves as inept, they allow all decisions to be made by others and fail to learn independent living skills, resulting in significant impairment in occupational functioning (American Psychiatric Association, 2000b; Levy & Scott, 2006). This is further exacerbated by their fear of appearing too competent, since this may result in abandonment. When a relationship ends, they may replace it indiscriminately with another that often involves a negligent, exploitive partner (American Psychiatric Association, 2000b; Widiger & Bornstein, 2001).

Abusive Relationships   Individuals with Dependent PD manage their fears of inadequacy by clinging to others and interpreting others' criticism and disapproval as confirmation of their own worthlessness in a self-critical, denigrating manner (First & Tasman, 2004). As these individuals frequently become involved in submissive, abusive, unbalanced relationships, this differentiation may at times be difficult to make (Levy & Scott, 2006).

Onset, Course, and Life Span Considerations

As children, individuals with Dependent PD may have had separation anxiety or a physical illness or been excessively clingy and submissive (First & Tasman, 2004). As adolescents, they often defer to their parents for everyday decisions, including what to wear, whom to be friends with, and which activities to join; they continue as submissive and clingy, often learning few independent living skills (American Psychiatric Association, 2000b). They have difficulty initiating action or following through on decisions, and considering themselves inept and incapable, they continually depend on others. They dread autonomy and may be productive only under others' supervision (Maxmen & Ward, 1995). Dependent PD was found to be a significant predictor of disability (B. F. Grant et al., 2004). These individuals' need for others' approval and intense fear of loss of others' concern result in their going to excessive lengths to secure nurturance from others, including attaching indiscriminately (Bornstein, 1999; Widiger & Bornstein, 2001). Their excessive neediness may drive others away and make them vulnerable to exploitive, rejecting, and abusive relationships (First & Tasman, 2004). Their personal histories include recurrent themes of self-sacrifice, inadequacy, insecurity, fears of abandonment, and an extreme reliance on others (American Psychiatric Association, 2000b; Bornstein, 1999; McClanahan et al., 2003). The symptoms may decrease if they find a reliable, understanding partner; however, if the relationship ends, they may frantically seek out a replacement relationship or experience prolonged impairment (First & Tasman, 2004). The development of comorbid anxiety and mood disorders negatively impacts the prognosis.

Obsessive-Compulsive Personality Disorder

Individuals with Obsessive-Compulsive PD have consistently been described as present-ing with extreme rigidity, perfectionism, a preoccupation with details and orderliness, and a need for cognitive and interpersonal control (American Psychiatric Association, 2000b; First et al., 2004; McCann, 1999). These personality features often result in relationship and occupational difficulties, yet they are not only ego-syntonic but often are valued by the individual in a self-righteous, moralistic manner (First & Tasman, 2004). Obsessive-Compulsive PD is one of the less frequently diagnosed PDs, occurring in 5% to 25% of psychiatric patients, and has a high overlap with other PDs (First & Tasman, 2004; McCann, 1999). These individuals may present as drab, monotonous, overcontrolled in-tellectualizers with a chronic sense of time pressure and excessive devotion to work (American Psychiatric Association, 2000b; Skodol, 2005). They are prone to depression, particularly as they age, and they become dissatisfied with their overvalued careers (First et al., 2004). This disorder, unlike Axis I Obsessive-Compulsive Disorder, does not have obsessions and compulsions as part of its clinical presentation; however, some re-searchers contend that both disorders are better conceptualized as on a spectrum rather than as discrete entities (McCann, 1999). Some individuals' cultural reference groups en-dorse and encourage an overemphasis on competitiveness, work, and status, and these cultural values must be considered when assessing for this disorder (American Psychiatric Association, 2000b).

Clinical Presentation

Need for Control   The characteristic features of Obsessive-Compulsive PD are a preoccu-pation with orderliness, perfectionism, and interpersonal control (American Psychiatric As-sociation, 2000b). This pervasive pattern is at the expense of flexibility, openness, and efficiency, has an onset in early adulthood, is stable, and occurs across situations (American Psychiatric Association, 2000b). The clinical presentation involves a level of preoccupation with rules and structure to the extent that the purpose of activities is lost; perfectionism that interferes with completion; and excessive devotion to work or a workaholic approach (American Psychiatric Association, 2000b; Fauman, 2002). Individuals with Obsessive-Compulsive PD are also cognitively inflexible and moralistic. Unable to delegate or let go, they clutter their lives with the hoarding of meaningless and worthless objects (Levy & Scott, 2006). Their excessive need to control, rigid adherence to rules, preoccupation with often irrelevant, trivial details, and insistence that others comply make it difficult for these individuals to work with others (Fauman, 2002; A. Roth & Fonagy, 2005). Their lives are joyless, with the constant postponement of pleasurable activities; everything becomes a task or a project to be accomplished; they are miserly with their money, time, and affection (LaBruzza & Mendez-Villarrubia, 1997). They have difficulty expressing their highly con-trolled emotions. Thus they appear formal, stiff, and dour, what Reich (1949) described as "living machines." They may be preoccupied with intellect and logic and intolerant of af-fection, rarely expressing tenderness; they are hypersensitive to status and vacillate between excessive deference and resistance to authority (First & Tasman, 2004).

Perfectionism   Individuals with Obsessive-Compulsive PD are scrupulously moralistic, rigidly imposing high standards on themselves and others, and when they are unable to follow these standards they become mercilessly self-critical (American Psychiatric Association, 2000b). Their extreme adherence to perfectionism contributes to difficulty with decision making and initiating activities, which results in unproductive procrastination (McCann, 1999). As with the Dependent PD, they use dichotomous thinking to imagine catastrophe and magnify the potential negative outcomes (Bailey, 1998). Their self-imposed perfectionism results in obsessively and repeatedly checking for errors and in procrastination, which often antagonizes others. Individuals with Obsessive-Compulsive PD manage their anxiety about others' criticism by a rigid adherence to strict rule-based standards (American Psychiatric Association, 2000b; McClanahan et al., 2003; Scott & Levy, 2006).

Onset, Course, and Life Span Considerations

During childhood and adolescence, individuals with Obsessive-Compulsive PD may have been conscientious, well-behaved, overly serious, and rigid (First & Tasman, 2004). As adults, they may be very successful in their occupation because they tend to be workaholics, showing excessive diligence and perfectionism and refusing free time. There is also an overlap with Type A characteristics, including competitiveness, time urgency, and a preoccupation with work (American Psychiatric Association, 2000b). On the other hand, these individuals may procrastinate and show poor time management, with excessive attention to inconsequential details, resulting in missed deadlines (American Psychiatric Association, 2000b). Their rigid adherence to rules, lack of flexibility, excessive perfectionism, inability to delegate, and need for control all adversely impact their occupational functioning (Levy & Scott, 2006). Their avoidance of emotion makes it difficult in turn for them to empathize with others, and their relationship history is often very restricted and controlled, with limited spontaneity, few pleasurable activities, and an excessive devotion to work (American Psychiatric Association, 2000b). Family relationships may be strained by the avoidance of leisure activities and by an authoritarian, domineering parenting style and detached uninvolvement. In middle age these individuals may be vulnerable to depression secondary to occupational failures or a realization of the personal sacrifices made for work (First & Tasman, 2004). Some individuals also experience difficulty discarding things and become packrats or hoarders.

PERSONALITY DISORDER NOT OTHERWISE SPECIFIED

If the individual presents with mixed features for several PDs but does not fulfill any one disorder, or if the individual meets the criteria for a disorder proposed for further study (Depressive PD or Passive-Aggressive PD), then the diagnosis PD-NOS should be assigned (American Psychiatric Association, 2000b). This is the most common PD diagnosed in clinical practice (L. A. Clark et al., 1995). As there are no diagnostic criteria, this tends to be a very heterogeneous group, making it difficult to conduct research or make inferences about it. Maladaptive personality traits that are relevant but that do not meet the threshold for a PD should be coded in the following manner: V71.09 NO diagnosis on Axis II, paranoid personality traits.

EPIDEMIOLOGY

Using a nationally representative epidemiological sample and structured diagnostic interviews in 2000–2001, B. F. Grant and colleagues (2004) found that 30.8 million Americans (14.79%) had at least one PD. They reported the following prevalence rates for the general population: Paranoid, 4.41%; Schizoid, 3.13%; Antisocial, 3.63%; Histrionic, 1.84%; Avoidant, 2.36%; Dependent, 0.49%; and Obsessive-Compulsive, 7.88%. Women were found to have a higher risk for Avoidant, Dependent, and Paranoid PDs, whereas men were at higher risk for Antisocial PD. After reviewing epidemiological studies, Levy and Scott (2006) report the prevalence rates for PDs among the general population to be 6% to 20%. The *DSM-IV-TR* notes the following prevalence rates in the general population and community samples: Paranoid, .5% to 2.5%; Schizoid, no data; Schizotypal, 3%; Antisocial, 3% of males and 1% of females; Borderline, 2%; Histrionic, 2% to 3%; Narcissistic, 1%; Avoidant, .5% to 1%; Dependent, no data; and Obsessive-Compulsive, 1% (American Psychiatric Association, 2000b). The prevalence rates in community samples are lower when semistructured interviews are used, resulting in the following range of rates: Paranoid, 0% to 2.4%; Schizoid, 0% to 4.1%; Schizotypal, 0% to 3.9%; Antisocial, 0% to 2.6%; Borderline, 0% to 5.5%; Histrionic, .3% to 3.9%; Narcissistic, 0% to 3.9%; Avoidant, 0% to 5.2%; Dependent, .1% to 10.3%; and Obsessive-Compulsive, .5% to 10.8% (First & Tasman, 2004). In England, 52% of the individuals seen by community mental health teams were found to meet the criteria for one or more PDs (Keown, Holloway, & Kuipers, 2002).

In clinical settings, the prevalence of PDs is reported to be considerably higher, with the highest number—20% to 40% of psychiatric outpatients and 50% of psychiatric inpatients—meeting criteria for a PD when structured diagnostic assessments were used (Levy & Scott, 2006). With psychiatric outpatients, M. Zimmerman, Rothschild, and Chelminski (2005) used a structured interview for the *DSM-IV* and found a prevalence rate of 31.4% for PDs; this rate increased to 45.5% when the NOS disorder was included. They also found that 60.4% of those meeting the criteria for one PD had more than one, and 25.2% had two or more PDs, and that Avoidant and NOS were the most frequent disorders assigned. When standardized interviews were used with psychiatric inpatients and outpatients, at least half of the individuals were diagnosed as having a PD. Cluster B PDs, particularly Borderline PD, tended to be the most frequently diagnosed. Cluster A PDs, notably Schizoid PD, were the most infrequent (M. Zimmerman et al., 2005). The *DSM-IV-TR* notes the following prevalence rates for psychiatric inpatients and mental health outpatients, respectively: Paranoid (10% to 30%, 2% to 10%), Antisocial (3% to 30%), Borderline (20%, 10%), Histrionic (10% to 15%), Narcissistic (2% to 16%), Avoidant (10% outpatient), and Obsessive-Compulsive (3% to 10%; American Psychiatric Association, 2000b). No data are provided on the prevalence of Schizoid and Schizotypal PDs, which are the least frequently diagnosed disorders in clinical settings, and no data are provided on Dependent PD, which is the most frequently diagnosed PD in clinical settings (American Psychiatric Association, 2000b). Reviewing epidemiological studies, Mattia and Zimmerman (2001) note that Cluster C was the most common cluster and that the most common PD was Obsessive-Compulsive. Moran and colleagues (2000) also found in primary care settings that Cluster C PDs are the most common.

In a study on a small sample (103) of Australian female offenders, 36% were diagnosed with a PD (Tye & Mullen, 2006). In a larger study in Australia comparing a community and a prison sample, A. C. Butler and colleagues (2006) found for the prisoners a 12-month prevalence of 43.1% for any PD (Cluster A, 27.3%; Cluster B, 30.9%; and Cluster C, 28.6%). In contrast, community members had a weighted 12-month prevalence of 9.2% for any PD (Cluster A, 4.1%; Cluster B, 3.8%; and Cluster C, 5.6%). In reviewing epidemiological studies of psychiatric disorders in correctional settings, Brink (2005) reported that out of 22 studies, only 3 studies noted personality disorders as separate, and the rates varied from 17% to 78%, with the highest rate being for male prisoners who were remanded into custody.

Summarizing the research, Levy and Scott (2006) note that individuals diagnosed with PDs are more likely to be single and younger (25 to 44) and equally likely to be male or female, with the exception of Antisocial PD, which occurs more frequently in males. They also note that in community samples the individuals with PDs were more likely to have alcohol and substance abuse problems and to experience adverse life events, including relationship and housing problems and long-term unemployment (Moran, 1999).

There is a lack of studies on the prevalence of PDs in older adults. Earlier studies found inconsistent results in determining the prevalence of PDs in the elderly, with some showing these disorders decreasing with age (Ekselius, Tillfors, Furmark, & Fredrickson, 2001). In contrast, Abrams and Horowitz (1996) found no such decline and the prevalence of PDs to be 10% in those older than 50. This rate may be an underestimation, as health care providers for this population are more likely to diagnose and treat an Axis I disorder than recognize a PD (Lynch & Aspnes, 2001). In a small sample of older adults (30) and younger adults (30) who were chronically mentally ill, Coolidge and colleagues (Coolidge, Segal, Pointer, Knaus, Yamazaki, & Silberman, 2000) found a high prevalence rate for PDs: 58% for the older and 66% for the younger group. The difference between the two groups was nonsignificant. Those in the younger group were more likely to receive Antisocial, Borderline, Passive-Aggressive, Sadistic, and Schizotypal PD diagnoses, and there was no difference between the two groups in the rate of Obsessive-Compulsive PD.

ETIOLOGY

Personality disorders are a heterogeneous group. Early theories of etiology were based on psychoanalytic theory or clinical inferences, often lacking empirical support and only recently including research findings (Levy & Scott, 2005). In reviewing the genetic research, Cloninger (2005) concluded that substantial research now exists that personality disorders are complex biopsychosocial phenomena. Paris (2005) proposes that they are best understood using an integrative stress-diathesis model. This allows for the consideration of the role of heritability, gene-environment interactions, temperament and biological factors, and the cumulative effects of multiple risk factors, including childhood adversities and sociocultural factors in their etiology and course (Magnavita, 2005; Paris, 2005). The research in this area has been limited by comorbidity and the trend for studies to use dimensional models rather than *DSM-IV-TR* diagnostic categories (Cloninger, 2005). Diagnostic definitional differences have contributed to what Jang and Vernon (2001, p. 177) aptly describe as "the elusive phenotype." Also, whereas some disorders, like Antisocial and Borderline PDs, have been the subject of decades of research, others, like Paranoid and Dependent PDs, have been virtually ignored.

Biological Theories

Cluster A PDs were originally thought to be on a spectrum with Schizophrenia, as both Schizoid and Schizotypal PDs are frequently found in the relatives of chronic schizophrenics (Kety et al., 1968; Kety & Wender, 1994; Torgersen, Onstad, Skre, Edvardsen, & Kringlen, 1993; Torgersen, Lygren, Oien, Shre, Onstad, Edvardsen, et al., 2000). The shared phenotypic resemblance was related to an underlying genetic vulnerability, or schizotypy, which was associated with schizotaxia, the synaptic slippage that was proposed to occur as a result of the combination of the Schizophrenia gene(s) with social learning influences (Lenzenweger, 1999; Meehl, 1962; M. B. Miller et al., 2001). Subsequent family and genetic studies have found that Schizotypal PD is related to Schizophrenia and the presence of more negative features in family samples, in contrast to clinical samples (Bergman, Silverman, Harvey, Smith, & Siever, 2000; Fanous, Gardner, Walsh, & Kendler, 2001; Jang & Vernon, 2001). There is little evidence, however, to suggest that Schizoid and Paranoid PDs are genetically related to Schizophrenia or are heritable (Bernstein & Travaglini, 1999). There is also weak evidence of a relationship between Paranoid PD and Delusional Disorder (Kazdin, 2000; Levy & Scott, 2006; M. B. Miller et al., 2001; Nigg & Goldsmith, 1994). Heritability research does suggest that the traits of suspiciousness, mistrust, and introversion, which are central to Paranoid and Schizoid PDs, are inherited (First & Tasman, 2004). M. B. Miller and colleagues (2001) suggest that for Cluster A PDs, the most relevant psychobiological risk factors are attention or selection deficits that contribute to the individual's mistrust, misunderstanding, and social isolation. On a neurotransmitter level, Coccaaro (2004) hypothesizes that dopamine may be inversely related with the characteristic Schizotypal deficit symptoms of interpersonal isolation and constricted affect.

In terms of Cluster B disorders, there is consistent research from adoption, family, and twin studies supporting the inheritance of antisocial tendencies (Sutker & Allain, 2001). The research discussed earlier in Chapter 6 on the etiology of Conduct Disorder is relevant here, including that of Farrington and colleagues (2001) on the aggregation of antisocial behavior in families and Foley and colleagues' (2004) work showing the impact of environment on the expression of genetic vulnerabilities. Biological theories have also focused on the role of temperament and deficits in behavioral inhibition in the development of Conduct Disorder and subsequent Antisocial PD (Fowles, 2001; Fowles & Kokanska, 2000; Frick & Morris, 2004; Moffitt, 2003). Family history and adoption studies suggest the possibility of a genetic association between Somatization Disorder, Histrionic PD, and Antisocial PD and sensation seeking and impulsive behavior (Lilienfeld & Hess, 2001). Some have described Histrionic and Antisocial PDs as phenotypic variants that are shaped by culture, hormones, and socialization and that share a similar genetic vulnerability that also occurs in Somatization Disorder (First et al., 2004; LaBruzza & Mendez-Villarrubia, 1997; Lilienfeld & Hess, 2001). Widiger and colleagues (2002) have theorized that Histrionic PD may be a maladaptive form of the personality traits of extraversion and neuroticism. They suggest that a hyperresponsiveness of the noradrenergic system may contribute to the pronounced emotional reactivity for Histrionic PD (Widiger & Bornstein, 2001). The genetic research for Borderline PD is very limited; there are no adoption studies, and to date only two twin studies, which had small samples and methodological limitations (Trull et al., 2006). H. E. Adams and colleagues (2001) note that individuals with Borderline PD are 5 times more likely to have first-degree relatives with the disorder. Family studies show significantly higher rates of impulse spectrum disorders, with a higher family aggregation for alcoholism, substance abuse, and antisocial and impulsive behaviors in the relatives of individuals with Borderline PD (White, Gunderson, Zanarini, & Hudson, 2003). The personality traits of impulsivity and emotional dysregulation that underline Borderline PD have also been found to be inherited and have a genetic basis (Paris, 2000; Silk, 2000). Trull and colleagues (2006) hypothesize that the eventual Borderline PD phenotype is so heterogeneous because its development relates to multiple genetic personality traits that vary in their level of effect. Reduced serotonergic activity in Borderline PD has been related to the clinical features of impulsivity and affective instability (Skodol, Siever, et al., 2002). Although there is evidence of the heritability of the traits of arrogance and conceit, to date, there is no evidence for the genetic basis of Narcissistic PD (First & Tasman, 2004; Jang & Vernon, 2001; Widiger & Bornstein, 2001).

Genetics and familial research on Cluster C PDs is very limited and has tended to focus on the inheritance of the traits of introversion, neuroticism, agreeableness (submissiveness), and obsessionality (Widiger & Bornstein, 2001; Widiger et al., 2002). Torgersen and colleagues (2000) note that although earlier research studies suggest evidence of a genetic basis for these disorders, they frequently had very small numbers and several methodological limitations (Trull et al., 2006). Studies have also focused on the role of temperament, such as shyness and inhibition, and lower limbic system reactivity, particularly for Avoidant PD (Bernstein & Travaglini, 1999). Reviewing the research, Villemarette-Pittman and colleagues, (Villemarette-Pitman, Stanford, Greve, Houston & Mathias, 2004) note the continued controversy over considering Obsessive-Compulsive PD as an obsessive-compulsive spectrum disorder. Research by both Posner and colleagues, (Posner, Rothbart, Vizueta, Thomas, Levy, et al., 2002) and Depue and Lenzenweger (2005) has focused on the role of temperamental and behavioral factors in the development of personality disorders.

Psychological Theories

The lack of longitudinal and empirical studies on Cluster A PDs currently limits our understanding of the role of psychosocial factors in the development of these disorders (First & Tasman, 2004). Early clinical studies focused on the individual's reliance on the defense mechanism of projection and the development of a hyperalert or vigilant cognitive style as indicative of Paranoid PD (M. B. Miller et al., 2001; D. Shapiro, 1965). Beck, Freeman, and Davis (2003) hypothesized that beliefs and feelings of inadequacy and being unable to cope interpersonally are central to Paranoid PD, and that the irrational beliefs are maintained by biased information processing. Earlier theories of the influence of excessive parental criticism and rejection lack empirical support, and there is no evidence of the role of childhood home environmental factors in the development of Paranoid PD (First & Tasman, 2004; M. B. Miller et al., 2001). Very little empirical research exists on the psychological factors associated with Schizoid and Schizotypal PDs (M. B. Miller et al., 2001). An earlier retrospective recall study suggested the role of childhood emotional depravation, but apart from methodological limitation it is not clear if the reported parental disengagement related to the presence of a familial genetic vulnerability for these traits (M. B. Miller et al., 2001). More recently, the relationship between Schizoid PD and autism spectrum disorders has been raised (Fitzgerald, 1999). Unfortunately, as Towbin (2005) notes, there are too few studies of the developmental histories of adults with Schizoid, Schizotypal, and Avoidant PDs to know if the behaviors characteristic of the pervasive developmental disorders are present during these individuals' childhood.

Cluster B PDs are the most widely studied of the PDs in terms of psychological factors. There is a long history of extensive research, including longitudinal studies, on the role of familial, social, and environmental factors in the development of antisocial behaviors. Risk factors are believed to be cumulative and interactional, and there are a range of developmental pathways that may lead to Antisocial PD (Hill, 2002; Loeber & Stouthamer-Loeber, 1998; Moffitt, 2003). Significant risk factors are temperamental style, maternal depression, parental psychopathology, coercive parenting relationships, deviant peers, and psychosocial and community factors (J. D. Burke et al., 2002; Dodge & Pettit, 2003; Kimonis & Frick, 2006).

Attachment theory has been used to describe the development of the characteristic interpersonal patterns of Histrionic, Borderline, and Narcissistic PDs. According to this theory, secondary to inconsistent caretaking, individuals with Histrionic PD develop a "preoccupied" attachment style, characterized by an intrusive and demanding interpersonal style (Bartholomew, Kwong, & Hart, 2001). Their characteristic exaggerated emotionality can be understood as a means to engage and maintain others' interest (Gunderson & Gabbard, 2000). S. M. Johnson (1994) describes family patterns associated with the development of Histrionic PD as including a domineering parent, a weaker, ineffectual parent, and blurred boundaries between the parent and child.

Individuals with Borderline PD have been described as having insecure attachments following unresolved, preoccupied, and fearful attachments (Agrawal, Gunderson, Holmes, & Lyon-Ruth, 2004). As Trull and colleagues (2006) note, there are different views in the field; they quote Nickell and colleagues (2002), who found that parental bonding and attachment variables predicted Borderline PD over and above childhood adversity. In contrast, Fossati and colleagues (2001) found that temperament was more important than attachment in discriminating borderline symptoms from other clinical symptoms. Some individuals with Borderline PD have a history of childhood sexual and physical abuse, and the severity of the abuse and the chaotic nature of the home may play a role in the development of their disorder (H. E. Adams et al., 2001; Paris, 1999; Sabo, 1997). In reviewing the role of psychological adversity in the development of Borderline PD, Paris (2004a) notes that a third of individuals with this disorder report severe abuse experiences, including incestuous perpetrators, that are likely to play an etiological role. Family histories of individuals with Borderline PD have found dysfunctional family environments characterized by emotional neglect, conflict, and hostility (Gunderson, 2001; Paris, 1999). Linehan (1993a) describes these invalidating environments as contributing to the child's difficulties in learning to trust and regulate their own emotions and tolerate emotional distress.

Early theories of narcissism described unempathic, devaluing parents who failed to mirror or idealized their child (Kernberg, 1975a,b; Kohut, 1968; Millon, 1996). Family settings where the child is overindulged or given a role or function that is special have been linked to the individual's sense of entitlement and the need for omnipotent control (Ronningstam, 1999). Caregiver-child interaction patterns and attachment have also been associated with affect under- and overregulation and hypersensitivity and the development of Narcissistic PD (Schore, 1994). Based on A. T. Beck and Freeman's (1990) earlier work, Young (1998) identified the core characteristic cognitive schema of the narcissistic individual, including entitlement, which are clustered to represent aspects of the self, including the "special self."

The shyness and interpersonal inhibition of the Avoidant PD has been related to childhood parental overprotectiveness, extreme cautiousness, a distress-prone temperament, and a history of embarrassing or devaluing experiences (Burgess, Rubin, Chea, & Nelson, 2001; Schmidt, Polak, & Spooner, 2001). Children as young as 2 years have been found to show patterns of heightened sympathetic sensitivity to environmental changes that remain stable throughout childhood and are believed to be inherited (Bartholomew, Kwong, & Hart, 2001; Kantor, 2003). Benjamin (2003) suggests that a biological predisposition alone is insufficient to account for the emergence of Avoidant PD, and posits that it is environmental factors that change the predisposition into a pervasive pattern. Bernstein and Travaglini (1999) describe how temperamental vulnerability, low self-esteem, early adverse experiences, parental guilt-engendering and rejecting experiences, and verbal emotional abuse all relate to the development of Avoidant PD. The child may experience relentless parental control, emphasizing the need to create an impressive appearance (Benjamin, 2003). The fear of parental and peer rejection results in avoidance behaviors, including a hypersensitivity to rejection and a restriction of social experiences (Eskedal & Demetri, 2006). After reviewing the research, Alden and colleagues (Alden, Laposa, Taylor, & Ryder, 2000) note that despite being the most prevalent PD, there is a paucity of research on Avoidant PD, and they suggest that future research focus on the role of the aspects of avoidance, specifically the avoidance of novelty, and the variability in interpersonal problems associated with this disorder.

Insecure attachment and helplessness associated with inconsistent, unreliable, or overprotective parenting has been linked to the development of Dependent PD (Gabbard, 2000a; Pincus & Wilson, 2001). These factors are thought to combine with an anxious fearful temperament to result in an internalized self-concept as weak and a preoccupation with fears of abandonment and insecurity (Widiger & Bornstein, 2001). Millon and Davis (2000) hypothesized that the child's fearful, sad, withdrawing temperament elicits overconcern and overprotection from the parent, and that prolonged childhood illnesses may be associated with the development of Dependent PD. Others note that authoritarian or overprotective parenting may exacerbate these feelings and, by discouraging autonomy, individuation, and the development of independence skills, contribute further to continued infantilization and dependency (Bornstein, 1999; Eskedal & Demetri, 2006). It may also be that these dependency-fostering behaviors reflect parents who are themselves dependent (Kochanska, Friesenberg, Lange, & Martel, 2004). Additionally, the individual's irrational cognitive schema are believed to perpetuate this lack of self-worth, sense of powerlessness, intense neediness, and inadequacy, resulting in the individual indiscriminately attaching to others who are often exploitive (Widiger & Bornstein, 2001).

To date there is no research for the evidence of a biological predisposition for Obsessive-Compulsive PD (Eskedal & Demetri, 2006; Millon & Davis, 2000). Clinical theories of the development of this disorder focus on the role of shame and guilt, the struggles for autonomy and control, and the conflict between defiance and obedience (Gunderson & Gabbard, 2000; McCann, 1999). Other theorists emphasize parental overcontrol, learned compulsive behaviors, and a focus on perfectionism and rigidity in childhood (Anderluh, Tchanturia, Rabe-Hesketh, & Tresure, 2003; Sperry, 1995). Parent-child relationships are described as deferential, often lacking nurturance and loving, supportive sentiments, with an emphasis on flawlessness, control, and avoiding punishment (Sperry, 1995). To avoid failure and falling short of the ideal, the individual becomes preoccupied with minutiae and anticipating the future (Eskedal & Demetri, 2006). A. T. Beck and colleagues (2003) describe the cognitive rigidity, perfectionism, and strict moralistic code characteristic of these individuals, which is applied to their interpersonal relationships and which accounts for their need to control and assume responsibility.

DIVERSITY CONSIDERATIONS

Personality disorders are closely tied to cultural expectations, and the first criterion in diagnostic determination explicitly states that evaluation of a PD must start with the clinician's awareness of what is expected by the individual's particular culture (American Psychiatric Association, 2000b). Overall, there is limited research on the impact of culture on PDs, but the research that does exist indicates that although *DSM-IV-TR* PDs have been identified in diverse cultures around the world, there are cultural variations in the expression of these disorders (Alarcon, 1996, 2005; Cooke, 1996). It is critical that the clinician considers the individual's clinical presentation in his or her unique cultural and social context to avoid pathologizing culturally condoned behaviors (Millon & Grossman, 2005). Reviewing the research on paranoid conditions and the different cultures' associations between suspiciousness and pathological behaviors, Blaney (1999) notes that, in contrast to Caucasians in the United States, mistrust for African Americans is more closely associated with depression than with paranoid disorders. He also quotes earlier research that found trust has a qualitatively different role in interpersonal relationships in the United States and Japan (Whaley, 1997; Yamagishi & Yamagishi, 1994). The *DSM-IV-TR* cautions the clinician that when diagnosing Paranoid PD it is crucial to consider the individual's ethnic and cultural background and not "erroneously label" individuals from minority groups, immigrants, political refugees, asylum seekers, or members of persecuted and disenfranchised groups as paranoid (American Psychiatric Association, 2000b; Blaney, 1999). Narcissistic PD, which is not included in the *ICD-10*, has a very low prevalence in some countries, which may be accounted for by cultural differences in the expression of self-esteem and narcissistic behaviors (Ronningstam, 1999; M. H. Stone, 1998). Bornstein (1999) reports profound cultural attitudinal differences in the expression of autonomy and dependence, with Western societies valuing independence and self-reliance. In contrast, he describes how affiliative and dependent behaviors are not only expected but are the norm in Japan and India. One study on Histrionic PD and ethnicity found that it was more frequently diagnosed in Latin American than in Asian cultures (Bornstein, 1999). Chavira, Grilo, Shea, Yen, Gunderson, Morey, et al., (2003) found that Borderline PD was also assigned to Hispanics more than Caucasians or African Americans. However, given scarcity of research, these findings must be interpreted with caution.

In terms of gender differences, both Paranoid and Schizoid PD are more frequently diagnosed in males, which may relate to societal expectations for men to be emotionally constricted (American Psychiatric Association, 2000b; Blaney, 1999). Whereas Schizoid PD is more common in males, Avoidant PD is more common in females (Bernstein & Travaglini, 1999). Histrionic PD tends to be diagnosed in women more than men, and the behavioral expression of Histrionic PD in males may include attempts to attract attention by bragging about physical prowess or athletic skills; overall, there has been a lack of research on gender expressions of this disorder (Bornstein, 1999). The current diagnostic criteria may be biased more toward expressions of histrionic behavior in women, and male Histrionic PD features are subsumed under Antisocial PD. The *DSM-IV-TR* notes that Borderline PD tends to be more frequently diagnosed in females, whereas Antisocial PD is more frequently diagnosed in males (American Psychiatric Association, 2000b). However, reviews of previous studies indicate inconsistent results for the gender difference with Borderline PD, particularly when diagnostic interviews or nonclinical community samples are used (D. M. Johnson et al., 2003; Skodol & Bender, 2003; Torgersen et al., 2001). In looking at the similarities in psychopathology in Borderline and Antisocial PD, Paris (1997) hypothesizes that there may be gender differences in the expressions of the same disorder and differences in the prominence of the affective components.

When considering age or life span, clinical practice is to rarely, if ever, assign a PD to a child and never assign an Antisocial PD to a child under 18 years (American Psychiatric Association, 2000b). For many individuals, personality traits often mellow with age. Edelstein and colleagues (2003) note that older adults with PDs have had them for several decades, and there are no longitudinal studies on this group. They describe two alternate theories. The first is the predisposition hypothesis, by which older adults who experience age-related stressors such as loss or physical illness present with decreased independence, impaired coping, and increasing problems (Sadavoy & Leszcz, 1987). The second theory, the maturation hypothesis, divides PDs into immature types (Histrionic, Narcissistic, Antisocial, and Borderline) and mature types (Obsessive-Compulsive, Schizoid, and Paranoid). Edelstein et al. (2003) theorize that the immature types tend to improve with age, which may be related to the decrease in activity level, making impulsive acting-out and high-risk behaviors such as reckless driving less likely (Abrams, 1990). In contrast, the mature type PDs worsen with age (Kernberg, 1984; Tyer, 1988). Early research by J. C. Perry (1993) showed that the prevalence of Antisocial and Borderline PDs decrease dramatically with age, whereas Zweig and Hillman (1999) found that as individuals with Borderline PD age, they continue to have high levels of Axis I comorbidity and present at increased risk for suicide. Bornstein (1999) noted that dependence varies with age, and especially in older adults it is important to differentiate between what he describes as health-related vulnerabilities and health-oriented support from Dependent PD.

INTAKE AND INTERVIEWING CONSIDERATIONS

Rapport

Interviewing individuals with PDs can be challenging, as they rarely seek treatment of their own volition and many have none or limited insight into the nature of their problems, which are enduring and ego-syntonic (Bender, 2005; Othmer & Othmer, 2002). The nature of these disorders, by definition, implies the presence of maladaptive, pervasive patterns that negatively impact the individual's capacity to interpret the world and establish interpersonal relationships (American Psychiatric Association, 2000b). Depending on the disorder, the clinician may be confronted with everything from hostility to superficial charm to idealization followed by devaluation (Gutheil, 2005). Individuals with PDs may present with extreme distress and insist on immediate relief. It is important to be flexible and adjust the interview style to match the individual's clinical presentation while staying focused enough to gather the necessary information (McClanahan et al., 2003). It is also critical to be continually mindful of the role of cultural factors in the expression of clinical symptoms and on the establishment of the therapeutic alliance (Alarcon, 2005). Given the range of symptomatology and rapport-challenging behaviors, disorder-specific intake strategies will be discussed in more detail.

Interview and Assessment Strategies

Clinical Interview

With PDs it is crucial to be prepared with a very organized approach for the intake interview (see Table 14.2), and to remember the mnemonic CLIENTS (Cause, Length, Impairment, Extinguished, Noticed, Tried anything, and Stopped) to assess the clinical symptoms. Given the long-standing nature of these disorders, the clinician needs to conduct a thorough developmental history, paying particular attention to the nature of the individual's relational experiences and early friendships. Any underlying reasons for patterns of isolation and poor peer relationships should be explored, while remaining alert for recurrent difficulties, themes, patterns, or styles of coping such as avoidance, leaving, attributions of responsibility, blaming others, and lack of insight (Othmer & Othmer, 2002).

McClanahan and colleagues (2003) suggest a series of questions that can be helpful in assessing the quality of the individual's relationships with others (see Table 14.3). When querying the individual's history, listen for and ask about patterns that occur across situa-

---

Table 14.2   Intake issues for personality disorders

Rapport is difficult, and there is a lack of insight.
Assess impulsivity and suicide risk.
Be alert for and monitor countertransference.
Attend to the interpersonal process in the interview.
Evaluate cognitions, behaviors, emotions, interpersonal skills.
Consider cultural and developmental factors in symptom presentation.
Obtain a detailed personal and relationship history.
Screen and remain alert for themes and patterns.
Determine if symptoms are pervasive and long-standing.
Evaluate impairment and distress at home, work, and in relationships.
Collateral information is essential.
Obtain releases and consents.
Assess for comorbid disorders.
Determine need for adjunct services.
Assess for recent and past stressors or trauma.
Evaluate context of symptom occurrence.
Consider using self-report measure and structured interview.
Document.

Table 14.3 Interview questions for personality disorders

Questions to Consider[*]

How would you describe yourself?

Do you experience yourself differently in different settings?

How would someone who knows you well describe you?

How would this description differ from that of a brief acquaintance?

What types of people are attracted to or gravitate to you?

Who do you avoid or not like and how would you describe them?

Describe the beginnings and endings of important past relationships.

Do you notice any common themes in your relationships?

Are there any behaviors that trigger particular responses?

In the past, what did and didn't work for you?

What did you like or dislike about prior clinicians?

Relationship Questions to Consider

How did you meet?

How would you describe your partner (be alert for idealization or devaluation)?

How would you describe the nature of the relationship?

Was it satisfying?

Was the individual monogamous or promiscuous?

Were high-risk behaviors or substance use involved?

How did it end, and what was the nature of the ending?

What has been the nature of the contact since then?

Source: [*]From "Personality Disorders" (pp. 173–202), by J. Z. McClanahan, S. A. Kim, and M. Bobowick, in *Diagnostic Interviewing,* third edition, M. Hersen and S. M. Turner (Eds.), 2003, New York: Kluwer Academic. Adapted with kind permission of Springer Science and Business Media.

tions, that appear to be inflexible, and that are repeated and not modified despite adverse consequences, indicating an inability to learn from experience. In terms of the individual's behavior, it is helpful to look for any preferred patterns, the individual's modus operandi, or the dominant threads in the fabric of his or her experience (McClanahan et al., 2003; Millon & Elevery, 1985). When evaluating these patterns it is crucial to consider the role of friends, family, and culture in influencing the expression of these behaviors.

The presence of a PD is determined by the content of individuals' responses and by their interpersonal interplay, including their nonverbal behaviors and the clinician's reaction to them. Thus the interview itself may trigger individuals' maladaptive responses, and their reaction to you will provide additional diagnostic information (Othmer & Othmer, 2002). In most cases, it is safe to assume that how clients respond to you and make you feel is how they react to others in their life. In this way, the clinical interview provides you with a unique perspective into the nature of the individual's relationships with others. It allows for consideration of how these clients deal with ambiguity and social anxiety and for an understanding of their reaction to perceived authority, structure, and emotional issues (Othmer & Othmer, 2002). The relationship between the content of their responses and their reaction provides invaluable information on their insight, judgment, planning, coping strategies, and resources. By gathering a detailed personal history, patterns and stressors that the individual is sensitive to and chronic coping deficits across different settings may be apparent. The number of similar conflicts the individual has within a year indicates the severity of these behaviors (Othmer & Othmer, 2002).

Central to the identification of pervasive maladaptive patterns is the impact of these patterns on the individual's relationships. Othmer and Othmer (2002) recommend identifying the triggers for the individual's maladjusted responses, which are apparent in intimate, familial, and sexual relationships, in social organized groups or the individual's leisure activities, and at work. They suggest asking clients to describe their relationships in these settings and also the situations they avoid, dread, or have difficulty dealing with. They note that these trigger-response patterns reoccur throughout the individual's life, indicating a pattern of chronic, repetitive coping deficits and series of situations the individual is sensitive to or actively avoids. The individual's academic and employment history will also further identify these patterns. Consideration should be given to whether clients' achievements are consistent with their abilities, how jobs were obtained, their level of satisfaction, themes of being appreciated or valued and devalued, job stability, reasons for leaving, conflict and resolution skills, and the presence of any ongoing resentments and grudges.

As the information these individuals provide will be colored by their experiences and emotions, obtaining collateral information is essential to understand the clinical presentation in context (McClanahan et al., 2003). Obtaining a wide range of sources can help counter the extreme subjectivity of the individual's report and corroborate as much information as possible (McClanahan et al., 2003). An informative technique involves asking the same questions asked earlier of the individual to significant others and looking at the disparities. Conducting a chart review of previous treatment records can identify patterns of prior impulsivity, previous diagnostic considerations, treatment challenges, failures, or noncompliance, and any conflicts with treating professionals. Some individuals, specifically those with Antisocial PD, may not always be forthcoming with information. For these individuals factors concerning the client's veracity, discussed in Chapter 12, should be reviewed and considered.

Disorder-Specific Interview Considerations

Cluster A

Cluster A individuals present with a lack of long-standing meaningful relationships and impoverished emotional expression, and, when stressed, are at risk for transient, psychotic episodes, all of which need to be fully evaluated (Maxmen & Ward, 1995; McClanahan et al., 2003). For these individuals the triggers for their maladaptive responses are close interpersonal relationships (Othmer & Othmer, 2002). They are difficult to engage, appearing cold, suspicious, and restricted, rarely talking spontaneously, relying on yes and no answers, and despite the clinician's best efforts, it may feel impossible to truly relate to or connect with them (Bender, 2005). Thus the clinician's primary challenge is the establishment of rapport, although the usual strategies, such as eye contact, body language, light conversation, interest, and empathy, may be ineffective. A more effective approach is to recognize from the beginning the individual's need for interpersonal distance and respect and to acknowledge the individual's social discomfort and review clearly the purpose of the interview, while keeping expressions of empathy and overt interest to a minimum (McClanahan et al., 2003; McWilliams, 1994).

Paranoid   Paranoid individuals are reluctant to confide for fear the information will be shared with others and used against them (American Psychiatric Association, 2000b). They may present as provocative, quarrelsome, guarded, and uncooperative, becoming hostile, refusing to answer questions, reading hidden meaning and conspiratorial content into innocuous questions and benign remarks, and scanning continually for malevolent intent on your part (Maxmen & Ward, 1995; McClanahan et al., 2003; Othmer & Othmer, 2002; Skodol, 2005). While they may see themselves as highly rational, they are quick to adopt an aggressive stance if they feel threatened, and it may be particularly difficult to directly question their misinterpretations and false suspiciousness (Bender, 2005; McClanahan et al., 2003). Asking whether or not they have friends they can trust or if they feel they can be open with others may help identify paranoid features (Othmer & Othmer, 2002). Genuine openness on your part may result in a temporary trust, but this may be followed by a hostile counterattack at any moment, and apart from anger, there may be overall emotional restriction (Maxmen & Ward, 1995; Othmer & Othmer, 2002). If there is a misunderstanding about scheduling or you make a mistake, an honest, formal, direct, and apologetic response is best, as defensiveness will only increase their distrust (H. I. Kaplan & Saddock, 1996). Typically, these individuals do not tolerate confrontation. Their hostility emerges early, making this interview particularly delicate and challenging, and smooth transitions during the interview are essential (Othmer & Othmer, 2002). An effective strategy is to be respectful and straightforward, maintain a professional stance, and avoid warmth and deep interpretations (Maxmen & Ward, 1995). Gathering collateral information may be compromised by the individual's unwillingness to sign releases of information or allow you to contact significant others, which may point to pathological jealousy and the individual's need to control all information and remain hypervigilant to perceived harmful intentions (American Psychiatric Association, 2000b). These clients are at high risk for dropping out, and many are litigious, so it is crucial to follow your clinic's procedures, fully inform the individual about informed consents and releases of information, and clearly document actions taken (Maxmen & Ward, 1995).

Schizoid   On intake individuals with Schizoid PD may appear reserved, serious, and task-orientated, answering questions succinctly with minimal information. They present with bland affect, showing little or no change in posture or facial expression and few social gestures and appearing oblivious to subtle, social, interactional cues (American Psychiatric Association, 2000b; H. I. Kaplan & Saddock, 1996; McClanahan et al., 2003). Rapport from the onset may be compromised by a pervasive, affective withdrawal and emptiness, which, combined with the lack of emotional warmth, makes it impossible to assess the individual's innermost concerns and feelings (Othmer & Othmer, 2002). Questions concerning the individual's level of concern or disinterest in others can elucidate the diagnostic picture (Othmer & Othmer, 2002). No matter what interview strategy is adopted, the flow of information is restricted, their answers monotonous and short. Although the clinical symptomatology can resemble the negative signs of Schizophrenia, their reality testing remains intact, and there is no evidence of a psychotic thought disorder (Othmer & Othmer, 2002). Because vague, superficial responses make information gathering about close relationships difficult, the quality of the interpersonal process and the nature of the individual's presentation are more informative than the actual content of the answers (McClanahan et al., 2003; Millon & Everly, 1985). In rare circumstances when sufficient trust is established, they may reveal and acknowledge painful experiences related to social interactions (American Psychiatric Association, 2000b).

Schizotypal Individuals with Schizotypal PD present with unusual, eccentric behaviors, mannerisms, speech, perceptual experiences, and beliefs, such as ideas of reference and magical thinking (American Psychiatric Association, 2000b). They may arrive to the interview strangely or sloppily attired in mismatched, wrinkled clothing, with talismans, displaying inappropriate affect, giggling, talking about special powers, including ESP, telepathy, and paranormal experiences, using idiosyncratic phrasing, and appear extremely anxious around others (American Psychiatric Association, 2000b; McClanahan et al., 2003; Othmer & Othmer, 2002). The clinician can build rapport with these individuals by being receptive, understanding, and empathic and by listening, clarifying, and appreciating their unique experiences. Questions about ESP experiences, special powers, or superstitious beliefs can often facilitate the individual's sharing unique experiences (Othmer & Othmer, 2002). It is important to realize that the individual's level of social discomfort may increase with familiarity; therefore, structuring the intake will help minimize tangential and loose thinking (First & Tasman, 2004).

Cluster B

The primary challenges for the clinician upon intake with Cluster B disorders are the issues of impulse control and countertransference reactions (Gutheil, 2005; Links & Kolla, 2005). The characteristic features of emotional lability, behavioral impulsivity, and interpersonal exploitiveness make these clients the most challenging, difficult, and emotionally draining for the clinician. It is important to assess issues of suicide risk and danger to others, to clearly document interventions, and to review the strategies provided in Chapter 2. With these clients, the clinician needs to be constantly mindful of boundary issues and to consider obtaining professional consultation or supervision from the beginning (First & Tasman, 2004).

Antisocial Individuals with Antisocial PD may present as callous, deceitful, manipulative, contemptuous, and lacking empathy, with an inflated, arrogant self-appraisal and a disregard for the rights of others (First et al., 2004; Skodol, 2005). Initially they may appear glib and disarmingly or seductively charming and resourceful, yet it is important to consider the veracity of the information provided, as they frequently lie, use aliases, and con others indiscriminately (American Psychiatric Association, 2000b). The triggers for their maladaptive behaviors are social standards and rules (Othmer & Othmer, 2002). Obtaining additional sources of information and considering the earlier discussed factors related to malingering is crucial (American Psychiatric Association, 2000b). When questioned, these individuals may provide superficial rationalizations for their behaviors and become easily angered, and their lack of sincerity makes rapport difficult (Bender, 2005; Othmer & Othmer, 2002). Rapport can be established if the clinician is felt to be an ally who is nonjudgmental and understanding of their difficulties following rules. Asking them to talk about themselves and their history provides them the opportunity to get attention and boast about their deeds. In order to encourage them to be forthcoming, it is important to maintain an interested but neutral stance, despite their pattern of lack of remorse and externalizing blame (McClanahan et al., 2003).

Borderline   Initially, rapport may appear easy to establish with these individuals as they may idealize the clinician as "the best therapist ever" or the only one who truly understands them. However, this can rapidly change to devaluation and hostility (First & Tasman, 2004). Individuals with Borderline PD present with a low tolerance of frustration, rapidly fluctuating moods, and hypersensitivity to interpersonal cues, particularly evidence of rejection (McClanahan et al., 2003). At the onset, a determination of the chronicity and pervasiveness of the hyperemotionality and lack of stable relationships is crucial (Othmer & Othmer, 2002). They may vacillate from appearing very competent to expressing sarcasm, enduring bitterness, intense panic, and despair at the end of the interview (American Psychiatric Association, 2000b). According to Othmer and Othmer (2002), the challenges for individuals with Borderline PD are close relationships and personal goals that are expressed with extreme ambivalence. Their emotional intensity, constant crises, array of problems, and behavioral impulsivity may be overwhelming, especially for the novice clinician (McClanahan et al., 2003). Their fear of abandonment may spur frequent calls and requests, which, if refused, may result in self-destructive acts, leaving the clinician feeling angered and emotionally blackmailed. A complete assessment of suicidal ideation and behavior and self-harming behaviors such as cutting should be obtained on intake. It is important from the outset to adopt a very structured approach with clear limits and crisis backup plans and to be alert to their tendency to be divisive with other care providers (Guthiel, 2005; H. I. Kaplan & Saddock, 1996). By being empathic, understanding, firm, and clear, and by asking open-ended questions but providing structure and guidance for staying on topic, relevant information can be gathered (Othmer & Othmer, 2002). The presence of dissociative symptoms is often difficult to identify, and individuals may experience repeated hospitalizations for years before they are recognized. These symptoms increase the individual's experience of fragmentation and complicate treatment (Maldonado & Spiegel, 2005). Lowenstein (1991) suggests that on intake the clinician inquire about amnesia, posttraumatic, and pseudo-psychotic symptoms and a history of trauma. Othmer and Othmer (2002) recommend asking about experiences of memory loss, feelings of depersonalization, derealization, and trance states. Administering a measure such as the Dissociative Experiences Scale (Bernstein & Putnam, 1986) may also be useful.

Histrionic   For the clinician the major challenge with Histrionic PD is monitoring one's own reaction to individuals who may be flamboyant, sexually provocative, and flirtatious and exude inappropriate displays of emotion (American Psychiatric Association, 2000b; H. I. Kaplan & Saddock, 1996). For these individuals heterosexual relationships are the trigger for emotional response and maladaptive behavior (Othmer & Othmer, 2002). They may initially appear deceptively easy to interview and engage, and rapport may seem instantly established because they can provide fascinating, dramatic answers to questions. Nonetheless, the level of superficiality and exaggerated emotionality make the establishment of true rapport very difficult (McClanahan et al., 2003; Othmer & Othmer, 2002). They may present with multiple exaggerated, unexplained physical complaints, and at the onset, a determination of the chronicity and pervasiveness of their hyperemotionality and lack of stable relationships is crucial (Bender, 2005; Othmer & Othmer, 2002). They are easily hurt and angered by interpretations. It is important not to underestimate the clinician's influence on these highly suggestible individuals or to minimize any suicidal behavior as attention-seeking attempts (First & Tasman, 2004). Their answers are often vague, evasive, excessively impressionistic, and emotionally shallow. Maxmen and Ward (1995) aptly described trying to get details from these individuals as like trying to nail Jell-O to a wall. An effective strategy is to take a more active, directive approach that emphasizes staying focused on the issues of concern while at the same time validating the individual's experience to maintain engagement (McClanahan et al., 2003).

Narcissistic   Individuals with Narcissistic PD present as arrogant, self-absorbed, and entitled. They may deign to answer questions on their terms, yet it is difficult for them to admit to having a problem or needing help (First & Tasman, 2004). Initially, they may adopt a collegial stance, appearing socially adept and extremely charming, idealizing the clinician and expecting validation of their inflated sense of importance (Othmer & Othmer, 2002). However, they do not suffer fools gladly and may question your competence, voicing a desire to be associated with only the best, and they may devalue you with disdain and contempt if you fail to meet their expectations (American Psychiatric Association, 2000b; McClanahan et al., 2003). They are egocentric and grandiose and will monopolize the interview with their achievements. In answering questions, they use impressionistic language, take liberties with the facts, and engage in prevarication and self-deception to preserve their grandiose self-concept, which triggers their maladaptive behavior (McClanahan et al., 2003; Othmer & Othmer, 2002). Hence, it is crucial to verify information with collateral sources. They appear at ease and exude self-confidence, but this is a facade that belies a damaged, fragile self-image that, if challenged, results in intense narcissistic rage (American Psychiatric Association, 2000b; Maxmen & Ward, 1995; McClanahan et al., 2003). Their sense of entitlement and uniqueness, lack of empathy, and interpersonal exploitive and envious style make the establishment of true rapport difficult (Bender, 2005). The clinician's empathic stance may allow these individuals to temporarily gain insight, which is often followed by a need for a grandiose repair of their damaged image (Othmer & Othmer, 2002). A very strong rapport is needed to gather information and to have the individual with a Narcissistic PD follow through on treatment recommendations.

Cluster C

The large overlap of Cluster C PDs with Axis I disorders, including anxiety, mood, and somatoform disorders, means that their clinical presentation may be masked by more florid Axis I symptomatology. Thus the major challenge for the clinician is the assessment of comorbid conditions and differential diagnosis. The predominant features of anxiety and fearfulness for Cluster C individuals contribute to high levels of interpersonal timidity, hypersensitivity, a strong need to please, and an emphasis on interpersonal control (American Psychiatric Association, 2000b). The gathering of accurate information upon intake may be hampered by the individual's need to minimize and not offend, which may be accompanied by a reluctance to discuss issues (First & Tasman, 2004). While these individuals may have more insight than individuals in the preceding clusters, the insight may be accompanied by a critical self-consciousness (Othmer & Othmer, 2002).

Avoidant   Avoidant individuals may act with restraint, appear tense and guarded, withhold feelings, and say little, fearing that whatever they say will be wrong and they will be judged negatively, and they may misinterpret benign statements as criticism (American

Psychiatric Association, 2000b; Maxmen & Ward, 1995; McClanahan et al., 2003). They may speak reluctantly, and their responses may be brief, circumstantial, overcontrolled, and lacking in details, causing the clinician to have to work hard to gather information (Morrison, 1995b; Othmer & Othmer, 2002). Close interpersonal relationships and public scrutiny will trigger their maladaptive patterns (Othmer & Othmer, 2002). These individuals may report feeling embarrassed or silly about their fears. It is very important that the clinician not identify with this, as it may be perceived as criticism and result in withdrawal (Othmer & Othmer, 2002). Conversations with significant others, if available, may be helpful in obtaining information (Bernstein & Travaglini, 1999). Overall, an empathic, validating, firm but gentle, reassuring, understanding, and patient approach, proceeding at a pace that is comfortable for the individual, will be most effective (First & Tasman, 2004; McClanahan et al., 2003). These individuals are likely to attend to the clinician's cues and responses and, once assured of acceptance, may respond in a more natural, relaxed manner, providing explicit details about social fears, injuries, and rejection (Othmer & Othmer, 2002; Sperry, 1995).

Dependent   Individuals with Dependent PD present as passive, pessimistic, self-doubting, submissive, naive, suggestible, and inept, with a strong need to be taken care of and for excessive advice and reassurance (American Psychiatric Association, 2000b; McClanahan et al., 2003; Morrison, 1995b). Self-reliance and being alone will trigger their maladaptive responses (Othmer & Othmer, 2002). Usually no difficulty will be found in establishing rapport. In fact, they may be overly agreeable and deferential, seeking to discern the clinician's expectations (Bender, 2005; McClanahan et al., 2003). They may elevate the clinician to a position of authority, be excessively compliant, and make unrealistic requests for time and availability, calling the office incessantly. Consequently, from the outset it is important to have clear expectations and firm limits (First & Tasman, 2004; Maxmen & Ward, 1995; Othmer & Othmer, 2002). When questioned, they provide elaborate, detailed answers but at times fall silent, awaiting your response (McClanahan et al., 2003). These clients have difficulty with confrontation and the interpretation of their dependency, and if they feel a lack of sympathy or understanding, they will find another clinician (Othmer & Othmer, 2002).

Obsessive-Compulsive   Within Cluster C, individuals with Obsessive-Compulsive PD are the most difficult to interview. They discount expressions of empathy and concern as irrelevant, and attempts to build rapport may backfire, resulting in their withdrawal from treatment (McClanahan et al., 2003; Othmer & Othmer, 2002). Many are bright, but they lack insight; they may attempt to control the session, frequently rambling, overwhelming the clinician with details, and becoming angry if interrupted or redirected (First & Tasman, 2004; Skodol, 2005). They value rule-based behaviors, showing significant cognitive and behavior inflexibility and preferring clinicians who pay attention to detail and are careful and precise (Maxmen & Ward, 1995; McClanahan et al., 2003). They are uncomfortable with ambivalence and may answer very concretely to unstructured questions, as they need to be sure what they say is perfect. They may appear preoccupied with intellectualization, logic, and status, avoiding affective experiences and the expression of emotion (American Psychiatric Association, 2000b; McClanahan et al., 2003). Initially, they may present in a pseudo-collaborative role; then, depending on whether they respect the clinician as an authority figure, their behavior will range from obsequious approval seeking to condescension (McClanahan et al., 2003). Close relationships, unstructured situations, and dealing with individuals in authority will trigger maladaptive responses (Othmer & Othmer, 2002). An effective clinical approach is to emphasize your competence and experience in problem solving, focus on discussing the basis for treatment, setting concrete goals, contracting for change and problem-solving strategies, and actively involving the individual in treatment planning (H. I. Kaplan & Saddock, 1996; McClanahan et al., 2003).

Assessment Measures

There are several excellent structured and semistructured assessment measures (see Table 14.4) that can facilitate the types of questions to ask when assessing for a PD. Given the wealth of information needed and the time limitations that many clinicians have to deal with, these measures can be extremely beneficial (McDermut & Zimmerman, 2005). In describing evidence-based assessment of PDs, Widiger and Samuel (2005) recommend a two-step procedure: First, administer a self-report measure to identify which PDs should be emphasized during the interview, then conduct a clinical interview using a semi-structured interview. This strategy also ensures that all of the PDs are systematically assessed, and it allows you to focus your interview on the most pertinent PDs (First & Tasman, 2004). It also compensates for the clinician's preferential attending to a particular PD based on idiosyncratic interests, and it increases diagnostic reliability (Widiger & Samuel, 2005). An excellent resource on diagnostic and structured interviewing is R. Rogers (2001).

Self-Report Scales

The most widely used self-report measures that include methods to assess for response sets and biases are the Minnesota Multiphasic Personality Inventory 2 (MMPI-2) and the Millon Clinical Multiaxial Inventory III (MCMI-III; Millon, Millon, & Davis, 1997). The MMPI-2 has excellent psychometric properties, and though it does not provide *DSM-IV* diagnoses, there is extensive information on its assessment of Axis I and Axis II disorders (Butcher, Dahlstrom, Graham, Tellegen, & Kaemmer, 1989; Colligan, Morey, & Offord, 1994). Graham's (2006) and Butcher's (2005) are excellent texts on this measure. Morey and colleagues (1985) have developed a two-step empirical procedure for identifying *DSM* personality disorder scales, which has been updated by Colligan and colleagues (1994). The major limitation of the MMPI-2 is that it is not coordinated with the *DSM-IV* (McDermut & Zimmerman, 2005). The MCMI-III provides *DSM* diagnoses, and though it does not have the extensive empirical or clinical findings associated with the MMPI-2, it is becoming more widely used. It does have a tendency to overpathologize normal individuals and should be used only with clinical populations for which it was normed. Excellent texts on the use of the MCMI-III include Choca and Van Denburg (1997) and Strack (1999).

The Coolidge Axis II Inventory (CATI; Coolidge & Merwin, 1992) is a 200-item self-report measure composed of items specifically selected to measure *DSM* Axis II clinical symptoms. The CATI has two validity scales and includes measures of anxiety, depression, and cognitive deficits, but it is not currently compatible with the *DSM-IV* (L. A.

Table 14.4   Assessment measures for personality disorders

Assessment Measure	Format (Administration Time)	Technical Support
Omnibus Self-Report Scales		**Computerized Report**
Minnesota Multiphasic Personality Inventory—Personality Disorder Scales (MMPI-PD)	Self-report; 157 items embedded in 567 items; 60–90 minutes	No
Millon Clinical Multiaxial Inventory III	Self-report; 175 items; 20–30 minutes	Yes
Coolidge Axis II Inventory (CATI)	Self-report; 200 items; 45–60 minutes	No
Personality Diagnostic Questionnaire 4	Self-report; 85 items; 20–30 minutes	Yes
Schedule for Nonadaptive and Adaptive Personality (SNAP)	Self-report; 375 items; 45–75 minutes	Yes
Wisconsin Personality Inventory	Self-report; 214 items; under 60 minutes	Yes
Omnibus Interviews		**Training video or workshop**
Structured Clinical Interview for *DSM-IV* Axis II Personality Disorder (SCID-II) (Screener: self-administered 119 items T-F)	Semistructured interview; 119 items; 105 items; under 60 minutes	Yes
Structured Interview for *DSM-IV* Personality-IV (SIDP-IV) (Screener: brief clinical interview)	Semistructured interview; 101 items; 90 minutes	Yes
International Personality Disorder Examination (PDE), for *DSM-IV* (Screener: self-administered 77 items T-F)	Semistructured interview; 537 items; 90 minutes	Yes
Diagnostic Interview for *DSM-IV* Personality Disorders (DIPD-IV)	Structured interview; 398 items; 90 minutes	Yes
Personality Disorder Interview IV (PDI-IV)	Semistructured interview; 93 items; 90–120 minutes	Detailed manual

Clark & Harrison, 2001; McDermut & Zimmerman, 2005). The Personality Diagnostic Questionnaire 4 (Hyler, 1994) is an 85-item questionnaire that provides diagnoses consistent with the *DSM-IV-TR*. The Schedule for Nonadaptive and Adaptive Personality is a 375-item questionnaire developed specifically to assess *DSM* Axis II clinical features. It includes validity, trait, and temperament scales, some of which reflect Axis I disorders (McDermut & Zimmerman, 2005). The Wisconsin Personality Inventory IV (Klein, Benjamin, Rosenfeld, Treece, Husted, & Greist, 1993) is a 214-item self-report measure that provides categorical *DSM* PD data and dimensional information on personality functioning. It is based on interpersonal and object relations theories (Benjamin, 1996). Two other widely used self-report measures that use models other than the *DSM* are the Personality Assessment Inventory (Morey, 1991) and the Dimensional Assessment of Personality Pathology—Basic Questionnaire (Livesley, Jackson, & Schroeder, 1992; Livesley, Reiffer, Sheldon, & West, 1987).

Structured and Semistructured Interviews

One of the most widely used structured interviews is the Structured Clinical Interview for the *DSM-IV* Axis II, which was developed by First and colleagues (1997). It consists of 119 questions specifically organized around the diagnostic criteria in the *DSM-IV* and is useful in streamlining the evaluation. It has adequate reliability and validity, but it takes approximately an hour to administer, which may cause difficulty given time constraints (R. Rogers, 2001). There is a computerized version, and training videos and workshops are available (L. A. Clark & Harrison, 2001).

The natural flow and phrasing of the items in the Structured Interview for *DSM* Personality Disorders by Pfohl, Blum, and Zimmerman (1995, 1997) are advantageous. It consists of 101 items, takes 90 minutes to administer, discriminates between Axis I and Axis II psychopathology, has empirically supported reliability and validity, and has training videos and workshops (L. A. Clark & Harrison, 2001; R. Rogers, 2001).

Loranger (1999) modified the earlier Personality Disorders Examination (PDE) to reflect *DSM-IV* changes and developed the International Personality Disorder Examination *DSM-IV*, which has 99 questions; training courses are available (L. A. Clark & Harrison, 2001). The PDE has been used in outpatient settings and validated for this clinical population; however, its use is contraindicated for severe Axis I psychopathology. It is suitable for multicultural settings and useful for noting clinical changes over time and allowing the interviewer to differentiate between early and late onset (McClanahan et al., 2003).

The Diagnostic Interview for Personality Disorders-IV (Zanarini, Frankenberg, Sickel, & Young 1996) is a 398-item interview that takes 90 minutes to administer; training videos and workshops are available (L. A. Clark & Harrison, 2001). It is currently being used in the collaborative Longitudinal Personality Disorders Study on the course and treatment of Avoidant, Borderline, Schizotypal, and Obsessive-Compulsive PDs (Gunderson et al., 2000). It includes a monthly assessment of PD symptoms, which can be used to measure improvement with treatment (Gunderson et al., 2000).

Widiger and colleagues (1995) developed the Personality Disorder Interview IV to assess each *DSM-IV* personality disorder. It has 93 items and takes 90 to 120 minutes to administer (L. A. Clark & Harrison, 2001). According to R. Rogers (2001), the major disadvantage is the length of administration time, which makes it difficult to use in settings with time constraints. There are also issues with reliability and validity that still need to be addressed. Nonetheless, it does provide a useful template for standard questions that reflect the *DSM* diagnostic criteria for PDs.

In describing evidence-based assessment of PDs, Widiger and Samuel (2005) note the use of the five aforementioned semistructured interviews and provide information on the psychometric properties of these interviews. It should be noted that to date none of these interviews provides information on norms (Widiger & Samuel, 2005). There is also a wide range of interviews that focus on specific disorders or personality features such as the Diagnostic Interview for Borderlines (Gunderson, Kolb, & Austin, 1981), the Diagnostic Interview for Narcissism (Gunderson, Ronningstam, & Bodkin, 1990), and the

Psychopathy Check List—Revised (Hare, 1991). See L. A. Clark and Harrison (2001) for a more detailed discussion of these measures.

If the clinician chooses to use an unstructured interview to assess for the presence of a PD, the Shedler-Western Assessment Procedure 200, developed by Westen and Shedler (1999a,b), may be helpful. This method has some methodological limitations, but it does allow the clinician to ask questions in a less structured manner, is based on psychodynamic and PD literature, and shows convergence with *DSM-IV* diagnoses (Westen & Muderrisoglu, 2003; Widiger & Samuel, 2005).

CRISIS, LEGAL, AND ETHICAL ISSUES

For individuals with Cluster A disorders, interpersonal trust is a major issue. These individuals tend to be interpersonally wary, and it is important to take time to explain issues relating to confidentiality and consent to talk to significant others and treating professionals (Bender, 2005).

Issues of substance abuse, impulse control, and suicidal and self-harming behaviors need to be assessed and continually monitored for all individuals with PDs, particularly those with Borderline and Histrionic PDs (Links & Kolla, 2005; Verheul, van den Bosch, & Ball, 2005). The clinician's challenge with many individuals with Borderline PD is managing the behavioral impulsivity, constant crisis, suicidal behavior, self-mutilation, engagement in high-risk behaviors, and comorbid substance abuse (Gabbard, 2000a,b; Kernberg, 2004). For those individuals with Narcissistic and Antisocial PDs, the clinician also needs to be mindful of interpersonal exploitiveness and the potential for engagement in antisocial and high-risk activities (M. H. Stone, 2005). Many individuals with Antisocial PD are financially irresponsible, and they may disrupt and sabotage treatment, so billing arrangements should be addressed at the onset (First & Tasman, 2004).

The need for hospitalization to prevent self-harm or harm to others is a consideration for many individuals with Cluster B disorders (Gunderson et al., 2005). However, individuals with Borderline PD often regress or do worse when initially hospitalized.

As described earlier, treating individuals with PDs can be challenging, and it is important to be aware of your boundaries and feelings about the client to ensure that you do not engage in unethical behavior. It is your responsibility as the treating clinician to set and maintain professional boundaries (Gutheil, 2006). Boundary problems are often precursors to sexual misconduct, and the clinical presentation of individuals with Histrionic, Dependent, Antisocial, and Borderline PDs often increases the clinician's risk for these behaviors (Gutheil, 2006). These individuals often require a high degree of experience and can be emotionally draining, resulting in clinicians feeling overwhelmed. In such cases, consultations with colleagues or involvement in a peer supervision group can be very helpful.

DIAGNOSTIC CONSIDERATIONS

Common Comorbidities

Comorbidity is the rule rather than the exception for PDs and both Axis I and other Axis II disorders (Dolan-Sewell, Kreuger, & Shea, 2001; McClanahan et al., 2003). An overview of common comorbid disorders is presented in Table 14.5.

Table 14.5 Personality disorders: common comorbidities

Personality Disorder	Substance Related	Mood Disorders	Anxiety Disorders	Other Disorder	Personality Disorders
Paranoid	Substance related	Major Depressive Disorder (MDD)	Agoraphobia OCD	Delusional Disorder	Schizotypal Narcissistic Dependent Obsessive-Compulsive
Schizoid		MDD	Social Phobia	Schizophrenia	Paranoid Schizotypal Dependent
Schizotypal		Major depressive episode 30%–50%		Schizophrenia	Paranoid Schizoid 38% Dependent Obsessive-Compulsive
Antisocial	Substance related	MDD	Anxiety Disorders	Impulse control Gambling Somatoform	Histrionic
Borderline	Substance related Substance abuse 57%	MDD Bipolar II		Eating Disorders Bulimia Posttraumatic Stress Disorder (PTSD) Attention-Deficit/ Hyperactivity Disorder (ADHD)	Paranoid Avoidant Antisocial Histrionic Dependent Obsessive-Compulsive

Personality Disorder	Substance Use	Mood Disorder	Anxiety Disorders	Other	Comorbid Personality Disorders
Histrionic	Substance use	MDD Dysthymia		Somatoform Dissociative disorders	Avoidant Borderline Antisocial Dependent Obsessive-Compulsive
Narcissistic	Substance abuse (SA) 5%–12% 12%–38% SA History 24%–50% Cocaine	MDD Depressive Mood Disorder 42%–50% Bipolar 5%–12%		Eating disorders Anorexia Nervosa	Histrionic 53% Borderline 47% Paranoid 36% Avoidant 36% Antisocial 16% Obsessive-Compulsive
Avoidant		Mood Disorder	Anxiety disorders Social Phobia 90%	Eating disorders	Dependent 71% Schizoid 53% Paranoid Obsessive-Compulsive
Dependent		MDD	Anxiety disorders	Adjustment Somatoform Eating disorders	Avoidant 50% Histrionic
Obsessive-Compulsive		MDD		Eating disorders	Dependent

Mood Disorders

Comorbid Axis I mood disorders are often the reason individuals with PDs seek treatment. The presence of Major Depressive Disorder is common for all three clusters (Dolan-Sewell et al., 2001; McClanahan et al., 2003). The *DSM-IV-TR* notes that individuals with Paranoid, Schizoid, Antisocial, Borderline, Histrionic, Narcissistic, Dependent, and Obsessive-Compulsive PDs may develop Major Depressive Disorder or other mood disorders (American Psychiatric Association, 2000b). Among individuals with Schizotypal PD admitted to a clinical setting, 30% to 50% have had a major depressive episode (American Psychiatric Association, 2000b). Histrionic PD can co-occur with Dysthymia (Bornstein, 1999). In looking at the comorbidity of diagnoses, Ronningstam (1999) notes that in clinical samples of individuals with Narcissistic PD, 42% to 50% also had a depressive mood disorder and 5% to 12% had Bipolar Disorder. Trull and colleagues (2006) found that Borderline PD has a high rate of comorbidity with Bipolar II. In reviewing earlier research on Borderline PD and depression, Paris (1999) describes how these disorders co-occur but are not related. He also notes that the more Axis I disorders an individual has, the more the clinician should consider a Borderline PD diagnosis. The co-occurrence of a mood disorder is also noted for Avoidant and Dependent PDs (Levy & Scott, 2000).

Substance-Related Disorders

According to the *DSM-IV-TR*, substance abuse and dependence frequently co-occur with Paranoid, Antisocial, and Borderline PDs, and individuals with Narcissistic PD are at high risk for using cocaine (American Psychiatric Association, 2000b). Dolan-Sewell and colleagues (2001) report on earlier research that found that the Cluster B PDs' association with alcohol abuse and dependence was 5 times greater than chance. Ronningstam (1999) found that, of individuals with Narcissistic PD, 12% to 38% were substance abusers and 24% to 50% had substance abuse histories. For individuals with a Borderline PD, Trull, Sher, Minks-Brown, Durbin, and Burr (2000) found that 57% also had substance abuse, with the most frequent being alcohol abuse or dependence. Of those with a substance abuse diagnosis, 27% also met the criteria for Borderline PD. Levy and Scott (2006) report that there is a strong association between Antisocial PD and substance abuse disorders, and some association between Histrionic PD and Narcissistic PD and substance use.

Anxiety Disorders

The *DSM-IV-TR* notes that individuals with Paranoid PD are at increased risk for developing Agoraphobia and Obsessive-Compulsive Disorder, and individuals with Antisocial and Dependent PDs may have associated anxiety disorders (American Psychiatric Association, 2000b). Most individuals with anxiety disorders are at increased risk for Obsessive-Compulsive PD. Dependent PD has been noted to co-occur with Anxiety Disorders, as has Avoidant PD, which is particularly associated with Social Phobia, generalized type (Bornstein, 1999). In general, there is a lack of studies in this area, and the relationship between Obsessive-Compulsive PD and Axis I disorders is not clear (McCann, 1999).

Other Disorders

Paranoid PD was originally thought to be a Schizophrenia spectrum disorder; however, current research suggests it may be closer to Delusional Disorder (Levy & Scott, 2006).

First and Tasman (2004) describe Schizoid PD as being characterized by subthreshold negative schizophrenic symptoms such as flattened affect, anhedonia, and avolition. In contrast, Schizotypal PDs' clinical presentation consists of the subthreshold positive schizophrenic symptoms of cognitive slippage and idiosyncratic or bizarre behavior, cognitions, and language. The *DSM-IV-TR* notes the association between Borderline PD and Bulimia Nervosa, Narcissistic PD and Anorexia Nervosa, and Obsessive-Compulsive PD and eating disorders (American Psychiatric Association, 2000b). It can be difficult to determine if eating problems reflect a separate eating disorder or the emotional dysregulation characteristic of Borderline PD (S. A. Kim & Goff, 2000). Cluster B disorders have also been found to co-occur more frequently with impulse control disorders, with Antisocial PD co-occurring with pathological gambling (American Psychiatric Association, 2000b; Dolan & Sewell, 2001; McClanahan et al., 2003). Histrionic PD and Antisocial PD have been associated with elevated rates of Somatization Disorder, and Histrionic PD is often comorbid with Conversion Disorder and dissociative disorders (American Psychiatric Association, 2000b; Bornstein, 1999). Borderline PD has been linked to higher rates of ADHD and PTSD, particularly for those individuals who have a history of childhood abuse (American Psychiatric Association, 2000b; Paris, 1999). Dependent PD has been found to co-occur with Adjustment, Somatization, and eating disorders (Bornstein, 1999; Dolan-Sewell et al., 2001; Levy & Scott, 2006). While Avoidant PD may be comorbid with anxiety and eating disorders (Levy & Scott, 2006; Oldham et al., 1995).

Among the Personality Disorders

Two thirds of individuals with Paranoid PD met criteria for another PD. The *DSM-IV-TR* notes that the most frequently co-occurring PDs are Schizotypal, Schizoid, Narcissistic, Avoidant, and Borderline (American Psychiatric Association, 2000b; Levy & Scott, 2006). Schizoid PD co-occurs most often with Schizotypal and Avoidant PDs, whereas Schizotypal PDs are most frequently comorbid with Schizoid and Paranoid PDs (American Psychiatric Association, 2000b). Bernstein and Travaglini (1999) quote earlier research which found that, of individuals with Avoidant PD, 53% received a Schizoid PD diagnosis, and 38% of individuals with Schizotypal PD also had a Schizoid PD. The large overlap between Schizoid and Avoidant PDs has resulted in controversy around their status as discrete diagnostic entities. Avoidant, Borderline, and Antisocial PDs have been associated with Histrionic and Narcissistic PDs (American Psychiatric Association, 2000b). Of psychiatric inpatients with a diagnosis of Avoidant PD, 71% also had Dependent PD, and 50% of individuals with Dependent also had Avoidant PD (Bernstein & Travaglini, 1999).

Borderline PD rarely occurs alone on Axis II (Trull et al., 2000). However, the comorbidity of Borderline PD with other PDs may be an artifact of a diagnostic rules system that encourages multiple diagnoses (Paris, 1999). To avoid this overlap, Paris recommends restricting the diagnosis to the one that meets the largest number of diagnostic criteria. For individuals with Narcissistic PD, the highest rates of comorbidity occur with other Cluster B PDs. Of those individuals with Narcissistic PD, 53% also had a diagnosis of Histrionic, 47% has a diagnosis of Borderline, 36% had a diagnosis of Paranoid, 36% had a diagnosis of Avoidant, and 16% had a diagnosis of Antisocial PD (Levy & Scott, 2006; Ronningstam, 1999). Histrionic PD was found to co-occur with Borderline,

Narcissistic, Antisocial, and Dependent PDs (American Psychiatric Association, 2000b; Bornstein, 1999; Levy & Scott, 2006). Individuals with Narcissistic PD present with other Cluster B PDs and Paranoid PD (Becker, Grilo, Edell, & McGlashan, 2000; Levy & Scott, 2006).

In terms of Cluster C disorders, Dependent PD was found to co-occur with Borderline, Avoidant, Paranoid, and Obsessive-Compulsive PDs (Marinangeli, Butti, Scinto, Di Cicco, Petruzzi, et al., 2000). Despite the superficial dissimilarity between Avoidant and Dependent PDs, there is a lack of discriminant validity between the two (Bernstein & Travaglini, 1999). The *DSM-IV-TR* notes that Dependent PD occurs with Borderline, Avoidant, and Histrionic PDs, and Bornstein (1999) reports it can also co-occur with Schizoid and Schizotypal PDs. Individuals with Obsessive-Compulsive PD also present with Borderline, Narcissistic, Histrionic, Paranoid, Schizotypal, and Avoidant PDs (Levy & Scott, 2006; Marinangeli et al., 2000; McCann, 1999).

DIFFERENTIAL DIAGNOSIS

Personality Disorders versus Other Psychiatric Disorders

Given the high levels of comorbidity of the PDs with Axis I disorders, diagnostic differentiation can be extremely complex. Considering the seven steps in making a diagnosis presented in Chapter 3 and the overview of discriminating clinical features (see Table 14.6) can facilitate this process.

Psychotic Disorders

Individuals with Cluster A PDs, by definition, will experience transient psychotic episodes under stress, which may last from a few minutes to hours (American Psychiatric Association, 2000b). The transitory psychotic symptoms are not of the severity of a psychotic disorder and are not associated with the negative or positive features and deteriorated functioning characteristic of Schizophrenia (American Psychiatric Association, 2000b; Kazdin, 2000). In Paranoid PD, the transitory psychotic episodes do not have delusions or hallucinations, and the prominent suspicious features and paranoid ideation are not odd or bizarre, or systematized as in Delusional Disorder (First et al., 2002; First & Tasman, 2004; Kazdin, 2000). Cluster A PDs do share some clinical features with the prodrome of Schizophrenia, including the presence of paranoid ideation and restricted and constricted affect, and it is not unusual for these PDs to coexist with Axis I psychotic disorders (Dolan-Sewell et al., 2001; First & Tasman, 2004; McClanahan et al., 2003). The clinical features of Schizoid PD are similar to Schizophrenia's prodromal, negative, and residual symptoms and the presence of these features is associated with a more negative prognosis for Schizophrenia (First et al., 2002; First & Tasman, 2004). Despite the similarities in clinical features, few individuals with Schizoid PD develop psychosis (Bernstein & Travaglini, 1999; Maxmen & Ward, 1995).

The symptoms of Schizotypal PD can be conceptualized as schizophrenic-like in that they are positive (cognitive and perceptual abnormalities) and negative (social avoidance and withdrawal). The bizarre cognitions or magical thinking of the Schizotypal PD are not of the intensity of a Delusional Disorder (M. B. Miller et al., 2001). In Schizotypal PD,

Table 14.6   Between-category diagnostic differential

Disorder	Similarities with Personality Disorders	Differences from Personality Disorders
Psychotic disorders	Cluster A Stress-induced brief psychotic episodes	Prominent positive symptoms, including hallucinations and delusions
Schizophrenia	Odd thoughts and behavior	Negative and positive features Deteriorated functioning Characteristic language deficits
Delusional Disorder	Paranoid ideation Constricted affect Interpersonal detachment	Delusions highly systematized
Anxiety disorders	Clusters A and C Anxiety and social discomfort	Associated with anxiety episodes
Social Phobia	Avoidance of social situations Interpersonal difficulties Hypersensitive to others' evaluations	More circumscribed in focus Lack of personality features such as pervasiveness
Obsessive-Compulsive	Perfectionism; ritualistic behaviors Ego-syntonic	Intrusive thoughts, compulsive behaviors are ego-dystonic
Pervasive developmental disorders Autism (HFA) and Asperger's	Cluster A Detachment Lack of relationships Poor social reciprocal skills Impaired conversational skills	Earlier age of onset Characteristic range of deficits, including linguistic, symbolic play, and behavior stereotypes
Mood disorders	Cluster B	Mood symptoms predominant
Bipolar Disorder	Impulsivity and emotional lability Grandiosity Interpersonally exploitive	Symptoms linked to mood episode Mood not interpersonally reactive Self-concept intact
Impulse control disorders	Cluster B Deficits in impulse control May include antisocial acts	Characteristic clinical presentation Not a pervasive pattern of antisocial behaviors
Dissociative disorders	Cluster B Impairment in consciousness, memory, or perception May be unaware of memory deficit	Impairments likely to begin after traumatic experience Forgotten material often has emotionally symbolic meaning

unlike Schizophrenia, speech is not typically incoherent or derailed and there are no loose associations or neologisms (Zuckerman, 1999). Also, though individuals with Schizotypal PD may experience subtle perceptual distortions and stress-induced brief psychotic episodes, they do not have the fully developed syndrome of prominent hallucinations and delusions associated with Schizophrenia (First et al., 2002; M. B. Miller et al., 2001). In the small proportion of individuals who do develop Schizophrenia, the Schizotypal PD features may reflect part of the prodrome of this disorder, which is indicated by noting (Premorbid) after the diagnosis (First et al., 2004). For individuals with Borderline PD who experience stress-induced transitory psychotic episodes, their reality testing remains intact, and the psychotic symptoms resolve with the removal of stressors (H. E. Adams et al., 2001).

Anxiety Disorders

Anxiety disorders are common among Clusters A and C PDs (Dolan & Sewell, 2001). In fact, for individuals with a Cluster C PD, anxiety is a fundamental feature (Dolan-Sewell et al., 2001; McClanahan et al., 2003). In both Avoidant PD and generalized Social Phobia, there are similar fears of initiating interactions and others' criticism or negative evaluation. Maxmen and Ward (1995) describe Social Phobia as specific to certain situations, whereas Avoidant PD pervades all social relationships and presents as a more general self-conscious social introversion, not simply social discomfort (Widiger, 2000). Bernstein and Travaglini (2000) note that Avoidant PD is characterized by a pervasive avoidance, whereas Social Phobia is a circumscribed impairment. Earlier studies by Marteinsdottir and colleagues (2003) and by Fahlen (1995) showed that both Social Phobia and Avoidant PD had similar underlying personality traits, and the differentiation of the two disorders on a clinical level may be virtually impossible (A. Frances et al., 1995). This distinction is often blurred in clinical practice, and the use of the generalized subtype of social anxiety has further blurred the boundaries. R. Grossman (2004) notes that there is 90% comorbidity between Avoidant PD and generalized Social Phobia and suggests they may be a single disorder. Bernstein and Travaglini (1999) report that although Schizoid and Avoidant PDs are frequently comorbid with Social Phobia, the disorders can be differentiated at a theoretical level by determining if the focus of the problem is relating to others or involves performance. However, this discrimination has become more difficult with the introduction of the generalized subtype of Social Phobia. Individuals with Avoidant PD present with greater impairment and more distress than individuals with Social Phobia (Bernstein & Travaglini, 1999). In fact, some theorize that Avoidant PD may represent a more severe form of Social Phobia (Dolan-Sewell et al., 2001; Levy & Scott, 2006).

Obsessive-Compulsive PD can be differentiated from the Axis I Obsessive-Compulsive Disorder by the lack of intrusive thoughts or compulsive rituals, which are ego-dystonic (First et al., 2002). The ritualistic behavior, perfectionism, and attention to order of those with Obsessive-Compulsive PD are ego-syntonic and often valued (American Psychiatric Association, 2000b).

Pervasive Developmental Disorders

There has been an increased focus on the difficulty differentiating Schizoid PD from the pervasive development disorders (PDDs), specifically Asperger's and high-functioning or mild Autism (American Psychiatric Association, 2000b; Fitzgerald, 1999). Individuals with Schizoid and Schizotypal PDs have significant difficulties with interpersonal relationships and may present as detached and lacking in social reciprocal skills. Unlike individuals with PDDs, there is later onset and a lack of the pervasive delays in language and symbolic play. The differentiation of Schizotypal PD from solitary or odd children with language and social challenges characteristic of autism, Asperger's Disorder, or communication disorders such as Mixed Receptive-Expressive Disorder can be particularly challenging (American Psychiatric Association, 2000b; First et al., 2002). The nature of the clinical symptoms, the lack of compensatory gestures, and a comprehensive assessment can help determine the most appropriate diagnosis (see Chapter 5).

Mood Disorders

The differentiation of Borderline PD from Bipolar Disorder can be very difficult (Dolan-Sewell et al., 2001). The mood shifts in Bipolar Disorder are seen as independent of environment; in contrast, the mood shifts in individuals with Borderline PD are often reactive or responsive to environmental or interpersonal stressors. Gunderson (2001) describes how individuals with Borderline PD are often sensitive and reactive to hostility and separations and have a very negative self-concept or a lack of sense of identity. In contrast, individuals with Bipolar II Disorder are often insensitive interpersonally and have a grandiose or inflated sense of self.

Antisocial Behaviors

Antisocial PD can be differentiated from adult antisocial behavior by the long-standing pervasive pattern that has an onset in adolescence. Individuals who engage in criminal, aggressive, or antisocial behavior for gain that is not due to a mental disorder or does not meet the full criteria for Antisocial PD are assigned the diagnosis of adult antisocial behavior. This is described in the *DSM-IV-TR* under other conditions that may be a focus of clinical attention (American Psychiatric Association, 2000b).

Impulse control disorders are characterized by problems with impulse control or the failure to resist the temptation to perform an act that is harmful to oneself or others (American Psychiatric Association, 2000b; First et al., 2002). Many of these behaviors, including Intermittent Explosive Disorder, Kleptomania, and Pyromania, have severe legal repercussions. However, they have a very characteristic presentation that is different from Antisocial PD. Typically, the individual experiences a buildup of tension, which is relieved by the commission of the act, and the individual may feel accompanying guilt or self-reproach (American Psychiatric Association, 2000b).

Antisocial PD is the only diagnosis in the *DSM-IV-TR* that cannot be assigned to a child or adolescent; the individual has to be at least 18 years old. There must also be earlier (before 15) evidence of a Conduct Disorder (Sutker & Allain, 2001). If the individual is over 18 but does not meet the criteria for Antisocial PD, a diagnosis of Conduct Disorder may still be assigned (American Psychiatric Association, 2000b). It is important to *not* assign a more severe disorder with more negative prognosis to younger individuals.

Dissociative Disorders

Individuals with Borderline PD may experience dissociative states; however, these are often not the most prominent clinical features, as they are for individuals with dissociative disorders.

Among the Personality Disorders

Compounding the difficulty of differential diagnosis is the fact that individuals who are diagnosed with one PD are more likely to meet the criteria of another, and currently the *DSM-IV-TR* encourages clinicians to assign multiple diagnoses (First & Tasman, 2004). The extent of the diagnostic overlap has fueled the call for a dimensional model of personality (Cloninger, 2000; Widiger, 2000).

Paranoid versus Schizoid

Both Paranoid and Schizoid PDs are characterized by an interpersonal coldness. They differ in their expression of anger. Those with Paranoid PD may appear rational and unemotional; they often also express a hostile labile affect in angry outbursts characterized by sarcasm and hostility (American Psychiatric Association, 2000b; M. B. Miller et al., 2001). In contrast, individuals with Schizoid PD have difficulty expressing anger even when provoked, responding passively to hostility and adverse events; and they appear not to experience strong emotions (American Psychiatric Association, 2000b; Levy & Scott, 2006).

Schizoid versus Schizotypal

The diagnostic criteria for Schizotypal PD are more schizophrenic-like than those for Schizoid PD in that they include disturbances of perception and bizarre and idiosyncratic behavior, speech, and cognitions (First et al., 2002; M. B. Miller et al., 2001). There is some overlap in the clinical presentation of both disorders in terms of social isolation, poor interpersonal relationships, and odd and inappropriate affect, leading some to question the validity of two separate diagnoses (Bernstein & Travaglini, 1999). The interpersonal histories of individuals with Schizotypal PD may reflect a few long-standing relationships, and unlike Schizoid PD, these individuals experience high levels of social anxiety and cognitive and perceptual distortions, including reports of heightened intuition (American Psychiatric Association, 2000b; First & Tasman, 2004; McClanahan et al., 2003). Both Schizoid and Schizotypal PDs have difficulty with social reciprocity, often failing to respond with appropriate facial expressions, missing the subtleties of social interaction and social cues and nuances; they appear socially inept and are perceived by others as odd and self-absorbed (M.B. Miller et al., 2001). Individuals with Schizoid PD appear bland, with limited emotional reactivity, whereas those with Schizotypal PD present with a stiff, constricted style, often accompanied by an odd, eccentric appearance and peculiar, idiosyncratic behaviors and unusual mannerisms (American Psychiatric Association, 2000b; First & Tasman, 2004).

Schizoid versus Avoidant

Earlier Millon (1981) hypothesized that Avoidant PD describes an active detachment, whereas Schizoid PD describes a more passive disinterest and detachment. Bernstein and Travaglini (1999) note that, when interacting with an individual with Schizoid PD, one has the feeling that something is missing, a sense of depersonalization or coldness. Those with Avoidant PD, unlike individuals with Schizoid PD, desire affection and human companionship and express strong needs for certainty and security but are too shy and insecure to seek relationships out (Levy & Scott, 2006).

Cluster B

There is considerable clinical overlap in this cluster, and differentiating between the disorders can be difficult. For Antisocial PD it may be helpful to focus on the number of antisocial behaviors and a prior diagnosis of Conduct Disorder rather than impulsivity and lack of empathy. Individuals with Histrionic PD may also be interpersonally exploitive, but they typically do not have a history of associated antisocial acts. Their rapidly shifting emotionality is usually not accompanied by the chronic sense of emptiness and loneliness and the level of anger and self-destructive acts seen in Borderline PD (Levy & Scott, 2006; McClanahan et al., 2003). Discriminating between Borderline and Narcissistic PDs may also be difficult. Differences in self-concept and identity, the level of self-destructive behaviors, and the role others serve as a source of admiration or nurturance may help with this differentiation. For individuals with Borderline PD, their fear of abandonment triggers impulsive behavior, rage, and feelings of emptiness, whereas for those with Dependent PD, their fear of interpersonal loss results in overly submissive behaviors (Levy & Scott, 2005). Both Histrionic and Antisocial PDs tend to be interpersonally manipulative, but the former relies on extroverted seductive flirtation, and the latter relies on antagonistic intimidation (Widiger & Bornstein, 2001b).

Cluster C

Avoidant PD is placed within the Cluster C PDs because of its characteristic features of interpersonal anxiety, hypersensitivity, and fear of rejection (M. B. Miller et al., 2001). Avoidant and Dependent PDs have a large overlap in terms of clinical symptoms, such as a lack of self-assertion and low self-esteem; yet the Avoidant PD shuns interpersonal intimacy, whereas the Dependent PD seeks it (Bernstein & Travaglini, 1999). Multidimensional scaling indicates that Avoidant PD can be discriminated from Schizoid PD, but it cannot be differentiated from Dependent PD (Levy & Scott, 2006).

TREATMENT

General Principles in Treating Personality Disorders

Many individuals with PDs not only misinterpret social information, but also present with significant impairments in personal, social, and work relationships (M. H. Stone, 2001). Consequently, the establishment and maintenance of a therapeutic relationship can be challenging (Gunderson & Gabbard, 2000; Kernberg, 2004). For individuals with Cluster A disorders, there may be a lack of interests or a paranoid unwillingness to establish a therapeutic relationship (Bender, 2005). In contrast, individuals in Cluster B may establish instant rapport only to follow with devaluing criticism (Gabbard, 2000b; Paris, 2000b; Stanley & Brodsky, 2005a,b). Cluster C individuals' anxiety and dependence may result in an overly dependent or controlling relationship (J. E. Young & Klosko, 2005). Individuals with Cluster C PDs have been described as the least dysfunctional, being more amenable to treatment, having greater insight, and having the best outcome with every type of short-term psychotherapy (Eskedal & Demetri, 2006).

The PDs represent chronic, long-standing, pervasive patterns that for many individuals are ego-syntonic, entrenched, and central to how they define themselves (First & Tasman,

2004). As mentioned earlier, these individuals frequently seek treatment for comorbid Axis I disorders (Skodol, 2005). Thus it may be natural for the clinician to focus on treating the presenting Axis I disorder; however, not considering the underlying personality disorder will result in treatment being ineffective (Levy & Scott, 2006). One of the major challenges for the clinician is addressing noncompliance and the potential that the individual may drop out of treatment before completion (Gutheil, 2005). Techniques described earlier in the treatment chapter may help to decrease these behaviors, and an overview of general interventions for PDs is presented in Table 14.7.

Despite early preconceptions that personality disorders were unchangeable and untreatable, research indicates that they are in fact amenable to a range of psychological and psychopharmacological interventions (Markovitz, 2001; J. C. Perry, Bannon, & Ianni, 1999; Tickle, Heatherton, & Wittenberg, 2001). Long-term longitudinal research also indicates that many of these disorders improve over time, with individuals developing more adaptive coping strategies and support systems and consequently experience decreases in impulsive, self-destructive behaviors (Grilo & McGlashan, 2005; M. H. Stone, 2001). These improvements can result in significant benefits to the individual, the public health system, and society as a whole (Linehan, 2000).

For many years the treatment of choice for those who could afford it was long-term psychotherapy (Gabbard, 2005). However, current resources for long-term treatment are limited, and many individuals have insurance plans that cap the number of individual therapy sessions. From the onset, part of the clinician's challenge will be to develop a treatment plan that will address clients' needs, given their limited resources. This may involve adjunct referral to low-fee or clinic programs with long-term treatment or

Table 14.7   General treatment interventions for personality disorders

Area	Interventions
Therapeutic interventions	Establish and maintain a therapeutic alliance and rapport.
	Remain alert for dropout and compliance issues.
	Evaluate and monitor impulsivity and high-risk behavior.
	Determine level of care and intervention.
	Consider diagnostic overlap and comorbidity.
	Assess and treat comorbid disorders and associated features.
	Be alert for boundary, ethical, and countertransference issues.
	Address pervasive chronic patterns and resistance to change.
	Evaluate need for a structured or long-term approach.
	Determine intervention approach.
Adjunctive referrals	Consider medication referral for comorbid disorders.
	Establish collaborative relationship with physician.
	Refer to low-fee long-term clinic.
	Refer to social skills group or training.
	If appropriate, refer to group therapy.
	Refer to vocational counseling.
Family interventions	Psychoeducation.
	Family or couples therapy.
	Refer to family support group.

providing care within a collaborative treatment framework (Gunderson et al., 2005; Schlesinger & Silk, 2005). Meta-analyses show that psychodynamic and cognitive-behavior therapies are effective treatments for PDs and may be associated with a rate of recovery 7 times greater than that of the natural course of the disorders, and longer treatment resulted in increased effect size (Leichsenring & Leibling, 2003; J. C. Perry et al., 1999). Psychoeducation and family support have been found to be crucial elements in the recovery of individuals with PDs (Hoffman & Fruzzetti, 2005; Pirooz & Sholevar, 2005).

One of the major challenges the clinician working with individuals with PDs confronts is the lack of information on empirically supported specific interventions. An overview of treatment interventions that have been demonstrated to be effective for each of the PDs are presented in the following tables (14.8, 14.9, and 14.10). Providing these services for older adults can be particularly challenging, Snapp Kean and colleagues (2004) describe how to facilitate treatment for these individuals in a community mental health setting.

Disorder-Specific Treatments

Paranoid

Individuals with Paranoid PD rarely seek treatment, and the primary challenge for the therapist will be the establishment of a therapeutic alliance and the development of trust (Gabbard, 2000). Bender (2005) describes the alliance challenges for the clinician as including the individual's expectation of being harmed or exploited, their hypersensitivity to perceived criticism, and their tendency to withdraw or attack. She recommends using the individual's underlying need for affirmation as a point of engagement for treatment. There are few empirical studies on treatment effectiveness for individuals with Paranoid PD, and most of the available information comes from clinical case studies (M. B. Miller et al., 2001; Piper & Joyce, 2001; Pretzer, 2004). These clients may have limited insight into their problems, externalize the blame to others, and are reluctant to address their own role in their maladaptive behaviors. Many form adversarial relationships with clinicians and often drop out prior to treatment completion (First & Tasman, 2004; Maxmen & Ward, 1995). Gabbard (2005) notes that difficulty with trust experienced by individuals with Paranoid PD makes them unsuitable for psychoanalytic therapy. The presence of paranoid personality features also makes treating comorbid Axis I disorders more difficult (Dolan-Sewell et al., 2001). A direct, consistent, honest approach is the most effective (see Table 14.8).

It is crucial to focus on problem identification and problem solving and use a very structured approach accompanied by sincere respect for the individual's autonomy, interpersonal space, and desire to play a role in decision making and treatment planning (Gabbard, 2000). Deep psychological interpretation and challenging or confronting the individual's paranoid beliefs, especially at the onset of treatment, are countertherapeutic, as is an overly compliant stance, which may be interpreted as patronizing (First & Tasman, 2004; Maxmen & Ward, 1995). The very nature of therapy, which requires trust, disclosure, compliance, and follow-through, may be experienced as overwhelming (M. B. Miller et al., 2001). A neutral, accepting stance and a willingness to discuss and consider logical explanations may help them develop a more self-reflective or observant style. Recognizing that these clients will re-create their conflicts with others in the context of the therapeutic relationship enables the clinician to respond in a nondefensive

Table 14.8   Specific treatment interventions for personality disorders

Personality Disorder	Interventions
Paranoid	Use a direct, consistent, honest, structured approach.
	Point of engagement client's need for affirmation.
	Focus on problem identification and solving.
	Respect autonomy.
	Involve client in decision making and treatment planning.
	Consider schema therapy, CBT, or short-term dynamic psychotherapy.
	Document consent and interventions.
Schizoid	Use a direct, supportive, professional approach.
	Point of engagement client's underlying neediness and sensitivity.
	Focus on education, feedback, social skills, and communication.
	Establish goal of increasing social contact.
	Use role-play and videos to facilitate self-observation.
	Employ behavioral interventions and homework assignments.
	Consider referral to group psychotherapy.
Schizotypal	Use a supportive, structured approach.
	Point of engagement client's motivation for human connection.
	Focus on practical advice and decreasing isolation.
	Use sympathetic listening, psychoeducation.
	Model considering alternatives.
	Use social skills training, role-play, concrete feedback.
	Refer to structured supportive group therapy.

manner and understand the individual's suspicious, litigious, contentious manner (Gabbard, 2000).

A. T. Beck and colleagues (2001) have described the role of cognitive distortion in Paranoid PD, and cognitive therapy techniques have been found to be effective for this disorder. However, most of the research is on single case studies or from uncontrolled clinical reports (Piper & Joyce, 2001; Pretzer, 2004). Schema therapy, which blends cognitive-behavioral techniques and elements from attachment, object relations, gestalt, and psychodynamic theories to address the individual's underlying core psychological themes (schema), maladaptive coping style, and coping responses (modes), may also be helpful (J. Young & Klosko, 2005). Short-term psychodynamic interventions that focus on the development of insight, anger control, and interpersonal relationships, as developed by Luborsky (1984) and Strupp and Binder (1984), may also be applicable. Cognitive-behavioral and interpersonal techniques also have been found to be effective (Beck et al., 2003; Turkat, 1990), though the research on Paranoid PDs has been limited. These individuals' difficulty trusting others and tendency to be accusatory and alienating to others make them poor candidates for group psychotherapy (Piper & Joyce, 2001). There has been considerable research on medication for paranoid ideation, but little has been conducted on the effectiveness of medication for long-standing paranoid personality patterns, and the efficacy of such treatment is unknown (R. Grossman, 2004; Markovitz, 2001; M. B. Miller et al., 2001). Given the level of distrust these individuals experience, they may be reluctant to take medication, seeing it as a method of control, though they may consider medication for coexisting anxiety and depression (First & Tasman, 2004). As these individuals tend to be litigious, it is important to clearly document consent, confidentiality, and discharge plans (Maxmen & Ward, 1995).

Schizoid

These individuals are comfortable in their interpersonal detachment, have little or no interest in establishing relationships with others, and consequently rarely seek treatment (American Psychiatric Association, 2000b). Their social detachment and emotional aloofness make the establishment of a therapeutic alliance difficult; a point of engagement for the clinician is the individual's underlying neediness and sensitivity (Bender, 2005). Millon and Davis (2000) note that the prognosis for individuals with Schizoid PD is poor. They typically seek treatment for comorbid Axis I conditions and tend to drop out of treatment as soon as the Axis I disorder is alleviated (M. B. Miller et al., 2001). Their difficulty with empathy, discomfort with emotional issues, and difficulty engaging or maintaining an interpersonal connection make the establishment of rapport challenging (Bender, 2005).

They are rarely suitable for long-term analytic psychotherapy and respond best to a direct, more professional, supportive approach that emphasizes education and feedback about interpersonal skills and communication (First & Tasman, 2004; Gabbard, 2005; Piper & Joyce, 2001). The main goals of treatment are typically to increase social contact and improve interpersonal and social skills (Millon & Davis, 2000). An effective approach to treatment is to focus on teaching more effective interpersonal and communication skills, using role-playing and video to encourage self-observation (First & Tasman, 2004). While no specific psychoeducation programs exist for individuals with Schizoid PD, Hoffman and Fruzzetti (2005) note that there are no contraindications for psychoeducation's effectiveness, and its utility is obvious. Behavioral techniques involving homework assignments of gradual involvement with social groups and using dysfunctional thought records (A. T. Beck et al., 2003) may also be effective, though the research is limited and confined to clinical reports (Maxmen & Ward, 1995; Piper & Joyce, 2001).

Involvement in group therapy can be effective, if the individual is not rejected by other members because of his or her emotional and interpersonal detachment, passivity, and silence (Piper & Joyce, 2001; Piper & Orgrodniczuk, 2000). Yalom (1975) describes techniques that are useful for these individuals in long-term group psychotherapy. According to First and Tasman (2004), there is no available information on the effectiveness of medication for individuals with Schizoid PD. R. Grossman (2004) reports on only one open-label study with only four individuals who were treated with risperidone, and though improvements were noted in all, the group was too small to be broadly representative, and standardized measures were not used for diagnosis. Therapeutic progress can be very slow, and it is important to monitor feelings of discouragement and frustration (Millon & Davis, 2000).

Schizotypal

Individuals with Schizotypal PD may seek treatment for comorbid anxiety and mood disorders (American Psychiatric Association, 2000b). They may have little insight into their bizarre behaviors or self-presentation, seeing themselves as creative and eccentric (First & Tasman, 2004). Their suspiciousness, distrust, profound interpersonal discomfort, and bizarre cognitions significantly impact the development of a therapeutic alliance, yet their motivation for human connection may serve as a point of therapeutic engagement (Bender, 2005). They tend to be uncomfortable with intimacy and emotions, and this discomfort may increase with time, making the establishment of a therapeutic relationship difficult (American Psychiatric Association, 2000b). They are more comfortable with a supportive, structured approach that curtails their cognitive slippage and emphasizes practical advice and decreasing social isolation (Piper & Joyce, 2001). M. H. Stone (1993) describes the clinician as functioning as these clients' auxiliary ego, helping them to consider alternative, more likely interpretations for events and to stay on track. Supportive interventions can be helpful, as can focusing on sympathetic listening, advice giving, and problem-solving psychoeducation focusing on restoring and maintaining functioning to adaptation (Applebaum, 2005).

Social skills training, using role-playing, scripts, and concrete feedback, can help the individual develop better social strategies in such areas as how to make small talk, how to establish appropriate eye contact, and how to be more accepted in social settings (First & Tasman, 2004). Cognitive-behavioral techniques may help address some of the cognitive distortions characteristic of Schizotypal PD, such as "Things happen for a reason" and "Relationships are not safe." However, there is a lack of empirically supported research on the effectiveness of both cognitive-behavioral and other methods for this PD (M. B. Miller et al., 2001; Piper & Joyce, 2001). Therapy is likely to proceed at a slow pace, and confronting the individual with emotionally laden material may be overwhelming and result in withdrawal from treatment. As psychodynamic psychotherapy requires a high degree of motivation and psychological-mindedness, M. H. Stone (1993) recommends it be limited to those individuals who appear predominantly avoidant, rather than those showing more of an indifference to human relationships and contact.

For some individuals, very structured, supportive group therapy may be helpful and can provide additional opportunities to address social anxiety and to engage in reality testing of negative assumptions (Piper & Ogrodniczuk, 2005). Nevertheless, the individual is likely to need significant preparation in one-to-one treatment before entering a group. Prolonged silences or exceptionally marked eccentricities may turn off others in the group. There is limited research on the effectiveness of medication for these individuals; few studies have a sufficient sample size or control groups to make meaningful conclusions. First and Tasman (2004) and Markovitz (2001) suggest that low-dose neuroleptics such as thiothixene may be helpful for individuals with ideas of reference or who are prone to psychotic thinking and social anxieties. A. Roth and Fonagy (2005) note that individuals with moderately severe schizotypal symptoms may also benefit from neuroleptics, and Soloff (2005) notes improvement in general schizotypal symptoms with neuroleptics. In contrast, R. Grossman's (2004) research review found that thiothixene shows limited efficacy and suggested it should be considered only for those individuals with marked psychotic features. A small ($N = 23$) double-blind controlled study by Koeningsberg and colleagues (2003) found risperidone improved both positive and negative symptoms.

Antisocial

Individuals with Antisocial PD, by definition, are interpersonally manipulative, superficially charming, and often lacking in empathy and concern for others. They are regarded as the most difficult PD to treat (First & Tasman, 2004; Gunderson & Gabbard, 2000).

What few studies of treatment effectiveness there are suggest that individuals with Antisocial PD without comorbid depression have a poorer prognosis, improving on only three of 22 outcome variables (Pretzer, 2004; A. Roth & Fonagy, 2005). These individuals typically lack the motivation or interest in change and are rarely self-referred, usually entering treatment secondary to external factors such as pending legal cases, divorce, or termination actions, and they are often seen in drug and alcohol treatment settings (Rounsaville, Kranzker, Ball, Tennen, et al., 1998). When comorbid substance abuse is treated in intensive psychosocial intervention and behavioral incentive contingencies and a cognitive-behavioral coping skills approach are used, these individuals do better than in interactional group therapy (Ball, 2004).

The most effective treatment is early intensive intervention, often in the preschool or grade school years when the child is first diagnosed as ODD or CD (Kazdin, 1998). These individuals are not considered appropriate for psychoanalysis, as they tend to be controlling, disingenuous, and often establish a pseudo-alliance for their personal advantage (Bender, 2005; Gabbard, 2005). They may engage in treatment if it is in their self-interest or to address distressing comorbid Axis I disorders (Bender, 2005). Individual therapy involving concrete interventions, a reality-based approach, and anger management and cognitive-behavioral techniques (see Table 14.9) is recommended over an insight-oriented approach (Kraus & Reynolds, 2001). Focusing on the issues that precipitated treatment

Table 14.9 Specific treatment interventions for personality disorders

Personality Disorder	Interventions
Antisocial	Requires early intensive intervention.
	Consider a concrete, reality-based approach.
	Employ anger management and cognitive-behavioral therapy (CBT).
	Treat comorbid substance-related disorders—12-step groups.
	Refer to residential, wilderness, or therapeutic programs.
	Refer to group programs in incarceration settings.
Borderline	Requires intensive supportive psychotherapy.
	Refer for medication consultation.
	Address and contain impulsivity and self-destructive behaviors.
	Consider empirically based intervention (DBT, STEPPS, or TFT).
	Provide individual and family psychoeducation.
	Refer to family support and skills training groups.
	Obtain clinical consultation.
Histrionic	Requires warm, supportive style.
	Maintain a structured, detailed approach.
	Point of engagement client's need for relationships.
	Consider psychodynamic and behavioral techniques.
	Use long-term psychodynamic or psychoanalytic psychotherapy.
	Consider integrative configural analysis.
	Refer to group psychotherapy.
Narcissistic	Requires a clear, professional approach.
	Point of engagement client's need for affirmation.
	Consider long-term psychodynamic psychotherapy, psychoanalysis.
	Consider CBT.

and comorbid alcohol and substance abuse may also be effective (Cottler, Compton, Ridenour, Ben Abdallah & Gallaher, 1998; Ruegg, Haynes, & Frances, 1997). In non-psychopathic individuals, marital and family therapy can be effective (Melroy, 1995).

For young adults with late onset and less pervasive forms of this disorder, residential wilderness programs may be effective (Gabbard, 2000). Therapeutic communities have shown some limited success. Many adults with Antisocial PD spend a considerable amount of time incarcerated, where treatment tends to focus on 12-step groups for comorbid alcohol and substance abuse conditions, or group psychotherapy addressing anger management and the long-term consequences of antisocial acts (Coid, 2005; Dolan, 1998). A. Roth and Fonagy (2005) note that the few existing studies on the impact of treatment during incarceration tend to focus on psychopathic individuals, and many lack adequate control groups and appropriate outcome measures. C. T. Taylor's (2000) research found the length of stay on a therapeutic community unit within a prison was associated with a better outcome than for those on a wait-list or in the general population. According to R. Grossman (2004), the core features of Antisocial PD are resistant to both psychotherapy and medication. Medication can be used to control explosive-impulsive type aggression, and depending on the nature of the aggression, SSRIs, beta-blockers, lithium, anticonvulsant mood stabilizers, or antipsychotics may be considered. However, the availability of controlled trials on the treatment of Antisocial PD with medication is limited (R. Grossman, 2004; Markovitz, 2001). These individuals often engender strong reactions in treating clinicians, so it is important to be aware of these feelings and the potential for boundary violations (Gunderson & Gabbard, 2000; Gutheil, 2005).

Borderline

The American Psychiatric Association (2001a) has provided specific guidelines and treatment recommendations for individuals with Borderline PD, and the National Institute of Mental Health has designated funds for research in this area (Trull et al., 2006). Individuals with Borderline PD are often highly motivated to seek treatment, but are also impulsive, emotionally unstable, self-destructive, and suicidal, form intense volatile relationships with treating clinicians, and are extremely difficult and stressful to treat (Gabbard, 2000a; Gunderson, 2001; M. H. Stone, 2000). Their emotional and cognitive instability, demanding nature, and tendency to act out make the establishment of a therapeutic alliance difficult, and they sometimes worsen in treatment, resulting in the clinician's increased frustration and sense of hopelessness (Bender, 2005; Robins & Koons, 2004). These individuals are often relationship seeking and respond well to a combination of psychotherapy, medication, and support (Bender, 2005; Gabbard, 2005). A solid therapeutic alliance, the clinician's commitment to treatment, and a safe setting where the client can express anger without retaliation have been linked to a more positive outcome (Bender, 2005; Gabbard, 2000b; Gunderson, 2001). Maintaining and repairing any damage to the therapeutic alliance and sustaining professional boundaries are essential ongoing tasks for the clinician, as well as not reacting precipitously, without careful consideration for the individual's impulsivity, constant chaos, and crises (Gutheil, 2005). These clients often engender intense reactions in their treating clinician and provide the most noteworthy examples of boundary problems and difficulties with clinician limit setting (Gutheil, 2005). For many clients, the unstable, intense relationships they experience with others are re-created in the therapeutic relationship, and it is essential for the clinician to have ongoing collegial consultation to prevent burnout and the development of countertherapeutic reactions (First & Tasman, 2004).

Addressing and containing impulsivity and self-destructive behaviors, including suicidality and substance abuse, are paramount (Gunderson et al., 2005; Verheul et al., 2005). It is helpful to assess the individual's chronic level and acute exacerbation of risk for suicide (Links & Kolla, 2005). Considering the severity of the individual's prior attempts and the factors discussed in Chapter 2 can assist in assessing the individual's chronic risk. Stanley and Brodsky (2005b) found that many of these individuals underestimated the lethality of their suicidal behaviors and often experienced significant depression, hopelessness, and impulsivity. Increasing depression and substance abuse often precede a suicide attempt. These clients are at high risk prior to hospital admission, discharge, or when the clinician or significant others are unavailable or on vacation (Yen et al., 2003).

Some individuals experience dissociation, a pathological process that keeps memories associated with a personal trauma out of consciousness (Koopman, Classen, Cardena, & Spiegel, 1995; Maldonado & Spiegel, 2005; Marmar, Weiss, & Metzler, 1998). In these scenarios, the clinician needs to ensure safety, develop a trusting alliance, and adopt a crisis intervention approach, as described in Chapter 4 (Cloitre et al., 2004; Westefeld & Heckman-Stone, 2003). The American Psychiatric Association (2001a) practice guidelines for Borderline PD recommend that clinicians treating individuals with dissociative symptoms treat the trauma, educate the individual, and help him or her develop control techniques. Hypnosis, relaxation techniques, and dialectical behavior therapy (DBT) have also been found to be effective for these symptoms.

Intensive psychotherapy is not only effective for those with Borderline PD, but also cost-effective (Chiesa, Fonagy, Holmes, Drahorad, & Harrison-Hall, 2002). One of the most widely used therapeutic interventions is DBT, which was developed by Linehan (1993a,b; 2000). It has demonstrated effectiveness for individuals who are suicidal and have Borderline PD in more than a dozen empirical studies (Hoffman & Fruzzetti, 2005). Dialectical behavior therapy is discussed further in the "Advanced Topics" section. Another form of cognitive-behavior therapy that has been found to be effective is Blum, Pfohl, St. John, Monahan, and Black's (2002) Systems Training for Emotional Predictability and Problem Solving (STEPPS), which focuses on behavior and emotion management skills. Individuals with Borderline PD also benefit from psychodynamic psychotherapy. Effective manualized models include Clarkin, Foelsch, Levy, Hull, Delaney, and Kernberg's (2001) transference-focused therapy (TFT), which focuses on the self-harming and therapy-interfering behaviors, and Bateman and Fonagy's (2004a,b) mentalization-based treatment that involves individual and group therapy.

Educating and providing support for family members of individuals with Borderline PD is crucial and decreases reported levels of depression, distress, and perceived burden (Hoffman, Buteau, Hooley, Fruzzetti, & Bruce, 2003). Dialectical behavior therapy provides both patient and family education components, including family skills training (Hoffman, Fruzzettii, & Swenson, 1999). Over the past 20 years, Gunderson (2001) has developed a very effective multifamily group program that includes excellent family guidebooks that describe Borderline PD (Gunderson & Berkowitz, 2002; Gunderson & Hoffman, 2005).

In reviewing the empirical research, Crits-Christoph and Barber (2004) note a wide range of medication used for Borderline PD; the most researched ones are the antidepressants fluoxetine and nefazodone and typical and atypical antipsychotics. R. Grossman (2004) provides a more detailed description of the American Psychiatric Association's (2001a) recommendations for the pharmacological treatment of Borderline PD. This includes medical algorithms for the three symptom clusters of affective dysregulation, impulsive-behavioral dyscontrol, and cognitive-perceptual symptoms. Zanarini (2004) provides a useful review of medications for individuals with Borderline PD. When more than one clinician is involved with the treatment of an individual with Borderline PD, there needs to be open communication and coordination of care to avoid splitting or the devaluing and idealization of care providers, resulting in fragmented treatment.

Histrionic

The Histrionic PD individual's emotional lability, unfocused cognitive style, and attempts to charm and entertain may undermine the therapeutic alliance. An effective approach involves adopting a warm and supportive therapeutic style and using the individual's intense need for relationships as an area of possible engagement for treatment (Bender, 2005). Individuals with Histrionic PD establish rapport rapidly, but it is often superficial and not sustained (First & Tasman, 2004).

A structured and detailed approach that combines psychodynamic and behavioral techniques focusing on immediate daily problems can be helpful (Gunderson & Gabbard, 2000; Piper & Joyce, 2005). In the past this disorder has typically been treated with long-term dynamic or psychoanalytic psychotherapy (Maxmen & Ward, 1995). Gabbard (2005) notes that individuals with good impulse control, stable object relations, and intact superegos can benefit from psychoanalysis, while other individuals may benefit from a modified psychoanalytic approach. These individuals respond well to supportive psychotherapy and collaborative treatment; however, all providers should have a clear plan for dealing with emotional outbursts and attention-seeking behaviors (Applebaum, 2005; Schlesinger & Silk, 2005).

A frequently used therapeutic approach for individuals with Histrionic PD is Horowitz's (1991, 1997) integrative configural analysis. This is rooted in psychodynamic approaches, but also incorporates CBT elements for identifying irrational cognitions. The treatment plan involves a problem list summarizing the individual's difficulties with impulsive behavior, frustration tolerance, and unsatisfying relationships. The individual's states of mind, the situations in which problems occur, and the defenses used to ward off uncomfortable feelings and thoughts are also incorporated. Understanding the clients' concepts of self and others, their personal schemas, and why certain roles (such as "wounded hero") are reenacted is essential. Clinicians also attend to the ways in which these repetitive role relationships are played out in the treatment and their own countertransference (Horowitz, 1991). Configural analysis starts with stabilizing the acute symptoms, including depression, anxiety, and substance use. Medications may be included at this stage. This is followed by a stage focusing on modification of communicative style and defensive control processes. Here clients learn how to think about conflict and to reflect on their intentions and motives and those of others. In the third phase of treatment the focus is on the modification and integration of interpersonal patterns and personal schemas. Here the clinician helps clients identify concepts of self and others and the ways these are repeatedly reenacted in relationships. The last stage, or termination, focuses on separation and addresses the individual's feelings of loss and developing coping strategies.

Individuals with Histrionic PD may also find group psychotherapy helpful, but the clinician needs to monitor the individual's involvement, attention-seeking behaviors, and suicidal gestures (First & Tasman, 2004). According to R. Grossman (2004), there are no psychopharmacological trials reported for the treatment of Histrionic PD. For individuals with comorbid mood disorders, antidepressant medication may be considered (Markovitz, 2001).

Narcissistic

These individuals rarely seek treatment, and when they do, it's usually only for comorbid depression or difficulties with intimate relationships (Kraus & Reynolds, 2001; Maxmen & Ward, 1995). Establishing rapport and a working relationship can be difficult, as grandiosity is the central feature, and they need constant positive regard and are often contemptuous of others (Bender, 2005; Paris, 2005). They are also very concerned that the clinician be the best and most competent, and they will quickly shift from idealizing to devaluing a clinician they find less than superior (First & Tasman, 2004). The clinician will need to find a balance between acknowledging the individual's specialness while setting appropriate limits and maintaining clear professional boundaries. These clients' lack of empathy, tendency to respond with rage to feedback, and distorted self-serving interpretation of events make therapy difficult and often ineffective. They often require confrontation, and the most difficult aspect of treatment is getting them to identify their maladaptive patterns and consequences (Paris, 2005). Over time they may respond to empathy and affirmation, and this may serve as a point of engagement for treatment (Bender, 2005).

Long-term psychodynamic psychotherapy or psychoanalysis focusing on the underlying anger and developing empathy and insight has been the treatment of choice for this disorder (Gabbard, 2000, 2005; Piper & Joyce, 2005). Cognitive-behavioral approaches that involve awareness of narcissistic behaviors and their impact on relationships have also been used. As they tend to monopolize and dominate psychotherapy groups, this therapeutic modality is not recommended (Yalom, 1985). There is no research on the effectiveness of medication for Narcissistic PD (R. Grossman, 2004; Markovitz, 2001). Treating these individuals can be challenging, and the clinician is likely to experience considerable countertransference (Gabbard, 2005). It is also important to be mindful of the individual's potential for aggression and interpersonally exploitive behaviors (M. H. Stone, 2005).

Avoidant

For individuals with Avoidant PD, the expectation of others' criticism and rejection, reluctance to disclose information, and tendency to feel shame and humiliation are challenges to the establishment of a therapeutic alliance. In general, these individuals will respond to empathy, unconditional acceptance, and warmth, and their desire for interpersonal relationships can be a motivator for treatment (Bender, 2005; Eskedal & Demetri, 2006). Earlier research by Barber and colleagues (1997) suggests a supportive, expressive psychodynamic approach is effective. If they are motivated to understand the origins of their anxieties, fears, and insecurities, they may do well in psychoanalysis or psychodynamic psychotherapy (Gabbard, 2005; Gunderson & Gabbard, 2000). They are at high risk for dropping out of treatment. In one follow-up study, 50% dropped out; their fear of ridicule may contribute to premature termination (Pretzer, 2004; A. Roth & Fonagy, 2005). The triggers for these individuals' avoidant behaviors include stressors related to close relationships and public appearances (Cottraux & Blackburn, 2001). They may be reluctant, embarrassed, and afraid of being ridiculed if they express their concerns, so a patient, accepting, understanding stance is vital.

Cognitive techniques can be helpful in addressing their distortions and irrational beliefs at the onset of treatment (A. T. Beck et al., 2003; D. M. Clark, 2001). Individuals with Avoidant PD may respond well to social skills training and behavioral or cognitive-behavioral techniques (See table 14.10), including systematic desensitization and in vivo gradual exposure to social situations (A. T. Beck et al., 2003; D. M. Clark, 2001; Levy & Scott, 2005; Millon & Davis, 2000). A combination of skills training and systematic desensitization in the form of schema therapy has been found to be effective in addressing interpersonal problems (Young, Klosko, & Weishaar, 2003). Psychoeducation programs that include social skills training have shown significant improvement that has been maintained on 3-month follow-up; referral to social skills and assertive training groups may also be helpful (Hoffman & Fruzzetti, 2005; Pretzer, 2004).

These clients may benefit from group psychotherapy, particularly after a course of individual therapy, as they are often very motivated (Piper & Ogrodniczuk, 2005). Those who benefit most from group therapy are those who value and desire personal change, and involvement with both cognitive-behavioral and short-term behavioral group therapy has been associated with significant improvements (Eskedal & Demetri, 2006). There is minimal information on medication for Avoidant PD, but there is considerable research on medication for Social Phobia and Social Anxiety Disorder. The SSRI antidepressants

Table 14.10   Specific treatment interventions for personality disorders

Personality Disorder	Interventions
Avoidant	Requires empathy, unconditional acceptance, patience, and warmth. Point of engagement client's desire for interpersonal relationships. Use supportive, expressive psychodynamic approach. Consider CBT. Consider social skills training and schema therapy. Assess need for systematic desensitization or in vivo gradual exposure. Include psychoeducation. Refer to group psychotherapy.
Dependent	Requires clear limits on out-of-session behavior. Consider psychodynamic or psychoanalytic psychotherapy. Consider CBT and assertiveness training. Consider brief adaptational therapy. Refer to group psychotherapy. Be alert for overmedication.
Obsessive-Compulsive	Requires supportive, expressive approach. Focus on here-and-now, feelings, self-awareness, and empathy. Consider short-term psychodynamic psychotherapy. Consider CBT. Include interpersonal skills training.

have been found to be effective and are regarded as first-line treatment; benzodiazepines are regarded as second-line treatment (Blanco, Anita, & Liebowitz, 2002; Markovitz, 2001). Individuals with Avoidant PD have also been found to respond to MAOIs, but there are fewer data for these medications, which are not often used because of side effects and risks (R. Grossman, 2004).

Dependent

Individuals with Dependent PD are considered the easiest to engage in therapy, as they often quickly develop a pseudo-alliance and willingly allow the clinician to make decisions, demonstrating hesitance to take any initiative for themselves (Bender, 2005; Eskedal & Demetri, 2006). They are friendly, at times excessively compliant, prefer to remain in treatment, and have unrealistic expectations of the therapist, calling incessantly and making inappropriate demands (Bender, 2005; First & Tasman, 2004). Clear limits and appointment times need to be established from the beginning to prevent later angry and hurt feelings. Given the intensity of neediness and difficulty with initiative it is important for clinicians to monitor any irritation, disdain, and countertransference they may experience toward these individuals (Benjamin, 2003). Their constant need for reassurance and need not to offend may result in withholding important information, and their interpersonal style is to want others, including the clinician, to assume the responsibility for change (Wessler, Hankin, & Stern, 2001). They may do well in psychodynamic psychotherapy or psychoanalysis, and discussion of the origin of their need to be taken care of, excessive need for support, low self-esteem, and fears of autonomy are important (Gabbard, 2005; Gunderson & Gabbard, 2000). Individuals with high levels of separation anxiety and lower ego strength may do better with more supportive treatment (Harper, 2004). As they may become involved in exploitive and abusive relationships, it is important to discuss their interpersonal choices and patterns, and if there are comorbid avoidant features the use of desensitization techniques can be helpful (Alden et al., 2002). Cognitive-behavioral techniques and assertiveness training may also be beneficial (A. T. Beck et al., 2003). Brief adaptational therapy, which uses a cognitive focus on the individual's maladaptive interpersonal relationships and the therapeutic relationship, and short-term psychodynamic psychotherapy have also been found to be effective (Piper & Joyce, 2005; Svartberg, Stiles, & Seltzer, 2004).

Group psychotherapy has been found to decrease the use of medication and crisis visits for these individuals (Piper & Joyce, 2005; Piper & Ogrodniczuk, 2005). As Eskedal and Demetri (2006) note, group psychotherapy allows individuals with Dependent PD to obtain nurturance and support, while experimenting with more adaptive behaviors and new ways of self-expression and having their needs met. Interactional groups expose these individuals to a broader range of interpersonal interactions, and by refusing to fulfill the individual's dependency needs, the group encourages the development of more appropriate coping (Corey & Corey, 2002). They benefit the most from homogeneous groups in which all members have a similar diagnosis and are addressing similar issues but are at different stages of recovery; such groups should be structured, with clearly defined goals (Rutan & Stone, 2000).

To date there is no specific psychopharmacological intervention for Dependent PD (R. Grossman, 2004; Markovitz, 2001; Rector, Bagby, Segal, Joffee, & Levitt, 2000). Despite this, individuals with this disorder are frequently prescribed medication for their help-seeking behaviors. On psychiatric inpatient programs, they have been found to be prescribed almost 50% more medication than individuals with similar Axis I disorders who do not have Dependent PD (O'Neill & Bornstein, 2001; Tyer, Mitchard, Methuen, & Ranger, 2003).

Obsessive-Compulsive

In general, the PD most amenable to treatment is Obsessive-Compulsive PD. Individuals with this disorder are often self-referred, as they are acutely aware of their own suffering (Chessick, 2001). Their preoccupation with small details and indecisiveness result in occupational impairment, which often precipitates their seeking treatment (Eskedal & Demetri, 2006). Their need for control, perfectionism, difficulty dealing with and avoidance of affect, and fear of the clinician's criticism may make the establishment of a therapeutic alliance difficult (Bender, 2005). The level of obsessiveness, overreliance on intellectualization, and lack of insight may also make therapy challenging (Gunderson & Gabbard, 2000). An effective approach is to focus on the here and now and on feelings rather than thoughts (Maxmen & Ward, 1995; Sperry, 1995). Despite being stubborn and controlling, these individuals tend to follow through, are conscientious and hard-working, and at times their use of intellectualization can be helpful (Bender, 2005; Eskedal & Demetri, 2006).

Barber and colleagues' (1997) earlier research suggests that a supportive, expressive, psychodynamic approach is successful; on follow-up 1 year later 85% no longer met diagnostic criteria. Short-term psychodynamic therapy focusing on particular goals and issues may also be effective, as can cognitive-behavioral techniques that are structured and present- and problem-focused (A. T. Beck et al., 2003). However, these individuals often like cognitive-behavior therapies, and clinicians may find themselves engaged in time-consuming, unproductive ruminations (First & Tasman, 2004). Gabbard (2000) suggests using techniques that encourage the recognition, acknowledgment, and expression of feelings. Self-awareness, empathy, and interpersonal skills training are also useful techniques to consider (Eskedal & Demetri, 2006). The goals for treatment may be helping these individuals to replace their unrealistic self-expectations with a more realistic self-appraisal and to increase their productivity by learning to relinquish their inflexible patterns of control (Eskedal & Demetri, 2006). They often do not benefit from group psychotherapy, as they can be domineering and critical, tending to monopolize the group session and lacking in empathic interpersonal interest in others (First & Tasman, 2004; Yalom, 1995). To date there are no controlled medication studies for this PD (R. Grossman, 2004; Markovitz, 2001).

ADVANCED TOPIC: DIALECTICAL BEHAVIOR THERAPY

One of the most widely used therapeutic interventions for individuals with Borderline PD and for those struggling with suicide is dialectical behavior therapy. This approach was developed over 20 years ago by Marsha Linehan (1993a,b; 2000) and has demonstrated effectiveness in more than a dozen empirical studies (Hoffman & Fruzzetti, 2005). It combines individual therapy, structured social skills training, and family or support groups. It is a very active approach that involves cognitive, behavioral, client-centered, and Zen

Buddhism techniques that are grounded in an acceptance of the client and a mindfulness orientation (Robins & Koons, 2004; Stanley & Brodsky, 2005a). Key elements of DBT are summarized in Table 14.11.

Dialectical behavior therapy is based on the theory that individuals with Borderline PD experience dysregulation in five areas: emotional, interpersonal, self, behavioral, and cognitive. These difficulties are theorized to occur because the individual has an inherent emotional sensitivity or vulnerability that makes the modulation of affect difficult (Robins, Ivanoff, & Linchan, 2001). Compounding these emotional regulation challenges, the individual grows up in an emotionally invalidating environment, where his or her feelings and thoughts are dismissed, trivialized, and ignored, and where problem solving and goal attainment are oversimplified. These factors contribute to both the development and the maintenance of the clinical features of Borderline PD. Emotional dysregulation is conceptualized as the clinical core feature that drives all of the other symptoms (Robins et al., 2001).

Table 14.11   Dialectic behavior therapy

Theoretical Concepts

Dysregulation: Emotional (central); interpersonal; self, behavioral, and cognitive
Inherent emotional sensitivity or vulnerability and an invalidating environment
Dialectics: Radical acceptance and commitment to change
Core strategies: Validation and problem solving
Principles: Interrelatedness and wholeness, polarity and continuous change
Communication style: Warm, reciprocal, and irreverent

Treatment Interventions

Individual therapy, skills training group, telephone coaching, consultation, case management, clinicians' team meeting, hierarchy of treatment goals, cross-session therapy agenda, diary cards

Treatment Stages

Pretreatment: Commitment
Stage 1 (control):
   Treatment targets:
   1) Decreasing self-harm and suicidal and violent behaviors
   2) Reducing therapy-interfering behaviors
   3) Decreasing quality of life interfering behaviors
   4) Increasing skill acquisition and implementation of life-enhancing skills
Stage 2 (order): Uncovering and addressing prior traumas
Stage 3 (synthesis): Mastery, self-efficacy
Stage 4 (transcendence): Integration and capacity for joy

Dialectic Strategies

Balancing treatment strategies (validation and problem solving), use of metaphor, entering the paradox, devil's advocate, allowing natural change, extending, wise mind, making lemonade out of lemons, and dialectical assessment

Skills training
   1) Mindfulness
   2) Distress tolerance
   3) Emotional regulation
   4) Interpersonal effectiveness

Dialectical behavior therapy emphasizes dialectics, the synthesis of opposites or apparent polarities, the primary being acceptance and change. This involves a worldview that embraces the beliefs that everything is connected and that our sense of self is determined by our relationships with others (the principle of interrelatedness and wholeness). Nature is seen as composed of opposites, the synthesis of which results in growth (principle of polarity), and everything continually changes (principle of continuous change; Robins & Koons, 2004). There is a recognition that individuals want to and are trying to improve; that their understanding of their past includes an invalidating environment; that they are vulnerable to experience emotional, relationship, self, behavioral, and cognitive dysregulation; and that their current lives are intolerable. For individuals to get better, they have to solve their problems and there has to be a radical acceptance and an active commitment to change.

Treatment involves a balancing of two core strategies: validation (acceptance) and problem solving (change; Robins & Koons, 2004). The therapist is encouraged to adopt a warm, reciprocal, genuine interpersonal style (acceptance), combined with a more irreverent case management consultant approach (change). Problem solving includes behavioral analysis, skills training, contingency management, exposure, and cognitive modification (Robins & Koons, 2004). Starting with pretreatment and followed by four active treatment stages (control, order, synthesis, and transcendence), DBT addresses treatment goals that are hierarchical within each session and that relate to a within- and across-session treatment agenda (Robins et al., 2001).

In pretreatment the philosophy, format, and principles of DBT are presented, and individuals commit to change, agree to treatment goals, and agree not to kill themselves. In Stage 1 the focus is on control and four areas are targeted: (1) decreasing self-harm, suicidal, or violent behaviors; (2) reducing therapy-interfering behaviors; (3) decreasing quality of life interfering behaviors; and (4) increasing the individual's knowledge and implementation of skills to make life changes.

Clients participate in individual therapy focusing on problem solving and therapy-interfering behaviors and obstacles to motivation, such as inconsistent attendance and recurrent crises (Pretzer, 2004). Diary cards are used to keep track of problems and set the therapy agenda (Stanley & Brodsky, 2005a). Skills training is provided in a group format focusing on the acquisition of life-changing behavioral skills. These skills include mindfulness, or learning to focus on the moment and to be nonjudgmentally aware; distress tolerance, including crisis survival skills and a radical acceptance of reality; emotion regulation; and interpersonal effectiveness skills (Stanley & Brodsky, 2005a). The clinician also provides telephone consultation to facilitate the generalization of learning. On an ongoing basis the clinician actively participates in team meetings for supervision and consultation aimed at enhancing his or her skills and providing support (Robins & Koons, 2004). Linehan (1993a,b; 2000) provides detailed descriptions of techniques and dialectal strategies, such as the use of metaphor, entering the paradox, the devil's advocate, allowing natural change, the use of the individual's inherent wisdom or wise mind, and "making lemonade out of lemons."

Stage 2 (order) focuses on the individual uncovering and addressing prior traumatic events and reconnecting with the world. This may include targeting denial, distortions, or self-invalidating behaviors and often increases the individual's risk for suicide. Consequently, it is important that these issues be addressed only when the individual has mastered the strategies for emotional regulation and distress tolerance (Robins, Ivanoff, & Linehan, 2001). Stage 3 focuses on synthesis, self-respect, mastery, self-efficacy, quality of life issues, and the achievement of life's goals through an integration and implementation of skills learned earlier. Stage 4 targets transcendence by integrating the past, present, and future to develop the capacity for joy and acceptance of reality.

Dialectical behavior therapy has been found to result in fewer days of hospitalization and to decrease parasuicidal behavior. These results have been maintained on follow-up, and DBT results in fewer individuals (16.7%) dropping out of treatment compared to 58.3% who received treatment as usual (Crits-Christoph & Barber, 2004; Koerner & Linehan, 2000; Robbins & Chapman, 2004). This approach has also been modified for use with adolescents and older adults (Lynch & Aspnes, 2001; Lynch, Morse, Mendelson, & Robins, 2003; Rathus & Miller, 2002).

Appendix A

PSYCHOPHARMACOLOGY

Disclaimer: This table represents an overview of psychopharmacologic treatments for various mental disorders. This information **should not** be used to make medication decisions for any client. Such decisions should only be made by a licensed medical professional.

Med Name/Generic Trade Name	Class Typical Dosage	Conditions Used to Treat (off label uses in italics)	Side Effects; Used with Children; FDA Pregnancy Rating; Breastfeeding Issues	Specific Special Precautions
Acamprosate *Campral*	Glutaminergic (blockage); 1–2 g/day	Alcohol dependence	Diarrhea, dyspepsia, headache, nausea and vomiting, rash, itching	
Alprazolam *Xanax*	Benzodiazepine; 0.25–2.0 mg	Panic Disorder, GAD, alcohol withdrawal, convulsions, insomnia, Dystonia *MDD, Social Phobia, PMDD*	Sedation, dizziness, weakness, nausea, incoordination, memory problems, clumsiness; Safety not established; D; Do not breastfeed.	High abuse potential (short-acting); Falls and disinhibition a concern in the elderly
Amantadine *Symmetrel*	Antiviral; 200 mg	Parkinsonism, drug-induced extrapyramidal reactions	Neuroleptic Malignant Syndrome, blurry vision, Anticholinergic effects; Safety not established in children under 1 year; C; Do not breastfeed.	Avoid alcohol; People with congestive heart failure or epilepsy should be closely monitored.
Amitriptyline *Elavil, Endep*	TCA; 150–300 mg	MDD *Bipolar*	May induce mania, weight gain; Safety not established.	See TCA in Common Side Effects section.
Amoxapine *Dexedrine, Asendin*	NonMAOI Antidepressant; 150–400 mg	Depression *MDD, Bipolar Disorder*	Risk of Tardive Dyskinesia; May induce mania; Safety not established.	Never combine with MAOI.
Aripiprazole *Abilify*	2nd (or possibly 3rd) generation antipsychotic; 10–30 mg/day	Schizophrenia; *Manic and Mixed Bipolar Disorder episodes, maintenance treatment of Bipolar Disorder*	Nausea, tremor, insomnia, headache, agitation, constipation; NMS Tardive Dyskinesia, Use in children not officially recommended but might be safe; C; Breast milk unknown, assume secreted	Unique mechanism of action; Avoid alcohol.

(Continued)

(*Continued*)

Med Name/Generic Trade Name	Class Typical Dosage	Conditions Used to Treat (off label uses in italics)	Side Effects; Used with Children; FDA Pregnancy Rating; Breastfeeding Issues	Specific Special Precautions
Atomoxetine *Strattera*	Selective Norepinephrine Reuptake Inhibitor; 0.5–1.2 mg/kg/day	ADHD	Increased anxiety/ excitability, headache, nausea, abdominal pain, vomiting, appetite/ weight loss, drowsiness/fatigue, dry mouth, dizziness, trouble remembering; Safety not established in children under 6; C; Unknown whether excreted in breast milk.	Can mask fatigue; May interact with dental medication
Benztropine *Cogentin*	Antiparkinsonin; 0.5–2 mg	Parkinsonism, treatment of extrapyramidal side effects (EPS), *Hypersalivation associated with first-generation antipsychotics*	Anhidrosis, Tachycardia, gastrointestinal issues, disorientation, nausea; Contraindicated in children under 3.	Not recommended for use in patients with Tardive Dyskinesia; Avoid sunlight exposure; Increased effects of alcohol.
Biperiden *Akineton*	Antidyskinetic; 2– 6 mg	Parkinson's Disease *Treatment of extrapyramidal side effects associated with first-generation antipsychotics*	Allergic reaction, unusual fever, irregular heartbeat, seizures, rash, eye pain, drowsiness, dry mouth, anxiety, upset stomach, decreased sweating; side effects aggravated in children; C; Unknown whether excreted in breast milk.	Eye exams before and during treatment; Report all medication to physician; Increases effects of alcohol; Avoid becoming overheated; Do not take within 1 hour of antidiarrheal medication.
Bromazepam *Lectopam*	Anxiolytic/ Benzodiazepine; 3– 6 mg	GAD, alcohol withdrawal, insomnia, convulsions, Dystonia *Sedation*	See Benzodiazepine in Common Side Effects section.	See Benzodiazepine in Common Side Effects section.
Bromocriptine *Parlodel*	Ergot Alkaloid; 1.25–2.5 mg	*Cocaine abuse may help with management of Neuroleptic Malignant Syndrome*	Dizziness, drowsiness, dry mouth, constipation, leg cramps at night, stomach pain, tingling in extremities; Contact physician immediately if heartbeat changes, fainting, vision changes, or black stool; Not approved for children under 15; Do not use during pregnancy.	This medication stops milk production in females. Takes several weeks to become effective; Avoid alcohol; Oral contraceptives decrease effectiveness.

Med Name/Generic Trade Name	Class Typical Dosage	Conditions Used to Treat (off label uses in italics)	Side Effects; Used with Children; FDA Pregnancy Rating; Breastfeeding Issues	Specific Special Precautions
Buprenorphine **Buprenex** **Temgesic, Subutex**	Narcotic; 0.3–0.6 mg/ml (injectable) 8–16 mg (oral)	*Pain relief Opiate abuse*	Energized, insomnia, abdominal pain, nausea, drowsiness, constipation, sweating, joint/ muscle pain; Pain relief in children ages 2–12; C; Do not breastfeed.	Store safely—can be poisonous to others; Stopping suddenly can result in withdrawal symptoms; Can cause dependence; Can cause death in overdose or if injected.
Buprenorphine plus naloxone **Suboxone**	Narcotic; 8–16 mg	Maintenance treatment of opiate dependence	Cold or flulike symptoms, headaches, sweating, sleeping difficulties, dizziness, fatigue, nausea, mood swings; Not approved for children. C; Do not breastfeed.	Store safely—can be poisonous to others; Stopping suddenly can result in withdrawal symptoms; Can cause dependence; Can cause death in overdose or if injected.
Bupropion **Wellbutrin, Zyban**	NDRI; 150–450 mg	MDD, Smoking cessation *ADHD, Atypical depression, Bipolar Disorder, May ameliorate sexual dysfunction in patients taking SSRIs*	Seizure, possible liver damage, agitation, tremor, Hypertension (particularly when used for smoking cessation); May exacerbate tics in ADHD and Tourette's, rash reported in 17%; B; do not breastfeed.	Contraindicated for those w/history of anorexia, bulimia, those undergoing alcohol or behzodiazepine withdrawal, or those w/seizure disorders; Do not combine with MAOI.
Buspirone **Buspar**	Anxiolytic; 5– 20 mg	Chronic anxiety *PTSD, social phobia, BDD, agitation, irritability, aggression antisocial behavior, smoking cessation, alcohol withdrawal, depression*	Drowsiness, headache, nausea/ heartburn, dizziness, energized/agitated, tingling or numbing in extremities.	Take consistently; Do not take with grapefruit juice; Avoid excessive caffeinated drinks; Check w/MD before taking over-the-counter or other drugs; Takes weeks to become effective; Little abuse/ overdose potential; Do not combine with MAOI.
Carbamazepine **Tegretol**	Anticonvulsant; 400–1200 mg	Bipolar Disorder, Impulse-control Disorders, aggression, alcohol/ drug withdrawal, cocaine addiction, Depression *Seizure Disorders, Chronic Pain*	Aplastic anemia, Agranulocytosis, fatigue, gait instability, headache, light headedness, rash; Used to treat Epilepsy, may be less effective than valproate, but few controlled studies;	Less weight gain, tremor, and hair loss than valproate; Less memory impairment than lithium; Regular blood tests first few months; Avoid grapefruit juice; Transient leucopenia in 10% of patients; Typically well-tolerated

(Continued)

(*Continued*)

Med Name/Generic Trade Name	Class Typical Dosage	Conditions Used to Treat (off label uses in italics)	Side Effects; Used with Children; FDA Pregnancy Rating; Breastfeeding Issues	Specific Special Precautions
			D; Potential for serious adverse reactions when breastfeeding.	Supplement to lithium therapy, but monitor carefully for signs/symptoms of toxicity; More likely to cause neurotoxicity in the elderly.
Chloral hydrate *Notec*	1st generation Sedative Hypnotic; 500–1000 mg	*Short-term (2–3 nights) treatment of insomnia*	GI side effects, intoxication; Used in painful pediatric procedures.	Lethal dose is only 5–10 times the therapeutic dose; Tolerance develops after 2 weeks of treatment; Limited use in modern medicine.
Chlordiazepoxide *Librium*	Benodiazepine Anxiolytic; 15–100 mg	GAD, insomnia, alcohol withdrawal, *Nocturnal myoclonus, Night terrors*	Paradoxical reactions; Used to treat GAD; Safety not established in children under 6.	Low abuse potential as compared to other drugs in its class.
Chlorpromazine *Thorazine*	Neuroleptic Antipsychotic; 150–1000 mg	Positive symptoms of Schizophrenia, nausea, vomiting, presurgery apprehension, MDD *Binge-eating disorder, OCD, Panic Disorder, PTSD*	See Antipsychotics in Common Side Effects section.	Used for short-term treatment of severe behavioral disorders, (i.e., explosive hyperactivity and combativeness).
Citalopram *Celexa*	SSRI; 10–60 mg		Abnormal bleeding, Hyponatremia; Used to treat MDD; C; Do not breastfeed.	Do not combine with MAOI.
Clomipramine *Anafranil*	TCA; 150–250 mg	OCD *MDD, Bipolar Disorder*	In high doses, may increase risk of seizures; May induce mania. Safety not established.	See TCA in Common Side Effects section.
Clonazepam *Klonopin*	Benzodiazepine Anxiolytic; 0.5–2.0 mg	GAD, alcohol withdrawal, insomnia *seizures, Social Phobia, Panic Disorder, Tardive dyskinesia, Bipolar Disorder, Tourette's Syndrome*	Increased salivation, dizziness, treatment-emergent Depression; Used to treat Panic Disorder; Social Phobia, Separation Anxiety Disorder; D; Do not breastfeed.	Avoid taking with grapefruit juice.
Clonidine *Catapres*	Anti-hypertensive; 0.1–0.3 mg	Hypertension *Tourette's syndrome, ADHD, impulsivity, aggression, Schizophrenia, Anxiety*	Drowsiness/fatigue, dizziness, dry mouth, headache, increased anxiety/excitability, difficulty remembering; Used to treat Hypertension; Safety not established in children under 12; C; Exercise caution when breastfeeding.	May cause fatigue; Stopping suddenly may cause withdrawal; Do not miss doses; Increases effects of alcohol; If having surgery, tell surgeon you are taking this medication

Med Name/Generic Trade Name	Class Typical Dosage	Conditions Used to Treat (off label uses in italics)	Side Effects; Used with Children; FDA Pregnancy Rating; Breastfeeding Issues	Specific Special Precautions
Clorazepate **Tranxene**	Benzodiazepine Anxiolytic; 3.75–15 mg	GAD, convulsions, alcohol withdrawal, Panic Disorder, insomnia	Drowsiness; Used to treat GAD, convulsions, Panic disorder; Not recommended for use in children under 9; No rating, however, increased risk of congenital malformations in first trimester.	Not recommended for use in patients with psychotic features or Depression; Blood and liver counts necessary.
Clozapine **Clozaril**	Atypical (2nd generation) Antipsychotic; 300–900 mg	Schizophrenia, treatment-resistant Schizophrenia, Reduce risk of suicide in those with psychosis	Agranulocytosis, seizures, Myocarditis, drowsiness/fatigue, dizziness, dry mouth, blurred vision, constipation, excess salivation/drooling, weight gain, nausea/heartburn; safety in children not established but used to treat Tic Disorders, PDD, Schizophrenia; B; Assume secreted in breast milk, do not breastfeed.	Weekly or biweekly monitoring required of white blood cell count for signs of agranulocytosis. Medication given a week at a time.
Cyproheptadine **Periactin**	Antihistamine; 50–100 mg	Anorexia nervosa, Anxiety	Sore throat, fever, irregular heartbeat, seizures, redness of skin, drowsiness, dry mouth, swelling around the face; Approved for use in children— serious side effects more likely in younger children (confusion, nightmares, nervousness, urination pain, irritability); Not recommended for use during first trimester or while breastfeeding.	May cover up signs of aspirin overdose, appendicitis, or allergies; Do not drive until medication effects are determined
Desipramine **Norpramin, Pertofane**	TCA; 150–300 mg	MDD *Bipolar Disorder*	Safety not established in children, during pregnancy, or while breastfeeding.	May induce mania.
Dextroamphe-tamine & Amphetamine **Adderall**	Stimulant; 5–40 mg	ADHD	Used to treat ADHD; Not recommended for children under 3; C; Do not breastfeed.	Impotence.

(Continued)

(*Continued*)

Med Name/Generic Trade Name	Class Typical Dosage	Conditions Used to Treat (off label uses in italics)	Side Effects; Used with Children; FDA Pregnancy Rating; Breastfeeding Issues	Specific Special Precautions
Diazepam *Valium*	Benzodiazepine Anxiolytic; 2–10 mg	GAD, Tetanus, insomnia, Dystonia *Social Phobia, Delirium tremens*	Confusion, constipation; No rating, however, avoid use during pregnancy and while breastfeeding.	See Benzodiazepine in Common Side Effects section.
Disulfiram *Antabuse*	Alcohol Antagonist; 125–500 mg	Alcohol use/abuse	Drowsiness, fatigue, Depression, energized/agitation, headache, skin rash, garliclike taste in mouth; Safety not established with children, during pregnancy, or while breastfeeding.	Avoid all food/drugs containing alcohol, alcohol-containing products (rubs, solvents) may cause reaction.
Divalproex sodium valproic acid valproate *Depakote, Depakene*	Anticonvulsant; 750–1500 mg	Bipolar Disorder	Hyperammonemia, changes in hair texture/hair loss, menstrual changes; Used to treat Bipolar Disorder; Not for use in children under 2. D; Excreted in breast milk, effects unknown.	Regular blood tests first few months; Toxicity is life threatening.
Donepezil *Aricept*	Cholinesterase inhibitor	Alzheimer's Disease	Nausea, diarrhea, appetite/weight loss, dyspepsia, insomnia, dizziness; Use in children not established; C; Breast milk unknown, assume secreted.	
Doxepin *Adapin, Sinequan*	TCA; 150–300 mg	*MDD, Bipolar Disorder*	See TCA in Common Side Effects sections.	May induce mania.
Duloxetine *Cymbalta*	SNRI; 20–40 mg	MDD, GAD, Pain management	Hepatoxicity, increase in blood pressure, activation of mania; Used to treat MDD; May cause behavior activation; C; Do not breastfeed.	Withdraw gradually after prolonged use.
Escitalopram *Lexapro*	SSRI; 5-mg	GAD, MDD	Abnormal bleeding, Hyponatremia, seizures; Used to treat MDD; C; Do not breastfeed.	Use caution with patients with diseases or conditions that produce altered metabolism or hemodynamic responses.
Estazolam *Prosom*	Benzodiazepine Anxiolytic; 1.0–2.0 mg	GAD, insomnia, Dystonia	Safety not established; X; Do not breastfeed.	Interacts with fluoxetine.

Med Name/Generic Trade Name	Class Typical Dosage	Conditions Used to Treat (off label uses in italics)	Side Effects; Used with Children; FDA Pregnancy Rating; Breastfeeding Issues	Specific Special Precautions
Fluoxetine **Prozac, Sarafem**	SSRI; 20–80 mg	MDD, Bulimia Nervosa, OCD, Panic Disorder, PMDD *Social phobia*	Tardive dyskinesia—more likely in older patients; May induce mania in Bipolar Disordered patients; Higher doses cause delirium in elderly; Used to treat MDD and OCD in ages 8 and up; C; Do not breastfeed.	See SSRI in Common Side Effects section.
Fluphenazine **Prolixin, Permitil**	Neuroleptic Antipsychotic 2-40mg	Schizophrenia and psychotic disorders	Tardive Dyskinesia, EPS, NMS. Safety not established. C; Do not breastfeed.	See Antipsychotics in Common Side Effects section.
Flurazepam **Dalmane**	Benzodiazepine Anxiolytic; 15–60 mg	GAD, alcohol withdrawal, insomnia, convulsions *sedation*	No rating, but not recommended during pregnancy and breastfeeding.	See Benzodiazepine in Common Side Effects section.
Fluvoxamine **Luvox**	SSRI; 50–300 mg	OCD *Panic Disorder, Binge-eating disorder, Bulimia Nervosa, Social phobia, MDD*	>8 for OCD.	See SSRI in Common Side Effects section.
Gabapentin **Neurontin**	Anticonvulsant Mood Stabilizer; 300–2400 mg	Epilepsy	Partial seizures in children 3–12 years; C; Do not breastfeed.	Don't take within 2 hours of an antacid; Do not withdraw abruptly.
glamantamine **Reminyl,** renamed **Razadyne** in 2005, **Nivalin**	cholinesterase inhibitor; 16–24 mg/day	Alzheimer's Disease	Gastrointestinal side effects including nausea, diarrhea, weight loss, dizziness, headaches; dyspepsia, fatigue, depression; Use in children not established; B; Breast milk unknown, assume secreted.	
Halazepam **Paxipam**	Benzodiazepine Anxiolytic	GAD, alcohol withdrawal, insomnia, convulsions *sedation*	See Benzodiazepine in Common Side Effects section.	See Benzodiazepine in Common Side Effects section.
Haloperidol **Haldol**	Neuroleptic Antipsychotic; 2–40 mg	Schizophrenia and other psychoses	Tardive Dyskinesia, NMS; EPS; Safety not established; C; Do not breastfeed.	See Antipsychotics in Common Side Effects section.

(Continued)

(Continued)

Med Name/Generic Trade Name	Class Typical Dosage	Conditions Used to Treat (off label uses in italics)	Side Effects; Used with Children; FDA Pregnancy Rating; Breastfeeding Issues	Specific Special Precautions
Imipramine *Tofranil*	TCA; 150–300 mg	*MDD, Bipolar Disorder, Enuresis*	Safety not established.	See TCA in Common Side Effects section.
Isocarboxzaid *Marplan*	monoamine oxidase inhibitor; 40–60 mg/day	Depression	Dizziness, nausea, dry mouth, weight gain, headaches, fatigue, tremor, weakness, blurred vision, sweating, movement problem, sexual dysfunction, sleep disturbances, orthostatic hypotension; C; Breast milk unknown, assume secreted.	Foods with high levels of tyramine and fermented foods, must be avoided.
Levo-alpha acetyl methadol (LAAM)	60–100 mg three days per week	Opiate agonist used in the maintenance treatment of opiate dependence	Weakness, loss of energy, nervousness, abdominal pain, constipation, sweating, sexual dysfunction, joint pain.	Dose can last up to 72 hours which is advantage over methadone.
Lamotrigine *Lamictal*	Anticonvulsant; 200–500 mg	*Bipolar Disorder*	Rash, Stevens-Johnson syndrome, Nausea, Vomiting, Constipation; Used to treat Bipolar Disorder, but risk of Stevens-Johnson syndrome is greater in children; No rating, but not recommended during pregnancy and breastfeeding.	See Anticonvulsants in Common Side Effects section.
Lithium *Eskalith, Lithonate, Lithotabs, Cibalith*	600–2400 mg	Mood stabilizer; acute Mania, Bipolar; not approved but augments effects of antidepressants in Depression and OCD, useful in treatment of cluster headaches, chronic aggression/impulsivity.	Fatigue, concentration difficulty, nausea/heartburn, muscle shakiness/weakness, sex drive changes, weight changes, skin changes, increased thirst/urination; Used to treat Bipolar Disorder in ages 12–17; No rating, but not recommended during pregnancy and breastfeeding.	Regular blood tests early on; Drink lots of fluids; May impair skills needed for driving; Stopping suddenly can lead to withdrawal symptoms; Report mood changes to MD; Limit caffeine and alcohol; Swallow pills whole; Watch salt intake and profuse sweating, which can lead to changes in levels in the body.

Med Name/Generic Trade Name	Class Typical Dosage	Conditions Used to Treat (off label uses in italics)	Side Effects; Used with Children; FDA Pregnancy Rating; Breastfeeding Issues	Specific Special Precautions
Lorazepam *Ativan*	Benzodiazepine Anxiolytic; 0.5–2.0 mg	GAD, alcohol withdrawal, insomnia, Dystonia *Social Phobia, catatonia, violent outbursts/ aggression.*	See Benzodiazepine in Common Side Effects section.	See Benzodiazepine in Common Side Effects section.
Memantine *Namenda*	Glutamatergic; 40 mg/day	Alzheimer's Disease	Dizziness, headache, constipation, hallucinations; B; Breast milk unknown, assume secreted.	
Mephobarbital *Mebaral*	Barbiturate; 400–600 mg	Anxiety, apprehension, seizures	No information regarding children; Exercise caution when breastfeeding.	Increase intake of Vitamins D and K.
Methadone *Dolophine Hydrochloride, Methadose*	Narcotic Analgesic; 2 mg	*Opiate addiction*	Fatigue, confusion, depression, energized, insomnia, dizziness, joint/muscle pain, nausea/vomiting, appetite/weight loss, sex drive change, sweating, constipation.	Mixed with OJ; Taken daily; Can be toxic to those who don't take opiates; Avoid driving if feel drowsy.
Methamphetamine *Desoxyn*	Sympathomimetic Amine; 20–25 mg (lowest effective dosage)	ADHD	Used to treat ADHD in children under 12; C; Do not breastfeed.	High abuse potential.
Methylphenidate *Ritalin*	Stimulant; 5–50 mg	ADHD, ADD, narcolepsy *Depression in the elderly*	Used to treat ADD, ADHD in children over age 6; C; Effects unknown	See Stimulants in Common Side Effects section.
Methylphenidate *Concerta*	Stimulant; 18–54 mg	ADHD	Used to treat ADHD in children over 6; C; Exercise caution when breastfeeding.	Visual disturbances.
Methylphenidate *Metadate*	Stimulant; 5–40 mg	ADHD	Used to treat ADHD in children over 6; Should not be prescribed for women of childbearing age.	Visual disturbances.
Midazolam *Versed, Hypnovel, Dormicum*	Benzodiazepine Anxiolytic	GAD, insomnia, alcohol withdrawal, Dystonia	See Benzodiazepine in Common Side Effects section.	May lower blood pressure. Acute use only.
Mirtazapine *Remeron*	Noradrenergic/ Specific Serotonergic Antidepressant; 15–60 mg	MDD *Bipolar Disorder, OCD, Panic Disorder, GAD, PTSD*	Minimal SSRI-like effects, somnolence, dizziness, increased appetite/weight gain.	Episodes of self-harm and suicidal behaviors reported.

(Continued)

(*Continued*)

Med Name/Generic Trade Name	Class Typical Dosage	Conditions Used to Treat (off label uses in italics)	Side Effects; Used with Children; FDA Pregnancy Rating; Breastfeeding Issues	Specific Special Precautions
Modafinil *Provigil*	Stimulant; 100–200 mg	*Narcolepsy*	Limited information regarding children; ages 16 and under not studied.	May increase alcohol effects; Stopping suddenly may result in withdrawal effects; May interact with dental medications; Minimal risk of agranulocytosis.
Molindone *Moban*	Neuroleptic Antipsychotic; 20–225 mg	Schizophrenia	Tardive Dyskinesia, NMS, EPS; Used to treat Schizophrenia in children over age 12; Studies on pregnant patients have not been carried out.	See Antipsychotics in Common Side Effects section.
Naltrexone *ReVia, Vivitrol*	Antinarcotic (opioid receptor antagonist); 350 mg per week	Opiate addiction, alcohol abuse *Impulse-control disorder, OCD*	Fatigue, confusion, depression, nervousness, anxiety, insomnia, headache, joint/ muscle pain, abdominal pain, cramps, nausea, dyspepsia, vomiting, weight loss; Use in children not established; B; Breast milk uknown, assume secreted.	Patient must be clean of narcotics for at least 10 days; Large doses may cause liver failure.
Nefazodone *Serzone*	SARI; 100–500 mg	*MDD, Bipolar Disorder, Bulimia Nervosa, insomnia, delirium*	Used to treat MDD and Bipolar Disorder in children.	Risk of hepatoxicity.
Nortriptyline *Aventyl, Pamelor*	TCA; 75–125 mg	*MDD, Bipolar Disorder*	May induce mania; Safety not established.	See TCA in Common Side Effects section.
Olanzapine *Zyprexa*	Atypical Antipsychotic; 5–20 mg	Schizophrenia and other psychoses Maintenance of treatment response in Schizophrenia, maintenance of Bipolar Disorder, agitation/acute Mania *MDD, OCD, PTSD.*	Insomnia, weight gain, diabetes, Tardive Dyskinesia, NMS; Used to treat Tic Disorders, Schizophrenia, PDD in children; C; Do not breastfeed.	Prescribe SSRIs simultaneously with caution.
Oxcarbazepine *Trileptal*	Antiepileptic; 1200–2400 mg	Seizures	Hyponatremia; Used to treat Epilepsy in children over 4 years; C; Do not breastfeed.	Withdraw gradually.
Paroxetine *Paxil*	SSRI; 20–50 mg (up to 60 for anti-obsessional)	MDD, OCD, Panic Disorder, Social Phobia, PTSD, GAD, PMDD *Bulimia Nervosa*	Used to treat MDD in children; C; Exercise caution when breastfeeding.	Tardive dyskinesia —more likely in older patients; Do not combine with MAOI.

Med Name/Generic Trade Name	Class Typical Dosage	Conditions Used to Treat (off label uses in italics)	Side Effects; Used with Children; FDA Pregnancy Rating; Breastfeeding Issues	Specific Special Precautions
Pemoline *Cylert*	Stimulant; 37.5–112.5 mg	ADHD *Narcolepsy*	Hepatic side effects (jaundice, hepatitis); Used to treat ADHD in children over 6 years; B; Exercise caution when breastfeeding.	Due to its association with life threatening hepatic failure, not be considered first line treatment.
Pentobarbital *Nembutal*	Barbiturate; 150–200 mg	Insomnia	D; Exercise caution when breastfeeding.	
Phenelzine *Nardil*	MAOI; 30–90 mg		See MAOI in Common Side Effects section.	See MAOI in Common Side Effects section.
Pimozide *Orap*	Neuroleptic Antipsychotic; 1–10 mg	Tourette's Syndrome	Anticholinergic side effects, EPS, NMS, Tardive Dyskinesia; Used to treat Tourette's Syndrome in children over 2 years; C; Unknown if excreted in breast milk.	Do not take with grapefruit juice; Monitor liver and kidney function.
Protriptyline *Vivactil*	TCA; 15–40 mg	MDD, *Bipolar Disorder*	May induce mania; Safety not established with children, during pregnancy or while breastfeeding.	See TCA in Common Side Effects section.
Quetiapine *Seroquel*	Atypical Antipsychotic; 150–400 mg	Schizophrenia and other psychoses Acute Mania and depressive episodes in Bipolar Disorder *OCD*	Tardive Dyskinesia, NMS Diabetes; Muscle Tics; Used to treat Tic Disorders, PDD, Schizophrenia in children; C; Do not breastfeed.	Avoid dehydration/ heat exposure.
Reboxetine *Edronax, Norebox, Prolift, Solvex, Vestra*	SNRI 8–10 mg/day	Alzheimer's Disease	Dry mouth, constipation, headache, drowsiness, dizziness, excessive sweating, anxiety, agitation, insomnia, urinary hesitancy, sexual dysfunction; Use in children not established; B; Secreted in breast milk.	
Risperidone *Risperdal*	Atypical Antipsychotic; 4–16 mg	Tardive Dyskinesia, NMS Schizophrenia, Acute and Chronic psychoses, maintenance of treatment in Schizophrenia, Acute Mania *MDD, OCD, PTSD PDD, Tic disorders*	Insomnia, nightmares, improved working memory, Hypotension; Used to treat Tic Disorders, PDD, Schizophrenia in children; C; Do not breastfeed.	Contains phenylalanine.

(Continued)

(*Continued*)

Med Name/Generic Trade Name	Class Typical Dosage	Conditions Used to Treat (off label uses in italics)	Side Effects; Used with Children; FDA Pregnancy Rating; Breastfeeding Issues	Specific Special Precautions
Rivastigmine *Exelon*	Cholinesterase inhibitors; 6–12 mg/day	Alzheimer's Disease	Nausea, diarrhea, appetite/weight loss, dyspepsia, headaches, fatigue, dizziness; Use in children not established; B; Breast milk unknown, assume secreted.	
Selegiline *Eldepryl*	Irreversible MAOI; 5–10 mg	Parkinsonism	Limited information on side effects; Safety not established in children; C; Do not use while breastfeeding unless essential.	See MAOI in Common Side Effects section.
Sertraline *Zoloft*	SSRI; 50–200 mg	MDD, Bulimia Nervosa, OCD, Panic Disorder, PTSD, Social Phobia, Premenstrual Dysphoric Disorder	Tardive dyskinesia—more likely in older patients; Used to treat MDD; Used to treat OCD in children over 7; C; Exercise caution when breastfeeding.	See SSRI in Common Side Effects section.
Thioridazine *Mellaril*	Neuroleptic Antipsychotic; 150–800 mg	Psychotic disorders, *severe behavioral problems in children*	Tardive Dyskinesia, NMS, EPS, Arrythymia; Used to treat psychosis in children; No information on pregnancy or breastfeeding.	No research on efficacy in refractory Schizophrenia.
Thiothixene *Navane*	Neuroleptic Antipsychotic; 10–60 mg	Schizophrenia, behavior management in children with mental retardation	Used to treat Tardive Dyskinesia, EPS, NMS, Schizophrenia, and other psychoses; behavior management in children over 12 years; No rating; safety not established during pregnancy or breastfeeding.	See Antipsychotics in Common Side Effects section.
Topiramate *Topomax*	Anticonvulsant; 50–300 mg	Seizures	Myopia, Hyperthermia, Kidney Stones; Used to treat seizures in children ages 2–16; C; Exercise caution when breastfeeding.	Decreases efficacy of oral contraceptives.

Med Name/Generic Trade Name	Class Typical Dosage	Conditions Used to Treat (off label uses in italics)	Side Effects; Used with Children; FDA Pregnancy Rating; Breastfeeding Issues	Specific Special Precautions
Tranylcypromine *Parnate*	MAOI; 20–60 mg	MDD	See MAOI in Common Side Effects section.	See MAOI in Common Side Effects section.
Trazodone *Desyrel*	SARI; 150–400 mg	MDD, Bipolar Disorder *insomnia, Bulimia Nervosa*	Drowsiness, sexual side effects; Used to treat MDD, night terrors, insomnia in children.	May lower seizure threshold.
Trimipramine *Surmontil*	TCA; 100–300 mg	MDD, *Bipolar Disorder*	May induce mania; Safety not established; C; Use caution when breastfeeding.	See TCA in Common Side Effects section.
Venlafaxine *Effexor*	SNRI; 75–350 mg	MDD, Social Phobia, GAD *OCD, Panic Disorder, Bipolar Disorder, ADHD*	Abnormal dreams, loss of appetite; Used to treat MDD and anxiety in children, but may adversely affect height and weight; C; Do not breastfeed.	Can cause increased blood pressure—use w/caution with those with hypertension; May induce manic reactions; Do not combine with MAOI.
Verapamil *Calan, Isoptin*	Calcium Channel Blocker; 120–480 mg;	*Bipolar Disorder*	Constipation, vertigo, headache, cardiac conduction problems, hypotension, elevated liver enzymes; Safety not established; C; Do not breastfeed.	Interacts with lithium and carbamazepine, as well as other drugs.
Zaleplon *Sonata*	Nonbenzodiazepine Hypnotic; 5–10 mg	*Insomnia*	Headache, abdominal pain; Safety not established; C; Do not breastfeed.	Discontinue after 7–10 nights; Check for drug interactions; Overdose can be fatal.
Ziprasidone *Geodon*	Atypical Antipsychotic; 60–160 mg	Schizophrenia and other psychoses, mania or mixed episodes in Bipolar Disorder	Drowsines, dizziness, dyspepsia, EPS, nausea, constipation, slight risk in increase of seizure, risk of NMS, rash, orthostatic hypotension, hyperprolactemia, priaprism, problems with body temperature regulation, Dysphagia; Safety not established; C; Breast milk unknown, assume secreted do not breastfeed.	In individuals with heart problems, may cause serious heartbeat irregularities (do not combine with diuretics or other drugs that prolong the QT interval of heartbeat); Check for drug interactions. Potential serious skin rash.

(Continued)

(Continued)

Med Name/Generic Trade Name	Class Typical Dosage	Conditions Used to Treat (off label uses in italics)	Side Effects; Used with Children; FDA Pregnancy Rating; Breastfeeding Issues	Specific Special Precautions
Zolpidem *Ambien*	Nonbenzodiazepine Hypnotic; 5–10 mg	Insomnia	Sleep-eating, Sleep-driving, Sleep-rages, Amnesia; Safety not established; B; Small percentage excreted into breast milk, but impact unknown.	Do not use for longer than 7–10 nights; Only use 5 mg in elderly; Schedule IV controlled substance.

Note: Side effects appearing in at least 15% of patients.

COMMON SIDE EFFECTS AND SPECIAL PRECAUTIONS BY CLASS OF MEDICATION

Anticonvulsant/Mood Stabilizers

Side Effects: Drowsiness/fatigue, concentration difficulty, dizziness, ataxia (unsteadiness), blurred vision, dry mouth, nausea/heartburn, muscle tremor, sex drive changes, weight changes.

Special Precautions: Swallow pills whole. Do not drive if drowsy. Sudden stop may result in withdrawal symptoms. Avoid aspirin. Report mood changes.

Anti-Parkinsonian Agents

Side Effects: Dry mouth, blurred vision, constipation, drowsiness/fatigue, nausea/heartburn.

Special Precautions: Check with physician before taking over-the-counter or other drugs. Do not drive if drowsy. May increase alcohol effects. Avoid extreme heat/humidity (for temperature regulation).

Antipsychotics/Neuroleptics

Side Effects: Muscle spasms, shaking, restlessness, rigidity, fatigue/drowsiness, dizziness, nausea or heartburn, blurred vision, dry mouth, constipation, stuffy nose, weight changes, increased thirst, frequent urination, bladder control problems, breast tenderness, missed periods, Tardive dyskinesia.

Special Precautions: Take with meals/water but not apple or grapefruit juice. Do not break/crush pills. Do not drive if drowsy. May increase alcohol effects. Avoid extreme heat/humidity (may affect temperature regulation and blood pressure). Antacids may interfere with drug absorption. Risk of serious sunburn with light sun exposure. Excessive caffeinated drinks can cause anxiety and counteract some of the med effects. Report cigarette smoking changes (can affect med amount in bloodstream). Sudden stop may result in withdrawal symptoms.

Benzodiazepine/Anxiolytics

Side Effects: Drowsiness/fatigue, muscle incoordination, weakness, dizziness, forgetfulness, memory lapse, slurred speech, nausea/heartburn.

Special Precautions: Take with meals/water but not grapefruit juice. Check with physician before taking over-the-counter or other drugs. Do not drive if drowsy. May increase alcohol effects. Excessive caffeinated drinks may counteract some of the med effects. Sudden stop may result in withdrawal symptoms.

Hypnotics/Sedatives

Side Effects: Morning hangover/drowsiness/fatigue, muscle incoordination, weakness, dizziness, forgetfulness, memory lapse, slurred speech, nausea/heartburn, bitter taste in mouth.

Special Precautions: Tolerance or loss of effectiveness can occur if used consistently for > 4 months. Long-term use = risk of dependence. Check with physician before taking over-the-counter or other drugs. Do not drive if drowsy. May increase alcohol effects. Excessive caffeinated drinks may counteract some of the med effects. Sudden stop may result in withdrawal symptoms. May have carry-over effect the following day (drive with caution until impact is known).

Monoamine Oxidase Inhibitor (MAOI)

Side Effects: Fatigue/drowsiness, agitation/nervousness, headache, dizziness, nausea or heartburn, muscle tremor/twitching, blurred vision, dry mouth, constipation, sweating, appetite loss.

Special Precautions: Must avoid certain foods to avoid hypertensive crisis and must avoid certain over-the-counter and prescription drugs—check with physician. Avoid driving if feeling drowsy/slowed down. Do not stop drug suddenly as may result in withdrawal symptoms. May interact with dental medication. Report mood changes.

Norepinephrine–Dopamine Reuptake Inhibitor (NDRI)

Side Effects: Agitation/nervousness, headache, nausea or heartburn, muscle tremor/twitching, dry mouth, sweating, nightmares, appetite loss, blood pressure increase.

Special Precautions: Swallow pills whole/do not chew. Avoid driving if feeling drowsy/slowed down. May increase effects of alcohol. Do not stop drug suddenly as may result in withdrawal symptoms. Report mood changes.

Psychostimulants

Side Effects: Agitation/excitability, increased heart rate/blood pressure, headache, nausea/heartburn, blurred vision, dry mouth, mild hair loss, respiratory problems (sinusitis, sore throat, coughing), appetite/weight loss.

Special Precautions: Report mood/sleep/appetite changes. Can affect or be affected by other meds. Do not chew/crush pills. Can mask fatigue and impair concentration. Stopping suddenly can result in withdrawal symptoms. May interact with dental meds.

Seratonin–Norepinephrine Reuptake Inhibitor (SNRI)

Side Effects: Agitation/nervousness, headache, nausea or heartburn, dry mouth, constipation, sweating, blood pressure increase, sex drive changes.

Special Precautions: Avoid driving if feeling drowsy/slowed down. May increase effects of alcohol. Do not stop drug suddenly as may result in withdrawal symptoms. May interact with dental medication. Swallow sustained release pill whole/do not chew. Report mood changes.

Selective Seratonin Reuptake Inhibitor (SSRI)

Side Effects: Fatigue/drowsiness, psychomotor agitation/nervousness, headache, heartburn, frequent gastrointestinal side effects (nausea, diarrhea), muscle tremor/twitching, changes in sex drive, blurred vision, dry mouth, insomnia, nightmares, appetite loss or weight gain. Less likely than TCA's to cause anticholinergic or cardiac/autonomic side effects. Occasional extrapyramidal reactions. Less commonly, may cause abnormal bleeding.

Special Precautions: Take with meals or liquids. Avoid driving if feeling drowsy/slowed down. May increase effects of alcohol. Do not stop drug suddenly as may result in withdrawal symptoms. Report mood changes. Have been associated w/increased SI in children/adolescents. May induce manic reactions in bipolar patients. Children are more prone to adverse behavioral (agitation) effects. Chronic use in children may reduce growth rates.

Serotonin Antagonist and Reuptake Inhibitor (SARI)

Side Effects: Fatigue/drowsiness, agitation/nervousness, headache, nausea or heartburn, muscle tremor/twitching, changes in sex drive, dry mouth, appetite loss.

Special Precautions: Take with meals or liquids. Avoid driving if feeling drowsy/slowed down. May increase effects of alcohol. Do not stop drug suddenly as may result in withdrawal symptoms. May interact with dental medication. Report mood changes. May lower seizure threshold or induce manic reactions.

Tricyclic Antidepressant (TCA)

Side Effects: Orthostatic hypotension, dizziness; hypertension and tachycardia are less common; anticholinergic effects, exacerbation of psychosis and mania, memory impairment, psychomotor stimulation, myoclonic twitches, tremors, weight gain, significant sedation, hepatic dysfunction, and sexual dysfunction.

Special Precautions: NOTE: TCAs have been associated with the sudden death of six children due to cardiac effects. This, coupled with their significant, uncomfortable side effects, leads to their being rarely prescribed in children. However, some early case reports did show TCA efficacy in severely depressed, hospitalized children.

Common Terms

Extrapyramidal side effects (EPS): Pseudoparkinsonism (tremors, shuffling gate, muscle rigidity, cog-wheeling); akathesia; acute dystonic reaction (facial grimaces, spasms in neck, tongue, back, and face); tardive dyskenisia (abnormal movements of head and extremities).

Neuroleptic Malignant Syndrome (NMS): High fever, muscle rigidity, irregular pulse or blood pressure, rapid heartbeat, excessive perspiration, changes in heart rhythm.

Anticholinergic side effects: Dry mouth, blurred vision, constipation, tachycardia, urine retention, confusion, and memory impairment.

FOOD AND DRUG ADMINISTRATION USE-IN-PREGNANCY RATINGS (A-D, X)

A. **Controlled Studies Show No Risk.** Adequate, well-controlled studies in pregnant women have failed to demonstrate a risk to the fetus in any trimester of pregnancy.

B. **No Evidence of Risk in Humans.** Adequate, well-controlled studies in pregnant women have not shown increased risk of fetal abnormalities despite adverse findings in animals, or, in the absence of adequate human studies, animal studies show no fetal risk. The chance of fetal harm is remote, but remains a possibility.

C. **Risk Cannot be Ruled Out.** Adequate, well-controlled human studies are lacking, and animal studies have shown a risk to the fetus or are lacking as well. There is a chance of fetal harm if the drug is administered during pregnancy; but the potential benefits may outweigh the potential risk.

D. **Positive Evidence of Risk.** Studies in humans, or investigational or postmarketing data, have demonstrated fetal risk. Nevertheless, potential benefits from the use of the drug may outweigh the potential risk. For example, the drug may be acceptable if needed in a life threatening situation or in the case of a serious disease for which safer drugs cannot be used or are ineffective.

X. **Contraindicated in Pregnancy.** Studies in animals or humans, or investigational or postmarketing reports have demonstrated positive evidence of fetal abnormalities or risk which clearly outweighs any possible benefit to the patient.

References

Abbott, D. W., de Zwann, M., Mussell, M. P., Raymond, N. C., Seim, H. C., Crow, S. J., et al. (1998). Onset of binge eating and dieting in overweight women: Implications for etiology, associated features and treatment. *Journal of Psychosomatic Research, 44*, 367–374.

Abi-Dargham, A., Jaskiw, G., Suddath, R., & Weinberger, D. R. (1991). Evidence against progression of in vivo anatomical abnormalities in schizophrenia. *Schizophrenia Research, 5*, 210.

Abraham, G., Milev, R., & Lawson, J. S. (2006). T3 augmentation of SSRI resistant depression. *Journal of Affective Disorders, 91*, 211–215.

Abraham, K. (1921). Contributions to the theory of the anal character. D. Bryan & A. Strachey, Trans. In E. Jones (Ed.), *Selected papers of Karl Abraham* (pp. 370–392). London: Hogarth.

Abraham, K. (1927). The influence of oral eroticism on character formation. In C. A. D. Bryan & A. Strachey (Eds.), *Selected papers on psychoanalysis* (pp. 393–406). London: Hogarth.

Abraham, K. (1927). Notes on the psychoanalytical investigation and treatment of manic-depressive insanity and allied conditions. In E. Jones (Ed.), *Selected papers of Karl Abraham, MD* (D. Byran & A. Strachey, Trans., pp. 137–156). London: Hogarth Press. (Original work published 1911).

Abraham, S. F., & Beumont, P. J. (1982). How patients describe bulimia or binge eating. *Psychological Medicine, 12*(3), 625–635.

Abramowitz, J. S. (1997). Effectiveness of psychological and pharmacologic treatments for obsessive compulsive disorder: A quantitative review. *Journal of Consulting and Clinical Psychology, 65*, 44–52.

Abrams, K. K., Allen, L. R., & Gray, J. J. (1993). Disordered eating attitudes and behaviors, psychological adjustment, and ethnic identity: A comparison of Black and White female college students. *International Journal of Eating Disorders, 14*(1), 49–57.

Abrams, R. (1990). Personality disorders in the elderly. In D. Binenfeld (Ed.), *Verwoerdt's clinical geropsychiatry* (pp. 151–163). Baltimore: Wilkins & Wilkins.

Abrams, R. C., & Horowitz, S. V. (1996). Personality disorders after age 50: A meta-analysis. *Journal of Personality Disorders, 10*(3), 271–281.

Abramson, L. Y., Alloy, L. B., & Metalsky, G. I. (1989). Hopeless depression: A theory-based subtype of depression. *Psychological Review, 96*, 358–372.

Abramson, L. Y., Seligman, M. E. P., & Teasdale, J. (1978). Learned helplessness in humans: Critique and reformulation. *Journal of Abnormal Psychology, 87*, 49–74.

Abushua'leh, K., & Abu-Akel, A. (2006). Association of psychopathic traits and symptomatology with violence in patients with schizophrenia. *Psychiatry Research, 143*, 205–211.

Achenbach, T. M., McConaughy, S. H., & Howell, C. T. (1987). Child/adolescent behavioral and emotional problems: Implications of cross-informant correlations for situational specificity. *Psychological Bulletin, 101*, 213–232.

Acierno, R., Hersen, M., & Van Hasselt, V. B. (1998). Prescriptive assessment and treatment. In A. S. Bellack & M. Hersen (Eds.), *Behavioral assessment: A practical handbook* (pp. 47–62). Boston: Allyn & Bacon.

Ackenheil, M. (2001). Neurotransmitters and signal transduction processes in bipolar affective disorders: A synopsis. *Journal of Affective Disorders, 62*, 101–111.

Ackerman, S. J., & Hilsenroth, M. J. (2003). A review of therapist characteristics and techniques positively impacting the therapeutic alliance. *Clinical Psychology Review, 23*, 1–33.

Acosta, F. J., Aguilar, E. J., Cejas, M. R., Gracia, R., Caballero-Hidalgo, A., & Siris, S. (2006). Are there subtypes of suicidal schizophrenia? A prospective study. *Schizophrenia Research, 86*, 215–220.

Acosta, M. C., Haller, D. L., & Schnoll, S. H. (2005). Cocaine and stimulants. In R. J. Frances, S. I. Miller, & A. H. Mack (Eds.), *Clinical textbook of addictive disorders* (3rd ed., pp. 184–218). New York: Guilford Press.

Adak, S., Illouz, K., Gorman, W., Tandon, R., Zimmerman, E. A., Guariglia, R., et al. (2004). Predicting the rate of cognitive decline in aging and early Alzheimer disease. *Neurology, 63*, 108–114.

Adams, H. E., Bernaty, J. A., & Luscher, K. A. (2001). Borderline personality disorder: An overview. In H. E. Adams & P. B. Sutker (Eds.), *Comprehensive handbook of psychopathology* (3rd ed., pp. 491–507). New York: Kluwer Academic/Plenum.

Adams, H. E., Luscher, K. A., & Bernat, J. A. (2001). The classification of abnormal behavior: An overview. In H. E. Adams & P. S. Sutker (Eds.), *Comprehensive handbook of psychopathology* (pp. 3–28). New York: Kluwer Academic/Plenum Press.

Adams, J. B., Heath, A. J., Young, S. E., Hewitt, J. K., Corley, R. P., & Stallings, M. C. (2003). Relationships between personality and preferred substance and motivations for use among adolescent substance abusers. *American Journal of Drug and Alcohol Abuse, 29*, 691–712.

Ad-Dab'bagh, Y., & Greenfield, B. (2001). Multiple complex developmental disorder: the "multiple and complex" evolution of the "childhood borderline syndrome" construct. *Journal of American Academy of Child and Adolescent Psychiatry, 40*, 954–964.

Adler, D. A., McLaughlin, T. J., Rogers, W. H., Chang, H., Lapitsky, L., & Lerner, D. (2006). Job performance deficits due to depression. *American Journal of Psychiatry, 163*, 1569–1576.

Adler, L. A. (2004). Clinical presentations of adult patients with ADHD. *Journal of Clinical Psychiatry, 65*(3), 8–11.

Aggarwal, N. T., Neelum, T., Wilson, R. S., Beck, T. L., Bienias, J., Berry-Kravis, E., et al. (2005). The apolipoprotein E 4 allele and incident Alzheimer's disease in persons with mild cognitive impairment. *Neurocase, 11*, 3–7.

Agras, W. S., & Apple, R. F. (2002). Understanding and treating eating disorders. In F. W. Kaslow & T. Patterson (Eds.), *Comprehensive handbook of psychotherapy: Vol. 2. Cognitive-behavioral approaches* (pp. 189–212). Hoboken, NJ: Wiley.

Agras, W. S., Walsh, T., Fairburn, C. G., Wilson, C. T., & Kraemer, H. C. (2000). A multicenter comparison of cognitive-behavioral therapy and interpersonal psychotherapy for bulimia nervosa. *Archives of General Psychiatry, 57*(5), 459–466.

Agrawal, H. R., Gunderson, J. G., Holmes, B. M., & Lyon-Ruth, K. (2004). Attachment studies with borderline patients: A review. *Harvard Review of Psychiatry, 12*, 94–104.

Agüero-Torres, H., Winblad, B., & Fratiglioni, L. (1999). Epidemiology of vascular dementia: Some results despite research limitations. *Alzheimer's Disease and Associated Disorders, 13*, 15–20.

Ahrens, B., & Stieglitz, R. D. (1998). Psychopathological assessment and diagnosis: A study of the specificity of single symptoms. *Psychopathology, 31*, 138–152.

Aichorn, A. (1935). *The wayward youth.* New York: Viking.

Aisen, P. S., Schafer, K. A., Grundman, M., Pfeiffer, E., Sano, M., Davis, K. L., et al. (2003). Effects of rofecoxib or naproxen vs placebo on Alzheimer disease progression: A randomized controlled trial. *Journal of the American Medical Association, 289*, 2819–2826.

Aizenberg, D., Zemishlany, Z., Dorfman-Etrog, P., & Weizman, A. (1995). Sexual dysfunction in male schizophrenic patients. *Journal of Clinical Psychiatry, 56*(4), 137–141.

Akhtar, S. (1990). Paranoid personality disorder: A synthesis of developmental, dynamic, and descriptive features. *American Journal of Psychotherapy, 44*, 5–25.

Akishita, M., Yamada, S., Nishiya, H., Sonohara, K., Nakai, R., Toba, K., et al. (2005). Effects of physical exercise on plasma concentrations of sex hormones in elderly women with dementia. *Journal of the American Geriatric Society, 53*, 1072–1076.

Akiskal, H. S., & Benazzi, F. E. (2005). Atypical depression: A variant of bipolar II or a bridge between unipolar and bipolar II? *Journal of Affective Disorders, 84*, 209–217.

Akiskal, H. S., Bourgeois, M. L., Angst, J., Post, R., Moller, H. J., & Hirschfeld, R. M. A. (2000). Re-evaluating the prevalence of and diagnostic composition within the broad clinical spectrum of bipolar disorders. *Journal of Affective Disorders, 59*, 5–30.

Akiskal, H. S., Maser, J. D., Zeller, P. J., Endicott, J., Coryell, W., Keller, M., et al. (1995). Switching from "unipolar" to bipolar: II. An 11-year prospective study of clinical and temperamental predictors in 559 patients. *Archives of General Psychiatry, 52*, 114–123.

Akiskal, H. S., & Pinto, O. (1999). The evolving bipolar spectrum: Prototypes I, II, III, IV. *Psychiatric Clinics of North America, 22*, 517–534.

Akiskal, H. S., Walker, P., Puzantian, V. R., King, D., Rosenthal, T. L., & Dranon, M. (1983). Bipolar outcome in the course of depressive illness: Phenomenologic, familial, and pharmacologic predictors. *Journal of Affective Disorders, 5*, 115–128.

Alarcon, R. D. (1995). Culture and psychiatric diagnosis: Impact of the DSM-IV and ICD-10. *Psychiatric Clinics of North America, 18*(3), 449–465.

Alarcon, R. D. (1996). Personality disorders and culture in the DSM-IV: A critique. *Journal of Personality Disorders, 10*, 260–270.

Alarcon, R. D. (2005). Cross-cultural issues. In J. M. Oldham, A. E. Skodol, & D. S. Bender (Eds.), *Textbook of Personality Disorders* (pp. 561–578). Washington, DC: American Psychiatric Publishing.

Alarcon, R. D., & Foulks, E. F. (1997). Cultural factors and personality disorders: A review of the literature. In T. A. Widiger, A. J. Frances, & H. A. Pincus (Eds.). *DSM-IV Sourcebook, Vol. 3* (pp. 975–982). Washington, DC: American Psychiatric Association.

Albano, A. M., Chorpita, B. F., & Barlow, D. (2003). Childhood anxiety disorders. In E. J. Mash & R. A. Barkley (Eds). *Child psychopathology* (2nd ed.) (pp. 279–329). New York: Guilford Press.

Albertini, R. S., & Phillips, K. A. (2001). Thirty–three cases of body dysmorphic disorder in children and adolescents. In M. E. Herzig & M. E. A. Farber (Eds.), *Annual progress in child psychiatry and child development* (pp. 335–348). New York: Brunner-Routledge.

Albinsson, L., & Strang, P. (2003). Differences in supporting families of dementia and cancer patients: A palliative perspective. *Palliative Medicine, 17*, 359–367.

Albucher, R. C., & Liberzon, I. (2002). Psychopharmacological treatment in PTSD: A critical review. *Journal of Psychiatric Research, 36*, 355–367.

Alcoholics Anonymous. (1983). *Questions and answers about sponsorship.* New York: Alcoholics Anonymous World Services.

Alcoholics Anonymous. (2002). *The twelve steps and twelve traditions.* Center City, MN: Hazelden.

Alcoholics Anonymous General Service Office. (2005). *A.A. Fact File.* New York: A.A. World Services Incorporated.

Alden, L. E., Laposa, J. M., Taylor, C. T., & Ryder, A. G. (2002). Avoidant personality disorder: Current status and future directions. *Journal of Personality Disorder, 16*(1), 1–29.

Aldarondo, E., & Sugarman, D. B. (1996). Risk marker analysis of the cessation and persistence of wife assault. *Journal of Consulting and Clinical Psychology, 64*, 1010–1019.

Alden, L. E., & Wallace, S. T. (1995). Social phobia and social appraisal in successful and unsuccessful social interactions. *Behaviour Research and Therapy, 33*, 497–505.

Aldridge, S. L. (2000). First person account: How the first wave of deinstitutionalization saved my mother from the "snake pit." *Schizophrenia Bulletin, 26*, 933–938.

Alegria, M., Canino, G., Rios, R., Vera, M., Calderon, J., Dana, R., et al. (2002). Inequalities in use of specialty mental health services among Latinos, African Americans, and non-Latino Whites. *Psychiatric Services, 53*, 1547–1555.

Aleman, A., de Haan, E. H. F., & Kahn, R. (2002). Insight and neurocognitive function in schizophrenia. *Journal of Neuropsychiatry and Clinical Neuroscience, 14*, 241–242.

Alfano, C. A., Beidel, D. C., Turner, S. M., & Lewin, D. S. (2006). Preliminary evidence for sleep complaints among children referred for anxiety. *Sleep Medicine, 7*, 467–473.

Allen, D. A., & Mendelson, L. (2000). Parent, child, and professional: Meeting the needs of young autistic children and their families in a multidisciplinary therapeutic nursery model. In S. Epstein (Ed.), *Autistic spectrum disorders and psychoanalytic ideas: Reassessing the fit* (pp. 704–731). Hillsdale, NJ: Analytic Press.

Allen, D. N., & Landis, R. K. B. (1998). Neuropsychological correlates of substance use disorders. In P. J. Snyder, P. Jeffrey, & P. D. Nussbaum (Eds.), *Clinical neuropsychology: A pocket handbook for assessment* (pp. 591–612). Washington, DC: American Psychological Association.

Allen, I. M. (1996). PTSD among African-Americans. In A. J. Marsella, M. J. Friedman, E. T. Gerrity, & R. M. Scurfield (Eds.), *Ethnocultural aspects of posttraumatic stress disorder: Issues, research, and clinical applications* (pp. 209–238). Washington, DC: American Psychological Association.

Allen, J. G., Buskirk, J. R., & Sebastian, L. M. (1992). A psychodynamic approach to the master treatment plan. *Bulletin of the Menninger Clinic, 56*, 487–510.

Allen, J. G., & Lewis, L. (1996). A conceptual framework for treating traumatic memories and its application to EMDR. *Bulletin of the Menninger Clinic, 60*, 238–263.

Allen, L. A., Woolfolk, R. L., Lehrer, P. M., Gara, M. A., & Escobar, J. I. (2001). Cognitive behavior therapy for somatization disorder: A preliminary investigation. *Journal of Behavior Therapy and Experimental Psychiatry, 32*, 53–62.

Allgulander, C., & Lavori, P. W. (1993). Causes of death among 936 elderly patients with "pure" anxiety neurosis in Stockholm County, Sweden, and in patients with depressive neurosis or both diagnoses. *Comprehensive Psychiatry, 34*, 299–302.

Allgulander, C., Dahl, A. A., Austin, C., Morris, L. P., Sogaard, J. A., Fayyad, R, et al. (2004). Efficacy of sertraline in a 12-week trial for generalized anxiety disorder. *American Journal of Psychiatry, 161*, 1642–1649.

Almeida, O. P., & Fenner, S. (2002). Bipolar disorder: Similarities and differences between patients with illness onset before and after 65 years of age. *International Psychogeriatrics, 14*, 311–322.

Almkvist, O., Darreh-Shori, T., Stefanova, E., Spiegel, R., & Nordberg, A. (2004). Preserved cognitive function after 12 months of treatment with rivastigmine in mild Alzheimer's disease in comparison with untreated AD and MCI patients. *European Journal of Neurology, 11*, 253–261.

Alonso, J., Angermeyer, M. C., Bernert, S., Bruffaerts, R., Brugha, T. S., Bryson, H., et al. (2004). Disability and quality of life impact of mental disorders in Europe: Results from the European Study of the Epidemiology of Mental Disorders (ESEMeD) project. *Acta Psychiatrica Scandinavica, 109*, 38–46.

Alspaugh, M. E. L., Stephens, M. P., Townsend, A. L., Zarit, S. H., & Greene, R. (1999). Longitudinal patterns of risk for depression in dementia caregivers: Objective and subjective primary stress as predictors. *Psychology and Aging, 14*, 34–43.

Altamura, A. C., Mundo, E., Bassetti, R., Green, A., Lindemayer, P. D., Alphs, L., et al. (2007). Transcultural differences in suicide attempters: Analysis on a high-risk population of patients with schizophrenia or schizoaffective disorder. *Schizophrenia Research, 89*, 140–146.

Altshuler, L. L., Post, R. M., Leverich, G. S., Mikalauskas, K., Roseoff, A., & Ackerman, L. (1995). Antidepressant-induced mania and cycle acceleration: A controversy revisited. *American Journal of Psychiatry, 152*, 1130–1138.

Alvarez, J., Olson, B. D., Jason, L. A., Davis, M. I., & Ferrari, J. R. (2004). Heterogeneity among Latinas and Latinos entering substance abuse treatment: Findings from a national database. *Journal of Substance Abuse Treatment, 26*, 277–284.

Alzheimer's Association. (2005). *Statistics about Alzheimer's disease.* Retrieved September 14, 2006, from www.alz.org/alzheimers_disease_alzheimer_statistics.asp#6.

Amador, X. F., Strauss, D. H., Yale, S. A., Flaum, M. M., Endicott, J., & Gorman, J. M. (1993). Assessment of insight in psychosis. *American Journal of Psychiatry, 150*, 873–879.

Amaro, H., Whitaker, R., Coffman, G., & Hereen, T. (1990). Acculturation and marijuana and cocaine use: Findings from H-HANES 1982–1984. *American Journal of Public Health, 80*(Suppl.), 54–60.

Amato, P. R. (2001). Children of divorce in the 1990s: An update of the Amato and Keith's 1991 meta-analysis. *Journal of Family Psychology, 15*, 355–370.

American Association on Intellectual and Developmental Disabilities. (2007). *Definition of mental retardation.* Washington, DC: Author. Retrieved September 20, 2007, from www.aamr.org?Policies?faq_Mental_retardation.shtml.

American Association of Marriage and Family Therapists. (2001). *AAMFT code of ethics.* Washington, DC: Author. Retrieved March 7, 2006, from www.aamft.org/resources/lrmplan/ethics/ethicscode2001.asp.

American Association on Mental Retardation. (2002). *Mental retardation: Definition, classification, and systems of support.* Washington, DC: Author.

American Counseling Association. (2005). *ACA code of ethics.* Alexandria, VA: Author. Retrieved March 7, 2006, from www.cacd.org/ACA_2005_Ethical_Code10405.pdf.

American Medical Association. (1992). *Diagnostic and treatment guidelines on domestic violence.* Chicago: Author.

American Methadone Treatment Association. (1999). *1998 Methadone maintenance program and patient census in the U.S.* New York: Author.

American Psychiatric Association. (1952). *Diagnostic and statistical manual of mental disorders.* Washington, DC: Author.

American Psychiatric Association. (1968). *Diagnostic and statistical manual of mental disorders* (2nd ed.). Washington, DC: Author.

American Psychiatric Association. (1980). *Diagnostic and statistical manual of mental disorders* (3rd ed.). Washington, DC: Author.

American Psychiatric Association. (1987). *Diagnostic and statistical manual of mental disorders* (3rd ed., rev.). Washington, DC: Author.

American Psychiatric Association. (1992). *Clinician safety* (Task force report No. 33). Washington, DC: Author.

American Psychiatric Association. (1993). Practice guidelines for major depressive disorder in adults. *American Journal of Psychiatry, 150*, 1–26.

American Psychiatric Association. (1994). *Diagnostic and statistical manual of mental disorders* (4th ed.). Washington, DC: Author.

American Psychiatric Association. (1996). *U.S. health official puts schizophrenia costs at $65 billion.* Retrieved June 10, 2005, from www.schizophrenia.com/news/costs1.html.

American Psychiatric Association. (1997). Practice guidelines for the treatment of patients with Alzheimer's disease and other dementias of late life. *American Journal of Psychiatry, 154*, 1–39.

American Psychiatric Association. (1999). *Practice guideline for the treatment of patients with delirium.* Washington, DC: Author.

American Psychiatric Association. (2000a). *American Psychiatric Association work group on eating disorders.* Washington, DC: Author.

American Psychiatric Association. (2000b). *Diagnostic and statistical manual of mental disorders* (4th ed., text rev.). Washington, DC: Author.

American Psychiatric Association. (2000c). Practice guidelines for the treatment of patients with eating disorders (Rev. ed.). *American Journal of Psychiatry, 157*(Suppl. 1), 1–39.

American Psychiatric Association. (2001a). Practice guideline for the treatment of patients with borderline personality disorder. *American Journal of Psychiatry, 158*(Suppl. 10), 1–52.

American Psychological Association. (2001b). *End of life issues and care: Historical changes affecting end of life care.* Retrieved March 3, 2006, from www.apa.org/pi/eol/historical.html.

American Psychiatric Association. (2001c). *The practice of electroconvulsive therapy: Recommendations for treatment, training and privileging* (2nd ed.). Washington, DC: Author.

American Psychological Association. (2002). *APA code of ethics.* Washington, DC: Author. Retrieved March 7, 2006, from www.apa.org/ethics/code2002.html.

Americans With Disabilities Act of 1990. Retrieved September 20, 2007, from www.ada.gov/pubs/ada.htm.

Amir, N., Foa, E. B., & Coles, M. E. (1998). Negative interpretation bias in social phobia. *Behaviour Research and Therapy, 36,* 945–957.

Amir, R. E., Van den Veyver, I. B., Wan, M., Tran, C. Q., Francke, U., & Zoghbi, H. Y. (1999). Rett syndrome is caused by mutations in X-linked MECP2, encoding methyl-CpG-binding protein 2. *Nature Genetics, 23,* 185–188.

Ancelin, M. N. L., De Roquefeuil, G., Ledesert, B., Bonnel, F., Cheminal, J. C., & Ritchie, K. (2001). Exposure to anaesthetic agents, cognitive functioning, and depressive symptomatology in the elderly. *British Journal of Psychiatry, 178,* 360–366.

Ancoli-Israel, S., & Roth, T. (1999). Characteristics of insomnia in the United States: Results of the 1991 National Sleep Foundation Survey I. *Sleep, 22* (Suppl. 2), S347–S353.

Anderluh, M. B., Tchanturia, K., Rabe-Hesketh, S., & Treasure, J. (2003). Childhood obsessive-compulsive personality traits in adult women with eating disorders: Defining a broader eating disorder phenotype. *American Journal of Psychiatry, 160,* 242–247.

Andersen, A. E. (1999). Eating disorders in gay males. *Psychiatric Annals, 29*(4), 206–212.

Andersen, A. E., & Holman, J. E. (1997). Males with eating disorders: Challenges for treatment and research. *Psychopharmacology Bulletin, 33*(3), 391–397.

Andersen, K., Lolk, A., Nielsen, H., Andersen, J., Olsen, C., & Kragh-Sorensen, P. (1997). The prevalence of very mild to severe dementia in Denmark. *Acta Neurologica Scandinavica, 96,* 82–87.

Anderson, D. A., Lundgren, J. D., Shapiro, J. R., & Paulosky, C. A. (2004). Assessment of eating disorders: Review and recommendations for clinical use. *Behavior Modification, 28*(6), 763–782.

Anderson, G. M., & Hoshino, Y. (2005). Neurochemical aspects of autism. In F. R. Volkmar, R. Paul, A. Klin, & D. Cohen (Eds.), *Handbook of autism and pervasive developmental disorders* (3rd ed., pp. 453–472). Hoboken, NJ: Wiley.

Anderson, K., Launer, L. J., Dewey, M. E., Letenneur, L., Ott, A., Copeland, J. R. M., et al. (1999). Gender differences in the incidence of AD and vascular dementia. *Neurology, 53,* 1992–1997.

Andreasen, N. C. (1981). *The Scale for the Assessment of Negative Symptoms (SANS).* Iowa City: University of Iowa, Department of Psychiatry.

Andreasen, N. C. (1984). *The Scale for the Assessment of Positive Symptoms (SAPS).* Iowa City: University of Iowa, Department of Psychiatry.

Andreasen, N. C. (2001). *Brave new brain: Conquering mental illness in the era of the genome.* New York: Oxford University Press.

Andreasen, N. C., & Flaum, M. (1991). Schizophrenia: The characteristic symptoms. *Schizophrenia Bulletin, 17,* 27–49.

Andreasen, N. C., Flaum, M., & Schultz, S. (1997). Diagnosis, methodology, and subtypes of schizophrenia. *Neuropsychobiology, 35,* 61–63.

Andrews, G., Slade, T., & Peters, L. (1999). Classification in psychiatry: ICD-10 versus DSM-IV. *British Journal of Psychiatry, 174,* 3–5.

Andrews, J. A., Tildesley, E., Hops, H., Duncan, S. C., & Severson, H. H. (2003). Elementary school age children's future intentions and use of substances. *Journal of Clinical Child and Adolescent Psychology, 32,* 556–567.

Angermeyer, M. C., & Kühn, L. (1988). Gender differences in age at onset of schizophrenia. *European Archives of Psychiatry and Neurological Sciences, 237,* 351–364.

Angold, A., & Costello, E. J. (1996). Toward establishing an empirical basis for the diagnosis of oppositional defiant disorder. *Journal of the American Academy of Child and Adolescent Psychiatry, 35,* 1205–1212.

Angold, A., & Costello, E. J. (2001). The epidemiology of disorders of conduct: Nosological issues and comorbidity. In J. Hill & B. Maughan (Eds.), *Conduct disorders in childhood and adolescence* (pp. 478–506). Cambridge: Cambridge University Press.

Angrist, B., Rotrosen, J., & Gershon, S. (1980). Differential effects of amphetamine and neuroleptics on negative vs. positive symptoms in schizophrenia. *Psychopharmacology, 72,* 17–19.

Angst, F., Stassen, H. H., Clayton, P. J., & Angst, J. (2002). Mortality of patients with mood disorders: Follow-up over 34–38 years. *Journal of Affective Disorders, 68,* 167–181.

Angst, J. (1998). The emerging epidemiology of hypomania and bipolar II disorder. *Journal of Affective Disorders, 50,* 143–151.

Angst, J., Gamma, A., Sellaro, R., Lavori, P., & Zhang, H. (2003). Recurrence of bipolar disorders and major depression: A life long perspective. *European Archives of Psychiatry and Clinical Neuroscience, 253,* 236–240.

Angst, J., & Marneros, A. (2001). Bipolarity from ancient to modern times: Conception, birth and rebirth. *Journal of Affective Disorders, 67,* 3–19.

Anonymous. (1990). First person account: Birds of a psychic feather. *Schizophrenia Bulletin, 16,* 165–168.

Anonymous. (2006). Treatment recommendations for patients with eating disorders. *American Journal of Psychiatry, 163*(7), 5–54.

Anthony, J. C., Warner, L. A., & Kessler, R. C. (1994). Comparative epidemiology of dependence on tobacco, alcohol, controlled substances, and inhalants: basic findings from the National Cormorbidity Survey. *Experimental and Clinical Psychopharmacology, 2,* 244–268.

Antony, M. M., & Barlow, D. H. (2002). Specific phobias. In D. H. Barlow (Ed.), *Anxiety and its disorders: The nature and treatment of anxiety and panic* (2nd ed., pp. 380–417). New York: Guilford Press.

Antony, M. M., Brown, T. A., & Barlow, D. H. (1997). Heterogeneity among specific phobia types in the DSM-IV. *Behaviour Research and Therapy, 35,* 1089–1100.

Antony, M. M., Orsillo, S. M., & Roemer, L. (2001). *Practitioner's guide to empirically based measures of anxiety.* Dordrecht, Netherlands: Kluwer Academic Publishers.

Antshel, K. M. (2002). Integrating culture as a means of improving treatment adherence in the Latino population. *Psychology, Health, and Medicine, 7,* 435–449.

Applebaum, A. H. (2005). Supportive psychotherapy. In J. M. Oldham, A. E. Skodol, & D. S. Bender (Eds.), *Textbook of Personality Disorders* (pp. 335–346). Washington, DC: American Psychiatric Publishing.

Applebaum, P., & Gutheil, T. (1991). *Clinical handbook of psychiatry and the law* (2nd ed.). Baltimore: Williams & Wilkins.

Appleby, L. (1998). A controlled study of fluoxetine and cognitive-behavioural counselling in the treatment of postnatal depression. *European Psychiatry, 13,* 178s.

Arick, J. R., Krug, D. A., Fullerton, A., Loos, L., & Falco, R. (2005). School-based programs. In F. R. Volkmar, R. Paul, A. Klin, & D. Cohen (Eds.), *Handbook of autism and pervasive developmental disorders* (3rd ed., pp. 1003–1028). Hoboken, NJ: Wiley.

Armstrong, D. (2001). Rett syndrome neuropathology review. *Brain and Development, 23,* S72–S76.

Armstrong, T. D., & Costello, E. J. (2002). Community studies on adolescent substance use, abuse and dependence and psychiatric comorbidity. *Journal of Consulting and Clinical Psychology, 70,* 1224–1239.

Arndt, S., Gunter, T. D., & Acion, L. (2005). Older admissions to substance abuse treatment in 2001. *American Journal of Geriatric Psychiatry, 13,* 385–392.

Arnold, L. M., McElroy, S. L., Hudson, J. I., Welge, J., & Bennett, A. (2002). A placebo-controlled randomized trial of fluoxetine in the treatment of binge eating disorder. *Journal of Clinical Psychiatry, 63,* 1028–1033.

Aronson, R., Offman, H., Joffe, R., & Naylor, C. (1996). Triiodothyronine augmentation in treatment of refractory depression. *Archives of General Psychiatry, 53,* 842–848.

Arroll, B., Macgillivray, S., Ogston, S., Reid, I., Sukkivan, F., Williams, B., et al. (2005). Efficacy and tolerability of tricyclic antidepressants and SSRIs compared with placebo for treatment of depression in primary care: A meta-analysis. *Annals of Family Medicine, 3,* 449–456.

Arvanitakis, A., Wilson, R. S., Bienias, J. L., Evans, D. A., & Bennet, D. A. (2004). Diabetes mellitus and risk of Alzheimer's disease and decline in cognitive function. *Archives of Neurology, 61,* 661–666.

Asaad, G. (2000). Somatization disorder. In M. Hersen & M. Biaggio (Eds.), *Effective brief therapies: A clinician's guide* (pp. 179–190). New York: Academic Press.

Asarnow, J. R., Tompson, M. C., & Goldstein, M. J. (1994). Childhood-onset schizophrenia: A follow-up study. *Schizophrenia Bulletin, 29*, 599–617.

Asarnow, R. F., Asamen, J., Granholm, E., Sherman, T., Watkins, J. M., & Williams, M. E. (1994). Cognitive/neuropsychological studies of children with schizophrenic disorder. *Schizophrenia Bulletin, 20*, 647–669.

Aserinsky, E., & Kleitman, N. (1953). Regularly occurring periods of eye motility, and concomitant phenomena, during sleep. *Science, 118*, 273–274.

Ashenberg-Straussner, S. L. (2004). Assessment and treatment of clients with alcohol and other drug abuse problems: An overview. In S. L. Ashenberg-Straussner (Ed.), *Clinical work with substance abusing clients* (2nd ed., pp. 3–35). New York: Guilford Press.

Asher, R. (1951). Munchausen's syndrome. *Lancet, 1*, 339–341.

Asnis, G. M., McGinn, L. K., & Sanderson, W. C. (1995). Atypical depression: Clinical aspects and noradrenergic function. *American Journal of Psychiatry, 152*, 31–36.

Asperger, H. (1991). Autistic psychopathy in childhood. In U. Frith (Ed. & Trans.), *Autism and Asperger syndrome*. Cambridge: Cambridge University Press. (Original work published 1944)

Atkins, M. S., & McKay, M. M. (1996). DSM-IV diagnosis of conduct disorder and oppositional defiant disorder: Implications and guidelines for school mental health teams. *School Psychology Review, 25*(3), 274–285.

Atkinson, R. M., Turner, J. A., Kofoed, L. L., & Tolson, R. L. (1985). Early versus late onset alcoholism in older persons: Preliminary findings. *Alcoholism: Clinical and Experimental Research, 9*, 513–515.

Atwood, J. (2003). New directions in sex therapy: Innovations and alternatives. *American Journal of Family Therapy, 31*(4), 318–321.

Auchus, A. P. (1997). Dementia in urban Black outpatients: Initial experience at the Emory Satellite Clinics. *Gerontologist, 37*, 25–29.

Auerswald, K. B., Charpentier, P. A., & Inouye, S. K. (1997). The informed consent process in older patients who developed delirium: A clinical epidemiologic study. *American Journal of Medicine, 103*, 410–418.

August, G. J., Realmuto, G. M., MacDonald, A. W., Nugent, S. M., & Crosby, R. (1996). Prevalence of ADHD and comorbid disorders among elementary school children screened for disruptive behavior. *Journal of Abnormal Child Psychology, 24*(5), 571–595.

Auld, F., Hyman, M., & Rudzinski, D. (2005). *Resolution of inner conflict: An introduction to psychoanaltyic therapy* (2nd ed.). Washington, DC: American Psychological Association.

Austen, J. (1997). *Persuasion*. Ann Arbor, MI: Tally Hall Press. (Original work published 1817)

Averill, P. M., & Beck, J. G. (2000). Posttraumatic stress disorder in older adults: A conceptual review. *Journal of Anxiety Disorders, 14*, 133–156.

Avina, C., & O'Donohue, W. (2002). Sexual harassment and PTSD: Is sexual harassment diagnosable trauma? *Journal of Traumatic Stress, 15*, 69–75.

Awad, G. A. (1996). The use of selective serotonin re-uptake inhibitors in young children with pervasive developmental disorders: Some clinical observations. *Canadian Journal of Psychiatry, 41*, 361–366.

Aylward, E. H., Minshew, N. J., Field, K., Sparks, B. F., & Singh, N. (2002). Effects of age on brain volume and head circumference in autism. *Neurology, 59*, 175–183.

Ayuso-Gutierrez, J. L., & Ramos-Brieva, J. A. (1982). The course of manic depressive illness: A comparative study of bipolar I and bipolar II patients. *Journal of Affective Disorders, 4*, 9–14.

Bacaltchuk, J., Hay, P., & Mari, J. J. (2000). Antidepressants versus placebo for the treatment of bulimia nervosa: A systematic review. *Australian and New Zealand Journal of Psychiatry, 34*(2), 310–317.

Bachman, R., & Pillemer, K. A. (1992). Epidemiology and family violence involving adults. In R. T. Ammerman & M. Hersen (Eds.), *Assessment of family violence: A clinical and legal sourcebook* (pp. 108–120). New York: Wiley.

Bäckman, L., Small, B. J., & Fratiglioni, L. (2001). Stability of the preclinical episodic memory deficit in Alzheimer's disease. *Brain, 124*, 96–102.

Bacon, A. L., Fein, D., Morris, R., Waterhouse, L., & Allen, D. (1998). The responses of children with autism to the distress of others. *Journal of Autism and Developmental Disorders, 28*, 129–142.

Bae, C. J., & Golish, J. A. (2006). The sleep interview and sleep questionnaires. In T. Lee-Chiong (Ed.), *Sleep: A comprehensive handbook* (pp. 967–971). Hoboken, NJ: Wiley.

Baer, L. (2000). *Getting control: Overcoming your obsessions and compulsions* (Rev. ed.). New York: Plume.

Baerger, D. R. (2001). Risk management with the suicidal patient: Lessons from case law. *Professional Psychology: Research and Practice, 32*, 359–366.

Baethge, C., Smolka, M. N., Grushka, P., Berhöfer, A., Schlattmann, P., Altschuler, L., et al. (2003). Does prophylaxis-delay in bipolar disorder influence outcome? Results from a long-term study of 147 patients. *Acta Psychiatrica Scandinavica, 107*, 260–267.

Baird, G., Charman, T., Cox, A., Baron-Cohen, S., Swettenham, J., Wheelwright, S., et al. (2000). A screening instrument for autism at 18 months of age: A 6-year follow-up study. *Journal of the American Academy of Child and Adolescent Psychiatry, 39*, 694–702.

Bailey, G. R. (1998). Cognitive-behavioral treatment of obsessive-compulsive personality disorder. *Journal of Psychological Practice, 4*(1), 51–59.

Baker, L., Cross, S., Greaver, L., Wei, G., Lewis, R., & Healthy Start CORPS. (2005). Prevalence of postpartum depression in a Native American population. *Maternal and Child Health Journal, 9*, 21–25.

Baker, D. B., Taylor, C. J., & Leyva, C. (2006). Continous performance tests: A comparison of modalities. *Journal of Clinical Psychology, 51*(4), 548–551.

Bakker, A., van Dyck, R., Spinhoven, P., & van Balkom, A. J. L. M. (1999). Paroxetine, clomipramine, and cognitive therapy in the treatment of panic disorder. *Journal of Clinical Psychiatry, 60*, 831–838.

Baldessarini, R. J., Tondo, L., Floris, G., & Hennen, J. (2000). Effects of rapid cycling on response to lithium maintenance treatment in 360 bipolar I and II disorder patients. *Biological Psychiatry, 48*, 445–457.

Baldessarini, R. J., Tondo, L., & Hennen, J. (1999). Treatment delays in bipolar disorders. *American Journal of Psychiatry, 156*, 811–812.

Baldessarini, R. J., Tondo, L., & Hennen, J. (2003a). Lithium treatment and suicide risk in major affective disorders: Update and new findings. *Journal of Clinical Psychiatry, 64*, 44–52.

Baldessarini, R. J., Tondo, L., & Hennen, J. (2003b). Treatment-latency and previous episodes: Relationships to pretreatment morbidity and response to maintenance treatment in bipolar I and II disorders. *Bipolar Disorders, 5*, 169–179.

Baldwin, B. B. (1979). Crisis intervention: An overview of theory and practice. *Counseling Psychologist, 8*, 43–52.

Ball, J. C., Lange, W. R., Myers, C. P., & Friedman, S. R. (1988). Reducing the risk of AIDS through methadone maintenance treatment. *Journal of Health and Social Behavior, 29*, 214–226.

Ball, S. A. (2004). Treatment of personality disorder with Co-occurring substance dependence: Dual focus schema therapy. In J. J. Magnavita (Ed.), *Handbook of Personality: Theory and practice* (pp. 398–425). Hoboken, NJ: Wiley.

Ballard, C., Waite, J., & Birks, J. (2006). Atypical antipsychotics for aggression and psychosis in Alzheimer's disease. *Cochrane Database of Systematic Reviews* (1), CD003476.

Bancroft, J., Janssen, E., Strong, D., Carnes, L., Vukadinovic, Z., & Long, J. S. (2003). The relation between mood and sexuality in heterosexual men. *Archives of Sexual Behavior, 32*(3), 217–230.

Bandura, A. (1977). *Social learning theory.* Englewood Cliffs, NJ: Prentice-Hall.

Bandura, A. (1999). A sociocognitive analysis of substance abuse: An agentic perspective. *Psychological Science, 10,* 214–217.

Bank, A. L., Arguelles, S., Rubert, M., Eisdorfer, C., & Czaja, S. J. (2006). The value of telephone support groups among ethnically diverse caregivers of persons with dementia. *Gerontologist, 46,* 134–138.

Bank, P. A., & Silk, K. (2001). Axis I and Axis II interactions. *Current Opinions in Psychiatry, 14,* 137–142.

Barak, Y., & Aizenberg, D. (2002). Suicide amongst Alzheimer's disease patients: A 10-year survey. *Dementia and Geriatric Cognitive Disorders, 14,* 101–103.

Baranek, G. T. (2002). Efficacy of sensory and motor interventions for children with autism. *Journal of Autism and Developmental Disorders, 5,* 397–422.

Baranek, G. T., Parham, L. D., & Bodfish, J. W. (2005). Sensory and motor features in autism: Assessment and intervention. In F. R. Volkmar, R. Paul, A. Klin, & D. Cohen (Eds.), *Handbook of autism and pervasive developmental disorders* (3rd ed., pp. 831–861). Hoboken, NJ: Wiley.

Barber, J. P., Morse, J. Q., Krakauer, I. D., Chittams, J., & Crits-Christoph, K. (1997). Change in obsessive-compulsive and avoidant personality disorders following time-limited supportive-expressive therapy. *Psychotherapy, 34*(2), 133–143.

Barbini, B., Bertelli, S., Colombo, C., & Smeraldi, E. (1996). Sleep loss, a possible factor in augmenting manic episode. *Psychiatric Research, 65,* 121–125.

Bardenstein, K. K., & McGlashan, T. H. (1990). Gender differences in affective, schizoaffective, and schizophrenic disorders: A review. *Schizophrenia Research, 3,* 159–172.

Barker, M. J., Greenwood, K. M., Jackson, M., & Crowe, S. F. (2004). Cognitive effects of long-term benzodiazepine use: A meta-analysis. *CNS Drugs, 18,* 37–48.

Barker, M. J., Greenwood, K. M., Jackson, M., & Crowe, S. F. (2005). An evaluation of persisting cognitive effects after withdrawal from long-term benzodiazepine use. *Journal of the International Neuropsychological Society, 11,* 281–289.

Barker, P. (1990). *Clinical interviews with children and adolescents.* New York: Norton.

Barkley, R. A. (1997a). *ADHD and the nature of self-control.* New York: Guilford Press.

Barkley, R. A. (1997b). Behavioral inhibition, sustained attention, and executive functions: Constructing a unifying theory of ADHD. *Psychological Bulletin, 121,* 65–94.

Barkley, R. A. (1997c). *Defiant children: A clinician's manual for assessment and parent training* (2nd ed.). New York: Guilford Press.

Barkley, R. A. (2005). *ADHD: A handbook for diagnosis and treatment* (3rd ed.). New York: Guilford.

Barkley, R. A., Fischer, M., Smallish, L., & Fletcher, K. (2002). The persistence of attention-deficit/hyperactivity disorder into young adulthood as a function of reporting source and definition of the disorder. *Journal of Abnormal Psychology, 111,* 279–289.

Barkley, R. A., Fischer, M., Smallish, L., & Fletcher, K. (2003). Does the treatment of attention-deficit/hyperactivity disorder with stimulants contribute to drug use/abuse? A 13-year prospective study. *Pediatrics, 111,* 97–109.

Barlow, D. H. (1991). Introduction to the special issue on diagnoses, dimensions, and the DSM-IV: The science of classification. *Journal of Abnormal Psychology, 100*(3), 243–244.

Barlow, D. H. (2002a). The experience of anxiety: Shadow of intelligence or specter of death? In D. H. Barlow (Ed.), *Anxiety and its disorders: The nature and treatment of anxiety and panic* (2nd ed., pp. 1–36). New York: Guilford Press.

Barlow, D. H. (2002b). Fear, anxiety, and theories of emotion. In D. H. Barlow (Ed.), *Anxiety and its disorders: The nature and treatment of anxiety and panic* (2nd ed., pp. 37–63). New York: Guilford Press.

Barlow, D. H. (2002c). The nature of anxious apprehension. In D. H. Barlow (Ed.), *Anxiety and its disorders: The nature and treatment of anxiety and panic* (2nd ed., pp. 64–104). New York: Guilford Press.

Barlow, D. H. (2002d). The phenomena of panic. In D. H. Barlow (Ed.), *Anxiety and its disorders: The nature and treatment of anxiety and panic* (2nd ed., pp. 105–179). New York: Guilford Press.

Barlow, D. H. (2002e). Biological aspects of anxiety and panic. In D. H. Barlow (Ed.), *Anxiety and its disorders: The nature and treatment of anxiety and panic* (2nd ed., pp. 180–218). New York: Guilford Press.

Barlow, D. H., Craske, M. G., Cerny, J. A., & Klosko, J. S. (1989). Behavioral treatment of panic disorder. *Behavior Therapy, 20,* 261–282.

Barlow, D. H., Gorman, J. M., Shear, M. K., & Woods, S. W. (2000). Cognitive-behavioral therapy, imipramine, or their combination for panic disorder: A randomized controlled trial. *Journal of the American Medical Association, 283,* 2529–2536.

Barlow, D. H., Raffa, S. D., & Cohen, E. M. (2002). Psychosocial treatments for panic disorders, phobias, and generalized anxiety disorder. In P. E. Nathan & J. M. Gordon (Eds.), *A guide to treatments that work* (2nd ed., pp. 301–335). New York: Oxford University Press.

Barnes, G. M., Reifman, A. S., Farrell, M. P., & Dintcheff, B. A. (2000). The effects of parenting on the development of adolescent alcohol misuse: A six wave latent growth model. *Journal of Marriage and Family, 54,* 763–776.

Baron, D. A., Baron, D. A., & Baron, S. H. (2005). Laboratory testing for substance abuse. In R. J. Frances, S. I. Miller, & A. H. Mack (Eds.), *Clinical textbook of addictive disorders* (pp. 63–71). New York: Guilford Press.

Baron-Cohen, S. (1995). *Mindblindness: An essay on autism and theory.* Cambridge, MA: MIT Press.

Baron-Cohen, S. (2002). The extreme male brain theory of autism. *Trends in Cognitive Sciences, 6,* 248–254.

Baron-Cohen, S., Allen, J., & Gillberg, C. (1992). Can autism be detected at 18 months? The needle, the haystack, and the CHAT. *British Journal of Psychiatry, 161,* 839–843.

Baron-Cohen, S., Bolton, P., Wheelwright, S., Short, L., Mead, G., Smith, A., et al. (1998). Does autism occur more often in families of physicists, engineers, and mathematicians? *Autism, 2,* 296–301.

Baron-Cohen, S., Cox, A., Baird, G., Swettenham, J., Nightingale, N., Morgan, K., et al. (1996). Psychological markers in the detection of autism in infancy in a large population. *British Journal of Psychiatry, 168,* 1–6.

Baron-Cohen, S., Leslie, A. M., & Frith, U. (1985). Does the autistic child have a "theory of mind?" *Cognition, 21,* 37–46.

Baron-Cohen, S., & Wheelright, S. (2003). The Friendship Questionnaire: An investigation of adults with Asperger syndrome or high-functioning autism, and normal sex differences. *Journal of Autism Developmental Disorders, 33,* 509–517.

Baron-Cohen, S., Wheelwright, S., Lawson, J., Griffin, R., Ashwin, C., Billington, J., et al. (2005). Empathizing and systemizing in autism spectrum conditions. In F. R. Volkmar, R. Paul, A. Klin, & D. Cohen (Eds.), *Handbook of autism and pervasive developmental disorders* (3rd ed., pp. 628–639). Hoboken, NJ: Wiley.

Baron-Cohen, S., Wheelwright, S., Scott, C., Bolton, P., & Goodyer, I. (1997). Is there a link between engineering and autism? *Autism: An International Journal of Research and Practice, 1,* 153–163.

Baron-Cohen, S., Wheelwright, S., Stone, V., & Rutherford, M. (1999). A mathematician, a physicist, and a computer scientist with Asperger syndrome: Performance of folk psychology and folk physics tests. *Neurocase, 5*(6), 475–483.

Barr, C. L. (2001). Genetics of childhood disorders: XXII. ADHD: Pt. 6. The dopamine D4 receptor gene. *Journal of the American Academy of Child and Adolescent Psychiatry, 40*(1), 118–121.

Barriga, A. Q., Doran, J. W., Newell, S. E. R., Morrison, E. M., Barbetti, V., & Robbins, B. D. (2002). Relationships between problem behaviors and academic achievement in adolescents: The unique role of attention problems. *Journal of Emotional and Behavioral Disorders, 10,* 233–240.

Barrow, S., & Linden, M. (2000). Epidemiology and psychiatric morbidity of suicidal ideation among the elderly. *Crisis, 21*, 171–180.

Barry, C. T., Frick, P. J., DeShazo, T. M., McCoy, M. G., Ellis, M., & Loney, B. R. (2000). The importance of callous-unemotional traits for extending the concept of psychopathy to children. *Journal of Abnormal Psychology, 109*, 335–340.

Barsky, A. J., & Ahern, D. K. (2004). Cognitive behavior therapy for hypochondriasis. *Journal of the American Medical Association, 12*, 1464–1470.

Barsky, A. J., Orav, E. J., & Bates, D. W. (2005). Somatization increases medical utilization and costs independent of psychiatric and medical comorbidity. *Archives of General Psychiatry, 62*, 903–910.

Bartels, S. J., Mueser, K. T., & Miles, K. M. (1997). Functional impairments in elderly patients with schizophrenia and major affective illness in the community: Social skills, living skills, and behavior problems. *Behavior Therapy, 28*, 43–63.

Barthauer, L. (1999). Domestic violence in the psychiatric emergency service. In G. W. Currier (Ed.), *New developments in emergency psychiatry: Medical, legal, and economic* (pp. 29–42). San Francisco: Jossey-Bass.

Bartholomew, K., Kwong, M. J., & Hart, S. D. (2001). Attachment. In J. J. Magnavita (Ed.), *Handbook of personality: Theory and practice* (pp. 196–230). New York: Wiley.

Barton, L. (2001). Attention deficit hyperactivity disorder (ADHD) and bipolar disorder in children and their coexisting comorbidity: A challenge for family counselors. *Family Journal: Counseling and Therapy for Couples and Families, 9*(4), 424–430.

Barzega, G., Maina, G., Venturello, S., & Bogetto, F. (2001). Dysthymic disorder: Clinical characteristics in relation to age at onset. *Journal of Affective Disorders, 66*, 39–46.

Basco, M. R., & Rush, A. J. (1996). *Cognitive-behavioral therapy for bipolar disorder.* New York: Guilford Press.

Basco, M. R., & Rush, A. J. (2007). *Cognitive-behavioral therapy for bipolar disorder.* (2nd ed.). New York: Guilford Press.

Bashiri, N., & Spielvogel, A. M. (1999). Postpartum depression: A cross-cultural perspective. *Primary Care Update for OB/GYNS, 6*, 82–87.

Bassarath, L. (2001). Conduct disorder: A biopsychosocial review. *Canadian Journal of Psychiatry, 46*, 609–616.

Bassett, S. S., Chase, G. A., Folstein, M. F., & Regier, D. A. (1998). Disability and psychiatric disorders in an urban community: Measurement, prevalence, and outcomes. *Psychological Medicine, 28*, 509–517.

Bassiony, M. M., & Lyketsos, C. G. (2003). Delusions and hallucinations in Alzheimer's disease: A review of the brain decade. *Psychosomatics, 44*, 388–401.

Bateman, A., & Fonagy, P. (2004a). Mentalization-based treatment of BPD. *Journal of Personality Disorders, 18*(1), 36–51.

Bateman, A., & Fonagy, P. (2004b). *Psychotherapy for borderline personality disorder: Mentalization-based treatment.* Oxford, England: Oxford University.

Baucom, D. H., & Epstein, N. (1990). *Cognitive-behavioral marital therapy.* New York: Brunner/Mazel.

Bauer, M., & Boegner, F. (1996). Neurological syndromes in factitious disorders. *Journal of Nervous and Mental Diseases, 184*(5), 281–288.

Baving, L., Laucht, M., & Schmidt, M. H. (2000). Oppositional children differ from healthy children in frontal brain activation. *Journal of Abnormal Child Psychology, 28*, 267–275.

Bayley, N. (1993). *The Bayley Scales of Infant Development* (2nd ed.). San Antonio, TX: Psychological Corporation.

Beach, D. A. (1989). The behavioral interview. In R. J. Craig (Ed.), *Clinical and diagnostic interviewing* (pp. 79–83). Northvale, NJ: Aronson.

Beach, S. R., Wamboldt, M. Z., Kaslow, N. J., Heyman, R. E., First, M. B., Underwood, L. G., et al. (Eds.). (2006). *Relational processes and DSM-V: Neuroscience, assessment, prevention, and treatment.* Washington, DC: American Psychiatric Association.

Beach, S. R. H. (2001). Marital therapy for co-occurring marital discord and depression. In S. R. H. Beach (Ed.), *Marital and family processes in depression: A scientific foundation for clinical practice* (pp. 205–224). Washington, DC: American Psychological Association.

Beals, J., Novins, D. K., Spicer, P., Whitesell, N. R., Mitchell, C. M., & Manson, S. M. (2006). Help seeking for substance use problems in two American Indian reservation populations. *Psychiatric Services, 57,* 512–520.

Bebbington, P. (1995). The content and context of compliance. *International Clinical Psychopharmacology, 9*(Suppl. 5), 41–50.

Bebko, J. M., & Weiss, J. A. (2006). Mental retardation. In M. Hersen, J. C. Thomas, & R. T. Ammermam (Eds.), *Comprehensive handbook of personality and psychopathology: Child psychopathology* (Vol. 3, pp. 233–253). Hoboken, NJ: Wiley.

Bech, P., & Angst, J. (1996). Quality of life in anxiety and social phobia. *International Clinical Psychopharmacology, 11,* 97–100.

Bech, P., Ciadella, P., Haugh, M. C., Birkett, M. A., Hours, A., Boissel, J. P., et al. (2000). Meta-analysis of randomised controlled trials of fluoxetine vs. placebo and tricyclic antidepressants in the short-term treatment of major depression. *British Journal of Psychiatry, 176,* 421–428.

Beck, A. T. (1967). *Depression: Causes and treatment.* Philadelphia. University of Pennsylvania Press.

Beck, A. T., Brown, G. K., Berchick, R. J., Stewart, B. L., & Steer, R. A. (1990). Relationship between hopelessness and ultimate suicide: A replication with psychiatric outpatients. *Behavior Research and Therapy, 35*(11), 1039–1046.

Beck, A. T., Brown, G. K., Steer, A., Dahlsgaard, K. K., & Grisham, J. R. (1999). Suicidal ideation at its worst point: A prediction of eventual suicide in psychiatric outpatients. *Suicide and Life Threatening Behavior, 29,* 1–29.

Beck, A. T., & Emery, G. (1985). *Anxiety disorders and phobias: A cognitive perspective.* New York: Basic Books.

Beck, A. T., Butler, A. C., Brown, G. K., Dahlsgaard, K. K., Newman, C. F., & Beck, J. S. (2001). Dysfunctional beliefs discriminate personality disorders. *Behavior Research and Therapy, 39,* 1213–1225.

Beck, A., & Freeman, A. (1990). *Cognitive therapy of personality disorders.* New York: Guilford Press.

Beck, A., Freeman, A., & Davis, D. (2003). *Cognitive therapy of personality disorders* (2nd ed.). New York: Guilford Press.

Beck, A. T., Kovacs, M., & Weisman, A. (1979). Assessment of suicidal ideation: The Scale for Suicidal Ideation. *Journal of Consulting and Clinical Psychology, 47*(2), 343–352.

Beck, A. T., Shaw, B. F., Emery, G., & Rush, A. J. (1979). *Cognitive therapy of depression.* New York: Guilford Press.

Beck, A. T., & Steer, R. A. (1988). *Manual for Beck Hopelessness Scale.* San Antonio, TX: Psychological Corporation.

Beck, A. T., & Steer, R. A. (1989). Clinical prediction of eventual suicide: A 5- to 10-year prospective study of suicide attempters. *Journal of Affective Disorders, 17,* 203–209.

Beck, A. T., & Steer, R. A. (1991). *Manual for Beck Scale for Suicidal Ideation.* San Antonio, TX: Psychological Corporation.

Beck, A. T., Steer, R. A., Beck, J. S., & Newman, C. F. (1993). Hopelessness, depression, suicidal ideation and clinical diagnosis of depression. *Suicide and Life-Threatening Behavior, 23,* 139–145.

Beck, A. T., Steer, R. A., & Brown, G. K. (1996). *Manual for the Beck Depression Inventory* (2nd ed.). San Antonio TX: Psychological Corporation.

Beck, A. T., Ward, C. H., Mendelson, M., Mock, J., & Erbaugh, J. (1961). An inventory for measuring depression. *Archives of General Psychiatry, 4,* 53–63.

Beck, A. T., Ward, C. H., Mendelson, M., Mock, J. E., & Erbaugh, J. (1962). Reliability of psychiatric diagnosis: Pt. II. A study of consistency of clinical judgments and ratings. *American Journal of Psychiatry, 119,* 351–357.

Beck, A. T., Wright, F. W., Newman, C. F., & Liese, B. (1993). *Cognitive therapy of substance abuse*. New York: Guilford Press.

Beck, J. S. (1995). *Cognitive therapy: Basics and beyond*. New York: Guilford Press.

Becker, A. E., Burwell, R. A., Gilman, S. E., Herzog, D. G., & Hamburg, P. (2002). Eating behaviours and attitudes following prolonged exposure to television among ethnic Fijian adolescent girls. *British Journal of Psychiatry, 180*, 509–514.

Becker, A. E., & Fay, K. (2006). Sociocultural issues and eating disorders. In S. Wonderlich, J. E. Mitchell, M. de Zwaan, & H. Steiger (Eds.), *Annual review of eating disorders* (Pt. 2 pp. 35–64). Oxford: Radcliffe Publishing.

Becker, A. E., Grinspoon, S. K., & Klibanski, A. (1999). Current concepts: Eating disorders. *New England Journal of Medicine, 340*(14), 1092–1098.

Becker, D., Drake, R., Farabaugh, A., & Bond, G. R. (1996). Job preferences of clients with severe psychiatric disorders participating in supported employment programs. *Psychiatric Services, 47*, 1223–1226.

Becker, D. F., Grilo, C. M., Edell, W. S., & McGlashan, T. H. (2000). Comorbidity of borderline personality disorders in hospitalized adolescents and adults. *American Journal of Psychiatry, 157*(12), 2011–2016.

Becker, E. S., Rinck, M., Turke, V., Kause, P., Goodwin, R., Neumer, S., et al. (2007). Epidemiology of specific phobia subtypes: Findings from the Dresden Mental Health Study. *European Psychiatry, 22*, 69–74.

Becker, J. V., & Johnson, B. R. (2004). Sexual and gender identity disorders. In R. E. Hales & S. C. Yudofsky (Eds.), *Essentials of clinical psychiatry* (2nd ed., pp. 505–525). Washington, DC: American Psychiatric Publishing.

Becker, P. M. (2005). Pharmacologic and nonpharmacologic treatments of insomnia. *Neurologic Clinics, 23*, 1149–1163.

Becker, R. E., Singh, M. M., Meisler, N., & Shillcutt, S. (1985). Clinical significance, evaluation, and management of secondary depression in schizophrenia. *Journal of Clinical Psychiatry, 46*, 26–32.

Beekman, A. T., Bremmer, M. A., Deeg, D. J., van Balkom, A. J. L. M., Snut, J. H., van Dyck, R., et al. (1998). Anxiety disorder in later life: A report from the Longitudinal Aging Study Amsterdam. *International Journal of Geriatric Psychiatry, 13*, 717–726.

Beesley, D., & Stoltenberg, C. D. (2002). Control, attachment style, and relationship satisfaction among adult children of alcoholics. *Journal of Mental Health Counseling, 24*, 281–298.

Beglin, S. J., & Fairburn, C. G. (1992). What is meant by the term "binge"? *American Journal of Psychiatry, 149*(1), 123–124.

Behar, E., & Borkovec, T. D. (2006). The nature and treatment of generalized anxiety disorder. In B. Olasov-Rothbaum (Ed.), *Pathological anxiety: Emotional processing in etiology and treatment* (pp. 181–193). New York: Guilford Press.

Beidel, D. C., Morris, T. L., & Turner, M. W. (2004). Social phobia. In T. L. Morris & J. S. March (Eds.), *Anxiety disorders in children and adolescents* (pp. 141–163). New York: Guilford Press.

Beidel, D. C., & Turner, S. M. (1998). *Shy children, phobic adults: Nature and treatment of social phobia*. Washington, DC: American Psychological Association.

Beidel, D. C., Turner, S. M., & Morris, T. L. (1995). A new inventory to assess childhood social anxiety and phobia: The Social Phobia and Anxiety Inventory for Children. *Psychological Assessment, 7*, 73–79.

Beitchman, J. H., & Young, A. R. (1997). Learning disorders with a special emphasis on reading disorders. *Journal of the American Academy of Child and Adolescent Psychiatry, 36*, 1020–1032.

Belitsky, R., & McGlashan, T. H. (1993). The manifestation of schizophrenia in late life: A dearth of data. *Schizophrenia Bulletin, 4*, 683–689.

Bell, B., Chalkin, L., Mills, M., Browne, G., Steiner, M., Roberts, J., et al. (2004). Burden of dysthymia and comorbid illness in adults in a Canadian primary care setting: High rates of psychiatric illness in the offspring. *Journal of Affective Disorders, 78*, 73–80.

Bell, K. E., & Stein, D. M. (1992). Behavioral treatments of pica: A review of empirical studies. *International Journal of Eating Disorders, 11*, 377–389.

Bell, M. D., Lysaker, P. H., Beam-Goulet, J. L., Milstein, R. M., & Lindenmayer, J. P. (1994). Five-component model of schizophrenia: Assessing the factorial invariance of the positive and negative syndrome scale. *Psychiatry Research, 52*, 295–303.

Bell, Q. (1992). *Virginia Woolf: A biography.* New York: Quality Paperback Book Club.

Bemporad, J. R. (1996). Self-starvation through the ages: Reflections on the pre-history of anorexia nervosa. *International Journal of Eating Disorders, 19*, 217–237.

Benazon, N. R., & Coyne, J. C. (2000). Living with a depressed spouse. *Journal of Family Psychology, 14*, 71–79.

Benazzi, F. (1998). Schizophreniform disorder with good prognostic features: A 6-year follow-up. *Canadian Journal of Psychiatry, 43*, 180–182.

Benazzi, F. (2001). Depressive and mixed state: Testing different definitions. *Psychiatry and Clinical Neuroscience, 55*, 647–652.

Bender, D., Dolan, R., Skodol, A., Sanislow, C., Dyck, I., McGlasgan, T., et al. (2001). Treatment utilization by patients with personality disorders. *American Journal of Psychiatry, 158*(2), 295–302.

Bender, D. S. (2005). Therapeutic alliance. In J. M. Oldham, A. E. Skodol, & D. S. Bender (Eds.), *Textbook of personality disorders* (pp. 405–420). Washington, DC: American Psychiatric Publishing.

Benes, F. M., & Berretta, S. (2001). GABAergic interneurons: Implications for understanding schizophrenia and bipolar disorder. *Neuropsychopharmacology, 25*, 1–27.

Benjamin, L. S. (1996). A clinician-friendly version of the interpersonal circumplex: Structural Analysis of Social Behavior (SASB). *Journal of Personality Assessment, 66*, 248–266.

Benjamin, L. S. (2003). *Interpersonal diagnosis and treatment of personality disorders* (2nd ed.). New York: Guilford Press.

Bennett, D. S., Ambrosini, P. J., Kudes, D., Metz, C., & Rabinovich, H. (2005). Gender differences in adolescent depression: Do symptoms differ for boys and girls? *Journal of Affective Disorders, 89*, 35–44.

Benoit, D. (2000). Feeding disorders, failure to thrive, and obesity. In C. H. Zeanah Jr. (Ed.), *Handbook of infant mental health* (2nd ed., pp. 339–352). New York: Guilford Press.

Benson, D. F., Djenderedjian, A., Miller, B. L., Pachana, N. A., Chang, L., Itti, L., et al. (1996). Neural basis of confabulation. *Neurology, 45*, 1239–1243.

Benton, M. K., & Schroeder, H. E. (1990). Social skills training with schizophrenics: A meta-analytic evaluation. *Journal of Counseling and Clinical Psychology, 58*, 741–747.

Bérard, A., Ramos, E., Rey, E., Blais, L., St.-André, M., & Oraichi, D. (2006). First trimester exposure to paroxetine and risk of cardiac malformations in infants: The importance of dosage. *Birth Defects Research Part B: Developmental and Reproductive Toxicology.* Retrieved December 22, 2006, from http://www.3.interscience.wiley.com/cgi-bin/fulltext/ 113493580/HTMLSTART.

Berg, C. Z., Rapoport, J. L., Whitaker, A., Davies, M., Leonard, H., Swedo, S. E., et al. (1989). Childhood obsessive compulsive disorder: A 2-year prospective follow-up of a community sample. *Journal of the American Academy of Child and Adolescent Psychiatry, 8*, 528–533.

Berglund, M., & Nilsson, K. (1987). Mortality in severe depression: A prospective study including 103 suicides. *Acta Psychiatrica Scandinavica, 76*, 372–380.

Bergman, A. J., Silverman, J. M., Harvey, P. D., Smith, C. J., & Siever, L. J. (2000). Schizotypal symptoms in the relatives of schizophrenic patients: An empirical analysis of the factor structure. *Schizophrenia Bulletin, 26*(3), 577–586.

Bergner, R. M. (1998). Characteristics of optimal clinical case formulations: The linchpin concept. *American Journal of Psychotherapy, 52*(3), 287–300.

Berk, M., & Dodd, S. (2005). Bipolar II disorder: A review. *Bipolar Disorders, 7*, 11–21.

Berkowitz, A., & Perkins, H. W. (1988). Personality characteristics of children of alcoholics. *Journal of Consulting and Clinical Psychology, 56*, 206–209.

Berlin, I. N. (1987). Suicide among American Indian adolescents: An overview. *Suicide and Life Threatening Behavior, 17*(3), 218–232.

Berlin, R. M., & Qayyum, U. (1986). Sleepwalking: Diagnosis and treatment through the life cycle. *Psychosomatics, 27*, 755–760.

Berman, J. R., Berman, L. A., Lin, H., Flaherty, E., Lahey, N., Goldstein, I., et al. (2001). Effect of sildenafil on subjective and physiologic parameters of the female sexual response in women with sexual arousal disorders. *Journal of Sex and Marital Therapy, 27*(5), 411–420.

Berman, L. A., Berman, J. R., Bruck, D., Pawar, R. V., & Goldstein, I. (2001). Pharmacotherapy or psychotherapy? Effective treatment for FSD related to unresolved childhood sexual abuse. *Journal of Sex and Marital Therapy, 27*(5), 421–425.

Bernheimer, L. P., Weisner, T. S., & Lowe, E. D. (2003). Impacts of children with troubles on working poor families: Mixed-method and experimental evidence. *Mental Retardation, 41*(6), 403–419.

Bernstein, D. P., & Travaglini, L. (1999). Schizoid and avoidant personality disorders. In T. Millon, P. H. Blaney, & R. D. Davis (Eds.), *Oxford textbook of psychopathology* (pp. 523–534). New York: Oxford University Press.

Bernstein, D. P., Useda, D., & Siever, L. J. (1993). Paranoid personality disorder: Review of the literature and recommendations for DSM-IV. *Journal of Personality Disorders, 7*, 53–62.

Bernstein, E., & Putnam, F. W. (1986). Development, reliability and validity of a dissociation rating scale. *Journal of Nervous and Mental Disorders, 174*, 727–735.

Berrettini, W. H. (2000). Are schizophrenic and bipolar disorders related? A review of family and molecular studies. *Biological Psychiatry, 48*, 531–538.

Berrios, G. E. (1999). Mood disorders: Clinical section. In G. E. Berrios & R. Porter (Eds.), *A history of clinical psychiatry* (pp. 384–408). New Brunswick, NJ: Athlone Press.

Berrios, G. E. (2001). Hypochondriasis: History of the concept. In V. Starcevic & D. R. Lipsitt (Eds.), *Hypochondriasis: Modern perspectives on an ancient malady* (pp. 3–20). New York: Oxford University Press.

Berrios, G. E., & Link, C. (1999). Anxiety disorders: Clinical section. In G. E. Berrios & R. Porter (Eds.), *A history of clinical psychiatric disorders* (pp. 543–562). New Brunswick, NJ: Athlone Press.

Berrios, G. E., & Mumford, D. (1995). Somatoform disorders. In G. E. Berrios & R. Porter (Eds.), *A history of clinical psychiatry: The origin and history of psychiatric disorder* (pp. 451–489). New York: New York University Press.

Berry, E. M., & Marcus, E. L. (2000). Disorders of eating in the elderly. *Journal of Adult Development, 7*(2), 87–99.

Berry, J. W., & Sam, D. L. (1997). Acculturation and adaptation. In J. W. Berry, M. S. Segall, & C. Kagitcibasi (Eds.), *Handbook of cross-cultural psychology: Vol. 3. Social behavior and applications* (2nd ed., pp. 291–326). Needham Heights, MA: Allyn & Bacon.

Bertelsen, A. (1999). Reflections on the clinical utility of the ICD-10 and the DSM-IV classifications and their diagnostic criteria. *Australian and New Zealand Journal of Psychiatry, 33*, 166–173.

Bertrand, J., Mars, A., Boyle, C., Bove, F., Yeargin-Allsopp, M., & Decoufle, P. (2001). Prevalence of autism in a United States population: The Brick Township, New Jersey, investigation. *Pediatrics, 108*, 1155–1161.

Berument, S. K., Rutter, M., Lord, C., Pickles, A., & Bailey, A. (1999). Autism screening questionnaire: Diagnostic validity. *British Journal of Psychiatry, 175*, 444–451.

Bettelheim, B. (1967). *The empty fortress.* New York: Free Press.

Beumont, P. J. V. (2002). Clinical presentation of anorexia nervosa and bulimia nervosa. In C. G. Fairburn & K. D. Brownell (Eds.), *Eating disorders and obesity: A comprehensive handbook* (2nd ed., pp. 162–170). New York: Guilford Press.

Beutler, L. E., Brookman, L., Harwood, T. M., Alimohamed, S., & Malik, M. (2001). Functional impairment and coping style. *Psychotherapy, 38*(4), 437–442.

Beutler, L. E., Consoli, A. J., & Lane, G. (2005). Systematic treatment selection and prescriptive psychotherapy. In J. C. Norcross & M. R. Goldfrieds (Eds.), *Handbook of psychotherapy integration* (2nd ed., pp. 121–143). New York: Oxford University Press.

Beutler, L. E., & Harwood, T. M. (2000). *Prescriptive psychotherapy: A practical guide to systematic treatment selection*. New York: Oxford University Press.

Beutler, L. E., Moleiro, C., & Talebi, H. (2002). How practitioners can systematically use empirical evidence in treatment selection. *Journal of Clinical Psychology, 58*(10), 1199–1212.

Beuzen, J. N., Ravily, V. F., Souetre, E. J., & Thomander, L. (1993). Impact of fluoxetine on work loss in depression. *International Clinical Psychopharmacology, 8*, 319–321.

Bhalla, R. K., Butters, M. A., Mulsant, B. H., Begley, A. E., Zmuda, M. D., Schoderbek, B., et al. (2006). Persistence of neuropsychologic deficits in the remitted state of late-life depression. *American Journal of Geriatric Psychiatry, 14*, 419–427.

Bidder, T. G., Strain, J. J., & Brunschwig, L. (1970). Bilateral and unilateral ECT: Follow-up study and critique. *American Journal of Psychiatry, 127*, 737–745.

Bieber Nielsen, J., Henriksen, K. F., Hanses, C., Siahtaroglu, A., Schwartz, M., & Tommerup, N. (2001). MECP2 mutations in Danish patients with Rett syndrome: High frequency of mutations but no consistent correlations with clinical severity or with X chromosome inactivation pattern. *European Journal of Human Genetics, 9*, 178–184.

Biederman, J., Faraone, S., & Mick., E. (1996). Attention-deficit hyperactivity disorder and juvenile mania: An overlooked comorbidity? *Journal of American Academy Child and Adolescent Psychiatry, 35*, 997–1008.

Biederman, J., Mick, E., & Faraone, S. V. (2000). Age-dependent decline of symptoms of attention deficit hyperactivity disorder: Impact of remission definition and symptom type. *American Journal of Psychiatry, 157*, 816–818.

Biederman, J., Petty, C., Faraone, S. V., Hirshfeld-Becker, D. R., Henin, A., Dougherty, M., et al. (2005). Parental predictors of pediatric panic disorder/agoraphobia: A controlled study in high-risk offspring. *Depression and Anxiety, 22*, 114–120.

Biederman, J., Rosenbaum, J., Hirshfeld, D. R., Faraone, S. V., Bolduc, E. A., Gersten, M., et al. (1990). Psychiatric correlates of behavioral inhibition in young children of parents with and without psychiatric disorders. *Archives of General Psychiatry, 47*, 21–26.

Biederman, J., & Spencer, T. (2000). Non-stimulant treatment for ADHD. *European Child and Adolescent Psychiatry, 9*, 51–59.

Bienvenu, O. J., Samuels, J. F., Riddle, M. A., Hoehn-Saric, R., Liang, K. Y., Cullen, B. A., et al. (2000). The relationship of obsessive-compulsive disorder to possible spectrum disorders: Results from a family study. *Biological Psychiatry, 48*, 287–293.

Bilder, R. M., Mukherjee, S., Rieder, R. O., & Pandurangi, A. K. (1985). Symptomatic and neuropsychological components of defect states. *Schizophrenia Bulletin, 11*, 409–419.

Bilj, R. V., Ravelli, A., & van Zessen, G. (1998). Prevalence of psychiatric disorder in the general population: Results from the Netherlands Mental Health Survey and Incidence Study. *Social Psychiatry and Psychiatric Epidemiology, 33*, 587–595.

Billiard, M. (2003). Hypersomnias: Introduction. In M. Billiard (Ed.) & A. Kent (Trans.), *Sleep: Physiology, investigations, and medicine* (pp. 333–336). New York: Kluwer Academic/Plenum Press.

Billing, L., Eriksson, M., Jonsson, B., Steneroth, G., & Zatterstrom, R. (1994). The influence of environmental factors on behavioural problems in 8-year-old children exposed to amphetamine during fetal life. *Child Abuse and Neglect, 18*, 3–9.

Binder, R. L., & McNeil, D. E. (1986). Victims and families of violent psychiatric patients. *Bulletin of the American Academy of Psychiatry Law, 14*, 131–139.

Binder, R. L., & McNeil, D. E. (1990). The relationship of gender to violent behavior in acutely disturbed psychiatric patients. *Journal of Clinical Psychology, 51*, 110–114.

Birket-Smith, M., & Mortensen, E. L. (2002). Pain in somatoform disorders: Is somatoform pain disorder a valid diagnosis? *Acta Psychiatrica Scandinavica, 1067*, 103–108.

Birmaher, B., & Ollendick, T. H. (2004). Childhood-onset panic disorder. In T. S. Ollendick & J. S. March (Eds.), *Phobic and anxiety disorders in children and adolescents* (pp. 306–333). New York: Oxford University Press.

Bishop, D. V. M., & Baird, G. (2001). Parent and teacher report of pragmatic aspects of communication: Use of the Children's Communication Checklist in a clinical setting. *Developmental Medicine and Child Neurology, 43*, 809–818.

Bittner, A., Goodwin, R. D., Wittchen, H.-U., Beesdo, K., Höfler, M., & Lieb, R. (2004). What characteristics of primary anxiety disorders predict subsequent major depressive disorder? *Journal of Clinical Psychiatry, 65*, 618–626.

Bjorkly, S. (1997). Clinical assessment of dangerousness in psychotic patients: Some risk indicators and pitfalls. *Aggression and Violent Behavior, 2*, 167–178.

Blachman, D. R., & Hinshaw, S. P. (2002). Patterns of friendship among girls with and without attention-deficit/hyperactivity disorder. *Journal of Abnormal Child Psychology, 30*, 625–640.

Black, C. (1982). *It will never happen to me.* Denver, CO: MAC Publishing.

Black, D. W., Yates, W., Petty, F., Noyes, R., & Brown, K. (1986). Suicidal behavior in alcoholic males. *Comprehensive Psychiatry, 27*, 227–233.

Black, K. J., Compton, W. M., Wetzel, M., Minchin, S., & Farber, N. B. (1994). Assaults by patients on psychiatric residents at three training sites. *Hospital and Community Psychiatry, 45*, 706–710.

Black, S. A., & Markides, K. (1993). Acculturation and alcohol consumption in Puerto Rican, Cuban American, and Mexican-American women in the United States. *American Journal of Public Health, 83*, 890–893.

Blackwood, D. H., & Muir, W. J. (2004). Clinical phenotypes associated with DISCI, a candidate gene for schizophrenia. *Neurotoxicity Research, 6*, 35–41.

Blair, R. J. R., Colledge, E., Murray, L., & Mitchell, D. G. V. (2001). A selective impairment in the processing of sad and fearful expressions in children with psychopathic tendencies. *Journal of Abnormal Child Psychology, 29*, 491–498.

Blair-West, G. W., Cantor, S. H., Mellsop, G. W., & Eyeson-Annan, M. L. (1999). Lifetime suicide risk in major depression: Sex and age determinants. *Journal of Affective Disorders, 55*, 171–178.

Blanco, C., Anita, S. X., & Liebowitz, M. R. (2002). Pharmacotherapy of social anxiety disorder [Review]. *Biological Psychiatry, 51*(1), 109–120.

Blanco, C., García, C., & Liebowitz, M. R. (2004). Pharmacological treatment of social phobia. *Psychiatry, 3*, 60–64.

Bland, R. C., Newman, S. C., & Orn, H. (1988). Prevalence of psychiatric disorders in the elderly in Edmonton. *Acta Psychiatrica Scandinavica, 77*, 57–63.

Blaney, P. H. (1999). Paranoid conditions. In T. Millon, P. H. Blaney, & R. D. Davis (Eds.), *Oxford textbook of psychopathology* (pp. 339–361). New York: Oxford University Press.

Blansjaar, B. A., Takens, H., & Zwinderman, A. H. (1992). The course of alcohol amnestic disorder: A 3-year follow-up study of clinical signs and social disabilities. *Acta Psychiatrica Scandinavica, 86*, 240–246.

Blanton, H., Gibbons, F. X., Gerrard, M., Jewsbury-Conger, K., & Smith, G. A. (1997). Role of family and peers in the development of prototypes associated with substance use. *Journal of Family Psychology, 11*, 271–288.

Blashfield, R. K., & Livesley, W. J. (1999). Classification. In T. Millon, P. H. Blaney, & R. D. Davis (Eds.), *Oxford textbook of psychopathology* (pp. 3–28). New York: Oxford University Press.

Blazer, D. G. (2004). The epidemiology of depressive disorders in late life. In S. P. Roose & H. A. Sackheim (Eds.), *Late life depression* (pp. 3–11). New York: Oxford University Press.

Blazer, D. G., Federspiel, C. F., Ray, W. A., & Schaffner, W. (1983). The risk of anticholinergic toxicity in the elderly: A study of prescribing practices in two populations. *Journal of Gerontology, 38*, 31–35.

Blazer, D. G., George, L. K., & Hughes, D. (1991). The epidemiology of anxiety disorders: An age comparison. In C. Salzman & B. D. Lebowitz (Eds.), *Anxiety in the elderly: Treatment and research* (pp. 17–30). New York: Springer.

Blazer, D. G., Kessler, R. C., & Swartz, M. S. (1998). Epidemiology of recurrent major and minor depression with a seasonal pattern: The National Comorbidity Survey. *British Journal of Psychiatry, 172*, 164–167.

Bleuler, E. (1922). Die probleme der schizoidie und der syntonie: Zeitschrift fuer die gesamte. *Nurologie und Psychiatrie, 78*, 373–388.

Bleuler, E. (1950). *Dementia praecox or the group of schizophrenias* (J. Zinkin, Trans.). New York: International Universities Press. (Original work published 1911)

Bleuler, M. (1978). *The schizophrenic disorders: Long-term patient and family studies.* New Haven, CT: Yale University Press.

Bliwise, D. L. (1994). What is sundowning? *Journal of the American Geriatric Society, 42*, 1009–1011.

Blomhoff, S., Haug, T. T., Hellstöm, K., Holme, I., Humble, M., Madsbu, H. P., et al. (2001). Randomised controlled general practice trial of sertraline, exposure therapy and combined treatment in generalised social phobia. *British Journal of Psychiatry, 179*, 23–30.

Bloom, B. S., de Pouvourville, N., & Straus, W. L. (2003). Cost of illness of Alzheimer's disease: How useful are current estimates? *Gerontologist, 43*, 158–164.

Bloom, P. (2001). Treating adolescent conversion disorders: Are hypnotic techniques reusable? *International Journal of Clinical and Experimental Hypnosis, 49*(3), 243–256.

Blow, F. C., Brower, K. J., Schulenberg, J. E., Demo-Dananberg, L. M., Young, J. P., & Beresford, T. P. (1992). The Michigan Alcoholism Screening Test—Geriatric Version (MAST-G): A new elderly-specific screening instrument. *Alcoholism: Clinical and Experimental Research, 16*, 372.

Blum, N., Pfohl, B., St. John, D., Monahan, P., & Black, D. W. (2002). STEPPS: A cognitive-behavioral systems-based group treatment for outpatients with borderline personality disorder: A preliminary report. *Comprehensive Psychiatry, 43*, 301–310.

Blume, S. B., & Zilberman, M. L. (2005). Addictive disorders in women. In R. I. Frances, S. I. Miller, & A. H. Mack (Eds.), *Clinical textbook of addictive disorders* (3rd ed., pp. 437–453). New York: Guilford Press.

Boachie, A., Goldfield, G. S., & Spettigue, W. (2003). Olanzapine use as an adjunctive treatment for hospitalized children with anorexia nervosa: Case reports. *International Journal of Eating Disorders, 33*(1), 98–103.

Bobo, J. K., McIlvain, H. E., & Leed-Kelly, A. (1998). Depression screening scores during residential drug treatment and risk of drug use after discharge. *Psychiatric Services, 49*, 693–695.

Bogduk, N. (2004). Diagnostic blocks: A truth serum for malingering. *Clinical Journal of Pain, 20*(6), 409–414.

Bögels, S. M., van der Vleuten, C. P. M., Kreutzkamp, R., Melles, R., & Schmidt, H. G. (1995). Assessment and validation of diagnostic interviewing skills for the mental health professions. *Journal of Psychopathology and Behavioral Assessment, 17*, 217–230.

Boggs, K. M., Griffin, R. S., & Gross, A. M. (2003). Children. In M. Hersen & S. M. Turner (Eds.), *Diagnostic interviewing* (3rd ed., pp. 393–414). New York: Kluwer Academic.

Bohman, M. (1995). Predisposition to criminality: Swedish adoption studies in retrospect. In R. Bock & J. A. Goode (Eds.), *Genetics of criminal and antisocial behavior* (pp. 99–114). Chichester, West Sussex, England: Wiley.

Bohman, M., Cloninger, R., Sigvardsson, S., & von Knorring, A. L. (1987). The genetics of alcoholism and related disorders. *Journal of Psychiatric Research, 21*, 447–452.

Bohne, A., Keuthen, N. J., Wilhelm, S., Deckersbach, T., & Jenike, M. A. (2002). Prevalence of symptoms of body dysmorphic disorder and its correlates: A cross-cultural comparison. *Psychosomatics, 43*(6), 487–490.

Bolger, J. P., Carpenter, B. D., & Strauss, M. E. (1994). Behavior and affect in Alzheimer's disease. *Clinics in Geriatric Medicine, 10*, 315–337.

Bolland, R. J., & Keller, M. B. (1999). Mixed state bipolar disorders: Outcome data from the NIMH collobrative program on the psychobiology of depression. In J. F. Goldberg & M. Harrow (Eds.), *Bipolar disorders: Clinical course and outcome* (pp. 115–128). Washington, DC: American Psychiatric Press.

Boller, F., Becker, J. T., Holland, A. L., Forbes, M. M., Hood, P. C., & McGonigle-Gibson, K. L. (1991). Predictors of decline in Alzheimer's disease. *Cortex, 27*, 9–17.

Boller, F., & Forbes, M. M. (1998). History of dementia and dementia in history: An overview. *Journal of Neurological Sciences, 158*, 125–133.

Bolton, E. E., Mueser, K. T., & Rosenberg, S. D. (2006). Symptom correlates of posttraumatic stress disorder in clients with borderline personality disorder. *Comprehensive Psychiatry, 47*, 357–361.

Bolton, P. F., Murphy, M. M., MacDonald, H., Whitlock, B., Pickles, A., & Rutter, M. (1997). Obstetric complications in autism: Consequences or causes of the condition? *Journal of the American Academy of Child and Adolescent Psychiatry, 36*, 272–281.

Bombardier, C. H., Temkin, N., Machamer, J., & Dikmen, S. S. (2003). The natural history of drinking and alcohol-related problems after traumatic brain injury. *Archives of Physical Medicine and Rehabilitation, 84*, 185–191.

Bömmer, I., & Brüne, M. (2006). Social cognition in "pure" delusional disorder. *Cognitive Neuropsychiatry, 11*, 493–503.

Bonanno, G. A. (2006). Is complicated grief a valid construct? *Clinical Psychology Science and Practice, 13*, 129–140.

Bond, G. R., McGrew, J. H., & Fekete, D. M. (1995). Assertive outreach for frequent users of psychiatric hospitals: A meta analysis. *Journal of Mental Health Administration, 22*, 4–16.

Bongar, B. (1991). *The suicidal patient: Clinical and legal standards of care.* Washington, DC: American Psychological Association.

Bongar, B. (1992). *Suicide: Guidelines for assessment, management, and treatment.* New York: Oxford University Press.

Bongar, B., Greaney, S., & Peruzzi, N. (1998). Risk management with the suicidal patient. In P. M. Kleespies (Ed.), *Emergencies in mental health practice: Evaluation and management* (pp. 199–216). New York: Guilford Press.

Bongar, B., Maris, R. W., Berman, A. L., & Litman, R. E. (1998). Outpatient standards of care and the suicidal patient. In B. Bongar, A. L. Berman, R. W. Maris, M. M. Silverman, E. A. Harris, & W. L. Packman (Eds.), *Risk management with suicidal patients* (pp. 4–33). New York: Guilford Press.

Bonner, A. P., Cousins, A. P., & O'Brien, S. (1996). Exercise and Alzheimer's disease: Benefits and barriers. *Activities, Adaptation and Aging, 20*, 21–34.

Bonner, R. L. (1990). A "M.A.P." to the clinical assessment of suicide risk. *Journal of Mental Health Counseling, 12*, 232–236.

Boothby, L. A., & Doering, P. L. (2005). Acamprosate for the treatment of alcohol dependence. *Clinical Therapeutics, 27*, 695–714.

Bordini, E. J., Chaknis, M. M., Ekman-Turner, R. M., & Perna, R. B. (2002). Advances and issues in the diagnostic differential of malingering versus brain injury. *NeuroRehabilitation, 17*, 93–104.

Borkovec, T. D., & Mathews, A. M. (1988). Treatment of nonphobic anxiety disorders: A comparison of nondirective, cognitive, and coping desensitization therapy. *Journal of Consulting and Clinical Psychology, 56*, 877–884.

Borkovec, T. D., Mathews, A. M., Chambers, A., Ebrahimi, S., Lytle, R., & Nelson, R. (1987). The effects of relaxation training with cognitive therapy or non-directive therapy and the role of relaxation-induced anxiety in the treatment of generalized anxiety. *Journal of Consulting and Clinical Psychology, 55*, 883–888.

Borkovec, T. D., Newman, M. G., Pincus, A. L., & Lytle, R. (2002). A component analysis of cognitive-behavioral therapy for generalized anxiety disorder and the role of interpersonal problems. *Journal of Consulting and Clinical Psychology, 70*, 288–298.

Borkovec, T. D., & Ruscio, A. M. (2001). Psychotherapy for generalized anxiety disorder. *Journal of Clinical Psychiatry, 62*(Suppl. 11), 37–42.

Bornstein, R. F. (1996). Beyond orality: Towards an object relations/interactionist reconceptualization of the etiology and dynamics of dependency. *Psychoanalytic Psychology, 13*, 177–203.

Bornstein, R. F. (1999). Dependent and histrionic personality disorders. In T. Millon, P. H. Blaney, & R. D. Davis (Eds.), *Oxford textbook of psychopathology* (pp. 535–553). New York: Oxford University Press.

Borum, R. (1996). Improving the clinical practice of violence risk assessment: Technology, guidelines, and training. *American Psychologist, 51*, 945–956.

Bostwick, J. M., & Masterson, B. J. (1998). Psychopharmacological treatment of delirium to restore mental capacity. *Psychosomatics, 39*, 112–117.

Botteron, K., Figiel, G. S., & Zorumski, C. F. (1991). Electroconvulsive therapy in patients with late-onset psychosis and structured brain changes. *Journal of Geriatric Psychiatry and Neurology, 4*, 44–47.

Bouchard, C., Rhéaume, J., & LaDouceur, R. (1999). Responsibility and perfectionism in OCD: An experimental study. *Behaviour Research and Therapy, 37*, 239–248.

Bouman, T. (2002). A community-based psychoeducational group approach to hypochondriasis. *Psychotherapy and Psychosomatics, 71*, 326–332.

Bouman, T. K., Eifert, G. H., & Lejuez, C. W. (1999). Somatoform disorders. In T. Millon, P. H. Blaney, & R. D. Davis (Eds.), *Oxford textbook of psychopathology* (pp. 444–465). New York: Oxford University Press.

Bourgeois, M. S., Dijkstra, K., & Burgio, L. (2001). Memory aids as an augmentative and alternative communication strategy for nursing home residents with dementia. *AAC: Augmentative and Alternative Communication, 17*, 196–210.

Bourland, S. L., Stanley, M. A., Snyder, A. G., Novy, D. M., Beck, J. G., Averill, P. M., et al. (2000). Quality of life in older adults with generalized anxiety disorder. *Aging and Mental Health, 4*, 315–323.

Bowden, C. L. (2005). A different depression: Clinical distinctions between bipolar and unipolar depression. *Journal of Affective Disorders, 84*, 117–125.

Bowden, C. L., Calbabrese, J. R., Sachs, G., Yatham, L. N., Asghar, S. A., Hompland, M., et al. (2003). A placebo-controlled 18-month trial of lamotrigine and lithium maintenance treatment in recently manic or hypomanic patients with bipolar I disorder. *Archives of General Psychiatry, 60*, 392–400.

Bowden, C. L., & McElroy S. L. (1995). History of the development of valproate for treatment of bipolar disorder. *Journal of Clinical Psychiatry, 56*, 3–5.

Bowden, C. L., & Singh, V. (2005). Long-term management of bipolar disorder. In T. A. Ketter (Ed.), *Advances in the treatment of bipolar disorder* (pp. 111–146). Washington, DC: American Psychiatric Publishing.

Bowen, L., Wallace, C. J., Glynn, S. M., Nuechterlein, K. H., Lutzker, J. R., & Kuehnel, T. G. (1994). Schizophrenic individuals' cognitive functioning and performance in interpersonal interactions and skills training procedures. *Journal of Psychiatric Research, 28*, 289–301.

Bowers, M. B., Mazure, C. M., Nelson, J. C., & Jatlow, P. I. (1990). Psychotogenic drug use and neuroleptic response. *Schizophrenia Bulletin, 16*, 81–85.

Bowers, T. G., & Derr Bailey, M. (1998). Specific learning disorders: Neuropsychological aspects of psychoeducational remediation. *Innovations in Clinical Practice: A Sourcebook, 19*, 49–62.

Bowers, W. A., Evans, K., LeGrange, D., & Andersen, A. E. (2003). Treatment of adolescent eating disorders. In M. A. Reinecke, F. M. Dattilio, & A. Freeman (Eds.), *Cognitive therapy with children and adolescents: A casebook for clinical practice* (2nd ed., pp. 247–279). New York: Guilford Press.

Bowker, L. H., & Maurer, L. (1986). The effectiveness of counseling services utilized by battered women. *Women and Therapy, 5*, 65–82.

Bowlby, J. (1944). Forty-four juvenile thieves: Their characters and home-life. *International Journal of Psychoanalysis, 25*, 19–52, 107–127.

Bowlby, J. (1951). *Maternal care and mental health.* Geneva, Switzerland: World Health Organization.

Bowser, B. P., & Word, C. O. (1993). Comparison of African-American adolescent crack cocaine users and non-users: Background factors in drug use and HIV sexual risk behaviors. *Psychology of Addictive Behaviors, 7*, 155–161.

Boyce, P., & Judd, F. (1999). The place for the tricyclic antidepressants in the treatment of depression. *Australian and New Zealand Journal of Psychiatry, 33*, 323–327.

Braaten, E. B., & Rosen, L. A. (2000). Self-regulation of affect in attention deficit-hyperactivity disorder (ADHD) and non-ADHD boys: Differences in empathic responding. *Journal of Consulting and Clinical Psychology, 68*, 313–321.

Bradizza, C. M., Stasiewicz, P. R., & Paas, N. D. (2006). Relapse to alcohol and drug use among individuals diagnosed with co-occurring mental health and substance use disorders: A review. *Clinical Psychology Review, 26*, 162–178.

Brådvik, L., & Berglund, M. (2006). Long-term treatment and suicidal behavior in severe depression: ECT and antidepressant pharmacotherapy may have different effects on the occurrence and seriousness of suicide attempts. *Depression and Anxiety, 23*, 34–41.

Brady, J. P. (1966). Brevital-relaxation treatment of frigidity. *Behaviour Research and Therapy, 4*(2), 71–77.

Brady, M. (1995). Culture in treatment, culture as treatment: A critical appraisal of developments in addictions programs for indigenous North Americans and Australians. *Social Science and Medicine, 41*, 1487–1498.

Braff, D. L., Saccuzzo, D. P., & Geyer, M. A. (1991). Information processing dysfunctions in schizophrenia: Studies of visual backward masking, sensorimotor gating, and habituation. In S. R. Steinhauer & J. H. Gruzelier (Eds.), *Handbook of schizophrenia: Neuropsychology, psychophysiology, and information processing* (Vol. 5, pp. 303–334). New York: Elsevier Science.

Braga, R. J., Mendlowicz, M. V., Marrocos, R., & Figueira, I. L. (2005). Anxiety disorders in outpatients with schizophrenia: Prevalence and impact on the subjective quality of life. *Journal of Psychiatric Research, 39*, 409–414.

Braga, R. J., Petrides, G., & Figueira, I. (2004). Anxiety disorders in schizophrenia. *Comprehensive Psychiatry, 45*, 460–468.

Bragier, D. K., & Venning, H. E. (1997). Conversion disorders in adolescents: A practical approach to rehabilitation. *British Journal of Rheumatology, 36*, 594–598.

Brand, M., Fujiwara, E., Kalve, Z., Steingrass, H. P., Kessler, J., & Markowitsch, H. J. (2003). Cognitive estimation and affective judgments in alcoholic Korsakoff patients. *Journal of Clinical and Experimental Neuropsychology, 25*, 324–334.

Brasic, J. R. (2002). Conversion disorder in childhood. *German Journal of Psychiatry, 5*, 54–61.

Brassard, M., & Gelardo, M. (1987). Psychological maltreatment: The unifying construct in child abuse and neglect. *School Psychology Review, 16*, 127–136.

Braun, D. L., Sunday, S. R., & Halmi, K. A. (1994). Psychiatric comorbidity in patients with eating disorders. *Psychological Medicine, 24*(4), 859–867.

Braun, D. L., Sunday, S. R., Huang, A., & Halmi, K. A. (1999). More males seek treatment for eating disorders. *International Journal of Eating Disorders, 25*(4), 415–424.

Bray, J. H., Adams, G. J., Getz, J. G., & Baer, P. E. (2001). Developmental, family, and ethnic influences on adolescent alcohol usage: A growth curve approach. *Journal of Family Psychology, 15*, 301–314.

Brecht, M. L., O'Brien, A. O., von Mayrhauser, C., & Anglin, M. D. (2004). Methamphetamine use behaviors and gender differences. *Addictive Behaviors, 29*, 89–106.

Breckman, R. S., & Adelman, R. D. (1992). Elder abuse and neglect. In R. T. Ammerman & M. Hersen (Eds.), *Assessment of family violence: A clinical and legal sourcebook* (pp. 236–252). New York: Wiley.

Breen, M. J., & Altepeter, T. S. (1990). Situational variability in boys and girls identified as ADHD. *Journal of Clinical Psychology, 46*, 486–490.

Bregman, J. D., Zager, D., & Gerdtz, J. (2005). Behavioral interventions. In F. R. Volkmar, R. Paul, A. Klin, & D. Cohen (Eds.), *Handbook of autism and pervasive developmental disorders* (3rd ed., pp. 897–924). Hoboken, NJ: Wiley.

Breier, A., Charney, D. S., & Heninger, G. R. (1985). The diagnostic validity of anxiety disorders and their relationship to depressive illness. *American Journal of Psychiatry, 142*, 787–797.

Breitbart, W., Marotta, R., Platt, M. M., Weisman, H., Derevenco, M., Grau, C., et al. (1996). A double-blind trial of haloperidol, chlorpromazine, and lorazepam in the treatment of delirium in hospitalized AIDS patients. *American Journal of Psychiatry, 153*, 231–237.

Breitbart, W., Gibson, C., & Tremblay, A. (2002). The delirium experience: Delirium recall and delirium-related distress in hospitalized patients with cancer, their spouses/caregivers, and their nurses. *Psychosomatics, 43*, 183–194.

Breitbart, W., Tremblay, A., & Gibson, C. (2002). An open trial of olanzapine for the treatment of delirium in hospitalized cancer patients. *Psychosomatics, 43*, 175–182.

Breitner, J. C., & Zandi, P. P. (2003). Effects of estrogen plus progestin on risk of dementia. *Journal of the American Medical Association, 290*, 1706–1707.

Bremner, J. D. (2002). *Does stress damage the brain?* New York: Norton.

Brendel, R. W., & Bryan, E. (2004). HIPAA for psychiatrists. *Harvard Review of Psychiatry, 12*, 177–183.

Brennan, P. A., Mendick, S. A., & Jacobsen, B. (1995). Assessing the role of genetics in crime using adoption cohorts. In G. R. Bock & J. A. Goode (Eds.), *Genetics of criminal and antisocial behavior* (Ciba Foundation Symposium 194, pp. 115–128). Chichester, West Sussex, England: Wiley.

Brent, B. A., Birmhauer, B., Kolko, D., Baugher, M., & Bridge, J. (2000). Subsyndromal depression in adolescents after a brief psychotherapy trial: Course and outcome. *Journal of Affective Disorders, 63*, 51–58.

Brent, D. A., Perper, J. A., Moritz, G., Allman, C., Friend, A., Roth, C., et al. (1993). Psychiatric risk factors for adolescent suicide: A case-control study. *Journal of the American Academy of Child and Adolescent Psychiatry, 32*, 521–529.

Breslau, N., Davis, G. C., Andreski, P., & Peterson, E. L. (1991). Traumatic events and posttraumatic stress disorder in an urban population of young adults. *Archives of General Psychiatry, 48*, 216–222.

Breslau, N., Johnson, E. O., & Lucia, V. C. (2001). Academic achievement of low birthweight children at age 11: The role of cognitive abilities at school entry–statistical data included. *Journal of Abnormal Child Psychology, 29*, 273–279.

Brestan, E. V., & Eyberg, S. M. (1998). Effective psychosocial treatments for conduct disordered children and adolescents: 29 years, 82 studies and 5272 kids. *Journal of Clinical Child Psychology, 27*, 180–189.

Brewerton, T. D., Lydiard, R. B., Herzog, D. B., Brotman, A. W., O'Neil, P. M., & Ballenger, J. C. (1995). Comorbidity of Axis I psychiatric disorders in bulimia nervosa. *Journal of Clinical Psychiatry, 56*(2), 77–80.

Brieger, P., Ehrt, U., Bloeink, R., & Marneros, A. (2002). Consequences of comorbid personality disorders in major depression. *Journal of Nervous and Mental Diseases, 190*, 304–309.

Briere, J. (1995). *Trauma Symptom Inventory professional manual.* Odessa, FL: Psychological Assessment Resources.

Briere, J. (2004). *Psychological assessment of adult posttraumatic states* (2nd ed.). Washington, DC: American Psychological Association.

Brink, J. (2005). Epidemiology of mental illness in a correctional setting. *Current Opinion in Psychiatry, 18*, 536–541.

Brinkmeyer, M. Y., & Eyberg, S. M. (2003). Parent-child interaction therapy for oppositional children. In A. E. Kazdin & J. R. Weisz (Eds.), *Evidence-based psychotherapies for children and adolescents* (pp. 204–223). New York: Guilford Press.

Bristol-Powers, M. M., & Spinella, G. (1999). Research on screening and diagnosis in autism: A work in progress. *Journal of Autism and Developmental Disorders, 29*(6), 435–438.

Broadhurst, D. D. (1984). *The educator's role in the prevention and treatment of child abuse and neglect.* Washington, DC: National Center on Child Abuse and Neglect, U.S. Department of Health and Human Services.

Broderick, G. A. (2006). Premature ejaculation: On defining and quantifying a common male sexual dysfunction. *Journal of Sexual Medicine, 3*(4), 295–302.

Brodsky, B. S., Cloitre, M., & Dulit, R. A. (1995). Relationship of dissociation to self-mutilitation and childhood abuse in borderline personality disorder. *American Journal of Psychiatry, 152*(12), 1788–1792.

Brodsky, C. M. (1984). Sociocultural and interactional influences on somatization. *Psychosomatics, 25*, 673–680.

Brogan, M., & Prochaska, J. (1999). Predicting termination and continuation status in psychotherapy using the transtheoretical model. *Psychotherapy: Theory, Research, Practice Training, 36*, 105–113.

Brook, J. S., Brook, D. W., Arencibia-Mireles, O., Richter, L., & Whiteman, M. (2001). Risk factors for adolescent marijuana use across cultures and across time. *Journal of Genetic Psychology, 162*, 357–374.

Brook, J. S., Whiteman, M., Gordon, A. S., & Brook, D. W. (1990). The role of older brothers in younger brothers' drug use viewed in the context of parent and peer influence. *Journal of Genetic Psychology, 151*, 59–75.

Brouette, T., & Anton, R. (2001). Clinical review of inhalants. *American Journal on Addictions, 10*, 79–94.

Brower, M. C., & Price, B. H. (2001). Neuropsychiatry of frontal lobe dysfunction in violent and criminal behavior: A critical review. *Journal of Neurology Neurosurgical Psychiatry, 71*, 720–726.

Brown, C., Schulberg, H. C., & Madonia, M. J. (1996). Clinical presentations of major depression by African Americans and whites in primary medical care practice. *Journal of Affective Disorders, 41*, 181–191.

Brown, C., Schulberg, H. C., Madonia, M., Shear, M. K., & Houck, P. (1996). Treatment outcomes for primary care patients with major depression and lifetime anxiety disorders. *American Journal of Psychiatry, 153*, 1293–1300.

Brown, E. (1999). Post-traumatic stress disorder and shell shock. In G. E. Berrios & R. Porter (Eds.), *A history of clinical psychiatric disorders* (pp. 501–508). New Brunswick, NJ: Athlone Press.

Brown, E., Dawson, G., Osterling, J., & Dinno, J. (1998). *Early identification of 8–10 month old infants with autism based on observation from home videotapes* [Abstract]. Paper presented at the International Society for Infant Studies, Atlanta, GA.

Brown, G. K. (2000). *A review of suicide assessment measures for intervention research with adults and older adults* (Technical Report submitted to NIMH). Bethesda, MD: National Institute of Mental Health.

Brown, G. K., Beck, A. T., Steer, R. A., & Grisham, J. R. (2000). Risk factors for suicide in psychiatric out-patients: A 20 year prospective study. *Journal of Consulting and Clinical Psychology, 68*, 371–377.

Brown, G. R. (2001). Transvestism and gender identity disorders. In G. O. Gabbard (Ed.), *Treatments of psychiatric disorders.* (3rd ed., pp. 2007–2068). Washington, DC: American Psychiatric Press.

Brown, M. Z., Comtois, K. A., & Linehan, M. M. (2002). Reasons for suicide attempts and nonsuicidal self-injury in women with borderline personality disorder. *Journal of Abnormal Psychology, 111*, 198–202.

Brown, P. J., & Ouimette, P. C. (1999). Introduction to the special section on substance use disorder and posttraumatic stress disorder comorbidity. *Psychology of Addictive Behaviors, 13*, 75–77.

Brown, T. A., & Barlow, D. H. (2002). Classification of anxiety and mood disorders. In D. H. Barlow (Ed.), *Anxiety and its disorders: The nature and treatment of anxiety and panic* (2nd ed., pp. 292–327). New York: Guilford Press.

Brown, T. A., DiNardo, P. A., & Barlow, D. H. (1994). *Anxiety disorders interview schedule for DSM-IV (ADIS-IV).* San Antonio, TX: Psychological Corporation.

Brown, T. A., Di Nardo, P. A., Lehman, C. L., & Campbell, L. A. (2001). Reliability of DSM-IV anxiety and mood disorders: Implications for the classification of emotional disorders. *Journal of Abnormal Psychology, 110*, 49–58.

Browne, A. (1987). *Battered women who kill.* New York: Free Press.

Brownell, K. D., & Rodin, J. (1992). Prevalence of eating disorders in athletes. In K. D. Brownell, J. Rodin, & J. H. Wilmore (Eds.), *Eating, body weight, and performance in athletes: Disorders of modern society* (pp. 128–145). Philadelphia: Lea & Febiger.

Bruce, M. L. (2002). Psychosocial risk factors for depressive disorders in late life. *Biological Psychiatry, 52*, 175–184.

Brunello, N., & Tascedda, F. (2003). Cellular mechanisms and second messengers: Relevance to the psychopharmacology of bipolar disorders. *International Journal of Neuropsychopharmacology, 6*, 181–189.

Bryant, R. (2003). Early predictors of posttraumatic stress disorder. *Biological Psychiatry, 53*, 789–795.

Bryant, R. A., & Harvey, A. G. (2002). Delayed-onset posttraumatic stress disorder: A prospective evaluation. *Australian and New Zealand Journal of Psychiatry, 36*, 205–209.

Bryant-Waugh, R. J., & Lask, B. D. (2002). Childhood-onset eating disorders. In C. G. Fairburn & K. D. Brownell (Eds.), *Eating disorders and obesity: A comprehensive handbook* (2nd ed., pp. 210–214). New York: Guilford Press.

Bryant-Waugh, R. J., Lask, B. D., Shafran, R. L., & Fosson, A. R. (1992). Do doctors recognize eating disorders in children? *Archives of Disease in Childhood, 67*(1), 103–105.

Bryson, G., & Bell, M. D. (2003). Initial and final work performance in schizophrenia: Cognitive and symptom predictors. *Journal of Nervous and Mental Diseases, 191*, 87–92.

Buchanan, R. W., Strauss, M. E., Kirkpatrick, B., Holstein, C., Breier, A., & Carpenter, W. T. (1994). Neuropsychological impairments in deficit vs. non-deficit forms of schizophrenia. *Archives of General Psychiatry, 51*, 804–811.

Buchanan, W. L. (1997). Children's mental health services and managed care. In R. S. Sauber (Ed.), *Managed health care: Major diagnostic and treatment approaches* (pp. 187–215). London: Brunner-Routledge.

Buckley, T. C., Blanchard, E. B., & Hickling, E. J. (1996). A prospective examination of delayed onset PTSD secondary to motor vehicle accidents. *Journal of Abnormal Psychology, 105*, 617–625.

Buckwalter, K. C., Smith, M., Maas, M., & Kelley, L. (1998). Family and staff: Partners in caregiving. In M. Kaplan & S. B. Hoffman (Eds.), *Behaviors in dementia: Best practices for successful management* (pp. 89–103). Baltimore: Health Professions Press.

Budney, A. J. (2006). Are specific dependence criteria necessary for different substances: How can research on cannabis inform this issue? *Addiction, 101*, 125–133.

Budney, A. J., Higgins, S. T., Radonvich, K. J., & Novy, P. L. (2000). Adding voucher-based incentives to coping-skills and motivational enhancement improves outcomes during treatment for marijuana dependence. *Journal of Consulting and Clinical Psychology, 68*, 1051–1061.

Budney, A. J., Moore, B. A., Rocha, H. L., & Higgins, S. T. (2006). Clinical trial of abstinence-based vouchers and cognitive-behavioral therapy for cannabis dependence. *Journal of Consulting and Clinical Psychology, 74*, 307–316.

Budney, A. J., Moore, B. A., Vandrey, R. G., & Hughes, J. R. (2003). The time course and significance of cannabis withdrawal. *Journal of Abnormal Psychology, 112*, 393–402.

Budney, A. J., Novy, P., & Hughes, J. R. (1999). Marijuana withdrawal among adults seeking treatment for marijuana dependence. *Addiction, 94*, 1311–1322.

Buitelaar, J. K., & Van der Gaag, R. J. (1998). Diagnostic rules for children with PDD-NOS and multiple complex developmental disabilities. *Journal of Child Psychology and Psychiatry, 39*(6), 911–919.

Buitelaar, J. K., Van der Gaag, R., Klin, A., & Volkmar, F. (1998). Exploring the boundaries of pervasive developmental disorder not otherwise specified: Analyses of the data from the DSM-IV autistic disorder field trial. *Journal of Autism and Developmental Disorders, 29*, 33–43.

Bulik, C. M., & Kendler, K. S. (2000). "I am what I (don't) eat": Establishing an identity independent of an eating disorder. *American Journal of Psychiatry, 157*(11), 1755–1760.

Bulik, C. M., Sullivan, P. F., Joyce, P. R., Carter, F. A., & McIntosh, V. V. (1998). Predictors of 1-year treatment outcome in bulimia nervosa. *Comprehensive Psychiatry, 39*(4), 206–214.

Bulik, C. M., Sullivan, P. F., & Kendler, K. S. (2000). An empirical study of the classification of eating disorders. *American Journal of Psychiatry, 157*(6), 886–895.

Bulik, C. M., Sullivan, P. F., Wade, T. D., & Kendler, K. S. (2000). Twin studies of eating disorders: A review. *International Journal of Eating Disorders, 27*(1), 2–20.

Bullock, R. (2006). Efficacy and safety of memantine in moderate-to-severe Alzheimer disease: The evidence to date. *Alzheimer Disease and Associated Disorders, 20*, 23–29.

Burack, J. A., Iarocci, G., Bowler, D., & Mottron, L. (2002). Benefits and pitfalls in the merging of disciplines: The example of developmental psychopathology and the study of persons with autism. *Development and Psychopathology, 14*, 225–237.

Burch, E. A. (1994). Suicide attempt histories in alcohol-dependent men: Differences in psychological profiles. *International Journal of the Addictions, 29*, 1477–1486.

Burd, L., Fisher, W., & Kerbeshian, J. (1989). Pervasive disintegrative disorder: Are Rett syndrome and Hellar dementia infantilis subtypes? *Developmental Medicine and Child Neurology, 31*(5), 609–616.

Burford, B., Kerr, A. M., & Macleod, H. A. (2003). Nurse recognition of early deviation in development in home videos of infants with Rett disorder. *Journal of Intellectual Disability Research, 47*, 588–589.

Burgess, K. D., Rubin, K. H., Cheah, C. S. L., & Nelson, J. L. (2001). Behavioral inhibition, social withdrawal, and parenting. In W. R. Crozier & L. E. Alden (Eds.), *International handbook of social anxiety* (pp. 137–158). New York: Wiley.

Burgoon, J. K., Beutler, L. E., LePoire, B. A., Engle, D., Bergan, J., Salvio, M. A., et al. (1993). Nonverbal indices of arousal in group psychotherapy. *Psychotherapy, 30*, 635–645.

Burke, J. D., Loeber, R., & Birmaher, B. (2002). Oppositional defiant disorder and conduct disorder: Pt. II. A review of the past 10 years. *Journal of the American Academy of Child and Adolescent Psychiatry, 41*(11), 1275–1293.

Burke, K. C., Burke, J. D., Regier, D. A., & Rae, D. S. (1990). Age of onset of selected mental disorders in five community populations. *Archives of General Psychiary, 47*, 511–519.

Burke, W. J., & Bohac, D. L. (2001). Amnestic disorder due to a general medical condition and amnestic disorder not otherwise specified. In G. O. Gabbard (Ed.), *Treatment of psychiatric disorders* (3rd ed., pp. 609–624). Washington, DC: American Psychiatric Press.

Burke, W. J., Roccaforte, W. H., Wengel, S. P., MacArthur-Miller, D., Folks, D. G., & Potter, J. F. (1998). Disagreement in the reporting of depressive symptoms between patients with dementia of the Alzheimer type and their collateral sources. *American Journal of Geriatric Psychiatry, 6*, 308–319.

Burns, D. D. (1984). The Burns Anxiety Inventory. In D. Burns (1989), *The feeling good handbook*. New York: Plume.

Burns, R., Nichols, L. O., Martindale-Adams, J., Graney, M. J., & Lummus, A. (2003). Primary care interventions for dementia caregivers: Two-year outcomes from the REACH study. *Gerontologist, 43*, 547–555.

Buroughs, M., & Thompson, J. K. (2001). Exercise status and sexual orientation as moderators of body image disturbance and eating disorders in males. *International Journal of Eating Disorders, 31*(3), 307–311.

Burroughs, V. J., Maxey, R. W., & Levy, R. A. (2002). Racial and ethnic differences in response to medicines: Towards individualized pharmaceutical treatment. *Journal of the National Medical Association, 94*, 1–26.

Burruss, J. W., Travella, J. I., & Robinson, R. G. (2001). Vascular dementia. In G. O. Gabbard (Ed.), *Treatments of psychiatric disorders* (3rd ed., pp. 515–534). Washington, DC: American Psychiatric Press.

Bursch, B. (2006). Somatization disorders. In M. Hersen, J. C. Thomas, & R. T. Ammerman (Eds.), *Comprehensive handbook of personality and psychopathology: Vol. 2. Child psychopathology* (pp. 403–421). Hoboken, NJ: Wiley.

Bursch, B., Ingman, K., Vitti, L., Hyman, P. E., & Zeltzer, L. K. (2004). Chronic pain in individuals with previously undiagnosed autistic spectrum disorders. *Journal of Pain, 5*, 290–295.

Burt, S. A., Krueger, R. F., & McGue, M. (2001). Sources of covariation among attention-deficit/hyperactivity disorder, oppositional defiant disorder, and conduct disorder: The importance of shared environment. *Journal of Abnormal Psychology, 110*(4), 516–525.

Burton, C. J., Crow, T. J., Firth, C. D., Johnstone, E. C., Owens, D. G. C., & Roberts, G. W. (1990). Schizophrenia and the brain: A prospective clinico-neuropathological study. *Psychological Medicine, 20,* 285–304.

Busen, N. H., Marcus, M. T., & von Sternberg, K. L. (2006). What African-American middle school youth report about risk-taking behaviors. *Journal of Pediatric Care, 20,* 393–400.

Bush, G., Fink, M., Petrides, G., & Francis, A. (1996). Catatonia I: Rating scale and standardized examination. *Acta Psychiatrica Scandinavica, 93,* 129–136.

Bushman, B. J., & Cooper, H. M. (1990). Effects of alcohol on human aggression: An intergrative research review. *Psychological Bulletin, 107,* 341–354.

Bussing, R., Gary, F. A., Mason, D. M., Leon, C. E., Sinha, K., & Gasrvan, C. W. (2003). Child temperament, ADHD, and caregiver strain: Exploring relationships in an epidemiological sample. *Journal of the American Academy of Child and Adolescent Psychiatry, 42,* 184–192.

Butcher, J. N. (2005). *MMPI-2: A beginner's guide* (2nd ed.). Washington, DC: American Psychological Association.

Butcher, J. N., Dahlstrom, W. G., Grahan, J. R., Tellegen, A., & Kaemmer, B. (1989). *Minnesota Multiphasic Personality Inventory-2 (MMPI-2): Manual for administration and scoring.* Minneapolis: University of Minnesota Press.

Butler, A. C., Chapman, J. E., Forman, E. M., & Beck, A. T. (2006). The empirical status of cognitive-behavioral therapy: A review of meta-analyses. *Clinical Psychology Review, 26,* 17–31.

Butler, R. W., & Braff, D. L. (1991). Delusions: A review and integration. *Schizophrenia Bulletin, 17,* 643–647.

Butler, T., Andrews, G., Allnut, S., Sakashita, C., & Smith, N. E. (2006). *Australian and New Zealand Journal of Psychiatry, 40,* 272–276.

Butzlaff, R. L., & Hooley, J. M. (1998). Expressed emotion and psychiatric relapse: A meta-analysis. *Archives of General Psychiatry, 55,* 547–552.

Bux, D. A., Lamb, R. J., & Iguchi, M. Y. (1995). Cocaine use and HIV risk behavior in methadone maintenance patients. *Drug and Alcohol Dependence, 37,* 29–35.

Buysse, D. J., Reynolds, C. F., & Monk, T. H. (1989). The Pittsburgh Sleep Quality Index: A new instrument for psychiatric practice and research. *Psychiatry Research, 28*(2), 193–213.

Byrd, R. (2002). *Report to the legislature on the principal findings from the epidemiology of autism in California: A comprehensive pilot study.* Retrieved January 6, 2007, from University of California Davis, MIND Institute Web site: http//www.ucdmc.ucdavis.edu/mindinstitue/hmtl/news/autismreport.htm.

Byrne, S. M. (2002). Sport, occupation, and eating disorders. In C. G. Fairburn & K. D. Brownell (Eds.), *Eating disorders and obesity: A comprehensive handbook* (2nd ed., pp. 256–259). New York: Guilford Press.

Caballero, J., & Nahata, M. C. (2003). Atomexetine hydrochloride for the treatment of attention-deficit/hyperactivity disorder. *Clinical Therapeutics, 25,* 3065–3083.

Cachelin, F. M., & Maher, B. A. (1998). Is amenorrhea a critical criterion for anorexia nervosa? *Journal of Psychosomatic Research, 44*(3/4), 435–440.

Cade, J. F. (1949). Lithium salts in the treatment of psychotic excitement. *Medical Journal of Australia, 2,* 349–352.

Cadoret, R. (1986). Adoption studies: Historical and methodological critique. *Psychiatric Developments, 1,* 45–64.

Cadoret, R. J. (1978). Evidence for genetic inheritance of primary affective disorder in adoptees. *American Journal of Psychiatry, 135,* 463–466.

Caine, E. D. (1981). Pseudodementia. *Archives of General Psychiatry, 38,* 1359–1364.

Calebrese, J. R., Markovitz, P. J., Kimmel, S. E., & Wagner, S. C. (1992). Spectrum of efficacy of calproate in 78 rapid-cycling bipolar patients. *Journal of Clinical Psychopharmacology, 12,* 53–56.

Calebrese, J. R., Shelton, M. D., Rapport, D. J., Youngstrom, E. A., Jackson, K., Bilali, S., et al. (2005). A 20-month, double-blind, maintenance trial of lithium versus divalproex in rapid-cycling bipolar disorder. *American Journal of Psychiatry, 162,* 2152–2161.

Calebrese, J. R., Suppes, T., Bowden, C. L., Sachs, G. S., Swann, A. C., McElroy, S. L. (2000). A double-blind, placebo controlled prophylaxis study of lamotrigine, in rapid cycling bipolar disorder. *Journal of Clinical Psychiatry, 61,* 841–850.

California Department of Developmental Services (CDD). (2002). *Autistic spectrum disorders: Best practice guidelines for screening, diagnosis and assessment.* Retrieved October 11, 2007, www.ddhealthinfo.org.

California Department of Developmental Services (CDD). (2003). *Autistic spectrum disorders: Changes in the California caseload. An update: 1999–2002.* Retrieved October 11, 2007, from www.dds.ca.gov.

Callahan, C. M., Boustani, M. A., Unverzagt, F. W., Austrom, M. G., Damush, T. M., Perkins, A. J., et al. (2006). Effectiveness of collaborative care for older adults with Alzheimer disease in primary care: A randomized controlled trial. *Journal of the American Medical Association, 295,* 2148–2157.

Callahan, J. (1993). Blueprint for an adolescent suicidal crisis. *Psychiatric Annals, 23,* 263–270.

Camp, C. J., Foss, J. W., O'Hanlon, A. M., & Stevens, A. B. (1996). Memory interventions for persons with dementia. *Applied Cognitive Psychology, 10,* 193–210.

Campbell, M., Schopler, E., Cueva, J. E., & Hallin, A. (1996). Treatment of autistic disorder. *Journal of the American Academy of Child and Adolescent Psychiatry, 35,* 134–143.

Campo, J. V., Comer, D. M., Jansen-McWilliams, L., Gardner, W., & Kelleher, K. J. (2002). Recurrent pain, emotional distress, and health services use in childhood. *Journal of Pediatrics, 141,* 76–83.

Campo, J. V., & Fritz, G. (2001). A management model for pediatric somatization. *Psychosomatics, 42,* 1221–1226.

Cannistraro, P. A., Wright, C. I., Wedig, M. M., Martis, B., Shin, L. M., Wilhelm, S., et al. (2004). Amygdala responses to human faces in obsessive-compulsive disorder. *Biological Psychiatry, 56,* 916–920.

Cannon, M., Caspi, A., Moffitt, T. E., Harrington, H. L., Taylor, A., Murray, R. M., et al. (2002). Evidence for early-childhood pan-developmental impairment specific to schizophreniform disorder: Results from a longitudinal birth cohort. *Archives of General Psychiatry, 59,* 449–457.

Cantwell, D. P. (1997). Introduction to the scientific study of child and adolescent psychopathology: The attention deficit disorder syndrome. *Journal of the American Academy of Child and Adolescent Psychiatry, 36,* 1033–1035.

Capaldi, D. M., Dishion, T. J., Stoolmiller, M., & Yoerger, K. (2001). Aggression towards female partners by at-risk young men: The contribution of male adolescent friendships. *Developmental Psychology, 27,* 489–504.

Capaldi, D. M., & Shortt, J. W. (2003). Understanding conduct problems in adolescence from a lifespan perspective. In G. R. Adams & M. D. Berzonsky (Eds.), *Blackwell handbook of adolescence* (pp. 470–493). Malden, MA: Blackwell Publishing.

Caparrotta, L., & Ghaffari, K. (2006). A historical overview of the psychodynamic contributions to the understanding of eating disorders. *Psychoanalytic Psychotherapy, 20*(3), 175–196.

Caplan, G. (1964). *Principles of preventive psychiatry.* New York: Basic Books.

Caplan, P. J. (1991). How do they decide who is normal? The bizarre, but true, tale of the DSM process. *Canadian Psychology, 32,* 162–170.

Caraceni, A., & Grassi, L. (2003). *Delirium: Acute confusional states in palliative medicine.* New York: Oxford University Press.

Cardemil, E. V., & Battle, C. L. (2003). Guess who's coming to therapy? Getting comfortable with conversations about race and ethnicity in psychotherapy. *Professional Psychology: Research and Practice, 34,* 278–286.

Cardno, A. G., & McGuffin, P. (2006). Genetics and delusional disorder. *Behavioral Sciences and the Law, 24,* 257–276.

Carey, K. B. (1997). Reliability and validity of the Time-Line Follow-Back Interview among psychiatric outpatients: A preliminary report. *Psychology of Addictive Behaviors, 11*, 26–33.

Carlat, D. J., Camargo, C. A., Jr., & Herzog, D. B. (1997). Eating disorders in males: A report on 135 patients. *American Journal of Psychiatry, 154*(8), 1127–1132.

Carlson, C. L., & Mann, M. (2000). Attention deficit hyperactivity disorder, predominately inattentive subtype. *Child and Adolescent Psychiatric Clinics of North America, 9*, 499–510.

Carlson, C. L., Shin, M., & Booth, J. (1999). The case for DSM-IV subtypes in ADHD. *Mental Retardation and Developmental Disabilities Research Reviews, 5*, 199–206.

Carlson, G. A. (2002). Bipolar disorder in children and adolescents: A critical review. In D. Shaffer & B. D. Waslick (Eds.), *The many faces of depression in children and adolescents* (pp. 105–128). Washington, DC: American Psychiatric Publishing.

Carlson, G. A., & Goodwin, F. K. (1973). The stages of mania: A longitudinal analysis of the manic episode. *Archives of General Psychiatry, 28*, 221–228.

Carlson, G. A., & Weisbrot, D. M. (2004). Where are all the fearful children? In M. Maj, H. S. Akiskal, J. J. López-Ibor, & A. Okasha (Eds.), *Phobias* (pp. 285–288). Hoboken, NJ: Wiley.

Carlsson, A. (2001). Neurotransmitters: Dopamine and beyond. In A. Breier & P. V. Tran (Eds.), *Current issues in the psychopharmacology of schizophrenia* (pp. 3–11). Philadelphia: Lippincott, Williams, & Wilkins.

Carney, S. M., & Goodwin, G. M. (2005). Lithium: A continuing story in the treatment of bipolar disorder. *Acta Psychiatrica Scandinavica, 111*, 7–12.

Carpenter, W., Strauss, J., & Bartko, J. (1973). Flexible system for the diagnosis of schizophrenia: Report from the WHO international pilot study of schizophrenia. *Science, 182*, 1275–1277.

Carpenter, W. T., & Conley, R. R. (1999). Sense and nonsense: an essay on schizophrenia research ethics. *Schizophrenia Research, 35*, 219–225.

Carpenter, W. T., Heinrichs, D. W., & Wagman, A. M. (1988). Deficit and non-deficit forms of schizophrenia: The concept. *American Journal of Psychiatry, 145*, 578–583.

Carpenter, W. T., & Strauss, J. (1991). The prediction of outcome in schizophrenia: Pt. IV. Eleven-year follow-up of the Washington IPSS cohort. *Journal of Nervous and Mental Diseases, 179*, 517–525.

Carrns, A. (1999, October 5). Cyberchondriacs get what goes around on the Internet now. *Wall Street Journal,* pp. A1–A6.

Carroll, E. M., & Foy, D. W. (1992). Assessment and treatment of combat-related post-traumatic stress disorder in a medical center setting. In D. W. Foy (Ed.), *Treating PTSD: Cognitive-behavioral strategies* (pp. 39–68). New York: Guilford Press.

Carroll, J. M., Touyz, S. W., & Beumont, P. J. V. (1996). Specific comorbidity between bulimia nervosa and personality disorders. *International Journal of Eating Disorders, 19*(2), 159–170.

Carroll, K. M. (1996). Relapse prevention as a psychosocial treatment: A review of controlled clinical trials. *Experimental and Clinical Psychopharmacology, 4*, 46–54.

Carroll, K. M., Easton, C. J., Nich, C., Hunkele, K. A., Neavins, T. M., Sinha, R., et al. (2006). The use of contingency management and motivational/skills-building therapy to treat young adults with marijuana dependence. *Journal of Consulting and Clinical Psychology, 74*, 955–966.

Carroll, K. M., & Rawson, R. A. (2005). Relapse prevention for stimulant dependence. In G. A. Marlatt & D. M. Donovan (Eds.), *Relapse prevention: Maintenance strategies in the treatment of addictive behaviors* (2nd ed., pp. 130–150). New York: Guilford Press.

Carroll, K. M., Sinha, R., Nich, C., Babuscio, T., & Rounsaville, B. J. (2002). Contingency management to enhance naltrexone treatment of opioid dependence: A randomized clinical trial of reinforcement magnitude. *Experimental and Clinical Psychopharmacology, 10*, 54–63.

Carroll, R. A. (2000). Assessment and treatment of gender dysphoria. In S. R. Leiblum & R. C. Rosen (Eds.), *Principles and practice of sex therapy* (3rd ed., pp. 368–397). New York: Guilford Press.

Carskadon, M., Wolfson, A., Acebo, C., Tzischinsky, O., & Seifer, R. (1998). Adolescent sleep patterns, circadian timing, and sleepiness at a transition to early school days. *Sleep, 21*, 871–881.

Carson, R. C. (1991). Dilemmas in the pathway of the DSM-IV. *Journal of Abnormal Psychology, 100*(3), 302–307.

Carter, A. S., Ornstein Davis, N., Klin, A., & Volkmar, F. R. (2005). Social development in autism. In F. R. Volkmar, R. Paul, A. Klin, & D. Cohen (Eds.), *Handbook of autism and pervasive developmental disorders* (3rd. ed., pp. 312–334). Hoboken, NJ: Wiley.

Carter, A. S., Volkmar, F. R., Sparrow, S. S., Wang, J. J., Lord, C., Dawson, G., et al. (1998). The Vineland Adaptive Behavior Scales: Supplementary norms for individuals with autism. *Journal of Autism and Developmental Disorders, 28*(4), 287–302.

Carter, J. C., Bewell, C., Blackmore, E., & Wodside, D. B. (2006). The impact of childhood sexual abuse in anorexia nervosa. *Child Abuse and Neglect, 20*, 257–269.

Cartwright, D. (2004). Anticipatory interpretations: Addressing "cautionary tales" and the problem of premature termination. *Bulletin of the Menninger Clinic, 682*, 95–114.

Carty, J., O'Donnell, M., & Creamer, M. (2006). Delayed-onset PTSD: A prospective study of injury survivors. *Journal of Affective Disorders, 90*, 257–261.

Carver, L. J., & Dawson, G. (2002). Development and neural bases of facial recognition in autism. *Molecular Psychiatry, 7*, S18–S20.

Casey, P., Birbeck, G., McDoagh, C., Horgan, A., Dowrick, C., Dalgard, O., et al. (2004). Personality disorder, depression and functioning: Results from the ODIN study. *Journal of Affective Disorders, 82*, 277–283.

Cassidy, F., & Carroll, B. J. (2002). Vascular risk factors in late onset mania. *Psychological Medicine, 32*, 359–362.

Cassidy, F., McEvoy, J. P., Yang, Y. K., & Wilson, W. H. (2001). Insight is greater in mixed than in pure manic episodes of bipolar I disorder. *Journal of Nervous and Mental Diseases, 189*, 398–399.

Castle, D. J., Wessely, S., & Murray, R. M. (1993). Sex and schizophrenia: Effects of diagnostic stringency and association with premorbid variables. *British Journal of Psychiatry, 162*, 658–664.

Castonguay, L. G., & Beutler, L. E. (2006). *Principles of therapeutic change that work*. New York: Oxford University Press.

Castro-Fornieles, J., Parellada, M., Gonzalez-Pinto, A., Moreno, D., Graell, M., Baeza, I., et al. (2007). The child and adolescent first-episode psychosis study (CAFEPS): Design and baseline results. *Schizophrenia Research, 91*, 226–237.

Cavanagh, J., Smyth, R., & Goodwin, G. M. (2004). Relapse into mania or depression following lithium discontinuation: A 7-year follow-up. *Acta Psychiatrica Scandinavica, 109*, 91–95.

Centers for Disease Control. (1998). Youth risk behavior surveillance United States, CDC surveillance summaries, August 14, 1998. *Morbidity and Mortality Weekly Report, 47*, No. SS-3.

Centers for Disease Control. (2003). Deaths: Preliminary data for 2001. *National Vital Statistics Reports, 51*. Retrieved January 13, 2005, from www.cdc.gov/nchs/data/nvsr/nvsr51/nvsr51_05.pdf.

Centers for Disease Control. (2005). Acute public health consequences of methamphetamine laboratories: 16 states, January 2000–June 2004. *Morbidity and Mortatlity Weekly Report, 54*, 356–359.

Centers for Disease Control. (2006). Fact sheet: CDC examines autism among children. Retrieved December 27, 2006, from www.cdc.gov/ncbdd/fact/autism1.htm.

Chadwick, P. D. J., & Lowe, C. F. (1990). Measurement and modification of delusional beliefs. *Journal of Consulting and Clinical Psychology, 58*, 225–232.

Chahine, L. M., & Chemali, Z. N. (2006). Restless legs syndrome: A review. *CNS Spectrums, 11*(7), 511–520.

Chaiken, J. M., & Chaiken, M. R. (1990). Drugs and predatory crime. In M. Tonry & J. Q. Wilson (Eds.), *Drugs and crime: Crime and justice, a review of research* (pp. 203–240). Chicago: University of Chicago Press.

Chaimowitz, G. A., & Moscovitch, A. (1991). Patient assaults on psychiatric residents: The Canadian experience. *Canadian Journal of Psychiatry, 36*, 107–117.

Chang, L., Ernst, T., Speck, O., Patel, H., DeSilva, M., Leonido-Yee, M., et al. (2002). Perfusion MRI and computerized cognitive test abnormalities in abstinent methamphetamine users. *Psychiatry Research, 114*, 65–79.

Chaplin, S. (1997). Somatization. In W.-S. Tseng & J. Streltzer (Eds.), *Culture and psychopathology: A guide to clinical assessment* (pp. 67–86). New York: Brunner/Mazel.

Charcot, J. M. (1889). *Lectures on the diseases of the nervous system* (Vol. 3, G. Sigerson, Trans.). London: New Sydenham Society.

Charman, T., & Baird, G. (2002). Practitioner review: Diagnosis of autism spectrum disorder in 2- and 3-year-old children. *Journal of Child Psychology and Psychiatry and Allied Disciplines, 43*(3), 289–305.

Charney, D. S., Nelson, J. C., & Quinlan, D. M. (1981). Personality traits and disorder in depression. *American Journal of Psychiatry, 138*, 1601–1604.

Chatoor, I., Ganiban, J., Colin, V., Plummer, N., & Harmon, R. J. (1998). Attachment and feeding problems: A reexamination of nonorganic failure to thrive and attachment insecurity. *Journal of the American Academy of Child and Adolescent Psychiatry, 37*(11), 1217–1224.

Chavira, D. A., Grilo, C. M., Shea, M. T., Yen, S., Gunderson, J., Morey, L. C. et al. (2003). Ethnicity and four personality disorders. *Comprehensive Psychiatry, 44*(6), 483–491.

Chawarska, K., & Volkmar, F. R. (2005). Autism in infancy and early childhood. In F. R. Volkmar, R. Paul, A. Klin, & D. Cohen (Eds.), *Handbook of autism and pervasive developmental disorders* (3rd ed., pp. 223–246). Hoboken, NJ: Wiley.

Chen, Y. W., & Dilsaver, S. C. (1995). Comorbidity of panic disorder in bipolar illness: Evidence from the epidemiological catchment area survey. *American Journal of Psychiatry, 152*, 280–282.

Cherland, E., & Fitzpatrick, R. (1999). Psychotic side effects of psychostimulants: A 5-year review. *Canadian Journal of Psychiatry, 44*, 811–813.

Chervin, R. D., Dillon, J. E., Bassetti, C., Ganoczy, D. A., & Pituch, K. J. (1997). Symptoms of sleep disorders, inattention and hyperactivity in children. *Sleep, 20*, 1185–1192.

Chess, S. (1960). Diagnosis and treatment of the hyperactive child. *New York State Journal of Medicine, 60*, 2379–2385.

Chessick, R. (2001). Acronyms do not make a disease. *Psychoanalytic Inquiry, 21*(2), 183–208.

Chesson, A. L., Jr., Anderson, W. M., Littner, M., Davila, D., Hartse, K., Johnson, S., et al. (1999). Practice parameters for the non-pharmacologic treatment of chronic insomnia: An American Academy of Sleep Medicine report—Standards of Practice Committee of the American Academy of Sleep Medicine. *Sleep, 22*(8), 1128–1133.

Chesson, A. L., Jr., Ferber, R. A., Fry, J. M., Grigg-Damberger, M., Hartse, K. M., Hurwitz, T. D., et al. (1997). The indications for polysomnography and related procedures. *Sleep, 20*(6), 423–487.

Chesson, A. L., Littner, M., Davila, D., Anderson, W. M., Grigg-Damberger, M., Hartse, K., et al. (2000). Practice parameters for the use of light therapy in the treatment of sleep disorders. *Sleep, 22*(5), 641–660.

Cheyne, G. (1733). *The English malady: Or a treatise of nervous diseases of all kinds, as spleen, vapours, lowness of spirits, hypochondriacal, and hysterical distempers, etc.* London: J. Strachan.

Chi, T. C., & Hinshaw, S. P. (2002). Mother-child relationships of children with ADHD: The role of maternal depressive symptoms and depression-related disorders. *Journal of Abnormal Child Psychology, 30*, 387–400.

Chick, J. (1999). Safety issues concerning the use of disulfiram in treating alcohol dependence. *Drug Safety, 20*, 427–435.

Chiesa, M., Fonagy, P., Holmes, J., Drahorad, C., & Harrison-Hall, A. (2002). Health services use costs by personality disorder following specialist and nonspecialist treatment: A comparative study. *Journal of Personality Disorders, 16*, 160–173.

Chilcott, L. A., & Shapiro, C. M. (1996). The socioeconomic impact of insomnia: An overview. *Pharmacoeconomics, 10*(Suppl. 1), 1–14.

Chioqueta, A. P., & Stiles, T. C. (2003). Suidied risk in outpatients with specific mood and anxiety disorders. *Crisis, 24*, 105–112.

Choca, J. P., & Van Denburg, E. (1997). *Interpretive guide to the Millon Clinical Multiaxial Inventory* (2nd ed.). Washington, DC: American Psychological Association.

Chorpita, B. F., Tracey, S. A., Brown, T. A., Collica, T. J., & Barlow, D. H. (1997). Assessment of worry in children and adolescents: An adaptation of the Penn State Worry Questionnaire. *Behaviour Research and Therapy, 35*, 569–581.

Choy, Y., Fyer, A. J., & Lipsitz, J. D. (2007). Treatment of specific phobia in adults. *Clinical Psychology Review, 27*, 266–286.

Christensen, H., Low, L. F., & Anstey, K. (2006). Prevalence, risk factors and treatment for substance abuse in older adults. *Current Opinion in Psychiatry, 19*, 587–592.

Chronis, A. M., Chacko, A., Fabiano, G. A., Wymbs, B. T., & Pelham, W. E. (2004). Enhancements to the behavioral parent training paradigm for families of children with ADHD: Review and future directions. *Clinical Child and Family Psychology Review, 7*(1), 1–27.

Chuba, H., Paul, R., Miles, S., Klin, A., & Volkmar, F. (2003). *Assessing pragmatic skills in individuals with autism spectrum disorders.* Poster presented at the National Convention of the American Speech-Language-Hearing Association, Chicago.

Chudley, A. E., Guitierrez, E., Jocelyn, L. J., & Chodirker, B. N. (1998). Outcomes of genetic evaluation in children with pervasive developmental disorder. *Developmental and Behavioral Pediatrics, 19*, 321–325.

Chung, R. C. Y., & Singer, M. K. (1995). Interpretation of symptom presentation and distress: A Southeast Asian refugee example. *Journal of Nervous Mental Disease, 183*, 639–648.

Churchill, J. C., Broida, J. P., & Nicholson, N. L. (1990). Locus of control and self-esteem of adult children of alcoholics. *Journal of Studies on Alcohol, 51*, 373–376.

Cimbora, D. M., & McIntosh, D. N. (2003). Emotional responses to antisocial acts in adolescent males with conduct disorder: A link to affective morality. *Journal of Clinical Child and Adolescent Psychology, 32*(2), 296–301.

Ciompi, L. (1980). Catamnestic long-term study on the course of life and aging of schizophrenics. *Schizophrenia Bulletin, 6*, 606–618.

Clapper, R. L., Buka, S. L., & Goldfield, E. C. (1995). Adolescent problem behaviors as predictors of adult alcohol diagnoses. *International Journal of the Addictions, 30*, 507–523.

Clare, L., Wilson, B. A., Carter, G., Hodges, J. R., & Adams, M. (2001). Long-term maintenance of treatment gains following a cognitive rehabilitation intervention in early dementia of Alzheimer type: A single case study. *Neuropsychological Rehabilitation, 11*, 477–494.

Clare, L., Wilson, B. A., Carter, G., Roth, I., & Hodges, R. (2004). Awareness in early-stage Alzheimer's disease: Relationship to outcome of cognitive rehabilitation. *Journal of Clinical and Experimental Neuropsychology, 26*, 215–226.

Clare, L., & Woods, R. T. (2004). Cognitive training and cognitive rehabilitation for people with early-stage Alzheimer's disease: A review. *Neuropsychological Rehabilitation, 14*, 385–401.

Clare, L., Woods, B., Moniz-Cook, E., Orrell, M., & Spector, A. (2003). Cognitive rehabilitation and cognitive training interventions targeting memory functioning in early-stage Alzheimer's disease and vascular dementia. *Cochrane Library,* (Issue 4).

Clark, C. M., & Karlawish, J. H. T. (2003). Alzheimer disease: Current concepts and emerging diagnostic and therapeutic strategies. *Annals of Internal Medicine, 138*, 400–410.

Clark, D. B., DeBellis, M. D., Lynch, K. G., Cornelius, J. R., & Martin, C. S. (2003). Physical and sexual abuse, depression and alcohol use disorders in adolescents: Onsets and outcomes. *Drug and Alcohol Dependence, 69*, 51–60.

Clark, D. C. (1998). The evaluation and management of the suicidal patient. In P. M. Kleepies (Ed.), *Emergencies in mental health practice* (pp. 75–94). New York: Guilford Press.

Clark, D. M. (2001). A cognitive perspective on social phobia. In W. R. Crozier & L. E. Alden (Eds.), *International handbook of social anxiety.* (pp. 405–430). New York: Wiley.

Clark, D. M., & Wells, A. (1995). A cognitive model of social phobia. In R. G. Heimberg, M. Liebowitz, D. Hope, & F. Schneier (Eds.), *Social phobia: Diagnosis, assessment, and treatment* (pp. 69–93). New York: Guilford Press.

Clark, L. A., & Harrison, J. A. (2001). Assessment Instruments. In W. J. Livesley (Ed.), *Handbook of personality disorders* (pp. 277–306). New York: Guilford Press.

Clark, L. A., Watson, D., & Reynolds, S. (1995). Diagnosis and classification of psychopathology: Challenges to the current system and future directions. *Annual Review of Psychology, 46*, 121–153.

Clark, M. J. (1999). Anxiety disorders: Social section. In G. E. Berrios & R. Porter (Eds.), *A history of clinical psychiatric disorders* (pp. 563–572). New Brunswick, NJ: Athlone Press.

Clark, N., Lintzeris, N., Gijsbers, A., Whelan, G., Dunlop, A., Ritter, A., et al. (2002). LAAM maintenance vs. methadone maintenance for heroin dependence. *Cochrane Database of Systematic Reviews,* CD002210.

Clarkin, J. F., Foelsch, P. A., Levy, K. N., Hull, J. W., Delaney, J. C., & Kernberg, O. F. (2001). The development of a psychodynamic treatment for patients with borderline personality disorder: A preliminary study of behavioral change. *Journal of Personality Disorders, 15,* 487–495.

Clayton, A. H. (2001). Assessment of female sexual dysfunction. *Primary Psychiatry, 8*(4), 36–52.

Clayton, A. H. (2003). Sexual function and dysfunction. *Primary Psychiatry, 10*(6), 21–22.

Cleare, A. J. (2004). Biological models and issues in depression. In M. Power (Ed.), *Mood disorders: A handbook of science and practice* (pp. 29–46). Hoboken, NJ: Wiley.

Cleckley, H. (1976). *The mask of sanity* (5th ed.). St Louis, MO: Mosby. (Original work published in 1941)

Cloitre, M., Stovall-McClough, K. C., & Chemtob, C. M. (2004). Therapeutic alliance, negative mood regulation, and treatment outcome in child abuse-related posttraumatic stress disorder. *Journal of Consulting and Clinical Psychology, 72,* 411–416.

Cloninger, C. R. (1993). Somatoform and dissociative disorders. In G. Winokur & P. J. Clayton (Eds.), *Medical basis of psychiatry* (2nd ed., pp. 162–192). Philadelphia: Saunders.

Cloninger, C. R. (2000). A practical way to diagnosis personality disorders: A proposal. *Journal of Personality Disorders, 14,* 99–108.

Cloninger, C. R. (2004). Genetics of substance abuse. In M. Galanter & H. D. Kleber (Eds.), *American Psychiatric Publishing textbook of substance abuse treatment* (3rd ed., pp. 73–79). Washington, DC: American Psychiatric Publishing.

Cloninger, C. R. (2005). Genetics. In J. M. Oldham, A. E. Skodol, & D. S. Bender (Eds.), *Textbook of personality disorders* (pp. 143–154). Washington, DC: American Psychiatric Publishing.

Cloninger, C. R., Bohman, M., & Sigvardsson, S. (1981). Inheritance of alcohol abuse: Cross-fostering analysis of adopted men. *Archives of General Psychiatry, 38,* 861–868.

Cloninger, C. R., Reich, T., & Guze, S. B. (1975). The mutifactorial model of disease transmission III: Familial relationship between sociopathy and hysteria (Briquet's syndrome). *British Journal of Psychiatry, 127,* 23–32.

Cloninger, C. R., & Yutz, S. (1993). Somatoform and dissociative disorders: A summary of changes for DSM-IV. In D. L. Dunner (Ed.), *Current psychiatric therapy* (pp. 310–313). Philadelphia: Saunders.

Coccaro, E. F. (2004). Biological treatment correlates. In J. J. Magnavita (Ed.), *Handbook of personality: Theory and practice* (pp. 124–135). Hoboken, NJ: Wiley.

Coccaro, E. F., & Siever, L. J. (2005). Neurobiology. In J. M. Oldham, A. E. Skodol, & D. S. Bender (Eds.), *Textbook of Personality Disorders* (pp. 155–170). Washington, DC: American Psychiatric Publishing.

Coffin, P. O., Galea, S., Ahern, J., Leon, A. C., Vlahov, P., & Tardiff, K. (2003). Opiates, cocaine and alcohol combinations in accidental drug overdose deaths in New York City, 1990–1998. *Addiction, 98,* 739–747.

Cohen, L. S., Nonacs, R. M., Bailey, J. W., Viguera, A. C., Reminick, A. M., Altshuler, L. L., et al. (2004). Relapse of depression during pregnancy following antidepressant discontinuation: A preliminary prospective study. *Archives of Women's Mental Health, 7,* 217–221.

Cohen, D., Nicolas, J. D., Flament, M. F., Perisse, D., Dubos, P. F., Bonnot, O., et al. (2005). Clinical relevance of chronic catatonic schizophrenia in children and adolescents: Evidence from a prospective naturalistic study. *Schziophrenia Resarch, 76*, 301–308.

Cohen, J. A., & Mannarino, A. P. (2004). Post-traumatic stress disorder. In T. H. Ollendick & J. S. March (Eds.), *Phobic and anxiety disorders in children and adolescents* (pp. 405–432). New York: Oxford University Press.

Cohen, L. M., & Chang, K. (2004). Case report: Comorbid factitious and conversion disorders. *Psychosomatics, 45*(3), 243–246.

Cohen, M. A. (1998). The monetary value of saving a high-risk youth. *Journal of Quantative Criminology, 14*, 5–33.

Cohen, M. B., Baker, G., Cohen, R. A., Fromm-Reichmann, F., & Weigert, E. V. (1954). An intensive study of twelve cases of manic depressive psychosis. *Psychiatry, 17*, 103–137.

Cohen, P., & Crawford, T. (2005). Developmental issues. In J. M. Oldham, A. E. Skodol, & D. S. Bender (Eds.), *Textbook of personality disorders* (pp. 171–186). Washington, DC: American Psychiatric Publishing.

Cohen, P., Chen, H., Crawford, T. N., Brook, J. S., & Gordon, K. (2007). Personality disorders in early adolescence and the development of later substance use disorders in the general population. *Drug Alcohol Dependence.* Vol. 88, pgs. S71–S84.

Cohen, S. (1998). *Targeting autism.* Berkeley: University of California Press.

Cohen, S. (2002). Psychosocial stress, social networks, and susceptibility to infection. In H. G. Koenig & H. J. Cohen (Eds.), *The link between religion and health: Psychoneuroimmunology and the faith factor* (pp. 101–123). New York: Oxford University Press.

Cohen-Mansfield, J. (2003). Nonpharmacologic interventions for psychotic symptoms in dementia. *Journal of Geriatric Psychiatry and Neurology, 16*, 219–224.

Cohn, J. E., Campbell, S. B., Matias, R., & Hopkins, J. (1990). Face-to-face interactions of postpartum depressed and nondepressed mother-infant pairs at two months. *Developmental Psychology, 26*, 15–23.

Coid, J. (2005). Correctional populations: Criminal careers and recidivism. In J. M. Oldham, A. E. Skodol, & D. S. Bender (Eds.), *Textbook of personality disorders* (pp. 579–606). Washington, DC: American Psychiatric Publishing.

Cole, M. G., McCusker, J., Dendukuri, N., & Han, L. (2002). Symptoms of delirium in elderly medical inpatients with and without dementia. *Journal of Neuropsychiatry and Clinical Neurosciences, 14*, 167–175.

Coleman, D., & Baker, F. M. (1994). Misdiagnosis of schizophrenia in older, Black veterans. *Journal of Nervous and Mental Diseases, 182*, 527–528.

Coleman, H. L. K., Wampold, B. E., & Casali, S. L. (1995). Ethnic minorities' ratings of ethnically similar and European American counselors: A meta-analysis. *Journal of Counseling Psychology, 42*, 55–64.

Coles, M. E., & Horng, B. (2006). Social anxiety disorder. In M. Hersen & J. C. Thomas (Eds.), *Andrasik comprehensive handbook of personality and psychopathology: Adult psychopathology* (Vol. 2, pp. 138–153). Hoboken, NJ: Wiley.

Collier, D. A. (2002). Molecular genetics of eating disorders. In C. G. Fairburn & K. D. Brownell (Eds.), *Eating disorders and obesity: A comprehensive handbook* (2nd ed., pp. 243–246). New York: Guilford Press.

Colligan, R. C., Morey, L. C., & Offord, K. P. (1994). MMPI/MMPI-2 Personality Disorder Scales: Contemporary norms for adults and adolescents. *Journal of Clinical Psychology, 50*, 168–200.

Collins, E. D., & Kleber, H. D. (2004). Opioids: Detoxification. In M. Galanter & H. D. Kleber (Eds.), *Textbook of substance abuse treatment* (pp. 265–289). Washington, DC: American Psychiatric Press.

Commission on Adolescent Eating Disorders. (2005). Defining eating disorders. In D. L. Evans, E. B. Foa, R. E. Gur, H. Hendin, C. P. O'Brien, M. E. P. Seligman, et al. (Eds.), *Treating and preventing adolescent mental health disorders: What we know and what we don't know: A research agenda for improving the mental health of our youth* (pp. 257–281). New York: Oxford University Press.

Compas, B. E., & Boyer, M. C. (2001). Coping and attention for children's health and pediatric conditions. *Journal of Developmental and Behavioral Pediatrics, 22,* 1–11.

Compas, B. E., & Gotlib, I. H. (2002). *Introduction to clinical psychology: Science and practice.* Boston, MA: McGraw-Hill.

Conduct Problems Prevention Research Group. (1992). A developmental and clinical model for the prevention of conduct disorder: The FAST Track program. *Development and Psychopathology, 4,* 509–527.

Conduct Problems Prevention Research Group. (1999a). Initial impact of the FAST Track prevention trial for conduct problems: Pt. I. The high-risk sample. *Journal of Consulting and Clinical Psychology, 67,* 631–647.

Conduct Problems Prevention Research Group. (1999b). Initial impact of the FAST Track prevention trial for conduct problems: Pt. II. Classroom effects. *Journal of Consulting and Clinical Psychology, 67,* 648–657.

Connor, D. F. (2004). *Aggression and antisocial behavior in children and adolescents: Research and training.* New York: Guilford Press.

Connor, D. F., Glatt, S. J., Lopez, I. D., Jackson, D., & Melloni, R. H. J., Jr. (2002). Psychopharmacology and aggression: Pt. I. A meta-analysis of stimulant effects on overt/covert aggression-related behaviors in ADHD. *Journal of the American Academy of Child and Adolescent Psychiatry, 41,* 253–261.

Constantino, M. J., Castonguay, L. G., & Schut, A. J. (2002). The working alliance: A flagship for the "scientist-practitioner" model in psychotherapy. In G. Tryon (Ed.), *Counseling based on process research* (pp. 81–131). New York: Allyn & Bacon.

Conus, P., Abdel-Baki, A., Harrigan, A., Lambert, M., & McGorry, P. D. (2004). Schneiderian first rank symptoms predict poor outcome within first episode manic psychosis. *Journal of Affective Disorders, 81,* 259–268.

Conway, K. P., Compton, W., Stinson, F. S., & Grant, B. F. (2006). Lifetime comorbidity of DSM-I mood and anxiety disorders and specific drug use disorders: Results from the National Epidemiological Survey on Alcohol and Related Conditions. *Journal of Clinical Psychiatry, 67,* 247–257.

Cook, E. H. (2001). Genetics of autism. *Child and Adolescent Psychiatric Clinics of North America, 10,* 333–350.

Cook, J. A., & Razzano, L. A. (1995). Discriminant function analysis of competitive employment outcomes in a transitional employment program. *Journal of Vocational Rehabilitation, 5,* 127–139.

Cook, J. A., & Razzano, L. A. (2000). Vocational rehabilitation for persons with schizophrenia: Recent research and implications for practice. *Schizophrenia Bulletin, 26,* 87–103.

Cooke, D. J. (1996). Psychopathic personality in different cultures: What do we know? What do we need to find out? *Journal of Personality Disorders, 10,* 23–40.

Coolidge, F. L., & Merwin, M. M. (1992). Reliability and validity of the Coolidge Axis II Inventory: A new inventory for the assessment of personality disorders. *Journal of Personality Assessment, 59,* 223–238.

Coolidge, F. L., Segal, D. L., Pointer, J. C., Knaus, E. A., Yamazaki, T. G., & Silberman, C. S. (2000). Personality disorders in older adult inpatients with chronic mental illness. *Journal of Clinical Geropsychology, 6*(1), 63–72.

Coombs, R. H., & Howatt, W. A. (2005). *The addiction counselor's desk reference.* Hoboken, NJ: Wiley.

Coon, D. W., Rubert, M., Soano, N., Mausbach, B., Kraemer, H., Arguelles, T., et al. (2004). Well-being, appraisal, and coping in Latina and Caucasian female dementia caregivers: Findings from the REACH study. *Aging and Mental Health, 8,* 335–345.

Coonrod, E. C., & Stone, W. L. (2005). Screening for autism in young children. In F. R. Volkmar, R. Paul, A. Klin, & D. Cohen (Eds.), *Handbook of autism and pervasive developmental disorders* (3rd ed., pp. 707–729). Hoboken, NJ: Wiley.

Cooper, A. J. (1969). "Sex drive" and male potency disorders. *Psychosomatics, 10*(4), 230–235.

Cooper, J. E., Kendell, R. E., Gurland, B. J., Sharpe, L., Copeland, J. R. M., & Simon, R. (1972). *Psychiatric diagnosis in New York and London. Maudsley Monograph (No. 20)*. London: Oxford University Press.

Cooper, J. M., Shanks, M. F., & Venneri, A. (2006). Provoked confabulations in Alzheimer's disease. *Neuropsychologia, 44*, 1697–1707.

Cooper, P. J., Coker, S., & Fleming, C. (1994). Self-help for bulimia nervosa: A preliminary report. *International Journal of Eating Disorders, 16*(4), 401–404.

Cooper, P. J., Murray, L., Wilson, A., & Romaniuk, H. (2003a). Controlled trial of short- and long-term effect of psychological treatment of post-partum depression: Pt. 1. Impact on maternal mood. *British Journal of Psychiatry, 182*, 412–419.

Copenhaver, M. M., Johnson, B. T., Lee, I. C., Harman, J. J., Carey, M. P., & Research SHARP Team. (2006). Behavioral HIV risk reduction among people who inject drugs: Meta-analytic evidence of efficacy. *Journal of Substance Abuse Treatment, 31*, 163–171.

Corey, M. S., & Corey, G. (2002). *Groups: Process and practice* (6th ed.). New York: Brooks/Cole.

Cornblatt, B. A., Green, M. F., & Walker, E. F. (1999). Schizophrenia: Etiology and neurocognition. In T. Millon, P. H. Blaney, & R. D. Davis (Eds.), *Oxford textbook of psychopathology* (pp. 277–310). New York: Oxford University Press.

Cornelius, J. R., Salloum, I. M., Mezzich, J., Cornelius, M. D., Fabrega, H., Ehler, J. G., et al. (1995). Disproportionate suicidality in patients with comorbid major depression and alcoholism. *American Journal of Psychiatry, 152*, 358–364.

Corning, A., & Malofeeva, E. (2004). The application of survival analysis to the study of psychotherapy termination. *Journal of Counseling Psychology, 51*(3), 354–367.

Cororve, M. B., & Gleaves, D. H. (2001). Body dysmorphic disorder: A review of conceptualizations, assessment, and treatment strategies. *Clinical Psychology Review, 21*(6), 949–970.

Coryell, W. (2005). Rapid cycling bipolar disorder: Clinical characteristics and treatment options. *CNS Drugs, 19*, 557–569.

Coryell, W., Keller, M., Endicott, J., Andreason, N., Clayton, P., & Hirschfeld, R. (1989). Bipolar II illness: Course and outcome over a 5-year period. *Psychological Medicine, 19*, 129–141.

Coryell, W., Leon, A., Winokur, G., Endicott, J., Keller, M., Akiskal, H., et al. (1996). Importance of psychotic features to long-term course in major depressive disorder. *American Journal of Psychiatry, 153*, 483–48.

Coryell, W., Noyes, R., & House, J. D. (1986). Mortality among outpatients with anxiety disorders. *American Journal of Psychiatry, 143*, 508–510.

Coryell, W., Solomon, D., Tuvey, C., Keller, M., Leon, A., Endicott, J., et al. (2003). The long-term course of rapid cycling bipolar disorder. *Archives of General Psychiatry, 60*, 914–920.

Cosgrove, J., & Newell, T. G. (1991). Recovery of neuropsychological functions during reduction in use of phencyclidine. *Journal of Clinical Psychology, 47*, 159–169.

Costello, E. J., & Angold, A. (2000). Bad behavior: An historical perspective on disorders of conduct. In J. Hill & B. Maughan (Eds.), *Conduct disorders in childhood and adolescence* (pp. 1–31). New York: Cambridge University Press.

Costello, J., Mustillo, S., Erkanli, A., Keeler, G., & Angold, A. (2003). Prevalence and development of psychiatric disorders in childhood and adolescence. *Archives of General Psychiatry, 60*, 837–844.

Costello, R. M. (2006). Long-term mortality from alcoholism: A descriptive analysis. *Journal of Studies on Alcohol, 67*, 694–699.

Cote, T. R., Biggar, R. J., & Dannenberg, A. L. (1992). Risk of suicide among persons with AIDS: A national assessment. *Journal of the American Medical Association, 268*, 2066–2068.

Cottler, L. B., Compton, W. M., Ridenour, T. A., Ben Abdallah, A., & Gallagher, T. (1998). Reliability with self-reported antisocial personality symptoms among substance users. *Drug and Alcohol Dependence, 49*, 189–199.

Cottraux, J., & Blackburn, I. M. (2001). Cognitive therapy. In W. J. Livesley (Ed.), *Handbook of personality disorders: Theory, research and treatment* (pp. 377–399). New York: Guilford Press.

Courchesne, E., Carper, R., & Akshoomoff, N. (2003). Evidence of brain overgrowth in the first year of life in autism. *Journal of the American Medical Association, 290*, 337–344.

Courchesne, E., Karns, C. M., Davis, H. R., Zicardi, R., Carper, R. A., Tigue, Z. D., et al. (2001). Unusual brain growth patterns in early life in patients with autistic disorder. *Neurology, 57*, 245–254.

Coursey, R. D., Keller, A. B., & Farrell, E. W. (1995). Individual psychotherapy and persons with serious mental illness: The client's perspective. *Schizophrenia Bulletin, 21*, 283–301.

Coverdale, J., Gale, C., Weeks, S., & Turbott, S. (2001). A survey of threats and violent acts by patients against training physicians. *Medical Education, 35*, 154–160.

Covington, E. C. (2000). Psychogenic pain: What it means, why it does not exist and how to diagnose it. *Pain Medicine, 1*(4), 287–294.

Covinsky, K. E., Newcomer, R., Fox, P., Wood, J., Sands, L., Dane, K., et al. (2003). Patient and caregiver characteristics associated with depression in caregivers of patients with dementia. *Journal of General Internal Medicine, 18*, 1006–1014.

Cowles, E. L., Castellano, T. C., & Gransky, L. A. (1995). *"Boot camp" drug treatment and aftercare interventions: An evaluation review.* (NCJ 155062). Washington, DC: U.S. Department of Justice, National Institute of Justice.

Cox, A., Holbrook, D., & Rutter, M. (1981). Psychiatric interviewing techniques: Pt. VI. Experimental study: Eliciting feelings. *British Journal of Psychiatry, 139*, 144–152.

Cox, A., Hopkinson, K., & Rutter, M. (1981). Psychiatric interviewing techniques: Pt. II. Naturalistic study: Eliciting factual information. *British Journal of Psychiatry, 138*, 283–291.

Cox, A., Klein, K., Charman, T., Baird, G., Baron-Cohen, S., Swetenham, J., et al. (1999). Autism spectrum disorders at 20 and 42 months of age: Stability of clinical and ADI-R diagnosis. *Journal of Child Psychology and Psychiatry, 40*, 719–732.

Cox, A., Rutter, M., & Holbrook, D. (1981). Psychiatric interviewing techniques: Pt. V. Eliciting factual information. *British Journal of Psychiatry, 139*, 29–37.

Cox, B. J., Norton, G. R., & Swinson, R. P. (1992). *Panic Attack Questionnaire—Revised.* Toronto: Clarke Institute of Psychiatry.

Cox, C. (1997). Findings from a statewide program of respite care: A comparison of service users, stoppers, and nonusers. *Gerontologist, 37*, 511–517.

Cox, C. J., Endler, N. S., Lee, P. S., & Swinson, R. P. (1992). A meta-analysis of treatments for panic disorder with agoraphobia: Imipramine, alprazolam, and in vivo exposure. *Journal of Behavior Therapy and Experimental Psychiatry, 23*, 175–182.

Coyne, J. C., Thompson, R., & Palmer, S. C. (2002). Marital quality, coping with conflict, marital complaints, and affection in couples with a depressed wife. *Journal of Family Psychology, 16*, 26–37.

Cozolino, L. (2006). *The neuroscience of human relationships: Attachment and the developing social brain.* New York: Norton.

Crago, M., Shisslak, C. M., & Estes, L. S. (1996). Eating disturbances among American minority groups: A review. *International Journal of Eating Disorders, 19*(3), 239–248.

Craighead, W. E., Hart, A. B., Craighead, L. W., & Ilardi, S. S. (2002). Psychosocial treatments of major depressive disorder. In P. E. Nathan & J. M. Gorman (Eds.), *A guide to treatments that work* (2nd ed., pp. 245–261). New York: Oxford University Press.

Craney, J. L., & Geller, B. (2003). A prepubertal and early adolescent bipolar disorder I phenotype: Review of phenomenology and longitudinal course. *Bipolar Disorders, 4*, 243–256.

Craske, M. G., Barlow, D. H., & Meadows, E. A. (2000). *Mastery of your anxiety and panic* (3rd ed.). San Antonio, TX: Graywind/Psychological Corporation.

Craske, M. G., Brown, T. A., & Barlow, D. H. (1991). Behavioral treatment of panic disorder: A 2-year follow-up. *Behavior Therapy, 22*, 289–304.

Craske, M. G., & Rachman, S. (1987). Return of fear: Perceived skill and heart-rate responsivity. *British Journal of Clinical Psychology, 26*, 187–199.

Craske, M. G., Rapee, R. M., Jackel, L., & Barlow, D. H. (1989). Qualitative dimensions of worry in DSM-III-R generalized anxiety disorder subjects and nonanxious controls. *Behaviour Research and Therapy, 27,* 397–402.

Creed, F. (1985). Life events and physical illness. *Journal of Psychosomatic Research, 29,* 113–123.

Cretzmeyer, M., Sarrazin, M. V., Huber, D. L., Block, R. I., & Hall, J. A. (2003). Treatment of methamphetamine abuse: Research findings and clinical directions. *Journal of Substance Abuse Treatment, 24,* 267–277.

Crisp, A. H. (1997). Anorexia nervosa as flight from growth: Assessment and treatment based on the model. In D. M. Garner & P. E. Garfinkel (Eds.), *Handbook of treatment for eating disorders* (2nd ed., pp. 248–277). New York: Guilford Press.

Crits-Christoph, P., & Barber, J. P. (2004). Empirical research on the treatment of personality disorders. In J. J. Magnavita (Ed.), *Handbook of Personality: Theory and practice* (pp. 513–527). New York: Wiley.

Croen, L., Grether, J. K., Hoogstrate, J., & Selvin, S. (2002a). The changing prevalence of autism in California. *Journal of Autism and Developmental Disorders, 32*(3), 207–215.

Croen, L., Grether, J. K., Hoogstrate, J., & Selvin, S. (2002b). Descriptive epidemiology of autism in a California population: Who is at risk? *Journal of Autism and Developmental Disorders, 32*(3), 217–224.

Cromer, R. J. (1995). *Abnormal psychology* (2nd ed.). New York: Freeman.

Crow, S. J., Agras, W. S., & Halmi, K. (2002). Full syndromal versus subthreshold anorexia nervosa, bulimia nervosa, and binge eating disorder: A multicenter study. *International Journal of Eating Disorders, 32*(3), 309–318.

Crowley, T. J., & Sakai, J. T. (2004). Inhalants. In M. Galanter & H. D. Kleber (Eds.), *The American Psychiatric Publishing textbook of substance abuse treatment* (3rd ed., pp. 247–255). Washington, DC: American Psychiatric Publishing.

Cubic, B., & Bluestein, D. (2004). Eating disorders. In L. J. Haas (Ed.), *Handbook of primary care psychology* (pp. 329–343). New York: Oxford University Press.

Cuffe, S. P., McCullough, E. L., & Pumariega, A. J. (1994). Comorbidity of attention-deficit/hyperactivity disorder and posttraumatic stress disorder. *Journal of Child and Family Studies, 3,* 327–336.

Cuffe, S. P., McKeown, R. E., Jackson, K. L., Addy, C. L., Abramson, R., & Garrison, C. Z. (2001). Prevalence of attention-deficit/hyperactivity disorder in a community sample of older adolescents. *Journal of the American Academy of Child and Adolescent Psychiatry, 40,* 1037–1044.

Cuffel, B. J. (1996). Co-morbid substance use disorders: Prevalence, patterns of use, and course. In R. E. Drake & K. T. Mueser (Eds.), *Dual diagnosis of major mental illness and substance disorder: Recent research and clinical implications* (pp. 93–105). San Francisco: Jossey-Bass.

Cullen, W. (1827). *The works of William Cullen* (Vols. 1–2, J. Thompson, Ed.), London: William Blackwood & Sons.

Cully, J. A., Molinari, V. A., Snow, A. L., Buruss, J., Kotrla, K. J., Kunik, M. E., et al. (2005). Utilization of emergency center services by older adults with a psychiatric diagnosis. *Aging and Mental Health, 9,* 172–176.

Cunningham, C. E., Bremner, R., & Secord, M. (1997). *COPE: The Community Parent Education Program: A school-based family systems oriented workshop for parents of children with disruptive behavior disorders.* Hamilton, Ontario, Canada: COPE Works.

Cunningham, P. B., & Henggeler, S. W. (2001). Healthy children through healthy schools: Implementing empirically-based drug and violence prevention and intervention programs in public school settings. *Journal of Clinical Child Psychology, 30,* 221–232.

Cummings, J. D. (1944). The incidence of emotional symptoms in school children. *British Journal of Educational Psychology, 14,* 151–161.

Cummings, J. L. (2003). *The neuropsychiatry of Alzheimer's disease and related dementias.* London: Martin Dunitz.

Cummings, J. L., & Benson, D. F. (1992). *Dementia: A clinical approach.* Boston: Butterworth-Heinemann.

Curran, G. M., Flynn, H. A., Kirchner, J., & Booth, B. M. (2000). Depression after alcohol treatment as a risk factor for relapse among male veterans. *Journal of Substance Abuse Treatment, 19*, 259–265.

Curtis, G. C., Magee, W. J., Eaton, W. W., Wittchen, H.-U., & Kessler, R. C. (1998). Specific fears and phobias: Epidemiology and classification. *British Journal of Psychiatry, 173*, 212–217.

Cusack, K., & Spates, C. R. (1999). The cognitive dismantling of eye movement desensitization and reprocessing (EMDR) treatment of posttraumatic stress disorder (PTSD). *Journal of Anxiety Disorders, 13*, 87–99.

Cyranowski, J. M., Frank, E., Winter, E., Rucci, P., Nocak, D., Pilkonis, P., et al. (2004). Personality pathology and outcome in recurrently depressed women over 2 years of maintenance interpersonal psychotherapy. *Psychological Medicine, 34*, 659–669.

Czajkowski, L. A., Casey, K. R., & Jones, C. R. (2004). Sleep disorders. In L. J. Haas (Ed.), *Handbook of primary care psychology* (pp. 511–526). New York: Oxford University Press.

Dackis, C. A., & O'Brien, C. P. (2003). Neurobiology of cocaine dependence limits development of pharmacologic treatment. *Psychiatric Annals, 33*, 565–570.

Dahlsgaard, K. K., Beck, A. T., & Brown, G. K. (1998). Inadequate response to therapy as a predictor of suicide. *Suicide and Life Threatening Behavior, 28*, 197–204.

Dales, L., Hammer, S., & Smith, N. N. (2001). Trends in autism and MMR immunization coverage in California. *Journal of the American Medical Association, 285*(9), 1183–1185.

Daley, S. E., Burge, D., & Hammen, C. (2000). Borderline personality disorder symptoms as predictors of 4-year romantic relationship dysfunction in young women: Addressing issues of specificity. *Journal of Abnormal Psychology, 109*, 451–460.

D'Amico, E. J., Ellickson, P. L., Collins, R. L., Martino, S., & Klein, D. J. (2005). Processes linking adolescent problems to substance-use problems in late young adulthood. *Journal of Studies on Alcohol, 66*, 766–775.

D'Amico, E. J., Ellickson, P. L., Wagner, E. F., Turrisi, R., Fromme, K., Ghosh-Dastidar, B., et al. (2005). Developmental considerations for substance use interventions from middle school through college. *Alcoholism: Clinical and Experimental Research, 29*, 474–483.

D'Amico, E. J., & McCarthy, D. M. (2006). Escalation and initiation of younger adolescents' substance use: The impact of perceived peer use. *Journal of Adolescent Health, 39*, 481–487.

Damon, L. L., Card, J. A., & Todd, J. (1992). Incest in young children. In R. T. Ammerman & M. Hersen (Eds.), *Assessment of family violence: A clinical and legal sourcebook* (pp. 148–207). New York: Wiley.

Dana, R. (1993). *Multicultural assessment perspectives for professional psychology.* Boston: Allyn & Bacon.

Dansky, B. S., Brewerton, T. D., Kilpatrick, D. G., & O'Neil, P. M. (1997). The National Women's Study: Relationship of victimization and posttraumatic stress disorder to bulimia nervosa. *International Journal of Eating Disorders, 21*(3), 213–228.

Dassori, A. M., Miller, A. L., Velligan, D., Saldana, S., Diamond, P., & Mahurin, R. (1998). Ethnicity and negative symptoms in patients with schizophrenia. *Cultural Diversity and Mental Health, 4*, 65–69.

D'Avanzo, D., Dunn, P., Murdock, J., & Naegle, M. (2000). Developing culturally informed strategies for substance-related interventions. In M. Naegle & D. D'Avanzo (Eds.), *Addictions and substance abuse: Strategies for advanced practice nursing* (pp. 59–104). Upper Saddle River, NJ: Prentice-Hall.

Davey, G. C., Forster, L., & Mayhew, G. (1993). Familial resemblances in disgust sensitivity and animal phobias. *Behaviour Research and Therapy, 31*, 41–50.

Davey, G. C. L. (1992). Some characteristics of individuals with fear of spiders. *Anxiety Research, 4*, 299–314.

Davey, G. C. L. (2004). Psychopathology of specific phobias. *Psychiatry, 3*, 83–86.

David, A. S. (1990). Insight and psychosis. *British Journal of Psychiatry, 156*, 798–808.

Davidovitch, M., Glick, L., Holtzman, G., Tirosh, E., & Safir, M. P. (2000). Developmental regression in autism: Maternal perception. *Journal of Autism and Developmental Disorders, 30*, 113–119.

Davidson, C., Gow, A. J., Lee, T. H., & Ellinwood, E. H. (2001). Methamphetamine neurotoxicity: Necrotic and apoptotic mechanisms and relevance to human abuse and treatment. *Brain Research Reviews, 36*, 1–22.

Davidson, J. R. (2004). Use of benzodiazepines in social anxiety disorder, GAD, and posttraumatic stress disorder. *Journal of Clinical Psychiatry, 65*(Suppl. 5), 29–33.

Davidson, J. R., Bose, A., Korotzer, A., & Zheng, H. (2004). Escitalopram in the treatment of generalized anxiety disorder: Double-blind, placebo controlled, flexible-dose study. *Depression and Anxiety, 19*, 234–240.

Davidson, J. R., Bose, A., & Wang, Q. (2005). Safety and efficacy of escitalopram in the long-term treatment of generalized anxiety disorder. *Journal of Clinical Psychiatry, 66*, 1441–1446.

Davidson, J. R. T. (2006). Social phobia: Then, now, the future. In B. O. Rothbaum (Ed.), *Pathological anxiety: Emotional processing in etiology and treatment* (pp. 115–131). New York: Guilford Press.

Davidson, J. R. T., Potts, N. L. S., Richichi, E. A., Ford, S. M., Krishnan, R. R., Smith, R., et al. (1993). Treatment of social phobia with clonazepam and placebo. *Journal of Clinical Psychopharmacology, 13*, 423–428.

Davidson, P. R., & Parker, K. C. H. (2001). Eye movement desensitization and reprocessing (EMDR): A meta-analysis. *Journal of Consulting and Clinical Psychology, 69*, 305–316.

Davidson, R. J., Putnam, K. M., & Larson, C. L. (2000). Dysfunction in the neural circuitry of emotion regulation: A possible prelude to violence. *Science, 289*, 591–594.

Davies, D. (1999). *Child development: A practitioner's guide*. New York: Guilford Press.

Davies, D. (2004). *Child development: A practitioner's guide*. New York: Guilford Press.

Davies, S. J., Pandit, S. A., Feeney, A., Stevenson, B. J., Kerwin, R. W., Nutt, D. J., et al. (2005). Is there cognitive impairment in clinically "healthy" abstinent alcohol dependence? *Alcohol and Alcoholism, 40*, 498–503.

Davis, J. M., Janicak, P. G., & Hogan, D. M. (1999). Mood stabilizers in the prevention of recurrent affective disorders: A meta-analysis. *Acta Psychiatrica Scandinavica, 100*, 406–417.

Davis, L. L., Frazer, E., Husain, M., Warden, D., Trivedi, M., Fava, M., et al. (2006). Substance use disorder comorbidity in major depressive disorder: A confirmatory analysis of the STAR*D cohort. *American Journal on Addictions, 15*, 178–185.

Davis, L. L., Rush, J. A., Wisniewski, S. R., Rice, K., Cassano, P., Jewell, M. E., et al. (2005). Substance use disorder comorbidity in major depressive disorder: An exploratory analysis of the sequenced treatment alternatives to relieve depression cohort. *Comprehensive Psychiatry, 46*, 81–89.

Davis, P. E., Liddiard, H., & McMillan, T. M. (2002). Neuropsychological deficits and opiate abuse. *Drug and Alcohol Dependence, 67*, 105–108.

Dawson, D. D., Grant, B. F., Stinson, F. S., Chou, P. S., Huang, B., & Ruan, W. J. (2005). Recovery from DSM-IV alcohol dependence: United States, 2001–2002. *Addiction, 100*, 281–292.

Dawson, G., Meltzoff, A. N., Osterling, J., Rinaldi, J., & Brown, E. (1998). Children with autism fail to orientate to naturally occurring social stimuli. *Journal of Autism and Developmental Disabilities, 28*, 479–485.

Dawson, G., & Osterling, J. (1997). Early intervention in autism: Effectiveness and common elements of current approaches. In M. J. Guralnick (Ed.), *The effectiveness of early intervention: Second generation research* (pp. 307–326). Baltimore: Paul H. Brookes.

Dearing, R. L., Stuewig, J., & Tangney, J. (2005). On the importance of distinguishing shame from guilt: Relations to problematic alcohol and drug use. *Addictive Behaviors, 30*, 1392–1404.

DeBettignies, B. H., Swihart, A. A., Green, L. A., & Pirozzolo, F. J. (1997). The neuropsychology of normal aging and dementia: An introduction. In A. M. Horton, D. Wedding, & J. Webster (Eds.), *Neuropsychology handbook: Vol. 2. Treatment issues and special populations* (pp. 173–210). New York: Springer.

Debnath, M., Das, S., Bera, N., Nayak, C. R., & Tapas, C. (2006). Genetic associations between delusional disorder and paranoid schizophrenia: A novel etiologic approach. *Canadian Journal of Psychiatry, 51*, 342–349.

De Giacomo, A., & Frombonne, E. (1998). Parental recognition of developmental abnormalities in autism. *European Child and Adolescent Psychiatry, 7*(3), 131–136.

De Girolamo, G., & Dotto, P. (2000). Epidemiology of personality disorders. In M. G. Gelder, J. J. Lopez-Ibor, & N. C. Andreasen (Eds.), *New Oxford textbook of psychiatry* (pp. 959–964). New York: Oxford University Press.

De Gucht, V., & Fischler, B. (2002). Somatization: A critical review of conceptual and methodological issues. *Psychosomatics, 43,* 1–9.

DeHert, M., McKenzie, K., & Peuskens, J. (2001). Risk factors for suicide in young people suffering from schizophrenia: A long-term follow-up study. *Schizophrenia Research, 47,* 127–134.

Delahanty, J., Ram, R., Postrado, L., Balis, T., Green-Paden, L., & Dixon, L. (2001). Differences in rates of depression in schizophrenia by race. *Schizophrenia Bulletin, 27,* 29–38.

DelBello, M. P., Lopez-Larson, M. P., Soutullo, C. A., & Strakowski, S. M. (2001). Effects of race on psychiatric diagnosis of hospitalized adolescents: A retrospective chart review. *Journal of Child and Adolescent Psychopharmacology, 11,* 95–103.

Delligatti, N., Akin-Little, A., & Little, S. (2003). Conduct disorder in girls: Diagnostic and intervention issues. *Psychology in the Schools, 40*(2), 183–192.

De Los Reyes, A., & Kazdin, A. E. (2005). Informant discrepancies in the assessment of childhood psychopathology: A critical review, theoretical framework, and recommendations for further study. *Psychological Bulletin, 131,* 483–509.

Deltito, J., Martin, L., Riefkohl, J., Austria, B., Kissilenko, A., & Corless, C. M. P. (2001). Do patients with borderline personality disorder belong to the bipolar spectrum? *Journal of Affective Disorders, 67,* 221–228.

DeMyer, M. K., Pontius, W., Norton, J. A., Barton, S., Allen, J., & Steele, R. (1972). Parental practices and innate activity in normal, autistic, and brain-damaged infants. *Journal of Autism and Childhood Schizophrenia, 2,* 49–66.

Dengiz, A. N., & Kershaw, P. (2004). The clinical efficacy and safety of galantamine in the treatment of Alzheimer's disease. *CNS Spectrums, 9,* 377–92.

DeOliveira, I. R., & Juruena, M. F. (2006). Treatment of psychosis: 30 years of progress. *Journal of Clinical Pharmacy and Therapeutics, 31,* 523–534.

Depp, C. A., & Jeste, D. V. (2004). Bipolar disorder in adults: A critical review. *Bipolar Disorders, 6,* 343–367.

Depp, C. A., Jin, H., Mohamed, S., Kaskow, J., Moore, D. J., & Jeste, D. V. (2004). Bipolar disorder in middle-aged and elderly adults: Is age of onset important? *Journal of Nervous and Mental Diseases, 192,* 796–799.

Depue, R. A., & Lenzenweger, M. F. (2005). A neurobehavioral dimensional model of personality disorders. In J. F. Clarkin & M. F. Lenzenweger (Eds.), *Major theories of personality disorders* (2nd ed., pp. 391–453). New York: Guilford Press.

de Renzi, E. (2000). The amnesic syndrome. In G. E. Berrios (Ed.), *Memory disorders in psychiatric practice* (pp. 164–186). New York: Cambridge University Press.

Derogatis, L. R. (1983). The SCL-90: Administration scoring and procedures for the SCL-90. Baltimore: Clinical Psychometric Research.

de Toledo-Morrell, L., Goncharova, I., Dickerson, B., Wilson, R. S., & Bennett, D. A. (2000). From healthy aging to early Alzheimer's disease: In vivo detection of entorhinal cortex atrophy. In H. E. Sharfman, M. F. Witter, & R. Schwartz (Eds.), *The parahippocampal region: Implications for neurological and psychiatric diseases* (Annals of the New York Academy of Sciences, Vol. 911, pp. 240–253). New York: New York Academy of Sciences.

Deutsch, C. (1982). *Broken bottles and dreams: Understanding and helping the children of alcoholics.* New York: Teachers College Press.

Devlin, M. J., Jahraus, J. P., & Dobrow, I. (2005). Eating disorders. In J. Levenson (Ed.), *American Psychiatric Publishing textbook of psychosomatic medicine* (pp. 311–334). Washington, DC: American Psychiatric Publishing.

De Vreese, L. P., Neri, M., Fioravanti, M., Belloi, L., & Zanetti, O. (2001). Memory rehabilitation in Alzheimer's disease: A review of progress. *International Journal of Geriatric Psychiatry, 16,* 794–809.

Dew, M. A., & Bromet, E. J. (1991). Effects of depression on support in a community sample of women. In J. Eckenrode (Ed.), *The social context of coping* (pp. 189–219). New York: Plenum Press.

Dew, M. A., Reynolds, C. F., Houck, P. R., Hall, M., Buysse, D. J., Frank, E., et al. (1997). Temporal profiles of the course of depression during treatment: Predictors of pathways toward recovery in the elderly. *Archives of General Psychiatry, 54*, 1016–1024.

De Waal, M. W., Arnold, I. A., Eekhof, J. A. H., & Van Hemert, A. M. (2004). Somatoform disorders in general practice: Prevalence, functional impairment, and comorbidity with anxiety and depressive disorders. *British Journal of Psychiatry, 184*, 470–476.

De Wolfe, N., Byrne, J., & Bawden, H. (2000). ADHD in preschool children: Parent-rated psychosocial correlates. *Developmental Medicine and Child Neurology, 42*, 825.

Deykin, E. Y., & MacMahon, B. (1979). The incidence of seizures among children with autistic symptoms. *American Journal of Psychiatry, 136*, 1310–1312.

Dhossche, D., van der Steen, F., & Ferdinand, R. (2002). Somatoform disorders in children and adolescents: A comparison with other internalizing disorders. *Annals of Clinical Psychiatry, 14*(1), 23–31.

Diaz-Marsá, M., Carrasco, J. L., & Sáiz, J. (2000). A study of temperament and personality in anorexia and bulimia nervosa. *Journal of Personality Disorders, 14*(4), 352–359.

Dickens, C. (2002). *Great expectations* (Rev. ed,). London: Penguin.

Dickens, C. (2003). *Oliver Twist* (Rev. ed.). London: Peguin.

Dick, D. M., Viken, R. J., Kaprio, J., Pulkkinen, L., & Rose, R. J. (2005). Understanding the covariation among childhood externalizing symptoms: Genetic and environmental influences on conduct disorder, attention deficit hyperactivity disorder and oppositional defiant disorder symptoms. *Journal of Abnormal Child Psychology, 33*(2), 219–229.

Dickerson, K. A., & Pincus, A. L. (2003). Interpersonal analysis of grandiose and vulnerable narcissism. *Journal of Personality Disorder, 17*, 188–207.

Dickerson, F., Boronow, J., Ringel, N., & Parente, F. (1997). Lack of insight among outpatients with schizophrenia. *Psychiatric Services, 48*, 195–199.

Didde, R., & Sigafoos, J. (2001). A review of the nature and treatment of sleep disorders in individuals with developmental disabilities. *Research in Developmental Disabilities, 22*(4), 255–272.

Dijkman-Caes, C. I. M., Kraan, H. F., & DeVries, M. W. (1993). Research on panic disorder and agoraphobia in daily life: A review of current studies. *Journal of Anxiety Disorders, 7*, 235–247.

DiLavore, P., Lord, C., & Rutter, M. (1995). Pre-linguistic Autism Diagnostic Observation Schedule (PLADOS). *Journal of Autism and Developmental Disorders, 25*(4), 355–379.

Dilk, M. N., & Bond, G. R. (1996). Meta-analytic evaluation of skills training research for individuals with severe mental illness. *Journal of Consulting and Clinical Psychology, 64*, 1337–1346.

Dilsaver, S. C., & Akiskal, H. S. (2005). High rate of unrecognized bipolar mixed states among destitute Hispanic adolescents referred for major depressive disorder. *Journal of Affective Disorders, 84*, 179–186.

Di Nardo, P. A., O'Brien, G. T., Barlow, D. H., Waddell, M. T., & Blanchard, E. B. (1983). Reliability of DSM-III anxiety disorder categories using a new structured interview. *Archives of General Psychiatry, 40*, 1070–1074.

Dippel, B., Kemper, J., & Berger, M. (1991). Folie à six: A case report on induced psychotic disorder. *Acta Psychiatrica Scandinavica, 83*, 137–141.

Dixon, L., Adams, C., & Lucksted, A. (2000). Update on family psychoeducation for schizophrenia. *Schizophrenia Bulletin, 26*, 5–20.

Dixon, L., Haas, G., Weiden, P. J., & Frances, A. J. (1991). Drug abuse in schizophrenic patients: Clinical correlates and reasons for use. *American Journal of Psychiatry, 148*, 224–230.

Dixon, L., Weiden, P. J., Haas, G., Sweeney, J., & Frances, A. J. (1992). Increased tardive dyskinesia in alcohol-abusing schizophrenic patients. *Comprehensive Psychiatry, 33*, 121–122.

Dobkin de Rios, M. D. (1990). *Hallucinogens: Cross-cultural perspectives.* Houston, TX: Prism Press.

Dobson, A. R. (2006). SSRI use during pregnancy is associated with fetal abnormalities. *British Medical Journal, 333,* 824.

Dobson, K. S. (1989). A meta-analysis of the efficacy of cognitive therapy of depression. *Journal of Consulting and Clinical Psychology, 57,* 414–419.

Docherty, N. M., Cohen, A. S., Nienow, T. M., Dinzeo, T. J., & Dangelmaier, R. E. (2003). Stability of formal thought disorder and referential communication disturbances in schizophrenia. *Journal of Abnormal Psychology, 112,* 469–475.

Dodes, L. (1996). Compulsion and addiction. *Journal of the American Psychoanalytic Association, 44,* 815–835.

Dodge, K. A., & Pettit, G. S. (2003). A biopsychosocial model of the development of chronic conduct problems in adolescence. *Development and Psychopathology, 39,* 349–371.

Dodson, W. W. (2005). Pharmacotherapy of adult ADHD. *Journal of Clinical Psychology/In session, 61*(5), 568–606.

Doggett, A. M. (2004). ADHD and drug therapy: Is it still a valid treatment? *Journal of Child Health Care, 8*(1), 69–81.

Dolan, B. (1998). Therapeutic community treatment for severe personality disorders. In T. Millon, E. Simonsen, M. Birket-Smith, & R. D. Davis (Eds.), *Psychopathy: Antisocial, criminal and violent behavior* (pp. 407–430). New York: Guilford Press.

Dolan, M., & Doyle, M. (2000). Violence risk prediction: Clinical and actuarial measures and the role of the Psychopathy Checklist. *British Journal of Psychiatry, 177,* 303–311.

Dolan-Sewell, R. G., Krueger, R. F., & Shea, M. T. (2001). Co-occurrence with syndrome disorders. In W. J. Livesley (Ed.), *Handbook of personality disorders* (pp. 84–104). New York: Guilford Press.

Dole, V. P., Nyswander, M. E., & Keek, M. J. (1966). Narcotic blockade. *Archives of Internal Medicine, 118,* 304–309.

Dombroski, A. Y., Blakesley-Call, R. E., Mulsant, B. H., Mazumdar, S., Houck, P. A., & Szanto, K. (2006). Speed of improvement in sleep disturbance and anxiety compared with core mood symptoms during acute treatment of depression in old age. *American Journal of Geriatric Psychiatry, 14,* 550–554.

Donny, E. C., Brasser, S. M., Bigelow, G. E., Stitzer, M. L., & Walsh, S. L. (2005). Methadone doses of 100 mg or greater are more effective than lower doses at suppressing heroin self-administration in opioid-dependent volunteers. *Addiction, 100,* 1496–1509.

Donovan, D. (2005). Assessment of addictive behaviors for relapse prevention. In D. Donovan & G. A. Marlatt (Eds.), *Assessment of addictive behaviors* (2nd ed., pp. 1–48). New York: Guilford Press.

Dorenlot, P., Harboun, M., Bige, V., Henrard, J. C., & Ankri, J. (2005). Major depression as a risk factor for early institutionalization of dementia patients living in the community. *International Journal of Geriatric Psychiatry, 25,* 471–478.

DosReis, S., Zito, J. M., Safer, D. J., Soeken, K. L., Mitchell, J. W., Jr., & Ellwood, L. C. (2003). Parental perceptions and satisfaction with stimulant medication for attention-deficit/hyperactivity disorder. *Journal of Developmental and Behavioral Pediatrics, 24,* 155–162.

Douglas, K. S., Yeomans, M., & Boer, D. P. (2005). Comparative validity analysis of multiple measures of violence risk in a sample of criminal offenders. *Criminal Justice and Behavior, 32*(5), 479–510.

Douglas, V. I. (1980). Higher mental processes in hyperactive children: Implications for training. In R. Knights & D. Bakker (Eds.), *Treatment of hyperactive and learning disordered children* (pp. 280–329). Baltimore: University Park Press.

Douglas, V. I. (1983). Attention and cognitive problems. In M. Rutter (Ed.), *Developmental neuropsychiatry* (pp. 280–329). New York: Guilford Press.

Drake, R., & Lewis, S. W. (2003). Insight and neurocognition in schizophrenia. *Schizophrenia Research, 62,* 165–173.

Drake, R. E., Osher, F. C., Noordsy, D. L., Hurlburt, S. C., Teague, G. B., & Beaudett, M. S. (1990). Diagnosis of alcohol use disorders in schizophrenia. *Schizophrenia Bulletin, 16*, 57–67.

Drake, R. E., Osher, F. C., & Wallach, M. A. (1989). Alcohol use and abuse in schizophrenia: A prospective community study. *Journal of Nervous and Mental Diseases, 177*, 408–414.

Drake, R. E., Osher, F. C., & Wallach, M. A. (1991). Homelessness and dual diagnosis. *American Psychologist, 46*, 1149–1158.

Drebing, C. E., Van Ormer, E. A., Krebs, C., Rosenheck, R., Rounsaville, B., Herz, L., et al. (2005). The impact of enhanced incentives on vocational rehabilitation outcomes for dually diagnosed veterans. *Journal of Applied Behavior Analysis, 38*, 359–372.

Drotar, D. (1995). Failure to thrive (growth deficiency). In M. C. Roberts (Ed.), *Handbook of pediatric psychology* (2nd ed., pp. 516–536). New York: Guilford Press.

Drug Enforcement Administration. (n.d.). Fast facts about meth. Retrieved November 21, 2006, from www.dea.gov/pubs/pressrel/methfact03.html.

Du, A. T., Schuff, N., Kramer, J. H., Ganzer, S., Zhu, W. J., Miller, B. L., et al. (2004). Higher atrophy rate in entorhinal cortex than hippocampus in Alzheimer's disease. *Neurology, 62*, 422–427.

Duberstein, P., & Conwell, Y. (1997). Personality disorders and completed suicide: A methodological and conceptual review. *Clinical Psychology: Science and Practice, 4*, 359–376.

Dugas, M. J., Buhr, K., & Ladouceur, R. (2004). The role of intolerance of uncertainty in etiology and maintenance. In R. G. Heimberg, C. L. Turk, & D. S. Mennin (Eds.), *Generalized anxiety disorder: Advances in research and practice* (pp. 143–163). New York: Guilford Press.

Dugas, M. J., & Ladouceur, R. (2000). Treatment of GAD: Targeting intolerance of uncertainty in two types of worry. *Behavior Modification, 24*, 635–657.

Dugas, M. J., Ladouceur, R., Léger, E., Freeston, M. H., Langlois, F., Provencher, M. D., et al. (2003). Group cognitive-behavioral therapy for generalized anxiety disorder: Treatment outcome and long-term follow-up. *Journal of Consulting and Clinical Psychology, 71*, 821–825.

Dunayevich, E., Sax, K. W., Keck, P. E., McElroy, S. L., Sorter, M. T., McConville, B. J., et al. (2000). Twelve-month outcome in bipolar patients with and without personality disorders. *Journal of Clinical Psychiatry, 61*, 134–139.

Dunitz, M., Scheer, P. J., Kvas, E., & Macari, S. (1996). Psychiatric diagnoses in infancy: A comparison. *Infant Mental Health Journal, 17*(1), 12–23.

Dunlap, E., Golub, A., & Johnson, B. D. (2006). The severely-distressed African American family in the crack era: Empowerment is not enough. *Journal of Sociology & Social Welfare, 33*, 115–139.

Dunn, L. M., & Dunn, L. M. (1997). *Peabody Picture Vocabulary Test* (3rd ed.). Circle Pines, MN: American Guidance Service.

Dunn, M. (2004). *SOS: Social skills in our schools: A social skills program for children with pervasive developmental disorders and their typical peers.* Shawnee Mission, KS: Autism Asperger.

Dunner, D. L. (1999). Rapid cycling bipolar affective disorder. In J. F. Goldberg & M. Harrow (Eds.), *Bipolar disorders: Clinical course and outcome* (pp. 199–217). Washington, DC: American Psychiatric Press.

Dunner, D. L., & Fieve, R. R. (1974). Clinical factors in lithium prophylaxis failure. *Archives of General Psychiatry, 30*, 229–233.

DuPaul, G. J., & Eckert, T. L. (1997). The effects of school based interventions for children with attention deficit hyperactivity disorder: A meta-analysis. *School Psychology Review, 26*, 5–27.

DuPaul, G. J., Schaughency, E. A., Weyandt, L. L., Tripp, G., Kiesner, J., Ota, K., et al. (2001). Self-report of ADHD symptoms in university students: Cross-gender and cross-national prevalence. *Journal of Learning Disabilities, 34*(4), 370–379.

Dupont, R. L., & Dupont, C. M. (2005). Sedative/hypnotics and benzodiazapines. In R. J. Frances, S. I. Miller, & A. H. Mack (Eds.), *Clinical handbook of addictive disorders* (pp. 219–242). New York: Guilford Press.

Duthie, E. H. J., & Glatt, S. L. (1988). Understanding and treating multiinfarct dementia. *Clinical Geriatric Medicine, 4,* 749–766.

Dutton, D., & Painter, S. L. (1981). Traumatic bonding: The development of emotional attachments in battered women and other relationships of intermittent abuse. *Victimology: An International Journal, 6,* 139–155.

Dutton, D. G., Saunders, K., Starzomski, A., & Bartholomew, K. (1994). Intimacy, anger, and insecure attachment as precursors of abuse in intimate relationships. *Journal of Applied Social Psychology, 24,* 1367–1386.

Duval, F., Mikrani, M. C., Monreal-Ortiz, J. A., Fattah, S., Champeval, C., Schulz, P., et al. (2006). Cortisol hypersecretion in unipolar major depression with melancholic and psychotic features: Dopaminergic, noradrenergic, and thyroid correlates. *Psychoneuroendocrinology, 31,* 876–888.

Dykens, E. M. (2000). Psychopathology in children with intellectual disability. *Journal of Child Psychology and Psychiatry and Allied Disciplines, 41*(4), 407–417.

Dykens, E. M., & Hodapp, R. M. (2001). Research in mental retardation: Towards an etiologic approach. *Child Psychology and Psychiatry, 42,* 49–71.

Eaton, W. W., Kessler, R. C., Wittchen, H.-U., & Magee, W. J. (1994). Panic and panic disorder in the United States. *American Journal of Psychiatry, 151,* 413–420.

Eaves, L., Rutter, M., Silberg, J. L., Shillady, L., Maes, H., & Pickles, A. (2000). Genetic and environmental causes of covariance in interview assessments of disruptive behavior in child and adolescent twins. *Behavior Genetics, 30,* 321–334.

Eaves, L. C., & Ho, H. H. (1996). Brief report: Stability and change in cognitive and behavioral characteristics of autism through childhood. *Journal of Autism and Developmental Disorders, 26,* 557–569.

Ebmeier, K. P., Berge, A., Semple, D., Shah, P. J., & Steele, J. D. (2003). Biological treatments of mood disorders. In M. Power (Ed.), *Mood disorders: A handbook of science and practice* (pp. 143–166). Hoboken, NJ: Wiley.

Eckardt, M. J., Stapleton, J. M., Rawlings, R. R., & Grodin, D. M. (1995). Neuropsychological functioning in detoxified alcoholics between 18 and 35 years of age. *American Journal of Psychiatry, 152,* 45–52.

Eddy, J. M., Leve, L. D., & Fagot, B. I. (2001). Coercive family process: A replication and extension of Paterson's coercion model. *Aggressive Behavior, 27,* 14–25.

Eddy, K. T., Keel, P. K., Dorer, D. J., Delinsky, S. S., Franko, D. L., & Herzog, D. B. (2002). Longitudinal comparison of anorexia nervosa subtypes. *International Journal of Eating Disorders, 31*(2), 191–201.

Eddy, S., & Harris, E. (1998). Risk management with the violent patient. In P. M. Kleespies (Ed.), *Emergencies in mental health practice: Evaluation and management* (pp. 217–231). New York: Guilford Press.

Edelbrock, C., Costello, A. J., Dulcan, M. K., Connover, N. C., & Kalas, R. (1986). Parent-child agreement on child psychiatric symptoms assessed via structured interview. *Journal of Child Psychology and Psychiatry, 27,* 181–190.

Edelstein, B., Koven, L., Spira, A., & Shreve-Neiger, A. (2003). Older adults. In M. Hersen & S. M. Turner (Eds.), *Diagnostic interviewing* (3rd ed., pp. 433–454). New York: Kluwer Academic.

Edinger, J. D., & Means, M. K. (2005). Cognitive-behavioral therapy for primary insomnia. *Clinical Psychology Review, 25*(5), 539–558.

Edwards, J. G., & Anderson, I. (1999). Systematic review and guide to selection of selective serotonin reuptake inhibitors. *Drugs, 57,* 507–533.

Eells, T. D. (1997). *Handbook of psychotherapy case formulation.* New York: Guilford Press.

Egbert, A. M. (1993). Clinical clues to active alcoholism in the older patient. *Geriatrics, 48,* 63–69.

Eggermont, L., Swaab, D., & Luiten, P. (2006). Exercise, cognition, and Alzheimer's disease: More is not necessarily better. *Neuroscience and Biobehavioral Reviews, 30,* 562–575.

Ehlers, A., & Clark, D. M. (2006). Predictors of chronic post-traumatic stress disorder. In B. O. Rothbaum (Ed.), *Pathological anxiety: Emotional processing in etiology and treatment* (pp. 39–55). New York: Guilford Press.

Ehlers, A., Mayou, R. A., & Bryant, B. (1998). Psychological predictors of chronic posttraumatic stress disorder after motor vehicle accidents. *Journal of Abnormal Psychology, 107,* 508–519.

Ehlers, S., Gillberg, C., & Wing, L. (1999). A screening questionnaire for Asperger syndrome and other high-functioning autism spectrum disorders in school age children. *Journal of Autism and Developmental Disorders, 29,* 129–141.

Ehrman, R. N., & Robbins, S. J. (1994). Reliability and validity of 6-month timeline reports of cocaine and heroin use in a methadone population. *Journal of Consulting and Clinical Psychology, 62,* 843–850.

Eichleman, B. S. (1996). Violent patients. In J. V. Vaccaro & G. H. Clark (Eds.), *Practicing psychiatry in the community: A manual* (pp. 277–292). Washington, DC: American Psychiatric Press.

Eichleman, B. S., & Hartwig, A. C. (Eds.). (1995). *Patient violence and the clinician.* Washington, DC: American Psychiatric Press.

Eichstedt, J. A., & Arnold, S. L. (2001). Childhood-onset obsessive-compulsive disorder: A tic-related subtype of OCD? *Clinical Psychology Review, 21,* 137–158.

Eikelenboom, P., & Hoogenijk, W. J. G. (1999). Do delirium and Alzheimer's dementia share specific pathogenetic mechanisms? *Dementia and Geriatric Cognitive Disorders, 10,* 319–324.

Eiraldi, R. B., Power, T. J., & Maguth Nezu, C. (1997). Patterns of comorbidity associated with subtypes of attention deficit/hyperactivity disorder among 6- to 12-year-old children. *Journal of the American Academy of Child and Adolescent Psychiatry, 36*(4), 503–514.

Eisen, J. L., Mancebo, M. A., Pinto, A., Coles, M. E., Pagano, M. E., Stout, R., et al. (2006). Impact of obsessive-compulsive disorder on quality of life. *Comprehensive Psychiatry, 47,* 270–275.

Eisenberg, N. (2000). Emotion, regulation and moral development. In S. T. Finke, D. I. Schacter, & C. Zahn-Waxler (Eds.), *Annual review of psychology* (pp. 665–697). Palo Alto, CA: Annual Reviews.

Eisendrath, S. J. (2001). Factitious disorders and malingering. In G. O. Gabbard (Ed.), *Treatment of psychiatric disorders* (3rd ed., pp. 1825–1844). Washington, DC: American Psychiatric Publishing.

Eisendrath, S. J., & McNeil, D. E. (2004). Case report: Factitious physical disorders, litigation, and mortality. *Psychosomatics, 45*(3), 350–353.

Eisenmajer, R., Prior, M., Leekman, S., Wing, L., Ong, B., Gould, J., et al. (1998). Delayed language onset as a predictor of clinical symptoms in pervasive developmental disorders. *Journal of Autism and Developmental Disorders, 28*(6), 527–533.

Eisler, I., Le Grange, D., & Asen, E. (2003). Family interventions. In J. Treasure, U. Schmidt, E. van Furth (Eds.), *Handbook of eating disorders* (2nd ed., pp. 291–310). Chichester, West Sussex, England: Wiley.

Ekselius, L., Tillfors, M., Furmark, T., & Fredrikson, M. (2001). Personality disorders in the general population: DSM-I and ICD-10 defined prevalence as related to sociodemographic profile. *Personality and Individual Differences, 30,* 311–320.

El-Ad, B., & Lavie, P. (2005). Effect of sleep apnea on cognition and mood. *International Review of Psychiatry, 17*(4), 277–282.

Elkin, I., Shea, M. T., Watkins, J. T., Imber, S. D., Sotsky, S. M., Collins, J. F., et al. (1989). National Institute of Mental Health Treatment of Depression Collaborative Research Program: General effectiveness of treatments. *Archives of General Psychiatry, 46,* 971–982.

Ellaway, C., & Christodoulou, J. (1999). Rett syndrome: Clinical update and review of recent genetic advances. *Journal of Pediatric and Child Health, 35,* 419–426.

Elliott, C. (1990). *Differential Abilities Scale.* San Antonio TX: Psychological Corporation.

Elliott, R., Watson, J. C., Goldman, R. N., & Greenberg, L. S. (2004). *Learning emotion-focused therapy: The process-experiential approach to change.* Washington, DC: American Psychological Association.

Ellis, H. (1898). Auto-erotism: A psychological study. *Alienst and Neurologist, 19,* 260–299.

Elmstahl, S., Ingvad, B., & Annerstedt, L. (1998). Family caregiving in dementia: Prediction of caregiver burden 12 months after relocation to group-living care. *International Psychogeriatrics, 10,* 127–146.

El-Sayeh, H. G., & Morganti, C. (2004). Aripiprazole for schizophrenia. *Cochrane Database of Systematic Reviews, 19,* CD004578.

El-Shikh, H., Fahmy, E., Michael, V. S., & Moshelhy, H. F. A. (2004). Life events and addiction: A review of literature. *European Journal of Psychiatry, 18,* 163–170.

Ely, E. W., Shintani, A., Truman, B., Speroff, T., Gordon, S., Harrell, F. E., et al. (2004). Delirium as a predictor of mortality in mechanically ventilated patients in the intensive care unit. *Journal of the American Medical Association, 291,* 1753–1762.

Emery, R. E., Waldron, M., Kitzman, K. M., & Aaron, J. (1999). Delinquent behavior, future divorce or nonmarital childbearing, and externalizing behavior among offspring: A 14-year prospective study. *Journal of Family Psychology, 13,* 568–579.

Emes, C. (1997). Is Mr. Pac Man eating our children? A review of the effects of videogames on children. *Canadian Journal of Psychiatry, 42,* 409–414.

Emmelkamp, P. M. G., & Scholing, A. (1997). Anxiety disorders. In C. A. Essau & F. Petermann (Eds.), *Developmental psychopathology: Epidemiology, diagnostics and treatment* (pp. 219–263). London: Harwood.

Endicott, J., & Spitzer, R. L. (1978). A diagnostic interview: The schedule for affective disorders and schizophrenia. *Archives of General Psychiatry, 35,* 837–844.

Engel, G. E. (1959). Psychogenic pain and the pain-prone patient. *American Journal of Medicine, 16,* 899–918.

Engelhart, M. J., Ruitenberg, A., Meijer, J., Kiliaan, A., van Swieten, J. C., Hofman, A., et al. (2005). Plasma levels of antioxidants are not associated with Alzheimer's disease or cognitive decline. *Dementia and Geriatric Cognitive Disorders, 19,* 134–139.

Engstrom, C., Brandstrom, S., Sigvardsson, S., Cloninger, R., & Nylander, P. O. (2003). Bipolar disorder II: Personality and age of onset. *Bipolar Disorders, 5,* 340–348.

Erba, H. W. (2000). Early intervention programs for children with autism: Conceptual frameworks for implementation. *American Journal of Orthopsychiatry, 70*(1), 82–94.

Erickson, E. H. (1950). *Childhood and society.* New York: Norton.

Erickson, K., Drevets, W. C., Clark, L., Cannon, D. M., Bain, E. E., Zarate, C. A., et al. (2005). Mood-congruent bias in affective go/no-go performance of unmedicated patients with major depressive disorder. *American Journal of Psychiatry, 162,* 2171–2173.

Erk, R. R. (1997). Mutlidimensional treatment of attention deficit disorder: A family oriented approach. *Journal of Mental Health Counselling, 19*(1), 3–23.

Erkinjuntti, T., & Pantoni, U. (2000). Subcortical vascular dementia. In S. Gauthier & J. L. Cummings (Eds.), *Yearbook of Alzheimer's disease and related disorders* (pp. 101–133). London: Marin Dunitz.

Ernst, R. L., & Hay, J. W. (1994). The U.S. economic and social costs of Alzheimer's disease revisited. *American Journal of Public Health, 84,* 1261–1264.

Ersche, K. D., Clark, L., London, M., Robbins, T. W., & Sahakian, B. J. (2006). Profile of executive and memory function associated with amphetamine and opiate dependence. *Neuropsychopharmacology, 31,* 1036–1047.

Escobar, J. I. (1996). Pharmacological treatment of somatization/hypochondriasis—Overview of somatization: Diagnosis, epidemiology, and management. *Psychopharmacology Bulletin, 32*(4), 589–596.

Escobar, J. I., Nervi, C. H., & Gara, M. A. (2000). Immigration and mental health: Mexican-Americans in the United States. *Harvard Review of Psychiatry, 8,* 64–72.

Escobar, J. I., Randolph, E. T., & Hill, M. (1986). Symptoms of schizophrenia in Hispanic and Anglo veterans. *Culture, Medicine, and Psychiatry, 10,* 259–276.

Eskedal, G. A., & Demetri, J. M. (2006). Etiology and treatment of cluster c personality disorders. *Journal of Mental Health Counseling, 28*(1), 1–18.

Espie, C. A. (2000). Assessment and differential diagnosis. In K. L. Lichstein & C. M. Morin (Eds.), *Treatment of late-life insomnia* (pp. 81–108). Thousand Oaks, CA: Sage.

Espie, C. A., Inglis, S. J., Tessier, S., & Harvey, L. (2001). The clinical effectiveness of cognitive behavior therapy for chronic insomnia: Implementation and evaluation of a sleep clinic in general medical practice. *Behaviour Research and Therapy, 39*(1), 34–60.

Esquirol, J. (1838). *Mental maladies: A treatise on insanity.* Birmingham, AL: Classics of Medicine Library.

Essau, C. A. (2003). Epidemiology and comorbidity. In C. A. Essau (Ed.), *Conduct and oppositional defiant disorders: Epidemiology, risk factors, and treatment* (pp. 33–59). Mahwah, NJ: Erlbaum.

Essau, C. A., Conradt, J., & Petermann, F. (1999). Frequency and comorbidity of social phobia and social fears in adolescents. *Behaviour Research and Therapy, 37*, 831–843.

Essau, C. A., Conradt, J., & Petermann, F. (2000). Frequency, comorbidity, and psychosocial impairment of specific phobia in adolescents. *Journal of Clinical and Child Psychology, 29*, 221–231.

Essen-Moller, E., & Wohlfarht, S. (1947). Suggestions for the amendment of the official Swedish classification of mental disorders. *Acta Psychiatrica Scandinavica, 47*(Suppl.), 551.

Estroff, S. E., & Zimmer, C. (1994). Social networks, social support, and violence among persons with severe, persistent mental illness. In J. Monahan & H. Steadman (Eds.), *Violence and mental disorder* (pp. 259–295). Chicago: University of Chicago Press.

Estroff, S. E., Zimmer, C., Lachicotte, W. S., & Benoit, J. (1994). The influence of social networks and social support on violence by persons with serious mental illness. *Hospital and Community Psychiatry, 45*, 669–679.

Ethier, L., Lacharite, C., & Couture, G. (1995). Childhood adversity, parental stress, and depression of negligent mothers. *Child Abuse and Neglect, 19*, 619–632.

Evans, J. J., Levine, B., & Bateman, A. (2004). Research digest: Errorless learning. *Neuropsychological Rehabilitation, 14*, 467–476.

Evans, M. D., Hollon, S. D., DeRubeis, R. J., Piasecki, J. M., Grove, W. M., & Garvey, M. J. (1992). Differential relapse following cognitive therapy and pharmacotherapy for depression. *Archives of General Psychiatry, 49*, 802–808.

Ewing, J. A. (1984). Detecting alcoholism. The CAGE Questionnaire. *Journal of the American Medical Association, 252*, 1905–1907.

Eyberg, S. M., & Boggs, S. R. (1998). Parent-child interaction therapy: A psychosocial intervention for the treatment of young conduct-disordered children. In J. M. Briesmeister & C. E. Schafers (Eds.), *Handbook of parent training: Parents as co-therapists for children's behavior problems* (2nd ed., pp. 61–97). New York: Wiley.

Eyman, J. R., Mikawa, J. K., & Eyman, S. K. (1990). The problem of adolescent suicide: Issues and assessment. In P. McReynolds, J. C. Rosen, & G. J. Chelune (Eds.), *Advances in psychological assessment* (Vol. 7, pp. 165–201). New York: Plenum Press.

Faber, E., & Keating-O'Connor, B. (1991). Planned family intervention: Johnson Institute method. *Journal of Chemical Dependency Treatment, 4*, 61–71.

Fabrega, H. (2001). Culture and history in psychiatric diagnosis and practice. *Psychiatric Clinics of North America, 24*(3), 391–405.

Fabrega, H., Mezzich, J., & Ulrich, R. F. (1988). Black-White differences in psychopathology in an urban psychiatric population. *Comprehensive Psychiatry, 29*, 285–297.

Factor, R. M., & Diamond, R. J. (1996). Emergency psychiatry and crisis resolution. In J. V. Vaccaro & G. H. Clark (Eds.), *Practicing psychiatry in the community: A manual* (pp. 51–76). Washington, DC: American Psychiatric Press.

Fadden, G., Bebbington, P., & Kuipers, L. (1987). Caring and its burdens. *British Journal of Psychiatry, 151*, 660–667.

Faedda, G. L., Tondo, L., Teicher, M. H., Baldessarini, R. J., Gelbard, H. A., & Floris, G. F. (1993). Seasonal mood disorders: Patterns of seasonal recurrence in mania and depression. *Archives of General Psychiatry, 50*, 17–23.

Fagot, B. I., & Leve, L. D. (1998). Teacher rating of externalizing behavior at school entry for boys and girls: Similar early predictors and different correlates. *Journal of Child Psychology and Psychiatry, 39,* 555–566.

Fahlen, T. (1995). Personality traits in social phobia II: Changes during drug treatment. *Journal of Clinical Psychiatry, 56,* 569–573.

Fahy, T. J., O'Rourke, D., Brophy, J., Schazmann, W., & Sciascia, S. (1992). The Galway study of panic disorder: Pt. I. Clomipramine and lofepramine in DSM-III-R panic disorder: A placebo controlled trial. *Journal of Affective Disorders, 25,* 63–76.

Fainsinger, R. L., Tapper, M., & Bruera, E. (1993). A perspective on the management of delirium in terminally ill patients on a palliative care unit. *Palliative Care, 9,* 4–8.

Fairbairn, W. R. D. (1952). *Psychoanalytical studies of the personality.* London: Routledge & Kegan Paul.

Fairburn, C. G. (1985). Cognitive-behavioral treatment for bulimia. In D. M. Garner & P. E. Garfinkel (Eds.), *Handbook of psychotherapy for anorexia nervosa and bulimia* (pp. 160–192). New York: Guilford Press.

Fairburn, C. G., & Cooper, Z. (1993). The eating disorder examination. In C. G. Fairburn & G. T. Wilson (Eds.), *Binge eating: Nature, assessment, and treatment* (12th ed., pp. 317–360). New York: Guilford Press.

Fairburn, C. G., Cooper, Z., & Doll, H. A. (1999). Risk factors for anorexia nervosa: Three integrated case-control comparisons. *Archives of General Psychiatry, 56*(5), 468–476.

Fairburn, C. G., Cooper, Z., & Doll, H. A. (2000). The natural course of bulimia nervosa and binge eating disorder in young women. *Archives of General Psychiatry, 57*(7), 659–665.

Fairburn, C. G., Cooper, Z., & Shafran, R. (2003). Cognitive behavior therapy for eating disorders: A "transdiagnostic" theory and treatment. *Behaviour Research and Therapy, 41*(5), 509–528.

Fairburn, C. G., Cowen, P. J., & Harrison, P. J. (1999). Twin studies and the etiology of eating disorders. *International Journal of Eating Disorders, 26*(4), 349–358.

Fairburn, C. G., Doll, H. A., Welch, S. L., Hay, P. J., Davies, B. A., & O'Connor, M. E. (1998). Risk factors for binge eating disorder: A community-based, case-control study. *Archives of General Psychiatry, 55*(5), 425–432.

Fairburn, C. G., & Harrison, P. J. (2003). Eating disorders. *Lancet, 361*(9355), 407–416.

Fairburn, C. G., Shafran, R., & Cooper, Z. (1999). A cognitive behavioural theory of anorexia nervosa. *Behaviour Research and Therapy, 37*(1), 1–13.

Fairburn, C. G., Stice, E., Cooper, Z., Doll, H. A., Norman, P. A., & O'Connor, M. E. (2003). Understanding persistence in bulimia nervosa: A 5-year naturalistic study. *Journal of Consulting and Clinical Psychology, 71*(1), 103–109.

Fakhoury, W., & Priebe, S. (2002). The process of deinstitutionalization: An international overview. *Current Opinions in Psychiatry, 15,* 187–192.

Fallon, B. (2004). Pharmacotherapy of somatoform disorders. *Journal of Psychosomatic Research, 56,* 455–460.

Fallon, B. A., & Feinstein, S. (2001). Hypochondriasis. In K. A. Phillips (Ed.), *Somatoform and factitious disorders* (pp. 27–65). Washington, DC: American Psychiatric Publishing.

Falloon, I. R. (2002). Cognitive-behavioral family and educational interventions for schizophrenic disorders. In S. G. Hofmann & M. C. Tompson (Eds.), *Treating chronic and severe mental disorders: A handbook of empirically supported interventions* (pp. 3–17). New York: Guilford Press.

Falloon, I. R., Hahlweg, K., & Tarrier, N. (1990). Family interventions in the community management of schizophrenia: Methods and results. In E. R. Straube & K. Hahlweg (Eds.), *Schizophrenia: Concepts, vulnerability and intervention* (pp. 217–240). New York: Springer-Verlag.

Falloon, I. R., & Liberman, R. P. (1983). Interactions between drug and psychosocial therapy in schizophrenia. *Schizophrenia Bulletin, 9,* 543–554.

Falloon, I. R., & Talbot, R. (1981). Persistent auditory hallucinations: Coping mechanisms and implications for management. *Psychological Medicine, 11,* 329–339.

Fals-Stewart, W., & O'Farrell, T. J. (2003). Family therapy techniques. In F. Rotgers, J. Morgenstern, & S. T. Walters (Eds.), *Treating substance abuse: Theory and technique* (2nd ed., pp. 140–165). New York: Guilford Press.

Fanous, A., Gardner, C., Walsh, D., & Kendler, K. (2001). Relationship between positive and negative symptoms of schizotypal symptoms in nonpsychotic relatives. *Archives of General Psychiatry, 58*, 669–673.

Faraone, S. V. (2000). Attention-deficit hyperactivity disorder in adults: Implications for theory of diagnosis. *Current Directions in Psychological Science, 9*, 33–36.

Faraone, S. V., Biderman, J., & Monuteaux, M. C. (2002). Further evidence for the diagnostic continuity between child and adolescent ADHD. *Journal of Attention Disorders, 6*, 5–13.

Faraone, S. V., Biederman, J., Weber, W., & Russell, R. L. (1998). Psychiatric, neuropsychological, and psychosocial features of DSM-IV subtypes of attention-deficit/ hyperactivity disorder: Results from a clinical referred sample. *Journal of the American Academy of Child and Adolescent Psychiatry, 37*, 185–193.

Faraone, S. V., Green, A. I., Sidman, L. J., & Tsuang, M. T. (2001). "Schizotaxia": Clinical implications and new directions for research. *Schizophrenia Bulletin, 27*, 1–18.

Faraone, S. V., Spenser, T., Aleardi, M., Pagano, C., & Biederman, J. (2004). Meta-analysis of the efficacy of methylphenidate for treating adult attention-deficit/hyperactivity disorder. *Journal of Clinical Psychopharmacology, 24*, 24–29.

Faraone, S. V., & Wilens, T. E. (2003). Does stimulant treatment lead to substance abuse disorder? *Journal of Clinical Psychiatry, 64*(Suppl. 11), 9–13.

Faravelli, C., Paterniti, S., & Servi, P. (1997). Stressful life events and panic disorder. In T. W. Miller (Ed.), *Clinical disorders and stressful life events* (pp. 143–147). Madison, CT: International Universities Press.

Farias, M., Claridge, G., & Lalljee, M. (2005). Personality and cognitive predictors of new age practices and beliefs. *Personality and Individual Differences, 39*, 979–989.

Farkas, K. (2004). Substance abuse problems among older adults. In S. L. Ashenberg-Smith (Ed.), *Clinical work with substance-abusing clients* (2nd ed., pp. 330–346). New York: Guilford Press.

Farrington, D. P. (1995). The development of offending and antisocial behavior from childhood: Key findings from the Cambridge study in delinquent behavior. *Journal of Child Psychology and Psychiatry, 36*, 929–964.

Farrington, D. P., Jolliffe, D., Loeber, R., Stouthamer-Loeber, M., & Kalb, L. M. (2001). The concentration of offenders in families, and family criminality in the prediction of boys' delinquency. *Journal of Adolescence, 24*, 579–596.

Farrington, D. P., & Loeber, R. (1998). Transatlantic reliability of risk factors in the development of delinquency. In P. Cohen, C. Slomkowski, & L. M. Robbins (Eds.), *Where and when: The influence of history and geography on aspects of psychopathology* (pp. 299–329). Mahwah, NJ: Erlbaum.

Faul, L. A., & Gross, A. M. (2006). Diagnosis and classification. In M. Hersen, J. C. Thomas, & R. T. Ammerman (Eds.), *Comprehensive handbook of personality and psychopathology: Vol. 3. Child psychopathology* (pp. 3–15). Hoboken, NJ: Wiley.

Faulk, M. (1994). *Basic forensic psychiatry* (2nd ed.). London: Blackwell Scientific.

Fauman, M. A. (2002). *Study guide to the DSM-IV-TR*. Washington, DC: American Psychiatric Press.

Fava, G. A., Grandi, S., Zielezny, M., Rafanelli, C., & Canastrari, R. (1996). Four year outcome for cognitive behavioral treatment of residual symptoms in major depression. *American Journal of Psychiatry, 153*, 945–947.

Fava, G. A., Rafanelli, C., Grandi, S., Canastrari, R., & Morphy, M. A. (1998). Six year outcome for cognitive behavioral treatment of residual symptoms in major depression. *American Journal of Psychiatry, 155*, 1443–1445.

Favaro, A., & Santonastaso, P. (1997). Suicidality in eating disorders: Clinical and psychological correlates. *Acta Psychiatrica Scandinavica, 95*, 508–514.

Favaro, A., Zanetti, T., Tenconi, E., Degortes, D., Ronzan, A., Veronese, A., et al. (2005). The relationship between temperament and impulsive behaviors in eating disordered subjects. *Eating Disorders: Journal of Treatment and Prevention, 13*(1), 61–70.

Fawcett, J. (1995). Compliance: Definitions and key issues. *Journal of Clinical Psychiatry, 56*(Suppl. 1), 4–10.

Fawcett, J., Clark, D. C., & Busch, K. A. (1993). Assessing and treating the patient at risk for suicide. *Psychiatric Annals, 23*, 245–255.

Fawcett, J., Scheftner, W., Clark, D., Hedeker, D., Gibbons, R., & Coryell, W. (1987). Clinical predictors of suicide in patients with major affective disorders: a controlled prospective study. *American Journal of Psychiatry, 144*, 35–40.

Fazey, J. A., & Hardy, L. (1988). The inverted-U hypothesis: A catastrophe for sport psychology. *British Association for Sports Sciences Monograph No. 1.* Leeds, UK: National Coaching Foundation.

Fedororf, I. C., & Taylor, S. S. (2001). Psychological and pharmacological treatments of social phobia. *Journal of Clinical Psychopharmacology, 21*, 311–324.

Feighner, J. P., Robins, E., Guze, S. B., Woodruff, R. A., Winokur, G., & Munoz, R. (1972). Diagnostic criteria for use in psychiatric research. *Archives of General Psychiatry, 26*, 57–63.

Feinstein, R., & Carey, L. (1995). Crisis intervention in office practice. In R. Rakel (Ed.), *Textbook for family practice* (5th ed., pp. 1502–1509). Philadelphia: Saunders.

Feldman, J., & Rust, J. (1989). Religiosity, schizotypal thinking, and schizophrenia. *Psychological Reports, 65*, 587–593.

Fenichel, O. (1945). *The psychoanalytic theory of neurosis.* New York: Norton.

Fenton, W., Blyler, C., & Heinssen, R. (1997). Determinants of medication compliance in schizophrenia: Empirical and clinical findings. *Schizophrenia Bulletin, 23*(4), 637–651.

Fenton, W., & McGlashan, T. H. (1987). Prognostic scale for chronic schizophrenia. *Schizophrenia Bulletin, 13*, 277–286.

Fenton, W. S., & McGlashan, T. H. (1991). Natural history of schizophrenia subtypes: Pt. II. Positive and negative symptoms and long-term course. *Archives of General Psychiatry, 48*, 978–986.

Ferguson, C. P., & Pigott, T. A. (2000). Anorexia and bulimia nervosa: Neurobiology and pharmacotherapy. *Behavior Therapy, 31*(2), 237–263.

Fergusson, D. M., & Lynskey, M. T. (1995). Childhood circumstances, adolescent adjustment, and suicide attempts in a New Zealand cohort. *Journal of the American Academy of Child and Adolescent Psychiatry, 34*, 612–622.

Fergusson, D. M., Swain, N. R., & Horwood, L. J. (2002). Deviant peer affiliations, crime and substance use: A fixed effects regression analysis. *Journal of Abnormal Child Psychology, 30*, 419–430.

Feske, U., & Chambless, D. L. (1995). Cognitive behavioral versus exposure only treatment for social phobia: A meta-analysis. *Behavior Therapy, 26*, 695–720.

Feske, U., & Goldstein, A. J. (1997). Eye movement desensitization and reprocessing treatment for panic disorder: A controlled outcome and partial dismantling study. *Journal of Consulting and Clinical Psychology, 65*, 1026–1035.

Fichter, M. M., & Daser, C. (1987). Symptomatology, psychosexual development and gender identity in 42 anorexic males. *Psychological Medicine, 17*(2), 409–418.

Fichter, M. M., Elton, M., Sourdi, L., Weyerer, S., & Koptagel-Ilal, G. (1998). Anorexia nervosa in Greek and Turkish adolescents. *European Archives of Psychiatry and Neurological Sciences, 237*(4), 200–208.

Fichter, M. M., & Krenn, H. (2003). Eating disorders in males. In J. Treasure, U. Schmidt, & E. van Furth (Eds.), *Handbook of eating disorders* (2nd ed., pp. 369–383). Chichester, West Sussex, England: Wiley.

Field, D., Garland, M., & Willams, K. (2003). Correlates of specific childhood feeding problems. *Journal of Pediatrics and Child Health, 39*(4), 299–304.

Filipek, P. A. (2005). Medical aspects of autism. In F. R. Volkmar, R. Paul, A. Klin, & D. Cohen (Eds.), *Handbook of autism and pervasive developmental disorders* (3rd ed., pp. 534–578). Hoboken, NJ: Wiley.

Filipek, P. A., Accardo, P. J., Baranek, G. T., Cook, E. H, Jr., Dawson, G., Gordon, B., et al. (1999). Practice parameters: Screening and diagnosis of autistic spectrum disorders (A multi-society consensus statement). *Neurology, 55*, 468–479.

Finch, A. E., Lambert, M. J., & Schaaljie, B. J. (2001). Psychotherapy quality control: The statistical generation of expected recovery curves for integration into an early warning system. *Clinical Psychology and Psychotherapy, 8*, 231–242.

Fink, D., Shoyer, B., & Dubin, W. R. (1991). A study of assaults against psychiatric residents. *Academic Psychiatry, 15*, 94–103.

Fink, P. (1996). From hysteria to somatization: A historical perspective. *Norwegian Journal of Psychiatry, 50*, 353–363.

Fink, P., Hansen, M., & Oxhoj, M. L. (2004). The prevalence of somatoform disorders among internal medical patients. *Journal of Psychosomatic Research, 56*, 413–418.

Fink, P., Hansen, M., & Soudergaard, L. (2005). Somatoform disorders among first time referrals to a neurology service. *Psychosomatics, 46*, 540–548.

Fink, P., Ornbol, E., Toft, T., Christensen Sparle, K., Frostholm, L., & Olesen, F. (2004). A new, empirically established hypochondriasis diagnosis. *American Journal of Psychiatry, 161*(9), 1680–1691.

Fink, P., Sorensen, L., Enberg, M., Holm, M., & Munk-Jorgensen, P. (1999). Somatization in primary care: Prevalence, health care utilization, and the general practitioner recognition. *Psychosomatics, 40*(4), 330–338.

Finn, M., & Rubin, J. B. (2000). Psychotherapy with Buddhists. In P. S. Richards & A. E. Bergin (Eds.), *Handbook of psychotherapy and religious diversity* (pp. 317–340). Washington, DC: American Psychological Association.

Finney, J. W., Moos, R. H., & Timkno, C. (1999). The course of treated and untreated substance use disorders: Remission and resolution, relapse and mortality. In B. S. McCrady & E. E. Epstein (Eds.), *Addictions: A comprehensive guidebook* (pp. 30–49). New York: Oxford University Press.

First, M. B. (2002). The DSM series and experience with DSM-IV. *Psychopathology, 35*, 67–71.

First, M. B., Frances, A., & Pincus, H. A. (2002). *DSM-IV-TR: Handbook of differential diagnosis.* Washington, DC: American Psychiatric Press..

First, M. B., Frances, A., & Pincus, H. A. (2004). *DSM-IV-TR guidebook.* Washington, DC: American Psychiatric Press.

First, M., Gibbon, M., Spitzer, R. L., Williams, J. B. W., & Benjamin, L. S. (1997). *User's guide for the Structured Clinical Interview for the DSM-I Axis II personality disorders.* Washington, DC: American Psychiatric Press.

First, M. B., & Pincus, H. A. (1999). Classification in psychiatry: ICD-10 vs. DSM-IV. *British Journal of Psychiatry, 175*, 205–209.

First, M. B., & Pincus, H. A. (2002). The DSM-I text revision: Rationale and potential impact on clinical practice. *Psychiatric Services, 53*(3), 288–292.

First, M. B., Spitzer, R. L., Williams, J. B. W., & Gibbon, M. (1995). *Structured Clinical Interview for DSM-IV (SCID)*, Washington, DC: American Psychiatric Association.

First, M. B., & Tasman, A. (2004). *DSM-IV-TR mental disorders: Diagnosis, etiology and treatment.* Hoboken, NJ: Wiley.

Fish, B. (1987). Infant predictors of the longitudinal course of schizophrenic development. *Schizophrenia Bulletin, 13*, 395–409.

Fishbain, D. A., Cutler, R. B., Rosomoff, H. L., & Rosomoff, R. S. (1998). Do antidepressants have an analgesic effect in psychogenic pain and somatoform pain disorder? A meta-analysis. *Psychosomatic Medicine, 60*, 503–509.

Fishbain, D. A., Cutler, R. B., Rosomoff, H. L., & Rosomoff, R. S. (2004). Is there a relationship between nonorganic physical findings (Waddell) signs and secondary gain/malingering? *Clinical Journal of Pain, 20*(6), 399–408.

Fisher, L. A., Elias, J. W., & Ritz, K. (1998). Predicting relapse to substance abuse as a function of personality dimensions. *Alcoholism: Clinical and Experimental Research, 22*, 1041–1047.

Fisher, W. W., Piazza, C. C., Bowman, L. G., Kurty, P. F., Sherer, M. R., & Lachman, S. R. (1994). A preliminary evaluation of empirically derived consequences for the treatment of pica. *Journal of Applied Behavior Analysis, 27,* 447–457.

Fitting, M., Rabins, P., Lucas, M. J., & Eastham, J. (1986). Caregivers for dementia patients: A comparison of husbands and wives. *Gerontologist, 26,* 248–252.

Fitzgerald, M. (1999). Differential diagnosis of adolescent and adult pervasive developmental disorders/autism spectrum disorders (PDD/ASD): A not uncommon diagnostic dilemma. *Irish Journal of Psychological Medicine, 16*(4), 145–148.

Flacker, J. M., & Marcantonio, E. R. (1998). Delirium in the elderly: Optimal management. *Drugs and Aging, 13,* 119–130.

Flament, M. F., Whitaker, A., Rapoport, J. L., Davies, M., Berg, C. Z., Kalikow, K., et al. (1988). Obsessive compulsive disorder in adolescence: An epidemiological study. *Journal of the American Academy of Child and Adolescent Psychiatry, 27,* 764–771.

Flannery-Schroeder, E. C. (2004). Generalized anxiety disorder. In T. L. Morris & J. S. March (Eds.), *Anxiety disorders in children and adolescents* (pp. 125–140). New York: Guilford Press.

Flaskerud, J. H., & Liu, P. Y. (1991). Effects of an Asian client-therapist language, ethnicity, gender match on utilization and outcome of therapy. *Community Mental Health Journal, 27,* 31–42.

Fleishhacker, W., Meise, U., Gunther, V., & Kurz, M. (1994). Compliance with antipsychotic drug treatment: Influence of side effects. *Acta Psychiatrica Scandinavica, 89*(Suppl. 382), 11–15.

Fleming, S. K., Blasey, C., & Schatzberg, A. F. (2004). Neuropsychological correlates of psychotic features in major depressive disorders: A review and meta-analysis. *Journal of Psychiatric Research, 38,* 27–35.

Fleminger, S. (2002). Remembering delirium. *British Journal of Psychiatry, 180,* 4–5.

Fleminger, S., Oliver, D. L., Lovestone, S., Rabe-Hesketh, S., & Giora, A. (2003). Head injury as a risk factor for Alzheimer's disease: The evidence 10 years on a partial replication. *Journal of Neurology, Neurosurgery, and Psychiatry, 74,* 857–862.

Flint, A. J., & Rifat, S. L. (1996). The effect of sequential antidepressant treatment on geriatric depression. *Journal of Affective Disorders, 36,* 95–105.

Flint, A. J., & Rifat, S. L. (1997). Anxious depression in elderly patients: Response to antidepressant treatment. *American Journal of Geriatric Psychiatry, 5,* 107–115.

Flor, F., Birbaumer, N., & Turk, D. C. (1990). The psychobiology of chronic pain. *Advances in Behavior Research and Therapy, 12,* 47–84.

Foa, E. B., Cashman, L. A., Jaycox, L., & Perry, K. (1997). The validation of a self-report measure of post-traumatic stress disorder: The Posttraumatic Diagnostic Scale. *Psychological Assessment, 4,* 445–451.

Foa, E. B., Huppert, J. D., & Cahill, S. P. (2006). Emotional processing theory: An update. In B. O. Rothbaum (Ed.), *Pathological anxiety: Emotional processing in etiology and treatment* (pp. 3–24). New York: Guilford Press.

Foa, E. B., & Kozak, M. J. (1986). Emotional processing of fear: Exposure to corrective information. *Psychological Bulletin, 99,* 20–35.

Foa, E. B., & Rothbaum, B. O. (1998). *Treating the trauma of rape: Cognitive-behavioral therapy for PTSD.* New York: Guilford Press.

Foa, E. B., Steketee, G., & Rothbaum, B. O. (1989). Behavioral/cognitive conceptualizations of post-traumatic stress disorder. *Behavior Therapy, 20,* 155–176.

Foa, E. B., Zoellner, L. A., Feeny, N. C., Hembree, E. A., & Alvarez-Conrad, J. (2002). Does imaginal exposure exacerbate PTSD symptoms? *Journal of Consulting and Clinical Psychology, 70,* 1022–1028.

Foley, D. L., Eaves, L. J., Wormley, B., Silberg, J. L., Maes, H. H., Kuhn, J., et al. (2004). Childhood adversity, monoamine oxidase, a genotype and risk for conduct disorder. *Archives of General Psychiatry, 61,* 738–744.

Foley, D. L., Goldston, D. B., Costello, E. J., & Angold, A. (2006). Proximal psychiatric risk factors for suicidality in youth: The Great Smoky Mountains study. *Archives of General Psychiatry, 63,* 1017–1024.

Foley, D. J., Monjan, A. A., Brown, S. L., Simonsick, E. M., Wallace, R. B., & Blazer, D. G. (1995). Sleep complaints among elderly persons: An epidemiologic study of three communities. *Sleep: Journal of Sleep Research and Sleep Medicine, 18*(6), 425–432.

Foley, D. J., Monjan, A., Simonsick, E. M., Wallace, R. B., & Blazer, D. G. (1999). Incidence and remission of insomnia among elderly adults: An epidemiologic study of 6,800 persons over 3 years. *Sleep, 22*(Suppl. 2), S366–S372.

Folkman, S. (1984). Personal control and stress and coping processes: Atheoretical analysis. *Journal of Personality and Social Psychology, 46,* 839–852.

Folks, D. G. (1995). Munchausen's syndrome and other factitious disorders. *Neurologic Clinics, 13*(2), 267–281.

Folstein, M. F. (1997). Differential diagnosis of dementia: The clinical process. *Psychiatric Clinics of North America, 20,* 45–57.

Folstein, M. F., Folstein, S. E., & McHugh, P. R. (1975). Mini-mental state. *Journal of Psychiatric Research, 12,* 189–198.

Folstein, S. E., & Mankoski, R. E. (2000). Chromosome 7q: Where autism meets language disorder? *American Journal of Human Genetics, 67,* 278–281.

Fombonne, E. (1997). Epidemiological studies of autism. In F. R. Volkmar (Ed.), *Autism and developmental disorders* (pp. 32–63). New York: Cambridge University Press.

Fombonne, E. (2003a). Epidemiological surveys of autism and other pervasive developmental disorders: An update. *Journal of Autism and Developmental Disorders, 33,* 365–382.

Fombonne, E. (2003b). The prevalence of autism. *Journal of the American Medical Association, 289*(1), 87–88.

Fombonne, E. (2005). Epidemiological studies of pervasive developmental disorders. In F. R. Volkmar, R. Paul, A. Klin, & D. Cohen (Eds.), *Handbook of autism and pervasive developmental disorders* (3rd ed., pp. 42–69). Hoboken, NJ: Wiley.

Fombonne, E., & Chakrabarti, S. (2001). No evidence for a new variant of measles-mumps-rubella-induced autism. *Pediatrics, 108*(4), E58.

Fombonne, E., & Tidmarsh, L. (2003). Epidemiologic data on Asperger disorder. *Child and Adolescent Psychiatric Clinics of North America, 12,* 15–22.

Fonagy, P., & Bateman, A. W. (2005). Attachment theory and mentalization-orientation model of borderline personality disorder. In J. M. Oldham, A. E. Skodol, & D. S. Bender (Eds.), *Textbook of personality disorders* (pp. 187–208). Washington, DC: American Psychiatric Publishing.

Fonagy, P., Target, M., Cottrell, D., Phillips, J., & Kurtz, Z. (2002). *What works for whom? A critical review of treatment for children and adolescents.* New York: Guilford Press.

Fontenelle, L. F., Mendlowicz, M. V., & Versiani, M. (2006). The descriptive epidemiology of obsessive-compulsive disorder. *Progress in Neuro-Psychopharmacology and Biological Psychiatry, 30,* 327–337.

Ford, C. (1995). Dimensions of somatization and hypochondriasis. *Neurologic Clinics, 13*(2), 241–253.

Ford, D. E., & Kamerow, D. B. (1989). Epidemiologic study of sleep disturbances and psychiatric disorders. *Journal of the American Medical Association, 262,* 1479–1484.

Ford, G. R., Goode, K. T., Barrett, J. J., Harrell, L. E., & Haley, W. E. (1997). Gender roles and caregiving stress: An examination of subjective appraisals of specific primary stressors in Alzheimer's caregivers. *Aging and Mental Health, 1,* 158–165.

Forrette, F., Seux, M. L., Staessen, J. A., Thijs, L., Babarskiene, M. R., Babeanu, S., et al. (2002). The prevention of dementia with antihypertensive treatment: New evidence from the Systolic Hypertension in Europe (Syst-Eur) Study. *Archives of Internal Medicine, 162,* 2046–2052.

Fossati, A., Donati, D., Donini, M., Novella, L., Bagnato, M., & Maffei, C. (2001). Temperament, character, and attachment patterns in borderline personality disorder. *Journal of Personality Disorders, 15,* 390–402.

Fowler, I. L., Carr, V., Carter, N., & Lewin, T. J. (1998). Patterns of current and lifetime substance use in schizophrenia. *Schizophrenia Bulletin, 24,* 443–455.

Fowles, D. C. (2001) Biological variables in psychopathology: A psychobiological perspective. In H. E. Adams & P. B. Sutker (Eds.), *Comprehensive handbook of psychopathology* (3rd ed., pp. 85–104). New York: Kluwer Academic/Plenum.

Fowles, D. C., & Kochanska, G. (2000). Temperament as a moderator of pathways to conscience in children: The contribution of electrodermal activity. *Psychophysiology, 37*, 788–795.

Frances, A., First, M. B., & Pincus, H. A. (1995). *DSM-IV guidebook.* Washington, DC: American Psychiatric Association.

Frances, A., First, M. B., & Pincus, H. A. (1999). *DSM-IV guidebook.* Washington, DC: American Psychiatric Press.

Frances, A., Manning, D., Marin, D., Kocsis, J., McKinney, K., Hall, W., et al. (1992). Relationship of anxiety and depression. *Psychopharmacology, 106*, S82–S86.

Frances, A., & Ross, R. (2001). *DSM-IV-TR case studies: A clinical guide to differential diagnosis.* Washington, DC: American psychiatric Press.

Frances, A. J. (1980). The DSM-III personality disorders section: A commentary. *American Journal of Psychiatry, 137*, 1050–1054.

Frances, J., & Kapoor, W. N. (1990). A prospective study of delirium in hospitalized elderly. *Journal of the American Medical Association, 263*, 1097–1101.

Franchini, L., Zanardi, R., Smeraldi, E., & Gasperini, M. (1998). Early onset of lithium prophylaxis as a predictor of good longterm outcome. *European Archives of Psychiatry and Clinical Neuroscience, 249*, 227–230.

Franco, K. S. N., & Branson, D. (2005). Diabetes mellitus and Alzheimer disease. *Archives of Neurology, 62*, 330.

Frank, E. (2005). *Treating bipolar disorder: A clinician's guide to interpersonal and social rhythm therapy.* New York: Guilford Press.

Frank, E., Hlastala, S., Ritenour, A., Houck, P., Tu, X. M., Monk, T. H., et al. (1997). Inducing lifestyle regularity in recovering bipolar disorder patients: Results from the maintenance therapies in bipolar disorder protocol. *Biological Psychiatry, 41*, 1165–1173.

Frank, E., Kupfer, D., & Siegel, L. (1995). Alliance not compliance: A philosophy of outpatient care. *Journal of Clinical Psychiatry, 56*(Suppl. 1), 11–17.

Frank, E., Swartz, H. A., & Kupfer, D. (2000). Interpersonal and social rhythm therapy: Managing the chaos of bipolar disorder. *Biological Psychiatry, 48*, 593–604.

Frank, N. C., Spirito, A., Stark, L., & Owens-Stively, J. (1997). The use of scheduled awakenings to eliminate childhood sleepwalking. *Journal of Pediatric Psychology, 22*(3), 345–353.

Frank, Y., & Pavlakis, S. G. (2001). Brain imaging in neurobehavioral disorders. *Pediatric Neurology, 25*, 278–287.

Franklin, J., & Markarian, M. (2005). Substance abuse in minority populations. In R. J. Frances, S. I. Miller, & A. H. Mack (Eds.), *Clinical textbook of addictive disorders* (3rd ed., pp. 321–339). New York: Guilford Press.

Franklin, M. E., Abramowitz, J. S., Brux, D. A., Zoellner, L. A., & Feeny, N. (2002). Cognitive-behavioral therapy with and without medication in the treatment of obsessive-compulsive disorder. *Professional Psychology: Research and Practice, 33*, 162–168.

Franklin, M. E., Abramowitz, J. S., Kozak, M. J., Levitt, J. T., & Foa, E. B. (2000). Effectiveness of exposure and ritual prevention for obsessive compulsive disorder: Randomized compared with non-randomized samples. *Journal of Consulting and Clinical Psychology, 68*, 594–602.

Franklin, M. E., Rynn, M. A., Foa, E. B., & March, J. S. (2004). Pediatric obsessive-compulsive disorder. In T. H. Ollendick & J. S. March (Eds.), *Phobic and anxiety disorders in children and adolescents: A clinician's guide to effective psychosocial and pharmacological interventions* (pp. 381–404). New York: Oxford University Press.

Franko, D. L., & Keel, P. K. (2006). Suicidality in eating disorders: Occurrence, correlates, and clinical implications. *Clinical Psychology Review, 26*(6), 769–782.

Frawley, P., & Smith, J. (1992). One-year follow-up after multimodal inpatient treatment for cocaine and methamphetamine dependencies. *Journal of Substance Abuse Treatment, 9*, 271–286.

Frazee, J. C., Chicota, C. L., Templer, D. I., & Arikawa, H. (2003). The usefulness of the Axis v diagnosis: Opinions of health care professionals. *Journal of Nervous and Mental Disorders, 191*(10), 692–694.

Frederikson, L. G., Chamberlain, K., & Long, N. (1996). Unacknowledged casualties of the Vietnam War: Experiences of the partners of New Zealand veterans. *Qualitative Health Research, 6*, 49–70.

Fredrikson, M., Annas, P., Fischer, H., & Wik, G. (1996). Gender and age differences in the prevalence of specific fears and phobias. *Behavioural Research and Therapy, 34*, 33–39.

Freeman, B. J. (1997). Guidelines for evaluating intervention programs for children with autism. *Journal of Autism and Developmental Disorders, 27*, 641–651.

Freeman, R. Q., Giovannetti, T., Lamar, M., Cloud, B. S., Stern, R. A., Kaplan, E., et al. (2000). Visuoconstructional problems in dementia: Contribution of executive systems functions. *Neuropsychology, 14*, 415–426.

French, S. A., Story, M., Remafedi, G., Resnick, M. D., & Blum, R. W. (1996). Sexual orientation and prevalence of body dissatisfaction and eating disordered behaviors: A population-based study of adolescents. *International Journal of Eating Disorders, 19*(2), 119–126.

Freud, S. (1917). Mourning and melancholia. In P. Gay (Ed.), *The Freud reader* (pp. 584–589). New York: Norton.

Freud, S. (1952). *Collected papers: Case histories.* Oxford, England: Hogarth. (Original work published in 1909)

Freud, S. (1955). The standard edition of the complete works of Sigmund Freud (J. Strachey, Trans.). London: Hogarth Press.

Frueh, C. B., Elhai, J. D., & Hamner, M. B. (2003). Post-traumatic stress disorder (combat). In M. Hersen & S. M. Turner (Eds.), *Diagnostic interviewing* (3rd ed., pp. 321–343). New York: Kluwer Academic.

Frick, P. J. (1998). *Conduct disorders and severe antisocial behavior.* New York: Plenum Press.

Frick, P. J. (2001). Effective interventions for children and adolescents with conduct disorder. *Canadian Journal of Psychiatry, 46*, 597–608.

Frick, P. J., Cornell, A. H., Bodin, S. D., Dane, H. A., Barry, C. T., & Loney, B. R. (2003). Callous-unemotional traits and developmental pathways to severe conduct problems. *Developmental Psychology, 39*, 246–260.

Frick, P. J., & Ellis, M. (1999). Callous-unemotional traits and developmental pathways to severe conduct disorder. *Clinical Child and Family Psychology Review, 2*, 149–168.

Frick, P. J., & Morris, A. S. (2004). Temperament and developmental pathways to conduct problems. *Journal of Child Psychology and Psychiatry, 33*, 54–68.

Frick, P. J., & Silverthorn, P. (2001). Psychopathology in children. In H. E. Adams & P. B. Sutker (Eds.), *Comprehensive handbook of psychopathology* (3rd ed.). New York: Kluwer Academic/Plenum Press.

Fridell, M., & Hesse, M. (2006). Psychiatric severity and mortality in substance abusers: A 15-year follow-up of drug users. *Addictive Behaviors, 31*, 559–565.

Friedman, E. G., & Wilson, R. (2004). Treatment of opiate addiction. In S. L. Ashenberg-Straussner (Ed.), *Clinical work with substance-abusing clients* (2nd ed., pp. 187–208). New York: Guilford Press.

Friedman, M. J., & Marsella, A. J. (1996). Posttraumatic stress disorder: An overview of the concept. In A. J. Marsella, M. J. Friedman, E. T. Gerrity, & R. M. Scurfield (Eds.), *Ethnocultural aspects of posttraumatic stress disorder: Issues, research, and clinical applications* (pp. 11–32). Washington, DC: American Psychological Association.

Frith, U. (1989). *Autism: Explaining the enigma.* Oxford: Blackwell.

Frith, U. (2004). Emmanual Miller lecture: Confusion and controversies about Asperger syndrome. *Journal of Child Psychology and Psychiatry, 45*(4), 672–686.

Frost, D. O., & Cadet, J. L. (2000). Effects of methamphetamine-induced neurotoxicity on the development of neural circuitry: A hypothesis. *Brain Research Reviews, 34*, 103–108.

Frost, R. O., Williams, N., & Jenter, C. (1995). *Perfectionism and body dysmorphic disorder.* Paper presented at the World Congress of Behavioral and Cognitive Therapies, Copenhagen, Denmark.

Frye, M. A., Altschuler, L. L., McElroy, S. L., Suppes, T., Keck, P. E., Denicoff, K., et al. (2003). Gender differences in prevalence, risk, and clinical correlates of alcoholism comorbidity in bipolar disorder. *American Journal of Psychiatry, 160*, 883–889.

Frye, M. A., Gitlin, M. J., & Altshuler, L. L. (2004). Unmet needs in bipolar depression. *Depression and Anxiety, 19*, 199–208.

Fujino, D. C., Okazaki, S., & Young, K. (1994). Asian-American women in the mental health system: An examination of ethnic and gender match between therapist and client. *Journal of Community Psychology, 22*, 164–176.

Furst, P. T. (1990). *Flesh of the gods: The ritual use of hallucinogens.* Long Grove, IL: Waveland Press.

Fyer, A. J. (1998). Current approaches to etiology and pathophysiology of specific phobia. *Biological Psychiatry, 44*, 1295–1304.

Gabbard, G. O. (2000a). Combining medication with psychotherapy in the treatment of personality disorders. In J. G. Gunderson & G. O. Gabbard (Eds.), *Psychotherapy for Personality Disorders.* (pp. 65–94). Washington, DC: American Psychiatric Press.

Gabbard, G. O. (2000b). *Psychodynamic psychiatry in clinical practice* (3rd ed.). Washington, DC: American Psychiatric Association.

Gabbard, G. O. (2005). Psychoanalysis. In J. M. Oldham, A. E. Skodol, & D. S. Bender (Eds.), *Textbook of personality disorders* (pp. 257–273). Washington, DC: American Psychiatric Publishing.

Gadow, K. D., & Nolan, E. E. (2002). Differences between preschool children with ODD, ADHD, and ODD+ADHD symptoms. *Journal of Child Psychology and Psychiatry, 43*(2), 191–201.

Gadow, K. D., & Weiss, M. (2001). Attention-deficit/hyperactivity disorder in adults: Beyond controversy. *Archives of General Psychiatry, 58*, 784–785.

Gainetdinov, R. R., & Caron, M. G. (2001). Genetics of childhood disorders: XXIV. ADHD, Part 8: Hyperdopaminergic mice as an animal model of ADHD. *Journal of the American Academy of Child and Adolescent Psychiatry, 40*(3), 380–382.

Gallagher, R., & Blader, J. (2001). The diagnosis and neuropsychological assessment of adult attention deficit/hyperactivity disorder: Scientific study and practical guidelines. *Annals of the New York Academy of Sciences, 931*, 148–171.

Gallant, D., Smith, D. E., & Wesson, D. R. (2001). Alcohol and other depressant drugs. In G. O. Gabbard (Ed.), *Treatments of psychiatric disorders.* (3rd ed., pp. 663–690). Washington, DC: American Psychiatric Press.

Gallassi, R., Monrreale, A., & Pagni, P. (2001). The relationship between depression and cognition. *Archives of Gerontology and Geriatrics, 7*, 163–171.

Galovski, T., & Lyons, J. A. (2004). Psychological sequelae of combat violence: A review of the impact of PTSD on the veteran's family and possible interventions. *Aggression and Violent Behavior, 9*, 477–501.

Gamst, G., Dana, R. H., Der-Karabetian, A., & Kramer, T. (2000). Ethnic match and client ethnicity effects on global assessment and visitation. *Journal of Community Psychology, 28*, 547–564.

Gans, A. M., Kenny, M. C., & Ghany, D. L. (2003). Comparing the self-concept of students with and without learning disabilities. *Journal of Learning Disabilities, 36*, 287–295.

Gao, K., Gajwani, P., Elhai, O., & Calabrese, J. R. (2005). Typical and atypical antipsychotics in bipolar depression. *Journal of Clinical Psychiatry, 66*, 1376–1385.

Garber, J., Keiley, M. K., & Martin, N. C. (2002). Developmental trajectories of adolescents' depressive symptoms: Predictors of change. *Journal of Consulting and Clinical Psychology, 70*, 79–95.

Garber, M. D., & Garber, S. W. (1998). Beyond Ritalin: A multimodal approach to assessment and treatment of attention deficit/hyperactivity disorder. *Innovations in Clinical Practice: A Source Book* (16), 109–126.

Garcia-Lawson, K., & Lane, R. (1997). Thoughts on termination: Practical considerations. *Psychoanalytic Psychology, 14*(2), 239–257.

Gard, M. C. E., & Freeman, C. P. (1996). The dismantling of a myth: A review of eating disorders and socioeconomic status. *International Journal of Eating Disorders, 20*(1), 1–12.

Gardner, F. E. M., Sonuga-Barke, E. J. S., & Sayal, K. (1999). Parents anticipating misbehavior: An observational study of strategies parent use to prevent conflict with behavioral problem children. *Journal of Child Psychology and Psychiatry, 40*, 1185–1196.

Gardner, W., Lidz, C., Mulvey, E. P., & Shaw, E. C. (1996). A comparison of actuarial methods for identifying repetitively-violent patients. *Law and Human Behavior, 20*, 443–497.

Gardos, G., Casey, D. E., Cole, J. O., Perenyi, A., Kocsis, E., Arato, M., et al. (1994). Ten-year outcome of tardive dyskinesia. *American Journal of Psychiatry, 151*, 836–841.

Garety, P. A., Fowler, D., & Kuipers, E. (2000). Cognitive-behavioral therapy for medication resistant symptoms. *Schizophrenia Bulletin, 26*, 73–86.

Garfield, S. L. (2001). Methodological issues in clinical diagnosis. In H. E. Adams & P. S. Sutker (Eds.), *Comprehensive handbook of psychopathology* (3rd ed., pp. 29–53). New York: Kluwer Academic/Plenum Press.

Garfinkel, P. E. (2002). Classification and diagnosis of eating disorders. In C. G. Fairburn & K. D. Brownell (Eds.), *Eating disorders and obesity: A comprehensive handbook* (2nd ed., pp. 155–161). New York: Guilford Press.

Garfinkel, P. E., Lin, E., Goering, P., Spegg, C., Goldbloom, D., Kennedy, S., et al. (1995). Bulimia nervosa in a Canadian community sample: Prevalence and comparison of subgroups. *American Journal of Psychiatry, 152*(7), 1052–1058.

Garfinkel, P. E., Lin, E., Goering, P., Spegg, C., Goldbloom, D., Kennedy, S., et al. (1996). Should amenorrhoea be necessary for the diagnosis of anorexia nervosa? Evidence from a Canadian community sample. *British Journal of Psychiatry, 168*(40), 500–506.

Garfinkel, P. E., & Newman, A. (2001). The Eating Attitudes Test: Twenty-five years later. *Eating and Weight Disorders, 6*(1), 1–24.

Garner, D. M. (1993). Binge eating in anorexia nervosa. In C. G. Fairburn & G. T. Wilson (Eds.), *Binge eating: Nature, assessment, and treatment* (pp. 50–76). New York: Guilford Press.

Garner, D. M., & Bemis, K. M. (1982). A cognitive-behavioral approach to anorexia nervosa. *Cognitive Therapy and Research, 6*(2), 123–150.

Garner, D. M., & Magana, C. (2002). Bulimia nervosa. In M. Hersen & L. K. Porzelius (Eds.), *Diagnosis, conceptualization, and treatment planning for adults: A step-by-step guide* (pp. 251–269). Mahwah, NJ: Erlbaum.

Garner, D. M., Rosen, L. W., & Barry, D. (1998). Eating disorders among athletes: Research and recommendations. *Child and Adolescent Psychiatric Clinics of North America, 7*(4), 839–857.

Garner, J. (2003). Psychotherapies and older adults. *Australian and New Zealand Journal of Psychiatry, 37*, 537–548.

Garno, J. L., Goldberg, J. E., Ramirez, P. M., & Ritzler, B. A. (2005). Bipolar disorder with comorbid Cluster B personality disorder features: Impact on suicidality. *Journal of Clinical Psychiatry, 66*, 339–345.

Garralda, M. E. (1996). Somatization in children. *Journal of Child Psychological Psychiatry, 37*(1), 13–33.

Garrison, C. Z. (1992). Demographic predictors of suicide. In R. W. Maris, A. L. Berman, J. T. Maltsberger, & R. I. Yufit (Eds.), *Assessment and prediction of suicide* (pp. 484–496). New York: Guilford Press.

Gasper, M. C., Ott, B. R., & Lapane, K. L. (2005). Is donepezil therapy associated with reduced mortality in nursing home residents with dementia? *American Journal of Geriatric Pharmacotherapy, 3*, 1–7.

Gatz, J. L., Tyas, S. L., St. John, P., & Montgomery, P. (2005). Do depressive symptoms predict Alzheimer's disease and dementia? *Journals of Gerontology, Series A: Biological Sciences and Medical Sciences, 60*, 744–747.

Gaub, M., & Carlson, C. L. (1997). Gender differences in ADHD: A meta-analysis and critical review. *Journal of the American Academy of Child and Adolescent Psychiatry, 36*(8), 1036–1045.

Gaudiano, B. A., & James, H. D. (2006). Believability of hallucinations as a potential mediator of their frequency and associated distress in psychotic inpatients. *Behavioural and Cognitive Psychotherapy, 34,* 497–502.

Gaugler, J. E., Anderson, K. A., Leach, C. R., Smith, C. D., Schmitt, F. A., & Mendiondo, M. (2004). The emotional ramifications of unmet need in dementia caregiving. *American Journal of Alzheimer's Disease and Other Dementias, 19,* 369–378.

Gaugler, J. E., Davey, A., Pearlin, L. I., & Zarit, S. H. (2000). Modeling caregiver adaptation over time: The longitudinal impact of behavior problems. *Psychology and Aging, 15,* 437–450.

Gaugler, J. E., Kane, R. L., Kane, R. A., & Newcomer, R. (2005). The longitudinal effects of early behavior problems in the dementia caregiving career. *Psychology and Aging, 20,* 100–116.

Gaugler, J. E., Leach, C. R., Clay, T., & Newcomer, R. C. (2004). Predictors of nursing home placement in African-Americans with dementia. *Journal of the American Geriatric Society, 52,* 445–452.

Gaugler, J. E., Zarit, S. H., & Pearlin, L. I. (2003). The onset of dementia caregiving and its longitudinal implications. *Psychology and Aging, 18,* 171–180.

Geddes, J. R., Burgess, S., Hawton, K., Jamison, K., & Goodwin, G. M. (2004). Long-term lithium therapy for bipolar disorder: Systematic review and meta-analysis of randomized controlled trials. *American Journal of Psychiatry, 161,* 217–222.

Geer, J. H. (1965). The development of a scale to measure fear. *Behaviour Research and Therapy, 3,* 45–53.

Gekker, G., Hu, S. X., Wentland, M. P., Bidlack, J. M., Lokensgard, J. R., & Peterson, P. K. (2004). Kappa-opioid receptor ligands inhibit cocaine-induced HIV-1 expression in microglial cells. *Journal of Pharmacology and Experimental Therapeutics, 309,* 600–606.

Geldmacher, D. S., Provenzano, G., McRae, T., Mastey, V., & Ieni, J. R. (2003). Donepezil is associated with delayed nursing home placement in patients with Alzheimer's disease. *Journal of the American Geriatric Society, 51,* 937–944.

Gelernter, C. S., Uhde, T. W., Cimbolic, P., Arnkoff, D. B., Vittone, B. J., Tancer, M. E., et al. (1991). Cognitive-behavioral and pharmacological treatments of social phobia: A controlled study. *Archives of General Psychiatry, 48,* 938–945.

Geller, B., & Luby, J. (1997). Child and adolescent bipolar disorder: A review of the past 10 years. *Journal of the American Academy of Child and Adolescent Psychiatry, 36,* 1168–1176.

Geller, B., Tillman, R., Craney, J. L., & Bolhofner, K. (2004). Four-year prospective outcome and natural history of mania in children with a prepubertal and early adolescent bipolar disorder phenotype. *Archives of General Psychiatry, 61,* 459–467.

Geller, B., Zimermann, B., Williams, M., Bolhofner, K., & Craney, J. L. (2001). Bipolar disorder at prospective follow-up of adults who had prepubertal major depressive disorder. *American Journal of Psychiatry, 158,* 125–127.

Geller, B., Zimerman, B., Williams, M., Delbello, M. P., Frazier, J., & Beringer, L. (2002). Phenomenology of pre-pubertal and early adolescent bipolar disorder: Examples of elated mood, decreased need for sleep, racing thoughts, and hypersexuality. *Journal of Child and Adolescent Psychopharmacology, 12,* 3–9.

Geller, J., Williams, K. D., & Srikameswaran, S. (2001). Clinician stance in the treatment of chronic eating disorders. *European Eating Disorders Review, 9*(6), 365–373.

Gelso, C. J., & Hayes, J. A. (2001). Countertransference management. *Psychotherapy, 38,* 418–422.

George, E. L., Miklowitz, D. J., Richards, J. A., Simoneau, T. L., & Taylor, D. O. (2003). The comorbidity of bipolar disorder and Axis II personality disorders: Prevalence and clinical correlates. *Bipolar Disorders, 5,* 115–122.

George, W. H., LaMarr, J., Barrett, K., & McKinnon, T. (1999). Alcoholic parentage, self-labeling, and endorsement of ACOA-codependent traits. *Psychology of Addictive Behaviors, 13,* 39–48.

Gerber, B. J., & Brown, D. A. (Eds). (1997). *Learning disabilities and employment.* Austin, TX: ProEd.

Gerhardt, P. F., & Holmes, D. L. (2005). Employment: Options and issues for adolescents and adults with autism spectrum disorders. In F. R. Volkmar, R. Paul, A. Klin, & D. Cohen (Eds.), *Handbook of autism and pervasive developmental disorders* (3rd ed., pp. 1087–1101). Hoboken, NJ: Wiley.

Geroldi, C., Frisoni, G. B., Paolisso, G., Bandinelli, S., Lamponi, M., Abbatecola, A. M., et al. (2005). Insulin resistance in cognitive impairment: The InCHIANTI Study. *Archives of Neurology, 62*, 1067–1072.

Gerrard, M., Gibbons, F. X., Stock, M. L., & Vande Lune, L. S. (2005). Images of smokers and willingness to smoke among African-American pre-adolescents: An application of the prototype/willingness model of adolescent health risk behavior to smoking initiation. *Journal of Pediatric Psychology, 30*, 305–318.

Gershon, E. S., DeLisi, L. E., Hamovit, J., Nurnberger, J. I., Maxwell, M. E., Schreiber, J., et al. (1988). A controlled family study of chronic psychoses: Schizophrenia and schizoaffective disorder. *Archives of General Psychiatry, 45*, 328–336.

Gershon, E. S., Hamovit, J. H., Guroff, J. J., & Nurnberger, J. I. (1987). Birth-cohort changes in manic and depressive disorders in relatives of bipolar and schizoaffective patients. *Archives of General Psychiatry, 44*, 314–319.

Gerson, A. R. (2002). Beyond DSM-IV: A meta-review of the literature on malingering. *American Journal of Forensic Psychology, 20*(1), 57–69.

Gerson, J., & Stanley, B. (2002). Suicidal and self-injurous behavior in personality disorder: Controversies and treatment directions. *Current Psychiatry Reports, 4*, 30–38.

Gesell, A., & Ilg, F. L. (1940). *The first five years of life: A guide to the study of the preschool child.* New York: Harper & Brothers.

Ghaemi, S. N., Sachs, G. S., Chiou, A. M., Pandurangi, A. K., & Goodwin, K. (1999). Is bipolar disorder still underdiagnosed? Are antidepressants overutilized? *Journal of Affective Disorders, 52*, 135–144.

Ghaziuddin, M. (1991). Folie a deux and mental retardation: Review and case report. *Canadian Journal of Psychiatry, 36*, 48–49.

Ghaziuddin, M., & Gerstein, L. (1996). Pedantic speaking style differentiates Asperger's syndrome from high-functioning autism. *Journal of Autism and Developmental Disorders, 32*(4), 299–306.

Ghaziuddin, M., & Mountain-Kimchi, K. (2004). Defining the intellectual profile of Asperger syndrome: Comparison with high functioning autism. *Journal of Autism and Developmental Disorders, 34*, 279–284.

Gibbs, J. T. (1997). African-American suicide: A cultural paradox. *Suicide and Life-Threatening Behavior, 27*, 68–79.

Gibson, R. (1958). The family background and early life experiences of the manic-depressive patient. *Psychiatry, 21*, 71–90.

Gilboa-Schechtman, E., Franklin, M. E., & Foa, E. (2000). Anticipated reactions to social events: Differences among individuals with generalized social phobia, obsessive compulsive disorder, and nonanxious controls. *Cognitive Therapy and Research, 24*, 731–746.

Gilchrist, A., Cox, A., Rutter, M., Green, J., Burton, D., & Le Couteur, A. (2001). Development and current functioning in adolescents with Asperger syndrome: A comparative study. *Journal of Child Psychology and Psychiatry, 42*, 227–240.

Gill, S. S., Rochon, P. A., Guttman, M., & Laupacis, A. (2003). The value of positron emission tomography in the clinical evaluation of dementia. *Journal of the American Geriatric Society, 51*, 258–264.

Gillberg, C. (1990). Autism and the pervasive developmental disorders. *Journal of Child Psychology and Psychiatry, 31*(1), 99–119.

Gillberg, C. (1998). Asperger syndrome and high functioning autism. *British Journal of Psychiatry, 172*, 200–209.

Gillberg, C., & Coleman, M. (2000). *The biology of the autistic syndromes* (3rd ed.). London: Mac Keith Press.

Gilliam, C. M., & Cottone, R. (2005). Couple or individual therapy for the treatment of depression? An update of the empirical literature. *American Journal of Family Therapy, 33*, 265–272.

Gilliam, J. E. (1995). *Gilliam Autism Rating Scale (GAR)*. Austin, TX: ProEd.

Gilliam, J. E. (2001). *Gilliam Asperger Disorder Scale*. Austin, TX: ProEd.

Gilliland, B. E., & James, R. K. (1988). *Crisis intervention strategies*. Pacific Grove, CA: Brooks/Cole.

Ginsberg, D. L. (2003). Anticonvulsants may reduce suicidality in bipolar disorder. *Primary Psychiatry, 10*, 19.

Girolamo, G., & McFarlane, A. C. (1996). The epidemiology of PTSD: A comprehensive review of the international literature. In A. J. Marsella, M. J. Friedman, E. T. Gerrity, & R. M. Scurfield (Eds.), *Ethnocultural aspects of posttraumatic stress disorder: Issues, research, and clinical applications* (pp. 33–86). Washington, DC: American Psychological Association.

Gitlin, L. N., Corcoran, M., Winter, L., Boyce, A., & Hauck, W. W. (2001). Randomized, controlled trial of a home environmental intervention: Effect on efficacy and upset in caregivers and on daily function of persons with dementia. *Gerontologist, 41*, 4–14.

Gitlin, L. N., Hauck, W. W., Dennis, M. P., & Winter, L. (2005). Maintenance of effects of the home environmental skill-building program for family caregivers and individuals with Alzheimer's disease and related disorders. *Journals of Gerontology, Series A: Biological Sciences and Medical Sciences, 60A*, 368–374.

Gitlin, L. N., Winter, L., Corcoran, M., Dennis, M. P., Schinfeld, S., & Hauck, W. W. (2003). Effects of the home environmental skill-building program on the caregiver-care recipient dyad: 6-month outcomes from the Philadelphia REACH initiative. *Gerontologist, 43*, 532–546.

Gitlin, M. J. (1996). *The psychotherapist's guide to psychopharmacology* (2nd ed.). New York: Free Press.

Gitlin, M. J. (2006, March). Treatment-resistant bipolar disorder. *Molecular Psychiatry, 11*, 227–240.

Gitlin, M. J., & Hammen, C. (1999). Subsyndromal and psychosocial outcome in bipolar disorder: A complex and circular relationship. In J. F. Goldberg & M. Harrow (Eds.), *Bipolar disorders: Clinical course and outcome* (pp. 39–55). Washington, DC: American Psychiatric Press.

Gladstone, T. R. G., & Kaslow, N. J. (1995). Depression and attributions in children and adolescents: A meta-analytic review. *Journal of Abnormal Child Psychology, 23*, 597–606.

Gloaguen, V., Cottraux, J., Cucherat, M., & Blackburn, I. (1998). A meta-analysis of the effects of cognitive therapy in depressed patients. *Journal of Affective Disorders, 49*, 59–72.

Glosoff, H. L., Herlihy, B., & Spence, E. B. (2000). Privileged communication in the counselor-client relationship. *Journal of Counseling and Development, 78*, 454–463.

Glosoff, H. L., Herlihy, S. B., Herlihy, B., & Spence, E. B. (1997). Privileged communication in the psychologist-client relationship. *Professional Psychology: Research and Practice, 28*, 573–581.

Glovinsky, I. (2002). A brief history of childhood-onset bipolar disorder through 1980. *Child and Adolescent Psychiatric Clinics of North America, 11*, 443–460.

Goate, A. M., Hardy, J. A., & Owen, M. J. (1991). The genetic aetiology of Alzheimer's disease. *International Review of Psychiatry, 1*, 243–248.

Godart, N. T., Flament, M. F., Perdereau, F., & Jeammet, P. (2002). Comorbidity between eating disorders and anxiety disorders: A review. *International Journal of Eating Disorders, 32*, 253–270.

Godley, M. D., Kahn, J. H., Dennis, M. L., Godley, S. H., & Funk, R. (2005). The stability and impact of environmental factors on substance use and problems after adolescent outpatient treatment for cannabis abuse or dependence. *Psychology of Addictive Behaviors, 19*, 62–70.

Goisman, R. M., Goldenberg, I., Vasile, R. G., & Keller, M. B. (1995). Comorbidity of anxiety disorders in a multicenter anxiety study. *Comprehensive Psychiatry, 36*, 303–311.

Gold, M. S., Frost-Pineda, K., & Jacobs, W. (2004). Cannabis. In M. Galanter & H. D. Kleber (Eds.), *The American Psychiatric Publishing textbook of substance abuse treatment* (3rd ed., pp. 167–188). Washington, DC: American Psychiatric Publishing.

Gold, P. W. (2005). The neurobiology of stress and its relevance to psychotherapy. *Clinical Neuroscience Research, 4*, 315–324.

Gold, S. D., Marx, B. P., Soler-Baillo, J. M., & Sloan, D. M. (2005). Is life stress more traumatic than traumatic stress? *Journal of Anxiety Disorders, 19*, 687–698.

Goldberg, J. F., Harrow, M., & Whiteside, J. E. (2001). Risk for bipolar illness in patients initially hospitalized for unipolar depression. *American Journal of Psychiatry, 158*, 1265–1270.

Goldberg, R. W., Green-Paden, L. D., Lehman, A. F., & Gold, J. M. (2001). Correlates of insight in serious mental illness. *Journal of Nervous and Mental Diseases, 189*, 137–145.

Goldberg, T. E., Hyde, T. M., Kleinman, J. E., & Weinberger, D. R. (1993). Course of schizophrenia: Neuropsychological evidence for a static encephalopathy. *Schizophrenia Bulletin, 19*, 797–804.

Goldbloom, D. S., Garfinkel, P. E., & Shaw, B. F. (1991). Biochemical aspects of bulimia nervosa. *Journal of Psychosomatic Research, 35*(Suppl. 1), 11–22.

Golden, N. H., & Shenker, I. R. (1994). Amenorrhea in anorexia nervosa: Neuroendocrine control of hypothalamic dysfunction. *International Journal of Eating Disorders, 16*(1), 53–60.

Goldfried, M. R., & Davila, J. (2005). The role of the relationship and technique in therapeutic change. *Psychotherapy, Theory, Research, Practice Training, 42*(4), 421–430.

Goldman, W. P., Baty, J. D., & Buckles, V. D. (1999). Motor dysfunction in mildly impaired AD individuals without extrapyramidal signs. *Neurology, 53*, 956–962.

Goldstein, A. B. (1998). Identification and classification of factitious disorders: An analysis of cases reported during a 10-year period. *International Journal of Psychiatry in Medicine, 28*(2), 221–241.

Goldstein, D. J., Wilson, M. C., Ashcroft, R. C., & Al-Banna, M. (1999). Effectiveness of fluoxetine therapy in bulimia nervosa regardless of comorbid depression. *International Journal of Eating Disorders, 25*(1), 19–27.

Goldstein, H. (2002). Communication intervention for children with autism: A review of treatment efficacy. *Journal of Autism and Developmental Disorders, 32*, 373–396.

Goldstein, I., Lue, T. F., Padma-Nathan, H., Rosen, R. C., Steers, W. D., & Wicker, P. A. (1998). Oral sildenafil in the treatment of erectile dysfunction. *New England Journal of Medicine, 338*(20), 1397–1404.

Goldstein, J. M. (1988). Gender differences in the course of schizophrenia. *American Journal of Psychiatry, 145*, 684–689.

Goldstein, N. A., Post, J. C., Rosenfeld, R. M., & Campbell, T. F. (2000). Impact of tonsillectomy and adenoidectomy on child behavior. *Archives of Otolaryngology-Head and Neck Surgery, 126*, 494–498.

Goldstein, T. R., Birmaher, B., Axelson, D., Ryan, N. D., Strober, M. A., & Gill, M. K. (2005). History of suicide attempts in pediatric bipolar disorder: Factors associated with increased risk. *Bipolar Disorders, 7*, 525–535.

Goldston, D. (2000, August 14). *Assessment of suicidal behaviors and risk among children and adolescents.* Technical Report submitted to NIMH under contract No. 263-MD-909995.

Golier, J. A., Yehuda, R., Bierer, L. M., Mitropoulou, V., New, A. S., Schmeidler, J., et al. (2003). The relationship of borderline personality disorder to posttraumatic stress disorder and traumatic events. *American Journal of Psychiatry, 160*, 2018–2024.

Goodman, C., Knoll, G., Isakov, V., & Silver, H. (2005). Insight into illness in schizophrenia. *Comprehensive Psychiatry, 46*, 284–290.

Goodman, E., & Capitman, J. (2000). Depressive symptoms and cigarette smoking among teens. *Pediatrics, 106*, 748–755.

Goodman, G. S., Rudy, L., Bottoms, B. L., & Aman, C. (1990). Children's concerns and memory: Issues of ecological validity in the study of children's eyewitness testimony. In R. Fivush & J. Hudson (Eds.), *Knowing and remembering in young children* (pp. 249–284). New York: Cambridge University Press.

Goodman, W. K., Price, L. H., Rasmussen, S. A., Mazure, C., Fleischmann, R. L., Hill, C., et al. (1989). The Yale-Brown Obsessive Compulsive Scale: Pt. I. Development, use, and reliability. *Archives of General Psychiatry, 46*, 1006–1011.

Goodsitt, A. (1997). Eating disorders: A self-psychological perspective. In D. M. Garner & P. E. Garfinkel (Eds.), *Handbook of treatment for eating disorders* (2nd ed., pp. 205–228). New York: Guilford Press.

Goodwin, F. K. (2002). Rationale for long-term treatment of bipolar disorder and evidence for long-term lithium treatment. *Journal of Clinical Psychiatry, 63*, 5–12.

Goodwin, D. W., Alderson, P., & Rosenthal, R. (1971). Clinical significance of hallucinations in psychiatric disorders: A study of 116 hallucinatory patients. *Archives of General Psychiatry, 24*, 76–80.

Goodwin, F. K., & Jamison, K. R. (1990). *Manic depressive illness.* New York: Oxford University Press.

Goodwin, R. D., Faravelli, C., Rosi, S., Cosci, F., Truglia, E., deGraaf, R., et al. (2005). The epidemiology of panic disorder and agoraphobia in Europe. *European Neuropsychopharmacology, 15*, 435–443.

Gordon, A. (2001). Eating disorders: Pt. 1. Anorexia nervosa. *Hospital Practice, 37*, 36–38.

Gorelick, P. B., Erkinjuntti, T., Hofman, A., Rocca, W. A., Skoog, I., & Winblad, B. (1999). Prevention of vascular dementia. *Alzheimer's Disease and Associated Disorders, 13*, S131–S139.

Gorman-Smith, D., & Tolan, P. (1998). The role of exposure to community violence and developmental problems among inner-city youth. *Development and Psychopathology, 10*, 101–116.

Gosselin, P., Ladouceur, R., Morin, C. M., Dugas, M. J., & Baillargeon, L. (2004). Discontinuation among adults with GAD: A randomized trial of cognitive-behavioral therapy. *Journal of Consulting and Clinical Psychology, 74*, 908–919.

Gotlib, I. H., & Hammen, C. L. (1992). *Psychological aspects of depression: Toward a cognitive-interpersonal integration.* Oxford, England: Wiley.

Gottesman, I. I. (1991). *Schizophrenia genesis: The origins of madness.* New York: Freeman.

Gottesman, I. I., & Gould, T. D. (2003). The endophenotype concept in psychiatry: Etymology and strategic intentions. *American Journal of Psychiatry, 160*, 636–645.

Gottesman, I. I., & Moldin, S. O. (1998). Genotypes, genes, genesis, and pathogenesis in schizophrenia. In M. F. Lenzenweger & R. H. Dworkin (Eds.), *Origins and development of schizophrenia* (pp. 5–26). Washington, DC: American Psychological Association.

Gottesman, I. I., & Moldin, S. O. (1999). *Schizophrenia and genetic risks: A guide to genetic counseling for consumers, their families, and mental health workers* (2nd ed.). Arlington, VA: National Alliance for the Mentally Ill.

Gottlieb, B. H., & Johnson, J. (2000). Respite programs for caregivers of persons with dementia: A review with practice implications. *Aging and Mental Health, 4*, 119–129.

Gould, M. S., King, R., Greenwald, S., Fisher, P., Schwab-Stone, M., Kramer, R., et al. (1998). Psychopathology associated with suicidal ideation and attempts among children and adolescents. *Journal of the American Academy of Child and Adolescent Psychiatry, 37*, 915–923.

Gould, R. A., Buckminster, S., Pollack, M. H., Otto, M. W., & Yap, L. (1997). Cognitive-behavioral and pharmacological treatment for social phobia: A meta-analysis. *Clinical Psychology Science and Practice, 4*, 291–306.

Gowers, S. G. (2006). Evidence based research in CBT with adolescent eating disorders. *Child and Adolescent Mental Health, 11*, 9–12.

Grabe, H. J., Meyer, C., Hapke, U., Rumpf, H. J., Freyberger, H. J., Dilling, H., et al. (2003). Somatoform pain disorder in the general population. *Psychotherapy and Psychosomatics, 72*(2), 88–94.

Grabe, H. J., Meyer, C., Hapke, U., Rumpf, H. J., Juergen, H., Freyberger, H. J., et al. (2003). Specific somatoform disorder in the general population. *Psychosomatics, 44,* 304–311.

Grady, T. A., Pigott, T. A., L'Heureux, F., Hill, J. L., Bernstein, S. E., & Murphy, D. L. (1993). Double-blind study of adjuvant buspirone for fluoxetine-treated patients with obsessive-compulsive disorder. *American Journal of Psychiatry, 150,* 819–821.

Graham, J. R. (2006). *MMPI-2: Assessing personality and psychopathology* (4th ed.). New York: Oxford University Press.

Grandin, T. (1995). *Thinking in pictures and other reports from my life with autism.* New York: Doubleday.

Grant, B. F., Dawson, D. A., Stinson, F. S., Chou, P. S., Dufour, M. C., & Pickering, R. P. (2004). The 12-month prevalence and trends in DSM-I alcohol abuse and dependence: United States, 1991–1992 and 2001–2002. *Drug and Alcohol Dependence, 74,* 223–234.

Grant, B. F., Hasin, D. S., Stinson, F. S., Dawson, D. A., Chou, P., Ruan, W. J., et al. (2005). Co-occurrence of 12-month mood and anxiety disorders and personality disorders in the United States: Results from the National Epidemiologic Survey on alcohol and related conditions. *Journal of Psychiatric Research, 39,* 1–9.

Grant, B. F., Hasin, D. S., Stinson, F. S., Dawson, D. A., Chou, S. P., Ruan, W. J., et al. (2004). Prevalence, correlates, and disability of personality disorders in the United States: Results from the national epidemiologic survey on alcohol and related conditions. *Journal of Clinical Psychiatry, 65*(7), 948–958.

Grant, B. F., Hasin, D. S., Stinson, F. S., Dawson, D. A., Goldstein, R. B., Smith, S., et al. (2006). The epidemiology of DSM-I panic disorder and agoraphobia in the United States: Results from the National Epidemiologic Survey on alcohol and related conditions. *Journal of Clinical Psychiatry, 67,* 363–374.

Grant, J. E., Kim, S. W., & Eckert, E. D. (2002). Body dysmorphic disorder in patients with anorexia nervosa: Prevalence, clinical features, and delusionality of body image. *International Journal of Eating Disorders, 32,* 291–300.

Gray, M. J., & Acierno, R. (2002). Symptom presentation of older adult crime victims: Description of a clinical sample. *Anxiety Disorders, 16,* 299–309.

Green, M. F. (2001). *Schizophrenia revealed: From neurons to social interactions.* New York: Norton.

Green, M. F., Marshall, B. D., Wirshing, W. C., Ames, D., Marder, S. R., McGurk, S. R., et al. (1997). Does risperidone improve verbal working memory in schizophrenia? *American Journal of Psychiatry, 154,* 799–804.

Green, R. C., Cupples, A., Go, R., Benke, K. S., Edeki, T., Griffith, P. A., et al. (2002). Risk of dementia among White and African American relatives of patients with Alzheimer disease. *Journal of the American Medical Association, 287,* 329–336.

Greenberg, P. E., Sisitsky, T., Kessler, R. C., Finkelstein, S. N., Berndt, E. R., Davidson, J. R. T., et al. (1999). The economic burden of anxiety disorders in the 1990s. *Journal of Clinical Psychiatry, 60,* 427–435.

Greene, R. W. (2006). Oppositional defiant disorder. In M. Hersen, J. C. Thomas, & R. T. Ammerman (Eds.), *Comprehensive handbook of personality and psychopathology: Vol 3. Child psychopathology* (pp. 285–298). Hoboken, NJ: Wiley.

Greene, R. W., Biederman, J., Faraone, S., Sienna, M., & Garcia-Jetton, J. (1997). Adolescent outcome of boys with attention-deficit/hyperactivity disorder and social disability: Results from a 4-year longitudinal follow-up study. *Journal of Consulting and Clinical Psychology, 65,* 758–767.

Greene, R. W., Biederman, J., Zerwas, S., Monteaux, M., Goring, J. C., & Faraone, S. V. (2002). Psychiatric comorbidity, family dysfunction, and social impairment in referred youth with oppositional defiant disorder. *American Journal of Psychiatry, 159*(7), 1214–1224.

Greene, R. W., & Doyle, A. E. (1999). Towards a transactional conceptualization of oppositional defiant disorder: Implications for assessment and treatment. *Clinical Child Family Psychology Review, 2,* 129–148.

Greenfield, S. F., & Hennessy, G. (2004). Assessment of the patient. In M. Galanter & H. D. Kleber (Eds.), *The American Psychiatric Publishing textbook of substance abuse treatment* (3rd ed., pp. 101–119). Washington, DC: American Psychiatric Publishing.

Greenhalgh, J., Knight, C., Hind, D., Beverley, C., & Walters, S. (2005). Clinical and cost-effectiveness of electroconvulsive therapy for depressive illness, schizophrenia, catatonia and mania: Systematic reviews and economic modeling studies. *Health Technology Assessment, 9,* 1–156.

Greenhill, L. L., Swanson, J. M., Vitiello, B., Davies, M., Clevebger, W., Wu, M., et al. (2001). Impairment and deportment responses to different methylphenidate doses in children with ADHD: The MTA titration trial. *Journal of the American Academy of Child and Adolescent Psychiatry, 40,* 180–187.

Greenspan, S. I. (1981). *The clinical interview of the child.* Washington, DC: American Psychiatric Press.

Greenspan, S. I., & Wieder, S. (1998). *The child with special needs: Encouraging intellectual and emotional growth.* Reading, MA: Perseus Books.

Grenier, J. (2003). A decision tree approach to the differential diagnosis of insomnia. In M. Billiard & A. Kent (Ed., Trans.), *Sleep: Physiology, investigations, and medicine* (pp. 191–199). New York: Kluwer Academic/Plenum Press.

Gresham, F. M., Beebe-Frankenberger, M. E., MacMillan, D. L. (1999). A selective review of treatment for children with autism: Description and methodological considerations. *School Psychology Review, 28*(4), 559–575.

Gretarsdottir, E., Woodruff-Borden, J., Meeks, S., & Depp, C. A. (2004). Social anxiety in older adults: Phenomenology, prevalence, and measurement. *Behaviour Research and Therapy, 42,* 459–475.

Griffin, K. W., Botvin, G. J., Scheier, L. M., & Nichols, T. R. (2002). Factors associated with regular marijuana use among high school students: A long-term follow-up study. *Substance Use and Misuse, 37,* 225–238.

Griffith, H. R., Neston, K. L., Harrell, L. E., Zamrini, E. Y., Brockington, J. C., & Mason, D. C. (2006). Amnestic mild cognitive impairment: Diagnostic outcomes and clinical prediction over a 2-year time period. *Journal of the International Neuropsychological Society, 12,* 166–175.

Griffith, J. D., Rowan-Szal, G. A., Roark, R. R., & Simpson, D. D. (2000). Contingency management in outpatient methadone treatment: A meta-analysis. *Drug and Alcohol Dependence, 58,* 55–56.

Griffiths, R. R., Richards, W. A., McCann, U., & Jesse, R. (2006). Psilocybin can occasion mystical-type experiences having substantial and sustained personal meaning and spiritual significance. *Psychopharmacology, 187,* 268–283.

Grilo, C. M., & McGlashan, T. M. (2005). Course and outcome of personality disorders. In J. M. Oldham, A. E. Skodol, & D. S. Bender (Eds.), *Textbook of personality disorders* (pp. 103–115). Washington, DC: American Psychiatric Publishing.

Grilo, C. M., McGlashan, T. H., & Skodol, A. E. (2000). Stability and course of personality disorders: The need to consider comorbidities and continuities between Axis I psychiatric disorders and Axis II personality disorders. *Psychiatric Quarterly, 71*(4), 291–307.

Grilo, C. M., Sanislow, C. A., Shea, M. T., Skodol, A. E., Stout, R. L., Gunderson, J. G., et al. (2005). Two-year prospective naturalistic study of remission from major depressive disorder as a function of personality disorder comorbidity. *Journal of Consulting and Clinical Psychology, 73,* 78–85.

Grisso, T., & Appelbaum, P. S. (1998). *MacArthur Competence Assessment Tool for Treatment (MacCAT-T).* Sarasota, FL: Professional Resource Press/Professional Resource Exchange.

Grisso, T., & Tomkins, A. J. (1996). Communicating violence risk assessments. *American Psychologist, 51,* 928–930.

Groholt, E. K., Stigum, H., Nordhagen, R., & Kohler, L. (2003). Recurrent pain in children, socio-economic factors and accumulation in families. *European Journal of Epidemiology, 18,* 965–975.

Grossman, H. (2003). Does diabetes protect or provoke Alzheimer disease? Insights into the pathobiology and future treatment of Alzheimer's disease. *CNS Spectrum, 8,* 815–822.

Grossman, L. S., Harrow, M., Fudala, J. L., & Meltzer, H. Y. (1984). The longitudinal course of schizoaffective disorders. *Journal of Nervous and Mental Diseases, 172,* 140–149.

Grossman, R. (2004). Pharmacotherapy of personality disorders. In J. J. Magnavita (Ed.), *Handbook of personality: Theory and practice* (pp. 331–355). Hoboken, NJ: Wiley.

Grosz, D. E., Zimmerman, J. K., & Asnis, G. M. (1995). Suicidal behavior in adolescents: A review of risk and protective factors. In J. K. Zimmerman & G. M. Asnis (Eds.), *Treatment approaches with suicidal adolescents* (pp. 17–43). New York: Wiley.

Groth-Marnat, G. (2003). *Handbook of psychological assessment* (4th ed.). Hoboken, NJ: Wiley.

Grunebaum, M. F., Galfalvy, H. C., Oquendo, M. A., Burke, A. K., & Mann, J. J. (2004). Melancholia and the probability and lethality of suicide attempts. *British Journal of Psychiatry, 184,* 534–535.

Gudmumdsson, O., Prendgast, M., Foreman, D., & Cowley, S. (2001). Outcome of pseudoseizures in children and adolescents: A 6-year symptom survival analysis. *Developmental Medicine and Child Neurology, 43,* 547–551.

Guedeney, N., Guedeney, A., Rabouam, C., Mintz, A. S., Danon, G., Morales-Huet, M., et al. (2003). The zero-to-three diagnostic classification: A contribution to the validation of this classification from a sample of 85 under threes. *Infant Mental Health Journal, 24*(4), 313–336.

Guérin, F., Belleville, S., & Ska, B. (2002). Characterization of visuoconstructional disabilities in patients with probable dementia Alzheimer's type. *Journal of Clinical and Experimental Neuropsychology, 24,* 1–17.

Guertin, T. L. (1999). Eating behavior of bulimics, self-identified binge eaters, and non-eating-disordered individuals: What differentiates these populations? *Clinical Psychology Review, 19*(1), 1–23.

Guilleminault, C., & Bliwise, D. L. (1994). Behavioral perspectives on abnormalities of breathing during sleep. In B. H. Timmons & R. Ley (Eds.), *Behavioral and psychological approaches to breathing disorders* (pp. 59–66). New York: Plenum Press.

Gunderson, J. G. (2001). *Borderline personality disorder: A clinical guide.* Washington, DC: American Psychiatric Press.

Gunderson, J. G., Bender, D., Sanislow, C., Yen, S., Rettew, J. B., Dolan-Sewell, R., et al. (2003). Plausibility and possible determinants of sudden "remissions" in borderline patients. *Psychiatry, 66,* 111–119.

Gunderson, J. G., & Berkowitz, C. (2002). *Family guidelines.* Belmont, MA: New England Personality Association.

Gunderson, J. G., & Gabbard, G. O. (2000). *Psychotherapy for personality disorders.* Washington, DC: American Psychiatric Press.

Gunderson, J. G., Gratz, K. L., Neuhaus, E. C., & Smith, G. W. (2005). Levels of care in treatment. In J. M. Oldham, A. E. Skodol, & D. S. Bender (Eds.), *Textbook of personality disorders* (pp. 239–256). Washington, DC: American Psychiatric Publishing.

Gunderson, J. G., & Hoffman, P. D. (Eds.). (2005). *Understanding and treating borderline personality disorder: A guide for professionals and families.* Washington, DC: American Psychiatric Publishing.

Gunderson, J. G., & Kolb, J. E. (1978). Discriminating features of borderline patients. *American Journal of Psychiatry, 135,* 1–9.

Gunderson, J. G., Kolb, J. E., & Austin, V. (1981). The diagnostic interview for borderline patients. *American Journal of Psychiatry, 138,* 896–903.

Gunderson, J. G., Morey, L. C., Stout, R. L., Skodol, A. E., Shea, M. T., McGashan, T. H., et al., (2004). Major depressive disorder and borderline personality revisited: Longitudinal interactions. *Journal of Clinical Psychiatry, 65,* 1049–1056.

Gunderson, J. G., Ronningstam, E., & Bodkin, A. (1990). The diagnostic interview for narcissistic patients. *Archives of General Psychiatry, 47,* 676–680.

Gunderson, J. G., Shea, M. T., Skodol, A. E., McGlashan, T. H., Morey, L. C., Stout, R. L., et al. (2000). The collaborative longitudinal personality disorders study I: Development, aims, design, and sample characteristics. *Journal of Personality Disorders, 14*, 300–315.

Gunderson, J. S., & Singer, M. T. (1975). Defining borderline patients: An overview. *American Journal of Psychiatry, 132*, 1–10.

Gunstad, J., & Phillips, K. (2003). Axis I comorbidity in body dysmorphic disorder. *Comprehensive Psychiatry, 44*(4), 270–276.

Gunter, T. (2004, May 31). Special needs, crushing costs. *Newsweek*, 94–97.

Guntrip, H. (1969). *Schizoid phenoma, object-relations, and the self.* New York: International Universities Press.

Gureje, O. (2004). What can we learn from a cross-national study of somatic distress? *Journal of Psychosomatic Research, 56*, 409–412.

Gureje, O., Simon, G. E., Ustun, T. B., & Goldberg, D. P. (1997). Somatization in cross-cultural perspective: A World Health Organization study in primary care. *American Journal of Psychiatry, 1254*(7), 989–995.

Gurland, B. J., Wilder, D. E., Lantigua, R., Stern, Y., Chen, J., Killeffer, E. H., et al. (1999). Rates of dementia in three ethnoracial groups. *International Journal of Geriatric Psychiatry, 14*, 481–493.

Gurney, J. G., Fritz, M. S., Ness, K. K., Sievers, P., Newschaffer, C. J., & Shapiro, E. G. (2003). Analysis of prevalence trends of autism spectrum disorder in Minnesota (Comment). *Archives of Pediatrics and Adolescent Medicine, 157*(7), 622–627.

Gurvits, I. G., Koenigsberg, H. W., & Siever, L. J. (2000). Neurotransmitter dysfunction in patients with borderline personality disorder. *Psychiatric Clinics of North America, 23*, 27–40.

Gutheil, T. G. (2005). Boundary issues. In J. M. Oldham, A. E. Skodol, & D. S. Bender (Eds.), *Textbook of personality disorders* (pp. 421–429). Washington, DC: American Psychiatric Publishing.

Gutierrez-Cebollada, J., de la Torre, R., Ortufio, J., Garces, J. M., & Cami, J. (1994). Psychotropic drug consumption and other factors associated with heroin overdose. *Drug and Alcohol Dependence, 35*, 169–174.

Guze, S. B. (1993). Genetics of Briquet's syndrome and somatization disorder: A review of family, adoption, and twin studies. *Annals of Clinical Psychiatry, 5*, 225–230.

Guze, S. B., & Robins, F. (1970). Suicide and primary affective disorders. *British Journal of Psychiatry, 117*, 437–438.

Haan, M. N., & Wallace, R. (2004). Can dementia be prevented? Brain aging in a population-based context. *Annual Review of Public Health, 25*, 1–24.

Hachinski, V. C., Lassen, N. A., & Marshall, J. (1974). Multi-infarct dementia: A cause of mental deterioration in the elderly. *Lancet, 27*, 207–210.

Haddock, G., McCarron, J., Tarrier, N., & Faragher, E. B. (1999). Scales to measure dimensions of hallucinations and delusions: The psychotic symptom rating scales (PSYRATS). *Psychological Medicine, 29*(4), 879–89.

Haddon, M. (2003). *The curious incident of the dog in the night-time.* New York: Doubleday.

Häffner, H. (2003). Gender differences in schizophrenia. *Psychoneuroendocrinology, 28*, 17–54.

Häfner, H., Heiden, W., Behrens, S., Gattaz, W., Hambrecht, M., Löeffler, W., et al. (1998). Causes and consequences of the gender difference in age at onset of schizophrenia. *Schizophrenia Bulletin, 24*, 99–113.

Hagberg, B., Aicardi, J., Dias, K., & Ramos, O. (1983). A progressive syndrome of autism, dementia, ataxia and loss of purposeful hand movements in girls: Rett's syndrome: Report of 35 cases. *Annals of Neurology, 14*(4), 471–479.

Hagberg, B., & Witt-Engerstrom, I. (1986). Rett syndrome: A suggested staging system for describing impairment profile with increasing age towards adolescence. *American Journal of Medical Genetics, 24*(Suppl. 1), 47–59.

Hahm, H. C., Lahiff, M., & Guterman, N. B. (2003). Acculturation and parental attachment in Asian-American adolescents' alcohol use. *Journal of Adolescent Health, 33*, 119–129.

Haight, W., Ostler, T., Black, J., Sheridan, K., & Kingery, L. (2007). A child's-eye view of parent methamphetamine abuse: Implications for helping foster families to succeed. *Children and Youth Services Review, 29*, 1–15.

Hakim-Larson, J., Voelker, S., Thomas, C., & Reinstein, L. (1997). Feeding and eating disorders. In C. A. Essau & F. Petermann (Eds.), *Developmental psychopathology: Epidemiology, diagnostics, and treatment* (pp. 351–410). Amsterdam, The Netherlands: Harwood Academic.

Halbreich, U. (2005). Postpartum disorders: Multiple interacting underlying mechanisms and risk factors. *Journal of Affective Disorders, 88*, 1–7.

Hale, T. S., Hariri, A. R., & McCracken, J. T. (2000). Attention-deficit/hyperactivity disorder: Perspectives from neuroimagining. *Mental Retardation and Developmental Disabilities Research Reviews, 6*, 214–219.

Haley, W. E., Gitlin, L. N., Wisniewski, S. R., Mahoney, D. F., Coon, D. W., Winter, L., et al. (2004). Well-being, appraisal, and coping in African-American and Caucasian dementia caregivers: Findings from the REACH study. *Aging and Mental Health, 8*, 316–329.

Hall, C. I. (1995). Asian eyes: Body image and eating disorders of Asian and Asian American women. *Eating Disorders: Journal of Treatment and Prevention, 3*, 8–19.

Hall, C. I., & Turner, T. C. (2001). The diversity of biracial individuals: Asian-White and Asian-minority biracial identity. In T. Williams-Leon & C. Nakashima (Eds.), *The sum of our parts: Mixed heritage Asian Americans* (pp. 81–91). Philadelphia: Temple University Press.

Hall, J. A., Harrigan, J. A., & Rosenthal, R. (1995). Nonverbal behavior in clinician-patient interaction. *Applied and Preventive Psychology, 4*, 21–37.

Hallberg, I. R. (2002). The role of families, family caregivers, and nurses. In J. Lindesay, R. Rockwood, & A. MacDonald (Eds.), *Delirium in old age* (pp. 187–212). New York: Oxford University Press.

Halmi, K. A. (2004). Anorexia nervosa: Dual therapy can bring patients back from the brink. *Current Psychiatry, 3*, 39–56.

Halmi, K. A., Sunday, S. R., Strober, M., Kaplan, A., Woodside, D. B., Fichter, M., et al. (2000). Perfectionism in anorexia nervosa: Variation by clinical subtype, obsessionality, and pathological eating behavior. *American Journal of Psychiatry, 157*, 1799–1805.

Halpern, J. K., & Glassman, A. H. (1990). Adequate tricyclic treatment: Defining the tricyclic nonresponder. In S. P. Roose & A. H. Glassman (Eds.), *Treatment strategies for refractory depression* (pp. 11–32). Washington, DC: American Psychiatric Press.

Hamilton, B., & Coates, J. (1993). Perceived helpfulness and use of professional services by abused women. *Journal of Family Violence, 8*, 313–324.

Hamilton, M. (1960). A rating scale for depression. *Journal of Neurology, Neurosurgery, and Psychiatry, 23*, 56–62.

Hammen, C. (2005). Stress and depression. *Annual Review of Clinical Psychology, 1*, 293–319.

Han, C. S., & Kim, Y. K. (2004). A double-blind trial of risperidone and haloperidol for the treatment of delirium. *Psychosomatics, 45*, 297–301.

Handelman, J. S., Harris, S. L., & Martins, M. P. (2005). Helping children with autism enter the mainstream. In F. R. Volkmar, R. Paul, A. Klin, & D. Cohen (Eds.), *Handbook of autism and pervasive developmental disorders* (3rd ed., pp. 1003–1028). Hoboken, NJ: Wiley.

Handelsman, M. M. (2001). Accurate and effective informed consent. In E. R. Welfel & R. E. Ingersoll (Eds.), *The mental health desk reference* (pp. 453–458). New York: Wiley.

Handleman, J. S., & Harris, S. L. (2001). *Preschool education programs for children with autism* (2nd ed.) Austin, TX: ProEd.

Haney, M. (2004). Neurobiology of stimulants. In M. Galanter & H. D. Kleber (Eds.), *The American Psychiatric Publishing textbook of substance abuse treatment.* (3rd ed., pp. 31–40). Washington, DC: American Psychiatric Publishing.

Hanna, F. J., Bemak, F. F., & Chung, R. C.-Y. (1999). Toward a new paradigm for multicultural counseling. *Journal of Counseling and Development, 77*, 125–134.

Hannon, L., & Cuddy, M. M. (2006). Neighborhood ecology and drug dependence mortality: An analysis of New York City census tracts. *American Journal of Drug and Alcohol Abuse, 32*, 453–463.

Hansell, N., & Willis, G. L. (1977). Outpatient treatment of schizophrenia. *American Journal of Psychiatry, 134,* 1082–1086.

Hansen, D. J., & Warner, J. (1992). Child physical abuse and neglect. In R. T. Ammerman & M. Hersen (Eds.), *Assessment of family violence: A clinical and legal sourcebook* (pp. 123–147). New York: Wiley.

Hansen, P. E. B., Wang, A. G., Stage, K. B., & Kragh-Sorensen, P. (2003). Comorbid personality disorder predicts suicide after major depression: A 10-year follow-up. *Acta Psychiatrica Scandinavica, 107,* 436–440.

Hansen, R., Struthers, J., & Gospe, S. J. (1993). Visual evoked potentials and visual processing in stimulant drug-exposed infants. *Developmental Medicine and Child Neurology, 35,* 798–805.

Hanson, S. L., Kerkhoff, T. R., & Bush, S. S. (2005). *Health care ethics for psychologists: A casebook.* Washington, DC: American Psychological Association.

Happe, F. G. (1995). The role of age and verbal ability in the theory of mind task performance of subjects with autism. *Child Development, 66*(3), 843–855.

Happe, F. G. (1996). Studying weak central coherence at low levels: Children with autism do not succumb to visual illusions (A research note). *Journal of Child Psychology and Psychiatry 37,* 873–877.

Happe, F. G. (1998). *Autism: An introduction to psychological theory* (3rd ed.). Cambridge, MA: Harvard University Press.

Happe, F. G. (2000). Parts and wholes, meaning and minds: Central coherence and its relation to theory of mind. In S. Baron-Cohen, H. Tager-Flusberg, & D. Cohen (Eds.), *Understanding other minds: Perspectives from autism and developmental cognitive neuroscience* (pp. 203–221). Oxford: Oxford University Press.

Happe, F. G. (2005). The weak central coherence account of autism. In F. R. Volkmar, R. Paul, A. Klin, & D. Cohen (Eds.), *Handbook of autism and pervasive developmental disorders* (3rd ed., pp. 640–649). Hoboken, NJ: Wiley.

Haput, M., Romero, B., & Kurtz, A. (1996). Delusions and hallucinations in Alzheimer's disease: Results from a 2-year longitudinal study. *International Journal of Geriatric Psychiatry, 11,* 965–972.

Hare, R. D. (1970). *Psychopathy: Theory and research.* New York: Wiley.

Hare, R. D. (1991). *The Hare Psychopathy Checklist—Revised.* Toronto: Multi-Health Systems.

Hare, R. D. (1998). Psychopathy, affect and behavior. In D. J. Cooke, A. E. Forth, & R. D. Hare (Eds.), *Psychopathy: Theory, research, and implications for society* (pp. 105–138). Dordrecht, The Netherlands: Kluwer Press.

Hare, R. D. (1999). *Without conscience: The disturbing world of psychopaths among us.* New York: Guilford Press.

Hare, R. D., Cooke, D. J., & Hart, S. D. (1999). Psychopathy and sadistic personality disorder. In T. Millon, P. H. Blaney, & R. D. Davis (Eds.), *Oxford textbook of psychopathology* (pp. 555–584). New York: Oxford University Press.

Harford, T. C., Grant, B. F., Yi, H., & Chen, C. M. (2005). Patterns of DSM-IV alcohol abuse and dependence criteria among adolescents and adults: Results from the 2001 National Household Survey on Drug Abuse. *Alcoholism: Clinical and Experimental Research, 29,* 810–828.

Harkness, K. L., & Monroe, S. M. (2006). Severe melancholic depression is more vulnerable than non-melancholic depression to minor precipitating life events. *Journal of Affective Disorders, 91,* 257–263.

Harper, R. G. (2004). *Personality-guided therapy in behavioral medicine.* Washington, DC: American Psychological Association.

Harris, E., & Barrowclough, C. B. (1997). Suicide as an outcome for mental disorders: A meta analysis. *British Journal of Psychiatry, 170,* 205–228.

Harris, E. C., & Barraclough, B. (1998). Excess mortality of mental disorder. *British Journal of Psychiatry, 173,* 11–53.

Harris, M. J., & Jeste, D. V. (1988). Late-onset schizophrenia: An overview. *Schizophrenia Bulletin, 14,* 39–55.

Harris, N. V., Thiede, H., McGough, J. P., & Gordon, D. (1993). Risk factors for HIV infection among injection drug users: Results of blinded surveys in drug treatment centers, King County, Washington 1988–1991. *Journal of Acquired Immune Deficiency Syndromes, 6,* 1275–1282.

Harris, S. L., & Handleman, J. S. (2000). Age and IQ at intake as predictors of placement for young children with autism: A 4- to 6-year follow up. *Journal of Autism and Developmental Disorders, 30*(2), 137–142.

Harris, S. L., Handleman, J. S., Arnold, M. S., & Gordon, R. F. (2001). The Douglass Developmental Disabilities Center. In J. S. Handleman & S. L. Harris (Eds.), *Preschool education programs for children with autism* (2nd ed., pp. 233–260). Austin, TX: ProEd.

Harris, S. L., Handleman, J., Gordon, R., Kristoff, B., & Fuentes, F. (1991). Changes in cognitive and language functioning of preschool children with autism. *Journal of Autism and Developmental Disorders, 21,* 281–290.

Harris, S. L., Handleman, J. S., & Jennett, H. K. (2005). Models of educational intervention for students with autism: Home, center, and school-based programming. In F. R. Volkmar, R. Paul, A. Klin & D. Cohen (Eds.), *Handbook of autism and pervasive developmental disorders* (3rd ed., pp. 1043–1054). Hoboken, NJ: Wiley.

Harrison, C., & Sofronoff, K. (2002). ADHD and parental psychological distress: Role of demographics, child behavioral characteristics, and parental cognitions. *Journal of the American Academy of Child and Adolescent Psychiatry, 41,* 703–711.

Harrison, G., Croudace, T., Mason, P., Glazebrook, C., & Medley, I. (1996). Predicting the long-term outcome of schizophrenia. *Psychological Medicine, 26,* 697–705.

Harrow, M., & Grossman, L. S. (1984). Outcome in schizoaffective disorder: A critical review and reevaluation of the literature. *Schizophrenia Bulletin, 10,* 87–108.

Harrow, M., & Marengo, J. T. (1986). Schizophrenic thought disorder at follow-up: Its persistence and prognostic significance. *Schizophrenia Bulletin, 12,* 373–393.

Harry, R. D., & Zakzanis, K. K. (2005). A comparison of donepezil and galantamine in the treatment of cognitive symptoms of Alzheimer's disease: A meta-analysis. *Human Psychopharmacology, 20,* 183–187.

Harvey, A. G., Schmidt, D. A., Scarná, A., Semler, C. N., & Goodwin, G. M. (2005). Sleep-related functioning in euthymic patients with bipolar disorder, patients with insomnia, and subjects without sleep problems. *American Journal of Psychiatry, 162,* 50–59.

Harvey, L., Inglis, S. J., & Espie, C. A. (2002). Insomniacs' reported use of CBT components and relationship to long-term clinical outcomes. *Behaviour Research and Therapy, 40*(1), 75–83.

Harvey, P. D. (2006). Cognitive and functional effects of atypical antipsychotic medications. *Journal of Clinical Psychiatry, 67,* e13.

Harvey, P. D., Bowie, C. R., & Lobel, A. (2006). Neuropsychological normalization with long-term atypical antipsychotic treatment: Results of a 6-month randomized, double-blind comparison of ziprasidone vs. olanzapine. *Journal of Neuropsychiatry and Clinical Neurosciences, 18,* 54–63.

Harvey, P. D., Green, M. F., McGurk, S. R., & Meltzer, H. Y. (2003). Changes in cognitive functioning with risperidone and olanzapine treatment: A large-scale, double-blind, randomized study. *Psychopharmacology, 169,* 414–411.

Harwood, D. G., Barker, W. W., Ownby, R. L., & Duara, R. (1999). The prevalence and correlates of Capgras syndrome in Alzheimer's disease. *International Journal of Geriatric Psychiatry, 14,* 415–420.

Harwood, D. G., & Sultzer, D. L. (2002). 'Life is not worth living': Hopelessness in Alzheimer's disease. *Journal of Geriatric Psychiatry and Neurology, 15,* 38–43.

Hasin, D. S., Tsai, W. Y., Endicott, J., Mueller, T. I., Coryell, W., & Keller, M. (1996). The effects of major depression on alcoholism. *American Journal on Addictions, 5,* 144–155.

Hasin, D. S., Van Rossem, R., McCloud, S., & Endicott, J. (1997). Differentiating DSM-IV alcohol dependence and abuse by course: Community heavy drinkers. *Journal of Substance Abuse, 9,* 127–135.

Hastings, R. P. (2003). Behavioral adjustment of siblings of children engaged in applied behavior analysis early intervention programs: The moderating role of social support. *Journal of Autism and Developmental Disorders, 33*, 141–150.

Hatchett, G. T., & Park, H. L. (2003). Comparison of four operational definitions of premature termination. *Psychotherapy: Theory, Research, Practice, Training, 40*(3), 226–231.

Haug, N. A., Sorensen, J. L., & Gruber, V. A. (2005). Relapse prevention for opioid dependence. In G. A. Marlatt & D. M. Donovan (Eds.), *Relapse prevention: Maintenance strategies in the treatment of addictive behaviors* (2nd ed., pp. 151–178). New York: Guilford Press.

Haugaard, J. J. (2004). Recognizing and treating uncommon behavioral and emotional disorders in children and adolescents who have been severely maltreated: Somatization and other somatoform disorders. *Child Maltreatment, 9*(2), 169–178.

Hauser-Cram, P., Warfield, M. E., Shonkoff, J. P., Krauss, M. W., Sayer, A., & Upsher, C. C. (2001). Children with disabilities: A longitudinal study of child development and parent well-being. *Monographs of the Society for Research in Child Development, 66*, 1–131.

Hawkins, J. D., Herrenkohl, T., Farrington, D. P., Brewer, D., Catalano, R. F., & Harachi, T. W. (1998). A review of predictors of youth violence. In R. Loeber & D. P. Farrington (Eds.), *Serious and violent juvenile offenders: Risk factors and successful interventions* (pp. 107–146). Thousand Oaks, CA: Sage.

Hawley, K. M., & Weisz, J. R. (2003). Child, parent, and therapist (dis)agreement on target problems in outpatient therapy: The therapist's dilemma and its implications. *Journal of Consulting and Clinical Psychology, 71*, 62–70.

Hay, P., Katsikitis, M., Begg, J., Da Costa, J., & Blumenfeld, N. (2003). A 2-year follow-up study and prospective evaluation of the DSM-IV Axis V. *Psychiatric Services, 54*(7), 1028–1030.

Hayes, J. A., & Gelso, C. J. (2001). Clinical implications of research on countertransference: Science informing practice. *Psychotherapy in Practice/In Session, 57*, 1041–1051.

Hayes, J. A., Gelso, C., Van Magoner, S., & Diemer, R. (1991). Managing countertransference: What the experts think. *Psychological Reports, 69*, 139–148.

Hayes, J. A., Riker, J. R., & Ingram, K. M. (1997). Countertransference behavior and management in brief counseling: A field study. *Psychotherapy Research, 7*, 145–153.

Haynes, P. L. (2005). The role of behavioral sleep medicine in the assessment and treatment of sleep disordered breathing. *Clinical Psychology Review, 25*(5), 673–705.

Hays, P. A. (2007). *Addressing cultural complexities in practice: Assessment, diagnosis, and Therapy.* Washington, DC: American Psychological Association.

Hazen, A. L., & Stein, M. B. (1995). Clinical phenomenology and comorbidity. In M. B. Stein (Ed.), *Social phobia: Clinical and research perspectives* (pp. 3–42). Washington, DC: American Psychiatric Press.

Healy, W. (1915). *The individual delinquent: A text-book of diagnosis and prognosis for all concerned in understanding offenders.* Boston: Little, Brown.

Heath, N. L., & Ross, S. (2000). Prevalence and expression of depressive symptomatology in students with and without learning disabilities. *Learning Disability Quarterly, 23*, 24–36.

Hebert, R., & Brayne, C. (1995). Epidemiology of vascular dementia. *Neuroepidemiology, 14*, 250–257.

Hechtmen, L. (1999). Predictors of long-term outcome in children with attention-deficit/ hyperactivity disorder. *Pediatric Clinics of North America, 46*, 1039–1052.

Hedayat-Diba, Z. (2000). Psychotherapy with Muslims. In P. S. Richards & A. E. Bergin (Eds.), *Handbook of psychotherapy and religious diversity* (pp. 289–314). Washington, DC: American Psychological Association.

Heilä, H., Isometsä, E. T., Henriksson, M. M., Heikkinen, M. E., Marttunen, M. J., & Lönnqvist. J. K. (1997). Suicide and schizophrenia: A nationwide psychological autopsy study on age- and sex-specific clinical characteristics of 92 suicide victims with schizophrenia. *American Journal of Psychiatry, 154*, 1235–1242.

Heilemann, M. V., Lee, K. A., Stinson, J., Koshar, J. H., & Goss, G. (2000). Acculturation and perinatal health outcomes among rural women of Mexican descent. *Research in Nursing and Health, 23*, 118–125.

Heim, C., Newport, D. J., Heit, S., Graham, Y. P., Wilcox, M., & Bonsall, R. (2000). Increased pituitary-adrenal and autonomic responses to stress in adult women after sexual and physical abuse in childhood. *Journal of the American Medical Association, 284*, 592–597.

Heimberg, R. G. (2002). Cognitive-behavioral therapy for social anxiety disorder: Current status and future directions. *Biological Psychiatry, 51*, 101–108.

Heimberg, R. G., Liebowitz, M. R., Hope, D. A., Schneier, F. R., Holt, C. S., & Welkowitz, L. A. (1998). Cognitive-behavioral group therapy vs. phenelzine therapy for social phobia. *Archives of General Psychiatry, 55*, 1133–1141.

Heinrichs, R. W., & Awad, A. W. (1993). Neurocognitive subtypes of chronic schizophrenia. *Schizophrenia Research, 9*, 49–58.

Heinssen, R. K., Liberman, R. P., & Kopelowicz, A. (2000). Psychosocial skills training for schizophrenia: Lessons from the laboratory. *Schizophrenia Bulletin, 26*, 21–46.

Heise, L. L. (1998). Violence against women: An integrated, ecological framework. *Violence Against Women, 4*, 262–290.

Hellawell, S. J., & Brewin, C. R. (2002). A comparison of flashbacks and ordinary autobiographical memories of trauma: Cognitive resources and behavioural observations. *Behaviour Research and Therapy, 40*, 1143–1156.

Heller, T. (1908). Dementia infantilis. *Zeitschrift fur die Erforschung und Behandling des Jugenlichen Schwachsinns, 2*, 141–165.

Heller, T. (1930). Urber Dementia infantalis. *Zeitschrift fur Kinderforschung, 37*, 661–667.

Hellström, K., Fellenius, J., & Öst, L.-G. (1996). One versus five sessions of applied tension in the treatment of blood phobia. *Behaviour Research and Therapy, 34*, 101–112.

Helzer, J. E., & Hudziak J. J. (Eds.). (2002). *Defining psychopathology in the 21st century: DSM-V and beyond.* Washington, DC: American Psychiatric Association.

Hembree, E. A., & Feeny, N. C. (2006). Cognitive-behavioral perspectives on theory and treatment of post-traumatic stress disorder. In B. O. Rothbaum (Ed.), *Emotional processing in etiology and treatment* (pp. 197–211). New York: Guilford Press.

Henderson, V. W., Paganini-Hill, A., Miller, B. L., Elble, R. J., Reyes, P. F., & Shoupe, D., (2000). Estrogen for Alzheimer's disease in women: Randomized, double-blind, placebo-controlled trial. *Neurology, 54*, 295–301.

Hendrie, H. C., Albert, M. S., Butters, M. A., Gao, S., Knopman, D. S., Launer, L. J., et al. (2006). The NIH cognitive and emotional health project: Report of the critical evaluation study committee. *Alzheimer's and Dementia, 2*, 12–32.

Hening, W. A., Allen, R. P., Earley, C. J., Picchietti, D. L., & Silber, M. H. (2004). An update on the dopaminergic treatment of restless legs syndrome and periodic limb movement disorder. *Sleep: Journal of Sleep and Sleep Disorders Research, 27*(3), 560–567.

Henkel, V., Mergl, R., Allgaier, A. K., Kohnen, R., Möller, H. J., & Hegerl, U. (2006). Treatment of depression with atypical features: a meta-analytic approach. *Psychiatry Research, 141*, 89–101.

Herbert, J. D., Gaudiano, B. A., Rheingold, A. A., Myers, V. H., Dalrymple, K., & Nolan, E. M. (2005). Social skills training augments the effectiveness of cognitive behavioral group therapy for social anxiety disorder. *Behavior Research, 36*, 125–138.

Herbert, M. R., Harris, G. J., Adrien, K. T., Ziegler, D. A., Markis, N., Kennedy, D., et al. (2002). Abnormal asymmetry in language associated cortex in autism. *Annals of Neurology, 52*, 588–596.

Herman, J. L. (1992). Complex PTSD: A syndrome in survivors of prolonged and repeated trauma. *Journal of Traumatic Stress, 5*, 377–392.

Herman, J. L. (1997). *Trauma and recovery.* New York: Basic Books.

Herpetz-Dahlmann, B. M., Wewetzer, C., Schulz, E., & Remschmidt, H. (2001). Course and outcome in adolescent anorexia nervosa. *International Journal of Eating Disorders, 19*(4), 335–345.

Herrán, A., Sierra-Biddle, D., Santiago, A., Artal, J., Diez-Manrique, J. F., & Vázquez-Barquero, J. L. (2001). Diagnostic accuracy in the first 5 min of a psychiatric interview. *Psychotherapy and Psychosomatics, 70*, 141–144.

Herrenkohl, T. I., Maguin, E., Hill, K. G., Hawkins, J. D., Abbott, R. D., & Catalano, R. F. (2000). Developmental risk factors for youth violence. *Journal of Adolescent Health, 26,* 1176–1186.

Hersen, M., & Turner, S. M. (2003). *Diagnostic interviewing* (3rd ed.). New York: Kluwer Academic.

Heru, A. M., & Ryan, C. E. (2004). Burden, reward, and family functioning of caregivers for relatives with mood disorders: One-year follow-up. *Journal of Affective Disorders, 83,* 221–225.

Herz, M. I., & Lamberti, J. S. (1995). Prodromal symptoms and relapse prevention in schizophrenia. *Schizophrenia Bulletin, 21,* 541–551.

Herz, M. I., & Marder, S. R. (2001). *Schizophrenia: Comprehensive treatment and management.* Philadelphia: Lippincott, Williams, & Wilkins.

Herz, M. I., & Marder, S. R. (2002). *Schizophrenia: Comprehensive treatment and management.* New York: Lippincott, Williams & Wilkins.

Herz, M. I., & Melville, C. (1980). Relapse in schizophrenia. *American Journal of Psychiatry, 137,* 801–807.

Herzog, D. B., Dorer, D. J., Keel, P. K., Selwyn, S. E., Ekeblad, E. R., Flores, A. T., et al. (1999). Recovery and relapse in anorexia and bulimia nervosa: A 7.5-year follow-up study. *Journal of the American Academy of Child and Adolescent Psychiatry, 38*(7), 829–837.

Herzog, D. B., Field, A. E., Keller, M. B., West, J. C., Robbins, W. M., Staley, J., et al. (1996). Subtyping eating disorders: Is it justified? *Journal of the American Academy of Child and Adolescent Psychiatry, 35*(7), 928–936.

Herzog, D. B., Greenwood, D. N., Dorer, D. J., Flores, A. T., Ekeblad, E. R., & Richards, A. (2000). Mortality in eating disorders: A descriptive study. *International Journal of Eating Disorders, 28,* 20–26.

Herzog, D. B., Keller, M. B., Lavori, P. W., & Kenny, G. M. (1992). The prevalence of personality disdorders in 210 women with eating disorders. *Journal of Clinical Psychiatry, 53*(5), 147–152.

Herzog, D. B., Keller, M. B., Sacks, N. R., Yeh, C. J., & Lavori, P. W. (1992). Psychiatric comorbidity in treatment-seeking anorexics and bulimics. *Journal of the American Academy of Child and Adolescent Psychiatry, 31*(5), 810–817.

Herzog, D. B., Nussbaum, K. M., & Marmor, A. K. (1996). Comorbidity and outcome in eating disorders. *Psychiatric Clinics of North America, 19*(4), 843–859.

Heston, L. L. (1966). Psychiatric disorders in foster home reared children of schizophrenic mothers. *British Journal of Psychiatry, 112,* 819–825.

Hettema, J. M., Neale, M. C., & Kendler, K. S. (2001). A review and meta-analysis of the genetic epidemiology of anxiety disorders. *American Journal of Psychiatry, 158,* 1568–1578.

Heydebrand, G. (2002). Psychosocial and cognitive rehabilitation. In J. G. Csernansky (Ed.), *Schizophrenia: A new guide for clinicians* (pp. 183–211). New York: Marcel Dekker.

Heyman, A., Fillenbaum, G., Prosnitz, B., & Raiford, K. (1991). Estimated prevalence of dementia among elderly Black and White community residents. *Archives of Neurology, 48,* 594–598.

Heyman, A., Peterson, B., Fillenbaum, G., & Pieper, C. (1996). The Consortium to Establish a Registry for Alzheimer's Disease (CERAD): Pt. XIV. Demographic and clinical predictors of survival in patients with Alzheimer's disease. *Neurology, 46,* 656–660.

Heyman, I. (2005). Challenges in child and adolescent obsessive-compulsive disorder. *Psychiatry, 4,* 73–77.

Heyman, I., Fombonne, E., Simmons, H., Ford, T., Meltzer, H., & Goodman, R. (2001). Prevalence of obsessive-compulsive disorder in the British nationwide survey of child mental health. *British Journal of Psychiatry, 179,* 324–329.

Hier, D. B., Warach, J. D., Gorelilck, P. B., & Thomas, J. (1989). Predictors of survival in clinically diagnosed Alzheimer's disease and multi-infarct dementia. *Archives of Neurology, 46,* 1213–1216.

Hierholzer, R. (2001). Suicide in dementia: Case studies of faiure as a risk factor. *Clinical Gerontologist, 24,* 159–164.

Higgins, S. T., Budney, A. J., Bickel, W. K., Foerg, R., Dunham, R., & Badger, G. J. (1994). Incentives improve outcome in outpatient behavioral treatment of cocaine dependence. *Archives of General Psychiatry, 51*, 568–576.

Higgins, S. T., Roll, J. M., Wong, C. J., Tidey, J. W., & Datona, R. (1999). Clinic and laboratory studies on the use of incentives to decrease cocaine and other substance use. In S. T. Higgins & K. Silverman (Eds.), *Motivating behavior change among illicit-drug abusers: Research on contingency management interventions* (pp. 35–56). Washington, DC: American Psychological Association.

Hill, C. E., & O'Brien, D. M. (1999). *Helping skills: Facilitating exploration, insight, and action*. Washington, DC: American Psychological Association.

Hill, J. (2002). Biological, psychological, and social processes in the conduct disorders. *Journal of Child Psychology and Psychiatry, 43*(1), 133–164.

Hill, S. K., Ragland, J. D., Gur, R. C., & Gur, R. E. (2001). Neuropsychological differences among empirically derived clinical subtypes of schizophrenia. *Neuropsychology, 15*, 492–501.

Hiller, W., Leibbrand, R., Rief, W., & Fitcher, M. (2002). Predictors of course and outcome in hypochondriasis after cognitive-behavioral treatment. *Psychotherapy and Psychosomatics, 71*, 318–325.

Hilsenroth, M. J., Ackerman, S. J., Blagys, M. D., Baumann, B. D., Baity, M. R., & Smith, S. R. (2000). Reliability and validity of the DSM-IV Axis V. *American Journal of Psychiatry, 157*(11), 1858–1863.

Himle, J. A., McPhee, K., Cameron, O. G., & Curtis, G. C. (1989). Simple phobia: Evidence for heterogeneity. *Psychiatry Research, 28*, 25–30.

Hines, A. M., & Caetano, R. (1997). Alcohol and AIDS-related sexual behavior among Hispanics: Acculturation and gender differences. *AIDS Education and Prevention, 10*, 533–547.

Hinshaw, S. P. (1992). Externalizing behavior problems and academic underachievment in childhood and adolescence: Causal relationships and underlying mechanisms. *Psychological Bulletin, 3*, 137–155.

Hinshaw, S. P. (2002). Preadolescent girls with attention-deficit/hyperactivity disorder: Pt. I. Background characteristics, comorbidity, cognitive and social functioning, and parenting practices. *Journal of Counsulting and Clinical Psychology, 70*, 1086–1098.

Hinshaw, S. P., Owens, E. B., Wells, K. C., Kraemer, H. C., Abikoff, H. B., Arnold, L. E., et al. (2000). Family process and treatment outcome in the MTA: Negative and ineffective parenting practices in relation to mutimodal treatment. *Journal of Abnormal Child Psychology, 28*, 555–568.

Hinton, D., Hsia, C., Um, K., & Otto, M. W. (2003). Anger-associated panic attacks in Cambodian refugees with PTSD: A multiple baseline examination of clinical data. *Behaviour Research and Therapy, 41*, 647–654.

Hipple, J. L., & Hipple, L. B. (1983). *Diagnosis and management of psychological emergencies: A manual for hospitalization*. Springfield, IL: Charles C Thomas.

Hippler, K., & Klicpera, C. (2003). A retrospective analysis of the clinical case records of "autistic psychopaths" diagnosed by Hans Asperger and his team at the University Children's Hospital at Vienna [Philosophical transactions of the Royal Society]. *Biological Sciences, 358*, 291–301.

Hippocrates. (1972). *Works* (W. H. S. Jones, Trans.). London: Loeb Classical Library, William Heinemann.

Hirsch, C. R., & Clark, D. M. (2004). Information-processing bias in social phobia. *Clinical Psychology Review, 24*, 799–825.

Hirschfeld, R. M., Lewis, L., & Vornik, L. A. (2003). Perceptions and impact of bipolar disorder: How far have we really come? Results of the national Depressive and Manic-Depressive Association 2000 survey of individuals with bipolar disorder. *Journal of Clinical Psychiatry, 64*, 161–174.

Hirschfeld, R. M., Williams, J. B., Spitzer, R. L., Calabrese, J. R., Flynn, L., Keck, P. E., et al. (2000). Development and validation of a screening instrument for bipolar spectrum disorder: The Mood Disorder Questionnaire. *American Journal of Psychiatry, 157*, 1873–1875.

Hirschowitz, J., Casper, R., Garver, D. L., & Chang, S. (1980). Lithium response in good prognosis schizophrenia. *American Journal of Psychiatry, 137*, 916–920.

Hoagwood, K., Kelleher, K. J., Feil, M., & Comer, D. M. (2000). Treatment services for children with ADHD: A national perspective. *Journal of the American Academy of Child and Adolescent Psychiatry, 39*(2), 198–206.

Hobson, P. (2005). Autism and emotion. In F. Volkmar, R. Paul, A. Klin, & D. Cohen (Eds.), *Handbook of autism and pervasive developmental disorders* (3rd ed., pp. 406–422). Hoboken, NJ: Wiley.

Hoch, A. (1910). Constitutional factors in the dementia praecox group. *Review of Neurology and Psychiatry, 8*, 463–475.

Hodgens, J. B., Cole, J., & Boldizar, J. (2000). Peer-differences among boys with ADHD. *Journal of Clinical Child Psychology, 29*, 443–452.

Hodson, C., Newcomb, M. D., Locke, T. F., & Goodyear, R. K. (2006). Childhood adversity, poly-substance use, and disordered eating in adolescent Latinas: Mediated and indirect paths. *Child Abuse and Neglect, 30*, 1017–1036.

Hoehn-Saric, R., McLeod, D. R., & Zimmerli, W. D. (1989). Somatic manifestations in women with generalized anxiety disorder: Psychophysiological responses to psychological stress. *Archives of General Psychiatry, 46*, 1113–1119.

Hoek, H. W. (1993). Review of the epidemiological studies of eating disorders. *International Review of Psychiatry, 5*(1), 61–74.

Hoek, H. W. (2006). Incidence, prevalence and mortality of anorexia nervosa and other eating disorders. *Current Opinion in Psychiatry, 19*(4), 389–394.

Hoek, H. W., & van Hoeken, D. (2003). Review of the prevalence and incidence of eating disorders. *International Journal of Eating Disorders, 34*(4), 383–396.

Hoff, A. L., Riordan, H., O'Donnell, D. W., & DiLisi, L. E. (1991). Cross sectional and longitudinal neuropsychological test findings in first episode schizophrenic patients. *Schizophrenia Research, 5*, 197–198.

Hoffbuhr, K., Devaney, J. M., La Fleur, B., Sirianni, N., Scacheri, C., Giron, J., et al. (2001). MECP2 mutations in children with and without the phenotype of Rett syndrome. *Journal of Intellectual and Developmental Disabilities, 27*, 57–71.

Hoffman, P. D., Buteau, E., Hooley, J. M., Fruzzetti, A. E., & Bruce, M. L. (2003). Family members' knowledge about borderline personality disorder: correspondence with their levels of depression, burden, distress, and expressed emotion. *Family Process, 42*, 469–478.

Hoffman, P. D., & Fruzzetti, A. E. (2005). Psychoeducation. In J. M. Oldham, A. E. Skodol, & D. S. Bender (Eds.), *Textbook of personality disorders.* (pp. 375–386). Washington, DC: American Psychiatric Publishing.

Hoffman, P. D., Fruzzetti, A. E., & Swenson, C. R. (1999). Dialectial behavior therapy: Family skills training. *Family Process, 38*, 399–414.

Hofmann, S. G., & Barlow, D. H. (2002). Social phobia (social anxiety disorder). In D. H. Barlow (Ed.), *Anxiety and its disorders: The nature and treatment of anxiety and panic* (2nd ed., pp. 454–476). New York: Guilford Press.

Hogan, A. E. (1999). Cognitive functioning in children with oppositional defiant disorder. In H. C. Quay & A. E. Hogan (Eds.), *Handbook of disruptive behavior disorders* (pp. 317–335). New York: Kluwer Academic/Plenum Press.

Hohagen, F., Käppler, C., Schramm, E., Riemann, D., Weyerer, S., & Berger, M. (1994). Sleep onset insomnia, sleep maintaining insomnia and insomnia with early morning awakening: Temporal stability of subtypes in a longitudinal study on general practice attenders. *Sleep: Journal of Sleep Research and Sleep Medicine, 17*(6), 551–554.

Hokanson, J. E., Rubert, M. P., Welker, R. A., Hollander, G. R., & Hedeen, C. (1989). Interpersonal concomitants and antecedents of depression among college students. *Journal of Abnormal Psychology, 98*, 209–217.

Holden, N. L., & Robinson, P. H. (1988). Anorexia nervosa and bulimia nervosa in British Blacks. *British Journal of Psychiatry, 152*, 544–549.

Holder-Perkins, V., & Wise, T. N. (2001). Somatization disorder. In K. A. Phillips (Ed.), *Somatoform and factitious disorders* (pp. 1–26). Washington, DC: American Psychiatric Publishing.

Holland, A. J., & Oliver, C. (1995). Down's syndrome and the links with Alzheimer's disease. *Journal of Neurology, Neurosurgery, and Psychiatry, 59,* 111–114.

Hollon, S. D., DeRubeis, R. J., & Evans, M. D. (1992). Cognitive therapy and pharmacotherapy for depression: Singly and in combination. *Archives of General Psychiatry, 49,* 774–781.

Holmes, C., Cairns, N., & Lantos, P. (1999). Validity and current clinical criteria for Alzheimer's disease, vascular dementia, and dementia with Lewy bodies. *British Journal of Psychiatry, 174,* 45–50.

Holmes, D. S. (2001). *Abnormal psychology* (4th ed.). Boston: Allyn & Bacon.

Holmes, T. H., & Rahe, R. H. (1967). The Social Readjustment Rating Scale. *Journal of Psychosomatic Research, 11,* 213–218.

Holoway, R. M., Heimberg, R. G., & Coles, M. E. (2006). A comparison of intolerance of uncertainty in analogue obsessive compulsive disorder and generalized anxiety disorder. *Anxiety Disorders, 20,* 158–174.

Honda, H., Shimizu, Y., & Rutter, M. (2005). No effect of MMR withdrawal on the incidence of autism: A total population study. *Journal of Child Psychology and Psychiatry, 46*(6), 572–579.

Hooper, R. G. (2001). *Sleep and its disorders: What you should know.* Scottsdale, AZ: Just Peachy Press.

Hope, T., & Fairburn, C. G. (1992). The Present Behavioural Examination (PBE): The development of an interview to measure current behavioural abnormalities. *Psychological Medicine, 22,* 223–230.

Hope, T., Keene, J., Fairburn, C. G., Jacoby, R., & McShane, R. (1999). Natural history of behavioral changes and psychiatric symptoms in Alzheimer's disease: A longitudinal study. *British Journal of Psychiatry, 174,* 39–44.

Horne, R. (1998). Adherence to medication: A review of existing research. In L. B. Myers & K. Midence (Eds.), *Adherance to treatment in medical conditions* (pp. 285–310). Australia, UK: Harwood Academic Publishers.

Horner, G. H. (2000). Mapping the road to quality collaborative patient care in a behavioral health community treatment center: Avoiding the detours of managed care. *Psychiatric Clinics of North America, 23*(2), 363–382.

Horney, K. (1939). *New ways in psychoanalysis.* New York: Norton.

Horowitz, M. J. (1991). Hysterical personality style and the histrionic personality disorder. Northvale, NJ: Jason Aronson.

Horowitz, M. J. (1997). Psychotherapy for histrionic personality disorder. In G. O. Gabbard (Ed.), *Treatment of psychiatric disorders* (pp. 23–26). Washington, DC: American Psychiatric Press.

Horton, A. M., Wedding, D., & Webster, J. (1997). *Neuropsychology handbook* (Vols. 1–2). New York: Springer.

Horvath, A. O. (1994). Research on the alliance. In A. O. Horvath & L. S. Greenberg (Eds.), *The working alliance: Theory, research, and practice* (pp. 259–286). New York: Wiley.

Horvath, A. O. (2000). The therapeutic relationship: From transference to alliance. *Journal of Clinical Psychology/In Session, 56,* 163–173.

Hough, R. L., Canino, G. J., Abueg, F. R., & Gusman, F. D. (1996). PTSD and stress related disorders among Hispanics. In A. J. Marsella, M. J. Friedman, E. T. Gerrity, & R. M. Scurfield (Eds.), *Ethnocultural aspects of posttraumatic stress disorder: Issues, research, and clinical applications* (pp. 105–130). Washington, DC: American Psychological Association.

Howard, K. A., & Tryon, G. S. (2002). Depressive symptoms in and type of classroom placement for adolescents with LD. *Journal of Learning Disabilities, 35,* 185–190.

Howland, R. H., & Thase, M. E. (1999). Affective disorders: Biological aspects. In T. Millon, P. H. Blaney, & R. D. Davis (Eds.), *Oxford textbook of psychopathology* (pp. 166–202). New York: Oxford University Press.

Howlin, P. (1998a). Outcome in adult life for more able individuals with autism or Asperger syndrome. *Autism, 4*, 63–83.

Howlin, P. (1998b). Practitioner review: Psychological and educational treatments for autism. *Journal of Child Psychology and Psychiatry and Allied Disciplines, 39*(3), 307–322.

Howlin, P. (2003). Outcomes in high functioning adults with autism with and without early language delays: Implications for the differentiation between autism and Asperger syndrome. *Journal of Autism and Developmental Disorders, 33*, 3–13.

Howlin, P. (2005). Outcomes in autism spectrum disorders. In F. R. Volkmar, R. Paul, A. Klin, & D. Cohen (Eds.), *Handbook of autism and pervasive developmental disorders* (3rd ed., pp. 201–220). Hoboken, NJ: Wiley.

Howlin, P., & Asgharian, A. (1999). The diagnosis of autism and Asperger syndrome: Findings from a survey of 770 families. *Developmental Medicine and Child Neurology, 41*, 834–839.

Howlin, P., & Goode, S. (1998). Outcome in adult life for individuals with autism. In F. Volkmar (Ed.), *Autism and developmental disorders* (pp. 209–241). New York: Cambridge University Press.

Howlin, P., Goode, S., Hutton, J., & Rutter, M. (2004). Adult outcomes for children with autism. *Journal of Child Psychology and Psychiatry, 45*, 212–229.

Howlin, P., Mawhood, L., & Rutter, M. (2000). Autism and developmental receptive language disorders: Pt. II. Social, behavioral and psychiatric outcomes. *Journal of Child Psychology, 41*, 561–578.

Hoyert, D. L., Smith, B. L., Murphy, S. L., & Kochanek, M. A. (2001). *Deaths: Final data for 1999—National vital statistics report.* Hyattsville, MD: National Center for Health Statistics.

Hoyt, M. (1995). *Brief therapy and managed care: Readings for contemporary practice.* San Francisco: Jossey-Bass.

Hoyt, M., & Austad, C. (1995). Psychotherapy in a staff-model HMO: Providing and assuring quality care in the future. In M. Hoyt (Ed.), *Brief therapy and managed care: Readings for contemporary practice* (pp. 23–40). San Francisco: Jossey-Bass.

Hoza, B., Owens, J. S., Pelham, W. E., Swanson, J., Conners, C. K., Hinshaw, S. P., et al., (2000). Effect of parent cognitions on child treatment response in attention deficit/hyperactivity disorder. *Journal of Abnormal Child Psychology, 28*, 569–583.

Hoza, B., Waschbush, D. A., Pelham, W. E., Molina, B. S., & Milich, R. (2000). Attention-deficit/hyperactivity disordered and controls' responses to social success and failure. *Child Development, 71*, 432–446.

Hser, Y. I., Evans, E., & Huang, Y. C. (2005). Treatment outcomes among women and men methamphetamine abusers in California. *Journal of Substance Abuse Treatment, 28*, 77–85.

Hsiung, G. R., Sadovnick, A. D., & Feldman, H. (2004). Apolipoprotein E e4 genotype as a risk factor for cognitive decline and dementia: Data from the Canadian Study of Health and Aging. *Canadian Medical Association Journal, 171*, 863–867.

Huang, B., Grant, B. F., Dawson, D. A., Stinson, F. S., Chou, P., Saha, T. D., et al. (2006). Race-ethnicity and the prevalence and co-occurrence of Diagnostic and Statistical Manual of Mental Disorders (4th ed.) alcohol and drug use disorders and Axis I and II disorders: United States, 2001 to 2002. *Comprehensive Psychiatry, 47*, 252–257.

Hubbard, J. A., Smithmyer, C. M., Ramsden, S. R., Parker, E. H., Flanagan, K. D., Dearing, K. F., et al. (2002). Observational physiological and self-report measures of children's anger: Relation to reactive versus proactive aggression. *Child Development, 73*, 1101–1118.

Huff, F. J., Belle, S. H., Shim, Y. K., Ganguli, M., & Boller, F. (1990). Prevalence of neurologic abnormalities in Alzheimer's disease. *Dementia, 1*, 32–40.

Hughes, J. N., & Baker, D. B. (1990). *The child clinical interview.* New York: Guilford Press.

Hugo, V. (1982). *Les miserables.* London: Penguin.

Hulse, G. K., English, D. R., Milne, E., & Holman, C. D. J. (1999). The quantification of mortality resulting from the regular use of illicit opiates. *Addiction, 94*, 221–229.

Hunfeld, J. A., Perquin, C. W., Hazebroek-Kampschreur, A. A., Passchier, J., van Suijlekom-Smit, L. W., & van der Wouden, J. C. (2002). Physically explained chronic pain and its impact on children and their families: The mother's perception. *Psychology and Psychotherapy, 75*, 251–260.

Hung, Y. Y., & Huang, T. L. (2006). Lorazepam and diazepam rapidly relieve catatonic features in major depression. *Clinical Neuropharmacology, 29*, 144–147.

Huppert, J. D., & Smith, T. E. (2001). Longitudinal analysis of subjective quality of life in schizophrenia: Anxiety as the best symptom predictor. *Journal of Nervous and Mental Diseases, 189*, 669–675.

Hurwitz, T. A. (2004). Somatization and conversion disorder. *Canadian Journal of Psychiatry, 49*(3), 172–178.

Hutton, J. (1998). *Cognitive decline and new problems arising with autism.* Unpublished doctoral dissertation, University of London.

Hybels, C. F., Blazer, D. G., & Steffens, D. C. (2005). Predictors of partial remission in older patients treated for major depression: The role of comorbid dysthymia. *American Journal of Geriatric Psychiatry, 13*, 713–721.

Hyler, S. E. (1994). *Personality Diagnostic Questionnaire—4 (PDQ-4).* New York: New York State Psychiatric Institute.

Hyman, P. E., Bursch, B., Lopez, E., Schwankovsky, L., Cocjin, J., & Zeltzer, L. K. (2002). Visceral pain associated disability syndrome: A descriptive analysis. *Journal of Pediatric Gastroenerology and Nutrition, 35*, 663–668.

Hyman, S. E. (2002). Neuroscience, genetics, and the future of psychiatric diagnosis. *Psychopathology, 35*, 139–144.

ICSD. (1990). *International classification of sleep disorders: Diagnostic and coding manual* (Diagnostic Classification Steering Committee, Chairman M.J. Thorpy). Rochester, MN: American Sleep Disorders Association.

Iezzi, T., Duckworth, M. P., & Adams, H. E. (2001). Somatoform and factitious disorders. In H. E. Adams & P. B. Sutker (Eds.), *Comprehensive handbook of psychopathology* (pp. 211–258). New York: Kluwer Academic.

Ihara, H., Berrios, G. E., & London, M. (2000). Group and case study of the dysexecutive syndrome in alcoholism without amnesia. *Journal of Neurology, Neurosurgery, and Psychiatry, 68*, 731–737.

Ihara, H., Berrios, G. E., & McKenna, P. J. (2003). The association between negative and dysexecutive syndromes in schizophrenia: A cross cultural study. *Behavioural Neurology, 14*, 63–74.

Ingram, B. L. (2006). *Clinical case formulations: Matching the integrative treatment plan to the client.* Hoboken, NJ: Wiley.

Ingram, R. E., Scott, A., & Siegle, G. (1999). Depression: Social and cognitive aspects. In T. Millon, P. H. Blaney, & R. D. Davis (Eds.), *Oxford textbook of psychopathology* (pp. 203–226). New York: Oxford University Press.

Inouye, S. K., Rushing, J. T., Foreman, M. D., Palmer, R. M., & Pompei, P. (1998). Does delirium contribute to poor hospital outcomes? A three-site epidemiologic study. *Journal of General Internal Medicine, 13*, 234–242.

Inouye, S. K., van Dyck, C., Alessi, C. A., Balkin, S., Siegal, A. P., & Horowitz, R. I. (1990). Clarifying confusion: The confusion assessment method—A new method for detection of delirium. *Annals of Internal Medicine, 113*, 941–948.

Institute of Medicine. (2004). *Vaccines and autism.* Retrieved on October 14, 2007, from www.fda.gov/cber/vaccine/thimerosal.htm#iomsafe/.

International Association for the Study of Pain. (1986). Classification of chronic pain: Description of pain syndromes definition of pain terms. *Pain Supplement,* S3.

in t' Veld, B. A., Ruitenberg, A., Hofman, A., Launer, L. J., van Duijn, C. M., Stijnen, T., et al. (2001). Nonsteroidal antiinflammatory drugs and the risk of Alzheimer's disease. *New England Journal of Medicine, 22*(345), 1515–1521.

Irvin, J. E., Bowers, C. A., Dunn, M. E., & Wang, M. C. (1999). Efficacy of relapse prevention: A meta-analytic review. *Journal of Consulting and Clinical Psychology, 67*, 563–570.

Isager, T., Mouridsen, S. E., & Rich, B. (1999). Mortality and causes of death in pervasive developmental disorders. *Autism: International Journal of Research and Practice, 3*, 7–16.

Issac, M., Janca, A., & Orley, J. (1996). Somatization: A culture bound or universal syndrome? *Journal of Mental Health, 5*(3), 219–223.

Ivey, A., & Ivey, M. B. (1999). *Intentional interviewing and counseling.* New York: Brooks/Cole.

Ivey, A. E., & Matthews, W. J. (1984). A meta-model for structuring the clinical interview. *Journal of Counseling and Development, 63*, 237–243.

Iwata, N., & Buka, S. (2002). Race/ethnicity and depressive symptoms: A cross-cultural/ethnic comparison among university students in East Asia, North and South America. *Social Science and Medicine, 55*, 2243–2252.

Jablensky, A. (1995). Schizophrenia: Recent epidemiologic issues. *Epidemiologic Reviews, 17*, 10–20.

Jablensky, A. (1997). The 100-year epidemiology of schizophrenia. *Schizophrenia Research, 28*, 111–125.

Jablensky, A. (1998). The nature of psychiatric classification: Issues beyond ICD-10 and DSM-IV. *Australian and New Zealand Journal of Psychiatry, 33*, 137–144.

Jablensky, A. (2002). The classification of personality disorders: Critical review and need for rethinking. *Psychopathology, 35*, 112–116.

Jablensky, A. (2006). Subtyping schizophrenia: Implications for genetic research. *Molecular Psychiatry, 11*, 815–836.

Jablensky, A., Sartorius, N., Ernberg, G., Anker, M., Korten, A., & Cooper, J. (1992). Schizophrenia: Manifestations, incidence, and course in different countries: A World Health Organization 10-country study. *Psychological Medicine,* (Suppl. 20), 1–97.

Jackson, C. T., Fein, D., Wolf, J., Jones, G., Hauck, M., Waterhouse, L., et al. (2003). Responses and sustained interactions in children with mental retardation and autism. *Journal of Autism and Developmental Disorders, 33*(2), 115–121.

Jackson, J. C., Gordon, S. M., Hart, R. P., Hopkins, R. O., & Ely, E. W. (2004). The association between delirium and cognitive decline: A review of the empirical literature. *Neuropsychology Review, 14*, 87–98.

Jackson, S., Thompson, R. A., Christiansen, E. H., Colman, R. A., Wyatt, J., & Buckendahl, C. W. (1999). Predicting abuse-prone parental attitudes and discipline practices in a nationally representative sample. *Child Abuse and Neglect, 23*(1), 15–29.

Jackson, S. W. (1986). *Melancholia and depression: From Hippocratic times to modern times.* New Haven, CT: Yale University Press.

Jacob, T., Wiindle, M., Seilhamer, R. A., & Bost, J. (1999). Adult children of alcoholics: Drinking, psychiatric, and social status. *Psychology of Addictive Behavior, 13*, 3–21.

Jacobs, D. G. (1995). *The Harvard Medical School guide to suicide assessment and intervention.* San Francisco: Jossey-Bass.

Jacobson, J. W., & Mulick, J. A. (1996). Definitions of mental retardation. In J. W. Jacobson & J. A. Mulick (Eds.), *Manual of diagnosis and professional practice in mental retardation* (pp. 15–53). Washington, DC: American Psychological Association.

Jacobson, J. W., & Mulick, J. A. (2000). System and cost research issues in treatments for people with autistic disorders. *Journal of Autism and Developmental Disorders, 30*(6), 585–593.

Jacobson, N. S., Dobson, K., Fruzzetti, A. E., Schmaling, D. B., & Salusky, S. (1991). Marital therapy as a treatment for depression. *Journal of Consulting and Clinical Psychology, 59*, 547–557.

Jacobson, S. A. (1997). Delirium in the elderly. *Psychiatric Clinics of North America, 20*, 91–111.

Jaffe, J. H., & Jaffe, A. B. (2004). Neurobiology of opioids. In M. Galanter & H. D. Kleber (Eds.), *American Psychiatric Publishing textbook of substance abuse treatment* (3rd ed., pp. 17–30). Washington, DC: American Psychiatric Press.

James, R. K., & Gilliland, B. E. (2005). *Crisis intervention strategies* (5th ed.). Belmont, CA: Brooks/Cole.

Jamison, K. R. (1999). *Night falls fast: Understanding suicide.* New York: Knopf.

Janet, P. (1889). *L'Automatisme Psychologique.* Doctoral dissertation. Paris: Felix Alcan.

Janet, P. (1920). *The major symptoms of hysteria.* New York: Macmillan.

Jang, K. L., & Vernon, P. A. (2001). Genetics. In W. J. Livesley (Ed.), *Handbook of Personality disorders: Theory, research and treatment* (pp. 177–195). New York: Guilford Press.

Janowsky, D. S., Boone, A., Morter, S., & Howe, L. (1999). Personality and alcohol/substance-use disorder patient relapse and attendance at self-help group meetings. *Alcohol and Alcoholism, 34,* 359–369.

Jansen, A., van den Hout, M., & Griez, E. (1990). Clinical and non-clinical binges. *Behavioural Research and Therapy 28*(5), 439–444.

Jansson, L., & Öst, L.-G. (1982). Behavioral treatments for agoraphobia: An evaluative review. *Clinical Psychology Review, 2,* 311–336.

Jarmas, A. L., & Kazak, A. E. (1992). Young adult children of alcoholic fathers: Depressive experiences, coping styles, and family systems. *Journal of Consulting and Clinical Psychology, 60,* 244–251.

Jaudes, P., Ekwo, E., & Voorhis, J. (1995). Association of drug abuse and child abuse. *Child Abuse and Neglect, 19,* 1065–1075.

Jehu, D. (1992). Adult survivors of sexual abuse. In R. T. Ammerman & M. Hersen (Eds.), *Assessment of family violence: A clinical and legal sourcebook* (pp. 348–370). New York: Wiley.

Jellinek, E. M. (1960). *The disease concept of alcoholism.* Highland Park, NJ: Hillhouse Press.

Jenkins, J. H. (1996). Ethnocultural considerations in the assessment of PTSD. In A. J. Marsella, M. J. Friedman, E. T. Gerrity, & R. M. Scurfield (Eds.), *Ethnocultural aspects of posttraumatic stress disorder: Issues, research, and clinical applications* (pp. 183–205). Washington, DC: American Psychological Association.

Jenner, J. A., Niehuis, F. J., van de Willige, G., & Wiersma, D. (2006). Hitting voices of schizophrenia patients may lastingly reduce persistent auditory hallucinations and their burden: 18-month outcome of a randomized controlled trial. *Canadian Journal of Psychiatry, 51,* 169–177.

Jensen, M. P., & Karoly, P. (2001). Self report scales and procedures for assessing pain in adults. In D. C. Turk & R. Melzack (Eds.), *Handbook of pain assessment* (2nd ed., pp. 170–187). New York: Guilford Press.

Jensen, P. S., Hinshaw, S. P., Kraemer, H. C., Lenora, N., Newcorn, J. H., Abikoff, H. B., et al. (2001). ADHD comorbidity findings from the MTA study: Comparing comorbid subgroups. *Journal of the American Academy of Child and Adolescent Psychiatry, 40*(2), 147–158.

Jensen, P. S., Martin, D., & Cantwell, D. (1997). Cormorbidity in ADHD: Implications for research, practice, and DSM-IV. *Journal of the American Academy of Child and Adolescent Psychiatry, 36*(8), 1065–1079.

Jensen, P. S., Rubio-Stipec, M., Canino, G., Bird, H. R., Dulcan, M. K., Schwab-Stone, M. E., et al. (1999). Parent and child contributions to diagnosis of mental disorder: Are both informants always necessary? *Journal of the American Academy of Child and Adolescent Psychiatry, 38*(12), 1569–1579.

Jeste, D. V., Dunn, L. B., Palmer, B. W., Saks, E., Halpain, M., Cook, A., et al. (2003). A collaborative model for research on decisional capacity and informed consent in older patients with schizophrenia: Bioethics unit of a geriatric psychiatry intervention research center. *Psychopharmacology, 171,* 68–74.

Johansson, B. A., Berglund, M., & Lindgren, A. (2006). Efficacy of maintenance treatment with naltrexone for opioid dependence: A meta-analytical review. *Addiction, 101,* 491–503.

Johnson, D. M., Shea, M. T., Yen, S., Battle, C. L., Zlotnick, C., Sanislow, C. A., et al. (2003). Gender differences in borderline personality disorder: Findings from the Collaborative Longitudinal Personality Disorders Study. *Comprehensive Psychiatry, 44,* 284–292.

Johnson, J. G., Bromley, E., & McGeoch, P. G. (2005) Role of childhood experiences in the development of maladaptive and adaptive personality traits. In J. M. Oldham, A. E. Skodol, & D. S. Bender (Eds.) *Textbook of personality disorders* (pp. 209–222). Washington, DC: American Psychiatric Publishing.

Johnson, J. G., Cohen, P., Smailes, E., Kasen, S., Oldham, J. M., & Skodol, A. E. (2000). Adolescent personality disorders associated with violence and criminal behavior during adolescence and early adulthood. *American Journal of Psychiatry, 157,* 1406–1412.

Johnson, M. B. (1998). Psychological differential diagnosis: Alternatives to the DSM system. *Journal of Contemporary Psychotherapy, 28*(1), 91–95.

Johnson, S. M. (1994). *Character styles.* New York: Norton.

Johnson, W. G., Jarrell, M. P., Chupurdia, K. M., & Williamson, D. A. (1994). Repeated binge/purge cycles in bulimia nervosa: Role of glucose and insulin. *International Journal of Eating Disorders, 15*(4), 331–341.

Johnston, C., & Marsh, E. J. (2001). Families of children with attention-deficit/hyperactivity disorder: Review and recommendations for future research. *Clinical Child and Family Psychology Review, 4,* 183–207.

Johnston, L. D., O'Malley, P. M., Bachman, J. G., & Schulenberg, J. E. (2005). *Monitoring the Future national survey results on drug use, 1975–2004: Vol. I. Secondary school students.* Bethesda, MD: National Institute on Drug Abuse.

Johnston, L. D., O'Malley, P. M., Bachman, J. G., & Schulenberg, J. E. (2006). *Monitoring the future national results on adolescent drug use: Overview of key findings, 2005* (NIH Publication No. 06-5882). Bethesda, MD: National Institute on Drug Abuse.

Johnstone, E. C., Crow, T. J., Frith, C. D., Stevens, M., Kreel, L., & Husband, J. (1978). The dementia of dementia praecox. *Acta Psychiatrica Scandinavica, 57,* 305–324.

Johr, G., Hartstein, J., & Miller, A. L. (2002). Challenges in the field of adolescent suicide research. *Behavioral Emergencies Update, 4*(6) and 11.

Joiner, T. E. (1999). A test of interpersonal theory of depression in youth psychiatric inpatients. *Journal of Abnormal Child Psychology, 27,* 77–85.

Joiner, T. E., Alfano, M. S., & Metalsky, G. I. (1992). When depression breeds contempt: Reassurance seeking, self-esteem, and rejection of depressed college students by their roommates. *Journal of Abnormal Psychology, 101,* 165–173.

Joiner, T. E., Pettit, J. W., & Rudd, M. D. (2004). Is there a window of heightened suicide risk if patients gain energy in the context of continued depressive symptoms? *Professional Psychology: Research and Practice, 35,* 84–89.

Joiner, T. E., & Rudd, M. D. (2000). Intensity and duration of suicidal crises vary as a function of previous suicide attempts and negative life events. *Journal of Consulting and Clinical Psychology, 68*(5), 909–916.

Joiner, T. E., Rudd, M. D., & Rajab, M. H. (1998). Agreement between self and clinician-rated suicidal symptoms in a clinical sample of young adults: Explaining discrepancies. *Journal of Consulting and Clinical Psychology, 67*(2), 171–176.

Joiner, T. E., Walker, R. L., Rudd, M. D., & Jobes, D. A. (1999). Scientizing and routinizing the assessment of suicidality in outpatient practice. *Professional Psychology: Research and Practice, 30,* 447–453.

Joint Commission on Accreditation of Healthcare Organizations (JCAHO). (2004). *Standards for behavioral healthcare.* Joint Commission Resources.

Jones, B. S., Brody, D., Roper, M., & Narrow, W. E. (2003). Prevalence of mood disorders in a national sample of young American adults. *Social Psychiatry and Psychiatric Epidemiology, 38,* 618–624.

Jones, D. (1994). Editorial: The syndrome of Munchausen by proxy. *Child Abuse and Neglect, 18,* 769–771.

Jones, D., & McGraw, J. (1987). Reliable and fictitious accounts of sexual abuse to children. *Journal of Interpersonal Violence, 2,* 27–45.

Jones, S. S. (2006). Are atypical antipsychotics safe in patients with Alzheimer's disease? *American Family Physician, 74.* Retrieved September 17, 2006, from www.aafp.org/afp/20060801/cochrane.html#c3/.

Jongsma, A. E., & Peterson, L. M. (2003). *The complete adult psychotherapy treatment planner* (3rd ed.). Hoboken, NJ: Wiley.

Jonsson, H., & Nyman, A. K. (1990). Predicting long-term outcome in schizophrenia. *Acta Psychiatrica Scandinavica, 83*, 342–346.

Jordon, J. V. (2004). Personality disorder or relational disconnection? In J. J. Magnavita (Ed.), *Handbook of personality: Theory and practice* (pp. 120–134). Hoboken, NJ: Wiley.

Jorgensen, P., Bennedsen, B., Christensen, J., & Hyllested, A. (1996). Acute and transient psychotic disorder: Comorbidity with personality disorder. *Acta Psychiatrica Scandinavica, 94*, 460–464.

Jorm, A. F., & Jolley, D. (1998). The incidence of dementia: A meta-analysis. *Neurology, 51*, 728–733.

Jorm, A. F., Korten, A. E., & Henderson, A. S. (1987). The prevalence of dementia: A quantitative integration of the literature. *Acta Psychiatrica Scandinavica, 76*, 465–479.

Jost, B. C., & Grossberg, G. T. (1996). The evolution of psychiatric symptoms in Alzheimer's disease: A natural history. *Journal of the American Geriatrics Society, 44*, 1978–1981.

Joyce, J. N., Lexow, N., Bird, E., & Winkour, A. (1988). Organization of dopamine D1 and D2 receptors in human striatum: Receptor audiographic studies in Huntington's disease and schizophrenia. *Synapse, 2*, 546–557.

Judd, L. L., & Akiskal, H. S. (2003). The prevalence and disability of bipolar spectrum disorders in the U.S. population: Re-analysis of the ECA database taking into account subthreshold cases. *Journal of Affective Disorders, 73*, 123–131.

Judd, L. L., Akiskal, H. S., Schettler, P. J., Coryell, W., Endicott, J., Maser, J. D., et al. (2003). A prospective investigation of the natural history of the long-term weekly symptomatic status of bipolar II disorder. *Archives of General Psychiatry, 60*, 261–269.

Judd, L. L., Akiskal, H. S., Schettler, P. J., Endicott, J., Maser, J. D., Solomon, D., et al. (2002). The long-term natural history of the weekly symptomatic status of bipolar I disorder. *Archives of General Psychiatry, 59*, 530–537.

Judd, L. L., Kessler, R. C., Paulus, M. P., Zeller, P. V., Wittchen, H. U., & Kunovac, J. L. (1998). Comorbidity as a fundamental feature of generalized anxiety disorders: Results from the National Comorbidity Study (NCS). *Acta Psychiatrica Scandinavica, 98*, 6–11.

Judd, L. L., Schettler, P. J., Akiskal, H. S., Maser, J., Coryell, W., Solomon, D., et al. (2003). Long-term symptomatic status of bipolar I vs. bipolar II disorders. *International Journal of Neuropsychopharmacology, 6*, 127–137.

Juhnke, G. A. (1994). Sad Persons Scale review. *Measurement and Evaluation in Counseling and Development, 27*, 325–328.

Junginger, J. (1990). Predicting compliance with command hallucinations. *American Journal of Psychiatry, 147*, 245–247.

Juster, H. R., & Heimberg, R. G. (1995). Social phobia: Longitudinal course and long-term outcome of cognitive-behavioral treatment. *Psychiatric Clinics of North America, 18*, 821–842.

Kadden, R. M., & Cooney, N. L. (2005). Treating alcohol problems. In G. A. Marlatt & D. M. Donovan (Eds.), *Relapse prevention: Maintenance strategies in the treatment of addictive behaviors* (2nd ed., pp. 65–91). New York: Guilford Press.

Kaduson, H. G., & Schaefer, C. G. (Eds.). (2000). *Short-term play therapy for children.* New York: Guilford Press.

Kagan, J. (1994). *Galen's prophecy.* New York: Basic Books.

Kalechstein, A. D., Newton, T. F., & Green, M. (2003). Methamphetamine dependence is associated with neurocognitive impairment in the initial phases of abstinence. *Journal of Neuropsychiatry and Clinical Neuroscience, 15*, 215–220.

Kales, E. F. (1990). Macronutrient analysis of binge eating in bulimia. *Physiology and Behavior, 48*, 837–840.

Kales, H. C., Chen, P., Blow, F. C., Welsh, D. E., & Mellow, A. M. (2005). Rates of clinical depression diagnosis, functional impairment, and nursing home placement in coexisting dementia and depression. *American Journal of Geriatric Psychiatry, 13*, 441–449.

Kallner, G., Lindelius, R., Petterson, U., Stockman, O., & Tham, A. (2000). Mortality in 497 patients with affective disorders attending a lithium clinic or after having left it. *Pharmacopsychiatry, 33*, 8–13.

Kaminer, Y., & Bukstein, O. G. (2005). Treating adolescent substance abuse. In R. J. Frances, S. I. Miller, & A. H. Mack (Eds.), *Clinical textbook of addictive disorders*. (3rd ed., pp. 559–587). New York: Guilford Press.

Kampman, K. M., Volpicelli, J. R., Mulvaney, F., Rukstalis, M., Alterman, A. I., Pettinati, H., et al. (2002). Cocaine withdrawal severity and urine toxicology results from treatment entry predict outcome in medication trials for cocaine dependence. *Addictive Behaviors, 27*, 251–260.

Kane, J. M., Honigfeld, G., Singer, J., Meltzer, H., & The Clozaril Collaborative Study Group. (1988). Clozapine for the treatment-resistant schizophrenic. *Archives of General Psychiatry, 45*, 789–796.

Kaneda, Y. (2006). Suicidality in schizophrenia as a separate symptom domain that may be independent of depression or psychosis. *Schizophrenia Research, 81*, 113–114.

Kanel, K. (2006). *A guide to crisis intervention*. (3rd ed.). Belmont, CA: Wadsworth.

Kanner, L. (1943). Autistic disturbances of affective contact. *Nervous Child, 2*, 217–250.

Kanner, L., Rodriguez, A., & Ashenden, B. (1972). How far can autistic children go in matters of social adaptation? *Journal of Autism and Childhood Schizophrenia, 2*, 9–33.

Kantor, M. (2003). Distancing: *A guide to avoidance and avoidant personality disorder*. London: Praeger.

Kaplan, A. S., Olmsted, M. P., Carter, J. C., & Woodside, B. (2001). Matching patient variables to treatment intensity: The continuum of care. *Psychiatric Clinics of North America, 24*(2), 281–292.

Kaplan, H. I., & Sadock, B. J. (1995). *Pocket handbook of clinical psychiatry* (2nd ed.). Philadelphia: Lippincott, Williams & Wilkins.

Kaplan, H. I., & Saddock, B. J. (1996). *Pocket handbook of primary care psychiatry*. Philadelphia: Lippincott, Williams, & Wilkins.

Kaplan, H. I., & Saddock, B. J. (1998). *Synopsis of psychiatry* (8th ed.). Philadelphia: Lippincott, Williams, & Wilkins.

Kaplan, M. J. (2002). Approaching sexual issues in primary care. *Primary Care, 29*(1), 113–124.

Karacan, I., Williams, R. L., & Moore, C. A. (1989). Sleep disorders. In H. I. Kaplan & B. J. Saddock (Eds.), *Comprehensive textbook of psychiatry* (Vols. 1–2, 5th ed., pp. 1105–1135). Baltimore: Williams & Wilkins.

Karlin, N. J. (2004). An analysis of religiosity and exercise as predictors of support group attendance and caregiver burden while caring for a family member with Alzheimer's disease. *Journal of Mental Health and Aging, 10*, 99–106.

Karlsson, I. (1999). Drugs that induce delirium. *Dementia and Geriatric Cognitive Disorders, 10*, 412–415.

Karno, M., Golding, J. M., Sorenson, S. B., & Burnam, M. A. (1988). The epidemiology of obsessive-compulsive disorder in five U.S. communities. *Archives of General Psychiatry, 45*, 1094–1099.

Karow, A., Schnedler, D., & Naber, D. (2006). What would the patient choose? Subjective comparison of atypical and typical neuroleptics. *Pharmacopsychiatry, 39*, 47–51.

Karvonen, J. T., Veijola, J., Jokelainen, J., Laksy, K., Jarvelin, M.-R., & Joukamaa, M. (2004). Somatization disorder in young adult population. *General Hospital Psychiatry, 26*, 9–12.

Kashikar-Zuck, S., Vaught, M. H., Goldschneider, K. R., Graham, T. B., & Miller, J. C. (2002). Depression, coping, and functional disability in juvenile primary fibromyalgia syndrome. *Journal of Pain, 3*, 412–419.

Kashner, T. M., Rost, K., Smith, G. R., & Lewis, S. (1992, September 30). An analysis of panel data: The impact of a psychiatric consultation letter on the expenditure and outcomes of care for patients with somatization disorder. *Medical Care,* (9), 811–821.

Kashubeck, S., & Christensen, S. A. (1992). Differences in distress among adult children of alcoholics. *Journal of Counseling Psychology, 39*, 356–362.

Kasper, S., & Resinger, E. (2001). Panic disorder: The place of benzodiazepines and selective serotonin reuptake inhibitors. *European Neuropsychopharmacology, 11*, 307–321.

Kastrup, M. (2002). Experience with current multiaxial diagnostic systems: A critical review. *Psychopathology, 35*, 122–126.

Katsanis, J., & Iacono, W. G. (1991). Clinical, neuropsychological, and brain structural correlates of smooth-pursuit eye tracking performance in chronic schizophrenia. *Journal of Abnormal Psychology, 100*, 526–534.

Katzelnick, D. J., Kobak, K. A., Greist, J. H., & Jefferson, J. W. (1997). Effect of primary care treatment of depression on service use by patients with medical expenditures. *Psychiatric Services, 48*, 59–64.

Kaufman, E., & Brook, D. W. (2004). Family therapy: Other drugs. In M. Galanter & H. D. Kleber (Eds.), *American Psychiatric Publishing textbook of substance abuse treatment* (3rd ed., pp. 417–431). Washington, DC: American Psychiatric Press.

Kaufman, J., Birmaher, B., Brent, D., Rao, U., Flynn, C., Moreci, P., et al. (1997). Schedule for Affective Disorders and Schizophrenia for School-Age Children-Present and Lifetime Version (K-SADS-PL): Initial reliability and validity data. *Journal of the American Academy Of Child and Adolescent Psychiatry, 36*, 980–988.

Kausch, O., & Resnick, P. J. (1999). Psychiatric assessment of the violent offender. In V. B. Van Hasselt & H. Hersen (Eds.), *Handbook of psychological approaches with violent offenders: Contemporary strategies and issues* (pp. 439–457). New York: Kluwer Academic/Plenum Press.

Kay, J. H., Altshuler, L. L., Ventura, J., & Mintz, J. (2002). Impact of Axis II comorbidity on the course of bipolar illness in men: A retrospective chart review. *Bipolar Disorders, 4*, 237–242.

Kay, S. R., & Sevy, S. (1990). Pyramidal model of schizophrenia. *Schizophrenia Bulletin, 16*, 537–545.

Kaye, J., Melero-Montes, M., & Jick, H. (2001). Mumps, measles, and rubella vaccine and the incidence of autism recorded by general practitioners: A time trend analysis. *British Medical Journal, 322*, 460–463.

Kaye, W. H., Bulik, C. M., Thornton, L., Barbarich, N., & Masters, K. (2004). Cormorbidity of anxiety disorders with anorexia and bulimia nervosa. *American Journal of Psychiatry, 161*, 2215–2221.

Kaye, W. H., Gendall, K., & Strober, M. (1998). Serotonin neuronal function and selective serotonin reuptake inhibitor treatment in anorexia and bulimia nervosa. *Biological Psychiatry, 44*, 825–838.

Kaye, W. H., & Strober, M. (2004). Biology of eating disorders. In A. F. Schatzberg & C. B. Nemeroff (Eds.), *American Psychiatric Publishing textbook of psychopharmacology.* (3rd ed., pp. 819–832). New York: American Psychoanalytic Association.

Kaye, W. H., & Weltzin, T. E. (1991). Neurochemistry of bulimia nervosa. *Journal of Clinical Psychiatry, 52*(Suppl. 10), 21–28.

Kazdin, A. (2000). Paranoid personality disorder. In A. E. Kazdin (Ed.), *Encyclopedia of psychology* (pp. 39–41). New York: Oxford University Press.

Kazdin, A. E. (1987). Assessment of depression: Current issues and strategies. *Behavioral Assessment, 9*, 291–319.

Kazdin, A. E. (1997a). Conduct disorder across the life span. In S. S. Luthar, J. A. Burback, D. Cicchetti, & J. R. Weisz (Eds.), *Developmental psychopathology: Perspectives on adjustment, risk, and disorder* (pp. 248–272). New York: Cambridge University Press.

Kazdin, A. E. (1997b). A model for developing effective treatment: Progression and interplay of theory, research and practice. *Journal of Clinical Child Psychology, 26*, 114–129.

Kazdin, A. E. (1998). Conduct disorders. In R. J. Morris & T. R. Kratochwill (Eds.), *The practice of child therapy* (3rd ed., pp. 199–230). Boston: Allyn & Bacon.

Kazdin, A. E., Siegel, T. C., & Bass, D. (1992). Cognitive problem-solving skills training and parent management training in the treatment of antisocial behavior in children. *Journal of Consulting and Clinical Psychology, 60*, 733–747.

Kazdin, A. E., & Wassell, G. (1999). Barriers to treatment and therapeutic change among children referred for conduct disorder. *Journal of Clinical Child Psychology, 28*(2), 160–172.

Kazdin, A. E. & Weisz, J. R. (Eds.). (2003). *Evidence-based psychotherapies for children and adolescents.* New York: Guilford Press.

Keane, T. M., & Barlow, D. H. (2002). Posttraumatic stress disorder. In D. H. Barlow (Ed.), *Anxiety and its disorders: The nature and treatment of anxiety and panic* (2nd ed., pp. 418–453). New York: Guilford Press.

Keck, P. E., Corya, S. A., Altshuler, L. L., Ketter, T. A., McElroy, S. L., Case, M., et al. (2005). Analyses of treatment-emergent mania with olanzapine/fluoxetine combination in the treatment of bipolar depression. *Journal of Clinical Psychiatry, 66*, 611–616.

Keck, P. E., McElroy, S. L., Havens, J. R., Altshuler, L. L., Nolen, W. A., Frye, M. A., et al. (2003). Psychosis in bipolar disorder: Phenomenology and impact on morbidity and course of illness. *Comprehensive Psychiatry, 44*, 263–239.

Keel, J. H., Mesibov, G., & Woods, A. V. (1997). TEACCH/Supported employment program. *Journal of Autism and Developmental Disorders, 27*, 3–10.

Keel, P. K., Dorer, D. J., Eddy, K. T., Franko, D., Charatan, D. L., & Herzog, D. B. (2003). Predictors of mortality in eating disorders. *Archives of General Psychiatry, 60*, 179–183.

Keel, P. K., & Klump, K. L. (2003). Are eating disorders culture-bound syndromes? Implications for conceptualizing their etiology. *Psychological Bulletin, 129*, 747–769.

Keel, P. K., Mitchell, J. E., Miller, K. B., Davis, T. L., & Crow, S. J. (1999). Long-term outcome of bulimia nervosa. *Archives of General Psychiatry, 56*, 63–69.

Keiley, M. (2002). Attachment and affect regulation: A framework for family treatment of conduct disorder. *Family Process, 41*(3), 477–493.

Keller, M. B., Klein, D. N., Hirschfeld, R. M. A., Kocsis, J. H., McCullough, J. P., Miller, I., et al. (1995). Results of the DSM-IV mood disorders field trial. *American Journal of Psychiatry, 152*, 843–849.

Keller, M. B., Lavori, P. W., Coryell, W., Endicott, J., & Mueller, T. I. (1992). Bipolar I: A 5-year prospective follow up. *Journal of Nervous and Mental Diseases, 181*, 238–245.

Keller, M. B., Lavori, P. W., Lewis, C. E., & Klerman, G. K. (1983). Predictors of relapse in major depressive disorder. *Journal of the American Medical Association, 250*, 3299–3304.

Kellogg, S. H. (2003). On "gradualism" and the building of the harm reduction-abstinence continuum. *Journal of Substance Abuse Treatment, 25*, 241–247.

Kelly, B. D. (2005). Erotomania: Epidemiology and management. *CNS Drugs, 19*, 657–669.

Kelly, K. G., Zisselman, M., Cutillo-Schmitter, T., Reichard, R., Payne, D., & Denman, S. J. (2001). Severity and course of delirium in medically hospitalized nursing facility residents. *American Journal of Geriatric Psychiatry, 9*, 72–77.

Kelsoe, J. R. (1999). Recent progress in the search for genes for bipolar disorder. *Current Psychiatry Reports*, 135–140.

Kelsoe, J. R. (2003). Arguments for the genetic basis of the bipolar spectrum. *Journal of Affective Disorders, 73*, 183–197.

Kempf, L., Hussain, N., & Potash, J. B. (2005). Mood disorder with psychotic features, schizoaffective disorder, and schizophrenia with mood features: Trouble at the borders. *International Review of Psychiatry, 17*, 9–19.

Kendall, P. C., & Pimentel, S. S. (2003). On the physiological symptom constellation in youth with generalized anxiety disorder. *Anxiety Disorders, 17*, 211–221.

Kendall, P. C., Reber, M., Mcleer, S., Epps, J., & Ronan, K. R. (1990). Cognitive-behavioral treatment of conduct disordered children. *Cognitive Therapy and Research, 14*, 279–297.

Kendall, P. C., & Warman, M. (1996). Anxiety disorders in youth: Diagnostic consistency across DSM-III-R and DSM-IV. *Journal of Anxiety Disorders, 10*, 453–463.

Kendell, R., & Jablensky, A. (2003). Distinguishing between validity and utility of psychiatric diagnoses. *American Journal of Psychiatry, 160*, 4–12.

Kendler, K. S. (1985). Diagnostic approaches to schizotypal personality disorder: A historical perspective. *Schizophrenia Bulletin, 11*(4), 538–553.

Kendler, K. S., & Diehl, S. R. (1993). The genetics of schizophrenia: A current, genetic-epidemiologic perspective. *Schizophrenia Bulletin, 19*, 261–285.

Kendler, K. S., & Hays, P. (1981). Paranoid psychosis (delusional disorder) and schizophrenia: A family history study. *Archives of General Psychiatry, 38*, 547–551.

Kennedy, G. J. (2000). *Geriatric mental health care: A treatment guide for professionals.* New York: Guilford Press.

Kennedy, N., Boydell, J., Kalidindi, S., Fearon, P., Jones, P. B., van Os, J., et al. (2005). Gender differences in the incidence and age at onset of mania and bipolar disorder over a 25-year period in Camberwell, England. *American Journal of Psychiatry, 162,* 257–262.

Kennedy, N., Boydell, J., & Murray, R. M. (2004). Ethnic differences in first clinical presentation of bipolar disorder: Results from an epidemiological study *Journal of Affective Disorder, 83,* 161–168.

Kennedy, N., Boydell, J., van Os, J., & Murray, R. M. (2004). Ethnic differences in first clinical presentation of bipolar disorder: Results from an epidemiological study. *Journal of Affective Disorders, 83,* 161–168.

Kent, D. A., Tomasson, K., & Coryell, W. (1995). Course and outcome of conversion and somatization disorder: A 4-year follow-up. *Psychosomatics, 36,* 138–144.

Keown, P., Holloway, F., & Kuipers, E. (2002). The prevalence of personality disorders, psychotic disorders and affective disorders amongst the patients seen by a community mental health team in London. *Social Psychiatry Psychiatric Epidemiology,* 37225–37229.

Kern, R. S., Green, M. F., Cornblatt, B. A., Owen, J. R., McQuade, R. D., Carson, W. H., et al. (2006). The neurocognitive effects of aripiprazole: An open-label comparison with olanzapine. *Psychopharmacology, 187,* 312–320.

Kern, R. S., Green, M. F., Marshall, B. D., Wirshing, W. C., Wirshing, D., McGurk, S. R., et al. (1999). Risperidone versus haloperidol on secondary memory: Can newer medications aid learning? *Schizophrenia Bulletin, 25,* 223–232.

Kern, R. S., Green, M. F., & Satz, P. (1992). Neuropsychological predictors of skills training for chronic psychiatric patients. *Psychiatric Research, 43,* 223–230.

Kernberg, O. F. (1975a). *Borderline conditions and pathological narcissism.* New York: Jason Aronson.

Kernberg, O. (1975b). Further contributions to the treatment of narcissistic personalities: A reply to the discussion by Paul H. Orenstein. *International Journal of Psychoanalysis, 56*(2), 245–247.

Kernberg, O. (1984). *Severe personality disorders: Psychotherapeutic strategies.* New Haven, CT: Yale University Press.

Kernberg, O. (1999). Acute and chronic countertransference reactions. In P. Fonagy, A. M. Cooper, & R. S. Wallerstein (Eds.), *Psychoanalysis on the move: The work of Joseph Sandler* (pp. 171–186). New York: Routledge.

Kernberg, O. F. (1989). The narcissistic personality disorder and the differential diagnosis of antisocial behavior. *Psychiatric Clinics of North America, 12,* 671–694.

Kernberg, O. F. (1990). Narcissistic personality disorder. In Michaels (Eds.) *Psychiatry.* Philadelphia: Lippincott-Raven.

Kernberg, O. F. (2004). Borderline personality disorder and borderline personality organization: Psychopathology and psychotherapy. In J. J. Magnavita (Ed.), *Handbook of personality: theory practice* (pp. 92–119). Hoboken, NJ: Wiley.

Kerns, R. D., Rosenberg, R., Jamison, R. N., Caudill, M. A., & Haythornthwaite, J. (1997). Readiness to adopt a self-management approach to chronic pain: The Pain Stages of Change Questionnaire (PSOCQ). *Pain, 72,* 227–234.

Kerns, R. D., Turk, D. C., & Rudy, T. E. (1985). The West Haven-Yale Multidimensional Pain & Inventory (WHYPI). *Pain, 23,* 345–356.

Kesey, K. (1962). *One flew over the cuckoo's nest.* Essex, UK: Signet Publishers.

Kessler, R. C., Berglund, P., Demler, O., Jin, R., Koretz, D., Merikangas, K. R., et al. (2003). The epidemiology of major depressive disorder (Results from the National Comorbidity Survey Replication [NCS-R]). *Journal of the American Medical Association, 289,* 3095–3105.

Kessler, R. C., Crum, R. M., Warner, L. A., Nelson, C. B., Schulenberg, J., & Anthony, J. C. (1997). Lifetime co-occurrence of DSM-III-R alcohol abuse and dependence with other psychiatric disorders in the National Comorbidity Survey. *Archives of General Psychiatry,* *54,* 313–321.

Kessler, R. C., McGonagle, K. A., Zhao, S., Nelson, C. B., Hughes, M., Eshelman, S., et al. (1994). Lifetime and 12 month prevalence of DSM-III-R psychiatric disorders in the United States: Results from the National Comorbidity Survey. *Archives of General Psychiatry, 51,* 8–19.

Kessler, R. C., Molnar, B. E., Feurer, I. D., & Applebaum, M. (2001). Patterns and mental health predictors of domestic violence in the United States: Results from the National Co-morbidity Survey [Special double issue on epidemiology, forensic psychiatry, and public policy]. *International Journal of Law and Psychiatry, 24*(4/5), 487–508.

Kessler, R. C., Nelson, C. B., McGonagle, K. A., Edmund, M. J., Frank, R. G., & Leaf, P. J. (1996). The epidemiology of co-occurring addictive and mental disorders: Implications for prevention and service utilization. *American Journal of Orthopsychiatry, 66,* 17–31.

Kessler, R. C., Nelson, C. B., McGonagle, K. A., Liu, J., Swartz, M., & Blazer, D. G. (1996). Comorbidity of DSM-III-R major depressive disorder in the general population: Results from the U.S. National Comorbidity Survey. *British Journal of Psychiatry, 168,* 17–30.

Kessler, R. C., Rubinow, D. R., Holmes, C., Abelson, J. M., & Zhao, S. (1997). The epidemiology of DSM-III-R bipolar I disorder in a general population survey. *Psychological Medicine, 27,* 1079–1089.

Kessler, R. C., Sonnega, A., Bromet, E., Hughes, M., & Nelson, C. B. (1995). Posttraumatic stress disorder in the National Comorbidity Survey. *Archives of General Psychiatry, 52,* 1048–1060.

Kessler, R. C., Stang, P., Wittchen, H. U., Stein, M., & Walters, E. E. (1999). Lifetime comorbidity between social phobia and mood disorders in the U.S. National Comorbidity Survey. *Psychological Medicine, 29,* 555–567.

Kessler, R. C., Stein, M. B., & Berglund, P. (1998). Social phobia subtypes in the National Comorbidity Survey. *American Journal of Psychiatry, 155,* 613–619.

Kessler, R. C., Walters, E. E., & Wittchen, H. U. (2004). Epidemiology. In R. G. Heimberg, C. L. Turk, & D. S. Mennin (Eds.), *Generalized anxiety disorder: Advances in research and practice* (pp. 29–50). New York: Guilford Press.

Ketter, T. A., Nowakowska, C., Marsh, W. K., Bonner, J., & Wang, P. W. (2005). Treatment of acute mania in bipolar disorder. In T. A. Ketter (Ed.), *Advances in treatment of bipolar disorder* (pp. 11–55). Washington, DC: American Psychiatric Publishing.

Kety, S. (1988). Schizophrenic illness in the families of schizophrenic adoptees: Findings from the Danish national sample. *Schizophrenia Bulletin, 14,* 217–222.

Kety, S. S., Rosenthal, D., Wender, P. H., & Schulsinger, F., (1968). The types and prevalence of mental illness in the biological and adoptive families of adopted schizophrenics. *Journal of Psychiatric Research, 6,* 345–362.

Kety, S. S., Wender, P. H., Jacobsen, B., Ingraham, L. J., Jansson, L., Farber, B., et al., (1994). Mental illness in the biological and adoptive relatives of schizophrenic adoptees. *Archives of General Psychiatry, 51,* 442–455.

Khachaturian, A. S., Zandi, P. P., Lyketsos, C. G., Hayden, K. M., Skoog, I., Norton, M. C., et al. (2006). Antihypertensive medication use and incident Alzheimer disease: The Cache County Study. *Archives of Neurology, 63,* 686–692.

Khan, A., Leventhal, R. M., Khan, S., & Brown, W. A. (2002). Suicide risk in patients with anxiety disorders: A meta-analysis of the FDA database. *Journal of Affective Disorders, 68,* 183–190.

Khandelwal, S. K., Sharan, P., & Saxena, S. (1995). Eating disorders: An Indian perspective. *International Journal of Social Psychiatry, 41,* 132–146.

Khantzian, E. J. (1980). An ego/self theory of substance dependence: A contemporary psychoanalytic perspective. In D. J. Lettieri, M. Sayers, & H. W. Pearson (Eds.), *Theories on drug abuse: Selected contemporary perspectives* (NIDA Research Monograph, 30, pp. 184–191). Rockville, MD: National Institute on Drug Abuse.

Kiecolt-Glaser, J., & Glaser, R. (1994). Caregivers, mental health, and immune function. In E. Light, G. Niederehe, & B. D. Lebowitz (Eds.), *Stress effects on family caregivers of Alzheimer's patients: Research and interventions* (pp. 64–75). New York: Springer.

Kiefer, F., & Wiedemann, K. (2004). What does acamprosate and naltrexone combination tell us? *Alcohol and Alcoholism, 39*, 542–547.

Kientz, M. A., & Dunn, W. (1997). A comparison of the performance of children with and without autism on the sensory profile. *American Journal of Occupational Therapy, 51*, 530–537.

Kiessling, N. K., Faulner, T., & Blair, R. L. (1990). *Robert Burton: The anatomy of melancholy* (Vol. 1–3). New York: Oxford University Press.

Kilbourne, A. M., Bauer, M. A., Pincus, H., Williford, W. O., Kirk, G. F., & Beresford, T. (2005). Clinical, psychosocial, and treatment differences in minority patients with bipolar disorder. *Bipolar Disorder, 7*, 89–97.

Kilbourne, A. M., Haas, G., Mulsant, B. H., Bauer, M. S., & Pincus, H. A. (2004). Concurrent psychiatric diagnoses by age and race among persons with bipolar disorder. *Psychiatric Services, 55*, 931–933.

Kilmer, J. R., Palmer, R. S., & Cronce, J. M. (2005). Assessment of club drug, hallucinogen, inhalant, and steroid use and misuse. In D. M. Donovan & A. G. Marlatt (Eds.), *Assessment of addictive behaviors* (2nd ed., pp. 274–304). New York: Guilford Press.

Kiloh, L. G., Andrews, G., & Neilson, M. (1988). The long-term outcome of depressive illness. *British Journal of Psychiatry, 153*, 752–757.

Kilpatrick, D. G., Acierno, R., Saunders, B., Resnick, H. S., Best, C. L., Schnurr, P. P., et al. (2000). Risk factors of adolescent substance abuse and dependence: Data from a national sample. *Journal of Consulting and Clinical Psychology, 68*, 19–30.

Kilpatrick, D. G., & Best, C. L. (1984). Some cautionary remarks on treating sexual assault victims with implosion. *Behavior Therapy, 15*, 421–423.

Kilts, C. D., Gross, R. E., Ely, T. D., & Drexler, K. P. G. (2004). The neural correlates of cue-induced craving in cocaine-dependent women. *American Journal of Psychiatry, 161*, 223–241.

Kim, B. N., Lee, J. S., Cho, S. C., & Lee, D. S. (2001). Methylphenidate increased regional cerebral blood flow in subjects with attention deficit/hyperactivity disorder. *Yonsei Medical Journal, 42*, 19–29.

Kim, C. H., Jayathilake, K., & Meltzer, H. Y. (2003). Hopelessness, neurocognitive function, and insight in schizophrenia: Relationship to suicidal behavior. *Schizophrenia Research, 60*, 71–80.

Kim, E. Y., & Miklowitz, D. J. (2002). Childhood mania, attention deficit hyperactivity disorder and conduct disorder: A critical review of diagnostic dilemmas. *Bipolar Disorders, 4*, 215–225.

Kim, J., & Gorman, J. (2005). The psychobiology of anxiety. *Clinical Neuroscience Research, 4*, 335–347.

Kim, K., Li, D., Jiang, Z., Cui, X., Lin, L., Kang, J., et al. (1993). Schizophrenic delusions among Koreans, Korean-Chinese, and Chinese: A transcultural study. *International Journal of Social Psychiatry, 39*, 190–199.

Kim, S. A., & Goff, B. C. (2000). Borderline personality disorder. In M. Hersen & M. Biaggio (Eds.), *Effective brief therapies: A clinician's guide*. New York: Academic Press.

Kim-Cohen, J., Caspi, A., Moffitt, T. E., Harrington, H., Milne, B. J., & Poulton, R. (2003). Prior juvenile diagnosis in adults with mental disorders. *Archives of General Psychiatry, 60*, 709–717.

Kimonis, E. R., & Frick, P. J. (2006). Conduct disorder. In M. Hersen, J. C. Thomas, & R. T. Ammerman (Eds.), *Comprehensive handbook of personality and psychopathology: Vol. 3. Child psychopathology* (pp. 299–315). Hoboken, NJ: Wiley.

King, A. C., Baumann, K., O'Sullivan, P., Wilcox, S., & Castro, C. (2002). Effects of moderate-intensity exercise on physiological, behavioral, and emotional responses to family caregiving: A randomized controlled trial. *Journals of Gerontology, Series A: Biological Sciences and Medical Sciences, 57A*, M26–M36.

King, C. A. (1999). Connect five: An innovative youth suicide prevention strategy (News Link). *American Association of Suicidology, 25*(1), 11–12.

King, D. A., Caine, E. D., Conwell, Y., & Cox, C. (1990). The neuropsychology of depression in the elderly: A comparative study of normal aging and Alzheimer's disease. *Journal of Neuropsychiatry, 3*, 163–168.

King, N. (2000). Sexually abused children and post-traumatic stress disorder. *Counseling Psychology Quarterly, 13*(4), 365–376.

King, N. J., Muris, P., & Ollendick, T. (2004). Specific phobia. In T. L. Morris & J. S. March (Eds.), *Anxiety disorders in children and adolescents* (2nd ed., pp. 263–279). New York: Guilford Press.

Kinsbourne, M., De Quiros, G. B., & Tocci Rufo, D. (2001). Adult ADHD: Controlled medication assessment. *Annals of the New York Academy of Sciences, 931*, 287–296.

Kinsella, P. (2001). Factitious disorder: A cognitive behavioral perspective. *Behavioral and Cognitive Psychotherapy, 29*, 195–202.

Kirby, K. C., Benishek, L. A., Dugosh, K. L., & Kerwin, M. E. (2006). Substance abuse treatment providers' beliefs and objections regarding contingency management: Implications for dissemination. *Drug and Alcohol Dependence, 85*, 19–27.

Kirk, S. A., & Kutchins, H. (1992). *The selling of DSM: The rhetoric of science in psychiatry.* Hawthorne, NY: Aldine de Gruyter.

Kirkpatrick, B., Buchanan, R. W., Ross, D. E., & Carpenter, W. T. (2001). A separate disease within the syndrome of schizophrenia. *Archives of General Psychiatry, 58*, 165–171.

Kirkpatrick, B., Ross, D. E., Walsh, D., Karkowski, L., & Kendler, K. S. (2000). Family characteristics of deficit and non-deficit schizophrenia in the Roscommon Family Study. *Schizophrenia Research, 45*, 57–64.

Kirkpatrick, D. W. (1984). Age, gender, and patterns of common intense fears among adults. *Behaviour Research and Therapy, 22*, 141–150.

Kirmayer, L. J. (1996). Confusion of the senses: Implications of ethnocultural variations in somatoform and dissociative disorders for PTSD. In A. J. Marsella, M. J. Friedman, E. T. Gerrity, & R. M. Scurfield (Eds.), *Ethnocultural aspects of posttraumatic stress disorder: Issues, research, and clinical applications* (pp. 131–164). Washington, DC: American Psychological Association.

Kirmayer, L. J., & Tillefer, S. (1997). Somatoform disorders. In S. Turner & M. Hersen (Eds.), *Adult psychopathology* (pp. 410-472). New York: Wiley.

Kirmayer, L. J., & Young, A. (1998). Culture and somatization: Clinical, epidemiological, and ethnographic perspectives. *Psychosomatic Medicine, 60*, 420–430.

Kirov, G., & Murray, R. M. (1999). Ethnic differences in the presentation of bipolar affective disorder. *European Psychiatry, 14*, 199–204.

Klassen, D., O'Conner, W. A. (1994). Demographic and case history variables in risk assessment. In J. Monahan & H. J. Steadman (Eds.), *Violence and mental disorder: Developments in risk assessment* (pp. 229–257). Chicago: University of Chicago Press.

Klatka, L. A., Schiffer, R. B., Powers, J. M., & Kazee, A. M. (1996). Incorrect diagnosis of Alzheimer's disease: A clinicopathological study. *Archives of Neurology, 53*, 35–42.

Klatte, E. T., Scharre, D. W., Nagaraja, H. N., Davis, R. A., & Beversdorf, D. Q. (2003). Combination therapy of donepezil and vitamin E in Alzheimer's disease. *Alzheimer's Disease and Associated Disorders, 17*, 113–116.

Klausner, E., & Alexopoulos, G. (1999). The future of psychosocial treatments for elderly patients. *Psychiatric Services, 50*(9), 1198–1204.

Kleber, H. D. (2001). Detoxification. In G. O. Gabbard (Ed.), *Treatments of psychiatric disorders* (3rd ed., pp. 783–797). Washington, DC: American Psychiatric Press.

Kleespies, P. M., Deleppo, J. D., Mori, D. L., & Niles, B. L. (1998). The emergency interview. In P. M. Kleespies (Ed.), *Emergencies in mental health practice: Evaluation and management* (pp. 41–72). New York: Guilford Press.

Klein, D. A., & Walsh, B. T. (2003). Eating disorders. *International Review of Psychiatry, 15*(3), 205–216.

Klein, D. A., & Walsh, B. T. (2004). Eating disorders: Clinical features and pathophysiology. *Physiology and Behavior, 81*, 359–374.

Klein, D. N., Dickstein, S., Taylor, E. B., & Harding, K. (1989). Identifying chronic affective disorders in outpatients: Validation of the General Behavior Inventory. *Journal of Consulting and Clinical Psychology, 57*, 106–111.

Klein, D. N., & Santiago, N. J. (2003). Dysthymia and chronic depression: Introduction, classification, risk factors, and course. *Journal of Clinical Psychology, 59*, 807–816.

Klein, D. N., Schatzberg, A. F., McCullough, J. P., Dowling, F., Goodman, D., Howland, R. H., et al. (1999). Age of onset in chronic major depression: Relation to demographic and clinical variables, family history, and treatment response. *Journal of Affective Disorders, 55*, 149–157.

Klein, D. N., Schatzberg, A. F., McCullough, J. P., Keller, M. B., Dowling, F., Goodman, D., et al. (1999). Early- versus late-onset dysthymic disorder: Comparison in outpatients with superimposed major depressive episodes. *Journal of Affective Disorders, 52*, 187–196.

Klein, D. N., Schwartz, J. E., Rose, S., & Leader, J. B. (2000). Five-year course and outcome of dysthymic disorder: A prospective, naturalistic follow-up study. *American Journal of Psychiatry, 157*, 931–939.

Klein, D. N., Schwartz, J. E., Santiago, N. J., Vivian, D., Vocisano, C., Castonguay, L. G., et al. (2003). Therapeutic alliance in depression treatment: Controlling for prior change and patient characteristics. *Journal of Consulting and Clinical Psychology, 71*, 997–1006.

Klein, D. N., Shankman, S., & Rose, S. (2006). Ten-year prospective follow-up study of the naturalistic course of dysthymic disorder and double depression. *American Journal of Psychiatry, 163*, 872–880.

Klein, M. (1940). Mourning and its relation to manic-depressive states. In *The Writings of Melanie Klein,* (Vol. 1, pp. 344–369). London: Hogarth Press.

Klein, M. H., Benjamin, L. S., Rosenfeld, R., Treece, C., Husted, J., & Greist, J. H. (1993). The Wisconsin Personality Disorders Inventory: I. Development, reliability, and validity. *Journal of Personality Disorders, 7*, 285–303.

Klein, S., & Alexander, D. A. (2006). Epidemiology and presentation of post-traumatic disorders. *Psychiatry, 5*, 225–227.

Kleinman, A. (1988). *Rethinking psychiatry: From cultural category to personal experience.* New York: Free Press.

Klerman, G. (1978). Affective disorders. In A. Nicholi (Ed.), *Harvard guide to modern psychiatry* (pp. 253–281). Cambridge, MA: Belknap Press.

Klin, A., Jones, W., Schultz, R., & Volkmar, F. R. (2003). The enactive mind, or from actions to cognitions: Lessons from autism. *Philosophical Transactions of the Royal Society of London, Series B: Biological Science, 358*(1430), 345–360.

Klin, A., Jones, W., Schultz, R. T., & Volkmar, F. R. (2005). The enactive mind—From actions to cognitions: Lessons from autism. In F. R. Volkmar, R. Paul, A. Klin, & D. Cohen (Eds.), *Handbook of autism and pervasive developmental disorders* (3rd ed., pp. 682–703). Hoboken, NJ: Wiley.

Klin, A., Lang, J., Cicchetti, D. V., & Volkmar, F. R. (2000). Brief report: Interrater reliability of clinical diagnosis and DSM-IV criteria for autistic disorder: Results of the DSM-IV autism field trial. *Journal of Autism and Developmental Disorders, 30*(2), 163–167.

Klin, A., McPartland, J., & Volkmar, F. R. (2005). Asperger syndrome. In F. R. Volkmar, R. Paul, A. Klin, & D. Cohen (Eds.), *Handbook of autism and pervasive developmental disorders* (3rd ed., pp. 88–125). Hoboken, NJ: Wiley.

Klin, A., Salnier, C., Tsatsanis, K., & Volkmar, F. R. (2005). Clinical evaluation in autism spectrum disorders: Psychological assessment within a transdisciplinary framework. In F. R. Volkmar, R. Paul, A. Klin, & D. Cohen (Eds.), *Handbook of autism and pervasive developmental disorders* (3rd ed., pp. 772–798). Hoboken, NJ: Wiley.

Klin, A., Volkmar, F. R., & Sparrow, S. S. (1992). Autistic social dysfunction: Some limitations of the theory of mind hypothesis. *Journal of Child Psychology and Psychiatry and Applied Disciplines, 35*(5), 861–876.

Klin, A., Volkmar, F. R., & Sparrow S. S. (Eds.). (2000). *Asperger syndrome.* New York: Guilford Press.

Klinger, L. G., & Dawson, G. (1996). Autistic disorder. In E. J. Mash & R. A. Barkley (Eds.), *Child psychopathology* (pp. 311–339). New York: Guilford Press.

Klosko, J. S., Barlow, D. H., Tassinari, R., & Cerny, J. A. (1990). A comparison of alprazolam and behavior therapy in treatment of panic disorder. *Journal of Consulting and Clinical Psychology, 58*, 77–84.

Klump, K. L., Bulik, C. M., Pollice, C., Halmi, K. A., Fichter, M. M., Berrettini, W. H., et al. (2000). Temperament and character in women with anorexia nervosa. *Journal of Nervous and Mental Diseases, 188*(9), 559–567.

Klump, K. L., Kaye, W. H., & Strober, M. (2001). The evolving genetic foundations of eating disorders. *Psychiatric Clinics of North America, 24*(2), 215–225.

Knopman, D. (2002). Pharmacotherapy for Alzheimer's disease: 2002. *Clinical Neuropharmacology, 26*, 93–101.

Knopman, D., & Selnes, O. (2003). Neuropsychology of dementia. In K. M. Heilman & E. Valenstein (Eds.), *Clinical neuropsychology* (4th ed., pp. 574–616). London: Oxford University Press.

Kobayashi, R., Murata, T., & Yoshinaga, K. (1992). A follow-up study of 201 children with autism in Kyushu and Yamaguchi areas, Japan. *Journal of Autism and Developmental Disorders, 22*, 395–411.

Kochanska, G., Friesenberg, A. E., Lange, L. A., & Martel, M. M. (2004). Parents' personality and infants' temperament as contributors to their emerging relationship. *Journal of Personality Disorders, 15*, 195–208.

Koegel, R. L., & Koegel, L. K. (Eds.). (1995). *Teaching children with autism.* Baltimore: Paul H. Brooks.

Koegel, R. L., Koegel, L. K., & McNerney, E. K. (2001). Pivotal areas in intervention for autism. *Journal of Clinical Child Psychology, 30*(1), 19–32.

Koeningsberg, H. W., Reynolds, D., Goodman, M., New, A., Mitropoulou, V., Treatment, R., et al. (2003). Risperidone in the treatment of schizotypal personality disorder. *Journal of Clinical Psychiatry, 64*, 628–634.

Koerner, K., & Linehan, M. M. (2000). Research on dialectical behavior therapy for patients with borderline personality disorder. *Psychiatric Clinics of North America, 23*, 151–167.

Kohut, H. (1968). The psychoanalytic treatment of narcissistic personality disorder. *Psychoanalytic Study of the Child, 23*, 86–113.

Kohut, H. (1971). *The analysis of the self.* New York: International Universities Press.

Kohut, H. (1972). Thoughts on narcissism and narcissistic rage. *Psychoanalytic Study of the Child, 27*, 360–400.

Kohut, H. (1977). *The restoration of the self.* New York: International Universities Press.

Kohut, H., & Wolf, E. D. (1978). The disorders of the self and their treatment: An outline. *International Journal of Psychoanalysis, 59*, 413–425.

Kolb, B., & Winshaw, I. Q. (1990). *Fundamentals of human neuropsychology* (3rd ed.). New York: Freeman.

Koob, G. F., Caine, S. B., Hyytia, P., Markou, A., Parsons, L. H., Roberts, A. J., et al. (1999). Neurobiology of drug addiction. In M. D. Glantz & C. R. Hartek (Eds.), *Drug abuse: Origins and interventions* (pp. 161–190). Washington, DC: American Psychological Association.

Koopman, C., Classen, C., Cardena, E., & Spiegel, D. (1995). When disaster strikes, acute stress disorders may follow. *Journal of Trauma Stress, 8*, 29–46.

Kopelman, M. D., Lasserson, D., Kingsley, D., Bello, F., Rush, C., Stanhope, N., et al. (2001). Structural MRI volumetric analysis in patients with organic amnesia: Pt. 2. Correlations with anterograde memory and executive tests in 40 patients. *Journal of Neurology, Neurosurgery, and Psychiatry, 71*, 23–28.

Kopelowicz, A., Zarate, R., Gonzalez, V., Lopez, S. R., Ortega, P., Obregon, N., et al. (2002). Evaluation of expressed emotion in schizophrenia: A comparison of Caucasians and Mexican-Americans. *Schizophrenia Research, 55*, 179–186.

Koponen, H. J., & Riekkinen, P. J. (1993). A prospective study of delirium in elderly persons admitted to a psychiatric hospital. *Psychological Medicine, 23*, 103–109.

Koponen, H. J., Rockwood, K., & Powell, C. (2002). Clinical assessment and diagnosis. In J. Lindesay, K. Rockwood, & A. MacDonald (Eds.), *Delirim in old age* (pp. 91–100). New York: Oxford University Press.

Koponen, H., Stenbäck, U., Mattila, E., Soininen, H., Reinikainen, K., & Riekkinen, P. J. (1989). Delirium among elderly persons admitted to a psychiatric hospital: Clinical course during the acute stage and one-year follow-up. *Acta Psychiatrica Scandinavica, 79,* 579–585.

Kosloski, K., & Montgomery, J. J. V. (1993). The effects of respite on caregivers of Alzheimer's patients: One year evaluation of the Michigan model respite program. *Journal of Applied Gerontology, 12,* 4–17.

Kosmin, B. A., Mayer, E., & Keysar, A. (2001). *American Religious Identification Survey.* New York: City University of New York.

Kosten, T. R., George, T. P., & Kleber, H. D. (2005). The neurobiology of substance dependence: Implications for treatment. In R. I. Frances, S. I. Miller, & A. H. Mack (Eds.), *Clinical textbook of addictive disorders* (3rd ed., pp. 3–15). New York: Guilford Press.

Kosten, T. R., Rounsaville, B., & Kleber, H. D. (1983). Concurrent validity of the Addiction Severity Index. *Journal of Nervous and Mental Diseases, 171,* 606–610.

Kosten, T. R., & Sofuoglu, M. (2004). Stimulants. In M. Galanter & H. D. Kleber (Eds.), *The American Psychiatric Publishing textbook of substance abuse treatment* (3rd ed., pp. 189–197). Washington, DC: American Psychiatric Publishing.

Kotagal, S., & Silber, M. H. (2004). Childhood-onset restless legs syndrome. *Annals of Neurology, 56*(6), 803–807.

Kotler, L. A., Cohen, P., Davies, M., Pine, D. S., & Walsh, B. T. (2001). Longitudinal relationships between childhood, adolescent, and adult eating disorders. *Journal of the American Academy of Child and Adolescent Psychiatry, 40,* 1434–1440.

Kovacs, M., Akiskal, H. S., Gastonis, C., & Parrone, P. L. (1994). Childhood-onset dythymic disorder: Clinical features and prospective natural outcome. *Archives of General Psychiatry, 51,* 365–374.

Kowatch, R. A., & Fristad, M. A. (2006). Bipolar disorders. In M. Hersen, J. C. Thomas, & R. T. Ammerman (Eds.), *Comprehensive handbook of personality and psychopathology: Vol. 3 Child psychopathology* (pp. 217–232). Hoboken, NJ: Wiley.

Kowatch, R. A., Suppes, T., Carmody, T. J., Bucci, J. P., Hume, J. H., Kromelis, M., et al. (2000). Effect size of lithium, divalproex sodium, and carbamazepine in children and adolescents with bipolar disorder. *Journal of the American Academy of Child and Adolescent Psychiatry, 39,* 713–720.

Kozlowska, K. (2003). Good children with conversion disorder: Breaking the silence. *Clinical Child Psychology and Psychiatry, 8*(1), 73–90.

Kraepelin, E. (1913). *Psychiatrie: Ein lehrbuch.* Leipzig: Barth.

Kraepelin, E. (1919). *Dementia pracox and paraphrenia.* New York: Krieger.

Kraepelin, E. (1921). *Manic-depressive insanity and paranoia* (R. M. Barclay, Trans.). Edinburgh, Scotland: Churchill Livingstone.

Krahn, L. E., Li, H., & O'Connor, M. K. (2003). Patients who strive to be ill: Factitious disorder with physical symptoms. *American Journal of Psychiatry, 160*(6), 1163–1168.

Krakowski, M. I., Convit, A., Jaeger, J., Shang, L., & Volka, V. (1989). Neurological impairment in violent schizophrenic outpatients. *American Journal of Psychiatry, 146,* 849–853.

Kral, M. J., & Sakinofsky, I. (1994). Clinical models for suicide risk assessment. *Death Studies, 18,* 311–326.

Kranzler, H. R., & VanKirk, J. (2001). Efficacy of naltrexone and acamprosate for alcoholism treatment: A meta-analysis. *Alcoholism: Clinical and Experimental Research, 25,* 1335–1341.

Kraus, G., & Reynolds, D. J. (2001). The A-B-C's of the cluster B's: Identifying, understanding and treating cluster B personality disorders. *Clinical Psychology Review, 21*(3), 345–373.

Krem, M. M. (2004). Motor conversion disorders reviewed from a neuropsychiatric perspective. *Journal of Clinical Psychiatry, 65*(6), 783–790.

Kretschmer, H. (1925). *Physique and character* (2nd ed., rev.). Oxford, England: Harcourt, Brace.

Krill, D. F. (1968). Family interviewing as an intake diagnostic method. *Social Work, 56*–63.

Kroenke, K., & Swindle, R. (2000). Cognitive-behavioral therapy for somatization and symptom syndromes: A critical review of controlled clinical trials. *Psychotherapy and Psychosomatics, 69*, 205–215.

Krueger, H. K., & Wollersheim, J. P. (1993). Suicide assessment. In J. Sommers-Flanagan & R. Sommers-Flanagan (Eds.), *Foundations of therapeutic interviewing* (pp. 243–267). Boston: Allyn & Bacon.

Krug, D. A., Arick, J., & Almond, P. (1980). Behavior checklist for identifying severely handicapped individuals with high levels of autistic behavior. *Journal of Child Psychology and Psychiatry, 21*, 221–229.

Krüger, S., Young, L. T., & Braünig, P. (2005). Pharmacotherapy of bipolar mixed states. *Bipolar Disorders, 5*, 205–215.

Kruh, I. P., Frick, P. J., & Clements, C. B. (2005). Historical and personality correlates to the violence patterns of juveniles tried as adults. *Criminal Justice and Behavior, 32*, 69–96.

Krupinski, M., Fischer, A., Grohmann, R., Engel, R., Hollweg, M., & Möller, H. J. (1998). Risk factors for suicides of inpatients with depressive psychoses. *European Archives of Psychiatry and Clinical Neuroscience, 248*, 141–147.

Kryger, M., Lavie, P., & Rosen, R. (1999). Recognition and diagnosis of insomnia. *Sleep: Journal of Sleep Research and Sleep Medicine, 22*(Suppl. 3), S421–S426.

Krystal, A. D., Walsh, J. K., Laska, E., Caron, J., Amato, D. A., Wessel, T. C., et al. (2003). Sustained efficacy of eszopiclone over 6 months of nightly treatment: Results of a randomized, double-blind, placebo-controlled study in adults with chronic insomnia. *Sleep: Journal of Sleep and Sleep Disorders Research, 26*(7), 793–799.

Krystal, H. (1978). Self-representation and the capacity for self-care. *Annual Psychoanalysis, 6*, 209–246.

Krystal, H. (1995). Disorders of emotional development in addictive behavior. In S. Dowling (Ed.), *The psychology and treatment of addictive behavior* (pp. 65–100). Madison, CT: International Universities Press.

Kuczynski, K., & Gibbs-Wahlberg, P. (2005). HIPAA the health care hippo: Despite the rhetoric, is privacy still an issue? *Social Work, 50*, 283–287.

Kukull, W. A., & Ganguli, M. (2000). Epidemiology of dementia: Concepts and overview. *Neurology Clinics, 18*, 923–949.

Kulka, R. A., Schlenger, W. E., Fairbank, J. A., Hough, R. L., Jordan, B. K., Marmar, C. R., et al. (1990). *Trauma and the Vietnam War generation: Report of findings from the National Vietnam Veterans Readjustment Study.* New York: Brunner/Mazel.

Kumar, S., Thara, R., & Rajkumar, S. (1989). Coping with the symptoms of relapse in schizophrenia. *European Archives of Psychiatry and Neurological Sciences, 239*, 213–215.

Kumra, S., Wiggs, E., Bedwell, J., Smith, A. K., Arling, E., Albus, K., et al. (2000). Neuropsychological deficits in pediatric patients with childhood-onset schizophrenia and psychotic disorder not otherwise specified. *Schizophrenia Research, 42*, 135–144.

Kuntsi, J., & Stevenson, J. (2000). Hyperactivity in children: A focus on genetic research and psychological theories. *Clinical Child and Family Psychological Review, 3*, 1–33.

Kupfer, D. J., First, M. B., & Regier, D. A. (Eds.). (2002). *A research agenda for DSM-V.* Washington, DC: American Psychiatric Association.

Kupfer, D. J., Frank, E., Grochocinski, V. J., Cluss, P. A., Houck, P. R., & Stapf, D. A. (2002). Demographic and clinical characteristics of individuals in a bipolar disorder case registry. *Journal of Clinical Psychiatry, 63*, 120–125.

Kupfer, D. J., Frank, E., Grochocinski, V. J., Houck, P. R., & Brown, C. (2005). African-American participants in a bipolar disorder registry: Clinical and treatment characteristics. *Bipolar Disorders, 7*, 82–88.

Kuriansky, J. B., Deming, W. E., & Gurland, B. J. (1974). On trends in the diagnosis of schizophrenia. *American Journal of Psychiatry, 131*, 402–408.

Kurz, A., Farlow, M., Quarg, P., & Spiegel, R. (2004). Disease stage in Alzheimer disease and treatment effects of rivastigmine. *Alzheimer Disease and Associated Disorders, 18*, 123–128.

Kurz, A. F., Erkinjuntti, T., Small, G. W., Lilienfeld, S., & Damaraju, C. R. (2003). Long-term safety and cognitive effects of galantamine in the treatment of probable vascular dementia or Alzheimer's disease with cerebrovascular disease. *European Journal of Neurology, 10*, 633–640.

Kushner, M. G., Abrams, K., & Borchardt, C. (2000). The relationship between anxiety disorders and alcohol use disorders: A review of major perspectives and findings. *Clinical Psychology Review, 20*, 149–171.

Kwapil, T. R. (1996). A longitudinal study of drug and alcohol use by psychosis-prone and impulsive-nonconforming individuals. *Journal of Abnormal Psychology, 105*, 114–123.

L'Abate, L., & Bagarozzim, D. A. (1993). *Sourcebook of marriage and family evaluation.* New York: Brunner/Mazel.

LaBruzza, A. L., & Mendez-Villarrubia, J. M. (1997). *Using the DSM-IV: A clinician's guide to psychiatric diagnosis.* Northvale, NJ: Aronson.

Lacks, P., Bertelson, A., Sugerman, J., & Kunkel, J. (1983). The treatment of sleep-maintenance insomnia with stimulus-control techniques. *Behavioural Research and Therapy, 2*, 291–295.

Lacro, J. P., Dunn, L. B., Dolder, C. R., Leckband, S. G., & Jeste, D. V. (2002). Prevalence of and risk factors for medication nonadherence in patients with schizophrenia. *Journal of Clinical Psychiatry, 63*, 892–909.

Ladwig, K. H., Marten-Mittag, B., Erazo, N., & Gundel, H. (2001). Identifying somatization disorder in a population-based health examination survey: Psychosocial burden and gender differences. *Psychosomatics, 24*(6), 511–518.

Lahey, B. B., Applegate, B., McBurnett, K., Biedermen, J., Greenhill, L., Hynd, G. W., et al. (1994). DSM-IV field trials for attention deficit/hyperactivity disorder in children and adolescents. *American Journal of Psychiatry, 15*, 1673–1685.

Lahey, B. B., Goodman, S. H., Canino, G., Schwab-Stone, M., Waldman, J. D., Rathouz, P. J., et al. (2000). Age and gender differences in oppositional behavior and conduct problems: A cross-sectional household survey of middle childhood and adolescence. *Journal of Abnormal Psychology, 109*(3), 488–503.

Lahey, B. B., Loeber, R., Burke, J., & Rathouz, P. J. (2002). Adolescent outcomes of childhood conduct disorder among clinic-referred boys: Predictors of improvement. *Journal of Abnormal Child Psychology, 30*(4), 333–348.

Lahey, B. B., Miller, T. L., Gordon, R. A., & Riley, A. W. (1999). Developmental epidemiology of the disruptive behavior disorders. In H. C. Quay, A. E. Dordrecht, P. S. Jensen, & J. Cooper (Eds.), *Handbook of disruptive behavior disorders* (pp. 23–48). New York: Academic/Plenum.

Lahey, B. B., & Willcutt, E. G. (2002). The validity of attention-deficit/hyperactivity disorder among children and adolescents. In P. S. Jensen & J. Cooper (Eds.), *Attention deficit hyperactivity disorder: State of the science, best practices* (pp. 1–23). Kingston, NJ: Civic Research Institute.

Lainhart, J. E. (1999). Psychiatric problems in individuals with autism, their parents and siblings. *International Review of Psychiatry, 11*, 278–298.

Lainhart, J. E. (2003). Increased rate of head growth during infancy in autism. *Journal of the American Medical Association, 290*, 393–394.

Laitinen, M. H., Ngandu, T., Rovio, S., Helkala, E. L., Uusitalo, U., Viitanen, M., et al. (2006). Fat intake at midlife and risk of dementia and Alzheimer's disease: A population-based study. *Dementia and Geriatric Cognitive Disorders, 22*, 99–107.

Lake, C. R., & Hurwitz, N. (2006). Schizoaffective disorders are psychotic mood disorders; there are no schizoaffective disorders. *Psychiatry Research, 143*, 255–287.

Lam, D., & Wong, G. (1997). Prodromes, coping strategies, insight and social functioning in bipolar affective disorders. *Psychological Medicine, 27*, 1091–1100.

Lam, D. H., Hayward, P., Watkins, E. R., Wright, K., & Sham, P. (2005). Relapse prevention in patients with bipolar disorder: Cognitive therapy outcome after 2 years. *American Journal of Psychiatry, 162*, 324–329.

Lam, D. H., Jones, S. H., Hayward, P., & Bright, J. A. (1999). *Cognitive therapy for bipolar disorder: A therapist's guide to concepts, methods, and practice.* New York: Wiley.

Lam, D. H., Watkins, E. R., Hayward, P., Bright, J., Wright, K., Kerr, N., et al. (2003). A randomized controlled study of cognitive therapy for relapse prevention for bipolar affective disorder: Outcome of the first year. *Archives of General Psychiatry, 60*, 145–152.

Lam, R. W., & Levitan, R. D. (2000). Pathophysiology of seasonal affective disorder: A review. *Journal of Psychiatry and Neuroscience, 25*, 469–480.

Lamar, M., Swenson, R., Kaplan, E., & Libon, D. J. (2004). Characterizing alterations in executive functioning across distinct subtypes of cortical and subcortical dementia. *Clinical Neuropsychologist, 18*, 22–31.

Landheim, A. S., Bakken, K., & Vaglum, P. (2006). What characterizes substance abusers who commit suicide attempts? Factors related to Axis I disorders and patterns of substance use disorders: A study of treatment-seeking substance abusers in Norway. *European Addiction Research, 12*, 102–108.

Landrø, N. I., Stiles, T. C., & Sletvold, H. (2001). Neuropsychological function in nonpsychotic unipolar major depression. *Neuropsychiatry, Neuropsychology, and Behavioral Neurology, 14*, 233–240.

Lang, A. J. (2004). Treating generalized anxiety disorder with cognitive-behavioral therapy. *Journal of Clinical Psychiatry, 65*, 14–19.

Lang, P. J. (1977). Imagery in therapy: An information processing analaysis of fear. *Behavior Therapy, 8*, 862–886.

Langa, K. M., Foster, N. L., & Larson, E. B. (2004). Mixed dementia: Emerging concepts and therapeutic implications. *Journal of the American Medical Association, 292*, 2901–2908.

Langenbucher, J. W., & Nathan, P. E. (2006). Diagnosis and classification. In M. Hersen, J. C. Thomas, & R. T. Ammerman (Eds.), *Comprehensive handbook of personality and psychopathology: Vol. 2. Adult psychopathology* (pp. 3–20). Hoboken, NJ: Wiley.

Langer, E. K., & Abelson, R. P. (1974). A patient by any other name . . . : Clinician group difference and labeling bias. *Journal of Consulting and Clinical Psychology, 42*, 4–9.

LaPierre, D., Braun, C. M. J., Hodgins, S., Toupin, J., Leveillee, S., & Constantineau, C. (1995). Neuropsychological correlates of violence in schizophrenia. *Schizophrenia Bulletin, 21*, 253–262.

La Roche, M. J. (2005). The cultural context and the psychotherapeutic process: Towards a culturally sensitive psychotherapy. *Journal of Psychotherapy Integration, 15*(2), 169–185.

Larrabee, G. J., Largen, J. W., & Levin, H. S. (1985). Sensitivity of age-decline resistant ("hold") WAIS subtests to Alzheimer's disease. *Journal of Clinical and Experimental Neuropsychology, 7*, 497–504.

Larsson, J.-O., Larsson, H., & Lichtenstein, P. (2004). Genetic and environmental contributions to stability and change of ADHD symptoms between 8 and 13 years of age: A longitudinal twin study. *Journal of the American Academy of Child and Adolescent Psychiatry, 43*(10), 1267–1275.

Lasègue, C., & Falret, J. (1964). Folie a deux ou folie communiqué (R. Michaud, Trans.). *American Journal of Psychiatry, 121*(Suppl. 4), S2–S23. (Original work published 1877)

Last, C. G. (2006). *Help for worried kids.* New York: Guilford Press.

Last, C. G., Perrin, S., Hersen, M., & Kazdin, A. E. (1996). A prospective study of childhood anxiety disorders. *Journal of the American Academy of Child and Adolescent Psychology, 35*, 1502–1510.

Laub, J. H., & Valliant, G. E. (2000). Deliquency and mortality: A 50-year follow-up study of 1,000 delinquent and nondelinquent boys. *American Journal of Psychiatry, 157*, 96–102.

Lauer, C. J., Schreiber, W., Holsboer, F., & Krieg, J. C. (1995). In quest of identifying vulnerability markers for psychiatric disorders by all-night polysomnography. *Archives of General Psychiatry, 52*, 145–153.

Laumann, E. O., Paik, A., & Rosen, R. C. (1999). Sexual dysfunction in the United States: Prevalence and predictors. *Journal of the American Medical Association, 281*(6), 537–544.

Launer, L. J., Andersen, K., Dewey, M. E., Letenneur, L., Ott, A., Amaducci, L. A., et al. (1999). Rates and risk factors for dementia and Alzheimer's disease: Results from EURODEM pooled analyses. *Neurology, 52*, 78–84.

Laurila, J. V., Pitkala, K. H., Strandberg, T. E., & Tilvis, R. S. (2004a). Detection and documentation of dementia and delirium in acute geriatric wards. *General Hospital Psychiatry, 26,* 31–35.

Laurila, J. V., Pitkala, K. H., Strandberg, T. E., & Tilvis, R. S. (2004b). Impact of different diagnostic criteria on prognosis of delirium: A prospective study. *Dementia and Geriatric Cognitive Disorders, 28,* 240–244.

Laurin, D., Verreault, R., Lindsay, J., MacPherson, K., & Rockwood, K. (2001). Physical activity and risk of cognitive impairment and dementia in elderly persons. *Archives of Neurology, 58,* 498–504.

La Via, M. C., Gray, N., & Kaye, W. H. (2000). Case reports of olanzapine treatment of anorexia nervosa. *International Journal of Eating Disorders, 27*(3), 363–366.

Lavigne, J. V., Cicchetti, C., Gibbons, R. D., Binns, H. J., Larsen, L., & DeVito, C. (2001). Oppositional defiant disorder with onset in preschool years: Longitudinal stability and pathways to other disorders. *Journal of the American Academy of Child and Adolescent Psychiatry, 40*(12), 1393–1400.

Lavigne, J. V., Gibbons, R. D., Christoffel, K. K., Arend, R., Rosenbaum, D., Binns, H., et al. (1996). Prevalence rates and risk factors for psychiatric disorder among preschool children. *Journal of the American Academy of Child and Adolescent Psychiatry, 35,* 204–214.

Leahy, R. L. (2004). Cognitive behavioral therapy. In R. G. Heimberg, C. L. Turk, & D. S. Mennin (Eds.), *Generalized anxiety disorder: Advances in research and practice* (pp. 265–292). New York: Guilford Press.

Leahy, R. L., Holland, S. J. (2000). *Treatment plans and interventions for depression and anxiety disorders.* New York: Guilford Press.

Leary, P. M. (2003). Conversion disorder in childhood: Diagnosed too late, investigated too much? *Journal of the Royal Society of Medicine, 96*(9), 436–438.

Le Blanc, M. (1994). Family, school, delinquency and criminality, the predictive power of an elaborated social control theory for males. *Criminal Behavior and Mental Health, 4,* 101–117.

Leboyer, M., Paillere-Martinot, M. L., & Bellivier, F. (2005). Age at onset in bipolar affective disorders: A review. *Bipolar Disorders, 7,* 111–118.

Le Couteur, A., Lord, C., & Rutter, M. (2003). *The Autism Diagnostic Interview: Revised.* Los Angeles: Western Psychological Services.

Lee, H. K., Villar, O., Juthani, N., & Bluestone, H. (1989). Characteristics and behavior of patients involved in psychiatric ward incidents. *Hospital and Community Psychiatry, 40,* 1295–1297.

Lee, S. (2002). Socio-cultural and global health perspectives for the development of future psychiatric diagnostic systems. *Psychopathology, 35,* 152–157.

Lee, S., Ho, T. P., & Hsu, L. K. G. (1993). Fat phobic and non-fat phobic anorexia nervosa: A comparative study of 70 Chinese patients in Hong Kong. *Psychological Medicine, 23,* 999–1017.

Lee-Chiong, T., & Sateia, M. (2006). Pharmacologic therapy of insomnia. In T. Lee-Chiong (Ed.), *Sleep: A comprehensive handbook* (pp. 125–132). Hoboken, NJ: Wiley.

Leeds, J., & Morgenstern, J. (2003). Psychoanalytic theories of substance abuse. In F. Rogers, J. Morgenstern, & S. T. Walters (Eds.), *Treating substance abuse: Theory and technique* (pp. 67–81). New York: Guilford Press.

Leenaars, A. A. (1994). Crisis intervention with highly lethal suicidal people. In A. A. Leenaars, J. T. Maltsberger, & R. A. Neimeyer (Eds.), *Treatment of suicidal people* (pp. 45–59). Philadelphia: Taylor & Francis.

Leenaars, A. A., & Lester, D. (1995). Assessment and prediction of suicide risk in adolescents. In J. K. Zimmerman & G. M. Asnis (Eds.), *Treatment approaches with suicidal adolescents* (pp. 47–70). New York: Wiley.

Leff, J. (2001). *The unbalanced mind.* New York: Columbia University Press.

Leger, D., Guilleminault, C., Bader, G., Levy, E., & Paillard, M. (2002). Medical and socioprofessional impact of insomnia. *Sleep, 25*(6), 625–629.

Le Grange, D., Lock, J., & Dymek, M. (2003). Family-based therapy for adolescents with bulimia nervosa. *American Journal of Psychotherapy, 57*(2), 237–251.

Lehfeld, H., & Erzigkeit, H. (2000). Functional aspects of dementia. In S. Gauthier & J. L. Cummins (Eds.), *Alzheimer's disease and related disorders* (pp. 155–177). London: Martin Dunitz.

Lehman, A. E., Dixon, L. B., Kernan, E., DeForge, B. R., & Postrado, L. T. (1997). A randomized trial of assertive community treatment for homeless persons with severe mental illness. *Archives of General Psychiatry, 54,* 1038–1043.

Lehman, A. F., Steinwachs, D. M., & PORT Co-investigators. (1998). At issue: Translating research into practice: The schizophrenia Patient Outcomes Research Team (PORT) treatment recommendations. *Schizophrenia Bulletin, 24,* 1–10.

Liebenluft, E. (2000). Women and bipolar disorder: An update. *Bulletin of the Menninger Clinic, 64,* 5–17.

Leibert, T. W. (2006). Assessment and diagnosis: Making change visible—The possibilities in assessing mental health counseling outcomes. *Journal of Counseling and Development, 84,* 108–113.

Leiblum, S. R., & Rosen, R. C. (2000). *Principles and practice of sex therapy* (3rd ed.). New York: Guilford Press.

Leiblum, S. R., & Segraves, R. T. (2000). Sex therapy with aging adults. In S. R. Leiblum & R. C. Rosen (Eds.), *Principles and practice of sex therapy* (3rd ed., pp. 423–448). New York: Guilford Press.

Leibson, C. L., Katusic, S. K., Barbaresi, A. J., Ransom, J., & O'Brien, P. C. (2001). Use and costs of medical care for children and adolescents with and without attention deficit/ hyperactivity. *Journal of the American Medical Association, 285,* 60–66.

Leichsenring, F., & Leibing, E. (2003). The effectiveness of psychodynamic psychotherapy and cognitive behavior therapy in the treatment of personality disorders: A meta-analysis. *American Journal of Psychiatry, 160,* 1223–1232.

Lemke, S., & Moos, R. H. (2003). Outcomes at 1 and 5 years for older patients with alcohol use disorders. *Journal of Substance Abuse Treatment, 24,* 43–50.

Lennox, R., Dennis, M. L., Scott, C. K., & Funk, R. (2006). Combining psychometric and biometric measures of substance use. *Drug and Alcohol Dependence, 83,* 95–103.

Lenze, E. J., Mulsant, B. H., Shear, M. K., Schulberg, H. C., Dew, M. A., Begley, A. E., et al. (2000). Comorbid anxiety disorders in depressed elderly patients. *American Journal of Psychiatry, 157,* 722–728.

Lenzenweger, M., Johnson, M., & Willett, J. (2004). Individual growth curve analysis illuminates stability and change in personality disorder features: The longitudinal study of personality disorders. *Archives of General Psychiatry, 61,* 1015–1024.

Lenzenweger, M. F. (1998). Schizotypy and schizotypic psychopathology: Mapping an alternative expression of schizophrenia liability. In M. F. Lenzenweger & R. H. Dworkin (Eds.), *Origins and development of schizophrenia: Advances in experimental psychopathology* (pp. 93–121). Washington, DC: American Psychological Association.

Lenzenweger, M. F. (1999a). Schizotypic psychopathology. In T. Millon, P. H. Blaney, & R. D. Davis, (Eds.), *Oxford textbook of psychopathology* (pp. 605–627). New York: Oxford University Press.

Lenzenweger, M. F., (1999b). Stability and change in personality disorder features: The Longitudinal Study of Personality Disorders. *Archives of General Psychiatry, 56,* 1009–1015.

Leon, R. L. (1982). *Psychiatric interviewing: A primer.* St. Louis, MO: Elsevier.

Leonard, H. L., Lenane, M. C., Swedo, S. E., Rettew, D. C., Gershon, E. S., & Rapoport, J. L. (1992). Tics and Tourette's disorder: A 2- to 7-year follow-up of 54 obsessive-compulsive children. *American Journal of Psychiatry, 149,* 1244–1251.

Leonard, K. (1959). *Die auftenlung der endogen psychosen.* Berlin: Akademie.

Leonardo, E. D., & Hen, R. (2006). Genetics of affective and anxiety disorders. *Annual Review of Psychology, 57,* 117–137.

Lepine, J. P., & Pelissolo, A. (1996). Comorbidity and social phobia: Clinical and epidemiological issues. *International Clinical Psychopharmacology, 11*(Suppl. 3), 35–41.

Lerner, D., Adler, D. A., Chang, H., Lapitsky, L., Hood, M. Y., Perissinotto, C., et al. (2004). Unemployment, job retention, and productivity loss among employees with depression. *Psychiatric Services, 55*, 1371–1378.

Leroi, I., Voulgari, A., Breitner, J. C. S., & Lyketsos, C. G. (2003). The epidemiology of psychosis in dementia. *American Journal of Geriatric Psychiatry, 11*, 83–91.

Lessa, N. R., & Scanlon, W. F. (2006). *Wiley concise guides to mental health: Substance use disorders.* Hoboken, NJ: Wiley

Lester, D. (2001). *Suicide prevention: Resources for the millennium.* Philadelphia: Brunner/ Routledge.

Lettsom, J. C. (1789). *History of some of the effects of hard drinking.* London.

Leucht, S., Wahlbeck, K., Hamann, J., & Kissling, W. (2003). New generation antipsychotics versus low-potency conventional antipsychotics: A systematic review and meta-analysis. *Lancet, 361*, 1581–1590.

Leung, N., Waller, G., & Thomas, G. (2000). Outcome of group cognitive-behavior therapy for bulimia nervosa: The role of core beliefs. *Behaviour Research and Therapy, 38*(2), 145–156.

Levenson, A. J. (1981). *Basic psychopharmacology.* New York: Springer.

Levenson, J. L., & Bostwick, J. M. (2005). Suicidality in the medically ill. *Primary Psychiatry, 12*, 16–18.

Leventhal, A. M., & Rehm, L. P. (2005). The empirical status of melancholia: Implications for psychology. *Clinical Psychology Review, 25*, 25–44.

Levin, P. M. (1938). Restlessness in children. *Archives of Neurology and Psychiatry, 39*, 764–770.

Levine, A. J., & Battista, M. (2004). Estrogen replacement therapy: Effects on the cognitive functioning and clinical course of women with Alzheimer's disease. *Archives of Clinical Neuropsychology, 19*, 769–778.

Levine, M. D. (2002). *A mind at a time.* New York: Simon & Schuster.

Levine, S. B., Brown, G., Coleman, E., Cohen-Kettenis, P., Hage, J. J., Van Maasdam, J., et al. (1998). Harry Benjamin International Gender Dysphoria Association's the standards of care for gender identity disorders. *International Journal of Transgenderism, 2*(2).

Levkoff, S. E., Evans, D. A., Liptzin, B., Clear, P. D., Lipsitz, L. A., Wetle, T. T., et al. (1992). Delirium: The occurrence and persistence of symptoms among elderly hospitalized patients. *Archives of Internal Medicine, 152*, 334–340.

Levy, F., Barr, C., & Sunhohara, G. (1998). Directions of aetiologic research on attention deficit hyperactivity disorder. *Australian and New Zealand Journal of Psychiatry, 32*, 97–103.

Levy, K. N., & Scott, L. N. (2006). Other personality disorders. In M. Hersen, J. C. Thomas, & F. Andrasis (Eds.), *Comprehensive handbook of personality and psychopathology: Adult psychopathology* (Vol. 2, pp. 316–336). New York: Wiley.

Levy-Lahad, E., Tsuang, D., & Bird, T. D. (1998). Recent advances in the genetics of Alzheimer's disease. *Journal of Geriatric Psychiatry and Neurology, 11*, 42–54.

Lewinsohn, P. M. (1974). Clinical and theoretical aspects of depression. In K. S. Calhoun, H. E. Adams, & K. M. Mitchell (Eds.), *Innovative treatment methods in psychopathology* (pp. 63–120). New York: Wiley.

Lewinsohn, P. M., & Clarke, G. N. (1999). Psychosocial treatments for adolescent depression. *Clinical Psychology Review, 19*, 329–342.

Lewinsohn, P. M., Hoberman, H. M., Teri, L., & Hautzinger, M. (1985). An integrated theory of depression. In S. Reiss & R. Bootzin (Eds.), *Theoretical issues in behavior therapy* (pp. 331–359). New York: Academic Press.

Lewinsohn, P. M., Hops, H., Roberts, R. E., Seeley, J. R., & Andrews, J. A. (1993). Adolescent psychopathology I: Prevalence and incidence of depression, and other DSM-III-R disorders in high school students. *Journal of Abnormal Psychology, 102*, 133–144.

Lewinsohn, P. M., Muñoz, R. F., Youngren, M. A., & Zeiss, A. M. (1986). *Control your depression.* New York: Fireside.

Lewinsohn, P. M., Rohde, P., & Brown, R. A. (1999). Level of current and past adolescent cigarette smoking as predictors of future substance use disorders in young adulthood. *Addiction, 94*, 913–921.

Lewinsohn, P. M., Rohde, P., Seely, J. R., & Fischer, S. A. (1993). Age-cohort changes in the lifetime occurrence of depression and other mental disorders. *Journal of Abnormal Psychology, 102,* 110–120.

Lewinsohn, P. M., Rohde, P., Seeley, J. R., Klein, D. N., & Gotlib, I. H. (2000). Natural course of adolescent major depressive disorder in a community sample: Predictors of recurrence in young adults. *American Journal of Psychiatry, 157,* 1584–1591.

Lewinsohn, P. M., Seeley, J. R., Buckley, M. E., & Klein, D. N. (2002). Bipolar disorder in adolescence and young adulthood. *Child and Adolescent Psychiatric Clinics of North America, 11,* 461–475.

Lewinsohn, P. M., Seeley, J. R., & Klein, D. N. (2003). Bipolar disorders in adolescence. *Acta Psychiatrica Scandinavica, 108,* 47–58.

Lewinsohn, P. M., Striegel-Moore, R. H., & Seeley, J. R. (2000). Epidemiology and natural course of eating disorders in young women from adolescence to young adulthood. *Journal of the American Academy of Child and Adolescent Psychiatry, 39,* 1284–1292.

Lewis, A. (1970). Paranoia and paranoid: A historical perspective. *Psychological Medicine, 1,* 2–12.

Lewis, S. A., Johnson, J., Cohen, P., Garcia, M., & Velez, C. N. (1988). Attempted suicide in youth: Its relationship to school achievement, education goals, and socioeconomic status. *Journal of Abnormal Child Psychology, 16,* 459–471.

Lewis-Harter, S. (2000). Psychosocial adjustment of adult children of alcoholics: A review of the recent empirical literature. *Clinical Psychology Review, 20,* 311–337.

Li, G., Shen, Y. C., Chen, C. H., & Zhao, Y. W. (1989). An epidemiological survey of age related dementia in an urban area of Beijing. *Acta Psychiatrica Scandinavica, 79,* 557–563.

Libby, A. M., Orton, H. D., Stover, S. K., & Riggs, P. (2005). What came first, major depression or substance use disorder? Clinical characteristics and substance use—Comparing teens in a treatment cohort. *Addictive Behaviors, 30,* 1649–1662.

Libon, D. J., Malamut, B. L., Swenson, R., & Cloud, B. S. (1996). Further analyses of clock drawings among demented and non-demented subjects. *Archives of Clinical Neuropsychology, 11,* 193–211.

Libow, J. (2003). Illness falsification in children: Pathways to prevention. In P. W. Halligan, C. Bass, & D. A. Oakley (Eds.), *Malingering and illness deception* (pp. 147–155). New York: Oxford University Press.

Libow, J., & Schreier, H. (1986). Three forms of factitious illness in children: When is it Munchausen syndrome by proxy? *American Journal of Orthopsychiatry, 56*(4), 602–610.

Libow, J. A. (2002). Beyond collusion: An active illness falsification. *Child Abuse and Neglect, 26,* 525–536.

Liddell, A., & Lyons, M. (1978). Thunderstorm phobias. *Behavior Research and Therapy, 16,* 306–308.

Lidz, C. W., Mulvey, E. P., & Gardner, W. (1993). The accuracy of predictions of violence to others. *Journal of the American Medical Association, 269,* 1007–1011.

Lieb, R., Zimmermann, P., Friis, R. H., Hofler, M., Tholen, S., & Wittchen, H. U. (2002). The natural course of DSM-IV somatoform disorders and syndromes among adolescents and young adults: A prospective-longitudinal community study. *European Psychiatry, 17,* 321–331.

Lieberman, J. A., & Koreen, A. R. (1993). Neurochemistry and neuroendocrinology of schizophrenia: A selective review. *Schizophrenia Bulletin, 19,* 371–428.

Lilenfeld, L. R., Kaye, W. H., Greeno, C. G., Merikangas, K. R., Plotnicov, K., Pollice, C., et al. (1998). A controlled family study of anorexia nervosa and bulimia nervosa: Psychiatric disorders in first-degree relatives and effects of proband comorbidity. *Archives of General Psychiatry, 55*(7), 603–610.

Lilenfeld, L. R., Stein, D., Bulik, C. M., Strober, M., Plotnicov, K., Pollice, C., et al. (2000). Personality traits among current eating disordered, recovered and never ill first-degree female relatives of bulimic and control women. *Psychological Medicine, 30*(6), 1399–1410.

Lilienfeld, S. O., & Hess, T. H. (2001). Psychopathic personality traits and somatization: Sex differences and the mediating role of negative emotionality. *Journal of Psychopathology Behavior and Assessment, 23,* 11–24.

Lillienfeld, S. (2003). Comorbidity between and within childhood externalizing and internalizing disorders: Reflections and directions. *Journal of Abnormal Child Psychology, 31*, 285–291.

Limandri, B. J., & Sheridan, D. J. (1995). Prediction of intentional interpersonal violence: An introduction. In J. C. Campbell (Ed.), *Assessing dangerousness: Violence by sexual offenders, batterers, and child abusers* (pp. 1–19). Thousand Oaks, CA: Sage.

Lin, D., Mok, H., & Yatham, L. N. (2006). Polytherapy in bipolar disorder. *CNS Drugs, 20*, 29–42.

Lin, K., & Cheung, F. (1999). Mental health issues for Asian Americans. *Psychiatric Services, 50*, 774–780.

Lin, K., Inui, T. S., Kleinman, A. M., & Womack, W. M. (1982). Sociocultural determinants of the help-seeking behavior of patients with mental illness. *Journal of Nervous and Mental Diseases, 170*, 78–85.

Lin, K. M., & Kleinman, A. M. (1988). Psychopathology and the clinical course of schizophrenia: A cross-cultural perspective. *Schizophrenia Bulletin, 14*, 555–567.

Lin, K. M., & Lin, M. T. (2001). Ethnic issues in schizophrenia. In A. Brier, P. V. Tran, J. M. Herrera, G. D. Tollefson, & F. P. Bymaster (Eds.), *Current issues in the psychopharmacology of schizophrenia* (pp. 459–469). Philadelphia: Lippincott, Williams, & Wilkins.

Linde, J. A., & Clark, L. E. A. (1998). Diagnostic assignment of criteria: Clinicians and the DSM-IV. *Journal of Personality Disorders, 12*, 126–137.

Lindemann, E. (1994). Symptomatology and management of acute grief. *American Journal of Psychiatry, 101*, 141–148.

Lindqvist, G., & Malmgren, H. (1993). Organic mental disorders as hypothetical pathogenetic processes. *Acta Psychiatrica Scandinavica, 88*(Suppl. 373), 5–13.

Lindsay, J., Laurin, D., Verreault, R., Hebert, R., Helliwell, B., Hill, G. B., et al. (2002). Risk factors for Alzheimer's disease: A prospective analysis from the Canadian Study of Health and Aging. *American Journal of Epidemiology, 156*, 445–453.

Linehan, M. M. (1993a). *Cognitive behavior therapy of borderline personality disorder.* New York: Guilford Press.

Linehan, M. M. (1993b). *Skills training manual for treating borderline personality disorder.* New York: Guilford Press.

Linehan, M. M. (1996). *Suicidal Behaviors Questionnaire (SBQ).* Unpublished manuscript, University of Washington at Seattle.

Linehan, M. M. (1997). Behavioral treatments of suicidal behaviors: Definitional obfuscation and treatment outcomes. In D. M. Stoff & J. J. Mann (Eds.), *Neurobiology of suicide: From bench to the clinic* (pp. 302–328). New York: Annals of the New York Academy of Sciences.

Linehan, M. M. (2000). The empirical basis of dialectial behavior therapy: Development of new treatments vs. evaluation of existing treatment. *Clinical Psychology: Science Practice, 7*, 113–119.

Link, B. G., Andrews, H., & Cullen, F. T. (1992). The violent and illegal behavior of mental patients reconsidered. *American Sociological Review, 57*, 275–292.

Link, B. G., & Stueve, A. (1994). Psychotic symptoms and the violent/illegal behavior of mental patients compared to community controls. In J. Monahan & H. J. Steadman (Eds.), *Violence and mental disorder: Developments in risk assessment* (pp. 137–159). Chicago: University of Chicago Press.

Links, P. S., Heslegrave, R. J., Mitton, J. E., van Reekum, R., & Patrick, J. (1995). Borderline personality disorder and substance abuse: Consequences of comorbidity. *Candadian Journal of Psychiatry, 40*, 9–14.

Links, P. S., & Kolla, N. (2005). Assessing and managing suicide risk. In J. M. Oldham, A. E. Skodol, & D. S. Bender (Eds.), *Textbook of personality disorders* (pp. 449–475). Washington, DC: American Psychiatric Publications.

Linscheid, T. R., & Bennett-Murphy, L. B. (1999). Feeding disorders of infancy and early childhood. In S. D. Netherton, D. Holmes, & C. E. Walker (Eds.), *Child and adolescent psychological disorders: A comprehensive textbook* (pp. 139–155). New York: Oxford University Press.

Lipowsky, Z. J. (1990). *Delirium: Acute confusional states.* New York: Oxford University Press.

Lipowsky, Z. J. (1992). Update on delirium. *Psychiatric Clinics of North America, 15*, 335–346.

Lipsitt, D. R. (2001). The patient-physician relationship in the treatment of hypochondriasis. In V. Starcevic & D. R. Lipsitt (Eds.), *Hypochondriasis: Modern perspectives on an ancient malady* (pp. 265–290). New York: Oxford University Press.

Lipsitz, J. D., Barlow, D. H., Mannuzza, S., Hofmann, S. G., & Fyer, A. J. (2002). Clinical features of four DSM-IV-specific phobia subtypes. *Journal of Nervous and Mental Diseases, 190*, 471–478.

Liptzin, B., & Levkoff, S. E. (1992). An empirical study of delirium subtypes. *British Journal of Psychiatry, 161*, 843–845.

Lish, J. D., Dime-Meenan, S., Whybrow, P. C., Price, R. A., & Hirshfeld, R. M. (1994). The national Depressive and Manic Depressive Association (DMDA) survey of bipolar members. *Journal of Affective Disorders, 31*, 281–294.

Lishman, W. A. (1987). The senile dementias, presenile dementias, and pseudodementias. In W. A. Lishman (Ed.), *Organic psychiatry: The psychological consequences of cerebral disorder* (2nd ed., pp. 370–427). Oxford: Blackwell Scientific.

Little, S. G., Akin-Little, K. A., & Mocniak, U. H. (in press). Conduct disorders and impulse control in children. In R. Laws, C. Hollin, & W. O'Donohue (Eds.), *Handbook of forensic psychology*. New York: Basic Books.

Little, J. T., Satlin, A., Sunderland, T., & Volicer, L. (1995). Sundown syndrome in severely demented patients with probable Alzheimer's disease. *Journal of Geriatric Psychiatry and Neurology, 8*, 103–106.

Litwack, T. R., & Schlesinger, L. B. (1999). Dangerousness risk assessment: Research, legal, and clinical considerations. In A. K. Hess & I. B. Weiner (Eds.), *The handbook of forensic psychology* (pp. 171–217). New York: Wiley.

Litz, B., Orsillo, S., Kaloupek, D., & Weathers, F. (2000). Emotional processing in post traumatic stress disorder. *Journal of Abnormal Psychology, 109*, 26–39.

Liu, C. Y., Juang, Y. Y., Liang, H. Y., Lin, E. C., & Yeh, N. K. (2004). Efficacy of risperidone in treating the hyperactive symptoms of delirium. *International Clinical Psychopharmacology, 19*, 165–168.

Liu, W. M., & Clay, D. L. (2002). Multicultural counseling competencies: Guidelines in working with children and adolescents. *Journal of Mental Health Counseling, 24*(2), 177–187.

Livesley, W., Jackson, D. N., & Schroeder, M. L. (1992) Factorial structure of traits delinating personality disorders in clinical and general populations samples. *Journal of Abnormal Psychology, 101*(3), 432–440.

Livesley, W., Schroeder, M. L., Jackson, D. N., & Jang, K. L. (1994). Categorical distinctions in the study of personality disorder: Implications for classification. *Journal of Abnormal Psychology, 103*(1), 6–17.

Livesley, W. J. (2001). Conceptual and taxonomic issues. In W. J. Livesley (Ed.), *Handbook of personality disorders: Theory, research treatment* (pp. 3–38). New York: Guilford Press.

Livesley, W. J., Reiffer, L. I., Sheldon, A. E., & West, M. (1987). Prototypicality rating of DSM-III criteria for personality disorders. *Journal of Nervous and Mental Disorders, 103*(1), 6–17.

Lo, H.-T., & Fung, K. P. (2003). Culturally competent psychotherapy. *Canadian Journal of Psychiatry, 48*(3), 161–170.

Lochman, J. E., Barry, T. D., & Pardini, D. A. (2003). Anger control training for aggressive youth. In A. E. Kazdin & J. R. Weisz (Eds.), *Evidence-based psychotherapies for children and adolescents* (pp. 263–281). New York: Guilford Press.

Lochman, J. E., Coie, J. D., Underwood, M. K., & Terry, R. (1993). Effectiveness of a social relations intervention program for aggressive and nonaggressive, rejected children. *Journal of Consulting and Clinical Psychology, 61*, 1053–1058.

Lock, J., Le Grange, D., Agras, W. S., & Dare, C. (2001). *Treatment manual for anorexia nervosa: A family-based approach*. New York: Guilford Press.

Lock, J., & Steiner, H. (1999). Gay, lesbian, and bisexual youth risks for emotional, physical, and social problems: Results from a community-based survey. *Journal of the American Academy of Child and Adolescent Psychiatry, 38*(3), 297–304.

Locke, T. F., Newcomb, M. D., & Goodyear, R. K. (2005). Childhood experiences and psychosocial influences on risky sexual behavior, condom use, and HIV attitudes-behaviors among Latino males. *Psychology of Men and Masculinity, 6*, 25–38.

Loeber, R. (1991). Oppositional defiant disorder and conduct disorder. *Hospital Community Psychiatry, 42*, 1099–1100.

Loeber, R., Burke, J. D., Lahey, B. B., Winters, A., & Zera, M. (2000). Oppositional defiant and conduct disorder: Pt. I. A review of the past 10 years. *Journal of the American Academy of Child and Adolescent Psychiatry, 39*, 1468–1484.

Loeber, R., & Farrington, D. P. (2000). Young children who commit crime: Epidemiology, developmental origins, risk factors, early interventions and policy implications. *Development and Psychopathology, 12*, 737–762.

Loeber, R., Farrington, D. P., Stouthamer-Loeber, M., & Van Kammen, W. B. (Eds.). (1998). *Antisocial behavior and mental health problems: Explanatory factors in childhood and adolescence.* Mahwah, NJ: Erlbaum.

Loeber, R., Green, S. M., & Lahey, B. B. (2003). Risk factors for antisocial personality. In D. P. Farrington & J. Coid (Eds.), *Early prevention of adult antisocial personality* (pp. 79–108). Cambridge: Cambridge University Press.

Loeber, R., Green, S. M., Lahey, B. B., & Kalb, L. (2000). Physical fighting in childhood as a later mental health risk. *Journal of the American Academy of Child and Adolescent Psychiatry, 39*, 421–428.

Loeber, R., Keenan, K., Lahey, B. B., Green, S. M., & Thomas, C. (1993). Evidence for developmentally based diagnoses of oppositional defiant disorder and conduct disorder. *Journal of Abnormal Child Psychology, 21*, 377–410.

Loeber, R., Lahey, B. B., & Thomas, C. (1991). Diagnostic conundrum of oppositional disorder and conduct disorder. *Journal of Abnormal Psychology, 100*, 379–390.

Loeber, R., & Stouthamer-Loeber, M. (1998). Development of juvenile aggression and violence: Some common misconceptions and controversies. *American Psychologist, 53*, 242–259.

Logie, R. H., Cocchini, G., Delia Sala, S., & Baddeley, A. D. (2004). Is there a specific executive capacity for dual task coordination? Evidence from Alzheimer's disease. *Neuropsychology, 18*, 504–513.

Logue, M. B., Sher, K. J., & Frensch, P. A. (1992). Purported characteristics of adult children of alcoholics: A possible "Barnum effect." *Professional Psychology: Research and Practice, 23*, 226–232.

Looi, J. C. L., & Sachdev, P. S. (1999). Differentiation of vascular dementia from AD on neuropsychological tests. *Neurology, 53*, 670–678.

Loomis, J. W. (2006). Learning disabilities. In M. Hersen, J. C. Thomas, & R. T. Ammermam (Eds.), *Comprehensive handbook of personality and psychopathology: Vol. 3. Child psychopathology* (pp. 272–284). Hoboken, NJ: Wiley.

Looney, B. R., Frick, P. J., Clements, C. B., Ellis, M. L., & Kerlin, K. (2003). Callous unemotional traits, impulsivity, and emotional processing in antisocial adolescents. *Journal of Psychopathology and Behavioral Assessment, 20*, 231–247.

Looper, K. J., & Kirmayer, L. J. (2002). Behavioral medicine approaches to somatoform disorders. *Journal of Consulting and Clinical Psychology, 70*(3), 810–827.

Lopatka, C., & Rachman, S. J. (1995). Perceived responsibility and compulsive checking: An experimental analysis. *Behaviour Research and Therapy, 33*, 673–684.

López, S. R., Nelson-Hipke, K., Polo, A. J., Jenkins, J. H., Karno, M., Vaughn, C., et al. (2004). Ethnicity, expressed emotion, attributions, and course of schizophrenia: Family warmth matters. *Journal of Abnormal Psychology, 113*, 428–439.

Lopez-Pousa, S., Turon-Estrada, A., Garre-Olmo, J., Pericot-Nierga, I., Lozano-Gallego, M., Vilalta-Franch, M., et al. (2005). Differential efficacy of treatment with acetylcholinesterase inhibitors in patients with mild and moderate Alzheimer's disease over a 6-month period. *Dementia and Geriatric Cognitive Disorders, 19*, 189–95.

LoPiccolo, C. J., Goodkin, K., & Baldewicz, T. T. (1999). Current issues in the diagnosis and management of malingering. *Annals of Medicine, 31*, 166–174.

Loranger, A. W. (1999). *International Personality Disorder Examination (IPDE)*. Odessa, FL: Psychological Assessment Resources.

Lord, C. (1995). Follow-up of 2-year-olds referred for possible autism. *Journal of Child Psychology and Psychiatry, 36*, 1365–1382.

Lord, C., & Bailey, A. (2002). Autism spectrum disorders. In M. Rutter & E. Taylor (Eds.), *Child and adolescent psychiatry* (4th ed., pp. 636–663). Malden, MA: Blackwell Scientific.

Lord, C., & Corsello, C. (2005). Diagnostic instruments in autistic spectrum disorders. In F. R. Volkmar, R. Paul, A. Klin, & D. Cohen (Eds.), *Handbook of autism and pervasive developmental disorders* (3rd ed., pp. 730–771). Hoboken, NJ: Wiley.

Lord, C., & Magill-Evans, J. (1995). Peer interactions of autistic children and adolescents. *Development and Psychopathology, 7*, 611–626.

Lord, C., Risi, S., Lambrecht, L., Cook, E. H., Leventhal, B. L., DiLavore, P. C., et al. (2000). The Autism Diagnostic Observation Schedule—Generic: A standard measure of social and communicative deficits associated with the spectrum of autism. *Journal of Autism and Developmental Disorders, 30*, 205–223.

Lord, C., & Rutter, M. (1994). Autism and pervasive developmental disorders. In M. Rutter, E. Taylor, & L. Hersov (Eds.), *Child and adolescent psychiatry: Modern approaches* (3rd ed., pp. 569–593). Oxford: Blackwell.

Lotspeich, L., Kwon, H., Schumann, C., Fryer, S. L., Goodlin-Jones, B. L., Buoncore, M. H., et al. (2004). Investigation of neuroanatomical differences between autism and Asperger syndrome. *Archives of General Psychiatry, 61*(3), 291–298.

Lovaas, O. I. (1981). *Teaching developmentally disabled children: The me book*. Baltimore: University Park Press.

Lovaas, O. I. (1987). Behavioral treatment and normal educational and intellectual functioning in young autistic children. *Journal of Consulting and Clinical Psychology, 55*, 3–9.

Loveland, K. A., & Tunali-Kotoski, B. (2005). The school age child with autistic spectrum disorder. In F. R. Volkmar, R. Paul, A. Klin, & D. Cohen (Eds.), *Handbook of autism and pervasive developmental disorders* (3rd ed., pp. 247–287). Hoboken, NJ: Wiley.

Lovinger, R. J. (1996). Considering the religious dimension in assessment and treatment. In E. Shafrankse (Ed.), *Religion and the clinical practice of psychology* (pp. 327–364). Washington, DC: American Psychological Association.

Lowe, M., & Costello, A. J. (1995). *Symbolic Play Test—Revised*. Windsor, England: NFER-Nelson Publishing.

Loewenstein, R. J. (1991). An office mental status examination for complex chronic dissociative symptoms and multiple personality disorder. *Psychiatric Clinics of North America, 4*, 567–604.

Lowing, P. A., Mirsky, A. F., & Pereira, R. (1983). The inheritance of schizophrenic spectrum disorders: A re-analysis of the Danish adoptee study data. *American Journal of Psychiatry, 140*, 1167–1171.

Lubin, H., Loris, M., Burt, J., & Johnson, D. R. (1998). The efficacy of psychoeducational group therapy in reducing the symptoms of posttraumatic stress disorder among multiply traumatized women. *American Journal of Psychiatry, 155*, 1172–1177.

Luborsky, L. (1984). *Principles of psychoanalytic psychotherapy: A manual for supportive-expressive treatment*. New York: Basic Books.

Luborsky, L. (2001). The meaning of empirically supported treatment research for psychoanalytic and long-term therapies. *Psychoanalytic Dialogues, 11*, 583–604.

Luborsky, L., Rosenthal, R., Diguer, L., Andrusyna, T. P., Levitt, J. T., Seligman, D. A., et al. (2003). Are some psychotherapies much more effective than others? *Journal of Applied Psychoanalytic Studies, 5*, 455–460.

Lucas, A. R., Crowson, C. S., O'Fallon, W. M., & Melton, L. J. (1999). The ups and downs of nervosa. *International Journal of Eating Disorders, 26*(4), 397–405.

Lucock, M. P., & Salkovskis, P. M. (1988). Cognitive factors in social anxiety and its treatment. *Behaviour Research and Therapy, 26*, 297–302.

Lukas, S. (1993). *Where to start and what to ask: An assessment handbook*. New York: Norton.

Lukoff, D., Nuechterlein, K. H., & Ventura, J. (1986). Appendix A: Manual for Expanded Brief Psychiatric Rating Scale (BPRS). *Schizophrenia Bulletin, 12*, 594–602.

Lundh, L. G., & Öst, L. G. (1996). Recognition bias for critical faces in social phobia. *Behaviour Research and Therapy, 34*, 787–794.

Lundy, M., & Grossman, S. (2001). Clinical research and practice with battered women: What we know, what we need to know. *Trauma, Violence, and Abuse, 2*(2), 120–141.

Lydiard, R. B., Brawman-Mintzer, O., & Ballenger, J. C. (1996). Recent developments in the psychopharmacology of anxiety disorders. *Journal of Consulting and Clinical Psychology, 64*, 660–668.

Lydiard, R. B., & Monnier, J. (2004). Pharmacological treatment. In R. G. Heimberg, C. L. Turk, & D. S. Mennin (Eds.), *Generalized anxiety disorder: Advances in research and practice.* (pp. 351–379). New York: Guilford Press.

Lyketsos, C. G., Lopez, O., Jones, B., Fitzpatrick, A. L., Britner, J., & DeKosky, S. (2002). Prevalence of neuropsychiatric symptoms in dementia and mild cognitive impairment: Results from the cardiovascular health study. *Journal of the American Medical Association, 288*, 1475–1483.

Lyketsos, C. G., Reichman, W. E., Kershaw, P., & Zhu, Y. (2004). Long-term outcomes of galantamine treatment in patients with Alzheimer disease. *American Journal of Geriatric Psychiatry, 12*, 473–482.

Lynam, D. R. (1996). Early identification of chronic offenders: Who is the fledgling psychopath? *Psychological Bulletin, 120*, 209–234.

Lynam, D. R. (1997). Pursuing the psychopath: Capturing the fledgling psychopath in an nomological net. *Journal of Abnormal Psychology, 106*, 425–438.

Lynam, D. R. (1998). Early identification of the fledgling psychopath: Locating the psychopathic child in the current nomenclature. *Journal of Abnormal Psychology, 107*, 566–575.

Lynam, D. R., & Henry, V. (2001). The role of neuropsychological deficits in conduct disorders. In J. Hill & B. Maughan (Eds.), *Conduct disorders in childhood and adolescence* (pp. 235–263). Cambridge: Cambridge University Press.

Lynch, T. R., & Aspnes, A. (2001). Personality disorders in older adults: Diagnostic and theoretic issues. *Clinical Geriatrics, 9*(101), 64–68.

Lynch, T. R., Morse, J. Q., Mendelson, T., & Robins, C. J. (2003). Dialectical behavior therapy for depressed older adults: A randomized pilot study. *American Journal of Geriatric Psychiatry, 11*, 1–13.

Lynskey, M. T., Heath, A. C., Bucholz, K. K., Slutske, W. S., Madden, P. A., Nelson, E. C., et al. (2003). Escalation of drug use in early-onset cannabis users vs. co-twin controls. *Journal of the American Medical Association, 289*, 427–433.

Lyons, J. S., & McGovern, M. P. (1989). Use of mental health services by dually diagnosed patients. *Hospital and Community Psychiatry, 40*, 1067–1069.

Lysaker, P. H., & Bell, M. D. (1995). Work rehabilitation and improvements in insight in schizophrenia. *Journal of Nervous and Mental Diseases, 183*, 103–106.

Lysaker, P. H., Bell, M. D., Bryson, G. J., & Kaplan, E. (1998). Insight and interpersonal function in schizophrenia. *Journal of Nervous and Mental Disease, 186*, 432–436.

Lysaker, P. H., Bryson, G. J., & Bell, M. D. (2002). Insight and work performance in schizophrenia. *Journal of Nervous and Mental Diseases, 190*, 142–146.

Lysaker, P. H., Bryson, G. J., Lancaster, R. S., Evans, J. D., & Bell, M. D. (2003). Insight in schizoprenia: Associations with executive function and coping style. *Schizophrenia Research, 59*, 41–47.

Lystad, M., Rice, M., & Kaplan, S. J. (1996). Domestic violence. In S. J. Kaplan (Ed.), *Family violence: A clinical and legal guide* (pp. 139–180). Washington, DC: American Psychiatric Press.

MacDonald, J. (1961). *The murderer and his victim.* Springfield, IL: Charles C. Thomas.

Mack, A. H., Frances, R. J., & Miller, S. I. (2005). Addiction and the law. In R. J. Frances, S. I. Miller, & A. H. Mack (Eds.), *Clinical textbook of addictive disorders* (3rd ed., pp. 354–366). New York: Guilford Press.

MacLeod, C., & Rutherford, E. (2004). Information-processing approaches: Assessing the selective functioning of attention, interpretation, and retrieval. In R. G. Heimberg, C. L. Turk, & D. S. Mennin (Eds.), *Generalized anxiety disorder: Advances in research and practice* (pp. 109–142). New York: Guilford Press.

MacQueen, G. M., Young, L. T., Robb, J. C., Cooke, R. G., & Joffe, R. T. (1997). Levels of functioning and well-being in recovered psychotic versus non-psychotic mania. *Journal of Affective Disorders, 46*, 69–72.

Macritchie, K. A., Geddes, J. R., Scott, J., Haslam, D. R., & Goodwin, G. M. (2001). Valproic acid, valproate, and divalproex in the maintenance treatment of bipolar disorder. *Cochrane Database Systematic Review, 3*, CD004052.

Madden, J. S. (1999). Substance use disorders: Clinical section. In G. E. Berrios & R. Porter (Eds.), *A history of clinical psychiatry: The origin and history of psychiatric disorders*. New Brunswick, NJ: Athelon Press.

Madsen, K. M., Hviid, A., Vestergaard, M., Schendel, D., Wohlfahrt, J., Thorsen, P., et al. (2002). A population-based study of measles, mumps, and rubella vaccination and autism. *New England Journal of Medicine, 347*(19), 1477–1482.

Magarinos, M., Zafar, U., Nissenson, K., & Blanco, C. (2002). Epidemiology and treatment of hypochondriasis. *CNS Drugs, 16*(1), 9–22.

Magee, W. J., Eaton, W. W., Wittchen, H. U., McGonagle, K. A., & Kessler, R. C. (1996). Agoraphobia, simple phobia and social phobia in the National Comorbidity Survey. *Archives of General Psychiatry, 53*, 159–168.

Magnavita, J. J. (2005). Classification, prevalence, and etiology of personality disorders: Related issues and controversy. In J. J. Magnavita, (Ed.), *Handbook of personality disorders: Theory practice* (pp. 3–23). Hoboken, NJ: Wiley.

Mahalik, J. R., van Ormer, E. A., & Simi, N. L. (2000). Ethical issues in using self-disclosure in feminist therapy. In M. M. Brabeck (Ed.), *Practicing feminist ethics in psychology* (pp. 189–202). Washington, DC: American Psychological Association.

Maher, B. A. (2001). Delusions. In P. B. Sutker & H. E. Adams (Eds.), *Comprehensive handbook of psychopathology* (3rd ed., pp. 309–339). New York: Kluwer Academic/Plenum Publishers,

Maher, L., Jalaludin, B., & Chant, K. G. (2006). Incidence and risk factors for hepatitis C seroconversion in injecting drug users in Australia. *Addiction, 101*, 1499–1508.

Mahoney, D. F., Tarlow, B. J., & Jones, R. N. (2003). Effects of an automated telephone support system on caregiver burden and anxiety: Findings from the REACH for TLC Intervention Study. *Gerontologist, 43*, 556–567.

Mahoney, E. K., Volicer, L., & Hurley, A. C. (2000). *Mangement of challenging behaviors in dementia*. Baltimore, MD: Health Professions Press.

Mahoney, W. J., Szatmari, P., Maclean, J. E., Bryson, S. E., Bartolucci, G., Walters, S. D., et al. (1998). Reliability and accuracy of differentiating pervasive developmental disorder subtypes. *Journal of the American Academy of Child and Adolescent Psychiatry, 37*, 278–285.

Mahowald, M. W., & Schenck, C. H. (2005). Non-rapid eye movement sleep parasomnias. *Neurologic Clinics, 23*(4), 1077–1106.

Maisto, S. A., Sobell, L. C., Cooper, A. M., & Sobell, M. B. (1982). Comparison of two techniques to obtain retrospective reports of drinking behavior from alcohol abusers. *Addictive Behaviors, 7*, 33–38.

Maj, M., Magliano, L., Pirozzi, R., Marasco, C., & Guarneri, M. (1994). Validity of rapid cycling as a course specifier for bipolar disorder. *American Journal of Psychiatry, 51*, 1015–1019.

Makover, R. B. (2004). *Treatment planning for psychotherapists: A practical guide to better outcomes* (2nd ed.). Washington, DC: American Psychiatric Publishing.

Malchiodi, C. A. (1998). *Interpreting children's drawings*. New York: Guilford Press.

Maldonado, J. R., & Spiegel, D. (2001). Conversion disorder. In K. A. Phillips (Ed.), *Somatoform and factitious disorders* (pp. 95–128). Washington, DC: American Psychiatric Publishing.

Maldonado, J. R., & Spiegel, D. (2002). Dissociative disorder. In R. E. Hale & S. C. Yudofsky (Eds.), *Textbook of clinical psychiatry* (4th ed., pp. 709–742). Washington, DC: American Psychiatric Publishing.

Maldonado, J. R., & Spiegel, D. (2005). Dissociative states. In J. M. Oldham, A. E. Skodol, & D. S. Bender (Eds.), *Textbook of personality disorders* (pp. 493–521). Washington, DC: American Psychiatric Publishing.

Maldonado-Duran, M., Helmig, L., Moody, C., Fonagy, P., Fulz, J., Lartigue, T., et al. (2003). The zero-to-three diagnostic classification in an infant mental health clinic: Its usefulness and challenges. *Infant Mental Health Journal, 24*(4), 378–397.

Maletzky, B. M. (2002). The paraphilias: Research and treatment. In P. E. Nathan & J. M. Gorman (Eds.), *A guide to treatments that work* (2nd ed., pp. 525–558). New York: Oxford University Press.

Malhotra, S., & Gupta, N. (2002). Childhood disintegrative disorder: Re-examination of the current concept. *European Child and Adolescent Psychiatry, 11*(3), 108–114.

Malloy, P., Belanger, H., Hall, S., Aloia, M., & Salloway, S. (2003). Assessing visuoconstructive performance in AD, MCI, and normal elderly using the Beery Visual-Motor Integration Test. *Clinical Neuropsychologist, 17*, 544–550.

Malouf, R., & Birks, J. (2004). Donepezil for vascular cognitive impairment. *Cochrane Database Systematic Review.* CD004395.

Maltby, J., & Day, L. (2002). Religious experience, religious orientation, and schizotypy. *Mental Health, Religion, and Culture, 5*, 163–174.

Maltsberger, J. T. (2001). The formulation of suicide risk. In J. M. Ellison (Ed.), *Treatment of suicidal patients in managed care* (pp. 189–196). Washington, DC: American Psychiatric Press.

Maltsberger, J. T., & Buie, D. H. (1974). Countertransferance hate in the treatment of suicidal patients. *Archives of General Psychiatry, 30*, 625–633.

Maltsberger, J. T., & Buie, D. H. (1989). Common errors in the management of suicidal patients. In D. Jacobs & H. N. Brown (Eds.), *Suicide: Understanding and responding* (pp. 59–72). Madison, CT: International Universities Press.

Mandalawitz, M. R. (2005). Educating children with autism: Current legal issues. In F. R. Volkmar, R. Paul, A. Klin, & D. Cohen (Eds.), *Handbook of autism and pervasive developmental disorders* (3rd ed., pp. 1161–1173). Hoboken, NJ: Wiley.

Mandel, M. R., Severe, J. B., Schooler, N. R., Gelenberg, A. J., & Mieske, M. (1982). Developmental and prediction of post-psychotic depression in neuroleptic treated schizophrenics. *Archives of General Psychiatry, 39*, 197–203.

Manfro, G. G., Otto, M. W., McArdle, E. T., Wothington, J. J., Rosenbaum, J. F., & Pollack, M. H. (1996). Relationship of antecedent stressful life events to childhood and family history of anxiety and the course of panic disorder. *Journal of Affective Disorders, 41*, 135–139.

Manji, H. K., & Potter, W. Z. (1997). Monoaminergic mechanism. In R. T. Joffe & L. T. Young (Eds.), *Biological models and their clinical application* (pp. 1–40). New York: Marcel Dekker.

Mann, J. J., Waternaux, C., Haas, G. L., & Malone, K. M. (1999). Towards a clinical model of suicidal behavior in psychiatric patients. *American Journal of Psychiatry, 156*, 181–189.

Mann, K., Lehert, P., & Morgan, M. Y. (2004). The efficacy of acamprosate in the maintenance of abstinence in alcohol-dependent individuals: Results of a meta-analysis. *Alcoholism Clinical and Experimental Research, 28*, 51–63.

Manschrek, T. C. (1979). The assessment of paranoid features. *Comprehensive Psychiatry, 20*, 370–377.

Manschreck, T. C. (1992). Delusional disorder: Clinical concepts and diagnostic strategies. *Psychiatric Annals, 22*, 241–251.

Manschreck, T. C., & Khan, N. L. (2006). Recent advances in the treatment of delusional disorder. *Canadian Journal of Psychiatry, 51*, 114–119.

Mantero, M., & Crippa, L. (2002). Eating disorders and chronic post traumatic stress disorder: Issues of psychopathology and comorbidity. *European Eating Disorders Review, 10*(1), 1–16.

Marans, W. D., Rubin, E., & Laurent, A. (2005). Addressing social communication skills in individuals with high-functioning autism and Asperger syndrome: Critical priorities in educational programming. In F. R. Volkmar, R. Paul, A. Klin, & D. Cohen (Eds.), *Handbook of autism and pervasive developmental disorders* (3rd ed., pp. 977–1002). Hoboken, NJ: Wiley.

Marazziti, D., Dell'Osso, L., Gemignani, A., Presta, S., Nasso, E. D., Pfanner, C., et al. (2001). Citalopram in refractory obsessive-compulsive disorder: An open study. *International Journal of Clinical Psychopharmacology, 16*, 215–219.

Marcantonio, E. (2002). The management of delirium. In J. Lindesay & K. Rockwood (Eds.), *Delirium in old age* (pp. 123–151). New York: Oxford University Press.

March, J. S., & Franklin, M. E. (2006). Cognitive-behavioral therapy for pediatric obsessive-compulsive disorder. In B. O. Rothbaum (Ed.), *Pathological anxiety: Emotional processing in etiology and treatment* (pp. 147–165). New York: Guilford Press.

Marcus, L. M., Kunce, L. J., & Schopler, E. (2005). Working with families. In F. R. Volkmar, R. Paul, A. Klin, & D. Cohen (Eds.), *Handbook of autism and pervasive developmental disorders* (3rd ed., pp. 1055–1086). Hoboken, NJ: Wiley.

Marcus, L. M., Schopler, E., & Lord, C. (2001). TEACCH services for preschool children. In J. S. Handelman & S. L. Harris (Eds.), *Preschool programs for children with autism* (pp. 215–232). Austin, TX: ProEd.

Marengo, J. T., & Harrow, M. (1987). Schizophrenic thought disorder at follow-up. A persistent or episodic course? *Archives of General Psychiatry, 44*, 651–659.

Marengo, J. T., & Harrow, M. (1997). Longitudinal courses of thought disorder in schizophrenia and schizoaffective disorder. *Schizophrenia Bulletin, 23*, 273–285.

Marengo, J. T., Harrow, M., & Edell, W. S. (1993). Thought disorder. In C. G. Costello (Ed.), *Symptoms of schizophrenia* (pp. 27–55). New York: Wiley.

Marin, R. S. (1990). Differential diagnosis and classification of apathy. *American Journal of Psychiatry, 147*, 22–30.

Marinangeli, M. G., Butti, G., Scinto, A., Di Cicco, L., Petruzzi, C., Daneluzzo, E., et al. (2000). Patterns of comorbidity among DSM-III-R personality disorder. *Psychopathology, 33*(2), 69–74.

Maris, R. (1992). The relationship of nonfatal suicide attempts to completed suicide. In R. Maris, A. Berman, J. Maltsberger, & R. Yufit (Eds.), *Assessment and prediction of suicide* (pp. 362–380). New York: Guilford Press.

Maris, R. W., Berman, A. L., & Silverman, M. M. (2000). *Comprehensive textbook of suicidology.* New York: Guilford Press.

Markowitz, J. C., Moran, M. E., Kocsis, J. H., & Francis, A. J. (1992). Prevalence and comorbidity of dysthymic disorder among psychiatric outpatients. *Journal of Affective Disorders, 24*, 63–71.

Marks, I. M., & Gelder, M. G. (1966). Different ages of onset in varieties of phobia. *American Journal of Psychiatry, 123*, 218–221.

Marks, R. C., & Luchins, D. J. (1990). Relationship between brain imaging findings in schizophrenia and psychopathology: A review of the literature relating to positive and negative symptoms. In N. C. Andreasen (Ed.), *Modern problems of pharmacopsychiatry: Vol. 24. Positive and negative syndromes* (pp. 89–123). Basel, Switzerland: S. Karger.

Markesbery, W. R. (1999). The role of oxidative stress in Alzheimer disease. *Archives of Neurology, 56*, 1449–1152.

Markovitz, P. (2001). Pharmacotherapy. In W. J. Livesley (Ed.), *Handbook of personality disorders: Theory, research treatment* (pp. 475–493). New York: Guilford Press.

Marlatt, G. A., Somers, J. M., & Tapert, S. F. (1993). Harm reduction: Application to alcohol abuse problems [Monograph]. *National Institute on Drug Abuse, 137*, 144–166.

Marlatt, G. A., & Witkiewitz, K. (2005). Relapse prevention for alcohol and drug problems. In G. A. Marlatt & D. M. Donovan (Eds.), *Relapse prevention: Maintenance strategies in the treatment of addictive behaviors* (2nd ed., pp. 1–44). New York: Guilford Press.

Marmar, C. R., Weiss, D. S., & Metzler, T. (1998). Peritraumatic dissociation and posttraumatic stress disorder. In J. D. Bremner & D. R. Marmar (Eds.), *Trauma, memory and dissociation* (pp. 229–252). Washington, DC: American Psychiatric Press.

Marmer, S. (1999). Variations on a factitious theme. *Journal of Psychiatry and Law, 27*, 459–481.

Marmor, J. (1953). Orality in the hysterical personality. *Journal of the American Psychoanalytic Association, 1*, 656–671.

Marmorstein, N. R., & Iacono, W. G. (2004). Major depression and conduct disorder in youth: Associations with parental psychopathology and parent-child conflict. *Journal of Child Psychology and Psychiatry, 45*(2), 377–386.

Marsch, L. A., Chutuape-Stephens, M. A., Mudric, T., Strain, E. C., Bigelow, G. E., & Johnson, R. E. (2005). Predictors of outcome in LAAM, buprenorphine, and methadone treatment for opioid dependence. *Experimental and Clinical Psychopharmacology, 13*, 293–302.

Marshal, M., Molina, B. S. G., & Pelham, W. E. (2003). Childhood ADHD and adolescent substance use: An examination of deviant peer group affiliation as a risk factor. *Psychology of Addictive Behaviors, 17*(4), 293–302.

Marson, D. C., Cody, H. A., & Ingram, K. K. (1995). Neuropsychologic predictors of competency in Alzheimer's disease using a rational reasons legal standard. *Archives of Neurology, 52*, 955–959.

Marteinsdottir, I., Tillfors, M., Furmark, T., Andenberg, U. M., & Ekselius, L. (2003). Personality dimensions measured by the Temperament and Character Inventory (TCI) in subjects with social phobia. *Nordic Journal of Psychiatry, 57*, 29–35.

Martin, A., Scahill, L., Klin, A., & Volkmar, F. R. (1999). Higher-functioning pervasive developmental disorders: Rates and patterns of psychotropic drug use. *Journal of the American Academy of Child and Adolescent Psychiatry, 38*, 923–931.

Martin, G., & Pear, J. (1999). *Behavior modification: What it is and how to do it*. Upper Saddle River, NJ: Prentice-Hall.

Martin, P. R., Adinoff, B., Lane, E., Stapleton, J. M., Bone, G. A. H., Weingartner, H., et al. (1995). Fluvoxamine treatment of alcoholic amnestic disorder. *European Neuropsychopharmacology, 5*, 27–33.

Martin, P. R., Singleton, C. K., & Hiller-Sturmhofel, S. (2003). The role of thiamine deficiency in alcoholic brain disease. *Alcohol Research and Health, 27*, 134–142.

Martin, R. L. (1995). DSM-I changes for the somatoform disorders. *Psychiatric Annals, 25*(1), 29–39.

Maruish, M. E. (Ed.). (1999). *The use of psychological testing for treatment planning: Vol. 2. Instruments for adults*. Mahwah, NJ: Erlbaum.

Maruish, M. E. (Ed.). (2004). *The use of psychological testing for treatment planning: Vol. 2. Instruments for children and adolescents* (3rd ed.). Mahwah, NJ: Erlbaum.

Marzuk, P. M. (1996). Editorial: Violence, crime and mental illness—How strong a link? *Archives of General Psychiatry, 53*, 481–486.

Maser, J. D., & Patterson, T. (2002). Spectrum and nosology: Implications for DSM-V. *Psychiatric Clinics of North America, 25*, 855–885.

Masheb, R. M., & Kerns, R. D. (2000). Pain disorder. In M. Hersen & M. Biaggio (Eds.), *Effective brief therapies: A clinician's guide* (pp. 191–214). New York: Academic Press.

Masi, G., Millepiedi, S., Mucci, M., Pascale, R. R., Perugi, G., & Akiskal, H. S. (2003). Phenomenology and comorbidity of dysthymic disorder in 100 consecutively referred children and adolescents: Beyond DSM-IV. *Canadian Journal of Psychiatry, 48*, 99–105.

Masi, G., Millepiedi, S., Mucci, M., Poli, P., Bertini, N., & Milantoni, L. (2004). Generalized anxiety disorder in referred children and adolescents. *Journal of the American Academy of Child Psychiatry, 43*, 752–760.

Mastero, S., Muratori, F., Cavallaro, M. C., Pei, F., Stern, D., Glose, B., et al. (2002). Attentional skills during the first 6 months of age in autism spectrum disorder. *Journal of the American Academy of Child and Adolescent Psychiatry, 41*(10), 1239–1245.

Matchett, G., & Davey, G. C. L. (1991). A test of a disease-avoidance model of animal phobias. *Behaviour Research and Therapy, 29*, 91–94.

Mathews, B. (1989). Terminating therapy: Implications for the private practitioner. *Psychotherapy in Private Practice, 7*(3), 29–39.

Matsuda, K., Yamaji, S., Ishii, K., Sasaki, M., Sakamoto, S., Kitagaki, H., et al. (1997). Regional cerebral blood flow and oxygen metabolism in a patient with Korsakoff syndrome. *Annals of Nuclear Medicine, 11*, 33–35.

Matsunaga, H., Kiriike, N., Nagata, T., & Yamagami, S. (1998). Personality disorders in patients with eating disorders in Japan. *International Journal of Eating Disorders, 23*(4), 399–408.

Matthews, J. R., & Walker, C. E. (Eds.). (2005). *Your practicum in psychology: A guide for maximizing knowledge and competence.* Washington, DC: American Psychological Association.

Mattia, J. I., & Zimmerman, J. (2001). Epidemiology. In W. J. Livesley (Ed.), *Handbook of personality disorders* (pp. 475–493). New York: Guilford Press.

Mattick, R. P., Kimber, J., Breen, C., & Davoli, M. (2004). Buprenorphine maintenance versus placebo or methadone maintenance for opioid dependence. *Cochrane Database of Systematic Reviews*, CD002207.

Mattis, S. (1976). Mental status examination for organic mental syndrome in the elderly patient. In L. Bellak & T. B. Karasu (Eds.), *Geriatric psychiatry* (pp. 77–101). New York: Grune & Stratton.

Mattis, S., Jurica, P. J., & Leitten, C. (2002). *Dementia Rating Scale-2.* Lutz, FL: Psychological Assessment Resources.

Maugh, T. (2001, March 7). Vaccine, surge in autism unrelated, study says. *Los Angeles Times,* B4–B6.

Maughan, B., Rowe, R., Messer, J., Goodman, R., & Meltzer, H. (2004). Conduct disorder and oppositional defiant disorder in a national sample: Developmental epidemiology. *Journal of Child Psychology and Psychiatry, 45*(3), 609–621.

Mausbach, B. T., Coon, D. W., Depp, C., Rabinowitz, Y. G., Wilson-Arias, E., Kraemer, H. C., et al. (2004). Ethnicity and time to institutionalization of dementia patients: A comparison of Latina and Caucasian female family caregivers. *Journal of the American Geriatrics Society, 52*, 1077–1084.

Mawhood, L. M., & Howlin, P. (1999). The outcome of a supported employment scheme for high functioning adults with autism or Asperger syndrome. *Autism: International Journal of Research and Practice, 3*, 229–253.

Maxmen, J. S., & Ward, N. G. (1995). *Essential psychopathology and its treatment.* New York: Norton.

Maxwell, J. C. (2005). Emerging research on methamphetamine. *Current Opinion in Psychiatry, 18*, 235–242.

Mayers, A. G., & Baldwin, D. S. (2006). The relationship between sleep disturbance and depression: A review. *International Journal of Psychiatry in Clinical Practice, 10*, 2–16.

Mayes, S. D., & Calhoun, S. L. (2003). Analysis of WICS-III, Stanford-Binet IV, and academic achievement scores in children with autism. *Journal of Autism and Developmental Disorders, 33*, 329–341.

Mayes, S. D., Calhoun, S. L., & Crites, D. L. (2001). Does DSM-IV Asperger's disorder exist? *Journal of Abnormal Child Psychology, 29*, 263–271.

Mayou, R., Levenson, J., & Sharpe, M. (2003). Somatoform disorders in the DSM-V. *Psychosomatics, 44*(6), 449–451.

Mayou, R., Kirmayer, L. J., Simon, G., Kroenke, K., & Sharpe, K. (2005). Somatoform disorders: Time for a new approach in the DSM-V. *American Journal of Psychiatry, 162*, 847–855.

Mayville, S., Katz, R. C., Gipson, M. T., & Carbal, K. (1999). Assessing the prevalence of body dysmorphic disorder in an ethnically diverse group of adolescents. *Journal of Child and Family Studies, 8*, 357–362.

Mazzoli, M. (1992). Folie a deux and mental retardation. *Canadian Journal of Psychiatry, 37*, 278–279.

McBurnett, K., Pfiffner, L. J., & Frick, P. J. (2001). Symptom properties as a function of ADHD type: An argument for continued study of sluggish cognitive tempo. *Journal of Abnormal Child Psychology, 29*, 207–213.

McCabe, M. P. (1992). A program for the treatment of inhibited sexual desire in males. *Psychotherapy: Theory, Research, Practice, Training, 29*(2), 288–296.

McCance-Katz, E. F., Hart, C. L., Boyarsky, B., Kosten, T., & Jatlow, P. (2005). Gender effects following repeated administration of cocaine and alcohol in humans. *Substance Use and Misuse, 40*, 511–528.

McCann, J. T. (1999). Obsessive-compulsive and negativistic personality disorders. In T. Millon, P. H. Blaney, & R. D. Davis (Eds.), *Oxford textbook of psychopathology* (pp. 585–603). New York: Oxford University Press.

McClanahan, J. Z., Kim, S. A., & Bobowick, M. (2003). Personality disorders. In M. Hersen & S. M. Turner (Eds.), *Diagnostic interviewing* (3rd ed., 173–202). New York: Kluwer Academic.

McCleary, L. (2002). Parenting adolescents with attention deficit hyperactivity disorder: Analysis of the literature for social work practice. *Health and Social Work, 27*, 285–292.

McConaghy, N. (1993). *Sexual behavior: Problems and management.* New York: Plenum Press.

McConaghy, N. (2002). Sexual dysfunction. In M. Hersen & L. Krug Porzelius (Eds.), *Diagnosis, conceptualization, and treatment planning for adults: A step-by-step guide* (pp. 291–310). Mahwah, NJ: Erlbaum.

McConaghy, N., & Lowy, M. (2000). Sexual dysfunction. In M. Hersen & M. Biaggio (Eds.), *Effective brief therapies: A clinician's guide* (pp. 215–228). San Diego, CA: Academic Press.

McCrae, C. S., & Lichstein, K. L. (2001). Secondary insomnia: A heuristic model and behavioral approaches to assessment, treatment, and prevention. *Applied and Preventive Psychology, 10*(2), 107–123.

McCreadie, R. G., Williamson, D. J., Athawes, R. W. B., & Connolly, M. (1994). The Nithsdale Schizophrenia Surveys XIII: Parental rearing patterns, current symptomatology and relatives' expressed emotion. *British Journal of Psychiatry, 165*, 347–352.

McCubbin, H. I., Patterson, J. M., & Wilson, L. P. (1983). *Family inventory of life events and changes.* St. Paul: University of Minnesota, Department of Family Social Sciences.

McCullagh, P. (1987). Model similarity effects on motor performance. *Journal of Sport Psychology, 9*, 249–260.

McCusker, J., Cole, M. G., Bellavance, F., & Primeau, F. (1998). Reliability and validity of a new measure of severity of delirium. *International Psychogeriatrics, 10*, 421–433.

McDermott, B. M., Harris, C., & Gibbon, P. (2002). Individual psychotherapy for children and adolescents with an eating disorder from historical precedent toward evidence-based practice. *Child and Adolescent Psychiatric Clinics of North America, 11*(2), 311–329.

McDermut, W., & Zimmerman, M. (2005). Assessment instruments and standardized evaluation. In J. M. Oldham, A. E. Skodol, & D. S. Bender (Eds.), *Textbook of personality disorders* (pp. 89–101). Washington, DC: American Psychiatric Publishing.

McEachin, J. J., Smith, T., & Lovaas, O. I. (1993). Long-term outcome for children with autism who received early intensive behavioral treatment. *American Journal on Mental Retardation, 97*, 359–372.

McElroy, S. L. (2004). Bipolar disorders: Special diagnostic and treatment considerations in women. *CNS Spectrums, 9*, 5–18.

McElroy, S. L., Hudson, J. I., Malhotra, S., Welge, J., & Nelson, E. (2003). Citalopram in the treatment of binge eating disorder: A placebo-controlled trial. *Journal of Clinical Psychiatry, 64*, 807–813.

McElroy, S. L., Kotwal, R., Keck, P. E., & Akiskal, H. (2005). Comorbidity of bipolar and eating disorders: Distinct or related disorders with shared dysregulations? *Journal of Affective Disorders, 86*, 107–127.

McElroy, S. L., Strakowski, S. M., Keck, P. E., Tugrul, K. L., West, S. A., & Lonczak, H. S. (1995). Differences and similarities in mixed and pure mania. *Comprehensive Psychiatry, 36*, 187–194.

McEvoy, J., Hartman, M., Gottlieb, D., Godwon, S., Apperson, L. J., & Wilson, W. (1996). Common sense, insight and neuropsychological test performance in schizophrenia patients. *Schizophrenia Bulletin, 22*, 635–641.

McFall, M. E., Mackay, P. W., & Donovan, D. M. (1992). Combat-related posttraumatic stress disorder and severity of substance abuse in Vietnam veterans. *Journal of Studies on Alcohol, 53,* 357–362.

McFie, B. S. (1934). Behavior and personality difficulties in school children. *British Journal of Educational Psychology, 4,* 34.

McGee, G. G., & Morrier, D. (2001). The Walden early childhood programs. In J. S. Handelman & S. L. Harris (Eds.), *Preschool programs for children with autism* (pp. 157–190). Austin, TX: Pro Ed.

McGee, R., & Williams, S. (1999). Environmental risk factors in oppositional-defiant disorders and conduct disorders. In H. C. Quay & A. E. Hogan (Eds.), *Handbook of disruptive behavior disorders* (pp. 419–440). New York: Kluwer Academic/Plenum Press.

McGeer, P. L., Schulzer, M., & McGeer, E. G. (1996). Arthritis and anti-inflammatory agents as possible protective factors for Alzheimer's disease: A review of 17 epidemiologic studies. *Neurology, 47,* 425–432.

McGlashan, T. H. (1986a). The Chestnut Lodge follow-up study III: Long-term outcome of borderline personality. *Archives of General Psychiatry, 43,* 2–30.

McGlashan, T. H. (1986b). The prediction and outcome of chronic schizophrenia: Pt. IV. The Chestnut Lodge follow-up study. *Archives of General Psychiatry, 143,* 167–176.

McGlashan, T. H. (1986c). Predictors of shorter-, medium-, and longer-term outcome in schizophrenia. *American Journal of Psychiatry, 143,* 50–55.

McGlashan, T. H. (1988). Selective review of recent North American long-term follow-up studies of schizophrenia. *Schizophrenia Bulletin, 14,* 515–542.

McGlashan, T. H., & Carpenter, W. T. (1976). Post-psychotic depression in schizophrenia. *Archives of General Psychiatry, 33,* 231–239.

McGlashan, T. H., Heinssen, R. K., & Fenton, W. S. (1990). Psychosocial treatment of negative symptoms in schizophrenia. In N. C. Andreasen (Ed.), *Positive and negative symptoms and syndromes* (pp. 175–200). Basel, Switzerland: Karger.

McGoey, K. E., Eckert, T. L., & Dupal, G. J. (2002). Early intervention for preschool-age children with ADHD: A literature review. *Journal of Emotional and Behavioral Disorders, 10*(1), 14.

McGoldrick, M., Gerson, R., & Shellenberger, S. (1999). *Genograms: Assessment and intervention.* New York: Norton.

McGovern, M. P., Wrisley, B. R., & Drake, R. E. (2005). Special section on relapse prevention: Relapse of substance use disorder and its prevention among persons with co-occurring disorders. *Psychiatric Services, 56,* 1270–1273.

McGue, M. (1999). The biological genetics of alcoholism. *Current Directions in Psychological Science, 8,* 109–115.

McGuire, T. G. (1991). Measuring the economic costs of schizophrenia. *Schizophrenia Bulletin, 17,* 375–388.

McIntosh, J. L. (1991). Epidemiology of suicide in the United States. In A. A. Leenars (Ed.), *Lifespan perspectives of suicide: Time-lines in the suicide process* (pp. 55–69). New York: Plenum Press.

McIntosh, V. V., Bulik, C. M., McKenzie, J. M., Luty, S. E., & Jordan, J. (2000). Interpersonal psychotherapy for anorexia nervosa. *International Journal of Eating Disorders, 27*(2), 125–139.

McIntyre, J. R. (2004). Family treatment of substance abuse. In S. L. Ashenberg-Straussner (Ed.), *Clinical work with substance-abusing clients* (2nd ed., pp. 237–263). New York: Guilford Press.

McIntyre, R. S., Mancini, D. A., Parikh, S., & Kennedy, S. (2001). Lithium revisited. *Canadian Journal of Psychiatry, 46,* 322–327.

McKellar, J., Stewart, E., & Humphreys, K. (2003). Alcoholics Anonymous involvement and positive alcohol-related outcomes: Cause, consequence, or just a correlate? A prospective 2-year study of 2,319 alcohol-dependent men. *Journal of Consulting and Clinical Psychology, 71,* 302–308.

McKenna, K., Gordon, C. T., & Rapoport, J. L. (1994). Childhood-onset schizophrenia: Timely neurobiological research. *Journal of the American Academy of Child and Adolescent Psychiatry, 33,* 771–781.

McKhann, G., Drachman, D., Folstein, M., Katzman, R., Price, D., & Stadlan, E. M. (1984). Clinical diagnosis of Alzheimer's disease: Report of the NINCDS-ADRDA work group under the auspices of Department of Health and Human Services Task Force on Alzheimer's disease. *Neurology, 34,* 939–944.

McKnight, C. D., Compton, S. N., & March, J. S. (2004). Posttraumatic stress disorder. In T. L. Morris & J. S. March (Eds.), *Anxiety disorders in children and adolescents* (2nd ed., pp. 241–262). New York: Guilford Press.

McKinley, M. G. (2005). Alcohol withdrawal syndrome overlooked and mismanaged? *Critical Care Nursing, 25,* 40–48.

McKitrick, D. S., & Jenkins, S. Y. (2000). Considerations for ethnically diverse clients. In W. Hersen & M. Biaggo (Eds.), *Effective brief therapies: A clinician's guide* (pp. 411–431). New York: Academic Press.

McLeer, S. V., & Rose, M. (1992). Extrafamilial child sexual abuse. In R. T. Ammerman & M. Hersen (Eds.), *Assessment of family violence: A clinical and legal sourcebook* (pp. 148–207). New York: Wiley.

McLellan, A. T., Luborsky, L., O'Brien, C. P., & Woody, G. E. (1980). An improved diagnostic instrument for substance abuse patients: The Addiction Severity Index. *Journal of Nervous and Mental Diseases, 168,* 26–33.

McLeod, J. D., & Shanahan, M. J. (1996). Trajectories of poverty and children's mental health. *Journal of Health and Social Behavior, 37,* 207–220.

McMahon, R. J., & Frick, P. J. (2005). Evidence-based assessment of conduct problems in children and adolescents. *Journal of Clinical Child and Adolescent Psychology, 34,* 477–505.

McMahon, R. J., & Forehand, R. I. (2005). *Helping the noncompliant child.* New York: Guilford Press.

McNally, R. J. (2003). Progress and controversy in the study of posttraumatic stress disorder. *Annual Review of Psychology, 54,* 229–252.

McNeil, D. E. (1998). Empirically based clinical evaluation and management of the potentially violent patient. In P. M. Kleespies (Ed.), *Emergencies in mental health practice: Evaluation and management* (pp. 95–116). New York: Guilford Press.

McNeil, D. E., & Binder, R. L. (1994). Screening for risk of inpatient violence: Validation of an actuarial tool. *Law and Human Behavior, 18,* 579–586.

McWilliams, N. (1994). *Psychoanalytic diagnosis.* New York: Guilford Press.

McWilliams, N. (2004). *Psychoanalytic psychotherapy: A practitioner's guide.* New York: Guilford Press.

Meadow, R. (1977). Munchausen syndrome by proxy: The hinterland of child abuse. *Lancet, 2,* 342–345.

Meadow, R. (1982). Munchausen syndrome by proxy. *Archives of Disease in Childhood, 57,* 92–98.

Meagher, D. J. (2001). Delirium: Optimising management. *British Medical Journal, 322,* 144–149.

Meagher, D. J., O'Hanlon, D., O'Mahony, E., & Casey, P. R. (1996). The use of environmental strategies and psychotropic medication in the management of delirium. *British Journal of Psychiatry, 168,* 512–515.

Meagher, D. J., O'Hanlon, D., O'Mahony, E., Casey, P. R., & Trzepacz, P. T. (2000). Relationship between symptoms and motoric subtype of delirium. *Journal of Neuropsychiatry and Clinical Neurosciences, 12,* 51–56.

Meagher, D. J., & Trzepacz, T. P. (1998). Delirium phenomenology illuminates pathophysiology, management, and course. *Journal of Geriatric Psychiatry and Neurology, 11,* 150–156.

Means, M., & Edinger, J. (2006). Nonpharmacologic therapy of insomnia. In T. Lee-Chiong (Ed.), *Sleep: A comprehensive handbook* (pp. 125–132). Hoboken, NJ: Wiley.

Mednick, S. A., Watson, J. B., Huttunen, M., Cannon, T. D., Katila, H., Parnas, J., et al. (1998). A two-hit working model of the etiology of schizophrenia. In M. F. Lenzenweger & R. H. Dworkin (Eds.), *Origins and development of schizophrenia* (pp. 27–66). Washington, DC: American Psychological Association.

Meehl, P. E. (1962). Schizotaxia, schizotypy, schizophrenia. *American Psychologist, 17,* 827–838.

Meehl, P. E. (1990). Towards an integrated theory of schizotaxia, schizotypy, and schizophrenia. *Journal of Personality Disorders, 4*, 1–99.

Mehler, P. S. (2003). Bulimia nervosa. *New England Journal of Medicine, 349*(9), 875–881.

Mehler, C., & Warnke, A. (2002). Structural brain abnormalities specific to childhood-onset schizophrenia identified by neuroimaging techniques. *Journal of Neural Transmission, 109*, 219–234.

Meissner, W. W. (1996). The pathology of beliefs and the beliefs of pathology. In E. P. Shafranske (Ed.), *Relgion and the clinical practice of psychology* (pp. 241–267). Washington, DC: American Psychological Association.

Melartin, T. K., Leskelä, U., Rystälä, H., Sokero, P., Lestelä-Mielonen, P., & Isomestä, E. (2004). Co-morbidity and stability of melancholic features in DSM-IV major depressive disorder. *Psychological Medicine, 34*, 1443–1552.

Melartin, T. K., Rystälä, H. J., Leskelä, U. S., Lestelä-Mielonen, P. S., Sokero, T. P., & Isometsä, E. T. (2004). Severity and comorbidity predict episode duration and recurrence of DSM-IV major depressive disorder. *Journal of Clinical Psychiatry, 65*, 810–819.

Mellor, C. S. (1992). Dermatoglyphic evidence of fluctuating asymmetry in schizophrenia. *British Journal of Psychiatry, 160*, 467–472.

Meloy, J. R. (1995). Antisocial personality disorder. In G. O. Gabbard (Ed.), *Treatment of psychiatric disorders* (2nd ed., pp. 2273–2290). Washington, DC: American Psychiatric Association.

Meloy, J. R. (1995). *The psychopathic mind: Origins, dynamics, and treatment.* Northvale, NJ: Aronson.

Meltzer, H. Y., Gatward, R., Goodman, R., & Ford, R. T. (2003). Mental health of children and adolescents in Great Britain. *International Review of Psychiatry, 15*, 185–187.

Meltzer, H. Y., & McGurk, S. R. (1999). The effects of clozapine, risperidone, and olanzapine on cognitive function in schizophrenia. *Schizophrenia Bulletin, 25*, 233–255.

Melzack, R. (1975). The McGill Pain Questionnaire: Major properties and scoring methods. *Pain, 1*, 277–299.

Mendlewicz, J., & Rainer, J. D. (1977). Adoption study supporting genetic transmission in manic-depressive illness. *Nature, 268*, 327–329.

Mennin, D. S., Heimberg, R. G., & Turk, C. L. (2004). Clinical presentation and diagnostic features. In R. G. Heimberg, C. L. Turk, & D. S. Mennin (Eds.), *Generalized anxiety disorder: Advances in research and practice* (pp. 3–28). New York: Guilford Press.

Menninger, K. (1963). *The vital balance.* New York: Viking.

Mercer, C. H., Fenton, K. A., Johnson, A. M., Wellings, K., Macdowall, W., & McManus, S. (2003). Sexual function problems and help seeking behaviour in Britain: National Probability Sample Survey. *British Medical Journal, 327*(7412), 426–427.

Meredith, C. W., Jaffe, C., Ang-Lee, K., & Saxon, A. J. (2005). Implications of chronic methamphetamine use: A literature review. *Harvard Review of Psychiatry, 13*, 141–154.

Merikangas, K. R., & Angst, J. (1995). Comorbidity and social phobia: Evidence from clinical, epidemiologic, and genetic studies. *European Archives of Psychiatry and Clinical Neuroscience, 244*, 297–303.

Merikangas, K. R., Avenevoli, S., Acharyya, S., Zhang, H., & Angst, J. (2002). The spectrum of social phobia in the Zurich cohort study of young adults. *Biological Psychiatry, 51*, 81–91.

Merikangas, K. R., Mehta, R. L., Molnar, B. E., Walters, E. E., Swendsen, J. D., Auilar-Gaziola, S., et al. (1998). Comorbidity of substance use disorders with mood and anxiety disorders: Results of the international consortium in psychiatric epidemiology. *Addictive Behaviors, 23*, 893–908.

Mermelstein, H. T., & Basu, R. (2001). Can you ever be too old to be too thin? Anorexia nervosa in a 92-year-old woman. *International Journal of Eating Disorders, 30*(1), 123–126.

Merry, S. N., & Werry, J. S. (2001). Course and prognosis. In H. Remschmidt (Ed.), *Schizophrenia in children and adolescents* (pp. 268–297). New York: Cambridge University Press.

Messier, C. (2005). Impact of impaired glucose tolerance and Type 2 diabetes on cognitive aging. *Neurobiology of Aging, 26*(Suppl. 1), 26–30.

Messinis, L., Kyprianidou, A., Malefaki, S., & Papathanasopoulos, P. (2006). Neuropsychological deficits in long-term frequent cannabis users. *Neurology, 66,* 737–739.

Meyer, A. (1951–1952). *Collected papers* (Vols. 1–4, E. Winters, Ed.). Baltimore: Johns Hopkins University Press.

Meyer, A. (1957). *Psychobiology: A science of man.* Springfield, IL: Charles C. Thomas.

Meyer, J. M., Rutter, M., Silberg, J. L., Maes, H. H., Simonoff, E., Shillady, L. L., et al. (2000). Familial aggregation for conduct disorder symptomology: The role of genes, marital discord and family adaptability. *Psychological Medicine, 30,* 759–774.

Meyer, R. G., & Deitsch, S. E. (1996). *The clinician's handbook: Integrated diagnostics, assessment and intervention in adult and adolescent psychopathology* (4th ed.). Needham, MA: Allyn & Bacon.

Meyer, T. J., Miller, M. L., Metzger, R. L., & Borkovec, T. D. (1990). Development and validation of the Penn State Worry Questionnaire. *Behaviour Research and Therapy, 28,* 487–495.

Mezzich, J. E., Berganza, C. E., & Ruiperez, M. A. (2001). Culture in DSM-IV: ICD-10 and evolving diagnostic systems. *Psychiatric Clinics of North America, 24*(3), 407–419.

Mezzich, J. E., & Schmolke, M. M. (1995). Multiaxial diagnosis and psychotherapy planning: On the relevance of ICD-10, DSM-IV and complementary schemas. *Psychotherapy and Psychosomatics, 63,* 71–80.

Michel, D. M. (2002). Psychological assessment as a therapeutic intervention in patients hospitalized with eating disorders. *Professional Psychology: Research and Practice, 33*(5), 470–477.

Michelson, D., Faries, D., Wernicke, J., Kelsey, D., Kendrick, K., Sallee, F. R., et al. (2001). Atomoxetine in the treatment of children and adolescents with attention deficit/hyperactivity disorder: A randomized, placebo-controlled, dose-response study. *Pediatrics, 108,* E83.

Mick, E., Biederman, J., Faraone, S. V., Sayer, J., & Kleinman, S. (2002). Case-control study of attention-deficit hyperactivity disorder and maternal smoking, alcohol use, and drug use during pregnancy. *Journal of the American Academy of Child and Adolescent Psychiatry, 41,* 378–385.

Miida, T., Takahasi, A., Tanabe, N., & Ikeuchi, T. (2005). Can statin therapy really reduce the risk of Alzheimer's disease and slow its progression? *Current Opinion in Lipidology, 16,* 619–623.

Miklowitz, D. J. (1992). Longitudinal outcome and medication noncompliance among manic patients with and without mood-incongruent psychotic features. *Journal of Nervous and Mental Diseases, 180,* 703–711.

Miklowitz, D. J. (2002). *The bipolar disorder survival guide.* New York: Guilford Press.

Miklowitz, D. J., & Goldstein, M. J. (1990). Behavioral family treatment for patients with bipolar affective disorder. *Behavior Modification, 14,* 457–489.

Miklowitz, D. J., & Goldstein, M. J. (1997). *Bipolar disorder: A family-focused treatment approach.* New York: Guilford Press.

Miklowitz, D. J., Goldstein, M. J., Nuechterlein, K. H., Snyder, K. S., & Mintz, J. (1988). Family factors and the course of bipolar affective disorder. *Archives of General Psychiatry, 45,* 225–231.

Miklowitz, D. J., Simoneau, T. L., George, E. L., Suddath, R., & Wendel, J. S. (2000). Family focused treatment of bipolar disorder: One year effects of a psychoeducational program in conjunction with pharmacotherapy. *Biological Psychiatry, 48,* 582–592.

Miles, J. H., Hadden, L. L., Tahashashi, T. N., & Hillman, R. E. (2000). Head circumference is an independent clinical finding associated with autism. *American Journal of Medical Genetics, 95,* 339–350.

Milich, R., Balentine, A. C., & Lynam, D. R. (2001). ADHD combined type and ADHD predominately inattentive type are distinct and unrelated disorders. *Clinical Psychology: Science and Practice, 8*(4), 463–488.

Militerni, R., Bravaccio, C., Falco, C., Fico, C., & Palermo, M. T. (2002). Repetitive behaviors in autistic disorder. *European Journal of Child and Adolescent Psychiatry, 11*(5), 210– 218.

Millar, A., Espie, C. A., & Scott, J. (2004). The sleep of remitted bipolar outpatients: A controlled naturalistic study using actigraphy. *Journal of Affective Disorders, 80,* 145–153.

Miller, A. L., & Glinski, J. (2000). Youth suicidal behavior: Assessment and intervention. *Journal of Clinical Psychology, 56*(9), 1131–1152.

Miller, A. L., Rathus, J. H., Linehan, M. M., Wetzler, S., & Leigh, E. (1997). Dialectial behavior therapy adapted for suicidal adolescents. *Journal of Practical Psychiatry and Behavioral Health, 3*(2), 78–86.

Miller, D. J., & Thelen, M. H. (1986). Knowledge and beliefs about confidentiality in psychotherapy. *Professional Psychology: Research and Practice, 17*, 15–19.

Miller, I. W., Uebelacker, L. A., Keitner, G. I., Ryan, C. E., & Solomon, D. A. (2004). Longitudinal course of bipolar I disorder. *Comprehensive Psychiatry, 45*, 431–440.

Miller, J., & Ozonoff, S. (2000). The external validity of Asperger disorder: Lack of evidence from the domain of neuropsychology. *Journal of Abnormal Psychology, 109*, 227–238.

Miller, M. (1985). *Information center: Training workshop manual.* San Diego, CA: Information Center.

Miller, M. B., Useda, J. D., Trull, T. J., Burr, R. M., & Minks-Brown, C. (2001). Paranoid, schizoid, and schizotypal personality disorders. In H. E. Adams & P. B. Sutker (Eds.), *Comprehensive handbook of psychopathology* (3rd. ed., pp. 535–557). New York: Kluwer Academic/Plenum.

Miller, M. N., & Pumariega, A. J. (2001). Eating disorders: Bulimia and anorexia nervosa. In H. B. Vance & A. J. Pumariega (Eds.), *Clinical assessment of child and adolescent behavior* (pp. 307–327). New York: Wiley.

Miller, M. N., Verhegge, R., Miller, B. E., & Pumariega, A. J. (1999). Assessment of risk of eating disorders among adolescents in Appalachia. *Journal of the American Academy of Child and Adolescent Psychiatry, 38*(4), 437–443.

Miller, S. B. (1987). A comparison of methods of inquiry: The testing and interviewing contributions to the diagnostic process. *Bulletin of the Menninger Clinic, 51*, 505–518.

Miller, W. R., & Rollnick, S. (2002). *Motivational interviewing: Preparing people to change* (2nd ed.). New York: Guilford Press.

Miller, W. R., Wilbourne, P. L., & Hettema, J. E. (2003). What works? A summary of alcohol treatment outcome research. In R. K. Hester & W. R. Miller (Eds.), *Handbook of alcoholism treatment approaches* (pp. 13–63). Boston: Pearson Education.

Millon, T. (1981). *Disorders of personality: DSM-III, Axis II.* New York: Wiley.

Millon, T. (1991). Classification in psychopathology: Rationale, alternatives, and standards. *Journal of Abnormal Psychology, 100*(3), 245–261.

Millon, T., & Elevery, G. S., Jr. (1985). *Personality and its disorders.* New York: Wiley.

Millon, T., & Grossman, S. D. (2005). Sociocultural factors. In J. M. Oldham, A. E. Skodol, & D. S. Bender (Eds.), *Textbook of personality disorders* (pp. 223–235) Washington, DC: American Psychiatric Publishing.

Millon, T., Millon, C., & Davis, R. (1997). *MCMI-III manual* (2nd ed.). Minneapolis, MN: National Computer Systems.

Millon, T. H. (1996). *Disorders of personality: DSM-IV and beyond.* New York: Wiley.

Millon, T. H. (1998). The DSM narcissistic personality: Historical reflections and future directions. In E. Ronningstam (Ed.), *Disorders of narcissism: Diagnostic, clinical and empirical implications* (pp. 75–102). Washington, DC: American Psychiatric Press.

Millon, T. H., & Davis, R. (2000). *Personality disorders in modern life.* New York: Wiley.

Milos, G. F., Spindler, A. M., Buddeberg, C., & Crameri, A. (2003). Axes I and II comorbidity and treatment experiences in eating disorder subjects. *Psychotherapy and Psychosomatics, 72*, 276–285.

Mimica, N., Folnegovic-Smale, V., & Folnegovic, Z. (2001). Catatonic schizophrenia in Croatia. *European Archives of Psychiatry and Clinical Neuroscience, 251*, 17–20.

MIND Institute. (2002, October). *Report to the legislature on the principal findings from the epidemiology of autism in California: A comprehensive pilot study.* Davis: University of California.

Mineka, S., & Cook, M. (1993). Mechanisms involved in the observational conditioning of fear. *Journal of Experimental Psychology, 122*, 23–38.

Minshew, N. J., Sweeney, J. A., Bauman, M. L., & Webb, S. J. (2005). Neurologic aspects of autism. In F. R. Volkmar, R. Paul, A. Klin, & D. Cohen (Eds.), *Handbook of autism and pervasive developmental disorders* (3rd ed., pp. 473–514). Hoboken, NJ: Wiley.

Mintzer, M. Z., & Stitzer, M. L. (2002). Cognitive impairment in methadone maintenance patients. *Drug and Alcohol Dependence, 67*, 41–51.

Mitchell, J. E., Raymond, N., & Specker, S. M. (1993). A review of the controlled trials of pharmacotherapy and psychotherapy in the treatment of bulimia nervosa. *International Journal of Eating Disorders, 14*(3), 229–247.

Mitchell, P. B., Parker, G. B., Jaimeson, K., Wilhelm, K., Hickie, I., Brodaty, H., et al. (1992). Are there any differences between bipolar and unipolar melancholia? *Journal of Affective Disorders, 25*, 92–105.

Mitchell, P. B., Wilhelm, K., Parker, G., Austin, M. P., Rutgers, P., & Mahli, G. S. (2001). The clinical features of bipolar depression: A comparison with matched major depressive disorder patients. *Journal of Clinical Psychiatry, 62*, 212–216.

Mitrany, E., Lubin, F., Chetrit, A., & Modan, B. (1995). Eating disorders among Jewish female adolescents in Israel: A 5-year study. *Journal of Adolescent Health, 16*(6), 454–457.

Mittelman, M. S., Roth, D. L., Coon, D. W., & Hayley, M. E. (2004). Sustained benefit of supportive intervention for depressive symptoms in caregivers of patients with Alzheimer's disease. *American Journal of Psychiatry, 61*, 850–856.

Mittenberg, W., Patton, C., Canyock, E. M., & Condit, D. C. (2002). Base rates of malingering and symptom exaggeration. *Journal of Clinical and Experimental Neuropsychology, 24*(8), 1094–1102.

Mizes, J. S., & Bonifazi, D. Z. (2000). Bulimia nervosa. In M. Hersen & M. Biaggio (Eds.), *Effective brief therapies: A clinician's guide* (pp. 257–285). New York: Academic Press.

Modestin, J., Matutat, B., & Wurmle, O. (2001). Antecedents of opioid dependence and personality disorder: Attention-deficit/hyperactivity disorder and conduct disorder. *European Archives of Clinical Neuroscience, 251*, 42–47.

Modesto-Lowe, V., Brooks, D., & Ghani, M. (2006). Alcohol dependence and suicidal behavior: From research to clinical challenges. *Harvard Review of Psychiatry, 14*, 241–248.

Modesto-Lowe, V., & VanKirk, J. (2002). Clinical uses of naltrexone: A review of the evidence. *Experimental and Clinical Psychopharmacology, 10*, 213–227.

Moene, F. C., Landberg, E. H., Hoogduin, K. A. L., Spinhoven, P., Hertzberger, L. I., Kleyweg, R. P., et al. (2000). Organic syndromes diagnosed as conversion disorder: Identification and frequency in a study of 85 patients. *Journal of Psychosomatic Research, 49*, 7–12.

Moffitt, T. E. (2003). Life course persistent and adolescence-limited antisocial behavior: A 10-year research review and research agenda. In B. B. Lahey, T. E. Moffitt, & A. Caspi (Eds.), *Causes of conduct disorder and juvenile delinquency* (pp. 49–75). New York: Guilford Press.

Moffitt, T. E., & Caspi, A. (2001). Childhood predictors differentiate life-course persistent and adolescence-limited antisocial pathways among males and females. *Development and Psychopathology, 13*, 355–375.

Moffitt, T. E., Caspi, A., Dickson, N., Silva, P., & Stanton, W. (1996). Childhood-onset versus adolescent-onset antisocial conduct problems in males: Natural history from ages 3 to 18 years. *Development and Psychopathology, 14*, 179–207.

Moffitt, T. E., Caspi, A., Harrington, H., & Milne, B. J. (2002). Males on life-course-persistent and adolescence-limited antisocial pathways: Follow-up at 26 years. *Development and Psychopathology, 14*, 179–207.

Mogg, K., Millar, N., & Bradley, B. P. (2000). Biases in eye movements to threatening facial expressions in generalized anxiety disorder and depressive disorder. *Journal of Abnormal Psychology, 109*, 695–704.

Mohammadi, M. R., Ghanizadeh, A., Rahgozar, M., Noorbala, A. A., Davidian, H., Afzali, H. M., et al. (2004). Prevalence of obsessive–compulsive disorder in Iran. *BMC Psychiatry, 4*(1), 2.

Mohlman, J., deJesus, M., Gorsenstein, E. E., Kleber, M., Gorman, J. M., & Papp, L. A. (2004). Distinguishing generalized anxiety disorder, panic disorder, and mixed anxiety states in older treatment-seeking adults. *Anxiety Disorders, 18*, 275–290.

Mojtabi, R., Nicholson, R. A., & Carpenter, B. N. (1998). Role of psychosocial treatments in management of schizophrenia: A meta-analytic review of controlled outcome studies. *Schizophrenia Bulletin, 24*, 569–587.

Mol, S. S. L., Arntz, A., Metsemakers, J. F. M., Dinant, G. J., Vilters-Van Montfort, P. A. P., & Knottnerus, J. A. (2005). Symptoms of post-traumatic stress disorder after non-traumatic events: Evidence from an open population study. *British Journal of Psychiatry, 128*, 494–499.

Moldin, S. O. (2000). Gender and schizophrenia: An overview. In E. Frank (Ed.), *Gender and its effects on psychopathology* (pp. 169–186). Washington, DC: American Psychiatric Press.

Molero, A. E., Pino-Ramirez, G., & Maestre, G. E. (2001). Modulation by age and gender of risk for Alzheimer's disease and vascular dementia associated with the apolipoprotein Evarepsilon4 allele in Latin Americans: Findings from the Maracaibo Aging Study. *Neuroscience Letters, 307*, 5–8.

Monahan, J. (1993). Limiting therapist exposure to Tarasoff liability: Guidelines for risk containment. *American Psychologist, 48*, 242–250.

Monahan, J. (1994). *MacArthur community violence instrument.* Charlottesville: University of Virginia.

Monahan, J. (2003). Violence risk assessment. In A. M. Goldstein (Ed.), *Handbook of psychology: Vol. 11. Forensic psychology* (pp. 527–540). Hoboken, NJ: Wiley.

Monahan, J., & Steadman, H. J. (1996). Violent storms and violent people: How meteorology can inform risk communication in mental health law. *American Psychologist, 51*, 931– 938.

Monahan, J. Steadman, H. S., & Silver, E. (2001). *Rethinking risk assessment: The MacArthur study of mental disorder and violence.* Oxford, Oxford University Press.

Mondrego, P. J., & Fernandez, J. (2004). Depression in patients with mild cognitive impairment increases the risk of developing dementia of Alzheimer type: A prospective cohort study. *Archives of Neurology, 61*, 1290–1293.

Monteleone, P., Brambilla, F., Bortolotti, F., & Maj, M. (2000). Serotonergic dysfunction across the eating disorders: Relationship to eating behaviour, purging behaviour, nutritional status and general psychopathology. *Psychological Medicine, 30*, 1099–1110.

Monterosso, J. R., Aron, A. R., Cordoova, X., Xu, J., & London, E. D. (2005). Deficits in response inhibition associated with chronic methamphetamine abuse. *Drug and Alcohol Dependence, 79*, 273–277.

Moore, V., & Goodson, S. (2003). How well does early diagnosis of autism stand the test of time? Follow-up study of children assessed for autism at age 2 and development of an early diagnostic service. *Autism: International Journal of Research and Practice, 7*(1), 47–63.

Moorhead, S. R., & Young, A. H. (2003). Evidence for a late onset bipolar-I disorder subgroup from 50 years. *Journal of Affective Disorders, 73*, 271–277.

Moos, R. H., & Billings, A. G. (1982). Conceptualizing and measuring coping resources and processes. In L. Goldberger & S. Breznitz (Eds.), *Handbook of stress: Theoretical and clinical aspects* (pp. 212–230). New York: Free Press.

Moos, R. H., Brennan, P. L., & Mertens, J. R. (1994). Mortality rates and predictors of mortality among late-middle-aged and older substance abuse patients. *Alcoholism: Clinical and Experimental Research, 18*, 187–195.

Moos, R. H., & Moos, B. S. (2005). Paths of entry into Alcoholics Anonymous: Consequences for participation and remission. *Alcoholism: Clinical and Experimental Research, 29*, 1858–1868.

Moran, M., & Lawlor, B. (2005). Late-life schizophrenia. *Psychiatry, 4*, 51–55.

Moran, P. (1999). The epidemiology of antisocial personality disorder. *Social Psychiatry and Psychiatric Epidemiology, 34*(5), 231–242.

Moran, P., Jenkins, R., Tylee, A., Blizard, R., & Munn, A., (2000). The prevalence of personality disorder among UK primary care attenders. *Acta Psychiatrica Scandinavica, 102*, 52–57.

Moran, P. W. (2000). The adaptive practice of psychotherapy in the managed care era. *Psychiatric Clinics of North America, 23*(2), 383–902.

Morel, B. A. (1860). *Traite des maladies mentales*. Paris, France: Librairie Victor Masson.

Morey, L. C. (1991). *The Personality Assessment Inventory professional manual*. Odessa, FL: Psychological Assessment Resources.

Morey, L. C., & Jones, J. K. (1998). Empirical studies of the construct validity of narcissistic personality disorder. In E. Ronningstam (Ed.), *Disorders of narcissism: Theoretical, empirical, and clinical implications* (pp. 351–374). Washington, DC: American Psychiatric Press.

Morey, L. C., Waugh, M. H., & Blashfield, R. K. (1985). MMPI scales for DSM-III personality disorders: Their derivation and correlates. *Journal of Personality Assessment, 49*, 245–251.

Morgan, A. E., Hynd, G. W., Riccio, C. A., & Hall, J. (1996). Validity of the DSM-IV ADHD predominantly inattentive and combined types: Relationship to previous DSM diagnoses/ subtype differences. *Journal of the American Academy of Child and Adolescent Psychiatry, 35*, 325–333.

Morgan, R. D., Olson, K. R., Krueger, R. M., Schellenberg, R. P., & Jackson, T. T. (2000). Do the DSM decision trees improve diagnostic ability? *Journal of Clinical Psychology, 56*(1), 73–88.

Morgenstern, J., Labouvie, E., McCrady, B. S., Kahler, C. W., & Frey, R. M. (1997). Affiliation with Alcoholics Anonymous after treatment: A study of its therapeutic effects and mechanisms of action. *Journal of Consulting and Clinical Psychology, 65*, 768–777.

Morgenstern, J., Langenbucher, J., Labouvie, E., & Miller, K. J. (1997). The comorbidity of alcoholism and personality disorders in a clinical population: Prevalence and relation to alcohol typology variables. *Journal of Abnormal Psychology, 106*, 74–84.

Morin, C. M. (2003). Primary insomnia (A. Kent, Trans.). In M. Billiard (Ed.), *Sleep: Physiology, investigations, and medicine* (pp. 133–136). New York: Kluwer Academic/ Plenum Press.

Morin, C. M., Colecchi, C., Stone, J., Sood, R., & Brink, D. (1999). Behavioral and pharmacological therapies for late-life insomnia: A randomized controlled trial. *Journal of the American Medical Association, 281*(11), 91–99.

Morin, C. M., Hauri, P. J., Espie, C. A., Spielman, A. J., Buysse, D. J., & Bootzin, R. R. (1999). Nonpharmacological treatment of chronic insomnia. *Sleep, 22*, 1134–1156.

Morin, C. M., Savard, J., Ouellet, M. C., & Daley, M. (2003). Insomnia. In A. M. Nezu, C. Maguth, & P. A. Geller (Eds.), *Handbook of psychology: Vol. 9. Health psychology* (pp. 317–337). Hoboken, NJ: Wiley.

Morrell, J., & Murray, L. (2003). Parenting and the development of conduct disorder and hyperactive symptoms in childhood: A prospective longitudinal study from 2 months to 8 years. *Journal of Child Psychology and Psychiatry and Allied Disciplines, 44*, 348–508.

Morris, M. C., Evans, D. A., Tangney, C. C., Bienias, J. L., Schneider, J. A., Wilson, R. S., et al. (2006). Dietary copper and high saturated and trans fat intakes associated with cognitive decline. *Archives of Neurology, 63*, 1085–1088.

Morrison, J. (1995a). *DSM-IV made easy: The clinician's guide to diagnosis*. New York: Guilford Press.

Morrison, J. (1995b). *The first interview: Revised for the DSM-IV*. New York: Guilford Press.

Morrison, J., & Anders, T. F. (1999). *Interviewing children and adolescents: Skills and strategies for effective DSM-IV diagnosis*. New York: Guilford Press.

Morrow, A. L., Suzdak, P. D., Karanian, J. W., & Paul, S. M. (1988). Chronic ethanol administration alters gamma-aminobutyric acid, pentobarbitol and ethanol-induced 36CL-uptake in cerebral cortical synaptoneurosomes. *Journal of Pharmacology and Experimental Therapeutics, 246*, 158–164.

Morselli, E. (1886). Sulla dismorfofobia e sulla tafefobia [On dysmorphobia and on phobias]. *Bolletinno della Accademia di Genova, 6*, 110–119.

Mortimer, A. M., Lund, C. E., & McKenna, P. J. (1990). The positive: Negative dichotomy in schizophrenia. *British Journal of Psychiatry, 157*, 41–49.

Moscicki, E. K. (1997). Identification of suicide risk factors using epidemiologic studies. *Psychiatric Clinics of North America, 20*, 499–517.

Motto, J. A. (1989). Problems in suicide risk assessment. In D. Jacobs & H. N. Brown (Eds.), *Suicide: Understanding and responding* (pp. 129–142). Madison, CT: International Universities Press.

Moul, D. E., & Buysse, D. J. (2006). Evaluation of insomnia. In T. Lee-Chiong (Ed.), *Sleep: A comprehensive handbook* (pp. 117–123). Hoboken, NJ: Wiley.

Moutier, C. Y., & Stein, M. B. (1999). The history, epidemiology, and differential diagnosis of social anxiety disorder. *Journal of Clinical Psychiatry, 60,* 4–8.

Mowrer, O. H. (1939). A stimulus-response analysis of anxiety and its role as a reinforcing agent. *Psychological Review, 46,* 553–565.

Moye, J., Karel, M., Gurrera, R. J., & Azar, A. R. (2006). Neuropsychological predictors of decision-making capacity over 9 months in mild-to-moderate dementia. *Journal of General Internal Medicine, 21,* 78–83.

Mpofu, E. (2002). Psychopharmacology in the treatment of conduct disorder children and adolescents: Rationale, prospects, and ethics. *South African Journal of Psychology, 32*(4), 9–21.

Mpofu, E., & Conners, L. M. (2003). Neurochemistry in the comorbidity of conduct disorder with other disorders of childhood and adolescence: Implications for counseling. *Counseling Psychology Quarterly, 16*(1), 37–41.

Mpofu, E., & Crystal, R. (2001). Conduct disorder in children: Challenges and prospective cognitive behavioral treatments. *Counseling Psychology Quarterly, 14*(1), 21–32.

MTA Cooperative Committee. (1999a). A 14 month randomized clinical trial of treatment strategies for attention deficit/hyperactivity disorder. *Archives of General Psychiatry, 56,* 1073–1086.

MTA Cooperative Committee. (1999b). Moderators and mediators of treatment response for children with attention deficit/hyperactivity disorder. *Archives of General Psychiatry, 56,* 1088–1096.

Mueser, K. T., Bellack, A. S., Douglas, M. S., & Wade, J. H. (1991). Prediction of social skill acquisition in schizophrenic and major affective disorder patients from memory and symptomatology. *Psychiatry Research, 37,* 281–296.

Mueser, K. T., Doonan, R., Penn, D. L., Blanchard, J. J., Bellack, A. S., Nithith, P., et al. (1996). Emotion recognition and social competence in chronic schizophrenia. *Journal of Abnormal Psychology, 105,* 271–275.

Mueser, K. T., Drake, R. E., & Bond, G. R. (1997). Recent advances in psychiatric rehabilitation for patients with severe mental illness. *Harvard Review of Psychiatry, 5,* 123–137.

Mueser, K. T., Drake, R. E., & Wallach, M. A. (1998). Dual diagnosis: A review of etiological theories. *Addictive Behaviors, 23,* 717–734.

Mueser, K. T., & Gingrich, S. (1994). *Coping with schizophrenia.* Oakland, CA: New Harbinger.

Mueser, K. T., & Glynn, S. M. (1995). *Behavioral family therapy for psychiatric disorders.* Boston: Allyn & Bacon.

Mueser, K. T., Goodman, L. A., Trumbettam, S. L., Rosenberg, S. D., Osher, F. C., Vidaver, R., et al. (1998). Trauma and posttraumatic stress disorder in severe mental illness. *Journal of Consulting and Clinical Psychology, 66,* 493–499.

Mueser, K. T., Yarnold, P. R., Levinson, D. F., Singh, H., Bellack, A. S., Kee, K., et al. (1990). Prevalence of substance abuse in schizophrenia: Demographic and clinical correlates. *Schizophrenia Bulletin, 16,* 31–56.

Mukaddes, N. M., Abali, O., & Kaynak, N. (2003). Citalopram treatment of children and adolescents with obsessive-compulsive disorder: A preliminary report. *Psychiatric and Clinical Neurosciences, 57,* 405–408.

Mukherjee, S., Shukla, S., Woodle, J., Rosen, A. M., & Olarte, S. (1983). Misdiagnosis of schizophrenia in bipolar patients: A multiethnic comparison. *American Journal of Psychiatry, 140,* 1571–1574.

Mulkens, S. A. N., de Jong, P. L., & Merckelbach, H. (1996). Disgust and spider phobia. *Journal of Abnormal Psychology, 105,* 464–468.

Mullen, E. M. (1995). *Mullen scales of early language.* Circle Pines, MN: American Guidance Service.

Mulnard, R. A., Cotman, C. W., Kawas, C., van Dyck, C. H., Sano, M., Doody, R., et al. (2000). Estrogen replacement therapy for treatment of mild to moderate Alzheimer disease: A randomized controlled trial: Alzheimer's Disease Cooperative Study. *Journal of the American Medical Association, 283,* 1007–1015.

Mulsant, B. H., Pollock, B. G., Nebes, R., Miller, M. D., Sweet, R. A., Stack, J., et al. (2001). A 12-week, double blind randomized comparison of nortriptyline and paroxetine in older depressed patients and outpatients. *American Journal of Psychiatry, 9,* 406–414.

Mulsant, B. H., Stergiou, A., Keshavan, M. S., Sweet, R. A., Rifai, H., Pasternak, R., et al. (1993). Schizophrenia in late life: Elderly patients admitted to an acute care psychiatric hospital. *Schizophrenia Bulletin, 19,* 709–721.

Munaka, M., Kohshi, K., Kawamoto, T., Takasawa, S., Nagata, N., Itoh, H., et al. (2003). Genetic polymorphisms of tobacco and alcohol related metabolizing enzymes and the risk of hepatocellular carcinoma. *Journal of Cancer Research and Clinical Oncology, 129,* 355–360.

Mundy, P., & Burnette, C. (2005). Joint attention and neurodevelopmental models of autism. In F. R. Volkmar, R. Paul, A. Klin, & D. Cohen (Eds.), *Handbook of autism and pervasive developmental disorders* (3rd ed., pp. 650–681). Hoboken, NJ: Wiley.

Mundy, P., Sigman, M., & Kasari, C. (1994). Joint attention, developmental level, and symptom presentation in young children with autism. *Developmental and Psychopathology, 6,* 387–401.

Munro, A. (1982). *Delusional hypochondriasis: Clarke Institute of Psychiatry* [Monograph Series No. 5]. Toronto, Ontario, Canada: Clarke Institute of Psychiatry.

Munro, A. (1999). *Delusional disorder: Paranoia and related illnesses.* New York: Cambridge University Press.

Munro, A., & Mok, H. (2006). An overview of treatment in paranoia/delusional disorder. *Canadian Journal of Psychiatry, 40,* 616–622.

Murch, S. H., Anthony, A., Casson, D. H., Malik, M., Berelowitz, M., Dhillon, A. P., et al. (2004). Retraction of an interpretation. *Lancet, 363*(9411), 750.

Murphy, C. M., & O'Farrell, T. J. (1994). Factors associated with marital aggression in male alcoholics. *Journal of Family Psychology, 8,* 321–335.

Murphy, D. G. M., Critchley, H. D., Schmitz, N., McAlonan, G., van Amelsvoort, T., Robertson, D., et al. (2002). Asperger syndrome: A proton magnetic resonance spectroscopy study of the brain. *Archives of General Psychiatry, 59*(10), 885–892.

Murphy, F. C., Sahakian, B. J., Rubinsztein, J. S., Michael, A., Rogers, R. D., Robbins, T. W., et al. (1999). Emotional bias and inhibitory control processes in mania and depression. *Psychological Medicine, 29,* 1307–1321.

Murphy, G. E., & Wetzel, R. D. (1990). The lifetime risk of suicide in alcoholism. *Archives of General Psychiatry, 47,* 383–392.

Murphy, J. (2005). Psychosocial treatments for ADHD in teens and adults: A practice-friendly review. *Journal of Clinical Psychology/In Session, 61,* 607–619.

Murphy, K. R., & Barkley, R. A. (1996). ADHD adults: Comorbidity and adaptive functioning. *Comprehensive Psychiatry, 37,* 393–401.

Murphy, K. R., Barkley, R. A., & Bush, T. (2002). Young adults with attention deficit hyperactivity disorder: Subtype differences in comorbidity, educational and clinical histories. *Journal of Nervous and Mental Diseases, 190,* 147–157.

Murray, C. J. L., & Lopez, A. D. (Eds.) (1996). *The global burden of disease and injury series: Vol. 1. A comprehensive assessment of mortality and disablity from disease, injuries, and risk factors in 1990 and projected to 2020.* Cambridge, MA: Harvard University Press.

Murray, L., Cooper, P. J., Wilson, A., & Romaniuk, H. (2003). Controlled trial of short- and long-term effect of psychological treatment of post-partum depression: Pt. 2. Impact on the mother-child relationship and child outcome. *British Journal of Psychiatry, 182,* 420–427.

Murray, L. L. (2002). Cognitive distinctions between depression and early Alzheimer's disease in the elderly. *Aphasiology, 16,* 573–585.

Murtagh, D. R., & Greenwood, K. M. (1995). Identifying effective psychological treatments for insomnia: A meta-analysis. *Journal of Consulting and Clinical Psychology, 63,* 79–89.

Myers, C. S. (1915). A contribution to the study of shell shock: Being an account of three cases of loss of memory, vision, smell and taste, admitted into the duchess of Westminster's War Hospital, Le Touquet. *The Lancet, 1,* 316–320.

Myhr, G. (1998). Autism and other pervasive developmental disorders: Exploring the dimensional view. *Canadian Journal of Psychiatry, 43,* 589–595.

Myles, B. S., Bock, S. J., & Simpson, R. (2001). *Asperger Syndrome Diagnostic Scale.* Austin, TX: ProEd.

Nacke, P. (1899). Die sexuellen Perversitaten in der Irrenanstalt. *Psychiatriche en Neurologische Bladen, 3,* 20–30.

Nadaoka, T., Oiji, A., Takahashi, S., Morioka, Y., Kashiwakura, M., & Totsuka, S. (1996). An epidemiological study of eating disorders in a northern area of Japan. *Acta Psychiatrica Scandinavica, 93*(4), 305–310.

Nadder, T. S., Rutter, M., Silberg, J. L., Maes, H. H., & Eaves, L. J. (2002). Genetic effects on the variation and covariation of attention-deficit hyperactivity disorder (ADHD) and oppositional defiant/conduct disorder (ODD/CD) symptomatologies across informant and occasion of measurement. *Psychological Medicine, 32,* 39–53.

Nadeau, K. (2002). *Understanding women with AD/HD.* Silver Springs, MD. Advantage Books.

Nadeau, L., Boivin, M., Tessier, R., Lefebrve, F., & Robaey, P. (2001). Mediators of behavioral problems in 7-year-old children born after 24 to 28 weeks of gestation. *Journal of Developmental Pediatrics, 22,* 1–10.

Nader, R., Oberlander, T. F., Chambers, C. T., & Craig, K. D. (2004). Expression of pain in children with autism. *Clinical Journal of Pain, 20*(2), 88–97.

Nagin, D. S., & Tremblay, R. E. (1999). Trajectories of boys' physical aggression, opposition, and hyperactivity on the path to physically violent and non violent juvenile delinquency. *Child Development, 70,* 1181–1196.

Nagin, D. S., & Tremblay, R. E. (2001). Parental and early childhood predictors of persistent physical aggression in boys from kindergarten to high school. *Archives of General Psychiatry, 58,* 389–394.

Nakada, T., & Knight, R. T. (1984). Alcohol and the central nervous system. *Medical Clinics of North America, 68,* 121–131.

Narash-Eisikovits, O., Dierberger, A., & Westen, D. (2002). A multidimensional meta-analysis of pharmacotherapy for bulimia nervosa: Summarizing the range of outcomes in controlled clinical trials. *Harvard Review of Psychiatry, 10*(4), 193–211.

Nasman, B., Bucht, G., Eriksson, S., & Sandman, P. O. (1993). Behavioral symptoms in the institutionalized elderly: Relationship to dementia. *International Journal of Geriatric Psychiatry, 8,* 843–849.

Nasser, M. (1986). Comparative study of the prevalence of abnormal eating attitudes among Arab female students of both London and Cairo universities. *Psychological Medicine, 16*(3), 621–625.

Nasser, M. (1993). A prescription of vomiting: Historical footnotes. *International Journal of Eating Disorders, 13*(1), 129–131.

Nathan, P. E., Andberg, M. M., Behan, P. O., & Patch, V. D. (1969). Thirty-two observers and one patient: A study of diagnostic reliability. *Journal of Clinical Psychology, 25,* 9–15.

Nation, M., & Heflinger, C. A. (2006). Risk factors for serious alcohol and drug use: The role of psychosocial variables in predicting the frequency of substance use among adolescents. *American Journal of Drug and Alcohol Abuse, 32,* 415–433.

National Association of Social Workers. (1999). *Code of ethics of the National Association of Social Workers.* Washington, DC: Author.

National Center for Health Statistics. (1996). Advance report of final mortality statistics. *NCHS Monthly Vital Statistics Report, 45,* 63.

National Institute on Aging. (2005). *Alzheimer's disease fact sheet.* Washington, DC: National Institutes of Health.

National Institute on Alcohol Abuse and Alcoholism. (2005). *A pocket guide for alcohol screening and intervention.* Rockville, MD: NIAAA Publications.

National Institute on Alcohol Abuse and Alcoholism (NIAAA) (1989). *Alcohol alert: Alcohol withdrawal*. Retrieved March 13, 2007, from http://pubs.niaaa.nih.gov/publications/aa05.htm.

National Institute for Clinical Excellence (NICE). (2004). *Eating disorders: Core interventions in the treatment and management of anorexia nervosa, bulimia nervosa and related eating disorders*. London: National Collaborating Centre for Mental Health.

National Institute on Drug Abuse. (2000a). Gender differences in drug abuse risks and treatment. *NIDA Notes, 15*(4). Retrieved December 7, 2006, from www.drugabuse.gov/NIDA_Notes/NNVol15N4/tearoff.html.

National Institute on Drug Abuse. (2000b). *Inhalant abuse* (NIH Publication No. 00-3818). Retrieved April 14, 2007, from http://teens.drugabuse.gov/facts/facts_inhale2.asp.

National Institute on Drug Abuse. (2001). *Hallucinogens and dissociative drugs*. Retrieved June 12, 2006, from www.nida.nih.gov/PDF/RRHalluc.pdf.

National Institute on Drug Abuse. (2003). *Drug use among ethnic/racial minorities*. Retrieved June 14, 2006, from www.nida.nih.gov/pdf/monographs/115.pdf.

National Institute on Drug Abuse. (2004). *NIDA info facts*. Retrieved June 10, 2006, from www.drugabuse.gov/pdf/infofacts/NationTrends.pdf.

National Institute on Drug Abuse. (2005). *NIDA info facts heroin*. Retrieved June 19, 2006, from www.nida.nih.gov/PDF/RRHeroin.pdf.

National Institute on Drug Abuse. (2006a). *Monitoring the future survey press release*. Retrieved October 19, 2006, from www.nida.nih.gov/Newsroom/06/MTF2006Drug.pdf.

National Institute on Drug Abuse. (2006b). *NIDA info facts: Cocaine and crack*. Retrieved June 13, 2006, from www.nida.nih.gov/infofacts/cocaine.html.

National Institute on Drug Abuse. (2006c). *NIDA info facts: Inhalants*. Retrieved June 15, 2006, from www.nida.nih.gov/PDF/Infofacts/Inhalants06.pdf.

National Institute on Drug Abuse. (2006d). *NIDA info facts: Marijuana*. Retrieved June 12, 2006, from www.nida.nih.gov/Infofacts/marijuana.html.

National Institute on Drug Abuse. (2006e). *NIDA info facts*. Retrieved June 12, 2006, from www.drugabuse.gov/pdf/infofacts/HSYouthTrends06.pdf.

National Institute on Drug Abuse. (2006f). *Research report series: Methamphetamine abuse and addiction*. Retrieved June 14, 2006, from www.nida.nih.gov/PDF/RRMetham.pdf.

National Institute on Drug Abuse. (n.d.). *Principles of drug addiction treatment: A research based guide*. Retrieved September 21, 2006, from www.drugabuse.gov/PODAT/PODAT9.html.

National Research Council. (Eds.). (2001). *Educating children with autism*. Washington, DC: National Academy Press.

Naz, B., Bromet, E. J., & Mojtabai, R. (2003). Distinguishing between first-admission schizophreniform disorder and schizophrenia. *Schizophrenia Research, 62*, 51–58.

Neighbors, H. W., Jackson, J. J., Campbell, L., & Williams, D. (1989). The influence of racial factors on psychiatric diagnosis: A review and suggestions for research. *Community Mental Health Journal, 25*, 301–311.

Neimeyer, R. A., & Pfeiffer, A. M. (1994). The ten most common errors of suicide interventionists. In A. A. Leenaars, J. T. Maltsberger, & R. A. Neimeyer (Eds.), *Treatment of suicidal people* (pp. 207–224). Philadelphia: Taylor & Francis.

Nelles, W. B., & Barlow, D. H. (1988). Do children panic? *Clinical Psychology Review, 8*, 359–372.

Nelson, J. C., Kennedy, J. S., Pollock, B. G., Lahgrissi-Thode, F., Narayan, J. M., Nobler, M. S., et al. (1999). Treatment of major depression with nortriptyline and paroxetine in patients with ischemic heart disease. *American Journal of Psychiatry, 156*, 1024–1028.

Nelson-Gray, R. O. (1991). DSM-IV: Empirical guidelines from psychometrics. *Journal of Abnormal Psychology, 100*(3), 308–315.

Nemeroff, C. B., Bremner, J. D., Foa, E. B., Mayberg, H. S., North, C. S., & Stein, M. B. (2006). Posttraumatic stress disorder: A state-of-the-science review. *Journal of Psychiatric Research, 40*, 1–21.

Nemeroff, C. B., Evans, D., Gyulai, L., Sachs, G. S., Bowden, C. L., Gergel, I. P., et al. (2001). Double-blind, placebo-controlled comparison of imipramine and paroxetine in the treatment of bipolar depression. *American Journal of Psychiatry, 158,* 906–909.

Neubauer, D. N. (2003). *Understanding sleeplessness: Perspectives on insomnia.* Baltimore: Johns Hopkins University Press.

Newcomb, M. D., & Bentler, P. M. (1986). Substance use and ethnicity: Differential impact of peer and adult models. *Journal of Psychology: Interdisciplinary and Applied, 120,* 83–95.

Newcorn, J. H., Spencer, T. J., Biederman, J., Milton, D. R., & Michelson, D. (2005). Atomoxetine treatment in children and adolescents with attention-deficit/hyperactivity disorder and comorbid oppositional defiant disorder. *Journal of the American Academy of Child and Adolescent Psychiatry, 44*(3), 240–248.

Newman, J. P., & Brinkley, C. A. (1998). Psychopathy: Rediscovering Cleckley's construct. *Psychopathology Research: The Newsletter of the Society for Research in Psychopathology, 9*(1), 1–5, 7–8.

Newman, M. G., Zuellig, A. R., Kachin, K. E., Constantino, M. J., Przeworksi, A., Erikson, T., et al. (2002). Preliminary reliability and validity of the Generalized Anxiety Disorder Questionnaire-IV: A revised self-report diagnostic measure of generalized anxiety disorder. *Behavior Therapy, 33,* 215–233.

Newman, S. C., & Bland, R. C. (1994). Life events and the 1-year prevalence of major depressive episode, generalized anxiety disorder, and panic disorder in a community sample. *Comprehensive Psychiatry, 35,* 76–82.

Nezu, A. M., Ronan, G. F., & Meadows, E. A. (2006). *Practitioner's guide to empirically based measures of depression.* Hoboken, NJ: Wiley.

Ngai, E. S. W., Lee, S., & Lee, A. M. (2000). The variability of phenomenology in anorexia nervosa. *Acta Psychiatrica Scandinavica, 102*(4), 314–317.

Nicholas, L. M., & Lindsey, B. A. (1995). Delirium presenting with symptoms of depression. *Psychosomatics, 36,* 471–479.

Nicholls, D., & Bryant-Waugh, R. (2003). Children and young adolescents. In J. Treasure, U. Schmidt, & E. van Furth (Eds.), *Handbook of eating disorders* (2nd ed., pp. 415–433). Chichester, West Sussex, England: Wiley.

Nicholls, D., & Stanhope, R. (2000). Medical complications of anorexia nervosa in children and young adults. *European Eating Disorders Review, 8*(2), 170–180.

Nicholson, N., & Trautman, J. (1980). *Virginia Woolf: The letters.* London: Hogarth Press.

Nickell, A. D., Waudby, C. J., & Trull, T. J. (2002). Attachment, parental bonding and borderline personality features in young adults. *Journal of Personality Disorders, 16,* 148–159.

Nielsen, S. (2001). Epidemiology and mortality of eating disorders. *Psychiatric Clinics of North America, 24*(2), 201–214.

Niemi, L. T., Suvisaari, J. M., Tuulio-Henriksson, A., & Lönnqvist, J. K. (2003). Childhood developmental abnormalities in schizophrenia: Evidence from high-risk studies. *Schizophrenia Research, 60,* 239–258.

Nigg, J. T., Blaskey, L., Huang-Pollock, C., & Rappley, M. D. (2002). Neuropsychological executive functions and ADHD DSM-IV subtypes. *Journal of the American Academy of Child and Adolescent Psychiatry, 41,* 59–66.

Nigg, J. T., & Goldsmith, H. H. (1994). Genetics of personality disorders: Perspectives from personality and psychopathology research. *Psychological Bulletin, 115,* 346–380.

Nigg, J. T., & Hinshaw, S. P. (1998). Parent personality traits and psychopathology associated with antisocial behaviors in childhood attention-deficit hyperactivity disorder. *Journal of Child Psychiatry and Human Development and Allied Disciplines, 39,* 145–159.

NIH Consensus Developmental Panel. (2000). National Institutes of Health consensus development conference statement: Diagnosis and treatment of attention-deficit/hyperactivity disorder (ADHD). *Journal of the American Academy of Child and Adolescent Psychiatry, 39,* 182–193.

Nixon, S. J. (1996). Alzheimer's disease and vascular dementia. In R. L. Adams, O. A. Parsons, J. L. Culbertson, & S. J. Nixon (Eds.), *Neuropsychology for clinical practice* (pp. 65–105). Washington, DC: American Psychological Association.

Nobile, M., Cataldo, G. M., Marino, C., & Molteni, M. (2003). Diagnosis and treatment of dysthymia in children and adolescents. *CNS Drugs, 17*, 927–946.

Noble, P., & Rodger, S. (1989). Violence by psychiatric inpatients. *British Journal of Psychiatry, 155*, 384–390.

Nocon, A., Wittchen, H. U., Pfister, H., Zimmerman, P., & Lieb, R. (2006). Dependence symptoms in young cannabis users? A prospective epidemiological study. *Journal of Psychiatric Research, 40*, 394–403.

Noel, X., Van der Linden, M., Schmidt, N., Sferrazza, R., Hanak, C., Le Bon, O., et al. (2001). Supervisory attentional system in nonamnesic alcoholic men. *Archives of General Psychiatry, 58*, 1152–1158.

Nofzinger, E. A., Buysse, D. J., Reynolds, C. F., & Kupfer, D. J. (1993). Sleep disorders related to another mental disorder (nonsubstance/primary): A DSM-IV literature review. *Journal of Clinical Psychiatry, 54*(7), 244–259.

Nolan, E. E., Volpe, R. J., Gadow, K. D., & Sprafkin, J. (1999). Developmental, gender, and comorbidity differences in clinically referred children with ADHD. *Journal of Emotional and Behavioral Disorders, 7*(1), 11–20.

Nolen, W. A., Luckenbaugh, D. A., Altshuler, L. L., Suppes, T., McElroy, S. L., Frye, M. A., et al. (2004). Correlates of 1-year prospective outcome in bipolar disorder: Results from the Stanley Foundation Bipolar Network. *American Journal of Psychiatry, 161*, 1447–1454.

Nolen-Hoeksema, S. (1987). Sex differences in unipolar depression: Evidence and theory. *Psychological Bulletin, 101*(2), 259–282.

Nonacs, R. (2005). Postpartum mood disorders. In L. S. Cohen & R. M. Nonacs (Eds.), *Mood and anxiety disorders during pregnancy and postpartum* (pp. 77–103). Washington, DC: American Psychiatric Publishing.

Nonacs, R. M., Cohen, L. S., Viguera, A. C., & Mogielnicki, J. (2005). Diagnosis and treatment of mood and anxiety disorders in pregnancy. In L. S. Cohen & R. M. Ninacs (Eds.), *Mood disorders during pregnancy and postpartum* (pp. 17–51). Washington, DC: American Psychiatric Publishing.

Norcross, J. C. (1999). Collegially validated limitations of empirically validated treatments. *Clinical Psychology: Practice and Science, 6*(4), 472–476.

Norcross, J. C. (2002a). Empirically supported therapy relationships. In J. C. Norcross (Ed.), *Psychotherapy relationships that work* (pp. 3–16). New York: Oxford University Press.

Norcross, J. C. (Ed.). (2002b). *Psychotherapy relationships that work*. New York: Oxford University Press.

Nordhus, I., Nielsen, G., & Kvale, G. (2003). Psychotherapy with older adults. In G. Stricker & T. Widiger (Eds.), *Handbook of psychology: Vol. 8. Clinical psychology*. Hoboken, NJ: Wiley.

Nordin, V., & Gillberg, C. (1998). The long-term course of autistic disorders: Update on follow up studies. *Acta Psychiatrica Scandinavica, 97*, 99–108.

Norman, R. M., & Malla, A. K. (1993). Stressful life events and schizophrenia: A review of the research. *British Journal of Psychiatry, 162*, 161–166.

Nowell, P. D., Buysse, D. J., Morin, C., Reynolds, C. F., & Kupfer, D. J. (2002). Effective treatments for selected sleep disorders. In P. E. Nathan & J. M. Gorman (Eds.), *A guide to treatments that work* (2nd ed., pp. 593–609). New York: Oxford University Press.

Nowinski, J. (2003). Facilitating 12-step recovery from substance abuse and addiction. In F. Rotgers, J. Morgenstern, & S. T. Walters (Eds.), *Treating substance abuse: Theory and technique* (pp. 31–66). New York: Guilford Press.

Noyes, R. (2001). Epidemiology of hypochondriasis. In V. Starcevic & D. R. Lipsitt (Eds.), *Hypochondriasis: Modern perspectives on an ancient malady* (pp. 127–154). New York: Oxford University Press.

Noyes, R., Kathol, R. G., Fisher, M. M., Phillips, B., Suelzer, M. T., & Woodman, C. L. (1994). Psychiatric comorbidity among patients with hypochondriasis. *General Hospital Psychiatry, 16*, 78–87.

Noyes, R., Langbehn, R., Happel, R. L., Sieren, L. R., & Muller, B. A., (1999). Health attidude survey. *Psychosomatics, 40*, 470–478.

Noyes, R., Stuart, S., Langbehn, D. R., Happel, R. L., Longley, S., Muller, B. A. et al. (2003). Test of an interpersonal model of hypochondriasis. *Psychosomatic Medicine, 65*, 292– 300.

Noyes, R., Woodman, C., Garvey, M. J., Cook, B. L., Suelzer, M., Clancy, J., et al. (1992). Generalized anxiety disorder vs. panic disorder: Distinguishing characteristics and patterns of comorbidity. *Journal of Nervous and Mental Diseases, 180*, 369–379.

Nuechterlein, K. H. (1985). Converging evidence for vigilance deficit as a vulnerability indicator for schizophrenic disorders. In A. Alpert (Ed.), *Controversies in schizophrenia: Changes and constancies* (pp. 175–198). New York: Guilford Press.

Nutt, D., Argyropoulos, S., Hood, S., & Potokar, J. (2006). Generalized anxiety disorder: A co-morbid disease. *European Neuropsychopharmacology, 16*, S109–S118.

Nyman, K. A., & Jonsson, H. (1986). Patterns of self-destructive behaviour in schizophrenia. *Acta Psychiatrica Scandinavica, 73*, 252–262.

O'Brien, C. P., Charney, D. S., Lewis, L., Cornish, J. W., Post, R. M., & Woody, G. E. (2004). Priority actions to improve the care of persons with co-occurring substance abuse and other mental disorders: A call to action. *Biological Psychiatry, 56*, 703–713.

O'Brien, K. M., & Vincent, N. K. (2003). Psychiatric comorbidity in anorexia and bulimia nervosa: Nature, prevalence, and causal relationships. *Clinical Psychology Review, 23*, 57–74.

O'Carroll, R. (1991). Sexual desire disorders: A review of controlled treatment studies. *Journal of Sex Research, 28*(4), 607–624.

O'Carroll, R. E., Moffoot, A. P., Ebmeier, K. P., & Goodwin, G. M. (1994). Effects of fluvoxamine treatment on cognitive functioning in the alcoholic Korsakoff syndrome. *Psychopharmacology, 116*, 85–88.

Ockert, D., Baier, A. R., & Coons, E. E. (2004). Treatment of stimulant dependence. In S. L. Ashenberg-Straussner (Ed.), *Clinical work with substance-abusing clients* (2nd ed., pp. 209–233). New York: Guilford Press.

O'Conner, K. J., & Braverman, L. M. (1996). *Play therapy theory and practice: A comparative presentation.* New York: Wiley.

O'Connor, K. J., & Schaefer, C. E. (1994). *Handbook of play therapy* (Wiley series on personality processes). New York: Wiley.

Odejide, A. O. (1981). Some clinical aspects of criminology: A study of criminal psychiatric patients at the Lantoro Psychiatric Institution. *Acta Psychiatrica Scandinavica, 63*, 208–224.

O'Farrell, T. J., & Fals-Stewart, W. (2003a). Alcohol abuse. *Journal of Marital and Family Therapy, 29*, 121–146.

O'Farrell, T. J., & Fals-Stewart, W. (2003b). Marital and family therapy. In R. K. Hester & W. R. Miller (Eds.), *Handbook of alcoholism treatment approaches: Effective alternatives* (3rd ed., pp. 188–212). Boston: Pearson Education.

Offord, D. R., Boyle, M. H., Campbell, D., Goering, P., Lin, E., Wong, M., et al. (1996). One-year prevalence of psychiatric disorder in Ontarians 15–64 years of age. *Canadian Journal of Psychiatry, 41*, 559–563.

Ogunniyi, A. O., Osuntokun, B. O., Lekwauwa, U. G., & Falope, Z. F. (1992). Rarity of dementia (DSM-III-R) in an urban community in Nigeria. *East African Medical Journal, 69*, 10–14.

O'Hara, M. N., Neunaber, D. J., & Zekoski, E. M. (1984). Prospective study of post-partum depression: Prevalence, course, and predictive factors. *Journal of Abnormal Psychology, 93*, 158–171.

Ohayon, M. M., & Caulet, M. (1996). Psychotropic medication and insomnia complaints in two epidemiological studies. *Canadian Journal of Psychiatry, 41*(7), 457–464.

Ohayon, M. M., Caulet, M., & Lemoine, P. (1998). Comorbidity of mental and insomnia disorders in the general population. *Comprehensive Psychiatry, 39*(4), 185–197.

Ohayon, M. M., & Okun, M. L. (2006). Occurrence of sleep disorders in the families of narcoleptic patients. *Neurology, 67*(4), 703–705.

Ohayon, M. M., Priest, R. G., Caulet, M., & Guilleminault, C. (1996). Hypnagogic and hypnopompic hallucinations: Pathological phenomena? *British Journal of Psychiatry, 169*(4), 459–467.

Ohayon, M. M., & Roth, T. (2002). Prevalence of restless legs syndrome and periodic limb movement disorder in the general population. *Journal of Psychosomatic Research, 53*(1), 547–554.

Ohayon, M. M., & Roth, T. (2003). Place of chronic insomnia in the course of depressive and anxiety disorders. *Journal of Psychiatric Research, 37*(1), 9–15.

Ohayon, M. M., & Schatzberg, A. F. (2002). Prevalence of depressive episodes with psychotic features in the general population. *American Journal of Psychiatry, 159*, 1855–1861.

Okazaki, S. (2000). Treatment delay among Asian-American patients with severe mental illness. *American Journal of Orthopsychiatry, 70*, 58–64.

O'Keefe, S., & Lavan, J. (1997). The prognostic significance of delirium in older hospital patients. *Journal of the American Geriatric Society, 45*, 174–178.

O'Keefe, S., & Lavan, J. (1999). Clinical significance of delirium subtypes in older people. *Age and Aging, 28*, 115–119.

Oldham, J. M. (2005). Personality disorders: Recent history and future directions. In J. M. Oldham, A. E. Skodol, & D. S. Bender (Eds.), *Textbook of personality disorders* (pp. 3–16). Washington, DC: American Psychiatric Publishing.

Oldham, J. M., Skodol, A. E., Kellman, H. D., Hyler, S. E., Doidge, N., Rosnick, L., et al. (1995). Comorbidity of Axis I and Axis II disorders. *American Journal of Psychiatry, 152*(4), 571–578.

O'Leary, K. D. (2002). Treatment of marital discord and coexisting depression. In S. G. Hofmann & M. C. Tompson (Eds.), *Treating chronic and severe mental disorders: A handbook of empirically supported interventions* (pp. 175–190). New York: Guilford Press.

O'Leary, K. D., Barling, J., Arias, I., Rosenbaum, A., Malone, J., & Tyree, A. (1989). Prevalence and stability of physical aggression between spouses: A longitudinal analysis. *Journal of Consulting and Clinical Psychology, 57*, 263–268.

O'Leary, K. D., & Beach, S. R. (1990). Marital therapy: A viable treatment for depression and marital discord. *American Journal of Psychiatry, 147*, 183–186.

O'Leary, K. D., & Murphy, C. (1992). Clinical issues in the assessment of spouse abuse. In R. T. Ammerman & M. Hersen (Eds.), *Assessment of family violence: A clinical and legal sourcebook* (pp. 26–46). New York: Wiley.

Olin, J., & Keatinge, C. (1997). *Rapid psychological assessment.* New York: Wiley.

Olivardia, R., Pope, H. G., Mangweth, B., & Hudson, J. I. (1995). Eating disorders in college men. *American Journal of Psychiatry, 152*(9), 1279–1285.

Ollendick, T. H. (1983). Reliability and validity of the Revised Fear Survey Schedule for Children (FSSC-R). *Behaviour Research and Therapy, 21*, 685–692.

Ollendick, T. H., Mattis, S. G., & King, N. J. (1994). Panic in children and adolescents: A review. *Journal of Child Psychology and Psychiatry, 35*, 113–134.

Olley, J. G. (2005). Curriculum and classroom structure. In F. R. Volkmar, R. Paul, A. Klin, & D. Cohen (Eds.), *Handbook of autism and pervasive developmental disorders* (3rd ed., pp. 863–881). Hoboken, NJ: Wiley.

Olson, E. J., Boeve, B. F., & Silber, M. H. (2000). Rapid eye movement sleep behaviour disorder: Demographic, clinical and laboratory findings in 93 cases. *Brain: A Journal of Neurology, 123*(2), 331–339.

O'Malley, S., Adamse, M., Heaton, R. K., & Gawin, F. H. (1992). Neuropsychological impairment in chronic cocaine abusers. *American Journal of Drug and Alcohol Abuse, 18*, 131–144.

O'Neal, J. H., Talaga, M. C., & Preston, J. D. (2002). *Handbook of clinical psychopharmacology for therapists* (3rd ed.). Oakland, CA: New Harbinger.

O'Neill, R. M., & Bornstein, R. F. (2001). The dependent patient in psychiatric inpatient setting: Relationship of interpersonal dependency to consultation and medication frequencies. *Journal of Clinical Psychology, 57*, 289–298.

Opjordsmoen, S. (1991). Long-term clinical outcome of schizophrenia with special reference to gender differences. *Acta Psychiatrica Scandinavica, 83*, 307–313.

Oquendo, M. A., Malone, K. M., & Mann, J. J. (1997). Suicide: Risk factors and prevention in refractory major depression. *Depression and Anxiety, 5,* 202–211.

Oregon Social Learning Center Program (OSLC). (2007). Retrieved September 20, 2007, from www.oslc.org.

Organista, P. B., Organista, K. C., & Kurasaki, K. (2003). The relationship between acculturation and ethnic minority mental health. In K. M. Chun, P. B. Organista, & G. Marín (Eds.), *Acculturation: Advances in theory, measurement, and applied research* (pp. 139–161). Washington, DC: American Psychological Association.

Orr, S., & Miller, C. (1995). Maternal depressive symptoms and the risk of poor pregnancy outcome: Review of the literature and preliminary findings. *Epidemiologic Reviews, 17,* 165–171.

Orr, W. C. (1997). Obstructive sleep apnea: Natural history and varieties of the clinical presentation. In M. R. Pressman & W. C. Orr (Eds.), *Understanding sleep: The evaluation and treatment of sleep disorders* (pp. 267–281). Washington, DC: American Psychological Association.

Orsmond, G., Krauss, M. W., & Seltzer, M. M. (2004). Peer relationships and social and recreational activities among adolescents and adults with autism. *Journal of Autism and Developmental Disorders, 24,* 247–257.

Ortmeyer, I. S. (2001). Individual psychotherapy: A long journey of growth and change. In B. P. Kinoy (Ed.), *Eating disorders: New directions in treatment and recovery* (2nd ed., pp. 133–147). New York: Columbia University Press.

Oscar-Berman, M., Kirkley, S. M., Gansler, D. A., & Couture, A. (2004). Comparisons of Korsakoff and non-Korsakoff alcoholics on neuropsychological tests of prefrontal brain functioning. *Alcoholism Clinical and Experimental Research, 667–675.*

O'Shea, B. (2003). Factitious disorders: The baron's legacy. *International Journal of Clinical Practice, 7,* 33–39.

Oshodi, A., Bangaru, R., & Benbow, J. (2005). A paranoid migrant family: Folie à famille. *Irish Journal of Psychological Medicine, 22,* 26–29.

Oslin, D. W., Pettinati, H., & Volpicelli, J. R. (2002). Alcoholism treatment adherence: Older age predicts better adherence and drinking outcomes. *American Journal of Geriatric Psychiatry, 10,* 740–747.

Öst, L.-G. (1987). Age of onset in different phobias. *Journal of Abnormal Psychology, 96,* 223–229.

Öst, L.-G. (1991). Acquisition of blood and injection phobia and anxiety response patterns in clinical patients. *Behaviour Research and Therapy, 29,* 323–332.

Öst, L.-G., Fellenius, J., & Sterner, U. (1991). Applied tension, exposure in vivo, and tension-only in the treatment of blood phobia. *Behaviour Research and Therapy, 29,* 561–574.

Öst, L.-G., Sterner, U., & Fellenius, J. (1989). Applied tension, applied relaxation, and the combination in the treatment of blood phobia. *Behaviour Research and Therapy, 27,* 109–121.

Öst, L.-G., Sterner, U., & Lindahl, I.-L. (1984). Physiological responses in blood phobics. *Behaviour Research and Therapy, 22,* 109–117.

Oster, G. D., & Gould, P. (1987). *Using drawings in assessment and therapy: A guide for mental health professionals.* New York: Brunner-Routledge.

Osterling, J., & Dawson, G. (1994). Early recognition of children with autism: A study of first birthday home videotapes. *Journal of Autism and Developmental Disorders, 24*(3), 247–258.

Osterling, J., Dawson, G., & McPartland, J. (2001). Autism. In C. E. Walker & M. C. Roberts (Eds.), *Handbook of clinical child psychology* (3rd ed., pp. 432–452). New York: Wiley.

Ota, M., Mizukhami, K., Katano, T., Sato, S., Takeda, T., & Asada, T. (2003). A case of delusional disorder, somatic type with remarkable improvement of clinical symptoms and single photon emission computed tomograpy findings following modified electroconvulsive therapy. *Progress in Neuro-Psychopharmacology and Biological Psychiatry, 27,* 881–884.

Othmer, E., & Othmer, S. C. (1989). *The clinical interview using the DSM-III-R.* Washington, DC: American Psychiatric Press.

Othmer, E., & Othmer, S. C. (2002a). *The clinical interview using the DSM-IV: Vol. 1. Fundamentals* (2nd ed.). Washington, DC: American Psychiatric Press.

Othmer, E., & Othmer, S. C. (2002b). *The clinical interview using the DSM-IV: Vol. 2. The difficult patient.* Washington, DC: American Psychiatric Press.

Otto, R. K. (1992). Prediction of dangerous behavior: A review and analysis of second generation research. *Forensic Reports, 5,* 103–133.

Ottosson, H., Ekselius, L., Grann, M., & Kullgren, G. (2002). Cross-system concordance of personality disorders diagnoses of DSM-IV and diagnostic criteria for research of ICD-10. *Journal of Personality Disorders, 16*(3), 283–292.

Ouimette, P. C., Ahrens, C., Moos, R. H., & Finney, J. W. (1997). Posttraumatic stress disorder in substance abuse patients: Relationship to 1-year posttreatment outcomes. *Psychology of Addictive Behaviors, 11,* 34–41.

Ouimette, P. C., Finney, J. W., & Moos, R. H. (1999). Two-year post-treatment functioning and coping of substance abuse patients with posttraumatic stress disorder. *Psychology of Addictive Behaviors, 13,* 105–114.

Ouimette, P. C., Moos, R. H., & Finney, J. W. (2003). PTSD treatment and 5-year remission among patients with substance use and posttraumatic stress disorders. *Journal of Consulting and Clinical Psychology, 71,* 410–414.

Overall, J. E., & Gorham, D. R. (1962). The Brief Psychiatric Rating Scale. *Psychological Reports, 10,* 799–812.

Owen, C., Tarantello, C., Jones, M., & Tennant, C. (1998). Violence and aggression in psychiatric units. *Psychiatric Services, 49,* 1452–1457.

Owens, J., & Hoza, B. (2003). Diagnostic utility of the DSM-IV-TR symptoms in the prediction of DSM-IV-TR ADHD subtypes and ODD. *Journal of Attention Disorders, 7*(1), 11–27.

Oxford, M., Cavell, T. A., & Hughes, J. N. (2003). Callous-unemotional traits moderate the relation between ineffective parenting and child externalizing problems: A partial replication and extention. *Journal of Clinical Child and Adolescent Psychology, 32,* 577–585.

Ozonoff, S., Dawson, G., & McPartland, J. (2002). *A parent's guide to Asperger syndrome and high functioning autism.* New York: Guilford Press.

Ozonoff, S., Goodlin-Jones, B., & Solomon, M. (2005). Evidence-based assessment of autism spectrum disorders in children and adolescents. *Journal of Child and Adolescent Psychology, 34*(3), 523–540.

Ozonoff, S., South, M., & Miller, J. (2000). DSM-IV-defined Asperger's syndrome: Cognitive, behavioral and early history differentiation from high-functioning autism. *Autism, 4,* 29–46.

Ozonoff, S., South, M., & Provencal, S. (2005). Executive functions. In F. R. Volkmar, R. Paul, A. Klin, & D. Cohen (Eds.), *Handbook of autism and pervasive developmental disorders.* (3rd ed., pp. 606–627). Hoboken, NJ: Wiley.

Paelecke-Habermann, V., Pohl, J., & Leplow, B. (2005). Attention and executive functions in remitted major depression patients. *Journal of Affective Disorders, 89,* 125–135.

Pagani, L., & Pinard, G. F. (2001). Clinical assessment of dangerousness: An overview of the literature. In L. Pagani & G. F. Pinard (Eds.), *Clinical assessment of dangerousness: Empirical contributions* (pp. 1–22). Cambridge: Cambridge University Press.

Page, M., Wilson, B. A., Shiel, A., Carter, G., & Norris, D. (2006). What is the locus of the errorless-learning advantage? *Neuropsychologia, 44,* 90–100.

Pagnin, D., de Queiroz, V., Pini, S., & Cassano, G. B. (2004). Efficacy of ECT in depression: A meta-analytic review. *Journal of ECT, 20,* 13–20.

Paleacu, D., Mazeh, D., Mirecki, I., Even, M., & Barak, Y. (2002). Donepezil for the treatment of behavioral symptoms in patients with Alzheimer's disease. *Clinical Neuropharmacolgy, 25,* 313–317.

Pallanti, S., Quercioli, L., & Hollander, E. (2004). Social anxiety in outpatients with schizophrenia: A relevant cause of disability. *American Journal of Psychiatry, 16,* 53–58.

Palmer, B., Dunn, L. B., Applebaum, P. S., & Jeste, D. V. (2004). Correlates of treatment-related decision making capacity among middle aged and older patients with schizophrenia. *Archives of General Psychiatry, 61,* 230–236.

Paludszny, M., Davenport, C., & Kim, W. J. (1991). Suicide attempts and ideation: Adolescents evaluated on a pediatric ward. *Adolescence, 26*, 209–215.

Pan, H. S., Neidig, P. H., & O'Leary, K. D. (1994). Predicting mild and severe husband-to-wife physical aggression. *Journal of Consulting and Clinical Psychology, 62*, 975–981.

Pandina, R. J., & Johnson, V. L. (1999). Why people use, abuse, and become dependent on drugs: Progress toward a heuristic model. In M. D. Glantz & C. R. Hartel (Eds.), *Drug abuse: Origins and Interventions* (pp. 119–147). Washington, DC: American Psychological Association.

Panisset, M., Roudier, M., Saxton, J., & Boller, F. (1994). Severe impairment battery: A neuropsychological test for severely demented patients. *Archives of Neurology, 51*, 41–45.

Pankratz, L. (1999). Factitious disorders and factitious disorder by proxy. In S. Netherton, D. Holmes, & C. E. Walker (Eds.), *Child and adolescent psychological disorders: A comprehensive textbook* (pp. 304–319). New York: Oxford University Press.

Papolos, D., & Papolos, J. (1999). *The bipolar child.* New York: Broadway Books.

Pardini, D. A., & Lochman, J. (2003). Treatments for oppositional defiant disorder. In M. A. Reinecke, F. M. Dattilio, & A. Freeman (Eds.), *Cognitive therapy with children and adolescents: A case book for clinical practice* (2nd ed., pp. 43–69). New York: Guilford Press.

Pardini, D. A., Lochman, J. E., & Frick, J. P. (2003). Callous/unemotional traits and social cognitive processes in adjudicated youth. *Journal of the American Academy of Child and Adolescent Psychiatry, 42*, 364–371.

Paris, J. (1997). Antisocial and borderline personality disorders: Two separate diagnoses or two aspects of the same psychopathology? *Comprehensive Psychiatry, 38*, 237–242.

Paris, J. (1999). Borderline personality disorder. In T. Millon, P. H. Blarney, & R. D. Davis (Eds.), *Oxford textbook of psychopathology* (pp. 625–652). New York: Oxford University Press.

Paris, J. (2000). Childhood precursors of borderline personality disorder. *Psychiatric Clinics of North America, 23*, 77–88.

Paris, J. (2001). Psychosocial adversity. In J. J. Magnavita (Ed.), *Handbook of personality: Theory and practice* (pp. 231–241). New York: Wiley.

Paris, J. (2002a). Chronic suicidality among patients with borderline personality disorder. *Psychiatric Services, 53*, 738–742.

Paris, J. (2002b). Clinical practice guidelines for borderline personality disorder. *Journal of Personality Disorders, 16*, 107–108.

Paris, J. (2003). Personality disorders over time: Precursors, course and outcome. *Journal of Personality Disorders, 17*(6), 479–488.

Paris, J. (2004a). Psychosocial adversity. In J. J. Magnavita (Ed.), *Handbook of personality: Theory and practice* (pp. 231–241). Hoboken, NJ: Wiley.

Paris, J. (2004b). Sociocultural factors in the treatment of personality disorders In J. J. Magnavita (Ed.), *Handbook of personality: Theory and practice* (pp. 135–147). Hoboken, NJ: Wiley.

Paris, J. (2005). A current integrative perspective of personality disorders. In J. M. Oldham, A. E. Skodol, & D. S. Bender (Eds.), *Textbook of personality disorders* (pp. 119–128). Washington, DC: American Psychiatric Publishing.

Paris, J., & Zweig-Frank, H. (2001). The 27-year follow-up of patients with borderline personality disorder. *Comprehensive Psychiatry, 42*, 482–487.

Paris, M., Añez, L. M., Begregal, L. E., Andrés-Hyman, R. C., & Davidson, L. (2005). Help seeking and satisfaction among Latinas: The roles of setting, ethnic identity, and therapeutic alliance. *Journal of Community Psychology, 33*, 299–312.

Parker, G., & Hadzi-Pavlovic, D. (2001). Is any female preponderance in depression secondary to a primary female preponderance in anxiety disorders? *Acta Psychiatrica Scandinavica, 103*, 252–256.

Parker, G., Roussos, J., Eyers, K., Wilhem, K., Mitchell, P., & Hadzi-Pavlovic, D. (1997). How distinct is "distinct" quality of mood? *Psychological Medicine, 27*, 445–453.

Parker, G., Roy, K., Wilhelm, K., & Mitchell, P. (2001). Assessing the comparative effectiveness of antidepressant therapies: A prospective clinical practice study. *Journal of Clinical Psychiatry, 62,* 117–125.

Parks, G. A., Anderson, B. K., & Marlatt, A. G. (2004). Cognitive-behavioral alcohol treatment. In N. Heather & T. Stockwell (Eds.), *The essential handbook of treatment and prevention of alcohol problems* (pp. 87–104). Hoboken, NJ: Wiley.

Partonen, T., & Lönnqvist, J. (1998). Seasonal affective disorder: A guide to diagnosis and management. *CNS Drugs, 9,* 203–212.

Patatanian, E., & Gales, M. A. (2005). The future of statins: Alzheimer's disease? *Consultant Pharmacologist, 20,* 663–673.

Patel, D. R., Greydanus, D. E., Pratt, H. D., & Phillips, E. L. (2003). Eating disorders in adolescent athletes. *Journal of Adolescent Research, 18*(3), 280–296.

Paternite, C. E., Loney, J., & Roberts, M. A. (1996). A preliminary validation of the subtypes of DSM-IV attention-deficit/hyeractivity disorder. *Journal of Attention Disorders, 1,* 70–86.

Patterson, G. R. (1982). *Coercive family process.* Eugene, OR: Castalia.

Patterson, G. R. (1986). Performance models for antisocial boys. *American Psychologist, 41,* 432–444.

Patterson, G. R., Capaldi, D. M., & Bank, L. (1991). An early starter model for predicting delinquency. In D. J. Pepler & K. H. Rubin (Eds.), *The development and treatment of childhood aggression* (pp. 139–168). Hillsdale, NJ: Elbaum.

Patterson, G. R., DeGarmo, D. S., & Knutson, N. (2000). Hyperactive and antisocial behaviors: Comorbid or two points in the same process? *Development and Psychopathology, 12,* 91–106.

Patterson, G. R., Reid, J. B., & Dishion, T. J. (1992). *Antisocial boys.* Eugene, OR: Castalia.

Patterson, W. M., Dohn, H. H., Bird, J., & Patterson, G. A. (1983). Evaluations of suicidal patients: The SAD PERSONS scale. *Psychometrics, 24*(4), 343–349.

Patton, G. C., Coffey, C., Carlin, J. B., Degenhardt, L., Lynskey, M. T., & Hall, W. D. (2002). Cannabis use and mental health in young people: Cohort study. *British Medical Journal, 325,* 1195–1198.

Paul, G. L. (1967). Strategy of outcome research in psychotherapy. *Journal of Consulting Psychology, 31,* 109–119.

Paul, R. (2005). Assessing communication in autism spectrum disorders. In F. R. Volkmar, R. Paul, A. Klin, & D. Cohen (Eds.), *Handbook of autism and pervasive developmental disorders* (3rd ed., pp. 799–816). Hoboken, NJ: Wiley.

Paul, R., & Sutherland, D. (2005). Enhancing early language in children with autism spectrum disorder. In F. R. Volkmar, R. Paul, A. Klin, & D. Cohen (Eds.), *Handbook of autism and pervasive developmental disorders* (3rd ed., pp. 946–976). Hoboken, NJ: Wiley.

Paykel, E. S. (1995). Psychotherapy, medication combinations and compliance. *Journal of Clinical Psychiatry, 56,* 24–30.

Paykel, E. S. (2003). Affective disorders and life events. *Acta Psychiatrica Scandinavica, 108,* 61–66.

Pearce, J. M. S. (2004). Richard Morton: Origins of anorexia nervosa. *European Neurology, 52*(4), 191–192.

Pearlstein, T. (2002). Eating disorders and comorbidity. *Archives of Women's Mental Health, 4*(3), 67–78.

Pearson, J. L., Teri, L., Reifler, B. V., & Raskind, M. A. (1989). Functional status and cognitive impairment in Alzheimer's patients with and without depression. *Journal of the American Geriatrics Society, 37,* 1117–1121.

Pechnick, R. N., & Ungerleider, J. T. (2004). Hallucinogens. In M. Galanter & H. D. Kleber (Eds.), *The American Psychiatric Publishing textbook of substance abuse treatment* (3rd ed., pp. 199–209). Washington, DC: American Psychiatric Publishing.

Peck, R. C. (1968). Psychological development in the second half. In B. L. Neugarten (Ed.), *Middle age and aging: A reader in social psychology* (pp. 88–92). Chicago: University of Chicago Press.

Pecknold, J. C. (1993). Discontinuation reactions to alprazolam in panic. *Journal of Psychiatric Research, 27,* 155–170.

Pederson, P. B., & Ivey, A. E. (1993). *Culture centered counseling and interviewing skills.* Westport, CN: Praeger.

Peet, M. (1994). Induction of mania with selective serotonin reuptake inhibitors and tricyclic antidepressants. *British Journal of Psychiatry, 164,* 549–550.

Pehlivanturk, B., & Unal, F. (2002). Conversion disorder in children and adolescents: A 4-year follow-up study. *Journal of Psychosomatic Research, 52,* 187–191.

Pelham, W. E., Fabiano, G. A., Gnagy, E. M., Greiner, A. R., & Hoza, B. (2005). The role of summer treatment programs in the context of comprehensive treatment for attention-deficit/ hyperactivity disorder. In E. D. Hibbs & P. S. Jensen (Eds.), *Psychosocial treatments for child and adolescent disorders: Empirically based strategies for clinical practice* (2nd ed., pp. 377–409). Washington, DC: American Psychological Association.

Pelham, W. E., Fabino, G. A., & Massetti, G. M. (2005). Evidence-based assessment of attention-deficit/hyperactivity disorder in children and adolescents. *Journal of Clinical Child and Adolescent Psychology, 34,* 449–476.

Pelham, W. E., Greiner, A. R., & Gnagy, E. M. (1997). *Summer treatment program manual.* Buffalo, NY: Comprehensive Treatment for Attention Deficit Disorders.

Pelham, W. E., & Lang, A. R. (1999). Can your children drive you to drink? Stress and parenting in adults interacting with children with ADHD. *Alcohol Research and Health: Journal of the National Institute on Alcohol Abuse and Alcoholism, 23,* 292–298.

Pelham, W. E., Jr., Wheeler, T., & Chronis, A. (1998). Empirically supported psychosocial treatments for attention deficit hyperactivity disorder. *Journal of Clinical Child Psychology, 27*(2), 190–205.

Pennington, B. F., & Ozonoff, S. (1996). Executive functions and developmental psychopathologies. *Journal of Child Psychology and Psychiatry, 37,* 51–87.

Perkins, D. (1999). Adherence to antipsychotic medications. *Journal of Clinical Psychiatry, 60*(Suppl. 21), 25–30.

Perkins, D. (2002). Predictors of noncompliance in patients with schizophrenia. *Journal of Clinical Psychiatry, 63*(12), 1121–1128.

Perlis, M. L., McCall, W. V., Krystal, A. D., & Walsh, J. K. (2004). Long-term, non-nightly administration of zolpidem in the treatment of patients with primary insomnia. *Journal of Clinical Psychiatry, 65*(8), 1128–1137.

Perlis, R. H., Miyahara, S., Marangell, L. B., Wisniewski, M. O., Ostacher, M., DelBello, M. P., et al. (2004). Long-term implications of early onset bipolar disorder: Data from the first 1,000 participants in the Systematic Treatment Enhancement Program for Bipolar Disorder (STEP-BD). *Biological Psychiatry, 55,* 875–881.

Perquin, C. W., Hazebroek-Kampscheur, A. A., Hunfeld, J. A., van Suijlekom-Smit, L. W., Passchier, J., & Koes, B. W. (2003). The natural course of chronic benign pain in childhood and adolescence: A 2-year population-based follow-up study. *European Journal of Pain, 7,* 551–559.

Perquin, C. W., Hunfeld, J. A., Hazebroek-Kampscheur, A. A., van Suijlekom-Smit, L. W., Passchier, J., & van der Wouden, J. C. (2000). Chronic pain among children and adolescents: Physician consultation and medication use. *Clinical Journal of Pain, 16,* 229–235.

Perry, E. K. (1980). The cholinergic system in old age and Alzheimer's disease. *Age and Ageing, 9,* 1–8.

Perry, J. C. (1993). Longitudinal studies of personality disorders. *Journal of Personality Disorders, 7*(Suppl.), 63–85.

Perry, J. C. (2001). A pilot study of defenses in adults with personality disorders entering psychotherapy. *Journal of Nervous and Mental Diseases, 189,* 651–660.

Perry, J. C., Banon, E., & Ianni, F. (1999). Effectiveness of psychotherapy for personality disorders. *American Journal of Psychiatry, 156*(9), 1312–1321.

Perry, J. C., & Bond, M. (2000). Empirical studies of psychotherapy for personality disorders. In J. G. Gunderson & G. O. Gabbard (Eds.), *Psychotherapy for personality disorders* (pp. 1–31). Washington, DC: American Psychiatric Press.

Perry, J. C., & Klerman, G. L. (1978). Clinical features of borderline personality disorder. *American Journal of Psychiatry, 137*, 165–173.

Perry, P. (1996). Pharmacotherapy for major depression with melancholic features: Relative efficacy of tricyclic versus selective serotonin reuptake inhibitor antidepressants. *Journal of Affective Disorders, 39*, 1–6.

Perry, R. J., & Hodges, J. R. (1999). Attention and executive deficits in Alzheimer's disease: A critical review. *Brain, 122*, 383–404.

Persons, J. B. (1989). *Cognitive therapy in practice: A case formulation approach.* New York: Norton.

Peskind, E. R., Potkin, S. G., Pomara, N., Ott, B. R., Graham, S. M., Olin, J. T., et al. (2005). Memantine treatment in mild to moderate Alzheimer disease: A 24-week randomized, controlled trial. *American Journal of Geriatric Psychiatry, 14*, 704–715.

Petersen, R. C., Smith, G. E., Waring, S. C., Ivnik, R. J., Tangalos, E. G., & Kokmen, E. (1999). Mild cognitive impairment: Clinical characterisation and outcome. *Archives of Neurology, 56*, 303–308.

Peterson, C. B., & Mitchell, J. E. (1999). Psychosocial and pharmacological treatment of eating disorders: A review of research findings. *Journal of Clinical Psychology, 55*, 685–697.

Petrillo, L. F., Nonacs, R., Viguera, A. C., & Cohen. L. S. (2005). Course of psychiatric illness during pregnancy and the post-partum. In J. M. Oldham, M. B. Riba (Eds.), *Review of psychiatry: Vol. 24 Mood and anxiety disorders during pregnancy and postpartum* (pp. 1–15). Washington, DC: American Psychiatric Publishing.

Petry, N. M., Martin, B., Cooney, J. L., & Kranzler, H. R. (2000). Give them prizes and they will come: Contingency management for treatment of alcohol dependence. *Journal of Consulting and Clinical Psychology, 68*, 250–257.

Petty, D. M. (1990). Respite care: A flexible response to service fragmentation. In N. L. Mace (Ed.), *Dementia care: Patient, family and community* (pp. 243–269). Baltimore: Johns Hopkins University Press.

Petty, F., Kramer, G. L., Fulton, M., Moeller, F. G., & Rush, A. J. (1993). Low plasma GABA is a trait-like marker for bipolar illness. *Neuropsychopharmacology, 9*, 125–132.

Petty, F., & Sherman, A. D. (1984). Plasma GABA levels in psychiatric illness. *Journal of Affective Disorders, 6*, 131–138.

Pfohl, B., Blum, N., & Zimmerman, M. (1995). *The structured interview for the DSM-IV Personality: SIDP-IV.* Iowa City: University of Iowa.

Pfohl, B., Blum, N., & Zimmerman, M. (1997). *Structured interview for DSM-IV personality.* Washington, DC: American Psychiatric Press.

Phares, E. J. (1992). *Clinical psychology: Concepts, methods, and profession.* Pacific Grove, CA: Brooks-Cole.

Phelan, J. C., Link, B. G., Stueve, A., & Pescosolido, B. A. (2000). Public conceptions of mental illness in 1950 and 1996: Has sophistication increased? Has stigma declined? *Journal of Health and Social Behavior, 41*, 188–207.

Phillips, B. K., Ingram, M. V., & Grammer, G. C. (2004). Wernicke-Korsakoff syndrome and galantamine. *Psychosomatics, 45*, 366–368.

Phillips, K. A. (2000). Body dysmorphic disorder: Diagnostic controversies and treatment challenges. *Bulletin of the Menninger Clinic, 64*(1), 18–35.

Phillips, K. A. (2001). Body dysmorphic. In K. A. Phillips (Ed.), *Somatoform, and factitious disorders* (pp. 67–94). Washington, DC: American Psychiatric Publishing.

Phillips, K. A., Albertini, R. S., Siniscalchi, J. M., Khan, A., & Robinson, M. (2001). Effectiveness of pharmacotherapy for body dysmorphic disorder: A chart review study. *Journal of Clinical Psychiatry, 62*(9), 721–727.

Phillips, K. A., First, M. B., & Pincus, H. A. (Eds.). (2003). *Advancing DSM: Dilemmas in psychiatric diagnosis.* Washington, DC: American Psychiatric Association.

Phillips, K. A., & McElroy, S. L. (2000). Personality disorders and traits in patients with body dysmorphic disorder. *Comprehensive Psychiatry, 41*(4), 229–236.

Phillips, K. A., McElroy, S. L., Keck, P. E., Hudson, J. I., & Pope, H. G. (1994). A comparison of delusional and nondelusional body dysmorphic disorder in 100 cases. *Psychopharmacology Bulletin, 30*(2), 179–186.

Phillips, K. A., & Menard, W. (2006). Suicidality in body dysmorphic disorder: A prospective study. *American Journal of Psychiatry, 163*, 1280–1282.

Phillips, K. A., Menard, W., Fay, C., & Pagano, M. E. (2005). Psychosocial functioning and quality of life in body dysmorphic disorder. *Comprehensive Psychiatry, 46*(4), 254–260.

Phillips, L. R. (1987). The relationship between confusion and abuse. In H. J. Altman (Ed.), *Alzheimer's disease problems: Prospects and perspectives* (pp. 219–223). New York: Plenum Press.

Physician's desk reference. (2005). (60th ed.). Stamford, CT: Wadsworth/Thomson Learning.

Physician's desk reference. (2006). (61st ed.). Stamford, CT: Wadsworth/Thomson Learning.

Pickles, A., Starr, E., Kazak, S., Bolton, P., Papanikolau, K., Bailey, A. J., et al. (2000). Variable expression of the autism broader phenotype: Findings from extended pedigrees. *Journal of Child Psychology and Psychiatry, 41*, 491–502.

Pigott, T. A., Carson, W. H., Saha, A. R., Torbeyns, A. F., Stock, E. G., Ingenito, G. G., et al. (2003). Aripiprazole for the prevention of relapse in stabilized patients with chronic schizophrenia: A placebo-controlled 26-week study. *Clinical Psychiatry, 64*, 1048–1056.

Pilcher, J. J., & Huffcutt, A. J. (1996). Effects of sleep deprivation on performance: A meta-analysis. *Sleep: Journal of Sleep Research and Sleep Medicine, 19*(4), 318–326.

Pillemer, K. A. (1986). Risk factors in elder abuse: Results from a case control study. In K. A. Pillemer & R. Wold (Eds.), *Elder abuse: Conflict in the family* (pp. 239–263). Dover, MA: Auburn House.

Pillmann, F., Balzuweit, S., Haring, A., Bloink, R., & Marneros, A. (2003). Suicidal behavior in acute and transient psychotic disorders *Psychiatry Research, 117*, 199–209.

Pillmann, F., Haring, A., Balzuweit, S., Bloink, R., & Marneros, A. (2002). The concordance of ICD-10 acute and transient psychosis and DSM-IV brief psychotic disorder. *Psychological Medicine, 32*, 525–533.

Pillmann, F., & Marneros, A. (2005). Longitudinal follow-up in acute and transient psychotic disorders and schizophrenia. *British Journal of Psychiatry, 187*, 286–287.

Pillon, B., Deweer, B., Agid, R., & DuBois, B. (1993). Explicit memory in Alzheimer's, Huntington's, and Parkinson's diseases. *Archives of Neurology, 50*, 374–379.

Pillow, D. R., Pelham, W. E., Hoza, B., Molina, B. S. G., & Schultz, C. H. (1998). Confirmatory factor analyses examining attention deficit hyperactivity disorder symptoms and other hildhood disruptive behaviors. *Journal of Abnormal Child Psychology, 26*, 293–309.

Pilowsky, I. (1967). Dimensions of hypochondriasis. *British Journal of Psychiatry, 113*, 89–93.

Pilowsky, I. (2001). Hypochondriasis, abnormal illness behavior, and social context. In V. Starcevic & D. R. Lipsitt (Eds.), *Hypochondriasis: Modern perspectives on an ancient malady* (pp. 249–264). New York: Oxford University Press.

Pina, A., Silverman, W. K., Alfano, C. A., & Saavedra, L. (2002). Diagnostic efficiency of symptoms in the diagnosis of DSM-IV generalized anxiety disorder in youth. *Journal of Child Psychology and Psychiatry, 43*, 959–967.

Pinard, G. F., & Pagani, L. (2001). Discussion and clinical commentary on issues in the assessment and prediction of dangerousness. In L. Pagani & G. F. Pinard (Eds.), *Clinical assessment of dangerousness: Empirical contributions* (pp. 258–278). Cambridge: Cambridge University Press.

Pincus, A. L., & Wilson, K. R. (2001). Interpersonal variability in dependent personality. In L. Pervin & O. John (Eds.) *Handbook of personality* (pp. 251–276). New York: Guilford Press.

Pini, S., Cassano, G. B., Savino, M., Russo, A., & Montgomery, S. A. (1997). Prevalence of anxiety disorders comorbidity in bipolar depression, unipolar depression and dysthymia. *Journal of Affective Disorders, 42*, 145–153.

Piper, W. E., & Joyce, A. S. (2001). Psychosocial treatment outcome. In W. J. Livesley (Ed.), *Handbook of personality disorders: Theory, research and treatment* (pp. 323–343). New York: Guilford Press.

Piper, W. E., McCallum, M., Joyce, A. S., Azim, H. F., & Ogrodnickzuk, J. S. (1999). Follow-up findings for interpretive and supportive forms of psychotherapy and patient personality variables. *Journal of Consulting and Clinical Psychology, 67*, 267–273.

Piper, W. E., & Ogrondniczuk, J. S. (2005). Group treatment. In J. M. Oldham, A. E. Skodol, & D. S. Bender (Eds.), *Textbook of personality disorders* (pp. 347–373). Washington, DC: American Psychiatric Publishing.

Pipes, R. B., & Davenport, D. S. (1990). *Introduction to psychotherapy: Common clinical wisdom*. Englewood Cliffs, NJ: Prentice-Hall.

Pirke, K. M. (1996). Central and peripheral noradrenalin regulation in eating disorders. *Psychiatry Research, 62*(1), 43–49.

Pirooz Sholevar, G. (2005). Family therapy. In J. M. Oldham, A. E. Skodol, & D. S. Bender (Eds.), *Textbook of personality disorders* (pp. 359–374). Washington, DC: American Psychiatric Publishing.

Piven, J., Harper, J., Palmer, P., & Arndt, S. (1996). Course of behavioral change in autism: A retrospective study of high IQ adolescents and adults. *Journal of the American Academy of Child and Adolescent Psychiatry, 35*, 523–529.

Pliszka, S. R. (1999). The psychobiology of oppositional defiant disorder and conduct disorder. In H. C. Quay & A. E. Hogan (Eds.), *Handbook of disruptive behavior disorders* (pp. 371–395). New York: Kluwer Academic/Plenum Press.

Pliszka, S. R., Greenhill, L. L., Crismon, M. L., Sedillo, A., Carson, C., Conners, C. K., et al. (2000a). The Texas Children's Medication Algorithm Project: Report of the Texas Consensus Conference panel on medication treatment of childhood attention-deficit/hyperactivity disorder: Pt. I. Attention-deficit/hyperactivity disorder. *Journal of the American Academy Child and Adolescent Psychiatry, 39*, 908–919.

Pliszka, S. R., Greenhill, L. L., Crismon, M. L., Sedillo, A., Carlson, C., Conners, C. K., et al. (2000b). The Texas Children's Medication Algorithm Project: Report of the Texas Consensus Conference panel on medication treatment of childhood attention-deficit/hyperactivity disorder: Pt. II. Tactics. *Journal of the American Academy Child and Adolescent Psychiatry, 39*, 920–927.

Plutchik, R., & van Praag, H. M. (1995). The nature of impulsivity: Definitions, ontology, genetics, and relations to aggression. In E. Hollander & D. J. Stein (Eds.), *Impulsivity and aggression* (pp. 7–24). Chichester, West Sussex, England: Wiley.

Pobee, K. A., & LaPalio, L. R. (1996). Anorexia nervosa in the elderly: A multidisciplinary diagnosis. *Clinical Gerontologist, 16*, 3–9.

Podolski, C. L., & Nigg, J. T. (2001). Parental stress and coping in relation to child ADHD severity and associated child disruptive behavior problems. *Journal of Clinical Child Psychology, 30*, 503–513.

Pogue-Geile, M. F., & Harrow, M. (1984). Negative and positive symptoms in schizophrenia and depression: A follow-up. *Schizophrenia Bulletin, 10*, 371–387.

Pogue-Geile, M. F., & Harrow, M. (1985). Negative symptoms in schizophrenia: Their longitudinal course and prognostic importance. *Schizophrenia Bulletin, 11*, 427–439.

Polatin, P. (1975). Paranoid states. In A. M. Kaplanv, H. I. Kaplam, & B. J. Saddock (Eds.), *Comprehensive textbook of psychiatry-II* (Vol. 1, pp. 992–1002). Baltimore: Williams & Wilkins.

Polidori, M. C., Mattioli, P., Aldred, S., Cecchetti, R., Stahl, W., Griffiths, H., et al. (2004). Plasma antioxidant status, immunoglobulin g oxidation and lipid peroxidation in demented patients: Relevance to Alzheimer disease and vascular dementia. *Dementia and Geriatric Cognitive Disorders, 18*, 265–270.

Polimeni, M. A., Richdale, A. L., & Francis, A. J. P. (2005). A survey of sleep problems in autism, Asperger's disorder, and typically developing children. *Journal of Intellectual Disability Research, 49*(4), 260–268.

Polivy, J., & Herman, C. P. (2002). Causes of eating disorders. *Annual Review of Psychology, 53*, 187–213.

Polivy, J., & Herman, C. P. (2004). Sociocultural idealization of thin female body shapes: An introduction to the special issue on body image and eating disorders. *Journal of Social and Clinical Psychology, 23*(1), 1–6.

Polivy, J., Herman, C. P., & Boivin, M. (2005). Eating disorders. In J. E. Maddux & B. A. Winstead (Eds.), *Psychopathology: Foundations for a contemporary understanding* (pp. 229–254). Mahwah, NJ: Erlbaum.

Pollack, M. H., Zaninelli, R., Goddard, A., McCafferty, J. P., Bellew, K. M., Burnham, D. B. et al. (2001). Paroxetine in the treatment of generalized anxiety disorder: Results of a placebo-controlled, flexible-dosage trial. *Journal of Clinical Psychiatry, 62*, 350–357.

Pomerantz, A. M. (2005). Increasingly informed consent: Discussing distinct aspects of psychotherapy at different points in time. *Ethics and Behavior, 15*, 351–360.

Pomery, E. A., Gibbons, F. X., Gerrard, M., Cleveland, M. J., Brody, G. H., & Wills, T. A. (2005). Families and risk: Prospective analyses of familial and social influences on adolescent substance use. *Journal of Family Psychology, 19*, 560–570.

Pompili, M., Mancinelli, I., Girardi, P., Ruberto, A., & Tatarelli, R. (2004). Suicide in anorexia nervosa: A meta-analysis. *International Journal of Eating Disorders, 36*(1), 99–103.

Pope, H., McElroy, S., Keck, P., & Hudson, J. I. (1991). Valproate in the treatment of acute mania: A placebo controlled study. *Archives of General Psychiatry, 46*, 62–68.

Pope, K. S., & Vasquez, M. J. T. (2001). *Ethics in psychotherapy and counseling: A practical guide* (2nd ed.). San Francisco: Jossey-Bass.

Popper, C. W. (1997). Antidepressants in the treatment of attention-deficit/hyperactivity disorder. *Journal of Clinical Psychiatry, 58*(Suppl. 14), 14–29.

Porter, R. (1999). Mood disorders: Social section. In G. E. Berrios & R. Porter (Eds.), *A history of clinical psychiatry* (pp. 409–420). New Brunswick, NJ: Athlone Press.

Posner, M. I., Rothbart, M., Vizueta, N., Thomas, K., Levy, K., Fosella, J., et al. (2003). An approach to the psychobiology of personality disorders. *Development and Psychopathology, 15*, 1093–1106.

Post, R., Rubinow, D., & Ballenger, J. (1986). Conditioning, sensitization, and the longitudinal course of affective disorder. *British Journal of Psychiatry, 149*, 191–201.

Potenza, M. N. (2003). Should addictive disorders include non-substance-related conditions? *Addiction, 101*, 142–151.

Potkin, S. G., Saha, A. R., Kujawa, M. J., Ali, M., Stringfellow, J., & Ingenito, G., et al. (2003). Aripiprazole, an antipsychotic with a novel mechanism of action, and risperidone vs. placebo in patients with schizophrenia and schizoaffective disorder. *Archives of General Psychiatry, 60*, 681–690.

Poulton, R., Caspi, A., Moffitt, T. E., Cannon, M., Murray, R., & Harrington, H. (2000). Children's self-reported psychotic symptoms and adult schizophreniform disorder: A 15-year longitudinal study. *Archives of General Psychiatry, 57*, 1053–1058.

Powell, A. L., Cummings, J. L., Hill, M. A., & Benson, D. F. (1988). Speech and language alterations in multi-infarct dementia. *Neurology, 38*, 717–719.

Powell, J., Ewards, A., Ewards, M., Pandit, B. S., Sungum-Paliwal, S. R., & Whitehouse, W. (2000). Changes in the incidence of childhood autism and other autistic spectrum disorders in preschool children from two areas of the West Midlands. *UK Developmental Medicine and Child Neurology, 42*, 624–628.

Powell-Smith, K. A., & Stollar, S. A. (1997). Families of children with disabilities. In G. G. Bear, K. M. Minke, & A. Thomas (Eds.), *Children's needs II: Development, problems and alternatives* (pp. 667–680). Bethesda, MD: National Association of School Psychologists.

Power, M. (2004). Cognitive behavioural therapy for depression. In M. Power (Ed.), *Mood disorders: A handbook of science and practice* (pp. 167–181). Hoboken, NJ: Wiley.

Powers, P. S., Santana, C. A., & Bannon, Y. S. (2002). Olanzapine in the treatment of anorexia nervosa: An open label trial. *International Journal of Eating Disorders, 32*(2), 146–154.

Prager, S., & Jeste, D. V. (1993). Sensory impairment in late-life schizophrenia. *Schizophrenia Bulletin, 19*, 755–772.

Pratt, E. M., Niego, S. H., & Agras, W. S. (1998). Does the size of a binge matter? *International Journal of Eating Disorders, 24*(3), 307–312.

Pratt, S., & Mueser, K. T. (2002). Social skills training for schizophrenia. In S. G. Hofmann & M. C. Tompson (Eds.), *Treating chronic and severe mental disorders: A handbook of empirically supported interventions* (pp. 18–49). New York: Guilford Press.

Prendergast, M., Podus, D., Finney, J., Greenwell, L., & Roll, J. (2006). Contingency management for treatment of substance use disorders: A meta-analysis. *Addiction, 101*, 1546–1560.

Prentice, K. J., Bellack, A. S., Gold, J. M., & Carpenter, W. T. (2003). Improving decisional capacity for informed consent in schizophrenia. *Schizophrenia Research, 60*, 327–328.

Preskorn, S. H. (1995). Beyond DSM-IV: What is the cart and what is the horse? *Psychiatric Annals, 25*(1), 53–62.

Preston, P., & Goodfellow, M. (2006). Cohort comparisons: Social learning explanations for alcohol use among adolescents and older adults. *Addictive Behaviors, 31*, 2268–2283.

Pretzer, J. (2004). Cognitive therapy of personality disorders. In J. J. Magnavita (Ed.), *Handbook of personality: Theory and practice* (pp. 169–193). New York: Wiley

Preuss, U. W., & Soyka, M. (1999). Paroxetine treatment in alcohol amnestic disorder. *Journal of Neuropsychiatry and Clinical Neurosciences, 11*, 286–287.

Price, R. K., Risk, N. K., & Spitznagel, E. L. (2001). Remission from drug abuse over a 25-year period: Patterns of remission and treatment use. *American Journal of Public Health, 91*, 1107–1113.

Prichard, J. C. (1837). *A treatise on insanity and other disorders affecting the mind.* Philadelphia: Haswell, Barrington & Haswell.

Prigerson, H. G., Maciejewski, P. K., & Rosenheck, R. A. (2001). Combat trauma: Trauma with highest risk of delayed onset and unresolved posttraumatic stress disorder symptoms, unemployment, and abuse among men. *Journal of Nervous and Mental Diseases, 189*, 99–108.

Prince, J. D. (2006). Ethnicity and life quality of recently discharged inpatients with schizophrenia. *American Journal of Orthopsychiatry, 76*, 202–205.

Pringle, K. E., Ahern, F. M., Heller, D. A., Gold, C. H., & Brown, T. V. (2005). Potential for alcohol and prescription drug interactions in older people. *Journal of the American Geriatric Society, 53*, 1930–1936.

Pritts, S. D., & Susman, J. (2003). Diagnosis of eating disorders in primary care. *American Family Physician, 67*(2), 297–304.

Prizant, B. M., & Wetherby, A. M. (2005). Critical issues in enhancing communication abilities for persons with autistic spectrum disorders. In F. R. Volkmar, R. Paul, A. Klin, & D. Cohen (Eds.), *Handbook of autism and pervasive developmental disorders* (3rd ed., pp. 925–945). Hoboken, NJ: Wiley.

Prizant, B. M., Wetherby, A. M., & Rydell, P. J. (2000). Communication intervention issues for young children with autism spectrum disorders. In A. M. Wetherby & B. M. Prizant (Eds.), *Autism spectrum disorders: A transactional developmental perspective* (pp. 193–224). Baltimore: Paul H. Brookes.

Project MATCH Research Group. (1993). Project MATCH: Rationale and methods for a multisite clinical trial matching patients to alcoholism treatment. *Alcoholism: Clinical and Experimental Research, 17*, 1130–1145.

Project MATCH Research Group. (1997). Project MATCH: Secondary a-priori hypotheses. *Addiction, 92*, 1671–1698.

Project MATCH Research Group.(1998). Matching alcoholism treatments to client heterogeneity: Project MATCH 3-year drinking outcomes. *Alcoholism: Clinical and Experimental Research, 22*, 1300–1311.

Prugh, D. G., Wagonfeld, S., Metcalf, D., & Jordan, K. (1980). A clinical study of delirium in children and adolescents. *Psychosomatic Medicine, 42*, 177–195.

Pulver, S. E. (1970). Narcissism: The term and the concept. *Journal of American Psychoanalytic Association, 18*, 319–341.

Pumariega, A. J., Gustavson, C. R., Gustavson, J. C., Motes, P. S., & Ayers, S. (1994). Eating attitudes in African-American women: The Essence eating disorders survey. *Eating Disorders: Journal of Treatment and Prevention, 2*(1), 5–16.

Purdie, F. R., Honigman, B., & Rosen, P. (1981). Acute organic brain syndrome: A review of 100 cases. *Annals of Emergency Medicine, 10,* 455–461.

Purdie, N., Hattie, J., & Carroll, A. (2002). A review of the research on interventions for attention-deficit hyperactivity disorder: What works best? *Review of Educational Research, 72*(1), 61–99.

Pyne, J. M., Rost, K. M., Zhang, M., Williams, D. K., Smith, J., & Fortney, J. (2003). Cost-effectiveness of a primary care depression intervention. *Journal of General Internal Medicine,* 432–441.

Quayle, M., & Moore, E. (1998). Evaluating the impact of structured group work with men in a high security hospital. *Criminal Behavior and Mental Health, 8,* 77–92.

Quill, T. E. (1985). Somatization disorder: One of medicine's blind spots. *Journal of the American Medical Association, 254,* 3075–3079.

Quinn, P. O. (2005). Treating adolescent girls and women with ADHD: Gender-specific issues. *Journal of Clinical Psychology/In Session, 61*(5), 579–587.

Quintana, S., & Holahan, W. (1992). Termination in short-term counseling: Comparison of successful and unsuccessful cases. *Journal of Counseling Psychology, 39*(3), 299–305.

Quist, J. F., & Kennedy, J. L. (2001). Genetics of childhood disorders: XXIII. ADHD, P. 7. The serotonin system. *Journal of the American Academy of Child and Adolescent Psychiatry, 40*(2), 253–256.

Raber, J., Huang, Y., & Ashford, J. W. (2004). ApoE genotype accounts for the vast majority of AD risk and AD pathology. *Neurobiology of Aging, 25,* 641–650.

Rabins, P. V., Lyketsos, C. G., & Steele, C. (1999). *Practical dementia care.* New York: Oxford University Press.

Rachman, S. J. (1977). The conditioning theory of fear acquisition: A critical examination. *Behaviour Research and Therapy, 15,* 375–387.

Rachman, S. J., & de Silva, P. (1978). Abnormal and normal obsessions. *Behaviour Research and Therapy, 16,* 233–248.

Radant, A., Tsuang, D., Peskind, E. R., McFall, M., & Raskind, W. (2001). Biological markers and diagnostic accuracy in the genetics of posttraumatic stress disorder. *Psychiatry Research, 102,* 203–214.

Radloff, L. (1977). The CES-D scale: A self-report depression scale for research in the general population. *Applied Psychological Measurement, 1*(3), 385–401.

Rado, S. (1953). Dynamics and classification of disordered behavior. *American Journal of Psychiatry, 110,* 406–416.

Raffi, A. R., Rondini, M., Grandi, S., & Fava, G. A. (2000). Life events and prodromal symptoms in bulimia nervosa. *Psychological Medicine, 30,* 727–731.

Raine, A., Lencz, T., & Mendick, S. A. (Eds.). (1995). *Schizotypal personality.* New York: Cambridge University Press.

Raja, M., & Azzoni, A. (2004). Suicide attempts: Differences between unipolar and bipolar patients and among groups with different lethality risk. *Journal of Affective Disorders, 82,* 437–442.

Ram, R., Bromet, E. J., Eaton, W. W., Pato, C., & Schwarz, J. E. (1992). The natural course of schizophrenia: A review of first admission studies. *Schizophrenia Bulletin, 18,* 185–207.

Ramaswamy, K., Masand, P. S., & Nasrallah, H. A. (2006). Do certain atypical antipsychotics increase the risk of diabetes? A critical review of 17 pharmacoepidemiologic studies. *Annals of Clinical Psychiatry, 18,* 183–194.

Ramirez Basco, M., & Rush, J. (1995). Compliance with pharmacotherapy in mood disorders. *Psychiatric Annals, 25*(5), 269–279.

Randall, P., & Parker, J. (1999). *Supporting the families of children with autism.* New York: Wiley.

Rank, O. (1911). Ein Beitrag zum Narzissismus. *Jahrbuch fur Psychoanalytische und Psychopathologische Forschungen, 3*, 401–426.

Rapee, R., & Heimberg, R. G. (1997). A cognitive-behavioral model of anxiety in social phobia. *Behaviour Research and Therapy, 35*, 741–756.

Rapee, R. M., & Lim, L. (1992). Discrepancy between self- and observer ratings of performance in social phobics. *Journal of Abnormal Psychology, 101*, 728–731.

Rapee, R. M., McCallum, S. L., Melville, L. F., Ravenscroft, H., & Rodney, J. M. (1992). Memory bias in social phobia. *Behaviour Research and Therapy, 32*, 89–99.

Rapee, R. M., Sanderson, W. C., McCauley, P. A., & DiNardo, P. A. (1992). Differences in reported symptom profile between panic disorder and other DSM-III-R anxiety disorders. *Behavior Research and Therapy, 30*, 45–52.

Rapin, I. (2005). Autism: Where we have been, where we are going. In F. R. Volkmar, R. Paul, A. Klin, & D. Cohen (Eds.), *Handbook of autism and pervasive developmental disorders* (3rd ed., pp. 1304–1317). Hoboken, NJ: Wiley.

Rapp, S. R., Espeland, M. A., Shumaker, S. A., Henderson, V. W., Brunner, R. L., Manson, J. E., et al. (2003). Effect of estrogen plus progestin on global cognitive function in postmenopausal women: The Women's Health Initiative Memory Study: A randomized controlled trial. *Journal of the American Medical Association, 289*, 2663–2672.

Räsänen, P., Tiihonen, J., Isohanni, M., Rantakallio, P., Lehtonen, J., & Moring, J. (1998). Schizophrenia, alcohol abuse, and violent behavior: A 26-year follow-up study of an unselected birth cohort. *Schizophrenia Bulletin, 24*, 437–441.

Rasmussen, S. A., & Eisen, J. L. (1989). Clinical features and phenomenology of obsessive compulsive disorder. *Psychiatric Annals, 19*, 67–73.

Rasmussen, S. A., & Tsuang, M. T. (1986). Epidemiological and clinical findings of significance to the design or neuropharmacologic studies of obsessive compulsive disorder. *Psychopharmacological Bulletin, 22*, 723–733.

Ratey, J. J., Dymek, M. P., Fein, D., Joy, S., Green, L. A., & Waterhouse, L. (2000). Neurodevelopmental disorders. In B. S. Fogel, R. B. Schiffer, & S. M. Rao (Eds.), *Synopsis of neuropsychiatry* (pp. 245–271). Philadelphia: Lippincott, Willams & Wilkins.

Rathus, J. H., & Miller, A. L. (2002). Dialetical behavior therapy adapted for suicidal adolescents. *Suicide and Life Threatening Behavior, 32*, 146–157.

Rauch, S. L., Shin, L. M., & Phelps, E. A. (2006). Neurocircuitry models of posttraumatic stress disorder and extinction: Human neuroimaging research—Past, present, and future. *Biological Psychiatry, 60*, 376–382.

Rawson, R. A., McCann, M. J., Flammino, F., Shoptaw, S., Miotto, K., Reiber, C., et al. (2006). A comparison of contingency management and cognitive-behavioral approaches for stimulant-dependent individuals. *Addiction, 101*, 267–274.

Rayfield, A., Monaco, L., & Eyberg, S. M. (1999). Parent-child interaction therapy with oppositional children: Review and clinical strategies. In S. W. Russ & T. H. Ollendick (Eds.), *Handbook of psychotherapies with children and families* (pp. 327–343). New York: Kluwer Academic/Plenum Press.

Rea, M. M., Tompson, M. C., Miklowitz, D. J., Goldstein, M. J., Hwang, S., & Mintz, J. (2003). Family-focused treatment versus individual treatment for bipolar disorder: Results of a randomized clinical trial. *Journal of Consulting and Clinical Psychology, 71*, 482–492.

Read, J., Agar, K., Barker-Collo, S., Davies, E., & Moskowitz, A. (2001). Assessing suicidality in adults: Integrating childhood trauma as a major risk factor. *Professional Psychology: Research and Practice, 32*, 367–372.

Reamer, F. G. (2005). Update on confidentiality issues in practice with children: Ethics risk management. *Children and Schools, 27*, 117–120.

Rector, N. A., Bagby, R. M., Segal, Z. V., Joffee, R. T., & Levitt, A. (2000). Self-criticism and dependency in depressed patients treated with cognitive therapy and pharmacotherapy. *Cognitive Therapy and Research, 24*, 571–584.

Regan, C., Katona, C., Walker, Z., & Livingston, G. (2005). Relationship of exercise and other risk factors to depression of Alzheimer's disease: The LASER-AD study. *International Journal of Geriatric Psychiatry, 20*, 261–268.

Regehr, C., & Glancy, G. D. (1999). Paranoid disorders. In F. J. Turner (Ed.), *Adult psychopathology: A social work perspective* (pp. 488–506). New York: Free Press.

Regestein, Q. R., & Monk, T. H. (1995). Delayed sleep phase syndrome: A review of its clinical aspects. *American Journal of Psychiatry, 152*(44), 602–608.

Regier, D. A., Farmer, M. E., Rae, D. S., Locke, B. Z., Keith, S. J., Judd, L. L., et al. (1990). Comorbidity of mental disorders with alcohol and other drug abuse: Results from the Epidemiologic Catchment Area (ECA) Study. *Journal of the American Medical Association, 264*, 2511–2518.

Regier, D. A., Narrow, W. E., First, M. B., & Marshall, T. (2002). The APA classification of mental disorders: Future perspectives. *Psychopathology, 35*, 166–170.

Reich, A. (1960). Pathological forms of self-esteem regulation. *Psychoanalytic Study of the Child, 15*, 215–232.

Reich, J. (2000). The relationship of social phobia to avoidant personality disorder: A proposal to reclassify avoidant personality disorder based on clinical empirical findings. *European Psychiatry, 15*, 151–159.

Reich, J. (2003). The effect of Axis II disorders on the outcome of treatment of unipolar depressive disorders: A review. *Journal of Personality Disorders, 17*(5), 387–405.

Reich, J., Goldenberg, I., Vasile, R., Goisman, R., & Keller, M. (1994). A prospective follow-along study of the course of social phobia. *Psychiatry Research, 54*, 249–258.

Reich, W. (1933/1949). *Character analysis* (T. P. Wolfe, Trans.). New York: Oregon Institute Press.

Reichenberg, A., Gross, M., Weiser, M., Bernahan, M., Silverman, S., Harlap, S., et al. (2006). Advancing paternal age and autism. *Archives of General Psychiatry, 63*(9), 1026–1032.

Reinecke, M. A., Ryan, N. E., & DuBois, D. L. (1998). Cognitive-behavioral therapy of depression and depressive symptoms during adolescence: A review and meta-analysis. *Journal of the American Academy of Child and Adolescent Psychiatry, 37*, 26–34.

Reines, S. A., Block, G. A., Morris, J. C., Liu, G., Nessly, M. L., Lines, C. R., et al. (2004). Rofecoxib: No effect on Alzheimer's disease in a 1-year, randomized, blinded, controlled study. *Neurology, 62*, 66–71.

Reinherz, H. Z., Giaconia, R. M., Silverman, A. B., Friedman, A., Pakiz, B., Frost, A. K., et al. (1995). Early psychosocial risks for adolescent suicidal ideation and attempts. *Journal of the American Academy of Child and Adolescent Psychiatry, 34*, 599–611.

Reisberg, B., Ferris, S. H., Leon, J. J., & Crook, T. (1982). The Global Deterioration Scale for the assessment of primary degenerative dementia. *American Journal of Psychiatry, 139*, 1136–1139.

Reiser, D. E., & Levenson, H. (1984). Abuses of the borderline diagnosis: A clinical problem with teaching opportunities. *American Journal of Psychiatry, 141*, 1528–1532.

Reiss, D., & Neiderhiser, J. M. (2000). The interplay of genetic influences and social processes in developmental theory: Specific mechanisms are coming into view. *Developmental Psychopathology, 12*, 357–374.

Reite, M. (1998). Sleep disorders presenting as psychiatric disorders. *Psychiatric Clinics of North America, 21*(3), 591–607.

Reite, M., Ruddy, J., & Nagel, K. (2002). *Concise guide to evaluation and management of sleep disorders* (3rd ed.). Washington, DC: American Psychiatric Publishing.

Reitzel, J. A., & Szatmari, P. (2003). Cognitive and academic problems. In M. Prior (Ed.), *Learning and behavioral problems in Asperger syndrome* (pp. 35–54). New York: Guilford Press.

Remschmidt, H. E., Schulz, E., Martin, M., Warnke, A., & Trott, G. E. (1994). Childhood-onset schizophrenia: History of the concept and recent studies. *Schizophrenia Bulletin, 20*, 727–745.

Research Units on Pediatric Psychopharmacology Autism Network. (2002). Risperidone in children with autism and serious behavioral problems. *New England Journal of Medicine, 347*, 314–321.

Resnick, P. J. (1997). Malingered psychosis. In R. Rogers (Ed.), *Clinical assessment of malingering and deception* (pp. 47–67). New York: Guilford Press.

Rettew, D. C. (2000). Avoidant personality disorder, generalized social phobia, and shyness: Putting the personality back into personality disorders. *Harvard Review of Psychiatry, 8*(6), 283–297.

Rey, J., Walter, G., Plapp, J., & Denshire, C. (2000). Family environment in attention deficit hyperactivity, oppositional defiant and conduct disorders. *Australian and New Zealand Journal of Psychiatry, 34*, 453–457.

Rey, J. M., & Walter, G. (1999). Oppositional defiant disorder. In R. L. Hendren (Ed.), *Disruptive behavior disorders in children and adolescents: Review of psychiatry*, (pp. 99–132). Washington, DC: American Psychiatric Press.

Reynolds, C. F., III. (1999). Pharmacotherapy for concomitant insomnia and depression. *Primary Care Psychiatry, 5*(3), 101–108.

Reynolds, W. K. (2006). Sexual dysfunction in major depression. *CNS Spectrums, 11*(8, Suppl. 9), 19–23.

Reynolds, W. M. (1991). *Adult Suicide Ideation Questionnaire: Professional manual.* Odessa, FL: Psychological Assessment Resources.

Rheingold, A. A., & Acierno, R. A. (2003). Post-traumatic stress disorder (noncombat). In M. Hersen & S. M. Turner (Eds.) *Diagnostic interviewing* (3rd ed., pp. 345–362). New York: Kluwer Academic.

Ribeiro, M., Dunn, J., Laranjeira, R., & Sesso, R. (2004). High mortality among young crack cocaine users in Brazil: A 5-year follow-up study. *Addiction, 99*, 1133–1135.

Ricciardelli, L. A., Williams, R. J., & Kiernan, M. J. (1999). Bulimic symptoms in adolescent girls and boys. *International Journal of Eating Disorders, 26*(2), 217–221.

Richards, P. S., & Bergin, A. E. (1997). *A spiritual strategy for counseling and psychotherapy.* Washington, DC: American Psychological Association.

Richdale, A. (1999). Sleep problems in autism: Prevalence, cause, and intervention. *Developmental Medicine and Child Neurology, 41*(1), 60–66.

Richdale, A. (2001). Sleep in autism and Asperger's syndrome. In G. Stores & L. Wiggs (Eds.), *Sleep disturbances in children and adolescents with disorders of development: Its significance and management* (pp. 181–191). London: Mac Keith Press.

Richdale, A., Francis, A., Gavidia-Payne, S., & Cotton, S. (2000). Stress, behavior, and sleep problems in children with intellectual disabilities. *Journal of Intellectual and Developmental Disability, 25*, 147–161.

Rich-Edwards, J. W., Kleinman, K., Abrams, A., Harlow, B., McLaughlin, T. J., & Joffe, H. (2006). Sociodemographic predictors of antenatal and postpartum depressive symptoms among women in a medical group practice. *Journal of Epidemiology and Community Health, 60*, 221–227.

Rickels, K., Zaninelli, R., McCafferty, J., Bellew, K., Iyengar, M., & Sheehan, D. (2003). Paroxetine treatment of generalized anxiety disorder: A double-blind, placebo-controlled study. *American Journal of Psychiatry, 160*, 749–756.

Riddle, M. A., Scahill, L., King, R., Hardin, M. T., Towbin, K. E., Ort, S. I., et al. (1990). Obsessive compulsive disorder in children and adolescents: Phenomenology and family history. *Journal of the American Academy of Child and Adolescent Psychiatry, 29*, 766–772.

Rief, W., Hessel, A., & Braehler, E. (2001). Somatization symptoms and hypochondriacal features in the general population. *Psychosomatic Medicine, 63*, 595–602.

Rief, W., & Hiller, W. (2003). A new approach to the assessment of the treatment effects of somatoform disorders. *Psychosomatics, 44*(6), 492–498.

Rief, W., Pilger, F., Ihle, D., Verkerk, R., Scharpe, S., & Maes, M. (2004). Psychobiological aspects of somatoform disorders: Contributions of monoaminergic transmitter systems. *Neuropsychobiology, 49*, 24–29.

Rief, W., & Sharpe, M. (2004). Somatoform disorders: New approaches to classification, conceptualization, and treatment. *Journal of Psychosomatic Research, 56,* 387–390.

Riemann, D., & Voderholzer, U. (2003). Primary insomnia: A risk factor to develop depression? *Journal of Affective Disorders, 76*(1/3), 255–259.

Riggs, D. S., Caulfield, M. B., & Street, A. E. (2000). Risk for domestic violence: Factors associated with perpetuation and victimization. *Journal of Clinical Psychology, 56*(10), 1289–1316.

Righetti-Veltema, M., Conne-Perreard, E., Bousquet, A., & Manzano, J. (2002). Postpartum depression and mother-infant relationships at 3 months old. *Journal of Affective Disorders, 70,* 291–306.

Rihmer, A. (2007). Suicide risk in mood disorders. *Current Opinion in Psychiatry, 20,* 17–22.

Rihmer, Z., & Pestality, P. (1999). Bipolar II disorder and suicidal behavior. *Psychiatric Clinics of North America, 22,* 667–673.

Rimland, B. (1964). *Infantile autism.* New York: Appleton-Century-Crofts.

Risen, C. B. (1995). A guide to taking a sexual history. *Psychiatric Clinics of North America, 18*(1), 39–53.

Ritchie, C. W., Ames, D., Clayton, T., & Lai, R. (2004). Metaanalysis of randomized trials of the efficacy and safety of donepezil, galantamine, and rivastigmine for the treatment of Alzheimer disease. *American Journal of Geriatric Psychiatry, 12,* 358–369.

Ritchie, K., Ledésert, B., & Touchon, J. (2000). Subclinical cognitive impairment: Epidemiology and clinical characteristics. *Comprehensive Psychiatry, 41,* 61–65.

Rivera, R. P., & Borda, T. (2001). The etiology of body dysmorphic disorder. *Psychiatric Annals, 31,* 559–563.

Rivers, J. W., & Stoneman, Z. (2003). Sibling relationships when a child has autism: Marital stress and support coping. *Journal of Autism and Developmental Disorders, 33,* 383–394.

Robbins, J. M. & Kirmayer, L. J., (1996). Patients who somatize in primary care: A longitudinal study of cognitive and social characteristics. *Psychological Medicine, 26,* 937–951.

Robbins, J. M., & Kirmayer, L. J. (1996). Transient and persistent hyprochondriacal worry in primary care. *Psychological Medicine, 26,* 575–589.

Robbins, L. N. (1966). *Deviant children grown up: A sociological and psychiatric study of sociopathic personality.* Baltimore: Williams & Wilkins.

Robert, P. H., Berr, C., Volteau, M., Bertogliati, C., Benoit, M., & Sarazin, M. (2006). Apathy in patients with mild cognitive impairment and the risk of developing dementia of Alzheimer's disease: A 1-year follow-up study. *Clinical Neurology and Neurosurgery, 108,* 733–736.

Roberts, A. R. (2000). *Crisis intervention handbook: Assessment, treatment, and research* (2nd ed.). New York: Oxford University Press.

Roberts, J. (2005). Transparency and self-disclosure in family therapy: Dangers and possibilities. *Family Process, 44,* 45–63.

Roberts, R. E., Alegria, M., Roberts, C. R., & Chen, I. G. (2005). Concordance of reports of mental health functioning by adolescents and their caregivers: A comparison of European, African and Latino Americans. *Journal of Nervous and Mental Disease, 193,* 528–534.

Roberts, S. L., Bushnell, J. A., Collins, S. C., & Purdie, G. L. (2006). Psychological health of men with partners who have post-partum depression. *Australian and New Zealand Journal of Psychiatry, 40,* 704–711.

Robertsson, B. (2003). The instrumentation of delirium. In J. Lindesay & K. Rockwood (Eds.), *Delirium in old age* (pp. 9–25). New York: Oxford University Press.

Robin, A. L., Siegel, P. T., Moye, A. W., Gilroy, M., Dennis, A. B., & Sikand, A. (1999). A controlled comparison of family versus individual therapy for adolescents with anorexia nervosa. *Journal of the American Academy of Child and Adolescent Psychiatry, 38*(12), 1482–1489.

Robins, C. J., & Chapman, A. L. (2004). Dialectial behavior therapy: Current status, recent developments, and future directions. *Journal of Personality Disorders, 16,* 122–129.

Robins, C. J., Ivanoff, A., & Linehan, M. M. (2001). Dialectical behavior therapy. In W. J. Livesley (Ed.), Handbook of personality disorders. (pp. 437–459). New York: Guilford Press.

Robins, C. J., & Koons, C. R. (2004). Dialectial behavior therapy of severe personality disorders. In J. J. Magnavita (Ed.), *Handbook of personality: Theory and practice.* (pp. 221–253). Hoboken, NJ: Wiley.

Robins, D. L., Fein, D., Barton, M. L., & Green, J. A. (2001). The Modified Checklist for Autism in toddlers: An initial study investigating the early detection of autism and pervasive developmental disorders. *Journal of Autism and Developmental Disabilities, 31,* 131–144.

Robins, L. N. (1966). *Deviant children grown up.* Baltimore: Williams & Wilkins.

Robins, L. N. (1999). A 70-year history of conduct disorder: Variations in definition, prevalence and correlates. In S. Cohen, C. Slomkowski, & L. N. Robins (Eds.), *Historical and geographical influences on psychopathology* (pp. 37–56). Mahwah, NJ: Erlbaum.

Robins, L. N., Helzer, J. E., Croughan, J., & Ratcliff, K. S. (1981). National Institute of Mental Health Diagnostic Interview Schedule: Its history, characteristics, and validity. *Archives of General Psychiatry, 38,* 381–389.

Robins, L. N., & McEvoy, L. (1990). Conduct problems as predictors of substance abuse. In L. N. Roins & M. Rutter (Eds.), *Straight and devious pathways from childhood to adulthood* (pp. 182–204). Cambridge: Cambridge University Press.

Robins, L. N., Wing, J., Wittchen, H. U., Helzer, J. E., Babor, T. F., Burke, J., et al. (1988). The Composite International Diagnostic Interview: An epidemiologic instrument suitable for use in conjunction with different diagnostic systems and in different cultures. *Archives of General Psychiatry, 45,* 69–1077.

Robins, L. N., & Regier, D. A. (1991). *Psychiatric disorders in America: The Epidemiologic Catchment Area study.* New York: Free Press.

Robins, R. S., & Post, J. M. (1997). *Political paranoia: The psychopolitics of hatred.* New Haven: Yale University Press.

Rocca, W. A., & Kokmen, E. (1999). Frequency and distribution of vascular dementia. *Alzheimer's Disease and Associated Disorders, 13,* S9–S14.

Roccataliata, G. (1986). *History of ancient psychiatry.* New York: Greenwood Press.

Rockwood, K., & Lindesay, J. (2003). The concept of delirium: Historical antecedents and present meanings. In J. Lindesay & K. Rockwood (Eds.), *Delirium in old age* (pp. 1–8). New York: Oxford University Press.

Roelofs, K., Keijsers, G. P., Hoogduin, K. A., Naring, G. W., & Moene, F. C. (2002). Childhood abuse in patients with conversion disorder. *American Journal of Psychiatry, 159,* 1908–1913.

Roerig, J. L., Mitchell, J. E., Myers, T. C., & Glass, J. B. (2002). Pharmacotherapy and medical complications of eating disorders in children and adolescents. *Child and Adolescent Psychiatric Clinics of North America, 11*(2), 365–385.

Rogers, C. (1992). The processes of therapy. *Journal of Consulting and Clinical Psychology, 60,* 163–164.

Rogers, M. P., Liang, M. H., Daltroy, L. H., Eaton, E., Peteet, J., Wright, E., et al. (1989). Delirium after elective orthopedic surgery: Risk factors and natural history. *International Journal of Psychiatry in Medicine, 19,* 109–121.

Rogers, R. (1997). *Clinical assessment of malingering and deception* (2nd ed.). New York: Guilford Press.

Rogers, R. (2001). *Handbook of diagnostic and structured interviewing.* New York: Guilford Press.

Rogers, R. (2004). Diagnostic, explanatory, and detection models of Munchausen by proxy: Extrapolations from malingering and deception. *Child Abuse and Neglect, 28,* 225–238.

Rogers, R., Gillis, J. R., Turner, R. E., & Freise-Smith, T. (1990). The clinical presentation of command hallucinations in a forensic population. *American Journal of Psychiatry, 147,* 1304–1307.

Rogers, R. D., Everitt, B. J., Baldacchino, A., Blackshaw, A. J., Swainson, R., Wynne, K., et al. (1999). Dissociable deficits in the decision-making cognition of chronic amphetamine abusers, opiate abusers, patients with focal damage to prefrontal cortex, and tryptophan-depleted normal volunteers: Evidence for monoaminergic mechanisms. *Neuropsychopharmacology, 20,* 322–339.

Rogers, S. (2000). Interventions that facilitate socialization in children with autism. *Journal of Autism and Developmental Disabilities, 30,* 399–409.

Rogers, S. J. (1998). Empirically supported comprehensive treatments for young children with autism. *Journal of Clinical Child Psychology, 27*(2), 168–179.

Rogers, S. J., Cook, I., & Meryl, A. (2005). Imitation and play in autism. In F. R. Volkmar, R. Paul, A. Klin, & D. Cohen (Eds.), *Handbook of autism and pervasive developmental disorders* (3rd ed., pp. 382–405). Hoboken, NJ: Wiley.

Rogers, S. J., Hall, T., Osaki, D., Reavan, J., & Herbison, J. (2001). The Denver model: A comprehensive, integrated educational approach to young children with autism and their families. In J. S. Handleman & S. L. Harris (Eds.), *Preschool education programs for children with autism* (2nd ed., pp. 95–134). Austin, TX:ProEd.

Rogers, S. J., & Lewis, H. C. (1989). An effective day treatment model for young children with pervasive developmental disorders. *Journal of the American Academy of Child and Adolescent Psychiatry, 28,* 207–214.

Rogers, M. P., Warshaw, M. G., Goisman, R. M., Goldenberg, I., Rodriguez-Villa, F., Mallya, G., et al. (1999). Comparing primary and secondary generalized anxiety disorder in a long-term naturalistic study of anxiety disorders. *Depression and Anxiety, 10,* 1–7.

Rohde, L. A. (2002). ADHD in Brazil: The DSM-IV criteria in a culturally different population. *Journal of the American Academy of Child and Adolescent Psychiatry, 41*(9), 1131–1133.

Rohrbaugh, M. J., & Shoham, V. (2002). Couple treatment for alcohol abuse: A systemic family-consultation model. In S. G. Hofmann & M. C. Tompson (Eds.), *Treating chronic and severe mental disorders: A handbook of empirically supported interventions* (pp. 277–295). New York: Guilford Press.

Roid, G. H. (2003). *Stanford-Binet Intelligence Scale manual* (5th ed.). Itasca, IL: Riverside.

Roid, G., & Miller, L. (1997). *Leiter International Test of Intelligence—Revised.* Chicago: Stoelting.

Rolfson, D. (2002). The causes of delirium. In J. Lindesay, K. Rockwood, & A. MacDonald (Eds.), *Delirium in old age* (pp. 101–122). New York: Oxford University Press.

Román, G. C., Tatemichi, T. K., Erkinjuntti, T., Cummings, J. L., Masdeu, J. C., Garcia, J. H., et al. (1993). Vascular dementia diagnostic criteria for research studies (Report to the NINDS-AIREN International Workgroup) *Neurology, 43,* 250–260.

Romano, S. J., Halmi, K. A., Sarkar, N. P., Koke, S., & Lee, J. S. (2002). A placebo-controlled study of fluoxetine in continued treatment of bulimia nervosa after successful acute fluoxetine treatment. *American Journal of Psychiatry, 159*(1), 96–102.

Romanowski Bashe, P., & Kirby, B. L. (2001). *The OASIS guide to Asperger syndrome: Advice, support and inspiration.* New York: Crown.

Ron, M. A. (1986). Volatile substance abuse: A review of possible long-term neurological, intellectual, and psychiatric sequelae. *British Journal of Psychiatry, 148,* 235–246.

Ronningstam, E. (1999). Narcissistic personality disorder. In T. Millon, P. H. Blaney, & R. D. Davis (Eds.), *Oxford textbook of psychopathology* (pp. 674–693). New York: Oxford University Press.

Ronningstam, E., & Gunderson, J. G. (1990). Identifying criteria for narcissistic personality disorder. *American Journal of Psychiatry, 147,* 918–922.

Ronningstam, E., & Maltzberger, J. (1998). Suicide attempts in patients with pathological affect regulation and narcissistic disorders. *Suicide and Life Threatening Behavior, 28,* 261–271.

Roof, W. C. (1999). *Spiritual marketplace.* Princeton, NJ: Princeton University Press.

Roose, S. P., Glassman, A. H., Walsh, B. T., Woodring, S., & Vital-Herne, J. (1983). Depression, delusions, and suicide. *American Journal of Psychiatry, 140,* 1159–1162.

Roose, S. P., & Sackheim, H. A. (2004). Antidepressant medication for the treatment of late life depression. In S. P. Roose & H. A. Sackheim (Eds.), *Late life depression* (pp. 192–202). New York: Oxford University Press.

Rosen, G. M., Ferber, R., & Mahowald, M. W. (1996). Evaluation of parasomnias in children. *Child and Adolescent Psychiatric Clinics of North America, 5*(3), 601–616.

Rosen, G. M., Kohen, D. P., & Mahowald, M. W. (2003). Parasomnias. In M. L. Perlis & K. L. Lichstein (Eds.), *Treating sleep disorders: Principles and practice of behavioral sleep medicine* (pp. 393–414). Hoboken, NJ: Wiley.

Rosen, J. C. (1997). Cognitive-behavioral body image therapy. In D. M. Garner & P. E. Garfinkel (Eds.), *Handbook of treatment for eating disorders* (pp. 188–201). New York: Guilford Press.

Rosen, R. C., & Leiblum, S. R. (1995). Treatment of sexual disorders in the 1990s: An integrated approach. *Journal of Consulting and Clinical Psychology, 63*(6), 877–890.

Rosenberg, M. (1965). *Society and the adolescent self-image*. Princeton, NJ: Princeton University Press.

Rosenberg, R. P. (2006). Sleep maintenance insomnia: Strengths and weaknesses of current pharmacologic therapies. Annals of Clinical Psychiatry, *18*(1), 49–56.

Rosenberger, E., & Hayes, J. (2002). Therapist as subject: A review of the empirical countertransference literature. *Journal of Counseling and Development, 80*, 264–271.

Rosenblum, J., & Forman, S. (2002). Evidence-based treatment of eating disorders. *Current Opinion in Pediatrics, 14*(4), 379–383.

Rosenfarb, I., Goldstein, M. J., & Nuechterlein, K. H. (1995). Expressed emotion and subclinical psychopathology observable within the transactions between schizophrenic patients and their family members. *Journal of Abnormal Psychology, 104*, 259–267.

Rosenhan, D. L. (1973). On being sane in insane places. *Science, 179*, 250–258.

Rosenheck, R., Fontana, A., & Cottrol, C. (1995). Effect of clinician-veteran racial pairing in the treatment of post-traumatic stress disorder. *American Journal of Psychiatry, 152*, 555–563.

Rosenheck, R., & Thomson, J. (1986). Detoxification of Vietnam War trauma: A combined family-individual approach. *Family Process, 25*, 559–570.

Rosenthal, C. J., Sulman, J., & Marshall, V. W. (1993). Depressive symptoms in family caregivers of long-stay patients. *Gerontologist, 33*, 249–257.

Rosenthal, R., & Akiskal, H. S. (1985). Mental status examination. In M. Hersen & S. M. Turner (Eds.), *Diagnostic interviewing*. New York: Plenum Press.

Rosenthal, R. N., & Levounis, P. (2005). Polysubstance use, abuse, and dependence. In R. J. Frances, S. I. Miller, & A. H. Mack (Eds.), *Clinical textbook of addictive disorders* (3rd ed., pp. 245–270). New York: Guilford Press.

Rosenstiel, A. K., & Keefe, F. J. (1983). The use of coping strategies in chronic low back pain patients: Relationship to patient characteristics and current adjustment. *Pain, 17*, 33–44.

Rosenvinge, J. H., & Gresko, R. B. (1997). Do we need a prevention model for eating disorders? Recent developments in the Norwegian school-based prevention model. *Eating Disorders: Journal of Treatment and Prevention, 5*(2), 110–118.

Rosenvinge, J. H., Martinussen, M., & Ostensen, E. (2000). The comorbidity of eating disorders and personality disorders: A meta-analytic review of studies published between 1983 and 1998. *Eating and Weight Disorders, 5*(2), 52–61.

Roses, A. D. (1997). A model for susceptibility polymorphisms for complex diseases: Apolipoprotein E and Alzheimer disease. *Neurogenetics, 1*, 3–11.

Ross, C. A., Peyser, C. E., Shapiro, I., & Folstein, M. F. (1991). Delirium: Phenomenologic and etiologic subtypes. *International Psychogeriatrics, 3*, 135–147.

Ross, S., Dermatis, H., Levounis, P., & Galanter, M. (2003). A comparison between dually diagnosed inpatients with and without Axis II comorbidity and the relationship to treatment outcome. *American Journal of Drug and Alcohol Abuse, 29*, 263–279.

Rossell, S. L., Coakes, J., Shapleske, J., Woodruff, P. W. R., & David, A. S. (2003). Insight: Its relationship with cognitive function, brain volume, and symptoms in schizophrenia. *Psychological Medicine, 33*, 111–119.

Rotgers, F. (2003). Cognitive-behavioral theories of substance abuse. In F. Rotgers, J. Morgenstern, & S. T. Walters (Eds.), *Treating substance abuse: Theory and technique* (2nd ed., pp. 166–189). New York: Guilford Press.

Roth, A., & Fonagy, P. (2006). *What works for whom? A critical review of psychotherapy research* (2nd ed.). New York: Guilford Press.

Roth, D., Haley, W., Owen, J., Clay, O., & Goode, K. (2001). Latent growth models of the longitudinal effects of dementia caregiving: A comparison of African American and White family caregivers. *Psychology and Aging, 16*, 427–436.

Rothbaum, B. O. (2006). Virtual reality exposure therapy. In B. O. Rothbaum (Ed.), *Emotional processing in etiology and treatment* (pp. 227–244). New York: Guilford Press.

Rothbaum, B. O., Meadows, E. A., Resick, P., & Foy, D. W. (2000). Cognitive-behavioral therapy. In E. D. Foa, T. M. Keane, & M. J. Friedman (Eds.), *Effective treatments for PTSD: Practice guidelines from the international society for traumatic stress studies* (pp. 60–83). New York: Guilford Press.

Rounsaville, B. J. (1995). Can psychotherapy rescue naltrexone treatment of opioid addiction? *NIDA Research Monograph, 150*, 37–52.

Rounsaville, B. J., Alarcon, R. D., Andrews, G., Jackson, J. S., Kendell, R. E., & Kendler, K. (2002). Basic nomenclature issues for DSM-V. *American Journal of Psychiatry, 126*, 983–986.

Rounsaville, B. J., Kranzker, H. R., Ball, S. A., Tennen, H., Poling, J. C., et al., (1998). Personality disorders in substance users: Relation to substance abuse. *Journal of Nervous and Mental Diseases, 186*, 87–95.

Rowland, A. S., Umbach, D. M., Stallone, L., Naftel, J., Bohlig, E. M., & Sandler, D. P. (2002). Prevalence of medication treatment for attention deficit-hyperactivity disorder among elementary school children in Johnston County, North Carolina. *American Journal of Public Health, 92*, 231–234.

Roy, A. (1989). Suicide. In H. I. Kaplan & B. J. Saddock (Eds.), *Comprehensive textbook of psychiatry* (3rd ed., pp. 2031–2039). Baltimore: Williams & Wilkins.

Roy, A. (1992). Genetics, biology, and suicide in the family. In R. W. Maris, A. L. Berman, J. T. Mattsberger, & R. I. Yufit (Eds.), *Assessment and prediction of suicide* (pp. 553–573). New York: Guilford Press.

Roy-Byrne, P., Post, R. M., Uhde, T. W., Porcu, T., & Davis, D. (1985). The longitudinal course of recurrent affective illness: Life chart data from patients at the NIMH. *Acta Psychiatrica Scandinavica, 317*(Suppl.), 1–34.

Roy-Byrne, P. P., Stang, P., Wittchen, H. U., Ustun, B., Walters, E. E., & Kessler, R. C. (2000). Lifetime panic-depression comorbidity in the National Comorbidity Survey: Association with symptoms, impairment, course and help-seeking. *British Journal of Psychiatry, 176*, 229–235.

Rozzini, L., Chilovi, B. V., Bertoletti, E., Conti, M., DelRio, I., & Trabucchi, M. (2006). Angiotensin converting enzyme (ACE) inhibitors modulate the rate of progression of amnestic mild cognitive impairment. *International Journal of Geriatric Psychiatry, 21*, 550–555.

Rubinsztein, J. S., Michael, A., Underwood, B. R., Tempest, M., & Sahakian, B. J. (2006). Impaired cognition and decision-making in bipolar depression but no "affective bias" evident. *Psychological Medicine, 36*, 629–639.

Rubio, G., & López-Ibor, J. J. (2007). What can be learnt from the natural history of anxiety disorders? *European Psychiatry, 22*, 80–86.

Rudd, M. D., Joiner, T., & Rajab, M. H. (2001). *Treating suicidal behavior: An effective, time-limited approach.* New York: Guilford Press.

Rudolph, C. D., & Link, D. T. (2002). Feeding disorders in infants and children. *Pediatric Clinics of North America, 49*, 97–112.

Ruegg, R. G., Haynes, C., & Frances, A. (1997). Assessment and management of antisocial personality disorder. In M. Rosenbluth & I. Yalom (Eds.), *Treating difficult personality disorder* (pp. 123–172). San Francisco: Jossey-Bass.

Ruffolo, J. S., Phillips, K. A., Menard, W., Fay, C., & Weisberg, R. B. (2006). Comorbidity of body dysmorphic disorder and eating disorders: Severity of psychopathology and body image disturbance. *International Journal of Eating Disorders, 39*(1), 11–19.

Rupp, A., & Keith, S. J. (1993). The costs of schizophrenia: Assessing the burden. *Psychiatric Clinics of North America, 16*, 413–423.

Ruscio, A. M., Chiu, W. T., Roy-Byrne, P., Stang, P. E., Stein, D. J., Wittchen, H. U., et al. (2006). Broadening the definition of generalized anxiety disorder: Effects on prevalence and associations with other disorders in the National Comorbidity Survey Replication. *Journal of Anxiety Disorders, 21*, 662–676.

Ruscio, A. M., Lane, M., Roy-Byrne, P., Stang, P. E., Stein, D. J., Wittchen, H. U., et al. (2005). Should excessive worry be required for a diagnosis of generalized anxiety disorder? Results from the U.S. National Comorbidity Survey Replication. *Psychological Medicine, 35*, 1761–1772.

Ruscio, M. M., & Borkovec, T. D. (2004). Experience and appraisal of worry among high worriers with and without generalized anxiety disorder. *Behaviour Research and Therapy, 42*, 1469–1482.

Rush, B. (1973). *An inquiry into the effects of ardent spirits upon the human body and mind* (Reprinted in Medical Inquiries and Observations, Vol. 2). Philadelphia: Kimber and Richardson.

Russell, A. T. (1994). The clinical presentation of childhood-onset schizophrenia. *Schizophrenia Bulletin, 20*, 631–646.

Russell, G. (1979). Bulimia nervosa: An ominous variant of anorexia nervosa. *Psychological Medicine, 9*(3), 429–448.

Russell, M. (1990). Prevalence of alcoholism among children of alcoholics. In M. Windle & J. S. Searles (Eds.), *Children of alcoholics: Critical perspectives* (pp. 9–38). New York: Guilford Press.

Russell, M., Martier, S. S., & Sokol, R. J. (1994). Screening for pregnancy risk-drinking: Tweaking the tests. *Alcoholism: Clinical and Experimental Research, 18*, 1157–1161.

Russo, D., Purohit, V., Foudin, L., & Salin, L. (2004). Workshop on alcohol use and health disparities 2002: A call to arms. *Alcohol, 32*, 37–43.

Rutan, J. S., & Stone, W. N. (2000). *Psychodynamic group psychotherapy* (3rd ed.). New York: Guilford Press.

Rutter, M. (1994). Debate and argument: There are connections between brain and mind and it is important that Rett syndrome be classified somewhere. *Journal of Child Psychiatry and Allied Disciplines, 35*(2), 379–381.

Rutter, M. (1997a). Autistic children: Infancy to adulthood. *Seminars in Psychiatry, 2*, 435–450.

Rutter, M. (1997b). Comorbidity: Concepts, claims, and choices. *Criminal Behavior and Mental Health, 7*, 265–285.

Rutter, M. (2002). Classification: Conceptual issues and substantive findings. In E. Taylor & M. Rutter (Eds.), *Child and adolescent psychiatry* (4th ed., pp. 3–17). Oxford: Blackwell.

Rutter, M. (2005). Genetic influences and autism. In F. R. Volkmar, R. Paul, A. Klin, & D. Cohen (Eds.) *Handbook of autism and pervasive developmental disorders* (3rd ed., 425–452). Hoboken, NJ: Wiley.

Rutter, M., Bailey, A., Bolton, P., & Le Couteur, A. (1994). Autism and known medical conditions: Myth and substance. *Journal of Child Psychology and Psychiatry, 33*(2), 311–322.

Rutter, M., Bailey, A., & Lord, C. (2003). *Social Communication Questionnaire (SCQ) manual.* Los Angeles: Western Psychological Services.

Rutter, M., Greenfeld, D., & Lockyer, L. (1967). A 5- to 15-year follow-up study of infantile psychosis: Pt. II. Social and behavioral outcome. *British Journal of Psychiatry, 113*, 1183–1199.

Rutter, M., & Gould, M. (1985). Classification. In M. Rutter & L. Hesov (Eds.), *Child and adolescent psychiatry: Modern approaches* (pp. 775–911). Oxford: Blackwell.

Rutter, M., Silberg, J., O'Conner, T., & Simonoff, E. (1999). Genetics and child psychiatry: Pt. II. Empirical research findings. *Journal of Child Psychology and Psychiatry, 40*, 19–55.

Sabo, A. N. (1997). Etiological significance of associations between childhood trauma and borderline personality disorder: Conceptual and clinical implications. *Journal of Personality Disorders, 11*, 50–70.

Sachs, G. S., Baldassano, C. F., Truman, C. J., & Guille, C. (2000). Comorbidity of attention deficit hyperactivity disorder with early- and late-onset bipolar disorder. *American Journal of Psychiatry, 157*(3), 466–467.

Sackeim, H. A., Prudic, J., Devanand, D. P., Nobler, M. S., Lisanby, S. H., Peyser, S., et al. (2000). A prospective, randomized, double-blind comparison of bilateral and right unilateral electroconvulsive therapy at different stimulus intensities. *Archives of General Psychiatry, 57*, 425–434.

Sacks, J. A., Drake, R. E., Williams, V. F., Banks, S. M., & Herrell, J. M. (2003). Utility of the time-line follow-back to assess substance use among homeless adults. *Journal of Nervous and Mental Diseases, 191*, 145–153.

Sadavoy, J., & Leszcz, M. (1987). *Treating the elderly with psychotherapy: The scope for change in late life.* Madison, CT: International Universities Press.

Safer, D. J., Zito, J. M., & Gardner, J. F. (2001). Pemoline hepatotoxicity and postmarketing surveillance. *Journal of the American Academy of Child and Adolescent Psychiatry, 40*, 622–629.

Safer, D. L., Telch, C. F., & Agras, S. (2001). Dialectical behavior therapy for bulimia nervosa. *American Journal of Psychiatry, 158*, 632–634.

Saha, T. D., Chou, S. P., & Grant, B. F. (2006). Toward an alcohol use disorder continuum using item response theory: Results from the National Epidemiologic Survey on alcohol and related conditions. *Psychological Medicine, 36*, 931–941.

Sahin, H. A., Gurvit, I. H., Bilgic, B., Hanagasi, H. A., & Emre, M. (2002). Therapeutic effects of an acetylcholinesterase inhibitor (donepezil) on memory in Wernicke-Korsakoff's disease. *Clinical Neuropharmacology, 25*, 16–20.

Saitz, R. (1998). Introduction to alcohol withdrawal. *Alcohol Health and Research World, 22*, 5–12.

Sajatovic, M., Blow, F. C., Ignacio, R. V., & Kales, H. C. (2005). New-onset bipolar disorder in later life. *American Journal of Geriatric Psychiatry, 13*, 282–289.

Sakai, J. T., Ho, P. M., Shore, J. H., Risk, N. K., & Price, R. K. (2005). Asians in the United States: Substance dependence and use of substance-dependence treatment. *Journal of Substance Abuse Treatment, 29*, 75–84.

Salaspuro, M. (2003). Alcohol consumption and cancer of the gastrointestinal tract. *Best Practice and Research Clinical Gastroenterology, 17*, 679–694.

Sales, B. D., Miller, M. O., & Hall, S. R. (2005). *Laws effecting clinical practice.* Washington, DC: American Psychological Association.

Salkovskis, P. M. (1985). Obsessional-compulsive problems: A cognitive behavioural analysis. *Behaviour Research and Therapy, 23*, 571–583.

Salkovskis, P. M. (1989). Cognitive behavioural factors and the persistence of intrusive thoughts in obsessional problems. *Behaviour Research and Therapy, 27*, 677–682.

Salloum, I. M., & Thase, M. E. (2000). Impact of substance abuse on the course and treatment of bipolar disorder. *Bipolar Disorders, 2*, 269–280.

Salzman, L. (1980). *Treatment of the obsessive personality.* New York: Jason Aronson.

Samuels, J., Eaton, W. W., Bienvenue, O. J., III, Brown, C. H., Costa, P. T., Jr., & Nestadt, G. (2002). Prevalence and correlates of personality disorders in a community sample. *British Journal of Psychiatry, 180*, 536–542.

Sampson, R. J., Raudenbaush, S. W., & Earls, F. (1997). Neighborhoods and violent crime: A multilevel study of collective efficacy. *Science, 277*, 918–924.

Samson, J. A., Simpson, J. C., & Tsuang, M. T. (1988). Outcome studies of schizoaffective disorders. *Schizophrenia Bulletin, 14*, 543–554.

Sanchez, H. (2001). Risk factor model for suicide assessment and intervention. *Professional Psychology Research and Practice, 32*(4), 351–358.

Sandberg, O., Gustafson, Y., Brännström, B., & Buch, G. (1999). Clinical profile of delirium in older patients. *Journal of the American Geriatrics Society, 47*, 1300–1306.

Sandell, R., Blomberg, J., & Lazar, A. (2002). Time matters: On temporal interactions in long-term follow-up of psychotherapies. *Psychotherapy Research, 12*, 39–58.

Sanders, J. L., & Morgan, S. B. (1997). Family stress and adjustment as perceived by parents of children with autism or Down's syndrome: Implications for intervention. *Child and Family Behavior Therapy, 19*, 15–32.

Sano, M., Ernesto, C., Thomas, R. G., Klauber, M. R., Schafer, K., Grundman, M., et al. (1997). A controlled trial of selegiline, alpha-tocopherol, or both as treatment for Alzheimer's disease: The Alzheimer's Disease Cooperative Study. *New England Journal of Medicine, 336*, 1216–22.

Sanson, A., & Prior, M. (1999). Temperament and behavioral precursors to oppositional defiant disorder and conduct disorder. In H. C. Quay & A. E. Hogan (Eds.), *Handbook of disruptive behavior disorders* (pp. 397–417). New York: Kluwer Academic/Plenum Press.

Sansone, R. A., Gaither, G. A., & Rytwinski, D. (2004). Major depression versus dysthymia: Comorbid psychiatric disorders, psychotropic medication patterns, and psychotherapy sessions. *International Journal of Psychiatry in Clinical Practice, 8*, 61–63.

Santos, M., Schwarz, M., & Aladjem, A. (2002). Outcome measurements in somatoform disorders. In W. W. IsHak, T. Burt, & L. Sederer (Eds.), *Outcome measurement in psychiatry: A critical review* (pp. 221–235). Washington, DC: American Psychiatric Publishing.

Sapolsky, R. M., Krey, L. C., & McEwen, B. S. (1986). The neuroendocrinology of stress and aging: The glucocorticoid cascade hypothesis. *Endocrine Reviews, 7*, 284–301.

Saravanan, B. (2002). Postnatal depression in India. *American Journal of Psychiatry, 159*, 1437–1438.

Saravay, S. M., Kaplowitz, M., Kurek, J., Zeman, D., Pollack, S., & Novik, S. (2004). How do delirium and dementia increase length of stay of elderly general medical inpatients? *Psychosomatics, 45*, 235–242.

Sartorius, N., Gulbinat, W., Harrison, G., Laska, E., & Siegel, C. (1996). Long-term follow-up of schizophrenia in different cultures. *Psychological Medicine, 16*, 909–928.

Sarwer, D. B., Creand, C. E., & Didie, E. R. (2003). Body dysmorphic disorder in cosmetic surgery patients. *Facial and Plastic Surgery, 19*(1), 7–17.

Sassin, J. F., & Mitler, M. M. (1987). An historical perspective on sleep disorders medicine. *Psychiatric Clinics of North America, 10*(4), 517–523.

Sauber, S. (1997). Introduction to managed mental health care: Provider survival. *Mental Health Practice under Managed Care*, 1–39.

Saunders, D. G. (1992). Woman battering. In R. T. Ammerman & M. Hersen (Eds.), *Assessment of family violence: A clinical and legal sourcebook* (pp. 208–235). New York: Wiley.

Saunders, J. B., Aasland, O. G., Babor, T. F., de la Fuente, J. R., & Grant, M. (1993). Development of the Alcohol Use Disorders Identification Test (AUDIT): Pt. II. WHO collaborative project on early detection of persons with harmful alcohol consumption. *Addiction, 88*, 791–804.

Saxena, S., Winograd, A., Dunkin, J., Maidment, K., Rosen, R., Vapnik, T., et al. (2001). A retrospective review of clinical characteristics and treatment response in body dysmorphic disorder versus obsessive-compulsive disorder. *Journal of Clinical Psychiatry, 62*, 67–74.

Saxon, S. V., & Etten, M. J. (2002). *Physical change and aging: A guide for the helping professions*. New York: Tiresias Press.

Scaer, R. C. (2001). *The body bears the burden: Trauma, dissociation, and disease*. Binghamton, NY: Hayworth Medical Press.

Scahill, L., & Martin, A. (2005). Psychopharmacology. In F. R. Volkmar, R. Paul, A. Klin, & D. Cohen (Eds.), *Handbook of autism and pervasive developmental disorders* (3rd. ed., 1102–1117). Hoboken, NJ: Wiley.

Scahill, L., Riddle, M. A., McSwiggin-Hardin, M., Ort, S. I., King, R. A., Goodman, W., et al. (1997). Yale-Brown Obsessive Compulsive Scale: Reliability and validity. *Journal of the American Academy of Child and Adolescent Psychiatry, 36*, 844–852.

Scahill, L., & Schwab Stone, M. (2000). Epidemiology of ADHD in school-age children. *Child and Adolescent Psychiatric Clinics of North America, 9*, 185–190.

Schaar, I., & Oejahagen, A. (2001). Severely mentally ill substance abusers: An 18-month follow-up study. *Social Psychiatry and Psychiatric Epidemiology, 36*, 70–78.

Schacht, J., Binder, J., & Strupp, H. (1984). The dynamic focus. In H. Strupp & J. Binder (Eds.), *Psychotherapy in a new key* (pp. 65–109). New York: Basic Books.

Schaefer, C. E., & Cangelosi, D. M. (2002). *Play therapy techniques* (2nd ed.). Northvale, NJ: Aronson.

Schaefer, J., Caetano, R., & Clark, C. L. (1998). Rates of intimate partner violence in the United States. *American Journal of Public Health, 88,* 1702–1704.

Schaeffer, J. C., & Ross, R. G. (2002). Childhood-onset schizophrenia: Premorbid and prodromal diagnostic and treatment histories. *Journal of the American Academy of Child and Adolescent Psychiatry, 41,* 538–545.

Schain, R., & Freedman, D. X. (1961). Studies on 5-hydroxyindole metabolism in autistic and other mentally retarded children. *Journal of Pediatrics, 58,* 315–320.

Schall, C. (2000). Family perspectives on raising a child with autism. *Journal of Child and Family Studies, 9,* 409–423.

Schanda, H., Berner, P., Gabriel, E., Kronberger, M. L., & Kufferle, B. (1983). The genetics of delusional psychoses. *Schizophrenia Bulletin, 9,* 563–570.

Shaner, A., Tucker, D. E., Roberts, L. J., & Eckman, T. (1999). Disability income, cocaine use, and contingency management among patients with cocaine dependence and schizophrenia. In S. T. Higgins & K. Silverman (Eds.), *Motivating behavior change among illicit-drug abusers: Research on contingency management interventions* (pp. 95–121). Washington, DC: American Psychological Association.

Schatzberg, A. F., Cole, J. O., & Debattista, C. (2005). *Manual of clinical psychopharmacology* (4th ed.). Washington, DC: American Psychiatric Publishing.

Scheinkopf, S. J., & Siegel, B. (1998). Home-based behavioral treatment of young children with autism. *Journal of Autism and Developmental Disorders, 28,* 15–23.

Schiavi, R. C., & Segraves, R. T. (1995). The biology of sexual function. *Psychiatric Clinics of North America, 18,* 7–23.

Schiavone, P., Dorz, S., Conforti, D., Scarso, C., & Borgherini, G. (2004). Comorbidity of DSM-IV Personality Disorders in unipolar and bipolar affective disorders: A comparative study. *Psychological Reports, 95,* 121–128.

Shibayama, H., Kasahara, Y., & Kobayashi, H. (1986). Prevalence of dementia in a Japanese elderly population. *Acta Psychiatrica Scandinavica, 74,* 144–151.

Schinke, S. P., Tepavac, L., & Cole, K. C. (2000). Preventing substance use among Native American youth: Three-year results. *Addictive Behaviors, 25,* 387–397.

Schlesinger, A., & Silk, K. (2005). Collaborative care. In J. M. Oldham, A. E. Skodol, & D. S. Bender (Eds.), *Textbook of personality disorders* (pp. 431–446). Washington, DC: American Psychiatric Publishing.

Schmidt, L. A., Polak, C. P., & Spooner, A. L. (2001) Biological and environmental contributions to childhood shyness: A diathesis-stress model. In W. R. Crozier & L. E. Alden (Eds.), *International handbook of social anxiety* (pp. 29–52). New York: Wiley.

Schmidt, N. B., & Telch, M. J. (1990). Prevalence of personality disorders among bulimics, nonbulimic binge eaters, and normal controls. *Journal of Psychopathology and Behavioral Assessment, 12,* 169–185.

Schmitt, B., & Mauro, R. (1989). Nonorganic failure to thrive: An outpatient approach. *Child Abuse and Neglect, 13,* 235–248.

Schneck, C. D., Miklowitz, D. J., Calabrese, J. R., Allen, M. H., Thomas, M. R., Wisniewski, S. R., et al. (2004). Phenomenology of rapid-cycling bipolar disorder: Data from the first 500 participants in the Systematic Treatment Enhancement Program. *American Journal of Psychiatry, 161,* 1902–1908.

Schneider, B., Philipp, M., & Müller, M. J. (2001). Psychopathological predictors of suicide in patients with major depression during a 5-year follow-up. *European Psychiatry, 16,* 283–288.

Schneider, K. (1923). *Psychopathic personalities.* London: Cassell.

Schneider, K. (1959). *Clinical psychopathology.* New York: Grune and Stratton.

Schneider, L. S., Pollack, V. E., & Lyness, S. A. (1990). A meta-analysis of controlled trials of neuroleptic treatment in dementia. *Journal of the American Geriatric Society, 38,* 553–563.

Schneier, F. R., Johnson, J., Hornig, C. D., Liebowitz, M. R., & Weissman, M. M. (1992). Social phobia: Comorbidity and morbidity in an epidemiologic sample. *Archives of General Psychiatry, 49,* 282–288.

Schnider, A. (2001). Spontaneous confabulation, reality monitoring, and the limbic system—A review. *Brain Research, 36,* 150–160.

Schnoll, S. H., & Weaver, M. F. (2004). Phencyclidine and ketamine. In M. Galanter & H. D. Kleber (Eds.), *The American Psychiatric Publishing textbook of substance abuse treatment* (3rd ed., pp. 211–215). Washington, DC: American Psychiatric Publishing.

Shoptaw, S., Huber, A., Peck, J., Yang, X., Liu, J., Dang, J., et al. (2006). Randomized, placebo-controlled trial of sertraline and contingency management for the treatment of methamphetamine dependence. *Drug and Alcohol Dependence, 85,* 12–18.

Schnyder, U., Klaghfor, R., Leuthold, A., & Buddeberg, C. (1999). Characteristics of psychiatric emergencies and their choice of intervention strategies. *Acta Psychiatrica Scandinavia, 99,* 179–187.

Schoenwald, S. K., & Henggeler, S. W. (1999). Treatment of oppositional defiant disorder and conduct disorder in home and community samples. In H. C. Quay & A. E. Hogan (Eds.), *Handbook of disruptive behavior disorders* (pp. 475–493). New York: Kluwer Academic/ Plenum Press.

Schooler, N. R., & Keith, S. J. (1993). The clinical research base for the treatment of schizophrenia. *Psychopharmacology Bulletin, 29,* 431–446.

Schopler, E., Reichler, R. J., & Renner, B. R. (1988). *The Childhood Autism Rating Scale.* Los Angeles: Western Psychological Services.

Schore, A. (1994). *Affect regulation and the origin of the self: The neurobiology of emotional development.* Hillsdale, N. J.: Erlbaum.

Schork, N. J., & Schork, C. M. (1998). Issues and strategies in the genetic analysis of alcoholism and related addictive behaviors. *Alcohol, 16,* 71–83.

Schreck, K. A., & Mulick, J. A. (2000). Parental reports of sleep problems in children with autism. *Journal of Autism and Developmental Disorders, 30*(2), 127–135.

Schreibman, L., & Charlop-Christy, M. H. (1998). Autistic disorder. In T. H. Ollendick & M. Hersen (Eds.), *Handbook of child psychopathology* (3rd ed., pp. 157–179). New York: Plenum Press.

Schreier, H. (2002). Munchausen by proxy defined. *Pediatrics, 110,* 985–988.

Schreier, H. A., & Libow, J. A. (1994, December). Munchausen by proxy syndrome: A modern pediatric challenge. *Journal of Pediatrics, 125*(6, Pt. 2), S110–S115.

Schuckit, M. A., Danko, G. P., Raimo, E. B., Smith, T. L., Eng, M. V., Carpenter, K. K. T., et al. (2001). A preliminary evaluation of the potential usefulness of the diagnoses of polysubstance dependence. *Journal of Studies on Alcohol, 62,* 54–61.

Schuckit, M. A., Smith, T. L., Danko, G. P., Bucholz, K. K., Reich, T., & Bierut, L. (2001). Five-year clinical course associated with DSM-I alcohol abuse or dependence in a large group of men and women. *American Journal of Psychiatry, 158,* 1084–1090.

Schuckit, M. A., Smith, T. L., & Landi, N. (2000). The 5-year clinical course of high functioning men with DSM-IV alcohol abuse or dependence. *American Journal of Psychiatry, 157,* 2028–2035.

Schuckit, M. A., & Tapert, S. (2004). Alcohol. In M. Galanter & H. D. Kleber (Eds.), *Textbook of substance abuse treatment* (3rd ed., pp. 151–166). Washington, DC: American Psychiatric Press.

Schuler, A. L., Peck, C. A., Willard, C., & Theimer, K. (1989). Assessment of communicative means and functions through interview: Assessing the communicative capabilities of individuals with limited language. *Seminars in Speech and Language, 10,* 51–61.

Schulmann, E. M., Foote, R. C., Eyberg, S. M., Boggs, S. R., & Algina, J. (1998). Efficacy of parent-child interaction therapy: Interim report of a randomized trial with short-term maintenance. *Journal of Clinical Child Psychology, 27,* 35–45.

Schultz, R. T., & Robins, D. L. (2005). Functional neuroimaging studies of autism spectrum disorders. In F. R. Volkmar, R. Paul, A. Klin, & D. Cohen (Eds.), *Handbook of autism and pervasive developmental disorders* (3rd ed., pp. 515–533). Hoboken, NJ: Wiley.

Schulz, R., Drayer, R. A., & Rollman, B. L. (2002). Depression as a risk factor for non-suicide mortality in the elderly. *Biological Psychiatry, 52*, 205–225.

Schulz, R., & Matire, L. M. (2004). Family caregiving of persons with dementia: Prevalence, health effects, and support strategies. *American Journal of Geriatric Psychiatry, 12*, 240–249.

Schulze, T. G., Müller, D. J., Krauss, H., Gross, M., Fangerau-Lefvre, H., Illes, F., et al. (2002). Further evidence for age of onset being an indicator for severity of bipolar disorder. *Journal of Affective Disorders, 68*, 343–345.

Schumacher, J. E., Milby, J. B., Wallace, D., Simpson, C., Frison, S., McNamara, C., et al. (2003). Diagnostic compared with abstinence outcomes of day treatment and contingency management among cocaine-dependent homeless persons. *Experimental and Clinical Psychopharmacology, 11*, 146–157.

Schwannauer, M. (2004). Cognitive behavioral therapy for bipolar affective disorder. In M. Power (Ed.), *Mood disorders: A handbook of science and practice* (pp. 259–273). Hoboken, NJ: Wiley.

Schwartz, E. (1989). The mental status examination. In R. Craig (Ed.), *Clinical and diagnostic interviewing* (pp. 269–287). Northvale, NJ: Aronson.

Schwartz, J. E., Fennig, S., Tanenberg-Karant, M., Carlson, G., Craig, T., Galambos, N., et al. (2000). Congruence of diagnosis 2 years after a first-admission diagnosis of psychosis. *Archives of General Psychiatry, 57*, 593–600.

Schwartz, M. B., & Brownell, K. D. (1998, April). *How do clients match themselves to treatment? A study of participants in Overeaters Anonymous and Jenny Craig.* Paper presented at the International Conference for Eating Disorders, New York.

Schwartz, M. B., & Brownell, K. D. (2001). Vulnerability to eating disorders in adulthood. In R. E. Ingram & J. M. Price (Eds.), *Vulnerability to psychopathology: Risk across the lifespan* (pp. 412–446). New York: Guilford Press.

Schwartz, T. L., & Park, T. L. (1999). Assaults by patients on psychiatric residents: A survey and training recommendations. *Psychiatric Services, 50*, 381–384.

Schweizer, E., & Rickels, K. (1988). Buspirone in the treatment of panic disorder: A controlled pilot comparison with clorazepate. *Journal of Clinical Psychopharmacology, 8*, 303.

Schwiebert, V. L., & Myers, J. E. (2001). Counseling older adults. In E. R. Welfel & R. E. Ingersoll (Eds.), *The mental health desk reference* (pp. 320–325). New York: Wiley.

Scott, J., Stanton, B., Garland, A., & Ferrier, I. N. (2000). Cognitive vulnerability in patients with bipolar disorder. *Psychological Medicine, 30*, 467–472.

Scott, J. E., & Dixon, L. B. (1995). Assertive community treatment and case management for schizophrenia. *Schizophrenia Bulletin, 21*, 657–668.

Scott, S. (1994). Mental retardation. In M. Rutter, E. Taylor, & L. Hersov (Eds.), *Child and adolescent psychiatry: Modern approaches* (3rd ed., pp. 618–646). Oxford, England: Blackwell Scientific Publications.

Scoville, W. B., & Milner, B. (1957). Loss of recent memory after bilateral hippocampal lesions. *Journal of Neurology, Neurosurgery, and Psychiatry, 20*, 11–21.

Secker, D., Kazantzis, N., & Pachana, N. (2004). Cognitive behavior therapy for older adults: Practical guidelines for adapting therapy structure. *Journal of Rational-Emotive and Cognitive-Behavior Therapy, 21*(2), 93–109.

Seeman, M. V., & Lang, M. (1990). The role of estrogens in schizophrenia gender differences. *Schizophrenia Bulletin, 16*, 185–194.

Segal, D. L. (1997). Structured interviewing and DSM classification. In S. M. Turner & M. Hersen (Eds.), *Adult psychopathology and diagnosis* (pp. 24–57). New York: Wiley.

Segal, H. (1979). *Melanie Klein.* New York: Viking Press.

Segal, Z. V., Pearson, J. L., & Thase, M. E. (2003). Challenges in preventing relapse in major depression: Report of a National Institute of Mental Health workshop on the state and science of relapse prevention in major depression. *Journal of Affective Disorders, 77*, 97–108.

Segraves, K. B., & Segraves, R. T. (1991). Multiple-phase sexual dysfunction. *Journal of Sex Education and Therapy, 17*(3), 153–156.

Segraves, R. T., Croft, H., Kavoussi, R., Ascher, J. A., Batey, S. R., Foster, V. J., et al. (2001). Bupropion sustained release (SR) for the treatment of hypoactive sexual desire disorder (HSDD) in nondepressed women. *Journal of Sex and Marital Therapy, 27*(3), 303–316.

Segraves, T., & Althof, S. (2002). Psychotherapy and pharmacotherapy for sexual dysfunctions. In P. E. Nathan & J. M. Gorman (Eds.), *A guide to treatments that work* (2nd ed., pp. 497–524). New York: Oxford University Press.

Segre, L. S., Losch, M. E., & O'Hara, M. W. (2006). Race/ethnicity and perinatal depressed mood. *Journal of Reproductive and Infant Psychology, 24*, 99–106.

Segrin, C., & Abramson, L. Y. (1994). Negative reactions to depressive behaviors: A communication theories analysis. *Journal of Abnormal Psychology, 103*, 655–668.

Seivewright, H., Tyrer, P., & Johnson, T., (2002). Change in personality status in neurotic disorders. *Lancet, 359*, 2253–2254.

Seligman, L. (1998). *Selecting effective treatments: A comprehensive systematic guide to treating mental disorders.* San Francisco: Jossey-Bass.

Seligman, M. E. (1971). Phobias and preparedness. *Behavior Therapy, 2*, 307–320.

Seligman, M. E. (1975). *Helplessness: On depression, development, and death.* San Francisco: Freeman.

Seligman, M. E., Abramson, L. Y., Semmel, A., & von Baeyer, C. (1979). Depressive attributional style. *Journal of Abnormal Psychology, 88*, 242–247.

Selten, J., Wiersma, D., & van den Bosch, R. J. (2000). Distress attributed to negative symptoms in schizophrenia. *Schizophrenia Bulletin, 26*, 737–744.

Seltzer, M. M., Krauss, M. W., Orsmond, G. I., & Vestal, C. (2001). Families of adolescents and adults with autism: Uncharted territory. In L. M. Glidden (Ed.), *International review of research in mental retardation: Vol 23. Autism* (pp. 267–294). San Diego, CA: Academic Press.

Seltzer, M. M., Krauss, M. W., Shattuck, P. T., Orsmond, G., Sweet, A., & Lord, C. (2003). The symptoms of autism spectrum disorder in adolescence and adulthood. *Journal of Autism and Developmental Disabilities, 33*, 565–581.

Selzer, M. L. (1971). The Michigan Alcoholism Screening Test (MAST): The quest for a new diagnostic instrument. *American Journal of Psychiatry, 127*, 1653–1658.

Serretti, A., Jori, M. C., Casadei, G., Ravizza, L., Smeraldi, E., & Akiskal, H. (1999). Delineating psychopathologic clusters within dysthymia: A study of 512 out-patients without major depression. *Journal of Affective Disorders, 56*, 17–25.

Seto, M. C. (2004). Pedophilia and sexual offenses against children. *Annual Review of Sex Research, 15*, 321–361.

Sevincok, L., Akoglu, A., & Kokcu, F. (2007). Suicidality in schizophrenic patients with and without obsessive-compulsive disorder. *Schizophrenia Research, 90*, 198–202.

Sevy, S., Kay, S. R., Opler, L. A., & Van Praag, H. M. (1990). Significance of cocaine history in schizophrenia. *Journal of Nervous and Mental Diseases, 178*, 642–648.

Shader, R. I., Ciraulo, D. A., & Greenblatt, D. J. (2003). Treatment of physical dependence on barbiturates, benzodiazepines, and other sedative-hypnotics. In R. I. Shader (Ed.), *Manual of psychiatric therapeutics* (3rd ed., pp. 103–114). Philadelphia: Lippincott, Williams, & Wilkins.

Shafii, M. (1989). Completed suicide in children and adolescents. In C. R. Pfeiffer (Ed.), *Suicide among youth: Perspectives on risk and prevention* (pp. 1–20). Washington, DC: American Psychiatric Press.

Shafrankse, E. P. (2000). Psychotherapy with Roman Catholics. In P. S. Richards & A. E. Bergin (Eds.), *Handbook of psychotherapy and religious diversity* (pp. 59–88). Washington, DC: American Psychological Association.

Shafrankse, E. P., & Maloney, H. N. (1990). Clinical psychologists' religious and spiritual orientations and their practice of psychotherapy. *Psychotherapy, 27*, 72–78.

Shaner, A., Mintz, J., Eckman, T. A., Roberts, L. J., Wilkins, J. N., Tucker, D. E., et al. (1995). Disability income, cocaine use, and repeated hospitalizations among schizophrenic cocaine abusers: A government sponsored revolving door? *New England Journal of Medicine, 333*, 777–783.

Shaner, A., Tucker, D. E., Roberts, L. J., & Eckman, T. A. (1999). Disability income, cocaine use, and contingency management among patients with cocaine dependence and schizophrenia. In S. T. Higgins & K. Silverman (Eds.), *Motivating behavior change among illicit-drug abusers: Research on contingency management interventions* (pp. 95–121). Washington, DC: American Psychological Association.

Shannon, M., & Graef, J. W. (1997). Lead intoxication in children with pervasive developmental disorders. *Journal of Toxicology-Clinical Toxicology, 34,* 177–181.

Shapiro, D. (1965). *Neurotic styles.* New York: Basic Books.

Shapiro, D. A., Barkham, M., Stiles, W. B., Hard, G. E., Rees, A., Reynolds, S., et al. (2003). Time is of the essence: A selective review of the fall and rise of brief therapy research. *Psychology and Psychotherapy, 76,* 211–235.

Shapiro, F. (1989). Eye movement desensitization: A new treatment for posttraumatic stress disorder. *Journal of Behavior Therapy and Experimental Psychiatry, 51,* 323–329.

Shapiro, F. (1995). *Eye movement desensitization and reprocessing: Basic principles, protocols, and procedures.* New York: Guilford Press.

Sharkansky, E. J., Brief, B. J., Peirce, J. M., Meehan, J. C., & Mannix, L. M. (1999). Substance use patients with posttraumatic stress disorder: Identifying specific triggers for substance use and their associations with PTSD symptoms. *Psychology of Addictive Behaviors, 13,* 89–97.

Sharma, T., & Antonova, L. (2003). Cognitive function in schizophrenia: Deficits, functional consequences, and future treatment. *Psychiatric Clinics of North America. 26,* 25–40.

Sharma, V. (2001). The effect of electroconvulsive therapy on suicide risk in patients with mood disorders. *Canadian Journal of Psychiatry, 46,* 704–709.

Sharp, C. W., Clark, S. A., Dunan, J. R., Blackwood, D. H. R., & Shapiro, C. M. (1994). Clinical presentation of anorexia nervosa in males: 24 new cases. *International Journal of Eating Disorders, 15*(2), 125–134.

Sharpe, M., & Mayou, R. (2004). Somatoform disorders: A help or hindrance to good patient care? *British Journal of Psychiatry, 184,* 465–467.

Sharpe, M., & Williams, A. C. (2002). Treating patients with somatoform pain disorder and hypochondriasis. In D. C. Turk & R. J. Gatchel (Eds.), *Psychological approaches to pain management* (2nd ed., pp. 515–533). New York: Guilford Press.

Sharpley, C. F., & McNally, J. (1997). Effects of level of academic training on client-perceived rapport and use of verbal response modes in counseling dyads. *Counselling Psychology Quarterly, 10,* 449–460.

Sharpley, C. F., Munro, D., & Elly, M. J. (2005). Silence and rapport during initial interviews. *Counselling Psychology Quarterly, 18,* 149–159.

Shavelle, R. M., Strauss, D. J., & Pickett, J. (2001). Causes of death in autism. *Journal of Autism and Developmental Disorders, 6,* 569–576.

Shea, M. T., Pilkonis, P. A., Beckham, E., Collins, J. F., Elkin, I., & Sotsky, S. M. (1990). Personality disorders and treatment outcome in the NIMH treatment of depression collaborative research program. *American Journal of Psychiatry, 147,* 711–718.

Shea, M. T., Stout, R. L., Gunderson, J. G., Morey, L. C., Grilo, C. M., McGlashan, T. H. et al., (2002). Short-term diagnostic stability of schizotypal, borderline, avoidant and obsessive-compulsive personality disorders. *American Journal of Psychiatry, 169,* 2036–2041.

Shea, M. T., & Yen, S. (2003). Stability as a distinction between Axis I and Axis II disorders. *Journal of Personality Disorders, 17*(5), 373–386.

Shea, S. C. (1999). *The practical art of suicide assessment: A guide for mental health professionals and substance abuse counselors.* New York: Wiley.

Shea, V., & Mesibov, G. B. (2005). Adolescents and adults with autism. In F. R. Volkmar, R. Paul, A. Klin, & D. Cohen (Eds.), *Handbook of autism and pervasive developmental disorders* (3rd ed., 288–311). Hoboken, NJ: Wiley.

Shear, M. K., Brown, T. A., Sholomskas, D. E., Barlow, D. H., Gorman, J. M., Woods, S. W. et al. (1992). *Panic Disorder Severity Scale (PDSS).* Pittsburgh, PA: University of Pittsburgh Medical School, Department of Psychiatry.

Shearer, S., & Gordon, L. (2006). The patient with excessive worry. *American Family Physician, 73*(6), 1049–1057.

Sheehan, B., & Banerjee, S. (1999). Review: Somatization in the elderly. *International Journal of Geriatric Psychiatry, 14*, 1044–1049.

Sheikh, J. I., Swales, P. J., Carlson, E. B., & Lindley, S. E. (2004). Aging and panic disorder: Phenomenology, comorbidity, and risk factors. *American Journal of Geriatric Psychiatry, 12*, 102–109.

Shelder, J., & Westen, D. (2004). Dimensions of personality pathology: An alternative to the Five-Factor Model. *American Journal of Psychiatry, 161*, 1743–1754.

Sheldrick, C. (1999). Practitioner review: The assessment and management of risk in adolescents. *Journal of Psychology and Psychiatry, 49*(4), 507–518.

Shepherd, M. (1961). Morbid jealousy: Some clinical and social aspects of psychiatric symptoms. *British Journal of Psychiatry, 107*, 678–714.

Sher, L., Oquendo, M. A., & Mann, J. J. (2001). Risk of suicide in mood disorders. *Clinical Neuroscience Research, 1*, 337–344.

Sherman, A., Amery, C., Duffield, B., Ebb, N., & Weinstein, D. (1998). *Early findings on family hardship and well-being.* Washington, DC: Children's Defense Fund and National Coalition for the Homeless.

Sherwood, N. E., Crowther, J. H., & Wills, L. (2000). The perceived function of eating for bulimic, subclinical bulimic, and non-eating disordered women. *Behavior Therapy, 31*(4), 777–793.

Shibayama, H., Kasahara, Y., & Kobayashi, H. (1986). Prevalence of dementia in a Japanese elderly population. *Acta Psychiatrica Scandinavica, 74*, 144–151.

Shifren, J. L., Braunstein, G. D., Simon, J. A., Casson, P. R., Buster, J. E., Redmond, G. P., et al. (2000). Transdermal testosterone treatment in women with impaired sexual function after oophorectomy. *New England Journal of Medicine, 343*(10), 682–688.

Shih, R. A., Belmonte, P. L., & Zandi, P. P. (2004). A review of the evidence from family, twin and adoption studies for a genetic contribution to adult psychiatric disorders. *International Review of Psychiatry, 16*, 260–283.

Shinnar, S., Rapin, I., Arnold, S., Tuchman, R., Shulman, L., Ballabasn-Gil, K., et al. (2001). Language regression in childhood. *Pediatric Neurology, 24*, 183–194.

Shiperd, J. C., Stafford, J., & Tanner, L. R. (2005). Predicting alcohol and drug abuse in Persian Gulf War veterans: What role do PTSD symptoms play? *Addictive Behaviors, 30*, 595–599.

Shneidman, E. S. (1981). Psychotherapy with suicidal patients. *Suicide and Life-Threatening Behavior, 11*, 341–348.

Shneidman, E. S. (1985). *Definition of suicide.* New York: Wiley.

Shneidman, E. S. (1993). Suicide as a psycheache. *Journal of Nervous and Mental Disorders, 181*, 145–147.

Shoptaw, S., Jarvik, M. E., Ling, W., & Rawson, R. A. (1996). Contingency management of tobacco smoking in methadone-maintained opiate addicts. *Addictive Behaviors, 21*, 409–412.

Shoptaw, S., Reback, C. J., Peck, J. A., Yang, X., Rotheram-Fuller, E. J., Larkins, S., et al. (2005). Behavioral treatment approaches for methamphetamine dependence and HIV-related sexual risk behaviors among urban gay and bisexual men. *Drug and Alcohol Dependence, 78*, 125–134.

Siassi, I. (1984). Psychiatric interview and the mental status examination. In G. Goldstein & M. Hersen (Eds.), *Handbook of psychological assessment* (pp. 259–275). New York: Pergamon Press.

Siegel, B. (1996). *The world of the autistic child: Understanding and treating autistic spectrum disorders.* New York: Oxford University Press.

Siegel, B. (2003). *Helping children with autism learn: Treatment approaches for parents and professional.* New York: Oxford University Press.

Siegel, B. (2004). *The Pervasive Developmental Disorder Screening Test-II.* San Antonio, TX: Psychological Corp.

Siegel, B., & Ficcaglia, M. (2006). Pervasive developmental disorders. In M. Hersen, J. Thomas, & R. T. Ammerman (Eds.), *Comprehensive handbook of personality and psychopathology* (Vol. 3, pp. 254–271). Hoboken, NJ: Wiley.

Siegel, B., & Hayer, C. (1999, April). *Detection of autism in the 2nd and 3rd year: The Pervasive Developmental Disorders Screening Test (PDDST).* Poster presented at the biennal meeting for the Society for Research in Child Development, Albuquerque, NM.

Siegel, B., Hayer, C., & Tanguay, P. (2001). Treatment of pervasive developmental disorders. In E. Weller, J. McDermott, & G. Gabbard (Eds.), *Treatment of psychiatric disorders* (3rd ed., Vol. 1, pp. 65–90). Washington, DC: American Psychiatric Association.

Siegel, S. (2001). Pavlovian conditioning and drug overdose: When tolerance fails. *Addiction Research and Theory, 9,* 503–513.

Siegel, S., Hinson, R. E., Krank, M. D., & McCully, J. (1982). Heroin "overdose" death: Contribution of drug-associated environmental cues. *Science, 216,* 436–437.

Silber, M. H. (2001). Sleep disorders. *Neurologic Clinics, 19*(1), 173–186.

Silberg, J., Rutter, M., Meyer, J., Maes, H., Hewitt, J., Simonoff, E., et al. (1996). Genetic and environmental covariation between hyperactivity and conduct disturbance in juvenile twins. *Journal of Child Psychology Psychiatry, 37,* 803–816.

Silberg, J. L., Rutter, M., Tracy, K., Maes, H. H., & Eaves, L. (1996). Heterogeneity in the development of antisocial behavior: The Virginia twin study of adolescents' behavioral development and young adult follow-up. *Psychological Medicine, 26,* 1119–1133.

Silk, K. S. (2000). Overview of biologic factors. *Psychiatric Clinics of North America, 23,* 61–75.

Silveira, J. M., & Seeman, M. V. (1995). Shared psychotic disorder: A critical review of the literature. *Canadian Journal of Psychiatry, 40,* 389–395.

Silver, A. A., & Hagin, R. A. (2002). *Disorders of learning in childhood* (2nd ed.). Hoboken, NJ: Wiley.

Silver, R. C., Holman, E. A., McIntosh, D. N., Poulin, M., & Gil-Rivas, V. (2002). Nationwide longitudinal study of psychological responses to September 11. *Journal of the American Medical Association, 288,* 1235–1244.

Silverman, W. K., & Albano, A. M. (1996). *Anxiety disorders interview schedule (ADIS-IV) child/parent version.* New York: Oxford University Press.

Silverman, J. A. (1997). Anorexia nervosa: Historical perspective on treatment. In D. M. Garner & P. E. Garfinkel (Eds.), *Handbook of eating disorders* (2nd ed., pp. 6–7). New York: Guilford Press.

Silverman, K., Svikis, D., Robles, E., Stitzer, M. L., & Bigelow, G. E. (2001). A reinforcement-based therapeutic workplace for the treatment of drug abuse: Six-month abstinence outcomes. *Experimental and Clinical Psychopharmacology, 9,* 14–23.

Silverman, W. K., & Ollendick, T. H. (2005). Evidence-based assessment of anxiety and its disorders in children and adolescents. *Journal of Clinical Child and Adolescent Psychology, 34,* 380–411.

Silverstein, M. L., Mavrolefteros, G., & Close, D. (2002). Premorbid adjustment and neuropsychological performance in schizophrenia. *Schizophrenia Bulletin, 28,* 157–165.

Simon, G. E. (2002). Management of somatoform and factitious disorders. In P. E. Nathan, & J. M. Gorman (Eds.), *A guide to treatments that work* (2nd ed., pp. 447–462). New York: Oxford University Press.

Simon, G. E., Gureje, O., & Fullerton, C. (2001). Course of hypochondriasis in an international primary care study. *General Hospital Psychiatry, 23,* 51–55.

Simon, G. E., Hunkeler, E., Fireman, B., Lee, J. Y., & Savarino, J. (2007). Risk of suicide attempt and suicide death in patients treated for bipolar disorder. *Bipolar Disorders, 9,* 526–530.

Simon, G. E., & Von Korff, M. (1997). Prevalence, burden, and treatment of insomnia in primary care. *American Journal of Psychiatry, 154*(10), 1417–1423.

Simon, R. I., & Gutheil, T. G. (2002). A recurrent pattern of suicide risk factors observed in litigated cases: Lessons in risk management. *Psychiatric Annals, 32*(7), 384–387.

Simon, S. L., Davey, J., Glynn, S., Rawson, R., & Ling, W. (2004). The effect of relapse on cognition in abstinent methamphetamine abusers. *Journal of Substance Abuse Treatment, 27*, 59–66.

Simon, S. L., Domier, C., Carnell, J., Brethen, P., Rawson, R., & Ling, W. (2000). Cognitive impairment in individuals currently using methamphetamine. *American Journal on Addictions, 9*, 222–231.

Simonoff, E. (2001a). Gene-environment interplay in oppositional defiant and conduct disorder. *Child and Adolescent Clinics of North America, 10*(2), 351–374.

Simonoff, E. (2001b). Genetic influences on conduct disorder. In J. Hill & B. Maughan (Eds.), *Conduct disorders in childhood and adolescence* (pp. 202–234). Cambridge: Cambridge University Press.

Simons, A. D., Murphy, G. E., Levine, J. L., & Wetzel, R. D. (1986). Cognitive therapy and pharmacotherapy for depression: Sustained improvement over one year. *Archives of General Psychiatry, 43*, 43–48.

Simons-Morton, B. G., Crump, A. D., Haynie, D. L., Saylor, K. E., Eitel, P., & Yu, K. (1999). Psychosocial, school, and parent factors associated with recent smoking among early adolescent boys and girls. *Preventive Medicine: An International Journal Devoted to Practice and Theory, 28*, 138–148.

Simpson, S. G., McMahon, F. J., McInnis, M. G., MacKinnon, D. F., Edwin, D., Folstein, S. E., et al. (2002). Diagnostic reliability of bipolar II disorder. *Archives of General Psychiatry, 59*, 736–740.

Sipahimalani, A., & Massand, P. S. (1998). Use of risperidone in delirium: Case reports. *Annals of Clinical Psychiatry, 9*, 105–107.

Siperstein, R., & Volkmar, F. R. (2004). Parental reporting of regression in children with pervasive developmental disorders. *Journal of Autism and Developmental Disorders, 34*, 731–734.

Siris, S. G. (1991). Diagnosis of secondary depression in schizophrenia: Implications for DSM-IV. *Schizophrenia Bulletin, 16*, 75–98.

Siris, S. G. (1995). Depression in schizophrenia. In C. L. Shriqui & H. A. Nasrallah (Eds.), *Contemporary issues in the treatment of schizophrenia* (pp. 155–166). Washington, DC: American Psychiatric Press.

Siris, S. G., Mason, S. E., & Shuwall, M. A. (1993). Histories of substance abuse, panic and suicidal ideation in schizophrenic patients with histories of post-psychotic depressions. *Progress in Neuro-Psychopharmacology and Biological Psychiatry, 17*, 609–617.

Sirles, E., & Franke, P. (1989). Factors influencing mothers' reactions to intra familial sexual abuse. *Child Abuse and Neglect, 13*, 131–140.

Sirois, F. (1988). Delirium: 100 cases. *Canadian Journal of Psychiatry, 33*, 375–378.

Sivertsen, B., Omvik, S., Pallesen, S., Bjorvatn, B., Havik, O. E., Kvale, G., et al. (2006). Cognitive behavioral therapy vs. zopiclone for treatment of chronic primary insomnia in older adults: A randomized controlled trial. *Journal of the American Medical Association, 295*(24), 2851–2858.

Skodol, A. E. (2005). Manifestations, clinical diagnosis, and comorbidity. In J. M. Oldham, A. E. Skodol, & D. S. Bender (Eds.), *Textbook of personality disorders* (pp. 57–87). Washington, DC: American Psychiatric Publishing.

Skodol, A. E., & Bender, D. S. (2003). Why are more women diagnosed borderline than men? *Psychiatric Quarterly, 74*, 349–360.

Skodol, A. E., Gunderson, J. G., McGlashan, T. H., Dyck, I. R., Stout, R. L., Bender, D. S., et al. (2002). Functional impairment in patients with schizotypal, borderline, avoidant or obsessive-compulsive personality disorders. *American Journal of Psychiatry, 159*, 276–283.

Skodol, A. E., Gunderson, J. G., Pfohl, B., Widiger, T. A., Livesley, W. J., & Siever, L. J. (2002). The borderline diagnosis I: Psychopathology, comorbidity, and personality structure. *American Journal of Psychiatry, 159*, 276–283.

Skodol, A. E., Siever, L. J., Livesley, J., Gunderson, J. G., Pfohl, B., & Widiger, T. A. (2002). The borderline diagnosis II: Biology, genetics, and clinical course. *Biological Psychiatry, 51*, 951–963.

Skodol Wilson, H., & Skodol, A. (1994). Special report: DSM-IV: Overview and examination of major changes. *Archives of Psychiatric Nursing, 8,* 340–347.

Skoog, G., & Skoog, I. (1999). A 40-year follow-up of patients with obsessive-compulsive disorder. *Archives of General Psychiatry, 56,* 121–127.

Skoog, I. (1998). Status of risk factors for vascular dementia. *Neuroepidemiology, 17,* 2–9.

Skoog, I. K., Raj, N., & Breteler, M. B. (1999). Vascular factors in Alzheimer's disease. *Alzheimer Disease and Associated Disorders, 13*(Suppl. 3), S106–S114.

Slade, M., Daniel, L. J., & Hoisler, C. J. (1991). Application of forensic toxicology to the problem of domestic violence. *Journal of Forensic Science, 36,* 708–713.

Slade, T., & Andrews, G. (2002). Exclusion criteria in the diagnostic classification of DSM-IV and ICD-10: Revisiting the co-occurrence of psychiatric syndromes. *Psychological Medicine, 32,* 1203–1211.

Slaikeu, K. (1990). *Crisis intervention* (2nd ed.). Boston: Allyn & Bacon.

Sloan, D. M., Mizes, J. S., & Epstein, E. M. (2005). Empirical classification of eating disorders. *Eating Behaviors, 6*(1), 53–62.

Slooter, A. J., Tang, M. X., van Duijn, C. M., Stern, Y., Ott, A., & Bell, K. (1997). Apolipoprotein E epsilon 4 and the risk of dementia with stroke: A population-based investigation. *Journal of the American Medical Association, 277,* 818–821.

Slutske, W. S., Heath, A. C., Dinwiddie, S. H., Madden, P. A. F., Bucholz, K. K., Dunne, M. P., et al. (1997). Modeling genetic and environmental influences in the etiology of conduct disorder: A study of 2,682 adult twin pairs. *Journal of Abnormal Psychology, 106,* 269–279.

Small, G. W., Rabins, P. V., Barry, P. P., Buckholtz, N. S., DeKosky, S. T., Ferris, S. H., et al. (1997). Diagnosis and treatment of Alzheimer disease and related disorders: Consensus statement of the American Association for Geriatric Psychiatry, the Alzheimer's Association, and the American Geriatrics Society. *Journal of the American Medical Association, 278,* 1363–1371.

Smeeth, L., Cook, C., Fombonne, E., Heavey, L., Rodrigues, L., Smith, P., et al. (2004). Rate of first recorded diagnosis of autism and other pervasive developmental disorders in the United Kingdom general practice, 1988–2001. *Biomed Central Medicine (BMC), 2*(39) 10.1186/1741-7015-2-39.

Smith, B. H., Waschbusch, D. A., Willoughby, M. T., & Evans, S. (2000). The efficacy, safety, and predictability of treatments for adolescents with attention-deficit/hyperactivity disorder (ADHD). *Clinical Child and Family Psychology Review, 3*(4), 243–267.

Smith, D. J. (1995). Youth crime and conduct disorders. In M. Rutter & D. J. Smith (Eds.), *Psychosocial disorders in young people: Time trends and their causes* (pp. 389–489). Chichester, West Sussex, England: Wiley.

Smith, I. M. (2000). Motor functioning in Asperger syndrome. In A. Klin & F. R. Volkmar (Eds.), *Asperger syndrome* (pp. 97–124). New York: Guilford Press.

Smith, M. T., & Perlis, M. L. (2002). Primary insomnia. In M. Hersen & L. K. Porzelius (Eds.), *Diagnosis, conceptualization, and treatment planning for adults: A step-by-step guide* (pp. 225–250). Mahwah, NJ: Erlbaum.

Smith, M. T., Smith, L. J., Nowakowski, S., & Perlis, M. L. (2003). Primary insomnia: Diagnostic issues, treatment, and future directions. In M. L. Perlis & K. L. Lichstein (Eds.), *Treating sleep disorders: Principles and practice of behavioral sleep medicine* (pp. 214–261). Hoboken, NJ: Wiley.

Smith, T., Groen, A., & Wynn, J. (2002). Randomized trial of intensive early intervention for children with pervasive developmental disorder. *American Journal of Mental Retardation, 105,* 259–285.

Smith, T. E., Hull, J. M., Israel, L. M., & Wilson, D. F. (2000). Insight, symptoms and neurocognitive functioning in schizophrenia and schizoaffective disorder. *Schizophrenia Bulletin, 26,* 193–200.

Smolak, L., Murnen, S. K., & Ruble, A. E. (2000). Female athletes and eating problems: A meta-analysis. *International Journal of Eating Disorders, 27*(4), 371–380.

Smolak, L., & Striegel-Moore, R. H. (2001). Challenging the myth of the golden girl: Ethnicity and eating disorders. In R. H. Striegel-Moore & L. Smolak (Eds.), *Eating disorders: Innovative directions in research and practice* (pp. 111–132). Washington, DC: American Psychological Association.

Snapp Kean, R., Hoey, K. M., & Pinals, S. l. (2004). Treatment of personality disorders in older adults: A community Mental Health model. In J. J. Magnavita (Ed.), *Handbook of personality: Theory and practice*. (pp. 498–510). Hoboken, NJ: Wiley

Snow, A. L., Kunik, M. E., Molinari, V. A., Orengo, C. A., Doody, R., Graham, D. P., et al. (2005). Accuracy of self-reported depression in persons with dementia. *Journal of the American Geriatric Society, 53*, 389–396.

Snowdon, D. A., Greiner, L. H., Mortimer, J. A., Riley, K. P., Greiner, P. A., & Markesbery, W. R. (1997). Brain infarction and the clinical expression of Alzheimer's disease: The nun study. *Journal of the American Medical Association, 277*, 813–817.

Snyder, H. (2001). Epidemiology of official offending. In R. Loeber & D. P. Farrington (Eds.), *Child delinquents: Development, interventions and service needs* (pp. 25–46). Thousand Oaks, CA: Sage.

Snyder, H. (2002). Juvenile arrest 2002. Office of Justice Program: U.S. Dept. of Justice. Retrieved October 14, 2007, from www.ncjrs.gov/pdffiles1/ojjdp/204608.pdf.

Snyder, H. N., & Sickmund, M. (2006). *Juvenile offenders and victims: 2006 national report.* Washington, DC: U.S. Department of Justice, Office of Justice Programs, Office of Juvenile Justice and Delinquency Prevention.

Sobell, L. C., Cunningham, J. A., & Sobell, M. B. (1996). Recovery from alcohol problems with and without treatment: Prevalence in two population surveys. *American Journal of Public Health, 86*, 966–972.

Sobell, L. C., & Sobell, M. B. (1992). Timeline follow-back: A technique for assessing self-reported alcohol consumption. In R. Litten & J. Allen (Eds.), *Measuring alcohol consumption* (pp. 41–72). Totowa, NJ: Humana Press.

Sofuoglu, M., Dudish-Poulsen, S., Brown, S. B., & Hatsukami, D. K. (2003). Association of cocaine withdrawal symptoms with more severe dependence and enhanced subjective response to cocaine. *Drug and Alcohol Dependence, 69*, 273–282.

Soloff, P. H. (2005). Somatic treatments. In J. M. Oldham, A. E. Skodol, & D. S. Bender (Eds.), *Textbook of personality disorders* (pp. 387–403). Washington, DC: American Psychiatric Publishing.

Solomon, D. A., Keller, M. B., Leon, A. C., Mueller, T. I., Lavori, P. W., Shea, T., et al. (2000). Multiple recurrences of major depressive disorder. *American Journal of Psychiatry, 157*, 229–233.

Solomon, P., Drain, J., & Delaney, M. A. (1995). The working alliance and consumer case management. *Journal of Mental Health Administration, 22*, 126–134.

Solomon, Z. (1988). The effect of combat-related posttraumatic stress disorder on the family. *Psychiatry, 51*, 323–329.

Sommers-Flanagan, J., & Sommers-Flanagan, R. (1993). *Foundations of therapeutic interviewing.* Boston: Allyn & Bacon.

Sommers-Flanagan, J., & Sommers-Flanagan, R. (1995). Intake interviewing with suicidal patients: A systematic approach. *Professional Psychology: Research and Practice, 26*(1), 41–47.

Sommers-Flanagan, R., & Sommers-Flanagan, J. (1999). *Clinical interviewing.* New York: Wiley.

Sonuga-Barke, E. J., Dalen, L., Daley, D., & Remington, B. (2002). Are planning, working memory and inhibition associated with individual differences in preschool ADHD symptoms? *Developmental Neuropsychology, 21*, 255–272.

Sörensen, A., Pinquart, M., & Duberstein, P. (2002). How effective are interventions with caregivers? An updated meta-analysis. *Gerontologist, 42*, 356–372.

Sorenson, S. B., Upchurch, D. M., & Shen, H. (1996). Violence and injury in marital arguments: Risk patterns and gender differences. *American Journal of Public Health, 86*, 35–40.

Sotsky, S. M., Glass, D. R., Shea, M. T., Pilkonis, P. A., Collins, J. F., Elkin, I., et al. (1991). Patient predictors of response to psychotherapy and pharmacotherapy: Findings in the NIMH Treatment of Depression Collaborative Research Program. *American Journal of Psychiatry, 148*, 997–1008.

Soundy, T. J., Lucas, A. R., Suman, V. J., & Melton, L. J. (1995). Bulimia nervosa in Rochester, Minnesota from 1980 to 1990. *Psychological Medicine, 25*(5), 1065–1071.

Spahic-Mihajlovic, A., Crayton, J. W., & Neafsey, E. J. (2005). Selective numbing and hyperarousal in male and female refugees with PTSD. *Anxiety Disorders, 19*, 282–402.

Sparrevohn, R., & Howie, P. M. (1995). Theory of mind in children with autistic disorder: Evidence of developmental progression and the role of verbal ability. *Journal of Child Psychology and Psychiatry, 36*(2), 249–263.

Sparrow, S., Balla, D., & Cicchetti, D. (1984). *Vineland Adaptive Behavior Scales*. Circle Pines, MN: American Guidance Service.

Speckens, A. E. M., Spinhoven, P., Sloekers, P. P. A., Bolk, J. H., & van Hemert, A. M. (1996). A validation study of the Whitley Index, the Illness Attitude Scales, and the Somatosensory Amplification Scale in general medical and general practice patients. *Journal of Psychosomatic Research, 40*(1), 95–104.

Speckens, A. E. M., van Hemert, A. M., Spinhoven, P., & Bolk, J. H. (1996). The diagnostic and prognostic significance of the Whitley Index, the Illness Attitude Scales, and the Somatosensory Amplification Scale. *Psychological Medicine, 26*, 1085–1090.

Spector, A., Thorgrimsen, L., Woods, B., Royan, L., Davies, S., Butterworth, M., et al. (2003). Efficacy of an evidence-based cognitive stimulation therapy programme for people with dementia. *British Journal of Psychiatry, 183*, 248–254.

Speltz, M. L., McClellan, J., De Klyen, M., & Jones, K. (1999). Preschool boys with oppositional defiant disorder: Clinical presentation and diagnostic change. *Journal of the American Academy of Child and Adolescent Psychiatry, 38*(7), 838–845.

Spence, S. H., Donovan, C., & Brechman-Toussaint, M. (1999). Social skills, social outcomes, and cognitive features of childhood social phobia. *Journal of Abnormal Psychology, 108*, 211–221.

Spencer, E. K., & Campbell, M. (1994). Children with schizophrenia: Diagnosis, phenomenology, and pharmacotherapy. *Schizophrenia Bulletin, 20*, 713–725.

Spencer, T. J. (2004). ADHD treatment across the life cycle. *Journal of Clinical Psychiatry, 65*(Suppl. 3), 22–26.

Sperry, L. (1995) Personality disorders. In L. Sperry & I. Carlson (Eds.), *Psychopathology and psychotherapy: From DSM-IV diagnosis to treatment* (2nd ed., pp. 279–336). Washington, DC: Accelerated Development/Taylor & Francis.

Sperry, L. (1999). *Cognitive behavioral therapy of DSM-IV personality disorders*. Philadelphia: Burner/Mazel.

Spiegel, B. R., & Fewell, C. H. (2004). 12-Step programs as a treatment modality. In S. L. Ashenberg-Straussner (Ed.), *Clinical work with substance-abusing clients* (2nd ed., pp. 125–145). New York: Guilford Press.

Spiegel, D., Koopman, C., Cardeña, E., & Classen, C. (1996). Dissociative symptoms in the diagnosis of acute stress disorder. In L. K. Michelson & W. J. Ray (Eds.), *Handbook of dissociation: Theoretical, empirical, and clinical perspectives* (pp. 367–380). New York: Plenum Press.

Spielman, A. J., Caruso, L. S., & Glovinsky, P. B. (1987). A behavioral perspective on insomnia treatment. *Psychiatric Clinics of North America, 10*(4), 541–553.

Spielman, A. J., & Glovinsky, P. B. (1997). The diagnostic interview and differential diagnosis for complaints of insomnia. In M. R. Pressman & W. C. Orr (Eds.), *Understanding sleep: The evaluation and treatment of sleep disorders* (pp. 125–160). Washington, DC: American Psychological Association.

Spielman, A. J., Nunes, J., & Glovinsky, P. B. (1996). Insomnia. *Neurologic Clinics, 14*(3), 513–543.

Spielman, A. J., Saskin, J. P., & Thorpy, J. J. (1987). Treatment of chronic insomnia by restriction of time in bed. *Sleep, 10*, 45–56.

Spitzer, R. L. (1991). An outsider-insider's views about revising the DSMs. *Journal of Abnormal Psychology, 100*(3), 294–296.

Spitzer, R. L., Devlin, M., Walsh, B. T., Hasin, D., Wing, R., Marcus, M., et al. (1992). Binge eating disorder: A multisite field trial of the diagnostic criteria. *International Journal of Eating Disorders, 11*, 191–203.

Spitzer, R. L., Endicott, J., & Gibbon, M. (1979). Crossing the border into borderline personality and boderline schizophrenia: The development of criteria. *Archives of General Psychiatry, 36*, 17–24.

Spitzer, R. L., Endicott, J. J., & Robins, E. (1975). *Research diagnostic criteria (RDC) for a select group of functional disorders.* New York: New York State Psychiatric Institute.

Spitzer, R. L., Endicott, J. J., & Robins, E. (1978). Research diagnostic criteria: Rationale and reliability. *Archives of General Psychiatry, 35*, 773–782.

Spitzer, R. L., Kroenke, K., & Williams, J. B. (1999). Validation and utility of a self-report version of PRIME-MD: The PHQ primary care study. *Journal of the American Medical Association, 282*, 1737–1744.

Spitzer, R. L., & Wakefield, J. C. (1999). DSM-IV diagnostic criterion for clinical significance: Does it help solve the false positive problem? *American Journal of Psychiatry, 156*(12), 1856–1864.

Spitzer, R. L., Yanovski, S., Wadden, T., Wing, R., Marcus, M., Stunkard, A., et al. (1993). Binge eating disorder: Its further validation in a multisite study. *International Journal of Eating Disorders, 13*, 137–153.

Sponheim, E. (1996). Changing criteria of autistic disorders: A comparison of the ICD-10 research criteria and DSM-IV with DSM-III-R, CARS and ABC. *Journal of Autism and Developmental Disorders, 26*(5), 513–525.

Spooner, A. L., Evans, M., & Santos, R. (2005). Hidden shyness in children: Discrepancies between self-perceptions and the perceptions of parents and teachers. *Merrill-Palmer Quarterly, 51*, 437–466.

Squires-Wheeler, E., Friedman, D., & Amminger, G. P., (1997). Negative and positive dimensions of schizotypal personality disorder. *Journal of Personality Disorders, 11*, 285–300.

Stahl, N. D., & Clarizio, H. F. (1999). Conduct disorder and comorbidity. *Psychology in the Schools, 36*(1), 41–50.

Stahl, S. M. (2006). *Essential psychopharmacology: The prescriber's guide—Revised and updated edition.* New York: Cambridge University Press.

Stanford, E. J., Goetz, R. R., & Bloom, J. D. (1994). The no harm contract in the emergency assessment of suicidal risk. *Journal of Clinical Psychiatry, 55*, 344–348.

Stanley, B., & Brodsky, B. (2005a). Dialectical behavior therapy. In J. M. Oldham, A. E. Skodol, & D. S. Bender (Eds.), *Textbook of personality disorders* (pp. 307–320). Washington, DC: American Psychiatric Publishing.

Stanley, B., & Brodsky, B. S. (2005b). Suicidal and self-injurious behavior in borderline personality disorder. In J. G. Gunderson & P. D. Hoffman (Eds.), *Understanding and treating borderline personality disorder: A guide for professionals* (pp. 43–63). Washington, DC: American Psychiatric Press.

Stanley, M. A., Beck, J. G., Novy, D. M., Averill, P. M., Swann, A. C., Diefenbach, G. J., et al. (2003). Cognitive-behavioral treatment of late-life generalized anxiety disorder. *Journal of Consulting and Clinical Psychology, 71*, 309–319.

Stanton, M. (2005). Relapse prevention needs more emphasis on interpersonal factors. *American Psychologist, 60*, 340–341.

Stanton, M. D., & Heath, A. W. (2005). In R. J. Miller, S. I. Miller, & A. H. Mack (Eds.), *Clinical textbook of addictive disorders* (3rd ed., pp. 528–558). New York: Guilford Press.

Stapleton, J. M., Eckardt, M. J., Martin, P., Adinoff, B., Roehrich, L., Bone, G., et al. (1988). Treatment of alcoholic organic brain syndrome with the serotonin reuptake inhibitor fluvoxamine: A preliminary study. *Advances in Alcohol and Substance Abuse, 7*, 47–51.

Starcevic, V. (2001). Clinical features and diagnosis of hypochondriasis. In V. Starcevic & D. R. Lipsitt (Eds.), *Hypochondriasis: Modern perspectives on an ancient malady* (pp. 21–57). New York: Oxford University Press.

Starr, E., Szatmari, P., Bryson, S., & Zwaigenbaum, L. (2003). Stability and change among high-functioning children with pervasive developmental disorders: A 2-year outcome study. *Journal of Autism and Developmental Disorders, 33*, 15–22.

Startup, M. (1996). Insight and cognitive deficits in schizophrenia: Evidence for a curvilinear relationship. *Psychological Medicine, 26*, 1277–1281.

Startup, M., Jackson, M. C., & Bendix, S. (2002). The concurrent validity of the global assessment of functioning (GAF). *British Journal of Clinical Psychology, 41*, 417–422.

Staton, M., Leukefeld, C., Logan, T. K., Zimmerman, R., Lynam, D., Milich, R., et al. (1999). Risky sex behavior and substance use among young adults. *Health and Social Work, 24*, 147–154.

Stattin, H., & Kerr, M. (2000). Parental monitoring: A reinterpretation. *Child Development, 71*, 1072–1085.

Stayton, W. R. (1996). Sexual and gender identity disorders in a relational perspective. In F. W. Kaslow (Ed.), *Handbook of relational diagnosis and dysfunctional family patterns* (pp. 357–370). Oxford: Wiley.

Steadman, H. J., Mulvey, E. P., Monahan, J., Clark Robbins, P., Applebaum, P. S., Grisso, T., et al. (1998). Violence by people discharged from acute psychiatric inpatient facilities and by others in the same neighborhoods. *Archives of General Psychiatry, 55*, 393–401.

Steffens, D. C., Snowden, M., Fan, M. Y., Hendrie, H., Katon, W. J., & Unützer, J. (2006). Cognitive impairment and depression outcomes in the IMPACT study. *American Journal of Geriatric Psychiatry, 14*, 401–409.

Stein, K. F., & Corte, C. (2003). Reconceptualizing causative factors and intervention strategies in the eating disorders: A shift from body image to self-concept impairments. *Archives of Psychiatric Nursing, 17*(2), 57–66.

Stein, L. I., & Test, M. A. (1980). Alternative mental hospital treatment: Pt. I. Conceptual model, treatment program, and clinical evaluation. *Archives of General Psychiatry, 37*, 392–397.

Stein, M. B., Fyer, A. J., Davidson, J. R. T., Pollack, M. H., & Wiita, B. (1999). Fluvoxamine treatment of social phobia (social anxiety disorder): A double-blind placebo-controlled study. *American Journal of Psychiatry, 156*, 756–760.

Stein, M. B., & Heimberg, R. G. (2004). Well-being and life satisfaction in generalized anxiety disorder: Comparison to major depressive disorder in a community sample. *Journal of Affective Disorders, 79*, 161–166.

Stein, M. B., McQuaid, J. R., Laffaye, C., & McCahill, M. E. (1999). Social phobia in the primary care medical setting. *Journal of Family Practice, 48*, 514–519.

Steiner, H., Petersen, M. L., Saxena, K., Ford, S., & Matthews, Z. (2003). Divalproex sodium for the treatment of conduct disorder: A randomized controlled clinical trial. *Journal of Clinical Psychiatry, 64*(10), 1183–1191.

Steinhausen, H. C. (2002). The outcome of anorexia nervosa in the 20th century. *American Journal of Psychiatry, 159*, 1284–1293.

Steinhausen, H. C., Drechsler, R., Foldenyi, M., Imhof, K., & Brandeis, D. (2003). Clinical course of attention-deficit/hyperactivity disorder from childhood towards early adolescence. *Journal of the American Academy of Child and Adolescent Psychiatry, 42*, 1085–1092.

Stekel, W. (1943). *The interpretation of dreams.* New York: Liveright.

Steketee, G. S. (1993). *Treatment of obsessive compulsive disorder.* New York: Guilford Press.

Steketee, G. S., & Barlow, D. H. (2002). Obsessive-compulsive disorder. In D. H. Barlow (Ed.), *Anxiety and its disorders: The nature and treatment of anxiety and panic* (2nd ed., pp. 516–550). New York: Guilford Press.

Steketee, G. S., Frost, R. O., & Cohen, I. (1998). Beliefs in obsessive-compulsive disorder. *Journal of Anxiety Disorders, 12*, 525–537.

Steketee, G., Frost, R. O., & Kim, H. J. (2001). Hoarding by elderly people. *Health and Social Work, 26,* 176–184.

Steketee, G. S., & Pigott, T. (2006). *Obsessive-compulsive disorder: The latest assessment and treatment strategies.* Kansas City, MO: Compact Clinicals.

Stengel, E. (1959). Classification of mental disorders. *Bulletin of the World Health Organization, 21,* 601–663.

Stepanski, E. J., & Perlis, M. L. (2003). A historical perspective and commentary on practice issues. In M. L. Perlis & K. L. Lichstein (Eds.), *Treating sleep disorders: Principles and practice of behavioral sleep medicine* (pp. 3–26). Hoboken, NJ: Wiley.

Stephan, C. W. (1992). Mixed heritage individuals: Ethnic identity and trait characteristics. In M. Root (Ed.), *Racially mixed people in America* (pp. 50–63). Newbury Park, CA: Sage.

Stern, A. (1938). Psychoanalytic investigation of and therapy in the borderline group of neuroses. *Psychoanalytic Quarterly, 7,* 467–489.

Stevens, J. R. (1982). Neuropathology of schizophrenia. *Archives of General Psychiatry, 39,* 1131–1139.

Stevens, J., & Ward-Estes, J. (2006). Attention-deficit/hyperactivity disorder. In M. Hersen, J. C. Thomas, & R. T. Ammerman (Eds.), *Comprehensive handbook of personality and psychopathology: Vol. 3. Child psychopathology* (pp. 316–329). Hoboken, NJ: Wiley.

Steward, S. H., Pihl, R. O., Conrod, P. J., & Dongier, M. (1998). Functional associations among trauma, PTSD, and substance related disorders. *Addictive Behaviors, 23,* 797–812.

Stewart, D. E. (1988). Prophylactic lithium in postpartum affective psychosis. *Journal of Nervous and Mental Diseases, 176,* 485–489.

Stewart, R. (1998). Cardiovascular factors in Alzheimer's disease. *Journal of Neurology, Neurosurgery, and Psychiatry, 65,* 143–147.

Stewart, T. M., & Williamson, D. A. (2004a). Assessment of eating disorders. In M. Hersen (Ed.), *Psychological assessment in clinical practice: A pragmatic guide* (pp. 175–195). New York: Brunner-Routledge.

Stewart, T. M., & Williamson, D. A. (2004b). Multidisciplinary treatment of eating disorders, Part. 2. *Behavior Modification, 28*(6), 831–853.

St. George-Hyslop, P. H. (2000). Genetic factors in the genesis of Alzheimer's disease. *Annals of the New York Academy of Sciences, 924,* 1–7.

Stice, E. (2001). A prospective test of the dual-pathway model of bulimic pathology: Mediating effects of dieting and negative affect. *Journal of Abnormal Psychology, 110*(1), 124–135.

Stice, E. (2002). Risk and maintenance factors for eating pathology: A meta-analytic review. *Psychological Bulletin, 128*(5), 825–848.

Stice, E., Myers, M. G., & Brown, S. A. (1998). A longitudinal grouping analysis of adolescent substance use escalation and de-escalation. *Psychology of Addictive Behaviors, 12,* 14–27.

Stice, E., & Shaw, H. E. (1994). Adverse effects of the media portrayed thin-ideal on women and linkages to bulimic symptomatology. *Journal of Social and Clinical Psychology, 13*(3), 288–308.

Stice, E., Telch, C. F., & Rizvi, S. L. (2000). Development and validation of the eating disorder diagnostic scale: A brief self-report measure of anorexia, bulimia, and binge eating disorder. *Psychological Assessment, 12*(2), 123–131.

Stierlin, H., Weber, G., Schmidt, G., & Simon, F. B. (1986). Features of families with major affective disorders. *Family Process, 25,* 325–336.

Still, G. F. (1902). Some abnormal psychical conditions in children. *Lancet, 1,* 1008–1012, 1077–1082, 1163–1168.

Stinson, F. S., & DeBakey, S. F. (1992). Alcohol-related mortality in the United States, 1979–1988. *British Journal of Addiction, 87,* 777–783.

Stinson, F. S., Grant, B. F., Dawson, D. A., Ruan, W. J., Huang, B., & Saha, T. (2005). Comorbidity between DSM-IV alcohol and specific drug use disorders in the United States: Results from the National Epidemiologic Survey on Alcohol and Related Conditions. *Drug and Alcohol Dependence, 80,* 105–116.

Stirling, J., Hellewell, J., Blakely, A., & Deakin, W. (2006). Thought disorder in schizophrenia is associated with both executive dysfunction and circumscribed impairments in semantic function. *Psychological Medicine, 36,* 475–484.

Stöber, J., & Bittencourt, J. (1998). Weekly assessment of worry: An adaptation of the Penn State Worry Questionnaire. *Behaviour Research and Therapy, 30,* 33–37.

Stock, S. L., Goldberg, E., & Corbett, S. (2002). Substance use in female adolescents with eating disorders. *Journal of Adolescent Health, 31*(2), 176–182.

Stöffelmayr, B. E., Mavis, B. E., & Kasim, R. M. (1994). The longitudinal stability of the Addiction Severity Index. *Journal of Substance Abuse Treatment, 11,* 373–378.

Stone, J., Wojcik, W., Durrance, D., Carson, A., Lewis, S., MacKenzie, L., et al. (2002). What should we say to patients with symptoms unexplained by disease? The "number needed to offend." *British Medical Journal, 325,* 1449–1450.

Stone, M. H. (1993). *Abnormalities of personality.* New York: Norton.

Stone, M. H. (2001). Natural history and long-term outcome. In W. J. Livesley (Ed.), *Handbook of personality disorders: Theory, research and treatment* (pp. 259–273). New York: Guilford Press:

Stone, M. H. (2005). Violence. In J. M. Oldham, A. E. Skodol, & D. S. Bender (Eds.), *Textbook of personality disorders* (pp. 477–491). Washington, DC: American Psychiatric Publishing.

Stone, W. L., Coonrod, E. E., & Ousley, O. Y. (2000). Brief report: Screening Tool for Autism in 2-year-olds (STAT): Development and preliminary data. *Journal of Autism and Developmental Disorders, 30*(6), 607–612.

Stone, W. L., Coonrod, E. E., Turner, L. M., & Pozdol, S. L. (2004). Psychometric properties of the STAT for early autism screening. *Journal of Autism and Developmental Disorders, 34,* 691–701.

Stone, W. L., Lee, E. B., Ashford, L., Brissie, J., Hepburn, S. L., Coonrod, E. E., et al. (1999). Can autism be diagnosed accurately in children under 3 years? *Journal of Child Psychology and Psychiatry, 40,* 219–226.

Stone, W. L., & Ousley, O. Y. (1997). *STAT manual: Screening Tool for Autism in 2-year-olds.* Unpublished manuscript, Vanderbilt University, Nashville, TN.

Stopa, L., & Clark, D. M. (1993). Cognitive processes in social phobia. *Behaviour Research and Therapy, 31,* 255–267.

Stores, G. (2001). *A clinical guide to sleep disorders in children and adolescents.* New York: Cambridge University Press.

Stores, G., & Wiggs, L. (1998). Abnormal sleep patterns associated with autism. *Autism: Journal of Research and Practice, 2,* 157–169.

Stormshak, E. A., Bierman, K. L., McMahon, R. J., & Lengua, L. J. (2000). Parenting practices and child disruptive behavior problems in early elementary school. *Journal of Clinical Child Psychology, 29,* 17–29.

Storr, A. (1980). *The art of psychotherapy.* New York: Metheun.

Stoudemire, A., Wallack, L., & Hedenark, N. (1987). Alcohol dependence and abuse. In R. W. Amler & H. B. Dull (Eds.), *Enclosing the gap: The burden of unnecessary illness* (pp. 9–18). New York: Oxford University Press.

Stout, C. E., & Hayes, R. A. (Ed.). (2005). *The evidence-based practice: Methods, models and tools for mental health professionals.* Hoboken, NJ: Wiley.

Strack, S. (1999). *Essentials of Millon inventories assessment.* New York: Wiley.

Strahan, E. Y., & Conger, A. J. (1998). Social anxiety and its effects on performance and perception. *Journal of Anxiety Disorders, 12,* 293–305.

Strahan, E. Y., & Conger, A. J. (1999). Social anxiety and social performance: Why don't we see more catastrophes? *Journal of Anxiety Disorders, 13,* 399–416.

Strain, P., McGee, G. G., & Kohler, F. W. (2001). Inclusion of children with autism in early intervention environments: An example of rationale, myths and procedures. In M. J. Guralnick (Ed.), *Early childhood inclusion: Focus on change* (pp. 337–363). Baltimore: Paul H. Brookes.

Strakowski, S. M. (1994). Diagnostic validity of schizophreniform disorder. *American Journal of Psychiatry, 151*, 815–824.

Strakowski, S. M., Flaum, M., Amador, X., Bracha, H., Pandurangi, A., Robinson, D., et al. (1996). Racial differences in the diagnosis of psychosis. *Schizophrenia Research, 21*, 117–124.

Strakowski, S. M., McElroy, S. L., Keck, P. E., & West, S. A. (1996). Suicidality among patients with mixed and manic bipolar disorder. *American Journal of Psychiatry, 153*, 674–676.

Strakowski, S. M., Tohen, M., Stoll, A. L., Faedda, G. L., Mayer, P. V., Kolbrener, M. L., et al. (1993). Comorbidity in psychosis at first hospitalization. *American Journal of Psychiatry 150*, 752–757.

Strakowski, S. M., Williams, J. R., Sax, K. W., Fleck, D. E., DeBello, M. P., & Bourne, M. L. (2000). Is impaired outcome following a first manic episode due to mood-incongruent psychosis? *Journal of Affective Disorders, 61*, 87–94.

Straus, M. A., & Gelles, R. J. (Eds.,)(1990). *Physical violence in American families: Risk factors and adaptations to violence in 8,145 families.* New Brunswick, NJ: Transaction.

Strauss, C., Lease, C., Last, C., & Francis, G. (1988). Overanxious disorder: An examination of developmental differences. *Journal of Abnormal Child Psychology, 16*, 433–443.

Strauss, J. S., & Carpenter, W. T. (1974). Prediction of outcome in schizophrenia: Pt. II. Relationships between predictor and outcome variables. *Archives of General Psychiatry, 31*, 37–42.

Strauss, J. S., & Carpenter, W. T. (1977). Prediction of outcome in schizophrenia. *Archives of General Psychiatry, 34*, 159–163.

Strauss, M. E., & Ogrocki, P. K. (1996). Confirmation of an association between family history of affective disorder and the depressive syndrome in Alzheimer's disease. *American Journal of Psychiatry, 153*, 1340–1342.

Striegel-Moore, R. H. (1993). Etiology of binge eating: A developmental perspective. In C. G. Fairburn & G. T. Wilson (Eds.), *Binge eating: Nature, assessment, and treatment* (pp. 144–172). New York: Guilford Press.

Striegel-Moore, R. H., & Cachelin, F. M. (2001). Etiology of eating disorders in women. *Counseling Psychologist, 29*(5), 635–661.

Striegel-Moore, R. H., & Smolak, L. (2002). Gender, ethnicity, and eating disorders. In C. G. Fairburn & K. D. Brownell (Eds.), *Eating disorders and obesity: A comprehensive handbook* (2nd ed., pp. 251–255). New York: Guilford Press.

Strober, M. (1991). Disorders of the self in anorexia nervosa: An organismic-developmental paradigm. In C. L. Johnson (Ed.), *Psychodynamic treatment of anorexia nervosa and bulimia* (pp. 354–373). New York: Guilford Press.

Strober, M. (2004). Managing the chronic, treatment-resistant patient with anorexia nervosa. *International Journal of Eating Disorders, 36*, 245–255.

Strober, M., Freeman, R., Lampert, C., Diamond, J., & Kaye, W. (2000). Controlled family study of anorexia nervosa and bulimia nervosa: Evidence of shared liability and transmission of partial syndromes. *American Journal of Psychiatry, 157*(3), 393–401.

Strober, M., Freeman, R., & Morrell, W. (1997). The long-term course of severe anorexia nervosa in adolescents: Survival analysis of recovery, relapse, and outcome predictors over 10–15 years in a prospective study. *International Journal of Eating Disorders, 22*(4), 339–360.

Strober, M., Freeman, R., & Morrell, W. (1999). Atypical anorexia nervosa: Separation from typical cases in course and outcome in a long-term prospective study. *International Journal of Eating Disorders, 25*(2), 135–142.

Strupp, H. L., & Binder, J. L. (1984). *Psychotherapy in a new key: A guide to time-limited dynamic psychotherapy.* New York: Basic Books.

Stuart, S., & Noyes, R. (1999). Attachment and interpersonal communication in somatization. *Psychosomatics, 40*, 34–43.

Stuart, S., & O'Hara, M. W. (1995). Treatment of postpartum depression with interpersonal psychotherapy. *Archives of General Psychiatry, 52*, 75–76.

Stueve, A., & Link, B. G. (1997). Violence and psychiatric disorders: Results from an epidemiological study of young adults in Israel. *Psychiatric Quarterly, 68*(4), 327–342.

Subotnik, K. L., & Nuechterlein, K. H. (1988). Prodromal signs and symptoms of schizophrenic relapse. *Journal of Abnormal Psychology, 97*, 405–412.

Subotnik, K. L., Nuechterlein, K. H., Irzhevsky, V., Kitchen, C. M., Woo, S. M., & Mintz, J. (2005). Is unawareness of psychotic disorder a neurocognitive or psychological defensiveness problem? *Schizophrenia Research, 75*, 147–157.

Substance Abuse and Mental Health Services Administration. (2006). *Results from the 2005 National Survey on Drug Use and Health: National findings* (Office of Applied Studies, NSDUH Series H-30, DHHS Publication No. SMA 06-4194). Rockville, MD: Author.

Sue, S. (1988). Psychotherapeutic services for ethnic minorities: Two decades of research findings. *American Psychologist, 43*, 301–308.

Sue, S., Fujino, D. C., Hsu, L., Takeuchi, D. T., & Zane, N. (1991). Community mental health services for minority groups: A test of the cultural responsiveness hypothesis. *Journal of Consulting and Clinical Psychology, 59*, 533–540.

Suh, G. H., & Shah, A. (2001). A review of the epidemiological transition in dementia: Cross-national comparisons of the indices related to Alzheimer's disease and vascular dementia. *Acta Psychiatrica Scandinavica, 104*, 4–11.

Sullivan, M. D. (2000). DSM-IV pain disorder: A case against the diagnosis. *International Review of Psychiatry, 12*(2), 91–99.

Sullivan, M. J., Thorn, B., Haythornthwaite, J. A., Keefe, F., Martin, M., Bradley, L. A., et al. (2001). Theoretical perspectives on the relationship between catastrophizing and pain. *Clinical Journal of Pain, 17*, 52–64.

Sullivan, P. F. (1995). Mortality in anorexia nervosa. *American Journal of Psychiatry, 152*(7), 1073–1074.

Sullivan, P. F., Bulik, C. M., & Kendler, K. S. (1998). Genetic epidemiology of binging and vomiting. *British Journal of Psychiatry, 173*, 75–79.

Sullivan, P. F., Neale, M. C., & Kendler, K. S. (2000). Genetic epidemiology of major depression: Review and meta-analysis. *American Journal of Psychiatry, 157*, 1552–1562.

Summit, R. (1983). The child sexual abuse accomodation syndrome. *Child Abuse and Neglect, 7*, 177–193.

Sumner, D. D. (1998). Benzodiaepine-induced persisting amnestic disorder: Are older adults at risk? *Archives of Psychiatric Nursing, 12*, 119–125.

Sun, P., Cameron, A., Seftel, A., Shabsigh, R., Niederberger, C., & Guay, A. (2006). Erectile dysfunction—An observable marker of diabetes mellitus? A large national epidemiological study. *Journal of Urology, 176*(3), 1081–1085.

Sundgot-Borgen, J. (1994). Eating disorders in female athletes. *Sports Medicine, 17*(3), 176–188.

Sundgot-Borgen, J., Skarderud, F., & Rodgers, S. (2003). Athletes and dancers. In J. Treasure, U. Schmidt, & Evan Furth (Eds.), *Handbook of eating disorders* (2nd ed., 385–400). Chichester, West Sussex, England: Wiley.

Sutker, P. B., & Allain, A. N. (1996). Assessment of PTSD and other mental disorders in World War II and Korean conflict survivors and combat veterans. *Psychological Assessment, 8*, 18–25.

Sutker, P. B. & Allain, A. N. (2001). Antisocial personality disorder. In H. E. Adams, & P. B. Sutker (Eds.), *Comprehensive Handbook of psychopathology* (3rd. ed., 445–490). New York: Kluwer Academic/Plenum.

Suwaki, H. (1997). Methamphetamine abuse in Japan: Its 45 year history and the current situation. In H. Klee (Ed.), *Amphetamine misuse: International perspectives on current trends* (pp. 191–214). Reading, England: Harwood Academic Press.

Svartberg, M., Stiles, T., & Seltzer, M. (2004). Randomized, controlled trial of the effectiveness of short-term dynamic psychotherapy and cognitive therapy for Cluster C personality disorders. *American Journal of Psychiatry, 161*(5), 810–817.

Swainston, H. T., & Perry, C. M. (2004). Aripiprazole: A review of its use in schizophrenia and schizoaffective disorder. *Drugs, 64*, 1715–1736.

Swan, A. (1998). Some child abuse victims are more vulnerable than others to child abuse. *NIDA Notes, 13*(2). Retrieved January 20, 2007, from www.drugabuse.gov/NIDA_Notes/NNVol13N2/vulnerable.html.

Swann, A. C. (2005). Long-term treatment in bipolar disorder. *Journal of Clinical Psychiatry, 66*, 7–12.

Swann, A. C., Dougherty, D. M., Pazzaglia, P. J., Pham, M., & Moeller, F. G. (2004). Impulsivity: A link between bipolar disorder and substance abuse. *Bipolar Disorders, 6*, 204–212.

Swanson, J. W. (1994). Mental disorder, substance abuse, and community violence: An epidemiological approach. In J. Monahan & H. Steadman (Eds.), *Violence and mental disorder: Developments in risk assessment* (pp. 101–136). Chicago: University of Chicago Press.

Swanson, J. W., Borum, R., Swartz, M. S., & Monahan, J. (1996). Psychotic symptoms and disorders and the risk of violent behavior in the community. *Criminal Behavior and Mental Health, 6*, 309–329.

Swanson, J. W., Holzer, C. E., Ganju, V. K., & Jono, R. T. (1990). Violence and psychiatric disorder in the community: Evidence from the Epidemiologic Catchment surveys. *Hospital and Community Psychiatry, 41*(7), 761–770.

Swartz, H. A., Frank, E., Spielvogle, H. N., & Kupfer, D. J. (2004). Interpersonal social rhythm therapy. In M. Power (Ed.), *Mood disorders: A handbook of science and practice* (pp. 275–293). Hoboken, NJ: Wiley.

Swartz, H. A., Markowitz, J. C., & Frank, E. (2002). Interpersonal psychotherapy for unipolar and bipolar disorders. In S. G. Hofmann & M. C. Tompson (Eds.), *Treating chronic and severe mental disorders* (pp. 131–158). New York: Guilford Press.

Swedo, S., & Grant, P. J. (2004). PANDAS: A model for autoimmune neuropsychiatric disorders. *Primary Psychiatry, 11*, 28–33.

Sweeney, P. D., Anderson, K., & Bailey, S. (1986). Attributional style in depression: A meta-analytic review. *Journal of Personality and Social Psychology, 50*, 974–991.

Sweet, J. (1999). Malingering: Differential diagnosis. In J. Sweet (Ed.), *Forensic neuropsychology fundamentals and practice* (pp. 255–286). Lisse, The Netherlands: Swets & Zeitlinger.

Summit, R. (1983). The child sexual abuse accommodation syndrome. *Child Abuse and Neglect, 7*, 177–193.

Sydenham, T. (1666). *Methodus curandi ferbres, propriss observationibus superstructura.* London: Transactions of the Royal Society.

Sydenham, T. (1850). *The works of Thomas Sydenham, M.D.* (G. Latham, Trans., Vols. 1–2). London: Sydenham Society.

Szanto, K., Mulsant, B. H., Houck, P. R., Dew, M. A., & Reynolds, C. F. (2003). Occurrence and course of suicidality during short-term treatment of late life depression. *Archives of General Psychiatry, 60*, 610–617.

Szanto, K., Mulsant, B. H., Houck, P. R., Miller, M. D., Mazumdar, S., & Reynolds, C. F. (2001). Treatment outcome in suicidal versus non-suicidal elderly. *American Journal of Geriatric Psychiatry, 9*, 261–268.

Szasz, T. (1961). *The myth of mental illness.* New York: Harper & Row.

Szatmari, P. (2000a). The classification of autism, Asperger's syndrome, and pervasive developmental disorder. *Canadian Journal of Psychiatry, 45*, 731–738.

Szatmari, P. (2000b). Perspectives on the classification of Asperger syndrome. In A. Klin & F. R. Volkmar (Eds.), *Asperger syndrome* (pp. 403–417). New York: Guilford Press.

Szatmari, P., Archer, L., Fisman, S., Streiner, D. L., & Wilson, F. (1995). Asperger's syndrome and autism: Differences in behavior, cognition, and adaptive functioning. *Journal of the American Academy of Child and Adolescent Psychiatry, 34*, 1662–1671.

Szatmari, P., Jones, M. B., Zwaigenbaum, L., & McLean, J. E. (1998). Genetics of autism: Overview and new directions. *Journal of Autism and Developmental Disorder, 28*(5), 351–368.

Szmukler, G. (2001). Violence risk prediction in practice. *British Journal of Psychiatry, 178*, 84–85.

Tager-Flusberg, H., Paul, P., & Lord, C. (2005). Language and communication in autism. In F. R. Volkmar, R. Paul, A. Klin, & D. Cohen (Eds.), *Handbook of autism and pervasive developmental disorders* (3rd ed., pp. 335–364). Hoboken, NJ: Wiley.

Tait, R. C., & Chibnall, J. T. (1997). Development of a brief version of the Survey of Pain Attitudes. *Pain, 70,* 229–235.

Takeshita, T., & Morimoto, K. (1999). Self-reported alcohol-associated symptoms and drinking behavior in three ALDH2 genotypes among Japanese university students. *Alcoholism: Clinical and Experimental Research, 23,* 1065–1069.

Talay-Ongan, A., & Wood, K. (2000). Unusual sensory sensitivities in autism: A possible crossroads. *International Journal of Disability, Development, and Education, 47*(2), 201–212.

Tang, M. X., Cross, P., Andrews, H., Jacobs, D. M., Small, S., Bell, K., et al. (2001). Incidence of AD in African-Americans, Caribbean Hispanics, and Caucasians in northern Manhattan. *Neurology, 56,* 49–56.

Tannock, R. (1998). Attention deficit hyperactivity disorder: Advances in cognitive, neurobiological, and genetic research. *Journal of Child Psychology and Psychiatry and Allied Disciplines, 39,* 65–99.

Tantam, D. (1988). Annotation: Asperger's syndrome. *Journal of Child Psychology and Psychiatry, 29*(3), 245–255.

Tardiff, K. (1989). *Concise guide to assessment and management of violent patients.* Washington, DC: American Psychiatric Press.

Tardiff, K. (1991). Violence by psychiatric patients. In R. I. Simon (Ed.), *Review of clinical psychiatry and the law* (pp. 175–233). Washington, DC: American Psychiatric Press.

Tarasoff v. Regents of University of California, 529 P.2d 553, 118 Cal. Rptr. 129 (1974).

Tarasoff v. Regents of University of California, 17 Cal.3d 425, 551 P.2d 334, 131 Cal. Rptr. 14 (1976).

Targum, S. D., Dibble, E. D., Davenport, Y. B., & Gershon, E. S. (1981). The Family Attitudes Questionnaire: Patients' and spouses views of bipolar disorder. *Archives of General Psychiatry, 38,* 562–568.

Tarrier, N., & Haddock, G. (2002). Cognitive behavioral therapy for schizophrenia: A case formulation approach. In S. G. Hofmann & M. C. Tompson (Eds.), *Treating chronic and severe mental disorders: A handbook of empirically supported interventions* (pp. 69–95). New York: Guilford Press.

Tatarsky, A. (2003). Harm reduction psychotherapy: Extending the reach of traditional substance use treatment. *Journal of Substance Abuse Treatment,* 249–256.

Taylor, B., Miller, E., Farrington, C. P., Petropoulos, M. C., Favot-Mayaud, I., Li., J., et al., (1999). Autism and measles, mumps and rubella vacinne: No epidemiological evidence for a causal association. *Lancet, 353,* 2026–2029.

Taylor, B., Miller, E., Lingam, R., Andrews, N., Simmons, A., & Stowe, J. (2002). Measles, mumps, and rubella vaccination and bowel problems or developmental regression in children with autism: Population study. *British Medical Journal, 324*(7334), 393–396.

Taylor, C. B., Sharpe, T., Shisslak, C., Bryson, S., Estes, L. S., Gray, N., et al. (1998). Factors associated with weight concerns in adolescent girls. *International Journal of Eating Disorders, 24*(1), 31–42.

Taylor, R. (2000). *A seven year reconviction study of HMP Grendon Therapeutic Community.* London: Home Office Research, Development and Statistics Directorate.

Taylor, G. (2003). Somatization and conversion disorder: Distinct or overlapping constructs? *Journal of the American Academy of Psychoanalysis and Dynamic Psychiatry, 31*(3), 487–508.

Taylor, P. J. (1995). Schizophrenia and the risk of violence. In S. R. Hirsch & D. R. Weinberger (Eds.), *Schizophrenia* (pp. 163–183). Oxford: Blackwell Science..

Taylor, P. J., Mullen, P., & Wessely, S. (1993). Psychosis, violence, and crime. In J. Gunn & P. J. Taylor (Eds.), *Forensic psychiatry: Clinical, legal, and ethical issues* (pp. 330–371). London: Butterworth and Heinemann.

Taylor, C. T., Laposa, J. M., & Alden, L. E. (2004). Is avoidant personality disorder more than just social avoidance? *Journal of Personality Disorders, 18*(6), 571–594.

Taylor, S. (1996). Meta-analysis of cognitive-behavioral treatment for social phobia. *Journal of Behavior Therapy and Experimental Psychiatry, 27,* 1–9.

Teachman, B. A. (2007). Linking obsessional beliefs to OCD symptoms in older and younger adults. *Behaviour Research and Therapy.*

Tedde, A., Nacmias, B., Ciantelli, M., Forelo, P., Cellini, E., Bagnoli, S., et al. (2003). Identification of new presenilin gene mutations in early-onset Alzheimer disease. *Archives of Neurology, 60,* 1541–1544.

Tedlow, J., Smith, M., Neault, N., Polania, L., Alpert, J., Nierenberg, A., et al. (2002). Melancholia and Axis II comorbidity. *Comprehensive Psychiatry, 43,* 331–335.

Tentler, D., Johannesson, T. M., Johansson, M., Rastamm, M., Gillberg, C., Orsmark, C., et al. (2003). A candidate gene for Asperger syndrome defined by two 17p breakpoints. *European Journal of Human Genetics, 11*(2), 189–195.

Teplin, L. A., Abram, K. M., & McClelland, G. M. (1994). Does psychiatric disorder predict violent crime among released jail detainees? A 6-year longitudinal study. *American Psychologist, 49,* 335–342.

Tepper, D. T., & Haase, R. F. (1978). Verbal and nonverbal communication of facilitative conditions. *Journal of Counseling Psychology, 25,* 35–44.

Teri, L., Gibbons, L. E., McCurry, S. M., Logsdon, R. G., Buchner, D. M., Barlow, W. E., et al. (2003). Exercise plus behavioral management in patients with Alzheimer disease: A randomized controlled trial. *Journal of the American Medical Association, 290,* 2015–2022.

Teri, L., McKenzie, G., & LaFazia, D. (2005). Psychosocial treatment of depression in older adults with dementia. *Clinical Psychology: Science and Practice, 12,* 303–316.

Terre, L., & Ghiselli, W. (1997). A developmental perspective on family risk factors in somatization. *Journal of Psychosomatic Research, 42*(2), 197–208.

Terrell, M. D. (1993). Ethnocultural factors and substance abuse: Toward culturally sensitive treatment models. *Psychology of Addictive Behaviors, 7,* 162–167.

Terry, C. (2005). History of treatment of people with mental illness. In J. R. Matthews & C. E. Walker (Eds.), *Your practicum in psychology: A guide for maximizing knowledge and competence* (pp. 81–103). Washington, DC: American Psychological Association.

Test, M. A. (1992). Training in community living. In R. P. Liberman (Ed.), *Handbook of psychiatric rehabilitation* (pp. 153–179). New York: Macmillan.

Thangavelu, R., & Martin, R. L. (1995). ICD-10 and DSM-IV: Depiction of the diagnostic elephant. *Psychiatric Annals, 25*(1), 20–28.

Thomas, D. A., Libon, D. J., & Ledakis, G. E. (2005). Treating dementia patients with vascular lesions with donepezil: A preliminary analysis. *Applied Neuropsychology, 12,* 12–18.

Thomas, J., & Clark, R. (1998). Disruptive behaviors in the very young child: Diagnostic classifications: 0–3 guides identification of risk factors and relational intervention. *Infant Mental Health Journal, 19,* 229–244.

Thomas, J. M., & Guskin, K. A. (2001). Disruptive behavior in young children: What does it mean? *Journal of the American Academy Child and Adolescent Psychiatry, 40,* 44–51.

Thomassen, R., van Hemert, A. M., Huyse, F. J., van der Mast, R. C., & Hengeveld, M. W. (2003). Somatoform disorders in consultation-liaison psychiatry: A comparison with other mental disorders. *General Hospital Psychiatry, 25,* 8–13.

Thombs, D. L. (2006). *Introduction to addictive behaviors* (3rd ed.). New York: Guilford Press.

Thompson, J. K., Heinberg, L. J., & Altabe, M. (1999). The scope of body image disturbance: The big picture. In J. K. Thompson, L. J. Heinberg, M. Altabe, & S. Tantleff-Dunn (Eds.), *Exacting beauty: Theory, assessment, and treatment of body image disturbance* (pp. 19–50). Washington, DC: American Psychological Association.

Thordarson, D. S., Radomsky, A. S., Rachman, S., Shafran, R., Sawchuk, C. N., & Hakstian, A. (2004). The Vancouver Obsessional Compulsive Inventory (VOCI). *Behavior Research and Therapy, 42,* 1289–1314.

Thornton, C., & Russell, J. (1997). Obsessive compulsive comorbidity in the dieting disorders. *International Journal of Eating Disorders, 21*(1), 83–87.

Thornton, M. (1991). *Alcohol prohibition was a failure* (Cato Policy Analysis, No. 157). Retrieved May 17, 2006, from www.cato.org/pubs/pas/pa-157.html.

Thunstrom, M. (2002). Severe sleep problems in infancy associated with subsequent development of attention deficit/hyperactivity disorder at 5.5 years. *Acta Paediatrica, 91*, 584–592.

Thurstin, A. H., Alfano, A. M., & Nerviano, V. J. (1987). The efficacy of Alcoholics Anonymous attendance for aftercare of inpatient alcoholics: Some follow-up data. *International Journal of Addiction, 22*, 1083–1090.

Tibbo, P., Swainson, J., Chue, P., & LeMelledo, J. M. (2003). Prevalence and relationship to delusions and hallucinations of anxiety disorders in schizophrenia. *Depression and Anxiety, 17*, 65–72.

Tickle, J. J., Heatherton, T. F., & Wittenberg, L. G. (2001). Can personality change? In W. J. Livesley, (Ed.), *Handbook of personality disorders: Theory research and treatment* (pp. 242–258). New York: Guilford Press.

Tillet, R. (1996). Psychotherapy assessment and treatment selection. *British Journal of Psychiatry, 168*, 10–15.

Timko, C., Finney, J. W., & Moos, R. H. (2005). The 8-year course of alcohol abuse: Gender differences in social context and coping. *Alcoholism: Clinical and Experimental Research, 29*, 612–621.

Todd, D. M., Deane, F. P., & Bragdon, R. A. (2003). Client and therapist's reasons for termination: A conceptualization and preliminary validation. *Journal of Clinical Psychology, 59*(1), 133–147.

Tohen, M., Tsuang, M. T., & Goodwin, D. C. (1992). Prediction of outcome in mania by mood-congruent or mood-incongruent psychotic features. *American Journal of Psychiatry, 149*, 1580–1584.

Tohen, M., Vieta, E., Calabrese, J., Ketter, T. A., Sachs, G., Bowden, C., et al. (2003). Efficacy of olanzapine and olanzapine-fluoxetine combination in the treatment of bipolar I depression. *Archives of General Psychiatry, 60*, 1079–1088.

Tohen, M., Waternaux, C., & Tsuang, M. T. (1990). Outcome in mania: A 4-year prospective follow-up of 75 patients utilizing survival analysis. *Archives of General Psychiatry, 47*, 1106–1111.

Tolin, D. F., Abramowitz, J. S., Brigidi, B. D., & Foa, E. B. (2003). Intolerance of uncertainty in obsessive-compulsive disorder. *Journal of Anxiety Disorders, 17*, 233–242.

Tolman, R. M. (1992). Psychological abuse of women. In R. T. Ammerman & M. Hersen (Eds.), *Assessment of family violence: A clinical and legal sourcebook* (pp. 291–310). New York: Wiley.

Tondo, L., & Baldessarini, R. J. (1998). Rapid cycling in women and men with bipolar manic-depressive disorders. *American Journal of Psychiatry, 155*, 1434–1436.

Tondo, L., & Baldessarini, R. J. (2000). Reduced suicide risk during lithium maintenance treatment. *Journal of Clinical Psychiatry, 61*, 97–104.

Tondo, L., Isacsson, G., & Baldesaarini, R. J. (2003). Suicidal behaviour in bipolar disorder: Risk and prevention. *CNS Drugs, 17*, 491–511.

Tonge, B. J., & Enfield, S. L. (2003). Psychopathology and intellectual disability: The Australian child to adult longitudinal study. *International Review of Research in Mental Retardation, 26*, 61–91.

Tonigan, J. S., Miller, W. R., & Schermer, C. (2002). Atheists, agnostics, and Alcoholics Anonymous. *Journal of Studies on Alcohol, 63*, 534–541.

Toomery, R., Lyons, M. J., Eisen, S. A., Xian, H., Chantarujikapong, S., Seidman, L. J., et al. (2003). A twin study of the neuropsychological consequences of stimulant abuse. *Archives of General Psychiatry, 60*, 303–310.

Torack, R. (1983). The early history of senile dementia. In B. Reisberg (Ed.), *Alzheimer's disease: The standard reference* (pp. 23–28). New York: Free Press.

Torgersen, S. (2005). Epidemiology. In J. M. Oldham, A. E. Skodol, & D. S. Bender (Eds.), *Textbook of personality disorders* (pp. 129–141). Washington, DC: American Psychiatric Publishing.

Torgersen, S., Kringlen, E., & Cramer, V. (2001). The prevalence of personality disorders in a community sample. *Archives of General Psychiatry, 58*, 590–596.

Torgersen, S., Lygren, S., Oien, P. A., Skre, I., Onstad, S., Edvardsen, J., et al. (2000). A twin study of personality disorders. *Comprehensive Psychiatry, 41*(6), 416–425.

Torgersen, S., Onstad, S., Skre, I., Edvardsen, J., & Kringlen, E. (1993). "True" schizotypal personality disorder: A study of co-twins and relatives of schizophrenic probands. *American Journal of Psychiatry, 150*(11), 1661–1667.

Torrey, E. F. (1998). Violent behavior by individuals with serious mental illness. In X. F. Amador & A. S. David (Eds.), *Insight and psychosis* (pp. 269–285). New York: Oxford University Press.

Torrey, E. F. (2006). Violence and schizophrenia. *Schizophrenia Research, 88*, 3–4.

Tortu, S., McCoy, H. V., Beardsley, M., Deren, S., & McCoy, C. B. (1998). Predictors of HIV infection among women drug users in New York and Miami. *Women and Health, 27*, 191–204.

Toseland, R. W., Rossiter, C. M., Peak, T., & Smith, P. (1990). Therapeutic processes in peer led and professionally led support groups for caregivers. *International Journal of Group Psychotherapy, 40*, 279–303.

Toupin, J., Dery, M., Pauze, R., Mercier, H., & Fortlin, L. (2000). Cognitive and familial contributions to conduct disorder in children. *Journal of Psychological Psychiatry, 41*(3), 333–344.

Towbin, K. E. (2005). Pervasive developmental disorder not otherwise specified. In F. R. Volkmar, R. Paul, A. Klin, & D. Cohen (Eds.), *Handbook of autism and pervasive developmental disorders* (3rd ed., pp. 165–200). Hoboken, NJ: Wiley.

Tozzi, F., Thornton, L. M., Klump, K. L., Fichter, M. M., Halmi, K. A., Kaplan, A. S., et al. (2005). Symptom fluctuation in eating disorders: Correlates of diagnostic crossover. *American Journal of Psychiatry, 162*, 732–740.

Traykov, L., Baudic, S., Thibaudet, M. C., Rigaud, A. S., Smagghe, A., & Boller, F. (2002). Neuropsychological deficit in early subcortical vascular dementia: Comparison to Alzheimer's disease. *Dementia and Geriatric Cognitive Disorders, 14*, 26–32.

Traykov, L., Rigaud, A. S., Caputo, L., Couderc, R., Coste, J., Michot, J. L., et al. (1999). Apolipoprotein E phenotypes in demented and cognitively impaired patients with and without cerebrovascular disease. *European Journal of Neurology, 6*, 415–421.

Treasure, J., & Bauer, B. (2003). Assessment and motivation. In J. Treasure, U. Schmidt, & E. van Furth (Eds.), *Handbook of eating disorders* (2nd ed., pp. 219–231). Chichester, West Sussex, England: Wiley.

Treatment for Adolescents with Depression Study Team. (2004). Fluoxetine, cognitive-behavioral therapy, and their combination for adolescents with depression. *Journal of the American Medical Association, 292*, 807–820.

Treves, T. A., Bornstein, N. M., Chapman, J., Klimovitzki, S., Verchovsky, R., Asherov, A., et al. (1996). APOE-epsilon 4 in patients with Alzheimer's disease and vascular dementia. *Alzheimer's Disease and Associated Disorders, 10*, 189–191.

Trillat, E. (1995). Conversion disorder and hysteria. In G. E. Berrios & R. Porter (Eds.), *The history of clinical psychiatry*. London: Athlone Press.

Trinh, N.H., Hoblyn, J., Mohanty, S., & Yaffe, K. (2003). Efficacy of cholinesterase inhibitors in the treatment of neuropsychiatric symptoms and functional impairment in Alzheimer disease: a meta-analysis. *Journal of the American Medical Association, 289*, 210–216.

Truant, G. S. (1998a). Assessment of suitability for psychotherapy: Pt. I. Introduction and the assessment process. *American Journal of Psychotherapy, 52*(4), 397–411.

Truant, G. S. (1998b). Assessment of suitability for psychotherapy: Pt. II. Assessment based on basic process goals. *American Journal of Psychotherapy, 53*(1), 17–34.

True, W. R., Rice, J., Eisen, S. A., Heath, A. C., Goldberg, J., Lyons, M. J., et al. (1993). A twin study of genetic and environmental contributions to liability for posttraumatic stress symptoms. *Archives of General Psychiatry, 50*, 257–264.

Trull, T. J., Sher, K. J., Minks-Brown, C., Durbin, J., & Burr, R. (2000). Borderline personality disorder and substance abuse disorders: A review and integration. *Clinical Psychology Review, 20*, 235–253.

Trull, T. J., Stepp, S. D., & Solhan, M. (2006). Borderline personality disorder. In M. Hersen, J. C. Thomas, & F. Andrasik (Eds.), *Comprehensive handbook of personality and psychopathology: Adult psychopathology* (Vol. 2, pp. 299–315). Hoboken, NJ: Wiley.

Truscott, D., Evans, J., & Mansell, S. (1995). Outpatient psychotherapy with dangerous clients: A model for clinical decision making. *Professional Psychology: Research and Practice, 26,* 484–490.

Trzepacz, P. T. (1996). Delirium: Advances in diagnosis, pathophysiology, and treatment. *Consultation Liaison Psychiatry, 19,* 429–448.

Trezpacz, P. T. (1999a). The Delirium Rating Scale: Its use in consultation liaison research. *Psychosomatics, 49,* 193–204.

Trzepacz, P. T. (1999b). Update on the neuropathogenesis of delirium. *Dementia and Geriatric Cognitive Disorders, 10,* 330–334.

Trzepacz, P. T. (2000). Is there a final common neural pathway in delirium? Focus on acetylcholine and dopamine. *Seminars in Clinical Neuropsychiatry, 5,* 132–148.

Trzepacz, P. T., & Breitbart, W. (1999). Practice guideline for the treatment of patients with delirium. *American Journal of Psychiatry, 156,* 11.

Trzepacz, P. T., Mulsant, B. H., Dew, M. A., Pasternak, R., Sweet, R. A., & Zubenko, G. S. (1998). Is delirium different when it occurs in dementia? A study using the Delirium Rating Scale. *Journal of Neuropsychiatry and Clinical Neurosciences, 10,* 199–204.

Tsai, S., Kuo, C., Chen, C., & Lee, H. (2002). Risk factors for completed suicide in bipolar disorder. *Journal of Clinical Psychiatry, 63,* 469–476.

Tsatsanis, K. D. (2005). Neuropsychological characteristics in autism and related conditions. In F. R. Volkmar, R. Paul, A. Klin, & D. Cohen (Eds.), *Handbook of autism and pervasive developmental disorders* (3rd ed., pp. 365–381). Hoboken, NJ: Wiley.

Tsolaki, M., Kokarida, K., Iakovidou, V., Stilopoulis, E., Meimaris, J., & Kazis, A. (2001). Extrapyramidal signs and symptoms in Alzheimer's disease: Prevalence and correlation with the first symptom. *American Journal of Alzheimer's Disease, 16,* 268–278.

Tsuang, M. T., Bar, J. L., Harley, R. M., & Lyons, M. J. (2001). The Harvard Twin Study of Substance Abuse: What we have learned so far. *Harvard Review of Psychiatry, 9,* 267–279.

Tsuang, M. T., Simpson, J. C., & Kronfol, Z. (1982). Subtypes of drug abuse with psychosis. *Archives of General Psychiatry, 39,* 141–147.

Tsuang, M. T., Woolson, R. F., & Fleming, J. A. (1979). Long-term outcome of major psychoses: Pt. I. Schizophrenia and affective disorders compared with psychiatrically symptom-free, surgical conditions. *Archives of General Psychiatry, 39,* 1295–1301.

Tucker, J. S., D'Amico, E. J., Wenzel, S. L., Golinelli, D., Elliott, M. N., & Williamson, S. (2005). A prospective study of risk and protective factors for substance use among impoverished women living in temporary shelter settings in Los Angeles County. *Drug and Alcohol Dependence, 80,* 35–43.

Tune, L. E. (2001). Anticholinergic effects of medication in elderly patients. *Journal of Clinical Psychiatry, 62*(Suppl. 21), 11–14.

Tune, L. E., Wong, D. F., Pearlson, G., Strauss, M., Young, T., Shaya, E. K., et al. (1993). Dopamine D2 receptor density estimates in schizophrenia: A positron emission tomography study with 11C-N-methylspiperone. *Psychiatry Research, 29,* 219–237.

Turk, C. L., Heimberg, R. G., & Mennin, D. S. (2004). Assessment. In R. G. Heimberg, C. L. Turk, & D. S. Mennin (Eds.), *Generalized anxiety disorder: Advances in research and practice* (pp. 219–247). New York: Guilford Press.

Turk, D. C., & Melzack, R. (2001). *Handbook of pain assessment* (2nd ed.). New York: Guilford Press.

Turk, D. C., & Okifuji, A. (2001). Measuring treatment to assessment of patients with chronic pain. In D. C. Turk & R. Melzack (Eds.), *Handbook of pain assessment* (2nd ed.). New York: Guilford Press.

Turkat, I. (1990). *The personality disorders: A psychological approach to clinical management.* Elmsford, NY: Pergamon Press.

Turkel, S. B., Braslow, K., Tavaré, C. J., & Trzepacz, P. T. (2003). The Delirium Rating Scale in children and adolescents. *Psychosomatics, 44*, 126–129.

Turkel, S. B., & Tavaré, C. J. (2003). Delirium in children and adolescents. *Journal of Neuropsychiatry and Clinical Neurosciences, 15*, 431–435.

Turley, B., Bates, G. W., Edwards, J., & Jackson, H. J. (1992). MCMI-II personality disorders in recent-onset bipolar disorders. *Journal of Clinical Psychology, 48*, 320–329.

Turnbull, S., Ward, A., Treasure, J., Jick, H., & Derby, L. (1996). The demand for eating disorder care: An epidemiological study using the General Practice Research Database. *British Journal of Psychiatry, 169*(6), 705–712.

Turnbull, Q., Wolf, A., & Holroyd, S. (2003). Attitudes of elderly toward 'truth telling' for the diagnosis of Alzheimer's disease. *Journal of Geriatric Psychiatry and Neurology, 16*, 90–93.

Turner, M. (1997). Towards an executive dysfunction account of repetitive behavior in autism. In J. Russell (Ed.), *Autism as an executive disorder* (pp. 57–100). New York: Oxford University Press.

Turner, M. (1999a). Malingering, hysteria, and the factitious disorders. *Cognitive Neuropsychiatry, 4*(3), 193–201.

Turner, M. (1999b). Repetitive behavior in autism: A review of psychological research. *Journal of Child Psychology and Psychiatry, 40*, 839–849.

Turner, S. M., Beidel, D. C., Borden, J. W., Stanley, M. A., & Jacob, R. G. (1991). Social phobia: Axis I and II correlates. *Journal of Abnormal Psychology, 100*, 102–106.

Turner, S. M., Beidel, D. C., & Dancu, C. V. (1996). *SPAI: Social Phobia and Anxiety Inventory.* North Tonawanda, NY: Multi-Health Systems.

Turner, S. M., Beidel, D. C., & Townsley, R. M. (1992). Behavioral treatment of social phobia. In S. M. Turner, K. S. Calhoun, & H. E. Adams (Eds.), *Handbook of clinical behavior therapy* (pp. 13–37). New York: Wiley.

Turner, S. M., Hersen, M., & Heiser, N. (2003). The interviewing process. In M. Hersen (Ed.), *Diagnostic interviewing* (pp. 1–20). New York: Kluwer Academic/Plenum Press.

Twemlow, S. W. (1995). DSM-I from a cross-cultural perspective. *Psychiatric Annals, 25*, 46–52.

Twemlow, S. W. (2001). Interviewing violent patients. *Bulletin of the Menninger Clinic, 65*, 503–521.

Tye, C. S., & Mullen, P. E. (2006). Mental disorders in female prisoners. *Australian and New Zealand Journal of Psychiatry, 40*, 266–271.

Tyer, P. (Ed.) (1988). Personality disorder: Diagnosis, management, and course. London: Wright.

Tyer, P., & Alexander, J. (1988). Personality assessment schedule. In P. Tyrer (Ed.), Personality disorders: Diagnostic management and course (pp. 43–62). London: Wright.

Tyer, P., Mitchard, S., Methuen, C., & Ranger, M. (2003). Treatment rejecting and treatment seeking personality disorders: Type R and Type S. *Journal of Personality Disorders, 17*, 263–268.

Uhlenhuth, E. H., Leon, A. C., & Matuzas, M. (2006). Psychopathology of panic attacks in panic disorder. *Journal of Affective Disorders, 92*, 55–62.

Ungvari, G. S., Leung, S. K., Ng, F. S., Cheung, H. K., & Leung, T. (2005). Schizophrenia with prominent catatonic features ("catatonic schizophrenia"): Pt. I. Demographic and clinical correlates in the chronic phase. *Progress in Neuro-Psychopharmacology and Biological Psychiatry, 29*, 27–38.

Unnever, J. D., & Cornell, D. G. (2003). Bullying, self-control and ADHD. *Journal of Interpersonal Violence, 18*(2), 128–147.

U.S. Congress, Office of Technology Assessment. (1987). *Losing a million minds: Confronting the tragedy of Alzheimer's disease and other dementias* (Report No. OTA-BA-324). Washington, DC: U.S. Government Printing Office.

U.S. Department of Health and Human Services. (1999). *Mental health: A report of the surgeon general—Executive summary.* Rockville, MD: U.S. Department of Health and Human Services, Substance Abuse and Mental Health Services Administration, Center for Mental Health Services, National Institutes of Health, National Institute of Mental Health.

U.S. Department of Health and Human Services. (2003). *Code of federal regulations 45 CFR Parts 160, 162, and 164: Health insurance reform: Security standards—Final rule.* Retrieved March 8, 2006, from www.cms.hhs.gov/SecurityStandard/Downloads/securityfinalrule.pdf.

U.S. Department of Justice. (1998). *Violence by intimates: An analysis of data on crimes by current or former spouses, boyfriends, or girlfriends.* Washington, DC: Bureau of Justice Statistics.

U.S. Food and Drug Administration. (2004). *FDA launches a multi-pronged strategy to strengthen safeguards for children treated with antidepressant medications.* Retrieved September 27, 2006, from www.fda.gov/bbs/topics/news/2004/NEW01124.html.

U.S. Food and Drug Administration & Public Health Advisory. (2005). *Deaths with antipsychotics in elderly patients with behavioral disturbances.* Retrieved September 16, 2006, from www.fda.gov/cder/drug/advisory/antipsychotics.htm.

Utay, J., & Utay, C. (1999). The ABCs of rapport building: An organizing strategy for training counselors. *Psychology: A Journal of Human Behavior, 36,* 34–39.

Valan, M. N., & Hilty, D. M. (1996). Incidence of delirium in patients referred for evaluation of depression. *Psychosomatics, 37,* 190–191.

Valenzuela, M. (1990). Attachment in chronically underweight young children. *Child Development, 61*(6), 1984–1996.

Vaillant, G. (2003). A 60-year follow-up of alcoholic men. *Addiction, 98,* 1043–1051.

Vaillant, G. E. (1964). Prospective prediction of schizophrenic remission. *Archives of General Psychiatry, 11,* 509–518.

Vaillant, G. E. (1996). A long-term follow-up of male alcohol abuse. *Archives of General Psychiatry, 53,* 243–249.

Valtonen, H., Suominen, K., Mantere, O., Leppämäki, S., Arvilommi, P., & Isometsä, E., (2005). Suicidal ideation and attempts in bipolar I and II disorders. *Journal of Clinical Psychiatry, 66,* 1456–1462.

Van Acker, R., Loncola, J. A., & Van Acker, E. Y. (2005). Rett syndrome: A pervasive developmental disorder. In F. R. Volkmar, R. Paul, A. Klin, & D. Cohen (Eds.), *Handbook of autism and pervasive developmental disorders* (3rd ed., pp. 126–164). Hoboken, NJ: Wiley.

Van Amerigen, M., Mancini, C., & Farvolden, P. (2003). The impact of anxiety disorders on educational achievement. *Anxiety Disorders, 17,* 561–571.

Van Balkom, A. J. M., van Oppen, P., Vermeulen, A. W. A., van Dyck, R., Nauta, M. C. E., & Vorst, H. C. M. (1994). A meta-analysis on the treatment of obsessive-compulsive disorder: A comparison of antidepressants, behavior, and cognitive therapy. *Clinical Psychology Review, 14,* 359–381.

Van Brunt, D. L., & Lichstein, K. L. (2000). Primary insomnia. In M. Hersen & M. Biaggio (Eds.), *Effective brief therapies: A clinician's guide* (pp. 283–302). New York: Academic Press.

van de Loo, E. L. H. M., & Eurelings-Bontekoe, E. H. M. (1990). Psychotic disorders. In D. F. Peck & C. M. Shapiro (Eds.), *Measuring human problems: A practical guide* (pp. 217–240). Oxford: Wiley.

Vandereycken, W. (1985). "Bulimia" has different meanings. *American Journal of Psychiatry, 142*(1), 141–142.

van der Kolk, B. (1997). The psychobiology of posttraumatic stress disorder. *Journal of Clinical Psychiatry, 58,* 16–24.

Vanderlinden, J., Grave, R. D., Fernandez, F., Vandereycken, W., Pieters, G., & Noorduin, C. (2004). Which factors do provoke binge eating? An exploratory study in eating disorder patients. *Eating and Weight Disorders, 9*(4), 300–305.

Vanderlinden, J., Vandereycken, W., & Probst, M. (1995). Dissociative symptoms in eating disorders: A follow-up study. *European Eating Disorders Review, 3*(3), 174–184.

Van Deth, R., & Vandereycken, W. (1995). Was late-nineteenth-century nervous vomiting an early variant of bulimia nervosa? *History of Psychiatry, 6*(23, Pt. 3), 333–347.

Van Deth, R., Vandereycken, W., & Parry-Jones, W. L. L. (1995). Eating disorders. In G. E. Berrios & R. Porter (Eds.), *A history of clinical psychiatry: The origin and history of psychiatric disorders* (pp. 593–611). New York: New York University Press.

Vandrey, R., Budney, A. J., Kamon, J. L., & Stanger, C. (2005). Cannabis withdrawal in adolescent treatment seekers. *Drug and Alcohol Dependence, 78*, 205–210.

Van Etten, M. L., & Anthony, J. C. (1999). Comparative epidemiology of initial drug opportunities and transitions to first use: Marijuana, cocaine, hallucinogens, and heroin. *Drug and Alcohol Dependence, 54*, 117–125.

Van Etten, M. L., Neumark, Y. D., & Anthony, J. C. (1999). Male-female differences in the earliest stages of drug involvement. *Addiction, 94*, 1413–1419.

Van Gerpen, M., Johnson, J. E., & Winstead, D. K. (1999). Mania in the geriatric population: A review of the literature. *American Journal of Geriatric Psychiatry, 7*, 188–202.

Van Gorp, W. G., Root, J. C., & Sackheim, H. A. (2004). Neuropsychological assessment of late-life depression. In S. P. Roose & H. A. Sackheim (Eds.), *Late life depression* (pp. 81–94). New York: Oxford University Press.

Van Hemert, A. M., van der Mast, R. C., Hengeveld, M. W., & Vorstenbosch, M. (1994). Excess mortality in general hospital patients with delirium: A 5-year follow-up study of 519 patients seen in psychiatric consultation. *Journal of Psychosomatic Research, 38*, 339–346.

van Hoeken, D., Seidell, J., & Hoek, H. (2003). Epidemiology. In J. Treasure, U. Schmidt, & E. van Furth (Eds.), *Handbook of eating disorders* (2nd ed., pp. 11–34). Chichester, West Sussex, England: Wiley.

Van Krevelen, D. A. (1971). Early infantile autism and autistic psychopathy. *Journal of Autism and Child Schizophrenia, 1*(1), 82–86.

Vannicelli, M. (2001). Leader dilemmas and countertransference considerations in group psychotherapy with substance abusers. *International Journal of Group Psychotherapy, 51*, 43–62.

van Vliet, I. M., den Boer, J. A., & Westenberg, H. G. M. (1994). Psychopharmacological treatment of social phobia: A double-blind placebo controlled study with fluvoxamine. *Psychopharmacology, 115*, 128–134.

van Vliet, I. M., den Boer, J. A., Westenberg, H. G., & Pian, K. L. (1997). Clinical effects of buspirone in social phobia: A double-blind placebo-controlled study. *Journal of Clinical Psychiatry, 58*, 164–168.

Van Wagoner, S. L., Gelso, C. J., Hayes, J. A., & Diemer, R. A. (1991). Countertransference and the reputedly excellent therapist. *Psychotherapy, 28*, 411–421.

Varma, A. R., Snowden, J. S., Lloyd, J. J., Talbot, P. R., Mann, D. M. A., & Neary, D. (1999). Evaluation of the NINCDS-ADRDA criteria in the differentiation of Alzheimer's disease and frontotemporal dementia. *Journal of Neurology, Neurosurgery, and Psychiatry 66*, 184–188.

Varma, D., Chandra, P. S., Thomas, T., & Carey, M. P. (2007). Intimate partner violence and sexual coercion among pregnant women in India: Relationship with depression and post-traumatic stress disorder. *Journal of Affective Disorders*.

Vasudev, K., Macritchie, K., Geddes, J., Watson, S., & Young, A. (2006). Topiramate for acute affective episodes in bipolar disorder. *Cochrane Database of Systematic Reviews, 25*, CD003384.

Veale, D., Boocock, A., Gournay, K., Dryden, W., Shah, F., Wilson, R., et al. (1996). Body dysmorphic disorder: A survey of fifty cases. *British Journal of Psychiatry, 169*, 196–201.

Vecchierini, M. F. (2003). Parasomnias. In M. Billiard (Trans.), *Sleep: Physiology, investigations, and medicine* (pp. 51–541). New York: Kluwer Academic/Plenum Press.

Vega, W. A., Gil, A., Warheit, G., Apospori, E., & Zimmerman, R. (1993). The relationship of drug use to suicide ideation and attempts among African American. Hispanic, and White non-Hispanic male adolescents. *Suicide and Life-Threatening, Behavior, 23*(2), 110–119.

Veltkamp, L. J., & Miller, T. W. (1994). *Clinical handbook of child abuse and neglect*. Madison, CT: International Universities Press.

Venable, W., & Thompson, B. (1998). Caretaker psychological factors predicting premature termination of children's counseling. *Journal of Counseling and Development, 76*, 286–293.

Verhaak, P. F. M., Kerssens, J. J., Decker, J., Sorbi, M. J., & Bensing, J. M. (1998). Prevalence of chronic benign pain disorder among adults: A review of the literature. *Pain, 77*, 231–239.

Verheul, R., van der Bosch, L. M. C., & Ball, S. A. (2005). Substance abuse. In J. M. Oldham, A. E. Skodol, & D. S. Bender (Eds.), *Textbook of personality disorders* (pp. 463–477). Washington, DC: American Psychiatric Publishing.

Viding, E., Blair, R. J., Moffitt, T. E., & Plomin, R. (2003, July). *Psycopathic syndrome in indexes strong genetic risk for antisocial behavior in 7-year-olds.* Paper presented at the conference Developmental and Neuroscience Perspectives on Psychopathy conference, Madison, WI.

Vieweg, W. V., Julius, D. A., Fernandez, A., Beatty-Brooks, M., Hettema, J. M., & Pandurangi, A. K. (2006). Posttraumatic stress disorder: Clinical features, pathophysiology, and treatment. *American Journal of Medicine, 119*, 383–390.

Vig, S., & Jedrysek, E. (1999). Autistic features in young children with significant cognitive impairment: Autism or mental retardation? *Journal of Autism and Developmental Disorders, 29*(3), 235–247.

Viguera, A., Baldessarini, R., & Tondo, L. (2001). Response to lithium maintenance treatment in bipolar disorders: Comparison of women and men. *Bipolar Disorders, 3*, 245–252.

Viguera, A. C., Cohen, L. S., Baldessarini, R. J., & Nonacs, R. (2002). Managing bipolar disorder during pregnancy: Weighing the risks and benefits. *The Canadian Journal of Psychiatry, 47*, 426–436.

Viguera, A. C., Cohen, L. S., Nonacs, R. M., & Bladessarini, R. J. (2005). Management of bipolar disorder during pregnancy and the postpartum period: Weighing the risks and benefits. In L. S. Cohen & R. M. Nonacs (Eds.), *Review of psychiatry: Vol. 24. Mood and anxiety disorders during pregnancy and postpartum* (pp. 53–76). Washington, DC: American Psychiatric Press.

Viguera, A. C., Nonacs, R., Cohen, L. S., Tondo, L., Murray, A., & Baldessarini, R. J. (2000). Risk of recurrence of bipolar disorder in pregnant and nonpregnant women after discontinuing lithium maintenance. *American Journal of Psychiatry, 157*, 179–184.

Vik, P. W., Cellucci, T., Jarchow, A., & Hedt, J. (2004). Cognitive impairment in substance abuse. *Psychiatric Clinics of North America, 27*, 97–109.

Villemarette-Pitman, N. R., Stanford, M. S., Greve, K. W., Houston, R. J., & Mathias, C. W. (2004). Obsessive-compulsive personality disorder and behavioral dsinhibition. *Journal of Psychology, 138*(1), 5–22.

Vinkers, D. J., Stek, M. L., Gussekbi, J., van der Mast, R. C., & Westendorp, R. G. J. (2004). Does depression in old age increase only cardiovascular mortality? The Leiden 85-Plus Study. *International Journal of Geriatric Psychiatry, 19*, 852–857.

Visser, S., & Bouman, T. (2001). The treatment of hypochondriasis: Exposure plus response prevention vs. cognitive therapy. *Behavior Research and Therapy, 39*, 423–442.

Vitaliano, P. P., Zhang, J., & Scanlan, J. M. (2003). Is caregiving hazardous to one's health? A meta-analysis. *Psychological Bullentin, 129*.

Vitaro, F., Tremblay, R. E., & Bukowski, W. M. (2001). Friends, friendships, and conduct disorders. In J. Hill & B. Maughan (Eds.), *Conduct disorders in childhood and adolescence* (pp. 346–376). Cambridge: Cambridge University Press.

Vitousek, K. M. (1996). The current status of cognitive-behavioral models of anorexia nervosa and bulimia nervosa. In P. M. Salkovskis (Ed.), *Frontiers of cognitive therapy* (pp. 383–418). New York: Guilford Press.

Volkmar, F. R. (2005). International perspectives. In. F. R. Volkmar, R. Paul, A. Klin, & D. Cohen (Eds.), *Handbook of autism and pervasive developmental disorders* (3rd ed., pp. 1193–1252), Hoboken, NJ: Wiley.

Volkmar, F. R., Cohen, D., & Paul, R. (1986). An evaluation of the DSM-III criteria for infantile autism. *Journal of the American Academy of Child Psychiatry, 25*(2), 190–197.

Volkmar, F. R., & Cohen, D. J. (1989). Disintergrative disorder or "late onset" autism. *Journal of Child Psychology and Psychiatry and Allied Disciplines, 30*(5), 717–724.

Volkmar, F. R., Cook, E. H., Jr., Pomeroy, J., Realmuto, G., & Tanguay, P. (1999). Practice parameters for the assessment and treatment of children, adolescents and adults with autism and other pervasive developmental disorders. *Journal of the American Academy of Child and Adolescent Psychiatry, 38*, S32–S34.

Volkmar, F. R., & Klin, A. (2000). Diagnostic issues in Asperger syndrome. In A. Klin, F. R. Volkmar, & S. S. Sparrow (Eds.), *Asperger syndrome* (pp. 25–71). New York: Guilford Press.

Volkmar, F. R., & Klin, A. (2005). Issues in classification of autism and related conditions. In F. R. Volkmar, R. Paul, A. Klin, & D. Cohen (Eds.), *Handbook of autism and pervasive developmental disorders* (3rd ed., 5–41). Hoboken, NJ: Wiley.

Volkmar, F. R., Klin, A., & Paul, R. (2005). Preface. In F. R. Volkmar, R. Paul, A. Klin, & D. Cohen (Eds.), *Handbook of autism and pervasive developmental disorders* (3rd ed., pp. xv–xix). Hoboken, NJ: Wiley.

Volkmar, F. R., Koeing, K., & State, M. (2005). Childhood disintegrative disorder. In F. R. Volkmar, R. Paul, A. Klin, & D. Cohen (Eds.), *Handbook of autism and pervasive developmental disorders* (3rd ed., 70–87). Hoboken, NJ: Wiley.

Volkmar, F. R., Lord, C., Bailey, A., Schultz, R. T., & Klin, A. J. (2004). Autism and pervasive developmental disorders. *Journal of Child Psychology and Psychiatry, 45*(1), 135–170.

Volkmar, F. R., Paul, R. R., Klin, A., & Cohen, D. (2005). *Handbook of autism and pervasive developmental disorders* (3rd ed.). Hoboken, NJ: Wiley.

Volkow, N. D., Wang, G. J., Fischman, M. W., Foltin, R., Fowler, J. S., Franceschi, D., et al. (2000). Effects of route of administration on cocaine induced dopamine transporter blockade in the human brain. *Life Sciences, 67*, 1507–1515.

Vondra, J. I., Kolar, A. B., & Radigan, B. L. (1992). Psychological maltreatment of children. In R. T. Ammerman & M. Hersen (Eds.), *Assessment of family violence: A clinical and legal sourcebook* (pp. 253–290). New York: Wiley.

Von Hahn, L., Harper, G., McDaniel, S., Siegel, D. M., Feldman, M. D., & Libow, J. A. (2001). A case of factitious disorder by proxy: The role of the health-care system, diagnostic dilemmas, and family dynamics. *Harvard Review of Psychiatry, 9*, 124–135.

von Knorring, A. L., Cloninger, C. R., Bohman, M., & Sigvardsson, S. (1983). An adoption study of depressive disorders and substance abuse. *Archives of General Psychiatry, 40*, 943–950.

Voruganti, L., Heslegrave, R. J., & Awad, A. G. (1997). Neurocognitive correlates of positive and negative syndromes in schizophrenia. *Canadian Journal of Psychiatry, 42*, 1066–1071.

Wachtel, P. L. (2002). Termination of therapy: An effort at integration. *Journal of Psychotherapy Integration, 12*(3), 373–383.

Wade, T. D., Bulik, C. M., Neale, M., & Kendler, K. S. (2000). Anorexia nervosa and major depression: Shared genetic and environmental risk factors. *American Journal of Psychiatry, 157*(3), 469–471.

Waelde, L. C., Thompson, L., & Gallagher-Thompson, D. (2004). A pilot study of a yoga and meditation intervention for dementia caregiver stress. *Journal of Clinical Psychology, 60*, 677–687.

Wagner, R., Silove, D., Marnane, C., & Rouen, D. (2006). Delays in referral of patients with social phobia, panic disorder, and generalized anxiety disorder attending a specialist anxiety clinic. *Anxiety Disorders, 20*, 363–371.

Wakefield, A. J., Murch, S. H., Anthony, A., Linell, J., Casson, D. M., Malik, M., et al. (1998). Ileal-lymphoid-nodular hyperplasia, non-specific colitis, and pervasive developmental disorder in children. *Lancet, 351*(9103), 637–641.

Wakeling, A. (1996). Epidemiology of anorexia nervosa. *Psychiatry Research, 62*, 3–9.

Walcott, D. D., Pratt, H. D., & Patel, D. R. (2003). Adolescents and eating disorders: Gender, racial, ethnic, sociocultural, and socioeconomic issues. *Journal of Adolescent Research, 18*(3), 223–243.

Waldinger, R. J., Schulz, M. S., Barsky, A. J., & Ahern, D. K. (2006). Mapping the road from childhood trauma to adult somatization: The role of attachment. *Psychosomatic Medicine, 68*, 129–135.

Waldman, I. D., & Lilienfeld, S. O. (1991). Diagnostic efficiency of symptoms for oppositional defiant disorder and attention-deficit hyperactivity disorder. *Journal of Consulting Clinical Psychology, 59*, 732–738.

Walitzer, K. S., & Dearing, R. L. (2006). Gender differences in alcohol and substance use relapse. *Clinical Psychology Review, 26*, 128–148.

Walker, D. R., Thompson, A., Zwaigenbaum, L., Goldberg, J., Bryson, S. E., Makoney, W. J., et al. (2004). Specifying PDD-NOS: A comparison of PDD-NOS, Asperger syndrome and autism. *Journal of the American Academy of Child and Adolescent Psychiatry, 43*(2), 72–80.

Walker, E. F., Grimes, K. E., Davis, D. M., & Smith, A. J. (1993). Childhood precursors of schizophrenia: Facial expressions of emotion. *American Journal of Psychiatry, 150,* 1654–1660.

Walker, L. E. (1989). *Terrifying love: Why battered women kill and how society responds.* New York: Harper & Row.

Walker, L. S., Claar, R. L., & Garber, J. (2002). Social consequences of children's pain: When do they encourage symptom maintenance? *Journal of Pediatric Psychology, 27,* 689–698.

Walker, L. S., Smith, C. A., Garber, J., Van Slyke, D. A., & Claar, R. L. (2001). The relation of daily stressors to somatic and emotional symptoms in children with recurrent abdominal pain. *Journal of Consulting and Clinical Psychology, 69,* 85–91.

Wall, T. L., Shea, S. H., Chan, K. K., & Carr, L. G. (2001). A genetic association with the development of alcohol and other substance use behavior in Asian Americans. *Journal of Abnormal Psychology, 110,* 173–178.

Wallace, S. T., & Alden, L. E. (1997). Social phobia and positive social events: The price of succes. *Journal of Abnormal Psychology, 106,* 416–424.

Waller, G. (1997). Drop-out and failure to engage in individual outpatient cognitive behavior therapy for bulimic disorders. *International Journal of Eating Disorders, 22,* 35–41.

Waller, G., & Kennerley, H. (2003). Cognitive-behavioral treatments. In J. Treasure, U. Schmidt, & Evan Furth (Eds.), *Handbook of eating disorders* (2nd ed., pp. 233–251). Chichester, West Sussex, England: Wiley.

Wallin, A. K., Blennow, K., Andreasen, N., & Minthon, L. (2006). CSF biomarkers for Alzheimer's disease: Levels of beta-amyloid, tau, phosphorylated tau relate to clinical symptoms and survival. *Dementia and Geriatric Cognitive Disorders, 21,* 131–138.

Walsh, A. E., Oldman, A. D., Franklin, M., Fairburn, C. G., & Cowen, P. J. (1995). Dieting decreases plasma tryptophan and increases the prolactin response to d-fenfluramine in women but not men. *Journal of Affective Disorders, 33*(2), 89–97.

Walsh, B. T. (1993). Binge eating in bulimia nervosa. In C. G. Fairburn & G. T. Wilson (Eds.), *Binge eating: Nature, assessment, and treatment* (pp. 37–49). New York: Guilford Press.

Walsh, B. T., & Devlin, M. J. (1998). Eating disorders: Progress and problems. *Science, 280*(5368), 1387–1390.

Walsh, B. T., Kissileff, H. R., Cassidy, S. M., & Dantzic, S. (1989). Eating behavior of women with bulimia. *Archives of General Psychiatry 46,* 54–58.

Walsh, B. T., Wilson, G. T., Loeb, K. L., Devlin, M. J., Pike, K. M., Roose, S. P., et al. (1997). Medication and psychotherapy in the treatment of bulimia nervosa. *American Journal of Psychiatry, 154*(4), 523–531.

Walsh, J. K., & Üstün, T. B. (1999). Prevalence and health consequences of insomnia. *Sleep: Journal of Sleep Research and Sleep Medicine, 22*(Suppl. 3), S427–S436.

Walters, A. (1969). Psychogenic regional pain and motor disorders alias hysteria. *Canadian Psychiatric Association Journal, 14,* 573–590.

Walters, G. D. (2002). The heritability of alcohol abuse and dependence: A meta-analysis of behavior genetic research. *American Journal of Drug and Alcohol Abuse, 28,* 557–584.

Waraich, P., Goldner, E. M., Somers, J. M., & Hsu, L. (2004). Prevalence and incidence studies of mood disorders: A systematic review of the literature. *Canadian Journal of Psychiatry, 49,* 124–138.

Ward, A., Ramsay, R., Turnbull, S., Benedettini, M., & Treasure, J. (2000). Attachment patterns in eating disorders: Past in the present. *International Journal of Eating Disorders, 28*(4), 370–376.

Ward, C. H., Beck, A. T., Mendelson, M., Mock, J. E., & Erbaugh, J. K. (1962). The psychiatric nomenclature. *Archives of General Psychiatry, 7,* 198–205.

Ward, J., Mattick, R. P., & Hall, W. (1998). The effectiveness of methadone maintenance treatment: Pt 2. HIV and infectious hepatitis. In J. Ward, R. P. Mattick, & W. Hall (Eds.),

Methadone maintenance treatment and other opioid replacement therapies (pp. 59–73). Amsterdam, The Netherlands: Harwood Academic.

Warren, F., Preedy-Fasyers, K., McGauley, G., Pickering, A., Norton, K., Geddes, J. R., et al., (2003). *Review of treatments for severe personality disorder.* Home Office Online Report, 30/03. Available from www.homeoffice.gov.uk/rds/pdfs2/rdsolr3003.pdf.

Warzok, R. W., Kessler, C., Apel, G., Schwarz, A., Egensperger, R., Schreiber, D., et al. (1998). Apolipoprotein E4 promotes incipient Alzheimer pathology in the elderly. *Alzheimer Disease and Associated Disorders, 12,* 33–39.

Waslick, B. D., Kandel, R., & Kakouros, A. (2002). Depression in children and adolescents. In D. Scaffer & B. D. Waslick (Eds.), *The many faces of depression in children and adolescents* (pp. 1–36). Washington, DC: American Psychiatric Publishing.

Wasserstein, J. (2005). Diagnostic issues for adolescents and adults with ADHD. *Journal of Clinical Psychology In Session, 61*(5), 535–547.

Waterhouse, L., Morris, R., Allen, D., Dunn, M., Fein, D., Feinstein, C., et al. (1996). Diagnosis and classification in autism. *Journal of Autism and Developmental Disorders, 26*(1), 59–85.

Watkins, B., & Lask, B. (2002). Eating disorders in school-aged children. *Child and Adolescent Psychiatric Clinics, 11,* 185–199.

Watson, J. B., & Raynor, R. (1920). Conditioned emotional reactions. *Journal of Experimental Psychology, 3*(1), 1–14.

Ways, B., & Banks, S. (2001). Clinical factors related to admission and release decisions in psychiatric emergency services. *Psychiatric Services, 52,* 214–218.

Wayte, A., Bebbington, P., Skelton-Robinson, M., & Orrell, M. (2004). Social factors and depression in carers of people with dementia. *International Journal of Geriatric Psychiatry, 19,* 582–587.

Webster, C. D., Harris, G., Rice, M., Cormier, C., & Quinsey, V. (1994). *The violence prediction scheme: Assessing dangerousness in high risk men.* Toronto, Ontario, Canada: University of Toronto, Center of Criminology.

Webster's. (1999). *The New International Webster's Compact Dictionary of the English Language.* Trident Press International.

Webster-Stratton, C. (1996). Early intervention with videotape modeling: Programs for families of children with oppositional defiant disorder or conduct disorder. In M. J. Guralnick (Ed.), *The effectiveness of early intervention: Second generation research* (pp. 429–454). Baltimore, MD: Paul H. Brookes.

Webster-Stratton, C. (2005). The incredible years: A training series for the prevention and treatment of conduct problems in young children. In E. D. Hibbs & P. S. Jernsen (Eds.), *Psychosocial treatments for child and adolescent disorders: Empirically based strategies for clinical practice* (2nd ed., pp. 507–555). Washington, DC: American Psychological Association.

Webster-Stratton, C., & Reid, M. J. (2003). The Incredible Years parents, teachers and children training series: A multifaceted treatment approach for young children with conduct problems. In A. E. Kazdin & J. R. Weisz (Eds.), *Evidence-based psychotherapies for children and adolescents* (pp. 224–262). New York: Guilford Press.

Webster-Stratton, C., Reid, M. J., & Hammond, M. (2001a). Preventing conduct problems, promoting social competence: A parent and teacher training partnership in Head Start. *Journal of Clinical Child Psychology, 30,* 283–302.

Webster-Stratton, C., Reid, M. J., & Hammond, M. (2001b). Social skills and problem-solving training for children with early-onset conduct problems: Who benefits? *Journal of Child Psychology and Applied Disciplines, 42,* 943–952.

Wechsler, D. (2002). *Wechsler Intelligence Preschool and Primary Scale of Intelligence* (3rd ed.). San Antonio, TX: Psychological Corporation.

Wechsler, D. (2003). *Wechsler Intelligence Scale for Children* (4th. ed.). San Antonio, TX: Psychological Corporation.

Wefel, J. S., Hoyt, B. D., & Massman, P. J. (1999). Neuropsychological functioning in depressed vs. non-depressed participants with Alzheimer's disease. *Clinical Neuropsychologist, 13,* 249–257.

Wegscheider, S. (1981). *Another chance: Hope and health for the alcoholic family.* Palo Alto, CA: Science and Behavior Books.

Wehman, P., & Moon, M. (1988). *Vocational rehabilitation and supported employment.* Baltimore: Paul H. Brookes.

Wehmeier, P. M., Barth, N., & Remschmidt, H. (2003). Induced delusional disorder: A review of the concept and an unusual case of folie à famille. *Psychopathology, 36,* 37–45.

Wehr, T. A., Sack, D. A., & Rosenthal, N. E. (1987). Sleep reduction as a final common pathway in the genesis of mania. *American Journal of Psychiatry, 144,* 201–204.

Weiden, P. J., Mott, T., & Curcio, N. (1995). Recognition and management of neuroleptic noncompliance. In C. L. Shriqui & H. A. Nasrallah (Eds.), *Contemporary issues in the treatment of schizophrenia* (pp. 411–434). Washington, DC: American Psychiatric Press.

Weiderhold, B. K., & Weiderhold, M. D. (2005). Anxiety disorders and their treatment. In B. K. Weiderhold & M. D. Weiderhold (Eds.), *Virtual reality therapy for anxiety disorders: Advances in evaluation and treatment* (pp. 31–45). Washington, DC: American Psychological Association.

Weimer, A. K., Schatz, A. M., Lincoln, A., Ballantyne, A. O., & Trauner, D. A. (2001). "Motor" impairment in Asperger syndrome: Evidence for a deficit in proprioception. *Journal of Developmental and Behavioral Pediatrics, 22*(20), 92–101.

Weinberger, D. R., Berman, F., & Zec, R. F. (1986). Physiological dysfunction of dorsolateral prefrontal cortex in schizophrenia: Pt. I. Regional cerebral blood flow evidence. *Archives of General Psychiatry, 43,* 114–124.

Weinberger, D. R., Jeste, D. V., & Wyatt, R. J. (1987). Cerebral atrophy in elderly schizophrenic patients: Effects of aging and of long-term institutionalization and neuroleptic therapy. In N. E. Miller & G. D. Cohen (Eds.), *Schizophrenia and ageing: Schizophrenia, paranoia and schizophreniform disorders in later life* (pp. 109–118). New York: Guilford Press.

Weiner, I. (1998). *Principles of psychotherapy* (2nd ed.). New York: Wiley.

Weiner, R. D., Rogers, H. J., Davidson, J. R., & Squire, L. R. (1986). Effects of stimulus parameters on cognitive side effects. *Annals of the New York Academy of Science, 462,* 315–325.

Weisman, A. G., Lopez, S. R., Ventura, J., Nuechterlein, K. H., Goldstein, M. J., & Hwang, S. (2000). A comparison of psychiatric symptoms between Anglo-Americans and Mexican-Americans with schizophrenia. *Schizophrenia Bulletin, 26,* 817–824.

Weisner, C., Ray, G. T., Mertens, J. R., Satre, D. D., & Moore, C. (2003). Short-term alcohol and drug treatment outcomes predict long-term outcome. *Drug and Alcohol Dependence, 71,* 281–294.

Weiss, M., Worling, D., & Wasdell, M. (2003). A chart review study of the inattentive and combined types of ADHD. *Journal of Attention Disorders, 7*(1), 1–9.

Weiss, M. D., & Weiss, J. R. (2004). A guide to the treatment of adults with ADHD. *Journal of Clinical Psychiatry, 65*(Suppl. 3), 27–37.

Weissman, M. M., Bland, R. C., Canino, G. J., Greenwald, S., Hwu, H. G., Lee, C. K., et al. (1994). The cross national epidemiology of obsessive compulsive disorder (The Cross National Collaborative Group). *Journal of Clinical Psychiatry, 55,* 5–10.

Weissman, M. M., & Bothwell, S. (1976). Assessment of social adjustment by patient self-report. *Archives of General Psychiatry, 33,* 1111–1115.

Weissman, M. M., Klerman, G. L., Markowitz, J. S., & Ouellette, M. (1989). Suicidal ideation and suicide attempts in panic disorder. *New England Journal of Medicine, 321,* 1209–1214.

Weissman, M. M., Leaf, P. J., Bruce, M. L., & Florio, L. (1988). The epidemiology of dysthymia in five communities: Rates, risks, comorbidity, and treatment. *American Journal of Psychiatry, 145,* 815–819.

Weissman, M. M., Markowitz, J. C., & Klerman, G. L. (2000). *Comprehensive guide to interpersonal psychotherapy.* New York: Basic Books.

Weissman, M. M., Merikangas, K. R., & Wickramaratne, P. (1986). Understanding the clinical heterogeneity of major depression using family data. *Archives of General Psychiatry, 43,* 430–434.

Weissman, M. M., Wolk, S., Goldstein, R. B., Moreau, D., Adams, P., Greenwald, S., et al. (1999). Depressed adolescents grow up. *Journal of the American Medical Association, 281,* 1707–1713.

Weisz, J. R., McCarty, C. A., & Valeri, S. A. (2006). Effects of psychotherapy for depression in children and adolescents: A meta-analysis. *Psychological Bulletin, 132,* 132–149.

Welch, L. W., Cunningham, A. T., Eckardt, M. J., & Martin, P. R. (1997). Fine motor speed deficits in alcoholic Korsakoff's syndrome. *Alcoholism Clinical and Experimental Research, 21,* 134–139.

Welch, L. W., Nimmerrichter, A., Gilliland, R., King, D. E., & Martin, P. R. (1997). Wineglass confabulations among brain-damaged alcoholics on the Wechsler Memory Scale—Revised visual reproduction subtest. *Cortex, 33,* 543–551.

Welfel, E. R. (2005). *Ethics in counseling and psychotherapy: Standards, research, and emerging issues* (3rd ed.). Belmont, CA: Wadsworth Publishing.

Welfel, E. R. (2006). *Ethics in counseling and psychotherapy: Standards, research, and emerging issues* Belmont, CA: Thomson Brooks/Cole.

Wells, K. B., Burnam, M. A., Rogers, W., & Hays, R. (1992). The course of depression in adult outpatients: Results from the Medical Outcomes Study. *Archives of General Psychiatry, 49,* 788–794.

Wender, P., Kety, S. S., Rosenthal, D., Schulsinger, F., Ortmann, J., & Lunde, I. (1986). Psychiatric disorders in the biological and adoptive families of adopted individuals with affective disorders. *Archives of General Psychiatry, 43,* 923–929.

Werner, E., Dawson, G., Osterling, J., & Dinno, N. (2000). Brief report: Recognition of autism spectrum disorders before one year of age: A retrospective study based on home video tapes. *Journal of Autism and Developmental Disorders, 30,* 157–162.

Werry, J. S. (1996). Pervasive development, psychotic, and allied disorders. In L. Hetchman (Ed.), *Do they grow out of it? Long term outcomes of childhood disorders* (pp. 195–223). Washington, DC: American Psychiatric Association.

Wessely, S. C., Castle, D., & Douglas, A. J. (1994). The criminal careers of incident cases of schizophrenia. *Psychological Medicine, 24,* 483–502.

Wessler, R., Hankin, S., & Stern, J. (2001). *Succeeding with difficult clients: Applications of cognitive appraisal therapy.* New York: Academic Press.

West, S. L., Vinikoor, L. C., & Zolnoun, D. (2004). A systematic review of the literature on female sexual dysfunction prevalence and predictors. *Annual Review of Sex Research, 15,* 40–172.

Westefeld, J., & Heckman-Stone, C. (2003). The integrated problem-solving model of crisis intervention: Overview and application. *Counseling Psychologist, 3,* 221–239.

Westen, D., & Muderrisoglu, S. (2003). Assessing personality disorders using a systematic clinical interview: Evaluation of an alternative to structured interviews. *Journal of Personality Disorders, 4,* 351–369.

Westen, D., & Shedler, J. (1999a). Revising and assessing Axis II: Pt. I. Developing a clinically and empirically valid assessment method. *American Journal of Psychiatry, 156,* 258–272.

Westen, D., & Shedler, J. (1999b). Revising and assessing Axis II: Pt. II. Towards an empirically based and clinically useful classification of personality disorders. *American Journal of Psychiatry, 160,* 952–966.

Westermeyer, J. (2005). Historical and social context of psychoactive substance use disorders. In R. J. Frances, S. I. Miller, & A. H. Mack (Eds.), *Clinical textbook of addictive disorders* (3rd ed., pp. 16–34), New York: Guilford Press.

Westermeyer, J. F., & Harrow, M. (1988). Course and outcome in schizophrenia. In M. T. Tsuang & J. C. Simpon (Eds.), *Handbook of schizophrenia: Vol. 3. Nosology, epidemiology, and genetics of schizophrenia* (pp. 205–244). Amsterdam, The Netherlands: Elsevier.

Westermeyer, J. F., Harrow, M., & Marengo, J. T. (1991). Risk of suicide in schizophrenia and other psychotic and nonpsychotic disorders. *Journal of Nervous Mental Disorders, 179,* 259–266.

Westermeyer, J., Yargic, I., & Thuras, P. (2004). Michigan Assessment-Screening Test for Alcohol and Drugs (MAST/AD): Evaluation in a clinical sample. *American Journal on Addictions, 13,* 151–162.

Wetherell, J. L., Gatz, M., & Craske, M. G. (2003). Treatment of generalized anxiety disorder in older adults. *Journal of Consulting and Clinical Psychology, 71*, 31–40.

Wetherell, J. L., Hopko, D. R., Diefenbach, G. J., Averill, P. M., Beck, J. G., Craske, M. G., et al. (2005). Cognitive-behavioral therapy for late-life generalized anxiety disorder: Who gets better? *Behavior Therapy, 36*, 147–156.

Wetherell, J. L., Le Roux, H., & Gatz, M. (2003). DSM-IV criteria for generalized anxiety disorder in older adults: Distinguishing the worried from the well. *Psychology and Aging, 18*, 622–627.

Whalen, C. K., Jamner, L. D., Henker, B., Delfino, R. J., & Lozano, J. M. (2002). The ADHD spectrum and everyday life: Experience sampling of adolescent moods, activities, smoking and drinking. *Child Development, 73*, 209–227.

Whaley, A. L. (1997). Ethnicity/race, paranoia, and psychiatric diagnoses: Clinician bias versus sociocultural difference. *Journal of Psychopathology and Behavioral Assessment, 19*, 1–20.

Whisman, M. A., & Bruce, M. L. (1999). Marital dissatisfaction and incidence of major depressive episode in a community sample. *Journal of Abnormal Psychology, 108*, 674–678.

Whisman, M. A., Weinstock, L. M., & Uebelacker, L. A. (2002). Mood reactivity to marital conflict: The influence of marital dissatisfaction and depression. *Behavior Therapy, 33*, 299–314.

White, C. N., Gunderson, J. G., Zanarini, M. C., & Hudson, J. I. (2003) Family studies of borderline personality disorder: A review. *Harvard Review of Psychiatry, 11*, 8–19.

White, K. G., & Ruske, A. C. (2002). Memory deficits in Alzheimer's disease: The encoding hypothesis and cholinergic function. *Psychonomic Bulletin and Review, 9*, 426–437.

White, K. S., & Barlow, D. H. (2002). Panic disorder and agoraphobia. In D. H. Barlow (Eds.), *Anxiety and its disorders: The nature and treatment of anxiety and panic* (2nd ed., pp. 328–379). New York: Guilford Press.

Whitehead, A., Perdomo, C., Pratt, R. D., Birks, J., Wilcock, G. K., Evans, J. G., et al. (2004). Donepezil for the symptomatic treatment of patients with mild to moderate Alzheimer's disease: A meta-analysis of individual patient data from randomised controlled trials. *International Journal of Geriatric Psychiatry, 19*, 624–633.

Whittal, M. L., Agras, W. S., & Gould, R. A. (1999). Bulimia nervosa: A meta-analysis of psychosocial and pharmacological treatments. *Behavior Therapy, 30*(1), 117–135.

Whittington, C. J., Kendall, T., Fonagy, P., Cottrell, D., Cotgrove, A., & Boddington, E. (2004). Selective serotonin reuptake inhibitors in childhood depression: Systematic review of published versus unpublished data. *Lancet, 363*, 1341–1345.

Widiger, T. A. (2000). Personality disorders in the 21st century. *Journal of Personality Disorders, 14*, 3–16.

Widiger, T. A. (2001). Offical classification systems. In W. J. Livesley (Ed.), *Handbook of personality disorders: Theory, research, and treatment* (pp. 60–83). New York: Guilford Press.

Widiger, T. A. (2005). Five Factor Model of personality disorder: Integrating science and practice. *Journal of research in Personality, 39*, 67–83.

Widiger, T. A., & Bornstein, R. F. (2001) Histrionic, narcissistic and dependent personality disorders. In H. E. Adams & P. B. Sutker (Eds.) *Comprehensive handbook of psychopathology* (3rd. ed., pp. 509–531). New York: Kluwer Academic/Plenum.

Widiger, T. A., & Clark, L. A. (2000). Towards DSM-V and the classification of psychopathology. *Psychological Bulletin, 126*, 946–963.

Widiger, T. A., & Corbitt, E. M. (1995). Antisocial personality disorder. In W. J. Livesley (Ed.), *The DSM-IV personality disorders* (pp. 103–126). New York: Guilford Press.

Widiger, T. A., Frances, A. J., Pincus, H. A., First, M. B., Ross, R., & Davis, W. (Eds.). (1994). *DSM-IV sourcebook* (Vol. 1). Washington, DC: American Psychiatric Association.

Widiger, T. A., Frances, A. J., Pincus, H. A., First, M. B., Ross R., & Davis, W. (Eds.). (1996). *DSM-IV sourcebook* (Vol. 2). Washington, DC: American Psychiatric Association.

Widiger, T. A., Frances, A. J. Pincus, H. A. First, M. B., Ross, R., & Davis, W. (Eds.). (1997). *DSM-IV sourcebook* (Vol. 3). Washington, DC: American Psychiatric Association.

Widiger, T. A., Frances, A. J., Pincus, H. A., First, M. B., Ross, R., & Davis, W. (Eds.). (1998). *DSM-IV sourcebook* (Vol. 4). Washington, DC: American Psychiatric Association.

Widiger, T. A., & Lynam, D. R. (1998). Psychopathy from the perspective of the five factor model of personality. In T. Millon, E. Simonsen, & M. Birket-Smith (Eds.), *Psychopathy: Antisocial, criminal, and violent behaviors* (pp. 171–187). New York: Guilford Press.

Widiger, T. A., Manigne, S., Corbitt, E. M., Ellis, C. G., & Thomas, G. V. (1995). *Personality Disorder Interview-IV: A semistructured interview for the assessment of personality disorders, professional manual.* Odessa, FL: Psychological Assessment Resources.

Widiger, T. A., & Mullins-Sweatt, S. N. (2005). Categorical and dimensional models of personality disorders. In J. M. Oldham, A. E. Skodol, & D. S. Bender (Eds.), *Textbook of personality disorders* (pp. 35–53). Washington, DC: American Psychiatric Publishing.

Widiger, T. A., & Samuel, D. B. (2005). Evidence-based assessment of personality disorders. *Psychological Assessment, 17, 3,* 278–287.

Widiger, T. A., Simonsen, E., Sirovatka, P., & Regier, D. A. (Eds.). (2007). *Dimensional models of personality disorders: Refining the research agenda for DSM-V.* Washington, DC: American Psychiatric Association.

Widiger, T. A., & Trull, T. J. (1993). The scholarly development of the DSM-IV. In J. A. C. E. Silva & C. C. Nadelson (Eds.), *International review of psychiatry* (pp. 59–78). Washington, DC: American Psychiatric Association.

Widiger, T. A., Trull, T. J., Clarkin, J. F., Sanderson, C., & Costa, P. T. (2002). A description of the DSM-IV personality disorders with the Five Factor Model of personality. In T. A. Widiger & P. T. Costa, Jr. (Eds.), *Personality disorders and the five factor model of personality* (2nd ed., pp. 89–99). Washington, DC: American Psychological Association.

Wiederman, M. W., & Pryor, T. (1996). Multi-impulsivity among women with bulimia nervosa. *International Journal of Eating Disorders, 20*(4), 359–365.

Wiehe, V. R. (1996). *Working with child abuse and neglect: A primer—Interpersonal violence* (The Practice Series). Thousand Oaks, CA: Sage.

Wiger, D. E. (2005). *The psychotherapy documentation primer* (2nd ed.). Hoboken, NJ: Wiley.

Wiger, D. E., & Huntly, D. K. (2003). *Essentials of interviewing.* Hoboken, NJ: Wiley.

Wiggs, L., & Stores, G. (2004). Sleep patterns and sleep disorders in children with autistic spectrum disorder: Insights using parent reports and actigraphy. *Developmental Medicine and Child Neurology, 46*(6), 372–380.

Wijeratne, C., Brodaty, H., & Hickie, I. (2003). The neglect of somatoform disorders by old age psychiatry: Some explanations and suggestions for further research. *International Journal of Geriatric Psychiatry, 18,* 812–819.

Wikstrom, P. O., & Loeber, R. (2000). Do disadvantaged neighborhoods cause well-adjusted children to become adolescent delinquents? A study of male juvenile serious offending, risk and protective factors and neighborhood context. *Criminology, 38,* 1109–1142.

Wilcock, G., Möbius, H. J., & Stöffler, A. (2002). A double-blind, placebo-controlled multicentre study of memantine in mild to moderate vascular dementia (MMM500). *Journal of Clinical Psychopharmacology, 17,* 297–305.

Wilcox, H. C., Conner, K. R., & Caine, E. D. (2004). Association of alcohol and drug use disorders and completed suicide: An empirical review of cohort studies. *Drug and Alcohol Dependence, 76,* S11–S19.

Wildgoose, A., Waller, G., Clarke, S., & Reid, A. (2000) Psychiatric symptomology in borderline and other personality disorders: Dissociation and fragmentation as mediators. *Journal of Nervous and Mental Disorders, 188,* 757–763.

Wilens, T. E., Biederman, J., Brown, S., Tanguay, S., Monteaux, M. C., Blake, C., et al. (2002). Psychiatric comorbidity and functioning in clinically referred preschool children and school-age youths with ADHD. *Journal of the American Academy of Child and Adolescent Psychiatry, 41*(3), 262–268.

Wilens, T. E., Biederman, J., & Spencer, T. J. (2002). Attention deficit/hyperactivity disorder across the life span. *Annual Review of Medicine, 53,* 113–131.

Wilens, T. E., & Spencer, T. (2000). The stimulants revisited. In C. Stubbe (Ed.), *Child and adolescent psychiatric clinics of North America* (pp. 573–603). Philadelphia: Saunders.

Wilfley, D. E., & Saelens, B. E. (2002). Epidemiology and causes of obesity in children. In C. G. Fairburn & K. D. Brownell (Eds.), *Eating disorders and obesity: A comprehensive handbook* (2nd ed., pp. 429–432). New York: Guilford Press.

Wilhelmsen, K. C., & Ehlers, C. (2005). Heritability of substance dependence in a Native American population. *Psychiatric Genetics, 15*, 101–107.

Wilkins, J. N. (1997). Pharmacotherapy of schizophrenia patients with co-morbid substance abuse. *Schizophrenia Bulletin, 23*, 215–228.

Wilkinson, D., & Murray, J. (2001). Galantamine: A randomized, double-blind, dose comparison in patients with Alzheimer's disease. *International Journal of Geriatric Psychiatry, 16*, 852–857.

Wilkinson-Ryan, T., & Westen, D. (2000). Identity disturbance in borderline personality disorder: An empirical investigation. *American Journal of Psychiatry, 158*, 1–52.

Willemsen-Swinkles, S. H. N., & Buitelaar, J. K. (2002). The autistic spectrum: Subgroups, boundaries and treatment. *Psychiatric Clinics of North America, 25*, 811–836.

Williams, D. A., & Thorn, B. E. (1989). An empirical assessment of pain beliefs. *Pain, 36*, 351–358.

Williams, J. M., & Dunlop, L. C. (1999). Pubertal timing and self-reported delinquency among male adolescents. *Journal of Adolescence, 22*, 157–171.

Williamson, D. A., Cubic, B. A., & Gleaves, D. H. (1993). Equivalence of body image disturbance in anorexia and bulimia nervosa. *Journal of Abnormal Psychology, 102*, 177–180.

Williamson, D. A., White, M. A., York-Crowe, E., & Stewart, T. A. (2004). Cognitive-behavioral theories of eating disorders. *Behavior Modification, 28*(6), 711–738.

Willoughby, M. T. (2003). Developmental course of ADHD symptomatology during the transition from childhood to adolescence: A review with recommendations. *Journal of Child Psychology and Psychiatry, 44*(1), 88–106.

Wills, L., & Garcia, J. (2002). Parasomnias: Epidemiology and management. *CNS Drugs, 16*(12), 803–810.

Wilson, G. T. (1987). Cognitive studies in alcoholism. *Journal of Consulting and Clinical Psychology, 55*, 325–331.

Wilson, G. T. (1999). Cognitive behavior therapy for eating disorders: Progress and problems. *Behaviour Research and Therapy, 37*(Suppl. 1), S79–S85.

Wilson, G. T., & Abrams, D. B. (1977). Effects of alcohol on social anxiety and physiological arousal: Cognitive versus pharmacological processes. *Cognitive Therapy and Research, 1*, 195–210.

Wilson, G. T., Becker, C. B., & Heffernan, K. (2003). Eating disorders. In E. J. Mash & R. A. Barkley (Eds.), *Child psychopathology* (2nd ed., pp. 687–715). New York: Guilford Press.

Wilson, G. T., & Fairburn, C. G. (2002). Treatments for eating disorders. In P. E. Nathan & J. M. Gorman (Eds.), *A guide to treatments that work* (2nd ed., pp. 559–592). New York: Oxford University Press.

Wilson, M., & Daly, M. (1993). Spousal homicide risk and estrangement. *Violence and Victims, 8*, 3–16.

Winblad, B., & Jelic, V. (2003). Treating the full spectrum of dementia with memantine. *International Journal of Geriatric Psychiatry, 18*(Suppl.), S41–S46.

Windle, M., Miller-Tutzauer, C., & Domenico, D. (1992). Alcohol use, suicidal behavior, and risky activities among adolescents. *Journal of Research on Adolescence, 2*, 317–330.

Wing, L. (1981). Asperger's syndrome: A clinical account. *Psychological Medicine, 11*(1), 115–129.

Wing, L. (1991). The relationship between Asperger's syndrome and Kanner's autism. In U. Frith (Ed.), *Autism and Asperger syndrome* (pp. 93–121). Cambridge: Cambridge University Press.

Wing, L. (1993). The definition and prevalence of autism: A review. *European Child Adolescent Psychiatry, 2*, 61–74.

Wing, L. (1996). Autistic spectrum disorders. *British Medical Journal, 312*, 327–328.

Wing, L. (2005). Problems of categorical classification systems. In F. R. Volkmar, R. Paul, A. Klin, & D. Cohen (Eds.), *Handbook of autism and pervasive developmental disorders* (3rd ed., pp. 583–605). Hoboken, NJ: Wiley.

Wing, L., & Gould, J. (1979). Severe impairments of social interaction and associated abnormalities in children: Epidemiology and classification. *Journal of Autism and Developmental Disorders, 9*(1), 11–29.

Wing, L., Gould, J., Yeates, S. R., & Brierley, L. M. (1977). Symbolic play in severely mentally retarded and in autistic children. *Journal of Child Psychology and Psychiatry, 18*(2), 167–178.

Winnicott, D. W. (1991). Psychotherapy of character disorders. In M. Kets de Vries & S. Perzow (Eds.), *Handbook of character studies: Psychoanalytic explorations* (pp. 461–475). Madison, CT: International Universities Press.

Wirshing, D. A., Sergi, M. J., & Mintz, J. (2005). A videotape intervention to enhance the informed consent process for medical and psychiatric treatment research. *American Journal of Psychiatry, 162*, 186–188.

Wirshing, D. A., Wirshing, W. C., Marder, S. R., Liberman, R. P., & Mintz, J. (1998). Informed consent: Assessment of comprehension. *American Journal of Psychiatry, 155*, 1508–1511.

Wise, M. G., Hilty, D. M., & Cerda, G. M. (2001). Delirium due to a general medication condition, delirium due to multiple etiologies, and delirium not otherwise specified. In G. O. Gabbard (Ed.), *Treatments of psychiatric disorders* (3rd ed., pp. 387–412). Washington, DC: American Psychiatric Publishing.

Wise, T. N., & Birket-Smith, M. (2002). The somatoform disorders for DSM-V: The need for changes in process and content. *Psychosomatics, 43*(6), 437–440.

Wisniewski, S. R., Belle, S. H., Coon, D. W., Marcus, S. M., Ory, M. G., & Burgio, L. D. (2003). The Resources for Enhancing Alzheimer's Caregiver Health (REACH): Project design and baseline characteristics. *Psychology and Aging, 18*, 375–384.

Witbrodt, J., & Kaskutas, L. A. (2005). Does diagnosis matter? Differential effects of 12-step participation and social networks on abstinence. *American Journal of Drug and Alcohol Abuse, 31*, 685–707.

Wittchen, H.-U., Carter, R. M., Pfister, H., Montgomery, S. A., & Kessler, R. C. (2000). Disabilities and quality of life in pure and comorbid generalized anxiety disorder and major depression in a national survey. *International Clinical Psychopharmacology, 15*, 319–328.

Wittchen, H.-U., & Essau, C. A. (1993). Comorbidity and mixed anxiety-depressive disorders: Is there epidemiologic evidence? *Journal of Clinical Psychiatry, 54*, 9–15.

Wittchen, H.-U., & Fehm, L. (2001). Epidemiology, patterns of comorbidity, and associated disabilities of social phobia. *Psychiatric Clinics of North America, 24*, 617–641.

Wittchen, H.-U., & Fehm, L. (2003). Epidemiology and natural course of social fears and social phobia. *Acta Psychiatrica Scandinavica, 108*, 4–18.

Wittchen, H.-U., Fuetsch, M., Sonntag, H., Müller, N., & Liebowitz, M. (2000). Disability and quality of life in pure and comorbid social phobia: Findings from a controlled study. *European Psychiatry, 15*, 46–58.

Wittchen, H.-U., & Hoyer, J. (2001). Generalized anxiety disorder: Nature and course. *Journal of Clinical Psychiatry, 62*, 15–19.

Wittchen, H.-U., Stein, M. B., & Kessler, R. C. (1999). Social fears and social phobia in a community sample of adolescents and young adults: Prevalence, risk factors and co-morbidity. *Psychological Medicine, 29*, 309–323.

Wittchen, H.-U., Zhao, S., Kessler, R., & Eaton, W. W. (1994). DSM-III-R generalized anxiety disorder in the National Comorbidity Survey. *Archives of General Psychiatry, 51*, 355–364.

Woell, C., Fichter, M. M., Pirke, K. M., & Wolfram, G. (1989). Eating behavior of patients with bulimia nervosa. *International Journal of Eating Disorders, 8*, 557–568.

Wohl, M., Lesser, I., & Smith, M. (1997). Clinical presentations of depression in African American and White outpatients. *Cultural Diversity and Mental Health, 3*, 279–284.

Wolf, L. E., & Wasserstein, J. (2001). Adult ADHD: Concluding thoughts. *Annals of the New York Academy of Sciences, 931*, 396–408.

Wolfe, D. A., & McEachran, A. (1997). Child abuse and neglect. In E. J. Mash & L. G. Terdal (Eds.), *Assessment of childhood disorders* (3rd ed., pp. 523–568). New York: Guilford Press.

Wolpe, J. (1958). *Psychotherapy by reciprocal inhibition.* Palo Alto, CA: Stanford University Press.

Wolpe, J., & Lang, P. J. (1997). *Manual for the Fear Survey Schedule* (Rev.). San Diego, CA: Education and Industrial Testing Service.

Wolraich, M. L., Hanah, J. N., Pinnock, T. V., Baumgaertel, A., & Brown, J. (1996). Comparisons of diagnostic criteria for attention-deficit hyperactivity disorder in a country wide sample. *Journal of the American Academy of Child and Adolescent Psychiatry, 35*, 319–324.

Wonderlich, S. A., Fullerton, D., Swift, W. J., & Klein, M. H. (1994). Five-year outcome from eating disorders: Relevance of personality disorders. *International Journal of Eating Disorders, 15*(3), 233–243.

Wonderlich, S. A., & Mitchell, J. E. (1997). Eating disorders and comorbidity: Empirical conceptual, and clinical implications. *Psychopharmacology Bulletin, 33*(3), 381–390.

Wonderlich, S. A., & Mitchell, J. E. (2001). The role of personality in the onset of eating disorders and treatment implications. *Psychiatric Clinics of North America, 24*(2), 249–258.

Woo, S. M., Goldstein, M. J., & Nuechterlein, K. H. (1997). Relatives' expressed emotion and non-verbal signs of subclinical psychopathology in schizophrenic patients. *British Journal of Psychiatry, 170*, 58–61.

Woodcock, R. W., McGrew, K. S., & Mather, N. (2001a). *Woodcock-Johnson III: Tests of achievement.* Itasca, IL: Riverside.

Woodcock, R. W., McGrew, K. S., & Mather, N. (2001b). *Woodcock-Johnson III: Tests of cognitive abilities.* Itasca, IL: Riverside.

Woods, C. M., Vevea, J. L., Chambless, D. L., & Bayen, U. J. (2002). Are compulsive checkers impaired in memory? A meta-analytic review. *Clinical Psychology Science and Practice, 9*, 353–366.

Woody, S. R., Detweiler-Bedell, J., Teachman, B. A., & O'Hearn, T. (2003). *Treatment planning in psychotherapy: Taking the guesswork out of clinical care.* New York: Guilford Press.

Work Group on Quality Issues. (1998). Summary of the practice parameters for the assessment and treatment of children and adolescents with language and learning disorders. *Journal of the Academy of Child and Adolescent Psychiatry, 37*(10), 1117–1119.

World Health Organization. (1948). *International classification of diseases* (6th rev.). Geneva, Switzerland: Author.

World Health Organization. (1992). *The ICD-10 classification of mental and behavioral disorders: Clinical descriptions and diagnostic guidelines.* Geneva, Switzerland: Author.

World Health Organization. (1993). *The ICD-10 classification of mental and behavioral diseases.* Geneva, Switzerland: Author.

World Health Organization. (1993). *The ICD–10 classification of mental and behavioral disorders: Diagnostic criteria for research.* Geneva, Switzerland: Author.

Wozniak, J. (2005). Recognizing and managing bipolar disorder in children. *Journal of Clinical Psychiatry, 66*, 18–23.

Wozniak, J., Crawford, M., Biederman, J., Faraone, S., Spencer, T., Taylor, A., et al. (1999). Antecedents and complications of trauma in boys with ADHD: Findings from a longitudinal study. *Journal of the American Academy of Child and Adolescent Psychiatry, 38*, 48–55.

Wray, J. N. (2000). Psychophysiological aspects of methamphetamine abuse. *Journal of Addictions Nursing, 12*, 143–147.

Wren, F. J., & Tarbell, S. E. (1998). Feeding and growth disorders. In R. T. Ammerman & J. V. Campo (Eds.), *Handbook of pediatric psychology and psychiatry: Vol. 2. Disease, injury, and illness* (pp. 133–165). Needham Heights, MA: Allyn & Bacon.

Wright, F. D., Beck, A. T., Newman, C. F., & Liese, B. S. (1993). Cognitive therapy of substance abuse: Theoretical rationale. *NIDA Research Monograph, 137*, 123–146.

Wright, K., & Lam, D. (2004). Bipolar affective disorder: Current perspectives on psychological theory and treatment. In M. Powers (Ed.), *Mood disorders: A handbook of science and practice* (pp. 235–246). Hoboken, NJ: Wiley.

Wurtele, S. K., & Miller-Perrin, C. L. (1992). *Preventing child sexual abuse: Sharing the responsibility.* Lincoln: University of Nebraska Press.

Wurmser, L. (1985). The role of superego conflicts in substance abuse and their treatment. *International Journal of Psychoanalytic Psychotherapy, 10*, 227–258.

Wyatt, R. J., & Henter, I. (1991). An economic evaluation of manic-depressive illness, 1991. *Social Psychiatry and Psychiatric Epidemiology, 30*, 213–219.

Wykes, T., & Sturt, E. (1986). The measurement of social behavior in psychiatric patients: An assessment of the reliability and validity of the S.S. schedule. *British Journal of Psychiatry, 148*, 1–11.

Wyllie, E., Glazer, J. P., Benbadis, S., Kotagal, P., & Wolgamuth, B. (1999). Psychiatric features of children and adolescents with pseudoseizures. *Archives of Pediatric and Adolescent Medicine, 153*, 244–248.

Yaffe, K., Edwards, E. R., Covinksy, K. E., Lui, L., & Eng, C. (2003). Depressive symptoms and risk of mortality in frail, community-living elderly persons. *American Journal of Geriatric Psychiatry, 11*, 561–567.

Yaffe, K., Krueger, K., Cummings, S. R., Blackwell, T., Henderson, V. W., Sarkar, S., et al. (2005). Effect of raloxifene on prevention of dementia and cognitive impairment in older women: The Multiple Outcomes of Raloxifene Evaluation (MORE) randomized trial. *American Journal of Psychiatry, 162*, 683–690.

Yager, J., & Andersen, A. E. (2005). Anorexia nervosa. *New England Journal of Medicine, 353*(14), 1481–1488.

Yalom, I. (1975). *The theory and practice of group psychotherapy.* New York: Basic Books.

Yalom, I. D. (2002). *The gift of therapy.* New York: HarperCollins.

Yamagishi, T., & Yamagishi, M. (1994). Trust and commitment in the United States and Japan. *Motivation and Emotion, 18*, 129–166.

Yamashiro, G., & Matsuoka, K. (1997). Help-seeking among Asian and Pacific Americans: A multiperspective analysis. *Social Work, 42*, 176–186.

Yates, A. (1989). Current perspectives on the eating disorders: Pt. I. History, psychological and biological aspects. *Journal of the American Academy of Child and Adolescent Psychiatry, 28*(6), 813–828.

Yeargin-Allsopp, M., Rice, C., Karapurkar, T., Doernberg, N., Boyle, C., & Murphy, C. (2003). Prevalence of autism in a U.S. metropolitan area. *Journal of the American Medical Association, 289*, 49–55.

Yeh, M., Eastman, K., & Cheung, M. K. (1994). Children and adolescents in community mental health centers: Does ethnicity or the language of the therapist matter? *Journal of Community Psychology, 22*, 153–163.

Yeh, M., & Weisz, J. R. (2001). Why are we here at the clinic? Parent-child (dis)agreement on referral problems at outpatient treatment entry. *Journal of Consulting and Clinical Psychology, 69*, 1018–1025.

Yehuda, R., Kahana, B., Schmeidler, J., Southwick, S., Wilson, S., & Giller, E. (1995). Impact of cumulative lifetime trauma and recent stress on current posttraumatic stress disorder symptoms in Holocaust survivors. *American Journal of Psychiatry, 152*, 1815–1818.

Yen, S., Shea, T., Pagano, M., Sanislow, C. A., Crilo, C. M., McGlashan, T. H., et al. (2003). Axis I and Axis II disorders as predictors of prospective suicide attempts: Finding from the Collaborative Longitudinal Personality Disorders study. *Journal of Abnormal Psychology, 112*, 375–381.

Yerevanian, B. I., Koek, R. J., Feusner, J. D., Hwang, S., & Mintz, J. (2004). Antidepressants and suicidal behaviour in unipolar depression. *Acta Psychiatrica Scandinavica, 110*, 452–458.

Yerevanian, B., Koek, R. J., & Mintz, J. (2003). Lithium, anticonvulsants and suicidal behavioral in bipolar disorder. *Journal of Affective Disorders, 73*, 223–228.

Yerevanian, B., Koek, R. J., & Ramdev, S. (2001). Anxiety disorders comorbidity in mood disorder subgroups: Data from a mood disorders clinic. *Journal of Affective Disorders, 67*, 167–173.

Yokoyama, A., & Omori, T. (2003). Genetic polymorphisms of alcohol and aldehyde dehydrogenase and risk for esophageal and head and neck cancers. *Japanese Journal of Clinical Oncology, 33*, 111–121.

Yonkers, K. A., Warshaw, M. G., Massion, A. O., & Keller, M. B. (1996). Phenomenology and course of generalised anxiety disorder. *British Journal of Psychiatry, 168*, 308–313.

Yorulmaz, O., Karanci, N., & Tekok-Kiliç, A. (2006). What are the roles of perfectionism and responsibility in checking and cleaning, compulsions? *Anxiety Disorders, 20*, 312–327.

Young, A. S., & Magnabosco, A. S. (2004). Services for adults with mental illness. In L. Luborsky, B. Levin, J. Petrila, & K. Hennesasy (Eds.), *Mental health services: A public health perspective* (pp. 177–208). New York: Oxford University Press.

Young, A. S., Nuechterlein, K. H., Mintz, J., Ventura, J., Gitlin, M., & Liberman, R. P. (1998). Suicidal ideation and suicide attempts in recent-onset schizophrenia. *Schizophrenia Bulletin, 24*, 629–634.

Young, J. (1998). Schema-focused therapy for narcissistic patients. In S. Ronningstam (Ed.), *Disorders of narcissism: Diagnostic, clinical and empirical implications* (pp. 239–268). Washington, DC: American Psychiatric Press.

Young, J., & Klosko, B. S. (2005). Schema therapy. In J. M. Oldham, A. E. Skodol, & D. S. Bender (Eds.), *Textbook of personality disorders* (pp. 289–306). Washington, DC: American Psychiatric Publishing.

Young, J. E., Klosko, K. S., & Weishaar, M. E. (2003). *Schema therapy: A practitioner's guide.* New York: Guilford Press.

Young, L. T., Cooke, R. G., Robb, J. C., Levitt, A. J., & Joffe, R. T. (1993). Anxious and non-anxious bipolar disorder. *Journal of Affective Disorders, 29*, 49–52.

Young, R. C., Biggs, J. T., Ziegler, V. E., & Meyer, D. A. (1978). A rating scale for mania: Reliability, validity, and sensitivity. *British Journal of Psychiatry 133*, 429–435.

Young, R. C., & Meyers, B. S. (2004). Psychopharmacology. In J. Sadavoy, L. F. Jarvik, G. T. Grossberg, & B. S. Meyers (Eds.), *Comprehensive textbook of geriatric psychiatry* (pp. 903–993). New York: Norton.

Young, S. (2000). ADHD children grown up: An empirical review. *Counseling Psychology Quarterly, 13*(2), 191–200.

Young, S. E., Corley, R. P., Stallings, M. C., Rhee, S. H., Crowley, T. J., & Hewitt, J. K. (2002). Substance use, abuse, and dependence in adolescence: Prevalence, symptom profiles, and correlates. *Drug and Alcohol Dependence, 68*, 309–322.

Young, T. J. (1988). Substance use among Native Americans. *Clinical Psychology Review, 8*, 125–138.

Zalewski, C., Johnson-Selfridge, M. T., Ohriner, O., Zarrella, Z., & Seltzer, J. C. (1998). A review of neuropsychological differences between paranoid and nonparanoid schizophrenia patients. *Schizophrenia Bulletin, 24*, 127–145.

Zanarini, M., Frankenberg, F. R., Sickel, A. E., & Young, L. (1996). *Diagnostic interview for the DSM-IV personality disorders.* Laboratory for the study of adult development, McLean Hospital and the Department of psychiatry, Harvard University.

Zanarini, M. C. (2004). Update on pharmacotherapy of borderline personality disorder. *Current Psychiatric Reports, 61*, 66–70.

Zanarini, M. C. (2005). The longitudinal course of Borderline personality disorder. In J. G. Gunderson & P. D. Hoffman (Eds.), *Understanding and treating borderline personality disorder: A guide for professionals and families* (pp. 83–101). Washington, DC: American Psychiatric Publishing.

Zanarini, M. C., Frankenburg, F. R., Dubo, E. D., Sickel, A. E., Trikha, A., Levin, A., et al. (1998). Axis I comorbidity of borderline personality disorder. *American Journal of Psychiatry, 155*, 1733–1739.

Zanarini, M. C., Frankenberg, F. R., Hennen, J., & Silk, K. R. (2004). Mental health utilization by borderline personality disorder patients and Axis II comparison subjects followed prospectively for 6 years. *Journal of Clinical Psychiatry, 65*, 28–36.

Zanarini, M. C., Ruser, T., Frankenburg, F. R., Hennen, J., & Gunderson, J. G. (2000). The dissociative experiences of borderline patients. *Comprehensive Psychiatry, 41*, 223–227.

Zandi, P. P., Anthony, J. C., Khachaturian, A. S., Stone, S. V., Gustafson, D., Tschanz, J. T., et al. (2004). Reduced risk of Alzheimer disease in users of antioxidant vitamin supplements: The Cache County Study. *Archives of Neurology, 61*, 82–88.

Zarit, S. H., Todd, P. A., & Zarit, J. M. (1986). Subjective burden of husbands and wives as caregivers: A longitudinal study. *Gerontologist, 26*, 260–266.

Zarit, S. H., & Zarit, J. M. (1998). *Mental disorders in older adults.* New York: Guilford Press.

Zarit, S. H., & Zarit, J. M. (2006). *Mental disorders in older adults: Fundamentals of assessment and treatment* (2nd ed.). New York: Guilford Press.

Zeiss, A. M., Lewinsohn, P. M., & Muñoz, R. F. (1979). Nonspecific improvement effects in depression using interpersonal skills training, pleasant activity schedules, or cognitive training. *Journal of Consulting and Clinical Psychology, 47*, 427–439.

Zero to Three National Center for Clinical Infant Programs. (1994). *Diagnostic classification: 0–3.* Arlington, VA: Author.

Zhang, A. Y., & Snowden, L. R. (1999). Ethnic characteristics of mental disorders in five U.S. communities. *Cultural Diversity and Ethnic Minority Psychology, 5*(2), 134–146.

Zhu, A. J., & Walsh, B. T. (2002). Pharmacologic treatment of eating disorders. *Canadian Journal of Psychiatry, 47*(3), 227–234.

Ziedonis, D. M., & George, T. P. (1997). Schizophrenia and nicotine use: Report of a pilot smoking cessation program and review of neurobiological and clinical issues. *Schizophrenia Bulletin, 23*, 247–254.

Zigler, E. (2001). Looking back 40 years and still seeing the person with mental retardation as a whole person In H. N. Switzky (Ed.), *Personality and motivation differences in persons with mental retardation* (pp. 3–55). Mahwah, NJ: Erlbaum.

Zilbergeld, B., & Hammond, D. C. (1988). The use of hypnosis in treating desire disorders. In S. R. Leiblum & R. C. Rosen (Eds.), *Sexual desire disorders* (pp. 192–225). New York: Guilford Press.

Zimberg, S. (2005). Alcoholism and substance abuse in older adults. In R. J. Frances, S. I. Miller, & A. H. Mack (Eds.), *Clinical textbook of addictive disorders* (3rd ed., pp. 396–410). New York: Guilford Press.

Zimmerman, B. J., & Koussa, R. (1979). Social influences on children's toy preferences: Effects of model rewardingness and affect. *Contemporary Educational Psychology, 4*, 55–66.

Zimmerman, I. L., Steiner, V. G., & Pond, R. E. (2002). *Preschool Language Scales 4.* San Antonio, TX: Psychological Corporation.

Zimmerman, J. K., & Asnis, G. M. (1995). *Treatment approaches with suicidal adolescents.* New York: Wiley.

Zimmerman, M. (1994). *Interview guide for evaluating DSM-IV psychiatric disorders and the mental status exam.* East Greenwich, RI: Psych Products Press.

Zimmerman, M., Coryell, W., Pfohl, B. M., & Stangl, D. (1986). The validity of four definitions of endogenous depression: Pt. II. Clinical, demographic, familial, and psychosocial correlates. *Archives of General Psychiatry, 43*, 234–244.

Zimmerman, M., & Mattia, J. (1998). Body dysmorphic disorder in psychiatric outpatients: Recognition, prevalence, comorbidity, demographics, and clinical correlates. *Comprehensive Psychiatry, 39*(5), 265–270.

Zimmerman, M., Rothschild, L., & Chelminski, I. (2005). The prevalence of DSM-IV personality disorders in psychiatric outpatients. *American Journal of Psychiatry, 162* (10), 1911–1918.

Zipfel, S., Lowe, B., Reas, D. L., Deter, H.-C., & Herzog, W. (2000). Long-term prognosis in anorexia nervosa: Lessons from a 21-year follow-up study. *Lancet, 355*(9205), 721–722.

Zisook, S., Nyer, M., Kasckow, J., Golshan, S., Lehman, D., & Montross, L. (2006). Depressive symptom patterns in patients with chronic schizophrenia and subsyndromal depression. *Schizophrenia Research, 86*, 226–233.

Zisook, S., Rush, J. A., Albala, A., Alpert, J., Balasubramani, G. K., Fava, M., et al. (2004). Factors that differentiate early vs. later onset of major depression disorder. *Psychiatry Research, 129*, 127–140.

Zoccolillo, M., Tremblay, R., & Vitaro, F. (1996). DSM-III-R and DSM-III criteria for conduct disorder in preadolescent girls: Specific but insensitive. *Journal of the American Academy of Child and Adolescent Psychiatry, 35*, 461–470.

Zozula, R., & Rosen, R. (2001). Compliance with continuous positive airway pressure therapy: Assessing and improving treatment outcomes. *Current Opinion in Pulmonary Medicine, 7*, 391–398.

Zubin, J. (1967). Classification of behavior disorders. *Annual Review of Psychology, 18*, 373–406.

Zubin, J., & Spring, B. (1977). Vulnerability: A new view of schizophrenia. *Journal of Abnormal Psychology, 86*, 103–126.

Zuckerman, B., Amaro, H., Bauchner., H., & Cabral, H. (1989). Depressive symptoms during pregnancy: relationship to poor health behaviors. *American Journal of Obstetrics and Gynecology, 160*, 1107–11.

Zuckerman, M. (1999). *Vulnerability to psychopathology: A biosocial model.* Washington, DC: American Psychological Association.

Zur, J., & Yule, W. (1990). Chronic solvent abuse: Pt. I. Cognitive sequelae. *Child Care, Health and Development, 16*, 1–20.

Zweig, R. A., & Hillman, J. (1999). Personality disorders in adults: A review. In E. Rosowsky R. C. Abrams, & R. A. Zweig (Eds.), *Personality disorders in older adults: Emerging issues in diagnosis and treatment* (pp. 31–54). Mahwah, NJ: Lawrence Erlbaum Associates.

Zygmunt, A., Olfson, M., Boyer, C., & Mechanic, D. (2002). Interventions to improve medication adherence. *American Journal of Psychiatry, 159*, 1653–1664.

Zywiak, W. H., Longabaugh, R., & Wirtz, P. W. (2002). Decomposing the relationships between pretreatment social network characteristics and alcohol treatment outcome. *Journal of Studies on Alcohol, 63*, 114–121.

Author Index

Subject Index

of ADHD, 304–307
of anxiety disorders, 652–659
of autism, 205
within category differentiation,
145–147
of children, 121
clinical skills for, 122–128
of cognitive disorders, 364–365,
368–374
of conduct disorder, 280–281
correlates with treatment, 121
deferred, 150
determination of, 135–154
of disruptive behavior disorders,
304–307
DSM-IV and, 116–122
of eating disorders, 766–770
exclusion criteria, 125–126
functions of, 122
history of classification and, 111–
113
interclinician agreement on, 120
modern classification systems,
114–122
monothetic approach, 125
of mood disorders, 573–580
multiaxial, 131–135
multiple, 127–128
not otherwise specified, 149
openness concerning, 4–5
of PDDs, 241–244
of personality disorders, 809–811,
851–861
polythetic approach, 125
principle, 128
provisional, 128, 149–150
revisions to, 122
as self-fulfilling prophecy, 121
severity modifiers, 126
of sleep disorders, 786–787
of somatoform disorders, 685,
717–724
of substance use disorders, 446–
450
therapeutic relationship and, 135–
136
tips and strategies for, 154
*Diagnostic and Statistical Manual of
Mental Disorders (DSM-I)*,
112–113
*Diagnostic and Statistical Manual of
Mental Disorders (DSM-II)*, 113
*Diagnostic and Statistical Manual of
Mental Disorders (DSM-III)*,
114–115
*Diagnostic and Statistical Manual of
Mental Disorders (DSM-IV)*,
115–116
*Diagnostic and Statistical Manual of
Mental Disorders (DSM-IV-TR)*,
115–116
appendixes, 130
categorical model in, 118–119
clinical judgment and, 119–120
as communication tool, 117–118
compatibility of, with *ICD-10*, 122
correlates with treatment, 121
diagnostic categories, 123–124
diagnostic criteria, 119–120, 124–
125, 128

diagnostic principles, 127–128
diagnostic process and, 122–128
exclusion criteria, 125–126
multiaxial and diversity
considerations, 120–121
multiaxial diagnosis, 131–135
organization of, 128–130
reliability of, 120
strengths and limitations of, 116–
122
syndromes, 124
terminology, 123
*Diagnostic and Statistical Manual of
Mental Disorders (DSM-V)*, 116
Diagnostic categories, 123–124, 126–
127
Diagnostic conceptualization models,
136–137
Diagnostic criteria:
for Alzheimer's disease, 341–343
DSM-IV and, 119–120
DSM-IV-TR, 124–125
DSM-IV versus *ICD-10*, 122
familiarization with, 4
provisional diagnosis and, 128
subtypes and specifiers, 126–127
within-category diagnostic
differentiation and, 145
Diagnostic decision making, 143,
145
Diagnostic errors, 136
Diagnostic Interview for Children
(DICA), 47
Diagnostic Interview for Personality
Disorders-IV, 850
Diagnostic interviews, 306–307. *See
also* Interviewing; *specific
interviews*
Diagnostic Interview Schedule (DIS),
46
Diagnostic Interview Schedule for
Children (DISC-IV), 47
Diagnostic principles, 127–128
Diagnostic process:
Step 1: rule out medical or physical
causes, 137–139
Step 2: rule out substances or
toxins, 138, 140–141
Step 3: consider cultural and
developmental factors, 138,
141–143
Step 4: determine Axis I and Axis
II disorders, 138, 143–147
Step 5: resolve diagnostic
uncertainty, 138, 147–150
Step 6: consider comorbidity, 138,
150–152
Step 7: asses level of distress and/or
impairment, 138, 152–154
Diagnostic terminology, 123
Diagnostic uncertainty, resolution of,
147–150
Dialectical behavior therapy (DBT),
80, 869, 874–877
Diaphragmatic breathing, 788
Diathesis-stress model, of
schizophrenia, 497
Diazepam, 661
Dieting, 759
Differential Abilities Scales, 261

Differential diagnosis. *See also*
Diagnosis
of anxiety disorders, 654–659
of cognitive disorders, 368–374
of depression versus dementia,
393–395
diagnostic differentiation and, 145
diagnostic principles, 127–128
of disruptive behavior disorders,
310–314
of eating disorders, 768–770
of factitious disorders, 742–744
of mood disorders, 575–580
of PDDs, 241–244
of personality disorders, 856–861
of schizophrenia, 515–519
of sleep disorders, 786–787
of somatoform disorders, 685,
719–724, 737
steps in, 135–154
of substance use disorders, 449–
450
Dimensional Assessment of
Personality Pathology, 850
Dimensional model, 118–119
Dinosaur School, 328
Directive guidance, 21–22
Disability benefits, for psychotic
patients, 530–531
Discharge summary, 191
Discrepancy, developing, 444
Discrete-trial training (DTT), 250–
251
Discriminate validity, 182
Disease model, 113
Disease-moral model, of substance
use, 399
Disgust sensitivity, 611
Disinhibition, 341, 343
Disordered eating. *See* Eating
disorders
Disorganized thinking or speech, 473,
476–477, 505–506
Disorganized type schizophrenia,
478–479
Disorientation, 334
Disruptive behavior disorders. *See
also specific disorders*
comorbidities with, 308–310
conduct disorder, 279–286
differential diagnosis, 310–314
early intervention for, 327–328
gender differences in, 301–302
historical overview, 266–267
intake and interviewing
considerations, 302–304
introduction to, 265
not otherwise specified, 288
oppositional defiant disorder, 286–
289
relationships among, 312–314
risk factors for, 296–301
treatment, 314–327
Dissociation, 868
Dissociative anesthetic, 416
Dissociative disorders:
versus cognitive disorders, 371,
373
versus personality disorders, 859
Dissociative states, 821